T H E
1989
Elias Baseball
Analyst

T H E
1989
Elias Baseball
Analyst

Seymour Siwoff, Steve Hirdt, Peter Hirdt & Tom Hirdt

COLLIER BOOKS
Macmillan Publishing Company
New York
COLLIER MACMILLAN PUBLISHERS
London

Collier Books
Macmillan Publishing Company
866 Third Avenue, New York, NY 10022
Collier Macmillan Canada, Inc.

"The Library of Congress has cataloged this
serial publication as follows:".

The . . . Elias baseball analyst.—1985–   —New York:
  Collier Books, c1985–

    v.; 28 cm.

    Annual.
    Re-arrangement of material issued in a series of computerized reports called: The
Player analysis.
    Produced by the Elias Sports Bureau.
    Editors for 1989–   by S. Siwoff, S. Hirdt, P. Hirdt, and T. Hirdt.

    1. Baseball—United States—Statistics—Periodicals. 2. National League of Profes-
sional Baseball Clubs—Statistics—Periodicals. 3. Baseball—Statistics—
    1. Baseball—United States—Statistics—Periodicals. 2. National League of Peri-
odicals. 4. Baseball—Miscellanea—Periodicals. I. Siwoff,   Seymour. II. Hirdt,
Steve. III. Hirdt, Peter. IV. Hirdt, Tom. V. Elias Sports Bureau. VI. Player
analysis. VII. Title: Baseball analyst.
GV877.E44   85-643022
                        796.357'0973—dc19
                                                       AACR 2   MARC-S

BOMC offers recordings and compact discs, cassettes
and records. For information and catalog write to
BOMR, Camp Hill, PA 17012.

Contents

ACKNOWLEDGEMENTS

Regular readers of the *Analyst* will note that another name has been added to our front cover this year. Call us madcap, but we thought that writing most of the individual player notes for each of the past three years had earned Tom Hirdt something more than a page-vii thank you.

We've calculated that, at the current rate of one additional name every five years, by the time we publish *The 2189 Elias Baseball Analyst*, we'll have filled the cover with the names of a long list of associates equally indispensable to its production. Of course, there won't be any room left for the title, but what the heck. Every one of those listed would be deserving of mention.

In truth, the publication of each edition of the *Analyst* has been possible only with the help of those whose names follow. Their work has been invaluable, and their willingness to spend countless hours on the project has been essential to its success. The grind of producing such a large volume under deadline often makes it seem that we take their efforts for granted. But believe us, without their help, we'd be nowhere.

Thanks to all of you:

From the Elias staff, chief researchers John Chymczuk, John Labombarda, Alex Stern, and Bob Waterman. We appreciate the care with which Alex, John C. and John L. double- and triple-check our work, and often contribute some worthwhile nuggets of their own. Of course, Bob doesn't have to work as hard, since he long ago committed *The Baseball Encyclopedia* to memory. But we appreciate his work just the same.

The summer-long, day-to-day work of many others at Elias forms the basis of much of the data in this book. Thanks to Rocky Avakian, Jay Chesler, Frank Labombarda, Santo Labombarda, and Bob Rosen. Thanks, also, to the boys in the computer room: Chris Thorn, Andy Serp, and Chris Lasch. Each has provided on-the-spot assistance countless times for seemingly insoluble problems.

They aren't the only ones who make sure our bits don't turn into bytes, and vice versa. The *Analyst* also requires the expertise of several consultants. We'd hereby like to thank Warren Bannerman, Larry Meisner, and Bernie Schanker. Especially Bernie, who bore the brunt of our adorable little habit of demanding to have work done by yesterday.

As always, Macmillan provided generous and capable assistance, which was gratefully accepted. All we can say is thank God for Angels pitcher Willie Fraser. There might be a baseball fan or two somewhere who doesn't know the story of Willie's role in sending editor Rick Wolff our way. (Frankly, we don't know how they could call themselves fans. But for the uninformed, check the comments on Fraser on page 276.) Had Rick's Mercy College team beaten Fraser back in '85, Wolff would now be managing the Yankees, and Billy Martin editing our book. We know who'd have gotten the worst of that deal, and it ain't Steinbrenner.

And anyone who thinks the 1988 rookie crop was below par didn't consider Rick's free-agent additions to the Mac team, Jeanine Bucek and Ken Samelson. We'll take them over Sabo and Weiss anyday.

Copy editors David Frost and Paul Heacock were relentless in their pursuit of stray hyphens and misplaced boldface. Some of the best writing in our manuscript went unpublished—Paul's query notes on questionable facts.

The Macmillan crew at Riverside once again took our material and beautified it. Casey Lee, Fred Richardson, Bob Keefe, and Jackie Dickens are the ones responsible for the print design of the *Analyst*, and we're proud to call their work our own. Keefe deserves special mention in that regard. Bob has a knack for taking our data in its raw form and presenting it in an intelligent and comprehensible format. And after five years of Elias nit-picking, he's remained a prince to work with. Thanks a million, guy.

Finally, we'd like to thank the folks at Mike Cohen Communications for the outstanding job they did publicizing our book last year. Unfortunately, Mike passed away last autumn, and so we join a long line of those whom he helped, but who never thanked him appropriately. He was, quite simply, a great guy and the best at what he did. Mike's colleagues, Bryan Harris and Tony Signore, also won our appreciation with their hard work.

On a personal note, we'd like to dedicate this edition

of the *Analyst* to Emil Hirdt. He was Most Valuable Player in New York's German-American Soccer League several times in the mid-1950s, so he scored his share of goals in Late-Game Pressure Situations. But he never won a more important match than he did last November. Dad, this one's for you.

T H E
1989
Elias Baseball
Analyst

I
Introduction

INTRODUCTION

The is the fifth edition of *The Elias Baseball Analyst.* To some of you, who are familiar with the series, this won't come as a surprise. But to others, especially to those who like their baseball straight (hold the arithmetic, please), the notion that a book of baseball numbers could thrive is about as welcome as an ice-water bath.

Actually, it's that latter group that we'd like to address first.

The Elias Sports Bureau has been in the business of compiling statistics for more than three-quarters of a century. We're now the official statistician not only for major league baseball, but also for the National Football League and the National Basketball Association. But for about half of our existence, baseball was our only business. And for most of that time, being the official statistician first for the National League and later for all major league baseball meant taking each day's box scores and updating the year-to-date totals for each player. When a writer or a broadcaster or a general manager needed to know, for instance, whether Pie Traynor was still leading the National League in doubles, Elias was the place to call. That role, crucial to number-*philes* and number-*phobes* alike, remains the meat and potatoes of our work.

But about 20 years ago, an explosion took place in the field of sports information. The proliferation of televised sports, the increasing availability and use of computers, and the emphasis on numerical data generated by the emphasis on the business of sports all served to propel the sports data business into high gear. At Elias, we caught the computer fever in the mid–1970s, with the result being a voluminous series of reports called *The Player Analysis*—the first reports ever to classify every major leaguer's performance into game-situation categories. When we first developed the reports, we figured that the teams themselves would be the most interested parties, and they were. But as we approached the middle of this decade, we decided to use *The Player Analysis* as the basis for a book. Nine months later, the *Analyst* was born.

Still, we are sometimes asked, don't you guys think that there are *too many* numbers in baseball? Our answer to that is usually, "Yes and no."

Yes, if you think that the only value of baseball statistics is in memorizing them so that you can prove to your buddies that you really *know* baseball. To those individuals, our new wave of statistics must be terribly frustrating, in that we have expanded their annual memorization project.

But if you accept the premise that in sports, just as in other social sciences, statistics are reference material, then the answer to the question is *No.* Sports statistics are there to be drawn on when needed. They enhance our portrait of each player's strengths and weaknesses, supplying shadings and depth-of-field to what otherwise might be a rather flat and lifeless form. At a time when it's become nearly impossible to follow each and every major league player merely through observation —as our parents and grandparents did during the era of eight-team leagues—statistics are our most valuable resource for tracking the progress of nearly 1000 players each summer.

Think of statistics as the 3–D glasses through which the game and its players may be more fully enjoyed. It may not be necessary information, in the cosmic sense, to know that Ozzie Virgil has never had a hit off Sid Fernandez. But even *that* information adds to the enjoyment of those few times each season when you watch Virgil bat against Fernandez. Of course, it takes on even further importance if you're managing Virgil or Fernandez. And it's vital if you happen to be Virgil or Fernandez.

Now, like everyone else, we're aware that statistics are often abused, used for evil instead of good. If you're tired of statistics used as "filler" material in newspapers and magazines, on radio and television, well, so are we. But that's part of the price we pay for living in a free society. It's an annoyance, but look at it this way: If after 200 years of the Constitution, we still can't keep guns out of the hands of the wrong people, how can we expect to do that with baseball statistics?

The 1989 *Analyst* is different from previous editions in a couple of prominent respects. But first, let us assure our returning readers that all of the features that were here last year are back again this year: the team essays and tables, the statistics and comments on individual batters, pitchers, and teams, the league leaders and rankings, the stadium profiles and ballpark effects, and the batter-pitcher matchups for selected superstars. We've tried to augment the player comments with increased references to "fly-ball" and "ground-ball" hitters and pitchers, since one of the discoveries that we made in recent years has to do with how such players perform against opponents of similar or dissimilar tendencies. See the Cleveland essay on page 35 for details.

We've also created a new section, *Player Tendencies,* which identifies those players whose performance rises or falls depending upon the circumstances of the game. If you look at page 359, for example, you'll discover that Tim Raines's batting average in Late-Inning Pressure Situations is 56 points better than it is at other times. That 56-point increase is the largest in the majors over the past 10 years. And you'll learn that his opposite number, Danny Heep, has hit .194 in LIPS, but .265 at other times.

In addition to that new section, we've also taken our first step backward into baseball history by generating *Analyst*-type statistics for a team that redefined the word *Cinderella* a generation ago: the Miracle Mets of 1969. One of the things that we've always wanted to do in the *Analyst* was to look at some great teams of the past through the prism of the new statistics. Our 39-page section on the '69 Mets—to paraphrase a famous line of the time—may seem at first like one small step. But it represented a giant leap, statistically speaking, to reconstruct a season from the past in such detail.

What do we know now, 20 years later, that would have heightened our appreciation of that team and those players? Our answers begin on page 431. If you like what you see, let us know. The historical section could become an annual feature of the *Analyst*.

II
Team Section

Team Section

The Team Section consists of comments and statistics for each of the twenty-six major-league teams. The examples here, and in all of the section introductions, just happen to be taken from the 1985 season.

WON-LOST RECORD BY STARTING POSITION

BALTIMORE 83-78	C	1B	2B	3B	SS	LF	CF	RF	P	DH	Leadoff	Relief	Starts
Don Aase	·	·	·	·	·	·	·	·	·	·	·	26-28	·
Eric Bell	·	·	·	·	·	·	·	·	·	·	·	0-4	·
Mike Boddicker	·	·	·	·	·	·	·	·	13-19	·	·	·	13-19
Fritz Connally	·	1-0	·	12-15	·	·	·	·	·	1-0	·	·	14-15
Rich Dauer	·	·	32-31	4-4	·	·	·	·	·	·	·	·	36-35
Storm Davis	·	·	·	·	·	·	·	·	16-12	·	·	0-3	16-12
Rick Dempsey	57-56	·	·	·	·	·	·	·	·	·	·	·	57-56
Ken Dixon	·	·	·	·	·	·	·	·	10-8	·	·	2-14	10-8
Jim Dwyer	·	·	·	·	·	·	16-20	·	16-9	·	0-1	9-6	32-30
Mike Flanagan	·	·	·	·	·	·	·	·	7-8	·	·	·	7-8
Dan Ford	·	·	·	·	·	·	·	·	·	10-6	5-5	·	10-6
Wayne Gross	·	0-5	·	30-27	·	·	·	·	1-3	·	·	·	31-35
John Habyan	·	·	·	·	·	·	·	·	·	·	·	1-1	·
Brad Havens	·	·	·	·	·	·	·	·	0-1	·	·	2-5	0-1
Leo Hernandez	·	·	·	·	·	·	·	·	·	0-4	·	·	0-4
Phil Huffman	·	·	·	·	·	·	·	·	1-0	·	·	0-1	1-0
Lee Lacy	·	·	·	·	·	·	51-61	·	·	3-1	16-20	·	54-62
John Lowenstein	·	·	·	·	1-3	·	·	·	·	2-2	·	·	3-5

The first table following the team comments is the Won-Lost Record by Starting Position chart. This chart lists, for each player on a team, the team's won-lost record in games started by that player at each position, in the leadoff spot in the lineup, and in games in which a pitcher appeared in relief. (This last is included to give some insight into how the manager chose to use his relief staff.) The players are listed in alphabetical order.

Following this table is a series of eight charts detailing the performance of each player and pitcher on the team who played at least semiregularly. Included are all players who had at least 200 plate appearances in the season, all pitchers who faced at least 200 batters, and selected individuals who did not meet the standard but were still significant enough to merit inclusion.

Overall Batting Compared to Late Inning Pressure Situations

		BA	Rank	SA	Rank	OBA	Rank	HR %	Rank	BB %	Rank	SO %	Rank	RDI %	Rank
Rich Dauer	Overall	.202	155	.264	154	.275	148	0.96	129	8.55	73	2.99	1	.200	--
	Pressure	.118	--	.118	--	.118	--	0.00	--	0.00	--	0.00	--	.000	--
Rick Dempsey	Overall	.254	99	.406	88	.345	50	3.31	61	11.90	30	20.71	149	.318	48
	Pressure	.171	149	.293	124	.286	118	2.44	77	14.00	30	24.00	146	.286	--
Jim Dwyer	Overall	.249	106	.399	95	.353	36	3.00	73	13.50	16	11.31	50	.324	43
	Pressure	.344	13	.563	10	.500	2	3.13	56	23.81	2	14.29	82	.455	12
Wayne Gross	Overall	.235	134	.424	69	.369	17	5.07	17	17.42	2	18.18	133	.118	163
	Pressure	.184	143	.316	113	.225	149	2.63	69	5.00	124	20.00	133	.100	155
Lee Lacy	Overall	.293	22	.409	82	.343	52	1.83	105	7.22	103	17.59	124	.262	113
	Pressure	.297	40	.453	44	.378	33	4.69	38	10.81	56	16.22	100	.167	128
Fred Lynn	Overall	.263	78	.449	41	.339	63	5.13	15	10.43	40	19.69	140	.285	88
	Pressure	.231	104	.481	34	.333	73	7.69	11	13.33	35	23.33	143	.214	117
Eddie Murray	Overall	.297	16	.523	4	.383	6	5.32	13	12.41	24	10.04	42	.428	4
	Pressure	.333	15	.682	3	.400	23	9.09	4	10.67	57	8.00	23	.636	1
Floyd Rayford	Overall	.306	9	.521	5	.324	84	5.01	19	2.69	156	18.55	136	.214	143
	Pressure	.268	64	.585	8	.333	73	7.32	12	8.89	79	24.44	149	.250	87
Cal Ripken	Overall	.282	39	.469	25	.347	47	4.05	44	9.33	57	9.47	37	.378	9
	Pressure	.292	43	.528	23	.366	41	6.94	15	10.98	54	9.76	37	.250	87
Gary Roenicke	Overall	.218	151	.458	30	.342	57	6.67	4	16.06	4	13.14	77	.364	19
	Pressure	.043	--	.174	--	.185	--	4.35	--	14.81	--	14.81	--	.167	--
Larry Sheets	Overall	.262	81	.442	49	.323	90	5.18	14	7.76	92	14.40	98	.330	35
	Pressure	.235	102	.412	71	.291	116	5.88	25	7.27	101	20.00	133	.273	78
John Shelby	Overall	.283	38	.434	57	.307	121	3.41	60	3.27	154	20.56	147	.333	31
	Pressure	.200	130	.286	127	.222	150	0.00	113	2.78	143	25.00	150	.250	87
Alan Wiggins	Overall	.285	35	.349	130	.353	38	0.00	154	8.66	68	4.78	2	.339	29
	Pressure	.308	32	.346	94	.438	9	0.00	113	18.18	7	3.03	4	.400	22
Mike Young	Overall	.273	59	.513	11	.348	43	6.22	6	9.52	52	20.63	148	.293	73
	Pressure	.222	114	.426	56	.311	93	5.56	30	11.48	52	18.03	118	.333	55

Column Headings Information

BA   Batting Average

SA   Slugging Average

OBA   On-Base Average

HR%   Home Run Percentage (home runs per 100 at bats)

BB%   Base-on-Balls Percentage (bases on balls per 100 plate appearances)

SO%   Strikeout Percentage (strikeouts per 100 plate appearances)

RBI%   Percentage of Runs Batted In (per 100 opportunities)

Each chart provides a statistical breakdown of player performance in a selected category. For each category, the player's average or percentage is given, along with his ranking within the league. This enables us to see at a glance that while Jim Dwyer ranked 95th in the league in slugging overall in 1985, he ranked tenth in pressure situations (see below). Rankings in each category are listed for the 162 players and 145 pitchers with the most plate appearances or batters faced in the category (plus ties) in the American League, and the top 136 batters and 125 pitchers (plus ties) in the National League. If a player does not qualify under this standard, no ranking is listed. (For a more detailed description of the methods used in determining the number of qualifiers for a given category, see the introduction to the Leaders Section.)

The batter charts list breakdowns against left-handed and right-handed pitching, performance with bases empty and runners on base, and overall performance for the season compared with performance in pressure situations (all at bats occurring in the seventh inning or later with the score tied or the batter's team trailing by one, two, or three runs, or four runs with the bases loaded).

The final batter chart lists miscellaneous comparisons for each player, giving his batting average on grass fields and artificial turf; in home games and in road games; with runners in scoring position and with runners in scoring position and two out; on-base average leading off an inning; and the percentage of runners he drove in from third base with less than two out. (For players who played for more than one team in a league, all totals are combined. The "home" totals for Ken Phelps, for example, include all games played in Seattle when he was with the Mariners, and all games played in New York while he was with the Yankees.)

On each chart, following the individual batter totals, are the team's averages for each category, and the team's ranking within the league. For purposes of comparison, the overall league average is also included.

The pitcher charts list breakdowns against left-handed and right-handed batters, performance with bases empty and runners on base, and overall performance for the season compared with performance in pressure situations (against all batters in the seventh inning or later with the score tied or the pitcher's team leading or trailing by one or two runs).

The final pitcher chart lists miscellaneous comparisons for each pitcher giving his opponents' batting average on grass fields and artificial turf; in home games and in road games; with runners in scoring position and with runners in scoring position and two out; and opponents' on-base average leading off an inning.

On each chart, following the individual pitcher statistics, are the team's averages for each category, and the team's ranking within the league. For purposes of comparison, the overall league average is also included.

For a detailed discussion of the use of opposing batters' records to examine pitching performance, see the introduction to the Pitcher Section.

American League

BALTIMORE ORIOLES

- **Can anyone fill Eddie Murray's shoes?**
- **Does Murray have Hall of Fame credentials?**

Psst! Looking for a job? There's a good one available, if you're willing to relocate. Lots of travel and vacation time, good benefits, get to meet celebrities, all that stuff. Oh, and the pay's OK, too, a couple of million a year if you're good enough.

Where do you sign up? Call Memorial Stadium, Baltimore. Ask for Roland Hemond. Trouble is, we're talking about Eddie Murray's old job, so you might as well be trying to replace Iacocca at Chrysler. Or Lennon with the Beatles. Or Carson on "The Tonight Show." Big shoes to fill.

We've spent the last decade calling Eddie Murray the most underrated superstar in baseball. Now the Orioles have sent him from the major leagues' worst team to the National League champs, from the heat and humidity of the east coast summer to the year-round comfort of Lalaland, from the city of crab cakes to the land of sushi. To console the poor lad, we'd like to suggest that the maligned Mr. Murray might have been baseball's most valuable player during his 12 years in Baltimore.

We'll start with a fact that might surprise those who don't read the box scores every day. Since Murray joined the Orioles in 1977, he's played 1820 games, the highest total in the majors during that time, 32 more than his nearest competitor, Dave Winfield. So while Cal, Jr., has earned the lion's share of publicity by counting his contributions in innings rather than home runs, RBIs, or clutch performance, Murray has danced just about every dance as well, although under a much softer spotlight.

But it's what Murray's done in those games that really separates him from most of his peers. Only three players have driven in more runs since 1977, and only two have hit more home runs. The leaders over the past 12 seasons:

Player	HR	Player	RBI
Mike Schmidt	411	Jim Rice	1223
Dale Murphy	334	Dave Winfield	1206
Eddie Murray	333	Mike Schmidt	1194
Jim Rice	331	Eddie Murray	1190
Dave Winfield	306	Andre Dawson	1047

Murray's career batting average has remained near the .300 mark as well, currently residing at the .295 level. Among the players listed above, only Rice can match that figure. The others don't even come close.

But Murray's most spectacular talent has without question been his ability to rise to the occasion, to increase his productivity in proportion to the pressure of the moment. Look at the following table of Murray's career batting statistics, and notice how his performance swells in response to the pressure:

Category	AB	H	HR	RBI	BA
Overall statistics	6845	2021	333	1222	.295
Runners in scoring position	1700	505	87	849	.297
Late-Inning Pressure Situations	922	280	56	187	.303
LIPS/Runners on base	390	138	24	155	.353
LIPS/Runners in scoring pos.	193	72	11	124	.373
LIPS/2 outs, scoring pos.	82	31	5	52	.378

And, of course, let's not forget his 61-for-149 performance with the bases loaded, a .409 batting average that includes 14 grand-slam home runs. Quite simply, Murray has been the quintessential clutch hitter of the past decade.

Consistency? He's never hit below .277, nor above .316. With the exception of the strike-shortened 1981 season and an injury-plagued 1986 season, he's hit between 25 and 33 home runs every year.

Reliability? Murray's productivity with runners in scoring position was nearly unmatched during the five seasons from 1982 through 1986. He batted .341, to rank second in the majors during that time (behind Wade Boggs's .367 mark). But the past two seasons represented a severe decline for a player of such remarkable consistency as Murray's. His year-by-year performance with runners in scoring position (the final column represents the percentage of runners in scoring position that he drove in):

Year	AB	H	BA	RBI%	Year	AB	H	BA	RBI%
1977	154	36	.234	.273	1983	129	43	.333	.345
1978	165	40	.242	.272	1984	142	44	.310	.382
1979	164	52	.317	.315	1985	138	51	.370	.428
1980	184	55	.299	.326	1986	123	45	.366	.374
1981	103	26	.252	.339	1987	136	39	.287	.305
1982	134	44	.328	.401	1988	128	30	.234	.252

Given Murray's age, the enormity of his contract, and his marked decline in the clutch, it's hard to argue that the decision to trade him was unsound. After all, Baltimore is more than a left-handed middle-innings reliever from contention. But Dodgers fans, who reaped no benefit from Murray's Cooperstown performance over the past 12 seasons, are left to wonder whether the good Eddie Murray is gone forever.

The answer to that question can't be found in the following table, but it makes for some interesting speculation.

Five players in major league history compiled similar statistics in a variety of categories and at a comparable age to those Murray had accumulated by the end of the 1986 season. (For batters, we restricted our comparisons to players who fell within 10 percent of the player in question in at-bats, RBIs, home runs per at-bat, and extra-base hits per at-bat, within 12.5 percent in walk and strikeout percentages, and within 2.5 percent in batting average.)

While some of the comparable players prospered in the years after that, others declined steadily:

Player	Through	AB	H	2B	3B	HR	RBI	BB	SO	BA
Eddie Murray	1986	5624	1679	296	20	275	1015	709	769	.299
Frank Robinson	1965	5527	1673	318	50	324	1009	698	789	.303
Duke Snider	1956	4809	1470	263	59	276	911	615	770	.306
Vern Stephens	1951	5481	1588	260	39	224	1046	598	565	.290
Billy Williams	1969	5695	1656	263	70	249	855	557	650	.291
Carl Yastrzemski	1970	5741	1703	347	37	242	869	879	774	.297

Of those players, Robinson won the triple crown a year later, and Williams led the N.L. in hits and runs scored the next season. Snider hit 40 home runs in 1957, his last season in Brooklyn, prior to the steady slide toward retirement that accompanied him from the east coast to Los Angeles.

But the other two, like Murray, suffered marked declines in each of the two seasons that followed. Stephens never recovered from his slide, which actually began with the 1951 season. He slipped from 30 home runs in 1950 to 17 in 1951, and he never again reached double figures. Yaz appeared to be on the same track after disappointing seasons in 1971 (.254, 15 HRs) and 1972 (.264, 12 HRs). And although he rarely displayed the home run swing of his early years thereafter, he did compile a .284 batting average over his last six seasons with an average of 84 RBI per year.

Those comparisons leave little doubt that Murray is traveling in Hall of Fame company. His Cooperstown credentials might be borderline at the moment, but only if you fail to consider his enormous contributions in the clutch. Was he the best hitter of his time? Possibly, though trying to choose from among Murray, Rice, Schmidt, and Winfield is as pointless as it is difficult. But Murray's productivity over the past 12 seasons alone—like that of the others—should be enough to earn all of them a place in the Hall.

Nevertheless, the parallels to Snider and Stephens also suggest that a strong rebound from two seasons that were mediocre by previous standards is far from a foregone conclusion. Murray's best days are probably behind him. The question is, how good will those to follow be?

What will it take for Baltimore to replace Murray? If you're an Orioles fan, it's a frightening prospect. Cal Ripken notwithstanding, Murray has been Mr. Everything to Baltimore since 1977. Like Boog Powell, Murray has been a fixture at first base, playing more games there (1602) than

any other player in the team's history. In fact, with the exception of Powell, no other four Baltimore Orioles first basemen combined have played as many games there as Murray. The all-time team leaders:

Eddie Murray	1602	Tony Muser	248
Boog Powell	1265	Norm Siebern	225
Jim Gentile	561	Gus Triandos	155
Bob Boyd	417	Walt Dropo	133
Lee May	361	Bob Hale	104

Incidentally, trivia experts in baseball folklore and firearms will be interested to know that the only other player in Orioles history to play 100 games at first base is Eddie Waitkus.

But the problem of replacing Murray at first base will be nothing compared to that of finding a bat to fill the cleanup spot that Murray manned almost totally on his own for most of his career. Over the past seven seasons, Murray made 4582 plate appearances batting cleanup, compared to 349 for the rest of the Orioles team combined. Murray's total is 1300 more—which is to say, two full season's worth—than any other player in the majors. He also led cleanup hitters in home runs and RBIs, all while batting .300 in the number-four hole. Major league leaders batting cleanup since 1982:

Player	PA	Player	HR	Player	RBI
Eddie Murray	4582	Eddie Murray	198	Eddie Murray	707
Mike Schmidt	3230	Mike Schmidt	172	Mike Schmidt	524
Andre Thornton	2902	Dale Murphy	145	Lance Parrish	447
Dale Murphy	2858	Lance Parrish	138	Dale Murphy	437
Lance Parrish	2759	Jack Clark	120	Andre Thornton	422

The absence of Murray from the number-four slot may also have a detrimental effect on Cal Ripken, Baltimore's perennial third-place hitter. To gain an appreciation for the support Ripken received by hitting with Murray in the on-deck circle, consider that Orioles number-three hitters have been intentionally walked only 12 times in the past seven seasons. The other major league teams averaged 46 intentional passes to their third-slot hitters. Ripken himself was intentionally walked 17 times since 1982, the lowest total among the 33 players with at least 500 RBIs during that period. Opposing pitchers will certainly exercise more care working to Ripken this season than ever before.

Nevertheless, the effectiveness of Baltimore's offense in 1989 won't depend solely on the question of filling Murray's shoes or supporting Ripken in the middle of the order. Larry Sheets and Phil Bradley had uncharacteristically poor years in 1988, and if both were to rebound to their 1987 levels, the Orioles would certainly score more runs than anyone suspected in the wake of the Murray trade. (For a discussion of players bouncing back from off seasons, see the Philadelphia Phillies essay, page 140.)

That's not to say Baltimore could contend for a division title this season. But turnarounds by Sheets and Bradley would certainly restore some dignity to a team with a proud heritage but a humbling recent past.

WON-LOST RECORD BY STARTING POSITION

BALTIMORE 54-107	C	1B	2B	3B	SS	LF	CF	RF	P	DH	Leadoff	Relief	Starts
Don Aase	·	·	·	·	·	·	·	·	·	·	·	7-28	·
Brady Anderson	·	·	·	·	·	·	15-28	·	·	·	2-3	·	15-28
Jeff Ballard	·	·	·	·	·	·	·	·	10-15	·	·	·	10-15
Jose Bautista	·	·	·	·	·	·	·	·	9-16	·	·	0-8	9-16
Mike Boddicker	·	·	·	·	·	·	·	·	7-14	·	·	·	7-14
Butch Davis	·	·	·	·	·	·	·	4-3	·	0-1	·	·	4-4
Gordon Dillard	·	·	·	·	·	·	·	·	0-1	·	·	0-1	0-1
Jim Dwyer	·	·	·	·	·	·	·	·	·	5-6	·	·	5-6
Ken Gerhart	·	·	·	·	·	3-14	19-30	2-4	·	1-0	3-9	·	25-48
Rene Gonzales	·	0-1	3-5	24-39	·	·	·	·	·	·	·	·	27-45
John Habyan	·	·	·	·	·	·	·	·	·	·	·	1-6	·
Pete Harnisch	·	·	·	·	·	·	·	·	0-2	·	·	·	0-2
Keith Hughes	·	·	·	·	·	·	·	9-20	·	·	4-4	·	9-20
Terry Kennedy	20-55	·	·	·	·	·	·	·	·	·	·	·	20-55
Tito Landrum	·	·	·	·	·	0-1	·	1-5	·	·	0-1	·	1-6
Fred Lynn	·	·	·	·	·	·	20-40	7-11	·	1-1	0-3	·	28-52
Scott McGregor	·	·	·	·	·	·	·	·	0-4	·	·	·	0-4
Bob Milacki	·	·	·	·	·	·	·	·	3-0	·	·	·	3-0
Mike Morgan	·	·	·	·	·	·	·	·	1-9	·	·	2-10	1-9
Eddie Murray	·	27-76	·	·	·	·	·	·	·	27-31	·	·	54-107
Carl Nichols	2-9	·	·	·	·	·	·	1-2	·	·	·	·	3-11
Tom Niedenfuer	·	·	·	·	·	·	·	·	·	·	·	29-23	·
Dickie Noles	·	·	·	·	·	·	·	·	0-2	·	·	·	0-2
Gregg Olson	·	·	·	·	·	·	·	·	·	·	·	3-7	·
Joe Orsulak	·	·	·	·	·	12-17	0-9	11-38	·	·	20-46	·	23-64
Oswaldo Peraza	·	·	·	·	·	·	·	·	8-7	·	·	0-4	8-7
Billy Ripken	·	·	51-95	·	·	·	·	·	·	·	0-2	·	51-95
Cal Ripken	·	·	·	·	54-107	·	·	·	·	·	·	·	54-107
Wade Rowdon	·	·	·	2-2	·	0-3	·	·	·	0-1	·	·	2-6
Bill Scherrer	·	·	·	·	·	·	·	·	·	·	·	0-4	·
Curt Schilling	·	·	·	·	·	·	·	·	1-3	·	·	·	1-3
Dave Schmidt	·	·	·	·	·	·	·	·	6-3	·	·	11-21	6-3
Rick Schu	·	1-3	·	22-46	·	·	·	·	·	2-5	·	·	25-54
Larry Sheets	·	1-1	·	·	·	11-26	·	15-18	·	11-38	·	·	38-83
Doug Sisk	·	·	·	·	·	·	·	·	·	·	·	8-44	·
Pete Stanicek	·	·	0-7	·	28-31	·	·	·	·	·	25-29	·	28-38
Jeff Stone	·	·	·	·	·	0-14	·	0-1	·	0-1	0-10	·	0-16
Mickey Tettleton	32-43	·	·	·	·	·	·	·	·	·	·	·	32-43
Mark Thurmond	·	·	·	·	·	·	·	·	0-6	·	·	11-26	0-6
Jay Tibbs	·	·	·	·	·	·	·	·	7-17	·	·	0-6	7-17
Jim Traber	·	25-26	·	·	·	0-1	·	4-5	·	7-23	·	·	36-55
Mark Williamson	·	·	·	·	·	·	·	·	2-8	·	·	9-18	2-8
Craig Worthington	·	·	·	6-20	·	·	·	·	·	·	·	·	6-20

Batting vs. Left and Right Handed Pitchers

		BA	Rank	SA	Rank	OBA	Rank	HR %	Rank	BB %	Rank	SO %	Rank
Brady Anderson	vs. Lefties	.200	155	.247	157	.277	134	0.00	140	6.12	99	24.49	157
	vs. Righties	.217	150	.300	149	.270	155	0.42	153	6.39	117	19.17	139
Ken Gerhart	vs. Lefties	.186	158	.329	115	.243	159	3.11	56	6.78	86	16.95	118
	vs. Righties	.208	--	.366	--	.277	--	3.96	--	7.89	--	23.68	--
Rene Gonzales	vs. Lefties	.326	17	.407	64	.383	24	1.16	116	8.42	67	11.58	70
	vs. Righties	.152	169	.185	170	.193	170	0.66	139	3.03	165	12.73	70
Terry Kennedy	vs. Lefties	.231	--	.308	--	.268	--	2.56	--	4.76	--	26.19	--
	vs. Righties	.226	139	.296	152	.269	158	0.88	131	5.35	135	17.28	121
Eddie Murray	vs. Lefties	.230	126	.371	89	.288	121	3.29	51	7.73	75	13.73	84
	vs. Righties	.313	14	.531	7	.400	8	5.38	14	12.72	19	10.27	43
Joe Orsulak	vs. Lefties	.235	114	.235	163	.321	72	0.00	140	8.64	62	8.64	36
	vs. Righties	.299	25	.463	31	.333	75	2.57	76	4.78	149	6.87	12
Billy Ripken	vs. Lefties	.220	138	.263	152	.281	127	0.00	140	7.28	79	9.71	47
	vs. Righties	.199	162	.255	165	.249	166	0.61	143	5.10	142	12.18	61
Cal Ripken	vs. Lefties	.316	24	.500	25	.430	8	4.74	27	16.96	6	10.43	55
	vs. Righties	.239	124	.397	73	.342	61	3.64	42	13.73	14	9.80	37
Rick Schu	vs. Lefties	.252	88	.387	81	.305	101	2.52	71	6.25	93	15.63	103
	vs. Righties	.258	84	.344	120	.325	85	0.66	139	7.83	90	17.47	123
Larry Sheets	vs. Lefties	.202	153	.237	162	.305	97	0.88	129	11.45	35	14.50	91
	vs. Righties	.240	121	.379	90	.300	124	2.66	71	7.24	98	14.21	93
Pete Stanicek	vs. Lefties	.236	111	.340	111	.311	88	2.78	62	8.54	63	15.85	106
	vs. Righties	.222	142	.274	161	.316	104	0.00	140	10.37	49	14.07	88
Mickey Tettleton	vs. Lefties	.252	89	.463	44	.313	86	6.12	14	7.98	72	21.47	147
	vs. Righties	.272	58	.382	87	.349	46	1.47	106	9.80	61	22.88	156
Jim Traber	vs. Lefties	.233	122	.302	137	.289	118	1.72	98	6.98	84	13.95	86
	vs. Righties	.216	151	.335	126	.247	167	3.39	52	4.05	159	9.72	36
Team Average	vs. Lefties	.231	14	.337	14	.300	12	2.30	9	8.60	4	15.63	10
	vs. Righties	.242	14	.371	12	.308	13	2.69	6	8.34	9	13.94	5
League Average	vs. Lefties	.259		.391		.321		2.47		7.97		14.12	
	vs. Righties	.259		.391		.326		2.47		8.51		14.39	

Batting with Runners on Base and Bases Empty

		BA	Rank	SA	Rank	OBA	Rank	HR %	Rank	BB %	Rank	SO %	Rank
Brady Anderson	Runners On	.220	150	.288	157	.283	146	0.76	138	6.41	122	17.95	135
	Bases Empty	.207	148	.285	146	.264	155	0.00	156	6.25	109	22.60	149
Ken Gerhart	Runners On	.155	170	.233	166	.235	167	1.94	90	8.26	87	12.40	76
	Bases Empty	.220	138	.415	56	.271	150	4.40	31	6.47	102	24.71	155
Rene Gonzales	Runners On	.253	108	.275	160	.314	117	0.00	148	6.54	119	10.28	51
	Bases Empty	.192	161	.260	162	.229	167	1.37	112	3.92	159	13.73	78
Terry Kennedy	Runners On	.185	164	.222	168	.231	168	0.00	148	5.88	133	20.17	150
	Bases Empty	.255	84	.350	110	.295	109	1.91	93	4.82	142	17.47	121
Eddie Murray	Runners On	.279	67	.504	17	.365	45	5.43	10	12.26	37	9.75	44
	Bases Empty	.287	32	.450	36	.358	30	3.98	37	9.92	44	12.95	63
Joe Orsulak	Runners On	.252	109	.357	122	.299	134	1.74	95	5.19	146	5.19	11
	Bases Empty	.303	14	.451	35	.345	43	2.27	82	5.69	121	8.19	18
Billy Ripken	Runners On	.185	164	.222	168	.249	165	0.53	142	6.05	129	7.44	20
	Bases Empty	.220	139	.279	151	.267	151	0.31	154	5.81	116	13.66	77
Cal Ripken	Runners On	.258	104	.443	47	.376	35	4.07	34	16.85	10	7.53	23
	Bases Empty	.268	51	.424	45	.368	22	3.95	39	13.41	12	11.71	53
Rick Schu	Runners On	.305	32	.415	72	.349	66	1.69	97	5.56	138	15.87	117
	Bases Empty	.217	142	.322	130	.292	120	1.32	115	8.33	71	17.26	117
Larry Sheets	Runners On	.260	102	.391	92	.315	116	2.60	75	7.51	100	15.49	112
	Bases Empty	.208	147	.308	136	.292	118	1.92	92	8.93	63	13.40	75
Pete Stanicek	Runners On	.276	69	.310	149	.385	25	0.00	148	14.68	17	10.09	50
	Bases Empty	.207	150	.310	135	.274	146	2.30	80	6.32	105	17.89	128
Mickey Tettleton	Runners On	.230	140	.405	77	.340	83	3.97	36	13.91	20	23.84	160
	Bases Empty	.287	34	.439	38	.321	73	3.82	41	4.24	151	20.61	145
Jim Traber	Runners On	.270	87	.417	69	.299	135	4.29	29	4.57	153	12.00	68
	Bases Empty	.180	165	.243	165	.229	166	1.59	105	5.47	125	10.45	39
Team Average	Runners On	.234	14	.353	14	.307	14	2.55	5	9.39	5	13.25	4
	Bases Empty	.241	13	.363	13	.304	11	2.56	7	7.74	6	15.45	10
League Average	Runners On	.268		.401		.336		2.45		9.09		13.68	
	Bases Empty	.253		.383		.315		2.48		7.76		14.81	

Overall Batting Compared to Late Inning Pressure Situations

		BA	Rank	SA	Rank	OBA	Rank	HR %	Rank	BB %	Rank	SO %	Rank	RDI %	Rank
Brady Anderson	Overall	.212	159	.286	160	.272	157	0.31	161	6.32	117	20.60	146	.205	157
	Pressure	.106	170	.128	170	.176	169	0.00	110	1.92	166	34.62	167	.000	165
Ken Gerhart	Overall	.195	169	.344	122	.256	168	3.44	50	7.22	100	19.59	141	.217	145
	Pressure	.163	153	.279	134	.250	148	2.33	66	10.42	53	16.67	91	.000	165
Rene Gonzales	Overall	.215	157	.266	167	.263	165	0.84	141	5.00	151	12.31	67	.231	131
	Pressure	.289	49	.316	111	.289	120	0.00	110	0.00	168	20.00	110	.250	--
Terry Kennedy	Overall	.226	143	.298	157	.269	162	1.13	122	5.26	137	18.60	137	.182	166
	Pressure	.171	149	.268	139	.244	151	2.44	63	8.89	77	17.78	98	.000	165
Eddie Murray	Overall	.284	36	.474	23	.361	33	4.64	25	11.01	38	11.45	53	.252	102
	Pressure	.229	109	.365	80	.308	98	2.08	74	10.28	54	18.69	104	.250	72
Joe Orsulak	Overall	.288	34	.422	54	.331	67	2.11	91	5.53	133	7.21	13	.221	141
	Pressure	.281	59	.375	74	.329	81	0.00	110	7.04	102	5.63	11	.222	85
Billy Ripken	Overall	.207	167	.258	169	.260	167	0.39	159	5.90	125	11.27	52	.240	116
	Pressure	.243	94	.300	122	.299	109	0.00	110	6.49	116	15.58	85	.235	80
Cal Ripken	Overall	.264	67	.431	44	.372	22	4.00	32	14.80	6	10.01	37	.333	17
	Pressure	.278	61	.400	64	.381	29	2.22	69	13.33	21	10.48	39	.313	49
Rick Schu	Overall	.256	90	.363	108	.316	91	1.48	109	7.14	101	16.67	119	.210	152
	Pressure	.316	32	.395	66	.422	14	2.63	58	15.56	11	17.78	98	.000	165
Larry Sheets	Overall	.230	136	.343	123	.302	123	2.21	82	8.33	78	14.29	88	.248	109
	Pressure	.325	24	.413	58	.396	21	1.25	104	9.89	61	13.19	63	.300	53
Pete Stanicek	Overall	.230	137	.310	150	.313	100	1.53	106	9.36	58	15.05	102	.228	134
	Pressure	.159	154	.182	164	.240	152	0.00	110	10.00	57	18.00	101	.350	37
Mickey Tettleton	Overall	.261	77	.424	51	.330	69	3.89	34	8.86	69	22.15	156	.233	129
	Pressure	.214	120	.357	86	.267	136	3.57	43	6.67	112	31.67	163	.130	137
Jim Traber	Overall	.222	148	.324	140	.261	166	2.84	67	5.05	149	11.17	50	.221	139
	Pressure	.150	163	.150	167	.203	163	0.00	110	6.25	121	7.81	22	.214	90
Team Average	Overall	.238	14	.359	14	.305	13	2.56	7	8.43	7	14.53	7	.229	14
	Pressure	.224	14	.303	14	.298	13	1.24	13	9.36	3	18.01	9	.195	13
League Average	Overall	.259		.391		.324		2.47		8.35		14.31		.269	
	Pressure	.249		.365		.319		2.28		8.71		17.04		.246	

Additional Miscellaneous Batting Comparisons

	Grass Surface BA	Rank	Artificial Surface BA	Rank	Home Games BA	Rank	Road Games BA	Rank	Runners in Scoring Position BA	Rank	Runners in Scoring Pos and Two Outs BA	Rank	Leading Off Inning OBA	Rank	Runners on 3B with less than 2 Outs RDI %	Rank
Brady Anderson	.216	148	.193	155	.195	162	.232	128	.250	101	.107	168	.211	164	.429	147
Ken Gerhart	.202	161	.163	165	.231	133	.159	170	.191	160	.241	78	.227	159	.667	33
Rene Gonzales	.230	125	.152	169	.220	148	.210	150	.214	145	.174	147	.213	162	.667	33
Terry Kennedy	.222	139	.257	--	.176	169	.279	48	.179	166	.147	158	.397	11	.556	89
Eddie Murray	.289	31	.255	98	.283	48	.284	40	.234	121	.207	119	.335	58	.391	160
Joe Orsulak	.288	33	.288	57	.287	39	.288	34	.246	103	.243	74	.359	33	.818	4
Billy Ripken	.214	153	.156	168	.222	144	.191	163	.219	141	.273	51	.273	129	.571	81
Cal Ripken	.253	89	.329	17	.263	80	.266	67	.267	75	.180	144	.375	19	.828	3
Rick Schu	.247	100	.333	--	.234	126	.279	48	.235	116	.160	153	.229	157	.333	--
Larry Sheets	.223	137	.268	83	.206	156	.252	92	.235	116	.302	32	.319	74	.464	139
Pete Stanicek	.249	97	.094	--	.252	97	.206	152	.273	67	.333	--	.228	158	.364	167
Mickey Tettleton	.258	79	.277	70	.278	60	.247	107	.214	145	.273	51	.288	115	.467	137
Jim Traber	.227	129	.189	156	.239	116	.202	155	.230	127	.214	110	.247	150	.500	115
Team Average	.241	13	.222	14	.238	14	.238	14	.217	14	.204	12	.301	9	.537	12
League Average	.256		.267		.262		.257		.262		.239		.311		.570	

Pitching vs. Left and Right Handed Batters

		BA	Rank	SA	Rank	OBA	Rank	HR %	Rank	BB %	Rank	SO %	Rank
Don Aase	vs. Lefties	.250	52	.417	94	.434	125	2.78	95	24.75	130	13.86	55
	vs. Righties	.232	--	.368	--	.318	--	2.11	--	11.11	--	12.96	--
Jeff Ballard	vs. Lefties	.287	98	.437	104	.340	87	3.45	113	6.38	30	12.77	62
	vs. Righties	.277	98	.425	95	.329	82	2.34	55	6.43	42	5.18	126
Jose Bautista	vs. Lefties	.258	62	.432	103	.314	43	3.90	122	6.37	29	9.97	91
	vs. Righties	.257	64	.384	66	.306	47	2.42	60	6.11	38	11.11	109
Mike Morgan	vs. Lefties	.317	118	.492	119	.372	112	3.17	109	7.97	47	9.42	99
	vs. Righties	.203	15	.297	9	.267	11	1.35	17	7.45	59	9.94	119
Tom Niedenfuer	vs. Lefties	.291	104	.473	115	.371	110	3.64	118	9.52	77	12.70	66
	vs. Righties	.229	--	.356	--	.270	--	3.39	--	5.56	--	19.05	--
Oswaldo Peraza	vs. Lefties	.239	41	.381	68	.324	62	2.58	85	10.67	97	17.42	26
	vs. Righties	.318	127	.495	120	.376	126	3.13	95	8.41	78	14.02	71
Dave Schmidt	vs. Lefties	.266	74	.393	81	.300	31	2.78	95	4.81	10	13.33	58
	vs. Righties	.258	71	.388	69	.335	92	2.92	85	9.23	95	11.44	104
Doug Sisk	vs. Lefties	.358	129	.415	93	.450	129	0.63	12	13.54	121	5.73	129
	vs. Righties	.264	77	.330	25	.329	83	1.02	8	8.72	86	6.88	125
Mark Thurmond	vs. Lefties	.241	45	.342	38	.330	70	2.53	83	10.64	95	12.77	62
	vs. Righties	.290	114	.510	123	.342	98	3.81	112	7.46	60	7.46	123
Jay Tibbs	vs. Lefties	.299	111	.461	111	.367	106	2.69	91	9.55	78	12.47	68
	vs. Righties	.285	108	.431	101	.344	104	3.05	94	8.16	73	10.57	113
Mark Williamson	vs. Lefties	.265	73	.426	100	.337	82	3.14	106	9.96	87	12.35	70
	vs. Righties	.280	102	.436	106	.327	79	2.97	88	5.86	32	14.84	59
Team Average	vs. Lefties	.278	13	.422	13	.350	13	2.83	13	9.52	9	11.76	11
	vs. Righties	.272	14	.419	13	.331	13	2.75	8	7.72	9	11.38	14
League Average	vs. Lefties	.262		.387		.331		2.24		9.12		13.21	
	vs. Righties	.258		.393		.320		2.63		7.80		15.09	

Pitching with Runners on Base and Bases Empty

		BA	Rank	SA	Rank	OBA	Rank	HR %	Rank	BB %	Rank	SO %	Rank
Jeff Ballard	Runners On	.240	36	.370	51	.301	30	2.85	84	6.91	29	6.55	122
	Bases Empty	.305	125	.466	119	.351	114	2.26	67	6.07	40	6.07	128
Jose Bautista	Runners On	.249	50	.449	105	.291	18	4.91	125	5.23	6	9.41	113
	Bases Empty	.263	81	.381	68	.323	79	2.01	50	6.91	56	11.29	100
Mike Morgan	Runners On	.381	--	.598	--	.459	--	4.12	--	11.61	--	4.46	--
	Bases Empty	.186	3	.271	8	.230	2	1.13	13	5.35	25	12.83	78
Tom Niedenfuer	Runners On	.269	72	.370	50	.323	56	2.52	73	6.06	16	10.61	98
	Bases Empty	.248	--	.459	--	.317	--	4.59	--	9.17	--	21.67	--
Oswaldo Peraza	Runners On	.322	121	.523	125	.402	125	4.03	119	12.43	115	11.86	83
	Bases Empty	.253	63	.384	71	.312	63	2.02	52	6.98	58	18.60	29
Dave Schmidt	Runners On	.235	24	.359	41	.296	23	2.30	65	7.35	33	12.65	77
	Bases Empty	.284	108	.415	98	.334	97	3.27	101	6.76	53	12.16	85
Doug Sisk	Runners On	.337	125	.400	73	.413	128	1.05	19	11.21	104	4.93	126
	Bases Empty	.271	96	.331	24	.353	115	0.60	4	10.70	116	8.02	124
Mark Thurmond	Runners On	.266	69	.459	110	.354	95	3.67	110	11.54	107	5.38	125
	Bases Empty	.283	107	.467	120	.328	89	3.33	103	6.25	43	11.46	96
Jay Tibbs	Runners On	.347	128	.531	126	.399	123	3.05	123	8.28	54	11.92	82
	Bases Empty	.253	65	.387	76	.325	84	2.72	88	9.36	94	11.33	99
Mark Williamson	Runners On	.344	127	.550	129	.408	127	4.23	123	9.68	87	13.36	64
	Bases Empty	.222	24	.348	37	.276	17	2.22	62	6.55	50	13.79	69
Team Average	Runners On	.288	14	.447	14	.356	14	3.15	14	9.25	9	10.31	14
	Bases Empty	.264	11	.399	11	.326	12	2.51	6	7.92	8	12.54	13
League Average	Runners On	.268		.401		.336		2.45		9.09		13.68	
	Bases Empty	.253		.383		.315		2.48		7.76		14.81	

Overall Pitching Compared to Late Inning Pressure Situations

		BA	Rank	SA	Rank	OBA	Rank	HR %	Rank	BB %	Rank	SO %	Rank
Don Aase	Overall	.240	--	.389	--	.374	--	2.40	--	17.70	--	13.40	--
	Pressure	.361	123	.583	126	.405	119	2.78	85	8.89	64	15.56	52
Jeff Ballard	Overall	.278	103	.427	106	.330	80	2.50	74	6.42	23	6.27	126
	Pressure	.235	51	.412	89	.278	89	3.92	105	5.26	20	8.77	113
Jose Bautista	Overall	.258	63	.408	89	.310	41	3.16	105	6.24	22	10.54	105
	Pressure	.266	88	.375	70	.299	38	3.13	95	4.48	13	5.97	123
Mike Morgan	Overall	.255	57	.387	68	.315	49	2.19	62	7.69	52	9.70	116
	Pressure	.146	4	.220	6	.186	1	0.00	1	4.65	15	11.63	96
Tom Niedenfuer	Overall	.259	65	.412	92	.320	59	3.51	115	7.54	46	15.87	44
	Pressure	.264	84	.368	64	.336	73	1.89	58	9.09	66	14.88	60
Oswaldo Peraza	Overall	.282	109	.444	113	.352	113	2.88	92	9.44	92	15.56	48
	Pressure	.333	--	.500	--	.467	--	0.00	--	13.33	--	20.00	--
Dave Schmidt	Overall	.262	68	.390	74	.317	55	2.85	92	7.02	35	12.38	84
	Pressure	.273	94	.384	76	.345	87	3.03	91	8.85	63	15.93	51
Doug Sisk	Overall	.306	126	.368	48	.385	127	0.84	4	10.98	114	6.34	125
	Pressure	.446	129	.554	122	.538	129	1.54	42	15.48	120	4.76	126
Mark Thurmond	Overall	.277	102	.464	120	.339	92	3.46	113	8.39	70	9.01	121
	Pressure	.209	24	.403	84	.341	82	4.48	113	15.85	121	13.41	80
Jay Tibbs	Overall	.293	118	.447	114	.356	116	2.86	93	8.90	84	11.58	96
	Pressure	.250	67	.438	98	.379	109	4.17	110	16.95	125	15.25	57
Mark Williamson	Overall	.272	92	.431	108	.332	81	3.05	98	7.89	58	13.61	68
	Pressure	.329	118	.512	119	.409	122	2.44	71	11.58	95	6.32	122
Team Average	Overall	.274	14	.420	14	.340	14	2.79	14	8.52	8	11.55	14
	Pressure	.274	13	.431	14	.358	14	3.09	13	10.84	13	12.11	14
League Average	Overall	.259		.391		.324		2.47		8.35		14.31	
	Pressure	.249		.369		.324		2.26		9.33		15.69	

Additional Miscellaneous Pitching Comparisons

	Grass Surface		Artificial Surface		Home Games		Road Games		Runners in Scoring Position		Runners in Scoring Pos and Two Outs		Leading Off Inning	
	BA	Rank	BA	Rank	BA	Rank	BA	Rank	BA	Rank	BA	Rank	OBA	Rank
Don Aase	.240	42	.237	--	.197	--	.275	--	.321	--	.345	--	.302	--
Jeff Ballard	.280	108	.274	68	.280	100	.276	86	.306	115	.317	117	.329	87
Jose Bautista	.262	70	.226	20	.258	70	.257	67	.228	35	.236	65	.319	75
Mike Morgan	.238	38	.317	113	.204	9	.320	127	.371	128	.321	120	.225	6
Tom Niedenfuer	.274	97	.184	--	.256	67	.262	--	.250	--	.171	24	.244	--
Oswaldo Peraza	.276	102	.316	112	.264	81	.302	114	.333	123	.302	110	.330	88
Dave Schmidt	.265	73	.247	39	.285	103	.238	37	.250	54	.250	78	.361	107
Doug Sisk	.301	123	.353	--	.289	109	.322	129	.283	86	.161	17	.338	92
Mark Thurmond	.268	84	.311	110	.252	58	.293	108	.230	36	.216	52	.205	3
Jay Tibbs	.293	120	.289	88	.277	94	.321	128	.318	120	.321	119	.304	59
Mark Williamson	.270	90	.292	93	.241	49	.308	118	.336	126	.327	123	.252	16
Team Average	.272	14	.288	13	.261	9	.288	14	.285	14	.270	13	.308	6
League Average	.256		.267		.257		.262		.262		.239		.311	

BOSTON RED SOX

- Joe Morgan made all the right moves—restoring Boggs to the leadoff spot included.
- Winning at Fenway calls for finesse, not power.

Last year, we published the results of a study that took us nearly two years to complete, and pronounced Billy Martin the best manager in major league history. Some of our readers disagreed. Some of our colleagues disagreed. Even within our office, the survey created its share of disagreement.

Shortly after the 1988 *Analyst* reached the bookstores, the principles themselves got into the act. George Steinbrenner voiced *his* disagreement in the only way he knows how. *Sayonara,* Billy. And a month after that, Boston named Joe Morgan to replace John McNamara as manager. Morgan immediately set about the task of proving to all the world that *he,* in fact, was the best of all time. It took him about two months.

Morgan took over at the All-Star break, with the Sox in fourth place, nine games behind the division-leading Tigers. The Sox won their next 12 games, 24 in a row at home (an A.L. record), caught the Tigers by the first week in September, and drew away to a division title.

Well, we were wondering a few weeks ago, what was it, exactly, that made Morgan the best manager ever? So we took a look at the differences between his Red Sox and those who played under McNamara during the first half of the season, and here's what we found.

Morgan, of course, benefited from the arrival of several players after McNamara's departure, most notably Mike Boddicker and Larry Parrish. He reduced the roles of Spike Owen and Jim Rice, and defined roles for everyone—even Randy Kutcher (pinch runner). But more important, Morgan made better and more frequent use of several players that Mac underutilized, particularly rookie shortstop Jody Reed and Todd Benzinger. Did those moves win the pennant for Boston? You tell us. But before you decide, consider these facts:

- Reed, who made only 21 starts under McNamara, started all but seven games after Morgan took over. He batted .314 during that time, to rank 6th in the A.L. after the All-Star break.

- Benzinger started only 39 of 85 games for McNamara; Morgan gave him 61 starts. And despite sitting 16 games even after Morgan took over, Benzinger managed to tie Mike Greenwell for the team lead in RBI after the break with 48, good for 7th place in the A.L.

Playing Benzinger at first base allowed Morgan to move Dwight Evans back to right field. Morgan also promoted Wes Gardner from the bullpen to the starting rotation in place of Jeff Sellers, and utilized Tom Bolton as his southpaw relief specialist against left-handed hitters (as McNamara himself had used Joe Sambito so effectively in 1986).

And finally, Morgan restored Wade Boggs to the leadoff spot in the batting order, where he'd appeared only occasionally since taking a regular turn there in 1984. Boston talk-show hosts like Eddie Andelman and Chuck Wilson spent the intervening years regularly debating the pros and cons of Boggs as leadoff hitter with incensed callers. But the statistics of the past five years indicate that Boggs batting in the leadoff spot, like Evans playing in right field, is exactly where he belongs.

The table below classifies Boggs's starts from 1984 through 1988 according to whether or not he batted leadoff. It shows the difference between (1) the number of runs Boston scored in those games; and (2) the runs they "should have scored" based on an analysis of each game's totals (AB, H, 2B, 3B, HR, BB, SB, etc.). After all, a player's position in the batting order can only affect his team's performance in two ways: by getting him to the plate more often (and on that count, batting Boggs leadoff is obviously desirable), or by creating more runs from the hits and walks the team gets through some sort of dynamic interaction with the other players in the lineup. Simply stated, with Boggs batting leadoff, the Sox have scored more runs than expected; with Boggs elsewhere, they've underperformed those expectations:

Batting Order Slot	Games	Expected Runs	Actual Runs	Diff.
Batting leadoff	339	1732	1744	+ 12
Not batting leadoff	426	2137	2121	− 16

The differences aren't massive, but, as with most of Morgan's moves, the facts tend to support his decision to restore Boggs to the leadoff spot.

Boston's turnaround under Morgan last July was so spectacular that it prompted the widespread knee-jerk reaction that no manager could possibly have caused such a turn of events. True enough, but Morgan was hardly a *laissez-faire* leader. He made lots of changes, and almost all of them helped. Morgan wasn't simply along for the ride; he was in the driver's seat.

Funny thought: What if, after decades of hoarding right-handed home run hitters, the Red Sox discovered that they'd have been better off stocking up on contact hitters with high batting averages, power be damned? Hard to believe? Consider these facts:

- Red Sox batters accumulated the fewest strike-outs in the American League in each of the past three seasons, a category in which they hadn't led the league for 67 years. Their reward: two A.L. championships in those three years, as many as they won in the previous 67 seasons.

- Boston has won four pennants in the last 22 years. In three of those four seasons, the Sox ranked higher in batting average than in home runs. They led the league in both categories in 1967.

- Boston led the A.L. in home runs seven times in 13 years from 1967 through 1979, but won only one pennant during that time. When the Sox won the A.L. title in 1975, they ranked fifth in homers.

A more thorough analysis provides further evidence that Boston has indeed benefited more from slap hitters than from thumpers (with a small *t*, that is). That won't surprise the many Sox fanatics who have contended for years that the team's ponderous lineup of slow power hitters was a greater liability in road games than it was an advantage at Fenway Park. (Is *ponderous* another of those marvelous Boston adjectives, George?) What *will* probably surprise them is what shocked us: *Even in the shadow of the Green Monster,* Boston derived no more benefit from the home run hitters than from the contact hitters.

See for yourself: The Red Sox led the league in batting average 17 times since the construction of the Olive Ogre. They compiled a winning percentage 144 points higher at home than on the road in those seasons. That figure represents their home-field advantage in those years. Now compare that spread to Boston's margins in seasons in which it led the league in home runs or in strikeouts. The differences are nearly identical:

Category	Home Games W–L	Pct.	Road Games W–L	Pct.	Diff.
Fewest Strikeouts	289–178	.619	213–237	.473	+.146
Most Home Runs	442–278	.614	338–382	.469	+.144
Highest Batting Average	827–482	.632	641–672	.488	+.144

By contrast, the home-run hitters proved to be more of a liability on the road than did the high-batting average hitters, just as the Fenway faithful suspected through so many seasons of frustration. The following tables show that the 17 Red Sox teams that led the A.L. in batting average scored an average of 4.68 runs per game on the road, more than half a run per game more than the home-run leaders. Some of that margin can be explained by the fact that Boston often led the league in batting average in seasons that were generally high-scoring years on a league wide basis. But even comparing Boston's road-game scoring averages to the corresponding *league* averages in those seasons, the batting average teams outscored the power-hitting teams on the road:

Category	Years	Boston Runs/G	League Runs/G	Diff.
Highest Batting Average	17	4.68	4.41	+0.27
Most Home Runs	9	4.16	4.04	+0.12
Fewest Strikeouts	6	4.37	4.50	−0.13

The differences between the groups aren't extreme enough to conclude with certainty that contact-hitting, high-batting-average teams are more suited to Fenway Park than power-hitting teams. But the numbers clearly trend in that direction, and they make it nearly impossible to support the opposite point of view—a viewpoint that we espoused as recently as three years ago.

But since then, the Sox have strung together three consecutive seasons of 50 or more wins at home, something only one other team has accomplished during the 1980s (the New York Yankees from 1983 through 1985). Along the way, Boston fashioned a streak of 24 straight wins at Fenway Park, the longest home winning streak in American League history. The Red Sox achieved all that with an uncharacteristic disdain for the long ball, and much of the credit goes to Walt Hriniak, the team's batting coach. But just as Hriniak's philosophy—frequently criticized in Boston during his tenure—has been vindicated, he has ended his 12–year association with the Sox.

Hriniak joined the team as a bullpen coach in 1977. And although he didn't replace Johnny Pesky as the official batting coach until 1985, Hriniak's influence over Boston's personnel has grown constantly since the early 1980s. The effect of the Hriniak hitting philosophy, embodied in the exaggerated helicopter swings of Dwight Evans and Rich Gedman, is clearly illustrated in the following tables. Look at where Boston ranked in the American League in home runs, batting average, and strikeouts in each of the last three Olympiads. The bottom line, the average ranks for each four-year period, paints a vivid picture:

Year	HR	BA	SO	Year	HR	BA	SO	Year	HR	BA	SO
1977	1	2	10	1981	5	1	10	1985	5	1	5
1978	2	4	11	1982	9	3	4	1986	11	3	1
1979	1	1	7	1983	7	6	5	1987	9	1	1
1980	3	3	6	1984	2	1	8	1988	10	1	1
Avg.	2	3	8	Avg.	6	3	7	Avg.	9	2	2

Boston's rank in home runs decreased in proportion to Hriniak's increasing influence as the team's hitting instructor, official or otherwise. It's worth noting that the team's performance not only reflected the coach's philosophy, but to some degree mirrored his own brief major league career. You see, Hriniak doesn't pronounce the first letter of his last name, and as a player he totally ignored the first *two*: He didn't hit a HR in 99 career at-bats. In fact, he didn't have an extra-base hit of any sort. With the exception of pitchers, only one player in major league history had more at-bats and no extra-base hits: Ossie Blanco (102 AB).

While his career as a player was meager, Boston's success of the past few seasons places Hriniak in the batting coach Hall of Fame, alongside guys like Charley Lau and Harry Walker. Whether the Hriniak style would have been suited to other teams playing 81 games a season somewhere other than Fenway Park is as irrelevant as it is uncertain. Hriniak succeeded by challenging the wisdom of a decades-old rule—namely, that to win at Fenway, you need right-handed power hitters swinging for the Green Monster. We like guys like that.

WON-LOST RECORD BY STARTING POSITION

BOSTON 89-73	C	1B	2B	3B	SS	LF	CF	RF	P	DH	Leadoff	Relief	Starts
Brady Anderson	-	-	-	-	-	7-10	14-10	-	-	-	8-6	-	21-20
Marty Barrett	-	-	83-65	-	-	-	-	-	-	-	-	1-2	83-65
Todd Benzinger	-	33-24	-	-	-	1-1	-	19-21	-	1-0	-	-	54-46
Mike Boddicker	-	-	-	-	-	-	-	-	7-7	-	-	1-0	7-7
Wade Boggs	-	-	-	84-67	-	-	-	-	-	2-1	50-41	-	86-68
Tom Bolton	-	-	-	-	-	-	-	-	-	-	-	11-17	-
Oil Can Boyd	-	-	-	-	-	-	-	-	13-10	-	-	-	13-10
Ellis Burks	-	-	-	-	-	-	81-58	-	-	-	18-13	-	81-58
Rick Cerone	35-34	-	-	-	-	-	-	-	-	1-0	-	-	36-34
Roger Clemens	-	-	-	-	-	-	-	-	22-13	-	-	-	22-13
Zack Crouch	-	-	-	-	-	-	-	-	-	-	-	0-3	-
Steve Curry	-	-	-	-	-	-	-	-	2-1	-	-	-	2-1
Pat Dodson	-	5-7	-	-	-	-	-	-	-	-	-	-	5-7
Steve Ellsworth	-	-	-	-	-	-	-	-	2-5	-	-	0-1	2-5
Dwight Evans	-	32-29	-	-	-	-	-	43-35	-	4-2	-	-	79-66
Wes Gardner	-	-	-	-	-	-	-	-	8-10	-	-	8-10	8-10
Rich Gedman	50-35	-	-	-	-	-	-	-	-	1-0	-	-	51-35
Mike Greenwell	-	-	-	-	-	80-60	-	4-3	-	3-8	-	-	87-71
Sam Horn	-	-	-	-	-	-	-	-	-	9-7	-	-	9-7
Bruce Hurst	-	-	-	-	-	-	-	-	22-10	-	-	0-1	22-10
Randy Kutcher	-	-	0-1	-	-	1-1	1-0	-	-	-	-	-	2-2
Dennis Lamp	-	-	-	-	-	-	-	-	-	-	-	23-23	-
John Marzano	4-4	-	-	-	-	-	-	-	-	-	-	-	4-4
Spike Owen	-	-	-	-	35-36	-	-	-	-	-	3-5	-	35-36
Larry Parrish	-	19-13	-	-	-	-	-	-	9-4	-	-	-	28-17
Carlos Quintana	-	-	-	-	-	-	0-1	-	-	-	-	-	0-1
Jody Reed	-	-	4-7	2-0	51-32	-	-	-	-	-	9-6	-	57-39
Jim Rice	-	-	-	-	-	7-11	-	-	-	59-51	-	-	66-62
Mike Rochford	-	-	-	-	-	-	-	-	-	-	-	0-2	-
Ed Romero	-	-	2-1	3-5	3-5	-	-	-	-	-	-	-	8-11
Kevin Romine	-	-	-	-	-	-	1-5	8-3	-	-	-	-	9-8
Jeff Sellers	-	-	-	-	-	-	-	-	2-10	-	-	1-5	2-10
Lee Smith	-	-	-	-	-	-	-	-	-	-	-	44-20	-
Mike Smithson	-	-	-	-	-	-	-	-	11-7	-	-	4-9	11-7
Bob Stanley	-	-	-	-	-	-	-	-	-	-	-	28-29	-
John Trautwein	-	-	-	-	-	-	-	-	-	-	-	0-9	-
Rob Woodward	-	-	-	-	-	-	-	-	-	-	-	0-1	-

Batting vs. Left and Right Handed Pitchers

		BA	Rank	SA	Rank	OBA	Rank	HR %	Rank	BB %	Rank	SO %	Rank
Marty Barrett	vs. Lefties	.254	83	.298	139	.292	113	0.00	140	4.55	127	5.05	8
	vs. Righties	.295	32	.353	113	.345	53	0.23	160	6.34	118	5.11	6
Todd Benzinger	vs. Lefties	.212	146	.308	134	.259	147	0.96	126	6.14	98	10.53	56
	vs. Righties	.269	62	.465	29	.305	114	3.99	32	4.66	152	21.12	146
Wade Boggs	vs. Lefties	.331	14	.453	50	.458	3	1.16	116	18.06	4	7.87	27
	vs. Righties	.381	1	.505	14	.483	1	0.73	137	17.10	2	3.38	1
Ellis Burks	vs. Lefties	.324	18	.486	33	.410	16	3.52	48	12.65	24	10.84	59
	vs. Righties	.284	42	.480	18	.351	42	3.27	55	9.13	71	15.81	107
Rick Cerone	vs. Lefties	.307	32	.404	66	.333	60	0.88	129	3.33	155	7.50	20
	vs. Righties	.240	120	.327	132	.321	92	1.33	112	9.47	67	13.61	81
Dwight Evans	vs. Lefties	.333	12	.521	19	.439	4	4.17	31	16.18	9	12.72	75
	vs. Righties	.280	46	.475	22	.351	40	3.61	44	10.17	52	16.31	116
Rich Gedman	vs. Lefties	.243	--	.378	--	.326	--	0.00	--	6.67	--	13.33	--
	vs. Righties	.229	134	.366	103	.271	153	3.44	48	5.23	139	14.98	99
Mike Greenwell	vs. Lefties	.289	45	.416	59	.332	65	2.03	85	3.74	147	7.48	19
	vs. Righties	.344	2	.588	2	.453	2	4.58	22	16.49	6	4.59	5
Spike Owen	vs. Lefties	.276	59	.480	37	.324	71	4.08	33	6.67	88	11.43	69
	vs. Righties	.233	128	.302	148	.324	86	0.63	141	10.58	43	7.94	18
Larry Parrish	vs. Lefties	.222	137	.325	121	.272	138	2.38	74	5.15	120	25.74	159
	vs. Righties	.214	153	.375	92	.269	156	3.93	34	6.89	108	24.92	159
Jody Reed	vs. Lefties	.226	133	.262	153	.301	104	0.00	140	9.28	53	8.25	32
	vs. Righties	.315	13	.413	62	.405	6	0.39	154	11.88	27	4.29	3
Jim Rice	vs. Lefties	.290	41	.477	39	.349	45	3.87	39	7.10	83	17.16	120
	vs. Righties	.252	98	.373	95	.322	91	2.73	68	9.65	65	16.09	112
Team Average	vs. Lefties	.287	2	.408	4	.357	1	1.87	14	8.89	3	10.54	1
	vs. Righties	.281	1	.425	2	.357	1	2.38	9	10.22	1	11.88	1
League Average	vs. Lefties	.259		.391		.321		2.47		7.97		14.12	
	vs. Righties	.259		.391		.326		2.47		8.51		14.39	

Batting with Runners on Base and Bases Empty

		BA	Rank	SA	Rank	OBA	Rank	HR %	Rank	BB %	Rank	SO %	Rank
Marty Barrett	Runners On	.303	37	.358	118	.343	75	0.32	147	5.54	139	4.71	8
	Bases Empty	.262	70	.315	134	.316	84	0.00	156	6.13	111	5.52	7
Todd Benzinger	Runners On	.245	119	.420	65	.278	153	3.00	61	4.59	152	19.27	149
	Bases Empty	.263	69	.429	42	.307	101	3.41	46	5.50	123	17.43	120
Wade Boggs	Runners On	.339	8	.452	39	.455	1	0.42	146	18.15	4	4.95	10
	Bases Empty	.386	1	.516	14	.490	1	1.16	126	16.83	2	4.57	4
Ellis Burks	Runners On	.326	15	.547	8	.396	17	3.75	43	10.58	52	11.86	67
	Bases Empty	.264	67	.418	52	.337	52	2.93	62	9.57	49	17.16	115
Rick Cerone	Runners On	.270	84	.402	80	.328	97	1.64	98	6.67	116	11.85	66
	Bases Empty	.268	55	.324	128	.325	69	0.70	145	7.14	90	10.39	37
Dwight Evans	Runners On	.316	22	.549	6	.396	18	4.61	23	12.29	35	14.80	106
	Bases Empty	.267	58	.412	57	.348	36	2.75	68	11.15	28	16.03	100
Rich Gedman	Runners On	.232	136	.387	96	.273	157	3.52	49	5.52	140	14.11	99
	Bases Empty	.229	129	.350	110	.284	134	2.55	73	5.33	129	15.38	98
Mike Greenwell	Runners On	.326	14	.541	10	.418	10	4.75	21	13.23	25	5.82	12
	Bases Empty	.325	4	.518	13	.413	2	2.55	72	11.75	21	5.08	5
Spike Owen	Runners On	.216	152	.320	142	.330	95	1.03	123	12.30	34	9.02	37
	Bases Empty	.269	50	.400	69	.320	76	2.50	76	6.98	92	9.30	31
Larry Parrish	Runners On	.225	143	.335	138	.279	152	2.20	85	6.47	121	20.40	153
	Bases Empty	.210	146	.379	89	.263	156	4.46	29	6.25	109	29.17	166
Jody Reed	Runners On	.290	56	.370	113	.383	26	0.72	139	10.98	47	6.94	19
	Bases Empty	.295	24	.380	88	.379	13	0.00	156	11.45	25	3.96	1
Jim Rice	Runners On	.273	77	.442	48	.343	73	3.90	39	9.81	60	14.72	105
	Bases Empty	.256	78	.374	91	.318	80	2.36	78	7.94	76	18.05	131
Team Average	Runners On	.288	1	.437	2	.363	1	2.61	4	10.29	1	11.13	1
	Bases Empty	.279	1	.404	3	.351	1	1.90	13	9.40	1	11.85	1
League Average	Runners On	.268		.401		.336		2.45		9.09		13.68	
	Bases Empty	.253		.383		.315		2.48		7.76		14.81	

Overall Batting Compared to Late Inning Pressure Situations

		BA	Rank	SA	Rank	OBA	Rank	HR %	Rank	BB %	Rank	SO %	Rank	RDI %	Rank
Marty Barrett	Overall	.283	37	.337	126	.330	70	0.16	164	5.82	126	5.09	4	.296	48
	Pressure	.194	136	.224	147	.270	132	0.00	110	7.79	92	5.19	8	.318	48
Todd Benzinger	Overall	.254	92	.425	47	.293	138	3.21	56	5.05	150	18.35	134	.296	47
	Pressure	.286	51	.518	17	.310	94	5.36	21	3.33	151	23.33	134	.500	6
Wade Boggs	Overall	.366	1	.490	15	.476	1	0.86	140	17.39	3	4.73	3	.333	17
	Pressure	.271	67	.339	98	.427	10	0.00	110	20.00	3	12.00	52	.143	128
Ellis Burks	Overall	.294	26	.481	18	.367	26	3.33	53	10.08	52	14.47	94	.303	41
	Pressure	.323	28	.484	27	.425	12	1.61	87	13.70	17	17.81	100	.217	89
Rick Cerone	Overall	.269	60	.360	109	.326	76	1.14	120	6.92	105	11.07	48	.227	135
	Pressure	.156	157	.188	162	.206	162	0.00	110	2.94	156	11.76	49	.125	138
Dwight Evans	Overall	.293	28	.487	16	.375	19	3.76	37	11.78	24	15.35	105	.349	10
	Pressure	.243	94	.386	69	.299	109	4.29	33	7.69	93	23.08	133	.125	138
Rich Gedman	Overall	.231	134	.368	102	.279	153	3.01	63	5.42	139	14.76	99	.261	93
	Pressure	.171	148	.371	76	.189	166	5.71	16	2.63	159	23.68	136	.083	159
Mike Greenwell	Overall	.325	3	.531	8	.416	2	3.73	39	12.55	18	5.48	6	.328	23
	Pressure	.257	82	.329	106	.341	69	0.00	110	12.20	32	10.98	41	.174	112
Spike Owen	Overall	.249	106	.370	98	.324	81	1.95	95	9.18	61	9.18	30	.164	167
	Pressure	.222	116	.333	103	.317	87	2.78	57	12.20	32	14.63	74	.500	--
Larry Parrish	Overall	.217	155	.360	111	.270	160	3.45	48	6.35	115	25.17	163	.248	108
	Pressure	.200	128	.300	122	.250	148	3.33	47	6.25	121	21.88	122	.190	106
Jody Reed	Overall	.293	29	.376	94	.380	14	0.30	162	11.25	34	5.25	5	.234	125
	Pressure	.324	25	.378	72	.359	46	0.00	110	5.00	136	2.50	2	.333	39
Jim Rice	Overall	.264	68	.406	68	.330	68	3.09	61	8.86	70	16.42	113	.287	57
	Pressure	.254	85	.328	107	.306	100	1.49	91	6.94	105	18.06	102	.320	47
Team Average	Overall	.283	1	.420	2	.357	1	2.24	10	9.84	1	11.49	1	.287	2
	Pressure	.243	9	.355	9	.321	8	2.10	10	9.55	2	16.10	5	.263	5
League Average	Overall	.259		.391		.324		2.47		8.35		14.31		.269	
	Pressure	.249		.365		.319		2.28		8.71		17.04		.246	

Additional Miscellaneous Batting Comparisons

	Grass Surface BA	Rank	Artificial Surface BA	Rank	Home Games BA	Rank	Road Games BA	Rank	Runners in Scoring Position BA	Rank	Runners in Scoring Pos and Two Outs BA	Rank	Leading Off Inning OBA	Rank	Runners on 3B with less than 2 Outs RDI %	Rank
Marty Barrett	.285	37	.273	77	.295	30	.270	57	.296	38	.224	100	.324	69	.750	8
Todd Benzinger	.264	66	.196	153	.270	72	.239	121	.238	109	.243	74	.307	88	.630	56
Wade Boggs	.363	1	.383	4	.382	2	.351	2	.325	21	.264	57	.476	1	.680	30
Ellis Burks	.302	19	.256	96	.325	8	.269	62	.333	14	.274	50	.341	48	.633	54
Rick Cerone	.283	38	.184	161	.308	18	.220	140	.230	128	.265	56	.319	73	.500	115
Dwight Evans	.292	29	.300	36	.318	11	.270	59	.326	20	.362	8	.328	64	.659	42
Rich Gedman	.235	119	.205	149	.256	92	.213	148	.221	138	.158	154	.268	135	.625	58
Mike Greenwell	.332	4	.289	54	.331	7	.319	4	.332	17	.309	25	.441	4	.667	33
Spike Owen	.244	106	.273	77	.279	58	.229	134	.158	168	.000	172	.328	62	.500	115
Larry Parrish	.222	141	.178	164	.247	105	.175	168	.259	88	.246	70	.264	139	.409	155
Jody Reed	.294	27	.286	--	.309	17	.273	52	.253	100	.233	91	.371	23	.647	46
Jim Rice	.278	46	.187	159	.276	62	.254	88	.270	72	.290	40	.310	85	.526	109
Team Average	.287	1	.261	9	.303	1	.263	6	.285	1	.259	4	.350	1	.607	2
League Average	.256		.267		.262		.257		.262		.239		.311		.570	

Pitching vs. Left and Right Handed Batters

		BA	Rank	SA	Rank	OBA	Rank	HR %	Rank	BB %	Rank	SO %	Rank
Mike Boddicker	vs. Lefties	.272	80	.370	59	.338	84	1.74	53	8.29	56	10.60	86
	vs. Righties	.251	58	.363	49	.313	53	2.07	43	7.05	53	20.95	20
Oil Can Boyd	vs. Lefties	.292	106	.468	113	.328	68	3.60	117	5.86	21	13.19	60
	vs. Righties	.286	110	.560	128	.352	111	6.18	128	8.68	84	12.15	97
Roger Clemens	vs. Lefties	.256	56	.363	52	.308	37	1.59	45	6.39	31	24.09	8
	vs. Righties	.183	3	.276	5	.229	1	1.87	32	5.24	21	30.87	1
Wes Gardner	vs. Lefties	.239	42	.382	70	.331	73	2.57	84	12.54	114	14.11	51
	vs. Righties	.200	9	.344	39	.272	15	3.70	108	7.97	71	20.27	26
Bruce Hurst	vs. Lefties	.279	88	.374	64	.327	66	1.36	35	6.10	22	16.46	35
	vs. Righties	.260	74	.391	72	.314	54	2.73	72	7.26	57	18.34	35
Dennis Lamp	vs. Lefties	.313	115	.422	99	.357	104	1.36	35	5.66	16	13.84	56
	vs. Righties	.260	73	.339	34	.300	39	0.56	3	5.24	20	14.14	68
Jeff Sellers	vs. Lefties	.318	119	.414	91	.443	127	1.27	28	18.13	128	9.33	101
	vs. Righties	.223	27	.377	59	.317	62	4.00	117	10.50	110	26.00	6
Lee Smith	vs. Lefties	.232	33	.317	24	.321	56	1.83	54	11.11	102	24.87	6
	vs. Righties	.218	22	.359	46	.289	30	2.56	65	9.20	94	28.16	4
Mike Smithson	vs. Lefties	.291	103	.472	114	.338	83	3.90	121	6.51	33	14.33	50
	vs. Righties	.293	115	.511	124	.353	113	6.11	127	6.69	46	11.42	105
Bob Stanley	vs. Lefties	.263	71	.339	35	.332	74	0.58	10	9.79	85	11.86	76
	vs. Righties	.224	28	.333	28	.281	23	2.49	62	4.44	11	15.11	56
Team Average	vs. Lefties	.275	11	.402	10	.340	9	2.12	7	8.95	7	15.91	1
	vs. Righties	.246	2	.386	5	.307	2	3.02	13	7.39	5	19.41	1
League Average	vs. Lefties	.262		.387		.331		2.24		9.12		13.21	
	vs. Righties	.258		.393		.320		2.63		7.80		15.09	

Pitching with Runners on Base and Bases Empty

		BA	Rank	SA	Rank	OBA	Rank	HR %	Rank	BB %	Rank	SO %	Rank
Mike Boddicker	Runners On	.256	57	.376	55	.325	61	2.18	57	8.69	63	15.02	47
	Bases Empty	.266	86	.361	49	.327	87	1.71	37	6.96	57	16.00	51
Oil Can Boyd	Runners On	.294	105	.467	112	.335	73	3.05	91	6.33	22	13.12	71
	Bases Empty	.285	114	.545	127	.344	110	6.09	129	7.94	73	12.35	84
Roger Clemens	Runners On	.238	31	.361	44	.291	19	2.19	59	6.19	19	27.23	1
	Bases Empty	.210	16	.297	9	.256	7	1.45	25	5.61	29	27.47	2
Wes Gardner	Runners On	.203	7	.308	8	.278	9	2.20	63	9.09	73	15.53	38
	Bases Empty	.232	34	.403	89	.320	75	3.81	110	11.24	118	18.26	31
Bruce Hurst	Runners On	.280	88	.427	89	.324	58	2.88	86	6.23	21	16.88	25
	Bases Empty	.253	63	.362	51	.311	59	2.22	62	7.64	68	18.81	28
Dennis Lamp	Runners On	.280	89	.360	42	.333	68	0.61	5	7.65	42	9.84	107
	Bases Empty	.288	117	.394	83	.317	69	1.25	17	2.99	3	18.56	30
Jeff Sellers	Runners On	.291	101	.418	84	.388	120	1.90	43	12.97	118	15.14	45
	Bases Empty	.247	55	.374	60	.370	124	3.45	104	15.38	127	20.19	19
Lee Smith	Runners On	.249	49	.416	82	.313	42	4.05	120	8.72	65	22.05	9
	Bases Empty	.197	6	.245	2	.298	40	0.00	1	11.90	121	31.55	1
Mike Smithson	Runners On	.325	122	.535	127	.384	115	5.50	127	7.02	31	12.72	76
	Bases Empty	.270	94	.460	115	.318	71	4.50	123	6.31	45	13.21	76
Bob Stanley	Runners On	.246	43	.355	37	.311	40	2.19	59	7.48	35	13.55	62
	Bases Empty	.238	42	.317	16	.298	39	1.06	11	6.34	46	13.66	70
Team Average	Runners On	.270	8	.410	9	.332	8	2.62	10	8.10	3	16.62	1
	Bases Empty	.250	5	.380	7	.314	6	2.61	10	8.09	9	18.78	1
League Average	Runners On	.268		.401		.336		2.45		9.09		13.68	
	Bases Empty	.253		.383		.315		2.48		7.76		14.81	

Overall Pitching Compared to Late Inning Pressure Situations

		BA	Rank	SA	Rank	OBA	Rank	HR %	Rank	BB %	Rank	SO %	Rank
Mike Boddicker	Overall	.262	67	.367	45	.326	76	1.90	35	7.69	52	15.58	46
	Pressure	.238	54	.417	90	.304	44	3.57	101	7.61	43	16.30	49
Tom Bolton	Overall	.285	--	.398	--	.355	--	0.81	--	10.00	--	15.00	--
	Pressure	.325	115	.425	94	.417	124	2.50	73	14.29	116	18.37	30
Oil Can Boyd	Overall	.289	115	.515	128	.341	97	4.91	128	7.31	40	12.66	80
	Pressure	.265	86	.471	112	.359	95	5.88	125	12.20	99	14.63	63
Roger Clemens	Overall	.220	16	.320	13	.270	5	1.72	24	5.83	16	27.38	1
	Pressure	.179	8	.250	9	.243	6	0.71	25	7.74	48	36.77	1
Wes Gardner	Overall	.220	15	.363	42	.302	26	3.14	103	10.32	105	17.10	34
	Pressure	.256		.436	97	.396	118	5.13	118	18.37	128	16.33	46
Bruce Hurst	Overall	.264	72	.388	70	.316	51	2.49	73	7.05	36	18.00	28
	Pressure	.234	49	.312	33	.302	41	1.30	35	9.09	66	13.64	79
Dennis Lamp	Overall	.284	112	.377	58	.326	75	0.93	5	5.43	11	14.00	62
	Pressure	.288	105	.384	75	.369	101	1.37	39	11.63	96	12.79	86
Jeff Sellers	Overall	.268	83	.395	80	.379	125	2.71	88	14.25	126	17.81	30
	Pressure	.259	--	.481	--	.355	--	7.41	--	12.90	--	9.68	--
Lee Smith	Overall	.225	19	.338	20	.306	31	2.19	61	10.19	101	26.45	2
	Pressure	.238	56	.368	63	.323	64	2.07	63	10.76	86	26.91	2
Mike Smithson	Overall	.292	117	.489	126	.345	105	4.89	127	6.60	27	13.01	74
	Pressure	.368	--	.947	--	.368	--	15.79	--	0.00	--	10.53	--
Bob Stanley	Overall	.242	38	.336	19	.304	30	1.61	19	6.92	33	13.60	69
	Pressure	.247	64	.322	39	.319	62	0.68	24	8.19	55	17.54	37
Team Average	Overall	.259	8	.393	7	.322	5	2.61	9	8.10	6	17.82	1
	Pressure	.247	8	.366	8	.327	7	2.22	7	10.26	11	21.37	1
League Average	Overall	.259		.391		.324		2.47		8.35		14.31	
	Pressure	.249		.369		.324		2.26		9.33		15.69	

Additional Miscellaneous Pitching Comparisons

	Grass Surface		Artificial Surface		Home Games		Road Games		Runners in Scoring Position		Runners in Scoring Pos and Two Outs		Leading Off Inning	
	BA	Rank	BA	Rank	BA	Rank	BA	Rank	BA	Rank	BA	Rank	OBA	Rank
Mike Boddicker	.259	65	.283	79	.272	89	.254	62	.211	19	.227	59	.317	73
Oil Can Boyd	.288	117	.291	91	.284	102	.292	106	.263	68	.255	84	.341	98
Roger Clemens	.225	21	.183	4	.230	35	.211	10	.222	29	.213	50	.236	7
Wes Gardner	.216	14	.239	31	.201	7	.240	40	.195	11	.169	22	.390	120
Bruce Hurst	.252	57	.339	119	.260	72	.270	80	.288	92	.189	34	.281	43
Dennis Lamp	.287	115	.269	61	.313	124	.255	64	.279	83	.250	78	.342	99
Jeff Sellers	.269	89	.263	56	.291	111	.246	46	.297	107	.372	127	.300	54
Lee Smith	.205	7	.378	--	.207	10	.248	52	.206	14	.158	15	.247	12
Mike Smithson	.291	119	.294	99	.295	116	.286	102	.301	111	.246	76	.316	70
Bob Stanley	.241	43	.250	42	.226	32	.262	71	.240	45	.224	57	.268	30
Team Average	.256	8	.275	11	.261	8	.256	7	.258	6	.224	4	.307	5
League Average	.256		.267		.257		.262		.262		.239		.311	

CALIFORNIA ANGELS

- **What's high in the middle and round on the ends? Besides Ohio.**
- **Why is Moose Stubing answering to "double zero"?**

We're sure that most of you are familiar with ancient Greek literature—especially the *Iliad* and the *Odyssey,* the great works of the ninth century before Christ. Perhaps composed by the poet Homer, these works each consisted of lengthy chapters that were recited orally before appreciative crowds in an early day version of Willie Nelson's Las Vegas act.

Part of the allure of those works, and one that really stood the old Athenians on their ears, was the bard's use of palindromic symmetry in his telling of the tale. For example, in the 24–book *Iliad,* the incidents and imagery contained in book one corresponded to what appeared in book 24, book two corresponded to book 23, and so on. Hey, these ancient Greeks didn't know from miniseries, this was their entertainment. We guess you had to be there. If you enjoy this stuff, on your next trip to Istanbul, check out the inscription on the sacred font in the courtyard of Hagia Sophia and you'll find the longest palindrome of the Greek world:

νιψον ανομημα μη μοναν οψιν

Translation: wash away your sins, not only your face. Take that, "Able was I ere I saw Elba"!

If Homer were still around, he may have written an epic poem about the 1988 Angels, who not only went about their business with an unusual sense of symmetry, but also had a roller-coaster season unprecedented in the modern history of major league baseball. The Angels' 1988 season was divided not into 24 parts, as was the *Iliad,* but into three parts (as was Gaul, for you Latin scholars).

In the 1988 *Analyst,* we discussed California's penchant for fast starts. In the 10–year period from 1978 through 1987, the Angels had a .594 won-lost percentage in April games, the best by any American League team, compared with a .491 mark in games played after April.

The ink was hardly dry on those pages before the Angels went out and had their worst April since 1977, winning only 10 of 23 games. And they didn't stop there. By June 4, when they played their 54th game of the season, and lost it, their record had fallen to 19–35, worst in the division. Only once before (in 1969) had they been 16 games below .500 this early in the season. Never before, at the one-third mark of the season, had they stood 19½ games out of first place.

But then, the Angels began a remarkable turnaround. Over the middle one-third of the season, the Angels won 37 games and lost 17. At the 108–game mark, they stood four games above .500, in third place, eleven games behind Oakland. The second-place Twins were within their sight, and as the curtain fell on act two, Southland fans wondered if their team were properly poised for a run at the Athletics.

No way. California treaded water for a while, splitting its next 34 games, but then lost 18 of its last 20, including the last 12 in succession. Cookie Rojas was fired in the midst of that final streak and his replacement, Moose Stubing, never won a game. Stubing now carries the unusual distinction of having played in the majors without getting a hit and having managed in the majors without winning a game. He was 0–for–5, with four strikeouts, as a batter; he was 0–for–8 as a manager.

When it was all over, the Angels' season looked like this, taking it one-third at a time:

First 54 Games	19–35	.352
Next 54 Games	37–17	.685
Last 54 Games	19–35	.352

The Angels won 37 games in the middle third of the season; they won a combined total of 38 games on either side.

We looked at the pattern of every major league team in this century, and found none whose pendulum swung to the extremes exhibited by Cookie Rojas's team. There were very few that even swung to a degree that approached the Angels. Listed here are the 14 teams that played under .500 ball over the first third, over .600 in the middle third, and under .500 in the homestretch. Only seasons of 130 or more decisions were considered, and any surplus or shortfall in games played (due to rain, strikes, playoffs, etc.) was considered as part of the "final third."

	First Third		Middle Third		Final Third	
	W–L	Pct.	W–L	Pct.	W–L	Pct.
1905 Yankees	21–30	.412	33–18	.647	17–30	.362
1917 Reds	23–28	.451	31–20	.608	24–28	.462

1922 White Sox	22–29	.431	31–20	.608	24–28	.462
1922 Tigers	24–27	.471	31–20	.608	24–28	.462
1940 Pirates	20–31	.392	33–18	.647	25–27	.481
1941 Pirates	23–28	.451	35–16	.686	23–29	.442
1955 Red Sox	21–30	.412	38–13	.745	25–27	.481
1972 Yankees	25–29	.463	33–21	.611	21–26	.447
1973 Cardinals	25–29	.463	33–21	.611	23–31	.426
1982 Pirates	25–29	.463	33–21	.611	26–28	.481
1983 Brewers	26–28	.481	35–19	.648	26–28	.481
1985 Athletics	26–28	.481	33–21	.611	18–36	.333
1988 Expos	26–28	.481	33–21	.611	22–32	.407
1988 Angels	19–35	.352	37–17	.685	19–35	.352

No team in major league history had ever blazed the trail followed by last year's Angels: under .400, over .600, under .400. And the Angels didn't just sneak within the boundaries of those parameters. They played *well below* .400 at the beginning and the end, and nearly .700 in between.

Step back for a better view: A .685 percentage, over the course of a 162–game season, would produce 111 wins. Since the 162–game schedule was adopted (1961 in A.L., 1962 in N.L.), no team has won that many games; the 1961 Yankees and the 1969 Orioles (both were 109–53) have had the best records.

A .352 percentage is equivalent to 57 wins over a 162–game season. While there have been teams (such as last year's Orioles and Braves) that have played that poorly over a full year, the juxtaposition of such teams with the '61 Yankees and '69 Orioles sharpens the schizophrenic nature of the Angels.

From now on, the riddle, "What's high in the middle and round on the end?" will have two answers. Ohio and the 1988 Angels.

We broke the season's statistics into three segments reflecting the Angels' season, to identify the ingredients that allowed them to play better in the middle of the season:

	First Third			Middle Third			Final Third		
	Avg.	HR	R	Avg.	HR	R	Avg.	HR	R
Angels	.249	30	223	.277	55	279	.257	39	212
Opponents	.275	47	270	.264	44	254	.271	44	247

From the "opponents' runs" totals, it's evident that the team's pitching showed only slight improvement from the first 54 games to the next 54 games, and then it again improved slightly during the final third of the season, when the team played poorly. The big difference in the middle of the season was in California's run production. The Angels averaged better than one run per game more during the middle third of the season than they did either before or after that segment. A look at the individual batting statistics of the team's principal players leads to the conclusion that it was a classic case of everyone in the lineup getting hot together. Seven of the nine regulars (excluding the disabled Mark McLemore) increased their first-third RBI total in the middle third of the season; then, the RBI total for eight of those nine players decreased over the final third:

	First Third				Middle Third				Final Third			
	GS	Avg.	HR	BI	GS	Avg.	HR	BI	GS	Avg.	HR	BI
Armas	31	.216	2	9	38	.273	4	21	26	.327	7	19
?ne	37	.205	0	7	37	.383	4	22	37	.296	1	10

C. Davis	52	.262	6	30	53	.312	11	41	51	.231	4	22
Downing	38	.259	8	19	47	.259	9	25	46	.211	8	20
Howell	50	.269	3	24	47	.245	7	25	45	.247	6	14
Joyner	52	.281	2	20	48	.322	6	41	48	.282	5	24
McLemore	40	.251	1	12	0	Injured			12	.212	1	4
Ray	50	.296	2	30	48	.285	1	21	51	.335	3	32
Schofield	53	.237	2	13	48	.235	3	12	53	.246	1	9
White	26	.245	2	11	50	.273	7	24	34	.250	2	16

Over the first third of the season, the Angels ranked 12th in the league in batting average and 11th in runs scored. Over the final third, they were eighth in batting average and 10th in runs scored. But during their hot streak, the Angels ranked third in team batting average and second in runs scored.

So for the Angels last season, the equation was a simple one: when they hit, they won.

After all was said and done, the Angels wound up with the same 75–87 record in 1988 that they had in 1987. That's a bit unusual in itself, because trying to follow the Angels' up-and-down movement in the standings in recent seasons has produced more dizziness among sports fans than anything this side of John Madden's Coaches' Clicker. Prior to 1988, the Angels' won-lost percentage had fluctuated more than 50 points eight times in the 10 previous seasons, including four shifts of more than 100 percentage points. No American League team could match either of those figures.

The following table measures year-to-year mood swings among the major league teams since 1977, the first year for Seattle and Toronto. By virtue of finishing with identical records in the past two seasons, the Angels have lost the American League lead in the Most Unstable Team (or "MUT") rankings. The figures under the average column represent the average year-to-year change in a team's won-lost percentage. Also noted are the number of times that a team fluctuated at least 50 or at least 100 points.

	Avg. Change	50+	100+		Avg. Change	50+	100+
Oakland	71.2	5	3	St. Louis	86.8	9	5
California	70.4	8	4	San Diego	70.4	9	2
Texas	68.3	5	2	Los Angeles	62.8	6	2
Toronto	62.7	8	1	Pittsburgh	60.7	7	1
Chicago	62.6	6	2	San Francisco	60.6	4	2
Cleveland	62.5	5	3	Cincinnati	57.0	4	2
Kansas City	59.3	6	1	Houston	54.0	4	1
Milwaukee	57.4	4	2	Chicago	53.7	4	2
Seattle	56.3	6	0	Atlanta	50.3	4	0
Minnesota	52.5	6	1	New York	45.1	4	1
Detroit	50.0	6	1	Philadelphia	41.9	4	0
Boston	49.0	5	1	Montreal	41.5	3	1
New York	47.9	6	0				
Baltimore	47.2	5	0				

What the Angels need in 1989 is another one of their 100–point swings, one that would lift a 75–87 team to, oh, 92–70 or so. Which just happened to be their record when they last won a division title in 1986. And the Athletics, the only team in the league with a higher MUT rating than California, could fall back. In a division where four of the last five champions have lost at least 70 games, anything is possible.

WON-LOST RECORD BY STARTING POSITION

CALIFORNIA 75-87	C	1B	2B	3B	SS	LF	CF	RF	P	DH	Leadoff	Relief	Starts
Tony Armas	·	·	·	·	·	32-23	10-19	5-3	·	1-2	·	·	48-47
Dante Bichette	·	·	·	·	·	0-2	1-12	·	·	·	·	·	1-14
Bob Boone	55-56	·	·	·	·	·	·	·	·	·	·	·	55-56
Thad Bosley	·	·	·	·	·	11-8	·	·	·	1-0	·	·	12-8
Mike Brown	·	·	·	·	·	4-8	·	0-1	·	·	·	·	4-9
Bill Buckner	·	·	·	·	·	·	·	·	·	5-5	·	·	5-5
Dewayne Buice	·	·	·	·	·	·	·	·	·	·	·	9-23	·
Terry Clark	·	·	·	·	·	·	·	·	7-8	·	·	·	7-8
Stu Cliburn	·	·	·	·	·	·	·	·	0-1	·	·	11-28	0-1
Mike Cook	·	·	·	·	·	·	·	·	·	·	·	0-3	·
Sherman Corbett	·	·	·	·	·	·	·	·	·	·	·	13-21	·
Chili Davis	·	·	·	·	·	·	1-1	69-82	·	1-2	·	·	71-85
Doug Davis	1-0	·	·	2-0	·	·	·	·	·	·	·	·	3-0
Frank DeMichele	·	·	·	·	·	·	·	·	·	·	·	2-2	·
Brian Dorsett	1-2	·	·	·	·	·	·	·	·	·	·	·	1-2
Brian Downing	·	·	·	·	·	·	·	·	·	60-71	10-23	·	60-71
Jim Eppard	·	1-2	·	·	·	7-8	·	·	·	5-2	·	·	13-12
Chuck Finley	·	·	·	·	·	·	·	·	14-17	·	·	·	14-17
Willie Fraser	·	·	·	·	·	·	·	·	16-16	·	·	1-1	16-16
Bryan Harvey	·	·	·	·	·	·	·	·	·	·	·	35-15	·
George Hendrick	·	5-6	·	·	·	4-8	·	1-1	·	0-1	·	·	10-16
Jack Howell	·	·	·	65-77	·	·	·	·	·	·	·	·	65-77
Wally Joyner	·	69-79	·	·	·	·	·	·	·	·	·	·	69-79
Ray Krawczyk	·	·	·	·	·	·	·	·	0-1	·	·	2-11	0-1
Jack Lazorko	·	·	·	·	·	·	·	·	1-2	·	·	1-6	1-2
Vance Lovelace	·	·	·	·	·	·	·	·	·	·	·	0-3	·
Urbano Lugo	·	·	·	·	·	·	·	·	·	·	·	0-1	·
Kirk McCaskill	·	·	·	·	·	·	·	14-9	·	·	·	·	14-9
Mark McLemore	·	·	19-29	2-2	·	·	·	·	·	·	13-21	·	21-31
Darrell Miller	12-20	·	·	·	2-2	·	·	·	·	·	·	·	14-22
Greg Minton	·	·	·	·	·	·	·	·	·	·	·	17-27	·
Rich Monteleone	·	·	·	·	·	·	·	·	·	·	·	0-3	·
Donnie Moore	·	·	·	·	·	·	·	·	·	·	·	15-12	·
Junior Noboa	·	·	1-5	·	·	·	·	·	·	·	·	·	1-5
Dan Petry	·	·	·	·	·	·	·	·	8-14	·	·	·	8-14
Gus Polidor	·	·	0-2	5-5	7-1	·	·	·	·	·	·	·	12-8
Domingo Ramos	·	·	·	1-2	·	·	·	·	·	·	1-0	·	1-2
Johnny Ray	·	·	52-50	·	·	14-27	·	·	·	2-4	0-1	·	68-81
Joe Redfield	·	·	·	0-1	·	·	·	·	·	·	·	·	0-1
Dick Schofield	·	·	·	·	68-86	·	·	·	·	·	18-16	·	68-86
Chico Walker	·	·	3-1	·	·	1-1	4-4	·	·	·	0-2	·	8-6
Devon White	·	·	·	·	·	·	59-51	·	·	·	33-24	·	59-51
Mike Witt	·	·	·	·	·	·	·	·	15-19	·	·	·	15-19
Butch Wynegar	6-9	·	·	·	·	·	·	·	·	·	·	·	6-9

Batting vs. Left and Right Handed Pitchers

		BA	Rank	SA	Rank	OBA	Rank	HR %	Rank	BB %	Rank	SO %	Rank
Tony Armas	vs. Lefties	.297	38	.515	21	.345	49	4.85	25	6.78	86	14.69	93
	vs. Righties	.251	99	.384	85	.284	141	2.46	77	4.63	153	28.24	163
Bob Boone	vs. Lefties	.264	70	.336	112	.318	77	0.71	134	7.14	81	5.19	10
	vs. Righties	.316	11	.420	60	.375	19	1.89	91	7.56	94	7.56	15
Chili Davis	vs. Lefties	.256	78	.429	55	.307	94	3.65	45	7.14	81	18.49	134
	vs. Righties	.276	50	.433	49	.336	68	3.41	51	9.09	72	17.25	120
Brian Downing	vs. Lefties	.223	136	.383	82	.382	25	4.57	29	17.65	5	9.50	44
	vs. Righties	.252	95	.476	21	.351	41	5.50	13	11.38	32	11.38	54
George Hendrick	vs. Lefties	.276	58	.368	90	.296	107	2.63	66	3.66	150	8.54	35
	vs. Righties	.196	--	.255	--	.263	--	1.96	--	7.02	--	22.81	--
Jack Howell	vs. Lefties	.237	109	.397	70	.296	110	2.56	69	4.05	141	26.01	161
	vs. Righties	.262	78	.433	48	.335	71	3.49	47	10.13	55	22.08	152
Wally Joyner	vs. Lefties	.264	71	.321	125	.309	91	0.47	139	5.22	118	6.09	13
	vs. Righties	.312	59	.473	24	.381	16	3.12	59	9.93	59	8.55	23
Mark McLemore	vs. Lefties	.200	155	.246	158	.268	143	0.00	140	8.33	68	13.89	85
	vs. Righties	.256	89	.363	106	.328	82	1.19	114	9.84	60	9.33	31
Darrell Miller	vs. Lefties	.311	29	.467	43	.354	39	2.22	76	6.12	99	8.16	31
	vs. Righties	.179	--	.232	--	.264	--	1.05	--	5.56	--	23.15	--
Johnny Ray	vs. Lefties	.281	52	.395	73	.327	70	0.95	127	5.63	111	3.90	2
	vs. Righties	.319	9	.446	38	.354	38	1.02	124	5.37	134	6.78	11
Dick Schofield	vs. Lefties	.228	129	.344	108	.302	103	2.22	76	7.39	77	9.85	50
	vs. Righties	.245	113	.303	146	.303	121	0.58	147	6.48	116	9.59	34
Devon White	vs. Lefties	.247	99	.420	58	.289	116	4.00	36	4.97	124	14.91	96
	vs. Righties	.266	70	.374	94	.301	123	1.64	100	4.62	154	18.46	134
Team Average	vs. Lefties	.252	10	.376	12	.312	9	2.29	10	7.09	12	11.92	3
	vs. Righties	.266	4	.390	6	.326	7	2.18	11	7.79	11	13.85	4
League Average	vs. Lefties	.259		.391		.321		2.47		7.97		14.12	
	vs. Righties	.259		.391		.326		2.47		8.51		14.39	

Batting with Runners on Base and Bases Empty

		BA	Rank	SA	Rank	OBA	Rank	HR %	Rank	BB %	Rank	SO %	Rank
Tony Armas	Runners On	.276	71	.449	42	.311	120	3.85	40	5.36	142	17.26	131
	Bases Empty	.269	49	.439	40	.311	91	3.30	50	5.78	118	25.78	162
Bob Boone	Runners On	.333	12	.417	70	.381	28	1.28	108	6.78	112	3.95	2
	Bases Empty	.265	64	.362	100	.330	60	1.53	107	7.91	78	8.84	27
Chili Davis	Runners On	.293	50	.481	26	.349	69	3.83	41	9.15	70	18.60	144
	Bases Empty	.246	96	.387	84	.304	103	3.19	52	7.67	85	16.81	112
Brian Downing	Runners On	.275	74	.420	65	.391	20	3.50	50	13.44	23	10.67	54
	Bases Empty	.218	140	.458	30	.341	47	6.34	9	13.95	8	10.68	43
Jack Howell	Runners On	.295	47	.486	23	.379	32	3.64	46	10.51	53	18.68	145
	Bases Empty	.221	137	.371	93	.276	144	2.86	65	6.31	106	27.24	164
Wally Joyner	Runners On	.292	51	.438	54	.369	42	3.20	58	10.15	56	8.00	28
	Bases Empty	.297	21	.402	68	.343	44	1.27	116	6.51	101	7.40	15
Mark McLemore	Runners On	.161	169	.230	167	.227	169	1.15	113	7.84	94	8.82	34
	Bases Empty	.288	31	.390	81	.362	26	0.68	146	10.43	36	11.66	52
Johnny Ray	Runners On	.342	6	.469	29	.374	38	0.77	137	5.08	148	4.41	4
	Bases Empty	.278	41	.398	72	.321	72	1.17	123	5.77	120	6.87	11
Dick Schofield	Runners On	.240	125	.310	150	.316	115	1.00	126	7.20	105	10.59	52
	Bases Empty	.239	114	.321	131	.295	110	1.22	117	6.52	100	9.07	28
Devon White	Runners On	.266	97	.399	82	.312	119	2.31	81	5.24	144	14.66	104
	Bases Empty	.255	82	.383	86	.288	129	2.48	77	4.41	148	18.98	137
Team Average	Runners On	.277	5	.403	8	.341	7	2.30	10	8.22	11	12.20	2
	Bases Empty	.250	7	.372	10	.306	10	2.16	12	7.01	11	13.96	6
League Average	Runners On	.268		.401		.336		2.45		9.09		13.68	
	Bases Empty	.253		.383		.315		2.48		7.76		14.81	

Overall Batting Compared to Late Inning Pressure Situations

		BA	Rank	SA	Rank	OBA	Rank	HR %	Rank	BB %	Rank	SO %	Rank	RDI %	Rank
Tony Armas	Overall	.272	55	.443	34	.311	107	3.53	45	5.60	131	22.14	155	.266	87
	Pressure	.203	126	.424	55	.299	111	5.08	22	11.94	38	28.36	155	.125	138
Bob Boone	Overall	.295	23	.386	87	.352	40	1.42	112	7.40	97	6.63	12	.306	39
	Pressure	.269	70	.288	128	.367	40	0.00	110	13.11	24	4.92	6	.267	67
Chili Davis	Overall	.268	62	.432	43	.326	78	3.50	46	8.40	76	17.69	130	.289	56
	Pressure	.200	128	.316	111	.269	133	3.16	49	8.57	81	20.00	110	.174	112
Brian Downing	Overall	.242	121	.442	35	.362	31	5.17	15	13.73	11	10.68	45	.233	129
	Pressure	.309	41	.691	2	.412	17	9.88	1	12.00	36	15.00	80	.375	27
Jim Eppard	Overall	.283	--	.327	--	.347	--	0.00	--	8.73	--	11.90	--	.255	--
	Pressure	.333	16	.400	64	.394	23	0.00	110	9.09	71	9.09	28	.308	50
George Hendrick	Overall	.244	--	.323	--	.283	--	2.36	--	5.04	--	14.39	--	.275	77
	Pressure	.324	25	.324	108	.372	35	0.00	110	6.82	107	9.09	28	.429	14
Jack Howell	Overall	.254	93	.422	55	.323	83	3.20	57	8.24	84	23.30	159	.261	95
	Pressure	.165	151	.241	142	.221	159	1.27	103	5.81	129	38.37	171	.222	85
Wally Joyner	Overall	.295	25	.419	59	.356	35	2.18	84	8.30	79	7.69	15	.354	7
	Pressure	.347	9	.449	46	.404	20	2.04	75	9.17	70	7.34	18	.440	12
Mark McLemore	Overall	.240	123	.330	133	.312	105	0.86	139	9.43	57	10.57	43	.188	164
	Pressure	.250	87	.295	124	.298	112	0.00	110	6.00	127	12.00	52	.250	72
Darrell Miller	Overall	.221	--	.307	--	.292	--	1.43	--	5.73	--	18.47	--	.152	--
	Pressure	.200	128	.233	143	.273	129	0.00	110	2.94	156	23.53	135	.000	165
Johnny Ray	Overall	.306	14	.429	45	.345	49	1.00	132	5.46	136	5.77	9	.314	29
	Pressure	.278	61	.344	93	.302	108	1.11	108	2.97	155	3.96	3	.244	77
Dick Schofield	Overall	.239	127	.317	146	.303	117	1.14	119	6.79	108	9.68	35	.220	142
	Pressure	.358	6	.433	52	.442	7	0.00	110	11.90	39	7.14	15	.231	82
Devon White	Overall	.259	82	.389	86	.297	130	2.42	75	4.73	156	17.28	128	.271	80
	Pressure	.250	87	.375	74	.304	104	1.56	89	5.63	132	16.90	93	.350	37
Team Average	Overall	.261	6	.385	9	.321	7	2.22	11	7.55	11	13.18	3	.274	7
	Pressure	.264	3	.377	5	.332	5	2.20	8	8.37	9	15.29	3	.296	2
League Average	Overall	.259		.391		.324		2.47		8.35		14.31		.269	
	Pressure	.249		.365		.319		2.28		8.71		17.04		.246	

Additional Miscellaneous Batting Comparisons

	Grass Surface BA	Rank	Artificial Surface BA	Rank	Home Games BA	Rank	Road Games BA	Rank	Runners in Scoring Position BA	Rank	Runners in Scoring Pos and Two Outs BA	Rank	Leading Off Inning OBA	Rank	Runners on 3B with less than 2 Outs RDI %	Rank
Tony Armas	.264	63	.320	23	.241	114	.308	17	.264	80	.300	33	.337	52	.381	165
Bob Boone	.270	55	.429	1	.282	50	.309	15	.361	3	.289	41	.344	45	.619	60
Chili Davis	.255	84	.337	16	.251	99	.285	38	.255	98	.216	106	.273	128	.585	77
Brian Downing	.240	111	.250	101	.238	118	.245	112	.204	154	.216	107	.289	113	.583	78
Jim Eppard	.283	--	.286	--	.290	--	.275	--	.262	82	.318	18	.389	--	.400	156
George Hendrick	.246	102	.231	--	.257	--	.228	--	.282	52	.280	46	.296	--	.750	--
Jack Howell	.224	136	.413	2	.238	119	.270	58	.288	52	.208	118	.298	97	.542	102
Wally Joyner	.296	25	.289	54	.279	56	.309	14	.294	40	.211	115	.333	59	.694	22
Mark McLemore	.245	105	.212	--	.216	154	.260	86	.196	159	.174	147	.310	84	.438	145
Darrell Miller	.220	145	.235	--	.281	--	.171	--	.172	--	.118	--	.293	--	.500	--
Johnny Ray	.297	24	.355	10	.296	27	.314*	8	.274	65	.280	46	.331	61	.635	53
Dick Schofield	.236	118	.260	93	.230	137	.249	101	.225	134	.213	112	.298	97	.450	142
Devon White	.254	86	.282	63	.237	122	.279	50	.257	92	.140	161	.326	66	.563	87
Team Average	.253	9	.308	1	.251	11	.270	1	.258	9	.228	10	.306	8	.576	6
League Average	.256		.267		.262		.257		.262		.239		.311		.570	

Pitching vs. Left and Right Handed Batters

		BA	Rank	SA	Rank	OBA	Rank	HR %	Rank	BB %	Rank	SO %	Rank
Dewayne Buice	vs. Lefties	.338	126	.465	112	.427	124	1.41	38	12.64	116	19.54	14
	vs. Righties	.244	--	.430	--	.302	--	4.65	--	8.33	--	21.88	--
Terry Clark	vs. Lefties	.351	127	.511	124	.400	122	2.30	71	8.67	62	6.63	125
	vs. Righties	.298	120	.424	93	.343	101	2.02	41	6.54	43	12.15	98
Stu Cliburn	vs. Lefties	.286	97	.511	123	.375	115	6.77	129	10.46	92	9.15	104
	vs. Righties	.251	59	.318	17	.317	63	1.12	11	7.69	64	13.46	78
Sherman Corbett	vs. Lefties	.240	44	.307	17	.314	44	0.00	1	10.34	90	16.09	39
	vs. Righties	.299	--	.423	--	.377	--	2.06	--	11.97	--	11.97	--
Chuck Finley	vs. Lefties	.289	102	.370	59	.374	114	0.74	14	10.06	88	11.95	74
	vs. Righties	.257	67	.387	68	.330	87	2.37	57	9.82	104	13.69	74
Willie Fraser	vs. Lefties	.275	85	.551	128	.348	96	5.96	128	9.83	86	7.64	115
	vs. Righties	.257	66	.394	74	.331	88	2.51	64	8.68	85	12.66	90
Bryan Harvey	vs. Lefties	.147	2	.217	2	.212	3	1.40	37	7.59	43	28.48	2
	vs. Righties	.286	110	.376	56	.326	77	1.50	22	5.52	25	15.17	55
Jack Lazorko	vs. Lefties	.321	121	.474	116	.393	120	5.13	125	11.11	102	6.67	124
	vs. Righties	.179	--	.269	--	.257	--	1.49	--	8.00	--	17.33	--
Kirk McCaskill	vs. Lefties	.267	76	.351	45	.336	80	1.04	22	9.63	81	12.73	64
	vs. Righties	.281	104	.417	84	.348	107	2.16	48	9.58	101	18.21	37
Greg Minton	vs. Lefties	.241	46	.308	18	.325	64	0.75	15	11.18	104	7.89	114
	vs. Righties	.227	33	.260	2	.313	51	0.00	1	9.50	99	18.99	33
Dan Petry	vs. Lefties	.288	99	.417	94	.377	116	2.65	90	11.97	112	8.74	106
	vs. Righties	.239	39	.432	102	.303	42	4.17	119	7.46	61	12.54	91
Mike Witt	vs. Lefties	.261	68	.357	48	.324	60	1.34	32	8.55	60	11.45	80
	vs. Righties	.285	109	.398	75	.343	102	1.58	24	7.47	62	13.33	81
Team Average	vs. Lefties	.270	9	.407	11	.343	10	2.61	11	9.77	11	11.48	12
	vs. Righties	.270	12	.396	8	.334	14	2.27	2	8.37	11	14.25	12
League Average	vs. Lefties	.262		.387		.331		2.24		9.12		13.21	
	vs. Righties	.258		.393		.320		2.63		7.80		15.09	

Pitching with Runners on Base and Bases Empty

		BA	Rank	SA	Rank	OBA	Rank	HR %	Rank	BB %	Rank	SO %	Rank
Terry Clark	Runners On	.329	124	.470	114	.385	117	3.05	92	9.52	84	8.99	115
	Bases Empty	.317	126	.462	117	.357	118	1.44	24	5.88	36	9.95	115
Stu Cliburn	Runners On	.247	44	.387	64	.343	82	3.33	101	9.73	89	7.03	121
	Bases Empty	.284	110	.414	97	.341	107	3.70	108	7.95	74	16.48	46
Sherman Corbett	Runners On	.258	60	.340	28	.306	34	1.03	18	7.83	49	16.52	30
	Bases Empty	.293	--	.413	--	.404	--	1.33	--	15.73	--	10.11	--
Chuck Finley	Runners On	.271	75	.407	76	.342	81	1.69	35	10.03	96	13.18	69
	Bases Empty	.258	71	.369	56	.336	99	2.32	70	9.75	104	13.49	74
Willie Fraser	Runners On	.284	94	.502	122	.354	96	4.29	124	9.38	81	10.51	100
	Bases Empty	.255	69	.461	116	.330	93	4.37	122	9.23	92	9.63	117
Bryan Harvey	Runners On	.200	6	.274	1	.265	3	0.74	8	8.44	60	22.08	7
	Bases Empty	.227	30	.312	13	.268	12	2.13	57	4.70	13	22.15	9
Kirk McCaskill	Runners On	.290	100	.373	53	.355	97	0.78	9	9.97	93	14.78	49
	Bases Empty	.260	75	.392	80	.331	95	2.25	66	9.30	93	15.99	52
Greg Minton	Runners On	.268	70	.319	13	.377	112	0.00	1	14.12	124	11.76	85
	Bases Empty	.201	9	.248	3	.256	6	0.67	6	6.21	42	16.15	50
Dan Petry	Runners On	.283	92	.484	120	.343	83	4.11	122	8.30	56	12.25	79
	Bases Empty	.249	56	.382	69	.339	104	2.91	94	10.83	117	9.40	118
Mike Witt	Runners On	.300	107	.397	70	.363	104	1.03	17	9.21	75	10.53	99
	Bases Empty	.253	66	.361	50	.311	58	1.74	41	7.21	64	13.62	72
Team Average	Runners On	.283	13	.416	12	.352	12	2.24	5	9.71	11	12.47	12
	Bases Empty	.260	9	.390	9	.327	13	2.57	9	8.43	12	13.39	11
League Average	Runners On	.268		.401		.336		2.45		9.09		13.68	
	Bases Empty	.253		.383		.315		2.48		7.76		14.81	

Overall Pitching Compared to Late Inning Pressure Situations

		BA	Rank	SA	Rank	OBA	Rank	HR %	Rank	BB %	Rank	SO %	Rank
Dewayne Buice	Overall	.287	--	.446	--	.360	--	3.18	--	10.38	--	20.77	--
	Pressure	.312	113	.452	105	.409	123	2.15	66	13.91	114	16.52	43
Terry Clark	Overall	.323	128	.465	121	.370	124	2.15	56	7.56	47	9.51	118
	Pressure	.344	--	.438	--	.364	--	0.00	--	2.86	--	5.71	--
Stu Cliburn	Overall	.266	76	.401	85	.342	101	3.53	116	8.86	83	11.63	94
	Pressure	.235	51	.255	11	.344	85	0.00	1	14.52	117	14.52	64
Sherman Corbett	Overall	.273	--	.372	--	.350	--	1.16	--	11.27	--	13.73	--
	Pressure	.250	67	.375	70	.373	105	2.08	64	16.13	122	14.52	64
Chuck Finley	Overall	.263	70	.384	66	.339	93	2.07	45	9.87	99	13.36	71
	Pressure	.269	93	.410	87	.383	111	2.56	77	13.40	110	10.31	105
Willie Fraser	Overall	.267	80	.477	124	.340	96	4.34	125	9.29	88	9.99	113
	Pressure	.231	43	.431	96	.286	27	4.62	116	7.14	35	7.14	120
Bryan Harvey	Overall	.214	10	.293	5	.267	4	1.45	11	6.60	28	22.11	8
	Pressure	.191	4	.263	16	.250	8	1.55	43	6.98	31	24.65	7
Kirk McCaskill	Overall	.274	96	.383	64	.342	102	1.59	18	9.61	96	15.43	49
	Pressure	.262	79	.277	23	.319	63	0.00	1	8.33	56	9.72	110
Greg Minton	Overall	.233	28	.282	4	.318	56	0.35	2	10.27	103	13.90	64
	Pressure	.221	34	.262	15	.315	57	0.00	1	10.50	84	14.50	66
Donnie Moore	Overall	.343	--	.486	--	.373	--	2.86	--	5.33	--	14.67	--
	Pressure	.333	119	.485	114	.366	100	3.03	91	5.63	21	18.31	33
Dan Petry	Overall	.263	71	.424	103	.341	98	3.41	111	9.77	97	10.60	104
	Pressure	.296	107	.465	110	.346	88	4.23	111	7.59	42	12.66	87
Mike Witt	Overall	.272	91	.376	57	.332	84	1.45	11	8.06	62	12.31	85
	Pressure	.281	100	.353	53	.346	88	0.72	26	9.49	72	13.92	74
Team Average	Overall	.270	12	.401	11	.338	13	2.42	6	9.02	12	12.97	12
	Pressure	.255	9	.355	6	.330	8	1.76	3	9.70	9	15.05	10
League Average	Overall	.259		.391		.324		2.47		8.35		14.31	
	Pressure	.249		.369		.324		2.26		9.33		15.69	

Additional Miscellaneous Pitching Comparisons

	Grass Surface		Artificial Surface		Home Games		Road Games		Runners in Scoring Position		Runners in Scoring Pos and Two Outs		Leading Off Inning	
	BA	Rank	BA	Rank	BA	Rank	BA	Rank	BA	Rank	BA	Rank	OBA	Rank
Dewayne Buice	.280	109	.357	--	.338	--	.234	--	.294	103	.310	112	.355	--
Terry Clark	.339	129	.242	36	.339	128	.306	117	.263	68	.267	94	.414	126
Stu Cliburn	.282	112	.193	7	.286	106	.253	59	.298	108	.229	62	.351	104
Sherman Corbett	.272	95	.286	--	.211	--	.341	--	.226	--	.296	--	.429	--
Chuck Finley	.268	87	.235	25	.273	90	.253	61	.292	99	.149	10	.333	90
Willie Fraser	.266	79	.270	63	.261	74	.271	81	.295	104	.329	124	.300	53
Bryan Harvey	.211	10	.235	--	.199	6	.231	25	.169	3	.100	2	.371	113
Kirk McCaskill	.271	92	.300	104	.259	71	.292	107	.301	110	.317	117	.327	84
Greg Minton	.232	32	.242	--	.257	69	.210	9	.231	37	.204	44	.299	52
Dan Petry	.258	64	.304	109	.262	77	.265	75	.236	41	.135	8	.338	94
Mike Witt	.269	88	.294	99	.243	50	.303	115	.298	109	.267	94	.305	60
Team Average	.270	13	.272	10	.265	12	.275	11	.275	12	.246	11	.330	13
League Average	.256		.267		.257		.262		.262		.239		.311	

CHICAGO WHITE SOX

• *Deja vu:* Like 10 years ago, Chicago's pitching staff is loaded with rookies.

• A "rookie record book" for pitchers.

It's never easy to give up what you've got and start all over again, even if what you've got doesn't add up to all that much in the first place. So give the White Sox' new management credit. They've indicated that the days of the quick fix are over, at least on the south side of town.

Only five players who closed the 1985 season with the Sox remained on their roster at the end of last season. And if you were going to pick a five-man nucleus from that '85 team around which to rebuild, you couldn't do too much better than Harold Baines, Carlton Fisk, Ozzie Guillen, Jerry Hairston, and Greg Walker. (Of course, Scott Fletcher for Jerry Hairston would have been a nice substitution.) But the turnover in the pitching staff was even more drastic. The only White Sox pitcher to finish last season that was around at the start of the 1987 season was relief ace Bobby Thigpen.

Last season, Chicago's pitching staff was the second youngest in the American League, on average just 51 days older than that of Seattle. The White Sox average of 27 years, three months, was nearly three years younger than that of their 1984 staff, despite the addition of Jerry Reuss, whose resurrection in the Windy City makes him a contender for four-decade status in 1990.

Reuss is an interesting character. He'll turn 40 in June, and provides a textbook lesson in survival. The strangest we've seen, in fact since the Bee Gees crossed over from "I've Gotta Get A Message to You" to "Jive Talkin'." He led the Sox with 13 wins last season, a year after losing what seemed like last-chance tryouts with the Dodgers, Reds, and Angels. And this wasn't the first time his career was in jeopardy either. It was only the first time in this decade.

Nine years ago, Reuss appeared to be on shaky ground following seasons of 3–2 as a seldom-used reliever with the Pirates and then 7–14 starting for the Dodgers. But the dawn of the 1980s breathed new life into his arm. He pitched a no-hitter against the Giants in June 1980, and still remains one of the winningest pitchers of the decade. (He needs four more wins to reach the 100–mark for the decade, a level only 24 pitchers have attained to date.)

Still, the fate of Chicago's fortunes, both short- and long-term, will reside with the team's deep crop of rookie pitchers, many of whom made their major league debuts in 1988.

The Sox used 10 different rookie pitchers in 1988, the highest total in the American League since 1983, when Oakland used 11. And while many of last season's White Sox rookies will never see their names in *The Book of Baseball Records,* several very well may. Many fans probably remember Chicago's baby staffs of 1979 and 1980, when the Sox tossed Britt Burns, Richard Dotson, LaMarr Hoyt, Ross Baumgarten, Steve Trout, and several others out of the nest. Well, last season's rookies compiled stats comparable at least in sheer volume (although not necessarily in quality) to those of the 1979 and 1980 teams:

Year	No.	W	L	Pct.	IP	H	BB	SO	ERA
1979	11	29	35	.453	595.0	600	252	270	4.04
1980	6	38	27	.585	635.0	603	231	357	3.66
1988	10	20	32	.385	552.2	579	253	338	4.64

If any of the 1988 rookies are going to establish themselves as front-line starters the way Hoyt, Dotson, and Trout did (in some cases, temporarily), the most likely contenders are Melido Perez and Jack McDowell. Both took regular turns in the Chicago rotation for most of the season. Only one rookie in either league won more games than Perez (Milwaukee's Don August). Only one struck out more batters (Los Angeles' Tim Belcher). And while McDowell won only five games, he pitched better than his record suggests. Their statistics:

Player	GS	CG	W	L	IP	H	HR	BB	SO	ERA
McDowell	26	1	5	10	158.2	147	12	68	84	3.97
Perez	32	3	12	10	197.0	186	26	72	138	3.79

McDowell's ERA was only slightly higher than the league-wide mark; so close, in fact, that if he'd pitched another third of an inning without allowing an earned run, his own ERA would have fallen below the A.L. average. That's significant because few rookie pitchers compile ERAs lower than the league average in 25 or more starts. Last season, Perez was the only American League rookie to do it. And no team has had two such rookies since 1978, when Oakland's John Henry Johnson and Matt Keough did it. The following table shows that only eight other teams have equalled that feat since earned runs were first compiled in 1912. The list proves not only how rare that accomplishment is, but that it's hardly a guide to future success:

Year	Team	Pitchers
1912	Chicago Cubs	Larry Cheney and Jimmy Lavender
1914	Washington Senators	Doc Ayers and Jim Shaw
1922	Chicago White Sox	Dixie Leverett and Charlie Robertson
1927	Washington Senators	Bump Hadley and Hod Lisenbee
1935	Chicago White Sox	Vern Kennedy and John Whitehead
1937	Boston Braves	Lou Fette and Jim Turner
1943	Boston Braves	Nate Andrews and Red Barrett
1960	Baltimore Orioles	Steve Barber and Chuck Estrada
1978	Oakland Athletics	John Henry Johnson and Matt Keough

While the complete list of rookies who bettered their league's ERAs in at least 25 starts includes the names of many forgettable players, you'll find the names of several Hall of Famers, present and future, as well, such as Dazzy Vance, Dizzy Dean, and Tom Seaver. The list of 10 qualifiers from the four seasons prior to 1988 indicates both the upside potential and the downside risk: Dwight Gooden, Mark Langston, and Ron Romanick (1984); Tim Birtsas, Tom Browning, Joe Hesketh, and Ted Higuera (1985); Jim Deshaies (1986); and Joe Magrane and Les Straker (1987).

This seemed like a good opportunity to examine the best rookie pitchers, both individually and on a team basis, on a historical scale. A few ground rules: For the purposes of this section, we ignored the rule that denies rookie status to players who spent 45 days on a major league roster prior to September 1. We simply had no record of those figures. We considered any pitcher to be a rookie if he had pitched 50 innings or less in his career prior to a given season. And in all cases, we considered only the "modern" era (since 1900).

Only two teams since 1900 got more than 50 wins from their rookies: the 1911 Cleveland Indians (51–40) and the 1952 Brooklyn Dodgers (51–36). The Indians' top rookies were Vean Gregg (23–7) and Gene Krapp (13–9). The Dodgers' best were Joe Black (15–4), Billy Loes (13–8), and Ben Wade (11–9). But a better indicator of the best teams would be the *combined winning percentage* of rookies. The following table shows the top 10 teams among those with at least 30 rookie wins:

Year	Team	W–L	Pct.	Winningest Rookie
1941	St. Louis Cardinals	42–14	.750	Ernie White (17–7)
1976	Cincinnati Reds	32–12	.727	Pat Zachry (14–7)
1924	Pittsburgh Pirates	38–16	.704	Roy Kremer (18–10)
1910	New York Yankees	47–22	.681	Russ Ford (26–6)
1947	New York Yankees	34–16	.680	Spec Shea (14–5)
1927	Washington Senators	36–18	.667	Hod Lisenbee (18–9)
1945	St. Louis Cardinals	35–19	.648	Ken Burkhart (19–8)
1952	St. Louis Cardinals	34–18	.654	Eddie Yuhas (12–2)
1912	Boston Red Sox	41–22	.651	Hugh Bedient (20–9)
1944	St. Louis Cardinals	35–19	.648	Ted Wilks (17–4)

Notice the remarkable performance of the Cardinals rookies during the 1940s and early 1950s. From 1941 through 1952, St. Louis rookies won 257 games, losing only 142, for an outstanding .644 winning percentage.

The record for most rookie pitchers used in a single season is 22, set in 1914 by the Philadelphia Athletics. That's six more than any other team in modern major league history. The record for losses, 71, has stood since 1902. It belongs to the St. Louis Cardinals, thanks in no small part to Stan Yerkes, who lost 20 all by himself.

The highest individual totals for wins and losses were drawn mainly from the early years, when starting pitchers worked to a decision in most games. The ERA leaders are based on 154 innings prior to expansions, 162 innings thereafter.

Most wins by a rookie: 28, Grover Cleveland Alexander (1911); 26, Russ Ford (1910) and Larry Cheney (1912); 24, Ed Summers (1908); 23, Roscoe Miller and Jack Harper (1901), George McQuillan (1908), Vean Gregg (1911), and Jeff Pfeffer (1914); 22, Reb Russell (1913) and Monte Weaver (1932)

Most losses by a rookie: 26, Bob Groom (1909); 25, Harry McIntyre (1905) and Stoney McGlynn (1907); 23, Beany Jacobson (1904), Vive Lindaman (1906), and Elmer Myers (1916); 22, Orval Overall (1905) and Joe Lake (1908); 21, Ed Scott (1900), Long Tom Hughes (1901), Irv Young (1905), Joe Harris (1906), and Ed Brandt (1928).

Highest winning percentage by a rookie (minimum: 10 wins): 1.000, Howie Krist (10–0, 1941); .923, Jim Nash (12–1, 1966); .875, Ron Davis (14–2, 1979); .857, Eddie Yuhas (12–2, 1952) and Mike Nagy (12–2, 1969); .846, Charlie Kerfeld (11–2, 1986); .842, Emil Yde (16–3, 1924); .833, King Cole (20–4, 1910), Hoyt Wilhelm (15–3, 1952), and Dick Farrell (10–2, 1957).

Most strikeouts by a rookie: 276, Dwight Gooden (1984); 245, Herb Score (1955); 227, Grover Cleveland Alexander (1911); 225, Long Tom Hughes (1901); 221, Christy Mathewson (1901); 215, John Montefusco (1975); 209, Russ Ford (1910) and Don Sutton (1966); 206, Gary Nolan (1967) and Bob Johnson (1970).

Lowest earned run averages by a rookie: 1.91, Reb Russell (1913); 1.96, Jeff Tesreau (1912); 1.97, Jeff Pfeffer (1914); 1.98, Scott Perry (1918); 2.06, Stan Bahnsen (1968); 2.09, Jerry Koosman (1968); 2.13, Johnny Beazley (1942); 2.14, Joe Boehling (1913); 2.21, Al Demaree (1913); 2.23, Erv Lange (1914).

WON-LOST RECORD BY STARTING POSITION

CHICAGO 71-90	C	1B	2B	3B	SS	LF	CF	RF	P	DH	Leadoff	Relief	Starts
Harold Baines								4-4		65-81			69-85
Jeff Bittiger									1-6			6-12	1-6
Daryl Boston						12-20	16-23					5-12	28-43
Ivan Calderon						3-1		30-34		1-2			34-37
Joel Davis									0-2			0-3	0-2
John Davis									0-1			10-23	0-1
Mike Diaz		17-22								0-1			17-23
Carlton Fisk	31-37												31-37
Dave Gallagher						2-2	26-41	8-5			25-33		36-48
Ozzie Guillen					67-86								67-86
Jerry Hairston													
Donnie Hill			21-28	4-6						1-2			26-36
Shawn Hillegas									4-2				4-2
Ricky Horton									3-6			21-22	3-6
Lance Johnson						17-10					16-10		17-10
Barry Jones												8-9	
Ron Karkovice	17-20												17-20
Dave LaPoint									10-15				10-15
Bill Long									8-10			11-18	8-10
Steve Lyons			2-0	44-58			5-3	1-4			0-1		52-65
Fred Manrique			39-59		4-4								43-63
Ravelo Manzanillo									1-1				1-1
Carlos Martinez				5-10									5-10
Tom McCarthy												3-3	
Jack McDowell									11-15				11-15
Russ Morman		4-4				2-8				1-1			7-13
Donn Pall												4-13	
Kelly Paris		3-5		3-0									6-5
Dan Pasqua		1-5				30-29		21-24		1-1			53-59
Ken Patterson									1-1			1-6	1-1
John Pawlowski												1-5	
Melido Perez									15-17				15-17
Adam Peterson									0-2				0-2
Jim Randall		1-1						0-1		1-0			2-2
Gary Redus						22-30	5-8	0-1			23-32		27-39
Jerry Reuss									17-12			2-1	17-12
Steve Rosenberg												5-28	
Mark Salas	23-33									0-1			23-34
Jose Segura												0-4	
Bobby Thigpen												45-23	
Greg Walker		45-53											45-53
Ken Williams					15-16		2-5	7-17		1-1	0-2		25-39
Carl Willis												1-5	
Mike Woodard			9-3								2-0		9-3

Batting vs. Left and Right Handed Pitchers

		BA	Rank	SA	Rank	OBA	Rank	HR %	Rank	BB %	Rank	SO %	Rank
Harold Baines	vs. Lefties	.253	87	.358	99	.316	84	1.05	122	8.96	58	18.40	133
	vs. Righties	.289	36	.435	47	.361	29	2.69	69	10.39	48	15.15	101
Daryl Boston	vs. Lefties	.250	--	.393	--	.241	--	0.00	--	0.00	--	23.33	--
	vs. Righties	.213	154	.439	42	.274	150	5.93	8	7.64	93	13.45	78
Ivan Calderon	vs. Lefties	.238	108	.488	31	.347	47	6.25	11	14.74	16	16.84	117
	vs. Righties	.201	161	.397	74	.277	147	4.89	21	9.71	63	24.27	157
Mike Diaz	vs. Lefties	.233	119	.350	104	.233	162	3.33	50	0.00	168	13.33	80
	vs. Righties	.239	--	.326	--	.286	--	1.09	--	5.10	--	22.45	--
Carlton Fisk	vs. Lefties	.290	41	.667	1	.427	10	10.75	1	18.80	3	11.11	63
	vs. Righties	.269	64	.469	28	.344	56	5.63	12	8.29	84	14.92	97
Dave Gallagher	vs. Lefties	.271	63	.335	113	.331	66	0.65	137	8.72	60	9.88	51
	vs. Righties	.328	6	.464	30	.374	21	2.08	86	6.60	113	10.85	49
Ozzie Guillen	vs. Lefties	.263	73	.287	143	.285	123	0.00	140	3.26	156	8.15	30
	vs. Righties	.261	79	.327	133	.297	132	0.00	161	4.50	155	5.92	7
Donnie Hill	vs. Lefties	.180	161	.246	159	.320	73	1.64	99	16.88	7	18.18	129
	vs. Righties	.231	130	.294	155	.286	138	0.63	142	7.39	97	10.23	42
Ron Karkovice	vs. Lefties	.164	166	.273	147	.193	169	1.82	91	3.45	153	29.31	165
	vs. Righties	.183	--	.300	--	.258	--	3.33	--	7.35	--	19.12	--
Steve Lyons	vs. Lefties	.266	68	.374	87	.305	102	2.16	80	5.70	109	13.29	78
	vs. Righties	.270	60	.372	96	.317	101	0.60	145	6.25	119	10.33	44
Fred Manrique	vs. Lefties	.248	95	.329	116	.289	116	1.34	107	5.59	112	16.15	110
	vs. Righties	.224	140	.352	114	.278	146	1.53	103	5.31	137	12.39	67
Russ Morman	vs. Lefties	.258	76	.273	147	.279	130	0.00	140	2.86	159	20.00	142
	vs. Righties	.111	--	.222	--	.200	--	0.00	--	10.00	--	30.00	--
Dan Pasqua	vs. Lefties	.123	169	.160	170	.217	165	0.00	140	7.53	76	25.81	160
	vs. Righties	.252	96	.478	20	.328	81	5.87	11	10.21	51	19.90	144
Gary Redus	vs. Lefties	.248	97	.390	79	.333	60	2.86	61	10.83	38	15.00	97
	vs. Righties	.274	53	.408	68	.348	50	1.91	89	10.87	41	18.48	136
Mark Salas	vs. Lefties	.250	--	.375	--	.294	--	0.00	--	0.00	--	17.65	--
	vs. Righties	.250	102	.328	130	.304	118	1.67	98	6.19	120	7.22	14
Greg Walker	vs. Lefties	.232	124	.321	124	.269	140	0.89	128	4.17	136	18.33	131
	vs. Righties	.253	93	.396	95	.318	75	2.64	74	8.22	85	18.84	137
Ken Williams	vs. Lefties	.208	147	.354	101	.255	151	3.13	54	3.92	142	21.57	148
	vs. Righties	.121	170	.266	164	.196	169	4.03	31	4.26	158	29.79	166
Team Average	vs. Lefties	.238	13	.349	13	.296	14	2.13	12	7.32	10	16.36	12
	vs. Righties	.246	13	.380	9	.306	14	2.56	7	7.42	12	14.42	9
League Average	vs. Lefties	.259		.391		.321		2.47		7.97		14.12	
	vs. Righties	.259		.391		.326		2.47		8.51		14.39	

Batting with Runners on Base and Bases Empty

		BA	Rank	SA	Rank	OBA	Rank	HR %	Rank	BB %	Rank	SO %	Rank
Harold Baines	Runners On	.288	61	.420	65	.373	39	2.00	88	12.54	32	15.25	110
	Bases Empty	.269	48	.404	67	.327	65	2.29	81	7.92	77	16.89	113
Daryl Boston	Runners On	.194	160	.361	116	.261	161	4.63	22	8.26	87	13.22	90
	Bases Empty	.231	128	.480	23	.277	142	5.78	15	5.98	114	15.22	97
Ivan Calderon	Runners On	.174	167	.347	130	.264	160	4.96	15	11.43	44	23.57	159
	Bases Empty	.245	102	.490	19	.329	63	5.59	16	11.18	27	20.50	144
Carlton Fisk	Runners On	.270	84	.459	36	.381	28	4.92	17	12.84	28	12.16	73
	Bases Empty	.282	37	.618	1	.373	16	9.92	2	12.00	18	14.67	86
Dave Gallagher	Runners On	.317	21	.382	101	.381	27	0.81	136	9.66	63	7.59	24
	Bases Empty	.295	25	.420	49	.339	49	1.79	97	6.28	108	12.13	57
Ozzie Guillen	Runners On	.309	28	.378	107	.326	99	0.00	148	2.95	170	4.22	3
	Bases Empty	.232	125	.275	152	.274	145	0.00	156	4.88	138	8.13	17
Donnie Hill	Runners On	.170	168	.216	170	.276	155	0.00	148	12.96	27	12.04	69
	Bases Empty	.248	93	.323	129	.310	95	1.50	109	8.28	73	13.10	67
Steve Lyons	Runners On	.272	80	.398	86	.319	107	1.05	122	7.02	107	7.46	21
	Bases Empty	.267	57	.356	107	.309	99	1.07	127	5.37	127	14.09	84
Fred Manrique	Runners On	.234	132	.348	129	.276	154	1.42	101	5.36	142	9.52	40
	Bases Empty	.235	119	.338	120	.288	131	1.47	110	5.48	124	17.35	119
Dan Pasqua	Runners On	.194	161	.311	148	.301	132	3.06	59	12.99	26	23.38	158
	Bases Empty	.257	76	.509	16	.311	90	6.19	11	6.56	99	18.85	136
Gary Redus	Runners On	.228	141	.391	91	.284	145	3.26	57	9.17	69	20.18	151
	Bases Empty	.282	38	.406	65	.374	15	1.76	99	11.79	20	15.38	98
Mark Salas	Runners On	.211	--	.268	--	.291	--	1.41	--	8.86	--	6.33	--
	Bases Empty	.272	45	.368	94	.311	93	1.60	104	3.79	161	9.09	29
Greg Walker	Runners On	.306	31	.425	61	.369	43	1.25	109	8.33	83	16.67	123
	Bases Empty	.203	156	.336	122	.254	161	2.76	67	6.03	112	20.26	143
Ken Williams	Runners On	.188	163	.400	81	.245	166	5.88	7	4.12	163	26.80	166
	Bases Empty	.141	171	.244	164	.205	170	2.22	84	4.11	155	26.03	163
Team Average	Runners On	.246	13	.363	12	.312	13	2.14	11	8.54	10	14.13	9
	Bases Empty	.242	12	.375	8	.296	14	2.62	6	6.54	13	15.69	11
League Average	Runners On	.268		.401		.336		2.45		9.09		13.68	
	Bases Empty	.253		.383		.315		2.48		7.76		14.81	

Overall Batting Compared to Late Inning Pressure Situations

		BA	Rank	SA	Rank	OBA	Rank	HR %	Rank	BB %	Rank	SO %	Rank	RDI %	Rank
Harold Baines	Overall	.277	46	.411	61	.347	46	2.17	85	9.94	53	16.17	111	.337	16
	Pressure	.333	16	.570	9	.421	15	4.30	32	13.08	26	14.02	70	.379	26
Daryl Boston	Overall	.217	154	.434	40	.271	159	5.34	12	6.89	106	14.43	93	.186	165
	Pressure	.200	128	.340	96	.268	135	2.00	76	8.93	76	21.43	120	.100	149
Ivan Calderon	Overall	.212	160	.424	49	.299	127	5.30	13	11.30	33	21.93	153	.227	137
	Pressure	.211	124	.316	111	.302	106	0.00	110	11.63	43	34.88	168	.167	114
Mike Diaz	Overall	.237	--	.336	--	.266	--	1.97	--	3.16	--	18.99	--	.231	--
	Pressure	.281	59	.406	62	.324	83	3.13	50	5.88	128	20.59	115	.222	85
Carlton Fisk	Overall	.277	47	.542	6	.377	15	7.51	3	12.42	20	13.42	78	.284	63
	Pressure	.296	45	.574	8	.377	31	7.41	7	11.29	47	14.52	72	.263	69
Dave Gallagher	Overall	.303	20	.406	67	.354	37	1.44	111	7.55	93	10.42	40	.289	55
	Pressure	.322	29	.458	41	.365	42	1.69	84	6.35	119	12.70	58	.278	61
Ozzie Guillen	Overall	.261	77	.314	147	.294	137	0.00	165	4.13	161	6.60	11	.238	121
	Pressure	.237	102	.312	117	.276	126	0.00	110	4.85	139	4.85	5	.280	60
Donnie Hill	Overall	.217	153	.281	162	.296	132	0.90	136	10.28	47	12.65	69	.233	128
	Pressure	.213	122	.213	151	.339	71	0.00	110	16.07	10	12.50	56	.200	95
Steve Lyons	Overall	.269	59	.373	97	.313	98	1.06	125	6.08	123	11.22	51	.273	79
	Pressure	.273	66	.338	101	.329	80	1.30	100	8.14	88	8.14	24	.208	93
Fred Manrique	Overall	.235	131	.342	124	.283	151	1.45	110	5.43	138	13.95	86	.274	78
	Pressure	.158	156	.281	133	.186	167	1.75	82	3.28	152	11.48	44	.167	114
Dan Pasqua	Overall	.227	141	.417	60	.307	111	4.74	22	9.68	55	21.05	148	.192	161
	Pressure	.189	138	.338	100	.286	121	4.05	39	10.71	46	20.24	114	.161	121
Gary Redus	Overall	.263	71	.401	75	.342	52	2.29	79	10.86	43	17.11	126	.289	54
	Pressure	.214	120	.333	103	.353	55	2.38	64	17.65	7	27.45	153	.385	24
Mark Salas	Overall	.250	102	.332	132	.303	116	1.53	107	5.69	130	8.06	18	.130	--
	Pressure	.300	--	.333	--	.300	--	0.00	--	0.00	--	6.67	--	.167	--
Greg Walker	Overall	.247	111	.374	95	.304	115	2.12	89	7.04	102	18.69	138	.283	65
	Pressure	.222	116	.286	129	.290	119	1.59	88	7.14	100	28.57	156	.100	149
Ken Williams	Overall	.159	170	.305	153	.221	170	3.64	42	4.12	162	26.34	165	.235	124
	Pressure	.231	108	.308	119	.279	123	0.00	110	6.82	107	36.36	169	.200	95
Team Average	Overall	.244	13	.370	12	.303	14	2.42	9	7.39	12	15.04	11	.247	13
	Pressure	.240	10	.354	10	.309	10	1.99	11	8.81	6	17.23	8	.224	11
League Average	Overall	.259		.391		.324		2.47		8.35		14.31		.269	
	Pressure	.249		.365		.319		2.28		8.71		17.04		.246	

Additional Miscellaneous Batting Comparisons

	Grass Surface BA	Rank	Artificial Surface BA	Rank	Home Games BA	Rank	Road Games BA	Rank	Runners in Scoring Position BA	Rank	Runners in Scoring Pos and Two Outs BA	Rank	Leading Off Inning OBA	Rank	Runners on 3B with less than 2 Outs RDI %	Rank
Harold Baines	.281	42	.260	92	.281	51	.273	53	.301	33	.215	108	.350	38	.683	28
Daryl Boston	.211	158	.265	--	.181	166	.252	93	.237	111	.222	101	.282	122	.500	--
Ivan Calderon	.197	167	.333	--	.191	164	.233	126	.221	139	.111	166	.311	83	.471	136
Mike Diaz	.213	--	.295	44	.231	--	.241	--	.286	--	.333	--	.302	93	.000	--
Carlton Fisk	.254	87	.375	6	.273	65	.280	45	.250	101	.156	155	.421	6	.750	8
Dave Gallagher	.322	6	.244	110	.298	23	.307	18	.310	25	.143	160	.328	62	.917	1
Ozzie Guillen	.247	98	.337	15	.261	83	.262	76	.305	30	.228	95	.255	145	.500	115
Donnie Hill	.231	122	.143	--	.236	124	.205	153	.190	161	.172	149	.340	49	.474	132
Lance Johnson	.196	--	.118	--	.143	--	.230	--	.160	--	.154	--	.250	147	.400	--
Steve Lyons	.268	56	.272	80	.269	73	.269	61	.274	66	.239	81	.283	121	.696	20
Fred Manrique	.242	108	.203	151	.222	147	.249	103	.275	63	.250	61	.243	153	.526	109
Dan Pasqua	.224	135	.246	107	.225	142	.230	133	.186	164	.190	135	.283	120	.414	153
Gary Redus	.267	60	.243	111	.286	42	.231	129	.204	153	.185	140	.349	41	.600	65
Mark Salas	.236	116	.314	--	.264	78	.233	--	.167	--	.048	171	.309	86	.800	--
Greg Walker	.231	123	.354	11	.229	138	.267	63	.282	59	.229	94	.258	143	.563	87
Ken Williams	.156	170	.200	--	.156	170	.162	169	.189	163	.105	--	.186	168	.412	154
Team Average	.239	14	.265	7	.238	13	.249	11	.245	13	.193	14	.293	12	.533	13
League Average	.256		.267		.262		.257		.262		.239		.311		.570	

Pitching vs. Left and Right Handed Batters

		BA	Rank	SA	Rank	OBA	Rank	HR %	Rank	BB %	Rank	SO %	Rank
Jeff Bittiger	vs. Lefties	.242	47	.442	108	.354	99	5.26	126	14.78	125	9.57	98
	vs. Righties	.265	79	.500	121	.318	66	4.41	122	7.84	69	14.38	64
John Davis	vs. Lefties	.324	122	.529	125	.459	130	2.94	101	21.05	129	9.77	93
	vs. Righties	.280	103	.382	65	.380	127	1.27	14	11.83	121	12.90	87
Shawn Hillegas	vs. Lefties	.200	9	.318	26	.327	65	3.53	114	14.85	118	11.88	75
	vs. Righties	.217	--	.350	--	.246	--	1.67	--	4.62	--	21.54	--
Ricky Horton	vs. Lefties	.280	92	.390	78	.327	67	1.00	19	6.84	35	11.11	81
	vs. Righties	.295	116	.429	99	.356	117	1.60	25	7.91	70	4.24	128
Dave LaPoint	vs. Lefties	.259	64	.376	66	.293	23	1.18	26	5.32	13	9.57	97
	vs. Righties	.242	42	.336	31	.300	38	1.69	26	7.20	56	12.01	99
Bill Long	vs. Lefties	.311	114	.486	118	.370	108	2.77	94	7.73	44	8.56	110
	vs. Righties	.250	56	.422	87	.278	18	3.49	105	4.05	7	12.43	93
Jack McDowell	vs. Lefties	.274	83	.384	73	.356	102	1.95	59	11.20	105	11.48	78
	vs. Righties	.216	20	.332	27	.294	33	2.05	42	8.48	80	13.03	84
Melido Perez	vs. Lefties	.232	34	.385	75	.299	28	3.02	103	9.01	67	16.22	37
	vs. Righties	.267	85	.435	104	.329	84	3.98	116	8.16	74	16.84	44
Jerry Reuss	vs. Lefties	.266	75	.415	92	.314	42	3.19	110	4.90	11	6.86	121
	vs. Righties	.262	76	.369	52	.306	45	1.99	36	5.86	31	10.17	117
Bobby Thigpen	vs. Lefties	.315	116	.345	42	.384	117	0.61	11	11.05	100	10.53	87
	vs. Righties	.235	35	.337	32	.294	34	2.67	70	5.77	28	20.19	27
Team Average	vs. Lefties	.277	12	.418	12	.350	14	2.59	10	10.15	12	11.26	14
	vs. Righties	.259	9	.389	6	.319	7	2.44	5	7.65	7	12.69	13
League Average	vs. Lefties	.262		.387		.331		2.24		9.12		13.21	
	vs. Righties	.258		.393		.320		2.63		7.80		15.09	

Pitching with Runners on Base and Bases Empty

		BA	Rank	SA	Rank	OBA	Rank	HR %	Rank	BB %	Rank	SO %	Rank
Jeff Bittiger	Runners On	.242	39	.429	92	.348	89	3.30	100	14.66	127	12.93	72
	Bases Empty	.264	83	.507	126	.322	78	5.71	128	7.89	72	11.84	91
John Davis	Runners On	.310	114	.458	109	.400	124	1.94	46	12.30	113	10.16	103
	Bases Empty	.279	103	.413	96	.432	129	1.92	46	20.45	129	13.64	71
Ricky Horton	Runners On	.292	103	.451	106	.324	59	2.05	51	5.75	13	5.75	124
	Bases Empty	.290	119	.392	79	.371	125	0.92	9	9.39	96	6.12	127
Dave LaPoint	Runners On	.261	66	.343	29	.316	45	0.82	10	7.58	39	11.55	88
	Bases Empty	.234	36	.341	29	.288	22	2.15	58	6.50	48	11.75	94
Bill Long	Runners On	.272	78	.462	111	.309	38	3.45	105	5.85	15	8.92	116
	Bases Empty	.285	113	.446	110	.334	96	2.90	93	5.90	38	11.79	93
Jack McDowell	Runners On	.237	27	.361	45	.323	55	2.81	83	9.76	90	12.79	74
	Bases Empty	.251	62	.357	46	.328	90	1.43	23	10.00	110	11.79	92
Melido Perez	Runners On	.239	34	.389	65	.291	17	2.61	76	7.54	38	16.23	35
	Bases Empty	.255	68	.422	103	.328	88	4.06	115	9.37	95	16.70	43
Jerry Reuss	Runners On	.255	56	.378	59	.294	22	2.52	72	4.93	3	10.86	95
	Bases Empty	.268	89	.373	59	.315	65	1.91	45	6.26	44	8.95	121
Bobby Thigpen	Runners On	.261	65	.320	15	.332	67	1.48	28	8.47	61	14.41	54
	Bases Empty	.289	118	.369	57	.346	111	2.01	51	8.02	76	17.28	37
Team Average	Runners On	.266	4	.402	7	.329	5	2.47	7	8.61	6	11.80	13
	Bases Empty	.265	14	.397	10	.332	14	2.52	7	8.57	13	12.44	14
League Average	Runners On	.268		.401		.336		2.45		9.09		13.68	
	Bases Empty	.253		.383		.315		2.48		7.76		14.81	

Overall Pitching Compared to Late Inning Pressure Situations

		BA	Rank	SA	Rank	OBA	Rank	HR %	Rank	BB %	Rank	SO %	Rank
Jeff Bittiger	Overall	.255	56	.476	123	.333	86	4.76	126	10.82	111	12.31	86
	Pressure	.233	46	.395	81	.340	79	2.33	69	14.00	115	12.00	94
John Davis	Overall	.297	121	.440	112	.413	128	1.93	36	15.67	128	11.60	95
	Pressure	.238	54	.369	67	.375	107	2.38	70	16.19	123	16.19	50
Ricky Horton	Overall	.291	116	.420	98	.349	111	1.46	13	7.64	49	5.94	128
	Pressure	.327	116	.481	113	.385	112	1.92	60	8.06	50	8.06	117
Barry Jones	Overall	.170	--	.284	--	.302	--	3.41	--	16.04	--	16.04	--
	Pressure	.196	15	.314	35	.305	48	3.92	105	13.56	111	15.25	57
Dave LaPoint	Overall	.245	41	.342	24	.299	23	1.62	20	6.94	34	11.67	93
	Pressure	.362	124	.617	127	.380	110	4.26	112	3.70	6	5.56	124
Bill Long	Overall	.280	105	.453	116	.323	70	3.14	104	5.87	18	10.52	106
	Pressure	.257	74	.368	65	.301	40	2.08	64	4.46	12	8.92	112
Jack McDowell	Overall	.245	44	.359	37	.326	77	2.00	40	9.90	100	12.23	88
	Pressure	.269	92	.448	104	.359	95	2.99	89	12.50	102	11.25	100
Melido Perez	Overall	.248	49	.409	90	.313	47	3.47	114	8.61	79	16.51	37
	Pressure	.328	117	.638	129	.391	116	5.17	119	9.23	70	15.38	53
Jerry Reuss	Overall	.263	69	.375	54	.307	35	2.16	57	5.73	15	9.72	115
	Pressure	.175	7	.263	17	.203	4	1.75	52	3.33	4	13.33	82
Steve Rosenberg	Overall	.298	--	.444	--	.360	--	2.81	--	9.36	--	13.79	--
	Pressure	.255	72	.298	29	.271	19	0.00	1	2.04	3	22.45	13
Bobby Thigpen	Overall	.273	95	.341	23	.338	90	1.70	23	8.29	65	15.58	47
	Pressure	.275	97	.328	42	.345	86	1.15	32	9.33	71	14.00	72
Team Average	Overall	.266	9	.399	10	.331	12	2.50	7	8.59	10	12.15	13
	Pressure	.272	12	.397	11	.339	12	2.27	8	8.78	5	12.26	13
League Average	Overall	.259		.391		.324		2.47		8.35		14.31	
	Pressure	.249		.369		.324		2.26		9.33		15.69	

Additional Miscellaneous Pitching Comparisons

	Grass Surface BA	Rank	Artificial Surface BA	Rank	Home Games BA	Rank	Road Games BA	Rank	Runners in Scoring Position BA	Rank	Runners in Scoring Pos and Two Outs BA	Rank	Leading Off Inning OBA	Rank
Jeff Bittiger	.242	45	.302	106	.237	44	.274	83	.241	--	.167	--	.306	63
John Davis	.304	124	.211	--	.309	123	.278	--	.291	97	.167	19	.453	127
Shawn Hillegas	.186	--	.250	42	.133	--	.240	--	.207	--	.083	--	.286	--
Ricky Horton	.281	111	.343	121	.273	91	.316	125	.292	98	.265	92	.455	128
Dave LaPoint	.250	53	.214	16	.252	57	.237	36	.266	74	.262	89	.260	21
Bill Long	.285	113	.241	35	.296	117	.263	72	.296	105	.284	102	.333	90
Jack McDowell	.241	44	.348	--	.214	15	.280	93	.199	12	.138	9	.347	102
Melido Perez	.258	61	.214	15	.251	56	.246	47	.253	57	.213	49	.325	83
Jerry Reuss	.267	81	.246	38	.262	78	.264	74	.273	79	.262	89	.294	49
Steve Rosenberg	.308	125	.211	--	.310	--	.282	--	.291	--	.241	--	.421	--
Bobby Thigpen	.280	110	.185	--	.288	108	.250	54	.256	62	.220	55	.394	122
Team Average	.269	12	.251	1	.264	11	.267	10	.264	9	.238	8	.336	14
League Average	.256		.267		.257		.262		.262		.239		.311	

CLEVELAND INDIANS

- **A new basis for platooning. Is anybody out there listening?**
- **Quick now—who was the dominant team in the A.L. East early last season? Surprise!**

A colleague of ours once wrote that the greatest contribution a statistician could make to baseball would be to uncover a new basis for platooning, one that would complement the traditional lefty-righty maneuvers. So we took pride three years ago in presenting the results of a 10–year study that did just that. Our figures proved that ground-ball hitters enjoyed greater success against fly-ball pitchers than they did against ground-ball pitchers. Conversely, fly-ball hitters generally hit better against ground-ballers than they did against fly-ballers.

The rule was simple to remember because it mirrored the lefty-righty rules: Matchups of opposites (right-handed batters vs. southpaws, or ground-ball hitters vs. fly-ball pitchers) favor the batter; matchups of like types favor the pitcher.

Each edition of the *Analyst* has been liberally sprinkled with information on which batters and pitchers tend toward ground outs and which tend toward fly outs. (This year, we've even included ground-out and air-out data in our new "Player Tendencies" section.) And we supplemented the results of that initial study in each subsequent edition of the *Analyst*.

Two years ago, we pointed out that San Diego's bias toward fly-ball hitters made them vulnerable to fly-ball pitchers, and that manager Larry Bowa would be wise to start a few extra ground-ball hitters against pitchers who induced lots of fly balls. In last year's edition, we pointed out that Seattle manager Dick Williams ought to exploit the ground ball-fly ball rules, since the Mariners had the American League's strongest bias toward ground outs in 1986. Both managers ignored us. Both are history.

Now we're not presumptuous enough to think that Doc Edwards's fate will be determined by whether or not he heeds our warning. But it is our "unhappy duty" (fans of TV's "Superman", identify that quote and earn membership in the Elias trivia Hall of Fame) to point out that last season's Cleveland Indians had the strongest tendency in either league toward hitting fly outs.

And since we've had no luck convincing managers that there might be a few extra wins in exploiting this recently discovered tendency, we're going to appeal this time to the baser instincts of our readers. Frankly, we think there's some money to be made by those who have a nodding acquaintance with the neighborhood bookie. But first, let's take a step back. The ground outs-to-air outs ratios for each team's hitters last season (the higher the ratio, the greater the tendency toward ground outs):

Cleveland	0.99	New York	0.96
Seattle	0.99	Houston	1.09
Boston	1.00	San Francisco	1.09
Texas	1.00	Cincinnati	1.14
Oakland	1.02	Chicago	1.17
Chicago	1.02	Pittsburgh	1.18
California	1.03	Montreal	1.20
Minnesota	1.06	Atlanta	1.22
Detroit	1.08	Los Angeles	1.23
Toronto	1.08	San Diego	1.26
Kansas City	1.09	St. Louis	1.28
Baltimore	1.12	Philadelphia	1.31
New York	1.14		
Milwaukee	1.21		

The departure of Franco (1.77 last season), to be replaced by Jerry Browne (1.09), the substitution of Pete O'Brien (0.90) for Upshaw (0.88), and the addition of Oddibe McDowell (0.94) suggest that Cleveland's average could fall to an even lower level in 1989. And that means that the Indians may be even a better bet this season than last when facing a ground-ball pitcher. Their opponents are likely to have an edge once again when throwing a fly-baller. Look at the difference in Cleveland's performance last season, with opposing pitchers of decision classified according to whether they fell above or below the American League G/A ratio of 1.06:

	W	L	Pct.
Indians vs. ground-ball pitchers	47	40	.540
Indians vs. fly-ball pitchers	31	44	.413

Cleveland's team of fly-ball hitters played seven games over .500 against ground-ball pitchers, 13 games below against fly-ball pitchers. The Milwaukee Brewers, who had the league's highest G/A ratio (that is, the strongest tendency toward ground outs) were a much better bet against fly-ball pitchers than against ground-ballers:

	W	L	Pct.
Brewers vs. ground-ball pitchers	38	37	.507
Brewers vs. fly-ball pitchers	49	38	.563

The trend is significant on a team level because it's so prevalent at the player level. Among the 414 players with at least 500 at-bats over the past five seasons, we classified those with G/A ratios below 1.00 as fly-ball hitters, those above 1.25 as ground-ball hitters, and those in between as neutral. The group performances are illustrated in the following table, showing how many members of each group had higher batting averages against each type of pitcher. "GBP" stands for ground-ball pitchers (G/A ratios above the major league average), "FBP" for fly-ball pitchers (below the average):

Group of batters	Better vs. GBP	Better vs. FBP	Pct. Better vs. GBP
Ground-ball hitters	66	58	.532
Neutral hitters	104	55	.654
Fly-ball hitters	96	35	.733

The differences were significant, though not as striking, when slugging average rather than batting average was used as the basis for comparison:

Group of batters	Better vs. GBP	Better vs. FBP	Pct. Better vs. GBP
Ground-ball hitters	45	79	.363
Neutral hitters	71	88	.447
Fly-ball hitters	64	67	.489

You might be wondering how those figures compare to the corresponding numbers for classification by "handedness." Using that same group of 414 players (with 500 or more at-bats since 1984), we compiled five-year figures against lefty and righty pitchers, and found those differences to be more pronounced, especially those based on slugging percentage:

Group of batters	Better vs. LHP	Better vs. RHP	Pct. Better vs. LHP
Left-handed hitters	9	117	.071
Switch hitters	42	33	.560
Right-handed hitters	170	43	.798

Clearly, the lefty-righty trend is more closer to a universal trait than the ground out-air out tendencies. That makes it all the more important for managers to know which players conform to the general rule for ground outs and air outs, which don't, and—most important of all—which exaggerate it. The following table shows the career batting averages of the 1989 Indians roster (as we went to press) against ground-ball and fly-ball pitchers:

Player	G/A Ratio	Vs. GBP	Vs. FBP	Diff.
Joe Carter	0.69	.265	.280	−.015
Cory Snyder	0.81	.269	.249	+.020
Mel Hall	0.92	.287	.275	+.012
Luis Aguayo	0.98	.244	.238	+.006
Pete O'Brien	0.98	.270	.274	−.004
Brook Jacoby	1.01	.271	.274	−.003
Jay Bell	1.06	.200	.242	−.042
Oddibe McDowell	1.12	.269	.236	+.033
Carmen Castillo	1.16	.270	.249	+.021
Denny Gonzalez	1.18	.201	.198	+.003
Andy Allanson	1.20	.287	.222	+.065
Paul Zuvella	1.39	.215	.215	.000

Jerry Browne	1.50	.335	.217	+.118
Dave Clark	2.27	.289	.211	+.078

The figures above make it clear that Allanson, Browne, and Clark should play against all ground-ball pitchers, whether they throw right-handed, left-handed, or with their feet. Only six players outhit Browne against ground-ballers over the past three years: Boggs, Mattingly, Greenwell, Yount, Puckett, and Trillo (minimum: 250 AB). Jay Bell, on the other hand, might be a poor choice against ground-ball pitchers (although his career stats are basically only one season's worth).

As we've said in the past, this data shouldn't be the sole guide for choosing a lineup. But three years after the figures were first published, it's become downright inexcusable for a manager to disregard it.

Although it now seems like ancient history, Cleveland won 16 of its first 20 games last season. The Indians' long and nearly unprecedented slide toward a losing record made that start noteworthy but entirely forgettable. Actually, with each year it's becoming easier to forget about fast starts in general, because teams breaking from the gate with the speed of Dr. Fager, once a rarity, have become almost commonplace.

The Indians were the 22d team in modern major league history to win at least 16 of its first 20 games. Ten of those teams played during a 21–year stretch from 1902 to 1922. Only seven more followed during a 58–year drought from 1923 through 1980, leaving the remaining five teams to the last eight years. The following table summarizes the fast-starting teams by decade:

1900s	1910s	1920s	1930s	1940s	1950s	1960s	1970s	1980s
3	5	2	1	3	1	1	1	5

(Incidentally, despite the Orioles' record slow start last season, there hasn't been a corresponding increase in the number of slow starts during the 1980s. In fact, only three teams in the past 15 years have lost as many as 16 of their first 20 games: the 1981 Cubs, the 1988 Braves, and the 1988 Orioles.)

As for fast-starting teams failing to play .500 for the season, last season's Indians have little company. Only their 1941 Cleveland ancestors also managed that trick. The table below shows that most of the other teams played at least .600 for the season:

	Teams	Above .600	.500–.600	Below .500
16 wins in first 20 games	13	7	2	2
17 wins in first 20 games	6	3	3	0
18 wins in first 20 games	5	2	3	0

Cleveland was also the first team ever to win 16 of its first 20 games coming off a sub-.400 season. Now the Tribe can become the first to do it coming off successive losing seasons. Good luck!

WON-LOST RECORD BY STARTING POSITION

CLEVELAND 78-84	C	1B	2B	3B	SS	LF	CF	RF	P	DH	Leadoff	Relief	Starts
Andy Allanson	66-65												66-65
Rod Allen										2-1			2-1
Scott Bailes									8-13			6-10	8-13
Chris Bando	9-14												9-14
Jay Bell					30-38								30-38
Bud Black									3-4			4-5	3-4
Tom Candiotti									16-15				16-15
Joe Carter							75-81						75-81
Carmen Castillo						12-11		6-6		3-4			21-21
Dave Clark						3-4		4-6		9-12			16-22
Chris Codiroli									0-2			4-8	0-2
Jeff Dedmon												3-18	
John Farrell									14-16			0-1	14-16
Dan Firova													
Julio Franco			70-81							0-1	63-72		70-82
Terry Francona		2-2				1-4				21-17	3-0		24-23
Don Gordon												11-27	
Mel Hall						58-61	1-2	1-1		1-4			61-68
Brad Havens												6-22	
Brook Jacoby				74-75									74-75
Houston Jimenez			4-0								1-0		4-0
Doug Jones												41-10	
Scott Jordan						2-0	1-0						3-0
Jeff Kaiser												1-2	
Ron Kittle										26-32			26-32
Tom Lampkin	1-0												1-0
Bill Laskey												4-13	
Luis Medina		9-6											9-6
Rod Nichols									3-7			0-1	3-7
Jon Perlman												1-9	
Domingo Ramos		0-4	2-2	0-1	0-2						0-1		2-9
Rick Rodriguez									1-4			0-5	1-4
Dan Schatzeder												5-10	
Cory Snyder						0-1	66-71						66-72
Greg Swindell									19-14				19-14
Pat Tabler		9-1								16-13			25-14
Ron Tingley	2-5												2-5
Willie Upshaw		58-71									2-1		58-71
Mike Walker									0-1			0-2	0-1
Ron Washington			2-1	0-5	27-21							9-10	29-27
Eddie Williams				4-3									4-3
Reggie Williams						4-4							4-4
Rich Yett									14-8			0-1	14-8
Paul Zuvella					21-23								21-23

Batting vs. Left and Right Handed Pitchers

		BA	Rank	SA	Rank	OBA	Rank	HR %	Rank	BB %	Rank	SO %	Rank
Andy Allanson	vs. Lefties	.269	66	.308	134	.306	95	0.00	140	4.39	130	11.40	68
	vs. Righties	.261	81	.327	131	.304	117	1.52	104	5.56	131	13.89	84
Jay Bell	vs. Lefties	.350	--	.425	--	.386	--	0.00	--	6.67	--	13.33	--
	vs. Righties	.187	165	.246	168	.267	160	1.17	117	9.42	68	24.61	158
Joe Carter	vs. Lefties	.311	30	.553	10	.348	46	5.30	20	5.67	110	12.06	72
	vs. Righties	.260	82	.458	33	.305	115	4.09	29	5.10	141	12.29	63
Carmen Castillo	vs. Lefties	.257	77	.352	103	.291	114	1.90	87	3.64	151	16.36	112
	vs. Righties	.296	--	.437	--	.306	--	2.82	--	1.39	--	18.06	--
Dave Clark	vs. Lefties	.200	--	.200	--	.167	--	0.00	--	0.00	--	16.67	--
	vs. Righties	.265	72	.364	104	.339	64	1.99	87	10.12	56	16.07	111
Julio Franco	vs. Lefties	.383	2	.624	4	.461	2	3.76	42	12.50	25	5.26	11
	vs. Righties	.281	44	.350	115	.333	77	1.04	122	7.06	105	12.21	62
Terry Francona	vs. Lefties	.375	--	.375	--	.444	--	0.00	--	11.11	--	11.11	--
	vs. Righties	.309	16	.363	107	.319	94	0.49	150	1.88	170	7.98	19
Mel Hall	vs. Lefties	.109	170	.196	167	.163	170	2.17	79	5.88	102	13.73	83
	vs. Righties	.296	29	.412	66	.327	84	1.07	121	4.98	145	8.57	25
Brook Jacoby	vs. Lefties	.233	123	.357	100	.277	133	2.33	75	5.84	106	16.06	109
	vs. Righties	.243	115	.329	128	.307	113	1.42	107	8.53	80	16.84	119
Ron Kittle	vs. Lefties	.236	112	.562	9	.333	60	10.11	2	9.52	51	22.86	151
	vs. Righties	.272	58	.515	11	.315	105	6.62	6	4.03	160	27.52	162
Cory Snyder	vs. Lefties	.342	6	.667	1	.400	20	8.11	4	9.60	49	16.80	116
	vs. Righties	.253	94	.433	50	.305	116	4.25	27	6.93	106	18.48	135
Willie Upshaw	vs. Lefties	.203	151	.216	165	.280	129	0.00	140	8.54	63	14.63	92
	vs. Righties	.253	92	.396	76	.338	65	2.63	75	11.41	31	11.20	53
Ron Washington	vs. Lefties	.255	82	.382	83	.281	128	1.82	91	1.72	166	10.34	54
	vs. Righties	.256	89	.357	111	.304	119	0.60	146	4.37	156	15.85	108
Team Average	vs. Lefties	.275	3	.444	2	.331	5	3.69	1	7.23	11	14.00	9
	vs. Righties	.257	9	.371	13	.309	12	2.09	12	6.78	14	14.41	8
League Average	vs. Lefties	.259		.391		.321		2.47		7.97		14.12	
	vs. Righties	.259		.391		.326		2.47		8.51		14.39	

Batting with Runners on Base and Bases Empty

		BA	Rank	SA	Rank	OBA	Rank	HR %	Rank	BB %	Rank	SO %	Rank
Andy Allanson	Runners On	.305	32	.379	105	.349	68	1.13	116	5.91	132	12.32	75
	Bases Empty	.233	123	.284	147	.273	148	1.17	124	4.80	143	14.02	82
Jay Bell	Runners On	.234	132	.298	156	.288	140	1.06	120	7.62	98	21.90	156
	Bases Empty	.205	153	.265	159	.290	125	0.85	136	9.92	43	22.90	151
Joe Carter	Runners On	.288	60	.502	18	.338	86	3.91	37	6.73	114	13.14	88
	Bases Empty	.256	80	.459	29	.293	112	4.71	25	3.91	160	11.45	50
Julio Franco	Runners On	.274	76	.385	98	.340	81	0.96	131	9.32	67	14.41	101
	Bases Empty	.319	6	.422	47	.373	17	1.98	90	7.73	84	8.64	24
Terry Francona	Runners On	.390	1	.429	57	.402	14	0.00	148	3.53	168	4.71	7
	Bases Empty	.267	58	.326	126	.277	141	0.74	142	1.46	171	10.22	36
Mel Hall	Runners On	.291	53	.405	78	.339	84	0.91	134	8.00	90	8.00	28
	Bases Empty	.271	46	.383	85	.290	123	1.36	114	2.64	168	9.90	32
Brook Jacoby	Runners On	.236	130	.302	154	.311	121	0.89	135	10.12	57	16.73	125
	Bases Empty	.245	103	.358	105	.292	116	2.14	87	6.30	107	16.62	111
Ron Kittle	Runners On	.248	115	.448	43	.317	111	5.71	8	7.32	102	26.02	164
	Bases Empty	.267	58	.608	2	.328	64	10.00	1	5.34	128	25.19	159
Cory Snyder	Runners On	.266	96	.495	20	.328	98	5.50	9	8.61	78	18.44	143
	Bases Empty	.276	43	.474	25	.325	68	4.78	23	6.69	95	17.83	127
Willie Upshaw	Runners On	.231	137	.333	139	.317	110	1.39	102	11.11	46	13.10	86
	Bases Empty	.256	77	.397	73	.340	48	2.89	64	10.90	30	10.58	42
Ron Washington	Runners On	.245	120	.383	99	.280	149	1.06	120	3.88	166	15.53	113
	Bases Empty	.264	68	.349	112	.312	89	0.78	141	3.62	162	13.77	79
Team Average	Runners On	.262	9	.387	10	.320	12	2.10	12	7.83	13	14.88	12
	Bases Empty	.260	3	.386	5	.310	9	2.67	5	6.17	14	13.90	5
League Average	Runners On	.268		.401		.336		2.45		9.09		13.68	
	Bases Empty	.253		.383		.315		2.48		7.76		14.81	

Overall Batting Compared to Late Inning Pressure Situations

		BA	Rank	SA	Rank	OBA	Rank	HR %	Rank	BB %	Rank	SO %	Rank	RDI %	Rank
Andy Allanson	Overall	.263	74	.323	141	.305	113	1.15	118	5.27	143	13.29	76	.320	25
	Pressure	.226	113	.274	137	.304	104	0.00	110	10.14	56	15.94	88	.455	10
Jay Bell	Overall	.218	150	.280	163	.289	140	0.95	134	8.90	67	22.46	157	.239	117
	Pressure	.174	--	.174	--	.240	--	0.00	--	7.69	--	19.23	--	.000	--
Joe Carter	Overall	.271	56	.478	19	.314	94	4.35	27	5.22	145	12.24	66	.317	27
	Pressure	.202	127	.381	70	.256	144	3.57	43	4.44	142	15.56	84	.250	72
Carmen Castillo	Overall	.273	--	.386	--	.297	--	2.27	--	2.75	--	17.03	--	.243	--
	Pressure	.235	105	.353	88	.235	153	2.94	54	0.00	168	32.35	164	.375	27
Dave Clark	Overall	.263	--	.359	--	.333	--	1.92	--	9.77	--	16.09	--	.313	--
	Pressure	.149	164	.213	151	.167	170	2.13	73	2.08	165	27.08	152	.091	154
Julio Franco	Overall	.303	19	.409	63	.361	32	1.63	102	8.28	82	10.65	44	.267	86
	Pressure	.333	16	.500	21	.376	32	3.85	41	6.98	103	13.95	69	.263	69
Terry Francona	Overall	.311	8	.363	107	.324	80	0.47	156	2.25	170	8.11	19	.313	--
	Pressure	.452	1	.516	19	.452	5	0.00	110	0.00	168	9.68	33	.571	1
Mel Hall	Overall	.280	43	.392	85	.312	103	1.17	117	5.06	148	9.04	25	.333	17
	Pressure	.304	42	.435	50	.347	63	2.90	55	6.67	112	13.33	64	.308	50
Brook Jacoby	Overall	.241	122	.335	128	.300	126	1.63	103	7.92	87	16.67	119	.238	121
	Pressure	.176	146	.203	154	.235	154	0.00	110	7.41	97	22.22	127	.154	125
Ron Kittle	Overall	.258	84	.533	7	.323	85	8.00	2	6.30	118	25.59	164	.269	85
	Pressure	.250	87	.469	36	.316	89	6.25	13	10.53	51	28.95	157	.200	95
Cory Snyder	Overall	.272	54	.483	17	.326	77	5.09	18	7.53	95	18.10	131	.248	107
	Pressure	.237	101	.553	12	.275	127	9.21	4	5.00	136	26.25	151	.267	67
Willie Upshaw	Overall	.245	115	.369	99	.330	71	2.23	81	10.99	39	11.70	60	.224	138
	Pressure	.176	145	.191	160	.250	148	0.00	110	8.97	74	11.54	47	.107	147
Ron Washington	Overall	.256	89	.363	106	.298	128	0.90	137	3.73	164	14.52	96	.281	68
	Pressure	.265	75	.412	59	.306	100	0.00	110	2.63	159	15.79	86	.571	1
Team Average	Overall	.261	7	.387	8	.314	11	2.43	8	6.88	14	14.32	6	.273	8
	Pressure	.233	12	.351	11	.286	14	2.59	5	6.60	14	18.49	13	.241	9
League Average	Overall	.259		.391		.324		2.47		8.35		14.31		.269	
	Pressure	.249		.365		.319		2.28		8.71		17.04		.246	

Additional Miscellaneous Batting Comparisons

	Grass Surface BA	Rank	Artificial Surface BA	Rank	Home Games BA	Rank	Road Games BA	Rank	Runners in Scoring Position BA	Rank	Runners in Scoring Pos and Two Outs BA	Rank	Leading Off Inning OBA	Rank	Runners on 3B with less than 2 Outs RDI %	Rank
Andy Allanson	.271	54	.215	138	.274	64	.251	94	.307	27	.373	5	.264	138	.500	115
Jay Bell	.200	162	.323	--	.197	161	.245	113	.236	113	.296	37	.209	165	.571	81
Joe Carter	.264	64	.302	35	.281	52	.261	80	.291	45	.308	26	.272	131	.588	75
Carmen Castillo	.304	16	.158	166	.388	--	.202	156	.235	--	.278	--	.296	--	.500	--
Dave Clark	.254	88	.333	--	.228	139	.313	--	.297	--	.235	--	.308	--	.556	89
Julio Franco	.318	8	.233	121	.364	3	.251	97	.270	71	.217	105	.363	28	.636	50
Terry Francona	.303	17	.353	--	.333	5	.290	31	.370	--	.500	--	.304	89	.375	--
Mel Hall	.278	47	.289	53	.289	37	.271	56	.288	53	.246	68	.256	144	.750	8
Brook Jacoby	.240	112	.244	109	.239	117	.243	115	.225	135	.186	139	.298	100	.571	81
Ron Kittle	.236	117	.340	13	.247	103	.264	70	.226	133	.244	72	.293	108	.667	33
Cory Snyder	.276	50	.246	106	.233	127	.315	7	.238	110	.228	95	.261	141	.520	113
Willie Upshaw	.240	110	.274	76	.238	119	.253	90	.202	156	.250	61	.314	82	.533	108
Ron Washington	.247	99	.293	48	.233	130	.280	44	.255	97	.231	92	.359	32	.667	33
Paul Zuvella	.198	165	.375	--	.204	--	.247	--	.226	--	.176	--	.333	--	.250	--
Team Average	.261	4	.260	10	.266	5	.256	8	.253	11	.254	6	.300	10	.582	4
League Average	.256		.267		.262		.257		.262		.239		.311		.570	

Pitching vs. Left and Right Handed Batters

		BA	Rank	SA	Rank	OBA	Rank	HR %	Rank	BB %	Rank	SO %	Rank
Scott Bailes	vs. Lefties	.243	48	.270	7	.315	46	0.00	1	8.59	61	10.94	83
	vs. Righties	.272	94	.465	118	.324	73	4.94	125	7.16	55	7.98	122
Bud Black	vs. Lefties	.174	--	.217	--	.298	--	1.45	--	12.94	--	17.65	--
	vs. Righties	.289	113	.417	85	.354	115	2.89	83	8.42	79	17.58	41
Tom Candiotti	vs. Lefties	.280	93	.383	71	.333	76	1.53	43	7.30	41	12.03	72
	vs. Righties	.262	75	.359	47	.301	41	2.16	49	4.04	6	19.19	31
John Farrell	vs. Lefties	.270	79	.376	65	.341	90	1.13	24	9.20	71	10.20	88
	vs. Righties	.267	86	.410	82	.315	55	2.75	73	5.32	22	10.38	114
Don Gordon	vs. Lefties	.227	28	.330	30	.299	29	1.03	21	8.26	55	8.26	112
	vs. Righties	.326	128	.508	122	.372	124	3.03	91	6.58	45	7.24	124
Brad Havens	vs. Lefties	.254	--	.338	--	.286	--	1.41	--	5.06	--	16.46	--
	vs. Righties	.282	105	.481	119	.337	94	3.85	113	7.69	64	10.06	118
Doug Jones	vs. Lefties	.203	11	.266	5	.254	9	0.56	9	6.35	28	18.52	18
	vs. Righties	.236	37	.271	3	.267	12	0.00	1	2.68	1	24.83	8
Rod Nichols	vs. Lefties	.261	66	.362	51	.320	55	1.45	40	7.74	45	7.10	117
	vs. Righties	.285	--	.415	--	.345	--	2.31	--	7.75	--	14.08	--
Greg Swindell	vs. Lefties	.274	84	.372	62	.301	32	1.83	54	4.00	3	16.57	32
	vs. Righties	.247	50	.361	48	.283	28	1.96	34	4.67	13	18.57	34
Rich Yett	vs. Lefties	.295	108	.447	110	.346	93	1.86	57	7.18	38	9.77	94
	vs. Righties	.244	46	.373	54	.340	96	2.39	59	12.40	126	15.29	54
Team Average	vs. Lefties	.273	10	.387	7	.334	8	1.62	2	8.06	3	11.43	13
	vs. Righties	.268	11	.400	11	.321	9	2.53	7	6.58	1	14.47	11
League Average	vs. Lefties	.262		.387		.331		2.24		9.12		13.21	
	vs. Righties	.258		.393		.320		2.63		7.80		15.09	

Pitching with Runners on Base and Bases Empty

		BA	Rank	SA	Rank	OBA	Rank	HR %	Rank	BB %	Rank	SO %	Rank
Scott Bailes	Runners On	.321	120	.544	128	.375	108	5.58	128	7.76	47	9.39	114
	Bases Empty	.232	35	.351	41	.288	23	2.90	92	7.26	65	8.06	123
Bud Black	Runners On	.258	58	.409	78	.377	111	3.79	114	13.69	121	15.48	39
	Bases Empty	.268	90	.346	33	.311	56	1.68	35	5.79	33	19.47	23
Tom Candiotti	Runners On	.246	42	.344	31	.302	31	2.02	49	6.87	27	16.54	28
	Bases Empty	.291	120	.393	82	.331	94	1.66	33	5.10	22	14.12	67
John Farrell	Runners On	.258	59	.373	53	.317	49	2.24	64	7.39	34	11.58	87
	Bases Empty	.277	100	.407	91	.339	105	1.57	28	7.57	67	9.20	120
Don Gordon	Runners On	.252	54	.383	63	.328	63	0.87	11	10.00	94	6.43	123
	Bases Empty	.316	--	.482	--	.355	--	3.51	--	4.13	--	9.09	--
Brad Havens	Runners On	.275	82	.402	75	.339	77	0.98	15	9.40	82	17.09	24
	Bases Empty	.272	98	.464	118	.305	50	4.80	125	4.58	12	7.63	125
Doug Jones	Runners On	.229	20	.276	2	.280	12	0.00	1	5.41	7	21.08	11
	Bases Empty	.204	9	.259	4	.235	3	0.68	7	3.92	8	21.57	12
Rod Nichols	Runners On	.287	97	.443	100	.349	91	3.48	107	7.63	41	9.92	105
	Bases Empty	.261	77	.346	34	.319	73	0.65	5	7.83	70	10.84	107
Greg Swindell	Runners On	.274	80	.411	80	.312	41	2.33	66	5.56	9	15.34	42
	Bases Empty	.239	43	.335	27	.270	13	1.71	38	3.93	9	20.00	20
Rich Yett	Runners On	.294	104	.430	94	.352	93	2.19	61	7.94	50	11.51	89
	Bases Empty	.261	76	.409	93	.337	101	1.98	49	10.36	113	12.43	83
Team Average	Runners On	.278	12	.414	11	.339	9	2.38	6	7.95	2	13.01	11
	Bases Empty	.264	12	.379	6	.316	8	1.99	2	6.56	2	13.39	12
League Average	Runners On	.268		.401		.336		2.45		9.09		13.68	
	Bases Empty	.253		.383		.315		2.48		7.76		14.81	

Overall Pitching Compared to Late Inning Pressure Situations

		BA	Rank	SA	Rank	OBA	Rank	HR %	Rank	BB %	Rank	SO %	Rank
Scott Bailes	Overall	.266	78	.425	104	.322	67	3.93	122	7.46	43	8.59	122
	Pressure	.260	78	.425	93	.325	65	4.11	109	8.54	60	12.20	93
Bud Black	Overall	.264	73	.373	53	.341	99	2.57	82	9.50	93	17.60	31
	Pressure	.250	67	.250	9	.346	88	0.00	1	12.50	102	26.25	3
Tom Candiotti	Overall	.272	90	.372	52	.319	57	1.81	27	5.87	17	15.17	52
	Pressure	.257	75	.343	49	.331	70	0.95	30	9.76	76	13.82	76
Jeff Dedmon	Overall	.276	--	.425	--	.383	--	2.36	--	13.38	--	10.83	--
	Pressure	.300	108	.375	70	.375	107	2.50	73	12.00	98	8.00	118
John Farrell	Overall	.269	86	.392	77	.330	79	1.87	32	7.49	45	10.28	109
	Pressure	.316	114	.439	99	.371	103	1.75	52	6.35	25	9.52	111
Don Gordon	Overall	.284	111	.432	109	.341	100	2.18	60	7.28	38	7.66	123
	Pressure	.268	91	.402	83	.354	94	2.44	71	10.00	78	8.00	118
Brad Havens	Overall	.273	--	.436	--	.321	--	3.08	--	6.85	--	12.10	--
	Pressure	.262	79	.492	115	.304	44	4.62	116	5.71	23	12.86	85
Doug Jones	Overall	.218	14	.268	1	.260	2	0.32	1	4.73	6	21.30	11
	Pressure	.233	47	.267	19	.288	29	0.00	1	6.35	25	21.03	19
Rod Nichols	Overall	.272	94	.388	69	.332	82	1.87	32	7.74	54	10.44	108
	Pressure	.346	--	.385	--	.400	--	0.00	--	9.38	--	12.50	--
Greg Swindell	Overall	.252	54	.363	41	.286	11	1.94	37	4.55	4	18.22	27
	Pressure	.286	103	.411	88	.317	59	1.79	55	4.03	8	13.71	78
Rich Yett	Overall	.275	98	.418	97	.344	103	2.07	46	9.32	89	12.03	90
	Pressure	.340	120	.528	121	.386	113	1.89	58	7.02	33	10.53	103
Team Average	Overall	.270	13	.394	8	.326	8	2.16	3	7.19	1	13.21	11
	Pressure	.278	14	.383	10	.338	11	1.55	2	7.78	1	14.38	11
League Average	Overall	.259		.391		.324		2.47		8.35		14.31	
	Pressure	.249		.369		.324		2.26		9.33		15.69	

Additional Miscellaneous Pitching Comparisons

	Grass Surface		Artificial Surface		Home Games		Road Games		Runners in Scoring Position		Runners in Scoring Pos and Two Outs		Leading Off Inning	
	BA	Rank	BA	Rank	BA	Rank	BA	Rank	BA	Rank	BA	Rank	OBA	Rank
Scott Bailes	.265	77	.273	67	.252	60	.284	99	.342	127	.382	128	.265	27
Bud Black	.276	102	.241	34	.294	114	.230	23	.241	47	.238	66	.321	76
Tom Candiotti	.270	91	.286	80	.245	51	.305	116	.249	53	.235	63	.306	62
Jeff Dedmon	.293	--	.229	--	.304	--	.241	--	.333	123	.382	129	.360	--
John Farrell	.268	83	.278	74	.261	75	.277	89	.267	77	.315	115	.357	105
Don Gordon	.278	106	.310	--	.268	--	.295	110	.282	85	.281	99	.377	116
Brad Havens	.274	98	.263	--	.269	--	.276	87	.254	58	.289	105	.250	--
Doug Jones	.238	36	.091	--	.270	85	.165	1	.186	8	.111	4	.277	41
Rod Nichols	.272	94	.275	69	.269	84	.278	--	.278	82	.290	--	.366	111
Greg Swindell	.242	46	.303	108	.234	41	.267	77	.290	94	.281	98	.262	24
Rich Yett	.262	69	.337	118	.271	86	.279	92	.250	54	.197	39	.324	82
Team Average	.267	11	.286	12	.264	10	.277	12	.276	13	.276	14	.315	8
League Average	.256		.267		.257		.262		.262		.239		.311	

DETROIT TIGERS

- **The Tigers took a record-tying tumble in '88: Who stole the strawberries?**
- **Sparky Anderson: He's a winner.**

What goes around comes around. What's good for the goose is good for the gander. Let's find out how the other half lives. Turnabout is fair play. And, as Maynard G. Krebs might add, "Tippecanoe and Tyler, too!"

In 1987, the Tigers became the first American League team ever to win a league or division title after trailing by as much as three and one-half games with as few as eight games remaining. But in 1988, only Michael Dukakis blew a bigger lead than the Tigers, who led by four games on August 21 and still led by two games 10 days later. But Detroit became only the sixth team in the league's history to lose a title after holding a lead of two or more games entering September:

Year	Leader	Sept. 1 Lead	Winner
1940	Cleveland	2.5	Detroit
1974	Boston	3	Baltimore
1978	Boston	6.5	New York
1984	Minnesota	2	Kansas City
1985	California	2.5	Kansas City
1988	Detroit	2	Boston

A brief recap of the race (readers in Detroit have permission to skip ahead): The Tigers took over first place from the Yankees on June 20 by winning the first game of a three-game series that marked the end of Billy Martin's fifth term as New York manager. Except for three days in late July, Detroit held first place continuously until September 5. Its largest lead was 4½ games on August 11, and following a four-game sweep of Chicago, the Tigers still led by four games on August 21. But then, disaster: 17 losses in their next 20 games, as the Red Sox overtook them on September 5 and held on until the end. The Tigers, after being eliminated, won their last three games of the season to capture second place, one game behind Boston.

Before we go any farther, let's get something straight. This is not going to be a criticism of Sparky Anderson. Sparky knows a little bit about the ebb and flow of pennant races; his teams have now finished above the .500 mark in 17 consecutive seasons. That shows us something. The last (and only)

time that Sparky finished below .500 was with the Reds in 1971, when he club-sandwiched a 79–83 team among three division championships. No, his hair wasn't dark then, but if you don't think that's a long time ago, consider that Sparky's National League managerial brethren that season included Leo Durocher, Red Schoendienst, Gil Hodges, and Danny Murtaugh.

Those 17 consecutive winning seasons are not a record; Anderson will have to stick around a while longer to catch Joe McCarthy, who never had a losing season in 24 years as a major league manager. But Sparky's right behind him:

Joe McCarthy	24	Cubs 1926–30; Yankees 1931–46; Red Sox 1948–50
Sparky Anderson	17	Reds 1972–78; Tigers 1979–88
Earl Weaver	16	Orioles 1968–82, 1985
Al Lopez	15	Indians 1951–56; White Sox 1957–65
Fred Clarke	14	Pirates 1900–13
Steve O'Neill	14	Indians 1935–37; Tigers 1943–48; Red Sox 1950–51; Phillies 1952–54

We went down to 14 consecutive seasons to include O'Neill, who never had a losing season in his major league managerial career. He and McCarthy are the only managers with 14 or more years of service who can make that claim.

Some pretty important managers are not on the list at all. The longest streak of finishes above .500 by either John McGraw or Casey Stengel was 12 years; by Connie Mack, 10; Whitey Herzog, eight; Hall-of-Famer Walter Alston, eight; Leo Durocher, seven; Billy Martin, six; Gene Mauch, six; Tommy Lasorda, four; Ralph Houk, three. Davey Johnson would have to keep managing—and winning—through the year 2000 just to match Anderson's streak.

Instead of construing anything here as a criticism of Sparky, let's emulate the approach taken by the Jose Ferrer character in cross-examining Bogart's Captain Queeg in *The Caine Mutiny.* Ferrer told the court–martial tribunal that it was not his intention to disparage Queeg or to suggest cowardice in the performance of his duties. Rather, it was his assumption that any man who had risen to a United States naval command during wartime could not possibly be a coward, and so the explanation for any questionable actions on the captain's part must reside elsewhere.

Now, there's a big difference between the navy's Captain Queeg and baseball's Captain Hook. No one has observed Sparky rolling little steel balls in his hand, and if he's caught muttering under his breath about "missing the strawberries," he'll likely be musing about never having had the opportunity to manage Daaaaaarryyyyyyl and his brothers. And there's no chance that Alex Grammas, Billy Consolo, and Dick Tracewski will conspire against him the way that Van Johnson and Fred MacMurray undercut Queeg in the film.

But no one could blame Sparky if he felt a bit betrayed by the baseball gods in 1988. He entered the season with what looked like the best five-man starting staff in the league, but they never were humming on all five cylinders. The Tigers won only *half* of the games that Doyle Alexander started, after winning *all* of his regular-season starts in 1987; Jack Morris's ERA didn't settle below five until the last day of July; Frank Tanana and Walt Terrell combined for an 0–10 record in 16 starts after August 20; and Jeff Robinson, the team's best pitcher, didn't throw a ball after August 23 due to numbness in his fingers.

Then Sparky had to contend with a sub par year from Matt Nokes, injuries that limited Alan Trammell to 128 games, and the pièce de résistance, torn knee cartilage suffered by Lou Whitaker while disco dancing on September 3; he didn't play again in 1988.

So there were problems. Nevertheless, it's safe to assume that other teams throughout baseball history that have been in first place in a pennant race have also had problems. But no team has ever gone belly-up quite like the 1988 Tigers did.

We looked at the records of every major league team in this century that held first place in its league or division for at least one day on or after August 1 of a given season. Next, we looked at every span of 20 games played by each of those teams in August, September, and October, as long as they were still in first place for the first of the 20 games. What we found was startling: *No team in major league history that was in first place in its league or division on or after August 1 has ever had a worse record over a 20–game span than last year's Tigers.* Detroit went 3–17 from August 22 to September 11.

There was only one team that had an equally-sudden demise: the 1925 Philadelphia Athletics. On the morning of August 15, 1925, the Athletics were in first place with a 71–36 record and a two-game lead over Washington. But Philadelphia lost 17 of its next 20 games, dropping out of first place on August 20, never to return. By the time the 3–17 tailspin ended, the Senators held a nine-game lead en route to what turned out to be their second consecutive American League title.

Before last season, two teams had come close to the Athletics' 1925 August collapse. In 1932, Pittsburgh held a 5½-

game lead at the start of the month, but lost 16 of its next 20 games and finished the season four games behind the pennant-winning New York Giants.

The other team to undergo an August depression was the 1982 Atlanta Braves, who lost 16 of their first 20 games in August, turning a seven-game lead into a four-game deficit in record time. (The Braves at their worst actually lost 19 of 21 games, but that span started with a doubleheader loss to the Dodgers on July 30, two days before the starting point for our current study.) But Atlanta righted itself and came back to win the division title, appropriately, as the second-place Dodgers lost to the Giants on the final day of the season, after the Braves had lost to San Diego.

For those fans (and national newspapers) who demand their information in tabular form—and you know who you are—we've assembled this list of the worst 20–game spans by league-leading teams on or after August 1. Note that in four cases, teams were able to withstand the slump to finish in first place:

Year	Team	Slump Start	Before Slump	20-Game Record	Finish Position	GB
1925	Athletics	Aug. 15	71–36	3–17	2nd	8.5
1988	Tigers	Aug. 21	73–50	3–17	2nd	1
1932	Pirates	Aug. 1	59–40	4–16	2nd	4
1982	Braves	Aug. 1	61–40	4–16	1st	—
1920	Reds	Sept. 9	73–54	5–15	3rd	10.5
1927	Cubs	Aug. 17	69–40	5–15	4th	8.5
1930	Dodgers	Aug. 9	66–41	5–15	4th	6
1944	Cardinals	Sept. 1	91–30	5–15	1st	—
1969	Cubs	Sept. 3	84–52	5–15	2nd	8
1971	Giants	Sept. 5	82–56	5–15	1st	—
1973	Dodgers	Aug. 27	81–49	5–15	2nd	3.5
1974	Red Sox	Aug. 28	71–56	5–15	3rd	7
1976	Phillies	Aug. 27	83–42	5–15	1st	—
1980	Pirates	Aug. 25	70–54	5–15	3rd	8
1987	Reds	Aug. 7	58–50	5–15	2nd	6

Sparky was even on the other end of one of these things. In 1973, it was his Cincinnati team that overtook the Dodgers to win the National League West. And here's one more consolation for Sparky. You know who managed that 1925 Philadelphia team? A guy named Connie Mack, who went on to manage 25 more seasons in the big leagues. Let's see, Sparky has expressed a renewed interest in being a "lifer"; 25 more years would bring him through the year 2013.

Then again, Mack may have had an unfair advantage in his pursuit of managerial longevity. He also owned his team. (Don't get any ideas, George.)

WON-LOST RECORD BY STARTING POSITION

DETROIT 88-74	C	1B	2B	3B	SS	LF	CF	RF	P	DH	Leadoff	Relief	Starts
Doyle Alexander	-	-	-	-	-	-	-	-	17-17	-	-	-	17-17
Chris Bando	-	-	-	-	-	-	-	-	-	-	-	-	-
Bill Bean	-	-	-	-	-	-	0-1	-	-	-	0-1	-	0-1
Billy Beane	-	-	-	-	-	2-0	-	-	-	-	-	-	2-0
Dave Bergman	-	24-20	-	-	-	8-3	-	-	-	10-13	9-10	-	42-36
Tom Brookens	-	-	-	71-55	-	-	-	-	-	-	10-5	-	71-55
Ivan DeJesus	-	-	-	-	3-4	-	-	-	-	-	-	-	3-4
Darrell Evans	-	34-29	-	-	-	-	-	-	-	32-22	-	-	66-51
Paul Gibson	-	-	-	-	-	-	-	-	1-0	-	-	13-26	1-0
Mike Heath	34-28	-	-	-	-	-	-	1-2	-	-	-	-	35-30
Don Heinkel	-	-	-	-	-	-	-	-	-	-	-	6-15	-
Mike Henneman	-	-	-	-	-	-	-	-	-	-	-	43-22	-
Willie Hernandez	-	-	-	-	-	-	-	-	-	-	-	36-27	-
Larry Herndon	-	-	-	-	-	8-2	-	-	-	23-23	-	-	31-25
Mark Huismann	-	-	-	-	-	-	-	-	-	-	-	1-4	-
Eric King	-	-	-	-	-	-	-	-	3-2	-	-	9-9	3-2
Ray Knight	-	30-23	-	4-2	-	-	-	-	-	11-9	-	-	45-34
Chet Lemon	-	-	-	-	-	-	76-65	-	-	-	-	-	76-65
Salvatore Lovullo	-	-	3-1	-	-	-	-	-	-	-	-	-	3-1
Scott Lusader	-	-	-	-	-	0-1	-	-	-	-	0-1	-	0-1
Fred Lynn	-	-	-	-	-	7-10	0-3	-	-	1-2	-	-	8-15
Jack Morris	-	-	-	-	-	-	-	-	19-15	-	-	-	19-15
Jim Morrison	-	0-2	-	0-1	-	0-1	-	-	-	-	9-4	-	9-8
Dwayne Murphy	-	-	-	-	-	-	20-12	4-3	-	0-1	-	-	24-16
Matt Nokes	54-46	-	-	-	-	-	-	-	-	2-0	-	-	56-46
Gary Pettis	-	-	-	-	-	-	63-52	-	-	-	53-39	-	63-52
Ted Power	-	-	-	-	-	-	-	-	0-2	-	-	1-1	0-2
Jeff M. Robinson	-	-	-	-	-	-	-	-	16-7	-	-	1-0	16-7
Luis Salazar	-	-	2-1	13-16	14-14	21-23	3-2	3-0	-	-	-	-	56-56
Steve Searcy	-	-	-	-	-	-	-	-	0-2	-	-	-	0-2
Pat Sheridan	-	-	-	-	-	42-35	2-3	4-4	-	-	5-3	-	48-42
Frank Tanana	-	-	-	-	-	-	-	-	21-11	-	-	-	21-11
Walt Terrell	-	-	-	-	-	-	-	-	11-18	-	-	-	11-18
Alan Trammell	-	-	-	-	68-55	-	-	-	-	-	-	-	68-55
Mike Trujillo	-	-	-	-	-	-	-	-	-	-	-	2-4	-
Jim Walewander	-	-	28-24	3-1	-	-	-	-	-	-	3-1	-	31-25
Lou Whitaker	-	-	55-48	-	-	-	-	-	-	-	8-14	-	55-48

Batting vs. Left and Right Handed Pitchers

		BA	Rank	SA	Rank	OBA	Rank	HR %	Rank	BB %	Rank	SO %	Rank
Dave Bergman	vs. Lefties	.235	--	.294	--	.278	--	0.00	--	5.26	--	5.26	--
	vs. Righties	.298	27	.401	72	.377	18	1.84	92	11.78	29	10.51	46
Tom Brookens	vs. Lefties	.220	139	.311	131	.310	89	1.13	118	11.76	31	16.67	113
	vs. Righties	.258	86	.379	89	.315	106	1.14	118	6.80	111	13.61	80
Darrell Evans	vs. Lefties	.156	167	.188	169	.270	139	0.00	140	13.51	20	20.27	146
	vs. Righties	.217	148	.413	63	.348	49	5.90	10	16.52	5	16.52	117
Mike Heath	vs. Lefties	.243	101	.399	69	.300	105	3.38	49	6.83	85	8.70	37
	vs. Righties	.254	--	.296	--	.321	--	0.00	--	8.75	--	22.50	--
Larry Herndon	vs. Lefties	.236	113	.344	109	.328	68	2.55	70	12.02	28	18.03	127
	vs. Righties	.118	--	.118	--	.167	--	0.00	--	5.56	--	22.22	--
Ray Knight	vs. Lefties	.219	141	.325	120	.256	150	1.78	94	4.44	129	8.33	33
	vs. Righties	.215	152	.269	163	.290	137	0.00	161	8.16	86	10.20	41
Chet Lemon	vs. Lefties	.297	38	.539	11	.370	33	5.45	17	10.33	41	8.70	37
	vs. Righties	.248	108	.386	83	.335	72	2.31	82	10.05	57	12.31	66
Fred Lynn	vs. Lefties	.174	162	.349	106	.205	167	3.67	43	4.24	133	26.27	162
	vs. Righties	.273	55	.528	8	.338	66	7.45	3	8.92	74	16.24	115
Dwayne Murphy	vs. Lefties	.161	--	.290	--	.257	--	3.23	--	8.33	--	25.00	--
	vs. Righties	.274	52	.389	81	.388	13	2.65	72	15.56	8	12.59	68
Matt Nokes	vs. Lefties	.263	--	.500	--	.300	--	5.26	--	2.33	--	11.63	--
	vs. Righties	.250	102	.416	61	.314	107	4.07	30	8.64	77	13.87	83
Gary Pettis	vs. Lefties	.214	144	.250	156	.258	148	0.00	140	5.59	113	17.32	121
	vs. Righties	.207	158	.293	157	.299	129	1.03	123	11.11	37	16.22	113
Luis Salazar	vs. Lefties	.320	22	.500	25	.351	43	4.00	36	4.21	135	11.21	65
	vs. Righties	.230	133	.294	156	.269	157	1.59	101	4.36	157	16.73	118
Pat Sheridan	vs. Lefties	.308	--	.654	--	.379	--	3.85	--	9.68	--	19.35	--
	vs. Righties	.249	105	.383	86	.336	70	3.12	60	11.05	38	15.63	106
Alan Trammell	vs. Lefties	.348	5	.522	17	.420	13	3.62	47	11.46	34	7.64	23
	vs. Righties	.296	30	.439	41	.352	39	3.05	62	7.65	92	9.29	29
Jim Walewander	vs. Lefties	.226	133	.262	153	.250	153	0.00	140	3.26	156	9.78	49
	vs. Righties	.198	--	.220	--	.270	--	0.00	--	8.49	--	16.04	--
Lou Whitaker	vs. Lefties	.228	128	.272	149	.330	67	0.00	140	13.51	20	19.82	141
	vs. Righties	.289	35	.463	31	.390	12	3.86	37	13.93	12	10.66	47
Team Average	vs. Lefties	.250	11	.379	11	.313	8	2.48	7	8.19	7	13.43	7
	vs. Righties	.250	11	.378	10	.330	5	2.70	5	10.18	2	13.78	3
League Average	vs. Lefties	.259		.391		.321		2.47		7.97		14.12	
	vs. Righties	.259		.391		.326		2.47		8.51		14.39	

Batting with Runners on Base and Bases Empty

		BA	Rank	SA	Rank	OBA	Rank	HR %	Rank	BB %	Rank	SO %	Rank
Dave Bergman	Runners On	.286	63	.395	89	.355	56	2.52	79	10.71	50	12.14	72
	Bases Empty	.300	19	.394	75	.383	11	1.18	121	11.92	19	8.81	26
Tom Brookens	Runners On	.210	156	.274	161	.274	156	1.08	119	8.41	82	11.68	63
	Bases Empty	.267	58	.408	63	.342	46	1.18	121	9.15	59	17.25	116
Darrell Evans	Runners On	.211	155	.338	136	.349	67	3.29	56	17.44	8	16.28	120
	Bases Empty	.205	152	.420	49	.326	66	6.70	7	14.77	6	17.80	126
Mike Heath	Runners On	.225	152	.303	152	.289	139	0.00	148	7.00	108	14.00	98
	Bases Empty	.262	71	.408	64	.319	77	3.85	40	7.80	81	12.77	61
Larry Herndon	Runners On	.237	129	.316	146	.307	124	1.32	107	10.23	55	18.18	138
	Bases Empty	.214	143	.327	125	.319	79	3.06	58	12.39	16	18.58	134
Ray Knight	Runners On	.223	147	.360	117	.270	158	1.44	99	5.84	135	7.79	25
	Bases Empty	.213	144	.250	163	.272	149	0.63	147	6.36	103	10.40	38
Chet Lemon	Runners On	.279	66	.441	49	.363	49	3.60	47	10.12	57	12.06	70
	Bases Empty	.252	89	.431	41	.332	58	3.10	57	10.15	38	10.46	40
Fred Lynn	Runners On	.198	159	.358	119	.265	159	4.32	27	8.60	79	18.28	139
	Bases Empty	.279	40	.563	7	.329	62	7.86	3	6.91	94	19.51	139
Dwayne Murphy	Runners On	.250	111	.389	95	.372	40	4.17	31	14.77	16	13.64	95
	Bases Empty	.250	--	.347	--	.349	--	1.39	--	13.25	--	16.87	--
Matt Nokes	Runners On	.263	100	.406	76	.338	85	3.43	53	9.80	61	13.24	91
	Bases Empty	.242	112	.440	37	.290	127	4.83	22	6.33	104	14.03	83
Gary Pettis	Runners On	.246	118	.349	128	.316	114	1.14	114	9.05	72	15.08	109
	Bases Empty	.187	162	.233	170	.265	154	0.35	153	9.27	57	17.57	123
Luis Salazar	Runners On	.272	79	.376	108	.321	105	2.48	80	6.06	128	13.85	96
	Bases Empty	.268	53	.392	76	.291	121	2.80	66	2.71	166	14.73	87
Pat Sheridan	Runners On	.252	110	.415	73	.313	118	3.40	54	7.06	106	15.88	118
	Bases Empty	.255	83	.395	74	.358	31	3.00	60	13.79	10	15.95	103
Alan Trammell	Runners On	.311	26	.450	40	.375	37	2.70	68	9.77	62	11.33	58
	Bases Empty	.311	10	.475	24	.371	19	3.69	44	7.87	79	6.37	9
Jim Walewander	Runners On	.156	--	.172	--	.214	--	0.00	--	6.25	--	13.75	--
	Bases Empty	.243	109	.279	150	.288	129	0.00	156	5.93	115	12.71	60
Lou Whitaker	Runners On	.279	68	.461	34	.410	11	4.24	30	18.01	5	12.80	81
	Bases Empty	.273	44	.391	80	.350	35	2.10	89	10.53	34	12.78	62
Team Average	Runners On	.253	12	.376	11	.331	9	2.53	6	10.04	3	13.39	5
	Bases Empty	.248	9	.380	7	.320	5	2.71	3	9.16	3	13.89	4
League Average	Runners On	.268		.401		.336		2.45		9.09		13.68	
	Bases Empty	.253		.383		.315		2.48		7.76		14.81	

Overall Batting Compared to Late Inning Pressure Situations

		BA	Rank	SA	Rank	OBA	Rank	HR %	Rank	BB %	Rank	SO %	Rank	RDI %	Rank
Dave Bergman	Overall	.294	27	.394	81	.372	21	1.73	100	11.41	32	10.21	39	.313	30
	Pressure	.250	87	.357	86	.323	84	1.79	79	9.68	64	14.52	72	.222	85
Tom Brookens	Overall	.243	118	.351	117	.313	99	1.13	121	8.84	71	14.86	101	.234	126
	Pressure	.313	37	.453	44	.348	62	3.13	50	5.63	132	16.90	93	.200	95
Darrell Evans	Overall	.208	165	.380	92	.337	57	5.03	19	16.09	5	17.05	124	.238	123
	Pressure	.284	53	.507	20	.368	37	5.97	14	11.84	40	19.74	109	.278	61
Mike Heath	Overall	.247	112	.365	104	.307	110	2.28	80	7.47	96	13.28	75	.212	150
	Pressure	.119	169	.214	148	.196	165	2.38	64	8.51	82	12.77	59	.300	53
Larry Herndon	Overall	.224	145	.322	142	.313	96	2.30	78	11.44	30	18.41	135	.300	44
	Pressure	.276	64	.310	118	.382	28	0.00	110	14.71	14	29.41	159	.000	165
Ray Knight	Overall	.217	152	.301	155	.271	158	1.00	131	6.12	121	9.17	29	.255	99
	Pressure	.213	122	.277	135	.260	140	0.00	110	3.92	148	9.80	34	.333	39
Chet Lemon	Overall	.264	69	.436	39	.346	47	3.32	54	10.14	51	11.17	49	.264	90
	Pressure	.313	36	.614	4	.424	13	7.23	9	14.14	16	8.08	23	.077	161
Fred Lynn	Overall	.246	114	.478	19	.302	122	6.39	5	7.64	92	18.98	139	.190	163
	Pressure	.155	160	.282	132	.215	161	4.23	34	7.59	96	25.32	147	.154	125
Matt Nokes	Overall	.251	97	.424	50	.313	101	4.19	28	8.00	86	13.65	84	.255	100
	Pressure	.264	77	.472	34	.310	94	5.66	17	6.78	110	13.56	65	.400	20
Gary Pettis	Overall	.210	162	.277	164	.285	149	0.66	148	9.18	62	16.60	118	.256	97
	Pressure	.167	150	.183	163	.219	160	0.00	110	4.48	141	23.88	137	.091	154
Luis Salazar	Overall	.270	57	.385	89	.305	112	2.65	70	4.29	158	14.31	90	.302	42
	Pressure	.284	53	.358	85	.333	75	1.49	91	6.67	112	16.00	89	.407	19
Pat Sheridan	Overall	.254	95	.403	72	.339	55	3.17	60	10.95	40	15.92	109	.279	72
	Pressure	.295	47	.477	29	.367	39	4.55	27	10.20	55	22.45	129	.182	108
Alan Trammell	Overall	.311	9	.464	27	.373	20	3.22	55	8.80	72	8.80	24	.308	36
	Pressure	.403	3	.639	3	.449	6	6.94	11	7.69	93	7.69	21	.533	4
Lou Whitaker	Overall	.275	51	.419	57	.376	16	2.98	65	13.84	10	12.79	72	.278	75
	Pressure	.235	105	.275	136	.339	73	0.00	110	13.33	21	15.00	80	.211	92
Team Average	Overall	.250	12	.378	10	.324	6	2.63	6	9.56	2	13.67	5	.267	10
	Pressure	.261	5	.406	2	.332	4	3.43	1	9.07	4	15.87	4	.283	4
League Average	Overall	.259		.391		.324		2.47		8.35		14.31		.269	
	Pressure	.249		.365		.319		2.28		8.71		17.04		.246	

Additional Miscellaneous Batting Comparisons

	Grass Surface BA	Rank	Artificial Surface BA	Rank	Home Games BA	Rank	Road Games BA	Rank	Runners in Scoring Position BA	Rank	Runners in Scoring Pos and Two Outs BA	Rank	Leading Off Inning OBA	Rank	Runners on 3B with less than 2 Outs RDI %	Rank
Dave Bergman	.299	22	.271	82	.283	46	.302	24	.290	46	.367	7	.341	46	.556	89
Tom Brookens	.253	91	.185	160	.258	87	.227	137	.228	130	.182	142	.379	15	.591	74
Darrell Evans	.216	150	.158	166	.223	143	.194	161	.228	129	.150	157	.337	54	.700	17
Mike Heath	.215	151	.395	3	.179	168	.298	26	.234	122	.192	132	.180	169	.750	--
Larry Herndon	.225	133	.222	--	.198	160	.253	--	.273	67	.238	83	.293	--	.556	89
Ray Knight	.218	147	.214	141	.188	165	.248	104	.184	165	.147	158	.266	136	.500	115
Chet Lemon	.262	69	.271	81	.278	61	.251	96	.284	55	.315	20	.326	67	.429	147
Fred Lynn	.251	95	.205	149	.258	88	.234	125	.161	167	.111	166	.350	39	.545	99
Dwayne Murphy	.242	109	.300	--	.271	--	.230	--	.263	81	.250	61	.265	--	.833	--
Matt Nokes	.255	82	.226	128	.250	100	.253	91	.292	43	.333	15	.286	118	.438	145
Gary Pettis	.211	157	.203	152	.200	158	.218	141	.276	62	.265	55	.281	123	.474	132
Luis Salazar	.262	71	.306	31	.254	95	.285	39	.328	19	.352	10	.300	94	.483	129
Pat Sheridan	.262	70	.184	161	.233	128	.272	55	.259	88	.235	86	.422	5	.500	115
Alan Trammell	.308	13	.325	20	.312	16	.311	13	.290	46	.292	39	.380	14	.545	99
Jim Walewander	.208	160	.231	--	.220	149	.200	--	.097	--	.111	--	.298	101	.444	143
Lou Whitaker	.260	76	.348	12	.269	75	.281	43	.283	58	.200	126	.333	59	.636	50
Team Average	.249	11	.257	11	.245	12	.255	9	.262	7	.245	7	.315	4	.548	10
League Average	.256		.267		.262		.257		.262		.239		.311		.570	

Pitching vs. Left and Right Handed Batters

		BA	Rank	SA	Rank	OBA	Rank	HR %	Rank	BB %	Rank	SO %	Rank
Doyle Alexander	vs. Lefties	.293	107	.476	117	.337	81	2.62	89	5.82	20	9.24	103
	vs. Righties	.272	93	.435	105	.297	37	3.88	114	3.49	4	16.43	47
Paul Gibson	vs. Lefties	.234	39	.344	41	.273	12	1.56	44	5.67	18	10.64	85
	vs. Righties	.243	44	.358	45	.327	78	1.83	31	10.44	109	14.06	70
Mike Henneman	vs. Lefties	.218	22	.303	16	.293	22	1.41	38	8.92	64	17.83	25
	vs. Righties	.217	21	.312	15	.257	8	2.65	68	4.83	15	14.49	62
Willie Hernandez	vs. Lefties	.224	26	.365	55	.296	26	3.53	114	9.00	66	19.00	15
	vs. Righties	.200	9	.342	37	.311	50	3.23	97	11.96	124	21.74	19
Eric King	vs. Lefties	.213	17	.380	67	.331	71	2.78	95	14.73	124	14.73	46
	vs. Righties	.248	53	.342	38	.333	90	1.34	16	8.62	82	14.94	58
Jack Morris	vs. Lefties	.234	38	.337	33	.306	35	1.85	56	9.19	70	16.18	38
	vs. Righties	.272	95	.422	88	.330	86	2.70	71	7.28	58	17.66	40
Ted Power	vs. Lefties	.295	109	.432	102	.367	107	2.27	68	9.64	82	10.66	84
	vs. Righties	.314	124	.459	116	.367	122	1.82	30	7.72	67	14.63	60
Jeff M. Robinson	vs. Lefties	.197	6	.335	32	.291	20	2.90	99	11.80	110	16.57	31
	vs. Righties	.197	7	.328	22	.272	16	3.28	99	8.77	87	16.08	50
Frank Tanana	vs. Lefties	.210	15	.286	11	.248	7	1.68	47	4.72	8	18.11	22
	vs. Righties	.276	97	.440	109	.336	93	3.38	101	7.74	68	13.89	72
Walt Terrell	vs. Lefties	.257	57	.366	56	.319	52	1.94	58	8.46	57	6.72	123
	vs. Righties	.260	72	.402	78	.333	89	3.35	100	9.54	100	12.96	85
Team Average	vs. Lefties	.239	2	.367	5	.306	1	2.27	8	8.66	6	13.15	8
	vs. Righties	.255	6	.398	10	.317	5	3.09	14	7.72	8	15.64	5
League Average	vs. Lefties	.262		.387		.331		2.24		9.12		13.21	
	vs. Righties	.258		.393		.320		2.63		7.80		15.09	

Pitching with Runners on Base and Bases Empty

		BA	Rank	SA	Rank	OBA	Rank	HR %	Rank	BB %	Rank	SO %	Rank
Doyle Alexander	Runners On	.279	87	.453	107	.327	62	3.70	111	7.14	32	9.69	109
	Bases Empty	.284	109	.457	113	.310	55	2.98	97	3.04	4	14.84	59
Paul Gibson	Runners On	.237	28	.353	35	.290	16	1.73	38	7.65	43	10.71	96
	Bases Empty	.243	50	.353	42	.325	82	1.73	40	9.79	106	14.95	58
Mike Henneman	Runners On	.212	11	.364	47	.297	26	3.97	116	9.60	85	16.38	33
	Bases Empty	.222	24	.261	5	.251	5	0.56	3	3.74	5	15.51	56
Willie Hernandez	Runners On	.224	14	.353	36	.336	75	2.59	75	13.01	119	20.55	14
	Bases Empty	.194	5	.347	35	.275	16	4.03	114	8.70	82	21.01	15
Eric King	Runners On	.185	3	.296	3	.268	4	1.48	29	8.23	53	15.19	44
	Bases Empty	.287	116	.426	105	.400	126	2.46	81	14.48	125	14.48	63
Jack Morris	Runners On	.266	68	.410	79	.324	60	2.39	69	7.53	37	16.24	34
	Bases Empty	.241	45	.351	40	.311	61	2.12	56	8.92	85	17.31	36
Ted Power	Runners On	.317	119	.483	119	.377	113	3.33	101	9.22	77	15.05	46
	Bases Empty	.296	123	.417	99	.359	119	0.93	10	8.02	75	10.97	104
Jeff M. Robinson	Runners On	.175	1	.313	11	.272	7	2.76	80	11.72	110	16.41	32
	Bases Empty	.209	14	.342	30	.287	21	3.27	100	9.50	99	16.29	47
Frank Tanana	Runners On	.300	107	.474	115	.375	108	3.87	115	10.61	99	14.53	50
	Bases Empty	.245	53	.380	67	.288	24	2.66	87	5.02	19	14.48	64
Walt Terrell	Runners On	.269	71	.377	58	.340	78	1.97	47	9.72	88	8.61	117
	Bases Empty	.251	59	.386	75	.316	66	3.00	98	8.43	80	10.39	110
Team Average	Runners On	.252	2	.401	6	.323	2	3.00	13	9.27	10	13.82	9
	Bases Empty	.245	4	.373	4	.304	2	2.55	8	7.27	5	15.12	7
League Average	Runners On	.268		.401		.336		2.45		9.09		13.68	
	Bases Empty	.253		.383		.315		2.48		7.76		14.81	

Overall Pitching Compared to Late Inning Pressure Situations

		BA	Rank	SA	Rank	OBA	Rank	HR %	Rank	BB %	Rank	SO %	Rank
Doyle Alexander	Overall	.282	108	.456	119	.317	54	3.25	107	4.67	5	12.79	79
	Pressure	.217	31	.310	30	.257	12	1.55	44	4.35	10	13.04	83
Paul Gibson	Overall	.240	35	.353	29	.307	37	1.73	25	8.72	80	12.82	78
	Pressure	.225	40	.400	82	.289	31	2.50	73	8.89	64	11.11	101
Mike Henneman	Overall	.218	13	.308	8	.273	6	2.11	54	6.59	26	15.93	43
	Pressure	.227	41	.328	41	.287	28	2.62	81	7.03	34	16.41	44
Willie Hernandez	Overall	.208	7	.350	27	.306	32	3.33	109	10.92	112	20.77	13
	Pressure	.241	58	.393	80	.348	91	3.57	101	10.95	89	21.17	18
Eric King	Overall	.233	29	.358	34	.332	83	1.95	38	11.22	118	14.85	54
	Pressure	.276	98	.310	31	.405	120	0.00	1	15.38	118	17.95	34
Jack Morris	Overall	.251	52	.375	55	.317	52	2.23	65	8.32	67	16.85	35
	Pressure	.187	12	.260	14	.268	17	1.63	49	10.07	81	18.71	27
Ted Power	Overall	.306	125	.447	115	.367	123	2.02	42	8.58	77	12.87	76
	Pressure	.244	62	.289	27	.327	67	0.00	1	9.62	73	3.85	128
Jeff M. Robinson	Overall	.197	17	.332	17	.282	9	3.09	100	10.32	104	16.33	39
	Pressure	.198	17	.272	22	.244	7	0.00	1	5.81	24	18.60	28
Frank Tanana	Overall	.267	79	.417	96	.323	69	3.13	102	7.31	39	14.50	57
	Pressure	.221	34	.351	52	.310	53	2.60	80	11.24	92	12.36	90
Walt Terrell	Overall	.258	64	.383	62	.326	74	2.59	84	8.97	99	9.66	117
	Pressure	.280	99	.447	103	.340	80	3.79	104	7.43	40	11.49	98
Team Average	Overall	.248	4	.385	5	.312	2	2.73	12	8.13	7	14.56	8
	Pressure	.231	2	.346	4	.301	2	2.42	9	8.37	4	15.67	7
League Average	Overall	.259		.391		.324		2.47		8.35		14.31	
	Pressure	.249		.369		.324		2.26		9.33		15.69	

Additional Miscellaneous Pitching Comparisons

	Grass Surface BA	Rank	Artificial Surface BA	Rank	Home Games BA	Rank	Road Games BA	Rank	Runners in Scoring Position BA	Rank	Runners in Scoring Pos and Two Outs BA	Rank	Leading Off Inning OBA	Rank
Doyle Alexander	.267	82	.340	120	.256	68	.313	122	.286	88	.244	73	.324	81
Paul Gibson	.240	41	.238	--	.225	30	.258	68	.216	24	.200	40	.304	58
Mike Henneman	.219	18	.207	--	.223	28	.213	13	.170	4	.170	23	.178	2
Willie Hernandez	.205	6	.240	--	.172	2	.255	65	.176	5	.059	1	.208	4
Eric King	.238	35	.200	--	.221	26	.248	51	.152	1	.105	3	.463	129
Jack Morris	.249	51	.275	71	.274	92	.232	27	.267	76	.266	93	.317	72
Ted Power	.278	107	.322	115	.303	121	.309	119	.316	119	.171	24	.343	101
Jeff M. Robinson	.187	1	.231	23	.167	1	.234	29	.167	2	.120	5	.274	38
Frank Tanana	.263	71	.293	96	.255	66	.279	91	.287	90	.227	58	.261	23
Walt Terrell	.266	80	.209	11	.254	63	.261	70	.275	81	.282	100	.323	79
Team Average	.245	4	.268	8	.236	1	.260	8	.245	2	.217	3	.299	4
League Average	.256		.267		.257		.262		.262		.239		.311	

KANSAS CITY ROYALS

- **Kansas City's domination of Baltimore.**
- **Will Bob be a boon to the Royals' pitching staff?**

A lesson in patience and revenge: This year marks the 20th anniversary of one of the most one-sided matchups in the history of sports. On May 10, 1969, after losing their first game ever against the Royals the day before, the Baltimore Orioles began a streak of 23 consecutive wins over Kansas City.

That's still the longest winning streak by one team over another in major league history, and in a sense it symbolizes all that's wrong with expansion, not only in baseball, but in all sports. (Or have you already put the Miami Heat on the back burner?) The Orioles of 1969 and 1970 were among the greatest teams ever; the only one of the past 40 years, in fact, to win two-thirds of its games in two consecutive seasons. Kansas City was part of the four-team expansion of 1969, teams that won an average of 59 games in their first season. The Royals were the best of the group, winning 69 games. But matched against teams like the Orioles, they played the role of Michael Spinks to Baltimore's Mike Tyson.

Fans older than Iron Mike might have been reminded of that streak when, in 1987, Baltimore once again reeled off win after win against the Royals—eight of them, to be exact. But this time, the more mature Royals were able to strike back. They snapped that streak in their last meeting of the 1987 season and won all 12 games against Baltimore in 1988, an Orioles club that was itself reminiscent of some of baseball's weaker expansion teams.

Kansas City will try to continue its domination of Baltimore on April 10 this year. Here's what the Royals will be shooting for—the longest team-vs.-team winning streaks in modern major league history:

Years	Winner	Loser	Wins
1969–1970	Baltimore Orioles	Kansas City Royals	23
1903–1904	Boston Red Sox	Washington Senators	22
1927	New York Yankees	St. Louis Browns	21
1927–1928	St. Louis Cardinals	Philadelphia Phillies	20
1937–1938	Pittsburgh Pirates	Cincinnati Reds	20
1909	Chicago Cubs	Boston Braves	19
1938–1939	New York Yankees	Philadelphia Athletics	19
1908–1909	Pittsburgh Pirates	Boston Braves	18
1917–1918	New York Giants	Boston Braves	18
1930–1931	St. Louis Cardinals	Cincinnati Reds	18
1940–1941	Boston Red Sox	Philadelphia Athletics	18

As Kramden once told Norton (and repeated to him thousands of times more in syndication), "You've gotta be nice to people on the way up, 'cause you're gonna meet the same people on the way down." Now, with Kansas City's revenge in mind, who would like to guess when the Heat's going to run off 23 straight wins against the Lakers. We'll set the over/under at, oh, let's say mid–21st century.

The off-season addition of Bob Boone reminds us of the post-season success that Kansas City enjoyed after Jim Sundberg joined the team in 1985. Sundberg was asked to mold the Royals' young starting staff into a championship rotation, and he complied. Kansas City's pitchers led the A.L. in ERA (after ranking seventh in 1984), and they led the Royals to a World Series victory.

But since that time, the Royals have been frustrated in their attempts to develop a solid everyday backstop. First, Ed Hearn was, as the NFL might put it, physically unable to perform—a particularly bitter disappointment in light of the subsequent development of David Cone, whom the Mets extracted as payment for Hearn. Career minor leaguer Larry Owen and perennial utility player Jamie Quirk were asked to fill the void, which only accelerated the ascent of Mike Macfarlane as Kaycee's catcher of the future. That future lasted three months.

Shortly after last season's All-Star break, Kansas City sent Macfarlane to Omaha, and replaced him with Owen. Despite a .265 batting average and 26 RBI, Macfarlane was considered a liability on account of his defense. He had thrown out only 11 of 54 base runners, and there were rumblings that his handling of the pitching staff was inadequate.

On the other hand, Owen, whose 74 games for the Royals in 1987 were more than he had played in four previous seasons with Atlanta combined, was considered a good receiver. But ain't it funny how a .188 career batting average has a way of keeping even a great defensive catcher down on the farm.

Still, Kansas City's pitchers, wedded for better or for worse to Macfarlane for the first half of the season, posted a 3.77 ERA during his tenure, fifth best in the A.L. And a look at the staff's performance with each of its catchers behind the plate suggests that: (1) Macfarlane wasn't all that bad, (2) Owen wasn't all that great, and (3) maybe Jamie Quirk is the guy they should have been complaining about. The following figures include all runs, earned and unearned:

Catcher	Innings	Runs	Per 9 Inn.
Owen	259.2	106	3.67
Macfarlane	553.0	236	3.84
Quirk	543.2	273	4.52
Others	72.0	33	4.13

Incidentally, the biggest mystery surrounding the change behind the plate concerns how Owen developed his reputation in the first place. In 1987, when Owen and Quirk split the team's catching chores, the Royals' pitchers allowed 4.41 runs per nine innings with Owen, 4.50 with Quirk. Go figure.

All's well that ends well, however, and Boone should shore things up at least in the near term. Here's how he compared with California's other backstops over the past five seasons:

Year	With Boone Catching			With Other Catchers			
	Innings	Runs	Rate	Innings	Runs	Rate	Diff.
1984	1180.1	538	4.10	277.2	159	5.15	−1.05
1985	1214.1	595	4.41	243.0	108	4.00	+0.41
1986	1188.1	550	4.17	267.2	134	4.51	−0.34
1987	1034.0	555	4.83	423.1	248	5.27	−0.44
1988	928.0	485	4.70	527.2	286	4.88	−0.17
Totals	5545.0	2723	4.42	1739.1	935	4.84	−0.42

That margin of .42 runs per nine innings translates to 67 runs saved over the course of a 162–game season. If Boone can do for Kansas City what he did for California—and admittedly, at his age that's a big *if*—Saberhagen, Leibrandt, and Gubicza could pitch the Royals to a repeat of 1985.

Speaking of Gubicza, he may have generated less publicity than any 20–game winner in recent memory. We pointed out in the Mets essay that it's become difficult to determine exactly who the ace of their staff is. The days of Gooden and Co. in New York are long gone, and it appears that the times they are a changin' in Kansas City as well.

Like his New York counterpart and former teammate David Cone, Gubicza led his team in wins last season with 20. And like Cone, he ranked third in his league in victories.

Gubicza ranked fourth in the A.L. in ERA, Cone ranked second in the N.L. And both Gubicza and Cone pitch for teams with deep starting rotations, one in the shadow of Saberhagen and Leibrandt, the other obscured by the halos surrounding Gooden and Darling.

In fact, so little attention has been paid to Gubicza during his five-year career that a little historical perspective is in order. A search of every pitcher in major league history yielded seven who at some point in their careers had stats comparable to Gubicza's at a similar age. (Each came within a 20–percent margin of Gubicza's current career total for innings, and a 10–percent cushion in wins and losses, and hits, walks, and strikeouts per nine innings. Additionally, each was within a year of Gubicza's age.) Those pitchers and their statistics at the end of the seasons listed:

Year	Pitcher	Age	W	L	ERA	IP	H	BB	SO
1988	Mark Gubicza	26	69	56	3.62	1058.1	955	439	677
1963	Gary Bell	26	67	61	3.84	1025.2	897	464	696
1985	Richard Dotson	26	73	59	3.75	1097.2	1055	441	594
1971	Jim Nash	26	67	55	3.44	1038.1	969	359	746
1963	Jim O'Toole	26	69	57	3.52	1071.1	1005	381	690
1959	Johnny Podres	26	68	54	3.77	1027.1	1001	370	672
1963	Stan Williams	26	66	54	3.74	1018.1	897	486	755
1986	Mike Witt	25	71	59	3.52	1228.1	1146	424	821

Of concern to Royals fans is the fact that only two of the pitchers listed above had winning records beyond those points: O'Toole (29–27) and Podres (80–62). Their composite record after the seasons listed was only seven games above the .500 mark (269–262). But only one of those seven pitchers was coming off a season even vaguely comparable to Gubicza's 20–win performance last season. (Mike Witt went 18–10 in 1986.)

And therein lies the problem. Gubicza's 1988 season, in light of his modest career totals prior to last season, was almost unprecedented. Among pitchers who, at some points in their careers, matched Gubicza's stats *coming into 1988* (according to the parameters described above), only two won more than 15 games the next year: Jerry Reuss (16–13 in 1974) and Witt.

So it appears time to upgrade our evaluation of Gubicza. Granted, prior to last season, he'd given little indication that he'd ever be a 20–game winner. But history suggests that those 20 wins elevate Gubicza to the level of Reuss and Witt, so we shouldn't be surprised if he stays on the fast track.

WON-LOST RECORD BY STARTING POSITION

KANSAS CITY 84-77	C	1B	2B	3B	SS	LF	CF	RF	P	DH	Leadoff	Relief	Starts
Rick Anderson	·	·	·	·	·	·	·	·	0-3	·	·	2-2	0-3
Luis Aquino	·	·	·	·	·	·	·	·	5-0	·	·	0-2	5-0
Steve Balboni	·	·	·	·	·	·	·	·	·	2-4	·	·	6-10
Floyd Bannister	·	·	·	·	·	·	·	·	17-14	·	·	·	17-14
Bud Black	·	·	·	·	·	·	·	·	·	·	·	8-9	·
Thad Bosley	·	·	·	·	·	1-0	·	·	·	1-2	·	·	2-2
George Brett	·	66-58	·	·	·	·	·	·	·	15-18	·	·	81-76
Bill Buckner	·	6-12	·	·	·	·	·	·	·	20-21	·	·	26-33
Nick Capra	·	·	·	·	·	1-1	3-1	·	·	·	1-1	·	4-2
Jose DeJesus	·	·	·	·	·	·	·	·	0-1	·	·	0-1	0-1
Luis Delos Santos	·	2-1	·	·	·	·	·	·	·	2-1	·	·	4-2
Jim Eisenreich	·	·	·	·	·	10-7	4-2	2-8	·	8-4	3-0	·	24-21
Steve Farr	·	·	·	·	·	·	·	1-0	·	·	·	35-26	1-0
Gene Garber	·	·	·	·	·	·	·	·	·	·	·	10-16	·
Jerry Don Gleaton	·	·	·	·	·	·	·	·	·	·	·	19-23	·
Tom Gordon	·	·	·	·	·	·	·	·	0-2	·	·	2-1	0-2
Mark Gubicza	·	·	·	·	·	·	·	·	25-10	·	·	·	25-10
Ed Hearn	2-1	·	·	·	·	·	·	·	·	0-1	·	·	2-2
Bo Jackson	·	·	·	·	·	51-51	2-2	6-6	·	2-0	·	·	61-59
Mark Lee	·	·	·	·	·	·	·	·	·	·	·	1-3	·
Charlie Leibrandt	·	·	·	·	·	·	·	·	16-19	·	·	·	16-19
Mike MacFarlane	34-29	·	·	·	·	·	·	·	·	·	·	·	34-29
Scotti Madison	1-1	1-0	·	·	·	·	·	·	·	1-3	·	·	3-4
Jeff Montgomery	·	·	·	·	·	·	·	·	·	·	·	21-24	·
Dave Owen	·	·	·	·	0-2	·	·	·	·	·	·	·	0-2
Larry Owen	16-15	·	·	·	·	·	·	·	·	·	·	·	16-15
Rey Palacios	1-1	·	·	·	·	·	·	·	·	·	·	·	1-1
Bill Pecota	·	·	8-6	15-18	0-1	·	·	1-0	·	·	1-1	·	24-25
Ted Power	·	·	·	·	·	·	·	·	4-8	·	·	3-7	4-8
Jamie Quirk	30-30	·	·	·	·	·	·	·	·	·	·	·	30-30
Dan Quisenberry	·	·	·	·	·	·	·	·	·	·	·	8-12	·
Bret Saberhagen	·	·	·	·	·	·	·	·	15-20	·	·	·	15-20
Israel Sanchez	·	·	·	·	·	·	·	·	1-0	·	·	8-10	1-0
Kevin Seitzer	·	·	·	76-71	·	·	·	·	·	0-1	2-0	·	76-72
Kurt Stillwell	·	·	·	·	66-55	·	·	·	·	·	26-22	·	66-55
Pat Tabler	·	5-0	·	·	·	14-13	·	3-5	·	25-15	·	·	47-33
Danny Tartabull	·	·	·	·	·	·	72-58	·	·	6-6	·	·	78-64
Gary Thurman	·	·	·	·	·	7-4	2-4	·	·	·	2-4	·	9-8
Brad Wellman	·	·	11-11	3-2	·	·	·	·	·	·	·	·	14-13
Frank White	·	·	73-66	·	·	·	·	·	·	2-1	·	·	75-67
Willie Wilson	·	·	·	·	·	·	73-68	·	·	·	49-49	·	73-68

Batting vs. Left and Right Handed Pitchers

		BA	Rank	SA	Rank	OBA	Rank	HR %	Rank	BB %	Rank	SO %	Rank
George Brett	vs. Lefties	.313	27	.530	14	.379	28	5.05	23	9.82	48	7.14	15
	vs. Righties	.302	21	.499	17	.394	11	3.58	45	13.13	15	7.66	16
Bill Buckner	vs. Lefties	.281	--	.375	--	.314	--	0.00	--	5.71	--	2.86	--
	vs. Righties	.245	112	.324	134	.283	142	1.19	115	5.43	133	6.52	10
Jim Eisenreich	vs. Lefties	.368	--	.421	--	.385	--	0.00	--	2.56	--	17.95	--
	vs. Righties	.183	167	.250	166	.202	168	0.61	144	2.86	167	13.71	82
Bo Jackson	vs. Lefties	.276	57	.520	20	.315	85	6.50	9	5.38	117	35.38	170
	vs. Righties	.234	127	.453	36	.276	148	5.38	15	5.33	136	29.59	165
Mike Macfarlane	vs. Lefties	.238	106	.345	107	.250	153	1.19	114	2.27	163	18.18	129
	vs. Righties	.283	43	.425	56	.381	17	2.36	81	12.84	18	14.19	92
Bill Pecota	vs. Lefties	.239	105	.239	161	.308	92	0.00	140	6.17	95	13.58	82
	vs. Righties	.187	166	.299	151	.273	151	0.93	128	10.40	47	18.40	133
Jamie Quirk	vs. Lefties	.368	--	.474	--	.400	--	0.00	--	4.55	--	18.18	--
	vs. Righties	.226	138	.401	70	.327	83	4.52	23	12.86	17	17.62	126
Kevin Seitzer	vs. Lefties	.353	4	.477	40	.432	7	0.65	136	11.86	30	10.73	58
	vs. Righties	.286	40	.379	88	.371	24	0.99	127	10.94	39	9.66	35
Kurt Stillwell	vs. Lefties	.226	135	.323	123	.299	106	1.61	102	8.51	65	13.48	81
	vs. Righties	.260	83	.427	54	.331	78	2.39	80	9.28	69	15.12	100
Pat Tabler	vs. Lefties	.302	35	.403	67	.377	29	0.72	133	10.69	39	10.06	52
	vs. Righties	.272	57	.338	125	.336	69	0.33	157	8.53	79	15.29	103
Danny Tartabull	vs. Lefties	.289	46	.537	12	.404	19	5.37	19	16.29	8	16.29	111
	vs. Righties	.268	65	.506	12	.354	37	5.03	18	11.33	35	21.69	149
Frank White	vs. Lefties	.265	69	.368	92	.296	107	1.29	110	3.70	149	11.11	63
	vs. Righties	.223	141	.314	140	.254	163	1.57	102	3.63	163	11.86	58
Willie Wilson	vs. Lefties	.258	75	.366	94	.275	136	0.00	140	2.56	160	23.08	152
	vs. Righties	.264	73	.319	137	.295	133	0.25	159	3.93	161	14.09	89
Team Average	vs. Lefties	.272	4	.400	6	.331	4	1.96	13	7.91	8	16.04	11
	vs. Righties	.254	10	.387	8	.316	11	2.32	10	8.02	10	15.29	12
League Average	vs. Lefties	.259		.391		.321		2.47		7.97		14.12	
	vs. Righties	.259		.391		.326		2.47		8.51		14.39	

Batting with Runners on Base and Bases Empty

		BA	Rank	SA	Rank	OBA	Rank	HR %	Rank	BB %	Rank	SO %	Rank
George Brett	Runners On	.348	4	.593	2	.445	2	4.44	25	15.45	12	6.67	18
	Bases Empty	.270	47	.439	39	.336	53	3.76	42	8.83	66	8.26	20
Bill Buckner	Runners On	.357	2	.444	45	.407	12	0.00	148	9.40	66	6.04	15
	Bases Empty	.164	168	.239	168	.179	171	1.89	94	1.85	170	6.17	8
Jim Eisenreich	Runners On	.239	126	.337	137	.253	163	1.09	117	2.97	169	15.84	115
	Bases Empty	.200	158	.236	169	.221	168	0.00	156	2.65	167	13.27	73
Bo Jackson	Runners On	.232	135	.416	71	.280	149	4.32	26	5.97	130	32.34	169
	Bases Empty	.256	78	.512	15	.292	117	6.69	8	4.87	139	30.34	168
Mike Macfarlane	Runners On	.291	54	.465	32	.357	54	3.49	51	10.10	59	13.13	87
	Bases Empty	.248	94	.344	116	.314	86	0.80	139	8.03	74	17.52	122
Bill Pecota	Runners On	.257	105	.351	126	.333	89	0.00	148	8.79	76	16.48	122
	Bases Empty	.173	167	.221	171	.252	163	0.96	132	8.70	67	16.52	110
Jamie Quirk	Runners On	.210	--	.274	--	.333	--	0.00	--	15.85	--	15.85	--
	Bases Empty	.254	87	.470	27	.333	54	5.97	14	10.00	41	18.67	135
Kevin Seitzer	Runners On	.324	16	.407	75	.425	7	0.46	144	13.74	21	8.78	33
	Bases Empty	.292	29	.405	66	.362	25	1.17	125	9.45	53	10.76	45
Kurt Stillwell	Runners On	.308	30	.491	21	.362	50	2.96	62	6.70	115	12.89	83
	Bases Empty	.217	141	.345	115	.299	106	1.72	100	10.49	35	15.74	102
Pat Tabler	Runners On	.336	10	.441	51	.393	19	0.95	132	8.79	77	12.13	71
	Bases Empty	.232	126	.283	149	.309	97	0.00	156	9.62	47	15.00	92
Danny Tartabull	Runners On	.303	38	.545	9	.389	22	4.92	16	11.90	38	18.01	136
	Bases Empty	.243	111	.481	22	.348	37	5.35	17	13.83	9	22.34	148
Frank White	Runners On	.221	148	.317	144	.252	164	1.25	109	4.15	162	7.92	27
	Bases Empty	.246	98	.340	118	.277	140	1.68	101	3.23	164	14.84	88
Willie Wilson	Runners On	.295	48	.357	121	.317	113	0.00	148	3.93	165	17.90	134
	Bases Empty	.245	101	.320	132	.273	147	0.26	155	3.26	163	16.29	109
Team Average	Runners On	.287	2	.426	4	.351	2	2.09	13	8.92	9	14.28	10
	Bases Empty	.240	14	.365	12	.298	13	2.30	11	7.27	9	16.46	13
League Average	Runners On	.268		.401		.336		2.45		9.09		13.68	
	Bases Empty	.253		.383		.315		2.48		7.76		14.81	

Overall Batting Compared to Late Inning Pressure Situations

		BA	Rank	SA	Rank	OBA	Rank	HR %	Rank	BB %	Rank	SO %	Rank	RDI %	Rank
George Brett	Overall	.306	15	.509	13	.389	9	4.07	30	12.04	22	7.49	14	.356	5
	Pressure	.283	55	.446	47	.353	55	2.17	71	9.80	62	14.71	77	.421	17
Bill Buckner	Overall	.249	105	.330	134	.287	146	1.05	127	5.47	135	6.11	10	.374	1
	Pressure	.311	38	.344	94	.357	49	0.00	110	8.45	85	7.04	14	.458	9
Jim Eisenreich	Overall	.218	151	.282	161	.236	169	0.50	154	2.80	169	14.49	95	.231	131
	Pressure	.256	84	.282	131	.275	127	0.00	110	2.50	161	20.00	110	.200	95
Bo Jackson	Overall	.246	113	.472	24	.287	145	5.69	9	5.34	140	31.20	169	.250	104
	Pressure	.282	57	.366	78	.346	64	1.41	95	7.69	93	38.46	172	.167	114
Mike Macfarlane	Overall	.265	64	.393	82	.332	66	1.90	98	8.90	67	15.68	108	.279	73
	Pressure	.156	157	.313	116	.156	171	3.13	50	0.00	168	25.00	143	.200	--
Bill Pecota	Overall	.208	166	.275	165	.286	147	0.56	150	8.74	73	16.50	116	.207	154
	Pressure	.158	--	.158	--	.200	--	0.00	--	4.17	--	16.67	--	.333	--
Jamie Quirk	Overall	.240	124	.408	64	.333	63	4.08	29	12.07	21	17.67	129	.271	82
	Pressure	.125	167	.125	171	.344	67	0.00	110	22.86	2	22.86	131	.286	58
Kevin Seitzer	Overall	.304	17	.406	69	.388	10	0.89	138	11.20	36	9.95	36	.324	24
	Pressure	.227	112	.267	140	.310	94	0.00	110	11.24	49	12.36	55	.526	5
Kurt Stillwell	Overall	.251	100	.399	78	.322	86	2.18	83	9.07	65	14.67	98	.301	43
	Pressure	.322	29	.441	49	.429	9	1.69	84	13.70	17	21.92	124	.353	35
Pat Tabler	Overall	.282	42	.358	112	.349	43	0.45	158	9.22	60	13.63	82	.353	9
	Pressure	.180	140	.213	150	.257	143	0.00	110	10.00	57	14.29	71	.421	17
Danny Tartabull	Overall	.274	52	.515	12	.369	23	5.13	16	12.82	13	20.07	144	.286	60
	Pressure	.198	134	.321	109	.293	116	1.23	105	11.96	37	25.00	143	.167	114
Frank White	Overall	.235	132	.330	135	.266	164	1.49	108	3.65	166	11.65	58	.234	127
	Pressure	.174	147	.233	144	.226	156	1.16	107	5.26	134	21.05	118	.200	95
Willie Wilson	Overall	.262	76	.333	130	.289	142	0.17	163	3.50	167	16.88	122	.264	89
	Pressure	.286	51	.345	92	.302	106	0.00	110	2.30	163	11.49	45	.357	33
Team Average	Overall	.259	8	.391	7	.321	8	2.21	12	7.99	9	15.51	13	.278	4
	Pressure	.238	11	.313	13	.302	12	0.86	14	8.18	12	19.96	14	.302	1
League Average	Overall	.259		.391		.324		2.47		8.35		14.31		.269	
	Pressure	.249		.365		.319		2.28		8.71		17.04		.246	

Additional Miscellaneous Batting Comparisons

	Grass Surface BA	Rank	Artificial Surface BA	Rank	Home Games BA	Rank	Road Games BA	Rank	Runners in Scoring Position BA	Rank	Runners in Scoring Pos and Two Outs BA	Rank	Leading Off Inning OBA	Rank	Runners on 3B with less than 2 Outs RDI %	Rank
George Brett	.325	5	.294	47	.293	34	.318	6	.303	32	.305	29	.351	37	.743	11
Bill Buckner	.197	166	.294	46	.270	71	.230	132	.348	9	.310	24	.162	170	.778	5
Jim Eisenreich	.229	--	.212	143	.222	144	.214	146	.200	157	.167	152	.204	166	.500	115
Bo Jackson	.192	169	.281	65	.318	12	.180	167	.259	88	.250	61	.304	91	.421	150
Mike Macfarlane	.253	--	.275	74	.264	78	.267	64	.280	60	.276	48	.298	97	.583	78
Larry Owen	.212	--	.208	145	.189	--	.227	--	.091	--	.000	--	.360	--	.400	--
Bill Pecota	.188	--	.226	129	.226	--	.198	160	.244	106	.176	146	.278	--	.385	164
Jamie Quirk	.152	--	.285	60	.276	63	.204	154	.240	108	.273	51	.317	76	.600	--
Kevin Seitzer	.279	44	.320	22	.320	10	.289	32	.298	34	.245	71	.326	68	.655	45
Kurt Stillwell	.231	124	.262	91	.257	89	.243	116	.306	28	.208	117	.279	126	.667	33
Pat Tabler	.282	40	.281	66	.280	54	.283	41	.333	14	.339	14	.292	109	.688	25
Danny Tartabull	.265	62	.280	68	.289	37	.260	85	.287	54	.280	45	.366	27	.579	80
Brad Wellman	.280	--	.263	89	.238	--	.292	--	.143	--	.182	--	.227	--	.000	--
Frank White	.251	93	.224	132	.242	112	.228	136	.213	147	.203	125	.246	151	.525	112
Willie Wilson	.230	127	.282	64	.283	48	.241	119	.277	61	.241	79	.272	130	.444	143
Team Average	.244	12	.270	5	.274	3	.246	12	.268	6	.242	9	.283	14	.575	7
League Average	.256		.267		.262		.257		.262		.239		.311		.570	

Pitching vs. Left and Right Handed Batters

		BA	Rank	SA	Rank	OBA	Rank	HR %	Rank	BB %	Rank	SO %	Rank
Floyd Bannister	vs. Lefties	.214	18	.276	8	.253	8	0.00	1	4.43	5	15.82	40
	vs. Righties	.257	65	.437	107	.330	85	3.74	110	9.27	96	13.37	80
Steve Farr	vs. Lefties	.277	87	.406	83	.349	97	1.29	29	9.71	83	21.14	10
	vs. Righties	.203	14	.327	20	.268	13	1.96	33	7.69	64	20.71	23
Mark Gubicza	vs. Lefties	.252	53	.340	37	.318	50	1.34	33	8.09	50	12.56	67
	vs. Righties	.215	19	.299	11	.269	14	0.82	5	6.79	48	20.75	22
Charlie Leibrandt	vs. Lefties	.253	55	.360	50	.290	19	1.33	31	4.27	4	6.10	127
	vs. Righties	.266	84	.385	67	.315	58	2.33	54	6.56	44	13.72	73
Jeff Montgomery	vs. Lefties	.218	21	.347	43	.316	47	1.98	60	11.76	109	9.24	102
	vs. Righties	.241	41	.391	71	.325	75	3.01	90	10.53	111	23.68	10
Bret Saberhagen	vs. Lefties	.245	50	.343	40	.299	30	1.13	23	7.25	39	17.96	24
	vs. Righties	.295	117	.462	117	.320	69	2.51	63	3.33	3	13.14	83
Team Average	vs. Lefties	.256	5	.358	3	.318	4	1.40	1	7.92	2	14.38	4
	vs. Righties	.260	10	.391	7	.318	6	2.16	1	7.53	6	14.82	8
League Average	vs. Lefties	.262		.387		.331		2.24		9.12		13.21	
	vs. Righties	.258		.393		.320		2.63		7.80		15.09	

Pitching with Runners on Base and Bases Empty

		BA	Rank	SA	Rank	OBA	Rank	HR %	Rank	BB %	Rank	SO %	Rank
Floyd Bannister	Runners On	.277	84	.446	102	.345	87	3.04	90	8.28	55	13.31	65
	Bases Empty	.229	31	.378	65	.295	34	2.97	96	8.37	79	14.23	65
Steve Farr	Runners On	.231	22	.338	23	.296	25	1.88	42	8.33	57	20.56	13
	Bases Empty	.250	57	.399	85	.323	80	1.35	20	9.15	91	21.34	13
Mark Gubicza	Runners On	.232	23	.305	5	.275	8	0.94	14	5.41	8	16.88	25
	Bases Empty	.235	39	.331	23	.309	52	1.19	16	8.94	86	16.18	49
Charlie Leibrandt	Runners On	.270	73	.358	38	.332	65	1.45	27	8.44	59	13.30	66
	Bases Empty	.260	74	.395	84	.298	41	2.59	85	4.75	15	11.95	89
Jeff Montgomery	Runners On	.259	64	.398	72	.359	100	2.78	81	12.21	112	16.79	27
	Bases Empty	.206	11	.349	39	.286	20	2.38	76	10.00	110	17.86	33
Bret Saberhagen	Runners On	.296	106	.422	88	.333	68	1.51	30	6.09	18	13.77	59
	Bases Empty	.251	58	.385	73	.293	31	1.97	48	4.95	18	17.03	39
Team Average	Runners On	.268	6	.379	3	.330	6	1.75	1	8.20	4	14.64	4
	Bases Empty	.251	6	.377	5	.310	4	1.95	1	7.28	6	14.65	8
League Average	Runners On	.268		.401		.336		2.45		9.09		13.68	
	Bases Empty	.253		.383		.315		2.48		7.76		14.81	

Overall Pitching Compared to Late Inning Pressure Situations

		BA	Rank	SA	Rank	OBA	Rank	HR %	Rank	BB %	Rank	SO %	Rank
Floyd Bannister	Overall	.248	48	.405	86	.316	50	3.00	97	8.33	68	13.85	65
	Pressure	.219	32	.313	34	.359	95	0.00	1	17.95	126	15.38	53
Steve Farr	Overall	.240	36	.367	44	.309	39	1.62	21	8.72	81	20.93	12
	Pressure	.248	66	.366	60	.327	68	1.38	40	9.70	75	19.39	25
Gene Garber	Overall	.238	--	.352	--	.321	--	3.28	--	9.42	--	14.49	--
	Pressure	.233	48	.342	48	.309	52	2.74	83	7.32	38	13.41	80
Jerry Don Gleaton	Overall	.232	--	.338	--	.327	--	1.41	--	10.37	--	17.68	--
	Pressure	.244	60	.359	56	.337	74	2.56	77	9.89	77	17.58	36
Mark Gubicza	Overall	.234	31	.320	12	.294	16	1.09	6	7.47	44	16.47	38
	Pressure	.283	102	.408	85	.343	84	1.32	37	7.74	47	14.29	68
Charlie Leibrandt	Overall	.264	74	.381	59	.311	42	2.16	58	6.19	21	12.48	81
	Pressure	.225	38	.318	37	.275	21	1.55	44	5.67	22	14.18	71
Jeff Montgomery	Overall	.231	23	.372	51	.321	62	2.56	78	11.07	115	17.34	33
	Pressure	.244	61	.353	54	.308	51	0.84	28	8.33	56	16.67	42
Bret Saberhagen	Overall	.269	87	.400	84	.309	38	1.79	26	5.42	10	15.70	45
	Pressure	.234	49	.364	58	.252	10	1.30	35	1.88	2	14.38	67
Israel Sanchez	Overall	.265	--	.287	--	.348	--	0.00	--	11.46	--	8.92	--
	Pressure	.163	5	.163	2	.280	24	0.00	1	13.73	113	13.73	77
Team Average	Overall	.258	7	.378	4	.318	4	1.86	1	7.69	4	14.64	7
	Pressure	.242	5	.344	2	.309	4	1.25	1	8.03	3	15.20	9
League Average	Overall	.259		.391		.324		2.47		8.35		14.31	
	Pressure	.249		.369		.324		2.26		9.33		15.69	

Additional Miscellaneous Pitching Comparisons

	Grass Surface BA	Rank	Artificial Surface BA	Rank	Home Games BA	Rank	Road Games BA	Rank	Runners in Scoring Position BA	Rank	Runners in Scoring Pos and Two Outs BA	Rank	Leading Off Inning OBA	Rank
Rick Anderson	.342	--	.263	56	.263	--	.342	--	.306	--	.313	--	.343	--
Luis Aquino	.538	--	.252	48	.250	--	.393	--	.300	--	.333	--	.345	--
Floyd Bannister	.239	39	.254	49	.253	62	.243	42	.266	70	.314	114	.303	56
Steve Farr	.254	--	.231	22	.232	37	.248	53	.210	18	.157	14	.361	108
Gene Garber	.091	--	.292	94	.282	--	.159	--	.244	--	.286	--	.321	--
Jerry Don Gleaton	.159	--	.265	59	.224	--	.242	--	.172	--	.192	--	.313	--
Mark Gubicza	.229	26	.237	30	.240	47	.227	21	.232	40	.250	78	.313	66
Charlie Leibrandt	.227	23	.291	91	.277	95	.253	60	.256	63	.228	61	.296	50
Jeff Montgomery	.197	--	.247	40	.233	39	.228	22	.208	15	.176	28	.271	32
Dan Quisenberry	.200	--	.383	129	.442	--	.210	--	.265	--	.200	--	.417	--
Bret Saberhagen	.231	31	.290	90	.286	107	.251	57	.274	80	.245	75	.280	42
Israel Sanchez	.280	--	.256	52	.297	--	.236	--	.263	--	.176	--	.353	--
Team Average	.238	1	.271	9	.269	13	.248	2	.256	4	.235	7	.311	7
League Average	.256		.267		.257		.262		.262		.239		.311	

MILWAUKEE BREWERS

● Here's a bunch of newly-researched streak records to shoot for.

● Who is Bob Betts and why don't we hear much from him?

Baseball's streakiest team had a rather quiet year in 1988, in more ways than one.

That the Brewers finished only two games out of first place last season is a fact that may be known only to residents of Wisconsin, close friends of the Trebelhorn family, and Bob Uecker's buddies on the set of "Mr. Belvedere." As the infamous American League "swing team," the Brewers were given a strict diet of A.L. West teams over the last four weeks of the season. In newspapers in the East, the dreaded footnote, "Late Game Not Included in Standings," applied to the Brewers through much of the last month of the season.

Accordingly, the Brewers were able to sneak up on the other teams in their division, all of whom were playing among themselves over that same span. Few will recall that it was Milwaukee—not Detroit, not Toronto, and not New York—that had the last shot at catching the Red Sox, but the Brew Crew's loss on the final Friday of the season—typically, a night game at Oakland—clinched the title for the Sox, somewhere around 1:15 a.m., early Saturday morning, Boston time.

The Brewers wound up winning 14 of 22 games against the West in September; had they been able to win just three more, they would have spent the winter being hailed as the most remarkable Cinderella story in major league history. On the morning of September 1, they rested in fourth place in the East, with a 69–67 record. The Brewers were eight games behind division-leading Detroit, six games behind Boston, and two and one-half behind New York. No team going into September with that large a deficit has ever come back to win a league or division title. Here are the teams that overcame the largest August 31 deficits to finish in first place:

Year	Team	Through Aug. 31 W–L	Position	GB	Sept./Oct. W–L
1964	Cardinals	71–59	4th	7.5	22–10
1938	Cubs	67–56	4th	7	22–7
1951	Giants	76–53	2d	7	22–6
1930	Cardinals	71–58	4th	6.5	21–4
1978	Yankees	77–54	2d	6.5	23–9
1974	Orioles	66–65	3d	6	25–6
1934	Cardinals	74–51	2d	5.5	21–7
1973	Mets	62–71	5th	5.5	20–8
1969	Mets	76–54	2d	4.5	24–8
1942	Cardinals	85–44	2d	3.5	21–4

The largest deficit ever overcome *during* the month of September was eight and one-half games. Those 1964 Cardinals were that far behind the Phillies after games of September 5. The Brewers didn't win it, of course, but few remember how close they actually came.

In yet another respect, however, it was a quiet summer in the upper midwest: The Brewers didn't put together any eye-catching streaks. A year earlier, Milwaukee had captivated the baseball world with a season-opening 13–game winning streak, a 12–game losing streak that started less than two weeks later, and Paul Molitor's 39–game hitting streak. Last year, the best that the Brewers could do was a 10–game winning streak, a seven-game losing streak (just for old times' sake, they both began in April), and a puny little 12–game hitting streak by Robin Yount. Oh, sure, there were some other pedestrian streaks; you can't expect a team to go cold turkey. Chris Bosio did have an 11–game losing streak, longest in the majors last season. And Tom Filer, after winning his first 11 American League decisions, ended the season with a five-game losing streak. But these were small potatoes; certainly nothing that excited the general public.

But the excitement requirement for statisticians is somewhat lower than it is for the general public. And our interest was piqued by the fact that the Brewers did not allow an opponent to score 10 or more runs in a game for the first 100 games of the season. The Yankees finally broke the streak with a 16–3 win on July 27, and four other teams subsequently reached double figures against the Brewers, but we wondered what the record was for consecutive games without allowing a 10–run game. The record books were bare on this topic, so we did some research.

It turns out that even when you include Milwaukee's last 11 games of the 1987 season, the Brewers' total of 111 games was not even halfway to the modern record. The Chicago Cubs held their opponents to single figures for 257 consecutive games from August 3, 1908, to June 4, 1910. We always wondered what the big deal was about Tinker, Evers, and Chance; now we know why they were the saddest of possible words. Here are the top five streaks without allowing a 10–run game:

Cubs, 1908–10	257 games
Senators, 1917–19	203 games

Yankees, 1975–76	194 games	
Red Sox, 1916–17	181 games	
Phillies, 1978–79	177 games	

Allowing 7 or Less	89, Bos. 1917	93, Chi. 1919
Allowing 8 or Less	129, Bos. 1917	160, Pitt. 1908–09
Allowing 9 or Less	203, Wash. 1917–19	257, Chi. 1908–10

That Philadelphia team, by the way, had its single-digit streak snapped in that memorable 23–22 win over the Cubs at Wrigley Field on May 17, 1979.

While we were hot, we decided to keep going. The record books listed only the records for consecutive shutouts by a pitching staff, consecutive times shut out, and consecutive games without being shut out. To those records we were able to create the following companions, which date from 1900. We offer these as both a gift and a challenge to the Brewers, a team that lives by the credo, "There can never be enough streak records." Maybe they'll be able to mount a challenge to some of these in 1989:

Most Consecutive Games Since 1900

	American League	National League
Scoring 1 + Runs	308, N.Y. 1931–33	150, Pitt. 1924–25
Scoring 2 + Runs	86, N.Y. 1938	50, St.L. 1940–41
Scoring 3 + Runs	49, N.Y. 1950–51	39, Chi. 1930
Scoring 4 + Runs	28, Det. 1927	22, Pitt. 1929
Scoring 5 + Runs	19, Chi. 1901	17, Phil. 1934
Scoring 6 + Runs	14, Det. 1936	15, N.Y. 1929
Scoring 7 + Runs	11, Det. 1936	11, Phil. 1900
	11, N.Y. 1938	
Scoring 8 + Runs	9, Phil. 1930	8, Chi. 1929
Scoring 9 + Runs	9, Phil. 1930	6, Pitt. 1901
		6, N.Y. 1929
		6, Chi. 1930
Scoring 10 + Runs	5, Clev. 1925	6, Pitt. 1901
	5, N.Y. 1930	6, N.Y. 1929
Scoring 0 Runs	4, by 5 teams	4, by 7 teams
Scoring 1 or Less	8, Wash. 1909	9, Hou. 1963
Scoring 2 or Less	11, Wash. 1947	12, Bklyn. 1904
		12, Bklyn. 1907
Scoring 3 or Less	19, Clev. 1942	19, Bklyn. 1906–07
Scoring 4 or Less	26, Cal. 1969	26, Bos. 1906
		26, Bos. 1918–19
		26, Bos. 1931
Scoring 5 or Less	38, Cal. 1969	42, Atl. 1967–68
Scoring 6 or Less	65, N.Y. 1967–68	63, Bos. 1931
Scoring 7 or Less	95, Wash. 1909	106, Bklyn. 1917–18
Scoring 8 or Less	131, Wash. 1908–09	192, Phil. 1941–42
Scoring 9 or Less	203, Chi. 1913–15	284, Hou. 1981–83
Allowing 1 + Runs	199, St.L. 1939–40	197, Bos. 1928–29
Allowing 2 + Runs	80, St.L. 1925	63, L.A. 1979
Allowing 3 + Runs	38, Bos. 1925	40, Phil. 1927
Allowing 4 + Runs	25, St.L. 1937	26, Phil. 1923
Allowing 5 + Runs	17, Phil. 1901	20, Phil. 1924
Allowing 6 + Runs	10, by 6 teams	11, Phil. 1925
		11, N.Y. 1962
Allowing 7 + Runs	10, St.L. 1936	10, Phil. 1923
Allowing 8 + Runs	7, St.L. 1932	7, N.Y. 1901
Allowing 9 + Runs	6, St.L. 1949	7, N.Y. 1901
Allowing 10 + Runs	4, by 9 teams	7, N.Y. 1901
Allowing 0 Runs	5, Balt. 1974	6, Pitt. 1903
Allowing 1 or Less	8, K.C. 1966	8, N.Y. 1906
		8, Chi. 1919
Allowing 2 or Less	17, Chi. 1917	16, N.Y. 1916
Allowing 3 or Less	20, Chi. 1917	20, Cin. 1943–44
Allowing 4 or Less	28, Clev. 1904–05	30, Chi. 1909–10
Allowing 5 or Less	41, Chi. 1909	56, Phil. 1908
Allowing 6 or Less	61, Balt. 1961	65, Chi. 1905–06

There's a hilarious scene in the movie spoof *Airplane* in which Robert Hays plays the role of the passenger recruited to land a jumbo jet after the pilots fall ill. In the echo-chamber manner in which movies usually portray a person's thoughts, Hays hears his own voice resounding back to him as he thinks about his priorities. "I have to concentrate (concentrate, concentrate)." Upon realizing that he himself hears the echo, he plays around for a moment— "Hey (hey, hey). . . Echo (echo, echo) . . ."—before fulfilling the lifelong fantasy of many a baseball fan. While a planeload of passengers heads toward possible doom, Hays enthusiastically announces, "Now batting for Pedro Borbon, Manny Mota (Mota, Mota)."

Stadium public-address announcers are an important part of baseball's romance. The voices of longtime public-address announcers such as Fenway Park's Sherm Feller or Yankee Stadium's Bob Sheppard are easily recognized even outside their own cities. Bob Betts, who handles the Brewers' public-address system, is in his 14th season with the team, but through no fault of his own, he's not exactly a household name. No disrespect to Bob—he works hard at his job and we're sure that he'd like to work even harder, if only given the chance. But with Tom Trebelhorn sending up a major league low of only 40 pinch hitters last season, Betts just didn't get a lot of extra time at the mike. If Treb continues his laid-back pinch-hitting style, Bob will never get the acclaim of a Feller or a Sheppard. Maybe he'll have to take up singing the national anthem as a sideline, as has the Cubs' Wayne Messmer. On the other hand, Betts will be able to catch up on his reading.

The Brewers last season were among the most prolific nonusers of pinch hitters since managers regularly began to use them in the early years of this century. Only one major league team since Prohibition (that's 1920 for those of you without your constitutional amendments handy) has used fewer pinch hitters in a season: the 1973 Red Sox, who in the first year of the designated hitter rule, used only 32 of what *The Sporting News* used to call "emergency swingers." Although the DH rule certainly reduces the number of pinch hitters employed in the American League, the 13 other teams in the league averaged 136 pinch hitters last season, a figure that is 240 percent higher than Milwaukee's.

So when baseball statisticians of the future look back to the 1988 Brewers, they will see some very modest totals. The team had six hits in 33 pinch-hit at-bats. They also had five walks, and two pinch hitters were withdrawn without batting, due to pitching changes. No, those are not typographical errors. B.J. Surhoff *did* lead the team with nine pinch-hit appearances, and he *was* the only Milwaukee player with two pinch hits. And Jim Gantner *did* lead the team with the grand total of two pinch-hit runs batted in, generated by a single swing of the bat at Minnesota on July 9. In this era of specialized substitution in all sports, it's refreshing that there's at least one manager who's bucking the trend.

WON-LOST RECORD BY STARTING POSITION

MILWAUKEE 87-75	C	1B	2B	3B	SS	LF	CF	RF	P	DH	Leadoff	Relief	Starts
Jim Adduci	-	0-1	-	-	-	4-1	-	1-3	-	7-4	-	-	12-9
Don August	-	-	-	-	-	-	-	-	13-9	-	-	2-0	13-9
Mike Birkbeck	-	-	-	-	-	-	-	-	13-10	-	-	-	13-10
Chris Bosio	-	-	-	-	-	-	-	-	7-15	-	-	10-6	7-15
Glenn Braggs	-	-	-	-	-	-	-	28-26	-	8-10	-	-	36-36
Greg Brock	-	53-51	-	-	-	-	-	-	-	-	-	-	53-51
Juan Castillo	-	-	5-4	1-4	3-4	-	-	-	-	-	-	-	9-12
Mark Clear	-	-	-	-	-	-	-	-	-	-	-	7-18	-
Chuck Crim	-	-	-	-	-	-	-	-	-	-	-	38-32	-
Rob Deer	-	-	-	-	-	26-27	-	43-36	-	0-1	-	-	69-64
Mike Felder	-	-	-	-	-	6-3	1-0	2-1	-	2-1	1-0	-	11-5
Tom Filer	-	-	-	-	-	-	-	-	8-8	-	-	0-3	8-8
Jim Gantner	-	-	81-68	-	-	-	-	-	-	-	1-4	-	81-68
Darryl Hamilton	-	-	-	-	-	2-2	1-2	13-9	-	-	1-0	-	16-13
Ted Higuera	-	-	-	-	-	-	-	-	19-12	-	-	-	19-12
Odell Jones	-	-	-	-	-	-	-	-	2-0	-	-	6-20	2-0
Steve Kiefer	-	-	0-2	0-1	-	-	-	-	-	-	-	-	0-3
Mark Knudson	-	-	-	-	-	-	-	-	-	-	-	0-5	-
Jeffrey Leonard	-	-	-	-	-	49-42	-	-	-	1-1	1-0	-	50-43
Joey Meyer	-	12-14	-	-	-	-	-	-	-	39-26	-	-	51-40
Paul Mirabella	-	-	-	-	-	-	-	-	-	-	-	17-21	-
Paul Molitor	-	-	1-0	60-44	-	-	-	-	-	22-27	82-71	-	83-71
Juan Nieves	-	-	-	-	-	-	-	-	8-7	-	-	6-4	8-7
Charlie O'Brien	18-18	-	-	-	-	-	-	-	-	-	-	-	18-18
Dan Plesac	-	-	-	-	-	-	-	-	-	-	-	36-14	-
Ernest Riles	-	-	-	13-12	2-4	-	-	-	-	2-2	1-0	-	17-18
Billy Jo Robidoux	-	16-8	-	-	-	-	-	-	-	-	-	-	16-8
Bill Schroeder	11-16	6-1	-	-	-	-	-	-	-	1-0	-	-	18-17
Gary Sheffield	-	-	-	-	15-8	-	-	-	-	-	-	-	15-8
Dave E. Stapleton	-	-	-	-	-	-	-	-	-	-	-	2-4	-
B.j. Surhoff	58-41	-	-	13-14	-	-	-	-	-	-	-	-	71-55
Dale Sveum	-	-	0-1	-	67-59	-	-	-	-	0-1	-	-	67-61
Bill Wegman	-	-	-	-	-	-	-	-	17-14	-	-	0-1	17-14
Mike Young	-	-	-	-	-	-	-	-	-	3-0	-	-	3-0
Robin Yount	-	-	-	-	-	-	85-73	-	-	2-2	-	-	87-75

Batting vs. Left and Right Handed Pitchers

		BA	Rank	SA	Rank	OBA	Rank	HR %	Rank	BB %	Rank	SO %	Rank
Glenn Braggs	vs. Lefties	.247	98	.471	42	.283	125	5.88	15	4.35	132	22.83	150
	vs. Righties	.267	68	.401	71	.318	96	2.67	70	4.95	146	19.31	140
Greg Brock	vs. Lefties	.233	120	.320	126	.316	82	0.97	124	10.08	46	8.40	34
	vs. Righties	.203	160	.307	142	.334	73	1.92	88	16.04	7	11.95	60
Juan Castillo	vs. Lefties	.240	104	.240	160	.240	161	0.00	140	0.00	168	7.84	26
	vs. Righties	.200	--	.200	--	.256	--	0.00	--	6.98	--	23.26	--
Rob Deer	vs. Lefties	.255	79	.482	36	.366	35	5.84	16	14.63	17	18.90	135
	vs. Righties	.251	100	.425	55	.312	109	4.23	28	6.89	107	31.12	169
Jim Gantner	vs. Lefties	.274	61	.329	117	.318	76	0.00	140	4.88	125	6.71	14
	vs. Righties	.277	49	.338	124	.323	89	0.00	161	6.02	122	9.03	27
Jeffrey Leonard	vs. Lefties	.270	65	.441	52	.317	80	2.70	64	5.83	107	15.00	97
	vs. Righties	.221	145	.312	141	.249	164	1.90	90	3.24	164	17.99	127
Joey Meyer	vs. Lefties	.292	40	.507	24	.338	54	4.86	24	5.84	105	17.53	122
	vs. Righties	.240	118	.350	116	.293	134	2.19	84	7.07	104	30.81	168
Paul Molitor	vs. Lefties	.276	59	.393	77	.353	41	2.04	83	10.36	40	4.50	4
	vs. Righties	.329	5	.479	19	.399	9	2.18	85	10.23	50	9.38	32
Bill Schroeder	vs. Lefties	.135	168	.270	150	.200	168	4.05	35	6.17	95	30.86	166
	vs. Righties	.188	--	.333	--	.220	--	4.17	--	2.00	--	22.00	--
B.J. Surhoff	vs. Lefties	.191	157	.270	151	.256	149	1.74	97	6.11	101	9.16	43
	vs. Righties	.262	77	.333	127	.304	120	0.79	134	5.61	130	9.02	26
Dale Sveum	vs. Lefties	.251	91	.395	74	.278	131	2.40	73	3.39	154	23.16	154
	vs. Righties	.237	126	.320	136	.272	152	1.67	98	4.72	151	25.47	161
Robin Yount	vs. Lefties	.284	49	.448	51	.381	26	3.83	40	13.95	18	5.12	9
	vs. Righties	.315	12	.473	25	.363	27	1.37	111	6.86	110	10.81	48
Team Average	vs. Lefties	.245	12	.382	9	.308	11	2.81	3	7.67	9	13.30	6
	vs. Righties	.262	6	.372	11	.317	10	1.73	14	7.04	13	15.78	13
League Average	vs. Lefties	.259		.391		.321		2.47		7.97		14.12	
	vs. Righties	.259		.391		.326		2.47		8.51		14.39	

Batting with Runners on Base and Bases Empty

		BA	Rank	SA	Rank	OBA	Rank	HR %	Rank	BB %	Rank	SO %	Rank
Glenn Braggs	Runners On	.288	58	.481	27	.333	89	4.81	20	4.35	157	19.13	148
	Bases Empty	.244	107	.387	83	.291	122	2.98	61	5.03	136	21.23	146
Greg Brock	Runners On	.230	139	.358	120	.370	41	1.82	93	17.54	7	9.48	39
	Bases Empty	.196	160	.271	154	.292	119	1.51	108	11.50	23	12.39	58
Rob Deer	Runners On	.288	62	.500	19	.357	55	5.31	11	8.49	81	25.48	163
	Bases Empty	.222	135	.391	79	.303	104	4.14	35	9.76	46	29.29	167
Jim Gantner	Runners On	.263	99	.329	140	.318	109	0.00	148	6.77	113	9.96	48
	Bases Empty	.285	35	.340	117	.325	70	0.00	156	4.93	137	7.25	14
Jeffrey Leonard	Runners On	.225	145	.342	133	.259	162	2.67	71	3.96	164	15.84	115
	Bases Empty	.246	97	.358	104	.281	137	1.60	103	4.08	156	18.37	133
Joey Meyer	Runners On	.299	40	.445	44	.340	82	3.65	45	5.44	141	24.49	162
	Bases Empty	.237	117	.400	69	.293	114	3.16	55	7.32	88	25.37	160
Paul Molitor	Runners On	.357	3	.508	15	.438	3	2.70	68	12.61	31	5.86	13
	Bases Empty	.292	27	.427	43	.359	29	1.89	94	9.17	58	8.74	25
B.J. Surhoff	Runners On	.276	69	.350	127	.342	77	0.99	127	7.95	91	9.62	42
	Bases Empty	.224	133	.297	140	.255	160	1.03	128	3.97	158	8.61	23
Dale Sveum	Runners On	.270	86	.411	74	.299	133	2.70	68	4.50	155	24.00	161
	Bases Empty	.223	134	.305	137	.258	158	1.42	111	4.07	157	25.08	158
Robin Yount	Runners On	.321	18	.468	31	.378	34	1.37	104	9.01	73	9.61	41
	Bases Empty	.293	26	.463	28	.361	28	2.74	69	9.09	60	8.54	22
Team Average	Runners On	.273	6	.401	9	.333	8	2.38	9	7.82	14	15.13	13
	Bases Empty	.245	11	.356	14	.300	12	1.83	14	6.80	12	14.93	7
League Average	Runners On	.268		.401		.336		2.45		9.09		13.68	
	Bases Empty	.253		.383		.315		2.48		7.76		14.81	

Overall Batting Compared to Late Inning Pressure Situations

		BA	Rank	SA	Rank	OBA	Rank	HR %	Rank	BB %	Rank	SO %	Rank	RDI %	Rank
Jim Adduci	Overall	.266	--	.383	--	.258	--	1.06	--	0.00	--	15.46	--	.371	--
	Pressure	.231	--	.231	--	.231	--	0.00	--	0.00	--	30.77	--	.143	128
Glenn Braggs	Overall	.261	80	.423	52	.307	109	3.68	40	4.76	154	20.41	145	.338	15
	Pressure	.250	87	.477	29	.267	136	4.55	27	2.17	164	21.74	121	.364	31
Greg Brock	Overall	.212	161	.310	149	.329	72	1.65	101	14.42	7	10.98	47	.297	46
	Pressure	.314	34	.343	95	.500	1	0.00	110	26.53	1	10.20	37	.357	33
Rob Deer	Overall	.252	96	.441	37	.328	74	4.67	24	9.17	63	27.52	167	.312	31
	Pressure	.179	142	.321	110	.229	155	3.85	41	3.61	150	32.53	165	.200	95
Jim Gantner	Overall	.276	48	.336	127	.322	88	0.00	165	5.70	129	8.39	23	.291	53
	Pressure	.253	86	.360	84	.296	114	0.00	110	6.10	124	7.32	16	.375	27
Jeffrey Leonard	Overall	.235	129	.350	118	.270	161	2.14	87	4.02	163	17.09	125	.248	110
	Pressure	.294	48	.353	88	.308	99	0.00	110	0.00	168	19.23	106	.071	163
Joey Meyer	Overall	.263	73	.419	58	.313	102	3.36	52	6.53	113	25.00	162	.293	51
	Pressure	.224	115	.429	54	.264	139	4.08	37	5.66	131	33.96	166	.400	20
Paul Molitor	Overall	.312	6	.452	30	.384	12	2.13	88	10.27	48	7.81	17	.331	21
	Pressure	.282	57	.366	78	.350	58	1.41	95	9.76	63	7.32	16	.259	71
B.J. Surhoff	Overall	.245	115	.318	145	.292	139	1.01	130	5.73	128	9.06	27	.203	158
	Pressure	.189	138	.203	154	.259	141	0.00	110	8.33	86	11.90	51	.103	148
Dale Sveum	Overall	.242	119	.347	121	.274	156	1.93	96	4.24	159	24.65	161	.276	76
	Pressure	.338	15	.493	24	.356	51	1.41	95	2.70	158	25.68	149	.167	114
Robin Yount	Overall	.306	13	.465	26	.369	24	2.09	92	9.05	66	9.05	26	.346	12
	Pressure	.351	7	.468	37	.407	19	1.30	100	9.30	68	12.79	60	.333	39
Team Average	Overall	.257	10	.375	11	.314	12	2.06	13	7.24	13	15.02	10	.284	3
	Pressure	.261	4	.366	7	.321	7	1.57	12	7.67	13	18.04	11	.248	8
League Average	Overall	.259		.391		.324		2.47		8.35		14.31		.269	
	Pressure	.249		.365		.319		2.28		8.71		17.04		.246	

Additional Miscellaneous Batting Comparisons

	Grass Surface		Artificial Surface		Home Games		Road Games		Runners in Scoring Position		Runners in Scoring Pos and Two Outs		Leading Off Inning		Runners on 3B with less than 2 Outs	
	BA	Rank	BA	Rank	BA	Rank	BA	Rank	BA	Rank	BA	Rank	OBA	Rank	RDI %	Rank
Jim Adduci	.293	--	.083	--	.318	--	.220	--	.269	--	.333	--	.250	--	.700	17
Glenn Braggs	.268	58	.227	127	.259	85	.264	72	.333	14	.212	113	.271	132	.538	104
Greg Brock	.212	155	.205	147	.231	133	.189	164	.237	112	.188	138	.268	134	.696	20
Rob Deer	.250	96	.267	86	.256	91	.248	105	.284	56	.268	54	.296	102	.526	109
Jim Gantner	.275	51	.284	61	.273	65	.280	45	.256	94	.254	60	.345	44	.586	76
Darryl Hamilton	.147	--	.286	--	.176	--	.188	--	.207	--	.250	--	.200	--	.400	156
Jeffrey Leonard	.225	132	.311	28	.239	115	.231	130	.212	148	.191	133	.290	110	.500	115
Joey Meyer	.251	94	.309	30	.261	81	.264	69	.268	74	.361	9	.288	117	.421	150
Paul Molitor	.312	10	.313	27	.316	14	.307	19	.350	7	.300	33	.360	31	.632	55
Ernest Riles	.277	49	.067	--	.307	--	.173	--	.323	--	.250	--	.147	--	.500	--
B.J. Surhoff	.239	114	.286	59	.225	141	.265	68	.256	94	.231	92	.250	147	.389	162
Dale Sveum	.257	80	.145	170	.280	55	.202	157	.283	57	.263	58	.245	152	.565	85
Robin Yount	.302	18	.327	18	.307	19	.305	21	.364	2	.388	3	.289	112	.592	73
Team Average	.255	8	.265	8	.260	9	.254	10	.276	4	.261	3	.290	13	.544	11
League Average	.256		.267		.262		.257		.262		.239		.311		.570	

Pitching vs. Left and Right Handed Batters

		BA	Rank	SA	Rank	OBA	Rank	HR %	Rank	BB %	Rank	SO %	Rank
Don August	vs. Lefties	.268	77	.384	72	.324	61	2.11	65	7.99	48	8.63	108
	vs. Righties	.222	25	.327	21	.282	26	2.18	50	7.64	63	12.96	86
Mike Birkbeck	vs. Lefties	.262	69	.352	46	.323	59	1.23	27	8.24	54	11.61	77
	vs. Righties	.308	123	.444	112	.347	105	2.80	76	5.54	26	12.18	96
Chris Bosio	vs. Lefties	.259	65	.356	47	.294	24	1.73	51	4.78	9	9.11	105
	vs. Righties	.279	101	.390	70	.315	56	1.97	35	5.20	19	13.46	79
Chuck Crim	vs. Lefties	.253	54	.385	74	.320	53	2.87	98	9.18	69	13.78	57
	vs. Righties	.243	43	.381	63	.279	19	2.86	81	4.37	10	13.54	75
Tom Filer	vs. Lefties	.288	101	.438	105	.356	103	2.40	77	9.75	84	5.93	128
	vs. Righties	.271	91	.379	62	.306	44	1.69	27	5.13	16	12.82	88
Ted Higuera	vs. Lefties	.208	14	.315	23	.256	10	2.01	63	5.52	15	25.77	4
	vs. Righties	.206	16	.297	8	.265	9	1.81	29	6.83	50	20.49	24
Odell Jones	vs. Lefties	.230	30	.320	27	.317	48	2.46	81	11.89	111	13.99	54
	vs. Righties	.266	82	.424	91	.311	49	2.82	78	6.12	39	14.29	65
Paul Mirabella	vs. Lefties	.167	4	.211	1	.235	6	0.00	1	8.08	49	17.17	29
	vs. Righties	.230	--	.341	--	.298	--	2.38	--	9.15	--	11.27	--
Juan Nieves	vs. Lefties	.148	3	.250	4	.208	2	2.27	68	7.29	40	22.92	9
	vs. Righties	.225	29	.377	58	.319	67	3.48	104	11.88	122	14.09	69
Dan Plesac	vs. Lefties	.225	--	.375	--	.262	--	0.00	--	4.65	--	23.26	--
	vs. Righties	.236	36	.306	14	.281	25	1.27	14	5.95	33	25.00	7
Bill Wegman	vs. Lefties	.273	81	.407	84	.313	41	2.73	93	5.75	19	7.59	116
	vs. Righties	.257	68	.419	86	.306	43	3.45	103	6.07	37	12.38	94
Team Average	vs. Lefties	.251	4	.361	4	.306	2	2.00	5	7.51	1	11.87	10
	vs. Righties	.246	3	.369	1	.300	1	2.50	6	7.06	4	15.22	7
League Average	vs. Lefties	.262		.387		.331		2.24		9.12		13.21	
	vs. Righties	.258		.393		.320		2.63		7.80		15.09	

Pitching with Runners on Base and Bases Empty

		BA	Rank	SA	Rank	OBA	Rank	HR %	Rank	BB %	Rank	SO %	Rank
Don August	Runners On	.252	55	.358	39	.317	46	1.83	40	8.91	71	11.34	90
	Bases Empty	.240	44	.355	44	.294	33	2.35	73	7.08	62	10.35	112
Mike Birkbeck	Runners On	.308	112	.443	98	.371	106	1.99	48	9.21	75	13.16	70
	Bases Empty	.270	93	.369	55	.310	54	2.05	53	5.16	23	10.97	105
Chris Bosio	Runners On	.283	93	.377	57	.311	39	1.33	21	4.82	2	9.64	111
	Bases Empty	.256	70	.366	53	.297	38	2.20	60	5.07	21	11.98	88
Chuck Crim	Runners On	.207	8	.320	14	.271	6	2.37	67	7.61	40	13.71	60
	Bases Empty	.279	104	.433	106	.320	74	3.26	99	5.70	31	13.60	73
Tom Filer	Runners On	.311	116	.480	116	.384	116	4.05	121	11.54	107	8.24	118
	Bases Empty	.262	78	.367	54	.297	37	0.84	8	4.82	17	9.64	116
Ted Higuera	Runners On	.247	46	.360	43	.301	29	2.18	58	6.65	23	20.57	12
	Bases Empty	.186	2	.270	7	.244	4	1.67	34	6.56	51	21.93	10
Odell Jones	Runners On	.273	79	.414	81	.344	85	3.13	96	10.97	102	10.97	93
	Bases Empty	.234	37	.357	45	.288	26	2.34	72	6.52	49	16.85	42
Paul Mirabella	Runners On	.144	--	.189	--	.269	--	1.11	--	14.55	--	16.36	--
	Bases Empty	.246	54	.357	46	.275	15	1.59	30	3.82	7	11.45	97
Juan Nieves	Runners On	.238	30	.419	86	.307	35	3.75	113	8.89	70	15.00	48
	Bases Empty	.189	4	.303	11	.288	25	2.87	91	12.23	122	16.55	45
Dan Plesac	Runners On	.248	48	.367	49	.299	28	1.83	40	6.72	25	25.21	2
	Bases Empty	.216	--	.261	--	.250	--	0.00	--	4.35	--	23.91	--
Bill Wegman	Runners On	.301	110	.430	95	.348	88	2.10	53	7.69	45	8.00	120
	Bases Empty	.245	52	.403	88	.285	19	3.64	106	4.79	16	11.11	103
Team Average	Runners On	.266	5	.390	4	.327	4	2.24	4	8.58	5	13.23	10
	Bases Empty	.235	2	.350	2	.286	1	2.32	5	6.30	1	14.22	9
League Average	Runners On	.268		.401		.336		2.45		9.09		13.68	
	Bases Empty	.253		.383		.315		2.48		7.76		14.81	

Overall Pitching Compared to Late Inning Pressure Situations

		BA	Rank	SA	Rank	OBA	Rank	HR %	Rank	BB %	Rank	SO %	Rank
Don August	Overall	.245	42	.356	30	.303	29	2.15	55	7.82	55	10.75	102
	Pressure	.091	--	.364	--	.259	--	9.09	--	18.52	--	7.41	--
Mike Birkbeck	Overall	.285	113	.399	83	.335	89	2.02	43	6.88	32	11.90	91
	Pressure	.286	--	.286	--	.375	--	0.00	--	12.50	--	12.50	--
Chris Bosio	Overall	.268	81	.370	50	.303	28	1.83	28	4.96	7	10.97	100
	Pressure	.195	14	.247	8	.269	18	0.65	23	8.62	62	11.49	97
Chuck Crim	Overall	.247	46	.383	63	.298	21	2.86	94	6.59	24	13.65	67
	Pressure	.265	86	.382	74	.339	77	1.76	54	9.69	74	16.33	46
Tom Filer	Overall	.281	107	.410	91	.333	86	2.08	48	7.66	50	9.05	120
	Pressure	.286	--	.286	--	.375	--	0.00	--	8.00	--	12.00	--
Ted Higuera	Overall	.207	4	.300	6	.263	3	1.85	30	6.59	25	21.45	10
	Pressure	.258	76	.367	61	.318	61	2.50	73	8.09	53	17.65	35
Odell Jones	Overall	.251	51	.381	60	.313	48	2.68	87	8.55	76	14.16	60
	Pressure	.289	106	.500	116	.341	82	5.26	120	7.14	35	23.81	9
Paul Mirabella	Overall	.204	--	.287	--	.272	--	1.39	--	8.71	--	13.69	--
	Pressure	.282	101	.372	69	.329	69	1.28	34	6.98	31	8.14	116
Juan Nieves	Overall	.208	6	.349	25	.295	18	3.22	106	10.92	113	15.94	42
	Pressure	.102	1	.122	1	.262	14	0.00	1	18.03	127	19.67	23
Dan Plesac	Overall	.234	--	.320	--	.278	--	1.02	--	5.69	--	24.64	--
	Pressure	.266	88	.367	62	.299	38	1.56	46	4.44	11	21.48	16
Bill Wegman	Overall	.265	75	.413	93	.309	40	3.08	99	5.90	19	9.92	114
	Pressure	.305	111	.458	108	.349	92	3.39	98	6.35	25	11.11	101
Team Average	Overall	.248	3	.366	3	.303	1	2.29	4	7.25	2	13.80	9
	Pressure	.244	7	.349	5	.313	5	2.07	6	8.96	7	15.78	6
League Average	Overall	.259		.391		.324		2.47		8.35		14.31	
	Pressure	.249		.369		.324		2.26		9.33		15.69	

Additional Miscellaneous Pitching Comparisons

	Grass Surface		Artificial Surface		Home Games		Road Games		Runners in Scoring Position		Runners in Scoring Pos and Two Outs		Leading Off Inning	
	BA	Rank	BA	Rank	BA	Rank	BA	Rank	BA	Rank	BA	Rank	OBA	Rank
Don August	.251	54	.213	13	.226	31	.263	73	.218	26	.161	17	.314	68
Mike Birkbeck	.278	105	.314	111	.293	113	.277	88	.333	123	.217	53	.308	64
Chris Bosio	.265	76	.283	78	.251	55	.284	98	.256	61	.222	56	.273	35
Chuck Crim	.266	78	.162	2	.255	65	.239	39	.212	20	.241	71	.274	37
Tom Filer	.268	86	.344	122	.272	87	.288	104	.238	42	.189	34	.340	97
Ted Higuera	.206	8	.208	9	.193	5	.221	18	.257	64	.250	78	.264	25
Odell Jones	.240	40	.302	106	.265	82	.234	29	.272	78	.257	85	.243	10
Paul Mirabella	.200	4	.250	--	.167	--	.230	24	.125	--	.156	13	.208	4
Juan Nieves	.213	12	.180	3	.214	16	.201	5	.266	73	.188	33	.322	77
Dan Plesac	.234	33	.233	--	.188	--	.277	--	.288	91	.325	121	.206	--
Bill Wegman	.265	74	.270	62	.285	105	.239	38	.331	122	.316	116	.251	15
Team Average	.247	6	.255	3	.244	3	.252	4	.263	8	.240	9	.279	1
League Average	.256		.267		.257		.262		.262		.239		.311	

MINNESOTA TWINS

- The new Murderer's Row includes guys named Kirby and Kent?
- The guys who can't buy a hit off certain pitchers.
- Ballplayers' delight: No overtime.

The term "murderer's row" conjures up different images for different baseball fans. To many, it can only mean the middle of the order for the great Yankees teams of the late 1920s: Ruth, Gehrig, Meusel, and Lazzeri. To some more contemporary fans, the mid–1960s Giants trio of Mays, McCovey, and Cepeda comes to mind. And for even more recent fans, the Big Red Machine's crew of Foster, Perez, and Bench was the ultimate symbol of awesome offense.

No current team can boast a crew of sluggers to compare with those listed above. But in 1988, the middle of Minnesota's batting order—Kirby Puckett, Kent Hrbek, and Gary Gaetti—stood head and shoulders above the rest.

Last season, Minnesota's three, four, and five hitters were the most productive in the American League. Puckett started 138 games in the three slot, Hrbek started 96 as the cleanup hitter, and Gaetti started 79 batting fifth (and another 39 in the cleanup slot, with Gene Larkin usually behind him). The Twins' combined output from those three batting-order slots ranked first in the American League in batting average, and second in home runs and RBIs:

Team	AB	H	HR	RBI	BA
Minnesota	1900	592	79	322	.312
Boston	1857	568	60	335	.306
New York	1876	542	80	322	.289
Kansas City	1842	510	51	281	.277
California	1885	513	55	267	.272
Cleveland	1894	511	63	267	.270
Seattle	1820	488	74	248	.268
Oakland	1901	508	81	303	.267
Detroit	1869	493	75	289	.264
Baltimore	1798	471	65	231	.262
Milwaukee	1835	469	48	281	.256
Toronto	1883	481	71	266	.255
Texas	1873	464	60	236	.248
Chicago	1856	457	60	229	.246

A better indication of the strength of the middle of Minnesota's batting order: The Twins scored in 48 of the 109 innings in which their third hitter led off, the highest rate in either league last season (44 percent). They scored an average of 0.82 runs in those innings, also a major league-leading figure, and by a wide margin. The following table shows the batting-order slots that produced, on average, the most runs in the A.L. in 1988:

Team	Slots	Inns	Runs	Avg.	Most Common Batters
Minnesota	3-4-5	109	89	0.82	Puckett, Hrbek, Gaetti
Boston	1-2-3	279	206	0.74	Boggs, Barrett, Evans
New York	1-2-3	309	228	0.74	Henderson, Randolph, Mattingly
Milwaukee	8-9-1	142	102	0.72	Gantner, Sveum, Molitor
Seattle	2-3-4	150	106	0.71	Reynolds, Brantley, Davis
Oakland	1-2-3	307	209	0.68	Lansford, Henderson, Canseco
Cleveland	3-4-5	131	86	0.66	Carter, Kittle, Hall
Minnesota	9-1-2	161	104	0.65	Newman, Gladden, Herr
Boston	8-9-1	171	109	0.64	Reed, Gedman, Boggs
Oakland	9-1-2	141	89	0.63	Weiss, Lansford, Henderson

What's clear from the data above is that the scoring potential in a given inning doesn't depend as much as we might have thought on the three players due to bat. Nearly as important, it seems, is who bats behind those three. For instance, Minnesota wasn't effective when its ninth spot led off because Al Newman, Dan Gladden, and Tom Herr were due up; it was Puckett, Hrbek, and Gaetti hitting behind them that increased the likelihood of a big inning. The same can be said of Oakland's trio of Weiss, Lansford, and Henderson. Good hitters, sure. But Moe, Larry, and Curly could probably put up good numbers with Canseco and McGwire to follow.

Anyway, we thought you might want to know which were the most impotent due-up combinations as well. The least productive slots in the American League were Baltimore's fifth, sixth, and seventh slots. When that set led off an inning, the Orioles scored an average of 0.25 runs. Take a bow, Mickey Tettleton, Larry Sheets, and Terry Kennedy. But the major league low came from a surprising spot. When the Dodgers' ninth spot led off, they scored an average of 0.20 runs. The most common hitters: Orel Hershiser, Steve Sax, and Alfredo Griffin. And you thought Hershiser had a *good* season!

The king is dead. Long live the king.

Prior to last season, St. Paul native Jack Morris was the victor and Ken Phelps the victim in the longest current streak

59

of hitless at-bats between two active players. Phelps carried an 0–for–26 career mark against Morris into 1988. But he got the monkey off his back in his first shot at Morris last season, 12 at-bats short of the longest hitless streak since we began tracking these things in 1975. Butch Wynegar's 0–for–38 against Nolan Ryan from 1974 through 1976 (sandwiched by hits in Wynegar's first and last at-bats against Ryan) remains safe at least for another year. Or so it appears.

The longest current streak among active players stands little chance of an extension in 1989. Cleveland's Tom Candiotti may have been more upset over Spike Owen's trade to the Expos than anyone including the Spikester, given the fact that Owen is hitless in his last 27 at-bats against little Knucksie.

Among active players still in the same league, Mike Pagliarulo's 25-at-bat hitless streak against Mike Boddicker tops the list. But as you scan the list of other current streaks of 20 or more at-bats, you'll notice a distinctly Twin Cities flavor, both on the batter and pitcher sides. The most interesting matchup, in fact, may be Hrbek facing Moore, against whom he once toted a .406 batting average. Anyway, Twins fans who love the thumbs-down scenes in those old John Derek gladiator movies ought to enjoy these matchups in the months to come:

Lions	Christians	Current Streak	AB	H	HR	SO	BA
Tom Candiotti	Spike Owen	27	31	1	0	3	.032
Mike Boddicker	Mike Pagliarulo	25	38	4	2	8	.105
Sid Fernandez	Ozzie Virgil	24	24	0	0	6	.000
Storm Davis	Randy Bush	22	30	3	0	7	.100
Mark Gubicza	Dick Schofield	22	22	0	0	4	.000
Ted Higuera	Gary Pettis	22	22	0	0	7	.000
Roger Clemens	Steve Lombardozzi	21	21	0	0	8	.000
Jim Deshaies	Andres Thomas	21	22	1	0	4	.045
Mike Moore	Kent Hrbek	21	53	13	2	11	.245
Rick Reuschel	Shawon Dunston	21	35	7	1	8	.200
Frank Viola	Larry Parrish	21	43	7	1	21	.163
Tom Browning	Howard Johnson	20	20	0	0	4	.000
Orel Hershiser	Garry Templeton	20	45	7	0	10	.156
Mike Smithson	Ivan Calderon	20	23	1	0	3	.043

Remember straight-shootin' Twins manager Tom Kelly, the reluctant cause célèbre at the 1987 World Series. Nice guy, good manager, but—well, there's no other way to say it—dull. Nothing about his manner seemed to suggest that he spent his late-night hours doubled over with laughter over the latest list of "10 reasons why" on the Letterman show. But he must have something worthwhile to do after the witching hour, because his Twins sure don't work much overtime.

Last season, Minnesota played only eight extra-inning games, and six of those lasted 10 innings. In fact, the Twins played only 11 innings of overtime during 1988, to crack the list of the 10 lowest totals in modern major league history. The teams that played the fewest extra innings:

Year	Team	Games	Innings
1901	Baltimore Orioles	3	4
1900	New York Giants	5	5
1901	Cleveland Indians	5	6
1901	Washington Senators	6	6
1945	Chicago Cubs	6	8
1938	Philadelphia Athletics	6	9
1936	St. Louis Browns	3	9
1939	New York Yankees	7	10
1902	Cincinnati Reds	5	11
1939	New York Giants	6	11
1978	Chicago White Sox	9	11
1983	Seattle Mariners	8	11
1987	Kansas City Royals	8	11
1988	Boston Red Sox	10	11
1988	Minnesota Twins	8	11

Many of those teams rarely reached extra innings simply because they weren't good enough to remain competitive through the first nine. The 1901 Indians finished 28 games below the .500 mark; the 1936 Brownies played 38 below; and 1938 A's, 36. The 1983 Mariners lost 102 games. And despite a 70–70 mark, the 1902 Reds finished 33½ games out. Another three of the teams above won their leagues or divisions (the 1939 Yankees, 1945 Cubs, and 1988 Red Sox), seldom needing anything beyond regulation time to finish off their opposition.

But we think the presence of so many recent teams on the list also suggests another reason why some teams now play so little overtime. Managers are becoming increasingly reluctant to bring their top relievers into games unless they have a lead. Look at how Kelly used his top man, Jeff Reardon, last season. The table below shows whether the Twins were winning, tied, or losing when Reardon entered each of his 63 games; and, if winning, by how many runs:

+4 or More	+3	+2	+1	Tied	Losing
8	11	16	21	3	4

Kelly rarely called on Reardon when the Twins were losing. And among the three games in which Reardon was called on to protect a tie, two had already reached the tenth inning when he entered. In effect, the use of Reardon, one of baseball's best relievers, was restricted even in game situations.

The connection between using lesser relievers in tie games and not reaching extra innings is complex, and deserves further research. But if teams are blowing tie games while their stoppers watch from the bullpen, the current vogue to use those pitchers only to protect leads may have gone too far.

WON-LOST RECORD BY STARTING POSITION

MINNESOTA 91-71	C	1B	2B	3B	SS	LF	CF	RF	P	DH	Leadoff	Relief	Starts
Allan Anderson	·	·	·	·	·	·	·	·	18-12	·	·	·	18-12
Keith Atherton	·	·	·	·	·	·	·	·	·	·	·	25-24	·
Doug Baker	·	·	·	·	·	0-2	·	·	·	·	·	·	0-2
Juan Berenguer	·	·	·	·	·	·	·	·	1-0	·	·	29-27	1-0
Karl Best	·	·	·	·	·	·	·	·	·	·	·	2-9	·
Bert Blyleven	·	·	·	·	·	·	·	·	14-19	·	·	·	14-19
Tom Brunansky	·	·	·	·	·	0-1	·	4-8	·	0-1	·	·	4-10
Eric Bullock	·	·	·	·	·	2-0	·	·	·	·	·	·	2-0
Randy Bush	·	1-0	·	·	·	0-1	·	55-40	·	12-5	0-1	·	68-46
Steve Carlton	·	·	·	·	·	·	·	·	0-1	·	·	0-3	0-1
John Christensen	·	·	·	·	·	·	·	6-4	·	·	·	·	6-4
Mark Davidson	·	·	·	·	·	0-1	1-0	16-14	·	·	0-1	·	17-15
Jim Dwyer	·	·	·	·	·	·	·	·	·	8-5	·	·	8-5
Gary Gaetti	·	·	·	65-50	·	·	·	·	·	2-2	·	·	67-52
Greg Gagne	·	·	·	·	73-61	·	·	·	·	·	·	·	73-61
Dan Gladden	·	·	·	·	·	77-57	·	·	·	·	72-53	0-1	77-57
German Gonzalez	·	·	·	·	·	·	·	·	·	·	·	7-9	·
Brian Harper	25-16	·	·	·	·	·	·	·	·	0-3	·	·	25-19
Tom Herr	·	·	40-33	·	·	·	·	·	·	2-0	3-1	·	42-33
Kent Hrbek	·	60-43	·	·	·	·	·	·	·	18-16	·	·	78-59
Gene Larkin	·	29-27	·	·	·	·	·	·	·	48-37	·	·	77-64
Tim Laudner	56-46	·	·	·	·	·	·	·	·	1-2	·	·	57-48
Charlie Lea	·	·	·	·	·	·	·	·	12-11	·	·	0-1	12-11
Steve Lombardozzi	·	·	46-28	1-1	8-2	·	·	·	·	·	·	·	55-31
Dwight Lowry	0-1	·	·	·	·	·	·	·	·	·	·	·	0-1
Tippy Martinez	·	·	·	·	·	·	·	·	·	·	·	0-3	·
Mike Mason	·	·	·	·	·	·	·	·	·	·	·	2-3	·
John Moses	·	·	·	·	·	12-11	4-0	10-5	·	·	13-12	·	26-16
Al Newman	·	·	5-10	25-20	10-6	·	·	·	·	·	3-3	·	40-36
Joe Niekro	·	·	·	·	·	·	·	·	0-2	·	·	1-2	0-2
Tom Nieto	10-8	·	·	·	·	·	·	·	·	·	·	·	10-8
Mark Portugal	·	·	·	·	·	·	·	·	·	·	·	9-17	·
Kirby Puckett	·	·	·	·	·	·	86-71	·	·	·	·	·	86-71
Jeff Reardon	·	·	·	·	·	·	·	·	·	·	·	51-12	·
Dan Schatzeder	·	·	·	·	·	·	·	·	·	·	·	5-5	·
Roy Smith	·	·	·	·	·	·	·	·	2-2	·	·	3-2	2-2
Les Straker	·	·	·	·	·	·	·	·	6-8	·	·	1-1	6-8
Fred Toliver	·	·	·	·	·	·	·	·	11-8	·	·	0-2	11-8
Kelvin Torve	·	1-1	·	·	·	·	·	·	·	·	·	·	1-1
Frank Viola	·	·	·	·	·	·	·	·	27-8	·	·	·	27-8
Jim Winn	·	·	·	·	·	·	·	·	·	·	·	1-8	·

Batting vs. Left and Right Handed Pitchers

		BA	Rank	SA	Rank	OBA	Rank	HR %	Rank	BB %	Rank	SO %	Rank
Randy Bush	vs. Lefties	.182	--	.364	--	.333	--	0.00	--	20.00	--	20.00	--
	vs. Righties	.264	74	.436	44	.366	26	3.66	39	12.20	24	10.20	40
Mark Davidson	vs. Lefties	.215	143	.316	129	.267	144	1.27	111	5.75	108	18.39	132
	vs. Righties	.222	--	.296	--	.344	--	0.00	--	15.63	--	12.50	--
Gary Gaetti	vs. Lefties	.338	9	.592	8	.400	20	6.15	13	10.00	47	12.67	74
	vs. Righties	.287	39	.536	6	.334	74	5.92	9	5.74	127	18.03	129
Greg Gagne	vs. Lefties	.297	37	.477	38	.352	42	1.80	93	6.50	91	23.58	155
	vs. Righties	.217	149	.371	98	.267	159	3.43	49	4.94	147	21.04	145
Dan Gladden	vs. Lefties	.321	21	.509	22	.388	23	3.77	41	10.11	45	8.99	42
	vs. Righties	.249	104	.362	108	.300	125	1.20	113	6.15	121	12.75	71
Brian Harper	vs. Lefties	.286	47	.408	63	.345	48	2.04	83	7.27	80	3.64	1
	vs. Righties	.299	24	.436	45	.344	58	1.71	95	4.72	150	7.87	17
Tom Herr	vs. Lefties	.289	44	.395	75	.349	44	1.32	109	8.43	66	12.05	71
	vs. Righties	.254	91	.303	145	.349	47	0.00	161	12.60	21	14.12	90
Kent Hrbek	vs. Lefties	.250	93	.379	84	.336	58	1.52	104	11.69	33	11.04	62
	vs. Righties	.333	4	.569	4	.405	7	6.08	7	11.34	34	8.56	24
Gene Larkin	vs. Lefties	.307	33	.440	54	.380	27	1.33	108	9.36	52	8.77	39
	vs. Righties	.251	100	.358	110	.363	28	1.69	96	12.29	22	9.46	33
Tim Laudner	vs. Lefties	.321	20	.495	29	.359	37	2.75	41	5.88	102	10.92	61
	vs. Righties	.222	144	.372	97	.299	130	3.76	38	9.70	64	25.42	160
Steve Lombardozzi	vs. Lefties	.250	93	.319	128	.337	55	0.00	140	11.76	31	10.59	57
	vs. Righties	.195	164	.302	147	.280	144	1.40	109	10.00	58	15.60	104
John Moses	vs. Lefties	.222	--	.444	--	.300	--	0.00	--	10.00	--	10.00	--
	vs. Righties	.320	8	.421	58	.369	25	1.02	125	6.51	115	9.30	30
Al Newman	vs. Lefties	.174	163	.188	168	.260	146	0.00	140	10.13	44	11.39	67
	vs. Righties	.241	117	.272	162	.316	103	0.00	161	9.72	62	11.57	56
Kirby Puckett	vs. Lefties	.398	1	.614	6	.425	12	4.82	26	4.60	126	7.47	18
	vs. Righties	.342	3	.521	10	.358	33	3.26	56	2.90	166	13.54	79
Team Average	vs. Lefties	.294	1	.447	1	.356	2	2.45	8	8.48	5	11.83	2
	vs. Righties	.267	3	.412	3	.335	4	2.84	3	8.56	7	14.01	6
League Average	vs. Lefties	.259		.391		.321		2.47		7.97		14.12	
	vs. Righties	.259		.391		.326		2.47		8.51		14.39	

Batting with Runners on Base and Bases Empty

		BA	Rank	SA	Rank	OBA	Rank	HR %	Rank	BB %	Rank	SO %	Rank
Randy Bush	Runners On	.283	64	.444	45	.399	15	3.89	39	15.70	11	9.87	47
	Bases Empty	.243	110	.425	44	.333	54	3.27	51	9.47	51	11.11	47
Gary Gaetti	Runners On	.300	39	.524	12	.360	53	5.15	13	9.06	71	17.36	133
	Bases Empty	.302	15	.579	5	.347	40	6.81	5	4.78	145	15.54	100
Greg Gagne	Runners On	.212	154	.370	112	.283	147	2.88	63	6.61	118	21.90	155
	Bases Empty	.257	75	.419	51	.293	113	3.16	54	4.14	154	21.43	147
Dan Gladden	Runners On	.297	43	.427	58	.354	60	1.08	118	7.58	99	11.85	65
	Bases Empty	.256	81	.391	78	.310	94	2.30	79	7.11	91	11.61	51
Brian Harper	Runners On	.304	35	.402	79	.350	65	0.00	148	5.88	133	4.90	9
	Bases Empty	.284	--	.459	--	.338	--	4.05	--	5.00	--	8.75	--
Tom Herr	Runners On	.233	134	.275	159	.324	101	0.00	148	11.68	42	14.60	103
	Bases Empty	.283	36	.359	103	.365	24	0.54	150	11.54	22	12.98	65
Kent Hrbek	Runners On	.271	83	.441	50	.364	48	4.45	24	13.51	22	11.49	62
	Bases Empty	.350	3	.593	3	.410	3	5.32	18	9.31	55	6.90	12
Gene Larkin	Runners On	.267	93	.398	83	.368	44	1.99	89	12.33	33	9.33	38
	Bases Empty	.268	54	.366	54	.367	23	1.18	120	10.54	33	9.18	30
Tim Laudner	Runners On	.220	149	.341	134	.282	148	2.75	66	8.29	85	18.05	137
	Bases Empty	.280	39	.472	26	.347	38	4.15	34	8.92	64	24.41	154
Steve Lombardozzi	Runners On	.241	124	.362	115	.345	72	1.72	96	12.84	28	13.51	94
	Bases Empty	.187	163	.269	156	.257	159	0.58	148	8.56	68	14.97	91
John Moses	Runners On	.319	--	.449	--	.385	--	1.45	--	10.13	--	11.39	--
	Bases Empty	.314	9	.409	61	.356	32	0.73	143	4.79	144	8.22	19
Al Newman	Runners On	.242	121	.263	162	.306	127	0.00	148	7.89	92	8.77	32
	Bases Empty	.211	145	.242	166	.298	107	0.00	156	11.05	29	13.26	72
Kirby Puckett	Runners On	.344	5	.513	13	.364	46	2.60	76	4.22	161	12.95	84
	Bases Empty	.367	2	.573	6	.384	9	4.58	27	2.51	169	11.14	48
Team Average	Runners On	.270	7	.408	7	.344	6	2.44	8	9.76	4	13.83	8
	Bases Empty	.276	2	.430	1	.337	2	2.98	2	7.50	8	13.14	2
League Average	Runners On	.268		.401		.336		2.45		9.09		13.68	
	Bases Empty	.253		.383		.315		2.48		7.76		14.81	

Overall Batting Compared to Late Inning Pressure Situations

		BA	Rank	SA	Rank	OBA	Rank	HR %	Rank	BB %	Rank	SO %	Rank	RDI %	Rank
Randy Bush	Overall	.261	79	.434	41	.365	28	3.55	44	12.45	19	10.52	42	.284	62
	Pressure	.265	74	.469	35	.390	26	4.08	37	16.95	8	11.86	50	.200	95
Jim Dwyer	Overall	.255	--	.330	--	.410	--	2.13	--	20.49	--	15.57	--	.333	--
	Pressure	.208	125	.208	153	.323	84	0.00	110	16.13	9	19.35	107	.429	14
Gary Gaetti	Overall	.301	21	.551	3	.353	38	5.98	7	6.98	104	16.47	115	.308	35
	Pressure	.344	12	.719	1	.364	43	9.38	2	3.03	154	16.67	91	.400	20
Greg Gagne	Overall	.236	128	.397	80	.288	144	3.04	62	5.31	142	21.65	152	.197	159
	Pressure	.241	98	.463	38	.305	102	5.56	19	8.20	87	24.59	142	.143	128
Dan Gladden	Overall	.269	58	.403	73	.325	79	1.91	97	7.27	99	11.69	59	.331	20
	Pressure	.257	82	.371	76	.325	82	1.43	94	6.41	117	10.26	38	.353	35
Brian Harper	Overall	.295	--	.428	--	.344	--	1.81	--	5.49	--	6.59	--	.294	50
	Pressure	.263	--	.421	--	.333	--	5.26	--	4.55	--	4.55	--	.200	--
Tom Herr	Overall	.263	72	.326	138	.349	44	0.33	160	11.59	26	13.62	81	.241	115
	Pressure	.263	79	.263	141	.349	60	0.00	110	11.63	43	11.63	48	.333	39
Kent Hrbek	Overall	.312	7	.520	11	.387	11	4.90	21	11.43	31	9.22	31	.280	69
	Pressure	.348	8	.594	6	.425	11	7.25	8	12.35	29	11.11	43	.300	53
Gene Larkin	Overall	.267	63	.382	91	.368	25	1.58	105	11.45	29	9.26	33	.286	59
	Pressure	.323	27	.462	39	.432	8	1.54	90	14.81	13	9.88	35	.462	8
Tim Laudner	Overall	.251	99	.408	65	.316	93	3.47	47	8.61	74	21.29	151	.243	112
	Pressure	.240	99	.340	96	.309	97	2.00	76	7.14	100	25.00	143	.136	135
Steve Lombardozzi	Overall	.209	164	.307	151	.295	135	1.05	128	10.45	45	14.33	92	.242	114
	Pressure	.095	--	.095	--	.208	--	0.00	--	11.11	--	25.93	--	.000	--
John Moses	Overall	.316	5	.422	53	.366	27	0.97	133	6.67	111	9.33	34	.195	--
	Pressure	.333	16	.433	51	.355	53	3.33	47	0.00	168	12.90	61	.143	128
Al Newman	Overall	.223	147	.250	170	.301	124	0.00	165	9.83	54	11.53	55	.217	144
	Pressure	.259	--	.296	--	.310	--	0.00	--	6.90	--	13.79	--	1.000	--
Kirby Puckett	Overall	.356	2	.545	5	.375	18	3.65	41	3.33	168	12.01	65	.370	2
	Pressure	.346	11	.519	16	.368	38	1.23	105	4.60	140	11.49	45	.281	59
Team Average	Overall	.274	2	.421	1	.340	2	2.74	3	8.54	6	13.46	4	.276	5
	Pressure	.287	1	.447	1	.356	1	3.37	2	8.79	7	14.60	1	.295	3
League Average	Overall	.259		.391		.324		2.47		8.35		14.31		.269	
	Pressure	.249		.365		.319		2.28		8.71		17.04		.246	

Additional Miscellaneous Batting Comparisons

	Grass Surface BA	Rank	Artificial Surface BA	Rank	Home Games BA	Rank	Road Games BA	Rank	Runners in Scoring Position BA	Rank	Runners in Scoring Pos and Two Outs BA	Rank	Leading Off Inning OBA	Rank	Runners on 3B with less than 2 Outs RDI %	Rank
Randy Bush	.267	59	.258	94	.243	110	.278	51	.292	43	.171	151	.304	89	.480	130
Mark Davidson	.196	--	.233	120	.234	--	.203	--	.219	--	.333	--	.320	--	.333	169
Jim Dwyer	.228	--	.297	40	.279	--	.235	--	.333	--	.200	--	.300	--	.727	13
Gary Gaetti	.287	34	.311	29	.297	25	.305	22	.304	31	.323	17	.361	29	.600	65
Greg Gagne	.280	43	.206	146	.222	144	.250	98	.210	152	.194	131	.320	72	.333	169
Dan Gladden	.222	140	.297	43	.317	13	.217	142	.360	4	.328	16	.315	79	.680	30
Brian Harper	.279	--	.305	33	.293	--	.298	--	.256	--	.348	11	.313	--	.571	--
Tom Herr	.330	--	.232	124	.228	140	.307	20	.227	132	.238	83	.328	65	.688	25
Kent Hrbek	.340	2	.294	45	.304	20	.319	5	.235	119	.215	108	.376	18	.594	71
Gene Larkin	.246	101	.280	67	.283	46	.251	95	.267	76	.312	23	.377	17	.593	72
Tim Laudner	.279	45	.232	123	.231	133	.269	60	.225	135	.283	44	.337	53	.455	141
Steve Lombardozzi	.200	162	.215	139	.204	157	.213	147	.203	155	.189	136	.219	161	.556	89
John Moses	.327	--	.305	33	.259	--	.355	1	.235	--	.222	--	.338	51	.500	--
Al Newman	.211	156	.232	125	.234	125	.212	149	.227	131	.238	83	.321	71	.333	169
Kirby Puckett	.335	3	.370	7	.406	1	.308	16	.366	1	.300	33	.453	3	.725	15
Team Average	.272	2	.275	4	.279	2	.268	3	.269	5	.263	2	.337	3	.564	8
League Average	.256		.267		.262		.257		.262		.239		.311		.570	

Pitching vs. Left and Right Handed Batters

		BA	Rank	SA	Rank	OBA	Rank	HR %	Rank	BB %	Rank	SO %	Rank
Allan Anderson	vs. Lefties	.320	120	.368	57	.390	119	0.00	1	9.22	73	7.09	118
	vs. Righties	.249	55	.367	50	.280	22	2.19	51	3.56	5	10.83	112
Keith Atherton	vs. Lefties	.273	82	.500	120	.340	87	5.47	127	9.03	68	9.72	95
	vs. Righties	.201	12	.295	7	.252	6	2.01	40	5.45	24	17.58	42
Juan Berenguer	vs. Lefties	.212	16	.364	54	.344	92	3.26	111	16.74	127	18.06	23
	vs. Righties	.202	13	.283	6	.296	36	0.58	4	11.44	119	28.86	3
Bert Blyleven	vs. Lefties	.304	112	.441	106	.356	101	2.28	70	6.69	34	14.44	47
	vs. Righties	.283	107	.426	96	.333	90	2.91	84	4.56	12	18.23	36
Charlie Lea	vs. Lefties	.327	123	.559	130	.388	118	4.78	124	8.47	58	12.70	65
	vs. Righties	.272	96	.411	83	.339	95	2.44	61	8.63	83	11.87	102
Mark Portugal	vs. Lefties	.288	100	.542	127	.339	85	6.78	130	6.98	36	16.28	36
	vs. Righties	.257	--	.416	--	.310	--	2.97	--	7.08	--	8.85	--
Jeff Reardon	vs. Lefties	.264	72	.338	34	.313	39	1.35	34	6.10	22	14.02	53
	vs. Righties	.225	--	.380	--	.259	--	3.10	--	3.70	--	24.44	--
Les Straker	vs. Lefties	.259	63	.374	63	.297	27	1.72	48	5.41	14	8.65	107
	vs. Righties	.297	119	.449	113	.361	120	3.62	107	9.62	102	4.49	127
Fred Toliver	vs. Lefties	.280	94	.401	82	.355	100	2.59	86	10.23	89	15.53	44
	vs. Righties	.258	70	.328	23	.342	99	1.01	7	11.01	116	12.33	95
Frank Viola	vs. Lefties	.233	36	.368	58	.280	13	2.45	80	4.55	6	16.48	34
	vs. Righties	.248	52	.354	44	.287	29	2.00	37	5.38	23	19.18	32
Team Average	vs. Lefties	.283	14	.439	14	.348	12	3.11	14	8.65	5	13.56	6
	vs. Righties	.255	5	.377	4	.308	3	2.36	4	6.65	2	15.65	4
League Average	vs. Lefties	.262		.387		.331		2.24		9.12		13.21	
	vs. Righties	.258		.393		.320		2.63		7.80		15.09	

Pitching with Runners on Base and Bases Empty

		BA	Rank	SA	Rank	OBA	Rank	HR %	Rank	BB %	Rank	SO %	Rank
Allan Anderson	Runners On	.258	61	.318	12	.293	20	0.99	16	5.20	5	10.09	104
	Bases Empty	.262	79	.399	86	.303	49	2.39	78	4.10	10	10.25	113
Keith Atherton	Runners On	.270	74	.467	113	.333	68	4.92	126	7.69	45	11.19	92
	Bases Empty	.206	12	.329	22	.259	9	2.58	84	6.63	52	16.27	48
Juan Berenguer	Runners On	.198	5	.326	20	.317	48	2.91	87	14.55	126	22.07	8
	Bases Empty	.216	20	.324	19	.326	85	1.08	12	13.95	124	24.19	6
Bert Blyleven	Runners On	.343	126	.497	121	.391	121	3.20	98	5.68	10	16.54	29
	Bases Empty	.258	72	.388	78	.311	60	2.12	55	5.71	32	15.94	53
Charlie Lea	Runners On	.272	76	.418	85	.322	54	3.35	103	7.01	30	11.81	84
	Bases Empty	.326	128	.548	128	.401	127	3.94	112	9.87	108	12.74	81
Mark Portugal	Runners On	.238	32	.390	68	.278	10	2.86	85	5.13	4	14.53	51
	Bases Empty	.307	--	.570	--	.368	--	7.02	--	8.80	--	11.20	--
Jeff Reardon	Runners On	.225	16	.324	17	.279	11	2.11	54	5.70	11	16.46	31
	Bases Empty	.267	87	.393	81	.298	41	2.22	62	4.26	11	21.28	14
Les Straker	Runners On	.275	83	.325	19	.338	76	0.00	1	9.49	83	3.65	129
	Bases Empty	.276	99	.458	114	.319	72	4.17	116	5.88	36	8.82	122
Fred Toliver	Runners On	.291	102	.401	74	.375	108	2.20	62	11.63	109	13.95	58
	Bases Empty	.254	67	.343	31	.330	92	1.61	31	9.78	105	14.13	66
Frank Viola	Runners On	.236	25	.347	33	.269	5	2.44	70	4.25	1	18.25	21
	Bases Empty	.251	60	.363	52	.296	36	1.85	43	5.86	35	19.02	26
Team Average	Runners On	.271	9	.395	5	.330	7	2.55	8	7.85	1	14.31	5
	Bases Empty	.263	10	.408	13	.320	10	2.75	12	7.17	4	15.17	6
League Average	Runners On	.268		.401		.336		2.45		9.09		13.68	
	Bases Empty	.253		.383		.315		2.48		7.76		14.81	

Overall Pitching Compared to Late Inning Pressure Situations

		BA	Rank	SA	Rank	OBA	Rank	HR %	Rank	BB %	Rank	SO %	Rank
Allan Anderson	Overall	.261	66	.367	46	.299	24	1.83	29	4.54	3	10.18	111
	Pressure	.167	6	.205	4	.198	3	0.00	1	3.70	6	12.35	91
Keith Atherton	Overall	.235	32	.390	73	.293	15	3.61	117	7.12	37	13.92	63
	Pressure	.267	90	.519	120	.336	72	6.87	127	8.00	49	14.00	72
Juan Berenguer	Overall	.207	5	.325	14	.322	65	1.96	39	14.25	127	23.13	7
	Pressure	.245	63	.365	59	.371	104	1.26	33	16.33	124	20.41	21
Bert Blyleven	Overall	.294	119	.434	110	.345	107	2.57	83	5.70	14	16.20	41
	Pressure	.300	108	.500	116	.340	78	4.00	107	3.64	5	25.45	5
Charlie Lea	Overall	.301	123	.488	125	.365	118	3.67	118	8.55	75	12.31	87
	Pressure	.500	--	1.125	--	.556	--	12.50	--	11.11	--	22.22	--
Mark Portugal	Overall	.274	--	.484	--	.325	--	5.02	--	7.02	--	12.81	--
	Pressure	.273	94	.409	86	.327	66	2.27	68	8.16	54	14.29	68
Jeff Reardon	Overall	.245	45	.357	33	.288	13	2.17	59	5.02	8	18.73	21
	Pressure	.247	65	.368	66	.289	30	2.75	84	5.05	17	14.65	62
Les Straker	Overall	.276	100	.407	88	.326	78	2.56	78	7.33	41	6.74	124
	Pressure	.400	--	.467	--	.412	--	0.00	--	5.56	--	0.00	--
Fred Toliver	Overall	.270	88	.367	47	.349	110	1.86	31	10.59	109	14.05	61
	Pressure	.200	--	.300	--	.385	--	0.00	--	22.22	--	11.11	--
Frank Viola	Overall	.245	43	.357	32	.286	10	2.08	49	5.24	9	18.72	22
	Pressure	.198	19	.311	32	.261	13	2.83	87	7.69	45	15.38	53
Team Average	Overall	.266	10	.402	12	.325	6	2.67	11	7.47	3	14.79	4
	Pressure	.244	6	.378	9	.319	6	2.71	12	9.47	8	15.65	8
League Average	Overall	.259		.391		.324		2.47		8.35		14.31	
	Pressure	.249		.369		.324		2.26		9.33		15.69	

Additional Miscellaneous Pitching Comparisons

	Grass Surface		Artificial Surface		Home Games		Road Games		Runners in Scoring Position		Runners in Scoring Pos and Two Outs		Leading Off Inning	
	BA	Rank	BA	Rank	BA	Rank	BA	Rank	BA	Rank	BA	Rank	OBA	Rank
Allan Anderson	.258	63	.262	55	.262	79	.259	69	.214	22	.187	32	.316	71
Keith Atherton	.202	--	.251	45	.253	61	.211	11	.241	46	.167	19	.273	33
Juan Berenguer	.172	--	.224	18	.229	33	.185	3	.209	17	.173	26	.323	79
Bert Blyleven	.287	114	.298	103	.303	122	.284	100	.380	129	.356	126	.322	78
Steve Carlton	.000	--	.408	131	.435	--	.000	--	.400	--	.286	--	.455	--
German Gonzalez	.333	--	.192	6	.174	--	.333	--	.087	--	.077	--	.400	--
Charlie Lea	.312	127	.294	98	.291	112	.311	120	.221	28	.209	46	.373	114
Mark Portugal	.191	--	.336	117	.336	127	.191	--	.250	--	.194	--	.385	--
Jeff Reardon	.316	--	.209	10	.211	12	.281	95	.216	25	.176	28	.328	85
Dan Schatzeder	.322	--	.288	87	.308	--	.304	--	.250	--	.250	--	.320	--
Roy Smith	.238	--	.187	5	.187	--	.238	--	.207	--	.188	--	.237	--
Les Straker	.247	49	.301	105	.325	125	.246	48	.221	27	.242	72	.391	121
Fred Toliver	.253	58	.280	76	.299	118	.233	28	.239	44	.194	37	.374	115
Frank Viola	.276	104	.227	21	.216	21	.275	85	.232	39	.155	11	.247	13
Team Average	.264	10	.267	6	.270	14	.262	9	.258	5	.212	1	.321	11
League Average	.256		.267		.257		.262		.262		.239		.311	

NEW YORK YANKEES

- **Why say goodbye to T. J. and Rhoden? Dallas wants to win in October, not May.**
- **Southpaws in Yankee Stadium: Has the advantage survived?**

Ordinarily, the release of a 45–year-old pitcher wouldn't create a public debate. But let's face it—these days, even the influence of Robin Givens in Mike Tyson's life (positive or negative, 50 cents a call) prompted a nationwide referendum in our most colorful newspaper. So if the fans and media want to make an issue over the Yankees' decision last November not to re-sign Tommy John, who's going to stand in their way? After all, John led all Yankees pitchers in starts in 1988, he threw more innings than any teammate except Rick Rhoden, he won nine games, and he would have had five more wins had his bullpen not blown leads he turned over to them.

We think the decision made sense because it addressed one of the team's most glaring recent problems: For the past three years, the Yankees have been unable to sustain their fine early-season performances throughout the summer. And that gradual disintegration over the course of a long season was due in large part to the team's aging pitching staff.

First, let's examine the facts. In each of the past three seasons, the Yankees have posted winning percentages of .625 or better over the first two months. Here's where they stood on the morning of June 1:

Year	W	L	Pct.	Pos.
1986	30	18	.625	2
1987	31	18	.633	1
1988	33	16	.673	1

Over the past three seasons, the Yankees had a combined record of 94–52 during April and May. That's a winning percentage of .644—good enough to win all but four of the 80 division titles over the past 20 years. But New York has watched Boston, Detroit, and Boston again capture the last three A.L. East titles. No team since the Brooklyn Dodgers of the early 1940s failed to win a division or league title for three consecutive seasons in which it played at least .625 through the end of May.

The greatest factor in those June swoons was the perennial midseason collapse of the Yankees' staff. Over the past three years, the Yankees have compiled a 3.72 ERA during April and May, 4.46 thereafter. Of course, their offense also contributed to the fall, scoring 17 percent fewer runs per game after June 1 than before. But even that substantial decrease pales by comparison to the 25–percent increase in their opponents' scoring after the end of May.

That pattern of fast starts and steady summer-long declines is typical of teams with older pitching staffs. And the Yankees' staff over the past few years was nothing if not old. Only one team in modern major league history had an older starting rotation than that of last season's Yankees. We measured the average age of every team since 1900, weighting the averages by the number of starts each pitcher made. (In other words, on the 1988 Yankees, John accounted for a larger portion of the average age than Al Leiter did because he started more than twice as many games as Leiter did.) And only the 1983 California Angels—with Geoff Zahn, Bruce Kison, and T.J. himself—was older than the 1988 Yankees. The top 10:

Year	Team	Age
1983	California Angels	33.99
1988	New York Yankees	33.93
1988	Houston Astros	33.92
1987	New York Yankees	33.76
1947	Philadelphia Phillies	33.44
1983	Kansas City Royals	33.41
1947	Pittsburgh Pirates	33.36
1985	New York Yankees	33.27
1934	Chicago White Sox	33.26
1982	Houston Astros	33.26

The performances of those pitching staffs, as well as those of 12 other teams that averaged more than 33 years of age, indicate that fast starts and slow fades, like those of recent Yankees teams, are the rule for teams with old pitching staffs. The 22 teams with the oldest rotations (we excluded last season's Yankees and Astros, and the 1981 Atlanta Braves, whose season was divided by the strike) allowed an average of 4.17 runs per game during April and May, 4.48 from June through October. That's not as wide a spread as that of recent Yankees teams, but it's wide enough to support the contention that a pitching staff's age becomes a factor before the season is even half over.

A more telling set of figures are the composite won-lost records in each month for those teams:

April	May	June	July	August	Sept./Oct.
178–167	307–255	297–304	332–311	326–328	334–319
.516	.546	.494	.516	.498	.511

The performance of the Yankees over the past three seasons is simply an exaggeration of the general trend. As a group, the teams barely exceeded the .500 mark from June through October despite a collective fast start (.535 for the first two months). So while the decision to release Tommy John (as well as the subsequent trade of Rick Rhoden) addresses the long-term need to develop the organization's younger pitchers, it also may help solve the frustrating summer swoons of recent Yankees teams.

The Yankees' decision to jettison John does little to answer a related question: What was T.J. doing there in the first place? Forget that he pitched more innings for the team than any other player over the past two seasons. The fact of the matter is that three years ago John's career appeared to all the world, pinstriped or otherwise, to be over. The Yankees gave him a uniform and he went with it, a comeback for which he is to be congratulated, but one that surprised everyone. *Everyone.* So why would a team with such a deep (albeit unspectacular) pitching staff have even thought about making Yankee Stadium the venue for T.J.'s attempted resurrection?

Steinbrenner's penchant for playing the forgiving father to his prodigal sons (like Rick Cerone, Chris Chambliss, and, of course Billy Martin, among others) certainly played a part. But the key was probably the Yankees' love of left-handed pitchers. It's no coincidence that they subsequently denied similar comeback trials to right-handers Tom Seaver and Don Sutton.

Traditionally, the Yankees have gathered southpaws with even greater zeal than they've hired and fired managers. That fire burns as strongly today as ever. Here's a look at the number of games in which New York has started left-handed pitchers over the past seven seasons. Notice that only once during that time did they fail to compile one of the league's two highest totals:

1982	1983	1984	1985	1986	1987	1988
109	127	95	57	81	91	83
2d	1st	2d	7th	1st	1st	1st

Before the reconstruction of Yankee Stadium in the mid–1970s, you needed to look no further than the 457–foot sign on the left-center field fence—if you could see that far—to understand why the Yankees thought they were better off with a predominantly left-handed rotation. But the series of changes to the stadium's configuration over the past 13 years has substantially reduced the disadvantage to right-handed batters.

So two questions need to be answered: Did Yankees left-handers of the past really have a greater home-field advantage than their right-handers? And if so, does that edge still exist despite the changes to Yankee Stadium itself?

The answer to the first question is a resounding yes. From 1961 through 1973, when the Stadium was closed for alterations, the home-field advantage was worth an average of more than one win per season more to southpaws than to right-handers.

Here's the proof: We gathered the annual home and road records for any pitcher who accumulated at least 15 decisions in a season. The group was divided into lefties and righties. Pitchers with identical road-game records were paired, one from each group. For instance:

Throws	Year	Pitcher	Home	Road
Left-handed	1969	Fritz Peterson	12–4	5–12
Right-handed	1966	Mel Stottlemyre	7–8	5–12

When there wasn't an identical match, some right-handers were paired with similar lefties (same number of games above .500; same number of wins; one loss more or less; etc.). We came up with 21 pairs—21 left-handers and 21 right-handers—with nearly identical won-lost totals on the road. Any difference in home-game records should indicate a true difference in the home-field advantage between the groups. As you can see, the southpaws' composite winning percentage was nearly 80 points higher than that of the right-handers—a difference that translates into an average of 1.2 wins for a pitcher evenly dividing 30 starts between home and road games:

	Home Games		Road Games		
	W–L	Pct.	W–L	Pct.	Diff.
Left-handers	164–87	.653	127–134	.487	.167
Right-handers	148–110	.574	124–136	.477	.097

The corresponding figures for the years since the stadium's reconfiguration paints a similar portrait of the left-handers' extra edge there. During those 13 seasons, the home-field advantage has declined not just at Yankee Stadium, but throughout the major leagues in general. But notice that while Yankees right-handers now have little if any edge at home, their lefties still thrive there:

	Home Games		Road Games		
	W–L	Pct.	W–L	Pct.	Diff.
Left-handers	187–84	.690	144–102	.585	.105
Right-handers	130–88	.596	145–105	.580	.016

Although that edge looks substantial on paper, don't forget that it translates into an average of no more than two extra wins per season more for a left-handed pitcher than a right-hander. So if the Yankees are using the question of "handedness" as a sort of tie-breaker when making personnel decisions, they're handling the situation correctly, but if a southpaw journeyman looks better to the Yankees than an established right-handed starter, that's trouble. Based upon the acquisitions of the past few winters—Rick Rhoden, Richard Dotson, Andy Hawkins, and Jimmy Jones—we think the Yankees are headed in the *right* direction.

WON-LOST RECORD BY STARTING POSITION

NEW YORK 85-76	C	1B	2B	3B	SS	LF	CF	RF	P	DH	Leadoff	Relief	Starts
Luis Aguayo	·	·	4-3	11-18	0-1	·	·	·	·	·	·	·	15-22
Neil Allen	·	·	·	·	·	·	·	·	0-2	·	·	13-26	0-2
Jay Buhner	·	·	·	·	·	0-2	8-6	·	·	·	·	·	8-8
John Candelaria	·	·	·	·	·	·	·	·	16-8	·	·	1-0	16-8
Chris Chambliss	·	·	·	·	·	·	·	·	·	·	·	·	·
Jack Clark	·	6-4	·	·	·	4-1	·	4-10	·	55-52	·	·	69-67
Pat Clements	·	·	·	·	·	·	·	·	0-1	·	·	2-3	0-1
Jose Cruz	·	·	·	·	·	1-2	2-1	·	·	8-3	1-2	·	11-6
Richard Dotson	·	·	·	·	·	·	·	·	19-10	·	·	1-2	19-10
David Eiland	·	·	·	·	·	·	·	·	1-2	·	·	·	1-2
Alvaro Espinoza	·	·	0-1	·	·	·	·	·	·	·	·	·	0-1
Bob Geren	0-2	·	·	·	·	·	·	·	·	·	·	·	0-2
Cecilio Guante	·	·	·	·	·	·	·	·	·	·	·	27-29	·
Lee Guetterman	·	·	·	·	·	·	·	·	0-2	·	·	5-13	0-2
Ron Guidry	·	·	·	·	·	·	·	·	4-6	·	·	0-2	4-6
Rickey Henderson	·	·	·	·	·	70-62	3-0	·	·	1-2	74-64	·	74-64
Charles Hudson	·	·	·	·	·	·	·	·	6-6	·	·	8-8	6-6
Tommy John	·	·	·	·	·	·	·	·	19-13	·	·	0-3	19-13
Roberto Kelly	·	·	·	·	·	·	10-9	·	·	·	2-2	·	10-9
Al Leiter	·	·	·	·	·	·	·	·	7-7	·	·	·	7-7
Don Mattingly	·	74-67	·	·	·	1-0	·	·	·	0-1	·	·	75-68
Bobby Meacham	·	·	9-7	3-1	5-4	·	·	·	·	·	·	·	17-12
Dale Mohorcic	·	·	·	·	·	·	·	·	·	·	·	8-5	·
Hal Morris	·	·	·	·	·	0-2	·	·	·	·	·	·	0-2
Scott Nielsen	·	·	·	·	·	·	·	·	0-2	·	·	3-2	0-2
Mike Pagliarulo	·	·	·	63-49	·	·	·	·	·	·	·	·	63-49
Hipolito Pena	·	·	·	·	·	·	·	·	·	·	·	6-10	·
Ken Phelps	·	·	·	·	·	·	·	·	·	13-15	·	·	13-15
Willie Randolph	·	·	63-44	·	·	·	·	·	·	·	3-2	·	63-44
Rick Rhoden	·	·	·	·	·	·	·	·	13-17	1-0	·	·	14-17
Dave Righetti	·	·	·	·	·	·	·	·	·	·	·	41-19	·
Rafael Santana	·	·	·	·	80-67	·	·	·	·	·	·	·	80-67
Steve Shields	·	·	·	·	·	·	·	·	·	·	·	17-22	·
Joel Skinner	39-33	·	·	·	·	·	·	·	·	·	·	·	39-33
Don Slaught	46-41	·	·	·	·	·	·	·	·	1-0	·	·	47-41
Tim Stoddard	·	·	·	·	·	·	·	·	·	·	·	8-20	·
Wayne Tolleson	·	·	1-8	4-4	·	·	·	·	·	·	2-2	·	5-12
Randy Velarde	·	·	8-13	4-4	0-4	·	·	·	·	·	1-1	·	12-21
Gary Ward	·	5-5	·	·	·	6-4	14-20	0-1	·	4-1	·	·	29-31
Claudell Washington	·	·	·	·	·	3-3	50-41	0-2	·	·	2-3	·	53-46
Dave Winfield	·	·	·	·	·	·	·	79-62	·	2-2	·	·	81-64

Batting vs. Left and Right Handed Pitchers

		BA	Rank	SA	Rank	OBA	Rank	HR %	Rank	BB %	Rank	SO %	Rank
Luis Aguayo	vs. Lefties	.273	62	.394	76	.310	90	3.03	57	4.23	134	19.72	140
	vs. Righties	.230	--	.297	--	.269	--	1.35	--	5.13	--	24.36	--
Jack Clark	vs. Lefties	.248	95	.483	35	.435	5	6.71	7	25.00	1	24.00	156
	vs. Righties	.239	123	.412	64	.356	34	4.90	20	15.14	9	22.36	154
Rickey Henderson	vs. Lefties	.368	3	.521	18	.470	1	2.45	72	15.66	11	4.55	5
	vs. Righties	.279	47	.348	119	.360	30	0.51	149	11.36	33	10.02	39
Roberto Kelly	vs. Lefties	.241	103	.296	140	.268	142	0.00	140	3.51	152	17.54	123
	vs. Righties	.261	--	.522	--	.280	--	4.35	--	3.70	--	18.52	--
Don Mattingly	vs. Lefties	.290	43	.389	80	.316	81	1.36	106	3.80	145	4.64	6
	vs. Righties	.323	7	.505	13	.374	20	3.97	33	7.73	91	4.35	4
Bobby Meacham	vs. Lefties	.218	142	.327	118	.224	163	0.00	140	1.69	167	15.25	99
	vs. Righties	.217	--	.267	--	.373	--	0.00	--	17.33	--	17.33	--
Mike Pagliarulo	vs. Lefties	.170	164	.358	97	.224	163	4.72	28	5.13	121	26.50	163
	vs. Righties	.231	131	.370	101	.292	136	2.96	64	8.31	83	19.57	141
Ken Phelps	vs. Lefties	.100	--	.250	--	.174	--	5.00	--	8.70	--	39.13	--
	vs. Righties	.274	51	.570	3	.417	3	8.30	1	19.54	1	14.94	98
Willie Randolph	vs. Lefties	.208	148	.288	142	.318	79	0.80	132	13.91	19	7.95	28
	vs. Righties	.240	119	.305	144	.324	87	0.36	155	10.53	45	8.36	20
Rafael Santana	vs. Lefties	.234	132	.290	141	.268	141	0.69	135	4.55	127	7.79	25
	vs. Righties	.242	116	.296	153	.298	131	0.90	130	7.08	103	13.35	77
Joel Skinner	vs. Lefties	.226	132	.358	97	.328	68	1.89	88	12.90	23	19.35	137
	vs. Righties	.227	137	.328	129	.249	165	1.52	104	2.86	167	28.57	164
Don Slaught	vs. Lefties	.310	31	.474	41	.377	31	2.59	68	9.16	55	19.08	136
	vs. Righties	.267	69	.437	43	.309	110	2.91	67	5.29	138	12.78	72
Gary Ward	vs. Lefties	.227	131	.375	85	.313	87	3.13	54	10.27	42	17.81	125
	vs. Righties	.223	--	.233	--	.289	--	0.00	--	7.76	--	12.93	--
Claudell Washington	vs. Lefties	.313	28	.458	47	.333	60	2.08	81	3.92	142	19.61	138
	vs. Righties	.307	18	.440	40	.343	59	2.46	78	5.07	144	14.75	96
Dave Winfield	vs. Lefties	.331	13	.594	7	.432	6	6.29	10	15.05	14	9.71	47
	vs. Righties	.318	10	.500	16	.381	15	3.65	41	8.94	73	16.00	109
Team Average	vs. Lefties	.267	5	.412	3	.345	3	2.87	2	10.46	1	13.94	8
	vs. Righties	.261	7	.388	7	.328	6	2.55	8	8.84	6	15.26	11
League Average	vs. Lefties	.259		.391		.321		2.47		7.97		14.12	
	vs. Righties	.259		.391		.326		2.47		8.51		14.39	

Batting with Runners on Base and Bases Empty

		BA	Rank	SA	Rank	OBA	Rank	HR %	Rank	BB %	Rank	SO %	Rank
Jack Clark	Runners On	.239	127	.457	38	.379	33	6.48	4	18.65	3	20.26	152
	Bases Empty	.245	100	.410	60	.384	10	4.42	30	18.03	1	25.57	161
Rickey Henderson	Runners On	.289	57	.373	110	.380	31	1.20	112	13.37	24	8.42	30
	Bases Empty	.312	9	.410	59	.400	6	1.03	129	12.36	17	8.31	21
Don Mattingly	Runners On	.320	19	.474	28	.360	52	3.44	52	6.83	111	4.66	6
	Bases Empty	.302	17	.451	34	.347	41	2.60	71	5.78	119	4.26	2
Mike Pagliarulo	Runners On	.275	73	.468	30	.341	80	5.05	14	9.60	64	18.40	141
	Bases Empty	.159	170	.270	155	.208	169	1.77	98	5.42	126	24.17	153
Ken Phelps	Runners On	.273	77	.583	3	.434	4	9.09	1	22.86	1	13.14	89
	Bases Empty	.255	85	.521	12	.372	18	7.27	4	15.31	4	19.39	138
Willie Randolph	Runners On	.270	87	.356	123	.398	16	1.23	111	17.29	9	6.07	16
	Bases Empty	.203	155	.261	161	.262	157	0.00	156	6.92	93	10.00	33
Rafael Santana	Runners On	.242	121	.303	153	.286	142	1.01	125	5.96	131	11.47	61
	Bases Empty	.238	116	.287	145	.290	123	0.71	144	6.60	96	11.88	55
Joel Skinner	Runners On	.276	72	.398	85	.321	106	1.02	124	6.25	124	18.75	147
	Bases Empty	.196	159	.294	142	.231	165	1.96	91	4.38	149	31.88	170
Don Slaught	Runners On	.250	111	.321	141	.288	141	0.71	140	5.06	149	17.09	129
	Bases Empty	.308	11	.549	8	.370	21	4.40	32	8.00	75	13.50	76
Gary Ward	Runners On	.207	157	.319	143	.279	151	2.59	77	8.27	86	15.04	108
	Bases Empty	.243	108	.304	138	.326	67	0.87	135	10.08	40	16.28	108
Claudell Washington	Runners On	.299	41	.425	60	.333	89	1.87	91	4.76	150	12.99	85
	Bases Empty	.315	7	.456	32	.350	34	2.90	63	5.12	134	17.32	118
Dave Winfield	Runners On	.340	7	.556	5	.418	9	4.85	18	11.76	40	12.75	80
	Bases Empty	.306	12	.505	17	.378	14	4.12	36	10.15	38	15.08	94
Team Average	Runners On	.270	8	.411	5	.344	5	3.08	2	10.22	2	13.58	6
	Bases Empty	.257	4	.383	6	.324	4	2.30	10	8.61	4	15.91	12
League Average	Runners On	.268		.401		.336		2.45		9.09		13.68	
	Bases Empty	.253		.383		.315		2.48		7.76		14.81	

Overall Batting Compared to Late Inning Pressure Situations

		BA	Rank	SA	Rank	OBA	Rank	HR %	Rank	BB %	Rank	SO %	Rank	RDI %	Rank
Jack Clark	Overall	.242	120	.433	42	.381	13	5.44	11	18.34	2	22.89	158	.304	40
	Pressure	.179	144	.286	129	.338	74	3.57	43	19.72	5	29.58	160	.176	110
Jose Cruz	Overall	.200	--	.263	--	.273	--	1.25	--	9.09	--	9.09	--	.222	--
	Pressure	.143	--	.143	--	.143	--	0.00	--	0.00	--	28.57	--	.200	95
Rickey Henderson	Overall	.305	16	.399	77	.394	7	1.08	124	12.67	16	8.35	22	.353	8
	Pressure	.328	21	.361	83	.413	16	0.00	110	14.67	15	5.33	9	.571	1
Don Mattingly	Overall	.311	10	.462	28	.353	39	3.01	64	6.30	119	4.45	1	.317	27
	Pressure	.275	65	.420	56	.311	93	2.90	55	4.05	146	5.41	10	.300	53
Mike Pagliarulo	Overall	.216	156	.367	103	.276	155	3.38	51	7.55	94	21.22	149	.278	74
	Pressure	.180	140	.197	157	.254	147	0.00	110	8.82	78	20.59	115	.214	90
Ken Phelps	Overall	.263	75	.549	4	.402	4	8.08	1	18.87	1	16.44	114	.210	151
	Pressure	.222	116	.537	15	.311	92	9.26	3	11.48	46	27.87	154	.150	127
Willie Randolph	Overall	.230	135	.300	156	.322	87	0.50	154	11.60	25	8.23	21	.261	93
	Pressure	.156	159	.178	165	.255	145	0.00	110	9.43	66	9.43	32	.100	149
Rafael Santana	Overall	.240	125	.294	159	.289	141	0.83	142	6.33	116	11.71	61	.220	143
	Pressure	.315	33	.315	115	.339	71	0.00	110	1.72	167	8.62	25	.200	95
Joel Skinner	Overall	.227	142	.335	129	.267	163	1.59	104	5.15	147	26.47	166	.254	101
	Pressure	.385	--	.808	--	.467	--	11.54	--	13.33	--	23.33	--	.000	--
Don Slaught	Overall	.283	38	.450	31	.334	61	2.80	69	6.70	110	15.08	103	.286	61
	Pressure	.283	55	.565	10	.358	48	6.52	12	7.41	97	24.07	139	.381	25
Gary Ward	Overall	.225	144	.312	148	.302	118	1.73	99	9.16	64	15.65	107	.191	162
	Pressure	.382	4	.588	7	.462	4	5.88	15	7.32	99	14.63	74	.429	14
Claudell Washington	Overall	.308	11	.442	36	.342	51	2.42	75	4.95	153	15.26	104	.260	96
	Pressure	.328	20	.493	25	.366	41	4.48	30	4.23	144	19.72	108	.227	83
Dave Winfield	Overall	.322	4	.530	9	.398	5	4.47	26	10.94	41	13.95	85	.357	4
	Pressure	.296	46	.451	45	.375	33	4.23	34	11.25	48	20.00	110	.176	110
Team Average	Overall	.263	5	.395	6	.333	4	2.65	5	9.34	3	14.85	9	.274	6
	Pressure	.254	6	.368	6	.322	6	2.86	4	8.35	10	18.04	10	.255	7
League Average	Overall	.259		.391		.324		2.47		8.35		14.31		.269	
	Pressure	.249		.365		.319		2.28		8.71		17.04		.246	

Additional Miscellaneous Batting Comparisons

	Grass Surface BA	Rank	Artificial Surface BA	Rank	Home Games BA	Rank	Road Games BA	Rank	Runners in Scoring Position BA	Rank	Runners in Scoring Pos and Two Outs BA	Rank	Leading Off Inning OBA	Rank	Runners on 3B with less than 2 Outs RBI %	Rank
Luis Aguayo	.264	65	.200	--	.275	--	.225	--	.120	--	.077	--	.194	--	.400	--
Jack Clark	.230	126	.314	25	.233	130	.250	98	.245	105	.294	38	.372	21	.686	27
Rickey Henderson	.291	30	.364	8	.297	24	.312	11	.290	46	.209	116	.399	8	.870	2
Don Mattingly	.308	14	.323	21	.294	31	.327	3	.298	35	.206	121	.295	103	.689	24
Bobby Meacham	.183	--	.303	--	.280	--	.200	158	.125	171	.120	164	.357	--	.571	--
Mike Pagliarulo	.209	159	.250	101	.192	163	.237	123	.265	78	.212	113	.156	171	.600	65
Ken Phelps	.272	53	.250	101	.265	77	.261	80	.211	149	.222	101	.398	10	.462	140
Willie Randolph	.229	128	.238	117	.218	150	.242	117	.272	70	.200	126	.229	156	.737	12
Rafael Santana	.235	120	.263	89	.217	153	.263	75	.222	137	.222	101	.299	96	.476	131
Joel Skinner	.227	130	.226	--	.180	167	.264	70	.261	85	.250	61	.200	167	.727	13
Don Slaught	.285	36	.274	75	.279	57	.287	36	.233	125	.234	89	.385	13	.700	17
Gary Ward	.223	138	.237	118	.230	136	.221	138	.189	162	.152	156	.392	12	.429	147
Claudell Washington	.318	7	.246	107	.358	4	.262	78	.267	77	.239	82	.276	127	.645	47
Dave Winfield	.309	11	.380	5	.332	6	.312	10	.340	13	.304	30	.372	21	.535	106
Team Average	.258	7	.289	2	.261	7	.264	5	.254	10	.219	11	.313	5	.636	1
League Average	.256		.267		.262		.257		.262		.239		.311		.570	

Pitching vs. Left and Right Handed Batters

		BA	Rank	SA	Rank	OBA	Rank	HR %	Rank	BB %	Rank	SO %	Rank
Neil Allen	vs. Lefties	.328	124	.508	122	.399	121	3.83	120	11.00	99	8.61	109
	vs. Righties	.227	32	.375	55	.266	10	2.60	67	4.75	14	14.58	61
John Candelaria	vs. Lefties	.144	1	.268	6	.189	1	4.12	123	5.66	16	30.19	1
	vs. Righties	.268	88	.423	89	.292	32	2.76	74	3.18	2	16.67	46
Richard Dotson	vs. Lefties	.239	43	.392	80	.306	36	3.17	108	8.53	59	10.08	90
	vs. Righties	.295	118	.522	125	.372	123	4.97	126	10.60	113	10.33	116
Ron Guidry	vs. Lefties	.265	--	.449	--	.294	--	4.08	--	3.85	--	9.62	--
	vs. Righties	.257	69	.456	115	.316	59	2.92	86	6.95	51	14.44	63
Charles Hudson	vs. Lefties	.215	19	.298	14	.283	16	0.55	8	8.13	51	11.48	79
	vs. Righties	.252	60	.430	100	.316	61	3.74	109	7.98	72	14.29	65
Tommy John	vs. Lefties	.281	95	.418	96	.335	78	2.05	64	6.25	25	6.88	120
	vs. Righties	.315	125	.424	92	.359	118	1.40	18	5.84	30	11.36	106
Al Leiter	vs. Lefties	.152	--	.152	--	.333	--	0.00	--	19.05	--	23.81	--
	vs. Righties	.246	49	.425	94	.351	109	3.91	115	11.96	125	23.92	9
Dale Mohorcic	vs. Lefties	.315	117	.446	109	.352	98	0.77	16	6.34	27	14.08	52
	vs. Righties	.250	56	.393	73	.352	110	3.57	106	10.00	106	12.00	100
Rick Rhoden	vs. Lefties	.280	91	.409	86	.340	86	2.43	78	7.83	46	9.35	100
	vs. Righties	.256	63	.402	77	.300	40	2.81	77	5.17	18	13.18	82
Dave Righetti	vs. Lefties	.279	89	.442	107	.347	95	2.33	73	9.38	75	19.79	13
	vs. Righties	.249	54	.329	24	.327	81	1.20	12	9.96	105	18.15	38
Steve Shields	vs. Lefties	.336	125	.507	121	.416	123	2.99	102	11.61	107	15.48	45
	vs. Righties	.271	92	.367	51	.317	63	2.13	46	5.80	29	14.98	57
Tim Stoddard	vs. Lefties	.238	40	.381	69	.343	91	2.38	74	13.13	118	8.08	113
	vs. Righties	.316	126	.451	114	.373	125	2.26	53	9.09	90	16.23	48
Team Average	vs. Lefties	.262	7	.400	9	.331	6	2.68	12	8.98	8	11.91	9
	vs. Righties	.271	13	.422	14	.326	10	2.83	10	7.02	3	14.72	9
League Average	vs. Lefties	.262		.387		.331		2.24		9.12		13.21	
	vs. Righties	.258		.393		.320		2.63		7.80		15.09	

Pitching with Runners on Base and Bases Empty

		BA	Rank	SA	Rank	OBA	Rank	HR %	Rank	BB %	Rank	SO %	Rank
Neil Allen	Runners On	.227	18	.365	48	.305	32	2.37	68	10.00	94	12.80	73
	Bases Empty	.303	124	.485	125	.339	102	3.73	109	4.72	14	11.42	98
John Candelaria	Runners On	.259	63	.436	96	.296	23	3.64	108	5.74	12	20.49	15
	Bases Empty	.242	47	.377	63	.263	10	2.60	86	2.27	1	17.93	32
Richard Dotson	Runners On	.310	115	.504	123	.370	105	3.65	109	9.24	78	9.87	106
	Bases Empty	.235	38	.420	102	.315	64	4.30	121	9.75	103	10.43	109
Ron Guidry	Runners On	.213	--	.436	--	.272	--	4.26	--	6.73	--	17.31	--
	Bases Empty	.294	122	.468	122	.341	106	2.38	76	5.93	39	10.37	111
Charles Hudson	Runners On	.278	86	.417	83	.345	86	2.65	77	9.34	79	13.19	68
	Bases Empty	.209	15	.340	28	.272	14	2.05	54	7.17	63	12.83	79
Tommy John	Runners On	.288	99	.390	66	.359	99	0.64	6	8.43	58	10.96	94
	Bases Empty	.324	127	.448	111	.350	113	2.23	65	3.81	6	10.00	114
Al Leiter	Runners On	.263	--	.337	--	.320	--	1.05	--	6.73	--	22.12	--
	Bases Empty	.205	10	.419	101	.367	122	5.13	127	17.69	128	25.17	5
Dale Mohorcic	Runners On	.277	85	.428	91	.344	84	3.01	89	7.77	48	13.47	63
	Bases Empty	.280	106	.402	87	.362	121	1.52	26	9.40	97	12.08	87
Rick Rhoden	Runners On	.274	81	.448	104	.340	79	4.01	118	8.88	68	11.75	86
	Bases Empty	.265	85	.378	66	.309	53	1.71	38	5.02	20	10.64	108
Dave Righetti	Runners On	.284	95	.358	40	.360	102	1.14	20	10.45	98	17.91	23
	Bases Empty	.226	28	.358	48	.301	45	1.89	44	9.09	90	19.32	24
Steve Shields	Runners On	.313	117	.427	90	.382	114	1.33	21	9.66	86	13.64	61
	Bases Empty	.285	112	.424	104	.339	105	3.49	105	6.99	60	16.67	44
Tim Stoddard	Runners On	.309	113	.443	99	.407	126	2.06	52	14.52	125	12.10	80
	Bases Empty	.267	87	.408	92	.318	70	2.50	82	6.98	58	13.95	68
Team Average	Runners On	.271	11	.414	10	.341	10	2.57	9	9.11	8	13.98	6
	Bases Empty	.264	13	.414	14	.318	9	2.93	13	6.62	3	13.45	10
League Average	Runners On	.268		.401		.336		2.45		9.09		13.68	
	Bases Empty	.253		.383		.315		2.48		7.76		14.81	

Overall Pitching Compared to Late Inning Pressure Situations

		BA	Rank	SA	Rank	OBA	Rank	HR %	Rank	BB %	Rank	SO %	Rank
Neil Allen	Overall	.268	82	.429	107	.322	68	3.10	101	7.34	42	12.10	89
	Pressure	.214	29	.443	101	.267	15	7.14	128	5.19	19	10.39	104
John Candelaria	Overall	.248	47	.398	82	.275	7	2.98	96	3.59	1	18.91	20
	Pressure	.179	8	.214	5	.193	2	0.00	1	1.72	1	22.41	14
Richard Dotson	Overall	.266	77	.454	117	.338	91	4.04	124	9.54	95	10.20	110
	Pressure	.333	--	.333	--	.517	--	0.00	--	26.67	--	6.67	--
Charles Hudson	Overall	.235	33	.370	49	.301	25	2.28	66	8.05	61	12.98	75
	Pressure	.308	112	.508	118	.370	102	3.08	93	9.21	69	17.11	39
Tommy John	Overall	.308	127	.423	99	.354	115	1.53	16	5.93	20	10.44	107
	Pressure	.383	127	.447	102	.408	121	0.00	1	4.08	9	10.20	106
Al Leiter	Overall	.231	25	.382	61	.348	108	3.30	108	13.15	124	23.90	4
	Pressure	.333	--	.333	--	.333	--	0.00	--	0.00	--	33.33	--
Dale Mohorcic	Overall	.279	104	.416	94	.352	112	2.35	69	8.48	73	12.87	77
	Pressure	.273	94	.417	90	.353	93	1.52	41	8.61	61	11.92	95
Rick Rhoden	Overall	.269	84	.405	87	.322	66	2.61	85	6.61	29	11.10	97
	Pressure	.259	77	.389	79	.310	53	1.85	57	6.78	29	15.25	57
Dave Righetti	Overall	.257	61	.358	35	.332	85	1.49	15	9.81	98	18.57	24
	Pressure	.230	42	.333	44	.305	47	1.65	50	9.16	68	18.32	32
Steve Shields	Overall	.298	122	.425	105	.360	117	2.48	72	8.29	64	15.19	51
	Pressure	.231	44	.324	40	.297	34	2.78	85	7.44	41	14.88	60
Tim Stoddard	Overall	.286	114	.424	102	.361	118	2.30	68	10.67	110	13.04	73
	Pressure	.200	20	.260	13	.255	11	0.00	1	7.27	37	16.36	45
Team Average	Overall	.267	11	.414	13	.328	10	2.78	13	7.74	5	13.69	10
	Pressure	.238	3	.359	7	.304	3	2.46	10	7.79	2	16.04	5
League Average	Overall	.259		.391		.324		2.47		8.35		14.31	
	Pressure	.249		.369		.324		2.26		9.33		15.69	

Additional Miscellaneous Pitching Comparisons

	Grass Surface BA	Rank	Artificial Surface BA	Rank	Home Games BA	Rank	Road Games BA	Rank	Runners in Scoring Position BA	Rank	Runners in Scoring Pos and Two Outs BA	Rank	Leading Off Inning OBA	Rank
Neil Allen	.250	52	.361	127	.262	76	.272	82	.222	29	.155	12	.358	106
John Candelaria	.251	55	.235	28	.264	80	.220	17	.243	49	.254	83	.290	48
Richard Dotson	.251	56	.319	114	.236	43	.291	105	.259	65	.158	15	.348	103
Lee Guetterman	.310	126	.200	--	.315	--	.294	--	.255	--	.250	--	.395	--
Ron Guidry	.262	68	.241	--	.194	--	.285	101	.208	--	.240	--	.379	117
Charles Hudson	.234	34	.250	--	.224	29	.243	43	.305	113	.250	78	.306	61
Tommy John	.300	122	.388	130	.302	120	.314	123	.290	93	.268	96	.339	95
Al Leiter	.230	28	.235	28	.217	23	.245	45	.275	--	.231	--	.406	125
Dale Mohorcic	.268	85	.341	--	.268	83	.288	103	.245	51	.283	101	.266	28
Rick Rhoden	.265	75	.287	85	.251	54	.297	111	.293	102	.211	48	.269	31
Dave Righetti	.258	61	.250	--	.219	25	.299	113	.261	66	.300	109	.250	14
Steve Shields	.299	121	.296	101	.278	97	.316	124	.284	87	.286	103	.286	45
Tim Stoddard	.290	118	.271	64	.252	59	.318	126	.242	48	.206	45	.264	26
Team Average	.264	9	.288	14	.257	5	.278	13	.259	7	.232	6	.317	9
League Average	.256		.267		.257		.262		.262		.239		.311	

OAKLAND A's

- **The 40–40 club: Let's keep things in perspective.**
- **The World Series "upset" wasn't all that shocking.**

The sign outside the building said, "Meeting 12:00 a.m. Members only." At precisely midnight, we pressed our ear to the drinking glass held against the wall.

   "Roll call. Canseco?"
   "Here."
   "All present and accounted for."

Ah-hah! The first meeting of the 40–40 club. We'd always wondered: When, exactly, do these clubs meet anyway?

We don't mean to denigrate Canseco's unusual combination of speed and power. After all, anyone who doesn't know that baseball's version of Conan the Destroyer was the first player ever to hit 40 home runs and steal 40 bases in the same season is hereby sentenced to a week at the Arnold Schwarzenegger film festival. But a little perspective on its significance is in order.

The carnival atmosphere that surrounded Canseco's quest to be first was, it seemed to us, a bit extreme. But several factors combined to make this "first" attainable in 1988. Most important, the relationship of home runs to steals is one of an ever-increasing number of what might be called "coincidence" statistics. Double figures in doubles, triples, and home runs. One thousand yards each, rushing and receiving. And the worst offender of all: basketball's "triple double," which, in the absence of any definition at all, is molded to the desired shape to suit one's needs. Our favorite was the apparently serious inclusion of turnovers invoked by an overzealous publicist in order to award a triple-double to one of his protégés.

Canseco's accomplishment, although one that requires ample doses of talent and skill, also benefited from a generous dash of will. Which is to say that Jose announced his intention to seek enrollment in the 40–40 club long before he gained admission even to the 30–30 club—during spring training 1988, to be exact. The media then saw to it that the flame kept burning through the summer.

Finally, the combination of high totals in both home runs *and* stolen bases is a contemporary phenomenon, induced by generational influences in the same way that other biases produced batting averages in the 1930s that seem extraordinary by today's standards. Stolen bases fell into disfavor in the early 1920s as the frequency of home runs increased, and finally fell below the one-per-game mark for the first time in 1930—when home runs reached an all-time high rate (at the time) of one per 55 at-bats. The following table summarizes the relationship of home run and stolen base frequency:

Decade	AB per Home Run	Steals Per Game	Decade	AB per Home Run	Steals Per Game
1870s	497	11.97	1930s	64	0.78
1880s	164	7.46	1940s	65	0.72
1890s	140	3.54	1950s	40	0.60
1900s	243	2.40	1960s	41	0.84
1910s	193	2.34	1970s	45	1.24
1920s	86	1.17	1980s	41	1.54

As home run frequency has maintained its peak slightly below the level of one per 40 at-bats, stolen bases have steadily increased to a rate not seen since 1920—when home runs were hit at only one-third of the current rate. As a result, the 40–40 feat has only been a possibility in the contemporary era.

Trying to put Canseco's accomplishment into historical perspective can be as simple or complex an algebraic challenge as one wants. The following measures are both simple in their execution and satisfyingly similar in their results.

For every season in major league history, we've adjusted each player's HR and SB figures to raise or lower them to 1988 standards. A simple example: if, in a given year, home runs were hit at one-tenth the current rate, each player's total for that season would be multiplied by 10. After those adjustments, nine other players were awarded membership in the "club":

Year	Player	HR	SB
1903	Jimmy Sheckard	9	67
1908	Honus Wagner	10	53
1909	Ty Cobb	9	76
1920	George Sisler	19	42
1922	Ken Williams	39	37
1932	Chuck Klein	38	20
1933	Chuck Klein	28	15
1958	Mickey Mantle	42	18
1964	Willie Mays	47	19

Cobb (in 1911) and Mike Schmidt (1975) both missed by fractional amounts. Judged by standards that reflected the way baseball was played in their eras, each of the players above equalled or bettered Canseco's 40–40 parlay. It's easy to lose sight of the fact that Ty Cobb, in his day, was every bit the home run hitter that Canseco is a base stealer today.

Another piece of evidence corroborates that claim. Forgetting the totals involved, Canseco ranked fourth in the A.L. in steals while leading the league in home runs. No fewer than 39 other players in modern major league history have ranked as high as fourth in their leagues in both categories in the same season. (That figure also contains a generational bias: More than half of those seasons come prior to the 1920s. Increasing specialization has reduced the frequency of dual-category leaders over the past half-century.) Twelve other home-run leaders, like Canseco, ranked as high as fourth in steals. And three of the "adjusted" 40–40 club members listed above actually led their leagues in both categories: Sheckard, Cobb, and Klein (in 1932).

Of course, none of this changes the fact that Jose Canseco was and forever will be the first player to hit 40 home runs and steal 40 bases in the same season. But let's judge that feat in its proper perspective. Don't forget that in 1920, Babe Ruth became the first player ever to hit more than 30 home runs in a season, a feat that was virtually impossible during the dead-ball era, but one that has become commonplace today.

It's no big deal, but was anyone else bothered by the "Can the A's lose?" discussion prior to last year's World Series?

Let's start with the obvious. Upsets happen. Didn't Liston lose to Clay? Didn't the Colts lose to Namath? Didn't Dewey lose to Truman? Didn't Oprah beat the pants off Donahue?

Those are the grand examples. But on a lesser scale, upsets take place every night of the week, every week of the year. Did the Miami Heat lose *every* game last season? (Remember, close doesn't count.) Did Frank Viola win every start? Did Larry Bird make every free throw? The NFL has exploited the "anything can happen" philosophy by invading our psyches with the most quoted incomplete thought in the history of American culture, such as it is ("On any given Sunday . . .")? Anyone who approaches a sporting event with a deeply-held conviction that one side absolutely *cannot* lose either doesn't follow sports closely, or doesn't understand what he's watching.

So, alright, we've gone overboard. What's a little hyperbole among friends, you say? After all, won't you sell more papers with the headline "A's Can't Lose" than with "A's Probably Won't Lose"? Of course. But our problem isn't so much with the notion that one team can have virtually no chance against another. It's the notion that one of baseball's best teams has little more than a prayer in a short series against a somewhat superior team that bothers us.

Here's the extreme case. What do you think are the chances that in a game between a league's best and worst teams, the better team will win? We checked every season in modern major league history, accumulating the records of the best team in each league in head-to-head matchups against that league's worst team in the same season. The table below lists the combined records of the better teams in those games:

	W	L	Pct.
American League	1245	457	.731
National League	1275	483	.725
Major league totals	2520	940	.728

To put those numbers in World Series perspective: A team that wins roughly 73 percent of its games against a particular opponent stands a 91–percent chance of defeating that opponent in a best-of-seven series. Or, to state it conversely: The worst team in any league still has nearly one chance in 10 of defeating the best team in a best-of-seven competition. Yes, even *Baltimore* against the A's.

What does that suggest about the chances of one of the best teams in baseball defeating the A's in the 1988 World Series? Let's look at some empirical evidence on that issue. The following table represents the head-to-head record of teams that in a given season had winning percentages similar to that of the 1988 Oakland A's when playing head to head against teams with records similar to that of last season's Dodgers. (We allowed a margin of two wins in either direction for either team.)

	W	L	Pct.
American League	144	111	.565
National League	106	83	.561
Major league totals	250	194	.563

A 56–percent winning percentage translates to a 64–percent shot at winning a best-of-seven series. Simply stated, the Dodgers had roughly four chances in 11 of winning last year's World Series.

WON-LOST RECORD BY STARTING POSITION

OAKLAND 104-58	C	1B	2B	3B	SS	LF	CF	RF	P	DH	Leadoff	Relief	Starts
Don Baylor	.	.	.	.	.	.	.	.	.	36-37	.	.	36-37
Lance Blankenship	.	.	.	.	.	.	.	.	.	.	.	.	.
Rich Bordi	.	.	.	.	.	.	.	.	1-1	.	.	.	1-1
Todd Burns	.	.	.	.	.	.	.	.	10-4	.	.	2-1	10-4
Greg Cadaret	.	.	.	.	.	.	.	.	.	.	.	38-20	.
Jose Canseco	.	.	.	.	.	.	.	91-52	.	10-3	.	.	101-55
James Corsi	.	.	.	.	.	.	.	.	0-1	.	.	4-6	0-1
Storm Davis	.	.	.	.	.	.	.	.	22-11	.	.	.	22-11
Dennis Eckersley	.	.	.	.	.	.	.	.	.	.	.	55-5	.
Mike Gallego	.	.	33-23	4-3	11-10	.	.	.	.	.	1-1	.	48-36
Ron Hassey	58-20	.	.	.	.	.	.	.	5-4	.	.	.	63-24
Dave Henderson	.	.	.	.	.	.	81-46	.	.	.	.	.	81-46
Rick Honeycutt	.	.	.	.	.	.	.	.	.	.	.	38-17	.
Glenn Hubbard	.	.	59-27	.	.	.	.	.	.	.	.	1-1	59-27
Stan Javier	.	4-0	.	.	.	23-17	21-11	9-5	.	.	4-4	.	57-33
Doug Jennings	.	6-1	.	.	.	8-2	.	3-0	.	1-0	1-0	.	18-3
Felix Jose	.	.	.	.	.	.	.	.	.	.	.	.	.
Ed Jurak	.	.	.	.	.	.	.	.	.	.	.	.	.
Carney Lansford	.	.	.	85-49	.	.	.	.	0-1	.	38-29	.	85-50
Mark McGwire	.	90-56	.	.	.	.	.	.	.	.	.	.	90-56
Orlando Mercado	3-5	.	.	.	.	.	.	.	.	.	.	.	3-5
Gene Nelson	.	.	.	.	.	.	.	.	0-1	.	.	31-22	0-1
Steve Ontiveros	.	.	.	.	.	.	.	.	5-5	.	.	.	5-5
Dave Otto	.	.	.	.	.	.	.	.	2-0	.	.	0-1	2-0
Dave Parker	.	1-0	.	.	.	17-17	.	.	.	45-12	.	.	63-29
Tony Phillips	.	.	12-8	11-3	1-0	9-5	2-1	0-1	.	.	15-8	.	35-18
Eric Plunk	.	.	.	.	.	.	.	.	.	.	.	32-17	.
Luis Polonia	.	.	.	.	.	47-16	.	1-0	0-1	.	44-15	.	48-17
Jeff Shaver	.	.	.	.	.	.	.	.	.	.	.	0-1	.
Matt Sinatro	0-2	.	.	.	.	.	.	.	.	.	.	.	0-2
Terry Steinbach	43-31	3-1	.	4-3	.	0-1	.	.	7-0	.	.	.	57-36
Dave Stewart	.	.	.	.	.	.	.	.	23-14	.	.	.	23-14
Walt Weiss	.	.	.	.	92-48	.	.	.	.	.	.	.	92-48
Bob Welch	.	.	.	.	.	.	.	.	25-11	.	.	.	25-11
Curt Young	.	.	.	.	.	.	.	.	16-10	.	.	.	16-10

Batting vs. Left and Right Handed Pitchers

Player		BA	Rank	SA	Rank	OBA	Rank	HR %	Rank	BB %	Rank	SO %	Rank
Don Baylor	vs. Lefties	.220	140	.285	144	.305	100	0.81	131	9.22	54	15.60	102
	vs. Righties	.220	147	.362	109	.355	35	4.26	26	12.21	23	12.79	73
Jose Canseco	vs. Lefties	.340	8	.620	5	.412	15	6.67	8	8.82	59	17.65	124
	vs. Righties	.296	31	.552	5	.384	14	6.96	4	11.78	30	18.32	131
Mike Gallego	vs. Lefties	.233	120	.311	132	.336	57	0.97	124	12.40	27	14.05	89
	vs. Righties	.195	163	.230	169	.275	149	0.57	148	9.55	66	18.09	130
Ron Hassey	vs. Lefties	.121	--	.152	--	.194	--	0.00	--	5.41	--	16.22	--
	vs. Righties	.272	56	.393	78	.337	67	2.41	79	8.54	78	10.98	50
Dave Henderson	vs. Lefties	.306	34	.524	15	.372	32	4.08	33	8.98	57	12.57	73
	vs. Righties	.303	20	.525	9	.359	31	5.00	19	7.94	88	17.62	125
Glenn Hubbard	vs. Lefties	.278	55	.342	110	.337	56	1.27	111	8.14	69	12.79	76
	vs. Righties	.247	111	.340	122	.333	75	0.93	129	10.16	53	15.23	102
Stan Javier	vs. Lefties	.253	86	.308	134	.277	134	1.10	119	2.13	165	14.89	95
	vs. Righties	.258	85	.324	135	.324	88	0.33	158	8.67	76	14.16	91
Doug Jennings	vs. Lefties	.000	--	.000	--	.000	--	0.00	--	0.00	--	0.00	--
	vs. Righties	.210	156	.300	149	.349	45	1.00	126	16.54	4	22.05	151
Carney Lansford	vs. Lefties	.203	152	.222	164	.244	158	0.00	140	5.45	116	4.85	7
	vs. Righties	.308	17	.412	65	.358	32	1.74	93	5.88	124	6.11	8
Mark McGwire	vs. Lefties	.247	99	.533	13	.358	38	7.33	5	14.77	15	15.34	100
	vs. Righties	.265	71	.458	34	.349	43	5.25	16	10.89	40	19.61	143
Dave Parker	vs. Lefties	.182	159	.309	133	.274	137	3.64	46	11.29	36	22.58	149
	vs. Righties	.270	61	.422	57	.321	93	3.11	61	7.16	102	16.05	110
Tony Phillips	vs. Lefties	.282	51	.423	56	.427	11	0.00	140	20.00	2	16.67	113
	vs. Righties	.163	168	.248	167	.261	161	1.42	107	11.18	36	21.74	150
Luis Polonia	vs. Lefties	.167	--	.278	--	.158	--	0.00	--	0.00	--	15.00	--
	vs. Righties	.300	23	.385	84	.349	44	0.74	136	7.17	101	12.63	69
Terry Steinbach	vs. Lefties	.342	7	.421	57	.400	20	1.75	96	9.09	56	7.58	22
	vs. Righties	.228	136	.392	79	.302	122	2.95	65	7.89	89	13.91	85
Walt Weiss	vs. Lefties	.208	149	.257	155	.250	153	0.00	140	5.56	114	7.41	17
	vs. Righties	.262	76	.339	123	.329	79	0.85	132	7.20	99	11.91	59
Team Average	vs. Lefties	.256	8	.386	8	.329	6	2.56	5	9.27	2	13.25	5
	vs. Righties	.266	5	.404	4	.339	3	2.86	2	9.08	4	15.01	10
League Average	vs. Lefties	.259		.391		.321		2.47		7.97		14.12	
	vs. Righties	.259		.391		.326		2.47		8.51		14.39	

Batting with Runners on Base and Bases Empty

		BA	Rank	SA	Rank	OBA	Rank	HR %	Rank	BB %	Rank	SO %	Rank
Don Baylor	Runners On	.305	34	.419	68	.424	8	2.86	64	14.39	18	11.36	59
	Bases Empty	.164	168	.264	160	.265	153	2.52	75	8.29	72	16.02	105
Jose Canseco	Runners On	.313	24	.639	1	.391	21	8.93	2	10.91	48	16.22	119
	Bases Empty	.301	18	.505	18	.391	7	5.02	20	11.20	26	19.95	141
Mike Gallego	Runners On	.213	153	.241	165	.286	143	0.00	148	7.87	93	17.32	132
	Bases Empty	.207	149	.272	153	.306	102	1.18	119	12.44	15	16.06	107
Ron Hassey	Runners On	.267	94	.385	97	.342	79	2.22	83	9.32	68	11.80	64
	Bases Empty	.250	90	.356	106	.309	98	2.13	88	7.35	86	11.27	49
Dave Henderson	Runners On	.322	17	.512	14	.364	47	3.31	55	6.93	110	17.15	130
	Bases Empty	.287	33	.536	11	.361	27	6.04	11	9.46	52	15.20	96
Glenn Hubbard	Runners On	.294	49	.426	59	.351	63	2.21	84	6.21	127	11.18	57
	Bases Empty	.222	136	.266	158	.320	74	0.00	156	12.71	14	17.68	124
Stan Javier	Runners On	.247	116	.302	155	.307	123	0.00	148	7.21	104	12.50	77
	Bases Empty	.265	65	.335	123	.319	78	0.93	134	7.33	87	15.95	103
Carney Lansford	Runners On	.296	45	.372	111	.343	76	1.35	106	6.40	123	6.40	17
	Bases Empty	.267	56	.351	109	.317	83	1.20	118	5.32	130	5.32	6
Mark McGwire	Runners On	.296	46	.558	4	.403	13	7.08	15	14.78	15	16.84	127
	Bases Empty	.232	124	.416	53	.308	100	4.84	21	9.59	48	19.77	140
Dave Parker	Runners On	.290	55	.489	22	.343	74	4.84	19	7.84	94	15.69	114
	Bases Empty	.225	131	.325	127	.285	133	1.57	106	7.73	83	18.36	132
Tony Phillips	Runners On	.239	128	.398	87	.333	89	1.14	115	11.65	43	12.62	78
	Bases Empty	.177	166	.242	167	.311	92	0.81	138	16.22	3	25.00	157
Luis Polonia	Runners On	.291	52	.398	84	.336	87	0.97	129	6.96	109	13.91	97
	Bases Empty	.292	28	.368	95	.338	50	0.54	151	6.57	98	12.12	56
Terry Steinbach	Runners On	.281	65	.431	56	.347	70	2.61	74	8.94	75	13.41	92
	Bases Empty	.253	88	.379	90	.324	71	2.53	74	7.76	82	10.50	41
Walt Weiss	Runners On	.272	82	.345	132	.302	131	0.49	143	3.86	167	8.58	31
	Bases Empty	.232	127	.301	139	.320	75	0.81	137	9.35	54	12.95	64
Team Average	Runners On	.283	4	.440	1	.351	3	3.25	1	8.99	8	13.65	7
	Bases Empty	.248	10	.367	11	.324	3	2.42	9	9.23	2	15.32	9
League Average	Runners On	.268		.401		.336		2.45		9.09		13.68	
	Bases Empty	.253		.383		.315		2.48		7.76		14.81	

Overall Batting Compared to Late Inning Pressure Situations

		BA	Rank	SA	Rank	OBA	Rank	HR %	Rank	BB %	Rank	SO %	Rank	RDI %	Rank
Don Baylor	Overall	.220	149	.326	137	.332	65	2.65	71	10.86	42	14.06	87	.329	22
	Pressure	.200	128	.289	127	.357	49	2.22	69	12.50	28	10.71	40	.167	114
Jose Canseco	Overall	.307	12	.569	1	.391	8	6.89	4	11.06	37	18.16	132	.300	44
	Pressure	.258	81	.461	40	.340	70	5.62	18	10.00	57	17.00	95	.333	39
Mike Gallego	Overall	.209	163	.260	168	.298	129	0.72	144	10.63	44	16.56	117	.266	88
	Pressure	.143	165	.214	148	.226	156	0.00	110	9.38	67	12.50	56	.000	--
Ron Hassey	Overall	.257	86	.368	101	.323	82	2.17	86	8.22	85	11.51	54	.348	11
	Pressure	.288	50	.404	63	.333	75	1.92	78	6.90	106	15.52	83	.474	7
Dave Henderson	Overall	.304	18	.525	10	.363	30	4.73	23	8.25	83	16.14	110	.341	14
	Pressure	.302	44	.476	31	.378	30	4.76	25	12.16	34	14.86	79	.208	93
Glenn Hubbard	Overall	.255	91	.340	125	.334	60	1.02	129	9.65	56	14.62	97	.229	133
	Pressure	.227	111	.227	146	.277	125	0.00	110	4.00	147	12.00	52	.077	161
Stan Javier	Overall	.257	87	.320	144	.313	97	0.50	152	7.27	98	14.32	91	.270	84
	Pressure	.265	75	.338	99	.351	57	0.00	110	11.69	42	18.18	103	.375	27
Doug Jennings	Overall	.208	--	.297	--	.346	--	0.99	--	16.41	--	21.88	--	.333	--
	Pressure	.154	161	.192	158	.273	129	0.00	110	9.09	71	21.21	119	.400	20
Carney Lansford	Overall	.279	44	.360	110	.327	75	1.26	114	5.77	127	5.77	8	.309	34
	Pressure	.267	73	.347	91	.345	65	1.33	99	9.20	69	2.30	1	.100	149
Mark McGwire	Overall	.260	81	.478	21	.352	42	5.82	8	11.97	23	18.43	136	.307	38
	Pressure	.241	97	.494	23	.312	91	8.43	5	8.51	82	17.02	96	.333	39
Dave Parker	Overall	.257	85	.406	70	.314	95	3.18	58	7.79	89	17.03	123	.250	104
	Pressure	.268	71	.411	60	.305	102	1.79	79	5.08	135	13.56	65	.118	145
Tony Phillips	Overall	.203	168	.307	152	.320	90	0.94	135	14.34	8	19.92	143	.140	170
	Pressure	.088	172	.088	173	.184	168	0.00	110	10.53	51	28.95	157	.167	--
Luis Polonia	Overall	.292	32	.378	93	.338	56	0.69	145	6.71	109	12.78	71	.284	64
	Pressure	.342	13	.474	32	.359	46	2.63	58	2.44	162	14.63	74	.333	--
Terry Steinbach	Overall	.265	65	.402	74	.334	62	2.56	74	8.29	81	11.81	64	.318	26
	Pressure	.154	161	.192	158	.254	146	0.00	110	8.47	84	13.56	65	.273	63
Walt Weiss	Overall	.250	102	.321	143	.312	104	0.66	147	6.85	107	10.96	46	.215	148
	Pressure	.071	173	.107	172	.148	173	0.00	110	6.25	121	21.88	122	.000	165
Team Average	Overall	.263	4	.399	4	.336	3	2.78	2	9.13	4	14.57	8	.288	1
	Pressure	.228	13	.339	12	.305	11	2.44	6	8.58	8	15.02	2	.257	6
League Average	Overall	.259		.391		.324		2.47		8.35		14.31		.269	
	Pressure	.249		.365		.319		2.28		8.71		17.04		.246	

Additional Miscellaneous Batting Comparisons

	Grass Surface BA	Rank	Artificial Surface BA	Rank	Home Games BA	Rank	Road Games BA	Rank	Runners in Scoring Position BA	Rank	Runners in Scoring Pos and Two Outs BA	Rank	Leading Off Inning OBA	Rank	Runners on 3B with less than 2 Outs RDI %	Rank
Don Baylor	.220	144	.220	135	.200	158	.234	124	.293	42	.297	36	.288	115	.778	5
Jose Canseco	.300	21	.340	14	.313	15	.301	25	.297	36	.235	86	.375	19	.535	106
Mike Gallego	.193	168	.278	69	.218	151	.200	158	.269	73	.276	48	.360	30	.417	152
Ron Hassey	.252	92	.297	40	.253	96	.262	77	.260	86	.250	61	.319	75	.667	33
Dave Henderson	.305	15	.298	39	.293	35	.314	9	.317	22	.371	6	.410	7	.600	65
Glenn Hubbard	.260	77	.225	130	.267	76	.245	109	.256	96	.243	74	.289	111	.611	63
Stan Javier	.255	83	.266	87	.261	82	.253	89	.245	104	.200	126	.321	70	.467	137
Doug Jennings	.179	--	.353	--	.140	--	.275	--	.233	--	.250	--	.462	--	.556	89
Carney Lansford	.277	48	.292	49	.245	108	.312	12	.328	18	.313	22	.367	26	.692	23
Mark McGwire	.254	85	.291	50	.246	107	.272	54	.340	12	.214	110	.303	92	.682	29
Dave Parker	.263	67	.233	122	.271	69	.245	111	.241	107	.200	126	.316	77	.619	60
Tony Phillips	.200	162	.216	137	.217	152	.189	165	.216	144	.389	2	.378	16	.333	169
Luis Polonia	.281	41	.359	9	.322	9	.257	87	.305	29	.286	43	.349	40	.611	63
Terry Steinbach	.268	57	.250	101	.287	40	.244	114	.256	93	.244	72	.345	43	.565	85
Walt Weiss	.245	103	.273	77	.237	122	.261	79	.235	120	.224	99	.337	55	.517	114
Team Average	.260	6	.279	3	.261	8	.265	4	.281	3	.264	1	.343	2	.581	5
League Average	.256		.267		.262		.257		.262		.239		.311		.570	

Pitching vs. Left and Right Handed Batters

		BA	Rank	SA	Rank	OBA	Rank	HR %	Rank	BB %	Rank	SO %	Rank
Todd Burns	vs. Lefties	.244	49	.364	53	.313	39	2.30	72	8.75	63	13.33	58
	vs. Righties	.237	38	.331	26	.290	31	1.78	28	7.03	52	13.51	76
Greg Cadaret	vs. Lefties	.198	7	.217	3	.309	38	0.00	1	12.80	117	18.40	19
	vs. Righties	.244	45	.325	19	.322	72	1.25	13	10.75	114	22.04	17
Storm Davis	vs. Lefties	.263	70	.348	44	.336	79	1.01	20	10.44	91	15.56	43
	vs. Righties	.287	112	.442	110	.362	121	3.22	96	10.43	108	13.51	77
Dennis Eckersley	vs. Lefties	.198	8	.286	11	.229	5	2.38	74	3.82	2	19.85	12
	vs. Righties	.197	8	.255	1	.231	3	1.46	21	4.05	7	29.73	2
Rick Honeycutt	vs. Lefties	.227	28	.371	61	.282	14	3.09	104	6.31	26	18.92	16
	vs. Righties	.265	81	.378	60	.327	80	1.53	23	8.22	75	11.87	101
Gene Nelson	vs. Lefties	.232	35	.339	36	.314	45	2.38	74	10.47	93	10.99	82
	vs. Righties	.225	30	.342	36	.282	27	2.08	44	6.79	48	17.36	43
Steve Ontiveros	vs. Lefties	.276	86	.414	90	.359	105	1.72	48	11.28	106	12.03	73
	vs. Righties	.253	--	.343	--	.295	--	2.02	--	5.56	--	12.96	--
Eric Plunk	vs. Lefties	.205	12	.279	10	.305	33	0.82	17	12.59	115	25.17	5
	vs. Righties	.226	31	.348	41	.316	59	3.05	93	11.17	117	22.87	12
Dave Stewart	vs. Lefties	.224	27	.323	29	.305	34	1.60	46	10.49	94	17.37	27
	vs. Righties	.246	48	.345	40	.310	48	1.08	9	8.32	77	15.67	53
Bob Welch	vs. Lefties	.248	51	.386	76	.318	49	2.61	88	9.30	74	14.34	49
	vs. Righties	.265	80	.381	64	.324	74	2.16	47	6.37	40	16.22	49
Curt Young	vs. Lefties	.258	59	.392	79	.287	18	3.09	104	2.94	1	6.86	121
	vs. Righties	.278	100	.443	111	.342	97	4.07	118	8.56	81	11.29	108
Team Average	vs. Lefties	.237	1	.342	1	.311	3	1.83	3	9.60	10	15.67	2
	vs. Righties	.255	8	.374	2	.320	8	2.29	3	8.21	10	15.75	3
League Average	vs. Lefties	.262		.387		.331		2.24		9.12		13.21	
	vs. Righties	.258		.393		.320		2.63		7.80		15.09	

Pitching with Runners on Base and Bases Empty

		BA	Rank	SA	Rank	OBA	Rank	HR %	Rank	BB %	Rank	SO %	Rank
Todd Burns	Runners On	.196	4	.310	10	.254	1	1.90	43	6.86	26	14.29	56
	Bases Empty	.272	97	.377	64	.336	98	2.19	59	8.80	83	12.80	80
Greg Cadaret	Runners On	.225	15	.297	4	.313	42	1.45	26	11.52	106	19.39	19
	Bases Empty	.227	29	.266	6	.322	77	0.00	1	11.64	120	21.92	11
Storm Davis	Runners On	.249	51	.372	52	.340	80	2.46	71	12.47	116	13.25	67
	Bases Empty	.293	121	.410	94	.355	117	1.80	42	8.83	84	15.61	55
Dennis Eckersley	Runners On	.233	--	.359	--	.274	--	2.91	--	6.14	--	21.93	--
	Bases Empty	.175	1	.213	1	.200	1	1.25	17	2.42	2	27.27	3
Rick Honeycutt	Runners On	.221	13	.336	22	.282	13	1.34	23	7.51	36	16.18	36
	Bases Empty	.285	111	.417	99	.344	109	2.78	89	7.64	69	12.10	86
Gene Nelson	Runners On	.247	45	.322	16	.318	50	1.72	37	8.96	72	11.94	81
	Bases Empty	.214	19	.355	43	.278	18	2.56	83	7.84	71	16.86	41
Steve Ontiveros	Runners On	.247	--	.376	--	.333	--	2.15	--	10.91	--	11.82	--
	Bases Empty	.279	102	.385	73	.328	91	1.64	32	6.87	55	12.98	77
Eric Plunk	Runners On	.209	9	.326	20	.320	52	3.10	94	14.10	123	21.15	10
	Bases Empty	.223	26	.312	14	.303	48	1.27	19	9.71	101	26.29	4
Dave Stewart	Runners On	.239	35	.343	30	.315	44	1.62	30	10.22	97	15.43	40
	Bases Empty	.230	32	.326	20	.301	46	1.17	14	8.98	87	17.50	34
Bob Welch	Runners On	.236	26	.348	34	.328	64	2.56	74	11.11	103	16.08	37
	Bases Empty	.269	92	.406	90	.316	67	2.27	68	5.56	28	14.73	60
Curt Young	Runners On	.282	91	.421	87	.349	90	3.35	104	8.71	64	9.54	112
	Bases Empty	.271	95	.442	108	.324	81	4.21	117	7.07	61	11.22	102
Team Average	Runners On	.238	1	.349	1	.316	1	2.20	3	10.15	12	15.08	2
	Bases Empty	.254	7	.367	3	.315	7	2.00	3	7.83	7	16.20	3
League Average	Runners On	.268		.401		.336		2.45		9.09		13.68	
	Bases Empty	.253		.383		.315		2.48		7.76		14.81	

Overall Pitching Compared to Late Inning Pressure Situations

		BA	Rank	SA	Rank	OBA	Rank	HR %	Rank	BB %	Rank	SO %	Rank
Todd Burns	Overall	.241	37	.350	26	.303	27	2.07	47	8.00	59	13.41	70
	Pressure	.143	3	.167	3	.250	8	0.00	1	12.24	101	14.29	68
Greg Cadaret	Overall	.226	20	.282	3	.317	53	0.75	3	11.58	119	20.58	15
	Pressure	.225	38	.287	26	.306	49	0.78	27	10.07	80	22.82	12
Storm Davis	Overall	.274	97	.394	79	.349	109	2.08	50	10.44	107	14.56	56
	Pressure	.389	128	.630	128	.452	127	5.56	122	11.11	90	17.46	38
Dennis Eckersley	Overall	.198	2	.270	2	.230	1	1.90	34	3.94	2	25.09	3
	Pressure	.198	18	.271	21	.239	5	1.69	51	4.76	16	25.40	6
Rick Honeycutt	Overall	.253	55	.375	56	.312	44	2.05	44	7.58	48	14.24	59
	Pressure	.205	22	.362	57	.271	20	3.15	97	8.51	59	18.44	29
Gene Nelson	Overall	.228	22	.341	22	.296	19	2.21	64	8.33	68	14.69	55
	Pressure	.181	10	.260	12	.278	22	1.57	47	10.88	88	16.33	46
Eric Plunk	Overall	.217	12	.318	10	.311	43	2.10	52	11.78	120	23.87	5
	Pressure	.207	23	.293	28	.304	43	2.00	62	11.49	94	22.41	14
Dave Stewart	Overall	.234	30	.333	18	.307	36	1.36	10	9.52	94	16.61	36
	Pressure	.196	16	.271	20	.267	15	0.00	1	8.06	50	16.94	40
Bob Welch	Overall	.257	62	.384	65	.321	63	2.38	71	7.83	56	15.28	50
	Pressure	.262	81	.318	36	.307	50	0.93	29	5.17	18	12.93	84
Curt Young	Overall	.275	99	.435	111	.333	86	3.90	121	7.68	51	10.60	103
	Pressure	.220	33	.463	109	.304	44	7.32	129	10.87	87	4.35	127
Team Average	Overall	.247	2	.360	1	.316	3	2.08	2	8.84	11	15.71	3
	Pressure	.217	1	.313	1	.290	1	1.85	4	8.83	6	18.64	2
League Average	Overall	.259		.391		.324		2.47		8.35		14.31	
	Pressure	.249		.369		.324		2.26		9.33		15.69	

Additional Miscellaneous Pitching Comparisons

	Grass Surface		Artificial Surface		Home Games		Road Games		Runners in Scoring Position		Runners in Scoring Pos and Two Outs		Leading Off Inning	
	BA	Rank	BA	Rank	BA	Rank	BA	Rank	BA	Rank	BA	Rank	OBA	Rank
Todd Burns	.246	48	.195	--	.216	20	.280	94	.266	71	.242	--	.260	19
Greg Cadaret	.231	30	.195	--	.255	64	.186	4	.224	31	.261	88	.284	44
Storm Davis	.275	100	.271	65	.281	101	.268	79	.255	60	.247	77	.343	100
Dennis Eckersley	.198	3	.196	--	.182	3	.214	14	.268	--	.303	111	.167	1
Rick Honeycutt	.228	25	.344	124	.212	14	.278	90	.213	21	.227	60	.329	86
Gene Nelson	.213	13	.286	80	.212	13	.245	44	.281	84	.273	97	.275	39
Steve Ontiveros	.275	99	.227	--	.216	--	.299	112	.250	--	.308	--	.362	109
Eric Plunk	.209	9	.273	--	.222	27	.213	12	.178	6	.122	6	.268	29
Dave Stewart	.230	29	.249	41	.230	34	.237	34	.202	13	.174	27	.312	65
Bob Welch	.249	50	.330	116	.239	45	.283	97	.287	89	.296	107	.275	39
Curt Young	.273	96	.286	80	.300	119	.251	56	.290	95	.296	108	.287	46
Team Average	.243	3	.268	7	.241	2	.253	6	.244	1	.241	10	.297	3
League Average	.256		.267		.257		.262		.262		.239		.311	

SEATTLE MARINERS

● Can Alvin Davis learn from Cher?

● The "Homerdome" has moved west.

We don't usually think of Alvin Davis in the same context as Cher. (We don't usually think of *anyone* in the same context as Cher. Except maybe Jim McMahon.) But Alvin could learn a lesson from the way Cher campaigned for and won her Academy Award last year.

Davis and Bono Allman both faced the same obstacle—being in the right place at the wrong time. Cher might have won an Oscar sooner, for *Silkwood* or *Mask,* were it not for the fact that the 1980s have been a golden age for leading ladies. If Cher wasn't competing with Sally Field or Jane Fonda, then it was with Meryl Streep, or Glenn Close, or Kathleen Turner, or Jessica Lange. But even if she truly does think of herself as inhibited, Cher has a way of making people sit up and take notice. It ain't subtle, but it works.

Davis can't have his wardrobe designed by Bob Mackie, or be seen around town with an ex-bagel maker 10 years younger than himself. But if he wants to get the recognition he deserves, he'd better find *some* way to gain the public's attention. Because the 1980s are also the golden age of first basemen, especially in the American League.

Now Davis isn't the only A.L. first baseman of considerable talent to simply blend into the background over the past few years. Eddie Murray and Kent Hrbek have also been underexposed in the bright glare that's surrounded first Carew, then Mattingly, and now McGwire. But unlike Murray and Hrbek, Davis doesn't even have the consolation of knowing that the media recognizes his dilemma. Even as Murray spent year after year watching the start of the All-Star Game from either the clubhouse or his own house, stories about that inequity abounded. Davis, on the other hand, is simply ignored. For comparison's sake, here are the 1988 statistics for each A.L. team's regular first basemen:

Team	Player	AB	R	H	2B	3B	HR	RBI	BB	BA
Minn.	Kent Hrbek	510	75	159	31	0	25	76	67	.312
N.Y.	Don Mattingly	599	94	186	37	0	18	88	41	.311
K.C.	George Brett	589	90	180	42	3	24	103	82	.306
Cal.	Wally Joyner	597	81	176	31	2	13	85	55	.295
Sea.	Alvin Davis	478	67	141	24	1	18	69	95	.295
Bos.	Dwight Evans	559	96	164	31	7	21	111	76	.293
Balt.	Eddie Murray	603	75	171	27	2	28	84	75	.284
Tor.	Fred McGriff	536	100	151	35	4	34	82	79	.282
Tex.	Pete O'Brien	547	57	149	24	1	16	71	72	.272
Oak.	Mark McGwire	550	87	143	22	1	32	99	76	.260
Chi.	Greg Walker	377	45	93	22	1	8	42	29	.247
Clev.	Willie Upshaw	493	58	121	22	3	11	50	62	.245
Mil.	Greg Brock	364	53	77	16	1	6	50	63	.212
Det.	Darrell Evans	437	48	91	9	0	22	64	84	.208
	Averages	517	73	143	27	2	20	77	68	.277

By comparison to the league averages, Davis looks pretty good. He far exceeded the group batting average, and he led the group in walks. His extra-base hits were only slightly below the norm. He fell short in both runs and RBIs, but those totals are tied to team performance as well. When RBIs were judged in relation to the number of runners in scoring position, Davis ranked eighth among the 14 first basemen.

But as we said, American League first basemen are quite a select group. The following table shows the American League composite statistics of each game's starters for the past seven seasons, classified by starting position and expressed on a 162–game basis. First basemen led the league in batting average, runs scored, RBIs, and walks, and ranked second in extra-base hits. The differences in some categories might seem small. But remember that over more than 7000 games, even that lead of five RBIs represents nearly 500 runs batted in:

Pos.	AB	R	H	2B	3B	HR	RBI	BB	SB	BA	SA
1B	604	82	167	30	3	21	89	64	5	.277	.443
LF	605	85	165	28	5	19	80	57	19	.273	.431
3B	586	77	157	29	4	16	73	57	8	.268	.413
CF	619	89	165	27	6	16	70	58	25	.267	.406
RF	599	83	160	30	4	22	84	57	10	.266	.440
2B	591	76	155	26	4	8	56	54	16	.262	.360
SS	568	72	147	24	5	9	58	43	12	.260	.364
C	545	60	134	24	2	14	64	47	4	.246	.376

Davis's problem, as we see it, is simply one of context. For instance, if his performance were judged against the standards for another position, like shortstop, they'd look outrageous. Basically, in another place or another time, we might have judged Davis as favorably as we considered three other slugging first basemen of the past, each of whom at some point in his career had compiled career figures similar to Davis's current career totals. The years listed are the latest seasons included in each players stats:

Year	Player	AB	R	H	2B	3B	HR	RBI	BB	SO	BA
1952	Vic Wertz	2807	458	808	148	30	110	531	413	377	.288
1956	Joe Adcock	2977	389	840	151	21	125	469	220	361	.282
1962	Bill White	2813	408	818	143	40	91	406	252	374	.291
1988	Alvin Davis	2682	377	769	146	8	110	435	430	354	.287

The Davis dilemma doesn't show any signs of going away soon. In fact, the problem will probably get worse before it gets better, despite the exile of Eddie Murray to the National League. Each of the past three seasons has seen the emergence of a new, young potential All-Star: Joyner in 1986, followed by McGwire in 1987, and McGriff last year. George Brett and Dwight Evans have apparently decided to play out their remaining days at first base—and at a pretty high performance level.

Our advice to Alvin Davis? Try several rounds of plastic surgery, showing his navel, or calling Letterman an "asshole" on national television. You can't argue with success.

For the past several years, we've devoted a lot of energy to destroying the myth that Minnesota's Metrodome is among baseball's best home-run parks. A good hitters' park, yes. But the fact that Twins scores often resembled those of the Vikings had little to do with home runs. The Metrodome increases batting average, doubles, and triples to such a degree that those high scores merely perpetuated the misnomer, "Homerdome."

Over the past few years, we've added a Ballparks section to the *Analyst,* and expanded it to include a rating of each stadium based on how it increases or decreases things like scoring, home runs, and so forth. These tables were designed to demonstrate in black-and-white the differences between the parks, to put an end to speculation and misinformation. Among the most interesting trends we've uncovered has been the change in the character of Fenway Park as teams have deemphasized hitting balls *over* the Green Monster in favor of knocking doubles *against* it.

Nearly as dramatic has been the progressive increase in the home-run rate at the Kingdome.

Over the past five years, no American League ballpark has promoted home runs to the degree that the Kingdome has, increasing them by 34 percent over the rate at a hypothetical average stadium. Only one N.L. park, Wrigley Field, produced a higher rate of increase during that time (plus 46 percent). For a complete listing of the five-year figures, see page 426.

And over the past three years, the rate of increase at the Kingdome has soared to a rate more than double the increase at any other park in the majors with the exception of Cincinnati's Riverfront Stadium. To determine the rate of increase, the method is as follows: Find the home-run rate in all Mariners home games for both teams combined. Do the same for all Mariners road games. Then compare the two averages. Assuming that roughly the same set of players contributed to each figure, we'll treat the road-game average as a league standard and view the difference between the two marks as the effect of the home stadium.

The following table shows the home-run rates in Mariners home and road games for the past three seasons, expressed in terms of home runs per 100 at-bats:

Year	Mariners Home Games AB	HR	Rate	Mariners Road Games AB	HR	Rate	Diff.
1986	5703	196	3.44	5421	133	2.45	+40.1%
1987	5541	218	3.93	5500	142	2.58	+52.4%
1988	5485	178	3.25	5359	114	2.13	+52.6%
Totals	16729	592	3.54	16280	389	2.39	+48.1%

The figures show that the Mariners and their opponents hit 2.39 home runs per 100 at-bats (or one per 42 AB) in road games, at a cross-section of A.L. parks that we'll use as a yardstick against which to measure the corresponding figures at the Kingdome. In Mariners home games, the same teams hit home runs at a rate nearly 50 percent higher (one home run per 28 at-bats). Only seven other stadiums produced an increase of more than 10 percent during those three seasons. They are listed below, with the rate of increase based on home-run percentages (although the raw home-run totals, not those averages, are displayed). Notice not only that the Kingdome tops the list, but also the margin by which it leads:

Stadium	Home	Road	Increase
Kingdome	592	389	48.1%
Riverfront Stadium	494	391	25.1%
Wrigley Field	501	393	23.8%
Atlanta Stadium	430	344	22.1%
Jack Murphy Stadium	427	353	21.9%
Memorial Stadium	571	502	14.8%
Tiger Stadium	564	515	12.3%
Anaheim Stadium	505	458	11.4%

One thing to note about stadium trends: On a year-to-year basis, there's a considerable amount of fluctuation, not because ballparks have good and bad years (or so we assume), but because 81 games simply aren't enough to even out the rough edges in the methodology. That's why in the Ballparks section we base our rates of increase and decrease on five-year figures. The changes that occur in those lists are either subtle, or due to changes in the playing surfaces or configurations of the stadiums over time.

Since there haven't been any such changes at the Kingdome over the past three years, we're left to speculate as to whether this three-year home-run explosion in Seattle is nothing more than the law of averages gone haywire. Regardless, it's clear that there is, in fact, a Homerdome after all. Not in Minneapolis, but Seattle.

WON-LOST RECORD BY STARTING POSITION

SEATTLE 68-93	C	1B	2B	3B	SS	LF	CF	RF	P	DH	Leadoff	Relief	Starts
Steve Balboni	·	14-25	·	·	·	·	·	·	·	28-22	·	·	42-47
Scott Bankhead	·	·	·	·	·	·	·	·	10-11	·	·	·	10-11
Scott Bradley	34-46	·	1-1	·	·	·	·	3-1	·	·	·	·	38-48
Mickey Brantley	·	·	·	·	·	38-56	21-24	3-0	·	·	·	17-18	62-80
Greg Briley	·	·	·	·	·	5-5	·	·	·	·	·	·	5-5
Jay Buhner	·	·	·	·	·	0-1	0-2	24-30	·	·	·	·	24-33
Mike Campbell	·	·	·	·	·	·	·	·	8-12	·	·	·	8-12
Darnell Coles	·	·	·	·	·	20-23	·	1-3	·	1-6	·	·	22-32
Henry Cotto	·	·	·	·	·	·	42-53	·	·	·	20-20	·	42-53
Alvin Davis	·	50-64	·	·	·	·	·	·	·	9-15	·	·	59-79
Mario Diaz	·	·	0-1	0-1	10-8	·	·	·	·	·	·	·	10-10
Bruce Fields	·	·	·	·	·	4-4	0-1	2-3	·	·	2-3	·	6-8
Erik Hanson	·	·	·	·	·	·	·	·	2-4	·	·	·	2-4
Dave Hengel	·	·	·	·	·	0-1	·	2-5	3-4	·	·	·	5-10
Mike Jackson	·	·	·	·	·	·	·	·	·	·	·	28-34	·
Mike Kingery	·	0-1	·	·	·	1-3	5-13	6-4	·	·	4-9	·	12-21
Mark Langston	·	·	·	·	·	·	·	·	20-15	·	·	·	20-15
Edgar Martinez	·	·	·	3-5	·	·	·	·	·	·	1-2	·	3-5
Bill McGuire	1-4	·	·	·	·	·	·	·	·	·	·	·	1-4
Mike Moore	·	·	·	·	·	·	·	·	10-22	·	·	3-2	10-22
Edwin Nunez	·	·	·	·	·	·	·	·	0-3	·	·	2-9	0-3
Ken Phelps	·	2-1	·	·	·	·	·	·	·	16-39	·	·	18-40
Dennis Powell	·	·	·	·	·	·	·	·	1-1	·	·	2-8	1-1
Jim Presley	·	·	·	63-82	·	·	·	·	·	1-3	·	·	64-85
Rey Quinones	·	·	·	·	55-79	·	·	·	·	2-2	·	·	57-81
Johnny Rabb	·	·	·	·	·	·	·	1-0	0-1	·	·	·	1-1
Jerry Reed	·	·	·	·	·	·	·	·	·	·	·	8-38	·
Rich Renteria	·	·	2-1	1-4	3-6	·	·	·	4-1	·	2-1	·	10-12
Harold Reynolds	·	·	66-91	·	·	·	·	·	·	·	22-40	·	66-91
Mike Schooler	·	·	·	·	·	·	·	·	·	·	·	25-15	·
Rod Scurry	·	·	·	·	·	·	·	·	·	·	·	7-32	1-2
Brick Smith	·	1-2	·	·	·	·	·	·	·	·	·	5-12	·
Julio Solano	·	·	·	·	·	·	·	·	·	·	·	6-8	·
Bill Swift	·	·	·	·	·	·	·	·	9-15	·	·	·	9-15
Terry Taylor	·	·	·	·	·	·	·	·	2-3	·	·	·	2-3
Steve Trout	·	·	·	·	·	·	·	·	6-7	·	·	0-2	6-7
Dave Valle	33-43	1-0	·	·	·	·	·	·	·	3-0	·	·	37-43
Gene Walter	·	·	·	·	·	·	·	·	·	·	·	3-13	·
Bill Wilkinson	·	·	·	·	·	·	·	·	·	·	·	12-18	·
Glenn Wilson	·	·	·	·	·	·	·	26-47	·	1-0	·	·	27-47

Batting vs. Left and Right Handed Pitchers

		BA	Rank	SA	Rank	OBA	Rank	HR %	Rank	BB %	Rank	SO %	Rank
Steve Balboni	vs. Lefties	.201	154	.366	93	.243	160	3.66	44	5.20	119	23.12	153
	vs. Righties	.257	88	.502	15	.300	126	6.83	5	5.62	129	17.60	124
Scott Bradley	vs. Lefties	.152	--	.174	--	.152	--	0.00	--	0.00	--	8.33	--
	vs. Righties	.273	54	.377	91	.316	102	1.38	110	5.47	132	3.86	2
Mickey Brantley	vs. Lefties	.206	150	.329	114	.244	157	1.76	95	5.00	122	7.22	16
	vs. Righties	.287	38	.428	53	.317	100	2.95	66	3.92	162	11.75	57
Jay Buhner	vs. Lefties	.169	165	.326	119	.208	166	4.49	30	4.17	136	32.29	167
	vs. Righties	.238	125	.471	27	.347	52	5.23	17	11.82	28	30.54	167
Darnell Coles	vs. Lefties	.328	16	.638	3	.418	14	8.62	3	11.94	29	8.96	41
	vs. Righties	.277	48	.453	35	.329	80	3.65	40	5.84	125	12.99	75
Henry Cotto	vs. Lefties	.277	56	.412	61	.306	96	2.70	64	3.80	145	13.29	78
	vs. Righties	.248	107	.349	118	.300	127	1.68	97	6.54	114	12.31	65
Alvin Davis	vs. Lefties	.321	19	.496	28	.428	9	2.19	78	15.06	13	10.84	59
	vs. Righties	.284	41	.449	37	.406	4	4.40	25	16.83	3	8.41	21
Mike Kingery	vs. Lefties	.000	--	.000	--	.400	--	0.00	--	40.00	--	20.00	--
	vs. Righties	.208	157	.283	159	.309	111	0.83	133	12.06	26	15.60	105
Jim Presley	vs. Lefties	.232	125	.323	122	.278	131	1.22	113	6.25	93	14.77	94
	vs. Righties	.229	135	.368	102	.281	143	3.16	57	6.01	123	21.15	148
Rey Quinones	vs. Lefties	.260	74	.493	30	.282	126	4.00	36	2.56	143	16.03	108
	vs. Righties	.244	114	.350	117	.285	139	1.72	94	5.08	143	12.30	64
Harold Reynolds	vs. Lefties	.314	26	.411	62	.340	51	1.08	120	4.12	138	5.67	12
	vs. Righties	.269	63	.370	100	.340	63	0.48	151	9.17	70	8.53	22
Dave Valle	vs. Lefties	.264	72	.416	60	.316	83	3.20	53	6.62	90		
	vs. Righties	.206	159	.388	82	.279	145	3.64	42	4.84	148	13.98	87
Glenn Wilson	vs. Lefties	.317	23	.396	72	.340	52	0.99	123	3.74	147	14.02	88
	vs. Righties	.213	155	.284	158	.256	162	1.09	119	5.64	128	18.97	138
Team Average	vs. Lefties	.255	9	.397	7	.300	13	2.50	6	5.88	14	13.16	4
	vs. Righties	.258	8	.399	5	.325	8	2.82	4	8.40	8	13.04	2
League Average	vs. Lefties	.259		.391		.321		2.47		7.97		14.12	
	vs. Righties	.259		.391		.326		2.47		8.51		14.39	

Batting with Runners on Base and Bases Empty

		BA	Rank	SA	Rank	OBA	Rank	HR %	Rank	BB %	Rank	SO %	Rank
Steve Balboni	Runners On	.246	117	.482	24	.290	137	6.03	6	5.61	136	16.36	121
	Bases Empty	.224	132	.416	54	.265	152	5.14	19	5.31	131	23.01	152
Scott Bradley	Runners On	.266	95	.367	114	.307	125	1.44	99	5.23	145	4.58	5
	Bases Empty	.250	90	.337	121	.286	132	1.02	130	4.37	150	4.37	3
Mickey Brantley	Runners On	.269	89	.423	63	.297	136	2.56	78	4.33	158	11.02	56
	Bases Empty	.259	72	.382	87	.294	111	2.62	70	4.17	153	10.00	33
Jay Buhner	Runners On	.228	142	.439	52	.305	128	5.26	12	8.33	83	31.06	168
	Bases Empty	.204	154	.408	62	.299	105	4.76	24	10.18	37	31.14	169
Darnell Coles	Runners On	.275	74	.463	33	.322	103	3.75	42	6.52	120	9.78	46
	Bases Empty	.304	13	.539	10	.380	12	6.09	12	8.53	70	13.18	70
Henry Cotto	Runners On	.267	92	.390	93	.317	112	2.74	67	6.67	116	12.73	79
	Bases Empty	.254	86	.363	99	.292	115	1.67	102	4.74	146	12.65	59
Alvin Davis	Runners On	.304	36	.435	55	.425	6	2.80	65	17.54	6	5.97	14
	Bases Empty	.288	30	.485	21	.401	5	4.55	28	15.29	5	11.78	54
Jim Presley	Runners On	.224	146	.353	124	.286	143	3.02	60	7.63	97	18.32	140
	Bases Empty	.234	120	.356	108	.276	143	2.24	83	4.85	141	20.00	142
Rey Quinones	Runners On	.255	107	.382	100	.289	138	0.98	128	4.55	154	11.36	59
	Bases Empty	.244	106	.400	69	.281	136	3.39	48	4.19	152	14.84	88
Harold Reynolds	Runners On	.313	23	.421	64	.355	57	0.93	133	6.22	126	7.47	22
	Bases Empty	.266	62	.362	101	.332	59	0.52	152	8.53	69	7.82	16
Dave Valle	Runners On	.298	42	.548	7	.350	64	4.03	35	4.29	160	10.00	49
	Bases Empty	.181	164	.289	144	.253	162	3.01	59	6.59	97	13.19	71
Glenn Wilson	Runners On	.176	166	.259	163	.216	170	1.85	92	5.13	147	20.51	154
	Bases Empty	.295	23	.364	97	.330	61	0.57	149	4.86	140	15.14	95
Team Average	Runners On	.262	10	.410	6	.323	11	2.79	3	8.19	12	12.21	3
	Bases Empty	.254	6	.390	4	.313	8	2.67	4	7.26	10	13.72	3
League Average	Runners On	.268		.401		.336		2.45		9.09		13.68	
	Bases Empty	.253		.383		.315		2.48		7.76		14.81	

Overall Batting Compared to Late Inning Pressure Situations

		BA	Rank	SA	Rank	OBA	Rank	HR %	Rank	BB %	Rank	SO %	Rank	RDI %	Rank
Steve Balboni	Overall	.235	130	.448	32	.277	154	5.57	10	5.45	137	19.77	142	.246	111
	Pressure	.228	110	.456	43	.290	118	7.02	10	8.06	89	24.19	140	.125	138
Scott Bradley	Overall	.257	88	.349	119	.295	134	1.19	116	4.74	155	4.46	2	.271	83
	Pressure	.250	87	.500	21	.333	75	5.00	23	8.70	79	6.52	12	.273	63
Mickey Brantley	Overall	.263	70	.399	79	.296	133	2.60	72	4.23	160	10.42	41	.205	156
	Pressure	.342	13	.539	13	.375	33	3.95	40	4.94	138	8.64	26	.273	63
Jay Buhner	Overall	.215	158	.421	56	.302	120	4.98	20	9.36	58	31.10	168	.271	80
	Pressure	.093	171	.163	166	.152	172	2.33	66	6.52	115	41.30	173	.091	154
Darnell Coles	Overall	.292	31	.508	14	.356	34	5.13	16	7.69	90	11.76	62	.279	71
	Pressure	.217	--	.348	--	.308	--	4.35	--	10.71	--	25.00	--	.250	--
Henry Cotto	Overall	.259	83	.373	96	.302	121	2.07	93	5.50	134	12.68	70	.216	146
	Pressure	.122	168	.146	168	.200	164	0.00	110	8.70	79	17.39	97	.133	136
Alvin Davis	Overall	.295	24	.462	29	.412	3	3.77	36	16.32	4	9.11	28	.292	52
	Pressure	.317	31	.556	11	.463	3	4.76	25	20.00	3	5.00	7	.158	122
Dave Hengel	Overall	.167	--	.283	--	.177	--	3.33	--	1.61	--	24.19	--	.143	--
	Pressure	.250	--	.583	--	.250	--	8.33	--	0.00	--	25.00	--	.125	138
Jim Presley	Overall	.230	138	.355	114	.280	152	2.57	73	6.08	124	19.26	140	.239	119
	Pressure	.238	100	.338	102	.282	122	2.50	62	5.75	130	20.69	117	.167	114
Rey Quinones	Overall	.248	108	.393	84	.284	150	2.40	77	4.34	157	13.40	77	.264	91
	Pressure	.236	104	.417	57	.295	115	4.17	36	6.41	117	15.38	82	.143	128
Harold Reynolds	Overall	.283	38	.383	90	.340	54	0.67	146	7.69	90	7.69	15	.255	98
	Pressure	.276	63	.329	105	.321	86	0.00	110	6.10	124	10.98	41	.235	80
Dave Valle	Overall	.231	133	.400	76	.295	136	3.45	48	5.59	132	11.80	63	.310	32
	Pressure	.302	43	.442	48	.362	44	2.33	66	4.17	145	22.92	132	.438	13
Glenn Wilson	Overall	.250	102	.324	139	.286	148	1.06	126	4.97	152	17.22	127	.143	168
	Pressure	.190	137	.190	161	.222	158	0.00	110	4.35	143	23.91	138	.118	145
Team Average	Overall	.257	9	.398	5	.317	10	2.72	4	7.66	10	13.08	2	.249	12
	Pressure	.248	8	.396	3	.316	9	3.27	3	8.30	11	16.48	6	.210	12
League Average	Overall	.259		.391		.324		2.47		8.35		14.31		.269	
	Pressure	.249		.365		.319		2.28		8.71		17.04		.246	

Additional Miscellaneous Batting Comparisons

	Grass Surface BA	Rank	Artificial Surface BA	Rank	Home Games BA	Rank	Road Games BA	Rank	Runners in Scoring Position BA	Rank	Runners in Scoring Pos and Two Outs BA	Rank	Leading Off Inning OBA	Rank	Runners on 3B with less than 2 Outs RDI %	Rank
Steve Balboni	.221	143	.243	111	.237	121	.232	127	.264	79	.235	86	.221	160	.391	160
Scott Bradley	.263	67	.252	100	.247	103	.267	64	.275	63	.250	61	.280	124	.600	65
Mickey Brantley	.261	74	.265	88	.279	59	.249	100	.261	84	.220	104	.253	146	.484	128
Jay Buhner	.235	121	.188	157	.214	155	.215	143	.236	113	.115	165	.315	78	.600	65
Darnell Coles	.253	--	.317	24	.301	22	.283	41	.255	99	.261	59	.270	--	.667	33
Henry Cotto	.309	12	.228	126	.255	94	.263	74	.217	142	.205	122	.336	56	.556	89
Alvin Davis	.302	20	.290	52	.294	32	.296	28	.290	49	.288	42	.370	24	.542	102
Mario Diaz	.423	--	.239	116	.211	--	.412	--	.412	--	.500	--	.389	--	.667	--
Dave Hengel	.050	--	.225	130	.219	--	.107	--	.118	--	.000	--	.111	--	.500	--
Mike Kingery	.216	--	.194	154	.194	--	.213	--	.182	--	.222	--	.447	--	.375	--
Jim Presley	.221	142	.236	119	.245	109	.215	144	.235	116	.203	123	.260	142	.613	62
Rey Quinones	.261	73	.240	114	.251	98	.246	108	.288	51	.234	89	.280	125	.538	104
Rich Renteria	.323	--	.140	171	.143	--	.313	--	.190	--	.222	--	.238	--	.500	--
Harold Reynolds	.261	72	.297	42	.286	41	.279	47	.297	37	.314	21	.314	81	.625	58
Dave Valle	.196	--	.250	101	.241	113	.221	139	.350	6	.447	1	.270	133	.370	166
Glenn Wilson	.214	154	.275	73	.273	65	.230	131	.134	170	.138	162	.346	42	.389	162
Team Average	.261	5	.255	13	.257	10	.257	7	.260	8	.244	8	.309	7	.525	14
League Average	.256		.267		.262		.257		.262		.239		.311		.570	

Pitching vs. Left and Right Handed Batters

		BA	Rank	SA	Rank	OBA	Rank	HR %	Rank	BB %	Rank	SO %	Rank
Scott Bankhead	vs. Lefties	.258	61	.389	77	.330	69	0.82	17	9.59	79	17.34	28
	vs. Righties	.193	5	.319	18	.229	2	2.22	52	4.20	9	19.23	30
Mike Campbell	vs. Lefties	.257	58	.419	97	.335	77	3.73	119	10.66	96	12.13	71
	vs. Righties	.306	121	.532	126	.343	103	4.17	119	5.96	34	12.77	89
Mike Jackson	vs. Lefties	.258	60	.421	98	.340	87	3.14	107	11.64	108	8.47	111
	vs. Righties	.169	2	.272	4	.249	5	2.56	65	9.42	98	26.91	5
Mark Langston	vs. Lefties	.201	10	.286	11	.271	11	1.30	30	8.14	52	20.35	11
	vs. Righties	.239	40	.409	81	.320	70	3.75	111	10.60	112	22.08	16
Mike Moore	vs. Lefties	.233	37	.357	49	.292	21	2.43	79	7.43	42	18.22	20
	vs. Righties	.229	34	.371	53	.279	20	3.40	102	6.05	36	22.11	15
Jerry Reed	vs. Lefties	.355	128	.537	126	.437	126	3.31	112	13.19	119	6.25	126
	vs. Righties	.196	6	.302	12	.252	7	2.01	38	6.39	41	17.81	39
Mike Schooler	vs. Lefties	.282	96	.408	85	.374	113	2.91	100	13.82	123	26.83	3
	vs. Righties	.198	--	.247	--	.270	--	1.23	--	7.69	--	23.08	--
Bill Swift	vs. Lefties	.307	113	.410	87	.371	111	1.51	42	8.92	65	3.51	130
	vs. Righties	.283	106	.376	57	.353	114	1.46	19	8.27	76	8.79	121
Steve Trout	vs. Lefties	.244	--	.317	--	.380	--	0.00	--	12.00	--	14.00	--
	vs. Righties	.386	129	.584	129	.454	129	3.05	92	10.96	115	3.07	129
Team Average	vs. Lefties	.266	8	.398	8	.343	11	2.29	9	10.17	13	13.88	5
	vs. Righties	.249	4	.397	9	.315	4	2.93	12	8.42	12	17.75	2
League Average	vs. Lefties	.262		.387		.331		2.24		9.12		13.21	
	vs. Righties	.258		.393		.320		2.63		7.80		15.09	

Pitching with Runners on Base and Bases Empty

		BA	Rank	SA	Rank	OBA	Rank	HR %	Rank	BB %	Rank	SO %	Rank
Scott Bankhead	Runners On	.244	41	.381	61	.309	37	1.52	31	8.64	62	20.00	17
	Bases Empty	.211	18	.334	26	.258	8	1.58	29	5.64	30	17.21	38
Mike Campbell	Runners On	.300	107	.480	117	.356	98	4.00	117	8.81	66	9.69	110
	Bases Empty	.265	84	.467	121	.325	83	3.89	111	8.21	77	14.64	62
Mike Jackson	Runners On	.179	2	.310	9	.265	2	3.26	99	11.26	105	18.02	22
	Bases Empty	.241	46	.371	58	.321	76	2.35	74	9.47	98	18.95	27
Mark Langston	Runners On	.226		.391	69	.288	15	2.79	82	7.96	52	23.63	4
	Bases Empty	.237	40	.388	77	.327	86	3.69	107	11.54	119	20.71	17
Mike Moore	Runners On	.252	53	.429	92	.320	51	3.74	112	9.37	80	15.41	41
	Bases Empty	.221	23	.328	21	.267	11	2.36	75	5.45	27	22.32	8
Jerry Reed	Runners On	.272	77	.408	77	.360	101	2.72	79	11.80	111	14.61	50
	Bases Empty	.243	50	.376	61	.292	30	2.31	69	6.49	47	11.89	90
Bill Swift	Runners On	.327	123	.448	103	.392	122	1.63	34	8.88	68	4.87	128
	Bases Empty	.268	91	.347	36	.337	100	1.36	21	8.33	78	7.35	126
Steve Trout	Runners On	.371	129	.483	118	.461	129	0.00	1	12.68	117	4.93	127
	Bases Empty	.352	129	.590	129	.419	128	4.92	126	9.56	100	5.15	129
Team Average	Runners On	.271	10	.420	13	.348	11	2.66	11	10.37	13	14.77	3
	Bases Empty	.245	3	.381	8	.311	5	2.67	11	8.21	10	17.15	2
League Average	Runners On	.268		.401		.336		2.45		9.09		13.68	
	Bases Empty	.253		.383		.315		2.48		7.76		14.81	

Overall Pitching Compared to Late Inning Pressure Situations

		BA	Rank	SA	Rank	OBA	Rank	HR %	Rank	BB %	Rank	SO %	Rank
Scott Bankhead	Overall	.224	18	.352	28	.278	8	1.56	17	6.82	30	18.31	26
	Pressure	.371	125	.571	125	.450	126	2.86	88	12.20	99	9.76	109
Mike Campbell	Overall	.280	106	.473	122	.339	94	3.94	123	8.48	74	12.43	82
	Pressure	.125	--	.250	--	.125	--	4.17	--	0.00	--	16.67	--
Mike Jackson	Overall	.209	8	.339	21	.291	14	2.82	89	10.44	108	18.45	25
	Pressure	.209	25	.350	51	.298	37	3.39	98	11.11	90	18.36	31
Mark Langston	Overall	.233	27	.389	72	.313	45	3.35	110	10.20	102	21.80	9
	Pressure	.263	82	.429	95	.318	60	4.49	115	7.65	44	23.53	10
Mike Moore	Overall	.232	26	.363	40	.286	12	2.84	91	6.86	31	19.83	18
	Pressure	.236	53	.382	73	.282	26	4.07	108	4.58	14	11.45	99
Jerry Reed	Overall	.256	58	.391	76	.325	73	2.50	74	9.09	87	13.22	72
	Pressure	.239	57	.388	78	.338	75	4.48	113	11.39	93	12.66	87
Mike Schooler	Overall	.245	--	.337	--	.330	--	2.17	--	11.21	--	25.23	--
	Pressure	.301	110	.421	92	.392	117	3.01	90	13.13	109	20.00	22
Bill Swift	Overall	.295	120	.393	78	.362	119	1.48	14	8.59	78	6.21	127
	Pressure	.250	67	.442	100	.304	42	5.77	124	6.90	30	5.17	125
Steve Trout	Overall	.361	129	.538	129	.440	129	2.52	76	11.15	117	5.04	129
	Pressure	.000	--	.000	--	.000	--	0.00	--	0.00	--	0.00	--
Bill Wilkinson	Overall	.233	--	.367	--	.316	--	2.50	--	11.03	--	18.38	--
	Pressure	.344	121	.469	111	.436	125	3.13	95	15.38	118	15.38	53
Team Average	Overall	.256	6	.398	9	.327	9	2.66	10	9.16	13	16.10	2
	Pressure	.257	10	.411	13	.334	9	3.93	14	10.06	10	16.11	4
League Average	Overall	.259		.391		.324		2.47		8.35		14.31	
	Pressure	.249		.369		.324		2.26		9.33		15.69	

Additional Miscellaneous Pitching Comparisons

	Grass Surface		Artificial Surface		Home Games		Road Games		Runners in Scoring Position		Runners in Scoring Pos and Two Outs		Leading Off Inning	
	BA	Rank	BA	Rank	BA	Rank	BA	Rank	BA	Rank	BA	Rank	OBA	Rank
Scott Bankhead	.197	2	.245	37	.241	48	.209	8	.243	49	.176	28	.259	18
Mike Campbell	.287	116	.276	73	.278	98	.282	96	.254	59	.241	70	.364	110
Erik Hanson	.120	--	.252	47	.250	--	.208	--	.290	--	.250	--	.233	--
Mike Jackson	.203	5	.214	14	.218	24	.201	6	.181	7	.190	36	.338	92
Mark Langston	.230	27	.235	27	.231	36	.234	31	.227	33	.129	7	.298	51
Mike Moore	.243	47	.222	17	.202	8	.254	63	.292	99	.264	91	.273	34
Edwin Nunez	.407	--	.354	126	.359	--	.378	--	.333	--	.250	--	.452	--
Dennis Powell	.393	--	.346	125	.349	--	.378	--	.344	--	.143	--	.722	--
Jerry Reed	.241	--	.264	58	.272	88	.235	32	.312	117	.286	103	.301	55
Mike Schooler	.250	--	.239	31	.241	--	.248	49	.290	96	.294	106	.333	--
Rod Scurry	.321	--	.240	33	.241	--	.297	--	.250	--	.208	--	.393	--
Julio Solano	.214	--	.296	102	.304	--	.222	--	.217	--	.375	--	.300	--
Bill Swift	.316	128	.287	84	.279	99	.311	121	.305	114	.312	113	.318	74
Terry Taylor	.167	--	.344	122	.344	--	.167	--	.357	--	.250	--	.333	--
Steve Trout	.344	--	.372	128	.372	129	.344	--	.325	121	.231	--	.508	130
Gene Walter	.040	--	.278	74	.278	--	.040	--	.297	--	.235	--	.217	--
Bill Wilkinson	.133	--	.293	97	.292	--	.146	--	.167	--	.200	--	.250	--
Team Average	.245	5	.263	5	.260	7	.252	3	.268	10	.231	5	.318	10
League Average	.256		.267		.257		.262		.262		.239		.311	

TEXAS RANGERS

- Can the addition of baseball's all-time walk leader tame baseball's wildest pitching staff?
- How can a team lead its league in most strike-outs but fewest homers?

	1st	2d	3d	4th	5th	6th	7th	8th	9th	10th
12 years of 7-team divisions	0	1	0	1	2	3	5	—	—	—
8 years of 6-team divisions	0	0	2	0	3	3	—	—	—	—
8 years of 10-team league	0	0	1	0	0	1	1	2	2	1
60 years of 8-team league	*3	2	6	*6	8	9	11	16	—	—

* in 1947, 1st-place team and 4th-place team tied for lead in walks.

We're not absolutely certain where we saw it. It might have come from an old Three Stooges film. Maybe it was Curly: a guy who was simply standing in a room by himself, repeatedly pounding the back of his head against a solid wall. Someone walked in and asked him why he was knocking his own head against the wall. He responded, "'Cause it feels good when I stop, nyuk, nyuk, nyuk."

Now that his pitchers have led the major leagues in walks in each of the last three seasons, perhaps Bobby Valentine feels much the same way. Bobby, if you ever run into Gabby Street or Fred Haney in managers' heaven, they could commiserate with you. Those guys managed the last pitching staff to lead the majors in walks three years in a row, the St. Louis Browns from 1938 to 1940. Street managed in '38, Haney the next two years; in three years, the Brownies won 170 games and lost 290.

Valentine's team hasn't been *that* bad, but it's been no day at the beach, either. After a promising 87–75 mark in 1986, a year in which the team matched the second-highest win total in its Texas history, the Rangers have had a record of 145–178 (.449) over the past two years, the worst in their division. Over the three years, American League batters have received 2150 walks from the Texas pitching staff. How large a factor those walks have played in the Rangers' won-lost record is a matter of some speculation, but it's our impression that the destructive nature of walks is something that is underappreciated by most baseball followers. We were in that group ourselves until we did a study on the subject.

We compiled a list of the pitching staffs with the most walks in the American League in every season from 1901 through 1988, and then matched it against the final standings from each season. The results are summarized here, with the figure under each ordinal representing the total number of times that teams that led the league in walks have finished in that particular position in the standings. (We have given teams that were tied for a position the benefit of the doubt, and listed them at the higher of the two positions.)

The evidence is overwhelming. Only three teams that led the American League in walks have ever finished in first place: the 1913 Philadelphia Athletics and the Yankees in 1947 and 1949 (they tied for the lead in walks in '47). In only 20 of the 88 years in A.L. history has the team that allowed the most walks ever finished in the "first division." On the other hand, 25 of the teams allowing the most walks finished in last place—26 if you count the 1987 Rangers, who actually tied for last place. We computed the "average" finish for all of these teams; those of you enamored with half-sacks and quarter-horses will enjoy these fractional finishes:

In 7-team division:	5.75 out of 7
In 6-team division:	4.88 out of 6
In 10-team league:	7.50 out of 10
In 8-team league:	5.76 out of 8

The different numbers of teams in the league make the comparison a bit murky, but stay with it and you'll see a remarkable consistency. The averages show that teams leading the American League in walks have repeatedly finished among the bottom three teams in the league or their division. In recent years, the trend has accelerated, notwithstanding the Rangers' second-place finish in 1986. Since the beginning of divisional play in 1969, these teams averaged a fifth-place finish in a six-team division and a sixth-place finish in a seven-team division.

Consider, too, that the Rangers have not earned their status as league leaders in walks by the margin of just a stray walk or two. In 1988, they were 26 ahead of the Phillies, who finished second; in 1987, they led the second-place Cubs by 132; and in 1986, they finished 69 walks ahead of the nearest team, Oakland. Over the past three years, their total of 2,150 walks is 382 higher than the second-highest team, Philadelphia. And in just the last *two* seasons, the Rangers have had nearly as many walks as the Mets have had in the last *three* (Rangers 1,414; Mets 1,423).

Nor is there any significant cross section of data in which the Rangers were *not* last, (or first, depending on your point of view) in walks, at least in the American League. The tables at the end of this section show that their rate of walks was the highest in the league both overall and in Late-Inning Pressure Situations, against both left- and right-handed batters, and both with runners on base and with the bases empty.

What must have been doubly frustrating for the Rangers is that when they got the ball over the plate, the Texas pitchers were hard to hit. They allowed the fewest hits in the league, becoming the first team in either league to allow the most walks and the fewest hits since the Indians in 1968, when Sudden Sam McDowell was terrorizing both opposing hitters and Cleveland catchers.

But after three years' worth of head-knocking, the Rangers may have made some moves to escape the base-on-balls basement. First, those two months that Bobby Witt spent in the minor leagues last year seem to have turned him into a recovering walkaholic. His career rate of walks was 8.5 per nine innings before the trip to Oklahoma City; it was 4.3 per nine innings after his return. Then in the big off-season trade with the Cubs, Texas acquired two pitchers (Drew Hall and Jamie Moyer) with a combined career rate of 3.6 walks per nine innings, and they got rid of two (Mitch Williams and Paul Kilgus) with a combined rate of 5.1 walks per nine innings.

And then, of course, the Rangers signed free agent Nolan Ryan on December 7. We know what you're thinking, "Nolan Ryan has walked 2442 batters—more than 600 more walks than anyone else in the history of baseball." (Our readers are very exact.) Well, we know all that. But Ryan's rate of walks last year was 3.6 per nine innings; over the last five years it has been 3.7 per nine innings. He's joining a pitching staff that has averaged 4.5 walks per nine innings over the past three seasons. There's a word for that. Progress.

Despite all of the free passes, five teams in the American League allowed more runs that the Rangers last season. Which is more than Texas's batters can say: only two teams, the White Sox and the Orioles, scored fewer runs than the Rangers.

Sometimes we may get carried away with various arcane analyses. But you didn't need to look to batting averages with runners in scoring position, or on-base averages leading off an inning to determine the source of the Rangers' offensive problems in 1988. Ask any four year old and he'll tell you: The best thing that any batter can do is to hit a home run; the worst thing he can do is to strike out. And last year, Texas's hitters had the unusual distinction of hitting the fewest home runs in the American League while they struck out the most times.

Think about that combination for a minute; it's an odd one. If you have batters that don't hit a lot of home runs, wouldn't you think that they wouldn't strike out much, either? After all, there's a logical connection between the two categories. The hefty swings necessary to generate the long ball produce an unfortunate but natural by-product: an accumulation of strikeouts. It was a baseball theorem first discovered by Babe Ruth, and perpetuated through generations of sluggers to come. Meanwhile, banjo hitters who rarely struck out would hardly ever hit the ball out of the lot. The three toughest hitters to strike out in this century, Joe Sewell, Lloyd Waner, and Nellie Fox, combined for an average of one home run for every 215 at-bats.

Somewhere, the Rangers' hitters got their wires crossed. They were the only American League team to strike out more than 1000 times last season, but they could do no better than 112 home runs. There have been 13 other teams that have struck out *that many* times while hitting *that few* home runs. One of them, the 1969 Mets, even got a World Championship out of it. But only three of those 13 teams have played in the American League, and no other American League team has done it since the designated hitter rule was adopted in 1973. And that last one is the appropriate comparative yardstick, because of the high number of strikeouts, and low number of home runs, that are produced by a teamful of pitchers who bat.

Have any other teams ever led their league in those two categories, one positive and one negative, in the same season? Yes, but only six, and two of those actually tied for the fewest home runs in their league that year. And you won't be seeing this group of teams that the Rangers joined on the next edition of "Greats of the Game":

	HR	SO	W–L	Pct.	Pos.
1943 Braves	*39	604	68–85	.444	6th
1945 Reds	*56	532	61–93	.396	7th
1952 Pirates	92	724	42–112	.273	8th
1954 Pirates	76	737	53–101	.344	8th
1955 Orioles	54	742	57–97	.370	7th
1960 Phillies	99	1054	59–95	.383	8th
1988 Rangers	112	1022	70–91	.435	6th

* tied for fewest home runs

In acquiring Julio Franco and Rafael Palmeiro, Tom Grieve got a couple of men who should reduce the strikeout totals—particularly Palmeiro, who was the second-toughest regular player for National League pitchers to strike out last season (behind the Reds' Barry Larkin). Whether or not those additions will be enough to offset the annual gargantuan strikeout totals of Pete Incaviglia remains to be seen.

WON-LOST RECORD BY STARTING POSITION

TEXAS 70-91	C	1B	2B	3B	SS	LF	CF	RF	P	DH	Leadoff	Relief	Starts
Bob Brower	·	·	·	·	·	4-12	14-13	1-0	·	2-5	15-15	·	21-30
Kevin Brown	·	·	·	·	·	·	·	·	2-2	·	·	·	2-2
Jerry Browne	·	·	29-31	·	·	·	·	·	·	·	·	·	29-31
Steve Buechele	·	·	0-2	67-82	·	·	·	·	·	·	·	·	67-84
Jose Cecena	·	·	·	·	·	·	·	·	·	·	·	5-17	·
Cecil Espy	·	·	·	·	·	19-24	13-18	1-4	·	0-3	9-17	·	33-49
Scott Fletcher	·	·	·	·	59-76	·	·	·	·	·	·	·	59-76
Tony Fossas	·	·	·	·	·	·	·	·	·	·	·	0-5	·
Barbaro Garbey	·	1-3	·	·	·	3-1	·	·	·	0-3	·	·	4-7
Cecilio Guante	·	·	·	·	·	·	·	·	·	·	·	1-6	·
Jose Guzman	·	·	·	·	·	·	·	·	14-16	·	·	·	14-16
Ray Hayward	·	·	·	·	·	·	·	·	6-6	·	·	·	6-6
Dwayne Henry	·	·	·	·	·	·	·	·	·	·	·	2-9	·
Guy Hoffman	·	·	·	·	·	·	·	·	·	·	·	0-11	·
Charlie Hough	·	·	·	·	·	·	·	·	16-18	·	·	·	16-18
Pete Incaviglia	·	·	·	·	·	43-49	·	·	·	8-13	·	·	51-62
Mike Jeffcoat	·	·	·	·	·	·	·	·	0-2	·	·	0-3	0-2
Steve Kemp	·	·	·	·	·	0-2	·	·	·	3-3	·	·	3-5
Paul Kilgus	·	·	·	·	·	·	·	·	14-18	·	·	·	14-18
Chad Kreuter	5-10	·	·	·	·	·	·	·	·	·	·	·	5-10
Jeff Kunkel	·	·	10-12	1-4	3-9	0-2	·	·	·	1-1	·	0-1	15-28
Scott May	·	·	·	·	·	·	·	·	0-1	·	·	0-2	0-1
Oddibe McDowell	·	·	·	·	·	·	43-60	·	·	·	42-53	·	43-60
Craig McMurtry	·	·	·	·	·	·	·	·	·	·	·	10-22	·
Dale Mohorcic	·	·	·	·	·	·	·	·	·	·	·	14-29	·
Pete O'Brien	·	66-82	·	·	·	·	·	·	·	·	·	·	66-82
Larry Parrish	·	·	·	·	·	·	·	·	·	32-35	·	·	32-35
Geno Petralli	31-41	1-1	·	1-1	·	·	·	·	·	12-9	·	·	45-52
Kevin Reimer	·	·	·	·	·	·	·	·	·	1-4	·	·	1-4
Jeff Russell	·	·	·	·	·	·	·	·	9-15	·	·	2-8	9-15
Larry See	·	·	·	·	·	·	·	·	·	3-3	·	·	3-3
Ruben Sierra	·	·	·	·	·	·	·	67-85	·	0-1	·	·	67-86
Mike Stanley	23-26	1-3	·	0-1	·	·	·	·	·	8-9	·	·	32-39
James Steels	·	1-2	·	·	·	1-1	1-2	·	·	0-2	0-1	·	3-7
Jim Sundberg	11-14	·	·	·	·	·	·	·	·	·	·	·	11-14
Ed Vande Berg	·	·	·	·	·	·	·	·	·	·	·	6-20	·
Dewayne Vaughn	·	·	·	·	·	·	·	·	·	·	·	0-8	·
Curtis Wilkerson	·	·	31-46	1-3	8-6	·	·	·	·	·	·	·	40-55
Mitch Williams	·	·	·	·	·	·	·	·	·	·	·	26-41	·
Steve Wilson	·	·	·	·	·	·	·	·	·	·	·	1-2	·
Bobby Witt	·	·	·	·	·	·	·	·	9-13	·	·	·	9-13

Batting vs. Left and Right Handed Pitchers

		BA	Rank	SA	Rank	OBA	Rank	HR %	Rank	BB %	Rank	SO %	Rank
Bob Brower	vs. Lefties	.237	110	.275	146	.338	53	0.00	140	13.07	22	16.99	119
	vs. Righties	.200	--	.271	--	.273	--	1.43	--	8.64	--	14.81	--
Jerry Browne	vs. Lefties	.243	102	.300	138	.289	115	0.00	140	6.41	92	12.82	77
	vs. Righties	.222	142	.306	143	.317	99	0.69	138	12.12	25	13.33	76
Steve Buechele	vs. Lefties	.235	114	.392	78	.335	59	3.27	52	12.43	26	11.30	66
	vs. Righties	.257	87	.409	67	.345	54	3.14	58	10.70	42	14.68	95
Cecil Espy	vs. Lefties	.328	15	.508	23	.369	34	1.64	99	6.15	97	20.00	142
	vs. Righties	.231	131	.315	139	.271	154	0.35	156	5.14	140	22.51	155
Scott Fletcher	vs. Lefties	.337	10	.399	68	.407	18	0.00	140	9.57	50	4.26	3
	vs. Righties	.247	109	.295	154	.345	55	0.00	161	10.45	46	6.18	9
Pete Incaviglia	vs. Lefties	.254	84	.524	15	.319	75	7.14	6	7.97	73	33.33	168
	vs. Righties	.247	110	.442	39	.322	90	4.45	24	8.51	81	32.52	170
Jeff Kunkel	vs. Lefties	.316	24	.500	25	.333	60	2.63	66	2.56	160	16.67	113
	vs. Righties	.141	--	.218	--	.171	--	0.00	--	2.41	--	26.51	--
Oddibe McDowell	vs. Lefties	.229	127	.354	101	.288	119	2.08	81	6.67	88	18.10	128
	vs. Righties	.252	96	.355	112	.318	97	1.17	116	8.90	75	18.32	132
Pete O'Brien	vs. Lefties	.252	90	.350	105	.305	98	1.84	90	7.30	78	17.98	126
	vs. Righties	.281	44	.432	51	.371	23	3.39	53	13.11	16	9.11	28
Geno Petralli	vs. Lefties	.182	159	.205	166	.245	156	0.00	140	8.00	71	14.00	87
	vs. Righties	.296	28	.420	59	.371	22	2.28	83	10.57	44	12.86	74
Ruben Sierra	vs. Lefties	.285	48	.487	32	.305	99	4.15	32	3.00	158	7.50	20
	vs. Righties	.239	122	.396	77	.299	128	3.55	46	8.12	87	16.24	114
Mike Stanley	vs. Lefties	.238	107	.320	127	.354	39	1.64	99	15.28	12	20.14	145
	vs. Righties	.220	146	.276	160	.293	135	0.79	135	10.14	54	22.30	153
Curtis Wilkerson	vs. Lefties	.255	80	.277	145	.286	122	0.00	140	4.08	140	14.29	90
	vs. Righties	.299	26	.371	99	.354	36	0.00	161	7.45	95	11.18	52
Team Average	vs. Lefties	.258	7	.380	10	.321	7	2.21	11	8.25	6	16.45	13
	vs. Righties	.249	12	.363	14	.320	9	1.97	13	9.03	5	16.66	14
League Average	vs. Lefties	.259		.391		.321		2.47		7.97		14.12	
	vs. Righties	.259		.391		.326		2.47		8.51		14.39	

Batting with Runners on Base and Bases Empty

		BA	Rank	SA	Rank	OBA	Rank	HR %	Rank	BB %	Rank	SO %	Rank
Bob Brower	Runners On	.189	162	.257	164	.318	108	1.35	105	14.89	14	17.02	128
	Bases Empty	.244	105	.283	148	.314	85	0.00	156	9.29	56	15.71	101
Jerry Browne	Runners On	.218	151	.287	158	.303	129	0.00	148	10.78	49	10.78	55
	Bases Empty	.236	118	.315	133	.312	88	0.79	140	9.93	42	14.89	90
Steve Buechele	Runners On	.257	105	.378	106	.353	62	1.80	94	11.88	39	13.41	93
	Bases Empty	.246	99	.423	46	.333	54	4.27	33	10.69	32	13.84	80
Cecil Espy	Runners On	.313	25	.424	62	.346	71	1.39	102	5.59	137	14.91	107
	Bases Empty	.202	157	.296	141	.247	164	0.00	156	5.12	135	27.44	165
Scott Fletcher	Runners On	.311	27	.374	109	.386	23	0.00	148	8.55	80	3.72	1
	Bases Empty	.250	90	.294	143	.347	39	0.00	156	11.47	24	7.06	13
Pete Incaviglia	Runners On	.231	138	.379	103	.308	122	3.59	48	9.50	65	33.03	170
	Bases Empty	.265	66	.543	9	.333	54	6.73	6	7.32	88	32.52	171
Oddibe McDowell	Runners On	.248	114	.345	131	.303	130	0.00	148	7.49	101	18.72	146
	Bases Empty	.246	95	.360	102	.317	82	2.21	85	9.00	62	18.00	129
Pete O'Brien	Runners On	.265	98	.390	94	.361	51	2.24	82	14.07	19	9.63	43
	Bases Empty	.278	41	.420	48	.346	42	3.40	47	9.50	50	13.13	68
Geno Petralli	Runners On	.234	131	.316	145	.323	102	0.63	141	11.76	40	12.83	82
	Bases Empty	.321	5	.456	33	.385	8	3.11	56	8.92	64	13.15	69
Ruben Sierra	Runners On	.269	90	.458	37	.321	104	4.32	28	8.04	89	12.20	74
	Bases Empty	.239	113	.392	77	.280	138	3.18	53	5.12	133	15.06	93
Mike Stanley	Runners On	.262	101	.340	135	.336	88	0.97	129	11.38	45	26.02	164
	Bases Empty	.205	151	.267	157	.314	87	1.37	112	13.61	11	17.75	125
Curtis Wilkerson	Runners On	.288	58	.353	125	.354	59	0.00	148	8.99	74	8.99	36
	Bases Empty	.297	22	.363	98	.337	51	0.00	156	5.18	132	13.99	81
Team Average	Runners On	.256	11	.363	13	.326	10	1.51	14	9.32	7	15.48	14
	Bases Empty	.248	8	.373	9	.315	7	2.46	8	8.38	5	17.51	14
League Average	Runners On	.268		.401		.336		2.45		9.09		13.68	
	Bases Empty	.253		.383		.315		2.48		7.76		14.81	

Overall Batting Compared to Late Inning Pressure Situations

		BA	Rank	SA	Rank	OBA	Rank	HR %	Rank	BB %	Rank	SO %	Rank	RDI %	Rank
Bob Brower	Overall	.224	146	.274	166	.316	92	0.50	153	11.54	27	16.24	112	.143	168
	Pressure	.138	166	.138	169	.265	138	0.00	110	13.51	20	18.92	105	.091	154
Jerry Browne	Overall	.229	139	.304	154	.308	108	0.47	157	10.29	46	13.17	74	.227	135
	Pressure	.310	39	.379	71	.394	23	0.00	110	11.76	41	8.82	27	.333	39
Steve Buechele	Overall	.250	101	.404	71	.342	53	3.18	59	11.23	35	13.64	83	.239	117
	Pressure	.222	116	.378	73	.314	90	4.44	31	9.62	65	22.12	126	.125	138
Cecil Espy	Overall	.248	109	.349	120	.288	143	0.58	149	5.32	141	22.07	154	.367	3
	Pressure	.164	152	.230	145	.278	124	1.64	86	13.70	17	21.92	124	.308	50
Scott Fletcher	Overall	.276	50	.328	136	.364	29	0.00	165	10.18	50	5.58	7	.251	103
	Pressure	.247	93	.315	114	.385	27	0.00	110	14.89	12	7.45	19	.179	109
Pete Incaviglia	Overall	.249	107	.467	25	.321	89	5.26	14	8.35	77	32.76	170	.210	152
	Pressure	.268	71	.411	60	.369	36	1.79	79	12.31	31	30.77	161	.294	57
Jeff Kunkel	Overall	.227	--	.357	--	.250	--	1.30	--	2.48	--	21.74	--	.268	--
	Pressure	.348	--	.522	--	.400	--	4.35	--	8.00	--	12.00	--	.143	128
Oddibe McDowell	Overall	.247	110	.355	115	.311	106	1.37	113	8.42	75	18.28	133	.243	113
	Pressure	.313	35	.388	68	.356	51	0.00	110	6.76	111	24.32	141	.333	39
Pete O'Brien	Overall	.272	53	.408	66	.352	41	2.93	66	11.46	28	11.62	57	.308	36
	Pressure	.264	78	.538	14	.350	59	7.69	6	11.54	45	16.35	90	.091	154
Geno Petralli	Overall	.282	40	.393	83	.356	36	1.99	94	10.25	73	13.00	73	.239	120
	Pressure	.259	80	.362	82	.348	61	1.72	83	12.12	35	25.76	150	.083	159
Ruben Sierra	Overall	.254	94	.424	48	.301	125	3.74	38	6.59	112	13.62	80	.263	92
	Pressure	.237	102	.290	126	.297	113	1.08	109	7.92	91	14.85	78	.100	149
Mike Stanley	Overall	.229	140	.297	158	.323	84	1.20	115	12.67	17	21.23	150	.280	70
	Pressure	.179	142	.308	119	.333	75	2.56	60	18.75	6	25.00	143	.200	95
Jim Sundberg	Overall	.286	--	.462	--	.323	--	4.40	--	5.05	--	17.17	--	.296	--
	Pressure	.313	--	.750	--	.353	--	12.50	--	5.56	--	27.78	--	.000	165
Curtis Wilkerson	Overall	.293	29	.358	113	.345	48	0.00	165	7.01	103	11.59	56	.221	140
	Pressure	.328	22	.431	53	.391	25	0.00	110	9.09	71	4.55	4	.158	122
Team Average	Overall	.252	11	.368	13	.320	9	2.04	14	8.80	5	16.60	14	.251	11
	Pressure	.249	7	.361	8	.335	3	2.18	9	10.91	1	18.45	12	.169	14
League Average	Overall	.259		.391		.324		2.47		8.35		14.31		.269	
	Pressure	.249		.365		.319		2.28		8.71		17.04		.246	

Additional Miscellaneous Batting Comparisons

	Grass Surface BA	Rank	Artificial Surface BA	Rank	Home Games BA	Rank	Road Games BA	Rank	Runners in Scoring Position BA	Rank	Runners in Scoring Pos and Two Outs BA	Rank	Leading Off Inning OBA	Rank	Runners on 3B with less than 2 Outs RDI %	Rank
Bob Brower	.216	149	.256	95	.233	129	.214	145	.157	169	.087	169	.356	35	.400	156
Jerry Browne	.218	146	.308	--	.256	90	.194	162	.196	158	.083	170	.250	147	.500	--
Steve Buechele	.259	78	.211	144	.260	84	.241	120	.234	123	.177	145	.314	80	.667	33
Cecil Espy	.243	107	.268	83	.297	26	.208	151	.354	5	.341	13	.242	154	.778	5
Scott Fletcher	.265	61	.326	19	.286	42	.266	66	.308	26	.203	124	.352	36	.645	47
Pete Incaviglia	.257	81	.188	157	.249	102	.249	102	.211	150	.240	80	.336	57	.350	168
Jeff Kunkel	.215	152	.273	--	.238	--	.216	--	.219	--	.118	--	.324	--	.667	--
Oddibe McDowell	.253	90	.217	136	.246	106	.248	106	.258	91	.308	26	.299	95	.474	132
Pete O'Brien	.283	39	.223	133	.286	42	.260	84	.260	87	.246	69	.358	34	.629	57
Geno Petralli	.275	52	.313	26	.272	68	.291	30	.236	115	.224	98	.369	25	.556	89
Ruben Sierra	.261	75	.221	134	.281	52	.228	135	.233	124	.188	137	.283	119	.658	43
Mike Stanley	.237	115	.184	161	.259	85	.189	165	.273	67	.172	149	.294	105	.706	16
Curtis Wilkerson	.295	26	.284	62	.289	36	.296	29	.310	24	.184	141	.295	104	.571	81
Team Average	.251	10	.255	12	.262	6	.242	13	.250	12	.203	13	.310	6	.597	3
League Average	.256		.267		.262		.257		.262		.239		.311		.570	

Pitching vs. Left and Right Handed Batters

		BA	Rank	SA	Rank	OBA	Rank	HR %	Rank	BB %	Rank	SO %	Rank
Cecilio Guante	vs. Lefties	.231	32	.343	39	.318	51	2.24	67	9.21	72	17.11	30
	vs. Righties	.221	24	.429	98	.281	24	4.91	124	6.70	47	21.79	18
Jose Guzman	vs. Lefties	.205	13	.312	20	.286	17	2.13	66	9.62	80	15.73	42
	vs. Righties	.255	62	.403	79	.325	76	2.97	89	9.11	93	20.00	28
Ray Hayward	vs. Lefties	.314	--	.471	--	.390	--	1.96	--	11.67	--	11.67	--
	vs. Righties	.266	82	.401	76	.361	119	2.82	78	13.27	127	14.22	67
Charlie Hough	vs. Lefties	.220	23	.318	26	.321	57	2.00	61	12.19	113	16.57	32
	vs. Righties	.222	26	.335	30	.321	71	2.38	58	11.44	118	16.05	51
Paul Kilgus	vs. Lefties	.221	24	.279	9	.283	15	0.71	13	5.23	12	14.38	48
	vs. Righties	.248	51	.379	61	.319	68	2.65	69	8.77	88	9.19	120
Craig McMurtry	vs. Lefties	.214	--	.314	--	.321	--	1.43	--	12.35	--	11.11	--
	vs. Righties	.163	1	.304	13	.237	4	2.96	87	9.03	89	16.77	45
Jeff Russell	vs. Lefties	.292	105	.411	88	.370	109	2.70	92	10.79	98	9.83	92
	vs. Righties	.219	23	.297	10	.273	17	1.46	19	5.59	27	12.50	92
Mitch Williams	vs. Lefties	.185	--	.231	--	.337	--	0.00	--	14.29	--	22.62	--
	vs. Righties	.211	18	.333	28	.348	106	2.34	55	16.51	129	19.81	29
Bobby Witt	vs. Lefties	.223	25	.301	15	.331	72	1.16	25	13.73	122	18.14	21
	vs. Righties	.207	17	.341	35	.315	56	3.26	98	13.72	128	22.56	13
Team Average	vs. Lefties	.245	3	.349	2	.332	7	1.89	4	10.92	14	15.07	3
	vs. Righties	.243	1	.375	3	.327	11	2.76	9	10.34	14	14.54	10
League Average	vs. Lefties	.262		.387		.331		2.24		9.12		13.21	
	vs. Righties	.258		.393		.320		2.63		7.80		15.09	

Pitching with Runners on Base and Bases Empty

		BA	Rank	SA	Rank	OBA	Rank	HR %	Rank	BB %	Rank	SO %	Rank
Cecilio Guante	Runners On	.209	10	.338	24	.293	21	2.70	78	8.88	67	19.53	18
	Bases Empty	.242	48	.443	109	.302	47	4.70	124	6.79	54	19.75	22
Jose Guzman	Runners On	.241	37	.381	62	.317	47	2.93	88	9.89	92	14.41	54
	Bases Empty	.225	27	.345	32	.299	44	2.33	71	9.00	89	20.31	18
Ray Hayward	Runners On	.375	--	.597	--	.479	--	4.17	--	18.37	--	10.20	--
	Bases Empty	.231	33	.333	25	.306	51	1.92	46	9.83	107	15.61	54
Charlie Hough	Runners On	.241	38	.339	27	.362	103	1.79	39	15.00	128	15.24	43
	Bases Empty	.210	17	.319	17	.295	35	2.43	80	9.74	102	17.00	40
Paul Kilgus	Runners On	.281	90	.444	101	.334	72	3.19	97	6.90	28	11.21	91
	Bases Empty	.217	21	.305	12	.298	43	1.71	36	8.99	88	9.37	119
Jeff Russell	Runners On	.314	118	.441	97	.375	107	3.10	95	7.95	51	10.40	101
	Bases Empty	.217	22	.298	10	.290	28	1.42	22	8.58	81	11.59	95
Mitch Williams	Runners On	.218	12	.345	32	.350	92	2.11	54	15.00	128	23.89	3
	Bases Empty	.181	1	.245	--	.336	--	1.06	--	17.24	--	15.52	--
Bobby Witt	Runners On	.228	19	.324	18	.333	68	1.93	45	13.92	122	18.99	20
	Bases Empty	.207	13	.315	15	.317	68	2.21	61	13.57	123	20.95	16
Team Average	Runners On	.270	7	.404	8	.356	13	2.71	12	11.35	14	13.93	7
	Bases Empty	.225	1	.335	1	.309	3	2.17	4	9.98	14	15.41	4
League Average	Runners On	.268		.401		.336		2.45		9.09		13.68	
	Bases Empty	.253		.383		.315		2.48		7.76		14.81	

Overall Pitching Compared to Late Inning Pressure Situations

		BA	Rank	SA	Rank	OBA	Rank	HR %	Rank	BB %	Rank	SO %	Rank
Jose Cecena	Overall	.213	--	.319	--	.372	--	2.13	--	19.01	--	22.31	--
	Pressure	.132	2	.237	7	.389	115	2.63	82	25.93	129	25.93	4
Cecilio Guante	Overall	.226	21	.391	75	.298	22	3.70	119	7.85	57	19.64	19
	Pressure	.203	21	.353	55	.282	25	3.76	103	7.33	39	20.67	20
Jose Guzman	Overall	.231	24	.359	38	.306	34	2.57	81	9.36	91	17.92	29
	Pressure	.216	30	.336	46	.295	32	2.59	79	10.00	78	12.31	92
Ray Hayward	Overall	.276	101	.417	95	.367	122	2.63	86	12.92	123	13.65	66
	Pressure	.407	--	.556	--	.433	--	0.00	--	6.67	--	13.33	--
Charlie Hough	Overall	.221	17	.326	15	.321	64	2.19	63	11.81	121	16.31	40
	Pressure	.222	36	.281	25	.316	58	1.80	56	11.79	97	16.92	41
Paul Kilgus	Overall	.243	39	.361	39	.313	46	2.30	67	8.15	63	10.10	112
	Pressure	.211	27	.263	17	.310	53	1.32	37	12.64	106	3.45	129
Craig McMurtry	Overall	.180	--	.307	--	.266	--	2.44	--	10.17	--	14.83	--
	Pressure	.263	83	.456	107	.373	106	5.26	120	13.04	107	10.14	107
Jeff Russell	Overall	.257	60	.356	31	.324	72	2.10	53	8.32	66	11.10	98
	Pressure	.225	37	.281	24	.296	33	0.00	1	8.08	52	10.10	108
Berg Ed Vande	Overall	.308	--	.413	--	.353	--	1.40	--	6.92	--	11.32	--
	Pressure	.346	122	.385	77	.386	113	0.00	1	6.67	28	6.67	121
Mitch Williams	Overall	.203	3	.305	7	.345	106	1.69	22	15.88	129	20.61	14
	Pressure	.212	28	.338	47	.331	71	1.99	61	13.66	112	19.67	23
Bobby Witt	Overall	.216	11	.319	11	.324	71	2.09	51	13.72	125	20.11	16
	Pressure	.184	11	.333	44	.297	35	3.45	100	12.62	105	23.30	11
Team Average	Overall	.244	1	.364	2	.329	11	2.40	5	10.58	14	14.76	5
	Pressure	.239	4	.345	3	.338	10	1.96	5	11.89	14	14.36	12
League Average	Overall	.259		.391		.324		2.47		8.35		14.31	
	Pressure	.249		.369		.324		2.26		9.33		15.69	

Additional Miscellaneous Pitching Comparisons

	Grass Surface		Artificial Surface		Home Games		Road Games		Runners in Scoring Position		Runners in Scoring Pos and Two Outs		Leading Off Inning	
	BA	Rank	BA	Rank	BA	Rank	BA	Rank	BA	Rank	BA	Rank	OBA	Rank
Cecilio Guante	.226	22	.226	19	.233	38	.219	16	.189	10	.196	38	.288	47
Jose Guzman	.227	24	.250	42	.215	17	.251	58	.216	23	.200	40	.315	69
Ray Hayward	.271	93	.306	--	.337	--	.231	25	.359	--	.278	--	.243	9
Charlie Hough	.216	15	.252	46	.217	22	.226	19	.251	56	.260	87	.273	36
Paul Kilgus	.238	37	.275	69	.247	53	.237	35	.302	112	.338	125	.260	20
Craig McMurtry	.217	16	.075	1	.211	11	.146	--	.266	71	.257	85	.204	--
Jeff Russell	.255	59	.265	60	.261	73	.251	55	.308	116	.325	122	.260	22
Mitch Williams	.223	20	.116	--	.236	42	.168	2	.227	32	.167	19	.326	--
Bobby Witt	.218	17	.206	8	.216	19	.216	15	.267	75	.235	64	.303	57
Team Average	.242	2	.254	2	.248	4	.239	1	.271	11	.265	12	.287	2
League Average	.256		.267		.257		.262		.262		.239		.311	

TORONTO BLUE JAYS

- **Will the outfield of the 1980s stumble in the '90s?**
- **At what age does a player reach his peak? Guess again.**

Six years ago, the Toronto Blue Jays were baseball's symbol of futility. Their record of 348–566 during the franchise's first six seasons qualified as a slow start even by comparison to those of other expansion teams. The six-year records of baseball's 10 rookie teams, with the Jays ranking last among the six A.L. clubs:

Years	Team	W	L	Pct.
1969–74	Kansas City Royals	460	503	.478
1961–66	California Angels	463	507	.477
1969–74	Montreal Expos	424	540	.440
1969–74	Milwaukee Brewers II	413	552	.428
1962–67	Houston Astros	402	568	.414
1977–82	Seattle Mariners	366	551	.399
1961–66	Washington Senators II	380	587	.393
1977–82	Toronto Blue Jays	348	566	.381
1969–74	San Diego Padres	354	608	.368
1962–67	New York Mets	321	648	.331

But over the six seasons since then, the Blue Jays have been one of baseball's winningest clubs. Since 1983, only two teams have compiled a better winning percentage than Toronto's .562 mark: the New York Mets (.573) and the Detroit Tigers (.569). Toronto's turnaround of 182 percentage points from one six-year period to the next is almost unprecedented in modern major league history. The top 10 follows. Repetitions of the same teams in overlapping years have been eliminated. (For instance, Philadelphia from 1920 through 1931 would have ranked second to the same team one year earlier.)

		First 6 Years			Last 6 Years			
Years	Team	W	L	Pct.	W	L	Pct.	Diff.
1919–30	Philadelphia A's	342	563	.378	566	347	.620	.242
1962–73	New York Mets	321	648	.331	504	461	.522	.191
1977–88	Toronto Blue Jays	348	566	.381	546	425	.562	.181
1932–43	Cincinnati Reds	368	550	.401	530	387	.578	.177
1904–15	Washington Senators	315	592	.347	477	441	.520	.173
1952–63	Pittsburgh Pirates	333	591	.360	499	440	.531	.171
1928–39	Boston Red Sox	335	581	.366	485	426	.532	.166
1906–17	Boston Braves	312	598	.343	459	455	.502	.159
1962–73	Kansas City/Oakland	397	572	.410	547	417	.567	.157
1956–67	Washington/Minnesota	381	549	.410	543	428	.559	.149

The continued success of Dave Stieb and Jim Clancy was one reason for Toronto's dramatic about-face. But even in the early 1980s, those two gave the Blue Jays the nucleus of a formidable young starting rotation. More than anything, the metamorphosis of the Jays from losers to winners was driven by the emergence of Jesse Barfield, George Bell, and Lloyd Moseby as the best outfield of the decade.

Although all three were born within 16 days of each other in the autumn of 1959, Moseby won a starting spot in Toronto's outfield in 1981, a year before Barfield, and three years before Bell. So it wasn't until 1983 that Toronto's outfield gave a hint of what was to come. Moseby raised his batting average from .236 in 1982 to .315 that year; Barfield hit 27 home runs as a part-time starter; and Bell had 11 extra-base hits in 112 at-bats.

In fact, Barfield didn't win a regular, full-time starting position until 1985. But the combined contributions of the three players was substantial long before that, and continued to grow for several years. Eventually, Barfield and Bell both reached the 40–home-run plateau, and Moseby provided solid offense with 30 to 40 stolen bases a year and ever-increasing home-run totals. But all that ended last season, as the following table of their combined statistics indicates:

Year	AB	R	H	2B	3B	HR	RBI	BB	SO	SB	BA
1984	1518	233	434	81	20	58	228	137	289	58	.285
1985	1730	273	474	92	22	73	249	185	324	80	.273
1986	1819	297	517	97	13	92	302	174	330	47	.284
1987	1792	306	510	84	11	101	314	167	340	47	.284
1988	1554	217	392	65	17	52	195	145	267	42	.252

Home run production fell from 1987 by nearly half. None of the three batted as high as .270. Barfield and Moseby failed to drive in 100 runs between them. With the 1990s looming, it appears that baseball's outfield of the '80s might be just that. And while Toronto's minimal postseason exposure makes it hard to accept the Jays as an aging team, its outfield —like the nucleus of Canada's other major league entry a few years before them (Dawson, Carter, and Parrish)—has nonetheless matured to a point where another bad season will confer over-the-hill status upon it.

Cognizant of that fact, Toronto's management has already begun the rebuilding process, weaving an increasing mix of younger players into the picture before many of us realized it was even necessary. Last year, catcher Pat Borders pulled some playing time from Ernie Whitt. Infielders Manny Lee and Nelson Liriano made significant contributions in the role once played by Garth Iorg. Sil Campusano was the opening-day center fielder, creating the controversy surrounding Bell's DH status. And most important of all, Fred McGriff won the full-time starting first-base position. As a result, the average age of Toronto's starting lineup, with each player's contribution weighted according to how often he batted, fell to its lowest point since the Jays became perennial winners:

	1981	1982	1983	1984	1985	1986	1987	1988
Average age	26.3	27.0	28.3	28.2	28.2	28.8	28.2	27.8
A.L. rank	1	2	4	4	4	6	8	3

The collective off season by Barfield, Bell, and Moseby, none of whom had turned 29 by season's end, raises the question of when a player hits his peak. The increasing success of many veteran players into their 40s suggests that athletes may be exceptions to the generally accepted norm that one's physical peak occurs in his mid–20s.

A study of major league history indicates that Tommy John, Pete Rose, Phil Niekro, and their contemporaries are the exceptions. Baseball players in general prove the rule that the mid–20s are indeed the peak of physical prowess.

We examined the age at which players who retired before 1987 compiled their highest career totals in home runs, stolen bases, and hits for batters, and in wins for pitchers. Players who never achieved a reasonably successful total in those categories were eliminated from consideration. (Had we included everyone, the results would have been skewed toward younger peaks on account of the thousands of prospects who played a year or two in their mid–20s and failed.) The table below summarizes the age at which the players peaked in each area, if they ever hit 10 home runs in a season, accumulated 50 hits, stole 10 bases, or won 10 games:

	<23	23	24	25	26	27	28	29	30	31	32	33	34	35	36	>36
HR	41	66	76	115	111	111	105	101	72	52	56	30	22	14	4	7
Hits	229	232	298	400	371	384	337	290	240	148	104	68	39	31	7	16
SB	114	101	157	202	190	172	137	121	86	53	45	33	16	14	8	5
Wins	153	100	120	147	170	152	141	104	90	63	37	43	34	22	5	22

Lots of numbers, but one essential fact: In each of the batting categories, the age at which the most players established their career highs was 25; for pitchers, the most prevalent age for most wins was 26. And in every case, players were far more likely to compile their peak seasons at age 23 (generally considered as a formative stage) than at age 31 (traditionally considered to be near a player's peak age).

Could it be that we didn't eliminate enough of the young players who never made it, and whose careers accordingly ended before they turned 30? The following table is restricted to players who achieved levels of excellence in those categories (25 home runs, 25 steals, 150 hits, or 15 wins):

	<23	23	24	25	26	27	28	29	30	31	32	33	34	35	36	>36
HR	18	11	11	25	30	24	25	18	26	15	18	7	8	2	0	3
Hits	41	38	66	75	59	71	59	50	34	20	17	16	6	5	3	2
SB	45	57	88	116	122	111	104	94	57	45	31	14	15	1	3	3
Wins	83	54	66	87	95	79	84	59	61	40	25	35	24	11	4	9

The peaks shift only slightly to the right; on average, to the age of 26. And while we won't present the complete statistical breakdown here, we also examined only players with at least 10 years of major league experience, a group with a natural skew toward later peaks. And even *they* peaked well before their 30th birthdays—an average of age 27.

Among the 985 players in major league history who hit at least 10 home runs in a season and retired prior to 1987, only one reached his career high after his 40th birthday: Bob Thurman, who didn't make his big-league debut until age 38, a victim of the racial barrier. The 10 youngest and oldest home-run peaks among players with 10–HR seasons (ages as of October 1):

Year	Player	HR	Age	Year	Player	HR	Age
1929	Mel Ott	42	20	1957	Bob Thurman	16	40
1965	Ron Swoboda	19	21	1977	Ron Fairly	19	38
1901	Sam Crawford	16	21	1925	Ty Cobb	12	38
1949	Dick Kokos	23	21	1922	Jake Daubert	12	38
1966	Ed Kranepool	16	21	1952	Luke Easter	31	37
1953	Eddie Mathews	47	21	1971	Hank Aaron	47	37
1973	Bob Coluccio	15	21	1954	Hank Sauer	41	37
1958	Bill Mazeroski	19	21	1944	Phil Weintraub	13	36
1938	Buddy Lewis	12	21	1954	Mickey Vernon	20	36
1948	Whitey Lockman	18	21	1922	Zack Wheat	16	36

The incidence of players remaining competitive into their 40s is clearly increasing. But those players are performing far below the levels they established earlier in their careers. Fact is, we still aren't seeing career highs established by players in their late 30s or early 40s, and we probably never will.

WON-LOST RECORD BY STARTING POSITION

TORONTO 87-75	C	1B	2B	3B	SS	LF	CF	RF	P	DH	Leadoff	Relief	Starts
Doug Bair	-	-	-	-	-	-	-	-	-	-	-	1-9	-
Jesse Barfield	-	-	-	-	-	-	6-4	63-53	-	-	-	-	69-57
George Bell	-	-	-	-	-	82-65	-	-	-	2-5	-	-	84-70
Juan Beniquez	-	-	-	-	-	-	-	-	-	6-10	-	-	6-10
Pat Borders	13-20	-	1-0	-	-	-	-	-	0-2	-	-	-	14-22
Sal Butera	10-9	-	-	-	-	-	-	-	-	-	-	-	10-9
Sil Campusano	-	-	-	-	-	1-2	13-13	3-9	-	-	-	-	17-24
Tony Castillo	-	-	-	-	-	-	-	-	-	-	-	7-7	-
John Cerutti	-	-	-	-	-	-	-	-	6-6	-	-	11-23	6-6
Jim Clancy	-	-	-	-	-	-	-	-	13-18	-	-	2-3	13-18
Rob Ducey	-	-	-	-	-	11-4	-	-	-	-	-	-	11-4
Mark Eichhorn	-	-	-	-	-	-	-	-	-	-	-	10-27	-
Tony Fernandez	-	-	-	-	87-67	-	-	-	-	-	83-61	-	87-67
Cecil Fielder	-	4-10	-	0-1	-	-	-	-	-	16-12	-	-	20-23
Mike Flanagan	-	-	-	-	-	-	-	-	20-14	-	-	-	20-14
Kelly Gruber	-	-	0-2	81-66	-	-	-	-	-	-	0-1	-	81-68
Tom Henke	-	-	-	-	-	-	-	-	-	-	-	36-16	-
Alexis Infante	-	-	1-1	-	-	-	-	-	-	-	-	-	1-1
Jimmy Key	-	-	-	-	-	-	-	-	13-8	-	-	-	13-8
Rick Leach	-	1-1	-	-	-	2-4	-	17-11	-	8-7	-	-	28-23
Manny Lee	-	-	55-39	2-4	0-8	-	-	-	-	-	0-3	-	57-51
Nelson Liriano	-	-	31-34	-	-	-	-	-	-	1-0	4-10	-	32-34
Fred McGriff	-	82-64	-	-	-	-	-	-	-	-	-	-	82-64
Lloyd Moseby	-	-	-	-	-	2-4	57-54	4-2	-	0-1	-	-	63-61
Rance Mulliniks	-	-	-	3-3	-	-	-	-	-	54-38	-	-	57-41
Jeff Musselman	-	-	-	-	-	-	-	-	9-6	-	-	-	9-6
Jose Nunez	-	-	-	-	-	-	-	-	1-1	-	-	0-11	1-1
Mark Ross	-	-	-	-	-	-	-	-	-	-	-	1-2	-
Dave Stieb	-	-	-	-	-	-	-	-	20-11	-	-	0-1	20-11
Todd Stottlemyre	-	-	-	-	-	-	-	-	5-11	-	-	4-8	5-11
Lou Thornton	-	-	-	-	-	-	-	-	-	-	-	-	-
Duane Ward	-	-	-	-	-	-	-	-	-	-	-	40-24	-
David Wells	-	-	-	-	-	-	-	-	-	-	-	19-22	-
Ernie Whitt	64-46	-	-	-	-	-	-	-	-	-	-	-	64-46
Frank Wills	-	-	-	-	-	-	-	-	-	-	-	2-8	-

Batting vs. Left and Right Handed Pitchers

		BA	Rank	SA	Rank	OBA	Rank	HR %	Rank	BB %	Rank	SO %	Rank
Jesse Barfield	vs. Lefties	.212	145	.406	65	.284	124	5.45	17	8.70	61	20.11	144
	vs. Righties	.261	80	.436	46	.312	108	2.97	63	7.44	96	21.13	147
George Bell	vs. Lefties	.270	64	.485	34	.296	109	5.10	22	3.88	144	7.77	24
	vs. Righties	.268	67	.428	52	.308	112	3.35	54	5.75	126	11.06	51
Juan Beniquez	vs. Lefties	.302	36	.396	71	.377	30	1.89	88	11.29	36	9.68	46
	vs. Righties	.200	--	.200	--	.333	--	0.00	--	16.67	--	0.00	--
Pat Borders	vs. Lefties	.280	53	.455	49	.294	111	3.03	57	2.21	164	15.44	101
	vs. Righties	.227	--	.409	--	.227	--	4.55	--	0.00	--	12.50	--
Sal Butera	vs. Lefties	.255	81	.373	88	.255	151	1.96	86	0.00	168	9.62	45
	vs. Righties	.111	--	.222	--	.200	--	0.00	--	10.00	--	40.00	--
Sil Campusano	vs. Lefties	.235	114	.441	53	.264	145	2.94	59	4.11	139	24.66	158
	vs. Righties	.203	--	.284	--	.298	--	0.00	--	7.06	--	17.65	--
Tony Fernandez	vs. Lefties	.279	54	.374	86	.318	78	1.37	105	5.46	115	7.98	29
	vs. Righties	.291	34	.392	80	.344	57	0.47	152	6.87	109	9.87	38
Cecil Fielder	vs. Lefties	.228	130	.462	45	.294	112	6.21	12	8.13	70	28.75	164
	vs. Righties	.241	--	.276	--	.267	--	0.00	--	3.33	--	23.33	--
Kelly Gruber	vs. Lefties	.251	92	.364	95	.288	120	0.53	138	4.98	123	15.92	107
	vs. Righties	.291	34	.474	23	.348	51	3.93	35	6.64	112	14.22	94
Rick Leach	vs. Lefties	.133	--	.200	--	.188	--	0.00	--	6.25	--	25.00	--
	vs. Righties	.288	37	.364	105	.348	48	0.00	161	8.46	82	11.44	55
Manny Lee	vs. Lefties	.336	11	.458	48	.365	36	1.53	103	4.38	131	10.22	53
	vs. Righties	.268	66	.316	138	.318	98	0.00	161	7.19	100	17.99	127
Nelson Liriano	vs. Lefties	.269	67	.312	130	.320	73	1.08	121	5.88	102	19.61	138
	vs. Righties	.262	75	.344	121	.284	140	1.09	119	2.59	169	10.36	45
Fred McGriff	vs. Lefties	.234	118	.368	90	.307	93	2.92	60	7.94	74	33.86	169
	vs. Righties	.304	19	.638	1	.406	5	7.95	2	14.75	10	19.59	142
Lloyd Moseby	vs. Lefties	.253	85	.359	96	.344	50	1.18	115	10.20	43	15.82	105
	vs. Righties	.232	129	.374	93	.343	60	2.65	73	14.04	11	17.42	122
Rance Mulliniks	vs. Lefties	.267	--	.533	--	.389	--	6.67	--	16.67	--	22.22	--
	vs. Righties	.301	22	.472	26	.396	10	3.42	50	13.91	13	13.91	86
Ernie Whitt	vs. Lefties	.282	50	.462	46	.408	17	5.13	21	15.69	10	15.69	104
	vs. Righties	.248	106	.404	69	.341	62	3.90	36	12.71	20	7.19	13
Team Average	vs. Lefties	.260	6	.405	5	.311	10	2.81	4	6.46	13	17.14	14
	vs. Righties	.272	2	.427	1	.342	2	2.86	1	9.38	3	14.07	7
League Average	vs. Lefties	.259		.391		.321		2.47		7.97		14.12	
	vs. Righties	.259		.391		.326		2.47		8.51		14.39	

Batting with Runners on Base and Bases Empty

		BA	Rank	SA	Rank	OBA	Rank	HR %	Rank	BB %	Rank	SO %	Rank
Jesse Barfield	Runners On	.242	123	.379	104	.330	96	2.63	72	12.28	36	18.42	142
	Bases Empty	.245	104	.457	31	.281	135	4.68	26	4.45	147	22.60	150
George Bell	Runners On	.308	29	.481	25	.333	89	4.15	32	4.47	156	8.95	35
	Bases Empty	.234	121	.415	55	.278	139	3.69	43	5.80	117	11.01	46
Tony Fernandez	Runners On	.319	20	.450	41	.376	36	0.42	145	7.81	96	7.81	26
	Bases Empty	.268	52	.349	113	.310	95	0.98	131	5.52	122	10.11	35
Cecil Fielder	Runners On	.250	111	.395	90	.326	100	2.63	72	10.47	54	29.07	167
	Bases Empty	.214	--	.459	--	.260	--	7.14	--	4.81	--	26.92	--
Kelly Gruber	Runners On	.336	11	.525	11	.381	30	2.05	86	6.23	125	10.62	53
	Bases Empty	.234	121	.372	92	.289	128	3.38	49	6.00	113	18.00	129
Rick Leach	Runners On	.337	9	.382	102	.385	24	0.00	148	7.29	103	14.58	102
	Bases Empty	.227	130	.327	124	.298	108	0.00	156	9.09	60	10.74	44
Manny Lee	Runners On	.331	13	.396	88	.354	61	0.00	148	4.32	148	16.76	126
	Bases Empty	.259	73	.340	119	.317	81	0.94	133	7.83	80	14.35	85
Nelson Liriano	Runners On	.272	81	.316	146	.306	126	0.00	148	4.76	150	14.29	100
	Bases Empty	.259	74	.346	114	.290	126	1.85	96	2.96	165	13.02	66
Fred McGriff	Runners On	.258	103	.504	16	.342	78	6.36	5	10.66	51	22.79	157
	Bases Empty	.300	19	.590	4	.402	4	6.33	10	14.25	7	24.79	156
Lloyd Moseby	Runners On	.203	158	.310	151	.331	94	2.03	87	15.00	13	16.67	123
	Bases Empty	.265	63	.411	58	.353	33	2.18	86	10.90	30	16.99	114
Rance Mulliniks	Runners On	.296	44	.459	35	.428	5	3.70	44	19.43	2	15.43	111
	Bases Empty	.302	16	.485	20	.371	20	3.47	45	9.82	45	13.39	74
Ernie Whitt	Runners On	.269	91	.439	52	.355	58	4.09	33	12.68	30	9.76	45
	Bases Empty	.238	115	.388	82	.342	45	3.96	38	13.31	13	6.84	10
Team Average	Runners On	.284	3	.427	3	.350	4	2.50	7	9.33	6	14.82	11
	Bases Empty	.257	5	.414	2	.318	6	3.10	1	7.70	7	15.31	8
League Average	Runners On	.268		.401		.336		2.45		9.09		13.68	
	Bases Empty	.253		.383		.315		2.48		7.76		14.81	

Overall Batting Compared to Late Inning Pressure Situations

		BA	Rank	SA	Rank	OBA	Rank	HR %	Rank	BB %	Rank	SO %	Rank	RDI %	Rank
Jesse Barfield	Overall	.244	117	.425	46	.302	118	3.85	35	7.88	88	20.77	147	.206	155
	Pressure	.197	135	.393	67	.269	134	4.92	24	8.96	75	22.39	128	.125	138
George Bell	Overall	.269	61	.446	33	.304	114	3.91	33	5.17	146	10.03	38	.250	72
	Pressure	.270	68	.473	33	.316	88	5.41	20	6.33	120	10.13	36	.287	58
Pat Borders	Overall	.273	--	.448	--	.285	--	3.25	--	1.88	--	15.00	--	.245	--
	Pressure	.310	39	.517	18	.333	75	3.45	46	3.23	153	12.90	61	.188	107
Tony Fernandez	Overall	.287	35	.386	88	.335	59	0.77	143	6.39	114	9.23	148	.354	6
	Pressure	.364	5	.481	28	.412	18	1.30	100	6.98	103	6.98	13	.242	78
Cecil Fielder	Overall	.230	--	.431	--	.289	--	5.17	--	7.37	--	27.89	--	.250	104
	Pressure	.200	128	.200	156	.273	129	0.00	110	6.06	126	36.36	169	.250	72
Kelly Gruber	Overall	.278	45	.438	38	.328	73	2.81	68	6.10	122	14.77	100	.309	33
	Pressure	.346	10	.487	26	.395	22	2.56	60	6.82	107	9.09	28	.444	11
Rick Leach	Overall	.276	49	.352	116	.336	58	0.00	165	8.29	80	12.44	68	.282	66
	Pressure	.242	96	.364	81	.342	68	0.00	110	13.16	23	15.79	86	.143	128
Manny Lee	Overall	.291	33	.365	105	.333	63	0.52	151	6.27	120	15.42	106	.295	49
	Pressure	.270	69	.270	138	.361	45	0.00	110	12.33	30	13.70	68	.238	79
Nelson Liriano	Overall	.264	66	.333	130	.297	131	1.09	123	3.73	165	13.56	79	.212	149
	Pressure	.326	23	.457	42	.354	54	2.17	71	3.92	148	25.49	148	.364	31
Fred McGriff	Overall	.282	41	.552	2	.376	17	6.34	6	12.68	15	23.92	160	.216	146
	Pressure	.225	114	.352	90	.345	65	1.41	95	13.10	25	30.95	162	.050	164
Lloyd Moseby	Overall	.239	126	.369	100	.343	50	2.12	90	12.68	14	16.85	121	.193	160
	Pressure	.232	107	.304	121	.293	117	1.45	93	8.00	90	22.67	130	.158	122
Rance Mulliniks	Overall	.300	22	.475	22	.395	6	3.56	43	14.04	9	14.29	88	.282	67
	Pressure	.424	2	.606	5	.474	2	3.03	53	10.00	57	7.50	20	.273	63
Ernie Whitt	Overall	.251	98	.410	62	.348	45	4.02	31	13.03	12	8.12	20	.343	13
	Pressure	.159	154	.295	124	.259	141	4.55	27	12.73	27	9.09	28	.227	83
Team Average	Overall	.268	3	.419	3	.332	5	2.84	1	8.41	8	15.10	12	.271	9
	Pressure	.272	2	.393	4	.341	2	2.29	7	9.02	5	16.73	7	.233	10
League Average	Overall	.259		.391		.324		2.47		8.35		14.31		.269	
	Pressure	.249		.365		.319		2.28		8.71		17.04		.246	

Additional Miscellaneous Batting Comparisons

	Grass Surface BA	Rank	Artificial Surface BA	Rank	Home Games BA	Rank	Road Games BA	Rank	Runners in Scoring Position BA	Rank	Runners in Scoring Pos and Two Outs BA	Rank	Leading Off Inning OBA	Rank	Runners on 3B with less than 2 Outs RDI %	Rank
Jesse Barfield	.224	134	.255	98	.250	100	.237	122	.211	150	.130	163	.265	137	.500	115
George Bell	.226	131	.298	38	.296	28	.242	118	.294	39	.242	77	.212	163	.644	49
Juan Beniquez	.273	--	.306	32	.370	--	.226	--	.278	--	.182	--	.286	--	1.000	--
Pat Borders	.269	--	.276	72	.292	--	.256	--	.244	--	.182	--	.242	--	.556	89
Sal Butera	.286	--	.205	147	.174	--	.270	--	.267	--	.167	--	.200	--	.250	--
Sil Campusano	.224	--	.215	140	.229	--	.208	--	.243	--	.368	--	.282	--	.125	--
Tony Fernandez	.285	35	.289	56	.285	45	.289	33	.348	9	.386	4	.263	140	.556	89
Cecil Fielder	.254	--	.214	142	.190	--	.263	73	.262	82	.200	126	.340	50	.400	156
Kelly Gruber	.293	28	.267	85	.269	74	.287	35	.348	8	.308	26	.288	114	.676	32
Rick Leach	.226	--	.299	37	.294	33	.256	--	.344	11	.346	12	.233	155	.636	50
Manny Lee	.297	23	.288	58	.296	29	.286	37	.316	23	.318	18	.293	107	.485	127
Nelson Liriano	.297	--	.242	113	.270	70	.261	82	.293	41	.182	142	.309	87	.500	115
Fred McGriff	.289	32	.277	71	.256	92	.304	23	.220	140	.190	134	.460	2	.500	115
Lloyd Moseby	.239	113	.240	115	.232	132	.245	110	.217	143	.207	119	.293	106	.474	132
Rance Mulliniks	.313	9	.291	51	.303	21	.297	27	.232	126	.226	97	.341	46	.545	99
Ernie Whitt	.245	104	.255	97	.242	111	.260	83	.289	50	.304	31	.398	9	.656	44
Team Average	.268	3	.269	6	.268	4	.269	2	.281	2	.256	5	.300	11	.554	9
League Average	.256		.267		.262		.257		.262		.239		.311		.570	

Pitching vs. Left and Right Handed Batters

		BA	Rank	SA	Rank	OBA	Rank	HR %	Rank	BB %	Rank	SO %	Rank
John Cerutti	vs. Lefties	.190	5	.310	19	.226	4	1.72	48	4.69	7	18.75	17
	vs. Righties	.278	99	.426	97	.349	108	2.84	80	9.09	90	10.35	115
Jim Clancy	vs. Lefties	.280	90	.411	89	.324	63	2.48	82	6.16	24	12.79	61
	vs. Righties	.264	78	.438	108	.317	65	4.49	123	5.14	17	15.94	52
Mark Eichhorn	vs. Lefties	.299	110	.333	31	.346	94	0.00	1	7.03	37	7.03	119
	vs. Righties	.308	122	.434	103	.407	128	2.10	45	10.34	107	10.92	111
Mike Flanagan	vs. Lefties	.270	78	.426	101	.320	54	2.61	87	6.40	32	9.60	96
	vs. Righties	.271	90	.423	90	.342	100	2.87	82	9.10	92	11.00	110
Tom Henke	vs. Lefties	.261	67	.321	28	.322	58	1.49	41	8.22	53	24.66	7
	vs. Righties	.210	--	.412	--	.289	--	3.36	--	8.63	--	21.58	--
Jimmy Key	vs. Lefties	.147	--	.253	--	.200	--	1.33	--	2.44	--	14.63	--
	vs. Righties	.267	87	.408	80	.313	52	2.76	75	5.97	35	11.30	107
Jeff Musselman	vs. Lefties	.286	--	.408	--	.390	--	2.04	--	15.25	--	6.78	--
	vs. Righties	.245	47	.349	42	.306	46	1.12	10	7.12	54	11.86	103
Dave Stieb	vs. Lefties	.218	20	.315	22	.294	25	2.00	61	9.44	76	12.36	69
	vs. Righties	.201	11	.316	16	.296	35	2.01	39	9.27	97	23.06	11
Todd Stottlemyre	vs. Lefties	.371	130	.553	129	.444	128	3.55	116	11.06	101	10.18	89
	vs. Righties	.191	4	.351	43	.279	21	4.26	121	9.68	103	20.28	25
Duane Ward	vs. Lefties	.231	31	.312	21	.332	75	1.73	52	13.30	120	15.76	41
	vs. Righties	.254	61	.338	33	.352	112	0.83	6	11.62	120	20.77	21
David Wells	vs. Lefties	.265	--	.324	--	.351	--	0.00	--	8.97	--	14.10	--
	vs. Righties	.270	89	.557	127	.355	116	6.90	129	11.94	123	22.39	14
Team Average	vs. Lefties	.257	6	.371	6	.323	5	2.09	6	8.58	4	13.20	7
	vs. Righties	.255	7	.404	12	.327	12	2.90	11	8.54	13	15.46	6
League Average	vs. Lefties	.262		.387		.331		2.24		9.12		13.21	
	vs. Righties	.258		.393		.320		2.63		7.80		15.09	

Pitching with Runners on Base and Bases Empty

		BA	Rank	SA	Rank	OBA	Rank	HR %	Rank	BB %	Rank	SO %	Rank
John Cerutti	Runners On	.247	47	.376	56	.332	66	1.55	32	10.82	101	14.29	56
	Bases Empty	.263	80	.412	95	.311	57	3.28	102	5.80	34	10.92	106
Jim Clancy	Runners On	.286	96	.398	71	.335	74	2.04	50	6.08	17	9.77	108
	Bases Empty	.264	82	.440	107	.311	62	4.29	120	5.42	26	15.46	57
Mark Eichhorn	Runners On	.303	111	.379	60	.386	118	0.69	7	9.20	74	9.77	108
	Bases Empty	.304	--	.400	--	.375	--	1.74	--	8.59	--	8.59	--
Mike Flanagan	Runners On	.251	52	.362	46	.308	36	0.87	12	6.65	24	10.23	102
	Bases Empty	.286	115	.469	124	.362	120	4.26	118	10.29	112	11.24	101
Tom Henke	Runners On	.237	29	.339	26	.324	57	1.69	35	10.71	100	22.14	6
	Bases Empty	.237	41	.385	72	.290	27	2.96	95	6.21	41	24.14	7
Jimmy Key	Runners On	.262	67	.390	67	.305	33	2.14	56	5.80	14	10.63	97
	Bases Empty	.242	49	.382	70	.291	29	2.80	90	5.23	24	12.50	82
Jeff Musselman	Runners On	.243	40	.338	24	.288	14	1.35	24	6.21	20	8.07	119
	Bases Empty	.259	73	.376	62	.347	112	1.18	15	10.36	114	13.47	75
Dave Stieb	Runners On	.229	21	.308	7	.298	27	1.37	25	7.67	44	14.42	53
	Bases Empty	.197	7	.320	18	.293	32	2.41	79	10.42	115	19.31	25
Todd Stottlemyre	Runners On	.287	98	.454	108	.386	119	3.45	105	13.68	120	12.74	75
	Bases Empty	.280	105	.455	112	.342	108	4.27	119	7.36	66	17.32	35
Duane Ward	Runners On	.239	33	.307	6	.321	53	0.92	13	9.77	91	22.27	5
	Bases Empty	.251	61	.349	38	.368	123	1.54	27	15.15	126	14.72	61
David Wells	Runners On	.259	62	.517	124	.353	94	6.03	129	12.32	114	20.29	16
	Bases Empty	.278	101	.468	122	.355	116	3.97	113	9.93	109	19.86	21
Team Average	Runners On	.256	3	.375	2	.326	3	1.85	2	8.74	7	13.83	8
	Bases Empty	.256	8	.406	12	.326	11	3.19	14	8.42	11	15.31	5
League Average	Runners On	.268		.401		.336		2.45		9.09		13.68	
	Bases Empty	.253		.383		.315		2.48		7.76		14.81	

Overall Pitching Compared to Late Inning Pressure Situations

		BA	Rank	SA	Rank	OBA	Rank	HR %	Rank	BB %	Rank	SO %	Rank
John Cerutti	Overall	.256	59	.397	81	.320	58	2.56	78	8.02	60	12.40	83
	Pressure	.254	71	.349	50	.314	56	1.59	48	8.33	56	12.50	89
Jim Clancy	Overall	.272	93	.424	101	.321	61	3.42	112	5.68	13	14.27	58
	Pressure	.517	--	.690	--	.548	--	3.45	--	6.06	--	6.06	--
Mark Eichhorn	Overall	.304	124	.388	71	.381	126	1.15	7	8.94	85	9.27	119
	Pressure	.378	126	.556	123	.481	128	2.22	67	10.53	85	8.77	113
Mike Flanagan	Overall	.271	89	.424	100	.339	95	2.83	90	8.73	82	10.81	101
	Pressure	.264	84	.453	106	.361	99	5.66	123	13.11	108	8.20	115
Tom Henke	Overall	.237	34	.364	43	.306	33	2.37	70	8.42	71	23.16	6
	Pressure	.210	26	.370	68	.297	36	3.09	94	10.11	82	24.47	8
Jimmy Key	Overall	.250	50	.385	67	.296	20	2.55	77	5.44	12	11.80	92
	Pressure	.095	--	.095	--	.174	--	0.00	--	8.70	--	17.39	--
Jeff Musselman	Overall	.252	53	.358	36	.320	60	1.26	9	8.47	72	11.02	99
	Pressure	.000	--	.000	--	.000	--	0.00	--	0.00	--	22.22	--
Dave Stieb	Overall	.210	9	.316	9	.295	17	2.01	41	9.36	90	17.42	32
	Pressure	.232	45	.321	38	.338	76	0.00	1	7.69	45	13.85	75
Todd Stottlemyre	Overall	.283	110	.455	118	.363	120	3.90	120	10.38	106	15.12	53
	Pressure	.308	--	.500	--	.357	--	3.85	--	7.14	--	17.86	--
Duane Ward	Overall	.245	40	.327	16	.344	104	1.21	8	12.32	122	18.69	23
	Pressure	.241	59	.332	43	.340	81	1.01	31	12.61	104	21.43	17
David Wells	Overall	.269	85	.492	127	.354	114	4.96	129	11.11	116	20.07	17
	Pressure	.287	104	.559	124	.359	98	5.88	125	10.32	83	18.71	26
Team Average	Overall	.256	5	.392	6	.326	7	2.61	8	8.56	9	14.65	6
	Pressure	.259	11	.410	12	.345	13	2.68	11	10.36	12	17.78	3
League Average	Overall	.259		.391		.324		2.47		8.35		14.31	
	Pressure	.249		.369		.324		2.26		9.33		15.69	

Additional Miscellaneous Pitching Comparisons

	Grass Surface		Artificial Surface		Home Games		Road Games		Runners in Scoring Position		Runners in Scoring Pos and Two Outs		Leading Off Inning	
	BA	Rank	BA	Rank	BA	Rank	BA	Rank	BA	Rank	BA	Rank	OBA	Rank
Doug Bair	.000	--	.286	80	.325	--	.100	--	.056	--	.000	--	.500	--
John Cerutti	.256	60	.257	54	.247	52	.266	76	.227	33	.204	43	.244	11
Jim Clancy	.259	66	.282	77	.291	110	.257	66	.296	106	.215	51	.330	89
Mark Eichhorn	.329	--	.292	94	.295	115	.319	--	.292	101	.245	74	.400	123
Mike Flanagan	.264	72	.275	72	.275	93	.267	78	.238	43	.238	66	.339	96
Tom Henke	.242	--	.234	24	.233	39	.241	41	.247	52	.209	47	.259	17
Jimmy Key	.220	19	.271	66	.278	96	.227	20	.312	117	.239	68	.239	8
Jeff Musselman	.241	--	.255	51	.285	104	.205	7	.333	--	.148	--	.382	118
Jose Nunez	.263	--	.255	50	.282	--	.246	--	.172	--	.200	--	.407	--
Dave Stieb	.211	10	.209	12	.193	4	.235	33	.231	38	.200	40	.313	67
Todd Stottlemyre	.275	101	.289	89	.331	126	.248	50	.262	67	.239	68	.404	124
Duane Ward	.262	67	.235	26	.215	18	.275	84	.187	9	.178	31	.388	119
David Wells	.282	--	.256	53	.239	46	.295	109	.208	16	.219	54	.368	112
Frank Wills	.200	--	.288	86	.292	--	.188	--	.174	--	.250	--	.278	--
Team Average	.253	7	.258	4	.259	6	.253	5	.249	3	.213	2	.329	12
League Average	.256		.267		.257		.262		.262		.239		.311	

National League

ATLANTA BRAVES

- **The '88 Braves were a blast from the past.**
- **Really bad teams bounce back faster than you might think.**

Three years ago, Tom Shales, writing in *Esquire,* observed that just as the 1970s were known as the "Me Decade," the 80s should be christened the "Re Decade." Shales noted that the 80s "have no texture, no style, no tone of their own. (Their) texture and style and tone (is) of all the other decades, at least those that were recorded on film or tape, because the Re Decade is everything that preceded it thrown into one big electronic revue. (It's) the decade of replay, recycle, recall, retrieve, reprocess, and rerun." Shales was right, of course, and he has been proved even righter over the last three years. Cable television has given us reruns of "Mr. Ed" and "Car 54, Where Are You?"—programs that no right-thinking American thought that he would ever see again. The NFL has gotten into the swing of things by using replays of television pictures to aid in officiating its games.

One blast from the past that the 1980s lacked, however, was a really bad baseball team. We're not talking here about a chronically bad or perennially bad team, such as the Indians or the Cubs. We're talking about a team that is particularly dreadful for one given year, regardless of how well or poorly it plays before or after that season, making that team a metaphor for ineptitude. A team like the '62 Mets, the '52 Pirates, or the 1935 Boston Braves, who were so bad that they changed their nickname to the Bees for the next five years.

And then, voila; not only did we get one, we got two. Last year's Atlanta Braves and Baltimore Orioles provided us with what we had been missing during the 1980s. The Braves (54–106, .338) and the Orioles (54–107, .335) turned in the worst single-season records in the majors since 1979, when both Oakland (54–108) and Toronto (53–109) played doormat to the American League. The last National League teams with as bad a record as the '88 Braves were the Expos and Padres, who each finished at 52–110 as expansion teams in 1969.

Atlanta and Baltimore were the 68th and 69th major league teams to play below .340 ball in this century. Notwithstanding the fact that both teams played down to their potential in the same season, the frequency of teams of this ilk has actually been on the decrease. Below is a summary of how many teams didn't reach the .340 mark in each decade since 1900. We have included the total number of team-years for each decade to reflect major league expansion. In the 1920s, for example, 16 teams played for 10 years apiece, a total of 160 team-years.

	Total Team-Years	Below .340	Pct.
1900s	152	13	8.6
1910s	160	10	6.3
1920s	160	9	5.6
1930s	160	9	5.6
1940s	160	8	5.0
1950s	160	7	4.4
1960s	198	7	3.5
1970s	246	4	1.6
1980s	234	2	0.9

In every decade in this century, the rate of horrid teams has been less than it was in the previous decade. Now there's something that we can all feel good about, Republican and Democrat, black and white, American Leaguer and National Leaguer. We may not have figured out ways to feed the poor, reduce the deficit, or design an effective gas recycling system, but we've made progress in stamping out bad baseball teams. Want more proof, we'll give you more: In the 46 seasons from 1900 through 1945, there were 17 teams that played less than .300 ball; in the 43 seasons since the end of World War II, only two teams, the '52 Pirates and the '62 Mets, didn't hit .300. And some people still hail Judge Landis as the game's greatest commissioner. Hah! Happy Chandler, Ford Frick, Bowie Kuhn, and Peter Ueberroth have succeeded in reducing the incidence of bad ball playing. And under the direction of good ol' Spike Eckert, commissioner for three years in the 60s, nary a team played .360 or worse.

Not only have there been fewer bad teams in recent years; the good news for Braves' fans is that it seems to take fewer years than it once did for these teams to climb back up to the top of the standings. Let's look at the data that we earlier grouped by decade. For each of the 67 previous teams, how long, on average did it take before those teams next finished in first place?

We should note, incidentally, that each of those teams did indeed come back to win a pennant or division title. Some took a bit longer than others. The St. Louis Browns, who had a .305 percentage in 1910 and .296 in 1911, didn't win a pennant until 1944; the Phillies, .331 in 1921, didn't win a National League pennant until 1950; and the Athletics, a

.318 team in 1945, meandered through three cities until they next finished in first place, in Oakland in 1971.

But those cases are exceptional. The average span of time that it has taken to go from very bad to first place is shown here:

	Teams	Average
1900s	13	14.2 years
1910s	10	13.2 years
1920s	9	21.1 years
1930s	9	13.9 years
1940s	8	14.0 years
1950s	7	14.1 years
1960s	7	9.1 years
1970s	4	5.3 years
1980s	2	—

Since the introduction of divisional play, of course, there have been two "first places" in each league that teams may shoot for. But that advantage is somewhat mitigated by there being more teams to beat out now than there were before the first expansion in 1961. With four division titles to be won by any of 26 teams, the average team has one chance in 6.5 to finish first. In the old days, there was one chance in eight. That's a difference, but a comparatively slight one. The drop in the average turnaround time has been dramatic; here are the figures for teams that played less than .340 ball in the years since 1960, compared with teams that had done the same thing in olden days:

	Teams	Average
Before 1960	56	15.1 years
Since 1961	11	7.7 years

Here are the records of the 11 worst teams since 1961, along with the turnaround time until they next finished in first place:

	W–L	Pct.	Next in First	Span
1961 Phillies	47–107	.305	1976	15 years
1962 Mets	40–120	.250	1969	7 years
1963 Mets	51–111	.315	1969	6 years
1964 Mets	53–109	.327	1969	5 years
1965 Mets	50–112	.309	1969	4 years
1969 Expos	52–110	.321	1981	12 years
1969 Padres	52–110	.321	1984	15 years
1976 Expos	55–107	.3395	1981	5 years
1977 Blue Jays	54–107	.335	1985	8 years
1979 Athletics	54–108	.333	1981	2 years
1979 Blue Jays	53–109	.327	1985	6 years

So if the Braves are looking for a model team after which to pattern their comeback plans, how about the 1979 Athletics? It took only two years for Oakland to go from a .333 percentage to an American League West Division title. The Athletics' modus operandi: (1) the team was sold; (2) a 50-day players' strike that necessitated a split season; and (3) Billy Martin was brought in as manager.

Hmmmm, maybe it isn't worth all that trouble. . . .

Instead of bringing back Billy, here's a simpler plan for the Braves to follow if they are to improve in 1989. First, get off to a better start. Second, protect some late-inning leads.

Atlanta lost its first 10 games of last season, a modern National League record that was dwarfed by the Orioles'

21-game streak. Still, by the end of April, the Braves had lost 16 of 19 games, leaving them farther below .500 than all but two teams in major league history. The 1969 Astros (4–20) and the 1988 Orioles (1–22) were farther below the .500 mark on the morning of May 1.

Almost inevitably, a disastrous April leads to a disastrous season. Only three teams in history have wound up in first place after finishing April six or more games below .500: the 1908 Tigers, the 1951 Giants, and the 1974 Pirates. The Braves last season became the first team in major league history to open a season with eight straight home games and to lose every one. They were probably the first team in National League history to lose their pennant hopes before the income-tax deadline!

Protecting late-inning leads has been a cause for concern in Atlanta ever since Bruce Sutter came up lame and Steve Bedrosian was traded to Philadelphia. Last year, the Braves held a lead after six innings in only 51 games, the lowest total in the National League. Yet they wound up losing 15 of those games—the most losses by any team in the National League in games of that type, despite the "handicap" of having a pool of only 51 games to work with. Here are the National League standings for 1988 in games in which each team led going into the seventh inning:

	W–L	Pct.
Cincinnati	64–5	.928
Montreal	55–5	.917
New York	68–7	.907
Pittsburgh	63–7	.900
Los Angeles	67–8	.893
San Francisco	66–8	.892
Philadelphia	50–7	.877
San Diego	68–10	.872
Chicago	59–9	.868
Houston	58–10	.853
St. Louis	62–12	.838
Atlanta	36–15	.706

The 11 other National League teams lost one out of every 8.7 games in which they led after six innings; that's about as frequently as Larry Bird has missed a free throw over the past seven years with the Celtics. The Braves' rate of one loss every 3.4 such games is closer to Manute Bol's free-throw percentage than it is to Bird's. We've been keeping track of these things for every major league team since 1981, and only one team over that time has had a worse record in these games than the 1988 Braves (and that was in the strike-shortened 1981 season):

	W–L	Pct.
1981 Cubs	30–13	.698
1988 Braves	36–15	.706
1981 Pirates	32–13	.711
1985 Giants	40–16	.714
1986 Dodgers	54–18	.750

The boys in the Braves' bullpen must put up numbers closer to Bird than to Bol if America's cable watchers are to be spared another long summer.

WON-LOST RECORD BY STARTING POSITION

ATLANTA 54-106	C	1B	2B	3B	SS	LF	CF	RF	P	Leadoff	Relief	Starts
Jim Acker	·	·	·	·	·	·	·	·	0-1	·	2-18	0-1
Jose Alvarez	·	·	·	·	·	·	·	·	·	·	16-44	·
Paul Assenmacher	·	·	·	·	·	·	·	·	·	·	27-37	·
Bruce Benedict	26-50	·	·	·	·	·	·	·	·	·	·	26-50
Kevin Blankenship	·	·	·	·	·	·	·	·	0-2	·	·	0-2
Jeff Blauser	·	·	4-5	·	2-6	·	·	·	·	2-1	·	6-11
Terry Blocker	·	·	·	·	·	·	18-41	·	·	1-0	·	18-41
Joe Boever	·	·	·	·	·	·	·	·	·	·	4-12	·
Chuck Cary	·	·	·	·	·	·	·	·	·	·	0-7	·
Kevin Coffman	·	·	·	·	·	·	·	·	3-8	·	0-7	3-8
Jody Davis	1-1	·	·	·	·	·	·	·	·	·	·	1-1
Gary Eave	·	·	·	·	·	·	·	·	·	·	0-5	·
Juan Eichelberger	·	·	·	·	·	·	·	·	·	·	4-16	·
Ron Gant	·	·	41-79	7-15	·	·	·	·	·	26-63	·	48-94
Damaso Garcia	·	·	2-10	·	·	·	·	·	·	·	·	2-10
Tom Glavine	·	·	·	·	·	·	·	·	13-21	·	·	13-21
Tommy Gregg	·	·	·	·	·	1-4	1-1	·	·	·	·	2-5
Ken Griffey	·	2-5	·	·	·	8-29	·	1-1	·	·	·	11-35
Albert Hall	·	·	·	·	·	·	22-29	·	·	20-25	·	22-29
Dion James	·	·	·	·	·	23-41	7-28	0-2	·	5-17	·	30-71
German Jimenez	·	·	·	·	·	·	·	·	3-6	·	1-5	3-6
Mark Lemke	·	·	5-11	·	·	·	·	·	·	·	·	5-11
Rick Mahler	·	·	·	·	·	·	·	·	12-22	·	2-3	12-22
Jim Morrison	·	·	·	7-9	·	1-1	·	·	·	·	0-3	8-10
Dale Murphy	·	·	·	·	·	·	52-103	·	·	·	·	52-103
Ken Oberkfell	·	·	·	35-74	·	·	·	·	·	·	·	35-74
Ed Olwine	·	·	·	·	·	·	·	·	·	·	1-15	·
Gerald Perry	·	47-91	·	·	·	·	·	·	·	·	·	47-91
Charlie Puleo	·	·	·	·	·	·	·	·	·	1-2	12-38	1-2
Gary Roenicke	·	·	·	·	·	13-12	·	1-0	·	·	·	14-12
Jerry Royster	·	·	·	1-1	·	1-1	6-7	·	·	·	·	8-9
Paul Runge	·	·	2-1	4-7	0-2	·	·	·	·	·	·	6-10
Ted Simmons	0-1	5-10	·	·	·	·	·	·	·	·	·	5-11
Lonnie Smith	·	·	·	·	·	7-18	·	·	·	·	·	7-18
Pete Smith	·	·	·	·	·	·	·	·	10-22	·	·	10-22
Zane Smith	·	·	·	·	·	·	·	·	8-14	·	0-1	8-14
John Smoltz	·	·	·	·	·	·	·	·	4-8	·	·	4-8
Bruce Sutter	·	·	·	·	·	·	·	·	·	·	24-14	·
Andres Thomas	·	·	·	·	52-98	·	·	·	·	·	·	52-98
Ozzie Virgil	27-54	·	·	·	·	·	·	·	·	·	·	27-54

Batting vs. Left and Right Handed Pitchers

		BA	Rank	SA	Rank	OBA	Rank	HR %	Rank	BB %	Rank	SO %	Rank
Bruce Benedict	vs. Lefties	.182	122	.221	126	.247	120	0.00	103	8.14	66	9.30	36
	vs. Righties	.270	44	.296	109	.320	62	0.00	115	6.82	80	10.23	31
Terry Blocker	vs. Lefties	.217	--	.267	--	.230	--	0.00	--	1.59	--	20.63	--
	vs. Righties	.210	120	.290	114	.259	124	1.45	68	6.12	91	4.76	3
Jody Davis	vs. Lefties	.186	120	.255	119	.270	110	1.96	68	10.43	34	17.39	104
	vs. Righties	.258	63	.406	37	.331	46	3.23	27	9.60	40	18.08	106
Ron Gant	vs. Lefties	.280	40	.513	12	.352	37	4.66	10	10.14	40	18.43	113
	vs. Righties	.249	81	.400	40	.298	89	2.70	33	5.99	95	19.45	115
Albert Hall	vs. Lefties	.188	119	.225	124	.283	99	0.00	103	10.64	31	13.83	80
	vs. Righties	.278	31	.338	83	.331	47	0.66	102	6.75	82	13.50	60
Dion James	vs. Lefties	.114	--	.200	--	.205	--	0.00	--	10.00	--	22.50	--
	vs. Righties	.271	43	.365	64	.368	16	0.85	91	13.20	11	12.22	46
Jim Morrison	vs. Lefties	.152	127	.273	116	.224	126	3.03	41	9.21	53	5.26	8
	vs. Righties	.154	--	.154	--	.241	--	0.00	--	10.34	--	31.03	--
Dale Murphy	vs. Lefties	.256	71	.478	21	.379	15	5.00	9	16.89	3	15.07	91
	vs. Righties	.214	117	.396	44	.281	109	3.64	23	8.19	59	20.35	117
Gerald Perry	vs. Lefties	.270	53	.346	84	.279	103	1.42	78	1.82	128	10.91	56
	vs. Righties	.318	3	.435	24	.373	13	1.49	64	8.53	53	6.67	9
Gary Roenicke	vs. Lefties	.261	62	.352	79	.309	80	1.14	89	6.38	90	9.57	39
	vs. Righties	.115	--	.115	--	.179	--	0.00	--	7.14	--	21.43	--
Lonnie Smith	vs. Lefties	.253	74	.405	49	.306	83	3.80	22	7.06	73	18.82	117
	vs. Righties	.200	--	.200	--	.275	--	0.00	--	10.00	--	22.50	--
Andres Thomas	vs. Lefties	.240	91	.380	65	.267	113	3.65	24	3.96	118	12.87	71
	vs. Righties	.258	62	.350	75	.268	119	1.45	68	1.41	126	16.24	88
Ozzie Virgil	vs. Lefties	.279	42	.404	50	.345	43	2.88	44	9.40	49	8.55	30
	vs. Righties	.245	85	.356	68	.297	90	2.78	32	4.72	115	18.88	109
Team Average	vs. Lefties	.231	11	.351	9	.288	12	2.29	4	7.60	9	13.85	5
	vs. Righties	.248	6	.346	10	.303	10	1.51	11	6.98	11	14.23	4
League Average	vs. Lefties	.248		.367		.310		2.10		8.01		14.42	
	vs. Righties	.249		.360		.310		1.88		7.86		15.35	

Batting with Runners on Base and Bases Empty

		BA	Rank	SA	Rank	OBA	Rank	HR %	Rank	BB %	Rank	SO %	Ran!.
Bruce Benedict	Runners On	.295	31	.347	88	.330	78	0.00	104	5.56	112	14.81	83
	Bases Empty	.206	116	.220	124	.273	102	0.00	115	8.44	44	6.49	4
Terry Blocker	Runners On	.270	--	.365	--	.333	--	1.35	--	8.43	--	6.02	--
	Bases Empty	.177	126	.234	122	.197	127	0.81	97	2.36	120	11.81	44
Jody Davis	Runners On	.250	93	.348	87	.329	79	1.52	68	10.39	49	14.94	86
	Bases Empty	.208	114	.344	78	.283	95	4.00	18	9.42	28	21.01	115
Ron Gant	Runners On	.298	28	.466	20	.358	45	2.81	33	9.36	62	16.75	106
	Bases Empty	.242	78	.426	25	.296	79	3.64	23	6.51	70	20.24	110
Albert Hall	Runners On	.333	--	.406	--	.405	--	0.00	--	11.11	--	13.58	--
	Bases Empty	.210	113	.253	120	.273	102	0.62	107	6.82	64	13.64	53
Dion James	Runners On	.278	55	.353	83	.406	13	0.00	104	17.37	8	10.78	42
	Bases Empty	.245	73	.348	73	.323	44	1.19	84	10.28	18	14.54	67
Dale Murphy	Runners On	.198	121	.338	98	.327	81	2.66	37	15.72	17	16.67	104
	Bases Empty	.249	62	.486	9	.300	73	5.17	6	6.80	65	20.40	112
Gerald Perry	Runners On	.358	2	.492	13	.397	18	1.97	57	7.99	83	6.25	11
	Bases Empty	.249	64	.321	98	.283	94	1.02	88	4.23	108	10.10	26
Andres Thomas	Runners On	.247	98	.308	110	.267	121	0.81	90	3.44	124	11.07	48
	Bases Empty	.256	49	.396	38	.268	108	3.06	30	1.37	124	18.08	95
Ozzie Virgil	Runners On	.278	55	.338	99	.340	65	0.75	92	7.38	92	14.09	75
	Bases Empty	.241	80	.396	36	.294	83	4.28	17	5.47	89	16.42	85
Team Average	Runners On	.258	5	.359	11	.327	6	1.38	11	9.34	6	12.79	1
	Bases Empty	.232	11	.341	8	.279	12	2.01	5	5.69	11	15.01	4
League Average	Runners On	.257		.373		.329		1.91		9.45		14.09	
	Bases Empty	.242		.355		.297		1.98		6.73		15.80	

Overall Batting Compared to Late Inning Pressure Situations

		BA	Rank	SA	Rank	OBA	Rank	HR %	Rank	BB %	Rank	SO %	Rank	RDI %	Rank
Bruce Benedict	Overall	.242	97	.271	122	.296	99	0.00	118	7.25	76	9.92	29	.232	98
	Pressure	.133	--	.133	--	.188	--	0.00	--	5.88	--	14.71	--	.000	--
Terry Blocker	Overall	.212	121	.283	120	.250	126	1.01	91	4.76	116	9.52	26	.195	--
	Pressure	.282	35	.333	64	.349	44	0.00	79	8.89	53	8.89	22	.400	--
Jody Davis	Overall	.230	111	.346	89	.307	85	2.72	37	9.93	37	17.81	105	.253	82
	Pressure	.118	127	.206	120	.286	89	0.00	79	16.67	6	28.57	126	.077	125
Ron Gant	Overall	.259	63	.439	17	.317	70	3.37	23	7.44	72	19.09	115	.260	74
	Pressure	.242	66	.354	57	.303	76	1.01	75	8.18	65	19.09	90	.267	53
Albert Hall	Overall	.247	90	.299	114	.314	73	0.43	110	8.17	59	13.62	63	.277	--
	Pressure	.250	57	.333	64	.333	51	2.08	49	9.26	51	7.41	14	.250	--
Dion James	Overall	.256	69	.350	88	.353	22	0.78	96	12.92	10	13.14	57	.275	64
	Pressure	.235	76	.294	93	.354	39	0.00	79	15.48	14	10.71	34	.100	120
Jim Morrison	Overall	.152	--	.239	--	.229	--	2.17	--	9.52	--	12.38	--	.237	--
	Pressure	.133	--	.233	--	.229	--	3.33	--	11.43	--	8.57	--	.133	114
Dale Murphy	Overall	.226	113	.421	25	.313	78	4.05	15	11.03	27	18.63	109	.251	85
	Pressure	.204	99	.306	82	.275	101	1.85	54	8.33	63	20.00	97	.286	44
Gerald Perry	Overall	.300	8	.400	41	.338	41	1.46	75	6.05	98	8.24	12	.381	3
	Pressure	.267	48	.352	58	.313	66	0.95	76	6.19	89	9.73	26	.276	49
Ted Simmons	Overall	.196	--	.308	--	.293	--	1.87	--	12.20	--	7.32	--	.167	--
	Pressure	.146	121	.250	105	.268	105	2.08	49	14.29	18	10.71	34	.080	124
Andres Thomas	Overall	.252	78	.360	74	.268	120	2.15	49	2.23	126	15.15	83	.293	46
	Pressure	.197	102	.222	116	.215	120	0.00	79	2.48	122	21.49	109	.366	19
Ozzie Virgil	Overall	.256	71	.372	65	.313	76	2.81	34	6.29	96	15.43	86	.216	112
	Pressure	.316	19	.329	72	.372	24	0.00	79	7.95	67	15.91	74	.160	97
Team Average	Overall	.242	11	.348	11	.298	12	1.76	9	7.18	11	14.10	4	.257	6
	Pressure	.220	12	.284	12	.285	12	0.77	12	8.03	7	15.13	4	.227	9
League Average	Overall	.248		.363		.310		1.95		7.91		15.06		.256	
	Pressure	.242		.340		.310		1.70		8.47		15.93		.238	

Additional Miscellaneous Batting Comparisons

	Grass Surface		Artificial Surface		Home Games		Road Games		Runners in Scoring Position		Runners in Scoring Pos and Two Outs		Leading Off Inning		Runners on 3B with less than 2 Outs	
	BA	Rank	BA	Rank	BA	Rank	BA	Rank	BA	Rank	BA	Rank	OBA	Rank	RDI %	Rank
Bruce Benedict	.235	101	.264	--	.238	93	.245	81	.232	92	.233	67	.230	121	.385	125
Terry Blocker	.214	114	.205	--	.220	108	.204	118	.270	--	.300	--	.246	114	.286	--
Jody Davis	.205	119	.279	--	.181	124	.263	55	.211	108	.194	94	.373	14	.571	61
Ron Gant	.247	80	.288	27	.247	86	.270	40	.274	53	.255	54	.327	45	.526	85
Albert Hall	.251	71	.234	--	.212	113	.276	34	.324	--	.300	--	.265	98	.250	--
Dion James	.241	90	.304	18	.250	84	.263	57	.280	43	.286	37	.324	48	.563	67
Dale Murphy	.242	88	.184	123	.261	65	.194	127	.237	88	.212	84	.314	61	.541	78
Gerald Perry	.290	21	.331	4	.314	9	.285	22	.346	4	.358	7	.257	104	.750	6
Lonnie Smith	.241	91	.229	--	.237	--	.236	--	.250	--	.333	--	.258	--	.200	--
Andres Thomas	.247	81	.268	50	.263	63	.243	85	.292	30	.296	27	.253	108	.645	37
Ozzie Virgil	.285	27	.185	121	.315	8	.205	117	.243	82	.152	114	.333	39	.385	125
Team Average	.242	11	.243	8	.250	6	.235	11	.253	5	.246	2	.286	11	.519	12
League Average	.250		.246		.252		.244		.250		.231		.301		.554	

Pitching vs. Left and Right Handed Batters

Player		BA	Rank	SA	Rank	OBA	Rank	HR %	Rank	BB %	Rank	SO %	Rank
Jose Alvarez	vs. Lefties	.269	71	.374	64	.402	102	1.75	57	16.59	105	17.06	32
	vs. Righties	.215	28	.313	27	.288	49	2.05	58	8.00	76	20.00	20
Paul Assenmacher	vs. Lefties	.275	76	.385	72	.320	54	2.20	73	5.15	15	22.68	12
	vs. Righties	.240	54	.321	31	.330	86	1.02	20	11.64	105	21.12	16
Kevin Coffman	vs. Lefties	.277	77	.390	75	.412	107	1.42	41	17.42	106	5.62	108
	vs. Righties	.217	--	.321	--	.359	--	0.94	--	17.29	--	10.53	--
Tom Glavine	vs. Lefties	.244	40	.350	46	.343	73	2.44	81	11.56	84	9.52	92
	vs. Righties	.275	95	.376	72	.326	84	1.45	37	6.60	54	10.04	97
German Jimenez	vs. Lefties	.151	--	.170	--	.175	--	0.00	--	3.45	--	12.07	--
	vs. Righties	.339	109	.452	102	.374	107	2.38	76	5.46	37	10.38	93
Rick Mahler	vs. Lefties	.268	70	.352	48	.301	34	1.25	37	4.33	8	11.50	79
	vs. Righties	.301	103	.441	100	.334	91	2.33	73	3.46	10	13.39	76
Charlie Puleo	vs. Lefties	.298	96	.482	103	.390	97	3.66	103	12.89	98	13.33	60
	vs. Righties	.208	17	.288	16	.274	32	0.94	17	7.59	74	16.88	44
Pete Smith	vs. Lefties	.283	80	.424	89	.366	89	2.18	71	11.74	86	13.84	57
	vs. Righties	.207	16	.313	29	.281	39	1.88	50	8.89	83	16.11	49
Zane Smith	vs. Lefties	.238	36	.262	8	.297	28	0.00	1	7.53	37	11.83	74
	vs. Righties	.302	104	.395	83	.356	104	1.74	44	7.17	63	9.30	100
John Smoltz	vs. Lefties	.314	106	.487	105	.409	105	2.56	91	12.57	95	10.93	82
	vs. Righties	.240	--	.452	--	.307	--	5.77	--	8.77	--	14.91	--
Bruce Sutter	vs. Lefties	.273	74	.343	40	.301	35	2.02	66	3.85	4	23.08	9
	vs. Righties	.278	--	.430	--	.345	--	2.53	--	7.87	--	17.98	--
Team Average	vs. Lefties	.273	12	.386	10	.349	11	1.80	7	9.91	10	12.58	11
	vs. Righties	.264	12	.379	10	.322	11	2.07	4	7.26	10	13.26	12
League Average	vs. Lefties	.255		.365		.325		1.73		9.36		14.24	
	vs. Righties	.244		.361		.299		2.10		6.87		15.64	

Pitching with Runners on Base and Bases Empty

Player		BA	Rank	SA	Rank	OBA	Rank	HR %	Rank	BB %	Rank	SO %	Rank
Jose Alvarez	Runners On	.207	15	.244	6	.348	78	0.00	1	16.51	109	18.40	22
	Bases Empty	.267	91	.421	100	.339	98	3.47	102	8.04	80	18.75	24
Paul Assenmacher	Runners On	.243	45	.331	35	.331	59	1.35	38	10.73	75	19.77	17
	Bases Empty	.259	82	.353	51	.322	85	1.44	34	8.55	85	23.68	9
Kevin Coffman	Runners On	.283	87	.441	99	.397	107	2.36	78	15.09	105	6.29	107
	Bases Empty	.217	20	.275	6	.382	109	0.00	1	19.74	109	9.21	101
Tom Glavine	Runners On	.291	93	.385	68	.365	96	0.97	29	10.03	62	7.65	84
	Bases Empty	.255	74	.362	66	.301	65	2.06	61	5.38	30	11.83	85
Rick Mahler	Runners On	.319	107	.466	106	.368	97	2.09	69	5.94	8	12.33	74
	Bases Empty	.259	81	.343	43	.280	31	1.48	36	2.56	5	12.32	80
Charlie Puleo	Runners On	.257	61	.380	65	.369	99	2.23	75	15.32	107	13.06	64
	Bases Empty	.246	64	.379	79	.296	50	2.23	71	5.42	31	17.08	39
Pete Smith	Runners On	.259	63	.396	77	.356	86	1.80	58	12.72	92	13.31	61
	Bases Empty	.244	63	.363	67	.313	79	2.20	70	9.02	90	15.83	54
Zane Smith	Runners On	.301	102	.394	74	.351	80	1.61	52	6.64	11	10.84	85
	Bases Empty	.284	101	.358	58	.344	100	1.35	30	7.74	73	8.67	104
John Smoltz	Runners On	.292	96	.487	108	.407	108	3.54	105	16.06	108	8.76	102
	Bases Empty	.279	98	.463	106	.338	95	4.08	106	6.88	56	15.63	56
Team Average	Runners On	.286	12	.409	12	.366	12	1.95	6	10.62	11	12.00	12
	Bases Empty	.254	10	.362	8	.308	10	1.96	5	6.54	5	13.77	12
League Average	Runners On	.257		.373		.329		1.91		9.45		14.09	
	Bases Empty	.242		.355		.297		1.98		6.73		15.80	

Overall Pitching Compared to Late Inning Pressure Situations

Player		BA	Rank	SA	Rank	OBA	Rank	HR %	Rank	BB %	Rank	SO %	Rank
Jim Acker	Overall	.280	--	.435	--	.335	--	3.73	--	7.61	--	13.59	--
	Pressure	.314	100	.431	93	.373	95	1.96	66	8.06	45	14.52	56
Jose Alvarez	Overall	.240	45	.342	38	.343	96	1.91	52	12.16	103	18.58	23
	Pressure	.222	47	.302	38	.324	62	1.59	50	12.00	94	17.33	34
Paul Assenmacher	Overall	.251	62	.341	37	.327	81	1.39	32	9.73	85	21.58	12
	Pressure	.259	67	.371	70	.335	75	2.03	68	9.61	74	22.71	14
Joe Boever	Overall	.182	--	.242	--	.206	--	1.52	--	1.43	--	10.00	--
	Pressure	.189	16	.216	2	.231	8	0.00	1	2.44	2	9.76	92
Kevin Coffman	Overall	.251	63	.360	56	.390	109	1.21	24	17.36	109	7.72	109
	Pressure	.429	--	.429	--	.636	--	0.00	--	27.27	--	0.00	--
Tom Glavine	Overall	.270	87	.372	64	.329	86	1.61	38	7.46	46	9.95	99
	Pressure	.296	92	.537	106	.377	98	5.56	108	9.68	75	12.90	69
Rick Mahler	Overall	.282	102	.390	88	.315	61	1.72	44	3.95	1	12.32	82
	Pressure	.221	46	.286	27	.259	22	1.43	45	4.52	9	10.32	86
Charlie Puleo	Overall	.251	61	.380	77	.330	89	2.23	76	10.17	90	15.15	50
	Pressure	.275	83	.383	74	.370	92	1.67	55	11.43	91	14.29	59
Pete Smith	Overall	.250	59	.376	70	.330	87	2.05	62	10.51	93	14.81	56
	Pressure	.323	103	.484	102	.386	100	1.61	51	9.59	72	6.85	106
Zane Smith	Overall	.292	108	.374	69	.347	100	1.47	35	7.22	42	9.69	101
	Pressure	.266	73	.281	25	.319	56	0.00	1	6.94	34	11.11	80
John Smoltz	Overall	.285	103	.473	109	.369	108	3.85	105	11.11	95	12.46	77
	Pressure	.333	--	.733	--	.394	--	10.00	--	9.09	--	12.12	--
Bruce Sutter	Overall	.275	--	.382	--	.321	--	2.25	--	5.70	--	20.73	--
	Pressure	.303	96	.394	78	.348	81	1.52	48	5.59	15	20.98	18
Team Average	Overall	.268	12	.382	10	.334	11	1.95	5	8.39	11	12.97	12
	Pressure	.268	11	.378	10	.339	12	2.02	10	8.84	3	15.02	9
League Average	Overall	.248		.363		.310		1.95		7.91		15.06	
	Pressure	.243		.347		.315		1.72		9.12		15.69	

Additional Miscellaneous Pitching Comparisons

	Grass Surface BA	Rank	Artificial Surface BA	Rank	Home Games BA	Rank	Road Games BA	Rank	Runners in Scoring Position BA	Rank	Runners in Scoring Pos and Two Outs BA	Rank	Leading Off Inning OBA	Rank
Jim Acker	.266	71	.308	--	.305	--	.253	--	.395	--	.316	--	.349	--
Jose Alvarez	.261	65	.193	9	.275	86	.202	6	.185	14	.161	12	.316	70
Paul Assenmacher	.274	82	.158	--	.278	91	.216	13	.253	59	.261	86	.388	105
Kevin Coffman	.262	68	.235	40	.278	91	.230	32	.306	96	.235	68	.408	107
Juan Eichelberger	.303	100	.282	--	.258	--	.326	--	.352	--	.176	--	.353	--
Tom Glavine	.278	88	.251	63	.290	103	.253	55	.290	91	.232	65	.324	78
German Jimenez	.306	101	.255	--	.336	--	.252	54	.396	--	.440	--	.236	--
Rick Mahler	.283	90	.281	94	.290	104	.275	83	.307	97	.284	97	.253	11
Charlie Puleo	.252	57	.245	55	.260	73	.242	44	.294	92	.339	105	.276	32
Pete Smith	.241	38	.284	96	.237	50	.272	77	.242	46	.253	81	.275	30
Zane Smith	.268	75	.398	109	.278	94	.307	103	.313	99	.217	55	.303	62
John Smoltz	.270	76	.435	--	.278	91	.293	99	.242	48	.130	7	.368	100
Bruce Sutter	.252	56	.322	--	.272	--	.279	--	.393	--	.200	--	.349	--
Team Average	.267	10	.270	12	.274	12	.262	10	.291	12	.256	11	.306	10
League Average	.250		.246		.244		.252		.250		.231		.301	

CHICAGO CUBS

- The Cubs held true to form, just a little later than usual.
- The similarity between these Cubs and the Cubs of the early 1960s.

As a certain former Cubs' radio announcer might put it, "Well, now they've done it." The Cubbies have now gone 43 years without winning the championship of the National League, matching the major league record set from 1901 to 1943 by the team that we now know as the Baltimore Orioles. (When the American League was first recognized as a major league in 1901, that franchise was located in Milwaukee and was called the Brewers; the team moved in 1902, and spent the next 52 mostly futile seasons as the St. Louis Browns.)

As the division championship that the Cubs won in 1984 recedes into our memory, it's worthwhile to consider just how much of an aberration that season was. In no other season since 1973 have the Cubs finished above the .500 mark. Over the same time period, the Cleveland Indians, Atlanta Braves, and San Diego Padres, teams whose mere mention suggests what used to be called the "second division," have each finished above .500 four times. The South Side White Sox, themselves hardly perennial pennant contenders, have finished above .500 five times over those 16 years. So have the California Angels. In fact, every team in the majors has finished above .500 at least four times over the past 16 years except the Cubs and the Seattle Mariners. And in the Mariners' case, although they have never done better than .481, at least they have the excuse that they didn't start playing until 1977. The Cubs beat them into the majors by only 101 years.

Last year, it looked for a while as if the Cubs would break through their recent mediocrity. When Greg Maddux beat the Giants, 3–2, on July 4, the Cubs moved into second place and stood eight games above .500, 80 games into the season. But this first-half surprise was followed by a 33–49 swoon that left Don Zimmer's team eight games below the break-even point by season's end.

Now, the people of Chicago are not exactly babes in the woods; they've been down this road before. Cubs fans have been teased more often than a small-town conventioneer on his first trip down Bourbon Street. We wrote about this pattern in last year's *Analyst,* when we studied the records of all

major league teams that played .600 ball over the first 40 games of a season. From 1900 to 1987, we found that only 21 of 327 such teams finished the season below the .500 mark, but five of those 21 teams played on the North Side of Chicago. We resolved never again to be fooled by a fast Cubs' start. So much for resolutions.

The Cubs found a new twist in 1988, and wound up fooling us (and a lot of others) yet again. They did not roar to the top of the standings in the first 40 games; their record was just 19–21 at the first turn. But after winning 25 of their next 40 games, the Cubs seemed to have announced their arrival.

Even by Cubs' standards, this 1988 tease was an impressive one. Since 1900, there have been 537 major league teams that have played at least eight games above .500 through the first 80 games of a season. Only eight of those 537 teams—that's 1.5 percent—finished the season eight (or more) games *below* the .500 mark. These teams are the ultimate teases and have earned a place in the Belle Starr Hall of Fame:

	First 80 Games	Rest of Season	Final Record	Next Pennant
1909 Indians	45–35	26–47	71–82	1920
1940 Giants	44–36	28–44	72–80	1951
1955 Cubs	44–36	28–45	72–81	—
1963 Red Sox	44–36	32–49	76–85	1967
1974 Indians	45–35	32–50	77–85	—
1976 Rangers	44–36	32–50	76–86	—
1983 Rangers	44–36	33–49	77–85	—
1988 Cubs	44–36	33–49	77–85	—

As the Who sang twenty years ago, "We won't get fooled again." We've broadened our study of a year ago to look at where all teams since 1900 have stood at the 80–game mark: above, below, or at the .500 mark. Then we've followed their progress through the rest of the season to determine in which of those three categories they finished.

	Through 80 Games		
	Above .500	At .500	Below .500
Finished above .500	697	41	97
Finished at .500	23	6	6
Finished below .500	93	42	625

These figures show that 86 percent of the teams that played winning ball over the first 80 games finished the season in that same area. But over the 16–year span that we mentioned earlier, during which the Cubs have produced only one winning season, they have stood over .500 through 80 games eight times. Think about that: the Cubs have taken something with an 86 percent chance of happening and have done it one time in eight. Here are the figures:

	First 80 Games	Rest of Season	Final Record
1973 Cubs	47–33	30–51	77–84
1977 Cubs	51–29	30–52	81–81
1978 Cubs	42–38	37–45	79–83
1979 Cubs	44–36	36–46	80–82
1984 Cubs	45–35	51–30	96–65
1985 Cubs	42–38	35–46	77–84
1987 Cubs	42–38	34–47	76–85
1988 Cubs	44–36	33–49	77–85

But perhaps the worst news for the Cubs is that history allows little hope for a pennant any time soon. Our earlier chart of teams that had a strong first 80 games but finished well below .500 suggests that there is indeed a carryover effect to subsequent seasons. Only one team won its league's pennant any time within the next 10 years; that team was the aptly named Impossible Dream team in Boston in 1967.

Last year, the Cubs introduced a pair of 24–year-old rookies, first baseman Mark Grace and catcher Damon Berryhill. They joined 25–year old shortstop Shawon Dunston and left fielder Rafael Palmeiro, who turned 24 in September, in the regular lineup, giving the Cubs four regular everyday starters, each of them developed in the team's farm system, and each of them not yet 26 years old when the season ended.

You have to go back a quarter of a century to find the last time that the Cubs possessed four players of that pedigree. Two of the players in that earlier group, Billy Williams and Lou Brock, have already been inducted into the Hall of Fame, and another, Ron Santo, is a bonafide contender for that honor. The fourth player of that group, second baseman Ken Hubbs, had been the National League's Rookie of the Year in 1962, but played only one more season before his death in a plane crash.

Despite the second half collapse in 1988, Cubs' fans went into the off-season with the anticipation of good times to come. Even if expecting a couple of Hall of Famers might be regarded as pie-in-the-sky, the quartet of Grace, Palmeiro, Dunston, and Berryhill at least had the promise to be the backbone of Cubs' teams for years to come. Palmeiro and Dunston had already been selected to the 1988 National League All-Star team, Grace was a Rookie of the Year candidate, and Berryhill had done enough to allow the Cubs to trade Jody Davis to Atlanta.

And then came the winter meetings and the big trade with Texas: Palmeiro, Jamie Moyer, and Drew Hall to the Rangers for Mitch Williams, Paul Kilgus, Steve Wilson, Curtis Wilkerson, and two 18–year-old minor leaguers. While the players on the periphery added some spice, fans in both Chicago and Dallas quickly boiled the deal down to Palmeiro for Williams.

We think that the Cubs' need for a closer can be documented rather succinctly; one year without Lee Smith left the team gasping in the late innings. In 1987, Chicago had the National League's best record (67–1) when taking a lead into the ninth inning; in 1988, the Cubs were 69–5 in those games, the worst such record in the league. (If you can't bring yourself to accept a 69–5 record as being "bad," then think of it this way: Chicago lost one of every 15 games in which it took a lead into the ninth inning; the other 11 National League teams lost one of every 31 games of that type. The Cubs' rate of losses in this category was more than twice as high as the average for the rest of the league.) The team's leader in saves, 37–year-old Rich Gossage, was credited with only 13 of them, matching the lowest total for a team leader on any of the 26 major league teams.

Meanwhile, the trade regenerated the questions of what direction the Cubs were taking with their everyday lineup. The most commonly heard negative about the young Cubs was that while players such as Palmeiro and Grace are excellent strikers of the baseball, they did not produce the power numbers that first basemen and outfielders have usually generated in the best hitters' park in the major leagues. The Cubs' offense in 1988 reflected those skills. In a pitchers' year, Chicago had the highest batting average in the National League, even though its mark of .261 was the lowest to lead the senior circuit since 1915.

But the Cubs have tried before to win with power hitters, and have repeatedly failed. In 1987, the Cubs led the league in home runs, but won only 76 games. In 1986, the Cubs led the league in home runs, but won only 70 games. In 1985, the Cubs led the league in home runs, but won only 77 games. Meanwhile, teams that built their offenses around contact hitters were prospering. In the eight years from 1980 to 1987, the team that led the National League in batting average also led in runs scored six times; only once over that span did a team that led the league in home runs also lead the league in runs. In ridding themselves of Bull Durham, Keith Moreland, and Jody Davis before or during the 1988 season, the signal coming out of Wrigley Field seemed to be, "Read our lips; no more one-dimensional power hitters."

And then, Palmeiro was traded. Does this mean a reevaluation of the philosophy that the 1988 team reflected? Or is it just an illustration of how starved the Cubs were for a closer? We don't have the answers, but it will be very interesting to see if the next long-distance phone call out of Jim Frey's office will be directed toward Dave Kingman or to Matty Alou!

WON-LOST RECORD BY STARTING POSITION

CHICAGO 77-85	C	1B	2B	3B	SS	LF	CF	RF	P	Leadoff	Relief	Starts
Damon Berryhill	35-44	·	·	·	·	·	·	·	·	·	·	35-44
Mike Bielecki	·	·	·	·	·	·	·	·	3-2	·	4-10	3-2
Kevin Blankenship	·	·	·	·	·	·	·	·	1-0	·	·	1-0
Mike Capel	·	·	·	·	·	·	·	·	·	·	4-18	·
Doug Dascenzo	·	·	·	·	·	·	5-12	·	·	3-9	·	5-12
Jody Davis	35-33	·	·	·	·	·	·	·	·	·	·	35-33
Andre Dawson	·	·	·	·	·	·	72-74	·	·	·	·	72-74
Frank DiPino	·	·	·	·	·	·	·	·	·	·	21-42	·
Shawon Dunston	·	·	·	·	72-77	·	·	·	·	25-19	·	72-77
Leon Durham	·	7-12	·	·	·	·	·	·	·	·	·	7-12
Rich Gossage	·	·	·	·	·	·	·	·	·	·	24-22	·
Mark Grace	·	59-66	·	·	·	·	·	·	·	·	·	59-66
Drew Hall	·	·	·	·	·	·	·	·	·	·	5-14	·
Mike Harkey	·	·	·	·	·	·	·	·	0-5	·	·	0-5
Darrin Jackson	·	·	·	·	·	2-2	20-15	0-1	·	2-2	·	22-18
Les Lancaster	·	·	·	·	·	·	·	·	1-2	·	20-20	1-2
Bill Landrum	·	·	·	·	·	·	·	·	·	·	2-5	·
Vance Law	·	·	71-77	·	·	·	·	·	·	·	·	71-77
Greg Maddux	·	·	·	·	·	·	·	·	23-11	·	·	23-11
Dave Martinez	·	·	·	·	·	·	29-33	0-1	·	17-21	·	29-34
Dave Meier	·	·	0-1	·	·	·	·	·	·	·	·	0-1
Jamie Moyer	·	·	·	·	·	·	·	·	10-19	·	1-3	10-19
Jerry Mumphrey	·	·	·	·	·	1-3	·	·	·	·	·	1-3
Al Nipper	·	·	·	·	·	·	·	·	5-7	·	3-7	5-7
Rafael Palmeiro	·	2-1	·	·	·	68-72	·	1-1	·	1-0	·	71-74
Pat Perry	·	·	·	·	·	·	·	·	·	·	14-21	·
Jeff Pico	·	·	·	·	·	·	·	·	6-7	·	6-10	6-7
Rolando Roomes	·	·	·	·	·	0-3	·	·	·	0-1	·	0-3
Argenis Salazar	·	·	·	0-1	5-8	·	·	·	·	·	·	5-9
Ryne Sandberg	·	·	72-78	·	·	·	·	·	·	10-9	·	72-78
Scott Sanderson	·	·	·	·	·	·	·	·	·	·	2-9	·
Calvin Schiraldi	·	·	·	·	·	·	·	·	12-15	·	1-1	12-15
Jim Sundberg	7-7	·	·	·	·	·	·	·	·	·	·	7-7
Rick Sutcliffe	·	·	·	·	·	·	·	·	15-17	·	·	15-17
Bob Tewksbury	·	·	·	·	·	·	·	·	1-0	·	·	1-0
Manny Trillo	·	9-6	5-7	6-6	·	·	·	·	·	·	·	20-19
Gary Varsho	·	·	·	·	·	4-2	·	1-4	·	0-1	·	5-6
Mitch Webster	·	·	·	·	·	2-3	23-25	3-4	·	19-23	·	28-32
Rick Wrona	0-1	·	·	·	·	·	·	·	·	·	·	0-1

Batting vs. Left and Right Handed Pitchers

		BA	Rank	SA	Rank	OBA	Rank	HR %	Rank	BB %	Rank	SO %	Rank
Damon Berryhill	vs. Lefties	.247	84	.318	99	.261	117	1.18	86	2.27	127	10.23	49
	vs. Righties	.263	54	.424	30	.307	75	2.68	35	6.15	90	19.26	113
Andre Dawson	vs. Lefties	.296	22	.453	28	.339	51	2.52	51	6.32	66	12.07	66
	vs. Righties	.306	10	.523	5	.346	37	4.63	10	5.58	104	11.16	39
Shawon Dunston	vs. Lefties	.234	99	.371	71	.247	120	2.40	53	1.75	129	15.20	93
	vs. Righties	.255	68	.350	74	.280	110	1.23	77	3.04	124	19.16	112
Mark Grace	vs. Lefties	.286	32	.429	36	.373	17	2.04	66	12.43	20	13.02	73
	vs. Righties	.301	12	.392	48	.370	15	1.18	80	10.24	34	5.51	5
Darrin Jackson	vs. Lefties	.315	11	.568	2	.339	49	4.50	13	3.45	120	10.34	52
	vs. Righties	.195	--	.286	--	.213	--	1.30	--	1.23	--	19.75	--
Vance Law	vs. Lefties	.291	28	.464	24	.371	19	3.31	31	10.47	33	9.30	36
	vs. Righties	.294	17	.393	47	.353	28	1.48	65	8.24	58	14.03	65
Rafael Palmeiro	vs. Lefties	.333	3	.480	20	.364	24	1.17	87	4.84	110	5.91	12
	vs. Righties	.296	16	.418	32	.343	38	1.47	67	6.55	86	5.19	4
Ryne Sandberg	vs. Lefties	.293	25	.482	19	.363	26	4.27	18	9.34	50	13.74	78
	vs. Righties	.253	72	.396	42	.306	79	2.64	38	7.44	71	13.28	59
Manny Trillo	vs. Lefties	.269	54	.343	85	.338	52	1.49	74	9.33	51	17.33	103
	vs. Righties	.237	--	.268	--	.242	--	0.00	--	0.98	--	18.63	--
Mitch Webster	vs. Lefties	.238	93	.268	118	.290	95	0.00	103	5.95	99	13.51	76
	vs. Righties	.270	45	.397	41	.359	24	1.69	59	10.68	29	15.05	72
Team Average	vs. Lefties	.263	2	.397	2	.314	4	2.29	3	6.73	12	14.71	7
	vs. Righties	.260	2	.378	3	.308	7	1.87	5	6.40	12	14.66	5
League Average	vs. Lefties	.248		.367		.310		2.10		8.01		14.42	
	vs. Righties	.249		.360		.310		1.88		7.86		15.35	

Batting with Runners on Base and Bases Empty

		BA	Rank	SA	Rank	OBA	Rank	HR %	Rank	BB %	Rank	SO %	Rank
Damon Berryhill	Runners On	.266	70	.391	59	.298	108	2.37	44	4.89	117	14.13	76
	Bases Empty	.250	61	.400	34	.291	87	2.14	55	5.41	90	20.27	111
Andre Dawson	Runners On	.287	44	.469	19	.346	59	3.10	27	8.53	77	8.19	20
	Bases Empty	.315	4	.532	3	.343	22	4.80	10	3.46	114	14.12	60
Shawon Dunston	Runners On	.252	89	.363	77	.275	116	1.77	63	3.33	125	14.17	78
	Bases Empty	.246	71	.352	71	.267	109	1.43	75	2.23	123	20.61	113
Mark Grace	Runners On	.317	11	.431	38	.378	24	1.83	59	9.76	58	5.28	5
	Bases Empty	.280	24	.381	50	.365	8	1.12	86	11.84	9	9.87	25
Darrin Jackson	Runners On	.226	110	.323	105	.270	118	1.08	82	4.90	114	13.73	73
	Bases Empty	.305	--	.579	--	.305	--	5.26	--	0.00	--	14.74	--
Vance Law	Runners On	.294	32	.431	37	.358	44	3.05	28	8.42	79	13.47	71
	Bases Empty	.293	16	.395	40	.358	10	1.02	89	9.26	31	12.04	45
Rafael Palmeiro	Runners On	.261	75	.343	92	.327	80	0.82	89	8.93	69	5.71	9
	Bases Empty	.340	1	.504	5	.367	5	1.79	66	3.72	112	5.16	2
Ryne Sandberg	Runners On	.308	19	.484	16	.375	29	3.17	24	10.63	47	12.20	60
	Bases Empty	.239	83	.383	46	.289	88	3.02	32	6.35	74	14.12	59
Manny Trillo	Runners On	.269	65	.295	117	.310	97	0.00	104	5.68	109	15.91	100
	Bases Empty	.233	--	.302	--	.258	--	1.16	--	3.37	--	20.22	--
Mitch Webster	Runners On	.286	46	.376	68	.362	40	1.59	66	9.82	57	12.50	62
	Bases Empty	.246	72	.344	77	.323	45	0.90	94	8.85	38	15.82	81
Team Average	Runners On	.264	1	.382	4	.321	12	2.00	5	7.80	12	13.29	4
	Bases Empty	.259	1	.384	2	.301	4	1.99	6	5.47	12	15.76	6
League Average	Runners On	.257		.373		.329		1.91		9.45		14.09	
	Bases Empty	.242		.355		.297		1.98		6.73		15.80	

Overall Batting Compared to Late Inning Pressure Situations

		BA	Rank	SA	Rank	OBA	Rank	HR %	Rank	BB %	Rank	SO %	Rank	RDI %	Rank
Damon Berryhill	Overall	.259	64	.395	43	.295	103	2.27	45	5.12	111	16.87	99	.202	120
	Pressure	.361	4	.590	3	.403	9	4.92	11	7.35	76	11.76	44	.375	15
Andre Dawson	Overall	.303	5	.504	5	.344	36	4.06	14	5.78	104	11.41	42	.279	54
	Pressure	.330	11	.426	28	.390	15	2.13	46	9.52	49	15.24	71	.276	49
Shawon Dunston	Overall	.249	85	.357	78	.271	118	1.57	70	2.67	124	18.03	108	.236	95
	Pressure	.173	116	.204	121	.194	124	0.00	79	2.86	119	22.86	113	.281	45
Mark Grace	Overall	.296	9	.403	39	.371	9	1.44	78	10.91	28	7.82	11	.310	22
	Pressure	.329	12	.384	43	.432	7	0.00	79	15.91	11	5.68	7	.143	108
Darrin Jackson	Overall	.266	--	.452	--	.287	--	3.19	--	2.54	--	14.21	--	.183	124
	Pressure	.212	--	.303	--	.257	--	3.03	--	5.56	--	13.89	--	.167	95
Vance Law	Overall	.293	15	.412	34	.358	17	1.98	58	8.86	46	12.72	52	.307	24
	Pressure	.316	20	.389	42	.365	31	1.05	73	7.41	74	14.81	66	.455	4
Jerry Mumphrey	Overall	.136	--	.167	--	.219	--	0.00	--	9.59	--	21.92	--	.250	--
	Pressure	.121	--	.152	--	.216	--	0.00	--	10.81	--	24.32	--	.111	118
Rafael Palmeiro	Overall	.307	3	.436	18	.349	28	1.38	79	6.04	100	5.41	3	.240	91
	Pressure	.276	41	.391	41	.315	65	0.00	79	5.38	100	4.30	4	.156	104
Ryne Sandberg	Overall	.264	54	.419	26	.322	59	3.07	32	7.95	65	13.40	61	.278	57
	Pressure	.245	63	.383	44	.311	70	3.19	24	8.74	55	19.42	91	.217	71
Manny Trillo	Overall	.250	--	.299	--	.283	--	0.61	--	4.52	--	18.08	--	.240	--
	Pressure	.258	--	.323	--	.273	--	0.00	--	2.94	--	11.76	--	.364	20
Mitch Webster	Overall	.260	61	.356	79	.337	43	1.15	86	9.21	43	14.57	77	.252	84
	Pressure	.231	80	.279	97	.319	63	0.00	79	10.66	42	19.67	95	.200	82
Team Average	Overall	.261	1	.383	2	.310	5	1.99	5	6.50	12	14.67	5	.252	8
	Pressure	.257	2	.346	5	.314	6	1.20	9	7.65	10	15.90	6	.252	5
League Average	Overall	.248		.363		.310		1.95		7.91		15.06		.256	
	Pressure	.242		.340		.310		1.70		8.47		15.93		.238	

Additional Miscellaneous Batting Comparisons

	Grass Surface BA	Rank	Artificial Surface BA	Rank	Home Games BA	Rank	Road Games BA	Rank	Runners in Scoring Position BA	Rank	Runners in Scoring Pos and Two Outs BA	Rank	Leading Off Inning OBA	Rank	Runners on 3B with less than 2 Outs RDI %	Rank
Damon Berryhill	.279	31	.218	104	.291	26	.215	108	.202	113	.205	89	.236	120	.500	92
Andre Dawson	.290	20	.333	3	.314	11	.292	17	.235	89	.283	40	.362	19	.553	73
Shawon Dunston	.270	45	.204	115	.278	44	.224	102	.253	70	.250	56	.244	116	.516	89
Mark Grace	.292	19	.307	14	.296	23	.297	10	.290	32	.250	56	.387	9	.667	28
Darrin Jackson	.264	51	.271	--	.329	--	.214	111	.193	119	.226	74	.333	--	.308	129
Vance Law	.303	13	.272	46	.302	17	.284	26	.303	22	.297	26	.346	31	.571	61
Rafael Palmeiro	.304	11	.313	10	.321	6	.293	14	.260	65	.214	80	.388	7	.607	51
Ryne Sandberg	.271	43	.246	73	.279	39	.248	77	.276	48	.246	59	.333	39	.655	33
Manny Trillo	.237	96	.280	--	.231	--	.263	57	.220	--	.300	--	.412	--	.429	--
Mitch Webster	.237	98	.280	37	.282	36	.236	94	.299	27	.288	35	.335	38	.714	15
Team Average	.262	1	.259	1	.273	1	.249	3	.245	10	.237	6	.313	3	.552	7
League Average	.250		.246		.252		.244		.250		.231		.301		.554	

Pitching vs. Left and Right Handed Batters

		BA	Rank	SA	Rank	OBA	Rank	HR %	Rank	BB %	Rank	SO %	Rank
Mike Bielecki	vs. Lefties	.296	93	.380	68	.342	70	1.85	61	7.50	35	15.00	47
	vs. Righties	.267	--	.407	--	.319	--	2.33	--	7.37	--	15.79	--
Frank DiPino	vs. Lefties	.192	9	.248	6	.228	4	0.00	1	5.15	14	26.47	4
	vs. Righties	.335	108	.472	106	.396	109	2.58	82	9.54	88	12.60	83
Rich Gossage	vs. Lefties	.301	97	.422	88	.372	94	1.20	35	10.53	73	15.79	41
	vs. Righties	.281	--	.393	--	.340	--	2.25	--	5.05	--	15.15	--
Les Lancaster	vs. Lefties	.282	78	.404	83	.362	86	1.28	39	11.17	79	7.26	102
	vs. Righties	.265	86	.382	79	.314	74	1.18	26	7.29	65	11.98	85
Greg Maddux	vs. Lefties	.237	33	.321	26	.322	57	1.41	40	10.58	75	11.64	77
	vs. Righties	.252	71	.335	41	.294		1.35	32	4.38	22	15.42	58
Jamie Moyer	vs. Lefties	.228	27	.331	33	.267	11	2.36	80	5.11	12	21.17	15
	vs. Righties	.281	100	.419	97	.333	89	2.61	83	6.69	55	12.81	81
Al Nipper	vs. Lefties	.259	56	.386	73	.339	68	2.53	89	10.11	66	8.99	94
	vs. Righties	.217	29	.350	56	.302	64	3.50	100	9.82	90	6.75	108
Pat Perry	vs. Lefties	.352	--	.493	--	.355	--	2.82	--	1.32	--	11.84	--
	vs. Righties	.229	44	.408	94	.293	54	4.46	106	8.57	79	14.86	62
Jeff Pico	vs. Lefties	.296	92	.409	85	.358	84	1.74	56	8.95	57	6.61	104
	vs. Righties	.202	10	.283	12	.251	12	1.01	18	6.51	52	18.60	31
Calvin Schiraldi	vs. Lefties	.298	95	.439	95	.368	92	2.21	75	9.93	65	15.38	44
	vs. Righties	.204	13	.306	22	.265	24	1.76	45	7.32	66	24.84	6
Rick Sutcliffe	vs. Lefties	.263	64	.371	62	.329	62	1.54	45	8.98	58	12.11	73
	vs. Righties	.275	92	.407	93	.317	76	2.70	88	5.38	34	18.39	34
Team Average	vs. Lefties	.269	11	.377	8	.336	9	1.72	6	9.15	6	12.84	9
	vs. Righties	.261	10	.388	11	.315	10	2.31	8	6.67	6	15.52	6
League Average	vs. Lefties	.255		.365		.325		1.73		9.36		14.24	
	vs. Righties	.244		.361		.299		2.10		6.87		15.64	

Pitching with Runners on Base and Bases Empty

		BA	Rank	SA	Rank	OBA	Rank	HR %	Rank	BB %	Rank	SO %	Rank
Frank DiPino	Runners On	.308	104	.438	98	.356	85	2.16	72	8.10	31	16.67	30
	Bases Empty	.260	84	.347	48	.319	84	1.16	24	7.98	79	18.09	29
Les Lancaster	Runners On	.293	97	.435	96	.358	90	2.04	65	10.80	77	7.39	105
	Bases Empty	.257	78	.358	57	.318	83	0.56	7	7.69	71	11.79	86
Greg Maddux	Runners On	.271	72	.346	42	.338	66	1.30	35	8.70	39	9.84	92
	Bases Empty	.225	26	.315	23	.289	44	1.43	33	7.05	60	15.90	53
Jamie Moyer	Runners On	.256	58	.382	67	.316	44	2.52	85	8.22	34	15.07	44
	Bases Empty	.284	102	.421	101	.327	88	2.60	81	5.10	24	13.47	72
Al Nipper	Runners On	.213	21	.323	31	.299	25	2.36	78	10.34	69	8.97	98
	Bases Empty	.259	80	.402	92	.338	96	3.45	101	9.69	95	7.14	109
Jeff Pico	Runners On	.287	89	.420	91	.338	67	2.21	74	7.84	27	13.73	56
	Bases Empty	.227	31	.300	14	.287	42	0.81	15	7.84	76	10.82	95
Calvin Schiraldi	Runners On	.292	95	.467	107	.356	87	2.72	92	9.62	57	16.84	29
	Bases Empty	.234	43	.324	28	.300	63	1.54	38	8.22	82	21.36	15
Rick Sutcliffe	Runners On	.288	90	.397	79	.368	98	1.52	44	10.83	78	14.61	48
	Bases Empty	.257	77	.382	83	.292	48	2.43	78	4.81	21	15.33	59
Team Average	Runners On	.273	11	.399	11	.341	10	2.15	11	9.35	5	13.25	8
	Bases Empty	.259	11	.372	10	.312	11	1.95	4	6.56	6	15.14	9
League Average	Runners On	.257		.373		.329		1.91		9.45		14.09	
	Bases Empty	.242		.355		.297		1.98		6.73		15.80	

Overall Pitching Compared to Late Inning Pressure Situations

		BA	Rank	SA	Rank	OBA	Rank	HR %	Rank	BB %	Rank	SO %	Rank
Mike Capel	Overall	.293	--	.483	--	.379	--	4.31	--	9.70	--	14.18	--
	Pressure	.238	53	.333	51	.333	72	2.38	78	10.20	80	12.24	73
Frank DiPino	Overall	.285	105	.394	92	.338	93	1.68	43	8.04	60	17.34	28
	Pressure	.282	86	.379	72	.348	82	2.42	79	9.35	68	21.58	17
Rich Gossage	Overall	.291	--	.407	--	.356	--	1.74	--	7.73	--	15.46	--
	Pressure	.327	105	.455	97	.405	105	1.82	61	9.38	69	14.06	60
Drew Hall	Overall	.295	--	.523	--	.360	--	4.55	--	8.74	--	21.36	--
	Pressure	.359	108	.692	109	.386	101	5.13	107	6.38	26	17.02	36
Les Lancaster	Overall	.273	94	.393	91	.337	92	1.23	26	9.16	78	9.70	100
	Pressure	.298	94	.440	95	.395	102	2.84	90	13.61	100	10.65	83
Greg Maddux	Overall	.244	52	.328	26	.309	50	1.38	30	7.74	53	13.37	71
	Pressure	.231	49	.276	23	.307	45	0.75	24	9.80	76	14.38	58
Jamie Moyer	Overall	.272	93	.405	97	.322	72	2.57	91	6.43	27	14.15	65
	Pressure	.295	91	.475	101	.328	69	3.28	101	4.55	10	10.61	84
Al Nipper	Overall	.239	44	.369	63	.322	71	2.99	100	9.97	88	7.92	108
	Pressure	.231	--	.423	--	.259	--	3.85	--	3.70	--	11.11	--
Pat Perry	Overall	.268	82	.434	104	.312	56	3.95	109	6.37	25	13.94	67
	Pressure	.258	65	.430	92	.317	53	4.30	105	7.62	40	15.24	48
Jeff Pico	Overall	.252	65	.350	45	.309	49	1.40	33	7.84	55	12.08	84
	Pressure	.302	95	.413	89	.366	91	3.17	95	9.86	78	12.68	71
Calvin Schiraldi	Overall	.257	74	.381	78	.323	75	2.01	57	8.79	72	19.53	19
	Pressure	.200	23	.225	4	.238	11	0.00	1	4.76	11	26.19	6
Rick Sutcliffe	Overall	.269	86	.388	87	.323	74	2.08	57	7.31	43	15.03	52
	Pressure	.248	57	.314	43	.307	46	0.95	30	7.56	39	10.08	88
Team Average	Overall	.265	11	.383	11	.325	10	2.04	7	7.81	7	14.29	9
	Pressure	.272	12	.391	12	.339	11	2.24	12	8.87	4	14.16	11
League Average	Overall	.248		.363		.310		1.95		7.91		15.06	
	Pressure	.243		.347		.315		1.72		9.12		15.69	

Additional Miscellaneous Pitching Comparisons

	Grass Surface BA	Rank	Artificial Surface BA	Rank	Home Games BA	Rank	Road Games BA	Rank	Runners in Scoring Position BA	Rank	Runners in Scoring Pos and Two Outs BA	Rank	Leading Off Inning OBA	Rank
Mike Bielecki	.286	91	.280	--	.290	--	.277	--	.262	--	.250	78	.304	--
Mike Capel	.324	105	.000	--	.333	--	.100	--	.171	--	.105	--	.346	--
Frank DiPino	.251	54	.364	108	.229	35	.341	108	.345	107	.419	109	.282	43
Rich Gossage	.270	77	.340	--	.319	--	.270	--	.333	--	.280	--	.421	--
Mike Harkey	.238	35	.265	--	.238	--	.265	--	.159	--	.217	--	.361	--
Les Lancaster	.274	83	.265	--	.282	98	.258	64	.322	101	.327	102	.321	75
Greg Maddux	.244	42	.244	53	.256	71	.230	31	.266	77	.275	91	.277	34
Jamie Moyer	.276	86	.264	74	.276	88	.269	75	.233	43	.215	52	.314	69
Al Nipper	.234	31	.253	--	.253	67	.218	17	.190	--	.138	--	.337	87
Pat Perry	.294	95	.239	46	.313	--	.224	26	.293	--	.333	--	.315	--
Jeff Pico	.239	36	.299	102	.231	40	.282	89	.330	105	.333	103	.272	26
Calvin Schiraldi	.266	73	.231	33	.299	108	.221	24	.270	79	.217	55	.275	31
Rick Sutcliffe	.272	80	.261	67	.262	75	.274	82	.255	64	.208	47	.264	17
Team Average	.265	9	.265	10	.270	11	.259	9	.267	11	.258	12	.298	8
League Average	.250		.246		.244		.252		.250		.231		.301	

CINCINNATI REDS

- Still another 2d-place finish. Will the Reds ever win the title again?
- An evaluation of last season's top rookies, Sabo and Weiss.

Sure, they've finished second for four consecutive seasons. But things *could* be worse. At least the Reds weren't playing Russian roulette.

And there's hope, too. Pete Rose ought to sit his boys down and tell 'em the story of Lou Gehrig. He should explain how Gehrig became the only player in baseball history to finish four straight seasons as the runner-up in home runs (1927–1930), each time to the Bambino. And tell them how Gehrig rebounded to tie Ruth for the A.L. home-run title the next year, and win it outright twice after that.

Actually, Cincinnati's consistency over the past four seasons—coinciding with Rose's full-time status as the team's manager—has been unusual, Gehrig-like if you will. The Reds have won no more than 89 games, no fewer than 84 in each of those seasons. And that range of five wins over four seasons is the smallest in the National League in more than 10 years, since Cincinnati won between 88 and 92 games in each season from 1974 through 1977. (Incidentally, the all-time champs are the Cleveland Indians, who won either 92 or 93 games in each season from 1947 through 1950; and the New York Mets of 1970 through 1973, who won either 82 or 83 games each year.)

The following table shows the range of wins for each team over the past four seasons. Notice that only the Cubs have come close to matching Cincinnati's consistency. And in Chicago's case, that's no mark of honor:

American	Low	High	Range	National	Low	High	Range
New York	89	97	8	Cincinnati	84	89	5
Seattle	67	78	11	Chicago	70	77	7
Toronto	86	99	13	Montreal	78	91	13
Chicago	71	85	14	New York	92	108	16
Detroit	84	98	14	Atlanta	54	72	18
Kansas City	76	91	15	San Diego	65	83	18
Boston	78	95	17	Houston	76	96	20
California	75	92	17	Philadelphia	65	86	21
Milwaukee	71	91	20	Los Angeles	73	95	22
Minnesota	71	91	20	St. Louis	76	101	25
Cleveland	60	84	24	Pittsburgh	57	85	28
Texas	62	87	25	San Francisco	62	90	28
Oakland	76	104	28				
Baltimore	54	83	29				

What's truly remarkable about Cincinnati's consistency at a level that many teams envy is this: The Reds have placed second in the N.L. West for four consecutive seasons of what those lesser teams would call "rebuilding years." Of the players on the Reds' roster at the close of the 1984 season, only six remained with the team at the end of last season. Among those six, Dave Concepcion and Nick Esasky were cut loose over the winter, leaving Eric Davis, John Franco, Ron Oester, and Ron Robinson as the only players to predate Rose with the Reds.

Before we canonize Rose without properly acknowledging those who also contributed to this renaissance in the Rhineland, let's also give credit to general manager Murray Cook, his predecessor Bill Bergesch, and—alright—even Marge and Schottzie for a turnaround that has transformed the Reds from one of the oldest teams in baseball to one of the youngest, even while improving its on-the-field play. The following table shows the average age of Cincinnati's batters and pitchers over the past six seasons, and where they ranked in the N.L. A rank of 1 indicates the youngest team; 12, the oldest:

Year	W–L	Batters		Pitchers	
		Age	Rank	Age	Rank
1983	74–88	28.5	6	27.2	1
1984	70–92	30.0	10	26.8	2
1985	89–72	32.5	12	26.8	2
1986	86–76	31.5	12	28.4	5
1987	84–78	29.3	9	28.9	9
1988	87–74	27.8	3	27.0	2

The pattern is pretty clear. Rose took over a team in August 1984 with a young pitching staff, an aging lineup, and a bad habit of losing. He initially righted the team by placing an emphasis—many said an *over*emphasis, at the time—on veteran players. Then, over a period of three years, Reds players who had blown away more than 30 candles on a single cake became an endangered species. Cincinnati institutions like Tony Perez, Dan Driessen, Concepcion, and Mario Soto, and other aging players like Dave Parker, Buddy Bell, and Bo Diaz were traded or released. In their places arrived Eric Davis, Kal Daniels, Barry Larkin, Jeff Treadway, and Jose Rijo, to name a few.

The prognosis for the coming seasons is undeniably favorable. A look at some of the most successful young teams of the 1980s supports the contention that the Reds should be among the National League's elite into the 1990s.

From 1981 through 1987, 40 teams had lineups with an average age under 28. Most were losers. Of those 40 teams, only 13 posted winning records. We've listed those teams below, with their positions in the standings in each season since then:

Year	Team	Subsequent Position in Standings						
1981	Detroit Tigers	4	2	1	3	3	1	2
1981	Montreal Expos	3	3	5	3	4	3	3
1981	St. Louis Cardinals	1	4	3	1	3	1	5
1982	Detroit Tigers	2	1	3	3	1	2	—
1982	Atlanta Braves	2	2	5	6	5	6	—
1982	St. Louis Cardinals	4	3	1	3	1	5	—
1983	Atlanta Braves	2	5	6	5	6	—	—
1984	New York Mets	2	1	2	1	—	—	—
1985	St. Louis Cardinals	3	1	5	—	—	—	—
1986	Cleveland Indians	7	6	—	—	—	—	—
1986	Texas Rangers	6	6	—	—	—	—	—
1986	San Francisco Giants	1	4	—	—	—	—	—
1987	Montreal Expos	3	—	—	—	—	—	—

We'll save you the trouble of adding up all the divisional titles won by those teams. They reached the championship series a total of 13 times in 58 chances. That average was quite a bit higher than the corresponding figure for older teams coming off winning seasons:

Teams with Winning Records	Teams	Winners	Pct. of Winners
Lineups younger than 28 years	58	13	.224
Lineups older than 28 years	226	34	.150

So while Cincinnati has become only the second team in modern major league history to finish second in four consecutive seasons (the Giants did it five straight years starting in 1965), they've also positioned themselves for several more years at or near the top.

Hey, you don't think they could actually finish second four *more* times in a row, do you? Naaaah!

After the arrival over the two previous years of Jose Canseco, Wally Joyner, Mark McGwire, Kevin Seitzer, Mike Greenwell, Will Clark, Andres Galarraga, Benito Santiago, and Todd Worrell; not to mention Cory Snyder, Pete Incaviglia, Danny Tartabull, Ruben Sierra, Barry Bonds, Barry Larkin, Jim Deshaies, and Joe Magrane—*phew!*—last season's rookie crop seemed a notch below par. Chris Sabo and Walt Weiss seem like nice enough guys. And they might be capable major leaguers with promising careers to come. But we'll be the first to admit, we're spoiled.

There's no question that by the most recent standards, the Sabo and Weiss team was substandard. The question is, How do they rank over a more representative period of time? A look at the voting pattern of the past 20 years indicates that those electing each league's top rookie are partial to infielders. That's to say the electorate apparently asks less of second basemen, third basemen, and shortstops at the plate than they do of, let's say, outfielders or designated hitters. That's

only fair, given the greater contributions that infielders make defensively.

Prior to last season, 19 infielders finished first or second in their league's Rookie-of-the-Year voting during the divisional era. Here's how Sabo and Weiss compared to those players. Their totals are not included in the position averages. Runners-up are marked with asterisks:

Year	Player	Pos.	AB	R	H	2B	3B	HR	RBI	SB	BA
1969	Ted Sizemore	2B	590	69	160	20	5	4	46	5	.271
1973	*Pedro Garcia	2B	580	67	142	32	5	15	54	11	.245
1978	Lou Whitaker	2B	484	71	138	12	7	3	58	7	.285
1978	*Paul Molitor	2B	521	73	142	26	4	6	45	30	.273
1980	*Dave Stapleton	2B	449	61	144	33	5	7	45	3	.321
1982	Steve Sax	2B	638	88	180	23	7	4	47	49	.282
1982	*Johnny Ray	2B	647	79	182	30	7	7	63	16	.281
1984	*Juan Samuel	2B	701	105	191	36	19	15	69	72	.272
1986	*Rob Thompson	2B	549	73	149	27	3	7	47	12	.271
	Averages	2B	573	76	159	27	7	8	53	23	.277
1969	*Coco Laboy	3B	562	53	145	29	1	18	83	0	.258
1978	Bob Horner	3B	323	50	86	17	1	23	63	0	.266
1979	John Castino	3B	393	49	112	13	8	5	52	5	.293
1987	*Kevin Seitzer	3B	641	105	207	33	8	15	83	12	.323
1988	Chris Sabo	3B	538	74	146	40	2	11	44	46	.271
	Averages	3B	480	64	138	23	5	15	70	4	.287
1974	*Bucky Dent	SS	496	55	136	15	3	5	45	3	.274
1978	*Ozzie Smith	SS	590	69	152	17	6	1	46	40	.258
1979	Alfredo Griffin	SS	624	81	179	22	10	2	31	21	.287
1982	Cal Ripken	SS	598	90	158	32	5	28	93	3	.264
1983	*Julio Franco	SS	560	68	153	24	8	8	80	32	.273
1985	Ozzie Guillen	SS	491	71	134	21	9	1	33	7	.273
1988	Walt Weiss	SS	452	44	113	17	3	3	39	4	.250
	Averages	SS	560	72	152	22	7	8	55	18	.272

Sabo's offensive performance was comparable to that of the second basemen, particularly to that of Franco, Molitor, and Thompson—all of whom, it should be noted, were runners-up. But except for his stolen-base total, Sabo fell somewhat below the standard set by third basemen, where the offensive criteria are understandably higher. On the other hand, Sabo's speed is among his most valuable attributes, and he joined a rather select 40/40 club himself: Sabo became the first rookie since 1914, and only the third in major league history, to hit 40 doubles and steal 40 bases in the same season. The others were Shoeless Joe Jackson in 1911 and Benny Kauff three years later.

Weiss, on the other hand, had the poorest offensive season of the 21 players listed above. And it's tough to argue that Weiss is superior defensively to a group of shortstops that includes Ozzie Smith, Ozzie Guillen, Alfredo Griffin, and Bucky Dent.

So even allowing for the upgrade that infielders deserve for defensive contributions, Sabo and Weiss taken together must be considered among the poorer tandems to win top rookie honors, especially over the past 20 years. But given a better running mate, Sabo's election might have been judged more kindly. Now where have we heard that before?

WON-LOST RECORD BY STARTING POSITION

CINCINNATI 87-74	C	1B	2B	3B	SS	LF	CF	RF	P	Leadoff	Relief	Starts
Jack Armstrong	·	·	·	·	·	·	·	·	4-9	·	0-1	4-9
Buddy Bell	·	0-2	·	6-7	·	·	·	·	·	·	·	6-9
Tim Birtsas	·	·	·	·	·	·	·	·	0-4	·	7-25	0-4
Keith Brown	·	·	·	·	·	·	·	·	2-1	·	0-1	2-1
Marty Brown	·	·	·	0-2	·	·	·	·	·	·	·	0-2
Tom Browning	·	·	·	·	·	·	·	·	24-12	·	·	24-12
Norm Charlton	·	·	·	·	·	·	·	·	5-5	·	·	5-5
Dave Collins	·	0-1	·	·	·	2-5	0-4	6-7	·	2-1	·	8-17
Dave Concepcion	·	2-2	20-16	1-0	3-3	·	·	·	·	·	0-1	26-21
Kal Daniels	·	·	·	·	·	76-62	·	·	·	22-19	·	76-62
Eric Davis	·	·	·	·	·	·	70-55	1-4	·	·	·	71-59
Bo Diaz	42-39	·	·	·	·	·	·	·	·	·	·	42-39
Rob Dibble	·	·	·	·	·	·	·	·	·	·	14-23	·
Leon Durham	··	6-8	·	·	·	·	·	·	·	·	·	6-8
Nick Esasky	·	60-49	·	·	·	·	·	·	·	·	·	60-49
John Franco	·	·	·	·	·	·	·	·	·	·	52-18	·
Leo Garcia	·	·	·	·	·	·	1-2	·	·	·	·	1-2
Jeff Gray	·	·	·	·	·	·	·	·	·	·	0-5	·
Ken Griffey	·	7-2	·	·	·	·	·	·	·	·	·	7-2
Lenny Harris	·	·	3-1	8-0	·	·	·	·	·	·	·	11-1
Danny Jackson	·	·	·	·	·	·	·	·	26-9	·	·	26-9
Tracy Jones	·	·	·	·	·	0-1	12-6	·	·	·	·	12-7
Barry Larkin	·	·	·	·	81-67	·	·	·	·	54-50	·	81-67
Lloyd McClendon	5-5	3-3	·	·	·	2-4	·	1-3	·	·	·	11-15
Terry McGriff	12-16	·	·	·	·	·	·	·	·	·	·	12-16
Eddie Milner	·	·	·	·	·	0-1	4-4	1-0	·	1-1	·	5-5
Rob Murphy	·	·	·	·	·	·	·	·	·	·	31-45	·
Paul O'Neill	·	9-7	·	·	·	·	4-2	57-50	·	·	·	70-59
Ron Oester	·	·	27-13	0-2	·	·	·	·	·	·	·	27-15
Pat Pacillo	·	·	·	·	·	·	·	·	·	·	1-5	·
Pat Perry	·	·	·	·	·	·	·	·	·	·	2-10	·
Luis Quinones	·	0-1	·	3-1	3-2	·	·	·	·	1-1	·	6-4
Dennis Rasmussen	·	·	·	·	·	·	·	·	3-8	·	·	3-8
Jeff Reed	28-14	·	·	·	·	·	·	·	·	·	·	28-14
Jose Rijo	·	·	·	·	·	·	·	·	11-8	·	11-19	11-8
Ron Robinson	·	·	·	·	·	·	·	·	6-10	·	1-0	6-10
Ron Roenicke	·	·	·	·	·	·	1-1	3-3	·	·	·	4-4
Chris Sabo	·	·	·	68-63	·	·	·	·	·	3-2	·	68-63
Candy Sierra	·	·	·	·	·	·	·	·	·	·	0-1	·
Van Snider	·	·	·	·	·	3-0	·	3-0	·	·	·	6-0
Mario Soto	·	·	·	·	·	·	·	·	6-8	·	·	6-8
Randy St. Claire	·	·	·	·	·	·	·	·	·	·	2-8	·
Jeff Treadway	·	·	37-43	1-1	·	·	·	·	·	·	·	38-44
Frank Williams	·	·	·	·	·	·	·	·	·	·	20-40	·
Herm Winningham	·	·	·	·	·	4-1	7-6	3-1	·	4-0	·	14-8

Batting vs. Left and Right Handed Pitchers

		BA	Rank	SA	Rank	OBA	Rank	HR %	Rank	BB %	Rank	SO %	Rank
Dave Collins	vs. Lefties	.233	--	.317	--	.277	--	0.00	--	6.15	--	15.38	--
	vs. Righties	.237	95	.281	118	.290	99	0.00	115	5.65	101	13.71	63
Dave Concepcion	vs. Lefties	.202	113	.237	123	.278	104	0.00	103	9.52	48	8.73	34
	vs. Righties	.193	--	.253	--	.247	--	0.00	--	6.67	--	13.33	--
Kal Daniels	vs. Lefties	.267	55	.363	74	.387	9	2.22	60	15.95	5	17.79	107
	vs. Righties	.300	14	.500	8	.401	4	4.17	14	14.32	7	15.26	77
Eric Davis	vs. Lefties	.292	27	.517	10	.390	8	5.83	4	13.48	15	13.48	75
	vs. Righties	.267	49	.480	11	.353	29	5.40	5	11.44	25	26.12	128
Bo Diaz	vs. Lefties	.236	97	.393	59	.266	114	4.49	14	4.26	114	14.89	90
	vs. Righties	.212	118	.323	97	.224	128	2.65	37	1.29	127	11.59	42
Leon Durham	vs. Lefties	.286	--	.286	--	.375	--	0.00	--	12.50	--	50.00	--
	vs. Righties	.214	116	.410	36	.292	98	3.42	26	10.00	35	21.54	119
Nick Esasky	vs. Lefties	.250	78	.388	62	.357	32	2.59	49	14.29	10	18.57	115
	vs. Righties	.240	92	.422	31	.313	68	4.36	12	9.03	44	25.16	127
Ken Griffey	vs. Lefties	.250	--	.417	--	.250	--	4.17	--	0.00	--	20.83	--
	vs. Righties	.256	66	.320	98	.313	71	1.37	73	7.92	62	10.83	35
Barry Larkin	vs. Lefties	.352	1	.559	4	.421	3	3.45	28	10.24	38	2.41	1
	vs. Righties	.278	32	.386	51	.322	55	1.58	60	4.94	113	4.12	2
Lloyd McClendon	vs. Lefties	.206	111	.279	114	.247	122	1.47	75	5.48	101	17.81	108
	vs. Righties	.232	--	.348	--	.349	--	2.90	--	13.10	--	10.71	--
Paul O'Neill	vs. Lefties	.233	100	.349	82	.272	108	1.16	88	4.21	116	18.95	118
	vs. Righties	.256	67	.429	28	.313	70	3.76	20	7.76	64	10.73	34
Ron Oester	vs. Lefties	.231	--	.308	--	.300	--	0.00	--	9.68	--	16.13	--
	vs. Righties	.290	21	.331	92	.323	54	0.00	115	4.55	117	14.39	68
Jeff Reed	vs. Lefties	.130	--	.130	--	.259	--	0.00	--	14.81	--	22.22	--
	vs. Righties	.236	96	.302	107	.303	83	0.41	111	8.96	46	13.06	57
Chris Sabo	vs. Lefties	.286	32	.450	30	.338	53	2.86	45	6.45	86	7.10	15
	vs. Righties	.266	50	.402	39	.305	81	1.76	57	4.45	120	9.60	27
Jeff Treadway	vs. Lefties	.242	--	.333	--	.265	--	0.00	--	2.94	--	11.76	--
	vs. Righties	.254	71	.366	62	.320	61	0.75	96	8.47	55	8.47	16
Herm Winningham	vs. Lefties	.237	--	.342	--	.231	--	0.00	--	0.00	--	25.00	--
	vs. Righties	.230	100	.273	120	.301	85	0.00	115	9.19	42	18.92	110
Team Average	vs. Lefties	.254	3	.375	4	.323	2	2.20	5	8.89	2	15.08	8
	vs. Righties	.243	9	.365	6	.304	9	2.27	2	7.55	8	15.25	7
League Average	vs. Lefties	.248		.367		.310		2.10		8.01		14.42	
	vs. Righties	.249		.360		.310		1.88		7.86		15.35	

Batting with Runners on Base and Bases Empty

		BA	Rank	SA	Rank	OBA	Rank	HR %	Rank	BB %	Rank	SO %	Rank
Dave Concepcion	Runners On	.185	125	.210	127	.290	113	0.00	104	12.77	30	12.77	64
	Bases Empty	.207	115	.267	116	.246	122	0.00	115	4.92	98	9.02	18
Kal Daniels	Runners On	.296	29	.423	40	.436	2	2.12	51	20.16	2	15.23	91
	Bases Empty	.288	19	.487	8	.370	4	4.58	14	10.98	15	16.47	86
Eric Davis	Runners On	.327	5	.596	1	.425	3	6.28	4	14.29	20	20.30	118
	Bases Empty	.225	103	.394	41	.303	65	4.82	9	9.75	23	25.27	126
Bo Diaz	Runners On	.212	118	.295	115	.252	125	2.27	46	4.86	118	15.28	92
	Bases Empty	.224	105	.377	54	.224	126	3.83	20	0.00	127	10.38	31
Nick Esasky	Runners On	.233	105	.364	75	.327	82	2.84	32	11.85	40	23.70	126
	Bases Empty	.251	58	.451	16	.326	40	4.65	13	9.62	26	22.59	120
Ken Griffey	Runners On	.232	106	.326	104	.299	107	2.11	53	9.35	63	8.41	21
	Bases Empty	.270	30	.331	95	.312	56	1.35	79	5.73	84	14.01	58
Barry Larkin	Runners On	.313	14	.451	30	.366	37	1.65	64	7.44	90	3.72	2
	Bases Empty	.288	18	.419	28	.339	26	2.22	52	5.72	85	3.66	1
Paul O'Neill	Runners On	.251	91	.413	49	.309	98	3.59	19	7.54	87	11.51	54
	Bases Empty	.252	55	.416	29	.302	66	3.05	31	6.76	66	12.81	51
Jeff Reed	Runners On	.219	115	.267	123	.320	104	0.00	104	13.01	28	13.01	66
	Bases Empty	.231	94	.300	109	.285	93	0.63	106	6.98	63	14.53	66
Chris Sabo	Runners On	.250	93	.346	90	.313	94	0.96	86	7.14	97	10.50	37
	Bases Empty	.285	21	.458	15	.314	51	2.73	40	3.49	113	7.85	12
Jeff Treadway	Runners On	.271	63	.417	44	.392	20	0.00	104	17.05	9	7.75	18
	Bases Empty	.244	75	.337	87	.269	107	0.98	91	2.36	121	9.43	21
Herm Winningham	Runners On	.309	17	.407	51	.341	62	0.00	104	5.49	113	21.98	125
	Bases Empty	.180	125	.205	127	.254	117	0.00	115	8.96	36	18.66	104
Team Average	Runners On	.252	11	.373	8	.332	5	2.11	3	10.37	3	14.93	10
	Bases Empty	.242	6	.365	4	.292	10	2.34	2	6.07	10	15.41	5
League Average	Runners On	.257		.373		.329		1.91		9.45		14.09	
	Bases Empty	.242		.355		.297		1.98		6.73		15.80	

Overall Batting Compared to Late Inning Pressure Situations

		BA	Rank	SA	Rank	OBA	Rank	HR %	Rank	BB %	Rank	SO %	Rank	RDI %	Rank
Dave Collins	Overall	.236	--	.293	--	.286	--	0.00	--	5.82	--	14.29	--	.326	--
	Pressure	.179	115	.179	123	.270	104	0.00	79	7.94	68	12.70	50	.133	114
Dave Concepcion	Overall	.198	124	.244	125	.265	123	0.00	118	8.33	56	10.65	36	.157	--
	Pressure	.133	--	.133	--	.235	--	0.00	--	11.43	--	17.14	--	.000	--
Kal Daniels	Overall	.291	17	.463	13	.397	1	3.64	20	14.77	3	15.96	90	.306	26
	Pressure	.190	104	.302	86	.366	30	3.17	26	21.95	1	20.73	103	.375	15
Eric Davis	Overall	.273	35	.489	9	.363	16	5.51	2	11.97	16	22.84	124	.298	39
	Pressure	.309	27	.568	4	.398	11	6.17	5	11.83	33	26.88	63	.280	46
Bo Diaz	Overall	.219	116	.343	93	.236	127	3.17	28	2.14	127	12.54	51	.208	118
	Pressure	.188	110	.271	100	.216	119	2.08	49	3.85	114	17.31	84	.154	105
Nick Esasky	Overall	.243	94	.412	35	.327	51	3.84	17	10.67	33	23.11	125	.260	73
	Pressure	.246	62	.415	32	.306	74	3.08	30	8.33	63	20.83	105	.238	63
Ken Griffey	Overall	.255	72	.329	103	.307	86	1.65	67	7.20	78	11.74	43	.219	109
	Pressure	.214	90	.250	105	.241	113	0.00	79	3.45	115	17.24	83	.222	70
Barry Larkin	Overall	.296	11	.429	21	.347	30	2.04	53	6.29	94	3.68	2	.301	35
	Pressure	.319	16	.383	44	.369	29	1.06	72	6.54	86	7.48	15	.259	58
Lloyd McClendon	Overall	.219	--	.314	--	.301	--	2.19	--	9.55	--	14.01	--	.211	--
	Pressure	.132	124	.132	127	.233	116	0.00	79	11.36	37	20.45	101	.000	--
Paul O'Neill	Overall	.252	79	.414	32	.306	88	3.30	27	7.13	79	12.20	49	.257	78
	Pressure	.205	96	.436	25	.262	106	5.13	10	5.88	93	11.76	44	.280	46
Jeff Reed	Overall	.226	112	.287	117	.299	95	0.38	113	9.49	40	13.90	69	.209	117
	Pressure	.270	46	.351	60	.372	24	0.00	79	13.64	22	11.36	40	.429	--
Chris Sabo	Overall	.271	38	.414	31	.314	74	2.04	52	4.98	114	8.93	16	.217	110
	Pressure	.326	13	.478	14	.361	34	3.26	23	4.08	112	12.24	48	.231	66
Jeff Treadway	Overall	.252	77	.362	71	.315	71	0.66	101	7.92	66	8.80	15	.286	48
	Pressure	.309	25	.473	15	.350	43	0.00	79	4.92	104	8.20	18	.154	105
Herm Winningham	Overall	.232	109	.286	118	.288	108	0.00	118	7.56	71	20.00	119	.230	99
	Pressure	.304	28	.413	34	.340	48	0.00	79	5.88	93	23.53	115	.333	32
Team Average	Overall	.246	9	.368	6	.309	8	2.25	2	7.90	6	15.21	7	.250	9
	Pressure	.248	5	.361	4	.319	4	2.17	3	8.68	6	16.55	9	.232	7
League Average	Overall	.248		.363		.310		1.95		7.91		15.06		.256	
	Pressure	.242		.340		.310		1.70		8.47		15.93		.238	

Additional Miscellaneous Batting Comparisons

	Grass Surface		Artificial Surface		Home Games		Road Games		Runners in Scoring Position		Runners in Scoring Pos and Two Outs		Leading Off Inning		Runners on 3B with less than 2 Outs	
	BA	Rank	BA	Rank	BA	Rank	BA	Rank	BA	Rank	BA	Rank	OBA	Rank	RDI %	Rank
Dave Collins	.260	--	.226	98	.200	119	.274	--	.324	--	.313	--	.191	127	.700	19
Dave Concepcion	.128	--	.215	105	.240	91	.151	--	.159	125	.222	75	.277	89	.000	--
Kal Daniels	.252	70	.310	13	.330	4	.257	65	.319	14	.311	19	.350	29	.621	47
Eric Davis	.287	25	.267	51	.259	71	.285	23	.314	17	.338	12	.365	18	.533	81
Bo Diaz	.216	113	.221	101	.206	118	.230	99	.190	120	.163	112	.209	126	.533	81
Nick Esasky	.246	84	.242	77	.254	79	.230	98	.227	96	.197	93	.375	13	.528	84
Ken Griffey	.238	94	.291	--	.268	53	.242	87	.196	117	.207	88	.344	33	.500	92
Barry Larkin	.276	36	.304	18	.307	15	.284	25	.333	7	.314	18	.340	36	.667	28
Lloyd McClendon	.259	--	.209	112	.212	--	.225	--	.138	--	.100	--	.233	--	.500	92
Terry McGriff	.100	--	.209	111	.236	--	.146	--	.100	--	.000	--	.250	--	.400	--
Paul O'Neill	.293	17	.232	89	.245	87	.258	64	.221	104	.238	63	.266	97	.516	89
Ron Oester	.269	--	.286	30	.253	81	.313	--	.200	--	.286	--	.367	17	.500	--
Jeff Reed	.262	53	.204	116	.198	120	.252	72	.241	84	.115	122	.276	90	.412	119
Chris Sabo	.248	76	.281	36	.296	22	.248	78	.252	72	.200	91	.361	20	.560	70
Jeff Treadway	.198	120	.276	41	.299	20	.213	113	.260	65	.190	98	.293	81	.667	28
Herm Winningham	.200	--	.248	72	.271	51	.196	124	.281	42	.267	48	.237	119	.500	92
Team Average	.243	10	.247	6	.254	5	.238	9	.243	11	.227	7	.302	6	.551	8
League Average	.250		.246		.252		.244		.250		.231		.301		.554	

Pitching vs. Left and Right Handed Batters

		BA	Rank	SA	Rank	OBA	Rank	HR %	Rank	BB %	Rank	SO %	Rank
Jack Armstrong	vs. Lefties	.302	98	.481	102	.422	108	3.88	104	17.90	107	12.96	61
	vs. Righties	.205	--	.376	--	.258	--	2.56	--	6.87	--	18.32	--
Tim Birtsas	vs. Lefties	.233	29	.360	57	.287	20	2.33	77	6.32	22	18.95	24
	vs. Righties	.259	82	.380	76	.339	95	2.53	80	9.89	91	10.99	86
Tom Browning	vs. Lefties	.285	84	.536	108	.347	77	5.30	109	9.41	62	20.00	18
	vs. Righties	.212	24	.370	67	.263	20	3.66	101	5.78	43	10.83	88
Norm Charlton	vs. Lefties	.184	--	.289	--	.279	--	2.63	--	9.30	--	13.95	--
	vs. Righties	.270	90	.403	91	.326	83	2.55	81	7.41	70	15.28	59
Rob Dibble	vs. Lefties	.215	20	.323	27	.321	55	1.08	29	12.84	97	26.61	3
	vs. Righties	.200	--	.270	--	.242	--	0.87	--	5.56	--	23.81	--
John Franco	vs. Lefties	.137	--	.235	--	.167	--	1.96	--	3.64	--	14.55	--
	vs. Righties	.210	22	.242	3	.282	41	0.79	12	8.90	84	13.52	74
Danny Jackson	vs. Lefties	.261	60	.336	35	.299	31	0.75	19	5.48	19	16.44	37
	vs. Righties	.211	23	.308	23	.269	27	1.48	38	7.09	62	15.43	57
Rob Murphy	vs. Lefties	.207	--	.220	--	.270	--	0.00	--	7.78	--	23.33	--
	vs. Righties	.237	52	.338	45	.333	90	1.37	34	11.92	106	20.38	17
Jose Rijo	vs. Lefties	.231	28	.347	44	.327	61	1.95	64	12.26	93	25.07	6
	vs. Righties	.184	3	.244	4	.241	9	0.38	4	6.46	50	23.81	11
Ron Robinson	vs. Lefties	.331	108	.485	104	.402	103	2.45	84	9.68	64	5.91	107
	vs. Righties	.233	49	.288	15	.266	25	0.68	10	4.97	30	16.77	45
Mario Soto	vs. Lefties	.289	86	.399	80	.342	71	1.16	32	7.77	41	8.81	95
	vs. Righties	.242	58	.395	84	.308	70	3.82	105	7.47	73	9.77	98
Frank Williams	vs. Lefties	.286	85	.429	90	.404	104	3.30	99	16.51	104	10.09	86
	vs. Righties	.231	46	.343	50	.321	82	2.10	62	10.18	93	19.16	26
Team Average	vs. Lefties	.264	9	.398	12	.340	10	2.36	12	10.30	11	16.16	2
	vs. Righties	.225	1	.341	3	.286	4	2.21	5	7.49	11	15.23	7
League Average	vs. Lefties	.255		.365		.325		1.73		9.36		14.24	
	vs. Righties	.244		.361		.299		2.10		6.87		15.64	

Pitching with Runners on Base and Bases Empty

		BA	Rank	SA	Rank	OBA	Rank	HR %	Rank	BB %	Rank	SO %	Rank
Jack Armstrong	Runners On	.241	41	.422	93	.321	49	3.45	104	11.35	83	13.48	58
	Bases Empty	.269	94	.438	104	.375	108	3.08	97	14.47	108	17.11	38
Tim Birtsas	Runners On	.261	--	.359	--	.349	--	2.17	--	12.50	--	16.07	--
	Bases Empty	.243	59	.382	81	.303	70	2.63	83	6.06	42	12.12	83
Tom Browning	Runners On	.237	35	.449	101	.274	7	5.06	109	5.16	3	12.89	68
	Bases Empty	.217	20	.370	70	.279	30	3.33	98	7.06	61	12.12	84
Norm Charlton	Runners On	.278	--	.433	--	.350	--	3.33	--	10.58	--	12.50	--
	Bases Empty	.243	58	.354	53	.297	55	2.08	63	5.81	38	16.77	45
John Franco	Runners On	.205	12	.265	9	.274	6	1.52	44	8.61	38	16.56	31
	Bases Empty	.193	6	.222	2	.254	10	0.58	9	7.57	69	11.35	90
Danny Jackson	Runners On	.255	57	.346	41	.315	40	1.17	32	7.67	25	13.04	65
	Bases Empty	.198	8	.292	12	.249	5	1.50	37	6.38	62	17.11	37
Rob Murphy	Runners On	.243	44	.350	44	.335	62	2.14	71	11.18	81	17.06	27
	Bases Empty	.217	22	.267	5	.300	62	0.00	1	10.56	100	25.00	7
Jose Rijo	Runners On	.206	13	.271	12	.330	57	0.47	12	15.24	106	23.42	3
	Bases Empty	.211	19	.317	24	.260	16	1.67	46	5.73	36	25.26	6
Ron Robinson	Runners On	.336	109	.448	100	.397	106	1.60	51	9.27	52	5.96	109
	Bases Empty	.250	69	.353	52	.296	51	1.63	43	6.12	43	14.80	62
Mario Soto	Runners On	.296	100	.496	109	.358	89	4.44	108	8.33	36	9.62	94
	Bases Empty	.246	67	.395	90	.303	71	1.03	20	7.11	63	9.00	103
Frank Williams	Runners On	.241	39	.352	46	.354	84	2.78	97	12.88	94	14.39	52
	Bases Empty	.262	88	.397	90	.354	103	2.38	76	12.50	105	16.67	47
Team Average	Runners On	.255	7	.390	9	.328	7	2.65	12	9.74	9	14.57	4
	Bases Empty	.225	1	.338	3	.286	3	2.00	7	7.42	10	16.19	4
League Average	Runners On	.257		.373		.329		1.91		9.45		14.09	
	Bases Empty	.242		.355		.297		1.98		6.73		15.80	

Overall Pitching Compared to Late Inning Pressure Situations

		BA	Rank	SA	Rank	OBA	Rank	HR %	Rank	BB %	Rank	SO %	Rank
Jack Armstrong	Overall	.256	70	.431	103	.349	102	3.25	103	12.97	107	15.36	49
	Pressure	.250	--	.500	--	.625	--	0.00	--	50.00	--	0.00	--
Tim Birtsas	Overall	.250	59	.373	66	.321	70	2.46	86	8.66	69	13.72	69
	Pressure	.273	--	.364	--	.360	--	0.00	--	8.00	--	12.00	--
Tom Browning	Overall	.224	21	.397	95	.277	13	3.93	108	6.39	26	12.39	81
	Pressure	.208	31	.349	58	.254	19	2.83	89	6.09	23	16.52	38
Norm Charlton	Overall	.256	72	.385	84	.318	68	2.56	89	7.72	52	15.06	51
	Pressure	.263	--	.526	--	.300	--	5.26	--	5.00	--	10.00	--
Rob Dibble	Overall	.207	--	.293	--	.279	--	0.96	--	8.94	--	25.11	--
	Pressure	.198	20	.256	12	.239	12	1.16	39	5.38	14	26.88	5
John Franco	Overall	.198	5	.241	2	.263	9	0.99	14	8.04	59	13.69	70
	Pressure	.189	15	.235	9	.257	20	0.92	28	8.26	48	11.57	77
Danny Jackson	Overall	.218	20	.312	18	.273	9	1.38	30	6.87	35	15.57	42
	Pressure	.168	4	.264	17	.206	2	0.80	25	4.48	8	17.16	35
Rob Murphy	Overall	.229	29	.306	16	.317	63	1.00	15	10.86	94	21.14	14
	Pressure	.199	22	.261	15	.272	29	0.57	22	8.33	50	20.10	22
Jose Rijo	Overall	.209	9	.300	11	.288	29	1.22	25	9.65	84	24.50	6
	Pressure	.208	32	.315	44	.327	65	2.31	75	13.38	99	19.11	25
Ron Robinson	Overall	.285	104	.392	89	.339	94	1.62	39	7.49	47	10.95	89
	Pressure	.385	--	.462	--	.467	--	0.00	--	13.33	--	20.00	--
Mario Soto	Overall	.267	81	.397	94	.326	79	2.42	85	7.63	50	9.26	103
	Pressure	.421	--	.526	--	.429	--	0.00	--	4.76	--	4.76	--
Frank Williams	Overall	.252	64	.376	71	.354	105	2.56	89	12.68	106	15.58	41
	Pressure	.264	70	.396	80	.374	96	2.20	71	13.64	101	18.18	29
Team Average	Overall	.237	2	.359	4	.303	5	2.26	12	8.38	10	15.52	4
	Pressure	.214	2	.314	3	.288	2	1.69	6	8.90	5	16.49	4
League Average	Overall	.248		.363		.310		1.95		7.91		15.06	
	Pressure	.243		.347		.315		1.72		9.12		15.69	

Additional Miscellaneous Pitching Comparisons

	Grass Surface		Artificial Surface		Home Games		Road Games		Runners in Scoring Position		Runners in Scoring Pos and Two Outs		Leading Off Inning	
	BA	Rank	BA	Rank	BA	Rank	BA	Rank	BA	Rank	BA	Rank	OBA	Rank
Jack Armstrong	.284	--	.244	54	.279	95	.237	38	.194	20	.129	6	.444	109
Tim Birtsas	.293	--	.228	31	.209	17	.305	--	.273	--	.333	103	.266	20
Tom Browning	.204	12	.233	34	.242	58	.207	10	.245	53	.239	72	.272	28
Norm Charlton	.225	--	.263	72	.273	84	.232	--	.245	--	.280	--	.286	49
Rob Dibble	.185	--	.214	19	.228	31	.176	--	.138	--	.097	2	.220	--
John Franco	.267	74	.171	3	.159	4	.240	43	.210	--	.156	10	.256	13
Danny Jackson	.245	43	.208	15	.212	18	.225	27	.259	69	.278	92	.278	36
Rob Murphy	.258	62	.216	20	.222	26	.239	41	.215	29	.170	15	.269	22
Jose Rijo	.206	14	.210	16	.229	37	.179	1	.228	39	.177	22	.272	27
Ron Robinson	.318	104	.272	82	.286	101	.284	91	.325	102	.359	107	.265	19
Candy Sierra	.372	108	.333	--	.419	--	.300	--	.366	--	.458	--	.480	--
Mario Soto	.295	96	.250	61	.271	82	.264	69	.305	95	.316	101	.289	52
Frank Williams	.154	--	.280	91	.294	106	.187	--	.253	61	.343	106	.400	106
Team Average	.247	6	.233	2	.239	6	.235	2	.247	5	.247	10	.287	2
League Average	.250		.246		.244		.252		.250		.231		.301	

HOUSTON ASTROS

- Houston's home-field advantage rises and falls with the league scoring average. Bring back the lively ball!

- What trait is characteristic of all three domed stadiums?

- What was Nolan Ryan's secret advantage at the Astrodome?

There are days when everything at the office seems to go just right. You breeze through the day, and the first time you look at the clock it's already time to head home. You wolf down your dinner, watch another rerun of "My Mother The Car: The Early Years," and go to bed.

Then there are the bad days. You spend the first half-hour digging out from under the piles of work on your desk. By the time you get around to the coffee that's been sitting there, it's cold. The day drags on, and the commute home is terrible. But when you arrive, you appreciate everything that much more. Dinner tastes better, the sofa's more comfortable, Jerry Van Dyke goes for it, and you really believe that the ol' '28 Porter *is* dear old mom. Then time to hit the sack. Woof!

We're reminded of that dichotomy by the relative home-field effect of the Astrodome in high- and low-scoring years. (OK, so it's a stretch.) In those seasons in which runs are at a premium and games go by quickly without a lot of lead changes, the Astros' home-field advantage is minimal. But in high-scoring seasons, when every game seems to be a back-and-forth, survival-of-the-fittest struggle, and no win is easy, home is a welcome haven for the 'Stros.

The past two seasons provide a graphic example. Two years back, amid all the controversy about lively balls, tampered-with bats, and substandard pitching, Houston won 16 more games at home than on the road. Last season, when there were fewer runs per game in the National League than in any season since 1968, the Astros managed just six more wins in home games than in road games. The following table shows those figures. The runs-per-game average is a league-wide mark, and HFA refers to the home-field advantage expressed as the difference between home and road wins:

Year	Runs per Game	Home Games W–L	Pct.	Road Games W–L	Pct.	HFA
1987	4.52	47–34	.580	29–52	.358	+16
1988	3.88	44–37	.543	38–43	.469	+6

But the Astrodome's been open for more than 20 years, so we're not limited to an analysis of just two seasons to determine if this trend is ongoing or random. Actually, Houston's first four seasons at the Astrodome provided conflicting data. From 1965 through 1968, very low-scoring years, the Astros had an enormous home-field advantage:

Year	Runs per Game	Home Games W–L	Pct.	Road Games W–L	Pct.	HFA
1965	4.03	36–45	.444	29–52	.358	+.086
1966	4.09	45–36	.556	27–54	.333	+.222
1967	3.84	46–35	.568	23–58	.284	+.284
1968	3.43	42–39	.519	30–51	.370	+.148

But if you disregard the stadium's first five years of operation, Houston's home-field advantage has been consistently greater in high-scoring seasons, and lesser in low-scoring ones. The table below contrasts Houston's Astrodome edge in the five highest- and five lowest-scoring seasons since 1970.

	High-Scoring Years				Low-Scoring Years		
Year	Home	Road	HFA	Year	Home	Road	HFA
1970	.543	.432	+.111	1971	.481	.494	−.012
1977	.568	.432	+.136	1972	.532	.566	−.033
1979	.642	.457	+.185	1976	.561	.425	+.136
1986	.642	.543	+.099	1981	.608	.508	+.099
1987	.580	.358	+.222	1988	.543	.469	+.074
Totals	.595	.444	+.151	Totals	.548	.491	+.057

The home-field advantage in the high-scoring years was more than twice that in the low-scoring years. But can we reasonably disregard the contradictory evidence of the Astrodome's wonder years, when the team maximized its home-field edge despite a leaguewide scoring drought? We think so. Don't forget that the Astrodome, idiosyncratic even after 20 years, was unique when it opened. It wasn't only the first domed stadium; it had a unique playing surface as well. The stuff ain't called Astroturf for nothin'.

The other N.L. teams probably endured a learning curve of at least a few seasons before discovering how to take advantage of the Astrodome's unique characteristics. The Astros, on the other hand, probably learned those strategies in their first season or two, giving them an added home-field edge totally unrelated to scoring levels. And if we disregard those learning years, it's clear that Houston's home-field advantage rises and falls along with the National League's scoring level.

The three domed stadiums—the Astrodome, Kingdome, and Metrodome—are in some ways as dissimilar as could be. The Astrodome is one of the major leagues' best pitchers' parks, decreasing scoring by an average of 11 percent. The Kingdome and Metrodome are hitters' parks of different types: the Kingdome tends to increase home runs; the Metrodome increases batting average, doubles, and triples. (We've ignored Montreal's Olympic Stadium in this discussion, since it's only been capped for one season.)

There are similarities, as well, many of which are characteristic of most or all stadiums with artificial turf; for example, an increase in stolen-base percentage. But there is one trait of domed stadiums that has nothing to do with plastic grass. All of the domed stadiums increase the rate of strikeouts, and to a degree that supports the contention that a batter's visibility is adversely affected indoors.

By referring to the table of strikeout percentages on page 428, you'll note that among the 26 major league ballparks, the Metrodome ranks second in strikeout increase. The Astrodome ranks ninth, and the Kingdome 15th. That distribution isn't particularly significant. But the stadiums were grouped so closely that we expanded our analysis to include 1982 and 1983 as well, giving us seven seasons of data.

In the seven-year rankings, the Metrodome fell to third and the Astrodome to 10th, but the Kingdome rose to ninth place. And the placement of all three in the top ten provides a strong indication that there is a dome effect on strikeouts. The following table summarizes those seven years of statistics. The dome-game figures include the combined stats for all Astros, Twins, and Mariners home games. (You can guess what the road-game figures include.)

	PA	SO	SO/PA
Dome Games	130,177	19,375	.1499
Road Games	127,956	18,361	.1435

Strikeouts were 3.7 percent more frequent at the domes than in road games. That might not sound like a lot, but over so many plate appearances, it's huge by comparison to just about anything other than the national debt. A difference of that magnitude would only occur once in roughly 8000 trials.

In the 1988 *Analyst,* we demonstrated that power pitchers benefit from working in a ballpark that increases strikeouts. So the off-season addition of Jim Clancy and Rick Rhoden may not be enough to offset the loss of Nolan Ryan to the Astros' state rivals. While Ryan keeps hummin' along, neither of the new Astros pitchers can be considered a power pitcher. And Rhoden seems to be slipping at that:

Player	Through 1987			Last Season		
	IP	SO	Rate	IP	SO	Rate
Ryan	4327.0	4547	9.46	220.0	228	9.33
Clancy	2009.2	1119	5.01	196.1	118	5.41
Rhoden	2229.2	1284	5.03	197.0	94	4.29

The advantage that power pitchers gain in high-strikeout stadiums may also explain the phenomenal success that Ryan enjoyed at the Astrodome. Of course, all pitchers benefit from the fact that the Astrodome depresses almost all the various components of run scoring: batting average, extra-base hits, and most of all, home runs. But during Ryan's nine-year hitch with the Astros, he was a terror in the Dome, merely mortal elsewhere:

	GS	CG	W	L	Pct.	IP	H	HR	BB	SO	ERA
Home Games	141	20	58	39	.598	966.2	688	37	393	982	2.63
Road Games	141	18	48	55	.466	908.0	753	74	403	884	3.59

Ryan allowed twice as many home runs on the road as he did in the Astrodome. He allowed one more hit and one more run per nine innings on the road. And if that difference in his won-lost record doesn't impress you, consider that his home record is roughly equal to the career mark of Tom Browning (63–40) and Sid Fernandez (55–40). His road record is similar to Charles Hudson's career mark (49–55).

Houston's other strikeout king, Mike Scott, has also pitched far better at home than on the road during his six seasons wearing the fruit-flavored outfit that passes for an Astros uniform. Scott's breakdown since 1983:

	GS	CG	W	L	Pct.	IP	H	HR	BB	SO	ERA
Home Games	96	16	47	26	.644	653.0	504	36	160	541	2.55
Road Games	99	13	34	30	.531	609.1	555	56	213	481	3.90

During those six seasons, Scott had the fourth-best home-game ERA in the majors among pitchers who made at least 50 starts at home. Ryan ranked sixth with a 2.67 mark. But among the 94 pitchers who made at least 50 starts on the road, Scott ranked 36th, one notch above Ryan.

Of course, holding on to Ryan for one last hurrah at such a high price might not have made financial sense for Houston. And considering the price the Astros paid for Rhoden (three minor leaguers) and Clancy (signed as a free agent), who can fault them? But the facts indicate that Houston moved a pitcher who was made to pitch in the Astrodome, and acquired two others not particularly suited to their new home park.

WON-LOST RECORD BY STARTING POSITION

HOUSTON 82-80	C	1B	2B	3B	SS	LF	CF	RF	P	Leadoff	Relief	Starts
Juan Agosto	·	·	·	·	·	·	·	·	·	·	32-43	·
Larry Andersen	·	·	·	·	·	·	·	·	·	·	23-30	·
Joaquin Andujar	·	·	·	·	·	·	·	·	5-5	·	3-10	5-5
Alan Ashby	31-29	·	·	·	·	·	·	·	·	·	·	31-29
Mark Bailey	3-4	·	·	·	·	·	·	·	·	·	·	3-4
Kevin Bass	·	·	·	·	·	·	·	68-69	·	·	·	68-69
Buddy Bell	·	4-2	·	31-34	·	·	·	·	·	·	·	35-36
Craig Biggio	18-22	·	·	·	·	·	·	·	·	·	·	18-22
Ernie Camacho	·	·	·	·	·	·	·	·	·	·	5-8	·
Ken Caminiti	·	·	·	13-7	·	·	·	·	·	·	·	13-7
Casey Candaele	·	·	1-2	·	·	·	·	·	·	·	·	1-2
Rocky Childress	·	·	·	·	·	·	·	·	·	·	1-10	·
Danny Darwin	·	·	·	·	·	·	·	·	7-13	·	12-12	7-13
Glenn Davis	·	74-76	·	·	·	·	·	·	·	·	·	74-76
Jim Deshaies	·	·	·	·	·	·	·	·	15-16	·	·	15-16
Bill Doran	·	·	67-61	·	·	·	·	·	·	·	·	67-61
Cameron Drew	·	·	·	·	·	0-2	·	0-2	·	·	·	0-4
John Fishel	·	·	·	·	·	0-1	·	0-1	·	·	·	0-2
Bob Forsch	·	·	·	·	·	·	·	·	1-5	·	·	1-5
Billy Hatcher	·	·	·	·	·	59-56	9-9	·	·	10-12	·	68-65
Jeff Heathcock	·	·	·	·	·	·	·	·	0-1	·	1-15	0-1
Steve Henderson	·	·	·	·	·	1-1	·	1-1	·	·	·	2-2
Chuck Jackson	·	·	·	12-8	·	·	·	·	·	·	·	12-8
Bob Knepper	·	·	·	·	·	·	·	·	18-9	·	·	18-9
Louie Meadows	·	·	·	·	·	3-2	·	1-1	·	·	·	4-3
Dave Meads	·	·	·	·	·	·	·	·	1-1	·	4-16	1-1
Brian Meyer	·	·	·	·	·	·	·	·	·	·	1-7	·
Jim Pankovits	·	·	11-12	3-5	·	·	·	·	·	·	·	14-17
Terry Puhl	·	·	·	·	·	18-18	12-6	·	·	·	·	30-24
Rafael Ramirez	·	·	·	·	75-74	·	·	·	·	·	·	75-74
Craig Reynolds	·	3-2	3-5	4-3	7-6	·	·	·	·	·	·	17-16
Nolan Ryan	·	·	·	·	·	·	·	·	16-17	·	·	16-17
Mike Scott	·	·	·	·	·	·	·	·	19-13	·	·	19-13
Craig Smajstrla	·	·	·	·	·	·	·	·	·	·	·	·
Dave Smith	·	·	·	·	·	·	·	·	·	·	35-16	·
Harry Spilman	·	·	·	·	·	·	·	·	·	·	·	·
Alex Trevino	30-25	·	·	·	·	·	·	·	·	·	·	30-25
Denny Walling	·	1-0	·	19-23	·	1-0	·	·	·	·	·	21-23
Gerald Young	·	·	·	·	·	·	73-71	·	·	72-68	·	73-71

Batting vs. Left and Right Handed Pitchers

		BA	Rank	SA	Rank	OBA	Rank	HR %	Rank	BB %	Rank	SO %	Rank
Alan Ashby	vs. Lefties	.136	--	.159	--	.188	--	0.00	--	6.12	--	8.16	--
	vs. Righties	.262	55	.426	29	.349	32	3.83	19	12.26	17	15.09	74
Kevin Bass	vs. Lefties	.316	10	.503	15	.354	34	3.11	37	4.37	113	7.77	21
	vs. Righties	.221	111	.328	94	.293	96	2.30	43	8.48	54	12.60	51
Buddy Bell	vs. Lefties	.242	89	.363	75	.314	78	2.20	61	9.80	45	5.88	11
	vs. Righties	.241	89	.336	86	.288	104	2.16	49	6.40	87	10.40	32
Casey Candaele	vs. Lefties	.222	107	.349	81	.258	118	0.00	103	4.55	112	7.58	19
	vs. Righties	.131	--	.155	--	.207	--	0.00	--	8.42	--	12.63	--
Glenn Davis	vs. Lefties	.228	104	.395	56	.322	70	4.19	20	10.55	32	11.06	58
	vs. Righties	.289	22	.513	6	.349	31	5.84	2	7.36	72	12.64	52
Bill Doran	vs. Lefties	.263	58	.346	83	.372	18	1.28	83	13.98	12	8.60	32
	vs. Righties	.241	91	.327	96	.321	60	1.54	61	10.66	30	12.02	45
Billy Hatcher	vs. Lefties	.284	35	.415	43	.333	56	2.19	62	6.83	81	9.76	41
	vs. Righties	.259	61	.346	77	.314	67	0.86	90	5.96	97	9.33	23
Jim Pankovits	vs. Lefties	.213	109	.333	91	.263	116	2.67	48	4.94	108	14.81	88
	vs. Righties	.231	--	.323	--	.282	--	0.00	--	5.56	--	22.22	--
Terry Puhl	vs. Lefties	.211	--	.211	--	.250	--	0.00	--	4.76	--	23.81	--
	vs. Righties	.312	5	.405	38	.406	3	1.40	72	13.55	8	9.96	28
Rafael Ramirez	vs. Lefties	.306	17	.440	31	.322	70	1.04	92	2.48	126	7.92	26
	vs. Righties	.260	59	.346	76	.287	106	1.07	82	3.29	123	11.39	41
Craig Reynolds	vs. Lefties	.333	--	.333	--	.333	--	0.00	--	0.00	--	61.54	--
	vs. Righties	.248	82	.315	101	.287	107	0.67	101	5.10	111	9.55	26
Alex Trevino	vs. Lefties	.239	92	.398	52	.350	40	2.27	58	12.50	62	11.54	62
	vs. Righties	.257	--	.343	--	.333	--	0.00	--	9.24	--	14.29	--
Gerald Young	vs. Lefties	.273	47	.337	90	.339	49	0.00	103	8.23	65	9.96	43
	vs. Righties	.248	83	.318	99	.331	48	0.00	115	11.08	27	10.14	29
Team Average	vs. Lefties	.250	5	.366	7	.313	6	1.84	7	7.75	8	12.80	2
	vs. Righties	.241	10	.344	11	.303	11	1.71	10	7.73	7	14.14	3
League Average	vs. Lefties	.248		.367		.310		2.10		8.01		14.42	
	vs. Righties	.249		.360		.310		1.88		7.86		15.35	

Batting with Runners on Base and Bases Empty

		BA	Rank	SA	Rank	OBA	Rank	HR %	Rank	BB %	Rank	SO %	Rank
Alan Ashby	Runners On	.244	99	.372	71	.349	56	2.33	45	14.95	19	13.08	67
	Bases Empty	.234	88	.376	55	.299	77	3.55	24	8.44	44	14.29	64
Kevin Bass	Runners On	.277	57	.420	42	.366	38	3.03	29	12.18	35	10.70	41
	Bases Empty	.239	85	.368	63	.272	104	2.26	51	2.78	115	11.11	36
Buddy Bell	Runners On	.255	86	.340	95	.316	93	1.31	74	8.77	72	10.53	38
	Bases Empty	.229	100	.347	74	.276	99	2.94	36	6.08	77	7.73	9
Glenn Davis	Runners On	.260	76	.524	10	.352	51	7.87	1	12.17	36	9.54	27
	Bases Empty	.280	23	.440	18	.330	33	3.26	28	4.85	99	14.55	68
Bill Doran	Runners On	.289	40	.385	61	.372	32	1.60	65	11.87	38	10.05	30
	Bases Empty	.222	106	.300	107	.315	48	1.37	78	11.71	10	11.41	39
Billy Hatcher	Runners On	.292	35	.416	45	.360	42	1.49	70	9.43	61	10.66	39
	Bases Empty	.253	52	.341	82	.294	82	1.22	82	4.03	110	8.65	17
Terry Puhl	Runners On	.258	78	.270	122	.368	35	0.00	104	14.02	22	14.95	87
	Bases Empty	.331	2	.462	14	.412	1	2.07	59	12.12	7	8.48	15
Rafael Ramirez	Runners On	.295	30	.406	52	.321	88	1.28	76	3.91	122	10.16	32
	Bases Empty	.262	43	.358	67	.282	96	0.90	93	2.35	122	10.26	29
Alex Trevino	Runners On	.275	58	.413	50	.408	10	1.25	79	15.84	15	9.90	29
	Bases Empty	.230	99	.336	88	.287	90	0.88	95	6.56	67	15.57	77
Gerald Young	Runners On	.279	54	.364	75	.361	41	0.00	104	11.06	44	8.54	23
	Bases Empty	.248	68	.309	104	.322	47	0.00	115	9.65	25	10.75	34
Team Average	Runners On	.256	8	.373	7	.333	4	1.97	7	9.99	5	12.95	2
	Bases Empty	.236	10	.336	12	.287	11	1.60	11	6.10	9	14.26	3
League Average	Runners On	.257		.373		.329		1.91		9.45		14.09	
	Bases Empty	.242		.355		.297		1.98		6.73		15.80	

Overall Batting Compared to Late Inning Pressure Situations

		BA	Rank	SA	Rank	OBA	Rank	HR %	Rank	BB %	Rank	SO %	Rank	RDI %	Rank
Alan Ashby	Overall	.238	101	.374	61	.319	64	3.08	30	11.11	25	13.79	66	.353	6
	Pressure	.224	83	.449	21	.377	20	6.12	6	19.67	4	9.84	27	.400	9
Kevin Bass	Overall	.255	73	.390	47	.314	72	2.59	39	7.06	81	10.92	38	.314	18
	Pressure	.244	64	.314	80	.305	75	2.33	43	8.16	66	4.08	3	.241	62
Buddy Bell	Overall	.241	98	.344	90	.295	100	2.17	47	7.39	74	9.09	19	.256	80
	Pressure	.218	87	.255	103	.254	110	0.00	79	5.08	102	16.95	82	.208	79
Glenn Davis	Overall	.271	40	.478	11	.341	40	5.35	3	8.36	55	12.15	48	.278	58
	Pressure	.277	40	.436	24	.376	21	3.19	24	12.84	26	12.84	51	.304	40
Bill Doran	Overall	.248	88	.333	99	.338	42	1.46	76	11.78	18	10.87	37	.301	35
	Pressure	.172	117	.172	124	.293	86	0.00	79	14.29	18	12.99	53	.158	101
Billy Hatcher	Overall	.268	45	.370	68	.321	62	1.32	84	6.26	97	9.48	25	.263	68
	Pressure	.326	13	.467	16	.386	18	1.09	70	6.86	81	11.76	44	.273	51
Terry Puhl	Overall	.303	4	.389	49	.395	2	1.28	85	12.87	40	11.03	40	.276	62
	Pressure	.375	3	.500	12	.516	1	2.08	49	21.88	2	10.94	38	.500	--
Rafael Ramirez	Overall	.276	33	.378	56	.298	97	1.06	88	3.02	123	10.22	32	.244	88
	Pressure	.226	81	.301	87	.258	109	1.08	71	4.00	113	7.00	11	.182	88
Craig Reynolds	Overall	.255	--	.317	--	.290	--	0.62	--	4.71	--	13.53	--	.265	--
	Pressure	.306	--	.444	--	.390	--	0.00	--	12.20	--	7.32	--	.500	2
Alex Trevino	Overall	.249	84	.368	69	.341	39	1.04	90	10.76	32	13.00	56	.192	122
	Pressure	.250	57	.278	98	.341	47	0.00	79	11.63	35	18.60	88	.125	--
Gerald Young	Overall	.257	67	.325	107	.334	46	0.00	118	10.08	35	10.08	31	.285	50
	Pressure	.322	15	.379	46	.361	34	0.00	79	6.93	79	10.89	37	.389	10
Team Average	Overall	.244	10	.351	9	.306	9	1.75	11	7.74	8	13.71	2	.258	5
	Pressure	.246	6	.342	6	.321	3	1.54	8	9.57	3	13.49	2	.267	2
League Average	Overall	.248		.363		.310		1.95		7.91		15.06		.256	
	Pressure	.242		.340		.310		1.70		8.47		15.93		.238	

Additional Miscellaneous Batting Comparisons

	Grass Surface BA	Rank	Artificial Surface BA	Rank	Home Games BA	Rank	Road Games BA	Rank	Runners in Scoring Position BA	Rank	Runners in Scoring Pos and Two Outs BA	Rank	Leading Off Inning OBA	Rank	Runners on 3B with less than 2 Outs RDI %	Rank
Alan Ashby	.247	82	.234	86	.211	114	.269	42	.245	79	.304	22	.291	82	.750	6
Kevin Bass	.246	83	.260	61	.277	45	.236	93	.307	20	.379	4	.250	125	.500	92
Buddy Bell	.255	62	.235	85	.228	101	.253	70	.275	50	.322	16	.261	101	.400	121
Casey Candaele	.212	--	.158	126	.160	--	.181	--	.161	--	.083	--	.191	127	.125	--
Glenn Davis	.158	126	.311	12	.297	21	.244	84	.212	107	.183	103	.319	54	.694	23
Bill Doran	.283	29	.233	87	.249	85	.247	79	.274	51	.340	10	.279	88	.452	114
Billy Hatcher	.273	40	.266	54	.243	90	.292	16	.276	48	.172	108	.355	25	.720	14
Jim Pankovits	.184	--	.235	82	.206	--	.234	--	.219	--	.231	--	.241	--	.250	--
Terry Puhl	.306	--	.302	20	.377	1	.242	86	.302	24	.158	113	.393	5	.643	38
Rafael Ramirez	.289	23	.270	48	.255	76	.295	11	.310	19	.300	25	.257	103	.586	58
Craig Reynolds	.313	--	.213	108	.231	--	.277	--	.282	--	.214	--	.306	--	.636	40
Alex Trevino	.304	--	.226	96	.167	127	.312	6	.205	110	.176	105	.233	--	.333	128
Gerald Young	.312	7	.237	81	.236	94	.278	32	.339	5	.279	42	.328	43	.706	18
Team Average	.245	9	.243	9	.241	12	.246	5	.257	2	.246	3	.288	10	.571	4
League Average	.250		.246		.252		.244		.250		.231		.301		.554	

Pitching vs. Left and Right Handed Batters

		BA	Rank	SA	Rank	OBA	Rank	HR %	Rank	BB %	Rank	SO %	Rank
Juan Agosto	vs. Lefties	.140	1	.178	1	.184	1	0.93	26	5.13	13	15.38	44
	vs. Righties	.268	87	.400	87	.335	92	2.27	70	9.45	86	5.91	109
Larry Andersen	vs. Lefties	.293	91	.360	55	.359	85	0.67	17	8.82	54	12.94	62
	vs. Righties	.220	33	.312	26	.239	8	1.16	24	2.78	3	24.44	9
Joaquin Andujar	vs. Lefties	.284	81	.439	94	.345	75	2.70	95	8.38	46	5.99	106
	vs. Righties	.308	105	.467	104	.346	98	2.96	92	3.80	17	13.59	73
Danny Darwin	vs. Lefties	.264	64	.401	81	.313	47	2.58	92	6.28	21	13.95	56
	vs. Righties	.254	75	.382	77	.301	63	2.92	90	5.61	39	18.45	32
Jim Deshaies	vs. Lefties	.248	44	.465	100	.310	43	4.65	108	7.64	38	12.50	66
	vs. Righties	.212	25	.345	51	.278	36	2.25	68	8.68	81	15.50	55
Bob Forsch	vs. Lefties	.235	31	.298	5	.291	24	0.42	11	7.38	33	8.49	96
	vs. Righties	.334	107	.503	109	.386	108	3.10	95	7.38	68	9.54	99
Bob Knepper	vs. Lefties	.239	37	.348	45	.273	15	1.09	30	4.00	6	21.00	16
	vs. Righties	.244	60	.364	65	.321	81	2.18	67	10.06	92	13.10	78
Nolan Ryan	vs. Lefties	.215	19	.315	24	.301	37	1.83	60	11.29	80	22.77	11
	vs. Righties	.242	59	.384	80	.308	69	2.63	85	7.06	60	26.59	3
Mike Scott	vs. Lefties	.185	8	.311	23	.260	10	2.47	87	8.50	48	19.39	21
	vs. Righties	.224	37	.340	46	.260	16	2.32	71	3.37	7	24.28	10
Dave Smith	vs. Lefties	.306	100	.357	52	.367	90	0.00	1	9.17	59	10.09	86
	vs. Righties	.238	--	.349	--	.294	--	0.79	--	6.43	--	19.29	--
Team Average	vs. Lefties	.238	1	.352	5	.306	2	1.96	10	8.66	3	16.04	3
	vs. Righties	.246	8	.377	9	.303	8	2.41	10	7.10	8	17.58	3
League Average	vs. Lefties	.255		.365		.325		1.73		9.36		14.24	
	vs. Righties	.244		.361		.299		2.10		6.87		15.64	

Pitching with Runners on Base and Bases Empty

		BA	Rank	SA	Rank	OBA	Rank	HR %	Rank	BB %	Rank	SO %	Rank
Juan Agosto	Runners On	.211	19	.278	15	.299	26	0.75	21	11.45	85	9.64	93
	Bases Empty	.237	47	.361	61	.278	28	2.58	80	5.37	29	8.29	107
Larry Andersen	Runners On	.270	70	.322	30	.321	50	0.00	1	7.60	23	18.71	21
	Bases Empty	.240	51	.345	45	.274	26	1.75	49	3.91	10	18.99	22
Joaquin Andujar	Runners On	.295	98	.463	105	.331	58	3.36	103	5.39	5	11.98	79
	Bases Empty	.298	106	.446	105	.359	105	2.38	76	6.52	53	8.15	108
Danny Darwin	Runners On	.270	71	.402	83	.322	52	2.70	91	7.31	21	14.91	46
	Bases Empty	.251	70	.385	87	.297	54	2.76	89	4.98	23	16.88	43
Jim Deshaies	Runners On	.201	11	.355	48	.256	2	2.73	93	7.65	24	15.29	40
	Bases Empty	.229	37	.373	74	.302	69	2.61	82	9.07	92	14.79	63
Bob Forsch	Runners On	.282	85	.398	80	.341	71	2.31	77	9.20	50	6.13	108
	Bases Empty	.295	105	.420	98	.343	99	1.60	41	5.97	41	11.34	91
Bob Knepper	Runners On	.226	26	.330	34	.287	14	1.85	59	7.74	26	12.90	67
	Bases Empty	.255	76	.384	86	.334	93	2.15	68	10.34	99	15.14	61
Nolan Ryan	Runners On	.219	22	.304	20	.291	17	1.37	39	8.27	35	21.99	9
	Bases Empty	.234	44	.382	82	.316	81	2.87	93	10.26	98	26.63	4
Mike Scott	Runners On	.207	14	.347	43	.260	3	2.81	98	5.49	6	21.65	11
	Bases Empty	.203	12	.313	22	.260	14	2.17	69	6.40	51	21.76	13
Dave Smith	Runners On	.275	78	.358	49	.338	68	0.83	24	8.76	40	14.60	49
	Bases Empty	.260	--	.346	--	.313	--	0.00	--	6.25	--	16.07	--
Team Average	Runners On	.246	4	.362	5	.307	2	2.03	9	7.94	2	16.07	2
	Bases Empty	.240	6	.370	9	.302	9	2.37	10	7.56	11	17.65	3
League Average	Runners On	.257		.373		.329		1.91		9.45		14.09	
	Bases Empty	.242		.355		.297		1.98		6.73		15.80	

Overall Pitching Compared to Late Inning Pressure Situations

		BA	Rank	SA	Rank	OBA	Rank	HR %	Rank	BB %	Rank	SO %	Rank
Juan Agosto	Overall	.226	26	.327	25	.287	27	1.83	48	8.09	62	8.89	107
	Pressure	.215	41	.279	24	.279	32	0.46	19	8.30	49	8.70	98
Larry Andersen	Overall	.254	67	.334	31	.297	36	0.93	11	5.71	13	18.86	22
	Pressure	.221	45	.286	29	.278	31	1.01	32	6.85	33	18.72	26
Joaquin Andujar	Overall	.297	109	.454	107	.346	99	2.84	99	5.98	17	9.97	97
	Pressure	.277	84	.617	108	.346	79	8.51	110	9.43	71	13.21	67
Danny Darwin	Overall	.259	76	.392	90	.307	45	2.74	97	5.97	16	16.04	37
	Pressure	.167	3	.235	10	.265	25	1.96	66	10.66	85	15.57	46
Jim Deshaies	Overall	.218	19	.366	61	.284	20	2.66	95	8.50	67	14.99	53
	Pressure	.200	23	.338	53	.247	14	2.50	81	5.88	18	11.76	74
Bob Forsch	Overall	.290	107	.411	99	.342	95	1.89	51	7.38	45	9.06	106
	Pressure	.213	40	.311	42	.294	40	1.64	53	9.59	72	2.74	108
Jeff Heathcock	Overall	.275	--	.425	--	.360	--	1.67	--	11.19	--	8.39	--
	Pressure	.316	101	.553	107	.381	99	2.63	85	8.89	59	8.89	97
Bob Knepper	Overall	.243	49	.361	57	.314	60	2.02	59	9.23	79	14.19	64
	Pressure	.211	34	.316	45	.237	10	1.75	60	3.39	5	13.56	62
Nolan Ryan	Overall	.227	27	.347	41	.304	44	2.20	74	9.35	82	24.52	5
	Pressure	.187	13	.347	56	.282	33	2.67	87	10.59	84	28.24	1
Mike Scott	Overall	.204	7	.325	24	.260	4	2.40	84	6.06	20	21.71	11
	Pressure	.160	2	.226	5	.231	8	0.94	29	6.67	29	18.33	28
Dave Smith	Overall	.268	--	.353	--	.327	--	0.45	--	7.63	--	15.26	--
	Pressure	.256	62	.341	55	.314	51	0.57	22	7.73	41	15.98	42
Team Average	Overall	.243	6	.367	7	.304	7	2.23	11	7.73	4	16.96	3
	Pressure	.225	3	.328	4	.292	4	1.64	4	8.23	2	15.23	7
League Average	Overall	.248		.363		.310		1.95		7.91		15.06	
	Pressure	.243		.347		.315		1.72		9.12		15.69	

Additional Miscellaneous Pitching Comparisons

	Grass Surface		Artificial Surface		Home Games		Road Games		Runners in Scoring Position		Runners in Scoring Pos and Two Outs		Leading Off Inning	
	BA	Rank	BA	Rank	BA	Rank	BA	Rank	BA	Rank	BA	Rank	OBA	Rank
Juan Agosto	.261	66	.213	18	.196	12	.264	66	.185	14	.179	25	.341	91
Larry Andersen	.250	52	.255	65	.258	72	.250	51	.276	85	.250	78	.325	79
Joaquin Andujar	.347	106	.273	84	.276	89	.326	107	.283	90	.171	16	.354	96
Danny Darwin	.302	99	.239	47	.252	66	.265	71	.229	41	.181	27	.349	94
Jim Deshaies	.204	11	.223	25	.224	27	.211	12	.188	18	.179	23	.307	65
Bob Forsch	.379	109	.268	79	.254	70	.341	109	.264	75	.218	58	.342	92
Bob Knepper	.275	84	.234	36	.228	31	.264	67	.185	16	.147	9	.377	102
Dave Meads	.231	--	.245	56	.286	--	.202	--	.176	--	.154	--	.286	--
Nolan Ryan	.242	40	.220	22	.214	19	.240	42	.201	24	.224	62	.326	81
Mike Scott	.217	19	.199	12	.189	10	.216	14	.176	10	.195	36	.285	48
Dave Smith	.227	--	.285	97	.280	96	.255	--	.274	84	.256	84	.360	--
Team Average	.262	8	.234	3	.235	4	.250	5	.226	3	.203	1	.328	11
League Average	.250		.246		.244		.252		.250		.231		.301	

LOS ANGELES DODGERS

- **OK, so they weren't the best team, but they won. Does this happen more in baseball than in other sports?**
- **Remarkable, but true: The Dodgers didn't have a four-game losing streak last year.**

The most-asked question about the 1988 baseball champions of North America is not the usual one, "Can they do it again next year?" What people want to know about the Dodgers is, "How the heck did they win in the first place?"

Some of our readers may recall the decisions in 1968 by the American League and the National League to break into divisions for the 1969 season. (Okay, so it's not in the same class as "Where were you when Kennedy was shot?" but it made the sports headlines, take our word for it.) At the time, each league was expanding its membership from 10 to 12 teams, and although N.L. President Warren Giles at first resisted the move to divisional play, both leagues eventually went forward with it.

The objection raised by Giles and others was based on the possibility that teams with inferior records might get into (or win) the World Series. Given the proliferation of playoff teams in other sports in the years since 1968, those concerns seem of another century. But the goal of baseball traditionalists was a simple one, best expressed, albeit somewhat ungrammatically, by the wish of the old ring announcer Johnny Addie: "May the best man win."

The Dodgers weren't even supposed to get to the playoffs last season. They became only the 12th team in this century to win a league or division title following two consecutive sub-.500 finishes. Their subsequent upset victories in the playoffs and the World Series were extolled as triumphs of emotion over talent. Well, we suppose that's true; there's only one Mickey Hatcher, and he was playing for Los Angeles. But, as they say in Hollywood, isn't that story line wearing a little thin? Four of those 12 teams that won titles following two losing seasons did so during the Reagan Administration. In 1987, we saw the Twins win the Series with the worst regular-season record by any champion in Series history. And we all remember 1985, when Dick Howser's Royals, with the worst record among that season's Final Four, walked away with the title.

In fact, there have now been 20 seasons since divisional play went into effect, and in only six of them has the team with the best regular-season record won the World Series. We have marked those six teams with an asterisk on this chart:

1969 Mets	1974 A's	1979 Pirates	1984 Tigers*
1970 Orioles*	1975 Reds*	1980 Phillies	1985 Royals
1971 Pirates	1976 Reds*	1981 Dodgers	1986 Mets*
1972 A's	1977 Yankees	1982 Cardinals	1987 Twins
1973 A's	1978 Yankees*	1983 Orioles	1988 Dodgers

That's the type of thing that seems more startling the more you think about it. If you ranked the four division champions each year according to regular-season winning percentage, then over a 20–year period, mere chance would suggest that five top-ranked teams would win the World Series. Well, in 20 years of actual play, top-ranked teams have produced only one more World Series victory than would be suggested by chance.

Is this a pattern limited to baseball, or is it a condition that cuts across the lines of all professional sports? Let's check the other major sports during the corresponding time period. How often has the champion of the NBA Finals, the Stanley Cup or the Super Bowl been the team that had the best record during that regular season?

For the winter sports, we start with the 1968–69 season. Nine of the last 20 NBA champions were teams that also had the best regular-season record that year; however, six of the last eight champions have done it. In the NHL, 12 of the last 20 Stanley Cup champions had accumulated the most points during the regular season.

In the NFL, there is an even greater pattern of domination. Since 1969, thirteen of the 20 Super Bowls have been won by teams that had the best record (or tied for the best record) during the regular season. To some degree that total is inflated because with football's shorter schedule, it is much more common for two or more teams to be tied for the best record than it is in the other sports. (No, we did not apply the NFL's tie-breakers to determine a single best team. There's something profane about introducing that topic in this book, anyway. If baseball used a system of tie-breakers, we would never have seen Thomson's home run off Branca, Dent's home run off Torrez, or Stan Williams walking in the winning run of the '62 Dodgers-Giants playoff!) But even in seasons in which there was *not* a tie for the NFL's best record, the best team went on to win the Super Bowl six times out of eleven.

To summarize, over the past 20 years, the "best team," or

a team tied for the best, has won the postseason championship 13 times in football, 12 times in hockey, and nine times in basketball, but only six times in baseball. And consider the number of teams eligible to compete in postseason play in each of those sports. Football allows 10 teams into its playoff tournament; hockey and basketball let in 16 apiece; and baseball allows only four. With fewer teams in postseason play, it would seem at first glance that baseball should allow the greatest chance for dominance.

Why, then, has the best team gone on to win so few times in baseball? We don't know. One practice that varies between baseball and all other sports is the matter of the postseason home-field advantage. In all other sports, the home field for the odd game of any postseason series is awarded to the better team over the course of the regular season. In baseball, the home field for such games is awarded on a rotational basis, whether in the Championship Series or the World Series. This creates a more level playing field among all postseason competitors, rather than giving the best teams an additional advantage. But could this policy alone be responsible for the difference between baseball and other sports?

Probably not. But perhaps baseball's rigid admissions policy in postseason play—second-place teams need not apply— has contributed to the phenomenon. Every baseball team that gets into postseason play is already a champion. Of the 42 teams in the NFL, NBA, and NHL that annually reach the playoffs, only 14 are division champions for the regular season. The other 28 teams are competing against teams that have already beaten them out over the course of a four- to six-month regular season.

These runner-up teams may be at such a competitive and psychological disadvantage that their presence in the playoffs is merely decorative, in a competitive sense, or obligatory, in a financial sense. No non division champion has won the NBA Finals since the Washington Bullets in 1977–78, and only four have done it over the past 20 years. Only four of the last 20 Stanley Cup champions didn't have the most points (or tied for most) in their division during the regular season. And in the NFL, only one team, the 1969 Kansas City Chiefs, has won a Super Bowl after not having the best record (or tied for best) in its division during the regular season. (When the Oakland Raiders won as a "wild card" team in 1980, they had actually tied San Diego for the best record in the AFC West, but lost the division title because of—what else?—"best net points in division games." Ugh, we didn't mean to do it, those tiebreakers just slipped in there. Honest, officer.)

What we're saying is that in baseball, all four teams entered in postseason play seem to have an honest-to-goodness chance of winning the World Series. And over the past 20

years, that is indeed what has happened. If you ranked the four division champions according to regular-season won-lost percentage, you will find that teams ranked number one won six times; number-two teams won four times; number-three teams, seven times; and number-four four teams, three times. So while the story line may be wearing a bit thin lately, a wider view shows everything in balance.

Even before their October heroics, the Dodgers fashioned their 94–67 regular-season record in a rather remarkable manner. They never lost more than three games in a row. We embarked on some lengthy research, expecting to find that the Dodgers had at least tied a record for having the "shortest longest losing streak" in a season. But, lo and behold, there once was a team that never even lost *three* games in succession, even though it was done in a 140–game schedule in baseball's horse-and-buggy days.

The 1902 Pirates were one of the greatest teams in major league history. They won 103 games, lost 36, and won the National League pennant by 27½ games, still the greatest margin of victory by any league or division champion. And during that 1902 season, the Pirates never lost three games in a row. Two in a row, yes; they had eight streaks of two. But they are the only team in this century to go through a season without a three-game losing streak.

The Dodgers had ten three-game losing streaks in 1988, but they won their next game on each occasion. And they became only the second National League team to go through a full, 162–game season without a four-game losing streak. (The first was the 1968 Giants; the Mets did it in 1972 in a season that was shortened by 10 days due to a players' strike.)

The lack of a long losing streak was made possible by the Dodgers' superior pitching staff. That was never more evident than in the closing weeks of the campaign, when the Dodgers allowed only 101 runs (earned and unearned) over their final 40 games. Of course, Orel Hershiser's streak is included within those 40 games, but there were also about 300 innings that he did *not* pitch. Since the introduction of the "lively ball" in 1920, only one team had come into postseason play having allowed fewer runs over its last 40 regular-season games; the 1969 Mets allowed ninety-nine. The pitchers did enough to overcome the failures of the Dodgers' hitters, a group that was never confused with the 1927 Yankees. The Dodgers' batting average for September was .205, the lowest in the major leagues. They batted .214 in the Championship Series, and .246 in the World Series.

But mark it down: Every team that has had its ace pitcher throw 59 consecutive scoreless innings during a season has gone on to win the World Series.

WON-LOST RECORD BY STARTING POSITION

LOS ANGELES 94-67	C	1B	2B	3B	SS	LF	CF	RF	P	Leadoff	Relief	Starts
Dave Anderson			2-2	3-0	40-31					3-3		45-33
Tim Belcher									17-10		7-2	17-10
William Brennan									1-1		0-2	1-1
Tim Crews											14-28	
Mike Davis						13-6	25-19					38-25
Rick Dempsey	24-21											24-21
Mike Devereaux							2-2	1-0				3-2
Kirk Gibson						88-58						88-58
Jose Gonzalez							0-1					0-1
Alfredo Griffin					53-36					11-3		53-36
Pedro Guerrero		5-10		24-20								29-30
Chris Gwynn												
Jeff Hamilton				50-29								50-29
Mickey Hatcher		9-9		1-1		3-4		9-5			2-7	22-19
Brad Havens												
Danny Heep		5-5				2-5		8-6			0-1	15-16
Orel Hershiser									24-9		1-0	24-9
Shawn Hillegas									5-5		0-1	5-5
Brian Holton											14-31	
Ricky Horton											6-6	
Jay Howell											36-13	
Ken Howell									0-1		0-3	0-1
Bill Krueger									1-0			1-0
Tim Leary									20-14		1-0	20-14
Mike Marshall		31-20						51-36				82-56
Ramon Martinez									3-3		1-2	3-3
Jesse Orosco											30-25	
Alejandro Pena											36-24	
Gilberto Reyes	0-1											0-1
Steve Sax			91-64							80-61		91-64
Mike Scioscia	70-45											70-45
Mike Sharperson			1-1	0-1	1-0							2-2
John Shelby							79-58					79-58
Franklin Stubbs		35-19				1-0		0-1				36-20
Don Sutton									6-10			6-10
John Tudor									6-3			6-3
Fernando Valenzuela									11-11		1-0	11-11
Tracy Woodson		9-4		16-16								25-20

Batting vs. Left and Right Handed Pitchers

		BA	Rank	SA	Rank	OBA	Rank	HR %	Rank	BB %	Rank	SO %	Rank
Dave Anderson	vs. Lefties	.248	82	.299	110	.331	60	0.00	103	10.22	39	10.95	57
	vs. Righties	.250	77	.333	89	.321	59	1.19	79	9.57	41	15.96	87
Mike Davis	vs. Lefties	.172	123	.297	111	.229	125	0.00	103	7.04	75	29.58	129
	vs. Righties	.203	125	.263	122	.269	117	0.92	85	8.37	56	15.90	85
Rick Dempsey	vs. Lefties	.246	85	.434	33	.324	66	4.10	21	11.27	29	23.24	125
	vs. Righties	.267	--	.511	--	.375	--	4.44	--	16.07	--	19.64	--
Kirk Gibson	vs. Lefties	.294	24	.520	9	.344	46	5.39	7	6.55	84	21.83	123
	vs. Righties	.287	25	.462	15	.396	8	4.14	15	14.39	6	17.37	97
Alfredo Griffin	vs. Lefties	.167	124	.222	125	.269	111	0.00	103	11.82	24	7.27	17
	vs. Righties	.212	118	.265	121	.255	125	0.44	109	4.51	118	9.02	19
Jeff Hamilton	vs. Lefties	.205	112	.304	109	.231	124	2.68	47	2.54	124	13.56	77
	vs. Righties	.254	70	.381	55	.288	103	1.52	62	3.35	122	16.75	92
Mickey Hatcher	vs. Lefties	.261	63	.324	95	.282	100	0.70	99	3.36	121	3.36	3
	vs. Righties	.388	--	.429	--	.434	--	0.00	--	3.77	--	3.77	--
Danny Heep	vs. Lefties	.167	--	.167	--	.167	--	0.00	--	0.00	--	16.67	--
	vs. Righties	.245	86	.259	125	.347	35	0.00	115	13.17	12	7.19	12
Mike Marshall	vs. Lefties	.231	101	.366	72	.277	105	2.15	63	6.44	88	13.86	81
	vs. Righties	.301	13	.486	10	.333	42	4.49	11	2.93	125	17.33	96
Steve Sax	vs. Lefties	.290	29	.375	67	.352	38	1.50	73	8.56	62	5.86	10
	vs. Righties	.271	42	.329	93	.312	72	0.46	107	5.59	103	8.17	14
Mike Scioscia	vs. Lefties	.244	88	.244	121	.289	96	0.00	103	6.02	98	7.23	16
	vs. Righties	.261	58	.342	80	.325	53	0.91	87	8.94	48	6.78	11
John Shelby	vs. Lefties	.238	93	.323	96	.286	98	1.06	91	6.40	89	23.65	126
	vs. Righties	.279	30	.439	21	.340	40	2.62	40	9.06	43	23.39	125
Franklin Stubbs	vs. Lefties	.185	--	.222	--	.214	--	0.00	--	3.57	--	17.86	--
	vs. Righties	.228	103	.395	45	.296	91	3.72	22	8.98	45	22.86	123
Tracy Woodson	vs. Lefties	.250	78	.357	77	.300	90	2.38	54	6.67	83	13.33	74
	vs. Righties	.247	--	.315	--	.258	--	1.12	--	1.08	--	21.51	--
Team Average	vs. Lefties	.237	10	.339	12	.291	11	1.83	9	7.00	11	15.51	10
	vs. Righties	.253	4	.358	7	.312	4	1.82	7	7.35	9	15.75	9
League Average	vs. Lefties	.248		.367		.310		2.10		8.01		14.42	
	vs. Righties	.249		.360		.310		1.88		7.86		15.35	

Batting with Runners on Base and Bases Empty

		BA	Rank	SA	Rank	OBA	Rank	HR %	Rank	BB %	Rank	SO %	Rank
Dave Anderson	Runners On	.221	113	.254	124	.297	109	0.00	104	9.09	66	13.99	74
	Bases Empty	.270	31	.368	61	.346	19	1.23	81	10.44	16	13.74	56
Mike Davis	Runners On	.191	124	.300	113	.248	126	1.82	60	7.32	94	17.89	108
	Bases Empty	.199	118	.251	121	.267	110	0.00	115	8.56	42	19.79	108
Rick Dempsey	Runners On	.313	--	.567	--	.358	--	4.48		9.88		18.52	
	Bases Empty	.210	112	.380	51	.325	41	4.00	18	14.53	2	24.79	124
Kirk Gibson	Runners On	.285	47	.484	16	.391	21	4.52	11	13.87	25	15.33	94
	Bases Empty	.293	15	.483	11	.366	7	4.67	12	9.78	22	21.79	118
Alfredo Griffin	Runners On	.221	114	.301	112	.282	114	0.00	104	7.41	91	6.67	14
	Bases Empty	.187	121	.227	123	.247	120	0.49	110	6.39	73	9.59	22
Jeff Hamilton	Runners On	.268	66	.417	43	.301	103	3.15	25	3.62	123	11.59	55
	Bases Empty	.214	109	.308	105	.243	123	1.10	87	2.65	116	18.52	100
Mickey Hatcher	Runners On	.323	9	.376	67	.363	39	1.08	82	4.90	114	2.94	1
	Bases Empty	.265	--	.327	--	.280	--	0.00	--	2.00	--	4.00	--
Mike Marshall	Runners On	.286	45	.475	18	.332	76	3.99	15	5.65	110	14.29	81
	Bases Empty	.267	36	.414	31	.293	84	3.38	26	2.54	118	18.12	97
Steve Sax	Runners On	.333	3	.394	57	.402	16	1.01	85	9.96	54	5.63	8
	Bases Empty	.251	59	.320	99	.287	89	0.69	100	4.82	100	8.33	14
Mike Scioscia	Runners On	.267	69	.339	97	.351	54	1.21	80	11.86	39	7.22	17
	Bases Empty	.251	60	.313	102	.295	81	0.41	113	5.81	83	6.59	5
John Shelby	Runners On	.283	48	.415	47	.339	69	1.89	58	8.75	74	20.00	117
	Bases Empty	.248	67	.379	52	.305	62	2.13	56	7.54	56	26.23	127
Franklin Stubbs	Runners On	.213	117	.343	93	.268	119	2.78	34	7.20	96	25.60	127
	Bases Empty	.231	93	.403	33	.304	63	3.73	21	9.46	27	19.59	107
Tracy Woodson	Runners On	.283	--	.321	--	.333	--	0.00	--	6.67	--	16.67	--
	Bases Empty	.233	91	.342	81	.252	118	2.50	45	2.44	119	17.89	94
Team Average	Runners On	.260	3	.371	9	.324	10	2.00	6	8.17	11	14.48	7
	Bases Empty	.240	8	.339	11	.292	9	1.70	10	6.53	7	16.55	9
League Average	Runners On	.257		.373		.329		1.91		9.45		14.09	
	Bases Empty	.242		.355		.297		1.98		6.73		15.80	

Overall Batting Compared to Late Inning Pressure Situations

		BA	Rank	SA	Rank	OBA	Rank	HR %	Rank	BB %	Rank	SO %	Rank	RDI %	Rank
Dave Anderson	Overall	.249	82	.319	110	.325	53	0.70	100	9.85	38	13.85	67	.210	116
	Pressure	.281	36	.438	23	.359	37	3.13	29	11.90	32	9.52	25	.455	4
Mike Davis	Overall	.196	125	.270	123	.260	124	0.71	99	8.06	63	19.03	113	.174	126
	Pressure	.267	48	.333	64	.283	95	0.00	79	2.13	108	21.28	108	.214	73
Rick Dempsey	Overall	.251	--	.455	--	.338	--	4.19	--	12.63	--	22.22	--	.346	7
	Pressure	.211	93	.421	29	.286	89	5.26	8	9.52	49	23.81	116	.250	59
Kirk Gibson	Overall	.290	18	.483	10	.377	7	4.61	9	11.55	22	18.99	111	.278	58
	Pressure	.348	5	.536	6	.444	5	2.90	31	12.35	28	13.58	59	.375	15
Alfredo Griffin	Overall	.199	123	.253	124	.259	125	0.32	117	6.78	85	8.47	14	.253	82
	Pressure	.250	57	.333	64	.308	72	2.78	34	4.76	107	14.29	62	.000	128
Jeff Hamilton	Overall	.236	102	.353	83	.268	121	1.94	59	3.06	122	15.60	88	.280	53
	Pressure	.140	123	.300	88	.204	123	2.00	53	5.45	97	20.00	97	.143	108
Mickey Hatcher	Overall	.293	14	.351	86	.322	58	0.52	107	3.47	121	3.47	1	.328	10
	Pressure	.410	2	.564	5	.452	3	2.56	36	7.14	77	7.14	12	.455	4
Danny Heep	Overall	.242	--	.255	--	.341	--	0.00	--	12.72	--	7.51	--	.244	--
	Pressure	.061	--	.061	--	.200	--	0.00	--	15.00	--	10.00	--	.154	105
Mike Marshall	Overall	.277	31	.445	15	.314	74	3.69	19	4.16	120	16.12	92	.301	37
	Pressure	.257	52	.529	9	.297	83	7.14	2	5.41	99	21.62	111	.211	76
Steve Sax	Overall	.277	30	.343	92	.325	53	0.79	95	6.55	91	7.42	9	.324	11
	Pressure	.317	17	.329	71	.374	22	0.00	79	8.42	62	6.32	9	.429	8
Mike Scioscia	Overall	.257	65	.324	109	.318	68	0.74	98	8.41	53	6.86	6	.239	92
	Pressure	.278	37	.315	78	.391	14	0.00	79	15.63	12	9.38	23	.000	128
John Shelby	Overall	.263	58	.395	44	.320	63	2.02	56	8.07	61	23.49	127	.304	31
	Pressure	.312	23	.532	7	.354	39	5.19	9	6.02	90	22.89	114	.348	30
Franklin Stubbs	Overall	.223	115	.376	60	.288	111	3.31	25	8.42	52	22.34	122	.304	30
	Pressure	.167	118	.333	64	.239	114	4.76	13	8.70	56	26.09	122	.333	32
Team Average	Overall	.248	6	.352	8	.305	11	1.82	8	7.23	10	15.67	9	.276	1
	Pressure	.261	1	.391	1	.324	2	2.70	2	7.88	8	16.10	7	.269	1
League Average	Overall	.248		.363		.310		1.95		7.91		15.06		.256	
	Pressure	.242		.340		.310		1.70		8.47		15.93		.238	

Additional Miscellaneous Batting Comparisons

	Grass Surface BA	Rank	Artificial Surface BA	Rank	Home Games BA	Rank	Road Games BA	Rank	Runners in Scoring Position BA	Rank	Runners in Scoring Pos and Two Outs BA	Rank	Leading Off Inning OBA	Rank	Runners on 3B with less than 2 Outs RDI %	Rank
Dave Anderson	.231	104	.291	26	.227	102	.268	46	.182	123	.176	105	.446	1	.412	119
Mike Davis	.155	127	.311	--	.150	128	.236	92	.207	109	.188	100	.220	123	.333	--
Rick Dempsey	.250	73	.255	--	.277	--	.235	95	.357	--	.167	--	.298	78	.667	28
Kirk Gibson	.308	9	.245	74	.316	7	.266	51	.261	64	.236	65	.416	2	.500	92
Alfredo Griffin	.196	121	.210	--	.184	123	.215	109	.240	87	.238	63	.211	125	.556	--
Jeff Hamilton	.253	64	.193	--	.283	34	.199	123	.282	38	.310	21	.250	110	.429	117
Mickey Hatcher	.288	24	.316	--	.284	32	.303	--	.328	10	.269	46	.200	--	.800	3
Danny Heep	.252	69	.192	--	.267	--	.216	--	.216	--	.192	96	.387	--	.800	--
Mike Marshall	.261	55	.316	9	.261	66	.291	18	.284	36	.361	6	.321	52	.480	108
Steve Sax	.279	33	.272	47	.302	16	.252	71	.350	3	.419	1	.255	107	.636	40
Mike Scioscia	.263	52	.241	78	.264	61	.250	74	.233	90	.179	104	.287	84	.556	71
John Shelby	.274	38	.232	88	.309	14	.221	106	.288	34	.279	42	.311	65	.640	39
Franklin Stubbs	.209	117	.267	--	.220	107	.226	101	.241	84	.323	15	.327	46	.750	--
Tracy Woodson	.219	110	.305	--	.237	--	.258	--	.233	--	.214	--	.255	106	.571	--
Team Average	.248	6	.246	7	.258	3	.238	10	.263	1	.258	1	.289	9	.557	5
League Average	.250		.246		.252		.244		.250		.231		.301		.554	

Pitching vs. Left and Right Handed Batters

		BA	Rank	SA	Rank	OBA	Rank	HR %	Rank	BB %	Rank	SO %	Rank
Tim Belcher	vs. Lefties	.212	16	.306	20	.271	12	1.47	44	7.26	32	22.04	13
	vs. Righties	.223	36	.285	14	.279	37	0.94	16	6.92	57	20.17	19
Tim Crews	vs. Lefties	.304	99	.384	71	.364	87	0.72	18	8.50	48	9.80	88
	vs. Righties	.252	72	.345	52	.259	14	1.44	36	2.03	1	20.27	18
Orel Hershiser	vs. Lefties	.220	23	.343	39	.294	27	2.44	81	9.43	63	12.12	72
	vs. Righties	.206	14	.269	9	.238	7	1.13	23	3.59	12	22.36	13
Shawn Hillegas	vs. Lefties	.266	69	.376	65	.352	80	2.75	96	12.00	88	11.20	80
	vs. Righties	.234	--	.346	--	.265	--	1.87	--	1.75	--	14.04	--
Brian Holton	vs. Lefties	.252	47	.310	22	.339	68	0.65	15	11.11	78	7.78	100
	vs. Righties	.204	12	.272	10	.232	4	0.00	1	3.77	16	22.01	14
Jay Howell	vs. Lefties	.169	5	.226	3	.232	5	0.81	21	7.86	42	26.43	5
	vs. Righties	.209	--	.255	--	.281	--	0.00	--	8.20	--	27.05	--
Tim Leary	vs. Lefties	.237	34	.320	25	.304	39	0.95	27	8.58	51	18.88	25
	vs. Righties	.231	45	.336	43	.265	23	2.05	59	3.43	9	19.74	23
Jesse Orosco	vs. Lefties	.226	--	.306	--	.338	--	1.61	--	14.67	--	18.67	--
	vs. Righties	.209	19	.326	36	.316	75	2.33	72	12.34	109	18.83	28
Alejandro Pena	vs. Lefties	.251	46	.281	12	.326	59	0.00	1	10.42	72	19.27	22
	vs. Righties	.186	5	.277	11	.222	1	2.26	69	3.76	15	24.73	7
Don Sutton	vs. Lefties	.291	88	.401	82	.367	91	2.33	77	11.00	77	12.50	66
	vs. Righties	.248	67	.345	53	.282	42	1.82	48	4.44	23	10.56	91
John Tudor	vs. Lefties	.282	78	.487	105	.306	42	4.27	105	3.15	3	24.41	7
	vs. Righties	.252	73	.335	42	.293	55	0.81	14	5.55	38	8.40	106
Fernando Valenzuela	vs. Lefties	.313	104	.448	96	.391	98	3.13	98	11.30	81	9.57	91
	vs. Righties	.258	79	.357	60	.349	99	1.84	49	12.33	108	10.37	94
Team Average	vs. Lefties	.246	4	.337	2	.318	5	1.52	3	9.56	8	15.64	4
	vs. Righties	.230	3	.318	1	.282	2	1.56	2	6.30	3	18.20	2
League Average	vs. Lefties	.255		.365		.325		1.73		9.36		14.24	
	vs. Righties	.244		.361		.299		2.10		6.87		15.64	

Pitching with Runners on Base and Bases Empty

		BA	Rank	SA	Rank	OBA	Rank	HR %	Rank	BB %	Rank	SO %	Rank
Tim Belcher	Runners On	.243	43	.364	52	.313	38	1.67	54	9.23	51	22.51	7
	Bases Empty	.202	11	.257	4	.252	8	0.95	18	5.80	37	20.31	20
Tim Crews	Runners On	.268	66	.398	81	.336	63	2.44	81	10.27	66	15.75	36
	Bases Empty	.286	103	.338	37	.290	45	0.00	1	0.65	1	14.19	69
Orel Hershiser	Runners On	.187	4	.268	10	.273	5	1.46	41	10.22	65	16.46	33
	Bases Empty	.228	34	.332	36	.267	19	2.06	60	4.80	20	16.79	44
Shawn Hillegas	Runners On	.259	--	.376	--	.316	--	2.35	--	6.25	--	9.38	--
	Bases Empty	.244	62	.351	50	.308	75	2.29	72	7.69	71	14.69	64
Brian Holton	Runners On	.193	5	.230	3	.287	13	0.00	1	11.59	86	10.37	88
	Bases Empty	.257	79	.341	41	.291	47	0.60	10	4.00	11	18.29	28
Jay Howell	Runners On	.226	28	.321	28	.292	19	0.94	28	8.94	45	25.20	2
	Bases Empty	.156	1	.172	1	.223	1	0.00	1	7.19	64	28.06	2
Tim Leary	Runners On	.242	42	.303	19	.312	37	0.65	18	8.22	33	17.28	26
	Bases Empty	.229	38	.342	42	.268	21	2.00	57	4.66	17	20.55	18
Jesse Orosco	Runners On	.168	2	.221	2	.305	31	1.05	30	14.88	104	20.66	13
	Bases Empty	.260	--	.417	--	.343	--	3.13	--	11.11	--	16.67	--
Alejandro Pena	Runners On	.246	49	.275	13	.310	34	0.00	1	8.86	44	22.78	4
	Bases Empty	.199	9	.282	8	.250	6	1.94	54	5.91	40	21.36	14
Don Sutton	Runners On	.228	29	.315	24	.298	24	2.01	62	8.99	46	10.67	86
	Bases Empty	.303	107	.420	99	.351	102	2.13	64	6.93	58	12.38	79
John Tudor	Runners On	.230	31	.332	36	.294	20	1.46	42	8.49	37	8.81	100
	Bases Empty	.273	97	.375	75	.296	52	1.30	27	2.94	7	12.39	78
Fernando Valenzuela	Runners On	.283	86	.396	78	.359	91	2.08	68	10.65	74	8.93	99
	Bases Empty	.255	75	.355	54	.355	104	2.07	62	13.43	107	11.34	91
Team Average	Runners On	.238	2	.325	1	.314	4	1.41	1	9.76	10	16.02	3
	Bases Empty	.237	4	.328	2	.288	4	1.63	3	6.38	4	17.74	2
League Average	Runners On	.257		.373		.329		1.91		9.45		14.09	
	Bases Empty	.242		.355		.297		1.98		6.73		15.80	

Overall Pitching Compared to Late Inning Pressure Situations

		BA	Rank	SA	Rank	OBA	Rank	HR %	Rank	BB %	Rank	SO %	Rank
Tim Belcher	Overall	.217	16	.296	10	.275	11	1.21	23	7.09	39	21.14	15
	Pressure	.205	27	.295	32	.300	43	2.27	74	11.76	93	27.45	3
Tim Crews	Overall	.278	101	.365	59	.312	57	1.08	17	5.32	6	14.95	54
	Pressure	.207	29	.230	7	.258	21	0.00	1	6.38	26	11.70	75
Orel Hershiser	Overall	.213	13	.310	17	.269	7	1.85	50	6.84	33	16.67	34
	Pressure	.212	35	.300	35	.265	24	1.18	40	6.35	25	15.34	47
Brian Holton	Overall	.228	28	.291	7	.289	30	0.33	2	7.67	51	14.45	61
	Pressure	.172	6	.276	22	.250	15	1.72	58	9.09	63	15.15	50
Jay Howell	Overall	.188	1	.239	1	.255	3	0.43	4	8.02	57	26.72	1
	Pressure	.177	8	.222	3	.254	17	0.00	1	8.89	59	27.22	4
Tim Leary	Overall	.234	34	.328	27	.284	23	1.51	36	6.01	19	19.31	20
	Pressure	.182	10	.195	1	.264	23	0.00	1	9.20	67	14.94	52
Jesse Orosco	Overall	.215	--	.319	--	.323	--	2.09	--	13.10	--	18.78	--
	Pressure	.248	58	.355	63	.361	88	1.65	54	14.67	107	16.67	37
Alejandro Pena	Overall	.218	18	.279	5	.275	10	1.16	19	7.14	40	21.96	10
	Pressure	.205	28	.288	30	.266	26	1.46	47	7.14	37	23.21	11
Don Sutton	Overall	.270	89	.374	68	.327	80	2.08	66	7.89	56	11.58	87
	Pressure	.000	--	.000	--	.000	--	0.00	--	0.00	--	0.00	--
John Tudor	Overall	.257	75	.359	53	.295	35	1.36	29	5.16	5	10.96	88
	Pressure	.265	71	.347	57	.308	47	1.02	33	5.61	16	11.21	79
Fernando Valenzuela	Overall	.268	83	.374	67	.357	106	2.08	65	12.14	102	10.22	95
	Pressure	.269	77	.385	76	.397	103	1.92	64	17.19	108	1.56	109
Team Average	Overall	.237	3	.327	1	.299	3	1.54	2	7.82	8	17.01	2
	Pressure	.208	1	.281	1	.284	1	1.07	2	9.26	7	18.35	1
League Average	Overall	.248		.363		.310		1.95		7.91		15.06	
	Pressure	.243		.347		.315		1.72		9.12		15.69	

Additional Miscellaneous Pitching Comparisons

	Grass Surface BA	Rank	Artificial Surface BA	Rank	Home Games BA	Rank	Road Games BA	Rank	Runners in Scoring Position BA	Rank	Runners in Scoring Pos and Two Outs BA	Rank	Leading Off Inning OBA	Rank
Tim Belcher	.233	30	.179	4	.241	57	.197	4	.313	98	.283	96	.282	42
Tim Crews	.265	70	.333	--	.305	109	.230	--	.253	61	.243	76	.265	18
Orel Hershiser	.204	13	.235	38	.221	25	.207	9	.193	19	.200	39	.279	37
Shawn Hillegas	.260	64	.209	--	.254	68	.243	--	.238	--	.304	--	.283	46
Brian Holton	.231	25	.218	--	.254	69	.186	2	.161	6	.140	8	.351	95
Jay Howell	.190	6	.182	--	.176	--	.197	3	.247	55	.189	31	.211	1
Tim Leary	.245	45	.194	11	.244	59	.221	23	.242	46	.183	28	.268	21
Ramon Martinez	.200	9	.280	--	.213	--	.222	--	.182	--	.083	--	.368	--
Jesse Orosco	.177	4	.295	--	.178	--	.237	39	.143	1	.167	14	.348	--
Alejandro Pena	.210	16	.240	48	.216	23	.220	18	.271	82	.250	78	.213	3
Don Sutton	.282	89	.242	51	.266	79	.274	80	.198	22	.200	39	.419	108
John Tudor	.250	52	.262	69	.290	105	.217	15	.175	9	.173	18	.308	66
Fernando Valenzuela	.264	69	.282	95	.282	97	.256	59	.260	71	.282	95	.329	84
Team Average	.240	4	.228	1	.247	8	.227	1	.237	4	.223	5	.296	7
League Average	.250		.246		.244		.252		.250		.231		.301	

MONTREAL EXPOS

- Did the Expos have an extra home-field advantage in cold weather, like the Vikings and Packers did?
- Montreal's key to extra-inning success.
- Maximizing the offense with a traditional batting order.

Anyone who's ever placed a bet on a football game—and we're told there are several million of you out there—has at some time probably considered the weather as a factor in selecting the right side of the point spread. The Green Bay Packers of the 1960s, the Minnesota Vikings of the 1970s, and the contemporary Buffalo Bills all seemed to benefit from games played in their customary arctic climate.

Now that Olympic Stadium has finally donned its long-awaited chapeau, two questions arise: Did the Expos' home-field advantage increase due to the cold April weather in Montreal, as do those of NFL teams who play at cold-weather sites? And if so, will that extra edge disappear under the Big O's retract-a-dome?

We won't get to the second part, because a look at the home and road records of teams from five cold-weather cities indicates that the frigid air and frozen tundra (sounds like an NFL Films script, doesn't it?) wasn't an aid to the home team. It was the great equalizer, shrinking the home-field advantage. The following table shows those teams' home and road winning percentages for the past 20 seasons, in April and thereafter:

| Team | April | | | May through Oct. | | | |
	Home	Road	HFA	Home	Road	HFA	Diff.
Boston	.585	.577	+.008	.591	.483	+.108	−.100
Detroit	.560	.466	+.094	.555	.491	+.064	+.030
Milwaukee	.542	.485	+.058	.520	.442	+.078	−.020
Toronto	.441	.512	−.072	.519	.428	+.091	−.163
Montreal	.577	.531	+.047	.501	.445	+.056	−.009
Totals	.547	.513	+.034	.539	.461	+.078	−.044

The columns headed "HFA" represent the home-field advantages, the differences between the home and road figures. Notice, for instance, that during the month of April, the Blue Jays have had a higher winning percentage on the road than in Toronto. As a result, their HFA is a negative number (−.072).

The final column shows the difference between the home-field advantage in April and the corresponding figure for the rest on the season. Notice that of the five teams listed, only Detroit has a bigger edge at home in April; the other four teams increase their HFA's in later months. And as a whole, the group has more than double the edge from May through October that they have in April.

Throughout the Expos' history, the National League schedule makers have restricted the number of games played in Montreal during April, in the hope that fewer games will need to be rescheduled on account of bad weather. Unwittingly, that technique may have helped the Expos, whose home-field advantage bloomed in the warmer weather. Retract-a-dome may change all that.

The Expos won 18 extra-inning games last season, one short of the modern major league record set by the Pittsburgh Pirates in 1959. A list of the teams that won more than 15 overtime games in a season:

Year	Team	W	L
1959	Pittsburgh Pirates	19	2
1949	Cleveland Indians	18	1
1988	Montreal Expos	18	7
1922	Chicago White Sox	16	12
1957	St. Louis Cardinals	16	10
1967	Cleveland Indians	16	9
1970	Baltimore Orioles	16	9

The source of Montreal's late-season success was the performance of its pitching staff in Late-Inning Pressure Situations. Opposing batters hit .238 in LIPS, but only .206 with runners in scoring position, and even lower than that with two outs and runners in scoring position (.193).

And a part of that success was the caution that Expos pitchers exercised in the late innings of close games. Montreal was one of two teams last season (and only 13 over the last 14 years) that allowed more walks than hits with runners on base in LIP Situations. The Expos used the open base to their advantage particularly well: they issued 107 bases on balls with first base open in Late-Inning Pressure Situations.

The Expos lost only five games last season in which they led after six innings, tying the Reds for the lowest total in the National League. Cincinnati, of course, has John Franco. The Expos, on the other hand, have been without a bullpen ace since they traded Jeff Reardon to Minnesota two years ago. In his absence, the Expos have succeeded nonetheless by pitching with care with the game on the line.

The rules for constructing a batting order aren't written anywhere, but everybody knows them just the same. Given the same set of nine starters, most managers would probably write the names on their lineup cards in a similar or identical order: a base stealer to lead off, followed by a contact hitter and a high-average hitter; power in the cleanup spot, then the extra-base hitters; the automatic outs at the bottom of the order.

Those unwritten guidelines haven't changed much over the past 60 years. Just look at the opening-day starting lineup for the 1927 New York Yankees: Combs, Koenig, Ruth, Gehrig, Meusel, Lazzeri, Dugan, Grabowski, and Hoyt.

Combs gave the team speed at the top of the order; he led the league with 23 triples. Koenig was a classic contact hitter: moderate batting average (.285, slightly above the major league average that year) and few strikeouts (21). Ruth and Gehrig are probably familiar to many of you. Meusel and Lazzeri both hit over .300 with extra-base potential, Meusel on account of his speed, Lazzeri on account of his power. Dugan and Grabowski both hit below the league average.

Sixty years later, little has changed. Some teams experiment, but they don't stray too far. San Francisco, for example, bats Rob Thompson second despite his high strikeout total. The Cubs used Vance Law or Mark Grace in the five slot last season, although neither has home run power. Barry Bonds, a home run hitter with less speed than his daddy, leads off for the Pirates. But those are the exceptions. Pretty much, there is a consensus on batting orders to which every team adheres.

And last season, no team adhered as closely to these unwritten rules as the Montreal Expos did. The following table shows the player who batted most often in each batting-order position along with 1988 statistics for each one:

Slot	Player	AB	R	H	2B	3B	HR	RBI	BB	SO	SB	BA	SA	OBA
1	Raines	429	66	116	19	7	12	48	53	44	33	.270	.431	.350
2	Webster	523	69	136	16	8	6	39	55	87	22	.260	.355	.337
3	Galarraga	609	99	184	42	8	29	92	39	153	13	.302	.540	.352
4	Brooks	588	61	164	35	2	20	90	35	108	1	.278	.447	.318
5	Wallach	592	52	152	32	5	12	69	38	88	2	.256	.388	.301
6	Foley	377	33	100	21	3	5	43	30	49	2	.265	.376	.318
7	Santovenia	309	26	73	20	2	8	41	24	77	2	.236	.391	.294
8	Rivera	371	35	83	17	3	4	30	24	69	3	.223	.318	.270

Is the formula so successful that no one dares violate it? In last year's *Analyst*, we analyzed each of those batting order features independent of one another, and concluded that there was little if any benefit to most of them. However, closer scrutiny reveals that teams that closely adhere to *all* the traditional rules of batting orders may indeed create more runs out of the same number of hits, walks, and so on as do teams that don't follow them as strictly. But the benefit is rather small.

The following list represents the National League teams of the past seven seasons that most closely followed those rules. They all bunched their good hitters together, as far from the automatic outs as possible. (That might sound like a subjective evaluation, but the determination was actually made via an elaborate statistical process that we guarantee you wouldn't want to know the details of.) And each of these clubs generated a team-leading total of home runs from the cleanup spot, with its leadoff hitters ranked among the top three slots in walks. (The 1988 Expos missed the list by three cleanup home runs.)

We've compared the number of runs each of the teams scored to the number that they should have scored, based on their hits, extra-base hits, walks, stolen bases, and so on. If these teams benefited from their batting orders, they should have outscored those projections:

Year	Team	Actual Runs	Expected Runs	Diff.
1988	Cincinnati	641	649	−8
1988	Houston	617	611	+6
1987	Montreal	741	715	+26
1987	St. Louis	798	741	+57
1986	Philadelphia	739	741	−2
1984	Chicago	762	735	+27
1984	Houston	693	669	+24
1984	San Francisco	682	680	+2
1982	Cincinnati	545	580	−35
1982	Pittsburgh	724	739	−15

On average, the 10 teams outscored their projected run totals by 8.2 runs. (By contrast, four recent National League teams that ignored each of those guidelines collectively scored only two fewer runs than expected. The four teams were the 1983 Phillies, the 1984 Cardinals, the 1986 Braves, and the 1988 Padres.) Such a margin is probably worth only one win per season, so it's obvious that no team is going to steal a pennant by rigorously following those time-honored guidelines for constructing a batting order. Still, it's somewhat comforting to know that Nelson Santovenia really shouldn't bat leadoff, and that newly acquired shortstop Spike Owen isn't a candidate for the cleanup spot.

WON-LOST RECORD BY STARTING POSITION

MONTREAL 81-81	C	1B	2B	3B	SS	LF	CF	RF	P	Leadoff	Relief	Starts
Tim Barrett	·	·	·	·	·	·	·	·	·	·	1-3	·
Hubie Brooks	·	·	·	·	·	·	71-77	·	·	·	·	71-77
Tim Burke	·	·	·	·	·	·	·	·	·	·	34-27	·
Casey Candaele	·	·	17-15	·	·	·	·	·	·	·	·	17-15
John Dopson	·	·	·	·	·	·	·	·	8-17	·	·	8-17
Dave Engle	1-1	·	·	·	·	0-1	·	1-0	·	·	·	2-2
Mike R. Fitzgerald	19-17	·	·	·	·	1-1	·	0-1	·	·	·	20-19
Tom Foley	·	·	31-41	·	13-12	·	·	·	·	·	·	44-53
Andres Galarraga	·	77-73	·	·	·	·	·	·	·	·	·	77-73
Neal Heaton	·	·	·	·	·	·	·	·	5-6	·	6-15	5-6
Joe Hesketh	·	·	·	·	·	·	·	·	·	·	36-24	·
Brian Holman	·	·	·	·	·	·	·	·	7-9	·	0-2	7-9
Rex Hudler	·	·	22-11	·	14-12	·	·	·	·	5-4	·	36-23
Jeff Huson	·	·	·	·	6-5	·	·	·	·	·	·	6-5
Randy Johnson	·	·	·	·	·	·	·	·	3-1	·	·	3-1
Wallace Johnson	·	3-5	·	·	·	·	·	·	·	·	·	3-5
Tracy Jones	·	·	·	·	·	10-10	5-2	3-2	·	3-6	·	18-14
Dave Martinez	·	·	·	·	·	·	17-26	4-1	·	5-9	·	21-27
Dennis Martinez	·	·	·	·	·	·	·	·	18-16	·	·	18-16
Bob McClure	·	·	·	·	·	·	·	·	·	·	4-15	·
Andy McGaffigan	·	·	·	·	·	·	·	·	·	·	26-36	·
Graig Nettles	·	1-2	·	5-4	·	·	·	·	·	·	·	6-6
Otis Nixon	·	·	·	·	·	10-11	25-17	·	·	34-25	·	35-28
Tom O'Malley	·	·	·	1-5	·	·	·	·	·	·	·	1-5
Johnny Paredes	·	·	11-14	·	·	·	·	·	·	0-1	·	11-14
Jeff Parrett	·	·	·	·	·	·	·	·	·	·	27-34	·
Pascual Perez	·	·	·	·	·	·	·	·	16-11	·	·	16-11
Tim Raines	·	·	·	·	·	53-54	·	·	·	31-33	·	53-54
Jeff Reed	14-22	·	·	·	·	·	·	·	·	·	·	14-22
Luis Rivera	·	·	·	·	48-52	·	·	·	·	·	·	48-52
Nelson Santovenia	44-39	0-1	·	·	·	·	·	·	·	·	·	44-40
Rich Sauveur	·	·	·	·	·	·	·	·	·	·	1-3	·
Bryn Smith	·	·	·	·	·	·	·	·	18-14	·	·	18-14
Mike Smith	·	·	·	·	·	·	·	·	·	·	1-4	·
Randy St. Claire	·	·	·	·	·	·	·	·	·	·	0-6	·
Wil Tejada	3-2	·	·	·	·	·	·	·	·	·	·	3-2
Tim Wallach	·	·	·	75-72	·	·	·	·	·	·	·	75-72
Mitch Webster	·	·	·	·	·	7-4	25-26	2-0	·	2-1	·	34-30
Herm Winningham	·	·	·	·	·	·	9-10	·	·	1-2	·	9-10
Floyd Youmans	·	·	·	·	·	·	·	·	6-7	·	0-1	6-7

Batting vs. Left and Right Handed Pitchers

		BA	Rank	SA	Rank	OBA	Rank	HR %	Rank	BB %	Rank	SO %	Rank
Hubie Brooks	vs. Lefties	.314	12	.538	8	.366	21	4.49	15	7.56	69	12.79	68
	vs. Righties	.266	51	.414	34	.300	86	3.01	29	4.82	114	18.86	108
Mike Fitzgerald	vs. Lefties	.254	73	.313	103	.333	56	0.00	103	11.39	27	10.13	47
	vs. Righties	.284	--	.500	--	.357	--	5.68	--	9.90	--	13.86	--
Tom Foley	vs. Lefties	.150	--	.150	--	.143	--	0.00	--	0.00	--	28.57	--
	vs. Righties	.272	40	.389	49	.328	51	1.40	71	7.69	65	11.03	37
Andres Galarraga	vs. Lefties	.283	36	.543	7	.332	59	5.78	5	6.95	79	24.06	128
	vs. Righties	.310	2	.539	6	.361	22	4.36	13	5.49	107	22.78	122
Rex Hudler	vs. Lefties	.292	26	.415	44	.325	65	1.89	69	5.26	102	11.40	61
	vs. Righties	.255	--	.409	--	.281	--	1.82	--	3.48	--	18.26	--
Tracy Jones	vs. Lefties	.351	2	.459	26	.419	4	1.80	71	8.80	59	3.20	2
	vs. Righties	.239	93	.283	117	.295	92	0.88	89	7.26	75	11.29	40
Dave Martinez	vs. Lefties	.196	--	.348	--	.296	--	4.35	--	9.26	--	35.19	--
	vs. Righties	.262	57	.352	71	.315	64	1.00	84	7.50	69	17.05	94
Otis Nixon	vs. Lefties	.226	105	.280	113	.308	81	0.00	103	10.38	36	11.32	60
	vs. Righties	.253	73	.292	112	.315	65	0.00	115	8.54	52	15.08	73
Tim Raines	vs. Lefties	.264	57	.408	46	.321	72	3.20	33	7.30	71	8.03	27
	vs. Righties	.273	39	.441	20	.362	21	2.63	39	12.25	18	9.40	25
Luis Rivera	vs. Lefties	.221	108	.331	93	.268	112	1.30	82	6.10	95	18.29	111
	vs. Righties	.226	106	.309	103	.272	114	0.92	85	5.88	98	16.39	89
Nelson Santovenia	vs. Lefties	.278	43	.468	22	.370	20	3.80	22	11.83	23	18.28	110
	vs. Righties	.222	109	.365	63	.266	121	2.17	47	5.18	110	23.90	126
Tim Wallach	vs. Lefties	.262	60	.413	45	.310	79	2.33	57	6.95	79	10.16	48
	vs. Righties	.255	69	.379	58	.298	88	1.90	54	5.52	106	15.23	75
Team Average	vs. Lefties	.252	4	.379	3	.309	9	2.09	6	7.48	10	15.93	11
	vs. Righties	.251	5	.370	5	.309	5	1.85	6	7.31	10	17.52	12
League Average	vs. Lefties	.248		.367		.310		2.10		8.01		14.42	
	vs. Righties	.249		.360		.310		1.88		7.86		15.35	

Batting with Runners on Base and Bases Empty

		BA	Rank	SA	Rank	OBA	Rank	HR %	Rank	BB %	Rank	SO %	Rank
Hubie Brooks	Runners On	.293	33	.463	22	.337	72	3.83	17	6.73	102	19.87	116
	Bases Empty	.266	39	.432	22	.301	71	2.99	33	4.43	107	14.56	69
Tom Foley	Runners On	.281	51	.381	63	.341	64	0.63	95	8.94	68	11.73	57
	Bases Empty	.253	51	.373	58	.302	67	1.84	65	6.03	79	12.07	46
Andres Galarraga	Runners On	.290	37	.525	9	.357	47	4.71	8	8.39	80	21.68	124
	Bases Empty	.311	5	.551	2	.349	17	4.80	11	4.00	111	24.27	123
Rex Hudler	Runners On	.218	116	.385	62	.292	112	1.28	76	10.00	52	5.56	7
	Bases Empty	.304	8	.428	24	.309	59	2.17	54	0.72	126	20.86	114
Tracy Jones	Runners On	.293	33	.427	39	.376	27	2.44	40	10.42	48	6.25	11
	Bases Empty	.296	11	.338	86	.346	18	0.70	99	6.54	68	7.84	11
Dave Martinez	Runners On	.267	68	.377	65	.337	70	2.05	56	9.94	56	20.47	120
	Bases Empty	.249	63	.339	84	.300	72	1.00	90	6.50	71	18.27	99
Otis Nixon	Runners On	.254	--	.310	--	.267	--	0.00	--	2.53	--	12.66	--
	Bases Empty	.240	82	.280	114	.327	39	0.00	115	11.50	11	14.16	61
Tim Raines	Runners On	.317	10	.532	6	.421	5	4.32	13	15.79	16	5.85	10
	Bases Empty	.248	65	.383	47	.312	55	2.07	59	8.20	48	10.73	33
Luis Rivera	Runners On	.240	102	.353	84	.293	111	0.60	97	7.49	89	15.51	96
	Bases Empty	.211	111	.289	112	.251	119	1.47	74	4.65	103	18.60	103
Nelson Santovenia	Runners On	.288	42	.460	24	.340	66	2.16	50	7.50	88	19.38	115
	Bases Empty	.194	119	.335	89	.255	116	2.94	36	6.52	69	25.00	125
Tim Wallach	Runners On	.243	101	.333	101	.303	102	0.78	91	7.67	84	12.20	59
	Bases Empty	.267	35	.430	23	.300	73	2.97	35	4.53	105	15.01	72
Team Average	Runners On	.259	4	.383	3	.326	7	1.89	8	8.90	9	15.48	12
	Bases Empty	.246	4	.366	3	.297	7	1.94	7	6.21	8	18.25	12
League Average	Runners On	.257		.373		.329		1.91		9.45		14.09	
	Bases Empty	.242		.355		.297		1.98		6.73		15.80	

Overall Batting Compared to Late Inning Pressure Situations

		BA	Rank	SA	Rank	OBA	Rank	HR %	Rank	BB %	Rank	SO %	Rank	RDI %	Rank
Hubie Brooks	Overall	.279	27	.447	14	.318	69	3.40	22	5.57	107	17.20	103	.294	44
	Pressure	.289	34	.456	18	.311	69	3.51	19	3.36	117	16.81	81	.234	65
Mike Fitzgerald	Overall	.271	--	.419	--	.347	--	3.23	--	10.56	--	12.22	--	.232	96
	Pressure	.310	24	.429	27	.333	51	2.38	40	4.26	110	10.64	33	.353	27
Tom Foley	Overall	.265	49	.377	59	.319	66	1.33	83	7.30	75	11.92	44	.280	52
	Pressure	.264	51	.379	46	.312	68	1.15	68	6.45	87	16.13	77	.350	29
Andres Galarraga	Overall	.302	7	.540	2	.352	24	4.76	8	5.90	103	23.15	126	.275	63
	Pressure	.293	31	.603	2	.359	36	6.90	3	8.59	59	27.34	125	.192	85
Rex Hudler	Overall	.273	36	.412	33	.303	90	1.85	64	4.37	119	14.85	81	.145	128
	Pressure	.194	--	.361	--	.189	--	2.78	--	0.00	--	18.42	--	.125	--
Wallace Johnson	Overall	.309	--	.383	--	.387	--	0.00	--	11.21	--	14.02	--	.107	--
	Pressure	.340	7	.434	26	.397	12	0.00	79	8.47	60	13.56	58	.105	119
Tracy Jones	Overall	.295	12	.371	66	.358	18	1.34	82	8.03	64	7.23	8	.290	47
	Pressure	.271	45	.292	95	.364	33	0.00	79	12.28	30	10.53	31	.333	32
Dave Martinez	Overall	.255	74	.351	85	.313	77	1.34	81	7.69	68	19.03	112	.298	40
	Pressure	.212	92	.273	99	.303	77	0.00	79	11.69	34	27.27	124	.227	68
Graig Nettles	Overall	.172	--	.247	--	.240	--	1.08	--	8.65	--	18.27	--	.250	--
	Pressure	.214	90	.357	55	.283	95	2.38	40	8.70	56	19.57	92	.381	12
Otis Nixon	Overall	.244	92	.288	116	.312	80	0.00	118	9.18	44	13.77	65	.242	90
	Pressure	.300	29	.360	54	.340	49	0.00	79	5.45	97	20.00	97	.125	--
Tim Raines	Overall	.270	41	.431	19	.350	25	2.80	35	10.86	31	9.02	17	.316	15
	Pressure	.347	6	.480	13	.443	6	2.67	35	13.64	22	7.95	17	.381	12
Luis Rivera	Overall	.224	114	.318	112	.271	117	1.08	87	5.97	101	17.16	102	.189	123
	Pressure	.189	107	.257	102	.208	122	0.00	79	2.53	121	21.52	110	.174	90
Nelson Santovenia	Overall	.236	102	.392	46	.294	104	2.59	38	6.98	83	22.38	123	.270	65
	Pressure	.254	53	.444	22	.329	58	3.17	26	9.59	47	24.66	119	.222	--
Tim Wallach	Overall	.257	68	.389	51	.302	91	2.03	55	5.94	102	13.75	64	.306	27
	Pressure	.217	88	.279	96	.261	107	0.78	78	5.80	95	19.57	92	.364	20
Team Average	Overall	.251	3	.373	3	.309	7	1.92	7	7.36	9	17.07	12	.245	10
	Pressure	.254	3	.377	3	.314	7	1.88	4	7.78	9	18.60	12	.253	4
League Average	Overall	.248		.363		.310		1.95		7.91		15.06		.256	
	Pressure	.242		.340		.310		1.70		8.47		15.93		.238	

Additional Miscellaneous Batting Comparisons

	Grass Surface BA	Rank	Artificial Surface BA	Rank	Home Games BA	Rank	Road Games BA	Rank	Runners in Scoring Position BA	Rank	Runners in Scoring Pos and Two Outs BA	Rank	Leading Off Inning OBA	Rank	Runners on 3B with less than 2 Outs RDI %	Rank
Hubie Brooks	.305	10	.270	49	.260	67	.297	9	.302	25	.288	36	.341	35	.590	54
Mike Fitzgerald	.368	--	.239	79	.260	--	.282	--	.225	--	.250	--	.273	--	.500	92
Tom Foley	.260	56	.267	52	.264	62	.266	49	.293	29	.186	102	.314	61	.842	2
Andres Galarraga	.289	22	.307	15	.314	10	.291	19	.281	41	.273	45	.315	60	.468	110
Rex Hudler	.140	--	.306	16	.278	40	.267	47	.167	124	.083	126	.282	86	.375	--
Tracy Jones	.316	--	.287	28	.330	5	.264	53	.268	57	.241	62	.317	57	.500	92
Dave Martinez	.286	26	.221	101	.260	68	.251	73	.266	58	.292	30	.299	75	.565	65
Graig Nettles	.179	--	.169	--	.214	--	.137	--	.171	--	.118	--	.231	--	.571	61
Otis Nixon	.246	--	.243	76	.234	97	.254	68	.224	101	.200	91	.356	24	.778	--
Tim Raines	.242	87	.282	34	.282	35	.260	61	.325	11	.333	13	.312	63	.625	45
Luis Rivera	.189	124	.235	84	.243	89	.203	120	.202	114	.128	121	.253	109	.478	109
Nelson Santovenia	.189	--	.251	69	.276	46	.192	128	.225	99	.171	110	.250	110	.650	35
Tim Wallach	.247	79	.260	60	.253	80	.260	60	.270	55	.260	52	.321	51	.610	50
Team Average	.238	12	.256	3	.259	2	.244	7	.250	6	.223	9	.305	5	.528	11
League Average	.250		.246		.252		.244		.250		.231		.301		.554	

Pitching vs. Left and Right Handed Batters

		BA	Rank	SA	Rank	OBA	Rank	HR %	Rank	BB %	Rank	SO %	Rank
Tim Burke	vs. Lefties	.306	100	.449	97	.385	96	3.40	100	11.63	85	8.14	98
	vs. Righties	.241	56	.346	54	.272	30	1.23	28	2.81	4	15.73	52
John Dopson	vs. Lefties	.258	53	.363	58	.334	63	2.10	68	10.37	71	12.77	64
	vs. Righties	.210	20	.338	44	.258	13	2.62	84	5.79	44	16.16	47
Neal Heaton	vs. Lefties	.244	42	.433	92	.306	41	4.44	106	6.93	28	14.85	49
	vs. Righties	.280	99	.480	107	.365	106	3.69	102	11.46	104	8.92	104
Joe Hesketh	vs. Lefties	.205	--	.244	--	.300	--	0.00	--	11.96	--	25.00	--
	vs. Righties	.258	80	.357	60	.340	96	0.55	7	11.32	103	19.34	25
Brian Holman	vs. Lefties	.270	72	.379	67	.345	74	1.42	42	10.13	67	12.24	70
	vs. Righties	.257	78	.310	25	.297	60	0.00	1	5.41	35	15.68	53
Dennis Martinez	vs. Lefties	.233	29	.347	42	.291	23	1.69	54	7.72	40	11.58	78
	vs. Righties	.246	65	.411	95	.280	38	3.05	94	3.33	6	13.33	77
Andy McGaffigan	vs. Lefties	.192	10	.243	4	.284	19	0.56	13	11.39	83	20.79	17
	vs. Righties	.276	97	.400	87	.337	94	1.76	46	7.37	67	15.26	60
Jeff Parrett	vs. Lefties	.210	15	.254	7	.319	53	0.00	1	14.12	100	15.88	40
	vs. Righties	.218	30	.412	96	.304	66	4.71	108	10.55	96	17.59	41
Pascual Perez	vs. Lefties	.213	18	.339	38	.273	14	2.46	86	7.14	31	17.24	31
	vs. Righties	.177	2	.260	7	.227	3	1.93	52	4.48	24	18.21	35
Bryn Smith	vs. Lefties	.259	55	.360	54	.300	33	1.59	49	4.94	10	12.84	63
	vs. Righties	.226	39	.352	57	.263	21	2.51	79	3.11	5	18.13	37
Floyd Youmans	vs. Lefties	.241	38	.372	63	.346	76	2.19	72	14.20	101	14.81	50
	vs. Righties	.189	6	.341	47	.274	33	3.05	93	9.52	87	15.87	51
Team Average	vs. Lefties	.242	3	.350	4	.312	4	1.87	8	9.19	7	14.37	7
	vs. Righties	.234	5	.371	8	.290	5	2.53	12	6.45	5	15.70	5
League Average	vs. Lefties	.255		.365		.325		1.73		9.36		14.24	
	vs. Righties	.244		.361		.299		2.10		6.87		15.64	

Pitching with Runners on Base and Bases Empty

		BA	Rank	SA	Rank	OBA	Rank	HR %	Rank	BB %	Rank	SO %	Rank
Tim Burke	Runners On	.285	88	.409	86	.383	104	2.19	73	12.57	91	13.71	57
	Bases Empty	.262	86	.384	85	.274	27	2.33	74	1.71	3	10.29	97
John Dopson	Runners On	.222	24	.319	27	.296	21	1.61	53	9.57	55	12.77	72
	Bases Empty	.244	60	.372	72	.301	64	2.82	92	7.35	65	15.40	58
Neal Heaton	Runners On	.269	67	.392	72	.372	101	1.54	46	12.42	89	6.83	106
	Bases Empty	.273	96	.511	109	.339	97	5.19	109	9.06	91	12.60	77
Joe Hesketh	Runners On	.212	20	.280	16	.322	51	0.00	1	14.19	99	19.59	18
	Bases Empty	.268	92	.359	60	.333	91	0.70	13	8.97	89	22.44	12
Brian Holman	Runners On	.289	92	.388	69	.359	92	0.66	19	9.71	58	13.14	63
	Bases Empty	.248	68	.322	25	.300	60	0.87	16	6.88	57	14.17	70
Dennis Martinez	Runners On	.239	37	.376	63	.296	22	2.69	90	7.51	22	14.48	50
	Bases Empty	.239	50	.378	78	.279	29	2.13	64	4.54	16	11.09	94
Andy McGaffigan	Runners On	.247	50	.352	46	.337	65	1.23	33	10.99	80	19.37	19
	Bases Empty	.222	24	.292	11	.284	37	1.08	16	7.96	78	16.92	42
Jeff Parrett	Runners On	.195	8	.309	22	.314	39	2.44	81	14.20	100	14.81	47
	Bases Empty	.227	32	.362	64	.309	77	2.70	87	10.63	101	18.36	27
Pascual Perez	Runners On	.210	18	.297	17	.278	9	1.31	36	7.92	29	12.83	71
	Bases Empty	.190	3	.306	19	.237	2	2.68	85	4.83	22	20.38	19
Bryn Smith	Runners On	.245	48	.374	59	.281	11	2.56	86	3.31	1	13.25	62
	Bases Empty	.242	55	.346	46	.282	35	1.73	48	4.50	14	16.77	46
Floyd Youmans	Runners On	.172	3	.233	4	.281	10	0.86	25	11.97	88	18.31	23
	Bases Empty	.238	48	.432	103	.325	87	3.78	104	11.48	103	13.40	73
Team Average	Runners On	.237	1	.345	3	.314	3	1.71	4	9.47	7	14.36	5
	Bases Empty	.239	5	.372	11	.292	5	2.54	12	6.57	7	15.55	5
League Average	Runners On	.257		.373		.329		1.91		9.45		14.09	
	Bases Empty	.242		.355		.297		1.98		6.73		15.80	

Overall Pitching Compared to Late Inning Pressure Situations

		BA	Rank	SA	Rank	OBA	Rank	HR %	Rank	BB %	Rank	SO %	Rank
Tim Burke	Overall	.272	91	.395	93	.327	83	2.27	78	7.14	40	12.00	86
	Pressure	.267	76	.398	81	.328	68	2.26	73	7.84	43	11.37	78
John Dopson	Overall	.235	37	.351	46	.299	38	2.35	83	8.24	64	14.35	63
	Pressure	.283	87	.472	100	.333	72	3.77	103	6.78	32	8.47	101
Neal Heaton	Overall	.271	90	.468	108	.351	104	3.88	107	10.36	91	10.36	93
	Pressure	.266	74	.383	73	.352	85	3.19	99	10.71	88	9.82	90
Joe Hesketh	Overall	.242	47	.323	22	.328	84	0.38	3	11.51	97	21.05	16
	Pressure	.245	56	.319	47	.326	64	0.00	1	10.58	83	22.75	13
Brian Holman	Overall	.264	80	.348	42	.324	77	0.79	7	8.06	61	13.74	68
	Pressure	.321	--	.321	--	.345	--	0.00	--	3.45	--	10.34	--
Dennis Martinez	Overall	.239	43	.377	73	.286	24	2.34	80	5.68	11	12.40	79
	Pressure	.173	7	.276	21	.204	1	2.04	69	2.86	3	10.48	85
Andy McGaffigan	Overall	.233	33	.320	21	.309	52	1.15	18	9.44	83	18.11	25
	Pressure	.200	23	.267	18	.290	36	1.03	34	10.67	86	17.78	32
Jeff Parrett	Overall	.214	15	.341	35	.311	93	2.60	93	12.20	104	16.80	33
	Pressure	.212	37	.332	50	.320	57	2.07	70	13.81	103	18.41	27
Pascual Perez	Overall	.196	4	.303	13	.252	2	2.22	75	5.94	15	17.68	27
	Pressure	.159	1	.286	27	.209	3	3.17	95	5.88	18	13.24	66
Bryn Smith	Overall	.243	50	.356	51	.282	17	2.04	60	4.05	2	15.42	46
	Pressure	.325	104	.500	104	.372	94	2.50	81	6.98	35	9.30	96
Floyd Youmans	Overall	.213	11	.355	49	.307	46	2.66	94	11.68	100	15.38	47
	Pressure	.348	--	.739	--	.360	--	8.70	--	3.85	--	11.54	--
Team Average	Overall	.238	4	.361	5	.301	4	2.22	10	7.77	5	15.06	5
	Pressure	.238	5	.352	6	.313	5	1.94	8	9.52	9	14.83	10
League Average	Overall	.248		.363		.310		1.95		7.91		15.06	
	Pressure	.243		.347		.315		1.72		9.12		15.69	

Additional Miscellaneous Pitching Comparisons

	Grass Surface		Artificial Surface		Home Games		Road Games		Runners in Scoring Position		Runners in Scoring Pos and Two Outs		Leading Off Inning	
	BA	Rank	BA	Rank	BA	Rank	BA	Rank	BA	Rank	BA	Rank	OBA	Rank
Tim Burke	.243	--	.280	92	.283	99	.256	58	.242	50	.245	77	.239	5
John Dopson	.195	8	.248	59	.251	65	.217	16	.212	28	.278	93	.316	71
Neal Heaton	.254	59	.281	93	.275	87	.269	74	.224	35	.196	38	.272	25
Joe Hesketh	.254	--	.238	45	.233	44	.250	51	.205	26	.118	5	.338	89
Brian Holman	.277	--	.263	70	.264	76	.265	70	.233	44	.234	67	.302	60
Dennis Martinez	.273	81	.224	26	.235	45	.242	45	.224	36	.238	70	.276	33
Andy McGaffigan	.164	--	.250	61	.232	43	.235	36	.245	54	.255	83	.256	12
Jeff Parrett	.282	--	.191	8	.174	6	.255	57	.198	21	.205	44	.310	68
Pascual Perez	.232	27	.189	7	.190	11	.204	8	.180	12	.174	19	.253	10
Bryn Smith	.286	91	.223	24	.228	33	.255	56	.260	70	.194	34	.285	47
Floyd Youmans	.135	--	.229	32	.232	41	.173	--	.186	17	.103	4	.326	80
Team Average	.244	5	.236	4	.238	5	.238	3	.223	1	.213	3	.289	3
League Average	.250		.246		.244		.252		.250		.231		.301	

NEW YORK METS

- ● **What did the Mets fail to do that every similar team in baseball history accomplished?**
- ● **Has there ever been a starting staff to rival this one?**

Who are the Mets? Are they the postwar Brooklyn Dodgers, who played .616 ball and won six National League titles within a 10–year span, but whose Boys of Summer had worse autumns than Adlai Stevenson? Are they the Los Angeles Lakers of the 1960s, playing the role of the Washington Generals to the Celtics' version of the Globetrotters, despite the presence of Baylor, West, and finally Chamberlain? Are they baseball's equivalent of the current Chicago Bears: great regular-season records, larger-than-life personnel, darlings of the TV networks, and annual Super Bowl expectations, but, sorry folks, we're just a tad short of championship rings this week, can we interest you in these consolation prizes?

It's an old sports cliche that a tie is like kissing your sister, and unless you grew up with Heather Locklear, the same analogy applies to losing the Championship Series. It's somewhat remarkable that the loss of one game—Game Seven of the National League Championship Series—could produce a winter's worth of wailing in the world's greatest city. But then again, it's particularly stinging to lose to a team that, everyone agrees, is not the equal of yours. And in 1988, that opinion was held not just by the Mets, their fans, or the media; according to their public comments, it was shared by the Dodgers!

Even though they finished with a 94–67 regular-season record compared to the Mets' 100—60, Hershiser, Hatcher & Co. were able to ride their emotional wave past a befuddled (see Game 7, Inning 2) group of Mets. There have now been 40 Championship Series since 1969, and only three other times has a favorite lost the series despite so large a gap (six and one-half games) between their regular-season records: in 1973, when the Mets upset the Reds; in 1985, when the Royals overcame the Blue Jays; and in 1987, when the Twins defeated the Tigers.

So if the Mets thought that there was pressure to win it all *last year*, wait until the 1989 season starts. Think of what stands between them and the position in which they stood last October 12, the day of the final game against the Dodgers: six months of hard work against the five other teams in their division, all of the turmoil and back page headlines of a summer in New York, potentially unsettling contract problems, the winning of a division title, and three wins in the Championship Series. The Mets have to survive all of that just to get back to where they stood a year ago—one win away from the World Series. And they'd better pray that *this time,* Hershiser is not out there in the seventh game!

Why were the Mets such overwhelming favorites over the Dodgers? After all, as we discussed in the Oakland essay, upsets do happen in professional sports, even in cases where one team is clearly superior to the other. But if there ever were such a thing as a form chart to be followed, the Mets certainly had that opportunity in 1988. They possessed the best offense and the best defense in the National League: New York scored the most runs (703) and allowed the fewest (532). Thirty other teams in this century have led their league in both of those categories. Astute fans may well recognize a common thread in these teams:

1902	Pirates	1936	Yankees	1953	Yankees
1903	Red Sox	1937	Yankees	1955	Dodgers
1904	Giants	1938	Yankees	1957	Yankees
1906	Cubs	1939	Yankees	1960	Pirates
1911	Athletics	1942	Cardinals	1968	Tigers
1912	Red Sox	1942	Yankees	1970	Orioles
1917	Giants	1943	Yankees	1971	Orioles
1918	Cubs	1944	Cardinals	1974	Dodgers
1927	Yankees	1946	Cardinals	1978	Dodgers
1935	Cubs	1947	Yankees	1984	Tigers

Every one of the teams on this list won the pennant in its league. (We can't use the phrase "reached the World Series" only because the Series was not yet invented in 1902, and the Giants refused to play in the Series in 1904.) That means that each of the 25 teams on the list before divisional play began in 1969 won the pennant, and each of the five teams that did it since 1969 won not only a division title, but also the Championship Series. So when Hershiser fanned Howard Johnson to end the 1988 Championship Series, the Mets became the first team in this century to lead their league in most runs scored and fewest runs allowed without winning the league championship.

These 30 teams dominated their leagues in both phases of the game, and most of them were certainly heavy favorites to retain their title the next season. So even though the Mets broke the string of teams of this type reaching the World Series, perhaps we can get a line on their chances of winning in 1989 by looking at the performance of their 30 predecessors in the year following their dominant season. Thirteen of these 30 teams repeated as champions of their league the following year; here's how that rate of repeating compares to other league champions (since 1900 in the National League, and since 1901 in the American):

	Repeat Champs	Repeat Pct.
30 dominant champions	13	43.3%
145 other champions	45	31.0%

Teams that led their league in both offense and defense have repeated with greater frequency than other, less dominant pennant-winners. This bodes well for the Mets in 1989, as does the depth of their pitching staff.

A quick review of 1988: David Cone authored a 2.22 ERA, the lowest among the five starters. Bob Ojeda came in at 2.88, Sid Fernandez weighed in at 3.03 (with or without the decimal point?), Dwight Gooden at 3.19, and Ron Darling was high man at 3.25, or more precisely, 3.253. Only once in the history of major league baseball has a staff had five pitchers, each making more than 25 starts, each with an earned run average below 3.30. That was the 1976 Dodgers' staff, with Doug Rau (2.57), Rick Rhoden (2.98), Don Sutton (3.06), Tommy John (3.09), and Burt Hooton (3.251). (Special for statsquirrels: Before 1982, ERAs were calculated only after innings totals were rounded to the nearest whole number; under current rules, Hooton's ERA would have been calculated at 3.256, higher than Darling's in 1988, thereby qualifying the Mets' 1988 staff as unique in baseball history. Just another case of the Dodgers beating the Mets in a close one.)

Not only were their ERAs low, but the Mets did just as well in all of the component pitching departments. Here's how the Mets' *team* pitching statistics for 1988 looked:

	Value	N.L. Rank
Earned Run Average	2.91	1st
Hits Allowed	1,253	1st
Walks Allowed	404	1st
Home Runs Allowed	78	1st
Strikeouts	1,100	1st

There have been many overpowering pitching staffs throughout baseball history, but for across-the-board domination in these specific categories, again, only one staff was the Mets' equal. And once again it was, who else, a Dodgers team—this time the 1966 edition—that was the only other team in major league history to do what the 1988 Mets' staff did; in this case, to lead its league in ERA, fewest hits, walks and home runs, and most strikeouts in the same season. Koufax, Drysdale, Osteen and Sutton (in his rookie season) were the regular starters; Phil Regan, Ron Perranoski and Bob Miller were the principal relievers. That staff was so good that the Dodgers were able to win the National League pennant despite an offense that produced 56 fewer runs than the league average, and scored only the eighth-most runs in a 10-team league.

But the Mets have a couple of legs up on that Dodgers team. First, they can hit. And second, the Mets have already made it through the winter without abruptly losing their ace, as the Dodgers did when Koufax retired following the '66 season. The Dodgers went seven years without so much as a division title in the wake of Koufax's departure. But in the Mets' case, you might be hard pressed to identify with any degree of assurance exactly who the Mets ace is these days. A survey of one hundred Mets fans might produce votes for several different pitchers; if you're ever a contestant on "Family Feud," this is one of those questions on which it might be better to pass than to play.

And that in itself is a rather remarkable change. Despite the quality of Darling, Cone, Fernandez, and Ojeda, did you ever think that the day would come when the name of Gooden would not be the automatic answer to the question, "If you had to have one Mets' pitcher start one game for the pennant, whom would you choose?"

Gooden started last season by winning his first eight decisions, but he won only 10 of 19 decisions thereafter. He pitched well but didn't win a game against the Dodgers in the playoffs, heightening the feeling of frustration toward him on the part of some Mets' fans. More than thirty years ago, Don Newcombe had three 20-win seasons for the Dodgers, but had an 0-4 record and 8.59 ERA in five World Series starts, and was hounded by cries that he "couldn't win the big one." Will those same catcalls, however undeserved, follow Gooden?

In five seasons in the majors, Dwight Gooden has fashioned a career record of 91-35, for a percentage of .722. That is the highest won-lost percentage among all pitchers in major league history with 100 or more decisions. Here are the top ten won-lost percentages among pitchers with 100 or more decisions since 1900:

	W–L	Pct.
Dwight Gooden	91–35	.722
Spud Chandler	109–43	.717
Roger Clemens	78–34	.696
Whitey Ford	236–106	.690
Don Gullett	109–50	.686
Lefty Grove	300–141	.680
Babe Ruth	94–46	.671
Smokey Joe Wood	116–57	.671
Vic Raschi	132–66	.667
Christy Mathewson	373–188	.665

But what can we look for from Gooden from here on out? Can he reasonably be expected to continue to win over two-thirds of his decisions throughout his career?

To help us explore that question, we compiled a list of the pitchers since 1900 who reached 100 wins with the fewest losses. Gooden needs nine wins to reach 100, and may join this group, at age 24, before the 1989 All-Star Game. We have also listed each pitcher's age at the time of his 100th victory, and his career record thereafter.

	Age	First 100 Wins		Thereafter	
		W–L	Pct.	W–L	Pct.
Whitey Ford	32	100–36	.735	136–70	.660
Spud Chandler	39	100–38	.725	9–5	.643
Ron Guidry	32	100–39	.719	70–52	.574
Johnny Allen	34	100–40	.714	42–35	.545
Vic Raschi	33	100–40	.714	32–26	.552
Ed Reulbach	27	100–42	.704	81–63	.563
Bob Feller	22	100–45	.690	166–117	.587
Don Newcombe	30	100–46	.685	49–44	.527
Sal Maglie	39	100–47	.680	19–15	.559
Juan Marichal	27	100–47	.680	143–95	.601
Jim Palmer	26	100–47	.680	168–105	.615
Don Gullett	26	100–47	.680	9–3	.750
Average Rest of Career				77–53	.595
Average Rest of Career for Pitchers Under 30				113–77	.597

Of the 12 pitchers listed, four went on to have Hall-of-Fame careers (Ford, Feller, Marichal, and Palmer, who is not yet eligible but is odds-on to be a first-time electee in 1990). The other eight had a combined record of 311-243 for the remainder of their careers, for a percentage of .561. And while .561 might not sound Hall-of-Famish, keep in mind that Don Drysdale had a career percentage of .557; Don Sutton, .558; and Tommy John, .560. Drysdale is already in Cooperstown; Sutton and John are strong candidates for future induction. It's a measure of Gooden's success if keeping company with those pitchers is the worst that he can look forward to!

WON-LOST RECORD BY STARTING POSITION

NEW YORK 100-60	C	1B	2B	3B	SS	LF	CF	RF	P	Leadoff	Relief	Starts
Rick Aguilera	·	·	·	·	·	·	·	·	0-3	·	3-5	0-3
Wally Backman	·	·	53-31	·	·	·	·	·	·	·	·	53-31
Mark Carreon	·	·	·	·	·	·	·	·	·	·	·	·
Gary Carter	72-44	4-2	·	·	·	·	·	·	·	·	·	76-46
David Cone	·	·	·	·	·	·	·	·	22-6	·	5-2	22-6
Ron Darling	·	·	·	·	·	·	·	·	23-11	·	·	23-11
Len Dykstra	·	·	·	·	·	·	58-40	·	·	57-40	·	58-40
Kevin Elster	·	·	·	·	76-47	·	·	·	·	·	·	76-47
Sid Fernandez	·	·	·	·	·	·	·	·	17-14	·	·	17-14
Dwight Gooden	·	·	·	·	·	·	·	·	24-10	·	·	24-10
Keith Hernandez	·	62-29	·	·	·	·	·	·	·	·	·	62-29
Jeff Innis	·	·	·	·	·	·	·	·	·	·	1-11	·
Gregg Jefferies	·	·	6-2	14-5	·	·	·	·	·	·	·	20-7
Howard Johnson	·	·	·	67-42	21-13	·	·	·	·	·	·	88-55
Terry Leach	·	·	·	·	·	·	·	·	·	·	17-35	·
Barry Lyons	10-4	·	·	·	·	·	·	·	·	·	·	10-4
Dave Magadan	·	31-23	·	18-10	·	·	·	·	·	·	·	49-33
Lee Mazzilli	·	3-4	·	·	·	4-2	·	0-2	·	·	·	7-8
Bob McClure	·	·	·	·	·	·	·	·	·	·	6-8	·
Roger McDowell	·	·	·	·	·	·	·	·	·	·	39-23	·
Kevin McReynolds	·	·	·	·	·	91-53	·	·	·	·	·	91-53
Keith A. Miller	·	·	1-5	1-3	3-0	·	·	·	·	·	·	5-8
John Mitchell	·	·	·	·	·	·	·	·	·	·	1-0	·
Randy Myers	·	·	·	·	·	·	·	·	·	·	41-14	·
Edwin Nunez	·	·	·	·	·	·	·	·	·	·	3-7	·
Bob Ojeda	·	·	·	·	·	·	·	·	13-16	·	·	13-16
Mackey Sasser	18-12	·	·	·	·	·	·	·	·	·	·	18-12
Darryl Strawberry	·	·	·	·	·	·	·	96-53	·	·	·	96-53
Tim Teufel	·	0-2	40-22	·	·	·	·	·	·	·	·	40-24
Gene Walter	·	·	·	·	·	·	·	·	·	·	2-17	·
Dave West	·	·	·	·	·	·	·	·	1-0	·	0-1	1-0
Mookie Wilson	·	·	·	·	·	5-5	42-20	4-5	·	43-20	·	51-30

Batting vs. Left and Right Handed Pitchers

		BA	Rank	SA	Rank	OBA	Rank	HR %	Rank	BB %	Rank	SO %	Rank
Wally Backman	vs. Lefties	.257	--	.286	--	.333	--	0.00	--	10.00	--	17.50	--
	vs. Righties	.309	8	.351	72	.395	10	0.00	115	12.05	20	13.68	61
Gary Carter	vs. Lefties	.256	70	.396	54	.295	92	3.05	40	5.11	105	6.82	14
	vs. Righties	.234	98	.337	85	.304	82	2.06	51	7.65	67	12.23	47
Len Dykstra	vs. Lefties	.270	51	.365	73	.321	79	1.35	79	4.94	108	14.81	88
	vs. Righties	.270	45	.389	50	.321	58	1.97	53	6.75	81	8.05	13
Kevin Elster	vs. Lefties	.228	103	.324	94	.304	85	2.07	64	9.09	54	7.88	24
	vs. Righties	.207	123	.307	105	.269	118	2.30	43	7.02	76	11.93	44
Keith Hernandez	vs. Lefties	.274	46	.452	29	.333	56	4.44	17	8.00	67	10.00	44
	vs. Righties	.277	33	.394	46	.333	42	2.35	42	8.12	60	17.95	103
Howard Johnson	vs. Lefties	.183	121	.338	87	.304	86	4.23	19	14.45	9	16.18	100
	vs. Righties	.249	79	.456	16	.359	25	5.10	8	14.49	5	18.05	105
Dave Magadan	vs. Lefties	.279	41	.314	102	.394	6	0.00	103	14.29	10	10.48	53
	vs. Righties	.276	34	.342	81	.393	11	0.44	110	16.36	3	10.18	30
Kevin McReynolds	vs. Lefties	.270	51	.546	6	.308	81	6.49	3	5.13	104	10.26	51
	vs. Righties	.297	15	.471	13	.349	33	4.09	16	6.91	77	8.89	17
Darryl Strawberry	vs. Lefties	.250	78	.560	3	.318	75	9.26	1	9.80	46	22.04	124
	vs. Righties	.281	28	.535	4	.395	9	5.81	3	15.44	4	18.48	107
Tim Teufel	vs. Lefties	.248	81	.394	58	.326	64	1.82	70	10.11	41	10.11	46
	vs. Righties	.213	--	.287	--	.275	--	0.93	--	8.26	--	18.18	--
Mookie Wilson	vs. Lefties	.282	37	.421	40	.335	55	2.05	65	7.04	75	14.08	83
	vs. Righties	.311	6	.443	19	.355	27	2.19	46	6.09	92	16.75	93
Team Average	vs. Lefties	.247	7	.413	1	.310	7	3.58	1	8.12	5	13.63	4
	vs. Righties	.261	1	.387	1	.332	1	2.41	1	9.32	1	13.88	2
League Average	vs. Lefties	.248		.367		.310		2.10		8.01		14.42	
	vs. Righties	.249		.360		.310		1.88		7.86		15.35	

Batting with Runners on Base and Bases Empty

		BA	Rank	SA	Rank	OBA	Rank	HR %	Rank	BB %	Rank	SO %	Rank
Wally Backman	Runners On	.274	61	.321	106	.378	25	0.00	104	13.97	23	15.44	95
	Bases Empty	.319	3	.356	70	.393	2	0.00	115	10.43	17	13.27	52
Gary Carter	Runners On	.256	83	.347	89	.335	74	2.27	46	9.66	59	11.11	49
	Bases Empty	.233	92	.366	64	.277	98	2.51	44	4.73	101	9.80	24
Len Dykstra	Runners On	.235	104	.353	85	.307	99	2.21	48	9.03	67	11.61	56
	Bases Empty	.287	20	.399	35	.328	38	1.71	68	5.14	95	8.04	13
Kevin Elster	Runners On	.251	90	.389	60	.345	61	3.43	22	11.65	41	10.19	33
	Bases Empty	.186	122	.255	119	.230	125	1.30	80	4.51	106	10.66	32
Keith Hernandez	Runners On	.308	18	.488	14	.356	48	4.65	9	7.33	93	14.14	77
	Bases Empty	.244	74	.347	75	.311	57	1.70	69	8.81	39	15.54	76
Howard Johnson	Runners On	.200	119	.333	101	.341	63	3.33	23	18.22	6	18.22	111
	Bases Empty	.253	53	.488	7	.345	20	5.96	2	11.38	12	16.92	90
Dave Magadan	Runners On	.316	12	.395	55	.422	4	0.66	93	16.13	14	10.22	34
	Bases Empty	.241	79	.278	115	.366	6	0.00	115	15.46	1	10.31	30
Kevin McReynolds	Runners On	.311	16	.502	12	.359	43	4.28	14	7.02	100	8.42	22
	Bases Empty	.268	34	.492	6	.314	50	5.42	3	5.71	86	10.16	28
Darryl Strawberry	Runners On	.258	80	.527	7	.376	28	7.81	2	16.61	12	18.50	112
	Bases Empty	.279	26	.561	1	.355	12	6.62	1	9.97	20	21.18	116
Tim Teufel	Runners On	.176	127	.311	109	.266	122	2.52	38	11.35	42	12.77	64
	Bases Empty	.279	25	.383	44	.339	25	0.65	103	7.74	52	13.69	55
Mookie Wilson	Runners On	.283	49	.421	41	.321	89	2.76	35	5.73	108	15.29	93
	Bases Empty	.305	6	.438	19	.360	9	1.72	67	7.11	59	15.42	73
Team Average	Runners On	.257	6	.396	1	.337	2	3.04	1	10.88	1	13.88	6
	Bases Empty	.256	2	.396	1	.316	1	2.64	1	7.32	5	13.72	2
League Average	Runners On	.257		.373		.329		1.91		9.45		14.09	
	Bases Empty	.242		.355		.297		1.98		6.73		15.80	

Overall Batting Compared to Late Inning Pressure Situations

		BA	Rank	SA	Rank	OBA	Rank	HR %	Rank	BB %	Rank	SO %	Rank	RDI %	Rank
Wally Backman	Overall	.303	6	.344	91	.388	5	0.00	118	11.82	17	14.12	75	.225	105
	Pressure	.314	--	.343	--	.368	--	0.00	--	7.69	--	17.95	--	.222	--
Gary Carter	Overall	.242	96	.358	76	.301	94	2.42	41	6.76	86	10.34	34	.212	114
	Pressure	.234	78	.364	53	.286	89	3.90	17	4.71	108	10.59	32	.292	43
Len Dykstra	Overall	.270	41	.385	52	.321	61	1.86	62	6.44	92	9.23	20	.214	113
	Pressure	.309	25	.400	37	.400	10	1.82	56	12.12	31	4.55	5	.263	57
Kevin Elster	Overall	.214	119	.313	113	.282	115	2.22	46	7.78	67	10.44	35	.198	121
	Pressure	.145	122	.255	103	.161	127	3.64	18	1.69	126	15.25	72	.200	--
Keith Hernandez	Overall	.276	32	.417	28	.333	47	3.16	29	8.07	62	14.84	80	.316	16
	Pressure	.317	17	.610	1	.391	13	9.76	1	8.70	56	19.57	92	.389	10
Howard Johnson	Overall	.230	110	.422	24	.343	37	4.85	7	14.48	5	17.51	104	.247	86
	Pressure	.235	76	.397	38	.389	16	4.41	16	20.00	3	16.67	79	.267	53
Dave Magadan	Overall	.277	29	.334	98	.393	4	0.32	116	15.79	2	10.26	33	.314	18
	Pressure	.189	109	.208	119	.338	50	0.00	79	18.18	5	12.12	47	.227	68
Lee Mazzilli	Overall	.147	--	.164	--	.227	--	0.00	--	9.09	--	12.12	--	.250	--
	Pressure	.163	119	.163	126	.208	121	0.00	79	6.25	88	10.42	29	.278	48
Kevin McReynolds	Overall	.288	20	.496	6	.336	45	4.89	6	6.33	93	9.33	23	.304	32
	Pressure	.333	9	.529	8	.352	42	4.60	15	2.17	123	10.87	36	.357	25
Mackey Sasser	Overall	.285	--	.407	--	.313	--	0.81	--	4.58	--	6.87	--	.300	--
	Pressure	.238	--	.333	--	.273	--	0.00	--	4.55	--	4.55	--	.250	59
Darryl Strawberry	Overall	.269	44	.545	1	.366	14	7.18	1	13.28	7	19.84	118	.259	75
	Pressure	.189	107	.419	31	.333	51	5.41	7	16.67	6	25.56	121	.167	95
Tim Teufel	Overall	.234	106	.352	84	.306	87	1.47	74	9.39	41	13.27	58	.226	104
	Pressure	.196	103	.239	112	.283	94	0.00	79	11.11	38	14.81	66	.200	82
Mookie Wilson	Overall	.296	9	.431	20	.345	35	2.12	50	6.59	90	15.37	85	.278	58
	Pressure	.290	33	.464	17	.388	17	2.90	31	12.35	28	11.11	39	.158	101
Team Average	Overall	.256	2	.396	1	.325	1	2.81	1	8.91	2	13.79	3	.256	7
	Pressure	.248	4	.385	2	.328	1	3.14	1	9.90	2	13.71	3	.255	3
League Average	Overall	.248		.363		.310		1.95		7.91		15.06		.256	
	Pressure	.242		.340		.310		1.70		8.47		15.93		.238	

Additional Miscellaneous Batting Comparisons

	Grass Surface BA	Rank	Artificial Surface BA	Rank	Home Games BA	Rank	Road Games BA	Rank	Runners in Scoring Position BA	Rank	Runners in Scoring Pos and Two Outs BA	Rank	Leading Off Inning OBA	Rank	Runners on 3B with less than 2 Outs RDI %	Rank
Wally Backman	.335	3	.215	105	.340	2	.267	48	.190	121	.094	124	.301	68	.727	12
Gary Carter	.237	97	.254	68	.211	115	.273	36	.226	98	.135	120	.300	72	.625	45
Len Dykstra	.251	72	.312	11	.254	78	.285	21	.195	118	.098	123	.301	69	.733	11
Kevin Elster	.218	111	.206	113	.194	121	.233	97	.204	111	.267	48	.281	87	.400	121
Keith Hernandez	.295	15	.231	91	.274	49	.277	33	.279	46	.227	73	.388	8	.696	22
Howard Johnson	.249	75	.190	120	.213	111	.245	82	.197	116	.141	119	.390	6	.548	75
Dave Magadan	.269	46	.297	24	.301	18	.250	74	.311	18	.294	29	.239	117	.588	55
Lee Mazzilli	.194	--	.068	--	.217	--	.100	--	.189	--	.188	--	.214	--	.462	111
Kevin McReynolds	.277	35	.320	6	.276	48	.300	8	.319	13	.289	33	.349	30	.441	116
Mackey Sasser	.277	34	.300	--	.276	--	.292	--	.293	--	.348	8	.286	--	1.000	--
Darryl Strawberry	.257	60	.297	23	.265	59	.272	38	.201	115	.186	101	.377	12	.595	53
Tim Teufel	.212	115	.286	30	.208	117	.259	63	.139	127	.143	118	.373	14	.611	49
Mookie Wilson	.294	16	.302	21	.259	70	.332	1	.318	15	.385	3	.354	27	.500	92
Team Average	.257	3	.256	2	.249	7	.264	1	.240	12	.217	10	.321	1	.579	2
League Average	.250		.246		.252		.244		.250		.231		.301		.554	

Pitching vs. Left and Right Handed Batters

		BA	Rank	SA	Rank	OBA	Rank	HR %	Rank	BB %	Rank	SO %	Rank
David Cone	vs. Lefties	.257	52	.351	47	.335	64	1.15	31	10.53	73	17.81	30
	vs. Righties	.165	1	.230	2	.225	2	1.25	29	6.33	47	28.28	1
Ron Darling	vs. Lefties	.254	49	.387	74	.304	38	2.65	94	7.01	29	17.03	33
	vs. Righties	.236	51	.378	74	.285	45	2.75	89	5.30	33	16.10	50
Sid Fernandez	vs. Lefties	.236	--	.347	--	.325	--	1.39	--	10.84	--	28.92	--
	vs. Righties	.185	4	.300	20	.264	22	2.36	75	9.13	85	24.70	8
Dwight Gooden	vs. Lefties	.236	32	.308	21	.290	21	0.81	23	6.74	25	16.85	35
	vs. Righties	.278	98	.360	63	.313	73	0.88	15	4.29	21	17.35	42
Terry Leach	vs. Lefties	.290	87	.399	79	.353	81	1.45	43	7.64	39	10.83	83
	vs. Righties	.255	77	.329	39	.294	57	1.39	35	5.11	31	14.47	65
Roger McDowell	vs. Lefties	.260	57	.325	29	.337	67	0.00	1	10.29	70	9.71	90
	vs. Righties	.220	34	.247	5	.275	34	0.55	7	6.40	49	14.29	67
Randy Myers	vs. Lefties	.180	--	.220	--	.250	--	0.00	--	7.02	--	28.07	--
	vs. Righties	.193	8	.294	18	.248	10	2.67	87	6.37	48	25.98	4
Bob Ojeda	vs. Lefties	.165	4	.283	14	.195	2	1.57	47	2.94	2	30.15	2
	vs. Righties	.238	53	.325	33	.276	35	0.69	11	4.71	27	14.94	61
Team Average	vs. Lefties	.247	5	.343	3	.308	3	1.30	2	7.92	2	17.41	1
	vs. Righties	.227	2	.321	2	.279	1	1.56	3	6.20	2	19.56	1
League Average	vs. Lefties	.255		.365		.325		1.73		9.36		14.24	
	vs. Righties	.244		.361		.299		2.10		6.87		15.64	

Pitching with Runners on Base and Bases Empty

		BA	Rank	SA	Rank	OBA	Rank	HR %	Rank	BB %	Rank	SO %	Rank
David Cone	Runners On	.220	23	.308	21	.301	27	1.26	34	10.19	64	22.52	6
	Bases Empty	.208	16	.284	10	.272	23	1.16	26	7.46	68	22.91	10
Ron Darling	Runners On	.248	51	.393	73	.291	18	2.76	95	5.99	9	18.26	24
	Bases Empty	.244	61	.377	77	.296	53	2.67	84	6.29	47	15.56	57
Sid Fernandez	Runners On	.193	7	.321	29	.267	4	2.47	83	7.89	28	20.79	12
	Bases Empty	.189	2	.296	13	.273	25	2.13	64	10.17	96	27.75	3
Dwight Gooden	Runners On	.276	81	.376	64	.328	56	1.32	37	6.78	14	17.76	25
	Bases Empty	.243	57	.303	17	.282	36	0.53	5	4.70	18	16.61	48
Terry Leach	Runners On	.253	54	.300	18	.309	32	0.00	1	6.63	10	13.78	55
	Bases Empty	.283	100	.408	94	.327	88	2.72	88	5.61	34	12.24	82
Roger McDowell	Runners On	.229	30	.255	7	.315	42	0.00	1	10.16	63	12.83	70
	Bases Empty	.246	65	.307	20	.293	49	0.56	7	6.28	46	11.52	88
Randy Myers	Runners On	.149	1	.198	1	.205	1	0.83	23	6.67	12	26.67	1
	Bases Empty	.233	--	.362	--	.294	--	3.45	--	6.35	--	26.19	--
Bob Ojeda	Runners On	.253	55	.343	40	.303	30	0.82	22	6.86	15	16.25	34
	Bases Empty	.210	18	.303	18	.238	3	0.87	17	2.95	8	18.53	25
Team Average	Runners On	.240	3	.336	2	.301	1	1.44	2	7.70	1	17.96	1
	Bases Empty	.231	2	.325	1	.283	2	1.47	2	6.28	2	19.26	1
League Average	Runners On	.257		.373		.329		1.91		9.45		14.09	
	Bases Empty	.242		.355		.297		1.98		6.73		15.80	

Overall Pitching Compared to Late Inning Pressure Situations

		BA	Rank	SA	Rank	OBA	Rank	HR %	Rank	BB %	Rank	SO %	Rank
David Cone	Overall	.213	12	.293	8	.283	18	1.20	22	8.55	68	22.76	8
	Pressure	.183	11	.267	18	.210	4	1.67	55	3.20	4	22.40	15
Ron Darling	Overall	.245	54	.383	80	.294	33	2.70	96	6.18	22	16.58	35
	Pressure	.187	14	.262	16	.243	13	1.87	62	6.03	21	18.10	31
Sid Fernandez	Overall	.191	3	.305	15	.271	8	2.25	77	9.32	81	25.17	4
	Pressure	.222	47	.333	51	.295	41	0.00	1	9.84	77	22.95	12
Dwight Gooden	Overall	.256	71	.333	29	.301	40	0.85	8	5.57	9	17.09	30
	Pressure	.305	99	.366	68	.356	87	1.22	41	6.67	29	10.00	89
Terry Leach	Overall	.268	85	.356	50	.318	67	1.41	34	6.12	21	13.01	75
	Pressure	.322	102	.356	64	.398	104	0.00	1	10.19	79	11.11	80
Roger McDowell	Overall	.238	40	.283	6	.304	43	0.30	1	8.20	63	12.17	83
	Pressure	.254	60	.306	41	.327	66	0.52	20	8.64	56	8.64	99
Randy Myers	Overall	.190	2	.278	4	.248	1	2.11	68	6.51	29	26.44	2
	Pressure	.171	5	.229	6	.219	5	1.14	38	5.79	17	27.89	2
Bob Ojeda	Overall	.225	22	.317	20	.261	5	0.85	10	4.39	4	17.69	26
	Pressure	.284	89	.338	54	.308	47	0.00	1	3.75	6	13.75	61
Team Average	Overall	.235	1	.329	2	.291	1	1.46	1	6.87	1	18.72	1
	Pressure	.238	4	.298	2	.291	3	0.83	1	6.57	1	16.70	3
League Average	Overall	.248		.363		.310		1.95		7.91		15.06	
	Pressure	.243		.347		.315		1.72		9.12		15.69	

Additional Miscellaneous Pitching Comparisons

	Grass Surface		Artificial Surface		Home Games		Road Games		Runners in Scoring Position		Runners in Scoring Pos and Two Outs		Leading Off Inning	
	BA	Rank	BA	Rank	BA	Rank	BA	Rank	BA	Rank	BA	Rank	OBA	Rank
David Cone	.200	9	.241	50	.180	8	.245	49	.179	11	.179	24	.249	9
Ron Darling	.238	34	.279	90	.224	28	.278	85	.259	68	.158	11	.289	53
Sid Fernandez	.175	3	.222	23	.152	2	.230	33	.157	3	.186	29	.303	61
Dwight Gooden	.252	55	.267	77	.237	51	.273	78	.272	83	.260	85	.282	41
Terry Leach	.271	79	.264	73	.284	100	.257	62	.212	27	.094	1	.299	59
Roger McDowell	.239	37	.237	43	.232	42	.242	46	.223	33	.224	63	.293	56
Randy Myers	.150	1	.273	--	.108	1	.274	79	.160	4	.216	53	.302	--
Bob Ojeda	.224	22	.228	30	.235	46	.210	11	.257	67	.243	75	.245	7
Team Average	.228	1	.253	8	.216	1	.254	6	.226	2	.203	2	.284	1
League Average	.250		.246		.244		.252		.250		.231		.301	

PHILADELPHIA PHILLIES

- "Juan" to win? Better bat Samuel second in the order.
- Who's most likely to rebound from a bad year in 1988?

Nick Leyva, Philadelphia's new manager, faces a dilemma that his three predecessors, Paul Owens, John Felske, and Lee Elia, all struggled with and lost to. On opening day, we'll know whether Leyva is on the right track simply by checking his lineup card. Unless Juan Samuel is listed in the second position in the batting order, he's in the wrong spot.

The problem isn't an easy one to solve according to the traditional rules of lineup construction because Samuel's combination of strengths and weaknesses are unique in baseball history.

Let's examine his statistical profile. First and foremost, Samuel is a great base stealer. Only six other players have stolen at least 30 bases in each of the past five seasons: Brett Butler, Rickey Henderson, Lloyd Moseby, Tim Raines, Ozzie Smith, and Willie Wilson. And of those players, only Henderson and Raines have outstolen Samuel during that period. World-class base stealers have traditionally batted in the leadoff position. Among the players who stole 30 or more bases last season, the number of games they started in each batting-order position is listed below:

1st	2d	3d	4th	5th	6th	7th	8th	9th
1724	600	709	125	123	90	46	112	73

The 30–steals players batted leadoff in nearly half of the more than 3600 games they started, and in one of the top three slots in the batting order in 84 percent of them. Problem is, a high on-base average is another component of the profile of desirable leadoff batters, and Samuel rarely walks, *especially for a base stealer*. Other leadoff hitters walk once in every 12 plate appearances; Samuel only once in every 18 trips to the plate. And Samuel's strikeout rate further distinguishes him from the profile of leadoff hitters in general. Last season, he struck out 151 times, nearly twice as often as the major leagues' other leadoff hitters would average in the same number of plate appearances.

That parlay—defined as 30 or more steals, 140 or more strikeouts, and fewer than 40 walks—is unprecedented in major league history. It's been done by only one player, and

Samuel has done it four times in his five seasons. For a more complete picture, compare Samuel's per-season averages to those of all 30–steals players from 1960 through 1987:

Player	AB	R	H	2B	3B	HR	RBI	BB	SO	SB	BA
Juan Samuel	647	95	170	34	13	18	78	37	152	47	.264
30-SB players	539	84	151	23	6	9	53	53	73	45	.279

The Phillies have moved Samuel around in the batting order quite a bit since he became a regular starter in 1984. In every season except 1986, he made a majority of his starts in the leadoff slot. But even in those seasons, he started anywhere from 29 games (in 1984) to 85 games (last season) batting elsewhere:

	1984	1985	1986	1987	1988	Total
Batting 1st	129	84	0	93	70	376
Batting 2nd	12	42	44	26	7	131
Batting 3d	17	30	76	40	52	215
Other starts	0	3	23	0	26	52

So what's a manager to do? A game-by-game analysis of the past five seasons indicates that Philadelphia makes the most of its offense with Samuel batting second. (That might surprise those who consider the ability to make contact a requirement for hitting behind the leadoff batter.)

The table below classifies the games that Samuel started according to where he batted in the order. (All games in which he batted below the third slot are grouped together.) For each group, the table below shows how many runs the Phillies actually scored, and how many they "should have scored", based on their building blocks of hits, walks, extra-base hits, and so on. As we pointed out in the Boston Red Sox essay, a player's position in the batting order can affect his team's performance in only two ways: (1) by getting him to the plate more often, or (2) by creating more runs from the hits and walks the team gets through some sort of interaction with the other players in the lineup. It's that second dynamic that this table illustrates:

Batting Order Slot	Games	Expected Runs	Actual Runs	Diff.
Batting 1st	376	1697	1634	−63
Batting 2d	131	529	547	+18
Batting 3d	215	944	924	−20
Other starts	52	198	198	0

Those figures leave little room for argument. With Samuel batting leadoff, the Phillies have failed to make the most of their hits and walks, scoring 63 fewer runs that they should have (an average of 27 per 162 games). That's an awful lot of runs to give away, especially considering that the team has overachieved with Samuel in the two hole.

The problem for 1989 isn't merely where to bat Samuel, but who to use in the leadoff slot. For what it's worth, Phil Bradley, another 100–strikeout candidate, appeared to be the more effective of last season's other leadoff hitters, but he now wears an Oriole uniform. The Phillies scored more than expected with Bradley in the top spot, less than expected with either Samuel or Milt Thompson (who has since been traded to St. Louis):

Leadoff Hitter	Games	Expected Runs	Actual Runs	Diff.
Bradley	60	197	210	+13
Thompson	21	71	65	−6
Samuel	70	288	280	−8

Bradley batted leadoff with Samuel behind him only six times last season, but those six games did include four consecutive wins the last week of September. It's ironic that those games were played under John Vukovich, who replaced Lee Elia with two weeks to go in the season. Keep an eye on those first-week Phillies box scores to see how Nick Leyva handles the situation.

Bradley and Lance Parrish both had disappointing seasons for the Phillies last season, raising the issue of what to expect from players coming off seasons that represent sharp declines from their career performances. Granted: On a world scale, solving this riddle ranks below feeding the hungry. But each season, decisions on such players are required not only from general managers in the major leagues, but also from thousands of fantasy-league general managers.

The Phillies apparently felt it wasn't worth waiting for either player, shipping both back to the American League before the off season was two months old. Bradley and Parrish were among the 14 players last season who hit at least 30 points below their career batting averages prior to 1988. (We considered only players with at least 400 at-bats last season, and 1000 or more before that.)

Player	Career	1988	Diff.
Larry Sheets	.289	.230	.059
Dale Murphy	.279	.226	.053
Lance Parrish	.266	.215	.051
Larry Parrish	.266	.217	.049
Willie Randolph	.277	.230	.047
Darrell Evans	.251	.208	.043
Brook Jacoby	.281	.241	.040
Tim Raines	.308	.270	.038
Jim Rice	.302	.264	.038
Phil Bradley	.301	.264	.037
Jack Clark	.276	.242	.034
Willie Wilson	.295	.262	.033
Jeffrey Leonard	.274	.242	.032
Gary Pettis	.242	.210	.032

How should players be judged when coming off bad seasons: according to their career marks, the off year, or something in between? We researched the entire history of modern major league baseball and found 739 players who met the same criteria by which we identified the players listed above. (They batted at least 30 points lower in a given season than they had in their careers prior to that point, with at least 400 at-bats in the poor season, and 1000 at-bats prior to it.) Then we checked how those players performed in the seasons following their off years.

The first thing to know is that 104 of those players, or one in seven, either never played again or failed to bat even 100 times the next season. Of those with at least 100 at-bats the next season, slightly more than half batted somewhere between the two figures. On the whole, they tended to hit closer to the lower figure (their previous year's average) than the higher career mark. About a quarter of the players rebounded to exceed the old career mark; the other quarter didn't even reach their averages for the last season.

What's interesting is that the prognosis for players who switched leagues during the off year or the season after it, as did both Bradley and Parrish, isn't quite as optimistic. That may come as a surprise in light of the success that some players have had subsequent to poor first seasons in their new leagues. (Von Hayes and Howard Johnson come to mind immediately.) The following table shows the number of players who rebounded the next season to a mark even higher than their old career marks; those who batted somewhere between the career mark and the off-season average; and those who failed to reach even the off-season average:

	Rebounds	Moderates	Declines
All players	148 (23%)	317 (51%)	160 (26%)
League changers	8 (16%)	27 (53%)	16 (31%)

Incidentally, among the 16 players who switched leagues, had an off year, and then declined further the year after that are six Hall of Famers who were nearing the ends of their careers: Hank Aaron, Jimmie Foxx, Hank Greenberg, Frank Robinson, Al Simmons, and Billy Williams. That suggested there might be an age skew in the figures as well. And as suspected, young players who experience off years bounce back much more often than older players.

The 625 players who batted at least 100 times in the seasons following off years are classified according to their age on April 1 of those following seasons.

	Rebounds	Moderates	Declines
Younger than 30	73 (30%)	129 (52%)	44 (18%)
Age 30 to 35	59 (22%)	138 (51%)	71 (26%)
Older than 35	16 (14%)	50 (45%)	45 (41%)

Parrish will be 32 on opening day; Bradley will have just turned the big three-oh. Expecting a rebound to previous levels by either this season might be considered wishful thinking. But certainly in the case of Parrish, who'll be 33 by midseason and has been slowed by injuries in recent years, the decision to cut bait appears to be a sound one. Among the other players, only Sheets, Jacoby, and Raines are young enough to make complete rebounds likely. And good luck to those teams considering an investment in Darrell Evans—fantasy leagues or otherwise.

WON-LOST RECORD BY STARTING POSITION

PHILADELPHIA	65-96	C	1B	2B	3B	SS	LF	CF	RF	P	Leadoff	Relief	Starts
Luis Aguayo		-	-	0-2	1-5	8-9	-	-	-	-	-	-	9-16
Bill Almon		-	0-1	-	2-1	-	-	-	-	-	-	-	2-2
Salome Barojas		-	-	-	-	-	-	-	-	-	-	1-5	-
Tom Barrett		-	-	3-6	-	-	-	-	-	-	-	-	3-6
Steve Bedrosian		-	-	-	-	-	-	-	-	-	-	38-19	-
Phil Bradley		-	-	-	-	-	60-89	-	1-0	-	22-38	-	61-89
Jeff Calhoun		-	-	-	-	-	-	-	-	-	-	1-2	-
Don Carman		-	-	-	-	-	-	-	-	15-17	-	1-3	15-17
Danny Clay		-	-	-	-	-	-	-	-	-	-	1-16	-
Darren Daulton		14-22	0-1	-	-	-	-	-	-	-	-	-	14-23
Bill Dawley		-	-	-	-	-	-	-	-	-	-	0-8	-
Bob Dernier		-	-	-	-	-	-	15-24	1-0	-	3-7	-	16-24
Marvin Freeman		-	-	-	-	-	-	-	-	3-8	-	-	3-8
Todd Frohwirth		-	-	-	-	-	-	-	-	-	-	2-10	-
Greg Gross		-	3-6	-	-	-	1-3	-	3-1	-	0-1	-	7-10
Kevin Gross		-	-	-	-	-	-	-	-	15-18	-	-	15-18
Jackie Gutierrez		-	-	2-6	11-4	-	-	-	-	-	-	-	13-10
Greg A. Harris		-	-	-	-	-	-	-	-	0-1	-	19-46	0-1
Von Hayes		-	35-46	-	1-1	-	0-1	5-7	-	-	-	-	41-55
Chris James		-	-	12-19	-	-	2-2	6-7	39-57	-	-	-	59-85
Steve Jeltz		-	-	-	46-82	-	-	-	-	-	-	-	46-82
Ron Jones		-	-	-	-	-	-	11-21	-	-	-	-	11-21
Ricky Jordan		-	27-42	-	-	-	-	-	-	-	-	-	27-42
Mike Maddux		-	-	-	-	-	-	-	-	6-5	-	4-10	6-5
Alex Madrid		-	-	-	-	-	-	-	-	1-1	-	0-3	1-1
N. Keith Miller		-	-	-	-	-	0-1	-	-	-	-	-	0-1
Brad Moore		-	-	-	-	-	-	-	-	-	-	1-4	-
David Palmer		-	-	-	-	-	-	-	-	10-12	-	-	10-12
Al Pardo		-	-	-	-	-	-	-	-	-	-	-	-
Lance Parrish		44-69	-	-	-	-	-	-	-	-	-	-	44-69
Shane Rawley		-	-	-	-	-	-	-	-	10-22	-	-	10-22
Wally Ritchie		-	-	-	-	-	-	-	-	-	-	2-17	-
Bruce Ruffin		-	-	-	-	-	-	-	-	4-10	-	14-26	4-10
John Russell		7-5	-	-	-	-	-	-	-	-	-	-	7-5
Juan Samuel		-	-	62-88	0-1	-	-	1-1	0-1	-	31-39	-	63-91
Bill Scherrer		-	-	-	-	-	-	-	-	-	-	1-7	-
Mike Schmidt		-	-	-	46-56	-	-	-	-	-	-	-	46-56
Bob Sebra		-	-	-	-	-	-	-	-	1-2	-	-	1-2
David Service		-	-	-	-	-	-	-	-	-	-	1-4	-
Kent Tekulve		-	-	-	-	-	-	-	-	-	-	20-50	-
Milt Thompson		-	-	-	-	-	38-57	-	-	-	9-11	-	38-57
Shane Turner		-	-	-	1-7	0-1	-	-	-	-	-	-	1-8
Mike Young		-	-	-	-	-	2-1	-	10-15	-	-	-	12-16

Batting vs. Left and Right Handed Pitchers

		BA	Rank	SA	Rank	OBA	Rank	HR %	Rank	BB %	Rank	SO %	Rank
Phil Bradley	vs. Lefties	.272	49	.420	41	.342	48	2.37	55	8.95	58	15.79	99
	vs. Righties	.260	60	.380	56	.341	39	1.75	58	8.06	61	16.56	90
Darren Daulton	vs. Lefties	.111	--	.111	--	.111	--	0.00	--	0.00	--	5.56	--
	vs. Righties	.222	108	.294	110	.310	73	0.79	95	11.72	23	17.24	95
Bob Dernier	vs. Lefties	.314	13	.372	70	.361	30	0.73	97	6.04	97	8.05	28
	vs. Righties	.172	--	.172	--	.172	--	0.00	--	0.00	--	23.33	--
Greg Gross	vs. Lefties	.125	--	.125	--	.125	--	0.00	--	0.00	--	0.00	--
	vs. Righties	.208	122	.216	128	.301	84	0.00	115	11.19	26	2.10	1
Von Hayes	vs. Lefties	.129	129	.238	122	.196	128	1.98	67	7.96	68	16.81	102
	vs. Righties	.327	2	.474	12	.413	2	1.50	63	12.90	13	12.90	55
Chris James	vs. Lefties	.229	102	.408	47	.265	115	4.46	16	4.22	115	10.24	50
	vs. Righties	.247	84	.381	53	.289	102	2.93	37	5.47	108	12.76	54
Steve Jeltz	vs. Lefties	.152	126	.203	127	.280	102	0.00	103	14.58	8	9.38	38
	vs. Righties	.197	127	.247	126	.300	87	0.00	115	12.71	15	13.84	64
Ricky Jordan	vs. Lefties	.309	16	.605	1	.349	42	7.41	2	5.81	100	12.79	68
	vs. Righties	.307	9	.443	18	.313	69	2.60	41	1.03	128	14.36	67
Lance Parrish	vs. Lefties	.252	76	.397	53	.336	54	3.05	39	10.07	42	12.75	67
	vs. Righties	.198	126	.358	67	.274	113	3.75	21	9.73	39	22.49	121
Juan Samuel	vs. Lefties	.244	87	.381	64	.319	74	1.19	85	8.51	63	18.62	116
	vs. Righties	.243	88	.380	57	.290	100	2.17	48	4.63	116	23.34	124
Mike Schmidt	vs. Lefties	.330	5	.516	11	.435	1	3.30	32	13.89	13	3.70	4
	vs. Righties	.224	107	.371	60	.306	80	3.01	28	9.91	36	11.08	38
Milt Thompson	vs. Lefties	.350	--	.400	--	.462	--	0.00	--	14.81	--	7.41	--
	vs. Righties	.285	26	.355	69	.347	36	0.56	104	8.84	49	14.39	68
Mike Young	vs. Lefties	.290	30	.464	23	.364	25	1.45	77	10.39	35	20.78	121
	vs. Righties	.169	--	.234	--	.327	--	0.00	--	18.37	--	27.55	--
Team Average	vs. Lefties	.246	9	.375	5	.310	8	2.34	2	7.86	7	13.97	6
	vs. Righties	.237	12	.348	9	.304	8	1.81	8	8.16	4	17.09	11
League Average	vs. Lefties	.248		.367		.310		2.10		8.01		14.42	
	vs. Righties	.249		.360		.310		1.88		7.86		15.35	

Batting with Runners on Base and Bases Empty

		BA	Rank	SA	Rank	OBA	Rank	HR %	Rank	BB %	Rank	SO %	Rank
Phil Bradley	Runners On	.274	60	.394	56	.346	60	1.44	71	8.61	75	15.57	97
	Bases Empty	.258	48	.391	42	.338	27	2.22	53	8.15	49	16.79	89
Bob Dernier	Runners On	.267	--	.283	--	.290	--	0.00	--	1.54	--	9.23	--
	Bases Empty	.302	9	.368	62	.351	16	0.94	92	7.02	62	11.40	38
Von Hayes	Runners On	.308	19	.455	28	.372	31	1.28	76	9.94	55	10.50	36
	Bases Empty	.246	70	.374	56	.343	21	1.90	64	12.81	5	16.53	87
Chris James	Runners On	.226	111	.362	79	.264	123	3.50	20	4.69	119	12.64	63
	Bases Empty	.256	50	.411	32	.299	76	3.24	29	5.49	88	11.59	42
Steve Jeltz	Runners On	.229	108	.271	121	.326	83	0.00	104	12.32	33	9.36	25
	Bases Empty	.155	127	.211	126	.271	105	0.00	115	13.77	3	15.79	80
Ricky Jordan	Runners On	.311	15	.557	3	.325	85	6.56	3	2.38	126	16.67	104
	Bases Empty	.305	7	.437	20	.323	45	1.99	61	2.58	117	11.61	43
Lance Parrish	Runners On	.255	84	.457	26	.347	58	4.79	7	13.06	27	15.77	98
	Bases Empty	.182	124	.301	106	.246	121	2.54	43	7.03	61	22.66	121
Juan Samuel	Runners On	.279	52	.449	31	.339	68	2.43	42	6.50	105	21.66	122
	Bases Empty	.220	107	.335	90	.270	106	1.57	72	5.15	94	22.30	119
Mike Schmidt	Runners On	.301	25	.486	15	.407	11	2.73	36	14.16	21	7.08	16
	Bases Empty	.203	117	.333	91	.267	111	3.38	27	7.56	54	11.56	41
Milt Thompson	Runners On	.323	8	.391	58	.404	15	0.00	104	12.66	32	11.39	52
	Bases Empty	.269	32	.339	85	.325	42	0.82	96	7.17	58	15.47	74
Mike Young	Runners On	.239	103	.296	114	.378	26	0.00	104	18.89	5	21.11	121
	Bases Empty	.213	--	.387	--	.306	--	1.33	--	10.59	--	28.24	--
Team Average	Runners On	.256	7	.378	5	.324	8	2.04	4	8.59	10	14.59	8
	Bases Empty	.227	12	.339	10	.292	8	1.91	8	7.68	3	17.43	10
League Average	Runners On	.257		.373		.329		1.91		9.45		14.09	
	Bases Empty	.242		.355		.297		1.98		6.73		15.80	

Overall Batting Compared to Late Inning Pressure Situations

		BA	Rank	SA	Rank	OBA	Rank	HR %	Rank	BB %	Rank	SO %	Rank	RDI %	Rank
Phil Bradley	Overall	.264	55	.392	45	.341	38	1.93	60	8.32	57	16.33	94	.232	96
	Pressure	.241	69	.373	49	.347	46	1.20	66	11.11	38	16.16	78	.212	75
Darren Daulton	Overall	.208	--	.271	--	.288	--	0.69	--	10.43	--	15.95	--	.234	--
	Pressure	.265	--	.265	--	.286	--	0.00	--	2.86	--	28.57	--	.308	38
Bob Dernier	Overall	.289	--	.337	--	.330	--	0.60	--	5.03	--	10.61	--	.200	--
	Pressure	.375	--	.375	--	.375	--	0.00	--	0.00	--	8.00	--	.273	51
Greg Gross	Overall	.203	--	.211	--	.291	--	0.00	--	10.60	--	1.99	--	.161	--
	Pressure	.333	9	.356	56	.446	4	0.00	79	16.07	10	3.57	2	.250	--
Von Hayes	Overall	.272	37	.409	37	.355	20	1.63	68	11.58	21	13.95	70	.306	27
	Pressure	.186	112	.305	84	.275	100	1.69	58	11.43	36	14.29	62	.320	36
Chris James	Overall	.242	95	.389	50	.283	113	3.36	24	5.12	110	12.07	46	.206	119
	Pressure	.253	55	.368	52	.330	56	2.11	48	10.38	44	13.21	54	.115	117
Steve Jeltz	Overall	.187	127	.237	127	.295	100	0.00	118	13.11	8	12.89	54	.243	89
	Pressure	.128	126	.170	125	.288	88	0.00	79	16.42	9	13.43	56	.300	41
Ricky Jordan	Overall	.308	2	.491	7	.324	55	4.03	16	2.49	125	13.88	68	.321	13
	Pressure	.333	--	.639	--	.368	--	5.56	--	5.26	--	18.42	--	.200	82
Lance Parrish	Overall	.215	118	.370	67	.293	105	3.54	21	9.83	39	19.46	117	.219	108
	Pressure	.187	111	.227	114	.299	81	0.00	79	13.79	21	18.39	87	.190	87
Juan Samuel	Overall	.243	93	.380	55	.298	98	1.91	61	5.69	106	22.04	121	.278	56
	Pressure	.200	100	.316	77	.238	115	1.05	73	4.95	103	20.79	104	.237	64
Mike Schmidt	Overall	.249	83	.405	38	.337	44	3.08	31	10.86	30	9.31	22	.296	43
	Pressure	.131	125	.197	122	.194	125	1.64	59	7.46	73	10.45	30	.160	97
Milt Thompson	Overall	.288	19	.357	77	.354	21	0.53	106	9.22	42	13.95	70	.337	9
	Pressure	.421	1	.526	10	.500	2	1.75	57	13.43	25	13.43	56	.353	27
Mike Young	Overall	.226	--	.342	--	.343	--	0.68	--	14.86	--	24.57	--	.250	--
	Pressure	.205	98	.318	76	.327	59	0.00	79	13.46	24	25.00	120	.211	76
Team Average	Overall	.239	12	.355	7	.306	10	1.96	6	8.08	5	16.20	10	.244	12
	Pressure	.238	7	.330	8	.318	5	1.15	11	10.02	1	16.33	8	.236	6
League Average	Overall	.248		.363		.310		1.95		7.91		15.06		.256	
	Pressure	.242		.340		.310		1.70		8.47		15.93		.238	

Additional Miscellaneous Batting Comparisons

	Grass Surface BA	Rank	Artificial Surface BA	Rank	Home Games BA	Rank	Road Games BA	Rank	Runners in Scoring Position BA	Rank	Runners in Scoring Pos and Two Outs BA	Rank	Leading Off Inning OBA	Rank	Runners on 3B with less than 2 Outs RDI %	Rank
Phil Bradley	.264	49	.264	55	.268	57	.260	62	.264	62	.254	55	.326	47	.552	74
Darren Daulton	.275	--	.183	124	.217	--	.200	--	.189	--	.211	--	.375	--	.833	--
Bob Dernier	.397	--	.231	90	.208	--	.351	--	.293	--	.227	--	.442	--	.714	--
Greg Gross	.263	--	.193	118	.197	--	.210	--	.069	--	.000	--	.300	--	.625	--
Von Hayes	.385	1	.228	94	.229	100	.313	5	.273	54	.282	41	.386	10	.542	77
Chris James	.250	73	.239	80	.262	64	.220	107	.204	112	.173	107	.275	91	.500	92
Steve Jeltz	.225	107	.172	125	.179	125	.195	126	.265	60	.213	83	.298	77	.737	10
Ron Jones	.174	--	.317	8	.333	--	.224	--	.346	--	.357	--	.241	--	.833	--
Ricky Jordan	.316	--	.305	17	.331	3	.282	29	.333	7	.194	95	.412	3	.524	86
Lance Parrish	.254	63	.199	117	.225	104	.204	119	.222	103	.218	78	.248	113	.565	65
Juan Samuel	.206	118	.256	66	.272	50	.214	111	.301	26	.229	72	.266	96	.677	27
Mike Schmidt	.232	103	.254	67	.290	27	.211	116	.282	38	.245	60	.301	70	.571	61
Milt Thompson	.273	40	.295	25	.295	24	.283	28	.304	21	.393	2	.320	53	.650	35
Mike Young	.265	--	.214	107	.250	--	.211	115	.225	99	.056	127	.367	--	.700	19
Team Average	.254	4	.234	12	.248	9	.232	12	.247	8	.212	11	.300	7	.584	1
League Average	.250		.246		.252		.244		.250		.231		.301		.554	

Pitching vs. Left and Right Handed Batters

		BA	Rank	SA	Rank	OBA	Rank	HR %	Rank	BB %	Rank	SO %	Rank
Steve Bedrosian	vs. Lefties	.292	89	.461	99	.366	88	2.60	93	10.86	76	16.57	36
	vs. Righties	.217	--	.297	--	.259	--	1.45	--	5.44	--	21.77	--
Don Carman	vs. Lefties	.262	62	.407	84	.319	52	3.45	101	8.07	45	12.42	69
	vs. Righties	.272	91	.407	92	.332	88	2.35	74	8.01	77	13.48	75
Marvin Freeman	vs. Lefties	.309	102	.415	87	.445	109	0.81	22	19.87	109	12.18	71
	vs. Righties	.224	--	.303	--	.337	--	1.32	--	12.90	--	19.35	--
Kevin Gross	vs. Lefties	.255	50	.383	69	.349	78	2.04	67	12.08	89	14.54	54
	vs. Righties	.218	32	.325	34	.270	28	2.08	60	4.78	28	18.90	27
Greg Harris	vs. Lefties	.209	13	.302	18	.316	51	1.65	51	12.62	96	14.49	55
	vs. Righties	.210	21	.300	21	.303	65	2.00	56	10.78	99	17.24	43
Mike Maddux	vs. Lefties	.313	104	.472	101	.393	99	2.27	76	10.24	69	13.66	58
	vs. Righties	.232	48	.316	30	.297	59	1.29	30	7.43	72	17.71	40
David Palmer	vs. Lefties	.272	73	.358	53	.337	66	1.57	47	9.41	61	16.03	39
	vs. Righties	.250	69	.371	68	.309	71	1.67	42	7.95	75	14.77	64
Shane Rawley	vs. Lefties	.265	67	.368	59	.299	32	2.21	74	5.30	17	14.57	53
	vs. Righties	.291	102	.464	103	.362	105	3.80	103	9.70	89	9.00	103
Bruce Ruffin	vs. Lefties	.274	75	.339	37	.412	106	0.00	1	17.95	108	14.74	52
	vs. Righties	.275	93	.387	81	.354	102	1.64	41	10.61	97	12.04	84
Kent Tekulve	vs. Lefties	.225	26	.278	11	.298	29	0.66	16	9.36	60	11.11	81
	vs. Righties	.323	106	.445	101	.353	101	1.22	27	3.41	8	13.64	72
Team Average	vs. Lefties	.268	10	.388	11	.359	12	1.92	9	12.35	12	13.47	8
	vs. Righties	.262	11	.390	12	.329	12	2.31	9	8.46	12	13.86	11
League Average	vs. Lefties	.255		.365		.325		1.73		9.36		14.24	
	vs. Righties	.244		.361		.299		2.10		6.87		15.64	

Pitching with Runners on Base and Bases Empty

		BA	Rank	SA	Rank	OBA	Rank	HR %	Rank	BB %	Rank	SO %	Rank
Steve Bedrosian	Runners On	.276	79	.372	55	.345	75	0.69	20	10.30	67	20.00	15
	Bases Empty	.238	49	.395	89	.287	40	3.40	99	6.37	49	17.83	32
Don Carman	Runners On	.271	73	.375	62	.351	79	1.89	60	10.88	79	12.20	77
	Bases Empty	.269	93	.428	102	.315	80	3.01	96	5.85	39	14.11	71
Marvin Freeman	Runners On	.323	108	.414	89	.429	109	0.00	1	14.52	103	15.32	38
	Bases Empty	.230	--	.330	--	.384	--	2.00	--	20.00	--	14.40	--
Kevin Gross	Runners On	.255	56	.350	45	.335	61	1.12	31	9.88	60	15.18	42
	Bases Empty	.227	33	.362	65	.301	66	2.70	86	8.36	84	17.25	35
Greg Harris	Runners On	.193	6	.238	5	.315	40	0.55	13	14.41	102	13.96	53
	Bases Empty	.224	25	.358	59	.304	72	2.99	95	8.93	88	17.86	31
Mike Maddux	Runners On	.289	91	.415	90	.377	102	2.11	70	10.34	69	13.79	54
	Bases Empty	.265	90	.386	88	.325	86	1.59	40	7.77	74	16.99	41
David Palmer	Runners On	.309	105	.411	87	.359	95	2.42	80	8.09	30	17.02	28
	Bases Empty	.226	30	.331	34	.297	56	1.05	21	9.18	93	14.24	68
Shane Rawley	Runners On	.259	65	.425	94	.337	64	3.61	106	10.78	76	11.03	83
	Bases Empty	.307	108	.463	107	.363	107	3.44	100	7.38	66	9.07	102
Bruce Ruffin	Runners On	.291	94	.394	75	.394	105	1.57	50	14.10	98	10.58	87
	Bases Empty	.260	85	.361	63	.344	101	1.01	19	10.78	102	14.67	65
Kent Tekulve	Runners On	.249	52	.325	33	.332	60	0.59	16	10.55	71	9.55	95
	Bases Empty	.308	109	.411	95	.318	82	1.37	32	0.68	2	16.22	51
Team Average	Runners On	.269	10	.383	7	.356	11	1.87	5	11.74	12	12.99	9
	Bases Empty	.261	12	.394	12	.328	12	2.40	11	8.47	12	14.34	10
League Average	Runners On	.257		.373		.329		1.91		9.45		14.09	
	Bases Empty	.242		.355		.297		1.98		6.73		15.80	

Overall Pitching Compared to Late Inning Pressure Situations

		BA	Rank	SA	Rank	OBA	Rank	HR %	Rank	BB %	Rank	SO %	Rank
Steve Bedrosian	Overall	.257	73	.384	82	.317	64	2.05	63	8.39	65	18.94	21
	Pressure	.242	54	.362	67	.309	49	1.93	65	9.13	66	16.52	38
Don Carman	Overall	.270	88	.407	98	.330	88	2.56	88	8.02	58	13.29	72
	Pressure	.283	88	.400	82	.348	83	1.67	55	9.09	63	7.58	104
Kevin Gross	Overall	.239	41	.357	52	.315	62	2.05	63	9.00	76	16.38	36
	Pressure	.189	16	.351	60	.268	27	4.05	104	8.24	47	16.47	40
Greg Harris	Overall	.209	10	.301	12	.309	48	1.83	47	11.66	99	15.92	39
	Pressure	.215	42	.325	49	.317	54	2.45	80	12.50	95	13.02	68
Mike Maddux	Overall	.275	96	.399	96	.349	101	1.81	46	8.95	75	15.53	43
	Pressure	.185	12	.259	13	.254	17	0.00	1	8.33	50	21.67	16
David Palmer	Overall	.261	79	.364	58	.324	76	1.62	40	8.71	70	15.43	45
	Pressure	.351	--	.541	--	.400	--	2.70	--	7.50	--	17.50	--
Shane Rawley	Overall	.286	106	.447	106	.351	103	3.52	104	8.93	74	9.97	98
	Pressure	.270	79	.492	103	.347	80	4.76	106	10.67	86	6.67	107
Bruce Ruffin	Overall	.275	95	.376	72	.368	107	1.27	27	12.38	105	12.69	76
	Pressure	.273	82	.355	61	.413	107	0.91	26	18.18	109	13.29	65
Kent Tekulve	Overall	.276	97	.365	60	.326	78	0.95	12	6.34	23	12.39	80
	Pressure	.285	90	.383	75	.336	76	1.55	49	6.98	35	11.63	76
Team Average	Overall	.265	10	.389	12	.341	12	2.16	9	10.02	12	13.70	10
	Pressure	.253	8	.376	9	.336	10	2.13	11	10.82	12	13.67	12
League Average	Overall	.248		.363		.310		1.95		7.91		15.06	
	Pressure	.243		.347		.315		1.72		9.12		15.69	

Additional Miscellaneous Pitching Comparisons

	Grass Surface		Artificial Surface		Home Games		Road Games		Runners in Scoring Position		Runners in Scoring Pos and Two Outs		Leading Off Inning	
	BA	Rank	BA	Rank	BA	Rank	BA	Rank	BA	Rank	BA	Rank	OBA	Rank
Steve Bedrosian	.200	--	.273	83	.276	90	.236	37	.223	33	.220	60	.277	34
Don Carman	.301	98	.258	66	.240	55	.304	102	.303	94	.265	89	.335	86
Marvin Freeman	.277	--	.276	87	.265	--	.287	97	.348	108	.314	100	.286	49
Kevin Gross	.249	50	.236	41	.218	24	.258	63	.231	42	.239	71	.293	57
Greg Harris	.158	2	.226	29	.215	22	.203	7	.172	8	.172	17	.280	38
Mike Maddux	.362	107	.235	37	.240	54	.311	104	.256	66	.200	39	.344	93
David Palmer	.307	102	.249	60	.228	34	.300	100	.325	103	.180	26	.379	103
Shane Rawley	.234	32	.310	104	.298	107	.276	84	.253	59	.223	61	.359	97
Bruce Ruffin	.275	85	.274	85	.266	78	.285	94	.329	104	.288	98	.384	104
Kent Tekulve	.271	--	.278	88	.287	102	.264	68	.205	25	.228	64	.368	100
Team Average	.275	12	.261	9	.252	10	.278	12	.264	10	.237	7	.344	12
League Average	.250		.246		.244		.252		.250		.231		.301	

PITTSBURGH PIRATES

- ● **From worst to first in four years?**
- ● **Pirates once again shrivel under pressure.**
- ● **Will the real Bobby Bonilla please stand up?**

Three years ago, the Pittsburgh Pirates lost 98 games and compiled the worst record in baseball for the second year in a row. Despite that, history suggested that a rebound might not be too far off. Five other teams of the previous 40 years posted the poorest record in either league for two years running. On average, those teams rebounded to winning records within three years, and—if you can believe this—to a World Series appearance within eight years:

Team	Years With Worst Record	Winning Season	World Series
Phillies	1944–1945	1949	1950
Pirates	1952–1953	1958	1960
Senators/Twins	1957–1959	1962	1965
Mets	1962–1965	1969	1969
Rangers	1972–1973	1974	—
Pirates	1984–1985	1988	—

If that doesn't surprise you, you might as well skip ahead to the Cardinals essay. But if you thought that teams in such dire straits might take a wee bit longer than eight years to earn the privilege of playing ball on wintry nights in late October, we're with you. When we originally presented the table above in the 1987 *Analyst*, we considered it not a guarantee, but simply a "hopeful sign for a franchise badly in need of some good news." Yeah, right!

In the two seasons since then, Syd Thrift, Jim Leyland, Andy Van Slyke, and Bobby Bonilla, among others, have provided more good news for Pirates fans than most of us imagined they'd receive for the rest of the century. (Or about half as much as they'd get watching a half-hour of one of those happy-talk news reports that refuse to go away.) And last season's second-place finish generated an appropriate amount of off-season speculation on whether or not the Pirates, like the Mets of the 1960s, can move from worst to first in four years. This time history tells us that a Pittsburgh pennant is unlikely, but hardly out of the question.

The Pirates have increased their total of wins by at least five for three years in a row. Twenty other teams in modern major league history have done that; only four of them moved up by another five wins or more the next season. But

as the following table shows, those four all made big leaps in that next season:

Years	Team	Wins in Each Season				
1912–16	Brooklyn Dodgers	58	65	75	80	94
1917–21	Pittsburgh Pirates	51	65	71	79	90
1918–22	St. Louis Browns	58	67	76	81	93
1972–76	Philadelphia Phillies	59	71	80	86	101

Notice that the four teams in the preceding table all moved up by more than 10 wins in the fifth season. Normally, we'd consider a continuous streak of substantial improvement to be a negative leading indicator for the upcoming season. No team improves continually, and few manage it even for more than a few seasons in a row. So it's probable that after a run of three seasons, each of which was at least five wins more successful than the last, the Pirates are ready for a fall.

But some examples from the past indicate that such a streak occasionally precedes yet another advance, one even stronger than the previous. And if the Pirates can tack an additional 10 wins onto last season's total of 85, they stand a good chance of taking the N.L. East title away from the Mets.

Once again last season, Pittsburgh's hitters failed miserably in the most crucial and detailed situations we track—Late-Inning Pressure Situations with two outs and runners in scoring position. The Pirates hit .157 in those situations in 1988, two points lower than they hit in 1986, three lower than in 1981. It was the fifth time in the past nine years that Pittsburgh failed to hit .200 under those conditions. In fact, since posting a .304 mark in 1979, the Pirates' best effort in those most crucial at-bats was a .227 batting average in 1985.

Actually, the league average with two outs and runners in scoring position in LIP Situations is quite low—.232 during the 1980s. With two outs, the tying or lead run on base or at bat, and first base often open, every batter is treated as though the name on the back of his uniform shirt reads "Handle with Care." The rate of bases on balls is 91 percent higher with two outs and runners in scoring position in LIPS than it is otherwise. And the caution that pitchers exercise in those situations is translated into lower batting averages.

But even compared to that .232 leaguewide mark, Pittsburgh's performance during the 1980s has been dreadful. Here's how they match up against the rest of the N.L. teams for the years 1981 through 1988. Notice how the batting averages correspond to the won-lost percentages in games in which the teams trailed after six innings. A poor clutch average severely reduces a team's come-from-behind potential:

Team	LIPS with 2 Outs & Men in Scoring Pos.			When Trailing After 6 Innings			
	AB	H	BA	W	L	Pct.	Rank
San Francisco	814	202	.248	93	477	.163	1
Montreal	778	192	.247	73	448	.140	7
Cincinnati	756	186	.246	88	481	.155	2
New York	724	177	.244	73	431	.145	6
Philadelphia	764	185	.242	80	458	.149	4
Houston	743	178	.240	70	438	.138	8
San Diego	846	202	.239	65	457	.125	9
Atlanta	768	178	.232	83	477	.148	5
Los Angeles	721	165	.229	54	410	.116	11
Chicago	761	164	.216	63	485	.115	12
St. Louis	776	161	.207	74	421	.149	3
Pittsburgh	809	156	.193	65	470	.121	10

Oddly, Pittsburgh's come-from-behind record wasn't too bad last year: The Pirates won eight games in which they trailed after six innings. By comparison, they lost only seven games in which they led at that point. But if Pittsburgh's pitchers hadn't held opposing batters to a .204 mark with two outs and runners in scoring position in Late-Inning Pressure Situations, those figures would certainly have been far more damaging.

Bobby Bonilla started the 1988 season with career statistics that, taken at face value, seemed unimpressive: a .279 batting average, 18 home runs, and 120 RBIs in roughly two seasons' worth of games. So it came as something of a surprise that at the end of May, all the talk about Triple Crowns concerned not Winning Colors or Risen Star, but Bonilla.

That's right. On the morning of June 1, Bobby Bonilla led the National League in batting average (.342), home runs (13), and runs batted in (43). Things were never quite the same after that for Bonilla, but he did finish the season with some impressive numbers (.274, 24 HRs, 100 RBIs), raising the question of which Bobby Bonilla would show up in 1989.

In retrospect, those two-year totals were actually pretty strong viewed in the context of a 24–year-old player. They were quite similar to those that some eventual stars compiled at comparable stages of their careers—Steve Garvey (through 1973), Chris Chambliss (1972), Jackie Jensen (1952), and Mickey Vernon (1941) among them. The downside was unspectacular, but still somewhat productive. Bonilla's stats were also like those of Ken Landreaux (through 1979), Milt May (1974), and Jorge Orta (1974), to name a few contemporaries.

But what truly separated Bonilla from most others was his sudden emergence as a power hitter last season. He hit six more home runs in 1988 (24) than he had in his career prior to that point (18). An examination of the careers of other players who had similar breakthrough years indicates that the prognosis for Bonilla's continued excellence is good.

Each of the breakthrough players listed below met the following criteria: (1) exceeded his prior career home-run total in a single season; (2) had hit at least as many home runs prior to the breakthrough season as Bonilla had (18); and (3) had between 800 and 1000 at-bats prior to that season (Bonilla had 892):

Year	Player	HR	Prior Career Totals
1941	Charlie Keller	33	32 HR in 898 AB
1965	Deron Johnson	32	29 HR in 802 AB
1985	Don Mattingly	35	27 HR in 894 AB
1980	Tony Armas	35	26 HR in 886 AB
1962	Tommy Davis	27	26 HR in 813 AB
1924	Joe Hauser	27	25 HR in 905 AB
1977	Gary Carter	31	24 HR in 841 AB
1947	Willard Marshall	36	24 HR in 911 AB
1962	Johnny Callison	23	22 HR in 911 AB
1944	Ron Northey	22	21 HR in 988 AB
1950	Ted Kluszewski	25	20 HR in 920 AB
1977	Sixto Lezcano	21	20 HR in 996 AB
1958	Lee Walls	24	19 HR in 942 AB
1988	Bobby Bonilla	24	18 HR in 892 AB

Among those players, only Hauser and Walls never again displayed the form of their breakthrough seasons. And in Hauser's case, a severe knee injury that forced him to miss the entire 1925 season was to blame. The group as a whole compiled the following average career statistics: a .276 batting average, with 177 home runs and 728 RBI. Those figures will increase as Armas and Carter wind down their careers and Mattingly makes his run at Cooperstown. Which all bodes well for the future of Bobby Bonilla.

WON-LOST RECORD BY STARTING POSITION

PITTSBURGH 85-75	C	1B	2B	3B	SS	LF	CF	RF	P	Leadoff	Relief	Starts
Rafael Belliard	·	·	0-1	·	48-44	·	·	·	·	·	·	48-45
Barry Bonds	·	·	·	·	·	71-58	·	·	·	71-58	·	71-58
Bobby Bonilla	·	·	·	82-75	·	·	·	·	·	·	·	82-75
Sid Bream	·	62-57	·	·	·	·	·	·	·	·	·	62-57
John Cangelosi	·	·	·	·	·	5-3	2-7	1-0	·	6-5	0-1	8-10
Darnell Coles	·	·	·	1-0	·	·	34-20	·	·	·	·	35-20
Orestes Destrade	·	2-4	·	·	·	·	·	·	·	·	·	2-4
Mike Diaz	·	2-3	·	·	·	2-3	·	4-2	·	·	·	8-8
Benny Distefano	·	3-2	·	·	·	·	·	0-1	·	·	·	3-3
Doug Drabek	·	·	·	·	·	·	·	·	18-14	·	0-1	18-14
Mike Dunne	·	·	·	·	·	·	·	·	15-13	·	1-1	15-13
Felix Fermin	·	·	·	·	19-13	·	·	·	·	1-1	·	19-13
Brian Fisher	·	·	·	·	·	·	·	·	9-13	·	5-6	9-13
Miguel Garcia	·	·	·	·	·	·	·	·	·	·	0-1	·
Denny Gonzalez	·	·	4-0	·	0-1	·	·	·	·	·	·	4-1
Jim Gott	·	·	·	·	·	·	·	·	·	·	46-21	·
Tommy Gregg	·	·	·	·	·	1-0	·	1-0	·	1-0	·	2-0
Dave Hostetler	·	1-0	·	·	·	·	·	·	·	·	·	1-0
Barry Jones	·	·	·	·	·	·	·	·	·	·	17-25	·
Bob Kipper	·	·	·	·	·	·	·	·	·	·	15-35	·
Randy Kramer	·	·	·	·	·	·	·	·	0-1	·	1-3	0-1
Dave LaPoint	·	·	·	·	·	·	·	·	5-3	·	·	5-3
Mike LaValliere	58-47	·	·	·	·	·	·	·	·	·	·	58-47
Jose Lind	·	·	77-68	·	·	·	·	·	·	1-1	·	77-68
Morris Madden	·	·	·	·	·	·	·	·	·	·	0-5	·
Scott Medvin	·	·	·	·	·	·	·	·	·	·	5-12	·
Randy Milligan	·	14-9	·	·	·	·	·	·	·	·	·	14-9
Ken Oberkfell	·	1-0	4-6	2-0	·	·	·	·	·	·	·	7-6
Junior Ortiz	18-15	·	·	·	·	·	·	·	·	·	·	18-15
Vicente Palacios	·	·	·	·	·	·	·	·	2-1	·	1-3	2-1
Al Pedrique	·	·	·	·	18-17	·	·	·	·	·	·	18-17
Tom Prince	9-12	·	·	·	·	·	·	·	·	·	·	9-12
Gary Redus	·	·	·	·	·	4-6	·	2-5	·	3-5	·	6-11
Rick Reed	·	·	·	·	·	·	·	·	2-0	·	·	2-0
R.j. Reynolds	·	·	·	·	·	2-5	1-0	29-31	·	2-5	·	32-36
Jeff D. Robinson	·	·	·	·	·	·	·	·	·	·	43-32	·
Ruben Rodriguez	0-1	·	·	·	·	·	·	·	·	·	·	0-1
Dave Rucker	·	·	·	·	·	·	·	·	·	·	6-25	·
John Smiley	·	·	·	·	·	·	·	·	18-14	·	1-1	18-14
Andy Van Slyke	·	·	·	·	·	·	81-67	·	·	·	·	81-67
Bob Walk	·	·	·	·	·	·	·	·	16-16	·	·	16-16
Glenn Wilson	·	·	·	·	·	·	1-1	14-16	·	·	·	15-17

Batting vs. Left and Right Handed Pitchers

		BA	Rank	SA	Rank	OBA	Rank	HR %	Rank	BB %	Rank	SO %	Rank
Rafael Belliard	vs. Lefties	.225	106	.270	117	.303	88	0.00	103	9.09	54	14.14	84
	vs. Righties	.208	121	.228	127	.281	108	0.00	115	7.66	66	14.86	71
Barry Bonds	vs. Lefties	.302	19	.556	5	.383	12	5.56	6	11.48	26	15.30	94
	vs. Righties	.274	37	.463	14	.362	20	3.99	18	11.83	22	12.53	49
Bobby Bonilla	vs. Lefties	.278	44	.420	42	.366	46	2.83	46	11.79	25	8.13	29
	vs. Righties	.272	41	.508	7	.366	18	4.84	9	12.87	14	14.25	66
Sid Bream	vs. Lefties	.190	118	.319	97	.220	127	2.59	49	4.00	117	17.60	106
	vs. Righties	.289	23	.439	22	.362	19	2.02	52	10.58	31	10.58	33
John Cangelosi	vs. Lefties	.267	55	.317	100	.353	36	0.00	103	10.00	43	10.00	44
	vs. Righties	.241	--	.293	--	.353	--	0.00	--	14.49	--	13.04	--
Darnell Coles	vs. Lefties	.260	65	.506	14	.344	44	5.19	8	12.22	21	15.56	96
	vs. Righties	.216	115	.299	108	.272	116	0.75	96	5.96	96	17.88	101
Mike LaValliere	vs. Lefties	.159	125	.190	128	.293	93	0.00	103	13.16	16	18.42	112
	vs. Righties	.284	27	.360	66	.366	17	0.69	100	12.01	21	6.01	7
Jose Lind	vs. Lefties	.248	83	.304	108	.305	84	0.00	103	7.47	70	11.62	63
	vs. Righties	.270	48	.335	87	.310	74	0.50	105	5.62	102	11.01	36
Randy Milligan	vs. Lefties	.196	115	.375	67	.366	22	3.57	25	19.72	2	21.13	122
	vs. Righties	.269	--	.423	--	.406	--	3.85	--	18.75	--	28.13	--
Ken Oberkfell	vs. Lefties	.260	64	.350	80	.288	97	0.00	103	5.26	103	7.89	25
	vs. Righties	.274	37	.354	70	.330	49	0.80	94	7.47	70	6.02	8
Junior Ortiz	vs. Lefties	.324	8	.432	35	.363	27	1.35	79	5.00	106	5.00	7
	vs. Righties	.205	--	.295	--	.294	--	2.27	--	9.62	--	9.62	--
R.J. Reynolds	vs. Lefties	.318	9	.489	16	.362	28	3.41	29	6.38	90	11.70	64
	vs. Righties	.221	110	.311	102	.261	123	1.28	76	5.53	105	20.16	116
Andy Van Slyke	vs. Lefties	.191	117	.319	98	.239	123	1.47	75	6.28	94	23.77	127
	vs. Righties	.339	1	.606	1	.399	7	5.74	4	9.84	38	16.70	91
Glenn Wilson	vs. Lefties	.254	72	.429	36	.277	106	3.17	34	3.03	123	10.61	54
	vs. Righties	.286	--	.333	--	.299	--	0.00	--	1.47	--	16.18	--
Team Average	vs. Lefties	.230	12	.343	11	.300	10	1.83	10	8.75	3	16.25	12
	vs. Righties	.255	3	.383	2	.326	2	2.16	4	9.25	2	15.18	6
League Average	vs. Lefties	.248		.367		.310		2.10		8.01		14.42	
	vs. Righties	.249		.360		.310		1.88		7.86		15.35	

Batting with Runners on Base and Bases Empty

		BA	Rank	SA	Rank	OBA	Rank	HR %	Rank	BB %	Rank	SO %	Rank
Rafael Belliard	Runners On	.244	100	.277	120	.318	91	0.00	104	7.30	95	10.95	44
	Bases Empty	.192	120	.216	125	.266	112	0.00	115	8.70	40	17.39	93
Barry Bonds	Runners On	.255	87	.398	54	.396	19	3.11	26	19.31	3	14.85	84
	Bases Empty	.294	12	.531	4	.354	13	5.04	7	8.01	51	12.62	50
Bobby Bonilla	Runners On	.288	41	.527	8	.406	12	4.62	10	16.92	10	12.00	58
	Bases Empty	.262	42	.435	21	.329	36	3.70	22	8.43	46	12.08	47
Sid Bream	Runners On	.302	24	.454	29	.371	33	2.44	40	10.66	46	10.66	39
	Bases Empty	.233	90	.374	57	.291	86	1.95	63	7.55	55	13.67	54
Darnell Coles	Runners On	.255	84	.362	80	.325	86	1.06	84	9.65	60	15.79	99
	Bases Empty	.214	110	.385	43	.276	100	3.42	25	7.09	60	18.11	96
Mike LaValliere	Runners On	.306	21	.433	36	.419	6	1.49	69	16.67	11	4.17	3
	Bases Empty	.234	89	.266	117	.307	61	0.00	115	9.13	35	11.20	37
Jose Lind	Runners On	.251	92	.313	108	.299	105	0.00	104	6.52	104	10.87	43
	Bases Empty	.269	33	.332	94	.314	52	0.54	109	6.12	76	11.48	40
Ken Oberkfell	Runners On	.289	38	.416	46	.351	55	0.60	96	10.00	52	5.50	6
	Bases Empty	.261	44	.319	100	.304	64	0.65	104	5.17	93	6.99	6
R.J. Reynolds	Runners On	.266	71	.377	66	.304	101	1.30	75	5.95	107	14.29	81
	Bases Empty	.231	95	.343	79	.274	101	2.37	47	5.59	87	21.23	117
Andy Van Slyke	Runners On	.300	26	.538	5	.349	56	3.61	18	8.78	71	18.18	109
	Bases Empty	.277	27	.477	12	.341	24	4.84	8	8.50	43	19.94	109
Team Average	Runners On	.253	10	.378	6	.335	3	1.79	9	10.82	2	14.61	9
	Bases Empty	.242	5	.363	5	.304	2	2.22	3	7.73	2	16.27	8
League Average	Runners On	.257		.373		.329		1.91		9.45		14.09	
	Bases Empty	.242		.355		.297		1.98		6.73		15.80	

Overall Batting Compared to Late Inning Pressure Situations

		BA	Rank	SA	Rank	OBA	Rank	HR %	Rank	BB %	Rank	SO %	Rank	RDI %	Rank
Rafael Belliard	Overall	.213	120	.241	126	.288	110	0.00	118	8.10	60	14.64	79	.143	129
	Pressure	.214	--	.286	--	.290	--	0.00	--	9.38	--	15.63	--	.000	--
Barry Bonds	Overall	.283	24	.491	8	.368	11	4.46	10	11.73	19	13.36	59	.261	71
	Pressure	.224	84	.294	93	.298	82	2.35	42	9.57	48	14.89	69	.130	116
Bobby Bonilla	Overall	.274	34	.476	12	.366	13	4.11	13	12.48	13	12.04	45	.311	21
	Pressure	.267	48	.378	48	.371	27	3.33	22	12.38	27	11.43	42	.455	4
Sid Bream	Overall	.264	53	.409	36	.328	49	2.16	48	9.00	45	12.26	50	.297	42
	Pressure	.314	22	.514	11	.378	19	2.86	33	10.59	43	9.41	24	.318	37
John Cangelosi	Overall	.254	--	.305	--	.353	--	0.00	--	12.23	--	11.51	--	.308	--
	Pressure	.216	89	.243	109	.370	28	0.00	79	16.67	6	18.75	89	.000	--
Darnell Coles	Overall	.232	108	.374	62	.299	96	2.37	44	8.30	58	17.01	100	.315	17
	Pressure	.207	--	.379	--	.303	--	3.45	--	12.12	--	15.15	--	.182	88
Mike Diaz	Overall	.230	--	.270	--	.367	--	0.00	--	17.78	--	14.44	--	.192	--
	Pressure	.136	--	.136	--	.240	--	0.00	--	12.00	--	28.00	--	.100	120
Mike LaValliere	Overall	.261	60	.330	102	.353	23	0.57	104	12.22	15	8.31	13	.368	4
	Pressure	.278	37	.352	59	.322	61	0.00	79	6.67	85	8.33	19	.381	12
Jose Lind	Overall	.262	59	.324	108	.308	83	0.33	115	6.29	95	11.23	41	.237	93
	Pressure	.242	68	.308	81	.278	98	1.10	69	4.85	106	12.62	49	.160	97
Ken Oberkfell	Overall	.271	39	.353	82	.321	60	0.63	102	6.99	82	6.43	4	.281	51
	Pressure	.238	73	.298	90	.301	79	0.00	79	7.14	77	7.14	12	.308	38
R.J. Reynolds	Overall	.248	89	.359	75	.288	109	1.86	63	5.76	105	17.87	106	.367	5
	Pressure	.244	65	.341	62	.300	80	2.44	39	7.78	69	15.56	73	.267	53
Andy Van Slyke	Overall	.288	21	.506	4	.345	33	4.26	11	8.64	49	19.09	114	.297	41
	Pressure	.253	55	.453	19	.308	72	3.16	28	7.69	70	29.81	127	.207	81
Team Average	Overall	.247	8	.369	4	.317	3	2.04	4	9.08	1	15.55	8	.266	2
	Pressure	.237	9	.336	7	.309	8	1.72	6	9.05	4	17.61	10	.220	10
League Average	Overall	.248		.363		.310		1.95		7.91		15.06		.256	
	Pressure	.242		.340		.310		1.70		8.47		15.93		.238	

Additional Miscellaneous Batting Comparisons

	Grass Surface BA	Rank	Artificial Surface BA	Rank	Home Games BA	Rank	Road Games BA	Rank	Runners in Scoring Position BA	Rank	Runners in Scoring Pos and Two Outs BA	Rank	Leading Off Inning OBA	Rank	Runners on 3B with less than 2 Outs RDI %	Rank
Rafael Belliard	.229	105	.205	114	.213	110	.213	114	.274	52	.172	108	.211	124	.455	112
Barry Bonds	.237	95	.298	22	.285	31	.280	30	.266	58	.231	70	.360	21	.533	81
Bobby Bonilla	.322	6	.257	64	.217	109	.329	2	.284	35	.291	32	.299	74	.522	87
Sid Bream	.274	39	.261	58	.235	96	.292	15	.289	33	.191	97	.245	115	.750	6
John Cangelosi	.231	--	.261	58	.246	--	.263	--	.318	--	.300	--	.222	122	.500	--
Darnell Coles	.253	--	.221	103	.184	122	.274	35	.277	47	.242	61	.319	55	.545	76
Mike LaValliere	.247	78	.266	53	.258	73	.264	54	.333	7	.375	5	.303	67	.667	28
Jose Lind	.221	109	.275	42	.300	19	.221	105	.243	82	.209	87	.260	102	.484	107
Ken Oberkfell	.284	28	.243	75	.290	28	.254	68	.264	63	.257	53	.268	95	.556	71
Junior Ortiz	.273	--	.282	35	.373	--	.186	--	.242	--	.125	--	.207	--	.727	12
Al Pedrique	.280	--	.155	127	.155	--	.200	--	.091	--	.000	--	.286	--	1.000	--
R.J. Reynolds	.300	--	.230	93	.213	112	.289	20	.283	37	.265	50	.239	117	.864	1
Andy Van Slyke	.356	2	.262	56	.293	25	.283	27	.232	93	.190	98	.331	42	.588	55
Glenn Wilson	.231	--	.274	43	.259	--	.278	--	.229	--	.200	--	.257	--	.500	92
Team Average	.260	2	.242	10	.241	11	.252	2	.248	7	.204	12	.284	12	.578	3
League Average	.250		.246		.252		.244		.250		.231		.301		.554	

Pitching vs. Left and Right Handed Batters

		BA	Rank	SA	Rank	OBA	Rank	HR %	Rank	BB %	Rank	SO %	Rank
Doug Drabek	vs. Lefties	.237	35	.325	30	.290	22	1.60	50	6.83	27	12.44	68
	vs. Righties	.240	55	.400	89	.283	44	3.43	98	4.68	26	16.17	46
Mike Dunne	vs. Lefties	.262	63	.355	49	.371	93	0.93	24	14.54	102	4.85	109
	vs. Righties	.247	66	.389	82	.317	77	3.80	103	8.61	80	14.17	68
Brian Fisher	vs. Lefties	.326	107	.502	107	.400	101	2.46	85	11.31	82	9.79	89
	vs. Righties	.227	41	.348	55	.287	48	2.13	64	6.29	46	10.69	90
Jim Gott	vs. Lefties	.220	24	.394	77	.293	25	4.55	107	8.78	53	22.97	10
	vs. Righties	.264	85	.378	73	.306	68	2.03	57	5.42	36	25.30	5
Barry Jones	vs. Lefties	.284	82	.346	41	.375	95	1.23	36	13.27	99	8.16	97
	vs. Righties	.266	--	.367	--	.309	--	1.56	--	5.59	--	16.08	--
Bob Kipper	vs. Lefties	.244	41	.326	31	.301	36	2.33	77	7.45	34	14.89	48
	vs. Righties	.228	43	.379	75	.320	79	3.45	99	10.98	100	14.45	66
Dave LaPoint	vs. Lefties	.321	--	.571	--	.387	--	7.14	--	9.38	--	9.38	--
	vs. Righties	.263	84	.368	66	.291	51	1.17	25	3.83	18	8.74	105
Jeff D. Robinson	vs. Lefties	.247	43	.328	32	.277	17	1.28	38	4.00	6	15.20	46
	vs. Righties	.241	57	.342	48	.328	85	1.32	31	11.03	101	18.63	30
John Smiley	vs. Lefties	.159	3	.243	5	.252	9	1.87	63	10.16	68	18.75	26
	vs. Righties	.255	76	.373	70	.290	50	1.97	53	4.67	25	14.85	63
Bob Walk	vs. Lefties	.255	51	.360	56	.322	56	0.48	12	8.90	56	9.32	93
	vs. Righties	.202	11	.285	13	.250	11	1.06	21	5.62	40	9.05	102
Team Average	vs. Lefties	.258	7	.371	6	.331	8	1.69	5	9.72	9	11.56	12
	vs. Righties	.245	6	.368	7	.297	6	2.23	7	6.34	4	14.23	9
League Average	vs. Lefties	.255		.365		.325		1.73		9.36		14.24	
	vs. Righties	.244		.361		.299		2.10		6.87		15.64	

Pitching with Runners on Base and Bases Empty

		BA	Rank	SA	Rank	OBA	Rank	HR %	Rank	BB %	Rank	SO %	Rank
Doug Drabek	Runners On	.244	47	.370	53	.289	15	2.64	89	4.76	2	12.20	76
	Bases Empty	.236	46	.363	68	.285	39	2.55	79	6.25	45	15.81	55
Mike Dunne	Runners On	.271	74	.371	54	.358	88	1.79	57	11.44	84	8.80	101
	Bases Empty	.242	54	.372	73	.336	94	2.78	90	11.92	104	9.73	98
Brian Fisher	Runners On	.270	69	.436	97	.359	94	2.49	84	11.22	82	12.24	75
	Bases Empty	.282	99	.417	97	.333	91	2.15	67	6.84	55	8.55	106
Jim Gott	Runners On	.296	99	.400	82	.354	83	0.87	26	8.76	40	22.63	5
	Bases Empty	.206	14	.376	76	.260	15	4.85	108	5.65	35	25.42	5
Barry Jones	Runners On	.275	77	.373	56	.345	74	1.96	61	9.60	56	15.20	41
	Bases Empty	.271	--	.346	--	.328	--	0.93	--	7.76	--	10.34	--
Bob Kipper	Runners On	.272	--	.391	--	.333	--	3.26	--	9.09	--	12.73	--
	Bases Empty	.209	17	.338	38	.299	59	2.88	94	10.19	97	15.92	52
Jeff D. Robinson	Runners On	.269	68	.373	58	.344	73	1.55	47	10.62	73	15.93	35
	Bases Empty	.226	27	.307	21	.272	24	1.11	23	5.23	27	17.77	33
John Smiley	Runners On	.276	80	.404	85	.312	35	2.02	63	5.37	4	12.84	69
	Bases Empty	.219	23	.323	27	.266	18	1.91	53	5.60	33	17.20	36
Bob Walk	Runners On	.222	25	.318	26	.290	16	0.93	27	8.78	42	8.51	103
	Bases Empty	.236	45	.329	33	.287	41	0.64	11	6.34	48	9.70	100
Team Average	Runners On	.264	8	.388	8	.330	8	1.98	8	8.81	4	12.14	11
	Bases Empty	.241	7	.357	6	.297	8	2.02	8	6.99	9	13.83	11
League Average	Runners On	.257		.373		.329		1.91		9.45		14.09	
	Bases Empty	.242		.355		.297		1.98		6.73		15.80	

Overall Pitching Compared to Late Inning Pressure Situations

		BA	Rank	SA	Rank	OBA	Rank	HR %	Rank	BB %	Rank	SO %	Rank
Doug Drabek	Overall	.239	42	.366	62	.286	25	2.59	92	5.68	11	14.43	62
	Pressure	.257	64	.378	71	.321	59	2.70	88	8.43	54	15.66	45
Mike Dunne	Overall	.255	68	.372	65	.345	98	2.34	82	11.70	101	9.31	102
	Pressure	.256	63	.385	76	.412	106	2.56	83	21.57	110	9.80	91
Brian Fisher	Overall	.277	98	.425	102	.345	97	2.29	79	8.84	73	10.23	94
	Pressure	.200	23	.275	20	.298	42	0.00	1	12.50	95	14.58	55
Jim Gott	Overall	.243	48	.386	86	.300	39	3.21	102	7.01	38	24.20	7
	Pressure	.265	71	.403	84	.329	70	3.06	93	8.41	53	24.34	8
Barry Jones	Overall	.273	--	.359	--	.336	--	1.44	--	8.71	--	12.86	--
	Pressure	.305	98	.410	87	.364	90	1.90	63	8.87	58	14.52	56
Bob Kipper	Overall	.234	35	.359	54	.313	59	3.03	101	9.74	86	14.61	59
	Pressure	.221	44	.284	26	.345	78	1.05	37	13.91	104	19.13	24
Jeff D. Robinson	Overall	.244	53	.335	32	.303	42	1.30	28	7.60	49	16.96	31
	Pressure	.233	50	.300	35	.304	44	1.00	31	8.63	55	18.15	30
John Smiley	Overall	.241	46	.355	48	.284	21	1.96	54	5.51	8	15.45	44
	Pressure	.212	35	.318	46	.227	6	2.35	76	2.20	1	7.69	103
Bob Walk	Overall	.230	30	.325	23	.288	28	0.75	6	7.38	44	9.19	105
	Pressure	.213	38	.300	35	.284	35	1.25	43	7.78	42	7.78	102
Team Average	Overall	.250	8	.369	8	.311	8	2.00	6	7.78	6	13.10	11
	Pressure	.239	6	.338	5	.314	6	1.68	5	9.40	8	16.33	5
League Average	Overall	.248		.363		.310		1.95		7.91		15.06	
	Pressure	.243		.347		.315		1.72		9.12		15.69	

Additional Miscellaneous Pitching Comparisons

	Grass Surface		Artificial Surface		Home Games		Road Games		Runners in Scoring Position		Runners in Scoring Pos and Two Outs		Leading Off Inning	
	BA	Rank	BA	Rank	BA	Rank	BA	Rank	BA	Rank	BA	Rank	OBA	Rank
Doug Drabek	.248	48	.235	38	.247	62	.231	34	.226	38	.164	13	.317	72
Mike Dunne	.289	93	.244	52	.237	49	.281	88	.251	58	.236	69	.305	63
Brian Fisher	.314	103	.270	80	.273	83	.283	90	.247	55	.195	35	.322	77
Jim Gott	.343	--	.211	17	.181	9	.303	101	.244	51	.211	49	.281	39
Barry Jones	.235	--	.291	99	.337	--	.210	--	.250	57	.207	--	.302	--
Bob Kipper	.406	--	.168	1	.164	5	.312	105	.273	--	.240	--	.309	67
Dave LaPoint	.000	--	.271	81	.230	38	.338	--	.224	--	.238	--	.340	--
Jeff D. Robinson	.257	61	.240	49	.270	81	.220	19	.256	65	.216	53	.211	1
Dave Rucker	.478	--	.292	100	.286	--	.429	--	.340	--	.286	--	.440	--
John Smiley	.226	23	.247	58	.239	52	.243	47	.280	87	.253	82	.282	44
Bob Walk	.212	17	.236	42	.237	47	.223	25	.199	23	.188	30	.271	24
Team Average	.271	11	.243	5	.244	7	.257	8	.249	7	.217	4	.295	6
League Average	.250		.246		.244		.252		.250		.231		.301	

ST. LOUIS CARDINALS

- **Whitey's auto shop needs to fix the choke and the clutch.**
- **Late-game losses in '88 could mean a surprise rebound in '89.**

Remember those puzzles in children's books in which you had to identify the item that didn't fit: a rolling landscape with farm land, barns, silos, and an elephant perched in a tree? Or similar questions on IQ tests: Which of the following doesn't belong? (*a*) mouse, (*b*) canary, (*c*) squirrel, (*d*) giraffe. Well, we're going to turn the tables on you. In the standings listed below, despite appearances, *nothing is wrong.* You tell us what set of circumstances makes them correct.

Team	W	L	Pct.	GB
New York	76	57	.571	—
St. Louis	74	64	.536	4.5
Pittsburgh	70	64	.522	6
Chicago	68	73	.482	12
Montreal	61	75	.449	16.5
Philadelphia	57	88	.393	25

Take your time. We're not going to rush you.

The solution: Had every game last season ended after the sixth inning, those would have been the final N.L. East standings, with St. Louis in striking distance, within five games of the Mets. So the next time you hear someone claim that the final few innings aren't all that important because *x* percent of all games are decided in the first *y* innings, tell him to make sure Whitey Herzog ain't hangin' around.

Last season's Cardinals finished 10 games below the .500 mark despite playing 10 games above that level through the first six innings of each game. That net loss of 20 games from the seventh inning on was the largest in either league. Can't tell you the last team to blow so many games after the sixth. Can tell you no team's lost that many over the seven years we checked from 1982 through last year.

We can also tell you that St. Louis won only seven of the 24 games in which it was tied after six innings, for the lowest percentage in the N.L. (.292). And that the Cards posted the same 7–17 mark in extra-inning games. And that they lost 10 games in which they led after the seventh, a league high. And

while it might seem reasonable, based on those numbers, to conclude that St. Louis's bullpen cost the team a shot at the division title, the fact is that it was poor clutch hitting that was really to blame.

St. Louis ranked last in the N.L. in 1988 with a .232 batting average in Late-Inning Pressure Situations, 17 points lower than its overall mark for the season. The team also ranked next-to-last in the N.L. with a .207 mark in extra innings:

Team	AB	H	BA	Team	AB	H	BA
Pittsburgh	126	38	.302	Los Angeles	117	28	.239
Montreal	213	63	.296	New York	156	39	.224
Cincinnati	148	41	.277	Houston	203	45	.222
Philadelphia	97	26	.268	San Diego	120	26	.217
Atlanta	197	51	.259	St. Louis	184	38	.207
Chicago	137	33	.241	San Francisco	148	27	.182

That poor performance under pressure alerted us to another general rule of clutch hitting: Contact-hitting teams are not as effective in Late-Inning Pressure Situations as are power-hitting teams.

Over the past 14 years, the team with the lowest strikeout percentage in the National League has hit lower in LIP Situations than in unpressured at-bats 10 times. The A.L. team with the lowest strikeout rate has underachieved in the clutch nine times in those 14 years. During that same period, the 28 leaders in home run percentage (one in each league for 14 years) were split: half had higher batting averages in the clutch, half had worse. Taken as a group, the home run leaders hit two points worse under pressure than they did in unpressured at-bats, which is the league standard:

Category	Better in LIPS	Worse in LIPS	Average Change in LIP Situations
Lowest strikeout rate	9	19	7 points worse
Highest home run rate	14	14	2 points worse

In last year's *Analyst,* we demonstrated that teams with imbalanced hitting (that is, much better against left-handers than right-handers, or vice versa) had an edge in Late-Inning Pressure Situations over teams with balance. This season, we've added another general rule in an ongoing attempt to develop a clearer picture of what it takes to seize control of close games.

St. Louis's dismal late-game performance actually has a silver lining for the 1989 season. Among teams with losing records, the ones most likely to improve the next season are those that often lost games in the later innings after holding early leads. Conversely, poor teams who were consistently behind early have little hope for a dramatic rebound; in fact, they are unlikely to improve by the five game bounce that losing teams average the next year.

Before we illustrate that trend, take a look at the teams with the best and worst records in the majors last year after the first, third, and sixth innings (according to games above or below .500):

Best After 1st		Best After 3d		Best After 6th	
Los Angeles	45–22	Boston	75–54	Oakland	86–56
Boston	53–33	N.Y. Mets	63–44	San Diego	78–55
N.Y. Yankees	52–37	San Francisco	72–54	Boston	85–62

Worst After 1st		Worst After 3d		Worst After 6th	
Atlanta	29–45	Atlanta	42–85	Baltimore	50–91
Seattle	29–45	Philadelphia	46–69	Atlanta	51–86
Montreal	31–43	Montreal	50–61	Philadelphia	57–88

We've already noted St. Louis's fine record through six innings. But that mark (74–64) pales by comparison to San Diego's 78–55 record, the best in the National League. And now we'll tell you why those records portend good things for both teams in 1989.

From 1982 through 1987, 76 teams compiled losing records. Those teams can be divided according to the part of the game in which they fared worst: first three innings, middle three innings, or after. For instance, last season the Cardinals suffered their worst decline in the late innings. The following table shows their records had the games ended at the end of each group of three innings (which we'll call the "truncated W–L record"), where the Cards stood in relation to the .500 mark through that point, and the team's net gain or loss relative to .500 during each three-inning group:

	After 3 Innings	After 6 Innings	End of Game
Truncated W–L Record	55–58	74–64	76–86
Cumulative +/– .500	–3	+10	–10
Net Gain or Loss	–3	+13	–20

By referring to the bottom line, it's clear that St. Louis was done in by its late-game failures. The Cardinals stood 10 games above .500 when their games were truncated after the sixth inning, 10 games below when we extended those games to their conclusions, for a net loss of 20 games during the late innings.

Each losing team of the past seven seasons was classified similarly, according to which of the three groups was the most costly. And as the following table shows, teams that faded over the last three innings were most likely to improve a year later, and rebounded most strongly of all three groups:

	No. of Teams	Next Season		
		Up	Down	Avg. Gain/Loss
First 3 innings	32	19	11	+2.5 games
Middle 3 innings	20	11	8	+3.7 games
Last 3/extra innings	24	18	5	+7.0 games

Among last season's losing teams, that tendency bodes well not only for the Cardinals, but also for the White Sox. Chicago played only two games below the .500 mark through the first six innings, but finished the season with 90 losses nonetheless. Here's a look at where 1988's losers went awry. The column headed "Diff." indicates the net gain or loss relative to .500 during that particular group of innings:

Team	After 3 Innings		After 6 Innings		End of Game	
	W–L	Diff.	W–L	Diff.	W–L	Diff.
Baltimore Orioles	59–68	–9	50–91	–32	54–107	–12
California Angels	61–64	–3	61–76	–12	75–87	3
Chicago White Sox	59–64	–5	69–71	3	71–90	–17
Cleveland Indians	56–61	–5	71–72	4	78–84	–5
Seattle Mariners	58–66	–8	65–78	–5	68–93	–12
Texas Rangers	64–61	3	66–81	–18	70–91	–6
Atlanta Braves	42–85	–43	51–86	8	54–106	–17
Chicago Cubs	66–57	9	68–73	–14	77–85	–3
Philadelphia Phillies	46–69	–23	57–88	–8	65–96	0
St. Louis Cardinals	55–58	–3	74–64	13	76–86	–20

Conversely, the Braves and Phillies, who gave their fans little reason to stay for the seventh-inning stretch last season, can be considered unlikely candidates for a strong turnaround in 1989.

WON-LOST RECORD BY STARTING POSITION

ST. LOUIS 76-86	C	1B	2B	3B	SS	LF	CF	RF	P	Leadoff	Relief	Starts
Gibson Alba	·	·	·	·	·	·	·	·	·	·	0-3	·
Luis Alicea	·	·	38-39	·	·	·	·	·	·	·	·	38-39
Scott Arnold	·	·	·	·	·	·	·	·	·	·	1-5	·
Rod Booker	·	·	·	3-3	·	·	·	·	·	·	·	3-3
Tom Brunansky	·	·	·	·	·	·	·	70-73	·	·	·	70-73
Cris Carpenter	·	·	·	·	·	·	·	·	3-5	·	·	3-5
Vince Coleman	·	·	·	·	·	56-69	14-10	·	·	70-79	·	70-79
John Costello	·	·	·	·	·	·	·	·	·	·	12-24	·
Danny Cox	·	·	·	·	·	·	·	4-9	·	·	·	4-9
Ken Dayley	·	·	·	·	·	·	·	·	·	·	26-28	·
Jose DeLeon	·	·	·	·	·	·	·	·	20-14	·	·	20-14
Mike P. Fitzgerald	·	3-9	·	·	·	·	·	·	·	·	·	3-9
Curt Ford	·	1-1	·	·	·	5-5	0-1	1-4	·	·	·	7-11
Bob Forsch	·	·	·	·	·	·	·	·	5-7	·	7-11	5-7
Pedro Guerrero	·	22-13	·	·	·	2-5	·	·	·	·	·	24-18
Tom Herr	·	·	4-11	·	·	·	·	·	·	·	·	4-11
Ken Hill	·	·	·	·	·	·	·	·	0-1	·	0-3	0-1
Bob Horner	·	30-27	·	·	·	·	·	·	·	·	·	30-27
Tim Jones	·	·	0-5	·	1-1	·	·	·	·	·	·	1-6
Mike Laga	·	9-15	·	·	·	·	·	·	·	·	·	9-15
Steve Lake	5-5	·	·	·	·	·	·	·	·	·	·	5-5
Tom Lawless	·	·	0-1	4-7	·	2-1	·	·	·	·	·	6-9
Jim Lindeman	·	0-1	·	·	·	2-1	·	2-6	·	·	·	4-8
Joe Magrane	·	·	·	·	·	·	·	·	8-16	·	·	8-16
Greg Mathews	·	·	·	·	·	·	·	·	6-7	·	·	6-7
Willie McGee	·	·	·	·	·	·	60-75	·	·	4-5	·	60-75
Larry McWilliams	·	·	·	·	·	·	·	·	6-11	·	6-19	6-11
John Morris	·	·	·	·	·	1-3	·	1-0	·	·	·	2-3
Randy O'Neal	·	·	·	·	·	·	·	·	5-3	·	0-2	5-3
Jose Oquendo	·	0-2	34-30	18-22	2-8	1-0	2-0	1-3	·	·	0-1	58-65
Tom Pagnozzi	7-12	11-15	·	1-1	·	·	·	·	·	·	·	19-28
Tony Pena	64-69	0-2	·	·	·	·	·	·	·	·	·	64-71
Terry Pendleton	·	·	·	49-50	·	·	·	·	·	·	·	49-50
Steve Peters	·	·	·	·	·	·	·	·	·	·	13-31	·
Dan Quisenberry	·	·	·	·	·	·	·	·	·	·	10-23	·
Ozzie Smith	·	·	·	·	73-77	·	·	·	·	2-2	·	73-77
Scott Terry	·	·	·	·	·	·	·	7-4	·	·	12-28	7-4
John Tudor	·	·	·	·	·	·	·	·	12-9	·	·	12-9
Duane Walker	·	·	·	·	·	·	·	·	·	·	·	·
Denny Walling	·	0-1	·	1-3	·	7-2	·	1-0	·	·	·	9-6
Todd Worrell	·	·	·	·	·	·	·	·	·	·	42-26	·

Batting vs. Left and Right Handed Pitchers

		BA	Rank	SA	Rank	OBA	Rank	HR %	Rank	BB %	Rank	SO %	Rank
Luis Alicea	vs. Lefties	.130	128	.152	129	.190	129	0.00	103	4.95	107	10.89	55
	vs. Righties	.249	80	.341	82	.314	66	0.49	106	8.73	51	9.17	21
Tom Brunansky	vs. Lefties	.281	38	.421	39	.376	16	2.34	56	13.79	14	8.87	35
	vs. Righties	.227	104	.432	25	.329	50	5.11	7	12.44	16	15.61	82
Vince Coleman	vs. Lefties	.273	48	.395	55	.324	67	0.91	95	6.97	78	18.03	109
	vs. Righties	.253	74	.308	104	.307	76	0.25	114	7.36	72	15.40	80
Curt Ford	vs. Lefties	.000	--	.000	--	.000	--	0.00	--	0.00	--	42.86	--
	vs. Righties	.205	124	.279	119	.250	126	0.82	93	6.06	94	17.42	99
Pedro Guerrero	vs. Lefties	.280	39	.392	60	.385	10	2.40	52	14.86	6	12.84	70
	vs. Righties	.289	24	.431	27	.358	26	2.93	31	8.76	50	14.60	70
Bob Horner	vs. Lefties	.309	15	.485	18	.402	5	2.94	43	14.63	7	9.76	41
	vs. Righties	.232	99	.290	114	.321	57	0.72	98	12.12	19	9.09	20
Willie McGee	vs. Lefties	.294	23	.355	78	.322	68	0.00	103	3.88	119	16.50	101
	vs. Righties	.290	20	.381	54	.333	42	0.82	92	6.09	92	12.69	53
Jose Oquendo	vs. Lefties	.299	21	.461	25	.343	47	4.55	11	7.06	73	4.71	5
	vs. Righties	.266	52	.293	111	.353	30	0.00	115	11.49	24	9.20	22
Tom Pagnozzi	vs. Lefties	.278	45	.315	101	.322	69	0.00	103	6.09	96	15.65	97
	vs. Righties	.287	--	.345	--	.315	--	0.00	--	4.26	--	14.89	--
Tony Pena	vs. Lefties	.331	4	.512	13	.380	14	3.01	42	7.26	72	7.82	23
	vs. Righties	.230	101	.304	106	.272	115	1.47	66	5.45	109	12.53	50
Terry Pendleton	vs. Lefties	.328	6	.429	36	.349	41	0.84	96	3.15	122	4.72	6
	vs. Righties	.221	112	.331	91	.268	120	1.84	56	5.78	99	15.31	78
Ozzie Smith	vs. Lefties	.259	66	.343	85	.355	33	1.00	93	12.50	18	5.83	9
	vs. Righties	.275	35	.332	90	.348	34	0.27	113	10.26	33	6.76	10
Denny Walling	vs. Lefties	.214	--	.286	--	.313	--	0.00	--	11.76	--	23.53	--
	vs. Righties	.241	90	.327	95	.289	101	0.45	108	6.38	88	8.94	18
Team Average	vs. Lefties	.269	1	.371	6	.328	1	1.47	12	7.93	6	12.61	1
	vs. Righties	.239	11	.320	12	.300	12	1.20	12	7.79	6	13.78	1
League Average	vs. Lefties	.248		.367		.310		2.10		8.01		14.42	
	vs. Righties	.249		.360		.310		1.88		7.86		15.35	

Batting with Runners on Base and Bases Empty

		BA	Rank	SA	Rank	OBA	Rank	HR %	Rank	BB %	Rank	SO %	Rank
Luis Alicea	Runners On	.178	126	.211	126	.257	124	0.00	104	8.57	76	11.43	53
	Bases Empty	.248	65	.359	66	.297	78	0.69	101	6.45	72	7.74	10
Tom Brunansky	Runners On	.226	109	.362	78	.358	46	2.88	31	16.50	13	14.19	79
	Bases Empty	.261	45	.486	10	.332	31	5.36	4	9.35	29	12.58	49
Vince Coleman	Runners On	.264	73	.368	74	.312	96	0.55	98	7.14	97	12.38	61
	Bases Empty	.258	47	.327	96	.313	54	0.46	112	7.25	57	18.12	98
Pedro Guerrero	Runners On	.327	6	.463	23	.411	9	2.47	39	12.69	31	13.71	72
	Bases Empty	.252	54	.381	49	.329	35	2.97	34	9.33	30	14.22	62
Bob Horner	Runners On	.248	96	.287	119	.354	50	0.00	104	15.38	18	9.23	24
	Bases Empty	.267	37	.419	27	.342	23	2.86	38	10.26	19	9.40	20
Willie McGee	Runners On	.289	38	.373	70	.326	84	0.40	102	5.58	111	16.36	103
	Bases Empty	.294	13	.371	60	.332	30	0.64	105	5.14	96	12.08	48
Jose Oquendo	Runners On	.279	53	.374	69	.340	67	2.11	53	8.48	78	9.38	26
	Bases Empty	.276	29	.333	91	.357	11	1.15	85	11.22	14	6.46	3
Tom Pagnozzi	Runners On	.267	67	.291	118	.297	110	0.00	104	4.30	121	15.05	89
	Bases Empty	.294	14	.358	68	.336	28	0.00	115	6.03	79	15.52	75
Tony Pena	Runners On	.265	72	.359	82	.317	92	1.79	62	7.63	85	6.83	15
	Bases Empty	.262	41	.383	45	.300	75	2.13	56	4.71	102	14.48	65
Terry Pendleton	Runners On	.259	77	.341	94	.300	104	0.54	99	4.90	114	13.24	68
	Bases Empty	.248	69	.379	53	.286	91	2.43	46	5.07	97	11.06	35
Ozzie Smith	Runners On	.314	13	.405	53	.406	14	0.95	87	13.91	24	4.51	4
	Bases Empty	.244	76	.296	111	.315	49	0.27	114	9.18	34	7.69	8
Denny Walling	Runners On	.253	88	.337	100	.330	77	0.00	104	10.28	50	10.28	35
	Bases Empty	.230	97	.317	101	.262	115	0.72	98	4.14	109	9.66	23
Team Average	Runners On	.252	12	.331	12	.322	11	0.99	12	9.08	8	13.07	3
	Bases Empty	.247	3	.341	7	.300	6	1.50	12	6.85	6	13.64	1
League Average	Runners On	.257		.373		.329		1.91		9.45		14.09	
	Bases Empty	.242		.355		.297		1.98		6.73		15.80	

Overall Batting Compared to Late Inning Pressure Situations

		BA	Rank	SA	Rank	OBA	Rank	HR %	Rank	BB %	Rank	SO %	Rank	RDI %	Rank
Luis Alicea	Overall	.212	121	.283	120	.276	116	0.34	114	7.58	70	9.70	27	.227	102
	Pressure	.190	104	.222	116	.271	103	0.00	79	8.45	61	8.45	20	.136	112
Tom Brunansky	Overall	.245	91	.428	22	.345	34	4.21	12	12.89	11	13.38	60	.258	77
	Pressure	.250	57	.452	20	.354	41	4.76	13	14.00	20	14.00	61	.208	79
Vince Coleman	Overall	.260	62	.339	95	.313	78	0.49	109	7.22	77	16.35	95	.221	107
	Pressure	.275	44	.319	75	.330	57	0.00	79	6.93	79	13.86	60	.172	93
Curt Ford	Overall	.195	--	.266	--	.239	--	0.78	--	5.76	--	18.71	--	.321	14
	Pressure	.139	--	.167	--	.184	--	0.00	--	5.13	--	15.38	--	.214	73
Pedro Guerrero	Overall	.286	23	.418	27	.367	12	2.75	36	10.90	29	13.98	72	.382	2
	Pressure	.233	79	.326	73	.320	62	2.33	43	10.00	45	6.00	8	.333	32
Bob Horner	Overall	.257	66	.354	80	.348	29	1.46	77	12.96	9	9.31	21	.306	25
	Pressure	.346	--	.423	--	.513	--	0.00	--	28.21	--	5.13	--	.364	20
Willie McGee	Overall	.292	16	.372	64	.329	48	0.53	105	5.33	108	14.00	73	.229	101
	Pressure	.299	30	.346	61	.312	67	0.93	77	1.83	125	12.84	51	.172	93
Jose Oquendo	Overall	.277	28	.350	87	.350	27	1.55	71	10.04	36	7.72	10	.263	68
	Pressure	.238	73	.298	90	.316	64	1.19	67	10.00	45	15.00	97	.160	97
Tom Pagnozzi	Overall	.282	25	.328	105	.319	65	0.00	118	5.26	109	15.31	84	.246	87
	Pressure	.250	57	.250	105	.283	95	0.00	79	4.17	111	20.83	105	.231	66
Tony Pena	Overall	.263	57	.372	63	.308	84	1.98	57	6.04	99	10.99	39	.217	110
	Pressure	.290	32	.419	30	.333	51	2.15	45	6.80	84	6.80	10	.346	31
Terry Pendleton	Overall	.253	76	.361	73	.293	106	1.53	72	4.99	113	12.11	47	.308	23
	Pressure	.182	113	.236	113	.220	118	0.00	79	4.92	104	19.67	95	.158	101
Ozzie Smith	Overall	.270	43	.336	97	.350	26	0.52	108	11.06	26	6.43	5	.263	70
	Pressure	.223	85	.298	89	.284	93	2.13	46	7.69	70	7.69	16	.174	90
Denny Walling	Overall	.239	100	.325	106	.291	107	0.43	111	6.75	87	9.92	28	.279	55
	Pressure	.162	--	.216	--	.205	--	0.00	--	5.13	--	12.82	--	.429	--
Team Average	Overall	.249	4	.337	12	.309	6	1.29	12	7.84	7	13.39	1	.244	11
	Pressure	.232	10	.300	11	.291	11	1.19	10	7.57	11	13.23	1	.197	12
League Average	Overall	.248		.363		.310		1.95		7.91		15.06		.256	
	Pressure	.242		.340		.310		1.70		8.47		15.93		.238	

Additional Miscellaneous Batting Comparisons

	Grass Surface BA	Rank	Artificial Surface BA	Rank	Home Games BA	Rank	Road Games BA	Rank	Runners in Scoring Position BA	Rank	Runners in Scoring Pos and Two Outs BA	Rank	Leading Off Inning OBA	Rank	Runners on 3B with less than 2 Outs RDI %	Rank
Luis Alicea	.216	112	.211	109	.229	99	.196	125	.215	106	.209	86	.300	72	.381	127
Tom Brunansky	.293	18	.227	95	.225	105	.263	56	.226	97	.232	69	.299	75	.455	112
Vince Coleman	.253	66	.262	57	.276	46	.241	88	.243	81	.203	90	.301	71	.500	92
Curt Ford	.222	--	.185	121	.250	--	.147	--	.282	--	.238	--	.242	--	.636	40
Pedro Guerrero	.330	4	.235	82	.313	12	.256	67	.371	1	.289	34	.289	83	.710	17
Bob Horner	.257	--	.257	63	.278	41	.235	96	.250	74	.148	115	.357	22	.769	5
Willie McGee	.327	5	.279	39	.283	33	.301	7	.252	73	.220	77	.322	50	.489	106
Jose Oquendo	.279	31	.277	40	.289	30	.265	52	.279	44	.218	78	.408	4	.652	34
Tom Pagnozzi	.316	--	.274	44	.317	--	.257	66	.292	30	.167	111	.264	99	.714	--
Tony Pena	.192	123	.287	29	.259	72	.268	45	.244	80	.295	28	.274	92	.452	114
Terry Pendleton	.236	100	.260	62	.280	38	.223	104	.303	23	.279	44	.269	94	.680	26
Ozzie Smith	.262	54	.272	45	.278	41	.261	59	.246	77	.222	75	.333	39	.588	55
Denny Walling	.293	--	.222	100	.239	92	.240	89	.246	78	.231	70	.263	100	.500	92
Team Average	.246	8	.250	4	.257	4	.241	8	.246	9	.224	8	.297	8	.531	10
League Average	.250		.246		.252		.244		.250		.231		.301		.554	

Pitching vs. Left and Right Handed Batters

		BA	Rank	SA	Rank	OBA	Rank	HR %	Rank	BB %	Rank	SO %	Rank
Danny Cox	vs. Lefties	.341	109	.545	109	.395	100	2.84	97	8.67	52	7.14	103
	vs. Righties	.192	7	.258	6	.236	6	0.66	9	4.85	29	20.00	20
Ken Dayley	vs. Lefties	.278	--	.333	--	.371	--	0.00	--	12.70	--	23.81	--
	vs. Righties	.224	38	.313	28	.281	39	1.36	33	6.75	56	14.11	69
Jose DeLeon	vs. Lefties	.260	58	.355	51	.349	79	1.16	33	12.13	91	16.90	34
	vs. Righties	.213	26	.334	40	.259	15	1.98	54	5.72	41	28.15	2
Joe Magrane	vs. Lefties	.177	6	.283	13	.242	6	1.77	59	8.00	44	19.20	23
	vs. Righties	.226	40	.309	24	.286	47	0.80	13	7.43	71	13.77	71
Greg Mathews	vs. Lefties	.200	--	.340	--	.273	--	2.00	--	9.09	--	12.73	--
	vs. Righties	.259	81	.396	85	.352	100	1.52	40	12.12	107	10.39	92
Larry McWilliams	vs. Lefties	.202	11	.336	36	.252	8	2.52	88	5.26	16	18.05	29
	vs. Righties	.269	89	.396	85	.336	93	1.78	47	8.48	47	10.27	95
Randy O'Neal	vs. Lefties	.204	12	.287	16	.225	3	0.93	24	2.68	1	8.04	99
	vs. Righties	.350	--	.580	--	.404	--	6.00	--	6.36	--	10.00	--
Scott Terry	vs. Lefties	.251	45	.355	50	.298	30	1.73	55	6.40	23	14.80	51
	vs. Righties	.244	61	.328	38	.293	52	0.40	6	6.57	53	10.22	96
Todd Worrell	vs. Lefties	.213	17	.397	78	.305	40	3.55	102	12.12	90	23.64	8
	vs. Righties	.214	27	.291	17	.271	29	1.10	22	6.97	58	19.40	24
Team Average	vs. Lefties	.254	6	.385	9	.322	6	2.00	11	9.13	5	14.89	5
	vs. Righties	.250	9	.361	5	.306	9	1.45	1	7.19	9	13.99	10
League Average	vs. Lefties	.255		.365		.325		1.73		9.36		14.24	
	vs. Righties	.244		.361		.299		2.10		6.87		15.64	

Pitching with Runners on Base and Bases Empty

		BA	Rank	SA	Rank	OBA	Rank	HR %	Rank	BB %	Rank	SO %	Rank
Danny Cox	Runners On	.273	76	.422	92	.342	72	1.56	48	9.27	52	11.26	82
	Bases Empty	.271	95	.407	93	.310	78	2.01	58	5.24	28	14.29	67
Jose DeLeon	Runners On	.244	46	.341	38	.316	43	1.47	43	9.85	59	19.95	16
	Bases Empty	.232	41	.347	49	.301	67	1.62	42	8.64	86	23.71	8
Joe Magrane	Runners On	.200	9	.271	11	.274	8	0.42	11	8.99	47	15.11	43
	Bases Empty	.228	36	.325	29	.281	32	1.34	29	6.52	52	14.54	66
Greg Mathews	Runners On	.237	34	.392	71	.347	76	2.06	67	14.29	101	10.08	91
	Bases Empty	.253	72	.380	80	.329	90	1.33	28	9.58	94	11.38	89
Larry McWilliams	Runners On	.281	84	.452	102	.339	69	2.76	96	7.03	19	11.72	80
	Bases Empty	.233	42	.331	35	.302	68	1.35	30	8.31	83	12.31	81
Randy O'Neal	Runners On	.314	--	.486	--	.368	--	2.86	--	5.13	--	7.69	--
	Bases Empty	.254	73	.399	91	.285	38	3.62	103	4.17	12	9.72	99
Scott Terry	Runners On	.314	106	.429	95	.359	93	1.57	49	6.98	17	12.09	78
	Bases Empty	.203	13	.283	9	.252	9	0.69	12	6.15	44	12.62	76
Todd Worrell	Runners On	.240	38	.380	66	.328	55	3.33	102	11.67	87	21.67	10
	Bases Empty	.191	4	.301	16	.247	4	1.16	24	6.99	59	20.97	16
Team Average	Runners On	.265	9	.397	10	.335	9	1.98	7	9.61	8	12.93	10
	Bases Empty	.242	8	.351	5	.294	7	1.42	1	6.59	8	15.39	7
League Average	Runners On	.257		.373		.329		1.91		9.45		14.09	
	Bases Empty	.242		.355		.297		1.98		6.73		15.80	

Overall Pitching Compared to Late Inning Pressure Situations

		BA	Rank	SA	Rank	OBA	Rank	HR %	Rank	BB %	Rank	SO %	Rank
John Costello	Overall	.235	--	.332	--	.324	--	1.60	--	11.68	--	17.76	--
	Pressure	.198	19	.296	33	.270	28	1.23	42	8.99	61	23.60	10
Danny Cox	Overall	.272	92	.413	101	.323	73	1.83	48	6.93	36	13.02	74
	Pressure	.267	--	.400	--	.313	--	3.33	--	5.71	--	14.29	--
Ken Dayley	Overall	.239	--	.318	--	.306	--	1.00	--	8.41	--	16.81	--
	Pressure	.253	59	.305	40	.326	63	0.00	1	9.09	63	15.91	43
Jose DeLeon	Overall	.237	39	.345	40	.308	47	1.56	37	9.15	77	22.13	9
	Pressure	.304	97	.435	94	.364	89	1.45	46	8.86	57	20.25	21
Joe Magrane	Overall	.217	17	.304	14	.278	14	0.98	13	7.53	48	14.77	57
	Pressure	.219	43	.292	31	.272	30	1.04	36	6.67	29	9.52	95
Greg Mathews	Overall	.247	55	.385	84	.337	91	1.62	40	11.54	98	10.84	90
	Pressure	.143	--	.143	--	.333	--	0.00	--	11.11	--	0.00	--
Larry McWilliams	Overall	.253	66	.382	79	.317	66	1.95	53	7.75	54	12.05	85
	Pressure	.333	106	.444	96	.375	97	0.00	1	5.94	20	10.89	82
Steve Peters	Overall	.313	--	.527	--	.382	--	4.40	--	10.33	--	14.08	--
	Pressure	.333	106	.460	99	.432	109	3.17	95	13.92	105	15.19	49
Dan Quisenberry	Overall	.344	--	.529	--	.364	--	2.55	--	3.57	--	11.31	--
	Pressure	.400	109	.514	105	.421	108	0.00	1	4.88	13	9.76	92
Scott Terry	Overall	.247	56	.341	36	.295	34	1.04	16	6.49	48	12.40	78
	Pressure	.236	51	.350	59	.317	52	1.63	52	10.49	82	12.59	72
Todd Worrell	Overall	.214	14	.337	34	.287	26	2.17	71	9.29	80	21.31	13
	Pressure	.209	33	.355	62	.292	38	2.99	91	10.37	81	23.70	9
Team Average	Overall	.252	9	.370	9	.312	9	1.65	3	7.90	9	14.32	8
	Pressure	.256	9	.366	8	.325	8	1.53	3	9.02	6	15.23	8
League Average	Overall	.248		.363		.310		1.95		7.91		15.06	
	Pressure	.243		.347		.315		1.72		9.12		15.69	

Additional Miscellaneous Pitching Comparisons

	Grass Surface BA	Rank	Artificial Surface BA	Rank	Home Games BA	Rank	Road Games BA	Rank	Runners in Scoring Position BA	Rank	Runners in Scoring Pos and Two Outs BA	Rank	Leading Off Inning OBA	Rank
Cris Carpenter	.234	--	.319	106	.360	--	.257	61	.326	--	.286	--	.380	--
John Costello	.242	--	.234	35	.213	--	.255	--	.208	--	.267	90	.229	--
Danny Cox	.289	--	.267	78	.265	77	.285	92	.244	52	.233	66	.318	73
Ken Dayley	.347	--	.204	13	.216	--	.267	--	.260	72	.212	50	.205	--
Jose DeLeon	.262	67	.225	28	.226	29	.248	50	.217	31	.191	32	.338	88
Joe Magrane	.208	15	.219	21	.214	20	.221	22	.161	5	.097	3	.271	23
Greg Mathews	.213	--	.262	68	.200	--	.285	93	.242	48	.241	--	.333	85
Larry McWilliams	.233	29	.263	71	.250	64	.256	60	.264	75	.306	99	.326	82
Randy O'Neal	.266	--	.278	89	.333	--	.238	40	.250	--	.286	--	.218	--
Steve Peters	.300	--	.318	105	.320	--	.305	--	.400	109	.448	--	.366	--
Dan Quisenberry	.412	--	.325	107	.325	--	.363	--	.357	--	.273	--	.278	--
Scott Terry	.291	94	.238	44	.245	61	.250	51	.333	106	.375	108	.281	39
Todd Worrell	.271	78	.193	10	.201	14	.228	30	.217	30	.203	43	.292	55
Team Average	.261	7	.249	6	.249	9	.255	7	.249	6	.243	9	.306	9
League Average	.250		.246		.244		.252		.250		.231		.301	

SAN DIEGO PADRES

- **What does Tony Gwynn have in common with Bobby Thomson, Gil Hodges and Al Michaels? Miracles.**

- **Will the Padres match the record of the St. Louis Browns?**

Someone out there in this kinder, gentler nation should go ahead and create a dictionary in which words are defined not in the traditional sense, but rather by a series of crosschecks and references. For example, if you looked up "miracle," you would find a subheading for "baseball," under which you'd see entries for the greatest comebacks in the sport's history. You know, the ones that we always refer to as "miracles,": the 1914 Miracle Braves, the 1951 Miracle-of-Coogan's-Bluff Giants, and the 1969 Miracle Mets. Under the subheading "hockey," you would find the Americans' 4–3 ("Do you believe in miracles?") win over the Soviets in the 1980 Olympic hockey tournament at Lake Placid. Under "dessert toppings," you'd find Miracle Whip.

Until this year, the subheading "Gwynn" would not have been needed. The closest entry to him would have been a listing for Edmund Gwenn, the grandfatherly actor who convinced the U.S. courts, the postal system, and a reluctant Natalie Wood that he was indeed the one and true Santa Claus in the 1947 film, *Miracle on 34th Street*. But after the turn of events in the race for the 1988 National League batting championship, ol' Edmund would have company in future editions: Miracle Tony Gwynn himself.

Not since Doug Williams ravaged the Denver Broncos with four touchdown passes in the second quarter of Super Bowl XXII had fans at Jack Murphy Stadium seen such a blitzkrieg. Gwynn shook off a first-half slump that had reduced his batting average to .237 in mid-June to win the batting title by six points over Rafael Palmeiro, .313 to .307. In so doing, he became the first National Leaguer since Roberto Clemente in the mid–1960s to win three batting titles within a five-year span.

If Gwynn had been a team instead of a player, his run for the championship have been revered along with the 1914 Braves, the '51 Giants, and the '69 Mets. But it's a team game, not a horse race, so while Silky Sullivan went down in history, Gwynn may be forgotten by it. Before that happens, let's review what he did in 1988 and try to uncover some

mileposts by which to measure his feat.

To start, let's review where Gwynn stood at various points in the season, compared with the league leaders on those dates. The Diff. column indicates the margin (in terms of batting average points) by which Gwynn trailed the leader:

Through games of	Gwynn	N.L. Leader	Diff.
April 15	.237	Kal Daniels, .410	−173
April 30	.299	Mike Scioscia, .404	−105
May 15	.275	Rafael Palmeiro, .356	−81
May 31	.263	Bobby Bonilla, .342	−79
June 13	*.237	Andres Galarraga, .331	−94
June 15	.250	Galarraga, .327	−77
June 30	.249	Gerald Perry, .332	−83
July 4	.253	Galarraga, .345	−92
July 15	.287	Perry, .338	−51
July 31	.300	Perry, .325	−25
August 15	.314	Perry, .321	−7
August 31	.317	Perry, .319	−2
Sept. 15	.307	Gwynn	—
October 2	.313	Gwynn	—

* Gwynn's lowest average after April 15.

Let's focus on the July 4 figures, since that date is the traditional midpoint of the season. One of the earliest forays into *Analyst*-type material was the observation made in the early years of this century that the team leading the league on July 4 will more often than not go on to win the pennant. (That trend was more pronounced in the days before divisional play, when 65 percent of such teams went on to win; since 1969, only 55 percent of July 4 leaders have gone on to finish in first place.)

How often, then, does the July 4 batting leader go on to win the batting title?

We researched this question going back to 1946, the first full season in the postwar era. The list of some of the July 4 leaders would make an interesting essay in itself. In 1957, for example, Dee Fondy of the Pirates was the July 4 National League leader; in 1958, the A.L. leader through July 4 was Preston Ward of the Athletics; his teammate, Bob Cerv, was second.

George Altman (1961), Manny Jimenez (1962), and Leon Wagner (1963) all led on July 4; so did Hawk Harrelson (1968), Cleon Jones (1969), and Roy White (1970). We got our biggest charge, though, out of some relatively recent names: Easy Ed Goodson (1973), Art Howe (1981), and, believe it or not, Barry Bonnell with Toronto in 1982. (Hey, if we're lyin' we're dyin'.)

There have been 86 batting titles contested in the 43 seasons since the end of World War II. Only 39 of those 86 titles were won by the player who was leading the league of July 4; the other 47 were won by guys playing catch-up. However, no batting champion in the postwar era overcame a July 4 deficit as large as the 92 points that Tony Gwynn made up. Here are the largest margins overcome:

Season	July 4 Leader, Avg.	Winner, July 4 Avg.	Diff.
1988 N.L.	Galarraga, .345	Gwynn, .253 (.313)	−92
1965 A.L.	Yastrzemski, .340	Oliva, .270 (.321)	−70
1979 A.L.	Smalley, .372	Lynn, .310 (.333)	−62
1947 A.L.	Boudreau, .361	Williams, .302 (.343)	−59
1976 N.L.	Oliver, .366	Madlock, .310 (.339)	−56

Not only did Gwynn have to overcome a huge deficit in order to win the batting title, he also had to overcome another imposing obstacle: his own home ballpark. Jack Murphy Stadium is one of the most difficult stadiums in the majors in which to fashion a good batting average. To past readers of the *Analyst,* our methodology is by now familiar: Over a five-year period, we have compared the batting averages in games played at each stadium with those of the home team's games played on the road. Since the statistics represent performance by the same players in roughly the same number of games, the differences can be attributed to the peculiarities of the ballpark.

And there's no doubt about it, Jack Murphy Stadium is a peculiar ballpark. Its outstanding characteristics: a good home run park, but one in which it's hard to hit for average due to apparent visibility problems, which in turn make it the stadium that has the most dramatic effect on strikeouts in the majors. Since we're dealing here with the effect on batting average, we have listed the National League stadiums in the order which, over the past five years, they have had the greatest positive effect on that category. (For details of Jack Murphy's other characteristics, and those of other parks, see the Ballpark Effects section, pages 426–429.)

	Home Games	Road Games	Points Diff.
Atlanta Stadium	.266	.250	+16
Wrigley Field	.273	.257	+16
Riverfront Stadium	.260	.248	+12
Veterans Stadium	.258	.255	+3
Busch Stadium	.254	.254	0
Dodger Stadium	.248	.250	−2
Three Rivers Stadium	.251	.253	−2
Olympic Stadium	.247	.254	−7
Astrodome	.246	.253	−7
Shea Stadium	.248	.255	−7
Jack Murphy Stadium	.249	.260	−11
Candlestick Park	.246	.258	−12

Jack Murphy Stadium has depressed batting averages more than all but one other National League park over the past five years. What Gwynn has accomplished is similar to a player on the Astros, playing half his games in the Astrodome, winning the National League home-run title. Or a pitcher on the Braves, pitching in the Launching Pad, leading the league in earned run average. He has flourished despite a hostile environment. Maybe we've found the perfect man to explore the outer planets!

San Diego fans encouraged by the off-season acquisitions of Jack Clark, Bruce Hurst, and Walt Terrell are no doubt thinking "pennant." But first things first. Truly aware Padres buffs should be thinking May 21, for that's the date that the Padres are scheduled to play their 45th game of the season. And as anyone who has followed the team over the past two years can tell you, those first 45 can be the roughest.

Two years ago, under Larry Bowa, San Diego won only 11 of its first 45 games, before climbing back to respectability and finishing with a .401 percentage. Then last season, the early season curse was back, as they won just 15 of their first 45 games. A couple days later, Bowa was gone, Jack McKeon was in the dugout, and the rest is history; okay, baseball history. The Pads finished at 83–78 (.516), and wound up in third place, ahead of the Giants and the Astros, whom they swept in a three-game season-ending series at the Dome. Moreover, of the 102 teams in this century that have played .333 or worse over the first 45 games, the 1988 Padres were the first ever to come back strong enough to finish the season above the .500 mark. Here are the Padres atop the list of best finishes among those teams:

Year, Team	First 45	Final	
1988 San Diego	15–30	83–78	.516
1927 Cincinnati	13–32	75–78	.490
1943 Chicago Cubs	15–30	74–79	.484
1946 Chi. White Sox	15–30	74–80	.481
1921 Cincinnati	15–30	70–83	.458
1951 Phil. Athletics	15–30	70–84	.455

So the key question in San Diego is, will the Pads fall victim to the Big One for the third year in a row? If they do, they'll go down in history; okay, National League history. No National League team in this century has ever suffered through three successive seasons in which they won 15 or fewer of their first 45 decisions. Only a handful of teams have even done that twice in a row:

Years, Team	Year One		Year Two	
	First 45	Final	First 45	Final
1903–04 Phil. Phillies	14–31	49–86	10–35	52–100
1905–06 Boston Braves	15–30	51–103	12–33	49–102
1911–12 Boston Braves	11–34	44–107	13–32	52–101
1922–23 Phil. Phillies	15–30	57–96	13–32	50–104
1941–42 Phil. Phillies	15–30	43–111	14–31	42–109
1954–55 Pittsburgh	13–32	53–101	14–31	60–94

Three American League teams have had at least three such seasons in a row; in each case, it was the St. Louis Browns. First, a three-year span from 1910 through 1912; then a five-year stretch from 1935 through 1939; and then another three-game span from 1949 through 1951. That '51 season was when Bill Veeck hired Eddie Gaedel, all three feet seven inches of him, as a pinch hitter. Here's hoping that with Clark, Hurst, and Co. on board, the Padres won't be tempted to use any players shorter than five-foot-eight-inch Joey Cora and five-foot-seven inch Bip Roberts.

WON-LOST RECORD BY STARTING POSITION

SAN DIEGO 83-78	C	1B	2B	3B	SS	LF	CF	RF	P	Leadoff	Relief	Starts
Shawn Abner							4-6	4-10				8-16
Roberto Alomar			74-63							14-12		74-63
Sandy Alomar												1-1
Greg Booker									1-1		4-28	
Chris Brown				30-40								30-40
Randell Byers												2-1
Jerald Clark						2-1						
Keith Comstock											0-7	
Mark Davis											39-23	
Tim Flannery			0-1	25-15						1-1		25-16
Mark Grant									1-10		2-20	1-10
Tony Gwynn							20-12	52-49		6-8		72-61
Greg W. Harris									1-0		1-1	1-0
Andy Hawkins									19-14			19-14
Stan Jefferson						1-1	12-12			9-11		13-13
Jimmy Jones									11-18			11-18
John Kruk		22-34				14-12		16-10		13-5		52-56
Dave Leiper											6-29	
Shane Mack						14-18	2-3			2-1		16-21
Carmelo Martinez		16-11				32-20		4-5				52-36
Lance McCullers											23-37	
Keith Moreland		41-32		1-1		25-39						67-72
Rob Nelson		4-1										4-1
Eric Nolte											0-2	
Mark Parent	18-15											18-15
Dennis Rasmussen									16-4			16-4
Randy Ready			9-13	26-22		5-4				0-3		40-39
Bip Roberts			1-0									1-0
Benito Santiago	65-63											65-63
Eric Show									18-14			18-14
Candy Sierra											0-15	
Garry Templeton					48-51					0-2		48-51
Dickie Thon			0-1		35-27					17-16		35-28
Ed Whitson									16-17		1-0	16-17
Marvell Wynne						4-1	33-30	5-1		21-19		42-32

Batting vs. Left and Right Handed Pitchers

Player		BA	Rank	SA	Rank	OBA	Rank	HR %	Rank	BB %	Rank	SO %	Rank
Roberto Alomar	vs. Lefties	.258	67	.382	63	.330	62	2.25	59	8.46	64	14.43	87
	vs. Righties	.270	47	.381	52	.327	52	1.36	74	7.32	74	13.17	58
Chris Brown	vs. Lefties	.245	86	.311	105	.298	91	0.94	94	7.02	77	14.04	82
	vs. Righties	.227	105	.262	123	.293	95	0.71	99	6.88	78	20.63	118
Tim Flannery	vs. Lefties	.125	--	.125	--	.300	--	0.00	--	19.05	--	14.29	--
	vs. Righties	.279	29	.364	65	.372	14	0.00	115	10.87	28	15.76	83
Tony Gwynn	vs. Lefties	.314	14	.358	76	.358	31	0.00	103	6.36	92	8.64	33
	vs. Righties	.312	4	.451	17	.382	12	2.21	45	10.34	32	5.87	6
John Kruk	vs. Lefties	.194	116	.337	89	.270	109	3.06	38	9.73	47	19.47	119
	vs. Righties	.257	64	.371	59	.401	5	2.14	50	19.55	1	13.03	56
Shane Mack	vs. Lefties	.236	96	.255	120	.354	35	0.00	103	11.94	22	7.46	18
	vs. Righties	.250	--	.281	--	.319	--	0.00	--	8.22	--	21.92	--
Carmelo Martinez	vs. Lefties	.234	98	.390	61	.318	76	4.55	11	11.30	28	11.86	65
	vs. Righties	.237	94	.436	23	.288	105	5.21	6	6.58	85	15.79	84
Keith Moreland	vs. Lefties	.240	90	.307	107	.303	88	1.12	90	8.59	61	8.59	31
	vs. Righties	.265	53	.343	79	.307	78	0.90	88	6.32	89	9.34	24
Randy Ready	vs. Lefties	.286	32	.456	27	.361	29	3.40	30	10.78	30	7.78	22
	vs. Righties	.250	77	.337	84	.333	42	1.09	81	9.86	37	11.74	43
Benito Santiago	vs. Lefties	.257	69	.407	48	.291	94	3.57	25	4.70	111	15.44	95
	vs. Righties	.244	87	.344	78	.278	112	1.42	70	4.50	119	15.61	81
Garry Templeton	vs. Lefties	.237	95	.289	112	.256	119	0.00	103	2.50	125	13.75	79
	vs. Righties	.252	76	.371	61	.293	94	1.05	83	5.77	100	12.50	48
Dickie Thon	vs. Lefties	.302	20	.403	51	.391	7	0.72	98	12.96	17	14.20	85
	vs. Righties	.218	113	.261	124	.293	93	0.00	115	8.96	46	19.40	114
Marvell Wynne	vs. Lefties	.327	--	.491	--	.413	--	1.82	--	12.50	--	14.06	--
	vs. Righties	.252	75	.414	35	.307	77	3.60	24	7.54	68	17.38	98
Team Average	vs. Lefties	.247	8	.345	10	.313	5	1.83	8	8.50	4	13.46	3
	vs. Righties	.247	8	.353	8	.309	6	1.71	9	8.03	5	15.46	8
League Average	vs. Lefties	.248		.367		.310		2.10		8.01		14.42	
	vs. Righties	.249		.360		.310		1.88		7.86		15.35	

Batting with Runners on Base and Bases Empty

		BA	Rank	SA	Rank	OBA	Rank	HR %	Rank	BB %	Rank	SO %	Rank
Roberto Alomar	Runners On	.291	36	.360	81	.351	53	0.49	101	7.14	97	10.08	31
	Bases Empty	.251	57	.395	39	.314	53	2.34	49	8.04	50	15.82	81
Chris Brown	Runners On	.223	112	.243	125	.299	106	0.00	104	9.17	65	21.67	123
	Bases Empty	.243	77	.313	103	.292	85	1.39	77	5.19	91	14.94	70
Tim Flannery	Runners On	.304	32	.443	32	.380	23	0.00	104	11.34	43	13.40	69
	Bases Empty	.231	--	.253	--	.352	--	0.00	--	12.04	--	17.59	--
Tony Gwynn	Runners On	.382	1	.516	11	.456	1	0.92	88	12.20	34	6.30	13
	Bases Empty	.263	40	.342	80	.309	60	1.64	71	6.17	75	7.41	7
John Kruk	Runners On	.248	95	.370	73	.414	8	1.82	60	22.42	1	13.45	70
	Bases Empty	.235	87	.357	69	.329	34	2.82	39	12.35	6	15.64	78
Carmelo Martinez	Runners On	.247	97	.438	33	.306	100	4.49	12	8.04	82	11.06	46
	Bases Empty	.225	104	.396	36	.296	80	5.35	5	9.22	32	16.99	91
Keith Moreland	Runners On	.231	107	.302	111	.276	115	0.39	103	6.67	103	8.07	19
	Bases Empty	.281	22	.359	65	.336	29	1.56	73	7.58	53	10.11	27
Randy Ready	Runners On	.273	62	.413	48	.367	36	2.10	55	12.14	37	10.98	45
	Bases Empty	.261	46	.372	59	.329	37	2.13	56	8.70	40	9.18	19
Benito Santiago	Runners On	.195	123	.295	115	.232	127	1.36	73	4.55	120	14.88	85
	Bases Empty	.290	17	.415	30	.323	43	2.57	42	4.56	104	16.14	83
Garry Templeton	Runners On	.282	50	.437	35	.352	52	2.11	52	10.06	51	11.24	50
	Bases Empty	.227	102	.300	109	.238	124	0.00	115	1.35	125	13.90	57
Dickie Thon	Runners On	.258	79	.333	101	.336	73	0.00	104	11.01	45	19.27	113
	Bases Empty	.267	37	.339	83	.353	14	0.61	108	11.23	13	14.97	71
Marvell Wynne	Runners On	.328	4	.569	2	.370	34	5.17	6	6.92	101	16.15	102
	Bases Empty	.230	96	.350	72	.301	69	2.30	50	9.21	33	17.15	92
Team Average	Runners On	.255	9	.365	10	.324	9	1.55	10	9.25	7	13.53	5
	Bases Empty	.241	7	.341	9	.300	5	1.90	9	7.34	4	15.79	7
League Average	Runners On	.257		.373		.329		1.91		9.45		14.09	
	Bases Empty	.242		.355		.297		1.98		6.73		15.80	

Overall Batting Compared to Late Inning Pressure Situations

		BA	Rank	SA	Rank	OBA	Rank	HR %	Rank	BB %	Rank	SO %	Rank	RDI %	Rank
Roberto Alomar	Overall	.266	47	.382	54	.328	50	1.65	66	7.69	68	13.58	62	.230	100
	Pressure	.240	71	.333	64	.296	84	1.33	63	7.41	74	14.81	66	.211	76
Chris Brown	Overall	.235	105	.283	119	.295	102	0.81	94	6.93	84	17.88	107	.236	94
	Pressure	.270	46	.297	92	.372	24	0.00	79	6.82	82	15.91	74	.071	126
Tim Flannery	Overall	.265	50	.341	94	.365	15	0.00	118	11.71	20	15.61	89	.320	--
	Pressure	.207	--	.276	--	.303	--	0.00	--	12.12	--	21.21	--	.143	--
Tony Gwynn	Overall	.313	1	.415	30	.373	8	1.34	80	8.82	47	6.92	7	.418	1
	Pressure	.338	8	.394	40	.373	23	0.00	79	5.26	101	5.26	6	.524	1
John Kruk	Overall	.241	99	.362	70	.369	10	2.38	43	17.17	1	14.59	78	.261	71
	Pressure	.241	70	.315	78	.354	38	1.85	54	14.93	16	20.90	107	.286	--
Carmelo Martinez	Overall	.236	104	.416	29	.301	93	4.93	5	8.64	48	14.07	74	.264	67
	Pressure	.242	67	.403	36	.309	71	4.84	12	8.82	54	14.71	65	.300	41
Keith Moreland	Overall	.256	70	.331	101	.305	89	0.98	92	7.12	80	9.07	18	.299	38
	Pressure	.277	39	.369	51	.290	87	1.54	61	2.86	119	8.57	21	.368	18
Randy Ready	Overall	.266	48	.390	48	.346	32	2.11	51	10.26	34	10.00	30	.257	79
	Pressure	.200	100	.243	110	.273	102	1.43	62	7.69	70	17.95	86	.174	90
Benito Santiago	Overall	.248	87	.362	72	.282	114	2.03	54	4.55	117	15.56	87	.175	125
	Pressure	.225	82	.338	63	.250	111	2.50	37	3.37	116	14.61	64	.136	112
Garry Templeton	Overall	.249	86	.354	81	.286	112	0.83	93	5.10	112	12.76	53	.302	33
	Pressure	.237	75	.373	50	.258	108	3.39	21	3.08	118	1.54	1	.267	53
Dickie Thon	Overall	.264	56	.337	96	.347	31	0.39	112	11.15	24	16.55	97	.258	76
	Pressure	.150	120	.225	115	.186	126	2.50	37	4.55	109	15.91	74	.125	--
Marvell Wynne	Overall	.264	51	.426	23	.325	52	3.30	26	8.40	54	16.80	98	.277	61
	Pressure	.180	114	.262	101	.231	117	1.64	59	5.97	92	23.88	117	.091	122
Team Average	Overall	.247	7	.351	10	.310	4	1.75	10	8.19	4	14.79	6	.259	4
	Pressure	.237	8	.323	9	.292	10	1.79	5	6.64	12	15.56	5	.229	8
League Average	Overall	.248		.363		.310		1.95		7.91		15.06		.256	
	Pressure	.242		.340		.310		1.70		8.47		15.93		.238	

Additional Miscellaneous Batting Comparisons

	Grass Surface BA	Rank	Artificial Surface BA	Rank	Home Games BA	Rank	Road Games BA	Rank	Runners in Scoring Position BA	Rank	Runners in Scoring Pos and Two Outs BA	Rank	Leading Off Inning OBA	Rank	Runners on 3B with less than 2 Outs RDI %	Rank
Roberto Alomar	.248	77	.317	7	.254	77	.278	31	.324	12	.339	11	.304	66	.417	118
Chris Brown	.253	67	.195	--	.268	53	.202	121	.224	102	.214	80	.322	49	.625	--
Tim Flannery	.222	108	.386	--	.260	69	.269	43	.256	69	.318	17	.419	--	.800	3
Tony Gwynn	.303	12	.341	1	.310	13	.315	3	.371	2	.286	37	.372	16	.750	6
Stan Jefferson	.160	125	.059	--	.191	--	.070	--	.067	--	.143	--	.190	--	.600	--
John Kruk	.238	93	.250	70	.253	82	.230	100	.228	94	.311	19	.350	28	.500	92
Shane Mack	.259	57	.211	--	.180	--	.290	--	.320	--	.286	--	.367	--	.750	--
Carmelo Martinez	.245	85	.210	110	.258	73	.214	110	.248	76	.211	85	.315	59	.517	88
Keith Moreland	.268	47	.226	97	.268	55	.246	80	.268	56	.263	51	.357	22	.633	44
Mark Parent	.195	122	.194	--	.204	--	.188	--	.152	--	.111	--	.290	--	.400	121
Randy Ready	.272	42	.243	--	.265	58	.266	49	.264	61	.234	66	.318	56	.600	52
Benito Santiago	.253	65	.231	91	.230	98	.268	44	.148	126	.085	125	.295	80	.400	121
Garry Templeton	.255	61	.224	--	.253	83	.244	83	.282	40	.333	13	.312	64	.563	67
Dickie Thon	.253	67	.284	32	.223	106	.295	11	.260	65	.233	67	.337	37	.375	--
Marvell Wynne	.259	58	.279	38	.280	37	.249	76	.338	6	.302	23	.298	79	.615	48
Team Average	.247	7	.248	5	.249	8	.245	6	.255	3	.242	4	.321	2	.546	9
League Average	.250		.246		.252		.244		.250		.231		.301		.554	

Pitching vs. Left and Right Handed Batters

		BA	Rank	SA	Rank	OBA	Rank	HR %	Rank	BB %	Rank	SO %	Rank
Greg Booker	vs. Lefties	.311	103	.429	90	.354	82	1.68	53	6.25	20	11.72	76
	vs. Righties	.246	--	.333	--	.303	--	2.38	--	7.64	--	19.44	--
Mark Davis	vs. Lefties	.209	14	.302	19	.277	16	1.16	34	8.51	50	30.85	1
	vs. Righties	.195	9	.226	1	.286	46	0.38	4	11.04	102	23.70	12
Mark Grant	vs. Lefties	.261	59	.378	66	.327	60	1.67	52	8.82	54	11.76	75
	vs. Righties	.275	94	.500	108	.342	97	6.04	109	8.74	82	17.96	38
Andy Hawkins	vs. Lefties	.259	54	.347	43	.355	83	0.95	28	12.53	94	7.60	101
	vs. Righties	.227	42	.352	58	.260	17	3.13	97	3.58	11	12.89	80
Jimmy Jones	vs. Lefties	.293	90	.439	93	.343	72	1.96	65	7.52	36	10.78	84
	vs. Righties	.260	83	.382	78	.293	53	2.09	61	3.88	19	10.80	89
Dave Leiper	vs. Lefties	.250	--	.344	--	.304	--	1.56	--	7.25	--	14.49	--
	vs. Righties	.221	35	.267	8	.262	18	0.00	1	6.08	45	15.54	54
Lance McCullers	vs. Lefties	.153	2	.178	2	.293	26	0.00	1	16.42	103	19.90	19
	vs. Righties	.251	70	.469	105	.332	87	4.47	107	10.68	98	19.90	22
Dennis Rasmussen	vs. Lefties	.297	94	.449	98	.336	65	2.54	90	5.43	18	15.50	42
	vs. Righties	.248	67	.371	69	.304	67	2.12	63	7.03	59	12.69	82
Eric Show	vs. Lefties	.253	48	.392	76	.316	50	2.16	70	8.41	47	12.52	65
	vs. Righties	.206	15	.324	32	.234	5	2.95	91	2.35	2	18.82	29
Ed Whitson	vs. Lefties	.266	68	.383	70	.312	44	1.75	57	6.44	24	10.34	85
	vs. Righties	.253	74	.374	71	.283	43	2.63	85	4.14	20	17.76	39
Team Average	vs. Lefties	.262	8	.377	7	.329	7	1.60	4	9.13	4	12.61	10
	vs. Righties	.234	4	.352	4	.282	2	2.47	11	5.84	1	16.63	4
League Average	vs. Lefties	.255		.365		.325		1.73		9.36		14.24	
	vs. Righties	.244		.361		.299		2.10		6.87		15.64	

Pitching with Runners on Base and Bases Empty

		BA	Rank	SA	Rank	OBA	Rank	HR %	Rank	BB %	Rank	SO %	Rank
Greg Booker	Runners On	.307	103	.395	76	.352	82	1.75	55	6.87	16	12.98	66
	Bases Empty	.252	71	.366	69	.305	74	2.29	72	7.09	62	18.44	26
Mark Davis	Runners On	.207	15	.262	8	.318	47	0.61	17	13.57	95	22.11	8
	Bases Empty	.191	5	.229	3	.251	7	0.53	5	7.39	67	28.57	1
Mark Grant	Runners On	.232	33	.374	60	.301	28	3.87	107	8.79	43	10.99	84
	Bases Empty	.295	104	.488	108	.360	106	3.86	105	8.77	87	17.98	30
Andy Hawkins	Runners On	.249	53	.364	51	.324	53	2.02	63	9.07	48	9.35	97
	Bases Empty	.241	52	.341	40	.304	73	1.97	55	7.96	77	10.49	96
Jimmy Jones	Runners On	.301	101	.457	103	.348	77	2.60	87	6.71	13	10.22	89
	Bases Empty	.262	87	.382	84	.300	61	1.65	45	5.15	25	11.19	93
Lance McCullers	Runners On	.208	17	.333	37	.317	46	3.14	101	13.78	96	20.41	14
	Bases Empty	.202	10	.328	30	.308	76	1.64	44	13.27	106	19.43	21
Dennis Rasmussen	Runners On	.272	75	.403	84	.326	54	2.76	94	6.99	18	13.37	60
	Bases Empty	.246	66	.371	71	.299	58	1.84	51	6.67	54	12.95	75
Eric Show	Runners On	.232	32	.358	50	.320	48	2.05	66	10.56	72	11.44	81
	Bases Empty	.231	40	.361	62	.255	11	2.78	90	2.86	6	17.65	34
Ed Whitson	Runners On	.259	64	.413	88	.297	23	2.62	88	5.49	7	15.32	39
	Bases Empty	.259	83	.357	56	.298	57	1.90	52	5.20	26	13.00	74
Team Average	Runners On	.252	5	.373	6	.319	5	2.15	10	8.75	3	13.90	6
	Bases Empty	.244	9	.357	7	.293	6	2.03	9	6.33	3	15.44	6
League Average	Runners On	.257		.373		.329		1.91		9.45		14.09	
	Bases Empty	.242		.355		.297		1.98		6.73		15.80	

Overall Pitching Compared to Late Inning Pressure Situations

		BA	Rank	SA	Rank	OBA	Rank	HR %	Rank	BB %	Rank	SO %	Rank
Greg Booker	Overall	.278	100	.380	76	.327	82	2.04	61	6.99	37	15.81	40
	Pressure	.471	110	.706	110	.537	110	5.88	109	13.95	106	0.00	110
Mark Davis	Overall	.199	6	.244	3	.284	19	0.57	5	10.45	92	25.37	3
	Pressure	.198	21	.241	11	.292	37	0.36	18	11.49	92	25.78	7
Mark Grant	Overall	.268	84	.439	105	.334	90	3.87	106	8.78	71	14.88	55
	Pressure	.259	66	.400	82	.337	77	2.35	76	9.38	69	13.54	63
Andy Hawkins	Overall	.244	51	.350	43	.312	55	1.99	55	8.39	66	10.04	96
	Pressure	.260	68	.302	39	.372	93	0.00	1	13.68	102	10.26	87
Jimmy Jones	Overall	.277	99	.411	100	.319	69	2.02	58	5.79	14	10.79	91
	Pressure	.271	81	.458	98	.317	54	3.39	102	6.06	22	7.58	104
Dave Leiper	Overall	.231	--	.292	--	.276	--	0.51	--	6.45	--	15.21	--
	Pressure	.178	9	.260	14	.228	7	1.37	44	6.10	24	14.63	53
Lance McCullers	Overall	.205	8	.330	28	.313	58	2.34	81	13.51	108	19.90	18
	Pressure	.207	30	.370	69	.309	50	3.25	100	12.67	97	20.55	20
Dennis Rasmussen	Overall	.256	69	.383	81	.309	51	2.19	73	6.79	32	13.11	73
	Pressure	.270	79	.429	91	.333	72	3.17	95	8.22	46	16.44	41
Eric Show	Overall	.231	32	.360	55	.279	15	2.53	87	5.66	10	15.38	47
	Pressure	.263	92	.404	85	.324	61	3.03	92	6.42	28	12.84	70
Ed Whitson	Overall	.259	77	.379	74	.298	37	2.18	72	5.32	7	13.95	66
	Pressure	.297	93	.422	90	.324	60	3.13	94	4.29	7	8.57	100
Team Average	Overall	.247	7	.363	6	.304	6	2.08	8	7.34	3	14.80	6
	Pressure	.241	7	.353	7	.322	7	1.99	9	10.15	11	17.10	2
League Average	Overall	.248		.363		.310		1.95		7.91		15.06	
	Pressure	.243		.347		.315		1.72		9.12		15.69	

Additional Miscellaneous Pitching Comparisons

	Grass Surface BA	Rank	Artificial Surface BA	Rank	Home Games BA	Rank	Road Games BA	Rank	Runners in Scoring Position BA	Rank	Runners in Scoring Pos and Two Outs BA	Rank	Leading Off Inning OBA	Rank
Greg Booker	.259	63	.313	--	.282	--	.274	81	.270	81	.115	--	.322	76
Mark Davis	.182	5	.269	--	.175	7	.220	21	.224	37	.241	73	.241	6
Mark Grant	.244	41	.349	--	.267	80	.269	73	.222	32	.195	36	.364	98
Andy Hawkins	.229	24	.292	101	.214	21	.285	95	.277	86	.263	87	.288	51
Jimmy Jones	.278	87	.275	86	.274	85	.280	87	.320	100	.242	74	.298	58
Dave Leiper	.216	18	.286	--	.196	--	.262	--	.224	--	.286	--	.320	--
Lance McCullers	.194	7	.243	--	.152	3	.272	76	.153	2	.176	20	.273	29
Dennis Rasmussen	.249	51	.265	75	.239	52	.268	72	.228	40	.220	59	.235	4
Eric Show	.242	39	.169	2	.231	39	.232	35	.236	45	.280	94	.259	15
Ed Whitson	.256	60	.266	76	.241	56	.279	86	.283	89	.208	47	.321	74
Team Average	.240	3	.268	11	.232	2	.262	11	.254	8	.240	8	.291	4
League Average	.250		.246		.244		.252		.250		.231		.301	

SAN FRANCISCO GIANTS

- Clark for Mattingly? A tough call.
- Need a hit? Forget how the batter did his last time up. It probably means nothing.

Back in 1946, there was reportedly an agreement reached between the Yankees and Red Sox to swap Joe DiMaggio for Ted Williams. Imagine the Splendid Splinter in pinstripes, shaking his stick at Yankee Stadium's inviting right-field seats. Or Joe D. donning Boston's red socks to mount an assault on Fenway Park's Green Monster.

The trade never happened. Perhaps it never was, in fact, discussed. But the rarity of a one-for-one swap of superstars has earned the story a place in baseball folklore. The most comparable one-for-one deal that we know of was the trade of Rocky Colavito for Harvey Kuenn in 1960, and even that would pale by comparison to a DiMaggio-for-Williams swap. Orlando Cepeda for Joe Torre (1969) and Bobby Bonds for Bobby Murcer (1974) also come to mind, but we're obviously in a lower class now.

Maybe that's why the rumor of a Don Mattingly for Will Clark trade that swept New York last winter just refused to go away. What surprised us was the harsh reaction that most Yankees fans had toward the possibility of swapping Donnie Baseball for Will the Thrill.

Nothing that will be written here should suggest that Mattingly is anything less than a Hall of Famer-to-be. Nor that his accomplishments have even been matched by Clark's. Dandy Don may well have been baseball's best hitter over the past five years. His fielding is exceptional. And his attitude is refreshing despite difficult working conditions. It's been three years since we first asked why so few observers considered him the best player in baseball. Since then, he's won a lot of that support by hitting .331 with an average of 26 home runs and 105 RBI per season.

All of that notwithstanding, it's about time the right most 99 percent of the country woke up to what the Bay Area has known for a while now. Will Clark has the potential for greatness normally attributed to two other Bay Area studs, fellow member of the class of '86, Jose Canseco, and his teammate, Olympian Mark McGwire.

Let's look at the facts. During his three seasons in the bigs, Clark has batted .292, with 75 home runs and 241 RBI. Only three other players can match the Thrill's figures in those

three categories: George Bell, Kirby Puckett, and Mattingly. Bell and Puckett play their home games in excellent hitters' ballparks, and not even Mattingly labors under the burden of a home field as unfriendly to hitters as Candlestick Park is.

But the best way to place Clark's accomplishments in a historical perspective—one that allows us to speculate on the shape of things to come as well—is to compare his three-year statistics to players who have compiled similar figures at comparable stages of their own careers. Toward that end, we've made some modifications in a system that was published in the Bill James Abstract a few years back, and identified the players whose statistical profiles at some point most resembled Clark's current line. They are listed below in alphabetical order, following Clark's stats. Each year represents the last season included in the corresponding player's stats. The ages are as of October 1 in those seasons:

Player	Year	Age	AB	R	H	2B	3B	HR	RBI	BB	SB	BA
Will Clark	1988	24	1512	257	442	87	13	75	241	183	18	.292
Ernie Banks	1956	25	1762	253	510	74	25	93	287	141	21	.289
Jim Ray Hart	1966	24	1755	251	508	69	16	87	272	145	13	.289
Jeff Heath	1940	25	1391	237	404	82	35	50	247	117	17	.290
Kent Hrbek	1984	24	1673	242	503	98	12	67	290	181	8	.301
Don Hurst	1930	24	1376	251	420	71	11	67	267	194	19	.305
Walt Judnich	1942	25	1522	265	455	89	19	55	254	208	16	.299
Mickey Mantle	1953	21	1351	260	398	72	15	57	244	197	20	.295
Frank Robinson	1958	22	1737	309	512	81	17	98	241	170	28	.295
Duke Snider	1950	23	1415	237	419	68	24	59	225	129	34	.296
Danny Tartabull	1987	24	1174	182	344	60	10	62	211	150	14	.293

The career performances of the players listed above loosely define the range of accomplishment Clark is capable of. And, as befits any player with only three years of major league experience, no matter how good, that range is fairly wide.

The low end of the spectrum includes Hurst, whose career rapidly deteriorated after leading the N.L. with 143 RBI in 1932 at age 27; Judnich, who never rebounded after missing three seasons in the military during World War II; Hart, who was hampered by numerous injuries throughout his career; and Heath, the topic of this slight digression.

Heath's talent as a hitter was surpassed only by his temper. Oscar Vitt, his manager at Cleveland, claimed Heath could have been "one of the greatest hitters [ever]. But he was his own worst enemy." Heath staged several holdouts during his career, and in 1940, he led some of his teammates in the "Crybabies' Rebellion", calling for Vitt's firing. His legendary temper, obedience to superstition, and lackadaisical base-running all reduced Heath's chances of ever fulfilling his enormous potential.

But back to Clark. His upside potential is enormous. Four of the 10 comparable players are Hall of Famers. Hrbek and Tartabull are All-Stars, capable of MVP seasons. Here are the career averages of the eight comparable players who have retired:

AB	R	H	2B	3B	HR	RBI	BA
6184	1037	1789	301	63	326	1098	.289

As to the question of whether Clark's potential matches that of his Bay Area rivals, Canseco and McGwire, we think he's in the same ballpark. In fact, at this stage of their careers, the comparable player method suggests that Canseco and Clark have an edge on McGwire.

The list of players comparable to Canseco includes, alphabetically, Johnny Bench, Rocky Colavito, Tony Conigliaro, Willie Horton, Frank Howard, Willie McCovey, Wally Post, Boog Powell, Willie Stargell, and Darryl Strawberry. Those similar to McGwire are: Jesse Barfield, Don Demeter, Joe Gordon, Jimmie Hall, Bob Horner, Horton, Ralph Kiner, Mike Marshall, McCovey, and Wagner. Compare the averages for the *retired* players in those groups to the Clark extrapolations:

	AB	R	H	2B	3B	HR	RBI	BA
Clark	6184	1037	1789	301	63	326	1098	.289
Canseco	6442	907	1741	285	31	353	1146	.270
McGwire	5303	782	1431	216	33	280	904	.270

Strawberry will raise those Canseco-group averages if he fulfills even a fraction of his own potential. But don't forget that the Clark averages above don't include Hrbek and Tartabull, so let's call it a standoff. But McGwire's line ranks one rung below the other two.

The range of players within each group emphasizes one of the realities not only of baseball, but of life. Trite though it is to say it, it's impossible to predict the future. The inclusion of Tony C. among the Canseco group is a painful reminder of that fact. But even given the limitations of this method of analysis, it's obvious that based on his first three seasons, Clark can take his place alongside Canseco and McGwire. And one day, maybe beside Mattingly as well.

"Jose Uribe to the plate for the Giants. Lined a single to center his first time up. They'll pitch him more carefully this time around."

Sounds good, but a hard-hit ball on his last at-bat is no reason to pitch carefully to Uribe, or to a lot of other players for that matter.

For the past two years, we've shown that when players put together strings of good or bad games, those streaks occur randomly—like tossing five straight heads or tails. A player's recent past performances, whether hitting or pitching, provide no clue as to how he'll perform his next time out. In effect, players don't get hot and cold, despite the illusion

perpetuated by random streaks of good and bad games.

Until now, all research on this topic had been done at the *game* level. For instance, is a player more likely to hit well in his next game coming a off a recent streak of good games or coming off a slump? Our data showed that there was no discernible trend. But this year, we've compiled 10 years' worth of data at the *play-by-play* level, allowing us to examine the relationship of one at-bat to the next. After all, the basis of any streak is how one action (whether an at-bat, a game, or a season) affects the next one.

The play-by-play study showed that, in general, a player is more likely to get a hit having hit safely in his previous at-bat than having made out. And while that might seem like "dog bites man," two points must be emphasized. First, the corresponding relationship does not exist from one *game* to the next. Generally speaking, players hit just as well coming off a single bad game as a good one; they hit as well when they come into game on a hot streak as they do off a slump. Second, the relationship of one at-bat to the next is probably smaller than you think.

For some players, like Uribe, the trend is significantly strong in the *opposite* direction. Take at look at his career statistics:

	AB	H	BA
At bats following hits	430	85	.198
At bats following outs	1315	347	.264

How many players are like Uribe, hitting better after outs than after hits? Quite a few, though not a majority. Among the 440 players with at least 1000 at-bats over the past 10 years, 204 hit better after outs, 236 hit better following hits.

Uribe provided the most extreme example of hitting better after outs—66 points better, in fact. But for nearly half of those 440 players (215 to be exact), the difference in batting average was less than 15 points. Among players active in 1988 with a career total of at least 1000 at-bats, here are the most extreme cases, in both directions:

Better After Outs			Better After Hits		
Player	After Hits	After Outs	Player	After Hits	After Outs
Jose Uribe	.198	.264	Jim Dwyer	.315	.250
Kevin Seitzer	.270	.334	Mike LaValliere	.304	.247
John Kruk	.244	.304	Eric Davis	.308	.260
Cory Snyder	.214	.274	Dion James	.317	.270
Tom O'Malley	.221	.268	Bob Dernier	.296	.249
Craig Reynolds	.220	.267	Tim Laudner	.261	.215
Randy Ready	.237	.283	Scott Fletcher	.304	.259
Len Dykstra	.247	.292	Dan Pasqua	.278	.232
Rick Dempsey	.201	.246	Ernest Riles	.301	.257
Andres Thomas	.215	.259	Terry Pendleton	.293	.251

Among Giants players, Brett Butler is the only other player to hit significantly better after outs (.290) than after hits (.258). Rob Thompson (.292 to .258) and Will Clark (.312 to .283) both hit better following hits than outs. But the rest of the team, like most major league players, hit about the same regardless of what they did in their last at-bat. So the notion of pitching carefully to a hitter based on what he did his last time up just doesn't make an awful lot of sense.

WON-LOST RECORD BY STARTING POSITION

SAN FRANCISCO 83-79	C	1B	2B	3B	SS	LF	CF	RF	P	Leadoff	Relief	Starts
Mike Aldrete	·	1-3	·	·	·	36-25	1-3	13-15	·	0-2	·	51-46
Randy Bockus	·	·	·	·	·	·	·	·	·	·	5-15	·
Jeff Brantley	·	·	·	·	·	·	·	·	0-1	·	2-6	0-1
Bob Brenly	29-26	·	·	·	·	·	·	·	·	·	·	29-26
Brett Butler	·	·	·	·	·	·	78-72	·	·	78-72	·	78-72
Will Clark	·	82-75	·	·	·	·	·	·	·	·	·	82-75
Dennis Cook	·	·	·	·	·	·	·	·	3-1	·	·	3-1
Ron Davis	·	·	·	·	·	·	·	·	·	·	2-7	·
Kelly Downs	·	·	·	·	·	·	·	·	15-11	·	0-1	15-11
Dave Dravecky	·	·	·	·	·	·	·	·	2-5	·	·	2-5
Angel Escobar	·	·	·	·	·	·	·	·	·	·	·	·
Phil Garner	·	·	·	·	·	·	·	·	·	·	·	·
Scott Garrelts	·	·	·	·	·	·	·	·	·	·	26-39	·
Atlee Hammaker	·	·	·	·	·	·	·	·	8-9	·	13-13	8-9
Charlie Hayes	·	·	·	·	·	1-1	·	·	·	·	·	1-1
Mike Krukow	·	·	·	·	·	·	·	·	11-9	·	·	11-9
Mike LaCoss	·	·	·	·	·	·	·	·	9-10	·	·	9-10
Craig Lefferts	·	·	·	·	·	·	·	·	·	·	25-39	·
Jeffrey Leonard	·	·	·	·	·	21-19	·	·	·	·	·	21-19
Candy Maldonado	·	·	·	·	·	·	·	66-62	·	·	·	66-62
Kirt Manwaring	18-15	·	·	·	·	·	·	·	·	·	·	18-15
Francisco Melendez	·	0-1	·	·	·	·	·	·	·	·	·	0-1
Bob Melvin	36-38	·	·	·	·	·	·	·	·	·	·	36-38
Kevin Mitchell	·	·	·	51-46	·	14-24	·	·	·	·	·	65-70
Terry Mulholland	·	·	·	·	·	·	·	·	3-3	·	0-3	3-3
Donell Nixon	·	·	·	·	·	7-4	3-3	·	·	3-3	·	10-7
Tony Perezchica	·	·	1-1	·	·	·	·	·	·	·	·	1-1
Joe Price	·	·	·	·	·	·	·	·	1-2	·	13-22	1-2
Jessie Reid	·	·	·	·	·	·	·	·	·	·	·	·
Rick Reuschel	·	·	·	·	·	·	·	·	21-15	·	·	21-15
Ernest Riles	·	·	8-3	14-10	3-3	·	·	·	·	1-1	·	25-16
Don Robinson	·	·	·	·	·	·	·	·	9-10	·	15-17	9-10
Roger Samuels	·	·	·	·	·	·	·	·	·	·	6-9	·
Lary Sorensen	·	·	·	·	·	·	·	·	·	·	5-7	·
Chris Speier	·	·	9-13	4-4	4-2	·	·	·	1-0	·	·	17-19
Harry Spilman	·	·	·	·	·	0-1	·	·	·	·	·	0-1
Rob Thompson	·	·	65-62	·	·	·	·	·	·	·	·	65-62
Rusty Tillman	·	·	·	·	·	·	·	·	·	·	·	·
Jose Uribe	·	·	·	·	71-69	·	·	·	·	·	·	71-69
Mark Wasinger	·	·	·	·	·	·	·	·	·	·	·	·
Matt Williams	·	·	·	14-19	5-5	·	·	·	·	·	·	19-24
Trevor Wilson	·	·	·	·	·	·	·	·	1-3	·	·	1-3
Joel Youngblood	·	·	·	·	·	4-5	1-1	4-2	·	0-1	·	9-8

Batting vs. Left and Right Handed Pitchers

		BA	Rank	SA	Rank	OBA	Rank	HR %	Rank	BB %	Rank	SO %	Rank
Mike Aldrete	vs. Lefties	.288	31	.375	67	.344	44	1.25	84	8.79	60	17.58	105
	vs. Righties	.262	56	.317	100	.360	23	0.65	103	13.41	9	13.69	62
Bob Brenly	vs. Lefties	.207	110	.310	106	.273	107	1.72	72	9.09	54	15.15	92
	vs. Righties	.182	128	.291	113	.262	122	2.70	33	8.33	57	17.86	100
Brett Butler	vs. Lefties	.253	75	.332	92	.380	13	0.53	102	16.09	4	11.30	59
	vs. Righties	.304	11	.431	26	.400	6	1.32	75	13.36	10	8.46	15
Will Clark	vs. Lefties	.262	59	.434	34	.331	61	3.17	35	9.27	52	20.16	120
	vs. Righties	.294	18	.554	2	.417	1	6.21	1	17.46	2	17.91	102
Candy Maldonado	vs. Lefties	.251	77	.311	104	.303	87	0.55	101	6.47	85	12.94	72
	vs. Righties	.256	65	.415	33	.316	63	3.48	25	6.84	79	17.95	103
Bob Melvin	vs. Lefties	.271	50	.435	32	.315	77	3.53	27	6.45	86	9.68	40
	vs. Righties	.218	114	.351	73	.246	127	2.66	36	3.59	121	18.97	111
Kevin Mitchell	vs. Lefties	.200	114	.338	88	.280	101	3.13	36	9.89	44	14.29	86
	vs. Righties	.275	36	.490	9	.337	41	4.06	17	7.81	63	15.36	79
Ernest Riles	vs. Lefties	.304	--	.435	--	.333	--	4.35	--	4.17	--	25.00	--
	vs. Righties	.293	19	.396	43	.322	56	1.22	78	5.08	112	15.25	76
Chris Speier	vs. Lefties	.258	68	.379	66	.425	2	0.00	103	21.35	1	15.73	98
	vs. Righties	.190	--	.305	--	.220	--	2.86	--	3.57	--	22.32	--
Rob Thompson	vs. Lefties	.325	7	.487	17	.385	11	0.65	100	8.99	57	18.54	114
	vs. Righties	.235	97	.334	88	.293	97	1.86	55	6.63	84	21.55	120
Jose Uribe	vs. Lefties	.303	18	.395	57	.350	39	1.32	81	6.71	82	6.10	13
	vs. Righties	.229	102	.284	116	.280	111	0.29	112	6.74	83	15.90	86
Joel Youngblood	vs. Lefties	.262	61	.277	115	.329	63	0.00	103	10.26	37	7.69	20
	vs. Righties	.241	--	.293	--	.279	--	0.00	--	3.28	--	18.03	--
Team Average	vs. Lefties	.249	6	.361	8	.321	3	1.70	11	9.40	1	15.47	9
	vs. Righties	.248	7	.372	4	.317	3	2.25	3	8.66	3	17.08	10
League Average	vs. Lefties	.248		.367		.310		2.10		8.01		14.42	
	vs. Righties	.249		.360		.310		1.88		7.86		15.35	

Batting with Runners on Base and Bases Empty

		BA	Rank	SA	Rank	OBA	Rank	HR %	Rank	BB %	Rank	SO %	Rank
Mike Aldrete	Runners On	.299	27	.379	64	.386	22	1.13	81	12.98	29	9.62	28
	Bases Empty	.241	81	.288	113	.332	32	0.47	111	12.03	8	18.67	105
Bob Brenly	Runners On	.198	122	.349	86	.268	120	3.49	21	8.08	81	15.15	90
	Bases Empty	.183	123	.258	118	.263	114	1.67	70	8.89	37	18.52	100
Brett Butler	Runners On	.256	82	.340	96	.398	17	0.64	94	17.65	7	11.27	51
	Bases Empty	.299	10	.420	26	.392	3	1.21	83	12.84	4	8.63	16
Will Clark	Runners On	.287	43	.549	4	.419	7	5.60	5	19.08	4	18.21	110
	Bases Empty	.277	28	.472	13	.353	15	4.56	15	9.91	21	19.24	106
Candy Maldonado	Runners On	.258	81	.371	72	.323	87	2.18	49	7.60	86	15.97	101
	Bases Empty	.252	56	.381	48	.301	70	2.59	41	5.88	82	16.26	84
Bob Melvin	Runners On	.262	74	.466	21	.274	117	3.88	16	1.87	127	14.95	87
	Bases Empty	.218	108	.324	97	.265	113	2.35	48	6.08	77	16.57	88
Kevin Mitchell	Runners On	.275	58	.438	34	.337	71	2.92	30	8.76	73	14.23	80
	Bases Empty	.230	98	.445	17	.301	16	4.53	16	8.22	79	15.75	79
Ernest Riles	Runners On	.325	7	.458	25	.355	49	2.41	43	6.45	106	19.35	114
	Bases Empty	.269	--	.356	--	.296	--	0.96	--	3.70	--	13.89	--
Chris Speier	Runners On	.200	119	.314	107	.313	95	1.43	72	13.64	26	20.45	119
	Bases Empty	.228	101	.347	76	.310	58	1.98	62	9.73	24	18.58	102
Rob Thompson	Runners On	.303	23	.456	27	.373	30	1.54	67	9.21	64	17.15	107
	Bases Empty	.238	86	.333	91	.286	91	1.42	76	5.98	81	23.26	122
Jose Uribe	Runners On	.270	64	.345	91	.333	75	0.50	100	8.85	70	11.06	47
	Bases Empty	.239	84	.300	107	.278	97	0.68	102	5.18	92	14.24	63
Team Average	Runners On	.262	2	.387	2	.340	1	2.11	2	10.19	4	15.43	11
	Bases Empty	.239	9	.355	6	.302	3	2.04	4	7.90	1	17.44	11
League Average	Runners On	.257		.373		.329		1.91		9.45		14.09	
	Bases Empty	.242		.355		.297		1.98		6.73		15.80	

Overall Batting Compared to Late Inning Pressure Situations

		BA	Rank	SA	Rank	OBA	Rank	HR %	Rank	BB %	Rank	SO %	Rank	RDI %	Rank
Mike Aldrete	Overall	.267	46	.329	104	.357	19	0.77	97	12.47	14	14.48	76	.341	8
	Pressure	.206	95	.222	116	.296	85	0.00	79	11.11	38	16.67	79	.071	126
Bob Brenly	Overall	.189	126	.296	115	.265	122	2.43	40	8.55	50	17.09	101	.268	66
	Pressure	.222	86	.306	82	.349	44	0.00	79	15.56	13	13.33	55	.364	20
Brett Butler	Overall	.287	22	.398	42	.393	3	1.06	89	14.29	6	9.43	24	.254	81
	Pressure	.211	93	.250	105	.333	51	0.00	79	14.89	17	11.70	43	.143	108
Will Clark	Overall	.282	26	.508	3	.386	6	5.04	4	14.51	4	18.72	110	.313	20
	Pressure	.253	54	.414	33	.365	31	3.45	20	15.38	15	24.04	118	.364	20
Jeffrey Leonard	Overall	.256	--	.356	--	.292	--	1.25	--	5.26	--	14.04	--	.305	29
	Pressure	.379	--	.483	--	.419	--	0.00	--	6.45	--	12.90	--	.500	2
Candy Maldonado	Overall	.255	75	.377	58	.311	81	2.40	42	6.70	89	16.12	93	.286	48
	Pressure	.190	106	.241	111	.247	112	1.27	64	5.68	96	20.45	101	.091	122
Bob Melvin	Overall	.234	106	.377	57	.268	119	2.93	33	4.51	118	15.97	91	.167	127
	Pressure	.239	72	.304	85	.286	89	0.00	79	6.00	91	10.00	28	.250	59
Kevin Mitchell	Overall	.251	81	.442	16	.319	67	3.76	18	8.48	51	15.02	82	.294	45
	Pressure	.205	96	.410	35	.276	99	6.41	4	9.09	52	22.73	112	.138	111
Ernest Riles	Overall	.294	13	.401	40	.323	56	1.60	69	4.98	115	16.42	96	.323	12
	Pressure	.241	--	.414	--	.281	--	3.45	--	6.25	--	21.88	--	.375	--
Chris Speier	Overall	.216	117	.333	99	.311	82	1.75	65	11.44	23	19.40	116	.212	115
	Pressure	.269	--	.346	--	.457	--	0.00	--	20.51	--	15.38	--	.167	--
Rob Thompson	Overall	.264	52	.384	53	.323	57	1.47	73	7.41	73	20.56	120	.227	103
	Pressure	.275	42	.333	64	.301	78	0.00	79	1.35	127	20.27	100	.192	85
Jose Uribe	Overall	.252	80	.318	111	.301	92	0.61	103	6.73	88	12.90	55	.222	106
	Pressure	.275	43	.325	74	.326	60	1.25	65	6.82	82	11.36	40	.217	71
Joel Youngblood	Overall	.252	--	.285	--	.307	--	0.00	--	7.19	--	12.23	--	.302	34
	Pressure	.316	20	.395	39	.409	8	0.00	79	10.87	41	17.39	85	.357	25
Team Average	Overall	.248	5	.368	5	.318	2	2.07	3	8.90	3	16.56	11	.262	3
	Pressure	.227	11	.315	10	.303	9	1.56	7	8.99	5	18.60	11	.213	11
League Average	Overall	.248		.363		.310		1.95		7.91		15.06		.256	
	Pressure	.242		.340		.310		1.70		8.47		15.93		.238	

Additional Miscellaneous Batting Comparisons

	Grass Surface BA	Rank	Artificial Surface BA	Rank	Home Games BA	Rank	Road Games BA	Rank	Runners in Scoring Position BA	Rank	Runners in Scoring Pos and Two Outs BA	Rank	Leading Off Inning OBA	Rank	Runners on 3B with less than 2 Outs RDI %	Rank
Mike Aldrete	.245	86	.327	5	.208	116	.315	4	.298	28	.302	24	.345	32	.583	59
Bob Brenly	.211	116	.130	--	.177	126	.200	122	.217	105	.105	--	.328	44	.583	59
Brett Butler	.298	14	.257	65	.290	29	.284	24	.252	71	.214	80	.384	11	.700	19
Will Clark	.281	30	.283	33	.269	52	.295	11	.316	16	.345	9	.343	34	.538	79
Jeffrey Leonard	.239	92	.294	--	.215	--	.296	--	.326	--	.391	--	.289	--	.636	40
Candy Maldonado	.257	59	.248	71	.236	95	.273	37	.250	74	.286	37	.317	58	.516	89
Kirt Manwaring	.274	37	.188	--	.250	--	.250	--	.290	--	.188	--	.261	--	.500	--
Bob Melvin	.236	99	.230	--	.245	88	.224	103	.183	122	.250	56	.270	93	.200	--
Kevin Mitchell	.270	44	.192	119	.265	59	.238	90	.279	45	.267	47	.256	105	.563	67
Ernest Riles	.308	8	.259	--	.321	--	.272	39	.260	65	.292	30	.262	--	.714	15
Chris Speier	.242	89	.157	--	.278	41	.148	--	.233	91	.176	--	.250	--	.375	--
Rob Thompson	.235	102	.338	2	.257	75	.270	41	.240	86	.146	117	.354	26	.536	80
Jose Uribe	.264	50	.222	99	.268	56	.238	91	.227	95	.148	115	.284	85	.688	25
Matt Williams	.229	106	.080	--	.227	103	.169	--	.179	--	.211	--	.313	--	.250	--
Joel Youngblood	.264	48	.222	--	.259	--	.246	--	.325	--	.316	--	.200	--	.692	24
Team Average	.252	5	.238	11	.247	10	.249	4	.254	4	.239	5	.311	4	.556	6
League Average	.250		.246		.252		.244		.250		.231		.301		.554	

Pitching vs. Left and Right Handed Batters

		BA	Rank	SA	Rank	OBA	Rank	HR %	Rank	BB %	Rank	SO %	Rank
Kelly Downs	vs. Lefties	.184	7	.269	9	.249	7	1.56	46	7.91	43	16.10	38
	vs. Righties	.268	88	.401	90	.312	72	1.99	55	5.74	42	18.43	33
Scott Garrelts	vs. Lefties	.217	22	.287	15	.313	46	0.64	14	11.89	87	19.46	20
	vs. Righties	.234	50	.299	19	.320	80	1.02	19	10.53	95	21.93	15
Atlee Hammaker	vs. Lefties	.264	66	.333	34	.313	45	0.00	1	5.05	11	18.18	28
	vs. Righties	.245	63	.355	59	.299	61	2.38	76	7.09	61	9.25	101
Mike Krukow	vs. Lefties	.261	61	.412	86	.314	49	2.45	83	6.79	26	13.58	59
	vs. Righties	.209	18	.342	49	.262	19	3.11	96	5.16	32	15.48	56
Mike LaCoss	vs. Lefties	.224	25	.276	10	.322	58	0.00	1	12.15	92	18.22	27
	vs. Righties	.244	62	.359	62	.300	62	2.39	78	7.39	69	10.87	87
Craig Lefferts	vs. Lefties	.242	39	.368	60	.280	18	2.11	69	3.96	5	21.78	14
	vs. Righties	.218	31	.325	35	.273	31	2.14	65	7.28	64	13.79	70
Terry Mulholland	vs. Lefties	.227	--	.273	--	.261	--	0.00	--	4.17	--	16.67	--
	vs. Righties	.288	101	.423	99	.319	78	1.92	51	3.59	13	8.38	107
Joe Price	vs. Lefties	.154	--	.250	--	.228	--	1.92	--	8.62	--	25.86	--
	vs. Righties	.276	96	.422	98	.356	103	2.16	66	10.43	94	16.11	48
Rick Reuschel	vs. Lefties	.284	83	.369	61	.313	48	0.78	20	4.56	9	6.02	105
	vs. Righties	.232	47	.328	37	.268	26	1.67	43	3.76	14	13.05	79
Don Robinson	vs. Lefties	.216	21	.324	28	.272	13	1.85	61	7.02	30	15.45	43
	vs. Righties	.246	64	.362	64	.296	58	1.50	39	6.50	51	18.16	36
Team Average	vs. Lefties	.238	2	.327	1	.295	1	1.22	1	7.39	1	14.41	6
	vs. Righties	.245	7	.366	6	.299	7	2.22	6	6.70	7	14.51	8
League Average	vs. Lefties	.255		.365		.325		1.73		9.36		14.24	
	vs. Righties	.244		.361		.299		2.10		6.87		15.64	

Pitching with Runners on Base and Bases Empty

		BA	Rank	SA	Rank	OBA	Rank	HR %	Rank	BB %	Rank	SO %	Rank
Kelly Downs	Runners On	.257	60	.389	70	.317	45	1.77	56	9.13	49	14.45	51
	Bases Empty	.207	15	.301	15	.256	12	1.77	50	5.45	32	18.96	23
Scott Garrelts	Runners On	.256	59	.313	23	.370	100	0.00	1	14.09	97	19.09	20
	Bases Empty	.197	7	.275	7	.259	13	1.69	47	7.77	75	22.80	11
Atlee Hammaker	Runners On	.278	82	.373	57	.351	81	1.42	40	9.52	54	9.52	96
	Bases Empty	.228	35	.338	39	.268	20	2.37	75	4.79	19	11.55	87
Mike Krukow	Runners On	.226	27	.316	25	.302	29	0.56	14	8.17	32	13.46	59
	Bases Empty	.242	56	.416	96	.282	33	4.10	107	4.53	15	15.21	60
Mike LaCoss	Runners On	.241	40	.276	14	.340	70	0.00	1	12.87	93	12.38	73
	Bases Empty	.229	39	.344	44	.291	46	1.98	56	7.64	70	16.36	50
Craig Lefferts	Runners On	.200	9	.323	32	.282	12	2.31	76	10.32	68	15.48	37
	Bases Empty	.241	53	.347	47	.271	22	2.01	58	3.38	9	16.43	49
Joe Price	Runners On	.280	83	.460	104	.379	103	3.00	99	12.50	90	15.00	45
	Bases Empty	.226	28	.328	32	.289	43	1.46	35	8.05	81	20.81	17
Rick Reuschel	Runners On	.259	62	.342	39	.310	33	0.57	15	7.18	20	10.15	90
	Bases Empty	.262	89	.355	54	.282	34	1.55	39	2.18	4	8.56	105
Don Robinson	Runners On	.238	36	.375	61	.312	36	3.13	100	9.93	61	16.56	31
	Bases Empty	.226	29	.323	26	.265	17	0.75	14	4.49	13	17.02	40
Team Average	Runners On	.254	6	.362	4	.326	6	1.57	3	9.43	6	13.49	7
	Bases Empty	.235	3	.342	4	.278	1	1.97	6	5.19	1	15.19	8
League Average	Runners On	.257		.373		.329		1.91		9.45		14.09	
	Bases Empty	.242		.355		.297		1.98		6.73		15.80	

Overall Pitching Compared to Late Inning Pressure Situations

		BA	Rank	SA	Rank	OBA	Rank	HR %	Rank	BB %	Rank	SO %	Rank
Kelly Downs	Overall	.225	24	.333	30	.279	16	1.77	45	6.86	34	17.23	29
	Pressure	.196	18	.232	8	.254	16	0.00	1	7.94	44	15.87	44
Scott Garrelts	Overall	.226	25	.294	9	.317	65	0.85	8	11.14	96	20.82	17
	Pressure	.254	60	.321	48	.351	84	0.52	20	12.88	98	20.60	19
Atlee Hammaker	Overall	.248	57	.352	47	.302	41	2.00	56	6.75	30	10.71	92
	Pressure	.266	75	.358	65	.328	67	0.92	27	8.33	50	13.33	64
Mike Krukow	Overall	.236	38	.379	75	.289	31	2.77	98	6.00	18	14.51	60
	Pressure	.360	--	.680	--	.500	--	4.00	--	18.18	--	3.03	--
Mike LaCoss	Overall	.234	36	.317	19	.311	54	1.18	20	9.85	87	14.68	58
	Pressure	.237	52	.395	79	.293	39	2.63	85	7.32	38	14.63	53
Craig Lefferts	Overall	.225	23	.337	33	.275	12	2.13	70	6.35	24	16.02	38
	Pressure	.213	39	.299	34	.284	34	1.72	58	9.00	62	15.00	51
Joe Price	Overall	.249	58	.384	83	.328	85	2.11	68	10.04	89	18.22	24
	Pressure	.269	77	.410	88	.352	86	2.56	83	11.11	89	20.00	23
Rick Reuschel	Overall	.261	78	.350	44	.293	32	1.19	21	4.20	3	9.20	104
	Pressure	.278	85	.361	66	.320	58	1.03	35	4.81	12	9.62	94
Don Robinson	Overall	.231	31	.343	39	.284	22	1.67	42	6.76	31	16.83	32
	Pressure	.244	55	.407	86	.329	71	2.22	72	11.18	90	17.39	33
Team Average	Overall	.242	5	.350	3	.298	2	1.81	4	6.98	2	14.47	7
	Pressure	.258	10	.381	11	.331	9	1.85	7	9.57	10	15.41	6
League Average	Overall	.248		.363		.310		1.95		7.91		15.06	
	Pressure	.243		.347		.315		1.72		9.12		15.69	

Additional Miscellaneous Pitching Comparisons

	Grass Surface BA	Rank	Artificial Surface BA	Rank	Home Games BA	Rank	Road Games BA	Rank	Runners in Scoring Position BA	Rank	Runners in Scoring Pos and Two Outs BA	Rank	Leading Off Inning OBA	Rank
Kelly Downs	.218	20	.245	57	.208	16	.245	48	.254	63	.191	33	.246	8
Dave Dravecky	.245	44	.231	--	.333	--	.177	--	.240	--	.083	--	.297	--
Scott Garrelts	.248	48	.179	4	.226	30	.226	29	.270	80	.207	45	.366	99
Atlee Hammaker	.246	46	.252	64	.237	48	.263	65	.282	88	.200	39	.264	16
Mike Krukow	.254	58	.189	6	.245	60	.225	28	.180	13	.176	20	.305	64
Mike LaCoss	.219	21	.289	98	.203	15	.289	98	.269	78	.214	51	.328	83
Craig Lefferts	.233	28	.206	14	.261	74	.199	5	.165	7	.217	55	.259	14
Terry Mulholland	.266	72	.315	--	.246	--	.344	--	.319	--	.333	--	.375	--
Joe Price	.231	25	.309	--	.197	13	.314	106	.297	93	.429	--	.338	90
Rick Reuschel	.246	47	.301	103	.229	36	.287	96	.262	74	.207	46	.290	54
Don Robinson	.234	33	.224	27	.248	63	.220	20	.260	72	.264	88	.282	45
Trevor Wilson	.298	97	.000	--	.317	--	.250	--	.333	--	.250	--	.292	--
Team Average	.239	2	.251	7	.235	3	.250	4	.256	9	.233	6	.292	5
League Average	.250		.246		.244		.252		.250		.231		.301	
League Average	.250		.246		.244		.252		.250		.231		.301	

III
Batter Section

Batter Section

The Batter Section is an alphabetical listing of every player who had at least 200 plate appearances in either the American or the National League last season. Also included are key players who did not meet the 200-plate-appearance requirement. Players are listed alphabetically within each league, followed by the totals for each team and the league as a whole.

Column Headings Information

Tony Armas											Bats Right	
Boston Red Sox	AB	H	2B	3B	HR	RRF	BB	SO	BA	SA	OBA

AB	At Bats
H	Hits
2B	Doubles
3B	Triples
HR	Home Runs
RBI	Runs Batted In
BB	Bases on Balls
SO	Strikeouts
BA	Batting Average
SA	Slugging Average
OBA	On-Base Average

For each player, information is provided in eleven offensive categories.

Season Summary Information

	AB	H	2B	3B	HR	RBI	BB	SO	BA	SA	OBA
Season	493	129	29	1	27	91	38	68	.262	.489	.341
vs. Left-Handed Pitchers	188	53	9	0	9	38	18	27	.282	.473	.366
vs. Right-Handed Pitchers	305	76	20	1	18	53	20	41	.249	.498	.326
Home	223	55	11	0	10	43	18	38	.247	.430	.325
Road	270	74	18	1	17	48	20	30	.274	.537	.354
Grass	409	106	26	0	21	79	33	57	.259	.477	.336
Artificial Turf	84	23	3	1	6	12	5	11	.274	.548	.365
April	74	16	6	0	3	7	0	9	.216	.419	.244
May	75	21	4	0	6	12	10	12	.280	.573	.386
June	87	23	3	0	7	24	11	9	.264	.540	.360
July	88	22	6	0	3	11	6	10	.250	.420	.316
August	98	25	4	1	5	21	7	14	.255	.469	.333
Sept./Oct.	71	22	6	0	3	16	4	14	.310	.521	.402

Each player's seasonal performance is broken down into a variety of special categories. The first line for each player gives his totals for the whole season. This is followed by breakdowns of his performance against left- and right-handed pitchers, in home and road games, on grass fields and on artificial turf, and in each month. (For players who played for more than one team within a league, all totals are combined. The "home" totals for Ken Phelps, for example, include all games he played in Seattle while with the Mariners, and all games played in New York while with the Yankees.)

	AB	H	2B	3B	HR	RBI	BB	SO	BA	SA	OBA
Leading Off Inn.	107	25	5	0	6	6	8	16	.234	.449	.311
Runners On	272	72	18	0	13	77	20	39	.265	.474	.343
Runners/Scor. Pos.	140	35	9	0	3	51	13	15	.250	.379	.337
Runners On/2 Out	133	29	6	0	5	26	11	19	.218	.376	.325
Scor. Pos./2 Out	60	11	2	0	0	12	7	7	.183	.217	.319

Following these breakdowns, each batter's performance is divided into specific game situations. Totals are given for each batter when he led off an inning and when he batted with runners on base. These are followed by his performance with runners in scoring position (on second or third base, or both), with runners on base and two out, and with runners in scoring position and two out.

	AB	H	2B	3B	HR	RBI	BB	SO	BA	SA	OBA
Late Inning Pressure	90	23	6	1	3	13	5	13	.256	.444	.299
Bases Empty	42	12	5	1	2	2	1	7	.286	.595	.318
Runners On	48	11	1	0	1	11	4	6	.229	.313	.283
Runners/Scor. Pos.	26	7	1	0	1	11	3	2	.269	.423	.333

The next group shows the batter's performance in late-inning pressure situations: any plate appearances occurring in the seventh inning or later with the score tied or with the batter's team trailing by one, two, or three runs (or four runs if the bases are loaded).

Each player's totals are listed for all late-inning pressure situations, then broken out for his performance when leading off an inning, with runners on base, and with runners in scoring position.

RUNS BATTED IN	From 1B	From 2B	From 3B	Scoring Position
Total	6/138	14/80	21/57	35/137
Percentage	4%	18%	37%	26%
Driving In Runners from 3B with Less than Two Out:		15/30		50%

The next section, labeled "Runs Batted In," is a measure of the player's ability to drive in runners from each base. For every base, two numbers are listed: the first is the number of RBIs credited to the batter for bringing home runners from that base; the second is the total number of opportunities the batter faced for that situation. (For example, the notation "14/31" under runners on second would mean that the player batted 31 times with runners on second and drove home 14 of the runners.) Plate appearances that result in a base on balls, hit batsman, sacrifice bunt, or an award of first base through catcher's interference are not treated as "opportunities" if they do not result in a run.

If there is more than one runner on base, there is an "opportunity" to drive in each base runner. A single with the bases loaded that scores only the runner from third is an opportunity and an RBI for the "From 3B" line, but an unsuccessful opportunity for the "From 2B" and "From 1B" lines. (The exception to this is when a base on balls, hit batsman, sacrifice bunt, or award through interference results in a run. A walk with the bases loaded would result in an RBI and an opportunity for the "From 3B" line, but would not be charged as an unsuccessful opportunity for the other two.)

Also given is the percentage of successful opportunities; runners driven in from scoring position (combining the "From 3B" and "From 2B" totals); and a line summarizing the batter's performance driving in runners from third with less than two out.

Following the "Runs Batted In" information are comments for each player. Included are the pitchers each batter loves to face and hates to face. The statistics listed for each individual match-up are from regular season games since 1975.

American League

Andy Allanson

Cleveland Indians	AB	H	2B	3B	HR	RBI	BB	SO	BA	SA	OBA
Season	434	114	11	0	5	50	25	63	.263	.323	.305
vs. Left-Handers	104	28	4	0	0	8	5	13	.269	.308	.306
vs. Right-Handers	330	86	7	0	5	42	20	50	.261	.327	.304
Home	223	61	6	0	4	34	14	35	.274	.354	.318
Road	211	53	5	0	1	16	11	28	.251	.289	.290
Grass	369	100	9	0	5	46	21	53	.271	.336	.311
Artificial Turf	65	14	2	0	0	4	4	10	.215	.246	.271
April	66	16	2	0	1	9	3	8	.242	.318	.286
May	83	22	5	0	1	12	7	15	.265	.361	.319
June	80	18	1	0	2	10	4	7	.225	.313	.267
July	38	9	1	0	0	3	4	6	.237	.263	.295
August	77	19	1	0	0	11	3	14	.247	.260	.275
Sept./Oct.	90	30	1	0	1	5	4	13	.333	.378	.368
Leading Off Inn.	119	30	2	0	1	1	2	9	.252	.294	.264
Runners On	177	54	7	0	2	47	12	25	.305	.379	.349
Runners/Scor. Pos.	101	31	5	0	2	46	12	13	.307	.416	.378
Runners On/2 Out	79	26	5	0	1	26	8	12	.329	.430	.398
Scor. Pos./2 Out	51	19	4	0	1	25	8	9	.373	.510	.467
Late Inning Pressure	62	14	3	0	0	6	7	11	.226	.274	.304
Leading Off	21	4	0	0	0	0	0	3	.190	.190	.190
Runners On	17	5	1	0	0	6	4	4	.294	.353	.429
Runners/Scor. Pos.	8	3	1	0	0	6	4	1	.375	.500	.583

RUNS BATTED IN	From 1B	From 2B	From 3B	Scoring Position
Totals	4/127	19/82	22/46	41/128
Percentage	3%	23%	48%	32%
Driving In Runners from 3B with Less than Two Out:			11/22	50%

Loves to face: Doyle Alexander (.600, 6-for-10, 1 HR)
Hates to face: Dave Stewart (0-for-11)
Led A.L. catchers in games, putouts, errors, and double plays; first Cleveland catcher since John Romano in 1961 to lead A.L. in games caught. . . . Fewest extra-base hits in A.L. among players with at least 400 at-bats. . . . Removed for a pinch hitter 20 times last season, tied with Jay Bell for most on club. . . . Batted .417 (5-for-12) with bases loaded last season, including first career grand slam. . . . Hit .450 (18-for-40) in 13 games vs. Detroit last year. . . . Career batting averages: .287 vs. ground-ball pitchers, .222 vs. fly-ball pitchers. That 65-point difference is greater than his batting average disparity vs. left-handed/right-handed pitchers, on grass/artificial fields, in day/night games, or in home/road games.

Brady Anderson

Red Sox/Orioles	AB	H	2B	3B	HR	RBI	BB	SO	BA	SA	OBA
Season	325	69	13	4	1	21	23	75	.212	.286	.272
vs. Left-Handers	85	17	2	1	0	2	6	24	.200	.247	.277
vs. Right-Handers	240	52	11	3	1	19	17	51	.217	.300	.270
Home	174	34	7	1	1	15	11	44	.195	.264	.259
Road	151	35	6	3	0	6	12	31	.232	.311	.287
Grass	268	58	12	4	1	21	17	61	.216	.302	.272
Artificial Turf	57	11	1	0	0	0	6	14	.193	.211	.270
April	47	13	2	1	0	3	6	15	.277	.362	.375
May	96	21	3	2	0	9	8	17	.219	.292	.292
June	5	0	0	0	0	0	1	3	.000	.000	.167
July	9	2	1	0	0	0	1	1	.222	.333	.222
August	91	16	1	0	1	6	6	25	.176	.220	.227
Sept./Oct.	77	17	6	1	0	3	2	14	.221	.325	.241
Leading Off Inn.	86	11	1	0	0	0	8	23	.128	.140	.211
Runners On	132	29	4	1	1	21	10	28	.220	.288	.283
Runners/Scor. Pos.	68	17	1	1	1	19	8	17	.250	.338	.342
Runners On/2 Out	44	7	0	1	0	5	6	13	.159	.205	.275
Scor. Pos./2 Out	28	3	0	1	0	5	6	8	.107	.179	.286
Late Inning Pressure	47	5	1	0	0	0	1	18	.106	.128	.176
Leading Off	9	1	0	0	0	0	1	5	.111	.111	.273
Runners On	21	1	0	0	0	0	0	7	.048	.048	.091
Runners/Scor. Pos.	11	0	0	0	0	0	0	4	.000	.000	.083

RUNS BATTED IN	From 1B	From 2B	From 3B	Scoring Position
Totals	3/100	8/53	9/30	17/83
Percentage	3%	15%	30%	20%
Driving In Runners from 3B with Less than Two Out:			6/14	43%

Loves to face: Jack Morris (.455, 5-for-11)
Hates to face: Charlie Hough (0-for-8, 4 SO)
Boston's leadoff hitter on opening day. Morris fanned him in his first major league at-bat before he stroked three straight singles off Tigers' ace. . . . His only home run came off Tom Filer. . . . Stole 10 bases in 12 attempts in night games, but was 0-for-4 under the sun. . . . Grounded into only three double plays in 78 DP situations last season, 5th-lowest rate in A.L. (min.: 40 opportunities). . . . Split time between right field and center field while playing under John McNamara, but was used exclusively in center by Frank Robinson. . . . Batted .230 in 41 games for Boston, .198 in 53 games for Baltimore. . . . Red Sox won eight of first ten games that he started, but Orioles lost 15 of his last 16 starts.

Tony Armas

California Angels	AB	H	2B	3B	HR	RBI	BB	SO	BA	SA	OBA
Season	368	100	20	2	13	50	22	87	.272	.443	.311
vs. Left-Handers	165	49	12	0	8	26	12	26	.297	.515	.345
vs. Right-Handers	203	51	8	2	5	24	10	61	.251	.384	.284
Home	199	48	12	1	5	21	12	49	.241	.387	.282
Road	169	52	8	1	8	29	10	38	.308	.509	.346
Grass	318	84	17	1	12	44	16	75	.264	.437	.298
Artificial Turf	50	16	3	1	1	6	6	12	.320	.480	.393
April	35	9	3	0	1	2	3	7	.257	.429	.316
May	70	13	2	1	1	7	6	13	.186	.286	.250
June	71	16	4	0	1	4	8	22	.225	.324	.304
July	73	22	3	1	2	13	0	15	.301	.452	.297
August	83	32	5	0	8	19	0	17	.386	.735	.381
Sept./Oct.	36	8	3	0	0	5	5	13	.222	.306	.317
Leading Off Inn.	79	22	7	1	2	2	7	21	.278	.468	.337
Runners On	156	43	9	0	6	43	9	29	.276	.449	.311
Runners/Scor. Pos.	91	24	5	0	3	35	8	22	.264	.418	.317
Runners On/2 Out	73	21	3	0	4	23	3	17	.288	.493	.316
Scor. Pos./2 Out	40	12	1	0	2	18	2	11	.300	.475	.333
Late Inning Pressure	59	12	4	0	3	6	8	19	.203	.424	.299
Leading Off	12	1	0	0	0	0	3	5	.083	.083	.267
Runners On	19	4	2	0	1	4	4	6	.211	.474	.348
Runners/Scor. Pos.	12	1	1	0	0	2	3	5	.083	.167	.267

RUNS BATTED IN	From 1B	From 2B	From 3B	Scoring Position
Totals	8/119	12/66	17/43	29/109
Percentage	7%	18%	40%	27%
Driving In Runners from 3B with Less than Two Out:			8/21	38%

Loves to face: Steve Trout (.435, 10-for-23, 3 HR)
Hates to face: Juan Berenguer (.120, 3-for-25, 12 SO)
Tied Rob Deer and Mark McGwire for majors' home-run lead in August. . . . Has hit .194 in Late-Inning Pressure Situations over past six years; in past three years, has driven in only three of 33 runners from scoring position in LIPS. . . . Career totals: 240 homers, 253 walks (including 35 intentional). His ratio of 1.05 walks per home run is lowest among the 149 guys with at least 200 career home runs; closest to him: Dick Stuart (1.32 BB per HR); closest among active players: Andre Dawson (1.42 BB per HR). . . . Went from June 20 to Sept. 2 between walks last year, a streak of 193 plate appearances that is 2d longest in majors in any season over past 10 years, behind Rob Picciolo's legendary 268-PA streak in 1980.

Harold Baines

Chicago White Sox	AB	H	2B	3B	HR	RBI	BB	SO	BA	SA	OBA
Season	599	166	39	1	13	81	67	109	.277	.411	.347
vs. Left-Handers	190	48	14	0	2	25	19	39	.253	.358	.316
vs. Right-Handers	409	118	25	1	11	56	48	70	.289	.435	.361
Home	295	83	27	0	5	41	41	48	.281	.424	.369
Road	304	83	12	1	8	40	26	61	.273	.398	.325
Grass	499	140	34	1	11	67	63	88	.281	.419	.358
Artificial Turf	100	26	5	0	2	14	4	21	.260	.370	.288
April	81	21	6	0	1	9	10	14	.259	.370	.337
May	95	23	1	0	5	10	11	13	.242	.411	.327
June	107	29	5	0	4	12	11	23	.271	.430	.336
July	99	31	9	0	1	15	16	19	.313	.434	.402
August	103	27	6	0	1	20	15	20	.262	.350	.350
Sept./Oct.	114	35	12	1	1	15	4	20	.307	.456	.328
Leading Off Inn.	106	30	8	0	5	5	11	20	.283	.500	.350
Runners On	250	72	16	1	5	73	37	45	.288	.420	.373
Runners/Scor. Pos.	146	44	12	1	1	61	28	31	.301	.418	.401
Runners On/2 Out	85	19	4	0	0	16	14	14	.224	.271	.340
Scor. Pos./2 Out	65	14	3	0	0	15	12	12	.215	.262	.346
Late Inning Pressure	93	31	8	1	4	17	14	15	.333	.570	.421
Leading Off	27	11	4	0	2	2	3	3	.407	.778	.467
Runners On	41	14	3	1	1	14	5	7	.341	.537	.413
Runners/Scor. Pos.	24	8	3	1	0	12	3	4	.333	.542	.407

RUNS BATTED IN	From 1B	From 2B	From 3B	Scoring Position
Totals	11/158	24/100	33/69	57/169
Percentage	7%	24%	48%	34%
Driving In Runners from 3B with Less than Two Out:			28/41	68%

Loves to face: Jay Tibbs (.667, 6-for-9, 2 HR)
Hates to face: Mark Langston (.139, 5-for-36, 1 HR)
Led all designated hitters with 160 hits and 76 RBI last season. . . . Broke a streak of six consecutive seasons of 20-or-more home runs; still alive: he's one of four players with at least 50 extra-base hits in each of past seven seasons (others: Brunansky, Murphy, Winfield). . . . Career total of 173 home runs is White Sox record. Mariners and Padres are only current franchises with lower home-run records. . . . Now needs eight home homers to break Bill Melton's record of 90 home runs at Comiskey Park. . . . Had batted over .300 with runners on base in each of the previous four seasons. Average with runners on base has been higher than bases-empty average in each of last six seasons.

Steve Balboni

Royals/Mariners — Bats Right

	AB	H	2B	3B	HR	RBI	BB	SO	BA	SA	OBA
Season	413	97	17	1	23	66	24	87	.235	.448	.277
vs. Left-Handers	164	33	7	1	6	18	9	40	.201	.366	.243
vs. Right-Handers	249	64	10	0	17	48	15	47	.257	.502	.300
Home	215	51	10	1	15	41	14	51	.237	.502	.286
Road	198	46	7	0	8	25	10	36	.232	.389	.268
Grass	154	34	6	0	6	15	9	28	.221	.377	.262
Artificial Turf	259	63	11	1	17	51	15	59	.243	.490	.286
April	26	4	1	0	1	2	0	6	.154	.308	.154
May	37	5	1	0	1	3	1	14	.135	.243	.158
June	44	7	2	0	2	5	5	12	.159	.341	.245
July	100	28	3	0	10	22	7	21	.280	.610	.333
August	104	22	3	1	4	14	5	15	.212	.375	.245
Sept./Oct.	102	31	7	0	5	20	6	19	.304	.520	.339
Leading Off Inn.	91	17	4	0	6	6	4	24	.187	.429	.221
Runners On	199	49	9	1	12	55	12	35	.246	.482	.290
Runners/Scor. Pos.	106	28	4	0	7	43	5	23	.264	.500	.292
Runners On/2 Out	92	22	3	1	8	29	4	16	.239	.554	.278
Scor. Pos./2 Out	51	12	2	0	5	22	1	9	.235	.569	.250
Late Inning Pressure	57	13	1	0	4	8	5	15	.228	.456	.290
Leading Off	10	2	1	0	1	1	1	3	.200	.600	.273
Runners On	29	9	0	0	2	6	3	8	.310	.517	.375
Runners/Scor. Pos.	13	3	0	0	1	4	2	4	.231	.462	.333

RUNS BATTED IN	From 1B	From 2B	From 3B	Scoring Position
Totals	12/156	17/78	14/48	31/126
Percentage	8%	22%	29%	25%
Driving In Runners from 3B with Less than Two Out:		9/23		39%

Loves to face: Joel Davis (.444, 4-for-9, 2 HR)
Hates to face: Willie Fraser (0-for-13)

Hit more homers at home than on road for first time in career; it took the Kingdome to do it.... Canseco was only righty batter in majors with higher home-run rate vs. right-handed pitchers.... Hit 10 homers in July, tying Canseco for the most homers in any month. ... Batted .338 with four home runs and 16 RBI in his last 19 games; ended season with eight-game hitting streak, and 37-game errorless streak at first base.... Career batting average of .192 (10-for-52) with the bases loaded, but has three homers and eight walks.... Has 2549 career at-bats, one stolen base. Since stolen bases were invented in 1887, only one player has had more at-bats with a max of one steal: Gus Triandos (3907 AB, 1 SB).

Jesse Barfield

Toronto Blue Jays — Bats Right

	AB	H	2B	3B	HR	RBI	BB	SO	BA	SA	OBA
Season	468	114	21	5	18	56	41	108	.244	.425	.302
vs. Left-Handers	165	35	5	0	9	20	16	37	.212	.406	.284
vs. Right-Handers	303	79	16	5	9	36	25	71	.261	.436	.312
Home	236	59	9	5	12	31	20	49	.250	.483	.309
Road	232	55	12	0	6	25	21	59	.237	.366	.296
Grass	174	39	6	0	4	16	12	43	.224	.328	.271
Artificial Turf	294	75	15	5	14	40	29	65	.255	.483	.320
April	80	19	3	1	2	13	8	15	.238	.375	.297
May	47	9	1	1	1	5	1	13	.191	.319	.208
June	87	18	2	1	3	7	8	20	.207	.356	.281
July	57	13	4	1	3	6	7	16	.228	.491	.313
August	100	29	6	0	6	14	8	20	.290	.530	.336
Sept./Oct.	97	26	5	1	3	11	9	24	.268	.433	.327
Leading Off Inn.	110	27	1		4	4	3	23	.245	.400	.265
Runners On	190	46	7	2	5	43	28	42	.242	.379	.330
Runners/Scor. Pos.	109	23	3	1	4	36	17	27	.211	.367	.303
Runners On/2 Out	72	11	3	0	0	8	9	14	.153	.194	.247
Scor. Pos./2 Out	46	6	2	0	0	7	6	9	.130	.174	.231
Late Inning Pressure	61	12	3	0	3		6	15	.197	.393	.269
Leading Off	19	3	0	0	1	1	0	5	.158	.316	.158
Runners On	20	3	0	0	0	2	5	6	.150	.150	.320
Runners/Scor. Pos.	13	1	0	0	0	2	5	5	.077	.077	.333

RUNS BATTED IN	From 1B	From 2B	From 3B	Scoring Position
Totals	10/139	12/83	16/53	28/136
Percentage	7%	14%	30%	21%
Driving In Runners from 3B with Less than Two Out:		14/28		50%

Loves to face: Rick Honeycutt (.444, 4-for-9, 3 HR)
Hates to face: Willie Hernandez (.077, 1-for-13, 9 SO)

Leads major league outfielders with 71 assists over last four seasons. ... Averaged 2.51 putouts per nine innings, most by any right fielder in majors last season. That could explain why Lloyd Moseby had lowest rate in majors among center fielders.... Batting average with runners in scoring position has fallen in each of last three years (.281, .276, .235, .211), as has his overall batting average (.2894, .2886, .263, .244). In each of last five seasons his average with RISP has been lower than his overall average.... One of six players with 100+ strikeouts in each of last four years.... May not be leading the cheers for the SkyDome; his career averages: .281 at Exhibition Stadium, .220 in domes.

Marty Barrett

Boston Red Sox — Bats Right

	AB	H	2B	3B	HR	RBI	BB	SO	BA	SA	OBA
Season	612	173	28	1	1	65	40	35	.283	.337	.330
vs. Left-Handers	181	46	6	1	0	14	9	10	.254	.298	.292
vs. Right-Handers	431	127	22	0	1	51	31	25	.295	.353	.345
Home	308	91	18	1	1	35	19	17	.295	.370	.338
Road	304	82	10	0	0	30	21	18	.270	.303	.321
Grass	513	146	25	1	1	56	36	29	.285	.343	.333
Artificial Turf	99	27	3	0	0	9	4	6	.273	.303	.311
April	86	25	5	0	0	16	5	10	.291	.349	.323
May	115	35	7	0	0	9	4	5	.304	.365	.341
June	100	33	5	1	0	12	11	5	.330	.400	.398
July	111	28	4	0	1	9	5	3	.252	.315	.280
August	93	22	3	0	0	7	6	8	.237	.269	.287
Sept./Oct.	107	30	4	0	0	12	9	4	.280	.318	.345
Leading Off Inn.	98	27	10	0	0	0	6	6	.276	.378	.324
Runners On	310	94	12	1	1	65	20	17	.303	.358	.343
Runners/Scor. Pos.	152	45	6	1	0	59	12	10	.296	.349	.339
Runners On/2 Out	128	34	3	1	1	21	9	10	.266	.328	.319
Scor. Pos./2 Out	76	17	2	1	0	18	8	9	.224	.276	.306
Late Inning Pressure	67	13	2	0	0	7	6	4	.194	.224	.270
Leading Off	14	3	1	0	0	0	2	1	.214	.286	.313
Runners On	36	8	1	0	0	7	1	2	.222	.250	.243
Runners/Scor. Pos.	17	4	1	0	0	7	1	2	.235	.294	.278

RUNS BATTED IN	From 1B	From 2B	From 3B	Scoring Position
Totals	6/241	22/126	36/70	58/196
Percentage	2%	17%	51%	30%
Driving In Runners from 3B with Less than Two Out:		27/36		75%

Loves to face: Dave Stewart (.469, 15-for-32, 1 HR)
Hates to face: Jack Morris (.125, 5-for-40)

First A.L. player to lead league in sacrifice bunts for three consecutive seasons since Phil Rizzuto did it four years in succession (1949–52).... And he's the first A.L. player to reach 65 RBI in a season in which he hit one or no home runs since Billy Goodman of Red Sox in 1948. Three N.L. players have done it in interim (Groat in '64, Foli in '79, Ozzie Smith in '87).... Drove in more runs (64) from the 2d slot in the batting order than any other major leaguer last season.... Batted higher vs. right-handers than vs. left-handers for first time in five full seasons in majors.... Leads A.L. with 736 games at second base over last five seasons.

Don Baylor

Oakland As — Bats Right

	AB	H	2B	3B	HR	RBI	BB	SO	BA	SA	OBA
Season	264	58	7	0	7	34	34	44	.220	.326	.332
vs. Left-Handers	123	27	5	0	1	15	13	22	.220	.285	.305
vs. Right-Handers	141	31	2	0	6	19	21	22	.220	.362	.355
Home	110	22	2	0	2	14	8	21	.200	.273	.268
Road	154	36	5	0	5	20	26	23	.234	.364	.374
Grass	214	47	5	0	6	27	30	38	.220	.327	.339
Artificial Turf	50	11	2	0	1	7	4	6	.220	.320	.304
April	50	9	2	0	0	6	8	8	.180	.220	.305
May	63	15	1	0	1	7	5	10	.238	.302	.310
June	41	8	0	0	2	5	1	8	.195	.341	.233
July	39	9	3	0	1	5	6	4	.231	.385	.362
August	32	7	1	0	2	4	10	6	.219	.438	.422
Sept./Oct.	39	10	0	0	1	7	4	8	.256	.333	.375
Leading Off Inn.	61	9	1	0	1	0		6	.148	.213	.288
Runners On	105	32	3	0	3	30	19	15	.305	.419	.424
Runners/Scor. Pos.	58	17	2	0	2	27	15	6	.293	.414	.443
Runners On/2 Out	52	16	1	0	1	14	7	10	.308	.385	.419
Scor. Pos./2 Out	37	11	1	0	1	14	7	10	.297	.405	.422
Late Inning Pressure	45	9	1	0	1	3	7	6	.200	.289	.357
Leading Off	17	5	1	0	1	1	2	2	.294	.529	.429
Runners On	13	3	0	0	0	2	4	2	.231	.231	.474
Runners/Scor. Pos.	10	2	0	0	0	2	3	1	.200	.200	.429

RUNS BATTED IN	From 1B	From 2B	From 3B	Scoring Position
Totals	3/75	13/50	11/23	24/73
Percentage	4%	26%	48%	33%
Driving In Runners from 3B with Less than Two Out:		7/9		78%

Loves to face: Odell Jones (.571, 8-for-14, 1 HR)
Hates to face: Frank Tanana (.159, 13-for-82, 18 SO)

Does he still hit in the clutch? His 1988 batting average with runners on base was his highest in the 14 years since we started keeping track in 1975. He hit 141 points higher with ROB than with bases empty, 2d largest difference in majors last year (minimum: 100 AB each way).... Started 47 of Oakland's 49 games against left-handers starters, but only 26 of 113 games vs. righties.... One of three nonpitchers who played in their 19th season in majors in 1988; others: Dave Concepcion and Carlton Fisk.... Holds A.L. record with 115 sacrifice flies; he's six shy of Hank Aaron's major league mark.... Has played in 28 L.C.S. games, tied with Hal McRae and Pete Rose for 2d behind Reggie's 45.

George Bell — Toronto Blue Jays

Bats Right

	AB	H	2B	3B	HR	RBI	BB	SO	BA	SA	OBA
Season	614	165	27	5	24	97	34	66	.269	.446	.304
vs. Left-Handers	196	53	8	2	10	31	8	16	.270	.485	.296
vs. Right-Handers	418	112	19	3	14	66	26	50	.268	.428	.308
Home	304	90	17	3	9	47	18	31	.296	.461	.329
Road	310	75	10	2	15	50	16	35	.242	.432	.280
Grass	248	56	6	2	8	39	9	28	.226	.363	.254
Artificial Turf	366	109	21	3	16	58	25	38	.298	.503	.338
April	83	31	8	1	4	11	6	9	.373	.639	.416
May	115	31	4	2	3	14	5	13	.270	.417	.300
June	99	21	4	0	2	18	5	15	.212	.313	.241
July	90	21	2	1	5	13	9	8	.233	.444	.303
August	108	26	3	1	4	18	5	11	.241	.398	.270
Sept./Oct.	119	35	6	0	6	23	4	10	.294	.496	.317
Leading Off Inn.	167	33	6	1	3	3	3	20	.198	.299	.212
Runners On	289	89	10	2	12	85	14	28	.308	.481	.333
Runners/Scor. Pos.	177	52	5	1	8	74	12	21	.294	.469	.328
Runners On/2 Out	129	37	3	2	5	31	8	16	.287	.457	.333
Scor. Pos./2 Out	91	22	1	1	4	26	7	13	.242	.407	.303
Late Inning Pressure	74	20	3	0	4	15	5	8	.270	.473	.316
Leading Off	19	6	2	0	1	1	0	3	.316	.579	.316
Runners On	41	10	1	0	2	13	2	4	.244	.415	.279
Runners/Scor. Pos.	31	8	1	0	2	13	1	3	.258	.484	.281

RUNS BATTED IN	From 1B	From 2B	From 3B	Scoring Position
Totals	11/200	26/136	36/80	62/216
Percentage	6%	19%	45%	29%
Driving In Runners from 3B with Less than Two Out:		29/45		64%

Loves to face: Scott Bankhead (.476, 10-for-21, 5 HR)
Hates to face: Mike Boddicker (.174, 8-for-46)
Started season with five hits (4 HR) in his first seven at-bats as a DH, but had only one hit in 19 DH at-bats after that.... Led major league left fielders with 15 errors (none in 54 games after Aug. 3) while averaging only 1.79 putouts per nine innings, lowest rate in majors (minimum: 500 innings).... Owns .340 career batting average with the bases loaded; has six grand-slam homers, but no grand-slam walks in 62 times up with sacks full.... Totals since 1984: 787 games, 156 home runs, 521 RBI, 1577 total bases; only Ripken and Murphy played in as many games, only Murphy and Strawberry hit as many homers, only Mattingly and Winfield had as many RBI, and only Mattingly had as many total bases.

Jay Bell — Cleveland Indians

Bats Right

	AB	H	2B	3B	HR	RBI	BB	SO	BA	SA	OBA
Season	211	46	5	1	2	21	21	53	.218	.280	.289
vs. Left-Handers	40	14	1	1	0	6	3	6	.350	.425	.386
vs. Right-Handers	171	32	4	0	2	15	18	47	.187	.246	.267
Home	117	23	3	1	2	14	11	28	.197	.291	.267
Road	94	23	2	0	0	7	10	25	.245	.266	.317
Grass	180	36	3	1	2	18	19	47	.200	.261	.277
Artificial Turf	31	10	2	0	0	3	2	6	.323	.387	.364
April	70	10	0	1	1	8	8	14	.143	.214	.241
May	58	17	2	0	0	4	9	17	.293	.328	.382
June	25	3	0	0	0	3	2	7	.120	.120	.185
July	14	1	1	0	0	0	1	6	.071	.143	.133
August	0	0	0	0	0	0	0	0	—	—	—
Sept./Oct.	44	15	2	0	1	6	1	9	.341	.455	.348
Leading Off Inn.	42	8	0	0	1	1	0	13	.190	.190	.209
Runners On	94	22	1	1	1	20	8	23	.234	.298	.288
Runners/Scor. Pos.	55	13	0	1	0	17	3	13	.236	.273	.267
Runners On/2 Out	45	11	0	1	0	8	5	12	.244	.289	.320
Scor. Pos./2 Out	27	8	0	1	0	8	2	6	.296	.370	.345
Late Inning Pressure	23	4	0	0	0	0	2	5	.174	.174	.240
Leading Off	5	0	0	0	0	0	0	1	.000	.000	.000
Runners On	8	1	0	0	0	0	1	3	.125	.125	.222
Runners/Scor. Pos.	4	0	0	0	0	0	1	2	.000	.000	.200

RUNS BATTED IN	From 1B	From 2B	From 3B	Scoring Position
Totals	2/62	5/41	12/30	17/71
Percentage	3%	12%	40%	24%
Driving In Runners from 3B with Less than Two Out:		8/14		57%

Loves to face: Jeff Musselman (.750, 3-for-4)
Hates to face: Dave Stieb (0-for-9)
Batted .186 before the All-Star break, lowest in majors (minimum: two PA per game).... Removed for a pinch hitter 20 times last season, tied with Andy Allanson for most on the club.... Led the Tribe with four appearances as a pinch runner. Indians used pinch runners only 19 times last season, fewest in the majors.... Average of 2.57 assists per nine innings was lowest among major league shortstops (minimum: 500 innings).... Major league career consists of just 350 at-bats, but has hit .333 in 87 at-bats vs. left-handers, .186 in 263 at-bats vs. right-handers.... Outhit George Bell in face-to-face matchups, batting .476 (10-for-21) in six games against the Blue Jays.

Todd Benzinger — Boston Red Sox

Bats Left and Right

	AB	H	2B	3B	HR	RBI	BB	SO	BA	SA	OBA
Season	405	103	28	1	13	70	22	80	.254	.425	.293
vs. Left-Handers	104	22	7	0	1	13	7	12	.212	.308	.259
vs. Right-Handers	301	81	21	1	12	57	15	68	.269	.465	.305
Home	204	55	18	0	6	33	13	36	.270	.446	.315
Road	201	48	10	1	7	37	9	44	.239	.403	.270
Grass	349	92	26	1	11	59	19	64	.264	.438	.302
Artificial Turf	56	11	2	0	2	11	3	16	.196	.339	.237
April	27	6	0	0	1	6	1	4	.222	.333	.241
May	53	15	6	0	1	10	2	14	.283	.453	.309
June	25	4	2	0	0	4	6	6	.160	.240	.276
July	108	35	9	0	5	20	7	17	.324	.546	.365
August	110	24	8	0	6	24	3	25	.218	.455	.237
Sept./Oct.	82	19	3	1	0	10	5	14	.232	.293	.284
Leading Off Inn.	96	26	5	1	2	2	4	15	.271	.406	.307
Runners On	200	49	17	0	6	63	10	42	.245	.420	.278
Runners/Scor. Pos.	130	31	9	0	5	57	9	29	.238	.423	.284
Runners On/2 Out	101	26	7	0	1	31	6	25	.257	.356	.299
Scor. Pos./2 Out	74	18	5	0	1	29	5	19	.243	.351	.291
Late Inning Pressure	56	16	4	0	3	14	2	14	.286	.518	.310
Leading Off	20	6	1	0	0	0	0	3	.300	.350	.300
Runners On	29	9	3	0	2	13	2	7	.310	.621	.355
Runners/Scor. Pos.	18	7	2	0	2	12	2	3	.389	.833	.450

RUNS BATTED IN	From 1B	From 2B	From 3B	Scoring Position
Totals	9/138	15/93	33/69	48/162
Percentage	7%	16%	48%	30%
Driving In Runners from 3B with Less than Two Out:		17/27		63%

Loves to face: Walt Terrell (.667, 4-for-6, 3 HR)
Hates to face: Mitch Williams (0-for-5)
His first home run of 1988 was hit batting right-handed, but all of the rest were hit from left side.... Career average of .371 (13-for-35, one HR) with the bags full. Eight hits with the bags full last season tied him for A.L. lead with Pat Tabler, who did it in only nine at-bats.... Career breakdown: .278 with bases empty, .247 with runners on base, .241 with runners in scoring position.... Five walks in 157 career plate appearances leading off innings.... Point of order: Benzinger has 113 RBI in 628 career at-bats, or 18.0 RBI for every 100 at-bats. Reds fans may recognize that rate: Johnny Bench averaged 18.0 RBI for every 100 at-bats throughout his 17-year career.

Dave Bergman — Detroit Tigers

Bats Left

	AB	H	2B	3B	HR	RBI	BB	SO	BA	SA	OBA
Season	289	85	14	0	5	34	38	34	.294	.394	.372
vs. Left-Handers	17	4	1	0	0	0	1	1	.235	.294	.278
vs. Right-Handers	272	81	13	0	5	34	37	33	.298	.401	.377
Home	127	36	6	0	4	15	25	20	.283	.425	.394
Road	162	49	8	0	1	19	13	14	.302	.370	.352
Grass	241	72	12	0	4	26	35	28	.299	.398	.382
Artificial Turf	48	13	2	0	1	8	3	6	.271	.375	.314
April	13	3	0	0	1	2	6	2	.231	.462	.474
May	35	7	0	0	0	2	2	6	.200	.200	.243
June	29	13	5	0	0	4	4	4	.448	.621	.486
July	59	22	2	0	2	5	10	9	.373	.508	.464
August	84	26	5	0	2	17	7	8	.310	.440	.355
Sept./Oct.	69	14	2	0	0	4	9	5	.203	.232	.295
Leading Off Inn.	74	20	4	0	1	1	8	6	.270	.365	.341
Runners On	119	34	0	0	3	32	15	17	.286	.395	.355
Runners/Scor. Pos.	62	18	3	0	1	27	11	5	.290	.387	.377
Runners On/2 Out	46	18	2	0	2	15	6	5	.391	.565	.451
Scor. Pos./2 Out	30	11	2	0	1	13	3	4	.367	.533	.424
Late Inning Pressure	56	14	3	0	1	6	6	9	.250	.357	.323
Leading Off	10	2	1	0	0	0	1	1	.200	.300	.273
Runners On	28	4	0	0	1	6	3	5	.143	.250	.226
Runners/Scor. Pos.	14	2	0	0	0	4	3	1	.143	.143	.294

RUNS BATTED IN	From 1B	From 2B	From 3B	Scoring Position
Totals	4/91	12/51	13/29	25/80
Percentage	4%	24%	45%	31%
Driving In Runners from 3B with Less than Two Out:		10/18		56%

Loves to face: Willie Fraser (.500, 6-for-12, 3 HR)
Hates to face: Dave Stewart (0-for-16)
Only player in majors who started at least two games in each of the nine batting-order positions last season; he was one of four to start at least 10 games in both the leadoff and cleanup spots.... Made 78 starts last season, all against right-handers, of course.... His last start against a left-hander: July 22, 1978, for Houston vs. Randy Lerch.... Career average of .262 vs. right-handers, .215 in 149 scattered at-bats vs. lefties.... His annual pinch-hit batting averages since 1983: .355, .286, .250, .227, .190, then .125 (3-for-24) last season, when he went hitless in his last 10 at-bats.... Batting average with runners on base has been lower than with bases empty in each of last four years.

Wade Boggs

Boston Red Sox   Bats Left

	AB	H	2B	3B	HR	RBI	BB	SO	BA	SA	OBA
Season	584	214	45	6	5	58	125	34	.366	.490	.476
vs. Left-Handers	172	57	11	2	2	19	39	17	.331	.453	.458
vs. Right-Handers	412	157	34	4	3	39	86	17	.381	.505	.483
Home	285	109	29	3	4	35	76	18	.382	.547	.512
Road	299	105	16	3	1	23	49	16	.351	.435	.438
Grass	490	178	38	3	4	45	113	31	.363	.478	.480
Artificial Turf	94	36	7	3	1	13	12	3	.383	.553	.453
April	77	23	6	0	0	7	14	9	.299	.377	.409
May	90	36	6	2	1	9	28	4	.400	.544	.542
June	97	33	8	0	0	10	16	5	.340	.423	.430
July	114	43	9	2	3	14	15	6	.377	.570	.439
August	109	38	8	2	0	9	24	6	.349	.459	.466
Sept./Oct.	97	41	8	0	1	9	28	4	.423	.536	.551
Leading Off Inn.	186	68	9	0	2	2	39	6	.366	.446	.476
Runners On	239	81	20	2	1	54	55	15	.339	.452	.455
Runners/Scor. Pos.	120	39	11	1	1	50	45	10	.325	.458	.494
Runners On/2 Out	96	28	6	0	0	16	24	6	.292	.354	.438
Scor. Pos./2 Out	53	14	2	0	0	15	22	3	.264	.302	.487
Late Inning Pressure	59	16	2	1	0	1	15	9	.271	.339	.427
Leading Off	16	4	1	0	0	0	6	1	.250	.313	.455
Runners On	24	4	0	0	0	1	7	4	.167	.167	.375
Runners/Scor. Pos.	7	1	0	0	0	1	7	1	.143	.143	.600

RUNS BATTED IN	From 1B	From 2B	From 3B	Scoring Position
Totals	5/184	24/93	24/51	48/144
Percentage	3%	26%	47%	33%
Driving In Runners from 3B with Less than Two Out:		17/25		68%

Loves to face: Bill Long (.750, 9-for-12)
Hates to face: Jose Bautista (.125, 1-for-8)

First player to hit .350 or higher for four straight years since Chuck Klein had five-year run, 1927–31. Cobb did it for 11 straight seasons, 1909–19. ... Career on-base average is .445, the only active player with OBA above .400; Ted Williams's all-time record of .482 seems out of reach. ... Owns .405 career average vs. right-handers at Fenway Park. ... Fanned only four times over last 156 regular-season at-bats, but whiffed three times in first five at-bats in A.L.C.S. ... Only second player to lead his league in both batting average and grounding into double plays (23) in same season; Ernie Lombardi did it in 1938. GIDPs weren't recorded before 1940 in A.L., 1933 in N.L.

Bob Boone

California Angels   Bats Right

	AB	H	2B	3B	HR	RBI	BB	SO	BA	SA	OBA
Season	352	104	17	0	5	39	29	26	.295	.386	.352
vs. Left-Handers	140	37	7	0	1	16	11	8	.264	.336	.318
vs. Right-Handers	212	67	10	0	4	23	18	18	.316	.420	.375
Home	177	50	10	0	3	19	13	13	.282	.390	.339
Road	175	54	7	0	2	20	16	13	.309	.383	.366
Grass	296	80	16	0	4	29	22	23	.270	.365	.325
Artificial Turf	56	24	1	0	1	10	7	3	.429	.500	.492
April	56	15	4	0	1	5	5	7	.268	.339	.328
May	54	7	0	0	0	2	2	5	.130	.130	.161
June	53	21	3	0	2	11	3	2	.396	.566	.439
July	69	23	4	0	1	7	5	4	.333	.435	.378
August	54	18	4	0	2	9	8	5	.333	.519	.419
Sept./Oct.	66	20	2	0	0	5	6	3	.303	.333	.370
Leading Off Inn.	89	26	5	0	1	7	8	7	.292	.382	.344
Runners On	156	52	7	0	2	36	12	7	.333	.417	.381
Runners/Scor. Pos.	97	35	6	0	1	34	8	5	.361	.454	.410
Runners On/2 Out	69	17	1	0	1	13	5	4	.246	.304	.297
Scor. Pos./2 Out	45	13	1	0	1	13	4	3	.289	.378	.347
Late Inning Pressure	52	14	1	0	0	4	8	3	.269	.288	.367
Leading Off	11	4	1	0	0	0	4	1	.364	.455	.533
Runners On	20	5	0	0	0	4	3	1	.250	.250	.348
Runners/Scor. Pos.	13	4	0	0	0	4	3	1	.308	.308	.438

RUNS BATTED IN	From 1B	From 2B	From 3B	Scoring Position
Totals	1/108	16/70	17/38	33/108
Percentage	1%	23%	45%	31%
Driving In Runners from 3B with Less than Two Out:		13/21		62%

Loves to face: Mike Boddicker (.452, 14-for-31, 1 HR)
Hates to face: Richard Dotson (.115, 3-for-26)

Oldest player in majors to start 100 games in the field last year. ... K.C.-bound, he led majors with .429 mark on synthetic turf (min.: 50 AB). ... Batted .368 vs. ground-ball pitchers, highest in majors (min.: 100 AB). ... Has struck out 559 times in 2093 games. Rob Deer has 40 more Ks in 1599 fewer games. ... Posted career-high batting average in 17th season in majors. Only one player in history had career high later in career (minimum: 300 AB for high season): Tris Speaker hit .389 in 1925, his 19th year. ... Family BA record: Dad Ray hit .308 in 1956. ... Bob and Ray joined Buddy and Gus Bell as only father/son duos with 100 HRs apiece. Barry Bonds needs 35 more to integrate that club.

Daryl Boston

Chicago White Sox   Bats Left

	AB	H	2B	3B	HR	RBI	BB	SO	BA	SA	OBA
Season	281	61	12	2	15	31	21	44	.217	.434	.271
vs. Left-Handers	28	7	2	1	0	2	0	7	.250	.393	.241
vs. Right-Handers	253	54	10	1	15	29	21	37	.213	.439	.274
Home	138	25	3	2	6	11	9	22	.181	.362	.231
Road	143	36	9	0	9	20	12	22	.252	.503	.308
Grass	247	52	9	2	15	28	18	37	.211	.445	.263
Artificial Turf	34	9	3	0	0	3	3	7	.265	.353	.324
April	19	3	2	0	0	0	0	1	.158	.263	.158
May	39	9	1	0	4	8	3	4	.231	.564	.286
June	52	10	1	2	3	7	3	8	.192	.462	.236
July	59	14	2	0	4	8	6	11	.237	.475	.308
August	75	18	3	0	4	7	6	13	.240	.440	.293
Sept./Oct.	37	7	3	0	0	1	3	7	.189	.270	.250
Leading Off Inn.	80	19	3	2	5	5	5	12	.238	.513	.282
Runners On	108	21	3	0	5	21	10	16	.194	.361	.261
Runners/Scor. Pos.	59	14	2	0	4	18	7	11	.237	.475	.313
Runners On/2 Out	50	9	1	0	3	10	1	8	.180	.380	.196
Scor. Pos./2 Out	36	8	1	0	2	8	1	6	.222	.417	.243
Late Inning Pressure	50	10	2	1	1	2	5	12	.200	.340	.268
Leading Off	12	4	0	1	0	0	1	1	.333	.500	.385
Runners On	19	2	0	0	0	1	3	4	.105	.105	.217
Runners/Scor. Pos.	8	0	0	0	0	0	3	2	.000	.000	.250

RUNS BATTED IN	From 1B	From 2B	From 3B	Scoring Position
Totals	3/79	6/45	7/25	13/70
Percentage	4%	13%	28%	19%
Driving In Runners from 3B with Less than Two Out:		3/6		50%

Loves to face: Jeff Russell (.667, 6-for-9, 1 HR)
Hates to face: Mike Moore (.087, 2-for-23)

Boston and Dan Pasqua combined for 35 home runs, all against right-handed pitchers. Boston's only career homer off a lefty came in 1986 off Mark Thurmond. ... Has come to plate 1233 times, has never been hit by pitch; among active players, only John Kruk has been up more without being hit. ... Daryl's favorite foe in 1988? Boston hit .333 vs. Boston. ... One of seven players since 1975 to drive in less than 20 percent of runners from scoring position in their careers (minimum: 275 RISP). ... Had only 31 RBI despite hitting 15 home runs, the fewest RBI in major league history for a player with 15 or more homers. Jim Dwyer had 15 HR, 33 RBI in 1987, Bernie Carbo had 15 & 34 in 1977, Mantle had 15 & 35 in 1963.

Scott Bradley

Seattle Mariners   Bats Left

	AB	H	2B	3B	HR	RBI	BB	SO	BA	SA	OBA
Season	335	86	17	1	4	33	17	16	.257	.349	.295
vs. Left-Handers	46	7	1	0	0	4	0	4	.152	.174	.152
vs. Right-Handers	289	79	16	1	4	29	17	12	.273	.377	.316
Home	170	42	10	1	3	18	7	5	.247	.371	.281
Road	165	44	7	0	1	15	10	11	.267	.327	.309
Grass	133	35	6	0	1	14	7	10	.263	.331	.301
Artificial Turf	202	51	11	1	3	19	10	6	.252	.361	.291
April	30	12	2	1	0	6	1	2	.400	.533	.406
May	65	14	3	0	1	5	4	2	.215	.308	.261
June	42	5	0	0	0	2	1	2	.119	.119	.140
July	68	19	4	0	0	8	6	2	.279	.338	.342
August	92	26	6	0	2	10	4	6	.283	.413	.330
Sept./Oct.	38	10	2	0	1	2	1	2	.263	.395	.282
Leading Off Inn.	79	20	4	0	1	1	2	4	.253	.342	.280
Runners On	139	37	6	1	2	31	8	7	.266	.367	.307
Runners/Scor. Pos.	80	22	6	0	2	30	4	3	.275	.425	.310
Runners On/2 Out	58	12	2	0	0	10	4	2	.207	.241	.258
Scor. Pos./2 Out	36	9	2	0	0	10	3	1	.250	.306	.308
Late Inning Pressure	40	10	2	1	2	7	4	3	.250	.500	.333
Leading Off	12	3	2	0	1	1	0	0	.250	.667	.250
Runners On	19	4	0	0	1	6	1	2	.211	.474	.286
Runners/Scor. Pos.	11	3	0	1	1	5	0	1	.273	.545	.333

RUNS BATTED IN	From 1B	From 2B	From 3B	Scoring Position
Totals	3/105	13/65	13/31	26/96
Percentage	3%	20%	42%	27%
Driving In Runners from 3B with Less than Two Out:		9/15		60%

Loves to face: Dave Stewart (.471, 8-for-17, 2 HR)
Hates to face: John Farrell (0-for-7)

A strong starter and a strong finisher: Bradley's a .357 career hitter in April, .271 in May, .203 in June; then .252 in July, .295 in August, .284 in September. ... Batted .424 (14-for-33) with two homers and seven RBI in eight games vs. New York last season. ... Has .281 career batting average vs. right-handers, .198 in 126 at-bats vs. left-handers. Has hit 13 of 14 home runs off right-handers. ... Career average of .214 with two outs and runners on base. ... Bradley has 1039 plate appearances, but only 47 strikeouts. That's a strikeout rate of one every 22.1 times up, second to Bill Buckner (one every 22.3) among players active in 1988 (minimum: 500 career PA).

Glenn Braggs

Bats Right

Milwaukee Brewers	AB	H	2B	3B	HR	RBI	BB	SO	BA	SA	OBA
Season	272	71	14	0	10	42	14	60	.261	.423	.307
vs. Left-Handers	85	21	4	0	5	14	4	21	.247	.471	.283
vs. Right-Handers	187	50	10	0	5	28	10	39	.267	.401	.318
Home	143	37	5	0	6	22	8	28	.259	.420	.305
Road	129	34	9	0	4	20	6	32	.264	.426	.309
Grass	228	61	10	0	8	33	14	47	.268	.417	.317
Artificial Turf	44	10	4	0	2	9	0	13	.227	.455	.255
April	72	19	4	0	2	12	5	17	.264	.403	.325
May	107	28	5	0	6	23	4	21	.262	.477	.298
June	93	24	5	0	2	7	5	22	.258	.376	.303
July	0	0	0	0	0	0	0	0	—	—	—
August	0	0	0	0	0	0	0	0	—	—	—
Sept./Oct.	0	0	0	0	0	0	0	0	—	—	—
Leading Off Inn.	63	12	2	0	1	1	6	15	.190	.270	.271
Runners On	104	30	5	0	5	37	5	22	.288	.481	.333
Runners/Scor. Pos.	63	21	4	0	3	32	4	11	.333	.540	.389
Runners On/2 Out	50	12	1	0	4	16	2	12	.240	.500	.283
Scor. Pos./2 Out	33	7	0	0	2	11	2	9	.212	.394	.278
Late Inning Pressure	44	11	4	0	2	8	1	10	.250	.477	.267
Leading Off	13	2	0	0	0	0	1	2	.154	.154	.214
Runners On	18	6	2	0	2	8	0	4	.333	.778	.333
Runners/Scor. Pos.	11	4	2	0	1	6	0	2	.364	.818	.364

RUNS BATTED IN	From 1B	From 2B	From 3B	Scoring Position
Totals	6/77	17/50	9/27	26/77
Percentage	8%	34%	33%	34%
Driving In Runners from 3B with Less than Two Out:		7/13		54%

Loves to face: Charlie Hough (.667, 4-for-6, 1 HR)
Hates to face: DeWayne Buice (0-for-7)
Appeared in 72 of Brewers' 76 games through June 28, but shoulder injury sidelined him for the remainder of the season. . . . His first 54 games were in right field, his last 18 games were as DH. Hit safely in his first seven starts as DH, matching longest streak of his career. . . . Has never hit a grand slam, but has a career average of .348 (8-for-23) with the bases full. . . . Homered in consecutive games twice within a week in May. . . . Batted .331 in 388 games in minors; has hit .260 in 262 games in majors. . . . Born October 17, 1962 in San Bernardino, California. In that day's newspapers: reports of Ralph Terry's 1–0 win over Giants in seventh game of World Series, played the previous day at Candlestick Park.

Mickey Brantley

Bats Right

Seattle Mariners	AB	H	2B	3B	HR	RBI	BB	SO	BA	SA	OBA
Season	577	152	25	4	15	57	26	64	.263	.399	.296
vs. Left-Handers	170	35	8	2	3	13	9	13	.206	.329	.244
vs. Right-Handers	407	117	17	2	12	44	17	51	.287	.428	.317
Home	280	78	15	4	11	34	14	29	.279	.479	.315
Road	297	74	10	0	4	23	12	35	.249	.323	.277
Grass	226	59	10	0	3	18	12	25	.261	.345	.297
Artificial Turf	351	93	15	4	12	39	14	39	.265	.433	.295
April	76	16	2	1	2	8	1	7	.211	.342	.218
May	108	40	9	1	8	22	3	10	.370	.694	.393
June	98	22	2	1	3	10	4	13	.224	.357	.255
July	87	20	5	1	1	5	6	11	.230	.345	.278
August	114	30	5	0	1	6	6	15	.263	.333	.300
Sept./Oct.	94	24	2	0	0	6	6	8	.255	.277	.300
Leading Off Inn.	158	37	6	2	3	3	4	13	.234	.354	.253
Runners On	234	63	14	2	6	48	11	28	.269	.423	.297
Runners/Scor. Pos.	134	35	8	1	3	39	10	18	.261	.403	.304
Runners On/2 Out	89	21	4	2	4	22	6	9	.236	.461	.284
Scor. Pos./2 Out	59	13	2	1	2	16	6	5	.220	.390	.292
Late Inning Pressure	76	26	6	0	3	9	4	7	.342	.539	.375
Leading Off	27	7	3	0	2	2	0	1	.259	.593	.259
Runners On	31	11	2	0	1	7	4	3	.355	.516	.429
Runners/Scor. Pos.	20	7	2	0	1	7	3	2	.350	.600	.435

RUNS BATTED IN	From 1B	From 2B	From 3B	Scoring Position
Totals	9/164	10/101	23/60	33/161
Percentage	5%	10%	38%	20%
Driving In Runners from 3B with Less than Two Out:		15/31		48%

Loves to face: Oil Can Boyd (.667, 6-for-9, 3 HR)
Hates to face: Mark Gubicza (.071, 1-for-14)
Led majors with 18 extra-base hits in May, but had only one extra-base hit (a double) in his final 85 at-bats of the season. . . . His grand slam off Rick Rhoden on May 28 is his only hit in 17 career at-bats with the bases loaded. . . . Career breakdown: .267 with bases empty, .274 with runners on base, .293 with runners in scoring position. . . . Batted 75 points higher vs. right-handers than he did against lefties, 3d largest difference among A.L. players last season (minimum: 100 AB each way). . . . Has never been intentionally walked, despite 29 homers over the past two years. Only other nonpitchers active in 1988 who have never been walked on purpose (minimum: 1000 plate appearances) are Jackie Gutierrez and Wayne Tolleson.

George Brett

Bats Left

Kansas City Royals	AB	H	2B	3B	HR	RBI	BB	SO	BA	SA	OBA
Season	589	180	42	3	24	103	82	51	.306	.509	.389
vs. Left-Handers	198	62	13	0	10	42	22	16	.313	.530	.379
vs. Right-Handers	391	118	29	3	14	61	60	35	.302	.499	.394
Home	290	85	19	1	13	52	39	16	.293	.500	.377
Road	299	95	23	2	11	51	43	35	.318	.518	.401
Grass	228	74	20	1	9	38	34	27	.325	.539	.414
Artificial Turf	361	106	22	2	15	65	48	24	.294	.490	.373
April	79	25	4	0	5	19	13	5	.316	.557	.400
May	116	39	11	2	3	23	12	7	.336	.543	.398
June	93	31	10	0	5	14	13	7	.333	.602	.426
July	101	36	7	1	5	21	14	12	.356	.594	.436
August	98	23	4	0	4	17	18	11	.235	.398	.347
Sept./Oct.	102	26	6	0	2	9	12	9	.255	.373	.330
Leading Off Inn.	121	36	11	0	4	4	10	7	.298	.488	.351
Runners On	270	94	24	3	12	91	51	22	.348	.593	.445
Runners/Scor. Pos.	152	46	10	1	8	74	40	17	.303	.539	.435
Runners On/2 Out	99	34	8	3	5	36	20	10	.343	.636	.458
Scor. Pos./2 Out	59	18	4	1	4	28	18	7	.305	.610	.474
Late Inning Pressure	92	26	7	1	2	11	10	15	.283	.446	.353
Leading Off	31	5	2	0	0	0	2	6	.161	.226	.212
Runners On	33	12	4	1	1	10	7	4	.364	.636	.475
Runners/Scor. Pos.	18	7	3	1	1	10	6	3	.389	.833	.542

RUNS BATTED IN	From 1B	From 2B	From 3B	Scoring Position
Totals	16/190	27/119	36/58	63/177
Percentage	8%	23%	62%	36%
Driving In Runners from 3B with Less than Two Out:		26/35		74%

Loves to face: Gene Nelson (.429, 9-for-21, 4 HR)
Hates to face: Ed Vande Berg (.053, 1-for-19)
Played 157 games last season, two short of his career high, set in 1975 and equalled a year later. Oldest players to establish career highs in games (with at least 100) were Joe Start (101 games at age 42 in 1885) and Honus Wagner (151 at 41 in 1915). . . . From 1977 to 1987, he averaged 127 games a year. . . . Stole 14 bases last season after having stolen only 16 in the previous five years combined. . . . Matched his previous career high with 51 strikeouts (1982). . . . Batted for a higher average vs. left-handed pitchers than he did against right-handers for the first time in last 15 years; related item: had highest slugging average in A.L. by a left-handed batter vs. left-handed pitchers.

Greg Brock

Bats Left

Milwaukee Brewers	AB	H	2B	3B	HR	RBI	BB	SO	BA	SA	OBA
Season	364	77	16	1	6	50	63	48	.212	.310	.329
vs. Left-Handers	103	24	6	0	1	17	12	10	.233	.320	.316
vs. Right-Handers	261	53	10	1	5	33	51	38	.203	.307	.334
Home	195	45	8	1	4	30	29	19	.231	.344	.335
Road	169	32	8	0	2	20	34	29	.189	.272	.324
Grass	325	69	14	1	6	45	54	40	.212	.317	.327
Artificial Turf	39	8	2	0	0	5	9	8	.205	.256	.347
April	59	16	3	0	1	10	9	9	.271	.373	.380
May	91	23	4	1	2	21	20	13	.253	.385	.384
June	16	2	2	0	0	1	3	4	.125	.250	.263
July	29	4	2	0	1	3	4	6	.138	.310	.235
August	90	17	2	0	0	6	16	6	.189	.211	.318
Sept./Oct.	79	15	3	0	2	9	11	10	.190	.304	.286
Leading Off Inn.	97	15	2	0	3	3	14	15	.155	.268	.268
Runners On	165	38	10	1	3	47	37	20	.230	.358	.370
Runners/Scor. Pos.	97	23	3	1	2	40	28	12	.237	.351	.400
Runners On/2 Out	79	14	3	0	0	12	22	10	.177	.215	.363
Scor. Pos./2 Out	48	9	0	0	0	9	15	5	.188	.188	.391
Late Inning Pressure	35	11	1	0	0	5	13	5	.314	.343	.500
Leading Off	7	1	0	0	0	0	2	1	.143	.143	.333
Runners On	14	5	0	0	0	5	9	2	.357	.357	.609
Runners/Scor. Pos.	10	4	0	0	0	5	6	1	.400	.400	.625

RUNS BATTED IN	From 1B	From 2B	From 3B	Scoring Position
Totals	9/120	17/76	18/42	35/118
Percentage	8%	22%	43%	30%
Driving In Runners from 3B with Less than Two Out:		16/23		70%

Loves to face: Frank Viola (.571, 4-for-7)
Hates to face: Bobby Witt (.091, 1-for-11)
The good news: his walk-to-strikeout ratio was the best of his major league career; the bad news: his home-run ratio was his personal worst. . . . Drew 16 intentional walks in 1988, equal to his combined total for the four previous seasons. . . . Missed 42 games in June and July with a back ailment. Sounds like he'd still fit right in with the Dodgers. . . . Career average of .252 vs. right-handers, .220 vs. left-handers. . . . Hitless in his last 13 at-bats with the bases loaded and two outs; he's 3-for-26 lifetime in that situation. . . . Six stolen bases last season leaves him 908 behind namesake Lou; at least he's 23 ahead of John Brock, outfielder with Cardinals in 1917–18.

Tom Brookens

Detroit Tigers — Bats Right

	AB	H	2B	3B	HR	RBI	BB	SO	BA	SA	OBA
Season	441	107	23	5	5	38	44	74	.243	.351	.313
vs. Left-Handers	177	39	8	1	2	13	24	34	.220	.311	.310
vs. Right-Handers	264	68	15	4	3	25	20	40	.258	.379	.315
Home	221	57	10	4	4	20	24	32	.258	.394	.331
Road	220	50	13	1	1	18	20	42	.227	.309	.295
Grass	376	95	21	5	5	36	36	59	.253	.375	.320
Artificial Turf	65	12	2	0	0	2	8	15	.185	.215	.274
April	52	18	5	0	1	10	7	9	.346	.500	.435
May	69	13	3	0	1	6	8	15	.188	.275	.269
June	85	25	5	1	2	11	6	14	.294	.447	.337
July	58	19	2	2	1	6	8	11	.328	.483	.412
August	78	12	4	0	0	2	9	15	.154	.205	.241
Sept./Oct.	99	20	4	2	0	3	6	10	.202	.283	.248
Leading Off Inn.	120	38	10	0	1	1	12	16	.317	.425	.379
Runners On	186	39	4	1	2	35	18	25	.210	.274	.274
Runners/Scor. Pos.	101	23	2	0	1	32	10	17	.228	.277	.287
Runners On/2 Out	76	11	1	1	1	12	7	9	.145	.224	.217
Scor. Pos./2 Out	44	8	1	0	0	9	4	5	.182	.205	.250
Late Inning Pressure	64	20	3	0	2	4	4	12	.313	.453	.348
Leading Off	25	12	3	0	0	0	2	5	.480	.600	.519
Runners On	23	3	0	0	0	2	0	3	.130	.130	.125
Runners/Scor. Pos.	8	1	0	0	0	2	0	2	.125	.125	.111

RUNS BATTED IN	From 1B	From 2B	From 3B	Scoring Position
Totals	4/146	11/83	18/41	29/124
Percentage	3%	13%	44%	23%
Driving In Runners from 3B with Less than Two Out:		13/22		59%

Loves to face: Stu Cliburn (4-for-4, 2 BB)
Hates to face: Mark Huismann (0-for-8, 4 SO)

Oldest A.L. player to start half his team's games at third base last season. He'll be 36 in August. . . . Wasn't in starting lineup on Sept. 25, but played three infield positions anyway (2B, SS, and 3B). . . . August batting average was lowest in A.L. (minimum: two PA per game). . . . One hit in last 47 AB (.021) vs. Minnesota, including 0-for-13 in 1987 A.L.C.S. . . . Batting average vs. right-handers was highest of career; average vs. southpaws was lowest. Career averages: .270 vs. LHP, .227 vs. RHP. . . . Batting average in LIP Situations has been higher than his overall mark in each of last six seasons, tying Steve Sax and Butch Wynegar for longest current streak.

Bob Brower

Texas Rangers — Bats Right

	AB	H	2B	3B	HR	RBI	BB	SO	BA	SA	OBA
Season	201	45	7	0	1	11	27	38	.224	.274	.316
vs. Left-Handers	131	31	5	0	0	5	20	26	.237	.275	.338
vs. Right-Handers	70	14	2	0	1	6	7	12	.200	.271	.273
Home	103	24	3	0	1	8	16	21	.233	.291	.336
Road	98	21	4	0	0	3	11	17	.214	.255	.294
Grass	162	35	4	0	1	10	21	31	.216	.259	.306
Artificial Turf	39	10	3	0	0	1	6	7	.256	.333	.356
April	7	1	0	0	0	0	1	2	.143	.143	.250
May	38	10	2	0	0	1	6	5	.263	.316	.364
June	57	13	3	0	0	2	4	10	.228	.281	.279
July	38	8	1	0	1	6	4	12	.211	.316	.286
August	31	8	1	0	0	2	5	4	.258	.290	.361
Sept./Oct.	30	5	0	0	0	0	7	5	.167	.167	.324
Leading Off Inn.	77	21	5	0	0	0	10	12	.273	.338	.356
Runners On	74	14	2	0	1	11	14	16	.189	.257	.318
Runners/Scor. Pos.	51	8	1	0	1	11	9	12	.157	.235	.283
Runners On/2 Out	35	5	0	0	1	4	4	7	.143	.229	.231
Scor. Pos./2 Out	23	2	0	0	1	4	4	6	.087	.217	.222
Late Inning Pressure	29	4	0	0	0	1	5	7	.138	.138	.265
Leading Off	8	1	0	0	0	0	3	3	.125	.125	.364
Runners On	10	1	0	0	0	1	2	2	.100	.100	.250
Runners/Scor. Pos.	8	1	0	0	0	1	2	2	.125	.125	.300

RUNS BATTED IN	From 1B	From 2B	From 3B	Scoring Position
Totals	1/52	4/45	5/18	9/63
Percentage	2%	9%	28%	14%
Driving In Runners from 3B with Less than Two Out:		4/10		40%

Loves to face: Steve Trout (.667, 6-for-9)
Hates to face: Cecilio Guante 0-for-4, 2 SO)

Started 41 of 50 games in which the Rangers faced a left-handed pitcher, 10 of 111 games vs. right-handers. . . . RBI total was 2d lowest among A.L. players with at least 200 plate appearances. More than half his season's total came in one six-RBI orgy vs. Baltimore. . . . Made only 11 appearances as a pinch hitter, but led A.L. with two pinch sac bunts. Hey, this is the age of specialization. . . . Career BA of .152 in LIP Situations, .257 otherwise. . . . Abused the lively balls of '87 for 14 home runs in 303 at-bats, but he's hit only one HR in 210 AB before or after. That's the difference between the career rates of Dave Winfield and Angel Bravo.

Jerry Browne

Texas Rangers — Bats Left and Right

	AB	H	2B	3B	HR	RBI	BB	SO	BA	SA	OBA
Season	214	49	9	2	1	17	25	32	.229	.304	.308
vs. Left-Handers	70	17	2	1	0	5	5	10	.243	.300	.289
vs. Right-Handers	144	32	7	1	1	12	20	22	.222	.306	.317
Home	121	31	7	1	1	12	16	14	.256	.355	.341
Road	93	18	2	1	0	5	9	18	.194	.237	.265
Grass	188	41	8	1	1	16	24	26	.218	.287	.305
Artificial Turf	26	8	1	1	0	1	1	6	.308	.423	.333
April	67	13	0	0	0	3	9	12	.194	.194	.289
May	51	12	1	1	0	3	5	8	.235	.294	.298
June	14	1	1	0	0	0	3	1	.071	.143	.235
July	0	0	0	0	0	0	0	0	—	—	—
August	0	0	0	0	0	0	0	0	—	—	—
Sept./Oct.	82	23	7	1	1	11	8	11	.280	.427	.344
Leading Off Inn.	48	9	1	0	0	0	4	3	.188	.208	.250
Runners On	87	19	4	1	0	16	11	11	.218	.287	.303
Runners/Scor. Pos.	56	11	4	1	0	16	7	7	.196	.304	.281
Runners On/2 Out	36	5	1	0	0	3	3	4	.139	.167	.205
Scor. Pos./2 Out	24	2	1	0	0	3	2	4	.083	.125	.154
Late Inning Pressure	29	9	2	0	0	4	4	3	.310	.379	.394
Leading Off	6	1	0	0	0	0	0	0	.167	.167	.167
Runners On	15	6	1	0	0	4	2	0	.400	.467	.471
Runners/Scor. Pos.	10	3	1	0	0	4	1	0	.300	.400	.364

RUNS BATTED IN	From 1B	From 2B	From 3B	Scoring Position
Totals	1/59	10/45	5/21	15/66
Percentage	2%	22%	24%	23%
Driving In Runners from 3B with Less than Two Out:		4/8		50%

Loves to face: Jerry Reuss (2-for-2, 1 2B)
Hates to face: Chris Bosio (0-for-7)

Hitless in 27 consecutive at-bats from April 23 to May 6. . . . Picked up first extra-base hit in his 83rd at-bat of season. . . . Ranked last among A.L. second baseman with an average of 2.28 assists per nine innigns (minimum: 500 inn.). Rangers allowed 3.96 runs per nine innings with Browne at second, 4.57 with Jeff Kunkel, and 5.12 with Curtis Wilkerson. . . . Ground outs-to-air outs ratio fell from 1.76 through 1987 to 1.09 in 1988. . . . Career BA of .335 vs. ground-ball pitchers, .217 vs. fly-ball pitchers. . . . Career BA of .296 at Arlington Stadium, .220 on the road. But Cleveland's not a bad place to go (statistically speaking, that is). He's hit .280 at Cleveland Stadium.

Bill Buckner

Angels/Royals — Bats Left

	AB	H	2B	3B	HR	RBI	BB	SO	BA	SA	OBA
Season	285	71	14	0	3	43	17	19	.249	.330	.287
vs. Left-Handers	32	9	3	0	0	8	2	1	.281	.375	.314
vs. Right-Handers	253	62	11	0	3	35	15	18	.245	.324	.283
Home	137	37	6	0	0	20	8	6	.270	.314	.306
Road	148	34	8	0	3	23	9	13	.230	.345	.269
Grass	132	26	5	0	1	19	9	11	.197	.258	.243
Artificial Turf	153	45	9	0	2	24	8	8	.294	.392	.325
April	30	7	0	0	0	7	4	0	.233	.233	.314
May	64	15	2	0	2	7	2	3	.234	.359	.254
June	66	16	4	0	1	14	3	4	.242	.348	.268
July	53	14	4	0	0	5	1	3	.264	.340	.278
August	31	7	1	0	0	2	2	4	.226	.258	.273
Sept./Oct.	41	12	3	0	0	8	5	5	.293	.366	.362
Leading Off Inn.	65	8	1	0	2	3	2	2	.123	.231	.162
Runners On	126	45	11	0	0	40	14	9	.357	.444	.407
Runners/Scor. Pos.	69	24	7	0	0	38	11	3	.348	.449	.412
Runners On/2 Out	49	18	5	0	0	16	6	2	.367	.469	.436
Scor. Pos./2 Out	29	9	3	0	0	15	5	1	.310	.414	.412
Late Inning Pressure	61	19	2	0	0	12	6	5	.311	.344	.357
Leading Off	12	2	0	0	0	0	1	0	.167	.167	.231
Runners On	33	12	2	0	0	12	5	4	.364	.424	.415
Runners/Scor. Pos.	15	6	1	0	0	11	3	2	.400	.467	.429

RUNS BATTED IN	From 1B	From 2B	From 3B	Scoring Position
Totals	3/93	17/65	20/34	37/99
Percentage	3%	26%	59%	37%
Driving In Runners from 3B with Less than Two Out:		14/18		78%

Loves to face: Bobby Thigpen (.714, 5-for-7)
Hates to face: Jeff M. Robinson (0-for-13)

One of five nonpitchers active last year who have reached the 20-year mark. Others: Graig Nettles (22), Ted Simmons (21), Rick Dempsey (20), and Darrell Evans (20). . . . Leads all active players with 2669 hits and 9178 at-bats. at-bats rank 33rd on the all-time list, 54 behind Nellie Fox. . . . Has appeared in only one All-Star Game (as a pinch hitter in 1981). . . . Tied with former teammates George Hendrick and Jim Eppard for league lead in pinch hits (8). Led A.L. with 11 pinch RBI, but was hitless in his last 10 pinch AB. . . . Had eight hits in 12 at-bats with bases loaded last season. Among all players in majors with at least five bases-loaded hits, only Pat Tabler (8-for-9) had higher average.

Steve Buechele

Texas Rangers — Bats Right

	AB	H	2B	3B	HR	RBI	BB	SO	BA	SA	OBA
Season	503	126	21	4	16	57	65	79	.250	.404	.342
vs. Left-Handers	153	36	7	1	5	15	22	20	.235	.392	.335
vs. Right-Handers	350	90	14	3	11	42	43	59	.257	.409	.345
Home	246	64	10	2	8	31	32	35	.260	.415	.352
Road	257	62	11	2	8	26	33	44	.241	.393	.332
Grass	413	107	17	4	11	47	56	63	.259	.400	.354
Artificial Turf	90	19	4	0	5	10	9	16	.211	.422	.283
April	65	17	1	0	4	6	7	15	.262	.462	.333
May	85	27	5	1	4	9	10	12	.318	.541	.389
June	88	18	3	0	2	9	16	16	.205	.307	.346
July	82	22	6	1	1	10	9	9	.268	.402	.341
August	86	22	2	1	4	16	12	11	.256	.442	.354
Sept./Oct.	97	20	4	1	1	7	11	16	.206	.299	.294
Leading Off Inn.	130	34	3	1	7	7	10	17	.262	.462	.314
Runners On	222	57	13	1	4	45	31	35	.257	.378	.353
Runners/Scor. Pos.	124	29	8	0	1	37	15	21	.234	.323	.321
Runners On/2 Out	102	22	4	0	3	19	16	17	.216	.343	.328
Scor. Pos./2 Out	62	11	3	0	1	14	6	10	.177	.274	.261
Late Inning Pressure	90	20	2	0	4	10	10	23	.222	.378	.314
Leading Off	22	6	0	0	2	3	4	7	.273	.545	.360
Runners On	44	9	1	0	2	8	4	13	.205	.364	.271
Runners/Scor. Pos.	27	3	1	0	0	4	2	8	.111	.148	.172

RUNS BATTED IN	From 1B	From 2B	From 3B	Scoring Position
Totals	7/170	19/96	15/46	34/142
Percentage	4%	20%	33%	24%
Driving In Runners from 3B with Less than Two Out:		14/21		67%

Loves to face: Bret Saberhagen (.636, 7-for-11, 1 HR)
Hates to face: Dave Schmidt (0-for-13)
Set career highs in games (155), batting average, and RBI. . . . Hadn't homered against the Blue Jays until 1988, but made up for lost time with four last season. . . . Reached base safely in 17 consecutive games (Aug. 17–Sept. 3). . . . Committed 13 of his 16 errors last season in road games. . . . Career average of .154 (4-for-26) with the bases loaded, even worse with two out and the bases full (1-for-14). . . . Has hit 47 home runs over past three seasons, one more than Von Hayes, one fewer than Jim Rice. But he's hit only 10 of them with runners on base. . . . Has driven in only 10 of 56 runners from scoring position in LIP Situations (18%). Bad, but not quite as bad as teammate Ruben Sierra (11-for-79, 14%).

Jay Buhner

Yankees/Mariners — Bats Right

	AB	H	2B	3B	HR	RBI	BB	SO	BA	SA	OBA
Season	261	56	13	1	13	38	28	93	.215	.421	.302
vs. Left-Handers	89	15	2	0	4	10	4	31	.169	.326	.208
vs. Right-Handers	172	41	11	1	9	28	24	62	.238	.471	.347
Home	126	27	6	0	8	22	11	42	.214	.452	.284
Road	135	29	7	1	5	16	17	51	.215	.393	.318
Grass	149	35	7	1	6	26	18	52	.235	.416	.333
Artificial Turf	112	21	6	0	7	12	10	41	.188	.429	.258
April	0	0	0	0	0	0	0	0	——	——	——
May	9	1	0	0	0	0	2	1	.111	.111	.182
June	57	11	0	0	3	11	1	23	.193	.351	.246
July	31	5	2	0	1	4	4	9	.161	.323	.297
August	98	30	10	1	5	16	15	32	.306	.582	.397
Sept./Oct.	66	9	1	0	4	8	7	28	.136	.333	.219
Leading Off Inn.	65	15	4	0	5	8	8	28	.231	.523	.315
Runners On	114	26	4	1	6	31	11	41	.228	.439	.305
Runners/Scor. Pos.	55	13	1	1	3	24	7	21	.236	.455	.328
Runners On/2 Out	44	7	2	0	1	7	3	18	.159	.273	.229
Scor. Pos./2 Out	26	3	0	0	0	5	3	12	.115	.115	.233
Late Inning Pressure	43	4	0	0	1	2	3	19	.093	.163	.152
Leading Off	9	2	0	0	1	1	3	4	.222	.556	.417
Runners On	16	1	0	0	0	1	0	7	.063	.063	.063
Runners/Scor. Pos.	10	1	0	0	0	1	0	3	.100	.100	.100

RUNS BATTED IN	From 1B	From 2B	From 3B	Scoring Position
Totals	6/90	10/47	9/23	19/70
Percentage	7%	21%	39%	27%
Driving In Runners from 3B with Less than Two Out:		6/10		60%

Loves to face: Mike Smithson (2-for-2, 1 BB, 1 HR)
Hates to face: Ted Higuera (0-for-7, 6 SO)
Batted .188 with three home runs in 25 games for the Yankees. . . . Sixteen extra-base hits in August, his first full month as a starter, tied Rob Deer for most in majors. . . . September batting average was lowest in A.L. (minimum: two PA per game). . . . Led A.L. rookies in home runs and strikeouts. . . . Struck out at least once in 20 consecutive games with the Mariners, longest streak in the majors. . . . Did the Yankees give up too soon? You bet. The following players had comparable stats at a similar age: Harmon Killebrew and Roger Maris (through 1957), Don Mincher (through 1961), Hawk Harrelson (through 1964), and Rico Petrocelli (through 1965). As Casey would say, you could look it up.

Ellis Burks

Boston Red Sox — Bats Right

	AB	H	2B	3B	HR	RBI	BB	SO	BA	SA	OBA
Season	540	159	37	5	18	92	62	89	.294	.481	.367
vs. Left-Handers	142	46	8	0	5	24	21	18	.324	.486	.410
vs. Right-Handers	398	113	29	5	13	68	41	71	.284	.480	.351
Home	246	80	23	1	8	47	33	44	.325	.524	.402
Road	294	79	14	4	10	45	29	45	.269	.446	.335
Grass	454	137	33	3	17	80	55	75	.302	.500	.376
Artificial Turf	86	22	4	2	1	12	7	14	.256	.384	.312
April	52	20	5	1	2	9	11	12	.385	.635	.492
May	62	16	4	0	1	6	5	14	.258	.371	.314
June	113	38	8	1	5	23	7	15	.336	.558	.372
July	110	35	9	3	5	23	15	19	.318	.591	.397
August	101	23	6	0	2	14	11	14	.228	.347	.301
Sept./Oct.	102	27	5	0	3	17	13	15	.265	.402	.356
Leading Off Inn.	124	33	6	1	3	3	14	21	.266	.403	.341
Runners On	267	87	23	3	10	84	33	37	.326	.547	.396
Runners/Scor. Pos.	162	54	9	2	8	78	23	23	.333	.562	.406
Runners On/2 Out	114	33	8	3	2	29	19	14	.289	.465	.391
Scor. Pos./2 Out	73	20	3	2	1	25	15	8	.274	.411	.398
Late Inning Pressure	62	20	5	1	6	10	13	.323	.484	.425
Leading Off	12	4	1	0	2	3	.333	.583	.429
Runners On	30	10	3	0	5	5	4	.333	.433	.444
Runners/Scor. Pos.	19	7	1	0	5	4	2	.368	.421	.478

RUNS BATTED IN	From 1B	From 2B	From 3B	Scoring Position
Totals	11/185	21/121	42/87	63/208
Percentage	6%	17%	48%	30%
Driving In Runners from 3B with Less than Two Out:		31/49		63%

Loves to face: Bill Wegman (.615, 8-for-13, 1 HR)
Hates to face: DeWayne Buice (0-for-7, 4 SO)
First player in major league history with 50 extra-base hits and 25 stolen bases in each of his first two seasons. Three others qualify if you discard crumbs of seasons prior to their rookie years: Kiki Cuyler, Shoeless Joe Jackson, and Juan Samuel. . . . Red Sox were 81–58 with Burks starting in center field, 8–15 with others there. . . . April batting average was 4th highest in A.L. . . . Hit the only regular season home run for the Red Sox in their 12 games against the Athletics. . . . Heir apparent to Pat Tabler as Mr. Bases Loaded. Career average of .400 (12-for-30), with three walks and four grand slams. . . . Has hit half of his 38 home runs at Fenway Park. Career averages: .307 at home, .263 on the road.

Randy Bush

Minnesota Twins — Bats Left

	AB	H	2B	3B	HR	RBI	BB	SO	BA	SA	OBA
Season	394	103	20	3	14	51	58	49	.261	.434	.365
vs. Left-Handers	11	2	0	1	0	1	3	3	.182	.364	.333
vs. Right-Handers	383	101	20	2	14	50	55	46	.264	.436	.366
Home	185	45	12	2	10	31	34	29	.243	.492	.372
Road	209	58	8	1	4	20	24	20	.278	.383	.358
Grass	161	43	6	1	3	18	23	16	.267	.373	.363
Artificial Turf	233	60	14	2	11	33	35	33	.258	.476	.366
April	38	14	3	0	2	6	7	4	.368	.605	.489
May	67	15	3	1	3	10	17	8	.224	.433	.376
June	73	18	6	0	2	8	7	10	.247	.411	.333
July	72	22	4	0	4	16	6	8	.306	.528	.358
August	71	14	3	1	2	6	12	7	.197	.352	.329
Sept./Oct.	73	20	1	1	1	5	9	12	.274	.356	.357
Leading Off Inn.	87	23	6	1	4	3	7	.264	.494	.304
Runners On	180	51	8	0	7	44	35	22	.283	.444	.399
Runners/Scor. Pos.	96	28	6	0	5	40	28	13	.292	.510	.447
Runners On/2 Out	58	14	2	0	4	14	14	10	.241	.483	.397
Scor. Pos./2 Out	35	6	1	0	2	10	13	6	.171	.371	.408
Late Inning Pressure	49	13	4	0	2	6	10	7	.265	.469	.390
Leading Off	10	4	2	0	0	0	3	1	.400	.600	.538
Runners On	23	6	1	0	1	5	5	.261	.435	.393
Runners/Scor. Pos.	14	4	1	0	1	4	3	.286	.357	.444

RUNS BATTED IN	From 1B	From 2B	From 3B	Scoring Position
Totals	4/135	19/80	14/36	33/116
Percentage	3%	24%	39%	28%
Driving In Runners from 3B with Less than Two Out:		12/25		48%

Loves to face: Bobby Thigpen (4-for-4, 1 HR)
Hates to face: Mark Eichhorn (.067, 1-for-15)
Slugging percentage of .889 vs. Baltimore was the highest by any player against any team last season. . . . Started 114 of 116 games in which Minnesota faced right-handed starters. Hasn't started against a left-hander since July 2, 1986. . . . Had a pinch hitter sent to the plate in his place 38 times last season, 2d-highest total in A.L. . . . Here's something to shoot for: During Jimmy Carter's administration, Gary Carter hit 102 home runs. . . . What's the most home runs hit by any player during a particular president's White House tenure? Jimmy Foxx hit 353 during FDR's 12 years in Washington. . . . The record for Republicans? Eddie Mathews hit 313 under Ike.

Ivan Calderon

Chicago White Sox — Bats Right

	AB	H	2B	3B	HR	RBI	BB	SO	BA	SA	OBA
Season	264	56	14	0	14	35	34	66	.212	.424	.299
vs. Left-Handers	80	19	5	0	5	10	14	16	.238	.488	.347
vs. Right-Handers	184	37	9	0	9	25	20	50	.201	.397	.277
Home	131	25	6	0	6	17	12	33	.191	.374	.255
Road	133	31	8	0	8	18	22	33	.233	.474	.340
Grass	234	46	11	0	10	30	28	57	.197	.372	.279
Artificial Turf	30	10	3	0	4	5	6	9	.333	.833	.444
April	73	15	2	0	6	14	14	22	.205	.479	.330
May	84	18	9	0	4	9	8	21	.214	.464	.283
June	76	19	2	0	4	9	5	13	.250	.434	.289
July	31	4	1	0	0	3	7	10	.129	.161	.289
August	0	0	0	0	0	0	0	0	—	—	—
Sept./Oct.	0	0	0	0	0	0	0	0	—	—	—
Leading Off Inn.	68	17	6	0	5	6	6	12	.250	.559	.311
Runners On	121	21	3	0	6	27	16	33	.174	.347	.264
Runners/Scor. Pos.	68	15	2	0	4	23	8	21	.221	.426	.291
Runners On/2 Out	49	5	1	0	1	4	5	15	.102	.184	.185
Scor. Pos./2 Out	27	3	0	0	1	4	4	10	.111	.222	.226
Late Inning Pressure	38	8	4	0	0	2	5	15	.211	.316	.302
Leading Off	8	4	1	0	0	0	0	1	.500	.625	.500
Runners On	20	2	1	0	0	2	2	8	.100	.150	.182
Runners/Scor. Pos.	12	2	1	0	0	2	0	6	.167	.250	.167

RUNS BATTED IN	From 1B	From 2B	From 3B	Scoring Position
Totals	4/86	7/46	10/29	17/75
Percentage	5%	15%	34%	23%
Driving In Runners from 3B with Less than Two Out:			8/17	47%

Loves to face: Dale Mohorcic (.750, 3-for-4, 2 HR)
Hates to face: Mike Witt (.100, 2-for-20)
A.L. home-run leaders through games of June 13, 1988: Canseco 16, Calderon 14, Snyder 14. Ivan was terrible after that: .175, with no home runs in 63 at-bats.... Drove in or scored a run in 13 consecutive games in April, 3d-longest streak in A.L.... Batted in the cleanup spot in 69 of 71 starts.... Career average of .302 in Late-Inning Pressure Situations, .260 in unpressured at-bats.... Unflattering breakdown to those LIP Situations: .343 with bases empty, .253 with runners on, .186 with runners in scoring position.... One of two A.L. players to hit 50 points lower with runners on than with bases empty in each of last two seasons (minimum: 100 AB each way). The other: Don Slaught.

Jose Canseco

Oakland As — Bats Right

	AB	H	2B	3B	HR	RBI	BB	SO	BA	SA	OBA
Season	610	187	34	0	42	124	78	128	.307	.569	.391
vs. Left-Handers	150	51	12	0	10	29	15	30	.340	.620	.412
vs. Right-Handers	460	136	22	0	32	95	63	98	.296	.552	.384
Home	288	90	17	0	16	59	43	62	.313	.538	.407
Road	322	97	17	0	26	65	35	66	.301	.596	.375
Grass	513	154	24	0	31	100	65	106	.300	.528	.385
Artificial Turf	97	33	10	0	11	24	13	22	.340	.784	.421
April	89	24	3	0	8	24	16	17	.270	.573	.380
May	106	33	3	0	4	17	15	21	.311	.453	.407
June	102	29	3	0	8	17	12	19	.284	.549	.365
July	106	31	7	0	10	25	16	27	.292	.642	.394
August	114	34	10	0	4	17	8	28	.298	.491	.350
Sept./Oct.	93	36	8	0	8	24	11	16	.387	.731	.454
Leading Off Inn.	105	30	7	0	6	6	12	19	.286	.524	.375
Runners On	291	91	17	0	26	108	37	55	.313	.639	.391
Runners/Scor. Pos.	175	52	10	0	13	81	28	38	.297	.577	.389
Runners On/2 Out	99	28	4	0	9	35	15	22	.283	.596	.383
Scor. Pos./2 Out	68	16	2	0	5	27	13	18	.235	.485	.358
Late Inning Pressure	89	23	3	0	5	17	10	17	.258	.461	.340
Leading Off	21	7	2	0	1	1	1	4	.333	.571	.364
Runners On	42	11	1	0	4	16	6	7	.262	.571	.354
Runners/Scor. Pos.	30	10	1	0	4	16	5	6	.333	.767	.429

RUNS BATTED IN	From 1B	From 2B	From 3B	Scoring Position
Totals	22/193	29/122	31/78	60/200
Percentage	11%	24%	40%	30%
Driving In Runners from 3B with Less than Two Out:			23/43	53%

Loves to face: Oil Can Boyd (.421, 8-for-19, 4 HR)
Hates to face: Mark Clear (0-for-7)
Leads active players (minimum: 500 games) with 73 RBIs per 100 games played. Only one other player is over 70 (Mattingly, 70.5). Among players since 1900, Lou Gehrig is the all-time leader with 92 RBIs per 100 games, with Hank Greenberg second at 91.5.... Grand slam in Game 1 of World Series was only 2d of 15 Series slams hit in a losing effort. The other: Yogi Berra in 1956.... Now that he's put the 40/40 stuff behind him, here's another goal to shoot for: No player has led A.L. in RBI in back-to-back seasons since Roger Maris (1960–1961).... Oddity: 40 stolen bases, no triples; only one other player in A.L. history has done that: Miguel Dilone (50 SBs, no 3Bs) in 1978.

Joe Carter

Cleveland Indians — Bats Right

	AB	H	2B	3B	HR	RBI	BB	SO	BA	SA	OBA
Season	621	168	36	6	27	98	35	82	.271	.478	.314
vs. Left-Handers	132	41	9	1	7	21	8	17	.311	.553	.348
vs. Right-Handers	489	127	27	5	20	77	27	65	.260	.458	.305
Home	299	84	13	2	16	52	22	35	.281	.498	.336
Road	322	84	23	4	11	46	13	47	.261	.460	.292
Grass	515	136	26	4	23	79	32	70	.264	.464	.313
Artificial Turf	106	32	10	2	4	19	3	12	.302	.547	.318
April	82	29	5	0	7	21	6	15	.354	.671	.407
May	114	31	8	1	3	18	6	16	.272	.439	.306
June	98	19	5	0	5	13	6	15	.194	.398	.252
July	115	33	5	3	5	22	8	9	.287	.513	.333
August	109	31	6	0	4	13	5	16	.284	.450	.316
Sept./Oct.	103	25	7	2	3	11	4	11	.243	.437	.282
Leading Off Inn.	129	30	4	1	4	4	6	13	.233	.372	.272
Runners On	281	81	19	4	11	82	21	41	.288	.502	.338
Runners/Scor. Pos.	158	46	11	3	8	73	16	25	.291	.551	.355
Runners On/2 Out	103	26	7	2	3	30	15	16	.252	.447	.353
Scor. Pos./2 Out	65	20	5	1	2	26	11	10	.308	.508	.416
Late Inning Pressure	84	17	6	0	3	11	4	14	.202	.381	.256
Leading Off	21	3	0	0	1	1	1	4	.143	.286	.182
Runners On	39	9	4	0	1	9	3	8	.231	.410	.302
Runners/Scor. Pos.	21	4	1	0	0	7	2	6	.190	.238	.292

RUNS BATTED IN	From 1B	From 2B	From 3B	Scoring Position
Totals	11/203	32/124	28/65	60/189
Percentage	5%	26%	43%	32%
Driving In Runners from 3B with Less than Two Out:			20/34	59%

Loves to face: Jose Nunez (2-for-2, 2 HR)
Hates to face: Ted Higuera (.103, 3-for-29, 1 HR)
Reached 27 homers and 27 steals in each of the last three seasons. Only one player previously earned continuous membership in four straight years: Willie Mays (1956–59). Others with three years: Darryl Strawberry (1986–88) and Kirk Gibson (1984–86).... Had 27 home runs and 94 RBI with 18 games remaining last season, but failed to reach 30 homers or 100 RBI.... Batting average in Late-Inning Pressure Situations has decreased in every season since 1984: .324, .296, .295, .241, .202.... Has batted higher in day games than he has at night in each of his five full seasons in the majors.... Career average of .320 (16-for-50, 4 HR) with the bases loaded.

Rick Cerone

Boston Red Sox — Bats Right

	AB	H	2B	3B	HR	RBI	BB	SO	BA	SA	OBA
Season	264	71	13	1	3	27	20	32	.269	.360	.326
vs. Left-Handers	114	35	6	1	1	14	4	9	.307	.404	.333
vs. Right-Handers	150	36	7	0	2	13	16	23	.240	.327	.321
Home	146	45	7	0	3	15	11	17	.308	.418	.357
Road	118	26	6	1	0	12	9	15	.220	.288	.290
Grass	226	64	12	1	3	25	17	25	.283	.385	.332
Artificial Turf	38	7	1	0	0	2	3	7	.184	.211	.295
April	33	14	2	0	1	5	5	4	.424	.576	.487
May	75	23	4	0	1	4	7	12	.307	.400	.373
June	49	14	2	1	0	7	3	4	.286	.367	.352
July	51	12	3	0	1	10	2	3	.235	.353	.264
August	25	4	1	0	0	1	2	3	.160	.200	.222
Sept./Oct.	31	4	1	0	0	0	1	6	.129	.161	.156
Leading Off Inn.	68	19	5	0	0	0	4	5	.279	.353	.319
Runners On	122	33	8	1	2	26	9	16	.270	.402	.328
Runners/Scor. Pos.	74	17	5	0	0	21	7	11	.230	.297	.301
Runners On/2 Out	54	17	5	1	1	13	5	4	.315	.500	.383
Scor. Pos./2 Out	34	9	3	0	0	10	5	3	.265	.353	.359
Late Inning Pressure	32	5	1	0	0	1	1	4	.156	.188	.206
Leading Off	14	1	0	0	0	0	0	1	.071	.071	.071
Runners On	9	2	1	0	0	1	0	2	.222	.333	.300
Runners/Scor. Pos.	6	1	0	0	0	1	0	2	.167	.167	.286

RUNS BATTED IN	From 1B	From 2B	From 3B	Scoring Position
Totals	4/92	9/60	11/28	20/88
Percentage	4%	15%	39%	23%
Driving In Runners from 3B with Less than Two Out:			8/16	50%

Loves to face: Eric King (.429, 3-for-7, 1 HR)
Hates to face: Mark Langston (.056, 1-for-18)
Led A.L. catchers with a perfect fielding percentage. Caught in 83 games, two above the minimum needed to qualify.... Has now committed only one error in his last 204 games behind the plate.... Started 36 of 47 games in which the Red Sox faced a left-handed starter during the regular season, but started only 34 of 115 games against right-handers.... Batting average with runners on base was his highest since he drove in 85 runs for the Yankees in 1980.... How would you like to be his real estate agent? He's played for a different ballclub in each of the past five seasons.... Did not play in A.L.C.S. last season.... Has stolen only four bases in 23 attempts, so last season he didn't bother trying.

Jack Clark
New York Yankees — Bats Right

	AB	H	2B	3B	HR	RBI	BB	SO	BA	SA	OBA
Season	496	120	14	0	27	94	113	141	.242	.433	.381
vs. Left-Handers	149	37	5	0	10	33	50	48	.248	.483	.435
vs. Right-Handers	347	83	9	0	17	61	63	93	.239	.412	.356
Home	232	54	5	0	13	47	58	71	.233	.422	.384
Road	264	66	9	0	14	47	55	70	.250	.443	.380
Grass	426	98	9	0	25	78	103	127	.230	.427	.379
Artificial Turf	70	22	5	0	2	16	10	14	.314	.471	.398
April	44	13	1	0	4	14	11	18	.295	.591	.429
May	90	20	4	0	5	15	27	23	.222	.433	.395
June	91	23	1	0	7	18	24	25	.253	.495	.410
July	99	24	4	0	3	21	14	27	.242	.374	.333
August	81	15	1	0	3	10	14	22	.185	.309	.313
Sept./Oct.	91	25	3	0	5	16	23	26	.275	.473	.421
Leading Off Inn.	118	27	2	0	5	5	26	36	.229	.373	.372
Runners On	247	59	6	0	16	83	58	63	.239	.457	.379
Runners/Scor. Pos.	139	34	4	0	7	63	30	35	.245	.424	.368
Runners On/2 Out	116	32	4	0	9	40	25	24	.276	.543	.404
Scor. Pos./2 Out	68	20	3	0	3	27	14	15	.294	.471	.415
Late Inning Pressure	56	10	0	0	2	5	14	21	.179	.286	.338
Leading Off	11	1	0	0	1	1	2	6	.091	.364	.231
Runners On	25	3	0	0	0	3	6	7	.120	.120	.281
Runners/Scor. Pos.	11	0	0	0	0	3	3	5	.000	.000	.200

RUNS BATTED IN	From 1B	From 2B	From 3B	Scoring Position
Totals	15/178	19/101	33/70	52/171
Percentage	8%	19%	47%	30%
Driving In Runners from 3B with Less than Two Out:		24/35		69%

Loves to face: Craig Lefferts (.571, 4-for-7, 4 BB, 4 HR)
Hates to face: Rick Reuschel (.122, 5-for-41)
Played 150 games last season, his highest total since 1982. ... Led designated hitters with 92 walks and 113 strikeouts. ... Walked at least once in 14 consecutive games, longest streak in majors last season, eight games shy of Roy Cullenbine's A.L. record. Jack holds the N.L. record of 16. ... Walked 19 times vs. Baltimore last season, the most of any player against any club. ... Batted .279 against fly-ball pitchers, .192 vs. ground-ballers, 2d-lowest mark in A.L. (minimum: 200 AB). Walt Weiss batted .180. ... Fielding percentage of .989 ranks 25th among the 27 first basemen with at least 300 career games. ... Made his first major league appearance in the field at third base.

Darnell Coles
Seattle Mariners — Bats Right

	AB	H	2B	3B	HR	RBI	BB	SO	BA	SA	OBA
Season	195	57	10	1	10	34	17	26	.292	.508	.356
vs. Left-Handers	58	19	3	0	5	11	8	6	.328	.638	.418
vs. Right-Handers	137	38	7	1	5	23	9	20	.277	.453	.329
Home	103	31	4	1	9	19	10	11	.301	.621	.371
Road	92	26	6	0	1	15	7	15	.283	.380	.340
Grass	75	19	4	0	1	12	5	11	.253	.347	.301
Artificial Turf	120	38	6	1	9	22	12	15	.317	.608	.390
April	0	0	0	0	0	0	0	0	—	—	—
May	0	0	0	0	0	0	0	0	—	—	—
June	0	0	0	0	0	0	0	0	—	—	—
July	37	12	1	0	2	6	2	7	.324	.514	.375
August	70	17	3	0	5	14	6	7	.243	.500	.304
Sept./Oct.	88	28	6	1	3	14	9	12	.318	.511	.390
Leading Off Inn.	35	8	1	1	2	2	2	6	.229	.486	.270
Runners On	80	22	6	0	3	27	6	9	.275	.463	.322
Runners/Scor. Pos.	55	14	3	0	2	23	4	8	.255	.418	.302
Runners On/2 Out	32	8	2	0	1	9	3	5	.250	.406	.314
Scor. Pos./2 Out	23	6	2	0	1	9	2	5	.261	.478	.320
Late Inning Pressure	23	5	0	0	1	2	3	7	.217	.348	.308
Leading Off	8	3	0	0	1	1	1	3	.375	.750	.444
Runners On	4	1	0	0	0	1	1	1	.250	.250	.400
Runners/Scor. Pos.	3	1	0	0	0	1	1	1	.333	.333	.500

RUNS BATTED IN	From 1B	From 2B	From 3B	Scoring Position
Totals	5/53	7/42	12/26	19/68
Percentage	9%	17%	46%	28%
Driving In Runners from 3B with Less than Two Out:		10/15		67%

Loves to face: Juan Nieves (.800, 4-for-5, 1 HR)
Hates to face: Curt Young (0-for-14)
Figures *above* are for A.L. only. ... Batted .232 with five home runs in 68 games for Pittsburgh. ... Has played in both leagues in each of the last two seasons. ... Hitless in 11 at-bats as a pinch hitter last season, all with the Pirates. ... One of three A.L. players to collect hits in eight consecutive at-bats last season, and one of two to reach base safely in 10 consecutive plate appearances. ... Had six hits in 11 at-bats with the bases loaded. ... Batting average in Late-Inning Pressure Situations has been lower than overall average in each of the last six seasons. Career batting averages: .187 in LIP Situations, .254 in unpressured at-bats.

Henry Cotto
Seattle Mariners — Bats Right

	AB	H	2B	3B	HR	RBI	BB	SO	BA	SA	OBA
Season	386	100	18	1	8	33	23	53	.259	.373	.302
vs. Left-Handers	148	41	6	1	4	12	6	21	.277	.412	.306
vs. Right-Handers	238	59	12	0	4	21	17	32	.248	.349	.300
Home	188	48	7	1	5	17	14	23	.255	.383	.307
Road	198	52	11	0	3	16	9	30	.263	.364	.297
Grass	149	46	9	0	3	15	8	22	.309	.430	.348
Artificial Turf	237	54	9	1	5	18	15	31	.228	.338	.273
April	66	29	5	0	2	12	4	7	.439	.606	.472
May	98	23	3	0	1	5	6	12	.235	.296	.279
June	65	9	1	1	0	4	3	14	.138	.185	.171
July	55	17	2	0	2	5	5	7	.309	.455	.367
August	68	15	4	0	2	6	3	9	.221	.368	.264
Sept./Oct.	34	7	3	0	1	1	2	4	.206	.382	.250
Leading Off Inn.	105	32	5	1	3	3	4	12	.305	.457	.336
Runners On	146	39	6	0	4	29	11	21	.267	.390	.317
Runners/Scor. Pos.	83	18	0	0	2	24	9	16	.289	.392	.292
Runners On/2 Out	66	14	1	0	1	12	7	10	.212	.273	.288
Scor. Pos./2 Out	44	9	0	0	0	6	6	9	.205	.205	.300
Late Inning Pressure	41	5	1	0	0	2	4	8	.122	.146	.200
Leading Off	9	1	0	0	0	0	1	1	.111	.111	.200
Runners On	18	2	0	0	0	2	2	3	.111	.111	.200
Runners/Scor. Pos.	11	1	0	0	0	2	2	3	.091	.091	.231

RUNS BATTED IN	From 1B	From 2B	From 3B	Scoring Position
Totals	3/90	4/68	18/34	22/102
Percentage	3%	6%	53%	22%
Driving In Runners from 3B with Less than Two Out:		10/18		56%

Loves to face: Jeff Ballard (.636, 7-for-11, 1 HR)
Hates to face: Jimmy Key (.077, 1-for-13)
Forced the pace down the backstretch in race for A.L. batting title. Through games of May 9, Cotto trailed only Dave Winfield, .409 to .406. ... June batting average was 2d lowest in A.L. (minimum: two PA per game). ... Stole 27 bases in 30 attempts, but only one in 29 games after August 19. ... Nine appearances as a pinch runner tied Mike Kingery for most on the club. ... Has batted higher with runners on base than he has with the bases empty in each of the last four seasons. ... Career batting average of .218 with runners in scoring position, .118 (2-for-17) with the bases loaded. ... Had 15 hits in his first 32 career at-bats in Late-Inning Pressure Situations, 6-for-66 since then.

Alvin Davis
Seattle Mariners — Bats Left

	AB	H	2B	3B	HR	RBI	BB	SO	BA	SA	OBA
Season	478	141	24	1	18	69	95	53	.295	.462	.412
vs. Left-Handers	137	44	13	1	3	21	25	18	.321	.496	.428
vs. Right-Handers	341	97	11	0	15	48	70	35	.284	.449	.406
Home	228	67	13	0	12	43	51	22	.294	.509	.423
Road	250	74	11	1	6	26	44	31	.296	.420	.403
Grass	199	60	5	1	6	22	34	22	.302	.427	.403
Artificial Turf	279	81	19	0	12	47	61	31	.290	.487	.419
April	68	20	2	0	2	10	13	6	.294	.412	.398
May	97	32	7	0	8	24	12	8	.330	.649	.405
June	75	17	6	1	2	4	16	13	.227	.413	.370
July	51	16	1	0	1	5	15	6	.314	.392	.470
August	97	29	2	0	4	11	20	13	.299	.443	.417
Sept./Oct.	90	27	6	0	1	15	19	7	.300	.400	.427
Leading Off Inn.	124	37	7	0	5	5	14	19	.298	.476	.370
Runners On	214	65	10	0	6	57	47	16	.304	.435	.425
Runners/Scor. Pos.	107	31	5	0	2	45	35	9	.290	.393	.453
Runners On/2 Out	91	29	4	0	2	24	21	4	.319	.429	.451
Scor. Pos./2 Out	52	15	2	0	1	20	20	4	.288	.385	.493
Late Inning Pressure	63	20	4	1	3	9	16	4	.317	.556	.463
Leading Off	18	6	0	0	1	1	2	1	.333	.833	.368
Runners On	27	8	4	0	0	6	4	1	.296	.444	.406
Runners/Scor. Pos.	16	3	2	0	0	4	3	0	.188	.313	.316

RUNS BATTED IN	From 1B	From 2B	From 3B	Scoring Position
Totals	13/154	18/81	20/49	38/130
Percentage	8%	22%	41%	29%
Driving In Runners from 3B with Less than Two Out:		13/24		54%

Loves to face: Roger Clemens (.385, 10-for-26, 2 HR)
Hates to face: Bert Blyleven (.146, 7-for-48, 1 HR)
.321 batting average vs. left-handers was second in A.L. to Wade Boggs among left-handed batters (minimum: 100 AB). ... Had an extra-base hit in six consecutive games (May 3–8), tied for longest streak in A.L. last season. One of four players, all in the A.L., to homer in four consecutive games. ... Batting average in Late-Inning Pressure Situations was the highest of his career. ... Has hit more home runs at the Kingdome than he has on the road in each of his five seasons in the majors. Career totals: .294 (70 HR) at home, .279 (40 HR) on the road. ... Career average of .407 (11-for-27, 4 HR) with two outs and the bases loaded. ... A career .300 hitter vs. ground-ball pitchers.

Chili Davis

California Angels — Bats Left and Right

California Angels	AB	H	2B	3B	HR	RBI	BB	SO	BA	SA	OBA
Season	600	161	29	3	21	93	56	118	.268	.432	.326
vs. Left-Handers	219	56	10	2	8	35	17	44	.256	.429	.307
vs. Right-Handers	381	105	19	1	13	58	39	74	.276	.433	.336
Home	291	73	10	1	11	38	23	65	.251	.405	.302
Road	309	88	19	2	10	55	33	53	.285	.456	.348
Grass	499	127	24	2	16	71	47	101	.255	.407	.314
Artificial Turf	101	34	5	1	5	22	9	17	.337	.554	.384
April	94	29	7	0	3	17	5	19	.309	.479	.337
May	103	23	2	2	3	11	6	27	.223	.369	.264
June	98	23	4	0	3	14	5	18	.235	.367	.264
July	93	35	7	0	7	25	14	18	.376	.677	.450
August	112	29	6	1	4	18	11	18	.259	.438	.320
Sept./Oct.	100	22	3	0	1	8	15	18	.220	.280	.322
Leading Off Inn.	143	34	8	0	4	4	7	27	.238	.378	.273
Runners On	287	84	15	3	11	83	30	61	.293	.481	.349
Runners/Scor. Pos.	157	40	10	1	6	67	22	37	.255	.446	.328
Runners On/2 Out	136	35	6	2	4	33	11	30	.257	.419	.313
Scor. Pos./2 Out	74	16	3	0	2	24	6	18	.216	.338	.275
Late Inning Pressure	95	19	2	0	3	7	9	21	.200	.316	.269
Leading Off	33	5	1	0	1	1	1	7	.152	.273	.176
Runners On	39	9	1	0	0	4	4	11	.231	.256	.302
Runners/Scor. Pos.	20	3	1	0	0	4	4	6	.150	.200	.292

RUNS BATTED IN	From 1B	From 2B	From 3B	Scoring Position
Totals	18/217	20/111	34/76	54/187
Percentage	8%	18%	45%	29%
Driving In Runners from 3B with Less than Two Out:			24/41	59%

Loves to face: Rick Honeycutt (.435, 10-for-23, 4 HR)
Hates to face: Frank Tanana (0-for-7)
Led the majors with 21 RBI during spring training 1988. . . . Tied Jose Canseco for major league lead in RBI during July, and set a personal career high for the season. . . . Homered from both sides of the plate in a single game on June 30. Davis holds the N.L. record with three such games in his career. Career record is 10 by Mickey Mantle. . . . Led major league outfielders with 19 errors, most since Lou Brock made 19 in 1966; and the most by an A.L. outfielder since Ted Williams made 19 in 1939. . . . It could have been worse: He had 14 errors by the end of June. . . . Has played 977 games in the outfield, not an inning elsewhere. Maybe it's about time.

Rob Deer

Milwaukee Brewers — Bats Right

Milwaukee Brewers	AB	H	2B	3B	HR	RBI	BB	SO	BA	SA	OBA
Season	492	124	24	0	23	85	51	153	.252	.441	.328
vs. Left-Handers	137	35	7	0	8	25	24	31	.255	.482	.366
vs. Right-Handers	355	89	17	0	15	60	27	122	.251	.425	.312
Home	246	63	13	0	12	44	28	77	.256	.455	.344
Road	246	61	11	0	11	41	23	76	.248	.427	.311
Grass	432	108	23	0	20	75	42	136	.250	.442	.323
Artificial Turf	60	16	1	0	3	10	9	17	.267	.433	.362
April	77	17	4	0	4	11	5	20	.221	.429	.268
May	87	18	2	0	2	14	9	27	.207	.299	.293
June	95	20	5	0	6	17	12	34	.211	.453	.315
July	34	10	4	0	0	1	2	11	.294	.412	.351
August	105	35	8	0	8	26	10	28	.333	.638	.397
Sept./Oct.	94	24	1	0	3	16	13	33	.255	.362	.336
Leading Off Inn.	128	28	9	0	3	3	12	38	.219	.359	.296
Runners On	226	65	12	0	12	74	22	66	.288	.500	.357
Runners/Scor. Pos.	148	42	8	0	9	67	13	44	.284	.520	.339
Runners On/2 Out	111	28	6	0	6	31	14	34	.252	.468	.341
Scor. Pos./2 Out	71	19	3	0	5	28	9	24	.268	.521	.358
Late Inning Pressure	78	14	2	0	3	10	3	27	.179	.321	.229
Leading Off	22	4	1	0	0	0	0	5	.182	.227	.217
Runners On	35	8	1	0	2	9	0	13	.229	.429	.250
Runners/Scor. Pos.	22	4	1	0	1	7	0	8	.182	.364	.217

RUNS BATTED IN	From 1B	From 2B	From 3B	Scoring Position
Totals	9/152	26/107	27/63	53/170
Percentage	6%	24%	43%	31%
Driving In Runners from 3B with Less than Two Out:			20/38	53%

Loves to face: Rob Woodward (2-for-2, 2 HR)
Hates to face: Mark Eichhorn (0-for-7, 6 SO)
Became the second player in baseball history to top 150 strikeouts in three consecutive seasons, 16 days after Pete Incaviglia blazed that trail. Until last season, only Reggie had reached the 150-mark three times in a *career*. . .Brewers had a 37–21 record with Deer batting cleanup, 50–54 with others in that spot. . . . Batting average with runners in scoring position has increased in every season in the majors. Since 1987 he has seven hits in 14 at-bats, including three home runs, with the bases loaded. . . . Career average of .197 during June. . . . Has driven in only 54 of 116 runners from 3d base with less than two outs (47%).

Brian Downing

California Angels — Bats Right

California Angels	AB	H	2B	3B	HR	RBI	BB	SO	BA	SA	OBA
Season	484	117	18	2	25	64	81	63	.242	.442	.362
vs. Left-Handers	175	39	4	0	8	13	39	21	.223	.383	.382
vs. Right-Handers	309	78	14	2	17	51	42	42	.252	.476	.351
Home	239	57	9	1	11	31	44	34	.238	.423	.365
Road	245	60	9	1	14	33	37	29	.245	.461	.360
Grass	416	100	15	2	24	58	67	55	.240	.459	.357
Artificial Turf	68	17	3	0	1	6	14	8	.250	.338	.395
April	36	4	0	0	1	4	12	5	.111	.194	.353
May	93	31	6	1	7	14	8	13	.333	.645	.410
June	86	19	4	0	1	7	16	14	.221	.302	.349
July	77	21	3	1	7	15	18	12	.273	.610	.424
August	101	20	2	0	4	13	10	12	.198	.337	.281
Sept./Oct.	91	22	3	0	5	11	17	7	.242	.440	.364
Leading Off Inn.	133	27	6	0	6	6	16	18	.203	.383	.289
Runners On	200	55	6	1	7	46	34	27	.275	.420	.391
Runners/Scor. Pos.	113	23	1	0	2	33	25	18	.204	.265	.356
Runners On/2 Out	83	22	2	0	3	18	14	8	.265	.398	.384
Scor. Pos./2 Out	51	11	0	0	0	12	12	6	.216	.216	.385
Late Inning Pressure	81	25	3	2	8	21	12	15	.309	.691	.412
Leading Off	16	4	1	0	2	2	3	3	.250	.688	.368
Runners On	38	15	2	1	3	16	5	5	.395	.737	.489
Runners/Scor. Pos.	21	7	0	0	2	12	3	3	.333	.619	.444

RUNS BATTED IN	From 1B	From 2B	From 3B	Scoring Position
Totals	9/136	8/82	22/47	30/129
Percentage	7%	10%	47%	23%
Driving In Runners from 3B with Less than Two Out:			14/24	58%

Loves to face: Charlie Leibrandt (.515, 17-for-33, 7 BB, 2 HR)
Hates to face: Tom Henke (0-for-14)
Lowest batting average since he hit .240 for the White Sox in 1975. . . . The A.L.'s April home run leader for 1982 through 1987 compiled its lowest batting average in April 1988 (minimum: two PA per game). . . . Didn't play a game in the field, but led all designated hitters with 25 home runs. . . . Only major leaguer to start at least 20 games in both the leadoff and cleanup spots. . . . Over the last 14 years, he's batted .294 against ground-ball pitchers, .248 vs. fly-ballers. . . . Needs seven more games to become the Angels' all-time leader. Jim Fregosi currently holds the lead with 1429 games. . . . How good a fielder was Bill Melton? Downing made his big-league debut as a defensive sub for him. At third base!

Jim Eisenreich

Kansas City Royals — Bats Left

Kansas City Royals	AB	H	2B	3B	HR	RBI	BB	SO	BA	SA	OBA
Season	202	44	8	1	1	20	6	31	.218	.282	.236
vs. Left-Handers	38	14	2	0	0	2	1	7	.368	.421	.385
vs. Right-Handers	164	30	6	1	1	18	5	24	.183	.250	.202
Home	99	22	4	1	0	14	3	12	.222	.283	.238
Road	103	22	4	0	1	6	3	19	.214	.282	.234
Grass	70	16	2	0	0	3	2	11	.229	.257	.247
Artificial Turf	132	28	6	1	1	17	4	20	.212	.295	.230
April	60	14	3	0	0	7	1	10	.233	.283	.238
May	39	5	2	1	0	3	1	7	.128	.231	.150
June	43	9	1	0	0	3	2	5	.209	.233	.234
July	1	0	0	0	0	0	1	0	.000	.000	.000
August	11	3	0	0	0	0	0	3	.273	.273	.273
Sept./Oct.	48	13	2	0	1	6	2	6	.271	.375	.300
Leading Off Inn.	52	9	2	0	0	0	2	7	.173	.212	.204
Runners On	92	22	4	1	1	20	3	16	.239	.337	.253
Runners/Scor. Pos.	60	12	4	0	1	19	3	11	.200	.317	.224
Runners On/2 Out	34	8	1	0	1	4	1	6	.235	.265	.257
Scor. Pos./2 Out	24	4	1	0	0	4	1	4	.167	.208	.200
Late Inning Pressure	39	10	1	0	0	2	1	8	.256	.282	.275
Leading Off	12	3	0	0	0	0	1	3	.250	.250	.308
Runners On	14	3	1	0	0	2	0	3	.214	.286	.214
Runners/Scor. Pos.	8	1	1	0	0	2	0	2	.125	.250	.125

RUNS BATTED IN	From 1B	From 2B	From 3B	Scoring Position
Totals	1/62	6/50	12/28	18/78
Percentage	2%	12%	43%	23%
Driving In Runners from 3B with Less than Two Out:			10/20	50%

Loves to face: Dennis Eckersley (3-for-3, 2 2B)
Hates to face: Chris Bosio (0-for-10)
Hitless streak of 32 consecutive at-bats vs. right-handed pitchers was the longest in the majors last season. . . . On-base average was 2d lowest among A.L. players with 200 or more plate appearances. . . . Started at four different positions (LF, CF, RF, DH) over a five-day span in April. . . . Most games (64) of any major league outfielder without an assist last season. In fairness, he played an average of less than six innings per game. . . . Career average of .300 in day games, .214 at night. . . . Has only two hits in 17 career at-bats with runners in scoring position in Late-Inning Pressure Situations. . . . No home runs in 81 career at-bats in Late-Inning Pressure Situations.

Cecil Espy
Texas Rangers — Bats Left and Right

	AB	H	2B	3B	HR	RBI	BB	SO	BA	SA	OBA
Season	347	86	17	6	2	40	20	83	.248	.349	.288
vs. Left-Handers	61	20	6	1	1	10	4	13	.328	.508	.369
vs. Right-Handers	286	66	11	5	1	30	16	70	.231	.315	.271
Home	155	46	7	5	2	23	4	37	.297	.445	.313
Road	192	40	10	1	0	17	16	46	.208	.271	.269
Grass	276	67	11	5	2	31	14	64	.243	.341	.279
Artificial Turf	71	19	6	1	0	9	6	19	.268	.380	.325
April	37	10	2	1	0	2	0	8	.270	.378	.263
May	25	8	2	1	0	1	1	3	.320	.480	.346
June	44	13	3	0	1	9	3	15	.295	.432	.327
July	70	14	3	1	0	7	4	15	.200	.271	.253
August	65	15	1	2	1	6	4	17	.231	.354	.275
Sept./Oct.	106	26	6	1	0	15	8	25	.245	.321	.298
Leading Off Inn.	91	19	5	2	0	0	4	24	.209	.308	.242
Runners On	144	45	6	2	2	40	9	24	.313	.424	.346
Runners/Scor. Pos.	79	28	4	2	2	38	6	16	.354	.532	.386
Runners On/2 Out	67	20	3	1	1	19	5	12	.299	.418	.347
Scor. Pos./2 Out	41	14	1	1	1	17	4	10	.341	.488	.400
Late Inning Pressure	61	10	1	0	1	5	10	16	.164	.230	.278
Leading Off	18	5	0	0	0	0	4	4	.278	.278	.409
Runners On	23	3	0	0	1	5	4	5	.130	.261	.250
Runners/Scor. Pos.	12	3	0	0	1	5	3	3	.250	.500	.375

RUNS BATTED IN	From 1B	From 2B	From 3B	Scoring Position
Totals	2/103	16/61	20/37	36/98
Percentage	2%	26%	54%	37%
Driving In Runners from 3B with Less than Two Out:			14/18	78%

Loves to face: Juan Nieves (3-for-3)
Hates to face: Jack Morris (0-for-6, 4 SO)
Led A.L. rookies in stolen bases (33) and triples.... Grounded into only two double plays in 66 opportunities, 2d-lowest rate in A.L. (min: 40 opp.).... Played seven different positions last season, failing to appear at third base or as a pitcher, but didn't start a game anywhere but in the outfield.... Attention rotisserie players: Espy stole 74 bases for Vero Beach in 1982, and has stolen at least 40 bases in five of his nine seasons in pro ball.... Of the players who've hit more than 100 points better with runners on than with the bases empty over the past 14 years, only one has more career at-bats than Espy: Pete Stanicek.

Dwight Evans
Boston Red Sox — Bats Right

	AB	H	2B	3B	HR	RBI	BB	SO	BA	SA	OBA
Season	559	164	31	7	21	111	76	99	.293	.487	.375
vs. Left-Handers	144	48	5	2	6	31	28	22	.333	.521	.439
vs. Right-Handers	415	116	26	5	15	80	48	77	.280	.475	.351
Home	277	88	21	4	11	58	39	52	.318	.542	.398
Road	282	76	10	3	10	53	37	47	.270	.433	.352
Grass	479	140	27	5	16	93	65	84	.292	.470	.374
Artificial Turf	80	24	4	2	5	18	11	15	.300	.588	.380
April	74	18	3	1	0	10	9	13	.243	.311	.318
May	105	37	7	0	3	23	13	13	.352	.505	.413
June	112	34	7	1	2	22	8	15	.304	.438	.350
July	81	25	5	2	4	15	11	14	.309	.568	.391
August	96	25	7	2	4	17	16	29	.260	.500	.366
Sept./Oct.	91	25	2	1	8	24	19	15	.275	.582	.398
Leading Off Inn.	115	29	5	0	6	6	13	23	.252	.452	.328
Runners On	304	96	15	7	14	104	44	53	.316	.549	.396
Runners/Scor. Pos.	172	56	10	5	5	83	29	27	.326	.529	.411
Runners On/2 Out	91	29	5	0	4	32	23	15	.319	.505	.456
Scor. Pos./2 Out	58	21	4	0	1	26	15	8	.362	.483	.493
Late Inning Pressure	70	17	1	0	3	6	6	18	.243	.386	.299
Leading Off	21	3	0	0	1	0	6	6	.143	.286	.143
Runners On	26	6	0	0	1	4	5	7	.231	.346	.344
Runners/Scor. Pos.	13	1	0	0	0	2	3	2	.077	.077	.235

RUNS BATTED IN	From 1B	From 2B	From 3B	Scoring Position
Totals	16/226	35/143	39/69	74/212
Percentage	7%	24%	57%	35%
Driving In Runners from 3B with Less than Two Out:			27/41	66%

Loves to face: Mike Morgan (.636, 7-for-11, 6 BB, 1 HR)
Hates to face: Mike Witt (.103, 4-for-39)
Has hit five opening-day home runs, one short of A.L. record shared by Babe Ruth, Brooks Robinson, and Carl Yastrzemski. Frank Robinson holds the major league record (8).... Reached base safely in 11 consecutive plate appearances, longest streak in the majors.... Needs 56 games to tie Ted Williams for 2d place in Red Sox history.... Is this guy the All-American Boy, or what? Last year, he went 2-for-2 on Memorial Day, 3-for-4 on Independence Day, and 3-for-5 on Labor Day, for a holiday batting average of .727. He had a home run and three RBI in *each* of those games, *including the game-winners in all three*. Evans may be the only player who would favor a return to holiday doubleheaders.

Darrell Evans
Detroit Tigers — Bats Left

	AB	H	2B	3B	HR	RBI	BB	SO	BA	SA	OBA
Season	437	91	9	0	22	65	84	89	.208	.380	.337
vs. Left-Handers	64	10	2	0	0	9	10	15	.156	.188	.270
vs. Right-Handers	373	81	7	0	22	56	74	74	.217	.413	.348
Home	215	48	5	0	14	32	48	48	.223	.442	.365
Road	222	43	4	0	8	33	36	41	.194	.320	.309
Grass	380	82	9	0	21	58	77	83	.216	.405	.349
Artificial Turf	57	9	0	0	1	7	7	6	.158	.211	.250
April	59	11	1	0	1	7	10	11	.186	.254	.304
May	69	13	1	0	2	8	5	10	.188	.290	.243
June	67	14	2	0	5	13	25	15	.209	.463	.430
July	84	19	1	0	5	11	11	19	.226	.417	.316
August	79	16	3	0	4	15	17	15	.203	.392	.344
Sept./Oct.	79	18	1	0	5	11	16	19	.228	.430	.358
Leading Off Inn.	82	17	2	0	6	6	16	16	.207	.451	.337
Runners On	213	45	6	0	7	50	45	42	.211	.338	.349
Runners/Scor. Pos.	127	29	4	0	4	43	21	22	.228	.354	.338
Runners On/2 Out	90	14	3	0	3	18	22	22	.156	.289	.321
Scor. Pos./2 Out	60	9	1	0	2	15	11	15	.150	.267	.282
Late Inning Pressure	67	19	3	0	4	12	9	15	.284	.507	.368
Leading Off	7	1	0	0	1	1	3	3	.143	.571	.400
Runners On	35	12	3	0	1	9	3	9	.343	.514	.395
Runners/Scor. Pos.	18	5	1	0	0	6	0	3	.278	.333	.278

RUNS BATTED IN	From 1B	From 2B	From 3B	Scoring Position
Totals	8/150	16/98	19/49	35/147
Percentage	5%	16%	39%	24%
Driving In Runners from 3B with Less than Two Out:			14/20	70%

Loves to face: Rick Mahler (.444, 4-for-9, 2 HR)
Hates to face: Bob Walk (.091, 1-for-11)
Oldest nonpitcher in A.L. last season, and the oldest major leaguer in an opening-day starting lineup.... Started all 107 games in which the Tigers faced a right-handed starter last season, but only 10 starts in 55 games vs. lefties.... Became 10th major league player to hit 20 home runs in a season in which he had less than 10 other extra-base hits. That sound familiar, Tigers fans? Lance Parrish was the last major leaguer to do it, in 1986.... Needs 36 games to move past Lou Brock into the all-time top 20.... Hit his first home run on May 29, 1971, off Bob Gibson. Ranks 4th in M.L. history with 182 home runs after his 35th birthday, behind Aaron (245), Ruth (198), and Ted Williams (189).

Tony Fernandez
Toronto Blue Jays — Bats Left and Right

	AB	H	2B	3B	HR	RBI	BB	SO	BA	SA	OBA
Season	648	186	41	4	5	70	45	65	.287	.386	.335
vs. Left-Handers	219	61	8	2	3	21	13	19	.279	.374	.318
vs. Right-Handers	429	125	33	2	2	49	32	46	.291	.392	.344
Home	316	90	21	3	3	41	24	32	.285	.399	.337
Road	332	96	20	1	2	29	21	33	.289	.373	.333
Grass	267	76	20	0	2	26	13	24	.285	.382	.322
Artificial Turf	381	110	21	4	3	44	32	41	.289	.388	.344
April	76	19	0	0	1	9	5	12	.250	.289	.301
May	122	34	9	0	1	13	7	14	.279	.377	.313
June	111	32	10	1	0	11	10	10	.288	.396	.347
July	101	28	5	0	2	8	7	8	.277	.386	.321
August	121	37	7	1	0	11	5	10	.306	.380	.339
Sept./Oct.	117	36	10	2	1	18	11	11	.308	.453	.377
Leading Off Inn.	247	56	9	1	1	1	12	29	.227	.283	.263
Runners On	238	76	22	3	1	66	21	21	.319	.450	.376
Runners/Scor. Pos.	138	48	16	1	0	61	15	14	.348	.478	.413
Runners On/2 Out	103	38	8	1	0	32	10	10	.369	.466	.430
Scor. Pos./2 Out	70	27	0	0	0	31	9	8	.386	.471	.463
Late Inning Pressure	77	28	6	0	1	10	6	6	.364	.481	.412
Leading Off	10	4	0	0	0	1	1	1	.400	.400	.455
Runners On	44	15	3	0	1	10	5	4	.341	.477	.412
Runners/Scor. Pos.	27	7	2	0	0	8	4	3	.259	.333	.364

RUNS BATTED IN	From 1B	From 2B	From 3B	Scoring Position
Totals	7/172	26/98	32/66	58/164
Percentage	4%	27%	48%	35%
Driving In Runners from 3B with Less than Two Out:			15/27	56%

Loves to face: Dale Mohorcic (.714, 5-for-7)
Hates to face: Melido Perez (0-for-10)
Better keep this guy healthy. Blue Jays have lost their last 15 games without him in the starting lineup.... Committed two errors in game of August 27, snapping a streak of 65 consecutive errorless games.... Batting averages in Late-Inning Pressure Situations, year by year since 1984: .273, .305, .363, .363, .364.... Career batting average of .341 with two outs and runners in scoring position.... Has increased his RBI total for five consecutive seasons. (Year by year since 1983: 2, 19, 51, 65, 67, 70.) Ben Oglivie had the only seven-year streak in major league history (1974–1980). Six players had six-year streaks: Lave Cross, Stuffy McInnis, Frank Snyder, Alvin Dark, Billy Williams, and Keith Moreland.

Carlton Fisk

Chicago White Sox   Bats Right

Chicago White Sox	AB	H	2B	3B	HR	RBI	BB	SO	BA	SA	OBA
Season	253	70	8	1	19	50	37	40	.277	.542	.377
vs. Left-Handers	93	27	3	1	10	23	22	13	.290	.667	.427
vs. Right-Handers	160	43	5	0	9	27	15	27	.269	.469	.344
Home	121	33	5	0	9	22	18	18	.273	.537	.371
Road	132	37	3	1	10	28	19	22	.280	.545	.382
Grass	205	52	6	1	14	39	29	34	.254	.498	.354
Artificial Turf	48	18	2	0	5	11	8	6	.375	.729	.474
April	59	18	3	0	5	9	6	6	.305	.610	.379
May	25	6	1	0	3	8	4	6	.240	.640	.345
June	0	0	0	0	0	0	0	0	——	——	——
July	10	3	1	0	1	2	1	0	.300	.700	.364
August	78	25	2	1	5	18	13	9	.321	.564	.415
Sept./Oct.	81	18	1	0	5	13	13	19	.222	.420	.351
Leading Off Inn.	48	15	2	1	5	5	9	7	.313	.708	.421
Runners On	122	33	5	0	6	37	19	18	.270	.459	.381
Runners/Scor. Pos.	68	17	2	0	1	26	15	10	.250	.324	.384
Runners On/2 Out	53	12	0	0	3	13	8	9	.226	.396	.359
Scor. Pos./2 Out	32	5	0	0	1	9	5	6	.156	.250	.289
Late Inning Pressure	54	16	3	0	4	11	7	9	.296	.574	.377
Leading Off	11	3	1	0	2	2	1	2	.273	.909	.333
Runners On	29	8	2	0	1	8	5	5	.276	.448	.382
Runners/Scor. Pos.	14	2	0	0	0	5	4	1	.143	.143	.333

RUNS BATTED IN	From 1B	From 2B	From 3B	Scoring Position
Totals	8/90	10/55	13/26	23/81
Percentage	9%	18%	50%	28%
Driving In Runners from 3B with Less than Two Out:		9/12		75%

Loves to face: Mark Langston (.364, 12-for-33, 4 HR)
Hates to face: Jack Morris (.122, 6-for-49)
Tied Cory Snyder for highest slugging average vs. left-handed pitchers in majors. His home-run rate vs. lefties beat everyone, Snyder included. . . . Hasn't appeared as a designated hitter since June 21, 1987. Hasn't played anywhere in fair territory since June 5, 1987. . . . Once considered the quintessential Red Soxer from New England, he's now played nearly as many games in white (960) as in red (1078). . . . Batted .301 against ground-ball pitchers last season, .254 vs. fly-ball pitchers. . . . Candidates for four-decade status: Buckner, Dempsey, Darrell Evans, Fisk, Nettles, and Simmons. All played in the 1960s. For list of pitchers, see Jerry Reuss comments.

Scott Fletcher

Texas Rangers   Bats Right

Texas Rangers	AB	H	2B	3B	HR	RBI	BB	SO	BA	SA	OBA
Season	515	142	19	4	0	48	62	34	.276	.328	.364
vs. Left-Handers	163	55	6	2	0	17	18	8	.337	.399	.407
vs. Right-Handers	352	87	13	2	0	31	44	26	.247	.295	.345
Home	252	72	12	1	0	23	29	16	.286	.341	.368
Road	263	70	7	3	0	25	33	18	.266	.316	.359
Grass	426	113	15	1	0	34	57	24	.265	.305	.365
Artificial Turf	89	29	4	3	0	14	5	10	.326	.438	.354
April	74	11	0	0	0	2	5	5	.149	.149	.213
May	104	39	6	1	0	15	10	4	.375	.452	.422
June	101	27	5	0	0	12	19	6	.267	.317	.387
July	102	31	4	0	0	7	9	7	.304	.343	.366
August	99	27	4	1	0	7	12	8	.273	.333	.371
Sept./Oct.	35	7	0	2	0	5	7	4	.200	.314	.391
Leading Off Inn.	89	21	1	0	0	0	15	4	.236	.247	.352
Runners On	219	68	8	3	0	48	23	10	.311	.374	.386
Runners/Scor. Pos.	143	44	5	3	0	47	16	7	.308	.385	.388
Runners On/2 Out	96	21	3	1	0	14	11	3	.219	.271	.312
Scor. Pos./2 Out	74	15	2	1	0	14	10	2	.203	.257	.314
Late Inning Pressure	73	18	1	2	0	7	14	7	.247	.315	.385
Leading Off	14	3	0	0	0	0	4	1	.214	.214	.389
Runners On	40	9	0	0	0	7	4	4	.225	.325	.319
Runners/Scor. Pos.	29	7	0	2	0	7	2	2	.241	.379	.324

RUNS BATTED IN	From 1B	From 2B	From 3B	Scoring Position
Totals	3/133	19/119	26/60	45/179
Percentage	2%	16%	43%	25%
Driving In Runners from 3B with Less than Two Out:		20/31		65%

Loves to face: Dave LaPoint (.615, 8-for-13, 4 BB)
Hates to face: Kirk McCaskill (0-for-13)
May batting average was 5th highest in A.L. . . . Led Rangers with 15 sac bunts. . . . One of three A.L. players with 500 or more at-bats and no home runs last season. Record for RBIs in a homerless season: 79, by Luke Appling (1940). . . . Committed only four errors after the All-Star break, three of them in a single game (Aug. 12). . . . Batting average with runners on base has been higher than with the bases empty in each of his eight seasons. Career averages: .254 with bases empty, .297 with runners on base, .312 with runners in scoring position. . . . Career batting average of .346 (74-for-214) vs. Yankees. . . . Career batting average of .217 during September.

Julio Franco

Cleveland Indians   Bats Right

Cleveland Indians	AB	H	2B	3B	HR	RBI	BB	SO	BA	SA	OBA
Season	613	186	23	6	10	54	56	72	.303	.409	.361
vs. Left-Handers	133	51	11	3	5	12	19	8	.383	.624	.461
vs. Right-Handers	480	135	12	3	5	42	37	64	.281	.350	.333
Home	286	104	15	2	3	27	27	31	.364	.462	.416
Road	327	82	8	4	7	27	29	41	.251	.364	.314
Grass	510	162	22	4	6	42	48	60	.318	.412	.375
Artificial Turf	103	24	1	2	4	12	8	12	.233	.398	.292
April	90	21	1	0	1	5	7	11	.233	.278	.293
May	119	37	5	3	3	14	8	18	.311	.479	.354
June	96	30	3	1	4	8	10	13	.313	.490	.374
July	105	41	7	0	1	14	12	8	.390	.486	.454
August	98	27	3	0	1	5	5	13	.276	.337	.308
Sept./Oct.	105	30	4	2	0	8	14	9	.286	.362	.370
Leading Off Inn.	227	69	8	2	5	5	20	23	.304	.423	.363
Runners On	208	57	9	4	2	46	22	34	.274	.385	.340
Runners/Scor. Pos.	111	30	6	2	1	41	16	24	.270	.387	.356
Runners On/2 Out	98	20	3	1	1	20	13	18	.204	.286	.297
Scor. Pos./2 Out	60	13	2	0	1	18	11	15	.217	.300	.338
Late Inning Pressure	78	26	2	1	3	11	6	12	.333	.500	.376
Leading Off	15	5	1	0	1	1	3	3	.333	.600	.375
Runners On	33	11	1	1	2	10	3	6	.333	.606	.378
Runners/Scor. Pos.	16	3	0	1	1	7	2	5	.188	.375	.263

RUNS BATTED IN	From 1B	From 2B	From 3B	Scoring Position
Totals	8/152	17/91	19/44	36/135
Percentage	5%	19%	43%	27%
Driving In Runners from 3B with Less than Two Out:		14/22		64%

Loves to face: Floyd Bannister (.433, 13-for-30, 3 HR)
Hates to face: Tom Henke (.077, 1-for-13)
Had the longest hitting streak in A.L. last season (22 games), and the longest by a Cleveland player since Mike Hargrove's 23-gamer in 1980. Franco was the first player with two streaks of 20 games or more in the same season since Mickey Rivers in 1980. . . . Led A.L. in batting average during July. . . . One of two A.L. players to bat 100 points higher vs. lefties than righties (minimum: 100 AB each way). The other: Terry Steinbach. . . . Percentage of runners driven in from scoring position, year by year since 1984: .349, .320, .315, .289, .274. . . . Ranks fifth with 898 hits over past five seasons, behind superstars Boggs, Mattingly, Puckett, and Gwynn. But he's never made an All-Star team.

Terry Francona

Cleveland Indians   Bats Left

Cleveland Indians	AB	H	2B	3B	HR	RBI	BB	SO	BA	SA	OBA
Season	212	66	8	0	1	12	5	18	.311	.363	.324
vs. Left-Handers	8	3	0	0	0	0	1	1	.375	.375	.444
vs. Right-Handers	204	63	8	0	1	12	4	17	.309	.363	.319
Home	105	35	4	0	1	9	3	9	.333	.400	.352
Road	107	31	4	0	0	3	2	9	.290	.327	.297
Grass	178	54	7	0	1	12	4	13	.303	.360	.331
Artificial Turf	34	12	1	0	0	0	1	5	.353	.382	.371
April	0	0	0	0	0	0	0	0	——	——	——
May	0	0	0	0	0	0	0	0	——	——	——
June	0	0	0	0	0	0	0	0	——	——	——
July	86	25	3	0	1	6	2	7	.291	.360	.303
August	89	31	4	0	0	3	3	9	.348	.393	.368
Sept./Oct.	37	10	1	0	0	3	0	2	.270	.297	.270
Leading Off Inn.	45	13	2	0	0	0	1	5	.289	.333	.304
Runners On	77	30	3	0	0	11	3	4	.390	.429	.402
Runners/Scor. Pos.	27	10	0	0	0	10	2	1	.370	.370	.414
Runners On/2 Out	30	10	0	0	0	2	0	2	.333	.333	.333
Scor. Pos./2 Out	12	6	0	0	0	4	0	0	.500	.500	.500
Late Inning Pressure	31	14	2	0	0	4	0	3	.452	.516	.452
Leading Off	10	6	2	0	0	0	0	0	.600	.800	.600
Runners On	11	5	0	0	0	4	0	0	.455	.455	.455
Runners/Scor. Pos.	7	4	0	0	0	4	0	0	.571	.571	.571

RUNS BATTED IN	From 1B	From 2B	From 3B	Scoring Position
Totals	1/61	6/19	4/13	10/32
Percentage	2%	32%	31%	31%
Driving In Runners from 3B with Less than Two Out:		3/8		38%

Loves to face: Dickie Noles (.556, 5-for-9, 1 HR)
Hates to face: Oswaldo Pereza (0-for-8)
August batting average was 6th best in A.L. . . . Averaged one walk per 44.4 plate appearances, lowest rate of any A.L. player with at least 200 plate appearances. . . . Batted .331 in 38 games as a designated hitter. . . . Six hits in 30 career at-bats with the bases loaded, but none for extra bases. . . . Started 47 games last season, but only once vs. a left-handed pitcher. . . . Set a career high with 24 runs scored last season, a few fewer than you might expect from an eight-year vet. . . . Terry is baseball's version of an Army brat. He and his Dad Tito have played for 12 different teams. No parent/child combo in major league history have called as many places home. Closest: Marty and Matt Keough (10).

Gary Gaetti
Minnesota Twins — Bats Right

	AB	H	2B	3B	HR	RBI	BB	SO	BA	SA	OBA
Season	468	141	29	2	28	88	36	85	.301	.551	.353
vs. Left-Handers	130	44	9	0	8	27	15	19	.338	.592	.400
vs. Right-Handers	338	97	20	2	20	61	21	66	.287	.536	.334
Home	219	65	13	1	9	39	21	41	.297	.489	.363
Road	249	76	16	1	19	49	15	44	.305	.606	.344
Grass	188	54	14	0	16	43	12	35	.287	.617	.330
Artificial Turf	280	87	15	2	12	45	24	50	.311	.507	.369
April	78	18	5	0	4	11	7	21	.231	.449	.299
May	107	32	7	0	5	18	6	14	.299	.505	.339
June	105	38	8	0	7	19	10	15	.362	.638	.419
July	87	28	5	0	8	20	6	20	.322	.655	.368
August	59	14	2	2	2	8	6	10	.237	.441	.303
Sept./Oct.	32	11	2	0	2	12	1	5	.344	.594	.371
Leading Off Inn.	113	37	10	0	13	13	4	16	.327	.761	.361
Runners On	233	70	12	2	12	72	24	46	.300	.524	.360
Runners/Scor. Pos.	135	41	5	1	9	63	17	31	.304	.556	.371
Runners On/2 Out	101	31	6	0	8	36	12	17	.307	.604	.386
Scor. Pos./2 Out	62	20	3	0	5	29	9	11	.323	.613	.417
Late Inning Pressure	64	22	6	0	6	21	2	11	.344	.719	.364
Leading Off	12	4	1	0	1	1	0	0	.333	.667	.333
Runners On	37	12	2	0	4	19	1	10	.324	.703	.342
Runners/Scor. Pos.	25	8	1	0	4	19	1	8	.320	.840	.346

RUNS BATTED IN	From 1B	From 2B	From 3B	Scoring Position
Totals	11/183	18/101	31/58	49/159
Percentage	6%	18%	53%	31%
Driving In Runners from 3B with Less than Two Out:			18/30	60%

Loves to face: Floyd Bannister (.471, 16-for-34, 7 HR)
Hates to face: Bobby Witt (0-for-9)
Hit 19 home runs outside of the Metrodome, 3d-highest road total of any major leaguer. The only two players with more homers on the road were the A's dynamic duo: Canseco and McGwire. Career totals: Metrodome, 78; road, 88. . . . Games played, year by year since 1984: 162, 160, 157, 154, 133. . . . Career batting average of .255 through 1987. His highest previous mark was .287 in 1986. . . . Although he topped the .300 mark for the first time last season, he's hit .300 or better with two outs and runners on base in each of the last three seasons. . . . One of three players to average 30 home runs and 100 RBI over the past three seasons. The others won the last two A.L. MVP awards: George Bell and Jose Canseco.

Greg Gagne
Minnesota Twins — Bats Right

	AB	H	2B	3B	HR	RBI	BB	SO	BA	SA	OBA
Season	461	109	20	6	14	48	27	110	.236	.397	.288
vs. Left-Handers	111	33	4	5	2	9	8	29	.297	.477	.352
vs. Right-Handers	350	76	16	1	12	39	19	81	.217	.371	.267
Home	225	50	10	3	5	28	14	50	.222	.360	.279
Road	236	59	10	3	9	20	13	60	.250	.432	.298
Grass	189	53	8	2	9	19	9	46	.280	.487	.320
Artificial Turf	272	56	12	4	5	29	18	64	.206	.335	.267
April	70	16	3	1	1	4	4	23	.229	.343	.289
May	72	14	2	2	3	8	3	20	.194	.403	.247
June	81	25	4	2	4	15	6	16	.309	.556	.371
July	84	22	4	0	3	8	5	10	.262	.417	.319
August	91	20	5	1	1	10	6	20	.220	.330	.265
Sept./Oct.	63	12	2	0	2	3	3	21	.190	.317	.239
Leading Off Inn.	99	31	2	3	5	5	1	21	.313	.545	.320
Runners On	208	44	9	3	6	40	16	53	.212	.370	.283
Runners/Scor. Pos.	124	26	5	3	3	34	11	34	.210	.371	.293
Runners On/2 Out	98	19	5	2	3	22	5	21	.194	.378	.248
Scor. Pos./2 Out	67	13	3	2	1	18	3	16	.194	.343	.250
Late Inning Pressure	54	13	1	1	3	7	5	15	.241	.463	.305
Leading Off	17	5	0	0	1	1	0	5	.294	.471	.294
Runners On	28	3	0	1	1	5	2	7	.107	.286	.167
Runners/Scor. Pos.	18	2	0	1	0	3	2	4	.111	.222	.200

RUNS BATTED IN	From 1B	From 2B	From 3B	Scoring Position
Totals	6/151	15/96	13/46	28/142
Percentage	4%	16%	28%	20%
Driving In Runners from 3B with Less than Two Out:			6/18	33%

Loves to face: Willie Fraser (.429, 3-for-7, 3 HR)
Hates to face: Dave Stieb (.174, 4-for-23, 8 SO)
First A.L. player since 1980 (when game-winning RBI received its statistical wings) to make 500 or more plate appearances without a game-winner. He obviously still savors the memory of his last GW-RBI, in the seventh game of the 1987 World Series. . . . Had an extra-base hit in six consecutive games (May 29–June 4), tied for longest streak in A.L. . . . A lover *and* a fighter: Only player in double figures in both sac bunts and home runs in each of the last two seasons. . . . Batting average with runners in scoring position has decreased in each of the last three seasons: .303, .267, .238, .210. . . . Has batted .282 vs. ground-ball pitchers, .222 vs. fly-ballers over the past two seasons.

Dave Gallagher
Chicago White Sox — Bats Right

	AB	H	2B	3B	HR	RBI	BB	SO	BA	SA	OBA
Season	347	105	15	3	5	31	29	40	.303	.406	.354
vs. Left-Handers	155	42	3	2	1	11	15	17	.271	.335	.331
vs. Right-Handers	192	63	12	1	4	20	14	23	.328	.464	.374
Home	168	50	9	2	1	16	13	15	.298	.393	.348
Road	179	55	6	1	4	15	16	25	.307	.419	.360
Grass	261	84	14	3	4	27	25	27	.322	.444	.380
Artificial Turf	86	21	1	0	1	4	4	13	.244	.291	.275
April	0	0	0	0	0	0	0	0	—	—	—
May	41	10	0	1	1	4	4	4	.244	.366	.311
June	48	11	1	1	2	4	4	5	.229	.417	.288
July	46	19	2	0	0	2	3	5	.413	.457	.449
August	107	30	5	1	0	13	4	17	.280	.346	.304
Sept./Oct.	105	35	7	0	2	8	14	7	.333	.457	.408
Leading Off Inn.	127	37	7	1	2	2	16	7	.291	.409	.328
Runners On	123	39	3	1	1	27	14	11	.317	.382	.381
Runners/Scor. Pos.	71	22	2	0	0	24	12	10	.310	.338	.400
Runners On/2 Out	51	9	2	0	1	7	7	7	.176	.275	.276
Scor. Pos./2 Out	35	5	2	0	0	5	7	6	.143	.200	.286
Late Inning Pressure	59	19	5	0	1	6	4	8	.322	.458	.365
Leading Off	13	4	3	0	0	0	0	2	.308	.538	.308
Runners On	23	8	1	0	0	5	4	4	.348	.391	.444
Runners/Scor. Pos.	14	5	1	0	0	5	4	4	.357	.429	.500

RUNS BATTED IN	From 1B	From 2B	From 3B	Scoring Position
Totals	2/82	9/54	15/29	24/83
Percentage	2%	17%	52%	29%
Driving In Runners from 3B with Less than Two Out:			11/12	92%

Loves to face: Jose Guzman (2-for-2, 1 HR)
Hates to face: Dave Stieb (0-for-4, 3 SO)
Led A.L. rookies in batting average (minimum: 100 PA). Eight rookies in White Sox history with as many AB as Gallagher had higher BAs. The top three: Hank Steinbacher, .331 (1938); Minnie Minoso, .324 (1951); Alex Metzler, .319 (1927). . . . Batted .324 after the All-Star break, 4th-highest in A.L. . . . Fielded 233 chances last season, the most of any outfielder without an error, but was 13 games shy of total of 108 required to qualify for fielding title. Teammate Dan Pasqua won it instead. . . . He led International League outfielders in fielding percentage in 1986. . . . Played 895 minor league games in Indians and Mariners organizations before being released following 1987 season.

Mike Gallego
Oakland As — Bats Right

	AB	H	2B	3B	HR	RBI	BB	SO	BA	SA	OBA
Season	277	58	8	0	2	20	34	53	.209	.260	.298
vs. Left-Handers	103	24	5	0	1	9	15	17	.233	.311	.336
vs. Right-Handers	174	34	3	0	1	11	19	36	.195	.230	.275
Home	142	31	5	0	2	13	17	23	.218	.296	.302
Road	135	27	3	0	0	7	17	30	.200	.222	.294
Grass	223	43	8	0	2	19	25	43	.193	.256	.277
Artificial Turf	54	15	0	0	0	1	9	10	.278	.278	.381
April	30	7	1	0	0	2	6	5	.233	.267	.361
May	52	8	1	0	1	7	6	11	.154	.231	.241
June	57	15	2	0	1	3	1	12	.263	.351	.276
July	67	12	2	0	0	1	9	14	.179	.209	.276
August	15	4	0	0	0	4	6	0	.267	.267	.500
Sept./Oct.	56	12	2	0	0	3	6	11	.214	.250	.290
Leading Off Inn.	74	19	3	0	2	12	15	.257	.378	.360	
Runners On	108	23	3	0	0	18	10	22	.213	.241	.286
Runners/Scor. Pos.	52	14	3	0	0	18	7	11	.269	.327	.367
Runners On/2 Out	59	12	0	0	0	8	7	12	.203	.203	.299
Scor. Pos./2 Out	29	8	0	0	0	8	5	5	.276	.276	.400
Late Inning Pressure	28	4	0	0	0	0	3	4	.143	.214	.226
Leading Off	6	2	1	0	0	0	2	0	.333	.500	.500
Runners On	9	1	0	0	0	0	1	2	.111	.111	.200
Runners/Scor. Pos.	3	0	0	0	0	0	0	2	.000	.000	.000

RUNS BATTED IN	From 1B	From 2B	From 3B	Scoring Position
Totals	1/85	7/36	10/28	17/64
Percentage	1%	19%	36%	27%
Driving In Runners from 3B with Less than Two Out:			5/12	42%

Loves to face: Charlie Leibrandt (.421, 8-for-19)
Hates to face: Greg Swindell (0-for-9)
Didn't commit an error in the last 36 games in which he was used as a defensive replacement. . . . A's allowed 3.53 runs per nine innings with Gallego at second, 3.73 with Hubbard, 4.58 with Phillips. . . . Has played 54 career games at third base without ever making an error there. A.L. record for consecutive errorless games by a third baseman is 88 by Don Money, who accepted 261 chances (slightly less than three per game) during streak. In 54 games (mostly as a late-inning defensive replacement), Gallego has accepted only 62 chances. . . . Removed for pinch hitters 35 times last season, the most of any Oakland player. . . . On the other hand, he led the A's with 13 pinch-running appearances.

Jim Gantner — Milwaukee Brewers · Bats Left

	AB	H	2B	3B	HR	RBI	BB	SO	BA	SA	OBA
Season	539	149	28	2	0	48	34	50	.276	.336	.322
vs. Left-Handers	146	40	8	0	0	13	8	11	.274	.329	.318
vs. Right-Handers	393	109	20	2	0	35	26	39	.277	.338	.323
Home	275	75	15	2	0	27	16	26	.273	.342	.311
Road	264	74	13	0	0	21	18	24	.280	.330	.333
Grass	465	128	21	2	0	35	34	42	.275	.329	.323
Artificial Turf	74	21	7	0	0	13	0	8	.284	.378	.312
April	60	13	1	0	0	3	2	4	.217	.233	.242
May	95	30	4	0	0	9	6	11	.316	.358	.359
June	95	27	6	0	0	7	7	6	.284	.347	.333
July	102	28	8	1	0	10	7	11	.275	.373	.321
August	96	25	3	1	0	9	4	8	.260	.313	.297
Sept./Oct.	91	26	6	0	0	10	8	10	.286	.352	.347
Leading Off Inn.	114	36	7	1	0	0	3	5	.316	.395	.345
Runners On	213	56	12	1	0	48	17	25	.263	.329	.318
Runners/Scor. Pos.	125	32	6	1	0	45	13	19	.256	.320	.326
Runners On/2 Out	98	25	7	0	0	21	7	9	.255	.327	.305
Scor. Pos./2 Out	63	16	5	0	0	20	6	7	.254	.333	.319
Late Inning Pressure	75	19	8	0	0	11	5	6	.253	.360	.296
Leading Off	18	3	1	0	0	0	0	0	.167	.167	.167
Runners On	30	10	5	0	0	11	3	3	.333	.500	.382
Runners/Scor. Pos.	18	5	1	0	0	9	3	2	.278	.333	.364

RUNS BATTED IN	From 1B	From 2B	From 3B	Scoring Position
Totals	5/135	16/87	27/61	43/148
Percentage	4%	18%	44%	29%
Driving In Runners from 3B with Less than Two Out:			17/29	59%

Loves to face: Curt Young (.526, 10-for-19)
Hates to face: Roger Clemens (.071, 2-for-28)

One of three A.L. players with 500 at-bats and no home runs last season.... Led A.L. second basemen with 325 putouts.... Career batting average of .275. His yearly batting averages since 1986: .274, .272, .276.... Has hit between .250 and .300 in every season during the 1980s. We didn't think that was too restrictive, but no one else has done it.... Career average of .226 in over 500 at-bats with two outs and runners in scoring position.... Hit 42 of 44 career homers against right-handed pitchers.... Hasn't hit a home run at County Stadium since Sept. 6, 1986.... Middle name is Elmer. Father must have been a Burt Lancaster fan with a warped sense of humor.

Rich Gedman — Boston Red Sox · Bats Left

	AB	H	2B	3B	HR	RBI	BB	SO	BA	SA	OBA
Season	299	69	14	0	9	39	18	49	.231	.368	.279
vs. Left-Handers	37	9	5	0	0	8	3	6	.243	.378	.326
vs. Right-Handers	262	60	9	0	9	31	15	43	.229	.366	.271
Home	125	32	7	0	5	23	9	18	.256	.432	.312
Road	174	37	7	0	4	16	9	31	.213	.322	.254
Grass	255	60	14	0	8	36	17	41	.235	.384	.288
Artificial Turf	44	9	0	0	1	3	1	8	.205	.273	.222
April	15	1	0	0	1	3	0	6	.067	.267	.118
May	25	5	0	0	0	3	3	6	.200	.200	.286
June	52	12	3	0	1	4	4	7	.231	.346	.298
July	60	15	2	0	1	8	0	6	.250	.333	.242
August	73	18	4	0	4	13	7	13	.247	.466	.313
Sept./Oct.	74	18	5	0	2	8	4	11	.243	.392	.291
Leading Off Inn.	66	14	4	0	3	3	5	9	.212	.409	.268
Runners On	142	33	7	0	5	35	9	23	.232	.387	.273
Runners/Scor. Pos.	77	17	4	0	2	27	6	15	.221	.351	.267
Runners On/2 Out	59	13	2	0	2	11	5	12	.220	.356	.281
Scor. Pos./2 Out	38	6	0	0	0	6	4	9	.158	.158	.238
Late Inning Pressure	35	6	1	0	2	3	1	9	.171	.371	.189
Leading Off	9	4	1	0	2	2	1	1	.444	1.222	.500
Runners On	17	1	0	0	0	1	0	5	.059	.059	.056
Runners/Scor. Pos.	10	0	0	0	0	1	0	3	.000	.000	.000

RUNS BATTED IN	From 1B	From 2B	From 3B	Scoring Position
Totals	6/108	13/69	11/23	24/92
Percentage	6%	19%	48%	26%
Driving In Runners from 3B with Less than Two Out:			10/16	63%

Loves to face: Bill Swift (.667, 6-for-9)
Hates to face: Charles Hudson (0-for-8, 4 SO)

Unlikely home run off Greg Cadaret in second game of A.L.C.S. Gedman hadn't homered against a southpaw since July 1987; Cadaret allowed only two HRs in 71.2 innings during regular season, neither to a lefty.... Started 80 of 115 games in which the Red Sox faced a right-handed pitcher, but only six of 47 games vs. left-handers.... Removed for a pinch hitter nine times last season, most of any player on the Red Sox.... Batted .307 vs. ground-ball pitchers last season, .174 against fly-ballers. Difference of 133 points was the largest of any player in majors.... Batting average vs. fly-ball pitchers, year by year since 1983: .287, .276, .269, .241, .190, .174. Could it be the helicopter swing?

Ken Gerhart — Baltimore Orioles · Bats Right

	AB	H	2B	3B	HR	RBI	BB	SO	BA	SA	OBA
Season	262	51	10	1	9	23	21	57	.195	.344	.256
vs. Left-Handers	161	30	6	1	5	15	12	30	.186	.329	.243
vs. Right-Handers	101	21	4	0	4	8	9	27	.208	.366	.277
Home	130	30	7	1	5	15	9	27	.231	.415	.285
Road	132	21	3	0	4	8	12	30	.159	.273	.228
Grass	213	43	8	1	6	20	17	43	.202	.333	.263
Artificial Turf	49	8	2	0	3	3	4	14	.163	.388	.226
April	24	2	0	0	1	1	1	3	.083	.208	.120
May	35	8	3	1	1	1	4	9	.229	.457	.308
June	51	7	1	0	3	5	5	12	.137	.333	.224
July	80	19	2	0	3	7	5	15	.238	.375	.282
August	30	5	2	0	0	3	2	11	.167	.233	.219
Sept./Oct.	42	10	2	0	1	6	4	7	.238	.357	.300
Leading Off Inn.	62	11	4	0	2	2	2	16	.177	.339	.227
Runners On	103	16	2	0	2	16	10	15	.155	.233	.235
Runners/Scor. Pos.	47	9	0	0	1	14	5	6	.191	.255	.263
Runners On/2 Out	43	9	1	0	2	10	5	4	.209	.372	.306
Scor. Pos./2 Out	29	7	0	0	1	8	3	3	.241	.345	.333
Late Inning Pressure	43	7	2	0	1	5	5	8	.163	.279	.250
Leading Off	7	1	0	0	1	1	1	2	.143	.571	.250
Runners On	21	3	0	0	0	0	3	2	.143	.143	.250
Runners/Scor. Pos.	9	1	0	0	0	0	1	1	.111	.111	.111

RUNS BATTED IN	From 1B	From 2B	From 3B	Scoring Position
Totals	1/81	3/38	10/22	13/60
Percentage	1%	8%	45%	22%
Driving In Runners from 3B with Less than Two Out:			6/9	67%

Loves to face: Charlie Hough (.278, 5-for-18, 3 HR)
Hates to face: Cecilio Guante (0-for-4, 4 SO)

Batting average was 2d lowest among A.L. players with at least 200 at-bats. He peaked at .203 on July 19, but didn't have long to celebrate—it occurred between games of a doubleheader.... June batting average was lowest in the A.L. (minimum: two PA per game).... Started 54 of 59 games in which the Orioles faced left-handed starters, but only 19 of 102 games vs. RHP.... Batted .094 (3-for-32) vs. Toronto, but two of the hits were home runs.... Won't make any O's fans forget Eddie Murray. He matched his previous career batting average in Late-Inning Pressure Situations with that .163 mark. Four hits in 39 career at-bats with runners on base in LIP Situations, 0-for-13 with two outs.

Dan Gladden — Minnesota Twins · Bats Right

	AB	H	2B	3B	HR	RBI	BB	SO	BA	SA	OBA
Season	576	155	32	6	11	63	46	74	.269	.403	.325
vs. Left-Handers	159	51	8	2	6	21	18	16	.321	.509	.388
vs. Right-Handers	417	104	24	4	5	42	28	58	.249	.362	.300
Home	300	95	17	3	8	36	24	36	.317	.473	.365
Road	276	60	15	3	3	27	22	38	.217	.326	.282
Grass	212	47	13	0	2	23	19	26	.222	.311	.291
Artificial Turf	364	108	19	6	9	40	27	48	.297	.456	.345
April	82	25	8	0	2	10	4	8	.305	.476	.348
May	102	31	11	2	1	9	6	15	.304	.480	.339
June	105	22	4	1	3	13	10	13	.210	.352	.278
July	88	24	7	1	0	11	8	13	.273	.375	.337
August	107	28	0	0	3	12	7	12	.262	.346	.313
Sept./Oct.	92	25	2	2	2	8	11	13	.272	.402	.343
Leading Off Inn.	230	60	12	1	6	6	17	29	.261	.400	.315
Runners On	185	55	10	4	2	54	16	25	.297	.427	.354
Runners/Scor. Pos.	111	40	10	2	1	50	12	14	.360	.514	.420
Runners On/2 Out	81	23	5	1	1	23	7	15	.284	.407	.341
Scor. Pos./2 Out	61	20	5	1	0	21	6	10	.328	.443	.388
Late Inning Pressure	70	18	5	0	1	8	5	8	.257	.371	.325
Leading Off	13	4	3	0	0	0	1	1	.308	.538	.400
Runners On	33	8	1	0	1	8	2	4	.242	.364	.306
Runners/Scor. Pos.	12	3	1	0	1	8	2	1	.250	.583	.400

RUNS BATTED IN	From 1B	From 2B	From 3B	Scoring Position
Totals	5/123	25/95	22/47	47/142
Percentage	4%	26%	47%	33%
Driving In Runners from 3B with Less than Two Out:			17/25	68%

Loves to face: Roger Clemens (.417, 5-for-12, 1 HR)
Hates to face: Bill Wegman (0-for-15)

Also loves to face Johnny Ray, Chico Walker, and Brian Downing. Retired them in order in his debut as a pitcher (June 27).... A man of strong likes and dislikes. Exhibit A: Late-Inning Pressure batting average has been lower than his overall average in each of his six seasons in the majors. Career average of .220 in LIPS, .281 otherwise.... Exhibit B: Has hit for a higher average vs. left-handers than against right-handers in all six seasons. Career average of .290 vs. lefties, .264 for righties.... Exhibit C: Has batted for a higher average on artificial turf than on grass five times in six years. Career averages: .259 on grass, .288 on artificial turf.

Rene Gonzales

Baltimore Orioles — Bats Right

	AB	H	2B	3B	HR	RBI	BB	SO	BA	SA	OBA
Season	237	51	6	0	2	15	13	32	.215	.266	.263
vs. Left-Handers	86	28	4	0	1	6	8	11	.326	.407	.383
vs. Right-Handers	151	23	2	0	1	9	5	21	.152	.185	.193
Home	118	26	5	0	1	5	8	21	.220	.288	.279
Road	119	25	1	0	1	10	5	11	.210	.244	.246
Grass	191	44	5	0	1	9	11	25	.230	.272	.278
Artificial Turf	46	7	1	0	1	6	2	7	.152	.239	.200
April	11	3	0	0	0	2	0	2	.273	.273	.333
May	35	9	0	0	2	4	3	3	.257	.429	.333
June	68	12	4	0	0	3	4	12	.176	.235	.230
July	11	2	1	0	0	0	1	2	.182	.273	.250
August	75	17	0	0	0	5	2	9	.227	.227	.244
Sept./Oct.	37	8	1	0	0	1	3	4	.216	.243	.275
Leading Off Inn.	58	10	1	0	1	1	3	13	.172	.241	.213
Runners On	91	23	2	0	0	13	7	11	.253	.275	.314
Runners/Scor. Pos.	42	9	1	0	0	12	5	6	.214	.238	.314
Runners On/2 Out	42	7	0	0	0	3	4	5	.167	.167	.255
Scor. Pos./2 Out	23	4	0	0	0	3	3	2	.174	.174	.296
Late Inning Pressure	38	11	1	0	0	1	0	8	.289	.316	.289
Leading Off	8	1	0	0	0	0	0	4	.125	.125	.125
Runners On	15	6	1	0	0	1	0	2	.400	.467	.400
Runners/Scor. Pos.	4	1	1	0	0	1	0	1	.250	.500	.250

RUNS BATTED IN	From 1B	From 2B	From 3B	Scoring Position
Totals	1/73	6/35	6/17	12/52
Percentage	1%	17%	35%	23%
Driving In Runners from 3B with Less than Two Out:		6/9		67%

Loves to face: Rick Honeycutt (.750, 3-for-4, 1 HR)
Hates to face: Jack Morris (0-for-5, 3 SO)
Started 72 games, all but one of them batting either 8th or 9th in the batting order.... Grounded into four DPs in eight at-bats with a runner on first and less than two outs between Aug. 26 and Sept. 4.... In tradition of O's third basemen, he led A.L. with an average of 2.41 assists per nine innings (minimum: 500 innings). Orioles allowed 4.85 runs per nine innings with Gonzales there, 5.13 with other third basemen.... Career breakdowns: .261 with runners on base, .190 with bases empty, .277 vs. left-handers, .176 vs. right-handers; .317 (19-for-60) in Late-Inning Pressure Situations.... Has hit three home runs in 52 at-bats during May, but hasn't homered in 301 AB any other month.

Mike Greenwell

Boston Red Sox — Bats Left

	AB	H	2B	3B	HR	RBI	BB	SO	BA	SA	OBA
Season	590	192	39	8	22	119	87	38	.325	.531	.416
vs. Left-Handers	197	57	13	0	4	25	8	16	.289	.416	.332
vs. Right-Handers	393	135	26	8	18	94	79	22	.344	.588	.453
Home	305	101	25	5	12	66	42	19	.331	.564	.417
Road	285	91	14	3	10	53	45	19	.319	.495	.414
Grass	500	166	35	7	20	102	76	30	.332	.550	.426
Artificial Turf	90	26	4	1	2	17	11	8	.289	.422	.356
April	66	22	7	0	1	12	15	6	.333	.485	.483
May	94	26	2	1	5	18	14	9	.277	.479	.376
June	104	42	10	1	8	31	11	3	.404	.750	.466
July	111	38	7	2	3	23	19	7	.342	.523	.425
August	104	35	9	2	2	19	16	4	.337	.519	.425
Sept./Oct.	111	29	4	2	3	16	12	7	.261	.414	.336
Leading Off Inn.	114	43	14	3	4	4	12	4	.377	.658	.441
Runners On	316	103	15	4	15	112	50	22	.326	.541	.418
Runners/Scor. Pos.	184	61	7	3	8	93	36	10	.332	.533	.435
Runners On/2 Out	146	46	6	2	3	40	26	11	.315	.445	.429
Scor. Pos./2 Out	94	29	1	1	2	34	20	7	.309	.404	.440
Late Inning Pressure	70	18	5	0	0	4	10	9	.257	.329	.341
Leading Off	12	6	4	0	0	2	1	1	.500	.833	.571
Runners On	29	6	1	0	0	4	5	6	.207	.241	.306
Runners/Scor. Pos.	16	3	1	0	0	4	4	4	.188	.250	.318

RUNS BATTED IN	From 1B	From 2B	From 3B	Scoring Position
Totals	22/252	33/141	42/88	75/229
Percentage	9%	23%	48%	33%
Driving In Runners from 3B with Less than Two Out:		30/45		67%

Loves to face: Mike Campbell (.800, 4-for-5, 2 HR)
Hates to face: Juan Nieves (0-for-12)
Reached base safely in 41 consecutive games (May 9–June 28), longest streak in majors.... Drove in 24 runners from 1st base, a major league high.... 31 RBI in June were most by any player in any month.... Range of players with comparable stats at a similar age runs gamut, from disappointments like Wally Berger and Leon Durham to standouts like Bob Meusel and Tony Oliva.... One of 14 players with career averages of at least 20 RBI per 100 at-bats (minimum: 1000 AB). Others: Babe Ruth, Lou Gehrig, Hank Greenberg, Ted Williams, Jimmie Foxx, Joe DiMaggio, Hack Wilson, Sam Thompson, Al Simmons, Johnny Mize, George Selkirk, Roy Campanella, Charlie Keller.

Kelly Gruber

Toronto Blue Jays — Bats Right

	AB	H	2B	3B	HR	RBI	BB	SO	BA	SA	OBA
Season	569	158	33	5	16	81	38	92	.278	.438	.328
vs. Left-Handers	187	47	12	3	1	23	10	32	.251	.364	.288
vs. Right-Handers	382	111	21	2	15	58	28	60	.291	.474	.348
Home	294	79	13	3	5	36	18	56	.269	.384	.316
Road	275	79	20	2	11	45	20	36	.287	.495	.341
Grass	232	68	18	2	10	42	19	28	.293	.517	.350
Artificial Turf	337	90	15	3	6	39	19	64	.267	.383	.313
April	66	19	6	1	3	11	3	16	.288	.545	.324
May	107	33	7	1	2	19	10	19	.308	.449	.368
June	107	34	7	1	6	19	6	15	.318	.570	.371
July	104	26	7	0	2	11	4	13	.250	.375	.288
August	86	21	3	1	1	7	5	12	.244	.337	.290
Sept./Oct.	99	25	3	1	2	14	10	17	.253	.364	.318
Leading Off Inn.	115	26	3	0	4	4	9	25	.226	.357	.288
Runners On	244	82	21	5	5	70	17	29	.336	.525	.381
Runners/Scor. Pos.	155	54	15	4	4	67	14	22	.348	.574	.397
Runners On/2 Out	108	33	6	4	2	25	9	18	.306	.491	.370
Scor. Pos./2 Out	78	24	5	3	1	22	8	15	.308	.487	.372
Late Inning Pressure	78	27	5	0	2	15	6	8	.346	.487	.395
Leading Off	14	2	0	0	1	1	2	2	.143	.357	.200
Runners On	34	14	3	0	1	14	4	1	.412	.588	.462
Runners/Scor. Pos.	21	11	3	0	1	14	3	1	.524	.810	.560

RUNS BATTED IN	From 1B	From 2B	From 3B	Scoring Position
Totals	9/169	28/120	28/61	56/181
Percentage	5%	23%	46%	31%
Driving In Runners from 3B with Less than Two Out:		23/34		68%

Loves to face: Tom Niedenfuer (4-for-4, 1 2B, 2 HR)
Hates to face: Kirk McCaskill (0-for-10)
Career batting average prior to 1988 was .218.... One of two players in majors who started at least one game in each of the nine batting-order spots. The other: Dave Bergman.... Had stolen only 14 bases in 21 attempts in two previous full seasons, 23-for-28 last season.... Led A.L. with 156 games at the hot corner, slamming the door on years of Jays platooning at that position. No Toronto third baseman had played as many as 120 games since Roy Howell set the previous team mark of 138 in 1980.... Career average of .292 with runners on base, .218 with the bases empty.... The only A.L. player to hit at least 10 points better on the road than at home in each of the last five seasons.

Ozzie Guillen

Chicago White Sox — Bats Left

	AB	H	2B	3B	HR	RBI	BB	SO	BA	SA	OBA
Season	566	148	16	7	0	39	25	40	.261	.314	.294
vs. Left-Handers	171	45	4	0	0	15	6	15	.263	.287	.285
vs. Right-Handers	395	103	12	7	0	24	19	25	.261	.327	.297
Home	280	73	8	3	0	25	17	25	.261	.311	.303
Road	286	75	8	4	0	14	8	15	.262	.318	.284
Grass	477	118	13	6	0	37	22	34	.247	.300	.282
Artificial Turf	89	30	3	1	0	2	3	6	.337	.393	.359
April	87	15	2	0	0	4	2	10	.172	.195	.189
May	106	32	7	0	0	4	6	6	.302	.368	.339
June	100	31	3	0	0	11	2	9	.310	.340	.327
July	79	20	0	2	0	9	4	8	.253	.304	.294
August	100	24	2	1	0	4	4	2	.240	.280	.269
Sept./Oct.	94	26	2	4	0	7	7	5	.277	.383	.327
Leading Off Inn.	149	32	4	1	0	0	8	10	.215	.255	.255
Runners On	217	67	5	5	0	39	7	10	.309	.378	.326
Runners/Scor. Pos.	128	39	4	0	0	38	6	5	.305	.398	.328
Runners On/2 Out	91	22	2	2	0	15	4	6	.242	.308	.274
Scor. Pos./2 Out	57	13	2	0	0	15	3	2	.228	.333	.267
Late Inning Pressure	93	22	3	2	0	7	5	5	.237	.312	.276
Leading Off	26	4	1	0	0	0	1	1	.154	.192	.185
Runners On	38	10	1	1	0	7	3	3	.263	.342	.317
Runners/Scor. Pos.	21	6	1	1	0	7	3	1	.286	.429	.375

RUNS BATTED IN	From 1B	From 2B	From 3B	Scoring Position
Totals	3/148	15/97	21/54	36/151
Percentage	2%	15%	39%	24%
Driving In Runners from 3B with Less than Two Out:		15/34		50%

Loves to face: Tom Bolton (4-for-5)
Hates to face: Curt Young (.056, 1-for-18)
One of three A.L. players with 500+ at-bats and no home runs last season. His last homer was Sept. 19, 1987.... All seven of his triples were hit after the All-Star break.... Batted .205 in 36 games in the 2d spot, .282 in 119 games when batting elsewhere in the order.... Walked twice in a game only once.... Of 33 players with 600+ games played over the last four seasons, only Vince Coleman (150) has fewer RBI than Guillen (170). Blame it on lack of opportunity: Ozzie has a career average of .302 with runners in scoring position. ... Led major league shortstops with 570 assists, and broke Luis Aparicio's team record in the final inning of the season finale.

Mel Hall

Cleveland Indians — Bats Left

	AB	H	2B	3B	HR	RBI	BB	SO	BA	SA	OBA
Season	515	144	32	4	6	71	28	50	.280	.392	.312
vs. Left-Handers	46	5	1	0	1	5	3	7	.109	.196	.163
vs. Right-Handers	469	139	31	4	5	66	25	43	.296	.412	.327
Home	249	72	15	4	3	36	15	24	.289	.418	.322
Road	266	72	17	0	3	35	13	26	.271	.368	.302
Grass	439	122	26	4	6	60	23	42	.278	.396	.309
Artificial Turf	76	22	6	0	0	11	5	8	.289	.368	.333
April	75	23	5	1	0	9	3	10	.307	.400	.333
May	85	21	5	0	0	9	6	10	.247	.306	.284
June	85	28	5	0	1	9	6	8	.329	.424	.370
July	102	34	6	2	3	19	4	15	.333	.520	.355
August	92	24	9	0	1	16	6	4	.261	.391	.300
Sept./Oct.	76	14	2	1	1	9	3	3	.184	.276	.215
Leading Off Inn.	115	28	4	1	0	0	2	10	.243	.296	.256
Runners On	220	64	15	2	2	67	20	20	.291	.405	.339
Runners/Scor. Pos.	139	40	14	1	2	66	14	14	.288	.446	.335
Runners On/2 Out	97	26	8	1	1	21	11	13	.268	.402	.343
Scor. Pos./2 Out	69	17	7	0	1	20	8	10	.246	.391	.325
Late Inning Pressure	69	21	3	0	2	7	5	10	.304	.435	.347
Leading Off	16	3	0	0	0	0	1	4	.188	.188	.235
Runners On	25	6	0	0	1	6	3	2	.240	.360	.310
Runners/Scor. Pos.	12	3	0	0	1	6	2	2	.250	.500	.333

RUNS BATTED IN	From 1B	From 2B	From 3B	Scoring Position
Totals	8/148	26/119	31/52	57/171
Percentage	5%	22%	60%	33%
Driving In Runners from 3B with Less than Two Out:			24/32	75%

Loves to face: Willie Fraser (.636, 7-for-11, 1 HR)
Hates to face: Tom Henke (0-for-8, 4 SO)

Batting average has decreased in each of the last three seasons: .318, .296, .2804, .2796.... Batted .270 in day games, the first time in five seasons he's dropped below the .300 mark. Career averages: day games, .301; night games, .267.... Only two players in either league had more doubles vs. left-handers: Wade Boggs (34) and Tony Fernandez (33).... Has driven in more than 33 percent of runners from scoring position in each of last four seasons.... Career average of .154 vs. lefties (2 HRs in 228 at-bats), .294 vs. righties (one HR per 32 AB).... Career average of .365 (19-for-52, one HR) with the bases loaded.... Has played 656 games in the outfield, but none at any other position.

Ron Hassey

Oakland As — Bats Left

	AB	H	2B	3B	HR	RBI	BB	SO	BA	SA	OBA
Season	323	83	15	0	7	45	30	42	.257	.368	.323
vs. Left-Handers	33	4	1	0	0	2	2	6	.121	.152	.194
vs. Right-Handers	290	79	14	0	7	43	28	36	.272	.393	.337
Home	174	44	5	0	3	19	10	20	.253	.333	.296
Road	149	39	10	0	4	26	20	22	.262	.409	.352
Grass	286	72	12	0	6	40	25	36	.252	.357	.314
Artificial Turf	37	11	3	0	1	5	5	6	.297	.459	.386
April	42	9	2	0	2	7	4	7	.214	.405	.265
May	75	25	6	0	1	19	6	6	.333	.453	.378
June	43	10	4	0	1	7	1	5	.233	.395	.244
July	64	8	1	0	0	2	5	11	.125	.141	.200
August	60	19	1	0	3	8	10	6	.317	.483	.431
Sept./Oct.	39	12	1	0	0	2	4	7	.308	.333	.386
Leading Off Inn.	83	21	2	0	2	2	7	13	.253	.349	.319
Runners On	135	36	7	0	3	41	15	19	.267	.385	.342
Runners/Scor. Pos.	73	19	4	0	2	37	7	12	.260	.397	.306
Runners On/2 Out	56	13	3	0	2	16	9	9	.232	.393	.348
Scor. Pos./2 Out	32	8	2	0	1	13	4	5	.250	.406	.333
Late Inning Pressure	52	15	3	0	1	12	4	9	.288	.404	.333
Leading Off	13	4	1	0	0	0	0	2	.308	.385	.308
Runners On	23	8	1	0	1	12	3	5	.348	.522	.407
Runners/Scor. Pos.	15	6	1	0	1	12	2	4	.400	.667	.444

RUNS BATTED IN	From 1B	From 2B	From 3B	Scoring Position
Totals	6/111	16/59	16/33	32/92
Percentage	5%	27%	48%	35%
Driving In Runners from 3B with Less than Two Out:			14/21	67%

Loves to face: Rob Woodward (3-for-3, 1 2B, 1 HR)
Hates to face: Bret Saberhagen (0-for-10)

Made his first postseason appearance in his 11th season.... Hit his first major league home run in 1978 off Nolan Ryan.... Has hit 56 of his 60 career home runs against right-handers. His last HR vs. a southpaw was hit in 1983 off the renowned Gorman Heimueller. ... Wasn't included in 1988 *Analyst*, so you may not know that he hit .070 (3-for-43) with runners in scoring position in 1987.... What catchers of the past have put up the most similar numbers to Hassey's? Think of him as a left-handed-hitting Bo Diaz. Tell your Dad he's something like Clint Courtney, without the glasses. Tell your Dad to tell his Dad that Hassey's another Gus Mancuso, at least as a hitter. (He'll know what it means.)

Mike Heath

Detroit Tigers — Bats Right

	AB	H	2B	3B	HR	RBI	BB	SO	BA	SA	OBA
Season	219	54	7	2	5	18	18	32	.247	.365	.307
vs. Left-Handers	148	36	4	2	5	12	11	14	.243	.399	.300
vs. Right-Handers	71	18	3	0	0	6	7	18	.254	.296	.321
Home	95	17	1	1	4	8	11	15	.179	.337	.264
Road	124	37	6	1	1	10	7	17	.298	.387	.341
Grass	181	39	4	1	5	15	15	29	.215	.331	.279
Artificial Turf	38	15	3	1	0	3	3	3	.395	.526	.439
April	27	5	0	1	0	3	4	7	.185	.259	.290
May	39	6	1	0	0	4	2	8	.154	.179	.214
June	38	13	2	0	1	3	4	5	.342	.474	.405
July	27	10	1	1	3	5	4	2	.370	.815	.452
August	48	16	3	0	1	3	2	4	.333	.458	.360
Sept./Oct.	40	4	0	0	0	0	2	6	.100	.100	.143
Leading Off Inn.	61	11	0	0	1	1	0	10	.180	.230	.180
Runners On	89	20	5	1	0	13	7	14	.225	.303	.289
Runners/Scor. Pos.	47	11	3	1	0	12	3	6	.234	.340	.294
Runners On/2 Out	47	7	1	1	0	6	3	9	.149	.213	.200
Scor. Pos./2 Out	26	5	1	1	0	6	1	5	.192	.308	.222
Late Inning Pressure	42	5	1	0	1	4	4	6	.119	.214	.196
Leading Off	15	1	0	0	0	0	0	1	.067	.067	.067
Runners On	16	2	1	0	0	3	1	3	.125	.188	.176
Runners/Scor. Pos.	8	2	1	0	0	3	0	0	.250	.375	.250

RUNS BATTED IN	From 1B	From 2B	From 3B	Scoring Position
Totals	2/66	7/38	4/14	11/52
Percentage	3%	18%	29%	21%
Driving In Runners from 3B with Less than Two Out:			3/4	75%

Loves to face: Eric Plunk (.625, 5-for-8, 1 HR)
Hates to face: Juan Berenguer (0-for-14)

Started all 55 games in which Detroit faced a southpaw, but only 10 of 107 games against right-handers.... Failed to reach base in 22 consecutive innings in which he led off, longest streak in the majors. Led off 61 innings altogether, didn't walk once.... Batting average with runners on was lowest of his career.... Hasn't homered off a right-hander since July 19, 1987. Career average of .280 vs. left-handers, .225 vs. right-handers.... Batting average in Late-Inning Pressure Situations has been .150 or lower in each of the last three seasons.... Has a higher batting average in day games than at night in each of last eight seasons, longest streak among active players.

Dave Henderson

Oakland As — Bats Right

	AB	H	2B	3B	HR	RBI	BB	SO	BA	SA	OBA
Season	507	154	38	1	24	94	47	92	.304	.525	.363
vs. Left-Handers	147	45	12	1	6	20	15	21	.306	.524	.372
vs. Right-Handers	360	109	26	0	18	74	32	71	.303	.525	.359
Home	246	72	18	0	12	44	23	51	.293	.512	.354
Road	261	82	20	1	12	50	24	41	.314	.536	.371
Grass	423	129	31	1	20	74	39	79	.305	.525	.365
Artificial Turf	84	25	7	0	4	20	8	13	.298	.524	.351
April	32	10	2	0	3	8	4	3	.313	.656	.368
May	90	27	8	0	3	13	4	19	.300	.489	.337
June	79	24	8	1	4	16	10	15	.304	.582	.396
July	103	30	7	0	5	20	5	22	.291	.505	.321
August	112	36	8	0	6	19	10	15	.321	.554	.373
Sept./Oct.	91	27	5	0	3	18	14	18	.297	.451	.387
Leading Off Inn.	98	36	10	0	8	8	6	12	.367	.714	.410
Runners On	242	78	20	1	8	78	19	47	.322	.512	.364
Runners/Scor. Pos.	139	44	10	1	4	66	14	30	.317	.489	.366
Runners On/2 Out	97	35	8	0	3	36	11	16	.361	.536	.426
Scor. Pos./2 Out	70	26	7	0	2	33	8	10	.371	.557	.436
Late Inning Pressure	63	19	2	0	3	8	9	11	.302	.476	.378
Leading Off	17	7	2	0	2	2	2	3	.412	.882	.474
Runners On	28	6	0	0	2	5	6	4	.214	.214	.333
Runners/Scor. Pos.	19	3	0	0	1	5	4	2	.158	.158	.280

RUNS BATTED IN	From 1B	From 2B	From 3B	Scoring Position
Totals	13/182	23/101	34/66	57/167
Percentage	7%	23%	52%	34%
Driving In Runners from 3B with Less than Two Out:			21/35	60%

Loves to face: Jay Tibbs (.417, 5-for-12, 2 HR)
Hates to face: Juan Berenguer (.056, 1-for-18)

A's had a 23–1 record in games in which he homered.... Didn't hit a HR in last 22 games, his longest drought of the season. But went 9-for-16 in the final four games to boost his average above .300, a career high.... One of six players to hit .300 or better vs. both lefties and righties last season (minimum: 100 AB each way). The others: Boggs, Brett, Gwynn, Puckett, and Winfield.... Has played for different division winners in each of the last three seasons. Same agent as Don Baylor?... Career batting average of .174 with runners on base in LIP Situations, lowest over the past 14 years (minimum: 200 AB). But you'll never convince Red Sox fans that he ain't Mr. Clutch.

Rickey Henderson

Bats Right
New York Yankees

	AB	H	2B	3B	HR	RBI	BB	SO	BA	SA	OBA
Season	554	169	30	2	6	51	82	54	.305	.399	.394
vs. Left-Handers	163	60	11	1	4	14	31	9	.368	.521	.470
vs. Right-Handers	391	109	19	1	2	37	51	45	.279	.348	.360
Home	256	76	16	1	2	24	38	20	.297	.391	.389
Road	298	93	14	1	4	27	44	34	.312	.406	.398
Grass	447	130	24	1	4	37	70	43	.291	.376	.388
Artificial Turf	107	39	6	1	2	14	12	11	.364	.495	.419
April	94	34	7	1	3	14	10	8	.362	.553	.411
May	89	24	3	0	1	8	15	7	.270	.337	.377
June	42	13	1	0	1	7	11	4	.310	.405	.453
July	100	33	7	0	1	4	14	10	.330	.430	.417
August	109	30	4	0	0	9	14	7	.275	.312	.357
Sept./Oct.	120	35	8	1	0	9	18	18	.292	.375	.384
Leading Off Inn.	227	69	14	1	3	3	35	24	.304	.414	.399
Runners On	166	48	8	0	2	47	27	17	.289	.373	.380
Runners/Scor. Pos.	93	27	5	0	0	42	14	7	.290	.344	.368
Runners On/2 Out	76	20	3	0	0	13	13	10	.263	.303	.378
Scor. Pos./2 Out	43	9	2	0	0	13	11	5	.209	.256	.382
Late Inning Pressure	61	20	2	0	0	13	11	4	.328	.361	.413
Leading Off	11	3	0	0	0	0	3	1	.273	.273	.429
Runners On	26	8	1	0	0	13	2	2	.308	.346	.323
Runners/Scor. Pos.	14	5	1	0	0	13	1	1	.357	.429	.333

RUNS BATTED IN	From 1B	From 2B	From 3B	Scoring Position
Totals	4/123	12/74	29/42	41/116
Percentage	3%	16%	69%	35%
Driving In Runners from 3B with Less than Two Out:			20/23	87%

Loves to face: Jimmy Key (.370, 17-for-46, 4 HR)
Hates to face: Ed Vande Berg (0-for-10)
Career rate of 80 runs scored per 100 games, best among active players (minimum: 500 games). Only three others have rates above 70, but none above 71: Paul Molitor (70.6), Tim Raines (70.2), and Eric Davis (70.1). Three players from the 1800s averaged more than a run a game: Billy Hamilton (1.06), George Gore (1.01), and Harry Stovey (1.00). . . . Hit only one home run leading off the first inning last season, tying career record holder Bobby Bonds at 35. . . . Stole 33 bases in 34 attempts after August 10. . . . Has stolen 794 bases, now trails only Lou Brock (938) and Ty Cobb (892). . . . Only two extra-base hits (both doubles) in 104 career plate appearances with the bases loaded.

Larry Herndon

Bats Right
Detroit Tigers

	AB	H	2B	3B	HR	RBI	BB	SO	BA	SA	OBA
Season	174	39	5	0	4	20	23	37	.224	.322	.313
vs. Left-Handers	157	37	5	0	4	18	22	33	.236	.344	.328
vs. Right-Handers	17	2	0	0	0	2	1	4	.118	.118	.167
Home	91	18	3	0	2	8	14	19	.198	.297	.302
Road	83	21	2	0	2	12	9	18	.253	.349	.326
Grass	138	31	4	0	3	14	21	30	.225	.319	.327
Artificial Turf	36	8	1	0	1	6	2	7	.222	.333	.256
April	25	4	1	0	0	2	6	6	.160	.200	.222
May	35	11	1	0	2	7	3	5	.314	.514	.350
June	36	8	0	0	0	1	4	8	.222	.222	.317
July	27	7	2	0	1	4	5	7	.259	.444	.375
August	23	2	0	0	0	0	3	5	.087	.087	.192
Sept./Oct.	28	7	1	0	1	6	2	6	.250	.393	.371
Leading Off Inn.	35	6	1	0	1	1	6	6	.171	.286	.293
Runners On	76	18	3	0	1	17	9	16	.237	.316	.307
Runners/Scor. Pos.	44	12	2	0	1	17	7	10	.273	.386	.352
Runners On/2 Out	30	9	0	0	1	7	4	6	.300	.400	.382
Scor. Pos./2 Out	21	5	0	0	1	7	3	4	.238	.381	.333
Late Inning Pressure	29	8	1	0	0	0	5	10	.276	.310	.382
Leading Off	5	1	1	0	0	0	2	0	.200	.400	.429
Runners On	11	1	0	0	0	0	1	6	.091	.091	.231
Runners/Scor. Pos.	7	0	0	0	0	0	1	4	.000	.000	.125

RUNS BATTED IN	From 1B	From 2B	From 3B	Scoring Position
Totals	1/51	8/34	7/16	15/50
Percentage	2%	24%	44%	30%
Driving In Runners from 3B with Less than Two Out:			5/9	56%

Loves to face: Jeff Reardon (.714, 5-for-7)
Hates to face: Storm Davis (0-for-13)
Has the most hits (1334) of any active player never selected to an All-Star Game. That distinction belonged to Carney Lansford until last year. . . . Sparky sent up 33 pinch hitters in his place last season, more than any other player on the Tigers. . . . Started all 55 games in which the Tigers faced a left-handed starter, but started only once in 107 games against right-handers. . . . at-bats vs. right-handers, year by year since 1985: 287, 94, 48, 17. . . . Over the last 10 years, he's batted 40 points higher in night games (.288) than in day games (.248), largest difference during that time (minimum: 500 AB both ways). Last season was an exception: .192 by day, .238 by night.

Tom Herr

Bats Left and Right
Minnesota Twins

	AB	H	2B	3B	HR	RBI	BB	SO	BA	SA	OBA
Season	304	80	16	0	1	22	40	47	.263	.326	.349
vs. Left-Handers	76	22	5	0	1	7	7	10	.289	.395	.349
vs. Right-Handers	228	58	11	0	0	15	33	37	.254	.303	.349
Home	167	38	6	0	0	10	21	29	.228	.263	.314
Road	137	42	10	0	1	12	19	18	.307	.401	.391
Grass	97	32	6	0	1	8	15	10	.330	.423	.420
Artificial Turf	207	48	10	0	0	14	25	37	.232	.280	.315
April	32	8	1	0	0	1	1	4	.250	.281	.273
May	96	24	4	0	1	6	11	16	.250	.323	.327
June	32	12	4	0	0	5	4	2	.375	.500	.444
July	3	2	1	0	0	0	0	0	.667	1.000	.667
August	47	8	2	0	0	2	5	10	.170	.213	.250
Sept./Oct.	94	26	4	0	0	8	19	15	.277	.319	.398
Leading Off Inn.	54	15	3	0	0	0	4	8	.278	.333	.328
Runners On	120	28	5	0	0	21	16	20	.233	.275	.324
Runners/Scor. Pos.	75	17	4	0	0	20	9	13	.227	.280	.310
Runners On/2 Out	31	7	2	0	0	5	10	5	.226	.290	.415
Scor. Pos./2 Out	21	5	2	0	0	5	5	4	.238	.333	.385
Late Inning Pressure	38	10	0	0	0	5	5	5	.263	.263	.349
Leading Off	10	4	0	0	0	0	0	1	.400	.400	.400
Runners On	19	5	0	0	0	5	4	2	.263	.263	.391
Runners/Scor. Pos.	12	3	0	0	0	5	1	1	.250	.250	.308

RUNS BATTED IN	From 1B	From 2B	From 3B	Scoring Position
Totals	1/72	8/61	12/22	20/83
Percentage	1%	13%	55%	24%
Driving In Runners from 3B with Less than Two Out:			11/16	69%

Loves to face: Mike Scott (.415, 17-for-41)
Hates to face: Ron Darling (.095, 4-for-42, 1 HR)
Figures *above* are for A.L. only. . . . Fielding percentage of .988 at second base is highest in major league history (minimum: 1000 games), three points better than runner-up Jim Gantner. . . . Played four innings at shortstop, his first appearance there since 1980. . . . Batted .340 on grass, .230 on artificial turf. Difference was 2d largest in majors (minimum: 100 AB both ways). . . . Same overall batting average in 1988 as in 1987, but 59 fewer RBI. Herr batted with 207 runners in scoring position for the 1987 Cardinals, but had only 96 such opportunities for Twins in 1988. . . . Hasn't hit a triple or a home run in 580 at-bats vs. right-handers over the past two seasons.

Donnie Hill

Bats Left and Right
Chicago White Sox

	AB	H	2B	3B	HR	RBI	BB	SO	BA	SA	OBA
Season	221	48	6	1	2	20	26	32	.217	.281	.296
vs. Left-Handers	61	11	1	0	1	5	13	14	.180	.246	.320
vs. Right-Handers	160	37	5	1	1	15	13	18	.231	.294	.286
Home	89	21	2	0	1	12	16	11	.236	.292	.346
Road	132	27	4	1	1	8	10	21	.205	.273	.259
Grass	186	43	5	1	1	17	25	26	.231	.285	.319
Artificial Turf	35	5	1	0	1	3	1	6	.143	.257	.162
April	53	12	0	0	0	9	7	6	.226	.226	.306
May	38	8	1	0	0	2	3	6	.211	.237	.268
June	34	6	0	0	0	2	7	4	.176	.176	.317
July	19	5	0	0	0	0	1	1	.263	.263	.263
August	57	13	4	0	2	5	7	10	.228	.404	.313
Sept./Oct.	20	4	1	1	0	2	2	5	.200	.350	.261
Leading Off Inn.	47	14	2	0	1	1	3	10	.298	.404	.340
Runners On	88	15	2	1	0	18	14	13	.170	.216	.276
Runners/Scor. Pos.	58	11	2	0	0	17	12	10	.190	.224	.315
Runners On/2 Out	41	7	1	0	0	5	10	6	.171	.195	.333
Scor. Pos./2 Out	29	5	1	0	0	5	8	4	.172	.207	.351
Late Inning Pressure	47	10	0	0	0	5	9	7	.213	.213	.339
Leading Off	11	1	0	0	0	0	2	1	.091	.091	.231
Runners On	25	5	0	0	0	5	5	5	.200	.200	.333
Runners/Scor. Pos.	21	4	0	0	0	5	4	4	.190	.190	.320

RUNS BATTED IN	From 1B	From 2B	From 3B	Scoring Position
Totals	1/53	7/45	10/28	17/73
Percentage	2%	16%	36%	23%
Driving In Runners from 3B with Less than Two Out:			9/19	47%

Loves to face: Doyle Alexander (.417, 5-for-12, 2 HR)
Hates to face: Richard Dotson (0-for-10)
Batting averages, year by year since 1985: .285, .283, .239, 217. Decline is magnified with runners in scoring position, .337, .266, .241, .190. . . . Has hit 22 career home runs, only three in home games (one while playing for Oakland, two for Chicago). He's hit more home runs at the Kingdome (five in 70 AB) than he has at either stadium he called home. . . . Only player to hit at least 40 points higher vs. ground-ball pitchers than vs. fly-ballers in each of the last five seasons. . . . Career breakdown with the bases loaded: .462 (6-for-13) with less than two out, .188 (3-for-16) with two out. . . . Has been hit by only one pitch in 1858 career plate appearances.

Jack Howell

California Angels   Bats Left

	AB	H	2B	3B	HR	RBI	BB	SO	BA	SA	OBA
Season	500	127	32	2	16	63	46	130	.254	.422	.323
vs. Left-Handers	156	37	13	0	4	16	7	45	.237	.397	.296
vs. Right-Handers	344	90	19	2	12	47	39	85	.262	.433	.335
Home	244	58	11	0	9	36	26	75	.238	.393	.318
Road	256	69	21	2	7	27	20	55	.270	.449	.329
Grass	420	94	21	2	12	46	40	118	.224	.369	.298
Artificial Turf	80	33	11	0	4	17	6	12	.413	.700	.455
April	81	24	4	1	2	14	7	20	.296	.444	.363
May	87	22	5	0	1	10	9	24	.253	.345	.320
June	81	17	5	0	1	8	10	19	.210	.309	.297
July	70	17	4	0	4	10	4	21	.243	.471	.303
August	96	28	8	1	6	17	10	24	.292	.583	.370
Sept./Oct.	85	19	6	0	2	4	6	22	.224	.365	.275
Leading Off Inn.	108	28	11	0	3	3	6	30	.259	.444	.298
Runners On	220	65	14	2	8	55	27	48	.295	.486	.379
Runners/Scor. Pos.	118	34	7	2	3	42	19	31	.288	.458	.399
Runners On/2 Out	81	21	5	0	5	21	13	21	.259	.506	.362
Scor. Pos./2 Out	53	11	2	0	2	14	8	15	.208	.358	.311
Late Inning Pressure	79	13	3	0	1	5	5	33	.165	.241	.221
Leading Off	22	1	0	0	0	0	0	11	.045	.045	.045
Runners On	25	6	1	0	1	5	4	10	.240	.400	.355
Runners/Scor. Pos.	12	4	0	0	1	5	4	7	.333	.583	.500

RUNS BATTED IN	From 1B	From 2B	From 3B	Scoring Position
Totals	10/160	19/90	18/52	37/142
Percentage	6%	21%	35%	26%
Driving In Runners from 3B with Less than Two Out:			13/24	54%

Loves to face: Dave Stieb (.500, 10-for-20, 3 HR)
Hates to face: Dave Righetti (0-for-8, 7 SO)
Fifteen extra-base hits in August was one shy of major league lead. ... Committed 13 of his 17 errors in home games. ... Struck out in seven consecutive plate appearances vs. left-handed pitchers, longest streak by a nonpitcher. ... Struck out seven times with the bases loaded last season, most by any player in majors, pitchers included. ... One of five A.L. players to bat 100 points higher against ground-ball pitchers than against fly-ball pitchers. ... Batting average vs. left-handers was his highest ever, but his career average against southpaws remains below the .200 mark (.198). ... Career average of .271 with runners on base, .229 with the bases empty.

Kent Hrbek

Minnesota Twins   Bats Left

	AB	H	2B	3B	HR	RBI	BB	SO	BA	SA	OBA
Season	510	159	31	0	25	76	67	54	.312	.520	.387
vs. Left-Handers	132	33	11	0	2	18	18	17	.250	.379	.336
vs. Right-Handers	378	126	20	0	23	58	49	37	.333	.569	.405
Home	253	77	17	0	13	43	36	33	.304	.526	.386
Road	257	82	14	0	12	33	31	21	.319	.514	.388
Grass	194	66	11	0	12	29	20	14	.340	.582	.398
Artificial Turf	316	93	20	0	13	47	47	40	.294	.481	.380
April	73	23	7	0	4	10	7	5	.315	.575	.370
May	97	26	3	0	8	20	14	9	.268	.546	.357
June	76	25	3	0	0	7	14	8	.329	.368	.433
July	96	25	5	0	6	11	13	10	.260	.500	.345
August	108	40	8	0	7	23	16	14	.370	.639	.438
Sept./Oct.	60	20	5	0	0	5	3	8	.333	.417	.365
Leading Off Inn.	144	46	9	0	6	6	13	16	.319	.507	.376
Runners On	247	67	9	0	11	62	40	34	.271	.441	.364
Runners/Scor. Pos.	132	31	6	0	5	50	31	21	.235	.394	.365
Runners On/2 Out	119	27	2	0	4	19	23	12	.227	.345	.352
Scor. Pos./2 Out	65	14	1	0	2	15	18	5	.215	.323	.386
Late Inning Pressure	69	24	2	0	5	12	10	9	.348	.594	.425
Leading Off	18	6	0	0	2	2	1	3	.333	.667	.368
Runners On	39	13	2	0	2	9	9	6	.333	.538	.449
Runners/Scor. Pos.	16	3	1	0	1	7	7	2	.188	.438	.417

RUNS BATTED IN	From 1B	From 2B	From 3B	Scoring Position
Totals	7/183	18/97	26/60	44/157
Percentage	4%	19%	43%	28%
Driving In Runners from 3B with Less than Two Out:			19/32	59%

Loves to face: Bill Wegman (.458, 11-for-24, 4 HR)
Hates to face: Wes Gardner (0-for-10)
Fielding percentage was highest of his career (.997), higher even than Fred McGriff's (who led A.L. first basemen). But Hrbek was three games shy of minimum qualification for title (108 games). ... Hit seven homers against the Brewers last season tying him with Canseco (vs. Seattle and Texas) and Winfield (vs. California) for the most by one player vs. any club. ... RBI total has decreased in each of the last four seasons: 107, 93, 91, 90, 76. Percentage of runners driven in from scoring position was the lowest of his career. ... Has batted .290 with 136 home runs and 457 RBI over past five seasons. Only two players can match him in all three categories: George Bell and Don Mattingly.

Glenn Hubbard

Oakland As   Bats Right

	AB	H	2B	3B	HR	RBI	BB	SO	BA	SA	OBA
Season	294	75	12	2	3	33	33	50	.255	.340	.334
vs. Left-Handers	79	22	2	0	1	4	7	11	.278	.342	.337
vs. Right-Handers	215	53	10	2	2	29	26	39	.247	.340	.333
Home	131	35	5	0	3	16	15	21	.267	.374	.351
Road	163	40	7	2	0	17	18	29	.245	.313	.321
Grass	254	66	10	1	3	30	26	45	.260	.343	.335
Artificial Turf	40	9	2	1	0	3	7	5	.225	.325	.333
April	30	7	2	1	0	4	3	3	.233	.367	.343
May	47	10	0	0	0	2	8	13	.213	.213	.339
June	60	14	3	0	0	3	6	4	.233	.283	.303
July	27	4	0	0	0	3	6	6	.148	.148	.233
August	93	31	6	0	3	19	10	18	.333	.495	.394
Sept./Oct.	37	9	1	1	0	5	3	6	.243	.324	.293
Leading Off Inn.	71	12	3	0	0	0	12	11	.169	.211	.289
Runners On	136	40	5	2	3	33	10	18	.294	.426	.351
Runners/Scor. Pos.	86	22	3	2	1	28	7	10	.256	.372	.320
Runners On/2 Out	51	14	1	0	2	13	6	5	.275	.412	.373
Scor. Pos./2 Out	37	9	1	0	1	11	5	4	.243	.351	.349
Late Inning Pressure	44	10	0	0	0	1	2	6	.227	.227	.277
Leading Off	11	0	0	0	0	0	1	1	.000	.000	.083
Runners On	20	7	0	0	0	1	0	1	.350	.350	.381
Runners/Scor. Pos.	13	3	0	0	0	1	0	1	.231	.231	.286

RUNS BATTED IN	From 1B	From 2B	From 3B	Scoring Position
Totals	6/95	10/70	14/35	24/105
Percentage	6%	14%	40%	23%
Driving In Runners from 3B with Less than Two Out:			11/18	61%

Loves to face: Shane Rawley (.455, 5-for-11)
Hates to face: Jimmy Jones (0-for-9)
Moved from the N.L.'s best batting-average stadium to the majors' worst, and batted 10 points above his previous career mark. ... His only home runs were hit in three consecutive games (Aug. 7–9). ... Ended the season with 32 consecutive errorless games at second base, to bump Red Schoendienst from the all-time top 10 in fielding percentage (minimum: 1000 games). The list: Tom Herr, Jim Gantner, Frank White, Bobby Grich, Jerry Lumpe, Cookie Rojas, Dave Cash, Nellie Fox, Tommy Helms, and Hubbard. ... Batting average in LIP Situations has been lower than overall average in each of last eight seasons. Batting average on grass has been higher than on artificial turf in each of the last 10.

Pete Incaviglia

Texas Rangers   Bats Right

	AB	H	2B	3B	HR	RBI	BB	SO	BA	SA	OBA
Season	418	104	19	3	22	54	39	153	.249	.467	.321
vs. Left-Handers	126	32	5	1	9	18	11	46	.254	.524	.319
vs. Right-Handers	292	72	14	2	13	36	28	107	.247	.442	.322
Home	193	48	9	1	12	30	17	70	.249	.492	.316
Road	225	56	10	2	10	24	22	83	.249	.444	.325
Grass	370	95	18	3	18	49	32	130	.257	.468	.320
Artificial Turf	48	9	1	0	4	5	7	23	.188	.458	.328
April	68	15	2	0	4	8	7	27	.221	.426	.293
May	95	26	7	0	8	19	14	28	.274	.600	.389
June	81	22	5	1	2	6	4	26	.272	.432	.314
July	84	21	3	2	5	9	3	36	.250	.512	.273
August	87	20	2	0	3	12	10	34	.230	.356	.317
Sept./Oct.	3	0	0	0	0	0	1	2	.000	.000	.250
Leading Off Inn.	100	25	5	1	7	7	12	29	.250	.530	.336
Runners On	195	45	8	0	7	39	21	73	.231	.379	.308
Runners/Scor. Pos.	109	23	5	0	4	32	13	41	.211	.367	.294
Runners On/2 Out	94	22	4	0	1	14	7	36	.234	.309	.301
Scor. Pos./2 Out	50	12	2	0	1	13	6	18	.240	.340	.321
Late Inning Pressure	56	15	3	1	1	7	8	20	.268	.411	.369
Leading Off	17	1	0	0	0	0	3	8	.059	.059	.200
Runners On	23	7	1	0	0	6	4	8	.304	.348	.407
Runners/Scor. Pos.	15	5	1	0	0	6	2	5	.333	.400	.412

RUNS BATTED IN	From 1B	From 2B	From 3B	Scoring Position
Totals	6/137	16/85	10/39	26/124
Percentage	4%	19%	26%	21%
Driving In Runners from 3B with Less than Two Out:			7/20	35%

Loves to face: Steve Trout (5-for-5, 2 2B)
Hates to face: Roger Clemens (0-for-7, 7 SO)
First player in major league history with 150+ strikeouts in three consecutive seasons. Rob Deer joined him three weeks later. ... Struck out in 21 consecutive starts (June 15–July 22). ... Committed two errors, compared to 27 over the two previous years. ... Career average with runners on (.241) is 31 points lower than with bases empty, 4th-largest difference over last 10 years (minimum: 500 AB each way). ... Career batting average of .306 with one home run per 13 at-bats vs. left-handers; .234, one HR per 22 AB vs. right-handers. The former stats approximate the overall career figures of Mickey Mantle (but slightly better); the latter are comparable to those of Marv Throneberry (but slightly worse).

Bo Jackson
Kansas City Royals   Bats Right

	AB	H	2B	3B	HR	RBI	BB	SO	BA	SA	OBA
Season	439	108	16	4	25	68	25	146	.246	.472	.287
vs. Left-Handers	123	34	4	1	8	28	7	46	.276	.520	.315
vs. Right-Handers	316	74	12	3	17	40	18	100	.234	.453	.276
Home	211	67	12	4	10	37	15	58	.318	.555	.362
Road	228	41	4	0	15	31	10	88	.180	.395	.214
Grass	172	33	2	0	10	23	7	62	.192	.378	.223
Artificial Turf	267	75	14	4	15	45	18	84	.281	.532	.326
April	72	20	3	1	4	11	3	23	.278	.514	.303
May	103	34	5	0	5	19	6	27	.330	.524	.373
June	0	0	0	0	0	0	0	0	---	---	---
July	95	16	2	0	6	16	3	32	.168	.379	.192
August	87	19	2	0	7	14	8	31	.218	.483	.284
Sept./Oct.	82	19	4	3	3	8	5	33	.232	.463	.276
Leading Off Inn.	106	28	4	2	9	9	6	33	.264	.594	.304
Runners On	185	43	8	1	8	51	12	65	.232	.416	.280
Runners/Scor. Pos.	108	28	6	1	5	42	11	36	.259	.472	.328
Runners On/2 Out	82	18	4	1	2	19	7	32	.220	.366	.281
Scor. Pos./2 Out	56	14	3	1	2	17	6	20	.250	.446	.323
Late Inning Pressure	71	20	1	1	1	5	6	30	.282	.366	.346
Leading Off	16	4	0	0	1	1	3	8	.250	.438	.368
Runners On	29	7	1	0	0	4	3	12	.241	.276	.333
Runners/Scor. Pos.	17	4	0	0	0	3	2	7	.235	.235	.350

RUNS BATTED IN	From 1B	From 2B	From 3B	Scoring Position
Totals	11/135	20/83	12/45	32/128
Percentage	8%	24%	27%	25%
Driving In Runners from 3B with Less than Two Out:			8/19	42%

Loves to face: Mike Moore (.571, 4-for-7, 2 HR)
Hates to face: Bill Wegman (0-for-11)

Tied major league record for nonpitchers by striking out in nine consecutive plate appearances.... Word travels fast. Bo had 11 assists in the outfield, but none after July 4.... Has batted below .200 on the road in each of his three seasons. Career averages: .296 at Royals Stadium, .181 on the road.... Career average of .282 vs. ground-ball pitchers, .206 vs. fly-ballers.... Bashed Seattle pitchers with the same gusto he used to level the Boz, hitting five home runs in last 19 at-bats at the Kingdome, scene of his 221-yard rushing game in 1987.... Gained 18,630 yards running out his hits last season.... Has two career sacrifice bunts, half as many 100-yard games.

Brook Jacoby
Cleveland Indians   Bats Right

	AB	H	2B	3B	HR	RBI	BB	SO	BA	SA	OBA
Season	552	133	25	0	9	49	48	101	.241	.335	.300
vs. Left-Handers	129	30	7	0	3	9	8	22	.233	.357	.277
vs. Right-Handers	423	103	18	0	6	40	40	79	.243	.329	.307
Home	264	63	16	0	3	26	27	50	.239	.333	.307
Road	288	70	9	0	6	23	21	51	.243	.337	.294
Grass	462	111	24	0	6	40	40	83	.240	.331	.298
Artificial Turf	90	22	1	0	3	9	8	18	.244	.356	.313
April	85	29	9	0	2	9	5	17	.341	.518	.380
May	107	23	4	0	1	5	7	18	.215	.280	.263
June	104	27	5	0	3	6	11	20	.260	.394	.330
July	85	21	1	0	1	15	6	16	.247	.294	.287
August	91	16	3	0	2	8	18	14	.176	.275	.309
Sept./Oct.	80	17	3	0	0	6	1	16	.213	.250	.222
Leading Off Inn.	141	35	8	0	2	2	10	20	.248	.348	.298
Runners On	225	53	9	0	2	42	26	43	.236	.302	.311
Runners/Scor. Pos.	120	27	4	0	2	40	22	29	.225	.308	.333
Runners On/2 Out	84	13	3	0	0	15	12	23	.155	.190	.260
Scor. Pos./2 Out	59	11	2	0	0	14	12	18	.186	.220	.324
Late Inning Pressure	74	13	2	0	0		6	18	.176	.203	.235
Leading Off	29	7	2	0	0	0	1	3	.241	.310	.267
Runners On	24	4	0	0	0	2	3	7	.167	.167	.250
Runners/Scor. Pos.	10	1	0	0	0	2	3	5	.100	.100	.286

RUNS BATTED IN	From 1B	From 2B	From 3B	Scoring Position
Totals	4/156	13/94	23/57	36/151
Percentage	3%	14%	40%	24%
Driving In Runners from 3B with Less than Two Out:			16/28	57%

Loves to face: Mark Langston (.382, 13-for-34, 4 HR)
Hates to face: Dan Plesac (0-for-7, 4 SO)

Had increased his batting average in each of the previous three seasons before dropping to a career low in 1988.... Walked only once in his last 91 plate appearances, directly following a 19-game period during which he walked 17 times.... Scored only one run over his last 22 games.... Had a streak of 52 consecutive games at third base without an error (May 25–July 27). A.L. record is 88 games by Don Money.... Career average of .297 on artificial surfaces, .268 on grass fields.... Cleveland Stadium is one of baseball's best hitters' parks. But Jacoby has hit for a higher average on the road than at home in each of his five seasons with the Tribe.

Stan Javier
Oakland As   Bats Left and Right

	AB	H	2B	3B	HR	RBI	BB	SO	BA	SA	OBA
Season	397	102	13	3	2	35	32	63	.257	.320	.313
vs. Left-Handers	91	23	2	0	1	8	2	14	.253	.308	.277
vs. Right-Handers	306	79	11	3	1	27	30	49	.258	.324	.324
Home	176	46	6	1	0	13	16	21	.261	.307	.323
Road	221	56	7	2	2	22	16	42	.253	.330	.305
Grass	318	81	10	3	2	30	28	54	.255	.324	.316
Artificial Turf	79	21	3	0	0	5	4	9	.266	.304	.301
April	59	18	5	0	1	8	6	6	.305	.441	.358
May	77	19	1	1	0	10	3	13	.247	.286	.272
June	83	23	3	0	0	4	6	10	.277	.313	.333
July	91	27	0	2	1	6	6	10	.297	.374	.340
August	23	4	1	0	0	2	3	3	.174	.217	.269
Sept./Oct.	64	11	3	0	0	5	8	11	.172	.219	.274
Leading Off Inn.	77	22	4	0	0	0	4	13	.286	.338	.321
Runners On	182	45	6	2	0	33	15	26	.247	.302	.307
Runners/Scor. Pos.	98	24	3	2	0	33	12	16	.245	.316	.330
Runners On/2 Out	72	14	2	0	0	10	9	11	.194	.222	.293
Scor. Pos./2 Out	40	8	1	0	0	10	7	5	.200	.225	.333
Late Inning Pressure	68	18	3	1	0	9	9	14	.265	.338	.351
Leading Off	14	4	0	0	0	0	1	1	.286	.286	.333
Runners On	27	7	2	0	0	9	3	4	.259	.333	.333
Runners/Scor. Pos.	22	7	2	0	0	9	3	4	.318	.409	.400

RUNS BATTED IN	From 1B	From 2B	From 3B	Scoring Position
Totals	0/133	12/76	21/46	33/122
Percentage	0%	16%	46%	27%
Driving In Runners from 3B with Less than Two Out:			14/30	47%

Loves to face: Scott Bailes (.750, 6-for-8)
Hates to face: Mike Henneman (0-for-4, 3 SO)

Played more than one position in 31 different games.... Last four starts were made at four different positions (1B, LF, CF, RF).... Only player in majors to start at least 10 games at each of the outfield positions. Started at all three over a two-day period in July.... Stole 20 bases in 21 attempts (.952), including his last 17 in a row, best percentage in A.L. (minimum: 10 SB).... Stole 16 of his 20 bases before the All-Star break.... Career average of .195 vs. left-handers, .249 vs. right-handers.... Led the league with a .469 average against the Indians last season. His 23 hits against them matched the most by any A.L. player against any one club.

Wally Joyner
California Angels   Bats Left

	AB	H	2B	3B	HR	RBI	BB	SO	BA	SA	OBA
Season	597	176	31	2	13	85	55	51	.295	.419	.356
vs. Left-Handers	212	56	9	0	1	25	12	14	.264	.321	.309
vs. Right-Handers	385	120	22	2	12	60	43	37	.312	.473	.381
Home	290	81	16	1	6	40	26	24	.279	.403	.339
Road	307	95	15	1	7	45	29	27	.309	.433	.372
Grass	507	150	27	2	11	73	50	43	.296	.422	.359
Artificial Turf	90	26	4	0	2	12	5	8	.289	.400	.337
April	80	20	7	0	1	6	12	8	.250	.375	.365
May	113	34	6	1	1	13	6	10	.301	.398	.342
June	96	27	2	0	2	16	7	8	.281	.365	.327
July	98	35	9	1	4	24	8	7	.357	.592	.398
August	100	30	5	0	4	15	16	4	.300	.470	.398
Sept./Oct.	110	30	2	0	1	11	6	14	.273	.318	.308
Leading Off Inn.	126	38	7	1	2	2	6	7	.302	.421	.333
Runners On	281	82	14	0	9	81	33	26	.292	.438	.369
Runners/Scor. Pos.	160	47	8	0	8	76	31	16	.294	.494	.405
Runners On/2 Out	109	26	5	0	1	21	22	10	.239	.312	.385
Scor. Pos./2 Out	71	15	3	0	1	19	13	4	.211	.296	.404
Late Inning Pressure	98	34	4	0	2	14	10	8	.347	.449	.404
Leading Off	29	10	2	0	0	0	1	1	.345	.414	.367
Runners On	39	13	1	0	2	14	8	6	.333	.513	.438
Runners/Scor. Pos.	21	9	0	0	2	13	8	3	.429	.714	.567

RUNS BATTED IN	From 1B	From 2B	From 3B	Scoring Position
Totals	8/204	32/111	32/70	64/181
Percentage	4%	29%	46%	35%
Driving In Runners from 3B with Less than Two Out:			25/36	69%

Loves to face: Todd Burns (.400, 2-for-5, 2 HR)
Hates to face: Bud Black (0-for-10)

Hit 21 fewer home runs last season than he did in 1987. Prior to 1988, only three players in major league history dropped 20 or more HRs from their previous season while increasing their at-bat total: Rogers Hornsby (1925–26), Boog Powell (1964–65), and John Mayberry (1975–76). Last season Joyner, George Bell, Brook Jacoby, and Dale Murphy joined the club.... Only two extra-base hits after Sept. 1.... Led major league first basemen in assists (143) and double plays (148). Started 21 of those DPs, also a major league high.... Career RBI% from scoring position (35.5%) is the 2d highest of any player over the past 14 years (minimum: 250 opportunities). Don Mattingly leads (36.5%).

Terry Kennedy
Bats Left

Baltimore Orioles

	AB	H	2B	3B	HR	RBI	BB	SO	BA	SA	OBA
Season	265	60	10	0	3	16	15	53	.226	.298	.269
vs. Left-Handers	39	9	0	0	1	3	2	11	.231	.308	.268
vs. Right-Handers	226	51	10	0	2	13	13	42	.226	.296	.269
Home	136	24	3	0	2	8	6	37	.176	.243	.211
Road	129	36	7	0	1	8	9	16	.279	.357	.326
Grass	230	51	6	0	3	14	13	48	.222	.287	.261
Artificial Turf	35	9	4	0	0	2	2	5	.257	.371	.316
April	60	11	1	0	0	3	2	13	.183	.200	.206
May	39	6	2	0	0	2	4	9	.154	.205	.233
June	43	11	3	0	0	3	1	11	.256	.326	.283
July	39	7	0	0	1	1	2	6	.179	.256	.220
August	42	16	3	0	2	6	5	6	.381	.595	.447
Sept./Oct.	42	9	1	0	0	1	1	8	.214	.238	.233
Leading Off Inn.	59	21	2	0	2	2	4	7	.356	.492	.397
Runners On	108	20	4	0	0	13	7	24	.185	.222	.231
Runners/Scor. Pos.	56	10	3	0	0	12	5	17	.179	.232	.238
Runners On/2 Out	50	11	1	0	0	7	3	13	.220	.240	.264
Scor. Pos./2 Out	34	5	1	0	0	6	3	11	.147	.176	.216
Late Inning Pressure	41	7	1	0	1	1	4	8	.171	.268	.244
Leading Off	9	2	0	0	1	1	1	3	.222	.556	.300
Runners On	19	2	0	0	0	0	2	2	.105	.105	.190
Runners/Scor. Pos.	6	0	0	0	0	0	1	1	.000	.000	.143

RUNS BATTED IN	From 1B	From 2B	From 3B	Scoring Position
Totals	1/85	3/46	9/20	12/66
Percentage	1%	7%	45%	18%
Driving In Runners from 3B with Less than Two Out:			5/9	56%

Loves to face: Bob Forsch (.448, 13-for-29, 1 HR)
Hates to face: Mark Davis (.048, 1-for-21, 12 SO)

Only A.L. player to bat 100 points higher in road games than at home last season (minimum: 100 AB both ways). . . . Started 70 of 102 games in which the Orioles faced a right-handed starter, but only five of 59 games vs. left-handers. . . . Hasn't worn any leather except a catcher's mitt (at least on the field) since Sept. 20, 1985, his last appearance at first base for Padres. . . . Grounded into 13 double plays in 57 opportunities, 3d-highest rate in A.L. last season (min: 40 opp.). . . . Has reached a fork in the road. Two catchers from the past had poor seasons at a comparable point in careers similar to Kennedy's. Frankie Hayes (1946) decided to hang 'em up. Tim McCarver (1972) played for nearly another decade.

Ron Kittle
Bats Right

Cleveland Indians

	AB	H	2B	3B	HR	RBI	BB	SO	BA	SA	OBA
Season	225	58	8	0	18	43	16	65	.258	.533	.323
vs. Left-Handers	89	21	2	0	9	18	10	24	.236	.562	.333
vs. Right-Handers	136	37	6	0	9	25	6	41	.272	.515	.315
Home	85	21	2	0	7	18	9	19	.247	.518	.340
Road	140	37	6	0	11	25	7	46	.264	.543	.312
Grass	178	42	5	0	11	29	13	49	.236	.449	.299
Artificial Turf	47	16	3	0	7	14	3	16	.340	.851	.415
April	13	4	1	0	1	3	1	4	.308	.615	.438
May	38	7	0	0	3	8	5	12	.184	.421	.279
June	68	18	2	0	7	15	5	15	.265	.603	.333
July	46	12	3	0	3	8	2	17	.261	.522	.308
August	35	12	2	0	3	6	1	8	.343	.657	.359
Sept./Oct.	25	5	0	0	1	3	2	9	.200	.320	.276
Leading Off Inn.	55	14	2	0	5	5	2	12	.255	.564	.293
Runners On	105	26	3	0	6	31	9	32	.248	.448	.317
Runners/Scor. Pos.	62	14	1	0	3	25	4	17	.226	.387	.293
Runners On/2 Out	59	14	1	0	4	17	5	17	.237	.458	.297
Scor. Pos./2 Out	41	10	1	0	3	15	2	11	.244	.488	.299
Late Inning Pressure	32	8	1	0	2	5	4	11	.250	.469	.316
Leading Off	7	2	0	0	1	1	1	0	.286	.714	.375
Runners On	13	1	0	0	0	3	3	6	.077	.077	.222
Runners/Scor. Pos.	10	1	0	0	0	3	0	4	.100	.100	.083

RUNS BATTED IN	From 1B	From 2B	From 3B	Scoring Position
Totals	4/74	13/58	8/20	21/78
Percentage	5%	22%	40%	27%
Driving In Runners from 3B with Less than Two Out:			6/9	67%

Loves to face: Bert Blyleven (.351, 13-for-37, 9 HR)
Hates to face: Roger Clemens (0-for-11, 7 SO)

Made his first appearance 10 days into the season against his personal victim, Bert Blyleven. He hit a home run his first time up, giving four in four consecutive plate appearances vs. Bert. . . . Started 31 of 40 games in which the Indians faced a left-handed starter, but only 27 of 122 games vs. right-handers. . . . Never went more than seven games or 32 at-bats without a home run last season. . . . Batted 41 times with a runner on first base and less than two out, but did not ground into a double play. . . . Led the majors with three pinch-hit home runs. . . . Has played only three games in the field over the last three seasons, none at all in 1988. . . . Career batting average of .186 in Late-Inning Pressure Situations.

Ray Knight
Bats Right

Detroit Tigers

	AB	H	2B	3B	HR	RBI	BB	SO	BA	SA	OBA
Season	299	65	12	2	3	33	20	30	.217	.301	.271
vs. Left-Handers	169	37	7	1	3	20	8	15	.219	.325	.256
vs. Right-Handers	130	28	5	1	0	13	12	15	.215	.269	.290
Home	154	29	4	1	3	16	10	17	.188	.286	.242
Road	145	36	8	1	0	17	10	13	.248	.317	.300
Grass	257	56	7	2	3	28	17	26	.218	.296	.271
Artificial Turf	42	9	5	0	0	5	3	4	.214	.333	.267
April	42	6	2	0	0	5	4	8	.143	.190	.217
May	53	16	2	1	1	4	5	1	.302	.434	.367
June	82	19	3	0	0	7	6	9	.232	.268	.292
July	49	13	3	0	1	7	1	5	.265	.388	.280
August	35	4	0	0	0	3	3	4	.114	.114	.175
Sept./Oct.	38	7	2	1	1	7	1	3	.184	.368	.225
Leading Off Inn.	61	14	2	0	0	3	3	5	.230	.262	.266
Runners On	139	31	9	2	2	32	9	12	.223	.360	.270
Runners/Scor. Pos.	76	14	6	1	1	29	7	7	.184	.329	.244
Runners On/2 Out	53	10	2	1	0	9	2	5	.189	.264	.218
Scor. Pos./2 Out	34	5	2	0	0	8	2	3	.147	.206	.194
Late Inning Pressure	47	10	3	0	0	6	4	5	.213	.277	.260
Leading Off	8	1	0	0	0	0	0	1	.125	.125	.125
Runners On	23	7	3	0	0	6	1	3	.304	.435	.333
Runners/Scor. Pos.	10	3	2	0	0	6	1	1	.300	.500	.364

RUNS BATTED IN	From 1B	From 2B	From 3B	Scoring Position
Totals	6/104	11/56	13/38	24/94
Percentage	6%	20%	34%	26%
Driving In Runners from 3B with Less than Two Out:			11/22	50%

Loves to face: Gene Nelson (.750, 3-for-4, 1 HR)
Hates to face: Mike Flanagan (0-for-12)

Major league's three longest streaks of plate appearances without a hit vs. left-handed pitchers last season all belonged to members of the Tigers: Knight (29 PA), Tom Brookens (28), and Jim Walewander (25). . . . RBI rate from third base with less than two outs represented an *improvement* from his 1987 figures (9-for-33). . . . Batting average with runners on base has been higher than with the bases empty in each of the last five seasons. . . . Ed Kranepool made his major league debut the day Maury Wills broke Ty Cobb's single-season record for steals. Knight debuted the day that Lou Brock broke Wills's mark. Mike Smithson made his debut the day Henderson surpassed Brock.

Carney Lansford
Bats Right

Oakland As

	AB	H	2B	3B	HR	RBI	BB	SO	BA	SA	OBA
Season	556	155	20	2	7	57	35	35	.279	.360	.327
vs. Left-Handers	153	31	3	0	0	10	9	8	.203	.222	.244
vs. Right-Handers	403	124	17	2	7	47	26	27	.308	.412	.358
Home	277	68	10	2	1	24	21	19	.245	.307	.299
Road	279	87	10	0	6	33	14	16	.312	.412	.355
Grass	484	134	18	2	6	53	29	29	.277	.360	.322
Artificial Turf	72	21	2	0	1	4	6	6	.292	.361	.358
April	95	32	1	2	1	14	6	4	.337	.495	.388
May	117	52	7	1	2	18	7	6	.444	.573	.480
June	100	16	0	0	1	5	8	4	.160	.190	.229
July	98	24	1	0	1	7	2	8	.245	.286	.262
August	78	18	3	0	1	9	7	6	.231	.308	.303
Sept./Oct.	68	13	2	0	0	4	5	7	.191	.221	.244
Leading Off Inn.	158	51	7	2	4	4	9	11	.323	.468	.367
Runners On	223	66	8	0	3	53	16	16	.296	.372	.343
Runners/Scor. Pos.	125	41	6	0	1	48	11	7	.328	.400	.362
Runners On/2 Out	98	27	4	0	0	21	10	9	.276	.316	.343
Scor. Pos./2 Out	67	21	3	0	0	21	7	4	.313	.358	.378
Late Inning Pressure	75	20	3	0	1	3	8	2	.267	.347	.345
Leading Off	15	5	1	0	1	3	1	0	.333	.600	.444
Runners On	24	5	0	0	0	2	5	1	.208	.208	.367
Runners/Scor. Pos.	17	3	0	0	0	2	5	1	.176	.176	.391

RUNS BATTED IN	From 1B	From 2B	From 3B	Scoring Position
Totals	3/163	18/91	29/61	47/152
Percentage	2%	20%	48%	31%
Driving In Runners from 3B with Less than Two Out:			18/26	69%

Loves to face: Mike Boddicker (.415, 17-for-41, 4 HR)
Hates to face: Don August (0-for-8)

Batted .331 before the All-Star break. Average of .185 after the break was 3d lowest in A.L. (minimum: two PA per game). . . . Was batting over .400 as late as June 6. The lesson to be learned is this: Don't even *think* about a player hitting .400 until you've seen the season's first Ickey Shuffle. . . . Made his first All-Star appearance in 1988. . . . Led major league third basemen with a .979 fielding percentage, but his average of 1.64 assists per nine innings ranked last (minimum: 500 innings). . . . Only A.L. player to bat 100 points higher against right-handers than against left-handers—and he's a right-handed batter! Career average vs. left-handers was .303 prior to 1988.

Gene Larkin
Bats Left and Right

Minnesota Twins	AB	H	2B	3B	HR	RBI	BB	SO	BA	SA	OBA
Season	505	135	30	2	8	72	68	55	.267	.382	.368
vs. Left-Handers	150	46	12	1	2	26	16	15	.307	.440	.380
vs. Right-Handers	355	89	18	1	6	46	52	40	.251	.358	.363
Home	254	72	18	1	5	43	37	23	.283	.421	.389
Road	251	63	12	1	3	29	31	32	.251	.343	.346
Grass	191	47	9	1	3	23	24	28	.246	.351	.339
Artificial Turf	314	88	21	1	5	49	44	27	.280	.401	.384
April	55	16	7	0	1	10	7	6	.291	.473	.391
May	95	25	5	0	0	13	6	10	.263	.316	.339
June	94	26	4	0	1	10	7	15	.277	.351	.324
July	90	29	7	1	1	12	17	8	.322	.456	.445
August	81	24	2	1	3	16	17	8	.296	.457	.436
Sept./Oct.	90	15	5	0	2	11	14	8	.167	.289	.280
Leading Off Inn.	94	28	5	1	0	0	7	11	.298	.372	.377
Runners On	251	67	16	1	5	69	37	28	.267	.398	.368
Runners/Scor. Pos.	161	43	10	1	4	63	25	19	.267	.416	.372
Runners On/2 Out	107	29	8	1	1	33	18	14	.271	.393	.386
Scor. Pos./2 Out	77	24	7	1	1	33	12	9	.312	.468	.411
Late Inning Pressure	65	21	6	0	1	16	12	8	.323	.462	.432
Leading Off	12	5	1	0	0	0	0	2	.417	.500	.462
Runners On	31	13	3	0	1	16	9	3	.419	.613	.535
Runners/Scor. Pos.	19	8	2	0	1	15	7	2	.421	.684	.552

RUNS BATTED IN	From 1B	From 2B	From 3B	Scoring Position
Totals	9/182	26/126	29/66	55/192
Percentage	5%	21%	44%	29%
Driving In Runners from 3B with Less than Two Out:			16/27	59%

Loves to face: Jack Lazorko (2-for-2, 1 HR)
Hates to face: Chuck Finley (0-for-7)

At age 26, he was youngest player to start half of his team's games as designated hitter. ... But this Columbia graduate started 12 of Minnesota's last 16 games at first base. Hey, Kent, does the name Wally Pipp ring a bell? ... Hitless in 33 consecutive at-bats, tied for longest streak in majors. ... Hit by 15 pitches, most in A.L., the first time since 1983 that Don Baylor didn't lead the league. ... Career batting average of .185 in September. ... Career average of .190 (4-for-21) with the bases loaded, but two of those hits were triples. ... Has driven in 18 of 43 runners from scoring position in Late-Inning Pressure Situations (42%), but only 24.2% in unpressured at-bats.

Tim Laudner
Bats Right

Minnesota Twins	AB	H	2B	3B	HR	RBI	BB	SO	BA	SA	OBA
Season	375	94	18	1	13	54	36	89	.251	.408	.316
vs. Left-Handers	109	35	10	0	3	14	7	13	.321	.495	.359
vs. Right-Handers	266	59	8	1	10	40	29	76	.222	.372	.299
Home	182	42	12	0	8	31	17	45	.231	.429	.299
Road	193	52	6	1	5	23	19	44	.269	.389	.332
Grass	147	41	6	1	5	20	15	32	.279	.435	.341
Artificial Turf	228	53	12	0	8	34	21	57	.232	.390	.299
April	50	16	5	0	3	9	4	12	.320	.600	.370
May	67	16	2	0	1	8	7	13	.239	.313	.307
June	66	21	4	1	4	13	8	16	.318	.591	.395
July	66	9	2	0	2	6	3	18	.136	.258	.174
August	63	21	3	0	2	13	10	13	.333	.476	.419
Sept./Oct.	63	11	2	0	1	5	4	17	.175	.254	.224
Leading Off Inn.	83	24	4	0	5	5	6	23	.289	.518	.337
Runners On	182	40	7	0	5	49	17	37	.220	.341	.282
Runners/Scor. Pos.	120	27	5	0	4	44	11	30	.225	.367	.284
Runners On/2 Out	82	19	3	0	3	27	11	13	.232	.378	.323
Scor. Pos./2 Out	60	17	3	0	2	27	7	12	.283	.483	.358
Late Inning Pressure	50	12	2	0	1	4	4	14	.240	.340	.309
Leading Off	14	7	1	0	0	0	1	3	.500	.571	.533
Runners On	24	2	1	0	0	3	3	8	.083	.125	.185
Runners/Scor. Pos.	19	2	1	0	0	3	2	8	.105	.158	.190

RUNS BATTED IN	From 1B	From 2B	From 3B	Scoring Position
Totals	5/130	18/100	18/48	36/148
Percentage	4%	18%	38%	24%
Driving In Runners from 3B with Less than Two Out:			10/22	45%

Loves to face: John Farrell (.625, 5-for-8, 1 HR)
Hates to face: Jose Guzman (0-for-8, 5 SO)

July batting average was 2d lowest in majors (minimum: two PA per game). ... Has caught 589 games for the Twins, more than any other player in team history except the granddaddy of all Twins catchers, Earl Battey (831), and Butch Wynegar (759). ... Hit below .225 with runners on base in each of past six seasons. Career averages: .213 with runners on, .236 with the bases empty. ... While major leaguers were on strike in 1981, Laudner was busy swatting 42 homers for Orlando in the Southern League. Made his major league debut in August 1981, and tied a major league record by homering in each of his first two games. ... Has averaged one home run per 25.3 AB, about the same rate as Wally Joyner.

Rick Leach
Bats Left

Toronto Blue Jays	AB	H	2B	3B	HR	RBI	BB	SO	BA	SA	OBA
Season	199	55	13	1	0	23	18	27	.276	.352	.336
vs. Left-Handers	15	2	1	0	0	2	1	4	.133	.200	.188
vs. Right-Handers	184	53	12	1	0	21	17	23	.288	.364	.348
Home	109	32	8	0	0	12	11	13	.294	.367	.358
Road	90	23	5	1	0	11	7	14	.256	.333	.309
Grass	62	14	1	1	0	4	5	13	.226	.274	.284
Artificial Turf	137	41	12	0	0	19	13	14	.299	.387	.360
April	43	12	4	0	0	6	4	7	.279	.372	.340
May	42	10	2	0	0	9	4	3	.238	.286	.304
June	15	2	0	0	0	0	5	4	.133	.133	.350
July	44	17	5	0	0	5	3	6	.386	.500	.426
August	32	8	1	0	0	1	0	3	.250	.281	.250
Sept./Oct.	23	6	1	1	0	2	2	4	.261	.391	.320
Leading Off Inn.	43	10	2	1	0	0	0	5	.233	.326	.233
Runners On	89	30	4	0	0	23	7	14	.337	.382	.385
Runners/Scor. Pos.	61	21	4	0	0	23	6	11	.344	.410	.403
Runners On/2 Out	36	12	3	0	0	11	3	6	.333	.417	.385
Scor. Pos./2 Out	26	9	3	0	0	11	3	5	.346	.462	.414
Late Inning Pressure	33	8	2	1	0	2	5	6	.242	.364	.342
Leading Off	11	4	1	1	0	0	0	2	.364	.636	.364
Runners On	16	3	0	0	0	2	2	2	.188	.188	.278
Runners/Scor. Pos.	12	3	0	0	0	2	2	2	.250	.250	.357

RUNS BATTED IN	From 1B	From 2B	From 3B	Scoring Position
Totals	3/57	11/54	9/17	20/71
Percentage	5%	20%	53%	28%
Driving In Runners from 3B with Less than Two Out:			7/11	64%

Loves to face: Bill Swift (.625, 5-for-8)
Hates to face: Doyle Alexander (0-for-7)

Started 48 *consecutive* games for Bo Schembechler at Michigan, but only 51 games total for Jimy Williams last season (only one against a southpaw). ... Batted .053 (1-for-19) as a pinch hitter; hitless in his last 14 at-bats. ... Played 376 games for Toronto, but never had a stolen base or sacrifice bunt. ... Career average of .315 with runners in scoring position is 67 points higher than his average otherwise, largest difference in majors over last 10 years (minimum: 300 AB with RISP). ... Has hit 69 points higher on artificial turf than on grass, also the largest difference during that time (minimum: 500 AB both ways). ... Career average of .212 at his new home, Arlington Stadium (7-for-33, no HRs).

Manny Lee
Bats Left and Right

Toronto Blue Jays	AB	H	2B	3B	HR	RBI	BB	SO	BA	SA	OBA
Season	381	111	16	3	2	38	26	64	.291	.365	.333
vs. Left-Handers	131	44	8	1	2	17	6	14	.336	.458	.365
vs. Right-Handers	250	67	8	2	0	21	20	50	.268	.316	.318
Home	196	58	9	3	2	20	14	28	.296	.403	.338
Road	185	53	7	0	0	18	12	36	.286	.324	.328
Grass	148	44	3	0	0	15	9	24	.297	.318	.335
Artificial Turf	233	67	13	3	2	23	17	40	.288	.395	.332
April	43	10	3	0	0	4	3	7	.233	.302	.277
May	19	3	0	0	0	1	0	2	.158	.158	.158
June	58	20	0	1	1	7	2	10	.345	.431	.361
July	90	29	6	0	0	12	11	17	.322	.389	.392
August	101	28	3	1	1	9	5	14	.277	.356	.311
Sept./Oct.	70	21	4	1	0	5	5	14	.300	.386	.342
Leading Off Inn.	70	17	3	0	1	1	5	13	.243	.329	.293
Runners On	169	56	7	2	0	36	8	31	.331	.396	.354
Runners/Scor. Pos.	98	31	4	2	0	36	3	22	.316	.398	.324
Runners On/2 Out	72	25	3	2	0	14	3	17	.347	.444	.373
Scor. Pos./2 Out	44	14	2	2	0	14	1	11	.318	.455	.333
Late Inning Pressure	63	17	0	0	0	5	9	10	.270	.270	.361
Leading Off	16	5	0	0	0	0	3	5	.313	.313	.421
Runners On	26	9	0	0	0	5	3	4	.346	.346	.414
Runners/Scor. Pos.	17	5	0	0	0	5	2	4	.294	.294	.368

RUNS BATTED IN	From 1B	From 2B	From 3B	Scoring Position
Totals	0/120	13/74	23/48	36/122
Percentage	0%	18%	48%	30%
Driving In Runners from 3B with Less than Two Out:			16/33	48%

Loves to face: Charlie Leibrandt (.556, 5-for-9)
Hates to face: Bob Welch (0-for-6)

Youngest A.L. player to start at least half of his team's games in the middle infield. He's a week younger than Kurt Stillwell, who started 121 games at shortstop for the Royals. ... Blue Jays have a 4–19 record with Lee as their starting shortstop over the last four seasons. ... Batted .312 vs. fly-ball pitchers, .254 against ground-ballers. ... at-bats and batting average have increased in each major league campaign: 40 (.200), 78 (.205), 121 (.256), 381 (.291). ... Career average of .308 vs. lefties, .247 vs. righties. ... Has been hit by only one pitch in seven years of pro ball (in 1983).

Chet Lemon

Bats Right

Detroit Tigers	AB	H	2B	3B	HR	RBI	BB	SO	BA	SA	OBA
Season	512	135	29	4	17	64	59	65	.264	.436	.346
vs. Left-Handers	165	49	11	1	9	26	19	16	.297	.539	.370
vs. Right-Handers	347	86	18	3	8	38	40	49	.248	.386	.335
Home	245	68	14	2	12	32	25	31	.278	.498	.349
Road	267	67	15	2	5	32	34	34	.251	.378	.343
Grass	442	116	23	3	16	56	45	54	.262	.437	.336
Artificial Turf	70	19	6	1	1	8	14	11	.271	.429	.402
April	75	24	5	1	0	5	8	14	.320	.413	.386
May	98	26	11	1	2	11	9	10	.265	.459	.333
June	56	13	2	1	2	8	7	4	.232	.411	.348
July	94	26	4	1	4	13	9	11	.277	.468	.333
August	96	22	1	0	1	10	14	12	.229	.271	.339
Sept./Oct.	93	24	6	0	8	17	12	14	.258	.581	.346
Leading Off Inn.	128	33	8	1	5	5	11	15	.258	.453	.326
Runners On	222	62	8	2	8	55	26	31	.279	.441	.363
Runners/Scor. Pos.	116	33	4	0	5	47	20	18	.284	.448	.403
Runners On/2 Out	94	30	4	1	4	25	12	13	.319	.511	.402
Scor. Pos./2 Out	54	17	2	0	3	22	11	9	.315	.519	.439
Late Inning Pressure	83	26	7	0	6	9	14	8	.313	.614	.424
Leading Off	29	8	3	0	1	1	5	4	.276	.483	.400
Runners On	27	9	1	0	3	6	5	2	.333	.704	.455
Runners/Scor. Pos.	12	2	0	0	1	2	5	2	.167	.417	.444

RUNS BATTED IN	From 1B	From 2B	From 3B	Scoring Position
Totals	9/180	20/96	18/48	38/144
Percentage	5%	21%	38%	26%
Driving In Runners from 3B with Less than Two Out:			12/28	43%

Loves to face: Bud Black (.435, 10-for-23, 1 HR)
Hates to face: Juan Nieves (.048, 1-for-21)
Tigers had a record of 14–1 in games in which he hit a home run. . . . Hit seven home runs in 84 at-bats vs. left-handed pitchers at Tiger Stadium. . . . Had hit only one home run in Late-Inning Pressure Situations over the previous two seasons. . . . Committed seven of his eight errors in home games. . . . Batting average with two outs and runners in scoring position was the highest of his career. . . . Has hit below .270 vs. left-handers only once in the past seven seasons; has hit above .270 vs. right-handers only once during that time. . . . Batted .288 with one home run per 38 at-bats over first seven seasons; .267, one HR per 26 AB over last seven.

Jeffrey Leonard

Bats Right

Milwaukee Brewers	AB	H	2B	3B	HR	RBI	BB	SO	BA	SA	OBA
Season	374	88	19	0	8	44	16	68	.235	.350	.270
vs. Left-Handers	111	30	10	0	3	16	7	18	.270	.441	.317
vs. Right-Handers	263	58	9	0	5	28	9	50	.221	.312	.249
Home	188	45	10	0	5	21	10	31	.239	.372	.286
Road	186	43	9	0	3	23	6	37	.231	.328	.253
Grass	329	74	15	0	6	33	14	60	.225	.325	.260
Artificial Turf	45	14	4	0	2	11	2	8	.311	.533	.340
April	0	0	0	0	0	0	0	0	——	——	——
May	0	0	0	0	0	0	0	0	——	——	——
June	75	19	1	0	2	13	3	13	.253	.347	.277
July	89	17	6	0	3	8	4	22	.191	.360	.234
August	123	34	8	0	1	11	4	18	.276	.366	.299
Sept./Oct.	87	18	4	0	2	12	5	15	.207	.322	.258
Leading Off Inn.	68	19	4	0	2	2	1	14	.279	.426	.290
Runners On	187	42	7	0	5	41	8	32	.225	.342	.259
Runners/Scor. Pos.	99	21	3	0	3	35	7	17	.212	.333	.261
Runners On/2 Out	83	18	4	0	1	15	4	11	.217	.301	.261
Scor. Pos./2 Out	47	9	2	0	1	14	3	4	.191	.298	.255
Late Inning Pressure	51	15	3	0	1	0	0	10	.294	.353	.308
Leading Off	12	3	1	0	0	0	0	4	.250	.333	.250
Runners On	23	6	0	0	0	0	0	5	.261	.261	.292
Runners/Scor. Pos.	13	2	0	0	0	0	0	5	.154	.154	.154

RUNS BATTED IN	From 1B	From 2B	From 3B	Scoring Position
Totals	6/135	14/74	16/47	30/121
Percentage	4%	19%	34%	25%
Driving In Runners from 3B with Less than Two Out:			13/26	50%

Loves to face: Dave Stewart (.429, 6-for-14, 2 HR)
Hates to face: Roger Clemens (0-for-8, 4 SO)
Figures *above* are for A.L. only. . . . On the day that Leonard was acquired from San Francisco, all three Brewers outfielders (Deer, Yount, and Hamilton) and the DH (Glenn Braggs) drove in two runs each in a victory over Seattle. Talk about a presence in the clubhouse! . . . What's with this lack of respect for postseason MVP winners? First, 1986 World Series MVP Ray Knight cut loose by the Mets. Then Leonard traded after his MVP performance in the 1987 N.L.C.S. How 'bout Hershiser for Eckersley? . . . Batting average vs. ground-ball pitchers has been higher than against fly-ballers in each of the last seven seasons. That matches Mike Marshall for longest streak among active players.

Nelson Liriano

Bats Left and Right

Toronto Blue Jays	AB	H	2B	3B	HR	RBI	BB	SO	BA	SA	OBA
Season	276	73	6	2	3	23	11	40	.264	.333	.297
vs. Left-Handers	93	25	1	0	1	7	6	20	.269	.312	.320
vs. Right-Handers	183	48	5	2	2	16	5	20	.262	.344	.284
Home	111	30	2	2	0	9	7	18	.270	.324	.317
Road	165	43	4	0	3	14	4	22	.261	.339	.282
Grass	111	33	2	0	1	10	4	11	.297	.342	.328
Artificial Turf	165	40	4	2	2	13	7	29	.242	.327	.276
April	59	12	0	0	1	4	1	12	.203	.254	.226
May	63	13	2	0	0	2	2	7	.206	.238	.231
June	48	15	1	0	1	4	3	3	.313	.396	.365
July	29	8	2	1	1	3	1	7	.276	.517	.300
August	40	10	1	0	0	2	2	5	.250	.275	.286
Sept./Oct.	37	15	0	1	0	8	2	6	.405	.459	.436
Leading Off Inn.	77	21	5	0	0	0	3	11	.273	.338	.309
Runners On	114	31	1	2	0	20	6	18	.272	.316	.306
Runners/Scor. Pos.	75	22	1	2	0	20	5	11	.293	.360	.333
Runners On/2 Out	51	10	0	0	0	5	2	3	.196	.196	.226
Scor. Pos./2 Out	33	6	0	0	0	5	1	1	.182	.182	.206
Late Inning Pressure	46	15	1	1	1	6	2	13	.326	.457	.354
Leading Off	10	3	1	0	0	0	0	1	.300	.400	.300
Runners On	17	6	0	1	0	5	1	7	.353	.471	.389
Runners/Scor. Pos.	10	4	0	1	0	5	1	5	.400	.600	.455

RUNS BATTED IN	From 1B	From 2B	From 3B	Scoring Position
Totals	2/76	9/56	9/29	18/85
Percentage	3%	16%	31%	21%
Driving In Runners from 3B with Less than Two Out:			8/16	50%

Loves to face: Doug Jones (3-for-3, 1 HR)
Hates to face: Dave Righetti (0-for-6)
Started and batted leadoff in each of Toronto's first 10 games, only four times thereafter. . . . Blue Jays allowed 3.96 runs per nine innings with Manny Lee at second base, 4.55 with Liriano there. . . . Career stolen base totals: 15-for-16 on artificial turf, 10-for-16 on grass fields. . . . Averaged over 25 stolen bases over five seasons in minors. Has stolen that many in 136 games in majors. . . . Has hit more home runs at the Metrodome (two in 18 at-bats) than at Exhibition Stadium (one in 210 AB). . . . Career average of one extra-base hit per 34 at-bats vs. left-handed pitchers, one per 18 at-bats vs. right-handers. . . . Has batted seven times with the bases loaded, driving in only one of 21 runners.

Steve Lombardozzi

Bats Right

Minnesota Twins	AB	H	2B	3B	HR	RBI	BB	SO	BA	SA	OBA
Season	287	60	15	2	3	27	35	48	.209	.307	.295
vs. Left-Handers	72	18	3	1	0	5	10	9	.250	.319	.337
vs. Right-Handers	215	42	12	1	3	22	25	39	.195	.302	.280
Home	137	28	7	2	3	15	17	20	.204	.350	.296
Road	150	32	8	0	0	12	18	28	.213	.267	.294
Grass	115	23	6	0	0	8	12	20	.200	.252	.271
Artificial Turf	172	37	9	2	3	19	23	28	.215	.343	.310
April	32	3	1	1	0	4	4	5	.094	.188	.194
May	26	11	1	0	0	2	3	8	.423	.462	.483
June	60	13	1	0	1	4	11	10	.217	.283	.276
July	69	14	5	0	1	6	7	8	.203	.319	.276
August	61	14	6	1	0	11	8	14	.230	.361	.311
Sept./Oct.	39	5	1	0	1	4	2	3	.128	.231	.167
Leading Off Inn.	70	13	3	1	0	0	3	12	.186	.257	.219
Runners On	116	28	6	1	2	26	19	20	.241	.362	.345
Runners/Scor. Pos.	69	14	3	1	1	24	17	14	.203	.319	.348
Runners On/2 Out	57	15	3	0	0	7	11	10	.263	.316	.400
Scor. Pos./2 Out	37	7	1	0	0	7	10	8	.189	.216	.375
Late Inning Pressure	21	2	0	0	0	0	3	7	.095	.095	.208
Leading Off	8	2	0	0	0	0	0	4	.250	.250	.250
Runners On	6	0	0	0	0	0	2	1	.000	.000	.250
Runners/Scor. Pos.	5	0	0	0	0	0	1	1	.000	.000	.167

RUNS BATTED IN	From 1B	From 2B	From 3B	Scoring Position
Totals	2/78	10/57	12/34	22/91
Percentage	3%	18%	35%	24%
Driving In Runners from 3B with Less than Two Out:			10/18	56%

Loves to face: Frank Tanana (.500, 5-for-10, 1 HR)
Hates to face: Roger Clemens (0-for 21, 8 SO)
Twins allowed 4.30 runs per nine innings with Tom Herr at second base, 3.98 with Lombardozzi there. Twins' fans made it clear: They wanted himm, not Herr. . . . Had 32 consecutive plate appearances in which he failed to reach base, longest streak in the majors by a nonpitcher last season. . . . Batted 51 times with a runner on first and less than two outs, but grounded into only three double plays. . . . Batting average vs. right-handed pitchers has declined every season. Year by year since 1985: .382, .235, .215, .195. . . . Same is true of his average at the Metrodome: .414, .251, .211, .204. . . . Career average of .269 vs. ground-ball pitchers, .207 vs. fly-ball pitchers.

Fred Lynn

Orioles/Tigers — Bats Left

	AB	H	2B	3B	HR	RBI	BB	SO	BA	SA	OBA
Season	391	96	14	1	25	56	33	82	.246	.478	.302
vs. Left-Handers	109	19	5	1	4	16	5	31	.174	.349	.205
vs. Right-Handers	282	77	9	0	21	40	28	51	.273	.528	.338
Home	194	50	8	0	13	34	19	40	.258	.500	.318
Road	197	46	6	1	12	22	14	42	.234	.457	.285
Grass	347	87	13	0	20	49	29	72	.251	.461	.305
Artificial Turf	44	9	1	1	5	7	4	10	.205	.614	.271
April	69	15	2	0	2	3	4	14	.217	.333	.260
May	89	26	6	1	6	12	10	20	.292	.584	.360
June	72	19	3	0	5	9	7	14	.264	.514	.325
July	21	6	1	0	4	7	2	4	.286	.905	.333
August	50	10	1	0	1	6	5	14	.200	.280	.268
Sept./Oct.	90	20	1	0	7	19	5	16	.222	.467	.265
Leading Off Inn.	95	28	4	0	8	8	8	17	.295	.589	.350
Runners On	162	32	3	1	7	38	16	34	.198	.358	.265
Runners/Scor. Pos.	87	14	3	0	2	27	9	23	.161	.264	.233
Runners On/2 Out	60	10	1	0	3	12	8	10	.167	.333	.265
Scor. Pos./2 Out	36	4	1	0	0	6	6	8	.111	.139	.238
Late Inning Pressure	71	11	0	0	3	9	6	20	.155	.282	.215
Leading Off	23	6	0	0	1	1	2	5	.261	.391	.320
Runners On	29	2	0	0	2	8	1	9	.069	.276	.094
Runners/Scor. Pos.	18	1	0	0	1	6	1	6	.056	.222	.095

RUNS BATTED IN	From 1B	From 2B	From 3B	Scoring Position
Totals	9/126	6/76	16/40	22/116
Percentage	7%	8%	40%	19%
Driving In Runners from 3B with Less than Two Out:		12/22		55%

Loves to face: Bert Blyleven (.404, 21-for-52, 6 HR)
Hates to face: Scott Bailes (0-for-8)
Tied Rick Monday's 1973 major league record for fewest RBI in a season of 25+ home runs.... Hit three of his seven Detroit homers off left-handers, after hitting only one of 18 with Orioles off a southpaw.... Hit nine homers in 41 at-bats from June 17 to July 14.... Has hit at least 21, but no more than 25 home runs in each of the last seven seasons.... Lowest ratio of walks to strikeouts in his 15-year career.... Batting average with runners in scoring position was the lowest of his career.... One of three players with a grand-slam homer in each of past four years.... Late-Inning Pressure average has been lower than his overall average in each of the last six seasons, and 13 of the last 14.

Steve Lyons

Chicago White Sox — Bats Left

	AB	H	2B	3B	HR	RBI	BB	SO	BA	SA	OBA
Season	472	127	28	3	5	45	32	59	.269	.373	.313
vs. Left-Handers	139	37	4	1	3	15	9	21	.266	.374	.305
vs. Right-Handers	333	90	24	2	2	30	23	38	.270	.372	.317
Home	227	61	11	3	1	23	18	24	.269	.357	.321
Road	245	66	17	0	4	22	14	35	.269	.388	.305
Grass	380	102	23	3	4	39	26	45	.268	.376	.313
Artificial Turf	92	25	5	0	1	6	6	14	.272	.359	.313
April	7	0	0	0	0	0	1	1	.000	.000	.125
May	45	12	1	0	1	5	6	4	.267	.356	.353
June	104	34	6	0	2	11	12	7	.327	.442	.390
July	115	25	6	2	2	13	3	17	.217	.357	.238
August	107	27	6	1	0	8	5	22	.252	.327	.286
Sept./Oct.	94	29	9	0	0	8	5	8	.309	.404	.340
Leading Off Inn.	86	20	6	1	0	0	6	13	.233	.326	.283
Runners On	191	52	14	2	2	42	16	17	.272	.398	.319
Runners/Scor. Pos.	106	29	10	2	0	36	10	9	.274	.406	.320
Runners On/2 Out	78	20	6	0	0	11	8	5	.256	.333	.326
Scor. Pos./2 Out	46	11	5	0	0	10	6	4	.239	.348	.327
Late Inning Pressure	77	21	2	0	1	7	7	7	.273	.338	.329
Leading Off	17	4	0	0	0	0	2	2	.235	.235	.316
Runners On	33	9	2	0	1	7	3	3	.273	.375	.326
Runners/Scor. Pos.	20	5	2	0	0	5	3	2	.250	.350	.333

RUNS BATTED IN	From 1B	From 2B	From 3B	Scoring Position
Totals	5/126	15/89	20/39	35/128
Percentage	4%	17%	51%	27%
Driving In Runners from 3B with Less than Two Out:		16/23		70%

Loves to face: Bret Saberhagen (.417, 5-for-12)
Hates to face: Dave Stieb (.059, 1-for-17, 7 SO)
Committed 29 errors last season, most in A.L. Despite that, 20 of his first 24 appearances were as a defensive replacement.... Kevin Seitzer led A.L. third basemen with 26 errors, but White Sox' third basemen combined for 46: Lyons (25), Williams (14), Martinez (4), Hill (2), and Paris (1).... Sox pitchers allowed fewer runs per nine innings with other third basemen (4.52) than with Lyons there (4.84).... On the plus side, Lyons led major league third basemen with 36 double plays, becoming first White Sox third baseman since Willie Kamm (1924) to lead A.L.... Played every position except left field, shortstop, and pitcher last season.... Was traded for Tom Seaver in 1986.

Mike Macfarlane

Kansas City Royals — Bats Right

	AB	H	2B	3B	HR	RBI	BB	SO	BA	SA	OBA
Season	211	56	15	0	4	26	21	37	.265	.393	.332
vs. Left-Handers	84	20	6	0	1	8	2	16	.238	.345	.250
vs. Right-Handers	127	36	9	0	3	18	19	21	.283	.425	.381
Home	106	28	6	0	2	12	9	14	.264	.377	.328
Road	105	28	9	0	2	14	12	23	.267	.410	.336
Grass	91	23	7	0	2	14	11	18	.253	.396	.327
Artificial Turf	120	33	8	0	2	12	10	19	.275	.392	.336
April	37	14	5	0	0	3	5	9	.378	.514	.452
May	63	14	3	0	1	7	8	10	.222	.317	.319
June	63	16	6	0	0	10	6	10	.254	.349	.310
July	48	12	1	0	3	6	2	8	.250	.458	.280
August	0	0	0	0	0	0	0	0	———	———	———
Sept./Oct.	0	0	0	0	0	0	0	0	———	———	———
Leading Off Inn.	52	12	1	0	1	1	5	7	.231	.308	.298
Runners On	86	25	6	0	3	25	10	13	.291	.465	.357
Runners/Scor. Pos.	50	14	4	0	2	21	9	9	.280	.480	.377
Runners On/2 Out	40	10	3	0	1	11	4	7	.250	.400	.318
Scor. Pos./2 Out	29	8	2	0	1	10	3	7	.276	.448	.344
Late Inning Pressure	32	5	2	0	1	2	0	8	.156	.313	.156
Leading Off	10	3	1	0	1	1	0	2	.300	.700	.300
Runners On	9	0	0	0	0	0	1	3	.000	.000	.000
Runners/Scor. Pos.	5	0	0	0	0	1	0	2	.000	.000	.000

RUNS BATTED IN	From 1B	From 2B	From 3B	Scoring Position
Totals	5/59	7/42	10/19	17/61
Percentage	8%	17%	53%	28%
Driving In Runners from 3B with Less than Two Out:		7/12		58%

Loves to face: Bill Wegman (.667, 2-for-3, 1 2B, 1 HR)
Hates to face: Ray Hayward (0-for-4, 3 SO)
Only rookie in A.L. to play as many as 50 games behind the plate. ... Demoted to Omaha (AAA) in late July before breaking his thumb there in mid-August.... Hit three home runs in his last 35 at-bats with the Royals.... Hitless in four at-bats as a pinch hitter. ... Started 63 games, all but five of them in the 7th batting order slot or lower.... Kansas City pitchers allowed 3.84 runs per nine innings with Mac catching, compared with 4.24 rate with others behind the plate. Caught 39 percent of Royals' innings last season, tops on team; Quirk had 38 percent, Larry Owen 18, and four other players split the remaining five percent. (Al Haig finished with less than one percent of the vote.)

Fred Manrique

Chicago White Sox — Bats Right

	AB	H	2B	3B	HR	RBI	BB	SO	BA	SA	OBA
Season	345	81	10	6	5	37	21	54	.235	.342	.283
vs. Left-Handers	149	37	4	1	2	17	9	26	.248	.329	.289
vs. Right-Handers	196	44	6	5	3	20	12	28	.224	.352	.278
Home	176	39	4	3	3	22	11	31	.222	.330	.274
Road	169	42	6	3	2	15	10	23	.249	.355	.293
Grass	281	68	9	4	5	32	18	47	.242	.356	.294
Artificial Turf	64	13	1	2	0	5	3	7	.203	.281	.235
April	18	5	0	0	1	1	3	3	.278	.444	.381
May	62	11	2	3	1	10	2	8	.177	.355	.203
June	47	11	0	1	0	2	0	8	.234	.277	.234
July	87	27	6	1	3	12	7	12	.310	.506	.362
August	73	15	2	1	0	7	4	13	.205	.260	.266
Sept./Oct.	58	12	0	0	0	5	5	10	.207	.207	.340
Leading Off Inn.	73	17	1	1	2	2	1	9	.233	.356	.243
Runners On	141	33	4	3	2	34	9	16	.234	.348	.276
Runners/Scor. Pos.	80	22	3	1	1	29	7	10	.275	.375	.326
Runners On/2 Out	68	17	1	3	1	18	5	8	.250	.397	.301
Scor. Pos./2 Out	40	10	1	1	1	15	4	5	.250	.375	.318
Late Inning Pressure	57	9	0	2	1	4	2	7	.158	.281	.186
Leading Off	16	1	0	0	0	0	0	1	.063	.063	.063
Runners On	21	4	0	1	0	3	1	2	.190	.286	.227
Runners/Scor. Pos.	11	2	0	1	0	3	1	2	.182	.364	.250

RUNS BATTED IN	From 1B	From 2B	From 3B	Scoring Position
Totals	6/104	10/57	16/38	26/95
Percentage	6%	18%	42%	27%
Driving In Runners from 3B with Less than Two Out:		10/19		53%

Loves to face: John Cerutti (.417, 5-for-12, 1 HR)
Hates to face: Roger Clemens (0-for-6, 5 SO)
Has batted .242 in 301 games in majors, but has .287 career average with runners in scoring position.... Has walked only three times in 161 career plate appearances leading off innings.... Started 48 of 51 games last season in which Chicago faced left-handed starters, but only 58 of 110 games vs. right-handers.... Has made only 15 errors in 233 games at second base, for a .9843 fielding percentage. Keep that up for a decade or so, Fred, and you'll challenge Tom Herr's major league record (.988).... Successor to Aparicio and Fox as White Sox leader in sacrifice bunts (16) last season. OK, so it's not exactly a papal line of succession, but at least those names are better than Al Weis and Ken Berry.

Don Mattingly
New York Yankees — Bats Left

	AB	H	2B	3B	HR	RBI	BB	SO	BA	SA	OBA
Season	599	186	37	0	18	88	41	29	.311	.462	.353
vs. Left-Handers	221	64	13	0	3	34	9	11	.290	.389	.316
vs. Right-Handers	378	122	24	0	15	54	32	18	.323	.505	.374
Home	296	87	14	0	11	42	18	17	.294	.453	.334
Road	303	99	23	0	7	46	23	12	.327	.472	.372
Grass	500	154	28	0	17	73	34	25	.308	.466	.349
Artificial Turf	99	32	9	0	1	15	7	4	.323	.444	.374
April	91	25	8	0	0	12	10	8	.275	.363	.340
May	84	31	8	0	4	17	10	3	.369	.607	.443
June	64	17	3	0	1	7	4	2	.266	.359	.309
July	117	44	8	0	5	20	3	2	.376	.573	.392
August	118	30	3	0	3	16	7	7	.254	.356	.295
Sept./Oct.	125	39	7	0	5	16	7	7	.312	.488	.343
Leading Off Inn.	100	26	10	0	0	0	5	4	.260	.360	.295
Runners On	291	93	15	0	10	80	22	15	.320	.474	.360
Runners/Scor. Pos.	168	50	11	0	5	68	20	10	.298	.452	.360
Runners On/2 Out	100	25	5	0	5	23	9	4	.250	.450	.318
Scor. Pos./2 Out	63	13	3	0	4	19	9	2	.206	.444	.315
Late Inning Pressure	69	19	4	0	2	9	3	4	.275	.420	.311
Leading Off	18	4	0	0	0	0	0	2	.222	.222	.222
Runners On	35	10	2	0	2	9	3	1	.286	.514	.333
Runners/Scor. Pos.	19	6	1	0	1	7	3	1	.316	.526	.391

RUNS BATTED IN	From 1B	From 2B	From 3B	Scoring Position
Totals	10/198	24/116	36/73	60/189
Percentage	5%	21%	49%	32%
Driving In Runners from 3B with Less than Two Out:		31/45		69%

Loves to face: Dave Stieb (.400, 20-for-50, 2 HR)
Hates to face: Les Straker (0-for-8)

His lifetime slugging percentage is .52875; Strawberry's is .52860. Let's just call it even.... Made four errors in last month of season to finish with career-low fielding percentage (.993).... Did not drive in a run in five plate appearances with the bases loaded last year, after picking up 34 RBIs in 21 times up with the bags full in his six-slam 1987 season.... Owns career batting average of .285, with only four homers in 403 at-bats, in April.... Has hit .239 in Late-Inning Pressure Situations over the last two years.... Leads majors with 571 RBI and 1677 total bases over last five years; he's 49 RBI ahead of runner-up Winfield, and he's 100 TB ahead of second-place George Bell.

Oddibe McDowell
Texas Rangers — Bats Left

	AB	H	2B	3B	HR	RBI	BB	SO	BA	SA	OBA
Season	437	108	19	5	6	37	41	89	.247	.355	.311
vs. Left-Handers	96	22	4	1	2	9	7	19	.229	.354	.288
vs. Right-Handers	341	86	15	4	4	28	34	70	.252	.355	.318
Home	211	52	9	3	4	20	24	42	.246	.374	.321
Road	226	56	10	2	2	17	17	47	.248	.336	.302
Grass	368	93	13	5	6	30	35	72	.253	.364	.315
Artificial Turf	69	15	6	0	0	7	6	17	.217	.304	.291
April	61	13	1	0	2	3	3	18	.213	.328	.246
May	75	14	2	1	1	8	13	10	.187	.280	.303
June	35	8	2	1	0	3	4	6	.229	.343	.308
July	66	19	1	2	0	7	5	12	.288	.364	.333
August	99	30	7	0	1	5	2	17	.303	.404	.324
Sept./Oct.	101	24	6	1	2	11	14	26	.238	.376	.331
Leading Off Inn.	175	44	7	1	4	4	12	32	.251	.371	.299
Runners On	165	41	8	4	0	31	14	35	.248	.345	.303
Runners/Scor. Pos.	89	23	3	3	0	27	10	28	.258	.360	.324
Runners On/2 Out	70	21	3	1	0	13	8	13	.300	.371	.380
Scor. Pos./2 Out	39	12	2	0	0	11	6	11	.308	.359	.413
Late Inning Pressure	67	21	3	1	0	10	5	18	.313	.388	.356
Leading Off	13	4	0	0	0	0	0	6	.308	.308	.308
Runners On	36	13	2	1	0	10	4	8	.361	.472	.415
Runners/Scor. Pos.	21	8	1	1	0	9	3	6	.381	.524	.440

RUNS BATTED IN	From 1B	From 2B	From 3B	Scoring Position
Totals	5/122	8/68	18/39	26/107
Percentage	4%	12%	46%	24%
Driving In Runners from 3B with Less than Two Out:		9/19		47%

Loves to face: Bert Blyleven (.355, 11-for-31, 5 HR)
Hates to face: Mike Birkbeck (0-for-10)

Batted .222 before the All-Star break, .264 after the break.... Had three hits on opening day last season, after homering on opening day in 1987.... Has batted .315 in Late-Inning Pressure Situations over last two seasons, but only .232 in unpressured at-bats over same period.... Averaged one home run every 27.7 at-bats from 1985 to 1987, but fell to average of one every 72.8 at-bats last season.... Has batted for a higher average against ground-ball pitchers than vs. fly-ballers in each of his four seasons in majors.... Season average of .247 was 2d-lowest among 14 A.L. players who were the most frequent leadoff batters for their teams. Scored only 51 runs in his 95 games as a leadoff hitter.

Fred McGriff
Toronto Blue Jays — Bats Left

	AB	H	2B	3B	HR	RBI	BB	SO	BA	SA	OBA
Season	536	151	35	4	34	83	79	149	.282	.552	.376
vs. Left-Handers	171	40	8	0	5	16	15	64	.234	.368	.307
vs. Right-Handers	365	111	27	4	29	67	64	85	.304	.638	.406
Home	250	64	14	1	18	41	42	64	.256	.536	.363
Road	286	87	21	3	16	42	37	85	.304	.566	.387
Grass	225	65	17	2	10	31	29	62	.289	.516	.370
Artificial Turf	311	86	18	2	24	52	50	87	.277	.579	.380
April	53	17	4	0	4	8	11	19	.321	.623	.446
May	93	32	10	0	6	18	17	22	.344	.645	.445
June	102	24	7	1	5	11	12	34	.235	.471	.322
July	83	24	4	0	8	21	15	24	.289	.627	.400
August	99	25	3	3	7	15	11	31	.253	.556	.330
Sept./Oct.	106	29	7	0	4	10	13	19	.274	.453	.347
Leading Off Inn.	115	41	13	2	4	4	21	28	.357	.609	.460
Runners On	236	61	11	1	15	64	29	62	.258	.504	.342
Runners/Scor. Pos.	127	28	4	0	4	40	19	41	.220	.346	.322
Runners On/2 Out	100	20	4	0	2	18	13	28	.200	.300	.304
Scor. Pos./2 Out	63	12	1	0	1	15	11	20	.190	.254	.311
Late Inning Pressure	71	16	6	0	1	2	11	26	.225	.352	.345
Leading Off	17	8	2	0	0	0	6	4	.471	.588	.609
Runners On	29	3	2	0	0	1	3	13	.103	.172	.235
Runners/Scor. Pos.	16	1	0	0	0	1	2	10	.063	.063	.211

RUNS BATTED IN	From 1B	From 2B	From 3B	Scoring Position
Totals	16/178	13/100	20/53	33/153
Percentage	9%	13%	38%	22%
Driving In Runners from 3B with Less than Two Out:		13/26		50%

Loves to face: Mark Gubicza (.455, 5-for-11, 3 HR)
Hates to face: Scott Bankhead (0-for-7, 6 SO)

Surprise: his .460 on-base average when leading off innings was 2d-best in majors to Boggs's .476 mark.... Longest home-run drought was 18 games between 33rd and 34th homers.... Career breakdown: .287 with bases empty, .247 with runners on base, .210 with runners in scoring position, .187 with two outs and runners in scoring position.... Finished second to Canseco in slugging average; was A.L.'s top slugger vs. right-handers.... Career average of .283, with one homer every 13.3 at-bats vs. right-handed pitchers; .223, one HR every 32.8 AB vs. lefties. Exhibition Stadium is effectively HR-neutral; considering his youth and power, McGriff could be the player most affected by move to SkyDome.

Mark McGwire
Oakland As — Bats Right

	AB	H	2B	3B	HR	RBI	BB	SO	BA	SA	OBA
Season	550	143	22	1	32	99	76	117	.260	.478	.352
vs. Left-Handers	150	37	8	1	11	31	26	27	.247	.533	.358
vs. Right-Handers	400	106	14	0	21	68	50	90	.265	.458	.349
Home	256	63	11	0	12	45	37	57	.246	.430	.347
Road	294	80	11	1	20	54	39	60	.272	.520	.356
Grass	464	118	18	1	28	84	68	95	.254	.478	.353
Artificial Turf	86	25	4	0	4	15	8	22	.291	.477	.347
April	85	24	3	0	6	16	10	18	.282	.529	.378
May	103	26	7	0	5	19	15	24	.252	.466	.345
June	87	15	2	1	2	7	14	16	.172	.287	.284
July	107	28	5	0	9	19	9	26	.262	.477	.316
August	106	31	3	0	8	25	16	21	.292	.547	.382
Sept./Oct.	62	19	2	0	5	13	12	12	.306	.581	.427
Leading Off Inn.	136	30	6	0	8	8	15	39	.221	.441	.303
Runners On	240	71	10	1	17	84	43	49	.296	.558	.403
Runners/Scor. Pos.	141	48	7	1	11	71	31	29	.340	.638	.458
Runners On/2 Out	109	23	5	0	6	29	22	29	.211	.422	.344
Scor. Pos./2 Out	70	15	3	0	5	26	14	18	.214	.471	.345
Late Inning Pressure	83	20	0	0	7	19	8	16	.241	.494	.312
Leading Off	21	3	0	0	2	2	0	5	.143	.429	.143
Runners On	35	12	0	0	2	14	8	7	.343	.514	.467
Runners/Scor. Pos.	23	9	0	0	2	14	6	4	.391	.652	.516

RUNS BATTED IN	From 1B	From 2B	From 3B	Scoring Position
Totals	16/175	28/111	23/55	51/166
Percentage	9%	25%	42%	31%
Driving In Runners from 3B with Less than Two Out:		15/22		68%

Loves to face: Mike Boddicker (.400, 6-for-15, 4 HR)
Hates to face: Tom Henke (0-for-6, 6 SO)

Career average of .323 vs. ground-ball pitchers, .228 vs. fly-ball pitchers: difference is largest in majors *by far* over past 10 years (minimum: 500 AB vs. each).... Career averages: .249 with bases empty, .299 with runners on base, .320 with men in scoring position.... Starts 1989 with 84 home runs in 1160 at-bats. Fewest at-bats to reach 100 at start of career: Ralph Kiner, 1351; Jim Gentile, 1419; Harmon Killebrew, 1420; Rocky Colavito, 1432; Eddie Mathews, 1442.... Has hit 50 of his 84 career homers in road games.... Next intentional walk will be 13th of his career, surpassing Bob Uecker's career total. Big difference: McGwire has 1,334 plate appearances; Uke had only 843.

Mark McLemore

California Angels — Bats Left and Right

	AB	H	2B	3B	HR	RBI	BB	SO	BA	SA	OBA
Season	233	56	11	2	2	16	25	28	.240	.330	.312
vs. Left-Handers	65	13	3	0	0	2	6	10	.200	.246	.268
vs. Right-Handers	168	43	8	2	2	14	19	18	.256	.363	.328
Home	102	22	3	1	1	5	12	11	.216	.294	.298
Road	131	34	8	1	1	11	13	17	.260	.359	.322
Grass	200	49	9	1	2	14	22	26	.245	.330	.318
Artificial Turf	33	7	2	1	0	2	3	2	.212	.333	.270
April	93	22	5	2	1	6	13	14	.237	.366	.330
May	74	20	3	0	0	6	8	8	.270	.311	.337
June	0	0	0	0	0	0	0	0	——	——	——
July	0	0	0	0	0	0	0	0	——	——	——
August	26	6	2	0	1	3	1	0	.231	.423	.259
Sept./Oct.	40	8	1	0	0	1	3	6	.200	.225	.250
Leading Off Inn.	78	18	4	2	0	0	9	10	.231	.333	.310
Runners On	87	14	3	0	1	15	8	9	.161	.230	.227
Runners/Scor. Pos.	51	10	2	0	0	13	7	7	.196	.235	.283
Runners On/2 Out	39	5	3	0	0	5	5	5	.128	.205	.227
Scor. Pos./2 Out	23	4	2	0	0	5	4	5	.174	.261	.296
Late Inning Pressure	44	11	2	0	0	3	3	6	.250	.295	.298
Leading Off	14	2	1	0	0	0	2	1	.143	.214	.250
Runners On	19	2	0	0	0	3	0	2	.105	.105	.105
Runners/Scor. Pos.	11	2	0	0	0	3	0	2	.182	.182	.182

RUNS BATTED IN	From 1B	From 2B	From 3B	Scoring Position
Totals	2/57	3/39	9/25	12/64
Percentage	4%	8%	36%	19%
Driving In Runners from 3B with Less than Two Out:			7/16	44%

Loves to face: Jerry Reed (3-for-3, 1 3B)
Hates to face: Frank Tanana (0-for-10)
Batted 88 points higher against fly-ball pitchers (.278) than he did against ground-ballers, 2d-largest difference in the A.L. last season. . . . Successful in eight of his last nine attempts to steal a base, after being thrown out in six of his first 11 tries. . . . Drove in only one run in his last 32 games, although he never came to the plate in seven of those games. . . . Started only 12 games after injuring his elbow in late May. Returned to active roster in mid-August, mostly as a pinch hitter, pinch runner, and defensive replacement. . . . Angels were only 19–29 (.396) in McLemore's starts at second base last season; they were 52–50 (.510) in games that Johnny Ray started there.

Joey Meyer

Milwaukee Brewers — Bats Right

	AB	H	2B	3B	HR	RBI	BB	SO	BA	SA	OBA
Season	327	86	18	0	11	45	23	88	.263	.419	.313
vs. Left-Handers	144	42	10	0	7	18	9	27	.292	.507	.338
vs. Right-Handers	183	44	8	0	4	27	14	61	.240	.361	.293
Home	153	40	11	0	5	21	17	48	.261	.431	.339
Road	174	46	7	0	6	24	6	40	.264	.408	.287
Grass	259	65	12	0	8	35	21	73	.251	.390	.310
Artificial Turf	68	21	6	0	3	10	2	15	.309	.529	.324
April	23	4	1	0	2	2	0	6	.174	.478	.174
May	51	9	4	0	1	4	3	14	.176	.314	.222
June	49	15	2	0	1	6	1	11	.306	.408	.320
July	42	12	2	0	2	7	4	11	.286	.476	.348
August	70	24	6	0	4	17	11	15	.343	.600	.434
Sept./Oct.	92	22	3	0	1	9	4	31	.239	.304	.271
Leading Off Inn.	75	18	4	0	3	3	5	16	.240	.413	.288
Runners On	137	41	5	0	5	39	8	36	.299	.445	.340
Runners/Scor. Pos.	82	22	4	0	3	34	6	26	.268	.427	.322
Runners On/2 Out	56	20	4	0	2	19	2	12	.357	.536	.390
Scor. Pos./2 Out	36	13	3	0	1	16	1	9	.361	.528	.395
Late Inning Pressure	49	11	4	0	2	8	3	18	.224	.429	.264
Leading Off	12	3	2	0	1	1	1	4	.250	.667	.308
Runners On	18	4	1	0	1	7	1	5	.222	.444	.250
Runners/Scor. Pos.	10	3	1	0	1	7	1	3	.300	.700	.333

RUNS BATTED IN	From 1B	From 2B	From 3B	Scoring Position
Totals	5/91	14/68	15/31	29/99
Percentage	5%	21%	48%	29%
Driving In Runners from 3B with Less than Two Out:			8/19	42%

Loves to face: Mike Henneman (2-for-2, 1 2B, 1 HR)
Hates to face: Dan Petry (0-for-4, 4 SO)
Led A.L. rookies in extra-base hits and RBI. . . . Batted .325 vs. ground-ball pitchers, .224 vs. fly-ballers. . . . Started 50 of 56 games in which the Brewers faced a left-handed starter, but only 41 of 106 games vs. right-handers. . . . Had 25 consecutive hitless at-bats with runners in scoring position, longest streak in A.L. . . . Played the most games (103) of any A.L. players who made their major league debuts in 1988. N.L. had three virgins with more games: Roberto Alomar (143), Chris Sabo (137), and Mark Grace (134). . . . Like Sid Fernandez, Meyer was born and raised in Hawaii. Meyer's weight is listed as 260. You know that line about this place ain't big enough for the both of us?

Paul Molitor

Milwaukee Brewers — Bats Right

	AB	H	2B	3B	HR	RBI	BB	SO	BA	SA	OBA
Season	609	190	34	6	13	60	71	54	.312	.452	.384
vs. Left-Handers	196	54	11	0	4	15	23	10	.276	.393	.353
vs. Right-Handers	413	136	23	6	9	45	48	44	.329	.479	.399
Home	316	100	17	2	9	39	35	31	.316	.468	.382
Road	293	90	17	4	4	21	36	23	.307	.433	.386
Grass	513	160	28	3	12	55	63	47	.312	.448	.387
Artificial Turf	96	30	6	3	1	5	8	7	.313	.469	.369
April	78	27	5	0	1	4	10	4	.346	.449	.420
May	111	27	5	0	1	8	13	6	.243	.315	.323
June	88	34	4	1	1	9	11	11	.386	.489	.455
July	116	38	9	3	2	10	4	8	.328	.509	.355
August	118	37	7	1	5	21	17	9	.314	.517	.396
Sept./Oct.	98	27	4	1	3	8	16	16	.276	.429	.377
Leading Off Inn.	257	74	15	3	7	7	28	25	.288	.451	.360
Runners On	185	66	11	1	5	52	28	13	.357	.508	.438
Runners/Scor. Pos.	103	36	5	0	4	48	17	8	.350	.515	.435
Runners On/2 Out	87	22	4	0	2	20	9	3	.253	.299	.330
Scor. Pos./2 Out	60	18	3	0	0	20	7	2	.300	.350	.382
Late Inning Pressure	71	20	3	0	1	9	8	6	.282	.366	.350
Leading Off	14	3	1	0	0	0	4	0	.214	.286	.389
Runners On	36	11	2	0	1	9	4	3	.306	.444	.366
Runners/Scor. Pos.	21	6	1	0	0	7	4	2	.286	.333	.385

RUNS BATTED IN	From 1B	From 2B	From 3B	Scoring Position
Totals	5/125	19/78	23/49	42/127
Percentage	4%	24%	47%	33%
Driving In Runners from 3B with Less than Two Out:			12/19	63%

Loves to face: Jose Guzman (.474, 9-for-19, 1 HR)
Hates to face: Mike Moore (.077, 2-for-26)
Ratio of walks to strikeouts was the highest of his career. By comparison, in 1986 he had 40 walks and 81 strikeouts. . . . Stole 41 bases, four short of his career high, set in 1987 at age 30. Oldest player to set a career high with at least 40 SBs was Nixey Callahan, who stole 45 in 1911 at age 37. . . . Has hit for a higher average against right-handers than he has against southpaws in each of the last three seasons, but career average remains higher against LHP (.310 to .294). . . . Average of .344 vs. RHP over past two seasons is 3d highest in majors (minimum: 300 AB), behind Boggs (.379), Gwynn (.346). . . . Current career batting average is .299. Would have to hit .314 in 500 at-bats to reach .300 mark.

Lloyd Moseby

Toronto Blue Jays — Bats Left

	AB	H	2B	3B	HR	RBI	BB	SO	BA	SA	OBA
Season	472	113	17	7	10	42	70	93	.239	.369	.343
vs. Left-Handers	170	43	8	2	2	14	20	31	.253	.359	.344
vs. Right-Handers	302	70	9	5	8	28	50	62	.232	.374	.343
Home	211	49	8	4	2	13	35	46	.232	.336	.345
Road	261	64	9	3	8	29	35	47	.245	.395	.341
Grass	209	50	4	2	5	18	29	38	.239	.349	.340
Artificial Turf	263	63	13	5	5	24	41	55	.240	.384	.345
April	76	21	2	1	3	7	8	21	.276	.447	.360
May	96	23	3	1	3	12	18	22	.240	.385	.364
June	94	19	3	2	1	8	20	16	.202	.309	.345
July	77	17	5	0	2	8	6	13	.221	.364	.286
August	53	17	3	1	0	3	10	11	.321	.415	.429
Sept./Oct.	76	16	1	2	1	4	8	10	.211	.316	.286
Leading Off Inn.	83	18	0	1	2	2	8	13	.217	.313	.293
Runners On	197	40	9	0	4	36	36	40	.203	.310	.331
Runners/Scor. Pos.	120	26	6	0	3	33	23	23	.217	.342	.345
Runners On/2 Out	81	18	2	0	1	14	13	20	.222	.284	.337
Scor. Pos./2 Out	58	12	2	0	1	14	10	15	.207	.293	.333
Late Inning Pressure	69	16	2	0	1	9	6	17	.232	.304	.293
Leading Off	14	5	0	0	0	0	0	2	.357	.357	.357
Runners On	37	7	1	0	1	9	5	9	.189	.297	.286
Runners/Scor. Pos.	31	6	1	0	1	9	4	8	.194	.323	.286

RUNS BATTED IN	From 1B	From 2B	From 3B	Scoring Position
Totals	4/129	13/95	15/50	28/145
Percentage	3%	14%	30%	19%
Driving In Runners from 3B with Less than Two Out:			9/19	47%

Loves to face: Frank Viola (.383, 18-for-47, 4 HR)
Hates to face: Steve Ontiveros (0-for-13)
Average of 2.57 putouts per nine innings was the lowest of any A.L. center fielder (minimum: 500 innings). . . . Hitless in 10 at-bats with the bases loaded, largest 0-for in A.L. . . . Needed 26 homers in 1988 to become the first player in baseball history to maintain or increase his total for eight consecutive years. . . . A.L. stolen base leaders over the past six seasons: Henderson, 475; Wilson, 277; Pettis, 230; Moseby, 205. . . . RBI totals, year by year since 1985: 70, 86, 96, 42. . . . 1988 totals aren't indicative of his career breakdown with runners on base (.270) and the bases empty (.255). . . . Only player to hit for the cycle against Frank Viola last season, and he did it before the end of April.

John Moses

Minnesota Twins — Bats Left and Right

	AB	H	2B	3B	HR	RBI	BB	SO	BA	SA	OBA
Season	206	65	10	3	2	12	15	21	.316	.422	.366
vs. Left-Handers	9	2	0	1	0	0	1	1	.222	.444	.300
vs. Right-Handers	197	63	10	2	2	12	14	20	.320	.421	.369
Home	85	22	4	3	0	6	8	11	.259	.376	.330
Road	121	43	6	0	2	6	7	10	.355	.455	.392
Grass	101	33	4	0	2	6	6	10	.327	.426	.367
Artificial Turf	105	32	6	3	0	6	9	11	.305	.419	.365
April	6	1	1	0	0	2	3	1	.167	.333	.444
May	24	5	0	1	0	0	2	3	.208	.292	.269
June	47	20	3	1	1	4	1	6	.426	.596	.449
July	38	8	1	0	0	1	3	2	.211	.237	.268
August	50	16	4	0	1	4	2	5	.320	.460	.352
Sept./Oct.	41	15	1	1	0	1	4	4	.366	.439	.422
Leading Off Inn.	75	24	3	2	0	0	2	2	.320	.413	.338
Runners On	69	22	4	1	1	11	8	9	.319	.449	.385
Runners/Scor. Pos.	34	8	1	1	0	8	6	6	.235	.324	.341
Runners On/2 Out	29	9	2	0	1	7	3	3	.310	.483	.375
Scor. Pos./2 Out	18	4	1	0	0	4	2	3	.222	.278	.300
Late Inning Pressure	30	10	0	0	1	2	0	4	.333	.433	.355
Leading Off	7	3	0	0	0	0	0	0	.429	.429	.429
Runners On	11	4	0	0	0	1	0	3	.364	.364	.364
Runners/Scor. Pos.	7	3	0	0	0	1	0	3	.429	.429	.429

RUNS BATTED IN	From 1B	From 2B	From 3B	Scoring Position
Totals	2/51	4/28	4/13	8/41
Percentage	4%	14%	31%	20%
Driving In Runners from 3B with Less than Two Out:	2/4			50%

Loves to face: Scott Bailes (.750, 3-for-4, 1 HR)
Hates to face: Dan Petry (0-for-10)

Career average of .271 on grass fields, .252 on artificial surfaces. Bad news, what with his playing every home game of his career under a dome. . . . Started 42 games last season, all against right-handed pitchers. Started 34 games vs. lefties for the Mariners in 1987. . . . Twins' leadoff batter of choice when Dan Gladden wasn't in the lineup. Moses made 25 starts in the one hole. . . . Five hits in 12 career at-bats with the bases loaded. . . . Has batted higher with runners on base than with the bases empty in each of his last five seasons. Career averages: .282 with runners on, .246 otherwise.

Rance Mulliniks

Toronto Blue Jays — Bats Left

	AB	H	2B	3B	HR	RBI	BB	SO	BA	SA	OBA
Season	337	101	21	1	12	48	56	57	.300	.475	.395
vs. Left-Handers	15	4	1	0	1	3	3	4	.267	.533	.389
vs. Right-Handers	322	97	20	1	11	45	53	53	.301	.472	.396
Home	165	50	13	1	7	30	23	31	.303	.521	.382
Road	172	51	8	0	5	18	33	26	.297	.430	.408
Grass	134	42	6	0	4	14	25	20	.313	.448	.419
Artificial Turf	203	59	15	1	8	34	31	37	.291	.493	.380
April	15	2	1	0	0	0	0	2	.133	.200	.133
May	68	23	2	0	5	12	10	13	.338	.588	.423
June	73	26	6	1	1	10	10	6	.356	.507	.429
July	69	20	2	0	3	10	9	8	.290	.449	.372
August	54	13	4	0	2	5	13	13	.241	.426	.388
Sept./Oct.	58	17	6	0	1	11	14	15	.293	.448	.413
Leading Off Inn.	74	20	3	1	2	2	8	10	.270	.419	.341
Runners On	135	40	7	0	5	41	34	27	.296	.459	.428
Runners/Scor. Pos.	82	19	3	0	2	32	23	19	.232	.341	.385
Runners On/2 Out	44	10	4	0	0	10	14	11	.227	.318	.414
Scor. Pos./2 Out	31	7	2	0	0	8	10	8	.226	.290	.415
Late Inning Pressure	33	14	3	0	1	5	4	3	.424	.606	.474
Leading Off	11	5	0	0	1	1	0	2	.455	.727	.455
Runners On	12	4	2	0	0	4	4	1	.333	.500	.471
Runners/Scor. Pos.	7	2	1	0	0	3	2	0	.286	.429	.400

RUNS BATTED IN	From 1B	From 2B	From 3B	Scoring Position
Totals	7/84	12/68	17/35	29/103
Percentage	8%	18%	49%	28%
Driving In Runners from 3B with Less than Two Out:	12/22			55%

Loves to face: Keith Atherton (.429, 6-for-14, 1 HR)
Hates to face: Steve Ontiveros (0-for-11)

Actual batting average: .2997 (see comments under Gerald Perry in N.L. Batters Section). . . . Started five games at third base during the first week of season, only once thereafter. . . . Started 98 games, all against right-handers. . . . Had 51 at-bats vs. left-handers in his rookie season (1977), but has never faced them more than 35 times in any season since then. . . . Career batting averages: .231 vs. left-handers (one home run per 59 at-bats); .281 vs. right-handers (one HR per 44 AB). . . . Has batted over .300 vs. ground-ball pitchers in five of last six seasons. . . . Batting average with runners in scoring position, year by year since 1985: .381, .310, .284, .232.

Eddie Murray

Baltimore Orioles — Bats Left and Right

	AB	H	2B	3B	HR	RBI	BB	SO	BA	SA	OBA
Season	603	171	27	2	28	84	75	78	.284	.474	.361
vs. Left-Handers	213	49	9	0	7	24	18	32	.230	.371	.288
vs. Right-Handers	390	122	18	2	21	60	57	46	.313	.531	.400
Home	297	84	9	1	14	39	41	48	.283	.461	.368
Road	306	87	18	1	14	45	34	30	.284	.487	.355
Grass	505	146	22	1	25	71	69	66	.289	.485	.373
Artificial Turf	98	25	5	1	3	13	6	12	.255	.418	.298
April	92	19	5	0	2	8	4	11	.207	.326	.240
May	103	28	2	0	2	9	13	10	.272	.350	.353
June	96	26	6	0	7	17	20	15	.271	.552	.397
July	98	26	1	0	7	16	13	15	.265	.490	.351
August	109	41	6	2	7	20	15	11	.376	.661	.448
Sept./Oct.	105	31	7	0	3	14	10	16	.295	.448	.350
Leading Off Inn.	164	47	4	0	5	5	12	22	.287	.402	.335
Runners On	276	77	15	1	15	71	39	31	.279	.504	.365
Runners/Scor. Pos.	128	30	6	0	7	48	22	18	.234	.445	.340
Runners On/2 Out	126	36	7	1	8	35	22	17	.286	.548	.392
Scor. Pos./2 Out	58	12	2	0	3	19	12	10	.207	.397	.343
Late Inning Pressure	96	22	5	1	2	9	11	20	.229	.365	.308
Leading Off	22	4	1	0	0	0	1	2	.182	.227	.217
Runners On	47	14	4	1	1	8	4	10	.298	.489	.353
Runners/Scor. Pos.	20	5	2	0	0	5	3	4	.250	.350	.348

RUNS BATTED IN	From 1B	From 2B	From 3B	Scoring Position
Totals	19/220	22/104	15/43	37/147
Percentage	9%	21%	35%	25%
Driving In Runners from 3B with Less than Two Out:	9/23			39%

Loves to face: Jose DeLeon (.444, 4-for-9, 3 HR)
Hates to face: Bob Ojeda (.182, 6-for-33, 1 HR)

Batted .320 after the All-Star break, 5th-highest in A.L. . . . Lowest fielding percentage (.989) of any A.L. first baseman (minimum: 100 games). But he was the only A.L. first baseman to average more than one assist (1.07) per nine innings. . . . Has played 602 games since the last time he was hit by a pitch. . . . Has two hits in 17 at-bats with the bases loaded over the past two years, after hitting .400+ with the bags full for seven straight seasons (1980–86). . . . Batting average vs. left-handers was the lowest of his career. Has hit better from left side of plate than from right side in each of last six seasons. . . . Ends his Baltimore career with 1820 games, third in team history, behind Brooks Robinson and Mark Belanger.

Al Newman

Minnesota Twins — Bats Left and Right

	AB	H	2B	3B	HR	RBI	BB	SO	BA	SA	OBA
Season	260	58	7	0	0	19	29	34	.223	.250	.301
vs. Left-Handers	69	12	1	0	0	6	8	9	.174	.188	.260
vs. Right-Handers	191	46	6	0	0	13	21	25	.241	.272	.316
Home	128	30	4	0	0	9	16	14	.234	.266	.319
Road	132	28	3	0	0	10	13	20	.212	.235	.283
Grass	109	23	3	0	0	8	13	17	.211	.239	.295
Artificial Turf	151	35	4	0	0	11	16	17	.232	.258	.305
April	19	4	0	0	0	1	2	2	.211	.211	.286
May	16	2	0	0	0	2	1	1	.125	.125	.176
June	22	6	0	0	0	0	2	4	.273	.273	.333
July	44	13	2	0	0	5	6	5	.295	.341	.380
August	66	18	2	0	0	5	5	8	.273	.303	.324
Sept./Oct.	93	15	3	0	0	6	13	14	.161	.194	.264
Leading Off Inn.	67	14	1	0	0	0	11	9	.209	.224	.321
Runners On	99	24	2	0	0	19	9	10	.242	.263	.306
Runners/Scor. Pos.	66	15	2	0	0	19	6	9	.227	.258	.292
Runners On/2 Out	59	15	1	0	0	14	3	7	.254	.271	.290
Scor. Pos./2 Out	42	10	1	0	0	14	3	6	.238	.262	.289
Late Inning Pressure	27	7	1	0	0	1	2	4	.259	.296	.310
Leading Off	11	2	0	0	0	0	2	3	.182	.182	.308
Runners On	5	1	1	0	0	1	0	0	.200	.400	.200
Runners/Scor. Pos.	1	1	1	0	0	1	0	0	1.000	2.000	1.000

RUNS BATTED IN	From 1B	From 2B	From 3B	Scoring Position
Totals	1/64	9/50	9/33	18/83
Percentage	2%	18%	27%	22%
Driving In Runners from 3B with Less than Two Out:	3/9			33%

Loves to face: Curt Young (.571, 4-for-7)
Hates to face: Mark Gubicza (0-for-13)

Slugging percentage was lowest of any A.L. player with at least 200 at-bats. . . . Started only three games at the hot corner prior to his 45 starts there in 1988, including 41 of Twins' last 45 games. . . . Twins allowed 3.70 runs per nine innings with Newman at third, 4.47 with Gaetti there. . . . Batted over .200 vs. right-handers for the first time in his career, under .200 vs. lefties for first time. . . . One home run in 781 career at-bats, lowest rate among active A.L. batters with 750+ at-bats. . . . One hit in 28 career at-bats in Chicago: 1-for-7 at Wrigley, 0-for-21 at Comiskey. . . . Lenn Sakata knows how he feels. He had three hits in 52 at-bats at Comiskey, including none in his first 30 AB.

Matt Nokes

Detroit Tigers — Bats Left

	AB	H	2B	3B	HR	RBI	BB	SO	BA	SA	OBA
Season	382	96	18	0	16	53	34	58	.251	.424	.313
vs. Left-Handers	38	10	3	0	2	4	1	5	.263	.500	.300
vs. Right-Handers	344	86	15	0	14	49	33	53	.250	.416	.314
Home	196	49	5	0	9	29	14	33	.250	.413	.302
Road	186	47	13	0	7	24	20	25	.253	.435	.324
Grass	329	84	14	0	15	51	25	51	.255	.435	.308
Artificial Turf	53	12	4	0	1	2	9	7	.226	.358	.339
April	57	13	0	0	5	11	4	8	.228	.491	.279
May	56	12	1	0	2	7	4	11	.214	.339	.267
June	70	18	5	0	2	9	4	15	.257	.414	.297
July	66	14	2	0	2	10	9	11	.212	.333	.316
August	59	18	4	0	4	10	9	7	.305	.576	.386
Sept./Oct.	74	21	6	0	1	6	4	6	.284	.405	.321
Leading Off Inn.	85	20	4	0	5	5	6	15	.235	.459	.286
Runners On	175	46	7	0	6	43	20	27	.263	.406	.338
Runners/Scor. Pos.	96	28	3	0	3	34	13	16	.292	.417	.375
Runners On/2 Out	72	19	3	0	2	17	8	10	.264	.389	.338
Scor. Pos./2 Out	42	14	1	0	1	14	5	6	.333	.429	.404
Late Inning Pressure	53	14	2	0	3	8	4	8	.264	.472	.310
Leading Off	13	3	0	0	1	1	3	3	.231	.462	.286
Runners On	20	5	0	0	1	6	2	3	.250	.400	.304
Runners/Scor. Pos.	9	3	0	0	0	4	1	2	.333	.333	.364

RUNS BATTED IN	From 1B	From 2B	From 3B	Scoring Position
Totals	9/134	17/77	11/33	28/110
Percentage	7%	22%	33%	25%
Driving In Runners from 3B with Less than Two Out:			7/16	44%

Loves to face: Steve Ellsworth (.600, 3-for-5, 3 HR)
Hates to face: Bob Welch (0-for-11)
Tigers pitchers allowed 3.91 runs per nine innings with Nokes catching, 4.41 with Heath. . . . Hit 10 of his 16 home runs against two teams: six vs. Boston, four vs. Seattle. . . . Had eight walks and 30 strikeouts through games of June 19, but 26 BBs, 28 SOs thereafter. . . . Started 100 of 107 games in which the Tigers faced a right-handed starter, but only two of 55 games vs. left-handers. Career totals with Detroit: 216 starts vs. right-handers, six vs. southpaws. . . . Career average is .217 with six HRs vs. left-handers, .278 with 45 HRs vs. right-handers. . . . Career batting averages: .283 on grass fields, .188 on artificial turf. . . . Career average of .414 (12-for-29, 6 HR) at Anaheim Stadium.

Pete O'Brien

Texas Rangers — Bats Left

	AB	H	2B	3B	HR	RBI	BB	SO	BA	SA	OBA
Season	547	149	24	1	16	71	72	73	.272	.408	.352
vs. Left-Handers	163	41	5	1	3	22	13	32	.252	.350	.305
vs. Right-Handers	384	108	19	0	13	49	59	41	.281	.432	.371
Home	266	76	11	1	6	37	39	37	.286	.402	.370
Road	281	73	13	0	10	34	33	36	.260	.413	.335
Grass	453	128	19	1	13	62	63	58	.283	.415	.365
Artificial Turf	94	21	5	0	3	9	9	15	.223	.372	.291
April	71	31	3	0	5	8	11	7	.437	.690	.512
May	98	18	1	1	2	10	10	17	.184	.276	.257
June	96	27	6	0	1	11	14	10	.281	.375	.366
July	95	29	8	0	2	12	7	10	.305	.453	.343
August	101	28	4	0	3	19	14	15	.277	.406	.365
Sept./Oct.	86	16	2	0	3	11	16	14	.186	.314	.308
Leading Off Inn.	137	42	6	0	3	3	11	17	.307	.416	.358
Runners On	223	59	11	1	5	60	38	26	.265	.390	.361
Runners/Scor. Pos.	131	34	6	1	2	51	31	18	.260	.366	.382
Runners On/2 Out	90	27	4	1	2	22	17	11	.300	.433	.411
Scor. Pos./2 Out	65	16	2	1	1	18	16	9	.246	.354	.395
Late Inning Pressure	91	24	4	0	7	12	12	17	.264	.538	.350
Leading Off	22	9	3	0	2	2	3	4	.409	.818	.480
Runners On	38	8	0	0	3	8	7	6	.211	.447	.333
Runners/Scor. Pos.	19	1	0	0	1	4	6	6	.053	.211	.280

RUNS BATTED IN	From 1B	From 2B	From 3B	Scoring Position
Totals	7/168	20/98	28/58	48/156
Percentage	4%	20%	48%	31%
Driving In Runners from 3B with Less than Two Out:			22/35	63%

Loves to face: Roger Clemens (.500, 12-for-24)
Hates to face: Willie Hernandez (0-for-18)
Hit two home runs on opening day, but trailed George Bell for the league lead. . . . April batting average was 2d highest in the majors. Was batting .500 (18-for-36) after hitting safely in his first 10 games. . . . Stop him before he tries to steal again. Career totals: 19 stolen bases, 31 times caught stealing. . . . Career totals: 304 BBs, 201 SOs vs. right-handers; 100 BBs, 162 SOs vs. left-handers. . . . Has driven in only 19 percent of runners in Late-Inning Pressure Situations for his career compared to 34 percent in unpressured at-bats. . . . Career batting average of .234 in September. . . . Only three other A.L. players have played at least 155 games in each of the last four seasons: George Bell, Kirby Puckett, and Cal Ripken.

Joe Orsulak

Baltimore Orioles — Bats Left

	AB	H	2B	3B	HR	RBI	BB	SO	BA	SA	OBA
Season	379	109	21	3	8	27	23	30	.288	.422	.331
vs. Left-Handers	68	16	0	0	0	3	7	7	.235	.235	.321
vs. Right-Handers	311	93	21	3	8	24	16	23	.299	.463	.333
Home	174	50	10	1	3	12	10	9	.287	.408	.326
Road	205	59	11	2	5	15	13	21	.288	.434	.335
Grass	320	92	18	2	6	19	20	22	.288	.413	.328
Artificial Turf	59	17	3	1	2	8	3	8	.288	.475	.344
April	62	15	2	0	0	2	4	5	.242	.274	.299
May	36	12	2	0	0	2	4	1	.333	.389	.415
June	72	19	4	0	0	1	3	6	.264	.319	.293
July	45	15	2	1	1	4	2	4	.333	.489	.347
August	92	30	7	2	4	10	6	5	.326	.576	.364
Sept./Oct.	72	18	4	0	3	8	4	9	.250	.431	.299
Leading Off Inn.	147	47	14	1	4	4	8	15	.320	.510	.359
Runners On	115	29	4	1	2	21	7	7	.252	.357	.299
Runners/Scor. Pos.	61	15	2	1	2	20	5	5	.246	.410	.310
Runners On/2 Out	62	13	1	1	2	10	4	4	.210	.355	.269
Scor. Pos./2 Out	37	9	1	1	2	10	3	2	.243	.486	.317
Late Inning Pressure	64	18	4	1	0	4	5	4	.281	.375	.329
Leading Off	15	6	3	0	0	0	4	1	.400	.600	.526
Runners On	23	4	0	0	0	4	1	2	.174	.174	.200
Runners/Scor. Pos.	13	3	0	0	0	4	1	1	.231	.231	.267

RUNS BATTED IN	From 1B	From 2B	From 3B	Scoring Position
Totals	2/91	4/51	13/26	17/77
Percentage	2%	8%	50%	22%
Driving In Runners from 3B with Less than Two Out:			9/11	82%

Loves to face: Mike Moore (.667, 4-for-6, 2 HR)
Hates to face: Charles Hudson (.167, 4-for-24)
Committed five errors (all on the road) in 49 games in right field, none in 38 games in left and center field. . . . Stole nine bases in 17 attempts in 1988; was 48-for-70 over his previous two seasons. . . . Started 26 games after August 15, all in the leadoff spot. . . . Things to leave off the resume: .300 career batting average with bases empty; .224 with runners on base; .211 with runners in scoring position; .203 with two outs and RISP. . . . Batting average with RISP has been lower than his overall average in each of his five seasons in the majors. . . . Has hit 10 home runs in his career, but none in 198 at-bats vs. left-handers, and none in 214 at-bats in Late-Inning Pressure Situations.

Spike Owen

Boston Red Sox — Bats Left and Right

	AB	H	2B	3B	HR	RBI	BB	SO	BA	SA	OBA
Season	257	64	14	1	5	18	27	27	.249	.370	.324
vs. Left-Handers	98	27	6	1	4	8	7	12	.276	.480	.324
vs. Right-Handers	159	37	8	0	1	10	20	15	.233	.302	.324
Home	104	29	9	0	2	7	10	8	.279	.423	.348
Road	153	35	5	1	3	11	17	19	.229	.333	.308
Grass	213	52	14	1	3	16	23	21	.244	.362	.319
Artificial Turf	44	12	0	0	2	2	4	6	.273	.409	.347
April	48	7	2	0	2	3	10	4	.146	.313	.293
May	31	9	1	0	1	5	3	2	.290	.419	.343
June	88	26	8	0	2	5	6	6	.295	.455	.347
July	33	8	0	1	0	0	5	6	.242	.303	.359
August	38	10	2	0	0	3	3	7	.263	.316	.317
Sept./Oct.	19	4	1	0	0	2	0	2	.211	.263	.211
Leading Off Inn.	60	15	3	0	2	2	7	6	.250	.400	.328
Runners On	97	21	7	0	1	14	15	11	.216	.320	.330
Runners/Scor. Pos.	57	9	4	0	0	12	8	6	.158	.228	.269
Runners On/2 Out	36	3	1	0	0	0	5	3	.083	.111	.233
Scor. Pos./2 Out	27	0	0	0	0	0	4	3	.000	.000	.156
Late Inning Pressure	36	8	1	0	1	3	5	6	.222	.333	.317
Leading Off	8	2	1	0	0	0	2	1	.250	.375	.400
Runners On	9	1	0	0	0	2	1	2	.111	.111	.200
Runners/Scor. Pos.	3	1	0	0	0	2	0	0	.333	.333	.333

RUNS BATTED IN	From 1B	From 2B	From 3B	Scoring Position
Totals	2/76	4/43	7/24	11/67
Percentage	3%	9%	29%	16%
Driving In Runners from 3B with Less than Two Out:			7/14	50%

Loves to face: Jim Gott (.429, 3-for-7)
Hates to face: Tim Leary (0-for-14)
Started 57 of 85 games under John McNamara, but only 14 of 77 under Joe Morgan. . . . Five home runs in his first 125 at-bats left him one shy of his career high, but he went 0-for-132 thereafter. . . . His 0-for-27 with two outs and runners in scoring position was the worst in the past 14 years. . . . Career average of .262 before the All-Star break, .218 after the break. . . . Batting average in Late-Inning Pressure Situations has been lower than his overall average in each of his six seasons in the majors. . . . Has hit for a higher average vs. fly-ball pitchers than he has against ground-ballers in each of the last four seasons. . . . Has never played a position other than shortstop in the majors.

Mike Pagliarulo

New York Yankees — Bats Left

	AB	H	2B	3B	HR	RBI	BB	SO	BA	SA	OBA
Season	444	96	20	1	15	67	37	104	.216	.367	.276
vs. Left-Handers	106	18	3	1	5	20	6	31	.170	.358	.224
vs. Right-Handers	338	78	17	0	10	47	31	73	.231	.370	.292
Home	203	39	7	1	8	34	16	50	.192	.355	.250
Road	241	57	13	0	7	33	21	54	.237	.378	.298
Grass	364	76	13	1	13	57	31	84	.209	.357	.270
Artificial Turf	80	20	7	0	2	10	6	20	.250	.413	.303
April	83	19	4	1	6	24	11	27	.229	.518	.323
May	95	21	5	0	2	13	7	22	.221	.337	.267
June	99	21	5	0	1	11	5	21	.212	.293	.250
July	34	9	2	0	0	5	4	5	.265	.324	.342
August	65	14	2	0	2	4	5	14	.215	.338	.271
Sept./Oct.	68	12	2	0	4	10	5	15	.176	.382	.233
Leading Off Inn.	93	12	3	0	0	0	3	25	.129	.161	.156
Runners On	218	60	9	0	11	63	24	46	.275	.468	.341
Runners/Scor. Pos.	136	36	6	0	7	54	18	30	.265	.463	.342
Runners On/2 Out	88	20	3	0	2	19	12	19	.227	.330	.320
Scor. Pos./2 Out	66	14	3	0	1	17	10	15	.212	.303	.316
Late Inning Pressure	61	11	1	0	0	3	6	14	.180	.197	.254
Leading Off	17	3	1	0	0	0	1	4	.176	.235	.222
Runners On	25	8	0	0	0	3	5	4	.320	.320	.433
Runners/Scor. Pos.	13	4	0	0	0	3	2	2	.308	.308	.400

RUNS BATTED IN	From 1B	From 2B	From 3B	Scoring Position
Totals	8/149	26/115	18/43	44/158
Percentage	5%	23%	42%	28%
Driving In Runners from 3B with Less than Two Out:		15/25		60%

Loves to face: Bret Saberhagen (.333, 7-for-21, 4 HR)
Hates to face: Dan Plesac (0-for-8, 5 SO)
One hit in 26 at-bats as a pinch hitter (including 0-for-his-last 18), since his pinch HR in 1985 season finale.... Time for the white flag: his career batting average vs. left-handers has dipped to .199.... Career average of .298 (14-for-47, four HR) with the bases loaded. ... On-base average leading off innings was the 2d lowest in the past 14 years (minimum: 75 PA). He can thank Doug Flynn for his .136 mark in 1977.... Career batting average of .187 in September.... Has already played more games (615) at third base for Yankees than all but seven others: Graig Nettles (1509), Red Rolfe (1084), Clete Boyer (909), Joe Dugan (774), Billy Johnson (673), Andy Carey (656), and Home Run Baker (652).

Dave Parker

Oakland As — Bats Left

	AB	H	2B	3B	HR	RBI	BB	SO	BA	SA	OBA
Season	377	97	18	1	12	55	32	70	.257	.406	.314
vs. Left-Handers	55	10	1	0	2	5	7	14	.182	.309	.274
vs. Right-Handers	322	87	17	1	10	50	25	56	.270	.422	.321
Home	177	48	6	0	6	23	14	36	.271	.407	.325
Road	200	49	12	1	6	32	18	34	.245	.405	.305
Grass	304	80	13	1	11	44	27	58	.263	.421	.321
Artificial Turf	73	17	5	0	1	11	5	12	.233	.342	.282
April	89	23	2	1	2	13	8	22	.258	.371	.320
May	82	26	6	0	4	14	6	17	.317	.537	.364
June	92	21	6	0	3	10	7	16	.228	.391	.280
July	5	0	0	0	0	0	1	1	.000	.000	.167
August	30	7	0	0	0	2	6	4	.233	.233	.351
Sept./Oct.	79	20	4	0	3	16	4	10	.253	.418	.289
Leading Off Inn.	72	18	4	1	1	1	7	10	.250	.375	.316
Runners On	186	54	10	0	9	52	16	32	.290	.489	.343
Runners/Scor. Pos.	112	27	5	0	4	39	11	21	.241	.393	.304
Runners On/2 Out	83	18	4	0	3	15	6	11	.217	.373	.270
Scor. Pos./2 Out	50	10	2	0	2	12	4	6	.200	.360	.259
Late Inning Pressure	56	15	5	0	1	3	3	8	.268	.411	.305
Leading Off	12	3	3	0	0	0	1	2	.250	.500	.308
Runners On	27	8	1	0	0	2	3	3	.296	.333	.345
Runners/Scor. Pos.	15	3	0	0	0	2	1	2	.200	.200	.250

RUNS BATTED IN	From 1B	From 2B	From 3B	Scoring Position
Totals	11/127	16/86	16/42	32/128
Percentage	9%	19%	38%	25%
Driving In Runners from 3B with Less than Two Out:		13/21		62%

Loves to face: Steve Shields (.467, 7-for-15, 3 HR)
Hates to face: Dennis Powell (0-for-10)
Homered in three consecutive games (June 19–21), which he hadn't done since 1986.... Had an extra-base hit in six consecutive games (May 14–20), tied for longest streak in A.L.... Grounded into only three DPs in 80 opportunities, 4th-lowest rate in A.L. (min: 40 opp.).... Played in the field only three times after the All-Star break, but started fourth game of A.L.C.S. in left field. Against a left-hander, no less!... Batting average vs. left-handers, year by year since 1986: .302, .239, .182.... Batted higher with runners on base than with the bases empty for the sixth straight season. But his batting average with runners in scoring position was his lowest in the past 14 years.

Larry Parrish

Rangers/Red Sox — Bats Right

	AB	H	2B	3B	HR	RBI	BB	SO	BA	SA	OBA
Season	406	88	14	1	14	52	28	111	.217	.360	.270
vs. Left-Handers	126	28	4	0	3	13	7	35	.222	.325	.272
vs. Right-Handers	280	60	10	1	11	39	21	76	.214	.375	.269
Home	235	58	11	1	7	33	13	62	.247	.391	.286
Road	171	30	3	0	7	19	15	49	.175	.316	.249
Grass	361	80	12	1	12	47	27	97	.222	.360	.275
Artificial Turf	45	8	2	0	2	5	1	14	.178	.356	.229
April	52	6	0	0	1	3	4	19	.115	.173	.193
May	88	23	6	0	4	14	4	29	.261	.466	.295
June	81	11	1	1	2	9	10	22	.136	.247	.228
July	67	18	3	0	2	9	3	18	.269	.403	.296
August	35	10	1	0	0	3	5	8	.286	.314	.375
Sept./Oct.	83	20	3	0	5	14	2	15	.241	.458	.267
Leading Off Inn.	85	18	2	0	5	5	5	23	.212	.412	.264
Runners On	182	41	6	1	4	42	13	41	.225	.335	.279
Runners/Scor. Pos.	108	28	4	1	2	38	7	24	.259	.370	.306
Runners On/2 Out	91	21	3	0	3	24	7	23	.231	.363	.300
Scor. Pos./2 Out	61	15	3	0	1	20	4	15	.246	.344	.313
Late Inning Pressure	60	12	0	0	2	6	4	14	.200	.300	.250
Leading Off	15	5	0	0	2	2	1	4	.333	.733	.375
Runners On	29	4	0	0	0	4	3	6	.138	.138	.219
Runners/Scor. Pos.	18	3	0	0	0	4	0	3	.167	.167	.167

RUNS BATTED IN	From 1B	From 2B	From 3B	Scoring Position
Totals	5/129	17/77	16/56	33/133
Percentage	4%	22%	29%	25%
Driving In Runners from 3B with Less than Two Out:		9/22		41%

Loves to face: Dave Stieb (.485, 16-for-33, 3 HR)
Hates to face: Charles Hudson (0-for-10, 6 SO)
Batted .190 in 68 games with the Rangers, .259 in 52 games with the Red Sox.... Had never played a game at first base before finding himself starting there in his Red Sox debut.... Batted higher with runners on base than with the bases empty for the sixth straight season.... Batting average with runners in scoring position, year by year since 1986: .393, .356, .259.... Pinch-hit against Eckersley in each of the first three games of A.L.C.S., came up empty each time.... Parrish has played 1891 regular-season games, 3d most among active players who have never been in a World Series. Buddy Bell (2371) and Chris Speier (2232) top that list, with Brian Downing (1876) and Andre Dawson (1753) close behind.

Dan Pasqua

Chicago White Sox — Bats Left

	AB	H	2B	3B	HR	RBI	BB	SO	BA	SA	OBA
Season	422	96	16	2	20	50	46	100	.227	.417	.307
vs. Left-Handers	81	10	3	0	0	6	7	24	.123	.160	.217
vs. Right-Handers	341	86	13	2	20	44	39	76	.252	.478	.328
Home	213	48	7	2	11	28	22	57	.225	.432	.297
Road	209	48	9	0	9	22	24	43	.230	.402	.316
Grass	357	80	14	2	15	41	41	88	.224	.401	.306
Artificial Turf	65	16	2	0	5	9	5	12	.246	.508	.310
April	63	14	2	0	2	9	8	21	.222	.349	.310
May	73	16	4	1	2	4	6	14	.219	.384	.284
June	59	20	4	0	4	11	4	13	.339	.610	.391
July	81	17	3	0	5	13	11	21	.210	.432	.301
August	87	14	3	0	3	5	9	18	.161	.299	.247
Sept./Oct.	59	15	0	1	4	8	8	13	.254	.492	.343
Leading Off Inn.	99	23	7	2	4	4	6	21	.232	.465	.283
Runners On	196	38	5	0	6	36	30	54	.194	.311	.301
Runners/Scor. Pos.	118	22	4	0	3	30	22	40	.186	.297	.315
Runners On/2 Out	92	15	1	0	3	15	15	32	.163	.272	.280
Scor. Pos./2 Out	58	11	1	0	2	13	12	24	.190	.310	.329
Late Inning Pressure	74	14	2	0	3	10	9	17	.189	.338	.286
Leading Off	11	3	0	0	0	0	2	2	.273	.273	.333
Runners On	42	7	1	0	2	9	6	9	.167	.333	.271
Runners/Scor. Pos.	28	3	1	0	0	5	3	8	.107	.143	.194

RUNS BATTED IN	From 1B	From 2B	From 3B	Scoring Position
Totals	5/140	8/82	17/48	25/130
Percentage	4%	10%	35%	19%
Driving In Runners from 3B with Less than Two Out:		12/29		41%

Loves to face: Bill Wegman (.462, 6-for-13, 3 HR)
Hates to face: Kirk McCaskill (0-for-6, 4 SO)
Led A.L. outfielders with a .996 fielding percentage, and earned it by leading major league left fielders with an average of 2.47 putouts per nine innings.... August batting average was 2d lowest in A.L. (minimum: two PA per game).... Batted .313 with 10 home runs in 112 at-bats in day games; .197, 10 HRs in 310 AB at night.... Started 99 of 110 games in which the White Sox faced a right-handed starter, but only 13 of 51 games against left-handers.... Batting average vs. left-handed pitchers, year by year since 1985: .133, .216, .164, .123. Three HRs in 202 career AB vs. southpaws. ... Career average of .160 (13-for-81) with runners on base in Late-Inning Pressure Situations.

Bill Pecota

Kansas City Royals   Bats Right

	AB	H	2B	3B	HR	RBI	BB	SO	BA	SA	OBA
Season	178	37	3	3	1	15	18	34	.208	.275	.286
vs. Left-Handers	71	17	0	0	0	3	5	11	.239	.239	.308
vs. Right-Handers	107	20	3	3	1	12	13	23	.187	.299	.273
Home	62	14	1	3	0	10	6	14	.226	.339	.300
Road	116	23	2	0	1	5	12	20	.198	.241	.279
Grass	85	16	1	0	1	4	10	16	.188	.235	.281
Artificial Turf	93	21	2	3	0	11	8	18	.226	.312	.291
April	3	0	0	0	0	0	0	1	.000	.000	.000
May	19	3	0	0	1	3	2	3	.158	.316	.238
June	13	3	0	0	0	1	0	1	.231	.231	.231
July	30	4	1	1	0	1	0	9	.133	.233	.133
August	42	11	0	1	0	6	5	5	.262	.310	.333
Sept./Oct.	71	16	2	1	0	4	11	15	.225	.282	.345
Leading Off Inn.	33	7	1	0	1	1	2	7	.212	.333	.278
Runners On	74	19	1	3	0	14	8	15	.257	.351	.333
Runners/Scor. Pos.	45	11	0	2	0	12	8	10	.244	.333	.364
Runners On/2 Out	31	6	0	2	0	5	6	6	.194	.323	.324
Scor. Pos./2 Out	17	3	0	1	0	4	6	4	.176	.294	.391
Late Inning Pressure	19	3	0	0	0	1	1	4	.158	.158	.200
Leading Off	6	0	0	0	0	0	0	2	.000	.000	.000
Runners On	4	1	0	0	0	1	0	1	.250	.250	.250
Runners/Scor. Pos.	2	0	0	0	0	1	0	1	.000	.000	.000

RUNS BATTED IN	From 1B	From 2B	From 3B	Scoring Position
Totals	2/45	5/35	7/23	12/58
Percentage	4%	14%	30%	21%
Driving In Runners from 3B with Less than Two Out:		5/13		38%

Loves to face: Mike Smithson (.500, 3-for-6, 1 HR)
Hates to face: Jerry Reuss (0-for-5)
Removed in favor of a pinch hitter 21 times, most of any player on the club.... His revenge: Used as a pinch runner 19 times, 4th most of any major leaguer. The top three: Mark Davidson, 23; Mike Felder, 20; Jim Walewander, 20.... Played every position except center field and pitcher. Played five different positions in six games (July 24–Aug. 7).... Didn't drive in a run in 16 games after Sept. 10.... Has failed to reach base safely in all 11 career plate appearances leading off innings in Late-Inning Pressure Situations.... Averaged 35 stolen bases a year in his four full seasons in the minors, but has stolen only 12 bases in 168 major league games.

Geno Petralli

Texas Rangers   Bats Left

	AB	H	2B	3B	HR	RBI	BB	SO	BA	SA	OBA
Season	351	99	14	2	7	36	41	52	.282	.393	.356
vs. Left-Handers	44	8	1	0	0	3	4	7	.182	.205	.245
vs. Right-Handers	307	91	13	2	7	33	37	45	.296	.420	.371
Home	169	46	5	2	1	15	25	26	.272	.343	.371
Road	182	53	9	0	6	21	16	26	.291	.440	.342
Grass	284	78	10	2	6	28	37	41	.275	.387	.359
Artificial Turf	67	21	4	0	1	8	4	11	.313	.418	.342
April	35	8	2	0	1	1	0	5	.229	.371	.229
May	44	14	3	0	0	7	7	4	.318	.386	.412
June	53	14	1	1	2	6	12	12	.264	.434	.403
July	69	25	1	0	2	5	8	13	.362	.464	.429
August	76	26	6	0	1	12	3	11	.342	.461	.358
Sept./Oct.	74	12	1	1	1	5	11	7	.162	.243	.273
Leading Off Inn.	76	23	4	0	2	2	8	11	.303	.434	.369
Runners On	158	37	8	1	1	30	22	24	.234	.316	.323
Runners/Scor. Pos.	89	21	6	1	1	29	15	14	.236	.360	.336
Runners On/2 Out	65	14	3	1	1	13	8	9	.215	.338	.311
Scor. Pos./2 Out	49	11	2	1	1	13	6	7	.224	.367	.321
Late Inning Pressure	58	15	3	0	1	3	8	17	.259	.362	.348
Leading Off	10	3	1	0	0	0	3	3	.300	.400	.462
Runners On	29	5	1	0	1	3	4	9	.172	.310	.273
Runners/Scor. Pos.	20	3	1	0	1	3	3	7	.150	.350	.261

RUNS BATTED IN	From 1B	From 2B	From 3B	Scoring Position
Totals	3/113	13/70	13/39	26/109
Percentage	3%	19%	33%	24%
Driving In Runners from 3B with Less than Two Out:		10/18		56%

Loves to face: Juan Berenguer (.429, 3-for-7, 1 HR)
Hates to face: Dave Stewart (0-for-12)
Batting average was at .300 as late as Sept. 15.... Career-high eight-game hitting streak was interrupted by the All-Star break.... Batted .182 vs. left-handers *as a left-handed batter*. Prior to 1988, as a switch-hitter, he batted .200 vs. southpaws.... Batted .211 in 71 at-bats as designated hitter, .300 in other at-bats.... Batted 87 points higher with bases empty than with runners on, 4th-largest difference in majors (minimum: 100 AB each way).... One of five A.L. players to bat 100 points higher vs. ground-ball pitchers than vs. fly-ball pitchers.... Rangers pitchers allowed 4.56 runs per nine innings with Petralli catching, 4.60 with Stanley, 4.91 with Sundberg.

Gary Pettis

Detroit Tigers   Bats Left and Right

	AB	H	2B	3B	HR	RBI	BB	SO	BA	SA	OBA
Season	458	96	14	4	3	36	47	85	.210	.277	.285
vs. Left-Handers	168	36	4	1	0	13	10	31	.214	.250	.258
vs. Right-Handers	290	60	10	3	3	23	37	54	.207	.293	.299
Home	210	42	6	2	0	14	23	37	.200	.248	.282
Road	248	54	8	2	3	22	24	48	.218	.302	.287
Grass	389	82	13	4	1	27	41	74	.211	.272	.288
Artificial Turf	69	14	1	0	2	9	6	11	.203	.304	.267
April	82	15	1	0	0	7	15	11	.183	.195	.309
May	105	25	4	0	1	4	8	21	.238	.305	.292
June	99	25	3	3	1	14	14	20	.253	.374	.345
July	82	14	2	0	1	9	4	12	.171	.232	.218
August	46	10	3	0	0	2	1	11	.217	.283	.234
Sept./Oct.	44	7	1	1	0	5	10	.159	.227	.245	
Leading Off Inn.	176	35	6	1	0	0	20	36	.199	.244	.281
Runners On	175	43	6	3	2	35	18	30	.246	.349	.316
Runners/Scor. Pos.	98	27	3	2	1	31	15	23	.276	.378	.372
Runners On/2 Out	76	16	3	2	0	15	8	9	.211	.303	.286
Scor. Pos./2 Out	49	13	1	1	0	13	8	7	.265	.327	.368
Late Inning Pressure	60	10	1	0	0	4	3	16	.167	.183	.219
Leading Off	17	2	0	0	0	1	4	.118	.118	.167	
Runners On	23	4	0	0	0	1	1	6	.174	.174	.208
Runners/Scor. Pos.	11	1	0	0	0	1	1	4	.091	.091	.167

RUNS BATTED IN	From 1B	From 2B	From 3B	Scoring Position
Totals	3/125	17/77	13/40	30/117
Percentage	2%	22%	33%	26%
Driving In Runners from 3B with Less than Two Out:		9/19		47%

Loves to face: Richard Dotson (.455, 10-for-22, 1 HR)
Hates to face: Ted Higuera (0-for-22, 7 SO)
Batted .166 after the All-Star break, lowest in A.L. (minimum: two PA per game).... Drove in only two runs in his last 110 at-bats. ... Stole 30 bases in 33 attempts in road games, but was only 14-for-21 at home. Raised his career average above 80 percent for first time ever.... Grounded into only three DPs in 81 opportunities last season, 3d-lowest rate in A.L. (min: 40 opp.).... Hit two home runs in his first 15 career at-bats in Late-Inning Pressure Situations, but none in 270 LIPS at-bats since then.... Career average of .371 (13-for-35, one HR) with the bases loaded.... Career batting average of .291 at Comiskey Park (34-for-117, 1 HR) is his highest at any stadium.

Ken Phelps

Mariners/Yankees   Bats Left

	AB	H	2B	3B	HR	RBI	BB	SO	BA	SA	OBA
Season	297	78	13	0	24	54	70	61	.263	.549	.402
vs. Left-Handers	20	2	0	0	1	2	2	9	.100	.250	.174
vs. Right-Handers	277	76	13	0	23	52	68	52	.274	.570	.417
Home	136	36	7	0	12	28	33	28	.265	.581	.407
Road	161	42	6	0	12	26	37	33	.261	.522	.397
Grass	169	46	5	0	16	35	34	38	.272	.586	.390
Artificial Turf	128	32	8	0	8	19	36	23	.250	.500	.416
April	56	21	2	0	5	12	11	7	.375	.679	.471
May	61	13	0	0	6	13	13	14	.213	.508	.351
June	49	9	1	0	1	1	20	11	.184	.265	.420
July	32	12	6	0	2	7	10	5	.375	.750	.512
August	57	14	1	0	6	13	9	12	.246	.579	.348
Sept./Oct.	42	9	3	0	4	8	7	12	.214	.571	.327
Leading Off Inn.	72	19	2	0	4	4	16	17	.264	.458	.398
Runners On	132	36	5	0	12	42	40	23	.273	.583	.434
Runners/Scor. Pos.	71	15	1	0	6	29	23	20	.211	.479	.392
Runners On/2 Out	59	15	3	0	6	21	17	9	.254	.610	.421
Scor. Pos./2 Out	36	8	1	0	3	15	10	7	.222	.500	.391
Late Inning Pressure	54	12	2	0	5	11	7	17	.222	.537	.311
Leading Off	12	2	0	0	0	0	0	5	.167	.167	.167
Runners On	29	8	1	0	4	10	6	7	.276	.724	.400
Runners/Scor. Pos.	18	3	0	0	2	6	2	7	.167	.500	.250

RUNS BATTED IN	From 1B	From 2B	From 3B	Scoring Position
Totals	13/109	6/48	11/33	17/81
Percentage	12%	13%	33%	21%
Driving In Runners from 3B with Less than Two Out:		6/13		46%

Loves to face: Mark Williamson (.500, 3-for-6, 3 BB, 3 HR)
Hates to face: Jack Morris (.032, 1-for-31, 13 SO)
Career rate of one home run every 13.4 at-bats is second to Babe Ruth (one every 11.8) among all players with 100 or more home runs. Of course, the Bambino was in lineup against lefties, too.... Didn't go more than three starts or 15 at-bats without a home run after August 1.... Of the nine Mariners to reach double figures in home runs (Phelps had 14 with Seattle), he was the only one to hit more on the road (8) than he did in the Kingdome (6).... Started 84 games vs. right-handed pitchers, two vs. lefties (one for Seattle, one for New York).... Batted .118 (2-for-17, no HR) as a pinch hitter, but led majors with 11 pinch walks.... Batting average, year by year since 1985: .207, .247, .259, .263.

Tony Phillips

Oakland As — Bats Left and Right

	AB	H	2B	3B	HR	RBI	BB	SO	BA	SA	OBA
Season	212	43	8	4	2	17	36	50	.203	.307	.320
vs. Left-Handers	71	20	4	3	0	5	18	15	.282	.423	.427
vs. Right-Handers	141	23	4	1	2	12	18	35	.163	.248	.261
Home	106	23	5	3	2	11	12	25	.217	.377	.297
Road	106	20	3	1	0	6	24	25	.189	.236	.341
Grass	175	35	6	4	2	16	25	43	.200	.314	.299
Artificial Turf	37	8	2	0	0	1	11	7	.216	.270	.408
April	61	13	2	1	0	2	15	17	.213	.279	.368
May	25	4	1	0	0	1	1	9	.160	.200	.185
June	0	0	0	0	0	0	0	0	—	—	—
July	37	7	2	1	0	7	4	7	.189	.297	.268
August	31	5	0	1	0	1	6	3	.161	.226	.297
Sept./Oct.	58	14	3	1	2	6	10	14	.241	.431	.362
Leading Off Inn.	61	15	2	0	1	1	13	19	.246	.328	.378
Runners On	88	21	5	3	1	16	12	13	.239	.398	.333
Runners/Scor. Pos.	51	11	0	2	0	10	7	7	.216	.294	.317
Runners On/2 Out	31	12	3	3	0	10	7	2	.387	.677	.500
Scor. Pos./2 Out	18	7	0	2	0	6	5	2	.389	.611	.522
Late Inning Pressure	34	3	0	0	0	1	4	11	.088	.088	.184
Leading Off	13	1	0	0	0	0	1	4	.077	.077	.143
Runners On	10	2	0	0	0	1	1	2	.200	.200	.273
Runners/Scor. Pos.	6	2	0	0	0	1	1	1	.333	.333	.429

RUNS BATTED IN	From 1B	From 2B	From 3B	Scoring Position
Totals	7/62	3/42	5/15	8/57
Percentage	11%	7%	33%	14%
Driving In Runners from 3B with Less than Two Out:			3/9	33%

Loves to face: Mike Flanagan (.471, 8-for-17)
Hates to face: Mark Eichhorn (0-for-10)
One of two A.L. players to start at six different positions last season. He played more than one position in a game 30 times, playing both an infield and an outfield position in 16 of those games. . . . Good thing he's versatile. His batting average was third lowest in A.L. (minimum: 200 AB). . . . Started only 53 games last season. But he started 13 of the last 16 regular-season games, the first two games of the A.L.C.S., and two games in the World Series. . . . A switch hitter in name only. Over last five years, he's batted .309 vs. left-handers, .222 vs. right-handers. . . . Career average of .229 in day games, .260 at night. Difference of 31 points is 5th largest in majors over the past 10 years.

Luis Polonia

Oakland As — Bats Left

	AB	H	2B	3B	HR	RBI	BB	SO	BA	SA	OBA
Season	288	84	11	4	2	27	21	40	.292	.378	.338
vs. Left-Handers	18	3	0	1	0	2	0	3	.167	.278	.158
vs. Right-Handers	270	81	11	3	2	25	21	37	.300	.385	.349
Home	152	49	7	1	1	12	16	20	.322	.401	.387
Road	136	35	4	3	1	15	5	20	.257	.353	.280
Grass	249	70	8	2	2	21	19	32	.281	.353	.330
Artificial Turf	39	14	3	2	0	6	2	8	.359	.538	.390
April	0	0	0	0	0	0	0	0	—	—	—
May	0	0	0	0	0	0	0	0	—	—	—
June	36	11	2	0	0	3	5	2	.306	.361	.390
July	78	25	1	1	1	5	1	14	.321	.397	.329
August	96	24	3	1	1	12	9	10	.250	.333	.308
Sept./Oct.	78	24	5	2	0	7	6	14	.308	.423	.357
Leading Off Inn.	116	34	5	1	0	0	10	16	.293	.353	.349
Runners On	103	30	4	2	1	26	8	16	.291	.398	.336
Runners/Scor. Pos.	59	18	2	0	0	21	4	13	.305	.339	.338
Runners On/2 Out	48	14	2	1	1	11	3	9	.292	.438	.333
Scor. Pos./2 Out	28	8	0	0	0	7	2	8	.286	.286	.333
Late Inning Pressure	38	13	2	0	0	3	1	6	.342	.474	.359
Leading Off	12	2	2	0	0	0	0	2	.167	.333	.167
Runners On	12	6	0	0	0	2	0	1	.500	.500	.500
Runners/Scor. Pos.	6	3	0	0	0	2	0	1	.500	.500	.500

RUNS BATTED IN	From 1B	From 2B	From 3B	Scoring Position
Totals	4/76	8/41	13/33	21/74
Percentage	5%	20%	39%	28%
Driving In Runners from 3B with Less than Two Out:			11/18	61%

Loves to face: Steve Shields (.800, 4-for-5)
Hates to face: Jay Tibbs (0-for-7)
Stole 20 bases after the All-Star break. . . . Batted .310 in 59 games as the leadoff hitter. Drove in at least one run in six consecutive games from the leadoff spot (August 14–21). . . . Started 65 games, but only two were against left-handed pitchers. . . . Career average of .224 vs. left-handers, .300 vs. right-handers. He's hit all six of his home runs vs. RHP. . . . Career average of .223 during August. . . . It'll take him years to live down a reputation as a poor fielder, all because of one bad inning on national television. But last season, the A's allowed 3.42 runs per nine innings with Polonia in left field, 3.97 with other left fielders. In 1987, it was Polonia 4.80, others 4.95.

Jim Presley

Seattle Mariners — Bats Right

	AB	H	2B	3B	HR	RBI	BB	SO	BA	SA	OBA
Season	544	125	26	0	14	62	36	114	.230	.355	.280
vs. Left-Handers	164	38	9	0	2	10	11	26	.232	.323	.278
vs. Right-Handers	380	87	17	0	12	52	25	88	.229	.368	.281
Home	269	66	19	0	7	30	18	56	.245	.394	.290
Road	275	59	7	0	7	32	18	58	.215	.316	.271
Grass	226	50	6	0	7	30	15	51	.221	.341	.273
Artificial Turf	318	75	20	0	7	32	21	63	.236	.365	.285
April	92	23	4	0	4	13	5	13	.250	.424	.289
May	84	19	2	0	2	10	7	23	.226	.321	.293
June	96	17	4	0	2	9	5	18	.177	.281	.214
July	84	17	5	0	3	8	9	22	.202	.369	.287
August	106	26	5	0	3	18	6	21	.245	.377	.293
Sept./Oct.	82	23	6	0	0	4	4	17	.280	.354	.310
Leading Off Inn.	124	27	5	0	1	1	7	23	.218	.282	.260
Runners On	232	52	9	0	7	55	20	48	.224	.353	.286
Runners/Scor. Pos.	136	32	2	0	4	47	15	28	.235	.338	.310
Runners On/2 Out	96	19	2	0	6	22	8	26	.198	.406	.260
Scor. Pos./2 Out	59	12	0	0	4	18	7	18	.203	.407	.288
Late Inning Pressure	80	19	2	0	2	6	5	18	.238	.338	.282
Leading Off	24	5	0	0	0	0	2	4	.208	.208	.269
Runners On	30	7	0	0	1	5	2	4	.233	.333	.281
Runners/Scor. Pos.	16	3	0	0	0	3	2	2	.188	.188	.278

RUNS BATTED IN	From 1B	From 2B	From 3B	Scoring Position
Totals	9/161	18/113	21/50	39/163
Percentage	6%	16%	42%	24%
Driving In Runners from 3B with Less than Two Out:			19/31	61%

Loves to face: Rich Yett (.500, 4-for-8, 2 HR)
Hates to face: Mark Clear (0-for-7, 5 SO)
Didn't hit a home run in his last 144 at-bats. . . . Batting average and home run output have declined in each of last three seasons. Year by year since 1985: .275, 28 HRs; .265, 27; .247, 24; .230, 14. Batting average vs. left-handers has dropped more drastically, from .344 to .232. . . . One of six players with 100+ strikeouts in each of the last four seasons. . . . Career HR totals: 51 at Kingdome, 52 on road. . . . Players with comparable career patterns at the same age as Presley: Ron Hansen, John Mayberry, Joe Pepitone, Boog Powell, Doug Rader, Pete Ward, Earl Williams. Prognosis: fair to good, if he remains healthier than Hansen and Ward did. Likely range: .240–.260, 15–25 HRs per year for next three to five years.

Kirby Puckett

Minnesota Twins — Bats Right

	AB	H	2B	3B	HR	RBI	BB	SO	BA	SA	OBA
Season	657	234	42	5	24	121	23	83	.356	.545	.375
vs. Left-Handers	166	66	12	0	8	28	8	13	.398	.614	.425
vs. Right-Handers	491	168	30	5	16	93	15	70	.342	.521	.358
Home	323	131	26	5	13	59	17	41	.406	.638	.436
Road	334	103	16	0	11	62	6	42	.308	.455	.314
Grass	257	86	13	0	9	53	5	31	.335	.490	.338
Artificial Turf	400	148	29	5	15	68	18	52	.370	.580	.398
April	87	25	8	0	1	10	4	16	.287	.414	.326
May	116	44	5	2	7	25	2	10	.379	.638	.387
June	106	38	6	0	2	25	3	9	.358	.472	.363
July	109	42	8	2	4	17	3	16	.385	.606	.391
August	114	36	5	0	7	20	7	13	.316	.544	.355
Sept./Oct.	125	49	10	1	3	24	4	19	.392	.560	.412
Leading Off Inn.	110	46	7	1	7	7	7	12	.418	.691	.453
Runners On	308	106	26	1	8	105	14	43	.344	.513	.364
Runners/Scor. Pos.	191	70	17	1	5	93	8	29	.366	.545	.378
Runners On/2 Out	107	31	10	0	3	34	2	19	.290	.467	.303
Scor. Pos./2 Out	80	24	7	0	3	33	1	17	.300	.500	.309
Late Inning Pressure	81	28	7	2	1	12	4	10	.346	.519	.368
Leading Off	19	7	0	1	0	0	1	2	.368	.474	.400
Runners On	45	14	6	0	0	11	3	8	.311	.444	.340
Runners/Scor. Pos.	24	6	4	0	0	10	1	4	.250	.417	.259

RUNS BATTED IN	From 1B	From 2B	From 3B	Scoring Position
Totals	13/210	32/139	52/88	84/227
Percentage	6%	23%	59%	37%
Driving In Runners from 3B with Less than Two Out:			37/51	73%

Loves to face: Juan Nieves (.619, 13-for-21, 1 HR)
Hates to face: Don August (0-for-5, 3 SO)
Read those numbers again: 234 hits, 121 runs batted in. No major-league player has had that many hits and that many RBI in the same season since Joe Medwick in 1937; last A.L. player who could match those figures was Al Simmons in 1925. . . . Third straight season of 200+ hits, 25+ homers. Only three others have done that: Jim Rice (1977–79), Lou Gehrig (1930–32), Chuck Klein (five years, 1929–33). . . . Batting average vs. left-handers was highest by a qualifying player since Sixto Lezcano's .411 mark in 1979. . . . Averaged one walk per 30 plate appearances, lowest rate among qualifiers for A.L. batting title. . . . Had an 11-game RBI streak in September, tying Andy Van Slyke for longest in the majors.

Rey Quinones
Seattle Mariners — Bats Right

	AB	H	2B	3B	HR	RBI	BB	SO	BA	SA	OBA
Season	499	124	30	3	12	52	23	71	.248	.393	.284
vs. Left-Handers	150	39	15	1	6	17	4	25	.260	.493	.282
vs. Right-Handers	349	85	15	2	6	35	19	46	.244	.350	.285
Home	235	59	10	2	9	30	11	34	.251	.426	.291
Road	264	65	20	1	3	22	12	37	.246	.364	.278
Grass	203	53	18	1	2	18	8	28	.261	.389	.288
Artificial Turf	296	71	12	2	10	34	15	43	.240	.395	.282
April	89	27	7	0	1	6	4	13	.303	.416	.333
May	77	17	4	1	1	8	1	12	.221	.338	.241
June	78	22	3	0	6	9	2	12	.282	.551	.300
July	79	20	5	0	0	5	7	10	.253	.316	.310
August	93	25	8	2	3	16	5	11	.269	.495	.300
Sept./Oct.	83	13	3	0	1	8	4	13	.157	.229	.213
Leading Off Inn.	114	29	5	1	3	3	4	18	.254	.395	.280
Runners On	204	52	16	2	2	42	10	25	.255	.382	.289
Runners/Scor. Pos.	111	32	8	1	1	37	6	16	.288	.405	.322
Runners On/2 Out	85	17	5	1	0	14	2	8	.200	.282	.227
Scor. Pos./2 Out	47	11	2	0	0	12	1	4	.234	.277	.265
Late Inning Pressure	72	17	4	0	3	6	5	12	.236	.417	.295
Leading Off	15	5	1	0	0	0	0	3	.333	.400	.333
Runners On	29	2	0	0	1	4	3	5	.069	.172	.156
Runners/Scor. Pos.	12	1	0	0	0	2	2	2	.083	.083	.214

RUNS BATTED IN	From 1B	From 2B	From 3B	Scoring Position
Totals	6/147	15/84	19/45	34/129
Percentage	4%	18%	42%	26%
Driving In Runners from 3B with Less than Two Out:			14/26	54%

Loves to face: Oil Can Boyd (.625, 5-for-8, 1 HR)
Hates to face: Mark Eichhorn (0-for-10)
Forget Magic Johnson. This guy had a *real* triple-double: three two-baggers in one game. Actually, there wasn't anything magic about it. So did nine others. . . . One of four shortstops to lead his team in doubles. The others: Tony Fernandez, Rafael Ramirez, and Ozzie Smith. . . . Grounded into double plays in four consecutive games (Aug. 20–24). . . . Committed eight errors in his last 26 games. . . . Unlikely but true: He was the only Mariner to hit two home runs in a game. . . . Hit five home runs in 70 at-bats vs. left-handed pitchers at the Kingdome. . . . Three hits, all singles, in 23 career at-bats with the bases loaded. . . . Career average of .192 during September.

Jamie Quirk
Kansas City Royals — Bats Left

	AB	H	2B	3B	HR	RBI	BB	SO	BA	SA	OBA
Season	196	47	7	1	8	25	28	41	.240	.408	.333
vs. Left-Handers	19	7	2	0	0	2	1	4	.368	.474	.400
vs. Right-Handers	177	40	5	1	8	23	27	37	.226	.401	.327
Home	98	27	4	1	2	12	15	19	.276	.398	.365
Road	98	20	3	0	6	13	13	22	.204	.418	.301
Grass	66	10	2	0	2	6	7	15	.152	.273	.240
Artificial Turf	130	37	5	1	6	19	21	26	.285	.477	.379
April	38	6	1	1	1	2	2	8	.158	.316	.200
May	19	5	0	0	1	3	6	4	.263	.421	.440
June	28	7	1	0	1	3	1	5	.250	.393	.267
July	21	2	0	0	0	3	4	4	.095	.095	.208
August	42	14	4	0	3	12	9	8	.333	.643	.453
Sept./Oct.	48	13	1	0	2	5	7	12	.271	.417	.357
Leading Off Inn.	56	15	0	1	5	5	4	11	.268	.571	.317
Runners On	62	13	4	0	0	17	13	13	.210	.274	.333
Runners/Scor. Pos.	50	12	4	0	0	17	9	9	.240	.320	.339
Runners On/2 Out	38	10	2	0	0	11	6	7	.263	.316	.364
Scor. Pos./2 Out	33	9	2	0	0	11	4	6	.273	.333	.351
Late Inning Pressure	24	3	0	0	0	2	8	8	.125	.125	.344
Leading Off	5	0	0	0	0	0	1	2	.000	.000	.167
Runners On	7	1	0	0	0	2	4	3	.143	.143	.455
Runners/Scor. Pos.	6	1	0	0	0	2	3	2	.167	.167	.444

RUNS BATTED IN	From 1B	From 2B	From 3B	Scoring Position
Totals	1/38	10/42	6/17	16/59
Percentage	3%	24%	35%	27%
Driving In Runners from 3B with Less than Two Out:			3/5	60%

Loves to face: Jeff Russell (.455, 5-for-11)
Hates to face: Bobby Witt (0-for-8, 5 SO)
Each of his last nine home runs has been a solo shot against a right-handed pitcher. . . . Started 60 games last season, all against right-handed pitchers. Last start against a lefty was Aug. 29, 1986, vs. Ted Higuera, 172 starts ago. . . . Has faced left-handers 121 times during a 14-year career. Set a career high with seven hits vs. south-paws last season, and equalled his career high in home runs vs. LHP—none. . . . Has hit 21 of his 28 career home runs over the past three years. Averages: one HR per 138 at-bats from 1975 through 1985, one per 34 AB since then. . . . Has five career stolen bases in 16 attempts. . . . Career batting average of .195 with two outs and runners in scoring position.

Willie Randolph
New York Yankees — Bats Right

	AB	H	2B	3B	HR	RBI	BB	SO	BA	SA	OBA
Season	404	93	20	1	2	35	55	39	.230	.300	.322
vs. Left-Handers	125	26	5	1	1	9	21	12	.208	.288	.318
vs. Right-Handers	279	67	15	0	1	26	34	27	.240	.305	.324
Home	206	45	7	0	1	14	29	25	.218	.287	.318
Road	198	48	13	1	1	21	26	14	.242	.333	.326
Grass	341	78	15	1	1	28	46	32	.229	.287	.320
Artificial Turf	63	15	5	0	1	7	9	7	.238	.365	.333
April	69	13	3	0	0	2	6	12	.188	.232	.260
May	90	18	5	1	1	9	15	4	.200	.311	.311
June	46	11	2	0	0	5	5	3	.239	.283	.314
July	83	25	6	0	0	8	18	9	.301	.373	.417
August	17	7	2	0	1	4	1	1	.412	.706	.444
Sept./Oct.	99	19	2	0	0	7	10	10	.192	.212	.270
Leading Off Inn.	78	14	5	0	0	0	5	10	.179	.244	.229
Runners On	163	44	8	0	2	35	37	13	.270	.356	.398
Runners/Scor. Pos.	92	25	4	0	2	35	26	11	.272	.380	.415
Runners On/2 Out	60	15	2	0	0	9	17	6	.250	.283	.416
Scor. Pos./2 Out	35	7	2	0	0	9	14	6	.200	.257	.429
Late Inning Pressure	45	7	1	0	1	5	5	5	.156	.178	.255
Leading Off	15	2	0	0	0	0	0	3	.133	.133	.133
Runners On	19	5	1	0	0	1	5	1	.263	.316	.440
Runners/Scor. Pos.	8	0	0	0	0	1	4	1	.000	.000	.333

RUNS BATTED IN	From 1B	From 2B	From 3B	Scoring Position
Totals	3/108	11/80	19/35	30/115
Percentage	3%	14%	54%	26%
Driving In Runners from 3B with Less than Two Out:			14/19	74%

Loves to face: Bruce Hurst (.403, 27-for-67, 1 HR)
Hates to face: Danny Jackson (0-for-4)
Yankees were 63–44 with him in the starting lineup, 22–32 without him. Over last four seasons: .585 with him, .465 without him. . . . Ended the season, and his Yankees career (or Phase I, at least) with 30 consecutive hitless at-bats, the team's longest over the past 10 years. . . . Had batted at least .310 vs. left-handers in each of the previous four seasons, but dropped 123 points from 1987 to 1988. . . . Batting average leading off innings was his lowest since 1975, when he went 2-for-23 for the Pirates. . . . Was hitless in seven at-bats with the bases loaded. . . . Failed to drive any of ten runners from scoring position in Late-Inning Pressure Situations. Was 20-for-49 over the two previous seasons.

Johnny Ray
California Angels — Bats Left and Right

	AB	H	2B	3B	HR	RBI	BB	SO	BA	SA	OBA
Season	602	184	42	7	6	84	36	38	.306	.429	.345
vs. Left-Handers	210	59	14	2	2	15	13	9	.281	.395	.327
vs. Right-Handers	392	125	28	5	4	69	23	29	.319	.446	.354
Home	287	85	15	4	4	37	21	22	.296	.418	.348
Road	315	99	27	3	2	47	15	16	.314	.438	.341
Grass	509	151	33	6	6	69	33	38	.297	.420	.339
Artificial Turf	93	33	9	1	0	15	3	0	.355	.473	.374
April	80	35	10	0	1	19	3	7	.438	.600	.442
May	107	22	6	1	1	11	8	8	.206	.308	.267
June	85	25	6	0	0	10	8	10	.294	.365	.351
July	113	29	5	2	1	12	3	5	.257	.363	.281
August	106	34	6	3	2	17	8	3	.321	.491	.368
Sept./Oct.	111	39	9	1	1	15	6	5	.351	.477	.387
Leading Off Inn.	116	33	6	1	1	1	8	7	.284	.379	.331
Runners On	260	89	21	3	2	80	15	13	.342	.469	.374
Runners/Scor. Pos.	164	45	7	1	2	70	9	6	.274	.366	.310
Runners On/2 Out	104	36	9	2	0	31	11	3	.346	.529	.414
Scor. Pos./2 Out	75	21	2	0	0	25	7	2	.280	.387	.349
Late Inning Pressure	90	25	3	0	1	12	3	4	.278	.344	.302
Leading Off	18	4	0	0	0	0	0	2	.222	.222	.222
Runners On	43	10	2	0	0	11	3	1	.233	.279	.286
Runners/Scor. Pos.	34	7	1	0	0	11	1	1	.206	.235	.237

RUNS BATTED IN	From 1B	From 2B	From 3B	Scoring Position
Totals	12/169	23/128	43/82	66/210
Percentage	7%	18%	52%	31%
Driving In Runners from 3B with Less than Two Out:			33/52	63%

Loves to face: Andy Hawkins (.517, 15-for-29)
Hates to face: Ted Power (.138, 4-for-29)
One of three players to appear in 150+ games in each of last seven seasons. The others: noted "iron men" Cal Ripken and Dale Murphy. . . . Led A.L. in batting through games of May 2. Big deal: Indians led the A.L. East through that point. . . . Angels' record was 52–50 with Ray starting at second base, 23–37 in other games. . . . Had lowest fielding percentage among A.L. second basemen (minimum: 100 games), and the lowest among left fielders (minimum: 40 games). But his average of 3.33 assists per nine innings led A.L. second baseman. . . . Set career highs in doubles and batting average with runners on base. . . . Has hit either five, six, or seven home runs in each of his seven full seasons in the majors.

Gary Redus

Chicago White Sox   Bats Right

	AB	H	2B	3B	HR	RBI	BB	SO	BA	SA	OBA
Season	262	69	10	4	6	34	33	52	.263	.401	.342
vs. Left-Handers	105	26	4	1	3	12	13	18	.248	.390	.333
vs. Right-Handers	157	43	6	3	3	22	20	34	.274	.408	.348
Home	154	44	8	4	1	19	23	31	.286	.409	.372
Road	108	25	2	0	5	15	10	21	.231	.389	.298
Grass	225	60	8	4	4	31	29	46	.267	.391	.344
Artificial Turf	37	9	2	0	2	3	4	6	.243	.459	.333
April	22	8	1	1	0	0	4	5	.364	.500	.462
May	46	10	0	2	2	7	3	10	.217	.435	.280
June	93	24	5	0	2	12	12	19	.258	.376	.339
July	85	24	4	1	2	14	11	14	.282	.424	.350
August	16	3	0	0	0	1	3	4	.188	.188	.316
Sept./Oct.	0	0	0	0	0	0	0	0	—	—	—
Leading Off Inn.	95	26	4	2	3	3	10	18	.274	.453	.349
Runners On	92	21	2	2	3	31	10	22	.228	.391	.284
Runners/Scor. Pos.	54	11	2	0	3	29	8	16	.204	.407	.275
Runners On/2 Out	43	10	0	1	2	11	4	11	.233	.419	.298
Scor. Pos./2 Out	27	5	0	0	2	10	4	9	.185	.407	.290
Late Inning Pressure	42	9	2	0	1	7	9	14	.214	.333	.353
Leading Off	10	1	0	0	0	0	3	5	.100	.100	.308
Runners On	19	4	0	0	1	7	2	8	.211	.368	.286
Runners/Scor. Pos.	9	3	0	0	1	7	2	5	.333	.667	.455

RUNS BATTED IN	From 1B	From 2B	From 3B	Scoring Position
Totals	6/63	6/43	16/33	22/76
Percentage	10%	14%	48%	29%
Driving In Runners from 3B with Less than Two Out:			12/20	60%

Loves to face: David Palmer (.667, 2-for-3, 2 HR)
Hates to face: Danny Jackson (0-for-17)
Figures *above* are for A.L. only. . . . Led A.L. with 14 stolen bases in June, the only month in which Rickey Henderson graciously declined to lead the league. . . . When traded to Pittsburgh, he had a streak of 24 consecutive steals without being caught, eight shy of A.L. record shared by Willie Wilson and Julio Cruz. Should he ever return to A.L. he could extend that streak and eventually break A.L. record. . . . Winner of the 1988 Tony Cloninger Award for hitting two grand slams within five days. . . . Only six players in baseball batted at least 80 points higher with the bases empty than with runners on base. The Pirates acquired two of them in midseason: Redus and Glenn Wilson.

Jody Reed

Boston Red Sox   Bats Right

	AB	H	2B	3B	HR	RBI	BB	SO	BA	SA	OBA
Season	338	99	23	1	1	28	45	21	.293	.376	.380
vs. Left-Handers	84	19	3	0	0	8	9	8	.226	.262	.301
vs. Right-Handers	254	80	20	1	1	20	36	13	.315	.413	.405
Home	188	58	14	0	1	19	26	13	.309	.399	.399
Road	150	41	9	1	0	9	19	8	.273	.347	.357
Grass	303	89	21	0	1	26	43	16	.294	.373	.386
Artificial Turf	35	10	2	1	0	2	2	5	.286	.400	.324
April	17	1	0	0	0	0	2	2	.059	.059	.158
May	37	10	2	1	0	2	6	5	.270	.378	.372
June	16	4	0	0	1	3	6	2	.250	.438	.435
July	90	35	8	0	0	13	10	4	.389	.478	.446
August	77	19	5	0	0	4	9	6	.247	.312	.333
Sept./Oct.	101	30	8	0	0	6	12	2	.297	.376	.388
Leading Off Inn.	92	26	9	0	0	0	13	4	.283	.380	.371
Runners On	138	40	8	0	1	28	19	12	.290	.370	.383
Runners/Scor. Pos.	91	23	4	0	1	27	12	6	.253	.330	.346
Runners On/2 Out	75	19	2	0	0	13	10	6	.253	.280	.356
Scor. Pos./2 Out	60	14	1	0	0	12	7	4	.233	.250	.333
Late Inning Pressure	37	12	1	0	0	4	2	1	.324	.378	.359
Leading Off	7	3	1	0	0	0	1	0	.429	.571	.500
Runners On	16	5	1	0	0	4	1	1	.313	.375	.353
Runners/Scor. Pos.	11	4	1	0	0	4	1	1	.364	.455	.417

RUNS BATTED IN	From 1B	From 2B	From 3B	Scoring Position
Totals	1/95	11/71	15/40	26/111
Percentage	1%	15%	38%	23%
Driving In Runners from 3B with Less than Two Out:			11/17	65%

Loves to face: Dave Schmidt (2-for-2)
Hates to face: Mike Witt (0-for-8)
One hit in his first 17 at-bats cost him his job early, but he ranked 6th in A.L. with .314 mark after All-Star break. . . . July average was 2d highest to Julio Franco's .390. . . . Batting average was .311 as late as Sept. 23, but three hits in last 29 at-bats dropped his final mark below .300. . . . Sox were 51–32 with Reed starting at shortstop. . . . Batted .252 vs. ground-ball pitchers, .325 vs. fly-ballers. . . . Another Red Sox contact hitter: Struck out twice in last 101 at-bats. . . . Led A.L. rookies in on-base average, runs, doubles, and walks. . . . All-time Red Sox rookie batting leaders (minimum: 300 AB): Wade Boggs, .349; Patsy Dougherty, .342; Ike Boone, .333; Fred Lynn, .331; Johnny Pesky, .331.

Harold Reynolds

Seattle Mariners   Bats Left and Right

	AB	H	2B	3B	HR	RBI	BB	SO	BA	SA	OBA
Season	598	169	26	11	4	41	51	51	.283	.383	.340
vs. Left-Handers	185	58	10	1	2	11	8	11	.314	.411	.340
vs. Right-Handers	413	111	16	10	2	30	43	40	.269	.370	.340
Home	290	83	11	6	4	22	25	21	.286	.407	.344
Road	308	86	15	5	0	19	26	30	.279	.360	.336
Grass	241	63	11	5	0	14	19	23	.261	.349	.317
Artificial Turf	357	106	15	6	4	27	32	28	.297	.406	.355
April	83	24	4	3	1	10	3	4	.289	.446	.310
May	93	25	2	2	1	7	2	10	.269	.366	.281
June	99	30	4	1	0	1	10	9	.303	.364	.367
July	102	27	1	2	0	4	9	10	.265	.314	.330
August	120	37	9	3	0	11	13	11	.308	.433	.376
Sept./Oct.	101	26	6	0	2	8	14	10	.257	.376	.353
Leading Off Inn.	174	45	5	3	0	0	12	19	.259	.322	.314
Runners On	214	67	11	3	2	39	15	18	.313	.421	.355
Runners/Scor. Pos.	118	35	6	2	1	36	10	12	.297	.407	.346
Runners On/2 Out	78	28	6	2	0	17	8	7	.359	.487	.419
Scor. Pos./2 Out	51	16	3	2	0	17	7	6	.314	.451	.397
Late Inning Pressure	76	21	4	0	0	4	5	9	.276	.329	.321
Leading Off	19	6	1	0	0	0	0	2	.316	.368	.316
Runners On	32	9	2	0	0	4	3	6	.281	.344	.343
Runners/Scor. Pos.	15	5	2	0	0	4	1	4	.333	.467	.375

RUNS BATTED IN	From 1B	From 2B	From 3B	Scoring Position
Totals	2/143	18/99	17/38	35/137
Percentage	1%	18%	45%	26%
Driving In Runners from 3B with Less than Two Out:			10/16	63%

Loves to face: Willie Fraser (.462, 6-for-13)
Hates to face: Neil Allen (0-for-10)
Caught stealing 29 times last season, 3d-highest single-season total in A.L. since the category's inception in 1920, behind Rickey Henderson (42 in 1982) and Sam Rice (30 in 1920). . . . Shared A.L. lead in triples. . . . Had five hits in eight at-bats with the bases loaded. Career average: .346 (9-for-26, no HR). . . . Yearly batting averages since 1985: .144, .222, .275, .283. . . . One of three A.L. players to collect hits in eight consecutive at-bats last season. . . . Led A.L. second basemen in assists, errors, total chances, and double plays. . . . Ranked last among the nine second basemen who qualified for the fielding title, but did that stop him from winning the Gold Glove Award?

Jim Rice

Boston Red Sox   Bats Right

	AB	H	2B	3B	HR	RBI	BB	SO	BA	SA	OBA
Season	485	128	18	3	15	72	48	89	.264	.406	.330
vs. Left-Handers	155	45	7	2	6	22	12	29	.290	.477	.349
vs. Right-Handers	330	83	11	1	9	50	36	60	.252	.373	.322
Home	225	62	9	2	9	40	30	38	.276	.453	.362
Road	260	66	9	1	6	32	18	51	.254	.365	.301
Grass	410	114	16	2	14	68	40	71	.278	.429	.341
Artificial Turf	75	14	2	1	1	4	8	18	.187	.280	.274
April	81	22	2	0	0	10	7	11	.272	.296	.322
May	70	14	1	0	0	3	4	16	.200	.214	.253
June	90	30	5	1	4	23	15	8	.333	.544	.429
July	96	27	7	2	2	11	9	22	.281	.458	.336
August	86	21	2	0	4	10	9	24	.244	.407	.313
Sept./Oct.	62	14	1	0	5	15	4	8	.226	.484	.290
Leading Off Inn.	117	28	6	1	1	1	11	22	.239	.333	.310
Runners On	231	63	10	1	9	66	26	39	.273	.442	.343
Runners/Scor. Pos.	141	38	7	1	7	60	20	27	.270	.482	.355
Runners On/2 Out	111	35	6	1	8	37	13	15	.315	.604	.392
Scor. Pos./2 Out	69	20	4	1	6	31	9	11	.290	.638	.380
Late Inning Pressure	67	17	2	0	1	9	5	13	.254	.328	.306
Leading Off	15	2	0	0	0	0	1	1	.133	.133	.188
Runners On	35	11	2	0	1	9	4	5	.314	.457	.385
Runners/Scor. Pos.	20	6	1	0	1	9	1	3	.300	.500	.333

RUNS BATTED IN	From 1B	From 2B	From 3B	Scoring Position
Totals	5/163	25/114	27/67	52/181
Percentage	3%	22%	40%	29%
Driving In Runners from 3B with Less than Two Out:			20/38	53%

Loves to face: John Cerutti (.545, 6-for-11, 2 HR)
Hates to face: Willie Hernandez (0-for-10)
Career batting average dropped to .29978. . . . Total of 1423 RBI ranks third among active players, behind Schmidt (1567) and Winfield (1438). . . . Started only one game in the field after June 11. . . . Opened the season with the longest home run drought of his career. Didn't hit his first home run until his 49th game, when he connected twice against Richard Dotson at Fenway. . . . Kept alive his streak of having hit for a higher average at Fenway than he has on the road in each of his 15 seasons in the majors. . . . Batting average in Late-Inning Pressure Situations has been lower than his overall average in each of the past 10 seasons, longest streak of its kind in the 14 years we've kept track.

Billy Ripken

Baltimore Orioles — Bats Right

	AB	H	2B	3B	HR	RBI	BB	SO	BA	SA	OBA
Season	512	106	18	1	2	34	33	63	.207	.258	.260
vs. Left-Handers	186	41	8	0	0	10	15	20	.220	.263	.281
vs. Right-Handers	326	65	10	1	2	24	18	43	.199	.255	.249
Home	261	58	9	1	0	14	20	29	.222	.264	.282
Road	251	48	9	0	2	20	13	34	.191	.251	.238
Grass	448	96	17	1	1	29	27	54	.214	.263	.265
Artificial Turf	64	10	1	0	1	5	6	9	.156	.219	.229
April	84	15	4	0	0	5	5	13	.179	.226	.231
May	78	13	4	0	0	6	7	9	.167	.218	.235
June	96	20	5	0	1	3	9	11	.208	.292	.290
July	86	20	3	1	0	7	5	8	.233	.291	.272
August	103	23	2	0	0	9	5	11	.223	.243	.264
Sept./Oct.	65	15	0	0	1	4	2	11	.231	.277	.265
Leading Off Inn.	112	24	4	0	1	1	9	19	.214	.277	.273
Runners On	189	35	4	0	1	33	13	16	.185	.222	.249
Runners/Scor. Pos.	105	23	4	0	1	33	7	12	.219	.286	.267
Runners On/2 Out	79	17	2	0	0	14	10	8	.215	.241	.319
Scor. Pos./2 Out	44	12	2	0	0	14	5	5	.273	.318	.347
Late Inning Pressure	70	17	2	1	0	4	5	12	.243	.300	.299
Leading Off	20	3	1	0	0	0	1	8	.150	.200	.190
Runners On	26	5	0	0	0	4	4	1	.192	.192	.313
Runners/Scor. Pos.	13	3	0	0	0	4	2	1	.231	.231	.313

RUNS BATTED IN	From 1B	From 2B	From 3B	Scoring Position
Totals	1/135	15/94	16/35	31/129
Percentage	1%	16%	46%	24%
Driving In Runners from 3B with Less than Two Out:		12/21		57%

Loves to face: Bill Wegman (.800, 4-for-5)
Hates to face: Mike Moore (0-for-10)
First player to hit as low as .207 in as many as 150 games since Jim Sundberg hit .199 for Texas in 1975. Ed Brinkman set the all-time 150-game low of .185 with Washington in 1965.... Slugging average was 2d lowest among A.L. players with 200 or more at-bats.... Didn't start Orioles' last eight games, as Frank Robinson looked at Rene Gonzales and Pete Stanicek at second base.... Removed in favor of a pinch hitter 25 times last season, highest total on team. ... His overall batting average fell 101 points from 1987 (.308); the fall was even steeper with runners on base (138 points).... One thing he did improve: his average in Late-Inning Pressure Situations, up 36 points from .207 in 1987.

Cal Ripken

Baltimore Orioles — Bats Right

	AB	H	2B	3B	HR	RBI	BB	SO	BA	SA	OBA
Season	575	152	25	1	23	84	102	69	.264	.431	.372
vs. Left-Handers	190	60	8	0	9	25	39	24	.316	.500	.430
vs. Right-Handers	385	92	17	1	14	59	63	45	.239	.397	.342
Home	285	75	10	0	11	50	51	37	.263	.414	.370
Road	290	77	15	1	12	34	51	32	.266	.448	.373
Grass	490	124	17	0	19	71	84	60	.253	.404	.358
Artificial Turf	85	28	8	1	4	13	18	9	.329	.588	.447
April	77	20	5	0	3	7	18	12	.260	.442	.396
May	96	23	4	0	6	15	20	10	.240	.469	.368
June	98	28	4	1	3	23	20	13	.286	.439	.408
July	96	30	4	0	6	17	13	10	.313	.542	.387
August	106	29	7	0	4	15	16	15	.274	.453	.362
Sept./Oct.	102	22	1	0	1	7	15	9	.216	.255	.314
Leading Off Inn.	105	30	4	0	4	15	12	12	.286	.438	.375
Runners On	221	57	12	1	9	70	47	21	.258	.443	.376
Runners/Scor. Pos.	131	35	7	1	6	63	35	16	.267	.473	.398
Runners On/2 Out	86	16	4	1	3	21	21	11	.186	.360	.346
Scor. Pos./2 Out	61	11	2	1	3	21	16	10	.180	.393	.351
Late Inning Pressure	90	25	3	1	2	14	14	11	.278	.400	.381
Leading Off	25	7	2	0	0	0	5	5	.280	.360	.400
Runners On	34	9	0	1	1	13	5	3	.265	.412	.375
Runners/Scor. Pos.	25	6	0	1	1	13	3	3	.240	.440	.321

RUNS BATTED IN	From 1B	From 2B	From 3B	Scoring Position
Totals	9/151	21/105	31/51	52/156
Percentage	6%	20%	61%	33%
Driving In Runners from 3B with Less than Two Out:		24/29		83%

Loves to face: Bret Saberhagen (.382, 13-for-34, 5 HR)
Hates to face: Scott Bailes (0-for-17)
Has hit 175 home runs as a shortstop, eight others as a third baseman. He should become A.L.'s all-time home-run leader among shortstops before he turns 30 in August 1990. Vern Stephens holds that record with 213.... Became first A.L. shortstop to start five consecutive All-Star Games when Alan Trammell missed game due to injury.... His team loses its first 21 games, while Cal struggles through a 1-for-41 slump, including a 29–at-bat hitless streak, the team's longest since Mark Belanger went 0-for-31 in 1979. Still, *The Streak* continues. Rip's now more than halfway to Gehrig's record. Barring another players' strike, or other stoppage, he could top "Old Biscuit Pants" in June 1995.

Mark Salas

Chicago White Sox — Bats Left

	AB	H	2B	3B	HR	RBI	BB	SO	BA	SA	OBA
Season	196	49	7	0	3	9	12	17	.250	.332	.303
vs. Left-Handers	16	4	2	0	0	1	0	3	.250	.375	.294
vs. Right-Handers	180	45	5	0	3	8	12	14	.250	.328	.304
Home	106	28	2	0	2	5	7	8	.264	.340	.322
Road	90	21	5	0	1	4	5	9	.233	.322	.281
Grass	161	38	3	0	3	5	12	13	.236	.292	.301
Artificial Turf	35	11	4	0	1	4	0	4	.314	.514	.314
April	20	4	0	0	1	3	0	1	.200	.350	.200
May	36	12	2	0	0	1	3	3	.333	.389	.385
June	44	8	1	0	1	3	2	2	.182	.273	.222
July	49	13	0	0	1	1	2	6	.265	.327	.321
August	25	7	3	0	0	0	3	1	.280	.400	.357
Sept./Oct.	22	5	1	0	0	1	1	4	.227	.273	.261
Leading Off Inn.	53	15	2	0	1	1	1	1	.283	.377	.309
Runners On	71	15	1	0	1	7	5	5	.211	.268	.291
Runners/Scor. Pos.	42	7	1	0	1	7	4	2	.167	.262	.239
Runners On/2 Out	29	2	0	0	0	1	3	3	.069	.069	.156
Scor. Pos./2 Out	21	1	0	0	0	1	2	2	.048	.048	.130
Late Inning Pressure	30	9	1	0	0	0	2	3	.300	.333	.300
Leading Off	8	2	0	0	0	0	0	1	.250	.250	.250
Runners On	10	4	0	0	0	1	0	0	.400	.400	.400
Runners/Scor. Pos.	5	1	0	0	0	1	0	0	.200	.200	.200

RUNS BATTED IN	From 1B	From 2B	From 3B	Scoring Position
Totals	0/53	2/34	4/12	6/46
Percentage	0%	6%	33%	13%
Driving In Runners from 3B with Less than Two Out:		4/5		80%

Loves to face: Jay Tibbs (5-for-5, 1 HR)
Hates to face: Dave Stewart (0-for-12)
Only A.L. player with at least 200 plate appearances to drive in fewer than 10 runs last season. Nevertheless, he started in the cleanup spot three times in September.... White Sox pitchers allowed 5.38 runs per nine innings with Salas catching compared to 4.15 with Fisk and 4.81 with Karkovice.... Started 57 games last year, but only one vs. a left-handed pitcher.... Has never homered off a lefty in 72 career at-bats.... Career average of .225 with runners in scoring position.... Made big-league debut with 1984 Cardinals, collecting his only two hits in his first three at-bats before ending the season 0-for-his-last-17.... Palindrome fans, take a look at the Angels' essay beginning on page 23.

Luis Salazar

Detroit Tigers — Bats Right

	AB	H	2B	3B	HR	RBI	BB	SO	BA	SA	OBA
Season	452	122	14	1	12	62	21	70	.270	.385	.305
vs. Left-Handers	200	64	10	1	8	37	9	24	.320	.500	.351
vs. Right-Handers	252	58	4	0	4	25	12	46	.230	.294	.269
Home	213	54	7	0	5	26	10	35	.254	.357	.292
Road	239	68	7	1	7	36	11	35	.285	.410	.316
Grass	367	96	10	1	10	51	16	51	.262	.376	.296
Artificial Turf	85	26	4	0	2	11	5	19	.306	.424	.344
April	29	9	2	0	1	6	1	7	.310	.483	.333
May	88	29	2	0	4	13	4	12	.330	.489	.362
June	103	33	2	0	3	21	3	13	.320	.427	.336
July	92	20	4	0	3	8	3	15	.217	.359	.250
August	75	16	1	0	1	7	3	11	.213	.267	.241
Sept./Oct.	65	15	3	1	0	7	7	12	.231	.308	.315
Leading Off Inn.	97	27	3	0	2	2	3	12	.278	.371	.300
Runners On	202	55	6	0	5	55	14	32	.272	.376	.321
Runners/Scor. Pos.	119	39	6	0	4	53	11	19	.328	.479	.385
Runners On/2 Out	82	24	3	0	2	23	6	11	.293	.402	.348
Scor. Pos./2 Out	54	19	3	0	2	23	6	6	.352	.519	.426
Late Inning Pressure	67	19	0	1	1	13	5	12	.284	.388	.333
Leading Off	10	3	0	0	0	0	0	2	.300	.300	.300
Runners On	37	14	0	0	1	13	3	7	.378	.459	.425
Runners/Scor. Pos.	22	10	0	0	0	11	3	4	.455	.455	.520

RUNS BATTED IN	From 1B	From 2B	From 3B	Scoring Position
Totals	5/150	19/96	26/53	45/149
Percentage	3%	20%	49%	30%
Driving In Runners from 3B with Less than Two Out:		14/29		48%

Loves to face: Curt Young (.500, 6-for-12, 2 HR)
Hates to face: Bob Welch (.095, 4-for-42)
One of two A.L. players to start at six different positions last season; most frequent starting spot: left field (44).... Batted .316 vs. ground-ball pitchers, .240 vs. fly-ballers.... Started all 55 games in which Tigers faced a left-handed starter, but only 57 of 107 games vs. right-handers.... Had five hits in nine at-bats as a pinch hitter last season, and has a .294 career mark in that role.... Served notice last March, when he had 20 RBI in spring training, 2d most by anyone in majors.... His career average at Exhibition Stadium (.417) is his highest at any A.L. ballpark; when last seen, Salazar was en route to Toronto hoping to foment labor unrest in construction of SkyDome.

Rafael Santana

New York Yankees   Bats Right

	AB	H	2B	3B	HR	RBI	BB	SO	BA	SA	OBA
Season	480	115	12	1	4	38	33	61	.240	.294	.289
vs. Left-Handers	145	34	5	0	1	5	7	12	.234	.290	.268
vs. Right-Handers	335	81	7	1	3	33	26	49	.242	.296	.298
Home	240	52	5	1	2	19	15	24	.217	.271	.261
Road	240	63	7	0	2	19	18	37	.263	.317	.317
Grass	404	95	10	1	3	32	26	51	.235	.287	.282
Artificial Turf	76	20	2	0	1	6	7	10	.263	.329	.325
April	50	8	2	0	1	2	8	7	.160	.260	.276
May	75	20	0	1	0	8	4	13	.267	.293	.305
June	90	26	5	0	1	8	6	8	.289	.378	.333
July	83	19	2	0	2	9	4	10	.229	.325	.264
August	98	25	1	0	0	5	4	9	.255	.265	.284
Sept./Oct.	84	17	2	0	0	6	7	14	.202	.226	.264
Leading Off Inn.	117	28	2	0	1	1	10	17	.239	.282	.299
Runners On	198	48	4	1	2	36	13	25	.242	.303	.286
Runners/Scor. Pos.	117	26	3	1	2	36	9	10	.222	.316	.273
Runners On/2 Out	93	23	2	0	1	15	9	12	.247	.269	.314
Scor. Pos./2 Out	63	14	1	0	0	15	5	7	.222	.238	.279
Late Inning Pressure	54	17	0	0	0	2	1	5	.315	.315	.339
Leading Off	17	3	0	0	0	0	1	2	.176	.176	.222
Runners On	15	7	0	0	0	2	0	2	.467	.467	.467
Runners/Scor. Pos.	9	3	0	0	0	2	0	2	.333	.333	.333

RUNS BATTED IN	From 1B	From 2B	From 3B	Scoring Position
Totals	3/133	12/90	19/51	31/141
Percentage	2%	13%	37%	22%
Driving In Runners from 3B with Less than Two Out:		10/21		48%

Loves to face: Rod Nichols (4-for-4, 1 2B, 1 BB)
Hates to face: Greg Swindell (0-for-9)

At age 30, Raffy was the oldest everyday shortstop in A.L. last season.... Committed seven errors in 79 games at Yankee Stadium, 15 errors in 69 games on the road. Had to do something to justify that .217 average at home.... Had only two extra-base hits (both doubles) in his last 49 games.... Batting average with runners in scoring position has been lower than his overall average in each of last five seasons.... Grounded into 17 double plays in 85 DP situations last season, 5th-highest rate in A.L. (min.: 40 opportunities).... Career average of .181 during April.... Was the major leaguer most often removed for pinch hitters last season, removed in favor of a bigger stick 40 times.

Dick Schofield

California Angels   Bats Right

	AB	H	2B	3B	HR	RBI	BB	SO	BA	SA	OBA
Season	527	126	11	6	6	34	40	57	.239	.317	.303
vs. Left-Handers	180	41	5	2	4	8	15	20	.228	.344	.302
vs. Right-Handers	347	85	6	4	2	26	25	37	.245	.303	.303
Home	274	63	5	3	3	21	9	31	.230	.303	.271
Road	253	63	6	3	3	13	31	26	.249	.332	.336
Grass	450	106	9	5	5	30	27	48	.236	.311	.290
Artificial Turf	77	20	2	1	1	4	13	9	.260	.351	.374
April	75	19	4	1	1	8	5	9	.253	.373	.296
May	93	20	0	1	1	4	5	11	.215	.269	.263
June	99	26	3	1	1	10	10	12	.263	.343	.339
July	82	16	0	2	2	3	5	8	.195	.317	.258
August	89	29	3	0	1	8	8	7	.326	.393	.388
Sept./Oct.	89	16	1	1	0	1	7	10	.180	.213	.263
Leading Off Inn.	162	42	2	2	1	1	7	12	.259	.315	.298
Runners On	200	48	6	1	2	30	17	25	.240	.310	.316
Runners/Scor. Pos.	111	25	3	1	2	30	11	16	.225	.324	.313
Runners On/2 Out	80	15	2	1	0	12	7	12	.188	.238	.278
Scor. Pos./2 Out	47	10	1	1	0	12	5	9	.213	.277	.327
Late Inning Pressure	67	24	1	2	0	3	10	6	.358	.433	.442
Leading Off	20	8	0	1	0	0	2	2	.400	.500	.455
Runners On	24	7	0	0	0	3	6	2	.292	.292	.433
Runners/Scor. Pos.	12	4	0	0	0	3	4	1	.333	.333	.500

RUNS BATTED IN	From 1B	From 2B	From 3B	Scoring Position
Totals	0/139	16/90	12/37	28/127
Percentage	0%	18%	32%	22%
Driving In Runners from 3B with Less than Two Out:		9/20		45%

Loves to face: Jerry Reuss (.800, 4-for-5, 1 HR)
Hates to face: Mark Gubicza (0-for-22)

Led A.L. shortstops in fielding percentage for second straight season, and for third time in past five years. That equals the total of A.L. fielding titles won by Mark Belanger, and it's one more than the total won by perennial Hall-of-Fame candidate Phil Rizzuto.... Career high total of hits (126) is a figure that Dick's dad topped only once in his 19-year career; Schofield Sr. had 211 career RBI, while Junior has 203 to start the '89 season.... Has a long way to go to equal dad's total of 247 pinch-hit at-bats. Young Dick has pinch-hit only once in his career.... Hit 136 points higher in Late-Inning Pressure Situations than in unpressured at-bats, biggest such difference among A.L. players in 1988.

Rick Schu

Baltimore Orioles   Bats Right

	AB	H	2B	3B	HR	RBI	BB	SO	BA	SA	OBA
Season	270	69	9	4	4	20	21	49	.256	.363	.316
vs. Left-Handers	119	30	5	1	3	14	8	20	.252	.387	.305
vs. Right-Handers	151	39	4	3	1	6	13	29	.258	.344	.325
Home	141	33	5	3	2	6	12	24	.234	.355	.299
Road	129	36	4	1	2	14	9	25	.279	.372	.336
Grass	243	60	8	4	4	19	17	41	.247	.362	.302
Artificial Turf	27	9	1	0	0	1	4	8	.333	.370	.438
April	43	9	2	2	1	5	5	8	.209	.419	.292
May	53	13	2	1	0	2	5	10	.245	.321	.310
June	34	11	0	0	1	3	7	7	.324	.412	.395
July	74	16	2	0	2	6	5	10	.216	.324	.275
August	21	4	1	1	0	3	3	3	.190	.333	.292
Sept./Oct.	45	16	2	0	0	6	0	11	.356	.400	.370
Leading Off Inn.	65	11	1	0	0	0	5	14	.169	.185	.229
Runners On	118	36	5	1	2	18	7	20	.305	.415	.349
Runners/Scor. Pos.	51	12	3	0	1	15	4	8	.235	.353	.304
Runners On/2 Out	48	11	0	1	1	8	4	9	.229	.333	.288
Scor. Pos./2 Out	25	4	0	0	1	7	3	5	.160	.280	.250
Late Inning Pressure	38	12	0	0	1	1	7	8	.316	.395	.422
Leading Off	11	2	0	0	0	0	2	1	.182	.182	.308
Runners On	17	5	0	0	0	0	3	4	.294	.294	.400
Runners/Scor. Pos.	6	0	0	0	0	0	2	2	.000	.000	.250

RUNS BATTED IN	From 1B	From 2B	From 3B	Scoring Position
Totals	3/94	9/44	4/18	13/62
Percentage	3%	20%	22%	21%
Driving In Runners from 3B with Less than Two Out:		2/6		33%

Loves to face: Jay Tibbs (.571, 4-for-7, 1 HR)
Hates to face: Dave LaPoint (0-for-10)

Hit Orioles' only grand-slam home run of 1988, a shot off Paul Kilgus on July 2; that extended Orioles' streak to 19 seasons in a row with at least one grand slam. Major league record: 40 years by Philadelphia/K.C. Athletics (1926–65).... Has hit 19 homers in 607 at-bats vs. ground-ball pitchers, nine in 512 AB vs. fly-ballers. He and Robin Yount are only A.L. players with higher home-run rate vs. ground-ball pitchers than vs. fly-ballers in each of last four years.... Career-high 12-game hitting streak, Birds' longest last season, was snapped by pinch-hit appearance in season finale. We're always heartened to see a manager who doesn't alter his strategy so that players can continue personal streaks. Now about Cal Jr....

Kevin Seitzer

Kansas City Royals   Bats Right

	AB	H	2B	3B	HR	RBI	BB	SO	BA	SA	OBA
Season	559	170	32	5	5	60	72	64	.304	.406	.388
vs. Left-Handers	153	54	10	3	1	19	21	19	.353	.477	.432
vs. Right-Handers	406	116	22	2	4	41	51	45	.286	.379	.371
Home	272	87	17	2	4	33	37	27	.320	.441	.401
Road	287	83	15	3	1	27	35	37	.289	.373	.374
Grass	222	62	10	2	1	19	24	27	.279	.356	.355
Artificial Turf	337	108	22	3	4	41	48	37	.320	.439	.408
April	85	29	4	1	1	14	9	7	.341	.447	.406
May	97	25	6	0	1	9	13	13	.258	.351	.351
June	95	32	4	2	2	7	10	7	.337	.484	.406
July	110	35	9	0	1	9	7	15	.318	.427	.364
August	63	15	3	1	0	11	12	8	.238	.317	.367
Sept./Oct.	109	34	6	1	0	10	21	14	.312	.385	.423
Leading Off Inn.	120	33	6	1	2	2	8	10	.275	.392	.326
Runners On	216	70	13	1	1	56	36	23	.324	.407	.425
Runners/Scor. Pos.	124	37	10	1	0	51	28	16	.298	.395	.430
Runners On/2 Out	81	20	6	1	0	17	14	10	.247	.346	.365
Scor. Pos./2 Out	53	13	6	1	0	17	13	7	.245	.396	.403
Late Inning Pressure	75	17	3	0	0	11	10	11	.227	.267	.310
Leading Off	19	3	0	0	0	0	3		.158	.158	.158
Runners On	24	7	2	0	0	11	5	4	.292	.375	.387
Runners/Scor. Pos.	15	6	2	0	0	11	2	0	.400	.533	.421

RUNS BATTED IN	From 1B	From 2B	From 3B	Scoring Position
Totals	8/147	26/96	21/49	47/145
Percentage	5%	27%	43%	32%
Driving In Runners from 3B with Less than Two Out:		19/29		66%

Loves to face: Richard Dotson (.533, 8-for-15)
Hates to face: Ted Higuera (.091, 1-for-11)

First player since Fred Lynn to bat .300 or better in both his rookie and sophomore seasons, while qualifying for batting title in each of those years. (Boggs had only 338 at-bats as a rookie in 1982).... Batting average was .300 or better from June 2 until the end of the season with the exception of one day (Sept. 14), when it slipped to .299.... Started 33 double plays in the field last season to lead major league third basemen.... Had no home runs in 261 at-bats after July 6.... Intentional walk on June 25 was the first of his career, coming in his 259th major league game.... Career average of .338 at Royals Stadium, .292 on the road.... Batted .342 in Late-Inning Pressure Situations in 1987.

Larry Sheets
Baltimore Orioles   Bats Left

	AB	H	2B	3B	HR	RBI	BB	SO	BA	SA	OBA
Season	452	104	19	1	10	47	42	72	.230	.343	.302
vs. Left-Handers	114	23	1	0	1	2	15	19	.202	.237	.305
vs. Right-Handers	338	81	18	1	9	45	27	53	.240	.379	.300
Home	218	45	9	1	6	26	20	40	.206	.339	.275
Road	234	59	10	0	4	21	22	32	.252	.346	.327
Grass	381	85	14	1	8	41	33	62	.223	.328	.289
Artificial Turf	71	19	5	0	2	6	9	10	.268	.423	.366
April	78	18	2	0	2	7	8	14	.231	.333	.326
May	91	16	7	0	1	14	10	17	.176	.286	.262
June	87	19	4	0	1	7	11	13	.218	.299	.303
July	77	22	2	1	1	4	6	10	.286	.377	.353
August	75	17	2	0	3	10	3	12	.227	.373	.250
Sept./Oct.	44	12	2	0	2	5	4	6	.273	.455	.333
Leading Off Inn.	109	28	6	0	2	2	10	15	.257	.367	.319
Runners On	192	50	10	0	5	42	16	33	.260	.391	.315
Runners/Scor. Pos.	102	24	5	0	2	34	12	16	.235	.343	.305
Runners On/2 Out	84	25	4	0	2	18	11	9	.298	.417	.385
Scor. Pos./2 Out	53	16	2	0	2	17	9	4	.302	.453	.403
Late Inning Pressure	80	26	4	0	1	8	9	12	.325	.413	.396
Leading Off	19	5	1	0	0	0	3	4	.263	.316	.364
Runners On	33	12	2	0	1	8	3	6	.364	.515	.405
Runners/Scor. Pos.	16	4	1	0	1	7	1	4	.250	.500	.278

RUNS BATTED IN	From 1B	From 2B	From 3B	Scoring Position
Totals	5/141	13/83	19/46	32/129
Percentage	4%	16%	41%	25%
Driving In Runners from 3B with Less than Two Out:		13/28		46%

Loves to face: Steve Farr (.625, 5-for-8, 1 HR)
Hates to face: Willie Hernandez (0-for-5, 4 SO)
1987 stats: Batted .316 with 31 home runs in 469 at-bats. Became third player in major league history to drop at least 75 batting-average points and at least 20 home runs in two straight 400–at-bat seasons. The others: Rogers Hornsby (1925–26) and Jimmy Wynn (1970–71). . . . Despite that drop in his overall batting average, he improved his mark in Late-Inning Pressure Situations 43 points from .282 in 1987. . . . Had batted over .300 with runners in scoring position in both 1986 and 1987; his average with RISP has been higher than his overall average in each of last five seasons. . . . One of four Birds to play in each of club's 21 losses to start season. The others: Murray and the Ripkens.

Pat Sheridan
Detroit Tigers   Bats Left

	AB	H	2B	3B	HR	RBI	BB	SO	BA	SA	OBA
Season	347	88	9	5	11	47	44	64	.254	.403	.339
vs. Left-Handers	26	8	0	3	1	3	3	6	.308	.654	.379
vs. Right-Handers	321	80	9	2	10	44	41	58	.249	.383	.336
Home	163	38	5	2	7	22	19	32	.233	.417	.321
Road	184	50	4	3	4	25	25	32	.272	.391	.355
Grass	309	81	8	5	9	40	34	55	.262	.408	.337
Artificial Turf	38	7	1	0	2	7	10	9	.184	.368	.354
April	35	12	0	1	1	2	5	8	.343	.486	.425
May	43	10	1	0	3	9	5	5	.233	.465	.306
June	61	16	3	1	4	17	8	15	.262	.508	.343
July	75	17	4	1	3	14	12	9	.227	.427	.341
August	88	26	3	1	0	5	7	16	.295	.352	.354
Sept./Oct.	45	7	0	1	0	0	7	11	.156	.200	.269
Leading Off Inn.	72	24	2	1	3	3	11	9	.333	.514	.422
Runners On	147	37	5	2	5	41	12	27	.252	.415	.313
Runners/Scor. Pos.	81	21	3	2	5	40	10	16	.259	.531	.347
Runners On/2 Out	49	10	2	1	1	15	3	11	.204	.347	.250
Scor. Pos./2 Out	34	8	2	1	1	15	3	8	.235	.441	.297
Late Inning Pressure	44	13	0	1	2	5	5	11	.295	.477	.367
Leading Off	10	3	0	0	1	1	3	1	.300	.600	.462
Runners On	21	7	0	0	1	4	0	6	.333	.476	.333
Runners/Scor. Pos.	9	2	0	0	1	4	0	3	.222	.556	.222

RUNS BATTED IN	From 1B	From 2B	From 3B	Scoring Position
Totals	7/106	15/64	14/40	29/104
Percentage	7%	23%	35%	28%
Driving In Runners from 3B with Less than Two Out:		12/24		50%

Loves to face: Keith Atherton (.444, 4-for-9, 2 HR)
Hates to face: Witts (2-for-24 vs. Bobby; 2-for-32 vs. Mike)
Through 1987, had one triple and one home run in 210 career at-bats vs. left-handers; then had three triples and a homer in 26 at-bats vs. lefties last year. Career: .208 vs. lefties, .267 vs. righties. . . . Batted .214 (3-for-14) with the bases loaded, but the three hits were two homers and a double. . . . Has driven in less than 20 percent of runners from scoring position in Late-Inning Pressure Situations in each of past five years. Five-year totals: 7-of-46 (15 percent). . . . Has batted higher in day games than at night in each of six full years in majors. . . . He and Daryl Boston are the only players who had at least 50 fewer at-bats in 1988 than in 1987, but who hit at least five more homers.

Ruben Sierra
Texas Rangers   Bats Left and Right

	AB	H	2B	3B	HR	RBI	BB	SO	BA	SA	OBA
Season	615	156	32	2	23	91	44	91	.254	.424	.301
vs. Left-Handers	193	55	15	0	8	31	6	15	.285	.487	.305
vs. Right-Handers	422	101	17	2	15	60	38	76	.239	.396	.299
Home	299	84	18	2	15	46	27	41	.281	.505	.336
Road	316	72	14	0	8	45	17	50	.228	.348	.266
Grass	502	131	28	2	19	77	38	71	.261	.438	.310
Artificial Turf	113	25	4	0	4	14	6	20	.221	.363	.261
April	66	11	3	1	2	5	7	12	.167	.333	.247
May	95	31	6	0	4	17	4	20	.326	.516	.360
June	119	29	7	1	5	22	9	15	.244	.445	.295
July	106	20	2	0	4	12	5	18	.189	.321	.219
August	112	32	6	0	5	18	8	13	.286	.473	.328
Sept./Oct.	117	33	8	0	3	17	11	13	.282	.427	.338
Leading Off Inn.	119	28	3	1	4	4	8	18	.235	.378	.283
Runners On	301	81	18	0	13	81	27	41	.269	.458	.321
Runners/Scor. Pos.	159	37	8	0	5	61	22	25	.233	.377	.312
Runners On/2 Out	106	24	7	0	6	28	17	17	.226	.462	.333
Scor. Pos./2 Out	69	13	5	0	3	21	16	13	.188	.391	.341
Late Inning Pressure	93	22	2	0	1	5	8	15	.237	.290	.297
Leading Off	23	4	0	0	0	0	0	5	.174	.174	.174
Runners On	48	14	2	0	1	5	8	5	.292	.396	.393
Runners/Scor. Pos.	26	6	1	0	0	3	5	2	.231	.269	.355

RUNS BATTED IN	From 1B	From 2B	From 3B	Scoring Position
Totals	17/222	20/124	31/70	51/194
Percentage	8%	16%	44%	26%
Driving In Runners from 3B with Less than Two Out:		25/38		66%

Loves to face: Bud Black (.667, 8-for-12, 2 HR)
Hates to face: Ted Higuera (.071, 1-for-14)
Owns career home-run rate of one every 23.8 at-bats; that is superior to career rates of 300-homer hitters Stargell, Yaz, Kaline, Perez, Santo, Baylor, Simmons, Hornsby. . . . Had stolen 23 of 42 bases (54.8 percent) in 1986–87, but improved his rate to 81.8 (18-for-22) last year, with 14 steals in his last 15 tries. . . . Batting average with runners in scoring position has been lower than his overall average in each of three seasons with Texas. . . . Had a higher average vs. righties than vs. lefties in both '86 and '87. . . . Played in all 132 of Rangers' games after May 10. . . . At 22, the youngest everyday player in A.L. last season. Born October 6, 1965; he's one day younger than Mario Lemieux.

Joel Skinner
New York Yankees   Bats Right

	AB	H	2B	3B	HR	RBI	BB	SO	BA	SA	OBA
Season	251	57	15	0	4	23	14	72	.227	.335	.267
vs. Left-Handers	53	12	4	0	1	9	8	12	.226	.358	.328
vs. Right-Handers	198	45	11	0	3	14	6	60	.227	.328	.249
Home	111	20	8	0	1	10	8	38	.180	.279	.233
Road	140	37	7	0	3	13	6	34	.264	.379	.295
Grass	220	50	14	0	4	19	13	67	.227	.345	.269
Artificial Turf	31	7	1	0	0	4	1	5	.226	.258	.250
April	23	2	2	0	0	2	2	8	.087	.174	.160
May	54	14	3	0	1	3	1	10	.259	.370	.268
June	77	17	4	0	1	6	3	24	.221	.312	.250
July	39	9	3	0	1	8	3	9	.231	.385	.286
August	26	4	1	0	0	2	2	9	.154	.192	.214
Sept./Oct.	32	11	2	0	1	4	3	12	.344	.500	.400
Leading Off Inn.	64	12	3	0	0	0	1	22	.188	.234	.200
Runners On	98	27	9	0	1	20	7	21	.276	.398	.321
Runners/Scor. Pos.	46	12	5	0	0	18	4	9	.261	.370	.314
Runners On/2 Out	43	11	5	0	0	9	2	9	.256	.372	.289
Scor. Pos./2 Out	24	6	3	0	0	9	1	5	.250	.375	.280
Late Inning Pressure	26	10	2	0	3	4	4	7	.385	.808	.467
Leading Off	4	1	0	0	0	0	0	1	.250	.250	.250
Runners On	8	3	0	0	1	2	1	2	.375	.750	.444
Runners/Scor. Pos.	1	1	0	0	0	0	0	0	1.000	1.000	1.000

RUNS BATTED IN	From 1B	From 2B	From 3B	Scoring Position
Totals	4/78	6/40	9/19	15/59
Percentage	5%	15%	47%	25%
Driving In Runners from 3B with Less than Two Out:		8/11		73%

Loves to face: Israel Sanchez (3-for-3)
Hates to face: Mike Morgan (0-for-9, 5 SO)
Career-high eight game hitting streak (May 22–30) could not have come at a better time. Then-manager Billy Martin's legendary patience had to be wearing thin with Skin, who was batting .098 (4-for-41) the day before streak began. . . . Batted 84 points higher on road than at home, 2d-largest such difference in A.L. last season (minimum: 100 at-bats at each). . . . Career averages: .267 with runners in scoring position, .176 in all other at-bats combined, and .125 during April. . . . It's time to play "Career Comparison." This week's guests: Skinner (.219, 13 home runs, 83 RBI, 234 strikeouts in 840 at-bats) and Uecker (.200, 14 home runs, 74 RBI, 167 strikeouts in 731 at-bats). Give us a call with your vote.

Don Slaught
New York Yankees   Bats Right

	AB	H	2B	3B	HR	RBI	BB	SO	BA	SA	OBA
Season	322	91	25	1	9	44	24	54	.283	.450	.334
vs. Left-Handers	116	36	10	0	3	19	12	25	.310	.474	.377
vs. Right-Handers	206	55	15	1	6	25	12	29	.267	.437	.309
Home	172	48	15	1	7	25	13	26	.279	.500	.330
Road	150	43	10	0	2	19	11	28	.287	.393	.339
Grass	260	74	21	1	9	36	17	42	.285	.477	.330
Artificial Turf	62	17	4	0	0	8	7	12	.274	.339	.352
April	60	22	5	0	4	15	7	14	.367	.650	.426
May	38	15	7	0	1	11	4	3	.395	.658	.477
June	20	6	2	0	0	2	0	4	.300	.400	.300
July	53	15	5	0	0	3	4	10	.283	.377	.322
August	81	18	2	0	3	8	8	12	.222	.358	.289
Sept./Oct.	70	15	4	1	1	5	1	11	.214	.343	.236
Leading Off Inn.	73	25	7	0	2	2	4	8	.342	.521	.385
Runners On	140	35	7	0	1	36	8	27	.250	.321	.288
Runners/Scor. Pos.	86	20	5	0	0	33	6	19	.233	.291	.278
Runners On/2 Out	71	19	1	0	0	13	3	15	.268	.282	.297
Scor. Pos./2 Out	47	11	1	0	0	13	3	10	.234	.255	.280
Late Inning Pressure	46	13	4	0	3	11	4	13	.283	.565	.358
Leading Off	11	3	0	0	1	1	0	2	.273	.545	.333
Runners On	19	3	1	0	0	8	2	10	.158	.211	.261
Runners/Scor. Pos.	15	3	1	0	0	8	2	8	.200	.267	.316

RUNS BATTED IN	From 1B	From 2B	From 3B	Scoring Position
Totals	3/107	12/68	20/44	32/112
Percentage	3%	18%	45%	29%
Driving In Runners from 3B with Less than Two Out:			14/20	70%

Loves to face: Ted Higuera (.391, 9-for-23, 2 HR)
Hates to face: Bert Blyleven (.033, 1-for-30)
Had seven consecutive hits, April 9–11. Strange, but true: the last four Yankees to get seven consecutive hits are not named Mattingly, Winfield, Randolph, and Henderson, but rather Slaught, Wayne Tolleson, Gary Roenicke, and Babe Hassey.... Started his Yankees' career with a 12-game hitting streak, matching his career best, but 44 games short of club record.... Season batting average dropped below .300 for first time on September 2.... Led A.L. with a .444 average vs. Brewers.... Caught 53 percent of team's innings last season; Skinner had 45 percent; Bob Geren, 2 percent. Yankees' pitchers allowed 4.68 runs per nine innings with Slaught catching, 4.54 with Skinner in the mask.

Cory Snyder
Cleveland Indians   Bats Right

	AB	H	2B	3B	HR	RBI	BB	SO	BA	SA	OBA
Season	511	139	24	3	26	75	42	101	.272	.483	.326
vs. Left-Handers	111	38	9	0	9	26	12	21	.342	.667	.400
vs. Right-Handers	400	101	15	3	17	49	30	80	.253	.433	.305
Home	270	63	9	1	11	35	19	48	.233	.396	.283
Road	241	76	15	2	15	40	23	53	.315	.581	.374
Grass	442	122	23	3	21	62	31	76	.276	.484	.322
Artificial Turf	69	17	1	0	5	13	11	25	.246	.478	.350
April	73	20	3	0	5	16	13	17	.274	.521	.382
May	93	22	3	1	5	13	6	17	.237	.452	.283
June	99	27	6	0	7	17	4	16	.273	.545	.301
July	97	31	5	0	2	11	6	19	.320	.433	.356
August	82	23	4	2	4	11	4	16	.280	.524	.310
Sept./Oct.	67	16	3	0	3	7	9	16	.239	.418	.329
Leading Off Inn.	134	32	3	2	7	7	4	23	.239	.448	.261
Runners On	218	58	12	1	12	61	21	45	.266	.495	.328
Runners/Scor. Pos.	126	30	6	0	7	48	15	28	.238	.452	.315
Runners On/2 Out	86	19	4	0	2	17	11	14	.221	.337	.316
Scor. Pos./2 Out	57	13	2	0	2	16	8	7	.228	.368	.333
Late Inning Pressure	76	18	3	0	7	16	4	21	.237	.553	.275
Leading Off	16	0	0	0	0	0	1	3	.000	.000	.059
Runners On	25	10	1	0	6	15	1	7	.400	1.160	.423
Runners/Scor. Pos.	14	4	0	0	2	7	1	5	.286	.714	.333

RUNS BATTED IN	From 1B	From 2B	From 3B	Scoring Position
Totals	12/146	22/95	15/54	37/149
Percentage	8%	23%	28%	25%
Driving In Runners from 3B with Less than Two Out:			13/25	52%

Loves to face: Mark Williamson (.625, 5-for-8, 2 HR)
Hates to face: Roger Clemens (0-for-16, 12 SO)
Tied Carlton Fisk for major league lead in slugging average vs. left-handers.... Career average of .238 at home, .277 on road. Difference of 39 points is 7th largest in majors over last 10 years (minimum: 500 AB each).... Career averages: .227 with runners in scoring position, but .385 (10-for-26) with bases loaded.... Led A.L. outfielders with 16 assists in 1988, and all outfielders in majors with 32 over last two years. Became first Indians' outfielder since Charlie Jamieson in 1928 to lead A.L. in assists.... Maybe we'll look back one day on his 52 games at shortstop the same way we look on Aaron's 43 games at second base, Mantle's seven at short, or Dale Murphy's 85 games as catcher.

Pete Stanicek
Baltimore Orioles   Bats Left and Right

	AB	H	2B	3B	HR	RBI	BB	SO	BA	SA	OBA
Season	261	60	7	1	4	18	28	45	.230	.310	.313
vs. Left-Handers	144	34	3	0	4	10	14	26	.236	.340	.311
vs. Right-Handers	117	26	4	1	0	8	14	19	.222	.274	.316
Home	135	34	5	0	2	8	14	28	.252	.333	.325
Road	126	26	2	1	2	10	14	17	.206	.286	.301
Grass	229	57	7	1	3	15	23	40	.249	.328	.324
Artificial Turf	32	3	0	0	1	3	5	5	.094	.188	.237
April	9	3	1	0	0	1	0	0	.333	.444	.400
May	44	15	2	1	0	2	4	5	.341	.432	.396
June	30	6	1	0	1	2	2	5	.200	.333	.250
July	54	9	0	0	0	2	8	11	.167	.167	.286
August	43	10	1	0	1	4	4	9	.233	.326	.292
Sept./Oct.	81	17	2	0	2	7	10	15	.210	.309	.312
Leading Off Inn.	106	18	1	0	2	2	6	17	.170	.236	.228
Runners On	87	24	3	0	0	14	16	11	.276	.310	.385
Runners/Scor. Pos.	44	12	2	0	0	13	9	8	.273	.318	.389
Runners On/2 Out	31	10	0	0	0	6	8	4	.323	.323	.462
Scor. Pos./2 Out	18	6	0	0	0	6	3	3	.333	.333	.429
Late Inning Pressure	44	7	1	0	0	7	5	9	.159	.182	.240
Leading Off	14	1	0	0	0	0	1	2	.071	.071	.133
Runners On	22	5	1	0	0	7	4	3	.227	.273	.333
Runners/Scor. Pos.	15	4	1	0	0	7	3	2	.267	.333	.368

RUNS BATTED IN	From 1B	From 2B	From 3B	Scoring Position
Totals	1/69	5/35	8/22	13/57
Percentage	1%	14%	36%	23%
Driving In Runners from 3B with Less than Two Out:			4/11	36%

Loves to face: Ted Higuera (.375, 3-for-8, 1 HR)
Hates to face: Frank Viola (0-for-5, 2 SO)
Secret to Orioles' success: Birds won 28 of 59 games in which Stanicek started in left field, but they won only 26 of 102 when other guys started in left.... Impressive career breakdown: .206 with bases empty, .317 with runners on base, .328 with runners in scoring position.... If he never plays another game at Exhibition Stadium it will be too soon: his career average there is .069 (2-for-29, 1 HR). Don't look for him to hit much better in the SkyDome. He has a career average of .200 in both the Metrodome and the Kingdome.... Staniceks are like Hirdts: Steve's the older one, Pete's second-oldest. (But despite having three other brothers, there's no Tom Stanicek in the family!)

Mike Stanley
Texas Rangers   Bats Right

	AB	H	2B	3B	HR	RBI	BB	SO	BA	SA	OBA
Season	249	57	8	0	3	27	37	62	.229	.297	.323
vs. Left-Handers	122	29	4	0	2	12	22	29	.238	.320	.354
vs. Right-Handers	127	28	4	0	1	15	15	33	.220	.276	.293
Home	143	37	6	0	1	17	18	35	.259	.322	.337
Road	106	20	2	0	2	10	19	27	.189	.264	.305
Grass	211	50	6	0	3	24	31	52	.237	.308	.328
Artificial Turf	38	7	2	0	0	3	6	10	.184	.237	.295
April	39	8	1	0	0	3	6	11	.205	.231	.304
May	56	14	2	0	2	8	9	18	.250	.393	.348
June	51	10	1	0	0	4	8	13	.196	.216	.295
July	28	7	1	0	0	4	1	5	.250	.286	.286
August	33	10	3	0	0	4	4	7	.303	.394	.378
Sept./Oct.	42	8	0	0	1	4	9	8	.190	.262	.327
Leading Off Inn.	59	11	2	0	1	1	9	13	.186	.271	.294
Runners On	103	27	5	0	1	25	14	32	.262	.340	.336
Runners/Scor. Pos.	55	15	4	0	0	23	8	22	.273	.345	.338
Runners On/2 Out	42	8	2	0	0	7	15	9	.190	.238	.306
Scor. Pos./2 Out	29	5	2	0	0	6	5	12	.172	.241	.294
Late Inning Pressure	39	7	2	0	1	4	9	12	.179	.308	.333
Leading Off	14	2	0	0	1	1	4	3	.143	.357	.333
Runners On	13	2	1	0	0	3	2	5	.154	.231	.267
Runners/Scor. Pos.	8	2	1	0	0	3	0	4	.250	.375	.250

RUNS BATTED IN	From 1B	From 2B	From 3B	Scoring Position
Totals	3/86	9/42	12/33	21/75
Percentage	3%	21%	36%	28%
Driving In Runners from 3B with Less than Two Out:			12/17	71%

Loves to face: Charlie Leibrandt (.625, 5-for-8, 2 HR)
Hates to face: Juan Berenguer (0-for-4, 4 SO)
One of three players in majors who had more at-bats in 1988 than in 1987, but whose performance declined in all eight of these categories: batting average, slugging average, on-base average, runs, hits, home runs, RBI, stolen bases; the other two guys were coming from a higher plateau: George Bell and Dale Murphy.... Had the most hits of any major leaguer without a three-hit game last season.... Finished the season hitless in his last 14 at-bats.... Had one hit in eight at-bats with the bases loaded last season, after a perfect 3-for-3 with two grand slams in 1987.... Career average of .286 vs. ground-ball pitchers, .235 vs. fly-ball pitchers; .281 at Arlington Stadium, .224 on road.

Terry Steinbach

Oakland As — Bats Right

	AB	H	2B	3B	HR	RBI	BB	SO	BA	SA	OBA
Season	351	93	19	1	9	50	33	47	.265	.402	.334
vs. Left-Handers	114	39	3	0	2	17	12	10	.342	.421	.400
vs. Right-Handers	237	54	16	1	7	33	21	37	.228	.392	.302
Home	171	49	8	0	6	25	14	19	.287	.439	.347
Road	180	44	11	1	3	25	19	28	.244	.367	.322
Grass	295	79	17	0	8	42	30	39	.268	.407	.341
Artificial Turf	56	14	2	1	1	8	3	8	.250	.375	.295
April	51	10	2	0	0	3	5	8	.196	.235	.293
May	8	2	0	0	1	3	1	3	.250	.625	.333
June	65	15	5	0	2	7	4	11	.231	.400	.292
July	72	21	1	0	3	11	6	4	.292	.431	.354
August	71	18	6	0	0	12	8	5	.254	.338	.321
Sept./Oct.	84	27	5	1	3	14	9	16	.321	.512	.385
Leading Off Inn.	79	22	4	0	2	2	7	4	.278	.405	.345
Runners On	153	43	11	0	4	45	16	24	.281	.431	.347
Runners/Scor. Pos.	82	21	5	0	3	40	11	14	.256	.427	.333
Runners On/2 Out	70	19	5	0	1	15	6	10	.271	.386	.346
Scor. Pos./2 Out	41	10	2	0	1	14	5	6	.244	.366	.340
Late Inning Pressure	52	8	2	0	0	4	5	8	.154	.192	.254
Leading Off	13	3	0	0	0	0	3	0	.231	.231	.375
Runners On	18	3	2	0	0	4	2	3	.167	.278	.286
Runners/Scor. Pos.	9	2	1	0	0	3	2	1	.222	.333	.417

RUNS BATTED IN	From 1B	From 2B	From 3B	Scoring Position
Totals	7/129	15/63	19/44	34/107
Percentage	5%	24%	43%	32%
Driving In Runners from 3B with Less than Two Out:		13/23		57%

Loves to face: John Farrell (.429, 3-for-7, 2 HR)
Hates to face: Bobby Witt (0-for-9)

First Athletics' catcher to start All-Star Game since Buddy Rosar in 1948—forty years and two cities ago. . . . Warmed up for his All-Star home run against Gooden by homering off of Doc's former teammate, Walt Terrell, the day before the break. . . . Nine of the last 18 All-Star Game MVP's have gone on to play in the World Series that October, but seven of those nine have been on the Series loser. . . . Batted .286 in 74 starts behind the plate, .214 in 19 starts at other positions (DH-1B-3B-LF). So much for the "Let's-keep-his-bat-in-the-lineup" Theory. . . . Batted 114 points higher vs. left-handers than vs. right-handers, largest difference in majors last season (minimum: 100 AB vs. each).

Kurt Stillwell

Kansas City Royals — Bats Left and Right

	AB	H	2B	3B	HR	RBI	BB	SO	BA	SA	OBA
Season	459	115	28	5	10	54	47	76	.251	.399	.322
vs. Left-Handers	124	28	6	0	2	13	12	19	.226	.323	.299
vs. Right-Handers	335	87	22	5	8	41	35	57	.260	.427	.331
Home	249	64	15	4	4	26	22	35	.257	.398	.320
Road	210	51	13	1	6	28	25	41	.243	.400	.325
Grass	169	39	10	0	2	12	18	31	.231	.325	.307
Artificial Turf	290	76	18	5	8	42	29	45	.262	.441	.331
April	72	20	3	2	2	9	4	10	.278	.458	.325
May	97	25	6	1	3	17	15	16	.258	.433	.353
June	100	26	8	1	2	9	11	14	.260	.420	.333
July	85	19	6	0	2	8	5	13	.224	.365	.275
August	99	24	5	1	1	11	12	21	.242	.343	.324
Sept./Oct.	6	1	0	0	0	0	0	2	.167	.167	.167
Leading Off Inn.	123	22	7	0	1	1	17	22	.179	.260	.279
Runners On	169	52	12	2	5	49	13	25	.308	.491	.362
Runners/Scor. Pos.	98	30	9	2	2	42	8	17	.306	.500	.366
Runners On/2 Out	72	16	4	0	2	14	5	14	.222	.361	.291
Scor. Pos./2 Out	48	10	3	0	0	10	2	10	.208	.271	.269
Late Inning Pressure	59	19	2	1	1	7	10	16	.322	.441	.429
Leading Off	12	3	1	0	0	0	2	3	.250	.333	.357
Runners On	19	9	0	0	0	6	3	4	.474	.474	.565
Runners/Scor. Pos.	15	7	0	0	0	6	1	4	.467	.467	.529

RUNS BATTED IN	From 1B	From 2B	From 3B	Scoring Position
Totals	7/116	18/82	19/41	37/123
Percentage	6%	22%	46%	30%
Driving In Runners from 3B with Less than Two Out:		16/24		67%

Loves to face: Jimmy Jones (.571, 4-for-7)
Hates to face: Roger Clemens (0-for-10, 6 SO)

Royals were 66–55 with Stillwell as their starting shortstop, 18–22 without him there. . . . Turned 23 in June: he was youngest major leaguer to start at least half of his team's games at shortstop. . . . Had a power surge during a visit to the Metrodome in May: homered in all three games of series there, with six hits in 10 at-bats. In his only other visit to Minnesota (in late September) he was hitless in two at-bats as a pinch hitter. . . . Batted .303 in day games, .232 at night. . . . Career batting average of .193 leading off innings. . . . Batting averages with runners on base and with runners in scoring position have been higher than his overall average in each of his three seasons in the majors.

B.J. Surhoff

Milwaukee Brewers — Bats Left

	AB	H	2B	3B	HR	RBI	BB	SO	BA	SA	OBA
Season	493	121	21	0	5	38	31	49	.245	.318	.292
vs. Left-Handers	115	22	3	0	2	6	8	12	.191	.270	.256
vs. Right-Handers	378	99	18	0	3	32	23	37	.262	.333	.304
Home	244	55	10	0	2	15	22	25	.225	.291	.294
Road	249	66	11	0	3	23	9	24	.265	.345	.291
Grass	423	101	17	0	5	35	26	43	.239	.314	.286
Artificial Turf	70	20	4	0	0	3	5	6	.286	.343	.333
April	60	14	1	0	0	5	3	8	.233	.250	.266
May	90	26	6	0	1	6	8	7	.289	.389	.347
June	78	19	4	0	1	2	4	8	.244	.333	.280
July	97	22	2	0	1	8	3	7	.227	.278	.257
August	88	20	6	0	0	7	6	12	.227	.295	.284
Sept./Oct.	80	20	2	0	2	10	7	7	.250	.350	.311
Leading Off Inn.	98	23	5	0	1	1	2	5	.235	.316	.250
Runners On	203	56	9	0	2	35	19	23	.276	.350	.342
Runners/Scor. Pos.	125	32	6	0	2	34	14	16	.256	.352	.333
Runners On/2 Out	98	24	5	0	0	16	9	10	.245	.296	.315
Scor. Pos./2 Out	65	15	4	0	0	16	9	8	.231	.292	.333
Late Inning Pressure	74	14	1	0	0	3	7	10	.189	.203	.259
Leading Off	19	2	0	0	0	0	1	2	.105	.105	.150
Runners On	32	5	1	0	0	3	5	7	.156	.188	.270
Runners/Scor. Pos.	25	4	1	0	0	3	5	6	.160	.200	.300

RUNS BATTED IN	From 1B	From 2B	From 3B	Scoring Position
Totals	4/133	15/103	14/40	29/143
Percentage	3%	15%	35%	20%
Driving In Runners from 3B with Less than Two Out:		7/18		39%

Loves to face: Jimmy Key (.714, 5-for-7, 1 HR)
Hates to face: Floyd Bannister (0-for-9)

Stole 21 bases last season; there were only 25 other stolen bases by starting catchers on the other 13 A.L. teams combined. . . . Batted .314 at County Stadium and .318 vs. left-handed pitchers in 1987; 1988 figures were .225 and .191, respectively. . . . Career averages: .303 with runners on base, and .244 with the bases empty, and .421 (16-for-38, 3 HR) at Tiger Stadium. . . . Opportunities to drive in runners from scoring position were similar in 1987 and 1988, but results were much different: 50 of 141 (35.5%) in 1987, 29 of 143 (20.3%) last year. . . . Milwaukee pitchers allowed only 3.58 runs per nine innings with Surhoff catching; with Bill Schroeder, 4.09; with Charlie O'Brien, 4.30.

Dale Sveum

Milwaukee Brewers — Bats Left and Right

	AB	H	2B	3B	HR	RBI	BB	SO	BA	SA	OBA
Season	467	113	14	4	9	51	21	122	.242	.347	.274
vs. Left-Handers	167	42	4	4	4	20	6	41	.251	.395	.278
vs. Right-Handers	300	71	10	0	5	31	15	81	.237	.320	.272
Home	239	67	9	4	2	26	11	57	.280	.377	.311
Road	228	46	5	0	7	25	10	65	.202	.316	.237
Grass	405	104	12	4	9	45	18	108	.257	.373	.289
Artificial Turf	62	9	2	0	0	6	3	14	.145	.177	.182
April	71	17	0	1	3	9	2	23	.239	.394	.260
May	97	27	2	2	3	16	8	26	.278	.433	.336
June	81	18	3	0	3	11	1	25	.222	.370	.226
July	104	19	5	1	0	4	5	30	.183	.250	.220
August	102	27	4	0	0	10	5	18	.265	.304	.299
Sept./Oct.	12	5	0	0	0	1	0	0	.417	.417	.417
Leading Off Inn.	105	22	4	1	2	2	4	23	.210	.324	.245
Runners On	185	50	5	3	5	47	9	48	.270	.411	.299
Runners/Scor. Pos.	113	32	3	2	3	42	7	31	.283	.425	.317
Runners On/2 Out	83	24	3	2	3	23	6	23	.289	.482	.337
Scor. Pos./2 Out	57	15	2	2	2	21	5	17	.263	.474	.323
Late Inning Pressure	71	24	4	2	1	6	2	19	.338	.493	.356
Leading Off	18	4	1	1	0	0	0	5	.222	.389	.222
Runners On	26	11	2	1	1	6	2	6	.423	.692	.464
Runners/Scor. Pos.	15	2	0	0	0	3	2	5	.133	.133	.235

RUNS BATTED IN	From 1B	From 2B	From 3B	Scoring Position
Totals	5/125	17/85	20/49	37/134
Percentage	4%	20%	41%	28%
Driving In Runners from 3B with Less than Two Out:		13/23		57%

Loves to face: Allan Anderson (.455, 5-for-11)
Hates to face: Joel Davis (0-for-7, 4 SO)

One of four A.L. switch-hitters to homer from both sides of the plate in a single game last season. . . . Career breakdown: .230 with bases empty, .270 with men on base, .287 with runners in scoring position, .299 with two outs and RISP. . . . Another in long line of Milwaukee players—both Braves and Brewers—who have hit more of his home runs on road (26) than at County Stadium (15). . . . Career batting average is under .200 at five different ballparks: California, Kansas City, Minnesota, New York, and Toronto. . . . Born on November 23, 1963, the day after JFK died. Four shortstops who were regular major league starters last year were born that month: Sveum, Andres Thomas, Rey Quinones, Walt Weiss.

Pat Tabler

Indians/Royals — Bats Right

	AB	H	2B	3B	HR	RBI	BB	SO	BA	SA	OBA
Season	444	125	22	3	2	67	46	68	.282	.358	.349
vs. Left-Handers	139	42	9	1	1	27	17	16	.302	.403	.377
vs. Right-Handers	305	83	13	2	1	40	29	52	.272	.338	.336
Home	214	60	12	3	0	30	26	30	.280	.364	.358
Road	230	65	10	0	2	37	20	38	.283	.352	.341
Grass	241	68	7	1	2	32	22	42	.282	.344	.346
Artificial Turf	203	57	15	2	0	35	24	26	.281	.374	.354
April	66	15	2	1	0	9	11	11	.227	.288	.338
May	74	17	3	0	1	8	11	16	.230	.311	.333
June	82	19	5	0	0	11	5	15	.232	.293	.270
July	63	25	2	1	0	9	1	8	.397	.460	.409
August	93	29	8	1	0	17	15	9	.312	.419	.404
Sept./Oct.	66	20	2	0	1	13	3	9	.303	.379	.343
Leading Off Inn.	92	17	7	0	0	0	13	14	.185	.261	.292
Runners On	211	71	12	2	2	67	21	29	.336	.441	.393
Runners/Scor. Pos.	126	42	8	2	2	63	16	22	.333	.476	.403
Runners On/2 Out	95	32	7	1	1	31	10	15	.337	.463	.406
Scor. Pos./2 Out	59	20	4	1	1	28	8	12	.339	.492	.426
Late Inning Pressure	61	11	2	0	0	9	7	10	.180	.213	.257
Leading Off	13	3	1	0	0	0	4	2	.231	.308	.412
Runners On	29	4	1	0	0	9	2	4	.138	.172	.182
Runners/Scor. Pos.	15	2	1	0	0	9	1	3	.133	.200	.167

RUNS BATTED IN	From 1B	From 2B	From 3B	Scoring Position
Totals	10/143	21/99	34/57	55/156
Percentage	7%	21%	60%	35%
Driving In Runners from 3B with Less than Two Out:			22/32	69%

Loves to face: Willie Hernandez (.417, 5-for-12, 3 HR)
Hates to face: Dennis Eckersley (.100, 1-for-10)

One of three major leaguers (along with Winfield and Brett) to drive in at least 30 percent of runners from scoring position in each of last six seasons. His RISP batting average has been over .300 in each of those years. . . . Career average of .302 on grass fields, .244 on carpets. That's the largest such difference in majors over past 10 years (minimum: 500 AB on each). Has hit better on grass fields in each of last six years. . . . Eight hits in nine at-bats with bases loaded last season raised his career average to .578 (37-for-64, two HR, seven BB). More than 20 percent of his career RBI have been produced in bases-loaded situations, which account for less than three percent of his plate appearances.

Danny Tartabull

Kansas City Royals — Bats Right

	AB	H	2B	3B	HR	RBI	BB	SO	BA	SA	OBA
Season	507	139	38	3	26	102	76	119	.274	.515	.369
vs. Left-Handers	149	43	13	0	8	27	29	29	.289	.537	.404
vs. Right-Handers	358	96	25	3	18	75	47	90	.268	.506	.354
Home	249	72	17	3	15	48	44	51	.289	.562	.397
Road	258	67	21	0	11	54	32	68	.260	.469	.341
Grass	200	53	17	0	7	43	22	51	.265	.455	.338
Artificial Turf	307	86	21	3	19	59	54	68	.280	.554	.389
April	80	24	9	0	4	17	9	14	.300	.563	.378
May	83	21	5	1	6	14	19	21	.253	.554	.398
June	76	23	5	0	3	10	13	11	.303	.487	.396
July	96	22	6	1	3	16	5	31	.229	.406	.279
August	86	23	8	1	4	24	22	21	.267	.523	.405
Sept./Oct.	86	26	5	0	6	21	8	21	.302	.570	.362
Leading Off Inn.	101	23	9	0	2	2	22	29	.228	.376	.366
Runners On	264	80	21	2	13	89	37	56	.303	.545	.389
Runners/Scor. Pos.	167	48	14	2	7	75	29	41	.287	.521	.390
Runners On/2 Out	126	38	12	1	4	36	21	28	.302	.508	.413
Scor. Pos./2 Out	82	23	8	1	0	26	16	19	.280	.402	.410
Late Inning Pressure	81	16	5	1	1	5	11	23	.198	.321	.293
Leading Off	15	2	2	0	0	0	4	6	.133	.267	.316
Runners On	39	7	2	0	0	4	3	10	.179	.231	.238
Runners/Scor. Pos.	20	4	1	0	0	4	2	7	.200	.250	.273

RUNS BATTED IN	From 1B	From 2B	From 3B	Scoring Position
Totals	17/185	30/132	29/74	59/206
Percentage	9%	23%	39%	29%
Driving In Runners from 3B with Less than Two Out:			22/38	58%

Loves to face: Bert Blyleven (.361, 13-for-36, 6 HR)
Hates to face: Tom Henke (0-for-10, 5 SO)

Combined statistics over last three years: .286 batting average, .516 slugging average, 85 home runs, 299 RBI. George Bell is only player in majors with totals that good in each of those categories. . . . Averaged 1.84 putouts per nine innings, lowest of any A.L. right fielder (minimum: 500 innings). . . . Had 93 RBI with eight games remaining on the schedule and proceeded to drive in at least one run in each of next six games to finish season with 102. . . . Daddy Jose had career totals of two home runs and 107 RBI in nine years in majors. . . . Hit three grand slams last season, has six over last three years. . . . Yearly batting averages with runners on base since 1986: .303, .302, .303.

Mickey Tettleton

Baltimore Orioles — Bats Left and Right

	AB	H	2B	3B	HR	RBI	BB	SO	BA	SA	OBA
Season	283	74	11	1	11	37	28	70	.261	.424	.330
vs. Left-Handers	147	37	4	0	9	24	13	35	.252	.463	.313
vs. Right-Handers	136	37	7	1	2	13	15	35	.272	.382	.349
Home	133	37	3	1	7	21	17	30	.278	.474	.358
Road	150	37	8	0	4	16	11	40	.247	.380	.305
Grass	236	61	9	1	11	34	24	59	.258	.445	.328
Artificial Turf	47	13	2	0	0	3	4	11	.277	.319	.340
April	0	0	0	0	0	0	0	0	—	—	—
May	46	11	0	0	0	8	1	6	.239	.370	.265
June	57	14	4	0	3	9	6	17	.255	.474	.313
July	55	14	2	0	4	7	5	14	.255	.509	.317
August	67	21	2	1	1	8	6	13	.313	.418	.378
Sept./Oct.	58	14	3	0	1	5	10	20	.241	.345	.353
Leading Off Inn.	71	19	0	1	1	1	1	12	.268	.338	.288
Runners On	126	29	7	0	5	31	21	36	.230	.405	.340
Runners/Scor. Pos.	70	15	4	0	2	25	14	21	.214	.357	.345
Runners On/2 Out	56	15	3	0	3	16	10	14	.268	.482	.379
Scor. Pos./2 Out	33	9	2	0	1	12	7	7	.273	.424	.400
Late Inning Pressure	56	12	2	0	2	6	4	19	.214	.357	.267
Leading Off	8	0	0	0	0	0	0	2	.000	.000	.000
Runners On	27	4	0	0	1	5	3	13	.148	.259	.233
Runners/Scor. Pos.	17	3	0	0	1	5	3	6	.176	.353	.300

RUNS BATTED IN	From 1B	From 2B	From 3B	Scoring Position
Totals	6/104	10/58	10/28	20/86
Percentage	6%	17%	36%	23%
Driving In Runners from 3B with Less than Two Out:			7/15	47%

Loves to face: Allan Anderson (.429, 3-for-7, 1 HR)
Hates to face: Bert Blyleven (0-for-11)

One of four A.L. switch-hitters, and probably the least likely among them, to hit home runs from both sides of plate in a single game last season. Hit four home runs over the course of 21 at-bats from July 7 to July 19. . . . One hit in 19 career pinch-hit at-bats, including 0-for-9 last year. . . . Ended the season with 50 consecutive errorless games behind plate. . . . Hit .302 vs. ground-ball pitchers last season, .229 vs. fly-ballers. . . . Has had 17 career chances to drive in runners from scoring position in Late-Inning Pressure Situations with two outs; he's 0-for-17. . . . Has .095 (2-for-21) career average with the bases loaded, lowest among active players with at least 20 at-bats. But he has driven in eight runs with bases-loaded walks.

Jim Traber

Baltimore Orioles — Bats Left

	AB	H	2B	3B	HR	RBI	BB	SO	BA	SA	OBA
Season	352	78	6	0	10	44	19	42	.222	.324	.261
vs. Left-Handers	116	27	2	0	2	12	9	18	.233	.302	.289
vs. Right-Handers	236	51	4	0	8	32	10	24	.216	.335	.247
Home	184	44	4	0	4	18	12	27	.239	.326	.288
Road	168	34	2	0	6	26	7	15	.202	.321	.232
Grass	299	68	5	0	8	37	18	34	.227	.324	.271
Artificial Turf	53	10	1	0	2	7	1	8	.189	.321	.204
April	11	1	0	0	0	0	0	1	.091	.091	.091
May	0	0	0	0	0	0	0	0	—	—	—
June	89	26	1	0	3	16	4	9	.292	.404	.319
July	95	17	1	0	4	12	6	11	.179	.316	.233
August	87	19	2	0	2	11	5	16	.218	.310	.253
Sept./Oct.	70	15	2	0	1	5	4	5	.214	.286	.253
Leading Off Inn.	76	15	1	0	1	1	5	7	.197	.250	.247
Runners On	163	44	3	0	7	41	8	21	.270	.417	.299
Runners/Scor. Pos.	100	23	2	0	2	30	5	14	.230	.310	.259
Runners On/2 Out	92	21	1	0	2	21	3	11	.228	.304	.253
Scor. Pos./2 Out	70	15	0	0	1	18	2	9	.214	.257	.236
Late Inning Pressure	60	9	0	0	0	3	4	5	.150	.150	.203
Leading Off	14	2	0	0	0	0	1	0	.143	.143	.200
Runners On	23	4	0	0	0	3	2	3	.174	.174	.240
Runners/Scor. Pos.	13	3	0	0	0	3	2	1	.231	.231	.333

RUNS BATTED IN	From 1B	From 2B	From 3B	Scoring Position
Totals	7/124	16/74	11/48	27/122
Percentage	6%	22%	23%	22%
Driving In Runners from 3B with Less than Two Out:			7/14	50%

Loves to face: Bret Saberhagen (.375, 3-for-8, 2 HR)
Hates to face: Mike Witt (0-for-8)

More than his name is similar to Tabler. He has eight hits in 19 career at-bats with the bases loaded. . . . Slugging percentage was 5th-lowest among A.L. players with 200 or more plate appearances. . . . Drove in at least one run in six consecutive games in June. . . . Orioles were 25–26 with Traber starting at first base, 4–6 in his outfield starts, and 7–23 when he was the starting DH. . . . Career averages: .266 vs. ground-ball pitchers, .209 vs. fly-ball pitchers; .281 with runners on base, .192 with the bases empty. . . . Born Dec. 26, 1961. Big sports question of that week: Would Vince Lombardi's Packers, who hadn't won NFL title since 1944, beat Giants in NFL Championship Game?

Alan Trammell

Bats Right

Detroit Tigers	AB	H	2B	3B	HR	RBI	BB	SO	BA	SA	OBA
Season	466	145	24	1	15	70	46	46	.311	.464	.373
vs. Left-Handers	138	48	9	0	5	16	18	12	.348	.522	.420
vs. Right-Handers	328	97	15	1	10	54	28	34	.296	.439	.352
Home	215	67	12	0	7	37	19	11	.312	.465	.364
Road	251	78	12	1	8	33	27	35	.311	.462	.380
Grass	389	120	19	0	15	60	35	39	.308	.473	.365
Artificial Turf	77	25	5	1	0	10	11	7	.325	.416	.411
April	82	20	4	1	3	12	9	10	.244	.427	.312
May	98	39	5	0	4	17	9	10	.398	.571	.444
June	87	29	4	0	3	11	7	6	.333	.483	.385
July	52	13	3	0	1	5	7	3	.250	.365	.339
August	96	34	7	0	3	19	7	6	.354	.521	.393
Sept./Oct.	51	10	1	0	1	6	7	11	.196	.275	.317
Leading Off Inn.	112	37	4	0	4	4	9	9	.330	.473	.380
Runners On	222	69	13	0	6	61	25	29	.311	.450	.375
Runners/Scor. Pos.	124	36	7	0	4	56	21	17	.290	.444	.379
Runners On/2 Out	89	26	4	0	2	22	11	14	.292	.404	.382
Scor. Pos./2 Out	48	14	2	0	2	22	10	7	.292	.458	.424
Late Inning Pressure	72	29	2	0	5	22	6	6	.403	.639	.449
Leading Off	23	7	0	0	1	1	1	3	.304	.435	.333
Runners On	35	15	2	0	3	20	4	3	.429	.743	.487
Runners/Scor. Pos.	24	11	2	0	3	20	4	2	.458	.917	.536

RUNS BATTED IN	From 1B	From 2B	From 3B	Scoring Position
Totals	7/167	21/97	27/59	48/156
Percentage	4%	22%	46%	31%
Driving In Runners from 3B with Less than Two Out:			18/33	55%

Loves to face: Ed Vande Berg (.563, 9-for-16, 4 HR)
Hates to face: Mark Williamson (0-for-7)
One of 10 batting-title qualifiers to hit .300 in both 1987 and 1988; six of the 10 are American League infielders.... Had 20 HR/20 SB seasons in both 1986 and 1987. He's the only shortstop in history to have two such seasons anytime during his career. ... Yearly batting averages in Late-Inning Pressure Situations since 1983: .358, .373, .213, .303, .431, .403. He is the only player to bat over .400 in LIPS in *either* of the last two seasons (minimum: 25 hits), and he's done it in *both*. ...Eight hits (including one grand slam) in 13 at-bats with the bases loaded last season. ... One of two active players with 100+ home runs and 100+ sacrifice bunts; Bob Boone is the other.

Willie Upshaw

Bats Left

Cleveland Indians	AB	H	2B	3B	HR	RBI	BB	SO	BA	SA	OBA
Season	493	121	22	3	11	50	62	66	.245	.369	.330
vs. Left-Handers	74	15	1	0	0	6	7	12	.203	.216	.280
vs. Right-Handers	419	106	21	3	11	44	55	54	.253	.396	.338
Home	244	58	9	3	3	24	32	29	.238	.336	.325
Road	249	63	13	0	8	26	30	37	.253	.402	.335
Grass	420	101	18	3	8	43	55	57	.240	.355	.327
Artificial Turf	73	20	4	0	3	7	7	9	.274	.452	.346
April	75	19	0	1	4	11	13	11	.253	.440	.364
May	84	17	5	1	0	3	9	8	.202	.286	.280
June	98	22	5	1	4	8	11	10	.224	.418	.309
July	91	29	6	0	1	15	9	11	.319	.418	.376
August	94	24	5	0	1	9	16	17	.255	.340	.363
Sept./Oct.	51	10	1	0	1	4	4	9	.196	.275	.250
Leading Off Inn.	89	19	4	0	2	2	12	11	.213	.326	.314
Runners On	216	50	9	2	3	42	28	33	.231	.333	.317
Runners/Scor. Pos.	124	25	2	1	2	35	22	25	.202	.282	.313
Runners On/2 Out	88	20	4	1	0	21	15	20	.227	.295	.340
Scor. Pos./2 Out	64	16	1	1	0	18	10	18	.250	.297	.351
Late Inning Pressure	68	12	1	0	0	3	7	9	.176	.191	.250
Leading Off	15	4	0	0	0	0	0	1	.267	.267	.267
Runners On	34	5	0	0	0	3	5	6	.147	.147	.250
Runners/Scor. Pos.	24	2	0	0	0	3	3	6	.083	.083	.179

RUNS BATTED IN	From 1B	From 2B	From 3B	Scoring Position
Totals	7/153	19/103	13/40	32/143
Percentage	5%	18%	33%	22%
Driving In Runners from 3B with Less than Two Out:			8/15	53%

Loves to face: Dan Petry (.432, 16-for-37, 3 HR)
Hates to face: Shane Rawley (.105, 2-for-19, 8 SO)
Led A.L. first basemen in errors (12), but ended the season with 36 consecutive errorless games. Stand by for special Records Committee ruling on whether or not such streaks remain alive from season to season across the International Date Line. ... RBI total decreased in each of last five seasons: 104, 84, 65, 60, 58, 50. ... Drove in only three of 28 runners from scoring position in Late-Inning Pressure Situations last season. ... Started 113 of 122 games in which Indians were opposed by right-handed starters, but only 16 of 40 games against lefties. ... Batted 41 points higher in day games than he did in night games last season. What better place for him than the Land of the Rising Sun?

Dave Valle

Bats Right

Seattle Mariners	AB	H	2B	3B	HR	RBI	BB	SO	BA	SA	OBA
Season	290	67	15	2	10	50	18	38	.231	.400	.295
vs. Left-Handers	125	33	7	0	4	15	9	12	.264	.416	.316
vs. Right-Handers	165	34	8	2	6	35	9	26	.206	.388	.279
Home	145	35	10	1	5	25	9	18	.241	.428	.304
Road	145	32	5	1	5	25	9	20	.221	.372	.285
Grass	102	20	3	1	4	19	6	15	.196	.363	.261
Artificial Turf	188	47	12	1	6	31	12	23	.250	.420	.313
April	72	11	2	0	2	10	5	11	.153	.264	.218
May	49	11	3	2	2	13	5	6	.224	.490	.304
June	56	16	1	0	2	5	4	8	.286	.411	.355
July	52	16	7	0	3	16	1	7	.308	.615	.345
August	0	0	0	0	0	0	0	0	—	—	—
Sept./Oct.	61	13	2	0	1	6	3	6	.213	.295	.279
Leading Off Inn.	57	11	0	0	4	4	4	7	.193	.404	.270
Runners On	124	37	12	2	5	45	6	14	.298	.548	.350
Runners/Scor. Pos.	80	28	7	2	4	42	4	12	.350	.638	.400
Runners On/2 Out	53	22	6	2	3	25	2	7	.415	.774	.456
Scor. Pos./2 Out	38	17	3	2	3	24	2	7	.447	.868	.488
Late Inning Pressure	43	13	3	0	1	9	2	11	.302	.442	.362
Leading Off	8	0	0	0	0	0	2	4	.000	.000	.200
Runners On	17	9	3	0	1	9	0	2	.529	.882	.556
Runners/Scor. Pos.	12	7	2	0	1	9	0	1	.583	1.000	.615

RUNS BATTED IN	From 1B	From 2B	From 3B	Scoring Position
Totals	5/79	20/69	15/44	35/113
Percentage	6%	29%	34%	31%
Driving In Runners from 3B with Less than Two Out:			10/27	37%

Loves to face: Scott Bailes (.429, 3-for-7, 2 HR)
Hates to face: Jimmy Key (0-for-10)
One of the clutch hitting stars of 1988. ... First, he hit 118 points higher with runners on base than with bases empty, 4th largest such difference in majors (minimum: 100 AB each way). Ahead of him: Buckner, Baylor, Gwynn. ... He was also the only player to hit at least 150 points higher with runners in scoring position than at other times (minimum: 50 AB with RISP). ... And he hit .447 with runners in scoring position and two outs, best in majors. Before you get too excited, remember that Al Pedrique led majors in that category in 1987. ... Grounded into 13 double plays in 56 DP situations, 2d-worst rate in A.L. (min.: 40 opportunities). A.L.'s highest rate? Brian Harper (12 GIDP in 50 chances).

Greg Walker

Bats Left

Chicago White Sox	AB	H	2B	3B	HR	RBI	BB	SO	BA	SA	OBA
Season	377	93	22	1	8	42	29	77	.247	.374	.304
vs. Left-Handers	112	26	5	1	1	10	5	22	.232	.321	.269
vs. Right-Handers	265	67	17	0	7	32	24	55	.253	.396	.318
Home	205	47	12	1	2	15	15	44	.229	.327	.288
Road	172	46	10	0	6	27	14	33	.267	.430	.323
Grass	329	76	19	1	7	37	29	75	.231	.359	.298
Artificial Turf	48	17	3	0	1	5	0	2	.354	.479	.354
April	84	20	7	0	1	10	6	14	.238	.357	.286
May	97	23	4	0	1	9	4	19	.237	.309	.267
June	108	31	7	0	2	11	7	16	.287	.407	.330
July	88	19	4	1	4	12	12	28	.216	.420	.327
August	0	0	0	0	0	0	0	0	—	—	—
Sept./Oct.	0	0	0	0	0	0	0	0	—	—	—
Leading Off Inn.	87	18	4	0	2	2	5	13	.207	.322	.258
Runners On	160	49	11	1	2	36	15	30	.306	.425	.369
Runners/Scor. Pos.	85	24	8	1	1	32	13	21	.282	.435	.382
Runners On/2 Out	67	18	4	1	0	12	6	14	.269	.358	.347
Scor. Pos./2 Out	35	8	4	1	0	12	4	11	.229	.400	.341
Late Inning Pressure	63	14	1	0	1	3	5	20	.222	.286	.290
Leading Off	12	1	0	0	0	0	1	6	.083	.083	.214
Runners On	32	7	0	0	0	2	4	10	.219	.219	.306
Runners/Scor. Pos.	20	4	0	0	0	2	2	6	.200	.200	.273

RUNS BATTED IN	From 1B	From 2B	From 3B	Scoring Position
Totals	6/118	16/69	12/30	28/99
Percentage	5%	23%	40%	28%
Driving In Runners from 3B with Less than Two Out:			9/16	56%

Loves to face: Bob Stanley (.643, 9-for-14, 2 HR)
Hates to face: John Cerutti (0-for-13)
Has made at least 100 plate appearances vs. left-handed pitchers in each of last four years, but his career average is 55 points lower vs. lefties (.227) than vs. right-handers (.282). ... Averaged 0.42 assists per nine innings last season, lowest in majors among first baseman (minimum: 500 innings). ... White Sox have 88-year A.L. history, but no first baseman has reached the 1000-game mark. Club leaders: Earl Sheehy, 938; Joe Kuhel, 880; Tom McCraw, 735; Mike Squires, 688; Jiggs Donahue, 646; Walker, 640. Walker passed Zeke Bonura and Frank Isbell in 1988. ... Will be 30 years old on Oct. 6; he was born the day the Sox had their last World Series win, a 1–0 triumph by Bob Shaw over Sandy Koufax.

Gary Ward

New York Yankees — Bats Right

	AB	H	2B	3B	HR	RBI	BB	SO	BA	SA	OBA
Season	231	52	8	0	4	24	24	41	.225	.312	.302
vs. Left-Handers	128	29	7	0	4	20	15	26	.227	.375	.313
vs. Right-Handers	103	23	1	0	0	4	9	15	.223	.233	.289
Home	100	23	4	0	3	13	10	18	.230	.360	.306
Road	131	29	4	0	1	11	14	23	.221	.275	.299
Grass	193	43	7	0	3	21	17	37	.223	.306	.291
Artificial Turf	38	9	1	0	1	3	7	4	.237	.342	.356
April	21	7	1	0	0	0	6	5	.333	.381	.500
May	49	9	0	0	1	5	2	6	.184	.245	.216
June	52	11	1	0	1	4	6	8	.212	.288	.293
July	42	5	3	0	0	5	3	7	.119	.190	.196
August	27	7	1	0	0	1	4	6	.259	.296	.355
Sept./Oct.	40	13	2	0	2	9	3	9	.325	.525	.364
Leading Off Inn.	43	12	2	0	1	1	7	10	.279	.395	.392
Runners On	116	24	4	0	3	23	11	20	.207	.319	.279
Runners/Scor. Pos.	74	14	2	0	3	23	7	13	.189	.338	.265
Runners On/2 Out	45	8	2	0	1	9	5	10	.178	.289	.260
Scor. Pos./2 Out	33	5	2	0	1	9	4	7	.152	.303	.243
Late Inning Pressure	34	13	1	0	2	6	3	6	.382	.588	.462
Leading Off	13	4	1	0	0	0	1	3	.308	.385	.400
Runners On	10	6	0	0	2	6	2	2	.600	1.200	.692
Runners/Scor. Pos.	7	3	0	0	2	6	0	2	.429	1.286	.500

RUNS BATTED IN	From 1B	From 2B	From 3B	Scoring Position
Totals	3/83	10/64	7/25	17/89
Percentage	4%	16%	28%	19%
Driving In Runners from 3B with Less than Two Out:		6/14		43%

Loves to face: Ed Vande Berg (.769, 10-for-13)
Hates to face: Eric Plunk (0-for-10)

Batting average in Late-Inning Pressure Situations was highest on Yankees and 4th-best in A.L. Ward has batted .329 in those situations over last three years, 12th-best in majors (minimum: 150 LIPS at-bats).... Batted .294 (5-for-17, one HR) as a pinch hitter.... Batting average with runners in scoring position was lowest of his career.... Has hit for higher average against ground-ball pitchers than vs. fly-ball pitchers in each of last six seasons. Career averages: .302 vs. ground-ballers, .263 vs. fly-ballers.... A couple of sad streaks: he's hitless in his last 30 at-bats against former mates from Texas, and over past two years he is 0-for-14 with the bases loaded and two outs.

Claudell Washington

New York Yankees — Bats Left

	AB	H	2B	3B	HR	RBI	BB	SO	BA	SA	OBA
Season	455	140	22	3	11	64	24	74	.308	.442	.342
vs. Left-Handers	48	15	4	0	1	12	2	10	.313	.458	.333
vs. Right-Handers	407	125	18	3	10	52	22	64	.307	.440	.343
Home	218	78	13	1	6	37	15	33	.358	.509	.397
Road	237	62	9	2	5	27	9	41	.262	.380	.290
Grass	390	124	18	3	9	55	21	66	.318	.449	.353
Artificial Turf	65	16	4	0	2	9	3	8	.246	.400	.279
April	50	14	4	0	2	10	4	9	.280	.480	.333
May	84	21	4	0	1	7	2	10	.250	.333	.267
June	82	34	3	3	1	15	3	13	.415	.561	.430
July	57	18	3	0	0	5	2	9	.316	.368	.355
August	89	33	4	0	3	17	7	16	.371	.517	.412
Sept./Oct.	93	20	4	0	4	10	6	17	.215	.387	.260
Leading Off Inn.	94	23	2	0	2	2	4	14	.245	.330	.276
Runners On	214	64	13	1	4	57	11	30	.299	.425	.333
Runners/Scor. Pos.	135	36	9	0	2	51	11	23	.267	.378	.322
Runners On/2 Out	94	24	5	1	0	18	3	14	.255	.330	.286
Scor. Pos./2 Out	67	16	4	0	0	17	3	11	.239	.299	.282
Late Inning Pressure	67	22	0	0	3	9	3	14	.328	.493	.366
Leading Off	16	5	0	0	1	1	2	3	.313	.500	.389
Runners On	32	9	1	0	1	7	0	8	.281	.406	.303
Runners/Scor. Pos.	18	6	1	0	0	5	0	5	.333	.389	.368

RUNS BATTED IN	From 1B	From 2B	From 3B	Scoring Position
Totals	9/151	14/109	30/60	44/169
Percentage	6%	13%	50%	26%
Driving In Runners from 3B with Less than Two Out:		20/31		65%

Loves to face: Dan Schatzeder (.636, 7-for-11)
Hates to face: Bill Long (0-for-10)

Highest batting average since he hit .308 in 148 games for Oakland in 1975.... June batting average was best in majors.... Batted .372 in day games, .287 at night.... Started 98 of 104 games in which Yankees faced right-handed starters, but only one of 57 games vs. lefties.... Only home run off a left-handed pitcher was 18th-inning game-winner off Willie Hernandez.... Career totals: 150 home runs, 295 stolen bases; needs five steals to become 10th player to reach 150 HR, 300 SB.... Has homered at 25 major league parks, including old Met Stadium in Minnesota. Among current stadiums, he has gone homerless at only County Stadium (115 career AB) and Busch Stadium (102 career AB).

Ron Washington

Cleveland Indians — Bats Right

	AB	H	2B	3B	HR	RBI	BB	SO	BA	SA	OBA
Season	223	57	14	2	2	21	9	35	.256	.363	.298
vs. Left-Handers	55	14	4	0	1	5	1	6	.255	.382	.281
vs. Right-Handers	168	43	10	2	1	16	8	29	.256	.357	.304
Home	116	27	8	0	0	10	5	19	.233	.302	.288
Road	107	30	6	2	2	11	4	16	.280	.430	.310
Grass	182	45	11	2	1	17	6	31	.247	.346	.289
Artificial Turf	41	12	3	0	1	4	3	4	.293	.439	.341
April	3	1	0	0	0	1	0	1	.333	.333	.500
May	41	12	1	1	0	3	1	7	.293	.366	.310
June	64	16	5	1	0	6	3	12	.250	.359	.304
July	88	16	5	0	2	11	4	12	.182	.307	.223
August	14	9	2	0	0	1	0	0	.643	.786	.667
Sept./Oct.	13	3	1	0	0	0	0	4	.231	.308	.286
Leading Off Inn.	59	18	4	0	0		4	10	.305	.373	.359
Runners On	94	23	6	2	1	20	4	16	.245	.383	.280
Runners/Scor. Pos.	51	13	3	1	1	18	2	9	.255	.412	.291
Runners On/2 Out	44	10	3	1	0	6	1	11	.227	.341	.244
Scor. Pos./2 Out	26	6	1	0	0	6	0	7	.231	.385	.231
Late Inning Pressure	34	9	3	1	0	4	1	6	.265	.412	.306
Leading Off	6	1	0	0	0	0	0	2	.167	.167	.167
Runners On	16	4	1	1	0	4	1	2	.250	.438	.294
Runners/Scor. Pos.	7	4	1	1	0	4	0	0	.571	1.000	.571

RUNS BATTED IN	From 1B	From 2B	From 3B	Scoring Position
Totals	3/68	8/39	8/18	16/57
Percentage	4%	21%	44%	28%
Driving In Runners from 3B with Less than Two Out:		6/9		67%

Loves to face: Chris Codiroli (.571, 4-for-7)
Hates to face: Keith Atherton (0-for-7, 4 SO)

Broke into majors with N.L. champion Dodgers in 1977. Returned to majors in 1981; since then, has not played on a team with a winning record (combined: 545–698, .438).... Committed six errors in his last seven games at shortstop. His .933 fielding percentage in 54 games there was lowest by any shortstop in majors last season (minimum: 50 games). It was lowest mark by any 50-game shortstop in A.L. since Billy Smith fielded .932 for Angels in 1975.... Batting average on artificial turf has been higher than on grass fields in each of last six years.... Career breakdown: .273 with the bases empty, .245 with runners on base, .237 with runners in scoring position, .221 with two outs and RISP.

Walt Weiss

Oakland As — Bats Left and Right

	AB	H	2B	3B	HR	RBI	BB	SO	BA	SA	OBA
Season	452	113	17	3	3	38	35	56	.250	.321	.312
vs. Left-Handers	101	21	3	1	0	7	6	8	.208	.257	.250
vs. Right-Handers	351	92	14	2	3	31	29	48	.262	.339	.329
Home	211	50	9	1	0	12	12	30	.237	.289	.292
Road	241	63	8	2	3	26	23	26	.261	.349	.330
Grass	375	92	14	3	2	26	32	46	.245	.315	.316
Artificial Turf	77	21	3	0	1	12	3	10	.273	.351	.293
April	58	10	1	0	0	6	3	2	.172	.190	.215
May	62	15	2	0	1	4	11	9	.242	.323	.355
June	91	27	3	0	1	7	3	9	.297	.363	.326
July	81	16	3	1	1	10	5	10	.198	.296	.253
August	80	22	3	2	0	2	6	12	.275	.363	.341
Sept./Oct.	80	23	5	0	0	9	7	14	.288	.350	.359
Leading Off Inn.	91	22	4	0	0	0	8	10	.242	.286	.337
Runners On	206	56	8	2	1	36	9	20	.272	.345	.302
Runners/Scor. Pos.	115	27	4	2	1	35	9	11	.235	.330	.286
Runners On/2 Out	102	23	4	2	1	15	4	8	.225	.333	.262
Scor. Pos./2 Out	58	13	3	2	1	15	4	5	.224	.397	.274
Late Inning Pressure	56	4	2	0	0	0	4	14	.071	.107	.148
Leading Off	19	3	1	0	0	0	2	5	.158	.211	.273
Runners On	14	0	0	0	0	0	0	1	.000	.000	.000
Runners/Scor. Pos.	9	0	0	0	0	0	0	1	.000	.000	.000

RUNS BATTED IN	From 1B	From 2B	From 3B	Scoring Position
Totals	3/152	12/92	20/57	32/149
Percentage	2%	13%	35%	21%
Driving In Runners from 3B with Less than Two Out:		15/29		52%

Loves to face: John Farrell (5-for-5, 2 2B, 1 BB)
Hates to face: Neil Allen (0-for-7)

Batted 131 points higher vs. fly-ball pitchers (.311) than vs. ground-ballers, largest difference in majors (minimum: 100 AB vs. each).... His .071 batting average in Late-Inning Pressure Situations was lowest among the 300 major league hitters who batted most frequently in those situations last season.... Made 140 starts, batting 8th or 9th in every one.... Similar stats to those of teammate Tony Phillips in his first full year.... Here goes another myth: Teams can win titles with rookies at shortstop. Three of last season's four division winners did it (Weiss, Jody Reed of Boston, and Mets' Kevin Elster). And there have been 11 others since divisional play began.

Lou Whitaker

Detroit Tigers — Bats Left

	AB	H	2B	3B	HR	RBI	BB	SO	BA	SA	OBA
Season	403	111	18	2	12	55	66	61	.275	.419	.376
vs. Left-Handers	92	21	2	1	0	12	15	22	.228	.272	.330
vs. Right-Handers	311	90	16	1	12	43	51	39	.289	.463	.390
Home	175	47	7	1	8	22	34	28	.269	.457	.388
Road	228	64	11	1	4	33	32	33	.281	.390	.366
Grass	334	87	11	2	11	44	60	50	.260	.404	.371
Artificial Turf	69	24	7	0	1	11	6	11	.348	.493	.400
April	64	17	4	1	2	10	18	6	.266	.453	.427
May	80	24	3	0	2	6	11	11	.300	.413	.380
June	89	24	3	1	1	13	13	19	.270	.360	.359
July	78	20	4	0	3	13	11	13	.256	.423	.348
August	79	23	2	0	3	10	12	10	.291	.430	.385
Sept./Oct.	13	3	2	0	1	3	1	2	.231	.615	.286
Leading Off Inn.	86	22	2	0	2	2	10	11	.256	.349	.333
Runners On	165	46	7	1	7	50	38	27	.279	.461	.410
Runners/Scor. Pos.	99	28	5	0	3	40	26	16	.283	.424	.425
Runners On/2 Out	61	14	2	1	2	17	13	10	.230	.393	.365
Scor. Pos./2 Out	45	9	1	0	2	15	6	8	.200	.356	.294
Late Inning Pressure	51	12	2	0	0	4	8	9	.235	.275	.339
Leading Off	13	4	1	0	0	0	3	1	.308	.385	.438
Runners On	23	5	1	0	0	4	5	6	.217	.261	.357
Runners/Scor. Pos.	15	4	1	0	0	4	4	3	.267	.333	.421

RUNS BATTED IN	From 1B	From 2B	From 3B	Scoring Position
Totals	8/108	15/84	20/42	35/126
Percentage	7%	18%	48%	28%
Driving In Runners from 3B with Less than Two Out:			64%	

Loves to face: Roger Clemens (.406, 13-for-32, 1 HR)
Hates to face: Tom Henke (0-for-15)
Hasn't topped .230 mark vs. left-handed pitchers since he hit .307 against them in 1983, but has a streak of eight consecutive seasons hitting above .280 vs. right-handers. . . . Led majors with five bases-loaded walks last season. . . . Has hit at least a dozen homers in each of last seven seasons; Joe Morgan's best streak in that category was eight years. . . . Has played 1522 games in the field, but has played only second base. All-time leaders in games played at each position among players who never played elsewhere: 1B, Jake Daubert (2001); 2B, Bobby Doerr (1852); 3B, Willie Kamm (1672); SS, Luis Aparicio (2581); OF, Lou Brock (2507), Max Carey (2422), and Zack Wheat (2350); C, Rick Ferrell (1805).

Devon White

California Angels — Bats Left and Right

	AB	H	2B	3B	HR	RBI	BB	SO	BA	SA	OBA
Season	455	118	22	2	11	51	23	84	.259	.389	.297
vs. Left-Handers	150	37	6	1	6	15	8	24	.247	.420	.289
vs. Right-Handers	305	81	16	1	5	36	15	60	.266	.374	.301
Home	211	50	13	0	3	27	13	46	.237	.341	.283
Road	244	68	9	2	8	24	10	38	.279	.430	.310
Grass	370	94	21	0	8	42	21	73	.254	.376	.297
Artificial Turf	85	24	1	2	3	9	2	11	.282	.447	.299
April	80	20	4	1	2	11	6	8	.250	.400	.307
May	18	4	1	0	0	3	4	8	.222	.278	.333
June	70	16	1	1	1	7	3	14	.229	.314	.260
July	119	34	4	0	5	15	4	21	.286	.445	.315
August	120	32	8	0	2	12	6	24	.267	.383	.302
Sept./Oct.	48	12	4	0	1	6	1	13	.250	.396	.265
Leading Off Inn.	140	43	5	5	4	5	4	23	.307	.471	.326
Runners On	173	46	9	1	4	44	10	28	.266	.399	.312
Runners/Scor. Pos.	113	29	6	1	3	42	7	23	.257	.407	.303
Runners On/2 Out	59	12	1	1	1	9	6	6	.203	.305	.277
Scor. Pos./2 Out	43	6	0	1	0	7	5	5	.140	.186	.229
Late Inning Pressure	64	16	3	1	1	8	4	12	.250	.375	.304
Leading Off	16	6	1	0	0	0	0	2	.375	.438	.375
Runners On	25	7	2	1	1	8	1	4	.280	.560	.333
Runners/Scor. Pos.	17	5	1	1	1	8	0	3	.294	.647	.294

RUNS BATTED IN	From 1B	From 2B	From 3B	Scoring Position
Totals	2/115	18/87	20/53	38/140
Percentage	2%	21%	38%	27%
Driving In Runners from 3B with Less than Two Out:			18/32	56%

Loves to face: Scott Bailes (.375, 3-for-8, 3 HR)
Hates to face: Rich Yett (0-for-9)
Led major league center fielders with average of 3.35 putouts per nine innings. . . . Successful on 11 of his last 13 stolen base attempts, after being thrown out on six of first 12 tries. . . . Career average of .299 leading off innings, but he has walked only 10 times in 274 innings led off in his major league career. Last season, Angels were 33–24 with White batting in leadoff spot, 42–63 with others there. . . . Has 11 hits (including two grand slams) in 24 career at-bats with the bases loaded. . . . Career average of .241 at Anaheim, .276 on road; among 14 current A.L. stadiums, only Oakland Coliseum and Tiger Stadium have depressed batting averages more than Anaheim Stadium over past five years.

Frank White

Kansas City Royals — Bats Right

	AB	H	2B	3B	HR	RBI	BB	SO	BA	SA	OBA
Season	537	126	25	1	8	58	21	67	.235	.330	.266
vs. Left-Handers	155	41	10	0	2	16	6	18	.265	.368	.296
vs. Right-Handers	382	85	15	1	6	42	15	49	.223	.314	.254
Home	269	65	15	1	3	29	12	25	.242	.338	.274
Road	268	61	10	0	5	29	9	42	.228	.321	.257
Grass	211	53	10	0	5	27	8	32	.251	.370	.281
Artificial Turf	326	73	15	1	3	31	13	35	.224	.304	.256
April	79	15	4	0	1	9	3	17	.190	.278	.217
May	88	18	3	0	1	6	7	9	.205	.273	.271
June	78	26	5	1	4	19	2	10	.333	.577	.349
July	97	34	8	0	1	9	4	10	.351	.464	.373
August	97	16	3	0	1	7	2	12	.165	.227	.194
Sept./Oct.	98	17	2	0	0	8	3	9	.173	.194	.198
Leading Off Inn.	121	29	4	0	3	3	1	21	.240	.347	.246
Runners On	240	53	12	1	3	50	11	21	.221	.317	.252
Runners/Scor. Pos.	155	33	8	1	3	51	9	18	.213	.335	.251
Runners On/2 Out	105	20	6	0	2	20	6	12	.190	.305	.241
Scor. Pos./2 Out	79	16	5	0	2	20	5	10	.203	.342	.259
Late Inning Pressure	86	15	2	0	1	5	5	20	.174	.233	.226
Leading Off	23	3	1	0	1	1	0	9	.130	.304	.130
Runners On	37	7	0	0	0	4	1	3	.189	.189	.205
Runners/Scor. Pos.	16	2	0	0	0	4	0	2	.125	.125	.118

RUNS BATTED IN	From 1B	From 2B	From 3B	Scoring Position
Totals	4/160	17/121	29/76	46/197
Percentage	3%	14%	38%	23%
Driving In Runners from 3B with Less than Two Out:			21/40	53%

Loves to face: Les Straker (.857, 6-for-7, 1 HR)
Hates to face: Dennis Eckersley (.085, 4-for-47, 13 SO)
Oldest major leaguer to play at least half of his team's games at second base. . . . Led major league second basemen with a .994 fielding percentage. He started the season with 62 consecutive error-less games at second base, 26 games shy of Jerry Adair's A.L. record. Then put together a streak of 56 consecutive errorless games, broken on last day of September. . . . Now ranks third in major league history with a career fielding percentage of .984. . . . August batting average was 3d lowest in A.L. (minimum: two PA per game). . . . Went 132 consecutive at-bats without an extra-base hit, longest streak in A.L. . . . Batting average with runners on base, year by year since 1984: .289, .281, .276, .269, .221.

Ernie Whitt

Toronto Blue Jays — Bats Left

	AB	H	2B	3B	HR	RBI	BB	SO	BA	SA	OBA
Season	398	100	11	2	16	70	61	38	.251	.410	.348
vs. Left-Handers	39	11	1	0	2	5	8	8	.282	.462	.408
vs. Right-Handers	359	89	10	2	14	65	53	30	.248	.404	.341
Home	194	47	5	1	9	34	37	23	.242	.418	.359
Road	204	53	6	1	7	36	24	15	.260	.402	.336
Grass	159	39	2	1	6	29	21	11	.245	.384	.328
Artificial Turf	239	61	9	1	10	41	40	27	.255	.427	.360
April	50	13	1	1	0	7	5	1	.260	.320	.327
May	63	11	1	0	1	9	9	7	.175	.238	.274
June	71	17	1	1	2	11	12	7	.239	.366	.341
July	69	18	4	0	2	10	10	5	.261	.406	.363
August	66	21	2	0	5	15	10	7	.318	.576	.397
Sept./Oct.	79	20	2	0	6	18	15	11	.253	.506	.368
Leading Off Inn.	85	26	3	0	4	4	13	6	.306	.482	.398
Runners On	171	46	4	2	7	61	26	20	.269	.439	.355
Runners/Scor. Pos.	114	33	3	2	6	59	18	12	.289	.500	.370
Runners On/2 Out	76	20	1	2	5	28	14	8	.263	.526	.378
Scor. Pos./2 Out	56	17	1	2	5	28	10	4	.304	.661	.409
Late Inning Pressure	44	7	0	0	2	7	7	5	.159	.295	.259
Leading Off	11	3	0	0	2	2	1	1	.273	.818	.333
Runners On	20	2	0	0	0	5	5	3	.100	.100	.250
Runners/Scor. Pos.	15	1	0	0	0	5	3	3	.067	.067	.150

RUNS BATTED IN	From 1B	From 2B	From 3B	Scoring Position
Totals	5/114	21/90	28/53	49/143
Percentage	4%	23%	53%	34%
Driving In Runners from 3B with Less than Two Out:			21/32	66%

Loves to face: Jeff Russell (.545, 6-for-11, 1 HR)
Hates to face: Frank Tanana (0-for-7, 6 SO)
Started all 110 games in which the Jays faced a right-handed starter last season, but did not start any of Toronto's 52 games vs. south-paws. Hasn't started against a southpaw since July 5, 1987. . . . Hitless in his last 19 at-bats as a pinch hitter, including 0-for-11 in 1988. . . . Batted .194 in day games, .280 at night. . . . Batting average with runners in scoring position, year by year since 1984: .198, .229, .234, .272, .289. . . . Has hit for a higher average in road games than he has at Exhibition Stadium in each of the last five seasons. . . . Interesting breakdown to his career with the bases loaded: .465 (20-for-43, two HR) with less than two out, .185 (5-for-27, no HR) with two out.

Curtis Wilkerson

Texas Rangers — Bats Left and Right

	AB	H	2B	3B	HR	RBI	BB	SO	BA	SA	OBA
Season	338	99	12	5	0	28	26	43	.293	.358	.345
vs. Left-Handers	47	12	1	0	0	1	2	7	.255	.277	.286
vs. Right-Handers	291	87	11	5	0	27	24	36	.299	.371	.354
Home	152	44	6	3	0	18	9	22	.289	.368	.331
Road	186	55	6	2	0	10	17	21	.296	.349	.356
Grass	271	80	10	4	0	25	20	36	.295	.362	.346
Artificial Turf	67	19	2	1	0	3	6	7	.284	.343	.342
April	11	2	0	0	0	1	1	1	.182	.182	.250
May	60	23	2	3	0	6	3	7	.383	.517	.422
June	63	20	4	1	0	9	10	7	.317	.413	.411
July	68	19	2	0	0	4	4	6	.279	.309	.315
August	79	20	1	1	0	3	4	10	.253	.291	.294
Sept./Oct.	57	15	3	0	0	5	4	12	.263	.316	.311
Leading Off Inn.	76	21	2	0	0	0	2	9	.276	.303	.295
Runners On	156	45	4	3	0	28	16	16	.288	.353	.354
Runners/Scor. Pos.	87	27	1	2	0	25	13	14	.310	.368	.398
Runners On/2 Out	70	14	1	2	0	13	8	10	.200	.271	.291
Scor. Pos./2 Out	49	9	0	2	0	12	8	9	.184	.265	.310
Late Inning Pressure	58	19	2	2	0	4	6	3	.328	.431	.391
Leading Off	13	5	1	0	0	0	1	0	.385	.462	.429
Runners On	32	9	0	2	0	4	4	1	.281	.406	.361
Runners/Scor. Pos.	17	6	0	1	0	3	4	1	.353	.471	.476

RUNS BATTED IN	From 1B	From 2B	From 3B	Scoring Position
Totals	5/108	12/73	11/31	23/104
Percentage	5%	16%	35%	22%
Driving In Runners from 3B with Less than Two Out:			8/14	57%

Loves to face: Jim Clancy (.500, 9-for-18)
Hates to face: Dennis Martinez (.091, 1-for-11, 5 SO)
Overall batting average, year by year since 1986: .237, .268, .293. . . . Started 89 of 111 games in which the Rangers faced a right-handed starter, but only six of 50 games vs. left-handers. . . . Made 90 of his 95 starts from either the 8th or 9th batting-order position. . . . Didn't hit a home run last season after hitting two, one from each side of the plate, in 1987. . . . Career breakdown: .255 with bases empty, .255 with runners on base, .256 with runners in scoring position. . . . No home runs in 603 career at-bats with runners on base. . . . Career batting average of .183 during April. . . . Leaves Texas ranking fifth in team history in games played at second base, third in games at shortstop.

Glenn Wilson

Seattle Mariners — Bats Right

	AB	H	2B	3B	HR	RBI	BB	SO	BA	SA	OBA
Season	284	71	10	1	3	17	15	52	.250	.324	.286
vs. Left-Handers	101	32	5	0	1	9	4	15	.317	.396	.340
vs. Right-Handers	183	39	5	1	2	8	11	37	.213	.284	.256
Home	132	36	7	0	2	11	5	21	.273	.371	.297
Road	152	35	3	1	1	6	10	31	.230	.283	.276
Grass	117	25	3	1	1	5	8	25	.214	.282	.262
Artificial Turf	167	46	7	0	2	12	7	27	.275	.353	.303
April	83	18	3	1	0	4	4	17	.217	.277	.250
May	72	21	3	0	2	4	7	14	.292	.417	.354
June	82	22	3	0	1	7	4	11	.268	.341	.302
July	47	10	1	0	0	2	0	10	.213	.234	.208
August	0	0	0	0	0	0	0	0	—	—	—
Sept./Oct.	0	0	0	0	0	0	0	0	—	—	—
Leading Off Inn.	79	26	5	1	0	0	2	12	.329	.418	.346
Runners On	108	19	3	0	2	16	6	24	.176	.259	.216
Runners/Scor. Pos.	67	9	1	0	2	15	2	17	.134	.239	.155
Runners On/2 Out	44	7	1	0	1	4	4	12	.159	.250	.229
Scor. Pos./2 Out	29	4	0	0	1	4	2	6	.138	.241	.194
Late Inning Pressure	42	8	0	0	0	2	2	11	.190	.190	.222
Leading Off	11	3	0	0	0	0	1	1	.273	.273	.333
Runners On	16	2	0	0	0	2	1	5	.125	.125	.167
Runners/Scor. Pos.	14	1	0	0	0	2	0	4	.071	.071	.067

RUNS BATTED IN	From 1B	From 2B	From 3B	Scoring Position
Totals	2/71	2/53	10/31	12/84
Percentage	3%	4%	32%	14%
Driving In Runners from 3B with Less than Two Out:			12/27	39%

Loves to face: Frank DiPino (.778, 7-for-9, 3 BB, 2 HR)
Hates to face: Craig Lefferts (.091, 1-for-11)
Figures *above* are for A.L. only. . . . Hitless in his first 17 at-bats of the season. . . . Drove in only 11 runs in his first 60 games. . . . Came to the plate 105 times between his last walk as a Mariner and his first walk as a Pirate. . . . Averaged 19 assists a year from 1985 through 1987, but collected only five assists (both leagues combined) in 1988. . . . Batted .195 with runners on base, .295 with the bases empty (combined leagues), 2d-largest difference in majors (minimum 100 AB each way). . . . Grounded into 17 double plays in 72 opportunities last season, 3d-highest rate in the majors (min.: 40 opp.). . . . At-bats, RBIs, and batting average have all decreased in each of the last three seasons.

Ken Williams

Chicago White Sox — Bats Right

	AB	H	2B	3B	HR	RBI	BB	SO	BA	SA	OBA
Season	220	35	4	2	8	28	10	64	.159	.305	.221
vs. Left-Handers	96	20	3	1	3	9	4	22	.208	.354	.255
vs. Right-Handers	124	15	1	1	5	19	6	42	.121	.266	.196
Home	109	17	3	1	3	13	6	32	.156	.284	.225
Road	111	18	1	1	5	15	4	32	.162	.324	.217
Grass	205	32	4	2	7	26	10	61	.156	.298	.222
Artificial Turf	15	3	0	0	1	2	0	3	.200	.400	.200
April	57	9	1	2	4	13	7	19	.158	.456	.290
May	70	12	2	0	1	6	1	20	.171	.243	.194
June	4	2	1	0	0	0	0	0	.500	.750	.500
July	34	5	0	0	3	0	10	.147	.147	.189
August	23	4	0	0	1	2	1	5	.174	.304	.240
Sept./Oct.	32	3	0	0	2	4	1	10	.094	.281	.121
Leading Off Inn.	64	7	1	0	1	1	3	18	.109	.172	.186
Runners On	85	16	1	1	5	25	4	26	.188	.400	.245
Runners/Scor. Pos.	53	10	1	1	3	21	3	17	.189	.415	.262
Runners On/2 Out	28	4	0	1	2	6	2	6	.143	.429	.226
Scor. Pos./2 Out	19	2	0	1	1	4	2	6	.105	.368	.227
Late Inning Pressure	39	9	3	0	0	3	3	16	.231	.308	.279
Leading Off	13	2	0	0	0	0	1	4	.154	.154	.214
Runners On	16	3	1	0	0	3	1	10	.188	.250	.222
Runners/Scor. Pos.	13	3	1	0	0	3	1	8	.231	.308	.267

RUNS BATTED IN	From 1B	From 2B	From 3B	Scoring Position
Totals	4/62	7/43	9/25	16/68
Percentage	6%	16%	36%	24%
Driving In Runners from 3B with Less than Two Out:			7/17	41%

Loves to face: Jeff Musselman (.800, 4-for-5)
Hates to face: Greg Cadaret (0-for-4, 4 SO)
No hit, no field? Batting average was lowest among all major leaguers with 200 or more at-bats. Also committed 14 errors in 32 games at third base. . . . Only 10 other players in this century (none with White Sox) had sub-.160 average in season of 200+ at-bats. Last one was Jim Mason of 1975 Yankees (.152). All-time records: .132 by Bill Bergen (1911 Dodgers) in N.L., .135 by Ray Oyler (1968 Tigers) in A.L. . . . From the "Since You Asked" Dept.: The record for errors by a third baseman in a single season is 91, by Charles Hickman of the New York Giants in 1900. . . . They keep telling us about this guy's potential. But his career totals are pretty similar to those of Joe Garagiola's through 1949.

Willie Wilson

Kansas City Royals — Bats Left and Right

	AB	H	2B	3B	HR	RBI	BB	SO	BA	SA	OBA
Season	591	155	17	11	1	37	22	106	.262	.333	.289
vs. Left-Handers	186	48	8	6	0	7	5	45	.258	.366	.275
vs. Right-Handers	405	107	9	5	1	30	17	61	.264	.319	.295
Home	297	84	8	8	0	21	10	45	.283	.364	.303
Road	294	71	9	3	1	16	12	61	.241	.303	.274
Grass	222	51	5	2	1	12	8	48	.230	.284	.262
Artificial Turf	369	104	12	9	0	25	14	58	.282	.363	.305
April	86	25	1	4	0	2	3	17	.291	.395	.322
May	118	37	5	0	1	16	2	20	.314	.381	.320
June	102	24	3	3	0	2	2	18	.235	.324	.257
July	105	23	3	0	0	8	3	22	.219	.248	.241
August	100	30	4	2	0	5	3	14	.300	.380	.320
Sept./Oct.	80	16	1	2	0	4	9	15	.200	.263	.272
Leading Off Inn.	206	51	7	5	1	1	6	37	.248	.345	.272
Runners On	207	61	7	3	0	36	9	41	.295	.357	.317
Runners/Scor. Pos.	101	28	3	1	0	34	7	22	.277	.327	.310
Runners On/2 Out	83	21	1	0	0	14	4	14	.253	.265	.287
Scor. Pos./2 Out	54	13	1	0	0	14	3	11	.241	.259	.281
Late Inning Pressure	84	24	3	1	0	10	2	10	.286	.345	.302
Leading Off	20	5	1	1	0	1	2	2	.250	.400	.286
Runners On	37	14	2	0	0	10	1	7	.378	.432	.395
Runners/Scor. Pos.	24	9	0	0	0	10	1	4	.375	.375	.400

RUNS BATTED IN	From 1B	From 2B	From 3B	Scoring Position
Totals	3/151	13/72	20/53	33/125
Percentage	2%	18%	38%	26%
Driving In Runners from 3B with Less than Two Out:			12/27	44%

Loves to face: Frank Viola (.348, 16-for-46, 1 HR)
Hates to face: Steve Ontiveros (0-for-14)
Fourth player in baseball history to have stolen 30+ bases in 11 consecutive seasons: Lou Brock (14 years), Ty Cobb (12), Honus Wagner (11), and Wilson. . . . Successful in 19 consecutive stolen-base attempts (May 17–August 21). . . . Shared A.L. lead in triples, his fifth season as leader, tying A.L. record set by Wahoo Sam Crawford. . . . Had one assist in 142 games. Only three other outfielders in major league history had so few assists in 140 or more games: Harmon Killebrew in 1964, Ken Singleton in 1978, Kirk Gibson in 1985. . . . His lone assist came on a triple play. . . . Batted .322 in day games, .241 at night. . . . Seven hits (all singles) in 57 at-bats, with one walk, with bases loaded since 1981.

Dave Winfield

Bats Right

New York Yankees	AB	H	2B	3B	HR	RBI	BB	SO	BA	SA	OBA
Season	559	180	37	2	25	107	69	88	.322	.530	.398
vs. Left-Handers	175	58	11	1	11	36	31	20	.331	.594	.432
vs. Right-Handers	384	122	26	1	14	71	38	68	.318	.500	.381
Home	274	91	15	0	12	45	34	38	.332	.518	.405
Road	285	89	22	2	13	62	35	50	.312	.540	.391
Grass	459	142	28	1	18	75	59	76	.309	.492	.390
Artificial Turf	100	38	9	1	7	32	10	12	.380	.700	.436
April	83	33	5	1	7	29	15	14	.398	.735	.485
May	95	32	5	0	5	19	11	15	.337	.547	.406
June	94	29	10	0	3	12	13	14	.309	.511	.398
July	89	31	4	1	5	18	13	15	.348	.584	.431
August	104	30	7	0	4	14	6	14	.288	.471	.327
Sept./Oct.	94	25	6	0	1	15	11	16	.266	.362	.349
Leading Off Inn.	127	36	8	0	3	3	18	17	.283	.417	.372
Runners On	268	91	17	1	13	95	36	39	.340	.556	.418
Runners/Scor. Pos.	153	52	10	1	7	81	29	23	.340	.556	.446
Runners On/2 Out	118	38	7	1	5	34	16	18	.322	.525	.403
Scor. Pos./2 Out	69	21	4	1	2	27	14	9	.304	.478	.422
Late Inning Pressure	71	21	2	0	3	7	9	16	.296	.451	.375
Leading Off	18	7	1	0	0	0	4	2	.389	.444	.500
Runners On	27	7	1	0	0	4	3	6	.259	.296	.333
Runners/Scor. Pos.	15	2	0	0	0	3	3	3	.133	.133	.278

RUNS BATTED IN	From 1B	From 2B	From 3B	Scoring Position
Totals	17/207	29/108	36/74	65/182
Percentage	8%	27%	49%	36%
Driving In Runners from 3B with Less than Two Out:			23/43	53%

Loves to face: Juan Nieves (.636, 7-for-11, 2 HR)
Hates to face: Jose Nunez (0-for-4, 4 SO)
Set A.L. record for RBIs during the month of April with 29; tied the M.L. mark, set by Ron Cey in 1977 and equalled by Dale Murphy in 1985. . . . Has a seven-game All-Star Game hitting streak, tying the mark shared by Mickey Mantle and Joe Morgan. . . . Has started six straight All-Star Games. The record for consecutive All-Star starts by an A.L. outfielder is seven, by Joe DiMaggio (1936–42). . . . Tied with Roger Maris for 7th place on Yankees' home-run list, 47 behind Graig Nettles. . . . Has driven in better than 30 percent of runners in scoring position in each of the last eight seasons. . . . Led majors with 744 RBIs during his first eight seasons with Yankees. Of course, for some that's not enough.

Robin Yount

Bats Right

Milwaukee Brewers	AB	H	2B	3B	HR	RBI	BB	SO	BA	SA	OBA
Season	621	190	38	11	13	91	63	63	.306	.465	.369
vs. Left-Handers	183	52	7	1	7	26	30	11	.284	.448	.381
vs. Right-Handers	438	138	31	10	6	65	33	52	.315	.473	.363
Home	300	92	14	4	7	46	33	19	.307	.450	.374
Road	321	98	24	7	6	45	30	44	.305	.480	.364
Grass	523	158	29	9	12	75	56	51	.302	.461	.368
Artificial Turf	98	32	9	2	1	16	7	12	.327	.490	.371
April	80	20	3	0	5	10	7	8	.250	.475	.310
May	112	33	5	1	2	13	14	7	.295	.411	.380
June	103	34	8	6	1	19	12	10	.330	.553	.390
July	110	34	7	2	1	11	13	17	.309	.436	.382
August	116	37	5	1	2	19	9	10	.319	.431	.365
Sept./Oct.	100	32	10	1	2	19	8	11	.320	.500	.369
Leading Off Inn.	122	31	7	2	4	4	5	13	.254	.443	.289
Runners On	293	94	17	7	4	82	30	32	.321	.468	.378
Runners/Scor. Pos.	176	64	14	6	2	77	24	22	.364	.545	.428
Runners On/2 Out	97	33	7	4	2	32	11	9	.340	.557	.407
Scor. Pos./2 Out	67	26	7	4	1	30	8	7	.388	.657	.453
Late Inning Pressure	77	27	4	1	1	9	8	11	.351	.468	.407
Leading Off	22	6	3	0	0	0	1	2	.273	.409	.304
Runners On	31	12	1	1	0	8	5	4	.387	.484	.459
Runners/Scor. Pos.	19	7	1	1	0	8	4	2	.368	.526	.458

RUNS BATTED IN	From 1B	From 2B	From 3B	Scoring Position
Totals	6/187	31/131	41/77	72/208
Percentage	3%	24%	53%	35%
Driving In Runners from 3B with Less than Two Out:			29/49	59%

Loves to face: Mike Flanagan (.436, 34-for-78, 4 HR)
Hates to face: Mark Langston (.114, 4-for-35)
One of only four "iron men" in the majors in 1988, joining Will Clark, Eddie Murray, and Cal Ripken as the only major leaguers to play in all of their teams' games. . . . Only three A.L. players have accumulated 100 or more doubles, triples, home runs, and stolen bases since World War II: Yount, George Brett, and Mickey Vernon. . . . Has played 2131 games, all for the Brewers. Among active players, only Dwight Evans has played more games, all for one A.L. club. . . . Batted above .300 at home in six of the past seven seasons, missed by one hit in 1986. . . . One of two right-handed batters to hit at least .320 vs. right-handed pitchers over the last two seasons (min: 300 AB). The other: teammate Paul Molitor.

Baltimore Orioles

	AB	H	2B	3B	HR	RBI	BB	SO	BA	SA	OBA
Season	5358	1275	199	20	137	520	504	869	.238	.359	.305
vs. Left-Handers	1869	432	58	5	43	165	180	327	.231	.337	.300
vs. Right-Handers	3489	843	141	15	94	355	324	542	.242	.371	.308
Home	2643	628	96	10	70	267	268	455	.238	.361	.308
Road	2715	647	103	10	67	253	236	414	.238	.358	.302
Grass	4535	1092	164	15	114	439	421	726	.241	.359	.306
Artificial Turf	823	183	35	5	23	81	83	143	.222	.361	.300
April	747	152	25	3	12	50	65	127	.203	.293	.272
May	885	205	37	5	22	91	108	139	.232	.359	.316
June	922	223	40	1	28	99	96	154	.242	.379	.316
July	854	207	23	3	33	90	76	125	.242	.392	.306
August	996	259	37	6	26	114	86	161	.260	.388	.317
Sept./Oct.	954	229	37	2	16	76	73	163	.240	.333	.296
Leading Off Inn.	1344	331	49	2	32	32	102	212	.246	.357	.301
Runners On	2158	504	81	6	55	438	234	330	.234	.353	.307
Runners/Scor. Pos.	1123	244	44	2	26	360	150	195	.217	.329	.303
Runners On/2 Out	938	210	27	4	26	185	120	146	.224	.344	.316
Scor. Pos./2 Out	565	115	13	2	14	150	81	93	.204	.308	.307
Late Inning Pressure	888	199	27	5	11	66	93	179	.224	.303	.298
Leading Off	212	43	8	0	2	2	24	46	.203	.269	.284
Runners On	387	79	9	3	4	59	44	79	.204	.274	.284
Runners/Scor. Pos.	197	34	5	1	3	54	27	39	.173	.254	.264

RUNS BATTED IN	From 1B	From 2B	From 3B	Scoring Position
Totals	68/1648	141/924	174/454	315/1378
Percentage	4%	15%	38%	23%
Driving In Runners from 3B with Less than Two Out:		122/227	54%	

Love to face: Nolan Ryan (13–5 against him)
Hate to face: Doyle Alexander (5–13 against him)

Had fewest runs, hits, and total bases in A.L. last season, but no A.L. team has repeated a league-low performance in any of those categories in 1980s.... Ranked last in A.L. in batting average and slugging average for first time since 1955 and 1959, respectively.... The O's have hit better on the road than at home for 10 straight years. No other team has a streak longer than three years.... Lowest day-game batting average in last 14 years; lowest with runners in scoring position in Late-Inning Pressure Situations since Giants hit .163 in 1976.... Five rookies accounted for 674 at-bats, highest total in A.L.... Used 108 different combinations of starting players, highest total in majors.

Boston Red Sox

	AB	H	2B	3B	HR	RBI	BB	SO	BA	SA	OBA
Season	5545	1569	310	39	124	760	623	728	.283	.420	.357
vs. Left-Handers	1602	460	82	11	30	198	161	191	.287	.408	.357
vs. Right-Handers	3943	1109	228	28	94	562	462	537	.281	.425	.357
Home	2750	833	194	18	68	421	333	349	.303	.461	.380
Road	2795	736	116	21	56	339	290	379	.263	.380	.333
Grass	4725	1355	280	28	109	666	550	605	.287	.427	.362
Artificial Turf	820	214	30	11	15	94	73	123	.261	.379	.326
April	673	179	36	3	8	88	87	102	.266	.364	.352
May	933	264	43	6	15	109	107	136	.283	.390	.361
June	926	283	62	7	24	142	100	104	.306	.465	.376
July	1041	320	65	12	28	158	103	122	.307	.474	.365
August	965	251	57	6	22	125	112	150	.260	.400	.337
Sept./Oct.	1007	272	47	5	27	138	114	114	.270	.407	.351
Leading Off Inn.	1280	357	83	6	28	28	134	152	.279	.419	.350
Runners On	2645	761	146	21	69	705	320	346	.288	.437	.363
Runners/Scor. Pos.	1527	435	78	15	39	616	229	206	.285	.432	.373
Runners On/2 Out	1137	313	53	10	26	276	157	145	.275	.408	.369
Scor. Pos./2 Out	734	190	27	7	13	235	125	97	.259	.368	.373
Late Inning Pressure	668	162	27	3	14	67	73	123	.243	.355	.321
Leading Off	166	43	12	1	6	6	19	23	.259	.452	.339
Runners On	291	68	12	0	4	57	37	53	.234	.316	.322
Runners/Scor. Pos.	157	39	7	0	3	54	25	26	.248	.350	.351

RUNS BATTED IN	From 1B	From 2B	From 3B	Scoring Position
Totals	94/1961	234/1204	308/686	542/1890
Percentage		19%	45%	29%
Driving In Runners from 3B with Less than Two Out:		216/356	61%	

Love to face: Mike Morgan (6–0)
Hate to face: Jimmy Key (1–6)

Led A.L. with 813 runs scored. No A.L. team has repeated in that category since Twins in 1976–77.... Since 1975, four teams have hit .300 or better at their own home parks. All four were the Red Sox: 1979 (.306), 1984 (.305), 1985 (.301), and last season.... Red Sox batters had the fewest strikeouts in the majors for the 3d consecutive season. Three of the four toughest A.L. players to fan were Boggs, Barrett, and Greenwell.... pinch hitters batted .256, but didn't have an extra-base hit.... Stole 65 bases, fewest in A.L. for 7th time in last 10 years.... Leadoff slot in batting order produced a .425 on-base average, best for number-one spot over past seven years in either league.

California Angels

	AB	H	2B	3B	HR	RBI	BB	SO	BA	SA	OBA
Season	5582	1458	258	31	124	663	469	819	.261	.385	.321
vs. Left-Handers	1962	495	91	8	45	199	154	259	.252	.376	.312
vs. Right-Handers	3620	963	167	23	79	464	315	560	.266	.390	.326
Home	2708	681	114	14	58	309	222	432	.251	.368	.312
Road	2874	777	144	17	66	354	247	387	.270	.401	.330
Grass	4721	1193	211	24	105	539	389	719	.253	.374	.313
Artificial Turf	861	265	47	7	19	124	80	100	.308	.445	.367
April	785	216	50	5	15	107	80	112	.275	.409	.343
May	956	222	33	8	15	91	74	143	.232	.331	.291
June	874	222	36	2	13	100	78	145	.254	.344	.317
July	944	261	44	8	35	136	67	130	.276	.451	.329
August	1033	294	55	5	34	141	87	142	.285	.446	.343
Sept./Oct.	990	243	40	3	12	88	83	147	.245	.328	.306
Leading Off Inn.	1368	353	71	6	25	25	92	188	.258	.376	.306
Runners On	2388	661	115	11	55	594	227	337	.277	.403	.341
Runners/Scor. Pos.	1408	363	60	6	33	517	164	222	.258	.379	.335
Runners On/2 Out	992	247	43	6	23	221	114	148	.249	.374	.334
Scor. Pos./2 Out	636	145	19	2	12	182	83	103	.228	.321	.327
Late Inning Pressure	908	240	32	5	20	110	87	159	.264	.377	.332
Leading Off	230	55	8	1	3	3	21	40	.239	.322	.303
Runners On	366	101	14	2	8	98	46	60	.276	.391	.361
Runners/Scor. Pos.	222	61	5	1	6	89	34	40	.275	.387	.373

RUNS BATTED IN	From 1B	From 2B	From 3B	Scoring Position
Totals	77/1689	194/1061	268/625	462/1686
Percentage	5%	18%	43%	27%
Driving In Runners from 3B with Less than Two Out:		197/342	58%	

Love to face: Mike Moore (8–3)
Hate to face: Bob Stanley (4–15)

Batting average on artificial turf was 2d highest in majors over past 14 years. Angels batted one point higher on plastic in 1979.... Led A.L. in batting average during August.... Fell four short of league lead in sac bunts, in which they'd led six times in seven previous seasons.... Faced 60 left-handed starters, highest total in majors.... Leadoff batter reached third base in nine innings, Angels scored in only three of them. Other A.L. teams scored 107 of 124 times under the same circumstances (86%).... Defeated the Yankees on Friday, May 13, last season. Angels once went 13 years between wins on Friday the 13th; career record is now 7–17, lowest among 26 teams.

Chicago White Sox

	AB	H	2B	3B	HR	RBI	BB	SO	BA	SA	OBA
Season	5449	1327	224	35	132	573	446	908	.244	.370	.303
vs. Left-Handers	1735	413	63	9	37	185	141	315	.238	.349	.296
vs. Right-Handers	3714	914	161	26	95	388	305	593	.246	.380	.306
Home	2695	642	115	22	55	281	242	454	.238	.358	.303
Road	2754	685	109	13	77	292	204	454	.249	.382	.302
Grass	4514	1079	184	32	106	482	396	769	.239	.364	.302
Artificial Turf	935	248	40	3	26	91	50	139	.265	.398	.303
April	708	155	28	4	21	84	71	129	.219	.359	.292
May	920	216	38	7	26	92	70	149	.235	.376	.291
June	954	249	37	5	25	102	74	139	.261	.389	.315
July	937	234	40	7	24	108	84	181	.250	.384	.314
August	974	230	38	5	19	99	79	156	.236	.344	.295
Sept./Oct.	956	243	43	7	17	88	68	154	.254	.367	.305
Leading Off Inn.	1361	331	67	12	37	37	87	205	.243	.392	.293
Runners On	2200	542	80	18	47	488	217	359	.246	.363	.312
Runners/Scor. Pos.	1271	312	59	11	24	423	162	239	.245	.366	.325
Runners On/2 Out	928	189	27	8	17	162	98	167	.204	.305	.285
Scor. Pos./2 Out	587	113	22	5	11	143	79	120	.193	.303	.294
Late Inning Pressure	904	217	37	6	18	90	89	174	.240	.354	.309
Leading Off	216	48	10	1	4	4	18	38	.222	.333	.288
Runners On	400	94	13	3	6	78	44	86	.235	.328	.309
Runners/Scor. Pos.	239	52	11	3	1	67	33	57	.218	.301	.309

RUNS BATTED IN	From 1B	From 2B	From 3B	Scoring Position
Totals	69/1535	155/964	217/543	372/1507
Percentage	4%	16%	40%	25%
Driving In Runners from 3B with Less than Two Out:		161/302	53%	

Love to face: Bob Stanley (11–4)
Hate to face: Dave Stieb (4–16)

First team to lead major leagues in both double plays and errors since the Montreal Expos in 1969, their first season.... Led A.L. with 67 sacrifice bunts.... Ranked last in A.L. in batting average during August.... Batting average with two outs and runners on base was lowest in majors since Dodgers batted .203 in 1975.... Compiled lowest pinch-hit batting average in A.L. (.172).... Runners advanced more than one base on singles 111 times in 268 opportunities, highest average in majors (41.4 percent).... Dan Pasqua's 20 home runs was lowest total among A.L. team leaders.... Scored four times as many runs per inning when leadoff batter reached base (0.93) as when he didn't (0.21).

Cleveland Indians

	AB	H	2B	3B	HR	RBI	BB	SO	BA	SA	OBA
Season	5505	1435	235	28	134	630	416	866	.261	.387	.314
vs. Left-Handers	1192	328	59	5	44	143	95	184	.275	.444	.331
vs. Right-Handers	4313	1107	176	23	90	487	321	682	.257	.371	.309
Home	2692	716	114	16	62	331	219	410	.266	.389	.323
Road	2813	719	121	12	72	299	197	456	.256	.384	.305
Grass	4622	1205	197	24	104	517	348	717	.261	.381	.314
Artificial Turf	883	230	38	4	30	113	68	149	.260	.414	.318
April	733	197	30	4	23	107	75	126	.269	.415	.342
May	964	243	41	7	18	101	80	168	.252	.365	.308
June	913	231	38	4	33	105	69	135	.253	.412	.310
July	974	270	46	5	20	133	68	146	.277	.396	.323
August	950	257	46	2	18	96	69	135	.271	.380	.319
Sept./Oct.	971	237	34	6	22	88	55	156	.244	.359	.289
Leading Off Inn.	1348	340	45	7	31	31	85	180	.252	.365	.300
Runners On	2286	599	107	17	48	544	203	386	.262	.387	.320
Runners/Scor. Pos.	1273	322	62	10	29	482	149	238	.253	.386	.326
Runners On/2 Out	981	230	44	8	14	213	106	189	.234	.338	.312
Scor. Pos./2 Out	627	159	31	5	10	193	80	130	.254	.367	.341
Late Inning Pressure	773	180	27	2	20	78	56	157	.233	.351	.286
Leading Off	198	42	5	0	3	3	12	35	.212	.283	.257
Runners On	297	66	9	2	10	68	30	64	.222	.367	.290
Runners/Scor. Pos.	163	32	4	1	4	55	19	44	.196	.307	.275

RUNS BATTED IN	From 1B	From 2B	From 3B	Scoring Position
Totals	74/1633	207/1027	215/518	422/1545
Percentage	5%	20%	42%	27%
Driving In Runners from 3B with Less than Two Out:		152/261		58%

Love to face: Floyd Bannister (11–3)
Hate to face: Jack Morris (7–22)
Home-run rate vs. left-handers (one every 27 at-bats) was best in A.L. last season. Home-run rate vs. right-handers (one every 48 at-bats) ranked 12th in league.... Faced only 40 left-handed starters, lowest total in majors.... Pinch hitters batted .307, best in major leagues. In 1987, Tribe ranked last in A.L. with .186 average. ... Used only 19 pinch runners, fewest in majors.... Top six batting-order spots batted .271, bottom three hit .237, a 34-point difference. League average: 22 points.... No surprise here: Platoon of Jay Bell and Ron Washington produced lowest BA for starting shortstops in A.L. (.230).

Detroit Tigers

	AB	H	2B	3B	HR	RBI	BB	SO	BA	SA	OBA
Season	5433	1358	213	28	143	651	588	841	.250	.378	.324
vs. Left-Handers	1733	434	71	11	43	202	158	259	.250	.379	.313
vs. Right-Handers	3700	924	142	17	100	449	430	582	.250	.378	.330
Home	2613	639	90	14	83	301	298	414	.245	.385	.323
Road	2820	719	123	14	60	350	290	427	.255	.372	.326
Grass	4608	1146	167	25	129	554	498	711	.249	.380	.323
Artificial Turf	825	212	46	3	14	97	90	130	.257	.371	.331
April	700	171	29	5	15	89	93	120	.244	.364	.333
May	910	239	39	2	24	101	75	132	.263	.389	.319
June	924	259	37	7	24	133	106	150	.280	.413	.356
July	890	221	34	5	30	112	96	135	.248	.399	.325
August	996	249	39	1	21	112	108	139	.250	.354	.323
Sept./Oct.	1013	219	35	8	29	104	110	165	.216	.352	.295
Leading Off Inn.	1323	331	51	4	36	36	124	193	.250	.376	.315
Runners On	2373	600	89	12	60	568	278	371	.253	.376	.331
Runners/Scor. Pos.	1310	343	53	6	35	501	188	212	.262	.392	.352
Runners On/2 Out	982	231	31	8	23	218	118	153	.235	.353	.320
Scor. Pos./2 Out	608	149	20	3	16	195	82	96	.245	.367	.338
Late Inning Pressure	817	213	31	2	28	104	84	147	.261	.406	.332
Leading Off	206	50	9	0	6	6	23	37	.243	.374	.322
Runners On	356	95	11	0	13	89	36	70	.267	.407	.334
Runners/Scor. Pos.	186	50	7	0	6	74	27	36	.269	.403	.361

RUNS BATTED IN	From 1B	From 2B	From 3B	Scoring Position
Totals	80/1755	201/1040	227/562	428/1602
Percentage	5%	19%	40%	27%
Driving In Runners from 3B with Less than Two Out:		161/294		55%

Love to face: Mike Boddicker (10–3)
Hate to face: Bret Saberhagen (3–11)
Scored in only 76 of the 310 innings in which their first hitter in batting order led off, lowest average in majors (25 percent). So it follows that their total of 55 runs in first inning was the lowest as well. ... Opening-day lineup combination defeated Boston, and never started together again (Heath, c; Evans, 1b; Whitaker, 2b; Trammell, ss; Brookens, 3b; Sheridan, lf; Pettis, cf; Lemon, rf; Nokes, dh).... Haven't started a rookie on opening day since 1985, when Sparky unveiled Chris Pittaro.... Lou Whitaker and Alan Trammell made their debuts together in nightcap of a doubleheader on Sept. 9, 1977. Detroit's keystone combo in first game that day? Tito Fuentes and Tom Veryzer.

Kansas City Royals

	AB	H	2B	3B	HR	RBI	BB	SO	BA	SA	OBA
Season	5469	1419	275	40	121	674	486	944	.259	.391	.321
vs. Left-Handers	1633	444	90	12	32	199	143	290	.272	.400	.331
vs. Right-Handers	3836	975	185	28	89	475	343	654	.254	.387	.316
Home	2676	732	143	30	55	345	250	391	.274	.411	.335
Road	2793	687	132	10	66	329	236	553	.246	.371	.307
Grass	2142	522	99	6	43	241	172	413	.244	.356	.303
Artificial Turf	3327	897	176	34	78	433	314	531	.270	.413	.333
April	756	202	38	9	19	96	54	135	.267	.417	.316
May	970	254	52	5	26	132	98	160	.262	.406	.332
June	886	241	52	7	18	103	71	120	.272	.407	.325
July	959	251	49	4	21	109	50	174	.262	.387	.302
August	910	227	43	7	20	128	114	165	.249	.378	.332
Sept./Oct.	988	244	41	8	17	106	99	190	.247	.356	.316
Leading Off Inn.	1329	304	61	9	33	33	96	227	.229	.363	.283
Runners On	2296	659	138	19	48	601	236	378	.287	.426	.351
Runners/Scor. Pos.	1363	365	88	13	30	531	186	252	.268	.413	.350
Runners On/2 Out	986	256	59	9	17	229	107	177	.260	.389	.338
Scor. Pos./2 Out	658	159	41	6	10	199	88	129	.242	.368	.339
Late Inning Pressure	816	194	30	5	7	77	75	183	.238	.313	.302
Leading Off	208	36	9	1	3	3	17	52	.173	.269	.236
Runners On	320	86	15	1	1	71	33	66	.269	.331	.334
Runners/Scor. Pos.	180	48	9	1	1	69	22	40	.267	.344	.341

RUNS BATTED IN	From 1B	From 2B	From 3B	Scoring Position
Totals	87/1591	217/1078	249/597	466/1675
Percentage	5%	20%	42%	28%
Driving In Runners from 3B with Less than Two Out:		181/315		57%

Love to face: Oil Can Boyd (7–1)
Hate to face: Roger Clemens (1–9)
Had two 100-RBI players for second time in team history: Darrell Porter (112) and George Brett (107) in 1979; Brett (103) and Danny Tartabull (102) in 1988.... Made the most of their hits: .287 batting average with runners on base was 2d best in A.L., .240 mark with bases empty was worst. That 47-point difference was the largest margin in the past 14 years. Previous high: 40, by Milwaukee in 1987.... Lowest batting average in A.L. leading off innings in LIPS for second consecutive season, with the league's lowest mark since 1976.... Didn't have an extra-base hit in 20 games, highest total in A.L.... Played 12 games above .500 vs. left-handers (29–17), five games below vs. right-handers (55–60).

Milwaukee Brewers

	AB	H	2B	3B	HR	RBI	BB	SO	BA	SA	OBA
Season	5488	1409	258	26	113	633	439	911	.257	.375	.314
vs. Left-Handers	1671	410	77	5	47	189	143	248	.245	.382	.308
vs. Right-Handers	3817	999	181	21	66	444	296	663	.262	.372	.317
Home	2711	704	129	15	60	325	231	434	.260	.385	.321
Road	2777	705	129	11	53	308	208	477	.254	.366	.307
Grass	4672	1193	209	21	101	535	386	774	.255	.374	.314
Artificial Turf	816	216	49	5	12	98	53	137	.265	.381	.313
April	670	167	25	1	20	72	51	120	.249	.379	.307
May	999	258	43	5	18	125	89	162	.258	.365	.322
June	933	247	45	7	20	104	69	173	.265	.392	.315
July	970	234	54	7	13	82	63	161	.241	.352	.291
August	1044	287	56	4	21	138	87	146	.275	.397	.333
Sept./Oct.	872	216	35	2	21	112	80	149	.248	.365	.311
Leading Off Inn.	1345	319	68	7	27	27	91	196	.237	.358	.290
Runners On	2272	621	103	13	54	574	203	393	.273	.401	.333
Runners/Scor. Pos.	1343	371	61	10	37	525	151	248	.276	.419	.346
Runners On/2 Out	998	251	48	6	21	233	97	168	.252	.375	.323
Scor. Pos./2 Out	647	169	32	6	15	213	75	112	.261	.399	.344
Late Inning Pressure	762	199	38	3	12	83	65	153	.261	.366	.321
Leading Off	188	39	11	1	1	1	13	28	.207	.293	.262
Runners On	320	94	17	2	9	80	35	66	.294	.444	.365
Runners/Scor. Pos.	201	51	10	1	4	67	30	45	.254	.373	.350

RUNS BATTED IN	From 1B	From 2B	From 3B	Scoring Position
Totals	66/1542	206/1021	248/575	454/1596
Percentage	4%	20%	43%	28%
Driving In Runners from 3B with Less than Two Out:		167/307		54%

Love to face: Charlie Hough (9–1)
Hate to face: Dave Stewart (0–8)
Won at least 10 straight games in both 1987 and 1988. The last team that won 10 in a row in two consecutive seasons: Philadelphia, 1983–84. Last A.L. team: Milwaukee, 1978–79. New York Giants won at least 10 games in a row in five consecutive seasons, 1904–08. And Chicago Cubs had four separate winning streaks of 10 or more games in 1906 season alone!... Brew Crew has quietly led A.L. in steals in each of last two years.... Ranked last in A.L. in batting average during July.... Only A.L. team to hit better in Late-Inning Pressure Situations than overall in each of the last three seasons.... Led A.L. in batting average with runners on base in LIPS for second year in a row.

Minnesota Twins

	AB	H	2B	3B	HR	RBI	BB	SO	BA	SA	OBA
Season	5510	1508	294	31	151	714	528	832	.274	.421	.340
vs. Left-Handers	1389	409	88	11	34	184	132	184	.294	.447	.356
vs. Right-Handers	4121	1099	206	20	117	530	396	648	.267	.412	.335
Home	2706	756	158	21	76	384	277	411	.279	.438	.350
Road	2804	752	136	10	75	330	251	421	.268	.404	.331
Grass	2165	588	106	5	67	276	197	321	.272	.418	.334
Artificial Turf	3345	920	188	26	84	438	331	511	.275	.422	.344
April	715	184	53	2	19	81	62	127	.257	.417	.324
May	935	254	46	8	30	126	79	138	.272	.434	.331
June	929	282	51	5	27	131	91	132	.304	.456	.369
July	930	259	54	4	30	123	83	127	.278	.442	.340
August	1012	279	50	7	29	140	106	144	.276	.425	.346
Sept./Oct.	989	250	40	5	16	113	107	164	.253	.352	.328
Leading Off Inn.	1324	380	67	10	49	49	87	185	.287	.464	.337
Runners On	2457	664	131	14	60	623	278	394	.270	.408	.344
Runners/Scor. Pos.	1466	395	83	11	38	559	196	267	.269	.419	.353
Runners On/2 Out	1036	269	57	4	28	263	127	165	.260	.403	.346
Scor. Pos./2 Out	696	183	41	4	17	238	94	120	.263	.407	.357
Late Inning Pressure	683	196	34	3	23	107	68	113	.287	.447	.356
Leading Off	161	54	8	1	4	4	11	26	.335	.472	.389
Runners On	337	91	17	1	10	94	44	66	.270	.415	.352
Runners/Scor. Pos.	197	50	12	1	6	84	30	44	.254	.416	.349

RUNS BATTED IN	From 1B	From 2B	From 3B	Scoring Position
Totals	72/1747	225/1152	266/624	491/1776
Percentage	4%	20%	43%	28%
Driving In Runners from 3B with Less than Two Out:		177/314		56%

Love to face: Dave Stewart (8–3)
Hate to face: Roger Clemens (1–9)
Big year for fielding feats: Minnesota was the first team to pull off an opening-day triple play since Cardinals in 1981. Then they went on to set major league records for fielding percentage (.986) and fewest errors (84). . . . Batting average vs. left-handers was 3d highest in A.L. over past 14 years. They've hit better vs. lefties than righties for nine years running. . . . Number-three hitters (primarily Kirby Puckett) batted .344, highest for any batting-order slot in A.L. over past seven years. . . . Won 30 of 35 home games in which they scored the first run. . . . Used 61 pinch runners, tying Oakland for highest total in majors. . . . Only one rookie batted last season: Kelvin Torve (16 AB).

New York Yankees

	AB	H	2B	3B	HR	RBI	BB	SO	BA	SA	OBA
Season	5592	1469	272	12	148	718	588	935	.263	.395	.333
vs. Left-Handers	1705	455	92	4	49	232	204	272	.267	.412	.345
vs. Right-Handers	3887	1014	180	8	99	486	384	663	.261	.388	.328
Home	2675	698	125	6	77	358	284	435	.261	.399	.332
Road	2917	771	147	6	71	360	304	500	.264	.392	.335
Grass	4683	1206	210	10	128	581	495	801	.258	.389	.329
Artificial Turf	909	263	62	2	20	137	93	134	.289	.428	.355
April	780	214	51	3	27	134	97	151	.274	.451	.352
May	902	238	46	3	22	119	103	128	.264	.395	.339
June	951	252	42	3	22	117	99	168	.265	.385	.338
July	895	254	52	1	19	118	94	131	.284	.408	.353
August	1012	254	34	0	28	109	88	163	.251	.368	.311
Sept./Oct.	1052	257	47	2	30	121	107	194	.244	.378	.315
Leading Off Inn.	1320	318	64	1	23	23	134	237	.241	.343	.313
Runners On	2464	665	113	3	76	646	292	388	.270	.411	.344
Runners/Scor. Pos.	1431	364	70	2	41	562	200	238	.254	.392	.340
Runners On/2 Out	1055	261	44	2	26	226	129	177	.247	.367	.332
Scor. Pos./2 Out	680	149	30	1	13	194	95	119	.219	.324	.322
Late Inning Pressure	733	186	21	0	21	81	69	149	.254	.368	.322
Leading Off	183	38	3	0	3	3	16	41	.208	.273	.279
Runners On	299	81	8	0	9	69	32	57	.271	.388	.342
Runners/Scor. Pos.	163	36	4	0	4	58	21	40	.221	.319	.309

RUNS BATTED IN	From 1B	From 2B	From 3B	Scoring Position
Totals	94/1786	189/1111	287/625	476/1736
Percentage	5%	17%	46%	27%
Driving In Runners from 3B with Less than Two Out:		208/327		64%

Love to face: Mike Morgan (7–0)
Hate to face: Ted Higuera (2–9)
If you had the Yankees in a "Yankees vs. Andy Van Slyke" triples pool, you lost. Those 12 triples were the fewest that the Yankees have ever hit, and a major league low by any team in 1988. . . . Had an extra-base hit in all but seven games, lowest total in majors. . . . Led A.L. with five pinch-hit home runs. . . . Drove in 64 percent of runners from third base with less than two outs, highest rate in majors. . . . Won all nine home games tied after eight innings. . . . Outscored opponents by 55 runs in first inning (135–80), were outscored by 31 thereafter. . . . Odd combination: Yankees committed 18 more errors than their opponents, but scored 88 unearned runs, compared to 59 scored against them.

Oakland A's

	AB	H	2B	3B	HR	RBI	BB	SO	BA	SA	OBA
Season	5602	1474	251	22	156	751	580	926	.263	.399	.336
vs. Left-Handers	1404	359	61	7	36	166	147	210	.256	.386	.329
vs. Right-Handers	4198	1115	190	15	120	585	433	716	.266	.404	.339
Home	2683	700	117	8	67	335	272	447	.261	.385	.333
Road	2919	774	134	14	89	416	308	479	.265	.412	.339
Grass	4691	1220	200	18	130	620	484	776	.260	.394	.334
Artificial Turf	911	254	51	4	26	131	96	150	.279	.429	.349
April	793	202	36	4	25	119	102	129	.255	.405	.343
May	937	265	44	2	24	137	94	170	.283	.411	.351
June	957	233	43	2	25	99	81	137	.243	.371	.307
July	976	242	33	5	29	118	79	174	.248	.381	.308
August	968	268	47	4	28	141	117	142	.277	.420	.358
Sept./Oct.	971	264	48	5	25	137	107	174	.272	.409	.349
Leading Off Inn.	1317	351	65	4	36	36	135	206	.267	.404	.343
Runners On	2461	696	121	13	80	675	257	390	.283	.440	.351
Runners/Scor. Pos.	1403	394	67	10	43	576	181	236	.281	.435	.359
Runners On/2 Out	1051	273	49	6	29	257	126	171	.260	.401	.346
Scor. Pos./2 Out	659	174	30	4	19	226	92	107	.264	.408	.360
Late Inning Pressure	819	187	29	1	20	89	80	140	.228	.339	.305
Leading Off	214	51	14	0	7	7	20	33	.238	.402	.315
Runners On	313	80	8	0	7	76	43	45	.256	.348	.352
Runners/Scor. Pos.	205	54	6	0	7	75	33	33	.263	.395	.372

RUNS BATTED IN	From 1B	From 2B	From 3B	Scoring Position
Totals	105/1810	217/1067	273/637	490/1704
Percentage	6%	20%	43%	29%
Driving In Runners from 3B with Less than Two Out:		190/327		58%

Love to face: Bill Wegman (5–0)
Hate to face: Charlie Leibrandt (2–8)
Record of 57–27 vs. A.L. East was best ever by a Western Division club. . . . Played 54 postseason games since the start of divisional play, one fewer than the leader, Baltimore. . . . Oakland A's had never lost a postseason game (24–0) in which they led after eight innings until Kirk Gibson's pinch HR in first game of 1988 Series. . . . Best record in the majors in games in which they scored the first run. . . . Were shut out in both games of doubleheader vs. Minnesota on June 26 for first time in exactly 24 years. They failed to score in a doubleheader at L.A. on June 26, 1964. . . . Won eight games of 13 innings or longer, breaking modern major league record (7), set in 1969 by Minnesota.

Seattle Mariners

	AB	H	2B	3B	HR	RBI	BB	SO	BA	SA	OBA
Season	5436	1397	271	27	148	618	461	787	.257	.398	.317
vs. Left-Handers	1642	418	97	7	41	161	104	233	.255	.397	.300
vs. Right-Handers	3794	979	174	20	107	457	357	554	.258	.399	.325
Home	2688	690	144	17	97	340	233	368	.257	.431	.319
Road	2748	707	127	10	51	278	228	419	.257	.366	.316
Grass	2137	557	103	10	44	228	181	319	.261	.380	.319
Artificial Turf	3299	840	168	17	104	390	280	468	.255	.410	.316
April	829	229	43	6	19	97	60	105	.276	.411	.324
May	903	233	39	6	32	118	72	125	.258	.421	.315
June	874	189	31	4	22	68	78	134	.216	.336	.281
July	895	246	50	3	27	110	85	134	.275	.428	.342
August	1023	272	58	7	29	126	87	147	.266	.421	.324
Sept./Oct.	912	228	50	1	19	99	79	142	.250	.370	.314
Leading Off Inn.	1347	352	63	9	36	36	87	185	.261	.402	.309
Runners On	2256	590	123	12	63	533	210	313	.262	.410	.323
Runners/Scor. Pos.	1269	330	59	7	35	452	140	202	.260	.400	.329
Runners On/2 Out	949	233	46	8	30	218	95	143	.246	.406	.317
Scor. Pos./2 Out	590	144	22	5	18	184	75	99	.244	.390	.332
Late Inning Pressure	733	182	32	2	24	81	68	135	.248	.396	.316
Leading Off	183	48	8	0	9	9	13	28	.262	.454	.315
Runners On	312	76	14	1	10	67	31	54	.244	.391	.317
Runners/Scor. Pos.	179	43	11	0	5	54	18	33	.240	.385	.315

RUNS BATTED IN	From 1B	From 2B	From 3B	Scoring Position
Totals	85/1582	169/1001	216/545	385/1546
Percentage	5%	17%	40%	25%
Driving In Runners from 3B with Less than Two Out:		149/284		52%

Love to face: Juan Berenguer (7–2)
Hate to face: Jimmy Key (0–6)
Scored fewer than two runs in four consecutive games for first time in team history (June 13–17). . . . Received major league low 24 intentional walks last season, three fewer than Will Clark had all by himself. . . . Lower batting average in LIP Situations than overall for 10th consecutive season. . . . Hit better with runners on base than with bases empty for 12th straight season. . . . Runners advanced more than one base on singles 71 times in 262 opportunities, lowest average in majors (27.1%). . . . Outscored by just 19 runs from 4th inning on, but 61-run deficit over first three was a killer. . . . Won two games in which they trailed after seven innings, lowest total in majors.

Texas Rangers

	AB	H	2B	3B	HR	RBI	BB	SO	BA	SA	OBA
Season	5479	1378	227	39	112	590	542	1022	.252	.368	.320
vs. Left-Handers	1630	420	72	10	36	175	149	297	.258	.380	.321
vs. Right-Handers	3849	958	155	29	76	415	393	725	.249	.363	.320
Home	2669	698	116	23	58	317	277	489	.262	.387	.331
Road	2810	680	111	16	54	273	265	533	.242	.351	.309
Grass	4537	1138	176	32	91	489	466	826	.251	.364	.321
Artificial Turf	942	240	51	7	21	101	76	196	.255	.391	.313
April	683	153	15	2	19	46	61	149	.224	.335	.288
May	948	267	46	9	25	124	98	173	.282	.428	.350
June	950	230	47	8	16	109	118	174	.242	.359	.327
July	914	238	37	6	15	89	64	174	.260	.363	.307
August	969	259	40	5	20	112	78	171	.267	.381	.325
Sept./Oct.	1015	231	42	9	17	110	123	181	.228	.337	.313
Leading Off Inn.	1334	332	50	7	33	33	115	229	.249	.371	.310
Runners On	2384	610	107	20	36	514	257	427	.256	.363	.326
Runners/Scor. Pos.	1350	337	61	15	18	453	174	276	.250	.357	.330
Runners On/2 Out	1020	230	38	9	15	184	118	193	.225	.325	.312
Scor. Pos./2 Out	664	135	25	7	9	161	91	137	.203	.303	.308
Late Inning Pressure	872	217	29	6	19	80	110	186	.249	.361	.335
Leading Off	209	54	7	0	7	7	30	47	.258	.392	.351
Runners On	415	99	10	5	8	69	53	82	.239	.345	.324
Runners/Scor. Pos.	247	51	8	4	3	57	34	59	.206	.308	.302

RUNS BATTED IN	From 1B	From 2B	From 3B	Scoring Position
Totals	67/1735	187/1062	224/578	411/1640
Percentage	4%	18%	39%	25%
Driving In Runners from 3B with Less than Two Out:			173/290	60%

Love to face: Dennis Eckersley (13–6)
Hate to face: Storm Davis (1–11)
Designated hitters batted .197, lowest in 16 years of DH history, and one point higher than the collective batting average of Mets' pitching staff last season. . . . Led A.L. in strikeouts for second straight season. . . . Ranked last in A.L. in home runs (see page 84 for analysis). . . . Didn't win more than three consecutive road games all season long. . . . Youngest batters in A.L.: Rangers, 27.2 years; Mariners, 27.6; Blue Jays, 27.8; White Sox, 27.9, Orioles, 28.1; Indians, 28.3; A's, 28.4; Twins, 28.8; Brewers, 29.0; Red Sox, 29.3; Royals, 30.0; Angels, 30.1; Yankees, 31.1; Tigers, 32.6. Pirates had lowest average in majors (26.5).

Toronto Blue Jays

	AB	H	2B	3B	HR	RBI	BB	SO	BA	SA	OBA
Season	5557	1491	271	47	158	707	521	935	.268	.419	.332
vs. Left-Handers	1885	491	79	17	53	220	133	353	.260	.405	.311
vs. Right-Handers	3672	1000	192	30	105	487	388	582	.272	.427	.342
Home	2702	723	129	30	78	342	268	456	.268	.424	.334
Road	2855	768	142	17	80	365	253	479	.269	.415	.330
Grass	2222	595	99	13	54	282	193	353	.268	.397	.327
Artificial Turf	3335	896	172	34	104	425	328	582	.269	.434	.335
April	764	201	39	7	22	94	63	139	.263	.419	.321
May	996	261	50	5	26	129	93	168	.262	.401	.325
June	946	255	45	9	27	127	98	156	.270	.422	.339
July	915	247	50	5	32	118	87	150	.270	.440	.336
August	953	252	37	9	27	106	80	161	.264	.407	.321
Sept./Oct.	983	275	50	12	24	133	100	161	.280	.428	.345
Leading Off Inn.	1347	336	57	10	33	33	91	207	.249	.380	.300
Runners On	2360	670	113	24	59	608	253	402	.284	.427	.350
Runners/Scor. Pos.	1431	402	70	18	34	539	171	263	.281	.426	.351
Runners On/2 Out	1007	266	41	12	16	220	113	177	.264	.376	.343
Scor. Pos./2 Out	683	175	28	9	13	204	81	126	.256	.381	.339
Late Inning Pressure	743	202	33	3	17	94	76	141	.272	.393	.341
Leading Off	175	53	6	1	7	7	13	33	.303	.469	.351
Runners On	346	88	13	2	5	82	46	70	.254	.347	.341
Runners/Scor. Pos.	230	56	8	2	4	78	33	51	.243	.348	.335

RUNS BATTED IN	From 1B	From 2B	From 3B	Scoring Position
Totals	82/1632	210/1107	257/616	467/1723
Percentage	5%	19%	42%	27%
Driving In Runners from 3B with Less than Two Out:			184/332	55%

Love to face: Frank Viola (12–3)
Hate to face: Ted Higuera (3–7)
Led league in home runs for first time in team history. . . . First team since 1955 Yankees to lead A.L. in both triples and home runs. . . . Tied Minnesota for most extra-base hits in A.L., the third year in past six they've earned at least a share of that title. . . . Led A.L. in batting average from Sept. 1 on. . . . Ranked last in A.L. in sacrifice bunts for fourth consecutive season. . . . Hit better with runners in scoring position than otherwise for fourth straight season. Only Oakland has a longer streak (8). . . . Fifth slot in batting order scored 108 runs. No other spot that low in any batting order, A.L. or N.L., hit the 100 mark. . . . Used only 61 combinations of starting players, lowest total in A.L.

American League

	AB	H	2B	3B	HR	RBI	BB	SO	BA	SA	OBA
Season	77005	19967	3558	425	1901	9202	7191	12323	.259	.391	.324
vs. Left-Handers	23052	5968	1080	122	570	2618	2044	3622	.259	.391	.321
vs. Right-Handers	53953	13999	2478	303	1331	6584	5147	8701	.259	.391	.326
Home	37611	9840	1784	244	964	4656	3674	5945	.262	.399	.329
Road	39394	10127	1774	181	937	4546	3517	6378	.257	.383	.320
Grass	54974	14089	2405	263	1325	6449	5176	8830	.256	.382	.322
Artificial Turf	22031	5878	1153	162	576	2753	2015	3493	.267	.412	.330
April	10336	2622	498	58	264	1264	1021	1771	.254	.390	.323
May	13158	3419	597	78	323	1595	1240	2091	.260	.391	.325
June	12939	3396	606	71	324	1539	1228	2021	.262	.395	.328
July	13094	3484	631	75	356	1604	1099	2064	.266	.407	.325
August	13805	3638	637	68	342	1687	1298	2122	.264	.394	.328
Sept./Oct.	13673	3408	589	75	292	1513	1305	2254	.249	.367	.317
Leading Off Inn.	18687	4735	861	96	459	459	1460	2802	.253	.383	.311
Runners On	33000	8842	1567	203	810	8111	3465	5214	.268	.401	.336
Runners/Scor. Pos.	18968	4977	915	136	462	7092	2441	3294	.262	.398	.342
Runners On/2 Out	14060	3459	607	100	311	3105	1625	2319	.246	.370	.329
Scor. Pos./2 Out	9034	2159	381	66	190	2717	1221	1588	.239	.359	.335
Late Inning Pressure	11119	2774	427	46	254	1207	1093	2139	.249	.365	.319
Leading Off	2749	654	118	7	65	65	250	507	.238	.357	.305
Runners On	4759	1198	170	22	104	1057	554	918	.252	.362	.330
Runners/Scor. Pos.	2766	657	107	15	57	935	386	587	.238	.349	.330

RUNS BATTED IN	From 1B	From 2B	From 3B	Scoring Position
Totals	1120/2364	2752/1481	3429/8185	6181/2300
Percentage	5%	19%	42%	27%
Driving In Runners from 3B with Less than Two Out:			2438/4278	57%

National League

Mike Aldrete

San Francisco Giants — Bats Left

	AB	H	2B	3B	HR	RBI	BB	SO	BA	SA	OBA
Season	389	104	15	0	3	50	56	65	.267	.329	.357
vs. Left-Handers	80	23	4	0	1	5	8	16	.288	.375	.344
vs. Right-Handers	309	81	11	0	2	45	48	49	.262	.317	.360
Home	173	36	4	0	3	16	28	36	.208	.283	.318
Road	216	68	11	0	0	34	28	29	.315	.366	.389
Grass	282	69	9	0	3	38	43	52	.245	.309	.341
Artificial Turf	107	35	6	0	0	12	13	13	.327	.383	.400
April	54	14	5	0	0	6	7	10	.259	.352	.339
May	39	14	0	0	0	2	3	8	.359	.359	.405
June	81	26	4	0	2	15	3	12	.321	.444	.341
July	76	17	2	0	1	9	16	16	.224	.289	.359
August	75	23	3	0	0	14	11	8	.307	.347	.391
Sept./Oct.	64	10	1	0	0	4	16	11	.156	.172	.325
Leading Off Inn.	96	24	1	0	1	1	14	23	.250	.292	.345
Runners On	177	53	8	0	2	49	27	20	.299	.379	.386
Runners/Scor. Pos.	104	31	8	0	0	44	26	13	.298	.375	.429
Runners On/2 Out	87	26	6	0	0	24	18	11	.299	.368	.419
Scor. Pos./2 Out	63	19	6	0	0	23	18	9	.302	.397	.457
Late Inning Pressure	63	13	1	0	0	1	8	12	.206	.222	.296
Leading Off	18	5	0	0	0	0	4	6	.278	.278	.409
Runners On	25	4	0	0	0	1	3	2	.160	.160	.250
Runners/Scor. Pos.	13	2	0	0	0	1	3	1	.154	.154	.313

RUNS BATTED IN	From 1B	From 2B	From 3B	Scoring Position
Totals	4/125	18/73	25/53	43/126
Percentage	3%	25%	47%	34%
Driving In Runners from 3B with Less than Two Out:			14/24	58%

Loves to face: Danny Cox (.583, 7-for-12, 1 HR)
Hates to face: Eric Show (0-for-11)
Hit all three of his home runs at Candlestick, but was one of only three major leaguers to bat 100 points higher on road than at home last season (minimum: 100 AB each way). . . . Batted .379 (11-for-29) as pinch hitter last season, 3d highest in majors (minimum: 20 PH AB); pinch-hit on-base average, including six walks, was .486. . . . Led N.L. left fielders with an average of 2.34 putouts per nine innings. . . . Reached base safely in eight consecutive innings in which he led off (May 27 to June 12), longest streak in majors last season. . . . Batting average at season's end was at its lowest point since late May. . . . Career average of .257 with the bases empty, .321 with runners on base.

Luis Alicea

St. Louis Cardinals — Bats Left and Right

	AB	H	2B	3B	HR	RBI	BB	SO	BA	SA	OBA
Season	297	63	10	4	1	24	25	32	.212	.283	.276
vs. Left-Handers	92	12	2	0	0	5	5	11	.130	.152	.190
vs. Right-Handers	205	51	8	4	1	19	20	21	.249	.341	.314
Home	144	33	5	3	1	12	14	16	.229	.326	.302
Road	153	30	5	1	0	12	11	16	.196	.242	.251
Grass	88	19	3	0	0	9	10	9	.216	.250	.300
Artificial Turf	209	44	7	4	1	15	15	23	.211	.297	.265
April	23	4	0	1	0	3	4	4	.174	.261	.296
May	108	25	6	0	1	12	13	11	.231	.315	.311
June	96	21	4	2	0	6	4	8	.219	.302	.255
July	38	7	0	1	0	1	2	4	.184	.237	.225
August	0	0	0	0	0	0	0	0	——	——	——
Sept./Oct.	32	6	0	0	0	2	2	5	.188	.188	.257
Leading Off Inn.	55	13	2	0	1	1	5	6	.236	.327	.300
Runners On	152	27	3	1	0	23	15	20	.178	.211	.257
Runners/Scor. Pos.	79	17	2	0	0	22	12	11	.215	.241	.319
Runners On/2 Out	73	14	2	0	0	9	10	11	.192	.219	.289
Scor. Pos./2 Out	43	9	1	0	0	9	8	7	.209	.233	.333
Late Inning Pressure	63	12	2	0	0	3	6	6	.190	.222	.271
Leading Off	14	4	1	0	0	0	1	1	.286	.357	.333
Runners On	28	5	0	0	0	3	4	4	.179	.179	.303
Runners/Scor. Pos.	18	4	0	0	0	3	3	1	.222	.222	.333

RUNS BATTED IN	From 1B	From 2B	From 3B	Scoring Position
Totals	1/117	9/57	13/40	22/97
Percentage	1%	16%	33%	23%
Driving In Runners from 3B with Less than Two Out:			8/21	38%

Loves to face: Kevin Gross (.800, 4-for-5, 2 2B)
Hates to face: Sid Fernandez (0-for-6)
Batting average was 5th lowest in N.L. (minimum: 200 AB). . . . Did his best work, three hits in seven at-bats, with the bases loaded. . . . Cardinals used five starting second basemen last season, but had a winning record with only one of them (Oquendo). . . . Batted .345 (10-for-29) in spring training, but was not on Cardinals' opening-day roster. Recalled after Tommy Herr was dealt, but was sent back to Louisville on July 26 after batting .215 in 78 games. . . . Tripled against the Mets in first game in majors, but don't look for the ball in his trophy case. Play was originally ruled a three-base error on Keith Hernandez (the man they love to hate in Busch Country), but was later changed to a hit.

Roberto Alomar

San Diego Padres — Bats Left and Right

	AB	H	2B	3B	HR	RBI	BB	SO	BA	SA	OBA
Season	545	145	24	6	9	40	47	83	.266	.382	.328
vs. Left-Handers	178	46	6	2	4	17	17	29	.258	.382	.330
vs. Right-Handers	367	99	18	4	5	23	30	54	.270	.381	.327
Home	279	71	9	2	5	20	19	47	.254	.355	.309
Road	266	74	15	4	4	20	28	36	.278	.410	.347
Grass	403	100	15	3	5	31	30	64	.248	.337	.305
Artificial Turf	142	45	9	3	4	9	17	19	.317	.507	.390
April	31	9	1	0	1	2	1	9	.290	.419	.333
May	120	28	1	1	3	8	5	14	.233	.333	.264
June	101	22	4	1	2	6	9	18	.218	.337	.282
July	81	19	3	1	0	5	6	10	.235	.296	.287
August	93	28	8	2	1	6	14	23	.301	.462	.404
Sept./Oct.	119	39	7	1	2	13	12	9	.328	.454	.389
Leading Off Inn.	149	39	6	1	5	5	9	18	.262	.416	.304
Runners On	203	59	7	2	1	32	17	24	.291	.360	.351
Runners/Scor. Pos.	105	34	5	0	1	30	10	15	.324	.400	.383
Runners On/2 Out	76	22	2	1	1	21	8	8	.289	.382	.357
Scor. Pos./2 Out	56	19	2	0	1	20	7	6	.339	.429	.413
Late Inning Pressure	75	18	4	0	1	5	6	12	.240	.333	.296
Leading Off	25	7	1	0	1	1	2	3	.280	.440	.333
Runners On	29	6	2	0	0	4	1	6	.207	.276	.233
Runners/Scor. Pos.	16	3	0	0	0	4	1	4	.188	.188	.235

RUNS BATTED IN	From 1B	From 2B	From 3B	Scoring Position
Totals	3/153	15/80	13/42	28/122
Percentage	2%	19%	31%	23%
Driving In Runners from 3B with Less than Two Out:			5/12	42%

Loves to face: Danny Jackson (.500, 5-for-10, 1 HR)
Hates to face: Bob Ojeda (.091, 1-for-11)
September batting average (.330) was 7th best in N.L.; Padres won 10 of last 12 games, which coincided with Alomar's insertion into leadoff spot. . . . In September, came to plate 22 times in a row with the bases empty, longest such streak in majors in '88. . . . Needs five home runs to surpass dad's total for 15 years in majors. . . . 3d-youngest player (born Feb. 1968) in majors last year, and the youngest regular; L.A.'s Ramon Martinez (March '68) played in nine games, and Brewers' Gary Sheffield (Nov. '68) in 24 games. . . . In last six years, San Diego has had six different opening-day second basemen: Juan Bonilla, Alan Wiggins, Mario Ramirez, Bip Roberts, Joey Cora, Randy Ready. Alomar could make it 7-for-7 in '89.

Dave Anderson

Los Angeles Dodgers — Bats Right

	AB	H	2B	3B	HR	RBI	BB	SO	BA	SA	OBA
Season	285	71	10	2	2	21	32	45	.249	.319	.325
vs. Left-Handers	117	29	6	0	0	5	14	15	.248	.299	.331
vs. Right-Handers	168	42	4	2	2	16	18	30	.250	.333	.321
Home	132	30	3	0	1	12	14	20	.227	.273	.301
Road	153	41	7	2	1	9	18	25	.268	.359	.345
Grass	199	46	4	0	1	15	21	32	.231	.266	.308
Artificial Turf	86	25	6	2	1	6	11	13	.291	.442	.364
April	5	2	0	0	0	0	1	2	.400	.400	.500
May	38	11	2	0	1	3	3	5	.289	.421	.326
June	85	26	4	2	0	11	16	14	.306	.400	.422
July	94	16	2	0	0	3	8	16	.170	.191	.235
August	39	13	2	0	1	3	3	5	.333	.462	.381
Sept./Oct.	24	3	0	0	0	1	1	3	.125	.125	.160
Leading Off Inn.	63	22	5	0	1	1	11	3	.349	.476	.446
Runners On	122	27	2	1	0	19	13	20	.221	.254	.297
Runners/Scor. Pos.	66	12	0	1	0	18	11	11	.182	.212	.300
Runners On/2 Out	63	15	2	1	0	9	5	7	.238	.302	.304
Scor. Pos./2 Out	34	6	0	1	0	8	4	3	.176	.235	.282
Late Inning Pressure	32	9	2	0	1	6	5	4	.281	.438	.359
Leading Off	8	3	1	0	1	1	1	0	.375	.875	.444
Runners On	11	4	0	0	0	5	2	1	.364	.364	.400
Runners/Scor. Pos.	6	3	0	0	0	5	1	0	.500	.500	.444

RUNS BATTED IN	From 1B	From 2B	From 3B	Scoring Position
Totals	2/86	6/51	11/30	17/81
Percentage	2%	12%	37%	21%
Driving In Runners from 3B with Less than Two Out:			7/17	41%

Loves to face: Walt Terrell (.500, 5-for-10, 1 HR)
Hates to face: Mark Davis (0-for-13)
Only N.L. player with 200+ at-bats in each of last four seasons who has not hit .250 or better in any of the four years. . . . Batting average with runners in scoring position has been lower than his overall batting average in each of the last six seasons. . . . Started 60 of 61 games at shortstop while Griffin was sidelined; L.A. went 36–24 during that span. . . . Batted .307 in day games, .217 at night. . . . Grounded into nine double plays in 49 opportunities last season, 4th-highest rate in N.L. (min.: 40 opp.). . . . Career average of less than 18 RBI per 100 games played is 6th lowest among batters active in 1988 with 500+ games. Who's lower? Tolleson, Wilkerson, G. Gross, Dernier, and Jeltz.

Alan Ashby

Bats Left and Right

Houston Astros

	AB	H	2B	3B	HR	RBI	BB	SO	BA	SA	OBA
Season	227	54	10	0	7	33	29	36	.238	.374	.319
vs. Left-Handers	44	6	1	0	0	1	3	4	.136	.159	.188
vs. Right-Handers	183	48	9	0	7	32	26	32	.262	.426	.349
Home	123	26	5	0	0	16	11	26	.211	.252	.270
Road	104	28	5	0	7	17	18	10	.269	.519	.374
Grass	73	18	3	0	3	10	14	9	.247	.411	.368
Artificial Turf	154	36	7	0	4	23	15	27	.234	.357	.295
April	66	18	3	0	2	10	8	7	.273	.409	.347
May	62	15	2	0	4	14	6	10	.242	.468	.304
June	49	12	3	0	1	6	8	6	.245	.367	.345
July	0	0	0	0	0	0	0	0	——	——	——
August	5	2	1	0	0	1	1	3	.400	.600	.429
Sept./Oct.	45	7	1	0	0	2	6	10	.156	.178	.255
Leading Off Inn.	51	12	2	0	3	3	4	5	.235	.451	.291
Runners On	86	21	5	0	2	28	16	14	.244	.372	.349
Runners/Scor. Pos.	53	13	2	0	1	25	11	10	.245	.340	.353
Runners On/2 Out	33	9	2	0	0	11	6	6	.273	.333	.385
Scor. Pos./2 Out	23	7	1	0	0	10	5	5	.304	.348	.429
Late Inning Pressure	49	11	2	0	3	7	12	6	.224	.449	.377
Leading Off	11	4	1	0	1	1	1	1	.364	.727	.417
Runners On	20	3	0	0	0	4	6	2	.150	.150	.346
Runners/Scor. Pos.	9	3	0	0	0	4	3	1	.333	.333	.500

RUNS BATTED IN	From 1B	From 2B	From 3B	Scoring Position
Totals	2/56	10/45	14/23	24/68
Percentage	4%	22%	61%	35%
Driving In Runners from 3B with Less than Two Out:		9/12		75%

Loves to face: Mark Grant (.571, 4-for-7, 2 HR)
Hates to face: Fernando Valenzuela (.091, 4-for-44)
Last 23 home runs have been hit batting left-handed. His last home run off a southpaw came against Dave LaPoint on Sept. 12, 1986. Career averages: .259 vs. righties, .215 vs. lefties. . . . Hasn't homered at the Astrodome since Sept. 6, 1987. . . . Only player in majors with 180+ at-bats and no triples in each of last five seasons. . . . Has driven in more than 30 percent of runners from scoring positon in four of last five years. . . . His last hit of 1988 was the 1000th of his career. He got there with only one 100-hit season (111 in 1987). Only three other players in history have had 1000 hits with only one 100-hit season: ex-Reds Heinie Peitz and Ivy Wingo, and the ancient Rick Dempsey, catchers all.

Wally Backman

Bats Left and Right

New York Mets

	AB	H	2B	3B	HR	RBI	BB	SO	BA	SA	OBA
Season	294	89	12	0	0	17	41	49	.303	.344	.388
vs. Left-Handers	35	9	1	0	0	0	4	7	.257	.286	.333
vs. Right-Handers	259	80	11	0	0	17	37	42	.309	.351	.395
Home	144	49	8	0	0	7	20	25	.340	.396	.424
Road	150	40	4	0	0	10	21	24	.267	.293	.353
Grass	215	72	10	0	0	12	25	34	.335	.381	.405
Artificial Turf	79	17	2	0	0	5	16	15	.215	.241	.344
April	17	1	0	0	0	0	1	4	.059	.059	.158
May	56	18	1	0	0	6	5	8	.321	.339	.377
June	72	22	2	0	0	4	10	15	.306	.333	.381
July	55	16	2	0	0	1	10	8	.291	.327	.400
August	59	21	4	0	0	2	5	10	.356	.424	.406
Sept./Oct.	35	11	3	0	0	4	10	4	.314	.400	.467
Leading Off Inn.	68	17	1	0	0	0	5	15	.250	.265	.301
Runners On	106	29	5	0	0	17	19	21	.274	.321	.378
Runners/Scor. Pos.	58	11	3	0	0	16	12	12	.190	.241	.319
Runners On/2 Out	40	6	0	0	0	4	7	10	.150	.150	.277
Scor. Pos./2 Out	32	3	0	0	0	4	6	8	.094	.094	.237
Late Inning Pressure	35	11	0	0	0	2	3	7	.314	.343	.368
Leading Off	10	3	0	0	0	0	1	1	.300	.300	.364
Runners On	16	5	0	0	0	2	1	4	.313	.313	.353
Runners/Scor. Pos.	9	2	0	0	0	2	1	2	.222	.222	.300

RUNS BATTED IN	From 1B	From 2B	From 3B	Scoring Position
Totals	1/69	6/51	10/20	16/71
Percentage	1%	12%	50%	23%
Driving In Runners from 3B with Less than Two Out:		8/11		73%

Loves to face: Charles Hudson (.600, 15-for-25)
Hates to face: Nolan Ryan (.139, 5-for-36)
Batted .320 and .308 in his two best seasons (1986 & 1988), but hit only .226 and .190 with runners in scoring position in those years. In other years he has hit .295 in those situations. . . . Ground-ball hitter who last year batted .255 vs. ground-ball pitchers, .346 vs. fly-ball pitchers, illustrating the rule. . . . Started 83 of 110 games in which Mets faced right-handed starters, but only one of 50 games vs. lefties. Career averages: .306 vs. right-handers, .150 vs. left-handers. . . . Committed two errors in a game on May 18, then only two more the rest of the regular season. . . . His .283 career batting average is second to Hernandez's .301 in Mets' history (minimum: 500 games).

Kevin Bass

Bats Left and Right

Houston Astros

	AB	H	2B	3B	HR	RBI	BB	SO	BA	SA	OBA
Season	541	138	27	2	14	72	42	65	.255	.390	.314
vs. Left-Handers	193	61	16	1	6	33	9	16	.316	.503	.354
vs. Right-Handers	348	77	11	1	8	39	33	49	.221	.328	.293
Home	249	69	13	0	5	31	25	26	.277	.390	.347
Road	292	69	14	2	9	41	17	39	.236	.390	.286
Grass	179	44	10	1	4	27	13	22	.246	.380	.301
Artificial Turf	362	94	17	1	10	45	29	43	.260	.395	.321
April	60	19	4	0	1	15	2	6	.317	.433	.344
May	105	27	7	0	2	9	4	17	.257	.381	.291
June	93	21	3	0	3	12	10	10	.226	.355	.321
July	92	27	4	1	4	11	10	11	.293	.489	.363
August	91	21	2	0	2	14	9	12	.231	.319	.304
Sept./Oct.	100	23	7	1	2	11	7	9	.230	.380	.278
Leading Off Inn.	129	30	5	0	3	3	2	18	.233	.341	.250
Runners On	231	64	10	1	7	65	33	29	.277	.420	.366
Runners/Scor. Pos.	127	39	7	0	4	57	23	18	.307	.457	.405
Runners On/2 Out	99	31	5	1	2	34	19	9	.313	.444	.429
Scor. Pos./2 Out	66	25	4	0	2	33	12	5	.379	.530	.474
Late Inning Pressure	86	21	0	0	2	9	8	4	.244	.314	.305
Leading Off	24	10	0	0	2	2	1	1	.417	.667	.440
Runners On	38	9	0	0	0	7	7	2	.237	.237	.348
Runners/Scor. Pos.	22	6	0	0	0	7	5	2	.273	.273	.393

RUNS BATTED IN	From 1B	From 2B	From 3B	Scoring Position
Totals	10/167	25/100	23/53	48/153
Percentage	6%	25%	43%	31%
Driving In Runners from 3B with Less than Two Out:		12/24		50%

Loves to face: Tom Browning (.400, 18-for-45, 3 HR)
Hates to face: Pascual Perez (0-for-19)
One of four players to have appeared in 150+ N.L. games in each of last four seasons; others: Coleman, Murphy, Ozzie. . . . From April to June, batted .400 vs. left-handers, .185 vs. right-handers; after that, .243 vs. lefties, .256 vs. righties. . . . Last year's .244 mark in Late-Inning Pressure Situations ended three-year streak batting over .300 in that category. . . . Has batted 61 times with the bases loaded but has never drawn a walk. . . . Only player in majors to bat 100+ points higher in night games (.280) than in day games (.179) last season (minimum: 100 AB each way). Career averages: .249 by day, .280 at night. Maybe he can get a Michelob commercial; is his Sinatra imitation as good as his Sammy?

Buddy Bell

Bats Right

Reds/Astros

	AB	H	2B	3B	HR	RBI	BB	SO	BA	SA	OBA
Season	323	78	10	1	7	40	26	32	.241	.344	.295
vs. Left-Handers	91	22	5	0	2	15	10	6	.242	.363	.314
vs. Right-Handers	232	56	5	1	5	25	16	26	.241	.336	.288
Home	149	34	5	1	1	17	11	16	.228	.295	.281
Road	174	44	5	0	6	23	15	16	.253	.385	.307
Grass	110	28	2	0	2	12	11	10	.255	.327	.317
Artificial Turf	213	50	8	1	5	28	15	22	.235	.352	.284
April	13	3	0	0	0	3	1	1	.231	.231	.250
May	37	7	0	0	0	0	6	2	.189	.189	.302
June	37	6	2	1	0	3	4	4	.162	.270	.244
July	100	30	5	0	3	18	4	13	.300	.440	.327
August	64	13	1	0	2	10	3	6	.203	.313	.239
Sept./Oct.	72	19	2	0	2	6	8	6	.264	.375	.333
Leading Off Inn.	65	14	0	1	2	2	4	6	.215	.338	.261
Runners On	153	39	7	0	2	35	15	18	.255	.340	.316
Runners/Scor. Pos.	102	28	7	0	2	35	11	11	.275	.402	.336
Runners On/2 Out	79	23	6	0	1	22	9	7	.291	.405	.364
Scor. Pos./2 Out	59	19	6	0	1	22	6	2	.322	.475	.385
Late Inning Pressure	55	12	2	0	0	6	3	10	.218	.255	.254
Leading Off	13	4	0	0	0	0	1	2	.308	.308	.357
Runners On	27	5	2	0	0	6	1	7	.185	.259	.207
Runners/Scor. Pos.	19	5	2	0	0	6	1	4	.263	.368	.286

RUNS BATTED IN	From 1B	From 2B	From 3B	Scoring Position
Totals	3/110	21/82	9/35	30/117
Percentage	3%	26%	26%	26%
Driving In Runners from 3B with Less than Two Out:		6/15		40%

Loves to face: Floyd Bannister (.350, 14-for-40, 3 HR)
Hates to face: Chris Codiroli (0-for-12)
Most regular-season games (2371) of any active player who has never appeared in a postseason game. All-time record (among players since World Series began in 1903) is 2528 by Ernie Banks. . . . Has driven in less than 30 percent of runners from scoring position each year since 1984, when his 42 percent led majors. . . . Needs one hit to become 26th player in major league history with 2500 hits and 200 home runs. Of others, 18 of 19 eligibles are in Hall of Fame, Vada Pinson is not; Garvey, Jackson, Morgan, Oliver, Perez, Staub not yet eligible. . . . Within space of six months, Texas reacquired Bell and Jim Sundberg, two of the three players to have 1000 hits with Rangers. Can Toby Harrah be far behind?

Rafael Belliard

Pittsburgh Pirates — Bats Right

	AB	H	2B	3B	HR	RBI	BB	SO	BA	SA	OBA
Season	286	61	0	4	0	11	26	47	.213	.241	.288
vs. Left-Handers	89	20	0	2	0	4	9	14	.225	.270	.303
vs. Right-Handers	197	41	0	2	0	7	17	33	.208	.228	.281
Home	136	29	0	4	0	6	11	26	.213	.272	.272
Road	150	32	0	0	0	5	15	21	.213	.213	.302
Grass	96	22	0	0	0	2	8	14	.229	.229	.295
Artificial Turf	190	39	0	4	0	9	18	33	.205	.247	.284
April	33	7	0	2	0	3	1	5	.212	.333	.257
May	27	11	0	0	0	1	2	4	.407	.407	.467
June	64	15	0	0	0	3	9	11	.234	.234	.338
July	84	18	0	2	0	2	2	14	.214	.262	.233
August	57	5	0	0	0	2	9	10	.088	.088	.224
Sept./Oct.	21	5	0	0	0	0	3	3	.238	.238	.333
Leading Off Inn.	64	8	0	1	0	0	6	16	.125	.156	.211
Runners On	119	29	0	2	0	11	10	15	.244	.277	.318
Runners/Scor. Pos.	62	17	0	2	0	11	7	8	.274	.339	.375
Runners On/2 Out	47	9	0	1	0	4	7	6	.191	.234	.333
Scor. Pos./2 Out	29	5	0	1	0	4	6	4	.172	.241	.368
Late Inning Pressure	28	6	0	1	0	0	3	5	.214	.286	.290
Leading Off	10	2	0	1	0	0	1	3	.200	.400	.273
Runners On	9	2	0	0	0	0	1	0	.222	.222	.300
Runners/Scor. Pos.	4	1	0	0	0	0	0	0	.250	.250	.250

RUNS BATTED IN	From 1B	From 2B	From 3B	Scoring Position
Totals	0/85	5/52	6/25	11/77
Percentage	0%	10%	24%	14%
Driving In Runners from 3B with Less than Two Out:		5/11		45%

Loves to face: Orel Hershiser (.364, 8-for-22)
Hates to face: Bryn Smith (0-for-7)
286 at-bats without a double were the most in major league history; over past 50 years, only two players had as many as 200 at-bats in a season without a double: Ozzie Virgil, Sr. (226 AB, 1957 Giants) and Choo Choo Coleman (247 AB, 1963 Mets). Even so, Belliard had four triples, so his feat falls into the "oddity" category (along with hitting for the cycle, home runs from both sides of the plate, achievements in each league, boy could we go on). The *real* champ is Bill Holbert, a catcher with Troy and Syracuse in N.L. in 1879; he had 244 at-bats with *no* extra-base hits. . . . Removed for pinch hitter 36 times, tied with Greg Harris for N.L. high. . . . Broke Oz's four-year reign as N.L. fielding leader at shortstop.

Bruce Benedict

Atlanta Braves — Bats Right

	AB	H	2B	3B	HR	RBI	BB	SO	BA	SA	OBA
Season	236	57	7	0	0	19	19	26	.242	.271	.296
vs. Left-Handers	77	14	3	0	0	4	7	8	.182	.221	.247
vs. Right-Handers	159	43	4	0	0	15	12	18	.270	.296	.320
Home	126	30	2	0	0	13	8	17	.238	.254	.279
Road	110	27	5	0	0	6	11	9	.245	.291	.314
Grass	183	43	4	0	0	16	10	19	.235	.257	.272
Artificial Turf	53	14	3	0	0	3	9	7	.264	.321	.371
April	24	3	1	0	0	1	2	3	.125	.167	.185
May	35	13	3	0	0	6	4	3	.371	.457	.436
June	36	7	0	0	0	2	2	5	.194	.194	.237
July	46	14	2	0	0	6	6	4	.304	.348	.377
August	58	13	1	0	0	1	4	7	.224	.241	.274
Sept./Oct.	37	7	0	0	0	3	1	4	.189	.189	.211
Leading Off Inn.	56	9	1	0	0	0	5	2	.161	.179	.230
Runners On	95	28	5	0	0	19	9	16	.295	.347	.330
Runners/Scor. Pos.	56	13	3	0	0	17	5	14	.232	.286	.286
Runners On/2 Out	45	11	2	0	0	9	3	2	.244	.289	.292
Scor. Pos./2 Out	30	7	1	0	0	8	3	2	.233	.267	.303
Late Inning Pressure	30	4	0	0	0	0	2	5	.133	.133	.188
Leading Off	9	1	0	0	0	0	1	2	.111	.111	.200
Runners On	9	1	0	0	0	0	0	2	.111	.111	.111
Runners/Scor. Pos.	4	0	0	0	0	0	0	2	.000	.000	.000

RUNS BATTED IN	From 1B	From 2B	From 3B	Scoring Position
Totals	3/67	7/47	9/22	16/69
Percentage	4%	15%	41%	23%
Driving In Runners from 3B with Less than Two Out:		5/13		38%

Loves to face: David Palmer (.462, 6-for-13)
Hates to face: Orel Hershiser (0-for-14)
Mamas, don't let your babies grow up to be cowboys. Let them be catchers. Here's one who is now a 10-year man in the majors. What would you think of totals of 216 hits, 82 RBI, and 64 runs scored? Not bad for one season, but those are Benedict's combined totals for *five* years since he hit career-high .298 in 1983. No matter; catchers are always in demand. . . . Batting average in Late-Inning Pressure Situations has been lower than in nonpressure situations in each of last eight seasons, and has hit under .200 in LIPS in each of last five seasons. . . . Has hit only one home run in his last 712 at-bats. . . . Removed for pinch hitters 27 times last season, tying Paul Assenmacher for team lead.

Damon Berryhill

Chicago Cubs — Bats Left and Right

	AB	H	2B	3B	HR	RBI	BB	SO	BA	SA	OBA
Season	309	80	19	1	7	38	17	56	.259	.395	.295
vs. Left-Handers	85	21	3	0	1	9	2	9	.247	.318	.261
vs. Right-Handers	224	59	16	1	6	29	15	47	.263	.424	.307
Home	179	52	13	1	5	25	11	29	.291	.458	.328
Road	130	28	6	0	2	13	6	27	.215	.308	.248
Grass	208	58	14	1	6	29	13	39	.279	.442	.317
Artificial Turf	101	22	5	0	1	9	4	17	.218	.297	.248
April	0	0	0	0	0	0	0	0	—	—	—
May	48	10	3	0	0	2	1	7	.208	.271	.224
June	38	15	2	0	1	6	2	3	.395	.526	.405
July	52	12	3	0	1	6	1	10	.231	.346	.245
August	72	20	7	1	3	14	6	15	.278	.528	.333
Sept./Oct.	99	23	4	0	2	10	7	21	.232	.333	.280
Leading Off Inn.	53	11	2	0	2	2	2	13	.208	.358	.236
Runners On	169	45	7	1	4	35	9	26	.266	.391	.298
Runners/Scor. Pos.	89	18	3	0	2	28	7	17	.202	.303	.253
Runners On/2 Out	70	15	3	0	1	15	6	8	.214	.300	.276
Scor. Pos./2 Out	44	9	2	0	1	14	5	3	.205	.318	.286
Late Inning Pressure	61	22	5	0	3	10	5	8	.361	.590	.403
Leading Off	16	3	0	0	1	0	0	3	.188	.375	.188
Runners On	29	11	3	0	1	8	3	4	.379	.586	.424
Runners/Scor. Pos.	13	5	2	0	1	8	3	2	.385	.769	.471

RUNS BATTED IN	From 1B	From 2B	From 3B	Scoring Position
Totals	9/124	9/71	13/38	22/109
Percentage	7%	13%	34%	20%
Driving In Runners from 3B with Less than Two Out:		10/20		50%

Loves to face: Eric Show (.600, 3-for-5, 1 HR)
Hates to face: Pete Smith (0-for-7)
First major league home run was a 10th-inning shot off David Cone on June 2, the only extra-inning home run hit by Cubs last season. Later in series, he broke up Doc Gooden's no-hit bid with 8th-inning single. . . . Batted 127 points higher in Late-Inning Pressure Situations than in other at-bats, 2d-largest difference in N.L. last season (minimum: 50 LIPS AB). . . . In minors at start of season, and started only 20 of first 59 games after his recall. From mid-July to end of season, started 60 times in 76 games. . . . Hit grand-slam homer at Philly on Sept. 13. Cubs have hit 31 slams over past 10 years, and nine of them have been hit by catchers; Jody Davis had five, Barry Foote, three.

Terry Blocker

Atlanta Braves — Bats Left

	AB	H	2B	3B	HR	RBI	BB	SO	BA	SA	OBA
Season	198	42	4	2	2	10	10	20	.212	.283	.250
vs. Left-Handers	60	13	1	1	0	1	1	13	.217	.267	.230
vs. Right-Handers	138	29	3	1	2	9	9	7	.210	.290	.259
Home	100	22	3	1	1	6	3	9	.220	.300	.243
Road	98	20	1	1	1	4	7	11	.204	.265	.257
Grass	159	34	3	1	1	7	9	15	.214	.264	.256
Artificial Turf	39	8	1	1	1	3	1	5	.205	.359	.225
April	5	0	0	0	0	0	0	1	.000	.000	.000
May	0	0	0	0	0	0	0	0	—	—	—
June	0	0	0	0	0	0	0	0	—	—	—
July	15	4	0	0	0	0	2	2	.267	.267	.353
August	101	18	1	1	1	6	5	8	.178	.238	.217
Sept./Oct.	77	20	3	1	1	4	3	9	.260	.364	.288
Leading Off Inn.	54	11	1	0	0	0	3	5	.204	.222	.246
Runners On	74	20	2	1	1	9	7	5	.270	.365	.333
Runners/Scor. Pos.	37	10	2	1	1	9	5	2	.270	.459	.357
Runners On/2 Out	37	11	2	1	1	7	6	3	.297	.486	.395
Scor. Pos./2 Out	20	6	2	1	1	7	4	1	.300	.650	.417
Late Inning Pressure	39	11	0	1	0	2	4	4	.282	.333	.349
Leading Off	8	5	0	0	0	1	0	0	.625	.625	.667
Runners On	12	3	0	1	0	2	3	2	.250	.417	.400
Runners/Scor. Pos.	4	1	0	1	0	2	2	1	.250	.750	.500

RUNS BATTED IN	From 1B	From 2B	From 3B	Scoring Position
Totals	0/60	3/27	5/14	8/41
Percentage	0%	11%	36%	20%
Driving In Runners from 3B with Less than Two Out:		2/7		29%

Loves to face: Jose Rijo (2-for-2, 2 BB)
Hates to face: Mike Scott (0-for-5)
Frequently mentioned in the same breath as Darryl Strawberry and Dwight Gooden. That happens whenever someone runs down the Mets' first-round choices in amateur draft from 1980 to 1982. Blocker was the '81 pick. . . . On-base average of .250 was 2d lowest in N.L. last season (minimum: 200 PA). . . . Sent to Richmond (AAA) after his five hitless at-bats in April; went 2-for-2 with a walk in his return to Atlanta on July 28. . . . Made 59 starts, all in center field; batted 8th in 58 of them, led off once. . . . Has never driven in a runner from first base (63 career opportunities). . . . Reached base six times in nine plate appearances leading off in Late-Inning Pressure Situations.

Barry Bonds

Bats Left

Pittsburgh Pirates

	AB	H	2B	3B	HR	RBI	BB	SO	BA	SA	OBA
Season	538	152	30	5	24	58	72	82	.283	.491	.368
vs. Left-Handers	162	49	10	2	9	23	21	28	.302	.556	.383
vs. Right-Handers	376	103	20	3	15	35	51	54	.274	.463	.362
Home	256	73	11	3	14	33	35	38	.285	.516	.374
Road	282	79	19	2	10	25	37	44	.280	.468	.363
Grass	139	33	7	1	4	8	14	26	.237	.388	.305
Artificial Turf	399	119	23	4	20	50	58	56	.298	.526	.389
April	92	23	9	2	5	7	4	18	.250	.554	.278
May	97	29	1	2	7	12	15	21	.299	.567	.393
June	100	31	8	0	2	6	15	14	.310	.450	.400
July	73	23	6	1	4	12	13	8	.315	.589	.425
August	107	29	4	0	4	13	11	10	.271	.421	.345
Sept./Oct.	69	17	2	0	2	8	14	11	.246	.362	.369
Leading Off Inn.	228	70	17	1	13	13	18	31	.307	.561	.360
Runners On	161	41	4	2	5	39	39	30	.255	.398	.396
Runners/Scor. Pos.	94	25	3	1	4	36	30	19	.266	.447	.437
Runners On/2 Out	81	17	1	1	3	21	20	17	.210	.358	.366
Scor. Pos./2 Out	52	12	1	1	2	19	17	11	.231	.404	.420
Late Inning Pressure	85	19	0	0	2	6	9	14	.224	.294	.298
Leading Off	19	6	0	0	0	0	3	1	.316	.316	.409
Runners On	40	7	0	0	1	5	4	9	.175	.250	.250
Runners/Scor. Pos.	20	2	0	0	0	3	3	6	.100	.100	.217

RUNS BATTED IN	From 1B	From 2B	From 3B	Scoring Position
Totals	5/113	15/79	14/32	29/111
Percentage	4%	19%	44%	26%
Driving In Runners from 3B with Less than Two Out:		8/15		53%

Loves to face: Tom Browning (.500, 7-for-14, 2 HR)
Hates to face: Dennis Martinez (.091, 3-for-33)
Hit eight homers leading off first inning, three shy of dad's one-season major league record. The Cardinals *as a team* had only two 1st-inning homers in 1988. . . . Reached base safely in 31 games in a row, longest N.L. streak. . . . Had 13 straight hits that were extra-base hits, longest streak in majors over past 10 years. . . . Career average of .208 with runners in scoring position is 63 points below his average at other times, widest disparity since 1979 (minimum: 300 AB with RISP). . . . Career average of .212 in Late-Inning Pressure Situations. . . . Combine LIPS with RISP and what do you get? Four singles in 58 at-bats. . . . Father and son have fanned 2,029 times, 572 shy of Reggie and his dad.

Bobby Bonilla

Bats Left and Right

Pittsburgh Pirates

	AB	H	2B	3B	HR	RBI	BB	SO	BA	SA	OBA
Season	584	160	32	7	24	100	85	82	.274	.476	.366
vs. Left-Handers	212	59	10	1	6	29	29	20	.278	.420	.366
vs. Right-Handers	372	101	22	6	18	71	56	62	.272	.508	.366
Home	286	62	10	1	9	44	42	41	.217	.353	.320
Road	298	98	22	6	15	56	43	41	.329	.594	.411
Grass	152	49	10	2	7	28	19	24	.322	.553	.395
Artificial Turf	432	111	22	5	17	72	66	58	.257	.449	.356
April	88	30	7	1	7	18	7	11	.341	.682	.381
May	96	33	6	0	6	25	20	14	.344	.594	.454
June	104	27	4	1	4	13	13	12	.260	.433	.345
July	91	21	2	1	1	9	15	14	.231	.308	.343
August	105	24	8	2	2	10	15	18	.229	.400	.331
Sept./Oct.	100	25	5	2	4	25	15	13	.250	.460	.342
Leading Off Inn.	165	41	6	2	4	4	11	24	.248	.382	.299
Runners On	260	75	20	3	12	88	55	39	.288	.527	.406
Runners/Scor. Pos.	169	48	9	1	9	76	44	29	.284	.509	.422
Runners On/2 Out	127	37	9	0	4	32	28	17	.291	.457	.427
Scor. Pos./2 Out	86	25	5	0	4	30	23	12	.291	.488	.450
Late Inning Pressure	90	24	1	0	3	15	15	12	.267	.378	.371
Leading Off	36	6	0	0	0	0	1	7	.167	.167	.211
Runners On	29	10	0	0	3	15	10	3	.345	.655	.513
Runners/Scor. Pos.	20	9	0	0	2	13	8	3	.450	.750	.607

RUNS BATTED IN	From 1B	From 2B	From 3B	Scoring Position
Totals	15/170	30/117	31/79	61/196
Percentage	9%	26%	39%	31%
Driving In Runners from 3B with Less than Two Out:		24/46		52%

Loves to face: Calvin Schiraldi (.545, 6-for-11, 2 HR)
Hates to face: Mike Scott (.067, 1-for-15)
Batted 112 points higher on road than at home last season, largest difference by anyone in majors (minimum: 100 AB each way). . . . Led N.L. in batting average and RBI in road games; missed "Road Triple Crown" by three home runs (Strawberry had 18). . . . First Pirates' infielder to start All-Star Game since Bill Mazeroski in 1967, and first Bucs' third baseman to start since Frank Thomas in 1958. . . . His seven home runs vs. Cubs tied Glenn Davis (vs. Reds) for most homers by any N.L. player vs. any club last season. . . . Drove in 100th run in next-to-last at-bat in final game of season, becoming first Buc to reach 100 RBI since Andy Van Slyke did it earlier in same inning.

Phil Bradley

Bats Right

Philadelphia Phillies

	AB	H	2B	3B	HR	RBI	BB	SO	BA	SA	OBA
Season	569	150	30	5	11	57	54	106	.264	.392	.341
vs. Left-Handers	169	46	13	0	4	14	17	30	.272	.420	.342
vs. Right-Handers	400	104	17	5	7	43	37	76	.260	.380	.341
Home	284	76	16	2	8	33	24	44	.268	.423	.339
Road	285	74	14	3	3	24	30	62	.260	.361	.344
Grass	163	43	11	2	0	15	12	37	.264	.356	.328
Artificial Turf	406	107	19	3	11	42	42	69	.264	.406	.346
April	70	16	1	1	0	3	9	14	.229	.271	.337
May	102	23	3	2	1	10	12	22	.225	.324	.322
June	98	22	4	1	1	6	10	19	.224	.316	.306
July	80	22	6	0	3	12	11	12	.275	.463	.385
August	114	36	11	0	4	17	6	17	.316	.518	.347
Sept./Oct.	105	31	5	1	2	9	6	22	.295	.419	.353
Leading Off Inn.	165	43	12	1	6	6	9	31	.261	.455	.326
Runners On	208	57	12	2	3	49	21	38	.274	.394	.346
Runners/Scor. Pos.	140	37	6	1	1	42	14	26	.264	.343	.331
Runners On/2 Out	91	21	5	0	1	21	10	19	.231	.319	.320
Scor. Pos./2 Out	67	17	3	0	1	19	6	12	.254	.343	.324
Late Inning Pressure	83	20	4	2	1	10	11	16	.241	.373	.347
Leading Off	19	3	1	0	1	1	2	4	.158	.368	.273
Runners On	35	9	1	2	0	9	6	5	.257	.400	.386
Runners/Scor. Pos.	27	6	0	1	0	8	5	4	.222	.296	.353

RUNS BATTED IN	From 1B	From 2B	From 3B	Scoring Position
Totals	7/127	16/112	23/56	39/168
Percentage	6%	14%	41%	23%
Driving In Runners from 3B with Less than Two Out:		16/29		55%

Loves to face: John Cerutti (.750, 6-for-8)
Hates to face: Jose Guzman (.111, 2-for-18)
Led majors by being hit by pitches 16 times, most in N.L. since Ron Hunt was hit 16 times in 1974, his last year in majors. . . . Led left fielders with .990 fielding percentage. . . . One of six players with 100+ whiffs in each of last four seasons. . . . Slow starter: .246 career April average is lowest in any month. Career breakdown: .270 before All-Star break, .316 after break. . . . One of five N.L. players to bat .300 or higher after break in '88, and led N.L. with 15 extra-base hits in August. . . . Change of scenery didn't change one thing: he's hit for a higher average at home than on road in each of five full years in majors. . . . Has never played on a team that finished higher than fourth. Good luck in Baltimore.

Sid Bream

Bats Left

Pittsburgh Pirates

	AB	H	2B	3B	HR	RBI	BB	SO	BA	SA	OBA
Season	462	122	37	0	10	65	47	64	.264	.409	.328
vs. Left-Handers	116	22	6	0	3	13	5	22	.190	.319	.220
vs. Right-Handers	346	100	31	0	7	52	42	42	.289	.439	.362
Home	226	53	25	0	6	28	19	34	.235	.425	.292
Road	236	69	12	0	4	37	28	30	.292	.394	.362
Grass	117	32	5	0	0	10	15	15	.274	.316	.356
Artificial Turf	345	90	32	0	10	55	32	49	.261	.441	.319
April	67	21	9	0	1	4	6	5	.313	.493	.370
May	70	14	3	0	2	11	6	11	.200	.329	.256
June	77	30	11	0	4	17	3	5	.390	.688	.306
July	73	16	3	0	0	7	11	16	.219	.260	.321
August	105	27	6	0	1	17	11	13	.257	.343	.325
Sept./Oct.	70	14	5	0	2	9	10	14	.200	.357	.296
Leading Off Inn.	102	22	4	0	2	2	4	15	.216	.314	.245
Runners On	205	62	16	0	5	60	26	26	.302	.454	.371
Runners/Scor. Pos.	128	37	8	0	1	50	17	18	.289	.375	.353
Runners On/2 Out	96	21	6	0	2	19	12	16	.219	.344	.306
Scor. Pos./2 Out	68	13	2	0	1	16	9	12	.191	.265	.286
Late Inning Pressure	70	22	8	0	2	11	9	8	.314	.514	.378
Leading Off	14	5	0	0	0	0	1	2	.357	.357	.400
Runners On	28	6	3	0	1	10	5	2	.214	.429	.306
Runners/Scor. Pos.	16	5	2	0	1	10	3	0	.313	.625	.364

RUNS BATTED IN	From 1B	From 2B	From 3B	Scoring Position
Totals	9/138	17/102	29/53	46/155
Percentage	6%	17%	55%	30%
Driving In Runners from 3B with Less than Two Out:		24/32		75%

Loves to face: Greg Maddux (.588, 10-for-17, 1 HR)
Hates to face: Dave Dravecky (0-for-11)
June batting average was best in N.L., lifting season mark to .304 at month's end. But he hit only .230 the rest of the way, including .176 over last seven weeks. . . . Led N.L. first basemen with 140 assists (26 short of own N.L. mark), and 20 double plays started. . . . Batted .314 in day games, .246 at night. . . . His 11 doubles vs. Phils were most in majors by any player vs. any single club. . . . Yearly batting averages with runners in scoring position and two outs since 1986: .212, .216, .191. . . . Batting average vs. lefties fell from .275 in '87 to .190 last year. . . . In April 1987, homered on consecutive days off Bruce Ruffin and Randy Myers. Neither of those lefties has allowed a homer to a lefty batter since.

Bob Brenly

San Francisco Giants	AB	H	2B	3B	HR	RBI	BB	SO	BA	SA	OBA
Season	206	39	7	0	5	22	20	40	.189	.296	.265
vs. Left-Handers	58	12	3	0	1	8	6	10	.207	.310	.273
vs. Right-Handers	148	27	4	0	4	14	14	30	.182	.291	.262
Home	96	17	1	0	2	8	9	22	.177	.250	.259
Road	110	22	6	0	3	14	11	18	.200	.336	.270
Grass	152	32	4	0	5	20	16	33	.211	.336	.291
Artificial Turf	54	7	3	0	0	2	4	7	.130	.185	.190
April	37	7	2	0	1	5	2	9	.189	.324	.231
May	44	7	1	0	2	5	2	7	.159	.318	.191
June	38	8	3	0	0	4	6	3	.211	.289	.340
July	35	6	0	0	1	1	3	9	.171	.257	.237
August	41	8	1	0	1	5	7	10	.195	.293	.313
Sept./Oct.	11	3	0	0	0	2	0	2	.273	.273	.273
Leading Off Inn.	54	13	1	0	0	0	6	10	.241	.259	.328
Runners On	86	17	4	0	3	20	8	15	.198	.349	.268
Runners/Scor. Pos.	46	10	3	0	2	18	5	7	.217	.413	.283
Runners On/2 Out	32	6	0	0	2	6	5	4	.188	.375	.297
Scor. Pos./2 Out	19	2	0	0	1	4	4	3	.105	.263	.261
Late Inning Pressure	36	8	3	0	0	4	7	6	.222	.306	.349
Leading Off	6	2	0	0	0	0	3	1	.333	.333	.556
Runners On	14	4	2	0	0	4	2	1	.286	.429	.375
Runners/Scor. Pos.	9	3	2	0	0	4	1	1	.333	.556	.400

RUNS BATTED IN	From 1B	From 2B	From 3B	Scoring Position
Totals	2/64	7/37	8/19	15/56
Percentage	3%	19%	42%	27%
Driving In Runners from 3B with Less than Two Out:			7/12	58%

Loves to face: Andy Hawkins (.588, 10-for-17, 2 HR)
Hates to face: Charles Hudson (.143, 2-for-14)
Batting average was 2d lowest in N.L. (minmum: 200 AB). . . . Joined Chuck Hiller (1964) and Matt Williams (1987) as only 200-at-bat players to hit below .190 in team's 31 years on left coast. . . . Collected 10 of his 22 RBI last season in 10 games vs. Braves, including eight in six games at Atlanta Stadium. Giants averaged 7.3 runs per game there, highest rate by any N.L. team at any visiting stadium. . . . Homered in every N.L. ballpark except Dodger Stadium. Now starts from scratch in A.L. . . . Career averages: .250 vs. left-handers, .251 vs. right-handers. . . . After three straight seasons of 500+ plate appearances, he dropped to 436 in 1987, and 234 last season.

Chris Brown

San Diego Padres	AB	H	2B	3B	HR	RBI	BB	SO	BA	SA	OBA
Season	247	58	6	0	2	19	19	49	.235	.283	.295
vs. Left-Handers	106	26	4	0	1	4	8	16	.245	.311	.298
vs. Right-Handers	141	32	2	0	1	15	11	33	.227	.262	.293
Home	123	33	3	0	1	11	15	17	.268	.317	.357
Road	124	25	3	0	1	8	4	32	.202	.250	.229
Grass	170	43	4	0	1	14	16	33	.253	.294	.323
Artificial Turf	77	15	2	0	1	5	3	16	.195	.260	.232
April	41	10	1	0	1	3	5	13	.244	.341	.326
May	45	10	1	0	0	1	3	8	.222	.244	.286
June	47	13	2	0	1	5	4	7	.277	.383	.327
July	62	15	0	0	0	9	3	11	.242	.242	.294
August	32	7	2	0	0	1	2	8	.219	.281	.265
Sept./Oct.	20	3	0	0	0	0	2	2	.150	.150	.227
Leading Off Inn.	56	16	1	0	2	2	2	8	.286	.411	.322
Runners On	103	23	2	0	0	17	11	26	.223	.243	.299
Runners/Scor. Pos.	58	13	1	0	0	17	8	14	.224	.241	.319
Runners On/2 Out	43	8	2	0	0	8	5	7	.186	.233	.271
Scor. Pos./2 Out	28	6	1	0	0	8	5	4	.214	.250	.333
Late Inning Pressure	37	10	1	0	0	1	3	7	.270	.297	.372
Leading Off	10	2	0	0	0	1	0	0	.200	.200	.333
Runners On	14	3	0	0	0	1	1	5	.214	.214	.313
Runners/Scor. Pos.	12	2	0	0	0	1	1	5	.167	.167	.286

RUNS BATTED IN	From 1B	From 2B	From 3B	Scoring Position
Totals	0/74	7/46	10/26	17/72
Percentage	0%	15%	38%	24%
Driving In Runners from 3B with Less than Two Out:			5/8	63%

Loves to face: Jamie Moyer (.429, 6-for-14, 1 HR)
Hates to face: Jimmy Jones (0-for-5)
Even though he hit only .223 with runners on base in 1988, owns career average of .304 in those situations, .249 with bases empty. That 55-point difference is the 3d largest by any player over the past 10 seasons (minimum: 500 AB both ways). Only Bruce Bochte and Willie Montanez rose to runners-on-base situations better. . . . Homered in first at-bat of 1988, but only once in 246 at-bats thereafter. . . . Hasn't hit .200 on artificial turf in either of last two seasons; his new team, Tigers, will play only 25 games on carpets in '89. . . . From 1984 to 1986, batted .258 vs. left-handers and .307 vs. right-handers; in 1987-88, he has hit .255 vs. lefties, but has dropped to .224 vs. righties.

Hubie Brooks

Montreal Expos	AB	H	2B	3B	HR	RBI	BB	SO	BA	SA	OBA
Season	588	164	35	2	20	91	35	108	.279	.447	.318
vs. Left-Handers	156	49	12	1	7	30	13	22	.314	.538	.366
vs. Right-Handers	432	115	23	1	13	61	22	86	.266	.414	.300
Home	292	76	15	1	9	50	18	55	.260	.411	.300
Road	296	88	20	1	11	41	17	53	.297	.483	.337
Grass	154	47	8	0	5	25	8	27	.305	.455	.340
Artificial Turf	434	117	27	2	15	66	27	81	.270	.445	.311
April	81	20	2	1	3	15	1	14	.247	.407	.256
May	119	33	5	0	2	17	5	25	.277	.370	.304
June	111	32	6	1	4	15	11	16	.288	.468	.352
July	91	22	7	0	4	18	6	17	.242	.451	.283
August	89	28	7	0	3	9	7	18	.315	.494	.367
Sept./Oct.	97	29	8	0	4	17	5	18	.299	.505	.333
Leading Off Inn.	122	37	10	0	4	4	7	14	.303	.484	.341
Runners On	287	84	16	0	11	82	21	62	.293	.463	.337
Runners/Scor. Pos.	169	51	8	0	9	73	14	39	.302	.509	.348
Runners On/2 Out	122	33	6	0	4	35	10	29	.270	.418	.326
Scor. Pos./2 Out	80	23	4	0	4	33	6	16	.288	.488	.337
Late Inning Pressure	114	33	5	1	4	18	4	20	.289	.456	.311
Leading Off	22	7	2	0	1	1	0	1	.318	.545	.318
Runners On	61	19	2	0	2	16	3	12	.311	.443	.338
Runners/Scor. Pos.	37	11	2	0	1	14	3	7	.297	.432	.341

RUNS BATTED IN	From 1B	From 2B	From 3B	Scoring Position
Totals	13/189	23/117	35/80	58/197
Percentage	7%	20%	44%	29%
Driving In Runners from 3B with Less than Two Out:			23/39	59%

Loves to face: David Cone (.455, 5-for-11, 3 HR)
Hates to face: Steve Bedrosian (.161, 5-for-31, 15 SO)
.314 average vs. lefties made it four straight years hitting .310+ vs. southpaws. Career lefty/righty numbers: batting .310, slugging .478 vs. LHP; .264 and .381 vs. RHP. Translation: He hits lefties like Jackie Robinson (career averages: .311, .474), righties like Gino Cimoli (.265, .383). . . . Attained career highs in home runs and strikeouts in '88. . . . A .347 career hitter with bases loaded, with grand slam in each of last four years. . . . Has hit .300 with runners in scoring position in three of last four years; he missed in 1986, which was the only one of the four years in which hit .300 overall (.340). . . . First player ever to play 140 games in different seasons at third base, shortstop, and outfield.

Tom Brunansky

St. Louis Cardinals	AB	H	2B	3B	HR	RBI	BB	SO	BA	SA	OBA
Season	523	128	22	4	22	80	79	82	.245	.428	.345
vs. Left-Handers	171	48	12	0	4	25	28	18	.281	.421	.376
vs. Right-Handers	352	80	10	4	18	55	51	64	.227	.432	.329
Home	253	57	8	3	7	43	42	36	.225	.364	.336
Road	270	71	14	1	15	37	37	46	.263	.489	.354
Grass	140	41	7	0	13	28	23	22	.293	.621	.393
Artificial Turf	383	87	15	4	9	52	56	60	.227	.358	.327
April	24	7	0	0	3	7	4	3	.292	.667	.393
May	109	36	5	0	4	27	20	14	.330	.486	.427
June	104	25	3	2	2	9	19	20	.240	.365	.363
July	88	16	1	0	5	14	13	20	.182	.364	.288
August	108	28	6	2	6	19	13	16	.259	.519	.341
Sept./Oct.	90	16	7	0	2	4	10	9	.178	.322	.265
Leading Off Inn.	142	32	10	2	2	2	15	23	.225	.366	.299
Runners On	243	55	8	2	7	65	50	43	.226	.362	.358
Runners/Scor. Pos.	168	38	5	1	5	60	42	27	.226	.357	.376
Runners On/2 Out	108	25	2	2	2	26	31	22	.231	.343	.415
Scor. Pos./2 Out	82	19	2	1	2	25	25	15	.232	.354	.422
Late Inning Pressure	84	21	3	1	4	9	14	14	.250	.452	.354
Leading Off	23	7	1	0	0	0	5	3	.304	.435	.429
Runners On	32	5	2	0	1	6	4	7	.156	.313	.243
Runners/Scor. Pos.	21	3	1	0	1	6	4	2	.143	.333	.269

RUNS BATTED IN	From 1B	From 2B	From 3B	Scoring Position
Totals	7/155	20/112	31/86	51/198
Percentage	5%	18%	36%	26%
Driving In Runners from 3B with Less than Two Out:			20/44	45%

Loves to face: Bruce Hurst (.577, 15-for-26)
Hates to face: David Cone (.071, 1-for-14)
Figures *above* are for N.L. only. . . . One of five guys with 20 homers in each of last seven years; others: Dwight Evans, Lynn, Murphy, Ripken. . . . Led majors in RBI during May, but at another point, he stranded eight straight runners at third base with less than two out, majors' longest streak of year. . . . Hit a rut of 30 hitless at-bats in September; among nonpitchers, only Steve Jeltz (33) had longer 0-for in N.L. last season. . . . Four home runs vs. left-handers represented a career low; did not homer off a lefty in Busch Stadium last year. . . . Made three errors in 13 outfield games with Twins, but then led N.L. outfielders in fielding (.996). Obviously, it's easier to field in N.L.

Brett Butler

San Francisco Giants — Bats Left

	AB	H	2B	3B	HR	RBI	BB	SO	BA	SA	OBA
Season	568	163	27	9	6	43	97	64	.287	.398	.393
vs. Left-Handers	190	48	6	3	1	18	37	26	.253	.332	.380
vs. Right-Handers	378	115	21	6	5	25	60	38	.304	.431	.400
Home	276	80	12	3	1	16	49	29	.290	.366	.401
Road	292	83	15	6	5	27	48	35	.284	.428	.387
Grass	416	124	20	6	5	34	72	47	.298	.411	.404
Artificial Turf	152	39	7	3	1	9	25	17	.257	.362	.365
April	94	27	3	2	1	6	11	11	.287	.394	.362
May	97	22	4	2	0	4	15	15	.227	.309	.330
June	89	30	3	1	2	9	18	6	.337	.461	.444
July	96	28	4	1	0	12	21	8	.292	.354	.419
August	102	30	4	1	2	7	19	15	.294	.412	.410
Sept./Oct.	90	26	9	2	1	5	13	9	.289	.467	.393
Leading Off Inn.	245	70	12	4	4	4	38	19	.286	.416	.384
Runners On	156	40	6	2	1	38	36	23	.256	.340	.398
Runners/Scor. Pos.	107	27	4	2	0	35	26	15	.252	.327	.401
Runners On/2 Out	71	15	2	1	1	16	17	10	.211	.310	.364
Scor. Pos./2 Out	56	12	1	1	0	13	15	7	.214	.268	.380
Late Inning Pressure	76	16	1	1	0	5	14	11	.211	.250	.333
Leading Off	22	4	1	0	0	0	1	2	.182	.227	.217
Runners On	31	6	0	1	0	5	8	5	.194	.258	.359
Runners/Scor. Pos.	25	5	0	1	0	5	5	4	.200	.280	.333

RUNS BATTED IN	From 1B	From 2B	From 3B	Scoring Position
Totals	4/91	15/91	18/39	33/130
Percentage	4%	16%	46%	25%
Driving In Runners from 3B with Less than Two Out:			14/20	70%

Loves to face: Charlie Puleo (.625, 5-for-8, 2 2B)
Hates to face: Tim Leary (0-for-9)
Has scored 506 runs and stolen 207 bases over last five years. Only players with more runs over that span are Henderson, Boggs, Dwight Evans; only players with more steals are Henderson, Coleman, Raines, Willie Wilson. . . . Has batted leadoff in each of his last 275 starts. . . . Grounded into only two double plays in 72 opportunities last season, 3d-lowest rate in N.L. (min: 40 opp.). . . . Career average of .354 (23-for-65, one HR) with the bases loaded. . . . Yearly batting averages vs. left-handers since 1985: .332, .306, .267, .253; however, he still has higher career batting average vs. lefties (.289) than vs. righties (.278). . . . First Giant to lead league in runs scored since Bobby Bonds in 1973.

Gary Carter

New York Mets — Bats Right

	AB	H	2B	3B	HR	RBI	BB	SO	BA	SA	OBA
Season	455	110	16	2	11	46	34	52	.242	.358	.301
vs. Left-Handers	164	42	6	1	5	18	9	12	.256	.396	.295
vs. Right-Handers	291	68	10	1	6	28	25	40	.234	.337	.304
Home	228	48	5	0	5	24	12	33	.211	.298	.258
Road	227	62	11	2	6	22	22	19	.273	.419	.343
Grass	321	76	10	1	8	35	21	41	.237	.349	.289
Artificial Turf	134	34	6	1	3	11	13	11	.254	.381	.329
April	66	22	2	0	7	15	11	4	.333	.682	.432
May	82	17	4	1	1	9	7	12	.207	.317	.283
June	90	21	2	1	0	8	2	16	.233	.278	.260
July	71	16	1	0	0	3	5	7	.225	.282	.276
August	78	18	1	0	2	8	4	8	.231	.321	.274
Sept./Oct.	68	16	6	0	1	3	5	5	.235	.324	.288
Leading Off Inn.	111	27	7	0	2	2	7	11	.243	.360	.300
Runners On	176	45	2	1	4	39	20	23	.256	.347	.335
Runners/Scor. Pos.	124	28	1	1	3	36	12	19	.226	.323	.292
Runners On/2 Out	69	14	1	0	0	6	7	11	.203	.217	.286
Scor. Pos./2 Out	52	7	1	0	0	6	4	11	.135	.154	.211
Late Inning Pressure	77	18	1	0	3	12	4	9	.234	.364	.286
Leading Off	16	2	1	0	0	0	1	3	.125	.188	.222
Runners On	33	13	0	0	2	11	3	1	.394	.576	.447
Runners/Scor. Pos.	21	8	0	0	1	9	2	1	.381	.524	.417

RUNS BATTED IN	From 1B	From 2B	From 3B	Scoring Position
Totals	4/113	12/103	19/43	31/146
Percentage	4%	12%	44%	21%
Driving In Runners from 3B with Less than Two Out:			15/24	63%

Loves to face: Joe Price (.500, 10-for-20, 4 HR)
Hates to face: Dave Smith (.063, 1-for-16)
Hard to believe, but true: At 34, Kid was oldest player with 120+ starts in N.L. last year. . . . Seven April homers tied him for N.L. lead with Bonilla and Glenn Davis. . . . Summerlong wait for 300th homer wasn't his first drought in anticipation of a personal goal: He froze at 98 RBI for seven days in '86 before reaching 100 on final weekend. . . . Led N.L. catchers in putouts for 8th time, extending own record; A.L. mark: nine by Ray Schalk. . . . Batted .280 vs. ground-ball pitchers, .201 vs. fly-ballers. . . . Batting average with runners on base has been higher than with bases empty in each of last 11 years. . . . Had four hits in seven pinch-hit at-bats, after entering 1988 hitless in last 28 pinch at-bats.

Will Clark

San Francisco Giants — Bats Left

	AB	H	2B	3B	HR	RBI	BB	SO	BA	SA	OBA
Season	575	162	31	6	29	109	100	129	.282	.508	.386
vs. Left-Handers	221	58	11	3	7	36	23	50	.262	.434	.331
vs. Right-Handers	354	104	20	3	22	73	77	79	.294	.554	.417
Home	283	76	13	3	14	64	46	61	.269	.484	.364
Road	292	86	18	3	15	45	54	68	.295	.531	.407
Grass	423	119	21	4	20	83	70	96	.281	.492	.380
Artificial Turf	152	43	10	2	9	26	30	33	.283	.553	.402
April	85	22	3	1	5	14	12	18	.259	.494	.350
May	102	24	9	1	6	19	15	22	.235	.520	.336
June	85	28	4	2	8	29	21	19	.329	.706	.458
July	101	29	5	1	3	17	20	25	.287	.446	.407
August	102	30	6	0	3	13	13	28	.294	.441	.373
Sept./Oct.	100	29	4	1	4	17	19	17	.290	.470	.393
Leading Off Inn.	95	28	4	1	7	7	7	14	.295	.579	.343
Runners On	268	77	19	3	15	95	66	63	.287	.549	.419
Runners/Scor. Pos.	171	54	14	2	11	85	50	43	.316	.614	.455
Runners On/2 Out	89	27	4	3	6	35	33	25	.303	.618	.496
Scor. Pos./2 Out	58	20	2	2	5	32	25	16	.345	.707	.548
Late Inning Pressure	87	22	5	0	3	16	16	25	.253	.414	.365
Leading Off	24	7	2	0	2	2	2	4	.292	.625	.346
Runners On	36	11	3	0	0	13	10	9	.306	.389	.447
Runners/Scor. Pos.	24	8	3	0	0	13	7	7	.333	.458	.469

RUNS BATTED IN	From 1B	From 2B	From 3B	Scoring Position
Totals	14/177	30/130	36/81	66/211
Percentage	8%	23%	44%	31%
Driving In Runners from 3B with Less than Two Out:			28/52	54%

Loves to face: Pete Smith (.417, 5-for-12, 3 HR)
Hates to face: John Smiley (0-for-13)
First nonpitcher from Giants to start All-Star Game since Chris Speier in 1973. . . . First Giant to lead the N.L. in RBI since McCovey in 1969. . . . Also led N.L. in on-base average vs. right-handed pitchers and home-run rate vs. RHP. . . . Only N.L. player to appear in all of his team's games last season. . . . Although he hit six fewer homers than he did in 1987, he had surpassed 1987's RBI total by end of August. . . . Career average of .135 (5-for-37, no HR, no BB) with the bases loaded. . . . Had hit over .330 at Candlestick in both '86 and '87; owns .313 career mark there. . . . Gets more respect than some entire teams: Clark led majors with 27 intentional walks last season; Seattle Mariners had 24.

Vince Coleman

St. Louis Cardinals — Bats Left and Right

	AB	H	2B	3B	HR	RBI	BB	SO	BA	SA	OBA
Season	616	160	20	10	3	39	49	111	.260	.339	.313
vs. Left-Handers	220	60	13	4	2	21	17	44	.273	.395	.324
vs. Right-Handers	396	100	7	6	1	18	32	67	.253	.308	.307
Home	326	90	12	7	2	27	27	58	.276	.374	.330
Road	290	70	8	3	1	12	22	53	.241	.300	.294
Grass	154	39	2	0	1	6	11	29	.253	.286	.301
Artificial Turf	462	121	18	10	2	33	38	82	.262	.357	.317
April	89	25	3	4	2	9	7	15	.281	.472	.337
May	134	44	3	0	0	10	4	19	.328	.403	.345
June	101	23	4	2	0	0	13	22	.228	.307	.316
July	103	20	2	1	0	4	10	22	.194	.233	.265
August	109	30	3	0	1	11	7	14	.275	.330	.316
Sept./Oct.	80	18	4	0	0	5	8	21	.225	.275	.299
Leading Off Inn.	277	70	8	4	1	1	18	56	.253	.321	.301
Runners On	182	48	8	4	1	37	15	26	.264	.368	.312
Runners/Scor. Pos.	115	28	6	2	1	35	10	19	.243	.357	.292
Runners On/2 Out	83	22	3	1	1	22	12	12	.265	.410	.358
Scor. Pos./2 Out	59	12	3	1	1	20	8	9	.203	.339	.299
Late Inning Pressure	91	25	2	1	0	5	7	14	.275	.319	.330
Leading Off	28	8	2	0	0	0	2	6	.286	.357	.355
Runners On	32	5	0	1	0	5	2	4	.156	.219	.200
Runners/Scor. Pos.	21	3	0	1	0	5	1	3	.143	.238	.174

RUNS BATTED IN	From 1B	From 2B	From 3B	Scoring Position
Totals	4/110	14/96	18/49	32/145
Percentage	4%	15%	37%	22%
Driving In Runners from 3B with Less than Two Out:			12/24	50%

Loves to face: Ron Robinson (.471, 8-for-17)
Hates to face: Tom Browning (0-for-16)
One of seven players in majors with 650+ plate appearances in each of last four years. . . . Has led N.L. in steals for four straight seasons; record is six by Maury Wills, 1960–65. . . . Has 39 steals in 39 career attempts vs. Mets. . . . Caught stealing 27 times last season, a personal high; he tied Gerald Young for N.L. lead. . . . Batted .226 vs. ground-ball pitchers last season, .301 vs. fly-ball pitchers. . . . Had 28 consecutive hitless at-bats with runners in scoring position, longest streak in majors last season; that came during his streak of 41 games without an RBI. . . . Has had 58 outfield assists in four years in majors; since 1985, only Jesse Barfield (71) and Glenn Wilson (61) have as many.

Dave Concepcion

Bats Right

Cincinnati Reds	AB	H	2B	3B	HR	RBI	BB	SO	BA	SA	OBA
Season	197	39	9	0	0	8	18	23	.198	.244	.265
vs. Left-Handers	114	23	4	0	0	5	12	11	.202	.237	.278
vs. Right-Handers	83	16	5	0	0	3	6	12	.193	.253	.247
Home	104	25	6	0	0	7	11	11	.240	.298	.313
Road	93	14	3	0	0	1	7	12	.151	.183	.210
Grass	39	5	2	0	0	0	3	6	.128	.179	.190
Artificial Turf	158	34	7	0	0	8	15	17	.215	.259	.283
April	33	7	3	0	0	2	4	2	.212	.303	.297
May	53	13	2	0	0	3	6	2	.245	.283	.322
June	48	9	1	0	0	1	2	10	.188	.208	.220
July	21	2	2	0	0	0	2	4	.095	.190	.174
August	38	8	1	0	0	2	2	4	.211	.237	.250
Sept./Oct.	4	0	0	0	0	0	2	1	.000	.000	.333
Leading Off Inn.	42	8	2	0	0	0	5	2	.190	.238	.277
Runners On	81	15	2	0	0	8	12	12	.185	.210	.290
Runners/Scor. Pos.	44	7	1	0	0	8	12	8	.159	.182	.339
Runners On/2 Out	42	13	2	0	0	7	7	6	.310	.357	.408
Scor. Pos./2 Out	27	6	1	0	0	7	7	5	.222	.259	.382
Late Inning Pressure	30	4	0	0	0	0	4	6	.133	.133	.235
Leading Off	7	2	0	0	0	0	0	1	.286	.286	.286
Runners On	13	1	0	0	0	0	3	3	.077	.077	.250
Runners/Scor. Pos.	7	0	0	0	0	0	3	1	.000	.000	.300

RUNS BATTED IN	From 1B	From 2B	From 3B	Scoring Position
Totals	0/60	3/37	5/14	8/51
Percentage	0%	8%	36%	16%
Driving In Runners from 3B with Less than Two Out:		0/5		0%

Loves to face: John Tudor (.471, 8-for-17)
Hates to face: Orel Hershiser (.048, 1-for-21)
Finished 1988 season 12 games shy of 2500, and 234 short of Rose's team record of 2722 games. Only six players in history have played 2500+ games, all for one club: Yastrzemski (3308), Musial (3026), Brooks Robinson (2896), Kaline (2834), Ott (2732), Banks (2528). . . . At 40, was oldest major leaguer to start a game at either second base or shortstop last season. . . . One of two players in majors with 200 plate appearances and fewer than 10 RBI in '88; other: Mark Salas. . . . Started 37 of 42 games in which Reds faced a left-handed starter, but only 10 of 119 vs. right-handers. . . . Threw one and one-third shutout innings vs. Dodgers on June 3; loves to face Franklin Stubbs, whom he fanned.

Kal Daniels

Bats Left

Cincinnati Reds	AB	H	2B	3B	HR	RBI	BB	SO	BA	SA	OBA
Season	495	144	29	1	18	64	87	94	.291	.463	.397
vs. Left-Handers	135	36	4	0	3	19	26	29	.267	.363	.387
vs. Right-Handers	360	108	25	1	15	45	61	65	.300	.500	.401
Home	227	75	15	0	12	35	43	37	.330	.555	.436
Road	268	69	14	1	6	29	44	57	.257	.384	.363
Grass	159	40	8	0	4	15	28	29	.252	.377	.367
Artificial Turf	336	104	21	1	14	49	59	65	.310	.503	.411
April	73	19	4	0	4	14	16	15	.260	.479	.391
May	101	30	7	1	1	10	20	20	.297	.416	.403
June	60	19	3	0	3	9	19	11	.317	.517	.469
July	96	25	6	0	2	8	11	28	.260	.385	.336
August	84	24	6	0	4	13	14	9	.286	.500	.388
Sept./Oct.	81	27	3	0	4	10	11	11	.333	.519	.413
Leading Off Inn.	130	37	10	1	4	4	11	23	.285	.469	.350
Runners On	189	56	12	0	4	50	49	37	.296	.423	.436
Runners/Scor. Pos.	113	36	8	0	2	46	42	25	.319	.442	.494
Runners On/2 Out	62	18	4	0	1	17	23	11	.290	.403	.482
Scor. Pos./2 Out	45	14	3	0	1	17	20	10	.311	.444	.523
Late Inning Pressure	63	12	1	0	2	9	18	17	.190	.302	.366
Leading Off	17	3	1	0	0	0	1	5	.176	.235	.222
Runners On	30	6	0	0	1	8	14	7	.200	.300	.444
Runners/Scor. Pos.	13	4	0	0	1	8	11	5	.308	.538	.600

RUNS BATTED IN	From 1B	From 2B	From 3B	Scoring Position
Totals	5/115	16/88	25/46	41/134
Percentage	4%	18%	54%	31%
Driving In Runners from 3B with Less than Two Out:		18/29		62%

Loves to face: Orel Hershiser (.500, 12-for-24, 4 HR)
Hates to face: Mark Davis (0-for-11)
Batted 115 points lower in Late-Inning Pressure Situations than other at-bats last season, 2d-largest difference in N.L. (minimum: 50 LIPS AB). . . . Batted .413 with six homers and 15 RBI in 13 games vs. Astros last season; hit .419 against them in 1987. . . . Streak of 19 straight stolen bases was snapped on his last attempt of the season (Sept. 24). . . . Owns .340 career batting average when leading off an inning. . . . Had 159 more plate appearances in '88 than in '87 as playing time vs. lefties increased; finished with eight fewer homers, same RBI total, one more steal. . . . There's a difference of 100 points between his career averages vs. right-handers (.335) and left-handers (.235).

Eric Davis

Bats Right

Cincinnati Reds	AB	H	2B	3B	HR	RBI	BB	SO	BA	SA	OBA
Season	472	129	18	3	26	93	65	124	.273	.489	.363
vs. Left-Handers	120	35	4	1	7	21	19	19	.292	.517	.390
vs. Right-Handers	352	94	14	2	19	72	46	105	.267	.480	.353
Home	212	55	7	0	14	53	40	61	.259	.491	.377
Road	260	74	11	3	12	40	25	63	.285	.488	.350
Grass	143	41	4	2	7	22	16	33	.287	.490	.363
Artificial Turf	329	88	14	1	19	71	49	91	.267	.489	.363
April	84	15	2	0	2	7	17	29	.179	.274	.317
May	75	20	5	0	4	16	7	19	.267	.493	.321
June	73	21	0	0	7	17	4	22	.288	.575	.342
July	76	25	5	1	5	14	7	15	.329	.618	.393
August	93	30	4	1	6	24	19	21	.323	.581	.434
Sept./Oct.	71	18	2	1	2	15	11	18	.254	.394	.354
Leading Off Inn.	114	34	5	0	8	8	11	26	.298	.553	.365
Runners On	223	73	12	3	14	81	38	54	.327	.596	.425
Runners/Scor. Pos.	153	48	10	2	6	63	32	38	.314	.523	.432
Runners On/2 Out	108	40	6	3	11	44	22	27	.370	.787	.481
Scor. Pos./2 Out	74	25	5	2	5	31	19	21	.338	.662	.479
Late Inning Pressure	81	25	6	0	5	15	11	25	.309	.568	.398
Leading Off	18	8	2	0	1	1	1	5	.444	.722	.474
Runners On	35	13	3	0	4	14	7	10	.371	.800	.488
Runners/Scor. Pos.	22	8	2	0	2	10	6	6	.364	.727	.517

RUNS BATTED IN	From 1B	From 2B	From 3B	Scoring Position
Totals	13/134	26/118	28/63	54/181
Percentage	10%	22%	44%	30%
Driving In Runners from 3B with Less than Two Out:		16/30		53%

Loves to face: Don Carman (.636, 7-for-11, 4 HR)
Hates to face: Charlie Puleo (0-for-7, 6 SO)
Club math: What's the 30/30 Club times three? The 90/90 Club. Over past three years, only Davis (90 HR, 165 SB) and his buddy Darryl (105 HR, 93 SB) are in it. . . . Although his total of steals has fallen every year since 1986 (80, 50, 35), his rate of success has improved (87.9, 89.3, 92.1). . . . Batting averages with runners on base and with men in scoring position were both career highs. . . . Career average of .413 (19-for-46, four HR) with bases loaded. . . . Has played in only five of Reds' 15 games at Astrodome since he fanned in nine straight plate appearances there, tying major league mark for nonpitchers, in 1987. . . . Has averaged 132 games (122 starts) in three years as "fulltime" player.

Glenn Davis

Bats Right

Houston Astros	AB	H	2B	3B	HR	RBI	BB	SO	BA	SA	OBA
Season	561	152	26	0	30	101	53	77	.271	.478	.341
vs. Left-Handers	167	38	7	0	7	27	21	22	.228	.395	.322
vs. Right-Handers	394	114	19	0	23	74	32	55	.289	.513	.349
Home	290	86	17	0	15	52	28	36	.297	.510	.363
Road	271	66	9	0	15	49	25	41	.244	.443	.317
Grass	146	23	2	0	5	17	10	26	.158	.274	.230
Artificial Turf	415	129	24	0	25	84	43	51	.311	.549	.378
April	70	20	2	0	7	20	9	7	.286	.614	.378
May	108	30	5	0	4	21	10	14	.278	.435	.336
June	106	19	1	0	6	17	5	12	.179	.358	.230
July	73	28	8	0	5	17	10	9	.384	.699	.453
August	92	28	3	0	4	14	11	18	.304	.467	.382
Sept./Oct.	112	27	7	0	4	12	8	17	.241	.411	.306
Leading Off Inn.	156	43	8	0	6	6	6	20	.276	.442	.319
Runners On	254	66	7	0	20	91	37	29	.260	.524	.352
Runners/Scor. Pos.	151	32	1	0	6	59	33	19	.212	.338	.347
Runners On/2 Out	129	29	2	0	9	35	23	17	.225	.450	.342
Scor. Pos./2 Out	82	15	0	0	3	21	21	12	.183	.293	.350
Late Inning Pressure	94	26	6	0	3	12	14	14	.277	.436	.376
Leading Off	24	8	0	0	1	1	0	2	.333	.458	.333
Runners On	36	9	2	0	2	11	10	5	.250	.472	.413
Runners/Scor. Pos.	18	4	0	0	0	9	9	2	.222	.222	.481

RUNS BATTED IN	From 1B	From 2B	From 3B	Scoring Position
Totals	21/174	22/110	28/70	50/180
Percentage	12%	20%	40%	28%
Driving In Runners from 3B with Less than Two Out:		25/36		69%

Loves to face: Dennis Martinez (.636, 7-for-11, 4 HR)
Hates to face: Mike Bielecki (0-for-9)
Has 88 home runs and 293 runs batted in over past three years; among N.L. players, only Strawberry and Dawson outrank him. . . . Imagine what those numbers would be if he hit better in clutch; annual batting averages with runners in scoring position since 1985: .316, .265, .245, .212. . . . One of two major leaguers to bat 100 points higher on rugs than on grass fields last season (minimum: 100 AB each way); career averages: .279 on artificial turf, .223 on grass. . . . Batting average vs. right-handers was a career high, average vs. lefties a career low. . . . One hit in 10 at-bats with bases loaded last season; career average: .184 (7-for-38). . . . Became first Houston first baseman to lead N.L. in fielding (.996).

Jody Davis

Cubs/Braves — Bats Right

	AB	H	2B	3B	HR	RBI	BB	SO	BA	SA	OBA
Season	257	59	9	0	7	36	29	52	.230	.346	.307
vs. Left-Handers	102	19	1	0	2	12	12	20	.186	.255	.270
vs. Right-Handers	155	40	8	0	5	24	17	32	.258	.406	.331
Home	105	19	3	0	3	11	12	27	.181	.295	.263
Road	152	40	6	0	4	25	17	25	.263	.382	.337
Grass	171	35	6	0	5	19	22	38	.205	.327	.296
Artificial Turf	86	24	3	0	2	17	7	14	.279	.384	.330
April	60	18	4	0	3	13	11	11	.300	.517	.403
May	36	13	2	0	3	10	4	7	.361	.667	.429
June	72	13	1	0	0	4	4	15	.181	.194	.221
July	32	6	1	0	0	1	5	7	.188	.219	.297
August	32	4	1	0	0	3	3	8	.125	.156	.200
Sept./Oct.	25	5	0	0	1	5	2	4	.200	.320	.259
Leading Off Inn.	52	15	1	0	3	3	7	11	.288	.481	.373
Runners On	132	33	7	0	2	31	16	23	.250	.348	.329
Runners/Scor. Pos.	76	16	3	0	2	27	12	16	.211	.329	.315
Runners On/2 Out	52	12	4	0	0	13	7	12	.231	.308	.333
Scor. Pos./2 Out	36	7	2	0	0	11	4	10	.194	.250	.293
Late Inning Pressure	34	4	3	0	0	2	7	12	.118	.206	.286
Leading Off	10	2	1	0	0	0	3	5	.200	.300	.385
Runners On	16	1	1	0	0	2	4	3	.063	.125	.286
Runners/Scor. Pos.	10	0	0	0	0	1	3	3	.000	.000	.286

RUNS BATTED IN	From 1B	From 2B	From 3B	Scoring Position
Totals	6/91	10/57	13/34	23/91
Percentage	7%	18%	38%	25%
Driving In Runners from 3B with Less than Two Out:			8/14	57%

Loves to face: Floyd Youmans (.455, 5-for-11, 2 HR)
Hates to face: John Tudor (.038, 1-for-26)
Fielding percentage (.995) was higher than Tony Pena's (who led N.L. catchers), but Davis was five games short of minimum qualification (81 games) for fielding title. . . . Played two games vs. Houston last season; went 5-for-7 with three homers. . . . Joined Braves for their pennant drive on Sept. 30. Batted only .113 (8-for-71) over last 32 games with Cubs. Hadn't homered in last 161 at-bats with Chicago, but hit one out in his first game with Braves. . . . Batted .118 in Late-Inning Pressure Situations, lowest in N.L. last season. Career average in LIPS is .213; .193 career average in LIPS with runners on base is 3d lowest over past 14 years among players with 200 times up in those spots.

Mike Davis

Los Angeles Dodgers — Bats Left

	AB	H	2B	3B	HR	RBI	BB	SO	BA	SA	OBA
Season	281	55	11	2	2	17	25	59	.196	.270	.260
vs. Left-Handers	64	11	4	2	0	7	5	21	.172	.297	.229
vs. Right-Handers	217	44	7	0	2	10	20	38	.203	.263	.269
Home	133	20	4	0	1	5	10	25	.150	.203	.210
Road	148	35	7	2	1	12	15	34	.236	.331	.294
Grass	207	32	6	0	2	9	17	41	.155	.213	.218
Artificial Turf	74	23	5	2	0	8	8	18	.311	.432	.373
April	64	12	2	0	0	3	10	16	.188	.219	.297
May	93	21	2	1	0	6	6	24	.226	.269	.273
June	26	4	1	0	1	2	1	1	.154	.308	.185
July	36	8	3	1	1	4	3	10	.222	.444	.275
August	31	7	1	0	0	1	4	5	.226	.258	.314
Sept./Oct.	31	3	2	0	0	1	1	3	.097	.161	.121
Leading Off Inn.	55	9	0	0	0	0	4	11	.164	.164	.220
Runners On	110	21	2	2	2	17	9	22	.191	.300	.248
Runners/Scor. Pos.	58	12	1	2	0	12	6	11	.207	.293	.273
Runners On/2 Out	54	9	1	1	0	8	3	12	.167	.222	.211
Scor. Pos./2 Out	32	6	0	1	0	7	2	6	.188	.250	.235
Late Inning Pressure	45	12	3	0	0	3	1	10	.267	.333	.283
Leading Off	8	2	0	0	0	0	0	1	.250	.250	.250
Runners On	18	5	0	0	0	3	0	5	.278	.278	.278
Runners/Scor. Pos.	13	4	0	0	0	3	0	4	.308	.308	.308

RUNS BATTED IN	From 1B	From 2B	From 3B	Scoring Position
Totals	3/78	8/47	4/22	12/69
Percentage	4%	17%	18%	17%
Driving In Runners from 3B with Less than Two Out:			3/9	33%

Loves to face: Danny Jackson (.400, 4-for-10, 1 HR)
Hates to face: Doug Drabek (0-for-8, 4 SO)
One of 10 major leaguers with at least 20 fewer home runs in 1988 than in 1987. Has only four homers since '87 All-Star Break after belting 39 in a season and a half before that. . . . Even though he hit only .155 on grass fields, his .311 average on phony ones lifted his career mark to .292. . . . Batted 86 points higher on road than he did at home, 3d largest difference in N.L. (minimum: 100 AB each way). . . . He and Alfredo Griffin were first Dodgers since Zoilo Versalles in 1968 to hit below .200 in a season of 250+ at-bats; before Versalles, no Dodger had done that since Mickey Doolan in 1918. . . . Went 1-for-29 vs. Giants during season, but took out his Bay Area frustrations on A's during World Series.

Andre Dawson

Chicago Cubs — Bats Right

	AB	H	2B	3B	HR	RBI	BB	SO	BA	SA	OBA
Season	591	179	31	8	24	79	37	73	.303	.504	.344
vs. Left-Handers	159	47	7	3	4	16	11	21	.296	.453	.339
vs. Right-Handers	432	132	24	5	20	63	26	52	.306	.523	.346
Home	293	92	15	4	12	40	20	40	.314	.515	.360
Road	298	87	16	4	12	39	17	33	.292	.493	.329
Grass	420	122	23	6	18	55	28	56	.290	.502	.335
Artificial Turf	171	57	8	2	6	24	9	17	.333	.509	.368
April	91	29	6	2	6	13	2	7	.319	.626	.337
May	102	29	6	0	5	15	8	13	.284	.490	.336
June	104	34	6	1	3	16	8	14	.327	.490	.383
July	96	33	6	1	2	13	6	13	.344	.490	.375
August	105	28	3	3	5	15	6	14	.267	.495	.304
Sept./Oct.	93	26	4	1	3	7	7	12	.280	.441	.330
Leading Off Inn.	132	44	5	3	8	8	6	18	.333	.598	.362
Runners On	258	74	17	3	8	63	25	24	.287	.469	.346
Runners/Scor. Pos.	132	31	3	1	4	49	23	11	.235	.364	.341
Runners On/2 Out	102	32	6	1	4	26	9	6	.314	.510	.375
Scor. Pos./2 Out	60	17	2	0	3	20	9	3	.283	.467	.386
Late Inning Pressure	94	31	3	0	2	10	10	16	.330	.426	.390
Leading Off	27	11	1	0	1	1	1	3	.407	.556	.429
Runners On	41	11	2	0	0	8	8	6	.268	.317	.380
Runners/Scor. Pos.	25	7	0	0	0	8	6	4	.280	.280	.406

RUNS BATTED IN	From 1B	From 2B	From 3B	Scoring Position
Totals	12/188	16/91	27/63	43/154
Percentage	6%	18%	43%	28%
Driving In Runners from 3B with Less than Two Out:			21/38	55%

Loves to face: Mark Grant (.667, 10-for-15, 3 HR)
Hates to face: Bob Kipper (0-for-10)
Clear out the trophy case: Andre needs two home runs to reach 300, 68 hits to reach 2000, 24 steals to reach 300. There have been 40 players that have reached 300 homers and 2,000 hits; 26 of the 40 are in the Hall of Fame; 10 are not yet eligible. Only Orlando Cepeda, Lee May, Ron Santo, and Reggie Smith have not made it. When you blend in the 300 steals, you have a club of one: Willie Mays. . . . First player in history to reach double figures in homers and steals for 12 straight seasons. . . . Hit .500 vs. Expos last season (27-for-54), best average by any player vs. any club in majors. . . . Batting average vs. right-handers was a career high, but average with runners in scoring position was his lowest since 1981.

Bo Diaz

Cincinnati Reds — Bats Right

	AB	H	2B	3B	HR	RBI	BB	SO	BA	SA	OBA
Season	315	69	9	0	10	35	7	41	.219	.343	.236
vs. Left-Handers	89	21	2	0	4	10	4	14	.236	.393	.266
vs. Right-Handers	226	48	7	0	6	25	3	27	.212	.323	.224
Home	141	29	5	0	5	18	4	18	.206	.348	.230
Road	174	40	4	0	5	17	3	23	.230	.339	.242
Grass	102	22	2	0	1	11	1	15	.216	.265	.223
Artificial Turf	213	47	7	0	9	24	6	26	.221	.380	.242
April	76	18	1	0	4	9	0	10	.237	.408	.234
May	68	15	2	0	2	5	3	11	.221	.338	.250
June	49	12	2	0	0	7	1	7	.245	.286	.260
July	66	14	1	0	2	5	0	5	.212	.318	.209
August	56	10	3	0	2	9	3	8	.179	.339	.233
Sept./Oct.	0	0	0	0	0	0	0	0	----	----	----
Leading Off Inn.	67	14	3	0	4	4	0	7	.209	.433	.209
Runners On	132	28	2	0	3	28	7	22	.212	.295	.256
Runners/Scor. Pos.	79	15	1	0	2	25	7	14	.190	.278	.256
Runners On/2 Out	60	12	1	0	2	14	5	8	.200	.317	.273
Scor. Pos./2 Out	43	7	0	0	2	13	5	7	.163	.302	.265
Late Inning Pressure	48	9	1	0	1	3	2	9	.188	.271	.216
Leading Off	9	1	0	0	0	0	0	1	.111	.111	.111
Runners On	16	3	0	0	0	2	2	5	.188	.188	.263
Runners/Scor. Pos.	10	1	0	0	0	2	2	3	.100	.100	.231

RUNS BATTED IN	From 1B	From 2B	From 3B	Scoring Position
Totals	3/95	11/63	11/43	22/106
Percentage	3%	17%	26%	21%
Driving In Runners from 3B with Less than Two Out:			8/15	53%

Loves to face: Greg Maddux (.667, 6-for-9, 1 HR)
Hates to face: Mike Dunne (0-for-10)
Had lowest on-base average of any N.L. player with 200 plate appearances last season. Among same group, he had lowest rate of walks. Averaged one walk every 46.7 plate appearances last season; four of his seven walks were intentional. . . . Grounded into 16 double plays in 55 opportunities, the highest rate in majors (min.: 40 opp.). . . . Hitless in 16 at-bats as pinch hitter since Aug. 20, 1983. . . . Made his major league debut on Sept. 6, 1977, replacing Carlton Fisk as Boston catcher after Pudge had driven in seven runs at Exhibition Stadium. . . . One hit in 14 at-bats with the bases loaded last season. . . . Had .315 average in Late-Inning Pressure Situations until last two years; he has hit .183 in LIPS over that span.

Bill Doran
Houston Astros — Bats Left and Right

	AB	H	2B	3B	HR	RBI	BB	SO	BA	SA	OBA
Season	480	119	18	1	7	53	65	60	.248	.333	.338
vs. Left-Handers	156	41	5	1	2	13	26	16	.263	.346	.372
vs. Right-Handers	324	78	13	0	5	40	39	44	.241	.327	.321
Home	229	57	9	1	2	25	36	30	.249	.323	.351
Road	251	62	9	0	5	28	29	30	.247	.343	.325
Grass	145	41	6	0	3	22	17	19	.283	.386	.358
Artificial Turf	335	78	12	1	4	31	48	41	.233	.310	.329
April	74	19	2	0	0	11	9	6	.257	.284	.345
May	40	10	1	0	0	3	6	3	.250	.275	.348
June	101	28	5	0	3	16	12	12	.277	.416	.354
July	103	30	2	0	3	15	11	18	.291	.398	.360
August	98	21	5	1	1	6	17	17	.214	.316	.328
Sept./Oct.	64	11	3	0	0	2	10	4	.172	.219	.280
Leading Off Inn.	103	23	5	0	2	2	8	11	.223	.330	.279
Runners On	187	54	9	0	3	49	26	22	.289	.385	.372
Runners/Scor. Pos.	113	31	2	0	3	45	22	19	.274	.372	.387
Runners On/2 Out	65	20	3	0	1	24	11	9	.308	.400	.408
Scor. Pos./2 Out	47	16	1	0	1	23	10	8	.340	.426	.456
Late Inning Pressure	64	11	0	0	0	3	11	10	.172	.172	.293
Leading Off	23	5	0	0	0	0	2	3	.217	.217	.280
Runners On	24	4	0	0	0	3	4	5	.167	.167	.286
Runners/Scor. Pos.	17	2	0	0	0	3	4	5	.118	.118	.286

RUNS BATTED IN	From 1B	From 2B	From 3B	Scoring Position
Totals	6/112	20/83	20/50	40/133
Percentage	5%	24%	40%	30%
Driving In Runners from 3B with Less than Two Out:			14/31	45%

Loves to face: Tim Crews (5-for-5)
Hates to face: Bob Ojeda (0-for-11)
Led N.L. second basemen with a .987 fielding percentage. With Glenn Davis leading first basemen, Houston became only second N.L. team in past 25 years to have both players on right side of infield win fielding titles; Hernandez and Backman did it for Mets in 1985. . . . Switch hitter has batted higher vs. lefties five years in a row. . . . Six consecutive years as Astros' main second baseman is longest stint in club history. Last player to hold that spot down for even two straight years was Doran's new boss, Art Howe, 1977–78. . . . We've seen him get many big hits, but his career batting average in Late-Inning Pressure Situations is .236, and it's .185 in LIPS with runners in scoring position.

Shawon Dunston
Chicago Cubs — Bats Right

	AB	H	2B	3B	HR	RBI	BB	SO	BA	SA	OBA
Season	575	143	23	6	9	56	16	108	.249	.357	.271
vs. Left-Handers	167	39	7	2	4	15	3	26	.234	.371	.247
vs. Right-Handers	408	104	16	4	5	41	13	82	.255	.350	.280
Home	263	73	11	4	5	29	8	52	.278	.407	.300
Road	312	70	12	2	4	27	8	56	.224	.314	.245
Grass	389	105	15	5	7	39	11	77	.270	.388	.291
Artificial Turf	186	38	8	1	2	17	5	31	.204	.290	.228
April	87	22	2	1	4	13	2	16	.253	.437	.270
May	87	26	5	1	0	8	3	20	.299	.379	.330
June	112	37	7	0	4	21	2	17	.330	.500	.339
July	104	17	2	0	0	4	2	19	.163	.183	.178
August	99	21	4	3	0	4	3	25	.212	.313	.235
Sept./Oct.	86	20	3	1	1	6	4	11	.233	.326	.275
Leading Off Inn.	176	40	6	3	1	1	3	33	.227	.313	.244
Runners On	226	57	9	2	4	51	8	34	.252	.363	.275
Runners/Scor. Pos.	146	37	3	1	4	48	8	23	.253	.370	.288
Runners On/2 Out	105	27	3	2	2	26	5	17	.257	.381	.291
Scor. Pos./2 Out	72	18	1	1	2	24	5	11	.250	.375	.299
Late Inning Pressure	98	17	1	1	0	10	3	24	.173	.204	.194
Leading Off	26	5	0	1	0	0	1	7	.192	.269	.222
Runners On	38	9	1	0	0	10	2	8	.237	.263	.262
Runners/Scor. Pos.	25	6	0	0	0	9	2	7	.240	.240	.276

RUNS BATTED IN	From 1B	From 2B	From 3B	Scoring Position
Totals	5/156	18/118	24/60	42/178
Percentage	3%	15%	40%	24%
Driving In Runners from 3B with Less than Two Out:			16/31	52%

Loves to face: Mike Scott (.435, 10-for-23)
Hates to face: Eric Show (.077, 1-for-13, 6 SO)
Had 16 walks and 108 strikeouts. Among all players in major league history with 100+ strikeouts, only two had fewer walks: John Bateman (13 BB, 103 SO with 1963 Astros) and Tommie Agee (15, 103 with '68 Mets). . . . Batted .202 after the All-Star break, 3d lowest in N.L. (minimum: two PA per game); over last two seasons, has averaged one homer every 43 at-bats before All-Star break, but has one home run (total) in 364 at-bats after it. . . . Failed to reach base in 29 consecutive times up in July, longest streak by a nonpitcher in N.L. last season, and longest by any Cubs' player (pitcher or no) in 1980s. . . . Yearly averages since 1986 vs lefties: .231, .231, .234; vs. righties: .256, .250, .255.

Len Dykstra
New York Mets — Bats Left

	AB	H	2B	3B	HR	RBI	BB	SO	BA	SA	OBA
Season	429	116	19	3	8	33	30	43	.270	.385	.321
vs. Left-Handers	74	20	2	1	1	5	4	12	.270	.365	.321
vs. Right-Handers	355	96	17	2	7	28	26	31	.270	.389	.321
Home	201	51	7	1	3	10	13	18	.254	.343	.306
Road	228	65	12	2	5	23	17	25	.285	.421	.335
Grass	291	73	11	1	6	23	16	29	.251	.357	.294
Artificial Turf	138	43	8	2	2	10	14	14	.312	.442	.377
April	45	14	2	1	3	8	4	7	.311	.600	.367
May	83	23	5	0	0	3	4	11	.277	.337	.310
June	99	33	4	1	0	3	6	5	.333	.394	.371
July	68	19	5	0	0	1	6	5	.279	.353	.347
August	85	17	2	1	2	9	4	10	.200	.318	.244
Sept./Oct.	49	10	1	0	3	9	6	5	.204	.408	.293
Leading Off Inn.	175	45	8	2	5	5	9	17	.257	.411	.301
Runners On	136	32	5	1	3	28	14	18	.235	.353	.307
Runners/Scor. Pos.	77	15	4	1	1	24	12	15	.195	.312	.304
Runners On/2 Out	65	12	0	1	2	8	8	9	.185	.308	.274
Scor. Pos./2 Out	41	4	0	1	1	6	8	6	.098	.220	.245
Late Inning Pressure	55	17	2	0	1	6	8	3	.309	.400	.400
Leading Off	12	4	0	0	0	1	2	0	.333	.583	.429
Runners On	24	4	1	0	0	5	4	3	.167	.208	.300
Runners/Scor. Pos.	13	2	1	0	0	5	2	3	.154	.231	.294

RUNS BATTED IN	From 1B	From 2B	From 3B	Scoring Position
Totals	4/92	8/67	13/31	21/98
Percentage	4%	12%	42%	21%
Driving In Runners from 3B with Less than Two Out:			11/15	73%

Loves to face: Randy O'Neal (.667, 6-for-9, 2 2B, 1 HR)
Hates to face: John Franco (0-for-9)
Home run in N.L.C.S. was 4th postseason HR of career, tying club record of Staub and Strawberry. . . . Career stolen-base rate (81.1) is superior to Rickey Henderson's (80.9). . . . Led N.L. center fielders with .996 percentage. . . . Career: .306 before All-Star break, .250 after it. . . . Despite like at-bat totals (431, 431, 429) over past three years, his hits, walks, and RBI have fallen in each of last two years. . . . Has .321 career mark as pinch hitter (17-for-53). Top career average by a pinch hitter (minimum: 50 PHAB) was .390 by Duke Farrell, who played from 1888 to 1905, and was 23-for-59 in pinch. (Before 1891, pinch hitters weren't even allowed, except for injury, without OK of opposing team!)

Kevin Elster
New York Mets — Bats Right

	AB	H	2B	3B	HR	RBI	BB	SO	BA	SA	OBA
Season	406	87	11	1	9	37	35	47	.214	.313	.282
vs. Left-Handers	145	33	3	1	3	12	15	13	.228	.324	.304
vs. Right-Handers	261	54	8	0	6	25	20	34	.207	.307	.269
Home	196	38	4	0	6	20	12	24	.194	.306	.248
Road	210	49	7	1	3	17	23	23	.233	.319	.312
Grass	280	61	8	0	6	27	19	33	.218	.311	.272
Artificial Turf	126	26	3	1	3	10	16	14	.206	.317	.301
April	65	16	2	0	2	8	5	8	.246	.369	.300
May	76	16	0	0	2	7	6	12	.211	.289	.268
June	74	14	5	0	2	9	8	8	.189	.338	.277
July	72	16	1	1	1	6	4	9	.222	.306	.282
August	62	13	1	0	0	2	6	5	.210	.226	.279
Sept./Oct.	57	12	2	0	2	5	6	5	.211	.351	.286
Leading Off Inn.	91	22	3	1	1	1	3	9	.242	.330	.281
Runners On	175	44	6	0	6	34	24	21	.251	.389	.345
Runners/Scor. Pos.	98	20	2	0	1	23	20	15	.204	.255	.339
Runners On/2 Out	72	17	4	0	1	13	16	10	.236	.333	.382
Scor. Pos./2 Out	45	12	1	0	1	12	13	6	.267	.356	.431
Late Inning Pressure	55	8	0	0	2	3	1	9	.145	.255	.161
Leading Off	19	3	0	0	0	0	0	3	.158	.158	.158
Runners On	10	1	0	0	0	1	0	3	.100	.100	.100
Runners/Scor. Pos.	4	1	0	0	0	1	0	1	.250	.250	.250

RUNS BATTED IN	From 1B	From 2B	From 3B	Scoring Position
Totals	7/127	12/75	9/31	21/106
Percentage	6%	16%	29%	20%
Driving In Runners from 3B with Less than Two Out:			6/15	40%

Loves to face: Tim Leary (.600, 3-for-5, 2 HR)
Hates to face: Bruce Ruffin (0-for-6)
Batted .215 before All-Star break, lowest among everyday N.L. players. And that was his *good* half; he hit .214 after the break. . . . Defense was better in second half; made only two of 13 errors after the break. Finished season with 60 consecutive errorless games at shortstop, breaking Roger Metzger's one-season N.L. record of 59 games. Elster, who was a defensive replacement in 16 of the 60 games, needs eight games to tie Buddy Kerr's N.L. record, and 12 games to tie Ed Brinkman's major league mark. . . . Mets were undefeated in the eight games in which he homered. . . . Led major league rookies in games (149). One of only three N.L. rookies who were opening day starters (others: Chris Sabo, Randy Milligan).

Nick Esasky
Cincinnati Reds — Bats Right

	AB	H	2B	3B	HR	RBI	BB	SO	BA	SA	OBA
Season	391	95	17	2	15	62	48	104	.243	.412	.327
vs. Left-Handers	116	29	5	1	3	15	20	26	.250	.388	.357
vs. Right-Handers	275	66	12	1	12	47	28	78	.240	.422	.313
Home	213	54	8	2	7	28	20	59	.254	.408	.321
Road	178	41	9	0	8	34	28	45	.230	.416	.333
Grass	114	28	6	0	6	23	14	27	.246	.456	.336
Artificial Turf	277	67	11	2	9	39	34	77	.242	.394	.323
April	68	20	3	0	4	13	8	21	.294	.515	.380
May	29	5	1	0	0	3	4	7	.172	.207	.273
June	71	16	6	0	1	12	10	20	.225	.352	.333
July	85	23	2	2	5	18	8	19	.271	.518	.326
August	76	16	4	0	2	8	13	17	.211	.342	.315
Sept./Oct.	62	15	1	0	3	8	5	20	.242	.403	.299
Leading Off Inn.	81	26	4	0	4	4	6	17	.321	.519	.375
Runners On	176	41	6	1	5	52	25	50	.233	.364	.327
Runners/Scor. Pos.	119	27	2	1	4	47	20	37	.227	.361	.336
Runners On/2 Out	86	18	4	1	1	16	11	27	.209	.314	.313
Scor. Pos./2 Out	66	13	2	1	1	15	9	24	.197	.303	.312
Late Inning Pressure	65	16	3	1	2	8	6	15	.246	.415	.306
Leading Off	15	5	0	0	0	0	1	2	.333	.333	.375
Runners On	22	3	1	0	1	7	3	8	.136	.318	.231
Runners/Scor. Pos.	15	3	1	0	1	7	3	6	.200	.467	.316

RUNS BATTED IN	From 1B	From 2B	From 3B	Scoring Position
Totals	7/116	15/91	25/63	40/154
Percentage	6%	16%	40%	26%
Driving In Runners from 3B with Less than Two Out:			19/36	53%

Loves to face: Jimmy Jones (.375, 6-for-16, 3 HR)
Hates to face: Dennis Eckersley (.154, 2-for-13, 6 SO)
Batted .337 in day games, .209 at night; difference of 127 points was 2d largest in majors last season (minimum: 100 AB each way).... Career: .267 vs. left-handers, .234 vs. right-handers, but has slightly better HR rate vs. righties.... Hit six homers vs. Atlanta last season, the most by any player; moves to A.L. after clubbing 18 homers in 196 career at-bats vs. Braves. Will he transfer his Braves-bashing to Indians?... Went 0-for-11 with eight strikeouts pinch hitting last season; he's 6-for-45 lifetime in that role. Even so, 0-for-11 is nowhere near all-time mark for hitless pinch-hit at-bats: Frank Gibson of Braves went 0-for-31 in 1924. At least Gibson didn't have to read about it in *1925 Elias Baseball Analyst*.

Tim Flannery
San Diego Padres — Bats Left

	AB	H	2B	3B	HR	RBI	BB	SO	BA	SA	OBA
Season	170	45	5	4	0	19	24	32	.265	.341	.365
vs. Left-Handers	16	2	0	0	0	0	4	3	.125	.125	.300
vs. Right-Handers	154	43	5	4	0	19	20	29	.279	.364	.372
Home	77	20	0	1	0	5	13	14	.260	.286	.367
Road	93	25	5	3	0	14	11	18	.269	.387	.364
Grass	126	28	2	1	0	10	17	24	.222	.254	.313
Artificial Turf	44	17	3	3	0	9	7	8	.386	.591	.500
April	16	4	0	0	0	0	0	3	.250	.250	.250
May	3	1	0	0	0	0	0	1	.333	.333	.333
June	34	7	2	0	0	6	5	9	.206	.265	.300
July	27	8	1	1	0	2	5	6	.296	.407	.406
August	31	11	1	3	0	4	4	6	.355	.581	.459
Sept./Oct.	59	14	1	0	0	7	10	7	.237	.254	.361
Leading Off Inn.	36	11	0	0	0	0	6	5	.306	.306	.419
Runners On	79	24	5	3	0	19	11	13	.304	.443	.380
Runners/Scor. Pos.	43	11	1	1	0	16	7	8	.256	.326	.346
Runners On/2 Out	35	9	2	1	0	8	5	8	.257	.371	.350
Scor. Pos./2 Out	22	7	1	1	0	7	4	5	.318	.455	.423
Late Inning Pressure	29	6	2	0	0	2	4	7	.207	.276	.303
Leading Off	6	1	0	0	0	0	1	2	.167	.167	.286
Runners On	11	2	2	0	0	2	2	1	.182	.364	.308
Runners/Scor. Pos.	7	0	0	0	0	0	1	1	.000	.000	.222

RUNS BATTED IN	From 1B	From 2B	From 3B	Scoring Position
Totals	3/61	7/33	9/17	16/50
Percentage	5%	21%	53%	32%
Driving In Runners from 3B with Less than Two Out:			8/10	80%

Loves to face: Pascual Perez (.409, 9-for-22, 3 3B)
Hates to face: Todd Worrell (0-for-7, 4 SO)
Started 41 games last season, all against right-handed pitchers, of course. Has not started a game against a lefty since July 26, 1987, 72 starts ago.... Why? His career average vs. left-handers is .159 after 309 at-bats, 2d lowest in majors over last 14 years (minimum: 300 AB); only Wally Backman (.150) is worse.... Batted .308 (8-for-26) as pinch hitter last season.... Career average of .279 with runners on base, .243 with the bases empty.... Among players without a home run in either of the last two seasons, only Steve Jeltz and Al Newman have more at-bats than Flannery's 446.... Has batted over .300 with runners on base in three of last four seasons.

Tom Foley
Montreal Expos — Bats Left

	AB	H	2B	3B	HR	RBI	BB	SO	BA	SA	OBA
Season	377	100	21	3	5	43	30	49	.265	.377	.319
vs. Left-Handers	20	3	0	0	0	1	0	6	.150	.150	.143
vs. Right-Handers	357	97	21	3	5	42	30	43	.272	.389	.328
Home	193	51	14	1	3	21	16	31	.264	.394	.319
Road	184	49	7	2	2	22	14	18	.266	.359	.318
Grass	96	25	2	0	2	8	4	8	.260	.344	.290
Artificial Turf	281	75	19	3	3	35	26	41	.267	.388	.328
April	32	6	0	0	0	5	0	5	.188	.188	.188
May	71	17	5	1	0	7	8	15	.239	.338	.313
June	52	13	2	1	0	5	1	4	.250	.327	.264
July	65	20	7	0	2	7	10	10	.308	.508	.408
August	80	21	2	1	3	10	6	6	.263	.425	.307
Sept./Oct.	77	23	5	0	0	9	5	9	.299	.364	.341
Leading Off Inn.	81	22	5	1	1	1	5	5	.272	.395	.314
Runners On	160	45	9	2	1	39	16	21	.281	.381	.341
Runners/Scor. Pos.	99	29	6	2	0	36	14	11	.293	.394	.371
Runners On/2 Out	58	12	3	1	0	11	10	8	.207	.293	.324
Scor. Pos./2 Out	43	8	3	1	0	11	9	4	.186	.302	.327
Late Inning Pressure	87	23	5	1	1	10	6	15	.264	.379	.312
Leading Off	17	4	1	0	0	0	2	1	.235	.294	.316
Runners On	37	11	2	1	1	10	4	9	.297	.486	.366
Runners/Scor. Pos.	18	6	2	1	0	4	4	4	.333	.444	.455

RUNS BATTED IN	From 1B	From 2B	From 3B	Scoring Position
Totals	5/113	14/83	19/35	33/118
Percentage	4%	17%	54%	28%
Driving In Runners from 3B with Less than Two Out:			16/19	84%

Loves to face: Brian Fisher (.524, 11-for-21, 1 HR)
Hates to face: Scott Garrelts (0-for-10)
Percentage of runners driven in from third base with less than two out was 2d highest in N.L. last season, behind R.J. Reynolds.... In a league in which base stealers were successful 71 percent of the time, Foley was 2-for-9 last year.... Batted .273 in 97 games as a starter.... Career average of .188 (6-for-32) with the bases loaded. ... Batting average vs. ground-ballers has been higher than against fly-ballers in each of the last four seasons.... Has played 25+ games at both second base and shortstop in each of last three years; only two other players (Mike Gallego and Rex Hudler) did that in 1988, and no one else has done it for even the last *two* years.

Andres Galarraga
Montreal Expos — Bats Right

	AB	H	2B	3B	HR	RBI	BB	SO	BA	SA	OBA
Season	609	184	42	8	29	92	39	153	.302	.540	.352
vs. Left-Handers	173	49	15	0	10	29	13	45	.283	.543	.332
vs. Right-Handers	436	135	27	8	19	63	26	108	.310	.539	.361
Home	296	93	23	8	14	51	20	73	.314	.588	.369
Road	313	91	19	0	15	41	19	80	.291	.495	.336
Grass	159	46	11	0	8	18	8	48	.289	.509	.329
Artificial Turf	450	138	31	8	21	74	31	105	.307	.551	.360
April	80	27	8	0	5	12	3	16	.338	.625	.384
May	114	37	8	2	6	13	2	30	.325	.588	.347
June	113	34	8	1	7	23	9	23	.301	.575	.358
July	101	31	8	2	3	11	9	27	.307	.515	.325
August	103	27	5	1	3	11	8	29	.262	.417	.325
Sept./Oct.	98	28	5	2	5	22	8	23	.286	.531	.339
Leading Off Inn.	118	33	9	0	4	4	4	35	.280	.458	.315
Runners On	255	74	16	4	12	75	24	62	.290	.525	.357
Runners/Scor. Pos.	160	45	9	4	6	58	19	41	.281	.500	.362
Runners On/2 Out	82	20	3	2	4	23	11	24	.244	.476	.340
Scor. Pos./2 Out	55	15	2	2	4	22	10	16	.273	.600	.385
Late Inning Pressure	116	34	10	1	8	18	11	35	.293	.603	.359
Leading Off	26	6	2	0	1	1	0	9	.231	.423	.231
Runners On	48	12	3	0	4	14	8	15	.250	.563	.368
Runners/Scor. Pos.	25	6	1	0	1	7	7	8	.240	.400	.424

RUNS BATTED IN	From 1B	From 2B	From 3B	Scoring Position
Totals	14/147	21/107	28/71	49/178
Percentage	10%	20%	39%	28%
Driving In Runners from 3B with Less than Two Out:			22/47	47%

Loves to face: Rick Sutcliffe (.481, 13-for-27, 2 HR)
Hates to face: Ron Robinson (0-for-11)
Led N.L. in total bases, hits, and strikeouts; since majors started compiling batters' strikeouts (N.L. in 1910, A.L. in 1913) no player had ever led his league in hits and whiffs in same year.... Also became 4th Montreal player in last six years to lead N.L. in doubles. (Wallach 1987, Raines '84, Oliver '83). Batted .346 vs. ground-ball pitchers, .247 vs. fly-ballers.... Had 11 consecutive hits vs. right-handed pitchers, June 30 to July 4, longest such streak over past 10 years.... Batted for a higher average vs. right-handers than vs. left-handers for first time in his career. Career averages: .301 vs. lefties, .287 vs. righties.... Ended season with 48 consecutive error-less games at first base.

Ron Gant
Atlanta Braves — Bats Right

	AB	H	2B	3B	HR	RBI	BB	SO	BA	SA	OBA
Season	563	146	28	8	19	60	46	118	.259	.439	.317
vs. Left-Handers	193	54	10	4	9	20	22	40	.280	.513	.352
vs. Right-Handers	370	92	18	4	10	40	24	78	.249	.400	.298
Home	267	66	12	7	7	27	25	51	.247	.423	.316
Road	296	80	16	1	12	33	21	67	.270	.453	.317
Grass	393	97	17	7	10	39	37	83	.247	.402	.315
Artificial Turf	170	49	11	1	9	21	9	35	.288	.524	.320
April	27	2	1	0	0	0	2	7	.074	.111	.138
May	95	22	5	1	3	14	4	29	.232	.400	.257
June	109	32	3	4	5	16	6	23	.294	.532	.328
July	124	34	7	2	4	12	10	20	.274	.460	.326
August	108	27	6	1	3	8	12	24	.250	.407	.341
Sept./Oct.	100	29	6	0	4	10	12	15	.290	.470	.366
Leading Off Inn.	195	53	10	3	6	6	14	38	.272	.446	.327
Runners On	178	53	11	2	5	46	19	34	.298	.466	.358
Runners/Scor. Pos.	106	29	5	0	3	40	14	18	.274	.406	.347
Runners On/2 Out	89	26	7	2	2	24	10	14	.292	.483	.364
Scor. Pos./2 Out	55	14	4	0	2	22	7	5	.255	.436	.339
Late Inning Pressure	99	24	6	1	1	11	9	21	.242	.354	.303
Leading Off	26	7	1	0	0	0	2	8	.269	.308	.321
Runners On	37	8	2	1	0	10	5	8	.216	.324	.302
Runners/Scor. Pos.	23	6	2	0	0	9	5	3	.261	.348	.379

RUNS BATTED IN	From 1B	From 2B	From 3B	Scoring Position
Totals	7/116	17/87	17/44	34/131
Percentage	6%	20%	39%	26%
Driving In Runners from 3B with Less than Two Out:			10/19	53%

Loves to face: Jim Deshaies (.385, 5-for-13, 2 HR)
Hates to face: Bryn Smith (0-for-12)

This one will surprise some people: Gant tied Kevin McReynolds for N.L. lead with 30 extra-base hits after the All-Star break. . . . Led major league rookies in games started, at-bats, home runs, runs, hits, extra-base hits, triples, strikeouts, and errors. . . . His 19 home runs were most by Braves rookie since Bob Horner hit 23 in 1978; the last rookie who was primarily a second baseman to hit that many was Joe Gordon, who hit 25 in 1938. . . . His 26 errors were the most by any second baseman in majors. . . . Only player in N.L. to score runs in 10 consecutive games last season. . . . Hit three home runs in 32 at-bats in the Astrodome last year; by contrast, Keith Hernandez has two home runs in 258 career at-bats there.

Kirk Gibson
Los Angeles Dodgers — Bats Left

	AB	H	2B	3B	HR	RBI	BB	SO	BA	SA	OBA
Season	542	157	28	1	25	76	73	120	.290	.483	.377
vs. Left-Handers	204	60	11	1	11	38	15	50	.294	.520	.344
vs. Right-Handers	338	97	17	0	14	38	58	70	.287	.462	.396
Home	256	81	10	1	14	42	30	61	.316	.527	.389
Road	286	76	18	0	11	34	43	59	.266	.444	.366
Grass	383	118	17	1	20	55	46	88	.308	.514	.387
Artificial Turf	159	39	11	0	5	21	27	32	.245	.409	.353
April	69	17	4	0	2	10	7	23	.246	.391	.333
May	102	33	8	1	7	17	11	20	.324	.627	.391
June	96	27	4	0	5	13	16	27	.281	.479	.385
July	108	36	4	0	5	14	14	9	.333	.509	.410
August	101	28	7	0	4	15	15	22	.277	.465	.368
Sept./Oct.	66	16	1	0	2	7	10	19	.242	.348	.350
Leading Off Inn.	116	43	7	1	5	5	9	21	.371	.578	.416
Runners On	221	63	14	0	10	61	38	42	.285	.484	.391
Runners/Scor. Pos.	115	30	9	0	4	46	28	29	.261	.443	.399
Runners On/2 Out	86	21	4	0	0	14	14	14	.244	.291	.356
Scor. Pos./2 Out	55	13	4	0	0	13	11	11	.236	.309	.373
Late Inning Pressure	69	24	7	0	2	8	10	11	.348	.536	.444
Leading Off	23	11	4	0	1	1	2	1	.478	.783	.520
Runners On	27	8	1	0	0	6	6	4	.296	.333	.441
Runners/Scor. Pos.	15	5	0	0	0	6	4	2	.333	.333	.500

RUNS BATTED IN	From 1B	From 2B	From 3B	Scoring Position
Totals	11/146	18/81	22/63	40/144
Percentage	8%	22%	35%	28%
Driving In Runners from 3B with Less than Two Out:			18/36	50%

Loves to face: Tom Browning (.500, 7-for-14, 3 HR)
Hates to face: Jose Rijo (.150, 3-for-20)

Five straight seasons with 20 home runs and 20 steals; only Strawberry has a concurrent streak that long. . . . Has hit 175 home runs without a grand slam, most homers by any slamless player in history. . . . Career numbers in 21 postseason games: .282, 7 HR, 21 RBI, 9 SB; he's the only player in postseason history to have 7 homers and 7 steals. . . . Became 3d player to hit home run in only at-bat in a World Series; others: George Shuba (1953) and Jim Mason (1976). . . . Bagged an MVP award without ever having been selected to All-Star Game. Since Dream Game's birth in 1933, only Hank Greenberg had been named league MVP (1935) before being named to All-Star squad; Hank was named for first time in 1939.

Mark Grace
Chicago Cubs — Bats Left

	AB	H	2B	3B	HR	RBI	BB	SO	BA	SA	OBA
Season	486	144	23	4	7	57	60	43	.296	.403	.371
vs. Left-Handers	147	42	6	3	3	24	21	22	.286	.429	.373
vs. Right-Handers	339	102	17	1	4	33	39	21	.301	.392	.370
Home	250	74	7	2	0	24	34	16	.296	.340	.378
Road	236	70	16	2	7	33	26	27	.297	.470	.364
Grass	346	101	14	2	2	31	41	27	.292	.361	.364
Artificial Turf	140	43	9	2	5	26	19	16	.307	.507	.388
April	0	0	0	0	0	0	0	0	—	—	—
May	97	32	5	1	3	10	11	6	.330	.495	.398
June	91	24	1	2	1	10	11	8	.264	.352	.343
July	83	24	2	0	1	11	14	6	.289	.349	.388
August	110	33	6	1	1	12	9	12	.300	.400	.350
Sept./Oct.	105	31	9	0	1	14	15	11	.295	.410	.377
Leading Off Inn.	98	33	6	0	1	1	8	12	.337	.429	.387
Runners On	218	69	7	3	4	54	24	13	.317	.431	.378
Runners/Scor. Pos.	138	40	2	3	4	54	17	11	.290	.435	.358
Runners On/2 Out	87	22	3	2	1	19	8	5	.253	.368	.316
Scor. Pos./2 Out	60	15	2	1	1	19	7	3	.250	.400	.328
Late Inning Pressure	73	24	4	0	0	3	14	5	.329	.384	.432
Leading Off	21	8	2	0	0	0	2	2	.381	.476	.435
Runners On	31	9	1	0	0	3	7	0	.290	.323	.410
Runners/Scor. Pos.	20	5	0	0	0	3	5	0	.250	.250	.385

RUNS BATTED IN	From 1B	From 2B	From 3B	Scoring Position
Totals	2/146	20/103	28/52	48/155
Percentage	1%	19%	54%	31%
Driving In Runners from 3B with Less than Two Out:			20/30	67%

Loves to face: Mike Maddux (.700, 7-for-10, 1 HR)
Hates to face: Ron Darling (0-for-9)

What have fans in San Diego, Philadelphia, Cincinnati, St. Louis, and Los Angeles seen that fans in Chicago have not? We mean *besides* a recent World Series. It's Mark Grace hitting a home run. All seven of his homers came on the road. . . . Had best batting average among five rookies who qualified for batting title last season; also led rookies in walks. . . . Lowest fielding percentage (.987) of any N.L. first baseman (minimum: 100 games). . . . Four hits in six at-bats with the bases loaded, including 3-for-3 with two outs. . . . Batted .269 vs. ground-ball pitchers, .320 vs. fly-ballers. . . . Went 16-for-41 over last 10 days of season, but his effort fell two hits shy of .300 mark.

Ken Griffey
Braves/Reds — Bats Left

	AB	H	2B	3B	HR	RBI	BB	SO	BA	SA	OBA
Season	243	62	6	0	4	23	19	31	.255	.329	.307
vs. Left-Handers	24	6	1	0	1	4	0	5	.250	.417	.250
vs. Right-Handers	219	56	5	0	3	19	19	26	.256	.320	.313
Home	123	33	4	0	3	14	9	13	.268	.374	.316
Road	120	29	2	0	1	9	10	18	.242	.283	.298
Grass	164	39	3	0	3	15	11	20	.238	.311	.284
Artificial Turf	79	23	3	0	1	8	8	11	.291	.367	.352
April	31	4	2	0	0	5	2	6	.129	.194	.176
May	61	20	2	0	1	7	6	7	.328	.410	.382
June	63	14	1	0	1	5	4	7	.222	.286	.269
July	38	10	0	0	0	2	5	6	.263	.263	.349
August	19	5	0	0	1	1	0	4	.263	.421	.263
Sept./Oct.	31	9	1	0	1	3	2	1	.290	.419	.333
Leading Off Inn.	60	18	1	0	2	4	5		.300	.417	.344
Runners On	95	22	3	0	2	21	10	9	.232	.326	.299
Runners/Scor. Pos.	56	11	2	0	0	16	8	5	.196	.232	.288
Runners On/2 Out	42	9	1	0	2	11	7	4	.214	.381	.327
Scor. Pos./2 Out	29	6	1	0	0	7	6	2	.207	.241	.343
Late Inning Pressure	56	12	2	0	0	5	2	10	.214	.250	.241
Leading Off	13	3	1	0	0	0	0	3	.231	.308	.231
Runners On	23	6	1	0	0	5	2	4	.261	.304	.320
Runners/Scor. Pos.	17	4	1	0	0	5	2	1	.235	.294	.316

RUNS BATTED IN	From 1B	From 2B	From 3B	Scoring Position
Totals	5/73	5/43	9/21	14/64
Percentage	7%	12%	43%	22%
Driving In Runners from 3B with Less than Two Out:			5/10	50%

Loves to face: Kevin Gross (.545, 6-for-11, 5 BB, 3 HR)
Hates to face: Neal Heaton (0-for-14)

What active player's career batting, slugging, and on-base averages are closest to Griffey's .298, .432, and .359? Answer below. . . . Made 55 starts last season, all against right-handed pitchers. Has not started a game against a lefty since July 31, 1987; that's 85 starts ago. . . . Had never batted lower than .273 in any full major league season, nor lower than .286 in any full N.L. campaign. . . . Batted .161 (5-for-31) as pinch hitter last season; career pinch-hit average fell from .338 to .316. . . . Paul Molitor is the Griffey impersonator: .299, .435, .360. . . . Who says you can't go home again? Not Marge Schott, who brought back Perez, Rose, and now Griffey. Anyone have George Foster's phone number?

Alfredo Griffin

Los Angeles Dodgers   Bats Left and Right

	AB	H	2B	3B	HR	RBI	BB	SO	BA	SA	OBA
Season	316	63	8	3	1	28	24	30	.199	.253	.259
vs. Left-Handers	90	15	1	2	0	12	13	8	.167	.222	.269
vs. Right-Handers	226	48	7	1	1	16	11	22	.212	.265	.255
Home	158	29	4	0	0	7	14	14	.184	.209	.254
Road	158	34	4	3	1	21	10	16	.215	.297	.265
Grass	235	46	7	2	0	19	19	24	.196	.243	.262
Artificial Turf	81	17	1	1	1	9	5	6	.210	.284	.253
April	82	15	5	2	0	13	3	8	.183	.293	.212
May	62	9	0	1	0	6	5	4	.145	.177	.217
June	0	0	0	0	0	0	0	0	—	—	—
July	7	1	0	0	0	2	1	0	.143	.143	.250
August	80	17	1	0	1	4	7	5	.213	.263	.276
Sept./Oct.	85	21	2	0	0	3	8	13	.247	.271	.319
Leading Off Inn.	89	14	3	0	0	0	5	12	.157	.191	.211
Runners On	113	25	3	3	0	27	10	9	.221	.301	.282
Runners/Scor. Pos.	75	18	2	3	0	27	10	7	.240	.347	.326
Runners On/2 Out	56	11	0	3	0	18	10	5	.196	.304	.318
Scor. Pos./2 Out	42	10	0	3	0	18	10	5	.238	.381	.385
Late Inning Pressure	36	9	0	0	1	1	2	6	.250	.333	.308
Leading Off	10	2	0	0	0	0	1	0	.200	.200	.333
Runners On	13	1	0	0	0	0	1	3	.077	.077	.143
Runners/Scor. Pos.	9	1	0	0	0	0	1	3	.111	.111	.200

RUNS BATTED IN	From 1B	From 2B	From 3B	Scoring Position
Totals	4/75	11/63	12/28	23/91
Percentage	5%	17%	43%	25%
Driving In Runners from 3B with Less than Two Out:			5/9	56%

Loves to face: Rick Sutcliffe (.353, 6-for-17)
Hates to face: Calvin Schiraldi (0-for-7, 4 SO)

Dodgers picked up three potential everyday players from A.L.; two of them hit under .200, the other won MVP.... Batting average was 4th lowest in N.L. (minimum: 200 AB). May batting average was lowest in N.L. (minimum: two PA per game).... Hit three bases-loaded triples, tying major league record; last to do it: Manny Sanguillen in 1971. Has 12 hits in last 25 at-bats with bases full.... For fifth straight year, spanning three cities, had higher average in road games than in whatever park he called home.... One of 10 players active in 1988 with 100 sacrifice bunts.... Had averaged over 155 games a year over previous six seasons, but didn't have to face Dwight Gooden in A.L.

Pedro Guerrero

Dodgers/Cardinals   Bats Right

	AB	H	2B	3B	HR	RBI	BB	SO	BA	SA	OBA
Season	364	104	14	2	10	65	46	59	.286	.418	.367
vs. Left-Handers	125	35	3	1	3	15	22	19	.280	.392	.385
vs. Right-Handers	239	69	11	1	7	50	24	40	.289	.431	.358
Home	192	60	8	2	5	42	20	34	.313	.453	.373
Road	172	44	6	0	5	23	26	25	.256	.378	.361
Grass	194	64	7	1	7	39	21	29	.330	.485	.396
Artificial Turf	170	40	7	1	3	26	25	30	.235	.341	.335
April	68	25	2	0	2	15	7	8	.368	.485	.429
May	78	20	2	1	1	12	11	10	.256	.346	.355
June	12	5	0	0	0	3	1	2	.417	.417	.462
July	9	3	1	0	0	0	0	1	.333	.444	.333
August	104	29	5	1	3	17	14	17	.279	.433	.364
Sept./Oct.	93	22	4	0	4	18	13	21	.237	.409	.330
Leading Off Inn.	86	22	2	0	3	3	4	13	.256	.384	.289
Runners On	162	53	8	1	4	59	25	27	.327	.463	.411
Runners/Scor. Pos.	97	36	8	1	3	56	22	17	.371	.567	.469
Runners On/2 Out	75	21	1	1	4	24	14	16	.280	.480	.400
Scor. Pos./2 Out	45	13	1	1	3	21	11	10	.289	.556	.439
Late Inning Pressure	43	10	1	0	1	6	5	3	.233	.326	.320
Leading Off	18	5	0	0	0	0	0	1	.278	.278	.278
Runners On	15	4	1	0	1	6	3	1	.267	.533	.400
Runners/Scor. Pos.	8	2	1	0	0	4	2	1	.250	.375	.364

RUNS BATTED IN	From 1B	From 2B	From 3B	Scoring Position
Totals	5/107	20/77	30/54	50/131
Percentage	5%	26%	56%	38%
Driving In Runners from 3B with Less than Two Out:			22/31	71%

Loves to face: Ron Darling (.444, 8-for-18, 2 HR)
Hates to face: Dwight Gooden (.129, 4-for-31, 2 HR)

Dodgers had 29–30 record with Pete in starting lineup; they were 65–37 otherwise.... Batted 116 points higher with runners in scoring position than in other at-bats, largest difference in N.L. last season (minimum: 75 AB with RISP).... Batting average with runners in scoring position was highest of his career.... Led league with 17 RBI and five game-winners vs. Braves last season; won't be seeing as much of them this year.... Batting average in Late-Inning Pressure Situations has been lower than overall average in each of last seven seasons.... Career average of .307 vs. right-handers, .307 vs. left-handers.... Anyone out there have any footage of his 12 games at second base in 1980?

Tony Gwynn

San Diego Padres   Bats Left

	AB	H	2B	3B	HR	RBI	BB	SO	BA	SA	OBA
Season	521	163	22	5	7	71	51	40	.313	.415	.373
vs. Left-Handers	204	64	7	1	0	26	14	19	.314	.358	.358
vs. Right-Handers	317	99	15	4	7	45	37	21	.312	.451	.382
Home	242	75	9	1	3	26	33	17	.310	.393	.393
Road	279	88	13	4	4	45	18	23	.315	.434	.355
Grass	386	117	13	3	4	45	46	26	.303	.383	.377
Artificial Turf	135	46	9	2	3	26	5	14	.341	.504	.359
April	77	23	2	0	1	4	8	7	.299	.364	.365
May	37	7	2	0	0	4	1	5	.189	.243	.200
June	107	25	3	1	2	14	17	4	.234	.336	.339
July	106	43	3	2	3	18	7	11	.406	.557	.442
August	108	40	10	1	1	19	9	9	.370	.509	.419
Sept./Oct.	86	25	2	1	0	13	9	4	.291	.337	.358
Leading Off Inn.	108	37	2	2	2	2	5	6	.343	.454	.372
Runners On	217	83	17	3	2	66	31	16	.382	.516	.456
Runners/Scor. Pos.	116	43	9	2	2	61	26	9	.371	.534	.479
Runners On/2 Out	58	19	2	1	0	12	13	2	.328	.397	.451
Scor. Pos./2 Out	35	10	1	1	0	12	10	2	.286	.371	.444
Late Inning Pressure	71	24	4	0	0	12	4	4	.338	.394	.373
Leading Off	17	5	1	0	0	0	0	0	.294	.353	.294
Runners On	30	14	2	0	0	12	2	1	.467	.533	.500
Runners/Scor. Pos.	15	7	0	0	0	11	2	0	.467	.467	.529

RUNS BATTED IN	From 1B	From 2B	From 3B	Scoring Position
Totals	8/150	28/86	28/48	56/134
Percentage	5%	33%	58%	42%
Driving In Runners from 3B with Less than Two Out:			24/32	75%

Loves to face: Tom Browning (.426, 23-for-54, 3 HR)
Hates to face: Mike Maddux (.091, 1-for-11)

Hit .423 in 168 at-bats from July 2 to Aug. 18, to take over N.L. batting lead from Gerald Perry.... Won 2d batting title in a row in '88; no N.L. player has won three straight since Musial, 1950–52.... Batted 119 points higher with runners on base than with bases empty, largest difference in N.L. last year (minimum: 100 AB each way). Batting average with ROB was highest in N.L. since his own .406 mark in 1984.... Rate of runners driven in from scoring position was best in majors in '88.... Only player in majors to hit .300+ with 20+ steals in each of last three years.... First player since 1930, when George Sisler and Eddie Collins retired, to have .330+ career batting average coupled with 150+ steals.

Albert Hall

Atlanta Braves   Bats Left and Right

	AB	H	2B	3B	HR	RBI	BB	SO	BA	SA	OBA
Season	231	57	7	1	1	15	21	35	.247	.299	.314
vs. Left-Handers	80	15	1	1	0	4	10	13	.188	.225	.283
vs. Right-Handers	151	42	6	0	1	11	11	22	.278	.338	.331
Home	104	22	3	1	1	11	10	13	.212	.288	.278
Road	127	35	4	0	0	4	11	22	.276	.307	.343
Grass	167	42	5	1	1	13	13	20	.251	.311	.308
Artificial Turf	64	15	2	0	0	2	8	15	.234	.266	.329
April	46	14	0	0	0	3	8	6	.304	.348	.418
May	69	16	3	0	1	6	6	15	.232	.319	.303
June	98	24	4	0	0	6	5	13	.245	.286	.279
July	7	1	0	0	0	0	2	1	.143	.143	.333
August	0	0	0	0	0	0	0	0	—	—	—
Sept./Oct.	11	2	0	0	0	0	0	0	.182	.182	.182
Leading Off Inn.	90	18	3	0	0	0	6	16	.200	.233	.265
Runners On	69	23	3	1	0	14	9	11	.333	.406	.405
Runners/Scor. Pos.	37	12	2	1	0	13	7	7	.324	.432	.422
Runners On/2 Out	32	12	2	1	0	8	3	3	.375	.500	.429
Scor. Pos./2 Out	20	6	1	0	0	7	2	2	.300	.450	.364
Late Inning Pressure	48	12	1	0	1	3	5	4	.250	.333	.333
Leading Off	13	2	0	0	0	0	0	1	.154	.154	.214
Runners On	15	6	0	0	0	2	3	2	.400	.400	.500
Runners/Scor. Pos.	7	3	0	0	0	2	2	1	.429	.429	.600

RUNS BATTED IN	From 1B	From 2B	From 3B	Scoring Position
Totals	1/50	9/32	4/15	13/47
Percentage	2%	28%	27%	28%
Driving In Runners from 3B with Less than Two Out:			2/8	25%

Loves to face: Tim Belcher (.750, 6-for-8)
Hates to face: Orel Hershiser (.095, 2-for-21)

Until last season, owned higher career average vs. left-handed pitchers than vs. right-handers; including 1988 figures, he's now batting .254 against each type.... Career average of .234 at home, .273 on the road.... Has five career home runs, all solo shots.... On-base average when leading off innings fell from .423 in 1987 to .265 last year.... Has driven in only two of 170 runners from first base in his career.... Led Braves with 10 appearances as a pinch runner last season.... Russ Nixon didn't shy away from using pitchers on basepaths; he used a hurler to pinch-run on 13 occasions. We guess that was done to balance off Jim Morrison's three pitching appearances!

Jeff Hamilton
Los Angeles Dodgers — Bats Right

	AB	H	2B	3B	HR	RBI	BB	SO	BA	SA	OBA
Season	309	73	14	2	6	33	10	51	.236	.353	.268
vs. Left-Handers	112	23	2	0	3	13	3	16	.205	.304	.231
vs. Right-Handers	197	50	12	2	3	20	7	35	.254	.381	.288
Home	138	39	4	1	4	19	5	18	.283	.413	.315
Road	171	34	10	1	2	14	5	33	.199	.304	.229
Grass	221	56	7	2	5	28	7	35	.253	.371	.284
Artificial Turf	88	17	7	0	1	5	3	16	.193	.307	.226
April	9	0	0	0	0	1	0	3	.000	.000	.000
May	30	6	1	0	1	3	0	4	.200	.333	.219
June	99	26	4	1	2	15	3	18	.263	.384	.291
July	80	21	6	1	1	6	4	9	.263	.400	.306
August	0	0	0	0	0	0	0	0	—	—	—
Sept./Oct.	91	20	3	0	2	8	3	17	.220	.319	.253
Leading Off Inn.	67	16	4	2	1	1	1	12	.239	.403	.250
Runners On	127	34	7	0	4	31	5	16	.268	.417	.301
Runners/Scor. Pos.	78	22	4	0	3	29	5	10	.282	.449	.333
Runners On/2 Out	49	12	1	0	2	11	3	6	.245	.388	.302
Scor. Pos./2 Out	29	9	1	0	2	11	3	2	.310	.552	.394
Late Inning Pressure	50	7	3	1	1	3	3	11	.140	.300	.204
Leading Off	13	3	1	1	0	0	0	2	.231	.462	.231
Runners On	17	3	2	0	1	3	1	4	.176	.471	.222
Runners/Scor. Pos.	9	2	1	0	1	3	1	2	.222	.667	.300

RUNS BATTED IN	From 1B	From 2B	From 3B	Scoring Position
Totals	1/90	13/59	13/34	26/93
Percentage	1%	22%	38%	28%
Driving In Runners from 3B with Less than Two Out:			9/21	43%

Loves to face: Zane Smith (.375, 6-for-16)
Hates to face: Mike Krukow (0-for-7, 5 SO)
Made only one start in L.A.'s first 39 games, but took over when Guerrero got hurt. Must have made those subtle contributions: Dodgers were 50–29–1 in his 80 starts.... Youngest National Leaguer to play at least half of his team's games at third base last season.... Batted 115 points lower in Late-Inning Pressure Situations than in other at-bats last season, 3d-largest difference in N.L. (minimum: 50 LIPS AB).... Career average of .264 with runners on base, .208 with the bases empty.... Has led off 125 innings in his career, but has drawn only one walk in that situation.... His throwing error allowed only run to score in Tom Browning's perfect game, eliminating chance for Harvey Haddix II.

Billy Hatcher
Houston Astros — Bats Right

	AB	H	2B	3B	HR	RBI	BB	SO	BA	SA	OBA
Season	530	142	25	4	7	52	37	56	.268	.370	.321
vs. Left-Handers	183	52	8	2	4	20	14	20	.284	.415	.333
vs. Right-Handers	347	90	17	2	3	32	23	36	.259	.346	.314
Home	263	64	11	3	2	25	21	29	.243	.342	.308
Road	267	78	14	1	4	27	16	27	.292	.397	.333
Grass	165	45	10	1	2	13	7	19	.273	.382	.303
Artificial Turf	365	97	15	3	5	39	30	37	.266	.364	.328
April	82	21	3	1	1	8	8	13	.256	.354	.322
May	108	35	5	0	1	9	3	7	.324	.398	.357
June	97	27	5	0	1	13	6	9	.278	.392	.324
July	89	20	5	0	0	5	8	12	.225	.281	.300
August	79	18	4	1	1	6	6	8	.228	.342	.282
Sept./Oct.	75	21	3	1	3	11	6	7	.280	.453	.329
Leading Off Inn.	114	34	6	1	1	6	6	10	.298	.395	.355
Runners On	202	59	10	3	3	48	23	26	.292	.416	.360
Runners/Scor. Pos.	127	35	6	1	2	43	19	17	.276	.386	.359
Runners On/2 Out	73	17	4	1	1	14	13	15	.233	.356	.349
Scor. Pos./2 Out	58	10	2	0	1	12	12	12	.172	.259	.314
Late Inning Pressure	92	30	8	1	1	10	7	12	.326	.467	.386
Leading Off	18	9	1	1	1	1	1	1	.500	.833	.526
Runners On	43	14	5	0	0	9	4	7	.326	.442	.396
Runners/Scor. Pos.	29	8	2	0	0	9	4	5	.276	.345	.382

RUNS BATTED IN	From 1B	From 2B	From 3B	Scoring Position
Totals	5/126	19/105	21/47	40/152
Percentage	4%	18%	45%	26%
Driving In Runners from 3B with Less than Two Out:			18/25	72%

Loves to face: Larry McWilliams (.625, 5-for-8, 1 HR)
Hates to face: Pat Perry (0-for-8)
One of seven players to hit .300 in Late-Inning Pressure Situations in each of last three years (minimum: 50 LIPS AB each year); he's in a good group: Fernandez, Gwynn, Rickey Henderson, Raines, Sax, Trammell. Hatch's career batting average in LIPS is .324; it's .263 at less intense moments.... Started 54 of 55 games in which Astros faced a left-handed starter, but only 79 of 107 games against right-handers.... Career averages: .311 in April, .304 in May, .230 in September.... Likes all artificial turfs except his own: .338 career average on road rugs, .263 on Dome rug, .259 on road grass fields.... Has 123 stolen bases over past three seasons, 8th in majors but first among Hatchers.

Mickey Hatcher
Los Angeles Dodgers — Bats Right

	AB	H	2B	3B	HR	RBI	BB	SO	BA	SA	OBA
Season	191	56	8	0	1	25	7	7	.293	.351	.322
vs. Left-Handers	142	37	6	0	1	18	5	5	.261	.324	.282
vs. Right-Handers	49	19	2	0	0	7	2	2	.388	.429	.434
Home	102	29	5	0	0	8	3	7	.284	.333	.302
Road	89	27	3	0	1	17	4	0	.303	.371	.344
Grass	153	44	5	0	1	15	5	7	.288	.340	.317
Artificial Turf	38	12	3	0	0	10	2	0	.316	.395	.341
April	15	5	2	0	0	1	0	0	.333	.467	.333
May	25	9	1	0	0	4	1	0	.360	.400	.370
June	50	14	2	0	0	4	1	0	.280	.320	.294
July	11	5	1	0	0	3	1	0	.455	.545	.500
August	27	10	2	0	0	4	1	2	.370	.444	.393
Sept./Oct.	63	13	0	0	1	9	3	5	.206	.254	.261
Leading Off Inn.	29	5	2	0	0	1	0	2	.172	.241	.200
Runners On	93	30	2	0	1	25	5	3	.323	.376	.363
Runners/Scor. Pos.	58	19	2	0	1	25	5	2	.328	.414	.388
Runners On/2 Out	39	10	1	0	1	10	2	0	.256	.359	.310
Scor. Pos./2 Out	26	7	1	0	1	10	2	0	.269	.423	.345
Late Inning Pressure	39	16	3	0	0	8	3	3	.410	.564	.452
Leading Off	9	4	1	0	0	0	0	1	.444	.556	.444
Runners On	20	9	1	0	0	8	3	0	.450	.650	.522
Runners/Scor. Pos.	10	5	1	0	0	8	3	1	.500	.900	.615

RUNS BATTED IN	From 1B	From 2B	From 3B	Scoring Position
Totals	2/62	8/44	14/23	22/67
Percentage	3%	18%	61%	33%
Driving In Runners from 3B with Less than Two Out:			12/15	80%

Loves to face: Rick Sutcliffe (.462, 6-for-13, 1 HR)
Hates to face: Tom Browning (.091, 1-for-11)
Started only six of 108 regular-season games in which Dodgers faced right-handed starters, but started 10 of 11 such games in postseason.... First player to hit more homers in World Series than in regular season since way back in 1987. Don't tell us you've already forgotten Tom Lawless.... Had five extra-base hits as pinch hitter last season, tying Wallace Johnson for major league lead.... Career average of .307 on artificial turf, .259 on grass; 48-point difference is largest by anyone over last 10 years (minimum: 750 AB each way).... Has hit better with runners on base than with bases empty for five straight years.... Went 116 plate appearances between strikeouts, longest such streak in N.L. in '88.

Von Hayes
Philadelphia Phillies — Bats Left

	AB	H	2B	3B	HR	RBI	BB	SO	BA	SA	OBA
Season	367	100	28	2	6	45	49	59	.272	.409	.355
vs. Left-Handers	101	13	3	1	2	15	9	19	.129	.238	.196
vs. Right-Handers	266	87	25	1	4	30	40	40	.327	.474	.413
Home	175	40	14	1	2	16	21	28	.229	.354	.310
Road	192	60	14	1	4	29	28	31	.313	.458	.396
Grass	104	40	8	0	2	17	14	15	.385	.519	.455
Artificial Turf	263	60	20	2	4	28	35	44	.228	.365	.316
April	70	18	7	0	0	8	6	14	.257	.357	.325
May	93	29	7	0	4	13	13	17	.312	.516	.396
June	109	27	10	2	0	13	17	14	.248	.376	.341
July	41	11	3	0	1	5	5	8	.268	.415	.340
August	0	0	0	0	0	0	0	0	—	—	—
Sept./Oct.	54	15	1	0	1	6	8	6	.278	.352	.365
Leading Off Inn.	75	21	8	0	0	0	13	16	.280	.387	.386
Runners On	156	48	15	1	2	41	18	19	.308	.455	.372
Runners/Scor. Pos.	88	24	10	1	0	35	16	10	.273	.409	.373
Runners On/2 Out	59	15	5	1	1	17	8	10	.254	.424	.343
Scor. Pos./2 Out	39	11	4	1	0	14	7	7	.282	.436	.391
Late Inning Pressure	59	11	4	0	1	9	8	10	.186	.305	.275
Leading Off	13	2	1	0	0	0	3	3	.154	.231	.313
Runners On	27	4	2	0	0	8	4	4	.148	.222	.242
Runners/Scor. Pos.	17	3	2	0	0	8	3	2	.176	.294	.273

RUNS BATTED IN	From 1B	From 2B	From 3B	Scoring Position
Totals	6/113	16/66	17/42	33/108
Percentage	5%	24%	40%	31%
Driving In Runners from 3B with Less than Two Out:			13/24	54%

Loves to face: Rick Sutcliffe (.523, 23-for-44, 3 HR)
Hates to face: Dave Smith (0-for-10)
Hit 10th-inning home run off Randy Bockus on May 28; that was Phillies' only home run after 8th inning last season.... That .129 average vs. left-handers was 2d-lowest mark for one season over last 14 years (minimum: 100 AB); Wally Backman hit .122 vs. LHP in 1985.... Had some of the most lopsided breakdowns of 1988: Hit 198 points higher vs. righties than vs. lefties, largest difference in majors (minimum: 100 AB each way).... Batted .362 in day games, .237 at night.... Only N.L. player to bat 100+ points higher on grass fields than on artificial turf (minimum: 100 AB each way).... Let's piece those parts together: Hayes hit .485 (16-for-33) vs. right-handers in day games on grass.

Keith Hernandez

New York Mets   Bats Left

	AB	H	2B	3B	HR	RBI	BB	SO	BA	SA	OBA
Season	348	96	16	0	11	55	31	57	.276	.417	.333
vs. Left-Handers	135	37	6	0	6	25	12	15	.274	.452	.333
vs. Right-Handers	213	59	10	0	5	30	19	42	.277	.394	.333
Home	146	40	5	0	2	14	17	23	.274	.349	.348
Road	202	56	11	0	9	41	14	34	.277	.465	.323
Grass	244	72	9	0	8	41	22	38	.295	.430	.353
Artificial Turf	104	24	7	0	3	14	9	19	.231	.385	.287
April	74	15	4	0	3	15	6	9	.203	.378	.259
May	96	37	7	0	2	18	16	16	.385	.521	.465
June	28	7	1	0	0	2	1	5	.250	.286	.276
July	0	0	0	0	0	0	0	0	—	—	—
August	87	22	4	0	3	10	6	15	.253	.402	.305
Sept./Oct.	63	15	0	0	3	10	2	12	.238	.381	.262
Leading Off Inn.	45	15	4	0	0	0	4	7	.333	.422	.388
Runners On	172	53	7	0	8	52	14	27	.308	.488	.356
Runners/Scor. Pos.	104	29	3	0	4	42	8	18	.279	.423	.325
Runners On/2 Out	61	15	3	0	3	17	4	11	.246	.443	.292
Scor. Pos./2 Out	44	10	1	0	2	13	3	9	.227	.386	.277
Late Inning Pressure	41	13	0	0	4	13	4	9	.317	.610	.391
Leading Off	4	1	0	0	0	0	0	2	.250	.250	.250
Runners On	22	10	0	0	4	13	3	5	.455	1.000	.538
Runners/Scor. Pos.	16	6	0	0	2	9	3	5	.375	.750	.500

RUNS BATTED IN	From 1B	From 2B	From 3B	Scoring Position
Totals	7/114	17/76	20/41	37/117
Percentage	6%	22%	49%	32%
Driving In Runners from 3B with Less than Two Out:		16/23		70%

Loves to face: Orel Hershiser (.438, 14-for-32, 1 HR)
Hates to face: John Franco (0-for-9)
May batting average was highest in N.L. . . . Season average of .276 dropped his career mark to .29979; he hadn't dipped below .300 since 1984. Same thing happened to Jim Rice, now at .29978. . . . Batting average with runners on base has been higher than with the bases empty in each of last 11 seasons. Only Graig Nettles (14 years) has a longer streak. . . . Walk-to-strikeout ratio was worst of his career. . . . Has played 1914 games at first base, 17th in history; needs 140 games there to move into top ten. . . . Won 11th consecutive Gold Glove Award despite playing only 93 games in field; only players to go for the gold more often: Brooks Robinson (16), Jim Kaat (16), Clemente (12), and Mays (12).

Bob Horner

St. Louis Cardinals   Bats Right

	AB	H	2B	3B	HR	RBI	BB	SO	BA	SA	OBA
Season	206	53	9	1	3	33	32	23	.257	.354	.348
vs. Left-Handers	68	21	6	0	2	11	12	8	.309	.485	.402
vs. Right-Handers	138	32	3	1	1	22	20	15	.232	.290	.321
Home	108	30	6	0	0	18	19	13	.278	.333	.379
Road	98	23	3	1	3	15	13	10	.235	.378	.313
Grass	70	18	1	1	1	11	6	4	.257	.343	.300
Artificial Turf	136	35	8	0	2	22	26	19	.257	.360	.371
April	69	20	2	1	2	9	11	8	.290	.435	.381
May	97	22	4	0	0	17	15	6	.227	.268	.319
June	40	11	3	0	1	7	6	9	.275	.425	.362
July	0	0	0	0	0	0	0	0	—	—	—
August	0	0	0	0	0	0	0	0	—	—	—
Sept./Oct.	0	0	0	0	0	0	0	0	—	—	—
Leading Off Inn.	52	16	1	0	2	2	4	3	.308	.442	.357
Runners On	101	25	4	0	0	30	20	12	.248	.287	.354
Runners/Scor. Pos.	64	16	3	0	0	30	15	8	.250	.297	.364
Runners On/2 Out	41	7	1	0	0	9	7	5	.171	.195	.333
Scor. Pos./2 Out	27	4	1	0	0	7	7	3	.148	.185	.343
Late Inning Pressure	26	9	0	1	0	4	11	2	.346	.423	.513
Leading Off	8	3	0	0	0	0	0	0	.375	.375	.375
Runners On	8	4	0	0	0	4	8	0	.500	.500	.667
Runners/Scor. Pos.	6	3	0	0	0	4	6	0	.500	.500	.643

RUNS BATTED IN	From 1B	From 2B	From 3B	Scoring Position
Totals	0/74	6/53	24/45	30/98
Percentage	0%	11%	53%	31%
Driving In Runners from 3B with Less than Two Out:		20/26		77%

Loves to face: Charles Hudson (.500, 5-for-10, 2 HR)
Hates to face: Tom Niedenfuer (.059, 1-for-17)
Averaged one home run every 16.6 at-bats in nine years with Braves; averaged one every 68.7 at-bats with Cards last season. Give or take a tenth of a point, that's the difference between career home-run rates of Ed Mathews and Ralph Garr. . . . One of four N.L. players to reach base safely in nine consecutive plate appearances last year. . . . One hit in 12 at-bats in the Far East last season. Shea Stadium, that is, which is as far east as the N.L. gets. . . . Became only 50th player in history to play in 1000+ games with career slugging average of .500 or better. Horner joined group when he played 1000th game on May 21, but on June 7 he fell below .500, finishing year at .499. Membership is back down to 49.

Rex Hudler

Montreal Expos   Bats Right

	AB	H	2B	3B	HR	RBI	BB	SO	BA	SA	OBA
Season	216	59	14	2	4	14	10	34	.273	.412	.303
vs. Left-Handers	106	31	5	1	2	10	6	13	.292	.415	.325
vs. Right-Handers	110	28	9	1	2	4	4	21	.255	.409	.281
Home	115	32	9	1	1	9	7	18	.278	.400	.317
Road	101	27	5	1	3	5	3	16	.267	.426	.286
Grass	43	6	1	0	0	0	1	7	.140	.163	.159
Artificial Turf	173	53	13	2	4	14	9	27	.306	.474	.337
April	0	0	0	0	0	0	0	0	—	—	—
May	0	0	0	0	0	0	0	0	—	—	—
June	17	4	0	0	0	0	4	3	.235	.235	.381
July	60	18	6	1	0	3	2	6	.300	.433	.323
August	85	24	6	1	3	4	3	16	.282	.482	.303
Sept./Oct.	54	13	2	0	1	7	1	9	.241	.333	.250
Leading Off Inn.	70	19	5	1	2	3	3	13	.271	.457	.282
Runners On	78	17	8	1	1	11	9	5	.218	.385	.292
Runners/Scor. Pos.	48	8	4	1	0	9	7	5	.167	.292	.263
Runners On/2 Out	37	5	2	0	0	2	6	1	.135	.189	.256
Scor. Pos./2 Out	24	2	0	0	0	2	5	1	.083	.083	.241
Late Inning Pressure	36	7	1	1	1	2	0	7	.194	.361	.189
Leading Off	12	3	0	1	0	0	0	2	.250	.417	.250
Runners On	11	1	1	0	0	1	0	1	.091	.182	.083
Runners/Scor. Pos.	6	0	0	0	0	1	0	1	.000	.000	.000

RUNS BATTED IN	From 1B	From 2B	From 3B	Scoring Position
Totals	2/47	4/36	4/19	8/55
Percentage	4%	11%	21%	15%
Driving In Runners from 3B with Less than Two Out:		3/8		38%

Loves to face: John Tudor (.556, 5-for-9)
Hates to face: Bob Ojeda (0-for-10)
Ranked fourth in N.L. with 22 stolen bases after the All-Star break. Successful on his first 19 stolen base attempts, after which he stole only 10 in 17 attempts. . . . The key to success? Expos were 36–23 with Hudler in starting lineup, 45–58 without him. . . . Made 10 appearances as a pinch runner last season, 2d most on club to Pascual Perez's 14. . . . Scored a run in nine consecutive games last season, one game shy of Ron Gant's N.L. high. That streak coincided with a nine-game hitting streak that raised his average to .330 on August 8, his high-water mark for season. . . . Six of his 10 walks were intentional. . . . Did not play in the majors in 1987, and had only one at-bat in 1986.

Chris James

Philadelphia Phillies   Bats Right

	AB	H	2B	3B	HR	RBI	BB	SO	BA	SA	OBA
Season	566	137	24	1	19	66	31	73	.242	.389	.283
vs. Left-Handers	157	36	7	0	7	21	7	17	.229	.408	.265
vs. Right-Handers	409	101	17	1	12	45	24	56	.247	.381	.289
Home	298	78	15	1	10	38	16	31	.262	.419	.300
Road	268	59	9	0	9	28	15	42	.220	.354	.264
Grass	152	38	5	0	5	19	5	21	.250	.382	.273
Artificial Turf	414	99	19	1	14	47	26	52	.239	.391	.286
April	63	13	2	0	1	7	3	15	.206	.286	.239
May	93	24	4	0	6	13	5	10	.258	.495	.293
June	110	31	9	0	4	11	7	15	.282	.473	.336
July	112	23	3	1	3	14	7	13	.205	.330	.252
August	85	22	2	0	2	7	5	7	.259	.353	.300
Sept./Oct.	103	24	4	0	3	14	4	13	.233	.359	.261
Leading Off Inn.	137	34	8	1	4	4	5	13	.248	.409	.275
Runners On	257	58	8	0	9	56	13	35	.226	.362	.264
Runners/Scor. Pos.	162	33	3	0	4	45	9	24	.204	.296	.243
Runners On/2 Out	111	21	1	0	4	20	9	12	.189	.306	.250
Scor. Pos./2 Out	81	14	1	0	2	16	6	11	.173	.259	.230
Late Inning Pressure	95	24	5	0	2	6	11	14	.253	.368	.330
Leading Off	26	4	2	0	0	0	1	3	.154	.231	.185
Runners On	36	10	2	0	1	5	4	4	.278	.417	.297
Runners/Scor. Pos.	21	2	0	0	1	3	1	3	.095	.095	.136

RUNS BATTED IN	From 1B	From 2B	From 3B	Scoring Position
Totals	7/172	18/120	22/74	40/194
Percentage	4%	15%	30%	21%
Driving In Runners from 3B with Less than Two Out:		19/38		50%

Loves to face: Les Lancaster (.455, 5-for-11, 2 HR)
Hates to face: David Cone (0-for-15)
Averaged 2.28 putouts per nine innings last year, tops among N.L. right fielders (minimum: 500 innings). . . . Made 114 starts in outfield, but started 31 of team's last 34 games at third base while Ron Jones played right. . . . Career average of .218 with runners in scoring position is 63 points lower than his average in other at-bats, 3d largest difference by any player over last 10 years (minimum: 250 AB with RISP). . . . Had an extra-base hit in seven straight games in June, majors' longest such streak of 1988. . . . In both '87 and '88, Chris's home-run totals (17 and 19) were higher than his brother Craig's rushing-yards totals (10 and 15) with Patriots. With John Stephens there, that trend could continue.

Dion James
Atlanta Braves — Bats Left

	AB	H	2B	3B	HR	RBI	BB	SO	BA	SA	OBA
Season	386	99	17	5	3	30	58	59	.256	.350	.353
vs. Left-Handers	35	4	1	1	0	1	4	9	.114	.200	.205
vs. Right-Handers	351	95	16	4	3	29	54	50	.271	.365	.368
Home	188	47	10	3	1	16	31	24	.250	.351	.357
Road	198	52	7	2	2	14	27	35	.263	.348	.350
Grass	294	71	11	5	1	21	46	42	.241	.323	.345
Artificial Turf	92	28	6	0	2	9	12	17	.304	.435	.381
April	54	12	1	1	0	3	9	7	.222	.278	.333
May	73	23	5	1	0	7	11	10	.315	.411	.412
June	80	23	5	1	0	9	14	14	.288	.413	.394
July	65	15	1	1	1	6	6	9	.231	.323	.292
August	79	20	4	0	1	5	9	15	.253	.342	.326
Sept./Oct.	35	6	1	1	0	0	9	4	.171	.257	.341
Leading Off Inn.	101	26	5	1	0	0	10	13	.257	.327	.324
Runners On	133	37	8	1	0	27	29	18	.278	.353	.406
Runners/Scor. Pos.	75	21	2	1	0	25	22	12	.280	.333	.434
Runners On/2 Out	50	13	2	0	0	11	15	11	.260	.300	.439
Scor. Pos./2 Out	35	10	1	0	0	11	13	9	.286	.314	.479
Late Inning Pressure	68	16	2	1	0	1	13	9	.235	.294	.354
Leading Off	20	4	0	1	0	0	4	2	.200	.300	.333
Runners On	22	5	0	0	0	1	3	5	.227	.227	.308
Runners/Scor. Pos.	9	0	0	0	0	1	3	3	.000	.000	.231

RUNS BATTED IN	From 1B	From 2B	From 3B	Scoring Position
Totals	2/90	11/59	14/32	25/91
Percentage	2%	19%	44%	27%
Driving In Runners from 3B with Less than Two Out:		9/16		56%

Loves to face: Bob Walk (.438, 7-for-16, 5 2B)
Hates to face: Juan Agosto (0-for-6, 2 SO)
Want to neutralize this .284 career hitter? Bring in a pitcher who throws wormkillers. There's a difference of 70 points between James's career averages vs. fly-ball pitchers (.318) and vs. ground-ball pitchers (.248); that's the largest such disparity by any player in majors over past 10 seasons (minimum: 500 AB vs. each). . . . Has hit for a higher average at night than he has in day games in each of his five seasons in majors. . . . Started 99 of Braves 109 games vs. a right-handed starter, but only two of 51 games in which a left-hander opposed them; had hit .303 in 89 at-bats vs. left-handers the year before. . . . Even though he hit only .250 at home last season, his career mark at Atlanta is .320.

Steve Jeltz
Philadelphia Phillies — Bats Left and Right

	AB	H	2B	3B	HR	RBI	BB	SO	BA	SA	OBA
Season	379	71	11	4	0	27	59	58	.187	.237	.295
vs. Left-Handers	79	12	2	1	0	3	14	9	.152	.203	.280
vs. Right-Handers	300	59	9	3	0	24	45	49	.197	.247	.300
Home	184	33	7	2	0	10	28	28	.179	.239	.288
Road	195	38	4	2	0	17	31	30	.195	.236	.303
Grass	111	25	1	1	0	9	15	16	.225	.252	.313
Artificial Turf	268	46	10	3	0	18	44	42	.172	.231	.288
April	46	9	2	1	0	3	11	7	.196	.283	.351
May	60	13	3	2	0	3	7	10	.217	.333	.299
June	62	18	3	1	0	7	18	9	.290	.371	.444
July	79	12	3	0	0	6	8	11	.152	.190	.230
August	75	11	0	0	0	5	15	11	.147	.147	.286
Sept./Oct.	57	8	0	0	0	3	0	10	.140	.140	.140
Leading Off Inn.	89	16	2	2	0	0	15	17	.180	.247	.298
Runners On	166	38	5	1	0	27	25	19	.229	.271	.326
Runners/Scor. Pos.	83	22	4	0	0	25	15	9	.265	.313	.370
Runners On/2 Out	75	15	4	0	0	9	14	7	.200	.253	.326
Scor. Pos./2 Out	47	10	3	0	0	8	11	4	.213	.277	.362
Late Inning Pressure	47	6	2	0	0	3	11	9	.128	.170	.288
Leading Off	11	1	1	0	0	0	3	3	.091	.182	.286
Runners On	19	4	0	0	0	3	6	2	.211	.211	.385
Runners/Scor. Pos.	7	1	0	0	0	3	2	1	.143	.143	.300

RUNS BATTED IN	From 1B	From 2B	From 3B	Scoring Position
Totals	2/126	5/62	20/41	25/103
Percentage	2%	8%	49%	24%
Driving In Runners from 3B with Less than Two Out:		14/19		74%

Loves to face: Tim Leary (.500, 7-for-14)
Hates to face: Atlee Hammaker (0-for-13)
Batting average (.187) and slugging average (.237) were lowest in N.L. (minimum: 200 AB); only one player in 1980s has had a lower slugging average in a 350–at-bat season: ol' buddy Ivan DeJesus (.231 with '81 Cubs). . . . Went hitless in 33 straight at-bats, Aug. 22 to Sept. 5, tying Jim Morrison and Gene Larkin for longest nonpitchers' streak in majors. . . . Had no extra-base hits in last 153 at-bats, also the longest streak in majors last season. . . . Removed for pinch hitters 35 times last year, one behind N.L. co-leaders Rafael Belliard and Greg Harris. . . . Our annual Steve Jeltz "Positive Note": He was one of three N.L. players to bat 100 points higher with men in scoring position than at other times in 1988.

Howard Johnson
New York Mets — Bats Left and Right

	AB	H	2B	3B	HR	RBI	BB	SO	BA	SA	OBA
Season	495	114	21	1	24	68	86	104	.230	.422	.343
vs. Left-Handers	142	26	4	0	6	17	25	28	.183	.338	.304
vs. Right-Handers	353	88	17	1	18	51	61	76	.249	.456	.359
Home	221	47	10	1	9	30	43	50	.213	.389	.339
Road	274	67	11	0	15	38	43	54	.245	.449	.346
Grass	337	84	16	1	15	47	63	67	.249	.436	.368
Artificial Turf	158	30	5	0	9	21	23	37	.190	.392	.288
April	70	12	2	0	3	9	16	16	.171	.329	.326
May	96	27	6	0	5	14	17	13	.281	.500	.395
June	98	26	5	0	6	16	7	21	.265	.500	.312
July	77	13	1	0	4	10	19	17	.169	.338	.327
August	81	20	2	0	4	9	19	15	.247	.420	.386
Sept./Oct.	73	16	5	1	2	10	8	22	.219	.397	.298
Leading Off Inn.	109	34	6	0	9	9	11	18	.312	.615	.390
Runners On	210	42	5	1	7	51	49	49	.200	.333	.341
Runners/Scor. Pos.	127	25	2	0	6	48	40	31	.197	.354	.371
Runners On/2 Out	94	13	1	0	3	15	28	26	.138	.245	.336
Scor. Pos./2 Out	64	9	1	0	3	15	22	19	.141	.297	.360
Late Inning Pressure	68	16	2	0	3	7	18	15	.235	.397	.389
Leading Off	23	6	1	0	1	1	4	4	.261	.435	.393
Runners On	18	4	0	0	1	5	11	6	.222	.389	.469
Runners/Scor. Pos.	10	2	0	0	1	5	10	3	.200	.500	.522

RUNS BATTED IN	From 1B	From 2B	From 3B	Scoring Position
Totals	6/157	15/98	23/56	38/154
Percentage	4%	15%	41%	25%
Driving In Runners from 3B with Less than Two Out:		17/31		55%

Loves to face: Danny Darwin (.474, 9-for-19, 3 HR)
Hates to face: Tom Browning (0-for-20)
Career postseason batting average of .038 (1-for-26) is 2d lowest in history (minimum: 25 AB); Gene Alley hit .037 (1-for-27) with Pirates in 1970s. . . . Averaged 1.71 assists per nine innings, lowest among N.L. third basemen last season (minimum: 500 innings). . . . One of three Mets with 20 home runs and 20 steals last season; they were first team in history of majors to have three such players. . . . Has hit for higher average on road than at home in each of last six seasons. . . . Yearly averages with runners in scoring position since 1986: .362, .277, .197. . . . In 1987, hit 15 homers in 194 at-bats vs. left-handers, but has only 13 in 397 at-bats vs. lefties for rest of his career.

Tracy Jones
Reds/Expos — Bats Right

	AB	H	2B	3B	HR	RBI	BB	SO	BA	SA	OBA
Season	224	66	6	1	3	24	20	18	.295	.371	.358
vs. Left-Handers	111	39	4	1	2	15	11	4	.351	.459	.419
vs. Right-Handers	113	27	2	0	1	9	9	14	.239	.283	.295
Home	103	34	4	0	0	8	13	12	.330	.369	.415
Road	121	32	2	1	3	16	7	6	.264	.372	.305
Grass	57	18	2	0	2	9	3	1	.316	.456	.350
Artificial Turf	167	48	4	1	1	15	17	17	.287	.341	.360
April	43	12	0	0	0	4	3	2	.279	.279	.326
May	6	2	1	0	0	1	0	1	.333	.500	.429
June	18	4	0	0	0	2	4	3	.222	.222	.364
July	45	12	0	0	1	3	3	4	.267	.333	.327
August	39	11	0	0	1	4	2	3	.282	.359	.317
Sept./Oct.	73	25	5	1	1	11	7	6	.342	.479	.407
Leading Off Inn.	59	16	2	0	0	0	4	8	.271	.305	.317
Runners On	82	24	3	1	2	23	10	6	.293	.427	.376
Runners/Scor. Pos.	56	15	2	1	1	21	9	5	.268	.393	.379
Runners On/2 Out	35	9	2	1	0	10	4	2	.257	.371	.333
Scor. Pos./2 Out	29	7	1	1	0	10	4	2	.241	.345	.333
Late Inning Pressure	48	13	1	0	0	5	7	6	.271	.292	.364
Leading Off	12	3	1	0	0	0	0	3	.250	.333	.250
Runners On	17	4	0	0	0	5	6	2	.235	.235	.435
Runners/Scor. Pos.	13	3	0	0	0	5	5	2	.231	.231	.444

RUNS BATTED IN	From 1B	From 2B	From 3B	Scoring Position
Totals	3/45	8/40	10/22	18/62
Percentage	7%	20%	45%	29%
Driving In Runners from 3B with Less than Two Out:		6/12		50%

Loves to face: Neal Heaton (.625, 5-for-8, 1 HR)
Hates to face: Mike Dunne (0-for-6)
Batted 112 points higher against left-handers than he did against right-handers last season, largest difference by any N.L. batter (minimum: 100 AB vs. each). Career averages: .344 vs. lefties, .252 vs. righties; vs. lefties, that's a Ted Williams average, vs. righties, a Mike Hershberger average. . . . Batted .229 in 37 games for Reds, but .333 in 53 games with Expos, reaching base safely in 19 consecutive games at one point. . . . Stole 10 bases in first 10 tries, but only 8-of-14 after that. . . . Career averages of .321 on artificial turf, .239 on grass fields. . . . In three years in majors, has driven in 40 percent of runners (17-of-43) from scoring position in Late-Inning Pressure Situations.

Ricky Jordan

Philadelphia Phillies — Bats Right

	AB	H	2B	3B	HR	RBI	BB	SO	BA	SA	OBA
Season	273	84	15	1	11	43	7	39	.308	.491	.324
vs. Left-Handers	81	25	4	1	6	17	5	11	.309	.605	.349
vs. Right-Handers	192	59	11	0	5	26	2	28	.307	.443	.313
Home	142	47	9	0	6	29	5	24	.331	.521	.351
Road	131	37	6	1	5	14	2	15	.282	.458	.293
Grass	76	24	2	1	3	6	0	9	.316	.487	.316
Artificial Turf	197	60	13	0	8	37	7	30	.305	.492	.327
April	0	0	0	0	0	0	0	0	—	—	—
May	0	0	0	0	0	0	0	0	—	—	—
June	0	0	0	0	0	0	0	0	—	—	—
July	53	17	1	0	3	11	2	9	.321	.509	.345
August	113	35	10	0	4	15	2	17	.310	.504	.322
Sept./Oct.	107	32	4	1	4	17	3	13	.299	.467	.315
Leading Off Inn.	64	24	4	1	2	2	4	6	.375	.563	.412
Runners On	122	38	6	0	8	40	3	21	.311	.557	.325
Runners/Scor. Pos.	69	23	4	0	5	33	3	16	.333	.609	.356
Runners On/2 Out	57	11	1	0	1	8	2	12	.193	.263	.220
Scor. Pos./2 Out	31	6	1	0	1	8	2	9	.194	.323	.242
Late Inning Pressure	36	12	3	1	2	6	2	7	.333	.639	.368
Leading Off	10	5	1	1	0	0	2	1	.500	.800	.583
Runners On	14	6	2	0	2	6	0	4	.429	1.000	.429
Runners/Scor. Pos.	8	2	1	0	1	3	0	3	.250	.750	.250

RUNS BATTED IN	From 1B	From 2B	From 3B	Scoring Position
Totals	6/82	11/48	15/33	26/81
Percentage	7%	23%	45%	32%
Driving In Runners from 3B with Less than Two Out:		11/21		52%

Loves to face: Bob Knepper (.500, 2-for-4, 2 HR)
Hates to face: Ron Darling (0-for-7)

Batted .308 after the All-Star break, 2d best in N.L. behind Gwynn. . . . Phillies' first-round choice in 1983 amateur draft. None of Phils' first-round choices in June draft since 1975 has had a 350–at-bat season in majors; the only pitcher among that group to start 20+ games is 1984 pick Pete Smith, now with Braves. . . . Homered in each of first two games in majors. Walked twice in his first game, but only five times (two intentional) in 68 games after that. . . . Phillies won the first four games he started last season. How many other people can you say that about? . . . That was supposed to be a rhetorical question, but we don't want to cause any sleepless nights; the answer is none.

John Kruk

San Diego Padres — Bats Left

	AB	H	2B	3B	HR	RBI	BB	SO	BA	SA	OBA
Season	378	91	17	1	9	44	80	68	.241	.362	.369
vs. Left-Handers	98	19	5	0	3	18	11	22	.194	.337	.270
vs. Right-Handers	280	72	12	1	6	26	69	46	.257	.371	.401
Home	182	46	8	0	8	31	53	29	.253	.429	.414
Road	196	45	9	1	1	13	27	39	.230	.301	.321
Grass	294	70	16	0	9	39	69	57	.238	.384	.379
Artificial Turf	84	21	1	1	0	5	11	11	.250	.286	.333
April	47	15	1	0	3	8	6	9	.319	.532	.396
May	75	19	6	0	1	12	19	16	.253	.373	.392
June	73	17	4	0	2	7	16	8	.233	.370	.367
July	48	9	2	0	1	3	16	9	.188	.292	.385
August	78	20	2	1	2	7	11	14	.256	.385	.348
Sept./Oct.	57	11	2	0	0	7	12	12	.193	.228	.333
Leading Off Inn.	106	30	3	1	4	4	11	12	.283	.443	.350
Runners On	165	41	11	0	3	38	50	30	.248	.370	.414
Runners/Scor. Pos.	92	21	6	0	1	32	36	18	.228	.326	.429
Runners On/2 Out	79	23	7	0	2	22	22	12	.291	.456	.446
Scor. Pos./2 Out	45	14	4	0	1	19	16	6	.311	.467	.492
Late Inning Pressure	54	13	1	0	1	3	10	14	.241	.315	.354
Leading Off	16	5	0	0	1	1	2	2	.313	.500	.389
Runners On	20	5	0	0	0	2	6	4	.250	.250	.407
Runners/Scor. Pos.	6	2	0	0	0	2	5	0	.333	.333	.583

RUNS BATTED IN	From 1B	From 2B	From 3B	Scoring Position
Totals	6/114	12/73	17/38	29/111
Percentage	5%	16%	45%	26%
Driving In Runners from 3B with Less than Two Out:		10/20		50%

Loves to face: Ron Darling (.471, 8-for-17, 2 HR)
Hates to face: Zane Smith (0-for-9)

.367 career batting average with runners in scoring position and two outs is highest in the 14 years since we've been keeping track (minimum: 50 hits). . . . With runners in scoring position in Late-Inning Pressure Situations, his career average is .391 (18-for-46). . . . Averaged one walk every 5.8 plate appearances last season, highest rate in N.L. . . . One of four major leaguers with 10+ starts in both leadoff and cleanup spots; Padres were 13–5 with Kruk leading off. . . . Started 90 of 104 games in which Padres faced a right-handed starter, but only 18 of 57 vs. lefties. . . . Has never been hit by a pitch in 1320 career plate appearances; among active players, that's the most PA without a HBP.

Barry Larkin

Cincinnati Reds — Bats Right

	AB	H	2B	3B	HR	RBI	BB	SO	BA	SA	OBA
Season	588	174	32	5	12	57	41	24	.296	.429	.347
vs. Left-Handers	145	51	13	1	5	20	17	4	.352	.559	.421
vs. Right-Handers	443	123	19	4	7	37	24	20	.278	.386	.322
Home	303	93	18	2	9	39	20	13	.307	.469	.353
Road	285	81	14	3	3	18	21	11	.284	.386	.342
Grass	174	48	8	0	0	11	12	6	.276	.322	.326
Artificial Turf	414	126	24	5	12	46	29	18	.304	.473	.356
April	97	30	4	1	3	10	4	4	.309	.464	.343
May	97	29	5	0	2	9	8	7	.299	.412	.358
June	98	29	3	1	4	17	7	4	.296	.469	.355
July	83	21	5	0	1	1	13	3	.253	.349	.367
August	109	30	11	3	0	11	5	3	.275	.431	.307
Sept./Oct.	104	35	4	0	2	9	4	3	.337	.433	.358
Leading Off Inn.	222	65	8	3	6	6	12	10	.293	.437	.340
Runners On	182	57	14	1	3	48	16	8	.313	.451	.366
Runners/Scor. Pos.	111	37	8	0	3	46	12	4	.333	.486	.383
Runners On/2 Out	77	23	9	1	2	27	9	3	.299	.519	.379
Scor. Pos./2 Out	51	16	6	0	2	25	7	2	.314	.549	.397
Late Inning Pressure	94	30	3	0	1	9	7	8	.319	.383	.369
Leading Off	20	6	0	0	0	0	2	1	.300	.300	.364
Runners On	41	11	1	0	1	9	1	3	.268	.366	.295
Runners/Scor. Pos.	23	8	0	0	1	9	1	1	.348	.478	.360

RUNS BATTED IN	From 1B	From 2B	From 3B	Scoring Position
Totals	5/115	19/93	21/40	40/133
Percentage	4%	20%	53%	30%
Driving In Runners from 3B with Less than Two Out:		12/18		67%

Loves to face: Zane Smith (.500, 6-for-12, 2 HR)
Hates to face: David Palmer (0-for-12)

Toughest player in majors to strike out last season; averaged one whiff every 27.2 plate appearances. No other N.L. player was close; Palmeiro was second (one every 18.5 times up). . . . Career average of .319 vs. left-handers, .258 vs. right-handers. . . . Stole a base in each of his first six games last season, tying Andres Thomas for major league lead; no Reds' shortstop had led N.L. in errors since Eddie Joost in 1942. . . . Ended season with a 21-game hitting streak, three games shy of John Shelby's 24-game streak, tops in majors last year. Barring rainouts, benchings, or hitless games, Larkin could tie Willie Keeler's N.L. record 45-game streak on May 1 at Montreal. Pete Rose's club mark is 44.

Mike LaValliere

Pittsburgh Pirates — Bats Left

	AB	H	2B	3B	HR	RBI	BB	SO	BA	SA	OBA
Season	352	92	18	0	2	47	50	34	.261	.330	.353
vs. Left-Handers	63	10	2	0	0	3	10	14	.159	.190	.293
vs. Right-Handers	289	82	16	0	2	44	40	20	.284	.360	.366
Home	178	46	11	0	0	20	21	14	.258	.320	.338
Road	174	46	7	0	2	27	29	20	.264	.339	.368
Grass	93	23	2	0	0	14	12	7	.247	.333	.333
Artificial Turf	259	69	16	0	2	33	38	27	.266	.328	.360
April	58	22	5	0	0	12	12	2	.379	.466	.486
May	49	10	2	0	0	7	11	4	.204	.245	.339
June	67	12	5	0	0	6	10	4	.179	.254	.282
July	55	19	3	0	1	10	8	7	.345	.455	.438
August	62	12	2	0	0	5	5	8	.194	.274	.254
Sept./Oct.	61	17	1	0	0	7	4	9	.279	.295	.328
Leading Off Inn.	98	22	4	0	0	0	10	12	.224	.265	.303
Runners On	134	41	11	0	2	47	28	7	.306	.433	.419
Runners/Scor. Pos.	87	29	11	0	2	47	22	4	.333	.529	.451
Runners On/2 Out	69	25	6	0	0	21	14	1	.362	.449	.476
Scor. Pos./2 Out	40	15	6	0	0	21	11	1	.375	.525	.510
Late Inning Pressure	54	15	4	0	0	9	4	5	.278	.352	.322
Leading Off	19	5	1	0	0	0	1	1	.263	.316	.300
Runners On	21	7	2	0	0	9	2	2	.333	.429	.375
Runners/Scor. Pos.	16	6	2	0	0	9	1	1	.375	.500	.389

RUNS BATTED IN	From 1B	From 2B	From 3B	Scoring Position
Totals	6/94	19/66	20/40	39/106
Percentage	6%	29%	50%	37%
Driving In Runners from 3B with Less than Two Out:		14/21		67%

Loves to face: Kelly Downs (.500, 10-for-20)
Hates to face: Pascual Perez (0-for-8)

At end of April, N.L. batting leaders were two catchers: Mike Scioscia (.404) and LaValliere (.379); Lav finished the year four points ahead of Scioscia. Only two catchers in major league history have won batting titles (Ernie Lombardi, who won two, and Bubbles Hargrave). . . . Started 96 of 112 games in which Bucs faced a right-handed starter, but only nine of 48 games vs. lefties. . . . Yearly averages with runners in scoring position since 1985: .182, .268, .290, .333. . . . Career breakdown: .276 vs. right-handers, but .196 vs. left-handers. . . . Stole three bases last year, his first three in majors; needs 10 more to equal career total of Smoky Burgess, who twice stole three in a season.

Vance Law

Chicago Cubs	AB	H	2B	3B	HR	RBI	BB	SO	BA	SA	OBA
Season	556	163	29	2	11	78	55	79	.293	.412	.358
vs. Left-Handers	151	44	9	1	5	24	18	16	.291	.464	.371
vs. Right-Handers	405	119	20	1	6	54	37	63	.294	.393	.353
Home	285	86	12	2	5	50	25	33	.302	.411	.362
Road	271	77	17	0	6	28	30	46	.284	.413	.354
Grass	383	116	16	2	5	59	34	54	.303	.394	.363
Artificial Turf	173	47	13	0	6	19	21	25	.272	.451	.349
April	84	24	4	1	2	8	4	9	.286	.429	.318
May	97	28	6	0	2	22	10	11	.289	.412	.349
June	98	34	4	1	1	9	9	15	.347	.439	.413
July	84	20	2	0	2	9	6	15	.238	.333	.297
August	96	29	5	0	1	13	9	16	.302	.385	.362
Sept./Oct.	97	28	8	0	3	17	17	13	.289	.464	.391
Leading Off Inn.	128	39	8	0	2	2	8	18	.305	.414	.346
Runners On	262	77	10	1	8	75	25	40	.294	.431	.358
Runners/Scor. Pos.	155	47	5	0	7	70	16	26	.303	.471	.369
Runners On/2 Out	109	33	2	1	4	30	13	17	.303	.450	.382
Scor. Pos./2 Out	74	22	1	0	3	27	12	12	.297	.432	.402
Late Inning Pressure	95	30	4	0	1	16	8	16	.316	.389	.365
Leading Off	27	8	1	0	0	0	1	4	.296	.333	.321
Runners On	42	15	1	0	0	15	3	6	.357	.381	.391
Runners/Scor. Pos.	26	11	1	0	0	15	2	4	.423	.462	.448

RUNS BATTED IN	From 1B	From 2B	From 3B	Scoring Position
Totals	9/180	28/123	30/66	58/189
Percentage	5%	23%	45%	31%
Driving In Runners from 3B with Less than Two Out:		24/42		57%

Loves to face: Jim Deshaies (.833, 5-for-6, 2 2B, 4 BB)
Hates to face: Bob Knepper (.103, 3-for-29, 1 HR)
The Pat Tabler of the N.L.: had nine hits in 15 at-bats with bases loaded last season, most such hits by anyone in majors. Pat himself went 8-for-9. . . . Started the season with a career-high 16-game hitting streak, and had 5th best average in N.L. in June. . . . Hitless in 25 consecutive at-bats vs. left-handed pitchers, longest such streak by any N.L. player last season, and longest by any Cubs' player in 1980s. . . . Has driven in over 45 percent of runners (23-of-51) from scoring position in Late-Inning Pressure Situations over last two seasons. . . . Season average fell below .300 right after All-Star break, but he finished at a career-high .293. His dad had three .300 seasons in 16 years in majors.

Jose Lind

Pittsburgh Pirates	AB	H	2B	3B	HR	RBI	BB	SO	BA	SA	OBA
Season	611	160	24	4	2	50	42	75	.262	.324	.308
vs. Left-Handers	214	53	12	0	0	12	18	28	.248	.304	.305
vs. Right-Handers	397	107	12	4	2	38	24	47	.270	.335	.310
Home	313	94	17	2	1	35	21	40	.300	.377	.342
Road	298	66	7	2	1	15	21	35	.221	.268	.272
Grass	145	32	1	0	1	4	9	18	.221	.248	.266
Artificial Turf	466	128	23	4	1	46	33	57	.275	.348	.321
April	95	20	4	0	0	5	4	8	.211	.253	.242
May	118	32	2	2	0	14	12	14	.271	.322	.338
June	115	28	5	0	1	13	9	17	.243	.313	.296
July	88	22	5	0	1	4	2	12	.250	.341	.267
August	113	27	4	1	0	9	11	15	.239	.292	.304
Sept./Oct.	82	31	4	1	0	5	4	9	.378	.451	.402
Leading Off Inn.	94	20	3	0	0	0	6	14	.213	.245	.260
Runners On	243	61	7	4	0	48	18	30	.251	.313	.299
Runners/Scor. Pos.	148	36	4	3	0	44	13	19	.243	.311	.299
Runners On/2 Out	96	21	1	1	0	18	8	11	.219	.250	.279
Scor. Pos./2 Out	67	14	1	1	0	18	6	8	.209	.254	.274
Late Inning Pressure	91	22	3	0	1	7	5	13	.242	.308	.278
Leading Off	17	2	1	0	0	0	2	0	.118	.176	.211
Runners On	39	9	1	0	0	6	3	8	.231	.256	.279
Runners/Scor. Pos.	22	6	0	0	0	4	2	5	.273	.273	.320

RUNS BATTED IN	From 1B	From 2B	From 3B	Scoring Position
Totals	7/165	21/120	20/53	41/173
Percentage	4%	18%	38%	24%
Driving In Runners from 3B with Less than Two Out:		15/31		48%

Loves to face: Orel Hershiser (.636, 7-for-11)
Hates to face: Randy Myers (0-for-8, 4 SO)
September batting average (.378) was highest in N.L.; that push enabled him to finish at .262, the highest his average had been since May 14. . . . Batted in the second spot in the order in all but three of his 145 starts. . . . Committed only one error in his last 53 games at second base; his .987 percentage ranked third in N.L. behind champion Bill Doran and runner-up Ryne Sandberg. . . . Career average of .303 at Three Rivers Stadium, .241 on road. . . . Before he jumped over Garagiola's head did he practice on Costas? Is he leading up to an attempt on 6′ 3′ Tony Kubek?

Dave Magadan

New York Mets	AB	H	2B	3B	HR	RBI	BB	SO	BA	SA	OBA
Season	314	87	15	0	1	35	60	39	.277	.334	.393
vs. Left-Handers	86	24	3	0	0	13	15	11	.279	.314	.394
vs. Right-Handers	228	63	12	0	1	22	45	28	.276	.342	.393
Home	166	50	7	0	1	22	30	22	.301	.361	.407
Road	148	37	8	0	0	13	30	17	.250	.304	.378
Grass	223	60	8	0	1	25	36	31	.269	.318	.369
Artificial Turf	91	27	7	0	0	10	24	8	.297	.374	.448
April	17	3	0	0	0	1	5	1	.176	.176	.364
May	26	6	0	0	0	2	5	8	.231	.231	.355
June	87	31	5	0	1	10	16	8	.356	.448	.457
July	82	20	4	0	0	12	15	8	.244	.293	.360
August	58	15	2	0	0	5	6	6	.259	.293	.328
Sept./Oct.	44	12	4	0	0	5	13	8	.273	.364	.439
Leading Off Inn.	58	7	2	0	0	0	9	6	.121	.155	.239
Runners On	152	48	9	0	1	35	30	19	.316	.395	.422
Runners/Scor. Pos.	90	28	7	0	1	33	19	13	.311	.422	.420
Runners On/2 Out	58	18	2	0	0	10	13	6	.310	.345	.437
Scor. Pos./2 Out	34	10	2	0	0	10	8	5	.294	.353	.429
Late Inning Pressure	53	10	1	0	0	5	12	8	.189	.208	.338
Leading Off	12	0	0	0	0	0	2	0	.000	.000	.143
Runners On	27	6	0	0	0	5	6	5	.222	.222	.364
Runners/Scor. Pos.	20	4	0	0	0	5	4	4	.200	.200	.333

RUNS BATTED IN	From 1B	From 2B	From 3B	Scoring Position
Totals	2/105	17/72	15/30	32/102
Percentage	2%	24%	50%	31%
Driving In Runners from 3B with Less than Two Out:		10/17		59%

Loves to face: Paul Assenmacher (.800, 4-for-5)
Hates to face: Orel Hershiser (0-for-8)
Owns .328 career batting average vs. left-handed pitchers, the highest by any left-handed batter against lefty pitchers over the past 14 years (minimum: 100 AB); the rest of the top five: Mike Greenwell .321, Tony Gwynn .318, Wade Boggs .317, Rod Carew .310. . . . Had N.L.'s 4th best batting average in June, filling in for injured Hernandez. . . . Career breakdown: .328 with runners on base, .269 with the bases empty. . . . Has been struck out twice by the same pitcher in the same game only once in his career: Eric Show did it, Aug. 19 last year. . . . Batted .239 vs. ground-ball pitchers last season, .314 vs fly-ball pitchers. . . . Has .338 career average at Shea, .254 elsewhere.

Candy Maldonado

San Francisco Giants	AB	H	2B	3B	HR	RBI	BB	SO	BA	SA	OBA
Season	499	127	23	1	12	68	37	89	.255	.377	.311
vs. Left-Handers	183	46	8	0	1	24	13	26	.251	.311	.303
vs. Right-Handers	316	81	15	1	11	44	24	63	.256	.415	.316
Home	246	58	12	0	5	28	14	47	.236	.346	.283
Road	253	69	11	1	7	40	23	42	.273	.407	.338
Grass	362	93	18	0	11	49	27	65	.257	.398	.314
Artificial Turf	137	34	5	1	1	19	10	24	.248	.321	.305
April	81	20	3	0	3	12	8	13	.247	.395	.315
May	103	28	5	0	3	15	3	14	.272	.408	.306
June	88	25	5	0	1	16	7	22	.284	.375	.340
July	81	21	2	1	0	5	6	14	.259	.309	.315
August	67	17	5	0	2	11	6	13	.254	.418	.316
Sept./Oct.	79	16	3	0	3	9	7	13	.203	.354	.276
Leading Off Inn.	113	31	3	1	3	3	7	18	.274	.398	.317
Runners On	229	59	11	0	5	61	20	42	.258	.371	.323
Runners/Scor. Pos.	136	34	8	0	2	54	20	28	.250	.353	.345
Runners On/2 Out	112	32	6	0	3	32	6	19	.286	.420	.339
Scor. Pos./2 Out	70	20	4	0	1	27	6	14	.286	.386	.359
Late Inning Pressure	79	15	1	0	1	3	5	18	.190	.241	.247
Leading Off	22	6	0	0	0	1	3	3	.273	.273	.304
Runners On	28	2	0	0	0	2	3	9	.071	.071	.188
Runners/Scor. Pos.	20	2	0	0	0	2	3	4	.100	.100	.217

RUNS BATTED IN	From 1B	From 2B	From 3B	Scoring Position
Totals	8/156	23/104	25/64	48/168
Percentage	5%	22%	39%	29%
Driving In Runners from 3B with Less than Two Out:		16/31		52%

Loves to face: Frank DiPino (.636, 7-for-11, 1 HR)
Hates to face: Dennis Rasmussen (0-for-13)
There's a 51-point difference between his career batting averages in home games (.232) and in road games (.283), largest by any player in majors over past 10 seasons (minimum: 750 AB each way). He currently plays home games in park which depresses batting averages more than any other in N.L. . . . Went 2-for-28 with runners on base in Late-Inning Pressure Situations in 1988; had hit .300+ in those situations in each of past two years. . . . Career average of .386 (17-for-44, three HR) with the bases loaded. . . . Led N.L. right fielders with 10 errors last season; .962 fielding percentage was 2d lowest in Giants' S.F. history among outfielders in 100+ games; remember Terry Whitfield's .959 in 1979?

Mike Marshall

Bats Right

Los Angeles Dodgers	AB	H	2B	3B	HR	RBI	BB	SO	BA	SA	OBA
Season	542	150	27	2	20	82	24	93	.277	.445	.314
vs. Left-Handers	186	43	11	1	4	19	13	28	.231	.366	.277
vs. Right-Handers	356	107	16	1	16	63	11	65	.301	.486	.333
Home	264	69	16	1	9	34	13	45	.261	.432	.299
Road	278	81	11	1	11	48	11	48	.291	.457	.328
Grass	387	101	19	1	12	58	17	70	.261	.408	.294
Artificial Turf	155	49	8	1	8	24	7	23	.316	.535	.361
April	78	21	2	0	1	11	5	11	.269	.333	.313
May	107	24	3	0	5	16	6	22	.224	.393	.265
June	104	34	8	1	3	17	4	17	.327	.510	.360
July	111	26	7	0	5	16	5	17	.234	.432	.283
August	87	32	3	1	4	15	3	14	.368	.563	.391
Sept./Oct.	55	13	4	0	2	7	1	12	.236	.418	.259
Leading Off Inn.	124	35	3	0	5	5	5	24	.282	.427	.321
Runners On	276	79	17	1	11	73	17	43	.286	.475	.332
Runners/Scor. Pos.	141	40	6	1	6	59	13	28	.284	.468	.344
Runners On/2 Out	128	43	7	0	7	43	4	19	.336	.555	.370
Scor. Pos./2 Out	72	26	4	0	5	38	4	13	.361	.625	.403
Late Inning Pressure	70	18	4	0	5	11	4	16	.257	.529	.297
Leading Off	17	6	0	0	2	2	1	7	.353	.706	.389
Runners On	37	8	2	0	2	8	3	5	.216	.432	.275
Runners/Scor. Pos.	19	4	1	0	1	5	3	5	.211	.421	.318

RUNS BATTED IN	From 1B	From 2B	From 3B	Scoring Position
Totals	13/203	24/108	25/55	49/163
Percentage	6%	22%	45%	30%
Driving In Runners from 3B with Less than Two Out:		12/25		48%

Loves to face: Dennis Martinez (.833, 5-for-6, 2 HR)
Hates to face: Kelly Downs (.067, 1-for-15)
Right-handed batter who has done much better vs. right-handed pitchers than vs. lefties, especially in recent years. Career figures: batting .280, slugging .461 vs. righties; .258 and .442 vs. southpaws. Last two years: batting .300 vs. RHP, .251 vs. LHP. . . . August batting average was 2d best in N.L. . . . Hit at least one home run vs. every N.L. foe except Mets; didn't hit any in playoffs, either. . . . Batting average with runners on base has been higher than with bases empty in each of last five years. . . . Has hit ground-ball pitchers for higher average than fly-ballers in each of six full years in majors. . . . Averaged 1.66 putouts per nine innings, lowest by any right fielder in majors last year (minimum: 500 innings).

Carmelo Martinez

Bats Right

San Diego Padres	AB	H	2B	3B	HR	RBI	BB	SO	BA	SA	OBA
Season	365	86	12	0	18	65	35	57	.236	.416	.301
vs. Left-Handers	154	36	3	0	7	26	20	21	.234	.390	.318
vs. Right-Handers	211	50	9	0	11	39	15	36	.237	.436	.288
Home	178	46	8	0	11	36	21	24	.258	.489	.337
Road	187	40	4	0	7	29	14	33	.214	.348	.266
Grass	265	65	10	0	15	46	24	33	.245	.453	.306
Artificial Turf	100	21	2	0	3	19	11	24	.210	.320	.288
April	38	4	1	0	1	2	2	3	.105	.211	.150
May	49	13	2	0	1	6	6	8	.265	.367	.345
June	49	11	3	0	1	11	1	6	.224	.347	.235
July	51	13	2	0	2	12	4	6	.255	.412	.309
August	66	20	1	0	7	18	9	12	.303	.636	.387
Sept./Oct.	112	25	3	0	6	16	13	22	.223	.411	.302
Leading Off Inn.	85	22	2	0	4	4	7	15	.259	.424	.315
Runners On	178	44	10	0	8	55	16	22	.247	.438	.306
Runners/Scor. Pos.	117	29	6	0	6	47	13	16	.248	.453	.318
Runners On/2 Out	78	18	7	0	3	22	6	10	.231	.436	.286
Scor. Pos./2 Out	57	12	4	0	2	17	5	10	.211	.386	.274
Late Inning Pressure	62	15	1	0	3	11	6	10	.242	.403	.309
Leading Off	14	2	0	0	0	0	1	5	.143	.143	.200
Runners On	28	9	1	0	1	9	3	2	.321	.464	.375
Runners/Scor. Pos.	18	7	1	0	1	9	3	1	.389	.611	.476

RUNS BATTED IN	From 1B	From 2B	From 3B	Scoring Position
Totals	9/121	14/86	24/58	38/144
Percentage	7%	16%	41%	26%
Driving In Runners from 3B with Less than Two Out:		15/29		52%

Loves to face: Atlee Hammaker (.444, 8-for-18, 7 BB, 4 HR)
Hates to face: Ron Robinson (0-for-14)
Hit 15 home runs after the All-Star break, third-most in N.L. behind Strawberry (18) and McReynolds (16). . . . Owns .181 career batting average in 276 at-bats with runners in scoring position and two outs; over the past 14 years, only two players with 250+ at-bats in those situations have lower batting averages: Johnnie LeMaster (.170) and Jeff Newman (.179). . . . On the other hand, Martinez's career average with two outs and a runner on first is .338, and he shows no dread of runners in scoring position with *less than* two outs, situations in which he has .306 career average. . . . Since joining the Padres he has averaged one home run every 21 at-bats at home, one every 38 at-bats on road.

Dave Martinez

Bats Left

Cubs/Expos	AB	H	2B	3B	HR	RBI	BB	SO	BA	SA	OBA
Season	447	114	13	6	6	46	38	94	.255	.351	.313
vs. Left-Handers	46	9	1	0	2	5	5	19	.196	.348	.296
vs. Right-Handers	401	105	12	6	4	41	33	75	.262	.352	.315
Home	200	52	5	4	2	18	20	39	.260	.355	.329
Road	247	62	8	2	4	28	18	55	.251	.348	.300
Grass	234	67	8	1	5	25	24	45	.286	.393	.354
Artificial Turf	213	47	5	5	1	21	14	49	.221	.305	.266
April	88	22	3	1	2	15	4	15	.250	.375	.295
May	75	18	3	0	0	11	9	18	.240	.280	.310
June	62	15	2	0	1	6	5	8	.242	.323	.299
July	63	14	2	0	1	5	7	16	.222	.302	.296
August	71	17	1	1	0	3	5	22	.239	.282	.289
Sept./Oct.	88	28	2	4	2	6	8	15	.318	.500	.375
Leading Off Inn.	150	40	3	1	2	2	6	28	.267	.340	.299
Runners On	146	39	5	1	3	43	17	35	.267	.377	.337
Runners/Scor. Pos.	94	25	5	1	1	39	13	23	.266	.372	.345
Runners On/2 Out	64	16	4	0	2	21	8	18	.250	.406	.342
Scor. Pos./2 Out	48	14	4	0	1	19	8	12	.292	.438	.404
Late Inning Pressure	66	14	4	0	0	5	9	21	.212	.273	.303
Leading Off	19	7	2	0	0	0	1	2	.368	.474	.400
Runners On	30	5	2	0	0	5	5	11	.167	.233	.278
Runners/Scor. Pos.	17	3	2	0	0	5	3	6	.176	.294	.286

RUNS BATTED IN	From 1B	From 2B	From 3B	Scoring Position
Totals	4/84	14/75	22/46	36/121
Percentage	5%	19%	48%	30%
Driving In Runners from 3B with Less than Two Out:		13/23		57%

Loves to face: Terry Leach (.455, 5-for-11, 1 HR)
Hates to face: Doug Drabek (.111, 3-for-27)
Had seven hits in 13 at-bats with the bases loaded last season. Five of those hits went for extra bases; Ellis Burks was the only other player with five bases-loaded XBHs, and Burks and Martinez were also the only guys who hit for the cycle with the bases loaded. . . . Started 105 games vs. right-handers last season, six vs. left-handers. Made only one start against a southpaw after being traded to Montreal. . . . Removed for pinch hitters 13 times last season: seven with Cubs, six with Expos. . . . Overall batting average dropped 37 points from 1987 to last season, but he experienced an even larger drop of 159 points (from .371 to .212) in Late-Inning Pressure Situations.

Willie McGee

Bats Left and Right

St. Louis Cardinals	AB	H	2B	3B	HR	RBI	BB	SO	BA	SA	OBA
Season	562	164	24	6	3	50	32	84	.292	.372	.329
vs. Left-Handers	197	58	8	2	0	14	8	34	.294	.355	.322
vs. Right-Handers	365	106	16	4	3	36	24	50	.290	.381	.333
Home	283	80	11	3	1	32	17	43	.283	.353	.322
Road	279	84	13	3	2	18	15	41	.301	.391	.337
Grass	153	50	7	2	0	7	6	23	.327	.399	.352
Artificial Turf	409	114	17	4	3	43	26	61	.279	.362	.321
April	88	24	5	2	0	8	4	15	.273	.375	.304
May	122	38	5	0	0	9	8	15	.311	.352	.351
June	115	42	6	1	1	16	8	15	.365	.461	.400
July	107	28	3	0	1	7	4	14	.262	.318	.288
August	83	16	0	2	1	6	7	15	.193	.277	.264
Sept./Oct.	47	16	5	1	0	4	1	10	.340	.489	.354
Leading Off Inn.	111	33	5	1	0	0	4	13	.297	.360	.322
Runners On	249	72	8	5	1	48	15	44	.289	.373	.326
Runners/Scor. Pos.	155	39	6	3	0	44	13	31	.252	.329	.304
Runners On/2 Out	76	17	3	2	0	11	8	6	.224	.316	.298
Scor. Pos./2 Out	59	13	3	2	0	11	7	5	.220	.339	.303
Late Inning Pressure	107	32	2	0	1	6	2	14	.299	.346	.312
Leading Off	30	9	1	0	0	0	0	3	.300	.333	.300
Runners On	39	11	1	0	0	5	2	7	.282	.308	.317
Runners/Scor. Pos.	23	5	0	0	0	5	2	4	.217	.217	.280

RUNS BATTED IN	From 1B	From 2B	From 3B	Scoring Position
Totals	4/159	17/120	26/68	43/188
Percentage	3%	14%	38%	23%
Driving In Runners from 3B with Less than Two Out:		22/45		49%

Loves to face: Mike Scott (.556, 15-for-27)
Hates to face: Rich Gossage (0-for-9)
In 1987, batted with 260 runners in scoring position (highest total in majors since 1975), and came up with bases loaded 33 times; in '88, he saw only 188 ducks on the pond, and only 14 times were the bags full. . . . Batted .353 in his MVP year (1985) but has never topped the .300 mark in any other season. . . . Career average of .320 in day games, .283 at night. . . . Has six bases-loaded triples in his career, one short of Stan Musial's N.L. record., two shy of Shano Collins's major league mark. . . . One of those players who, we are told, "is made for artificial turf." You'd think that if that were true, you'd see a bigger difference in his career batting figures: .296 on turf, .294 on grass fields.

Kevin McReynolds

Bats Right

New York Mets	AB	H	2B	3B	HR	RBI	BB	SO	BA	SA	OBA
Season	552	159	30	2	27	99	38	56	.288	.496	.336
vs. Left-Handers	185	50	11	2	12	26	10	20	.270	.546	.308
vs. Right-Handers	367	109	19	0	15	73	28	36	.297	.471	.349
Home	279	77	15	0	13	45	18	29	.276	.470	.320
Road	273	82	15	2	14	54	20	27	.300	.524	.351
Grass	405	112	21	1	18	64	26	40	.277	.467	.323
Artificial Turf	147	47	9	1	9	35	12	16	.320	.578	.369
April	66	21	3	0	3	9	3	6	.318	.500	.348
May	97	22	3	1	1	12	7	8	.227	.309	.283
June	104	30	3	1	5	18	9	9	.288	.481	.353
July	94	32	11	0	6	22	7	13	.340	.649	.386
August	99	24	4	0	5	16	6	9	.242	.434	.287
Sept./Oct.	92	30	6	0	7	22	6	11	.326	.620	.364
Leading Off Inn.	118	34	7	1	5	5	10	7	.288	.492	.349
Runners On	257	80	16	0	11	83	20	24	.311	.502	.359
Runners/Scor. Pos.	163	52	5	0	8	71	12	13	.319	.497	.359
Runners On/2 Out	127	33	7	0	6	39	11	13	.260	.457	.329
Scor. Pos./2 Out	83	24	2	0	5	35	9	6	.289	.494	.366
Late Inning Pressure	87	29	5	0	4	16	2	10	.333	.529	.352
Leading Off	24	11	2	0	3	3	1	0	.458	.917	.480
Runners On	38	14	2	0	1	13	0	6	.368	.500	.359
Runners/Scor. Pos.	24	9	0	0	1	12	0	3	.375	.500	.360

RUNS BATTED IN	From 1B	From 2B	From 3B	Scoring Position
Totals	14/187	33/131	25/60	58/191
Percentage	7%	25%	42%	30%
Driving In Runners from 3B with Less than Two Out:		15/34	44%	

Loves to face: John Tudor (.371, 13-for-35, 3 HR)
Hates to face: Brian Fisher (0-for-9)
Only three players in history have had three seasons of 95+ RBI without ever reaching 100: McReynolds, Donn Clendenon, and Arky Vaughan. Mac is the first to do it in three consecuitve years. . . . Led N.L. with 52 RBI after the All-Star break; tied Andy Van Slyke for N.L. lead in go-ahead RBI (32). . . . Has stolen 32 consecutive bases since being caught by Alex Trevino, June 2, 1987; 21-for-21 in 1988, breaking record of 16-for-16 by Jimmy Sexton of A's in 1982. . . . Led N.L. outfielders with 18 assists last season, but average of 1.79 putouts per nine innings was lowest among N.L. left fielders (minimum: 500 innings). . . . Yearly batting averages vs. right-handers since 1985: .223, .261, .268, .297.

Bob Melvin

Bats Right

San Francisco Giants	AB	H	2B	3B	HR	RBI	BB	SO	BA	SA	OBA
Season	273	64	13	1	8	27	13	46	.234	.377	.268
vs. Left-Handers	85	23	5	0	3	12	6	9	.271	.435	.315
vs. Right-Handers	188	41	8	1	5	15	7	37	.218	.351	.246
Home	139	34	7	1	4	15	7	25	.245	.396	.279
Road	134	30	6	0	4	12	6	21	.224	.358	.257
Grass	199	47	9	1	7	22	9	36	.236	.397	.268
Artificial Turf	74	17	4	0	1	5	4	10	.230	.324	.269
April	54	12	2	0	3	6	1	13	.222	.426	.236
May	59	9	2	0	2	6	5	8	.153	.288	.219
June	3	0	0	0	0	0	0	1	.000	.000	.000
July	66	18	4	1	2	8	4	11	.273	.455	.314
August	56	18	4	0	1	4	3	10	.321	.446	.356
Sept./Oct.	35	7	1	0	0	3	0	3	.200	.229	.194
Leading Off Inn.	71	17	3	0	3	3	3	13	.239	.408	.270
Runners On	103	27	7	1	4	23	2	16	.262	.466	.274
Runners/Scor. Pos.	60	11	2	1	2	17	1	11	.183	.350	.194
Runners On/2 Out	57	15	4	1	3	18	1	8	.263	.526	.276
Scor. Pos./2 Out	40	10	2	1	2	16	0	6	.250	.500	.250
Late Inning Pressure	46	11	1	0	4	3	5		.239	.304	.286
Leading Off	10	2	0	0	0	0	2	0	.200	.200	.333
Runners On	17	4	0	1	0	4	0	3	.235	.235	.235
Runners/Scor. Pos.	11	3	0	1	0	4	0	2	.273	.455	.273

RUNS BATTED IN	From 1B	From 2B	From 3B	Scoring Position
Totals	8/76	9/50	2/16	11/66
Percentage	11%	18%	13%	17%
Driving In Runners from 3B with Less than Two Out:		1/5	20%	

Loves to face: Jamie Moyer (.600, 3-for-5)
Hates to face: Fred Toliver (0-for-4, 3 SO)
Career average of .273 vs. left-handers, .188 vs. righties; vs. left-handers, Melvin made 27 starts, Brenly 15, Kirt Manwaring 11; vs. right-handers, Melvin 47, Brenly 40, Manwaring 22. . . . Hit the last home run allowed by Orel Hershiser in 1988; he did that on August 14 at Dodger Stadium. . . . Owns a .245 career batting average on artificial turf; his three best stadiums for batting average are all carpeted: .349 at Busch, .279 at Astrodome, .273 at Riverfront. . . . His career statistics (.220 average, one homer every 36.2 at-bats) remind you of Nettles—Jim Nettles, Graig's brother, who hit .220 with one homer every 36.7 at-bats with four American League teams.

Kevin Mitchell

Bats Right

San Francisco Giants	AB	H	2B	3B	HR	RBI	BB	SO	BA	SA	OBA
Season	505	127	25	7	19	81	48	85	.251	.442	.319
vs. Left-Handers	160	32	7	0	5	23	18	26	.200	.338	.280
vs. Right-Handers	345	95	18	7	14	58	30	59	.275	.490	.337
Home	253	67	14	4	10	46	20	46	.265	.470	.319
Road	252	60	11	3	9	35	28	39	.238	.413	.318
Grass	385	104	21	7	14	67	31	69	.270	.470	.325
Artificial Turf	120	23	4	0	5	14	17	16	.192	.350	.300
April	77	18	1	1	3	12	12	15	.234	.390	.326
May	103	24	8	4	4	16	10	14	.233	.505	.316
June	72	20	4	0	1	8	5	9	.278	.375	.325
July	87	20	2	0	7	22	7	13	.230	.494	.292
August	105	32	6	2	3	17	10	21	.305	.486	.359
Sept./Oct.	61	13	4	0	1	6	4	13	.213	.328	.273
Leading Off Inn.	121	25	6	1	6	6	8	22	.207	.421	.256
Runners On	240	66	10	4	7	69	24	39	.275	.438	.337
Runners/Scor. Pos.	154	43	7	2	5	63	21	29	.279	.448	.355
Runners On/2 Out	125	31	5	0	3	30	14	19	.248	.360	.324
Scor. Pos./2 Out	86	23	5	0	3	30	12	15	.267	.430	.357
Late Inning Pressure	78	16	1	0	5	10	8	20	.205	.410	.276
Leading Off	18	4	1	0	2	2	1	3	.222	.611	.263
Runners On	36	7	0	0	2	7	4	10	.194	.361	.268
Runners/Scor. Pos.	24	2	0	0	1	5	3	8	.083	.208	.179

RUNS BATTED IN	From 1B	From 2B	From 3B	Scoring Position
Totals	7/174	22/108	33/79	55/187
Percentage	4%	20%	42%	29%
Driving In Runners from 3B with Less than Two Out:		18/32	56%	

Loves to face: John Tudor (.643, 9-for-14, 2 HR)
Hates to face: Jim Gott (0-for-8)
Hit 75 points better vs. right-handers than vs. lefties last year, largest difference by any right-handed batter in N.L. (minimum: 100 AB vs. each). Through '87, his career marks were .319 vs. LHP, .247 vs. RHP. . . . Batted .304 vs. ground-ball pitchers, .187 vs. fly-ball pitchers; that 117-point disparity was also widest in N.L. (again 100 AB vs. each). He could have trouble holding on to that title in '89; Gary Redus, Mr. Fly Ball himself, is back in N.L., and fly-ball hitters hit well vs. ground-ball pitchers. . . . Career batting average of .100 (3-for-30) with bases loaded; among active N.L. players (minimum: 20 AB over last 14 years), he and Fernando Valenzuela (2-for-20) have lowest bases-loaded averages.

Keith Moreland

Bats Right

San Diego Padres	AB	H	2B	3B	HR	RBI	BB	SO	BA	SA	OBA
Season	511	131	23	0	5	64	40	51	.256	.331	.305
vs. Left-Handers	179	43	6	0	2	20	17	17	.240	.307	.303
vs. Right-Handers	332	88	17	0	3	44	23	34	.265	.343	.307
Home	235	63	7	0	3	26	23	23	.268	.336	.327
Road	276	68	16	0	2	38	17	28	.246	.326	.286
Grass	365	98	15	0	4	43	29	36	.268	.342	.317
Artificial Turf	146	33	8	0	1	21	11	15	.226	.301	.277
April	76	24	2	0	0	5	2	7	.316	.342	.333
May	77	17	4	0	2	8	11	7	.221	.351	.318
June	98	28	8	0	1	14	6	10	.286	.398	.321
July	89	25	6	0	0	15	6	7	.281	.348	.316
August	86	19	2	0	0	13	9	12	.221	.244	.289
Sept./Oct.	85	18	1	0	2	9	6	8	.212	.294	.258
Leading Off Inn.	117	36	2	0	1	1	9	11	.308	.350	.357
Runners On	255	59	15	0	1	60	19	23	.231	.302	.276
Runners/Scor. Pos.	149	40	13	0	1	60	15	16	.268	.376	.318
Runners On/2 Out	120	26	6	0	0	24	9	9	.217	.267	.271
Scor. Pos./2 Out	80	21	6	0	0	24	7	7	.263	.338	.322
Late Inning Pressure	65	18	3	0	1	9	2	6	.277	.369	.290
Leading Off	17	4	0	0	0	0	2	1	.235	.235	.316
Runners On	28	8	3	0	0	8	0	1	.286	.393	.267
Runners/Scor. Pos.	14	4	2	0	0	8	0	1	.286	.429	.250

RUNS BATTED IN	From 1B	From 2B	From 3B	Scoring Position
Totals	4/184	27/117	28/67	55/184
Percentage	2%	23%	42%	30%
Driving In Runners from 3B with Less than Two Out:		19/30	63%	

Loves to face: John Candelaria (.417, 10-for-24, 2 HR)
Hates to face: Cecilio Guante (0-for-14)
Home-run total fell from career-high 27 in 1987 to five in 1988. Had no home runs in 67 games from June 2 to Sept. 5, longest home-run drought of his career. . . . Started the season with 10-game hitting streak, ended it with two hits in last 29 at-bats. . . . Career average of .302 (one HR every 33 AB) vs. left-handers, .271 (one HR every 37 AB) vs. right-handers. That's essential information to Sparky watchers. . . . Through N.L. career, hit 75 home runs at home (Wrigley Field and Jack Murphy Stadium), 40 home runs on road. Has had the luxury of playing home games in two of N.L.'s best home-run parks, now gets his shot at one of A.L.'s best, Tiger Stadium. Can the Kingdome be far behind?

Dale Murphy
Atlanta Braves — Bats Right

	AB	H	2B	3B	HR	RBI	BB	SO	BA	SA	OBA
Season	592	134	35	4	24	77	74	125	.226	.421	.313
vs. Left-Handers	180	46	11	1	9	28	37	33	.256	.478	.379
vs. Right-Handers	412	88	24	3	15	49	37	92	.214	.396	.281
Home	283	74	23	2	14	50	42	54	.261	.505	.358
Road	309	60	12	2	10	27	32	71	.194	.343	.270
Grass	434	105	26	3	18	64	51	91	.242	.440	.322
Artificial Turf	158	29	9	1	6	13	23	34	.184	.367	.290
April	67	16	3	0	2	6	12	14	.239	.373	.354
May	105	21	6	2	3	7	17	17	.200	.381	.311
June	107	25	8	1	7	24	15	24	.234	.523	.328
July	109	31	9	1	7	14	13	26	.284	.578	.366
August	103	20	6	0	4	16	5	21	.194	.369	.234
Sept./Oct.	101	21	3	0	1	10	12	23	.208	.267	.289
Leading Off Inn.	162	44	7	2	9	9	10	32	.272	.506	.314
Runners On	263	52	12	2	7	60	50	53	.198	.338	.327
Runners/Scor. Pos.	156	37	7	2	7	58	41	33	.237	.442	.393
Runners On/2 Out	115	20	8	0	5	24	27	31	.174	.374	.336
Scor. Pos./2 Out	66	14	5	0	5	22	21	18	.212	.515	.402
Late Inning Pressure	108	22	5	0	2	10	10	24	.204	.306	.275
Leading Off	29	6	1	0	1	1	2	8	.207	.345	.258
Runners On	46	8	2	0	0	8	7	8	.174	.217	.291
Runners/Scor. Pos.	23	5	2	0	0	8	6	5	.217	.304	.387

RUNS BATTED IN	From 1B	From 2B	From 3B	Scoring Position
Totals	9/173	20/111	24/64	44/175
Percentage	5%	18%	38%	25%
Driving In Runners from 3B with Less than Two Out:		20/37		54%

Loves to face: Atlee Hammaker (.516, 16-for-31, 5 HR)
Hates to face: Greg Maddux (0-for-9)
Made only three errors last season, all vs. Expos within six-game span in May. Ended year with 128 errorless games, 98 shy of Curt Flood's N.L. record for outfielders. . . . Grounded into 24 double plays in 112 DP situations, 2d highest rate in N.L. (min.: 40 opportunities). . . . Batting average in Late-Inning Pressure Situations has been lower than overall average in each of last seven years. Other current streaks: Guerrero, seven years; Winfield, eight; Rice, ten. . . . Led N.L. outfielders in games for 6th time, tying major league mark held by Billy Williams and George Burns. No, not *that* George Burns. Hold on, this guy did it in six times between 1914 and 1923. Could it be? Say goodnight, Gracie.

Otis Nixon
Montreal Expos — Bats Left and Right

	AB	H	2B	3B	HR	RBI	BB	SO	BA	SA	OBA
Season	271	66	8	2	0	15	28	42	.244	.288	.312
vs. Left-Handers	93	21	3	1	0	4	11	12	.226	.280	.308
vs. Right-Handers	178	45	5	1	0	11	17	30	.253	.292	.315
Home	145	34	4	1	0	7	19	19	.234	.276	.321
Road	126	32	4	1	0	8	9	23	.254	.302	.301
Grass	65	16	2	0	0	3	2	13	.246	.277	.265
Artificial Turf	206	50	6	2	0	12	26	29	.243	.291	.326
April	0	0	0	0	0	0	0	0	---	---	---
May	0	0	0	0	0	0	0	0	---	---	---
June	44	10	0	1	0	1	4	3	.227	.273	.292
July	83	18	4	1	0	5	9	13	.217	.289	.290
August	62	15	2	0	0	6	4	15	.242	.274	.288
Sept./Oct.	82	23	2	0	0	3	11	11	.280	.305	.362
Leading Off Inn.	118	31	3	2	0	0	17	19	.263	.322	.356
Runners On	71	18	4	0	0	15	2	10	.254	.310	.267
Runners/Scor. Pos.	49	11	3	0	0	15	2	8	.224	.286	.245
Runners On/2 Out	41	11	2	0	0	6	1	8	.268	.317	.290
Scor. Pos./2 Out	30	6	2	0	0	6	1	6	.200	.267	.226
Late Inning Pressure	50	15	1	1	0	1	3	11	.300	.360	.340
Leading Off	18	6	1	1	0	0	1	5	.333	.500	.368
Runners On	14	4	0	0	0	1	0	2	.286	.286	.286
Runners/Scor. Pos.	6	1	0	0	0	1	0	1	.167	.167	.167

RUNS BATTED IN	From 1B	From 2B	From 3B	Scoring Position
Totals	0/46	8/42	7/20	15/62
Percentage	0%	19%	35%	24%
Driving In Runners from 3B with Less than Two Out:		7/9		78%

Loves to face: Danny Cox (.500, 4-for-8)
Hates to face: Jose Rijo (0-for-8)
One of four active players with more career stolen bases than strikeouts (minimum: 100 SB); others: Henderson, Raines, Ozzie. . . . Stole 18 bases in his first 18 games, 46 for the season. His 16 steals vs. Cardinals were the most by any player vs. any club in majors last season. . . . Batted .211 vs. ground-ball pitchers last season, .286 vs. fly-ball pitchers. . . . Batted only .214 in 63 games in starting lineup, but he batted .500 (14-for-28) coming off the bench, including six hits in 11 at-bats as pinch hitter. . . . Brother Donell, playing with Giants, led majors with 25 pinch running appearances, but didn't bat enough to get his own spot in Batter Section; Otis graciously lent him some space.

Ken Oberkfell
Braves/Pirates — Bats Left

	AB	H	2B	3B	HR	RBI	BB	SO	BA	SA	OBA
Season	476	129	22	4	3	42	37	34	.271	.353	.321
vs. Left-Handers	100	26	5	2	0	15	6	9	.260	.350	.288
vs. Right-Handers	376	103	17	2	3	27	31	25	.274	.354	.330
Home	224	65	9	2	1	24	17	14	.290	.362	.335
Road	252	64	13	2	2	18	20	20	.254	.345	.309
Grass	324	92	16	2	1	32	18	22	.284	.355	.317
Artificial Turf	152	37	6	2	2	10	19	12	.243	.349	.329
April	52	12	0	1	1	4	7	6	.231	.327	.328
May	94	26	4	1	1	11	9	4	.277	.372	.327
June	110	28	7	0	0	9	6	11	.255	.318	.288
July	88	29	3	0	1	6	5	5	.330	.398	.372
August	87	25	8	2	0	11	6	2	.287	.425	.330
Sept./Oct.	45	9	0	0	0	1	4	6	.200	.200	.265
Leading Off Inn.	106	24	2	0	1	1	6	11	.226	.274	.268
Runners On	166	48	10	4	1	40	20	11	.289	.416	.351
Runners/Scor. Pos.	91	24	4	3	1	35	18	10	.264	.407	.359
Runners On/2 Out	61	19	5	1	0	12	10	3	.311	.426	.408
Scor. Pos./2 Out	35	9	3	0	0	10	9	3	.257	.343	.409
Late Inning Pressure	84	20	3	1	0	9	7	7	.238	.298	.301
Leading Off	24	5	1	0	0	0	0	4	.208	.250	.208
Runners On	33	7	2	1	0	9	6	1	.212	.333	.325
Runners/Scor. Pos.	24	7	2	1	0	9	5	1	.292	.458	.400

RUNS BATTED IN	From 1B	From 2B	From 3B	Scoring Position
Totals	7/121	15/73	17/41	32/114
Percentage	6%	21%	41%	28%
Driving In Runners from 3B with Less than Two Out:		15/27		56%

Loves to face: Danny Jackson (.556, 5-for-9)
Hates to face: Mark Grant (0-for-10)
He's nothing if not consistent: Obie is the only player in majors to hit between .270 and .280 in each of last four years. Only two players in history have had more consecutive seasons in the .270s: Hod Ford (seven years, 1921–27) and Mookie Wilson (five years, 1981–85). . . . Add consistency: .282 career average, .282 vs. fly-ball pitchers, .282 vs. ground-ballers, .284 on artificial turf, .279 on grass fields, .284 in night games, .276 in daytime. . . . Had worst walk-to-strikeout ratio of his career, but he's one of only four players with more walks than strikeouts in each of past 10 seasons; others: George Brett, Greg Gross, Willie Randolph. . . . Hitless in last 15 at-bats as pinch hitter, back to 1986.

Paul O'Neill
Cincinnati Reds — Bats Left

	AB	H	2B	3B	HR	RBI	BB	SO	BA	SA	OBA
Season	485	122	25	3	16	73	38	65	.252	.414	.306
vs. Left-Handers	86	20	5	1	1	11	4	18	.233	.349	.272
vs. Right-Handers	399	102	20	2	15	62	34	47	.256	.429	.313
Home	237	58	9	0	12	32	18	39	.245	.435	.297
Road	248	64	16	3	4	41	20	26	.258	.395	.314
Grass	157	46	13	3	2	27	15	15	.293	.452	.353
Artificial Turf	328	76	12	0	14	46	23	50	.232	.396	.283
April	64	17	3	0	0	5	2	12	.266	.313	.299
May	75	16	4	0	2	11	6	10	.213	.347	.272
June	85	26	5	0	5	16	12	10	.306	.541	.394
July	83	20	3	1	3	11	7	10	.241	.410	.300
August	87	19	4	0	3	8	7	11	.218	.368	.271
Sept./Oct.	91	24	6	2	3	22	4	12	.264	.473	.289
Leading Off Inn.	123	29	6	0	5	5	5	17	.236	.407	.266
Runners On	223	56	8	2	8	65	19	29	.251	.413	.309
Runners/Scor. Pos.	145	32	5	1	3	52	18	25	.221	.331	.306
Runners On/2 Out	90	23	6	1	2	28	10	11	.256	.411	.343
Scor. Pos./2 Out	63	15	4	0	1	23	10	11	.238	.349	.360
Late Inning Pressure	78	16	6	0	4	13	5	16	.205	.436	.262
Leading Off	24	4	1	0	1	1	1	3	.167	.333	.200
Runners On	26	6	2	0	2	11	3	4	.231	.538	.333
Runners/Scor. Pos.	18	5	2	0	1	9	3	3	.278	.556	.409

RUNS BATTED IN	From 1B	From 2B	From 3B	Scoring Position
Totals	11/146	22/118	24/61	46/179
Percentage	8%	19%	39%	26%
Driving In Runners from 3B with Less than Two Out:		16/31		52%

Loves to face: Eric Show (.750, 6-for-8, 1 HR)
Hates to face: Steve Bedrosian (0-for-5)
What do the following have in common: Kevin Bass, Tim Wallach, Jim Presley, Brook Jacoby, Paul Molitor, Phil Bradley, Chris Sabo? All of them had more at-bats than O'Neill last season, but none had as many home runs or runs batted in. . . . Started 115 of 119 games against right-handed starters, only 14 of 42 vs. southpaws. . . . Only home run of his career against a left-handed pitcher was on June 25 off Fernando Valenzuela. Led N.L. with five home runs vs. Los Angeles last season, including homers in three straight games at Riverfront in August. . . . One of five N.L. players to have hits in seven consecutive at-bats last season. . . . Career averages: .306 on grass fields, .231 on artificial turf.

Jose Oquendo
St. Louis Cardinals — Bats Left and Right

	AB	H	2B	3B	HR	RBI	BB	SO	BA	SA	OBA
Season	451	125	10	1	7	46	52	40	.277	.350	.350
vs. Left-Handers	154	46	4	0	7	30	12	8	.299	.461	.343
vs. Right-Handers	297	79	6	1	0	16	40	32	.266	.293	.353
Home	228	66	4	0	4	24	26	19	.289	.360	.362
Road	223	59	6	1	3	22	26	21	.265	.341	.337
Grass	104	29	2	0	1	10	14	11	.279	.327	.361
Artificial Turf	347	96	8	1	6	36	38	29	.277	.357	.346
April	26	7	1	0	0	1	3	1	.269	.308	.345
May	59	18	0	0	1	6	8	2	.305	.356	.388
June	107	30	3	1	1	8	6	8	.280	.355	.316
July	79	21	1	0	1	8	12	9	.266	.316	.363
August	102	30	2	0	4	16	7	11	.294	.431	.339
Sept./Oct.	78	19	3	0	0	7	16	9	.244	.282	.365
Leading Off Inn.	102	31	3	0	2	2	18	10	.304	.392	.408
Runners On	190	53	4	1	4	43	19	21	.279	.374	.340
Runners/Scor. Pos.	111	31	2	1	3	41	13	17	.279	.396	.346
Runners On/2 Out	80	20	1	1	2	20	14	12	.250	.363	.362
Scor. Pos./2 Out	55	12	1	1	2	20	10	11	.218	.382	.338
Late Inning Pressure	84	20	2	0	1	6	10	15	.238	.298	.316
Leading Off	22	5	0	0	0	0	3	4	.227	.227	.320
Runners On	34	10	2	0	1	6	4	10	.294	.441	.359
Runners/Scor. Pos.	21	3	1	0	0	4	4	8	.143	.190	.269

RUNS BATTED IN	From 1B	From 2B	From 3B	Scoring Position
Totals	4/126	11/81	24/52	35/133
Percentage	3%	14%	46%	26%
Driving In Runners from 3B with Less than Two Out:	15/23			65%

Loves to face: Dave Dravecky (.467, 7-for-15)
Hates to face: Larry Andersen (0-for-9)
Started games at seven different positions last season; no other N.L. player started at more than four positions.... Did not start at either battery position, but played one game at each, pitching four innings on May 14, and catching one on Sept. 24.... Ended the season with one hit in his last 27 at-bats.... Has batted .283 in three seasons with Cardinals after .217 average in two years with Mets.... Committed seven errors in 36 games on grass fields, but only four in 102 games on artificial surfaces.... Had only two home runs in 903 career at-bats prior to last year's power surge. All nine homers have been hit off left-handed pitchers; also has one postseason home run (off a lefty, natch).

Tom Pagnozzi
St. Louis Cardinals — Bats Right

	AB	H	2B	3B	HR	RBI	BB	SO	BA	SA	OBA
Season	195	55	9	0	0	15	11	32	.282	.328	.319
vs. Left-Handers	108	30	4	0	0	9	7	18	.278	.315	.322
vs. Right-Handers	87	25	5	0	0	6	4	14	.287	.345	.315
Home	82	26	5	0	0	3	4	12	.317	.378	.345
Road	113	29	4	0	0	12	7	20	.257	.292	.300
Grass	38	12	3	0	0	6	2	6	.316	.395	.350
Artificial Turf	157	43	6	0	0	9	9	26	.274	.312	.311
April	5	0	0	0	0	0	0	0	.000	.000	.000
May	27	8	1	0	0	5	3	4	.296	.333	.367
June	45	10	4	0	0	0	2	11	.222	.311	.255
July	27	11	1	0	0	3	1	0	.407	.444	.429
August	43	9	1	0	0	3	1	9	.209	.233	.222
Sept./Oct.	48	17	2	0	0	4	4	8	.354	.396	.404
Leading Off Inn.	50	11	3	0	0	0	3	9	.220	.280	.264
Runners On	86	23	2	0	0	15	4	14	.267	.291	.297
Runners/Scor. Pos.	48	14	1	0	0	15	3	9	.292	.313	.327
Runners On/2 Out	38	9	1	0	0	4	3	6	.237	.263	.293
Scor. Pos./2 Out	24	4	0	0	0	4	2	4	.167	.167	.231
Late Inning Pressure	44	11	0	0	0	3	2	10	.250	.250	.283
Leading Off	12	2	0	0	0	0	1	2	.167	.167	.231
Runners On	17	3	0	0	0	3	0	5	.176	.176	.176
Runners/Scor. Pos.	10	2	0	0	0	3	0	4	.200	.200	.200

RUNS BATTED IN	From 1B	From 2B	From 3B	Scoring Position
Totals	1/61	7/39	7/18	14/57
Percentage	2%	18%	39%	25%
Driving In Runners from 3B with Less than Two Out:	5/7			71%

Loves to face: Terry Mulholland (.800, 4-for-5)
Hates to face: John Smiley (0-for-6, 3 SO)
Homered twice in 48 at-bats for St. Louis in 1987; pinch hit once in N.L.C.S., then was starting DH in opening game of World Series at Minnesota.... Had five hits in 14 at-bats with runners in scoring position in 1987. That combines with the figures above for a career average of .306 with RISP.... Batted .154 (4-for-26) as pinch hitter last season.... Batted .314 in 47 games in the starting lineup last season. Started 26 games at first base, 19 at catcher, two at third; started 26 of 58 games in which Redbirds faced left-handed starters, but only 21 of 104 vs. right-handers.... Born July 30, 1962, seven days before the death of Marilyn Monroe. Accordingly, Pag is among the few who is not a suspect.

Rafael Palmeiro
Chicago Cubs — Bats Left

	AB	H	2B	3B	HR	RBI	BB	SO	BA	SA	OBA
Season	580	178	41	5	8	54	38	34	.307	.436	.349
vs. Left-Handers	171	57	11	4	2	19	9	11	.333	.480	.364
vs. Right-Handers	409	121	30	1	6	35	29	23	.296	.418	.343
Home	290	93	16	4	8	35	19	19	.321	.486	.362
Road	290	85	25	1	0	19	19	15	.293	.386	.337
Grass	414	126	21	5	8	42	27	27	.304	.437	.347
Artificial Turf	166	52	20	0	0	12	11	7	.313	.434	.354
April	81	25	9	0	1	7	7	4	.309	.457	.360
May	106	39	9	0	4	13	8	3	.368	.566	.410
June	119	35	6	1	1	9	3	7	.294	.387	.320
July	103	27	3	1	0	2	5	5	.262	.311	.296
August	100	29	7	2	0	10	8	11	.290	.400	.336
Sept./Oct.	71	23	7	1	2	13	7	4	.324	.535	.385
Leading Off Inn.	111	40	10	1	3	3	4	7	.360	.550	.388
Runners On	245	64	12	1	2	48	25	16	.261	.343	.327
Runners/Scor. Pos.	150	39	9	1	2	47	24	13	.260	.373	.354
Runners On/2 Out	102	25	4	0	0	14	16	6	.245	.284	.347
Scor. Pos./2 Out	70	15	4	0	0	14	15	5	.214	.271	.353
Late Inning Pressure	87	24	6	2	0	6	5	4	.276	.391	.315
Leading Off	15	5	1	1	0	0	1	0	.333	.533	.375
Runners On	46	10	2	0	0	6	3	3	.217	.261	.265
Runners/Scor. Pos.	26	3	0	0	0	5	2	2	.115	.115	.179

RUNS BATTED IN	From 1B	From 2B	From 3B	Scoring Position
Totals	3/161	20/123	23/56	43/179
Percentage	2%	16%	41%	24%
Driving In Runners from 3B with Less than Two Out:	17/28			61%

Loves to face: Andy Hawkins (.500, 4-for-8, 1 HR)
Hates to face: John Dopson (.143, 1-for-7)
Only the second N.L. player to qualify for the batting title (502 PA) without a game-winning RBI since that category was born in 1980. The other: Alan Wiggins in 1984.... Palmeiro had eight game-tying RBI, and nine go-ahead RBI. Every other N.L. player with more than 15 RBI last season had at least one game-winner.... His only hit in 10 career at-bats with the bases loaded was a grand slam off Bob Kipper on Oct 1.... Career breakdown: .326 with the bases empty, .252 with runners on base, .244 with runners in scoring position, .208 with RISP and two outs.... Leading hitter in major leagues on Sundays last season (.371); now he'll have to get used to Sunday *night* games in Arlington.

Lance Parrish
Philadelphia Phillies — Bats Right

	AB	H	2B	3B	HR	RBI	BB	SO	BA	SA	OBA
Season	424	91	17	2	15	60	47	93	.215	.370	.293
vs. Left-Handers	131	33	5	1	4	19	15	19	.252	.397	.336
vs. Right-Handers	293	58	12	1	11	41	32	74	.198	.358	.274
Home	213	48	9	2	11	34	22	42	.225	.441	.294
Road	211	43	8	0	4	26	25	51	.204	.299	.292
Grass	118	30	5	0	3	17	13	33	.254	.373	.331
Artificial Turf	306	61	12	2	12	43	34	60	.199	.369	.278
April	66	16	5	1	4	17	11	17	.242	.530	.351
May	91	24	4	0	4	16	6	16	.264	.440	.307
June	86	17	2	0	3	12	14	18	.198	.326	.307
July	27	5	3	0	1	4	1	4	.185	.407	.214
August	74	13	0	0	1	6	7	15	.176	.216	.256
Sept./Oct.	80	16	3	1	2	5	8	23	.200	.338	.270
Leading Off Inn.	94	18	0	0	4	4	5	18	.191	.330	.248
Runners On	188	44	9	1	9	54	29	35	.255	.457	.347
Runners/Scor. Pos.	126	28	4	1	3	38	22	29	.222	.341	.327
Runners On/2 Out	77	21	5	0	5	24	10	15	.273	.532	.356
Scor. Pos./2 Out	55	12	2	0	2	16	6	13	.218	.364	.295
Late Inning Pressure	75	14	1	1	0	5	12	16	.187	.227	.299
Leading Off	24	3	0	0	0	0	1	4	.125	.125	.160
Runners On	26	7	1	0	0	5	8	7	.269	.308	.441
Runners/Scor. Pos.	20	4	1	0	0	5	6	7	.200	.250	.385

RUNS BATTED IN	From 1B	From 2B	From 3B	Scoring Position
Totals	13/123	11/99	21/47	32/146
Percentage	11%	11%	45%	22%
Driving In Runners from 3B with Less than Two Out:	13/23			57%

Loves to face: Jamie Moyer (.348, 8-for-23, 4 HR)
Hates to face: Dave Schmidt (.071, 1-for-14, 1 HR)
Home runs have decreased in every year since That Championship Season: 33, 28, 22, 17, 15.... Has driven in less than 20 percent of runners from scoring position in LIPS in four of last five seasons.... Batted .191 after the All-Star break, 2d lowest in N.L. (minimum: two PA per game).... Angels got seven years and 968 games out of last catcher they acquired from Phils.... A.L. totals: .263 batting average, one home run every 20 at-bats; N.L. totals: .230 batting average, one home run every 28 at-bats. Could it be that Parrish has been hiding out for two years, with his place being taken by ex-Red Sox and Braves catcher Bob Tillman (.232 career hitter with one homer every 29 at-bats)?

Tony Pena

St. Louis Cardinals — Bats Right

	AB	H	2B	3B	HR	RBI	BB	SO	BA	SA	OBA
Season	505	133	23	1	10	52	33	60	.263	.372	.308
vs. Left-Handers	166	55	15	0	5	18	13	14	.331	.512	.380
vs. Right-Handers	339	78	8	1	5	34	20	46	.230	.304	.272
Home	255	66	11	0	4	22	16	31	.259	.349	.301
Road	250	67	12	1	6	30	17	29	.268	.396	.314
Grass	125	24	5	1	1	13	10	19	.192	.272	.254
Artificial Turf	380	109	18	0	9	39	23	41	.287	.405	.326
April	67	15	2	0	2	3	3	12	.224	.343	.257
May	106	29	4	0	4	15	7	11	.274	.425	.322
June	99	26	2	1	1	11	4	10	.263	.333	.288
July	78	19	5	0	1	8	5	9	.244	.346	.286
August	77	19	3	0	1	6	10	8	.247	.325	.333
Sept./Oct.	78	25	7	0	1	9	4	10	.321	.449	.349
Leading Off Inn.	118	28	7	0	3	3	6	15	.237	.373	.274
Runners On	223	59	9	0	4	46	19	17	.265	.359	.317
Runners/Scor. Pos.	131	32	4	0	2	40	17	12	.244	.321	.322
Runners On/2 Out	94	31	3	0	2	20	10	9	.330	.426	.394
Scor. Pos./2 Out	61	18	1	0	1	17	9	8	.295	.361	.386
Late Inning Pressure	93	27	4	1	2	12	7	7	.290	.419	.333
Leading Off	28	6	2	0	0	0	1	5	.214	.286	.241
Runners On	38	14	1	0	2	12	5	0	.368	.553	.422
Runners/Scor. Pos.	22	9	1	0	1	10	4	0	.409	.591	.464

RUNS BATTED IN	From 1B	From 2B	From 3B	Scoring Position
Totals	7/166	11/105	24/56	35/161
Percentage	4%	10%	43%	22%
Driving In Runners from 3B with Less than Two Out:			14/31	45%

Loves to face: Don Carman (.478, 11-for-23, 2 HR)
Hates to face: Dwight Gooden (.152, 5-for-33)

8th different catcher in last eight years to lead N.L. in fielding percentage. No catcher has successfully defended that title since Johnny Edwards (1969–71). In the last 18 seasons, 17 different catchers have led league.... One of three N.L. players to bat 100+ points higher against left-handers than against right-handers last season (minimum: 100 AB vs. each). Career average of .302 vs. southpaws, .264 vs. right-handers.... Homered in each game of a three-game set with Astros at Busch Stadium in May, but hit only one other home homer all year.... One hit in 12 at-bats with the bases loaded last season, dropping his career average with the bases full to .217.

Terry Pendleton

St. Louis Cardinals — Bats Left and Right

	AB	H	2B	3B	HR	RBI	BB	SO	BA	SA	OBA
Season	391	99	20	2	6	53	21	51	.253	.361	.293
vs. Left-Handers	119	39	9	0	1	26	4	6	.328	.429	.349
vs. Right-Handers	272	60	11	2	5	27	17	45	.221	.331	.268
Home	207	58	15	2	3	32	14	26	.280	.415	.326
Road	184	41	5	0	3	21	7	25	.223	.299	.254
Grass	106	25	3	0	2	11	4	14	.236	.321	.268
Artificial Turf	285	74	17	2	4	42	17	37	.260	.375	.302
April	82	18	4	0	1	6	6	9	.220	.305	.270
May	56	21	7	0	1	12	8	9	.375	.554	.446
June	8	1	0	0	0	0	1	1	.125	.125	.222
July	93	24	4	1	2	17	0	11	.258	.387	.266
August	116	25	4	0	1	13	4	17	.216	.276	.246
Sept./Oct.	36	10	1	1	1	5	2	4	.278	.444	.316
Leading Off Inn.	76	19	5	0	1	1	2	10	.250	.355	.269
Runners On	185	48	10	1	1	48	10	27	.259	.341	.300
Runners/Scor. Pos.	119	36	9	1	0	45	9	15	.303	.395	.353
Runners On/2 Out	86	21	5	0	1	22	7	14	.244	.337	.301
Scor. Pos./2 Out	61	17	4	0	0	19	7	9	.279	.344	.353
Late Inning Pressure	55	10	3	0	0	3	3	12	.182	.236	.220
Leading Off	9	2	1	0	0	0	0	1	.222	.333	.222
Runners On	29	4	1	0	0	3	3	5	.138	.172	.212
Runners/Scor. Pos.	14	3	1	0	0	3	3	1	.214	.286	.333

RUNS BATTED IN	From 1B	From 2B	From 3B	Scoring Position
Totals	3/129	17/86	27/57	44/143
Percentage	2%	20%	47%	31%
Driving In Runners from 3B with Less than Two Out:			17/25	68%

Loves to face: Kelly Downs (.545, 6-for-11, 1 HR)
Hates to face: Randy Myers (0-for-5, 3 SO)

Average of 2.49 assists per nine innings was the highest among major league third basemen last season.... Career average of .344 (22-for-64, two HR) with the bases loaded.... One of three N.L. players to bat 100+ points higher against left-handers than against right-handers last season (minimum: 100 AB vs. each), but the other two (Tony Pena and Tracy Jones) are strictly right-handed batters. ... Batted .295 in day games, .234 at night. Has hit for a higher average in day games than after dark in each of his five seasons in majors. Career averages: .282 (one HR every 54 AB) in day games, .253 (one HR every 156 AB) at night. Obviously, the night doesn't belong to Pendleton.

Gerald Perry

Atlanta Braves — Bats Left

	AB	H	2B	3B	HR	RBI	BB	SO	BA	SA	OBA
Season	547	164	29	1	8	74	36	49	.300	.400	.338
vs. Left-Handers	211	57	7	0	3	27	4	24	.270	.346	.279
vs. Right-Handers	336	107	22	1	5	47	32	25	.318	.435	.373
Home	280	88	20	0	4	42	18	28	.314	.429	.351
Road	267	76	9	1	4	32	18	21	.285	.371	.325
Grass	414	120	23	1	4	56	28	42	.290	.379	.330
Artificial Turf	133	44	6	0	4	18	8	7	.331	.466	.364
April	61	14	2	0	1	8	5	5	.230	.311	.284
May	109	36	6	0	2	18	8	8	.330	.440	.376
June	71	30	1	1	2	14	3	5	.423	.549	.442
July	104	32	6	0	1	8	6	11	.308	.394	.354
August	100	30	5	0	0	15	6	7	.300	.350	.327
Sept./Oct.	102	22	9	0	2	11	6	13	.216	.363	.255
Leading Off Inn.	104	26	5	0	1	1	1	4	.250	.327	.257
Runners On	254	91	17	1	5	71	23	18	.358	.492	.397
Runners/Scor. Pos.	127	44	8	1	2	63	19	10	.346	.472	.404
Runners On/2 Out	97	36	4	1	2	25	9	7	.371	.495	.425
Scor. Pos./2 Out	53	19	1	1	1	23	8	4	.358	.472	.443
Late Inning Pressure	105	28	4	1	1	10	7	11	.267	.352	.313
Leading Off	21	5	1	0	0	0	0	2	.238	.286	.238
Runners On	48	16	2	1	1	10	6	1	.333	.479	.407
Runners/Scor. Pos.	24	6	0	1	1	9	6	0	.250	.458	.400

RUNS BATTED IN	From 1B	From 2B	From 3B	Scoring Position
Totals	7/176	33/107	26/48	59/155
Percentage	4%	31%	54%	38%
Driving In Runners from 3B with Less than Two Out:			21/28	75%

Loves to face: Jeff Parrett (4-for-4, 2 BB)
Hates to face: Larry McWilliams (0-for-8, 4 SO)

Hit 109 points higher with men on base than with bases empty, 2d widest difference in N.L. last season (min: 100 AB each way).... Only N.L. player to bat 100+ points higher vs. fly-ball pitchers (.351) than vs. ground-ballers (.250) in '88 (minimum: 100 AB vs. each).... Technically, Perry was not a .300 hitter: he was removed from game on final Saturday of season after his average fell to .2998. Those looking to protect .300 averages should remember that when it comes to "batting .300" (or similar plateaus), rounding up does not apply. Rounding is done merely for convenience, not for precision, in presentation of statistics. (Bob Uecker, who says he hit ".200" in his career, actually hit .1997. Sorry, Uke!)

Terry Puhl

Houston Astros — Bats Left

	AB	H	2B	3B	HR	RBI	BB	SO	BA	SA	OBA
Season	234	71	7	2	3	19	35	30	.303	.389	.395
vs. Left-Handers	19	4	0	0	0	2	1	5	.211	.211	.250
vs. Right-Handers	215	67	7	2	3	17	34	25	.312	.405	.406
Home	106	40	4	2	2	10	18	10	.377	.509	.464
Road	128	31	3	0	1	9	17	20	.242	.289	.336
Grass	72	22	1	0	0	6	8	9	.306	.319	.383
Artificial Turf	162	49	6	2	3	13	27	21	.302	.420	.400
April	20	4	1	0	0	0	5	5	.200	.250	.360
May	23	6	1	0	0	0	3	2	.261	.304	.346
June	43	19	0	0	0	5	7	4	.442	.442	.502
July	55	19	2	1	3	6	6	7	.345	.582	.419
August	61	16	3	1	0	8	10	6	.262	.344	.361
Sept./Oct.	32	7	0	0	0	0	4	6	.219	.219	.255
Leading Off Inn.	49	15	1	2	2	7	7	5	.306	.510	.393
Runners On	89	23	1	0	0	16	15	16	.258	.270	.368
Runners/Scor. Pos.	53	16	1	0	0	16	10	11	.302	.321	.415
Runners On/2 Out	34	5	0	0	0	4	7	11	.147	.147	.310
Scor. Pos./2 Out	19	3	0	0	0	4	6	8	.158	.158	.385
Late Inning Pressure	48	18	1	1	1	5	14	7	.375	.500	.516
Leading Off	22	9	1	0	1	1	3	3	.409	.591	.480
Runners On	15	4	0	0	0	4	8	4	.267	.267	.520
Runners/Scor. Pos.	7	3	0	0	0	4	6	2	.429	.429	.667

RUNS BATTED IN	From 1B	From 2B	From 3B	Scoring Position
Totals	0/63	5/38	11/20	16/58
Percentage	0%	13%	55%	28%
Driving In Runners from 3B with Less than Two Out:			9/14	64%

Loves to face: Charlie Puleo (.643, 9-for-14)
Hates to face: Paul Assenmacher (0-for-6, 4 SO)

Made two errors last season, dropping his career fielding percentage from .9931 to .9926; he's still all-time leader, but Brett Butler (.9918) is ready to take over if Puhl falters.... Only player in N.L. to bat at least 40 times in double-play situations without grounding into any double plays.... Career high batting average was a result of batting only 21 times vs. left-handers. His .301 mark in 1984 (when he came to plate over 500 times) carries more weight than his .303 average last season.... Batted 135 points higher at home than on road; among major league players with at least 100 at-bats in each, that's the largest difference by anyone who doesn't spend his autumns with the L.A. Raiders.

Tim Raines

Montreal Expos — Bats Left and Right

	AB	H	2B	3B	HR	RBI	BB	SO	BA	SA	OBA
Season	429	116	19	7	12	48	53	44	.270	.431	.350
vs. Left-Handers	125	33	4	1	4	15	10	11	.264	.408	.321
vs. Right-Handers	304	83	15	6	8	33	43	33	.273	.441	.362
Home	202	57	12	2	5	25	21	21	.282	.436	.350
Road	227	59	7	5	7	23	32	23	.260	.427	.351
Grass	128	31	4	3	4	12	20	15	.242	.414	.349
Artificial Turf	301	85	15	4	8	36	33	29	.282	.439	.351
April	84	23	1	1	3	11	11	8	.274	.417	.354
May	107	33	4	3	1	10	19	7	.308	.430	.414
June	86	20	6	2	3	9	12	7	.233	.453	.333
July	50	13	2	0	2	6	1	10	.260	.420	.275
August	96	24	5	1	3	11	10	12	.250	.417	.315
Sept./Oct.	6	3	1	0	0	1	0	0	.500	.667	.500
Leading Off Inn.	158	39	9	3	3	3	14	18	.247	.399	.312
Runners On	139	44	6	3	6	42	27	10	.317	.532	.421
Runners/Scor. Pos.	80	26	4	1	3	34	24	7	.325	.513	.463
Runners On/2 Out	54	19	2	2	3	17	14	5	.352	.630	.485
Scor. Pos./2 Out	36	12	2	1	1	12	13	4	.333	.528	.510
Late Inning Pressure	75	26	2	1	2	13	12	7	.347	.480	.443
Leading Off	24	5	1	0	0	0	3	4	.208	.250	.321
Runners On	31	15	1	1	2	13	6	1	.484	.774	.568
Runners/Scor. Pos.	16	9	1	0	0	8	6	1	.563	.625	.682

RUNS BATTED IN	From 1B	From 2B	From 3B	Scoring Position
Totals	5/92	8/57	23/41	31/98
Percentage	5%	14%	56%	32%
Driving In Runners from 3B with Less than Two Out:			15/24	63%

Loves to face: Tom Browning (.524, 11-for-21, 2 HR)
Hates to face: Todd Worrell (.077, 1-for-13)

Career average in Late-Inning Pressure Situations (.352) is 56 points higher than in other at-bats, largest difference of any player over the last 10 seasons (minimum: 250 LIPS AB). Next three on that list are Jeff Newman, Garth Iorg, and Glenn Hoffman. . . . From 1984 to 1987, became only eighth player, but the first since Ty Cobb (1909–13), to hit .300 and steal 50 bases for four straight seasons. He didn't reach either plateau in 1988 (.270, 33 SBs). . . . One of six players to hit home runs from both sides of plate in a single game last season; that was the first multi-HR game of his career. . . . Started only eight games in the 3d spot in the batting order last season, after 81 starts there in 1987.

Rafael Ramirez

Houston Astros — Bats Right

	AB	H	2B	3B	HR	RBI	BB	SO	BA	SA	OBA
Season	566	156	30	5	6	58	18	61	.276	.378	.298
vs. Left-Handers	193	59	14	3	2	20	5	16	.306	.440	.322
vs. Right-Handers	373	97	16	2	4	38	13	45	.260	.346	.287
Home	274	70	12	2	2	26	6	32	.255	.336	.274
Road	292	86	18	3	4	32	12	29	.295	.418	.321
Grass	173	50	9	1	2	17	8	15	.289	.387	.319
Artificial Turf	393	106	21	4	4	41	10	46	.270	.374	.290
April	74	17	4	1	1	4	2	11	.230	.351	.247
May	89	25	4	2	1	14	6	6	.281	.404	.323
June	85	22	3	1	0	12	4	8	.259	.318	.292
July	105	26	6	1	1	9	2	17	.248	.352	.257
August	104	30	5	0	1	8	2	8	.288	.365	.303
Sept./Oct.	109	36	8	0	2	11	4	11	.330	.459	.354
Leading Off Inn.	130	29	7	1	1	1	5	8	.223	.315	.257
Runners On	234	69	13	2	3	55	10	26	.295	.406	.321
Runners/Scor. Pos.	142	44	3	1	2	50	10	15	.310	.387	.346
Runners On/2 Out	113	34	5	0	1	24	8	16	.301	.352	.352
Scor. Pos./2 Out	80	24	3	0	0	21	8	9	.300	.338	.364
Late Inning Pressure	93	21	4	0	1	6	4	7	.226	.301	.258
Leading Off	25	2	1	0	0	0	2	0	.080	.120	.148
Runners On	33	8	1	0	1	6	1	3	.242	.364	.265
Runners/Scor. Pos.	18	4	0	0	0	4	1	2	.222	.222	.263

RUNS BATTED IN	From 1B	From 2B	From 3B	Scoring Position
Totals	8/168	21/117	23/63	44/180
Percentage	5%	18%	37%	24%
Driving In Runners from 3B with Less than Two Out:			17/29	59%

Loves to face: Jim Gott (.545, 6-for-11)
Hates to face: Joe Price (.056, 1-for-18)

After eight seasons on sunbaked infield at Atlanta, he posted the best fielding percentage of his career in his first season in the Astrodome. . . . Led N.L. shortstops with 154 games played, but his average of 2.73 assists per nine innings was the lowest in league (minimum: 500 innings). . . . Had six hits, including his first career grand slam, in 15 at-bats with the bases loaded last season. . . . RBI total edged his previous career high by one. He drove in 58 runs for the 1983 Braves, a team that led N.L. in runs and batting average that season. . . . Drove in eight runners from first base last season, one fewer than Dale Murphy. . . . September batting average (.337) was 4th highest in N.L.

Randy Ready

San Diego Padres — Bats Right

	AB	H	2B	3B	HR	RBI	BB	SO	BA	SA	OBA
Season	331	88	16	2	7	39	39	38	.266	.390	.346
vs. Left-Handers	147	42	8	1	5	23	18	13	.286	.456	.361
vs. Right-Handers	184	46	8	1	2	16	21	25	.250	.337	.333
Home	147	39	5	1	3	20	20	17	.265	.374	.353
Road	184	49	11	1	4	19	19	21	.266	.402	.340
Grass	257	70	11	2	5	26	28	32	.272	.389	.346
Artificial Turf	74	18	5	0	2	13	11	6	.243	.392	.345
April	58	12	1	0	2	5	8	8	.207	.328	.303
May	73	22	6	1	2	9	11	10	.301	.493	.395
June	54	15	4	0	1	6	5	8	.278	.407	.350
July	39	17	2	1	0	6	2	5	.436	.538	.465
August	51	6	0	0	0	1	5	5	.118	.118	.196
Sept./Oct.	56	16	3	0	2	12	8	2	.286	.446	.369
Leading Off Inn.	64	19	4	0	2	2	1	5	.297	.453	.318
Runners On	143	39	7	2	3	35	21	19	.273	.413	.367
Runners/Scor. Pos.	87	23	4	2	0	28	16	16	.264	.356	.380
Runners On/2 Out	63	14	2	0	0	11	10	8	.222	.286	.329
Scor. Pos./2 Out	47	11	0	0	0	11	8	6	.234	.319	.345
Late Inning Pressure	70	14	0	0	1	5	6	14	.200	.243	.273
Leading Off	18	6	0	0	1	1	0	2	.333	.500	.333
Runners On	31	3	0	0	0	4	5	9	.097	.097	.243
Runners/Scor. Pos.	19	3	0	0	0	4	3	7	.158	.158	.304

RUNS BATTED IN	From 1B	From 2B	From 3B	Scoring Position
Totals	4/94	15/73	13/36	28/109
Percentage	4%	21%	36%	26%
Driving In Runners from 3B with Less than Two Out:			9/15	60%

Loves to face: Bob Knepper (.667, 8-for-12, 1 HR)
Hates to face: Orel Hershiser (0-for-11)

Batted .452 in day games, .181 at night, the largest difference by any player in the majors last season (minimum: 100 AB each way). Started 25 day games and hit safely in 24 of them, including the last 20 in succession. . . . Batted .208 (5-for-24) as pinch hitter, but he was 4-for-9 pinch hitting in day games! . . . Career breakdown: .255 with the bases empty, .288 with runners on base, .297 with runners in scoring position, .303 with RISP and two outs. . . . Walked one more time than he struck out last season. In 1988, there were 239 players in majors with at least 300 plate appearances; only 43 had more free passes than strikeouts, while 188 had more whiffs than walks.

Jeff Reed

Expos/Reds — Bats Left

	AB	H	2B	3B	HR	RBI	BB	SO	BA	SA	OBA
Season	265	60	9	2	1	16	28	41	.226	.287	.299
vs. Left-Handers	23	3	0	0	0	0	4	6	.130	.130	.259
vs. Right-Handers	242	57	9	2	1	16	24	35	.236	.302	.303
Home	126	25	4	1	1	6	10	26	.198	.270	.255
Road	139	35	5	1	0	10	18	15	.252	.302	.338
Grass	103	27	4	0	0	5	14	12	.262	.301	.350
Artificial Turf	162	33	5	2	1	11	14	29	.204	.278	.266
April	37	11	1	1	0	3	9	4	.297	.378	.426
May	48	11	1	1	0	5	2	11	.229	.292	.260
June	38	5	1	0	0	1	2	7	.132	.158	.175
July	21	5	2	0	0	1	2	1	.238	.333	.304
August	39	9	1	0	0	4	4	5	.231	.256	.302
Sept./Oct.	82	19	3	0	1	2	9	13	.232	.305	.308
Leading Off Inn.	71	16	4	0	0	0	5	7	.225	.282	.276
Runners On	105	23	1	2	0	15	16	16	.219	.267	.320
Runners/Scor. Pos.	58	14	0	2	0	14	10	12	.241	.310	.348
Runners On/2 Out	42	8	1	0	0	4	9	6	.190	.214	.333
Scor. Pos./2 Out	26	3	0	0	0	3	7	5	.115	.115	.303
Late Inning Pressure	37	10	1	1	0	3	6	5	.270	.351	.372
Leading Off	14	2	1	0	0	0	1	1	.143	.214	.200
Runners On	13	5	0	1	0	3	2	3	.385	.538	.467
Runners/Scor. Pos.	7	4	0	1	0	3	1	2	.571	.857	.625

RUNS BATTED IN	From 1B	From 2B	From 3B	Scoring Position
Totals	1/69	4/36	10/31	14/67
Percentage	1%	11%	32%	21%
Driving In Runners from 3B with Less than Two Out:			7/17	41%

Loves to face: Danny Darwin (.417, 5-for-12, 3 2B)
Hates to face: Brian Fisher (0-for-9)

Started 78 games last season, all but one vs. right-handed pitchers. Has come to the plate 742 times in his career, but only 74 vs. lefties. . . . Batted .220 in 43 games for Expos, .232 in 49 games with Reds. . . . One of three players who, in each of last two seasons, has had at least 200 at-bats, but has not hit .230 or slugged .290; others: Rafael Belliard and Gary Pettis. . . . Hitless in nine of ten starts from June 7 to July 22. . . . Started 25 of Reds' last 29 games, but drove in only two runs during that span. . . . His career average is .139 (10-for-72) with runners in scoring position and two outs; at least's he's still ahead of Mario Soto, who batted .133 in those spots.

R.J. Reynolds
Pittsburgh Pirates | | | | | | | | | Bats Left and Right

Pittsburgh Pirates	AB	H	2B	3B	HR	RBI	BB	SO	BA	SA	OBA
Season	323	80	14	2	6	52	20	62	.248	.359	.288
vs. Left-Handers	88	28	6	0	3	12	6	11	.318	.489	.362
vs. Right-Handers	235	52	8	2	3	40	14	51	.221	.311	.261
Home	174	37	7	1	4	26	15	33	.213	.333	.274
Road	149	43	7	1	2	26	5	29	.289	.389	.306
Grass	80	24	4	1	2	16	2	18	.300	.450	.313
Artificial Turf	243	56	10	1	4	36	18	44	.230	.329	.280
April	44	11	2	0	3	11	6	6	.250	.500	.333
May	70	17	4	0	0	11	4	13	.243	.300	.284
June	38	9	0	0	1	4	2	6	.237	.316	.275
July	55	14	2	2	0	9	0	11	.255	.364	.250
August	80	21	6	0	2	8	4	13	.263	.413	.291
Sept./Oct.	36	8	0	0	0	9	4	13	.222	.222	.300
Leading Off Inn.	65	14	4	0	1	1	2	16	.215	.323	.239
Runners On	154	41	7	2	2	48	10	24	.266	.377	.304
Runners/Scor. Pos.	99	28	5	2	2	47	9	19	.283	.434	.330
Runners On/2 Out	70	17	2	2	1	17	6	14	.243	.371	.303
Scor. Pos./2 Out	49	13	2	2	1	17	5	12	.265	.449	.333
Late Inning Pressure	82	20	2	0	2	10	7	14	.244	.341	.300
Leading Off	15	4	1	0	0	0	2	3	.267	.333	.353
Runners On	43	8	0	0	0	8	2	7	.186	.186	.217
Runners/Scor. Pos.	25	4	0	0	0	8	2	6	.160	.160	.214

RUNS BATTED IN	From 1B	From 2B	From 3B	Scoring Position
Totals	2/114	22/81	22/39	44/120
Percentage	2%	27%	56%	37%
Driving In Runners from 3B with Less than Two Out:		19/22		86%

Loves to face: Orel Hershiser (.433, 13-for-30)
Hates to face: Danny Darwin (0-for-12, 6 SO)
Started only eight of 48 games in which Pirates faced a left-hander, despite his .331 batting average in 145 at-bats vs. southpaws over past two years; he has hit only .232 vs. right-handers during that span. Yearly batting averages vs. right-handers since 1985: .292, .286, .241, .221. . . . Batted only .214 (9-for-42) but drove in 11 runs as a pinch hitter last season, tying Bill Buckner for 2d most in the majors; Graig Nettles led with 13 pinch-hit RBI. . . . Drove in last 11 runners from third base with less than two out, longest streak in N.L. last season; had a similar streak of 11 in 1987. His career rate? 68 percent. . . . Started only six of Pirates' last 30 games.

Ernest Riles
San Francisco Giants | | | | | | | | | Bats Left

San Francisco Giants	AB	H	2B	3B	HR	RBI	BB	SO	BA	SA	OBA
Season	187	55	7	2	3	28	10	33	.294	.401	.323
vs. Left-Handers	23	7	0	0	1	4	1	6	.304	.435	.333
vs. Right-Handers	164	48	7	2	2	24	9	27	.293	.396	.322
Home	84	27	2	1	3	14	6	18	.321	.476	.367
Road	103	28	5	1	0	14	4	15	.272	.340	.288
Grass	133	41	4	1	3	17	9	24	.308	.421	.350
Artificial Turf	54	14	3	1	0	11	1	9	.259	.352	.259
April	0	0	0	0	0	0	0	0	—	—	—
May	0	0	0	0	0	0	0	0	—	—	—
June	40	13	4	0	0	6	1	8	.325	.425	.333
July	42	9	2	0	1	8	3	10	.214	.333	.261
August	45	14	0	0	1	10	1	7	.311	.378	.319
Sept./Oct.	60	19	1	2	1	4	5	8	.317	.450	.364
Leading Off Inn.	41	10	0	0	1	1	1	6	.244	.317	.262
Runners On	83	27	5	0	2	27	6	18	.325	.458	.355
Runners/Scor. Pos.	50	13	3	0	2	26	6	13	.260	.440	.317
Runners On/2 Out	37	12	3	0	1	11	4	9	.324	.486	.390
Scor. Pos./2 Out	24	7	2	0	1	10	4	8	.292	.500	.393
Late Inning Pressure	29	7	1	1	1	5	2	7	.241	.414	.281
Leading Off	12	1	0	0	0	0	0	1	.083	.083	.083
Runners On	13	5	0	1	1	5	1	5	.385	.615	.400
Runners/Scor. Pos.	5	2	0	0	1	5	1	3	.400	1.000	.429

RUNS BATTED IN	From 1B	From 2B	From 3B	Scoring Position
Totals	4/56	9/42	12/23	21/65
Percentage	7%	21%	52%	32%
Driving In Runners from 3B with Less than Two Out:		10/14		71%

Loves to face: Ed Whitson (.455, 5-for-11)
Hates to face: Dennis Rasmussen (.100, 1-for-10)
Figures *above* are for N.L. only. . . . Started 41 games for the Giants last season, all but one of them against right-handed pitchers. Career average of .222 vs. lefties, .282 vs. righties. . . . Yearly batting averages leading off innings: .307, .266, .204, .189. . . . Has hit for a higher average with runners on base than with bases empty in each of four seasons in majors. . . . Played exclusively at shortstop (257 games) in first two years in majors; over last two years, has logged 123 games at third, only 46 at short, and 17 at second. . . . Must like home cooking, be it knockwurst or sourdough bread: He hit .307 at County Stadium last season, .321 at Candlestick, .239 everywhere else.

Luis Rivera
Montreal Expos | | | | | | | | | Bats Right

Montreal Expos	AB	H	2B	3B	HR	RBI	BB	SO	BA	SA	OBA
Season	371	83	17	3	4	30	24	69	.224	.318	.271
vs. Left-Handers	154	34	9	1	2	14	10	30	.221	.331	.268
vs. Right-Handers	217	49	8	2	2	16	14	39	.226	.309	.272
Home	189	46	6	2	2	18	7	35	.243	.328	.266
Road	182	37	11	1	2	12	17	34	.203	.308	.275
Grass	90	17	4	0	2	8	14	19	.189	.300	.305
Artificial Turf	281	66	13	3	2	22	10	50	.235	.324	.259
April	65	13	2	0	1	4	2	12	.200	.277	.224
May	60	14	3	0	1	4	3	8	.233	.333	.266
June	80	18	3	0	2	9	5	13	.225	.338	.264
July	75	16	3	3	0	8	4	17	.213	.333	.263
August	45	13	3	0	0	2	7	6	.289	.356	.385
Sept./Oct.	46	9	3	0	0	3	3	13	.196	.261	.245
Leading Off Inn.	94	20	4	0	0	0	5	21	.213	.255	.253
Runners On	167	40	10	3	1	27	14	29	.240	.353	.293
Runners/Scor. Pos.	104	21	4	2	0	23	12	25	.202	.279	.277
Runners On/2 Out	62	11	4	0	1	8	6	14	.177	.290	.250
Scor. Pos./2 Out	39	5	1	0	0	6	4	13	.128	.154	.244
Late Inning Pressure	74	14	1	2	0	5	2	17	.189	.297	.208
Leading Off	19	2	0	0	0	0	1	5	.105	.105	.150
Runners On	33	8	1	2	0	5	0	7	.242	.394	.235
Runners/Scor. Pos.	20	5	1	1	0	4	0	5	.250	.400	.238

RUNS BATTED IN	From 1B	From 2B	From 3B	Scoring Position
Totals	3/111	10/81	13/41	23/122
Percentage	3%	12%	32%	19%
Driving In Runners from 3B with Less than Two Out:		11/23		48%

Loves to face: Jimmy Jones (.600, 3-for-5)
Hates to face: Jamie Moyer (.056, 1-for-18)
Joins Red Sox in 1989. Don't count him out on a team that has seen Jackie Gutierrez, Glenn Hoffman, Rey Quinones, Spike Owen, Ed Romero, and Jody Reed go through the revolving door at short, all in the past five years. . . . Career batting average of .214 is the same as Bob Forsch's. . . . Has batted under .200 on grass fields in each of his three seasons in majors. . . . Remember all the talk last April about the Expos using two rookies in the middle infield? Paredes and Rivera combined for a .216 batting average and were in the starting lineup as a duo only nine times. . . . His .962 fielding percentage left him 8th among 10 N.L. qualifiers at shortstop; he beat out Barry Larkin and Andres Thomas.

Chris Sabo
Cincinnati Reds | | | | | | | | | Bats Right

Cincinnati Reds	AB	H	2B	3B	HR	RBI	BB	SO	BA	SA	OBA
Season	538	146	40	2	11	44	29	52	.271	.414	.314
vs. Left-Handers	140	40	11	0	4	13	10	11	.286	.450	.338
vs. Right-Handers	398	106	29	2	7	31	19	41	.266	.402	.305
Home	260	77	18	2	8	21	16	20	.296	.473	.344
Road	278	69	22	0	3	23	13	32	.248	.360	.285
Grass	157	39	11	0	3	15	7	17	.248	.376	.292
Artificial Turf	381	107	29	2	8	29	22	35	.281	.430	.323
April	76	20	7	0	4	7	4	7	.263	.513	.305
May	87	25	7	0	2	11	2	7	.287	.437	.303
June	110	41	14	2	4	13	10	10	.373	.645	.430
July	98	18	5	0	1	9	6	11	.184	.265	.241
August	110	29	3	0	0	3	2	10	.264	.291	.289
Sept./Oct.	57	13	4	0	0	1	5	7	.228	.298	.292
Leading Off Inn.	102	33	9	0	5	5	6	3	.324	.559	.361
Runners On	208	52	14	0	2	35	17	25	.250	.346	.313
Runners/Scor. Pos.	115	29	8	0	2	35	14	12	.252	.374	.338
Runners On/2 Out	84	19	5	0	0	8	9	11	.226	.286	.316
Scor. Pos./2 Out	50	10	4	0	0	8	7	5	.200	.280	.310
Late Inning Pressure	92	30	5	0	3	9	4	12	.326	.478	.361
Leading Off	24	11	2	0	3	3	2	2	.458	.917	.519
Runners On	40	11	1	0	0	6	1	4	.275	.300	.293
Runners/Scor. Pos.	23	7	1	0	0	6	1	1	.304	.348	.333

RUNS BATTED IN	From 1B	From 2B	From 3B	Scoring Position
Totals	3/135	13/95	17/43	30/138
Percentage	2%	14%	40%	22%
Driving In Runners from 3B with Less than Two Out:		14/25		56%

Loves to face: Orel Hershiser (.500, 7-for-14)
Hates to face: Greg Maddux (0-for-7)
Batted .312 before All-Star break, 4th best in N.L., but batted only .216 during second half. . . . Had 44 extra-base hits at the break, second in majors to Galarraga (51). . . . Led major league rookies in doubles and stolen bases. . . . Led N.L. with 10 doubles and 12 stolen bases vs. Astros, and with five home runs vs. Giants. . . . The only rookie in majors to play in 25+ games at third base. . . . Interesting contrast to last year's N.L. rookie infielders: Mark Grace and Ron Gant each led majors in errors at their respective positions, while Sabo supplanted Buddy Bell as N.L. fielding percentage leader among third basemen. . . . Reds had had only two such leaders (Don Hoak in '57, Rose in '76) over prior 35 years.

Juan Samuel

Philadelphia Phillies — Bats Right

	AB	H	2B	3B	HR	RBI	BB	SO	BA	SA	OBA
Season	629	153	32	9	12	67	39	151	.243	.380	.298
vs. Left-Handers	168	41	13	2	2	16	16	35	.244	.381	.319
vs. Right-Handers	461	112	19	7	10	51	23	116	.243	.380	.290
Home	320	87	27	6	7	42	25	67	.272	.459	.339
Road	309	66	5	3	5	25	14	84	.214	.298	.253
Grass	165	34	1	1	3	13	6	53	.206	.279	.240
Artificial Turf	464	119	31	8	9	54	33	98	.256	.416	.318
April	81	19	4	3	0	7	6	19	.235	.358	.300
May	110	29	3	2	4	13	7	30	.264	.436	.311
June	124	27	5	1	2	14	10	30	.218	.323	.279
July	99	33	10	1	4	17	5	21	.333	.576	.394
August	108	17	4	0	0	8	6	32	.157	.194	.198
Sept./Oct.	107	28	6	2	2	8	5	19	.262	.411	.313
Leading Off Inn.	189	37	6	2	5	5	15	42	.196	.328	.266
Runners On	247	69	14	5	6	61	18	60	.279	.449	.339
Runners/Scor. Pos.	143	43	9	4	4	56	14	35	.301	.503	.371
Runners On/2 Out	102	23	4	3	2	23	11	26	.225	.382	.319
Scor. Pos./2 Out	70	16	3	3	2	23	8	16	.229	.443	.325
Late Inning Pressure	95	19	4	2	1	11	5	21	.200	.316	.238
Leading Off	25	3	1	1	0	0	1	3	.120	.240	.154
Runners On	50	13	2	1	1	10	3	10	.260	.400	.296
Runners/Scor. Pos.	32	8	1	0	1	10	3	9	.250	.375	.306

RUNS BATTED IN	From 1B	From 2B	From 3B	Scoring Position
Totals	6/157	22/117	27/59	49/176
Percentage	4%	19%	46%	28%
Driving In Runners from 3B with Less than Two Out:			21/31	68%

Loves to face: Walt Terrell (.500, 7-for-14, 2 HR)
Hates to face: Scott Terry (0-for-12)
Averaged 2.58 assists per nine innings, lowest among N.L. second basemen in 1988 (minimum: 500 innings). Started three games in outfield in September. Enter Tommy Herr. . . . Watch out, Cliff Johnson! Since 1986, Samuel is 3-for-3 with a double and two home runs as a pinch hitter. . . . One of three players with 100 whiffs in each of last five seasons. . . . His 151 strikeouts left him two short of N.L. leader Andres Galarraga, ending Sammy's four-year streak leading league. A fifth straight year would have broken major league record he shares with Hack Wilson, Vince DiMaggio, and Reggie Jackson. Samuel should actually thank teammate Don Carman, who fanned Galarraga twice in final game.

Ryne Sandberg

Chicago Cubs — Bats Right

	AB	H	2B	3B	HR	RBI	BB	SO	BA	SA	OBA
Season	618	163	23	8	19	69	54	91	.264	.419	.322
vs. Left-Handers	164	48	6	2	7	26	17	25	.293	.482	.363
vs. Right-Handers	454	115	17	6	12	43	37	66	.253	.396	.306
Home	312	87	10	7	10	42	31	44	.279	.452	.342
Road	306	76	13	1	9	27	23	47	.248	.386	.300
Grass	451	122	15	8	14	58	41	60	.271	.432	.329
Artificial Turf	167	41	8	0	5	11	13	31	.246	.383	.300
April	91	18	4	1	3	8	6	13	.198	.363	.245
May	98	28	3	3	3	14	7	13	.286	.469	.333
June	106	31	5	1	4	12	13	15	.292	.472	.370
July	91	21	1	0	1	7	9	6	.231	.275	.300
August	103	30	3	2	4	12	12	22	.291	.476	.362
Sept./Oct.	129	35	7	1	4	16	7	22	.271	.434	.307
Leading Off Inn.	160	44	7	3	8	8	14	18	.275	.506	.333
Runners On	221	68	8	5	7	57	27	31	.308	.484	.375
Runners/Scor. Pos.	127	35	1	3	5	49	20	21	.276	.449	.362
Runners On/2 Out	82	24	1	4	3	20	13	8	.293	.512	.389
Scor. Pos./2 Out	57	14	0	2	3	18	9	8	.246	.474	.348
Late Inning Pressure	94	23	2	1	3	8	9	20	.245	.383	.311
Leading Off	26	6	1	1	2	2	4	4	.231	.577	.333
Runners On	35	8	0	0	0	5	3	7	.229	.229	.289
Runners/Scor. Pos.	21	5	0	0	0	5	1	3	.238	.238	.273

RUNS BATTED IN	From 1B	From 2B	From 3B	Scoring Position
Totals	8/144	17/96	25/55	42/151
Percentage	6%	18%	45%	28%
Driving In Runners from 3B with Less than Two Out:			19/29	66%

Loves to face: Bob Ojeda (.615, 8-for-13, 3 HR)
Hates to face: Pete Smith (0-for-12)
Has come up to plate 4707 times over past seven years; that's 3d-highest total in majors over that span, behind more famous ironmen Cal Ripken and Dale Murphy. . . . One of four major leaguers to start at least 10 games in both the leadoff and cleanup spots last year, but his last 64 starts were all in the 2d spot in the order. . . . Led major league second basemen with 3.46 assists per nine innings last season. . . . Entering his 7th year as Cubs' regular second baseman, longest stint there since Glenn Beckert (1965-73). Sandberg was Cubs' regular third baseman in 1982. . . . Career average of .304 at Wrigley Field, .266 elsewhere. . . . Career average of .222 in April, .294 after it gets warmer.

Benito Santiago

San Diego Padres — Bats Right

	AB	H	2B	3B	HR	RBI	BB	SO	BA	SA	OBA
Season	492	122	22	2	10	46	24	82	.248	.362	.282
vs. Left-Handers	140	36	4	1	5	17	7	23	.257	.407	.291
vs. Right-Handers	352	86	18	1	5	29	17	59	.244	.344	.278
Home	261	60	12	2	3	23	9	45	.230	.326	.253
Road	231	62	10	0	7	23	15	37	.268	.403	.313
Grass	375	95	19	2	10	43	14	63	.253	.395	.277
Artificial Turf	117	27	3	0	0	3	10	19	.231	.256	.295
April	70	19	2	0	2	7	0	13	.271	.386	.268
May	91	17	5	0	1	6	5	13	.187	.275	.229
June	83	20	3	0	0	6	4	19	.241	.277	.273
July	77	24	6	1	1	2	7	7	.312	.455	.369
August	87	24	1	1	4	11	6	17	.276	.448	.323
Sept./Oct.	84	18	5	0	2	14	2	13	.214	.345	.230
Leading Off Inn.	106	27	4	0	1	1	6	13	.255	.321	.295
Runners On	220	43	11	1	3	39	11	36	.195	.295	.232
Runners/Scor. Pos.	115	17	2	0	1	28	5	25	.148	.191	.176
Runners On/2 Out	87	16	7	1	0	11	4	20	.184	.287	.220
Scor. Pos./2 Out	47	4	1	0	0	5	2	16	.085	.106	.122
Late Inning Pressure	80	18	3	0	2	6	3	13	.225	.338	.250
Leading Off	15	5	1	0	0	0	0	1	.333	.400	.333
Runners On	37	4	1	0	0	4	1	5	.108	.135	.128
Runners/Scor. Pos.	16	2	0	0	0	3	0	3	.125	.125	.118

RUNS BATTED IN	From 1B	From 2B	From 3B	Scoring Position
Totals	11/169	9/89	16/54	25/143
Percentage	7%	10%	30%	17%
Driving In Runners from 3B with Less than Two Out:			12/30	40%

Loves to face: Zane Smith (.429, 6-for-14, 3 HR)
Hates to face: Bob Walk (.067, 1-for-15)
Batted 95 points lower with runners on base than with bases empty last year, 2d largest difference in N.L. (minimum: 100 AB each way). A 41-point difference on career averages is 2d largest in majors over past 10 seasons (only Ivan Calderon has a larger disparity). . . . Career breakdown: .295 with bases empty, .254 with runners on base, .219 with runners in scoring position, .217 with RISP and two out; .308 vs. left-handers, .262 vs. righties. . . . Had hits in eight straight at-bats vs. left-handed pitchers (July 2-15), longest streak of any N.L. player last year. . . . Cut his errors from 22 (in 1987) to 12, but became first N.L. catcher to lead league two years in a row since Andy Seminick, 1949-50.

Nelson Santovenia

Montreal Expos — Bats Right

	AB	H	2B	3B	HR	RBI	BB	SO	BA	SA	OBA
Season	309	73	20	2	8	41	24	77	.236	.392	.294
vs. Left-Handers	79	22	4	1	3	16	11	17	.278	.468	.370
vs. Right-Handers	230	51	16	1	5	25	13	60	.222	.365	.266
Home	163	45	14	1	6	29	9	30	.276	.485	.318
Road	146	28	6	1	2	12	15	47	.192	.288	.268
Grass	74	14	3	0	0	5	9	24	.189	.230	.230
Artificial Turf	235	59	17	2	8	36	15	53	.251	.443	.301
April	0	0	0	0	0	0	0	0	—	—	—
May	42	14	4	0	1	6	6	10	.333	.500	.417
June	48	10	3	0	1	7	2	12	.208	.333	.250
July	69	15	3	1	1	9	5	17	.217	.333	.273
August	78	18	7	0	2	8	3	21	.231	.397	.256
Sept./Oct.	72	16	3	1	3	11	8	17	.222	.417	.309
Leading Off Inn.	60	12	3	0	2	2	4	17	.200	.350	.250
Runners On	139	40	11	2	3	36	12	31	.288	.460	.340
Runners/Scor. Pos.	80	18	5	1	3	30	10	24	.225	.350	.305
Runners On/2 Out	59	12	4	0	2	14	9	15	.203	.373	.319
Scor. Pos./2 Out	41	7	2	0	1	11	7	12	.171	.293	.306
Late Inning Pressure	63	16	6	0	2	5	7	18	.254	.444	.329
Leading Off	19	3	0	0	1	1	1	6	.158	.316	.200
Runners On	20	8	4	0	1	4	3	3	.400	.750	.500
Runners/Scor. Pos.	8	2	0	0	0	2	4	1	.250	.250	.500

RUNS BATTED IN	From 1B	From 2B	From 3B	Scoring Position
Totals	6/99	11/59	16/41	27/100
Percentage	6%	19%	39%	27%
Driving In Runners from 3B with Less than Two Out:			13/20	65%

Loves to face: Doug Drabek (3-for-3, 2 2B)
Hates to face: Jose Rijo (0-for-5, 4 SO)
Drove in 41 runs in only 309 at-bats; among N.L. catchers who caught at least 81 games, only Parrish and LaValliere had better ratios. Point of interest for Expos fans: Gary Carter had 46 RBI in 455 at-bats. . . . Batted 84 points higher in home games than on road last year, 5th-largest difference in N.L. (minimum: 100 AB each way). . . . Drafted, not signed, by Phillies in 29th round of 1979 amateur draft; that was draft in which Jays chose Jay Schroeder in 1st round, and Royals chose both Dan Marino (4th) and John Elway (18th). . . . Member of 1982 national champion Miami Hurricanes. No, he didn't block for Bernie Kosar, we're talking about the collegiate *baseball* champions; the football team was No. 1 in '83.

Steve Sax
Los Angeles Dodgers — Bats Right

	AB	H	2B	3B	HR	RBI	BB	SO	BA	SA	OBA
Season	632	175	19	4	5	56	45	51	.277	.343	.325
vs. Left-Handers	200	58	8	0	3	17	19	13	.290	.375	.352
vs. Right-Handers	432	117	11	4	2	39	26	38	.271	.329	.312
Home	311	94	8	1	2	27	22	20	.302	.354	.348
Road	321	81	11	3	3	29	23	31	.252	.333	.303
Grass	470	131	15	2	3	39	31	35	.279	.338	.322
Artificial Turf	162	44	4	2	2	17	14	16	.272	.358	.333
April	79	17	0	0	1	9	6	8	.215	.253	.267
May	109	35	6	2	4	16	11	6	.321	.523	.383
June	105	32	2	0	0	8	11	7	.305	.324	.371
July	126	43	5	2	0	7	4	9	.341	.413	.364
August	114	25	1	0	0	11	7	14	.219	.228	.264
Sept./Oct.	99	23	5	0	0	5	6	7	.232	.283	.276
Leading Off Inn.	259	57	5	1	3	3	12	22	.220	.282	.255
Runners On	198	66	4	1	2	53	23	13	.333	.394	.402
Runners/Scor. Pos.	120	42	2	1	1	50	21	4	.350	.408	.441
Runners On/2 Out	96	35	2	0	2	35	14	8	.365	.448	.450
Scor. Pos./2 Out	62	26	1	0	1	32	13	3	.419	.484	.520
Late Inning Pressure	82	26	1	0	0	13	8	6	.317	.329	.374
Leading Off	25	5	0	0	0		2	2	.200	.200	.259
Runners On	32	15	1	0	0	13	5	3	.469	.500	.526
Runners/Scor. Pos.	24	11	1	0	0	13	5	1	.458	.500	.533

RUNS BATTED IN	From 1B	From 2B	From 3B	Scoring Position
Totals	5/125	26/104	20/38	46/142
Percentage	4%	25%	53%	32%
Driving In Runners from 3B with Less than Two Out:		7/11		64%

Loves to face: Lee Smith (.389, 7-for-18)
Hates to face: John Dopson (.071, 1-for-14)

Start spreadin' the news: His .419 average with runners in scoring position and two outs was the best in majors last season. . . . Has hit .317 with runners in scoring position over last four years. . . . One of five players with 25 or more steals in each of last seven seasons. . . . Dodgers' leadoff hitter for all of 1988 except for three-week stretch in September. . . . Had first two-home-run game of his career on May 26 vs. Phillies; has not hit a homer since. . . . Batting average in Late-Inning Pressure Situations has been higher than his overall average in each of the last six seasons. But in 1989, he'll be stepping into the ultimate Pressure Situation: a big-money free agent signed by Yankees.

Mike Schmidt
Philadelphia Phillies — Bats Right

	AB	H	2B	3B	HR	RBI	BB	SO	BA	SA	OBA
Season	390	97	21	2	12	62	49	42	.249	.405	.337
vs. Left-Handers	91	30	8	0	3	13	15	4	.330	.516	.435
vs. Right-Handers	299	67	13	2	9	49	34	38	.224	.371	.306
Home	186	54	11	2	6	32	32	20	.290	.468	.401
Road	204	43	10	0	6	30	17	22	.211	.348	.284
Grass	95	22	2	0	4	11	7	11	.232	.379	.284
Artificial Turf	295	75	19	2	8	51	42	31	.254	.414	.352
April	73	18	2	1	3	15	11	9	.247	.425	.349
May	91	16	3	0	2	7	12	12	.176	.275	.269
June	112	31	8	0	1	17	10	10	.277	.375	.341
July	75	21	5	1	4	19	14	7	.280	.533	.404
August	39	11	3	0	2	4	2	4	.282	.513	.317
Sept./Oct.	0	0	0	0	0	0	0	0	—	—	—
Leading Off Inn.	91	19	3	0	5	5	12	10	.209	.407	.301
Runners On	183	55	15	2	5	55	32	16	.301	.486	.407
Runners/Scor. Pos.	117	33	7	2	4	48	26	13	.282	.479	.416
Runners On/2 Out	76	16	3	1	1	14	18	7	.211	.316	.375
Scor. Pos./2 Out	53	13	1	1	1	13	13	7	.245	.358	.412
Late Inning Pressure	61	8	1	0	1	5	5	7	.131	.197	.194
Leading Off	14	1	1	0	0	0	1	3	.071	.143	.133
Runners On	28	5	0	0	0	4	3	2	.179	.179	.250
Runners/Scor. Pos.	21	4	0	0	0	4	3	1	.190	.190	.280

RUNS BATTED IN	From 1B	From 2B	From 3B	Scoring Position
Totals	8/128	14/83	28/59	42/142
Percentage	6%	17%	47%	30%
Driving In Runners from 3B with Less than Two Out:		20/35		57%

Loves to face: Bob Knepper (.402, 33-for-82, 9 HR)
Hates to face: Dennis Martinez (0-for-11, 5 SO)

Oldest N.L. player to start at least half of his team's games in 1988; he turned 39 during final week of season. . . . Batted 139 points lower in Late-Inning Pressure Situations than in other at-bats, largest difference in N.L. last season (minimum: 50 LIPS AB). . . . Leads active players in homers, RBI, runs, total bases, intentional walks, and strikeouts (1,866); he's 70 whiffs shy of Stargell's N.L. record. Reggie is safe at 2,597. . . . Has hit 263 home runs at the Vet, four more than Babe Ruth hit in his own House; leaders at one park: Ott 323 at Polo Grounds; Banks 290 at Wrigley; Mantle 266 at Yankee Stadium. . . . Enters 1989 in third place on Phillies' all-time hit list, seven behind Ed Delahanty, 13 behind Rich Ashburn.

Mike Scioscia
Los Angeles Dodgers — Bats Left

	AB	H	2B	3B	HR	RBI	BB	SO	BA	SA	OBA
Season	408	105	18	0	3	35	38	31	.257	.324	.318
vs. Left-Handers	78	19	0	0	0	8	5	6	.244	.244	.289
vs. Right-Handers	330	86	18	0	3	27	33	25	.261	.342	.325
Home	208	55	7	0	1	20	15	17	.264	.313	.313
Road	200	50	11	0	2	15	23	14	.250	.335	.324
Grass	300	79	12	0	1	27	24	25	.263	.313	.315
Artificial Turf	108	26	6	0	2	8	14	6	.241	.352	.328
April	52	21	5	0	0	10	9	3	.404	.500	.484
May	82	18	2	0	1	5	10	7	.220	.280	.304
June	75	19	1	0	1	8	2	4	.253	.307	.269
July	63	16	6	0	0	4	12	6	.254	.349	.368
August	86	19	1	0	0	4	4	8	.221	.233	.256
Sept./Oct.	50	12	3	0	1	4	1	3	.240	.360	.255
Leading Off Inn.	98	21	3	0	0	0	10	6	.214	.245	.287
Runners On	165	44	6	0	2	34	23	14	.267	.339	.351
Runners/Scor. Pos.	90	21	5	0	0	29	16	9	.233	.289	.339
Runners On/2 Out	68	12	2	0	1	11	13	6	.176	.250	.309
Scor. Pos./2 Out	39	7	2	0	0	8	10	3	.179	.231	.347
Late Inning Pressure	54	15	2	0	0		10	6	.278	.315	.391
Leading Off	15	3	1	0	0	0	4	1	.200	.267	.368
Runners On	19	3	0	0	0	0	6	4	.158	.158	.360
Runners/Scor. Pos.	9	0	0	0	0	0	6	2	.000	.000	.400

RUNS BATTED IN	From 1B	From 2B	From 3B	Scoring Position
Totals	4/120	18/84	10/33	28/117
Percentage	3%	21%	30%	24%
Driving In Runners from 3B with Less than Two Out:		10/18		56%

Loves to face: Mike Krukow (.360, 18-for-50, 3 HR)
Hates to face: John Franco (0-for-10)

Led N.L. in batting in April. . . . Career average of .278 on grass fields, .221 on synthetic turf. That 56-point margin is largest grass-over-turf difference by any N.L. player over last 10 years (minimum: 500 AB on each). . . . Career rate of one strikeout every 17.9 plate appearances is 2d to Tony Gwynn among active N.L. players (minimum: 2000 at-bats). . . . Only player in majors who has hit below .200 with runners on base and two outs in each of past three years (minimum: 50 AB each year). . . . Owns .219 career batting average, with one home run in 146 at-bats, in Late-Inning Pressure Situations with runners on base. But, as Doc Gooden can attest, he's considerably better in such situations in postseason play.

John Shelby
Los Angeles Dodgers — Bats Left and Right

	AB	H	2B	3B	HR	RBI	BB	SO	BA	SA	OBA
Season	494	130	23	6	10	65	44	128	.263	.395	.320
vs. Left-Handers	189	45	4	3	2	21	13	48	.238	.323	.286
vs. Right-Handers	305	85	19	3	8	44	31	80	.279	.439	.340
Home	236	73	11	3	5	42	18	56	.309	.445	.351
Road	258	57	12	3	5	23	26	72	.221	.349	.291
Grass	369	101	16	3	8	51	30	90	.274	.398	.324
Artificial Turf	125	29	7	3	2	14	14	38	.232	.384	.307
April	41	7	1	0	0	1	6	8	.171	.195	.277
May	64	23	7	1	2	7	7	13	.359	.594	.423
June	101	32	6	1	2	17	14	22	.317	.455	.397
July	96	23	5	0	1	15	3	19	.240	.323	.263
August	100	23	2	4	1	11	8	36	.230	.360	.282
Sept./Oct.	92	22	2	0	4	14	6	30	.239	.391	.277
Leading Off Inn.	121	30	8	1	3	3	11	34	.248	.405	.311
Runners On	212	60	12	2	4	59	21	48	.283	.415	.339
Runners/Scor. Pos.	118	34	6	0	2	50	16	29	.288	.390	.357
Runners On/2 Out	100	27	6	0	3	30	9	24	.270	.420	.330
Scor. Pos./2 Out	68	19	4	0	2	26	6	18	.279	.426	.338
Late Inning Pressure	77	24	3	1	4	14	5	19	.312	.532	.354
Leading Off	25	7	1	0	2	2	1	7	.280	.560	.308
Runners On	30	11	2	1	1	11	2	7	.367	.600	.406
Runners/Scor. Pos.	19	7	1	0	1	9	2	5	.368	.579	.429

RUNS BATTED IN	From 1B	From 2B	From 3B	Scoring Position
Totals	10/160	22/98	23/50	45/148
Percentage	6%	22%	46%	30%
Driving In Runners from 3B with Less than Two Out:		16/25		64%

Loves to face: Tom Glavine (.467, 7-for-15, 1 HR)
Hates to face: Kelly Downs (.083, 1-for-12, 6 SO)

Easiest N.L. player to strike out last season (minimum: 50 SO), averaging one whiff per 4.3 plate appearances. Struck out at least once in 17 consecutive games, longest streak in N.L. in 1988. Then he went out and tied Strawberry's record of 12 K in an L.C.S. . . . Seems an unlikely candidate to have a 24-game hitting streak, longest in majors last season, but he did it, May 14 to June 9; that was longest streak by player hitting below .270 since 26-game by Glenn Beckert (.255) in 1973. . . . Batted 88 points higher at home than on road last year, 3d largest difference in N.L. (minimum: 100 AB each). . . . Had five GW-RBI vs. Astros last season. . . . Career averages: .239 in A.L., .270 in N.L.

Ozzie Smith
St. Louis Cardinals — Bats Left and Right

	AB	H	2B	3B	HR	RBI	BB	SO	BA	SA	OBA
Season	575	155	27	1	3	51	74	43	.270	.336	.350
vs. Left-Handers	201	52	11	0	2	15	30	14	.259	.343	.355
vs. Right-Handers	374	103	16	1	1	36	44	29	.275	.332	.348
Home	288	80	11	1	2	30	40	21	.278	.344	.366
Road	287	75	16	0	1	21	34	22	.261	.328	.334
Grass	145	38	4	0	0	9	12	11	.262	.290	.316
Artificial Turf	430	117	23	1	3	42	62	32	.272	.351	.361
April	82	26	5	0	0	7	12	5	.317	.378	.392
May	117	31	1	0	1	6	8	7	.265	.299	.312
June	106	27	5	0	1	12	15	9	.255	.330	.341
July	86	23	2	0	1	7	8	7	.267	.326	.333
August	102	26	6	1	0	8	15	12	.255	.333	.350
Sept./Oct.	82	22	8	0	0	11	16	3	.268	.366	.384
Leading Off Inn.	115	31	5	0	0	0	11	7	.270	.313	.333
Runners On	210	66	11	1	2	50	37	12	.314	.405	.406
Runners/Scor. Pos.	130	32	8	0	1	44	28	7	.246	.331	.364
Runners On/2 Out	88	24	4	1	1	19	20	8	.273	.375	.407
Scor. Pos./2 Out	63	14	3	0	1	17	15	5	.222	.317	.372
Late Inning Pressure	94	21	1	0	2	7	8	8	.223	.298	.284
Leading Off	24	6	0	0	0	0	2	2	.250	.250	.308
Runners On	37	8	0	0	1	6	3	4	.216	.297	.275
Runners/Scor. Pos.	21	3	0	0	0	4	2	1	.143	.143	.217

RUNS BATTED IN	From 1B	From 2B	From 3B	Scoring Position
Totals	6/118	12/99	30/61	42/160
Percentage	5%	12%	49%	26%
Driving In Runners from 3B with Less than Two Out:		20/34		59%

Loves to face: Larry Andersen (.538, 7-for-13, 8 BB)
Hates to face: Tom Browning (.053, 1-for-19)

Led N.L. shortstops in assists for 7th time, extending own N.L. record; tied Luke Appling and Luis Aparicio for major league mark for seasons leading league.... Also led N.L. with 3.51 assists per nine innings.... At 33, was oldest regular SS in majors last season; failed to lead N.L. shortstops in fielding percentage for first time in five years, ranking 5th behind Belliard, Elster, Jeltz, Dunston.... Batting average with runners on base has been higher than with bases empty in each of last six seasons.... Has hit .563 (18-for-32) with bases loaded over past three years.... Home run off Cubs' Greg Maddux on June 12 is his only one in 4612 regular season plate appearances vs. right-handed pitchers.

Chris Speier
San Francisco Giants — Bats Right

	AB	H	2B	3B	HR	RBI	BB	SO	BA	SA	OBA
Season	171	37	9	1	3	18	23	39	.216	.333	.311
vs. Left-Handers	66	17	6	1	0	7	19	14	.258	.379	.425
vs. Right-Handers	105	20	3	0	3	11	4	25	.190	.305	.220
Home	90	25	8	1	3	13	12	21	.278	.489	.363
Road	81	12	1	0	0	5	11	18	.148	.160	.255
Grass	120	29	9	1	3	16	13	24	.242	.408	.321
Artificial Turf	51	8	0	0	0	2	10	15	.157	.157	.290
April	17	3	1	0	0	1	4	3	.176	.235	.333
May	29	9	2	0	1	6	2	7	.310	.483	.344
June	45	6	1	0	0	4	8	12	.133	.156	.264
July	29	10	2	1	2	6	4	6	.345	.690	.424
August	23	6	3	0	0	1	2	3	.261	.391	.346
Sept./Oct.	28	3	0	0	0	0	3	8	.107	.107	.194
Leading Off Inn.	36	6	1	0	1	1	3	7	.167	.278	.250
Runners On	70	14	3	1	1	16	12	18	.200	.314	.313
Runners/Scor. Pos.	43	10	2	1	1	15	10	14	.233	.395	.370
Runners On/2 Out	25	3	1	0	0	5	7	9	.120	.160	.313
Scor. Pos./2 Out	17	3	1	0	0	5	7	8	.176	.235	.417
Late Inning Pressure	26	7	2	0	0	2	8	6	.269	.346	.457
Leading Off	5	1	0	0	0	0	2	1	.200	.200	.500
Runners On	13	3	1	0	0	2	4	3	.231	.308	.412
Runners/Scor. Pos.	6	1	0	0	0	1	3	2	.167	.167	.444

RUNS BATTED IN	From 1B	From 2B	From 3B	Scoring Position
Totals	4/47	6/34	5/18	11/52
Percentage	9%	18%	28%	21%
Driving In Runners from 3B with Less than Two Out:		3/8		38%

Loves to face: Bruce Ruffin (.455, 5-for-11, 1 HR)
Hates to face: Craig Lefferts (0-for-10)

Had a streak of 26 consecutive hitless at-bats that lasted for almost a full month (Aug. 26 to Sept. 21).... Needs 15 games to tie Hal Lanier for 5th place on S.F. Giants all-time list. Needs 18 games to tie McCovey for 4th place.... We're not big fans of "the cycle," but by popular demand, here we go. Speier hit for cycle on July 9, just after 38th birthday, becoming 3d oldest player since 1900 to do so: Cy Williams was 39 when he did it in 1927. Honus Wagner "cycled" in 1912 at age of 38 years, five months. Speier was only N.L. player to hit for cycle in 1988, and he had only 13 extra-base hits all year, fewest by a cyclist in N.L. history. There, that oughta hold you 'til the Tour de France.

Darryl Strawberry
New York Mets — Bats Left

	AB	H	2B	3B	HR	RBI	BB	SO	BA	SA	OBA
Season	543	146	27	3	39	101	85	127	.269	.545	.366
vs. Left-Handers	216	54	7	0	20	52	24	54	.250	.560	.318
vs. Right-Handers	327	92	20	3	19	49	61	73	.281	.535	.395
Home	253	67	11	3	21	55	46	64	.265	.581	.375
Road	290	79	16	0	18	46	39	63	.272	.514	.357
Grass	378	97	17	3	28	70	63	96	.257	.540	.362
Artificial Turf	165	49	10	0	11	31	22	31	.297	.558	.375
April	72	26	5	0	6	10	14	14	.361	.681	.460
May	94	26	6	1	5	18	11	22	.277	.521	.352
June	91	23	4	2	8	22	24	16	.253	.604	.398
July	97	27	5	0	8	20	10	23	.278	.577	.346
August	99	17	3	0	3	12	11	28	.172	.293	.257
Sept./Oct.	90	27	4	0	9	19	15	24	.300	.644	.402
Leading Off Inn.	148	44	11	2	10	10	18	32	.297	.601	.377
Runners On	256	66	7	1	20	82	53	59	.258	.527	.376
Runners/Scor. Pos.	139	28	1	0	7	53	38	33	.201	.360	.355
Runners On/2 Out	113	31	2	0	10	29	27	22	.274	.558	.418
Scor. Pos./2 Out	59	11	0	0	3	14	19	14	.186	.339	.385
Late Inning Pressure	74	14	5	0	4	8	15	23	.189	.419	.333
Leading Off	23	5	2	0	2	2	4	5	.217	.565	.333
Runners On	25	3	0	0	1	5	7	12	.120	.240	.333
Runners/Scor. Pos.	16	2	0	0	0	3	7	8	.125	.125	.391

RUNS BATTED IN	From 1B	From 2B	From 3B	Scoring Position
Totals	20/193	14/104	28/58	42/162
Percentage	10%	13%	48%	26%
Driving In Runners from 3B with Less than Two Out:		22/37		59%

Loves to face: Bob Forsch (.476, 10-for-21, 5 HR)
Hates to face: Scott Garrelts (0-for-5, 5 SO)

His 20 home runs off southpaws were the most by a lefty hitter against lefty pitchers since we started keeping such records in 1975. Out of curiosity, we went back and checked Maris in 1961 and Ruth in 1927: Maris had 12, Ruth 19.... Has had 25+ homers and 25+ steals in each of last five years, tying major league record shared by Willie Mays (1956–60) and Bobby Bonds (1969–73).... Leads active players with one extra-base hit every 8.1 at-bats (minimum: 1000 PA).... Career home-run rate of one every 15.5 at-bats is 9th best in major league history (minimum: 150 HR).... Batting average with runners in scoring position, and average in Late-Inning Pressure Situations, were lowest of career.

Franklin Stubbs
Los Angeles Dodgers — Bats Left

	AB	H	2B	3B	HR	RBI	BB	SO	BA	SA	OBA
Season	242	54	13	0	8	34	23	61	.223	.376	.288
vs. Left-Handers	27	5	1	0	0	2	1	5	.185	.222	.214
vs. Right-Handers	215	49	12	0	8	32	22	56	.228	.395	.296
Home	127	28	4	0	3	17	12	30	.220	.323	.284
Road	115	26	9	0	5	17	11	31	.226	.435	.292
Grass	182	38	8	0	5	25	19	46	.209	.335	.279
Artificial Turf	60	16	5	0	3	9	4	15	.267	.500	.313
April	9	3	0	0	1	1	4	3	.333	.667	.538
May	17	3	0	0	0	3	2	8	.176	.176	.238
June	63	12	4	0	2	7	7	13	.190	.349	.268
July	54	14	2	0	2	11	3	14	.259	.407	.298
August	45	12	4	0	1	7	1	11	.267	.422	.292
Sept./Oct.	54	10	3	0	2	5	6	12	.185	.352	.262
Leading Off Inn.	49	14	4	0	2	2	3	8	.286	.490	.327
Runners On	108	23	5	0	3	29	9	32	.213	.343	.268
Runners/Scor. Pos.	58	14	4	0	3	29	5	18	.241	.466	.279
Runners On/2 Out	44	12	3	0	2	15	5	12	.273	.477	.360
Scor. Pos./2 Out	31	10	3	0	2	16	3	9	.323	.613	.382
Late Inning Pressure	42	7	1	0	2	9	4	12	.167	.333	.239
Leading Off	7	1	1	0	0	0	0	1	.143	.286	.143
Runners On	19	4	0	0	2	9	1	7	.211	.526	.250
Runners/Scor. Pos.	14	4	0	0	2	9	1	4	.286	.714	.333

RUNS BATTED IN	From 1B	From 2B	From 3B	Scoring Position
Totals	5/78	12/53	9/16	21/69
Percentage	6%	23%	56%	30%
Driving In Runners from 3B with Less than Two Out:		6/8		75%

Loves to face: Bryn Smith (.500, 8-for-16, 4 HR)
Hates to face: Rick Aguilera (0-for-12)

Has hit 50 of 55 career home runs (and last 30 in a row) off right-handed pitchers. Last homer off a lefty: July 20, 1986, vs. Tim Conroy.... 1988 leaders in pinch-hit home runs: Ron Kittle, three; Darrin Jackson, Claudell Washington, and Stubbs, two each.... Had the most hits of any N.L. player without a three-hit game last season.... Had lowest fielding percentage (.978) of any first baseman in majors in '88 (minimum: 50 games); led N.L. first sackers with .994 mark in 1987.... Career averages: .255 vs. ground-ball pitchers, .186 vs. fly-ballers; 69-point disparity is largest by any N.L. player over last 10 years (minimum: 500 AB vs. each).... Went 3-for-3 with bases loaded last season: single, double, home run.

Garry Templeton
San Diego Padres   Bats Left and Right

	AB	H	2B	3B	HR	RBI	BB	SO	BA	SA	OBA
Season	362	90	15	7	3	36	20	50	.249	.354	.286
vs. Left-Handers	76	18	2	1	0	7	2	11	.237	.289	.256
vs. Right-Handers	286	72	13	6	3	29	18	39	.252	.371	.293
Home	186	47	10	4	3	20	15	25	.253	.398	.307
Road	176	43	5	3	0	16	5	25	.244	.307	.262
Grass	286	73	11	6	3	29	19	40	.255	.367	.301
Artificial Turf	76	17	4	1	0	7	1	10	.224	.303	.228
April	52	12	3	1	0	3	3	12	.231	.327	.268
May	55	8	1	0	0	1	2	5	.145	.164	.175
June	59	14	3	2	0	11	7	13	.237	.356	.309
July	67	19	3	1	3	10	3	2	.284	.493	.314
August	59	13	0	1	0	2	1	8	.220	.254	.233
Sept./Oct.	70	24	5	2	0	9	4	10	.343	.471	.378
Leading Off Inn.	107	32	6	1	0	0	2	12	.299	.374	.312
Runners On	142	40	7	3	3	36	17	19	.282	.437	.352
Runners/Scor. Pos.	71	20	3	1	2	29	14	11	.282	.437	.386
Runners On/2 Out	55	17	2	2	1	14	12	7	.309	.473	.433
Scor. Pos./2 Out	30	10	1	1	1	12	12	6	.333	.533	.524
Late Inning Pressure	59	14	0	1	2	7	2	1	.237	.373	.258
Leading Off	15	3	0	0	0	0	0	0	.200	.200	.200
Runners On	24	7	0	1	2	7	2	1	.292	.625	.333
Runners/Scor. Pos.	13	4	0	0	2	6	2	0	.308	.769	.375

RUNS BATTED IN	From 1B	From 2B	From 3B	Scoring Position
Totals	7/114	14/59	12/27	26/86
Percentage	6%	24%	44%	30%
Driving In Runners from 3B with Less than Two Out:			9/16	56%

Loves to face: Fernando Valenzuela (.348, 24-for-69, 2 HR)
Hates to face: Don Carman (0-for-12)
May batting average was 2d lowest in N.L. (minimum: two PA per game). . . . Ten of his 20 walks were intentional. . . . Two games at third base last season marked first time he has played anywhere but shortstop in 13 years in majors. . . . Yearly total of games since 1984: 148, 148, 147, 148, 110. Needs 149 games to tie Dave Winfield (1117 games), Padres' all-time leader; it's a good bet, however, that Tony Gwynn (902) will beat Templeton there. . . . In 6838 career plate appearances, Tempy has been hit by pitches only nine times (never more than once in any season). Ken Williams of White Sox has been hit 18 times in 690 plate appearances; yes, *that* Ken Williams—the guy who hit .159 last year.

Tim Teufel
New York Mets   Bats Right

	AB	H	2B	3B	HR	RBI	BB	SO	BA	SA	OBA
Season	273	64	20	0	4	31	29	41	.234	.352	.306
vs. Left-Handers	165	41	15	0	3	20	19	19	.248	.394	.326
vs. Right-Handers	108	23	5	0	1	11	10	22	.213	.287	.275
Home	130	27	7	0	1	7	8	18	.208	.285	.246
Road	143	37	13	0	3	24	21	23	.259	.413	.358
Grass	189	40	10	0	2	17	14	35	.212	.296	.261
Artificial Turf	84	24	10	0	2	14	15	6	.286	.476	.400
April	58	11	3	0	0	5	13	5	.190	.241	.342
May	47	14	3	0	2	8	7	7	.298	.489	.382
June	30	11	0	0	0	3	1	4	.367	.367	.375
July	46	9	2	0	1	2	5	8	.196	.304	.275
August	53	9	5	0	0	9	2	14	.170	.264	.196
Sept./Oct.	39	10	7	0	1	4	1	3	.256	.513	.275
Leading Off Inn.	54	17	3	0	1	1	5	4	.315	.426	.373
Runners On	119	21	7	0	3	30	16	18	.176	.311	.266
Runners/Scor. Pos.	72	10	6	0	1	25	12	12	.139	.264	.250
Runners On/2 Out	39	8	3	0	1	9	11	7	.205	.359	.380
Scor. Pos./2 Out	28	4	3	0	1	9	10	4	.143	.357	.368
Late Inning Pressure	46	9	2	0	0	4	6	8	.196	.239	.283
Leading Off	11	1	0	0	0	0	3	0	.091	.091	.286
Runners On	20	4	1	0	0	4	3	4	.200	.250	.292
Runners/Scor. Pos.	9	1	1	0	0	4	2	3	.111	.222	.250

RUNS BATTED IN	From 1B	From 2B	From 3B	Scoring Position
Totals	6/77	8/60	13/33	21/93
Percentage	8%	13%	39%	23%
Driving In Runners from 3B with Less than Two Out:			11/18	61%

Loves to face: Tom Browning (.500, 11-for-22, 3 HR)
Hates to face: Greg Mathews (.056, 1-for-18)
In 1987, hit .368 with runners in scoring position, 4th in N.L.; in 1988, hit .139 in those spots, last in N.L. (among 127 players). . . . Also ranked last with runners on base, when he had .176 average. . . . Started 46 of 50 games in which the Mets faced left-handed starters, but only 18 of 110 games vs. righties; with Backman traded, that could change this year. . . . Overall batting average, and average vs. right-handers, were career lows. Career averages: .267 vs. left-handers, .262 vs. right-handers. . . . Only player in majors last season who had fewer than 300 at-bats but had a score of doubles; Tuff also had 20 or more doubles without the benefit of 300 at-bats in both 1986 and 1987.

Andres Thomas
Atlanta Braves   Bats Right

	AB	H	2B	3B	HR	RBI	BB	SO	BA	SA	OBA
Season	606	153	22	2	13	68	14	95	.252	.360	.268
vs. Left-Handers	192	46	4	1	7	23	8	26	.240	.380	.267
vs. Right-Handers	414	107	18	1	6	45	6	69	.258	.350	.268
Home	289	76	12	0	6	30	10	49	.263	.367	.286
Road	317	77	10	2	7	38	4	46	.243	.353	.251
Grass	442	109	14	1	8	43	12	75	.247	.337	.265
Artificial Turf	164	44	8	1	5	25	2	20	.268	.421	.275
April	63	14	2	0	1	5	1	16	.222	.302	.234
May	123	29	6	0	2	13	2	11	.236	.333	.246
June	108	33	5	0	4	20	4	13	.306	.463	.330
July	123	32	2	0	4	12	2	21	.260	.374	.272
August	116	29	4	2	2	12	0	21	.250	.371	.248
Sept./Oct.	73	16	3	0	0	6	5	13	.219	.260	.263
Leading Off Inn.	148	36	7	1	3	3	1	21	.243	.365	.253
Runners On	247	61	7	1	2	57	9	29	.247	.308	.267
Runners/Scor. Pos.	144	42	5	0	1	53	8	18	.292	.347	.316
Runners On/2 Out	117	28	3	1	1	28	4	18	.239	.308	.264
Scor. Pos./2 Out	81	24	3	0	1	27	4	11	.296	.370	.329
Late Inning Pressure	117	23	3	0	0	15	3	26	.197	.222	.215
Leading Off	31	8	2	0	0	0	1	6	.258	.323	.281
Runners On	55	11	0	0	0	15	2	12	.200	.200	.224
Runners/Scor. Pos.	32	10	0	0	0	15	2	6	.313	.313	.343

RUNS BATTED IN	From 1B	From 2B	From 3B	Scoring Position
Totals	4/163	24/111	27/63	51/174
Percentage	2%	22%	43%	29%
Driving In Runners from 3B with Less than Two Out:			20/31	65%

Loves to face: John Franco (.455, 5-for-11, 1 HR)
Hates to face: Jim Deshaies (.045, 1-for-22)
Tied with Barry Larkin for most errors by a major league shortstop last season. Thomas had lowest fielding percentage in N.L. at that position (minimum: 100 games). . . . Teammates Ron Gant (2d base) and Gerald Perry (1st base) also earned a share of league lead in errors at their positions. Last N.L. team with leaders at all three positions was 1971 Giants (McCovey, Fuentes, and Speier). . . . Went 138 plate appearances between walks, longest streak of its kind in N.L. last season. Averaged one walk per 44.8 PAs, 2d lowest rate in majors (minimum: 200 PA). Six of his 14 walks were intentional. . . . Career batting average of .308 with two out and runners in scoring position.

Milt Thompson
Philadelphia Phillies   Bats Left

	AB	H	2B	3B	HR	RBI	BB	SO	BA	SA	OBA
Season	378	109	16	2	2	33	39	59	.288	.357	.354
vs. Left-Handers	20	7	1	0	0	3	4	2	.350	.400	.462
vs. Right-Handers	358	102	15	2	2	30	35	57	.285	.355	.347
Home	173	51	8	1	1	17	24	25	.295	.370	.377
Road	205	58	8	1	1	16	15	34	.283	.346	.333
Grass	110	30	5	0	0	8	8	17	.273	.318	.328
Artificial Turf	268	79	11	2	2	25	31	42	.295	.373	.364
April	71	21	3	0	0	5	10	15	.296	.338	.390
May	68	12	2	1	1	3	9	16	.176	.279	.273
June	69	22	3	0	0	6	5	7	.319	.362	.355
July	70	22	2	1	1	7	10	11	.314	.414	.395
August	80	26	4	0	0	11	4	8	.325	.375	.357
Sept./Oct.	20	6	2	0	0	1	1	2	.300	.400	.333
Leading Off Inn.	95	25	7	0	1	1	8	16	.263	.368	.320
Runners On	133	43	7	1	0	31	20	18	.323	.391	.404
Runners/Scor. Pos.	69	21	4	0	0	29	16	15	.304	.362	.420
Runners On/2 Out	51	20	3	1	0	14	4	13	.392	.490	.436
Scor. Pos./2 Out	28	11	2	0	0	13	3	11	.393	.464	.452
Late Inning Pressure	57	24	3	0	1	7	9	9	.421	.526	.500
Leading Off	15	7	2	0	1	1	1	3	.467	.800	.500
Runners On	22	11	1	0	0	6	7	3	.500	.545	.621
Runners/Scor. Pos.	13	6	1	0	0	6	4	3	.462	.538	.588

RUNS BATTED IN	From 1B	From 2B	From 3B	Scoring Position
Totals	2/89	10/55	19/31	29/86
Percentage	2%	18%	61%	34%
Driving In Runners from 3B with Less than Two Out:			13/20	65%

Loves to face: Jeff Pico (5-for-5)
Hates to face: Pete Smith (0-for-9)
He's no wimp: Batted 156 points higher in Late-Inning Pressure Situations than otherwise, largest difference in majors last season (minimum: 50 LIPS AB). His average with runners on base in LIPS was the best in majors. . . . Batted .342 vs. ground-ball pitchers, .236 vs. fly-ballers. . . . Career average of .254 before the All-Star break (.197 during May), .319 after. . . . . Acquired from Atlanta in same deal that brought Steve Bedrosian. For Ozzie Virgil? . . . Lives in South Carolina, in a town called Ninety Six—the number of games he started last season, all against right-handers. He'll have to raise his .211 career mark vs. southpaws if he wants to move to a town called One Sixty-Two.

Rob Thompson
San Francisco Giants — Bats Right

	AB	H	2B	3B	HR	RBI	BB	SO	BA	SA	OBA
Season	477	126	24	6	7	48	40	111	.264	.384	.323
vs. Left-Handers	154	50	16	3	1	17	16	33	.325	.487	.385
vs. Right-Handers	323	76	8	3	6	31	24	78	.235	.334	.293
Home	214	55	10	3	3	23	22	60	.257	.374	.326
Road	263	71	14	3	4	25	18	51	.270	.392	.321
Grass	341	80	13	5	4	32	32	87	.235	.337	.302
Artificial Turf	136	46	11	1	3	16	8	24	.338	.500	.379
April	74	20	4	1	0	5	6	14	.270	.351	.321
May	98	35	5	2	1	12	9	19	.357	.480	.422
June	55	14	4	1	0	5	12	20	.255	.364	.382
July	94	27	5	0	2	11	3	24	.287	.404	.306
August	92	19	5	1	2	7	4	22	.207	.348	.240
Sept./Oct.	64	11	1	1	2	8	6	12	.172	.313	.257
Leading Off Inn.	94	32	4	1	2		1	21	.340	.468	.354
Runners On	195	59	13	4	3	44	22	41	.303	.456	.373
Runners/Scor. Pos.	104	25	5	1	2	34	15	29	.240	.365	.333
Runners On/2 Out	61	11	3	1	1	10	10	18	.180	.311	.315
Scor. Pos./2 Out	41	6	2	0	1	8	6	14	.146	.268	.271
Late Inning Pressure	69	19	4	0	0	8	1	15	.275	.333	.301
Leading Off	11	5	1	0	0	0	0	2	.455	.545	.500
Runners On	31	9	3	0	0	8	1	8	.290	.387	.324
Runners/Scor. Pos.	19	2	1	0	0	6	0	7	.105	.158	.143

RUNS BATTED IN	From 1B	From 2B	From 3B	Scoring Position
Totals	12/130	10/86	19/42	29/128
Percentage	9%	12%	45%	23%
Driving In Runners from 3B with Less than Two Out:		15/28		54%

Loves to face: Paul Assenmacher (4-for-4, 1 2B)
Hates to face: David Palmer (0-for-14)

Consistency may be only a word in the dictionary. But look it up, and you'll see Thompson's face smiling back. He's never hit below .262 or above .271. He's hit between seven and 10 HRs, with between 37 and 42 XBHs, and between 44 and 48 RBIs each year. Stole between 12 and 16 bases each season. Walked 42 times as a rookie, 40 times each in 1987 and 1988.... The exception: One of two major leaguers to bat 100+ points higher on artificial turf than on grass fields last season (minimum: 100 AB each way), but in each of his previous two seasons he hit for a higher average on grass fields than on synthetics.... Career average of .306 vs. left-handed pitchers, .248 vs. right-handers.

Jeff Treadway
Cincinnati Reds — Bats Left

	AB	H	2B	3B	HR	RBI	BB	SO	BA	SA	OBA
Season	301	76	19	4	2	23	27	30	.252	.362	.315
vs. Left-Handers	33	8	1	1	0	3	1	4	.242	.333	.265
vs. Right-Handers	268	68	18	3	2	20	26	26	.254	.366	.320
Home	137	41	11	1	2	12	14	10	.299	.438	.370
Road	164	35	8	3	0	11	13	20	.213	.299	.268
Grass	91	18	4	1	0	3	6	14	.198	.264	.253
Artificial Turf	210	58	15	3	2	20	21	16	.276	.405	.340
April	60	13	7	1	0	6	7	6	.217	.367	.294
May	76	26	4	0	0	8	10	4	.342	.395	.411
June	74	16	4	1	1	4	6	14	.216	.338	.280
July	51	11	2	2	1	3	3	5	.216	.392	.259
August	40	10	2	0	0	2	1	1	.250	.300	.279
Sept./Oct.	0	0	0	0	0	0	0	0	———	———	———
Leading Off Inn.	90	25	4	1	2	2	1	8	.278	.411	.293
Runners On	96	26	10	2	0	21	22	10	.271	.417	.392
Runners/Scor. Pos.	50	13	7	0	0	18	15	7	.260	.400	.394
Runners On/2 Out	41	12	4	1	0	5	15	5	.293	.439	.482
Scor. Pos./2 Out	21	4	3	0	0	4	12	4	.190	.333	.485
Late Inning Pressure	55	17	5	2	0	4	3	5	.309	.473	.350
Leading Off	19	7	3	0	0	0	1	1	.368	.526	.400
Runners On	17	6	2	2	0	4	2	3	.353	.706	.429
Runners/Scor. Pos.	9	2	1	0	0	2	1	1	.222	.333	.333

RUNS BATTED IN	From 1B	From 2B	From 3B	Scoring Position
Totals	3/63	7/39	11/24	18/63
Percentage	5%	18%	46%	29%
Driving In Runners from 3B with Less than Two Out:		10/15		67%

Loves to face: Orel Hershiser (.417, 5-for-12, 1 HR)
Hates to face: Pascual Perez (0-for-12)

May batting average was 5th highest in N.L.... Batted 86 points higher in home games than on the road, 4th largest difference in N.L. (minimum: 100 AB each way).... Batted .200 in day games, .279 at night.... Ended the season with 46 consecutive errorless games at second base.... Career averages: .302 at Riverfront, .241 on the road.... Has hit all four of his career home runs at Riverfront.... Has started 103 games in his career, but has never been in the starting lineup vs. a left-handed pitcher.... Career batting average of .294 leading off innings, but has only one walk in 105 leadoff plate appearances.... Never hit below .302 in four seasons in minors.

Dickie Thon
San Diego Padres — Bats Right

	AB	H	2B	3B	HR	RBI	BB	SO	BA	SA	OBA
Season	258	68	12	2	1	18	33	49	.264	.337	.347
vs. Left-Handers	139	42	7	2	1	11	21	23	.302	.403	.391
vs. Right-Handers	119	26	5	0	0	7	12	26	.218	.261	.293
Home	112	25	3	1	0	8	18	28	.223	.268	.331
Road	146	43	9	1	1	10	15	21	.295	.390	.360
Grass	170	43	6	1	1	12	24	39	.253	.318	.345
Artificial Turf	88	25	6	1	0	6	9	10	.284	.375	.350
April	21	4	1	0	0	0	2	1	.190	.238	.261
May	69	16	3	1	0	6	9	20	.232	.304	.325
June	35	10	0	0	0	4	8	8	.286	.286	.419
July	37	12	3	0	0	2	2	7	.324	.405	.359
August	47	10	3	0	0	3	5	9	.213	.277	.283
Sept./Oct.	49	16	2	1	1	3	7	4	.327	.469	.411
Leading Off Inn.	89	24	3	1	1		8	16	.270	.360	.337
Runners On	93	24	5	1	0	17	12	21	.258	.333	.336
Runners/Scor. Pos.	50	13	2	0	0	16	11	12	.260	.300	.381
Runners On/2 Out	40	10	2	0	0	8	8	10	.250	.300	.375
Scor. Pos./2 Out	30	7	2	0	0	8	7	7	.233	.300	.378
Late Inning Pressure	40	6	0	0	0	2	2	7	.150	.225	.186
Leading Off	12	3	0	0	0	1	0	2	.250	.500	.250
Runners On	13	1	0	0	0	1	2	4	.077	.077	.188
Runners/Scor. Pos.	5	1	0	0	0	1	2	2	.200	.200	.375

RUNS BATTED IN	From 1B	From 2B	From 3B	Scoring Position
Totals	1/62	7/40	9/22	16/62
Percentage	2%	18%	41%	26%
Driving In Runners from 3B with Less than Two Out:		3/8		38%

Loves to face: Eric Show (.391, 9-for-23, 3 HR)
Hates to face: Bruce Sutter (0-for-11)

Started 41 of 57 games in which the Padres faced a southpaw starter, but only 22 of 104 games against right-handers.... Batted .158 (3-for-19) as a pinch-hitter. But his only home run came off Paul Assenmacher in that role.... Revenge factor? Batted .355 in ten games vs. Houston.... Hadn't played second or third base since 1982, but played both last season.... Hit by a Bryn Smith pitch on May 26, the only time he's been hit in 252 games since the Torrez beaning.... Career average of .279 at the time of the beaning, .251 since.... Where was Thon's career headed? Players with similar stats at a comparable age to Thon's in 1983: Lou Brock (through 1964), Ron Hunt (1966), Joe Morgan (1968).

Alex Trevino
Houston Astros — Bats Right

	AB	H	2B	3B	HR	RBI	BB	SO	BA	SA	OBA
Season	193	48	17	0	2	13	24	29	.249	.368	.341
vs. Left-Handers	88	21	8	0	2	7	13	12	.239	.398	.350
vs. Right-Handers	105	27	9	0	0	6	11	17	.257	.343	.333
Home	84	14	6	0	0	6	14	17	.167	.238	.293
Road	109	34	11	0	2	7	10	12	.312	.468	.380
Grass	56	17	6	0	2	6	6	7	.304	.518	.381
Artificial Turf	137	31	11	0	0	7	18	22	.226	.307	.325
April	0	0	0	0	0	0	0	0	———	———	———
May	26	8	4	0	0	2	5	3	.308	.462	.419
June	39	8	2	0	0	1	3	6	.205	.256	.295
July	32	8	4	0	1	4	4	5	.250	.469	.351
August	72	19	6	0	0	3	8	11	.264	.347	.338
Sept./Oct.	24	5	1	0	1	3	4	4	.208	.375	.321
Leading Off Inn.	41	8	3	0	0	0	2	9	.195	.268	.233
Runners On	80	22	8	0	1	12	16	10	.275	.413	.408
Runners/Scor. Pos.	44	9	4	0	0	10	13	5	.205	.295	.407
Runners On/2 Out	31	8	3	0	0	4	11	5	.258	.452	.452
Scor. Pos./2 Out	17	3	2	0	0	2	9	2	.176	.294	.462
Late Inning Pressure	36	9	1	0	0	1	5	8	.250	.278	.341
Leading Off	12	0	0	0	0	0	1	3	.000	.000	.077
Runners On	12	4	1	0	0	1	3	2	.333	.417	.467
Runners/Scor. Pos.	7	1	0	0	0	1	2	1	.143	.143	.333

RUNS BATTED IN	From 1B	From 2B	From 3B	Scoring Position
Totals	1/55	5/34	5/18	10/52
Percentage	2%	15%	28%	19%
Driving In Runners from 3B with Less than Two Out:		5/15		33%

Loves to face: Bob Forsch (.500, 6-for-12)
Hates to face: Steve Bedrosian (0-for-8)

Would you believe that he led the Astros with seven appearances as a pinch runner last season? ... Career average of .278 in day games, .229 at night. Difference is the largest of any active player over the last 10 years (minimum: 500 AB each way).... Hit both of his 1988 home runs against the Dodgers, who cut him in spring training in favor of Rick Dempsey. Can't argue with success, besides Trevino isn't as quotable.... Career average of .269 vs. ground-ball pitchers, .220 vs. fly-ballers.... Has now played for half of the current N.L. clubs. Here's the breakdown: Mets (247 games), Reds (200), Dodgers (161), Braves (79), Astros (78), Giants (57).

Jose Uribe

Bats Left and Right

San Francisco Giants	AB	H	2B	3B	HR	RBI	BB	SO	BA	SA	OBA
Season	493	124	10	7	3	35	36	69	.252	.318	.301
vs. Left-Handers	152	46	6	1	2	14	11	10	.303	.395	.350
vs. Right-Handers	341	78	4	6	1	21	25	59	.229	.284	.280
Home	224	60	5	2	1	12	13	32	.268	.321	.308
Road	269	64	5	5	2	23	23	37	.238	.316	.296
Grass	349	92	7	4	2	26	27	52	.264	.324	.315
Artificial Turf	144	32	3	3	1	9	9	17	.222	.306	.268
April	81	18	1	0	0	2	7	12	.222	.235	.284
May	92	24	1	2	2	5	7	10	.261	.380	.313
June	49	17	3	2	0	7	2	6	.347	.490	.373
July	85	19	2	0	0	2	3	10	.224	.247	.250
August	89	18	1	2	0	10	8	18	.202	.258	.265
Sept./Oct.	97	28	2	1	1	9	9	13	.289	.361	.346
Leading Off Inn.	128	32	4	1	1	1	6	16	.250	.320	.284
Runners On	200	54	4	4	1	33	20	25	.270	.345	.333
Runners/Scor. Pos.	110	25	3	3	0	29	16	17	.227	.309	.320
Runners On/2 Out	90	19	3	1	1	14	13	15	.211	.300	.311
Scor. Pos./2 Out	54	8	2	0	0	10	11	12	.148	.185	.292
Late Inning Pressure	80	22	1	0	1	8	6	10	.275	.325	.326
Leading Off	17	3	0	0	0	0	3	3	.176	.176	.300
Runners On	41	14	1	0	1	8	2	4	.341	.439	.372
Runners/Scor. Pos.	22	7	0	0	0	5	2	2	.318	.318	.375

RUNS BATTED IN	From 1B	From 2B	From 3B	Scoring Position
Totals	4/139	13/94	15/32	28/126
Percentage	3%	14%	47%	22%
Driving In Runners from 3B with Less than Two Out:			11/16	69%

Loves to face: Rick Mahler (.519, 14-for-27)
Hates to face: Ed Whitson (.059, 1-for-17)
Batted .289 vs. ground-ball pitchers, .207 vs. fly-ballers. Has hit for a higher average against ground-ballers than he has against fly-ballers in each of his five seasons in majors. . . . Grounded into only three double plays in 86 opportunities last season, 4th lowest rate in N.L. (min.: 40 opp.). Of the 146 players with at least 450 games played since 1985, Uribe has grounded into the fewest DPs (11). Vince Coleman is second on that list with 18. . . . Had only 35 RBI for season, but 10 game-winners (29%), highest average in majors (minimum: 5 GW). . . . Class-AA shortstop in St. Louis chain in 1982, one level above Bobby Meacham, one below Rafael Santana. Ozzie had the job with the big club.

Andy Van Slyke

Bats Left

Pittsburgh Pirates	AB	H	2B	3B	HR	RBI	BB	SO	BA	SA	OBA
Season	587	169	23	15	25	100	57	126	.288	.506	.345
vs. Left-Handers	204	39	5	6	3	25	14	53	.191	.319	.239
vs. Right-Handers	383	130	18	9	22	75	43	73	.339	.606	.399
Home	280	82	13	9	16	53	33	58	.293	.575	.364
Road	307	87	10	6	9	47	24	68	.283	.443	.327
Grass	160	57	5	3	8	29	10	28	.356	.575	.383
Artificial Turf	427	112	18	12	17	71	47	98	.262	.480	.331
April	78	17	1	3	3	12	10	19	.218	.423	.300
May	114	37	3	4	4	17	9	22	.325	.526	.368
June	105	31	6	4	5	25	10	28	.295	.571	.345
July	97	27	4	3	4	14	9	23	.278	.505	.340
August	103	32	4	1	6	16	8	19	.311	.544	.363
Sept./Oct.	90	25	5	0	3	16	11	15	.278	.433	.343
Leading Off Inn.	105	26	5	1	4	4	12	23	.248	.429	.331
Runners On	277	83	12	12	10	85	28	58	.300	.538	.349
Runners/Scor. Pos.	164	38	3	7	3	64	21	40	.232	.390	.298
Runners On/2 Out	100	22	3	3	3	24	14	24	.220	.400	.316
Scor. Pos./2 Out	63	12	1	2	1	18	11	17	.190	.317	.311
Late Inning Pressure	95	24	4	3	3	10	8	31	.253	.453	.308
Leading Off	21	5	1	0	0	0	2	9	.238	.286	.304
Runners On	43	9	1	2	1	8	3	14	.209	.395	.255
Runners/Scor. Pos.	27	5	0	2	1	8	2	9	.185	.444	.233

RUNS BATTED IN	From 1B	From 2B	From 3B	Scoring Position
Totals	18/190	20/112	37/80	57/192
Percentage	9%	18%	46%	30%
Driving In Runners from 3B with Less than Two Out:			30/51	59%

Loves to face: Rick Mahler (.529, 18-for-34, 3 HR)
Hates to face: Mike Scott (.036, 1-for-28)
Reached double figures in doubles, triples, and home runs for a second consecutive season. The longest streak ever: 7, by Stan Musial (1942–49). . . . Backstops, beware: this man has reached base 10 times on catcher's interference, the most among active players. . . . Led N.L. center fielders with 12 assists last season. . . . Had at least one RBI in 11 straight games in June, longest streak in majors last season (equalled by Kirby Puckett in Sept.). . . . RBI total has increased in each season in majors: 38, 50, 55, 61, 82, 100. . . . Career average of .208 vs. left-handers, .296 vs. right-handers. That 87-point difference is the largest over the past 10 seasons (minimum: 500 AB each way).

Ozzie Virgil

Bats Right

Atlanta Braves	AB	H	2B	3B	HR	RBI	BB	SO	BA	SA	OBA
Season	320	82	10	0	9	31	22	54	.256	.372	.313
vs. Left-Handers	104	29	4	0	3	13	11	10	.279	.404	.345
vs. Right-Handers	216	53	6	0	6	18	11	44	.245	.356	.297
Home	149	47	8	0	5	13	14	18	.315	.470	.389
Road	171	35	2	0	4	18	8	36	.205	.287	.243
Grass	228	65	9	0	7	23	17	32	.285	.417	.348
Artificial Turf	92	17	1	0	2	8	5	22	.185	.261	.224
April	40	8	0	0	1	3	3	5	.200	.275	.250
May	74	15	1	0	4	9	1	15	.203	.378	.224
June	64	18	5	0	2	6	2	14	.281	.453	.294
July	50	11	1	0	1	3	7	7	.220	.300	.316
August	35	12	2	0	0	3	5	4	.343	.400	.452
Sept./Oct.	57	18	1	0	1	7	4	9	.316	.386	.361
Leading Off Inn.	58	16	3	0	4	4	3	11	.276	.534	.333
Runners On	133	37	5	0	1	23	11	21	.278	.338	.340
Runners/Scor. Pos.	74	18	3	0	1	21	7	15	.243	.324	.313
Runners On/2 Out	54	12	3	0	0	8	4	10	.222	.278	.288
Scor. Pos./2 Out	33	5	1	0	0	6	2	7	.152	.182	.200
Late Inning Pressure	79	25	1	0	0	5	7	14	.316	.329	.372
Leading Off	15	5	0	0	0	0	2	1	.333	.333	.412
Runners On	36	13	1	0	0	5	3	6	.361	.389	.410
Runners/Scor. Pos.	23	5	0	0	0	4	2	5	.217	.217	.280

RUNS BATTED IN	From 1B	From 2B	From 3B	Scoring Position
Totals	3/96	12/61	7/27	19/88
Percentage	3%	20%	26%	22%
Driving In Runners from 3B with Less than Two Out:			5/13	38%

Loves to face: Dave Dravecky (.429, 6-for-14, 2 HR)
Hates to face: Sid Fernandez (0-for-24)
One of two N.L. players to bat 100 points higher in home games than on the road last season (minimum: 100 AB each way). . . . He's the only N.L. player other than Shane Rawley to hit at least 10 points higher at home than on the road in each of the last five seasons. . . . Batted .467 (7-for-15) as pinch hitter last season, including seven hits in his last 10 at-bats. . . . Batting average leading off innings was the highest of his career. . . . Drove in only four runs in 25 chances from scoring position in Late-Inning Pressure Situations. Previous career mark was 37 percent (41-for-110). . . . Braves pitchers allowed 4.81 runs per nine innings with Osvaldo catching, 4.23 with Eggs Benedict.

Tim Wallach

Bats Right

Montreal Expos	AB	H	2B	3B	HR	RBI	BB	SO	BA	SA	OBA
Season	592	152	32	5	12	71	38	88	.257	.389	.302
vs. Left-Handers	172	45	10	2	4	13	13	19	.262	.413	.310
vs. Right-Handers	420	107	22	3	8	58	25	69	.255	.379	.298
Home	292	74	14	2	3	32	22	37	.253	.346	.302
Road	300	78	18	3	9	39	16	51	.260	.430	.301
Grass	158	39	6	1	4	19	4	30	.247	.373	.268
Artificial Turf	434	113	26	4	8	52	34	58	.260	.394	.313
April	84	20	5	0	2	5	4	6	.238	.369	.273
May	101	27	4	3	1	11	7	15	.267	.396	.318
June	108	30	7	2	3	15	9	12	.278	.463	.331
July	100	25	6	0	2	12	7	15	.250	.370	.294
August	107	27	5	0	3	17	5	19	.252	.383	.284
Sept./Oct.	92	23	5	0	1	11	6	21	.250	.337	.303
Leading Off Inn.	154	44	9	1	5	5	8	20	.286	.455	.321
Runners On	255	62	13	2	2	61	22	35	.243	.333	.303
Runners/Scor. Pos.	152	41	8	2	1	57	15	23	.270	.368	.333
Runners On/2 Out	107	26	3	2	1	23	12	17	.243	.336	.331
Scor. Pos./2 Out	73	19	3	2	0	21	7	11	.260	.356	.341
Late Inning Pressure	129	28	5	0	1	17	8	27	.217	.279	.261
Leading Off	43	8	2	0	1	1	1	7	.186	.302	.205
Runners On	53	11	1	0	0	16	4	9	.208	.226	.259
Runners/Scor. Pos.	35	10	1	0	0	16	4	3	.286	.314	.350

RUNS BATTED IN	From 1B	From 2B	From 3B	Scoring Position
Totals	4/168	19/101	36/79	55/180
Percentage	2%	19%	46%	31%
Driving In Runners from 3B with Less than Two Out:			25/41	61%

Loves to face: Brian Fisher (.368, 7-for-19, 4 HR)
Hates to face: Kelly Downs (.063, 1-for-16, 7 SO)
Has led N.L. third basemen in putouts in six of last seven years; N.L. record is seven, shared by Pie Traynor, Willie Jones, and Ron Santo. That may not be a ticket to Cooperstown; it's just that there's a lot of foul territory at the Big O. . . . Career batting average of .299 leading off innings. . . . Has had five sacrifice bunts in his career, all during the 1982 season. . . . Hit only 12 home runs last season, his lowest total since becoming a regular in 1982; but he is one of 33 guys with 140 or more home runs, or 20 per year, since then. . . . Has hit only 13 home runs in 635 at-bats vs. left-handed pitchers over past four years; in 1982 alone, he had 13 circuit clouts in 163 at-bats vs. lefties.

Denny Walling

Astros/Cardinals — Bats Left

	AB	H	2B	3B	HR	RBI	BB	SO	BA	SA	OBA
Season	234	56	13	2	1	21	17	25	.239	.325	.291
vs. Left-Handers	14	3	1	0	0	2	2	4	.214	.286	.313
vs. Right-Handers	220	53	12	2	1	19	15	21	.241	.327	.289
Home	113	27	6	1	0	10	6	8	.239	.310	.277
Road	121	29	7	1	1	11	11	17	.240	.339	.303
Grass	58	17	4	1	1	8	6	8	.293	.448	.359
Artificial Turf	176	39	9	1	0	13	11	17	.222	.284	.267
April	46	14	4	2	0	6	3	4	.304	.478	.347
May	43	8	1	0	0	6	4	3	.186	.209	.255
June	57	14	3	0	1	6	6	7	.246	.351	.317
July	0	0	0	0	0	0	0	0	—	—	—
August	30	7	2	0	0	2	2	4	.233	.300	.281
Sept./Oct.	58	13	3	0	0	1	2	7	.224	.276	.250
Leading Off Inn.	56	14	4	0	0	0	1	4	.250	.321	.263
Runners On	95	24	4	2	0	20	11	11	.253	.337	.330
Runners/Scor. Pos.	57	14	4	1	0	19	8	8	.246	.351	.338
Runners On/2 Out	43	10	2	1	0	8	4	7	.233	.326	.298
Scor. Pos./2 Out	26	6	2	1	0	8	3	6	.231	.385	.310
Late Inning Pressure	37	6	2	0	0	3	2	5	.162	.216	.205
Leading Off	9	1	0	0	0	0	0	2	.111	.111	.111
Runners On	13	3	1	0	0	3	1	1	.231	.308	.286
Runners/Scor. Pos.	7	3	1	0	0	3	1	1	.429	.571	.500

RUNS BATTED IN	From 1B	From 2B	From 3B	Scoring Position
Totals	3/67	8/39	9/22	17/61
Percentage	4%	21%	41%	28%
Driving In Runners from 3B with Less than Two Out:			6/12	50%

Loves to face: Jeff D. Robinson (.643, 9-for-14, 1 HR)
Hates to face: Rich Gossage (0-for-10)
Started a total of 59 games last season, all vs. right-handed pitchers. Has not started against a lefty since June 7, 1987; that's 118 starts ago. . . . Hit .150 (3-for-20) as pinch hitter last season; he had hit .435 (20-for-46) over the previous two years. . . . Has a career average of .400 (22-for-55) with the bases loaded, but has never hit a grand slam. . . . Career average of .292 vs. ground-ball pitchers, .258 vs. fly-ballers. . . . What distinction do Ed Halicki and Dick Ruthven share? They're the only two guys who have ever hit Walling with a pitch in his 3005 plate appearances over 14 years in majors. The only active player with more plate appearances and as few HBP is Pete O'Brien (two in 3805).

Mitch Webster

Expos/Cubs — Bats Left and Right

	AB	H	2B	3B	HR	RBI	BB	SO	BA	SA	OBA
Season	523	136	16	8	6	39	55	87	.260	.356	.337
vs. Left-Handers	168	40	5	0	0	6	11	25	.238	.268	.290
vs. Right-Handers	355	96	11	8	6	33	44	62	.270	.397	.359
Home	273	77	8	5	3	23	33	46	.282	.381	.369
Road	250	59	8	3	3	16	22	41	.236	.328	.301
Grass	241	57	5	3	5	18	22	46	.237	.344	.310
Artificial Turf	282	79	11	5	1	21	33	41	.280	.365	.360
April	69	19	2	2	1	6	13	11	.275	.406	.386
May	83	21	0	0	0	2	9	9	.253	.253	.340
June	81	18	3	0	0	1	10	12	.222	.259	.323
July	90	27	2	2	1	7	9	14	.300	.400	.366
August	106	26	4	2	3	12	3	26	.245	.406	.290
Sept./Oct.	94	25	5	2	1	11	11	15	.266	.394	.343
Leading Off Inn.	161	46	8	4	2	2	8	26	.286	.422	.335
Runners On	189	54	4	2	3	36	22	28	.286	.376	.362
Runners/Scor. Pos.	107	32	2	1	3	35	20	18	.299	.421	.402
Runners On/2 Out	84	24	1	1	1	17	10	14	.286	.357	.362
Scor. Pos./2 Out	59	17	1	0	1	16	10	10	.288	.356	.391
Late Inning Pressure	104	24	1	2	0	7	13	24	.231	.279	.319
Leading Off	26	4	0	1	0	0	2	6	.154	.231	.214
Runners On	41	11	0	1	0	7	7	8	.268	.317	.380
Runners/Scor. Pos.	23	6	0	0	0	6	6	4	.261	.261	.400

RUNS BATTED IN	From 1B	From 2B	From 3B	Scoring Position
Totals	1/125	15/89	17/38	32/127
Percentage	1%	17%	45%	25%
Driving In Runners from 3B with Less than Two Out:			10/14	71%

Loves to face: Jim Gott (.571, 4-for-7, 2 HR)
Hates to face: Terry Leach (.091, 2-for-22)
Has played more than 150 games in each of last three seasons: his overall batting average has slipped since 1986 (.290, .281, .260), but his average with runners in scoring position has increased (.250, .287, .299). . . . Stole only one base in six tries last season against Mets, who allowed 79 percent success rate during season. . . . Had played for the Blue Jays prior to his days with the Expos. His debut with Cubs (July 15 vs. L.A.) marked the first time in his major league career that he heard only *one* anthem. . . . Attention, Mr. Giamatti: Webster was hit by pitches five times in 65 plate appearances vs. Atlanta last season. He was hit only three times by the rest of league.

Mookie Wilson

New York Mets — Bats Left and Right

	AB	H	2B	3B	HR	RBI	BB	SO	BA	SA	OBA
Season	378	112	17	5	8	41	27	63	.296	.431	.345
vs. Left-Handers	195	55	9	3	4	14	15	30	.282	.421	.335
vs. Right-Handers	183	57	8	2	4	27	12	33	.311	.443	.355
Home	185	48	9	1	1	13	8	31	.259	.335	.292
Road	193	64	8	4	7	28	19	32	.332	.523	.393
Grass	262	77	13	2	2	21	18	42	.294	.382	.343
Artificial Turf	116	35	4	3	6	20	9	21	.302	.543	.349
April	58	16	4	2	2	10	5	11	.276	.517	.333
May	56	14	4	0	0	3	4	6	.250	.321	.300
June	55	13	1	0	0	2	4	5	.236	.255	.283
July	51	9	2	1	1	4	6	14	.176	.314	.276
August	72	29	3	1	1	7	5	9	.403	.514	.442
Sept./Oct.	86	31	3	1	4	15	3	18	.360	.558	.385
Leading Off Inn.	137	42	4	2	2	9	22	9	.307	.409	.354
Runners On	145	41	6	1	4	37	9	24	.283	.421	.321
Runners/Scor. Pos.	88	28	3	1	2	33	5	16	.318	.443	.347
Runners On/2 Out	59	18	1	1	1	17	4	9	.305	.407	.349
Scor. Pos./2 Out	39	15	1	1	1	17	1	7	.385	.538	.400
Late Inning Pressure	69	20	2	2	2	6	10	9	.290	.464	.388
Leading Off	18	7	0	1	1	1	2	2	.389	.667	.450
Runners On	32	10	1	0	1	5	3	3	.313	.438	.371
Runners/Scor. Pos.	17	5	1	0	0	3	2	2	.294	.353	.368

RUNS BATTED IN	From 1B	From 2B	From 3B	Scoring Position
Totals	3/91	13/75	17/33	30/108
Percentage	3%	17%	52%	28%
Driving In Runners from 3B with Less than Two Out:			10/20	50%

Loves to face: Greg Mathews (.600, 15-for-25)
Hates to face: Ricky Horton (.042, 1-for-24)
First player in major league history to (a) have at least 300 at bats and (b) hit more than .270 but less than .300 (c) for eight straight years. . . . Hit .378 in September, 2d best in N.L. . . . Grounded into 12 double plays in 59 DP situations last year, 3d highest rate in N.L. (min.: 40 opportunities). . . . Averaged 2.21 putouts per nine innings, the low among major league center fielders in '88 (minimum: 500 innings). . . . Hey, Davey, Mookie has hit .324 vs. right-handers over past two years, 4th best mark in N.L. (minimum: 300 AB). Dykstra's at .287 vs. righties over those two years. . . . Batted .360 in day games, .270 at night last year. And you thought those shades only made him *look* cool!

Herm Winningham

Expos/Reds — Bats Left

	AB	H	2B	3B	HR	RBI	BB	SO	BA	SA	OBA
Season	203	47	3	4	0	21	17	45	.232	.286	.288
vs. Left-Handers	38	9	0	2	0	8	0	10	.237	.342	.231
vs. Right-Handers	165	38	3	2	0	13	17	35	.230	.273	.301
Home	96	26	2	3	0	9	6	19	.271	.354	.314
Road	107	21	1	1	0	12	11	26	.196	.224	.267
Grass	70	14	1	1	0	6	7	16	.200	.243	.273
Artificial Turf	133	33	2	3	0	15	10	29	.248	.308	.297
April	19	7	0	0	0	3	2	6	.368	.368	.455
May	33	7	2	0	0	1	4	6	.212	.273	.297
June	27	6	0	1	0	4	4	9	.222	.296	.313
July	22	4	0	1	0	2	1	5	.182	.273	.217
August	40	14	1	2	0	9	2	8	.350	.475	.372
Sept./Oct.	62	9	0	0	0	5	3	15	.145	.145	.185
Leading Off Inn.	54	9	2	0	0	5	10	16	.167	.204	.237
Runners On	81	25	0	4	0	21	5	20	.309	.407	.341
Runners/Scor. Pos.	57	16	0	1	0	18	4	18	.281	.316	.317
Runners On/2 Out	39	11	0	3	0	12	1	12	.282	.436	.300
Scor. Pos./2 Out	30	8	0	1	0	10	1	11	.267	.333	.290
Late Inning Pressure	46	14	1	2	0	6	3	12	.304	.413	.340
Leading Off	14	4	1	0	0	0	0	2	.286	.357	.286
Runners On	13	7	0	2	0	6	1	2	.538	.846	.533
Runners/Scor. Pos.	8	4	0	0	0	4	1	2	.500	.500	.500

RUNS BATTED IN	From 1B	From 2B	From 3B	Scoring Position
Totals	4/47	4/47	13/27	17/74
Percentage	9%	9%	48%	23%
Driving In Runners from 3B with Less than Two Out:			7/14	50%

Loves to face: Doug Drabek (.500, 5-for-10)
Hates to face: Rick Rhoden (.100, 1-for-10, 5 SO)
Batted .214 in 41 games as a starter and .190 (4-for-21) as a pinch hitter. In other games—those in which he entered as a defensive substitute—he batted .692 (9-for-13). . . . This left-handed hitter has a better career average vs. left-handers (.277 in 141 at-bats) than vs. righties (.232). . . . Batted .233 in 47 games with Montreal, .230 in 53 games with Reds. . . . One of three players, along with Dave Collins and Eddie Milner, who started at all three outfield positions for Reds last season. . . . Career average of .220 with the bases empty, .264 with runners on base. Those figures are even more lopsided in Late-Inning Pressure Situations: .195 with bases empty, .328 with runners on.

Marvell Wynne

San Diego Padres — Bats Left

San Diego Padres	AB	H	2B	3B	HR	RBI	BB	SO	BA	SA	OBA
Season	333	88	13	4	11	42	31	62	.264	.426	.325
vs. Left-Handers	55	18	4	1	1	8	8	9	.327	.491	.413
vs. Right-Handers	278	70	9	3	10	34	23	53	.252	.414	.307
Home	164	46	6	3	6	27	16	32	.280	.463	.343
Road	169	42	7	1	5	15	15	30	.249	.391	.308
Grass	247	64	7	3	6	30	22	46	.259	.385	.319
Artificial Turf	86	24	6	1	5	12	9	16	.279	.547	.344
April	28	7	2	1	2	7	5	4	.250	.607	.364
May	49	17	2	2	4	12	5	9	.347	.714	.407
June	85	24	1	1	3	9	7	15	.282	.424	.333
July	65	13	3	0	0	3	5	15	.200	.246	.257
August	42	10	2	0	1	3	4	7	.238	.357	.304
Sept./Oct.	64	17	3	0	1	8	5	12	.266	.359	.314
Leading Off Inn.	122	30	4	1	2	2	9	21	.246	.344	.298
Runners On	116	38	6	2	6	37	9	21	.328	.569	.370
Runners/Scor. Pos.	68	23	3	2	3	29	8	12	.338	.574	.397
Runners On/2 Out	60	18	2	2	4	22	6	13	.300	.600	.364
Scor. Pos./2 Out	43	13	1	2	3	19	6	8	.302	.628	.388
Late Inning Pressure	61	11	2	0	1	3	4	16	.180	.262	.231
Leading Off	21	1	0	0	0	0	2	6	.048	.048	.130
Runners On	19	4	1	0	1	3	2	4	.211	.421	.286
Runners/Scor. Pos.	10	2	0	0	1	2	2	1	.200	.500	.333

RUNS BATTED IN	From 1B	From 2B	From 3B	Scoring Position
Totals	8/74	11/48	12/35	23/83
Percentage	11%	23%	34%	28%
Driving In Runners from 3B with Less than Two Out:			8/13	62%

Loves to face: Rick Sutcliffe (.464, 13-for-28)
Hates to face: Dwight Gooden (0-for-19)
Started 68 of 104 games in which Padres faced a right-handed starter, but only six of 57 games against left-handers. . . . One of five N.L. players to have hits in seven consecutive at-bats last season. . . . Batted .087 (2-for-23) as pinch hitter last season, hitless in last 12 at-bats. That lowered his career pinch hitting average to .159. . . . Home-run and RBI totals were career highs. . . . Had 369 plate appearances last season, his highest total since he had 702 for 1984 Pirates. . . . Has batted .342 with runners in scoring position over last two years. . . . Career average of .274 before the All-Star break, .225 after the break. . . . He's a career .304 hitter in June, but .238 in other months.

Gerald Young

Houston Astros — Bats Left and Right

Houston Astros	AB	H	2B	3B	HR	RBI	BB	SO	BA	SA	OBA
Season	576	148	21	9	0	37	66	66	.257	.325	.334
vs. Left-Handers	205	56	9	2	0	11	19	23	.273	.337	.339
vs. Right-Handers	371	92	12	7	0	26	47	43	.248	.318	.331
Home	288	68	7	4	0	19	26	32	.236	.288	.302
Road	288	80	14	5	0	18	40	34	.278	.361	.365
Grass	154	48	8	3	0	10	23	20	.312	.403	.399
Artificial Turf	422	100	13	6	0	27	43	46	.237	.296	.309
April	88	23	4	0	0	4	5	10	.261	.307	.309
May	104	32	4	1	0	10	16	11	.308	.365	.397
June	96	20	4	1	0	5	13	10	.208	.271	.306
July	75	18	3	4	0	5	16	11	.240	.387	.370
August	100	27	2	2	0	7	10	12	.270	.330	.333
Sept./Oct.	113	28	4	1	0	6	6	12	.248	.301	.289
Leading Off Inn.	246	62	8	5	0	0	28	29	.252	.325	.328
Runners On	165	46	10	2	0	37	22	17	.279	.364	.361
Runners/Scor. Pos.	109	37	10	2	0	37	17	10	.339	.468	.421
Runners On/2 Out	88	24	5	2	0	18	13	8	.273	.375	.373
Scor. Pos./2 Out	68	19	5	2	0	18	11	6	.279	.412	.388
Late Inning Pressure	87	28	5	0	0	14	7	11	.322	.379	.361
Leading Off	21	7	0	0	0	0	2	2	.333	.333	.391
Runners On	42	14	2	0	0	14	3	6	.333	.429	.354
Runners/Scor. Pos.	28	11	4	0	0	14	3	3	.393	.536	.412

RUNS BATTED IN	From 1B	From 2B	From 3B	Scoring Position
Totals	0/98	21/92	16/38	37/130
Percentage	0%	23%	42%	28%
Driving In Runners from 3B with Less than Two Out:			12/17	71%

Loves to face: Frank DiPino (.667, 4-for-6)
Hates to face: Dennis Martinez (0-for-10)
Led major leagues with 47 stolen bases at the All-Star break, but stole only 18 bases in second half. . . . Youngest N.L. player to start at least half of his team's games in the outfield last season; he didn't turn 24 until October. . . . Only N.L. player with 500 or more at-bats and no home runs last season. Struck out 66 times in his homerless season; that's a far cry from Vince Coleman's major league record of 98 whiffs, no dingers, set in 1986. . . . One of three N.L. players to bat 100 points higher with men in scoring position than in other at-bats last season. . . . Career breakdown: .269 with the bases empty, .300 with runners on base, .336 with runners in scoring position.

Atlanta Braves

	AB	H	2B	3B	HR	RBI	BB	SO	BA	SA	OBA
Season	5440	1319	228	28	96	527	432	848	.242	.348	.298
vs. Left-Handers	1794	414	70	11	41	183	152	277	.231	.351	.288
vs. Right-Handers	3646	905	158	17	55	344	280	571	.248	.346	.303
Home	2675	669	131	16	48	281	224	394	.250	.365	.308
Road	2765	650	97	12	48	246	208	454	.235	.331	.289
Grass	3965	960	162	22	60	384	308	612	.242	.339	.297
Artificial Turf	1475	359	66	6	36	143	124	236	.243	.369	.301
April	615	125	20	3	8	48	61	99	.203	.285	.275
May	961	242	50	5	18	105	79	140	.252	.370	.309
June	988	274	45	7	22	126	71	161	.277	.404	.327
July	1000	256	35	4	21	88	82	152	.256	.362	.311
August	966	220	40	6	12	85	71	144	.228	.319	.282
Sept./Oct.	910	202	38	3	15	75	68	152	.222	.320	.275
Leading Off Inn.	1391	336	60	7	26	26	80	199	.242	.351	.286
Runners On	2105	544	98	13	29	460	230	315	.258	.359	.327
Runners/Scor. Pos.	1213	307	54	9	20	419	183	200	.253	.362	.342
Runners On/2 Out	923	232	49	7	13	199	117	157	.251	.362	.339
Scor. Pos./2 Out	589	145	31	3	11	183	94	99	.246	.365	.352
Late Inning Pressure	1040	229	32	5	8	80	94	177	.220	.284	.285
Leading Off	272	67	10	1	2	2	19	47	.246	.313	.298
Runners On	414	90	11	4	2	74	51	67	.217	.278	.301
Runners/Scor. Pos.	241	51	8	3	2	71	45	40	.212	.295	.331

RUNS BATTED IN	From 1B	From 2B	From 3B	Scoring Position
Totals	56/1461	184/961	191/500	375/1461
Percentage	4%	19%	38%	26%
Driving In Runners from 3B with Less than Two Out:		135/260		52%

Love to face: Mike Scott (10–6 against him)
Hate to face: Tim Leary (0–5 against him)

Talent pool has dried up. Last rookie to start on opening day was Brett Butler in 1982. Every other major league team has started at least one rookie on opening day since 1985. . . . Collective .232 batting average from 4th spot in order was lowest in N.L., and was lower than any other spot (except 9th) in Braves' order. . . . Batting average in Late-Inning Pressure Situations was lowest in N.L. over past 14 years. . . . One of three teams with fewer grand slams in 1988 than Steffi Graf. *Die anderen:* Pittsburgh and St. Louis. . . . Used 287 pinch hitters; only 184 were "by the book" (lefty for righty, or vice versa), lowest percentage in N.L. (64%).

Chicago Cubs

	AB	H	2B	3B	HR	RBI	BB	SO	BA	SA	OBA
Season	5675	1481	262	46	113	613	403	910	.261	.383	.310
vs. Left-Handers	1615	425	71	17	37	180	119	260	.263	.397	.314
vs. Right-Handers	4060	1056	191	29	76	433	284	650	.260	.378	.308
Home	2808	766	110	29	58	320	205	445	.273	.395	.314
Road	2867	715	152	17	55	293	198	465	.249	.372	.297
Grass	3991	1045	159	35	80	431	291	641	.262	.379	.312
Artificial Turf	1684	436	103	11	33	182	112	269	.259	.392	.304
April	777	194	40	8	24	92	49	124	.250	.414	.295
May	943	259	49	5	22	113	72	150	.275	.407	.325
June	950	265	38	9	17	105	66	146	.279	.392	.328
July	952	229	30	4	10	75	60	138	.241	.312	.286
August	956	249	48	14	21	109	65	185	.260	.406	.307
Sept./Oct.	1097	285	57	6	19	119	91	167	.260	.375	.315
Leading Off Inn.	1400	388	69	16	35	35	67	223	.277	.424	.313
Runners On	2404	635	99	20	48	548	213	363	.264	.382	.321
Runners/Scor. Pos.	1434	351	45	11	36	497	171	246	.245	.367	.319
Runners On/2 Out	1042	263	37	11	20	230	109	165	.252	.367	.326
Scor. Pos./2 Out	709	168	24	5	17	211	95	121	.237	.357	.330
Late Inning Pressure	919	236	37	6	11	89	78	162	.257	.346	.314
Leading Off	236	65	9	4	6	6	15	35	.275	.424	.319
Runners On	400	101	15	1	1	79	43	64	.253	.303	.322
Runners/Scor. Pos.	239	56	6	0	1	75	31	41	.234	.272	.315

RUNS BATTED IN	From 1B	From 2B	From 3B	Scoring Position
Totals	63/1636	188/1110	249/621	437/1731
Percentage	4%	17%	40%	25%
Driving In Runners from 3B with Less than Two Out:		175/317		55%

Love to face: Mark Davis (9–1)
Hate to face: Bob Walk (1–9)

Held to fewer than three runs in nine consecutive games (May 11-20) for first time in modern era. . . . First natural-turf team to lead N.L. in doubles since 1970 Giants. . . . Had fewest walks in majors last season, lowest total by any team in last four years. . . . Hitters in 3d spot in order batted .300, highest mark of any slot on any N.L. team. But batters hitting in number-one slot in order compiled .294 on-base average, lowest in majors. Maybe that explains 71 RBIs from cleanup slot, a seven-year N.L. low. . . . Outscored opponents by 39 runs over first three innings, not enough to overcome 73-run deficit thereafter. . . . Seven rookies combined for 20 HRs, 124 RBIs, highest totals in majors.

Cincinnati Reds

	AB	H	2B	3B	HR	RBI	BB	SO	BA	SA	OBA
Season	5426	1334	246	25	122	590	479	922	.246	.368	.309
vs. Left-Handers	1412	358	61	9	31	156	142	241	.254	.375	.323
vs. Right-Handers	4014	976	185	16	91	434	337	681	.243	.365	.304
Home	2648	672	122	10	75	307	248	464	.254	.392	.319
Road	2778	662	124	15	47	283	231	458	.238	.344	.298
Grass	1644	400	72	7	27	173	136	263	.243	.345	.303
Artificial Turf	3782	934	174	18	95	417	343	659	.247	.378	.311
April	793	194	37	2	22	86	76	138	.245	.380	.314
May	957	237	45	1	15	101	93	150	.248	.344	.316
June	922	234	50	4	26	112	89	170	.254	.401	.323
July	867	193	34	7	23	79	69	153	.223	.358	.283
August	930	228	46	7	18	105	80	141	.245	.368	.305
Sept./Oct.	957	248	34	4	18	107	72	170	.259	.359	.310
Leading Off Inn.	1361	347	62	6	40	40	81	196	.255	.398	.302
Runners On	2176	548	101	12	46	514	268	386	.252	.373	.332
Runners/Scor. Pos.	1305	317	63	5	24	451	216	251	.243	.354	.345
Runners On/2 Out	960	238	52	9	22	222	148	185	.248	.390	.355
Scor. Pos./2 Out	653	148	37	4	14	194	127	143	.227	.360	.359
Late Inning Pressure	876	217	34	4	19	86	86	164	.248	.361	.319
Leading Off	231	58	11	0	5	5	12	37	.251	.364	.294
Runners On	337	81	11	3	9	76	52	68	.240	.371	.345
Runners/Scor. Pos.	198	50	8	0	6	67	46	38	.253	.384	.391

RUNS BATTED IN	From 1B	From 2B	From 3B	Scoring Position
Totals	66/1455	161/1026	241/579	402/1605
Percentage	5%	16%	42%	25%
Driving In Runners from 3B with Less than Two Out:		162/294		55%

Love to face: Mark Grant (6–0)
Hate to face: Rick Sutcliffe (3–10)

Faced only 42 left-handed starters, fewest in N.L., but had a better record vs. right-handers (67–54) than southpaws (20–20). . . . Eighth slot in batting order produced only 30 RBIs, lowest total in N.L. over past seven seasons, excluding ninth positions. . . . Compiled a 38–48 record (.442) in games following wins, 48–26 (.649) following losses. . . . Posted their first 1–0 victory since 1985 when Tom Browning pitched a perfect game vs. Los Angeles. That snapped streak of nine consecutive losses in 1–0 contests, one short of modern N.L. record, coheld by Cardinals (1908–13), Dodgers (1912–13), and Mets (1978–81). . . . There were 66 1–0 games in N.L. last season, nearly twice as many as in 1987 (38).

Houston Astros

	AB	H	2B	3B	HR	RBI	BB	SO	BA	SA	OBA
Season	5494	1338	239	31	96	576	474	840	.244	.351	.306
vs. Left-Handers	1743	435	89	9	32	186	152	251	.250	.366	.313
vs. Right-Handers	3751	903	150	22	64	390	322	589	.241	.344	.303
Home	2636	636	111	17	33	271	228	410	.241	.334	.304
Road	2858	702	128	14	63	305	246	430	.246	.366	.307
Grass	1692	415	73	8	31	177	142	251	.245	.353	.306
Artificial Turf	3802	923	166	23	65	399	332	589	.243	.350	.306
April	707	176	31	4	12	88	62	106	.249	.355	.312
May	935	243	43	5	13	109	79	152	.260	.358	.321
June	977	225	37	4	17	108	85	135	.230	.329	.297
July	934	246	47	9	23	103	82	148	.263	.407	.324
August	948	220	39	5	13	88	91	158	.232	.325	.300
Sept./Oct.	993	228	42	4	18	80	75	141	.230	.334	.285
Leading Off Inn.	1379	328	55	11	26	26	86	193	.238	.350	.288
Runners On	2178	557	104	11	43	523	257	333	.256	.373	.333
Runners/Scor. Pos.	1322	340	59	6	22	458	202	222	.257	.361	.351
Runners On/2 Out	974	238	43	5	17	227	148	163	.244	.351	.346
Scor. Pos./2 Out	668	164	30	3	9	201	121	113	.246	.340	.363
Late Inning Pressure	912	224	40	3	14	90	100	141	.246	.342	.321
Leading Off	246	72	6	1	9	9	17	34	.293	.435	.338
Runners On	360	87	20	0	3	79	56	61	.242	.322	.342
Runners/Scor. Pos.	214	56	11	0	0	71	45	39	.262	.313	.386

RUNS BATTED IN	From 1B	From 2B	From 3B	Scoring Position
Totals	67/1468	201/1058	211/537	412/1595
Percentage	5%	19%	39%	26%
Driving In Runners from 3B with Less than Two Out:		152/266		57%

Love to face: Mike Krukow (13–7)
Hate to face: Dwight Gooden (2–10)

Turned only 124 double plays, fewest in N.L. for 3d straight year. It's 9th time in last 26 years that Houston has had fewest DPs in N.L. . . . Tied Atlanta for ninth in N.L. in home runs, but led the league with four grand slams. . . . Compiled N.L.'s lowest batting average in day games for second consecutive season. . . . Last season's Astros batters were young by comparison only to their pitchers. Average age of N.L. teams' batters: Pirates, 26.5; Padres, 27.5; Reds, 27.9; Giants, 28.2; Cubs, 28.2; Mets, 28.5; Expos, 28.6; Cardinals, 28.7; Braves, 29.3; Phillies, 29.4; Astros, 29.4; Dodgers, 29.5. Astros had N.L.'s oldest pitching staff (34.0).

Los Angeles Dodgers

	AB	H	2B	3B	HR	RBI	BB	SO	BA	SA	OBA
Season	5431	1346	217	25	99	589	437	947	.248	.352	.305
vs. Left-Handers	1860	441	70	9	34	210	145	321	.237	.339	.291
vs. Right-Handers	3571	905	147	16	65	379	292	626	.253	.358	.312
Home	2619	677	93	9	49	298	197	436	.258	.357	.310
Road	2812	669	124	16	50	291	240	511	.238	.347	.300
Grass	3981	989	144	14	72	431	306	687	.248	.346	.303
Artificial Turf	1450	357	73	11	27	158	131	260	.246	.368	.310
April	649	164	25	2	8	84	63	106	.253	.334	.320
May	944	239	39	7	22	111	85	154	.253	.379	.315
June	957	265	43	6	19	117	83	159	.277	.394	.336
July	991	247	50	4	16	103	75	152	.249	.356	.303
August	961	243	31	5	17	99	68	185	.253	.349	.303
Sept./Oct.	929	188	29	1	17	75	63	191	.202	.291	.256
Leading Off Inn.	1363	331	50	5	25	25	85	221	.243	.342	.289
Runners On	2205	573	93	10	44	534	211	374	.260	.371	.324
Runners/Scor. Pos.	1252	329	55	8	23	473	162	221	.263	.375	.341
Runners On/2 Out	997	248	36	5	21	246	110	174	.249	.358	.330
Scor. Pos./2 Out	636	164	26	5	14	223	86	113	.258	.381	.352
Late Inning Pressure	778	203	32	3	21	93	69	141	.261	.391	.324
Leading Off	208	62	11	1	6	6	12	32	.298	.447	.339
Runners On	316	83	10	1	9	81	41	60	.263	.386	.347
Runners/Scor. Pos.	192	54	6	0	7	74	33	38	.281	.422	.383

RUNS BATTED IN	From 1B	From 2B	From 3B	Scoring Position
Totals	71/1554	201/1011	218/508	419/1519
Percentage	5%	20%	43%	28%
Driving In Runners from 3B with Less than Two Out:			142/255	56%

Love to face: Danny Cox (7–2)
Hate to face: Craig Lefferts (0–7)
Batted .426 with two outs and bases loaded, highest mark in either league over past 14 years by wide margin (2d highest: .378 by 1980 Braves).... Had league's highest batting average and slugging average in Late-Inning Pressure Situations; on-base average in those situations was 2d best in N.L., as opposed to 2d-worst on-base average overall.... Finished 10th in N.L. in fielding percentage (.977), first time in four years that they haven't been last.... Had lowest batting average in majors (.205) in September. Thank God for Orel.... Played .630 ball (68–40) vs. right-handed starters, only .491 (26–27) vs. lefties. But in 12 postseason games, they saw only one lefty starter (Sid Fernandez).

Montreal Expos

	AB	H	2B	3B	HR	RBI	BB	SO	BA	SA	OBA
Season	5573	1400	260	48	107	578	454	1053	.251	.373	.309
vs. Left-Handers	1580	398	80	11	33	171	131	279	.252	.379	.309
vs. Right-Handers	3993	1002	180	37	74	407	323	774	.251	.370	.309
Home	2743	710	144	30	47	301	231	510	.259	.385	.317
Road	2830	690	116	18	60	277	223	543	.244	.361	.301
Grass	1460	348	53	5	32	138	112	297	.238	.347	.295
Artificial Turf	4113	1052	207	43	75	440	342	756	.256	.382	.314
April	703	177	27	5	16	73	65	106	.252	.373	.316
May	970	246	39	10	14	94	82	178	.254	.358	.316
June	984	232	47	10	20	100	86	164	.236	.365	.299
July	913	228	50	9	17	101	72	190	.250	.380	.306
August	984	248	49	5	21	94	67	212	.252	.376	.300
Sept./Oct.	1019	269	48	9	19	116	82	203	.264	.385	.320
Leading Off Inn.	1395	356	76	9	23	23	94	251	.255	.372	.305
Runners On	2272	589	108	22	43	514	234	407	.259	.383	.326
Runners/Scor. Pos.	1394	348	64	16	24	454	185	282	.250	.370	.333
Runners On/2 Out	927	210	35	10	19	197	121	184	.227	.347	.319
Scor. Pos./2 Out	628	140	24	7	12	175	101	125	.223	.341	.334
Late Inning Pressure	1120	285	52	11	21	119	97	232	.254	.377	.314
Leading Off	290	70	16	2	4	4	15	58	.241	.352	.281
Runners On	455	121	18	6	11	109	53	90	.266	.404	.339
Runners/Scor. Pos.	270	72	9	3	3	88	50	55	.267	.356	.375

RUNS BATTED IN	From 1B	From 2B	From 3B	Scoring Position
Totals	62/1474	160/1036	249/630	409/1666
Percentage	4%	15%	40%	25%
Driving In Runners from 3B with Less than Two Out:			178/337	53%

Love to face: Steve Bedrosian (6–1)
Hate to face: Joaquin Andujar (6–15)
All-time record of 20–6 in games played on July 4, the best record of any active franchise. Un-American, you say? Not really; after all, the team colors are red, white, and bleu.... Led N.L. in strikeouts for first time in team history.... Used 57 pinch runners, most in N.L. last season.... Runners advanced more than one base on singles 82 times in 270 opportunities, lowest average in N.L. (30.4 percent).... Had at least one extra-base hit in all but eight games, lowest total in N.L.... Compiled N.L.'s highest pinch-hit batting average (.251).... Lost 11 of 13 one-run games on grass, won 30 of 46 of artificial turf.

New York Mets

	AB	H	2B	3B	HR	RBI	BB	SO	BA	SA	OBA
Season	5408	1387	251	24	152	660	544	842	.256	.396	.325
vs. Left-Handers	1844	456	83	12	66	235	168	282	.247	.413	.310
vs. Right-Handers	3564	931	168	12	86	425	376	560	.261	.387	.332
Home	2612	650	113	12	67	300	248	406	.249	.378	.315
Road	2796	737	138	12	85	360	296	436	.264	.413	.334
Grass	3776	969	162	15	101	447	353	588	.257	.388	.321
Artificial Turf	1632	418	89	9	51	213	191	254	.256	.415	.334
April	679	171	31	3	29	99	86	103	.252	.434	.337
May	940	244	42	3	19	112	98	147	.260	.371	.330
June	989	268	39	7	23	117	92	138	.271	.394	.332
July	879	208	45	3	22	95	91	150	.237	.370	.310
August	977	235	39	4	21	97	83	149	.241	.353	.302
Sept./Oct.	944	261	55	4	38	140	94	155	.276	.464	.341
Leading Off Inn.	1318	349	62	9	39	39	96	186	.265	.414	.321
Runners On	2302	591	89	11	70	578	297	379	.257	.396	.337
Runners/Scor. Pos.	1390	333	48	6	35	487	211	251	.240	.358	.330
Runners On/2 Out	986	229	30	7	29	213	149	175	.232	.365	.336
Scor. Pos./2 Out	654	142	18	4	18	182	112	123	.217	.339	.333
Late Inning Pressure	797	198	28	3	25	94	91	126	.248	.385	.328
Leading Off	205	52	7	1	9	9	21	25	.254	.429	.329
Runners On	318	87	5	1	10	79	46	58	.274	.390	.363
Runners/Scor. Pos.	194	51	3	1	5	68	38	40	.263	.366	.374

RUNS BATTED IN	From 1B	From 2B	From 3B	Scoring Position
Totals	86/1598	190/1120	232/529	422/1649
Percentage	5%	17%	44%	26%
Driving In Runners from 3B with Less than Two Out:			168/290	58%

Love to face: Jose DeLeon (9–1)
Hate to face: Mike Krukow (7–20)
First team since 1949–53 Dodgers to lead N.L. in runs in three consecutive seasons.... Didn't allow a home run in 14 consecutive games from August 21 through Sept. 6, longest streak in majors last season.... Committed fewest errors in N.L. for first time in team's 27-year history.... Had N.L.'s best batting average from Sept. 1 on (.271). The worst belonged to the team that beat them in October.... Runners advanced more than one base on singles 109 times in 283 opportunities, highest average in N.L. (38.5 percent).... Led majors with 79 runs in 9th inning, quite an accomplishment for a team that had the majors' best home record.... Won 21 of 25 one-run games at home.

Phila. Phillies

	AB	H	2B	3B	HR	RBI	BB	SO	BA	SA	OBA
Season	5403	1294	246	31	106	569	489	981	.239	.355	.306
vs. Left-Handers	1539	379	76	7	36	165	135	240	.246	.375	.310
vs. Right-Handers	3864	915	170	24	70	404	354	741	.237	.348	.304
Home	2654	657	142	20	62	311	248	446	.248	.386	.315
Road	2749	637	104	11	44	258	241	535	.232	.326	.296
Grass	1459	371	47	5	23	141	108	302	.254	.341	.308
Artificial Turf	3944	923	199	26	83	428	381	679	.234	.361	.305
April	662	147	28	7	9	69	77	142	.222	.326	.310
May	920	213	37	7	23	90	94	184	.232	.362	.304
June	968	241	58	5	15	110	106	172	.249	.366	.325
July	958	235	47	6	23	111	99	152	.245	.379	.322
August	940	222	42	0	14	92	63	162	.236	.326	.284
Sept./Oct.	955	236	34	6	22	97	50	169	.247	.364	.289
Leading Off Inn.	1329	314	67	9	32	32	109	244	.236	.372	.300
Runners On	2254	578	109	14	46	509	225	382	.256	.378	.324
Runners/Scor. Pos.	1346	332	60	9	24	437	165	257	.247	.358	.327
Runners On/2 Out	965	214	38	6	17	185	108	182	.222	.326	.305
Scor. Pos./2 Out	655	139	23	5	11	162	77	135	.212	.313	.301
Late Inning Pressure	870	207	38	6	10	86	100	163	.238	.330	.318
Leading Off	221	48	14	2	2	2	19	38	.217	.326	.282
Runners On	371	97	14	3	5	81	50	63	.261	.355	.348
Runners/Scor. Pos.	234	54	9	1	3	74	36	46	.231	.316	.330

RUNS BATTED IN	From 1B	From 2B	From 3B	Scoring Position
Totals	68/1545	152/1033	243/588	395/1621
Percentage	4%	15%	41%	24%
Driving In Runners from 3B with Less than Two Out:			180/308	58%

Love to face: Walt Terrell (5–2)
Hate to face: Terry Leach (0–5)
Ranked last in N.L. in batting average for 11th time in team history, but only the second time in past 27 years.... Lost all 83 games in which they trailed after eight innings.... Used 290 pinch hitters; 261 were "by the book" (lefty for righty, or vice versa), highest average in N.L. (90%).... Of their 290 pinch hitters, 194 batted for pitchers, 2d highest total in N.L. The highest: 201, Montreal.... Used only 23 pinch runners, fewest in N.L. last season.... Opening-day starting lineup combination made 31 starts for the season, highest total for any set last season (Parrish, c; Hayes, 1b; Samuel, 2b; Schmidt, 3b; Jeltz, ss; Bradley, lf; Thompson, cf; James, rf).

Pittsburgh Pirates

	AB	H	2B	3B	HR	RBI	BB	SO	BA	SA	OBA
Season	5379	1327	240	45	110	621	553	947	.247	.369	.317
vs. Left-Handers	1862	429	84	12	34	179	183	340	.230	.343	.300
vs. Right-Handers	3517	898	156	33	76	442	370	607	.255	.383	.326
Home	2626	634	134	23	56	314	297	458	.241	.374	.319
Road	2753	693	106	22	54	307	256	489	.252	.365	.316
Grass	1394	362	44	10	31	152	109	254	.260	.372	.311
Artificial Turf	3985	965	196	35	79	469	444	693	.242	.368	.320
April	753	186	43	9	23	92	73	123	.247	.420	.314
May	946	246	35	9	20	126	115	173	.260	.379	.340
June	917	233	48	5	21	106	101	147	.254	.386	.328
July	846	197	34	10	13	91	76	166	.233	.343	.297
August	999	229	45	4	17	96	96	168	.229	.333	.301
Sept./Oct.	918	236	35	8	16	110	92	170	.257	.365	.324
Leading Off Inn.	1332	302	63	8	29	29	98	237	.227	.384	.284
Runners On	2231	565	101	29	40	551	288	389	.253	.378	.335
Runners/Scor. Pos.	1365	338	59	19	23	493	203	262	.248	.369	.336
Runners On/2 Out	969	208	38	8	15	194	134	172	.215	.317	.316
Scor. Pos./2 Out	646	132	27	7	10	179	102	126	.204	.314	.320
Late Inning Pressure	873	207	33	4	15	79	90	175	.237	.336	.309
Leading Off	222	49	8	1	1		19	39	.221	.279	.288
Runners On	360	75	11	2	6	70	45	79	.208	.300	.294
Runners/Scor. Pos.	211	46	6	2	4	63	28	51	.218	.322	.300

RUNS BATTED IN	From 1B	From 2B	From 3B	Scoring Position
Totals	75/1573	192/1053	244/589	436/1642
Percentage	5%	18%	41%	27%
Driving In Runners from 3B with Less than Two Out:			190/329	58%

Love to face: Greg Maddux (5-1)
Hate to face: Ron Darling (2-10)

Team batting average vs. right-handers was 3d highest in N.L.; average vs. left-handers was lowest in N.L. in past 14 years. . . . Compiled 58-46 (.558) record vs. righties, 27-29 (.482) vs. lefties. . . . Scored three runs or fewer in 11 consecutive games in late July, their longest such streak in 20 years. The modern major league record: 19 by the 1908 Dodgers and the 1942 Indians. . . . Led N.L. in walks; previous five teams that did that each won a division title. . . . Ninth slot in batting order produced more RBIs (37) than eighth slot (32). . . . Led N.L. with seven pinch-hit home runs. . . . Shortstops hit only six doubles.

St. Louis Cardinals

	AB	H	2B	3B	HR	RBI	BB	SO	BA	SA	OBA
Season	5518	1373	207	33	71	538	484	827	.249	.337	.309
vs. Left-Handers	1843	495	92	8	27	195	164	261	.269	.371	.328
vs. Right-Handers	3675	878	115	25	44	343	320	566	.239	.320	.300
Home	2733	702	104	20	29	294	255	406	.257	.341	.320
Road	2785	671	103	13	42	244	229	421	.241	.332	.299
Grass	1425	350	43	6	23	133	111	228	.246	.333	.300
Artificial Turf	4093	1023	164	27	48	405	373	599	.250	.338	.313
April	725	178	24	8	15	68	69	112	.246	.363	.310
May	1041	285	38	3	12	128	99	126	.274	.351	.336
June	965	240	36	9	8	79	84	152	.249	.330	.308
July	883	193	22	3	12	73	60	138	.219	.291	.270
August	971	245	31	6	16	107	80	147	.252	.346	.311
Sept./Oct.	933	232	56	4	8	83	92	152	.249	.343	.315
Leading Off Inn.	1379	339	62	7	17	17	98	196	.246	.338	.297
Runners On	2316	583	80	17	23	490	248	357	.252	.331	.322
Runners/Scor. Pos.	1415	348	54	9	15	459	199	232	.246	.329	.333
Runners On/2 Out	1020	238	28	10	12	203	147	165	.233	.316	.333
Scor. Pos./2 Out	702	157	20	6	10	191	117	119	.224	.312	.338
Late Inning Pressure	928	215	22	4	11	66	79	138	.232	.300	.291
Leading Off	246	57	9	1	1	1	17	37	.232	.289	.284
Runners On	357	80	9	1	5	60	41	59	.224	.297	.301
Runners/Scor. Pos.	211	43	5	1	2	54	34	33	.204	.265	.306

RUNS BATTED IN	From 1B	From 2B	From 3B	Scoring Position
Totals	42/1571	157/1074	268/670	425/1744
Percentage	3%	15%	40%	24%
Driving In Runners from 3B with Less than Two Out:			181/341	53%

Love to face: Don Carman (7-1)
Hate to face: Steve Bedrosian (2-9)

Led N.L. in steals for 7th straight season, longest streak since Dodgers did it in each of their first eight years in L.A. . . . How do you keep 'em off base? Throw right-handed pitchers against them. Cards had league's best on-base average vs. southpaws, its worst OBA vs. righties. . . . Led N.L. in singles, trailed in extra-base hits. . . . Ranked last in home runs for sixth time in past seven years. Hit only two in first inning. . . . Ranked next-to-last in N.L. in runs scored, but led league with 14 innings of five runs or more. . . . Eighth-place hitters batted .272, a major league high. A.L. average was .245, N.L., .239. . . . Led N.L. in fielding for record 5th straight year.

San Diego Padres

	AB	H	2B	3B	HR	RBI	BB	SO	BA	SA	OBA
Season	5366	1325	205	35	94	566	494	892	.247	.351	.310
vs. Left-Handers	1804	446	60	9	33	196	173	274	.247	.345	.313
vs. Right-Handers	3562	879	145	26	61	370	321	618	.247	.353	.309
Home	2605	648	90	17	56	292	281	431	.249	.361	.322
Road	2761	677	115	18	38	274	213	461	.245	.341	.299
Grass	3962	977	143	23	73	420	374	656	.247	.350	.311
Artificial Turf	1404	348	62	12	21	146	120	236	.248	.354	.309
April	656	155	18	3	13	51	47	115	.236	.332	.287
May	964	215	40	5	16	83	93	167	.223	.325	.293
June	936	228	42	5	14	115	97	153	.244	.344	.313
July	873	238	36	8	10	91	71	128	.273	.367	.328
August	910	228	33	9	20	96	86	168	.251	.373	.317
Sept./Oct.	1027	261	36	5	21	130	100	161	.254	.360	.319
Leading Off Inn.	1351	368	45	8	27	27	90	188	.272	.377	.321
Runners On	2265	577	110	17	35	507	247	361	.255	.365	.324
Runners/Scor. Pos.	1273	324	61	8	20	445	182	233	.255	.362	.339
Runners On/2 Out	974	232	46	10	14	209	121	161	.238	.349	.322
Scor. Pos./2 Out	631	153	29	7	9	184	96	121	.242	.353	.343
Late Inning Pressure	780	185	23	1	14	69	58	136	.237	.323	.292
Leading Off	204	51	4	0	4	4	13	30	.250	.328	.298
Runners On	310	71	12	1	5	60	30	51	.229	.323	.296
Runners/Scor. Pos.	163	38	3	0	4	53	23	29	.233	.325	.325

RUNS BATTED IN	From 1B	From 2B	From 3B	Scoring Position
Totals	69/1613	185/983	218/570	403/1553
Percentage	4%	19%	38%	26%
Driving In Runners from 3B with Less than Two Out:			147/269	55%

Love to face: Atlee Hammaker (8-3)
Hate to face: John Franco (0-7)

Didn't score in double figures in any game last season. Their streak of 181 consecutive games scoring fewer than 10 runs is the 12th longest in modern major league history, and the longest since Houston set the record of 284 from 1981 through 1983. . . . Didn't have an extra-base hit in 25 games, tying St. Louis for highest total in majors last season. . . . Ranked last in N.L. in batting average during May, first in July. . . . Cleanup hitters executed five sacrifice bunts, most by an N.L. team's number-four hitters over the past seven seasons. . . . Lost nine of 10 extra-inning road games. . . . Started 96 different lineup combinations, highest total in N.L. Cubs compiled major league low total of 56.

San Francisco Giants

	AB	H	2B	3B	HR	RBI	BB	SO	BA	SA	OBA
Season	5450	1353	227	44	113	630	550	1023	.248	.368	.318
vs. Left-Handers	1764	440	82	12	30	195	189	311	.249	.361	.321
vs. Right-Handers	3686	913	145	32	83	435	361	712	.248	.372	.317
Home	2634	651	103	19	58	304	259	521	.247	.367	.315
Road	2816	702	124	25	55	326	291	502	.249	.370	.322
Grass	3971	1001	160	32	88	480	400	762	.252	.375	.321
Artificial Turf	1479	352	67	12	25	150	150	261	.238	.350	.310
April	776	181	29	5	16	74	79	149	.233	.345	.303
May	952	235	42	12	23	111	79	163	.247	.389	.308
June	847	233	42	7	19	126	94	162	.275	.409	.347
July	925	234	37	6	20	111	100	179	.253	.371	.326
August	990	256	44	7	18	118	98	202	.259	.372	.327
Sept./Oct.	960	214	33	7	17	90	100	168	.223	.325	.299
Leading Off Inn.	1344	338	47	10	31	31	113	225	.251	.371	.311
Runners On	2270	594	102	19	48	565	276	418	.262	.387	.340
Runners/Scor. Pos.	1376	344	66	12	30	505	219	280	.254	.384	.351
Runners On/2 Out	1004	240	43	7	24	241	147	194	.239	.368	.341
Scor. Pos./2 Out	681	163	32	4	17	217	123	145	.239	.373	.360
Late Inning Pressure	836	190	28	3	13	80	86	178	.227	.315	.303
Leading Off	213	52	8	0	4	4	20	34	.244	.338	.315
Runners On	352	81	11	2	4	71	44	77	.230	.307	.319
Runners/Scor. Pos.	221	44	7	2	2	63	34	52	.199	.276	.308

RUNS BATTED IN	From 1B	From 2B	From 3B	Scoring Position
Totals	81/1573	195/1080	241/584	436/1664
Percentage	5%	18%	41%	26%
Driving In Runners from 3B with Less than Two Out:			168/302	56%

Love to face: Bruce Ruffin (5-1)
Hate to face: Orel Hershiser (4-12)

Only N.L. team to lose two games last season in which it led by five runs or more from the 6th inning on. Won their next game both times, supporting studies published in last two editions of the *Analyst* (1988, p. 40; 1987, p.36) that any after-effect from blowing such a lead is insiginifcant (if, in fact, one exists at all). Over past seven seasons, teams losing leads under those conditions have posted a composite record of 74-80 (.481) in their next games, only slightly worse than their composite winning percentage in all games (.500). . . . Will Clark and Brett Butler were first N.L. teammates to rank first and second outright in walks since Duke Snider and Junior Gilliam of 1956 Dodgers.

National League

	AB	H	2B	3B	HR	RBI	BB	SO	BA	SA	OBA
Season	65563	16277	2828	415	1279	7057	5793	11032	.248	.363	.310
vs. Left-Handers	20660	5116	918	126	434	2251	1853	3337	.248	.367	.310
vs. Right-Handers	44903	11161	1910	289	845	4806	3940	7695	.249	.360	.310
Home	31993	8072	1397	222	638	3593	2921	5327	.252	.370	.316
Road	33570	8205	1431	193	641	3464	2872	5705	.244	.356	.305
Grass	32720	8187	1262	182	641	3507	2750	5541	.250	.359	.309
Artificial Turf	32843	8090	1566	233	638	3550	3043	5491	.246	.366	.311
April	8495	2048	353	59	195	924	807	1423	.241	.365	.308
May	11473	2904	499	72	217	1283	1068	1884	.253	.366	.318
June	11400	2938	525	78	221	1321	1054	1859	.258	.376	.322
July	11021	2704	467	73	210	1121	937	1846	.245	.358	.306
August	11532	2823	487	72	208	1186	948	2021	.245	.354	.303
Sept./Oct.	11642	2860	497	61	228	1222	979	1999	.246	.358	.305
Leading Off Inn.	16342	4096	718	105	350	350	1097	2559	.251	.372	.301
Runners On	26978	6934	1194	195	515	6293	2994	4464	.257	.373	.329
Runners/Scor. Pos.	16085	4016	688	118	296	5578	2298	2937	.250	.362	.337
Runners On/2 Out	11741	2790	475	95	223	2566	1559	2077	.238	.351	.331
Scor. Pos./2 Out	7852	1815	321	60	152	2302	1251	1483	.231	.345	.341
Late Inning Pressure	10729	2596	399	53	182	1031	1028	1933	.242	.340	.310
Leading Off	2794	703	113	14	53	53	199	448	.252	.359	.305
Runners On	4350	1054	147	25	70	919	552	797	.242	.336	.326
Runners/Scor. Pos.	2588	615	81	13	39	821	443	502	.238	.324	.344

RUNS BATTED IN	From 1B	From 2B	From 3B	Scoring Position
Totals	807/1852	2166/1254	2805/6905	4971/1945
Percentage	4%	17%	41%	26%
Driving In Runners from 3B with Less than Two Out:			1978/3568	55%

IV
Pitcher Section

Pitcher Section

The Pitcher Section is an alphabetical listing of every pitcher who faced at least 300 batters in either the American or the National League last season. Also included are several key pitchers who did not face the required 300 batters, including all those who finished at least 20 games in relief. Pitchers are listed alphabetically within each league, followed by the totals for each team and the league as a whole.

Column Headings Information

Don Aase

Baltimore Orioles	W-L	ERA	AB	H	HR	BB	SO	BA	SA	OBA

- **W-L** Won-Lost Record
- **ERA** Earned-Run Average
- **AB** At Bats
- **H** Hits
- **HR** Home Runs
- **BB** Bases on Balls
- **SO** Strikeouts
- **BA** Batting Average
- **SA** Slugging Average
- **OBA** On-Base Average

In addition to the expected categories for pitchers (won-lost record, ERA, walks, and strikeouts), this book includes a unique perspective on each pitcher's season: the batting performance of the league against him. While this method may be unfamiliar at first, it enables us to look at the pitcher and his abilities in fascinating detail.

By compiling pitching statistics in this way, we can examine a pitcher's performance in the same "within the game" contexts we've used to look at batters. To take one example, we're all familiar with platoon differentials for batters; we know that some right-handed batters are far more effective against left-handed pitchers than they are against righties. The same must be true of pitchers, but because the specific information was never available before, who knew how big those differences were? Well, we know now, and the differences can be huge.

Moreover, by looking at the opponents' batting figures with runners on base or in scoring position, we can show conclusively who are those underrated pitchers who may give up a lot of hits or home runs, but rarely give them up with men on or in clutch situations. And we can also see those pitchers who (whisper the word, please) fold under the same pressure. (Bear in mind that overall batting averages increase with men on base. This makes any pitcher who holds opponents to a lower average with runners on all the more impressive.)

Season Summary Information

Season	19-7	2.87	910	204	19	74	170	.224	.330	.285
vs. Left-Handed Batters			475	95	7	42	93	.200	.282	.269
vs. Right-Handed Batters			435	109	12	32	77	.251	.382	.302
Home	10-2	3.23	468	118	10	30	86	.252	.357	.297
Road	9-5	2.50	442	86	9	44	84	.195	.301	.272
Grass	14-6	3.06	702	163	16	59	128	.232	.343	.291
Artificial Turf	5-1	2.22	208	41	3	15	42	.197	.284	.264
April	3-1	3.00	132	32	2	11	31	.242	.364	.301
May	1-1	4.26	103	29	1	13	20	.282	.379	.356
June	2-1	3.26	114	25	4	10	15	.219	.342	.291
July	4-1	2.93	163	32	7	16	30	.196	.337	.269
August	5-1	2.51	173	38	2	14	27	.220	.277	.282
Sept./Oct.	4-2	2.23	225	48	3	10	47	.213	.316	.249

Each pitcher's seasonal performance is broken down into a variety of special categories. The first line for each pitcher gives his totals for the whole season. This is followed by breakdowns of his performance against left- and right-handed hitters, in home and road games, on grass fields and on artificial turf, and by month. (For pitchers who pitched for more than one team within a league, all totals are combined. The "home" totals for John Tudor, for example, include all games he pitched in St. Louis while with the Cardinals, and all games he pitched in Los Angeles while with the Dodgers.)

Leading Off Inn.	240	59	6	14	37	.246	.367	.287
Runners On	350	79	8	32	63	.226	.343	.290
Runners/Scor. Pos.	178	40	4	21	41	.225	.343	.301
Runners On/2 Out	152	30	3	14	31	.197	.309	.278
Scor. Pos./2 Out	89	20	2	9	20	.225	.371	.310

Following these breakdowns, each pitcher's performance is divided into specific game situations.

Totals are given for each pitcher against batters who led off an inning, and against players batting with runners on base. These are followed by his performance with runners in scoring position (on second or third base, or both), with runners on base and two out, and with runners in scoring position and two out.

Late Inning Pressure	79	19	2	11	19	.241	.342	.333
Leading Off	24	7	1	3	5	.292	.458	.370
Runners On	26	7	1	3	4	.269	.385	.345
Runners/Scor. Pos.	10	1	0	3	2	.100	.100	.308

The next group shows the pitcher's performance in late-inning pressure situations, which are defined a little differently for pitchers than they are for batters. For pitchers, late-inning pressure is defined as any situation occurring in the seventh inning or later with the score tied, or with his team leading or trailing by one or two runs.

First 9 Batters	240	50	2	27	44	.208	.288	.288
Second 9 Batters	362	81	8	23	75	.224	.340	.272
All Batters Thereafter	308	73	9	24	51	.237	.351	.297

Each pitcher's totals are listed for all late-inning pressure situations, then broken out for his performance when facing a leadoff batter, with runners on base, and with runners in scoring position.

The last set of breakdowns tracks a pitcher's performance throughout each appearance by listing the opponents' batting record according to the number of batters he has faced, regardless of when he entered the game. This allows us to spotlight those pitchers who get stronger as the game progresses, and to pick out those who can breeze through the order once, but falter the second or third time around.

Following the statistics for each pitcher are a series of comments, beginning with the batter each pitcher loves to face and hates to face. The statistics listed for each individual match-up are from regular season games since 1975. Contained within the comments for each pitcher is his "Ground outs-to-air outs" ratio, which consists of his total of ground outs divided by outs on balls hit in the air. (Also included are plays in which the batter reaches base on an error.) An average figure is roughly 1.15. Pitchers with ratios below 0.75 have their games charted by NASA; those above 1.50 receive hate mail from burrowing animals.

American League

Doyle Alexander

Throws Right

Detroit Tigers	W–L	ERA	AB	H	HR	BB	SO	BA	SA	OBA
Season	14-11	4.32	922	260	30	46	126	.282	.456	.317
vs. Left-Handers			458	134	12	29	46	.293	.476	.337
vs. Right-Handers			464	126	18	17	80	.272	.435	.297
Home	9-5	3.09	503	129	18	22	77	.256	.421	.289
Road	5-6	5.88	419	131	12	24	49	.313	.496	.350
Grass	12-7	3.74	734	196	24	32	108	.267	.428	.298
Artificial Turf	2-4	6.80	188	64	6	14	18	.340	.564	.388
April	2-2	3.72	155	40	5	4	25	.258	.445	.281
May	2-2	3.38	169	46	6	16	22	.272	.444	.337
June	3-0	2.66	153	33	6	6	18	.216	.373	.245
July	3-1	4.97	126	41	3	4	16	.325	.524	.351
August	1-4	6.50	149	48	4	11	21	.322	.483	.370
Sept./Oct.	3-2	5.14	170	52	6	5	24	.306	.476	.318
Leading Off Inn.			235	70	8	5	30	.298	.502	.324
Runners On			351	98	13	28	38	.279	.453	.327
Runners/Scor. Pos.			185	53	8	18	21	.286	.470	.340
Runners On/2 Out			152	37	5	17	24	.243	.388	.320
Scor. Pos./2 Out			90	22	2	11	13	.244	.344	.327
Late Inning Pressure			129	28	2	6	18	.217	.310	.257
Leading Off			40	10	0	0	5	.250	.325	.250
Runners On			30	6	1	4	4	.200	.300	.314
Runners/Scor. Pos.			17	2	0	3	3	.118	.118	.286
First 9 Batters			283	83	9	18	50	.293	.470	.333
Second 9 Batters			274	80	11	15	36	.292	.489	.330
All Batters Thereafter			365	97	10	13	40	.266	.419	.294

Loves to face: Danny Tartabull (.118, 2-for-17)
Hates to face: Ken Phelps (.400, 8-for-20, 4 HR)
Ground outs-to-air outs ratio: 0.66 last season, 0.91 for career. . . .
Additional statistics: 10 double-play ground outs in 153 opportunities, 52 doubles, 9 triples in 229.0 innings last season. . . . Allowed 22 first-inning runs in 34 starts. . . . Batting support: 4.74 runs per start. . . . Faced 107 batters between walks (Sept. 6–25), longest streak in A.L. last season. . . . Career record of 46–21 during September (24–6 since 1982). . . . Has defeated every major league club at least twice except the Expos (1–2). . . . Has won his last seven decisions against Seattle. . . . One of six pitchers with more than 10 wins and a winning record in each of the past five years. The others: Darling, Gooden, Leibrandt, Morris, and Viola.

Neil Allen

Throws Right

New York Yankees	W–L	ERA	AB	H	HR	BB	SO	BA	SA	OBA
Season	5-3	3.84	452	121	14	37	61	.268	.429	.322
vs. Left-Handers			183	60	7	23	18	.328	.508	.399
vs. Right-Handers			269	61	7	14	43	.227	.375	.266
Home	0-1	3.93	195	51	6	19	22	.262	.421	.326
Road	5-2	3.76	257	70	8	18	39	.272	.436	.319
Grass	3-3	3.51	380	95	11	32	51	.250	.400	.308
Artificial Turf	2-0	5.71	72	26	3	5	10	.361	.583	.397
April			0	0	0	0	0	—	—	—
May	2-0	1.52	81	12	2	4	11	.148	.247	.195
June	0-2	4.50	97	28	2	9	15	.289	.454	.346
July	2-0	3.70	97	30	3	10	13	.309	.485	.367
August	0-0	7.36	90	30	4	6	11	.333	.544	.367
Sept./Oct.	1-1	2.31	87	21	3	8	11	.241	.391	.313
Leading Off Inn.			102	32	3	7	12	.314	.490	.358
Runners On			211	48	5	25	32	.227	.365	.305
Runners/Scor. Pos.			126	28	4	14	22	.222	.373	.293
Runners On/2 Out			90	14	1	11	15	.156	.233	.248
Scor. Pos./2 Out			58	9	1	5	11	.155	.259	.222
Late Inning Pressure			70	15	5	4	8	.214	.443	.267
Leading Off			21	4	1	0	1	.190	.381	.190
Runners On			17	3	1	2	4	.176	.353	.300
Runners/Scor. Pos.			8	1	0	1	4	.125	.125	.300
First 9 Batters			268	65	7	27	42	.243	.381	.310
Second 9 Batters			142	44	5	7	15	.310	.493	.344
All Batters Thereafter			42	12	2	3	4	.286	.524	.326

Loves to face: Mark McGwire (0-for-10)
Hates to face: Wade Boggs (.727, 8-for-11)
Ground outs-to-air outs ratio: 0.70 last season, 1.14 for career. . . .
Additional statistics: 8 double-play ground outs in 95 opportunities, 27 doubles, 2 triples in 117.1 innings last season. . . . Record of 0–2 (5.23 ERA) as a starter, 5–1 (3.70) in relief. . . . Opponents batted 75 points lower with runners on base than with the bases empty, 2d-largest difference among A.L. pitchers last season (minimum: 100 AB each way). . . . One of four pitchers whose left-handed opponents outhit right-handers by more than 100 points last season (minimum: 100 AB each way). . . . Ground-ball hitters batted .316 against him last season, fly-ballers hit .237. . . . One of five pitchers to appear both as a starter and in relief in each of the past six seasons.

Allan Anderson

Throws Left

Minnesota Twins	W–L	ERA	AB	H	HR	BB	SO	BA	SA	OBA
Season	16-9	2.45	763	199	14	37	83	.261	.367	.299
vs. Left-Handers			125	40	0	13	10	.320	.368	.390
vs. Right-Handers			638	159	14	24	73	.249	.367	.280
Home	9-2	2.29	381	100	5	19	43	.262	.352	.304
Road	7-7	2.60	382	99	9	18	40	.259	.382	.295
Grass	5-5	2.04	271	70	7	11	28	.258	.376	.290
Artificial Turf	11-4	2.67	492	129	7	26	55	.262	.362	.304
April	1-0	2.84	23	4	0	3	4	.174	.217	.269
May	1-3	4.62	148	45	6	6	14	.304	.459	.340
June	2-3	2.15	155	48	1	5	19	.310	.381	.329
July	4-1	1.96	153	39	2	11	15	.255	.379	.310
August	4-1	1.96	126	28	4	5	6	.222	.365	.252
Sept./Oct.	4-1	1.66	158	35	1	7	25	.222	.278	.265
Leading Off Inn.			203	58	3	8	16	.286	.379	.316
Runners On			302	78	3	17	33	.258	.318	.293
Runners/Scor. Pos.			159	34	1	12	24	.214	.258	.261
Runners On/2 Out			113	25	1	8	15	.221	.265	.273
Scor. Pos./2 Out			75	14	1	7	14	.187	.227	.256
Late Inning Pressure			78	13	0	3	10	.167	.205	.198
Leading Off			24	4	0	1	2	.167	.208	.200
Runners On			20	4	0	0	2	.200	.200	.200
Runners/Scor. Pos.			7	0	0	0	2	.000	.000	.000
First 9 Batters			248	60	3	14	26	.242	.335	.293
Second 9 Batters			254	77	10	10	31	.303	.480	.330
All Batters Thereafter			261	62	1	13	26	.238	.287	.275

Loves to face: Steve Balboni (.067, 1-for-15)
Hates to face: Fred Lynn (.667, 4-for-6, 2 2B, 1 HR)
Ground outs-to-air outs ratio: 1.05 last season, 1.05 for career. . . .
Additional statistics: 25 double-play ground outs in 154 opportunities, 33 doubles, 3 triples in 202.1 innings last season. . . . Allowed 10 first-inning runs in 30 starts. . . . Batting support: 3.90 runs per start. . . . Third pitcher to win ERA title while a teammate won Cy Young Award. Others: Bob Turley won Cy, Whitey Ford won ERA title on 1958 Yankees; Don Drysdale won Cy, Sandy Koufax won ERA title on 1962 Dodgers. . . . Only pitcher since 1945–46 to lead A.L. in ERA in consecutive seasons: Ron Guidry (1978–79). . . . Led A.L. with 11 wins after All-Star break. . . . Hasn't allowed a HR to a left-hander since May 23, 1987 (Lou Whitaker).

Keith Atherton

Throws Right

Minnesota Twins	W–L	ERA	AB	H	HR	BB	SO	BA	SA	OBA
Season	7-5	3.41	277	65	10	22	43	.235	.390	.293
vs. Left-Handers			128	35	7	13	14	.273	.500	.340
vs. Right-Handers			149	30	3	9	29	.201	.295	.252
Home	3-1	3.32	154	39	6	10	23	.253	.435	.293
Road	4-4	3.51	123	26	4	12	20	.211	.333	.292
Grass	1-4	4.21	94	19	4	7	15	.202	.362	.265
Artificial Turf	6-1	2.98	183	46	6	15	28	.251	.404	.307
April	0-0	1.23	54	11	1	4	11	.204	.296	.259
May	3-1	2.51	48	9	2	4	9	.188	.333	.259
June	2-1	6.08	53	14	2	4	10	.264	.453	.310
July	0-3	6.10	43	12	2	5	5	.279	.512	.367
August	1-0	1.93	54	12	2	5	3	.222	.370	.288
Sept./Oct.	1-0	3.68	25	7	1	0	5	.280	.400	.269
Leading Off Inn.			64	16	3	2	10	.250	.422	.273
Runners On			122	33	6	11	16	.270	.467	.333
Runners/Scor. Pos.			79	19	6	8	9	.241	.494	.308
Runners On/2 Out			54	12	0	9	7	.222	.315	.333
Scor. Pos./2 Out			42	7	0	7	5	.167	.190	.286
Late Inning Pressure			131	35	9	12	21	.267	.519	.336
Leading Off			32	10	2	1	4	.313	.531	.333
Runners On			61	18	6	6	8	.295	.639	.371
Runners/Scor. Pos.			42	14	6	5	3	.333	.810	.408
First 9 Batters			264	61	10	17	41	.231	.390	.280
Second 9 Batters			13	4	0	5	2	.308	.385	.500
All Batters Thereafter			0	0	0	0	0	—	—	—

Loves to face: Don Slaught (0-for-11)
Hates to face: Dan Pasqua (.750, 6-for-8, 2 HR)
Ground outs-to-air outs ratio: 0.64 last season, 0.56 for career. . . .
Additional statistics: 3 double-play ground outs in 62 opportunities, 11 doubles, 1 triple in 74.0 innings last season. . . . The A.L.'s 17 qualifying .300 hitters batted .156 against him (5-for-32). . . . Allowed 10 home runs, all with less than two outs. . . . Has faced decreasing number of batters in each of last four seasons: 453, 435, 431, 348, 309. . . . Has gone 294 games since committing the only balk of his major league career. . . . Opposing left-handed batters have outhit right-handers in all six seasons in majors. Career figures: left-handers, .274; right-handers, .230. . . . Opponents' career average of .194 with two out and runners in scoring position. . . . Has made 310 appearances in his career, all in relief.

Don August

Milwaukee Brewers — Throws Right

	W–L	ERA	AB	H	HR	BB	SO	BA	SA	OBA
Season	13-7	3.09	559	137	12	48	66	.245	.356	.303
vs. Left-Handers			284	76	6	25	27	.268	.384	.324
vs. Right-Handers			275	61	6	23	39	.222	.327	.282
Home	8-2	2.72	270	61	6	18	35	.226	.341	.274
Road	5-5	3.45	289	76	6	30	31	.263	.370	.329
Grass	12-5	3.06	479	120	10	37	54	.251	.363	.303
Artificial Turf	1-2	3.32	80	17	2	11	12	.213	.313	.308
April			0	0	0	0	0	—	—	—
May			0	0	0	0	0	—	—	—
June	4-2	2.65	139	29	2	12	13	.209	.302	.272
July	1-3	2.89	135	34	4	13	22	.252	.363	.311
August	3-1	4.13	129	35	3	13	17	.271	.388	.338
Sept./Oct.	5-1	2.85	156	39	3	10	14	.250	.372	.295
Leading Off Inn.			140	33	3	16	15	.236	.357	.314
Runners On			218	55	4	22	28	.252	.358	.317
Runners/Scor. Pos.			124	27	2	13	22	.218	.323	.286
Runners On/2 Out			88	20	1	9	11	.227	.295	.299
Scor. Pos./2 Out			56	9	0	6	10	.161	.196	.242
Late Inning Pressure			22	2	2	5	2	.091	.364	.259
Leading Off			6	1	1	3	1	.167	.667	.444
Runners On			4	0	0	1	0	.000	.000	.200
Runners/Scor. Pos.			0	0	0	0	0			
First 9 Batters			192	44	1	20	29	.229	.313	.300
Second 9 Batters			180	42	4	13	20	.233	.328	.284
All Batters Thereafter			187	51	7	15	17	.273	.428	.325

Loves to face: Carney Lansford (0-for-8)
Hates to face: Kent Hrbek (.750, 3-for-4, 2 HR)
Ground outs-to-air outs ratio: 1.28 last season, his first in majors. . . . Additional statistics: 16 double-play ground outs in 114 opportunities, 24 doubles, 1 triple in 148.1 innings last season. . . . Allowed 4 first-inning runs in 22 starts, 3d-lowest average in A.L. (minimum: 15 GS). . . . Batting support: 4.32 runs per start. . . . Led major league rookies in wins and complete games. . . . Won A.L. fielding title by narrowest margin, handling 46 chances without an error, one more than Ted Higuera, Dan Petry, and Dave Stieb. . . . Had a 3–0 record against Chicago and California. . . . Didn't allow a HR in first or second inning. . . . Rookie pitchers with most similar stats: Bernie Boland (13–7, 3.11), Dickie Kerr (13–7, 2.88), Rich Gale (14–8, 3.09). Sorry we mentioned it.

Scott Bailes

Cleveland Indians — Throws Left

	W–L	ERA	AB	H	HR	BB	SO	BA	SA	OBA
Season	9-14	4.90	560	149	22	46	53	.266	.425	.322
vs. Left-Handers			115	28	0	11	14	.243	.270	.315
vs. Right-Handers			445	121	22	35	39	.272	.465	.324
Home	7-6	3.72	317	80	10	24	34	.252	.382	.307
Road	2-8	6.56	243	69	12	22	19	.284	.481	.341
Grass	8-11	4.42	494	131	18	35	50	.265	.415	.314
Artificial Turf	1-3	8.64	66	18	4	11	3	.273	.500	.377
April	1-2	3.71	103	25	0	11	12	.243	.301	.322
May	3-2	4.91	122	26	8	9	11	.213	.426	.265
June	2-3	4.33	139	36	4	11	13	.259	.417	.314
July	1-3	6.14	121	43	7	6	5	.355	.537	.386
August	1-2	5.54	49	14	1	4	7	.286	.429	.333
Sept./Oct.	1-2	5.87	26	5	2	5	5	.192	.423	.323
Leading Off Inn.			146	32	3	9	11	.219	.322	.265
Runners On			215	69	12	19	23	.321	.544	.375
Runners/Scor. Pos.			111	38	5	12	14	.342	.541	.398
Runners On/2 Out			84	30	6	7	8	.357		.413
Scor. Pos./2 Out			55	21	4	7	4	.382	.655	.460
Late Inning Pressure			73	19	3	7	10	.260	.425	.325
Leading Off			19	2	0	1	4	.105	.158	.150
Runners On			30	10	3	2	3	.333	.667	.375
Runners/Scor. Pos.			17	4	1	1	2	.235	.412	.278
First 9 Batters			230	59	9	26	29	.257	.413	.332
Second 9 Batters			163	39	5	12	10	.239	.362	.292
All Batters Thereafter			167	51	8	8	14	.305	.503	.337

Loves to face: Cal Ripken (0-for-17)
Hates to face: Jim Rice (.636, 7-for-11, 1 HR)
Ground outs-to-air outs ratio: 1.23 last season, 1.12 for career. . . . Additional statistics: 17 double-play ground outs in 114 opportunities, 19 doubles, 2 triples in 145.0 innings last season. . . . Allowed 14 first-inning runs in 21 starts. . . . Batting support: 4.10 runs per start. . . . Starting pitcher in first 21 appearances (7–11, 4.95), used exclusively in relief thereafter (2–3, 4.58). . . . Opponents batted 89 points higher with runners on than with bases empty, 3d-largest gap in A.L. (minimum: 100 AB each way). . . . Opponents' career average of .310 with runners in scoring position, .269 in other at-bats. . . . Hasn't allowed a HR to a left-hander since August 22, 1987 (Lou Whitaker). . . . Career ERAs: 5.65 in day games, 4.48 at night.

Jeff Ballard

Baltimore Orioles — Throws Left

	W–L	ERA	AB	H	HR	BB	SO	BA	SA	OBA
Season	8-12	4.40	600	167	15	42	41	.278	.427	.330
vs. Left-Handers			87	25	3	6	12	.287	.437	.340
vs. Right-Handers			513	142	12	36	29	.277	.425	.329
Home	7-4	3.73	321	90	9	17	22	.280	.433	.322
Road	1-8	5.17	279	77	6	25	19	.276	.419	.340
Grass	8-8	4.26	483	135	14	35	38	.280	.437	.333
Artificial Turf	0-4	5.02	117	32	1	7	13	.274	.385	.320
April			0	0	0	0	0	—	—	—
May	1-1	3.00	60	20	1	3	4	.333	.467	.365
June	3-3	4.54	164	46	2	9	15	.280	.384	.316
July	0-5	9.00	95	33	4	2	9	.347	.547	.370
August	3-2	2.20	163	36	5	16	7	.221	.362	.302
Sept./Oct.	1-1	4.99	118	32	3	12	6	.271	.458	.341
Leading Off Inn.			154	46	5	7	11	.299	.506	.329
Runners On			246	59	7	19	18	.240	.370	.301
Runners/Scor. Pos.			124	38	4	11	11	.306	.476	.373
Runners On/2 Out			108	28	4	8	9	.259	.435	.322
Scor. Pos./2 Out			60	19	3	4	7	.317	.550	.379
Late Inning Pressure			51	12	2	3	5	.235	.412	.278
Leading Off			16	5	1	1	1	.313	.688	.353
Runners On			13	2	1	1	2	.154	.385	.214
Runners/Scor. Pos.			8	1	0	1	2	.125	.125	.222
First 9 Batters			208	61	5	13	18	.293	.457	.338
Second 9 Batters			178	58	6	14	10	.326	.522	.382
All Batters Thereafter			214	48	4	15	18	.224	.318	.278

Loves to face: Jeffrey Leonard (0-for-7)
Hates to face: Rey Quinones (.467, 7-for-15, 4 2B, 2 HR)
Ground outs-to-air outs ratio: 0.94 last season, 1.08 for career. . . . Additional statistics: 19 double-play ground outs in 116 opportunities, 34 doubles, 5 triples in 153.1 innings last season. . . . Allowed 19 first-inning runs in 25 starts. . . . Batting support: 4.12 runs per start. . . . Started 25 games, but won consecutive decisions only once. . . . Allowed extra-base hits to four consecutive batters (July 3–8), 2d-longest streak by any pitcher over the last 10 seasons. . . . Guy Hoffman gave up five in a row in 1987. . . . Opponents batted 65 points lower with runners on base than with the bases empty, 5th-largest difference among A.L. pitchers (minimum: 100 AB each way). . . . Opponents' career batting average is .340 with runners in scoring position.

Scott Bankhead

Seattle Mariners — Throws Right

	W–L	ERA	AB	H	HR	BB	SO	BA	SA	OBA
Season	7-9	3.07	514	115	8	38	102	.224	.352	.278
vs. Left-Handers			244	63	2	26	47	.258	.389	.330
vs. Right-Handers			270	52	6	12	55	.193	.319	.229
Home	3-5	4.06	241	58	6	16	47	.241	.390	.290
Road	4-4	2.22	273	57	2	22	55	.209	.319	.268
Grass	3-3	1.74	228	45	2	16	50	.197	.303	.250
Artificial Turf	4-6	4.19	286	70	6	22	52	.245	.392	.300
April			0	0	0	0	0	—	—	—
May	0-2	3.50	70	17	1	5	16	.243	.329	.289
June	2-1	2.23	134	28	0	12	25	.209	.276	.279
July	3-2	4.12	148	32	6	10	31	.216	.419	.266
August	2-4	2.61	162	38	1	11	30	.235	.364	.283
Sept./Oct.			0	0	0	0	0	—	—	—
Leading Off Inn.			131	25	1	12	29	.191	.290	.259
Runners On			197	48	3	19	44	.244	.381	.309
Runners/Scor. Pos.			115	28	2	17	28	.243	.409	.338
Runners On/2 Out			84	17	1	10	27	.202	.310	.287
Scor. Pos./2 Out			51	9	1	10	17	.176	.314	.311
Late Inning Pressure			35	13	1	5	4	.371	.571	.450
Leading Off			12	4	1	0	2	.333	.667	.333
Runners On			10	6	0	4	2	.600	.800	.714
Runners/Scor. Pos.			7	3	0	4	2	.429	.571	.636
First 9 Batters			174	26	3	13	44	.149	.259	.213
Second 9 Batters			176	44	2	11	29	.250	.364	.293
All Batters Thereafter			164	45	3	14	29	.274	.439	.331

Loves to face: Tom Brookens (0-for-9)
Hates to face: George Bell (.476, 10-for-21, 5 HR)
Ground outs-to-air outs ratio: 0.61 last season, 0.70 for career. . . . Additional statistics: 9 double-play ground outs in 70 opportunities, 34 doubles, 4 triples in 135.0 innings last season. . . . Allowed 8 first-inning runs in 21 starts. . . . Batting support: 3.05 runs per start. . . . One of three pitchers to shut out the Red Sox at Fenway last season. . . . Allowed one home run per 16.9 innings, compared to one per 5.5 innings during first two seasons in majors. . . . Walked either 37 or 38 batters and struck out between 94 and 102 in each of three seasons. . . . Only three other pitchers in major league history have won and lost between seven and nine games in three straight years: Tommy Thomas (1932–34), Marv Breuer (1940–42), and Dave Sisler (1956–58).

Floyd Bannister

Kansas City Royals — Throws Left

	W–L	ERA	AB	H	HR	BB	SO	BA	SA	OBA
Season	12-13	4.33	733	182	22	68	113	.248	.405	.316
vs. Left-Handers			145	31	0	7	25	.214	.276	.253
vs. Right-Handers			588	151	22	61	88	.257	.437	.330
Home	4-6	4.22	371	94	7	32	50	.253	.377	.315
Road	8-7	4.44	362	88	15	36	63	.243	.434	.316
Grass	7-4	4.14	272	65	8	28	45	.239	.393	.316
Artificial Turf	5-9	4.44	461	117	14	40	68	.254	.412	.315
April	3-1	3.66	116	23	2	16	20	.198	.319	.299
May	3-3	3.86	160	39	4	16	23	.244	.413	.311
June	2-2	6.48	102	31	6	10	8	.304	.549	.366
July	0-2	6.95	87	23	5	8	8	.264	.506	.333
August	1-3	3.66	126	30	1	11	29	.238	.302	.299
Sept./Oct.	3-2	2.97	142	36	4	7	25	.254	.394	.303
Leading Off Inn.			183	45	5	15	29	.246	.372	.303
Runners On			296	82	9	28	45	.277	.446	.345
Runners/Scor. Pos.			177	47	9	16	28	.266	.475	.333
Runners On/2 Out			135	43	6	11	16	.319	.556	.383
Scor. Pos./2 Out			86	27	6	9	10	.314	.605	.398
Late Inning Pressure			32	7	0	7	6	.219	.313	.359
Leading Off			12	1	0	0	2	.083	.083	.083
Runners On			8	4	0	1	0	.500	.625	.556
Runners/Scor. Pos.			4	2	0	1	0	.500	.750	.600
First 9 Batters			252	62	9	20	37	.246	.405	.301
Second 9 Batters			253	52	6	22	35	.206	.316	.277
All Batters Thereafter			228	68	7	26	41	.298	.504	.372

Loves to face: Bobby Meacham (0-for-13, 6 SO)
Hates to face: Gary Gaetti (.471, 16-for-34, 7 HR)
Ground outs-to-air outs ratio: 0.84 last season, 0.89 for career....
Additional statistics: 12 double-play ground outs in 123 opportunities, 39 doubles, 5 triples in 189.1 innings last season.... Allowed 13 first-inning runs in 31 starts.... Batting support: 4.06 runs per start.... Faced 34 consecutive A.L. batters without allowing a hit in April, longest streak in A.L. last season.... Held opponents below .200 with two outs and runners in scoring position in each of three previous seasons.... Has allowed 226 home runs during 1980s. Only Jack Morris has yielded more (242).... Has double-figure wins and losses in each of last seven seasons. Now he's more than halfway to Phil Niekro's major league "record" of 13 (1968–1980).

Juan Berenguer

Minnesota Twins — Throws Right

	W–L	ERA	AB	H	HR	BB	SO	BA	SA	OBA
Season	8-4	3.96	357	74	7	61	99	.207	.325	.322
vs. Left-Handers			184	39	6	38	41	.212	.364	.344
vs. Right-Handers			173	35	1	23	58	.202	.283	.296
Home	5-0	3.40	179	41	3	30	49	.229	.330	.338
Road	3-4	4.53	178	33	4	31	50	.185	.320	.305
Grass	2-4	4.13	116	20	1	19	32	.172	.259	.288
Artificial Turf	6-0	3.88	241	54	6	42	67	.224	.357	.338
April	3-3	5.57	78	20	0	16	27	.256	.321	.381
May	2-0	3.77	57	15	0	7	19	.263	.368	.344
June	2-0	0.00	61	5	0	9	22	.082	.098	.200
July	1-0	3.06	63	13	1	8	12	.206	.349	.292
August	0-1	9.18	65	17	5	12	11	.262	.523	.372
Sept./Oct.	0-0	1.64	33	4	1	9	8	.121	.242	.310
Leading Off Inn.			78	15	0	15	25	.192	.308	.323
Runners On			172	34	5	31	47	.198	.326	.317
Runners/Scor. Pos.			115	24	5	21	34	.209	.391	.326
Runners On/2 Out			71	12	1	15	18	.169	.268	.314
Scor. Pos./2 Out			52	9	1	11	14	.173	.308	.317
Late Inning Pressure			159	39	2	32	40	.245	.365	.371
Leading Off			36	8	0	9	8	.222	.417	.378
Runners On			86	19	2	17	25	.221	.337	.349
Runners/Scor. Pos.			58	14	2	12	15	.241	.414	.370
First 9 Batters			316	63	4	50	88	.199	.294	.308
Second 9 Batters			41	11	3	11	11	.268	.561	.415
All Batters Thereafter			0	0	0	0	0			

Loves to face: Pete Incaviglia (0-for-10, 8 SO)
Hates to face: Rickey Henderson (.429, 9-for-21, 3 2B, 3 3B)
Ground outs-to-air outs ratio: 0.55 last season, 0.61 for career....
Additional statistics: 6 double-play ground outs in 82 opportunities, 17 doubles, 2 triples in 100.0 innings last season.... Appeared in career-high 57 games.... Opposing batters were hitless in 39 consecutive plate appearances with runners in scoring position, longest streak in majors last season.... Batting average of opposing left-handers was lowest of his career.... Strikeouts per nine innings: 6.5 through 1984, 8.6 since 1985.... Has won 10 consecutive decisions at the Metrodome, 11 in a row on artificial turf.... Opposing fly-ball hitters have outhit ground-ballers in each of past eight seasons, longest streak in the 14 years we've been tracking that stuff.

Jose Bautista

Baltimore Orioles — Throws Right

	W–L	ERA	AB	H	HR	BB	SO	BA	SA	OBA
Season	6-15	4.30	664	171	21	45	76	.258	.408	.310
vs. Left-Handers			333	86	13	23	36	.258	.432	.314
vs. Right-Handers			331	85	8	22	40	.257	.384	.306
Home	4-7	4.48	333	86	13	23	35	.258	.414	.312
Road	2-8	4.11	331	85	8	22	41	.257	.402	.308
Grass	6-13	4.58	580	152	21	39	66	.262	.424	.314
Artificial Turf	0-2	2.42	84	19	0	6	10	.226	.298	.286
April	0-0	3.86	78	24	2	4	14	.308	.423	.349
May	2-3	5.06	85	23	2	4	7	.271	.365	.326
June	1-3	5.14	132	32	6	15	14	.242	.432	.324
July	2-3	5.06	105	29	4	12	12	.276	.438	.294
August	1-2	1.79	151	30	1	10	19	.199	.272	.248
Sept./Oct.	0-4	5.76	113	33	6	10	10	.292	.558	.349
Leading Off Inn.			168	44	4	14	24	.262	.387	.319
Runners On			265	66	13	15	27	.249	.449	.291
Runners/Scor. Pos.			149	34	6	12	17	.228	.409	.280
Runners On/2 Out			112	30	6	9	13	.268	.473	.328
Scor. Pos./2 Out			72	17	3	7	7	.236	.403	.304
Late Inning Pressure			64	17	2	3	4	.266	.375	.299
Leading Off			18	6	0	2	0	.333	.333	.400
Runners On			23	6	2	1	2	.261	.522	.292
Runners/Scor. Pos.			8	2	0	1	1	.250	.250	.333
First 9 Batters			260	68	7	19	32	.262	.388	.317
Second 9 Batters			215	57	9	10	26	.265	.460	.309
All Batters Thereafter			189	46	5	16	18	.243	.376	.303

Loves to face: Jim Gantner (0-for-8)
Hates to face: Mike Greenwell (.667, 6-for-9, 2 HR)
Ground outs-to-air outs ratio: 0.79 last season, his first in majors.
... Additional statistics: 14 double-play ground outs in 106 opportunities, 29 doubles, 4 triples in 171.2 innings last season.... Allowed 14 first-inning runs in 25 starts.... Batting support: 2.72 runs per start, lowest in majors (minimum: 15 GS).... Made eight appearances in relief, was used exclusively as a starter thereafter.... Tied with Braves' Pete Smith for most losses by a rookie.... Third rookie in Orioles history to lead the club in innings. McNally and Palmer? Nope. Chuck Estrada (1960) and Tom Phoebus (1967).... Orioles rookie record for innings was set by Wally Bunker in 1964 (214.1). Only Phoebus had more strikeouts (179) than Bautista.... Career record of 53–39 in minors.

Mike Birkbeck

Milwaukee Brewers — Throws Right

	W–L	ERA	AB	H	HR	BB	SO	BA	SA	OBA
Season	10-8	4.72	494	141	10	37	64	.285	.399	.335
vs. Left-Handers			244	64	3	22	31	.262	.352	.323
vs. Right-Handers			250	77	7	15	33	.308	.444	.347
Home	6-4	4.50	256	75	4	23	29	.293	.391	.354
Road	4-4	4.95	238	66	6	14	35	.277	.408	.315
Grass	9-6	4.50	389	108	9	32	52	.278	.393	.333
Artificial Turf	1-2	5.63	105	33	1	5	12	.314	.419	.345
April	0-2	9.95	25	10	0	6	4	.400	.440	.516
May	2-2	4.76	108	29	1	11	13	.269	.389	.331
June	0-1	9.00	25	8	0	3	2	.320	.400	.393
July	3-0	1.89	127	32	1	5	19	.252	.307	.286
August	4-1	5.55	145	43	6	10	20	.297	.469	.342
Sept./Oct.	1-2	5.28	64	19	2	2	6	.297	.422	.318
Leading Off Inn.			128	36	1	4	9	.281	.359	.308
Runners On			201	62	4	21	30	.308	.443	.371
Runners/Scor. Pos.			102	34	1	16	13	.333	.441	.417
Runners On/2 Out			79	22	1	7	10	.278	.367	.337
Scor. Pos./2 Out			46	10	0	4	6	.217	.239	.280
Late Inning Pressure			7	2	0	1	1	.286	.286	.375
Leading Off			2	1	0	0	0	.500	.500	.500
Runners On			3	0	0	1	1	.000	.000	.250
Runners/Scor. Pos.			1	0	0	0	0	.000	.000	.000
First 9 Batters			189	56	4	15	22	.296	.407	.346
Second 9 Batters			171	43	1	12	22	.251	.322	.299
All Batters Thereafter			134	42	5	10	20	.313	.485	.366

Loves to face: Oddibe McDowell (0-for-10)
Hates to face: Kirby Puckett (.778, 7-for-9)
Ground outs-to-air outs ratio: 1.82 last season, 1.73 for career....
Additional statistics: 12 double-play ground outs in 97 opportunities, 20 doubles, 3 triples in 124.0 innings last season.... Allowed 30 first-inning runs (2d most in A.L.) in 23 starts. Opposing batters hit .381 (40-for-105) with 3 HRs and 10 walks in the first.... Batting support: 4.83 runs per start.... Pitched an average of 5.39 innings per start, 4th-lowest mark in A.L. (minimum: 15 GS).... Only Tommy John started more games than Birkbeck without pitching a complete game in 1988. John started 38, Birkbeck 23.... Committed 11 balks in 124 innings. He's no Rod Scurry, who needed only 31.1 innings to accumulate his 11 balks.

Bud Black
Royals/Indians   Throws Left

	W–L	ERA	AB	H	HR	BB	SO	BA	SA	OBA
Season	4-4	5.00	311	82	8	34	63	.264	.373	.341
vs. Left-Handers			69	12	1	11	15	.174	.217	.298
vs. Right-Handers			242	70	7	23	48	.289	.417	.354
Home	1-2	5.88	163	48	3	13	32	.294	.387	.356
Road	3-2	4.08	148	34	5	21	31	.230	.358	.326
Grass	1-3	5.60	203	56	6	25	44	.276	.404	.363
Artificial Turf	3-1	3.86	108	26	2	9	19	.241	.315	.297
April	1-1	3.48	40	10	0	3	10	.250	.250	.302
May	1-0	6.17	46	13	2	8	9	.283	.457	.389
June	1-1	6.00	74	21	3	10	16	.284	.405	.365
July	1-1	7.20	62	18	1	5	8	.290	.435	.371
August	0-0	2.45	33	5	1	4	6	.152	.273	.237
Sept./Oct.	0-1	3.60	56	15	1	4	14	.268	.339	.323
Leading Off Inn.			75	20	0	6	11	.267	.320	.321
Runners On			132	34	5	23	26	.258	.409	.377
Runners/Scor. Pos.			83	20	3	14	16	.241	.373	.365
Runners On/2 Out			60	16	3	11	8	.267	.467	.389
Scor. Pos./2 Out			42	10	2	8	6	.238	.429	.373
Late Inning Pressure			68	17	0	10	21	.250	.250	.346
Leading Off			16	3	0	1	5	.188	.188	.235
Runners On			28	7	0	8	9	.250	.250	.417
Runners/Scor. Pos.			19	5	0	4	6	.263	.263	.391
First 9 Batters			190	50	5	20	44	.263	.363	.333
Second 9 Batters			84	23	2	10	12	.274	.405	.357
All Batters Thereafter			37	9	1	4	7	.243	.351	.341

Loves to face: Steve Balboni (0-for-10)
Hates to face: Ruben Sierra (.667, 8-for-12, 2 HR)
Ground outs-to-air outs ratio: 1.28 last season, 1.08 for career. . . .
Additional statistics: 5 double-play ground outs in 68 opportunities, 10 doubles, 0 triples in 81.0 innings last season. . . . Opposing batters were hitless in 34 consecutive plate appearances with runners on base, longest streak in the majors last season. . . . Batting average by opposing left-handed hitters was the lowest of any full season in his career, but the average by right-handed hitters was a career high. . . . Record of 27–35 with a 4.01 ERA since going 17–12 in 1984. . . . Career records: 39–30 on artificial turf, 19–30 on grass. . . . Has faced 70 batters with the bases loaded, hit four of them with pitches, highest total during the 1980s.

Bert Blyleven
Minnesota Twins   Throws Right

	W–L	ERA	AB	H	HR	BB	SO	BA	SA	OBA
Season	10-17	5.43	816	240	21	51	145	.294	.434	.345
vs. Left-Handers			438	133	10	32	69	.304	.441	.356
vs. Right-Handers			378	107	11	19	76	.283	.426	.333
Home	6-9	5.83	429	130	9	34	86	.303	.424	.367
Road	4-8	4.98	387	110	12	17	59	.284	.444	.320
Grass	2-7	5.19	300	86	9	14	42	.287	.443	.325
Artificial Turf	8-10	5.56	516	154	12	37	103	.298	.428	.357
April	1-2	6.75	107	33	5	10	25	.308	.458	.388
May	2-3	3.75	189	50	4	16	32	.265	.376	.327
June	4-1	3.98	163	47	2	4	37	.288	.387	.314
July	0-5	9.20	123	44	8	8	12	.358	.650	.397
August	2-1	2.70	71	16	1	5	15	.225	.310	.282
Sept./Oct.	1-5	6.64	163	50	1	8	24	.307	.423	.356
Leading Off Inn.			202	57	5	7	29	.282	.411	.322
Runners On			344	118	11	22	64	.343	.497	.391
Runners/Scor. Pos.			208	79	4	18	48	.380	.505	.435
Runners On/2 Out			139	45	5	10	29	.324	.504	.377
Scor. Pos./2 Out			90	32	0	9	21	.356	.456	.426
Late Inning Pressure			50	15	2	2	14	.300	.500	.340
Leading Off			13	2	0	1	3	.154	.231	.214
Runners On			17	8	1	0	5	.471	.706	.500
Runners/Scor. Pos.			11	5	1	0	4	.455	.818	.500
First 9 Batters			265	78	6	21	46	.294	.423	.364
Second 9 Batters			271	82	6	16	48	.303	.413	.345
All Batters Thereafter			280	80	9	14	51	.286	.464	.328

Loves to face: Don Slaught (.033, 1-for-30)
Hates to face: Ron Kittle (.351, 13-for-37, 9 HR)
Ground outs-to-air outs ratio: 1.05 last season, 1.21 for career. . . .
Additional statistics: 17 double-play ground outs in 170 opportunities, 39 doubles, 6 triples in 207.1 innings last season. . . . Allowed 25 first-inning runs (3d most in A.L.) in 33 starts. . . . Batting support: 4.18 runs per start. . . . Has an august August record of 20–6 over the past seven seasons. . . . Didn't allow a home run in his last 32 innings. For Blyleven, that's an eon. . . . Career record of 28–14 vs. his new team, California, is his best against any A.L. club. . . . Career record of 254–226 similar to that of Ted Lyons (260–230), who's in the Hall of Fame, and John Picus Quinn (247–217) and Gus Weyhing (264–235), who aren't. Bert's ERA is best of the four.

Mike Boddicker
Orioles/Red Sox   Throws Right

	W–L	ERA	AB	H	HR	BB	SO	BA	SA	OBA
Season	13-15	3.39	894	234	17	77	156	.262	.367	.326
vs. Left-Handers			459	125	8	43	55	.272	.370	.338
vs. Right-Handers			435	109	9	34	101	.251	.363	.313
Home	7-6	3.21	397	108	7	32	75	.272	.375	.333
Road	6-9	3.55	497	126	10	45	81	.254	.360	.320
Grass	13-12	3.21	781	202	15	64	134	.259	.359	.319
Artificial Turf	0-3	4.76	113	32	2	13	22	.283	.425	.369
April	0-5	6.75	113	35	3	12	23	.310	.434	.394
May	2-3	2.90	148	38	5	12	26	.257	.405	.315
June	1-2	3.52	145	34	3	13	26	.234	.338	.302
July	4-2	2.64	184	50	3	15	31	.272	.370	.332
August	3-3	4.03	146	42	3	15	25	.288	.425	.358
Sept./Oct.	3-0	1.85	158	35	0	10	25	.222	.253	.269
Leading Off Inn.			225	55	4	18	41	.244	.342	.317
Runners On			367	94	8	37	64	.256	.376	.325
Runners/Scor. Pos.			199	42	5	23	41	.211	.332	.287
Runners On/2 Out			152	37	3	22	28	.243	.329	.343
Scor. Pos./2 Out			97	22	3	16	20	.227	.340	.342
Late Inning Pressure			84	20	3	7	15	.238	.417	.304
Leading Off			23	3	1	2	8	.130	.304	.231
Runners On			25	4	1	3	3	.160	.280	.250
Runners/Scor. Pos.			9	0	0	2	1	.000	.000	.182
First 9 Batters			282	72	2	25	43	.255	.337	.330
Second 9 Batters			267	77	4	24	52	.288	.378	.349
All Batters Thereafter			345	85	11	28	61	.246	.383	.304

Loves to face: Ron Kittle (0-for-12, 6 SO)
Hates to face: Carney Lansford (.415, 17-for-41, 4 HR)
Ground outs-to-air outs ratio: 1.25 last season, 1.40 for career. . . .
Additional statistics: 22 double-play ground outs in 181 opportunities, 35 doubles, 4 triples in 236.0 innings last season. . . . Allowed 9 first-inning runs in 35 starts. . . . Batting support: 4.03 runs per start. . . . Hasn't allowed a first-inning home run in 45 starts since August 8, 1987. . . . Record of 6–12 with a 3.86 ERA with Baltimore, 7–3, 2.63 ERA with Boston. . . . One of three A.L. pitchers with 15 or more losses, but an ERA below 3.50. . . . Allowed only one home run in 47 innings at Fenway, to Mark McGwire. . . . One of eight pitchers to start at least 32 games in each of last six seasons.

Chris Bosio
Milwaukee Brewers   Throws Right

	W–L	ERA	AB	H	HR	BB	SO	BA	SA	OBA
Season	7-15	3.36	710	190	13	38	84	.268	.370	.303
vs. Left-Handers			405	105	7	21	40	.259	.356	.294
vs. Right-Handers			305	85	6	17	44	.279	.390	.315
Home	5-6	2.73	354	89	6	22	41	.251	.339	.291
Road	2-9	4.01	356	101	7	16	43	.284	.402	.315
Grass	6-12	3.23	611	162	12	32	71	.265	.373	.299
Artificial Turf	1-3	4.24	99	28	1	6	13	.283	.354	.327
April	3-2	2.20	149	32	2	5	17	.215	.309	.242
May	3-4	3.02	204	58	3	10	19	.284	.377	.318
June	0-2	4.28	135	35	5	4	13	.259	.407	.279
July	0-5	6.59	128	49	3	10	15	.383	.500	.421
August	0-1	0.87	37	8	0	6	7	.216	.270	.326
Sept./Oct.	1-1	1.53	57	8	0	3	13	.140	.193	.177
Leading Off Inn.			175	42	4	8	21	.240	.349	.273
Runners On			300	85	4	16	32	.283	.377	.311
Runners/Scor. Pos.			176	45	3	12	20	.256	.352	.289
Runners On/2 Out			134	31	0	6	17	.231	.269	.264
Scor. Pos./2 Out			90	20	0	5	9	.222	.267	.263
Late Inning Pressure			154	30	1	15	20	.195	.247	.269
Leading Off			39	5	0	4	2	.128	.179	.209
Runners On			66	15	0	6	10	.227	.258	.288
Runners/Scor. Pos.			35	6	0	6	7	.171	.171	.286
First 9 Batters			268	76	5	16	42	.284	.392	.321
Second 9 Batters			191	48	3	5	24	.251	.340	.265
All Batters Thereafter			251	66	5	17	18	.263	.371	.312

Loves to face: Willie Wilson (.059, 1-for-17)
Hates to face: Greg Walker (.636, 7-for-11, 1 HR)
Ground outs-to-air outs ratio: 1.24 last season, 1.37 for career. . . .
Additional statistics: 18 double-play ground outs in 141 opportunities, 30 doubles, 2 triples in 182.0 innings last season. . . . Allowed 10 first-inning runs in 22 starts. . . . Batting support: 3.05 runs per start, 2d lowest in A.L. (minimum: 15 GS). . . . First pitcher to complete five starts and earn five saves in same season since Bob Stanley in 1980. . . . Had a 1.23 ERA in 29.1 innings of relief. . . . Held 36 consecutive batters hitless in Late-Inning Pressure Situations, longest streak in majors. Opposing batters have a career average of .234 in LIP Situations, .283 otherwise. . . . Involved in seven double plays as a fielder last season, most of any major league pitcher.

Oil Can Boyd

Throws Right

Boston Red Sox	W–L	ERA	AB	H	HR	BB	SO	BA	SA	OBA
Season	9-7	5.34	509	147	25	41	71	.289	.515	.341
vs. Left-Handers			250	73	9	16	36	.292	.468	.328
vs. Right-Handers			259	74	16	25	35	.286	.560	.352
Home	4-2	5.96	211	60	10	18	31	.284	.517	.339
Road	5-5	4.90	298	87	15	23	40	.292	.513	.342
Grass	5-5	5.51	375	108	16	32	57	.288	.488	.342
Artificial Turf	4-2	4.86	134	39	9	9	14	.291	.590	.336
April	2-1	3.16	95	23	4	6	11	.242	.389	.291
May	3-2	8.68	121	42	9	13	16	.347	.678	.404
June	1-3	4.71	164	48	4	13	21	.293	.439	.343
July	2-1	4.97	97	27	5	7	20	.278	.557	.321
August	1-0	5.19	32	7	3	2	3	.219	.531	.286
Sept./Oct.			0	0	0	0	0	—	—	—
Leading Off Inn.			127	36	10	11	20	.283	.598	.341
Runners On			197	58	6	14	29	.294	.467	.335
Runners/Scor. Pos.			99	26	2	9	14	.263	.404	.313
Runners On/2 Out			83	24	2	8	8	.289	.446	.352
Scor. Pos./2 Out			51	13	0	5	5	.255	.333	.321
Late Inning Pressure			34	9	2	5	6	.265	.471	.359
Leading Off			10	3	1	1	3	.300	.600	.364
Runners On			8	2	0	3	1	.250	.375	.455
Runners/Scor. Pos.			3	0	0	3	0	.000	.000	.500
First 9 Batters			186	55	10	17	32	.296	.559	.348
Second 9 Batters			174	50	7	12	26	.287	.466	.335
All Batters Thereafter			149	42	8	12	13	.282	.517	.337

Loves to face: Pete Incaviglia (0-for-11, 8 SO)
Hates to face: Mickey Brantley (.667, 6-for-9, 3 HR)
Ground outs-to-air outs ratio: 0.79 last season, 1.04 for career. . . .
Additional statistics: 9 double-play ground outs in 93 opportunities, 30 doubles, 5 triples in 129.2 innings last season. . . . Allowed 9 first-inning runs in 23 starts. Didn't allow a first-inning home run. . . . Batting support: 5.09 runs per start. . . . Allowed hits to nine consecutive right-handed batters, the longest streak in the last 10 years. . . . Opponents' career average of .317 in Late-Inning Pressure Situations, .265 otherwise. . . . Has pitched 166.1 innings over the past two seasons, the most of any A.L. pitcher without a wild pitch during that time. . . . Opponents' career average is .069 (2-for-29) with the bases loaded. . . . Winless in his last six decisions vs. the Royals.

Greg Cadaret

Throws Left

Oakland As	W–L	ERA	AB	H	HR	BB	SO	BA	SA	OBA
Season	5-2	2.89	266	60	2	36	64	.226	.282	.317
vs. Left-Handers			106	21	0	16	23	.198	.217	.309
vs. Right-Handers			160	39	2	20	41	.244	.325	.322
Home	3-1	2.52	153	39	0	17	38	.255	.307	.328
Road	2-1	3.34	113	21	2	19	26	.186	.248	.303
Grass	5-2	2.83	225	52	0	32	52	.231	.267	.326
Artificial Turf	0-0	3.18	41	8	2	4	12	.195	.366	.267
April	0-0	3.27	41	8	1	6	13	.195	.317	.313
May	0-0	1.00	28	4	0	6	6	.143	.179	.286
June	1-1	3.55	49	12	0	6	10	.245	.327	.327
July	2-0	2.70	47	9	1	4	13	.191	.298	.255
August	1-1	1.80	57	16	0	6	11	.281	.281	.338
Sept./Oct.	1-0	5.06	44	11	0	8	11	.250	.250	.365
Leading Off Inn.			58	10	0	9	17	.172	.190	.284
Runners On			138	31	2	19	32	.225	.297	.313
Runners/Scor. Pos.			85	19	1	9	20	.224	.294	.289
Runners On/2 Out			62	14	0	6	12	.226	.274	.294
Scor. Pos./2 Out			46	12	0	2	7	.261	.304	.292
Late Inning Pressure			129	29	1	15	34	.225	.287	.306
Leading Off			32	6	0	5	10	.188	.219	.297
Runners On			57	14	1	6	13	.246	.333	.317
Runners/Scor. Pos.			32	7	0	3	9	.219	.281	.286
First 9 Batters			232	54	2	34	54	.233	.289	.330
Second 9 Batters			34	6	0	2	10	.176	.235	.222
All Batters Thereafter			0	0	0	0	0			

Loves to face: Wade Boggs (0-for-6, 2 SO)
Hates to face: Tony Fernandez (.750, 3-for-4, 1 HR)
Ground outs-to-air outs ratio: 0.64 last season, 0.80 for career. . . .
Additional statistics: 6 double-play ground outs in 82 opportunities, 9 doubles, 0 triples in 71.2 innings last season. . . . Faced only 28 batters protecting leads of three runs or fewer in 8th inning or later. That role belonged to Eckersley (209 BFP). . . . Ended regular season by facing 137 consecutive batters without allowing an extra-base hit, longest streak in A.L. last season. . . . Didn't allow a HR to a left-hander during season, but Rich Gedman clocked him in A.L.C.S. . . . Average of one HR per 35 innings was 3d best among A.L. pitchers (minimum: 50 IP). . . . Allowed only one hit in 13 at-bats with the bases loaded. . . . Career ERAs: 2.28 at Oakland Coliseum, 4.85 on the road.

Todd Burns

Throws Right

Oakland As	W–L	ERA	AB	H	HR	BB	SO	BA	SA	OBA
Season	8-2	3.16	386	93	8	34	57	.241	.350	.303
vs. Left-Handers			217	53	5	21	32	.244	.364	.313
vs. Right-Handers			169	40	3	13	25	.237	.331	.290
Home	5-0	1.68	236	51	4	19	35	.216	.284	.273
Road	3-2	5.63	150	42	4	15	22	.280	.453	.347
Grass	6-2	3.39	345	85	7	27	49	.246	.357	.301
Artificial Turf	2-0	1.46	41	8	1	7	8	.195	.293	.313
April			0	0	0	0	0	—	—	—
May	0-0	5.40	7	2	0	0	4	.286	.286	.286
June	0-0	2.00	64	15	1	6	11	.234	.297	.296
July	3-0	3.03	114	27	3	12	16	.237	.342	.315
August	3-1	4.25	114	29	2	11	12	.252	.365	.317
Sept./Oct.	2-1	2.66	86	20	2	5	14	.233	.384	.272
Leading Off Inn.			98	21	1	6	15	.214	.286	.260
Runners On			158	31	3	12	25	.196	.310	.254
Runners/Scor. Pos.			64	17	2	7	12	.266	.438	.338
Runners On/2 Out			72	11	0	1	14	.153	.194	.164
Scor. Pos./2 Out			33	8	0	1	6	.242	.303	.265
Late Inning Pressure			42	6	0	6	7	.143	.167	.250
Leading Off			11	0	0	1	2	.000	.000	.083
Runners On			15	1	0	2	2	.067	.067	.176
Runners/Scor. Pos.			6	0	0	2	1	.000	.000	.250
First 9 Batters			130	34	2	12	25	.262	.354	.319
Second 9 Batters			123	29	3	10	19	.236	.366	.299
All Batters Thereafter			133	30	3	12	13	.226	.331	.290

Loves to face: Rob Deer (0-for-5, 3 SO)
Hates to face: Ruben Sierra (.625, 5-for-8, 2 BB)
Ground outs-to-air outs ratio: 0.72 last season, his first in majors.
. . . Additional statistics: 4 double-play ground outs in 81 opportunities, 14 doubles, 2 triples in 102.2 innings last season. . . . Allowed 9 first-inning runs in 14 starts. . . . Batting support: 5.21 runs per start. . . . Was recalled from Tacoma on May 31, made his major league debut that night against the Yankees, and was sent back to Tacoma the following day. . . . Started only 14 games, but completed more (2) than either Curt Young (26 GS, 1 CG) or Storm Davis (33 GS, 1 CG). . . . Made his postseason debut with two outs in the ninth inning of final game of World Series. He retired Alfredo Griffin. Nice touch by LaRussa, who used all 24 players.

Mike Campbell

Throws Right

Seattle Mariners	W–L	ERA	AB	H	HR	BB	SO	BA	SA	OBA
Season	6-10	5.89	457	128	18	43	63	.280	.473	.339
vs. Left-Handers			241	62	9	29	33	.257	.419	.335
vs. Right-Handers			216	66	9	14	30	.306	.532	.343
Home	2-6	6.41	237	66	10	21	35	.278	.485	.336
Road	4-4	5.34	220	62	8	22	28	.282	.459	.341
Grass	3-3	6.00	167	48	6	19	22	.287	.467	.354
Artificial Turf	3-7	5.82	290	80	12	24	41	.276	.476	.329
April	2-2	3.75	131	29	3	12	21	.221	.359	.283
May	1-4	8.33	115	37	8	8	16	.322	.609	.366
June	0-2	6.60	65	23	2	5	11	.354	.554	.389
July			0	0	0	0	0	—	—	—
August	2-0	1.88	52	8	1	5	5	.154	.288	.228
Sept./Oct.	1-2	8.46	94	31	4	13	10	.330	.511	.407
Leading Off Inn.			110	33	5	11	15	.300	.555	.364
Runners On			200	60	8	20	22	.300	.480	.356
Runners/Scor. Pos.			118	30	5	14	12	.254	.441	.321
Runners On/2 Out			80	24	2	8	7	.300	.438	.364
Scor. Pos./2 Out			54	13	2	5	5	.241	.407	.305
Late Inning Pressure			24	3	1	0	4	.125	.250	.125
Leading Off			7	0	0	0	1	.000	.000	.000
Runners On			5	1	1	0	0	.200	.800	.200
Runners/Scor. Pos.			2	0	0	0	0	.000	.000	.000
First 9 Batters			157	41	4	20	28	.261	.414	.339
Second 9 Batters			160	31	9	9	21	.319	.550	.355
All Batters Thereafter			140	36	5	14	14	.257	.450	.321

Loves to face: Claudell Washington (.067, 1-for-15)
Hates to face: Mike Greenwell (.800, 4-for-5, 2 HR)
Ground outs-to-air outs ratio: 0.62 last season, 0.63 for career. . . .
Additional statistics: 5 double-play ground outs in 92 opportunities, 30 doubles, 2 triples in 114.2 innings last season. . . . Allowed 12 first-inning runs in 20 starts. . . . Batting support: 5.15 runs per start. . . . The A.L.'s 17 qualifying .300 hitters batted .416 against him, their highest mark vs. any pitcher (minimum: 50 AB). . . . Only Mike Smithson (5.97) had a higher ERA than Campbell's (minimum: 100 IP). . . . Ground-ball hitters have a career average of .299 against him, fly-ballers have hit .235. . . . Opposing batters have a career average of .230 on his first pass through batting order, .283 after that. . . . Career record of 32–12 in the minors, 7–14 in the majors.

John Candelaria

Throws Left

New York Yankees

	W–L	ERA	AB	H	HR	BB	SO	BA	SA	OBA
Season	13-7	3.38	605	150	18	23	121	.248	.398	.275
vs. Left-Handers			97	14	4	6	32	.144	.268	.189
vs. Right-Handers			508	136	14	17	89	.268	.423	.292
Home	7-5	3.28	387	102	9	13	84	.264	.393	.287
Road	6-2	3.55	218	48	9	10	37	.220	.408	.254
Grass	8-7	3.38	486	122	14	18	104	.251	.397	.279
Artificial Turf	5-0	3.38	119	28	4	5	17	.235	.403	.260
April	2-2	3.19	144	37	6	6	29	.257	.444	.291
May	5-0	1.66	130	23	3	3	29	.177	.292	.193
June	1-2	4.74	95	27	2	4	13	.284	.421	.311
July	4-2	3.41	143	29	6	6	36	.203	.357	.235
August	1-1	5.23	93	34	1	4	14	.366	.516	.388
Sept./Oct.			0	0	0	0	0	—	—	—
Leading Off Inn.			161	46	5	1	26	.286	.410	.290
Runners On			220	57	8	14	50	.259	.436	.296
Runners/Scor. Pos.			115	28	6	9	29	.243	.461	.285
Runners On/2 Out			90	23	4	7	22	.256	.456	.309
Scor. Pos./2 Out			59	15	3	5	15	.254	.475	.313
Late Inning Pressure			56	10	0	1	13	.179	.214	.193
Leading Off			16	3	0	0	4	.188	.188	.188
Runners On			17	2	0	1	3	.118	.118	.167
Runners/Scor. Pos.			7	1	0	0	2	.143	.143	.143
First 9 Batters			205	52	4	10	52	.254	.366	.287
Second 9 Batters			196	44	7	6	35	.224	.398	.242
All Batters Thereafter			204	54	7	7	34	.265	.431	.296

Loves to face: Jim Presley (.105, 2-for-19)
Hates to face: Scott Fletcher (.611, 11-for-18)
Ground outs-to-air outs ratio: 0.69 last season, 0.86 for career. . . .
Additional statistics: 7 double-play ground outs in 107 opportunities, 31 doubles, 3 triples in 157.0 innings last season. . . . Allowed 6 first-inning runs in 24 starts. . . . Batting support: 4.88 runs per start. . . . Won seven consecutive starts (Apr. 29–June 11), longest streak of his career. . . . Recorded a shutout and a save in the same month (May). Big deal, Hershiser did it in one series, and Neil Allen almost did it in the same *game*. . . . July record of 22–5 over past seven seasons. . . . Walked only one of 162 leadoff batters last season, 2d-best percentage in the past 14 years. Rick Langford walked one of 246 leadoff batters in 1982. . . . Four HRs by left-handers was a career *high*.

Tom Candiotti

Throws Right

Cleveland Indians

	W–L	ERA	AB	H	HR	BB	SO	BA	SA	OBA
Season	14-8	3.28	827	225	15	53	137	.272	.372	.319
vs. Left-Handers			457	128	7	37	61	.280	.383	.333
vs. Right-Handers			370	97	8	16	76	.262	.359	.301
Home	10-2	2.63	453	111	5	22	87	.245	.307	.285
Road	4-6	4.15	374	114	10	31	50	.305	.452	.359
Grass	13-7	3.25	729	197	13	40	122	.270	.366	.312
Artificial Turf	1-1	3.55	98	28	2	13	15	.286	.418	.366
April	4-0	2.13	158	45	2	12	34	.285	.348	.337
May	2-3	3.05	178	53	1	8	30	.298	.365	.330
June	1-4	5.70	143	42	5	11	24	.294	.448	.352
July	1-1	4.28	136	42	2	6	19	.309	.419	.338
August	3-0	1.59	61	13	1	8	8	.213	.279	.314
Sept./Oct.	3-0	2.51	151	30	4	8	22	.199	.331	.238
Leading Off Inn.			214	60	4	8	34	.280	.383	.306
Runners On			346	85	7	27	65	.246	.344	.302
Runners/Scor. Pos.			189	47	4	20	33	.249	.354	.319
Runners On/2 Out			150	39	4	14	28	.260	.400	.331
Scor. Pos./2 Out			98	23	3	10	17	.235	.378	.318
Late Inning Pressure			105	27	1	14	17	.257	.343	.331
Leading Off			31	11	1	0	5	.355	.516	.355
Runners On			41	7	0	9	8	.171	.220	.314
Runners/Scor. Pos.			27	3	0	8	5	.111	.148	.306
First 9 Batters			255	68	4	16	41	.267	.361	.311
Second 9 Batters			246	66	6	16	38	.268	.382	.318
All Batters Thereafter			326	91	5	21	58	.279	.374	.325

Loves to face: Tim Laudner (0-for-10)
Hates to face: George Bell (.583, 14-for-24, 2 HR)
Ground outs-to-air outs ratio: 1.40 last season, 1.25 for career. . . .
Additional statistics: 20 double-play ground outs in 161 opportunities, 32 doubles, 3 triples in 216.2 innings last season. . . . Allowed 15 first-inning runs in 31 starts. . . . Batting support: 4.48 runs per start. . . . Ended the season with a seven-game winning streak. . . . One of two A.L. pitchers to allow hits to seven consecutive opposing batters last season. . . . Career record of 13–4 (.765) during August, 30–40 (.429) in other months. . . . Opponents' career batting average of .241 with runners on base, .272 with the bases empty. . . . First Indians pitcher to accumulate 200 innings pitched in each of three consecutive seasons since Rick Waits (1978–80).

John Cerutti

Throws Left

Toronto Blue Jays

	W–L	ERA	AB	H	HR	BB	SO	BA	SA	OBA
Season	6-7	3.13	468	120	12	42	65	.256	.397	.320
vs. Left-Handers			116	22	2	6	24	.190	.310	.226
vs. Right-Handers			352	98	10	36	41	.278	.426	.349
Home	3-3	2.98	227	56	5	18	28	.247	.383	.306
Road	3-4	3.27	241	64	7	24	37	.266	.411	.332
Grass	2-4	3.40	199	51	6	20	36	.256	.397	.324
Artificial Turf	4-3	2.93	269	69	6	22	29	.257	.398	.316
April	1-1	2.59	97	28	2	5	14	.289	.464	.324
May	2-1	3.81	103	25	3	9	17	.243	.398	.316
June	1-2	7.02	79	26	4	10	9	.329	.519	.404
July	1-2	3.38	81	22	3	8	6	.272	.420	.326
August	0-0	0.00	45	8	0	6	7	.178	.178	.275
Sept./Oct.	1-1	1.45	63	11	0	4	12	.175	.270	.235
Leading Off Inn.			110	20	3	8	9	.182	.291	.244
Runners On			194	48	3	25	33	.247	.376	.332
Runners/Scor. Pos.			132	30	3	22	28	.227	.341	.335
Runners On/2 Out			78	18	1	12	18	.231	.333	.341
Scor. Pos./2 Out			54	11	1	12	16	.204	.296	.358
Late Inning Pressure			63	16	1	6	9	.254	.349	.314
Leading Off			16	1	0	0	0	.063	.063	.063
Runners On			21	7	0	5	4	.333	.429	.444
Runners/Scor. Pos.			16	5	0	5	3	.313	.375	.455
First 9 Batters			250	64	7	24	37	.256	.412	.327
Second 9 Batters			135	36	4	14	17	.267	.415	.331
All Batters Thereafter			83	20	1	4	11	.241	.325	.276

Loves to face: Greg Walker (0-for-13)
Hates to face: Gary Gaetti (.500, 6-for-12, 4 HR)
Ground outs-to-air outs ratio: 1.17 last season, 0.85 for career. . . .
Additional statistics: 11 double-play ground outs in 91 opportunities, 22 doubles, 4 triples in 123.2 innings last season. . . . Allowed 9 first-inning runs in 12 starts. . . . Batting support: 4.50 runs per start. . . . Record of 5–4 (4.12 ERA) in 12 starts, 1–3 (2.09) in 34 relief appearances. Allowed an average of one home run per 6.1 innings as a starter, one HR per 30 innings in relief. . . . Faced only seven batters protecting leads of three runs or fewer in 8th inning or later. Has recorded only two saves in 74 career relief appearances. . . . Opponents' career batting average of .224 with runners in scoring position, .245 with runners on base, .270 with the bases empty.

Jim Clancy

Throws Right

Toronto Blue Jays

	W–L	ERA	AB	H	HR	BB	SO	BA	SA	OBA
Season	11-13	4.49	760	207	26	47	118	.272	.424	.321
vs. Left-Handers			404	113	10	27	56	.280	.411	.324
vs. Right-Handers			356	94	16	20	62	.264	.438	.317
Home	6-6	5.26	351	102	9	17	55	.291	.433	.330
Road	5-7	3.83	409	105	17	30	63	.257	.416	.313
Grass	4-6	3.59	320	83	12	23	48	.259	.406	.314
Artificial Turf	7-7	5.15	440	124	14	24	70	.282	.436	.326
April	1-2	6.91	110	30	3	13	23	.273	.445	.347
May	1-4	3.66	153	41	4	12	20	.268	.386	.323
June	2-4	5.55	136	35	8	10	20	.257	.493	.322
July	0-1	6.35	68	21	3	4	6	.309	.500	.356
August	4-2	2.64	167	40	4	4	32	.240	.347	.266
Sept./Oct.	3-0	3.86	126	40	4	4	17	.317	.437	.344
Leading Off Inn.			199	59	9	7	34	.296	.477	.330
Runners On			294	84	6	20	41	.286	.398	.335
Runners/Scor. Pos.			152	45	3	12	23	.296	.401	.351
Runners On/2 Out			114	26	1	6	17	.228	.325	.267
Scor. Pos./2 Out			65	14	0	3	12	.215	.246	.250
Late Inning Pressure			29	15	1	2	2	.517	.690	.548
Leading Off			10	5	0	0	1	.500	.500	.500
Runners On			10	5	0	2	0	.500	.600	.583
Runners/Scor. Pos.			6	3	0	1	0	.500	.500	.571
First 9 Batters			293	87	13	13	49	.297	.478	.331
Second 9 Batters			243	55	7	15	44	.226	.374	.281
All Batters Thereafter			224	65	6	19	25	.290	.406	.351

Loves to face: Mickey Hatcher (.182, 4-for-22)
Hates to face: Lee Mazzilli (.438, 7-for-16, 1 HR)
Ground outs-to-air outs ratio: 1.29 last season, 1.05 for career. . . .
Additional statistics: 25 double-play ground outs in 153 opportunities, 29 doubles, 4 triples in 196.1 innings last season. . . . Allowed 25 first-inning runs (3d most in A.L.) in 31 starts. . . . Allowed seven first-inning HRs, tied for most in majors. . . . Batting support: 4.39 runs per start. . . . Opposing batters have hit better in LIP Situations than otherwise in each of last seven seasons. . . . Blew past Bob Knepper in race for losingest pitcher of 1980s. Clancy's lost 112, four more than Floyd Bannister and Frank Tanana. . . . Last remaining pitcher from the original Blue Jays finished his Toronto career with a .478 winning percentage. The club had a .474 mark during those 11 years.

Terry Clark

California Angels — Throws Right

California Angels	W–L	ERA	AB	H	HR	BB	SO	BA	SA	OBA
Season	6-6	5.07	372	120	8	31	39	.323	.465	.370
vs. Left-Handers			174	61	4	17	13	.351	.511	.400
vs. Right-Handers			198	59	4	14	26	.298	.424	.343
Home	4-3	4.82	189	64	5	13	19	.339	.481	.377
Road	2-3	5.32	183	56	3	18	20	.306	.448	.363
Grass	5-6	5.61	310	105	7	29	36	.339	.481	.391
Artificial Turf	1-0	2.65	62	15	1	2	3	.242	.387	.262
April			0	0	0	0	0	—	—	—
May			0	0	0	0	0	—	—	—
June			0	0	0	0	0	—	—	—
July	3-0	3.55	94	25	2	5	11	.266	.340	.303
August	3-2	4.97	163	50	5	19	21	.307	.509	.377
Sept./Oct.	0-4	6.67	115	45	1	7	7	.391	.504	.413
Leading Off Inn.			94	36	0	5	11	.383	.500	.414
Runners On			164	54	5	18	17	.329	.470	.385
Runners/Scor. Pos.			99	26	2	15	13	.263	.394	.345
Runners On/2 Out			62	21	4	4	10	.339	.581	.379
Scor. Pos./2 Out			45	12	2	4	8	.267	.444	.327
Late Inning Pressure			32	11	0	1	2	.344	.438	.364
Leading Off			10	4	0	0	1	.400	.400	.400
Runners On			12	4	0	1	0	.333	.500	.385
Runners/Scor. Pos.			6	2	0	1	0	.333	.667	.429
First 9 Batters			121	48	3	9	10	.397	.562	.429
Second 9 Batters			114	25	0	10	14	.219	.272	.280
All Batters Thereafter			137	47	5	12	15	.343	.540	.393

Loves to face: Jose Canseco (0-for-5, 4 SO)
Hates to face: Don Baylor (1-for-1, 2 BB, 1 HR)
Ground outs-to-air outs ratio: 1.29 last season, his first in majors. . . . Additional statistics: 14 double-play ground outs in 89 opportunities, 23 doubles, 3 triples in 94.0 innings last season. . . . Allowed 21 first-inning runs in 15 starts. Opposing batters hit .462 in first inning (30-for-65). . . . Batting support: 5.20 runs per start, 9th highest in A.L. (minimum: 15 GS). . . . Seven of the eight home runs he allowed were hit with two men out. . . . Right-handed batters had hits in each of their last six at-bats against him. . . . Made pro debut in 1979 in same rookie league as Kent Hrbek and Gary Gaetti, then saw the world en route to majors, with stops in Johnson City, Gastonia, St. Pete, Little Rock, Louisville, Midland, and Edmonton.

Roger Clemens

Boston Red Sox — Throws Right

Boston Red Sox	W–L	ERA	AB	H	HR	BB	SO	BA	SA	OBA
Season	18-12	2.93	986	217	17	62	291	.220	.320	.270
vs. Left-Handers			504	129	8	35	132	.256	.363	.308
vs. Right-Handers			482	88	9	27	159	.183	.276	.229
Home	6-8	3.91	460	106	9	30	141	.230	.354	.279
Road	12-4	2.09	526	111	8	32	150	.211	.291	.262
Grass	14-12	3.19	866	195	17	58	259	.225	.338	.277
Artificial Turf	4-0	1.09	120	22	0	4	32	.183	.192	.216
April	4-0	1.75	185	33	3	8	60	.178	.265	.212
May	4-2	1.88	184	31	4	13	56	.168	.288	.223
June	3-3	4.08	160	46	1	6	47	.288	.375	.318
July	4-0	1.64	182	36	2	8	69	.198	.258	.240
August	0-5	7.33	111	34	4	15	25	.306	.468	.395
Sept./Oct.	3-2	3.27	164	37	3	12	34	.226	.335	.278
Leading Off Inn.			258	51	2	12	78	.198	.267	.236
Runners On			366	87	8	25	110	.238	.361	.291
Runners/Scor. Pos.			198	44	5	14	64	.222	.348	.283
Runners On/2 Out			156	33	3	12	46	.212	.327	.268
Scor. Pos./2 Out			94	20	2	9	30	.213	.319	.282
Late Inning Pressure			140	25	1	12	57	.179	.250	.243
Leading Off			41	10	1	3	17	.244	.415	.295
Runners On			45	8	0	7	20	.178	.244	.288
Runners/Scor. Pos.			28	3	0	6	11	.107	.143	.265
First 9 Batters			289	58	6	23	95	.201	.311	.260
Second 9 Batters			289	69	5	14	75	.239	.360	.281
All Batters Thereafter			408	90	6	25	121	.221	.299	.268

Loves to face: Pete Incaviglia (0-for-7, 7 SO)
Hates to face: Carmen Castillo (.429, 9-for-21, 3 HR)
Ground outs-to-air outs ratio: 0.82 last season, 0.90 for career. . . . Additional statistics: 7 double-play ground outs in 169 opportunities, 36 doubles, 6 triples in 264.0 innings last season. . . . Allowed 12 first-inning runs in 35 starts. . . . Batting support: 4.37 runs per start. . . . Held opposing right-handers hitless in 37 consecutive plate appearances, longest streak in A.L. . . . Retired leadoff batters in 24 consecutive innings, longest in majors. . . . Struck out the leadoff batter in 78 innings, highest total in A.L. over past 14 years. . . . First pitcher since Blyleven and Ryan 14 years ago to pitch 250 innings with an ERA below 3.00 for three consecutive seasons. Christy Mathewson and Walter Johnson did it 13 and 12 seasons in a row, respectively.

Stu Cliburn

California Angels — Throws Right

California Angels	W–L	ERA	AB	H	HR	BB	SO	BA	SA	OBA
Season	4-2	4.07	312	83	11	32	42	.266	.401	.342
vs. Left-Handers			133	38	9	16	14	.286	.511	.375
vs. Right-Handers			179	45	2	16	28	.251	.318	.317
Home	1-0	5.94	126	36	6	12	17	.286	.468	.361
Road	3-2	2.84	186	47	5	20	25	.253	.355	.329
Grass	2-2	4.95	255	72	11	30	32	.282	.443	.365
Artificial Turf	2-0	0.54	57	11	0	2	10	.193	.211	.230
April	0-0	8.53	26	9	1	4	1	.346	.500	.452
May	1-0	1.76	56	15	0	8	8	.268	.268	.369
June	1-0	1.26	45	7	1	2	9	.156	.267	.200
July	2-0	5.95	79	24	6	3	8	.304	.570	.341
August	0-2	4.76	65	17	3	8	8	.262	.431	.347
Sept./Oct.	0-0	3.97	41	11	0	7	8	.268	.293	.375
Leading Off Inn.			71	21	2	6	13	.296	.394	.351
Runners On			150	37	5	18	13	.247	.387	.343
Runners/Scor. Pos.			84	25	3	14	8	.298	.452	.417
Runners On/2 Out			58	10	2	5	4	.172	.310	.273
Scor. Pos./2 Out			35	8	1	4	3	.229	.371	.357
Late Inning Pressure			51	12	0	9	9	.235	.255	.344
Leading Off			13	3	0	3	6	.231	.231	.375
Runners On			22	7	0	4	1	.318	.364	.407
Runners/Scor. Pos.			12	5	0	3	0	.417	.500	.500
First 9 Batters			238	62	7	24	33	.261	.378	.335
Second 9 Batters			59	17	4	6	8	.288	.525	.373
All Batters Thereafter			15	4	0	2	1	.267	.267	.333

Loves to face: Frank White (0-for-7)
Hates to face: Tom Brookens (4-for-4, 2 BB)
Ground outs-to-air outs ratio: 1.34 last season, 1.28 for career. . . . Additional statistics: 13 double-play ground outs in 88 opportunities, 9 doubles, 0 triples in 84.0 innings last season. . . . Ground-ball hitters batted .232 against him, fly-ballers .293. . . . Allowed only one home run in his first 35 innings pitched last season, but surrendered 10 over the next 35 innings. . . . Only starting assignment of his career was a loss to Oakland on August 13. . . . Career record of 3–0 with a 1.40 ERA on artificial turf (6 ER in 38.2 IP). . . . Hadn't pitched in the majors since the 1985 season when he established an Angels club record with six consecutive victories out of the bullpen.

Chuck Crim

Milwaukee Brewers — Throws Right

Milwaukee Brewers	W–L	ERA	AB	H	HR	BB	SO	BA	SA	OBA
Season	7-6	2.91	384	95	11	28	58	.247	.383	.298
vs. Left-Handers			174	44	5	18	27	.253	.385	.320
vs. Right-Handers			210	51	6	10	31	.243	.381	.279
Home	5-4	3.38	196	50	9	9	26	.255	.459	.292
Road	2-2	2.44	188	45	2	19	32	.239	.303	.303
Grass	5-6	3.39	316	84	10	20	47	.266	.415	.308
Artificial Turf	2-0	0.90	68	11	1	8	11	.162	.235	.250
April	0-1	4.09	37	10	1	2	4	.270	.378	.317
May	0-1	3.06	64	16	2	6	7	.250	.406	.306
June	0-2	1.37	59	8	1	8	8	.136	.237	.246
July	3-1	2.95	82	17	3	4	16	.207	.366	.244
August	3-1	2.70	79	22	2	3	14	.278	.392	.305
Sept./Oct.	1-0	4.11	63	22	2	5	9	.349	.508	.386
Leading Off Inn.			91	22	3	4	13	.242	.396	.274
Runners On			169	35	4	15	27	.207	.320	.271
Runners/Scor. Pos.			104	22	4	10	16	.212	.365	.279
Runners On/2 Out			86	20	3	9	13	.233	.407	.305
Scor. Pos./2 Out			58	14	3	7	9	.241	.448	.323
Late Inning Pressure			170	45	3	19	32	.265	.382	.339
Leading Off			46	7	1	2	8	.152	.261	.188
Runners On			65	15	0	11	14	.231	.323	.342
Runners/Scor. Pos.			33	8	0	8	8	.242	.333	.386
First 9 Batters			342	86	11	27	51	.251	.398	.305
Second 9 Batters			40	8	0	1	7	.200	.250	.220
All Batters Thereafter			2	1	0	0	0	.500	.500	.500

Loves to face: Don Mattingly (0-for-7)
Hates to face: Steve Lyons (.600, 3-for-5, 1 HR)
Ground outs-to-air outs ratio: 1.27 last season, 1.33 for career. . . . Additional statistics: 12 double-play ground outs in 71 opportunities, 17 doubles, 1 triple in 105.0 innings last season. . . . Made 70 appearances, equalling 2d-highest total in team history. Ken Sanders set the mark with 83 games in 1971. Tom Murphy made 70 appearances in 1974. . . . Recorded nine saves last season, but no more than two in any month. . . . Faced 64 batters protecting leads of three runs or fewer in 8th inning or later. Other Brewers relievers: Plesac, 121; Mirabella, 24; Jones, 16. . . . Opponents batted 72 points lower with runners on than with bases empty, 3d-largest difference in A.L. (minimum: 100 AB each way). . . . Opposing ground-ball hitters batted .196, fly-ballers hit .283.

John Davis

Throws Right

Chicago White Sox	W–L	ERA	AB	H	HR	BB	SO	BA	SA	OBA
Season	2-5	6.64	259	77	5	50	37	.297	.440	.413
vs. Left-Handers			102	33	3	28	13	.324	.529	.459
vs. Right-Handers			157	44	2	22	24	.280	.382	.380
Home	2-4	7.38	162	50	4	31	27	.309	.469	.426
Road	0-1	5.47	97	27	1	19	10	.278	.392	.392
Grass	2-5	6.75	240	73	5	46	35	.304	.450	.416
Artificial Turf	0-0	5.40	19	4	0	4	2	.211	.316	.375
April	1-1	2.35	51	8	1	11	7	.157	.255	.333
May	0-1	7.13	73	26	0	18	16	.356	.425	.478
June	0-0	11.57	27	10	0	5	0	.370	.519	.469
July	1-2	6.88	73	24	3	7	9	.329	.507	.378
August	0-1	9.00	17	4	0	4	0	.235	.471	.381
Sept./Oct.	0-0	11.25	18	5	1	5	5	.278	.611	.458
Leading Off Inn.			49	14	1	15	10	.286	.429	.453
Runners On			155	48	3	23	19	.310	.458	.400
Runners/Scor. Pos.			103	30	2	20	13	.291	.456	.408
Runners On/2 Out			50	11	0	11	12	.220	.280	.381
Scor. Pos./2 Out			36	6	0	11	9	.167	.194	.388
Late Inning Pressure			84	20	2	17	17	.238	.369	.375
Leading Off			19	2	0	6	6	.105	.158	.320
Runners On			38	8	1	8	7	.211	.368	.354
Runners/Scor. Pos.			20	5	1	7	3	.250	.550	.448
First 9 Batters			205	63	5	38	25	.307	.459	.416
Second 9 Batters			44	11	0	9	8	.250	.386	.389
All Batters Thereafter			10	3	0	3	4	.300	.300	.462

Loves to face: Wade Boggs (0-for-3, 2 SO)
Hates to face: Mike Stanley (2-for-2, 1 3B)
Ground outs-to-air outs ratio: 2.10 last season, 2.13 for career. . . .
Additional statistics: 10 double-play ground outs in 83 opportunities, 20 doubles, 1 triple in 63.2 innings last season. . . . Allowed runs in 11 consecutive relief appearances, longest streak in majors. . . . Average of 7.07 walks per nine innings was highest in A.L. (minimum: 60 IP). . . . Doesn't it seem like a 6'7" pitcher should have a career average of more than 4.37 strikeouts per nine innings? (Lee Guetterman probably doesn't think so). . . . He and teammate Joel Davis don't set the Elias record for most similar names on the same pro sports club. That distinction goes to the 1962 Mets, who had two Bob Millers. Runners-up: the 1987–88 New Jersey Nets, with Dwayne and Duane Washington.

Storm Davis

Throws Right

Oakland As	W–L	ERA	AB	H	HR	BB	SO	BA	SA	OBA
Season	16-7	3.70	769	211	16	91	127	.274	.394	.349
vs. Left-Handers			396	104	4	47	70	.263	.348	.336
vs. Right-Handers			373	107	12	44	57	.287	.442	.362
Home	7-3	3.71	370	104	6	43	61	.281	.384	.354
Road	9-4	3.70	399	107	10	48	66	.268	.404	.344
Grass	13-6	3.74	662	182	14	82	112	.275	.396	.352
Artificial Turf	3-1	3.49	107	29	2	9	15	.271	.383	.325
April	2-1	2.84	90	20	2	15	21	.222	.356	.333
May	2-1	3.48	136	41	1	18	21	.301	.382	.380
June	1-2	4.14	160	45	5	9	29	.281	.444	.318
July	5-0	2.41	136	31	2	13	20	.228	.324	.293
August	4-0	3.47	132	35	2	20	19	.265	.348	.362
Sept./Oct.	2-3	6.18	115	39	4	16	17	.339	.504	.410
Leading Off Inn.			198	58	5	15	27	.293	.439	.343
Runners On			325	81	8	48	51	.249	.372	.340
Runners/Scor. Pos.			165	42	4	29	32	.255	.394	.355
Runners On/2 Out			143	36	5	17	20	.252	.427	.331
Scor. Pos./2 Out			81	20	2	12	15	.247	.420	.344
Late Inning Pressure			54	21	3	7	11	.389	.630	.452
Leading Off			13	3	1	3	3	.231	.462	.375
Runners On			25	9	2	2	3	.360	.680	.393
Runners/Scor. Pos.			8	3	0	0	0	.375	.625	.333
First 9 Batters			258	68	3	35	45	.264	.345	.351
Second 9 Batters			267	63	8	27	46	.236	.378	.303
All Batters Thereafter			244	80	5	29	36	.328	.463	.395

Loves to face: Jack Howell (.077, 1-for-13, 7 SO)
Hates to face: Jim Rice (.467, 14-for-30, 2 HR)
Ground outs-to-air outs ratio: 0.87 last season, 1.12 for career. . . .
Additional statistics: 19 double-play ground outs in 165 opportunities, 36 doubles, 4 triples in 201.2 innings last season. . . . Allowed 8 first-inning runs in 33 starts, 4th-lowest average in A.L. (minimum: 15 GS). . . . Batting support: 5.30 runs per start, 7th highest in A.L. (minimum: 15 GS). . . . ERA is 3.12 through first five innings of his starts, but 6.02 ERA after that. . . . Opposing batters hit 123 points higher in Late-Inning Pressure Situations than otherwise, the largest difference in the majors last season (minimum: 50 AB both ways). . . . Career records: 8–16 during June, 18–3 during July. . . . Has now faced 2366 right-handers, still hasn't hit one with a pitch. What's he waiting for?

Richard Dotson

Throws Right

New York Yankees	W–L	ERA	AB	H	HR	BB	SO	BA	SA	OBA
Season	12-9	5.00	669	178	27	72	77	.266	.454	.338
vs. Left-Handers			347	83	11	33	39	.239	.392	.306
vs. Right-Handers			322	95	16	39	38	.295	.522	.372
Home	6-3	3.99	301	71	14	34	33	.236	.432	.314
Road	6-6	5.87	368	107	13	38	44	.291	.473	.357
Grass	10-6	4.44	525	132	21	57	59	.251	.436	.327
Artificial Turf	2-3	7.13	144	46	6	15	18	.319	.521	.378
April	3-0	3.48	126	25	7	14	12	.198	.389	.277
May	2-1	2.53	123	30	5	7	17	.244	.382	.290
June	2-2	7.62	109	34	5	10	10	.312	.560	.369
July	1-1	9.53	49	19	2	7	3	.388	.633	.448
August	1-4	5.35	139	39	6	15	18	.281	.504	.350
Sept./Oct.	3-1	4.96	123	31	2	19	17	.252	.374	.357
Leading Off Inn.			164	44	7	18	15	.268	.470	.348
Runners On			274	85	10	29	31	.310	.504	.370
Runners/Scor. Pos.			147	38	5	21	20	.259	.435	.341
Runners On/2 Out			95	19	3	11	13	.200	.316	.283
Scor. Pos./2 Out			57	9	2	9	8	.158	.263	.273
Late Inning Pressure			21	7	0	8	2	.333	.333	.517
Leading Off			4	0	0	2	0	.000	.000	.333
Runners On			10	5	0	5	1	.500	.500	.667
Runners/Scor. Pos.			5	4	0	4	0	.800	.800	.889
First 9 Batters			253	61	9	25	33	.241	.407	.308
Second 9 Batters			218	61	7	22	22	.280	.463	.340
All Batters Thereafter			198	56	11	25	22	.283	.505	.372

Loves to face: Scott Fletcher (.091, 2-for-22)
Hates to face: Rich Gedman (.417, 15-for-36, 2 HR)
Ground outs-to-air outs ratio: 1.16 last season, 1.31 for career. . . .
Additional statistics: 11 double-play ground outs in 141 opportunities, 37 doubles, 4 triples in 171.0 innings last season. . . . Allowed 12 first-inning runs in 29 starts. . . . Batting support: 5.66 runs per start, 3d highest in A.L. (minimum: 15 GS). . . . Yankees won each of his first six and last five starts. . . . One of two pitchers to allow seven consecutive hits with runners on base. Opponents batted 75 points higher with runners on than with bases empty, 5th-largest gap in A.L. (minimum: 100 AB each way). . . . He's younger than Righetti, Leary, or Hershiser. At the time of his 100th career victory (June 5), only one younger pitcher had that many: Fernando Valenzuela.

Dennis Eckersley

Throws Right

Oakland As	W–L	ERA	AB	H	HR	BB	SO	BA	SA	OBA
Season	4-2	2.35	263	52	5	11	70	.198	.270	.230
vs. Left-Handers			126	25	3	5	26	.198	.286	.229
vs. Right-Handers			137	27	2	6	44	.197	.255	.231
Home	3-1	2.33	137	25	3	5	43	.182	.263	.215
Road	1-1	2.38	126	27	2	6	27	.214	.278	.246
Grass	3-1	2.41	217	43	4	7	60	.198	.263	.225
Artificial Turf	1-1	2.08	46	9	1	4	10	.196	.304	.255
April	0-0	0.00	38	5	0	1	8	.132	.132	.154
May	1-1	3.21	50	9	0	1	13	.180	.200	.196
June	1-0	1.54	43	10	1	3	10	.233	.326	.292
July	0-1	3.18	45	10	2	1	13	.222	.378	.239
August	1-0	5.91	41	11	2	1	10	.268	.415	.273
Sept./Oct.	1-0	0.66	46	7	0	4	16	.152	.174	.220
Leading Off Inn.			59	9	0	1	16	.153	.153	.167
Runners On			103	24	3	7	25	.233	.359	.274
Runners/Scor. Pos.			56	15	3	5	16	.268	.500	.313
Runners On/2 Out			57	14	2	4	11	.246	.404	.295
Scor. Pos./2 Out			33	10	2	3	7	.303	.576	.361
Late Inning Pressure			177	35	3	9	48	.198	.271	.239
Leading Off			38	5	0	1	13	.132	.132	.154
Runners On			68	15	2	6	15	.221	.368	.280
Runners/Scor. Pos.			38	10	2	4	10	.263	.526	.326
First 9 Batters			258	49	5	11	69	.190	.264	.223
Second 9 Batters			5	3	0	0	1	.600	.600	.600
All Batters Thereafter			0	0	0	0	0	—	—	—

Loves to face: Frank White (.085, 4-for-47)
Hates to face: Kent Hrbek (.429, 9-for-21, 2 HR)
Ground outs-to-air outs ratio: 0.80 last season, 0.71 for career. . . .
Additional statistics: 3 double-play ground outs in 36 opportunities, 4 doubles, 0 triples in 72.2 innings last season. . . . Has allowed 284 career home runs. Only active pitchers with 300 are Blyleven (384) and Tanana (326). . . . Four saves in A.L.C.S set a career record, one shy of Tug McGraw's major league mark of five in playoff competition. . . . Pitched 72.2 innings to earn his 45 saves. Righetti needed 106.2 for his 46 saves in 1986; Sutter needed 122.2 for 45 saves in 1984. . . . Two other 20-game winners also had 20-save seasons: Mudcat Grant and Wilbur Wood. Ellis Kinder and Johnny Sain also qualify if you accept the pre-1969 save extrapolations in Macmillan's *Baseball Encyclopedia*.

Mark Eichhorn

Toronto Blue Jays — Throws Right

	W–L	ERA	AB	H	HR	BB	SO	BA	SA	OBA
Season	0-3	4.19	260	79	3	27	28	.304	.388	.381
vs. Left-Handers			117	35	0	9	9	.299	.333	.346
vs. Right-Handers			143	44	3	18	19	.308	.434	.407
Home	0-1	4.25	166	49	1	19	17	.295	.367	.376
Road	0-2	4.07	94	30	2	8	11	.319	.426	.390
Grass	0-2	4.43	82	27	2	7	10	.329	.427	.402
Artificial Turf	0-1	4.08	178	52	1	20	18	.292	.371	.371
April	0-1	3.98	73	19	0	11	13	.260	.315	.368
May	0-2	5.02	61	24	2	6	4	.393	.525	.456
June	0-0	2.51	55	14	0	4	5	.255	.291	.328
July	0-0	6.75	38	14	1	3	4	.368	.500	.429
August			0	0	0	0	0	—	—	—
Sept./Oct.	0-0	3.24	33	8	0	3	2	.242	.333	.306
Leading Off Inn.			53	17	0	6	7	.321	.396	.400
Runners On			145	44	1	16	17	.303	.379	.386
Runners/Scor. Pos.			106	31	1	13	11	.292	.377	.382
Runners On/2 Out			64	16	1	4	9	.250	.328	.294
Scor. Pos./2 Out			49	12	1	4	7	.245	.347	.302
Late Inning Pressure			45	17	1	6	5	.378	.556	.481
Leading Off			7	3	0	3	1	.429	.571	.636
Runners On			32	11	0	3	3	.344	.469	.432
Runners/Scor. Pos.			27	7	0	2	3	.259	.370	.333
First 9 Batters			201	59	2	20	22	.294	.363	.370
Second 9 Batters			55	17	1	7	6	.309	.455	.387
All Batters Thereafter			4	3	0	0	0	.750	.750	.800

Loves to face: Rob Deer (0-for-7, 6 SO)
Hates to face: Mark McGwire (.455, 5-for-11, 1 HR)
Ground outs-to-air outs ratio: 1.34 last season, 1.60 for career. . . . Additional statistics: 4 double-play ground outs in 71 opportunities, 11 doubles, 1 triple in 66.2 innings last season. . . . Faced only five batters protecting leads of three runs or fewer in 8th inning or later. Blue Jays had a record of 10–27 in games in which he appeared. . . . Sent to Syracuse during the All-Star break, after having appeared in 121 games over previous year and a half, 2d-highest total in A.L. during that time. . . . Strikeout-to-walk ratio, year by year since 1986: 3.69, 1.85, 1.04. Year by year ERA since 1986: 1.72, 3.17, 4.19. . . . Opponents' batting average had been under .200 in each of the two previous seasons.

Steve Farr

Kansas City Royals — Throws Right

	W–L	ERA	AB	H	HR	BB	SO	BA	SA	OBA
Season	5-4	2.50	308	74	5	30	72	.240	.367	.309
vs. Left-Handers			155	43	2	17	37	.277	.406	.349
vs. Right-Handers			153	31	3	13	35	.203	.327	.268
Home	4-1	1.54	151	35	0	11	35	.232	.318	.283
Road	1-3	3.46	157	39	5	19	37	.248	.414	.333
Grass	1-3	3.78	126	32	4	16	30	.254	.437	.343
Artificial Turf	4-1	1.64	182	42	1	14	42	.231	.319	.285
April	0-0	5.68	49	12	2	6	15	.245	.490	.327
May	0-0	0.47	64	10	0	4	24	.156	.203	.206
June	2-1	1.35	49	12	0	7	8	.245	.327	.333
July	1-1	2.84	48	12	3	4	7	.250	.521	.333
August	1-0	1.38	54	16	0	3	8	.296	.352	.333
Sept./Oct.	1-2	4.50	44	12	0	6	10	.273	.364	.346
Leading Off Inn.			63	17	1	9	15	.270	.476	.361
Runners On			160	37	3	15	37	.231	.338	.296
Runners/Scor. Pos.			105	22	1	12	27	.210	.305	.289
Runners On/2 Out			73	15	1	4	17	.205	.260	.256
Scor. Pos./2 Out			51	8	1	2	15	.157	.235	.204
Late Inning Pressure			145	36	2	16	32	.248	.366	.327
Leading Off			30	8	1	2	6	.267	.533	.313
Runners On			72	19	1	10	16	.264	.361	.353
Runners/Scor. Pos.			50	13	0	8	13	.260	.320	.361
First 9 Batters			273	64	4	26	64	.234	.359	.303
Second 9 Batters			28	7	1	3	7	.250	.393	.323
All Batters Thereafter			7	3	0	1	1	.429	.571	.500

Loves to face: Oddibe McDowell (.071, 1-for-14, 7 SO)
Hates to face: Bill Schroeder (.714, 5-for-7, 3 2B, 2 HR)
Ground outs-to-air outs ratio: 1.06 last season, 1.11 for career. . . . Additional statistics: 7 double-play ground outs in 70 opportunities, 20 doubles, 2 triples in 82.2 innings last season. . . . Faced 113 batters protecting leads of three runs or fewer in 8th inning or later. Other Royals relievers: Garber, 43; Gleaton, 41; Montgomery, 18; Quis, 17. . . . Recorded 16 saves in his last 34 games, after only four saves in his first 28 appearances. . . . Career record of 6–18 (4.41 ERA) on grass fields, 16–5 (2.83) on artificial turf. . . . Has had a winning record in each of last four seasons, but career record still stands one game below .500 (22–23) on account of his 3–11 rookie season with 1984 Indians. . . . Cleveland'll do that to you.

John Farrell

Cleveland Indians — Throws Right

	W–L	ERA	AB	H	HR	BB	SO	BA	SA	OBA
Season	14-10	4.24	804	216	15	67	92	.269	.392	.330
vs. Left-Handers			441	119	5	46	51	.270	.376	.341
vs. Right-Handers			363	97	10	21	41	.267	.410	.315
Home	7-5	4.38	429	112	9	39	40	.261	.399	.328
Road	7-5	4.07	375	104	6	28	52	.277	.384	.331
Grass	13-9	4.27	714	191	13	60	82	.268	.389	.330
Artificial Turf	1-1	3.97	90	25	2	7	10	.278	.411	.327
April	3-1	2.39	137	33	1	9	15	.241	.314	.293
May	2-2	3.45	178	45	2	12	18	.253	.343	.302
June	3-2	4.59	127	35	4	15	13	.276	.472	.363
July	3-2	6.43	170	56	6	13	27	.329	.506	.380
August	2-2	4.96	129	37	0	9	11	.287	.357	.338
Sept./Oct.	1-1	3.06	63	10	2	9	8	.159	.302	.264
Leading Off Inn.			207	65	4	14	17	.314	.435	.357
Runners On			357	92	8	30	47	.258	.373	.317
Runners/Scor. Pos.			187	50	5	18	28	.267	.390	.329
Runners On/2 Out			149	44	4	18	21	.295	.430	.382
Scor. Pos./2 Out			92	29	3	12	14	.315	.467	.406
Late Inning Pressure			57	18	1	4	6	.316	.439	.371
Leading Off			16	4	1	1	1	.250	.500	.294
Runners On			18	8	0	2	0	.444	.500	.524
Runners/Scor. Pos.			9	5	0	1	0	.556	.556	.636
First 9 Batters			247	71	3	22	33	.287	.389	.355
Second 9 Batters			249	58	6	23	28	.233	.365	.298
All Batters Thereafter			308	87	6	22	31	.282	.416	.334

Loves to face: Fred Lynn (0-for-8)
Hates to face: Walt Weiss (5-for-5, 2 2B)
Ground outs-to-air outs ratio: 0.82 last season, 0.86 for career. . . . Additional statistics: 14 double-play ground outs in 166 opportunities, 42 doubles, 6 triples in 210.1 innings last season. . . . Allowed 17 first-inning runs in 30 starts. . . . Batting support: 4.37 runs per start. . . . Faced the A.L.'s 14 25-HR hitters 74 times, highest total among pitchers who didn't allow a home run to them. . . . Indians lost all six of his no-decision starts. . . . Opposing ground-ball hitters batted .320, fly-ballers hit .231. . . . He has only 19 career victories, but has defeated every opposing A.L. club except Kansas City. . . . One of three Indians pitchers with 200 innings and a winning record, which hadn't happened since 1968 (McDowell, Tiant, and Siebert).

Tom Filer

Milwaukee Brewers — Throws Right

	W–L	ERA	AB	H	HR	BB	SO	BA	SA	OBA
Season	5-8	4.43	385	108	8	33	39	.281	.410	.333
vs. Left-Handers			208	60	5	23	14	.288	.438	.356
vs. Right-Handers			177	48	3	10	25	.271	.379	.306
Home	2-6	4.18	173	47	4	16	20	.272	.393	.326
Road	3-2	4.64	212	61	4	17	19	.288	.425	.339
Grass	4-8	4.17	321	86	6	29	34	.268	.371	.326
Artificial Turf	1-0	5.87	64	22	2	4	5	.344	.609	.371
April			0	0	0	0	0	—	—	—
May	2-0	1.00	64	10	0	5	5	.156	.156	.217
June	2-2	4.34	116	38	1	8	7	.328	.414	.370
July	1-2	5.66	78	23	4	5	15	.295	.513	.329
August	0-4	5.64	112	32	3	12	12	.286	.482	.346
Sept./Oct.	0-0	4.91	15	5	0	3	0	.333	.400	.444
Leading Off Inn.			102	32	1	4	9	.314	.431	.340
Runners On			148	46	6	21	15	.311	.480	.384
Runners/Scor. Pos.			80	19	5	16	9	.238	.475	.346
Runners On/2 Out			58	15	2	13	8	.259	.414	.394
Scor. Pos./2 Out			37	7	2	11	7	.189	.378	.375
Late Inning Pressure			21	6	0	2	3	.286	.286	.375
Leading Off			7	2	0	1	2	.286	.286	.375
Runners On			6	2	0	1	1	.333	.333	.500
Runners/Scor. Pos.			2	0	0	0	0	.000	.000	.333
First 9 Batters			143	38	0	8	18	.266	.329	.297
Second 9 Batters			126	39	3	12	11	.310	.452	.362
All Batters Thereafter			116	31	5	13	10	.267	.466	.346

Loves to face: Cal Ripken (0-for-9)
Hates to face: Lloyd Moseby (.800, 4-for-5)
Ground outs-to-air outs ratio: 1.66 last season, 1.41 for career. . . . Additional statistics: 11 double-play ground outs in 74 opportunities, 18 doubles, 4 triples in 101.2 innings last season. . . . Allowed 9 first-inning runs in 16 starts. . . . Batting support: 4.31 runs per start. . . . Pitched a five-hit shutout in his season debut (May 24 vs. Detroit), followed it with a complete-game victory (vs. Cleveland). Had a 4–0 record through games of June 14, but was 1–8 thereafter. . . . His 70 chances are 2d most of any active pitcher who has never committed an error. Jimmy Jones heads that list with 95 chances. . . . Has played three seasons in the majors: 1982 (Cubs), 1985 (Blue Jays), and 1988 (Brewers). Look for him to surface again in 1991.

Chuck Finley
California Angels   Throws Left

	W–L	ERA	AB	H	HR	BB	SO	BA	SA	OBA
Season	9-15	4.17	726	191	15	82	111	.263	.384	.339
vs. Left-Handers			135	39	1	16	19	.289	.370	.374
vs. Right-Handers			591	152	14	66	92	.257	.387	.330
Home	5-8	4.44	359	98	9	41	57	.273	.407	.347
Road	4-7	3.91	367	93	6	41	54	.253	.362	.330
Grass	7-14	4.40	611	164	13	72	98	.268	.388	.345
Artificial Turf	2-1	2.93	115	27	2	10	13	.235	.365	.302
April	2-3	3.23	134	27	1	13	24	.201	.276	.268
May	1-3	4.97	102	32	2	12	12	.314	.412	.397
June	2-2	3.54	151	35	3	15	28	.232	.358	.300
July	0-1	13.97	46	19	1	5	8	.413	.630	.453
August	3-3	3.46	144	40	5	16	18	.278	.417	.350
Sept./Oct.	1-3	3.54	149	38	3	21	21	.255	.383	.353
Leading Off Inn.			188	48	2	20	20	.255	.340	.333
Runners On			295	80	5	35	46	.271	.407	.342
Runners/Scor. Pos.			154	45	2	23	23	.292	.422	.364
Runners On/2 Out			117	21	1	15	23	.179	.282	.278
Scor. Pos./2 Out			67	10	0	11	16	.149	.209	.269
Late Inning Pressure			78	21	2	13	10	.269	.410	.383
Leading Off			25	7	0	3	2	.280	.320	.379
Runners On			26	5	0	7	2	.192	.308	.353
Runners/Scor. Pos.			13	1	0	5	1	.077	.154	.316
First 9 Batters			254	71	2	27	36	.280	.354	.346
Second 9 Batters			230	55	5	21	43	.239	.361	.301
All Batters Thereafter			242	65	8	34	32	.269	.438	.365

Loves to face: Greg Walker (.071, 1-for-14)
Hates to face: Chet Lemon (.800, 4-for-5, 1 HR)
Ground outs-to-air outs ratio: 1.13 last season, 1.14 for career. . . .
Additional statistics: 2 double-play ground outs in 150 opportunities, 27 doubles, 8 triples in 194.1 innings last season. . . . Allowed 17 first-inning runs in 31 starts. Has started 34 games in his career, but has never allowed a first-inning home run. . . . Batting support: 3.87 runs per start. . . . Made 31 appearances last season, all starts. Made only three starts in 60 games for California over two previous seasons. . . . Won consecutive decisions only once last season. . . . Only HR allowed to a left-hander was hit by George Brett. . . . One of two A.L. pitchers to allow hits in seven consecutive at-bats. . . . Opponents' career average is .287 by ground-ball hitters, .250 by fly-ballers.

Mike Flanagan
Toronto Blue Jays   Throws Left

	W–L	ERA	AB	H	HR	BB	SO	BA	SA	OBA
Season	13-13	4.18	812	220	23	80	99	.271	.424	.339
vs. Left-Handers			115	31	3	8	12	.270	.426	.320
vs. Right-Handers			697	189	20	72	87	.271	.423	.342
Home	6-6	3.76	415	114	13	38	49	.275	.429	.336
Road	7-7	4.62	397	106	10	42	50	.267	.418	.342
Grass	5-5	4.84	303	80	10	35	42	.264	.439	.346
Artificial Turf	8-8	3.78	509	140	13	45	57	.275	.415	.335
April	2-1	3.41	114	31	2	15	12	.272	.386	.356
May	2-2	6.32	130	39	6	12	15	.300	.531	.357
June	3-2	3.32	151	37	2	18	24	.245	.331	.325
July	3-2	3.38	146	33	4	12	11	.226	.370	.294
August	1-5	5.66	143	48	7	14	19	.336	.559	.399
Sept./Oct.	2-1	3.34	128	32	2	9	18	.250	.367	.307
Leading Off Inn.			206	56	12	20	26	.272	.519	.339
Runners On			343	86	3	26	40	.251	.362	.308
Runners/Scor. Pos.			172	41	2	14	24	.238	.349	.304
Runners On/2 Out			150	35	1	13	12	.233	.347	.303
Scor. Pos./2 Out			84	20	0	8	5	.238	.333	.319
Late Inning Pressure			53	14	3	8	5	.264	.453	.361
Leading Off			18	4	2	1	2	.222	.556	.263
Runners On			13	4	0	1	0	.308	.385	.357
Runners/Scor. Pos.			2	1	0	1	0	.500	.500	.667
First 9 Batters			272	69	8	27	34	.254	.419	.319
Second 9 Batters			264	72	8	21	39	.273	.417	.340
All Batters Thereafter			276	79	7	32	26	.286	.435	.358

Loves to face: Bob Boone (.111, 3-for-27)
Hates to face: Robin Yount (.436, 34-for-78, 4 HR)
Ground outs-to-air outs ratio: 1.20 last season, 1.28 for career. . . .
Additional statistics: 21 double-play ground outs in 162 opportunities, 49 doubles, 3 triples in 211.0 innings last season. . . . Allowed 16 first-inning runs in 34 starts. . . . Batting support: 5.00 runs per start. . . . Blue Jays had a 7–1 record in his no-decision starts. . . . Was 0–6 in day games after July 24. . . . Allowed 133 HRs over last eight seasons, only 12 to left-handers. . . . Had winning records for seven consecutive seasons through 1983, but hasn't had one since. . . . One of three pitchers to shut out the Mariners at the Kingdome last season, his only shutout since July 7, 1984. . . . How tough is it to win 300 games? Flanagan reached the halfway point last season.

Willie Fraser
California Angels   Throws Right

	W–L	ERA	AB	H	HR	BB	SO	BA	SA	OBA
Season	12-13	5.41	761	203	33	80	86	.267	.477	.340
vs. Left-Handers			403	111	24	45	35	.275	.551	.348
vs. Right-Handers			358	92	9	35	51	.257	.394	.331
Home	5-6	5.50	341	89	14	36	42	.261	.449	.333
Road	7-7	5.33	420	114	19	44	44	.271	.500	.345
Grass	11-11	5.62	613	163	29	70	71	.266	.475	.342
Artificial Turf	1-2	4.54	148	40	4	10	15	.270	.486	.331
April	3-0	3.91	94	23	5	17	11	.245	.468	.363
May	1-4	8.39	103	33	5	14	9	.320	.544	.398
June	1-3	5.86	111	30	3	9	15	.270	.468	.339
July	2-3	6.13	160	46	10	16	21	.288	.538	.356
August	3-0	4.97	142	34	9	11	12	.239	.493	.295
Sept./Oct.	2-3	3.89	151	37	1	13	18	.245	.364	.310
Leading Off Inn.			194	49	6	13	19	.253	.407	.300
Runners On			303	86	13	33	37	.284	.502	.354
Runners/Scor. Pos.			173	51	9	26	21	.295	.538	.385
Runners On/2 Out			135	41	6	13	12	.304	.548	.373
Scor. Pos./2 Out			85	28	4	11	7	.329	.600	.418
Late Inning Pressure			65	15	3	5	5	.231	.431	.286
Leading Off			21	4	1	1	2	.190	.333	.227
Runners On			11	3	1	3	0	.273	.636	.429
Runners/Scor. Pos.			3	1	1	3	0	.333	1.333	.667
First 9 Batters			261	68	9	33	35	.261	.456	.351
Second 9 Batters			250	67	13	25	29	.268	.480	.337
All Batters Thereafter			250	68	11	22	22	.272	.496	.331

Loves to face: Steve Balboni (0-for-13)
Hates to face: Dave Bergman (.500, 6-for-12, 3 HR)
Ground outs-to-air outs ratio: 0.89 last season, 0.78 for career. . . .
Additional statistics: 17 double-play ground outs in 130 opportunities, 47 doubles, 7 triples in 194.2 innings last season. . . . Allowed 19 first-inning runs in 32 starts. . . . Batting support: 4.63 runs per start. . . . Allowed the most home runs of any A.L. pitcher last season, despite only one in his last 44 innings. . . . Allowed the leadoff batter to reach base safely in seven consecutive innings (Apr. 21–27), tied for longest streak in A.L. . . . Career records: 7–12 at home, 15–11 on the road. . . . His 2–1, 10-inning victory for Concordia over Mercy in 1985 greased the skids for the losing team's manager. Rick Wolff took off his uniform, headed for Macmillan, and the rest is history.

Wes Gardner
Boston Red Sox   Throws Right

	W–L	ERA	AB	H	HR	BB	SO	BA	SA	OBA
Season	8-6	3.50	542	119	17	64	106	.220	.363	.302
vs. Left-Handers			272	65	7	40	45	.239	.382	.331
vs. Right-Handers			270	54	10	24	61	.200	.344	.272
Home	5-3	3.38	288	58	8	32	54	.201	.326	.282
Road	3-3	3.65	254	61	9	32	52	.240	.406	.325
Grass	8-5	3.65	454	98	15	58	86	.216	.359	.304
Artificial Turf	0-1	2.70	88	21	2	6	20	.239	.386	.292
April	0-1	1.46	40	5	1	7	9	.125	.200	.265
May	0-0	2.38	42	8	3	7	6	.190	.452	.320
June	2-0	0.96	64	12	1	6	8	.188	.266	.254
July	2-0	6.21	108	27	4	12	22	.250	.435	.320
August	1-3	4.03	140	32	5	23	24	.229	.371	.341
Sept./Oct.	3-2	3.18	148	35	3	9	27	.236	.365	.277
Leading Off Inn.			132	38	7	22	25	.288	.508	.390
Runners On			227	46	5	24	41	.203	.308	.278
Runners/Scor. Pos.			118	23	2	16	23	.195	.263	.284
Runners On/2 Out			98	16	0	9	13	.163	.184	.234
Scor. Pos./2 Out			59	10	0	7	9	.169	.186	.258
Late Inning Pressure			39	10	2	9	8	.256	.436	.396
Leading Off			10	5	2	3	1	.500	1.200	.615
Runners On			18	2	0	5	5	.111	.111	.304
Runners/Scor. Pos.			8	1	0	5	2	.125	.125	.462
First 9 Batters			235	44	5	29	54	.187	.289	.278
Second 9 Batters			167	43	8	17	31	.257	.467	.337
All Batters Thereafter			140	32	4	18	21	.229	.364	.316

Loves to face: Kent Hrbek (0-for-10)
Hates to face: Alvin Davis (.556, 5-for-9, 2 HR)
Ground outs-to-air outs ratio: 0.78 last season, 0.82 for career. . . .
Additional statistics: 10 double-play ground outs in 116 opportunities, 25 doubles, 1 triple in 149.0 innings last season. . . . Allowed 7 first-inning runs in 18 starts. . . . Batting support: 4.44 runs per start. . . . Red Sox had a 1–5 record in his no-decision starts. . . . Record of 7–5 with a 4.12 ERA in 18 starts; 1–1, 1.53 ERA in 18 relief appearances. Was shifted to starting rotation after managerial change. . . . Had made only one start in 80 career appearances prior to 1988. . . . Opponents' career batting average was .297 through 1987. Lowest single-season ERA during that time was 5.25 for the 1985 Mets. . . . Career strikeout-to-walk ratios: 2.45 vs. right-handers, 1.19 vs. left-handers.

Paul Gibson

Detroit Tigers — Throws Left

	W–L	ERA	AB	H	HR	BB	SO	BA	SA	OBA
Season	4-2	2.93	346	83	6	34	50	.240	.353	.307
vs. Left-Handers			128	30	2	8	15	.234	.344	.273
vs. Right-Handers			218	53	4	26	35	.243	.358	.327
Home	2-0	2.42	191	43	4	18	37	.225	.319	.299
Road	2-2	3.60	155	40	2	16	13	.258	.394	.318
Grass	4-1	2.67	304	73	5	26	46	.240	.342	.301
Artificial Turf	0-1	4.91	42	10	1	8	4	.238	.429	.353
April	1-0	4.50	33	10	1	3	4	.303	.424	.361
May	1-1	3.86	82	21	2	6	13	.256	.415	.311
June	1-0	1.20	54	10	0	2	11	.185	.185	.211
July	0-0	0.00	39	7	0	5	6	.179	.179	.273
August	0-1	5.52	61	21	1	7	4	.344	.574	.400
Sept./Oct.	1-0	2.42	77	14	2	11	12	.182	.286	.289
Leading Off Inn.			70	15	1	8	15	.214	.329	.304
Runners On			173	41	3	15	21	.237	.353	.290
Runners/Scor. Pos.			102	22	2	13	12	.216	.333	.292
Runners On/2 Out			82	18	1	5	10	.220	.293	.264
Scor. Pos./2 Out			50	10	1	5	5	.200	.260	.273
Late Inning Pressure			40	9	1	4	5	.225	.400	.289
Leading Off			9	2	0	1	2	.222	.222	.300
Runners On			17	4	0	2	1	.235	.412	.300
Runners/Scor. Pos.			10	1	0	2	1	.100	.200	.231
First 9 Batters			222	52	3	24	34	.234	.333	.308
Second 9 Batters			90	21	3	8	11	.233	.378	.297
All Batters Thereafter			34	10	0	2	5	.294	.412	.333

Loves to face: Mike Felder (0-for-7)
Hates to face: Ron Karkovice (2-for-2, 1 HR)
Ground outs-to-air outs ratio: 0.91 last season, his first in majors. . . . Additional statistics: 6 double-play ground outs in 75 opportunities, 17 doubles, 2 triples in 92.0 innings last season. . . . ERA was 2d lowest on Tigers staff (Henneman, 1.87). . . . Picked up a victory in his only start of the season, allowing two runs in seven innings against the Brewers on May 17. . . . A matter of trust? Faced 390 batters, but only one protecting a lead of three runs or fewer in 8th inning or later. Made 39 relief appearances, no saves. . . . Kicked around minors for 10 years before making his big-league debut last season. Was All-Star team pitcher in 1977 rookie league that included Steve Bedrosian, Dave Dravecky, Steve Farr, John Butcher. That dates him.

Jerry Don Gleaton

Kansas City Royals — Throws Left

	W–L	ERA	AB	H	HR	BB	SO	BA	SA	OBA
Season	0-4	3.55	142	33	2	17	29	.232	.338	.327
vs. Left-Handers			53	14	1	4	13	.264	.377	.339
vs. Right-Handers			69	19	1	13	16	.213	.315	.320
Home	0-1	2.53	76	17	0	8	13	.224	.276	.306
Road	0-3	4.86	66	16	2	9	16	.242	.409	.351
Grass	0-1	3.09	44	7	1	7	12	.159	.250	.275
Artificial Turf	0-3	3.76	98	26	1	10	17	.265	.378	.351
April			0	0	0	0	0	—	—	—
May	0-0	0.00	8	1	0	2	3	.125	.250	.300
June	0-1	3.60	34	9	1	5	3	.265	.412	.375
July	0-0	2.08	32	5	0	4	8	.156	.188	.250
August	0-1	4.00	35	8	0	4	12	.229	.257	.325
Sept./Oct.	0-2	5.63	33	10	1	2	3	.303	.515	.361
Leading Off Inn.			28	6	1	2	4	.214	.429	.313
Runners On			80	16	1	10	17	.200	.262	.297
Runners/Scor. Pos.			58	10	0	7	14	.172	.190	.273
Runners On/2 Out			31	5	0	4	5	.161	.161	.257
Scor. Pos./2 Out			26	5	0	3	4	.192	.192	.276
Late Inning Pressure			78	19	2	9	16	.244	.359	.337
Leading Off			14	3	1	2	1	.214	.429	.353
Runners On			42	10	1	4	8	.238	.333	.319
Runners/Scor. Pos.			27	7	0	4	6	.259	.296	.375
First 9 Batters			138	32	2	16	29	.232	.341	.325
Second 9 Batters			4	1	0	1	0	.250	.250	.400
All Batters Thereafter			0	0	0	0	0	—	—	—

Loves to face: Oddibe McDowell (0-for-5, 3 SO)
Hates to face: Fred Lynn (.625, 5-for-8, 1 2B, 1 3B, 1 HR)
Ground outs-to-air outs ratio: 1.15 last season, 1.02 for career. . . . Additional statistics: 3 double-play ground outs in 42 opportunities, 7 doubles, 1 triple in 38.0 innings last season. . . . Had three saves last season, but none after July 1. . . . Opponents' career batting average is .185 (5-for-27) with bases loaded. . . . Career ERAs: 3.06 in day games, 4.93 in night games. . . . Got his annual fix of bus travel by starting 1988 season with Omaha. Has spent part of eight seasons in majors, but never an entire one. . . . Loves that A.L. West. Has spent parts of two seasons each with Texas, Seattle, Chicago, and Kansas City. . . . Among pitchers active in 1988 with that many seasons in majors, only Ernie Camacho (7) has fewer career wins than Gleaton (10).

Cecilio Guante

Yankees/Rangers — Throws Right

	W–L	ERA	AB	H	HR	BB	SO	BA	SA	OBA
Season	5-6	2.82	297	67	11	26	65	.226	.391	.298
vs. Left-Handers			134	31	3	14	26	.231	.343	.318
vs. Right-Handers			163	36	8	12	39	.221	.429	.281
Home	4-1	2.50	146	34	6	11	32	.233	.411	.294
Road	1-5	3.15	151	33	5	15	33	.219	.371	.302
Grass	5-5	2.84	235	53	10	23	52	.226	.404	.304
Artificial Turf	0-1	2.76	62	14	1	3	13	.226	.339	.273
April	2-0	2.81	60	13	2	4	13	.217	.367	.277
May	1-2	2.42	76	14	2	6	18	.184	.289	.253
June	1-2	2.00	63	8	3	8	18	.127	.286	.179
July	0-2	2.45	29	7	1	2	5	.241	.379	.313
August	1-0	5.56	49	17	2	7	7	.347	.633	.431
Sept./Oct.	0-0	1.93	20	8	1	4	4	.400	.600	.500
Leading Off Inn.			60	13	2	5	10	.217	.383	.288
Runners On			148	31	4	15	33	.209	.338	.293
Runners/Scor. Pos.			95	18	1	11	16	.189	.274	.284
Runners On/2 Out			69	15	2	9	16	.217	.319	.333
Scor. Pos./2 Out			51	10	1	5	12	.196	.275	.293
Late Inning Pressure			133	27	5	11	31	.203	.353	.282
Leading Off			26	3	0	4	6	.115	.115	.258
Runners On			64	12	3	6	14	.188	.359	.274
Runners/Scor. Pos.			38	6	0	6	12	.158	.184	.283
First 9 Batters			277	63	8	24	61	.227	.368	.297
Second 9 Batters			20	4	3	2	4	.200	.700	.304
All Batters Thereafter			0	0	0	0	0	—	—	—

Loves to face: Keith Moreland (0-for-14)
Hates to face: Brian Downing (.800, 4-for-5, 2 HR)
Ground outs-to-air outs ratio: 0.54 last season, 0.65 for career. . . . Additional statistics: 5 double-play ground outs in 61 opportunities, 12 doubles, 2 triples in 79.2 innings last season. . . . Recorded nine of his 12 saves before the All-Star break. . . . The A.L.'s qualifying .300 hitters had only five hits in 32 AB against him (.156). . . . As usual, was nearly unhittable with game on line. Opponents' career batting average of .205 in Late-Inning Pressure Situations, .251 otherwise. LIPS batting average breaks down as follows: .222 with the bases empty, .180 with runners on base, .150 with runners in scoring position. . . . Despite that, has only 33 career saves in 287 games, having assumed set-up role for Righetti, Don Robinson, Candelaria, and Tekulve.

Mark Gubicza

Kansas City Royals — Throws Right

	W–L	ERA	AB	H	HR	BB	SO	BA	SA	OBA
Season	20-8	2.70	1012	237	11	83	183	.234	.320	.294
vs. Left-Handers			523	132	7	47	73	.252	.340	.318
vs. Right-Handers			489	105	4	36	110	.215	.299	.269
Home	8-5	2.99	537	129	5	40	93	.240	.345	.294
Road	12-3	2.38	475	108	6	43	90	.227	.293	.295
Grass	9-3	2.37	380	87	4	38	67	.229	.282	.302
Artificial Turf	11-5	2.91	632	150	7	45	116	.237	.343	.290
April	3-1	2.65	119	26	1	14	17	.218	.269	.304
May	3-4	4.03	211	63	3	18	29	.299	.417	.353
June	5-0	1.18	139	28	1	14	29	.201	.223	.275
July	1-1	2.41	142	31	4	13	19	.218	.345	.284
August	4-1	2.76	179	38	1	10	38	.212	.307	.255
Sept./Oct.	4-1	2.70	222	51	1	14	51	.230	.311	.283
Leading Off Inn.			255	64	3	22	34	.251	.341	.313
Runners On			426	99	4	25	78	.232	.305	.275
Runners/Scor. Pos.			233	54	2	18	45	.232	.300	.286
Runners On/2 Out			196	51	2	12	36	.260	.367	.310
Scor. Pos./2 Out			124	31	1	10	23	.250	.339	.316
Late Inning Pressure			152	43	2	13	24	.283	.408	.343
Leading Off			38	11	0	6	5	.289	.368	.386
Runners On			65	16	2	4	11	.246	.462	.300
Runners/Scor. Pos.			38	11	1	3	7	.289	.526	.357
First 9 Batters			283	64	4	23	51	.226	.307	.285
Second 9 Batters			291	66	2	21	53	.227	.299	.280
All Batters Thereafter			438	107	5	39	79	.244	.342	.310

Loves to face: Dick Schofield (0-for-22)
Hates to face: Fred McGriff (.455, 5-for-11, 3 HR)
Ground outs-to-air outs ratio: 1.69 last season, 1.56 for career. . . . Additional statistics: 24 double-play ground outs in 180 opportunities, 38 doubles, 8 triples in 269.2 innings last season. . . . Allowed 9 first-inning runs in 35 starts. . . . Batting support: 4.94 runs per start. . . . Pitched an average of 7.70 innings per start, 2d-highest mark in A.L. (minimum: 15 GS). . . . Completed eight games, and won all eight. . . . Ground-ball hitters batted .191 against him, fly-ballers .266. . . . Opposing batters have had a higher average in LIP Situations than otherwise in all five seasons in majors. . . . Has thrown 12 or more wild pitches in each of last four seasons. Only one other pitcher has done it for two years running: Willie Fraser.

Jose Guzman

Texas Rangers — Throws Right

	W–L	ERA	AB	H	HR	BB	SO	BA	SA	OBA
Season	11-13	3.70	779	180	20	82	157	.231	.359	.306
vs. Left-Handers			375	77	8	41	67	.205	.312	.286
vs. Right-Handers			404	103	12	41	90	.255	.403	.325
Home	6-7	3.14	433	93	13	41	90	.215	.339	.287
Road	5-6	4.40	346	87	7	41	67	.251	.384	.330
Grass	9-11	3.48	647	147	19	64	130	.227	.359	.300
Artificial Turf	2-2	4.75	132	33	1	18	27	.250	.364	.338
April	3-1	1.41	113	18	1	3	27	.159	.212	.181
May	2-2	3.55	176	40	3	26	40	.227	.335	.327
June	2-3	5.08	164	39	6	23	32	.238	.402	.333
July	2-2	3.49	149	39	5	13	22	.262	.436	.319
August	2-2	4.15	118	32	2	8	20	.271	.364	.313
Sept./Oct.	0-3	4.60	59	12	3	9	16	.203	.390	.338
Leading Off Inn.			202	52	4	15	39	.257	.391	.315
Runners On			307	74	9	35	51	.241	.381	.317
Runners/Scor. Pos.			167	36	3	31	31	.216	.335	.332
Runners On/2 Out			128	29	2	21	25	.227	.313	.340
Scor. Pos./2 Out			80	16	1	19	16	.200	.288	.354
Late Inning Pressure			116	25	3	13	16	.216	.336	.295
Leading Off			35	12	1	2	4	.343	.486	.378
Runners On			37	6	1	7	4	.162	.243	.295
Runners/Scor. Pos.			15	3	1	6	1	.200	.400	.429
First 9 Batters			241	38	4	25	62	.158	.245	.240
Second 9 Batters			237	55	4	24	45	.232	.333	.306
All Batters Thereafter			301	87	12	33	50	.289	.472	.359

Loves to face: Tim Laudner (0-for-8, 5 SO)
Hates to face: Jose Canseco (.391, 9-for-23, 3 HR)
Ground outs-to-air outs ratio: 1.24 last season, 1.29 for career. . . .
Additional statistics: 19 double-play ground outs in 133 opportunities, 34 doubles, 3 triples in 206.2 innings last season. . . . Allowed 9 first-inning runs in 30 starts. . . . Batting support: 3.97 runs per start. . . . Rangers lost nine of his 12 starts after the All-Star break. . . . Had an 0–3 record in four starts against the A.L. champs. . . . Faced 14 batters with bases loaded. Retired 13, walked the other—the only time in his career that he's walked in a run (40 BFP with bases loaded). . . . Career record of 24–23 with a 3.79 ERA at Arlington Stadium; 13–21, 4.75 on the road. . . . Opponents' batting average, year by year since 1986: .293, .253, .231.

Tom Henke

Toronto Blue Jays — Throws Right

	W–L	ERA	AB	H	HR	BB	SO	BA	SA	OBA
Season	4-4	2.91	253	60	6	24	66	.237	.364	.306
vs. Left-Handers			134	35	2	12	36	.261	.321	.322
vs. Right-Handers			119	25	4	12	30	.210	.412	.289
Home	2-1	2.48	120	28	4	12	37	.233	.350	.306
Road	2-3	3.31	133	32	2	12	29	.241	.376	.306
Grass	2-1	3.12	99	24	2	9	22	.242	.384	.303
Artificial Turf	2-3	2.79	154	36	4	15	44	.234	.351	.308
April	0-0	0.79	40	8	1	2	13	.200	.325	.233
May	0-1	3.46	52	15	0	4	10	.288	.404	.333
June	0-0	2.08	34	10	0	5	7	.294	.353	.385
July	1-2	4.40	51	10	2	4	11	.196	.392	.281
August	1-0	2.13	45	8	1	3	13	.178	.244	.229
Sept./Oct.	2-1	4.50	31	9	2	6	12	.290	.484	.405
Leading Off Inn.			55	12	2	2	10	.218	.436	.259
Runners On			118	28	2	15	31	.237	.339	.324
Runners/Scor. Pos.			81	20	1	9	22	.247	.346	.315
Runners On/2 Out			58	13	1	9	15	.224	.328	.338
Scor. Pos./2 Out			43	9	0	4	12	.209	.256	.277
Late Inning Pressure			162	34	5	19	46	.210	.370	.297
Leading Off			35	6	2	2	7	.171	.486	.237
Runners On			67	16	2	13	21	.239	.388	.361
Runners/Scor. Pos.			52	13	1	8	14	.250	.385	.339
First 9 Batters			236	56	6	21	60	.237	.369	.303
Second 9 Batters			17	4	0	3	6	.235	.294	.350
All Batters Thereafter			0	0	0	0	0	—	—	—

Loves to face: Lou Whitaker (0-for-15)
Hates to face: Don Mattingly (.462, 6-for-13, 1 HR)
Ground outs-to-air outs ratio: 0.80 last season, 0.69 for career. . . .
Additional statistics: 4 double-play ground outs in 48 opportunities, 10 doubles, 2 triples in 68.0 innings last season. . . . Recorded 16 saves by the end of June, but ended the season with only 25. . . . Opponents' batting average was under .200 in both of the two previous seasons. . . . Had a career average of 10.69 strikeouts per nine innings through 1987, but averaged only 8.73 last season. . . . Opponents' career average of .196 in Late-Inning Pressure Situations, .254 in other at-bats. That 58-point difference is the 6th largest of any pitcher over the past 10 seasons (minimum: 250 LIPS AB).

Bryan Harvey

California Angels — Throws Right

	W–L	ERA	AB	H	HR	BB	SO	BA	SA	OBA
Season	7-5	2.13	276	59	4	20	67	.214	.293	.267
vs. Left-Handers			143	21	2	12	45	.147	.217	.212
vs. Right-Handers			133	38	2	8	22	.286	.376	.326
Home	3-4	1.96	146	29	3	12	35	.199	.281	.256
Road	4-1	2.34	130	30	1	8	32	.231	.308	.279
Grass	5-4	2.00	242	51	3	15	61	.211	.281	.257
Artificial Turf	2-1	3.12	34	8	1	5	6	.235	.382	.333
April	1-0	0.00	20	2	0	3	5	.100	.100	.217
May	1-1	0.47	63	9	0	3	19	.143	.159	.176
June	0-1	2.93	56	11	0	6	14	.196	.286	.281
July	2-1	4.50	64	19	1	4	7	.297	.406	.338
August	2-1	1.50	47	13	1	2	15	.277	.340	.306
Sept./Oct.	1-1	2.45	26	5	2	2	7	.192	.423	.250
Leading Off Inn.			57	18	2	4	10	.316	.474	.371
Runners On			135	27	1	13	34	.200	.274	.265
Runners/Scor. Pos.			89	15	1	11	26	.169	.281	.252
Runners On/2 Out			56	8	0	3	18	.143	.214	.186
Scor. Pos./2 Out			40	4	0	3	16	.100	.200	.163
Late Inning Pressure			194	37	3	15	53	.191	.263	.250
Leading Off			40	10	2	4	8	.250	.450	.333
Runners On			88	16	0	9	27	.182	.216	.253
Runners/Scor. Pos.			50	7	0	8	20	.140	.200	.250
First 9 Batters			266	57	4	17	65	.214	.293	.262
Second 9 Batters			10	2	0	3	2	.200	.300	.357
All Batters Thereafter			0	0	0	0	0	—	—	—

Loves to face: Mel Hall (0-for-6)
Hates to face: Paul Molitor (3-for-3)
Ground outs-to-air outs ratio: 0.62 last season, 0.62 for career. . . .
Additional statistics: 6 double-play ground outs in 74 opportunities, 6 doubles, 2 triples in 76.0 innings last season. . . . Led major league rookies in saves (17) and fewest runners allowed per nine innings (9.47). . . . Faced 114 batters protecting leads of three runs or fewer in 8th inning or later. That's more than Donnie Moore (37) and Greg Minton (60) combined. . . . Opposing left-handed batters had a streak of 36 consecutive plate appearances without a hit against him, the longest in the majors last season. . . . One of four pitchers whose right-handed opponents outhit left-handers by 100 points (minimum: 100 AB each way). . . . He and Moore were the only Angels pitchers to win their last decision.

Mike Henneman

Detroit Tigers — Throws Right

	W–L	ERA	AB	H	HR	BB	SO	BA	SA	OBA
Season	9-6	1.87	331	72	7	24	58	.218	.308	.273
vs. Left-Handers			142	31	2	14	28	.218	.303	.293
vs. Right-Handers			189	41	5	10	30	.217	.312	.257
Home	7-3	2.28	157	35	4	11	28	.223	.331	.276
Road	2-3	1.50	174	37	3	13	30	.213	.287	.270
Grass	9-5	1.84	302	66	6	23	53	.219	.305	.277
Artificial Turf	0-1	2.25	29	6	1	1	5	.207	.345	.233
April	0-0	1.35	44	6	0	3	8	.136	.159	.191
May	0-1	2.16	27	4	0	5	4	.148	.185	.281
June	2-1	2.63	53	12	1	3	12	.226	.302	.268
July	3-0	2.51	49	10	2	6	10	.204	.388	.298
August	2-2	2.04	71	22	2	4	12	.310	.408	.351
Sept./Oct.	2-2	1.13	87	18	2	3	12	.207	.299	.233
Leading Off Inn.			73	13	1	0	10	.178	.233	.178
Runners On			151	32	6	17	29	.212	.364	.297
Runners/Scor. Pos.			94	16	2	13	20	.170	.277	.266
Runners On/2 Out			77	15	0	10	15	.195	.234	.295
Scor. Pos./2 Out			53	9	0	9	10	.170	.226	.290
Late Inning Pressure			229	52	6	18	42	.227	.328	.287
Leading Off			52	9	1	0	9	.173	.250	.173
Runners On			99	22	5	14	18	.222	.394	.325
Runners/Scor. Pos.			60	10	2	11	11	.167	.300	.288
First 9 Batters			302	67	7	20	52	.222	.321	.273
Second 9 Batters			22	3	0	4	5	.136	.136	.269
All Batters Thereafter			7	2	0	0	1	.286	.286	.286

Loves to face: Frank White (0-for-9)
Hates to face: Mel Hall (.500, 5-for-10, 1 HR)
Ground outs-to-air outs ratio: 1.18 last season, 1.29 for career. . . .
Additional statistics: 10 double-play ground outs in 67 opportunities, 9 doubles, 0 triples in 91.1 innings last season. . . . Had eight saves in April, but no more than four in any other month. . . . Faced 124 batters protecting leads of three runs or fewer in 8th inning or later. Willie Hernandez faced 80. . . . Not only didn't he walk a leadoff batter last season, but he's never walked a leadoff batter in Late-Inning Pressure Situations (78 BFP). . . . Career ERA of 2.44 is lower than that of any other A.L. pitcher with as many innings as Henneman during the last two years (188.0). . . . Opponents' career breakdown: .243 with the bases empty, .211 with runners on base, .178 with runners in scoring position.

Willie Hernandez — Throws Left

Detroit Tigers	W–L	ERA	AB	H	HR	BB	SO	BA	SA	OBA
Season	6-5	3.06	240	50	8	31	59	.208	.350	.306
vs. Left-Handers			85	19	3	9	19	.224	.365	.296
vs. Right-Handers			155	31	5	22	40	.200	.342	.311
Home	4-3	2.11	134	23	4	14	29	.172	.299	.263
Road	2-2	4.30	106	27	4	17	30	.255	.415	.357
Grass	6-5	3.41	215	44	8	28	52	.205	.358	.305
Artificial Turf	0-0	0.00	25	6	0	3	7	.240	.280	.310
April	1-1	3.86	32	8	0	5	4	.250	.375	.350
May	2-0	1.72	57	11	3	6	12	.193	.368	.270
June	2-1	1.59	37	5	1	3	11	.135	.216	.200
July	0-1	1.13	31	7	0	4	10	.226	.258	.333
August	0-0	7.56	34	10	1	4	12	.294	.500	.368
Sept./Oct.	1-2	3.60	49	9	3	9	10	.184	.367	.328
Leading Off Inn.			49	7	1	3	12	.143	.224	.208
Runners On			116	26	3	19	30	.224	.353	.336
Runners/Scor. Pos.			74	13	2	13	23	.176	.297	.304
Runners On/2 Out			48	6	1	6	14	.125	.208	.222
Scor. Pos./2 Out			34	2	1	4	10	.059	.147	.158
Late Inning Pressure			112	27	4	15	29	.241	.393	.348
Leading Off			22	6	1	2	5	.273	.455	.360
Runners On			63	15	3	10	17	.238	.429	.355
Runners/Scor. Pos.			42	8	2	7	13	.190	.357	.327
First 9 Batters			229	47	7	28	58	.205	.332	.299
Second 9 Batters			11	3	1	3	1	.273	.727	.429
All Batters Thereafter			0	0	0	0	0	—	—	—

Loves to face: Pete O'Brien (0-for-18)
Hates to face: Pat Tabler (.417, 5-for-12, 3 HR)
Ground outs-to-air outs ratio: 1.14 last season, 1.08 for career. . . .
Additional statistics: 8 double-play ground outs in 74 opportunities, 10 doubles, 0 triples in 67.2 innings last season. . . . Retired the leadoff batter in 22 consecutive innings that he started, longest streak among major league relievers last season. . . . Opponents' batting average was his lowest since his Cy Young season (1984): .194, .210, .251, .276, .208. . . . Opponents were hitless in 13 at-bats (five SO) with the bases loaded last season. . . . Opposing left-handers outhit right-handers for first time in 12-year career. . . . Opposing fly-ball hitters have hit below .220 for five consecutive seasons. Career marks: ground-ballers, .266; fly-ballers, .223.

Ted Higuera — Throws Left

Milwaukee Brewers	W–L	ERA	AB	H	HR	BB	SO	BA	SA	OBA
Season	16-9	2.45	813	168	15	59	192	.207	.300	.263
vs. Left-Handers			149	31	3	9	42	.208	.315	.256
vs. Right-Handers			664	137	12	50	150	.206	.297	.265
Home	9-4	2.15	429	83	6	26	95	.193	.261	.244
Road	7-5	2.80	384	85	9	33	97	.221	.344	.284
Grass	14-9	2.46	717	148	12	50	166	.206	.294	.262
Artificial Turf	2-0	2.39	96	20	3	9	26	.208	.344	.274
April	2-1	2.67	107	22	1	7	22	.206	.290	.256
May	2-2	2.43	152	34	4	8	36	.224	.316	.259
June	2-2	2.27	120	20	4	8	20	.167	.317	.231
July	1-2	2.63	134	29	3	10	40	.216	.336	.269
August	5-1	2.17	171	41	1	8	43	.240	.292	.271
Sept./Oct.	4-1	2.65	129	22	2	18	31	.171	.248	.287
Leading Off Inn.			218	45	4	16	53	.206	.307	.264
Runners On			275	68	6	21	65	.247	.360	.301
Runners/Scor. Pos.			144	37	4	16	35	.257	.382	.321
Runners On/2 Out			122	30	2	12	24	.246	.303	.324
Scor. Pos./2 Out			72	18	2	9	13	.250	.347	.341
Late Inning Pressure			120	31	3	11	24	.258	.367	.318
Leading Off			34	9	1	3	12	.265	.412	.324
Runners On			37	12	1	5	4	.324	.432	.395
Runners/Scor. Pos.			23	7	1	3	3	.304	.478	.370
First 9 Batters			248	43	4	18	60	.173	.254	.232
Second 9 Batters			247	42	2	18	64	.170	.231	.231
All Batters Thereafter			318	83	9	23	68	.261	.390	.312

Loves to face: Gary Pettis (0-for-22, 7 SO)
Hates to face: Mark McGwire (.462, 6-for-13, 2 HR)
Ground outs-to-air outs ratio: 0.81 last season, 0.79 for career. . . .
Additional statistics: 12 double-play ground outs in 121 opportunities, 29 doubles, 1 triple in 227.1 innings last season. . . . Allowed 5 first-inning runs in 31 starts, lowest average in A.L. (minimum: 15 GS). . . . Batting support: 4.23 runs per start. . . . Started season with seven shutout innings on opening day, and his ERA never rose above 2.69 at any point. . . . Had a 9–1 record with a 2.12 ERA over his last 10 starts. . . . Retired 26 consecutive batters (Aug. 25–30), longest streak in A.L. . . . Career record of 8–12 in May, 61–26 in other months. . . . At least seven games above .500 in each of last four seasons, a streak twice as long as that of any other A.L. pitcher.

Rick Honeycutt — Throws Left

Oakland As	W–L	ERA	AB	H	HR	BB	SO	BA	SA	OBA
Season	3-2	3.50	293	74	6	25	47	.253	.375	.312
vs. Left-Handers			97	22	3	7	21	.227	.371	.282
vs. Right-Handers			196	52	3	18	26	.265	.378	.327
Home	2-1	2.18	113	24	2	7	21	.212	.310	.256
Road	1-1	4.44	180	50	4	18	26	.278	.417	.347
Grass	3-2	3.18	232	53	5	21	38	.228	.349	.296
Artificial Turf	0-0	4.91	61	21	1	4	9	.344	.475	.373
April	0-0	1.69	59	15	0	5	11	.254	.356	.294
May	1-0	4.09	44	13	1	1	8	.295	.455	.333
June	1-1	6.43	53	15	2	3	9	.283	.453	.333
July	0-1	4.85	48	10	2	3	6	.208	.375	.255
August	1-0	1.88	49	10	1	7	9	.204	.306	.304
Sept./Oct.	0-0	2.38	40	11	0	6	4	.275	.300	.362
Leading Off Inn.			66	19	3	4	10	.288	.485	.329
Runners On			149	33	2	13	28	.221	.336	.282
Runners/Scor. Pos.			89	19	2	11	17	.213	.337	.296
Runners On/2 Out			69	16	2	6	13	.232	.333	.303
Scor. Pos./2 Out			44	10	2	5	7	.227	.364	.320
Late Inning Pressure			127	26	4	12	26	.205	.362	.271
Leading Off			33	7	2	1	6	.212	.515	.235
Runners On			58	10	1	6	15	.172	.276	.246
Runners/Scor. Pos.			31	5	1	6	8	.161	.355	.289
First 9 Batters			245	59	5	21	39	.241	.355	.303
Second 9 Batters			47	15	1	4	8	.319	.489	.365
All Batters Thereafter			1	0	0	0	0	.000	.000	.000

Loves to face: Ozzie Guillen (0-for-9)
Hates to face: Chili Davis (.435, 10-for-23, 4 HR)
Ground outs-to-air outs ratio: 2.40 last season, 1.91 for career. . . .
Additional statistics: 13 double-play ground outs in 56 opportunities, 16 doubles, 1 triple in 79.2 innings last season. . . . Combined with Eckersley for 115 relief appearances last season. Ten years earlier, they made a total of 59 starts. . . . The A.L.'s qualifying .300 batters had only three hits in 21 at-bats against him (.143). . . . Ground-ball hitters batted .297 against him, fly-ballers .223. . . . Opposing left-handers batted .308 (45-for-146) in 1982, but have hit only .211 since then, with fewer than 10 extra-base hits each of those six seasons. . . . Has defeated every A.L. team except the Orioles, and every N.L. team as well—if you include his World Series victory over the Dodgers.

Ricky Horton — Throws Left

Chicago White Sox	W–L	ERA	AB	H	HR	BB	SO	BA	SA	OBA
Season	6-10	4.86	412	120	6	36	28	.291	.420	.349
vs. Left-Handers			100	28	1	8	13	.280	.390	.327
vs. Right-Handers			312	92	5	28	15	.295	.429	.356
Home	4-6	3.97	238	65	5	21	12	.273	.403	.335
Road	2-4	6.18	174	55	1	15	16	.316	.443	.370
Grass	6-9	4.42	345	97	5	34	20	.281	.406	.348
Artificial Turf	0-1	7.47	67	23	1	2	8	.343	.493	.357
April	3-3	3.43	167	45	3	10	9	.269	.401	.317
May	0-3	9.64	55	19	1	10	1	.345	.527	.456
June	1-0	8.15	70	28	0	9	6	.400	.557	.457
July	1-3	5.19	66	16	2	4	6	.242	.394	.282
August	1-1	0.57	54	12	0	3	6	.222	.222	.259
Sept./Oct.			0	0	0	0	0	—	—	—
Leading Off Inn.			94	33	0	15	3	.351	.447	.455
Runners On			195	57	4	13	13	.292	.451	.324
Runners/Scor. Pos.			113	33	2	10	9	.292	.434	.328
Runners On/2 Out			78	21	1	6	5	.269	.385	.321
Scor. Pos./2 Out			49	13	1	4	3	.265	.388	.321
Late Inning Pressure			104	34	2	10	10	.327	.481	.385
Leading Off			28	11	0	4	1	.393	.500	.469
Runners On			47	16	1	4	3	.340	.489	.377
Runners/Scor. Pos.			28	10	1	3	3	.357	.571	.394
First 9 Batters			252	75	1	22	16	.298	.385	.354
Second 9 Batters			86	21	4	9	8	.244	.453	.320
All Batters Thereafter			74	24	1	5	4	.324	.500	.367

Loves to face: Mookie Wilson (.042, 1-for-24)
Hates to face: Glenn Davis (.455, 5-for-11, 2 HR)
Figures *above* are for A.L. only. . . . Ground outs-to-air outs ratio: 1.54 last season, 1.45 for career. . . . Additional statistics: 16 double-play ground outs in 106 opportunities, 32 doubles, 3 triples in 108.1 innings last season. . . . Opposing left-handers batted .226 prior to last season. . . . Opposing fly-ball hitters have a career average of .291, 53 points higher than ground-ballers, largest margin over past 14 years (minimum: 1000 AB each way). . . . Career records: 11–13 on grass, 20–10 on artificial turf; 7–9 in day games, 24–14 in night games. . . . Struck out 1.7 batters for every walk prior to last season. . . . Opposing batters have a career average of .255 on his first pass through the order, .276 the second time around, .293 after that.

Charlie Hough
Throws Right

Texas Rangers	W–L	ERA	AB	H	HR	BB	SO	BA	SA	OBA
Season	15-16	3.32	913	202	20	126	174	.221	.326	.321
vs. Left-Handers			450	99	9	64	87	.220	.318	.321
vs. Right-Handers			463	103	11	62	87	.222	.335	.321
Home	9-8	3.63	452	98	15	69	83	.217	.358	.325
Road	6-8	3.01	461	104	5	57	91	.226	.295	.317
Grass	13-14	3.07	782	169	19	102	148	.216	.329	.310
Artificial Turf	2-2	4.84	131	33	1	24	26	.252	.313	.381
April	3-3	2.01	172	30	5	24	35	.174	.297	.278
May	1-3	8.33	115	37	4	16	17	.322	.478	.426
June	4-1	1.26	202	37	3	24	44	.183	.243	.276
July	1-5	3.92	133	28	5	25	25	.211	.353	.333
August	2-2	4.75	134	34	2	18	27	.254	.366	.342
Sept./Oct.	4-2	2.68	157	36	1	19	26	.229	.299	.317
Leading Off Inn.			243	49	7	23	39	.202	.313	.273
Runners On			336	81	6	63	64	.241	.339	.362
Runners/Scor. Pos.			203	51	4	43	46	.251	.369	.377
Runners On/2 Out			148	34	1	33	25	.230	.304	.374
Scor. Pos./2 Out			96	25	1	27	18	.260	.365	.423
Late Inning Pressure			167	37	3	23	33	.222	.281	.316
Leading Off			50	14	2	5	8	.280	.400	.345
Runners On			52	10	0	11	9	.192	.192	.323
Runners/Scor. Pos.			28	5	0	4	9	.179	.179	.265
First 9 Batters			251	55	6	42	58	.219	.339	.336
Second 9 Batters			266	56	5	30	51	.211	.308	.297
All Batters Thereafter			396	91	9	54	65	.230	.331	.328

Loves to face: Jack Howell (0-for-16)
Hates to face: Mark Salas (.481, 13-for-27, 3 HR)
Ground outs-to-air outs ratio: 1.16 last season, 1.05 for career. . . .
Additional statistics: 12 double-play ground outs in 150 opportunities, 32 doubles, 2 triples in 252.0 innings last season. . . . Allowed 21 first-inning runs in 34 starts. . . . Batting support: 3.62 runs per start. . . . Over the last seven seasons, only Jack Morris (126) has won more games than Hough (111). . . . The only player to accumulate 60 saves and 60 complete games since saves became an official statistic in 1969. According to data in the *Baseball Encyclopedia,* Firpo Marbery (86 CGs, 101 saves) and Clint Brown (62 CGs, 64 saves) were ahead of their time. . . . No longer the oldest active Ranger in sports. He survived challenges from Marcel Dionne and Guy Lafleur, but succumbed to new teammate Nolan Ryan.

Charles Hudson
Throws Right

New York Yankees	W–L	ERA	AB	H	HR	BB	SO	BA	SA	OBA
Season	6-6	4.49	395	93	9	36	58	.235	.370	.301
vs. Left-Handers			181	39	1	17	24	.215	.298	.283
vs. Right-Handers			214	54	8	19	34	.252	.430	.316
Home	3-2	3.80	165	37	2	13	27	.224	.327	.286
Road	3-4	4.99	230	56	7	23	31	.243	.400	.312
Grass	5-6	4.39	363	85	8	34	52	.234	.369	.301
Artificial Turf	1-0	5.63	32	8	1	2	6	.250	.375	.294
April	2-1	3.50	69	16	1	4	12	.232	.319	.274
May	2-0	3.46	91	16	1	7	8	.176	.253	.238
June	1-2	3.81	107	28	3	10	15	.262	.421	.331
July	1-0	1.59	39	7	0	4	8	.179	.256	.244
August	0-2	31.50	22	13	1	4	2	.591	.864	.621
Sept./Oct.	0-1	3.86	67	13	3	7	13	.194	.403	.276
Leading Off Inn.			95	20	4	12	13	.211	.432	.306
Runners On			151	42	4	17	24	.278	.417	.345
Runners/Scor. Pos.			82	25	2	14	20	.305	.439	.390
Runners On/2 Out			67	15	1	8	11	.224	.328	.316
Scor. Pos./2 Out			40	10	0	7	10	.250	.350	.375
Late Inning Pressure			65	20	2	7	13	.308	.508	.370
Leading Off			18	8	2	2	6	.444	1.000	.500
Runners On			28	6	0	4	5	.214	.286	.303
Runners/Scor. Pos.			19	3	0	4	5	.158	.211	.292
First 9 Batters			203	45	4	20	34	.222	.320	.291
Second 9 Batters			121	29	2	9	15	.240	.372	.299
All Batters Thereafter			71	19	3	7	9	.268	.507	.329

Loves to face: Al Newman (.059, 1-for-17)
Hates to face: Alvin Davis (.625, 5-for-8, 1 HR)
Ground outs-to-air outs ratio: 0.43 last season, 0.80 for career. . . .
Additional statistics: 4 double-play ground outs in 76 opportunities, 20 doubles, 3 triples in 106.1 innings last season. . . . Allowed 6 first-inning runs in 12 starts. . . . Batting support: 5.08 runs per start. . . . Record of 4–4 (5.45 ERA) in 12 starts, 2–2 (2.79) in 16 relief appearances. . . . Batting average by opposing left-handers was the lowest of his career. Career breakdown: .269 by left-handers, .243 by right-handers. . . . Career record of 22–11 in day games, 27–44 at night. . . . Has allowed only four hits in 27 at-bats (.148) with the bases loaded since joining the Yankees, but two of those hits were grand slams.

Bruce Hurst
Throws Left

Boston Red Sox	W–L	ERA	AB	H	HR	BB	SO	BA	SA	OBA
Season	18-6	3.66	842	222	21	65	166	.264	.388	.316
vs. Left-Handers			147	41	2	10	27	.279	.374	.327
vs. Right-Handers			695	181	19	55	139	.260	.391	.314
Home	13-2	3.33	497	129	11	44	110	.260	.376	.321
Road	5-4	4.14	345	93	10	21	56	.270	.406	.309
Grass	17-4	3.34	727	183	18	58	145	.252	.373	.307
Artificial Turf	1-2	6.04	115	39	3	7	21	.339	.487	.377
April	4-0	2.92	142	34	0	11	35	.239	.317	.294
May	2-2	4.63	140	39	5	11	25	.279	.450	.331
June	3-1	4.68	169	50	9	14	30	.296	.479	.350
July	2-1	8.36	67	26	1	7	13	.388	.537	.453
August	5-0	2.27	163	35	3	10	29	.215	.294	.259
Sept./Oct.	2-2	2.42	161	38	3	12	34	.236	.335	.287
Leading Off Inn.			213	49	4	15	38	.230	.333	.281
Runners On			347	97	10	24	65	.280	.427	.324
Runners/Scor. Pos.			177	51	7	11	32	.288	.463	.325
Runners On/2 Out			145	34	3	14	28	.234	.359	.306
Scor. Pos./2 Out			74	14	2	7	16	.189	.311	.268
Late Inning Pressure			77	18	1	8	12	.234	.312	.302
Leading Off			21	2	0	3	4	.095	.095	.208
Runners On			25	7	1	3	5	.280	.440	.345
Runners/Scor. Pos.			12	5	1	1	1	.417	.750	.429
First 9 Batters			264	66	6	23	63	.250	.356	.308
Second 9 Batters			256	65	6	15	47	.254	.387	.298
All Batters Thereafter			322	91	9	27	56	.283	.416	.337

Loves to face: Brett Butler (.182, 4-for-22)
Hates to face: Tom Brunansky (.577, 15-for-26, 1 HR)
Ground outs-to-air outs ratio: 1.09 last season, 1.13 for career. . . .
Additional statistics: 15 double-play ground outs in 168 opportunities, 40 doubles, 1 triple in 216.2 innings last season. . . . Allowed 14 first-inning runs in 32 starts. . . . Batting support: 6.00 runs per start, highest in majors (minimum: 15 GS). . . . Ground-ball hitters batted .298 against him, the third time in the last four seasons they've topped the .290 mark. Fly-ballers hit .238. . . . Winningest Red Sox pitcher of decade? Hurst leaves Beantown with an 88–78 lead over Clemens. Past leaders, 1900s through 1970s: Cy Young (193), Joe Wood (104), Howard Ehmke (51), Lefty Grove (91), Tex Hughson (96), Frank Sullivan (84), Bill Monboquette (86), Luis Tiant (122).

Mike Jackson
Throws Right

Seattle Mariners	W–L	ERA	AB	H	HR	BB	SO	BA	SA	OBA
Season	6-5	2.63	354	74	10	43	76	.209	.339	.291
vs. Left-Handers			159	41	5	22	16	.258	.421	.340
vs. Right-Handers			195	33	5	21	60	.169	.272	.249
Home	5-3	3.00	165	36	7	21	35	.218	.388	.300
Road	1-2	2.32	189	38	3	22	41	.201	.296	.283
Grass	1-2	2.81	148	30	3	19	35	.203	.304	.289
Artificial Turf	5-3	2.50	206	44	7	24	41	.214	.364	.292
April	0-1	2.70	62	15	0	4	11	.242	.290	.275
May	1-0	2.70	49	10	2	8	9	.204	.408	.310
June	2-1	1.74	71	15	1	8	11	.211	.310	.293
July	3-0	5.00	71	17	3	9	20	.239	.408	.333
August	0-2	1.25	68	9	2	12	17	.132	.235	.263
Sept./Oct.	0-1	3.00	33	8	2	2	8	.242	.455	.286
Leading Off Inn.			73	20	0	6	12	.274	.315	.338
Runners On			184	33	6	25	40	.179	.310	.265
Runners/Scor. Pos.			116	21	3	24	28	.181	.302	.300
Runners On/2 Out			79	15	3	14	16	.190	.329	.312
Scor. Pos./2 Out			58	11	1	14	12	.190	.276	.347
Late Inning Pressure			177	37	6	23	38	.209	.350	.298
Leading Off			42	11	0	2	7	.262	.310	.295
Runners On			89	18	4	12	17	.202	.360	.286
Runners/Scor. Pos.			53	13	2	12	11	.245	.396	.362
First 9 Batters			318	63	9	37	69	.198	.330	.279
Second 9 Batters			35	10	1	6	7	.286	.400	.372
All Batters Thereafter			1	1	0	0	0	1.000	1.000	1.000

Loves to face: Rafael Santana (0-for-9)
Hates to face: Rafael Palmiero (3-for-3, 1 HR)
Ground outs-to-air outs ratio: 0.72 last season, 0.69 for career. . . .
Additional statistics: 7 double-play ground outs in 91 opportunities, 16 doubles, 0 triples in 99.1 innings last season. . . . Struck out six straight batters with runners in scoring position, matching Roger Clemens for the longest streak in the majors last season. . . . Allowed grand slams to Pat Sheridan (May 6) and Brook Jacoby (July 15). Opponents' career average is .393 (11-for-28, six XBH) with the bases loaded. . . . Opposing right-handed batters have hit below .180 in each of his three seasons in the majors. Career breakdowns: .265 by left-handers (one HR per 34 AB), .174 by right-handers (one HR per 25 AB).

Tommy John
New York Yankees — Throws Left

	W–L	ERA	AB	H	HR	BB	SO	BA	SA	OBA
Season	9-8	4.49	717	221	11	46	81	.308	.423	.354
vs. Left-Handers			146	41	3	10	11	.281	.418	.335
vs. Right-Handers			571	180	8	36	70	.315	.424	.359
Home	3-5	4.19	348	105	8	18	41	.302	.417	.337
Road	6-3	4.78	369	116	3	28	40	.314	.428	.370
Grass	8-8	4.31	650	195	11	39	76	.300	.418	.343
Artificial Turf	1-0	6.32	67	26	0	7	5	.388	.463	.453
April	1-0	4.91	73	21	3	5	9	.288	.438	.342
May	2-1	3.48	124	39	2	6	12	.315	.476	.346
June	3-1	2.48	156	44	0	10	18	.282	.314	.325
July	2-1	4.88	100	30	2	5	14	.300	.400	.333
August	0-3	6.82	138	44	1	9	9	.319	.449	.373
Sept./Oct.	1-2	5.17	126	43	3	11	19	.341	.484	.397
Leading Off Inn.			185	58	2	7	20	.314	.389	.339
Runners On			313	90	2	30	39	.288	.390	.359
Runners/Scor. Pos.			176	51	0	24	26	.290	.381	.383
Runners On/2 Out			118	30	0	12	18	.254	.339	.338
Scor. Pos./2 Out			82	22	0	11	15	.268	.341	.368
Late Inning Pressure			47	18	0	2	5	.383	.447	.408
Leading Off			13	5	0	1	2	.385	.385	.429
Runners On			21	7	0	1	1	.333	.476	.364
Runners/Scor. Pos.			8	2	0	1	0	.250	.375	.333
First 9 Batters			275	80	6	22	31	.291	.425	.350
Second 9 Batters			249	79	2	14	34	.317	.398	.358
All Batters Thereafter			193	62	3	10	16	.321	.451	.355

Loves to face: Ernie Whitt (.071, 1-for-14)
Hates to face: Don Slaught (.643, 9-for-14, 2 HR)
Ground outs-to-air outs ratio: 2.76 last season, 2.52 for career. . . .
Additional statistics: 29 double-play ground outs in 163 opportunities, 43 doubles, 3 triples in 176.1 innings last season. . . . Allowed 12 first-inning runs in 32 starts. . . . Batting support: 4.84 runs per start. . . . Made 15 no-decision starts, one short of Rudy May's A.L. record, set in 1970. . . . Most wins after 35th birthday (since 1900): Phil Niekro (208), Cy Young (193), Warren Spahn (180), Jack Quinn (168), Gaylord Perry (140), Eddie Plank (126), John (126). . . . One more game and he'll tie Deacon McGuire's record of 26 seasons in majors. Deacon reached 26 by playing one game at age 46, as "replacement catcher" during Detroit's one-game strike to protest A.L.'s suspension of Ty Cobb.

Doug Jones
Cleveland Indians — Throws Right

	W–L	ERA	AB	H	HR	BB	SO	BA	SA	OBA
Season	3-4	2.27	317	69	1	16	72	.218	.268	.260
vs. Left-Handers			177	36	1	12	35	.203	.266	.254
vs. Right-Handers			140	33	0	4	37	.236	.271	.267
Home	1-4	3.99	159	43	1	10	32	.270	.352	.318
Road	2-0	0.80	158	26	0	6	40	.165	.184	.200
Grass	3-4	2.70	273	65	1	13	58	.238	.297	.278
Artificial Turf	0-0	0.00	44	4	0	3	14	.091	.091	.149
April	0-0	0.00	24	1	0	3	10	.042	.083	.179
May	1-1	3.18	63	13	0	1	13	.206	.238	.219
June	0-0	0.77	40	5	1	2	15	.125	.200	.167
July	0-1	2.70	51	10	0	5	12	.196	.255	.268
August	1-1	2.18	84	21	0	3	13	.250	.286	.284
Sept./Oct.	1-1	3.38	55	19	0	2	9	.345	.418	.368
Leading Off Inn.			62	15	0	3	12	.242	.274	.277
Runners On			170	39	0	10	39	.229	.276	.280
Runners/Scor. Pos.			102	19	0	6	26	.186	.235	.245
Runners On/2 Out			77	15	0	5	18	.195	.208	.244
Scor. Pos./2 Out			54	6	0	3	14	.111	.130	.158
Late Inning Pressure			232	54	0	16	53	.233	.267	.288
Leading Off			43	11	0	3	9	.256	.279	.304
Runners On			134	32	0	10	29	.239	.291	.301
Runners/Scor. Pos.			80	14	0	6	19	.175	.225	.250
First 9 Batters			293	62	1	16	65	.212	.263	.257
Second 9 Batters			24	7	0	0	7	.292	.333	.292
All Batters Thereafter			0	0	0	0	0	—	—	—

Loves to face: Jim Presley (0-for-7)
Hates to face: Nelson Liriano (3-for-3, 1 HR)
Ground outs-to-air outs ratio: 1.31 last season, 1.49 for career. . . .
Additional statistics: 6 double-play ground outs in 80 opportunities, 7 doubles, 3 triples in 83.1 innings last season. . . . Faced 338 batters, 213 while protecting leads of three runs or fewer in 8th inning or later (63%). Only Eckersley had a higher average (75%). . . . Opponents batted 106 points higher at home than on road, largest difference in majors (minimum: 100 AB each way). . . . Set major league record by earning saves in 15 consecutive appearances. . . . Only two pitchers over last 14 years have faced more batters in LIP Situations in one season without allowing a HR: Dale Murray (337 in 1975) and Greg Minton (273 in 1980). Career totals: one HR to 474 batters faced in LIPS.

Odell Jones
Milwaukee Brewers — Throws Right

	W–L	ERA	AB	H	HR	BB	SO	BA	SA	OBA
Season	5-0	4.35	299	75	8	29	48	.251	.381	.313
vs. Left-Handers			122	28	3	17	20	.230	.320	.317
vs. Right-Handers			177	47	5	12	28	.266	.424	.311
Home	2-0	4.81	162	43	4	12	24	.265	.395	.315
Road	3-0	3.82	137	32	4	17	24	.234	.365	.312
Grass	4-0	4.30	246	59	6	21	40	.240	.362	.297
Artificial Turf	1-0	4.61	53	16	2	8	8	.302	.472	.387
April	0-0	0.00	9	1	0	3	0	.111	.222	.308
May	3-0	2.66	84	12	3	5	17	.143	.274	.191
June	0-0	6.00	56	16	0	4	10	.286	.321	.333
July	1-0	4.63	47	15	2	7	3	.319	.574	.407
August	1-0	3.66	76	21	1	7	13	.276	.342	.329
Sept./Oct.	0-0	10.80	27	10	2	3	5	.370	.667	.419
Leading Off Inn.			72	16	4	2	17	.222	.444	.243
Runners On			128	35	4	17	17	.273	.414	.344
Runners/Scor. Pos.			81	22	2	13	8	.272	.407	.350
Runners On/2 Out			56	15	3	5	7	.268	.482	.328
Scor. Pos./2 Out			35	9	1	5	4	.257	.429	.350
Late Inning Pressure			38	11	2	3	10	.289	.500	.341
Leading Off			13	4	1	0	6	.308	.692	.308
Runners On			11	3	1	2	1	.273	.545	.385
Runners/Scor. Pos.			6	2	1	2	0	.333	.833	.500
First 9 Batters			199	46	4	18	34	.231	.332	.288
Second 9 Batters			89	27	4	8	11	.303	.517	.367
All Batters Thereafter			11	2	0	3	3	.182	.182	.333

Loves to face: Brian Downing (0-for-10)
Hates to face: Don Baylor (.571, 8-for-14, 1 HR)
Ground outs-to-air outs ratio: 0.97 last season, 0.97 for career. . . .
Additional statistics: 7 double-play ground outs in 63 opportunities, 13 doubles, 1 triple in 80.2 innings last season. . . . His five victories were a career high, and the most of any undefeated pitcher in the A.L. last season. Not bad for a guy who started the season with a career winning percentage of .352 (19–35), the lowest among pitchers with at least 50 decisions when he last wore a big-league toga in 1986. . . . Started two games last season, the first time he'd listened to the national anthem from the pitcher's mound since 1981. . . . Only two other players that played in his major league debut (Sept. 11, 1975) were still active last season: Willie Randolph and Kent Tekulve.

Jimmy Key
Toronto Blue Jays — Throws Left

	W–L	ERA	AB	H	HR	BB	SO	BA	SA	OBA
Season	12-5	3.29	509	127	13	30	65	.250	.385	.296
vs. Left-Handers			75	11	1	2	12	.147	.253	.200
vs. Right-Handers			434	116	12	28	53	.267	.408	.313
Home	4-3	4.45	223	62	6	9	24	.278	.444	.309
Road	8-2	2.47	286	65	7	21	41	.227	.339	.286
Grass	6-2	2.61	218	48	6	19	29	.220	.326	.289
Artificial Turf	6-3	3.84	291	79	7	11	36	.271	.430	.302
April	2-1	3.31	67	20	3	2	12	.299	.552	.314
May			0	0	0	0	0	—	—	—
June	1-0	1.35	23	4	0	2	5	.174	.217	.240
July	3-1	2.23	151	35	1	6	16	.232	.298	.269
August	2-2	5.00	114	32	4	12	10	.281	.447	.354
Sept./Oct.	4-1	3.51	154	36	5	8	22	.234	.377	.279
Leading Off Inn.			131	26	5	5	19	.198	.328	.239
Runners On			187	49	4	12	22	.262	.390	.305
Runners/Scor. Pos.			93	29	3	8	8	.312	.505	.362
Runners On/2 Out			85	16	1	7	12	.188	.271	.258
Scor. Pos./2 Out			46	11	1	5	6	.239	.391	.327
Late Inning Pressure			21	2	0	2	4	.095	.095	.174
Leading Off			6	0	0	1	1	.000	.000	.143
Runners On			2	0	0	1	0	.000	.000	.333
Runners/Scor. Pos.			1	0	0	0	0	.000	.000	.000
First 9 Batters			170	40	2	10	30	.235	.347	.290
Second 9 Batters			175	44	6	9	20	.251	.423	.288
All Batters Thereafter			164	43	5	11	15	.262	.384	.311

Loves to face: Dave Valle (0-for-10)
Hates to face: Rickey Henderson (.370, 17-for-46, 4 HR)
Ground outs-to-air outs ratio: 1.01 last season, 1.36 for career. . . .
Additional statistics: 6 double-play ground outs in 85 opportunities, 26 doubles, 2 triples in 131.1 innings last season. . . . Allowed 9 first-inning runs in 21 starts. . . . Batting support: 4.62 runs per start. . . . Allowed a HR to George Brett in first inning on opening day, didn't allow another to a left-hander all season. . . . Here's an oddity. Key pitched two complete games: a pair of two-hitters, one vs. each division champ, in his only appearances vs. them. . . . Opposing ground-ball hitters batted .297, fly-ballers hit .213. . . . His 12 wins came against 12 different clubs. The only team he failed to beat: Chicago. . . . Career stats: 61–35, 3.23 ERA. Ted Higuera's: 69–38, 3.25.

Paul Kilgus

Texas Rangers   Throws Left

	W–L	ERA	AB	H	HR	BB	SO	BA	SA	OBA
Season	12-15	4.16	782	190	18	71	88	.243	.361	.313
vs. Left-Handers			140	31	1	8	22	.221	.279	.283
vs. Right-Handers			642	159	17	63	66	.248	.379	.319
Home	7-7	3.72	449	111	9	38	52	.247	.354	.311
Road	5-8	4.78	333	79	9	33	36	.237	.369	.315
Grass	10-13	3.79	680	162	15	60	79	.238	.349	.306
Artificial Turf	2-2	6.84	102	28	3	11	9	.275	.441	.357
April	2-2	2.87	115	23	3	10	10	.200	.313	.276
May	4-1	2.74	178	45	1	13	29	.253	.326	.316
June	1-3	3.74	130	31	3	13	13	.238	.385	.308
July	1-3	6.44	115	29	6	9	9	.252	.452	.312
August	3-3	4.71	132	31	1	18	15	.235	.303	.322
Sept./Oct.	1-3	5.40	112	31	4	8	12	.277	.411	.339
Leading Off Inn.			204	42	6	13	16	.206	.353	.260
Runners On			313	88	10	24	39	.281	.444	.334
Runners/Scor. Pos.			162	49	6	13	20	.302	.500	.350
Runners On/2 Out			143	40	7	14	17	.280	.503	.348
Scor. Pos./2 Out			80	27	5	9	9	.338	.613	.404
Late Inning Pressure			76	16	1	11	3	.211	.263	.310
Leading Off			24	2	0	3	0	.083	.083	.185
Runners On			20	6	0	3	1	.300	.350	.391
Runners/Scor. Pos.			6	2	0	2	0	.333	.333	.500
First 9 Batters			255	64	5	24	35	.251	.373	.327
Second 9 Batters			234	55	3	15	28	.235	.316	.286
All Batters Thereafter			293	71	10	32	25	.242	.386	.320

Loves to face: Todd Benzinger (0-for-5)
Hates to face: Gary Redus (.375, 3-for-8, 2 2B)
Ground outs-to-air outs ratio: 1.27 last season, 1.32 for career. . . .
Additional statistics: 15 double-play ground outs in 139 opportunities, 32 doubles, 3 triples in 203.1 innings last season. . . . Allowed 21 first-inning runs in 32 starts. . . . Batting support: 3.97 runs per start. . . . Only HR allowed to a left-hander was hit by Greg Brock. . . . Opponents batted 66 points higher in night games than in day games, largest difference in A.L. last season (minimum: 100 AB both ways). Career records: 7–2 (2.39 ERA) in day games, 7–20 (4.64) at night. The bad news is that there are 18 night games scheduled at Wrigley Field in 1989. . . . Opponents' career average is .063 (2-for-32) leading off innings in Late-Inning Pressure Situations.

Eric King

Detroit Tigers   Throws Right

	W–L	ERA	AB	H	HR	BB	SO	BA	SA	OBA
Season	4-1	3.41	257	60	5	34	45	.233	.358	.332
vs. Left-Handers			108	23	3	19	19	.213	.380	.331
vs. Right-Handers			149	37	2	15	26	.248	.342	.333
Home	2-1	2.82	140	31	1	23	32	.221	.314	.333
Road	2-0	4.15	117	29	4	11	13	.248	.410	.331
Grass	4-1	3.56	227	54	5	33	40	.238	.370	.346
Artificial Turf	0-0	2.25	30	6	0	1	5	.200	.267	.219
April			0	0	0	0	0	—	—	—
May	0-0	0.00	7	2	0	1	1	.286	.286	.375
June	1-0	4.30	57	16	1	11	9	.281	.404	.406
July	0-1	2.45	68	18	1	7	14	.265	.397	.333
August	2-0	4.50	82	16	2	11	14	.195	.341	.298
Sept./Oct.	1-0	2.25	43	8	1	4	7	.186	.279	.286
Leading Off Inn.			54	18	2	12	9	.333	.556	.463
Runners On			135	25	2	13	24	.185	.296	.268
Runners/Scor. Pos.			79	12	1	10	19	.152	.215	.250
Runners On/2 Out			56	7	0	5	7	.125	.196	.197
Scor. Pos./2 Out			38	4	0	3	6	.105	.132	.171
Late Inning Pressure			29	8	0	6	7	.276	.310	.405
Leading Off			5	1	0	2	2	.200	.200	.429
Runners On			18	4	0	3	4	.222	.222	.348
Runners/Scor. Pos.			16	3	0	2	4	.188	.188	.300
First 9 Batters			133	37	2	18	30	.278	.391	.366
Second 9 Batters			69	13	1	8	10	.188	.319	.282
All Batters Thereafter			55	10	2	8	5	.182	.327	.313

Loves to face: Wade Boggs (.100, 1-for-10)
Hates to face: Jesse Barfield (.500, 5-for-10, 2 HR)
Ground outs-to-air outs ratio: 0.86 last season, 1.06 for career. . . .
Additional statistics: 5 double-play ground outs in 66 opportunities, 13 doubles, 2 triples in 68.2 innings last season. . . . Faced only 10 batters protecting leads of three runs or fewer in 8th inning or later, compared to 86 in 1987. . . . The only home run he allowed at Tiger Stadium last season was hit by Mark McGwire. . . . Opponents batted 102 points lower with runners on base than with the bases empty, largest difference in majors last season (minimum: 100 AB each way). . . . Career average of .216 by opposing ground-ball hitters, .243 by fly-ballers. . . . Career records: 6–6, 5.06 ERA in day games; 15–8, 3.53 ERA at night.

Dennis Lamp

Boston Red Sox   Throws Right

	W–L	ERA	AB	H	HR	BB	SO	BA	SA	OBA
Season	7-6	3.48	324	92	3	19	49	.284	.377	.326
vs. Left-Handers			147	46	2	9	22	.313	.422	.357
vs. Right-Handers			177	46	1	10	27	.260	.339	.300
Home	5-0	3.73	163	51	3	11	23	.313	.423	.352
Road	2-6	3.24	161	41	0	8	26	.255	.329	.298
Grass	7-4	3.47	272	78	3	17	43	.287	.379	.329
Artificial Turf	0-2	3.55	52	14	0	2	6	.269	.365	.309
April	1-0	1.35	22	5	0	1	7	.227	.227	.250
May	0-1	3.65	50	14	0	2	9	.280	.320	.308
June	1-2	3.86	53	13	0	4	7	.245	.283	.310
July	3-0	3.38	112	29	2	4	15	.259	.402	.291
August	1-0	2.08	34	11	0	3	4	.324	.324	.378
Sept./Oct.	1-3	5.40	53	20	1	5	7	.377	.566	.424
Leading Off Inn.			69	21	0	2	12	.304	.406	.342
Runners On			164	46	1	14	18	.280	.360	.333
Runners/Scor. Pos.			111	31	1	13	16	.279	.369	.349
Runners On/2 Out			64	17	1	8	7	.266	.344	.347
Scor. Pos./2 Out			48	12	1	7	5	.250	.333	.345
Late Inning Pressure			73	21	1	10	11	.288	.384	.369
Leading Off			19	8	0	2	4	.421	.526	.476
Runners On			32	6	0	7	4	.188	.188	.325
Runners/Scor. Pos.			23	4	0	6	3	.174	.174	.333
First 9 Batters			282	79	3	16	44	.280	.372	.319
Second 9 Batters			39	12	0	3	5	.308	.410	.372
All Batters Thereafter			3	1	0	0	0	.333	.333	.333

Loves to face: Oddibe McDowell (.083, 1-for-12)
Hates to face: Kent Hrbek (.406, 13-for-32, 2 HR)
Ground outs-to-air outs ratio: 2.03 last season, 2.32 for career. . . .
Additional statistics: 12 double-play ground outs in 70 opportunities, 17 doubles, 2 triples in 82.2 innings last season. . . . The A.L.'s qualifying .300 hitters had 18 hits in 41 at bats against him (.439). . . . Opposing left-handed batters have hit over .300 against him in five of the last six seasons. . . . Opponents' career average is .300 with runners in scoring position. . . . Has defeated every A.L. club in his career except the Orioles (0–4). Has lost his last seven decisions to the Angels. . . . Has made 82 relief appearances without a save over past two seasons. Last season, he faced only 15 batters protecting leads of three runs or fewer in 8th inning or later.

Mark Langston

Seattle Mariners   Throws Left

	W–L	ERA	AB	H	HR	BB	SO	BA	SA	OBA
Season	15-11	3.34	954	222	32	110	235	.233	.389	.313
vs. Left-Handers			154	31	2	14	35	.201	.286	.271
vs. Right-Handers			800	191	30	96	200	.239	.409	.320
Home	8-6	3.48	493	114	19	58	125	.231	.396	.311
Road	7-5	3.18	461	108	13	52	110	.234	.382	.314
Grass	6-4	3.20	392	90	12	48	87	.230	.378	.315
Artificial Turf	9-7	3.44	562	132	20	62	148	.235	.397	.311
April	1-3	4.40	174	48	9	17	53	.276	.494	.339
May	4-1	2.78	169	41	6	17	42	.243	.420	.319
June	0-4	5.12	125	38	3	16	28	.304	.480	.378
July	2-1	4.19	160	37	7	16	39	.231	.413	.305
August	3-1	4.22	153	35	6	20	27	.229	.379	.314
Sept./Oct.	5-1	0.50	173	23	1	24	46	.133	.173	.239
Leading Off Inn.			244	51	10	31	53	.209	.365	.298
Runners On			358	81	10	32	95	.226	.391	.288
Runners/Scor. Pos.			176	40	5	17	52	.227	.420	.291
Runners On/2 Out			146	23	4	16	46	.158	.295	.241
Scor. Pos./2 Out			85	11	2	10	30	.129	.282	.221
Late Inning Pressure			156	41	7	13	40	.263	.429	.318
Leading Off			41	11	3	6	7	.268	.537	.362
Runners On			51	15	2	3	11	.294	.471	.327
Runners/Scor. Pos.			17	8	0	1	5	.471	.647	.474
First 9 Batters			274	58	9	34	80	.212	.336	.302
Second 9 Batters			267	56	7	37	71	.210	.356	.306
All Batters Thereafter			413	108	16	39	84	.262	.446	.324

Loves to face: Rick Cerone (.056, 1-for-18)
Hates to face: Brook Jacoby (.382, 13-for-34, 4 HR)
Ground outs-to-air outs ratio: 1.04 last season, 1.04 for career. . . .
Additional statistics: 29 double-play ground outs in 178 opportunities, 43 doubles, 5 triples in 261.1 innings last season. . . . Allowed 13 first-inning runs in 35 starts. . . . Batting support: 4.17 runs per start. . . . Led A.L. pitchers with 45 assists, a far cry from Ed Walsh's single-season record of 227. . . . Opposing batters hit 110 points higher in day games (.330) than night games (.220). Career records: day, 18–19; night, 52–43. . . . ERA has improved in each of last three seasons: 5.47, 4.85, 3.84, 3.34. Strikeouts per nine innings, year by year since 1986: 9.21, 8.67, 8.09. . . . Opponents' career average is .228 in his first two times through the batting order, .261 thereafter.

Dave LaPoint

Chicago White Sox — Throws Left

	W–L	ERA	AB	H	HR	BB	SO	BA	SA	OBA
Season	10-11	3.40	617	151	10	47	79	.245	.342	.299
vs. Left-Handers			85	22	1	5	9	.259	.376	.293
vs. Right-Handers			532	129	9	42	70	.242	.336	.300
Home	5-6	3.32	322	81	4	29	37	.252	.354	.316
Road	5-5	3.49	295	70	6	18	42	.237	.329	.279
Grass	8-9	3.55	519	130	6	43	65	.250	.337	.309
Artificial Turf	2-2	2.67	98	21	4	4	14	.214	.367	.243
April	3-1	0.94	131	20	1	10	23	.153	.221	.213
May	1-3	3.32	161	44	4	8	20	.273	.379	.306
June	2-4	4.34	144	38	1	14	18	.264	.368	.329
July	1-3	5.88	110	34	1	11	8	.309	.382	.376
August	3-0	3.32	71	15	3	4	10	.211	.366	.253
Sept./Oct.			0	0	0	0	0	—	—	—
Leading Off Inn.			161	36	5	8	18	.224	.342	.260
Runners On			245	64	2	21	32	.261	.343	.316
Runners/Scor. Pos.			124	33	1	17	17	.266	.355	.347
Runners On/2 Out			115	27	1	11	12	.235	.322	.302
Scor. Pos./2 Out			65	17	1	10	9	.262	.369	.360
Late Inning Pressure			47	17	2	2	3	.362	.617	.380
Leading Off			14	5	1	0	0	.357	.643	.357
Runners On			16	7	1	1	0	.438	.813	.444
Runners/Scor. Pos.			12	5	1	0	0	.417	.917	.385
First 9 Batters			208	47	5	14	35	.226	.313	.274
Second 9 Batters			200	44	1	15	29	.220	.285	.276
All Batters Thereafter			209	60	4	18	15	.287	.426	.345

Loves to face: Mark McGwire (.091, 1-for-11)
Hates to face: Scott Fletcher (.615, 8-for-13)
Figures *above* are for A.L. only. . . . Ground outs-to-air outs ratio: 1.18 last season, 1.31 for career. . . . Additional statistics: 13 double-play ground outs in 142 opportunities, 33 doubles, 5 triples in 213.1 innings last season. . . . Allowed 10 first-inning runs in 33 starts. . . . Batting support: 3.91 runs per start. . . . Faced the A.L.'s 25-HR hitters 68 times, 2d-highest total among pitchers who didn't allow a home run to them. . . . Has played in both the A.L. and the N.L. in each of the last three seasons. . . . Has defeated every N.L. club, but needs to beat the Orioles, White Sox, Indians, Tigers, and Royals to complete the major league circuit. . . . Earned the only save of his career in his major league debut on Sept. 10, 1980.

Charlie Lea

Minnesota Twins — Throws Right

	W–L	ERA	AB	H	HR	BB	SO	BA	SA	OBA
Season	7-7	4.85	518	156	19	50	72	.301	.488	.365
vs. Left-Handers			272	89	13	26	39	.327	.559	.388
vs. Right-Handers			246	67	6	24	33	.272	.411	.339
Home	2-3	5.07	254	74	11	30	45	.291	.488	.370
Road	5-4	4.62	264	82	8	20	27	.311	.489	.360
Grass	3-3	3.83	205	64	5	12	20	.312	.468	.355
Artificial Turf	4-4	5.47	313	92	14	38	52	.294	.502	.372
April	0-3	8.15	79	28	5	7	14	.354	.608	.407
May	1-0	5.95	77	27	1	7	15	.351	.506	.402
June	3-0	1.73	96	21	2	13	9	.219	.313	.321
July	2-1	3.86	121	37	4	10	19	.306	.504	.364
August	0-3	6.41	106	31	7	11	14	.292	.547	.361
Sept./Oct.	1-0	3.72	39	12	0	2	1	.308	.436	.333
Leading Off Inn.			122	38	4	12	19	.311	.533	.373
Runners On			239	65	8	19	32	.272	.418	.322
Runners/Scor. Pos.			145	32	1	13	25	.221	.290	.276
Runners On/2 Out			103	25	3	7	18	.243	.369	.297
Scor. Pos./2 Out			67	14	1	6	14	.209	.299	.274
Late Inning Pressure			8	4	1	1	2	.500	1.125	.556
Leading Off			1	0	0	1	1	.000	.000	.500
Runners On			4	1	0	0	1	.250	.250	.250
Runners/Scor. Pos.			0	0	0	0	0	—	—	—
First 9 Batters			189	62	10	20	33	.328	.561	.394
Second 9 Batters			186	52	3	16	22	.280	.419	.335
All Batters Thereafter			143	42	6	14	17	.294	.483	.365

Loves to face: Henry Cotto (0-for-7)
Hates to face: Chili Davis (.393, 11-for-28, 3 HR)
Ground outs-to-air outs ratio: 0.67 last season, 0.89 for career. . . . Additional statistics: 12 double-play ground outs in 99 opportunities, 32 doubles, 4 triples in 130.0 innings last season. . . . Allowed 10 first-inning runs in 23 starts. . . . Batting support: 5.52 runs per start. . . . Hasn't completed a start since August 11, 1984. (Of course, he missed most of three seasons during that time.) Only Tommy John (38 starts) started more games than Lea (23) without pitching a complete game in 1988. . . . Opponents' career average is .159 (7-for-44) with the bases loaded, and last season he performed the impossible. He induced Pat Tabler to ground into a double play with the bases loaded. Tabler was 8-for-8 vs. other pitchers with bags full last season.

Charlie Leibrandt

Kansas City Royals — Throws Left

	W–L	ERA	AB	H	HR	BB	SO	BA	SA	OBA
Season	13-12	3.19	924	244	20	62	125	.264	.381	.311
vs. Left-Handers			150	38	2	7	10	.253	.360	.290
vs. Right-Handers			774	206	18	55	115	.266	.385	.315
Home	8-3	2.94	422	117	5	22	49	.277	.370	.316
Road	5-9	3.39	502	127	15	40	76	.253	.390	.307
Grass	4-7	2.88	388	88	11	33	63	.227	.343	.286
Artificial Turf	9-5	3.42	536	156	9	29	62	.291	.409	.330
April	1-5	4.34	141	37	4	19	18	.262	.418	.350
May	1-3	5.25	141	47	4	8	19	.333	.475	.377
June	1-2	2.52	130	32	3	5	16	.246	.362	.270
July	3-1	1.99	170	41	5	10	30	.241	.371	.283
August	4-0	3.21	162	44	3	8	21	.272	.383	.306
Sept./Oct.	3-1	2.31	180	43	1	12	21	.239	.300	.285
Leading Off Inn.			237	63	5	9	25	.266	.380	.296
Runners On			344	93	5	33	52	.270	.358	.332
Runners/Scor. Pos.			199	51	2	25	36	.256	.322	.335
Runners On/2 Out			144	36	1	17	25	.250	.347	.333
Scor. Pos./2 Out			92	21	0	11	18	.228	.293	.317
Late Inning Pressure			129	29	2	8	20	.225	.318	.275
Leading Off			35	9	1	2	3	.257	.371	.297
Runners On			43	9	0	4	8	.209	.256	.277
Runners/Scor. Pos.			21	4	0	3	6	.190	.238	.292
First 9 Batters			288	77	2	23	42	.267	.351	.323
Second 9 Batters			288	80	8	20	31	.278	.413	.328
All Batters Thereafter			348	87	10	19	52	.250	.379	.287

Loves to face: Joel Skinner (0-for-10)
Hates to face: Mike Stanley (.625, 5-for-8, 2 HR)
Ground outs-to-air outs ratio: 1.33 last season, 1.21 for career. . . . Additional statistics: 27 double-play ground outs in 166 opportunities, 40 doubles, 4 triples in 243.0 innings last season. . . . Allowed 16 first-inning runs in 35 starts. . . . Batting support: 4.06 runs per start. . . . Won eight of his last nine decisions. . . . Finished with 43 assists, two behind A.L. leader Mark Langston, ending Leibrandt's dream of leading league for fourth year in a row. . . . Okay, he didn't dream about it. . . . Opponents' batting average with two outs and runners in scoring position was his highest over last five years. Only two other pitchers have held their opponents below .230 in each of those seasons: Nolan Ryan and Shane Rawley. . . . Has won his last six decisions against the A's.

Bill Long

Chicago White Sox — Throws Right

	W–L	ERA	AB	H	HR	BB	SO	BA	SA	OBA
Season	8-11	4.03	669	187	21	43	77	.280	.453	.323
vs. Left-Handers			325	101	9	28	31	.311	.486	.370
vs. Right-Handers			344	86	12	15	46	.250	.422	.278
Home	2-6	4.12	338	100	7	24	37	.296	.441	.341
Road	6-5	3.95	331	87	14	19	40	.263	.465	.304
Grass	6-10	4.07	582	166	19	39	68	.285	.462	.330
Artificial Turf	2-1	3.80	87	21	2	4	9	.241	.391	.280
April	0-1	2.25	47	13	2	5	7	.277	.447	.358
May	1-0	3.33	99	26	1	8	13	.263	.394	.315
June	2-2	6.67	117	42	5	10	9	.359	.590	.409
July	1-3	3.20	151	40	4	6	19	.265	.424	.289
August	2-3	5.63	129	39	5	8	16	.302	.465	.348
Sept./Oct.	2-2	2.55	126	27	4	6	13	.214	.397	.246
Leading Off Inn.			159	45	4	10	17	.283	.415	.333
Runners On			290	79	10	19	29	.272	.462	.309
Runners/Scor. Pos.			159	47	5	13	13	.296	.516	.333
Runners On/2 Out			128	33	4	10	14	.258	.445	.312
Scor. Pos./2 Out			81	23	2	6	6	.284	.481	.333
Late Inning Pressure			144	37	3	7	14	.257	.368	.301
Leading Off			36	13	2	1	1	.361	.611	.395
Runners On			70	12	1	5	7	.171	.243	.227
Runners/Scor. Pos.			46	7	1	5	5	.152	.261	.235
First 9 Batters			324	94	9	29	43	.290	.475	.345
Second 9 Batters			185	58	7	8	19	.314	.492	.342
All Batters Thereafter			160	35	5	6	15	.219	.363	.254

Loves to face: Claudell Washington (0-for-10)
Hates to face: Wade Boggs (.750, 9-for-12)
Ground outs-to-air outs ratio: 1.02 last season, 1.16 for career. . . . Additional statistics: 16 double-play ground outs in 128 opportunities, 37 doubles, 8 triples in 174.0 innings last season. . . . Allowed 7 first-inning runs in 18 starts. . . . Batting support: 3.50 runs per start, 4th lowest in A.L. (minimum: 15 GS). . . . Record of 6–9 (4.04 ERA) in 18 starts, 2–2 (4.02) in 29 relief appearances. . . . The A.L.'s 17 qualifying .300 hitters batted .414 against him, 2d-highest mark vs. any pitcher (minimum: 50 AB). . . . Career record of 4–11 at Comiskey Park, 12–9 elsewhere. . . . Opponents' career breakdown: .270 with bases empty, .297 with runners on base, .301 with runners in scoring position.

Kirk McCaskill

California Angels — Throws Right

	W-L	ERA	AB	H	HR	BB	SO	BA	SA	OBA
Season	8-6	4.31	566	155	9	61	98	.274	.383	.342
vs. Left-Handers			288	77	3	31	41	.267	.351	.336
vs. Right-Handers			278	78	6	30	57	.281	.417	.348
Home	5-5	3.90	316	82	5	29	62	.259	.354	.321
Road	3-1	4.83	250	73	4	32	36	.292	.420	.368
Grass	7-6	3.83	506	137	8	56	92	.271	.377	.341
Artificial Turf	1-0	8.59	60	18	1	5	6	.300	.433	.354
April	1-3	4.94	101	28	3	12	12	.277	.436	.357
May	1-1	3.22	139	43	3	14	24	.309	.432	.368
June	2-1	3.82	130	31	3	13	34	.238	.346	.308
July	4-0	3.73	160	39	0	14	26	.244	.313	.301
August	0-1	11.42	36	14	0	8	2	.389	.500	.489
Sept./Oct.			0	0	0	0	0	—	—	—
Leading Off Inn.			140	37	1	12	22	.264	.357	.327
Runners On			255	74	2	29	43	.290	.373	.355
Runners/Scor. Pos.			143	43	1	20	24	.301	.399	.373
Runners On/2 Out			100	29	1	9	17	.290	.340	.349
Scor. Pos./2 Out			60	19	1	5	11	.317	.383	.369
Late Inning Pressure			65	17	0	6	7	.262	.277	.319
Leading Off			17	5	0	1	1	.294	.294	.333
Runners On			29	9	0	4	2	.310	.310	.382
Runners/Scor. Pos.			9	6	0	3	0	.667	.667	.692
First 9 Batters			186	53	3	19	37	.285	.425	.350
Second 9 Batters			171	45	2	20	33	.263	.345	.340
All Batters Thereafter			209	57	4	22	28	.273	.378	.338

Loves to face: Scott Fletcher (0-for-13)
Hates to face: George Brett (.778, 7-for-9)
Ground outs-to-air outs ratio: 1.01 last season, 1.05 for career. . . .
Additional statistics: 14 double-play ground outs in 123 opportunities, 27 doubles, 4 triples in 146.1 innings last season. . . . Allowed 11 first-inning runs in 23 starts. . . . Batting support: 5.52 runs per start. . . . Drafted by Winnipeg in 4th round of 1981 NHL entry draft, before three now successful NHL goalies: John Vanbiesbrouck, Clint Malarchuk, Greg Stefan. . . . Scored 10 goals for Sherbrooke of the AHL in 1983-84. . . . Several NHL stars have played minor league ball, including Clark Gillies, Bob Bourne, and Doug ("Not The Umpire") Harvey. Harvey led the Border League in batting average (.351), runs (121), and RBIs (109) during the off-season after his first full year with the Canadiens.

Jack McDowell

Chicago White Sox — Throws Right

	W-L	ERA	AB	H	HR	BB	SO	BA	SA	OBA
Season	5-10	3.97	599	147	12	68	84	.245	.359	.326
vs. Left-Handers			307	84	6	40	41	.274	.384	.356
vs. Right-Handers			292	63	6	28	43	.216	.332	.294
Home	2-3	3.01	313	67	4	37	48	.214	.310	.299
Road	3-7	5.13	286	80	8	31	36	.280	.413	.356
Grass	5-9	4.01	576	139	11	66	82	.241	.352	.323
Artificial Turf	0-1	3.00	23	8	1	2	2	.348	.522	.400
April	1-2	5.93	108	28	3	13	18	.259	.426	.344
May	1-3	4.73	101	27	3	10	13	.267	.416	.327
June	1-1	3.16	113	25	2	14	15	.221	.310	.318
July	1-2	2.89	145	34	2	11	22	.234	.317	.296
August	1-2	3.75	132	33	2	20	16	.250	.348	.348
Sept./Oct.			0	0	0	0	0	—	—	—
Leading Off Inn.			152	41	2	17	20	.270	.382	.347
Runners On			249	59	7	29	38	.237	.361	.323
Runners/Scor. Pos.			146	29	4	23	24	.199	.315	.307
Runners On/2 Out			93	16	4	13	13	.172	.333	.287
Scor. Pos./2 Out			58	8	2	10	9	.138	.276	.286
Late Inning Pressure			67	18	2	10	9	.269	.448	.359
Leading Off			23	10	0	0	0	.435	.696	.435
Runners On			27	5	2	4	7	.185	.407	.281
Runners/Scor. Pos.			14	4	2	4	4	.286	.714	.421
First 9 Batters			200	45	5	21	36	.225	.345	.307
Second 9 Batters			187	44	2	25	29	.235	.321	.326
All Batters Thereafter			212	58	5	22	19	.274	.406	.345

Loves to face: Mark McGwire (0-for-8)
Hates to face: Don Mattingly (.625, 5-for-8, 1 HR)
Ground outs-to-air outs ratio: 1.38 last season, 1.35 for career. . . .
Additional statistics: 15 double-play ground outs in 128 opportunities, 28 doubles, 2 triples in 158.2 innings last season. . . . Allowed 17 first-inning runs in 26 starts. . . . Batting support: 3.58 runs per start, 6th lowest in A.L. (minimum: 15 GS). . . . Most starts by rookie pitchers in 1988: Melido Perez, 32; Pete Smith, 32; Tim Belcher, 27; John Dopson and McDowell, 26. . . . White Sox were the only A.L. club that had two rookies (McDowell and Perez) who each pitched 100 innings. . . . Faced only 12 batters protecting leads of three runs or fewer in 7th inning or later. . . . Lowest fielding percentage (.848) of any pitcher in the majors last season (minimum: 30 chances).

Greg Minton

California Angels — Throws Right

	W-L	ERA	AB	H	HR	BB	SO	BA	SA	OBA
Season	4-5	2.85	287	67	1	34	46	.233	.282	.318
vs. Left-Handers			133	32	1	17	12	.241	.308	.325
vs. Right-Handers			154	35	0	17	34	.227	.260	.313
Home	1-3	3.03	144	37	1	15	24	.257	.326	.329
Road	3-2	2.68	143	30	0	19	22	.210	.238	.307
Grass	2-4	2.87	254	59	1	29	39	.232	.283	.316
Artificial Turf	2-1	2.70	33	8	0	5	7	.242	.273	.333
April			0	0	0	0	0	—	—	—
May	0-1	5.59	42	14	0	7	3	.333	.405	.429
June	2-0	5.91	39	10	1	3	6	.256	.359	.318
July	1-0	0.86	73	14	0	9	14	.192	.205	.280
August	0-2	0.87	72	14	0	6	14	.194	.236	.253
Sept./Oct.	1-2	4.24	61	15	0	9	9	.246	.295	.356
Leading Off Inn.			62	15	1	5	9	.242	.306	.299
Runners On			138	37	0	24	20	.268	.319	.377
Runners/Scor. Pos.			91	21	0	19	17	.231	.275	.360
Runners On/2 Out			60	14	0	17	12	.233	.283	.403
Scor. Pos./2 Out			49	10	0	13	11	.204	.265	.371
Late Inning Pressure			172	38	0	21	29	.221	.262	.315
Leading Off			36	5	0	2	8	.139	.139	.184
Runners On			84	24	0	16	14	.286	.345	.408
Runners/Scor. Pos.			56	13	0	15	11	.232	.268	.397
First 9 Batters			263	64	1	32	44	.243	.297	.327
Second 9 Batters			24	3	0	2	2	.125	.125	.222
All Batters Thereafter			0	0	0	0	0	—	—	—

Loves to face: Joe Carter (0-for-9)
Hates to face: Rob Deer (4-for-4)
Ground outs-to-air outs ratio: 2.64 last season, 2.41 for career. . . .
Additional statistics: 13 double-play ground outs in 71 opportunities, 11 doubles, 0 triples in 79.0 innings last season. . . . Committed one balk last season, his first since 1981. . . . Career average of one home run per 27 innings is the lowest among active pitchers (minimum: 800 IP). . . . After 14 seasons, career high for strikeouts is 58. Only three players in major league history had careers as long as Minton's without striking out more than 58 batters in a season: Clarence Mitchell (18 years, 52 SOs), Dick Coffman (15, 55), and Jack Russell (15, 45). . . . Oldest active player in any of the four major team sports (sorry, indoor soccer fans) never to have played in a postseason game.

Dale Mohorcic

Rangers/Yankees — Throws Right

	W-L	ERA	AB	H	HR	BB	SO	BA	SA	OBA
Season	4-8	4.22	298	83	7	29	44	.279	.416	.352
vs. Left-Handers			130	41	1	9	20	.315	.446	.352
vs. Right-Handers			168	42	6	20	24	.250	.393	.352
Home	3-2	4.37	138	37	3	15	21	.268	.384	.352
Road	1-6	4.08	160	46	4	14	23	.288	.444	.352
Grass	3-6	3.99	254	68	7	26	42	.268	.406	.346
Artificial Turf	1-2	5.79	44	15	0	3	2	.341	.477	.388
April	0-0	0.00	8	2	0	0	1	.250	.250	.250
May	2-2	1.17	86	20	0	5	10	.233	.326	.280
June	0-3	7.59	48	19	3	3	5	.396	.646	.444
July	0-0	9.00	35	11	2	5	3	.314	.543	.405
August	0-1	8.31	33	10	1	7	6	.303	.485	.419
Sept./Oct.	2-2	2.78	88	21	1	9	19	.239	.318	.327
Leading Off Inn.			57	10	0	5	7	.175	.263	.266
Runners On			166	46	5	15	26	.277	.428	.344
Runners/Scor. Pos.			110	27	3	13	16	.245	.391	.331
Runners On/2 Out			76	20	1	5	9	.263	.382	.349
Scor. Pos./2 Out			53	15	0	5	5	.283	.377	.387
Late Inning Pressure			132	36	2	13	18	.273	.417	.353
Leading Off			26	6	0	3	0	.231	.346	.333
Runners On			72	20	2	8	10	.278	.458	.361
Runners/Scor. Pos.			53	15	2	7	7	.283	.509	.381
First 9 Batters			266	75	6	28	39	.282	.417	.357
Second 9 Batters			32	8	1	1	5	.250	.406	.306
All Batters Thereafter			0	0	0	0	0	—	—	—

Loves to face: Bo Jackson (0-for-8)
Hates to face: Ivan Calderon (.750, 3-for-4, 2 HR)
Ground outs-to-air outs ratio: 1.29 last season, 1.84 for career. . . .
Additional statistics: 5 double-play ground outs in 81 opportunities, 20 doubles, 0 triples in 74.2 innings last season. . . . ERAs had been below 3.00 in each of two previous seasons. . . . Hit eight batters with pitches last season, after hitting only three batters over the previous two seasons. . . . Rangers lost 24 of the last 26 games in which he appeared for them. . . . Opponents' career average is .294 in Late-Inning Pressure Situations, .241 in other at-bats. . . . Has allowed three grand slams over the last two seasons. . . . Opponents' career batting average is .232 in day games, .275 at night. ERAs: 2.53 by day, 3.38 by night.

Donnie Moore

California Angels　　Throws Right

	W-L	ERA	AB	H	HR	BB	SO	BA	SA	OBA
Season	5-2	4.91	140	48	4	8	22	.343	.486	.373
vs. Left-Handers			70	20	2	5	13	.286	.443	.333
vs. Right-Handers			70	28	2	3	9	.400	.529	.413
Home	1-1	6.00	64	22	1	4	12	.344	.438	.377
Road	4-1	4.00	76	26	3	4	10	.342	.526	.370
Grass	4-2	5.67	114	38	4	7	21	.333	.500	.366
Artificial Turf	1-0	1.50	26	10	0	1	1	.386	.423	.407
April	1-2	7.11	30	13	2	3	4	.433	.633	.471
May	1-0	6.75	19	8	0	2	2	.421	.421	.476
June	1-0	2.84	24	6	0	1	4	.250	.292	.280
July	2-0	5.02	59	19	2	2	12	.322	.542	.339
August	0-0	0.00	8	2	0	0	0	.250	.250	.250
Sept./Oct.			0	0	0	0	0	—	—	—
Leading Off Inn.			27	7	1	0	2	.259	.407	.259
Runners On			75	28	3	6	10	.373	.573	.410
Runners/Scor. Pos.			46	17	2	5	6	.370	.565	.415
Runners On/2 Out			35	14	2	2	4	.400	.714	.432
Scor. Pos./2 Out			22	8	1	1	3	.364	.591	.391
Late Inning Pressure			66	22	2	4	13	.333	.485	.366
Leading Off			13	2	0	0	2	.154	.154	.154
Runners On			34	13	2	3	6	.382	.647	.421
Runners/Scor. Pos.			21	9	0	1	7	.281	.313	.303
First 9 Batters			213	46	4	8	22	.333	.478	.365
Second 9 Batters			2	2	0	0	0	1.000	1.000	1.000
All Batters Thereafter			0	0	0	0	0	—	—	—

Loves to face: Dan Gladden (0-for-7)

Hates to face: George Bell (.600, 6-for-10, 2 HR)

Ground outs-to-air outs ratio: 1.38 last season, 1.09 for career. . . . Additional statistics: 4 double-play ground outs in 34 opportunities, 4 doubles, 2 triples in 33.0 innings last season. . . . Struck out 33 batters in between walks in August, longest streak in majors last season. . . . Only 47 percent of batters faced last season were in Late-Inning Pressure Situations. Here are his yearly percentages since 1984: 63.5, 70.0, 67.8, 77.0, 47.3. . . . Opponents' batting average topped the .300 mark for the third time in his career (.316 in 1975, .321 in '79). . . . Made his major league debut the same week as Jack Clark and Chet Lemon. Somehow, Moore seems younger than his 35 years indicates.

Mike Moore

Seattle Mariners　　Throws Right

	W-L	ERA	AB	H	HR	BB	SO	BA	SA	OBA
Season	9-15	3.78	846	196	24	63	182	.232	.363	.286
vs. Left-Handers			493	115	12	40	98	.233	.357	.292
vs. Right-Handers			353	81	12	23	84	.229	.371	.279
Home	6-4	3.31	366	74	6	28	74	.202	.301	.260
Road	3-11	4.16	480	122	18	35	108	.254	.410	.306
Grass	3-8	4.20	374	91	15	25	90	.243	.406	.293
Artificial Turf	6-7	3.46	472	105	9	38	92	.222	.328	.281
April	2-2	6.06	129	35	4	12	15	.271	.419	.336
May	0-4	4.96	126	32	7	15	14	.254	.452	.333
June	2-2	1.91	134	28	3	7	25	.209	.306	.254
July	0-4	6.43	135	38	5	13	37	.281	.459	.342
August	3-2	2.23	173	34	3	7	59	.197	.289	.231
Sept./Oct.	2-1	2.34	149	29	2	9	32	.195	.289	.241
Leading Off Inn.			225	52	5	13	51	.231	.320	.273
Runners On			294	74	11	31	51	.252	.429	.320
Runners/Scor. Pos.			154	45	6	14	28	.292	.474	.345
Runners On/2 Out			111	25	4	16	16	.225	.378	.323
Scor. Pos./2 Out			72	19	3	7	9	.264	.431	.329
Late Inning Pressure			123	29	5	6	15	.236	.382	.282
Leading Off			36	12	1	2	5	.333	.417	.368
Runners On			36	8	2	2	4	.222	.444	.263
Runners/Scor. Pos.			12	3	1	1	2	.250	.583	.308
First 9 Batters			284	68	9	20	62	.239	.387	.289
Second 9 Batters			259	53	6	21	59	.205	.317	.264
All Batters Thereafter			303	75	9	22	61	.248	.380	.303

Loves to face: Paul Molitor (.077, 2-for-26)

Hates to face: Dave Winfield (.600, 12-for-20, 2 HR)

Ground outs-to-air outs ratio: 1.08 last season, 1.28 for career. . . . Additional statistics: 20 double-play ground outs in 145 opportunities, 37 doubles, 1 triple in 228.2 innings last season. . . . Allowed 24 first-inning runs (5th most in A.L.) in 32 starts. Allowed seven first-inning home runs, tied for most in the majors. . . . Batting support: 3.69 runs per start. . . . Opponents' batting average was a career low, following a career high mark (.292) in 1987. . . . Opponents' career average is .293 with runners on base, .250 with the bases empty. . . . Career winning percentage with Seattle was .407 (66-96). M's played .444 ball (431-540) behind other pitchers during that time. . . . Opponents' career average is .198 (19-for-96, no HR) with the bases loaded.

Jack Morris

Detroit Tigers　　Throws Right

	W-L	ERA	AB	H	HR	BB	SO	BA	SA	OBA
Season	15-13	3.94	895	225	20	83	168	.251	.375	.317
vs. Left-Handers			487	114	9	50	88	.234	.337	.306
vs. Right-Handers			408	111	11	33	80	.272	.422	.330
Home	6-6	4.82	413	113	11	47	86	.274	.412	.351
Road	9-7	3.22	482	112	9	36	82	.232	.344	.287
Grass	14-11	3.61	815	203	15	75	155	.249	.360	.314
Artificial Turf	1-2	7.40	80	22	5	8	13	.275	.538	.348
April	2-3	5.27	169	50	3	21	39	.296	.414	.370
May	2-3	4.04	133	33	5	11	28	.248	.391	.313
June	3-2	5.28	126	38	3	16	16	.302	.468	.367
July	1-3	4.54	137	36	6	10	27	.263	.423	.322
August	4-1	1.85	170	29	1	12	28	.171	.241	.225
Sept./Oct.	3-1	3.46	160	39	2	16	30	.244	.350	.313
Leading Off Inn.			226	60	7	17	36	.265	.412	.317
Runners On			376	100	9	32	69	.266	.410	.324
Runners/Scor. Pos.			217	58	6	22	46	.267	.433	.333
Runners On/2 Out			166	47	5	15	40	.283	.446	.346
Scor. Pos./2 Out			109	29	4	11	27	.266	.468	.333
Late Inning Pressure			123	23	2	14	26	.187	.260	.268
Leading Off			33	6	1	4	5	.182	.273	.270
Runners On			46	9	1	4	10	.196	.304	.255
Runners/Scor. Pos.			20	2	0	3	5	.100	.200	.208
First 9 Batters			274	58	5	31	61	.212	.325	.296
Second 9 Batters			266	75	9	21	46	.282	.455	.337
All Batters Thereafter			355	92	6	31	61	.259	.355	.318

Loves to face: Ken Phelps (.032, 1-for-31, 13 SO)

Hates to face: Cal Ripken (.351, 20-for-57, 4 HR)

Ground outs-to-air outs ratio: 1.01 last season, 1.13 for career. . . . Additional statistics: 15 double-play ground outs in 161 opportunities, 43 doubles, 4 triples in 235.0 innings last season. . . . Allowed 10 first-inning runs in 34 starts. . . . Batting support: 4.35 runs per start. . . . Didn't allow an earned run in last 23 innings, retiring the leadoff batter in each. . . . Has won 156 games during 1980s, 33 more than runner-up Dave Stieb. Leaders in previous decades: 1870s, Tommy Bond (154); 1880s, Tim Keefe (292); 1890s, Kid Nichols (297); 1900s, Christy Mathewson (236); 1910s, Walter Johnson (264); 1920s, Burleigh Grimes (190); 1930s, Lefty Grove (199); 1940s, Hal Newhouser (170); 1950s, Warren Spahn (202); 1960s, Juan Marichal (191); 1970s, Jim Palmer (186).

Jeff Musselman

Toronto Blue Jays　　Throws Left

	W-L	ERA	AB	H	HR	BB	SO	BA	SA	OBA
Season	8-5	3.18	318	80	4	30	39	.252	.358	.320
vs. Left-Handers			49	14	1	9	4	.286	.408	.390
vs. Right-Handers			269	66	3	21	35	.245	.349	.306
Home	4-3	4.07	186	53	2	14	26	.285	.376	.340
Road	4-2	1.98	132	27	2	16	13	.205	.333	.293
Grass	2-2	2.82	87	21	1	11	7	.241	.368	.323
Artificial Turf	6-3	3.30	231	59	3	19	32	.255	.355	.319
April			0	0	0	0	0	—	—	—
May			0	0	0	0	0	—	—	—
June			0	0	0	0	0	—	—	—
July	3-0	0.87	74	14	1	7	11	.189	.297	.268
August	2-3	3.74	125	34	2	11	15	.272	.392	.333
Sept./Oct.	3-2	4.11	119	32	1	12	13	.269	.361	.338
Leading Off Inn.			78	23	1	9	11	.295	.372	.382
Runners On			148	36	2	10	13	.243	.338	.288
Runners/Scor. Pos.			63	21	1	8	6	.333	.429	.397
Runners On/2 Out			54	9	1	3	5	.167	.278	.211
Scor. Pos./2 Out			27	4	1	2	4	.148	.259	.207
Late Inning Pressure			9	0	0	0	2	.000	.000	.000
Leading Off			3	0	0	0	1	.000	.000	.000
Runners On			0	0	0	0	0	—	—	—
Runners/Scor. Pos.			0	0	0	0	0	—	—	—
First 9 Batters			114	35	0	16	14	.307	.404	.397
Second 9 Batters			112	22	1	10	17	.196	.268	.262
All Batters Thereafter			92	23	3	4	8	.250	.413	.290

Loves to face: Rick Cerone (0-for-8)

Hates to face: Darnell Coles (.667, 2-for-3, 1 HR)

Ground outs-to-air outs ratio: 1.08 last season, 1.57 for career. . . . Additional statistics: 12 double-play ground outs in 78 opportunities, 16 doubles, 3 triples in 85.0 innings last season. . . . Allowed 14 first-inning runs in 15 starts. . . . Batting support: 5.47 runs per start, 6th highest in A.L. (minimum: 15 GS). . . . Didn't complete any of his 15 starts last season. Had started only one game in his career prior to 1988, appearing in relief 73 times. . . . Opponents' batting average was 80 points higher in home games than in road games, the 2d-largest difference in A.L. last season (minimum: 100 AB each way). . . . Career records: 14-5 at Exhibition Stadium, 6-5 on the road. But ERA is much higher at home (4.53) than elsewhere (3.17).

Gene Nelson
Oakland As — Throws Right

	W–L	ERA	AB	H	HR	BB	SO	BA	SA	OBA
Season	9-6	3.06	408	93	9	38	67	.228	.341	.296
vs. Left-Handers			168	39	4	20	21	.232	.339	.314
vs. Right-Handers			240	54	5	18	46	.225	.342	.282
Home	5-4	3.79	208	44	6	25	37	.212	.341	.301
Road	4-2	2.30	200	49	3	13	30	.245	.340	.290
Grass	9-5	2.91	324	69	7	32	51	.213	.312	.287
Artificial Turf	0-1	3.68	84	24	2	6	16	.286	.452	.330
April	2-2	4.91	67	16	3	7	11	.239	.433	.316
May	1-0	1.50	41	8	0	5	8	.195	.220	.283
June	2-1	4.56	94	25	4	10	16	.266	.404	.343
July	0-0	2.53	76	18	1	8	11	.237	.316	.306
August	2-3	1.93	65	13	1	5	7	.200	.308	.257
Sept./Oct.	2-0	2.04	65	13	0	3	14	.200	.292	.239
Leading Off Inn.			96	22	1	6	15	.229	.344	.275
Runners On			174	43	3	18	24	.247	.322	.318
Runners/Scor. Pos.			114	32	3	14	18	.281	.377	.353
Runners On/2 Out			81	22	1	7	11	.272	.309	.337
Scor. Pos./2 Out			55	15	1	7	10	.273	.327	.355
Late Inning Pressure			127	23	2	16	24	.181	.260	.278
Leading Off			34	3	0	2	7	.088	.118	.139
Runners On			46	11	0	7	5	.239	.239	.340
Runners/Scor. Pos.			28	7	0	7	4	.250	.250	.400
First 9 Batters			325	70	5	32	54	.215	.314	.287
Second 9 Batters			78	21	4	5	13	.269	.449	.318
All Batters Thereafter			5	2	0	1	0	.400	.400	.500

Loves to face: Pat Sheridan (.067, 1-for-15)
Hates to face: George Brett (.429, 9-for-21, 4 HR)
Ground outs-to-air outs ratio: 0.92 last season, 1.15 for career. . . .
Additional statistics: 10 double-play ground outs in 66 opportunities, 13 doubles, 3 triples in 111.2 innings last season. . . . Has pitched exactly 54 games in each of the last three seasons. . . . One of two pitchers who's held opponents to a lower average in Late-Inning Pressure Situations than otherwise in each of the last six seasons. The other: Jeff Russell. Opponents' career averages: .226 LIPS, .268 in other at-bats. . . . Opponents' career batting average is .245 on grass fields, .300 on artificial turf. Difference of 55 points is the most of any pitcher over the last 10 seasons. . . . First A.L. pitcher to win two games in a four-game League Championship Series.

Tom Niedenfuer
Baltimore Orioles — Throws Right

	W–L	ERA	AB	H	HR	BB	SO	BA	SA	OBA
Season	3-4	3.51	228	59	8	19	40	.259	.412	.320
vs. Left-Handers			110	32	4	12	16	.291	.473	.371
vs. Right-Handers			118	27	4	7	24	.229	.356	.270
Home	2-1	4.06	121	31	5	10	25	.256	.446	.318
Road	1-3	2.89	107	28	3	9	15	.262	.374	.322
Grass	3-2	3.72	190	52	7	15	33	.274	.437	.333
Artificial Turf	0-2	2.53	38	7	1	4	7	.184	.289	.256
April	0-0	1.59	24	8	1	2	4	.333	.458	.385
May	0-0	5.91	42	11	1	5	8	.262	.452	.367
June	1-1	2.61	39	9	1	2	6	.231	.333	.268
July	0-0	0.00	33	6	0	0	8	.182	.182	.182
August	1-2	3.21	53	14	1	6	6	.264	.396	.333
Sept./Oct.	1-1	6.75	37	11	4	4	8	.297	.649	.366
Leading Off Inn.			40	6	1	5	12	.150	.250	.244
Runners On			119	32	3	8	14	.269	.370	.323
Runners/Scor. Pos.			64	16	2	6	9	.250	.359	.319
Runners On/2 Out			58	17	1	3	8	.293	.362	.349
Scor. Pos./2 Out			35	6	0	2	6	.171	.171	.237
Late Inning Pressure			106	28	2	11	18	.264	.368	.336
Leading Off			16	1	0	2	7	.063	.063	.167
Runners On			58	18	1	6	8	.310	.397	.379
Runners/Scor. Pos.			34	9	1	4	7	.265	.382	.333
First 9 Batters			225	57	8	18	40	.253	.404	.313
Second 9 Batters			3	2	0	1	0	.667	1.000	.750
All Batters Thereafter			0	0	0	0	0			

Loves to face: Nick Esasky (0-for-6, 4 SO)
Hates to face: Kelly Gruber (4-for-4, 2 HR)
Ground outs-to-air outs ratio: 0.40 last season, 0.53 for career. . . .
Additional statistics: 5 double-play ground outs in 59 opportunities, 7 doubles, 2 triples in 59.0 innings last season. . . . Has pitched 407 major league games, all in relief. . . . Saved 18 games last season for a team that won only 54. Career high in saves was 19 for 1985 Dodgers, when they won the N.L. West with 95 victories. . . . Ground-ball hitters batted .312 against him last season, fly-ballers hit .210. . . . Opponents' career breakdown: .264 by left-handed batters, .215 by right-handers. . . . Has allowed one home run per 6.7 innings over last three seasons, compared to one per 26.5 innings in five previous seasons. . . . Yearly totals of innings pitched since 1985: 106.1, 80.0, 68.2, 59.0.

Juan Nieves
Milwaukee Brewers — Throws Left

	W–L	ERA	AB	H	HR	BB	SO	BA	SA	OBA
Season	7-5	4.08	404	84	13	50	73	.208	.349	.295
vs. Left-Handers			88	13	2	7	22	.148	.250	.208
vs. Right-Handers			316	71	11	43	51	.225	.377	.319
Home	2-2	4.66	210	45	10	28	32	.214	.405	.307
Road	5-3	3.44	194	39	3	22	41	.201	.289	.282
Grass	4-5	4.44	343	73	12	44	59	.213	.362	.303
Artificial Turf	3-0	2.12	61	11	1	6	14	.180	.279	.254
April	2-2	7.78	80	23	3	12	14	.288	.463	.380
May	2-2	4.21	92	17	3	16	8	.185	.337	.309
June		—	0	0	0	0	0	—	—	—
July	0-0	0.00	18	4	0	0	2	.222	.278	.222
August	1-1	3.45	109	22	5	8	27	.202	.376	.256
Sept./Oct.	2-0	2.76	105	18	2	14	22	.171	.257	.267
Leading Off Inn.			99	21	3	16	13	.212	.323	.322
Runners On			160	38	6	16	27	.238	.419	.307
Runners/Scor. Pos.			79	21	3	9	16	.266	.443	.341
Runners On/2 Out			59	9	2	8	13	.153	.271	.254
Scor. Pos./2 Out			32	6	1	5	7	.188	.281	.297
Late Inning Pressure			49	5	0	11	12	.102	.122	.262
Leading Off			14	3	0	4	1	.214	.214	.389
Runners On			18	2	0	3	4	.111	.167	.227
Runners/Scor. Pos.			5	1	0	1	0	.200	.200	.286
First 9 Batters			185	39	5	19	43	.211	.341	.288
Second 9 Batters			134	25	5	15	18	.187	.328	.267
All Batters Thereafter			85	20	3	16	12	.235	.400	.353

Loves to face: Mike Greenwell (0-for-12)
Hates to face: Dave Winfield (.636, 7-for-11, 2 HR)
Ground outs-to-air outs ratio: 0.63 last season, 0.73 for career. . . .
Additional statistics: 7 double-play ground outs in 80 opportunities, 18 doubles, 0 triples in 110.1 innings last season. . . . Allowed 11 first-inning runs in 15 starts. . . . Batting support: 4.93 runs per start. . . . Record of 6–5 (4.75 ERA) in 15 starts, 1–0 (1.80) in 10 relief appearances. . . . Ground-ball hitters batted .160 against him last season, lowest mark of past 14 years in A.L. (minimum: 200 AB). Now get this: Over two prior seasons, ground-ballers batted .304 against him. . . . Shutout against the White Sox in September was his first since he no-hit the Orioles in April 1987. . . . Opponents' batting averages, year by year since 1986: .299, .264, .208.

Oswaldo Peraza
Baltimore Orioles — Throws Right

	W–L	ERA	AB	H	HR	BB	SO	BA	SA	OBA
Season	5-7	5.55	347	98	10	37	61	.282	.444	.352
vs. Left-Handers			155	37	4	19	31	.239	.381	.324
vs. Right-Handers			192	61	6	18	30	.318	.495	.376
Home	3-4	4.14	178	47	6	17	36	.264	.416	.328
Road	2-3	7.14	169	51	4	20	25	.302	.473	.377
Grass	4-7	5.10	290	80	8	26	50	.276	.424	.334
Artificial Turf	1-0	7.90	57	18	2	11	11	.316	.544	.435
April	0-2	7.07	55	16	3	10	9	.291	.527	.403
May			0	0	0	0	0	—	—	—
June	1-1	6.00	38	13	3	5	8	.342	.737	.432
July	2-1	5.40	121	33	4	8	18	.273	.430	.318
August	2-3	4.80	120	32	0	11	24	.267	.317	.323
Sept./Oct.	0-0	6.00	13	4	0	3	2	.308	.538	.452
Leading Off Inn.			83	22	3	8	12	.265	.458	.330
Runners On			149	48	6	22	21	.322	.523	.402
Runners/Scor. Pos.			105	35	5	19	15	.333	.581	.425
Runners On/2 Out			57	16	2	14	7	.281	.474	.423
Scor. Pos./2 Out			43	13	1	13	5	.302	.488	.464
Late Inning Pressure			12	4	0	2	3	.333	.500	.467
Leading Off			4	0	0	1	1	.000	.000	.000
Runners On			5	3	0	1	1	.600	.800	.667
Runners/Scor. Pos.			5	3	0	1	1	.600	.800	.667
First 9 Batters			143	39	4	14	27	.273	.441	.338
Second 9 Batters			114	32	5	16	23	.281	.465	.371
All Batters Thereafter			90	27	1	7	11	.300	.422	.350

Loves to face: Terry Francona (0-for-8)
Hates to face: Randy Bush (.600, 3-for-5, 2 2B, 1 HR)
Ground outs-to-air outs ratio: 1.11 last season, his first in majors. . . . Additional statistics: 6 double-play ground outs in 56 opportunities, 22 doubles, 2 triples in 86.0 innings last season. . . . Allowed 10 first-inning runs in 15 starts. . . . Batting support: 4.13 runs per start. . . . Pitched an average of 5.33 innings per start, 2d-lowest mark in A.L. (minimum: 15 GS). . . . Highest ERA by an A.L. rookie with 15 or more starts since 1977 (Phil Huffman, 5.77). Highest ever by that measure was 7.63, by Bill Rhodes in 1893. Since 1900: 6.80, by Hap Collard in 1930. . . . Compiled a nifty little 8.62 ERA in day games, losing all three decisions. Went 5–4 with a 4.86 ERA at night. . . . Born three days after Willie McCovey lined out to Bobby Richardson to end the 1962 World Series.

Melido Perez

Throws Right

Chicago White Sox

	W–L	ERA	AB	H	HR	BB	SO	BA	SA	OBA
Season	12-10	3.79	749	186	26	72	138	.248	.409	.313
vs. Left-Handers			397	92	12	40	72	.232	.385	.299
vs. Right-Handers			352	94	14	32	66	.267	.435	.329
Home	6-2	3.52	342	86	13	33	56	.251	.404	.316
Road	6-8	4.03	407	100	13	39	82	.246	.413	.310
Grass	8-7	3.92	590	152	19	59	103	.258	.415	.324
Artificial Turf	4-3	3.35	159	34	7	13	35	.214	.384	.273
April	1-0	2.70	70	13	3	8	18	.186	.314	.278
May	4-1	3.62	133	29	3	16	23	.218	.331	.298
June	1-4	5.29	133	41	7	13	23	.308	.556	.372
July	4-0	3.86	127	37	3	10	15	.291	.449	.341
August	1-3	5.12	134	41	9	10	29	.306	.567	.349
Sept./Oct.	1-2	2.30	152	25	1	15	30	.164	.217	.237
Leading Off Inn.			193	52	6	15	37	.269	.409	.325
Runners On			306	73	8	26	56	.239	.389	.291
Runners/Scor. Pos.			158	40	4	10	34	.253	.380	.284
Runners On/2 Out			130	27	3	10	25	.208	.346	.264
Scor. Pos./2 Out			80	17	1	4	18	.213	.313	.250
Late Inning Pressure			58	19	3	6	10	.328	.638	.391
Leading Off			18	4	0	1	4	.222	.444	.263
Runners On			14	5	0	2	0	.357	.714	.438
Runners/Scor. Pos.			8	4	0	1	0	.500	.875	.556
First 9 Batters			257	59	4	29	53	.230	.319	.308
Second 9 Batters			251	61	10	23	43	.243	.402	.305
All Batters Thereafter			241	66	12	20	42	.274	.510	.327

Loves to face: Tony Fernandez (0-for-10)
Hates to face: Johnny Ray (.800, 4-for-5, 1 2B, 1 3B, 1 HR)
Ground outs-to-air outs ratio: 0.83 last season, 0.85 for career. . . .
Additional statistics: 15 double-play ground outs in 147 opportunities, 28 doubles, 7 triples in 197.0 innings last season. . . . Allowed 12 first-inning runs in 32 starts. . . . Batting support: 4.34 runs per start. . . . Pitched more innings than any other rookie. Tied with Braves' Pete Smith for most games started. . . . Led A.L. rookies in strikeouts, even if you include Jay Buhner, who fanned 93 times. . . . Only one A.L. rookie won more games: Don August (13). . . . Most wins by a White Sox rookie since Richard Dotson won 12 in 1980. Highest rookie totals in team history: 22, Reb Russell (1913); 20, Roy Patterson (1901); 19, Gary Peters (1963). . . . Career record is perfect in day games (6–0), imperfect at night (7–11).

Dan Petry

Throws Right

California Angels

	W–L	ERA	AB	H	HR	BB	SO	BA	SA	OBA
Season	3-9	4.38	528	139	18	59	64	.263	.424	.341
vs. Left-Handers			264	76	7	37	27	.288	.417	.377
vs. Right-Handers			264	63	11	22	37	.239	.432	.303
Home	3-6	3.92	332	87	12	36	39	.262	.416	.332
Road	0-3	5.16	196	52	6	23	25	.265	.439	.354
Grass	3-8	3.96	472	122	17	47	60	.258	.417	.328
Artificial Turf	0-1	7.98	56	17	1	12	4	.304	.482	.437
April	1-1	6.00	109	28	3	17	13	.257	.422	.371
May	1-3	4.23	152	49	8	13	11	.322	.566	.371
June	1-1	1.55	99	15	2	8	16	.152	.232	.222
July			0	0	0	0	0	—	—	—
August	0-1	13.50	12	5	1	4	1	.417	.667	.563
Sept./Oct.	0-3	4.76	156	42	4	17	23	.269	.391	.341
Leading Off Inn.			133	35	5	13	10	.263	.414	.338
Runners On			219	62	9	21	31	.283	.484	.343
Runners/Scor. Pos.			123	29	3	14	17	.236	.423	.306
Runners On/2 Out			85	16	4	12	14	.188	.341	.296
Scor. Pos./2 Out			52	7	2	9	11	.135	.269	.262
Late Inning Pressure			71	21	3	6	10	.296	.465	.346
Leading Off			20	7	1	1	2	.350	.550	.381
Runners On			24	6	1	2	6	.250	.375	.296
Runners/Scor. Pos.			10	3	0	2	2	.300	.300	.385
First 9 Batters			169	41	5	20	18	.243	.361	.332
Second 9 Batters			171	43	7	21	18	.251	.439	.330
All Batters Thereafter			188	55	6	18	28	.293	.468	.359

Loves to face: Rob Deer (.091, 1-for-11, 7 SO)
Hates to face: Fred Lynn (.380, 19-for-50, 7 HR)
Ground outs-to-air outs ratio: 1.47 last season, 1.46 for career. . . .
Additional statistics: 12 double-play ground outs in 104 opportunities, 25 doubles, 3 triples in 139.2 innings last season. . . . Allowed 10 first-inning runs in 22 starts. . . . Batting support: 4.00 runs per start. . . . Lost a complete game in only appearance against his former teammates. Has yet to wear a halo at Tiger Stadium. . . . His only CG-win was his first shutout since 1984. . . . Opposing batters have hit below .230 with two outs and runners in scoring position seven times in his 10 seasons. Previous career low: .179 in 1979. . . . Has a record of 17–26 over the last three seasons, after posting winning records in each of his first seven seasons in the majors.

Dan Plesac

Throws Left

Milwaukee Brewers

	W–L	ERA	AB	H	HR	BB	SO	BA	SA	OBA
Season	1-2	2.41	197	46	2	12	52	.234	.320	.278
vs. Left-Handers			40	9	0	2	10	.225	.375	.333
vs. Right-Handers			157	37	2	10	42	.236	.306	.281
Home	0-0	1.69	96	18	1	9	30	.188	.302	.257
Road	1-2	3.16	101	28	1	3	22	.277	.337	.298
Grass	0-2	2.66	154	36	2	11	43	.234	.338	.285
Artificial Turf	1-0	1.54	43	10	0	1	9	.233	.256	.250
April	0-0	2.00	33	7	1	3	13	.212	.303	.278
May	1-0	1.32	48	9	1	1	17	.188	.250	.204
June	0-1	3.38	45	14	0	4	6	.311	.422	.367
July	0-0	3.09	45	10	0	1	7	.222	.311	.239
August	0-0	0.00	16	2	0	0	6	.125	.125	.125
Sept./Oct.	0-1	7.71	10	4	0	3	3	.400	.600	.538
Leading Off Inn.			31	4	0	3	6	.129	.161	.206
Runners On			109	27	2	8	30	.248	.367	.299
Runners/Scor. Pos.			73	21	2	7	20	.288	.452	.350
Runners On/2 Out			56	17	1	8	17	.304	.429	.391
Scor. Pos./2 Out			40	13	1	7	11	.325	.475	.426
Late Inning Pressure			128	34	2	6	29	.266	.367	.299
Leading Off			19	3	0	2	2	.158	.211	.238
Runners On			70	23	2	4	14	.329	.486	.365
Runners/Scor. Pos.			47	19	2	3	9	.404	.617	.440
First 9 Batters			196	46	2	12	52	.235	.321	.279
Second 9 Batters			1	0	0	0	0	.000	.000	.000
All Batters Thereafter			0	0	0	0	0			

Loves to face: Mike Pagliarulo (0-for-8, 5 SO)
Hates to face: Cory Snyder (.600, 3-for-5, 2 HR)
Ground outs-to-air outs ratio: 0.75 last season, 0.82 for career. . . .
Additional statistics: 2 double-play ground outs in 38 opportunities, 7 doubles, 2 triples in 52.1 innings last season. . . . Had recorded 25 of his 30 saves by July 19. Missed the Brewers' final 16 games last season, and with it a chance to break Ken Sanders's single-season club record of 31 saves. . . . Needs 30 saves to tie Rollie Fingers's club career record of 97. . . . Finished 48 of the 50 games in which he appeared. . . . Opponents' career batting average of .251 in Late-Inning Pressure Situations seems pretty good until you compare it to their .187 average against him in other at-bats. That difference of 65 points is the 4th-largest over the last 10 seasons (minimum: 250 LIPS AB).

Eric Plunk

Throws Right

Oakland As

	W–L	ERA	AB	H	HR	BB	SO	BA	SA	OBA
Season	7-2	3.00	286	62	6	39	79	.217	.318	.311
vs. Left-Handers			122	25	1	18	36	.205	.279	.305
vs. Right-Handers			164	37	5	21	43	.226	.348	.316
Home	4-1	4.93	126	28	3	17	32	.222	.341	.317
Road	3-1	1.45	160	34	3	22	47	.213	.300	.306
Grass	7-2	3.23	253	53	5	35	73	.209	.308	.306
Artificial Turf	0-0	1.08	33	9	1	4	6	.273	.394	.351
April	1-1	3.46	49	10	2	8	13	.204	.367	.316
May	2-0	1.46	43	7	0	6	14	.163	.209	.280
June	2-0	3.18	42	10	2	6	7	.238	.381	.327
July	0-0	1.23	23	2	0	6	10	.087	.087	.276
August	0-1	3.18	63	16	1	10	18	.254	.381	.351
Sept./Oct.	2-0	4.24	66	17	1	3	17	.258	.333	.290
Leading Off Inn.			68	16	1	3	22	.235	.309	.268
Runners On			129	27	4	22	33	.209	.326	.320
Runners/Scor. Pos.			90	16	1	17	25	.178	.222	.303
Runners On/2 Out			58	10	3	16	17	.172	.345	.351
Scor. Pos./2 Out			41	5	0	13	14	.122	.122	.333
Late Inning Pressure			150	31	3	20	39	.207	.293	.304
Leading Off			35	8	0	3	12	.229	.286	.289
Runners On			66	13	3	12	16	.197	.348	.321
Runners/Scor. Pos.			51	9	1	11	13	.176	.255	.323
First 9 Batters			246	50	5	36	71	.203	.289	.305
Second 9 Batters			39	12	1	3	8	.308	.513	.357
All Batters Thereafter			1	0	0	0	0	.000	.000	.000

Loves to face: Jack Howell (0-for-7, 6 SO)
Hates to face: Pete O'Brien (.333, 2-for-6, 8 BB, 1 HR)
Ground outs-to-air outs ratio: 0.77 last season, 0.87 for career. . . .
Additional statistics: 6 double-play ground outs in 53 opportunities, 7 doubles, 2 triples in 78.0 innings last season. . . . Faced 37 batters protecting leads of three runs or fewer in 8th inning or later. Eckersley faced 209; Honeycutt, 31; Cadaret, 28. . . . Had five of Oakland's 64 saves, a major league record. Burns, Cadaret, Honeycutt, and Plunk all had saves in late August or September as LaRussa used his entire bullpen in save opportunities, despite Eckersley's quest for the single-season record. A far cry from the shenanigans in the Bronx when Righetti broke Bruce Sutter's record. . . . Career totals: 103 BBs, 183 SOs on first pass through order; 100 BBs, 84 SOs after that.

Ted Power
Royals/Tigers   Throws Right

	W–L	ERA	AB	H	HR	BB	SO	BA	SA	OBA
Season	6-7	5.91	396	121	8	38	57	.306	.447	.367
vs. Left-Handers			176	52	4	19	21	.295	.432	.367
vs. Right-Handers			220	69	4	19	36	.314	.459	.367
Home	3-3	4.69	218	66	3	19	28	.303	.422	.358
Road	3-4	7.48	178	55	5	19	29	.309	.478	.378
Grass	3-2	6.69	151	42	4	15	25	.278	.411	.349
Artificial Turf	3-5	5.40	245	79	4	23	32	.322	.469	.379
April	1-0	5.40	30	8	1	2	4	.267	.433	.303
May	0-1	7.16	69	24	2	7	6	.348	.522	.418
June	3-0	2.22	106	25	1	7	19	.236	.330	.283
July	1-3	14.67	71	30	3	10	8	.423	.690	.494
August	0-2	2.25	45	11	0	4	7	.244	.356	.300
Sept./Oct.	1-1	5.79	75	23	1	8	13	.307	.373	.373
Leading Off Inn.			95	26	0	8	9	.274	.379	.343
Runners On			180	57	6	19	31	.317	.483	.377
Runners/Scor. Pos.			95	30	3	14	17	.316	.474	.395
Runners On/2 Out			64	14	1	6	14	.219	.313	.286
Scor. Pos./2 Out			35	6	0	5	8	.171	.171	.275
Late Inning Pressure			45	11	0	5	2	.244	.289	.327
Leading Off			11	1	0	1	0	.091	.091	.231
Runners On			19	3	0	3	1	.158	.158	.261
Runners/Scor. Pos.			9	1	0	2	1	.111	.111	.250
First 9 Batters			189	59	4	17	35	.312	.471	.373
Second 9 Batters			131	43	4	10	15	.328	.511	.373
All Batters Thereafter			76	19	0	11	7	.250	.276	.345

Loves to face: Johnny Ray (.138, 4-for-29)
Hates to face: Lance Parrish (.500, 3-for-6, 2 HR)
Ground outs-to-air outs ratio: 0.83 last season, 0.85 for career. . . .
Additional statistics: 8 double-play ground outs in 90 opportunities, 26 doubles, 3 triples in 99.0 innings last season. . . . Allowed 15 first-inning runs in 14 starts. . . . Batting support: 4.93 runs per start. . . . Record of 3–5 (6.42 ERA) in 14 starts, 3–2 (4.83) in 12 relief appearances. . . . Opposing ground-ball hitters batted .256, fly-ballers hit .344. . . . Despite last season, left-handed opponents have still outhit right-handers by 43 points for his career (.287 to .244). . . . ERA and opponents' batting average have both risen in each of the last three seasons. Opponents' batting averages, year by year since 1985: .227, .245, .267, .306.

Jeff Reardon
Minnesota Twins   Throws Right

	W–L	ERA	AB	H	HR	BB	SO	BA	SA	OBA
Season	2-4	2.47	277	68	6	15	56	.245	.357	.288
vs. Left-Handers			148	39	2	10	23	.264	.338	.313
vs. Right-Handers			129	29	4	5	33	.225	.380	.259
Home	1-4	2.58	142	30	3	9	27	.211	.310	.263
Road	1-0	2.34	135	38	3	6	29	.281	.407	.315
Grass	1-0	3.13	95	30	2	6	23	.316	.463	.359
Artificial Turf	1-4	2.16	182	38	4	9	33	.209	.302	.250
April	0-1	1.64	41	8	2	5	9	.195	.366	.298
May	0-1	3.21	50	12	1	1	7	.240	.400	.250
June	0-0	0.93	36	7	0	0	6	.194	.222	.194
July	0-1	3.75	45	10	0	5	14	.222	.267	.314
August	1-1	4.63	48	15	2	2	11	.313	.500	.340
Sept./Oct.	1-0	0.61	57	16	1	2	9	.281	.351	.305
Leading Off Inn.			54	15	2	4	14	.278	.463	.328
Runners On			142	32	3	9	26	.225	.324	.279
Runners/Scor. Pos.			97	21	3	8	20	.216	.361	.280
Runners On/2 Out			71	13	1	5	14	.183	.268	.247
Scor. Pos./2 Out			51	9	1	5	9	.176	.294	.250
Late Inning Pressure			182	45	5	10	29	.247	.368	.289
Leading Off			34	8	2	3	8	.235	.441	.297
Runners On			93	21	2	6	11	.226	.323	.277
Runners/Scor. Pos.			65	14	2	5	7	.215	.354	.268
First 9 Batters			274	68	6	15	55	.248	.361	.291
Second 9 Batters			3	0	0	0	1	.000	.000	.000
All Batters Thereafter			0	0	0	0	0	—	—	—

Loves to face: Cory Snyder (0-for-7, 6 SO)
Hates to face: Nick Esasky (.750, 3-for-4, 2 HR)
Ground outs-to-air outs ratio: 0.33 last season, 0.55 for career. . . .
Additional statistics: 3 double-play ground outs in 59 opportunities, 13 doubles, 0 triples in 73.0 innings last season. . . . Led A.L. with 42 saves. Only one other pitcher has hit the 30-mark in four consecutive seasons: Lee Smith, whose streak lives no more. . . . Twins beat the Mariners eight times, Reardon saved seven. . . . Had never committed a balk until last season, when he was called for three. . . . Has pitched in 582 games in his career, all in relief. . . . Career ERA of 2.93 is lowest of any active A.L. pitcher (minimum: 800 IP). . . . Appearances year by year since 1985: 63, 62, 63, 63. Last season's total of 73 innings was his lowest since 1981. (The strike strikes again!)

Jerry Reed
Seattle Mariners   Throws Right

	W–L	ERA	AB	H	HR	BB	SO	BA	SA	OBA
Season	1-1	3.96	320	82	8	33	48	.256	.391	.325
vs. Left-Handers			121	43	4	19	9	.355	.537	.437
vs. Right-Handers			199	39	4	14	39	.196	.302	.252
Home	0-1	3.31	184	50	5	23	25	.272	.424	.351
Road	1-0	4.82	136	32	3	10	23	.235	.346	.289
Grass	1-0	4.99	112	27	3	8	21	.241	.339	.293
Artificial Turf	0-1	3.40	208	55	5	25	27	.264	.418	.342
April	1-1	4.30	49	9	4	3	9	.184	.490	.222
May	0-0	6.14	57	17	1	5	9	.298	.386	.369
June	0-0	2.08	62	14	1	5	10	.226	.371	.284
July	0-0	1.04	57	10	0	7	9	.175	.211	.262
August	0-0	6.61	72	25	2	9	7	.347	.514	.420
Sept./Oct.	0-0	4.50	23	7	0	4	4	.304	.304	.393
Leading Off Inn.			68	17	3	5	7	.250	.441	.301
Runners On			147	40	4	21	26	.272	.408	.360
Runners/Scor. Pos.			93	29	3	16	20	.312	.484	.405
Runners On/2 Out			70	20	2	12	12	.286	.400	.390
Scor. Pos./2 Out			49	14	1	11	10	.286	.388	.417
Late Inning Pressure			67	16	3	9	10	.239	.388	.338
Leading Off			17	5	1	2	1	.294	.471	.368
Runners On			23	4	1	6	4	.174	.304	.367
Runners/Scor. Pos.			10	3	1	4	4	.300	.600	.533
First 9 Batters			259	66	8	26	38	.255	.402	.317
Second 9 Batters			58	16	0	7	9	.276	.362	.373
All Batters Thereafter			3	0	0	0	1	.000	.000	.000

Loves to face: Carlton Fisk (.083, 1-for-12, 1 HR)
Hates to face: Rich Gedman (.444, 4-for-9, 2 HR)
Ground outs-to-air outs ratio: 1.27 last season, 1.16 for career. . . .
Additional statistics: 9 double-play ground outs in 64 opportunities, 15 doubles, 2 triples in 86.1 innings last season. . . . Mariners had a record of 8–38 in games in which he appeared. At one point, they lost 26 consecutive games in which Reed was summoned from the pen. How's that for a confidence builder? . . . Opposing ground-ball hitters batted .218, fly-ballers hit .283. . . . Left-handers hit 159 points higher than right-handers last season, largest difference in majors (minimum: 100 AB each way). Career averages: .299 by left-handers, .234 by right-handers. . . . Record of 6–3 with a 3.60 ERA in more than 200 innings over past three seasons. Not bad.

Jerry Reuss
Chicago White Sox   Throws Left

	W–L	ERA	AB	H	HR	BB	SO	BA	SA	OBA
Season	13-9	3.44	696	183	15	43	73	.263	.375	.307
vs. Left-Handers			94	25	3	5	7	.266	.415	.314
vs. Right-Handers			602	158	12	38	66	.262	.369	.306
Home	7-4	3.72	385	101	7	30	51	.262	.358	.313
Road	6-5	3.10	311	82	8	13	22	.264	.395	.300
Grass	11-6	3.33	570	152	10	39	70	.267	.363	.314
Artificial Turf	2-3	3.93	126	31	5	4	3	.246	.429	.275
April	1-1	4.91	43	12	0	1	5	.279	.349	.295
May	2-1	2.38	122	26	2	8	18	.213	.361	.258
June	3-2	3.09	121	30	3	7	13	.248	.355	.287
July	1-3	6.32	127	44	5	15	18	.346	.504	.413
August	3-1	3.48	134	40	3	4	3	.299	.425	.329
Sept./Oct.	3-1	1.98	149	31	2	8	16	.208	.255	.253
Leading Off Inn.			173	41	2	14	14	.237	.312	.294
Runners On			278	71	7	15	33	.255	.378	.294
Runners/Scor. Pos.			143	39	6	7	13	.273	.448	.303
Runners On/2 Out			111	26	3	6	10	.234	.387	.280
Scor. Pos./2 Out			65	17	3	2	3	.262	.477	.294
Late Inning Pressure			57	10	1	2	8	.175	.263	.203
Leading Off			15	3	1	1	0	.200	.467	.250
Runners On			13	2	0	1	2	.154	.154	.214
Runners/Scor. Pos.			9	1	0	0	1	.111	.111	.111
First 9 Batters			252	59	4	19	34	.234	.329	.288
Second 9 Batters			235	69	4	13	20	.294	.391	.335
All Batters Thereafter			209	55	7	11	19	.263	.411	.299

Loves to face: Paul Molitor (.154, 2-for-13)
Hates to face: Alan Trammell (.750, 6-for-8, 1 HR)
Ground outs-to-air outs ratio: 1.48 last season, 1.88 for career. . . .
Additional statistics: 25 double-play ground outs in 145 opportunities, 29 doubles, 2 triples in 183.0 innings last season. . . . Allowed 12 first-inning runs in 29 starts. Didn't allow a first-inning home run. . . . Batting support: 4.48 runs per start. . . . Allowed one HR per 61 at-bats on first two passes through the order, one per 30 AB after that. . . . Made pro debut as teammate of Ted Simmons on Sarasota team that finished last in 1967 Gulf Coast league. ERA leader: Dave Goltz. . . . Made big-league debut on September 27, 1969. Other pitchers active in 1988 who debuted in 1960s: Carlton, Garber, John, Joe Niekro, Ryan, Sutton. Reuss should make the four-decade list; the rest are odds-on not to.

Rick Rhoden
New York Yankees — Throws Right

	W–L	ERA	AB	H	HR	BB	SO	BA	SA	OBA
Season	12-12	4.20	767	206	20	56	94	.269	.405	.322
vs. Left-Handers			411	115	10	36	43	.280	.409	.340
vs. Right-Handers			356	91	10	20	51	.256	.402	.300
Home	8-8	3.90	474	119	13	26	59	.251	.380	.298
Road	4-4	4.73	293	87	7	30	35	.297	.447	.359
Grass	10-10	4.20	645	171	18	46	82	.265	.403	.319
Artificial Turf	2-2	4.25	122	35	2	10	12	.287	.418	.336
April	1-3	6.04	104	28	3	8	15	.269	.423	.319
May	1-1	4.35	45	15	1	1	4	.333	.444	.348
June	1-2	3.97	134	38	3	11	17	.284	.425	.331
July	4-0	2.90	151	37	1	9	21	.245	.331	.286
August	1-4	5.40	163	45	5	13	18	.276	.429	.337
Sept./Oct.	4-2	3.38	170	43	7	14	19	.253	.412	.326
Leading Off Inn.			200	48	2	7	19	.240	.310	.269
Runners On			299	82	12	31	41	.274	.448	.340
Runners/Scor. Pos.			157	46	7	22	22	.293	.484	.370
Runners On/2 Out			131	31	5	11	22	.237	.374	.296
Scor. Pos./2 Out			76	16	2	8	14	.211	.329	.286
Late Inning Pressure			54	14	1	4	9	.259	.389	.310
Leading Off			17	6	0	0	2	.353	.471	.353
Runners On			18	4	1	4	3	.222	.389	.364
Runners/Scor. Pos.			10	4	1	3	0	.400	.700	.538
First 9 Batters			242	70	6	18	34	.289	.426	.342
Second 9 Batters			234	63	6	18	29	.269	.397	.324
All Batters Thereafter			291	73	8	20	31	.251	.395	.303

Loves to face: Mike LaValliere (.111, 2-for-18)
Hates to face: Mike Marshall (.391, 9-for-23, 2 HR)
Ground outs-to-air outs ratio: 1.14 last season, 1.32 for career. . . .
Additional statistics: 19 double-play ground outs in 147 opportunities, 41 doubles, 2 triples in 197.0 innings last season. . . . Allowed 31 first-inning runs (most in majors) in 30 starts. . . . Batting support: 4.33 runs per start. . . . Pitched at least 200 innings in each of his last five seasons with Pittsburgh, but failed to reach that mark in either of his two seasons in New York. . . . His only shutout in two years with the Yankees was a 3-hitter against Minnesota on opening day 1988. . . . Career record of 17–7 against the Cubs, including nine wins in his last three seasons with the Pirates. . . . The only pitcher whose left-handed opponents have outhit righties in each of the last 11 seasons.

Dave Righetti
New York Yankees — Throws Left

	W–L	ERA	AB	H	HR	BB	SO	BA	SA	OBA
Season	5-4	3.52	335	86	5	37	70	.257	.358	.332
vs. Left-Handers			86	24	2	9	19	.279	.442	.347
vs. Right-Handers			249	62	3	28	51	.249	.329	.327
Home	4-1	2.66	178	39	2	18	43	.219	.309	.294
Road	1-3	4.54	157	47	3	19	27	.299	.414	.375
Grass	4-3	3.67	295	76	4	31	62	.258	.356	.330
Artificial Turf	1-1	2.45	40	10	1	6	8	.250	.375	.348
April	1-0	3.00	49	13	1	4	10	.265	.347	.321
May	0-0	1.38	46	9	1	7	7	.196	.283	.302
June	2-0	6.92	53	15	1	9	6	.283	.434	.387
July	0-1	1.93	53	13	1	9	12	.245	.358	.365
August	2-2	5.65	57	17	1	3	10	.298	.386	.333
Sept./Oct.	0-1	2.61	77	19	0	5	25	.247	.338	.293
Leading Off Inn.			67	13	1	5	15	.194	.313	.250
Runners On			176	50	2	21	36	.284	.358	.360
Runners/Scor. Pos.			119	31	1	15	24	.261	.361	.343
Runners On/2 Out			87	25	1	10	15	.287	.356	.361
Scor. Pos./2 Out			60	18	1	7	9	.300	.400	.373
Late Inning Pressure			243	56	4	25	50	.230	.333	.305
Leading Off			53	10	0	4	13	.189	.283	.246
Runners On			117	25	2	13	23	.214	.282	.292
Runners/Scor. Pos.			75	13	1	9	15	.173	.227	.262
First 9 Batters			302	82	5	34	62	.272	.374	.347
Second 9 Batters			33	4	0	3	8	.121	.212	.194
All Batters Thereafter			0	0	0	0	0	——	——	——

Loves to face: Jack Howell (0-for-8, 7 SO)
Hates to face: Wally Joyner (.429, 3-for-7, 4 BB, 1 HR)
Ground outs-to-air outs ratio: 0.84 last season, 1.04 for career. . . .
Additional statistics: 8 double-play ground outs in 79 opportunities, 13 doubles, 3 triples in 87.0 innings last season. . . . Opposition batted 96 points lower in Late-Inning Pressure Situations than in other at-bats, 3d-largest difference among A.L. relievers last season (minimum: 50 AB both ways). . . . Has saved 162 games over past five seasons, to rank second to Jeff Reardon (172). . . . Career records: 42–17 at the Stadium, 21–32 elsewhere. . . . Over past three seasons, opposing left-handers have outslugged right-handers by 95 points (.410 to .315). Only 18 other pitchers have had a larger difference in that direction (minimum: 250 AB each way). All are right-handers.

Jeff M. Robinson
Detroit Tigers — Throws Right

	W–L	ERA	AB	H	HR	BB	SO	BA	SA	OBA
Season	13-6	2.98	615	121	19	72	114	.197	.332	.282
vs. Left-Handers			310	61	9	42	59	.197	.335	.291
vs. Right-Handers			305	60	10	30	55	.197	.328	.272
Home	9-2	2.19	341	57	8	33	74	.167	.276	.242
Road	4-4	4.05	274	64	11	39	40	.234	.401	.328
Grass	11-4	2.70	481	90	14	56	95	.187	.314	.274
Artificial Turf	2-2	4.08	134	31	5	16	19	.231	.396	.309
April	2-2	4.32	94	24	3	13	13	.255	.415	.339
May	3-0	4.80	112	24	5	15	23	.214	.393	.307
June	3-1	1.59	141	30	3	10	35	.213	.333	.266
July	4-1	1.77	133	15	3	13	19	.113	.195	.201
August	1-2	3.44	135	28	5	21	24	.207	.356	.312
Sept./Oct.			0	0	0	0	0	——	——	——
Leading Off Inn.			164	34	5	14	32	.207	.329	.274
Runners On			217	38	6	30	42	.175	.313	.272
Runners/Scor. Pos.			102	17	2	16	24	.167	.284	.272
Runners On/2 Out			90	12	2	15	16	.133	.289	.264
Scor. Pos./2 Out			50	6	0	9	10	.120	.180	.267
Late Inning Pressure			81	16	0	5	16	.198	.272	.244
Leading Off			26	4	0	1	4	.154	.231	.185
Runners On			22	4	0	1	6	.182	.318	.217
Runners/Scor. Pos.			9	1	0	1	3	.111	.111	.200
First 9 Batters			180	37	9	30	34	.206	.400	.326
Second 9 Batters			186	35	3	20	38	.188	.280	.266
All Batters Thereafter			249	49	7	22	42	.197	.321	.259

Loves to face: Bill Buckner (0-for-13)
Hates to face: Pete Incaviglia (3-for-3)
Ground outs-to-air outs ratio: 0.90 last season, 1.01 for career. . . .
Additional statistics: 10 double-play ground outs in 120 opportunities, 20 doubles, 3 triples in 172.0 innings last season. . . . Allowed 9 first-inning runs in 23 starts. . . . Batting support: 4.43 runs per start. . . . ERA dropped by more than two runs from 5.37 mark in 1987. . . . The A.L.'s 17 qualifying .300 hitters batted .169 against him (15-for-89), their lowest mark vs. any pitcher (minimum: 50 AB). . . . Career records: 16–5 vs. A.L. West, 6–7 vs. A.L. East. . . . Career stats: 22–12, 4.00 ERA. Contemporary pitchers with similar figures at a comparable age: Mike Nagy (20–13, 4.15 through 1974), Joe Cowley (22–10, 3.93 through 1985), Jim Deshaies (23–12, 4.09 through 1987).

Jeff Russell
Texas Rangers — Throws Right

	W–L	ERA	AB	H	HR	BB	SO	BA	SA	OBA
Season	10-9	3.82	713	183	15	66	88	.257	.356	.324
vs. Left-Handers			370	108	10	45	41	.292	.411	.370
vs. Right-Handers			343	75	5	21	47	.219	.297	.273
Home	6-6	3.75	410	107	9	33	43	.261	.356	.321
Road	4-3	3.91	303	76	6	33	45	.251	.356	.328
Grass	8-7	3.78	600	153	12	52	74	.255	.345	.319
Artificial Turf	2-2	3.99	113	30	3	14	14	.265	.416	.354
April	0-0	1.93	34	8	1	4	3	.235	.382	.325
May	4-0	2.51	106	25	2	9	14	.236	.292	.296
June	3-1	3.57	149	35	4	14	21	.235	.322	.301
July	1-2	4.32	133	39	3	13	15	.293	.391	.361
August	2-3	4.50	158	38	2	7	18	.241	.348	.284
Sept./Oct.	0-3	4.37	133	38	3	19	17	.286	.414	.381
Leading Off Inn.			179	37	2	13	20	.207	.274	.260
Runners On			290	91	9	26	34	.314	.441	.375
Runners/Scor. Pos.			169	52	5	20	25	.308	.426	.385
Runners On/2 Out			124	41	1	10	16	.331	.387	.390
Scor. Pos./2 Out			83	27	0	9	11	.325	.349	.398
Late Inning Pressure			89	20	0	8	10	.225	.281	.296
Leading Off			25	5	0	1	3	.200	.240	.231
Runners On			33	9	0	2	4	.273	.333	.333
Runners/Scor. Pos.			24	5	0	1	4	.208	.250	.269
First 9 Batters			248	67	8	22	29	.270	.407	.338
Second 9 Batters			198	47	1	17	21	.237	.288	.295
All Batters Thereafter			267	69	6	27	38	.258	.360	.333

Loves to face: Brook Jacoby (0-for-10)
Hates to face: Mike Greenwell (.667, 4-for-6, 2 BB, 2 HR)
Ground outs-to-air outs ratio: 1.29 last season, 1.16 for career. . . .
Additional statistics: 18 double-play ground outs in 139 opportunities, 26 doubles, 0 triples in 188.2 innings last season. . . . Allowed 11 first-inning runs in 24 starts. . . . Batting support: 4.29 runs per start. . . . Rangers lost all six of his no-decision starts. . . . Opponents had only three hits in 16 at-bats with bases loaded, but all three hits were grand slams. . . . Third A.L. pitcher in last 20 years to allow slams in consecutive games. The others: Dave LaPoint (1986) and John Henry Johnson (1979). . . . Opponents' career average is .210 in Late-Inning Pressure Situations, .274 in other at-bats, 2d-largest difference over past 10 seasons (minimum: 250 LIPS AB).

Bret Saberhagen

Throws Right

Kansas City Royals	W–L	ERA	AB	H	HR	BB	SO	BA	SA	OBA
Season	14-16	3.80	1008	271	18	59	171	.269	.400	.309
vs. Left-Handers			530	130	6	42	104	.245	.343	.299
vs. Right-Handers			478	141	12	17	67	.295	.462	.320
Home	6-9	4.36	510	146	7	23	80	.286	.425	.315
Road	8-7	3.24	498	125	11	36	91	.251	.373	.302
Grass	6-5	2.42	359	83	5	21	70	.231	.326	.276
Artificial Turf	8-11	4.61	649	188	13	38	101	.290	.441	.327
April	3-2	3.74	169	46	6	6	30	.272	.432	.299
May	3-3	3.54	180	45	1	13	32	.250	.361	.294
June	4-1	2.68	149	37	2	11	21	.248	.349	.302
July	1-4	5.63	162	45	4	8	24	.278	.444	.310
August	2-3	3.11	184	54	1	8	31	.293	.386	.325
Sept./Oct.	1-3	4.25	164	44	4	13	33	.268	.427	.322
Leading Off Inn.			252	59	4	14	46	.234	.369	.280
Runners On			398	118	6	27	61	.296	.422	.333
Runners/Scor. Pos.			230	63	3	20	36	.274	.396	.319
Runners On/2 Out			170	37	2	12	31	.218	.329	.269
Scor. Pos./2 Out			102	25	2	9	18	.245	.402	.306
Late Inning Pressure			154	36	2	3	23	.234	.364	.252
Leading Off			44	12	0	0	7	.273	.455	.289
Runners On			47	11	0	2	5	.234	.277	.260
Runners/Scor. Pos.			30	5	0	1	3	.167	.233	.188
First 9 Batters			288	83	5	23	60	.288	.420	.342
Second 9 Batters			282	72	4	20	43	.255	.351	.302
All Batters Thereafter			438	116	9	16	68	.265	.418	.291

Loves to face: Ron Hassey (0-for-10)
Hates to face: Steve Buechele (.636, 7-for-11, 1 HR)
Ground outs-to-air outs ratio: 1.03 last season, 1.16 for career. . . .
Additional statistics: 20 double-play ground outs in 177 opportunities, 46 doubles, 16 triples in 260.2 innings last season. . . . Allowed 21 first-inning runs in 35 starts. . . . Batting support: 3.80 runs per start. . . . The only starting pitcher in the majors (minimum: 800 IP) with a career average of less than two walks per nine innings (1.81). . . . Career record of 38–16 in odd-numbered years, 31–39 in even-numbered years. . . . Opposing batters have a career BA of .156 with runners in scoring position in Late-Inning Pressure Situations (12-for-77, no HRs). . . . Despite 69 career wins, he's younger than 148 of the 242 rookies who played last season, including both Weiss and Sabo.

Mike Schooler

Throws Right

Seattle Mariners	W–L	ERA	AB	H	HR	BB	SO	BA	SA	OBA
Season	5-8	3.54	184	45	4	24	54	.245	.337	.330
vs. Left-Handers			103	29	3	17	33	.282	.408	.374
vs. Right-Handers			81	16	1	7	21	.198	.247	.270
Home	3-2	3.74	83	20	2	5	28	.241	.337	.286
Road	2-6	3.38	101	25	2	19	26	.248	.337	.364
Grass	2-6	3.24	96	24	2	16	23	.250	.344	.354
Artificial Turf	3-2	3.86	88	21	2	8	31	.239	.330	.303
April			0	0	0	0	0	—	—	—
May			0	0	0	0	0	—	—	—
June	1-2	3.72	35	7	0	8	10	.200	.286	.341
July	1-2	3.77	51	12	2	3	20	.235	.373	.273
August	2-2	2.03	58	17	2	3	12	.293	.397	.339
Sept./Oct.	1-2	4.91	40	9	0	10	12	.225	.250	.373
Leading Off Inn.			36	8	1	6	9	.222	.306	.333
Runners On			94	30	2	13	27	.319	.426	.396
Runners/Scor. Pos.			62	18	1	9	19	.290	.387	.373
Runners On/2 Out			44	13	1	4	13	.295	.409	.354
Scor. Pos./2 Out			34	10	1	4	10	.294	.412	.368
Late Inning Pressure			133	40	4	21	32	.301	.421	.392
Leading Off			26	8	1	5	6	.308	.423	.419
Runners On			71	27	2	13	16	.380	.507	.466
Runners/Scor. Pos.			47	15	1	9	11	.319	.426	.417
First 9 Batters			175	43	4	23	53	.246	.343	.332
Second 9 Batters			9	2	0	1	1	.222	.222	.300
All Batters Thereafter			0	0	0	0	0	—	—	—

Loves to face: Geno Petralli (0-for-5, 3 SO)
Hates to face: Larry Sheets (2-for-2, 1 HR)
Ground outs-to-air outs ratio: 0.98 last season, his first in majors. . . . Additional statistics: 3 double-play ground outs in 55 opportunities, 5 doubles, 0 triples in 48.1 innings last season. . . . Only two rookies recorded more than four saves last season: Bryan Harvey (17) and Schooler (15). . . . Tied for 8th in A.L. with 11 saves after the All-Star break. . . . Didn't allow a hit in seven consecutive appearances in September, facing 28 batters during that streak, and saving shutouts for both Mark Langston and Erik Hanson in the process. . . . In Late-Inning Pressure Situations, opponents batted 170 points higher with runners on base than with the bases empty, largest difference in A.L. over past 14 years (minimum: 50 AB each way).

Dave Schmidt

Throws Right

Baltimore Orioles	W–L	ERA	AB	H	HR	BB	SO	BA	SA	OBA
Season	8-5	3.40	492	129	14	38	67	.262	.390	.317
vs. Left-Handers			252	67	7	13	36	.266	.393	.300
vs. Right-Handers			240	62	7	25	31	.258	.388	.335
Home	5-5	4.36	253	72	6	24	43	.285	.407	.350
Road	3-0	2.40	239	57	8	14	24	.238	.372	.281
Grass	7-5	3.30	419	111	10	36	56	.265	.375	.326
Artificial Turf	1-0	4.00	73	18	4	2	11	.247	.479	.263
April	0-1	5.00	75	21	1	8	8	.280	.387	.357
May	2-1	2.74	82	19	3	3	13	.232	.366	.267
June	1-1	4.40	53	15	2	9	7	.283	.434	.387
July	0-0	4.12	73	20	2	5	12	.274	.384	.313
August	4-0	1.95	140	33	4	7	14	.236	.350	.277
Sept./Oct.	1-2	4.08	69	21	2	6	13	.304	.478	.355
Leading Off Inn.			114	36	3	7	16	.316	.412	.361
Runners On			217	51	5	18	31	.235	.359	.296
Runners/Scor. Pos.			112	28	3	14	19	.250	.402	.336
Runners On/2 Out			95	23	2	12	16	.242	.358	.333
Scor. Pos./2 Out			52	13	2	10	8	.250	.404	.381
Late Inning Pressure			99	27	3	10	18	.273	.384	.345
Leading Off			27	11	1	1	5	.407	.519	.429
Runners On			44	9	1	5	8	.205	.273	.300
Runners/Scor. Pos.			24	5	1	5	6	.208	.333	.367
First 9 Batters			290	78	8	21	43	.269	.400	.320
Second 9 Batters			144	37	4	12	16	.257	.368	.314
All Batters Thereafter			58	14	2	5	8	.241	.397	.313

Loves to face: Steve Buechele (0-for-13)
Hates to face: Jesse Barfield (.500, 8-for-16, 1 HR)
Ground outs-to-air outs ratio: 1.33 last season, 1.43 for career. . . .
Additional statistics: 17 double-play ground outs in 102 opportunities, 17 doubles, 2 triples in 129.2 innings last season. . . . Record of 5–2 (2.63 ERA) in nine starts, 3–3 (3.96) in 32 relief appearances. . . . One of two A.L. pitchers involved in combined shutouts as both a starter and reliever. The other: Steve Farr. . . . Has started 37 games in his career, completed three of them. All were shutouts. . . . Opposing batters have hit only .169 with the bases loaded (10-for-59), with two walks and no extra-base hits. No pitcher has faced more batters with the bags full over the past 14 years without allowing an XBH. . . . Dave allowed more home runs than Mike hit, for first time in his career. Congrats!

Jeff Sellers

Throws Right

Boston Red Sox	W–L	ERA	AB	H	HR	BB	SO	BA	SA	OBA
Season	1-7	4.83	332	89	9	56	70	.268	.395	.379
vs. Left-Handers			157	50	2	35	18	.318	.414	.443
vs. Right-Handers			175	39	7	21	52	.223	.377	.317
Home	1-2	4.68	165	48	6	26	26	.291	.442	.394
Road	0-5	4.98	167	41	3	30	44	.246	.347	.364
Grass	1-5	4.54	275	74	8	43	55	.269	.400	.372
Artificial Turf	0-2	6.28	57	15	1	13	15	.263	.368	.408
April	0-1	2.40	55	10	1	7	15	.182	.236	.274
May	0-4	5.80	139	39	4	27	27	.281	.403	.405
June	0-1	6.57	53	19	1	14	11	.358	.509	.493
July			0	0	0	0	0	—	—	—
August	1-0	4.26	50	15	2	5	5	.300	.500	.364
Sept./Oct.	0-1	3.60	35	6	1	3	12	.171	.286	.256
Leading Off Inn.			81	18	4	9	16	.222	.370	.300
Runners On			158	46	3	24	28	.291	.418	.404
Runners/Scor. Pos.			91	27	1	21	20	.297	.418	.434
Runners On/2 Out			67	19	1	17	12	.284	.418	.435
Scor. Pos./2 Out			43	16	1	16	9	.372	.558	.550
Late Inning Pressure			27	7	2	4	3	.259	.481	.355
Leading Off			9	1	1	0	2	.111	.444	.111
Runners On			7	1	0	1	1	.143	.143	.250
Runners/Scor. Pos.			3	1	0	1	1	.333	.333	.500
First 9 Batters			137	31	2	19	38	.226	.314	.325
Second 9 Batters			103	34	4	25	20	.330	.515	.465
All Batters Thereafter			92	24	3	12	12	.261	.380	.352

Loves to face: Pete Incaviglia (0-for-6, 5 SO)
Hates to face: Dick Schofield (.800, 4-for-5, 2 BB, 1 HR)
Ground outs-to-air outs ratio: 1.14 last season, 1.18 for career. . . .
Additional statistics: 9 double-play ground outs in 72 opportunities, 13 doubles, 1 triple in 85.2 innings last season. . . . Allowed 5 first-inning runs in 12 starts. . . . Batting support: 3.08 runs per start. . . . Record of 0–7 (4.39 ERA) in 12 starts, 1–0 (6.50) in six relief appearances. . . . Lost his first six decisions in 1988, the longest losing streak by a Boston pitcher last season. . . . Batting average by opposing left-handers was a career high; by right-handers, a career low. . . . One of three pitchers whose opponents have hit at least 25 points higher with runners in scoring position than otherwise in each of the last four seasons. The others: Joel Davis and Pat Clemens.

Steve Shields

New York Yankees — Throws Right

	W–L	ERA	AB	H	HR	BB	SO	BA	SA	OBA
Season	5-5	4.37	322	96	8	30	55	.298	.425	.360
vs. Left-Handers			134	45	4	18	24	.336	.507	.416
vs. Right-Handers			188	51	4	12	31	.271	.367	.317
Home	3-0	3.79	151	42	3	17	24	.278	.404	.349
Road	2-5	4.93	171	54	5	13	31	.316	.444	.369
Grass	4-5	4.39	251	75	4	26	40	.299	.402	.367
Artificial Turf	1-0	4.32	71	21	4	4	15	.296	.507	.333
April			0	0	0	0	0	—	—	—
May	0-2	6.28	57	15	2	4	11	.263	.386	.323
June	1-0	2.16	58	13	1	5	8	.224	.293	.286
July	0-1	1.23	56	15	0	4	11	.268	.268	.317
August	2-1	7.59	98	41	5	10	17	.418	.684	.468
Sept./Oct.	2-1	3.52	53	12	0	7	8	.226	.302	.323
Leading Off Inn.			73	18	3	4	16	.247	.397	.286
Runners On			150	47	2	17	24	.313	.427	.382
Runners/Scor. Pos.			95	27	0	15	18	.284	.379	.375
Runners On/2 Out			64	20	2	9	12	.313	.469	.405
Scor. Pos./2 Out			42	12	0	8	8	.286	.357	.400
Late Inning Pressure			108	25	3	9	18	.231	.324	.297
Leading Off			31	6	1	1	8	.194	.290	.219
Runners On			38	7	1	3	5	.184	.263	.244
Runners/Scor. Pos.			15	2	0	3	3	.133	.133	.278
First 9 Batters			252	71	5	22	45	.282	.397	.337
Second 9 Batters			68	25	3	7	10	.368	.544	.442
All Batters Thereafter			2	0	0	1	0	.000	.000	.333

Loves to face: Jose Canseco (0-for-8)
Hates to face: Kirby Puckett (.833, 5-for-6, 2 HR)
Ground outs-to-air outs ratio: 1.67 last season, 1.64 for career. . . .
Additional statistics: 16 double-play ground outs in 73 opportunities, 11 doubles, 3 triples in 82.1 innings last season. . . . Allowed an average of 13.99 base runners per nine innings, 2d highest among A.L. relievers (min: 80 IP). . . . Faced 30 batters protecting leads of three runs or fewer in 8th inning or later. Other Yankees relievers: Righetti, 183; Guante, 69; Allen, 25; Stoddard, 25. . . . Opposing batters hit 100 points lower in LIP Situations than otherwise, the 2d-largest difference among A.L. relievers (minimum: 50 AB both ways). . . . Opposing batters have a career .333 BA with runners on base, tying Rich Hinton for highest in majors over the last 14 years (minimum: 350 AB).

Lee Smith

Boston Red Sox — Throws Right

	W–L	ERA	AB	H	HR	BB	SO	BA	SA	OBA
Season	4-5	2.80	320	72	7	37	96	.225	.338	.306
vs. Left-Handers			164	38	3	21	47	.232	.317	.321
vs. Right-Handers			156	34	4	16	49	.218	.359	.289
Home	3-2	2.66	179	37	4	15	58	.207	.318	.270
Road	1-3	2.97	141	35	3	22	38	.248	.362	.348
Grass	4-3	2.38	283	58	5	34	92	.205	.297	.291
Artificial Turf	0-2	6.75	37	14	2	3	4	.378	.649	.425
April	2-1	0.84	40	8	2	6	15	.200	.400	.304
May	0-1	6.00	36	11	0	5	6	.306	.389	.381
June	0-0	2.12	67	15	1	9	18	.224	.284	.316
July	2-2	5.94	67	20	3	6	21	.299	.493	.360
August	0-0	0.84	35	3	1	2	13	.086	.200	.135
Sept./Oct.	0-1	1.37	75	15	0	9	23	.200	.253	.286
Leading Off Inn.			64	9	0	8	20	.141	.172	.247
Runners On			173	43	7	17	43	.249	.416	.313
Runners/Scor. Pos.			102	21	5	12	29	.206	.422	.284
Runners On/2 Out			84	20	3	6	20	.238	.405	.289
Scor. Pos./2 Out			57	9	1	5	17	.158	.281	.226
Late Inning Pressure			193	46	4	24	60	.238	.368	.323
Leading Off			35	4	0	7	14	.114	.171	.279
Runners On			109	29	4	11	28	.266	.440	.328
Runners/Scor. Pos.			71	15	4	10	20	.211	.465	.301
First 9 Batters			312	71	7	35	92	.228	.340	.306
Second 9 Batters			8	1	0	2	4	.125	.250	.300
All Batters Thereafter			0	0	0	0	0	—	—	—

Loves to face: Dave Bergman (0-for-5, 3 SO)
Hates to face: Kent Hrbek (.750, 3-for-4)
Ground outs-to-air outs ratio: 0.81 last season, 1.18 for career. . . .
Additional statistics: 2 double-play ground outs in 81 opportunities, 11 doubles, 2 triples in 83.2 innings last season. . . . Fifth time in past six years that opposing batters hit below .200 with two outs and runners in scoring position. . . . Hasn't balked since 1983—one of the few balkless streaks to survive last season. . . . Struck out at least one batter in 30 consecutive games, an enormous feat for an enormous relief pitcher. Only one other pitcher had a streak of more than 20 games over the past seven seasons (Mark Eichhorn, 21 games in 1986). . . . The Goose never had a streak longer than 16 games. Some Red Sox fans may remember Dick Radatz's 27-game streak in 1963.

Doug Sisk

Baltimore Orioles — Throws Right

	W–L	ERA	AB	H	HR	BB	SO	BA	SA	OBA
Season	3-3	3.72	356	109	3	45	26	.306	.368	.385
vs. Left-Handers			159	57	1	26	11	.358	.415	.450
vs. Right-Handers			197	52	2	19	15	.264	.330	.329
Home	3-2	3.83	173	50	1	22	10	.289	.347	.371
Road	0-1	3.61	183	59	2	23	16	.322	.388	.399
Grass	3-2	3.96	322	97	3	39	25	.301	.360	.379
Artificial Turf	0-1	1.74	34	12	0	6	1	.353	.441	.439
April	0-1	1.84	49	13	0	5	3	.265	.327	.327
May	1-1	3.38	68	27	0	10	7	.397	.426	.468
June	2-0	4.12	80	24	2	6	6	.300	.413	.356
July	0-0	0.00	21	2	0	2	2	.095	.095	.174
August	0-1	6.63	73	27	0	10	5	.370	.425	.452
Sept./Oct.	0-0	3.38	65	16	1	12	3	.246	.308	.364
Leading Off Inn.			69	16	1	10	9	.232	.290	.338
Runners On			190	64	2	25	11	.337	.400	.413
Runners/Scor. Pos.			120	34	2	17	6	.283	.350	.371
Runners On/2 Out			78	21	0	10	6	.269	.269	.360
Scor. Pos./2 Out			56	9	0	6	4	.161	.161	.254
Late Inning Pressure			65	29	1	13	4	.446	.554	.538
Leading Off			11	3	0	3	3	.273	.273	.467
Runners On			40	22	1	8	0	.550	.650	.612
Runners/Scor. Pos.			28	14	1	5	0	.500	.607	.559
First 9 Batters			294	92	3	37	22	.313	.384	.391
Second 9 Batters			56	15	0	7	4	.268	.286	.349
All Batters Thereafter			6	2	0	1	0	.333	.333	.429

Loves to face: Terry Francona (0-for-10)
Hates to face: Greg Brock (.375, 3-for-8, 1 HR)
Ground outs-to-air outs ratio: 2.66 last season, 2.81 for career. . . .
Additional statistics: 21 double-play ground outs in 103 opportunities, 11 doubles, 1 triple in 94.1 innings last season. . . . Had a streak of 12 walks in between strikeouts, longest in the A.L. . . . Career totals: 255 BBs, 189 SOs, a ratio of 1.35 walks per strikeout. Would it surprise you to learn that among pitchers with at least 500 IP, 111 had ratios higher than Sisk's? And that 33 of them had winning records? And that four of those 33 won more than 100 games (Frank Dwyer, Duke Esper, Brickyard Kennedy, and Ed Stein)? . . . The group had a composite winning percentage of .460. . . . Among the notables: Jim Bagby, Tommy Byrne, Clint Hartung, and Spec Shea. . . . Highest ratio: 3.14, by Ernie Wingard.

Mike Smithson

Boston Red Sox — Throws Right

	W–L	ERA	AB	H	HR	BB	SO	BA	SA	OBA
Season	9-6	5.97	511	149	25	37	73	.292	.489	.345
vs. Left-Handers			282	82	11	20	44	.291	.472	.338
vs. Right-Handers			229	67	14	17	29	.293	.511	.353
Home	7-2	5.89	298	88	13	20	41	.295	.487	.339
Road	2-4	6.08	213	61	12	17	32	.286	.493	.353
Grass	9-5	5.83	460	134	22	32	64	.291	.487	.342
Artificial Turf	0-1	7.30	51	15	3	5	9	.294	.510	.368
April	0-0	9.82	20	8	0	4	1	.400	.450	.500
May	1-1	5.28	60	14	3	2	9	.233	.400	.270
June	2-1	5.63	96	27	7	9	15	.281	.552	.349
July	3-1	3.79	150	40	4	8	22	.267	.393	.315
August	0-2	8.89	108	35	8	8	14	.324	.602	.370
Sept./Oct.	3-1	6.52	77	25	3	6	12	.325	.519	.373
Leading Off Inn.			125	34	5	8	14	.272	.456	.316
Runners On			200	65	11	16	29	.325	.535	.384
Runners/Scor. Pos.			123	37	6	10	21	.301	.472	.360
Runners On/2 Out			87	24	3	7	15	.276	.425	.351
Scor. Pos./2 Out			61	15	3	4	11	.246	.410	.324
Late Inning Pressure			19	7	3	0	2	.368	.947	.368
Leading Off			6	1	0	0	0	.167	.167	.167
Runners On			2	0	0	0	1	.000	.000	.000
Runners/Scor. Pos.			0	0	0	0	0			
First 9 Batters			221	64	11	20	37	.290	.480	.348
Second 9 Batters			171	52	7	6	24	.304	.468	.339
All Batters Thereafter			119	33	7	11	12	.277	.538	.346

Loves to face: Ivan Calderon (.043, 1-for-23)
Hates to face: George Brett (.556, 20-for-36, 2 HR)
Ground outs-to-air outs ratio: 0.81 last season, 1.17 for career. . . .
Additional statistics: 8 DP ground outs in 97 opportunities, 24 doubles, 1 triple in 126.2 innings last season. . . . Allowed 17 first-inning runs in 18 starts, including seven HRs, tying Mike Moore and Jim Clancy for most in majors. . . . Batting support: 5.67 runs per start, 2d highest in A.L. (minimum: 15 GS). . . . Sweet revenge: Allowed only three hits in 34 at-bats to the team that cut him from its 1987 postseason roster. . . . Opposing lefties outhit righties by more than 30 points in each of six previous seasons. . . . One of two pitchers with an ERA over 4.50 in 100 or more innings in each of last three seasons. The other: Scott Bailes. . . . Career record of 5–15 in August, 64–57 in other months.

Bob Stanley
Throws Right

Boston Red Sox	W–L	ERA	AB	H	HR	BB	SO	BA	SA	OBA
Season	6-4	3.19	372	90	6	29	57	.242	.336	.304
vs. Left-Handers			171	45	1	19	23	.263	.339	.332
vs. Right-Handers			201	45	5	10	34	.224	.333	.281
Home	3-2	2.28	208	47	4	10	34	.226	.317	.276
Road	3-2	4.27	164	43	2	19	23	.262	.360	.339
Grass	6-4	3.02	320	77	4	24	54	.241	.325	.303
Artificial Turf	0-0	4.11	52	13	2	5	3	.250	.404	.310
April			0	0	0	0	0	—	—	—
May	1-0	2.35	53	10	2	2	12	.189	.321	.211
June	2-0	5.40	66	19	1	6	7	.288	.364	.373
July	1-0	1.57	78	17	0	7	12	.218	.256	.276
August	1-2	4.44	93	23	2	7	13	.247	.355	.321
Sept./Oct.	1-2	2.42	82	21	1	7	13	.256	.378	.315
Leading Off Inn.			81	21	1	1	10	.259	.358	.268
Runners On			183	45	4	16	29	.246	.355	.311
Runners/Scor. Pos.			104	25	3	12	13	.240	.394	.320
Runners On/2 Out			85	19	2	8	16	.224	.341	.313
Scor. Pos./2 Out			49	11	1	6	9	.224	.367	.333
Late Inning Pressure			146	36	1	14	30	.247	.322	.319
Leading Off			30	8	1	1	5	.267	.433	.290
Runners On			76	18	0	10	18	.237	.289	.330
Runners/Scor. Pos.			44	13	0	7	6	.295	.386	.393
First 9 Batters			316	79	5	26	44	.250	.345	.310
Second 9 Batters			48	8	1	3	11	.167	.271	.259
All Batters Thereafter			8	3	0	0	2	.375	.375	.375

Loves to face: Randy Bush (.063, 1-for-16)
Hates to face: Greg Walker (.643, 9-for-14, 2 HR)
Ground outs-to-air outs ratio: 1.39 last season, 2.18 for career. . . .
Additional statistics: 10 double-play ground outs in 88 opportunities, 15 doubles, 1 triple in 101.2 innings last season. . . . Opposing ground-ball hitters batted .204, fly-ballers hit .271. . . . Has appeared in 594 major-league games without ever getting an at-bat, a major league record. He inherited that distinction from Dan Quisenberry, who finally batted with the Cardinals last season after 573 games in his A.L. career. Record for nonpitchers is 104 games by Charley Finley's favorite pinch runner, Herb Washington. . . . Stanley is now the pitcher with the longest continuous service to his original team. Made his debut on April 16, 1977, three months before Jack Morris debuted with Detroit.

Dave Stewart
Throws Right

Oakland As	W–L	ERA	AB	H	HR	BB	SO	BA	SA	OBA
Season	21-12	3.23	1027	240	14	110	192	.234	.333	.307
vs. Left-Handers			563	126	9	67	111	.224	.323	.305
vs. Right-Handers			464	114	5	43	81	.246	.345	.310
Home	9-5	3.25	470	108	5	45	93	.230	.311	.295
Road	12-7	3.22	557	132	9	65	99	.237	.352	.317
Grass	15-11	3.20	838	193	12	87	159	.230	.329	.303
Artificial Turf	6-1	3.40	189	47	2	23	33	.249	.349	.327
April	6-0	2.98	176	39	1	18	27	.222	.313	.291
May	2-3	3.95	165	41	4	24	17	.248	.394	.344
June	2-3	4.15	163	41	2	18	31	.252	.356	.321
July	3-4	2.38	207	47	4	17	37	.227	.333	.289
August	3-1	2.42	159	31	2	17	35	.195	.277	.277
Sept./Oct.	5-1	3.89	157	41	1	16	45	.261	.325	.326
Leading Off Inn.			258	62	3	27	43	.240	.329	.312
Runners On			431	103	7	51	77	.239	.343	.315
Runners/Scor. Pos.			252	51	2	33	42	.202	.270	.286
Runners On/2 Out			171	32	3	22	28	.187	.304	.280
Scor. Pos./2 Out			115	20	1	14	16	.174	.252	.264
Late Inning Pressure			107	21	0	10	21	.196	.271	.267
Leading Off			32	10	0	3	3	.313	.438	.371
Runners On			36	7	0	5	7	.194	.250	.295
Runners/Scor. Pos.			24	4	0	3	5	.167	.208	.241
First 9 Batters			290	61	2	40	70	.210	.272	.308
Second 9 Batters			308	80	6	21	49	.260	.390	.305
All Batters Thereafter			429	99	6	49	73	.231	.333	.308

Loves to face: Dave Bergman (0-for-16)
Hates to face: Danny Tartabull (.636, 7-for-11, 4 BB, 1 HR)
Ground outs-to-air outs ratio: 0.84 last season, 0.86 for career. . . .
Additional statistics: 15 double-play ground outs in 208 opportunities, 46 doubles, 7 triples in 275.2 innings last season. . . . Allowed 12 first-inning runs in 37 starts. Hasn't allowed a first-inning HR in 49 starts since August 10, 1987. . . . Batting support: 4.76 runs per start. . . . Opposing batters have hit below .200 with two outs and runners in scoring position six times in last eight seasons. . . . Career record of 8–0 vs. the Brewers. Has won his last seven starts vs. Seattle. . . . Has won his last nine decisions during April, after losing the first ten April decisions of his career. . . . No pitcher has won 20 games in three consecutive seasons since Jim Palmer had four in a row (1975–78).

Dave Stieb
Throws Right

Toronto Blue Jays	W–L	ERA	AB	H	HR	BB	SO	BA	SA	OBA
Season	16-8	3.04	748	157	15	79	147	.210	.316	.295
vs. Left-Handers			400	87	8	42	55	.218	.315	.294
vs. Right-Handers			348	70	7	37	92	.201	.316	.296
Home	12-5	2.70	455	88	10	45	92	.193	.297	.277
Road	4-3	3.57	293	69	5	34	55	.235	.345	.322
Grass	4-1	3.18	242	51	1	28	48	.211	.281	.300
Artificial Turf	12-7	2.97	506	106	14	51	99	.209	.332	.293
April	1-3	3.86	99	26	2	11	18	.263	.384	.348
May	6-0	1.99	176	34	2	16	33	.193	.244	.265
June	3-1	4.10	99	25	4	17	24	.253	.475	.378
July	0-3	3.94	111	30	3	7	16	.270	.423	.322
August	2-1	4.24	125	24	4	15	29	.192	.312	.282
Sept./Oct.	4-0	1.50	138	18	0	13	27	.130	.159	.221
Leading Off Inn.			190	41	6	23	32	.216	.363	.313
Runners On			292	67	4	25	47	.229	.308	.298
Runners/Scor. Pos.			160	37	4	13	28	.231	.338	.291
Runners On/2 Out			120	24	2	9	21	.200	.292	.262
Scor. Pos./2 Out			75	15	2	5	13	.200	.307	.250
Late Inning Pressure			56	13	0	5	9	.232	.321	.338
Leading Off			17	3	0	1	4	.176	.353	.222
Runners On			20	5	0	1	2	.250	.250	.375
Runners/Scor. Pos.			10	3	0	0	0	.300	.300	.417
First 9 Batters			248	51	5	36	51	.206	.306	.314
Second 9 Batters			244	46	6	23	53	.189	.311	.266
All Batters Thereafter			256	60	4	20	43	.234	.328	.304

Loves to face: Steve Lyons (.059, 1-for-17, 7 SO)
Hates to face: Jack Howell (.500, 10-for-20, 3 HR)
Ground outs-to-air outs ratio: 1.18 last season, 1.14 for career. . . .
Additional statistics: 14 double-play ground outs in 142 opportunities, 24 doubles, 5 triples in 207.1 innings last season. . . . Allowed 11 first-inning runs in 31 starts. . . . Batting support: 4.71 runs per start. . . . The Johnny Vander Meer of Murphy's Law: He had no-hitters broken up with two out in the ninth inning of two consecutive starts. . . . A lock to record the A.L.'s lowest ERA during the 1980s (minimum: 1500 IP). Through 1988: 3.32. . . . Leaders in past decades: 1900s, Ed Walsh (1.68); 1910s, Walter Johnson (1.59); 1920s, Stan Coveleski (3.20); 1930s, Lefty Grove (2.91); 1940s, Hal Newhouser (2.84); 1950s, Whitey Ford (2.66); 1960s, Dean Chance (2.78); 1970s, Jim Palmer (2.58).

Todd Stottlemyre
Throws Right

Toronto Blue Jays	W–L	ERA	AB	H	HR	BB	SO	BA	SA	OBA
Season	4-8	5.69	385	109	15	46	67	.283	.455	.363
vs. Left-Handers			197	73	7	25	23	.371	.553	.444
vs. Right-Handers			188	36	8	21	44	.191	.351	.279
Home	1-4	7.22	163	54	10	22	26	.331	.546	.406
Road	3-4	4.70	222	55	5	24	41	.248	.387	.331
Grass	2-3	4.40	167	46	4	14	27	.275	.425	.339
Artificial Turf	2-5	6.71	218	63	11	32	40	.289	.477	.380
April	0-2	7.50	48	13	2	11	11	.271	.438	.407
May	1-5	5.28	124	33	3	7	26	.266	.419	.311
June	2-0	2.27	131	31	5	11	17	.237	.412	.299
July	0-1	10.91	67	25	5	11	11	.373	.612	.463
August			0	0	0	0	0	—	—	—
Sept./Oct.	1-0	13.50	15	7	0	6	2	.467	.467	.619
Leading Off Inn.			95	33	5	8	16	.347	.537	.404
Runners On			174	50	6	29	27	.287	.454	.386
Runners/Scor. Pos.			103	27	3	21	19	.262	.408	.383
Runners On/2 Out			65	18	3	9	15	.277	.538	.373
Scor. Pos./2 Out			46	11	1	7	9	.239	.370	.352
Late Inning Pressure			26	8	1	2	5	.308	.500	.357
Leading Off			9	3	1	1	2	.333	.667	.400
Runners On			5	3	0	1	0	.600	.600	.667
Runners/Scor. Pos.			3	2	0	1	0	.667	.667	.750
First 9 Batters			181	48	3	26	37	.265	.337	.362
Second 9 Batters			126	35	5	13	23	.278	.460	.345
All Batters Thereafter			78	26	7	7	7	.333	.718	.395

Loves to face: Joe Carter (0-for-8)
Hates to face: Ron Kittle (.750, 3-for-4, 2 HR)
Ground outs-to-air outs ratio: 0.86 last season, his first in majors. . . . Additional statistics: 10 double-play ground outs in 104 opportunities, 19 doubles, 1 triple in 98.0 innings last season. . . . Allowed 6 first-inning runs in 16 starts. . . . Batting support: 4.44 runs per start. . . . Pitched an average of 5.00 innings per start, lowest mark in A.L. (minimum: 15 GS). . . . Record of 2–7 (5.85 ERA) in 16 starts, 2–1 (5.00) in 12 relief appearances. . . . The last nine batters he faced all reached base safely, matching Jim Gott for the longest streak in the majors. . . . Committed more balks last season (three) than his father did in his 11-year career (one). . . . Maybe his dad's instructional video could help him with left-handed batters.

Les Straker

Minnesota Twins — Throws Right

	W–L	ERA	AB	H	HR	BB	SO	BA	SA	OBA
Season	2-5	3.92	312	86	8	25	23	.276	.407	.326
vs. Left-Handers			174	45	3	10	16	.259	.374	.297
vs. Right-Handers			138	41	5	15	7	.297	.449	.361
Home	0-4	6.52	117	38	6	14	8	.325	.547	.397
Road	2-1	2.52	195	48	2	11	15	.246	.323	.282
Grass	2-0	2.72	146	36	2	11	10	.247	.329	.296
Artificial Turf	0-5	5.02	166	50	6	14	13	.301	.476	.354
April	0-1	4.32	65	20	1	2	6	.308	.431	.314
May	2-1	3.00	96	21	0	12	8	.219	.250	.306
June	0-2	6.48	73	25	4	4	3	.342	.603	.377
July			0	0	0	0	0	—	—	—
August			0	0	0	0	0	—	—	—
Sept./Oct.	0-1	2.82	78	20	3	7	6	.256	.397	.318
Leading Off Inn.			78	25	4	9	4	.321	.526	.391
Runners On			120	33	0	13	5	.275	.325	.338
Runners/Scor. Pos.			68	15	0	10	4	.221	.265	.309
Runners On/2 Out			46	16	0	4	4	.348	.413	.400
Scor. Pos./2 Out			33	8	0	3	4	.242	.273	.306
Late Inning Pressure			15	6	0	1	0	.400	.467	.412
Leading Off			5	3	0	0	0	.600	.800	.600
Runners On			5	3	0	1	0	.600	.600	.571
Runners/Scor. Pos.			3	1	0	1	0	.333	.333	.400
First 9 Batters			126	30	3	12	7	.238	.381	.302
Second 9 Batters			108	30	4	9	9	.278	.398	.333
All Batters Thereafter			78	26	1	4	7	.333	.462	.357

Loves to face: Don Mattingly (0-for-8)
Hates to face: Frank White (.857, 6-for-7, 1 HR)
Ground outs-to-air outs ratio: 1.38 last season, 1.26 for career. . . .
Additional statistics: 14 double-play ground outs in 62 opportunities, 17 doubles, 0 triples in 82.2 innings last season. . . . Allowed 7 first-inning runs in 14 starts. . . . Batting support: 4.36 runs per start. . . . Opponents' batting average was 79 points higher in home games than in road games, 3d-largest difference in A.L. (minimum: 100 AB each way). . . . The last 10 home runs he's allowed have been solo shots. . . . Opposing batters hit .359 (14-for-39) in LIP Situations in 1987, giving them a healthy career average of .370. . . . Twins fans who thought Viola provided the pitching staff's only sweet music might be interested to know that Straker's middle name is Paul. . . . Think about it.

Bill Swift

Seattle Mariners — Throws Right

	W–L	ERA	AB	H	HR	BB	SO	BA	SA	OBA
Season	8-12	4.59	675	199	10	65	47	.295	.393	.362
vs. Left-Handers			332	102	5	33	13	.307	.410	.371
vs. Right-Handers			343	97	5	32	34	.283	.376	.353
Home	5-4	3.53	341	95	6	34	20	.279	.381	.350
Road	3-8	5.75	334	104	4	31	27	.311	.404	.375
Grass	2-3	6.32	190	60	3	23	18	.316	.411	.394
Artificial Turf	6-9	3.95	485	139	7	42	29	.287	.386	.350
April	1-0	4.76	95	30	1	7	8	.316	.389	.359
May	4-1	2.79	152	36	1	11	14	.237	.316	.297
June	1-3	4.00	138	43	3	11	9	.312	.449	.373
July	0-4	7.96	100	30	2	15	8	.300	.430	.398
August	0-2	5.79	116	43	2	14	3	.371	.448	.443
Sept./Oct.	2-2	3.15	74	17	1	7	5	.230	.311	.296
Leading Off Inn.			170	48	1	8	11	.282	.347	.318
Runners On			306	100	5	31	19	.327	.448	.392
Runners/Scor. Pos.			177	54	2	25	16	.305	.395	.394
Runners On/2 Out			119	37	3	15	9	.311	.454	.401
Scor. Pos./2 Out			77	24	2	12	9	.312	.455	.418
Late Inning Pressure			52	13	3	4	3	.250	.442	.304
Leading Off			14	4	0	1	1	.286	.357	.333
Runners On			20	4	1	1	1	.200	.350	.238
Runners/Scor. Pos.			13	2	0	1	1	.154	.154	.214
First 9 Batters			278	73	3	28	25	.263	.335	.334
Second 9 Batters			192	61	0	20	12	.318	.380	.389
All Batters Thereafter			205	65	7	17	10	.317	.483	.374

Loves to face: Rickey Henderson (.056, 1-for-18)
Hates to face: Alan Trammell (.625, 5-for-8, 1 HR)
Ground outs-to-air outs ratio: 2.78 last season, 2.46 for career. . . .
Additional statistics: 36 double-play ground outs (most in majors) in 152 opportunities, 32 doubles, 2 triples in 174.2 innings last season. . . . Allowed 15 first-inning runs in 24 starts. . . . Batting support: 4.67 runs per start. . . . Record of 5–11 (4.98 ERA) in 24 starts, 3–1 (2.54) in 14 relief appearances. . . . Completed six starts, including four in a row (May 17–June 2). . . . Faced 90 batters between strikeouts (Aug. 6–31), the longest streak in the majors. . . . Opposing left-handed batters have hit over .300 in each of his three seasons in the majors. . . . Career record of 16–31 (.340). Only one pitcher active in 1988 has a lower percentage (minimum: 40 decisions): Mike Morgan (.333).

Greg Swindell

Cleveland Indians — Throws Left

	W–L	ERA	AB	H	HR	BB	SO	BA	SA	OBA
Season	18-14	3.20	928	234	18	45	180	.252	.363	.286
vs. Left-Handers			164	45	3	7	29	.274	.372	.301
vs. Right-Handers			764	189	15	38	151	.247	.361	.283
Home	9-5	2.88	418	98	7	19	85	.234	.330	.267
Road	9-9	3.48	510	136	11	26	95	.267	.390	.302
Grass	16-10	2.87	776	188	13	36	150	.242	.341	.275
Artificial Turf	2-4	4.93	152	46	5	9	30	.303	.474	.342
April	5-0	2.53	163	39	3	4	26	.239	.362	.257
May	5-1	1.72	167	27	1	9	31	.162	.246	.207
June	0-5	7.00	119	46	6	5	18	.387	.588	.411
July	2-3	3.71	170	42	4	7	39	.247	.353	.275
August	2-4	3.02	162	44	1	12	34	.272	.352	.320
Sept./Oct.	4-1	2.70	147	36	3	8	32	.245	.340	.282
Leading Off Inn.			243	57	7	8	55	.235	.374	.262
Runners On			343	94	8	21	58	.274	.411	.312
Runners/Scor. Pos.			169	49	2	19	28	.290	.408	.352
Runners On/2 Out			153	43	3	11	27	.281	.431	.329
Scor. Pos./2 Out			89	25	0	11	17	.281	.382	.360
Late Inning Pressure			112	32	2	5	17	.286	.411	.317
Leading Off			32	14	2	0	4	.438	.750	.455
Runners On			47	9	0	3	9	.191	.255	.231
Runners/Scor. Pos.			24	5	0	3	4	.208	.292	.276
First 9 Batters			279	63	4	13	70	.226	.297	.259
Second 9 Batters			271	67	7	18	52	.247	.369	.293
All Batters Thereafter			378	104	7	14	58	.275	.407	.301

Loves to face: Pete Incaviglia (0-for-9, 5 SO)
Hates to face: Jose Canseco (.467, 7-for-15, 2 HR)
Ground outs-to-air outs ratio: 0.79 last season, 0.78 for career. . . .
Additional statistics: 12 double-play ground outs in 158 opportunities, 35 doubles, 7 triples in 242.0 innings last season. . . . Allowed 14 first-inning runs in 33 starts. . . . Batting support: 4.03 runs per start. . . . Lost eight straight decisions from June 5 to July 19. . . . Career record of 0–8 with a 7.88 ERA during June; 26–16, 3.29 in other months. . . . Opposing batters have a career batting average of .222 during his first pass through the batting order, .275 thereafter. . . . First Indians pitcher to win his first six starts of any season since 1920, when Stan Coveleski won his first seven starts, and Jim Bagby won his first eight.

Frank Tanana

Detroit Tigers — Throws Left

	W–L	ERA	AB	H	HR	BB	SO	BA	SA	OBA
Season	14-11	4.21	799	213	25	64	127	.267	.417	.323
vs. Left-Handers			119	25	2	6	23	.210	.286	.248
vs. Right-Handers			680	188	23	58	104	.276	.440	.336
Home	7-5	4.08	415	106	8	40	68	.255	.364	.322
Road	7-6	4.36	384	107	17	24	59	.279	.474	.324
Grass	13-9	4.11	700	184	21	58	117	.263	.407	.322
Artificial Turf	1-2	5.01	99	29	4	6	10	.293	.485	.333
April	5-0	3.01	141	37	4	12	24	.262	.418	.320
May	3-3	7.47	133	40	5	15	13	.301	.451	.372
June	2-1	3.09	136	37	4	12	26	.272	.434	.327
July	2-2	2.06	131	29	3	10	23	.221	.328	.280
August	2-2	5.73	92	27	3	8	11	.293	.457	.369
Sept./Oct.	0-3	4.25	166	43	6	7	30	.259	.422	.289
Leading Off Inn.			209	48	6	8	34	.230	.378	.261
Runners On			310	93	12	38	52	.300	.474	.375
Runners/Scor. Pos.			167	48	6	31	33	.287	.467	.393
Runners On/2 Out			125	30	5	22	25	.240	.392	.358
Scor. Pos./2 Out			75	17	3	17	16	.227	.373	.370
Late Inning Pressure			77	17	2	10	11	.221	.351	.310
Leading Off			24	4	1	2	3	.167	.333	.231
Runners On			21	6	1	6	3	.286	.476	.444
Runners/Scor. Pos.			12	3	0	5	2	.250	.333	.471
First 9 Batters			268	63	5	14	50	.235	.343	.277
Second 9 Batters			245	68	9	24	41	.278	.449	.341
All Batters Thereafter			286	82	11	26	36	.287	.458	.349

Loves to face: Ernie Whitt (0-for-7, 6 SO)
Hates to face: Rickey Henderson (.353, 24-for-68, 6 HR)
Ground outs-to-air outs ratio: 0.87 last season, 0.98 for career. . . .
Additional statistics: 14 double-play ground outs in 156 opportunities, 33 doubles, 6 triples in 203.0 innings last season. . . . Allowed 10 first-inning runs in 32 starts. . . . Batting support: 4.13 runs per start. . . . Winless in last eight starts, matching his longest streak since 1981. . . . Has lost 108 games during the 1980s, tying Floyd Bannister for 2d most, behind Jim Clancy (112). . . . Leaders in past decades: 1870s, George Bradley (82); 1880s, Pud Galvin (244); 1890s, Gus Weyhing (160); 1900s, Vic Willis (171); 1910s, Walter Johnson (143); 1920s, Dolf Luque (146); 1930s, Paul Derringer (137); 1940s, Dutch Leonard (123); 1950s, Robin Roberts (149); 1960s, Jack Fisher (133); 1970s, Phil Niekro (151).

Walt Terrell

Throws Right

Detroit Tigers	W–L	ERA	AB	H	HR	BB	SO	BA	SA	OBA
Season	7-16	3.97	771	199	20	78	84	.258	.383	.326
vs. Left-Handers			413	106	8	39	31	.257	.366	.319
vs. Right-Handers			358	93	12	39	53	.260	.402	.333
Home	4-5	3.76	315	80	13	22	30	.254	.406	.302
Road	3-11	4.11	456	119	7	56	54	.261	.366	.341
Grass	6-13	3.92	661	176	17	61	72	.266	.393	.328
Artificial Turf	1-3	4.26	110	23	3	17	12	.209	.318	.310
April	0-0	4.05	25	5	2	0	2	.200	.440	.200
May	2-2	3.96	135	32	2	15	14	.237	.333	.313
June	1-3	5.79	124	37	6	18	16	.298	.476	.389
July	2-3	2.89	139	32	1	11	20	.230	.317	.281
August	2-3	3.60	191	57	6	18	19	.298	.440	.355
Sept./Oct.	0-5	3.95	157	36	3	16	13	.229	.331	.305
Leading Off Inn.			196	49	5	20	17	.250	.362	.323
Runners On			305	82	6	35	31	.269	.377	.340
Runners/Scor. Pos.			153	42	5	26	21	.275	.425	.371
Runners On/2 Out			127	35	3	16	13	.276	.409	.357
Scor. Pos./2 Out			71	20	2	11	7	.282	.423	.378
Late Inning Pressure			132	37	5	11	17	.280	.447	.340
Leading Off			38	10	1	2	3	.263	.395	.300
Runners On			43	12	1	5	4	.279	.395	.367
Runners/Scor. Pos.			22	4	0	4	1	.182	.227	.333
First 9 Batters			231	55	5	23	36	.238	.325	.305
Second 9 Batters			217	60	4	27	21	.276	.382	.352
All Batters Thereafter			323	84	11	28	27	.260	.424	.322

Loves to face: Willie McGee (.071, 1-for-14)
Hates to face: Juan Samuel (.500, 7-for-14, 2 HR)
Ground outs-to-air outs ratio: 1.48 last season, 1.34 for career. . . .
Additional statistics: 26 double-play ground outs in 159 opportunities, 28 doubles, 4 triples in 206.1 innings last season. . . . Allowed 12 first-inning runs in 29 starts. . . . Batting support: 3.86 runs per start. . . . Completed 11 games, but lost seven of them. . . . Complete games, year by year since 1984: 3, 5, 9, 10, 11. . . . No matter where he may roam, Tiger Stadium will always be home to Terrell. His four-year A.L. breakdown: 36–12, 3.03 ERA at Tiger Stadium; 18–36, 5.22 ERA elsewhere. . . . Opponents have hit one home run per 60 at-bats on his first pass through the batting order, one per 48 AB on the second go-round, one per 32 AB after that.

Bobby Thigpen

Throws Right

Chicago White Sox	W–L	ERA	AB	H	HR	BB	SO	BA	SA	OBA
Season	5-8	3.30	352	96	6	33	62	.273	.341	.338
vs. Left-Handers			165	52	1	21	20	.315	.345	.384
vs. Right-Handers			187	44	5	12	42	.235	.337	.294
Home	5-4	3.27	212	61	2	22	31	.288	.340	.351
Road	0-4	3.34	140	35	4	11	31	.250	.343	.316
Grass	5-7	3.48	325	91	6	31	56	.280	.354	.345
Artificial Turf	0-1	1.23	27	5	0	2	6	.185	.185	.241
April	0-1	3.31	63	15	1	5	8	.238	.302	.300
May	1-4	6.75	53	17	2	8	9	.321	.434	.410
June	3-0	1.13	61	15	0	6	8	.246	.279	.319
July	1-0	1.13	62	15	0	3	12	.242	.258	.277
August	0-2	3.86	66	19	1	7	14	.288	.333	.364
Sept./Oct.	0-1	4.50	47	15	2	4	11	.319	.489	.365
Leading Off Inn.			64	21	2	7	9	.328	.438	.394
Runners On			203	53	3	20	34	.261	.320	.322
Runners/Scor. Pos.			125	32	2	11	22	.256	.328	.324
Runners On/2 Out			86	18	0	8	15	.209	.233	.299
Scor. Pos./2 Out			59	13	0	4	12	.220	.254	.303
Late Inning Pressure			262	72	3	28	42	.275	.328	.345
Leading Off			48	14	0	6	8	.292	.292	.370
Runners On			152	40	2	17	23	.263	.322	.337
Runners/Scor. Pos.			91	22	1	9	16	.242	.308	.311
First 9 Batters			338	96	6	33	59	.284	.355	.348
Second 9 Batters			14	0	0	0	3	.000	.000	.067
All Batters Thereafter			0	0	0	0	0	—	—	—

Loves to face: Frank White (0-for-8)
Hates to face: Randy Bush (4-for-4, 1 2B, 1 HR)
Ground outs-to-air outs ratio: 0.95 last season, 0.87 for career. . . .
Additional statistics: 6 double-play ground outs in 105 opportunities, 6 doubles, 0 triples in 90.0 innings last season. . . . Faced 209 batters protecting leads of three runs or fewer in 8th inning or later, four fewer than major league leader Doug Jones. . . . Sixth reliever in White Sox history to save 25 or more games in a season. None of the six have done it twice. . . . Yet. . . . Needs 19 saves to break Terry Forster's team record. . . . Only home run allowed to a left-handed batter last season was hit by Dave Bergman. . . . Opponents' career batting average is .319 leading off innings. . . . Career average is .211 by opposing ground-ball hitters, .281 by fly-ballers.

Mark Thurmond

Throws Left

Baltimore Orioles	W–L	ERA	AB	H	HR	BB	SO	BA	SA	OBA
Season	1-8	4.58	289	80	10	27	29	.277	.464	.339
vs. Left-Handers			79	19	2	10	12	.241	.342	.330
vs. Right-Handers			210	61	8	17	17	.290	.510	.342
Home	1-1	3.86	115	29	2	15	15	.252	.400	.341
Road	0-7	5.08	174	51	8	12	14	.293	.506	.337
Grass	1-7	4.80	228	61	7	25	24	.268	.443	.340
Artificial Turf	0-1	3.68	61	19	3	2	5	.311	.541	.333
April	0-5	6.23	109	36	4	6	10	.330	.550	.362
May	0-1	30.86	11	6	1	4	2	.545	1.091	.647
June	0-0	0.00	12	2	0	0	3	.167	.250	.167
July	0-0	0.63	50	10	0	4	3	.200	.260	.255
August	0-0	3.55	51	15	1	8	5	.294	.431	.393
Sept./Oct.	1-2	3.38	56	11	4	5	6	.196	.429	.262
Leading Off Inn.			75	13	2	3	14	.173	.280	.205
Runners On			109	29	4	15	7	.266	.459	.354
Runners/Scor. Pos.			61	14	2	9	5	.230	.426	.329
Runners On/2 Out			58	14	1	9	6	.241	.379	.343
Scor. Pos./2 Out			37	8	1	6	4	.216	.405	.326
Late Inning Pressure			67	14	3	13	11	.209	.403	.341
Leading Off			21	3	0	3	6	.143	.238	.250
Runners On			18	4	1	7	2	.222	.389	.444
Runners/Scor. Pos.			10	1	0	3	2	.100	.100	.333
First 9 Batters			206	56	5	19	21	.272	.408	.335
Second 9 Batters			59	16	4	5	6	.271	.559	.328
All Batters Thereafter			24	8	1	3	2	.333	.708	.393

Loves to face: Dan Pasqua (0-for-8)
Hates to face: Chris Brown (.625, 5-for-8, 2 HR)
Ground outs-to-air outs ratio: 0.96 last season, 1.32 for career. . . .
Additional statistics: 6 double-play ground outs in 46 opportunities, 16 doubles, 4 triples in 74.2 innings last season. . . . Opponents' batting average was his lowest in three seasons in the A.L. . . . One of 10 pitchers with a losing record in each of the last four seasons. To find another one, look to the right. . . . Record of 0–6 (7.76 ERA) in six starts, 1–2 (2.81) in 37 relief appearances. Didn't start a game after May 10. . . . Opponents' career batting average is .239 in Late-Inning Pressure Situations, .282 otherwise. . . . Career record of 13–26 (4.81 ERA) before the All-Star break, 23–13 (2.70) during the 2d half. Has won eight consecutive decisions during August, dating back to 1984.

Jay Tibbs

Throws Right

Baltimore Orioles	W–L	ERA	AB	H	HR	BB	SO	BA	SA	OBA
Season	4-15	5.39	629	184	18	63	82	.293	.447	.356
vs. Left-Handers			334	100	9	36	47	.299	.461	.367
vs. Right-Handers			295	84	9	27	35	.285	.431	.344
Home	4-8	4.59	408	113	10	39	57	.277	.407	.339
Road	0-7	6.91	221	71	8	24	25	.321	.520	.387
Grass	4-12	5.31	539	158	15	50	72	.293	.445	.353
Artificial Turf	0-3	5.87	90	26	3	13	10	.289	.456	.371
April			0	0	0	0	0	—	—	—
May	2-2	5.40	141	42	3	15	21	.298	.440	.369
June	1-2	3.34	121	28	1	13	18	.231	.314	.301
July	1-5	7.24	140	51	6	9	10	.364	.593	.411
August	0-3	4.89	130	33	5	16	17	.254	.423	.329
Sept./Oct.	0-3	6.38	97	30	3	10	16	.309	.443	.367
Leading Off Inn.			159	40	7	12	30	.252	.415	.304
Runners On			262	91	8	25	36	.347	.531	.399
Runners/Scor. Pos.			154	49	6	14	29	.318	.519	.367
Runners On/2 Out			117	41	2	8	17	.350	.504	.397
Scor. Pos./2 Out			78	25	2	7	15	.321	.487	.384
Late Inning Pressure			48	12	2	10	9	.250	.438	.379
Leading Off			17	5	2	2	3	.294	.647	.368
Runners On			12	2	0	5	2	.167	.250	.412
Runners/Scor. Pos.			6	0	0	3	2	.000	.000	.333
First 9 Batters			236	62	4	20	37	.263	.373	.320
Second 9 Batters			198	52	3	18	22	.263	.354	.323
All Batters Thereafter			195	70	11	25	23	.359	.631	.430

Loves to face: Luis Polonia (0-for-7)
Hates to face: Harold Baines (.667, 6-for-9, 2 HR)
Ground outs-to-air outs ratio: 0.95 last season, 1.40 for career. . . .
Additional statistics: 15 double-play ground outs in 127 opportunities, 35 doubles, 4 triples in 158.2 innings last season. . . . Allowed 8 first-inning runs in 24 starts. . . . Batting support: 3.54 runs per start, 5th lowest in A.L. (minimum: 15 GS). . . . Ended the season with a 10-game losing streak, one short of Chris Bosio's streak, longest in the majors in 1988. . . . One of two Orioles pitchers to win their first two decisions last season. The other was Bob Milacki, who won his only two decisions. . . . Opponents' career batting average is .298 with runners on base, .246 with the bases empty. . . . Year by year ERAs, 1984–1988: 2.86, 3.92, 3.97, 4.99, 5.39.

Fred Toliver
Minnesota Twins — Throws Right

	W–L	ERA	AB	H	HR	BB	SO	BA	SA	OBA
Season	7-6	4.24	430	116	8	52	69	.270	.367	.349
vs. Left-Handers			232	65	6	27	41	.280	.401	.355
vs. Right-Handers			198	51	2	25	28	.258	.328	.342
Home	2-3	4.75	241	72	4	26	40	.299	.415	.367
Road	5-3	3.67	189	44	4	26	29	.233	.307	.327
Grass	5-2	4.05	166	42	3	23	27	.253	.319	.346
Artificial Turf	2-4	4.37	264	74	5	29	42	.280	.398	.352
April			0	0	0	0	0	—	—	—
May			0	0	0	0	0	—	—	—
June	0-1	9.72	34	12	1	7	6	.353	.500	.452
July	2-0	2.81	115	30	2	13	21	.261	.357	.336
August	4-2	3.92	153	43	3	16	24	.281	.386	.349
Sept./Oct.	1-3	4.58	128	31	2	16	18	.242	.320	.331
Leading Off Inn.			111	34	1	12	15	.306	.405	.374
Runners On			182	53	4	25	30	.291	.401	.375
Runners/Scor. Pos.			92	22	3	17	22	.239	.348	.355
Runners On/2 Out			67	19	0	9	15	.284	.343	.368
Scor. Pos./2 Out			36	7	0	8	12	.194	.194	.341
Late Inning Pressure			20	4	0	6	3	.200	.300	.385
Leading Off			9	4	0	0	0	.444	.667	.444
Runners On			5	0	0	2	2	.000	.000	.286
Runners/Scor. Pos.			0	0	0	1	0	—	—	1.000
First 9 Batters			158	39	2	16	31	.247	.316	.320
Second 9 Batters			145	40	1	20	21	.276	.324	.361
All Batters Thereafter			127	37	5	16	17	.291	.480	.371

Loves to face: Wally Joyner (0-for-7)
Hates to face: Devon White (.800, 4-for-5, 1 HR)
Ground outs-to-air outs ratio: 1.09 last season, 1.05 for career. . . .
Additional statistics: 12 double-play ground outs in 104 opportunities, 18 doubles, 0 triples in 114.2 innings last season. . . . Allowed five first-inning runs in 19 starts. . . . Batting support: 4.53 runs per start. . . . Opponents' career breakdowns: .317 leading off innings; .130 (3-for-23) with the bases loaded; .244 by ground-ball hitters, .296 by fly-ball hitters. . . . Has started 32 games in his career, but has never completed one. . . . Lost first six decisions in majors, 8–7 since then. . . . Opposing batters have hit better than .300 in day games in each of the last three seasons. Career records: 1–6 with a 5.54 ERA in day games; 7–7, 3.81 at night.

Frank Viola
Minnesota Twins — Throws Left

	W–L	ERA	AB	H	HR	BB	SO	BA	SA	OBA
Season	24-7	2.64	962	236	20	54	193	.245	.357	.286
vs. Left-Handers			163	38	4	8	29	.233	.368	.280
vs. Right-Handers			799	198	16	46	164	.248	.354	.287
Home	14-2	2.18	490	106	11	30	103	.216	.327	.265
Road	10-5	3.14	472	130	9	24	90	.275	.388	.308
Grass	10-2	3.13	362	100	6	18	72	.276	.378	.307
Artificial Turf	14-5	2.36	600	136	14	36	121	.227	.343	.273
April	2-1	4.01	128	32	5	11	31	.250	.484	.312
May	6-0	1.53	176	40	2	6	39	.227	.278	.253
June	4-1	1.90	164	38	3	8	24	.232	.317	.272
July	4-1	2.25	131	29	5	9	27	.221	.374	.271
August	4-3	2.47	203	49	3	14	42	.241	.315	.291
Sept./Oct.	4-1	4.14	160	48	2	6	30	.300	.419	.320
Leading Off Inn.			242	44	2	21	50	.182	.260	.247
Runners On			369	87	9	17	73	.236	.347	.269
Runners/Scor. Pos.			190	44	4	6	42	.232	.337	.251
Runners On/2 Out			153	29	2	11	43	.190	.268	.248
Scor. Pos./2 Out			84	13	1	4	24	.155	.238	.202
Late Inning Pressure			106	21	3	9	18	.198	.311	.261
Leading Off			28	4	0	3	5	.143	.143	.226
Runners On			30	4	2	3	5	.133	.333	.212
Runners/Scor. Pos.			11	0	0	1	1	.000	.000	.083
First 9 Batters			303	78	2	10	80	.257	.320	.281
Second 9 Batters			292	64	7	15	59	.219	.342	.260
All Batters Thereafter			367	94	11	29	54	.256	.398	.311

Loves to face: Mickey Tettleton (0-for-14)
Hates to face: Lloyd Moseby (.383, 18-for-47, 4 HR)
Ground outs-to-air outs ratio: 0.79 last season, 0.80 for career. . . .
Additional statistics: 20 double-play ground outs in 173 opportunities, 37 doubles, 5 triples in 255.1 innings last season. . . . Allowed 6 first-inning runs in 35 starts, 2d-lowest average in A.L. (minimum: 15 GS). . . . Batting support: 5.29 runs per start. . . . Went 16–1 between losses to New York on opening day and to Toronto on July 27. . . . Career record of 3–12 vs. Jays, 101–69 vs. others. . . . Most wins since 1984: Viola, 93; Gooden, 91; Morris, 89; Hershiser, 83. . . . Sixth pitcher to win an L.C.S., World Series, and All-Star Game. Only pitcher to do it in same year: Don Sutton in 1977. Others: Steve Carlton, Jon Matlack, Bruce Sutter, and Rick Wise.

Duane Ward
Toronto Blue Jays — Throws Right

	W–L	ERA	AB	H	HR	BB	SO	BA	SA	OBA
Season	9-3	3.30	413	101	5	60	91	.245	.327	.344
vs. Left-Handers			173	40	3	27	32	.231	.312	.332
vs. Right-Handers			240	61	2	33	59	.254	.338	.352
Home	5-1	2.29	209	45	2	33	52	.215	.282	.327
Road	4-2	4.44	204	56	3	27	39	.275	.373	.362
Grass	4-1	4.35	149	39	3	22	34	.262	.356	.364
Artificial Turf	5-2	2.74	264	62	2	38	57	.235	.311	.332
April	0-0	1.80	38	9	0	6	8	.237	.263	.340
May	1-0	2.81	60	16	0	13	12	.267	.333	.413
June	4-0	3.00	85	20	2	9	17	.235	.353	.316
July	1-1	5.49	79	26	0	9	11	.329	.418	.389
August	2-1	3.63	81	17	2	11	18	.210	.309	.301
Sept./Oct.	1-1	2.29	70	13	1	12	25	.186	.243	.313
Leading Off Inn.			85	22	1	18	8	.259	.353	.388
Runners On			218	52	2	25	57	.239	.307	.321
Runners/Scor. Pos.			139	26	2	22	41	.187	.245	.298
Runners On/2 Out			95	22	1	11	25	.232	.295	.324
Scor. Pos./2 Out			73	13	1	10	20	.178	.233	.286
Late Inning Pressure			199	48	2	30	51	.241	.332	.340
Leading Off			44	10	1	10	5	.227	.364	.370
Runners On			100	29	1	11	29	.290	.400	.353
Runners/Scor. Pos.			61	15	1	10	23	.246	.311	.333
First 9 Batters			351	83	5	54	80	.236	.322	.344
Second 9 Batters			62	18	0	6	11	.290	.355	.343
All Batters Thereafter			0	0	0	0	0	—	—	—

Loves to face: Steve Buechele (0-for-4, 3 SO)
Hates to face: Rickey Henderson (.833, 5-for-6)
Ground outs-to-air outs ratio: 1.92 last season, 2.13 for career. . . .
Additional statistics: 12 double-play ground outs in 107 opportunities, 13 doubles, 3 triples in 111.2 innings last season. . . . Royals were hitless in 26 at-bats against him. . . . No major league saves before last season, when he had 15. Recorded five of Toronto's eight saves after Sept. 1. . . . Allowed one hit in 13 AB with bases loaded, but forced in four runs with walks. . . . Opponents' batting averages, year by year since 1986: .342, .326, .245. . . . Opposing right-handed batters have hit this fellow righty for a higher BA than left-handers have in each of his three seasons. . . . Opposing batters have a career BA of .303 but no HRs in 76 ABs after his first pass through the order.

Bill Wegman
Milwaukee Brewers — Throws Right

	W–L	ERA	AB	H	HR	BB	SO	BA	SA	OBA
Season	13-13	4.12	780	207	24	50	84	.265	.413	.309
vs. Left-Handers			403	110	11	25	33	.273	.407	.313
vs. Right-Handers			377	97	13	25	51	.257	.419	.306
Home	8-6	4.50	449	128	12	26	46	.285	.423	.322
Road	5-7	3.62	331	79	12	24	38	.239	.399	.292
Grass	12-12	4.03	717	190	20	49	76	.265	.404	.312
Artificial Turf	1-1	5.17	63	17	4	1	8	.270	.508	.281
April	2-3	3.03	134	34	2	9	9	.254	.358	.290
May	2-2	6.05	79	21	5	5	4	.266	.570	.310
June	2-1	2.20	122	27	1	9	11	.221	.254	.278
July	4-2	3.50	142	37	5	10	25	.261	.423	.323
August	0-3	8.07	134	45	5	9	14	.336	.515	.362
Sept./Oct.	3-2	3.14	169	43	6	9	21	.254	.408	.292
Leading Off Inn.			204	46	8	6	18	.225	.382	.251
Runners On			286	86	6	25	26	.301	.430	.348
Runners/Scor. Pos.			142	47	3	12	8	.331	.451	.364
Runners On/2 Out			130	40	3	16	10	.308	.438	.388
Scor. Pos./2 Out			76	24	3	7	4	.316	.461	.381
Late Inning Pressure			59	18	2	4	7	.305	.458	.349
Leading Off			16	2	0	0	0	.125	.125	.125
Runners On			19	7	2	3	2	.368	.737	.455
Runners/Scor. Pos.			6	4	1	1	0	.667	1.333	.714
First 9 Batters			264	62	6	17	38	.235	.348	.281
Second 9 Batters			251	72	9	17	21	.287	.450	.331
All Batters Thereafter			265	73	9	16	25	.275	.442	.317

Loves to face: Dan Gladden (0-for-15)
Hates to face: Kent Hrbek (.458, 11-for-24, 4 HR)
Ground outs-to-air outs ratio: 0.71 last season, 0.82 for career. . . .
Additional statistics: 14 double-play ground outs in 131 opportunities, 39 doubles, 2 triples in 199.0 innings last season. . . . Allowed 13 first-inning runs in 31 starts. . . . Batting support: 4.00 runs per start. . . . Pitched a complete game in each of his first two starts last season (both losses), but completed only two of 29 starts thereafter. . . . Combined 0–7 record vs. the division winners last season; 0–4 vs. Boston, 0–3 vs. Oakland. Career record of 0–5 vs. the A's. . . . The A.L.'s 17 qualifying .300 hitters batted .404 against him (42-for-104). . . . Opposing batters have a career BA of .300 with runners in scoring position, .261 in other at-bats.

Bob Welch

Throws Right

Oakland As

	W–L	ERA	AB	H	HR	BB	SO	BA	SA	OBA
Season	17-9	3.64	923	237	22	81	158	.257	.384	.321
vs. Left-Handers			459	114	12	48	74	.248	.386	.318
vs. Right-Handers			464	123	10	33	84	.265	.381	.324
Home	13-4	2.56	545	130	8	35	98	.239	.327	.286
Road	4-5	5.29	378	107	14	46	60	.283	.466	.368
Grass	17-7	3.31	832	207	18	68	140	.249	.361	.308
Artificial Turf	0-2	7.06	91	30	4	13	18	.330	.593	.430
April	3-2	5.45	141	40	4	17	25	.284	.440	.362
May	5-0	1.50	175	36	1	10	26	.206	.257	.249
June	2-2	3.79	149	45	3	11	19	.302	.409	.365
July	2-2	2.80	162	39	4	10	31	.241	.370	.291
August	3-1	4.81	154	43	6	15	28	.279	.435	.339
Sept./Oct.	2-2	4.26	142	34	4	18	29	.239	.415	.329
Leading Off Inn.			242	57	2	13	34	.236	.343	.275
Runners On			351	83	9	47	68	.236	.348	.328
Runners/Scor. Pos.			181	52	4	36	45	.287	.403	.402
Runners On/2 Out			172	48	2	26	37	.279	.366	.386
Scor. Pos./2 Out			98	29	1	20	24	.296	.388	.434
Late Inning Pressure			107	28	1	6	15	.262	.318	.307
Leading Off			31	10	0	0	4	.323	.355	.323
Runners On			45	8	0	4	7	.178	.200	.260
Runners/Scor. Pos.			17	5	0	4	3	.294	.353	.455
First 9 Batters			283	70	7	29	56	.247	.378	.324
Second 9 Batters			288	81	7	25	51	.281	.434	.343
All Batters Thereafter			352	86	8	27	51	.244	.347	.300

Loves to face: Matt Nokes (0-for-11)
Hates to face: Dick Schofield (.714, 5-for-7)
Ground outs-to-air outs ratio: 0.91 last season, 0.91 for career. . . .
Additional statistics: 14 double-play ground outs in 153 opportunities, 41 doubles, 5 triples in 244.2 innings last season. . . . Allowed 14 first-inning runs in 36 starts. . . . Batting support: 4.61 runs per start. . . . Record of 14–3 with a 2.63 ERA with Hassey behind the plate last season, 3–6 with a 6.64 ERA with Steinbach giving the signs. Yes, those numbers are correct. . . . Career record of 111–64 on grass fields, 21–31 on artificial turf. . . . Has lasted an average of 2.1 innings in his five career postseason starts. Has lasted through the third inning in just one of them. . . . Has won 120 games during the 1980s, to rank third in the majors during that time, behind Jack Morris (156) and Dave Stieb (123).

Mitch Williams

Throws Left

Texas Rangers

	W–L	ERA	AB	H	HR	BB	SO	BA	SA	OBA
Season	2-7	4.63	236	48	4	47	61	.203	.305	.345
vs. Left-Handers			65	12	0	12	19	.185	.231	.337
vs. Right-Handers			171	36	4	35	42	.211	.333	.348
Home	1-3	5.71	123	29	2	33	28	.236	.333	.400
Road	1-4	3.51	113	19	2	14	33	.168	.274	.288
Grass	2-6	5.24	193	43	3	43	47	.223	.332	.376
Artificial Turf	0-1	2.08	43	5	1	4	14	.116	.186	.188
April	0-1	2.08	26	3	0	5	8	.115	.154	.242
May	1-0	7.24	47	9	1	14	16	.191	.298	.371
June	0-1	3.52	51	7	2	7	16	.137	.275	.254
July	0-2	5.79	34	11	0	8	7	.324	.500	.489
August	1-0	3.65	46	11	0	9	7	.239	.283	.375
Sept./Oct.	0-3	5.19	32	7	1	4	7	.219	.313	.306
Leading Off Inn.			36	5	1	9	6	.139	.222	.326
Runners On			142	31	3	27	43	.218	.345	.350
Runners/Scor. Pos.			97	22	3	20	31	.227	.361	.368
Runners On/2 Out			65	9	1	8	18	.138	.215	.233
Scor. Pos./2 Out			48	8	1	6	13	.167	.271	.259
Late Inning Pressure			151	32	3	25	36	.212	.338	.331
Leading Off			20	0	0	6	4	.000	.000	.259
Runners On			90	24	3	14	24	.267	.444	.364
Runners/Scor. Pos.			62	16	3	11	16	.258	.435	.368
First 9 Batters			220	47	4	45	60	.214	.323	.356
Second 9 Batters			16	1	0	2	1	.063	.063	.167
All Batters Thereafter			0	0	0	0	0	—	—	—

Loves to face: Darrell Evans (0-for-8)
Hates to face: Tom Brunansky (.500, 2-for-4, 2 BB, 1 HR)
Ground outs-to-air outs ratio: 0.64 last season, 0.74 for career. . . .
Additional statistics: 4 double-play ground outs in 81 opportunities, 10 doubles, 1 triple in 68.0 innings last season. . . . Nine saves in first 16 appearances, but only nine more in 51 games thereafter. . . . Faced 96 batters protecting leads of three runs or fewer in 8th inning or later. Other Rangers relievers: Mohorcic, 48; McMurtry, 27; Cecena, 19. . . . Opposing batters were hitless in 20 at-bats leading off innings in LIP Situations. But the biggest 0-for of the past 14 years was undercut by six walks. . . . Opponents' career breakdown: .176 by left-handers, .199 by right-handers. . . . Opposing ground-ball hitters have never hit below .227; fly-ballers have never hit above .179.

Mark Williamson

Throws Right

Baltimore Orioles

	W–L	ERA	AB	H	HR	BB	SO	BA	SA	OBA
Season	5-8	4.90	459	125	14	40	69	.272	.431	.332
vs. Left-Handers			223	59	7	25	31	.265	.426	.337
vs. Right-Handers			236	66	7	15	38	.280	.436	.327
Home	2-4	3.20	245	59	7	15	34	.241	.376	.286
Road	3-4	6.96	214	66	7	25	35	.308	.495	.382
Grass	4-8	4.87	411	111	12	34	64	.270	.421	.328
Artificial Turf	1-0	5.11	48	14	2	6	5	.292	.521	.364
April	1-0	4.09	83	23	1	6	14	.277	.373	.319
May	0-4	5.65	143	39	8	5	22	.273	.524	.302
June	0-1	6.86	92	31	0	12	11	.337	.424	.413
July			0	0	0	0	0	—	—	—
August	3-1	2.79	34	7	0	7	8	.206	.324	.341
Sept./Oct.	1-2	3.81	107	25	5	10	14	.234	.393	.305
Leading Off Inn.			109	23	1	6	18	.211	.303	.252
Runners On			189	65	8	21	29	.344	.550	.408
Runners/Scor. Pos.			122	41	3	14	20	.336	.484	.403
Runners On/2 Out			81	26	3	8	10	.321	.494	.382
Scor. Pos./2 Out			55	18	0	5	9	.327	.382	.383
Late Inning Pressure			82	27	2	11	6	.329	.512	.409
Leading Off			20	8	0	1	2	.400	.500	.429
Runners On			44	13	2	9	4	.295	.500	.415
Runners/Scor. Pos.			33	9	0	7	3	.273	.364	.400
First 9 Batters			226	66	7	27	40	.292	.456	.371
Second 9 Batters			124	28	5	8	20	.226	.395	.271
All Batters Thereafter			109	31	2	5	9	.284	.422	.316

Loves to face: Jim Presley (0-for-9)
Hates to face: Ken Phelps (.500, 3-for-6, 3 BB, 3 HR)
Ground outs-to-air outs ratio: 0.95 last season, 1.33 for career. . . .
Additional statistics: 6 double-play ground outs in 78 opportunities, 29 doubles, 1 triple in 117.2 innings last season. . . . Allowed 6 first-inning runs in 10 starts. . . . Batting support: 2.80 runs per start. . . . Winning pitcher when Baltimore snapped its 21-game losing streak. . . . Record of 1–6 (4.04 ERA) in 10 starts, 4–2 (6.10) in 27 relief appearances. . . . Opponents hit 122 points higher with runners on than with bases empty, largest difference of 1988 (minimum 100 AB each way). . . . Opponents' career average of .321 in LIP Situations, .243 in other at bats, largest gap over last 10 years (minimum 250 LIPS AB). . . . Faced 39 batters with bases loaded, allowed 12 singles but no extra-base hits.

Bobby Witt

Throws Right

Texas Rangers

	W–L	ERA	AB	H	HR	BB	SO	BA	SA	OBA
Season	8-10	3.92	621	134	13	101	148	.216	.319	.324
vs. Left-Handers			345	77	4	56	74	.223	.301	.331
vs. Right-Handers			276	57	9	45	74	.207	.341	.315
Home	4-3	3.70	227	49	3	38	45	.216	.291	.326
Road	4-7	4.06	394	85	10	63	103	.216	.335	.322
Grass	7-10	4.21	524	114	12	89	121	.218	.323	.329
Artificial Turf	1-0	2.33	97	20	1	12	27	.206	.299	.294
April	0-4	6.97	117	28	3	30	27	.239	.342	.392
May	0-1	11.81	22	7	1	5	3	.318	.545	.444
June			0	0	0	0	0	—	—	—
July	3-1	1.29	118	23	1	15	32	.195	.254	.284
August	3-2	3.35	171	28	3	28	43	.164	.257	.282
Sept./Oct.	2-2	3.63	193	48	5	23	43	.249	.373	.326
Leading Off Inn.			157	33	6	21	32	.210	.357	.303
Runners On			259	59	5	44	60	.228	.324	.333
Runners/Scor. Pos.			135	36	4	27	32	.267	.400	.375
Runners On/2 Out			107	21	3	24	26	.196	.299	.344
Scor. Pos./2 Out			68	16	2	16	20	.235	.353	.381
Late Inning Pressure			87	16	3	13	24	.184	.333	.297
Leading Off			23	3	2	3	6	.130	.391	.231
Runners On			29	6	1	5	9	.207	.310	.342
Runners/Scor. Pos.			12	3	1	4	4	.250	.500	.438
First 9 Batters			171	38	2	23	44	.222	.310	.311
Second 9 Batters			163	35	3	32	43	.215	.288	.340
All Batters Thereafter			287	61	8	46	61	.213	.341	.321

Loves to face: Steve Lombardozzi (0-for-7, 5 SO)
Hates to face: Rob Deer (.500, 5-for-10, 6 BB, 2 HR)
Ground outs-to-air outs ratio: 1.09 last season, 0.96 for career. . . .
Additional statistics: 16 double-play ground outs in 128 opportunities, 17 doubles, 4 triples in 174.1 innings last season. . . . Allowed 21 first-inning runs in 22 starts. . . . Batting support: 3.73 runs per start. . . . Record of 0–6 with a 6.70 ERA at the All-Star break, 8–4, 2.98 ERA thereafter. . . . Completed only two of his first 62 career starts, then completed nine in a row (July 10–August 24), longest streak in the majors since Bert Blyleven had 10 straight in 1985. . . . Witt gives right-handed batters a case of happy feet. No pitcher who has faced as many RHB over the past 14 years has walked a higher percentage than Witt. But he's never hit one with a pitch.

Mike Witt

California Angels — Throws Right

	W–L	ERA	AB	H	HR	BB	SO	BA	SA	OBA
Season	13-16	4.15	966	263	14	87	133	.272	.376	.332
vs. Left-Handers			524	137	7	50	67	.261	.357	.324
vs. Right-Handers			442	126	7	37	66	.285	.398	.343
Home	6-7	2.77	498	121	6	37	74	.243	.315	.298
Road	7-9	5.71	468	142	8	50	59	.303	.440	.368
Grass	11-13	4.13	830	223	12	76	116	.269	.371	.330
Artificial Turf	2-3	4.24	136	40	2	11	17	.294	.404	.345
April	1-2	5.29	127	34	1	13	22	.268	.354	.340
May	1-4	4.50	166	41	3	21	28	.247	.386	.332
June	4-1	2.68	156	41	2	10	29	.263	.359	.307
July	2-3	5.02	159	51	3	10	16	.321	.434	.353
August	3-2	3.67	185	48	3	13	23	.259	.373	.313
Sept./Oct.	2-4	4.08	173	48	2	20	15	.277	.347	.350
Leading Off Inn.			248	66	6	13	38	.266	.411	.305
Runners On			390	117	4	42	48	.300	.397	.363
Runners/Scor. Pos.			215	64	0	24	26	.298	.363	.356
Runners On/2 Out			179	50	1	20	16	.279	.358	.355
Scor. Pos./2 Out			105	28	0	11	7	.267	.324	.336
Late Inning Pressure			139	39	1	15	22	.281	.353	.346
Leading Off			38	13	1	3	7	.342	.474	.390
Runners On			59	16	0	7	6	.271	.339	.338
Runners/Scor. Pos.			31	6	0	3	3	.194	.258	.250
First 9 Batters			281	70	2	20	41	.249	.345	.298
Second 9 Batters			272	73	7	24	32	.268	.408	.331
All Batters Thereafter			413	120	5	43	60	.291	.375	.356

Loves to face: Pat Sheridan (.063, 2-for-32)
Hates to face: Chet Lemon (.429, 15-for-35, 1 HR)
Ground outs-to-air outs ratio: 1.19 last season, 1.40 for career. . . .
Additional statistics: 24 double-play ground outs in 188 opportunities, 46 doubles, 6 triples in 249.2 innings last season. . . . Allowed 15 first-inning runs in 34 starts. Didn't allowed a first-inning home run. . . . Batting support: 3.88 runs per start. . . . Opposing ground-ball hitters batted .300, fly-ballers .250. . . . Strikeouts per nine innings fell from 7.00 in 1987 to 4.79 last season. . . . Has won his last six decisions against the Red Sox, has lost his last six against the Blue Jays. . . . Career record of 21–9 in June, 79–80 in other months (11–23 in September). . . . Opposing batters have hit one home run per 73 at-bats on his first pass through order, one per 40 AB after that.

Curt Young

Oakland As — Throws Left

	W–L	ERA	AB	H	HR	BB	SO	BA	SA	OBA
Season	11-8	4.14	589	162	23	50	69	.275	.435	.333
vs. Left-Handers			97	25	3	3	7	.258	.392	.287
vs. Right-Handers			492	137	20	47	62	.278	.443	.342
Home	2-5	4.32	290	87	9	22	35	.300	.434	.353
Road	9-3	3.98	299	75	14	28	34	.251	.435	.314
Grass	7-7	4.14	477	130	16	41	51	.273	.417	.332
Artificial Turf	4-1	4.15	112	32	7	9	18	.286	.509	.339
April	1-0	4.96	68	24	2	4	9	.353	.515	.389
May	3-2	2.88	125	28	4	13	14	.224	.352	.293
June	1-3	6.33	105	37	6	13	9	.352	.571	.417
July	1-2	15.83	44	18	8	4	5	.409	.977	.469
August	2-0	1.73	92	19	0	5	9	.207	.239	.255
Sept./Oct.	3-1	2.30	155	36	3	11	23	.232	.335	.290
Leading Off Inn.			151	34	6	12	17	.225	.377	.287
Runners On			209	59	7	21	23	.282	.421	.349
Runners/Scor. Pos.			100	29	4	14	12	.290	.440	.377
Runners On/2 Out			91	26	1	12	10	.286	.385	.381
Scor. Pos./2 Out			54	16	1	7	6	.296	.407	.397
Late Inning Pressure			41	9	3	5	2	.220	.463	.304
Leading Off			13	3	2	1	0	.231	.692	.286
Runners On			8	1	0	1	0	.125	.250	.222
Runners/Scor. Pos.			0	0	0	0	0	—	—	—
First 9 Batters			214	54	10	17	31	.252	.430	.312
Second 9 Batters			200	59	5	21	24	.295	.440	.366
All Batters Thereafter			175	49	8	12	14	.280	.434	.321

Loves to face: Darnell Coles (0-for-14)
Hates to face: Mike Young (.438, 7-for-16, 3 HR)
Ground outs-to-air outs ratio: 0.97 last season, 0.83 for career. . . .
Additional statistics: 22 double-play ground outs in 100 opportunities, 21 doubles, 2 triples in 156.1 innings last season. . . . Allowed 14 first-inning runs in 26 starts. . . . Batting support: 4.31 runs per start. . . . Ratio of strikeouts to walks fell from 2.82 in 1987 to 1.38 last season. . . . One of two pitchers to allow seven consecutive hits with runners on base last season. . . . One of six pitchers whose right-handed opponents have outhit left-handers by at least 20 points in each of the past five seasons. . . . Has played for the A's in each of the last six seasons. Among current players, only Tony Phillips has played with the club for more consecutive seasons.

Rich Yett

Cleveland Indians — Throws Right

	W–L	ERA	AB	H	HR	BB	SO	BA	SA	OBA
Season	9-6	4.62	531	146	11	55	71	.275	.418	.344
vs. Left-Handers			322	95	6	25	34	.295	.447	.346
vs. Right-Handers			209	51	5	30	37	.244	.373	.340
Home	6-3	4.01	266	72	5	27	40	.271	.387	.340
Road	3-3	5.24	265	74	6	28	31	.279	.449	.347
Grass	9-5	3.99	439	115	8	46	63	.262	.385	.333
Artificial Turf	0-1	7.89	92	31	3	9	8	.337	.576	.396
April	2-1	8.15	78	25	4	9	9	.321	.538	.391
May	1-2	4.72	135	38	2	15	21	.281	.437	.353
June	2-0	3.86	48	9	1	11	6	.188	.292	.339
July			0	0	0	0	0	—	—	—
August	3-1	2.88	124	26	0	11	17	.210	.274	.272
Sept./Oct.	1-2	4.76	146	48	4	9	18	.329	.500	.372
Leading Off Inn.			131	33	3	14	20	.252	.412	.324
Runners On			228	67	5	20	29	.294	.430	.352
Runners/Scor. Pos.			128	32	4	9	16	.250	.430	.302
Runners On/2 Out			95	24	1	10	14	.253	.347	.324
Scor. Pos./2 Out			61	12	1	4	11	.197	.311	.246
Late Inning Pressure			53	18	1	4	6	.340	.528	.386
Leading Off			15	3	0	2	3	.200	.333	.294
Runners On			17	6	0	1	1	.353	.471	.389
Runners/Scor. Pos.			8	3	0	0	0	.375	.625	.375
First 9 Batters			179	39	4	23	29	.218	.330	.307
Second 9 Batters			168	45	4	20	21	.268	.393	.349
All Batters Thereafter			184	62	3	12	21	.337	.527	.376

Loves to face: Harold Baines (0-for-10)
Hates to face: Brian Downing (.571, 4-for-7, 5 BB, 2 HR)
Ground outs-to-air outs ratio: 0.90 last season, 0.92 for career. . . .
Additional statistics: 10 double-play ground outs in 107 opportunities, 27 doubles, 8 triples in 134.1 innings last season. . . . Allowed 15 first-inning runs in 22 starts. . . . Batting support: 4.18 runs per start. . . . Opponents batted 98 points higher in day games than they did at night, 2d-largest difference in A.L. (minimum: 100 AB each way). . . . Allowed an average of one home run per 4.6 innings in 1987, one per 12.2 innings last season. . . . Has appeared in exactly 100 major league games and has never committed an error. . . . Opponents' career average is .228 the first time through the batting order, .311 thereafter. . . . Hey, Chris Berman: How 'bout Rich ("Is It Soup?") Yett.

Baltimore Orioles

	W–L	ERA	AB	H	HR	BB	SO	BA	SA	OBA
Season	54-107	4.54	5491	1506	153	523	709	.274	.420	.340
vs. Left-Handers			2400	666	68	259	320	.278	.422	.350
vs. Right-Handers			3091	840	85	264	389	.272	.419	.331
Home	34-46	3.80	2808	734	77	257	381	.261	.397	.326
Road	20-61	5.34	2683	772	76	266	328	.288	.444	.354
Grass	49-87	4.44	4660	1267	128	436	603	.272	.414	.337
Artificial Turf	5-20	5.12	831	239	25	87	106	.288	.457	.356
April	1-22	5.58	780	234	23	69	105	.300	.459	.360
May	10-17	4.69	931	268	28	76	128	.288	.441	.347
June	11-16	4.53	942	254	23	97	119	.270	.401	.340
July	10-16	4.80	899	255	26	63	117	.284	.434	.333
August	14-15	3.39	987	247	18	102	115	.250	.360	.322
Sept./Oct.	8-21	4.57	952	248	35	116	125	.261	.436	.340
Leading Off Inn.			1310	327	35	102	200	.250	.385	.308
Runners On			2384	687	75	254	283	.288	.447	.356
Runners/Scor. Pos.			1388	395	46	176	191	.285	.458	.362
Runners On/2 Out			1029	289	29	131	124	.281	.429	.368
Scor. Pos./2 Out			666	180	20	96	90	.270	.429	.369
Late Inning Pressure			809	222	25	102	114	.274	.431	.358
Leading Off			207	54	7	17	44	.261	.420	.323
Runners On			341	93	11	58	40	.273	.408	.378
Runners/Scor. Pos.			202	55	4	41	31	.272	.381	.392
First 9 Batters			2776	767	65	277	374	.276	.406	.344
Second 9 Batters			1447	409	49	134	180	.283	.446	.346
All Batters Thereafter			1268	330	39	112	155	.260	.421	.322

Starting pitchers: 37–89, 4.84 ERA
Relief pitchers: 17–18, 3.98 ERA
Ground outs-to-air outs ratio: 1.02.... Team's record has gotten worse in each of five years since 1983 World Series team: 98–64, 85–77, 83–78, 73–89, 67–95, 54–107. That equals major league record shared by Dodgers (1900–05), Athletics (1931–36), and Cubs (1937–42).... Compiled A.L.'s highest ERA for first time in team history. Also struck out the fewest batters in league for first time ever.... Record of 6–20 on artificial turf was worst in A.L. since Red Sox went 1–5 in 1976.... Used 15 different starting pitchers last season, the most of any team. Starters lasted an average of 5.85 innings, 2d worst in the majors.... Allowed six or more runs in an inning ten times last season, most of any team in the majors.

Boston Red Sox

	W–L	ERA	AB	H	HR	BB	SO	BA	SA	OBA
Season	89-73	3.97	5473	1415	143	493	1085	.259	.393	.322
vs. Left-Handers			2455	674	52	247	439	.275	.402	.340
vs. Right-Handers			3018	741	91	246	646	.246	.386	.307
Home	53-28	4.01	2827	738	73	245	572	.261	.398	.322
Road	36-45	3.93	2646	677	70	248	513	.256	.389	.322
Grass	80-58	3.88	4667	1193	119	426	946	.256	.386	.320
Artificial Turf	9-15	4.49	806	222	24	67	139	.275	.433	.334
April	14-6	2.64	674	149	16	56	160	.221	.334	.282
May	11-16	4.96	923	243	33	96	176	.263	.436	.334
June	14-12	4.31	914	257	25	86	177	.281	.415	.347
July	21-9	4.07	1012	271	23	78	215	.268	.402	.322
August	13-16	4.45	956	247	31	99	164	.258	.404	.332
Sept./Oct.	16-14	3.14	994	248	15	78	193	.249	.355	.304
Leading Off Inn.			1317	326	36	108	256	.248	.383	.307
Runners On			2366	639	62	218	447	.270	.410	.332
Runners/Scor. Pos.			1342	346	36	151	266	.258	.403	.331
Runners On/2 Out			1008	240	21	115	187	.238	.359	.321
Scor. Pos./2 Out			634	142	12	86	127	.224	.336	.323
Late Inning Pressure			809	200	18	96	200	.247	.366	.327
Leading Off			194	43	6	23	53	.222	.376	.307
Runners On			349	83	6	53	90	.238	.335	.335
Runners/Scor. Pos.			208	46	5	44	47	.221	.351	.351
First 9 Batters			2633	660	62	249	563	.251	.377	.316
Second 9 Batters			1446	390	40	120	269	.270	.416	.331
All Batters Thereafter			1394	365	41	124	253	.262	.400	.323

Starting pitchers: 68–51, 4.04 ERA
Relief pitchers: 21–22, 3.80 ERA
Ground outs-to-air outs ratio: 1.02.... Rookie pitchers combined for a 1–8 record and a 7.29 ERA. The ERA was the highest by the rookies on any A.L. team with that many innings pitched (66.2) since the 1950 St. Louis Browns. The one win went to Todd Ellsworth.... Led the A.L. in ERA during April, then compiled a 4.44 mark over next four months, including a league high in May.... Led A.L. in strikeouts for first time since 1954.... Won 10 consecutive games against Milwaukee from Oct. 4, 1987, through July 31, 1988, their longest streak ever against the Brewers.... Had the best record in baseball in games in which they led after eight innings (82–1).... Boston pitchers had the best walk-to-strikeout ratio in the majors last season, and the same is true of Boston batters.

California Angels

	W–L	ERA	AB	H	HR	BB	SO	BA	SA	OBA
Season	75-87	4.32	5568	1503	135	568	817	.270	.401	.338
vs. Left-Handers			2567	694	67	285	335	.270	.407	.343
vs. Right-Handers			3001	809	68	283	482	.270	.396	.334
Home	35-46	4.04	2838	751	71	265	441	.265	.387	.328
Road	40-41	4.60	2730	752	64	303	376	.275	.416	.349
Grass	61-77	4.34	4764	1284	119	495	722	.270	.399	.339
Artificial Turf	14-10	4.17	804	219	16	73	95	.272	.413	.337
April	10-13	4.84	750	195	20	93	112	.260	.403	.345
May	9-19	4.25	972	276	24	106	145	.284	.414	.355
June	15-11	3.56	886	212	16	81	174	.239	.352	.307
July	19-8	4.94	980	281	27	79	131	.287	.432	.338
August	15-14	4.12	986	268	30	97	132	.272	.421	.336
Sept./Oct.	7-22	4.26	994	271	18	112	123	.273	.383	.348
Leading Off Inn.			1342	365	29	108	172	.272	.396	.330
Runners On			2452	693	55	279	358	.283	.416	.352
Runners/Scor. Pos.			1418	390	28	198	224	.275	.406	.355
Runners On/2 Out			1039	265	25	123	160	.255	.387	.338
Scor. Pos./2 Out			662	163	14	91	114	.246	.372	.342
Late Inning Pressure			1138	290	20	127	197	.255	.355	.330
Leading Off			278	75	6	26	47	.270	.371	.337
Runners On			498	131	6	72	84	.263	.359	.351
Runners/Scor. Pos.			282	71	4	56	54	.252	.362	.365
First 9 Batters			2704	721	54	268	436	.267	.384	.333
Second 9 Batters			1387	354	40	142	193	.255	.395	.327
All Batters Thereafter			1477	428	41	158	188	.290	.440	.358

Starting pitchers: 50–68, 4.56 ERA
Relief pitchers: 25–19, 3.70 ERA
Ground outs-to-air outs ratio: 1.16.... Mike Witt's complete-game shutout vs. Baltimore on May 28 was the first by an Angels pitcher in 140 games since June 21, 1987 (by Jerry Reuss vs. Kansas City). That snapped the longest streak in the team's history, and the longest in the majors since 1977.... Lost their last seven home games and their last seven road games. Streak of 11 straight road victories (July 6–Aug. 2) was longest in majors last season.... Allowed one fewer home run to left-handed batters than they did to right-handers. The last team to allow more home runs to lefties than to righties was the 1984 Detroit Tigers (73 by LHB, 57 by RHB).... Worst record in the majors last season (1–8) in home games that were tied after eight innings.

Chicago White Sox

	W–L	ERA	AB	H	HR	BB	SO	BA	SA	OBA
Season	71-90	4.12	5520	1467	138	533	754	.266	.399	.331
vs. Left-Handers			2043	565	53	237	263	.277	.418	.350
vs. Right-Handers			3477	902	85	296	491	.259	.389	.319
Home	40-41	3.90	2854	754	64	283	402	.264	.392	.330
Road	31-49	4.36	2666	713	74	250	352	.267	.407	.332
Grass	59-75	4.15	4651	1249	109	456	641	.269	.399	.334
Artificial Turf	12-15	4.00	869	218	29	77	113	.251	.402	.314
April	11-10	3.29	717	164	15	67	100	.229	.344	.301
May	10-17	4.71	921	255	21	99	130	.277	.412	.345
June	13-15	4.81	962	281	26	98	118	.292	.453	.357
July	12-16	4.36	991	282	24	85	127	.285	.417	.340
August	12-17	4.20	999	280	33	92	130	.280	.425	.341
Sept./Oct.	13-15	3.21	930	205	19	92	149	.220	.327	.292
Leading Off Inn.			1314	354	28	124	163	.269	.389	.336
Runners On			2467	657	61	245	336	.266	.402	.329
Runners/Scor. Pos.			1400	370	34	168	197	.264	.403	.336
Runners On/2 Out			1019	239	26	108	138	.235	.370	.313
Scor. Pos./2 Out			647	154	16	80	93	.238	.372	.330
Late Inning Pressure			1057	287	24	106	148	.272	.397	.339
Leading Off			264	78	5	21	31	.295	.432	.350
Runners On			472	120	10	58	65	.254	.369	.333
Runners/Scor. Pos.			289	71	7	41	45	.246	.384	.335
First 9 Batters			2812	748	59	294	419	.266	.385	.335
Second 9 Batters			1500	389	41	139	205	.259	.397	.323
All Batters Thereafter			1208	330	38	100	130	.273	.436	.330

Starting pitchers: 53–66, 3.99 ERA
Relief pitchers: 18–24, 4.45 ERA
Ground outs-to-air outs ratio: 1.18, highest in the A.L.... Compiled fewest complete games in majors (11).... Didn't win more than four consecutive home games all season.... White Sox used 10 rookie pitchers last season, combining for 552.2 innings pitched, most of any club in the majors.... Only A.L. club to have five different pitchers lose at least 10 games last season.... Lost 10 games in which they led after seven innings; only the Yankees lost more (11).... A different pitcher has led the club in victories in each of the last six seasons: Hoyt, Seaver, Burns, Cowley, Bannister, and Reuss.... Longest droughts since last World Championship: White Sox (A.L.), Cubs (N.L.), Rangers (NHL), Cardinals (NFL), and Pistons (NBA).

Cleveland Indians

	W–L	ERA	AB	H	HR	BB	SO	BA	SA	OBA
Season	78-84	4.16	5555	1501	120	442	812	.270	.394	.326
vs. Left-Handers			2277	622	37	205	291	.273	.387	.334
vs. Right-Handers			3278	879	83	237	521	.268	.400	.321
Home	44-37	3.94	2832	747	52	216	411	.264	.371	.318
Road	34-47	4.40	2723	754	68	226	401	.277	.419	.334
Grass	69-68	3.97	4719	1262	93	354	691	.267	.381	.321
Artificial Turf	9-16	5.24	836	239	27	88	121	.286	.470	.356
April	16-6	3.14	753	191	12	58	116	.254	.356	.310
May	15-13	3.89	960	244	16	64	142	.254	.361	.303
June	10-17	5.03	931	267	29	98	137	.287	.446	.358
July	11-17	5.04	992	296	27	64	136	.298	.439	.344
August	12-16	4.00	939	248	14	70	139	.264	.368	.316
Sept./Oct.	14-15	3.72	980	255	22	88	142	.260	.388	.323
Leading Off Inn.			1350	366	29	82	193	.271	.391	.315
Runners On			2437	678	58	222	363	.278	.414	.339
Runners/Scor. Pos.			1401	386	28	154	217	.276	.410	.346
Runners On/2 Out			1060	302	28	112	160	.285	.438	.358
Scor. Pos./2 Out			696	192	16	88	107	.276	.424	.364
Late Inning Pressure			966	269	15	85	157	.278	.383	.338
Leading Off			239	77	8	9	39	.322	.498	.349
Runners On			441	112	5	57	72	.254	.349	.339
Runners/Scor. Pos.			270	63	2	43	48	.233	.319	.338
First 9 Batters			2507	655	46	217	405	.261	.365	.322
Second 9 Batters			1513	403	41	128	207	.266	.408	.325
All Batters Thereafter			1535	443	33	97	200	.289	.429	.333

Starting pitchers: 65–62, 4.12 ERA
Relief pitchers: 13–22, 4.38 ERA
Ground outs-to-air outs ratio: 1.05. . . . Allowed 20 innings of five runs or more, highest total in majors. . . . Lost four home games in which they led after eight innings. That tied them with the Yankees for most such losses in the majors last season. . . . Tied club record of 46 saves set in 1976. . . . One of three A.L. clubs (besides Mariners and Blue Jays) without a 20-game winner since the 1974 season. Jenkins (Rangers), Ryan (Angels), and Perry (Indians) were the last 20-game winners for their respective clubs, all in 1974. . . . Staff ERA on artificial turf was the highest of any team in the majors last season. . . . Allowed 4.46 runs per nine innings with Allanson catching, 5.16 per nine with Bando behind the plate.

Detroit Tigers

	W–L	ERA	AB	H	HR	BB	SO	BA	SA	OBA
Season	88-74	3.71	5489	1361	150	497	890	.248	.385	.312
vs. Left-Handers			2378	568	54	230	349	.239	.367	.306
vs. Right-Handers			3111	793	96	267	541	.255	.398	.317
Home	50-31	3.32	2771	654	76	244	492	.236	.365	.300
Road	38-43	4.12	2718	707	74	253	398	.260	.404	.324
Grass	80-58	3.49	4701	1150	122	417	784	.245	.374	.308
Artificial Turf	8-16	5.06	788	211	28	80	106	.268	.449	.334
April	13-8	3.95	722	185	18	63	143	.256	.399	.315
May	15-12	4.16	913	225	31	95	143	.246	.395	.319
June	18-9	3.38	907	225	26	81	159	.248	.387	.310
July	15-12	2.77	880	200	20	72	144	.227	.348	.290
August	14-16	4.15	1028	269	27	101	152	.262	.406	.329
Sept./Oct.	13-17	3.83	1039	257	28	85	164	.247	.373	.307
Leading Off Inn.			1346	330	36	94	210	.245	.383	.299
Runners On			2269	572	68	243	362	.252	.401	.323
Runners/Scor. Pos.			1243	305	40	175	231	.245	.400	.333
Runners On/2 Out			984	222	25	118	175	.226	.357	.311
Scor. Pos./2 Out			605	131	16	85	110	.217	.344	.314
Late Inning Pressure			993	229	24	94	176	.231	.346	.301
Leading Off			256	53	5	15	39	.207	.305	.254
Runners On			376	86	13	53	69	.229	.378	.330
Runners/Scor. Pos.			217	37	5	42	44	.171	.276	.311
First 9 Batters			2337	550	58	226	449	.235	.360	.305
Second 9 Batters			1453	375	44	137	221	.258	.409	.322
All Batters Thereafter			1699	436	48	134	220	.257	.397	.313

Starting pitchers: 67–61, 3.94 ERA
Relief pitchers: 21–13, 3.01 ERA
Ground outs-to-air outs ratio: 0.97. . . . Held opponents to two runs or less in eight straight games, longest streak in majors last season. . . . Batting average by opposing left-handed hitters was 2d lowest in A.L., two points higher than Oakland's. Detroit had led league in four previous seasons. . . . Opponents' BA with runners in scoring position in LIP Situations was lowest in majors over past 14 years. . . . Tigers made the fewest pitching changes (220) of any team in the majors last season. Used only nine pitchers out of the bullpen, tying the A's for the fewest in the majors. . . . Jack Morris is one shy of A.L. record for consecutive opening day starts for one club: 10, Walter Johnson for Senators, 1912–21. Robin Roberts has N.L. mark of 12 in a row for Phillies, 1950–61.

Kansas City Royals

	W–L	ERA	AB	H	HR	BB	SO	BA	SA	OBA
Season	84-77	3.65	5474	1415	102	465	886	.258	.378	.318
vs. Left-Handers			2148	550	30	189	343	.256	.358	.318
vs. Right-Handers			3326	865	72	276	543	.260	.391	.318
Home	44-36	3.70	2814	756	37	206	407	.269	.382	.320
Road	40-41	3.61	2660	659	65	259	479	.248	.374	.317
Grass	32-30	3.37	2015	479	42	203	367	.238	.348	.310
Artificial Turf	52-47	3.83	3459	936	60	262	519	.271	.395	.323
April	12-10	3.73	718	174	16	72	121	.242	.366	.313
May	11-17	4.06	974	268	17	81	161	.275	.402	.332
June	17-10	3.15	890	222	22	72	126	.249	.370	.308
July	12-15	4.27	930	247	25	86	128	.266	.415	.328
August	18-10	3.10	960	244	9	71	176	.254	.346	.307
Sept./Oct.	14-15	3.65	1002	260	13	83	174	.259	.366	.319
Leading Off Inn.			1327	340	29	98	194	.256	.378	.311
Runners On			2347	630	41	218	389	.268	.379	.330
Runners/Scor. Pos.			1405	359	25	147	250	.256	.367	.324
Runners On/2 Out			1003	245	16	93	168	.244	.356	.315
Scor. Pos./2 Out			656	154	12	67	117	.235	.348	.315
Late Inning Pressure			1037	251	13	93	176	.242	.344	.309
Leading Off			257	61	4	18	39	.237	.366	.295
Runners On			425	104	4	48	72	.245	.325	.326
Runners/Scor. Pos.			268	63	1	35	53	.235	.310	.330
First 9 Batters			2456	635	41	234	435	.259	.372	.325
Second 9 Batters			1431	369	29	118	200	.258	.374	.316
All Batters Thereafter			1587	411	32	113	251	.259	.391	.309

Starting pitchers: 64–57, 3.70 ERA
Relief pitchers: 20–20, 3.52 ERA
Ground outs-to-air outs ratio: 1.17, 3d highest in the A.L. . . . Allowed fewest home runs in A.L. for fourth consecutive season. The Orioles are the only team that has led the A.L. for more than four straight seasons, leading league for six straight from 1956 through 1961. . . . But they did allow the most triples of any A.L. club. . . . Allowed 151 multi-run innings, tying Milwaukee and Oakland for lowest total in A.L. . . . Led A.L. in ERA during June. . . . Opponents' batting average on grass surfaces was lowest in A.L. since 1975. . . . Have won 13 consecutive games against Baltimore, their longest winning streak ever against any particular opponent. . . . Haven't allowed an extra-inning HR since May 13, 1987 (Larry Sheets off Steve Farr), longest current streak in majors.

Milwaukee Brewers

	W–L	ERA	AB	H	HR	BB	SO	BA	SA	OBA
Season	87-75	3.45	5468	1355	125	437	832	.248	.366	.303
vs. Left-Handers			2305	578	46	191	302	.251	.361	.306
vs. Right-Handers			3163	777	79	246	530	.246	.369	.300
Home	47-34	3.37	2803	683	65	212	413	.244	.360	.296
Road	40-41	3.53	2665	672	60	225	419	.252	.372	.310
Grass	72-66	3.43	4655	1148	107	367	702	.247	.363	.301
Artificial Turf	15-9	3.56	813	207	18	70	130	.255	.385	.312
April	9-11	3.59	637	156	11	57	91	.245	.347	.306
May	17-13	3.33	1000	233	26	77	143	.233	.360	.287
June	12-15	3.15	915	220	15	74	108	.240	.338	.299
July	14-15	3.37	988	260	26	71	174	.263	.394	.313
August	17-13	4.14	1042	278	27	81	178	.267	.394	.316
Sept./Oct.	18-8	3.07	886	208	20	77	138	.235	.351	.296
Leading Off Inn.			1360	313	33	90	188	.230	.352	.279
Runners On			2189	583	49	216	333	.266	.390	.327
Runners/Scor. Pos.			1228	323	32	145	190	.263	.397	.331
Runners On/2 Out			958	240	20	114	153	.251	.362	.332
Scor. Pos./2 Out			609	146	15	83	95	.240	.356	.333
Late Inning Pressure			870	212	18	88	155	.244	.349	.313
Leading Off			223	42	5	19	37	.188	.305	.252
Runners On			340	90	8	45	56	.265	.385	.349
Runners/Scor. Pos.			180	54	7	31	29	.300	.472	.397
First 9 Batters			2585	622	50	218	452	.241	.347	.298
Second 9 Batters			1512	364	32	105	206	.241	.353	.289
All Batters Thereafter			1371	369	43	114	174	.269	.416	.326

Starting pitchers: 69–61, 3.69 ERA
Relief pitchers: 18–14, 2.82 ERA
Ground outs-to-air outs ratio: 1.05. . . . Starting pitchers compiled lowest ERA in A.L. . . . Milwaukee defeated Baltimore 12–0 on opening day, equalling the largest opening-day shutout margin in A.L. history, set by Angels and Twins, on April 7, 1970, against Milwaukee and Chicago, respectively. The modern major league record: 14–0, by Pirates over Reds on 4/12/11. . . . Held opponents to single figures in runs in 111 consecutive games (a club record) from Sept. 23, 1987, through July 26, 1988, when Yankees snapped streak. . . . Have won 116 straight home games in which they have led after eight innings (since Apr. 17, 1986). . . . Allowed only nine first-inning home runs last season, fewest of any A.L. club.

Minnesota Twins

	W–L	ERA	AB	H	HR	BB	SO	BA	SA	OBA
Season	91-71	3.93	5477	1457	146	453	897	.266	.402	.325
vs. Left-Handers			2219	627	69	215	337	.283	.439	.348
vs. Right-Handers			3258	830	77	238	560	.255	.377	.308
Home	47-34	4.11	2824	762	79	244	493	.270	.411	.332
Road	44-37	3.74	2653	695	67	209	404	.262	.392	.317
Grass	34-28	3.72	2049	541	49	158	312	.264	.388	.318
Artificial Turf	57-43	4.05	3428	916	97	295	585	.267	.411	.328
April	8-13	5.96	731	209	27	85	151	.286	.465	.363
May	17-10	3.81	917	247	24	66	158	.269	.400	.321
June	17-10	3.28	929	242	19	63	145	.260	.375	.309
July	15-12	3.73	896	240	27	76	140	.268	.431	.328
August	17-13	3.73	996	253	33	90	149	.254	.394	.317
Sept./Oct.	17-13	3.59	1008	266	16	73	154	.264	.367	.318
Leading Off Inn.			1322	347	32	106	206	.262	.399	.321
Runners On			2354	637	60	210	383	.271	.395	.330
Runners/Scor. Pos.			1378	355	32	150	270	.258	.375	.328
Runners On/2 Out			968	227	16	99	190	.235	.336	.309
Scor. Pos./2 Out			637	135	7	77	139	.212	.292	.300
Late Inning Pressure			850	207	23	92	152	.244	.378	.319
Leading Off			208	50	4	24	35	.240	.380	.319
Runners On			367	90	13	41	66	.245	.381	.325
Runners/Scor. Pos.			225	55	11	29	38	.244	.436	.331
First 9 Batters			2707	693	69	235	501	.256	.388	.319
Second 9 Batters			1479	410	44	123	222	.277	.419	.333
All Batters Thereafter			1291	354	33	95	174	.274	.414	.326

Starting pitchers: 68–53, 3.95 ERA
Relief pitchers: 23–18, 3.91 ERA
Ground outs-to-air outs ratio: 0.85, lowest in the majors. . . . ERA ranked 13th in home games, 4th on the road. . . . First A.L. club that did not get a win from a rookie pitcher since the 1985 Royals. German Gonzalez was the only rookie pitcher to appear in a game for Minnesota. . . . Have won their last 11 games against Detroit, their longest streak ever against the Tigers. . . . Used 17 different pitchers out of the bullpen last season, the most of any team in the majors. . . . Only team in the majors to have a winning record in one-run games on the road, but a losing record in such games at home. . . . No Twins' pitcher was removed from a game after facing only one batter last season. Relievers faced a single batter only four times, each in game-ending situations.

New York Yankees

	W–L	ERA	AB	H	HR	BB	SO	BA	SA	OBA
Season	85-76	4.24	5655	1512	157	487	861	.267	.414	.328
vs. Left-Handers			2052	537	55	208	276	.262	.400	.331
vs. Right-Handers			3603	975	102	279	585	.271	.422	.326
Home	46-34	3.83	2842	729	75	228	444	.257	.389	.314
Road	39-42	4.67	2813	783	82	259	417	.278	.439	.342
Grass	68-68	4.12	4781	1260	128	419	725	.264	.405	.326
Artificial Turf	17-8	4.94	874	252	29	68	136	.288	.465	.340
April	16-7	3.90	816	201	28	62	143	.246	.403	.305
May	17-9	3.02	877	200	21	65	140	.228	.344	.284
June	12-15	4.30	951	261	22	87	129	.274	.411	.335
July	15-11	3.59	898	234	21	70	151	.261	.392	.313
August	9-20	6.61	1073	352	38	94	131	.328	.521	.383
Sept./Oct.	16-14	3.82	1040	264	27	109	167	.254	.393	.332
Leading Off Inn.			1366	367	42	90	184	.269	.417	.317
Runners On			2450	665	63	258	396	.271	.414	.341
Runners/Scor. Pos.			1412	366	34	190	261	.259	.399	.344
Runners On/2 Out			1031	250	24	109	176	.242	.367	.324
Scor. Pos./2 Out			668	155	13	83	123	.232	.347	.324
Late Inning Pressure			975	232	24	85	175	.238	.359	.304
Leading Off			242	51	4	17	47	.211	.318	.265
Runners On			399	88	11	47	70	.221	.328	.308
Runners/Scor. Pos.			232	45	4	36	49	.194	.267	.308
First 9 Batters			2962	769	73	271	496	.260	.391	.324
Second 9 Batters			1578	432	47	127	224	.274	.433	.330
All Batters Thereafter			1115	311	37	89	141	.279	.448	.336

Starting pitchers: 56–53, 4.55 ERA
Relief pitchers: 29–23, 3.80 ERA
Ground outs-to-air outs ratio: 1.02. . . . Allowed the most home runs in the majors for the first time since 1919, when they were still tenants in the Polo Grounds. Yanks hadn't even led their own league in gophers since 1945. . . . August ERA was highest by any team, in either league, in any month last season except October. . . . Starters averaged only 5.62 innings per game last season, worst of any team in the majors. . . . Opponents scored at least one run in 428 different innings (most in majors), while Yanks scored in only 408 innings. . . . Yanks were the only undefeated team in the majors last season (9–0) in home games in which they were tied after eight innings. . . . Breakdown of one-run decisions: 17–8 at home, 6–17 on the road.

Oakland A's

	W–L	ERA	AB	H	HR	BB	SO	BA	SA	OBA
Season	104-58	3.44	5568	1376	116	553	983	.247	.360	.316
vs. Left-Handers			2511	595	46	272	444	.237	.342	.311
vs. Right-Handers			3057	781	70	281	539	.255	.374	.320
Home	54-27	3.21	2798	675	47	253	522	.241	.336	.304
Road	50-31	3.68	2770	701	69	300	461	.253	.384	.327
Grass	87-50	3.39	4705	1145	91	464	834	.243	.349	.312
Artificial Turf	17-8	3.72	863	231	25	89	149	.268	.416	.336
April	16-7	3.76	788	191	17	89	143	.242	.373	.319
May	19-8	2.87	914	214	12	91	151	.234	.323	.304
June	13-14	4.06	966	268	26	91	156	.277	.407	.341
July	16-12	3.26	967	226	28	85	173	.234	.364	.298
August	20-9	3.38	962	237	18	100	160	.246	.346	.316
Sept./Oct.	20-8	3.36	971	240	15	97	200	.247	.346	.315
Leading Off Inn.			1384	335	23	106	228	.242	.348	.297
Runners On			2322	553	51	276	410	.238	.349	.316
Runners/Scor. Pos.			1289	314	26	189	253	.244	.352	.334
Runners On/2 Out			1041	245	19	124	183	.235	.340	.321
Scor. Pos./2 Out			642	155	10	89	117	.241	.343	.340
Late Inning Pressure			1080	234	20	108	228	.217	.313	.290
Leading Off			277	57	5	21	60	.206	.307	.264
Runners On			433	90	9	52	84	.208	.312	.293
Runners/Scor. Pos.			242	50	4	41	54	.207	.314	.318
First 9 Batters			2654	613	48	286	541	.231	.326	.307
Second 9 Batters			1513	401	37	131	249	.265	.404	.324
All Batters Thereafter			1401	362	31	136	193	.258	.375	.323

Starting pitchers: 75–44, 3.70 ERA
Relief pitchers: 29–14, 2.81 ERA
Ground outs-to-air outs ratio: 0.94, 2d lowest in the majors. . . . Opponents' batting average in Late-Inning Pressure Situations was 2d lowest in A.L. in past 14 years. Detroit compiled .204 mark in 1984. . . . A's mark with runners on base was best in league during that period. . . . Rookie pitchers combined for a 3.13 ERA, lowest of any A.L. club. Give credit to Todd Burns, who pitched 76 percent of the A's "rookie innings". . . . Left-handed pitchers started 28 games, lowest total in A.L. . . . Won the opening games of eight of their 10 road trips. . . . Set major league record with 76 balks. Let's hope that one stands forever. . . . Used 10 pitchers, the most ever by an A.L. club in a five -game World Series, and one shy of the record for any length Series.

Seattle Mariners

	W–L	ERA	AB	H	HR	BB	SO	BA	SA	OBA
Season	68-93	4.15	5408	1385	144	558	981	.256	.398	.327
vs. Left-Handers			2270	603	52	263	359	.266	.398	.343
vs. Right-Handers			3138	782	92	295	622	.249	.397	.315
Home	37-44	4.30	2797	728	81	281	501	.260	.410	.329
Road	31-49	3.99	2611	657	63	277	480	.252	.384	.325
Grass	26-36	4.04	2030	498	52	225	392	.245	.378	.322
Artificial Turf	42-57	4.22	3378	887	92	333	589	.263	.410	.330
April	10-14	4.86	823	223	26	79	139	.271	.428	.334
May	12-15	4.60	909	244	31	101	149	.268	.431	.345
June	8-19	3.48	885	236	17	84	151	.267	.405	.330
July	10-16	5.21	887	232	32	92	184	.262	.436	.335
August	14-16	3.79	1017	254	22	107	180	.250	.368	.322
Sept./Oct.	14-13	3.16	887	196	16	95	178	.221	.325	.296
Leading Off Inn.			1314	336	31	114	225	.256	.384	.318
Runners On			2296	623	61	278	396	.271	.420	.348
Runners/Scor. Pos.			1360	365	35	203	259	.268	.418	.358
Runners On/2 Out			927	221	23	127	174	.238	.362	.334
Scor. Pos./2 Out			623	144	15	101	126	.231	.355	.343
Late Inning Pressure			890	229	35	103	165	.257	.411	.334
Leading Off			224	63	7	21	35	.281	.406	.343
Runners On			365	103	14	56	65	.282	.444	.372
Runners/Scor. Pos.			197	56	6	45	44	.284	.426	.405
First 9 Batters			2628	644	72	300	524	.245	.382	.323
Second 9 Batters			1425	371	30	142	241	.260	.389	.328
All Batters Thereafter			1355	370	42	116	216	.273	.437	.333

Starting pitchers: 47–71, 4.34 ERA
Relief pitchers: 21–22, 3.81 ERA
Ground outs-to-air outs ratio: 1.11. . . . Had the league's highest home-game ERA, and highest ERA during July. . . . Won the first game of nine of their 11 home stands. . . . Held opponents to seven runs or fewer in 42 straight games (Aug. 3–Sept. 17), longest streak in team history. . . . Composite relief stats were roughly the same as those of the Red Sox. . . . Staff allowed 109 1st-inning runs, most in the majors. . . . Mariners' relievers were summoned to face a single batter 31 times last season, most of any team in the majors. . . . Mariners and Blue Jays are only clubs in majors without a 20-game winner in their history. Both clubs are entering their 13th season. Royals and Brewers had 20-game winners in their fifth season, Padres in their seventh, Expos in their 10th.

Texas Rangers

	W–L	ERA	AB	H	HR	BB	SO	BA	SA	OBA
Season	70-91	4.05	5375	1310	129	654	912	.244	.364	.329
vs. Left-Handers			2219	543	42	279	385	.245	.349	.332
vs. Right-Handers			3156	767	87	375	527	.243	.375	.327
Home	38-43	3.92	2762	685	67	327	433	.248	.364	.331
Road	32-48	4.18	2613	625	62	327	479	.239	.364	.327
Grass	58-77	3.88	4500	1088	110	543	757	.242	.359	.326
Artificial Turf	12-14	4.92	875	222	19	111	155	.254	.391	.343
April	8-13	3.76	677	149	17	86	122	.220	.334	.312
May	17-11	4.34	963	248	17	125	163	.258	.368	.348
June	12-15	3.61	923	208	27	108	166	.225	.352	.309
July	9-18	3.96	871	220	25	105	134	.253	.392	.335
August	14-14	4.52	909	217	16	111	151	.239	.353	.322
Sept./Oct.	10-20	4.03	1032	268	27	119	176	.260	.379	.341
Leading Off Inn.			1315	284	34	121	191	.216	.344	.287
Runners On			2285	616	62	308	378	.270	.404	.356
Runners/Scor. Pos.			1341	363	36	222	245	.271	.410	.369
Runners On/2 Out			995	250	22	151	162	.251	.364	.356
Scor. Pos./2 Out			650	172	13	120	112	.265	.377	.384
Late Inning Pressure			967	231	19	135	163	.239	.345	.338
Leading Off			241	49	6	29	34	.203	.307	.297
Runners On			396	103	9	70	69	.260	.381	.374
Runners/Scor. Pos.			237	63	9	51	47	.266	.426	.397
First 9 Batters			2332	576	59	304	433	.247	.379	.338
Second 9 Batters			1361	315	24	146	216	.231	.326	.309
All Batters Thereafter			1682	419	46	204	263	.249	.375	.333

Starting pitchers: 60–72, 3.95 ERA
Relief pitchers: 10–19, 4.48 ERA
Ground outs-to-air outs ratio: 1.17, 2d highest in A.L. . . . Led A.L. in complete games (41) for first time in team history. . . . Opponents' batting average leading off innings was lowest in A.L. over past 14 seasons. . . . Relief pitchers compiled highest ERA in majors. . . . Starters averaged 6.87 innings pitched per game, highest of any team in the majors last season. . . . Lost seven games in which they led after eight innings, tying them with the Yankees for most in the majors last season. . . . Allowed the fewest triples in the majors last season (19). . . . Tied major league record by surrendering nine grand slam homers last season. . . . There were only four games last season in which Rangers' pitchers did not walk a batter, fewest of any team in the majors.

Toronto Blue Jays

	W–L	ERA	AB	H	HR	BB	SO	BA	SA	OBA
Season	87-75	3.80	5484	1404	143	528	904	.256	.392	.326
vs. Left-Handers			1964	505	41	188	289	.257	.371	.323
vs. Right-Handers			3520	899	102	340	615	.255	.404	.327
Home	45-36	3.83	2824	731	73	256	466	.259	.393	.325
Road	42-39	3.76	2660	673	70	272	438	.253	.391	.327
Grass	33-30	3.75	2077	525	56	213	354	.253	.387	.327
Artificial Turf	54-45	3.82	3407	879	87	315	550	.258	.395	.325
April	9-13	4.16	750	201	18	85	142	.268	.420	.344
May	13-16	3.70	984	254	22	98	162	.258	.383	.330
June	17-11	3.84	938	243	31	108	156	.259	.418	.341
July	12-14	4.08	903	240	25	73	108	.266	.405	.327
August	14-14	3.89	951	244	26	83	165	.257	.390	.319
Sept./Oct.	22-7	3.22	958	222	21	81	171	.232	.344	.298
Leading Off Inn.			1320	345	48	117	192	.261	.420	.329
Runners On			2382	609	44	240	380	.256	.375	.326
Runners/Scor. Pos.			1363	340	30	173	240	.249	.372	.334
Runners On/2 Out			998	224	17	101	169	.224	.302	.302
Scor. Pos./2 Out			639	136	11	75	118	.213	.319	.302
Late Inning Pressure			821	213	22	99	170	.259	.410	.345
Leading Off			202	48	8	25	28	.238	.431	.328
Runners On			340	100	7	48	77	.294	.444	.386
Runners/Scor. Pos.			221	60	4	38	53	.271	.398	.374
First 9 Batters			2752	704	68	292	516	.256	.388	.332
Second 9 Batters			1543	374	41	136	252	.242	.382	.308
All Batters Thereafter			1189	326	34	100	136	.274	.415	.336

Starting pitchers: 67–55, 3.91 ERA
Relief pitchers: 20–20, 3.59 ERA
Ground outs-to-air outs ratio: 1.16. . . . Lowest opponents' batting average with two outs and runners in scoring position for second consecutive season. . . . Opponents batted .114 with two outs and the bases loaded, lowest mark of the past 14 years. . . . One of four major league teams to use only eight starting pitchers last season. . . . Only A.L. team besides the Orioles and Yankees whose starters lasted an average of less than six innings per game last season. . . . Led the majors in hit batsmen (59) in 1988, after tying for the fewest in the majors (22) in the previous year. . . . Blue Jays and Cardinals were the only teams that did not play a doubleheader in 1988. Jays' last twin bill was July 2, 1987. . . . Only one of their league-leading ten shutouts was a complete game.

American League

	W–L	ERA	AB	H	HR	BB	SO	BA	SA	OBA
Season	1131-1131	3.96	77005	19967	1901	7191	12323	.259	.391	.324
vs. Left-Handers			31808	8327	712	3268	4732	.262	.387	.331
vs. Right-Handers			45197	11640	1189	3923	7591	.258	.393	.320
Home	614-517	3.81	39394	10127	937	3517	6378	.257	.383	.320
Road	517-614	4.13	37611	9840	964	3674	5945	.262	.399	.329
Grass	808-808	3.88	54974	14089	1325	5176	8830	.256	.382	.322
Artificial Turf	323-323	4.18	22031	5878	576	2015	3493	.267	.412	.330
April	153-153	4.09	10336	2622	264	1021	1771	.254	.390	.323
May	193-193	4.02	13158	3419	323	1240	2091	.260	.391	.325
June	189-189	3.89	12939	3396	324	1228	2021	.262	.395	.328
July	191-191	4.10	13094	3484	356	1099	2064	.266	.407	.325
August	203-203	4.10	13805	3638	342	1298	2122	.264	.394	.328
Sept./Oct.	202-202	3.62	13673	3408	292	1305	2254	.249	.367	.317
Leading Off Inn.			18687	4735	459	1460	2802	.253	.383	.311
Runners On			33000	8842	810	3465	5214	.268	.401	.336
Runners/Scor. Pos.			18968	4977	462	2441	3294	.262	.398	.342
Runners On/2 Out			14060	3459	311	1625	2319	.246	.370	.329
Scor. Pos./2 Out			9034	2159	190	1221	1588	.239	.359	.335
Late Inning Pressure			13262	3306	300	1413	2376	.249	.369	.324
Leading Off			3312	801	80	285	568	.242	.371	.305
Runners On			5542	1393	126	758	979	.251	.369	.342
Runners/Scor. Pos.			3270	789	73	573	636	.241	.363	.352
First 9 Batters			36845	9357	824	3671	6544	.254	.376	.323
Second 9 Batters			20588	5356	539	1828	3085	.260	.397	.322
All Batters Thereafter			19572	5254	538	1692	2694	.268	.412	.328

National League

Juan Agosto
Houston Astros   Throws Left

	W–L	ERA	AB	H	HR	BB	SO	BA	SA	OBA
Season	10-2	2.26	327	74	6	30	33	.226	.327	.287
vs. Left-Handers			107	15	1	6	18	.140	.178	.184
vs. Right-Handers			220	59	5	24	15	.268	.400	.335
Home	5-0	1.03	179	35	1	15	17	.196	.263	.254
Road	5-2	3.92	148	39	5	15	16	.264	.405	.327
Grass	2-2	4.63	92	24	4	6	8	.261	.413	.303
Artificial Turf	8-0	1.45	235	50	2	24	25	.213	.294	.281
April	1-0	2.25	29	6	0	1	4	.207	.207	.233
May	1-0	0.59	51	9	1	4	6	.176	.255	.228
June	3-0	3.42	83	23	3	11	10	.277	.386	.358
July	2-0	2.93	50	9	0	8	1	.180	.340	.288
August	3-1	1.72	63	18	1	3	9	.286	.381	.318
Sept./Oct.	0-1	1.98	51	9	1	3	3	.176	.294	.218
Leading Off Inn.			84	26	4	4	6	.310	.524	.341
Runners On			133	28	1	19	16	.211	.278	.299
Runners/Scor. Pos.			81	15	0	18	11	.185	.222	.317
Runners On/2 Out			62	17	1	5	5	.274	.355	.328
Scor. Pos./2 Out			39	7	0	5	3	.179	.205	.273
Late Inning Pressure			219	47	1	21	22	.215	.279	.279
Leading Off			61	21	1	4	5	.344	.492	.385
Runners On			85	16	0	14	9	.188	.235	.291
Runners/Scor. Pos.			56	10	0	14	6	.179	.214	.324
First 9 Batters			321	71	4	29	33	.221	.305	.282
Second 9 Batters			6	3	2	1	0	.500	1.500	.571
All Batters Thereafter			0	0	0	0	0			

Loves to face: Willie McGee (0-for-7)
Hates to face: Jody Davis (3-for-3, 2 HR)
Ground outs-to-air outs ratio: 2.62 last season, 2.72 for career. . . .
Additional statistics: 12 double-play ground outs in 60 opportunities, 9 doubles, 3 triples in 91.2 innings last season. . . . One of three major league relievers with 10 or more wins. . . . Ten wins equalled his total for previous seven seasons in majors. Could have won a spot in *The Book of Baseball Records* if he'd stopped there, tying Howie Krist's N.L. record for most wins in an undefeated season; then lost his last two decisions. . . . Average of 3.24 strikeouts per nine innings was lowest among N.L. relievers (minimum: 30 games). . . . Thirteen of his 30 walks were intentional. . . . Career batting average of .202 by opposing left-handed batters, .302 by right-handers.

Jose Alvarez
Atlanta Braves   Throws Right

	W–L	ERA	AB	H	HR	BB	SO	BA	SA	OBA
Season	5-6	2.99	366	88	7	53	81	.240	.342	.343
vs. Left-Handers			171	46	3	35	36	.269	.374	.402
vs. Right-Handers			195	42	4	18	45	.215	.313	.288
Home	2-3	3.52	193	53	5	27	40	.275	.409	.369
Road	3-3	2.40	173	35	2	26	41	.202	.266	.315
Grass	5-5	3.52	257	67	6	37	54	.261	.377	.358
Artificial Turf	0-1	1.76	109	21	1	16	27	.193	.257	.310
April	0-0		0	0	0	0	0	—	—	—
May	1-1	4.02	59	17	2	10	13	.288	.390	.411
June	1-1	3.20	69	16	0	10	12	.232	.333	.329
July	1-3	3.23	112	26	4	19	28	.232	.366	.351
August	0-1	3.93	71	21	1	10	15	.296	.408	.383
Sept./Oct.	2-0	0.50	55	8	0	4	13	.145	.164	.213
Leading Off Inn.			90	25	2	4	14	.278	.400	.316
Runners On			164	34	0	35	39	.207	.244	.348
Runners/Scor. Pos.			108	20	0	26	28	.185	.231	.345
Runners On/2 Out			76	14	0	17	25	.184	.250	.340
Scor. Pos./2 Out			56	9	0	15	19	.161	.232	.347
Late Inning Pressure			189	42	3	27	39	.222	.302	.324
Leading Off			49	16	2	2	4	.327	.490	.365
Runners On			83	13	0	17	22	.157	.181	.304
Runners/Scor. Pos.			55	8	0	12	14	.145	.182	.304
First 9 Batters			324	77	7	43	77	.238	.352	.330
Second 9 Batters			42	11	0	10	4	.262	.262	.436
All Batters Thereafter			0	0	0	0	0			

Loves to face: Rob Thompson (0-for-6, 4 SO)
Hates to face: Barry Bonds (2-for-2, 2 BB, 1 HR)
Ground outs-to-air outs ratio: 1.24 last season, 1.26 for career. . . .
Additional statistics: 8 double-play ground outs in 89 opportunities, 14 doubles, 1 triple in 102.1 innings last season. . . . Led major league rookie pitchers with 60 appearances. The only other N.L. rookie to record more than one save last season was Tim Belcher (4). Alvarez had 3. . . . Opponents' career breakdown: .269 with bases empty, .207 with runners on base, .192 with runners in scoring position. . . . Hadn't played a game in the majors since 1982. Had he postponed his return until 2004, he would have matched Paul Schreiber, a Yankees batting practice pitcher who tossed four innings in 1945, 22 years after he made his previous major league appearance with Brooklyn.

Larry Andersen
Houston Astros   Throws Right

	W–L	ERA	AB	H	HR	BB	SO	BA	SA	OBA
Season	2-4	2.94	323	82	3	20	66	.254	.334	.297
vs. Left-Handers			150	44	1	15	22	.293	.360	.359
vs. Right-Handers			173	38	2	5	44	.220	.312	.239
Home	1-2	2.03	159	41	0	9	36	.258	.308	.294
Road	1-2	3.80	164	41	3	11	30	.250	.360	.299
Grass	0-1	4.07	92	23	3	6	19	.250	.424	.296
Artificial Turf	2-3	2.47	231	59	0	14	47	.255	.299	.297
April	1-1	5.00	39	14	0	5	3	.359	.436	.432
May	0-1	7.20	20	6	1	1	1	.300	.450	.318
June	1-1	1.64	87	22	2	2	22	.253	.379	.270
July	0-0	3.14	59	16	0	6	15	.271	.356	.333
August	0-1	1.16	83	16	0	3	19	.193	.229	.227
Sept./Oct.	0-0	6.00	35	8	0	3	6	.229	.257	.289
Leading Off Inn.			71	19	1	6	12	.268	.338	.325
Runners On			152	41	0	13	32	.270	.322	.321
Runners/Scor. Pos.			98	27	0	11	26	.276	.316	.339
Runners On/2 Out			77	21	0	9	15	.273	.338	.349
Scor. Pos./2 Out			56	14	0	8	14	.250	.286	.344
Late Inning Pressure			199	44	2	15	41	.221	.286	.278
Leading Off			47	13	0	3	8	.277	.277	.320
Runners On			87	19	0	11	18	.218	.276	.303
Runners/Scor. Pos.			54	12	0	10	14	.222	.241	.338
First 9 Batters			296	76	3	16	61	.257	.345	.295
Second 9 Batters			27	6	0	4	5	.222	.222	.313
All Batters Thereafter			0	0	0	0	0	—	—	—

Loves to face: Shawon Dunston (0-for-10)
Hates to face: Ozzie Smith (.538, 7-for-13, 8 BB)
Ground outs-to-air outs ratio: 1.27 last season, 1.28 for career. . . .
Additional statistics: 7 double-play ground outs in 56 opportunities, 11 doubles, 3 triples in 82.2 innings last season. . . . Opponents batted .293 before the All-Star break, .214 after the break. . . . Didn't allow a home run in 55.1 innings after June 17. . . . Hasn't allowed a home run at the Astrodome since surrendering back-to-back shots to Juan Samuel and Mike Schmidt on May 11, 1987. . . . Made major league debut in 1975 for Frank Robinson's Cleveland Indians. . . . Started one game for Seattle in 1982, the only start of his 409-game career. . . . A human leading indicator: He joined Philadelphia in 1983; they went to the Series. Joined Houston in 1986, they reached the N.L.C.S.

Joaquin Andujar
Houston Astros   Throws Right

	W–L	ERA	AB	H	HR	BB	SO	BA	SA	OBA
Season	2-5	4.00	317	94	9	21	35	.297	.454	.346
vs. Left-Handers			148	42	4	14	10	.284	.439	.345
vs. Right-Handers			169	52	5	7	25	.308	.467	.346
Home	1-2	3.78	185	51	5	9	23	.276	.422	.322
Road	1-3	4.35	132	43	4	12	12	.326	.500	.378
Grass	0-1	4.37	101	35	3	6	12	.347	.515	.378
Artificial Turf	2-4	3.86	216	59	6	15	23	.273	.426	.331
April			0	0	0	0	0	—	—	—
May	0-2	9.00	33	12	3	3	3	.364	.727	.410
June	0-1	1.62	67	17	1	3	9	.254	.358	.315
July	1-1	3.73	122	39	3	12	11	.320	.484	.378
August	1-1	5.19	71	19	2	1	7	.268	.423	.288
Sept./Oct.	0-0	2.84	24	7	0	2	5	.292	.292	.333
Leading Off Inn.			74	21	0	6	8	.284	.311	.354
Runners On			149	44	5	9	20	.295	.463	.331
Runners/Scor. Pos.			99	28	5	9	18	.283	.495	.336
Runners On/2 Out			59	12	0	3	10	.203	.254	.242
Scor. Pos./2 Out			41	7	0	3	9	.171	.244	.227
Late Inning Pressure			47	13	4	5	7	.277	.617	.346
Leading Off			13	4	0	1	1	.308	.308	.357
Runners On			19	6	2	2	4	.316	.789	.381
Runners/Scor. Pos.			15	5	2	2	4	.333	.933	.412
First 9 Batters			147	46	4	12	13	.313	.456	.373
Second 9 Batters			93	29	4	5	12	.312	.516	.350
All Batters Thereafter			77	19	1	4	10	.247	.377	.284

Loves to face: R. J. Reynolds (0-for-10)
Hates to face: Tom Brunansky (.500, 4-for-8, 2 HR)
Ground outs-to-air outs ratio: 1.11 last season, 1.32 for career. . . .
Additional statistics: 4 double-play ground outs in 64 opportunities, 15 doubles, 4 triples in 78.2 innings last season. . . . Allowed 5 first-inning runs in 10 starts. . . . Batting support: 4.80 runs per start. . . . Record of 2-3 (3.59 ERA) as a starter, 0–2 (5.14) in 13 relief appearances. . . . Yearly total of wins since 1984: 20, 21, 12, 3, 2. . . . He was the last N.L. pitcher to win 20 or more games in consecutive seasons, something that Cone, Hershiser, and Jackson will be attempting to do in 1989. . . . Opponents' batting average was a career high. Previous high was .277 in 1980. . . . Has faced 158 batters with the bases loaded, but has never allowed a grand slam.

Paul Assenmacher

Throws Left

Atlanta Braves	W–L	ERA	AB	H	HR	BB	SO	BA	SA	OBA
Season	8-7	3.06	287	72	4	32	71	.251	.341	.327
vs. Left-Handers			91	25	2	5	22	.275	.385	.320
vs. Right-Handers			196	47	2	27	49	.240	.321	.330
Home	7-5	4.87	162	45	3	22	37	.278	.389	.366
Road	1-2	1.16	125	27	1	10	34	.216	.280	.274
Grass	7-6	3.86	230	63	4	28	55	.274	.383	.354
Artificial Turf	1-1	0.48	57	9	0	4	16	.158	.175	.213
April	0-2	5.25	42	10	1	6	9	.238	.381	.347
May	1-1	1.80	50	11	0	7	14	.220	.260	.316
June	1-1	5.63	58	19	1	7	10	.328	.483	.394
July	3-2	1.86	71	16	0	6	21	.225	.268	.286
August	0-0	1.50	20	2	1	5	4	.100	.250	.280
Sept./Oct.	3-1	1.64	46	14	1	1	13	.304	.370	.319
Leading Off Inn.			61	20	2	6	12	.328	.492	.388
Runners On			148	36	2	19	35	.243	.331	.331
Runners/Scor. Pos.			91	23	0	18	20	.253	.286	.378
Runners On/2 Out			66	16	0	6	16	.242	.318	.315
Scor. Pos./2 Out			46	12	0	6	9	.261	.304	.358
Late Inning Pressure			197	51	4	22	52	.259	.371	.335
Leading Off			43	13	2	5	9	.302	.512	.375
Runners On			101	25	2	12	26	.248	.356	.330
Runners/Scor. Pos.			60	15	0	12	14	.250	.283	.378
First 9 Batters			278	71	4	32	69	.255	.349	.331
Second 9 Batters			9	1	0	0	2	.111	.111	.200
All Batters Thereafter			0	0	0	0	0	—	—	—

Loves to face: Darryl Strawberry (.083, 1-for-12)
Hates to face: Eric Davis (4-for-4, 2 BB, 1 HR)
Ground outs-to-air outs ratio: 1.23 last season, 1.35 for career. . . .
Additional statistics: 10 double-play ground outs in 74 opportunities, 12 doubles, 1 triple in 79.1 innings last season. . . . Giants batted .483 (14-for-29) against him last season. Career record of 0–3 against them. . . . Has pitched 177 games in his career, but has never allowed more than one home run in a game. . . . Only one Braves pitcher—Boston, Milwaukee, or Atlanta—pitched more games over a three-year period: Gene Garber (179, 1978–1980; and 182, 1984–1986). . . . Opponents' career breakdown: .236 with the bases empty, .266 with runners on base. . . . Has faced 36 batters with bases loaded, striking out 14 of them, walking none. . . . Career record of 4–0 vs. the Pirates.

Steve Bedrosian

Throws Right

Philadelphia Phillies	W–L	ERA	AB	H	HR	BB	SO	BA	SA	OBA
Season	6-6	3.75	292	75	6	27	61	.257	.384	.317
vs. Left-Handers			154	45	4	19	29	.292	.461	.366
vs. Right-Handers			138	30	2	8	32	.217	.297	.259
Home	5-3	4.42	152	42	3	14	31	.276	.401	.337
Road	1-3	3.11	140	33	3	13	30	.236	.364	.295
Grass	0-1	2.50	65	13	1	4	14	.200	.277	.246
Artificial Turf	6-5	4.15	227	62	5	23	47	.273	.414	.336
April	0		0	0	0	0	0	—	—	—
May	0-1	5.14	29	8	1	2	2	.276	.483	.323
June	1-2	3.91	90	25	0	7	13	.278	.367	.323
July	0-1	3.60	57	13	2	7	14	.228	.421	.308
August	3-2	2.93	59	12	2	7	17	.203	.322	.288
Sept./Oct.	2-0	3.86	57	17	1	4	15	.298	.386	.344
Leading Off Inn.			62	15	2	3	10	.242	.371	.277
Runners On			145	40	1	17	33	.276	.372	.345
Runners/Scor. Pos.			94	21	0	15	25	.223	.266	.321
Runners On/2 Out			71	19	0	10	17	.268	.338	.358
Scor. Pos./2 Out			50	11	0	10	15	.220	.240	.350
Late Inning Pressure			207	50	4	21	38	.242	.362	.309
Leading Off			44	12	2	1	5	.273	.455	.289
Runners On			104	26	0	15	24	.250	.317	.339
Runners/Scor. Pos.			65	12	0	14	17	.185	.215	.321
First 9 Batters			287	74	6	26	61	.258	.380	.316
Second 9 Batters			5	1	0	1	0	.200	.600	.333
All Batters Thereafter			0	0	0	0	0	—	—	—

Loves to face: Mike Fitzgerald (0-for-13)
Hates to face: Glenn Davis (.467, 7-for-15, 1 HR)
Ground outs-to-air outs ratio: 0.63 last season, 0.82 for career. . . .
Additional statistics: 4 double-play ground outs in 56 opportunities, 13 doubles, 3 triples in 74.1 innings last season. . . . Phillies' staff recorded only two saves in 37 games before he made his season debut on May 20. Bedrock saved 28. . . Passed Ron Reed (90) and Tug McGraw (94) to become all-time Phillies saves leader with 97. . . . Allowed more than one hit per inning for first time in his career. . . . Opponents' batting average was the highest of his career, due to ineffectiveness against left-handers. Right-handers had their lowest average against him since 1984. . . . Opponents have hit better with bases empty than with runners on in seven straight seasons, longest current streak in majors.

Tim Belcher

Throws Right

Los Angeles Dodgers	W–L	ERA	AB	H	HR	BB	SO	BA	SA	OBA
Season	12-6	2.91	659	143	8	51	152	.217	.296	.275
vs. Left-Handers			340	72	5	27	82	.212	.306	.271
vs. Right-Handers			319	71	3	24	70	.223	.285	.279
Home	6-3	2.90	294	71	1	22	57	.241	.293	.294
Road	6-3	2.91	365	72	7	29	95	.197	.299	.259
Grass	7-5	2.98	463	108	3	35	96	.233	.305	.289
Artificial Turf	5-1	2.73	196	35	5	16	56	.179	.276	.241
April	1-1	2.82	82	15	1	6	24	.183	.256	.247
May	2-1	4.65	116	29	1	12	26	.250	.353	.318
June	2-2	4.05	80	21	1	9	19	.263	.363	.344
July	2-0	1.77	75	15	1	3	15	.200	.280	.231
August	3-0	3.50	162	38	4	13	33	.235	.333	.291
Sept./Oct.	2-2	1.06	144	25	0	8	35	.174	.201	.217
Leading Off Inn.			174	39	2	13	34	.224	.276	.282
Runners On			239	58	4	25	61	.243	.364	.313
Runners/Scor. Pos.			112	35	2	17	32	.313	.446	.400
Runners On/2 Out			101	26	2	12	27	.257	.347	.336
Scor. Pos./2 Out			60	17	1	10	18	.283	.383	.386
Late Inning Pressure			44	9	1	6	14	.205	.295	.300
Leading Off			13	4	0	0	2	.308	.308	.308
Runners On			15	2	1	5	7	.133	.400	.350
Runners/Scor. Pos.			8	1	1	3	4	.125	.500	.364
First 9 Batters			276	49	4	23	88	.178	.261	.245
Second 9 Batters			219	42	2	12	45	.192	.256	.234
All Batters Thereafter			164	52	2	16	19	.317	.409	.378

Loves to face: Chris James (0-for-8)
Hates to face: Albert Hall (.750, 6-for-8)
Ground outs-to-air outs ratio: 0.78 last season, 0.78 for career. . . .
Additional statistics: 9 double-play ground outs in 119 opportunities, 22 doubles, 3 triples in 179.2 innings last season. . . . Allowed 8 first-inning runs in 27 starts. . . . Batting support: 4.15 runs per start. . . . At 27, he's older than Roger Clemens, Storm Davis, Mark Gubicza, Danny Jackson, and Dwight Gooden. . . . Had N.L.'s lowest ERA (1.06) from Sept. 1 to end of season among pitchers whose initials aren't O.H. IV. . . . Opponents have averaged one home run per 133 at-bats against him at Dodger Stadium, one per 55 at-bats on the road. . . . Opponents' career average of .179 the first time around in the batting order, .202 during the second pass, and .313 thereafter.

Tom Browning

Throws Left

Cincinnati Reds	W–L	ERA	AB	H	HR	BB	SO	BA	SA	OBA
Season	18-5	3.41	916	205	36	64	124	.224	.397	.277
vs. Left-Handers			151	43	8	16	34	.285	.536	.347
vs. Right-Handers			765	162	28	48	90	.212	.370	.263
Home	5-3	4.40	434	105	19	32	62	.242	.445	.298
Road	13-2	2.55	482	100	17	32	62	.207	.355	.258
Grass	7-1	2.48	289	59	9	17	39	.204	.336	.249
Artificial Turf	11-4	3.85	627	146	27	47	85	.233	.426	.290
April	0-0	4.39	101	26	2	4	13	.257	.396	.294
May	2-2	3.48	126	29	4	10	19	.230	.405	.292
June	4-1	2.88	147	34	6	11	22	.231	.401	.288
July	4-1	2.81	171	36	7	11	19	.211	.374	.270
August	3-1	4.63	172	41	10	18	24	.238	.465	.304
Sept./Oct.	5-0	2.78	199	39	7	10	27	.196	.352	.233
Leading Off Inn.			241	54	5	14	31	.224	.349	.272
Runners On			316	75	16	18	45	.237	.449	.274
Runners/Scor. Pos.			147	36	5	15	27	.245	.442	.304
Runners On/2 Out			137	30	6	10	21	.219	.416	.272
Scor. Pos./2 Out			71	17	4	8	13	.239	.493	.316
Late Inning Pressure			106	22	3	7	19	.208	.349	.254
Leading Off			29	6	1	2	3	.207	.345	.258
Runners On			26	8	1	0	3	.308	.500	.296
Runners/Scor. Pos.			5	2	0	0	0	.400	.800	.333
First 9 Batters			291	49	6	22	44	.168	.285	.231
Second 9 Batters			299	70	13	18	38	.234	.401	.282
All Batters Thereafter			326	86	17	24	42	.264	.494	.315

Loves to face: Howard Johnson (0-for-20)
Hates to face: Tim Teufel (.500, 11-for-22, 3 HR)
Ground outs-to-air outs ratio: 0.65 last season, 0.66 for career. . . .
Additional statistics: 17 double-play ground outs in 138 opportunities, 43 doubles, 4 triples in 250.2 innings last season. . . . Allowed 12 first-inning runs in 36 starts. . . . ERA of 2.00 in the first two innings of his starts last season, 3.98 thereafter. . . . Batting support: 4.94 runs per start, 4th highest in N.L. (minimum: 15 GS). . . . Has stolen five bases without being caught in his major league career. . . . Career record of 18–4 during September. . . . Faced 40 consecutive batters (including 27 in his perfect game) without allowing one to reach base safely. No other pitcher in the last 10 years has had a streak of more than 33 batters. . . . Three of his five losses came in consecutive starts (May 22–June 1).

Tim Burke

Montreal Expos — Throws Right

	W–L	ERA	AB	H	HR	BB	SO	BA	SA	OBA
Season	3-5	3.40	309	84	7	25	42	.272	.395	.327
vs. Left-Handers			147	45	5	20	14	.306	.449	.385
vs. Right-Handers			162	39	2	5	28	.241	.346	.272
Home	3-2	4.50	184	52	5	13	22	.283	.440	.327
Road	0-3	1.85	125	32	2	12	20	.256	.328	.329
Grass	0-2	0.92	70	17	1	10	9	.243	.300	.333
Artificial Turf	3-3	4.19	239	67	6	15	33	.280	.423	.326
April	1-1	2.45	40	11	2	1	6	.275	.450	.293
May	0-0	4.32	63	17	3	6	8	.270	.460	.333
June	1-1	3.95	55	15	0	5	6	.273	.382	.339
July	1-0	3.86	43	14	0	1	4	.326	.372	.340
August	0-1	2.19	42	12	0	7	5	.286	.333	.385
Sept./Oct.	0-2	3.24	66	15	2	5	13	.227	.364	.282
Leading Off Inn.			70	16	2	1	3	.229	.371	.239
Runners On			137	39	3	22	24	.285	.409	.383
Runners/Scor. Pos.			95	23	1	21	18	.242	.326	.374
Runners On/2 Out			64	15	2	16	13	.234	.328	.388
Scor. Pos./2 Out			49	12	1	16	9	.245	.306	.431
Late Inning Pressure			221	59	5	20	29	.267	.398	.328
Leading Off			53	12	2	0	3	.226	.396	.226
Runners On			94	27	2	18	16	.287	.426	.398
Runners/Scor. Pos.			69	15	1	17	13	.217	.319	.363
First 9 Batters			290	81	7	19	39	.279	.410	.325
Second 9 Batters			19	3	0	6	3	.158	.158	.360
All Batters Thereafter			0	0	0	0	0	—	—	—

Loves to face: Kevin McReynolds (.063, 1-for-16)
Hates to face: Glenn Davis (.583, 7-for-12, 2 HR)
Ground outs-to-air outs ratio: 1.13 last season, 1.55 for career. . . .
Additional statistics: 8 double-play ground outs in 59 opportunities, 13 doubles, 2 triples in 82.0 innings last season. . . . Has pitched 262 games, 4th on Expos' all-time list behind Steve Rogers (399), Jeff Reardon (359), Woodie Fryman (297). . . . Thirteen of 25 walks were intentional. . . . Recorded 12 of 18 saves after the All-Star break. . . . Year by year innings pitched: 120.1 in 1985, then 101.1, 91.0, 82.0. . . . Opponents' career batting average: .270 by left-handers, .197 by right-handers. . . . Career records: 4–0 vs. Atlanta, 0–3 vs. Houston. . . . Among active pitchers with at least as many innings pitched as himself, only John Franco (2.37) has a lower career ERA than Burke (2.46).

Don Carman

Philadelphia Phillies — Throws Left

	W–L	ERA	AB	H	HR	BB	SO	BA	SA	OBA
Season	10-14	4.29	782	211	20	70	116	.270	.407	.330
vs. Left-Handers			145	38	5	13	20	.262	.407	.319
vs. Right-Handers			637	173	15	57	96	.272	.407	.332
Home	7-6	3.58	413	99	8	39	58	.240	.344	.306
Road	3-8	5.16	369	112	12	31	58	.304	.477	.357
Grass	2-5	5.16	209	63	6	14	36	.301	.469	.342
Artificial Turf	8-9	3.99	573	148	14	56	80	.258	.384	.326
April	3-2	3.27	120	27	3	16	19	.225	.358	.307
May	0-1	7.50	73	22	3	6	7	.301	.493	.363
June	1-1	5.03	144	46	4	16	22	.319	.451	.391
July	4-1	3.20	145	32	3	12	18	.221	.324	.280
August	1-4	4.65	121	37	3	6	23	.306	.479	.341
Sept./Oct.	1-5	3.91	179	47	4	14	27	.263	.385	.316
Leading Off Inn.			198	57	10	12	23	.288	.520	.335
Runners On			317	86	6	41	46	.271	.375	.351
Runners/Scor. Pos.			175	53	4	29	22	.303	.423	.387
Runners On/2 Out			133	35	2	21	17	.263	.353	.364
Scor. Pos./2 Out			83	22	1	16	9	.265	.337	.384
Late Inning Pressure			60	17	1	6	5	.283	.400	.348
Leading Off			19	4	0	0	1	.211	.368	.211
Runners On			18	5	0	2	2	.278	.278	.350
Runners/Scor. Pos.			6	2	0	1	1	.333	.333	.429
First 9 Batters			281	64	6	21	59	.228	.338	.288
Second 9 Batters			260	78	10	17	34	.300	.485	.341
All Batters Thereafter			241	69	4	32	23	.286	.402	.366

Loves to face: Garry Templeton (0-for-12)
Hates to face: Eric Davis (.636, 7-for-11, 3 BB, 4 HR)
Ground outs-to-air outs ratio: 0.56 last season, 0.57 for career. . . .
Additional statistics: 8 double-play ground outs in 162 opportunities, 37 doubles, 5 triples in 201.1 innings last season. . . . Allowed 15 first-inning runs in 32 starts. . . . Batting support: 3.84 runs per start. . . . His five-game winning streak was the longest by a Phillies pitcher last season, but was immediately followed by a six-game losing streak. . . . One of two pitchers to complete two starts against the Mets last season. The other: Rick Sutcliffe. . . . Held opposing batters to one hit in 16 at-bats with the bases loaded. . . . Has lost his last seven decisions against the Cardinals. . . . Career batting average of .050 (8-for-159, no XBH). . . . Born the same day as Magic Johnson (Aug. 14, 1959).

Kevin Coffman

Atlanta Braves — Throws Right

	W–L	ERA	AB	H	HR	BB	SO	BA	SA	OBA
Season	2-6	5.78	247	62	3	54	24	.251	.360	.390
vs. Left-Handers			141	39	2	31	10	.277	.390	.412
vs. Right-Handers			106	23	1	23	14	.217	.321	.359
Home	1-2	5.83	108	30	1	20	7	.278	.380	.389
Road	1-4	5.73	139	32	2	34	17	.230	.345	.390
Grass	1-3	5.90	145	38	1	34	8	.262	.366	.401
Artificial Turf	1-3	5.60	102	24	2	20	16	.235	.353	.373
April	0-2	6.92	48	12	0	10	6	.250	.354	.373
May	2-3	3.90	107	23	1	20	14	.215	.299	.353
June	0-1	8.71	82	25	2	21	3	.305	.463	.447
July			0	0	0	0	0	—	—	—
August			0	0	0	0	0	—	—	—
Sept./Oct.	0-0	0.00	10	2	0	3	1	.200	.200	.385
Leading Off Inn.			56	14	0	14	4	.250	.304	.408
Runners On			127	36	3	24	10	.283	.441	.397
Runners/Scor. Pos.			85	26	2	15	9	.306	.459	.404
Runners On/2 Out			44	8	1	15	4	.182	.318	.390
Scor. Pos./2 Out			34	8	1	11	4	.235	.412	.422
Late Inning Pressure			7	3	0	3	0	.429	.429	.636
Leading Off			3	2	0	0	0	.667	.667	.667
Runners On			3	1	0	2	0	.333	.333	.600
Runners/Scor. Pos.			3	1	0	2	0	.333	.333	.600
First 9 Batters			109	28	0	26	10	.257	.312	.403
Second 9 Batters			85	20	2	16	9	.235	.412	.356
All Batters Thereafter			53	14	1	12	5	.264	.377	.412

Loves to face: Gerald Young (0-for-8)
Hates to face: Pedro Guerrero (2-for-2, 1 HBP, 4 BB)
Ground outs-to-air outs ratio: 2.16 last season, 2.34 for career. . . .
Additional statistics: 7 double-play ground outs in 57 opportunities, 8 doubles, 5 triples in 67.0 innings last season. . . . Allowed 12 first-inning runs in 11 starts. . . . Batting support: 3.73 runs per start. . . . Opposing ground-ball hitters have career average of .218; fly-ball hitters have hit .320. . . . Had streaks of 13 and 10 walks between strikeouts, the two longest in N.L. last season. . . . Career ratio of 2.00 walks per strikeout (76 BB, 38 SO). No pitcher has finished a season with a career mark that high in as many innings as Coffman since 1957, when Laurin Pepper had 98 walks and 40 strikeouts (2.45). . . . Demoted from Braves to Class A team in Durham, N.C., on June 28.

David Cone

New York Mets — Throws Right

	W–L	ERA	AB	H	HR	BB	SO	BA	SA	OBA
Season	20-3	2.22	836	178	10	80	213	.213	.293	.283
vs. Left-Handers			436	112	5	52	88	.257	.351	.335
vs. Right-Handers			400	66	5	28	125	.165	.230	.225
Home	10-1	1.29	412	74	4	29	110	.180	.238	.236
Road	10-2	3.19	424	104	6	51	103	.245	.347	.327
Grass	15-2	1.56	575	115	5	45	163	.200	.261	.261
Artificial Turf	5-1	3.75	261	63	5	35	50	.241	.364	.330
April	2-0	3.63	61	12	1	12	17	.197	.311	.329
May	5-0	0.72	132	29	0	12	34	.220	.235	.288
June	2-1	2.76	163	32	3	16	39	.196	.313	.271
July	1-1	3.38	127	31	2	14	23	.244	.331	.313
August	4-1	1.66	173	33	2	14	48	.191	.272	.255
Sept./Oct.	6-0	2.08	180	41	2	12	52	.228	.306	.280
Leading Off Inn.			217	39	5	19	53	.180	.272	.249
Runners On			318	70	4	38	84	.220	.308	.301
Runners/Scor. Pos.			184	33	2	33	56	.179	.250	.300
Runners On/2 Out			142	31	3	16	38	.218	.317	.297
Scor. Pos./2 Out			95	17	2	15	27	.179	.242	.291
Late Inning Pressure			120	22	2	4	28	.183	.267	.210
Leading Off			37	7	2	0	7	.189	.351	.189
Runners On			32	4	0	0	7	.125	.156	.125
Runners/Scor. Pos.			13	1	0	0	3	.077	.077	.077
First 9 Batters			268	49	2	29	77	.183	.254	.268
Second 9 Batters			240	50	2	25	61	.208	.283	.280
All Batters Thereafter			328	79	6	26	75	.241	.332	.299

Loves to face: Chris James (0-for-15)
Hates to face: Hubie Brooks (.455, 5-for-11, 3 HR)
Ground outs-to-air outs ratio: 0.86 last season, 0.88 for career. . . .
Additional statistics: 11 double-play ground outs in 144 opportunities, 29 doubles, 4 triples in 231.1 innings last season. . . . Allowed 8 first-inning runs in 28 starts. . . . Batting support: 4.64 runs per start, 6th highest in N.L. (minimum: 15 GS). . . . Pitched an average of 7.64 innings per start, 2d highest mark in N.L. (minimum: 15 GS). . . . Batting average by right-handers was 2d lowest among pitchers with 20 or more starts in 14 years we've been keeping track. Best was Mike Scott in 1986 (.156). . . . Fewest losses by a 20-game winner in N.L. since Preacher Roe went 22–3 for 1951 Brooklyn Dodgers. No 20-game winner in baseball history ever lost fewer than three games.

Danny Cox
St. Louis Cardinals — Throws Right

	W-L	ERA	AB	H	HR	BB	SO	BA	SA	OBA
Season	3-8	3.98	327	89	6	25	47	.272	.413	.323
vs. Left-Handers			176	60	5	17	14	.341	.545	.395
vs. Right-Handers			151	29	1	8	33	.192	.258	.236
Home	3-3	3.67	204	54	4	11	29	.265	.417	.300
Road	0-5	4.50	123	35	2	14	18	.285	.407	.360
Grass	0-3	5.21	76	22	2	6	9	.289	.434	.349
Artificial Turf	3-5	3.63	251	67	4	19	38	.267	.406	.315
April	2-3	4.67	135	39	3	9	14	.289	.444	.331
May			0	0	0	0	0	—	—	—
June	0-0	0.00	19	3	0	1	3	.158	.211	.200
July	1-4	3.53	161	43	3	14	28	.267	.398	.328
August	0-1	9.00	12	4	0	1	2	.333	.583	.357
Sept./Oct.			0	0	0	0	0			
Leading Off Inn.			85	25	2	3	9	.294	.447	.318
Runners On			128	35	2	14	17	.273	.422	.342
Runners/Scor. Pos.			86	21	1	11	13	.244	.384	.320
Runners On/2 Out			61	14	2	10	10	.230	.459	.347
Scor. Pos./2 Out			43	10	1	8	6	.233	.465	.353
Late Inning Pressure			30	8	1	2	5	.267	.400	.313
Leading Off			9	4	1	1	1	.444	.778	.500
Runners On			10	1	0	1	1	.100	.100	.182
Runners/Scor. Pos.			8	1	0	1	1	.125	.125	.222
First 9 Batters			107	30	2	6	18	.280	.467	.319
Second 9 Batters			103	31	1	8	13	.301	.417	.348
All Batters Thereafter			117	28	3	11	16	.239	.359	.305

Loves to face: Rob Thompson (0-for-12)
Hates to face: Mike Aldrete (.583, 7-for-12, 4 BB, 1 HR)
Ground outs-to-air outs ratio: 1.42 last season, 1.39 for career....
Additional statistics: 7 double-play ground outs in 38 opportunities, 22 doubles, 3 triples in 86.0 innings last season. ... Allowed 11 first-inning runs in 13 starts.... Batting support: 2.77 runs per start. ... Hasn't won two consecutive decisions since the first half of the 1987 season.... Has pitched only one shutout in 97 starts since throwing back-to-back shutouts in June 1985.... Innings pitched, year by year since 1985: 241.0, 220.0, 199.1, 86.0.... ERAs have increased year by year from 2.88 in 1985 to 3.98 last season.... Left-handed batters have hit over .300 against him in each of the last two seasons.

Tim Crews
Los Angeles Dodgers — Throws Right

	W-L	ERA	AB	H	HR	BB	SO	BA	SA	OBA
Season	4-0	3.14	277	77	3	16	45	.278	.365	.312
vs. Left-Handers			138	42	1	13	15	.304	.384	.364
vs. Right-Handers			139	35	2	3	30	.252	.345	.259
Home	4-0	4.50	177	54	3	12	24	.305	.424	.342
Road	0-0	0.98	100	23	0	4	21	.230	.260	.257
Grass	4-0	3.34	226	60	3	14	31	.265	.363	.303
Artificial Turf	0-0	2.19	51	17	0	2	14	.333	.373	.352
April			0	0	0	0	0			
May	0-0	1.32	50	11	0	2	4	.220	.220	.250
June	2-0	2.82	84	25	1	7	12	.298	.393	.340
July	1-0	6.43	58	18	1	2	5	.310	.448	.333
August	0-0	4.50	41	13	0	3	14	.317	.390	.356
Sept./Oct.	1-0	0.77	44	10	1	2	10	.227	.341	.255
Leading Off Inn.			68	18	0	0	11	.265	.309	.265
Runners On			123	33	3	15	23	.268	.398	.336
Runners/Scor. Pos.			75	19	2	14	16	.253	.400	.351
Runners On/2 Out			51	14	1	8	11	.275	.392	.373
Scor. Pos./2 Out			37	9	0	7	9	.243	.297	.364
Late Inning Pressure			87	18	0	6	11	.207	.230	.258
Leading Off			24	4	0	0	3	.167	.167	.167
Runners On			31	6	0	5	3	.194	.194	.306
Runners/Scor. Pos.			16	4	0	5	1	.250	.250	.429
First 9 Batters			248	67	3	15	42	.270	.363	.306
Second 9 Batters			29	10	0	1	3	.345	.379	.367
All Batters Thereafter			0	0	0	0	0			

Loves to face: Barry Larkin (0-for-8)
Hates to face: Bill Doran (5-for-5, 1 BB, 2 2B)
Ground outs-to-air outs ratio: 1.13 last season, 1.13 for career....
Additional statistics: 3 double-play ground outs in 61 opportunities, 11 doubles, 2 triples in 71.2 innings last season. ... Pitched more innings vs. Mets (12.1) than anyone on Dodgers last season, and had lowest ERA of anyone in the league vs. Mets (0.73), but L.A. opted to make him ineligible for postseason play by removing him from Aug. 31 roster. Well, it worked! ... Astros batted .438 (21-for-48) against him last season. ... Opponents' career average is .308 at Dodger Stadium, .228 on the road. ... Has walked only one of 96 leadoff batters faced in his career, and has never allowed a home run to lead off an inning.

Ron Darling
New York Mets — Throws Right

	W-L	ERA	AB	H	HR	BB	SO	BA	SA	OBA
Season	17-9	3.25	888	218	24	60	161	.245	.383	.294
vs. Left-Handers			452	115	12	35	85	.254	.387	.304
vs. Right-Handers			436	103	12	25	76	.236	.378	.285
Home	14-1	2.29	539	121	11	31	100	.224	.330	.269
Road	3-8	4.83	349	97	13	29	61	.278	.464	.333
Grass	15-5	3.10	723	172	18	48	133	.238	.367	.287
Artificial Turf	2-4	3.98	165	46	6	12	28	.279	.455	.328
April	2-1	1.38	137	31	3	11	24	.226	.350	.284
May	4-2	2.87	165	31	3	10	33	.188	.303	.236
June	2-2	3.51	131	39	2	6	15	.298	.389	.328
July	3-2	5.55	143	41	7	13	36	.287	.497	.356
August	2-2	3.55	121	26	5	7	24	.215	.388	.256
Sept./Oct.	4-0	3.08	191	50	4	13	29	.262	.382	.306
Leading Off Inn.			236	59	6	10	40	.250	.386	.289
Runners On			326	81	9	22	67	.248	.393	.291
Runners/Scor. Pos.			170	44	5	17	38	.259	.412	.313
Runners On/2 Out			127	19	1	12	31	.150	.220	.229
Scor. Pos./2 Out			76	12	1	10	20	.158	.237	.256
Late Inning Pressure			107	20	2	7	21	.187	.262	.243
Leading Off			35	6	0	0	9	.171	.200	.171
Runners On			24	4	0	1	1	.167	.208	.231
Runners/Scor. Pos.			12	2	0	1	0	.167	.250	.231
First 9 Batters			278	71	6	17	54	.255	.360	.296
Second 9 Batters			267	66	7	21	52	.247	.412	.306
All Batters Thereafter			343	81	11	22	55	.236	.379	.284

Loves to face: Kal Daniels (.071, 1-for-14, 1 HR)
Hates to face: Jack Clark (.471, 8-for-17, 3 HR)
Ground outs-to-air outs ratio: 0.91 last season, 1.10 for career....
Additional statistics: 20 double-play ground outs in 162 opportunities, 38 doubles, 6 triples in 240.2 innings last season.... Allowed 22 first-inning runs (4th most in N.L.) in 34 starts.... Batting support: 4.24 runs per start.... Has played with Gary Carter for four years. In 1985 and 1986, opponents stole 27 bases in 52 attempts (52%). Over last two seasons, 38-for-42 (90%).... Career record of 19-1 in complete games.... Has double-figure wins and single-figure losses in each of the last five seasons. The only pitcher in baseball history to do that in six straight years is Whitey Ford (1953-1958), but Dwight Gooden could equal that streak this season as well.

Danny Darwin
Houston Astros — Throws Right

	W-L	ERA	AB	H	HR	BB	SO	BA	SA	OBA
Season	8-13	3.84	730	189	20	48	129	.259	.392	.307
vs. Left-Handers			387	102	10	27	60	.264	.401	.313
vs. Right-Handers			343	87	10	21	69	.254	.382	.301
Home	2-5	3.33	353	89	7	23	61	.252	.357	.298
Road	6-8	4.32	377	100	13	25	68	.265	.424	.316
Grass	5-6	4.88	232	70	7	14	42	.302	.444	.343
Artificial Turf	3-7	3.38	498	119	13	34	87	.239	.367	.291
April	1-1	3.07	114	29	3	5	15	.254	.395	.292
May	1-3	4.09	123	34	4	7	20	.276	.423	.306
June	1-3	6.08	152	49	5	10	25	.322	.526	.365
July	1-2	4.18	109	25	3	8	21	.229	.339	.282
August	2-2	3.65	139	35	4	9	30	.252	.353	.314
Sept./Oct.	2-2	1.30	93	17	1	9	18	.183	.247	.252
Leading Off Inn.			178	55	6	8	30	.309	.466	.349
Runners On			296	80	8	25	51	.270	.402	.322
Runners/Scor. Pos.			179	41	6	17	31	.229	.374	.286
Runners On/2 Out			127	29	3	8	28	.228	.370	.279
Scor. Pos./2 Out			83	15	3	7	18	.181	.337	.253
Late Inning Pressure			102	17	2	13	19	.167	.235	.265
Leading Off			29	8	1	3	3	.276	.414	.344
Runners On			28	5	0	6	7	.179	.179	.333
Runners/Scor. Pos.			17	3	0	5	3	.176	.176	.348
First 9 Batters			317	84	6	23	56	.265	.363	.309
Second 9 Batters			207	50	8	9	43	.242	.430	.280
All Batters Thereafter			206	55	6	16	30	.267	.398	.330

Loves to face: R.J. Reynolds (0-for-12, 6 SO)
Hates to face: Kal Daniels (.556, 10-for-18, 3 2B, 3 HR)
Ground outs-to-air outs ratio: 1.08 last season, 0.89 for career....
Additional statistics: 17 double-play ground outs in 143 opportunities, 27 doubles, 5 triples in 192.0 innings last season.... Allowed 13 first-inning runs in 20 starts.... Batting support: 3.70 runs per start.... Only major league pitcher to make the 20/20 Club in 1988: 20 starts, 24 relief games.... Credited with saves in three of his first four relief outings, but none thereafter.... Record of 4-10 (4.59 ERA) as a starter, 4-3 (2.15) in relief.... One of four Astros pitchers to lose five straight decisions last season.... Opposing batters hit better with runners on than with bases empty for 11th straight season. Last pitcher to do that: Steve Rogers.

Mark Davis

San Diego Padres — Throws Left

	W–L	ERA	AB	H	HR	BB	SO	BA	SA	OBA
Season	5-10	2.01	352	70	2	42	102	.199	.244	.284
vs. Left-Handers			86	18	1	8	29	.209	.302	.277
vs. Right-Handers			266	52	1	34	73	.195	.226	.286
Home	4-2	0.94	166	29	1	19	53	.175	.199	.259
Road	1-8	3.04	186	41	1	23	49	.220	.285	.305
Grass	4-7	1.44	285	52	1	33	87	.182	.214	.266
Artificial Turf	1-3	4.67	67	18	1	9	15	.269	.373	.355
April	1-0	0.92	69	11	0	7	29	.159	.188	.237
May	1-3	3.07	52	11	1	5	11	.212	.308	.281
June	0-3	4.86	62	16	1	12	18	.258	.371	.373
July	2-1	1.93	50	13	0	4	8	.260	.300	.315
August	1-0	0.00	60	7	0	9	15	.117	.117	.232
Sept./Oct.	0-3	1.84	59	12	0	5	21	.203	.203	.266
Leading Off Inn.			77	14	1	6	22	.182	.234	.241
Runners On			164	34	1	27	44	.207	.262	.318
Runners/Scor. Pos.			98	22	1	22	29	.224	.306	.364
Runners On/2 Out			80	15	1	16	22	.188	.275	.323
Scor. Pos./2 Out			54	13	1	13	17	.241	.370	.388
Late Inning Pressure			278	55	1	37	83	.198	.241	.292
Leading Off			62	12	0	5	14	.194	.210	.254
Runners On			128	25	1	25	38	.195	.266	.327
Runners/Scor. Pos.			77	18	1	20	24	.234	.338	.392
First 9 Batters			318	60	1	37	92	.189	.230	.272
Second 9 Batters			34	10	1	5	10	.294	.382	.385
All Batters Thereafter			0	0	0	0	0	—	—	—

Loves to face: Dave Anderson (0-for-13)
Hates to face: Willie McGee (.462, 6-for-13, 2 HR)
Ground outs-to-air outs ratio: 1.94 last season, 0.99 for career. . . .
Additional statistics: 12 double-play ground outs in 78 opportunities, 8 doubles, 1 triple in 98.1 innings last season. . . . Only reliever in the majors to reach double figures in losses last season. . . . Career record of 18–3 during July, 55–52 in other months. . . . Didn't allow a home run in 62 innings after June 3. . . . Ended the season by not allowing an extra-base hit to the last 158 batters he faced. That was the longest streak in the majors last season, and the 3d longest over the last 10 years. Bob Welch faced 223 consecutive batters without allowing an XBH in 1980. . . . Opponents' career average is .201 in Late-Inning Pressure Situations, .264 in other at-bats.

Ken Dayley

St. Louis Cardinals — Throws Left

	W–L	ERA	AB	H	HR	BB	SO	BA	SA	OBA
Season	2-7	2.77	201	48	2	19	38	.239	.318	.306
vs. Left-Handers			54	15	0	8	15	.278	.333	.371
vs. Right-Handers			147	33	2	11	23	.224	.313	.281
Home	2-3	1.71	111	24	0	11	17	.216	.252	.285
Road	0-4	4.18	90	24	2	8	21	.267	.400	.333
Grass	0-3	6.75	49	17	2	4	7	.347	.531	.407
Artificial Turf	2-4	1.66	152	31	0	15	31	.204	.250	.274
April			0	0	0	1	0	—	—	1.000
May	1-1	1.08	31	8	0	3	2	.258	.290	.324
June	1-2	3.86	51	11	0	7	7	.216	.294	.317
July	0-2	5.40	36	14	0	4	5	.389	.500	.450
August	0-1	3.14	47	9	2	3	11	.191	.340	.240
Sept./Oct.	0-1	0.00	36	6	0	1	13	.167	.167	.189
Leading Off Inn.			40	5	1	3	12	.125	.225	.205
Runners On			99	28	1	13	13	.283	.354	.363
Runners/Scor. Pos.			73	19	1	13	9	.260	.329	.368
Runners On/2 Out			40	8	1	5	5	.200	.275	.289
Scor. Pos./2 Out			33	7	1	5	3	.212	.303	.316
Late Inning Pressure			154	39	0	16	28	.253	.305	.326
Leading Off			31	4	0	2	8	.129	.161	.206
Runners On			75	22	0	11	9	.293	.333	.379
Runners/Scor. Pos.			53	13	0	11	6	.245	.264	.369
First 9 Batters			195	45	2	19	38	.231	.313	.301
Second 9 Batters			6	3	0	0	0	.500	.500	.500
All Batters Thereafter			0	0	0	0	0	—	—	—

Loves to face: Darryl Strawberry (.091, 1-for-11, 1 HR)
Hates to face: Jack Clark (.364, 4-for-11, 4 BB, 3 HR)
Ground outs-to-air outs ratio: 1.02 last season, 1.11 for career. . . .
Additional statistics: 5 double-play ground outs in 48 opportunities, 10 doubles, 0 triples in 55.1 innings last season. . . . Opposing batters leading off innings hit .134 (11-for-82) against him over the last two seasons. . . . Career average of .301 by opposing left-handed batters, .259 by right-handers. . . . Hasn't allowed a home run to a left-hander in the regular season since October 1985. (Kent Hrbek hit one in the '87 World Series). . . . Has pitched the most career innings (420) of any active pitcher who has never balked. . . . Most games (246) of any active pitcher who has never committed an error. N.L. record for consecutive errorless games on the mound is 364 by Lee Smith.

Jose DeLeon

St. Louis Cardinals — Throws Right

	W–L	ERA	AB	H	HR	BB	SO	BA	SA	OBA
Season	13-10	3.67	835	198	13	86	208	.237	.345	.308
vs. Left-Handers			431	112	5	61	85	.260	.355	.349
vs. Right-Handers			404	86	8	25	123	.213	.334	.259
Home	7-6	3.79	411	93	9	35	105	.226	.350	.284
Road	6-4	3.56	424	105	4	51	103	.248	.340	.330
Grass	4-3	3.31	279	73	1	29	70	.262	.337	.332
Artificial Turf	9-7	3.85	556	125	12	57	138	.225	.349	.295
April	1-2	5.88	103	29	4	13	22	.282	.466	.362
May	3-2	3.89	148	39	2	17	45	.264	.351	.337
June	1-1	3.09	129	31	1	12	29	.240	.333	.308
July	2-3	4.07	159	40	1	12	35	.252	.340	.301
August	2-0	3.79	129	28	3	15	35	.217	.364	.295
Sept./Oct.	4-2	2.28	167	31	2	17	42	.186	.263	.263
Leading Off Inn.			216	57	4	22	57	.264	.394	.338
Runners On			340	83	5	39	79	.244	.341	.316
Runners/Scor. Pos.			198	43	2	21	51	.217	.293	.283
Runners On/2 Out			141	30	3	15	45	.213	.340	.288
Scor. Pos./2 Out			89	17	1	11	32	.191	.281	.280
Late Inning Pressure			69	21	1	7	16	.304	.435	.364
Leading Off			20	5	0	4	5	.250	.400	.375
Runners On			22	9	1	2	5	.409	.591	.440
Runners/Scor. Pos.			15	6	1	2	3	.400	.667	.444
First 9 Batters			277	55	4	27	79	.199	.292	.270
Second 9 Batters			256	62	3	29	65	.242	.336	.316
All Batters Thereafter			302	81	6	30	64	.268	.401	.334

Loves to face: Jack Clark (0-for-7, 5 SO)
Hates to face: Eric Davis (.571, 4-for-7, 2 BB, 2 HR)
Ground outs-to-air outs ratio: 0.82 last season, 0.82 for career. . . .
Additional statistics: 15 double-play ground outs in 172 opportunities, 43 doubles, 4 triples in 225.1 innings last season. . . . Allowed 9 first-inning runs in 34 starts. . . . Batting support: 3.79 runs per start. . . . First winning season since his rookie year, when he posted a 7–3 mark for the 1983 Pirates. Was 25–52 from 1984 through 1987. . . . Has lost his last 11 decisions to the Reds, and his last nine against the Mets. . . . Career strikeout-to-walk ratio of 1.08 vs. left-handed batters, 3.11 vs. right-handers. . . . Batting average of .213 by opposing right-handers was the *highest* of his career. Has held right-handers under .200 in four of his six seasons in the majors.

Jim Deshaies

Houston Astros — Throws Left

	W–L	ERA	AB	H	HR	BB	SO	BA	SA	OBA
Season	11-14	3.00	752	164	20	72	127	.218	.366	.284
vs. Left-Handers			129	32	6	11	18	.248	.465	.310
vs. Right-Handers			623	132	14	61	109	.212	.345	.278
Home	7-8	2.91	406	91	13	45	59	.224	.401	.301
Road	4-6	3.10	346	73	7	27	68	.211	.324	.262
Grass	2-4	3.64	196	40	4	16	41	.204	.321	.259
Artificial Turf	9-10	2.77	556	124	16	56	86	.223	.381	.292
April	2-2	1.97	112	18	1	14	17	.161	.241	.254
May	2-0	2.15	103	18	3	6	9	.175	.301	.220
June	1-3	3.52	117	34	5	13	12	.291	.487	.353
July	2-3	5.15	138	34	5	12	33	.246	.428	.305
August	2-3	2.16	149	30	3	14	27	.201	.322	.265
Sept./Oct.	2-3	2.95	133	30	3	13	29	.226	.398	.291
Leading Off Inn.			191	44	7	21	28	.230	.398	.307
Runners On			293	59	8	26	52	.201	.355	.256
Runners/Scor. Pos.			165	31	6	17	38	.188	.345	.246
Runners On/2 Out			130	25	4	15	26	.192	.362	.276
Scor. Pos./2 Out			84	15	3	9	20	.179	.345	.258
Late Inning Pressure			80	16	2	5	10	.200	.338	.247
Leading Off			24	4	1	1	3	.167	.292	.200
Runners On			21	6	1	2	3	.286	.524	.348
Runners/Scor. Pos.			11	2	1	1	1	.182	.636	.250
First 9 Batters			240	46	3	27	49	.192	.279	.272
Second 9 Batters			246	55	10	21	47	.224	.419	.283
All Batters Thereafter			266	63	7	24	31	.237	.395	.295

Loves to face: Andres Thomas (.045, 1-for-22)
Hates to face: Vance Law (.833, 5-for-6, 4 BB, 2 2B)
Ground outs-to-air outs ratio: 0.55 last season, 0.59 for career. . . .
Additional statistics: 8 double-play ground outs in 122 opportunities, 35 doubles, 8 triples in 207.0 innings last season. . . . Allowed 10 first-inning runs in 31 starts. . . . Batting support: 2.90 runs per start, 3d lowest in N.L. (minimum: 15 GS). . . . Won back-to-back starts only once last season, but lost consecutive starts five times. . . . Had his first losing season in three full years with the Astros, despite the lowest ERA of his career. . . . Opponents' career average of .219 with runners on base, .249 with the bases empty. . . . Made major league debut for Yankees 1984, losing to the White Sox. Current teammate Juan Agosto earned a save for Chicago.

Frank DiPino

Chicago Cubs — Throws Left

	W–L	ERA	AB	H	HR	BB	SO	BA	SA	OBA
Season	2-3	4.98	358	102	6	32	69	.285	.394	.338
vs. Left-Handers			125	24	0	7	36	.192	.248	.228
vs. Right-Handers			233	78	6	25	33	.335	.472	.396
Home	2-1	3.72	179	41	3	15	35	.229	.313	.283
Road	0-2	6.43	179	61	3	17	34	.341	.475	.394
Grass	2-2	3.84	251	63	5	18	51	.251	.347	.297
Artificial Turf	0-1	8.03	107	39	1	14	18	.364	.505	.431
April	0-0	3.55	54	17	1	1	9	.315	.389	.327
May	0-1	4.82	69	18	2	8	15	.261	.406	.329
June	0-2	4.02	57	14	2	6	12	.246	.439	.308
July	1-0	4.76	51	16	0	3	8	.314	.373	.352
August	1-0	5.93	53	13	0	5	13	.245	.321	.305
Sept./Oct.	0-0	6.38	74	24	1	9	12	.324	.419	.393
Leading Off Inn.			73	17	1	5	9	.233	.329	.282
Runners On			185	57	4	17	35	.308	.438	.356
Runners/Scor. Pos.			110	38	1	12	17	.345	.436	.391
Runners On/2 Out			98	34	2	9	14	.347	.480	.402
Scor. Pos./2 Out			62	26	1	8	7	.419	.532	.486
Late Inning Pressure			124	35	3	13	30	.282	.379	.348
Leading Off			30	9	1	2	4	.300	.400	.344
Runners On			53	15	1	6	11	.283	.358	.350
Runners/Scor. Pos.			26	9	0	5	3	.346	.385	.438
First 9 Batters			310	91	6	29	61	.294	.413	.349
Second 9 Batters			46	10	0	2	8	.217	.261	.245
All Batters Thereafter			2	1	0	1	0	.500	.500	.667

Loves to face: Tony Gwynn (.077, 1-for-13)
Hates to face: Glenn Wilson (.778, 7-for-9, 2 HR)
Ground outs-to-air outs ratio: 0.93 last season, 1.16 for career. . . .
Additional statistics: 3 double-play ground outs in 75 opportunities, 19 doubles, 1 triple in 90.1 innings last season. . . . Career average of .213 by opposing left-handers, .270 by right-handers. . . . Hasn't allowed a home run to a left-handed batter since Jose Cruz connected against him on June 1, 1987. . . . Faced 21 batters in Reds' 17–0 shellacking of the Cubs at Wrigley on Sept. 4, the most batters he has ever faced in a relief appearance. . . . Career record of 0–6 vs. the Dodgers. First two losses of his career were to Los Angeles, in back-to-back starts during 1982 pennant race. . . . Has pitched in the majors for eight seasons, but has never had a winning record.

John Dopson

Montreal Expos — Throws Right

	W–L	ERA	AB	H	HR	BB	SO	BA	SA	OBA
Season	3-11	3.04	638	150	15	58	101	.235	.351	.299
vs. Left-Handers			333	86	7	39	48	.258	.363	.334
vs. Right-Handers			305	64	8	19	53	.210	.338	.258
Home	1-6	2.74	339	85	9	29	50	.251	.357	.308
Road	2-5	3.38	299	65	6	29	51	.217	.344	.289
Grass	1-2	3.50	159	31	3	16	26	.195	.289	.269
Artificial Turf	2-9	2.88	479	119	12	42	75	.248	.372	.309
April	0-0	3.60	16	2	0	3	5	.125	.250	.263
May	1-2	2.36	92	16	3	13	10	.174	.283	.276
June	0-3	3.76	153	42	4	8	26	.275	.418	.315
July	1-1	1.86	110	30	2	5	18	.273	.364	.304
August	1-2	3.38	138	32	5	16	21	.232	.370	.310
Sept./Oct.	0-3	3.34	129	28	1	13	21	.217	.302	.287
Leading Off Inn.			163	42	6	14	31	.258	.411	.316
Runners On			248	55	4	27	36	.222	.319	.296
Runners/Scor. Pos.			146	31	3	22	25	.212	.315	.312
Runners On/2 Out			112	30	1	13	14	.268	.375	.344
Scor. Pos./2 Out			79	22	1	13	9	.278	.380	.380
Late Inning Pressure			53	15	2	4	5	.283	.472	.333
Leading Off			18	7	1	0	1	.389	.611	.389
Runners On			16	3	0	3	3	.188	.313	.316
Runners/Scor. Pos.			12	2	0	3	3	.167	.167	.333
First 9 Batters			212	40	5	20	48	.189	.292	.259
Second 9 Batters			218	45	3	14	31	.206	.284	.258
All Batters Thereafter			208	65	7	24	22	.313	.481	.380

Loves to face: Rafael Palmeiro (.143, 1-for-7)
Hates to face: Greg Brock (2-for-2, 1 HR)
Ground outs-to-air outs ratio: 1.81 last season, 1.82 for career. . . .
Additional statistics: 13 double-play ground outs in 113 opportunities, 21 doubles, 4 triples in 168.2 innings last season. . . . Allowed 11 first-inning runs in 26 starts. . . . Batting support: 3.27 runs per start. Expos scored two or fewer runs in nine of his 11 losses, one run or fewer in six of them. . . . Eleven no-decision starts were the 2d most of any N.L. pitcher last season. . . . Ended the season with a five-game losing streak, Montreal's longest last season. . . . Completed only one game last season, a 2–1 loss to the Pirates in which his counterpart, John Smiley, threw a one-hitter. . . . Career average of .193 by opposing ground-ball hitters, .305 by fly-ballers.

Kelly Downs

San Francisco Giants — Throws Right

	W–L	ERA	AB	H	HR	BB	SO	BA	SA	OBA
Season	13-9	3.32	622	140	11	47	118	.225	.333	.279
vs. Left-Handers			320	59	5	28	57	.184	.269	.249
vs. Right-Handers			302	81	6	19	61	.268	.401	.312
Home	8-3	2.61	336	70	3	26	69	.208	.277	.261
Road	5-6	4.20	286	70	8	21	49	.245	.399	.300
Grass	11-4	3.02	459	100	6	30	87	.218	.296	.262
Artificial Turf	2-5	4.19	163	40	5	17	31	.245	.436	.326
April	0-2	3.12	88	13	1	5	21	.148	.216	.189
May	2-3	4.01	132	32	2	14	26	.242	.348	.318
June	4-2	3.49	137	31	4	9	21	.226	.372	.276
July	5-1	2.62	166	36	2	11	32	.217	.319	.264
August	2-1	3.60	99	28	2	8	18	.283	.384	.333
Sept./Oct.			0	0	0	0	0	—	—	—
Leading Off Inn.			162	33	5	7	28	.204	.333	.246
Runners On			226	58	4	24	38	.257	.389	.317
Runners/Scor. Pos.			126	32	3	14	21	.254	.397	.309
Runners On/2 Out			104	22	2	13	13	.212	.346	.299
Scor. Pos./2 Out			68	13	1	7	7	.191	.309	.267
Late Inning Pressure			56	11	0	5	10	.196	.232	.254
Leading Off			14	1	0	2	3	.071	.143	.188
Runners On			21	3	0	2	5	.143	.143	.200
Runners/Scor. Pos.			9	2	0	2	3	.222	.222	.308
First 9 Batters			221	45	2	11	55	.204	.281	.238
Second 9 Batters			202	54	6	19	32	.267	.391	.338
All Batters Thereafter			199	41	3	17	31	.206	.332	.262

Loves to face: Tim Wallach (.063, 1-for-16, 7 SO)
Hates to face: Chris Sabo (.800, 4-for-5, 2 2B, 1 HR)
Ground outs-to-air outs ratio: 1.25 last season, 1.35 for career. . . .
Additional statistics: 13 double-play ground outs in 99 opportunities, 32 doubles, 1 triple in 168.0 innings last season. . . . Allowed 11 first-inning runs in 26 starts. . . . Batting support: 5.42 runs per start, 2d highest in N.L. (minimum: 15 GS). . . . Held opposing left-handed batters hitless in 33 consecutive plate appearances, 2d longest streak of its kind in N.L. last season. . . . One of three N.L. pitchers with at least three shutouts in each of last two seasons. The others: Gooden and Scott. . . . Season ended on August 24 with shoulder injury. His final game was the first ever in which he allowed more than one home run at Candlestick Park.

Doug Drabek

Pittsburgh Pirates — Throws Right

	W–L	ERA	AB	H	HR	BB	SO	BA	SA	OBA
Season	15-7	3.08	812	194	21	50	127	.239	.366	.286
vs. Left-Handers			375	89	6	28	51	.237	.325	.290
vs. Right-Handers			437	105	15	22	76	.240	.400	.283
Home	7-3	3.22	392	97	10	23	64	.247	.367	.290
Road	8-4	2.95	420	97	11	27	63	.231	.364	.283
Grass	4-3	3.36	242	60	6	18	28	.248	.372	.303
Artificial Turf	11-4	2.95	570	134	15	32	99	.235	.363	.279
April	3-1	3.71	128	33	4	5	22	.258	.445	.289
May	2-2	4.05	147	36	5	12	17	.245	.374	.307
June	0-2	5.04	110	25	3	8	13	.227	.336	.286
July	4-0	1.93	128	26	4	9	28	.203	.313	.266
August	4-1	1.30	159	38	3	8	25	.239	.371	.275
Sept./Oct.	2-1	3.00	140	36	2	8	22	.257	.350	.290
Leading Off Inn.			211	56	5	16	28	.265	.379	.317
Runners On			303	74	8	16	41	.244	.370	.289
Runners/Scor. Pos.			164	37	4	12	24	.226	.341	.271
Runners On/2 Out			115	21	2	9	18	.183	.278	.248
Scor. Pos./2 Out			73	12	2	8	12	.164	.301	.247
Late Inning Pressure			74	19	2	7	13	.257	.378	.321
Leading Off			20	4	1	3	4	.200	.350	.304
Runners On			30	6	0	3	5	.200	.200	.273
Runners/Scor. Pos.			16	1	0	2	3	.063	.063	.167
First 9 Batters			271	53	5	18	48	.196	.306	.252
Second 9 Batters			263	61	5	16	43	.232	.319	.279
All Batters Thereafter			278	80	11	16	36	.288	.468	.328

Loves to face: Len Dykstra (.095, 2-for-21)
Hates to face: Pedro Guerrero (.714, 5-for-7, 2 BB, 2 HR)
Ground outs-to-air outs ratio: 1.04 last season, 0.96 for career. . . .
Additional statistics: 22 double-play ground outs in 159 opportunities, 30 doubles, 5 triples in 219.1 innings last season. . . . Allowed 8 first-inning runs in 32 starts. . . . Batting support: 4.50 runs per start, 9th highest in N.L. (minimum: 15 GS). . . . Pirates lost seven his 10 no-decision starts. . . . Completed three games last season, but none after May 8. . . . Won seven consecutive decisions, longest streak by a Pirates pitcher since 1983 (Candelaria, 8). . . . Career record of 8–15 (4.21 ERA) before All-Star break (including 0–7 in June), 25–12 (2.87) after the break. . . . Opponents have career batting averages of .221 on his first two passes through order, .298 thereafter.

Mike Dunne

Pittsburgh Pirates — Throws Right

	W–L	ERA	AB	H	HR	BB	SO	BA	SA	OBA
Season	7-11	3.92	640	163	15	88	70	.255	.372	.345
vs. Left-Handers			324	85	3	57	19	.262	.355	.371
vs. Right-Handers			316	78	12	31	51	.247	.389	.317
Home	5-6	3.44	380	90	11	57	42	.237	.363	.339
Road	2-5	4.63	260	73	4	31	28	.281	.385	.355
Grass	1-4	4.78	152	44	4	17	18	.289	.421	.357
Artificial Turf	6-7	3.67	488	119	11	71	52	.244	.357	.342
April	1-0	2.38	42	12	0	3	8	.286	.333	.333
May	2-3	5.52	132	40	5	10	18	.303	.455	.350
June	2-3	3.15	118	24	3	28	12	.203	.305	.358
July	1-2	3.51	121	27	2	19	10	.223	.298	.329
August	0-3	4.50	123	31	3	16	16	.252	.423	.343
Sept./Oct.	1-0	3.54	104	29	2	12	6	.279	.385	.353
Leading Off Inn.			157	34	4	19	18	.217	.344	.305
Runners On			280	76	5	39	30	.271	.371	.358
Runners/Scor. Pos.			175	44	3	28	21	.251	.349	.347
Runners On/2 Out			126	31	2	17	11	.246	.333	.345
Scor. Pos./2 Out			89	21	2	14	9	.236	.348	.352
Late Inning Pressure			39	10	1	11	5	.256	.385	.412
Leading Off			12	2	1	1	2	.167	.417	.231
Runners On			12	5	0	6	0	.417	.500	.579
Runners/Scor. Pos.			8	3	0	5	0	.375	.500	.571
First 9 Batters			211	55	5	36	22	.261	.389	.360
Second 9 Batters			218	51	4	19	23	.234	.330	.303
All Batters Thereafter			211	57	6	33	25	.270	.398	.372

Loves to face: Bo Diaz (0-for-10)
Hates to face: Dave Martinez (.538, 7-for-13, 2 3B)
Ground outs-to-air outs ratio: 1.30 last season, 1.54 for career. . . .
Additional statistics: 13 double-play ground outs in 135 opportunities, 28 doubles, 1 triple in 170.0 innings last season. . . . Allowed 25 first-inning runs (most in N.L.) in 28 starts. . . . Batting support: 3.93 runs per start. . . . Only N.L. pitcher with more walks than strikeouts (minimum: 162 IP). . . . One of three pitchers to walk five batters in a row last season. The others: Bob Walk (of course) and Steve Trout (of course). . . . First Pirates pitcher to walk 10 batters in a game since 1953, when outfielder Johnny Lindell walked 10 in his first pitching appearance in 11 years. . . . One of three N.L. pitchers to allow hits to left-handed batters in six consecutive at bats last season.

Sid Fernandez

New York Mets — Throws Left

	W–L	ERA	AB	H	HR	BB	SO	BA	SA	OBA
Season	12-10	3.03	666	127	15	70	189	.191	.305	.271
vs. Left-Handers			72	17	1	9	24	.236	.347	.325
vs. Right-Handers			594	110	14	61	165	.185	.300	.264
Home	8-4	1.83	336	51	5	37	116	.152	.232	.241
Road	4-6	4.36	330	76	10	33	73	.230	.379	.302
Grass	9-7	2.49	445	78	9	42	142	.175	.283	.252
Artificial Turf	3-3	4.18	221	49	6	28	47	.222	.348	.309
April	0-1	6.75	68	18	3	10	15	.265	.471	.366
May	2-3	3.18	105	23	1	9	29	.219	.314	.287
June	2-2	2.75	138	22	4	14	36	.159	.283	.239
July	2-2	1.64	109	17	1	14	41	.156	.202	.256
August	2-2	2.95	132	24	3	9	37	.182	.311	.239
Sept./Oct.	4-0	2.78	114	23	3	14	31	.202	.316	.285
Leading Off Inn.			175	39	4	19	54	.223	.349	.303
Runners On			243	47	6	22	58	.193	.321	.267
Runners/Scor. Pos.			134	21	3	14	41	.157	.254	.241
Runners On/2 Out			108	23	3	9	31	.213	.333	.286
Scor. Pos./2 Out			70	13	2	6	25	.186	.286	.269
Late Inning Pressure			54	12	0	6	14	.222	.333	.295
Leading Off			16	4	0	2	6	.250	.438	.333
Runners On			20	3	0	2	5	.150	.300	.217
Runners/Scor. Pos.			4	0	0	2	2	.000	.000	.286
First 9 Batters			243	51	7	25	75	.210	.354	.288
Second 9 Batters			225	39	5	27	67	.173	.284	.266
All Batters Thereafter			198	37	3	18	47	.187	.268	.256

Loves to face: Ozzie Virgil (0-for-24)
Hates to face: Tim Raines (.320, 8-for-25, 3 HR)
Ground outs-to-air outs ratio: 0.49 last season, 0.49 for career. . . .
Additional statistics: 8 double-play ground outs in 103 opportunities, 19 doubles, 6 triples in 187.0 innings last season. . . . Allowed 13 first-inning runs in 31 starts. . . . Batting support: 4.00 runs per start. . . . Lost first night game at Wrigley, but won all six decisions after that. . . . Opponents stole 36 bases in 42 attempts, including 32-of-35 with Carter catching. That combo threw out only one runner stealing second. . . . Opponents have batted below .200 at Shea Stadium in each of the last four seasons. . . . Career rate of 6.7 hits per nine innings is 3d lowest in history among pitchers with 800 or more innings. Only Herb Score (6.4) and Nolan Ryan (6.6) are ahead of him.

Brian Fisher

Pittsburgh Pirates — Throws Right

	W–L	ERA	AB	H	HR	BB	SO	BA	SA	OBA
Season	8-10	4.61	567	157	13	57	66	.277	.425	.345
vs. Left-Handers			285	93	7	37	32	.326	.502	.400
vs. Right-Handers			282	64	6	20	34	.227	.348	.287
Home	5-6	3.74	337	92	7	33	45	.273	.401	.340
Road	3-4	5.88	230	65	6	24	21	.283	.461	.351
Grass	0-2	5.64	86	27	4	9	10	.314	.547	.375
Artificial Turf	8-8	4.43	481	130	9	48	56	.270	.403	.340
April	3-0	1.84	112	30	1	7	12	.268	.348	.314
May	1-1	6.28	58	18	1	9	11	.310	.466	.406
June	0-5	7.27	143	46	7	13	11	.322	.594	.377
July	2-2	3.00	112	27	2	14	14	.241	.339	.325
August	1-2	6.92	105	31	2	10	13	.295	.438	.364
Sept./Oct.	1-0	0.75	37	5	0	4	5	.135	.162	.214
Leading Off Inn.			146	43	3	6	13	.295	.418	.322
Runners On			241	65	6	33	36	.270	.436	.359
Runners/Scor. Pos.			154	38	1	26	24	.247	.351	.358
Runners On/2 Out			109	24	2	17	20	.220	.330	.341
Scor. Pos./2 Out			77	15	0	13	16	.195	.260	.333
Late Inning Pressure			40	8	0	6	7	.200	.275	.298
Leading Off			11	2	0	1	1	.182	.182	.250
Runners On			15	2	0	3	5	.133	.133	.263
Runners/Scor. Pos.			12	1	0	2	4	.083	.083	.200
First 9 Batters			231	67	5	24	32	.290	.450	.362
Second 9 Batters			171	41	2	16	24	.240	.333	.312
All Batters Thereafter			165	49	6	17	10	.297	.485	.355

Loves to face: Kevin McReynolds (0-for-9)
Hates to face: Howard Johnson (.571, 4-for-7, 4 BB, 2 HR)
Ground outs-to-air outs ratio: 0.95 last season, 0.96 for career. . . .
Additional statistics: 9 double-play ground outs in 101 opportunities, 33 doubles, 6 triples in 146.1 innings last season. . . . Allowed 18 first-inning runs in 22 starts. . . . Batting support: 4.45 runs per start. . . . Pitched an average of 5.61 innings per start, 3d lowest mark in N.L. (minimum: 15 GS). . . . Record of 6–10 (5.33 ERA) in 22 starts, 2–0 (0.78) in 11 relief appearances. Didn't allow a home run in 23 innings as a reliever. . . . Recorded his only N.L. save on Sept. 30. Had 20 in partial seasons with Yankees. . . . Career record of 5–13 during June, 27–15 in other months. . . . Faced 71 batters between strikeouts (May 27–June 7), longest streak in N.L. last season.

Bob Forsch

Cardinals/Astros — Throws Right

	W–L	ERA	AB	H	HR	BB	SO	BA	SA	OBA
Season	10-8	4.29	528	153	10	44	54	.290	.411	.342
vs. Left-Handers			238	56	1	20	23	.235	.298	.291
vs. Right-Handers			290	97	9	24	31	.334	.503	.386
Home	7-4	2.79	311	79	2	23	30	.254	.331	.305
Road	3-4	6.71	217	74	8	21	24	.341	.525	.396
Grass	2-2	7.13	103	39	4	9	10	.379	.534	.425
Artificial Turf	8-6	3.69	425	114	6	35	44	.268	.381	.323
April	1-2	6.19	61	20	0	5	2	.328	.410	.373
May	3-1	3.32	73	18	2	5	3	.247	.356	.291
June	0-0	2.87	60	18	2	8	5	.300	.517	.371
July	0-0	6.00	72	20	2	4	9	.278	.389	.316
August	5-1	2.25	145	35	2	16	21	.241	.345	.321
Sept./Oct.	1-4	6.51	117	42	2	6	14	.359	.487	.385
Leading Off Inn.			141	45	3	5	18	.319	.461	.342
Runners On			216	61	5	24	16	.282	.398	.341
Runners/Scor. Pos.			121	32	3	19	14	.264	.380	.342
Runners On/2 Out			92	20	0	9	12	.217	.272	.287
Scor. Pos./2 Out			55	12	0	8	11	.218	.273	.317
Late Inning Pressure			61	13	1	7	2	.213	.311	.294
Leading Off			20	3	0	2	1	.150	.200	.227
Runners On			14	3	0	3	0	.214	.214	.353
Runners/Scor. Pos.			6	1	0	3	0	.167	.167	.444
First 9 Batters			265	74	6	23	29	.279	.400	.337
Second 9 Batters			162	50	4	15	14	.309	.469	.367
All Batters Thereafter			101	29	0	6	11	.287	.347	.318

Loves to face: Steve Jeltz (.050, 1-for-20)
Hates to face: Jim Gott (2-for-2, 2 HR)
Ground outs-to-air outs ratio: 1.31 last season, 1.43 for career. . . .
Additional statistics: 13 double-play ground outs in 111 opportunities, 30 doubles, 2 triples in 136.1 innings last season. . . . Allowed 7 first-inning runs in 18 starts. . . . Batting support: 3.33 runs per start. . . . Only left-hander to homer off Forsch last season was Kal Daniels. . . . Record of 6–6 (3.98 ERA) in 18 starts, 4–2 (5.08) in 18 relief appearances. . . . Won five of his last six starts for the Cardinals, but lost each of his last four with Houston. . . . Leads active pitchers with 12 HR, but he'll have to fight off Rick Rhoden (9), back in N.L. . . . Only Stan Musial (22), Jesse Haines (18), Bob Gibson (17), and Lou Brock (16) played more seasons for Cardinals than Forsch (15).

John Franco

Cincinnati Reds — Throws Left

	W–L	ERA	AB	H	HR	BB	SO	BA	SA	OBA
Season	6-6	1.57	303	60	3	27	46	.198	.241	.263
vs. Left-Handers			51	7	1	2	8	.137	.235	.167
vs. Right-Handers			252	53	2	25	38	.210	.242	.282
Home	4-2	0.99	157	25	0	8	22	.159	.185	.199
Road	2-4	2.23	146	35	3	19	24	.240	.301	.327
Grass	1-2	2.74	86	23	2	9	14	.267	.337	.337
Artificial Turf	5-4	1.14	217	37	1	18	32	.171	.203	.233
April	0-1	0.00	44	6	0	2	6	.136	.136	.174
May	1-3	2.30	54	13	1	8	6	.241	.296	.333
June	1-1	3.97	46	13	0	3	8	.283	.348	.327
July	0-0	0.61	49	6	1	5	7	.122	.184	.204
August	3-0	0.00	56	8	0	5	9	.143	.161	.213
Sept./Oct.	1-1	3.14	54	14	1	4	10	.259	.315	.310
Leading Off Inn.			75	17	0	3	9	.227	.240	.256
Runners On			132	27	2	13	25	.205	.265	.274
Runners/Scor. Pos.			62	13	1	10	11	.210	.274	.315
Runners On/2 Out			61	12	1	6	10	.197	.328	.269
Scor. Pos./2 Out			32	5	1	5	7	.156	.281	.270
Late Inning Pressure			217	41	2	20	28	.189	.235	.257
Leading Off			56	11	0	2	7	.196	.214	.224
Runners On			84	20	2	11	12	.238	.333	.326
Runners/Scor. Pos.			48	10	1	9	7	.208	.292	.333
First 9 Batters			301	60	3	26	45	.199	.243	.262
Second 9 Batters			2	0	0	1	1	.000	.000	.333
All Batters Thereafter			0	0	0	0	0			

Loves to face: Mike Scioscia (0-for-10)
Hates to face: Andre Dawson (.750, 6-for-8)
Ground outs-to-air outs ratio: 2.25 last season, 1.86 for career. . . .
Additional statistics: 8 double-play ground outs in 69 opportunities, 4 doubles, 0 triples in 86.0 innings last season. . . . Broke major league record for saves in a month with 13 in July. Previous record was 12 by Sparky Lyle (June 1973), Bruce Sutter (Aug. 1979), and Bob Stanley (Aug. 1980). . . . Fourth different Cincinnati pitcher to lead the league in saves. The others: Wayne Granger, Clay Carroll, and Rawly Eastwick. . . . Turned 28 last September with 110 career saves. Only Bruce Sutter (133) and Lee Smith (113) had more at that age. . . . One of five pitchers whose opponents have hit worse in LIP Situations than overall in each of the last five seasons.

Scott Garrelts

San Francisco Giants — Throws Right

	W–L	ERA	AB	H	HR	BB	SO	BA	SA	OBA
Season	5-9	3.58	354	80	3	46	86	.226	.294	.317
vs. Left-Handers			157	34	1	22	36	.217	.287	.313
vs. Right-Handers			197	46	2	24	50	.234	.299	.320
Home	1-7	4.20	159	36	0	21	40	.226	.283	.317
Road	4-2	3.06	195	44	3	25	46	.226	.303	.317
Grass	3-8	4.48	242	60	1	34	57	.248	.310	.341
Artificial Turf	2-1	1.71	112	20	2	12	29	.179	.259	.264
April	1-1	4.30	48	9	1	12	11	.188	.292	.349
May	0-2	3.31	57	15	1	8	11	.263	.333	.364
June	0-1	7.13	72	20	0	8	21	.278	.347	.350
July	2-1	4.73	47	10	0	4	12	.213	.298	.275
August	2-2	0.83	70	7	0	8	25	.100	.100	.192
Sept./Oct.	0-2	1.88	60	19	1	6	6	.317	.417	.379
Leading Off Inn.			73	21	3	9	16	.288	.452	.366
Runners On			176	45	0	31	42	.256	.313	.370
Runners/Scor. Pos.			126	34	0	28	31	.270	.333	.401
Runners On/2 Out			76	16	0	12	20	.211	.250	.333
Scor. Pos./2 Out			58	12	0	12	16	.207	.241	.352
Late Inning Pressure			193	49	1	30	48	.254	.321	.351
Leading Off			41	12	1	5	11	.293	.390	.370
Runners On			98	28	0	22	23	.286	.367	.410
Runners/Scor. Pos.			68	23	0	19	14	.338	.426	.472
First 9 Batters			306	67	3	40	72	.219	.294	.312
Second 9 Batters			48	13	0	6	14	.271	.292	.345
All Batters Thereafter			0	0	0	0	0			

Loves to face: Darryl Strawberry (0-for-5, 5 SO)
Hates to face: Mike Marshall (.480, 12-for-25, 4 HR)
Ground outs-to-air outs ratio: 1.53 last season, 1.34 for career. . . .
Additional statistics: 6 double-play ground outs in 83 opportunities, 13 doubles, 1 triple in 98.0 innings last season. . . . Collected 10 of his 13 saves during an eight-week period in midseason, but did not record one after August 20. . . . Pirates were hitless in 16 at-bats against him last season. . . . Allowed seven hits in 16 at-bats with the bases loaded. . . . Batting average of .219 by the first nine batters faced in a game last season, .271 after his first time through the order. . . . Average of 10.75 strikeouts per nine innings in 1987, 7.90 in 1988. . . . Career record of 27–13 in day games, 15–23 at night. . . . Has saved between 10 and 13 games in each of last four seasons.

Tom Glavine

Atlanta Braves — Throws Left

	W–L	ERA	AB	H	HR	BB	SO	BA	SA	OBA
Season	7-17	4.56	745	201	12	63	84	.270	.372	.329
vs. Left-Handers			123	30	3	17	14	.244	.350	.343
vs. Right-Handers			622	171	9	46	70	.275	.376	.326
Home	2-7	5.00	338	98	7	27	36	.290	.411	.345
Road	5-10	4.21	407	103	5	36	48	.253	.339	.316
Grass	4-12	4.73	514	143	8	40	56	.278	.374	.333
Artificial Turf	3-5	4.21	231	58	4	23	28	.251	.368	.321
April	0-3	4.44	88	23	3	9	13	.261	.409	.330
May	2-3	7.55	120	34	2	23	13	.283	.375	.388
June	1-3	4.64	125	41	2	8	13	.328	.416	.377
July	0-2	3.66	124	33	3	6	17	.266	.411	.308
August	2-4	4.63	137	36	1	9	13	.263	.387	.311
Sept./Oct.	2-2	2.93	151	34	1	8	15	.225	.265	.268
Leading Off Inn.			196	56	3	9	23	.286	.393	.324
Runners On			309	90	3	38	29	.291	.385	.365
Runners/Scor. Pos.			176	51	1	26	18	.290	.364	.373
Runners On/2 Out			116	24	2	17	14	.207	.302	.313
Scor. Pos./2 Out			69	16	1	12	9	.232	.348	.354
Late Inning Pressure			54	16	3	6	8	.296	.537	.377
Leading Off			16	4	1	0	2	.250	.500	.294
Runners On			20	4	1	3	2	.200	.400	.304
Runners/Scor. Pos.			10	1	0	2	1	.100	.100	.250
First 9 Batters			276	70	3	19	34	.254	.319	.300
Second 9 Batters			242	72	4	22	27	.298	.417	.361
All Batters Thereafter			227	59	5	22	23	.260	.388	.328

Loves to face: Jose Oquendo (0-for-6)
Hates to face: Gary Carter (.571, 4-for-7, 1 HR)
Ground outs-to-air outs ratio: 1.16 last season, 1.20 for career. . . .
Additional statistics: 18 double-play ground outs in 177 opportunities, 32 doubles, 4 triples in 195.1 innings last season. . . . Allowed 20 first-inning runs in 34 starts. . . . Batting support: 3.94 runs per start. . . . Tied Bert Blyleven for major league lead in losses. Only 20-game loser during 1980s: Brian Kingman (8–20 in 1980). . . . Faced Valenzuela, Hershiser, Scott, and Gooden in first four starts, and emerged 0–3. . . . Allowed only one home run in his last 71 innings. . . . Allowed nine hits (three doubles) in 15 at-bats with the bases loaded last season. . . . Career winning percentage of .300 (9–21) is lowest of any active pitcher with at least 30 decisions.

Dwight Gooden

New York Mets — Throws Right

	W–L	ERA	AB	H	HR	BB	SO	BA	SA	OBA
Season	18-9	3.19	944	242	8	57	175	.256	.333	.301
vs. Left-Handers			491	116	4	36	90	.236	.308	.290
vs. Right-Handers			453	126	4	21	85	.278	.360	.313
Home	8-4	2.46	434	103	4	22	89	.237	.297	.277
Road	10-5	3.84	510	139	4	35	86	.273	.363	.321
Grass	14-4	2.66	663	167	5	35	131	.252	.321	.292
Artificial Turf	4-5	4.46	281	75	3	22	44	.267	.359	.322
April	5-0	2.83	132	32	1	9	27	.242	.333	.296
May	3-1	3.42	208	53	3	12	40	.255	.332	.304
June	2-3	2.92	136	32	1	9	25	.235	.324	.284
July	3-1	2.11	147	36	0	7	22	.245	.299	.277
August	2-1	4.35	156	46	2	12	26	.295	.410	.343
Sept./Oct.	3-3	3.32	165	43	1	8	35	.261	.297	.297
Leading Off Inn.			238	57	2	13	37	.239	.328	.282
Runners On			380	105	5	29	76	.276	.376	.328
Runners/Scor. Pos.			254	69	4	25	61	.272	.374	.332
Runners On/2 Out			166	42	1	12	41	.253	.319	.311
Scor. Pos./2 Out			123	32	1	11	34	.260	.333	.326
Late Inning Pressure			82	25	1	6	9	.305	.366	.356
Leading Off			20	5	1	3	1	.250	.400	.348
Runners On			31	12	0	2	5	.387	.452	.429
Runners/Scor. Pos.			20	8	0	2	4	.400	.450	.435
First 9 Batters			279	53	1	16	65	.190	.251	.242
Second 9 Batters			277	74	3	21	47	.267	.357	.321
All Batters Thereafter			388	115	4	20	63	.296	.374	.329

Loves to face: Marvell Wynne (0-for-19)
Hates to face: Barry Bonds (.321, 9-for-28, 6 BB, 2 HR)
Ground outs-to-air outs ratio: 1.74 last season, 1.26 for career. Year by year, 1984–1987: 0.88, 1.01, 1.26, 1.54. . . . Additional statistics: 18 double-play ground outs in 149 opportunities, 40 doubles, 4 triples in 248.1 innings last season. . . . Allowed 10 first-inning runs in 34 starts. . . . Batting support: 5.59 runs per start, highest in N.L. (minimum: 15 GS). . . . Allowed 56 stolen bases and an 84-percent success rate. . . . Best regular-season record in history (91–35, .722), but 0–3 in six postseason starts. . . . Has never allowed a grand slam. Hasn't yielded a three-run HR since Sept. 12, 1986. Hasn't given up two in a game since June 20, 1987. . . . Has allowed four hits in 51 at-bats in LIP Situations with two outs and runners in scoring position.

Rich Gossage

Chicago Cubs — Throws Right

	W–L	ERA	AB	H	HR	BB	SO	BA	SA	OBA
Season	4-4	4.33	172	50	3	15	30	.291	.407	.356
vs. Left-Handers			83	25	1	10	15	.301	.422	.372
vs. Right-Handers			89	25	2	5	15	.281	.393	.340
Home	2-3	5.06	72	23	2	5	10	.319	.458	.364
Road	2-1	3.90	100	27	1	10	20	.270	.370	.351
Grass	2-3	3.16	122	33	2	6	21	.270	.352	.310
Artificial Turf	2-1	7.30	50	17	1	9	9	.340	.540	.452
April	1-1	4.00	33	11	1	5	8	.333	.455	.421
May	0-0	1.59	23	6	0	1	9	.261	.304	.292
June	0-0	4.50	29	8	0	1	3	.276	.345	.300
July	0-0	2.84	26	8	0	2	2	.308	.423	.367
August	1-1	9.95	27	8	2	1	3	.296	.630	.367
Sept./Oct.	2-2	3.24	34	9	0	5	5	.265	.294	.359
Leading Off Inn.			35	13	1	3	10	.371	.514	.421
Runners On			92	27	2	10	10	.293	.413	.371
Runners/Scor. Pos.			54	18	1	9	5	.333	.444	.439
Runners On/2 Out			38	12	2	6	4	.316	.526	.409
Scor. Pos./2 Out			25	7	1	5	4	.280	.400	.400
Late Inning Pressure			110	36	2	12	18	.327	.455	.405
Leading Off			21	10	1	3	6	.476	.667	.542
Runners On			67	21	1	7	4	.313	.418	.390
Runners/Scor. Pos.			40	16	1	6	3	.400	.550	.490
First 9 Batters			171	50	3	15	30	.292	.409	.358
Second 9 Batters			1	0	0	0	0	.000	.000	.000
All Batters Thereafter			0	0	0	0	0	—	—	—

Loves to face: Dale Murphy (.048, 1-for-21)
Hates to face: Kevin Bass (.727, 8-for-11)
Ground outs-to-air outs ratio: 0.88 last season, 0.83 for career. . . .
Additional statistics: 2 double-play ground outs in 44 opportunities, 9 doubles, 1 triple in 43.2 innings last season. . . . Who was the saves leader on the 1976 White Sox, for which Gossage completed 15 of his 29 starts? See below. . . . Fourth reliever in history to win 100 games. The all-time leaders: Hoyt Wilhelm (124), Lindy McDaniel (119), Rollie Fingers (107), Goose (101). . . . Strikeouts per nine innings, year by year since 1986: 8.77, 7.62, 6.18. . . . The only player since the start of divisional play to be selected for All-Star Games representing teams from each of baseball's four divisions. . . . Saves leader on '76 White Sox was Dave Hamilton (10). Clay Carroll had six.

Jim Gott

Pittsburgh Pirates — Throws Right

	W–L	ERA	AB	H	HR	BB	SO	BA	SA	OBA
Season	6-6	3.49	280	68	9	22	76	.243	.386	.300
vs. Left-Handers			132	29	6	13	34	.220	.394	.293
vs. Right-Handers			148	39	3	9	42	.264	.378	.306
Home	4-2	1.99	138	25	3	12	38	.181	.275	.245
Road	2-4	5.15	142	43	6	10	38	.303	.493	.353
Grass	0-3	6.89	67	23	3	6	16	.343	.567	.408
Artificial Turf	6-3	2.63	213	45	6	16	60	.211	.329	.264
April	1-0	3.18	39	8	2	1	11	.205	.410	.220
May	1-1	1.23	50	12	1	3	12	.240	.360	.283
June	2-1	4.50	43	11	1	6	14	.256	.372	.333
July	0-1	1.54	40	8	0	4	11	.200	.225	.289
August	2-2	5.40	64	15	4	6	16	.234	.438	.300
Sept./Oct.	0-1	4.91	44	14	1	2	12	.318	.477	.362
Leading Off Inn.			59	13	4	4	12	.220	.441	.281
Runners On			115	34	1	12	31	.296	.400	.354
Runners/Scor. Pos.			78	19	1	11	19	.244	.333	.326
Runners On/2 Out			50	10	0	7	18	.200	.220	.298
Scor. Pos./2 Out			38	8	0	7	10	.211	.237	.333
Late Inning Pressure			196	52	6	19	55	.265	.403	.329
Leading Off			42	8	2	4	8	.190	.333	.261
Runners On			81	30	1	10	24	.370	.506	.426
Runners/Scor. Pos.			51	17	1	9	13	.333	.471	.413
First 9 Batters			275	67	9	22	74	.244	.389	.301
Second 9 Batters			5	1	0	0	2	.200	.200	.200
All Batters Thereafter			0	0	0	0	0	—	—	—

Loves to face: Ozzie Smith (0-for-7)
Hates to face: Kal Daniels (.444, 4-for-9, 3 HR)
Ground outs-to-air outs ratio: 1.05 last season, 1.34 for career. . . .
Additional statistics: 4 double-play ground outs in 55 opportunities, 9 doubles, 2 triples in 77.1 innings last season. . . . Saved 34 games last season, breaking Kent Tekulve's club record of 31. Gott's 23 saves after the All-Star break were 2d most in the majors. John Franco had 25. . . . His seven saves against St. Louis tied him for most by any pitcher vs. any club. . . . Opponents' career average is .198 with two outs and runners in scoring position. . . . Career batting average only .167, but has more extra-base hits (6) than singles (5), and four HRs in 66 AB (one per 16.5 AB). That's roughly the same career rate as Aaron (16.4), Mays (16.3), and Gehrig (16.5).

Mark Grant

San Diego Padres — Throws Right

	W–L	ERA	AB	H	HR	BB	SO	BA	SA	OBA
Season	2-8	3.69	362	97	14	36	61	.268	.439	.334
vs. Left-Handers			180	47	3	18	24	.261	.378	.327
vs. Right-Handers			182	50	11	18	37	.275	.500	.342
Home	1-4	4.58	146	39	8	19	25	.267	.500	.345
Road	1-4	3.09	216	58	6	17	36	.269	.398	.326
Grass	2-6	3.26	279	68	12	32	48	.244	.427	.322
Artificial Turf	0-2	5.31	83	29	2	4	13	.349	.482	.379
April	0-3	5.50	68	18	5	6	7	.265	.559	.320
May	1-1	2.48	118	27	2	16	24	.229	.305	.331
June	0-2	5.79	93	29	5	10	18	.312	.570	.375
July	1-1	0.82	37	8	1	2	6	.216	.297	.256
August	0-1	11.57	13	7	1	0	2	.538	.923	.538
Sept./Oct.	0-0	0.87	33	8	0	2	4	.242	.273	.270
Leading Off Inn.			90	27	1	8	13	.300	.400	.364
Runners On			155	36	6	16	20	.232	.374	.301
Runners/Scor. Pos.			81	18	0	12	16	.222	.259	.309
Runners On/2 Out			64	15	3	10	11	.234	.391	.347
Scor. Pos./2 Out			41	8	0	8	9	.195	.195	.327
Late Inning Pressure			85	22	2	9	13	.259	.400	.337
Leading Off			23	8	1	3	4	.348	.478	.423
Runners On			35	6	1	4	3	.171	.286	.275
Runners/Scor. Pos.			15	3	0	4	2	.200	.267	.368
First 9 Batters			209	60	8	16	36	.287	.469	.332
Second 9 Batters			86	27	4	10	12	.314	.512	.392
All Batters Thereafter			67	10	2	10	13	.149	.254	.269

Loves to face: Ozzie Smith (0-for-11)
Hates to face: Glenn Davis (4-for-4, 2 BB, 2 HR)
Ground outs-to-air outs ratio: 1.48 last season, 1.23 for career. . . .
Additional statistics: 12 double-play ground outs in 78 opportunities, 18 doubles, 1 triple in 97.2 innings last season. . . . Allowed 8 first-inning runs in 11 starts. . . . Batting support: 2.36 runs per start. . . . Record of 1–5 (4.31 ERA) in 11 starts, 1–3 (2.57) in 22 relief appearances. . . . Padres had a record of 3–30 in games in which he appeared, 0–10 when he allowed a home run. . . . Opponents' career average of .246 on grass fields (8–13, 3.83 ERA), .324 on artificial turf (2–9, 6.16 ERA). . . . Had losing records in each of his four seasons in the majors. . . . His career winning percentage of .313 (10–22) is the lowest of any active pitcher with more than 30 decisions.

Kevin Gross

Philadelphia Phillies — Throws Right

	W–L	ERA	AB	H	HR	BB	SO	BA	SA	OBA
Season	12-14	3.69	876	209	18	89	162	.239	.357	.315
vs. Left-Handers			491	125	10	69	83	.255	.383	.349
vs. Right-Handers			385	84	8	20	79	.218	.325	.270
Home	6-6	3.64	422	92	9	48	85	.218	.327	.310
Road	6-8	3.74	454	117	9	41	77	.258	.385	.320
Grass	3-3	3.78	185	46	4	18	29	.249	.368	.317
Artificial Turf	9-11	3.67	691	163	14	71	133	.236	.355	.315
April	1-1	1.18	135	25	3	13	36	.185	.289	.257
May	4-1	2.80	173	38	2	18	29	.220	.301	.299
June	3-1	4.38	145	43	1	11	22	.297	.393	.350
July	2-4	5.05	158	36	6	17	27	.228	.424	.307
August	1-4	4.73	124	31	3	10	20	.250	.379	.319
Sept./Oct.	1-3	4.23	141	36	3	20	28	.255	.362	.360
Leading Off Inn.			223	54	7	14	42	.242	.413	.293
Runners On			357	91	4	41	63	.255	.350	.335
Runners/Scor. Pos.			234	54	4	30	52	.231	.346	.321
Runners On/2 Out			171	45	2	23	27	.263	.374	.357
Scor. Pos./2 Out			117	28	2	17	23	.239	.359	.341
Late Inning Pressure			74	14	3	7	14	.189	.351	.268
Leading Off			20	3	0	3	3	.150	.250	.261
Runners On			26	5	0	2	5	.192	.192	.250
Runners/Scor. Pos.			17	2	0	2	5	.118	.118	.211
First 9 Batters			267	51	1	23	66	.191	.258	.262
Second 9 Batters			266	66	7	21	37	.248	.376	.311
All Batters Thereafter			343	92	10	45	59	.268	.420	.359

Loves to face: Gerald Young (.063, 1-for-16)
Hates to face: Ken Griffey (.545, 6-for-11, 5 BB, 3 HR)
Ground outs-to-air outs ratio: 0.77 last season, 0.98 for career. . . .
Additional statistics: 8 double-play ground outs in 129 opportunities, 36 doubles, 7 triples in 231.2 innings last season. . . . Allowed 7 first-inning runs in 33 starts, 4th lowest average in N.L. (minimum: 15 GS). . . . Batting support: 3.61 runs per start. . . . Tied with Jamie Moyer for most losses in N.L. over last two seasons (30). . . . Hit 11 batters last season to lead N.L., his 3d straight season with a share of that title. One more and he ties Don Drysdale's N.L. record (1958–61). . . . Career record of 16–7 in June, 44–59 in other months. . . . Lowest previous opponents' batting average was .251 in 1985. . . . Career record against his new team, the Expos, is his best against any club (11–3).

Atlee Hammaker
San Francisco Giants — Throws Left

	W–L	ERA	AB	H	HR	BB	SO	BA	SA	OBA
Season	9-9	3.73	549	136	11	41	65	.248	.352	.302
vs. Left-Handers			87	23	0	5	18	.264	.333	.313
vs. Right-Handers			462	113	11	36	47	.245	.355	.299
Home	5-5	3.49	321	76	7	19	33	.237	.333	.279
Road	4-4	4.07	228	60	4	22	32	.263	.377	.331
Grass	6-6	3.56	394	97	8	26	44	.246	.340	.291
Artificial Turf	3-3	4.17	155	39	3	15	21	.252	.381	.326
April	1-0	3.86	70	19	2	4	7	.271	.400	.307
May	2-0	2.50	67	15	1	6	10	.224	.313	.284
June	1-1	6.75	72	24	1	6	15	.333	.444	.390
July	0-2	4.00	65	14	0	7	10	.215	.292	.301
August	3-3	3.53	138	34	1	8	9	.246	.304	.288
Sept./Oct.	2-3	2.92	137	30	6	10	14	.219	.372	.272
Leading Off Inn.			141	32	1	6	16	.227	.298	.264
Runners On			212	59	3	24	24	.278	.373	.351
Runners/Scor. Pos.			124	35	1	19	18	.282	.363	.376
Runners On/2 Out			83	16	1	11	10	.193	.301	.295
Scor. Pos./2 Out			45	9	1	8	7	.200	.333	.333
Late Inning Pressure			109	29	1	10	16	.266	.358	.328
Leading Off			29	7	0	0	3	.241	.310	.241
Runners On			44	13	1	7	7	.295	.432	.392
Runners/Scor. Pos.			29	9	1	4	4	.310	.483	.394
First 9 Batters			281	70	6	22	38	.249	.352	.308
Second 9 Batters			152	30	3	10	23	.197	.289	.244
All Batters Thereafter			116	36	2	9	4	.310	.431	.360

Loves to face: Von Hayes (.100, 2-for-20)
Hates to face: Dale Murphy (.516, 16-for-31, 5 HR)
Ground outs-to-air outs ratio: 1.62 last season, 1.43 for career. . . . Additional statistics: 15 double-play ground outs in 96 opportunities, 20 doubles, 2 triples in 144.2 innings last season. . . . Allowed 15 first-inning runs in 17 starts. . . . Batting support: 3.35 runs per start. . . . Record of 5–7 (3.56 ERA) in 17 starts, 4–2 (4.11) in 26 relief appearances. . . . Opposing left-handers had a higher batting average than right-handers for the first time in his career. . . . Last 32 home runs allowed have all been to right-handed batters. Last left-hander to take him deep was Darryl Strawberry, on May 27, 1987. . . . Career record of 31–15 at Candlestick, 17–33 in other N.L. stadiums. . . . Has had 266 career at-bats without an extra-base hit, the most by any active player.

Greg Harris
Philadelphia Phillies — Throws Right

	W–L	ERA	AB	H	HR	BB	SO	BA	SA	OBA
Season	4-6	2.36	382	80	7	52	71	.209	.301	.309
vs. Left-Handers			182	38	3	27	31	.209	.302	.316
vs. Right-Handers			200	42	4	25	40	.210	.300	.303
Home	1-6	2.18	205	44	4	29	39	.215	.302	.321
Road	3-0	2.55	177	36	3	23	32	.203	.299	.296
Grass	1-0	2.20	95	15	2	11	17	.158	.263	.241
Artificial Turf	3-6	2.41	287	65	5	41	54	.226	.314	.331
April	0-0	3.52	27	4	0	4	3	.148	.148	.281
May	1-1	2.60	60	10	1	11	8	.167	.233	.306
June	2-1	3.18	62	18	2	8	13	.290	.419	.371
July	0-1	1.17	85	22	2	7	15	.259	.353	.315
August	1-1	2.13	87	13	2	9	22	.149	.264	.242
Sept./Oct.	0-2	2.70	61	13	0	13	10	.213	.295	.347
Leading Off Inn.			84	17	2	7	17	.202	.333	.280
Runners On			181	35	1	32	31	.193	.238	.315
Runners/Scor. Pos.			116	20	1	26	20	.172	.216	.324
Runners On/2 Out			78	14	0	20	14	.179	.218	.347
Scor. Pos./2 Out			58	10	0	16	10	.172	.207	.351
Late Inning Pressure			163	35	4	24	25	.215	.325	.317
Leading Off			39	9	1	3	7	.231	.359	.286
Runners On			69	11	0	18	7	.159	.174	.330
Runners/Scor. Pos.			40	9	0	13	4	.225	.250	.407
First 9 Batters			337	68	7	45	62	.202	.300	.302
Second 9 Batters			36	10	0	7	8	.278	.333	.395
All Batters Thereafter			9	2	0	0	1	.222	.222	.222

Loves to face: Jose Canseco (0-for-10, 7 SO)
Hates to face: Mark McGwire (.600, 3-for-5, 2 HR)
Of course, those guys are history far as he's concerned. . . . Ground outs-to-air outs ratio: 1.09 last season, 1.25 for career. . . . Additional statistics: 8 double-play ground outs in 94 opportunities, 12 doubles, 1 triple in 107.0 innings last season. . . . Has pitched 89 games in relief over the past two seasons, but has saved only one of them. . . . No pitcher has won 10 games and saved 20 in same season since he and Roger McDowell did it in 1986. . . . Only one other Rangers pitcher saved 20 in a single season. Jim Kern holds club record (29). . . . Has completed only one of 45 career starts, and that game was halted by rain after seven innings (1982). . . . Opponents have a .220 career BA on his first pass through batting order, .291 after that.

Andy Hawkins
San Diego Padres — Throws Right

	W–L	ERA	AB	H	HR	BB	SO	BA	SA	OBA
Season	14-11	3.35	804	196	16	76	91	.244	.350	.312
vs. Left-Handers			421	109	4	61	37	.259	.347	.355
vs. Right-Handers			383	87	12	15	54	.227	.352	.260
Home	8-6	2.53	471	101	8	48	55	.214	.297	.291
Road	6-5	4.60	333	95	8	28	36	.285	.423	.341
Grass	11-6	2.71	619	142	11	57	69	.229	.323	.299
Artificial Turf	3-5	5.59	185	54	5	19	22	.292	.438	.354
April	3-1	4.31	115	29	2	13	16	.252	.357	.328
May	2-3	3.03	142	36	2	14	15	.254	.352	.321
June	2-2	2.70	120	26	2	9	18	.217	.283	.288
July	3-2	3.63	148	35	5	13	13	.236	.385	.296
August	3-2	3.79	148	36	2	16	16	.243	.338	.317
Sept./Oct.	1-1	2.62	131	34	3	11	13	.260	.374	.319
Leading Off Inn.			214	51	6	13	19	.238	.369	.288
Runners On			297	74	6	32	33	.249	.364	.324
Runners/Scor. Pos.			148	41	3	21	16	.277	.412	.362
Runners On/2 Out			138	31	5	18	18	.225	.399	.323
Scor. Pos./2 Out			76	20	3	13	9	.263	.461	.378
Late Inning Pressure			96	25	0	16	12	.260	.302	.372
Leading Off			29	11	0	2	2	.379	.483	.438
Runners On			42	8	0	7	7	.190	.214	.306
Runners/Scor. Pos.			19	3	0	6	4	.158	.211	.360
First 9 Batters			273	64	5	17	36	.234	.326	.281
Second 9 Batters			257	69	6	24	32	.268	.405	.336
All Batters Thereafter			274	63	5	35	23	.230	.321	.318

Loves to face: Rick Schu (0-for-11)
Hates to face: Johnny Ray (.517, 15-for-29)
Ground outs-to-air outs ratio: 0.90 last season, 0.99 for career. . . . Additional statistics: 13 double-play ground outs in 155 opportunities, 27 doubles, 5 triples in 217.2 innings last season. . . . Allowed 20 first-inning runs in 33 starts. . . . Batting support: 3.18 runs per start. . . . Held right-handed batters hitless in 40 consecutive plate appearances (June 26–July 14), 2d longest streak in the majors last season. Tom Browning had the longest (41). . . . Won his first 11 games in 1985, but lost his season debut every year since. Career record of 12–6 in April, 42–52 in other months. . . . Nine pitchers worked at least 200 innings with fewer than 100 strikeouts last season. The Yankees have signed two: Hawkins and LaPoint.

Neal Heaton
Montreal Expos — Throws Left

	W–L	ERA	AB	H	HR	BB	SO	BA	SA	OBA
Season	3-10	4.99	361	98	14	43	43	.271	.468	.351
vs. Left-Handers			90	22	4	7	15	.244	.433	.306
vs. Right-Handers			271	76	10	36	28	.280	.480	.365
Home	1-4	5.35	138	38	6	18	19	.275	.486	.354
Road	2-6	4.77	223	60	8	25	24	.269	.457	.349
Grass	1-4	5.24	126	32	3	16	14	.254	.413	.347
Artificial Turf	2-6	4.86	235	66	11	27	29	.281	.498	.353
April	0-1	14.54	18	7	2	4	1	.389	.833	.500
May	1-2	4.38	143	37	4	16	11	.259	.462	.337
June	1-2	5.70	90	25	7	10	15	.278	.578	.347
July	1-1	1.98	46	9	1	2	7	.196	.283	.225
August	0-4	5.40	64	20	0	11	9	.313	.359	.421
Sept./Oct.			0	0	0	0	0	—	—	—
Leading Off Inn.			92	17	4	11	13	.185	.380	.272
Runners On			130	35	2	20	11	.269	.392	.372
Runners/Scor. Pos.			85	19	2	14	9	.224	.341	.343
Runners On/2 Out			60	15	1	9	6	.250	.433	.348
Scor. Pos./2 Out			46	9	1	8	5	.196	.348	.315
Late Inning Pressure			94	25	3	12	11	.266	.383	.352
Leading Off			29	6	2	2	2	.207	.448	.258
Runners On			29	9	0	7	3	.310	.345	.447
Runners/Scor. Pos.			17	3	0	7	3	.176	.176	.423
First 9 Batters			203	59	5	20	28	.291	.448	.354
Second 9 Batters			92	19	5	13	12	.207	.446	.318
All Batters Thereafter			66	20	4	10	3	.303	.561	.362

Loves to face: Tom Brunansky (.136, 3-for-22, 1 HR)
Hates to face: Darryl Strawberry (.556, 5-for-9, 3 HR)
Ground outs-to-air outs ratio: 1.00 last season, 0.94 for career. . . . Additional statistics: 14 double-play ground outs in 63 opportunities, 19 doubles, 5 triples in 97.1 innings last season. . . . Allowed 13 first-inning runs in 11 starts. . . . Batting support: 4.09 runs per start. . . . Record of 2–6 (5.92 ERA) in 11 starts, 1–4 (3.34) in 21 relief appearances. . . . He and Mark Davis were the only N.L. pitchers with double figures in losses and fewer than 100 innings pitched last season. . . . Didn't allow a home run in his last 26.1 innings, after Ron Gant's 15th-inning game-winner beat him on July 2. . . . Won 12 of first 16 N.L. decisions, but has a 4–16 record since then. . . . Opponents' career average is .382 (26-for-68, 3 HR) with bases loaded.

Orel Hershiser
Los Angeles Dodgers — Throws Right

	W–L	ERA	AB	H	HR	BB	SO	BA	SA	OBA
Season	23-8	2.26	975	208	18	73	178	.213	.310	.269
vs. Left-Handers			533	117	13	56	72	.220	.343	.294
vs. Right-Handers			442	91	5	17	106	.206	.269	.238
Home	11-5	2.31	462	102	10	35	91	.221	.340	.277
Road	12-3	2.21	513	106	8	38	87	.207	.283	.263
Grass	17-5	1.95	690	141	11	48	127	.204	.299	.257
Artificial Turf	6-3	3.01	285	67	7	25	51	.235	.337	.298
April	5-0	1.56	142	23	1	10	24	.162	.232	.222
May	2-2	2.82	141	41	6	11	29	.291	.433	.342
June	5-1	2.72	180	37	4	18	29	.206	.322	.280
July	3-2	3.24	156	34	3	11	29	.218	.353	.269
August	3-3	3.86	169	43	4	14	33	.254	.367	.310
Sept./Oct.	5-0	0.00	187	30	0	9	34	.160	.176	.199
Leading Off Inn.			261	65	8	10	49	.249	.375	.279
Runners On			343	64	5	41	66	.187	.268	.273
Runners/Scor. Pos.			181	35	5	33	38	.193	.343	.315
Runners On/2 Out			159	28	3	27	27	.176	.302	.303
Scor. Pos./2 Out			100	20	3	22	20	.200	.400	.355
Late Inning Pressure			170	36	2	12	29	.212	.300	.265
Leading Off			50	14	0	0	7	.280	.380	.280
Runners On			62	11	2	9	13	.177	.290	.284
Runners/Scor. Pos.			36	7	2	9	8	.194	.389	.354
First 9 Batters			289	56	5	13	54	.194	.280	.230
Second 9 Batters			283	62	9	18	53	.219	.357	.271
All Batters Thereafter			403	90	4	42	71	.223	.298	.295

Loves to face: Bruce Benedict (0-for-14)
Hates to face: Kal Daniels (.500, 12-for-24, 4 HR)
Ground outs-to-air outs ratio: 1.89 last season, 2.15 for career....
Additional statistics: 18 double-play ground outs in 165 opportunities, 28 doubles, 6 triples in 267.0 innings last season.... Allowed 11 first-inning runs in 34 starts.... Batting support: 4.03 runs per start.... Pitched an average of 7.82 innings per start, highest mark in N.L. (minimum: 15 GS).... Didn't allow a hit to the last 31 batters he faced with runners in scoring position during regular season. Start of that streak coincided with start of The Streak.... First N.L. pitcher since Rick Reuschel in 1980 to lead league in both putouts and assists.... He and Gooden have same career totals in starts (158) and shutouts (19). Doc has 52 complete games, Orel 50.

Joe Hesketh
Montreal Expos — Throws Left

	W–L	ERA	AB	H	HR	BB	SO	BA	SA	OBA
Season	4-3	2.85	260	63	1	35	64	.242	.323	.328
vs. Left-Handers			78	16	0	11	23	.205	.244	.300
vs. Right-Handers			182	47	1	24	41	.258	.357	.340
Home	2-0	3.58	120	28	1	16	28	.233	.325	.321
Road	2-3	2.25	140	35	0	19	36	.250	.321	.333
Grass	1-2	3.26	67	17	0	7	15	.254	.299	.312
Artificial Turf	3-1	2.70	193	46	1	28	49	.238	.332	.333
April			0	0	0	0	0	—	—	—
May	1-0	3.00	44	13	0	6	11	.295	.386	.373
June	0-1	2.93	58	15	0	11	14	.259	.310	.371
July	2-0	2.25	51	9	0	6	12	.176	.216	.263
August	0-1	4.20	59	18	0	7	14	.305	.441	.368
Sept./Oct.	1-1	1.88	48	8	1	5	13	.167	.250	.245
Leading Off Inn.			63	16	0	8	16	.254	.302	.338
Runners On			118	25	0	21	29	.212	.280	.322
Runners/Scor. Pos.			78	16	0	17	24	.205	.244	.333
Runners On/2 Out			42	6	0	10	14	.143	.190	.308
Scor. Pos./2 Out			34	4	0	8	13	.118	.147	.286
Late Inning Pressure			163	40	0	20	43	.245	.319	.326
Leading Off			44	11	0	4	12	.250	.318	.313
Runners On			63	12	0	11	17	.190	.238	.307
Runners/Scor. Pos.			38	8	0	9	14	.211	.237	.354
First 9 Batters			254	62	1	33	64	.244	.323	.326
Second 9 Batters			6	1	0	2	0	.167	.333	.375
All Batters Thereafter			0	0	0	0	0	—	—	—

Loves to face: Keith Hernandez (.111, 2-for-18)
Hates to face: Glenn Davis (.364, 4-for-11, 3 HR)
Ground outs-to-air outs ratio: 1.58 last season, 1.13 for career....
Additional statistics: 10 double-play ground outs in 62 opportunities, 14 doubles, 2 triples in 72.2 innings last season.... Has allowed 26 home runs in his career, but only two to left-handed batters: Jose Cruz (1985) and John Kruk (1987).... Career record of 0–4 vs. the Phillies, 22–11 vs. the rest of the league.... Hitless in 49 at-bats with 34 strikeouts since June 19, 1985.... Career stats (22–15, 3.07 ERA) would be impressive if he weren't 30 years old. Pitchers with similar career numbers at a younger age include Lefty Gomez (through 1931), John Candelaria (1976), Luis Tiant (1965). Older pitchers with comparable stats: Rick Camp (1981), Mel Queen (1971), Minnie Rojas (1968).

Brian Holman
Montreal Expos — Throws Right

	W–L	ERA	AB	H	HR	BB	SO	BA	SA	OBA
Season	4-8	3.23	382	101	3	34	58	.264	.348	.324
vs. Left-Handers			211	57	3	24	29	.270	.379	.345
vs. Right-Handers			171	44	0	10	29	.257	.310	.297
Home	3-6	3.12	265	70	3	24	45	.264	.377	.325
Road	1-2	3.48	117	31	0	10	13	.265	.282	.320
Grass	0-1	3.75	47	13	0	4	2	.277	.298	.333
Artificial Turf	4-7	3.16	335	88	3	30	56	.263	.355	.322
April			0	0	0	0	0	—	—	—
May			0	0	0	0	0	—	—	—
June	1-1	2.19	46	10	0	7	8	.217	.304	.321
July	0-2	2.78	117	25	1	8	19	.214	.256	.264
August	1-3	4.70	89	25	0	7	18	.281	.360	.330
Sept./Oct.	2-2	3.03	130	41	2	12	13	.315	.438	.373
Leading Off Inn.			102	28	1	4	12	.275	.353	.302
Runners On			152	44	1	17	23	.289	.388	.359
Runners/Scor. Pos.			90	21	0	12	15	.233	.322	.320
Runners On/2 Out			65	16	0	10	15	.246	.323	.347
Scor. Pos./2 Out			47	11	0	8	11	.234	.340	.345
Late Inning Pressure			28	9	0	1	3	.321	.321	.345
Leading Off			9	3	0	0	1	.333	.333	.333
Runners On			8	3	0	1	0	.375	.375	.444
Runners/Scor. Pos.			2	0	0	1	0	.000	.000	.333
First 9 Batters			133	31	0	15	24	.233	.286	.311
Second 9 Batters			128	38	2	12	17	.297	.422	.355
All Batters Thereafter			121	32	1	7	17	.264	.339	.305

Loves to face: Dale Murphy (0-for-7)
Hates to face: Mookie Wilson (.667, 2-for-3, 1 HR)
Ground outs-to-air outs ratio: 0.90 last season, his first in majors.
... Additional statistics: 7 double-play ground outs in 70 opportunities, 15 doubles, 4 triples in 100.1 innings last season.... Allowed 8 first-inning runs in 16 starts.... Batting support: 2.81 runs per start, 2d lowest in N.L. (minimum: 15 GS).... Expos were one of two N.L. teams with two rookies (Holman and John Dopson) who each pitched 100 innings. The other: Atlanta (Jose Alvarez and Pete Smith).... Opposing ground-ball hitters batted .234, fly-ballers batted .285.... Faced 185 right-handed batters last season, the most of any pitcher who did not allow a homer to a righty. Alejandro Pena faced 344 right-handers without a HR in 1983, a 14-year major league high.

Brian Holton
Los Angeles Dodgers — Throws Right

	W–L	ERA	AB	H	HR	BB	SO	BA	SA	OBA
Season	7-3	1.70	302	69	1	26	49	.228	.291	.289
vs. Left-Handers			155	39	1	20	14	.252	.310	.339
vs. Right-Handers			147	30	0	6	35	.204	.272	.232
Home	1-2	1.58	189	48	0	14	29	.254	.312	.306
Road	6-1	1.89	113	21	1	12	20	.186	.257	.262
Grass	6-2	1.44	247	57	0	20	40	.231	.279	.289
Artificial Turf	1-1	2.81	55	12	1	6	9	.218	.345	.290
April	0-0	2.57	23	4	0	2	5	.174	.348	.240
May	1-0	1.35	47	12	0	4	5	.255	.277	.327
June	2-2	2.20	59	13	0	3	5	.220	.288	.254
July	3-1	2.50	66	13	1	6	13	.197	.258	.260
August	0-0	1.42	68	18	0	7	11	.265	.324	.329
Sept./Oct.	1-0	0.00	39	9	0	4	10	.231	.282	.302
Leading Off Inn.			75	25	0	1	13	.333	.413	.351
Runners On			135	26	0	19	17	.193	.230	.287
Runners/Scor. Pos.			93	15	0	14	9	.161	.204	.264
Runners On/2 Out			65	13	0	10	8	.200	.231	.307
Scor. Pos./2 Out			50	7	0	9	5	.140	.180	.271
Late Inning Pressure			58	10	1	6	10	.172	.276	.250
Leading Off			17	5	0	1	3	.294	.294	.333
Runners On			19	2	0	3	2	.105	.211	.227
Runners/Scor. Pos.			12	1	0	3	1	.083	.250	.267
First 9 Batters			261	58	1	23	46	.222	.295	.285
Second 9 Batters			36	11	0	3	2	.306	.306	.359
All Batters Thereafter			5	0	0	0	0	.000	.000	.000

Loves to face: Rafael Palmeiro (0-for-5)
Hates to face: Buddy Bell (.667, 4-for-6, 1 HR)
Ground outs-to-air outs ratio: 1.46 last season, 1.35 for career....
Additional statistics: 10 double-play ground outs in 58 opportunities, 10 doubles, 3 triples in 84.2 innings last season.... His 1.70 ERA was 2d lowest among N.L. relievers who appeared in 30 or more games.... Had a record of 3–0 in six relief appearances vs. the Cubs. Was the only visiting pitcher to win three games at Wrigley Field last season.... Finished season with 17.2 scoreless innings, not even worth a mention to Dodgers fans.... Only home run allowed last season was hit by Terry Pendleton.... Had allowed 11 home runs in 83.1 innings pitched in 1987.... Opposing batters have a career batting average of .309 leading off innings.... Has never committed an error (48 chances).

Jay Howell
Los Angeles Dodgers — Throws Right

	W-L	ERA	AB	H	HR	BB	SO	BA	SA	OBA
Season	5-3	2.08	234	44	1	21	70	.188	.239	.255
vs. Left-Handers			124	21	1	11	37	.169	.226	.232
vs. Right-Handers			110	23	0	10	33	.209	.255	.281
Home	3-0	1.61	102	18	0	6	35	.176	.216	.227
Road	2-3	2.43	132	26	1	15	35	.197	.258	.275
Grass	4-1	1.99	168	32	0	13	55	.190	.238	.251
Artificial Turf	1-2	2.29	66	12	1	8	15	.182	.242	.263
April	1-0	0.00	19	1	0	1	6	.053	.053	.100
May	1-1	4.05	50	14	0	8	12	.280	.320	.367
June	0-1	2.00	33	8	0	3	9	.242	.303	.306
July	0-0	1.42	49	11	0	4	14	.224	.286	.283
August	2-1	2.65	59	10	1	4	18	.169	.254	.231
Sept./Oct.	1-0	0.00	24	0	0	1	11	.000	.000	.040
Leading Off Inn.			55	10	0	2	16	.182	.200	.211
Runners On			106	24	1	11	31	.226	.321	.292
Runners/Scor. Pos.			77	19	0	5	23	.247	.325	.282
Runners On/2 Out			49	11	1	4	17	.224	.388	.283
Scor. Pos./2 Out			37	7	0	1	14	.189	.324	.211
Late Inning Pressure			158	28	0	16	49	.177	.222	.254
Leading Off			40	6	0	2	13	.150	.150	.190
Runners On			61	15	0	9	17	.246	.344	.333
Runners/Scor. Pos.			45	14	0	4	11	.311	.444	.353
First 9 Batters			231	43	1	21	69	.186	.238	.254
Second 9 Batters			3	1	0	0	1	.333	.333	.333
All Batters Thereafter			0	0	0	0	0	—	—	—

Loves to face: Tom Brunansky (.154, 2-for-13)
Hates to face: Paul O'Neill (3-for-3, 1 2B, 1 HR)
Ground outs-to-air outs ratio: 1.21 last season, 1.13 for career.... Additional statistics: 0 double-play ground outs in 46 opportunities, 7 doubles, 1 triple in 65.0 innings last season.... Held opposing left-handers hitless in last 33 plate appearances of regular season. ... Dodgers won 13 of last 14 regular-season games in which he appeared.... Finished season with 18 consecutive scoreless innings. ... Opponents' batting average was lowest of career. Previous low was .223 (1984.).... Opposing batters hit better with runners in scoring position than otherwise in every season of nine-year career. Breakdown: .278 with runners on, .236 with bases empty.... Middle name is Canfield. We say he can't. Two errors on 22 chances over last two seasons.

Danny Jackson
Cincinnati Reds — Throws Left

	W-L	ERA	AB	H	HR	BB	SO	BA	SA	OBA
Season	23-8	2.73	943	206	13	71	161	.218	.312	.273
vs. Left-Handers			134	35	1	8	24	.261	.336	.299
vs. Right-Handers			809	171	12	63	137	.211	.308	.269
Home	12-3	2.63	485	103	8	42	69	.212	.315	.276
Road	11-5	2.83	458	103	5	29	92	.225	.308	.270
Grass	8-2	2.84	278	68	5	16	56	.245	.331	.283
Artificial Turf	15-6	2.68	665	138	8	55	105	.208	.304	.269
April	3-1	2.83	128	25	2	17	21	.195	.289	.295
May	2-1	3.19	109	25	2	9	18	.229	.349	.288
June	3-2	4.17	137	32	1	9	32	.234	.307	.279
July	5-1	1.31	172	35	1	10	34	.203	.279	.245
August	6-1	2.23	229	46	2	14	35	.201	.271	.249
Sept./Oct.	4-2	3.38	168	43	5	12	21	.256	.399	.304
Leading Off Inn.			245	53	6	21	46	.216	.339	.278
Runners On			341	87	4	30	51	.255	.346	.315
Runners/Scor. Pos.			197	51	4	19	27	.259	.386	.323
Runners On/2 Out			148	39	3	16	22	.264	.385	.335
Scor. Pos./2 Out			97	27	3	12	11	.278	.464	.358
Late Inning Pressure			125	21	1	6	23	.168	.264	.206
Leading Off			36	5	0	2	7	.139	.222	.184
Runners On			34	7	1	2	4	.206	.382	.250
Runners/Scor. Pos.			20	5	1	1	1	.250	.450	.286
First 9 Batters			288	65	6	17	54	.226	.340	.269
Second 9 Batters			270	58	2	29	40	.215	.304	.291
All Batters Thereafter			385	83	5	25	67	.216	.296	.263

Loves to face: Gary Redus (0-for-17)
Hates to face: Roberto Alomar (.500, 5-for-10, cycle)
Ground outs-to-air outs ratio: 2.15 last season, 1.68 for career.... Additional statistics: 24 double-play ground outs in 158 opportunities, 39 doubles, 5 triples in 260.2 innings last season.... Allowed 16 first-inning runs in 35 starts. Batting support: 4.60 runs per start. ... Most wins by an N.L. pitcher who didn't win Cy Young Award since 1973, when Ron Bryant won 24 games and Tom Seaver won the award. Juan Marichal never won the Cy, despite 26 wins in 1968, and 25 in 1963 and 1966.... Went from nine games below .500 (9–18) in 1987 to 15 above in 1988. Gain of 24 games was most since Denny McLain went 17–16 year in 1967, 31–6 a year later. Last to improve his record by *more than* 24 games in one year was Don Larsen: 3–21 in 1954, 9–2 in 1955.

Jimmy Jones
San Diego Padres — Throws Right

	W-L	ERA	AB	H	HR	BB	SO	BA	SA	OBA
Season	9-14	4.12	693	192	14	44	82	.277	.411	.319
vs. Left-Handers			358	105	7	30	43	.293	.439	.343
vs. Right-Handers			335	87	7	14	39	.260	.382	.293
Home	5-7	3.34	354	97	5	23	39	.274	.379	.320
Road	4-7	4.95	339	95	9	21	43	.280	.445	.318
Grass	7-11	4.08	504	140	10	33	51	.278	.413	.322
Artificial Turf	2-3	4.22	189	52	4	11	31	.275	.407	.312
April	2-2	2.45	98	25	2	5	12	.255	.367	.291
May	2-3	3.27	159	42	3	9	19	.264	.434	.300
June	1-2	7.39	126	37	4	10	15	.294	.460	.350
July	2-2	1.80	112	27	2	7	13	.241	.348	.286
August	1-3	3.48	117	33	2	8	14	.282	.402	.323
Sept./Oct.	1-2	7.45	81	28	1	5	9	.346	.444	.378
Leading Off Inn.			182	48	2	9	16	.264	.368	.298
Runners On			269	81	7	21	32	.301	.457	.348
Runners/Scor. Pos.			150	48	4	14	16	.320	.480	.366
Runners On/2 Out			104	21	3	12	14	.202	.346	.297
Scor. Pos./2 Out			62	15	1	8	9	.242	.371	.338
Late Inning Pressure			59	16	2	4	5	.271	.458	.317
Leading Off			17	2	0	0	1	.118	.118	.118
Runners On			18	6	1	2	2	.333	.667	.400
Runners/Scor. Pos.			10	5	0	2	0	.500	.800	.583
First 9 Batters			233	52	4	19	37	.223	.339	.284
Second 9 Batters			238	69	4	10	22	.290	.424	.315
All Batters Thereafter			222	71	6	15	23	.320	.473	.361

Loves to face: Glenn Hubbard (0-for-9)
Hates to face: Nick Esasky (.375, 6-for-16, 3 HR)
Ground outs-to-air outs ratio: 1.35 last season, 1.51 for career.... Additional statistics: 15 double-play ground outs in 131 opportunities, 35 doubles, 8 triples in 179.0 innings last season.... Allowed 16 first-inning runs in 29 starts.... Batting support: 3.62 runs per start.... Opposing batters have a career batting average of .214 in his first pass through the batting order, .262 in his second pass, and .323 thereafter.... Other career averages: .241 with bases empty, .311 with runners on base.... Fly-ball hitters have hit 63 points higher than ground-ballers (.300 to .237).... One of four pitchers to hit a HR in both 1987 and 1988.... Has fielded 95 chances in his career, the most of any active pitcher who hasn't committed an error.

Bob Knepper
Houston Astros — Throws Left

	W-L	ERA	AB	H	HR	BB	SO	BA	SA	OBA
Season	14-5	3.14	642	156	13	67	103	.243	.361	.314
vs. Left-Handers			92	22	1	4	21	.239	.348	.273
vs. Right-Handers			550	134	12	63	82	.244	.364	.321
Home	9-3	2.36	369	84	6	38	60	.228	.331	.298
Road	5-2	4.25	273	72	7	29	43	.264	.403	.337
Grass	2-1	5.15	142	39	2	14	24	.275	.394	.340
Artificial Turf	12-4	2.60	500	117	11	53	79	.234	.352	.307
April	2-0	0.95	66	17	1	5	12	.258	.333	.310
May	4-1	1.66	164	40	4	12	22	.244	.354	.298
June	2-0	3.38	122	26	1	17	23	.213	.328	.305
July	3-2	5.74	121	32	5	17	22	.264	.463	.353
August	1-1	6.60	58	18	1	9	4	.310	.414	.397
Sept./Oct.	2-1	1.99	111	23	1	7	20	.207	.288	.261
Leading Off Inn.			162	48	6	21	21	.296	.506	.377
Runners On			270	61	5	24	40	.226	.330	.287
Runners/Scor. Pos.			151	28	4	16	21	.185	.285	.260
Runners On/2 Out			107	21	2	14	18	.196	.318	.295
Scor. Pos./2 Out			68	10	2	9	11	.147	.265	.256
Late Inning Pressure			57	12	1	2	8	.211	.316	.237
Leading Off			18	3	0	1	2	.167	.222	.211
Runners On			10	4	1	0	2	.400	.800	.400
Runners/Scor. Pos.			4	0	0	0	1	.000	.000	.000
First 9 Batters			212	52	3	23	29	.245	.349	.316
Second 9 Batters			208	43	5	23	40	.207	.317	.288
All Batters Thereafter			222	61	5	21	34	.275	.414	.337

Loves to face: Darrell Evans (.071, 1-for-14)
Hates to face: Mike Schmidt (.402, 33-for-82, 11 BB, 9 HR)
Ground outs-to-air outs ratio: 1.97 last season, 1.34 for career.... Additional statistics: 26 double-play ground outs in 132 opportunities, 31 doubles, 3 triples in 175.0 innings last season.... Allowed 8 first-inning runs in 27 starts.... Batting support: 4.63 runs per start.... Record of 6–0 with a 0.89 ERA after his first seven starts. ... Didn't lose consecutive decisions last season. Had streaks of three, four, and six losses in 1987.... Darryl Strawberry was the only left-hander to homer against him in 1988.... Opponents' average with runners in scoring position was lowest of his career. ... Leads active pitchers with nine sac flies. Career average of 37 percent driving in runners from 3d base with less than two outs (17-for-46).

Mike Krukow

Throws Right

San Francisco Giants	W–L	ERA	AB	H	HR	BB	SO	BA	SA	OBA
Season	7-4	3.54	470	111	13	31	75	.236	.379	.289
vs. Left-Handers			245	64	6	18	36	.261	.412	.314
vs. Right-Handers			225	47	7	13	39	.209	.342	.262
Home	4-2	3.54	257	63	7	16	44	.245	.381	.295
Road	3-2	3.54	213	48	6	15	31	.225	.376	.283
Grass	5-3	3.71	343	87	9	23	58	.254	.391	.306
Artificial Turf	2-1	3.09	127	24	4	8	17	.189	.346	.243
April	1-1	3.90	112	25	4	8	20	.223	.366	.276
May	3-2	3.89	139	31	6	11	23	.223	.403	.285
June	2-1	3.93	139	35	3	6	17	.252	.403	.293
July			0	0	0	0	0	—	—	—
August	1-0	1.71	80	20	0	6	15	.250	.313	.310
Sept./Oct.			0	0	0	0	0	—	—	—
Leading Off Inn.			127	36	6	4	17	.283	.457	.305
Runners On			177	40	1	17	28	.226	.316	.302
Runners/Scor. Pos.			111	20	1	14	16	.180	.261	.273
Runners On/2 Out			69	14	0	10	8	.203	.304	.329
Scor. Pos./2 Out			51	9	0	8	7	.176	.255	.300
Late Inning Pressure			25	9	1	6	1	.360	.680	.500
Leading Off			6	1	1	2	1	.167	.667	.375
Runners On			13	4	0	4	0	.308	.538	.471
Runners/Scor. Pos.			7	3	0	4	0	.429	.857	.636
First 9 Batters			165	32	4	8	28	.194	.309	.244
Second 9 Batters			165	41	5	6	29	.248	.400	.276
All Batters Thereafter			140	38	4	17	18	.271	.436	.354

Loves to face: Franklin Stubbs (.087, 2-for-23)
Hates to face: Kal Daniels (.500, 8-for-16, 2 HR)
Ground outs-to-air outs ratio: 0.99 last season, 1.20 for career. . . .
Additional statistics: 6 double-play ground outs in 82 opportunities, 18 doubles, 5 triples in 124.2 innings last season. . . . Allowed 6 first-inning runs in 20 starts. . . . Batting support: 4.00 runs per start. . . . Has a career record of 20–7 against the Mets (including 3–0 last season), but doesn't have more than 13 wins against any other club. . . . Career total of 146 batters faced with the bases loaded, but he has never allowed a grand slam. . . . Opponents' average with runners in scoring position has been under .200 in three of the last four seasons. . . . Most comparable stats to Krukow's at a similar age belonged to Earl Wilson and Milt Wilcox.

Mike LaCoss

Throws Right

San Francisco Giants	W–L	ERA	AB	H	HR	BB	SO	BA	SA	OBA
Season	7-7	3.62	423	99	5	47	70	.234	.317	.311
vs. Left-Handers			214	48	0	30	45	.224	.276	.322
vs. Right-Handers			209	51	5	17	25	.244	.359	.300
Home	7-2	2.25	271	55	3	18	48	.203	.266	.255
Road	0-5	6.34	152	44	2	29	22	.289	.408	.401
Grass	7-4	2.55	333	73	4	28	58	.219	.285	.281
Artificial Turf	0-3	7.94	90	26	1	19	12	.289	.433	.413
April	1-2	3.64	107	22	1	9	16	.206	.271	.267
May	2-2	3.05	144	37	2	14	23	.257	.354	.321
June	2-2	4.33	101	23	1	14	16	.228	.297	.328
July	2-1	3.72	71	17	1	10	15	.239	.338	.333
August			0	0	0	0	0	—	—	—
Sept./Oct.			0	0	0	0	0	—	—	—
Leading Off Inn.			106	26	1	13	20	.245	.340	.328
Runners On			170	41	0	26	25	.241	.276	.340
Runners/Scor. Pos.			104	28	0	19	15	.269	.308	.379
Runners On/2 Out			61	14	0	14	11	.230	.279	.373
Scor. Pos./2 Out			42	9	0	11	7	.214	.262	.377
Late Inning Pressure			38	9	1	3	6	.237	.395	.293
Leading Off			11	2	0	1	3	.182	.273	.250
Runners On			11	3	0	2	1	.273	.273	.385
Runners/Scor. Pos.			7	2	0	2	1	.286	.286	.444
First 9 Batters			146	36	1	18	31	.247	.308	.331
Second 9 Batters			145	25	1	17	24	.172	.221	.259
All Batters Thereafter			132	38	3	12	15	.288	.432	.347

Loves to face: R. J. Reynolds (.067, 1-for-15)
Hates to face: Ryne Sandberg (.467, 14-for-30, 3 HR)
Ground outs-to-air outs ratio: 2.16 last season, 1.91 for career. . . .
Additional statistics: 12 double-play ground outs in 91 opportunities, 16 doubles, 2 triples in 114.1 innings last season. . . . Allowed 11 first-inning runs in 19 starts. . . . Batting support: 3.32 runs per start. . . . Opponents' batting average was the lowest of his career. Previous low was .240 in 1986; career average is .271. . . . Faced 247 left-handed batters last season, the most of any pitcher who did not allow a homer to a lefty. . . . One of two pitchers to face 200+ batters with runners on base without allowing a home run last season (the other: Jose Alvarez). . . . Yearly batting averages of opposing left-handers since 1985: .229, .228, .302, .224.

Les Lancaster

Throws Right

Chicago Cubs	W–L	ERA	AB	H	HR	BB	SO	BA	SA	OBA
Season	4-6	3.78	326	89	4	34	36	.273	.393	.337
vs. Left-Handers			156	44	2	20	13	.282	.404	.362
vs. Right-Handers			170	45	2	14	23	.265	.382	.314
Home	2-3	3.98	202	57	3	19	25	.282	.401	.342
Road	2-3	3.48	124	32	1	15	11	.258	.379	.329
Grass	3-3	3.50	277	76	3	26	31	.274	.390	.334
Artificial Turf	1-3	5.27	49	13	1	8	5	.265	.408	.350
April	1-2	6.48	64	17	1	12	8	.266	.406	.377
May	2-2	1.80	111	30	1	4	10	.270	.360	.288
June	1-0	1.86	69	17	0	8	7	.246	.348	.316
July	0-1	6.75	69	23	1	7	8	.333	.478	.397
August	0-1	4.91	13	2	1	3	3	.154	.385	.313
Sept./Oct.			0	0	0	0	0	—	—	—
Leading Off Inn.			77	20	0	7	9	.260	.364	.321
Runners On			147	43	3	19	13	.293	.435	.358
Runners/Scor. Pos.			90	29	1	14	9	.322	.456	.387
Runners On/2 Out			72	22	1	8	6	.306	.431	.375
Scor. Pos./2 Out			49	16	0	5	4	.327	.449	.389
Late Inning Pressure			141	42	4	23	18	.298	.440	.395
Leading Off			35	10	0	5	6	.286	.371	.375
Runners On			66	22	3	12	6	.333	.515	.425
Runners/Scor. Pos.			39	14	1	8	5	.359	.513	.449
First 9 Batters			226	64	3	30	28	.283	.407	.360
Second 9 Batters			64	14	1	3	7	.219	.313	.254
All Batters Thereafter			36	11	0	1	1	.306	.444	.324

Loves to face: Billy Hatcher (0-for-7)
Hates to face: Darryl Strawberry (.545, 6-for-11, 2 HR)
Ground outs-to-air outs ratio: 0.96 last season, 0.93 for career. . . .
Additional statistics: 9 double-play ground outs in 68 opportunities, 21 doubles, 3 triples in 85.2 innings last season. . . . Fractured his right foot on August 19, didn't pitch again after that. . . . The only complete game in his 21 career starts was a tidy little 11-hitter vs. the Reds on May 30. . . . Career record of 8–3 with a 4.78 ERA as a starter; 4–6, 3.95 ERA in relief. . . . Career batting average of .305 by opposing left-handed batters, .235 by right-handers. . . . Opposing batters have a career average of .261 on grass fields, .301 on artificial turf. . . . Has never committed an error (49 career chances).

Terry Leach

Throws Right

New York Mets	W–L	ERA	AB	H	HR	BB	SO	BA	SA	OBA
Season	7-2	2.54	354	95	5	24	51	.268	.356	.318
vs. Left-Handers			138	40	2	12	17	.290	.399	.353
vs. Right-Handers			216	55	3	12	34	.255	.329	.294
Home	1-1	3.49	148	42	2	6	27	.284	.372	.316
Road	6-1	1.86	206	53	3	18	24	.257	.345	.319
Grass	4-1	2.41	229	62	3	8	37	.271	.345	.299
Artificial Turf	3-1	2.78	125	33	2	16	14	.264	.376	.350
April	0-0	6.92	54	19	0	3	8	.352	.444	.393
May	1-0	0.63	48	7	1	1	9	.146	.208	.163
June	1-1	3.31	68	19	0	8	10	.279	.338	.359
July	2-0	1.62	61	15	3	5	4	.246	.443	.303
August	2-1	2.45	85	26	1	3	14	.306	.376	.330
Sept./Oct.	1-0	0.00	38	9	0	4	6	.237	.263	.310
Leading Off Inn.			84	23	3	3	14	.274	.417	.299
Runners On			170	43	0	13	27	.253	.300	.309
Runners/Scor. Pos.			99	21	0	10	20	.212	.263	.289
Runners On/2 Out			77	13	0	9	16	.169	.221	.256
Scor. Pos./2 Out			53	5	0	7	12	.094	.132	.200
Late Inning Pressure			90	29	0	11	12	.322	.356	.398
Leading Off			25	9	0	1	4	.360	.400	.385
Runners On			50	12	0	4	7	.240	.260	.291
Runners/Scor. Pos.			29	4	0	4	6	.138	.138	.235
First 9 Batters			304	84	5	20	44	.276	.365	.324
Second 9 Batters			42	8	0	3	6	.190	.262	.244
All Batters Thereafter			8	3	0	1	1	.375	.500	.444

Loves to face: Casey Candaele (0-for-9)
Hates to face: Dave Martinez (.455, 5-for-11, 1 HR)
Ground outs-to-air outs ratio: 1.67 last season, 1.65 for career. . . .
Additional statistics: 8 double-play ground outs in 78 opportunities, 16 doubles, 0 triples in 92.0 innings last season. . . . Imagine a 20-game winner who didn't lose a game. That's Leach at night. He has a career mark of 20–0 in night games, 4–9 in day games. . . . His 12 appearances vs. the Cubs were the most by any pitcher vs. any team last season. And guess what? He didn't allow an earned run in 22.2 innings against them. . . . Has pitched 366 career innings without throwing a wild pitch. . . . Opposing batters have a career average of .162 with two outs and runners in scoring position. . . . Has allowed 26 home runs in his career, but only five of them with runners on base.

Tim Leary

Los Angeles Dodgers	W–L	ERA	AB	H	HR	BB	SO	BA	SA	Throws Right OBA
Season	17-11	2.91	860	201	13	56	180	.234	.328	.284
vs. Left-Handers			422	100	4	40	88	.237	.320	.304
vs. Right-Handers			438	101	9	16	92	.231	.336	.265
Home	11-6	2.66	480	117	5	32	101	.244	.321	.293
Road	6-5	3.22	380	84	8	24	79	.221	.337	.273
Grass	13-10	3.12	664	163	11	46	146	.245	.348	.297
Artificial Turf	4-1	2.28	196	38	2	10	34	.194	.260	.242
April	2-1	2.52	92	17	1	4	22	.185	.293	.219
May	2-3	2.75	144	34	1	10	34	.236	.285	.284
June	2-1	3.82	123	28	2	8	24	.228	.350	.280
July	4-2	0.96	174	39	1	10	37	.224	.276	.277
August	5-1	2.64	165	40	1	8	30	.242	.315	.286
Sept./Oct.	2-3	5.13	162	43	7	16	33	.265	.438	.330
Leading Off Inn.			227	52	4	11	41	.229	.335	.268
Runners On			310	75	2	29	61	.242	.303	.312
Runners/Scor. Pos.			178	43	1	25	38	.242	.309	.337
Runners On/2 Out			130	28	0	20	28	.215	.262	.333
Scor. Pos./2 Out			82	15	0	17	20	.183	.232	.337
Late Inning Pressure			77	14	0	8	13	.182	.195	.264
Leading Off			22	3	0	2	5	.136	.136	.208
Runners On			24	3	0	5	2	.125	.167	.290
Runners/Scor. Pos.			11	0	0	5	1	.000	.000	.294
First 9 Batters			293	68	4	16	70	.232	.321	.272
Second 9 Batters			274	61	4	17	55	.223	.328	.271
All Batters Thereafter			293	72	5	23	55	.246	.334	.308

Loves to face: Spike Owen (0-for-14)
Hates to face: Von Hayes (.600, 9-for-15)
Ground outs-to-air outs ratio: 1.62 last season, 1.30 for career. . . . Additional statistics: 21 double-play ground outs in 139 opportunities, 30 doubles, 6 triples in 228.2 innings last season. . . . Allowed 15 first-inning runs in 34 starts. . . . Batting support: 3.50 runs per start. . . . Never had a winning record in any of his six previous seasons. . . . Had best road ERA in N.L. . . . Started two games against the Expos, and shut them out both times. . . . Threw nine complete games, six of them shutouts. Had only two shutouts in 57 career starts prior to 1988. . . . Batted .269, highest among N.L. pitchers (minimum: 25 AB). . . . Drove in the winning runs in two consecutive games (Aug. 12–13), the second as a pinch hitter in the 11th inning.

Craig Lefferts

San Francisco Giants	W–L	ERA	AB	H	HR	BB	SO	BA	SA	Throws Left OBA
Season	3-8	2.92	329	74	7	23	58	.225	.337	.275
vs. Left-Handers			95	23	2	4	22	.242	.368	.280
vs. Right-Handers			234	51	5	19	36	.218	.325	.273
Home	2-3	2.84	138	36	3	11	22	.261	.362	.316
Road	1-5	2.98	191	38	4	12	36	.199	.319	.245
Grass	2-5	2.80	232	54	6	16	38	.233	.353	.283
Artificial Turf	1-3	3.21	97	20	1	7	20	.206	.299	.257
April	1-1	0.64	46	8	0	4	8	.174	.217	.255
May	0-1	2.50	65	13	0	4	10	.200	.292	.246
June	1-3	5.17	59	14	3	3	8	.237	.441	.270
July	0-2	5.11	44	11	2	2	10	.250	.455	.283
August	0-1	3.24	64	18	2	6	8	.281	.391	.343
Sept./Oct.	1-0	1.15	51	10	0	4	14	.196	.216	.246
Leading Off Inn.			83	20	2	1	11	.241	.373	.259
Runners On			130	26	3	16	24	.200	.323	.282
Runners/Scor. Pos.			79	13	1	13	13	.165	.253	.274
Runners On/2 Out			61	14	1	7	11	.230	.377	.309
Scor. Pos./2 Out			46	10	1	7	7	.217	.370	.321
Late Inning Pressure			174	37	3	18	30	.213	.299	.284
Leading Off			48	13	2	0	7	.271	.458	.271
Runners On			65	11	1	13	11	.169	.246	.300
Runners/Scor. Pos.			43	7	0	10	6	.163	.209	.309
First 9 Batters			302	70	6	22	52	.232	.344	.284
Second 9 Batters			27	4	1	1	6	.148	.259	.179
All Batters Thereafter			0	0	0	0	0	—	—	—

Loves to face: Chris Speier (0-for-10)
Hates to face: Jack Clark (.571, 4-for-7, 4 HR)
Ground outs-to-air outs ratio: 0.82 last season, 0.81 for career. . . . Additional statistics: 7 double-play ground outs in 69 opportunities, 10 doubles, 3 triples in 92.1 innings last season. . . . One of two N.L. pitchers to allow eight consecutive batters to reach base last season. . . . Career record of 7–0 against the Dodgers. . . . Career record of 0–11 during month of May, 30–24 in other months. . . . Career mark of 27–18 with a 2.63 ERA on grass fields; 3–17, 4.21 ERA on artificial turf. . . . Opponents' batting average has risen in each of the last three seasons: .191, .222, .228, .242. . . . Has pitched 402 games since debuting with the Cubs in 1983. During that time only one pitcher has appeared in more games than Lefferts: Kent Tekulve (442).

Greg Maddux

Chicago Cubs	W–L	ERA	AB	H	HR	BB	SO	BA	SA	Throws Right OBA
Season	18-8	3.18	943	230	13	81	140	.244	.328	.309
vs. Left-Handers			498	118	7	60	66	.237	.321	.322
vs. Right-Handers			445	112	6	21	74	.252	.335	.294
Home	8-6	3.66	508	130	8	42	73	.256	.346	.316
Road	10-2	2.63	435	100	5	39	67	.230	.306	.301
Grass	12-7	3.37	652	159	8	60	96	.244	.321	.311
Artificial Turf	6-1	2.75	291	71	5	21	44	.244	.344	.305
April	4-1	2.20	145	34	2	17	17	.234	.303	.319
May	4-2	2.06	170	32	0	9	36	.188	.235	.233
June	5-0	2.22	186	39	4	19	27	.210	.290	.286
July	2-2	4.00	170	41	1	13	26	.241	.312	.301
August	1-1	5.72	115	39	1	12	11	.339	.435	.408
Sept./Oct.	2-2	4.03	157	45	5	11	23	.287	.433	.341
Leading Off Inn.			242	54	4	15	39	.223	.335	.277
Runners On			384	104	5	38	43	.271	.346	.338
Runners/Scor. Pos.			218	58	2	29	27	.266	.317	.352
Runners On/2 Out			159	39	1	21	17	.245	.296	.337
Scor. Pos./2 Out			102	28	0	17	10	.275	.314	.383
Late Inning Pressure			134	31	1	15	22	.231	.276	.307
Leading Off			39	8	0	3	8	.205	.282	.262
Runners On			45	14	0	9	5	.311	.311	.418
Runners/Scor. Pos.			24	10	0	5	3	.417	.417	.500
First 9 Batters			271	65	1	25	47	.240	.295	.308
Second 9 Batters			279	79	5	21	44	.283	.405	.340
All Batters Thereafter			393	86	7	35	52	.219	.295	.289

Loves to face: Chris Sabo (0-for-7)
Hates to face: Sid Bream (.588, 10-for-17, 1 HR)
Ground outs-to-air outs ratio: 1.76 last season, 1.94 for career. . . . Additional statistics: 21 double-play ground outs in 183 opportunities, 34 doubles, 3 triples in 249.0 innings last season. . . . Allowed 8 first-inning runs in 34 starts. . . . Batting support: 4.18 runs per start. . . . He and Gooden were the only pitchers to beat every opposing club in N.L. in 1988. . . . Career record of 20–10 before the All-Star break, 6–16 after. . . . Held left-handers hitless in 35 consecutive plate appearances, longest N.L. streak of season. . . . Struck out six straight batters with runners on base, equalling longest streak of last 10 years. . . . Has made 159 career plate appearances without a walk. . . . Born April 14, 1966, the day Don Sutton made major league debut.

Mike Maddux

Philadelphia Phillies	W–L	ERA	AB	H	HR	BB	SO	BA	SA	Throws Right OBA
Season	4-3	3.76	331	91	6	34	59	.275	.399	.349
vs. Left-Handers			176	55	4	21	28	.313	.472	.393
vs. Right-Handers			155	36	2	13	31	.232	.316	.297
Home	2-0	2.93	167	40	3	15	28	.240	.371	.310
Road	2-3	4.64	164	51	3	19	31	.311	.427	.386
Grass	1-2	6.49	105	38	3	15	17	.362	.505	.448
Artificial Turf	3-1	2.60	226	53	3	19	42	.235	.350	.298
April	1-0	0.71	44	9	0	2	16	.205	.295	.234
May			0	0	0	0	0	—	—	—
June	1-0	2.79	35	11	1	3	6	.314	.486	.400
July	1-1	5.33	109	36	2	7	14	.330	.477	.376
August	0-2	5.08	103	29	3	13	16	.282	.408	.361
Sept./Oct.	1-0	1.42	40	6	0	9	7	.150	.200	.320
Leading Off Inn.			83	24	1	6	15	.289	.422	.344
Runners On			142	41	3	18	24	.289	.415	.377
Runners/Scor. Pos.			86	22	2	18	15	.256	.384	.380
Runners On/2 Out			53	12	1	6	8	.226	.340	.317
Scor. Pos./2 Out			35	7	0	6	6	.200	.257	.317
Late Inning Pressure			54	10	0	5	13	.185	.259	.254
Leading Off			13	2	0	3	4	.154	.231	.313
Runners On			17	4	0	2	4	.235	.353	.316
Runners/Scor. Pos.			8	1	0	2	2	.125	.250	.300
First 9 Batters			169	44	2	17	36	.260	.367	.337
Second 9 Batters			98	28	3	11	16	.286	.429	.360
All Batters Thereafter			64	19	1	6	7	.297	.438	.361

Loves to face: Tony Gwynn (.091, 1-for-11)
Hates to face: Bill Doran (.800, 4-for-5, 1 HR)
Ground outs-to-air outs ratio: 2.08 last season, 2.00 for career. . . . Additional statistics: 9 double-play ground outs in 69 opportunities, 23 doubles, 0 triples in 88.2 innings last season. . . . Allowed 11 first-inning runs in 11 starts. . . . Batting support: 4.36 runs per start. . . . Record of 2–3 (5.03 ERA) in 11 starts, 2–0 (1.21) in 14 relief appearances. . . . Relief wins came in season debut and season finale. . . . Has never pitched a complete game (29 career starts). . . . Started against and defeated his brother on July 31 at the Vet. . . . Opponents' career average is .325 on grass fields, .258 on artificial turf. . . . Prior to 1988, had allowed six home runs: five in first inning, one in second. Last season, only two of six opponents' HRs came on his first pass through batting order.

Joe Magrane
St. Louis Cardinals — Throws Left

	W–L	ERA	AB	H	HR	BB	SO	BA	SA	OBA
Season	5-9	2.18	612	133	6	51	100	.217	.304	.278
vs. Left-Handers			113	20	2	10	24	.177	.283	.242
vs. Right-Handers			499	113	4	41	76	.226	.309	.286
Home	1-6	1.95	322	69	3	25	55	.214	.320	.269
Road	4-3	2.43	290	64	3	26	45	.221	.286	.288
Grass	1-1	1.55	106	22	1	9	16	.208	.264	.265
Artificial Turf	4-8	2.31	506	111	5	42	84	.219	.312	.281
April	0-0	3.60	59	15	2	6	8	.254	.390	.318
May			0	0	0	0	0	—	—	—
June	1-2	2.83	111	25	0	8	21	.225	.288	.289
July	0-2	1.75	128	29	0	12	21	.227	.281	.289
August	1-4	2.03	159	29	3	13	28	.182	.308	.243
Sept./Oct.	3-1	1.74	155	35	1	12	22	.226	.297	.281
Leading Off Inn.			158	34	2	12	24	.215	.285	.271
Runners On			240	48	1	25	42	.200	.271	.274
Runners/Scor. Pos.			143	23	1	20	29	.161	.231	.262
Runners On/2 Out			105	14	1	7	16	.133	.190	.195
Scor. Pos./2 Out			72	7	1	4	12	.097	.181	.156
Late Inning Pressure			96	21	1	7	10	.219	.292	.272
Leading Off			26	3	0	2	2	.115	.115	.179
Runners On			35	5	1	2	3	.143	.229	.189
Runners/Scor. Pos.			18	3	1	2	1	.167	.333	.250
First 9 Batters			190	43	2	20	36	.226	.311	.300
Second 9 Batters			188	42	2	14	28	.223	.351	.276
All Batters Thereafter			234	48	2	17	36	.205	.261	.261

Loves to face: Mike Fitzgerald (0-for-10)
Hates to face: Ron Gant (.750, 3-for-4, 1 HR)
Ground outs-to-air outs ratio: 2.27 last season, 2.16 for career....
Additional statistics: 5 double-play ground outs in 107 opportunities, 25 doubles, 5 triples in 165.1 innings last season.... Allowed 12 first-inning runs in 24 starts.... Batting support: 2.75 runs per start, lowest in N.L. (minimum: 15 GS).... Became first pitcher to hit an opening-day home run since Rick Rhoden in 1982, and first Cardinals pitcher to do it since Jack Powell in 1901. Only pitcher to hit two opening-day homers: Don Drysdale (1959 and 1965).... First Cardinals pitcher to win ERA title since John Denny in 1976. ... Fourth pitcher to lead N.L. in ERA while posting losing record. Others: Dave Koslo (1949), Stu Miller (1958), Nolan Ryan (1987).

Rick Mahler
Atlanta Braves — Throws Right

	W–L	ERA	AB	H	HR	BB	SO	BA	SA	OBA
Season	9-16	3.69	989	279	17	42	131	.282	.390	.315
vs. Left-Handers			560	150	7	26	69	.268	.352	.301
vs. Right-Handers			429	129	10	16	62	.301	.441	.334
Home	4-6	3.96	455	132	8	12	59	.290	.389	.312
Road	5-10	3.46	534	147	9	30	72	.275	.391	.318
Grass	6-12	3.75	683	193	12	26	90	.283	.389	.311
Artificial Turf	3-4	3.54	306	86	5	16	41	.281	.392	.324
April	0-3	5.40	97	33	2	4	8	.340	.505	.375
May	6-1	2.80	177	47	0	6	18	.266	.316	.290
June	2-3	3.49	198	61	3	5	32	.308	.394	.322
July	0-3	5.23	168	56	3	12	24	.333	.458	.384
August	1-2	3.13	176	40	4	6	20	.227	.358	.257
Sept./Oct.	0-4	3.13	173	42	5	9	29	.243	.364	.288
Leading Off Inn.			252	60	5	5	23	.238	.321	.253
Runners On			382	122	8	26	54	.319	.466	.368
Runners/Scor. Pos.			241	74	4	19	39	.307	.444	.361
Runners On/2 Out			180	54	3	13	26	.300	.444	.357
Scor. Pos./2 Out			116	33	2	9	18	.284	.431	.346
Late Inning Pressure			140	31	2	7	16	.221	.286	.259
Leading Off			41	10	0	1	5	.244	.268	.262
Runners On			44	11	1	5	6	.250	.364	.327
Runners/Scor. Pos.			30	5	0	5	4	.167	.200	.286
First 9 Batters			319	90	4	10	50	.282	.367	.308
Second 9 Batters			297	85	8	13	37	.286	.438	.314
All Batters Thereafter			373	104	5	19	44	.279	.373	.322

Loves to face: Steve Lake (0-for-8)
Hates to face: Andy Van Slyke (.529, 18-for-34, 3 HR)
Ground outs-to-air outs ratio: 1.45 last season, 1.58 for career....
Additional statistics: 16 double-play ground outs in 152 opportunities, 46 doubles, 5 triples in 249.0 innings last season.... Allowed 24 first-inning runs (2d most in N.L.) in 34 starts.... Batting support: 4.12 runs per start.... Tied with Mike Moore for most losses in majors over last three years (47).... Allowed an average of 1.52 walks per nine innings last season, 2d lowest rate in majors. ... Faced 194 batters between walks (May 17–June 12), longest streak of last 10 years. (Moose Haas had 176 in 1982.).... Outspoken opponent of 1962 N.L. expansion. Has lost his last eight decisions to both Mets and Astros.... Career record of 54–45 before the All-Star break, 24–43 after it.

Dennis Martinez
Montreal Expos — Throws Right

	W–L	ERA	AB	H	HR	BB	SO	BA	SA	OBA
Season	15-13	2.72	899	215	21	55	120	.239	.377	.286
vs. Left-Handers			473	110	8	40	60	.233	.347	.291
vs. Right-Handers			426	105	13	15	60	.246	.411	.280
Home	6-4	2.50	366	86	10	25	43	.235	.393	.287
Road	9-9	2.87	533	129	11	30	77	.242	.366	.285
Grass	3-7	3.50	278	76	7	13	38	.273	.428	.306
Artificial Turf	12-6	2.39	621	139	14	42	82	.224	.354	.277
April	3-2	2.52	145	29	6	11	23	.200	.372	.256
May	1-4	2.78	147	44	3	7	19	.299	.469	.335
June	3-1	2.72	160	34	2	14	21	.213	.325	.281
July	5-0	1.57	168	38	2	7	18	.226	.321	.256
August	3-3	2.68	183	45	5	6	22	.246	.361	.272
Sept./Oct.	0-3	5.18	96	25	3	10	17	.260	.458	.336
Leading Off Inn.			230	54	6	11	29	.235	.387	.276
Runners On			335	80	9	28	54	.239	.376	.296
Runners/Scor. Pos.			192	43	5	18	31	.224	.333	.289
Runners On/2 Out			155	41	5	20	28	.265	.432	.356
Scor. Pos./2 Out			105	25	4	14	20	.238	.400	.339
Late Inning Pressure			98	17	2	3	11	.173	.276	.204
Leading Off			30	5	0	1	4	.167	.233	.194
Runners On			21	5	1	1	2	.238	.381	.261
Runners/Scor. Pos.			14	4	1	1	1	.286	.500	.313
First 9 Batters			278	68	5	20	35	.245	.374	.305
Second 9 Batters			277	73	8	19	38	.264	.430	.310
All Batters Thereafter			344	74	8	16	47	.215	.337	.250

Loves to face: Mike Schmidt (0-for-11, 5 SO)
Hates to face: Glenn Davis (.636, 7-for-11, 4 HR)
Ground outs-to-air outs ratio: 1.07 last season, 1.15 for career....
Additional statistics: 17 double-play ground outs in 130 opportunities, 39 doubles, 11 triples in 235.1 innings last season.... Allowed 17 first-inning runs in 34 starts.... Batting support: 4.35 runs per start.... Tied David Cone and Pascual Perez for N.L. lead with 10 balks. Even in the year of the balk, this trio came up one short of Steve Carlton's N.L. record of 11, set in 1979.... ERA of 5.00 or higher in each season from 1983 through 1985. Year by year since then: 4.72, 3.30, 2.72.... Only two pitchers have held left-handed batters to a lower batting average than right-handers in each of last eight seasons. The Martinezes: left-hander Tippy, and righty Dennis.

Lance McCullers
San Diego Padres — Throws Right

	W–L	ERA	AB	H	HR	BB	SO	BA	SA	OBA
Season	3-6	2.49	342	70	8	55	81	.205	.330	.313
vs. Left-Handers			163	25	0	33	40	.153	.178	.293
vs. Right-Handers			179	45	8	22	41	.251	.469	.332
Home	2-2	1.38	191	29	4	30	54	.152	.262	.263
Road	1-4	4.15	151	41	4	25	27	.272	.417	.375
Grass	2-4	2.09	268	52	5	42	66	.194	.310	.300
Artificial Turf	1-2	4.05	74	18	3	13	15	.243	.405	.356
April	0-2	4.73	49	11	2	5	15	.224	.469	.296
May	0-1	2.29	71	17	2	15	15	.239	.408	.368
June	1-1	2.55	67	15	1	12	11	.224	.328	.342
July	0-2	1.38	40	4	1	5	12	.100	.175	.200
August	2-0	0.63	47	8	1	9	14	.170	.234	.298
Sept./Oct.	0-0	3.20	68	15	1	9	14	.221	.309	.308
Leading Off Inn.			80	16	2	8	12	.200	.325	.273
Runners On			159	33	5	27	40	.208	.333	.317
Runners/Scor. Pos.			98	15	3	23	25	.153	.255	.306
Runners On/2 Out			70	12	3	17	18	.171	.300	.333
Scor. Pos./2 Out			51	9	3	15	12	.176	.353	.364
Late Inning Pressure			246	51	8	37	60	.207	.370	.309
Leading Off			59	14	2	6	11	.237	.407	.308
Runners On			109	23	5	20	29	.211	.394	.328
Runners/Scor. Pos.			70	10	3	18	20	.143	.286	.311
First 9 Batters			317	64	5	49	78	.202	.309	.306
Second 9 Batters			25	6	3	6	3	.240	.600	.387
All Batters Thereafter			0	0	0	0	0	—	—	—

Loves to face: Bob Brenly (0-for-7)
Hates to face: Chris Brown (.500, 4-for-8, 1 HR)
Ground outs-to-air outs ratio: 0.93 last season, 0.92 for career....
Additional statistics: 9 double-play ground outs in 80 opportunities, 15 doubles, 2 triples in 97.2 innings last season.... Walked 5.07 batters per nine innings last season, compared to Righetti's 3.83.... Allowed only one hit in 12 at-bats with the bases loaded last season. ... Lefty/righty breakdown for 1988 is not indicative of his career performance. Left-handers have a career average of .227 against him (with one home run per 76 AB) compared to .215 (one HR per 29 AB) by right-handers.... One of seven pitchers to appear in at least 200 games over the past three seasons.... Should like A.L.: fly-ball hitters have career average of .201; ground-ballers, .242.

Roger McDowell

New York Mets   Throws Right

	W–L	ERA	AB	H	HR	BB	SO	BA	SA	OBA
Season	5-5	2.63	336	80	1	31	46	.238	.283	.304
vs. Left-Handers			154	40	0	18	17	.260	.325	.337
vs. Right-Handers			182	40	1	13	29	.220	.247	.275
Home	2-1	1.53	138	32	0	9	18	.232	.283	.289
Road	3-4	3.35	198	48	1	22	28	.242	.283	.314
Grass	2-2	1.71	222	53	0	15	29	.239	.284	.293
Artificial Turf	3-3	4.35	114	27	1	16	17	.237	.281	.323
April	3-0	3.75	43	8	1	6	0	.186	.302	.275
May	0-0	1.06	61	11	0	2	11	.180	.180	.219
June	1-1	2.60	67	18	0	10	7	.269	.284	.364
July	0-1	1.84	51	11	0	7	7	.216	.294	.311
August	1-1	3.12	66	16	0	4	13	.242	.288	.296
Sept./Oct.	0-2	4.22	48	16	0	2	8	.333	.375	.353
Leading Off Inn.			76	18	0	6	10	.237	.276	.293
Runners On			157	36	0	19	24	.229	.255	.315
Runners/Scor. Pos.			94	21	0	16	18	.223	.245	.333
Runners On/2 Out			68	15	0	11	13	.221	.265	.346
Scor. Pos./2 Out			49	11	0	9	12	.224	.265	.356
Late Inning Pressure			193	49	1	19	19	.254	.306	.327
Leading Off			46	13	0	4	4	.283	.348	.340
Runners On			88	20	0	12	10	.227	.273	.333
Runners/Scor. Pos.			52	14	0	12	7	.269	.308	.412
First 9 Batters			311	72	1	28	42	.232	.277	.297
Second 9 Batters			24	7	0	3	4	.292	.333	.370
All Batters Thereafter			1	1	0	0	0	1.000	1.000	1.000

Loves to face: Jose Uribe (0-for-10)
Hates to face: Andy Van Slyke (.438, 7-for-16, 2 HR)
Ground outs-to-air outs ratio: 2.78 last season, 3.08 for career....
Additional statistics: 9 double-play ground outs in 83 opportunities, 4 doubles, 4 triples in 89.0 innings last season.... Faced 130 batters protecting leads of three runs or fewer in 8th inning or later. That's three more than Randy Myers faced.... Bo Diaz hit the only home run that he allowed during the regular season (April 29). Kirk Gibson's blast in 12th inning of N.L.C.S. Game Four will be remembered a little longer.... Career record of 7–0 in April.... Opponents' batting average with runners in scoring position was the lowest of his career, down 83 points from his .306 mark in 1987.... Has faced 923 right-handed batters in his career without allowing a triple.

Andy McGaffigan

Montreal Expos   Throws Right

	W–L	ERA	AB	H	HR	BB	SO	BA	SA	OBA
Season	6-0	2.76	347	81	4	37	71	.233	.320	.309
vs. Left-Handers			177	34	1	23	42	.192	.243	.284
vs. Right-Handers			170	47	3	14	29	.276	.400	.337
Home	4-0	2.92	194	45	2	15	38	.232	.314	.288
Road	2-0	2.57	153	36	2	22	33	.235	.327	.335
Grass	2-0	3.20	67	11	2	7	11	.164	.328	.253
Artificial Turf	4-0	2.64	280	70	2	30	60	.250	.318	.323
April	1-0	4.60	64	18	1	7	12	.281	.391	.352
May	2-0	4.67	71	20	2	9	12	.282	.451	.373
June	0-0	0.75	45	9	0	3	10	.200	.244	.245
July	0-0	1.80	40	10	0	6	11	.250	.300	.348
August	2-0	3.00	65	14	1	6	11	.215	.308	.282
Sept./Oct.	1-0	0.98	62	10	0	6	15	.161	.177	.235
Leading Off Inn.			80	16	0	6	17	.200	.238	.256
Runners On			162	40	2	21	37	.247	.352	.337
Runners/Scor. Pos.			102	25	2	16	26	.245	.363	.352
Runners On/2 Out			74	16	2	12	19	.216	.351	.326
Scor. Pos./2 Out			51	13	2	10	15	.255	.431	.377
Late Inning Pressure			195	39	2	24	40	.200	.267	.290
Leading Off			53	9	0	3	14	.170	.189	.214
Runners On			76	15	1	12	17	.197	.276	.311
Runners/Scor. Pos.			47	6	1	9	14	.128	.191	.276
First 9 Batters			321	74	3	33	69	.231	.305	.305
Second 9 Batters			24	5	1	4	2	.208	.417	.310
All Batters Thereafter			2	2	0	0	0	1.000	1.500	1.000

Loves to face: Dickie Thon (0-for-9)
Hates to face: Kevin McReynolds (.423, 11-for-26, 2 HR)
Ground outs-to-air outs ratio: 1.15 last season, 1.17 for career....
Additional statistics: 3 double-play ground outs in 72 opportunities, 14 doubles, 2 triples in 91.1 innings last season.... Has a career average of .040 (5-for-125) as a batter.... Had the most wins of any undefeated pitcher in the majors last season.... Career record of 20–6 in relief, 11–19 as a starter.... Career record of 8–15 (4.03 ERA) on grass fields, 23–10 (2.69) on artificial turf.... Career record of 24–11 as a member of the Expos, 7–14 with other clubs (Reds and Giants).... Ground-ball hitters have had a lower batting average against him than fly-ball hitters in seven of his eight seasons in the majors. Career averages: ground-ballers .212, fly-ballers .262.

Larry McWilliams

St. Louis Cardinals   Throws Left

	W–L	ERA	AB	H	HR	BB	SO	BA	SA	OBA
Season	6-9	3.90	513	130	10	45	70	.253	.382	.317
vs. Left-Handers			119	24	3	7	24	.202	.336	.252
vs. Right-Handers			394	106	7	38	46	.269	.396	.336
Home	3-3	3.98	236	59	5	22	35	.250	.369	.315
Road	3-6	3.84	277	71	5	23	35	.256	.394	.319
Grass	2-1	2.28	163	38	2	10	21	.233	.337	.284
Artificial Turf	4-8	4.66	350	92	8	35	49	.263	.403	.332
April	1-0	0.44	70	13	1	6	8	.186	.243	.250
May	3-0	2.48	148	35	1	19	23	.236	.324	.327
June	0-3	4.00	100	25	3	3	14	.250	.390	.269
July	0-1	5.02	55	16	0	4	7	.291	.400	.333
August	0-1	3.68	27	8	0	4	4	.296	.370	.387
Sept./Oct.	2-4	8.00	113	33	5	10	14	.292	.531	.360
Leading Off Inn.			128	33	2	13	14	.258	.359	.326
Runners On			217	61	6	18	30	.281	.452	.339
Runners/Scor. Pos.			121	32	3	16	16	.264	.463	.345
Runners On/2 Out			98	29	4	13	8	.296	.541	.384
Scor. Pos./2 Out			62	19	2	13	5	.306	.581	.427
Late Inning Pressure			90	30	0	6	11	.333	.444	.375
Leading Off			27	10	0	0	2	.370	.481	.370
Runners On			35	11	0	6	5	.314	.429	.415
Runners/Scor. Pos.			22	7	0	6	3	.318	.500	.464
First 9 Batters			246	63	5	22	35	.256	.390	.322
Second 9 Batters			147	36	2	14	20	.245	.340	.313
All Batters Thereafter			120	31	3	9	15	.258	.417	.313

Loves to face: Ryne Sandberg (.154, 8-for-52)
Hates to face: Mike Schmidt (.375, 18-for-48, 7 HR)
Ground outs-to-air outs ratio: 1.27 last season, 1.18 for career....
Additional statistics: 9 double-play ground outs in 100 opportunities, 28 doubles, 4 triples in 136.0 innings last season.... Allowed 11 first-inning runs in 17 starts.... Batting support: 3.65 runs per start.... Pitched an average of 5.71 innings per start, 4th-lowest mark in N.L. (minimum: 15 GS).... Record of 5–6 (4.36 ERA) in 17 starts, 1–3 (2.77) in 25 relief appearances.... One of 10 pitchers with a losing record in each of the last four years.... Has lost his last six decisions to the Mets. Seven of 10 HRs he allowed last season were hit by Mets.... Led N.L. in ERA through April 28. Allowed only one earned run in his first 29.2 innings pitched. After that, his mark was 4.91.

Jamie Moyer

Chicago Cubs   Throws Left

	W–L	ERA	AB	H	HR	BB	SO	BA	SA	OBA
Season	9-15	3.48	778	212	20	55	121	.272	.405	.322
vs. Left-Handers			127	29	3	7	29	.228	.331	.267
vs. Right-Handers			651	183	17	48	92	.281	.419	.333
Home	3-8	3.65	392	108	11	26	65	.276	.423	.322
Road	6-7	3.30	386	104	9	29	56	.269	.386	.322
Grass	6-12	3.38	566	156	13	43	88	.276	.401	.328
Artificial Turf	3-3	3.74	212	56	7	12	33	.264	.415	.307
April	1-2	5.09	93	26	5	6	9	.280	.484	.320
May	1-4	3.18	141	32	1	17	22	.227	.291	.314
June	2-1	2.27	129	26	4	4	31	.202	.326	.230
July	1-2	2.25	124	39	1	8	13	.315	.411	.353
August	2-4	4.35	167	50	6	15	24	.299	.467	.361
Sept./Oct.	2-2	4.15	124	39	3	5	22	.315	.468	.344
Leading Off Inn.			199	57	4	5	26	.286	.407	.314
Runners On			317	81	8	30	55	.256	.382	.316
Runners/Scor. Pos.			189	44	3	25	35	.233	.323	.317
Runners On/2 Out			142	33	6	16	23	.232	.394	.310
Scor. Pos./2 Out			93	20	3	14	16	.215	.344	.344
Late Inning Pressure			61	18	2	3	7	.295	.475	.328
Leading Off			16	5	0	1	1	.313	.438	.353
Runners On			23	7	1	1	2	.304	.565	.333
Runners/Scor. Pos.			12	4	0	1	1	.333	.500	.385
First 9 Batters			266	69	8	17	51	.259	.391	.305
Second 9 Batters			246	60	4	18	35	.244	.362	.303
All Batters Thereafter			266	83	8	20	35	.312	.459	.356

Loves to face: Luis Rivera (.056, 1-for-18)
Hates to face: Darnell Coles (.400, 4-for-10, 3 HR)
Ground outs-to-air outs ratio: 1.65 last season, 1.52 for career....
Additional statistics: 13 double-play ground outs in 132 opportunities, 33 doubles, 5 triples in 202.0 innings last season.... Allowed 12 first-inning runs in 30 starts.... Batting support: 3.27 runs per start, 10th lowest in N.L. (minimum: 15 GS).... Lost 30 games over last two seasons, tied with Kevin Gross for most in N.L.... Lowest ERA of five N.L. pitchers with 15 or more losses last season. ... ERA of 2.55 over the first four innings of his starts last season, 4.95 thereafter.... Was the only pitcher to shut out the Mets at Shea Stadium last season.... Opponents' career averages: .259 on his first two passes through batting order, .317 after that.

Rob Murphy

Throws Left

Cincinnati Reds

	W–L	ERA	AB	H	HR	BB	SO	BA	SA	OBA
Season	0-6	3.08	301	69	3	38	74	.229	.306	.317
vs. Left-Handers			82	17	0	7	21	.207	.220	.270
vs. Right-Handers			219	52	3	31	53	.237	.338	.333
Home	0-3	2.30	167	37	1	18	41	.222	.275	.301
Road	0-3	4.06	134	32	2	20	33	.239	.343	.335
Grass	0-2	4.32	97	25	1	12	27	.258	.330	.339
Artificial Turf	0-4	2.56	204	44	2	26	47	.216	.294	.306
April	0-1	1.23	49	11	0	10	11	.224	.265	.356
May	0-2	5.11	49	17	0	3	10	.347	.367	.385
June	0-0	0.55	52	4	0	7	19	.077	.077	.183
July	0-2	2.89	35	9	0	3	8	.257	.286	.316
August	0-0	5.94	60	16	2	9	11	.267	.467	.371
Sept./Oct.	0-1	2.93	56	12	1	6	15	.214	.339	.290
Leading Off Inn.			70	13	0	8	23	.186	.214	.269
Runners On			140	34	3	19	29	.243	.350	.335
Runners/Scor. Pos.			93	20	2	16	22	.215	.312	.333
Runners On/2 Out			65	15	1	11	16	.231	.308	.342
Scor. Pos./2 Out			47	8	0	9	13	.170	.213	.304
Late Inning Pressure			176	35	1	17	41	.199	.261	.272
Leading Off			44	11	0	4	15	.250	.295	.313
Runners On			76	12	1	10	13	.158	.237	.261
Runners/Scor. Pos.			48	6	1	9	11	.125	.188	.271
First 9 Batters			297	67	3	37	74	.226	.296	.313
Second 9 Batters			4	2	0	1	0	.500	1.000	.600
All Batters Thereafter			0	0	0	0	0	—	—	—

Loves to face: Stan Jefferson (0-for-4)
Hates to face: Jeffrey Leonard (.667, 2-for-3)
Ground outs-to-air outs ratio: 1.33 last season, 1.25 for career. . . .
Additional statistics: 8 double-play ground outs in 62 opportunities, 10 doubles, 2 triples in 84.2 innings last season. . . . Faced one batter nine times. Only Bob Kipper (12) and Ken Dayley (10) made more one-batter appearances. . . . Faced 40 batters last season protecting leads of three runs or fewer in 8th inning or later, compared to 185 by John Franco. Lee Smith's shadow may be bigger than Franco's, but at least it throws right-handed. . . . Murphy has career total of 199 games without committing an error. Smith holds N.L. record for consecutive errorless games (364). Now both can go wild in A.L. without N.L. impunity. . . . Has faced 273 left-handers, allowed only one HR (Barry Bonds).

Randy Myers

Throws Left

New York Mets

	W–L	ERA	AB	H	HR	BB	SO	BA	SA	OBA
Season	7-3	1.72	237	45	5	17	69	.190	.278	.248
vs. Left-Handers			50	9	0	4	16	.180	.220	.250
vs. Right-Handers			187	36	5	13	53	.193	.294	.248
Home	6-1	1.64	120	13	3	13	38	.108	.192	.200
Road	1-2	1.82	117	32	2	4	31	.274	.368	.301
Grass	6-3	1.66	160	24	4	15	51	.150	.250	.226
Artificial Turf	1-0	1.86	77	21	1	2	18	.273	.338	.296
April	1-0	0.00	26	5	0	1	5	.192	.192	.250
May	2-0	2.00	31	6	1	1	11	.194	.290	.219
June	2-0	1.93	48	9	1	2	13	.188	.313	.235
July	0-1	0.73	41	6	1	3	12	.146	.268	.205
August	0-2	2.92	46	11	0	6	13	.239	.239	.321
Sept./Oct.	2-0	2.08	45	8	2	4	15	.178	.333	.240
Leading Off Inn.			49	12	3	3	15	.245	.449	.302
Runners On			121	18	1	9	36	.149	.198	.205
Runners/Scor. Pos.			75	12	1	6	24	.160	.227	.217
Runners On/2 Out			57	10	0	2	15	.175	.228	.203
Scor. Pos./2 Out			37	8	0	1	10	.216	.270	.237
Late Inning Pressure			175	30	2	11	53	.171	.229	.219
Leading Off			37	9	2	3	12	.243	.405	.300
Runners On			87	11	0	5	28	.126	.161	.172
Runners/Scor. Pos.			50	7	0	2	18	.140	.180	.170
First 9 Batters			236	45	5	17	69	.191	.280	.249
Second 9 Batters			1	0	0	0	0	.000	.000	.000
All Batters Thereafter			0	0	0	0	0			

Loves to face: Jose Lind (0-for-8, 4 SO)
Hates to face: Dale Murphy (.667, 2-for-3, 2 HR)
Ground outs-to-air outs ratio: 0.64 last season, 0.72 for career. . . .
Additional statistics: 3 double-play ground outs in 57 opportunities, 4 doubles, 1 triple in 68.0 innings last season. . . . Rafael Palmeiro's triple was the only extra-base hit against him by a left-handed batter. Hasn't allowed a home run to a lefty since April 20, 1987 (Sid Bream). . . . Opposing left-handed batters had two hits in 23 at-bats at Shea Stadium, including an 0-for-19 streak from May 6 through Sept. 16. . . , Career record of 7–1 at Shea, 3–8 on the road. . . . Faced 32 batters in Late-Inning Pressure Situations without allowing a hit (May 13–June 15), longest streak by an N.L. reliever last season. . . . Opponents' career breakdown: .177 with runners on base, .241 with bases empty.

Al Nipper

Throws Right

Chicago Cubs

	W–L	ERA	AB	H	HR	BB	SO	BA	SA	OBA
Season	2-4	3.04	301	72	9	34	27	.239	.369	.322
vs. Left-Handers			158	41	4	18	16	.259	.386	.339
vs. Right-Handers			143	31	5	16	11	.217	.350	.302
Home	2-2	3.33	182	46	6	12	18	.253	.385	.306
Road	0-2	2.65	119	26	3	22	9	.218	.345	.343
Grass	2-2	2.64	222	52	6	20	22	.234	.351	.303
Artificial Turf	0-2	4.09	79	20	3	14	5	.253	.418	.368
April	0-0	2.21	69	14	2	18	5	.203	.319	.368
May	1-2	3.09	88	20	2	9	7	.227	.318	.306
June	0-0	8.10	16	5	1	0	2	.313	.625	.313
July	0-2	3.32	81	20	2	5	7	.247	.383	.295
August	1-0	2.38	47	13	2	2	6	.277	.426	.320
Sept./Oct.			0	0	0	0	0			
Leading Off Inn.			73	18	3	10	6	.247	.411	.337
Runners On			127	27	3	15	13	.213	.323	.299
Runners/Scor. Pos.			63	12	0	10	10	.190	.222	.307
Runners On/2 Out			51	7	0	6	7	.137	.176	.228
Scor. Pos./2 Out			29	4	0	4	5	.138	.138	.242
Late Inning Pressure			26	6	1	1	3	.231	.423	.259
Leading Off			7	3	1	1	0	.429	1.000	.500
Runners On			10	3	0	0	1	.300	.400	.300
Runners/Scor. Pos.			8	2	0	0	1	.250	.250	.250
First 9 Batters			135	33	3	12	15	.244	.370	.309
Second 9 Batters			97	22	3	12	5	.227	.340	.312
All Batters Thereafter			69	17	3	10	7	.246	.406	.358

Loves to face: Tim Teufel (.100, 1-for-10)
Hates to face: Mickey Hatcher (.571, 8-for-14)
Ground outs-to-air outs ratio: 1.05 last season, 1.12 for career. . . .
Additional statistics: 9 double-play ground outs in 70 opportunities, 10 doubles, 1 triple in 80.0 innings last season. . . . Allowed 9 first-inning runs in 12 starts. . . . Batting support: 4.17 runs per start. . . . Recorded the only save of his major league career on June 27 vs. the Phillies. . . . Last season's batting average by opposing right-handed batters was by far the lowest of his career (down 86 points from 1987). . . . One of 10 pitchers with a losing record in each of the last four years. . . . Get out your record books. Most career starts among pitchers without a shutout: Roy Mahaffey (120), Nipper (119), Roger Erickson (117), Jim Hughey (113), Dan Daub (102).

Bob Ojeda

Throws Left

New York Mets

	W–L	ERA	AB	H	HR	BB	SO	BA	SA	OBA
Season	10-13	2.88	703	158	6	33	133	.225	.317	.261
vs. Left-Handers			127	21	2	4	41	.165	.283	.195
vs. Right-Handers			576	137	4	29	92	.238	.325	.276
Home	6-9	3.15	408	96	3	20	66	.235	.321	.272
Road	4-4	2.53	295	62	3	13	67	.210	.312	.247
Grass	8-11	3.02	554	124	6	27	104	.224	.321	.263
Artificial Turf	2-2	2.40	149	34	0	6	29	.228	.302	.256
April	2-1	3.81	97	23	0	6	16	.237	.278	.282
May	2-3	3.31	123	21	2	6	25	.171	.293	.206
June	2-2	3.40	156	41	3	9	25	.263	.391	.318
July	2-2	2.03	107	20	0	2	16	.187	.252	.200
August	1-4	2.50	137	35	1	8	27	.255	.365	.295
Sept./Oct.	1-1	2.01	83	18	0	2	24	.217	.265	.233
Leading Off Inn.			188	40	3	7	33	.213	.346	.245
Runners On			245	62	2	19	45	.253	.343	.303
Runners/Scor. Pos.			144	37	1	16	29	.257	.306	.323
Runners On/2 Out			101	24	0	12	19	.238	.307	.319
Scor. Pos./2 Out			70	17	0	10	13	.243	.286	.338
Late Inning Pressure			74	21	0	3	11	.284	.338	.308
Leading Off			20	4	0	1	3	.200	.300	.238
Runners On			28	10	0	1	3	.357	.429	.367
Runners/Scor. Pos.			14	5	0	1	2	.357	.429	.375
First 9 Batters			236	46	2	12	52	.195	.284	.236
Second 9 Batters			237	53	3	11	43	.224	.316	.262
All Batters Thereafter			230	59	1	10	38	.257	.352	.287

Loves to face: Bruce Benedict (0-for-12)
Hates to face: Dale Murphy (.727, 8-for-11, 1 HR)
Ground outs-to-air outs ratio: 1.26 last season, 1.02 for career. . . .
Additional statistics: 10 double-play ground outs in 100 opportunities, 37 doubles, 5 triples in 190.1 innings last season. . . . Allowed 13 first-inning runs in 29 starts. . . . Batting support: 2.97 runs per start. Mets scored two runs or fewer in 10 of his 13 losses. . . . Five of his ten wins were complete-game shutouts. . . . Struck out the last seven left-handers faced last season, matching longest streak in majors over past 10 years. . . . Allowed only one hit in 15 at-bats with the bases loaded since joining the Mets. . . . Pitchers with comparable career stats (75–62, 3.68 ERA) at same age: Charlie Root, Rip Collins, Billy Loes, Stan Williams, Bob Shaw.

Jesse Orosco
Los Angeles Dodgers   Throws Left

	W–L	ERA	AB	H	HR	BB	SO	BA	SA	OBA
Season	3-2	2.72	191	41	4	30	43	.215	.319	.323
vs. Left-Handers			62	14	1	11	14	.226	.306	.338
vs. Right-Handers			129	27	3	19	29	.209	.326	.316
Home	1-0	2.75	73	13	1	7	14	.178	.260	.259
Road	2-2	2.70	118	28	3	23	29	.237	.356	.359
Grass	1-1	2.95	130	23	3	21	28	.177	.292	.290
Artificial Turf	2-1	2.20	61	18	1	9	15	.295	.377	.394
April	0-0	2.08	13	1	0	2	4	.077	.077	.188
May	2-1	2.57	52	11	0	5	12	.212	.231	.293
June	0-0	4.09	41	11	2	3	11	.268	.488	.311
July	0-0	5.14	29	8	1	5	6	.276	.483	.389
August	0-0	1.23	25	4	0	5	7	.160	.200	.300
Sept./Oct.	1-1	0.96	31	6	1	10	3	.194	.290	.390
Leading Off Inn.			42	12	2	4	6	.286	.429	.348
Runners On			95	16	1	18	25	.168	.221	.305
Runners/Scor. Pos.			63	9	1	11	17	.143	.206	.278
Runners On/2 Out			46	10	1	8	13	.217	.304	.345
Scor. Pos./2 Out			36	6	1	6	10	.167	.250	.302
Late Inning Pressure			121	30	2	22	25	.248	.355	.361
Leading Off			28	10	1	2	4	.357	.464	.400
Runners On			58	9	0	15	15	.155	.172	.325
Runners/Scor. Pos.			40	5	0	10	12	.125	.125	.296
First 9 Batters			188	41	4	29	43	.218	.324	.324
Second 9 Batters			3	0	0	1	0	.000	.000	.250
All Batters Thereafter			0	0	0	0	0	—	—	—

Loves to face: Nick Esasky (.100, 1-for-10, 5 SO)
Hates to face: Chili Davis (.471, 8-for-17, 1 HR)
Ground outs-to-air outs ratio: 1.23 last season, 0.89 for career. . . .
Additional statistics: 5 double-play ground outs in 49 opportunities, 6 doubles, 1 triple in 53.0 innings last season. . . . Earned a save in each of his first three games in Dodger Blue, but had only six saves in 52 appearances after that. . . . Left-handers had a higher batting average than right-handers for the first time in the last eight years, but still haven't tripled against him in 614 career ABs. . . . Only pitcher whose opponents have hit better with bases empty than with runners on in each of last eight seasons. . . . May not get a chance to spoil perfect career record vs. Reds (7–0). . . . Word of warning to the Indians this spring: Check inside your cap before putting it on.

David Palmer
Philadelphia Phillies   Throws Right

	W–L	ERA	AB	H	HR	BB	SO	BA	SA	OBA
Season	7-9	4.47	494	129	8	48	85	.261	.364	.324
vs. Left-Handers			254	69	4	27	46	.272	.358	.337
vs. Right-Handers			240	60	4	21	39	.250	.371	.309
Home	5-4	3.34	267	61	4	21	46	.228	.322	.283
Road	2-5	5.91	227	68	4	27	39	.300	.414	.370
Grass	1-2	6.75	101	31	2	12	18	.307	.455	.377
Artificial Turf	6-7	3.94	393	98	6	36	67	.249	.341	.309
April	0-0	4.50	16	6	0	3	1	.375	.438	.474
May	0-5	5.35	131	35	2	17	29	.267	.382	.347
June	3-1	3.27	125	31	2	12	21	.248	.336	.312
July	2-2	5.32	80	18	2	8	12	.225	.338	.292
August	2-1	4.21	142	39	2	8	22	.275	.380	.311
Sept./Oct.			0	0	0	0	0	—	—	—
Leading Off Inn.			124	37	2	16	16	.298	.452	.379
Runners On			207	64	5	19	40	.309	.411	.359
Runners/Scor. Pos.			123	40	4	18	22	.325	.463	.397
Runners On/2 Out			74	17	1	11	13	.230	.270	.329
Scor. Pos./2 Out			50	9	0	10	8	.180	.180	.317
Late Inning Pressure			37	13	1	3	7	.351	.541	.400
Leading Off			12	5	0	0	2	.417	.667	.417
Runners On			15	6	1	1	1	.400	.600	.438
Runners/Scor. Pos.			10	4	1	1	0	.400	.700	.455
First 9 Batters			180	36	1	13	35	.200	.256	.253
Second 9 Batters			175	47	6	18	29	.269	.417	.335
All Batters Thereafter			139	46	1	17	21	.331	.439	.396

Loves to face: Rob Thompson (0-for-14)
Hates to face: Gary Redus (.667, 2-for-3, 2 HR)
Ground outs-to-air outs ratio: 1.49 last season, 2.01 for career. . . .
Additional statistics: 9 double-play ground outs in 95 opportunities, 21 doubles, 3 triples in 129.0 innings last season. . . . Allowed 13 first-inning runs in 22 starts. . . . Batting support: 3.41 runs per start. . . . Only pitcher to hit two home runs last season, and the only one to hit at least one in each of the last three years. . . . Allowed leadoff batter to reach base safely in eight consecutive innings (May 25–June 5), longest streak by an N.L. pitcher last season. Seattle's Steve Trout allowed 10 straight leadoff batters to reach base. . . . Has completed only three of 125 starts since his five-inning "perfect game" in 1984. . . Career record: 31–16 through 1984, 33–40 since then.

Jeff Parrett
Montreal Expos   Throws Right

	W–L	ERA	AB	H	HR	BB	SO	BA	SA	OBA
Season	12-4	2.65	308	66	8	45	62	.214	.341	.311
vs. Left-Handers			138	29	0	24	27	.210	.254	.319
vs. Right-Handers			170	37	8	21	35	.218	.412	.304
Home	5-3	2.08	155	27	2	23	32	.174	.258	.277
Road	7-1	3.27	153	39	6	22	30	.255	.425	.347
Grass	2-1	4.57	78	22	3	8	15	.282	.410	.345
Artificial Turf	10-3	2.06	230	44	5	37	47	.191	.317	.300
April	1-0	2.08	44	7	2	5	10	.159	.295	.260
May	3-1	2.05	72	16	1	13	13	.222	.319	.341
June	3-1	2.50	59	12	1	14	14	.203	.322	.342
July	3-1	3.00	42	10	1	6	9	.238	.405	.333
August	1-0	1.86	29	5	1	2	7	.172	.276	.212
Sept./Oct.	1-1	4.24	62	16	2	5	9	.258	.403	.309
Leading Off Inn.			76	18	1	8	15	.237	.342	.310
Runners On			123	24	3	23	24	.195	.309	.314
Runners/Scor. Pos.			81	16	3	17	17	.198	.370	.317
Runners On/2 Out			57	12	2	11	14	.211	.368	.338
Scor. Pos./2 Out			44	9	2	8	10	.205	.409	.327
Late Inning Pressure			193	41	4	33	44	.212	.332	.320
Leading Off			51	12	1	6	10	.235	.373	.316
Runners On			76	16	2	16	17	.211	.329	.330
Runners/Scor. Pos.			55	12	2	12	11	.218	.382	.333
First 9 Batters			288	63	7	44	57	.219	.344	.319
Second 9 Batters			20	3	1	1	5	.150	.300	.190
All Batters Thereafter			0	0	0	0	0	—	—	—

Loves to face: Ken Oberkfell (0-for-7)
Hates to face: Kevin McReynolds (.500, 3-for-6, 3 HR)
Ground outs-to-air outs ratio: 0.99 last season, 0.92 for career. . . .
Additional statistics: 7 double-play ground outs in 62 opportunities, 11 doubles, 2 triples in 91.2 innings last season. . . . Led majors with 12 relief wins last season. Only 14 other pitchers in major league history won that many games without pitching at least 100 innings. . . . All six saves came in first half of season. . . . Allowed a home run to first batter he faced in 1988 (Kevin McReynolds). . . . Last 10 HRs allowed have all been hit by right-handers. Last homer by a left-hander was by Andy Van Slyke on August 9, 1987. . . . Opponents' batting average has decreased in each of his seasons in the majors: .247, .229, .214. . . . Lost four of first five career decisions, 18–7 since then.

Alejandro Pena
Los Angeles Dodgers   Throws Right

	W–L	ERA	AB	H	HR	BB	SO	BA	SA	OBA
Season	6-7	1.91	344	75	4	27	83	.218	.279	.275
vs. Left-Handers			167	42	0	20	37	.251	.281	.326
vs. Right-Handers			177	33	4	7	46	.186	.277	.222
Home	2-4	1.64	162	35	2	14	36	.216	.278	.278
Road	4-3	2.15	182	40	2	13	47	.220	.280	.271
Grass	5-5	1.71	248	52	3	19	56	.210	.262	.266
Artificial Turf	1-2	2.42	96	23	1	8	27	.240	.323	.296
April	1-0	0.00	31	6	0	1	5	.194	.194	.219
May	1-2	2.50	64	12	3	10	15	.188	.375	.293
June	0-1	2.30	57	13	0	4	16	.228	.246	.290
July	2-0	1.47	65	13	0	6	16	.200	.215	.268
August	1-3	4.20	67	25	0	3	17	.373	.418	.389
Sept./Oct.	1-1	0.49	60	6	1	3	14	.100	.167	.143
Leading Off Inn.			86	16	1	3	19	.186	.244	.213
Runners On			138	34	0	14	36	.246	.275	.310
Runners/Scor. Pos.			85	23	0	12	31	.271	.318	.350
Runners On/2 Out			71	20	0	10	19	.282	.324	.370
Scor. Pos./2 Out			52	13	0	9	17	.250	.308	.361
Late Inning Pressure			205	42	3	16	52	.205	.288	.266
Leading Off			57	12	0	1	13	.211	.246	.224
Runners On			68	15	0	8	18	.221	.265	.303
Runners/Scor. Pos.			39	12	0	7	15	.308	.385	.413
First 9 Batters			327	72	4	25	77	.220	.284	.275
Second 9 Batters			17	3	0	2	6	.176	.176	.263
All Batters Thereafter			0	0	0	0	0	—	—	—

Loves to face: Darryl Strawberry (0-for-9)
Hates to face: Billy Hatcher (.500, 5-for-10, 1 HR)
Ground outs-to-air outs ratio: 0.77 last season, 1.10 for career. . . .
Additional statistics: 4 double-play ground outs in 60 opportunities, 9 doubles, 0 triples in 94.1 innings last season. . . . Faced 80 batters protecting leads of three runs or less in the 8th inning or later. Other Dodgers relievers: Howell, 147; Orosco, 77. . . . All four home runs were yielded to right-handed batters, with bases empty, in 8th inning or later. . . . Opponents' batting average was his lowest since 1981. . . . Innings pitched have increased in every season since his 1985 surgery: 4.1, 70.0, 87.1, 94.1. . . . One of 10 pitchers with a losing record in each of the last four years. . . . Has faced 1427 right-handed batters without allowing a triple.

Pascual Perez

Montreal Expos — Throws Right

	W–L	ERA	AB	H	HR	BB	SO	BA	SA	OBA
Season	12-8	2.44	677	133	15	44	131	.196	.303	.252
vs. Left-Handers			366	78	9	29	70	.213	.339	.273
vs. Right-Handers			311	55	6	15	61	.177	.260	.227
Home	6-3	1.68	368	70	5	20	71	.190	.280	.239
Road	6-5	3.34	309	63	10	24	60	.204	.330	.266
Grass	1-2	4.18	112	26	4	14	20	.232	.393	.318
Artificial Turf	11-6	2.08	565	107	11	30	111	.189	.285	.238
April	3-2	1.66	136	26	2	12	36	.191	.265	.262
May	0-1	2.40	50	8	2	3	9	.160	.280	.208
June	1-0	0.00	59	11	0	3	9	.186	.203	.238
July	3-2	3.23	145	32	3	6	22	.221	.317	.260
August	2-1	3.46	144	33	3	8	27	.229	.368	.279
Sept./Oct.	3-2	2.41	143	23	5	12	28	.161	.308	.228
Leading Off Inn.			177	35	9	11	32	.198	.390	.253
Runners On			229	48	3	21	34	.210	.297	.278
Runners/Scor. Pos.			139	25	1	16	23	.180	.223	.264
Runners On/2 Out			96	19	1	11	16	.198	.281	.287
Scor. Pos./2 Out			69	12	0	9	11	.174	.217	.278
Late Inning Pressure			63	10	2	4	9	.159	.286	.209
Leading Off			18	3	2	0	3	.167	.556	.167
Runners On			16	0	0	3	1	.000	.000	.158
Runners/Scor. Pos.			12	0	0	2	1	.000	.000	.143
First 9 Batters			218	41	6	16	43	.188	.321	.254
Second 9 Batters			219	41	4	14	46	.187	.269	.243
All Batters Thereafter			240	51	5	14	42	.213	.317	.258

Loves to face: Kevin Bass (0-for-19)
Hates to face: Darryl Strawberry (.409, 9-for-22, 4 HR)
Ground outs-to-air outs ratio: 1.63 last season, 1.70 for career. . . . Additional statistics: 11 double-play ground outs in 108 opportunities, 19 doubles, 4 triples in 188.0 innings last season. . . . Allowed 12 first-inning runs in 27 starts. . . . Batting support: 3.63 runs per start. . . . Allowed 8.81 runners per nine innings, lowest rate in majors last season (minimum: 162 IP). . . . ERA breakdown by innings: 1st–3d innings: 3.00; 4th–6th: 2.20; 7th–9th: 1.53. . . . Lowest ERAs in majors over past two years (minimum: 250 IP): Perez 2.40, Hershiser 2.66, Cone 2.67. . . . Hasn't lost consecutive decisions since 1985, when he lost his last six. . . . 0-for-16 with runners on in Late-Inning Pressure Situations was best since Larry Gura posted 0-for-19 in 1976.

Jeff Pico

Chicago Cubs — Throws Right

	W–L	ERA	AB	H	HR	BB	SO	BA	SA	OBA
Season	6-7	4.15	428	108	6	37	57	.252	.350	.309
vs. Left-Handers			230	68	4	23	17	.296	.409	.358
vs. Right-Handers			198	40	2	14	40	.202	.283	.251
Home	4-2	3.51	251	58	4	16	38	.231	.331	.273
Road	2-5	5.09	177	50	2	21	19	.282	.379	.359
Grass	5-5	3.90	331	79	4	25	48	.239	.326	.289
Artificial Turf	1-2	5.04	97	29	2	12	9	.299	.433	.376
April			0	0	0	0	0	—	—	—
May	1-0	0.00	29	4	0	0	6	.138	.207	.138
June	2-2	4.85	117	33	1	13	10	.282	.385	.348
July	0-4	6.55	82	23	2	14	13	.280	.415	.385
August	2-0	0.91	105	20	0	3	18	.190	.200	.211
Sept./Oct.	1-1	6.85	95	28	3	7	10	.295	.463	.340
Leading Off Inn.			106	23	0	8	11	.217	.274	.272
Runners On			181	52	4	16	28	.287	.420	.338
Runners/Scor. Pos.			100	33	3	10	16	.330	.470	.377
Runners On/2 Out			76	19	3	6	13	.250	.395	.305
Scor. Pos./2 Out			42	14	2	3	5	.333	.476	.378
Late Inning Pressure			63	19	2	7	9	.302	.413	.366
Leading Off			16	2	0	1	2	.125	.125	.176
Runners On			27	10	2	3	3	.370	.630	.419
Runners/Scor. Pos.			12	7	2	2	0	.583	1.083	.600
First 9 Batters			205	56	3	15	30	.273	.356	.320
Second 9 Batters			122	21	0	13	19	.172	.213	.250
All Batters Thereafter			101	31	3	9	8	.307	.505	.360

Loves to face: Barry Larkin (0-for-10)
Hates to face: Milt Thompson (5-for-5)
Ground outs-to-air outs ratio: 1.42 last season, his first in majors. . . . Additional statistics: 11 double-play ground outs in 83 opportunities, 22 doubles, 1 triple in 112.2 innings last season. . . . Allowed 10 first-inning runs in 13 starts. . . . Batting support: 4.23 runs per start. . . . Record of 4–6 (4.67 ERA) in 13 starts, 2–1 (2.84) in 16 relief appearances. . . . Faced 472 batters, didn't hit any with a pitch. . . . Allowed hits to seven consecutive batters (Sept. 2–7), longest streak of any N.L. pitcher last season. . . . Shut out the Reds on four hits in his major league debut. Last Cubs pitcher to toss a shutout in his first major league start was Bill Lee, on May 7, 1934. . . . Two of his three complete games were shutouts.

Charlie Puleo

Atlanta Braves — Throws Right

	W–L	ERA	AB	H	HR	BB	SO	BA	SA	OBA
Season	5-5	3.47	403	101	9	47	70	.251	.380	.330
vs. Left-Handers			191	57	7	29	30	.298	.482	.390
vs. Right-Handers			212	44	2	18	40	.208	.288	.274
Home	2-0	4.06	196	51	4	25	32	.260	.372	.345
Road	3-5	2.93	207	50	5	22	38	.242	.386	.316
Grass	2-4	3.73	305	77	9	35	48	.252	.403	.328
Artificial Turf	3-1	2.70	98	24	0	12	22	.245	.306	.336
April	0-0	5.73	39	5	2	6	9	.128	.308	.244
May	0-1	3.63	72	22	0	12	15	.306	.389	.405
June	1-2	4.01	94	24	3	9	13	.255	.426	.324
July	1-0	1.69	80	18	3	5	16	.225	.350	.279
August	1-0	3.71	65	17	0	3	11	.262	.323	.286
Sept./Oct.	2-2	3.00	53	15	1	12	6	.283	.453	.418
Leading Off Inn.			91	20	3	5	19	.220	.352	.276
Runners On			179	46	4	34	29	.257	.380	.369
Runners/Scor. Pos.			102	30	3	28	19	.294	.441	.433
Runners On/2 Out			87	26	1	23	17	.299	.379	.445
Scor. Pos./2 Out			56	19	1	19	14	.339	.446	.507
Late Inning Pressure			120	33	2	16	20	.275	.383	.370
Leading Off			29	5	0	2	8	.172	.172	.250
Runners On			51	12	0	12	8	.235	.255	.381
Runners/Scor. Pos.			22	7	0	11	2	.318	.364	.545
First 9 Batters			309	74	6	40	55	.239	.340	.330
Second 9 Batters			80	23	3	6	14	.288	.513	.333
All Batters Thereafter			14	4	0	1	1	.286	.500	.333

Loves to face: Eric Davis (0-for-7, 6 SO)
Hates to face: Darryl Strawberry (.500, 6-for-12, 2 HR)
Ground outs-to-air outs ratio: 0.65 last season, 0.86 for career. . . . Additional statistics: 3 double-play ground outs in 81 opportunities, 23 doubles, 1 triple in 106.1 innings last season. . . . Record of 0–2 (7.84 ERA) in three starts, 5–3 (3.00) in 50 relief appearances. . . . His only save (July 2) was the second of his career, the first coming six years earlier in relief of Craig Swan. . . . Held right-handed batters hitless in 30 consecutive plate appearances (Aug. 15–Sept. 28). . . . Hasn't allowed two homers in a game since May 1987. . . . Had never walked in a run until last season, when he walked five of 23 batters faced with the bases loaded, a major league high. . . . Only N.L. pitcher to allow two grand slams in 1988.

Dennis Rasmussen

Reds/Padres — Throws Left

	W–L	ERA	AB	H	HR	BB	SO	BA	SA	OBA
Season	16-10	3.43	778	199	17	58	112	.256	.383	.309
vs. Left-Handers			118	35	3	7	20	.297	.449	.336
vs. Right-Handers			660	164	14	51	92	.248	.371	.304
Home	7-4	2.87	327	78	9	24	55	.239	.398	.294
Road	9-6	3.85	451	121	8	34	57	.268	.374	.320
Grass	10-5	3.19	442	110	9	29	69	.249	.369	.296
Artificial Turf	6-5	3.74	336	89	8	29	43	.265	.402	.327
April	1-2	4.70	86	25	2	10	8	.291	.465	.367
May	1-3	5.06	129	35	6	12	18	.271	.473	.331
June	4-1	3.82	129	32	3	7	21	.248	.372	.290
July	3-1	3.96	146	41	2	14	22	.281	.404	.350
August	3-1	1.50	105	22	0	7	18	.210	.276	.259
Sept./Oct.	4-2	2.25	183	44	4	8	25	.240	.333	.272
Leading Off Inn.			202	39	2	11	27	.193	.287	.235
Runners On			290	79	8	23	44	.272	.403	.326
Runners/Scor. Pos.			162	37	3	19	31	.228	.352	.306
Runners On/2 Out			139	34	1	19	26	.245	.324	.340
Scor. Pos./2 Out			91	20	1	16	21	.220	.341	.336
Late Inning Pressure			63	17	2	6	12	.270	.429	.333
Leading Off			18	5	0	2	3	.278	.333	.350
Runners On			19	3	1	2	4	.158	.316	.238
Runners/Scor. Pos.			8	2	0	1	2	.250	.250	.333
First 9 Batters			253	69	3	20	44	.273	.375	.329
Second 9 Batters			252	61	6	15	33	.242	.365	.286
All Batters Thereafter			273	69	8	23	35	.253	.407	.312

Loves to face: Candy Maldonado (0-for-13)
Hates to face: Pedro Guerrero (5-for-5)
Ground outs-to-air outs ratio: 0.84 last season, 0.72 for career. . . . Additional statistics: 9 double-play ground outs in 115 opportunities, 42 doubles, 3 triples in 204.2 innings last season. . . . Allowed 20 first-inning runs in 31 starts. . . . Batting support: 4.48 runs per start, 3d highest in N.L. (minimum: 15 GS). . . . Average of 7.42 innings per start, 4th highest mark in N.L. (minimum: 15 GS). . . . Had the highest ERA of any N.L. pitcher with 15 or more wins. . . . Never completed consecutive starts until he ended the season with three in a row. . . . Left-handers have hit .290 or better against this southpaw while right-handers have hit below .250 in each of the last two seasons. . . . Career record of 14–2 during July, 45–33 in other months.

Shane Rawley
Philadelphia Phillies — Throws Left

	W–L	ERA	AB	H	HR	BB	SO	BA	SA	OBA
Season	8-16	4.18	768	220	27	78	87	.286	.447	.351
vs. Left-Handers			136	36	3	8	22	.265	.368	.299
vs. Right-Handers			632	184	24	70	65	.291	.464	.362
Home	4-7	4.90	369	110	20	40	46	.298	.526	.363
Road	4-9	3.54	399	110	7	38	41	.276	.373	.340
Grass	4-4	2.63	239	56	6	20	22	.234	.326	.291
Artificial Turf	4-12	4.94	529	164	21	58	65	.310	.501	.377
April	0-4	3.77	118	30	6	12	13	.254	.449	.331
May	4-1	3.51	189	45	6	23	24	.238	.370	.318
June	1-3	3.38	150	38	2	11	22	.253	.367	.301
July	0-4	6.62	149	56	8	14	15	.376	.577	.425
August	1-1	3.60	39	11	0	5	5	.282	.333	.364
Sept./Oct.	2-3	4.15	123	40	5	13	8	.325	.537	.390
Leading Off Inn.			191	59	7	14	16	.309	.492	.359
Runners On			332	86	12	43	44	.259	.425	.337
Runners/Scor. Pos.			182	46	7	28	26	.253	.440	.339
Runners On/2 Out			147	35	5	23	19	.238	.395	.341
Scor. Pos./2 Out			94	21	4	13	13	.223	.426	.318
Late Inning Pressure			63	17	3	8	5	.270	.492	.347
Leading Off			20	5	0	1	2	.250	.350	.286
Runners On			20	4	1	6	1	.200	.400	.370
Runners/Scor. Pos.			12	1	0	5	1	.083	.083	.333
First 9 Batters			242	73	4	28	30	.302	.409	.374
Second 9 Batters			242	61	10	21	30	.252	.409	.312
All Batters Thereafter			284	86	13	29	27	.303	.511	.364

Loves to face: Jeffrey Leonard (.063, 1-for-16)
Hates to face: Keith Moreland (.447, 17-for-38, 1 HR)
Ground outs-to-air outs ratio: 1.02 last season, 1.20 for career....
Additional statistics: 14 double-play ground outs in 164 opportunities, 34 doubles, 4 triples in 198.0 innings last season.... Allowed 23 first-inning runs (3d most in N.L.) in 32 starts.... Batting support: 3.84 runs per start.... ERA was lower than when he posted a 17–11 record in 1987 (4.39).... Three HRs by left-handers equalled his career high.... Opponents' batting average was highest of his career for second consecutive season.... Only N.L. pitcher whose opponents hit better in day games than night games in each of last four seasons. During that time: 9–18, 5.64 ERA by day, 40–24, 3.23 ERA at night.... Career record of 25–12 during August, 10–23 in September.

Rick Reuschel
San Francisco Giants — Throws Right

	W–L	ERA	AB	H	HR	BB	SO	BA	SA	OBA
Season	19-11	3.12	928	242	11	42	92	.261	.350	.293
vs. Left-Handers			510	145	4	25	33	.284	.369	.313
vs. Right-Handers			418	97	7	17	59	.232	.328	.268
Home	8-5	2.63	419	96	4	15	40	.229	.313	.255
Road	11-6	3.55	509	146	7	27	52	.287	.381	.324
Grass	15-8	2.81	682	168	7	30	69	.246	.326	.279
Artificial Turf	4-3	4.04	246	74	4	12	23	.301	.419	.332
April	3-1	1.91	104	24	3	6	5	.231	.317	.270
May	4-2	3.50	177	51	3	15	19	.288	.379	.342
June	3-1	4.07	99	30	0	4	6	.303	.404	.330
July	4-1	2.38	167	40	1	6	13	.240	.323	.264
August	3-2	3.47	171	39	1	7	26	.228	.304	.262
Sept./Oct.	2-4	3.33	210	58	3	4	23	.276	.376	.291
Leading Off Inn.			243	64	2	7	18	.263	.329	.290
Runners On			348	90	2	29	41	.259	.342	.310
Runners/Scor. Pos.			172	45	1	16	24	.262	.355	.305
Runners On/2 Out			142	29	1	20	21	.204	.282	.307
Scor. Pos./2 Out			82	17	1	10	14	.207	.293	.293
Late Inning Pressure			97	27	1	5	10	.278	.361	.320
Leading Off			25	5	0	1	2	.200	.240	.231
Runners On			38	10	1	4	4	.263	.368	.349
Runners/Scor. Pos.			20	3	1	1	4	.150	.300	.190
First 9 Batters			301	71	1	13	36	.236	.299	.270
Second 9 Batters			300	84	5	9	20	.280	.387	.297
All Batters Thereafter			327	87	5	20	36	.266	.364	.310

Loves to face: Jack Clark (.122, 5-for-41)
Hates to face: Tim Raines (.436, 24-for-55)
Ground outs-to-air outs ratio: 1.08 last season, 1.91 for career....
Additional statistics: 25 double-play ground outs in 181 opportunities, 42 doubles, 4 triples in 245.0 innings last season.... Allowed 21 first-inning runs in 36 starts.... Batting support: 4.44 runs per start.... Tied Orel Hershiser for most sacrifice bunts (19) by any N.L. batter.... Allowed 14 sacrifice flies, most in N.L. since he allowed 14 in 1980. N.L. record is 15 by Randy Lerch in 1979.... Completed seven games, all after the All-Star break.... Could have become first pitcher in major league history to win 20 games more than 10 years after his last 20-win season. But Reuschel lost his final three starts, leaving Bert Cunningham's 10-year gap as the longest (1888–98).

Jose Rijo
Cincinnati Reds — Throws Right

	W–L	ERA	AB	H	HR	BB	SO	BA	SA	OBA
Season	13-8	2.39	574	120	7	63	160	.209	.300	.288
vs. Left-Handers			308	71	6	44	90	.231	.347	.327
vs. Right-Handers			266	49	1	19	70	.184	.244	.241
Home	6-7	3.12	340	78	5	35	96	.229	.338	.303
Road	7-1	1.42	234	42	2	28	64	.179	.244	.267
Grass	4-1	1.60	155	32	1	17	45	.206	.265	.280
Artificial Turf	9-7	2.69	419	88	6	46	115	.210	.313	.291
April	3-1	3.77	50	13	0	11	10	.260	.260	.381
May	2-0	1.84	98	17	2	13	22	.173	.286	.283
June	3-2	3.67	126	26	2	12	39	.206	.310	.273
July	3-2	1.47	149	29	1	17	45	.195	.268	.275
August	0-3	3.80	84	24	2	7	25	.286	.452	.337
Sept./Oct.	2-0	0.46	67	11	0	3	19	.164	.209	.211
Leading Off Inn.			148	33	6	9	37	.223	.412	.272
Runners On			214	44	1	41	63	.206	.271	.330
Runners/Scor. Pos.			123	28	0	27	36	.228	.260	.359
Runners On/2 Out			92	13	0	29	34	.141	.185	.352
Scor. Pos./2 Out			62	11	0	20	21	.177	.226	.386
Late Inning Pressure			130	27	3	21	30	.208	.315	.327
Leading Off			35	10	3	3	10	.286	.571	.359
Runners On			46	7	0	13	11	.152	.196	.350
Runners/Scor. Pos.			23	5	0	9	5	.217	.217	.455
First 9 Batters			297	63	3	38	82	.212	.290	.302
Second 9 Batters			158	32	2	11	42	.203	.310	.257
All Batters Thereafter			119	25	2	14	36	.210	.311	.293

Loves to face: Lonnie Smith (0-for-8, 5 SO)
Hates to face: Dale Murphy (.625, 5-for-8)
Ground outs-to-air outs ratio: 1.52 last season, 1.14 for career....
Additional statistics: 10 double-play ground outs in 100 opportunities, 23 doubles, 4 triples in 162.0 innings last season.... Allowed 3 first-inning runs in 19 starts, 2d lowest average in N.L. (minimum: 15 GS).... Batting support: 3.79 runs per start.... Record of 7–7 (2.47 ERA) in 19 starts, 6–1 (2.20) in 30 relief appearances.... Had the most starts of any N.L. pitcher without a complete game last season.... Opponents batting average was the lowest of his career, down 96 points from a career-high .305 in 1987.... Has made 73 career starts without a shutout. For list of all-time high totals, see Al Nipper.... Career records: 15–25 before the All-Star break, 17–13 after it.

Don Robinson
San Francisco Giants — Throws Right

	W–L	ERA	AB	H	HR	BB	SO	BA	SA	OBA
Season	10-5	2.45	658	152	11	49	122	.231	.343	.284
vs. Left-Handers			324	70	6	25	55	.216	.324	.272
vs. Right-Handers			334	82	5	24	67	.246	.362	.296
Home	4-0	2.47	254	63	4	21	47	.248	.350	.309
Road	6-5	2.43	404	89	7	28	75	.220	.339	.268
Grass	7-4	2.57	435	102	7	30	73	.234	.329	.286
Artificial Turf	3-1	2.21	223	50	4	19	49	.224	.372	.280
April	1-1	1.26	54	14	2	4	11	.259	.426	.310
May	1-0	3.50	73	23	3	10	20	.315	.548	.407
June	1-0	2.25	56	11	1	6	12	.196	.339	.270
July	0-0	2.72	140	33	1	15	33	.236	.314	.308
August	2-3	2.66	148	27	2	5	30	.182	.257	.210
Sept./Oct.	5-1	2.10	187	44	2	9	16	.235	.332	.268
Leading Off Inn.			165	38	1	11	32	.230	.321	.282
Runners On			256	61	8	30	50	.238	.375	.312
Runners/Scor. Pos.			146	38	5	23	30	.260	.418	.345
Runners On/2 Out			127	39	7	21	27	.307	.512	.409
Scor. Pos./2 Out			87	23	4	18	20	.264	.437	.390
Late Inning Pressure			135	33	3	18	28	.244	.407	.329
Leading Off			34	6	1	4	6	.176	.324	.263
Runners On			54	12	2	11	16	.222	.407	.343
Runners/Scor. Pos.			38	8	2	11	11	.211	.421	.373
First 9 Batters			314	80	7	23	70	.255	.408	.305
Second 9 Batters			180	35	2	12	33	.194	.256	.241
All Batters Thereafter			164	37	2	14	19	.226	.317	.291

Loves to face: Dave Anderson (0-for-12)
Hates to face: Jack Clark (.273, 12-for-44, 7 HR)
Ground outs-to-air outs ratio: 0.81 last season, 0.88 for career....
Additional statistics: 10 double-play ground outs in 98 opportunities, 27 doubles, 7 triples in 176.2 innings last season.... Allowed 11 first-inning runs in 19 starts.... Batting support: 3.79 runs per start.... Only pitcher in majors to start at least 15 games and average less than five innings per start (4.79).... Record of 8–4 (2.33 ERA) in 19 starts, 2–1 (2.78) in 32 relief appearances.... Retired leadoff batters in 24 consecutive innings (Aug. 10–20).... Opposing right-handers have hit better against this fellow righty than left-handers have in each of last five seasons.... Career batting average of .254 is highest of any active pitcher (minimum: 150 AB).

Jeff D. Robinson

Pittsburgh Pirates — Throws Right

	W–L	ERA	AB	H	HR	BB	SO	BA	SA	OBA
Season	11-5	3.03	463	113	6	39	87	.244	.335	.303
vs. Left-Handers			235	58	3	10	38	.247	.328	.277
vs. Right-Handers			228	55	3	29	49	.241	.342	.328
Home	2-4	3.64	222	60	2	18	40	.270	.342	.325
Road	9-1	2.48	241	53	4	21	47	.220	.328	.283
Grass	3-1	3.25	109	28	3	10	22	.257	.422	.317
Artificial Turf	8-4	2.97	354	85	3	29	65	.240	.308	.299
April	2-0	2.36	100	19	1	8	16	.190	.290	.250
May	1-1	3.38	91	24	1	3	16	.264	.330	.295
June	2-1	4.20	56	16	0	7	10	.286	.321	.364
July	3-0	2.20	65	18	0	6	17	.277	.385	.333
August	1-0	2.70	84	21	1	6	10	.250	.321	.304
Sept./Oct.	2-3	3.72	67	15	3	9	18	.224	.388	.308
Leading Off Inn.			110	20	0	3	18	.182	.218	.211
Runners On			193	52	3	24	36	.269	.373	.344
Runners/Scor. Pos.			133	34	2	19	31	.256	.368	.340
Runners On/2 Out			98	24	2	10	14	.245	.327	.315
Scor. Pos./2 Out			74	16	2	9	13	.216	.311	.301
Late Inning Pressure			300	70	3	29	61	.233	.300	.304
Leading Off			71	13	0	2	12	.183	.197	.216
Runners On			129	32	2	18	25	.248	.349	.338
Runners/Scor. Pos.			90	24	2	14	21	.267	.411	.361
First 9 Batters			422	104	5	38	83	.246	.332	.309
Second 9 Batters			41	9	1	1	4	.220	.366	.238
All Batters Thereafter			0	0	0	0	0	—	—	—

Loves to face: Dale Murphy (.107, 3-for-28)
Hates to face: Denny Walling (.643, 9-for-14, 1 HR)
Ground outs-to-air outs ratio: 1.41 last season, 1.64 for career. . . .
Additional statistics: 6 double-play ground outs in 73 opportunities, 20 doubles, 2 triples in 124.2 innings last season. . . . Eight of his nine saves were recorded by the end of June, before Jim Gott was established as Bucs' closer. . . . His three September losses came within eight days of each other. . . . Ended the season by holding hitless the last 30 right-handed batters to face him. . . . Won six straight decisions, 11 shy of ElRoy Face's record for Pirates' relievers. . . . Started 33 games for the Giants in 1984, but has started only one game since, while appearing in 228 games in relief. . . . Opponents' career average is .273 with runners on base, .236 with the bases empty.

Ron Robinson

Cincinnati Reds — Throws Right

	W–L	ERA	AB	H	HR	BB	SO	BA	SA	OBA
Season	3-7	4.12	309	88	5	26	38	.285	.392	.339
vs. Left-Handers			163	54	4	18	11	.331	.485	.402
vs. Right-Handers			146	34	1	8	27	.233	.288	.266
Home	2-3	5.35	133	38	3	9	16	.286	.436	.331
Road	1-4	3.20	176	50	2	17	22	.284	.358	.345
Grass	0-4	3.92	85	27	1	10	7	.318	.412	.388
Artificial Turf	3-3	4.19	224	61	4	16	31	.272	.384	.320
April	1-2	4.09	86	20	0	7	11	.233	.267	.284
May	1-2	4.45	117	37	4	8	15	.316	.479	.357
June	1-2	3.60	82	24	1	7	10	.293	.427	.356
July	0-0	0.00	6	1	0	0	1	.167	.167	.167
August			0	0	0	0	0	—	—	—
Sept./Oct.	0-1	6.23	18	6	0	4	1	.333	.333	.455
Leading Off Inn.			81	20	1	2	9	.247	.333	.265
Runners On			125	42	2	14	9	.336	.448	.397
Runners/Scor. Pos.			77	25	1	11	6	.325	.442	.394
Runners On/2 Out			60	22	2	6	3	.367	.567	.424
Scor. Pos./2 Out			39	14	1	5	1	.359	.538	.432
Late Inning Pressure			13	5	0	2	3	.385	.462	.467
Leading Off			4	1	0	0	0	.250	.250	.250
Runners On			4	2	0	1	2	.500	.500	.600
Runners/Scor. Pos.			3	2	0	1	1	.667	.667	.750
First 9 Batters			126	38	2	12	14	.302	.389	.366
Second 9 Batters			114	33	1	10	16	.289	.368	.344
All Batters Thereafter			69	17	2	4	8	.246	.435	.280

Loves to face: Jody Davis (0-for-14)
Hates to face: Will Clark (.615, 8-for-13, 1 HR)
Ground outs-to-air outs ratio: 1.00 last season, 0.96 for career. . . .
Additional statistics: 5 double-play ground outs in 58 opportunities, 12 doubles, 3 triples in 78.2 innings last season. . . . Allowed 12 first-inning runs in 16 starts. . . . Batting support: 3.25 runs per start. . . . Two of his three victories were recorded in back-to-back starts against the Expos. . . . Pitched 70 games in 1986, all in relief. Split time in 1987: 18 starts, 30 relief appearances. Pitched only once in relief last season, while starting 16 times. . . . Only pitcher whose left-handed opponents have outhit right-handers by more than 50 points in each of last four seasons. His smallest difference was 69 points. Career averages: .297 by left-handed batters, .223 by right-handers.

Bruce Ruffin

Philadelphia Phillies — Throws Left

	W–L	ERA	AB	H	HR	BB	SO	BA	SA	OBA
Season	6-10	4.43	550	151	7	80	82	.275	.376	.368
vs. Left-Handers			124	34	0	28	23	.274	.339	.412
vs. Right-Handers			426	117	7	52	59	.275	.387	.354
Home	3-5	3.75	301	80	5	40	44	.266	.372	.353
Road	3-5	5.31	249	71	2	40	38	.285	.382	.386
Grass	2-4	5.59	149	41	2	29	21	.275	.389	.394
Artificial Turf	4-6	4.00	401	110	5	51	61	.274	.372	.357
April	2-1	4.68	96	27	3	7	12	.281	.469	.327
May	2-3	2.43	142	36	0	14	18	.254	.310	.318
June	1-2	5.16	127	40	1	9	20	.315	.417	.365
July	1-2	4.50	95	25	2	17	16	.263	.389	.375
August	0-2	8.56	56	16	0	23	9	.286	.304	.494
Sept./Oct.	0-0	3.86	34	7	1	10	7	.206	.324	.404
Leading Off Inn.			130	37	0	19	20	.285	.377	.384
Runners On			254	74	4	44	33	.291	.394	.394
Runners/Scor. Pos.			140	46	2	32	14	.329	.443	.449
Runners On/2 Out			100	30	2	20	6	.300	.400	.417
Scor. Pos./2 Out			59	17	1	16	2	.288	.390	.440
Late Inning Pressure			110	30	1	26	19	.273	.355	.413
Leading Off			24	6	0	7	6	.250	.292	.438
Runners On			57	16	0	13	8	.281	.333	.408
Runners/Scor. Pos.			29	10	0	11	3	.345	.414	.512
First 9 Batters			307	81	5	54	56	.264	.365	.378
Second 9 Batters			126	37	1	16	15	.294	.381	.368
All Batters Thereafter			117	33	1	10	11	.282	.402	.339

Loves to face: Dave Anderson (0-for-7)
Hates to face: Pedro Guerrero (.833, 5-for-6)
Ground outs-to-air outs ratio: 2.47 last season, 2.45 for career. . . .
Additional statistics: 20 double-play ground outs in 144 opportunities, 31 doubles, 2 triples in 144.1 innings last season. . . . Allowed 6 first-inning runs in 15 starts. . . . Batting support: 2.93 runs per start, 4th lowest in N.L. (minimum: 15 GS). . . . Hasn't allowed a home run to a left-hander since April 19, 1987. . . . Faced 151 leadoff batters, most of any pitcher in the majors who didn't allow a HR. . . . First 70 career appearances, including 14 last season, were starts. But he appeared only in relief after the All-Star break. Record of 4–6 (4.18 ERA) in 15 starts, 2–4 (4.88) in 40 relief appearances. . . . Opposing fly-ball hitters have outhit ground-ballers by 64 points (.310 to .246).

Nolan Ryan

Houston Astros — Throws Right

	W–L	ERA	AB	H	HR	BB	SO	BA	SA	OBA
Season	12-11	3.52	818	186	18	87	228	.227	.347	.304
vs. Left-Handers			438	94	8	57	115	.215	.315	.301
vs. Right-Handers			380	92	10	30	113	.242	.384	.308
Home	7-4	2.91	388	83	8	36	105	.214	.340	.284
Road	5-7	4.08	430	103	10	51	123	.240	.353	.322
Grass	4-5	3.82	269	65	8	34	76	.242	.379	.327
Artificial Turf	8-6	3.38	549	121	10	53	152	.220	.332	.293
April	2-1	2.68	130	23	3	13	45	.177	.292	.247
May	3-1	3.86	142	34	2	18	32	.239	.324	.337
June	0-4	6.95	136	38	6	21	41	.279	.478	.381
July	3-1	2.80	136	33	0	19	28	.243	.331	.335
August	1-4	3.42	182	45	5	13	50	.247	.385	.297
Sept./Oct.	3-0	1.00	92	13	2	3	32	.141	.217	.168
Leading Off Inn.			206	55	7	17	58	.267	.422	.326
Runners On			365	80	5	35	93	.219	.304	.291
Runners/Scor. Pos.			234	47	2	29	67	.201	.261	.293
Runners On/2 Out			147	29	2	12	38	.197	.279	.272
Scor. Pos./2 Out			107	24	2	10	29	.224	.318	.308
Late Inning Pressure			75	14	2	9	24	.187	.347	.282
Leading Off			20	2	2	2	5	.100	.400	.182
Runners On			31	7	0	2	13	.226	.290	.294
Runners/Scor. Pos.			20	5	0	2	10	.250	.350	.348
First 9 Batters			255	55	2	32	73	.216	.286	.303
Second 9 Batters			256	54	6	21	70	.211	.324	.276
All Batters Thereafter			307	77	10	34	85	.251	.417	.328

Loves to face: Chet Lemon (.125, 4-for-32, 16 SO)
Hates to face: Ron Hassey (.429, 3-for-7, 1 HR)
Ground outs-to-air outs ratio: 0.99 last season, 1.09 for career. . . .
Additional statistics: 7 double-play ground outs in 154 opportunities, 36 doubles, 4 triples in 220.0 innings last season. . . . Allowed 16 first-inning runs in 33 starts. . . . Batting support: 3.88 runs per start. . . . Pitched four complete games last season, compared to one over the previous two years. Completed consecutive starts for first time since August 1983. . . . Has reached double figures in wins in 17 of the last 18 seasons. He won the ERA title in the only year he missed. . . . Only pitcher in major league history within 20 wins, 20 losses, and 20 ERA points of Ryan is Hall of Famer Eppa Rixey. . . . Youth is relative: Ryan is four days older than Vice President Quayle.

Calvin Schiraldi

Chicago Cubs — Throws Right

	W–L	ERA	AB	H	HR	BB	SO	BA	SA	OBA
Season	9-13	4.38	646	166	13	63	140	.257	.381	.323
vs. Left-Handers			362	108	8	40	62	.298	.439	.368
vs. Right-Handers			284	58	5	23	78	.204	.306	.265
Home	3-7	5.18	298	89	9	25	70	.299	.453	.356
Road	6-6	3.73	348	77	4	38	70	.221	.319	.296
Grass	7-9	4.19	477	127	10	41	115	.266	.388	.325
Artificial Turf	2-4	4.91	169	39	3	22	25	.231	.361	.318
April	1-2	6.27	78	23	5	13	16	.295	.538	.391
May	2-0	2.89	77	21	2	4	14	.273	.416	.317
June	1-4	3.82	128	30	2	15	32	.234	.328	.317
July	2-2	3.44	124	24	2	12	23	.194	.282	.265
August	2-1	3.42	103	27	0	11	27	.262	.330	.328
Sept./Oct.	1-4	6.48	136	41	2	8	28	.301	.449	.340
Leading Off Inn.			165	36	4	11	36	.218	.309	.275
Runners On			257	75	7	28	49	.292	.467	.356
Runners/Scor. Pos.			152	41	3	18	34	.270	.401	.339
Runners On/2 Out			109	24	1	10	23	.220	.321	.286
Scor. Pos./2 Out			69	15	0	5	18	.217	.275	.270
Late Inning Pressure			40	8	0	2	11	.200	.225	.238
Leading Off			12	4	0	0	3	.333	.417	.333
Runners On			13	3	0	1	3	.231	.231	.286
Runners/Scor. Pos.			11	1	0	1	3	.091	.091	.167
First 9 Batters			232	58	3	23	62	.250	.336	.315
Second 9 Batters			221	55	5	22	48	.249	.398	.320
All Batters Thereafter			193	53	5	18	30	.275	.415	.336

Loves to face: Darryl Strawberry (0-for-10)
Hates to face: Bobby Bonilla (.545, 6-for-11, 2 HR)
Ground outs-to-air outs ratio: 0.82 last season, 0.80 for career. . . .
Additional statistics: 5 double-play ground outs in 108 opportunities, 29 doubles, 6 triples in 166.1 innings last season. . . . Allowed 14 first-inning runs in 27 starts. . . . Batting support: 4.30 runs per start. . . . Won three consecutive starts (July 23–Aug. 4), including a 3-hit shutout of the Phillies. That shutout is one of only two complete games in 35 career starts. . . . Started only one game for Boston over the previous two seasons, but started 27 times for Chicago in 1988. . . . Opponents hit 90 points higher against Schiraldi at Wrigley Field last season than at Fenway Park in 1987. . . . Opponents' career strikeout rate: 25 percent on his first pass through batting order, 17 percent after that.

Mike Scott

Houston Astros — Throws Right

	W–L	ERA	AB	H	HR	BB	SO	BA	SA	OBA
Season	14-8	2.92	793	162	19	53	190	.204	.325	.260
vs. Left-Handers			405	75	10	39	89	.185	.311	.260
vs. Right-Handers			388	87	9	14	101	.224	.340	.260
Home	7-3	2.09	349	66	4	24	93	.189	.266	.248
Road	7-5	3.61	444	96	15	29	97	.216	.372	.269
Grass	3-3	4.06	230	50	8	15	47	.217	.370	.269
Artificial Turf	11-5	2.47	563	112	11	38	143	.199	.307	.256
April	4-0	1.94	144	25	3	11	43	.174	.278	.250
May	2-1	3.89	146	36	2	9	37	.247	.322	.288
June	2-1	3.18	104	19	4	8	22	.183	.346	.254
July	2-1	2.73	109	19	2	8	27	.174	.303	.231
August	3-1	1.54	150	32	2	5	30	.213	.287	.244
Sept./Oct.	1-4	4.42	140	31	6	12	31	.221	.421	.284
Leading Off Inn.			205	47	4	13	50	.229	.356	.285
Runners On			285	59	8	18	71	.207	.347	.260
Runners/Scor. Pos.			170	30	4	13	45	.176	.306	.238
Runners On/2 Out			124	22	2	9	33	.177	.290	.244
Scor. Pos./2 Out			82	16	2	6	26	.195	.354	.258
Late Inning Pressure			106	17	1	8	22	.160	.226	.231
Leading Off			29	5	0	2	5	.172	.207	.226
Runners On			31	6	1	4	6	.194	.323	.316
Runners/Scor. Pos.			25	5	1	4	5	.200	.360	.344
First 9 Batters			258	57	7	15	57	.221	.357	.269
Second 9 Batters			244	50	6	15	69	.205	.311	.252
All Batters Thereafter			291	55	6	23	64	.189	.309	.259

Loves to face: Andy Van Slyke (.036, 1-for-28)
Hates to face: Keith Hernandez (.377, 23-for-61, 6 HR)
Ground outs-to-air outs ratio: 1.04 last season, 1.17 for career. . . .
Additional statistics: 7 double-play ground outs in 122 opportunities, 23 doubles, 8 triples in 218.2 innings last season. . . . Allowed 17 first-inning runs in 32 starts. . . . Batting support: 4.25 runs per start. . . . Lost four consecutive starts in September. . . . Hadn't lost two in a row since 1984. . . . Struck out seven of 11 batters faced with bases loaded. . . . Batting average of opposing lefties was lowest of his career. . . . Strikeouts per nine innings, year by year since 1986: 10.00, 8.47, 7.82. . . . Career records: 23–36 on grass, 72–47 on rugs. . . . Opponents' average in LIP Situations below .200 in three of last four seasons; was above .300 in each of his first six seasons.

Eric Show

San Diego Padres — Throws Right

	W–L	ERA	AB	H	HR	BB	SO	BA	SA	OBA
Season	16-11	3.26	869	201	22	53	144	.231	.360	.279
vs. Left-Handers			462	117	10	43	64	.253	.392	.316
vs. Right-Handers			407	84	12	10	80	.206	.324	.234
Home	8-5	2.85	464	107	11	30	83	.231	.343	.279
Road	8-6	3.74	405	94	11	23	61	.232	.380	.279
Grass	12-11	3.57	745	180	20	48	125	.242	.377	.290
Artificial Turf	4-0	1.53	124	21	2	5	19	.169	.258	.208
April	1-3	5.09	88	28	3	6	10	.318	.466	.381
May	2-2	2.51	156	34	1	16	26	.218	.295	.295
June	3-3	4.54	148	34	6	10	25	.230	.399	.277
July	1-2	3.03	147	35	5	6	25	.238	.381	.273
August	4-1	2.05	178	39	3	7	26	.219	.337	.251
Sept./Oct.	5-0	3.43	152	31	4	8	32	.204	.336	.239
Leading Off Inn.			231	54	4	8	44	.234	.329	.259
Runners On			293	68	6	36	39	.232	.358	.320
Runners/Scor. Pos.			165	39	5	24	22	.236	.412	.332
Runners On/2 Out			127	34	4	18	15	.268	.457	.367
Scor. Pos./2 Out			82	23	3	15	8	.280	.512	.398
Late Inning Pressure			99	26	3	7	14	.263	.404	.324
Leading Off			28	9	1	0	4	.321	.464	.321
Runners On			32	6	1	6	3	.188	.313	.333
Runners/Scor. Pos.			23	5	0	3	2	.217	.261	.308
First 9 Batters			263	61	10	19	51	.232	.403	.284
Second 9 Batters			269	56	6	13	41	.208	.305	.253
All Batters Thereafter			337	84	6	21	52	.249	.371	.295

Loves to face: Ryne Sandberg (.122, 6-for-49)
Hates to face: Paul O'Neill (.750, 6-for-8, 1 HR)
Ground outs-to-air outs ratio: 1.18 last season, 0.98 for career. . . .
Additional statistics: 21 double-play ground outs in 140 opportunities, 36 doubles, 5 triples in 234.2 innings last season. . . . Allowed 20 first-inning runs in 32 starts. . . . Batting support: 3.59 runs per start. . . . Averaged 7.33 innings per start, 5th highest mark in N.L. (minimum: 15 GS). . . . Completed eight of his last 11 starts, and 13 for the season. Hadn't completed more than five starts in any previous year. . . . Retired leadoff batters in 27 consecutive innings (Aug. 2–19), longest streak of 1988. Streak was broken by a Sid Fernandez single. . . . Opponents' career average of .143 (11-for-77) with the bases loaded. . . . Career records: 16–3 vs. Atlanta, 70–70 vs. better teams.

John Smiley

Pittsburgh Pirates — Throws Left

	W–L	ERA	AB	H	HR	BB	SO	BA	SA	OBA
Season	13-11	3.25	767	185	15	46	129	.241	.355	.284
vs. Left-Handers			107	17	2	13	24	.159	.243	.252
vs. Right-Handers			660	168	13	33	105	.255	.373	.290
Home	5-6	3.61	327	78	4	24	46	.239	.352	.291
Road	8-5	2.98	440	107	11	22	83	.243	.357	.279
Grass	5-3	3.26	212	48	9	14	44	.226	.363	.278
Artificial Turf	8-8	3.24	555	137	6	32	85	.247	.351	.286
April	1-2	3.86	95	26	3	6	15	.274	.442	.324
May	3-2	2.81	156	36	1	10	22	.231	.301	.275
June	4-0	2.25	131	25	2	6	29	.191	.282	.226
July	1-3	3.03	127	25	2	14	30	.197	.299	.273
August	1-2	4.08	108	32	3	7	14	.296	.435	.339
Sept./Oct.	3-2	3.86	150	41	4	3	19	.273	.407	.286
Leading Off Inn.			197	47	4	11	30	.239	.360	.282
Runners On			297	82	6	18	43	.276	.404	.312
Runners/Scor. Pos.			175	49	4	16	25	.280	.417	.330
Runners On/2 Out			126	31	1	8	22	.246	.325	.291
Scor. Pos./2 Out			83	21	1	8	17	.253	.337	.319
Late Inning Pressure			85	18	2	2	7	.212	.318	.227
Leading Off			26	7	1	1	3	.269	.385	.296
Runners On			21	5	0	1	0	.238	.333	.261
Runners/Scor. Pos.			10	1	0	1	0	.100	.300	.167
First 9 Batters			264	58	5	20	55	.220	.326	.274
Second 9 Batters			252	65	4	14	45	.258	.393	.300
All Batters Thereafter			251	62	6	12	29	.247	.347	.278

Loves to face: Will Clark (0-for-13)
Hates to face: Andre Dawson (.643, 9-for-14, 2 HR)
Ground outs-to-air outs ratio: 1.03 last season, 1.10 for career. . . .
Additional statistics: 16 double-play ground outs in 137 opportunities, 34 doubles, 4 triples in 205.0 innings last season. . . . Allowed 11 first-inning runs in 32 starts. . . . Batting support: 3.47 runs per start. . . . Made 75 appearances prior to 1988, all in relief. Had never pitched more than three innings in a game when he made first major league start on April 10. . . . ERA of 3.75 over the first five innings of his starts, 1.73 thereafter. . . . Phillies batted .420 (29-for-69) against him. . . . Opponents' career average is .272 with runners on, .214 with bases empty. . . . Opposing fly-ball hitters have outhit ground-ballers, .254 to .217. . . . Has never committed an error (60 chances).

Bryn Smith
Montreal Expos — Throws Right

	W-L	ERA	AB	H	HR	BB	SO	BA	SA	OBA
Season	12-10	3.00	736	179	15	32	122	.243	.356	.282
vs. Left-Handers			378	98	6	20	52	.259	.360	.300
vs. Right-Handers			358	81	9	12	70	.226	.352	.263
Home	7-2	2.37	324	74	6	18	57	.228	.355	.277
Road	5-8	3.50	412	105	9	14	65	.255	.357	.286
Grass	2-6	4.31	238	68	8	7	37	.286	.412	.311
Artificial Turf	10-4	2.39	498	111	7	25	85	.223	.329	.268
April	0-2	4.68	94	22	4	3	16	.234	.415	.263
May	3-2	3.79	133	39	4	3	19	.293	.444	.319
June	2-1	4.06	122	34	1	5	17	.279	.352	.310
July	2-1	1.32	115	18	4	7	26	.157	.278	.205
August	2-2	2.35	146	38	1	5	20	.260	.329	.292
Sept./Oct.	3-2	2.38	126	28	1	9	24	.222	.325	.288
Leading Off Inn.			191	48	6	7	32	.251	.382	.285
Runners On			273	67	7	10	40	.245	.374	.281
Runners/Scor. Pos.			154	40	6	9	25	.260	.448	.298
Runners On/2 Out			108	19	2	5	19	.176	.287	.226
Scor. Pos./2 Out			67	13	2	5	12	.194	.373	.260
Late Inning Pressure			40	13	1	3	4	.325	.500	.372
Leading Off			10	2	0	0	1	.200	.200	.200
Runners On			19	6	1	1	3	.316	.579	.350
Runners/Scor. Pos.			11	3	1	1	3	.273	.727	.333
First 9 Batters			260	61	6	16	49	.235	.354	.289
Second 9 Batters			273	61	2	7	46	.223	.300	.245
All Batters Thereafter			203	57	7	9	27	.281	.433	.321

Loves to face: Ryne Sandberg (.098, 5-for-51)
Hates to face: Franklin Stubbs (.500, 8-for-16, 4 HR)
Ground outs-to-air outs ratio: 1.49 last season, 1.74 for career. . . .
Additional statistics: 22 double-play ground outs in 131 opportunities, 22 doubles, 8 triples in 198.0 innings last season. . . . Allowed 22 first-inning runs (4th most in N.L.) in 32 starts. . . . Batting support: 4.22 runs per start. . . . Allowed 1.45 walks per nine innings last season, lowest rate in majors. . . . Among active pitchers with 1000 innings in their careers, only Saberhagen (1.81) and Candelaria (2.18) have allowed fewer walks per nine innings than Smith (2.18). . . . Batting average of opposing left-handers was the same in 1987 and 1988, but right-handers dropped 69 points from .295 in 1987. . . . Career records: 12-2 vs. Atlanta, 59-58 vs. the rest of the league.

Dave Smith
Houston Astros — Throws Right

	W-L	ERA	AB	H	HR	BB	SO	BA	SA	OBA
Season	4-5	2.67	224	60	1	19	38	.268	.353	.327
vs. Left-Handers			98	30	0	10	11	.306	.357	.367
vs. Right-Handers			126	30	1	9	27	.238	.349	.294
Home	3-3	2.70	118	33	0	8	24	.280	.356	.325
Road	1-2	2.63	106	27	1	11	14	.255	.349	.328
Grass	1-1	1.56	66	15	0	4	12	.227	.273	.278
Artificial Turf	3-4	3.15	158	45	1	15	26	.285	.386	.347
April	1-1	2.00	33	6	0	2	6	.182	.182	.229
May	0-1	3.60	40	10	0	5	8	.250	.375	.333
June	2-2	2.79	44	17	0	7	10	.386	.500	.471
July	1-1	3.12	30	6	1	3	1	.200	.433	.294
August	0-0	0.00	25	3	0	0	3	.120	.120	.115
Sept./Oct.	0-0	3.65	52	18	0	2	10	.346	.385	.370
Leading Off Inn.			45	13	0	4	6	.289	.333	.360
Runners On			120	33	1	12	20	.275	.358	.338
Runners/Scor. Pos.			84	23	1	12	14	.274	.393	.361
Runners On/2 Out			53	13	1	6	8	.245	.340	.322
Scor. Pos./2 Out			43	11	1	6	6	.256	.372	.347
Late Inning Pressure			176	45	1	15	31	.256	.341	.314
Leading Off			38	10	0	4	6	.263	.316	.333
Runners On			89	24	1	8	15	.270	.348	.330
Runners/Scor. Pos.			63	15	1	8	10	.238	.349	.324
First 9 Batters			216	56	1	17	36	.259	.347	.315
Second 9 Batters			8	4	0	2	2	.500	.500	.600
All Batters Thereafter			0	0	0	0	0	—	—	—

Loves to face: Gary Carter (.063, 1-for-16)
Hates to face: Keith Hernandez (.600, 9-for-15)
Ground outs-to-air outs ratio: 1.93 last season, 1.44 for career. . . .
Additional statistics: 4 double-play ground outs in 58 opportunities, 10 doubles, 3 triples in 57.1 innings last season. . . . Made major league debut with Houston on April 11, 1980. At the end of 1988 he had the longest continuous service with his original major league club of any active N.L. pitcher. . . . Allowed seven runs, all unearned, in 0.2 innings pitched against the Braves on June 10. Had those runs been earned, his 1988 ERA would have been 3.77, not 2.67. . . . Hasn't allowed a home run in the Astrodome since July 1986. . . . Opposing left-handed batters, year by year since 1986: .167, .204, .306. . . . Opponents' batting average leading off innings was highest of his career.

Pete Smith
Atlanta Braves — Throws Right

	W-L	ERA	AB	H	HR	BB	SO	BA	SA	OBA
Season	7-15	3.69	732	183	15	88	124	.250	.376	.330
vs. Left-Handers			413	117	9	56	66	.283	.424	.366
vs. Right-Handers			319	66	6	32	58	.207	.313	.281
Home	6-9	3.46	464	110	10	57	77	.237	.375	.318
Road	1-6	4.09	268	73	5	31	47	.272	.377	.350
Grass	7-11	3.45	584	141	12	75	103	.241	.370	.326
Artificial Turf	0-4	4.66	148	42	3	13	21	.284	.399	.346
April	1-1	3.46	97	23	3	12	13	.237	.392	.321
May	0-4	6.21	133	39	2	18	23	.293	.436	.379
June	1-3	6.41	109	32	4	19	21	.294	.486	.395
July	1-3	2.70	134	32	5	19	21	.239	.373	.331
August	4-2	2.05	163	37	1	9	31	.227	.301	.266
Sept./Oct.	0-2	2.20	96	20	0	11	15	.208	.281	.290
Leading Off Inn.			190	42	3	14	32	.221	.342	.275
Runners On			278	72	5	43	45	.259	.396	.356
Runners/Scor. Pos.			178	43	3	32	36	.242	.360	.350
Runners On/2 Out			144	40	1	16	23	.278	.382	.350
Scor. Pos./2 Out			95	24	1	15	18	.253	.389	.355
Late Inning Pressure			62	20	1	7	5	.323	.484	.386
Leading Off			18	7	0	3	3	.389	.611	.476
Runners On			19	6	1	4	1	.316	.526	.417
Runners/Scor. Pos.			9	4	1	3	1	.444	.889	.538
First 9 Batters			256	62	4	30	58	.242	.332	.322
Second 9 Batters			246	63	7	25	45	.256	.419	.325
All Batters Thereafter			230	58	4	33	21	.252	.378	.343

Loves to face: Ryne Sandberg (0-for-12)
Hates to face: Mike Marshall (.800, 8-for-10, 1 HR)
Ground outs-to-air outs ratio: 0.80 last season, 0.81 for career. . . .
Additional statistics: 6 double-play ground outs in 103 opportunities, 37 doubles, 5 triples in 195.1 innings last season. . . . Allowed 12 first-inning runs in 32 starts. . . . Batting support: 3.03 runs per start, 6th lowest in N.L. (minimum: 15 GS). . . . Tied for major league lead among rookies in games started and losses, and led that group with five complete games and three shutouts. Led N.L. rookies in innings pitched. . . . Ranked 9th in N.L. with a 2.27 ERA after the All-Star break. . . . Didn't allow a home run in his last 55.2 innings. . . . Didn't allow a run in 25 innings against the Cubs, pitching shutouts against them in back-to-back starts (Aug. 21–26).

Zane Smith
Atlanta Braves — Throws Left

	W-L	ERA	AB	H	HR	BB	SO	BA	SA	OBA
Season	5-10	4.30	545	159	8	44	59	.292	.374	.347
vs. Left-Handers			84	20	0	7	11	.238	.262	.297
vs. Right-Handers			461	139	8	37	48	.302	.395	.356
Home	2-5	3.46	291	81	5	22	26	.278	.364	.330
Road	3-5	5.26	254	78	3	22	33	.307	.386	.366
Grass	5-7	3.19	447	120	5	34	49	.268	.329	.322
Artificial Turf	0-3	10.23	98	39	3	10	10	.398	.582	.455
April	1-3	3.55	126	33	1	6	14	.262	.333	.301
May	1-0	4.76	124	42	0	7	15	.339	.387	.374
June	1-2	2.77	93	25	2	9	11	.269	.344	.337
July	1-3	6.48	104	35	3	14	5	.337	.462	.412
August	1-2	4.18	98	24	2	8	14	.245	.347	.308
Sept./Oct.			0	0	0	0	0	—	—	—
Leading Off Inn.			132	33	2	9	12	.250	.311	.303
Runners On			249	75	4	19	31	.301	.394	.351
Runners/Scor. Pos.			150	47	3	12	21	.313	.407	.364
Runners On/2 Out			104	23	0	11	13	.221	.231	.302
Scor. Pos./2 Out			69	15	0	8	8	.217	.217	.308
Late Inning Pressure			64	17	0	5	8	.266	.281	.319
Leading Off			15	3	0	2	1	.200	.200	.294
Runners On			31	7	0	2	5	.226	.258	.273
Runners/Scor. Pos.			18	3	0	2	4	.167	.222	.250
First 9 Batters			180	59	3	16	16	.328	.433	.384
Second 9 Batters			175	46	3	11	24	.263	.349	.314
All Batters Thereafter			190	54	2	17	19	.284	.342	.341

Loves to face: Howard Johnson (.071, 1-for-14)
Hates to face: Junior Ortiz (.636, 7-for-11)
Ground outs-to-air outs ratio: 1.81 last season, 1.99 for career. . . .
Additional statistics: 18 double-play ground outs in 120 opportunities, 21 doubles, 0 triples in 140.1 innings last season. . . . Allowed 16 first-inning runs in 22 starts. . . . Batting support: 3.05 runs per start. . . . ERA of 6.02 during the first two innings of his starts last season, 3.28 thereafter. . . . Career ERAs, year by year: 2.25, 3.80, 4.05, 4.09, 4.30. . . . Career average of one home run per 18.9 innings, the best ever among Atlanta Braves pitchers (minimum: 500 IP). Second best: Carl Morton (one HR per 17.9 IP). . . . First home run he allowed in the majors was hit by Greg Brock. Since then 38 of 39 have been hit by right-handers. Last HR by a left-hander: August 21, 1987, by Barry Bonds.

Mario Soto

Cincinnati Reds — Throws Right

	W–L	ERA	AB	H	HR	BB	SO	BA	SA	OBA
Season	3-7	4.66	330	88	8	28	34	.267	.397	.326
vs. Left-Handers			173	50	2	15	17	.289	.399	.342
vs. Right-Handers			157	38	6	13	17	.242	.395	.308
Home	1-1	4.99	118	32	5	12	13	.271	.449	.344
Road	2-6	4.47	212	56	3	16	21	.264	.368	.316
Grass	1-4	5.28	122	36	3	8	8	.295	.426	.338
Artificial Turf	2-3	4.31	208	52	5	20	26	.250	.380	.319
April	1-1	2.94	124	31	2	10	16	.250	.363	.309
May	2-3	4.69	147	35	2	13	16	.238	.340	.298
June	0-3	9.00	59	22	4	5	2	.373	.610	.431
July			0	0	0	0	0	—	—	—
August			0	0	0	0	0	—	—	—
Sept./Oct.			0	0	0	0	0	—	—	—
Leading Off Inn.			85	21	0	5	9	.247	.306	.289
Runners On			135	40	6	13	15	.296	.496	.358
Runners/Scor. Pos.			82	25	4	10	9	.305	.512	.379
Runners On/2 Out			57	17	5	5	6	.298	.614	.355
Scor. Pos./2 Out			38	12	3	4	4	.316	.579	.381
Late Inning Pressure			19	8	0	1	1	.421	.526	.429
Leading Off			7	2	0	0	1	.286	.429	.286
Runners On			6	6	0	0	0	1.000	1.167	.857
Runners/Scor. Pos.			3	3	0	0	0	1.000	1.000	.750
First 9 Batters			108	32	3	11	9	.296	.454	.364
Second 9 Batters			108	26	4	10	15	.241	.389	.311
All Batters Thereafter			114	30	1	7	10	.263	.351	.303

Loves to face: Ryne Sandberg (.149, 7-for-47, 1 HR)
Hates to face: Will Clark (.700, 7-for-10, 2 HR)
Ground outs-to-air outs ratio: 1.05 last season, 0.85 for career. . . .
Additional statistics: 6 double-play ground outs in 55 opportunities, 13 doubles, 3 triples in 87.0 innings last season. . . . Allowed 11 first-inning runs in 14 starts. . . . Batting support: 3.86 runs per start. . . . His record was the worst of any pitcher who started on opening day in 1988. But only four of the 12 opening-day N.L. starters had winning records, and only two of the 12 led their teams in victories. . . . Lost his last five starts before being released by the Reds. . . . Was signed by Los Angeles, but immediately placed on the disabled list, where he spent the rest of the season. . . . Lost his last seven decisions vs. the Dodgers. Maybe they wanted him to pitch batting practice.

Rick Sutcliffe

Chicago Cubs — Throws Right

	W–L	ERA	AB	H	HR	BB	SO	BA	SA	OBA
Season	13-14	3.86	864	232	18	70	144	.269	.388	.323
vs. Left-Handers			456	120	7	46	62	.263	.371	.329
vs. Right-Handers			408	112	11	24	82	.275	.407	.317
Home	5-5	3.19	390	102	8	35	70	.262	.362	.322
Road	8-9	4.42	474	130	10	35	74	.274	.409	.324
Grass	8-9	3.80	588	160	15	53	100	.272	.391	.333
Artificial Turf	5-5	4.00	276	72	3	17	44	.261	.380	.302
April	1-3	4.53	179	51	6	13	29	.285	.441	.332
May	2-1	5.79	88	23	4	14	15	.261	.432	.363
June	3-1	3.28	94	27	1	8	19	.287	.362	.340
July	2-4	2.76	161	43	2	15	28	.267	.360	.333
August	3-2	2.64	176	40	1	10	24	.227	.301	.273
Sept./Oct.	2-3	4.89	166	48	4	10	29	.289	.440	.324
Leading Off Inn.			225	55	5	6	30	.244	.387	.264
Runners On			330	95	5	43	58	.288	.397	.368
Runners/Scor. Pos.			204	52	3	33	43	.255	.353	.354
Runners On/2 Out			150	39	2	22	25	.260	.333	.355
Scor. Pos./2 Out			96	20	1	17	19	.208	.271	.327
Late Inning Pressure			105	26	1	9	12	.248	.314	.307
Leading Off			31	5	0	0	2	.161	.161	.161
Runners On			31	7	0	8	4	.226	.258	.385
Runners/Scor. Pos.			20	4	0	5	4	.200	.250	.360
First 9 Batters			260	65	6	19	53	.250	.365	.301
Second 9 Batters			256	71	8	21	51	.277	.445	.332
All Batters Thereafter			348	96	4	30	40	.276	.362	.332

Loves to face: Gary Carter (.125, 5-for-40, 1 HR)
Hates to face: Von Hayes (.523, 23-for-44, 3 HR)
Ground outs-to-air outs ratio: 1.19 last season, 0.93 for career. . . .
Additional statistics: 12 double-play ground outs in 137 opportunities, 45 doubles, 2 triples in 226.0 innings last season. . . . Allowed 14 first-inning runs in 32 starts. . . . Batting support: 4.03 runs per start. . . . Allowed 97 runs last season, the 2d highest total ever without any scored as unearned. Dick Ruthven allowed 112 runs, all earned, in 1976. . . . Never won more than two consecutive decisions last season. . . . Record of 44–46 since his Cy Young season for Cubs in 1984. . . . Pitchers within 20 wins, 20 losses, and 20 ERA points of Sutcliffe at comparable ages: Doyle Alexander, Mike Flanagan, Mudcat Grant, Ross Grimsley, Pat Malone, Scott McGregor, Doc Medich, Charlie Root.

Bruce Sutter

Atlanta Braves — Throws Right

	W–L	ERA	AB	H	HR	BB	SO	BA	SA	OBA
Season	1-4	4.76	178	49	4	11	40	.275	.382	.321
vs. Left-Handers			99	27	2	4	24	.273	.343	.301
vs. Right-Handers			79	22	2	7	16	.278	.430	.345
Home	0-2	4.38	92	25	2	4	20	.272	.359	.302
Road	1-2	5.23	86	24	2	7	20	.279	.407	.340
Grass	0-2	3.98	119	30	2	5	25	.252	.319	.282
Artificial Turf	1-2	6.59	59	19	2	6	15	.322	.508	.394
April	1-0	3.24	29	6	0	2	8	.207	.310	.258
May	0-1	1.80	57	14	1	5	14	.246	.351	.306
June	0-1	4.50	31	8	0	0	5	.258	.258	.258
July	0-1	7.88	34	11	2	2	10	.324	.500	.378
August	0-1	21.00	17	9	1	2	2	.529	.765	.579
Sept./Oct.	0-0	0.00	10	1	0	0	1	.100	.100	.100
Leading Off Inn.			38	10	1	5	4	.263	.421	.349
Runners On			81	29	3	5	22	.358	.506	.402
Runners/Scor. Pos.			56	22	2	5	14	.393	.536	.443
Runners On/2 Out			26	5	2	2	12	.192	.423	.250
Scor. Pos./2 Out			20	4	2	2	8	.200	.500	.273
Late Inning Pressure			132	40	2	8	30	.303	.394	.348
Leading Off			28	10	1	3	3	.357	.571	.419
Runners On			64	23	1	4	17	.359	.453	.406
Runners/Scor. Pos.			43	18	0	4	10	.419	.465	.468
First 9 Batters			178	49	4	11	40	.275	.382	.321
Second 9 Batters			0	0	0	0	0	—	—	—
All Batters Thereafter			0	0	0	0	0	—	—	—

Loves to face: Dickie Thon (0-for-11)
Hates to face: Gary Redus (.667, 4-for-6)
Ground outs-to-air outs ratio: 1.94 last season, 1.95 for career. . . .
Additional statistics: 5 double-play ground outs in 42 opportunities, 5 doubles, 1 triple in 45.1 innings last season. . . . Faced 110 batters while protecting leads of three runs or fewer in the 8th inning or later. Other Braves relievers: Assenmacher, 43; Puleo, 23; Alvarez, 17. . . . Had 12 saves at the All-Star break, only two thereafter. . . . Allowed hits in six consecutive at-bats in LIP Situations (June 19–24). . . . Had his best strikeout-to-walk ratio since 1977, his 2d year in the majors. . . . Allowed 12 hits in last 19 at-bats with bases loaded. . . . Hasn't thrown a wild pitch since 1984, or committed a balk since 1983. . . . Record of 2–0 with two saves in his four All-Star games.

Don Sutton

Los Angeles Dodgers — Throws Right

	W–L	ERA	AB	H	HR	BB	SO	BA	SA	OBA
Season	3-6	3.92	337	91	7	30	44	.270	.374	.327
vs. Left-Handers			172	50	4	22	25	.291	.401	.367
vs. Right-Handers			165	41	3	8	19	.248	.345	.282
Home	2-3	3.27	158	42	2	18	22	.266	.342	.341
Road	1-3	4.50	179	49	5	12	22	.274	.402	.314
Grass	2-5	3.47	238	67	2	26	30	.282	.353	.349
Artificial Turf	1-1	5.04	99	24	5	4	14	.242	.424	.269
April	1-2	2.86	85	23	1	6	12	.271	.353	.319
May	2-1	4.68	133	38	4	7	15	.286	.436	.317
June	0-2	3.16	92	23	0	14	12	.250	.261	.345
July			0	0	0	0	0	—	—	—
August	0-1	6.43	27	7	2	3	5	.259	.519	.333
Sept./Oct.			0	0	0	0	0			
Leading Off Inn.			87	33	2	6	9	.379	.506	.419
Runners On			149	34	3	16	19	.228	.315	.298
Runners/Scor. Pos.			91	18	1	14	14	.198	.253	.291
Runners On/2 Out			59	13	1	9	9	.220	.305	.324
Scor. Pos./2 Out			45	9	1	8	7	.200	.267	.321
Late Inning Pressure			0	0	0	0	0	—	—	—
Leading Off			0	0	0	0	0	—	—	—
Runners On			0	0	0	0	0	—	—	—
Runners/Scor. Pos.			0	0	0	0	0	—	—	—
First 9 Batters			131	33	3	10	17	.252	.344	.301
Second 9 Batters			124	31	1	13	19	.250	.306	.321
All Batters Thereafter			82	27	3	7	8	.329	.524	.378

Loves to face: Manny Trillo (.089, 4-for-45)
Hates to face: Gary Gaetti (.400, 14-for-35, 6 2B, 4 HR)
Ground outs-to-air outs ratio: 1.04 last season, 0.88 for career. . . .
Additional statistics: 4 double-play ground outs in 68 opportunities, 12 doubles, 1 triple in 87.1 innings last season. . . . Allowed 1 first-inning run in 16 starts, lowest average in majors (minimum: 15 GS). . . . Batting support: 3.88 runs per start. . . . Opponents' career on-base average (.286) is 3d lowest among pitchers active in 1988 (minimum: 800 IP), behind Gooden (.279) and Clemens (.281). . . . Finished his career with 1354 at-bats, the most by any pitcher in major league history who never hit a homer. . . . 200-game winners within 20 percentage points and 20 ERA points of Sutton's career totals: Ferguson Jenkins, Tommy John, Jim Bunning, Jim Perry, and Billy Pierce.

Kent Tekulve

Throws Right

Philadelphia Phillies	W–L	ERA	AB	H	HR	BB	SO	BA	SA	OBA
Season	3-7	3.60	315	87	3	22	43	.276	.365	.326
vs. Left-Handers			151	34	1	16	19	.225	.278	.298
vs. Right-Handers			164	53	2	6	24	.323	.445	.353
Home	3-2	4.15	171	49	2	14	26	.287	.368	.342
Road	0-5	2.95	144	38	1	8	17	.264	.361	.305
Grass	0-2	2.08	70	19	0	3	10	.271	.343	.297
Artificial Turf	3-5	4.02	245	68	3	19	33	.278	.371	.333
April	0-2	3.00	54	17	1	3	7	.315	.444	.351
May	1-2	3.21	59	21	0	6	10	.356	.441	.415
June	1-0	6.48	30	7	0	5	2	.233	.233	.343
July	1-2	4.26	76	20	2	1	6	.263	.408	.282
August	0-0	2.20	54	10	0	3	13	.185	.241	.232
Sept./Oct.	0-1	3.48	42	12	0	4	5	.286	.333	.348
Leading Off Inn.			67	24	1	0	10	.358	.493	.368
Runners On			169	42	1	21	19	.249	.325	.332
Runners/Scor. Pos.			127	26	1	19	13	.205	.268	.309
Runners On/2 Out			68	14	1	5	8	.206	.265	.260
Scor. Pos./2 Out			57	13	1	5	6	.228	.298	.290
Late Inning Pressure			193	55	3	15	25	.285	.383	.336
Leading Off			46	19	1	0	8	.413	.587	.413
Runners On			100	23	1	15	10	.230	.300	.331
Runners/Scor. Pos.			73	16	1	14	5	.219	.301	.344
First 9 Batters			308	84	3	21	42	.273	.364	.321
Second 9 Batters			7	3	0	1	1	.429	.429	.500
All Batters Thereafter			0	0	0	0	0	—	—	—

Loves to face: Vince Coleman (0-for-12)
Hates to face: Kevin Bass (.692, 9-for-13)
Ground outs-to-air outs ratio: 1.96 last season, 2.23 for career. . . .
Additional statistics: 11 double-play ground outs in 80 opportunities, 15 doubles, 2 triples in 80.0 innings last season. . . . Faced 347 batters, only 47 while protecting leads of three runs or fewer in the 8th inning or later. . . . Allowed four home runs last season, all within a 10-inning span in May–June. Ended the season without allowing one in his last 49.1 innings. . . . Opposing ground-ball hitters batted .229, fly-ballers hit .314. . . . Was selected to one All-Star squad in his career (1980), but did not appear in the game. . . . Needs to pitch in 57 more games to tie Hoyt Wilhelm's all-time mark of 1070 games. He passed Lindy McDaniel in August to move into second place on that list.

John Tudor

Throws Left

Cardinals/Dodgers	W–L	ERA	AB	H	HR	BB	SO	BA	SA	OBA
Season	10-8	2.32	735	189	10	41	87	.257	.359	.295
vs. Left-Handers			117	33	5	4	31	.282	.487	.306
vs. Right-Handers			618	156	5	37	56	.252	.335	.293
Home	5-4	2.80	403	117	6	24	44	.290	.392	.329
Road	5-4	1.77	332	72	4	17	43	.217	.319	.254
Grass	3-6	2.87	292	73	6	16	35	.250	.360	.288
Artificial Turf	7-2	1.96	443	116	4	25	52	.262	.359	.300
April	0-0	0.00	21	4	0	0	2	.190	.238	.190
May	1-1	1.08	146	25	1	8	17	.171	.226	.212
June	3-1	1.85	160	45	2	13	12	.281	.413	.335
July	1-2	4.62	152	46	2	6	19	.303	.447	.329
August	3-2	2.43	139	35	2	7	18	.252	.324	.286
Sept./Oct.	2-2	2.08	117	34	3	7	19	.291	.402	.331
Leading Off Inn.			193	54	1	8	27	.280	.352	.308
Runners On			274	63	4	27	28	.230	.332	.294
Runners/Scor. Pos.			154	27	1	23	17	.175	.247	.275
Runners On/2 Out			115	26	0	19	11	.226	.287	.336
Scor. Pos./2 Out			75	13	0	15	7	.173	.253	.311
Late Inning Pressure			98	26	1	6	12	.265	.347	.308
Leading Off			26	11	0	1	2	.423	.577	.444
Runners On			39	9	1	5	6	.231	.333	.318
Runners/Scor. Pos.			27	6	0	4	4	.222	.259	.323
First 9 Batters			244	55	1	17	35	.225	.275	.275
Second 9 Batters			246	64	5	7	27	.260	.394	.283
All Batters Thereafter			245	70	4	17	25	.286	.408	.327

Loves to face: Jody Davis (.038, 1-for-26)
Hates to face: Kevin Mitchell (.643, 9-for-14, 2 HR)
Ground outs-to-air outs ratio: 1.11 last season, 0.92 for career. . . .
Additional statistics: 23 double-play ground outs in 125 opportunities, 37 doubles, 4 triples in 197.2 innings last season. . . . Allowed 5 first-inning runs in 30 starts, 3d lowest rate in N.L. (minimum: 15 GS). . . . Batting support: 3.60 runs per start. . . . Led N.L. with 10 pickoffs. . . . Held opponents hitless in 44 consecutive plate appearances (Apr. 26–May 7), longest streak of 1988. Streak was broken by Mike Marshall. . . . Opponents' average with runners in scoring position was lowest of his career. . . . Career record of 40–39 (.506) before the All-Star break, 65–29 (.691) after it. . . . One of two pitchers with a winning record in every season during the 1980s. The other: Jack Morris.

Scott Terry

Throws Right

St. Louis Cardinals	W–L	ERA	AB	H	HR	BB	SO	BA	SA	OBA
Season	9-6	2.92	481	119	5	34	65	.247	.341	.295
vs. Left-Handers			231	58	4	16	37	.251	.355	.298
vs. Right-Handers			250	61	1	18	28	.244	.328	.293
Home	5-3	3.10	269	66	2	19	36	.245	.342	.293
Road	4-3	2.70	212	53	3	15	29	.250	.340	.298
Grass	2-2	4.50	86	25	1	8	11	.291	.384	.351
Artificial Turf	7-4	2.60	395	94	4	26	54	.238	.332	.283
April	0-0	2.00	33	8	1	4	6	.242	.333	.316
May	2-3	4.57	82	21	1	8	12	.256	.415	.322
June	0-0	4.38	48	15	1	4	6	.313	.458	.358
July	0-0	0.00	14	1	0	1	1	.071	.071	.133
August	4-0	1.76	150	36	1	9	15	.240	.313	.283
Sept./Oct.	3-3	3.32	154	38	1	8	25	.247	.318	.282
Leading Off Inn.			122	30	1	6	14	.246	.311	.281
Runners On			191	60	3	15	26	.314	.429	.359
Runners/Scor. Pos.			108	36	2	13	19	.333	.472	.395
Runners On/2 Out			85	27	1	7	8	.318	.435	.370
Scor. Pos./2 Out			48	18	1	6	5	.375	.542	.444
Late Inning Pressure			123	29	2	15	18	.236	.350	.317
Leading Off			32	8	1	4	3	.250	.406	.333
Runners On			46	14	1	7	8	.304	.413	.389
Runners/Scor. Pos.			27	9	1	7	6	.333	.481	.457
First 9 Batters			287	73	4	23	41	.254	.369	.308
Second 9 Batters			100	23	1	6	16	.230	.310	.274
All Batters Thereafter			94	23	0	5	8	.245	.287	.280

Loves to face: Juan Samuel (0-for-12)
Hates to face: Mark Grace (.750, 3-for-4, 1 HR)
Ground outs-to-air outs ratio: 2.32 last season, 1.88 for career. . . .
Additional statistics: 13 double-play ground outs in 81 opportunities, 26 doubles, 2 triples in 129.1 innings last season. . . . Allowed 2 first-inning runs in 11 starts. . . . Batting support: 4.36 runs per start. . . . Record of 7–3 (2.40 ERA) in 11 starts, 2–3 (3.64) in 40 relief appearances. . . . Won seven consecutive starts (Aug. 16–Sept. 15), one short of longest streak of season (Cone, Stewart, Viola). . . . Allowed hits to right-handed batters in seven consecutive at-bats, longest streak in the N.L. It could have been worse. He retired pitcher Pete Smith to break streak. . . . Opponents' career average of .310 (one HR per 33 AB) with runners on, .227 (one HR per 140 AB) with bases empty.

Fernando Valenzuela

Throws Left

Los Angeles Dodgers	W–L	ERA	AB	H	HR	BB	SO	BA	SA	OBA
Season	5-8	4.24	530	142	11	76	64	.268	.374	.357
vs. Left-Handers			96	30	3	13	11	.313	.448	.391
vs. Right-Handers			434	112	8	63	53	.258	.357	.349
Home	1-5	5.34	241	68	5	38	29	.282	.390	.375
Road	4-3	3.33	289	74	6	38	35	.256	.360	.341
Grass	4-7	4.11	413	109	8	62	48	.264	.363	.357
Artificial Turf	1-1	4.70	117	33	3	14	16	.282	.410	.356
April	2-3	3.11	134	33	1	19	17	.246	.321	.331
May	1-2	4.28	123	33	1	19	16	.268	.350	.364
June	2-0	4.78	105	31	5	12	6	.295	.505	.368
July	0-3	5.50	144	41	3	22	21	.285	.361	.380
August			0	0	0	0	0	—	—	—
Sept./Oct.	0-0	1.29	24	4	1	4	4	.167	.292	.286
Leading Off Inn.			126	28	3	20	16	.222	.333	.329
Runners On			240	68	5	31	26	.283	.396	.359
Runners/Scor. Pos.			127	33	0	26	17	.260	.323	.373
Runners On/2 Out			110	33	1	18	16	.300	.373	.398
Scor. Pos./2 Out			71	20	0	16	13	.282	.338	.414
Late Inning Pressure			52	14	1	11	1	.269	.385	.397
Leading Off			12	2	0	4	1	.167	.250	.375
Runners On			19	8	1	6	0	.421	.684	.560
Runners/Scor. Pos.			11	3	0	6	0	.273	.364	.529
First 9 Batters			169	40	8	26	31	.237	.396	.337
Second 9 Batters			156	52	1	20	15	.333	.404	.402
All Batters Thereafter			205	50	2	30	18	.244	.332	.339

Loves to face: Alan Ashby (.091, 4-for-44)
Hates to face:Tom Brunansky (.625, 5-for-8, 5 BB, 1 HR)
Ground outs-to-air outs ratio: 1.33 last season, 1.34 for career. . . .
Additional statistics: 12 double-play ground outs in 126 opportunities, 17 doubles, 3 triples in 142.1 innings last season. . . . Allowed 16 first-inning runs in 22 starts. . . . Batting support: 4.86 runs per start, 5th highest in N.L. (minimum: 15 GS). . . . Dodgers' opponents hit only nine first-inning homers last season, but six of them were allowed by Fernando, most of any N.L. pitcher. . . . More walks than strikeouts for the first time in his career. . . . Five shutouts in first seven major league starts, four in last 105 starts. . . . One of two N.L. pitchers who pitched in 1980 and is still a member of his original major league club. The other: Dave Smith.

Bob Walk
Pittsburgh Pirates   Throws Right

	W–L	ERA	AB	H	HR	BB	SO	BA	SA	OBA
Season	12-10	2.71	795	183	6	65	81	.230	.325	.288
vs. Left-Handers			419	107	2	42	44	.255	.360	.322
vs. Right-Handers			376	76	4	23	37	.202	.285	.250
Home	6-4	3.12	410	97	2	32	45	.237	.339	.292
Road	6-6	2.27	385	86	4	33	36	.223	.309	.284
Grass	5-1	1.03	189	40	1	21	9	.212	.265	.292
Artificial Turf	7-9	3.26	606	143	5	44	72	.236	.343	.287
April	4-1	1.42	117	25	0	11	16	.214	.274	.279
May	1-2	4.06	119	28	0	8	11	.235	.311	.289
June	3-1	2.40	163	31	2	13	18	.190	.270	.250
July	3-2	2.84	147	40	1	9	9	.272	.388	.316
August	0-4	3.38	122	31	2	14	13	.254	.418	.328
Sept./Oct.	1-0	2.31	127	28	1	10	14	.220	.291	.273
Leading Off Inn.			208	47	2	13	21	.226	.332	.271
Runners On			324	72	3	33	32	.222	.318	.290
Runners/Scor. Pos.			191	38	1	27	23	.199	.298	.291
Runners On/2 Out			143	33	2	25	16	.231	.315	.345
Scor. Pos./2 Out			101	19	1	20	11	.188	.248	.322
Late Inning Pressure			80	17	1	7	7	.213	.300	.284
Leading Off			28	7	1	0	2	.250	.429	.250
Runners On			21	4	0	4	2	.190	.190	.320
Runners/Scor. Pos.			9	1	0	4	1	.111	.111	.385
First 9 Batters			255	61	4	23	31	.239	.373	.300
Second 9 Batters			263	61	0	16	29	.232	.278	.274
All Batters Thereafter			277	61	2	26	21	.220	.325	.291

Loves to face: Howard Johnson (0-for-11, 5 SO)
Hates to face: Hubie Brooks (.480, 12-for-25, 2 HR)
Ground outs-to-air outs ratio: 1.54 last season, 1.29 for career. . . .
Additional statistics: 12 double-play ground outs in 124 opportunities, 45 doubles, 6 triples in 212.2 innings last season. . . . Allowed 18 first-inning runs in 32 starts. . . . Batting support: 3.59 runs per start. . . . No need to bring your mitt to the park when he pitches. Allowed one home run per 35.4 innings, lowest rate in majors last season. . . . Nine straight hits allowed were extra-base hits (Aug. 10–15), longest streak of season. . . . What's in a name? He was one of three pitchers to walk five consecutive batters last season. . . . Pirates won 15 of the first 20 games he started, but lost 11 of his last 12 starts. . . . Opponents' yearly batting averages since 1985: .265, .251, .246, .230.

Ed Whitson
San Diego Padres   Throws Right

	W–L	ERA	AB	H	HR	BB	SO	BA	SA	OBA
Season	13-11	3.77	779	202	17	45	118	.259	.379	.298
vs. Left-Handers			399	106	7	28	45	.266	.383	.312
vs. Right-Handers			380	96	10	17	73	.253	.374	.283
Home	9-5	3.46	410	99	10	24	72	.241	.359	.283
Road	4-6	4.13	369	103	7	21	46	.279	.401	.314
Grass	12-5	3.44	520	133	11	30	80	.256	.365	.295
Artificial Turf	1-6	4.41	259	69	6	15	38	.266	.405	.303
April	2-0	3.33	101	27	3	5	13	.267	.406	.294
May	1-5	8.69	123	41	3	12	21	.333	.520	.387
June	4-0	3.05	142	37	2	7	17	.261	.359	.295
July	2-1	2.97	128	29	3	6	17	.227	.313	.261
August	2-2	2.55	150	33	3	10	33	.220	.300	.265
Sept./Oct.	2-3	3.06	135	35	3	5	17	.259	.400	.289
Leading Off Inn.			203	57	3	12	25	.281	.355	.321
Runners On			305	79	8	19	53	.259	.413	.297
Runners/Scor. Pos.			145	41	4	14	31	.283	.434	.333
Runners On/2 Out			118	22	3	15	24	.186	.288	.278
Scor. Pos./2 Out			72	15	2	10	14	.208	.333	.305
Late Inning Pressure			64	19	2	3	6	.297	.422	.324
Leading Off			20	9	1	1	1	.450	.600	.476
Runners On			21	4	0	2	2	.190	.190	.250
Runners/Scor. Pos.			9	1	0	1	1	.111	.111	.182
First 9 Batters			281	68	7	18	51	.242	.377	.286
Second 9 Batters			261	65	5	12	41	.249	.364	.280
All Batters Thereafter			237	69	5	15	26	.291	.397	.331

Loves to face: Jose Uribe (.059, 1-for-17)
Hates to face: Joel Youngblood (.517, 15-for-29)
Ground outs-to-air outs ratio: 1.20 last season, 1.00 for career. . . .
Additional statistics: 16 double-play ground outs in 163 opportunities, 36 doubles, 3 triples in 205.1 innings last season. . . . Allowed 12 first-inning runs in 33 starts. . . . Batting support: 3.76 runs per start. . . . Has defeated every major league team except the Yankees. Has beaten every National League club (including the Padres) at least four times. . . . Fewest intentional walks (one) of any N.L. pitcher with 200+ innings pitched last season. . . . Career record of 43–28 in June and July, 49–69 otherwise. . . . Has spent last 12 seasons in majors, but has never worn the same uniform for three full seasons in a row. He rejoined the Pads in June 1986.

Todd Worrell
St. Louis Cardinals   Throws Right

	W–L	ERA	AB	H	HR	BB	SO	BA	SA	OBA
Season	5-9	3.00	323	69	7	34	78	.214	.337	.287
vs. Left-Handers			141	30	5	20	39	.213	.397	.305
vs. Right-Handers			182	39	2	14	39	.214	.291	.271
Home	3-6	2.76	174	35	3	19	41	.201	.310	.281
Road	2-3	3.29	149	34	4	15	37	.228	.369	.293
Grass	1-2	4.37	85	23	4	8	20	.271	.447	.330
Artificial Turf	4-7	2.54	238	46	3	26	58	.193	.298	.271
April	0-2	4.85	48	11	3	4	10	.229	.479	.283
May	2-0	1.52	85	17	1	5	18	.200	.282	.244
June	1-2	1.62	55	10	0	8	17	.182	.291	.273
July	1-5	8.76	49	14	3	7	16	.286	.490	.379
August	1-0	1.38	42	4	0	7	9	.095	.119	.224
Sept./Oct.	0-0	1.59	44	13	0	3	8	.295	.386	.340
Leading Off Inn.			66	15	1	6	12	.227	.348	.292
Runners On			150	36	5	21	39	.240	.380	.328
Runners/Scor. Pos.			106	23	4	18	30	.217	.368	.323
Runners On/2 Out			74	17	2	13	26	.230	.351	.345
Scor. Pos./2 Out			59	12	2	12	22	.203	.339	.338
Late Inning Pressure			234	49	7	28	64	.209	.355	.292
Leading Off			44	9	1	5	9	.205	.364	.286
Runners On			112	27	5	19	33	.241	.411	.346
Runners/Scor. Pos.			83	17	4	17	27	.205	.373	.333
First 9 Batters			314	69	7	34	75	.220	.347	.295
Second 9 Batters			9	0	0	0	3	.000	.000	.000
All Batters Thereafter			0	0	0	0	0	—	—	—

Loves to face: Eric Davis (0-for-8)
Hates to face: Howard Johnson (.500, 4-for-8, 4 BB, 3 HR)
Ground outs-to-air outs ratio: 0.86 last season, 0.80 for career. . . .
Additional statistics: 8 double-play ground outs in 58 opportunities, 17 doubles, 1 triple in 90.0 innings last season. . . . Fourth pitcher in major league history to save at least 30 games in three consecutive seasons. The others all had four in a row: Dan Quisenberry, Lee Smith, and Jeff Reardon (whose streak is current). . . . Has saved at least one game against every opposing N.L. club in each of the last three seasons. . . . Made 13 consecutive appearances without a save (June 13–July 18). . . . Reds were hitless in 26 at-bats against him last season. . . . Opposing batters have compiled a higher average in road games than at Busch Stadium in each of his four seasons.

Floyd Youmans
Montreal Expos   Throws Right

	W–L	ERA	AB	H	HR	BB	SO	BA	SA	OBA
Season	3-6	3.21	301	64	8	41	54	.213	.355	.307
vs. Left-Handers			137	33	3	23	24	.241	.372	.346
vs. Right-Handers			164	31	5	18	30	.189	.341	.274
Home	2-5	4.04	203	47	5	30	39	.232	.384	.281
Road	1-1	1.59	98	17	3	11	15	.173	.296	.257
Grass	1-0	0.59	52	7	0	4	12	.135	.192	.196
Artificial Turf	2-6	3.80	249	57	8	37	42	.229	.390	.329
April	0-2	5.56	87	23	3	16	13	.264	.460	.385
May	1-1	2.20	101	20	3	11	25	.198	.327	.294
June	2-3	2.48	113	21	2	14	16	.186	.301	.271
July			0	0	0	0	0	—	—	—
August			0	0	0	0	0	—	—	—
Sept./Oct.			0	0	0	0	0	—	—	—
Leading Off Inn.			79	21	4	7	10	.266	.544	.326
Runners On			116	20	1	17	26	.172	.233	.281
Runners/Scor. Pos.			70	13	1	13	20	.186	.257	.315
Runners On/2 Out			49	5	1	10	13	.102	.204	.267
Scor. Pos./2 Out			29	3	1	7	9	.103	.207	.297
Late Inning Pressure			23	8	2	1	3	.348	.739	.360
Leading Off			6	3	1	0	1	.500	1.333	.500
Runners On			11	3	0	0	2	.273	.273	.250
Runners/Scor. Pos.			5	2	0	0	1	.400	.400	.333
First 9 Batters			104	17	2	16	25	.163	.298	.273
Second 9 Batters			102	19	4	11	16	.186	.363	.278
All Batters Thereafter			95	28	2	14	13	.295	.411	.375

Loves to face: Dale Murphy (.071, 1-for-14)
Hates to face: Eric Davis (.444, 4-for-9, 3 BB, 3 HR)
Ground outs-to-air outs ratio: 0.79 last season, 0.79 for career. . . .
Additional statistics: 5 double-play ground outs in 44 opportunities, 13 doubles, 3 triples in 84.0 innings last season. . . . Allowed 4 first-inning runs in 13 starts. . . . Batting support: 3.62 runs per start. . . . Average of 4.39 walks per nine innings was 7th highest among N.L. pitchers with at least 80 innings. . . . Strikeouts per nine innings, year by year since 1986: 8.30, 7.27, 5.79. . . . Opposing batters have a career average of .199 with runners in scoring position. . . . Only five players in major league history have pitched as many innings as Youmans (496.1) allowing fewer hits per nine innings than his 6.85 mark: Nolan Ryan, Sandy Koufax, Herb Score, Sid Fernandez, and Ryne Duren.

Atlanta Braves

	W–L	ERA	AB	H	HR	BB	SO	BA	SA	OBA
Season	54-106	4.09	5528	1481	108	524	810	.268	.382	.334
vs. Left-Handers			2337	638	42	264	335	.273	.386	.349
vs. Right-Handers			3191	843	66	260	475	.264	.379	.322
Home	28-51	4.32	2853	781	64	263	395	.274	.394	.336
Road	26-55	3.84	2675	700	44	261	415	.262	.369	.331
Grass	41-77	4.01	4087	1092	84	378	584	.267	.381	.330
Artificial Turf	13-29	4.32	1441	389	24	146	226	.270	.384	.342
April	3-16	5.03	649	173	15	65	89	.267	.408	.335
May	13-15	4.38	995	275	12	113	153	.276	.366	.352
June	10-18	4.56	961	286	17	97	128	.298	.413	.360
July	9-20	3.97	1024	273	28	92	163	.267	.403	.332
August	10-19	3.90	988	249	20	81	148	.252	.370	.310
Sept./Oct.	9-18	2.99	911	225	16	76	129	.247	.337	.310
Leading Off Inn.			1357	352	29	81	173	.259	.376	.306
Runners On			2360	675	46	301	340	.286	.409	.366
Runners/Scor. Pos.			1458	424	29	229	235	.291	.410	.382
Runners On/2 Out			1025	260	15	152	169	.254	.355	.355
Scor. Pos./2 Out			680	174	12	125	120	.256	.371	.377
Late Inning Pressure			1141	306	23	116	197	.268	.378	.339
Leading Off			290	87	8	22	42	.300	.455	.358
Runners On			487	124	9	69	91	.255	.345	.348
Runners/Scor. Pos.			295	78	3	60	54	.264	.332	.386
First 9 Batters			2921	758	54	276	494	.260	.364	.326
Second 9 Batters			1401	386	31	135	188	.276	.412	.341
All Batters Thereafter			1206	337	23	113	128	.279	.392	.344

Starting pitchers: 31–80, 4.33 ERA
Relief pitchers: 23–26, 3.64 ERA
Ground outs-to-air outs ratio: 1.15, 3d lowest in N.L. . . . First team since 1900 to play its first eight games of a season at home and to lose all eight. (Brooklyn in 1906 and Houston in 1983 had the old record: six games.). . . . Worst record in the majors in one-run games last season (24–36). Since 1969, 16 of the 19 teams that did that improved their records a year later. The average gain was 11 games. . . . Compiled N.L.'s highest ERA in each of first three months of season. . . . Won three consecutive games five times, never made it four in a row. Didn't win three consecutive road games all season. . . . Led N.L. in hit batters (43) for second straight year. . . . Braves' rookies combined for exactly 500 innings pitched. Only White Sox' rookies had more (522.2).

Chicago Cubs

	W–L	ERA	AB	H	HR	BB	SO	BA	SA	OBA
Season	77-85	3.84	5640	1494	115	490	897	.265	.383	.325
vs. Left-Handers			2560	689	44	263	369	.269	.377	.336
vs. Right-Handers			3080	805	71	227	528	.261	.388	.315
Home	39-42	3.87	2940	795	71	229	484	.270	.394	.325
Road	38-43	3.82	2700	699	44	261	413	.259	.371	.325
Grass	56-58	3.70	4058	1075	86	336	665	.265	.379	.322
Artificial Turf	21-27	4.21	1582	419	29	154	232	.265	.394	.330
April	10-12	4.30	767	208	25	95	115	.271	.415	.351
May	15-12	3.07	925	227	16	79	154	.245	.350	.306
June	16-11	3.27	922	226	18	82	154	.245	.352	.306
July	9-18	3.73	959	257	12	81	142	.268	.367	.327
August	16-12	3.72	961	252	18	70	156	.262	.369	.315
Sept./Oct.	11-20	4.93	1106	324	26	83	176	.293	.440	.342
Leading Off Inn.			1381	350	30	78	212	.253	.379	.298
Runners On			2413	658	52	262	371	.273	.399	.341
Runners/Scor. Pos.			1427	381	22	197	238	.267	.364	.350
Runners On/2 Out			1069	273	22	131	161	.255	.366	.339
Scor. Pos./2 Out			686	177	10	99	107	.258	.341	.355
Late Inning Pressure			1029	280	23	104	166	.272	.391	.339
Leading Off			265	71	7	20	44	.268	.408	.319
Runners On			427	128	10	57	56	.300	.426	.379
Runners/Scor. Pos.			250	85	6	43	34	.340	.472	.429
First 9 Batters			2688	724	54	232	484	.269	.386	.327
Second 9 Batters			1455	368	27	125	231	.253	.371	.314
All Batters Thereafter			1497	402	34	133	182	.269	.390	.330

Starting pitchers: 57–64, 3.69 ERA
Relief pitchers: 20–21, 4.40 ERA
Ground outs-to-air outs ratio: 1.23, 3d highest in N.L. . . . Defeated San Diego, 1–0, in 10 innings at Wrigley Field on May 11. It was the 20th time in the Cubs' 73 years at Wrigley Field that there had been a 1–0 extra-inning game within the friendly confines. The longest: the Phils beat the Cubs 1–0 in 15 innings back in 1955! Six days later, Cardinals beat Cubs, 3–0, in 11 innings at Wrigley. It marked first time in park's history that two extra-inning shutout games had been played there within the same calendar month. . . . Relief ERA was highest in N.L. Bring back Lee Smith! . . . Starters completed 30 games last season, most by a Cubs staff since 1972, when Durocher's staff racked up 35 by the All-Star break, and finished season with a total of 54.

Cincinnati Reds

	W–L	ERA	AB	H	HR	BB	SO	BA	SA	OBA
Season	87-74	3.35	5365	1271	121	504	934	.237	.359	.303
vs. Left-Handers			1654	437	39	195	306	.264	.398	.340
vs. Right-Handers			3711	834	82	309	628	.225	.341	.286
Home	45-35	3.46	2766	661	71	252	481	.239	.375	.304
Road	42-39	3.22	2599	610	50	252	453	.235	.342	.303
Grass	25-23	3.25	1555	384	31	146	275	.247	.350	.311
Artificial Turf	62-51	3.38	3810	887	90	358	659	.233	.362	.300
April	11-11	3.39	781	187	13	83	114	.239	.344	.313
May	12-16	3.77	948	239	25	94	149	.252	.386	.321
June	12-15	4.12	896	225	18	84	170	.251	.364	.317
July	16-11	2.45	856	181	20	80	170	.211	.335	.281
August	17-11	3.52	952	233	23	86	162	.245	.377	.306
Sept./Oct.	19-10	2.85	932	206	22	77	169	.221	.340	.281
Leading Off Inn.			1355	315	26	100	227	.232	.347	.287
Runners On			2111	538	56	242	362	.255	.390	.328
Runners/Scor. Pos.			1225	303	31	178	228	.247	.384	.336
Runners On/2 Out			943	231	29	137	167	.245	.397	.341
Scor. Pos./2 Out			616	152	21	106	110	.247	.420	.358
Late Inning Pressure			1067	228	18	108	200	.214	.314	.288
Leading Off			286	64	5	21	58	.224	.332	.279
Runners On			380	87	9	55	65	.229	.353	.327
Runners/Scor. Pos.			222	50	5	42	42	.225	.338	.349
First 9 Batters			2832	649	51	287	535	.229	.331	.301
Second 9 Batters			1330	319	29	116	215	.240	.363	.302
All Batters Thereafter			1203	303	41	101	184	.252	.419	.309

Starting pitchers: 66–56, 3.69 ERA
Relief pitchers: 21–18, 2.61 ERA
Ground outs-to-air outs ratio: 1.16. . . . Pitchers went 16 games without having an opposing batter ground into a double play (Sept. 11–Sept. 27), nearly twice the length of the season's 2d longest streak (9, by Houston). . . . Left-handed pitchers started 96 games, highest total in majors. . . . For the second straight season, Pete Rose led the majors in pitching changes, but his 1988 total of 343 didn't approach the major league record of 392 that he set in 1987. . . . Matched a modern-day club record with eight different pitchers starting at least 10 games for them last season. Reds had done that twice before in this century (1955 and 1977). . . . Only team in the majors without a 10-game loser on their staff last season.

Houston Astros

	W–L	ERA	AB	H	HR	BB	SO	BA	SA	OBA
Season	82-80	3.41	5521	1339	123	478	1049	.243	.367	.304
vs. Left-Handers			2196	522	43	216	400	.238	.352	.306
vs. Right-Handers			3325	817	80	262	649	.246	.377	.303
Home	44-37	2.85	2782	653	50	232	531	.235	.347	.295
Road	38-43	3.98	2739	686	73	246	518	.250	.387	.313
Grass	21-27	4.35	1646	432	45	141	313	.262	.402	.320
Artificial Turf	61-53	3.02	3875	907	78	337	736	.234	.351	.297
April	14-7	2.50	699	147	11	60	148	.210	.303	.276
May	13-14	3.35	909	222	24	77	153	.244	.370	.304
June	13-16	4.29	1016	279	28	103	189	.275	.428	.344
July	16-11	3.98	922	227	19	98	167	.246	.387	.318
August	15-14	2.77	985	231	20	61	191	.235	.339	.282
Sept./Oct.	11-18	3.35	990	233	21	79	201	.235	.354	.291
Leading Off Inn.			1362	367	40	109	240	.269	.420	.328
Runners On			2318	571	47	214	433	.246	.362	.307
Runners/Scor. Pos.			1419	321	31	165	301	.226	.340	.300
Runners On/2 Out			993	216	18	95	202	.218	.328	.290
Scor. Pos./2 Out			671	136	15	73	153	.203	.317	.287
Late Inning Pressure			1162	262	19	108	200	.225	.328	.292
Leading Off			309	79	5	23	41	.256	.362	.307
Runners On			441	110	8	58	82	.249	.363	.337
Runners/Scor. Pos.			294	71	6	54	58	.241	.367	.357
First 9 Batters			2697	665	45	244	485	.247	.351	.309
Second 9 Batters			1417	327	43	111	307	.231	.376	.288
All Batters Thereafter			1407	347	35	123	257	.247	.387	.310

Starting pitchers: 59–57, 3.45 ERA
Relief pitchers: 23–23, 3.29 ERA
Ground outs-to-air outs ratio: 1.17. . . . Ranked third in home-game ERA, next-to-last in road games. . . . Allowed most home runs in road games for second consecutive season, but most overall for first time in team history. . . . Brian Meyer was the only rookie pitcher to appear in a game for the Astros last season. The Astros and Twins, whose lone rookie hurler was German Gonzalez, were the only clubs not to get a victory from a rookie. . . . Pitchers' batting average of .085 was the worst in the N.L. last season. . . . Opponents' batting average with two outs and runners in scoring position was the lowest in the majors last season. . . . Lost five home games in which they led after seven innings, tied with Braves for most in N.L. last season.

Los Angeles Dodgers

	W–L	ERA	AB	H	HR	BB	SO	BA	SA	OBA
Season	94-67	2.96	5440	1291	84	473	1029	.237	.327	.299
vs. Left-Handers			2492	613	38	269	440	.246	.337	.318
vs. Right-Handers			2948	678	46	204	589	.230	.318	.282
Home	45-36	3.13	2784	688	38	246	509	.247	.333	.308
Road	49-31	2.80	2656	603	46	227	520	.227	.320	.289
Grass	67-52	3.00	4082	981	57	361	753	.240	.328	.302
Artificial Turf	27-15	2.87	1358	310	27	112	276	.228	.323	.288
April	13-7	2.33	639	129	6	52	122	.202	.280	.262
May	14-13	3.39	944	244	16	91	173	.258	.350	.323
June	17-11	3.39	940	237	16	85	159	.252	.355	.316
July	16-12	3.19	981	235	14	82	174	.240	.325	.301
August	17-12	3.31	996	254	16	80	206	.255	.347	.311
Sept./Oct.	17-12	2.02	940	192	16	83	195	.204	.287	.268
Leading Off Inn.			1372	339	23	90	239	.247	.335	.296
Runners On			2195	522	31	251	412	.238	.325	.314
Runners/Scor. Pos.			1263	299	16	192	260	.237	.330	.332
Runners On/2 Out			983	236	14	145	198	.240	.333	.342
Scor. Pos./2 Out			663	148	8	118	149	.223	.321	.346
Late Inning Pressure			1025	213	11	108	214	.208	.281	.284
Leading Off			279	62	1	14	56	.222	.262	.259
Runners On			369	76	5	65	78	.206	.293	.323
Runners/Scor. Pos.			225	48	3	52	53	.213	.311	.354
First 9 Batters			2775	619	42	238	595	.223	.310	.284
Second 9 Batters			1353	333	23	104	236	.246	.338	.302
All Batters Thereafter			1312	339	19	131	198	.258	.351	.326

Starting pitchers: 67-51, 3.22 ERA
Relief pitchers: 27-16, 2.35 ERA

Ground outs-to-air outs ratio: 1.25, 2d highest in N.L. . . . Lost three consecutive games 10 times, but won the next game in every case. Only one team since 1900 had more three-game losing streaks without ever dropping four in a row: the 1972 New York Mets (12). . . . Most shutouts (24) in either league since 1969 Mets led majors with 28. . . . Led N.L. in complete games for fifth straight season. N.L. record: 7, by Milwaukee (1955–61). . . . First team ever to lead either league in both complete games and saves. . . . Didn't hit a batter with a pitch in their last 47 regular-season games. Orosco hit Jefferies during Mets' game-winning rally in Game 3 of N.L.C.S. . . . Held Canseco and McGwire to two hits (both were HRs) in 36 at-bats during the Series.

New York Mets

	W–L	ERA	AB	H	HR	BB	SO	BA	SA	OBA
Season	100-60	2.91	5337	1253	78	404	1100	.235	.329	.291
vs. Left-Handers			2070	512	27	182	400	.247	.343	.308
vs. Right-Handers			3267	741	51	222	700	.227	.321	.279
Home	56-24	2.33	2696	581	34	176	588	.216	.295	.267
Road	44-36	3.53	2641	672	44	228	512	.254	.365	.314
Grass	75-38	2.59	3793	863	53	248	826	.228	.318	.278
Artificial Turf	25-22	3.71	1544	390	25	156	274	.253	.358	.321
April	15-6	3.81	683	171	11	65	125	.250	.360	.318
May	19-9	2.46	904	189	11	54	200	.209	.288	.257
June	15-13	2.97	992	235	14	79	185	.237	.331	.297
July	14-12	2.91	862	202	14	75	170	.234	.334	.297
August	15-14	2.99	968	231	16	65	209	.239	.347	.288
Sept./Oct.	22-6	2.61	928	225	12	66	211	.242	.323	.293
Leading Off Inn.			1347	314	26	87	273	.233	.344	.284
Runners On			2148	516	31	189	441	.240	.336	.301
Runners/Scor. Pos.			1274	288	18	151	304	.226	.309	.304
Runners On/2 Out			923	198	10	93	214	.215	.295	.292
Scor. Pos./2 Out			626	127	6	79	160	.203	.264	.296
Late Inning Pressure			967	230	8	70	178	.238	.298	.291
Leading Off			254	62	5	15	50	.244	.343	.286
Runners On			392	88	0	29	68	.224	.270	.281
Runners/Scor. Pos.			211	49	0	25	44	.232	.265	.309
First 9 Batters			2470	555	32	192	537	.225	.310	.284
Second 9 Batters			1363	321	21	114	283	.236	.343	.297
All Batters Thereafter			1504	377	25	98	280	.251	.349	.297

Starting pitchers: 76-46, 2.97 ERA
Relief pitchers: 24-14, 2.71 ERA

Ground outs-to-air outs ratio: 1.09, 2d lowest in N.L. . . . Walked fewest batters in N.L. for first time in team history. Led league in strikeouts for eighth time. . . . Ratio of 2.72 strikeouts per walk was 2d highest in modern history, behind 1966 Dodgers (3.04). . . . Held opponents to fewer than two runs for six consecutive games in August, 4th longest streak in this century. Three-way tie for record streak of eight games among 1906 Giants, 1919 Cubs, and—believe it or not—the 1966 Kansas City Athletics. . . . Didn't issue an intentional walk after August 31, and compiled league low (33) for third time in four years. . . . Won the last 11 day games of regular season, and would have faced Oakland in Series had they not split a pair of them in N.L.C.S.

Montreal Expos

	W–L	ERA	AB	H	HR	BB	SO	BA	SA	OBA
Season	81-81	3.08	5505	1310	122	476	923	.238	.361	.301
vs. Left-Handers			2622	634	49	271	424	.242	.350	.312
vs. Right-Handers			2883	676	73	205	499	.234	.371	.290
Home	43-38	3.04	2838	676	62	249	477	.238	.368	.308
Road	38-43	3.13	2667	634	60	227	446	.238	.355	.300
Grass	15-27	3.55	1360	332	32	111	216	.244	.364	.303
Artificial Turf	66-54	2.93	4145	978	90	365	707	.236	.360	.300
April	9-11	3.65	680	158	24	68	128	.232	.390	.305
May	14-14	3.42	954	243	28	91	143	.255	.412	.323
June	14-15	2.99	993	236	17	95	162	.238	.356	.305
July	18-8	2.31	898	200	14	54	149	.223	.308	.268
August	12-17	3.32	975	247	18	77	156	.253	.361	.310
Sept./Oct.	14-16	2.95	1005	226	21	91	185	.225	.346	.291
Leading Off Inn.			1388	331	42	93	218	.238	.387	.289
Runners On			2161	512	37	240	364	.237	.345	.314
Runners/Scor. Pos.			1323	295	25	186	248	.223	.329	.316
Runners On/2 Out			941	207	18	137	180	.220	.340	.324
Scor. Pos./2 Out			661	141	15	115	129	.213	.337	.335
Late Inning Pressure			1188	283	23	131	204	.238	.352	.313
Leading Off			325	75	9	17	52	.231	.369	.269
Runners On			441	104	7	76	83	.236	.338	.344
Runners/Scor. Pos.			291	60	6	64	65	.206	.313	.341
First 9 Batters			2766	652	55	275	523	.236	.354	.307
Second 9 Batters			1425	322	32	105	223	.226	.349	.282
All Batters Thereafter			1314	336	35	96	177	.256	.390	.307

Starting pitchers: 54-62, 3.05 ERA
Relief pitchers: 27-19, 3.21 ERA

Ground outs-to-air outs ratio: 1.22. . . . Different opening-day pitcher in each season since 1984: Charlie Lea, Steve Rogers, Bryn Smith, Floyd Youmans, and Dennis Martinez. From 1969 to 1976, Expos had eight different opening-day starters: Mudcat Grant, Joe Sparma, Carl Morton, Bill Stoneman, Mike Torrez, Steve Renko, Dave McNally, and Rogers, who then started every opener from 1976 to 1983. . . . Only 15 starts from left-handed pitchers, lowest total in majors. . . . Held opponents to six runs or less in 34 straight games (June 20–July 28), a team record. . . . Allowed five or more runs in only three innings, less than half the number of any other team in majors. . . . Pascual Perez led the majors in pinch running appearances (14) by a pitcher last season.

Phila. Phillies

	W–L	ERA	AB	H	HR	BB	SO	BA	SA	OBA
Season	65-96	4.14	5470	1447	118	628	859	.265	.389	.341
vs. Left-Handers			2136	572	41	310	338	.268	.388	.359
vs. Right-Handers			3334	875	77	318	521	.262	.390	.329
Home	38-42	3.90	2805	706	64	318	456	.252	.378	.330
Road	27-54	4.40	2665	741	54	310	403	.278	.400	.352
Grass	15-27	4.55	1378	379	32	163	201	.275	.399	.350
Artificial Turf	50-69	4.00	4092	1068	86	465	658	.261	.385	.338
April	7-12	3.31	665	162	20	74	116	.244	.397	.319
May	12-16	3.98	956	242	18	112	139	.253	.364	.332
June	15-13	4.08	1000	284	14	101	152	.284	.389	.350
July	11-18	4.59	988	269	30	93	142	.272	.425	.335
August	9-19	4.48	910	233	18	111	169	.256	.373	.339
Sept./Oct.	11-18	4.15	951	257	18	137	141	.270	.386	.362
Leading Off Inn.			1311	368	37	114	188	.281	.443	.344
Runners On			2464	663	46	348	385	.269	.383	.356
Runners/Scor. Pos.			1500	396	32	277	245	.264	.387	.371
Runners On/2 Out			1051	265	22	175	154	.252	.365	.365
Scor. Pos./2 Out			713	169	16	142	112	.237	.352	.366
Late Inning Pressure			1032	261	22	129	163	.253	.376	.336
Leading Off			256	68	5	19	41	.266	.406	.319
Runners On			453	110	4	85	69	.243	.318	.358
Runners/Scor. Pos.			278	63	2	73	42	.227	.291	.381
First 9 Batters			2861	704	49	335	516	.246	.353	.327
Second 9 Batters			1348	382	38	141	186	.283	.425	.350
All Batters Thereafter			1261	361	31	152	157	.286	.431	.362

Starting pitchers: 47-69, 4.26 ERA
Relief pitchers: 18-27, 3.93 ERA

Ground outs-to-air outs ratio: 1.06, lowest in the N.L. . . . First N.L. team to rank last in ERA and batting average since the 1978 Braves. . . . Compiled highest ERA for a league-record 31st time. No other team has led more than seven times. . . . Didn't win three consecutive road games all season. Had N.L.'s highest road-game ERA. . . . Lost 11 consecutive games to Los Angeles (May 14–Aug. 28), longest streak in teams' histories. Brooklyn Dodgers won 15 in a row vs. Phillies in 1945. . . . Only N.L. club with a losing record (9–11) in one-run games at home. . . . Phillies' opening-day starter has been a southpaw in each of the last 21 years: Carlton, 14; Short, 4; Rawley, 2; Kaat, 1. Last right-hander to start an opener for Phils: Jim Bunning in 1967.

Pittsburgh Pirates

	W–L	ERA	AB	H	HR	BB	SO	BA	SA	OBA
Season	85-75	3.47	5390	1349	108	469	790	.250	.369	.311
vs. Left-Handers			2247	579	38	249	296	.258	.371	.331
vs. Right-Handers			3143	770	70	220	494	.245	.368	.297
Home	43-38	3.28	2772	677	50	251	402	.244	.359	.308
Road	42-37	3.67	2618	672	58	218	388	.257	.380	.315
Grass	19-21	3.92	1324	359	38	128	185	.271	.406	.336
Artificial Turf	66-54	3.32	4066	990	70	341	605	.243	.357	.303
April	16-6	2.86	748	183	15	59	120	.245	.370	.302
May	14-14	3.89	963	251	18	70	133	.261	.369	.313
June	13-14	4.22	913	225	22	97	127	.246	.373	.318
July	15-11	2.62	836	190	12	84	136	.227	.318	.300
August	13-17	3.41	1005	255	21	88	144	.254	.387	.315
Sept./Oct.	14-13	3.64	925	245	20	71	130	.265	.392	.315
Leading Off Inn.			1347	330	28	88	172	.245	.367	.295
Runners On			2224	587	44	230	317	.264	.388	.330
Runners/Scor. Pos.			1373	342	24	181	214	.249	.367	.329
Runners On/2 Out			958	221	14	115	146	.231	.317	.318
Scor. Pos./2 Out			669	145	11	95	108	.217	.308	.319
Late Inning Pressure			1130	270	19	122	212	.239	.338	.314
Leading Off			297	62	7	19	43	.209	.327	.263
Runners On			433	116	6	64	83	.268	.363	.354
Runners/Scor. Pos.			268	68	5	52	57	.254	.377	.362
First 9 Batters			2726	679	54	258	463	.249	.371	.314
Second 9 Batters			1389	341	20	101	193	.246	.342	.300
All Batters Thereafter			1275	329	34	110	134	.258	.396	.317

Starting pitchers: 59–53, 3.52 ERA
Relief pitchers: 26–22, 3.35 ERA
Ground outs-to-air outs ratio: 1.16.... Led N.L. in wild pitches for third consecutive season (66).... Were the only N.L. club with a winning record (11–10) in one-run games played on the road.... Outscored their opponents 22–9 in extra innings.... Bucs have landed a different pitcher on the N.L. All-Star squad in each of the last three seasons (Walk, Reuschel, and Rhoden). That hasn't happened since 1971–1974 when they were represented in consecutive seasons by Dock Ellis, Steve Blass, Dave Giusti, and Ken Brett.... Set a club record for fewest complete games in a season (12).... Pitchers' batting average of .098 was 2d lowest in the N.L. last season. Whatever happened to Rick Rhoden and Don Robinson?

St. Louis Cardinals

	W–L	ERA	AB	H	HR	BB	SO	BA	SA	OBA
Season	76-86	3.47	5513	1387	91	486	881	.252	.370	.312
vs. Left-Handers			2002	509	40	206	336	.254	.385	.322
vs. Right-Handers			3511	878	51	280	545	.250	.361	.306
Home	41-40	3.25	2840	706	39	234	450	.249	.361	.304
Road	35-46	3.71	2673	681	52	252	431	.255	.379	.320
Grass	18-24	3.70	1347	351	30	112	214	.261	.385	.318
Artificial Turf	58-62	3.40	4166	1036	61	374	667	.249	.365	.310
April	8-14	3.91	729	187	16	68	104	.257	.381	.320
May	18-10	3.14	1016	249	11	94	156	.245	.344	.308
June	11-16	3.14	959	252	17	81	144	.263	.390	.320
July	8-19	4.29	903	248	16	73	151	.275	.400	.328
August	17-12	2.68	942	209	13	93	158	.222	.332	.290
Sept./Oct.	14-15	3.87	964	242	18	77	168	.251	.376	.308
Leading Off Inn.			1374	351	20	95	220	.255	.365	.306
Runners On			2276	603	45	257	346	.265	.397	.335
Runners/Scor. Pos.			1387	345	26	202	237	.249	.382	.336
Runners On/2 Out			1001	254	21	130	162	.254	.397	.344
Scor. Pos./2 Out			675	164	12	102	117	.243	.387	.344
Late Inning Pressure			1180	302	18	122	206	.256	.366	.325
Leading Off			299	77	4	23	43	.258	.388	.315
Runners On			480	125	11	73	81	.260	.373	.353
Runners/Scor. Pos.			315	82	9	65	58	.260	.394	.379
First 9 Batters			2820	690	52	257	499	.245	.366	.307
Second 9 Batters			1385	366	22	118	198	.264	.388	.323
All Batters Thereafter			1308	331	17	111	184	.253	.357	.311

Starting pitchers: 52–55, 3.33 ERA
Relief pitchers: 24–31, 3.80 ERA
Ground outs-to-air outs ratio: 1.26, highest in the majors.... Only team in majors not to lose more than three straight home games last season.... Had a record of 65–1 when leading after eight innings, but a 65–10 record when leading after seven. Were outscored 128–95 over the eighth and ninth innings last season.... But they haven't lost a home game in which they led after eight innings since June 29, 1986, vs. Philadelphia. Since then they are 100–0 in such games.... Whitey used a reliever to face a single batter 29 times last season, most of any N.L. manager.... Only one pitcher on their staff (DeLeon) started as many as 25 games last season.... Over the last 15 years (excluding 1981), only one team hasn't had any pitchers with 25 starts: the 1982 Mets.

San Diego Padres

	W–L	ERA	AB	H	HR	BB	SO	BA	SA	OBA
Season	83-78	3.28	5395	1332	112	439	885	.247	.363	.304
vs. Left-Handers			2435	638	39	249	344	.262	.377	.329
vs. Right-Handers			2960	694	73	190	541	.234	.352	.282
Home	47-34	2.83	2728	632	56	230	485	.232	.338	.292
Road	36-44	3.75	2667	700	56	209	400	.262	.389	.316
Grass	65-55	3.11	4058	974	88	333	673	.240	.356	.298
Artificial Turf	18-23	3.81	1337	358	24	106	212	.268	.384	.320
April	9-12	3.54	677	170	19	57	124	.251	.394	.310
May	9-20	3.93	984	271	18	100	164	.272	.401	.337
June	16-13	4.09	975	244	27	84	158	.250	.386	.311
July	14-12	2.70	856	201	20	59	126	.235	.346	.286
August	17-10	2.52	877	202	12	71	148	.230	.323	.286
Sept./Oct.	18-11	2.89	1012	244	16	68	165	.241	.333	.288
Leading Off Inn.			1368	337	23	83	199	.246	.344	.291
Runners On			2143	539	46	219	348	.252	.373	.319
Runners/Scor. Pos.			1171	298	23	161	212	.254	.377	.336
Runners On/2 Out			925	204	22	129	169	.221	.348	.321
Scor. Pos./2 Out			587	141	14	100	112	.240	.380	.354
Late Inning Pressure			1108	267	22	130	219	.241	.353	.322
Leading Off			287	80	6	22	44	.279	.380	.332
Runners On			454	102	10	75	92	.225	.337	.334
Runners/Scor. Pos.			267	59	5	62	59	.221	.330	.362
First 9 Batters			2589	623	50	233	507	.241	.353	.302
Second 9 Batters			1422	358	34	93	204	.252	.378	.299
All Batters Thereafter			1384	351	28	113	174	.254	.366	.311

Starting pitchers: 68–56, 3.46 ERA
Relief pitchers: 15–22, 2.78 ERA
Ground outs-to-air outs ratio: 1.17.... Won the opening game of all nine home stands last season, making it 17 of their last 18. Their five-year record in home-stand openers: 37–9.... Held opponents to fewer than eight runs in last 52 games of season, a team record.... Relievers were used to face a single batter eight times last season, four times to face the game's last batter. Jack McKeon removed a pitcher from a game after facing one batter only once (Dave Leiper, June 28).... Allowed 18 first-inning home runs, most in the N.L.... Only N.L. club with five different pitchers who lost at least ten games last season.... Had the best record in the N.L. in home games tied after eight innings (5–1).

San Francisco Giants

	W–L	ERA	AB	H	HR	BB	SO	BA	SA	OBA
Season	83-79	3.39	5459	1323	99	422	875	.242	.350	.298
vs. Left-Handers			2214	527	27	181	353	.238	.327	.295
vs. Right-Handers			3245	796	72	241	522	.245	.366	.299
Home	45-36	2.94	2766	649	42	192	447	.235	.324	.284
Road	38-43	3.86	2693	674	57	230	428	.250	.377	.311
Grass	66-54	3.13	4032	965	65	293	636	.239	.333	.291
Artificial Turf	17-25	4.13	1427	358	34	129	239	.251	.398	.316
April	11-12	3.17	778	173	20	61	118	.222	.339	.279
May	14-14	3.53	961	252	20	93	167	.262	.387	.328
June	14-11	4.09	833	209	13	66	131	.251	.364	.309
July	17-11	3.17	936	221	11	66	156	.236	.332	.287
August	14-15	3.15	973	227	13	65	174	.233	.314	.283
Sept./Oct.	13-16	3.26	978	241	22	71	129	.246	.363	.296
Leading Off Inn.			1380	342	26	79	198	.248	.356	.292
Runners On			2165	550	34	241	345	.254	.362	.326
Runners/Scor. Pos.			1265	324	19	179	215	.256	.360	.340
Runners On/2 Out			929	225	18	127	155	.242	.369	.339
Scor. Pos./2 Out			605	141	12	97	106	.233	.350	.343
Late Inning Pressure			1026	265	19	113	182	.258	.381	.331
Leading Off			261	61	6	19	43	.234	.368	.286
Runners On			418	111	10	75	77	.266	.411	.372
Runners/Scor. Pos.			268	73	6	62	47	.272	.414	.398
First 9 Batters			2774	668	50	227	518	.241	.349	.300
Second 9 Batters			1468	340	27	100	224	.232	.326	.280
All Batters Thereafter			1217	315	22	95	133	.259	.382	.313

Starting pitchers: 65–49, 3.22 ERA
Relief pitchers: 18–30, 3.82 ERA
Ground outs-to-air outs ratio: 1.19.... Used 12 different starting pitchers last season, most of any N.L. club.... One of four clubs (all in the N.L.) to commit fewer balks in 1988 than in 1987. The others: Phillies, Padres, and Cubs.... Worst record in N.L. last season in home games tied after eight innings (3–11). But they've won 43 straight games at Candlestick in which they led after eight innings.... Allowed six or more runs in an inning eight times, most of any N.L. staff.... Staff walked fewer batters than in any full season since 1968.... Only two Giants managers have lasted four full seasons since the move west: Al Dark (1961–64) and Herman Franks (1965–68). Roger Craig is starting his fourth season in 1989.

National League

	W–L	ERA	AB	H	HR	BB	SO	BA	SA	OBA
Season	969-969	3.45	65563	16277	1279	5793	11032	.248	.363	.310
vs. Left-Handers			26965	6870	467	2855	4341	.255	.365	.325
vs. Right-Handers			38598	9407	812	2938	6691	.244	.361	.299
Home	514-453	3.27	33570	8205	641	2872	5705	.244	.356	.305
Road	453-514	3.64	31993	8072	638	2921	5327	.252	.370	.316
Grass	484-484	3.42	32720	8187	641	2750	5541	.250	.359	.309
Artificial Turf	485-485	3.47	32843	8090	638	3043	5491	.246	.366	.311
April	127-127	3.47	8495	2048	195	807	1423	.241	.365	.308
May	167-167	3.53	11473	2904	217	1068	1884	.253	.366	.318
June	166-166	3.76	11400	2938	221	1054	1859	.258	.376	.322
July	164-164	3.34	11021	2704	210	937	1846	.245	.358	.306
August	172-172	3.31	11532	2823	208	948	2021	.245	.354	.303
Sept./Oct.	173-173	3.30	11642	2860	228	979	1999	.246	.358	.305
Leading Off Inn.			16342	4096	350	1097	2559	.251	.372	.301
Runners On			26978	6934	515	2994	4464	.257	.373	.329
Runners/Scor. Pos.			16085	4016	296	2298	2937	.250	.362	.337
Runners On/2 Out			11741	2790	223	1559	2077	.238	.351	.331
Scor. Pos./2 Out			7852	1815	152	1251	1483	.231	.345	.341
Late Inning Pressure			13055	3167	225	1361	2341	.243	.347	.315
Leading Off			3408	848	68	234	557	.249	.365	.299
Runners On			5175	1281	89	781	925	.248	.350	.344
Runners/Scor. Pos.			3184	786	56	654	613	.247	.352	.369
First 9 Batters			32919	7986	588	3054	6156	.243	.350	.308
Second 9 Batters			16756	4163	347	1363	2688	.248	.367	.307
All Batters Thereafter			15888	4128	344	1376	2188	.260	.383	.320

V
Rankings Section

Rankings Section

The Rankings Section consists of a series of lists ranking players in a wide variety of batting and pitching categories. Players are ranked in 24 batting categories and 24 pitching categories ranging from the simple (batting average, for example) to the more esoteric (like percentage of runners driven in from third base with less than two out). Listed are the players ranking in the top 20 and bottom 20 in each league.

The exact number of plate appearances required to qualify for ranking in each category varies. The number of eligible players for each ranking is determined by the number of players in each league who had 200 or more plate appearances, or who faced 200 or more batters. In the American League, the 175 players and 139 pitchers with the most plate appearances or batters faced in a given category are eligible for ranking; in the National League, the top 127 batters and 124 pitchers are eligible. (If there is a tie for the final position, all tied players are included.) In some categories, a large number of players tied for last place (as, for example, in Home Run Percentage vs. Left-Handed Pitchers). In such cases, a line indicating "42 players tied with 0.00" is used in place of the Bottom 20 list.

The intent here is to rank all players who qualify as at least semiregulars for the season. To do this properly, it is necessary to look at the number of plate appearances in each specific situation. Matt Nokes and Mike Heath platooned at catcher for Detroit last year, and both can be considered as at least "semiregulars." But the vast majority of Nokes's plate appearances were against right-handers, and Heath's were mostly against left-handers. Nokes was one of the 162 American League batters who faced righties most often, so he is ranked there, but he failed to meet this qualification against lefties, so he is not ranked in that category. Heath, of course, is ranked against lefties but not against righties.

The material in this section is generally based on the categories used in the Batter and Pitcher Sections. If any of the breakdowns are unfamiliar, detailed descriptions can be found in the introductions to the Batter and Pitcher Sections.

Batting Average vs. Left-Handed Pitchers

American League

Top 20				Bottom 20			
1. Kirby Puckett	MIN	.398		170. Mel Hall	CLE	.109
2. Julio Franco	CLE	.383		169. Dan Pasqua	CHI	.123
3. Rickey Henderson	NY	.368		168. Bill Schroeder	MIL	.135
4. Kevin Seitzer	KC	.353		167. Darrell Evans	DET	.156
5. Alan Trammell	DET	.348		166. Ron Karkovice	CHI	.164
6. Cory Snyder	CLE	.342		165. Jay Buhner	SEA	.169
7. Terry Steinbach	OAK	.342		164. Mike Pagliarulo	NY	.170
8. Jose Canseco	OAK	.340		163. Al Newman	MIN	.174
9. Gary Gaetti	MIN	.338		162. Fred Lynn	DET	.174
10. Scott Fletcher	TEX	.337		161. Donnie Hill	CHI	.180
11. Manny Lee	TOR	.336		159. Geno Petralli	TEX	.182
12. Dwight Evans	BOS	.333		159. Dave Parker	OAK	.182
13. Dave Winfield	NY	.331		158. Ken Gerhart	BAL	.186
14. Wade Boggs	BOS	.331		157. B.J. Surhoff	MIL	.191
15. Cecil Espy	TEX	.328		155. Mark McLemore	CAL	.200
16. Darnell Coles	SEA	.328		155. Brady Anderson	BAL	.200
17. Rene Gonzales	BAL	.326		154. Steve Balboni	SEA	.201
18. Ellis Burks	BOS	.324		153. Larry Sheets	BAL	.202
19. Alvin Davis	SEA	.321		152. Carney Lansford	OAK	.203
20. Tim Laudner	MIN	.321		151. Willie Upshaw	CLE	.203

National League

Top 20				Bottom 20			
1. Barry Larkin	CIN	.352		129. Von Hayes	PHI	.129
2. Tracy Jones	MTL	.351		128. Luis Alicea	STL	.130
3. Rafael Palmeiro	CHI	.333		127. Jim Morrison	ATL	.152
4. Tony Pena	STL	.331		126. Steve Jeltz	PHI	.152
5. Mike Schmidt	PHI	.330		125. Mike LaValliere	PIT	.159
6. Terry Pendleton	STL	.328		124. Alfredo Griffin	LA	.167
7. Rob Thompson	SF	.325		123. Mike Davis	LA	.172
8. Junior Ortiz	PIT	.324		122. Bruce Benedict	ATL	.182
9. R.J. Reynolds	PIT	.318		121. Howard Johnson	NY	.183
10. Kevin Bass	HOU	.316		120. Jody Davis	ATL	.186
11. Darrin Jackson	CHI	.315		119. Albert Hall	ATL	.188
12. Hubie Brooks	MTL	.314		118. Sid Bream	PIT	.190
13. Bob Dernier	PHI	.314		117. Andy Van Slyke	PIT	.191
14. Tony Gwynn	SD	.314		116. John Kruk	SD	.194
15. Bob Horner	STL	.309		115. Randy Milligan	PIT	.196
16. Ricky Jordan	PHI	.309		114. Kevin Mitchell	SF	.200
17. Rafael Ramirez	HOU	.306		113. Dave Concepcion	CIN	.202
18. Jose Uribe	SF	.303		112. Jeff Hamilton	LA	.205
19. Barry Bonds	PIT	.302		111. Lloyd McClendon	CIN	.206
20. Dickie Thon	SD	.302		110. Bob Brenly	SF	.207

Batting Average vs. Right-Handed Pitchers

American League

Top 20				Bottom 20			
1. Wade Boggs	BOS	.381		170. Ken Williams	CHI	.121
2. Mike Greenwell	BOS	.344		169. Rene Gonzales	BAL	.152
3. Kirby Puckett	MIN	.342		168. Tony Phillips	OAK	.163
4. Kent Hrbek	MIN	.333		167. Jim Eisenreich	KC	.183
5. Paul Molitor	MIL	.329		166. Bill Pecota	KC	.187
6. Dave Gallagher	CHI	.328		165. Jay Bell	CLE	.187
7. Don Mattingly	NY	.323		164. Steve Lombardozzi	MIN	.195
8. John Moses	MIN	.320		163. Mike Gallego	OAK	.195
9. Johnny Ray	CAL	.319		162. Billy Ripken	BAL	.199
10. Dave Winfield	NY	.318		161. Ivan Calderon	CHI	.201
11. Bob Boone	CAL	.316		160. Greg Brock	MIL	.203
12. Robin Yount	MIL	.315		159. Dave Valle	SEA	.206
13. Jody Reed	BOS	.315		158. Gary Pettis	DET	.207
14. Eddie Murray	BAL	.313		157. Mike Kingery	SEA	.208
15. Wally Joyner	CAL	.312		156. Doug Jennings	OAK	.210
16. Terry Francona	CLE	.309		155. Glenn Wilson	SEA	.213
17. Carney Lansford	OAK	.308		154. Daryl Boston	CHI	.213
18. Claudell Washington	NY	.307		153. Larry Parrish	BOS	.214
19. Fred McGriff	TOR	.304		152. Ray Knight	DET	.215
20. Dave Henderson	OAK	.303		151. Jim Traber	BAL	.216

National League

Top 20				Bottom 20			
1. Andy Van Slyke	PIT	.339		128. Bob Brenly	SF	.182
2. Von Hayes	PHI	.327		127. Steve Jeltz	PHI	.197
3. Gerald Perry	ATL	.318		126. Lance Parrish	PHI	.198
4. Tony Gwynn	SD	.312		125. Mike Davis	LA	.203
5. Terry Puhl	HOU	.312		124. Curt Ford	STL	.205
6. Mookie Wilson	NY	.311		123. Kevin Elster	NY	.207
7. Andres Galarraga	MTL	.310		122. Greg Gross	PHI	.208
8. Wally Backman	NY	.309		121. Rafael Belliard	PIT	.208
9. Ricky Jordan	PHI	.307		120. Terry Blocker	ATL	.210
10. Andre Dawson	CHI	.306		118. Alfredo Griffin	LA	.212
11. Brett Butler	SF	.304		118. Bo Diaz	CIN	.212
12. Mark Grace	CHI	.301		117. Dale Murphy	ATL	.214
13. Mike Marshall	LA	.301		116. Leon Durham	CIN	.214
14. Kal Daniels	CIN	.300		115. Darnell Coles	PIT	.216
15. Kevin McReynolds	NY	.297		114. Bob Melvin	SF	.218
16. Rafael Palmeiro	CHI	.296		113. Dickie Thon	SD	.218
17. Vance Law	CHI	.294		112. Terry Pendleton	STL	.221
18. Will Clark	SF	.294		111. Kevin Bass	HOU	.221
19. Ernest Riles	SF	.293		110. R.J. Reynolds	PIT	.221
20. Willie McGee	STL	.290		109. Nelson Santovenia	MTL	.222

Slugging Average vs. Left-Handed Pitchers

American League

Top 20				Bottom 20			
1. Carlton Fisk	CHI	.667		170. Dan Pasqua	CHI	.160
2. Cory Snyder	CLE	.667		169. Darrell Evans	DET	.188
3. Darnell Coles	SEA	.638		168. Al Newman	MIN	.188
4. Julio Franco	CLE	.624		167. Mel Hall	CLE	.196
5. Jose Canseco	OAK	.620		166. Geno Petralli	TEX	.205
6. Kirby Puckett	MIN	.614		165. Willie Upshaw	CLE	.216
7. Dave Winfield	NY	.594		164. Carney Lansford	OAK	.222
8. Gary Gaetti	MIN	.592		163. Joe Orsulak	BAL	.235
9. Ron Kittle	CLE	.562		162. Larry Sheets	BAL	.237
10. Joe Carter	CLE	.553		161. Bill Pecota	KC	.239
11. Chet Lemon	DET	.539		160. Juan Castillo	MIL	.240
12. Danny Tartabull	KC	.537		159. Donnie Hill	CHI	.246
13. Mark McGwire	OAK	.533		158. Mark McLemore	CAL	.246
14. George Brett	KC	.530		157. Brady Anderson	BAL	.247
15. Dave Henderson	OAK	.524		156. Gary Pettis	DET	.250
15. Pete Incaviglia	TEX	.524		155. Walt Weiss	OAK	.257
17. Alan Trammell	DET	.522		153. Jim Walewander	DET	.262
18. Rickey Henderson	NY	.521		153. Jody Reed	BOS	.262
19. Dwight Evans	BOS	.521		152. Billy Ripken	BAL	.263
20. Bo Jackson	KC	.520		151. B.J. Surhoff	MIL	.270

National League

Top 20				Bottom 20			
1. Ricky Jordan	PHI	.605		129. Luis Alicea	STL	.152
2. Darrin Jackson	CHI	.568		128. Mike LaValliere	PIT	.190
3. Darryl Strawberry	NY	.560		127. Steve Jeltz	PHI	.203
4. Barry Larkin	CIN	.559		126. Bruce Benedict	ATL	.221
5. Barry Bonds	PIT	.556		125. Alfredo Griffin	LA	.222
6. Kevin McReynolds	NY	.546		124. Albert Hall	ATL	.225
7. Andres Galarraga	MTL	.543		123. Dave Concepcion	CIN	.237
8. Hubie Brooks	MTL	.538		122. Von Hayes	PHI	.238
9. Kirk Gibson	LA	.520		121. Mike Scioscia	LA	.244
10. Eric Davis	CIN	.517		120. Shane Mack	SD	.255
11. Mike Schmidt	PHI	.516		119. Jody Davis	ATL	.255
12. Ron Gant	ATL	.513		118. Mitch Webster	CHI	.268
13. Tony Pena	STL	.512		117. Rafael Belliard	PIT	.270
14. Darnell Coles	PIT	.506		116. Jim Morrison	ATL	.273
15. Kevin Bass	HOU	.503		115. Joel Youngblood	SF	.277
16. R.J. Reynolds	PIT	.489		114. Lloyd McClendon	CIN	.279
17. Rob Thompson	SF	.487		113. Otis Nixon	MTL	.280
18. Bob Horner	STL	.485		112. Garry Templeton	SD	.289
19. Ryne Sandberg	CHI	.482		111. Mike Davis	LA	.297
20. Rafael Palmeiro	CHI	.480		110. Dave Anderson	LA	.299

Slugging Average vs. Right-Handed Pitchers

American League

Top 20				Bottom 20			
1.	Fred McGriff	TOR	.638	170.	Rene Gonzales	BAL	.185
2.	Mike Greenwell	BOS	.588	169.	Mike Gallego	OAK	.230
3.	Ken Phelps	NY	.570	168.	Jay Bell	CLE	.246
4.	Kent Hrbek	MIN	.569	167.	Tony Phillips	OAK	.248
5.	Jose Canseco	OAK	.552	166.	Jim Eisenreich	KC	.250
6.	Gary Gaetti	MIN	.536	165.	Billy Ripken	BAL	.255
7.	Eddie Murray	BAL	.531	164.	Ken Williams	CHI	.266
8.	Fred Lynn	DET	.528	163.	Ray Knight	DET	.269
9.	Dave Henderson	OAK	.525	162.	Al Newman	MIN	.272
10.	Kirby Puckett	MIN	.521	161.	Pete Stanicek	BAL	.274
11.	Ron Kittle	CLE	.515	160.	Mike Stanley	TEX	.276
12.	Danny Tartabull	KC	.506	159.	Mike Kingery	SEA	.283
13.	Don Mattingly	NY	.505	158.	Glenn Wilson	SEA	.284
14.	Wade Boggs	BOS	.505	157.	Gary Pettis	DET	.293
15.	Steve Balboni	SEA	.502	156.	Luis Salazar	DET	.294
16.	Dave Winfield	NY	.500	155.	Donnie Hill	CHI	.294
17.	George Brett	KC	.499	154.	Scott Fletcher	TEX	.295
18.	Ellis Burks	BOS	.480	153.	Rafael Santana	NY	.296
19.	Paul Molitor	MIL	.479	152.	Terry Kennedy	BAL	.296
20.	Dan Pasqua	CHI	.478	151.	Bill Pecota	KC	.299

National League

Top 20				Bottom 20			
1.	Andy Van Slyke	PIT	.606	128.	Greg Gross	PHI	.216
2.	Will Clark	SF	.554	127.	Rafael Belliard	PIT	.228
3.	Andres Galarraga	MTL	.539	126.	Steve Jeltz	PHI	.247
4.	Darryl Strawberry	NY	.535	125.	Danny Heep	LA	.259
5.	Andre Dawson	CHI	.523	124.	Dickie Thon	SD	.261
6.	Glenn Davis	HOU	.513	123.	Chris Brown	SD	.262
7.	Bobby Bonilla	PIT	.508	122.	Mike Davis	LA	.263
8.	Kal Daniels	CIN	.500	121.	Alfredo Griffin	LA	.265
9.	Kevin Mitchell	SF	.490	120.	Herm Winningham	CIN	.273
10.	Mike Marshall	LA	.486	119.	Curt Ford	STL	.279
11.	Eric Davis	CIN	.480	118.	Dave Collins	CIN	.281
12.	Von Hayes	PHI	.474	117.	Tracy Jones	MTL	.283
13.	Kevin McReynolds	NY	.471	116.	Jose Uribe	SF	.284
14.	Barry Bonds	PIT	.463	114.	Bob Horner	STL	.290
15.	Kirk Gibson	LA	.462	114.	Terry Blocker	ATL	.290
16.	Howard Johnson	NY	.456	113.	Bob Brenly	SF	.291
17.	Tony Gwynn	SD	.451	112.	Otis Nixon	MTL	.292
18.	Ricky Jordan	PHI	.443	111.	Jose Oquendo	STL	.293
19.	Mookie Wilson	NY	.443	110.	Darren Daulton	PHI	.294
20.	Tim Raines	MTL	.441	109.	Bruce Benedict	ATL	.296

Home Run Percentage vs. Left-Handed Pitchers

American League

Top 20				Bottom 20
1.	Carlton Fisk	CHI	10.75	31 players tied with .000
2.	Ron Kittle	CLE	10.11	
3.	Darnell Coles	SEA	8.62	
4.	Cory Snyder	CLE	8.11	
5.	Mark McGwire	OAK	7.33	
6.	Pete Incaviglia	TEX	7.14	
7.	Jack Clark	NY	6.71	
8.	Jose Canseco	OAK	6.67	
9.	Bo Jackson	KC	6.50	
10.	Dave Winfield	NY	6.29	
11.	Ivan Calderon	CHI	6.25	
12.	Cecil Fielder	TOR	6.21	
13.	Gary Gaetti	MIN	6.15	
14.	Mickey Tettleton	BAL	6.12	
15.	Glenn Braggs	MIL	5.88	
16.	Rob Deer	MIL	5.84	
17.	Jesse Barfield	TOR	5.45	
17.	Chet Lemon	DET	5.45	
19.	Danny Tartabull	KC	5.37	
20.	Joe Carter	CLE	5.30	

National League

Top 20				Bottom 20
1.	Darryl Strawberry	NY	9.26	27 players tied with .000
2.	Ricky Jordan	PHI	7.41	
3.	Kevin McReynolds	NY	6.49	
4.	Eric Davis	CIN	5.83	
5.	Andres Galarraga	MTL	5.78	
6.	Barry Bonds	PIT	5.56	
7.	Kirk Gibson	LA	5.39	
8.	Darnell Coles	PIT	5.19	
9.	Dale Murphy	ATL	5.00	
10.	Ron Gant	ATL	4.66	
11.	Carmelo Martinez	SD	4.55	
11.	Jose Oquendo	STL	4.55	
13.	Darrin Jackson	CHI	4.50	
14.	Bo Diaz	CIN	4.49	
15.	Hubie Brooks	MTL	4.49	
16.	Chris James	PHI	4.46	
17.	Keith Hernandez	NY	4.44	
18.	Ryne Sandberg	CHI	4.27	
19.	Howard Johnson	NY	4.23	
20.	Glenn Davis	HOU	4.19	

Home Run Percentage vs. Right-Handed Pitchers

American League

Top 20				Bottom 20			
1.	Ken Phelps	NY	8.30	161.	Scott Fletcher	TEX	0.00
2.	Fred McGriff	TOR	7.95	161.	Jim Gantner	MIL	0.00
3.	Fred Lynn	DET	7.45	161.	Ozzie Guillen	CHI	0.00
4.	Jose Canseco	OAK	6.96	161.	Tom Herr	MIN	0.00
5.	Steve Balboni	SEA	6.83	161.	Ray Knight	DET	0.00
6.	Ron Kittle	CLE	6.62	161.	Rick Leach	TOR	0.00
7.	Kent Hrbek	MIN	6.08	161.	Manny Lee	TOR	0.00
8.	Daryl Boston	CHI	5.93	161.	Al Newman	MIN	0.00
9.	Gary Gaetti	MIN	5.92	161.	Pete Stanicek	BAL	0.00
10.	Darrell Evans	DET	5.90	161.	Curtis Wilkerson	TEX	0.00
11.	Dan Pasqua	CHI	5.87	160.	Marty Barrett	BOS	0.23
12.	Carlton Fisk	CHI	5.63	159.	Willie Wilson	KC	0.25
13.	Brian Downing	CAL	5.50	158.	Stan Javier	OAK	0.33
14.	Eddie Murray	BAL	5.38	157.	Pat Tabler	KC	0.33
15.	Bo Jackson	KC	5.38	156.	Cecil Espy	TEX	0.35
16.	Mark McGwire	OAK	5.25	155.	Willie Randolph	NY	0.36
17.	Jay Buhner	SEA	5.23	154.	Jody Reed	BOS	0.39
18.	Danny Tartabull	KC	5.03	153.	Brady Anderson	BAL	0.42
19.	Dave Henderson	OAK	5.00	152.	Tony Fernandez	TOR	0.47
20.	Jack Clark	NY	4.90	151.	Harold Reynolds	SEA	0.48

National League

Top 20				Bottom 20			
1.	Will Clark	SF	6.21	115.	Wally Backman	NY	0.00
2.	Glenn Davis	HOU	5.84	115.	Rafael Belliard	PIT	0.00
3.	Darryl Strawberry	NY	5.81	115.	Bruce Benedict	ATL	0.00
4.	Andy Van Slyke	PIT	5.74	115.	Dave Collins	CIN	0.00
5.	Eric Davis	CIN	5.40	115.	Tim Flannery	SD	0.00
6.	Carmelo Martinez	SD	5.21	115.	Greg Gross	PHI	0.00
7.	Tom Brunansky	STL	5.11	115.	Danny Heep	LA	0.00
8.	Howard Johnson	NY	5.10	115.	Steve Jeltz	PHI	0.00
9.	Bobby Bonilla	PIT	4.84	115.	Otis Nixon	MTL	0.00
10.	Andre Dawson	CHI	4.63	115.	Ron Oester	CIN	0.00
11.	Mike Marshall	LA	4.49	115.	Jose Oquendo	STL	0.00
12.	Nick Esasky	CIN	4.36	115.	Dickie Thon	SD	0.00
13.	Andres Galarraga	MTL	4.36	115.	Herm Winningham	CIN	0.00
14.	Kal Daniels	CIN	4.17	115.	Gerald Young	HOU	0.00
15.	Kirk Gibson	LA	4.14	114.	Vince Coleman	STL	0.25
16.	Kevin McReynolds	NY	4.09	113.	Ozzie Smith	STL	0.27
17.	Kevin Mitchell	SF	4.06	112.	Jose Uribe	SF	0.29
18.	Barry Bonds	PIT	3.99	111.	Jeff Reed	CIN	0.41
19.	Alan Ashby	HOU	3.83	110.	Dave Magadan	NY	0.44
20.	Paul O'Neill	CIN	3.76	109.	Alfredo Griffin	LA	0.44

Batting Average, Day Games

American League

Top 20				Bottom 20			
1.	Dave Clark	CLE	.390	170.	Ken Gerhart	BAL	.127
2.	George Brett	KC	.374	169.	Ron Kittle	CLE	.138
3.	Claudell Washington	NY	.372	168.	Jim Walewander	DET	.152
4.	Paul Molitor	MIL	.361	167.	Ken Williams	CHI	.159
5.	Bob Boone	CAL	.357	166.	Donnie Hill	CHI	.161
6.	Dave Bergman	DET	.347	165.	Jerry Browne	TEX	.170
7.	John Moses	MIN	.346	164.	Jim Traber	BAL	.173
8.	Wade Boggs	BOS	.344	163.	Pete Incaviglia	TEX	.174
9.	Dave Gallagher	CHI	.344	162.	Jim Presley	SEA	.176
10.	Gary Redus	CHI	.344	161.	Tony Phillips	OAK	.179
11.	Don Slaught	NY	.333	160.	Bill Pecota	KC	.185
12.	Ellis Burks	BOS	.330	159.	Don Baylor	OAK	.186
13.	Rickey Henderson	NY	.329	158.	Billy Ripken	BAL	.186
14.	Kent Hrbek	MIN	.329	157.	Greg Gagne	MIN	.188
15.	Terry Francona	CLE	.329	156.	Greg Brock	MIL	.189
16.	Mark McLemore	CAL	.327	155.	Cecil Fielder	TOR	.190
17.	Luis Polonia	OAK	.324	154.	Cecil Espy	TEX	.192
18.	Willie Wilson	KC	.322	153.	Larry Herndon	DET	.192
19.	Don Mattingly	NY	.321	152.	Ernie Whitt	TOR	.194
20.	Johnny Ray	CAL	.321	151.	Steve Lombardozzi	MIN	.198

National League

Top 20				Bottom 20			
1.	Randy Ready	SD	.452	127.	Alfredo Griffin	LA	.141
2.	Ricky Jordan	PHI	.390	126.	Kevin Elster	NY	.159
3.	Von Hayes	PHI	.362	125.	Rafael Belliard	PIT	.176
4.	Mookie Wilson	NY	.360	124.	Kevin Bass	HOU	.179
5.	Nick Esasky	CIN	.337	123.	Carmelo Martinez	SD	.190
6.	Kevin McReynolds	NY	.333	122.	Bo Diaz	CIN	.194
7.	Wally Backman	NY	.330	120.	Mark Parent	SD	.194
8.	Andres Galarraga	MTL	.321	120.	Terry Puhl	HOU	.195
9.	Tracy Jones	MTL	.319	119.	Chris Brown	SD	.195
10.	Sid Bream	PIT	.314	118.	Jeff Treadway	CIN	.200
11.	Vance Law	CHI	.314	117.	Jeff Hamilton	LA	.202
12.	Gerald Perry	ATL	.308	116.	Jody Davis	ATL	.204
13.	Dave Anderson	LA	.307	115.	Steve Jeltz	PHI	.207
14.	Tony Gwynn	SD	.304	114.	Franklin Stubbs	LA	.213
15.	Rafael Palmeiro	CHI	.303	113.	Chris James	PHI	.213
15.	Mackey Sasser	NY	.303	112.	Gary Carter	NY	.214
17.	Steve Sax	LA	.303	110.	Luis Rivera	MTL	.214
18.	Brett Butler	SF	.302	110.	Mike Davis	LA	.214
19.	Dave Magadan	NY	.301	109.	Buddy Bell	HOU	.215
20.	Marvell Wynne	SD	.301	108.	Bob Melvin	SF	.216

Batting Average, Night Games

American League

Top 20				Bottom 20			
1.	Kirby Puckett	MIN	.380	170.	Ken Williams	CHI	.159
2.	Wade Boggs	BOS	.379	169.	Jay Buhner	SEA	.188
3.	Mike Greenwell	BOS	.329	168.	Jim Eisenreich	KC	.192
4.	Dave Winfield	NY	.324	167.	Gary Pettis	DET	.195
5.	Alan Trammell	DET	.313	166.	Dan Pasqua	CHI	.197
6.	Kevin Seitzer	KC	.307	165.	Al Newman	MIN	.203
7.	Don Mattingly	NY	.306	164.	Ivan Calderon	CHI	.203
8.	Jose Canseco	OAK	.305	163.	Joel Skinner	DET	.206
9.	Kent Hrbek	MIN	.304	161.	Gary Ward	NY	.209
10.	Robin Yount	MIL	.303	161.	Jay Bell	CLE	.209
11.	Terry Francona	CLE	.303	160.	Daryl Boston	CHI	.210
12.	Jody Reed	BOS	.302	159.	Brady Anderson	BAL	.210
13.	Alvin Davis	SEA	.302	158.	Rich Gedman	BOS	.212
14.	Darnell Coles	SEA	.301	157.	Billy Ripken	BAL	.213
15.	Rance Mulliniks	TOR	.301	156.	Terry Kennedy	BAL	.214
16.	Johnny Ray	CAL	.300	154.	Steve Lombardozzi	MIN	.214
17.	Curtis Wilkerson	TEX	.300	153.	Rene Gonzales	BAL	.215
18.	Wally Joyner	CAL	.300	152.	Mike Gallego	OAK	.216
19.	Ron Kittle	CLE	.299	151.	Larry Parrish	BOS	.216
20.	Geno Petralli	TEX	.299				

National League

Top 20				Bottom 20			
1.	Terry Puhl	HOU	.357	127.	Bob Brenly	SF	.152
2.	Andre Dawson	CHI	.319	126.	Randy Ready	SD	.181
3.	Tony Gwynn	SD	.317	125.	Steve Jeltz	PHI	.182
4.	Tom Pagnozzi	STL	.314	124.	Mike Davis	LA	.186
5.	Rafael Palmeiro	CHI	.313	123.	Dave Concepcion	CIN	.200
6.	Bob Dernier	PHI	.312	122.	Alex Trevino	HOU	.205
7.	Mickey Hatcher	LA	.304	121.	Tim Teufel	NY	.206
8.	Pedro Guerrero	STL	.304	120.	Darnell Coles	PIT	.207
9.	Mark Grace	CHI	.301	119.	Luis Alicea	STL	.209
10.	Barry Larkin	CIN	.300	118.	Nick Esasky	CIN	.209
11.	Eric Davis	CIN	.298	117.	Terry Blocker	ATL	.209
12.	Kal Daniels	CIN	.298	116.	Lance Parrish	PHI	.214
13.	Gerald Perry	ATL	.297	115.	Bruce Benedict	ATL	.214
14.	Rex Hudler	MTL	.297	114.	Howard Johnson	NY	.216
15.	Andres Galarraga	MTL	.295	113.	Mike Young	PHI	.216
16.	Willie McGee	STL	.293	112.	Dave Anderson	LA	.217
17.	Kirk Gibson	LA	.292	111.	Alfredo Griffin	LA	.218
18.	Chris Sabo	CIN	.291	110.	Alan Ashby	HOU	.222
19.	Wally Backman	NY	.290	109.	Jeff Reed	CIN	.225
20.	Andy Van Slyke	PIT	.288	108.	Rafael Belliard	PIT	.226

Batting Average, Grass Surfaces

American League

Top 20				Bottom 20			
1.	Wade Boggs	BOS	.363	170.	Ken Williams	CHI	.156
2.	Kent Hrbek	MIN	.340	169.	Bo Jackson	KC	.192
3.	Kirby Puckett	MIN	.335	168.	Mike Gallego	OAK	.193
4.	Mike Greenwell	BOS	.332	167.	Ivan Calderon	CHI	.197
5.	George Brett	KC	.325	166.	Bill Buckner	KC	.197
6.	Dave Gallagher	CHI	.322	165.	Paul Zuvella	CLE	.198
7.	Claudell Washington	NY	.318	162.	Steve Lombardozzi	MIN	.200
8.	Julio Franco	CLE	.318	162.	Tony Phillips	OAK	.200
9.	Rance Mulliniks	TOR	.313	162.	Jay Bell	CLE	.200
10.	Paul Molitor	MIL	.312	161.	Ken Gerhart	BAL	.202
11.	Dave Winfield	NY	.309	160.	Jim Walewander	DET	.208
12.	Henry Cotto	SEA	.309	159.	Mike Pagliarulo	NY	.209
13.	Alan Trammell	DET	.308	158.	Daryl Boston	CHI	.211
14.	Don Mattingly	NY	.308	157.	Gary Pettis	DET	.211
15.	Dave Henderson	OAK	.305	156.	Al Newman	MIN	.211
16.	Carmen Castillo	CLE	.304	155.	Greg Brock	MIL	.212
17.	Terry Francona	CLE	.303	154.	Glenn Wilson	SEA	.214
18.	Robin Yount	MIL	.302	153.	Billy Ripken	BAL	.214
19.	Ellis Burks	BOS	.302	152.	Jeff Kunkel	TEX	.215
20.	Alvin Davis	SEA	.302	151.	Mike Heath	DET	.215

National League

Top 20				Bottom 20			
1.	Von Hayes	PHI	.385	127.	Mike Davis	LA	.155
2.	Andy Van Slyke	PIT	.356	126.	Glenn Davis	HOU	.158
3.	Wally Backman	NY	.335	125.	Stan Jefferson	SD	.160
4.	Pedro Guerrero	STL	.330	124.	Luis Rivera	MTL	.189
5.	Willie McGee	STL	.327	123.	Tony Pena	STL	.192
6.	Bobby Bonilla	PIT	.322	122.	Mark Parent	SD	.195
7.	Gerald Young	HOU	.312	121.	Alfredo Griffin	LA	.196
8.	Ernest Riles	SF	.308	120.	Jeff Treadway	CIN	.198
9.	Kirk Gibson	LA	.308	119.	Jody Davis	ATL	.205
10.	Hubie Brooks	MTL	.305	118.	Juan Samuel	PHI	.206
11.	Rafael Palmeiro	CHI	.304	117.	Franklin Stubbs	LA	.209
12.	Tony Gwynn	SD	.303	116.	Bob Brenly	SF	.211
13.	Vance Law	CHI	.303	115.	Tim Teufel	NY	.212
14.	Brett Butler	SF	.298	114.	Terry Blocker	ATL	.214
15.	Keith Hernandez	NY	.295	113.	Bo Diaz	CIN	.216
16.	Mookie Wilson	NY	.294	112.	Luis Alicea	STL	.216
17.	Paul O'Neill	CIN	.293	111.	Kevin Elster	NY	.218
18.	Tom Brunansky	STL	.293	110.	Tracy Woodson	LA	.219
19.	Mark Grace	CHI	.292	109.	Jose Lind	PIT	.221
20.	Andre Dawson	CHI	.290	108.	Tim Flannery	SD	.222

Batting Average, Artificial Surfaces

American League

Top 20			Bottom 20		
1. Bob Boone	CAL	.429	171. Rich Renteria	SEA	.140
2. Jack Howell	CAL	.413	170. Dale Sveum	MIL	.145
3. Mike Heath	DET	.395	169. Rene Gonzales	BAL	.152
4. Wade Boggs	BOS	.383	168. Billy Ripken	BAL	.156
5. Dave Winfield	NY	.380	166. Carmen Castillo	CLE	.158
6. Carlton Fisk	CHI	.375	166. Darrell Evans	DET	.158
7. Kirby Puckett	MIN	.370	165. Ken Gerhart	BAL	.163
8. Rickey Henderson	NY	.364	164. Larry Parrish	BOS	.178
9. Luis Polonia	OAK	.359	161. Pat Sheridan	DET	.184
10. Johnny Ray	CAL	.355	161. Mike Stanley	TEX	.184
11. Greg Walker	CHI	.354	161. Rick Cerone	BOS	.184
12. Lou Whitaker	DET	.348	160. Tom Brookens	DET	.185
13. Ron Kittle	CLE	.340	159. Jim Rice	BOS	.187
14. Jose Canseco	OAK	.340	157. Pete Incaviglia	TEX	.188
15. Ozzie Guillen	CHI	.337	157. Jay Buhner	SEA	.188
16. Chili Davis	CAL	.337	156. Jim Traber	BAL	.189
17. Cal Ripken	BAL	.329	155. Brady Anderson	BAL	.193
18. Robin Yount	MIL	.327	154. Mike Kingery	SEA	.194
19. Scott Fletcher	TEX	.326	153. Todd Benzinger	BOS	.196
20. Alan Trammell	DET	.325	152. Gary Pettis	DET	.203

National League

Top 20			Bottom 20		
1. Tony Gwynn	SD	.341	127. Al Pedrique	PIT	.155
2. Rob Thompson	SF	.338	126. Casey Candaele	HOU	.158
3. Andre Dawson	CHI	.333	125. Steve Jeltz	PHI	.172
4. Gerald Perry	ATL	.331	124. Darren Daulton	PHI	.183
5. Mike Aldrete	SF	.327	123. Dale Murphy	ATL	.184
6. Kevin McReynolds	NY	.320	121. Ozzie Virgil	ATL	.185
7. Roberto Alomar	SD	.317	121. Curt Ford	STL	.185
8. Ron Jones	PHI	.317	120. Howard Johnson	NY	.190
9. Mike Marshall	LA	.316	119. Kevin Mitchell	SF	.192
10. Rafael Palmeiro	CHI	.313	118. Greg Gross	PHI	.193
11. Len Dykstra	NY	.312	117. Lance Parrish	PHI	.199
12. Glenn Davis	HOU	.311	116. Jeff Reed	CIN	.204
13. Kal Daniels	CIN	.310	115. Shawon Dunston	CHI	.204
14. Mark Grace	CHI	.307	114. Rafael Belliard	PIT	.205
15. Andres Galarraga	MTL	.307	113. Kevin Elster	NY	.206
16. Rex Hudler	MTL	.306	112. Lloyd McClendon	CIN	.209
17. Ricky Jordan	PHI	.305	111. Terry McGriff	CIN	.209
18. Dion James	ATL	.304	110. Carmelo Martinez	SD	.210
19. Barry Larkin	CIN	.304	109. Luis Alicea	STL	.211
20. Terry Puhl	HOU	.302	108. Craig Reynolds	HOU	.213

Batting Average, Home Games

American League

Top 20			Bottom 20		
1. Kirby Puckett	MIN	.406	170. Ken Williams	CHI	.156
2. Wade Boggs	BOS	.382	169. Terry Kennedy	BAL	.176
3. Julio Franco	CLE	.364	168. Mike Heath	DET	.179
4. Claudell Washington	NY	.358	167. Joel Skinner	NY	.180
5. Terry Francona	CLE	.333	166. Daryl Boston	CHI	.181
6. Dave Winfield	NY	.332	165. Ray Knight	DET	.188
7. Mike Greenwell	BOS	.331	164. Ivan Calderon	CHI	.191
8. Ellis Burks	BOS	.325	163. Mike Pagliarulo	NY	.192
9. Luis Polonia	OAK	.322	162. Brady Anderson	BAL	.195
10. Kevin Seitzer	KC	.320	161. Jay Bell	CLE	.197
11. Dwight Evans	BOS	.318	160. Larry Herndon	DET	.198
12. Bo Jackson	KC	.318	158. Gary Pettis	DET	.200
13. Dan Gladden	MIN	.317	158. Don Baylor	OAK	.200
14. Paul Molitor	MIL	.316	157. Steve Lombardozzi	MIN	.204
15. Jose Canseco	OAK	.313	156. Larry Sheets	BAL	.206
16. Alan Trammell	DET	.312	155. Jay Buhner	SEA	.214
17. Jody Reed	BOS	.309	154. Mark McLemore	CAL	.216
18. Rick Cerone	BOS	.308	153. Rafael Santana	NY	.217
19. Robin Yount	MIL	.307	152. Tony Phillips	OAK	.217
20. Kent Hrbek	MIN	.304	151. Mike Gallego	OAK	.218

National League

Top 20			Bottom 20		
1. Terry Puhl	HOU	.377	128. Mike Davis	LA	.150
2. Wally Backman	NY	.340	127. Alex Trevino	HOU	.167
3. Ricky Jordan	PHI	.331	126. Bob Brenly	SF	.177
4. Kal Daniels	CIN	.330	125. Steve Jeltz	PHI	.179
5. Tracy Jones	MTL	.330	124. Jody Davis	ATL	.181
6. Rafael Palmeiro	CHI	.321	123. Alfredo Griffin	LA	.184
7. Kirk Gibson	LA	.316	122. Darnell Coles	PIT	.184
8. Ozzie Virgil	ATL	.315	121. Kevin Elster	NY	.194
9. Gerald Perry	ATL	.314	120. Jeff Reed	CIN	.198
10. Andres Galarraga	MTL	.314	119. Dave Collins	CIN	.200
11. Andre Dawson	CHI	.314	118. Bo Diaz	CIN	.206
12. Pedro Guerrero	STL	.313	117. Tim Teufel	NY	.208
13. Tony Gwynn	SD	.310	116. Mike Aldrete	SF	.208
14. John Shelby	LA	.309	115. Gary Carter	NY	.211
15. Barry Larkin	CIN	.307	114. Alan Ashby	HOU	.211
16. Steve Sax	LA	.302	113. Albert Hall	ATL	.212
17. Vance Law	CHI	.302	112. R.J. Reynolds	PIT	.213
18. Dave Magadan	NY	.301	111. Howard Johnson	NY	.213
19. Jose Lind	PIT	.300	110. Rafael Belliard	PIT	.213
20. Jeff Treadway	CIN	.299	109. Bobby Bonilla	PIT	.217

Batting Average, Road Games

American League

Top 20			Bottom 20		
1. John Moses	MIN	.355	170. Ken Gerhart	BAL	.159
2. Wade Boggs	BOS	.351	169. Ken Williams	CHI	.162
3. Don Mattingly	NY	.327	168. Larry Parrish	BOS	.175
4. Mike Greenwell	BOS	.319	167. Bo Jackson	KC	.180
5. Kent Hrbek	MIN	.319	165. Mike Stanley	TEX	.189
6. George Brett	KC	.318	165. Tony Phillips	OAK	.189
7. Cory Snyder	CLE	.315	164. Greg Brock	MIL	.189
8. Johnny Ray	CAL	.314	163. Billy Ripken	BAL	.191
9. Dave Henderson	OAK	.314	162. Jerry Browne	TEX	.194
10. Dave Winfield	NY	.312	161. Darrell Evans	DET	.194
11. Rickey Henderson	NY	.312	160. Bill Pecota	KC	.198
12. Carney Lansford	OAK	.312	158. Bobby Meacham	NY	.200
13. Alan Trammell	DET	.311	158. Mike Gallego	OAK	.200
14. Wally Joyner	CAL	.309	157. Dale Sveum	MIL	.202
15. Bob Boone	CAL	.309	156. Carmen Castillo	CLE	.202
16. Kirby Puckett	MIN	.308	155. Jim Traber	BAL	.202
17. Tony Armas	CAL	.308	154. Jamie Quirk	KC	.204
18. Dave Gallagher	CHI	.307	153. Donnie Hill	CHI	.205
19. Paul Molitor	MIL	.307	152. Pete Stanicek	BAL	.206
20. Tom Herr	MIN	.307	151. Cecil Espy	TEX	.208

National League

Top 20			Bottom 20		
1. Mookie Wilson	NY	.332	128. Nelson Santovenia	MTL	.192
2. Bobby Bonilla	PIT	.329	127. Dale Murphy	ATL	.194
3. Tony Gwynn	SD	.315	126. Steve Jeltz	PHI	.195
4. Mike Aldrete	SF	.315	125. Luis Alicea	STL	.196
5. Von Hayes	PHI	.313	124. Herm Winningham	CIN	.196
6. Alex Trevino	HOU	.312	123. Jeff Hamilton	LA	.199
7. Willie McGee	STL	.301	122. Bob Brenly	SF	.200
8. Kevin McReynolds	NY	.300	121. Chris Brown	SD	.200
9. Hubie Brooks	MTL	.297	120. Luis Rivera	MTL	.203
10. Mark Grace	CHI	.297	119. Lance Parrish	PHI	.204
11. Will Clark	SF	.295	118. Terry Blocker	ATL	.204
11. Rafael Ramirez	HOU	.295	117. Ozzie Virgil	ATL	.205
11. Dickie Thon	SD	.295	116. Mike Schmidt	PHI	.211
14. Rafael Palmeiro	CHI	.293	115. Mike Young	PHI	.211
15. Sid Bream	PIT	.292	114. Rafael Belliard	PIT	.213
16. Billy Hatcher	HOU	.292	113. Jeff Treadway	CIN	.213
17. Andre Dawson	CHI	.292	111. Juan Samuel	PHI	.214
18. Mike Marshall	LA	.291	111. Darrin Jackson	CHI	.214
19. Andres Galarraga	MTL	.291	110. Carmelo Martinez	SD	.214
20. R.J. Reynolds	PIT	.289	109. Alfredo Griffin	LA	.215

Slugging Average, Home Games

American League

Top 20

1.	Kirby Puckett	MIN	.638
2.	Darnell Coles	SEA	.621
3.	Ken Phelps	NY	.581
4.	Mike Greenwell	BOS	.564
5.	Danny Tartabull	KC	.562
6.	Bo Jackson	KC	.555
7.	Wade Boggs	BOS	.547
8.	Dwight Evans	BOS	.542
9.	Jose Canseco	OAK	.538
10.	Carlton Fisk	CHI	.537
11.	Fred McGriff	TOR	.536
12.	Kent Hrbek	MIN	.526
13.	Ellis Burks	BOS	.524
14.	Rance Mulliniks	TOR	.521
15.	Dave Winfield	NY	.518
16.	Ron Kittle	CLE	.518
17.	Dave Henderson	OAK	.512
18.	Claudell Washington	NY	.509
19.	Alvin Davis	SEA	.509
20.	Ruben Sierra	TEX	.505

Bottom 20

170.	Jim Walewander	DET	.240
169.	Terry Kennedy	BAL	.243
168.	Gary Pettis	DET	.248
167.	Tom Herr	MIN	.263
165.	Billy Ripken	BAL	.264
165.	Brady Anderson	BAL	.264
164.	Al Newman	MIN	.266
163.	Willie Randolph	NY	.267
162.	Rafael Santana	NY	.271
161.	Don Baylor	OAK	.273
160.	Joel Skinner	NY	.279
159.	Jim Eisenreich	KC	.283
158.	Ken Williams	CHI	.284
157.	Ray Knight	DET	.286
156.	Rene Gonzales	BAL	.288
155.	Walt Weiss	OAK	.289
154.	Jay Bell	CLE	.291
153.	B.J. Surhoff	MIL	.291
152.	Bob Brower	TEX	.291
151.	Donnie Hill	CHI	.292

National League

Top 20

1.	Andres Galarraga	MTL	.588
2.	Darryl Strawberry	NY	.581
3.	Andy Van Slyke	PIT	.575
4.	Kal Daniels	CIN	.555
5.	Kirk Gibson	LA	.527
6.	Ricky Jordan	PHI	.521
7.	Barry Bonds	PIT	.516
8.	Andre Dawson	CHI	.515
9.	Glenn Davis	HOU	.510
10.	Terry Puhl	HOU	.509
11.	Dale Murphy	ATL	.505
12.	Eric Davis	CIN	.491
13.	Chris Speier	SF	.489
14.	Carmelo Martinez	SD	.489
15.	Rafael Palmeiro	CHI	.486
16.	Nelson Santovenia	MTL	.485
17.	Will Clark	SF	.484
18.	Matt Williams	SF	.474
19.	Chris Sabo	CIN	.473
20.	Kevin Mitchell	SF	.470

Bottom 20

128.	Mike Davis	LA	.203
127.	Alfredo Griffin	LA	.209
126.	Alex Trevino	HOU	.238
125.	Steve Jeltz	PHI	.239
124.	Bob Brenly	SF	.250
123.	Alan Ashby	HOU	.252
122.	Bruce Benedict	ATL	.254
121.	Dave Collins	CIN	.256
120.	Dickie Thon	SD	.268
119.	Jeff Reed	CIN	.270
118.	Rafael Belliard	PIT	.272
117.	Dave Anderson	LA	.273
116.	Otis Nixon	MTL	.276
115.	Ron Oester	CIN	.277
114.	Mike Aldrete	SF	.283
113.	Tim Teufel	NY	.285
111.	Tim Flannery	SD	.286
111.	Darnell Coles	PIT	.286
110.	Gerald Young	HOU	.288
109.	Albert Hall	ATL	.288

Slugging Average, Road Games

American League

Top 20

1.	Gary Gaetti	MIN	.606
2.	Jose Canseco	OAK	.596
3.	Cory Snyder	CLE	.581
4.	Fred McGriff	TOR	.566
5.	Carlton Fisk	CHI	.545
6.	Ron Kittle	CLE	.543
7.	Dave Winfield	NY	.540
8.	Dave Henderson	OAK	.536
9.	Ken Phelps	NY	.522
10.	Mark McGwire	OAK	.520
11.	George Brett	KC	.518
12.	Kent Hrbek	MIN	.514
13.	Tony Armas	CAL	.509
14.	Daryl Boston	CHI	.503
15.	Mike Greenwell	BOS	.495
16.	Kelly Gruber	TOR	.495
17.	Eddie Murray	BAL	.487
18.	Robin Yount	MIL	.480
19.	Ivan Calderon	CHI	.474
20.	Don Mattingly	NY	.472

Bottom 20

170.	Mike Gallego	OAK	.222
169.	Al Newman	MIN	.235
168.	Tony Phillips	OAK	.236
167.	Jerry Browne	TEX	.237
166.	Bill Pecota	KC	.241
165.	Rene Gonzales	BAL	.244
164.	Billy Ripken	BAL	.251
163.	Bob Brower	TEX	.255
162.	Mike Stanley	TEX	.264
161.	Jay Bell	CLE	.266
159.	Bobby Meacham	NY	.267
159.	Steve Lombardozzi	MIN	.267
158.	Cecil Espy	TEX	.271
157.	Greg Brock	MIL	.272
155.	Donnie Hill	CHI	.273
155.	Ken Gerhart	BAL	.273
154.	Gary Ward	NY	.275
153.	Jim Eisenreich	KC	.282
152.	Glenn Wilson	SEA	.283
151.	Carmen Castillo	CLE	.284

National League

Top 20

1.	Bobby Bonilla	PIT	.594
2.	Will Clark	SF	.531
3.	Kevin McReynolds	NY	.524
4.	Mookie Wilson	NY	.523
5.	Alan Ashby	HOU	.519
6.	Darryl Strawberry	NY	.514
7.	Andres Galarraga	MTL	.495
8.	Andre Dawson	CHI	.493
9.	Tom Brunansky	STL	.489
10.	Eric Davis	CIN	.488
11.	Hubie Brooks	MTL	.483
12.	Mark Grace	CHI	.470
13.	Barry Bonds	PIT	.468
14.	Alex Trevino	HOU	.468
15.	Keith Hernandez	NY	.465
16.	Von Hayes	PHI	.458
17.	Ricky Jordan	PHI	.458
18.	Mike Marshall	LA	.457
19.	Ron Gant	ATL	.453
20.	Darnell Coles	PIT	.451

Bottom 20

128.	Rafael Belliard	PIT	.213
127.	Herm Winningham	CIN	.224
126.	Steve Jeltz	PHI	.236
125.	Luis Alicea	STL	.242
124.	Chris Brown	SD	.250
123.	Terry Blocker	ATL	.265
122.	Jose Lind	PIT	.268
121.	Ken Griffey	CIN	.283
120.	Ozzie Virgil	ATL	.287
119.	Nelson Santovenia	MTL	.288
118.	Mike Young	PHI	.289
117.	Terry Puhl	HOU	.289
116.	Bruce Benedict	ATL	.291
115.	Tom Pagnozzi	STL	.292
114.	Wally Backman	NY	.293
113.	Alfredo Griffin	LA	.297
112.	Juan Samuel	PHI	.298
111.	Lance Parrish	PHI	.299
110.	Jeff Treadway	CIN	.299
109.	Terry Pendleton	STL	.299

Batting Average with Runners On Base

American League

Top 20

1.	Terry Francona	CLE	.390
2.	Bill Buckner	KC	.357
3.	Paul Molitor	MIL	.357
4.	George Brett	KC	.348
5.	Kirby Puckett	MIN	.344
6.	Johnny Ray	CAL	.342
7.	Dave Winfield	NY	.340
8.	Wade Boggs	BOS	.339
9.	Rick Leach	TOR	.337
10.	Pat Tabler	KC	.336
11.	Kelly Gruber	TOR	.336
12.	Bob Boone	CAL	.333
13.	Manny Lee	TOR	.331
14.	Mike Greenwell	BOS	.326
15.	Ellis Burks	BOS	.326
16.	Kevin Seitzer	KC	.324
17.	Dave Henderson	OAK	.322
18.	Robin Yount	MIL	.321
19.	Don Mattingly	NY	.320
20.	Tony Fernandez	TOR	.319

Bottom 20

170.	Ken Gerhart	BAL	.155
169.	Mark McLemore	CAL	.161
168.	Donnie Hill	CHI	.170
167.	Ivan Calderon	CHI	.174
166.	Glenn Wilson	SEA	.176
164.	Billy Ripken	BAL	.185
164.	Terry Kennedy	BAL	.185
163.	Ken Williams	CHI	.188
162.	Bob Brower	TEX	.189
161.	Dan Pasqua	CHI	.194
160.	Daryl Boston	CHI	.194
159.	Fred Lynn	DET	.198
158.	Lloyd Moseby	TOR	.203
157.	Gary Ward	NY	.207
156.	Tom Brookens	DET	.210
155.	Darrell Evans	DET	.211
154.	Greg Gagne	MIN	.212
153.	Mike Gallego	OAK	.213
152.	Spike Owen	BOS	.216
151.	Jerry Browne	TEX	.218

National League

Top 20

1.	Tony Gwynn	SD	.382
2.	Gerald Perry	ATL	.358
3.	Steve Sax	LA	.333
4.	Marvell Wynne	SD	.328
5.	Eric Davis	CIN	.327
6.	Pedro Guerrero	STL	.327
7.	Ernest Riles	SF	.325
8.	Milt Thompson	PHI	.323
9.	Mickey Hatcher	LA	.323
10.	Tim Raines	MTL	.317
11.	Mark Grace	CHI	.317
12.	Dave Magadan	NY	.316
13.	Ozzie Smith	STL	.314
14.	Barry Larkin	CIN	.313
15.	Ricky Jordan	PHI	.311
16.	Kevin McReynolds	NY	.311
17.	Herm Winningham	CIN	.309
18.	Keith Hernandez	NY	.308
19.	Von Hayes	PHI	.308
19.	Ryne Sandberg	CHI	.308

Bottom 20

127.	Tim Teufel	NY	.176
126.	Luis Alicea	STL	.178
125.	Dave Concepcion	CIN	.185
124.	Mike Davis	LA	.191
123.	Benito Santiago	SD	.195
121.	Bob Brenly	SF	.198
121.	Dale Murphy	ATL	.198
119.	Chris Speier	SF	.200
119.	Howard Johnson	NY	.200
118.	Bo Diaz	CIN	.212
117.	Franklin Stubbs	LA	.213
116.	Rex Hudler	MTL	.218
115.	Jeff Reed	CIN	.219
114.	Alfredo Griffin	LA	.221
113.	Dave Anderson	LA	.221
112.	Chris Brown	SD	.223
111.	Chris James	PHI	.226
110.	Darrin Jackson	CHI	.226
109.	Tom Brunansky	STL	.226
108.	Steve Jeltz	PHI	.229

Batting Average in Pressure Situations

American League

Top 20				Bottom 20		
1. Terry Francona	CLE	.452		173. Walt Weiss	OAK	.071
2. Rance Mulliniks	TOR	.424		172. Tony Phillips	OAK	.088
3. Alan Trammell	DET	.403		171. Jay Buhner	SEA	.093
4. Gary Ward	NY	.382		170. Brady Anderson	BAL	.106
5. Tony Fernandez	TOR	.364		169. Mike Heath	DET	.119
6. Dick Schofield	CAL	.358		168. Henry Cotto	SEA	.122
7. Robin Yount	MIL	.351		167. Jamie Quirk	KC	.125
8. Kent Hrbek	MIN	.348		166. Bob Brower	TEX	.138
9. Wally Joyner	CAL	.347		165. Mike Gallego	OAK	.143
10. Kelly Gruber	TOR	.346		164. Dave Clark	CLE	.149
11. Kirby Puckett	MIN	.346		163. Jim Traber	BAL	.150
12. Gary Gaetti	MIN	.344		161. Doug Jennings	OAK	.154
13. Mickey Brantley	SEA	.342		161. Terry Steinbach	OAK	.154
13. Luis Polonia	OAK	.342		160. Fred Lynn	DET	.155
15. Dale Sveum	MIL	.338		159. Willie Randolph	NY	.156
16. Harold Baines	CHI	.333		157. Rick Cerone	BOS	.156
16. Jim Eppard	CAL	.333		157. Mike Macfarlane	KC	.156
16. Julio Franco	CLE	.333		156. Fred Manrique	CHI	.158
16. John Moses	MIN	.333		154. Ernie Whitt	TOR	.159
20. Claudell Washington	NY	.328		154. Pete Stanicek	BAL	.159

National League

Top 20				Bottom 20		
1. Milt Thompson	PHI	.421		127. Jody Davis	ATL	.118
2. Mickey Hatcher	LA	.410		126. Steve Jeltz	PHI	.128
3. Terry Puhl	HOU	.375		125. Mike Schmidt	PHI	.131
4. Damon Berryhill	CHI	.361		124. Lloyd McClendon	CIN	.132
5. Kirk Gibson	LA	.348		123. Jeff Hamilton	LA	.140
6. Tim Raines	MTL	.347		122. Kevin Elster	NY	.145
7. Wallace Johnson	MTL	.340		121. Ted Simmons	ATL	.146
8. Tony Gwynn	SD	.338		120. Dickie Thon	SD	.150
9. Greg Gross	PHI	.333		119. Lee Mazzilli	NY	.163
9. Kevin McReynolds	NY	.333		118. Franklin Stubbs	LA	.167
11. Andre Dawson	CHI	.330		117. Bill Doran	HOU	.172
12. Mark Grace	CHI	.329		116. Shawon Dunston	CHI	.173
13. Billy Hatcher	HOU	.326		115. Dave Collins	CIN	.179
13. Chris Sabo	CIN	.326		114. Marvell Wynne	SD	.180
15. Gerald Young	HOU	.322		113. Terry Pendleton	STL	.182
16. Barry Larkin	CIN	.319		112. Von Hayes	PHI	.186
17. Keith Hernandez	NY	.317		111. Lance Parrish	PHI	.187
17. Steve Sax	LA	.317		110. Bo Diaz	CIN	.188
19. Ozzie Virgil	ATL	.316		109. Dave Magadan	NY	.189
20. Vance Law	CHI	.316		107. Luis Rivera	MTL	.189
20. Joel Youngblood	SF	.316		107. Darryl Strawberry	NY	.189

Home Run Percentage in Pressure Situations

American League

Top 20			Bottom 20
1. Brian Downing	CAL	9.88	64 players tied with .000
2. Gary Gaetti	MIN	9.38	
3. Ken Phelps	NY	9.26	
4. Cory Snyder	CLE	9.21	
5. Mark McGwire	OAK	8.43	
6. Pete O'Brien	TEX	7.69	
7. Carlton Fisk	CHI	7.41	
8. Kent Hrbek	MIN	7.25	
9. Chet Lemon	DET	7.23	
10. Steve Balboni	SEA	7.02	
11. Alan Trammell	DET	6.94	
12. Don Slaught	NY	6.52	
13. Ron Kittle	CLE	6.25	
14. Darrell Evans	DET	5.97	
15. Gary Ward	NY	5.88	
16. Rich Gedman	BOS	5.71	
17. Matt Nokes	DET	5.66	
18. Jose Canseco	OAK	5.62	
19. Greg Gagne	MIN	5.56	
20. George Bell	TOR	5.41	

National League

Top 20			Bottom 20
1. Keith Hernandez	NY	9.76	49 players tied with .000
2. Mike Marshall	LA	7.14	
3. Andres Galarraga	MTL	6.90	
4. Kevin Mitchell	SF	6.41	
5. Eric Davis	CIN	6.17	
6. Alan Ashby	HOU	6.12	
7. Darryl Strawberry	NY	5.41	
8. Rick Dempsey	LA	5.26	
9. John Shelby	LA	5.19	
10. Paul O'Neill	CIN	5.13	
11. Damon Berryhill	CHI	4.92	
12. Carmelo Martinez	SD	4.84	
13. Tom Brunansky	STL	4.76	
13. Franklin Stubbs	LA	4.76	
15. Kevin McReynolds	NY	4.60	
16. Howard Johnson	NY	4.41	
17. Gary Carter	NY	3.90	
18. Kevin Elster	NY	3.64	
19. Hubie Brooks	MTL	3.51	
20. Will Clark	SF	3.45	

% of Runners Driven in from Scoring Position, Pressure Situations

American League

Top 20				Bottom 20		
1. Terry Francona	CLE	.571		165. Brady Anderson	BAL	.000
1. Rickey Henderson	NY	.571		165. Ken Gerhart	BAL	.000
1. Ron Washington	CLE	.571		165. Larry Herndon	DET	.000
4. Alan Trammell	DET	.533		165. Terry Kennedy	BAL	.000
5. Kevin Seitzer	KC	.526		165. Darrell Miller	CAL	.000
6. Todd Benzinger	BOS	.500		165. Rick Schu	BAL	.000
7. Ron Hassey	OAK	.474		165. Jim Sundberg	TEX	.000
8. Gene Larkin	MIN	.462		165. Walt Weiss	OAK	.000
9. Bill Buckner	KC	.458		164. Fred McGriff	TOR	.050
10. Andy Allanson	CLE	.455		163. Jeffrey Leonard	MIL	.071
11. Kelly Gruber	TOR	.444		161. Glenn Hubbard	OAK	.077
12. Wally Joyner	CAL	.440		161. Chet Lemon	DET	.077
13. Dave Valle	SEA	.438		159. Rich Gedman	BOS	.083
14. Jim Dwyer	MIN	.429		159. Geno Petralli	TEX	.083
14. George Hendrick	CAL	.429		154. Bob Brower	TEX	.091
14. Gary Ward	NY	.429		154. Jay Buhner	SEA	.091
17. George Brett	KC	.421		154. Dave Clark	CLE	.091
17. Pat Tabler	KC	.421		154. Pete O'Brien	TEX	.091
19. Luis Salazar	DET	.407		154. Gary Pettis	DET	.091
20. Gary Gaetti	MIN	.400		149. Daryl Boston	CHI	.100
20. Doug Jennings	OAK	.400		149. Carney Lansford	OAK	.100
20. Joey Meyer	MIL	.400		149. Willie Randolph	NY	.100

National League

Top 20				Bottom 20		
1. Tony Gwynn	SD	.524		128. Alfredo Griffin	LA	.000
2. Jeffrey Leonard	SF	.500		128. Mike Scioscia	LA	.000
2. Craig Reynolds	HOU	.500		126. Mike Aldrete	SF	.071
4. Dave Anderson	LA	.455		126. Chris Brown	SD	.071
4. Bobby Bonilla	PIT	.455		125. Jody Davis	ATL	.077
4. Mickey Hatcher	LA	.455		124. Ted Simmons	ATL	.080
4. Vance Law	CHI	.455		122. Candy Maldonado	SF	.091
8. Steve Sax	LA	.429		122. Marvell Wynne	SD	.091
9. Alan Ashby	HOU	.400		120. Dion James	ATL	.100
10. Keith Hernandez	NY	.389		120. Mike Diaz	PIT	.100
10. Gerald Young	HOU	.389		119. Wallace Johnson	MTL	.105
12. Mike LaValliere	PIT	.381		118. Jerry Mumphrey	CHI	.111
12. Graig Nettles	MTL	.381		117. Chris James	PHI	.115
12. Tim Raines	MTL	.381		116. Barry Bonds	PIT	.130
15. Damon Berryhill	CHI	.375		114. Jim Morrison	ATL	.133
15. Kal Daniels	CIN	.375		114. Dave Collins	CIN	.133
15. Kirk Gibson	LA	.375		112. Luis Alicea	STL	.136
18. Keith Moreland	SD	.368		112. Benito Santiago	SD	.136
19. Andres Thomas	ATL	.366		111. Kevin Mitchell	SF	.138
20. Bob Brenly	SF	.364		108. Brett Butler	SF	.143
20. Will Clark	SF	.364		108. Mark Grace	CHI	.143
20. Bob Horner	STL	.364		108. Jeff Hamilton	LA	.143

On Base Average Leading Off the Inning

American League

Top 20				Bottom 20		
1. Wade Boggs	BOS	.476		171. Mike Pagliarulo	NY	.156
2. Fred McGriff	TOR	.460		170. Bill Buckner	KC	.162
3. Kirby Puckett	MIN	.453		169. Mike Heath	DET	.180
4. Mike Greenwell	BOS	.441		168. Ken Williams	CHI	.186
5. Pat Sheridan	DET	.422		167. Joel Skinner	NY	.200
6. Carlton Fisk	CHI	.421		166. Jim Eisenreich	KC	.204
7. Dave Henderson	OAK	.410		165. Jay Bell	CLE	.209
8. Rickey Henderson	NY	.399		164. Brady Anderson	BAL	.211
9. Ernie Whitt	TOR	.398		163. George Bell	TOR	.212
10. Ken Phelps	NY	.398		162. Rene Gonzales	BAL	.213
11. Terry Kennedy	BAL	.397		161. Steve Lombardozzi	MIN	.219
12. Gary Ward	NY	.392		160. Steve Balboni	SEA	.221
13. Don Slaught	NY	.385		159. Ken Gerhart	BAL	.227
14. Alan Trammell	DET	.380		158. Pete Stanicek	BAL	.228
15. Tom Brookens	DET	.379		157. Rick Schu	BAL	.229
16. Tony Phillips	OAK	.378		156. Willie Randolph	NY	.229
17. Gene Larkin	MIN	.377		155. Rick Leach	TOR	.233
18. Kent Hrbek	MIN	.376		154. Cecil Espy	TEX	.242
19. Jose Canseco	OAK	.375		153. Fred Manrique	CHI	.243
19. Cal Ripken	BAL	.375		152. Dale Sveum	MIL	.245

National League

Top 20				Bottom 20		
1. Dave Anderson	LA	.446		127. Casey Candaele	HOU	.191
2. Kirk Gibson	LA	.416		127. Dave Collins	CIN	.191
3. Ricky Jordan	PHI	.412		126. Bo Diaz	CIN	.209
4. Jose Oquendo	STL	.408		125. Alfredo Griffin	LA	.211
5. Terry Puhl	HOU	.393		124. Rafael Belliard	PIT	.211
6. Howard Johnson	NY	.390		123. Mike Davis	LA	.220
7. Rafael Palmeiro	CHI	.388		122. John Cangelosi	PIT	.222
8. Keith Hernandez	NY	.388		121. Bruce Benedict	ATL	.230
9. Mark Grace	CHI	.387		120. Damon Berryhill	CHI	.236
10. Von Hayes	PHI	.386		119. Herm Winningham	CIN	.237
11. Brett Butler	SF	.384		117. Dave Magadan	NY	.239
12. Darryl Strawberry	NY	.377		117. R.J. Reynolds	PIT	.239
13. Nick Esasky	CIN	.375		116. Shawon Dunston	CHI	.244
14. Jody Davis	ATL	.373		115. Sid Bream	PIT	.245
14. Tim Teufel	NY	.373		114. Terry Blocker	ATL	.246
16. Tony Gwynn	SD	.372		113. Lance Parrish	PHI	.248
17. Ron Oester	CIN	.367		110. Jeff Hamilton	LA	.250
18. Eric Davis	CIN	.365		110. Nelson Santovenia	MTL	.250
19. Andre Dawson	CHI	.362		110. Kevin Bass	HOU	.250
20. Chris Sabo	CIN	.361		109. Luis Rivera	MTL	.253

Batting Average with Runners in Scoring Position

American League

Top 20				Bottom 20		
1. Kirby Puckett	MIN	.366		171. Bobby Meacham	NY	.125
2. Robin Yount	MIL	.364		170. Glenn Wilson	SEA	.134
3. Bob Boone	CAL	.361		169. Bob Brower	TEX	.157
4. Dan Gladden	MIN	.360		168. Spike Owen	BOS	.158
5. Cecil Espy	TEX	.354		167. Fred Lynn	DET	.161
6. Dave Valle	SEA	.350		166. Terry Kennedy	BAL	.179
7. Paul Molitor	MIL	.350		165. Ray Knight	DET	.184
8. Kelly Gruber	TOR	.348		164. Dan Pasqua	CHI	.186
8. Bill Buckner	KC	.348		163. Ken Williams	CHI	.189
9. Tony Fernandez	TOR	.348		162. Gary Ward	NY	.189
11. Rick Leach	TOR	.344		161. Donnie Hill	CHI	.190
12. Mark McGwire	OAK	.340		160. Ken Gerhart	BAL	.191
13. Dave Winfield	NY	.340		159. Mark McLemore	CAL	.196
14. Glenn Braggs	MIL	.333		158. Jerry Browne	TEX	.196
14. Ellis Burks	BOS	.333		157. Jim Eisenreich	KC	.200
14. Pat Tabler	KC	.333		156. Willie Upshaw	CLE	.202
17. Mike Greenwell	BOS	.332		155. Steve Lombardozzi	MIN	.203
18. Carney Lansford	OAK	.328		154. Brian Downing	CAL	.204
19. Luis Salazar	DET	.328		153. Gary Redus	CHI	.204
20. Dwight Evans	BOS	.326		152. Greg Gagne	MIN	.210

National League

Top 20				Bottom 20		
1. Pedro Guerrero	STL	.371		127. Tim Teufel	NY	.139
2. Tony Gwynn	SD	.371		126. Benito Santiago	SD	.148
3. Steve Sax	LA	.350		125. Dave Concepcion	CIN	.159
4. Gerald Perry	ATL	.346		124. Rex Hudler	MTL	.167
5. Gerald Young	HOU	.339		123. Dave Anderson	LA	.182
6. Marvell Wynne	SD	.338		122. Bob Melvin	SF	.183
7. Ricky Jordan	PHI	.333		121. Wally Backman	NY	.190
7. Barry Larkin	CIN	.333		120. Bo Diaz	CIN	.190
7. Mike LaValliere	PIT	.333		119. Darrin Jackson	CHI	.193
10. Mickey Hatcher	LA	.328		118. Len Dykstra	NY	.195
11. Tim Raines	MTL	.325		117. Ken Griffey	CIN	.196
12. Roberto Alomar	SD	.324		116. Howard Johnson	NY	.197
13. Kevin McReynolds	NY	.319		115. Darryl Strawberry	NY	.201
14. Kal Daniels	CIN	.319		114. Luis Rivera	MTL	.202
15. Mookie Wilson	NY	.318		113. Damon Berryhill	CHI	.202
16. Will Clark	SF	.316		112. Chris James	PHI	.204
17. Eric Davis	CIN	.314		111. Kevin Elster	NY	.204
18. Dave Magadan	NY	.311		110. Alex Trevino	HOU	.205
19. Rafael Ramirez	HOU	.310		109. Mike Davis	LA	.207
20. Kevin Bass	HOU	.307		108. Jody Davis	ATL	.211

Batting Average with Runners in Scoring Position and Two Outs

American League

Top 20				Bottom 20		
1. Dave Valle	SEA	.447		172. Spike Owen	BOS	.000
2. Tony Phillips	OAK	.389		171. Mark Salas	CHI	.048
3. Robin Yount	MIL	.388		170. Jerry Browne	TEX	.083
4. Tony Fernandez	TOR	.386		169. Bob Brower	TEX	.087
5. Andy Allanson	CLE	.373		168. Brady Anderson	BAL	.107
6. Dave Henderson	OAK	.371		166. Fred Lynn	DET	.111
7. Dave Bergman	DET	.367		166. Ivan Calderon	CHI	.111
8. Dwight Evans	BOS	.362		165. Jay Buhner	SEA	.115
9. Joey Meyer	MIL	.361		164. Bobby Meacham	NY	.120
10. Luis Salazar	DET	.352		163. Jesse Barfield	TOR	.130
11. Brian Harper	MIN	.348		162. Glenn Wilson	SEA	.138
12. Rick Leach	TOR	.346		161. Devon White	CAL	.140
13. Cecil Espy	TEX	.341		160. Dave Gallagher	CHI	.143
14. Pat Tabler	KC	.339		158. Ray Knight	DET	.147
15. Matt Nokes	DET	.333		158. Terry Kennedy	BAL	.147
16. Dan Gladden	MIN	.328		157. Darrell Evans	DET	.150
17. Gary Gaetti	MIN	.323		156. Gary Ward	NY	.152
18. Jim Eppard	CAL	.318		155. Carlton Fisk	CHI	.156
18. Manny Lee	TOR	.318		154. Rich Gedman	BOS	.158
20. Chet Lemon	DET	.315		153. Rick Schu	BAL	.160

National League

Top 20				Bottom 20		
1. Steve Sax	LA	.419		127. Mike Young	PHI	.056
2. Milt Thompson	PHI	.393		126. Rex Hudler	MTL	.083
3. Mookie Wilson	NY	.385		125. Benito Santiago	SD	.085
4. Kevin Bass	HOU	.379		124. Wally Backman	NY	.094
5. Mike LaValliere	PIT	.375		123. Len Dykstra	NY	.098
6. Mike Marshall	LA	.361		122. Jeff Reed	CIN	.115
7. Gerald Perry	ATL	.358		121. Luis Rivera	MTL	.128
8. Mackey Sasser	NY	.348		120. Gary Carter	NY	.135
9. Will Clark	SF	.345		119. Howard Johnson	NY	.141
10. Bill Doran	HOU	.340		118. Tim Teufel	NY	.143
11. Roberto Alomar	SD	.339		117. Rob Thompson	SF	.146
12. Eric Davis	CIN	.338		115. Jose Uribe	SF	.148
13. Tim Raines	MTL	.333		115. Bob Horner	STL	.148
13. Garry Templeton	SD	.333		113. Ozzie Virgil	ATL	.152
15. Franklin Stubbs	LA	.323		113. Terry Puhl	HOU	.158
16. Buddy Bell	HOU	.322		112. Bo Diaz	CIN	.163
17. Tim Flannery	SD	.318		111. Tom Pagnozzi	STL	.167
18. Barry Larkin	CIN	.314		110. Nelson Santovenia	MTL	.171
19. Kal Daniels	CIN	.311		108. Rafael Belliard	PIT	.172
19. John Kruk	SD	.311		108. Billy Hatcher	HOU	.172

Batting Average with Runners On Base and Two Outs

American League							National League						
Top 20			**Bottom 20**				**Top 20**			**Bottom 20**			
1. Dave Valle	SEA	.415	172. Spike Owen	BOS	.083		1. Milt Thompson	PHI	.392	128. Rex Hudler	MTL	.135
2. Dave Bergman	DET	.391	171. Ivan Calderon	CHI	.102		2. Gerald Perry	ATL	.371	127. Howard Johnson	NY	.138
3. Tony Phillips	OAK	.387	170. Mark McLemore	CAL	.128		3. Eric Davis	CIN	.370	126. Terry Puhl	HOU	.147
4. Tony Fernandez	TOR	.369	169. Jerry Browne	TEX	.139		4. Steve Sax	LA	.365	125. Wally Backman	NY	.150
5. Bill Buckner	KC	.367	168. Bob Brower	TEX	.143		5. Mike LaValliere	PIT	.362	124. Mike Davis	LA	.167
6. Brian Harper	MIN	.366	167. Tom Brookens	DET	.145		6. Tim Raines	MTL	.352	123. Bob Horner	STL	.171
7. Dave Henderson	OAK	.361	166. Jim Walewander	DET	.147		7. Mike Marshall	LA	.336	122. Dale Murphy	ATL	.174
8. Harold Reynolds	SEA	.359	165. Mike Heath	DET	.149		8. Tony Pena	STL	.330	121. Mike Scioscia	LA	.176
9. Joey Meyer	MIL	.357	164. Jesse Barfield	TOR	.153		9. Tony Gwynn	SD	.328	120. Luis Rivera	MTL	.177
10. Manny Lee	TOR	.347	163. Brook Jacoby	CLE	.155		10. Ernest Riles	SF	.324	119. Rob Thompson	SF	.180
11. Johnny Ray	CAL	.346	162. Darrell Evans	DET	.156		11. Andre Dawson	CHI	.314	118. Benito Santiago	SD	.184
12. George Brett	KC	.343	159. Glenn Wilson	SEA	.159		12. Kevin Bass	HOU	.313	117. Len Dykstra	NY	.185
13. Carmen Castillo	CLE	.343	159. Brady Anderson	BAL	.159		13. Ken Oberkfell	PIT	.311	116. Chris Brown	SD	.186
14. Robin Yount	MIL	.340	159. Jay Buhner	SEA	.159		14. Dave Magadan	NY	.310	115. Bob Brenly	SF	.188
15. Pat Tabler	KC	.337	158. Dan Pasqua	CHI	.163		15. Dave Concepcion	CIN	.310	114. Chris James	PHI	.189
16. Rick Leach	TOR	.333	156. Fred Lynn	DET	.167		16. Garry Templeton	SD	.309	113. Jeff Reed	CIN	.190
17. Andy Allanson	CLE	.329	156. Rene Gonzales	BAL	.167		17. Bill Doran	HOU	.308	112. Rafael Belliard	PIT	.191
18. Pete Stanicek	BAL	.323	155. Donnie Hill	CHI	.171		18. Mookie Wilson	NY	.305	111. Luis Alicea	STL	.192
19. Dave Winfield	NY	.322	154. Dave Gallagher	CHI	.176		19. Will Clark	SF	.303	110. Ricky Jordan	PHI	.193
20. Chet Lemon	DET	.319	153. Greg Brock	MIL	.177		20. Vance Law	CHI	.303	109. Alfredo Griffin	LA	.196

% of Runners Driven in from Scoring Position

American League							National League						
Top 20			**Bottom 20**				**Top 20**			**Bottom 20**			
1. Bill Buckner	KC	.374	170. Tony Phillips	OAK	.140		1. Tony Gwynn	SD	.418	129. Rafael Belliard	PIT	.143
2. Kirby Puckett	MIN	.370	168. Glenn Wilson	SEA	.143		2. Pedro Guerrero	STL	.382	128. Rex Hudler	MTL	.145
3. Cecil Espy	TEX	.367	168. Bob Brower	TEX	.143		3. Gerald Perry	ATL	.381	127. Bob Melvin	SF	.167
4. Dave Winfield	NY	.357	167. Spike Owen	BOS	.164		4. Mike LaValliere	PIT	.368	126. Mike Davis	LA	.174
5. George Brett	KC	.356	166. Terry Kennedy	BAL	.182		5. R.J. Reynolds	PIT	.367	125. Benito Santiago	SD	.175
6. Tony Fernandez	TOR	.354	165. Daryl Boston	CHI	.186		6. Alan Ashby	HOU	.353	124. Darrin Jackson	CHI	.183
7. Wally Joyner	CAL	.354	164. Mark McLemore	CAL	.188		7. Rick Dempsey	LA	.346	123. Luis Rivera	MTL	.189
8. Rickey Henderson	NY	.353	163. Fred Lynn	DET	.190		8. Mike Aldrete	SF	.341	122. Alex Trevino	HOU	.192
9. Pat Tabler	KC	.353	162. Gary Ward	NY	.191		9. Milt Thompson	PHI	.337	121. Kevin Elster	NY	.198
10. Dwight Evans	BOS	.349	161. Dan Pasqua	CHI	.192		10. Mickey Hatcher	LA	.328	120. Damon Berryhill	CHI	.202
11. Ron Hassey	OAK	.348	160. Lloyd Moseby	TOR	.193		11. Steve Sax	LA	.324	119. Chris James	PHI	.206
12. Robin Yount	MIL	.346	159. Greg Gagne	MIN	.197		12. Ernest Riles	SF	.323	118. Bo Diaz	CIN	.208
13. Ernie Whitt	TOR	.343	158. B.J. Surhoff	MIL	.203		13. Ricky Jordan	PHI	.321	117. Jeff Reed	CIN	.209
14. Dave Henderson	OAK	.341	157. Brady Anderson	BAL	.205		14. Curt Ford	STL	.321	116. Dave Anderson	LA	.210
15. Glenn Braggs	MIL	.338	156. Mickey Brantley	SEA	.205		15. Tim Raines	MTL	.316	115. Chris Speier	SF	.212
16. Harold Baines	CHI	.337	155. Jesse Barfield	TOR	.206		16. Keith Hernandez	NY	.316	114. Gary Carter	NY	.212
17. Wade Boggs	BOS	.333	154. Bill Pecota	KC	.207		17. Darnell Coles	PIT	.315	113. Len Dykstra	NY	.214
17. Mel Hall	CLE	.333	152. Rick Schu	BAL	.210		18. Kevin Bass	HOU	.314	112. Ozzie Virgil	ATL	.216
17. Cal Ripken	BAL	.333	152. Pete Incaviglia	TEX	.210		18. Dave Magadan	NY	.314	110. Chris Sabo	CIN	.217
20. Dan Gladden	MIN	.331	151. Ken Phelps	NY	.210		20. Will Clark	SF	.313	110. Tony Pena	STL	.217

% of Runners Driven in from Third with Less than Two Out

American League							National League						
Top 20			**Bottom 20**				**Top 20**			**Bottom 20**			
1. Dave Gallagher	CHI	.917	169. Mark Davidson	MIN	.333		1. R.J. Reynolds	PIT	.864	129. Darrin Jackson	CHI	.308
2. Rickey Henderson	NY	.870	169. Greg Gagne	MIN	.333		2. Tom Foley	MTL	.842	128. Alex Trevino	HOU	.333
3. Cal Ripken	BAL	.828	169. Al Newman	MIN	.333		3. Tim Flannery	SD	.800	127. Luis Alicea	STL	.381
4. Joe Orsulak	BAL	.818	169. Tony Phillips	OAK	.333		3. Mickey Hatcher	LA	.800	125. Bruce Benedict	ATL	.385
5. Don Baylor	OAK	.778	168. Pete Incaviglia	TEX	.350		5. Bob Horner	STL	.769	125. Ozzie Virgil	ATL	.385
5. Bill Buckner	KC	.778	167. Pete Stanicek	BAL	.364		6. Alan Ashby	HOU	.750	121. Buddy Bell	HOU	.400
5. Cecil Espy	TEX	.778	166. Dave Valle	SEA	.370		6. Sid Bream	PIT	.750	121. Kevin Elster	NY	.400
7. Marty Barrett	BOS	.750	165. Tony Armas	CAL	.381		6. Tony Gwynn	SD	.750	121. Mark Parent	SD	.400
8. Carlton Fisk	CHI	.750	164. Bill Pecota	KC	.385		6. Gerald Perry	ATL	.750	121. Benito Santiago	SD	.400
8. Mel Hall	CLE	.750	162. B.J. Surhoff	MIL	.389		10. Steve Jeltz	PHI	.737	119. Dave Anderson	LA	.412
11. George Brett	KC	.743	162. Glenn Wilson	SEA	.389		11. Len Dykstra	NY	.733	119. Jeff Reed	CIN	.412
12. Willie Randolph	NY	.737	160. Eddie Murray	BAL	.391		12. Wally Backman	NY	.727	118. Roberto Alomar	SD	.417
13. Jim Dwyer	MIN	.727	160. Steve Balboni	SEA	.391		12. Junior Ortiz	PIT	.727	117. Jeff Hamilton	LA	.429
13. Joel Skinner	NY	.727	156. Darryl Hamilton	MIL	.400		14. Billy Hatcher	HOU	.720	116. Kevin McReynolds	NY	.441
15. Kirby Puckett	MIN	.725	156. Jim Eppard	CAL	.400		14. Ernest Riles	SF	.714	114. Bill Doran	HOU	.452
16. Mike Stanley	TEX	.706	156. Cecil Fielder	TOR	.400		15. Mitch Webster	CHI	.714	114. Tony Pena	STL	.452
17. Jim Adduci	MIL	.700	156. Bob Brower	TEX	.400		17. Pedro Guerrero	STL	.710	112. Tom Brunansky	STL	.455
17. Darrell Evans	DET	.700	155. Larry Parrish	BOS	.409		18. Gerald Young	HOU	.706	112. Rafael Belliard	PIT	.455
17. Don Slaught	NY	.700	154. Ken Williams	CHI	.412		19. Brett Butler	SF	.700	111. Lee Mazzilli	NY	.462
20. Greg Brock	MIL	.696	153. Dan Pasqua	CHI	.414		19. Dave Collins	CIN	.700	110. Andres Galarraga	MTL	.468
20. Steve Lyons	CHI	.696					19. Mike Young	PHI	.700			

Opponents' Batting Average

American League

Top 20			Bottom 20		
1. Jeff Robinson	DET	.197	129. Steve Trout	SEA	.361
2. Dennis Eckersley	OAK	.198	128. Terry Clark	CAL	.323
3. Mitch Williams	TEX	.203	127. Tommy John	NY	.308
4. Ted Higuera	MIL	.207	126. Doug Sisk	BAL	.306
5. Juan Berenguer	MIN	.207	125. Ted Power	DET	.306
6. Juan Nieves	MIL	.208	124. Mark Eichhorn	TOR	.304
7. Willie Hernandez	DET	.208	123. Charlie Lea	MIN	.301
8. Mike Jackson	SEA	.209	122. Steve Shields	NY	.298
9. Dave Stieb	TOR	.210	121. John Davis	CHI	.297
10. Bryan Harvey	CAL	.214	120. Bill Swift	SEA	.295
11. Bobby Witt	TEX	.216	119. Bert Blyleven	MIN	.294
12. Eric Plunk	OAK	.217	118. Jay Tibbs	BAL	.293
13. Mike Henneman	DET	.218	117. Mike Smithson	BOS	.292
14. Doug Jones	CLE	.218	116. Ricky Horton	CHI	.291
15. Wes Gardner	BOS	.220	115. Oil Can Boyd	BOS	.289
16. Roger Clemens	BOS	.220	114. Tim Stoddard	NY	.286
17. Charlie Hough	TEX	.221	113. Mike Birkbeck	MIL	.285
18. Scott Bankhead	SEA	.224	112. Dennis Lamp	BOS	.284
19. Lee Smith	BOS	.225	111. Don Gordon	CLE	.284
20. Greg Cadaret	OAK	.226	110. Todd Stottlemyre	TOR	.283

National League

Top 20			Bottom 20		
1. Jay Howell	LA	.188	109. Joaquin Andujar	HOU	.297
2. Randy Myers	NY	.190	108. Zane Smith	ATL	.292
3. Sid Fernandez	NY	.191	107. Bob Forsch	HOU	.290
4. Pascual Perez	MTL	.196	106. Shane Rawley	PHI	.286
5. John Franco	CIN	.198	105. Frank DiPino	CHI	.285
6. Mark Davis	SD	.199	104. Ron Robinson	CIN	.285
7. Mike Scott	HOU	.204	103. John Smoltz	ATL	.285
8. Lance McCullers	SD	.205	102. Rick Mahler	ATL	.282
9. Jose Rijo	CIN	.209	101. Tim Crews	LA	.278
10. Greg Harris	PHI	.209	100. Greg Booker	SD	.278
11. Floyd Youmans	MTL	.213	99. Jimmy Jones	SD	.277
12. David Cone	NY	.213	98. Brian Fisher	PIT	.277
13. Orel Hershiser	LA	.213	97. Kent Tekulve	PHI	.276
14. Todd Worrell	STL	.214	96. Mike Maddux	PHI	.275
15. Jeff Parrett	MTL	.214	95. Bruce Ruffin	PHI	.275
16. Tim Belcher	LA	.217	94. Les Lancaster	CHI	.273
17. Joe Magrane	STL	.217	93. Jamie Moyer	CHI	.272
18. Alejandro Pena	LA	.218	92. Danny Cox	STL	.272
19. Jim Deshaies	HOU	.218	91. Tim Burke	MTL	.272
20. Danny Jackson	CIN	.218	90. Neal Heaton	MTL	.271

Opponents' Slugging Average

American League

Top 20			Bottom 20		
1. Doug Jones	CLE	.268	129. Steve Trout	SEA	.538
2. Dennis Eckersley	OAK	.270	128. Oil Can Boyd	BOS	.515
3. Greg Cadaret	OAK	.282	127. David Wells	TOR	.492
4. Greg Minton	CAL	.282	126. Mike Smithson	BOS	.489
5. Bryan Harvey	CAL	.293	125. Charlie Lea	MIN	.488
6. Ted Higuera	MIL	.300	124. Willie Fraser	CAL	.477
7. Mitch Williams	TEX	.305	123. Jeff Bittiger	CHI	.476
8. Mike Henneman	DET	.308	122. Mike Campbell	SEA	.473
9. Dave Stieb	TOR	.316	121. Terry Clark	CAL	.465
10. Eric Plunk	OAK	.318	120. Mark Thurmond	BAL	.464
11. Bobby Witt	TEX	.319	119. Doyle Alexander	DET	.455
12. Mark Gubicza	KC	.320	118. Todd Stottlemyre	TOR	.455
13. Roger Clemens	BOS	.320	117. Richard Dotson	NY	.454
14. Juan Berenguer	MIN	.325	116. Bill Long	CHI	.453
15. Charlie Hough	TEX	.326	115. Ted Power	DET	.447
16. Duane Ward	TOR	.327	114. Jay Tibbs	BAL	.447
17. Jeff Robinson	DET	.332	113. Oswaldo Peraza	BAL	.444
18. Dave Stewart	OAK	.333	112. John Davis	CHI	.440
19. Bob Stanley	BOS	.336	111. Curt Young	OAK	.435
20. Lee Smith	BOS	.338	110. Bert Blyleven	MIN	.434

National League

Top 20			Bottom 20		
1. Jay Howell	LA	.239	109. John Smoltz	ATL	.473
2. John Franco	CIN	.241	108. Neal Heaton	MTL	.468
3. Mark Davis	SD	.244	107. Joaquin Andujar	HOU	.454
4. Randy Myers	NY	.278	106. Shane Rawley	PHI	.447
5. Alejandro Pena	LA	.279	105. Mark Grant	SD	.439
6. Roger McDowell	NY	.283	104. Pat Perry	CHI	.434
7. Brian Holton	LA	.291	103. Jack Armstrong	CIN	.431
8. David Cone	NY	.293	102. Brian Fisher	PIT	.425
9. Scott Garrelts	SF	.294	101. Danny Cox	STL	.413
10. Tim Belcher	LA	.296	100. Jimmy Jones	SD	.411
11. Jose Rijo	CIN	.300	99. Bob Forsch	HOU	.411
12. Greg Harris	PHI	.301	98. Don Carman	PHI	.407
13. Pascual Perez	MTL	.303	97. Jamie Moyer	CHI	.405
14. Joe Magrane	STL	.304	96. Mike Maddux	PHI	.399
15. Sid Fernandez	NY	.305	95. Tom Browning	CIN	.397
16. Rob Murphy	CIN	.306	94. Mario Soto	CIN	.397
17. Orel Hershiser	LA	.310	93. Tim Burke	MTL	.395
18. Danny Jackson	CIN	.312	92. Frank DiPino	CHI	.394
19. Mike LaCoss	SF	.317	91. Les Lancaster	CHI	.393
20. Bob Ojeda	NY	.317	90. Danny Darwin	HOU	.392

Opponents' Home Run Percentage

American League

Top 20			Bottom 20		
1. Doug Jones	CLE	0.32	129. David Wells	TOR	4.96
2. Greg Minton	CAL	0.35	128. Oil Can Boyd	BOS	4.91
3. Greg Cadaret	OAK	0.75	127. Mike Smithson	BOS	4.89
4. Doug Sisk	BAL	0.84	126. Jeff Bittiger	CHI	4.76
5. Dennis Lamp	BOS	0.93	125. Willie Fraser	CAL	4.34
6. Mark Gubicza	KC	1.09	124. Richard Dotson	NY	4.04
7. Mark Eichhorn	TOR	1.15	123. Mike Campbell	SEA	3.94
8. Duane Ward	TOR	1.21	122. Scott Bailes	CLE	3.93
9. Jeff Musselman	TOR	1.26	121. Curt Young	OAK	3.90
10. Dave Stewart	OAK	1.36	120. Todd Stottlemyre	TOR	3.90
11. Bryan Harvey	CAL	1.45	119. Cecilio Guante	TEX	3.70
11. Mike Witt	CAL	1.45	118. Charlie Lea	MIN	3.67
13. Ricky Horton	CHI	1.46	117. Keith Atherton	MIN	3.61
14. Bill Swift	SEA	1.48	116. Stu Cliburn	CAL	3.53
15. Dave Righetti	NY	1.49	115. Tom Niedenfuer	BAL	3.51
16. Tommy John	NY	1.53	114. Melido Perez	CHI	3.47
17. Scott Bankhead	SEA	1.56	113. Mark Thurmond	BAL	3.46
18. Kirk McCaskill	CAL	1.59	112. Jim Clancy	TOR	3.42
19. Bob Stanley	BOS	1.61	111. Dan Petry	CAL	3.41
20. Dave LaPoint	CHI	1.62	110. Mark Langston	SEA	3.35

National League

Top 20			Bottom 20		
1. Roger McDowell	NY	0.30	109. Pat Perry	CHI	3.95
2. Brian Holton	LA	0.33	108. Tom Browning	CIN	3.93
3. Joe Hesketh	MTL	0.38	107. Neal Heaton	MTL	3.88
4. Jay Howell	LA	0.43	106. Mark Grant	SD	3.87
5. Mark Davis	SD	0.57	105. John Smoltz	ATL	3.85
6. Bob Walk	PIT	0.75	104. Shane Rawley	PHI	3.52
7. Brian Holman	MTL	0.79	103. Jack Armstrong	CIN	3.25
8. Scott Garrelts	SF	0.85	102. Jim Gott	PIT	3.21
9. Dwight Gooden	NY	0.85	101. Bob Kipper	PIT	3.03
10. Bob Ojeda	NY	0.85	100. Al Nipper	CHI	2.99
11. Larry Andersen	HOU	0.93	99. Joaquin Andujar	HOU	2.84
12. Kent Tekulve	PHI	0.95	98. Mike Krukow	SF	2.77
13. Joe Magrane	STL	0.98	97. Danny Darwin	HOU	2.74
14. John Franco	CIN	0.99	96. Ron Darling	NY	2.70
15. Rob Murphy	CIN	1.00	95. Jim Deshaies	HOU	2.66
16. Scott Terry	STL	1.04	94. Floyd Youmans	MTL	2.66
17. Tim Crews	LA	1.08	93. Jeff Parrett	MTL	2.60
18. Andy McGaffigan	MTL	1.15	92. Doug Drabek	PIT	2.59
19. Alejandro Pena	LA	1.16	91. Jamie Moyer	CHI	2.57
20. Mike LaCoss	SF	1.18	89. Frank Williams	CIN	2.56
			89. Norm Charlton	CIN	2.56

Opponents' Extra Base Hits per 100 At Bats

American League

	Top 20				Bottom 20		
1.	Bobby Thigpen	CHI	3.41	129.	Oil Can Boyd	BOS	11.79
2.	Dennis Eckersley	OAK	3.42	128.	David Wells	TOR	11.57
3.	Doug Jones	CLE	3.47	127.	Willie Fraser	CAL	11.43
4.	Greg Cadaret	OAK	4.14	126.	Steve Trout	SEA	11.34
5.	Greg Minton	CAL	4.18	125.	Jeff Bittiger	CHI	11.26
6.	Doug Sisk	BAL	4.21	124.	Mike Campbell	SEA	10.94
7.	Bryan Harvey	CAL	4.35	123.	Charlie Lea	MIN	10.62
8.	Mike Henneman	DET	4.83	122.	Mark Thurmond	BAL	10.38
9.	Duane Ward	TOR	5.08	121.	Richard Dotson	NY	10.16
10.	Eric Plunk	OAK	5.24	120.	John Davis	CHI	10.04
11.	Bobby Witt	TEX	5.48	119.	Doyle Alexander	DET	9.87
12.	Ted Higuera	MIL	5.54	118.	Bill Long	CHI	9.87
13.	Mark Gubicza	KC	5.63	117.	Oswaldo Peraza	BAL	9.80
14.	Jeff Russell	TEX	5.75	116.	Mike Smithson	BOS	9.78
15.	Mark Eichhorn	TOR	5.77	115.	Mark Williamson	BAL	9.59
16.	Bud Black	CLE	5.79	114.	Neil Allen	NY	9.51
17.	Dave LaPoint	CHI	5.83	113.	Ted Power	DET	9.34
18.	Dave Stieb	TOR	5.88	112.	Mike Flanagan	TOR	9.24
19.	Bob Stanley	BOS	5.91	111.	Ricky Horton	CHI	9.22
20.	Charlie Hough	TEX	5.91	110.	Tim Stoddard	NY	9.22

National League

	Top 20				Bottom 20		
1.	John Franco	CIN	2.31	109.	Neal Heaton	MTL	10.53
2.	Roger McDowell	NY	2.68	108.	John Smoltz	ATL	10.38
3.	Mark Davis	SD	3.13	107.	Jack Armstrong	CIN	10.16
4.	Alejandro Pena	LA	3.78	106.	Danny Cox	STL	9.48
5.	Jay Howell	LA	3.85	105.	Greg Mathews	STL	9.31
6.	Randy Myers	NY	4.22	104.	Brian Fisher	PIT	9.17
7.	Brian Holton	LA	4.64	103.	Mark Grant	SD	9.12
8.	Scott Garrelts	SF	4.80	102.	Tom Browning	CIN	9.06
9.	Rob Murphy	CIN	4.98	101.	Joaquin Andujar	HOU	8.83
10.	Tim Belcher	LA	5.01	100.	Pat Perry	CHI	8.77
11.	David Cone	NY	5.14	99.	Mike Maddux	PHI	8.76
12.	Greg Harris	PHI	5.24	98.	Les Lancaster	CHI	8.59
13.	Larry Andersen	HOU	5.26	97.	Shane Rawley	PHI	8.46
14.	Greg Maddux	CHI	5.30	96.	Joe Price	SF	8.44
15.	Zane Smith	ATL	5.32	95.	Jim Deshaies	HOU	8.38
16.	Orel Hershiser	LA	5.33	94.	Jimmy Jones	SD	8.23
17.	Mike LaCoss	SF	5.44	93.	Charlie Puleo	ATL	8.19
18.	Juan Agosto	HOU	5.50	92.	Larry McWilliams	STL	8.19
19.	Dwight Gooden	NY	5.51	91.	Floyd Youmans	MTL	7.97
20.	Pascual Perez	MTL	5.61	90.	Dennis Rasmussen	SD	7.97

Opponents' Batting Average, Left-Handed Batters

American League

	Top 20				Bottom 20		
1.	John Candelaria	NY	.144	130.	Todd Stottlemyre	TOR	.371
2.	Bryan Harvey	CAL	.147	129.	Doug Sisk	BAL	.358
3.	Juan Nieves	MIL	.148	128.	Jerry Reed	SEA	.355
4.	Paul Mirabella	MIL	.167	127.	Terry Clark	CAL	.351
5.	John Cerutti	TOR	.190	126.	Dewayne Buice	CAL	.338
6.	Jeff Robinson	DET	.197	125.	Steve Shields	NY	.336
7.	Greg Cadaret	OAK	.198	124.	Neil Allen	NY	.328
8.	Dennis Eckersley	OAK	.198	123.	Charlie Lea	MIN	.327
9.	Shawn Hillegas	CHI	.200	122.	John Davis	CHI	.324
10.	Mark Langston	SEA	.201	121.	Jack Lazorko	CAL	.321
11.	Doug Jones	CLE	.203	120.	Allan Anderson	MIN	.320
12.	Eric Plunk	OAK	.205	119.	Jeff Sellers	BOS	.318
13.	Jose Guzman	TEX	.205	118.	Mike Morgan	BAL	.317
14.	Ted Higuera	MIL	.208	117.	Dale Mohorcic	NY	.315
15.	Frank Tanana	DET	.210	116.	Bobby Thigpen	CHI	.315
16.	Juan Berenguer	MIN	.212	115.	Dennis Lamp	BOS	.313
17.	Eric King	DET	.213	114.	Bill Long	CHI	.311
18.	Floyd Bannister	KC	.214	113.	Bill Swift	SEA	.307
19.	Charles Hudson	NY	.215	112.	Bert Blyleven	MIN	.304
20.	Dave Stieb	TOR	.218	111.	Jay Tibbs	BAL	.299

National League

	Top 20				Bottom 20		
1.	Juan Agosto	HOU	.140	109.	Danny Cox	STL	.341
2.	Lance McCullers	SD	.153	108.	Ron Robinson	CIN	.331
3.	John Smiley	PIT	.159	107.	Brian Fisher	PIT	.326
4.	Bob Ojeda	NY	.165	106.	John Smoltz	ATL	.314
5.	Jay Howell	LA	.169	104.	Fernando Valenzuela	LA	.313
6.	Joe Magrane	STL	.177	104.	Mike Maddux	PHI	.313
7.	Kelly Downs	SF	.184	103.	Greg Booker	SD	.311
8.	Mike Scott	HOU	.185	102.	Marvin Freeman	PHI	.309
9.	Frank DiPino	CHI	.192	100.	Dave Smith	HOU	.306
10.	Andy McGaffigan	MTL	.192	100.	Tim Burke	MTL	.306
11.	Larry McWilliams	STL	.202	99.	Tim Crews	LA	.304
12.	Randy O'Neal	STL	.204	98.	Jack Armstrong	CIN	.302
13.	Greg Harris	PHI	.209	97.	Rich Gossage	CHI	.301
14.	Mark Davis	SD	.209	96.	Charlie Puleo	ATL	.298
15.	Jeff Parrett	MTL	.210	95.	Calvin Schiraldi	CHI	.298
16.	Tim Belcher	LA	.212	94.	Dennis Rasmussen	SD	.297
17.	Todd Worrell	STL	.213	93.	Mike Bielecki	CHI	.296
18.	Pascual Perez	MTL	.213	92.	Jeff Pico	CHI	.296
19.	Nolan Ryan	HOU	.215	91.	Larry Andersen	HOU	.293
20.	Rob Dibble	CIN	.215	90.	Jimmy Jones	SD	.293

Opponents' Batting Average, Right-Handed Batters

American League

	Top 20				Bottom 20		
1.	Craig McMurtry	TEX	.163	129.	Steve Trout	SEA	.386
2.	Mike Jackson	SEA	.169	128.	Don Gordon	CLE	.326
3.	Roger Clemens	BOS	.183	127.	Oswaldo Peraza	BAL	.318
4.	Todd Stottlemyre	TOR	.191	126.	Tim Stoddard	NY	.316
5.	Scott Bankhead	SEA	.193	125.	Tommy John	NY	.315
6.	Jerry Reed	SEA	.196	124.	Ted Power	DET	.314
7.	Jeff Robinson	DET	.197	123.	Mike Birkbeck	MIL	.308
8.	Dennis Eckersley	OAK	.197	122.	Mark Eichhorn	TOR	.308
9.	Wes Gardner	BOS	.200	121.	Mike Campbell	SEA	.306
10.	Willie Hernandez	DET	.200	120.	Terry Clark	CAL	.298
11.	Dave Stieb	TOR	.201	119.	Les Straker	MIN	.297
12.	Keith Atherton	MIN	.201	118.	Richard Dotson	NY	.295
13.	Juan Berenguer	MIN	.202	117.	Bret Saberhagen	KC	.295
14.	Steve Farr	KC	.203	116.	Ricky Horton	CHI	.295
15.	Mike Morgan	BAL	.203	115.	Mike Smithson	BOS	.293
16.	Ted Higuera	MIL	.206	114.	Mark Thurmond	BAL	.290
17.	Bobby Witt	TEX	.207	113.	Bud Black	CLE	.289
18.	Mitch Williams	TEX	.211	112.	Storm Davis	OAK	.287
19.	Mark Gubicza	KC	.215	110.	Bryan Harvey	CAL	.286
20.	Jack McDowell	CHI	.216	110.	Oil Can Boyd	BOS	.286

National League

	Top 20				Bottom 20		
1.	David Cone	NY	.165	109.	German Jimenez	ATL	.339
2.	Pascual Perez	MTL	.177	108.	Frank DiPino	CHI	.335
3.	Jose Rijo	CIN	.184	107.	Bob Forsch	HOU	.334
4.	Sid Fernandez	NY	.185	106.	Kent Tekulve	PHI	.323
5.	Alejandro Pena	LA	.186	105.	Joaquin Andujar	HOU	.308
6.	Floyd Youmans	MTL	.189	104.	Zane Smith	ATL	.302
7.	Danny Cox	STL	.192	103.	Rick Mahler	ATL	.301
8.	Randy Myers	NY	.193	102.	Shane Rawley	PHI	.291
9.	Mark Davis	SD	.195	101.	Terry Mulholland	SF	.288
10.	Jeff Pico	CHI	.202	100.	Jamie Moyer	CHI	.281
11.	Bob Walk	PIT	.202	99.	Neal Heaton	MTL	.280
12.	Brian Holton	LA	.204	98.	Dwight Gooden	NY	.278
13.	Calvin Schiraldi	CHI	.204	97.	Andy McGaffigan	MTL	.276
14.	Orel Hershiser	LA	.206	96.	Joe Price	SF	.276
15.	Eric Show	SD	.206	95.	Tom Glavine	ATL	.275
16.	Pete Smith	ATL	.207	94.	Mark Grant	SD	.275
17.	Charlie Puleo	ATL	.208	93.	Bruce Ruffin	PHI	.275
18.	Mike Krukow	SF	.209	92.	Rick Sutcliffe	CHI	.275
19.	Jesse Orosco	LA	.209	91.	Don Carman	PHI	.272
20.	John Dopson	MTL	.210	90.	Norm Charlton	CIN	.270

Opponents' Slugging Average, Left-Handed Batters

American League								National League						
Top 20				*Bottom 20*				*Top 20*				*Bottom 20*		
1. Paul Mirabella	MIL	.211		130. Charlie Lea	MIN	.559		1. Juan Agosto	HOU	.178		109. Danny Cox	STL	.545
2. Bryan Harvey	CAL	.217		129. Todd Stottlemyre	TOR	.553		2. Lance McCullers	SD	.178		108. Tom Browning	CIN	.536
3. Greg Cadaret	OAK	.217		128. Willie Fraser	CAL	.551		3. Jay Howell	LA	.226		107. Brian Fisher	PIT	.502
4. Juan Nieves	MIL	.250		127. Mark Portugal	MIN	.542		4. Andy McGaffigan	MTL	.243		105. John Tudor	LA	.487
5. Doug Jones	CLE	.266		126. Jerry Reed	SEA	.537		5. John Smiley	PIT	.243		105. John Smoltz	ATL	.487
6. John Candelaria	NY	.268		125. John Davis	CHI	.529		6. Frank DiPino	CHI	.248		104. Ron Robinson	CIN	.485
7. Scott Bailes	CLE	.270		124. Terry Clark	CAL	.511		7. Jeff Parrett	MTL	.254		103. Charlie Puleo	ATL	.482
8. Floyd Bannister	KC	.276		123. Stu Cliburn	CAL	.511		8. Zane Smith	ATL	.262		102. Jack Armstrong	CIN	.481
9. Paul Kilgus	TEX	.279		122. Neil Allen	NY	.508		9. Kelly Downs	SF	.269		101. Mike Maddux	PHI	.472
10. Eric Plunk	OAK	.279		121. Steve Shields	NY	.507		10. Mike LaCoss	SF	.276		100. Jim Deshaies	HOU	.465
11. Dennis Eckersley	OAK	.286		120. Keith Atherton	MIN	.500		11. Kent Tekulve	PHI	.278		99. Steve Bedrosian	PHI	.461
11. Mark Langston	SEA	.286		119. Mike Morgan	BAL	.492		12. Alejandro Pena	LA	.281		98. Dennis Rasmussen	SD	.449
11. Frank Tanana	DET	.286		118. Bill Long	CHI	.486		13. Joe Magrane	STL	.283		97. Tim Burke	MTL	.449
14. Charles Hudson	NY	.298		117. Doyle Alexander	DET	.476		14. Bob Ojeda	NY	.283		96. Fernando Valenzuela	LA	.448
15. Bobby Witt	TEX	.301		116. Jack Lazorko	CAL	.474		15. Scott Garrelts	SF	.287		95. Calvin Schiraldi	CHI	.439
16. Mike Henneman	DET	.303		115. Tom Niedenfuer	BAL	.473		16. Randy O'Neal	STL	.287		94. Joaquin Andujar	HOU	.439
17. Sherman Corbett	CAL	.307		114. Mike Smithson	BOS	.472		17. Bob Forsch	HOU	.298		93. Jimmy Jones	SD	.439
18. Greg Minton	CAL	.308		113. Oil Can Boyd	BOS	.468		18. Greg Harris	PHI	.302		92. Neal Heaton	MTL	.433
19. John Cerutti	TOR	.310		112. Dewayne Buice	CAL	.465		19. Mark Davis	SD	.302		90. Frank Williams	CIN	.429
20. Jose Guzman	TEX	.312		111. Jay Tibbs	BAL	.461		20. Tim Belcher	LA	.306		90. Greg Booker	SD	.429

Opponents' Slugging Average, Right-Handed Batters

American League								National League						
Top 20				*Bottom 20*				*Top 20*				*Bottom 20*		
1. Dennis Eckersley	OAK	.255		129. Steve Trout	SEA	.584		1. Mark Davis	SD	.226		109. Bob Forsch	HOU	.503
2. Greg Minton	CAL	.260		128. Oil Can Boyd	BOS	.560		2. David Cone	NY	.230		108. Mark Grant	SD	.500
3. Doug Jones	CLE	.271		127. David Wells	TOR	.557		3. John Franco	CIN	.242		107. Neal Heaton	MTL	.480
4. Mike Jackson	SEA	.272		126. Mike Campbell	SEA	.532		4. Jose Rijo	CIN	.244		106. Frank DiPino	CHI	.472
5. Roger Clemens	BOS	.276		125. Richard Dotson	NY	.522		5. Roger McDowell	NY	.247		105. Lance McCullers	SD	.469
6. Juan Berenguer	MIN	.283		124. Mike Smithson	BOS	.511		6. Danny Cox	STL	.258		104. Joaquin Andujar	HOU	.467
7. Keith Atherton	MIN	.295		123. Mark Thurmond	BAL	.510		7. Pascual Perez	MTL	.260		103. Shane Rawley	PHI	.464
8. Ted Higuera	MIL	.297		122. Don Gordon	CLE	.508		8. Dave Leiper	SD	.267		102. German Jimenez	ATL	.452
9. Mike Morgan	BAL	.297		121. Jeff Bittiger	CHI	.500		9. Orel Hershiser	LA	.269		101. Kent Tekulve	PHI	.445
10. Jeff Russell	TEX	.297		120. Oswaldo Peraza	BAL	.495		10. Brian Holton	LA	.272		100. Rick Mahler	ATL	.441
11. Mark Gubicza	KC	.299		119. Brad Havens	CLE	.481		11. Alejandro Pena	LA	.277		99. Terry Mulholland	SF	.423
12. Jerry Reed	SEA	.302		118. Scott Bailes	CLE	.465		12. Jeff Pico	CHI	.283		98. Joe Price	SF	.422
13. Craig McMurtry	TEX	.304		117. Bret Saberhagen	KC	.462		13. Bob Walk	PIT	.285		97. Jamie Moyer	CHI	.419
14. Dan Plesac	MIL	.306		116. Ted Power	DET	.459		14. Tim Belcher	LA	.285		96. Jeff Parrett	MTL	.412
15. Mike Henneman	DET	.312		115. Ron Guidry	NY	.456		15. Ron Robinson	CIN	.288		95. Dennis Martinez	MTL	.411
16. Dave Stieb	TOR	.316		114. Tim Stoddard	NY	.451		16. Charlie Puleo	ATL	.288		94. Pat Perry	CHI	.408
17. Stu Cliburn	CAL	.318		113. Les Straker	MIN	.449		17. Todd Worrell	STL	.291		93. Rick Sutcliffe	CHI	.407
18. Scott Bankhead	SEA	.319		112. Mike Birkbeck	MIL	.444		18. Randy Myers	NY	.294		92. Don Carman	PHI	.407
19. Greg Cadaret	OAK	.325		111. Curt Young	OAK	.443		19. Scott Garrelts	SF	.299		91. Norm Charlton	CIN	.403
20. Steve Farr	KC	.327		110. Storm Davis	OAK	.442		20. Sid Fernandez	NY	.300		90. Kelly Downs	SF	.401

Opponents' Home Run Percentage, Left-Handed Batters

American League								National League						
Top 20				*Bottom 20*				*Top 20*				*Bottom 20*		
1. Allan Anderson	MIN	0.00		130. Mark Portugal	MIN	6.78		1. Frank DiPino	CHI	0.00		109. Tom Browning	CIN	5.30
1. Scott Bailes	CLE	0.00		129. Stu Cliburn	CAL	6.77		1. Atlee Hammaker	SF	0.00		108. Jim Deshaies	HOU	4.65
1. Floyd Bannister	KC	0.00		128. Willie Fraser	CAL	5.96		1. Mike LaCoss	SF	0.00		107. Jim Gott	PIT	4.55
1. Greg Cadaret	OAK	0.00		127. Keith Atherton	MIN	5.47		1. Lance McCullers	SD	0.00		106. Neal Heaton	MTL	4.44
1. Sherman Corbett	CAL	0.00		126. Jeff Bittiger	CHI	5.26		1. Roger McDowell	NY	0.00		105. John Tudor	LA	4.27
1. Mark Eichhorn	TOR	0.00		125. Jack Lazorko	CAL	5.13		1. Jeff Parrett	MTL	0.00		104. Jack Armstrong	CIN	3.88
1. Paul Mirabella	MIL	0.00		124. Charlie Lea	MIN	4.78		1. Alejandro Pena	LA	0.00		103. Charlie Puleo	ATL	3.66
8. Charles Hudson	NY	0.55		123. John Candelaria	NY	4.12		1. Bruce Ruffin	PHI	0.00		102. Todd Worrell	STL	3.55
9. Doug Jones	CLE	0.56		122. Jose Bautista	BAL	3.90		1. Dave Smith	HOU	0.00		101. Don Carman	PHI	3.45
10. Bob Stanley	BOS	0.58		121. Mike Smithson	BOS	3.90		1. Zane Smith	ATL	0.00		100. Tim Burke	MTL	3.40
11. Bobby Thigpen	CHI	0.61		120. Neil Allen	NY	3.83		11. Bob Forsch	HOU	0.42		99. Frank Williams	CIN	3.30
12. Doug Sisk	BAL	0.63		119. Mike Campbell	SEA	3.73		12. Bob Walk	PIT	0.48		98. Fernando Valenzuela	LA	3.13
13. Paul Kilgus	TEX	0.71		118. Tom Niedenfuer	BAL	3.64		13. Andy McGaffigan	MTL	0.56		97. Danny Cox	STL	2.84
14. Chuck Finley	CAL	0.74		117. Oil Can Boyd	BOS	3.60		14. Scott Garrelts	SF	0.64		96. Shawn Hillegas	LA	2.75
15. Greg Minton	CAL	0.75		116. Todd Stottlemyre	TOR	3.55		15. Brian Holton	LA	0.65		95. Joaquin Andujar	HOU	2.70
16. Dale Mohorcic	NY	0.77		115. Shawn Hillegas	CHI	3.53		16. Kent Tekulve	PHI	0.66		94. Ron Darling	NY	2.65
17. Scott Bankhead	SEA	0.82		114. Willie Hernandez	DET	3.53		17. Larry Andersen	HOU	0.67		93. Steve Bedrosian	PHI	2.60
17. Eric Plunk	OAK	0.82		113. Jeff Ballard	BAL	3.45		18. Tim Crews	LA	0.72		92. Danny Darwin	HOU	2.58
19. Ricky Horton	CHI	1.00		112. Jerry Reed	SEA	3.31		19. Danny Jackson	CIN	0.75		91. John Smoltz	ATL	2.56
20. Storm Davis	OAK	1.01		111. Juan Berenguer	MIN	3.26		20. Rick Reuschel	SF	0.78		90. Dennis Rasmussen	SD	2.54

Opponents' Home Run Percentage, Right-Handed Batters

American League

Top 20			Bottom 20		
1. Doug Jones	CLE	0.00	129. David Wells	TOR	6.90
1. Greg Minton	CAL	0.00	128. Oil Can Boyd	BOS	6.18
3. Dennis Lamp	BOS	0.56	127. Mike Smithson	BOS	6.11
4. Juan Berenguer	MIN	0.58	126. Richard Dotson	NY	4.97
5. Mark Gubicza	KC	0.82	125. Scott Bailes	CLE	4.94
6. Duane Ward	TOR	0.83	124. Cecilio Guante	TEX	4.91
7. Fred Toliver	MIN	1.01	123. Jim Clancy	TOR	4.49
8. Doug Sisk	BAL	1.02	122. Jeff Bittiger	CHI	4.41
9. Dave Stewart	OAK	1.08	121. Todd Stottlemyre	TOR	4.26
10. Jeff Musselman	TOR	1.12	119. Dan Petry	CAL	4.17
11. Stu Cliburn	CAL	1.12	119. Mike Campbell	SEA	4.17
12. Dave Righetti	NY	1.20	118. Curt Young	OAK	4.07
13. Greg Cadaret	OAK	1.25	117. Jeff Sellers	BOS	4.00
14. John Davis	CHI	1.27	116. Melido Perez	CHI	3.98
14. Dan Plesac	MIL	1.27	115. Al Leiter	NY	3.91
16. Eric King	DET	1.34	114. Doyle Alexander	DET	3.88
17. Mike Morgan	BAL	1.35	113. Brad Havens	CLE	3.85
18. Tommy John	NY	1.40	112. Mark Thurmond	BAL	3.81
19. Jeff Russell	TEX	1.46	111. Mark Langston	SEA	3.75
19. Bill Swift	SEA	1.46	110. Floyd Bannister	KC	3.74

National League

Top 20			Bottom 20		
1. Brian Holman	MTL	0.00	109. Mark Grant	SD	6.04
1. Brian Holton	LA	0.00	108. Jeff Parrett	MTL	4.71
1. Dave Leiper	SD	0.00	107. Lance McCullers	SD	4.47
4. Mark Davis	SD	0.38	106. Pat Perry	CHI	4.46
4. Jose Rijo	CIN	0.38	105. Mario Soto	CIN	3.82
6. Scott Terry	STL	0.40	103. Shane Rawley	PHI	3.80
7. Joe Hesketh	MTL	0.55	103. Mike Dunne	PIT	3.80
7. Roger McDowell	NY	0.55	102. Neal Heaton	MTL	3.69
9. Danny Cox	STL	0.66	101. Tom Browning	CIN	3.66
10. Ron Robinson	CIN	0.68	100. Al Nipper	CHI	3.50
11. Bob Ojeda	NY	0.69	99. Bob Kipper	PIT	3.45
12. John Franco	CIN	0.79	98. Doug Drabek	PIT	3.43
13. Joe Magrane	STL	0.80	97. Andy Hawkins	SD	3.13
14. John Tudor	LA	0.81	96. Mike Krukow	SF	3.11
15. Dwight Gooden	NY	0.88	95. Bob Forsch	HOU	3.10
16. Tim Belcher	LA	0.94	94. Dennis Martinez	MTL	3.05
17. Charlie Puleo	ATL	0.94	93. Floyd Youmans	MTL	3.05
18. Jeff Pico	CHI	1.01	92. Joaquin Andujar	HOU	2.96
19. Scott Garrelts	SF	1.02	91. Eric Show	SD	2.95
20. Paul Assenmacher	ATL	1.02	90. Danny Darwin	HOU	2.92

Opponents' Batting Average, Day Games

American League

Top 20			Bottom 20		
1. Jeff Montgomery	KC	.141	130. Don Gordon	CLE	.389
2. Keith Atherton	MIN	.162	129. Oswaldo Peraza	BAL	.368
3. Mike Jackson	SEA	.169	128. Scott Bailes	CLE	.362
4. Al Leiter	NY	.177	127. Jay Tibbs	BAL	.352
5. Roger Clemens	BOS	.184	126. Rich Yett	CLE	.348
6. Paul Kilgus	TEX	.192	125. Tommy John	NY	.343
7. Ted Higuera	MIL	.202	124. Mike Witt	CAL	.339
8. Duane Ward	TOR	.205	123. Mark Langston	SEA	.330
9. Bob Stanley	BOS	.206	122. Neil Allen	NY	.328
10. Jeff Reardon	MIN	.206	121. Bryan Harvey	CAL	.320
11. Dale Mohorcic	NY	.209	120. Todd Stottlemyre	TOR	.319
12. Eric Plunk	OAK	.210	119. Bill Long	CHI	.318
13. Luis Aquino	KC	.212	118. Bill Swift	SEA	.316
14. Jeff Robinson	DET	.213	117. Steve Shields	NY	.315
15. Charlie Hough	TEX	.218	116. Paul Gibson	DET	.314
16. Walt Terrell	DET	.218	115. John Davis	CHI	.313
17. Jeff Bittiger	CHI	.220	114. Curt Young	OAK	.313
18. Charlie Leibrandt	KC	.220	113. Tim Stoddard	NY	.310
19. Jerry Reed	SEA	.220	112. Mark Eichhorn	TOR	.308
20. Jose Guzman	TEX	.221	111. Dan Petry	CAL	.307

National League

Top 20			Bottom 20		
1. Alejandro Pena	LA	.152	109. Steve Peters	STL	.382
2. Greg Harris	PHI	.162	108. Tim Crews	LA	.353
3. Sid Fernandez	NY	.170	107. Dan Quisenberry	STL	.341
4. Doug Drabek	PIT	.173	106. Shane Rawley	PHI	.337
5. Larry Andersen	HOU	.180	105. Bob Forsch	HOU	.328
6. Mark Davis	SD	.184	104. Rick Mahler	ATL	.310
7. Scott Garrelts	SF	.186	103. Rich Gossage	CHI	.310
8. Danny Jackson	CIN	.189	102. Mario Soto	CIN	.309
9. Jack Armstrong	CIN	.190	101. Ron Robinson	CIN	.308
10. Jose Rijo	CIN	.190	100. Mike Capel	CHI	.306
11. Bob Ojeda	NY	.190	99. Jose Alvarez	ATL	.303
12. Andy McGaffigan	MTL	.193	98. Paul Assenmacher	ATL	.301
13. John Smoltz	ATL	.195	97. Brian Holton	LA	.297
14. John Franco	CIN	.200	96. Calvin Schiraldi	CHI	.295
15. Pascual Perez	MTL	.206	95. Bob Knepper	HOU	.293
16. Lance McCullers	SD	.208	94. Tom Browning	CIN	.292
17. Jim Deshaies	HOU	.210	93. Fernando Valenzuela	LA	.289
18. Zane Smith	ATL	.211	92. John Smiley	PIT	.288
19. Mike Scott	HOU	.211	91. Ed Whitson	SD	.286
20. Craig Lefferts	SF	.213	90. Terry Mulholland	SF	.286

Opponents' Batting Average, Night Games

American League

Top 20			Bottom 20		
1. Bryan Harvey	CAL	.174	129. Steve Trout	SEA	.364
2. Craig McMurtry	TEX	.175	128. Terry Clark	CAL	.341
3. Jeff Robinson	DET	.185	127. Doug Sisk	BAL	.326
4. Doug Jones	CLE	.188	126. Ted Power	DET	.318
5. Dave Stieb	TOR	.196	125. Dale Mohorcic	NY	.307
6. Juan Berenguer	MIN	.199	124. Charlie Lea	MIN	.305
7. Juan Nieves	MIL	.199	123. Bert Blyleven	MIN	.302
8. Bobby Witt	TEX	.202	122. Mike Smithson	BOS	.298
9. Mike Henneman	DET	.203	121. Tommy John	NY	.297
10. Eric King	DET	.209	120. Mark Thurmond	BAL	.297
11. Paul Mirabella	MIL	.210	119. Tom Filer	MIL	.294
12. Mitch Williams	TEX	.211	118. Steve Shields	NY	.293
13. Ted Higuera	MIL	.211	117. John Davis	CHI	.292
14. Wes Gardner	BOS	.214	116. Mike Birkbeck	MIL	.291
14. Lee Smith	BOS	.214	115. Ricky Horton	CHI	.289
16. Paul Gibson	DET	.215	114. Rod Nichols	CLE	.287
17. Scott Bankhead	SEA	.218	113. Dennis Lamp	BOS	.287
18. Mark Langston	SEA	.220	112. Bill Swift	SEA	.287
19. Greg Minton	CAL	.221	111. Doyle Alexander	DET	.286
20. Charles Hudson	NY	.221	110. Bobby Thigpen	CHI	.285

National League

Top 20			Bottom 20		
1. Randy Myers	NY	.167	109. Frank DiPino	CHI	.333
2. Jeff Parrett	MTL	.188	108. John Smoltz	ATL	.326
3. Pascual Perez	MTL	.192	107. Jeff Pico	CHI	.311
4. Todd Worrell	STL	.192	106. Zane Smith	ATL	.309
5. Brian Holton	LA	.194	105. Jimmy Jones	SD	.288
6. John Franco	CIN	.197	104. Rick Sutcliffe	CHI	.287
7. Tom Browning	CIN	.200	103. Kent Tekulve	PHI	.286
8. Juan Agosto	HOU	.200	102. Mike Maddux	PHI	.284
8. Rob Dibble	CIN	.200	101. Randy O'Neal	STL	.283
10. Joe Magrane	STL	.200	99. Don Sutton	LA	.283
11. Jay Howell	LA	.201	99. Joaquin Andujar	HOU	.283
12. Sid Fernandez	NY	.201	98. Tom Glavine	ATL	.282
13. Mike Scott	HOU	.202	97. Larry Andersen	HOU	.282
14. Lance McCullers	SD	.203	96. Brian Fisher	PIT	.281
15. Mark Davis	SD	.205	95. Jamie Moyer	CHI	.280
16. David Cone	NY	.208	94. Brian Holman	MTL	.279
17. Orel Hershiser	LA	.211	93. Mark Grant	SD	.278
18. Tim Belcher	LA	.216	92. Barry Jones	PIT	.278
19. Jose Rijo	CIN	.217	91. Steve Bedrosian	PHI	.276
20. Greg Maddux	CHI	.218	90. Rick Mahler	ATL	.275

Opponents' Batting Average, Grass Surfaces

American League

Top 20				Bottom 20		
1. Jeff Robinson	DET	.187		129. Terry Clark	CAL	.339
2. Scott Bankhead	SEA	.197		128. Bill Swift	SEA	.316
3. Dennis Eckersley	OAK	.198		127. Charlie Lea	MIN	.312
4. Paul Mirabella	MIL	.200		126. Lee Guetterman	NY	.310
5. Mike Jackson	SEA	.203		125. Steve Rosenberg	CHI	.308
6. Willie Hernandez	DET	.205		124. John Davis	CHI	.304
7. Lee Smith	BOS	.205		123. Doug Sisk	BAL	.301
8. Ted Higuera	MIL	.206		122. Tommy John	NY	.300
9. Eric Plunk	OAK	.209		121. Steve Shields	NY	.299
10. Bryan Harvey	CAL	.211		120. Jay Tibbs	BAL	.293
10. Dave Stieb	TOR	.211		119. Mike Smithson	BOS	.291
12. Juan Nieves	MIL	.213		118. Tim Stoddard	NY	.290
13. Gene Nelson	OAK	.213		117. Oil Can Boyd	BOS	.288
14. Wes Gardner	BOS	.216		116. Mike Campbell	SEA	.287
15. Charlie Hough	TEX	.216		115. Dennis Lamp	BOS	.287
16. Craig McMurtry	TEX	.217		114. Bert Blyleven	MIN	.287
17. Bobby Witt	TEX	.218		113. Bill Long	CHI	.285
18. Mike Henneman	DET	.219		112. Stu Cliburn	CAL	.282
19. Jimmy Key	TOR	.220		111. Ricky Horton	CHI	.281
20. Mitch Williams	TEX	.223		110. Bobby Thigpen	CHI	.280

National League

Top 20				Bottom 20		
1. Randy Myers	NY	.150		109. Bob Forsch	HOU	.379
2. Greg Harris	PHI	.158		108. Candy Sierra	CIN	.372
3. Sid Fernandez	NY	.175		107. Mike Maddux	PHI	.362
4. Jesse Orosco	LA	.177		106. Joaquin Andujar	HOU	.347
5. Mark Davis	SD	.182		105. Mike Capel	CHI	.324
6. Jay Howell	LA	.190		104. Ron Robinson	CIN	.318
7. Lance McCullers	SD	.194		103. Brian Fisher	PIT	.314
8. John Dopson	MTL	.195		102. David Palmer	PHI	.307
9. David Cone	NY	.200		101. German Jimenez	ATL	.306
9. Ramon Martinez	LA	.200		100. Juan Eichelberger	ATL	.303
11. Jim Deshaies	HOU	.204		99. Danny Darwin	HOU	.302
12. Tom Browning	CIN	.204		98. Don Carman	PHI	.301
13. Orel Hershiser	LA	.204		97. Trevor Wilson	SF	.298
14. Jose Rijo	CIN	.206		96. Mario Soto	CIN	.295
15. Joe Magrane	STL	.208		95. Pat Perry	CHI	.294
16. Alejandro Pena	LA	.210		94. Scott Terry	STL	.291
17. Bob Walk	PIT	.212		93. Mike Dunne	PIT	.289
18. Dave Leiper	SD	.216		91. Bryn Smith	MTL	.286
19. Mike Scott	HOU	.217		91. Mike Bielecki	CHI	.286
20. Kelly Downs	SF	.218		90. Rick Mahler	ATL	.283

Opponents' Batting Average, Artificial Surfaces

American League

Top 20				Bottom 20		
1. Craig McMurtry	TEX	.075		131. Steve Carlton	MIN	.408
2. Chuck Crim	MIL	.162		130. Tommy John	NY	.388
3. Juan Nieves	MIL	.180		129. Dan Quisenberry	KC	.383
4. Roger Clemens	BOS	.183		128. Steve Trout	SEA	.372
5. Roy Smith	MIN	.187		127. Neil Allen	NY	.361
6. German Gonzalez	MIN	.192		126. Edwin Nunez	SEA	.354
7. Stu Cliburn	CAL	.193		125. Dennis Powell	SEA	.346
8. Bobby Witt	TEX	.206		124. Rick Honeycutt	OAK	.344
9. Ted Higuera	MIL	.208		122. Terry Taylor	SEA	.344
10. Jeff Reardon	MIN	.209		122. Tom Filer	MIL	.344
11. Walt Terrell	DET	.209		121. Ricky Horton	CHI	.343
12. Dave Stieb	TOR	.209		120. Doyle Alexander	DET	.340
13. Don August	MIL	.213		119. Bruce Hurst	BOS	.339
14. Mike Jackson	SEA	.214		118. Rich Yett	CLE	.337
15. Melido Perez	CHI	.214		117. Mark Portugal	MIN	.336
16. Dave LaPoint	CHI	.214		116. Bob Welch	OAK	.330
17. Mike Moore	SEA	.222		115. Ted Power	DET	.322
18. Juan Berenguer	MIN	.224		114. Richard Dotson	NY	.319
19. Cecilio Guante	TEX	.226		113. Mike Morgan	BAL	.317
20. Jose Bautista	BAL	.226		112. Oswaldo Peraza	BAL	.316

National League

Top 20				Bottom 20		
1. Bob Kipper	PIT	.168		109. Zane Smith	ATL	.398
2. Eric Show	SD	.169		108. Frank DiPino	CHI	.364
3. John Franco	CIN	.171		107. Dan Quisenberry	STL	.325
4. Tim Belcher	LA	.179		106. Cris Carpenter	STL	.319
5. Scott Garrelts	SF	.179		105. Steve Peters	STL	.318
6. Mike Krukow	SF	.189		104. Shane Rawley	PHI	.310
7. Pascual Perez	MTL	.189		103. Rick Reuschel	SF	.301
8. Jeff Parrett	MTL	.191		102. Jeff Pico	CHI	.299
9. Jose Alvarez	ATL	.193		101. Andy Hawkins	SD	.292
10. Todd Worrell	STL	.193		100. Dave Rucker	PIT	.292
11. Tim Leary	LA	.194		99. Barry Jones	PIT	.291
12. Mike Scott	HOU	.199		98. Mike LaCoss	SF	.289
13. Ken Dayley	STL	.204		97. Dave Smith	HOU	.285
14. Craig Lefferts	SF	.206		96. Pete Smith	ATL	.284
15. Danny Jackson	CIN	.208		95. Fernando Valenzuela	LA	.282
16. Jose Rijo	CIN	.210		94. Rick Mahler	ATL	.281
17. Jim Gott	PIT	.211		93. Neal Heaton	MTL	.281
18. Juan Agosto	HOU	.213		92. Tim Burke	MTL	.280
19. Rob Dibble	CIN	.214		91. Frank Williams	CIN	.280
20. Rob Murphy	CIN	.216		90. Ron Darling	NY	.279

Opponents' Batting Average, Home Games

American League

Top 20				Bottom 20		
1. Jeff Robinson	DET	.167		129. Steve Trout	SEA	.372
2. Willie Hernandez	DET	.172		128. Terry Clark	CAL	.339
3. Dennis Eckersley	OAK	.182		127. Mark Portugal	MIN	.336
4. Dave Stieb	TOR	.193		126. Todd Stottlemyre	TOR	.331
5. Ted Higuera	MIL	.193		125. Les Straker	MIN	.325
6. Bryan Harvey	CAL	.199		124. Dennis Lamp	BOS	.313
7. Wes Gardner	BOS	.201		123. John Davis	CHI	.309
8. Mike Moore	SEA	.202		122. Bert Blyleven	MIN	.303
9. Mike Morgan	BAL	.204		121. Ted Power	DET	.303
10. Lee Smith	BOS	.207		120. Tommy John	NY	.302
11. Craig McMurtry	TEX	.211		119. Curt Young	OAK	.300
12. Jeff Reardon	MIN	.211		118. Fred Toliver	MIN	.299
13. Gene Nelson	OAK	.212		117. Bill Long	CHI	.296
14. Rick Honeycutt	OAK	.212		116. Mike Smithson	BOS	.295
15. Jack McDowell	CHI	.214		115. Mark Eichhorn	TOR	.295
16. Juan Nieves	MIL	.214		114. Bud Black	CLE	.294
17. Jose Guzman	TEX	.215		113. Mike Birkbeck	MIL	.293
18. Duane Ward	TOR	.215		112. Charlie Lea	MIN	.291
19. Bobby Witt	TEX	.216		111. Jeff Sellers	BOS	.291
20. Todd Burns	OAK	.216		110. Jim Clancy	TOR	.291

National League

Top 20				Bottom 20		
1. Randy Myers	NY	.108		109. Tim Crews	LA	.305
2. Sid Fernandez	NY	.152		108. Calvin Schiraldi	CHI	.299
3. Lance McCullers	SD	.152		107. Shane Rawley	PHI	.298
4. John Franco	CIN	.159		106. Frank Williams	CIN	.294
5. Bob Kipper	PIT	.164		105. John Tudor	LA	.290
6. Jeff Parrett	MTL	.174		104. Rick Mahler	ATL	.290
7. Mark Davis	SD	.175		103. Tom Glavine	ATL	.290
8. David Cone	NY	.180		102. Kent Tekulve	PHI	.287
9. Jim Gott	PIT	.181		101. Ron Robinson	CIN	.286
10. Mike Scott	HOU	.189		100. Terry Leach	NY	.284
11. Pascual Perez	MTL	.190		99. Tim Burke	MTL	.283
12. Juan Agosto	HOU	.196		98. Les Lancaster	CHI	.282
13. Joe Price	SF	.197		97. Fernando Valenzuela	LA	.282
14. Todd Worrell	STL	.201		96. Dave Smith	HOU	.280
15. Mike LaCoss	SF	.203		95. Jack Armstrong	CIN	.279
16. Kelly Downs	SF	.208		94. Zane Smith	ATL	.278
17. Tim Birtsas	CIN	.209		91. Kevin Coffman	ATL	.278
18. Danny Jackson	CIN	.212		91. John Smoltz	ATL	.278
19. Nolan Ryan	HOU	.214		91. Paul Assenmacher	ATL	.278
20. Joe Magrane	STL	.214		90. Steve Bedrosian	PHI	.276

Opponents' Batting Average, Road Games

American League

Top 20				Bottom 20			
1. Doug Jones	CLE	.165		129. Doug Sisk	BAL	.322
2. Mitch Williams	TEX	.168		128. Jay Tibbs	BAL	.321
3. Juan Berenguer	MIN	.185		127. Mike Morgan	BAL	.320
4. Greg Cadaret	OAK	.186		126. Tim Stoddard	NY	.318
5. Juan Nieves	MIL	.201		125. Ricky Horton	CHI	.316
6. Mike Jackson	SEA	.201		124. Steve Shields	NY	.316
7. Jeff Musselman	TOR	.205		123. Tommy John	NY	.314
8. Scott Bankhead	SEA	.209		122. Doyle Alexander	DET	.313
9. Greg Minton	CAL	.210		121. Bill Swift	SEA	.311
10. Roger Clemens	BOS	.211		120. Charlie Lea	MIN	.311
11. Keith Atherton	MIN	.211		119. Ted Power	DET	.309
12. Eric Plunk	OAK	.213		118. Mark Williamson	BAL	.308
13. Mike Henneman	DET	.213		117. Terry Clark	CAL	.306
14. Dennis Eckersley	OAK	.214		116. Tom Candiotti	CLE	.305
15. Bobby Witt	TEX	.216		115. Mike Witt	CAL	.303
16. Cecilio Guante	TEX	.219		114. Oswaldo Peraza	BAL	.302
17. John Candelaria	NY	.220		113. Dave Righetti	NY	.299
18. Ted Higuera	MIL	.221		112. Steve Ontiveros	OAK	.299
19. Charlie Hough	TEX	.226		111. Rick Rhoden	NY	.297
20. Jimmy Key	TOR	.227		110. Don Gordon	CLE	.295

National League

Top 20				Bottom 20			
1. Jose Rijo	CIN	.179		109. Bob Forsch	HOU	.341
2. Brian Holton	LA	.186		108. Frank DiPino	CHI	.341
3. Jay Howell	LA	.197		107. Joaquin Andujar	HOU	.326
4. Tim Belcher	LA	.197		106. Joe Price	SF	.314
5. Craig Lefferts	SF	.199		105. Bob Kipper	PIT	.312
6. Jose Alvarez	ATL	.202		104. Mike Maddux	PHI	.311
7. Greg Harris	PHI	.203		103. Zane Smith	ATL	.307
8. Pascual Perez	MTL	.204		102. Don Carman	PHI	.304
9. Orel Hershiser	LA	.207		101. Jim Gott	PIT	.303
10. Tom Browning	CIN	.207		100. David Palmer	PHI	.300
11. Bob Ojeda	NY	.210		99. John Smoltz	ATL	.293
12. Jim Deshaies	HOU	.211		98. Mike LaCoss	SF	.289
13. Paul Assenmacher	ATL	.216		97. Marvin Freeman	PHI	.287
14. Mike Scott	HOU	.216		96. Rick Reuschel	SF	.287
15. John Tudor	LA	.217		95. Andy Hawkins	SD	.285
16. John Dopson	MTL	.217		94. Bruce Ruffin	PHI	.285
17. Al Nipper	CHI	.218		93. Greg Mathews	STL	.285
18. Alejandro Pena	LA	.220		92. Danny Cox	STL	.285
19. Jeff Robinson	PIT	.220		91. Ron Robinson	CIN	.284
20. Don Robinson	SF	.220		90. Brian Fisher	PIT	.283

Opponents' Batting Average with Runners On Base

American League

Top 20				Bottom 20			
1. Jeff Robinson	DET	.175		129. Steve Trout	SEA	.371
2. Mike Jackson	SEA	.179		128. Jay Tibbs	BAL	.347
3. Eric King	DET	.185		127. Mark Williamson	BAL	.344
4. Todd Burns	OAK	.196		126. Bert Blyleven	MIN	.343
5. Juan Berenguer	MIN	.198		125. Doug Sisk	BAL	.337
6. Bryan Harvey	CAL	.200		124. Terry Clark	CAL	.329
7. Wes Gardner	BOS	.203		123. Bill Swift	SEA	.327
8. Chuck Crim	MIL	.207		122. Mike Smithson	BOS	.325
9. Eric Plunk	OAK	.209		121. Oswaldo Peraza	BAL	.322
10. Cecilio Guante	TEX	.209		120. Scott Bailes	CLE	.321
11. Mike Henneman	DET	.212		119. Ted Power	DET	.317
12. Mitch Williams	TEX	.218		118. Jeff Russell	TEX	.314
13. Rick Honeycutt	OAK	.221		117. Steve Shields	NY	.313
14. Willie Hernandez	DET	.224		116. Tom Filer	MIL	.311
15. Greg Cadaret	OAK	.225		115. Richard Dotson	NY	.310
16. Jeff Reardon	MIN	.225		114. John Davis	CHI	.310
17. Mark Langston	SEA	.226		113. Tim Stoddard	NY	.309
18. Neil Allen	NY	.227		112. Mike Birkbeck	MIL	.308
19. Bobby Witt	TEX	.228		111. Mark Eichhorn	TOR	.303
20. Doug Jones	CLE	.229		110. Bill Wegman	MIL	.301

National League

Top 20				Bottom 20			
1. Randy Myers	NY	.149		109. Ron Robinson	CIN	.336
2. Jesse Orosco	LA	.168		108. Marvin Freeman	PHI	.323
3. Floyd Youmans	MTL	.172		107. Rick Mahler	ATL	.319
4. Orel Hershiser	LA	.187		106. Scott Terry	STL	.314
5. Brian Holton	LA	.193		105. David Palmer	PHI	.309
6. Greg Harris	PHI	.193		104. Frank DiPino	CHI	.308
7. Sid Fernandez	NY	.193		103. Greg Booker	SD	.307
8. Jeff Parrett	MTL	.195		102. Zane Smith	ATL	.301
9. Craig Lefferts	SF	.200		101. Jimmy Jones	SD	.301
10. Joe Magrane	STL	.200		100. Mario Soto	CIN	.296
11. Jim Deshaies	HOU	.201		99. Jim Gott	PIT	.296
12. John Franco	CIN	.205		98. Joaquin Andujar	HOU	.295
13. Jose Rijo	CIN	.206		97. Les Lancaster	CHI	.293
14. Mike Scott	HOU	.207		96. John Smoltz	ATL	.292
15. Jose Alvarez	ATL	.207		95. Calvin Schiraldi	CHI	.292
16. Mark Davis	SD	.207		94. Bruce Ruffin	PHI	.291
17. Lance McCullers	SD	.208		93. Tom Glavine	ATL	.291
18. Pascual Perez	MTL	.210		92. Brian Holman	MTL	.289
19. Juan Agosto	HOU	.211		91. Mike Maddux	PHI	.289
20. Joe Hesketh	MTL	.212		90. Rick Sutcliffe	CHI	.288

Opponents' Batting Average with Bases Empty

American League

Top 20				Bottom 20			
1. Dennis Eckersley	OAK	.175		129. Steve Trout	SEA	.352
2. Ted Higuera	MIL	.186		128. Charlie Lea	MIN	.326
3. Mike Morgan	BAL	.186		127. Tommy John	NY	.324
4. Juan Nieves	MIL	.189		126. Terry Clark	CAL	.317
5. Willie Hernandez	DET	.194		125. Jeff Ballard	BAL	.305
6. Lee Smith	BOS	.197		124. Neil Allen	NY	.303
7. Dave Stieb	TOR	.197		123. Ted Power	DET	.296
8. Greg Minton	CAL	.201		122. Ron Guidry	NY	.294
9. Doug Jones	CLE	.204		121. Storm Davis	OAK	.293
10. Al Leiter	NY	.205		120. Tom Candiotti	CLE	.291
11. Jeff Montgomery	KC	.206		119. Ricky Horton	CHI	.290
12. Keith Atherton	MIN	.206		118. Bobby Thigpen	CHI	.289
13. Bobby Witt	TEX	.207		117. Dennis Lamp	BOS	.288
14. Jeff Robinson	DET	.209		116. Eric King	DET	.287
15. Charles Hudson	NY	.209		115. Mike Flanagan	TOR	.286
16. Roger Clemens	BOS	.210		114. Oil Can Boyd	BOS	.285
17. Charlie Hough	TEX	.210		113. Bill Long	CHI	.285
18. Scott Bankhead	SEA	.211		112. Steve Shields	NY	.285
19. Gene Nelson	OAK	.214		111. Rick Honeycutt	OAK	.285
20. Juan Berenguer	MIN	.216		110. Stu Cliburn	CAL	.284

National League

Top 20				Bottom 20			
1. Jay Howell	LA	.156		109. Kent Tekulve	PHI	.308
2. Sid Fernandez	NY	.189		108. Shane Rawley	PHI	.307
3. Pascual Perez	MTL	.190		107. Don Sutton	LA	.303
4. Todd Worrell	STL	.191		106. Joaquin Andujar	HOU	.298
5. Mark Davis	SD	.191		105. Bob Forsch	HOU	.295
6. John Franco	CIN	.193		104. Mark Grant	SD	.295
7. Scott Garrelts	SF	.197		103. Tim Crews	LA	.286
8. Danny Jackson	CIN	.198		102. Jamie Moyer	CHI	.284
9. Alejandro Pena	LA	.199		101. Zane Smith	ATL	.284
10. Lance McCullers	SD	.202		100. Terry Leach	NY	.283
11. Tim Belcher	LA	.202		99. Brian Fisher	PIT	.282
12. Mike Scott	HOU	.203		98. John Smoltz	ATL	.279
13. Scott Terry	STL	.203		97. John Tudor	LA	.273
14. Jim Gott	PIT	.206		96. Neal Heaton	MTL	.273
15. Kelly Downs	SF	.207		95. Danny Cox	STL	.271
16. David Cone	NY	.208		94. Jack Armstrong	CIN	.269
17. Bob Kipper	PIT	.209		93. Don Carman	PHI	.269
18. Bob Ojeda	NY	.210		92. Joe Hesketh	MTL	.268
19. Jose Rijo	CIN	.211		91. Jose Alvarez	ATL	.267
20. Tom Browning	CIN	.217		90. Mike Maddux	PHI	.265
20. Kevin Coffman	ATL	.217				

Opponents' Home Run Percentage with Runners On Base

American League							National League						
Top 20			**Bottom 20**				**Top 20**			**Bottom 20**			
1. Doug Jones	CLE	0.00	129. David Wells	TOR	6.03		1. Jose Alvarez	ATL	0.00	109. Tom Browning	CIN	5.06	
1. Greg Minton	CAL	0.00	128. Scott Bailes	CLE	5.58		1. Larry Andersen	HOU	0.00	108. Mario Soto	CIN	4.44	
1. Les Straker	MIN	0.00	127. Mike Smithson	BOS	5.50		1. Marvin Freeman	PHI	0.00	107. Mark Grant	SD	3.87	
1. Steve Trout	SEA	0.00	126. Keith Atherton	MIN	4.92		1. Scott Garrelts	SF	0.00	106. Shane Rawley	PHI	3.61	
5. Dennis Lamp	BOS	0.61	125. Jose Bautista	BAL	4.91		1. Joe Hesketh	MTL	0.00	105. John Smoltz	ATL	3.54	
6. Tommy John	NY	0.64	124. Willie Fraser	CAL	4.29		1. Brian Holton	LA	0.00	104. Jack Armstrong	CIN	3.45	
7. Mark Eichhorn	TOR	0.69	123. Mark Williamson	BAL	4.23		1. Mike LaCoss	SF	0.00	103. Joaquin Andujar	HOU	3.36	
8. Bryan Harvey	CAL	0.74	122. Dan Petry	CAL	4.11		1. Terry Leach	NY	0.00	102. Todd Worrell	STL	3.33	
9. Kirk McCaskill	CAL	0.78	121. Tom Filer	MIL	4.05		1. Roger McDowell	NY	0.00	101. Lance McCullers	SD	3.14	
10. Dave LaPoint	CHI	0.82	120. Lee Smith	BOS	4.05		1. Alejandro Pena	LA	0.00	100. Don Robinson	SF	3.13	
11. Don Gordon	CLE	0.87	119. Oswaldo Peraza	BAL	4.03		11. Joe Magrane	STL	0.42	99. Joe Price	SF	3.00	
12. Mike Flanagan	TOR	0.87	118. Rick Rhoden	NY	4.01		12. Jose Rijo	CIN	0.47	98. Mike Scott	HOU	2.81	
13. Duane Ward	TOR	0.92	117. Mike Campbell	SEA	4.00		13. Greg Harris	PHI	0.55	97. Frank Williams	CIN	2.78	
14. Mark Gubicza	KC	0.94	116. Mike Henneman	DET	3.97		14. Mike Krukow	SF	0.56	96. Larry McWilliams	STL	2.76	
15. Brad Havens	CLE	0.98	115. Frank Tanana	DET	3.87		15. Rick Reuschel	SF	0.57	95. Ron Darling	NY	2.76	
16. Allan Anderson	MIN	0.99	114. Bud Black	CLE	3.79		16. Kent Tekulve	PHI	0.59	94. Dennis Rasmussen	SD	2.76	
17. Mike Witt	CAL	1.03	113. Juan Nieves	MIL	3.75		17. Mark Davis	SD	0.61	93. Jim Deshaies	HOU	2.73	
18. Sherman Corbett	CAL	1.03	112. Mike Moore	SEA	3.74		18. Tim Leary	LA	0.65	92. Calvin Schiraldi	CHI	2.72	
19. Doug Sisk	BAL	1.05	111. Doyle Alexander	DET	3.70		19. Brian Holman	MTL	0.66	91. Danny Darwin	HOU	2.70	
20. Dave Righetti	NY	1.14	110. Mark Thurmond	BAL	3.67		20. Steve Bedrosian	PHI	0.69	90. Dennis Martinez	MTL	2.69	

Opponents' Home Run Percentage Bases Empty

American League							National League						
Top 20			**Bottom 20**				**Top 20**			**Bottom 20**			
1. Greg Cadaret	OAK	0.00	129. Oil Can Boyd	BOS	6.09		1. Kevin Coffman	ATL	0.00	109. Neal Heaton	MTL	5.19	
1. Lee Smith	BOS	0.00	128. Jeff Bittiger	CHI	5.71		1. Tim Crews	LA	0.00	108. Jim Gott	PIT	4.85	
3. Mike Henneman	DET	0.56	127. Al Leiter	NY	5.13		1. Jay Howell	LA	0.00	107. Mike Krukow	SF	4.10	
4. Doug Sisk	BAL	0.60	126. Steve Trout	SEA	4.92		1. Rob Murphy	CIN	0.00	106. John Smoltz	ATL	4.08	
5. Rod Nichols	CLE	0.65	125. Brad Havens	CLE	4.80		5. Mark Davis	SD	0.53	105. Mark Grant	SD	3.86	
6. Greg Minton	CAL	0.67	124. Cecilio Guante	TEX	4.70		5. Dwight Gooden	NY	0.53	104. Floyd Youmans	MTL	3.78	
7. Doug Jones	CLE	0.68	123. Mike Smithson	BOS	4.50		7. Les Lancaster	CHI	0.56	103. Randy O'Neal	STL	3.62	
8. Tom Filer	MIL	0.84	122. Willie Fraser	CAL	4.37		7. Roger McDowell	NY	0.56	102. Jose Alvarez	ATL	3.47	
9. Ricky Horton	CHI	0.92	121. Richard Dotson	NY	4.30		9. John Franco	CIN	0.58	101. Al Nipper	CHI	3.45	
10. Ted Power	DET	0.93	120. Jim Clancy	TOR	4.29		10. Brian Holton	LA	0.60	100. Shane Rawley	PHI	3.44	
11. Bob Stanley	BOS	1.06	119. Todd Stottlemyre	TOR	4.27		11. Bob Walk	PIT	0.64	99. Steve Bedrosian	PHI	3.40	
12. Juan Berenguer	MIN	1.08	118. Mike Flanagan	TOR	4.26		12. Scott Terry	STL	0.69	98. Tom Browning	CIN	3.33	
13. Mike Morgan	BAL	1.13	117. Curt Young	OAK	4.21		13. Joe Hesketh	MTL	0.70	97. Jack Armstrong	CIN	3.08	
14. Dave Stewart	OAK	1.17	116. Les Straker	MIN	4.17		14. Don Robinson	SF	0.75	96. Don Carman	PHI	3.01	
15. Jeff Musselman	TOR	1.18	115. Melido Perez	CHI	4.06		15. Jeff Pico	CHI	0.81	95. Greg Harris	PHI	2.99	
16. Mark Gubicza	KC	1.19	114. Willie Hernandez	DET	4.03		16. Brian Holman	MTL	0.87	94. Bob Kipper	PIT	2.88	
17. Dennis Eckersley	OAK	1.25	113. David Wells	TOR	3.97		17. Bob Ojeda	NY	0.87	93. Nolan Ryan	HOU	2.87	
17. Dennis Lamp	BOS	1.25	112. Charlie Lea	MIN	3.94		18. Tim Belcher	LA	0.95	92. John Dopson	MTL	2.82	
19. Eric Plunk	OAK	1.27	111. Mike Campbell	SEA	3.89		19. Bruce Ruffin	PHI	1.01	90. Eric Show	SD	2.78	
20. Steve Farr	KC	1.35	110. Wes Gardner	BOS	3.81		20. Mario Soto	CIN	1.03	90. Mike Dunne	PIT	2.78	

Opponents' On Base Average Leading Off the Inning

American League							National League						
Top 20			**Bottom 20**				**Top 20**			**Bottom 20**			
1. Dennis Eckersley	OAK	.167	130. Steve Trout	SEA	.508		1. Jay Howell	LA	.211	109. Jack Armstrong	CIN	.444	
2. Mike Henneman	DET	.178	129. Eric King	DET	.463		1. Jeff Robinson	PIT	.211	108. Don Sutton	LA	.419	
3. Mark Thurmond	BAL	.205	128. Ricky Horton	CHI	.455		3. Alejandro Pena	LA	.213	107. Kevin Coffman	ATL	.408	
4. Willie Hernandez	DET	.208	127. John Davis	CHI	.453		4. Dennis Rasmussen	SD	.235	106. Frank Williams	CIN	.400	
4. Paul Mirabella	MIL	.208	126. Terry Clark	CAL	.414		5. Tim Burke	MTL	.239	105. Paul Assenmacher	ATL	.388	
6. Mike Morgan	BAL	.225	125. Al Leiter	NY	.406		6. Mark Davis	SD	.241	104. Bruce Ruffin	PHI	.384	
7. Roger Clemens	BOS	.236	124. Todd Stottlemyre	TOR	.404		7. Bob Ojeda	NY	.245	103. David Palmer	PHI	.379	
8. Jimmy Key	TOR	.239	123. Mark Eichhorn	TOR	.400		8. Kelly Downs	SF	.246	102. Bob Knepper	HOU	.377	
9. Ray Hayward	TEX	.243	122. Bobby Thigpen	CHI	.394		9. David Cone	NY	.249	100. Kent Tekulve	PHI	.368	
10. Odell Jones	MIL	.243	121. Les Straker	MIN	.391		10. Pascual Perez	MTL	.253	100. John Smoltz	ATL	.368	
11. John Cerutti	TOR	.244	120. Wes Gardner	BOS	.390		11. Rick Mahler	ATL	.253	99. Scott Garrelts	SF	.366	
12. Lee Smith	BOS	.247	119. Duane Ward	TOR	.388		12. Andy McGaffigan	MTL	.256	98. Mark Grant	SD	.364	
13. Frank Viola	MIN	.247	118. Jeff Musselman	TOR	.382		13. John Franco	CIN	.256	97. Shane Rawley	PHI	.359	
14. Dave Righetti	NY	.250	117. Ron Guidry	NY	.379		14. Craig Lefferts	SF	.259	96. Joaquin Andujar	HOU	.354	
15. Bill Wegman	MIL	.251	116. Don Gordon	CLE	.377		15. Eric Show	SD	.259	95. Brian Holton	LA	.351	
16. Mark Williamson	BAL	.252	115. Fred Toliver	MIN	.374		16. Atlee Hammaker	SF	.264	94. Danny Darwin	HOU	.349	
17. Tom Henke	TOR	.259	114. Charlie Lea	MIN	.373		17. Rick Sutcliffe	CHI	.264	93. Mike Maddux	PHI	.344	
18. Scott Bankhead	SEA	.259	113. Bryan Harvey	CAL	.371		18. Tim Crews	LA	.265	92. Bob Forsch	HOU	.342	
19. Todd Burns	OAK	.260	112. David Wells	TOR	.368		19. Ron Robinson	CIN	.265	91. Juan Agosto	HOU	.341	
20. Paul Kilgus	TEX	.260	111. Rod Nichols	CLE	.366		20. Tim Birtsas	CIN	.266	90. Joe Price	SF	.338	

Opponents' Batting Average with Runners in Scoring Position

American League

#	Top 20			#	Bottom 20		
1.	Eric King	DET	.152	129.	Bert Blyleven	MIN	.380
2.	Jeff Robinson	DET	.167	128.	Mike Morgan	BAL	.371
3.	Bryan Harvey	CAL	.169	127.	Scott Bailes	CLE	.342
4.	Mike Henneman	DET	.170	126.	Mark Williamson	BAL	.336
5.	Willie Hernandez	DET	.176	123.	Jeff Dedmon	CLE	.333
6.	Eric Plunk	OAK	.178	123.	Oswaldo Peraza	BAL	.333
7.	Mike Jackson	SEA	.181	123.	Mike Birkbeck	MIL	.333
8.	Doug Jones	CLE	.186	122.	Bill Wegman	MIL	.331
9.	Duane Ward	TOR	.187	121.	Steve Trout	SEA	.325
10.	Cecilio Guante	TEX	.189	120.	Jay Tibbs	BAL	.318
11.	Wes Gardner	BOS	.195	119.	Ted Power	DET	.316
12.	Jack McDowell	CHI	.199	117.	Jerry Reed	SEA	.312
13.	Dave Stewart	OAK	.202	117.	Jimmy Key	TOR	.312
14.	Lee Smith	BOS	.206	116.	Jeff Russell	TEX	.308
15.	Jeff Montgomery	KC	.208	115.	Jeff Ballard	BAL	.306
16.	David Wells	TOR	.208	114.	Bill Swift	SEA	.305
17.	Juan Berenguer	MIN	.209	113.	Charles Hudson	NY	.305
18.	Steve Farr	KC	.210	112.	Paul Kilgus	TEX	.302
19.	Mike Boddicker	BOS	.211	111.	Mike Smithson	BOS	.301
20.	Chuck Crim	MIL	.212	110.	Kirk McCaskill	CAL	.301

National League

#	Top 20			#	Bottom 20		
1.	Jesse Orosco	LA	.143	109.	Steve Peters	STL	.400
2.	Lance McCullers	SD	.153	108.	Marvin Freeman	PHI	.348
3.	Sid Fernandez	NY	.157	107.	Frank DiPino	CHI	.345
4.	Randy Myers	NY	.160	106.	Scott Terry	STL	.333
5.	Joe Magrane	STL	.161	105.	Jeff Pico	CHI	.330
6.	Brian Holton	LA	.161	104.	Bruce Ruffin	PHI	.329
7.	Craig Lefferts	SF	.165	103.	David Palmer	PHI	.325
8.	Greg Harris	PHI	.172	102.	Ron Robinson	CIN	.325
9.	John Tudor	LA	.175	101.	Les Lancaster	CHI	.322
10.	Mike Scott	HOU	.176	100.	Jimmy Jones	SD	.320
11.	David Cone	NY	.179	99.	Zane Smith	ATL	.313
12.	Pascual Perez	MTL	.180	98.	Tim Belcher	LA	.313
13.	Mike Krukow	SF	.180	97.	Rick Mahler	ATL	.307
14.	Juan Agosto	HOU	.185	96.	Kevin Coffman	ATL	.306
15.	Jose Alvarez	ATL	.185	95.	Mario Soto	CIN	.305
16.	Bob Knepper	HOU	.185	94.	Don Carman	PHI	.303
17.	Floyd Youmans	MTL	.186	93.	Joe Price	SF	.297
18.	Jim Deshaies	HOU	.188	92.	Charlie Puleo	ATL	.294
19.	Orel Hershiser	LA	.193	91.	Tom Glavine	ATL	.290
20.	Jack Armstrong	CIN	.194	90.	Joaquin Andujar	HOU	.283

Opponents' Batting Average in Pressure Situations

American League

#	Top 20			#	Bottom 20		
1.	Juan Nieves	MIL	.102	129.	Doug Sisk	BAL	.446
2.	Jose Cecena	TEX	.132	128.	Storm Davis	OAK	.389
3.	Todd Burns	OAK	.143	127.	Tommy John	NY	.383
4.	Mike Morgan	BAL	.146	126.	Mark Eichhorn	TOR	.378
5.	Israel Sanchez	KC	.163	125.	Scott Bankhead	SEA	.371
6.	Allan Anderson	MIN	.167	124.	Dave LaPoint	CHI	.362
7.	Jerry Reuss	CHI	.175	123.	Don Aase	BAL	.361
8.	John Candelaria	NY	.179	122.	Berg Vande	TEX	.346
8.	Roger Clemens	BOS	.179	121.	Bill Wilkinson	SEA	.344
10.	Gene Nelson	OAK	.181	120.	Rich Yett	CLE	.340
11.	Bobby Witt	TEX	.184	119.	Donnie Moore	CAL	.333
12.	Jack Morris	DET	.187	118.	Mark Williamson	BAL	.329
13.	Bryan Harvey	CAL	.191	117.	Melido Perez	CHI	.328
14.	Chris Bosio	MIL	.195	116.	Ricky Horton	CHI	.327
15.	Barry Jones	CHI	.196	115.	Tom Bolton	BOS	.325
16.	Dave Stewart	OAK	.196	114.	John Farrell	CLE	.316
17.	Jeff Robinson	DET	.198	113.	Dewayne Buice	CAL	.312
18.	Dennis Eckersley	OAK	.198	112.	Charles Hudson	NY	.308
19.	Frank Viola	MIN	.198	111.	Bill Wegman	MIL	.305
20.	Tim Stoddard	NY	.200	110.	Mike Schooler	SEA	.301

National League

#	Top 20			#	Bottom 20		
1.	Pascual Perez	MTL	.159	110.	Greg Booker	SD	.471
2.	Mike Scott	HOU	.160	109.	Dan Quisenberry	STL	.400
3.	Danny Darwin	HOU	.167	108.	Drew Hall	CHI	.359
4.	Danny Jackson	CIN	.168	106.	Steve Peters	STL	.333
5.	Randy Myers	NY	.171	106.	Larry McWilliams	STL	.333
6.	Brian Holton	LA	.172	105.	Rich Gossage	CHI	.327
7.	Dennis Martinez	MTL	.173	104.	Bryn Smith	MTL	.325
8.	Jay Howell	LA	.177	103.	Pete Smith	ATL	.323
9.	Dave Leiper	SD	.178	102.	Terry Leach	NY	.322
10.	Tim Leary	LA	.182	101.	Jeff Heathcock	HOU	.316
11.	David Cone	NY	.183	100.	Jim Acker	ATL	.314
12.	Mike Maddux	PHI	.185	99.	Dwight Gooden	NY	.305
13.	Nolan Ryan	HOU	.187	98.	Barry Jones	PIT	.305
14.	Ron Darling	NY	.187	97.	Jose DeLeon	STL	.304
15.	John Franco	CIN	.189	96.	Bruce Sutter	ATL	.303
16.	Joe Boever	ATL	.189	95.	Jeff Pico	CHI	.302
17.	Kevin Gross	PHI	.189	94.	Les Lancaster	CHI	.298
18.	Kelly Downs	SF	.196	93.	Ed Whitson	SD	.297
19.	John Costello	STL	.198	92.	Tom Glavine	ATL	.296
20.	Rob Dibble	CIN	.198	91.	Jamie Moyer	CHI	.295

Strikeout Percentage in Pressure Situations

American League

#	Top 20			#	Bottom 20		
1.	Roger Clemens	BOS	36.77	129.	Paul Kilgus	TEX	3.45
2.	Lee Smith	BOS	26.91	128.	Ted Power	DET	3.85
3.	Bud Black	CLE	26.25	127.	Curt Young	OAK	4.35
4.	Jose Cecena	TEX	25.93	126.	Doug Sisk	BAL	4.76
5.	Bert Blyleven	MIN	25.45	125.	Bill Swift	SEA	5.17
6.	Dennis Eckersley	OAK	25.40	124.	Dave LaPoint	CHI	5.56
7.	Bryan Harvey	CAL	24.65	123.	Jose Bautista	BAL	5.97
8.	Tom Henke	TOR	24.47	122.	Mark Williamson	BAL	6.32
9.	Odell Jones	MIL	23.81	121.	Berg Vande	TEX	6.67
10.	Mark Langston	SEA	23.53	120.	Willie Fraser	CAL	7.14
11.	Bobby Witt	TEX	23.30	118.	Don Gordon	CLE	8.00
12.	Greg Cadaret	OAK	22.82	118.	Jeff Dedmon	CLE	8.00
13.	Steve Rosenberg	CHI	22.45	117.	Ricky Horton	CHI	8.06
14.	John Candelaria	NY	22.41	116.	Paul Mirabella	MIL	8.14
14.	Eric Plunk	OAK	22.41	115.	Mike Flanagan	TOR	8.20
16.	Dan Plesac	MIL	21.48	113.	Mark Eichhorn	TOR	8.77
17.	Duane Ward	TOR	21.43	113.	Jeff Ballard	BAL	8.77
18.	Willie Hernandez	DET	21.17	112.	Bill Long	CHI	8.92
19.	Doug Jones	CLE	21.03	111.	John Farrell	CLE	9.52
20.	Cecilio Guante	TEX	20.67	110.	Kirk McCaskill	CAL	9.72

National League

#	Top 20			#	Bottom 20		
1.	Nolan Ryan	HOU	28.24	110.	Greg Booker	SD	0.00
2.	Randy Myers	NY	27.89	109.	Fernando Valenzuela	LA	1.56
3.	Tim Belcher	LA	27.45	108.	Bob Forsch	HOU	2.74
4.	Jay Howell	LA	27.22	107.	Shane Rawley	PHI	6.67
5.	Rob Dibble	CIN	26.88	106.	Pete Smith	ATL	6.85
6.	Calvin Schiraldi	CHI	26.19	104.	Jimmy Jones	SD	7.58
7.	Mark Davis	SD	25.78	104.	Don Carman	PHI	7.58
8.	Jim Gott	PIT	24.34	103.	John Smiley	PIT	7.69
9.	Todd Worrell	STL	23.70	102.	Bob Walk	PIT	7.78
10.	John Costello	STL	23.60	101.	John Dopson	MTL	8.47
11.	Alejandro Pena	LA	23.21	100.	Ed Whitson	SD	8.57
12.	Sid Fernandez	NY	22.95	99.	Roger McDowell	NY	8.64
13.	Joe Hesketh	MTL	22.75	98.	Juan Agosto	HOU	8.70
14.	Paul Assenmacher	ATL	22.71	97.	Jeff Heathcock	HOU	8.89
15.	David Cone	NY	22.40	96.	Bryn Smith	MTL	9.30
16.	Mike Maddux	PHI	21.67	95.	Joe Magrane	STL	9.52
17.	Frank DiPino	CHI	21.58	94.	Rick Reuschel	SF	9.62
18.	Bruce Sutter	ATL	20.98	93.	Dan Quisenberry	STL	9.76
19.	Scott Garrelts	SF	20.60	92.	Joe Boever	ATL	9.76
20.	Lance McCullers	SD	20.55	91.	Mike Dunne	PIT	9.80

VI

Player
Tendencies

Player Tendencies

This isn't *X*-rated stuff. After all, we are a family publication. But if, after studying the statistics in other sections of this book, you wondered just which players had demonstrated the most pronounced differences in performance in day and night games, vs. left- and right-handers, or in several other category breakdowns, the Player Tendencies section will answer your questions.

We've examined eight different pairs of categories for batters and nine for pitchers. For each pair, we've ranked the players according to the differences in their batting averages (or, for pitchers, the averages of opposing batters). For example, we noted each player's difference in batting average with runners on base as opposed to bases-empty situations. The 25 with the largest differences in both directions are listed. And we've looked at the question not only for last season, but for the past ten years as well, adding some additional perspective.

Incidentally, the additional pair of categories we've included for pitchers illuminates an area that's never before been addressed in a comprehensive fashion: how a pitcher's performance varies from his first time through the batting order to subsequent passes. Take a look at page 375 to find out who thrives on those second and third at-bats, and whose performance deteriorates most noticeably.

For each pair of categories, we've established a minimum number of at-bats needed to qualify. A player had to qualify on both sides (for instance, in both home and road games) in order to be ranked.

In most cases, those minimums are the same: for batters, 100 at-bats to qualify for last season, 500 to qualify for the last 10 years. Pitchers qualify if opposing batters accumulated that many at-bats. The exceptions are for Late-Inning Pressure Situations (50 AB for last season, 250 for the last 10 years); runners in scoring position (75 and 250); and first time through the batting order (200 and 500).

Late-Inning Pressure Situations

LAST SEASON

BETTER UNDER PRESSURE

PLAYER	LATE-INNING PRESSURE AB	H	AVG	OTHER AT BATS AB	H	AVG	DIFF
Milt Thompson	57	24	.421	321	85	.265	.156
Dick Schofield	67	24	.358	460	102	.222	.136
Damon Berryhill	61	22	.361	248	58	.234	.127
Larry Sheets	80	26	.325	372	78	.210	.115
Dale Sveum	71	24	.338	396	89	.225	.113
Alan Trammell	72	29	.403	394	116	.294	.108
Jeffrey Leonard	80	26	.325	454	103	.227	.098
Tim Raines	75	26	.347	354	90	.254	.092
Mickey Brantley	76	26	.342	501	126	.251	.091
Darrell Evans	67	19	.284	370	72	.195	.089
Tony Fernandez	77	28	.364	571	158	.277	.087
Rafael Santana	54	17	.315	426	98	.230	.085
Kurt Stillwell	59	19	.322	400	96	.240	.082
Tom Brookens	64	20	.313	377	87	.231	.082
Brian Downing	81	25	.309	403	92	.228	.080
Ozzie Virgil	79	25	.316	241	57	.237	.080
Kelly Gruber	78	27	.346	491	131	.267	.079
Bill Buckner	61	19	.311	224	52	.232	.079
Oddibe McDowell	67	21	.313	370	87	.235	.078
Gerald Young	87	28	.322	489	120	.245	.076
Billy Hatcher	92	30	.326	438	112	.256	.070
Jeff Treadway	55	17	.309	246	59	.240	.069
Otis Nixon	50	15	.300	221	51	.231	.069
Kirk Gibson	69	24	.348	473	133	.281	.067
Harold Baines	93	31	.333	506	135	.267	.067

BETTER IN OTHER AT BATS

PLAYER	LATE-INNING PRESSURE AB	H	AVG	OTHER AT BATS AB	H	AVG	DIFF
Walt Weiss	56	4	.071	396	109	.275	.204
Mike Schmidt	61	8	.131	329	89	.271	.139
Terry Steinbach	52	8	.154	299	85	.284	.130
Pat Tabler	61	11	.180	383	114	.298	.117
Kal Daniels	63	12	.190	432	132	.306	.115
Jeff Hamilton	50	7	.140	259	66	.255	.115
Fred Lynn	71	11	.155	320	85	.266	.111
Dave Magadan	53	10	.189	261	77	.295	.106
Jack Howell	79	13	.165	421	114	.271	.106
Wade Boggs	59	16	.271	525	198	.377	.106
Marvell Wynne	61	11	.180	272	77	.283	.103
Von Hayes	59	11	.186	308	89	.289	.103
Cecil Espy	61	10	.164	286	76	.266	.102
Marty Barrett	67	13	.194	545	160	.294	.100
Darryl Strawberry	74	14	.189	469	132	.281	.092
Fred Manrique	57	9	.158	288	72	.250	.092
Danny Tartabull	81	16	.198	426	123	.289	.091
Shawon Dunston	98	17	.173	477	126	.264	.091
Kevin Seitzer	75	17	.227	484	153	.316	.089
Brett Butler	76	16	.211	492	147	.299	.088
Bill Doran	64	11	.172	416	108	.260	.088
Jim Traber	60	9	.150	292	69	.236	.086
Rob Deer	78	14	.179	414	110	.266	.086
Dave Collins	56	10	.179	118	31	.263	.084
Randy Ready	70	14	.200	261	74	.284	.084

LAST 10 YEARS

BETTER UNDER PRESSURE

PLAYER	LATE-INNING PRESSURE AB	H	AVG	OTHER AT BATS AB	H	AVG	DIFF
Tim Raines	671	236	.352	3660	1083	.296	.056
Jeff Newman	253	68	.269	1363	292	.214	.055
Garth Iorg	360	110	.306	2041	515	.252	.053
Glenn Hoffman	265	76	.287	1794	426	.237	.049
Thad Bosley	268	83	.310	813	212	.261	.049
Larry Milbourne	283	86	.304	1257	325	.259	.045
Chris Brown	269	83	.309	1197	316	.264	.045
Tony Fernandez	390	131	.336	2354	689	.293	.043
Ron Roenicke	260	70	.269	816	186	.228	.041
Steve Sax	617	196	.318	3695	1022	.277	.041
Milt May	277	81	.292	1299	334	.257	.035
Rick Manning	494	137	.277	2904	708	.244	.034
Vince Coleman	351	102	.291	2124	547	.258	.033
Bo Diaz	477	136	.285	2537	641	.253	.032
Rickey Henderson	693	221	.319	4290	1234	.288	.031
Alan Wiggins	299	85	.284	1948	496	.255	.030
Ron Oester	601	174	.290	3146	820	.261	.029
Rusty Staub	308	91	.295	976	261	.267	.028
Tom Foley	290	82	.283	1255	320	.255	.028
Bump Wills	256	74	.289	1694	443	.262	.028
Wayne Tolleson	342	93	.272	1766	432	.245	.027
Kurt Bevacqua	308	80	.260	627	146	.233	.027
Steve Yeager	252	60	.238	1350	286	.212	.026
Luis Salazar	482	138	.286	2295	597	.260	.026
Charlie Moore	453	131	.289	2224	585	.263	.026

BETTER IN OTHER AT BATS

PLAYER	LATE-INNING PRESSURE AB	H	AVG	OTHER AT BATS AB	H	AVG	DIFF
Danny Heep	330	64	.194	1230	326	.265	.071
Rick Burleson	325	70	.215	2021	570	.282	.067
Spike Owen	332	61	.184	2078	519	.250	.066
Larry Biittner	255	58	.227	651	191	.293	.066
Dan Gladden	355	78	.220	1917	539	.281	.061
Jim Rice	730	179	.245	4753	1449	.305	.060
Ron Kittle	295	55	.186	1859	455	.245	.058
Johnny Grubb	275	62	.225	1584	437	.276	.050
Mike Heath	541	114	.211	2674	693	.259	.048
Tim Foli	368	81	.220	1985	533	.269	.048
Fred Lynn	620	147	.237	3640	1039	.285	.048
Greg Brock	339	69	.204	2063	518	.251	.048
Mitch Webster	321	76	.237	1612	457	.283	.047
Bruce Benedict	405	83	.205	2261	569	.252	.047
Jody Davis	531	113	.213	2795	723	.259	.046
Lonnie Smith	484	120	.248	2941	864	.294	.046
Willie Randolph	625	147	.235	4198	1179	.281	.046
Brett Butler	492	119	.242	3293	945	.287	.045
Barry Bonnell	413	97	.235	1991	555	.279	.044
Jim Morrison	556	126	.227	2704	730	.270	.043
Bill Doran	492	116	.236	2921	813	.278	.043
Glenn Davis	334	76	.228	1790	481	.269	.041
Mike Scioscia	412	94	.228	2425	652	.269	.041
Miguel Dilone	261	63	.241	1412	398	.282	.040
Derrel Thomas	306	67	.219	1269	329	.259	.040

Runners On Base

LAST SEASON

BETTER WITH RUNNERS ON

PLAYER	RUNNERS ON AB	H	AVG	BASES EMPTY AB	H	AVG	DIFF
Bill Buckner	126	45	.357	159	26	.164	.194
Don Baylor	105	32	.305	159	26	.164	.141
Tony Gwynn	217	83	.382	304	80	.263	.119
Dave Valle	124	37	.298	166	30	.181	.118
Mike Pagliarulo	218	60	.275	226	36	.159	.116
Cecil Espy	144	45	.313	203	41	.202	.111
Gerald Perry	254	91	.358	293	73	.249	.109
Pat Tabler	211	71	.336	233	54	.232	.105
Greg Walker	160	49	.306	217	44	.203	.103
Eric Davis	223	73	.327	249	56	.225	.102
Kelly Gruber	244	82	.336	325	76	.234	.102
Mike Schmidt	183	55	.301	207	42	.203	.098
Marvell Wynne	116	38	.328	217	50	.230	.097
Nelson Santovenia	139	40	.288	170	33	.194	.094
Kurt Stillwell	169	52	.308	290	63	.217	.090
Jim Traber	163	44	.270	189	34	.180	.090
Rick Schu	118	36	.305	152	33	.217	.088
Steve Sax	198	66	.333	434	109	.251	.082
George Brett	270	94	.348	319	86	.270	.079
Ozzie Guillen	217	67	.309	349	81	.232	.077
Dave Magadan	152	48	.316	162	39	.241	.075
Pedro Guerrero	162	53	.327	202	51	.252	.075
George Bell	289	89	.308	325	76	.234	.074
Jack Howell	220	65	.295	280	62	.221	.074
Steve Jeltz	166	38	.229	213	33	.155	.074

BETTER WITH BASES EMPTY

PLAYER	RUNNERS ON AB	H	AVG	BASES EMPTY AB	H	AVG	DIFF
Tim Teufel	119	21	.176	154	43	.279	.103
Glenn Wilson	159	31	.195	251	74	.295	.100
Benito Santiago	220	43	.195	272	79	.290	.095
Geno Petralli	158	37	.234	193	62	.321	.087
Fred Lynn	162	32	.198	229	64	.279	.082
Gary Redus	117	23	.197	216	60	.278	.081
Rafael Palmeiro	245	64	.261	335	114	.340	.079
Kent Hrbek	247	67	.271	263	92	.350	.079
Ivan Calderon	121	21	.174	143	35	.245	.071
Luis Alicea	152	27	.178	145	36	.248	.071
Terry Kennedy	108	20	.185	157	40	.255	.070
Ken Gerhart	103	16	.155	159	35	.220	.065
Dan Pasqua	196	38	.194	226	58	.257	.063
Lloyd Moseby	197	40	.203	275	73	.265	.062
Tim Laudner	182	40	.220	193	54	.280	.060
Don Slaught	140	35	.250	182	56	.308	.058
Tom Brookens	186	39	.210	255	68	.267	.057
Mickey Tettleton	126	29	.230	157	45	.287	.056
Howard Johnson	210	42	.200	285	72	.253	.053
Dale Murphy	263	52	.198	329	82	.249	.052
Len Dykstra	136	32	.235	293	84	.287	.051
Joe Orsulak	115	29	.252	264	80	.303	.051
Keith Moreland	255	59	.231	256	72	.281	.050
Dave Anderson	122	27	.221	163	44	.270	.049
Wade Boggs	239	81	.339	345	133	.386	.047

LAST 10 YEARS

BETTER WITH RUNNERS ON

PLAYER	RUNNERS ON AB	H	AVG	BASES EMPTY AB	H	AVG	DIFF
Bruce Bochte	1409	451	.320	1809	471	.260	.060
Willie Montanez	557	160	.287	645	148	.229	.058
Chris Brown	618	188	.304	848	211	.249	.055
Jerry Royster	954	275	.288	1692	396	.234	.054
Graig Nettles	1640	442	.270	1880	406	.216	.054
Jose Canseco	893	266	.298	1043	256	.245	.052
Rick Leach	545	160	.294	761	184	.242	.052
Pat Tabler	1383	440	.318	1580	421	.266	.052
Scot Thompson	520	149	.287	717	169	.236	.051
Kevin Mitchell	597	176	.295	714	175	.245	.050
Mark McGwire	502	150	.299	658	164	.249	.050
Randy Bush	940	260	.277	1141	260	.228	.049
Dave Parker	2343	723	.309	2678	696	.260	.049
Carmelo Martinez	1013	281	.277	1134	260	.229	.048
Tony Phillips	812	225	.277	1325	306	.231	.046
Ted Simmons	1885	550	.292	2013	495	.246	.046
Jason Thompson	1529	433	.283	1687	403	.239	.044
Oscar Gamble	650	190	.292	776	193	.249	.044
Greg Brock	1105	296	.268	1297	291	.224	.044
Scott Fletcher	1063	316	.297	1659	421	.254	.044
Al Bumbry	1040	321	.309	1945	516	.265	.043
Ron LeFlore	623	189	.303	1169	304	.260	.043
Eric Davis	720	214	.297	937	238	.254	.043
Garth Iorg	1036	295	.285	1365	330	.242	.043
Gerald Perry	793	235	.296	981	249	.254	.043

BETTER WITH BASES EMPTY

PLAYER	RUNNERS ON AB	H	AVG	BASES EMPTY AB	H	AVG	DIFF
Ivan Calderon	546	131	.240	658	190	.289	.049
Benito Santiago	500	127	.254	600	177	.295	.041
Mickey Rivers	843	237	.281	1409	441	.313	.032
Pete Incaviglia	690	166	.241	777	211	.272	.031
Jim Wohlford	611	149	.244	648	178	.275	.031
Dan Pasqua	532	120	.226	636	163	.256	.031
Lee Lacy	1164	322	.277	1871	572	.306	.029
Dick Schofield	949	204	.215	1407	340	.242	.027
Ron Washington	633	155	.245	927	251	.271	.026
Bob Dernier	716	175	.244	1580	427	.270	.026
Jorge Orta	1223	315	.258	1370	387	.282	.025
Dave Engle	721	181	.251	857	236	.275	.024
Wayne Tolleson	803	188	.234	1305	337	.258	.024
Jeff Newman	706	148	.210	910	212	.233	.023
Damaso Garcia	1322	357	.270	2348	688	.293	.023
Tim Laudner	836	178	.213	963	227	.236	.023
Gary Redus	772	178	.231	1552	393	.253	.023
Terry Harper	653	157	.240	814	214	.263	.022
Jerry Morales	524	121	.231	557	141	.253	.022
Miguel Dilone	597	156	.261	1076	305	.283	.022
Doug Flynn	1207	274	.227	1454	360	.248	.021
Johnny Bench	826	211	.255	885	244	.276	.020
Billy Sample	933	241	.258	1568	436	.278	.020
Tom Paciorek	1221	343	.281	1588	474	.298	.018
Leon Roberts	673	168	.250	820	219	.267	.017

Runners In Scoring Position

LAST SEASON

BETTER WITH RUNNERS IN SCORING POSITION

PLAYER	SCORING POSITION			OTHER AT BATS			DIFF
	AB	H	AVG	AB	H	AVG	
Dave Valle	80	28	.350	210	39	.186	.164
Cecil Espy	79	28	.354	268	58	.216	.138
Pedro Guerrero	97	36	.371	267	68	.255	.116
Dan Gladden	111	40	.360	465	115	.247	.113
Mark McGwire	141	48	.340	409	95	.232	.108
Gerald Young	109	37	.339	467	111	.238	.102
Steve Jeltz	83	22	.265	296	49	.166	.100
Kelly Gruber	155	54	.348	414	104	.251	.097
Mike LaValliere	87	29	.333	265	63	.238	.096
Bob Boone	97	35	.361	255	69	.271	.090
Steve Sax	120	42	.350	512	133	.260	.090
Gary Pettis	98	27	.276	360	69	.192	.084
Robin Yount	176	64	.364	445	126	.283	.080
Luis Salazar	119	39	.328	333	83	.249	.078
Tony Fernandez	138	48	.348	510	138	.271	.077
Tony Gwynn	116	43	.371	405	120	.296	.074
Juan Samuel	143	43	.301	486	110	.226	.074
Pat Tabler	126	42	.333	318	83	.261	.072
Roberto Alomar	105	34	.324	440	111	.252	.072
Terry Pendleton	119	36	.303	272	63	.232	.071
Kurt Stillwell	98	30	.306	361	85	.235	.071
Mike Pagliarulo	136	36	.265	308	60	.195	.070
Kevin Bass	127	39	.307	414	99	.239	.068
Tim Raines	80	26	.325	349	90	.258	.067
Carney Lansford	125	41	.328	431	114	.265	.063

BETTER IN OTHER AT BATS

PLAYER	SCORING POSITION			OTHER AT BATS			DIFF
	AB	H	AVG	AB	H	AVG	
Benito Santiago	115	17	.148	377	105	.279	.131
Glenn Wilson	102	17	.167	308	88	.286	.119
Fred Lynn	87	14	.161	304	82	.270	.109
Kent Hrbek	132	31	.235	378	128	.339	.104
Len Dykstra	77	15	.195	352	101	.287	.092
Darryl Strawberry	139	28	.201	404	118	.292	.091
Rance Mulliniks	82	19	.232	255	82	.322	.090
Andre Dawson	132	31	.235	459	148	.322	.088
Glenn Davis	151	32	.212	410	120	.293	.081
Fred McGriff	127	28	.220	409	123	.301	.080
Damon Berryhill	89	18	.202	220	62	.282	.080
Andy Van Slyke	164	38	.232	423	131	.310	.078
Don Slaught	86	20	.233	236	71	.301	.068
Rafael Palmeiro	150	39	.260	430	139	.323	.063
Eddie Murray	128	30	.234	475	141	.297	.062
Geno Petralli	89	21	.236	262	78	.298	.062
Willie Upshaw	124	25	.202	369	96	.260	.059
Claudell Washington	135	36	.267	320	104	.325	.058
Dan Pasqua	118	22	.186	304	74	.243	.057
Willie McGee	155	39	.252	407	125	.307	.056
Tom Herr	86	19	.221	268	74	.276	.055
Jody Reed	91	23	.253	247	76	.308	.055
Henry Cotto	83	18	.217	303	82	.271	.054
Chris James	162	33	.204	404	104	.257	.054
Wade Boggs	120	39	.325	464	175	.377	.052

LAST 10 YEARS

BETTER WITH RUNNERS IN SCORING POSITION

PLAYER	SCORING POSITION			OTHER AT BATS			DIFF
	AB	H	AVG	AB	H	AVG	
Gary Allenson	272	75	.276	789	160	.203	.073
Rick Leach	308	97	.315	998	247	.247	.067
Rodney Scott	395	108	.273	1121	232	.207	.066
Mark McGwire	297	95	.320	863	219	.254	.066
Pat Tabler	806	272	.337	2157	589	.273	.064
Broderick Perkins	264	85	.322	774	203	.262	.060
Kelly Gruber	284	83	.292	798	187	.234	.058
Kurt Stillwell	261	76	.291	872	205	.235	.056
Oscar Gamble	390	120	.308	1036	263	.254	.054
Scott Fletcher	622	194	.312	2100	543	.259	.053
Larry Biittner	276	86	.312	630	163	.259	.053
Dale Sveum	335	96	.287	984	230	.234	.053
Mike Aldrete	257	83	.323	705	191	.271	.052
Chris Brown	353	110	.312	1113	289	.260	.052
Joe Rudi	287	75	.261	730	156	.214	.048
Ozzie Guillen	484	146	.302	1680	429	.255	.046
Jose Canseco	530	160	.302	1406	362	.257	.044
Dane Iorg	420	130	.310	1080	287	.266	.044
Scot Thompson	282	82	.291	955	236	.247	.044
Rob Wilfong	576	161	.280	1744	412	.236	.043
Larry Parrish	1189	355	.299	3537	905	.256	.043
Mike Ivie	293	84	.287	761	186	.244	.042
Ted Simmons	1129	336	.298	2769	709	.256	.042
Mike LaValliere	275	80	.291	761	190	.250	.041
Don Money	287	78	.272	926	214	.231	.041

BETTER IN OTHER AT BATS

PLAYER	SCORING POSITION			OTHER AT BATS			DIFF
	AB	H	AVG	AB	H	AVG	
Jackie Gutierrez	254	44	.173	703	183	.260	.087
Benito Santiago	270	59	.219	830	245	.295	.077
Chris James	280	61	.218	690	194	.281	.063
Barry Bonds	303	63	.208	1199	325	.271	.063
Bill Schroeder	267	53	.199	799	209	.262	.063
Jim Wohlford	369	82	.222	890	245	.275	.053
Lenn Sakata	271	55	.203	786	201	.256	.053
Don Slaught	501	117	.234	1515	432	.285	.052
Billy Sample	528	124	.235	1973	553	.280	.045
Tom O'Malley	273	61	.223	808	216	.267	.044
Mickey Rivers	476	127	.267	1776	551	.310	.043
Dave Anderson	340	68	.200	1136	275	.242	.042
Dan Pasqua	303	64	.211	865	219	.253	.042
Cory Snyder	374	85	.227	1130	303	.268	.041
Bill Robinson	273	64	.234	655	180	.275	.040
Floyd Rayford	261	56	.215	783	199	.254	.040
Lee Lacy	638	168	.263	2397	726	.303	.040
Wayne Tolleson	427	93	.218	1681	432	.257	.039
Ken Phelps	384	83	.216	1156	295	.255	.039
Juan Bonilla	348	79	.227	1114	296	.266	.039
Bob Bailor	423	94	.222	1384	360	.260	.038
Larry Milbourne	357	85	.238	1183	326	.276	.037
Chris Bando	349	70	.201	933	221	.237	.036
Greg Gross	378	95	.251	1169	336	.287	.036
Phil Bradley	659	175	.266	2069	624	.302	.036

Vs. Left- and Right-Handers

LAST SEASON

BETTER VS. LEFT-HANDERS

PLAYER	VS. LEFT-HANDERS			VS. RIGHT-HANDERS			DIFF
	AB	H	AVG	AB	H	AVG	
Terry Steinbach	114	39	.342	237	54	.228	.114
Tracy Jones	111	39	.351	113	27	.239	.112
Terry Pendleton	119	39	.328	272	60	.221	.107
Julio Franco	133	51	.383	480	135	.281	.102
Tony Pena	166	55	.331	339	78	.230	.101
Tim Laudner	109	35	.321	266	59	.222	.099
Kevin Bass	193	61	.316	348	77	.221	.095
Scott Fletcher	163	55	.337	352	87	.247	.090
Cory Snyder	111	38	.342	400	101	.252	.090
Luis Salazar	200	64	.320	252	58	.230	.090
Rob Thompson	154	50	.325	323	76	.235	.089
Rickey Henderson	163	60	.368	391	109	.279	.089
Dickie Thon	139	42	.302	119	26	.218	.084
Greg Gagne	111	33	.297	350	76	.217	.080
Cal Ripken	190	60	.316	385	92	.239	.077
Barry Larkin	145	51	.352	443	123	.278	.074
Jose Uribe	152	46	.303	341	78	.229	.074
Dan Gladden	159	51	.321	417	104	.249	.071
Manny Lee	131	44	.336	250	67	.268	.068
Kevin Seitzer	153	54	.353	406	116	.286	.067
Rick Cerone	114	35	.307	150	36	.240	.067
Glenn Wilson	164	48	.293	246	57	.232	.061
Dave Valle	125	33	.264	165	34	.206	.058
Gene Larkin	150	46	.307	355	89	.251	.056
Kirby Puckett	166	66	.398	491	168	.342	.055

BETTER VS. RIGHT-HANDERS

PLAYER	VS. LEFT-HANDERS			VS. RIGHT-HANDERS			DIFF
	AB	H	AVG	AB	H	AVG	
Von Hayes	101	13	.129	266	87	.327	.198
Andy Van Slyke	204	39	.191	383	130	.339	.148
Carney Lansford	153	31	.203	403	124	.308	.105
Sid Bream	116	22	.190	346	100	.289	.099
Fred Lynn	109	19	.174	282	77	.273	.099
Kent Hrbek	132	33	.250	378	126	.333	.083
Eddie Murray	213	49	.230	390	122	.313	.083
Mickey Brantley	170	35	.206	407	117	.287	.082
Kevin Mitchell	160	32	.200	345	95	.275	.075
Jody Davis	102	19	.186	155	40	.258	.072
B.J. Surhoff	115	22	.191	378	99	.262	.071
Fred McGriff	171	40	.234	365	111	.304	.070
Mike A. Marshall	186	43	.231	356	107	.301	.069
Howard Johnson	142	26	.183	353	88	.249	.066
Glenn Davis	167	38	.228	394	114	.289	.062
Mike Pagliarulo	106	18	.170	338	78	.231	.061
Todd Benzinger	104	22	.212	301	81	.269	.058
Dave Gallagher	155	42	.271	192	63	.328	.057
Steve Balboni	164	33	.201	249	64	.257	.056
Mike Diaz	107	22	.206	119	31	.261	.055
Walt Weiss	101	21	.208	351	92	.262	.054
Mike Greenwell	197	57	.289	393	135	.344	.054
Paul Molitor	196	54	.276	413	136	.329	.054
Bob Boone	140	37	.264	212	67	.316	.052
Brett Butler	190	48	.253	378	115	.304	.052

LAST 10 YEARS

BETTER VS. LEFT-HANDERS

PLAYER	VS. LEFT-HANDERS			VS. RIGHT-HANDERS			DIFF
	AB	H	AVG	AB	H	AVG	
Bill Stein	512	159	.311	589	142	.241	.069
Bob Bailor	620	183	.295	1187	271	.228	.067
Barry Bonnell	1035	318	.307	1369	334	.244	.063
Cliff Johnson	1099	326	.297	1533	361	.235	.061
Tim Laudner	701	182	.260	1098	223	.203	.057
Bob Dernier	810	241	.298	1486	361	.243	.055
Mike Heath	1455	408	.280	1760	399	.227	.054
Tony Phillips	711	202	.284	1426	329	.231	.053
Juan Beniquez	1092	339	.310	1385	357	.258	.053
Steve Yeager	626	155	.248	976	191	.196	.052
Jose Canseco	569	174	.306	1367	348	.255	.051
Julio Cruz	1094	295	.270	2016	441	.219	.051
Rick Dempsey	1214	323	.266	1785	385	.216	.050
Bucky Dent	732	194	.265	1147	248	.216	.049
Johnny Bench	529	158	.299	1182	297	.251	.047
Alan Wiggins	742	215	.290	1505	366	.243	.047
Hubie Brooks	1068	331	.310	2904	768	.264	.045
John Castino	860	264	.307	1460	382	.262	.045
Ron LeFlore	549	168	.306	1243	325	.261	.045
Lance Parrish	1696	490	.289	3133	766	.244	.044
Jim Wohlford	706	197	.279	553	130	.235	.044
Andre Thornton	1100	309	.281	2272	539	.237	.044
Tom Brookens	1521	411	.270	2022	460	.227	.043
Dave Lopes	997	286	.287	2116	518	.245	.042
Larry Herndon	1652	494	.299	2307	594	.257	.042

BETTER VS. RIGHT-HANDERS

PLAYER	VS. LEFT-HANDERS			VS. RIGHT-HANDERS			DIFF
	AB	H	AVG	AB	H	AVG	
Andy Van Slyke	697	145	.208	1966	581	.296	.087
Willie Aikens	636	139	.219	1765	518	.293	.075
Von Hayes	966	219	.227	2685	788	.293	.067
Jerry Mumphrey	1107	278	.251	2654	830	.313	.062
Mike Easler	759	190	.250	2819	866	.307	.057
Terry Puhl	994	236	.237	2634	775	.294	.057
Chris Chambliss	805	186	.231	2418	696	.288	.057
Al Oliver	1065	288	.270	2433	795	.327	.056
Wade Boggs	1193	378	.317	2720	1014	.373	.056
Greg Walker	721	164	.227	1871	527	.282	.054
Fred Lynn	1261	303	.240	2999	883	.294	.054
Mike Hargrove	937	236	.252	2133	648	.304	.052
Lou Whitaker	1606	391	.243	3590	1054	.294	.050
Ruppert Jones	819	175	.214	2476	649	.262	.048
Rod Carew	859	240	.279	2221	728	.328	.048
George Brett	1688	481	.285	3153	1048	.332	.047
Sid Bream	504	116	.230	1204	333	.277	.046
Darryl Strawberry	1055	250	.237	1830	518	.283	.046
Dwayne Murphy	1436	314	.219	2703	711	.263	.044
Wally Joyner	605	158	.261	1149	351	.305	.044
Mike Pagliarulo	502	100	.199	1549	377	.243	.044
Johnny Ray	1244	324	.260	3010	913	.303	.043
Rick Manning	1065	234	.220	2333	611	.262	.042
Ozzie Guillen	592	140	.236	1572	435	.277	.040
Ken Singleton	866	213	.246	2081	592	.284	.039

Vs. Ground- and Fly-Ballers

LAST SEASON

BETTER VS. GROUND-BALLERS

PLAYER	VS. GROUND-BALLERS			VS. FLY-BALLERS			DIFF
	AB	H	AVG	AB	H	AVG	
Rich Gedman	127	39	.307	172	30	.174	.133
Bob Boone	155	57	.368	197	47	.239	.129
Gary Redus	161	50	.311	172	33	.192	.119
Kevin Mitchell	280	85	.304	225	42	.187	.117
Jack Howell	198	64	.323	302	63	.209	.115
Milt Thompson	187	64	.342	191	45	.236	.107
Von Hayes	186	60	.323	181	40	.221	.102
Geno Petralli	140	48	.343	211	51	.242	.101
Andres Galarraga	338	117	.346	271	67	.247	.099
Steve Lyons	211	67	.318	261	60	.230	.088
Tony Armas	152	49	.322	216	51	.236	.086
Steve Lombardozzi	138	35	.254	149	25	.168	.086
Jose Uribe	266	77	.289	227	47	.207	.082
Terry Steinbach	181	55	.304	170	38	.224	.080
Andy Allanson	226	68	.301	208	46	.221	.080
Gary Carter	236	66	.280	219	44	.201	.079
Brian Downing	202	58	.287	282	59	.209	.078
Ken Gerhart	113	27	.239	149	24	.161	.078
Luis Salazar	177	56	.316	275	66	.240	.076
Curtis Wilkerson	136	46	.338	202	53	.262	.076
Mark McGwire	264	79	.299	286	64	.224	.075
Glenn Braggs	119	36	.303	153	35	.229	.074
Mickey Tettleton	126	38	.302	157	36	.229	.072
R.J. Reynolds	175	49	.280	148	31	.209	.071
Mike Diaz	124	33	.266	102	20	.196	.070

BETTER VS. FLY-BALLERS

PLAYER	VS. GROUND-BALLERS			VS. FLY-BALLERS			DIFF
	AB	H	AVG	AB	H	AVG	
Walt Weiss	211	38	.180	241	75	.311	.131
Gerald Perry	276	69	.250	271	95	.351	.101
Wally Backman	141	36	.255	153	53	.346	.091
Mark McLemore	100	19	.190	133	37	.278	.088
Jack Clark	213	41	.192	283	79	.279	.087
Dave Bergman	122	30	.246	167	55	.329	.083
Fred Lynn	192	39	.203	199	57	.286	.083
Howard Johnson	251	48	.191	244	66	.270	.079
Dave Magadan	155	37	.239	159	50	.314	.076
Vince Coleman	337	76	.226	279	84	.301	.076
Otis Nixon	152	32	.211	119	34	.286	.075
Dion James	192	42	.219	194	57	.294	.075
Darrell Evans	197	33	.168	240	58	.242	.074
John Kruk	178	36	.202	200	55	.275	.073
Roberto Alomar	272	63	.232	273	82	.300	.069
Jody Reed	145	37	.255	193	62	.321	.066
Claudell Washington	209	57	.273	246	83	.337	.065
Larry Sheets	191	37	.194	261	67	.257	.063
Al Newman	107	20	.187	153	38	.248	.061
Steve Buechele	196	42	.214	307	84	.274	.059
Paul Molitor	249	69	.277	360	121	.336	.059
John Shelby	263	62	.236	231	68	.294	.059
Glenn Hubbard	154	35	.227	140	40	.286	.058
Manny Lee	134	34	.254	247	77	.312	.058
Ellis Burks	222	58	.261	318	101	.318	.056

LAST 10 YEARS

BETTER VS. GROUND-BALLERS

PLAYER	VS. GROUND-BALLERS			VS. FLY-BALLERS			DIFF
	AB	H	AVG	AB	H	AVG	
Mark McGwire	523	169	.323	637	145	.228	.096
Franklin Stubbs	662	169	.255	612	114	.186	.069
Steve Lombardozzi	520	140	.269	706	146	.207	.062
Rick Dempsey	1262	341	.270	1737	367	.211	.059
Roy Smalley	1546	454	.294	2178	515	.236	.057
Lonnie Smith	1764	555	.315	1661	429	.258	.056
Donnie Hill	688	199	.289	1007	237	.235	.054
John Lowenstein	675	205	.304	835	209	.250	.053
Eddie Milner	1303	361	.277	1092	246	.225	.052
Broderick Perkins	514	156	.304	524	132	.252	.052
Alex Trevino	1217	328	.270	984	216	.220	.050
Brian Downing	1892	567	.300	2676	672	.251	.049
Eric Davis	932	273	.293	725	179	.247	.046
Terry Kennedy	2269	652	.287	1852	447	.241	.046
Rodney Scott	712	177	.249	804	163	.203	.046
Dave Stapleton	865	257	.297	1163	293	.252	.045
Andres Galarraga	854	266	.311	702	187	.266	.045
Alan Bannister	948	283	.299	1161	295	.254	.044
Randy Ready	527	154	.292	577	143	.248	.044
Gary Redus	1264	336	.266	1060	235	.222	.044
Cal Ripken	1837	562	.306	2572	674	.262	.044
Bob Kearney	507	132	.260	849	184	.217	.044
Jose Uribe	908	243	.268	842	189	.224	.043
Mitch Webster	1022	302	.295	911	231	.254	.042
Frank Taveras	776	216	.278	836	198	.237	.042

BETTER VS. FLY-BALLERS

PLAYER	VS. GROUND-BALLERS			VS. FLY-BALLERS			DIFF
	AB	H	AVG	AB	H	AVG	
Dion James	648	161	.248	688	219	.318	.070
Wayne Krenchicki	560	136	.243	503	147	.292	.049
Don Money	562	121	.215	651	171	.263	.047
John Kruk	572	152	.266	531	165	.311	.045
Lou Piniella	668	181	.271	768	241	.314	.043
Wally Backman	1234	326	.264	1135	344	.303	.039
Willie Montanez	568	134	.236	634	174	.274	.039
Rudy Law	1096	275	.251	1313	378	.288	.037
Rod Carew	1383	407	.294	1697	561	.331	.036
Wayne Tolleson	843	193	.229	1265	332	.262	.034
Darnell Coles	642	146	.227	847	219	.259	.031
Barry Larkin	633	165	.261	553	161	.291	.030
Spike Owen	917	204	.222	1493	376	.252	.029
Damaso Garcia	1496	400	.267	2174	645	.297	.029
Kevin Bass	1468	379	.258	1354	389	.287	.029
Tom Foley	815	201	.247	730	201	.275	.029
Howard Johnson	1121	265	.236	1113	295	.265	.029
Milt May	863	217	.251	713	198	.278	.026
Butch Hobson	585	134	.229	593	151	.255	.026
Dave Bergman	695	174	.250	812	224	.276	.026
Paul Householder	679	152	.224	647	161	.249	.025
Duane Kuiper	725	179	.247	623	169	.271	.024
Gene Richards	1218	333	.273	1251	372	.297	.024
Carl Yastrzemski	959	244	.254	1100	306	.278	.024
Buck Martinez	569	122	.214	946	224	.237	.022

Home and Road Games

LAST SEASON

BETTER IN HOME GAMES

	HOME GAMES			ROAD GAMES			
PLAYER	AB	H	AVG	AB	H	AVG	DIFF
Bo Jackson	211	67	.318	228	41	.180	.138
Terry Puhl	106	40	.377	128	31	.242	.135
Julio Franco	286	104	.364	327	82	.251	.113
Ozzie Virgil	149	47	.315	171	35	.205	.111
Dan Gladden	300	95	.317	276	60	.217	.099
Kirby Puckett	323	131	.406	334	103	.308	.097
Claudell Washington	218	78	.358	237	62	.262	.096
Cecil Espy	155	46	.297	192	40	.208	.088
John Shelby	236	73	.309	258	57	.221	.088
Rick Cerone	146	45	.308	118	26	.220	.088
Jeff Treadway	137	41	.299	164	35	.213	.086
Nelson Santovenia	163	45	.276	146	28	.192	.084
Jeff Hamilton	138	39	.283	171	34	.199	.084
Mike Schmidt	186	54	.290	204	43	.211	.080
Jose Lind	313	94	.300	298	66	.221	.079
Dale Sveum	239	67	.280	228	46	.202	.079
Ernest Riles	159	50	.314	155	37	.239	.076
Damon Berryhill	179	52	.291	130	28	.215	.075
Wally Backman	144	49	.340	150	40	.267	.074
Kal Daniels	227	75	.330	268	69	.257	.073
Ken Gerhart	130	30	.231	132	21	.159	.072
Larry Parrish	235	58	.247	171	30	.175	.071
Mike Stanley	143	37	.259	106	20	.189	.070
Dale Murphy	283	74	.261	309	60	.194	.067
Chris Brown	123	33	.268	124	25	.202	.067

BETTER IN ROAD GAMES

	HOME GAMES			ROAD GAMES			
PLAYER	AB	H	AVG	AB	H	AVG	DIFF
Bobby Bonilla	286	62	.217	298	98	.329	.112
Mike Aldrete	173	36	.208	216	68	.315	.107
Terry Kennedy	136	24	.176	129	36	.279	.103
Mike Davis	133	20	.150	148	35	.236	.086
Joel Skinner	111	20	.180	140	37	.264	.084
Von Hayes	175	40	.229	192	60	.313	.084
Jody Davis	105	19	.181	152	40	.263	.082
Cory Snyder	270	63	.233	241	76	.315	.082
Tom Herr	193	44	.228	161	49	.304	.076
R.J. Reynolds	174	37	.213	149	43	.289	.076
Mookie Wilson	185	48	.259	193	64	.332	.072
Dickie Thon	112	25	.223	146	43	.295	.071
Daryl Boston	138	25	.181	143	36	.252	.071
Tony Armas	199	48	.241	169	52	.308	.066
Carney Lansford	277	68	.245	279	87	.312	.066
Albert Hall	104	22	.212	127	35	.276	.064
Gary Carter	228	48	.211	227	62	.273	.063
Ray Knight	154	29	.188	145	36	.248	.060
Sid Bream	226	53	.235	236	69	.292	.058
Alan Ashby	123	26	.211	104	28	.269	.058
Jeff Reed	126	25	.198	139	35	.252	.053
Tim Teufel	130	27	.208	143	37	.259	.051
Billy Hatcher	263	64	.243	267	78	.292	.049
Fred McGriff	250	64	.256	286	87	.304	.048
Ron Washington	116	27	.233	107	30	.280	.048

LAST 10 YEARS

BETTER IN HOME GAMES

	HOME GAMES			ROAD GAMES			
PLAYER	AB	H	AVG	AB	H	AVG	DIFF
Carmen Castillo	566	169	.299	586	126	.215	.084
Ken Reitz	706	207	.293	692	152	.220	.074
Reid Nichols	616	182	.295	544	126	.232	.064
Rodney Scott	752	192	.255	764	148	.194	.062
Ernest Riles	764	227	.297	798	192	.241	.057
Wade Boggs	1955	750	.384	1958	642	.328	.056
Bobby Brown	606	166	.274	671	147	.219	.055
Butch Hobson	575	154	.268	603	131	.217	.051
Kirby Puckett	1606	555	.346	1603	473	.295	.051
Ozzie Virgil	1091	294	.269	1151	253	.220	.050
Al Oliver	1723	576	.334	1775	507	.286	.049
Pat Tabler	1467	462	.315	1496	399	.267	.048
Jim Rice	2721	874	.321	2762	754	.273	.048
Kevin Seitzer	639	216	.338	657	192	.292	.046
Rey Quinones	614	169	.275	675	155	.230	.046
Glenn Davis	1064	303	.285	1060	254	.240	.045
Jay Johnstone	562	161	.286	531	129	.243	.044
Jerry Royster	1259	348	.276	1387	323	.233	.044
Ellis Burks	502	154	.307	596	157	.263	.043
Floyd Rayford	515	137	.266	529	118	.223	.043
Will Clark	777	243	.313	735	199	.271	.042
Don Slaught	993	291	.293	1023	258	.252	.041
Ellis Valentine	854	247	.289	896	223	.249	.040
Scott Fletcher	1329	387	.291	1393	350	.251	.040
Leon Durham	1857	551	.297	1712	440	.257	.040

BETTER IN ROAD GAMES

	HOME GAMES			ROAD GAMES			
PLAYER	AB	H	AVG	AB	H	AVG	DIFF
Bobby Bonilla	709	175	.247	767	234	.305	.058
Todd Cruz	735	141	.192	787	193	.245	.053
Mike Ivie	522	120	.230	532	150	.282	.052
Candy Maldonado	933	216	.232	958	271	.283	.051
Dave Revering	633	153	.242	678	192	.283	.041
Benito Santiago	562	144	.256	538	160	.297	.041
Cory Snyder	732	174	.238	772	214	.277	.039
Mike R. Fitzgerald	689	154	.224	637	166	.261	.037
John Moses	639	154	.241	627	174	.278	.037
Devon White	548	132	.241	604	167	.276	.036
Wally Joyner	891	243	.273	863	266	.308	.035
George Wright	1051	239	.227	1109	290	.261	.034
David Green	676	169	.250	722	205	.284	.034
Rafael Santana	979	225	.230	1029	269	.261	.032
Rick Burleson	1157	298	.258	1189	342	.288	.030
Johnny Bench	838	210	.251	873	245	.281	.030
Gary Allenson	519	107	.206	542	128	.236	.030
Jeff Newman	767	159	.207	849	201	.237	.029
Ray Knight	2266	585	.258	2395	687	.287	.029
Rick Miller	933	246	.264	1061	310	.292	.029
Mike Squires	664	163	.245	698	191	.274	.028
Dwayne Murphy	2013	470	.233	2126	555	.261	.028
Harold Reynolds	860	207	.241	886	237	.267	.027
Jim Dwyer	820	207	.252	920	256	.278	.026
John Wockenfuss	693	176	.254	737	206	.280	.026

Grass and Artificial Surfaces

LAST SEASON

BETTER ON GRASS SURFACES

PLAYER	GRASS FIELDS AB	H	AVG	ARTIFICIAL TURF AB	H	AVG	DIFF
Von Hayes	104	40	.385	263	60	.228	.156
Tom Herr	106	36	.340	248	57	.230	.110
Pedro Guerrero	194	64	.330	170	40	.235	.095
Andy Van Slyke	160	57	.356	427	112	.262	.094
Julio Franco	510	162	.318	103	24	.233	.085
Henry Cotto	149	46	.309	237	54	.228	.081
Kevin Mitchell	385	104	.270	120	23	.192	.078
Gerald Young	154	48	.312	422	100	.237	.075
Greg Gagne	189	53	.280	272	56	.206	.075
Luis Aguayo	133	37	.278	104	22	.212	.067
Dave Martinez	234	67	.286	213	47	.221	.066
Shawon Dunston	389	105	.270	186	38	.204	.066
Bobby Bonilla	152	49	.322	432	111	.257	.065
Tom Brunansky	157	45	.287	415	92	.222	.065
Keith Hernandez	244	72	.295	104	24	.231	.064
Kirk Gibson	383	118	.308	159	39	.245	.063
Paul O'Neill	157	46	.293	328	76	.232	.061
Damon Berryhill	208	58	.279	101	22	.218	.061
Howard Johnson	337	84	.249	158	30	.190	.059
Jeff Reed	103	27	.262	162	33	.204	.058
Dale Murphy	434	105	.242	158	29	.184	.058
Lance Parrish	118	30	.254	306	61	.199	.055
Nelson Liriano	111	33	.297	165	40	.242	.055
Steve Jeltz	111	25	.225	268	46	.172	.054
Bill Doran	145	41	.283	335	78	.233	.050

BETTER ON ARTIFICIAL TURF

PLAYER	GRASS FIELDS AB	H	AVG	ARTIFICIAL TURF AB	H	AVG	DIFF
Glenn Davis	146	23	.158	415	129	.311	.153
Rob Thompson	341	80	.235	136	46	.338	.104
Bill Buckner	132	26	.197	153	45	.294	.097
Tony Pena	125	24	.192	380	109	.287	.095
Bo Jackson	172	33	.192	267	75	.281	.089
Mike Aldrete	282	69	.245	107	35	.327	.082
Chili Davis	499	127	.255	101	34	.337	.082
Dan Gladden	212	47	.222	364	108	.297	.075
Rickey Henderson	447	130	.291	107	39	.364	.074
George Bell	248	56	.226	366	109	.298	.072
Dave Winfield	459	142	.309	100	38	.380	.071
Roberto Alomar	403	100	.248	142	45	.317	.069
Barry Bonds	139	33	.237	399	119	.298	.061
Len Dykstra	291	73	.251	138	43	.312	.061
Glenn Wilson	130	28	.215	280	77	.275	.060
Kal Daniels	159	40	.252	336	104	.310	.058
Mike A. Marshall	387	101	.261	155	49	.316	.055
Jose Lind	145	32	.221	466	128	.275	.054
Dave Valle	102	20	.196	188	47	.250	.054
Willie Wilson	222	51	.230	369	104	.282	.052
Juan Samuel	165	34	.206	464	119	.256	.050
Mitch Webster	241	57	.237	282	79	.280	.044
Kevin McReynolds	405	112	.277	147	47	.320	.043
Andre Dawson	420	122	.290	171	57	.333	.043
Mike Diaz	121	26	.215	105	27	.257	.042

LAST 10 YEARS

BETTER ON GRASS SURFACES

PLAYER	GRASS FIELDS AB	H	AVG	ARTIFICIAL TURF AB	H	AVG	DIFF
Pat Tabler	2364	715	.302	599	146	.244	.059
Mike Scioscia	2083	579	.278	754	167	.221	.056
Bobby Bonilla	503	157	.312	973	252	.259	.053
Juan Beniquez	1875	551	.294	602	145	.241	.053
Kirk Gibson	3143	898	.286	609	144	.236	.049
Dale Murphy	4057	1178	.290	1447	350	.242	.048
Julio Franco	3033	914	.301	557	145	.260	.041
Jerry Royster	1992	524	.263	654	147	.225	.038
Brett Butler	2975	860	.289	810	204	.252	.037
Larry Milbourne	919	259	.282	621	152	.245	.037
Ryne Sandberg	3041	897	.295	1246	322	.258	.037
Richie Zisk	1296	382	.295	800	207	.259	.036
Jim Rice	4664	1408	.302	819	220	.269	.033
Mike R. Fitzgerald	512	134	.262	814	186	.229	.033
Mookie Wilson	2602	757	.291	1176	304	.259	.032
Glenn Hubbard	3124	790	.253	1023	226	.221	.032
Leon Durham	2388	688	.288	1181	303	.257	.032
Lance Parrish	3596	963	.268	1233	293	.238	.030
Andre Dawson	2080	635	.305	3541	975	.275	.030
Johnnie LeMaster	1892	443	.234	719	147	.204	.030
Wally Backman	1700	495	.291	669	175	.262	.030
Carmelo Martinez	1559	405	.260	588	136	.231	.028
Shawon Dunston	1214	314	.259	538	124	.230	.028
Greg Gagne	649	169	.260	1042	243	.233	.027
Jason Thompson	1441	396	.275	1775	440	.248	.027

BETTER ON ARTIFICIAL TURF

PLAYER	GRASS FIELDS AB	H	AVG	ARTIFICIAL TURF AB	H	AVG	DIFF
Rick Leach	729	172	.236	577	172	.298	.062
Glenn Davis	632	141	.223	1492	416	.279	.056
Mickey Hatcher	1585	411	.259	1436	441	.307	.048
Garry Templeton	2923	734	.251	2030	604	.298	.046
Cesar Cedeno	882	217	.246	1971	571	.290	.044
John Mayberry	699	159	.227	804	217	.270	.042
Bob Kearney	673	143	.212	683	173	.253	.041
Willie Upshaw	1834	444	.242	2145	606	.283	.040
Cal Ripken	3724	1021	.274	685	215	.314	.040
Mike Davis	2313	585	.253	513	150	.292	.039
Ruppert Jones	2400	575	.240	895	249	.278	.039
Tony Armas	3718	927	.249	636	183	.288	.038
Amos Otis	978	244	.249	1293	370	.286	.037
Tony Scott	591	133	.225	1550	403	.260	.035
Jim Gantner	3779	1026	.272	683	209	.306	.035
Darrell Evans	3814	928	.243	998	276	.277	.033
Julio Cruz	1745	388	.222	1365	348	.255	.033
Tony Pena	997	252	.253	2764	784	.284	.031
Ken Phelps	633	144	.227	907	234	.258	.031
Ozzie Smith	2183	518	.237	3141	836	.266	.029
Dan Gladden	1295	336	.259	977	281	.288	.028
Kirby Puckett	1220	370	.303	1989	658	.331	.028
Buck Martinez	781	168	.215	734	178	.243	.027
Dave Henderson	1474	367	.249	1412	390	.276	.027
Rance Mulliniks	1061	282	.266	1506	441	.293	.027

Day and Night Games

LAST SEASON

BETTER IN DAY GAMES

PLAYER	DAY GAMES			NIGHT GAMES			
	AB	H	AVG	AB	H	AVG	DIFF
Randy Ready	104	47	.452	227	41	.181	.271
Nick Esasky	104	35	.337	287	60	.209	.127
Von Hayes	105	38	.362	262	62	.237	.125
Dan Pasqua	112	35	.313	310	61	.197	.116
George Brett	155	58	.374	434	122	.281	.093
Mookie Wilson	111	40	.360	267	72	.270	.091
Mark McGwire	227	71	.313	323	72	.223	.090
Dave Anderson	101	31	.307	184	40	.217	.090
Claudell Washington	113	42	.372	342	98	.287	.085
Willie Wilson	152	49	.322	439	106	.241	.081
Kurt Stillwell	119	36	.303	340	79	.232	.070
Paul Molitor	183	66	.361	426	124	.291	.070
Kevin McReynolds	186	62	.333	366	97	.265	.068
Sid Bream	121	38	.314	341	84	.246	.068
Terry Steinbach	148	45	.304	203	48	.236	.068
Randy Bush	120	37	.308	274	66	.241	.067
Rick Cerone	107	33	.308	157	38	.242	.066
Steve Balboni	106	30	.283	307	67	.218	.065
Tom Brookens	132	38	.288	309	69	.223	.065
Rob Deer	152	45	.296	340	79	.232	.064
Terry Pendleton	122	36	.295	269	63	.234	.061
Carney Lansford	205	65	.317	351	90	.256	.061
Luis Polonia	136	44	.324	152	40	.263	.060
Tim Laudner	113	33	.292	262	61	.233	.059
Marvell Wynne	123	37	.301	210	51	.243	.058

BETTER IN NIGHT GAMES

PLAYER	DAY GAMES			NIGHT GAMES			
	AB	H	AVG	AB	H	AVG	DIFF
Kevin Bass	134	24	.179	407	114	.280	.101
Ernie Whitt	134	26	.194	264	74	.280	.086
Kevin Elster	132	21	.159	274	66	.241	.082
Kirby Puckett	197	59	.299	460	175	.380	.081
Jeff Treadway	100	20	.200	201	56	.279	.079
Eric Davis	157	35	.223	315	94	.298	.075
Jim Presley	125	22	.176	419	103	.246	.070
Greg Gagne	133	25	.188	328	84	.256	.068
Carmelo Martinez	121	23	.190	244	63	.258	.068
Pedro Guerrero	101	24	.238	263	80	.304	.067
Tim Raines	116	26	.224	313	90	.288	.063
Jody Davis	147	30	.204	110	29	.264	.060
Dan Gladden	171	39	.228	405	116	.286	.058
Cory Snyder	130	30	.231	381	109	.286	.055
Greg Walker	106	22	.208	271	71	.262	.054
Tim Wallach	165	36	.218	427	116	.272	.053
Ron Gant	124	27	.218	439	119	.271	.053
Lou Whitaker	133	32	.241	270	79	.293	.052
Dave Parker	142	32	.225	235	65	.277	.051
Bo Jackson	119	25	.210	320	83	.259	.049
Ken Oberkfell	135	32	.237	341	97	.284	.047
Tony Phillips	106	19	.179	106	24	.226	.047
Paul O'Neill	145	32	.221	340	90	.265	.044
Phil Bradley	143	33	.231	426	117	.275	.044
Ron Hassey	138	32	.232	185	51	.276	.044

LAST 10 YEARS

BETTER IN DAY GAMES

PLAYER	DAY GAMES			NIGHT GAMES			
	AB	H	AVG	AB	H	AVG	DIFF
Steve Kemp	879	287	.327	2045	538	.263	.063
Charlie Moore	908	274	.302	1769	442	.250	.052
Alex Trevino	789	220	.279	1412	324	.229	.049
Frank Taveras	668	190	.284	944	224	.237	.047
Duane Kuiper	513	147	.287	835	201	.241	.046
Thad Bosley	509	151	.297	572	144	.252	.045
Bake McBride	520	169	.325	1152	323	.280	.045
Scot Thompson	675	187	.277	562	131	.233	.044
Dave Lopes	1132	324	.286	1981	480	.242	.044
Dave Kingman	1526	402	.263	2099	464	.221	.042
Andre Dawson	2361	734	.311	3260	876	.269	.042
Wayne Gross	847	222	.262	1490	331	.222	.040
Pat Sheridan	627	180	.287	1398	346	.247	.040
Bob Boone	1113	304	.273	3025	710	.235	.038
Greg Gross	503	153	.304	1044	278	.266	.038
Rob Thompson	590	170	.288	856	215	.251	.037
Dave Engle	512	148	.289	1066	269	.252	.037
Willie McGee	1279	409	.320	2606	738	.283	.037
Ryne Sandberg	2778	825	.297	1509	394	.261	.036
Bruce Bochte	880	275	.313	2338	647	.277	.036
Mel Hall	977	294	.301	1439	384	.267	.034
U.L. Washington	707	195	.276	1941	470	.242	.034
Richie Hebner	696	200	.287	956	243	.254	.033
Will Clark	626	195	.312	886	247	.279	.033
Darrell Evans	1745	473	.271	3067	731	.238	.033

BETTER IN NIGHT GAMES

PLAYER	DAY GAMES			NIGHT GAMES			
	AB	H	AVG	AB	H	AVG	DIFF
Larry Herndon	1338	332	.248	2621	756	.288	.040
Al Cowens	797	191	.240	2468	671	.272	.032
Kevin Bass	743	185	.249	2079	583	.280	.031
Greg Gagne	505	112	.222	1186	300	.253	.031
Tony Phillips	795	182	.229	1342	349	.260	.031
Willie Aikens	661	166	.251	1740	491	.282	.031
Rafael Santana	665	150	.226	1343	344	.256	.031
Ron Jackson	633	153	.242	1225	333	.272	.030
Mickey Rivers	576	161	.280	1676	517	.308	.029
Rodney Scott	585	121	.207	931	219	.235	.028
Don Baylor	1415	338	.239	3279	876	.267	.028
Pedro Guerrero	1100	316	.287	2643	832	.315	.028
Alvin Davis	682	182	.267	2000	587	.294	.027
Gary Roenicke	707	162	.229	1853	473	.255	.026
Ron Kittle	654	143	.219	1500	367	.245	.026
Darrell Porter	878	204	.232	2010	519	.258	.026
George Vukovich	567	143	.252	1035	287	.277	.025
Amos Otis	560	141	.252	1711	473	.276	.025
Fred Lynn	1136	296	.261	3124	890	.285	.024
Denny Walling	655	171	.261	1750	499	.285	.024
Joe Morgan	738	173	.234	1699	438	.258	.023
Ron Oester	1160	289	.249	2587	705	.273	.023
Al Bumbry	782	206	.263	2203	631	.286	.023
Glenn Davis	618	152	.246	1506	405	.269	.023
Dave Parker	1717	460	.268	3304	959	.290	.022

Late-Inning Pressure Situations

LAST SEASON

BETTER IN OTHER AT BATS

PLAYER	LATE-INNING PRESSURE AB	H	AVG	OTHER AT BATS AB	H	AVG	DIFF
Doug Sisk	65	29	.446	291	80	.275	.171
Storm Davis	54	21	.389	715	190	.266	.123
Paul Mirabella	78	22	.282	138	22	.159	.123
Craig McMurtry	57	15	.263	148	22	.149	.115
Rich Gossage	110	36	.327	62	14	.226	.101
Dan Quisenberry	59	24	.407	203	62	.305	.101
Larry McWilliams	90	30	.333	423	100	.236	.097
Dan Plesac	128	34	.266	69	12	.174	.092
Jesse Orosco	121	30	.248	70	11	.157	.091
Charles Hudson	65	20	.308	330	73	.221	.086
Melido Perez	58	19	.328	691	167	.242	.086
Pete Smith	62	20	.323	670	163	.243	.079
Jim Gott	196	52	.265	84	16	.190	.075
Jose DeLeon	69	21	.304	766	177	.231	.073
Terry Leach	90	29	.322	264	66	.250	.072
Rich Yett	53	18	.340	478	128	.268	.072
Mark Williamson	82	27	.329	377	98	.260	.069
Juan Berenguer	159	39	.245	198	35	.177	.069
Dave LaPoint	67	21	.313	749	184	.246	.068
Bob Ojeda	74	21	.284	629	137	.218	.066
DeWayne Buice	93	29	.312	64	16	.250	.062
Keith Atherton	131	35	.267	146	30	.205	.062
Willie Hernandez	112	27	.241	128	23	.180	.061
Scott Garrelts	193	49	.254	161	31	.193	.061
Ted Higuera	120	31	.258	693	137	.198	.061

BETTER UNDER PRESSURE

PLAYER	LATE-INNING PRESSURE AB	H	AVG	OTHER AT BATS AB	H	AVG	DIFF
Tim Stoddard	50	10	.200	167	52	.311	.111
Mike Maddux	54	10	.185	277	81	.292	.107
Danny Darwin	102	17	.167	628	172	.274	.107
Allan Anderson	78	13	.167	685	186	.272	.105
Tim Crews	87	18	.207	190	59	.311	.104
Steve Shields	108	25	.231	214	71	.332	.100
Dave Righetti	243	56	.230	92	30	.326	.096
Jerry Reuss	57	10	.175	639	173	.271	.095
Chris Bosio	154	30	.195	556	160	.288	.093
Mark Thurmond	67	14	.209	222	66	.297	.088
John Davis	84	20	.238	175	57	.326	.088
Bob Forsch	61	13	.213	467	140	.300	.087
Larry Andersen	199	44	.221	124	38	.306	.085
Rick Honeycutt	127	26	.205	166	48	.289	.084
Dave Leiper	73	13	.178	122	32	.262	.084
Bryan Harvey	194	37	.191	82	22	.268	.078
John Candelaria	56	10	.179	549	140	.255	.076
Andy McGaffigan	195	39	.200	152	42	.276	.076
Tom Henke	162	34	.210	91	26	.286	.076
Doyle Alexander	129	28	.217	793	232	.293	.076
Jack Morris	123	23	.187	772	202	.262	.075
Dennis Martinez	98	17	.173	801	198	.247	.074
Rob Murphy	176	35	.199	125	34	.272	.073
Rick Mahler	140	31	.221	849	248	.292	.071
Randy Myers	175	30	.171	62	15	.242	.071

LAST 10 YEARS

BETTER IN OTHER AT BATS

PLAYER	LATE-INNING PRESSURE AB	H	AVG	OTHER AT BATS AB	H	AVG	DIFF
Mark Williamson	280	90	.321	647	157	.243	.079
Rich Bordi	316	101	.320	1139	282	.248	.072
Dennis Leonard	483	155	.321	3790	966	.255	.066
Dan Plesac	541	136	.251	289	54	.187	.065
Rich Gale	282	93	.330	2728	733	.269	.061
Dave Heaverlo	323	98	.303	327	80	.245	.059
Bill Castro	290	90	.310	744	188	.253	.058
Tom Tellmann	312	98	.314	553	142	.257	.057
Steve Rogers	657	195	.297	4755	1158	.244	.053
Tim Lollar	265	79	.298	3112	762	.245	.053
Jim Clancy	735	224	.305	6668	1682	.252	.053
Oil Can Boyd	407	129	.317	3319	881	.265	.052
Jim Acker	536	166	.310	1618	419	.259	.051
Terry Leach	289	85	.294	1096	268	.245	.050
Pat Clements	334	100	.299	567	142	.250	.049
David Palmer	344	101	.294	3649	901	.247	.047
Mark Gubicza	402	114	.284	3545	841	.237	.046
Dick Drago	490	142	.290	569	141	.248	.042
Atlee Hammaker	393	113	.288	3051	755	.247	.040
Barry Jones	308	85	.276	299	71	.237	.039
Jerry Koosman	513	157	.306	4466	1197	.268	.038
Bob Ojeda	449	129	.287	3978	993	.250	.038
Mike G. Marshall	476	131	.275	290	69	.238	.037
Steve Farr	471	128	.272	1161	273	.235	.037

BETTER UNDER PRESSURE

PLAYER	LATE-INNING PRESSURE AB	H	AVG	OTHER AT BATS AB	H	AVG	DIFF
Randy Myers	279	49	.176	278	68	.245	.069
Jeff Russell	353	74	.210	2264	621	.274	.065
Mark Davis	887	178	.201	1946	514	.264	.063
Sid Monge	916	198	.216	894	247	.276	.060
Vern Ruhle	487	106	.218	2803	776	.277	.059
Tom Henke	797	156	.196	489	124	.254	.058
Byron McLaughlin	304	75	.247	746	226	.303	.056
Randy Lerch	306	74	.242	2562	759	.296	.054
Bert Roberge	300	65	.217	508	135	.266	.049
Chris Bosio	286	67	.234	1241	351	.283	.049
Calvin Schiraldi	277	61	.220	1048	279	.266	.046
Cecilio Guante	791	162	.205	981	246	.251	.046
Jim Slaton	501	121	.242	3348	958	.286	.045
Mark Thurmond	284	68	.239	2368	667	.282	.042
John Franco	1140	254	.223	487	129	.265	.042
Gene Nelson	589	133	.226	2336	625	.268	.042
Doug Bair	1021	230	.225	1341	358	.267	.042
Ernie Camacho	499	128	.257	381	113	.297	.040
Don Aase	1053	249	.236	1725	477	.277	.040
Jay Howell	946	224	.237	971	267	.275	.038
Joe Sambito	845	188	.222	642	167	.260	.038
Bob Owchinko	429	104	.242	1547	433	.280	.037
Juan Agosto	547	134	.245	594	167	.281	.036
Tom Browning	282	61	.216	3336	839	.251	.035
Ken Schrom	327	80	.245	3157	883	.280	.035

Runners On Base

LAST SEASON

BETTER WITH BASES EMPTY

PLAYER	RUNNERS ON			BASES EMPTY			DIFF
	AB	H	AVG	AB	H	AVG	
Mark Williamson	189	65	.344	270	60	.222	.122
Scott Terry	191	60	.314	290	59	.203	.111
Jeff Russell	290	91	.314	423	92	.217	.096
Jay Tibbs	262	91	.347	367	93	.253	.094
Jim Gott	115	34	.296	165	34	.206	.090
Scott Bailes	215	69	.321	345	80	.232	.089
Ron Robinson	125	42	.336	184	46	.250	.086
Bert Blyleven	344	118	.343	472	122	.258	.085
David Palmer	207	64	.309	287	65	.226	.083
Richard Dotson	274	85	.310	395	93	.235	.075
Jay Howell	106	24	.226	128	20	.156	.070
Charles Hudson	151	42	.278	244	51	.209	.069
Kevin Coffman	127	36	.283	120	26	.217	.067
Greg Minton	138	37	.268	149	30	.201	.067
Doug Sisk	190	64	.337	166	45	.271	.066
Keith Atherton	122	33	.270	155	32	.206	.064
Paul Kilgus	313	88	.281	469	102	.217	.064
Ted Higuera	275	68	.247	538	100	.186	.061
Rick Mahler	382	122	.319	607	157	.259	.061
Scott Garrelts	176	45	.256	178	35	.197	.059
Bill Swift	306	100	.327	369	99	.268	.059
Dennis Eckersley	103	24	.233	160	28	.175	.058
Calvin Schiraldi	257	75	.292	389	91	.234	.058
Dave Righetti	176	50	.284	159	36	.226	.058
Danny Jackson	341	87	.255	602	119	.198	.057

BETTER WITH RUNNERS ON

PLAYER	RUNNERS ON			BASES EMPTY			DIFF
	AB	H	AVG	AB	H	AVG	
Eric King	135	25	.185	122	35	.287	.102
Randy Myers	121	18	.149	116	27	.233	.084
Neil Allen	211	48	.227	241	73	.303	.075
Don Sutton	149	34	.228	188	57	.303	.075
Chuck Crim	169	35	.207	215	60	.279	.072
Mark Portugal	105	25	.238	114	35	.307	.069
Floyd Youmans	116	20	.172	185	44	.238	.065
Jeff Ballard	246	59	.240	354	108	.305	.065
Brian Holton	135	26	.193	167	43	.257	.065
Don Gordon	115	29	.252	114	36	.316	.064
Rick Honeycutt	149	33	.221	144	41	.285	.063
Mark Grant	155	36	.232	207	61	.295	.062
Mike Jackson	184	33	.179	170	41	.241	.062
Jose Alvarez	164	34	.207	202	54	.267	.060
Kent Tekulve	169	42	.249	146	45	.308	.060
Joe Hesketh	118	25	.212	142	38	.268	.056
Charlie Lea	239	65	.272	279	91	.326	.054
Dave J. Schmidt	217	51	.235	275	78	.284	.049
Shane Rawley	332	86	.259	436	134	.307	.048
Al Nipper	127	27	.213	174	45	.259	.046
Tom Candiotti	346	85	.246	481	140	.291	.045
Storm Davis	325	81	.249	444	130	.293	.044
John Tudor	274	63	.230	461	126	.273	.043
Jeff Reardon	142	32	.225	135	36	.267	.041
Orel Hershiser	343	64	.187	632	144	.228	.041

LAST 10 YEARS

BETTER WITH BASES EMPTY

PLAYER	RUNNERS ON			BASES EMPTY			DIFF
	AB	H	AVG	AB	H	AVG	
Jimmy Jones	527	164	.311	797	192	.241	.070
Brad Havens	862	267	.310	1286	311	.242	.068
Frank LaCorte	529	140	.265	644	131	.203	.061
Dick Tidrow	909	259	.285	1088	252	.232	.053
Jay Tibbs	1175	350	.298	1680	413	.246	.052
Kirk McCaskill	1026	291	.284	1471	344	.234	.050
Danny Darwin	2558	712	.278	3583	825	.230	.048
Byron McLaughlin	532	165	.310	518	136	.263	.048
Frank Pastore	1591	474	.298	2214	555	.251	.047
Jesse Jefferson	555	177	.319	683	186	.272	.047
Vern Ruhle	1311	386	.294	1979	496	.251	.044
Nino Espinosa	531	161	.303	867	225	.260	.044
Jay Howell	920	256	.278	997	235	.236	.043
Mike Moore	2279	667	.293	3322	831	.250	.043
Rich Gossage	1282	316	.246	1356	278	.205	.041
LaMarr Hoyt	1924	550	.286	3117	763	.245	.041
Mike Armstrong	553	145	.262	699	155	.222	.040
Ken Kravec	722	200	.277	907	215	.237	.040
Jeff Sellers	581	178	.306	697	186	.267	.040
Don Schulze	536	174	.325	694	198	.285	.039
John Butcher	1338	410	.306	1942	521	.268	.038
Dave Goltz	1060	330	.311	1469	402	.274	.038
Jeff D. Robinson	834	228	.273	1174	277	.236	.037
Juan Eichelberger	955	263	.275	1292	308	.238	.037
Doc Medich	1090	323	.296	1549	402	.260	.037

BETTER WITH RUNNERS ON

PLAYER	RUNNERS ON			BASES EMPTY			DIFF
	AB	H	AVG	AB	H	AVG	
Todd Worrell	577	118	.205	555	140	.252	.048
Bill Lee	735	191	.260	1015	304	.300	.040
Rick Camp	1337	326	.244	1604	443	.276	.032
Jesse Orosco	1157	237	.205	1204	284	.236	.031
Steve McCatty	1904	456	.239	2493	674	.270	.031
Tom Candiotti	1222	295	.241	1680	457	.272	.031
Jim Deshaies	739	162	.219	1165	290	.249	.030
Bill Caudill	1234	275	.223	1244	312	.251	.028
Dave Rucker	618	162	.262	604	175	.290	.028
John Cerutti	661	162	.245	970	262	.270	.025
Ed Vande Berg	1054	288	.273	956	284	.297	.024
Craig Lefferts	926	211	.228	1184	296	.250	.022
Shane Rawley	2752	706	.257	3404	947	.278	.022
Ed Farmer	775	185	.239	661	172	.260	.022
Mark Huismann	506	127	.251	559	152	.272	.021
Tippy Martinez	1120	257	.229	1040	260	.250	.021
Pat Zachry	1107	284	.257	1322	366	.277	.020
Ron Darling	1745	393	.225	2588	635	.245	.020
Sid Monge	879	207	.235	931	238	.256	.020
Mark Bomback	569	161	.283	664	201	.303	.020
Pete Filson	588	145	.247	794	211	.266	.019
Jim Kaat	685	192	.280	724	216	.298	.018
Pete Redfern	774	208	.269	966	277	.287	.018
Kent Tekulve	1764	418	.237	1893	481	.254	.017
Lee Smith	1398	317	.227	1420	346	.244	.017

Runners In Scoring Position

LAST SEASON

BETTER IN OTHER AT BATS

PLAYER	SCORING POSITION AB	H	AVG	OTHER AT BATS AB	H	AVG	DIFF
Tim Belcher	112	35	.313	547	108	.197	.115
Bert Blyleven	208	79	.380	608	161	.265	.115
Scott Terry	108	36	.333	373	83	.223	.111
Scott Bailes	111	38	.342	449	111	.247	.095
Charles Hudson	82	25	.305	313	68	.217	.088
Jay Howell	77	19	.247	157	25	.159	.088
Frank DiPino	110	38	.345	248	64	.258	.087
Mark Williamson	122	41	.336	337	84	.249	.087
David Palmer	123	40	.325	371	89	.240	.085
Kevin Coffman	85	26	.306	162	36	.222	.084
Bill Wegman	142	47	.331	638	160	.251	.080
Jerry Reed	93	29	.312	227	53	.233	.078
Jimmy Key	93	29	.312	416	98	.236	.076
Paul Kilgus	162	49	.302	620	141	.227	.075
Mike Moore	154	45	.292	692	151	.218	.074
Gene Nelson	114	32	.281	294	61	.207	.073
Bruce Ruffin	140	46	.329	410	105	.256	.072
Juan Nieves	79	21	.266	325	63	.194	.072
Alejandro Pena	85	23	.271	259	52	.201	.070
Scott Garrelts	126	34	.270	228	46	.202	.068
Les Lancaster	90	29	.322	236	60	.254	.068
Jeff Russell	169	52	.308	544	131	.241	.067
Bobby Witt	135	36	.267	486	98	.202	.065
Ted Higuera	144	37	.257	669	131	.196	.061
Mike Birkbeck	102	34	.333	392	107	.273	.060

BETTER WITH RUNNERS IN SCORING POSITION

PLAYER	SCORING POSITION AB	H	AVG	OTHER AT BATS AB	H	AVG	DIFF
Kent Tekulve	127	26	.205	188	61	.324	.120
Eric King	79	12	.152	178	48	.270	.118
Charlie Lea	145	32	.221	373	124	.332	.112
John Tudor	154	27	.175	581	162	.279	.104
Don Sutton	91	18	.198	246	73	.297	.099
Brian Holton	93	15	.161	209	54	.258	.097
Duane Ward	139	26	.187	274	75	.274	.087
Craig Lefferts	79	13	.165	250	61	.244	.079
Jose Alvarez	108	20	.185	258	68	.264	.078
Terry Leach	99	21	.212	255	74	.290	.078
Bob Knepper	151	28	.185	491	128	.261	.075
Joe Magrane	143	23	.161	469	110	.235	.074
Mike Krukow	111	20	.180	359	91	.253	.073
Lance McCullers	98	15	.153	244	55	.225	.072
Bryan Harvey	89	15	.169	187	44	.235	.067
Mike Henneman	94	16	.170	237	56	.236	.066
Mike Boddicker	199	42	.211	695	192	.276	.065
Neil Allen	126	28	.222	326	93	.285	.063
Neal Heaton	85	19	.224	276	79	.286	.063
Jack McDowell	146	29	.199	453	118	.260	.062
Allan Anderson	159	34	.214	604	165	.273	.059
Mark Grant	81	18	.222	281	79	.281	.059
Eric Plunk	90	16	.178	196	46	.235	.057
Rick Honeycutt	89	19	.213	204	55	.270	.056
Juan Agosto	81	15	.185	246	59	.240	.055

LAST 10 YEARS

BETTER IN OTHER AT BATS

PLAYER	SCORING POSITION AB	H	AVG	OTHER AT BATS AB	H	AVG	DIFF
Mike Armstrong	360	105	.292	892	195	.219	.073
Jimmy Jones	300	97	.323	1024	259	.253	.070
Bert Roberge	255	75	.294	553	125	.226	.068
Pat Clements	256	81	.316	645	161	.250	.067
Steve Howe	402	122	.303	1034	245	.237	.067
Brad Havens	509	162	.318	1639	416	.254	.064
John Smiley	268	76	.284	820	182	.222	.062
Frank LaCorte	335	91	.272	838	180	.215	.057
Rich Wortham	272	84	.309	854	216	.253	.056
Jay Howell	563	166	.295	1354	325	.240	.055
Ken Howell	313	88	.281	809	185	.229	.052
Mark Williamson	257	78	.304	670	169	.252	.051
Luis DeLeon	298	80	.268	912	199	.218	.050
Grant Jackson	268	78	.291	602	147	.244	.047
Fred Norman	251	74	.295	867	215	.248	.047
Bill Krueger	458	142	.310	1281	339	.265	.045
Jesse Jefferson	328	107	.326	910	256	.281	.045
Scott Bailes	348	108	.310	1147	309	.269	.041
Dick Tidrow	581	165	.284	1416	346	.244	.040
Bill Wegman	486	146	.300	2005	524	.261	.039
Randy Jones	526	159	.302	1727	458	.265	.037
Jeff Sellers	320	100	.313	958	264	.276	.037
Don Schulze	303	100	.330	927	272	.293	.037
Larry Andersen	696	202	.290	1658	422	.255	.036
Don Carman	519	140	.270	1891	444	.235	.035

BETTER WITH RUNNERS IN SCORING POSITION

PLAYER	SCORING POSITION AB	H	AVG	OTHER AT BATS AB	H	AVG	DIFF
Tom Tellmann	254	58	.228	611	182	.298	.070
Steve Bedrosian	872	171	.196	2203	542	.246	.050
Jim Deshaies	411	82	.200	1493	370	.248	.048
John Cerutti	380	85	.224	1251	339	.271	.047
Tim Burke	445	89	.200	1005	248	.247	.047
Cecilio Guante	518	103	.199	1254	305	.243	.044
Todd Worrell	378	75	.198	754	183	.243	.044
Jeff Lahti	359	76	.212	691	176	.255	.043
Lee Smith	894	186	.208	1924	477	.248	.040
Jesse Orosco	675	130	.193	1686	391	.232	.039
Randy Martz	255	59	.231	861	233	.271	.039
Mike G. Brown	280	80	.286	754	244	.324	.038
Craig Lefferts	568	121	.213	1542	386	.250	.037
Tom Burgmeier	532	120	.226	1218	319	.262	.036
David Cone	301	60	.199	993	234	.236	.036
Rick Camp	816	192	.235	2125	577	.272	.036
Shane Rawley	1551	375	.242	4605	1278	.278	.036
Kent Tekulve	1193	265	.222	2464	634	.257	.035
Lee Guetterman	258	72	.279	672	211	.314	.035
Tippy Martinez	686	148	.216	1474	369	.250	.035
Pat Zachry	648	157	.242	1781	493	.277	.035
Renie Martin	550	132	.240	1375	377	.274	.034
Bob Sebra	313	76	.243	836	231	.276	.034
Mark Bomback	337	91	.270	896	271	.302	.032
Pete Falcone	748	176	.235	2395	641	.268	.032

Vs. Left- and Right-Handers

LAST SEASON

BETTER VS. RIGHT-HANDERS

PLAYER	VS. LEFT-HANDERS			VS. RIGHT-HANDERS			
	AB	H	AVG	AB	H	AVG	DIFF
Jerry Reed	121	43	.355	199	39	.196	.159
Danny Cox	176	60	.341	151	29	.192	.149
Mike Morgan	126	40	.317	148	30	.203	.115
Neil Allen	183	60	.328	269	61	.227	.101
Brian Fisher	285	93	.326	282	64	.227	.099
Ron Robinson	163	54	.331	146	34	.233	.098
Jeff Sellers	157	50	.318	175	39	.223	.096
Doug Sisk	159	57	.358	197	52	.264	.095
Calvin Schiraldi	362	108	.298	284	58	.204	.094
David Cone	436	112	.257	400	66	.165	.092
Charlie Puleo	191	57	.298	212	44	.208	.091
Mike Jackson	159	41	.258	195	33	.169	.089
Mike Maddux	176	55	.313	155	36	.232	.080
Bobby Thigpen	165	52	.315	187	44	.235	.080
Pete Smith	413	117	.283	319	66	.207	.076
Steve Bedrosian	154	45	.292	138	30	.217	.075
Steve Farr	155	43	.277	153	31	.203	.075
Larry Andersen	150	44	.293	173	38	.220	.074
Roger Clemens	504	129	.256	482	88	.183	.073
Jeff Russell	370	108	.292	343	75	.219	.073
Tom Browning	151	43	.285	765	162	.212	.073
Keith Atherton	128	35	.273	149	30	.201	.072
Allan Anderson	125	40	.320	638	159	.249	.071
Scott Bankhead	244	63	.258	270	52	.193	.066
Dale Mohorcic	130	41	.315	168	42	.250	.065

BETTER VS. LEFT-HANDERS

PLAYER	VS. LEFT-HANDERS			VS. RIGHT-HANDERS			
	AB	H	AVG	AB	H	AVG	DIFF
Randy O'Neal	108	22	.204	100	35	.350	.146
Frank DiPino	125	24	.192	233	78	.335	.143
Bryan Harvey	143	21	.147	133	38	.286	.139
Juan Agosto	107	15	.140	220	59	.268	.128
Bob Forsch	238	56	.235	290	97	.334	.099
Lance McCullers	163	25	.153	179	45	.251	.098
Kent Tekulve	151	34	.225	164	53	.323	.098
John Smiley	107	17	.159	660	168	.255	.096
John Cerutti	116	22	.190	352	98	.278	.089
Andy McGaffigan	177	34	.192	170	47	.276	.084
Kelly Downs	320	59	.184	302	81	.268	.084
Bob Ojeda	127	21	.165	576	137	.238	.072
Larry McWilliams	119	24	.202	394	106	.269	.067
Frank Tanana	119	25	.210	680	188	.276	.066
Richard Dotson	347	83	.239	322	95	.295	.056
Jamie Moyer	127	29	.228	651	183	.281	.053
Bret Saberhagen	530	130	.245	478	141	.295	.050
Jose Guzman	375	77	.205	404	103	.255	.050
Joe Magrane	113	20	.177	499	113	.226	.049
Mike Campbell	241	62	.257	216	66	.306	.048
Mike Birkbeck	244	64	.262	250	77	.308	.046
Greg Cadaret	106	21	.198	160	39	.244	.046
Jim Gott	132	29	.220	148	39	.264	.044
Floyd Bannister	145	31	.214	588	151	.257	.043
Dwight Gooden	491	116	.236	453	126	.278	.042

LAST 10 YEARS

BETTER VS. RIGHT-HANDERS

PLAYER	VS. LEFT-HANDERS			VS. RIGHT-HANDERS			
	AB	H	AVG	AB	H	AVG	DIFF
Mike Parrott	783	267	.341	814	202	.248	.093
Elias Sosa	590	183	.310	785	180	.229	.081
Salome Barojas	603	183	.303	853	191	.224	.080
Don Schulze	651	220	.338	579	152	.263	.075
Ron Robinson	913	271	.297	974	217	.223	.074
Tim Burke	708	191	.270	742	146	.197	.073
Bob Stoddard	748	228	.305	897	209	.233	.072
Frank Williams	625	175	.280	829	173	.209	.071
Bill Swift	847	280	.331	762	198	.260	.071
Bruce Kison	1348	390	.289	1361	298	.219	.070
David Cone	671	175	.261	623	119	.191	.070
Craig McMurtry	1083	312	.288	1141	251	.220	.068
Mike G. Brown	511	177	.346	523	147	.281	.065
Jerry Reed	539	161	.299	702	164	.234	.065
John Stuper	888	276	.311	1019	252	.247	.064
Larry Christenson	966	282	.292	1136	260	.229	.063
J.R. Richard	662	153	.231	780	132	.169	.062
Nino Espinosa	666	205	.308	732	181	.247	.061
Charlie Puleo	1131	330	.292	1144	265	.232	.060
Tommy Boggs	745	219	.294	793	186	.235	.059
Jose DeLeon	1818	457	.251	1791	344	.192	.059
Rich Gale	1417	433	.306	1593	393	.247	.059
Glenn Abbott	1324	410	.310	1160	291	.251	.059
Mark Huismann	506	148	.292	559	131	.234	.058
Terry Leach	572	165	.288	813	188	.231	.057

BETTER VS. LEFT-HANDERS

PLAYER	VS. LEFT-HANDERS			VS. RIGHT-HANDERS			
	AB	H	AVG	AB	H	AVG	DIFF
Tom Burgmeier	598	117	.196	1152	322	.280	.084
Atlee Hammaker	549	108	.197	2895	760	.263	.066
Matt Young	533	120	.225	2150	611	.284	.059
Frank DiPino	545	116	.213	1341	362	.270	.057
Ed Vande Berg	675	167	.247	1335	405	.303	.056
Mark Davis	641	129	.201	2192	563	.257	.056
Mark Langston	683	134	.196	3501	874	.250	.053
John Candelaria	921	197	.214	4928	1317	.267	.053
Dave Dravecky	627	127	.203	3273	833	.255	.052
Larry Gura	1052	232	.221	4029	1092	.271	.051
Gary Lavelle	767	165	.215	1671	441	.264	.049
Donnie Moore	913	227	.249	987	291	.295	.046
Mike Norris	1595	330	.207	1575	398	.253	.046
Tippy Martinez	736	154	.209	1424	363	.255	.046
Willie Hernandez	990	210	.212	2159	555	.257	.045
Bob Shirley	995	232	.233	2963	821	.277	.044
Bob McClure	823	190	.231	2425	663	.273	.043
Rick Honeycutt	1187	278	.234	5053	1396	.276	.042
Mike Flanagan	1268	293	.231	5756	1567	.272	.041
Jesse Orosco	614	117	.191	1747	404	.231	.041
Mark Thurmond	532	131	.246	2120	604	.285	.039
Jesse Jefferson	627	172	.274	611	191	.313	.038
John Curtis	524	124	.237	1857	507	.273	.036
Paul Splittorff	703	177	.252	2751	790	.287	.035
Randy Jones	511	126	.247	1742	491	.282	.035

Vs. Ground- and Fly-Ballers

LAST SEASON

BETTER VS. FLY-BALLERS

PLAYER	VS. GROUND-BALLERS			VS. FLY-BALLERS			DIFF
	AB	H	AVG	AB	H	AVG	
Randy Myers	102	26	.255	135	19	.141	.114
Brad Havens	124	43	.347	145	34	.234	.112
Tom Niedenfuer	109	34	.312	119	25	.210	.102
Shawn Hillegas	163	46	.282	198	38	.192	.090
John Farrell	341	109	.320	463	107	.231	.089
Jose Rijo	305	76	.249	269	44	.164	.086
Jimmy Key	222	66	.297	287	61	.213	.085
Neil Allen	174	55	.316	278	66	.237	.079
Lance McCullers	158	39	.247	184	31	.168	.078
Joe Price	118	34	.288	119	25	.210	.078
Frank Viola	372	109	.293	590	127	.215	.078
Mike Campbell	216	69	.319	241	59	.245	.075
Rick Honeycutt	118	35	.297	175	39	.223	.074
Bob Kipper	128	34	.266	103	20	.194	.071
Mike Maddux	161	50	.311	170	41	.241	.069
Steve Bedrosian	145	42	.290	147	33	.224	.065
Calvin Schiraldi	300	87	.290	346	79	.228	.062
Bryan Harvey	121	30	.248	155	29	.187	.061
Jeff Reardon	118	33	.280	159	35	.220	.060
Bruce Hurst	363	108	.298	479	114	.238	.060
Mario Soto	173	51	.295	157	37	.236	.059
Greg Minton	130	34	.262	157	33	.210	.051
Mike Witt	426	128	.300	540	135	.250	.050
Mark Davis	164	37	.226	188	33	.176	.050
Shane Rawley	390	121	.310	378	99	.262	.048

BETTER VS. GROUND-BALLERS

PLAYER	VS. GROUND-BALLERS			VS. FLY-BALLERS			DIFF
	AB	H	AVG	AB	H	AVG	
John Dopson	320	57	.178	318	93	.292	.114
Andy McGaffigan	147	25	.170	200	56	.280	.110
Frank Williams	116	23	.198	118	36	.305	.107
Frank DiPino	159	37	.233	199	65	.327	.094
Ted Power	172	44	.256	224	77	.344	.088
Chuck Crim	158	31	.196	226	64	.283	.087
Kent Tekulve	140	32	.229	175	55	.314	.086
Atlee Hammaker	263	54	.205	286	82	.287	.081
Mark Grant	176	40	.227	186	57	.306	.079
Greg Mathews	121	25	.207	126	36	.286	.079
Juan Nieves	156	25	.160	248	59	.238	.078
Mark Gubicza	425	81	.191	587	156	.266	.075
Mike Scott	391	65	.166	402	97	.241	.075
Kevin Coffman	126	27	.214	121	35	.289	.075
Joe Magrane	288	52	.181	324	81	.250	.069
Mike LaCoss	227	46	.203	196	53	.270	.068
Bob Stanley	162	33	.204	210	57	.271	.068
Mike Dunne	325	72	.222	315	91	.289	.067
Jerry Reed	133	29	.218	187	53	.283	.065
Dennis Rasmussen	358	79	.221	420	120	.286	.065
Fernando Valenzuela	289	69	.239	241	73	.303	.064
Jimmy Jones	336	82	.244	357	110	.308	.064
Alejandro Pena	162	30	.185	182	45	.247	.062
Ray Hayward	103	25	.243	125	38	.304	.061
Stu Cliburn	138	32	.232	174	51	.293	.061

LAST 10 YEARS

BETTER VS. FLY-BALLERS

PLAYER	VS. GROUND-BALLERS			VS. FLY-BALLERS			DIFF
	AB	H	AVG	AB	H	AVG	
Jerry Augustine	667	217	.325	720	192	.267	.059
Tom Niedenfuer	1035	277	.268	1008	212	.210	.057
Calvin Schiraldi	571	165	.289	754	175	.232	.057
Sid Monge	880	241	.274	930	204	.219	.055
Willie Hernandez	1453	394	.271	1696	371	.219	.052
Jimmy Key	1386	379	.273	1979	438	.221	.052
Luis Sanchez	585	171	.292	807	200	.248	.044
Dan Spillner	1415	418	.295	1924	484	.252	.044
Randy Martz	562	159	.283	554	133	.240	.043
Lance McCullers	695	168	.242	713	143	.201	.041
Wayne Garland	581	191	.329	624	181	.290	.039
Larry Gura	2178	615	.282	2903	709	.244	.038
Chuck Finley	550	158	.287	701	175	.250	.038
Ken Schrom	1497	445	.297	1987	518	.261	.037
Scott Bailes	609	183	.300	886	234	.264	.036
Juan Berenguer	1391	347	.249	1730	369	.213	.036
Dave Frost	812	237	.292	908	233	.257	.035
Willie Fraser	626	172	.275	818	197	.241	.034
Steve Renko	1296	375	.289	1482	379	.256	.034
Tug McGraw	672	175	.260	653	149	.228	.032
Len Barker	2091	572	.274	2523	611	.242	.031
Joe Beckwith	740	209	.282	885	223	.252	.030
Doyle Alexander	3325	929	.279	4001	1005	.251	.028
Jose Rijo	985	259	.263	1147	270	.235	.028
Glenn Abbott	1167	346	.296	1317	355	.270	.027

BETTER VS. GROUND-BALLERS

PLAYER	VS. GROUND-BALLERS			VS. FLY-BALLERS			DIFF
	AB	H	AVG	AB	H	AVG	
Terry Forster	650	138	.212	631	179	.284	.071
Mike Dunne	628	135	.215	608	171	.281	.066
Bruce Ruffin	943	232	.246	946	293	.310	.064
Jimmy Jones	654	155	.237	670	201	.300	.063
Ray Fontenot	855	217	.254	1066	334	.313	.060
Doug Corbett	869	182	.209	1181	315	.267	.057
Marty Bystrom	844	204	.242	847	250	.295	.053
Ricky Horton	1033	246	.238	1075	313	.291	.053
Andy McGaffigan	1235	262	.212	1248	327	.262	.050
Dave Goltz	1262	336	.266	1267	396	.313	.046
Mike LaCoss	2622	650	.248	2574	753	.293	.045
Floyd Youmans	923	175	.190	870	203	.233	.044
Joe Magrane	620	130	.210	632	160	.253	.043
Tom Griffin	635	139	.219	676	177	.262	.043
David Palmer	2099	484	.231	1894	518	.273	.043
Terry Leach	667	156	.234	718	197	.274	.040
Jeff Sellers	535	140	.262	743	224	.301	.040
David Cone	650	135	.208	644	159	.247	.039
Frank LaCorte	512	107	.209	661	164	.248	.039
Rick Wise	902	229	.254	997	291	.292	.038
Greg Maddux	864	217	.251	825	238	.288	.037
John Smiley	502	109	.217	586	149	.254	.037
Jesse Orosco	1159	234	.202	1202	287	.239	.037
Paul Moskau	684	172	.251	778	223	.287	.035
John Curtis	1168	289	.247	1213	342	.282	.035

Home and Road Games

LAST SEASON

BETTER IN ROAD GAMES

	HOME GAMES			ROAD GAMES			
PLAYER	AB	H	AVG	AB	H	AVG	DIFF
Doug Jones	159	43	.270	158	26	.165	.106
Barry Jones	152	44	.289	145	28	.193	.096
Pat Perry	112	35	.313	116	26	.224	.088
Jeff Musselman	186	53	.285	132	27	.205	.080
Les Straker	117	38	.325	195	48	.246	.079
Calvin Schiraldi	298	89	.299	348	77	.221	.077
Tim Crews	177	54	.305	100	23	.230	.075
John Tudor	403	117	.290	332	72	.217	.073
Jose Alvarez	193	53	.275	173	35	.202	.072
Dan Quisenberry	120	44	.367	142	42	.296	.071
Greg Cadaret	153	39	.255	113	21	.186	.069
Brian Holton	189	48	.254	113	21	.186	.068
Mitch Williams	123	29	.236	113	19	.168	.068
Fred Toliver	241	72	.299	189	44	.233	.066
Bud Black	163	48	.294	148	34	.230	.065
Craig Lefferts	138	36	.261	191	38	.199	.062
Paul Assenmacher	162	45	.278	125	27	.216	.062
Dennis Lamp	163	51	.313	161	41	.255	.058
Jimmy Key	223	62	.278	286	65	.227	.051
Jeff D. Robinson	222	60	.270	241	53	.220	.050
Jose Rijo	340	78	.229	234	42	.179	.050
Curt Young	290	87	.300	299	75	.251	.049
Kevin Coffman	108	30	.278	139	32	.230	.048
Greg Minton	144	37	.257	143	30	.210	.047
Bill Wegman	449	128	.285	331	79	.239	.046

BETTER IN HOME GAMES

	HOME GAMES			ROAD GAMES			
PLAYER	AB	H	AVG	AB	H	AVG	DIFF
Randy Myers	120	13	.108	117	32	.274	.165
Bob Kipper	122	20	.164	109	34	.312	.148
Jim Gott	138	25	.181	142	43	.303	.122
Lance McCullers	191	29	.152	151	41	.272	.120
Joe Price	132	26	.197	105	33	.314	.117
Mike Morgan	152	31	.204	122	39	.320	.116
Frank DiPino	179	41	.229	179	61	.341	.112
Tim Birtsas	139	29	.209	105	32	.305	.096
Bob Forsch	311	79	.254	217	74	.341	.087
Mike LaCoss	271	55	.203	152	44	.289	.087
Greg Mathews	110	22	.200	137	39	.285	.085
Willie Hernandez	134	23	.172	106	27	.255	.083
Jeff Parrett	155	27	.174	153	39	.255	.081
John Franco	157	25	.159	146	35	.240	.080
Dave Righetti	178	39	.219	157	47	.299	.080
Sid Fernandez	336	51	.152	330	76	.230	.079
Mike Maddux	167	40	.240	164	51	.311	.071
David Palmer	267	61	.228	227	68	.300	.071
Andy Hawkins	471	101	.214	333	95	.285	.071
Jeff Reardon	142	30	.211	135	38	.281	.070
Juan Agosto	179	35	.196	148	39	.264	.068
Mark Williamson	245	59	.241	214	66	.308	.068
Jeff M. Robinson	341	57	.167	274	64	.234	.066
Tim Stoddard	107	27	.252	110	35	.318	.066
David Cone	412	74	.180	424	104	.245	.066

LAST 10 YEARS

BETTER IN ROAD GAMES

	HOME GAMES			ROAD GAMES			
PLAYER	AB	H	AVG	AB	H	AVG	DIFF
Brian Fisher	1052	303	.288	956	221	.231	.057
Tom Griffin	614	164	.267	697	152	.218	.049
Kurt Kepshire	517	145	.280	504	118	.234	.046
Craig McMurtry	1233	337	.273	991	226	.228	.045
Manny Sarmiento	565	156	.276	567	132	.233	.043
Allen Ripley	703	216	.307	805	213	.265	.043
Jim Kern	738	189	.256	710	152	.214	.042
Calvin Schiraldi	577	161	.279	748	179	.239	.040
Ron Reed	948	254	.268	1014	239	.236	.032
Bill Long	646	192	.297	746	199	.267	.030
John Martin	547	138	.252	526	117	.222	.030
Gene Garber	1651	460	.279	1532	383	.250	.029
Brad Havens	1140	322	.282	1008	256	.254	.028
Bruce Kison	1309	351	.268	1400	337	.241	.027
Paul Mirabella	687	195	.284	845	217	.257	.027
Ken Dixon	1043	279	.267	834	201	.241	.026
Jeff Russell	1255	350	.279	1362	345	.253	.026
Tommy Boggs	764	211	.276	774	194	.251	.026
Oil Can Boyd	2045	577	.282	1681	433	.258	.025
Juan Nieves	793	222	.280	1114	285	.256	.024
Terry Leach	573	154	.269	812	199	.245	.024
Ken Dayley	816	229	.281	780	201	.258	.023
Lee Smith	1522	374	.246	1296	289	.223	.023
Allan Anderson	617	181	.293	532	144	.271	.023
John Stuper	1129	323	.286	778	205	.263	.023

BETTER IN HOME GAMES

	HOME GAMES			ROAD GAMES			
PLAYER	AB	H	AVG	AB	H	AVG	DIFF
Jeff M. Robinson	574	109	.190	545	144	.264	.074
Eric Rasmussen	722	178	.247	620	192	.310	.063
John Smiley	514	106	.206	574	152	.265	.059
Jesse Jefferson	721	194	.269	517	169	.327	.058
Bill Travers	792	193	.244	742	222	.299	.056
Dave Rucker	709	180	.254	513	157	.306	.052
Mike Armstrong	652	140	.215	600	160	.267	.052
Gary Lucas	1252	280	.224	1229	338	.275	.051
Steve Ontiveros	681	145	.213	648	170	.262	.049
Rich Bordi	900	220	.244	555	163	.294	.049
Sid Fernandez	1468	267	.182	1473	340	.231	.049
Chris Codiroli	1243	303	.244	1351	395	.292	.049
Sammy Stewart	1786	397	.222	1698	456	.269	.046
Don Schulze	710	202	.285	520	170	.327	.042
Ross Grimsley	752	228	.303	581	200	.344	.041
Joe Cowley	879	189	.215	880	225	.256	.041
Jim Kaat	749	203	.271	660	205	.311	.040
Tug McGraw	675	152	.225	650	172	.265	.039
Bob Sebra	570	141	.247	579	166	.287	.039
Ken Howell	550	123	.224	572	150	.262	.039
Walt Terrell	2425	587	.242	2365	663	.280	.038
Frank LaCorte	598	127	.212	575	144	.250	.038
Vida Blue	2471	574	.232	1787	482	.270	.037
Bryan Clark	1056	270	.256	877	257	.293	.037
Warren Brusstar	622	159	.256	611	179	.293	.037

Grass and Artificial Surfaces

LAST SEASON

BETTER ON ARTIFICIAL TURF

	GRASS FIELDS			ARTIFICIAL TURF			
PLAYER	AB	H	AVG	AB	H	AVG	DIFF
Mike Maddux	105	38	.362	226	53	.235	.127
Bob Forsch	103	39	.379	425	114	.268	.110
Joaquin Andujar	101	35	.347	216	59	.273	.073
Eric Show	745	180	.242	124	21	.169	.072
Scott Garrelts	242	60	.248	112	20	.179	.069
Jose Alvarez	257	67	.261	109	21	.193	.068
Mike Krukow	343	87	.254	127	24	.189	.065
Bryn Smith	238	68	.286	498	111	.223	.063
Danny Darwin	232	70	.302	498	119	.239	.063
David Palmer	101	31	.307	393	98	.249	.058
Walt Terrell	661	176	.266	110	23	.209	.057
Pat Perry	119	35	.294	109	26	.239	.056
Tim Belcher	463	108	.233	196	35	.179	.055
Tim Leary	664	163	.245	196	38	.194	.052
Frank Viola	362	100	.276	600	136	.227	.050
Dennis Martinez	278	76	.273	621	139	.224	.050
Mike Dunne	152	44	.289	488	119	.244	.046
Mario Soto	122	36	.295	208	52	.250	.045
Melido Perez	590	152	.258	159	34	.214	.044
Don Carman	209	63	.301	573	148	.258	.043
Pascual Perez	112	26	.232	565	107	.189	.043
Roger Clemens	866	195	.225	120	22	.183	.042
Bob Knepper	142	39	.275	500	117	.234	.041
Danny Jackson	278	68	.245	665	138	.208	.037
Jose DeLeon	279	73	.262	556	125	.225	.037

BETTER ON GRASS SURFACES

	GRASS FIELDS			ARTIFICIAL TURF			
PLAYER	AB	H	AVG	AB	H	AVG	DIFF
Frank DiPino	251	63	.251	107	39	.364	.113
Bruce Hurst	727	183	.252	115	39	.339	.087
Shane Rawley	239	56	.234	529	164	.310	.076
Barry Jones	134	27	.201	163	45	.276	.075
Doyle Alexander	734	196	.267	188	64	.340	.073
Richard Dotson	525	132	.251	144	46	.319	.068
Charlie Leibrandt	388	88	.227	536	156	.291	.064
Andy Hawkins	619	142	.229	185	54	.292	.062
Greg Swindell	776	188	.242	152	46	.303	.060
Bret Saberhagen	359	83	.231	649	188	.290	.058
Les Straker	146	36	.247	166	50	.301	.055
Rick Reuschel	682	168	.246	246	74	.301	.054
John Dopson	159	31	.195	479	119	.248	.053
Juan Berenguer	116	20	.172	241	54	.224	.052
Jimmy Key	218	48	.220	291	79	.271	.051
Scott Bankhead	228	45	.197	286	70	.245	.047
Sid Fernandez	445	78	.175	221	49	.222	.046
Ted Power	151	42	.278	245	79	.322	.044
Jeff M. Robinson	481	90	.187	134	31	.231	.044
Pete Smith	584	141	.241	148	42	.284	.042
David Cone	575	115	.200	261	63	.241	.041
Ron Darling	723	172	.238	165	46	.279	.041
Mike Birkbeck	389	108	.278	105	33	.314	.037
Paul Kilgus	680	162	.238	102	28	.275	.036
Charlie Hough	782	169	.216	131	33	.252	.036

LAST 10 YEARS

BETTER ON ARTIFICIAL TURF

	GRASS FIELDS			ARTIFICIAL TURF			
PLAYER	AB	H	AVG	AB	H	AVG	DIFF
Joe Sambito	636	180	.283	851	175	.206	.077
Mike Stanton	762	223	.293	632	155	.245	.047
Jesse Orosco	1747	406	.232	614	115	.187	.045
Kevin Gross	1008	292	.290	3212	796	.248	.042
Len Barker	3935	1031	.262	679	152	.224	.038
Mike Scott	2189	582	.266	3887	891	.229	.037
Joe Johnson	769	231	.300	514	136	.265	.036
Matt Keough	3005	821	.273	632	152	.241	.033
Pascual Perez	1868	500	.268	1754	413	.235	.032
Ken Schrom	1893	551	.291	1591	412	.259	.032
Bob Forsch	1639	472	.288	4861	1251	.257	.031
Jim Deshaies	501	130	.259	1403	322	.230	.030
Jay Tibbs	1006	287	.285	1849	476	.257	.028
Dan Schatzeder	1754	475	.271	2125	517	.243	.028
Pete Falcone	2240	599	.267	903	218	.241	.026
Phil Niekro	5685	1507	.265	1852	443	.239	.026
Tim Leary	1871	514	.275	562	140	.249	.026
Bryan Clark	887	254	.286	1046	273	.261	.025
Ken Dayley	787	222	.282	809	208	.257	.025
Dale Murray	946	280	.296	570	155	.272	.024
Dennis Martinez	4875	1333	.273	2009	503	.250	.023
Roger Clemens	3313	760	.229	546	113	.207	.022
David Palmer	1601	423	.264	2392	579	.242	.022
Bryn Smith	1344	358	.266	3161	775	.245	.021
Jeff D. Robinson	1192	310	.260	816	195	.239	.021

BETTER ON GRASS SURFACES

	GRASS FIELDS			ARTIFICIAL TURF			
PLAYER	AB	H	AVG	AB	H	AVG	DIFF
Gene Nelson	2174	533	.245	751	225	.300	.054
Craig Lefferts	1515	341	.225	595	166	.279	.054
Tim Conroy	1100	256	.233	640	179	.280	.047
Paul Mirabella	927	234	.252	605	178	.294	.042
Bob Welch	5904	1387	.235	1413	389	.275	.040
Frank Williams	742	163	.220	712	185	.260	.040
Chuck Rainey	2050	566	.276	548	172	.314	.038
Sparky Lyle	688	182	.265	501	150	.299	.035
Bob Owchinko	1427	374	.262	549	163	.297	.035
Rick Aguilera	1046	268	.256	509	148	.291	.035
Brian Fisher	874	212	.243	1134	312	.275	.033
Sid Fernandez	2011	395	.196	930	212	.228	.032
Rick Mahler	4351	1164	.268	1536	459	.299	.031
Milt Wilcox	3986	1018	.255	682	195	.286	.031
Richard Dotson	5474	1397	.255	925	263	.284	.029
Frank Tanana	6359	1636	.257	852	244	.286	.029
Ron Reed	737	173	.235	1225	320	.261	.026
Britt Burns	3499	861	.246	625	170	.272	.026
Jim Winn	531	137	.258	649	184	.284	.026
Mike Witt	5571	1393	.250	975	268	.275	.025
Ron Guidry	6269	1563	.249	872	239	.274	.025
Greg A. Harris	1720	400	.233	839	215	.256	.024
Steve Trout	4255	1192	.280	1355	411	.303	.023
Randy Jones	1594	426	.267	659	191	.290	.023
Lynn McGlothen	1355	383	.283	518	158	.305	.022

Day and Night Games

LAST SEASON

BETTER IN NIGHT GAMES

	DAY GAMES			NIGHT GAMES			
PLAYER	AB	H	AVG	AB	H	AVG	DIFF
Mark Langston	112	37	.330	842	185	.220	.111
Brian Holton	101	30	.297	201	39	.194	.103
Rich Yett	132	46	.348	399	100	.251	.098
Tom Browning	240	70	.292	676	135	.200	.092
Dennis Eckersley	113	28	.248	150	24	.160	.088
Mario Soto	165	51	.309	165	37	.224	.085
Juan Agosto	102	29	.284	225	45	.200	.084
Mike Witt	177	60	.339	789	203	.257	.082
Neil Allen	116	38	.328	336	83	.247	.081
Calvin Schiraldi	319	94	.295	327	72	.220	.074
Bob Knepper	191	56	.293	451	100	.222	.071
John Smiley	236	68	.288	531	117	.220	.068
Jim Gott	102	29	.284	178	39	.219	.065
Shane Rawley	163	55	.337	605	165	.273	.065
Chuck Crim	102	30	.294	282	65	.230	.064
Curt Young	227	71	.313	362	91	.251	.061
Odell Jones	107	31	.290	192	44	.229	.061
Joe Magrane	173	45	.260	439	88	.200	.060
Greg Swindell	240	71	.296	688	163	.237	.059
Bob Forsch	177	58	.328	351	95	.271	.057
Bill Long	201	64	.318	468	123	.263	.056
Jimmy Key	164	47	.287	345	80	.232	.055
Dave Stieb	212	52	.245	536	105	.196	.049
Mike Henneman	104	26	.250	227	46	.203	.047
Tommy John	169	58	.343	548	163	.297	.046

BETTER IN DAY GAMES

	DAY GAMES			NIGHT GAMES			
PLAYER	AB	H	AVG	AB	H	AVG	DIFF
Doug Drabek	196	34	.173	616	160	.260	.086
Frank DiPino	202	50	.248	156	52	.333	.086
Scott Garrelts	140	26	.186	214	54	.252	.067
Paul Kilgus	177	34	.192	605	156	.258	.066
Charlie Leibrandt	282	62	.220	642	182	.283	.064
Doug Sisk	114	30	.263	242	79	.326	.063
Tom Glavine	168	38	.226	577	163	.282	.056
Duane Ward	122	25	.205	291	76	.261	.056
Chuck Finley	163	36	.221	563	155	.275	.054
Roger Clemens	326	60	.184	660	157	.238	.054
Jerry Reed	100	22	.220	220	60	.273	.053
Bob Ojeda	231	44	.190	472	114	.242	.051
Bob Stanley	102	21	.206	270	69	.256	.050
Walt Terrell	119	26	.218	652	173	.265	.047
Rick Honeycutt	123	28	.228	170	46	.271	.043
Bobby Thigpen	110	27	.245	242	69	.285	.040
Jimmy Jones	197	49	.249	496	143	.288	.040
John Cerutti	184	43	.234	284	77	.271	.037
Bert Blyleven	170	45	.265	646	195	.302	.037
Pete Smith	179	40	.223	553	143	.259	.035
Danny Jackson	143	27	.189	800	179	.224	.035
Ron Darling	339	76	.224	549	142	.259	.034
Mike Dunne	182	42	.231	458	121	.264	.033
Sid Fernandez	224	38	.170	442	89	.201	.032
Joe Price	124	29	.234	113	30	.265	.032

LAST 10 YEARS

BETTER IN NIGHT GAMES

	DAY GAMES			NIGHT GAMES			
PLAYER	AB	H	AVG	AB	H	AVG	DIFF
Terry Leach	520	149	.287	865	204	.236	.051
Allen Ripley	552	174	.315	956	255	.267	.048
Joe Hesketh	502	136	.271	917	205	.224	.047
Ross Grimsley	527	184	.349	806	244	.303	.046
Dwight Gooden	1406	355	.252	2905	605	.208	.044
Calvin Schiraldi	565	159	.281	760	181	.238	.043
Eddie Solomon	551	165	.299	1260	324	.257	.042
Doug Corbett	666	180	.270	1384	317	.229	.041
Jerry Augustine	505	161	.319	882	248	.281	.038
Jeff D. Robinson	781	214	.274	1227	291	.237	.037
Dennis Rasmussen	1022	272	.266	2193	505	.230	.036
Ken Dixon	522	147	.282	1355	333	.246	.036
Tom Browning	1356	367	.271	2262	533	.236	.035
Rich Gossage	760	190	.250	1878	404	.215	.035
Jeff Sellers	515	157	.305	763	207	.271	.034
Mark Eichhorn	569	144	.253	864	190	.220	.033
Shane Rawley	1782	520	.292	4374	1133	.259	.033
Mike Mason	599	175	.292	1730	450	.260	.032
Lee Tunnell	617	178	.288	1180	303	.257	.032
Rick Wise	621	183	.295	1278	337	.264	.031
Tippy Martinez	608	159	.262	1552	358	.231	.031
Jesse Orosco	811	195	.240	1550	326	.210	.030
Dick Ruthven	2003	585	.292	2281	599	.263	.029
Greg Maddux	1138	317	.279	551	138	.250	.028
Jim Bibby	803	208	.259	1307	302	.231	.028

BETTER IN DAY GAMES

	DAY GAMES			NIGHT GAMES			
PLAYER	AB	H	AVG	AB	H	AVG	DIFF
John Cerutti	585	136	.232	1046	288	.275	.043
Craig Lefferts	785	169	.215	1325	338	.255	.040
Larry Andersen	654	155	.237	1700	469	.276	.039
Bruce Berenyi	846	189	.223	2066	541	.262	.038
Tim Lollar	1177	265	.225	2200	576	.262	.037
Ed Vande Berg	506	131	.259	1504	441	.293	.034
Silvio Martinez	529	127	.240	1091	299	.274	.034
David Palmer	1171	267	.228	2822	735	.260	.032
Joe Cowley	583	125	.214	1176	289	.246	.031
John Montefusco	896	218	.243	1860	508	.273	.030
Britt Burns	1045	238	.228	3079	793	.258	.030
Scott Garrelts	940	194	.206	1089	257	.236	.030
Jay Howell	606	143	.236	1311	348	.265	.029
Dave Frost	537	136	.253	1183	334	.282	.029
Keith Atherton	650	150	.231	1342	348	.259	.029
Frank Williams	566	126	.223	888	222	.250	.027
Rick Camp	843	204	.242	2098	565	.269	.027
Atlee Hammaker	1558	370	.237	1886	498	.264	.027
Charles Hudson	1178	281	.239	2422	641	.265	.026
Larry Christenson	559	134	.240	1543	408	.264	.025
John Stuper	585	152	.260	1322	376	.284	.025
Paul Moskau	549	140	.255	913	255	.279	.024
Mike Proly	793	196	.247	925	251	.271	.024
Bruce Kison	752	178	.237	1957	510	.261	.024
Don Robinson	1604	383	.239	2901	760	.262	.023

First Time Through Batting Order

LAST SEASON

BETTER FIRST TIME THROUGH

PLAYER	FIRST PASS			OTHER AT BATS			DIFF
	AB	H	AVG	AB	H	AVG	
Jose Guzman	241	38	.158	538	142	.264	.106
Dwight Gooden	281	53	.189	663	189	.285	.096
Jimmy Jones	234	52	.222	459	140	.305	.083
Tom Browning	292	49	.168	624	156	.250	.082
John Dopson	213	40	.188	425	110	.259	.071
Kevin Gross	267	51	.191	609	158	.259	.068
Tim Belcher	276	49	.178	383	94	.245	.068
Doug Drabek	272	53	.195	540	141	.261	.066
Don Carman	281	64	.228	501	147	.293	.066
Jose DeLeon	277	55	.199	558	143	.256	.058
Wes Gardner	235	44	.187	307	75	.244	.057
Bill Swift	278	73	.263	397	126	.317	.055
Jack Morris	271	58	.214	624	167	.268	.054
Frank Tanana	269	63	.234	530	150	.283	.049
Ted Higuera	248	43	.173	565	125	.221	.048
Jay Tibbs	236	62	.263	393	122	.310	.048
Bill Wegman	265	62	.234	515	145	.282	.048
David Cone	269	49	.182	567	129	.228	.045
Jerry Reuss	252	59	.234	444	124	.279	.045
Bob Ojeda	236	46	.195	467	112	.240	.045
John Tudor	245	56	.229	490	133	.271	.043
Richard Dotson	253	61	.241	416	117	.281	.040
Jim Deshaies	241	46	.191	511	118	.231	.040
Greg Swindell	279	63	.226	649	171	.263	.038
Rick Reuschel	301	71	.236	627	171	.273	.037

BETTER ON LATER AT BATS

PLAYER	FIRST PASS			OTHER AT BATS			DIFF
	AB	H	AVG	AB	H	AVG	
Don Robinson	315	80	.254	343	72	.210	.044
Jim Clancy	293	87	.297	467	120	.257	.040
Mark Williamson	226	66	.292	233	59	.253	.039
Bret Saberhagen	289	84	.291	719	187	.260	.031
Sid Fernandez	243	51	.210	423	76	.180	.030
John Farrell	247	71	.287	557	145	.260	.027
Rick Rhoden	244	70	.287	523	136	.260	.027
Chuck Finley	250	70	.280	476	121	.254	.026
Chris Bosio	268	76	.284	442	114	.258	.026
Dennis Rasmussen	253	69	.273	525	130	.248	.025
Mike Scott	258	57	.221	535	105	.196	.025
Jeff Ballard	208	61	.293	392	106	.270	.023
Shane Rawley	242	73	.302	526	147	.279	.022
Jeff Russell	248	67	.270	465	116	.249	.021
Bill Long	324	94	.290	345	93	.270	.021
Brian Fisher	233	67	.288	334	90	.269	.018
Dave J. Schmidt	290	78	.269	202	51	.252	.016
Doyle Alexander	283	83	.293	639	177	.277	.016
Frank Viola	298	76	.255	664	160	.241	.014
Bob Walk	257	61	.237	538	122	.227	.011
Ron Darling	281	71	.253	607	147	.242	.010
Paul Kilgus	256	64	.250	526	126	.240	.010
Mike Moore	285	68	.239	561	128	.228	.010
Danny Jackson	289	65	.225	654	141	.216	.009
Danny Darwin	318	84	.264	412	105	.255	.009

LAST 10 YEARS

BETTER FIRST TIME THROUGH

PLAYER	FIRST PASS			OTHER AT BATS			DIFF
	AB	H	AVG	AB	H	AVG	
Rich Yett	606	138	.228	607	189	.311	.084
Greg A. Harris	1816	399	.220	743	216	.291	.071
David Palmer	1522	327	.215	2471	675	.273	.058
Jose Guzman	808	176	.218	1558	426	.273	.056
Bob Kipper	592	139	.235	634	183	.289	.054
Odell Jones	1006	257	.255	634	196	.309	.054
Silvio Martinez	585	135	.231	1035	291	.281	.050
Kelly Downs	628	132	.210	1043	271	.260	.050
Bill Wegman	850	201	.236	1641	469	.286	.049
Eddie Solomon	726	176	.242	1085	313	.288	.046
Atlee Hammaker	1322	296	.224	2122	572	.270	.046
Steve Bedrosian	2302	508	.221	773	205	.265	.045
Neil Allen	2508	624	.249	1207	353	.292	.044
Bruce Ruffin	762	192	.252	1127	333	.295	.044
Bill Swift	673	183	.272	936	295	.315	.043
Moose Haas	1836	445	.242	3617	1032	.285	.043
Dave Goltz	905	237	.262	1624	495	.305	.043
Chris Welsh	885	228	.258	1210	363	.300	.042
Doug Drabek	716	156	.218	1265	329	.260	.042
Pete Falcone	1403	332	.237	1740	485	.279	.042
Steve Carlton	2305	494	.214	5117	1312	.256	.042
Luis Tiant	577	134	.232	1051	288	.274	.042
Mark Davis	1855	427	.230	978	265	.271	.041
Tom Hume	2630	666	.253	640	188	.294	.041
Ray Fontenot	900	239	.266	1021	312	.306	.040

BETTER ON LATER AT BATS

PLAYER	FIRST PASS			OTHER AT BATS			DIFF
	AB	H	AVG	AB	H	AVG	
Mike Parrott	631	201	.319	966	268	.277	.041
Eric King	669	167	.250	532	112	.211	.039
Fred Norman	514	142	.276	604	147	.243	.033
Rick Wise	676	197	.291	1223	323	.264	.027
Jack O'Connor	701	203	.290	532	140	.263	.026
Chuck Finley	589	163	.277	662	170	.257	.020
Dan Schatzeder	2154	569	.264	1725	423	.245	.019
Eric Rasmussen	688	196	.285	654	174	.266	.019
Bryan Clark	1027	289	.281	906	238	.263	.019
John Stuper	775	223	.288	1132	305	.269	.018
Vern Ruhle	1649	457	.277	1641	425	.259	.018
Bob Owchinko	1184	330	.279	792	207	.261	.017
Kirk McCaskill	805	214	.266	1692	421	.249	.017
Danny Cox	1226	340	.277	2496	651	.261	.017
John Curtis	1098	300	.273	1283	331	.258	.015
John Candelaria	2223	595	.268	3626	919	.253	.014
Lynn McGlothen	816	242	.297	1057	299	.283	.014
Ross Grimsley	572	188	.329	761	240	.315	.013
Charlie Leibrandt	1875	519	.277	3562	939	.264	.013
Guy Hoffman	742	208	.280	554	148	.267	.013
Steve Comer	1028	303	.295	1250	352	.282	.013
Paul Splittorff	1252	361	.288	2202	606	.275	.013
Bill Travers	574	160	.279	960	255	.266	.013
Pat Zachry	1215	333	.274	1214	317	.261	.013
Al Williams	912	253	.277	1569	417	.266	.012

VII
Single Season and Career Leaders

Single Season and Career Leaders

The Single Season and Career Leaders section lists, for a variety of batting and pitching categories, the top 25 performers since we began *The Player Analysis* in 1975.

When we began our analysis of play-by-play data from every game, we had a dual purpose: we recognized the value of the information for immediate use, and we knew we were accumulating and building a valuable resource for future study as well. This section gives us a chance to take stock of the results from our unparalleled files—files representing more than a million and a half plate appearances.

The leader categories for this section were chosen both for significance and for general interest (however quirky). The single season bests listed here provide an important context for evaluating the performances throughout this book. The career lists do considerably more; they provide the definitive look at situational statistics since 1975.

Minimum qualifiers for most batting categories are expressed in hits rather than in the equivalent number of plate appearances. As a general rule, the number of hits is one third the number of at bats of the qualifying range, if you're more comfortable thinking about it in those terms.

In dealing with last season's statistics in the Ranking Section of this book, we used a more inclusive level for rankings qualification: the equivalent of 200 plate appearances. The levels used here are more stringent, corresponding more to everyday play than part-time or "semiregular" status.

In the pitching categories, it should not be too surprising that relievers dominate. They allow consistently lower batting averages than starters for a variety of reasons, not only in traditional statistics but in these situational statistics as well. We have tried to set qualifying levels that are meaningful for both starters and relievers; the levels are the equivalent of about one and a half seasons as a full-time starter, or three as a primary reliever.

Bear in mind that *The Player Analysis* began in 1975. For the vast majority of active players, this poses no obstacle to calling these "career" statistics. In some cases, the missing information is very minor (67 at bats out of Jim Rice's career; a little under 500 from George Brett's); in the case of a Pete Rose or Tony Perez, obviously, a larger chunk is missing. We'd love to be able to fill in the gaps; we'd also love to know how Lou Gehrig hit with runners in scoring position in late-inning pressure. Maybe someday . . .

CAREER BATTING AVERAGE VS. LEFT-HANDED PITCHERS

Min. 150 Hits

Kirby Puckett	.346
Julio Franco	.324
Bob Watson	.318
Tony Gwynn	.318
Wade Boggs	.317
Jim Rice	.315
Rickey Henderson	.312
Pat Tabler	.310
Hubie Brooks	.310
Rod Carew	.310
Paul Molitor	.310
Ron LeFlore	.309
Don Mattingly	.308
Ellis Valentine	.307
Pedro Guerrero	.307
John Castino	.307
Jose Canseco	.306
Hal McRae	.305
Bill Madlock	.305
Gary Matthews	.305
Dwight Evans	.305
Buddy Bell	.304
Tim Raines	.304
Wayne Nordhagen	.304
Dave Cash	.304

CAREER SLUGGING AVERAGE VS. LEFT-HANDED PITCHERS

Min. 200 Total Bases

Pete Incaviglia	.592
Eric Davis	.591
Mike Schmidt	.579
Mark McGwire	.569
Ellis Valentine	.562
Jose Canseco	.561
Dave Winfield	.540
Jack Clark	.537
Dwight Evans	.534
Cory Snyder	.531
Johnny Bench	.531
George Foster	.530
Jim Rice	.528
Kirby Puckett	.528
George Bell	.527
Dale Murphy	.526
Ron Cey	.523
Rob Deer	.520
Cliff Johnson	.518
Dave Kingman	.518
Bill Robinson	.513
Cal Ripken	.512
Hal McRae	.511
Pedro Guerrero	.510
Danny Tartabull	.510

CAREER HOME RUN PCT. VS. LEFT-HANDED PITCHERS

Min. 20 Home Runs

Eric Davis	8.26
Mark McGwire	8.12
Dave Kingman	7.58
Pete Incaviglia	7.26
Rob Deer	6.97
Mike Schmidt	6.85
Ron Cey	6.56
Ron Kittle	6.54
Cecil Fielder	6.39
Gorman Thomas	6.12
Mike Diaz	6.10
Bill Schroeder	6.07
Ellis Valentine	6.07
Johnny Bench	6.03
Jose Canseco	5.98
George Foster	5.93
Gene Tenace	5.90
Darryl Strawberry	5.88
John Wockenfuss	5.85
Dale Murphy	5.82
Dave Winfield	5.63
Cory Snyder	5.61
Jack Clark	5.61
Cliff Johnson	5.57
Tom Brunansky	5.55

CAREER STRIKEOUT PCT. VS. LEFT-HANDED PITCHERS

Min. 500 PA

Ted Sizemore	2.90
Dave Cash	3.05
Tim Foli	3.08
Bob Bailor	3.41
Manny Sanguillen	3.48
Felix Millan	3.49
Marty Barrett	3.57
Doug Flynn	4.69
Rennie Stennett	4.72
Mickey Hatcher	4.89
Rich Dauer	4.96
Bucky Dent	5.09
Bob Boone	5.10
Pete Rose	5.21
Don Kessinger	5.30
Bill Russell	5.34
Mario Guerrero	5.46
Rob Andrews	5.48
Jerry Terrell	5.54
Bruce Benedict	5.57
Steve Nicosia	5.71
Willie Randolph	5.81
Bill Buckner	5.82
Tony Gwynn	6.00
Eric Soderholm	6.03

CAREER BATTING AVERAGE VS. RIGHT-HANDED PITCHERS

Min. 250 Hits

Wade Boggs	.373
Rod Carew	.341
Tony Gwynn	.339
Don Mattingly	.337
Kal Daniels	.335
George Brett	.328
Mike Greenwell	.327
Al Oliver	.326
Lyman Bostock	.325
Kevin Seitzer	.311
Kirby Puckett	.310
Pedro Guerrero	.307
Mike Easler	.307
Wally Backman	.306
Thurman Munson	.306
Bake McBride	.306
Wally Joyner	.305
Cecil Cooper	.305
Tim Raines	.305
Mickey Rivers	.305
Keith Hernandez	.304
Ken Griffey	.304
Jerry Mumphrey	.303
Johnny Ray	.303
Jose Cruz	.303

CAREER SLUGGING AVERAGE VS. RIGHT-HANDED PITCHERS

Min. 300 Total Bases

Kal Daniels	.589
Fred McGriff	.585
Mike Greenwell	.572
Darryl Strawberry	.568
Don Mattingly	.548
George Brett	.547
Will Clark	.540
Reggie Smith	.539
Ken Phelps	.535
Willie Stargell	.532
Fred Lynn	.529
Mark McGwire	.528
Kent Hrbek	.525
Mike Schmidt	.525
Danny Tartabull	.521
Wade Boggs	.511
Wally Joyner	.511
Alvin Davis	.508
Pedro Guerrero	.508
Kirk Gibson	.507
Eddie Murray	.507
Reggie Jackson	.503
Andy Van Slyke	.502
Jim Rice	.500
Leon Durham	.499

CAREER HOME RUN PCT. VS. RIGHT-HANDED PITCHERS

Min. 40 Home Runs

Ken Phelps	8.02
Fred McGriff	7.51
Ron Kittle	6.87
Mark McGwire	6.85
Darryl Strawberry	6.78
Mike Schmidt	6.70
Dave Kingman	6.35
Willie Stargell	6.19
Dan Pasqua	6.11
Reggie Jackson	6.10
Reggie Smith	5.99
Will Clark	5.97
Steve Balboni	5.90
Bob Horner	5.87
Gorman Thomas	5.80
Kal Daniels	5.74
Matt Nokes	5.69
Mike Pagliarulo	5.68
Oscar Gamble	5.67
Eric Davis	5.67
Jose Canseco	5.63
Danny Tartabull	5.61
Cory Snyder	5.49
Rob Deer	5.40
Graig Nettles	5.32

CAREER STRIKEOUT PCT. VS. RIGHT-HANDED PITCHERS

Min. 750 PA

Felix Millan	3.29
Bill Buckner	3.91
Scott Bradley	4.08
Dave Cash	4.30
Tony Gwynn	4.89
Johnny Ray	4.95
Larry Bowa	5.04
Jack Brohamer	5.17
Mike Squires	5.17
Ken Oberkfell	5.20
Greg Gross	5.20
Don Mattingly	5.26
Wade Boggs	5.29
Rich Dauer	5.31
Mike Scioscia	5.33
Ozzie Smith	5.36
Al Oliver	5.37
Rusty Staub	5.40
Terry Francona	5.69
Tom Poquette	5.72
George Brett	5.77
Pete Rose	5.83
Dan Meyer	5.95
Bob Bailor	5.98
Duane Kuiper	5.99

SINGLE-SEASON BATTING AVERAGE VS. LEFT-HANDED PITCHERS		SINGLE-SEASON BATTING AVERAGE VS. RIGHT-HANDED PITCHERS		SINGLE-SEASON BATTING AVERAGE IN HOME GAMES		SINGLE-SEASON BATTING AVERAGE IN ROAD GAMES	
Min. 40 Hits		*Min. 75 Hits*		*Min. 75 Hits*		*Min. 75 Hits*	
Rennie Stennett, 1977	.435	George Brett, 1980	.437	Wade Boggs, 1985	.418	George Brett, 1980	.388
Sixto Lezcano, 1979	.411	Wade Boggs, 1983	.398	Wade Boggs, 1987	.411	Cecil Cooper, 1980	.386
Kirby Puckett, 1988	.398	Rod Carew, 1977	.398	Kirby Puckett, 1988	.406	Rod Carew, 1977	.374
Tim Raines, 1987	.396	Wade Boggs, 1988	.381	Rod Carew, 1977	.401	Johnny Ray, 1984	.370
Steve Henderson, 1979	.395	Rod Carew, 1975	.379	Juan Beniquez, 1984	.399	Rod Carew, 1983	.369
Mike Vail, 1979	.395	Wade Boggs, 1985	.377	Wade Boggs, 1983	.397	Don Mattingly, 1986	.367
Ken Griffey, 1976	.393	Wade Boggs, 1987	.377	Paul Molitor, 1987	.394	Don Mattingly, 1984	.364
Gerald Young, 1987	.390	Tony Gwynn, 1987	.376	George Brett, 1980	.391	Kirby Puckett, 1987	.362
Bill Buckner, 1978	.389	Tony Gwynn, 1984	.371	Tony Gwynn, 1987	.390	Brian Downing, 1979	.360
Paul Molitor, 1979	.387	Oscar Gamble, 1979	.370	Rod Carew, 1975	.387	Bob Watson, 1975	.358
Brian Downing, 1979	.386	Kal Daniels, 1987	.370	Fred Lynn, 1979	.386	Mickey Rivers, 1977	.358
Chet Lemon, 1984	.384	Cecil Cooper, 1980	.365	Al Oliver, 1980	.385	Bill Madlock, 1975	.357
Julio Franco, 1988	.383	Fred Lynn, 1979	.364	Wade Boggs, 1988	.382	Wade Boggs, 1986	.356
Keith Moreland, 1983	.382	Paul Molitor, 1987	.363	Hal McRae, 1976	.382	Ken Singleton, 1977	.354
Buddy Bell, 1977	.382	Willie Wilson, 1982	.360	Miguel Dilone, 1980	.378	Ben Oglivie, 1980	.353
Rico Carty, 1975	.381	Wade Boggs, 1986	.359	Tony Gwynn, 1984	.376	Willie McGee, 1985	.353
Don Baylor, 1975	.380	Rod Carew, 1983	.358	Dion James, 1987	.376	Pedro Guerrero, 1987	.352
Jack Clark, 1980	.380	Bill Madlock, 1975	.357	Mike Easler, 1984	.375	Tony Gwynn, 1987	.352
Jeffrey Leonard, 1984	.380	Mike Easler, 1980	.357	George Brett, 1979	.373	Steve Sax, 1986	.352
Jose Cardenal, 1975	.379	Wade Boggs, 1982	.356	Bill Buckner, 1977	.372	Wade Boggs, 1988	.351
Ray Knight, 1986	.379	Wade Boggs, 1984	.356	Jim Rice, 1979	.369	Keith Hernandez, 1979	.350
Lee Lacy, 1980	.379	Willie McGee, 1985	.356	Fred Lynn, 1975	.368	Dave Winfield, 1984	.349
Gary Carter, 1977	.378	Rod Carew, 1982	.355	George Brett, 1985	.368	Enos Cabell, 1984	.348
Ken Singleton, 1977	.373	Al Oliver, 1979	.353	Dave Parker, 1977	.368	Al Oliver, 1978	.348
Larry Herndon, 1987	.373	Miguel Dilone, 1980	.353	George Brett, 1976	.367	Robin Yount, 1982	.347

CAREER HOME RUN PCT. IN HOME GAMES		CAREER HOME RUN PCT. IN ROAD GAMES		CAREER BATTING AVERAGE IN HOME GAMES		CAREER BATTING AVERAGE IN ROAD GAMES	
Min. 25 Home Runs		*Min. 25 Home Runs*		*Min. 200 Hits*		*Min. 200 Hits*	
Ken Phelps	8.46	Mark McGwire	8.26	Wade Boggs	.384	Don Mattingly	.332
Bob Horner	7.47	Ron Kittle	7.03	Kirby Puckett	.346	Wade Boggs	.328
Mike Schmidt	6.73	Dave Kingman	6.90	Tony Gwynn	.340	Rod Carew	.328
Dave Kingman	6.52	Eric Davis	6.85	Kevin Seitzer	.338	Tony Gwynn	.323
Ron Kittle	6.42	Darryl Strawberry	6.78	George Brett	.336	Pedro Guerrero	.308
Fred McGriff	6.41	Mike Schmidt	6.74	Rod Carew	.334	Wally Joyner	.308
Oscar Gamble	6.31	Steve Balboni	6.61	Al Oliver	.326	Mickey Rivers	.308
Willie Stargell	6.26	Fred McGriff	6.50	Jim Rice	.322	Lyman Bostock	.305
Greg Luzinski	6.25	Ken Phelps	6.45	Don Mattingly	.322	Bob Watson	.305
Dale Murphy	6.23	Jose Canseco	6.08	Lyman Bostock	.318	Bobby Bonilla	.305
Eric Davis	6.13	Bill Schroeder	6.01	Pat Tabler	.315	Manny Sanguillen	.303
Mark McGwire	6.13	Gorman Thomas	5.93	Julio Franco	.314	Cecil Cooper	.301
Darryl Strawberry	6.09	Rob Deer	5.71	Will Clark	.313	Tim Raines	.301
Rob Deer	6.03	Matt Nokes	5.64	Paul Molitor	.312	Bill Madlock	.301
Gorman Thomas	5.87	Cory Snyder	5.57	Dave Parker	.311	Tony Fernandez	.300
Jesse Barfield	5.85	Pedro Guerrero	5.52	Thurman Munson	.311	Keith Hernandez	.298
Reggie Jackson	5.80	Reggie Jackson	5.51	Kent Hrbek	.311	Thurman Munson	.297
George Foster	5.71	George Bell	5.43	Tim Raines	.308	Gene Richards	.297
Dan Pasqua	5.68	Glenn Davis	5.38	Mike Easler	.308	Dave Winfield	.297
Will Clark	5.53	Willie Stargell	5.35	Milt Thompson	.307	Ken Griffey	.296
Pete Incaviglia	5.53	Jack Clark	5.35	Thad Bosley	.307	Rickey Henderson	.296
Bo Jackson	5.53	Willie Aikens	5.29	Pedro Guerrero	.307	Ken Singleton	.296
Rick Monday	5.48	Tom Brunansky	5.25	Lou Brock	.306	Kirby Puckett	.295
Kal Daniels	5.47	Pete Incaviglia	5.24	Hal McRae	.306	George Brett	.294
Cory Snyder	5.46	Howard Johnson	5.22	Bill Madlock	.306	Eddie Murray	.294

CAREER BATTING AVERAGE WITH RUNNERS ON BASE

Min. 200 Hits

Wade Boggs	.358
Rod Carew	.348
Tony Gwynn	.346
Kirby Puckett	.329
Lyman Bostock	.326
Don Mattingly	.325
George Brett	.325
Thurman Munson	.321
Dave Parker	.321
Pete Rose	.319
Pat Tabler	.318
Keith Hernandez	.316
Al Oliver	.316
Cecil Cooper	.315
Bill Madlock	.313
Pedro Guerrero	.313
Tim Raines	.312
Bill Buckner	.310
Mike Easler	.307
Manny Sanguillen	.307
Wally Joyner	.307
Jim Rice	.306
Steve Garvey	.306
Bruce Bochte	.305
Andres Galarraga	.305

SINGLE-SEASON BATTING AVERAGE WITH RUNNERS ON BASE

Min. 75 Hits

Rod Carew, 1977	.422
Tony Gwynn, 1984	.406
George Brett, 1980	.400
Garry Templeton, 1979	.388
Wade Boggs, 1985	.387
Fred Lynn, 1979	.387
Keith Hernandez, 1979	.383
Dave Parker, 1978	.383
Tony Gwynn, 1988	.382
Wade Boggs, 1986	.379
Garry Templeton, 1977	.378
Rod Carew, 1975	.377
Robin Yount, 1987	.376
Mickey Rivers, 1977	.373
Bill Madlock, 1975	.370
Manny Sanguillen, 1975	.370
Bill Madlock, 1976	.368
Hal McRae, 1976	.368
George Brett, 1985	.367
Hal McRae, 1982	.366
Pete Rose, 1975	.366
Fred Lynn, 1975	.365
Ken Griffey, 1976	.362
Cecil Cooper, 1980	.362
Eddie Murray, 1985	.361

CAREER BATTING AVERAGE WITH RUNNERS IN SCORING POSITION

Min. 100 Hits

Wade Boggs	.356
Rod Carew	.345
Pat Tabler	.337
Tony Gwynn	.336
Thurman Munson	.329
Lyman Bostock	.324
Mike Greenwell	.323
Pete Rose	.323
Al Oliver	.323
Kirby Puckett	.322
George Brett	.321
Don Mattingly	.320
Tony Fernandez	.319
Broderick Perkins	.318
Rennie Stennett	.315
Cecil Cooper	.315
Lou Piniella	.314
Bill Madlock	.314
Dane Iorg	.313
Lamar Johnson	.312
Scott Fletcher	.312
Chris Brown	.312
Jim Rice	.312
Bake McBride	.309
Paul Molitor	.308

SINGLE-SEASON BATTING AVERAGE WITH RUNNERS IN SCORING POSITION

Min. 50 Hits

George Brett, 1980	.466
Cecil Cooper, 1980	.421
Tony Gwynn, 1984	.418
Bill Madlock, 1976	.414
Ken Griffey, 1976	.412
Pete Rose, 1975	.412
Don Mattingly, 1984	.405
Fred Lynn, 1975	.400
Mickey Rivers, 1977	.400
Kent Hrbek, 1982	.398
Wade Boggs, 1985	.392
Robin Yount, 1982	.392
Joe Morgan, 1976	.391
Willie McGee, 1985	.391
Hal McRae, 1982	.383
Pat Tabler, 1987	.383
Rod Carew, 1977	.382
Bake McBride, 1980	.380
Bill Robinson, 1977	.380
Garry Templeton, 1977	.379
Thurman Munson, 1975	.376
Rod Carew, 1978	.375
Ted Simmons, 1983	.375
Dave Winfield, 1979	.371
Eddie Murray, 1985	.370

CAREER BATTING AVERAGE WITH 2 OUTS AND RUNNERS ON BASE

Min. 75 Hits

Wade Boggs	.336
Kirby Puckett	.326
Tony Fernandez	.323
Larry Hisle	.321
Thurman Munson	.320
Eric Davis	.314
Tony Gwynn	.314
Mike Greenwell	.311
Al Oliver	.311
Larry Biittner	.307
Andres Galarraga	.305
Cecil Cooper	.305
Jose Cardenal	.304
Dave Parker	.303
Rico Carty	.303
Bill Madlock	.302
Rod Carew	.301
Ernest Riles	.301
Gene Richards	.301
Lyman Bostock	.301
Pat Tabler	.299
Chris Brown	.299
Alan Trammell	.298
Pete Rose	.298
Don Mattingly	.298

SINGLE-SEASON BATTING AVERAGE WITH 2 OUTS AND RUNNERS ON BASE

Min. 30 Hits

Barry Bonnell, 1977	.437
Lee Lacy, 1984	.432
Al Oliver, 1980	.424
Bruce Bochte, 1982	.418
Dave Parker, 1986	.412
Pat Tabler, 1987	.407
Ted Simmons, 1983	.404
Sixto Lezcano, 1979	.402
Garry Templeton, 1979	.400
Ray Knight, 1986	.400
Rod Carew, 1977	.398
Harold Baines, 1985	.391
Greg Gross, 1975	.390
Lee Mazzilli, 1979	.390
Larry Parrish, 1979	.388
Rod Carew, 1975	.388
Joe Rudi, 1976	.386
Frank Taveras, 1978	.386
Rennie Stennett, 1975	.383
Larry Hisle, 1978	.379
Steve Garvey, 1979	.377
Rod Carew, 1978	.376
Garry Templeton, 1977	.376
Steve Kemp, 1980	.375
Ozzie Guillen, 1986	.375

CAREER BATTING AVERAGE WITH 2 OUTS & RUNNERS IN SCORING POSITION

Min. 50 Hits

John Kruk	.367
Tony Fernandez	.341
Wade Boggs	.334
Larry Hisle	.332
Thurman Munson	.325
Al Oliver	.320
Kevin Mitchell	.312
Kirby Puckett	.312
Andres Galarraga	.312
Chris Brown	.308
Andres Thomas	.308
Lamar Johnson	.307
Pat Tabler	.306
Lyman Bostock	.304
Eric Davis	.304
Gene Richards	.303
Pete Rose	.303
Lou Piniella	.303
John Castino	.302
Dane Iorg	.302
Terry Harper	.302
Bill Madlock	.302
Jose Morales	.301
George Brett	.300
Dale Sveum	.299

SINGLE-SEASON BATTING AVERAGE WITH 2 OUTS & RUNNERS IN SCORING POSITION

Min. 20 Hits

Kent Hrbek, 1982	.466
Bruce Bochte, 1982	.457
Al Oliver, 1980	.446
Rod Carew, 1975	.440
Pat Tabler, 1987	.440
Ted Simmons, 1983	.437
George Foster, 1981	.426
Chris Speier, 1978	.426
Dave Parker, 1986	.419
Steve Sax, 1988	.419
Rod Carew, 1978	.414
Cecil Cooper, 1980	.414
Rod Carew, 1977	.412
Lee Mazzilli, 1978	.412
Joe Rudi, 1976	.410
Lyman Bostock, 1978	.407
Dave Winfield, 1979	.407
Mike Ivie, 1979	.404
Tony Fernandez, 1986	.404
Larry Hisle, 1978	.403
Lee Lacy, 1984	.400
Paul Molitor, 1986	.400
Rusty Staub, 1976	.397
Ray Knight, 1986	.396
Pete Rose, 1975	.395

CAREER BATTING AVERAGE IN LATE-INNING PRESSURE SITUATIONS

Min. 50 Hits

Tim Raines	.352
Tony Gwynn	.345
Wade Boggs	.339
Milt Thompson	.338
Tony Fernandez	.336
Billy Hatcher	.324
George Brett	.320
Joe Lefebvre	.320
Ed Romero	.319
Kirby Puckett	.319
Rickey Henderson	.319
Cecil Cooper	.318
Steve Sax	.318
Ken Griffey	.314
Barry Larkin	.312
Ron LeFlore	.312
Thad Bosley	.311
Tom Paciorek	.309
Thurman Munson	.309
Mickey Rivers	.309
Luis Aguayo	.309
Jose Cardenal	.309
Chris Brown	.309
Mike Ivie	.308
Benito Santiago	.307

SINGLE-SEASON BATTING AVERAGE IN LATE-INNING PRESSURE SITUATIONS

Min. 25 Hits

Manny Trillo, 1981	.466
Bill Madlock, 1975	.464
Mickey Rivers, 1977	.439
Wade Boggs, 1986	.433
George Brett, 1976	.433
Alan Trammell, 1987	.431
Steve Kemp, 1979	.429
Ken Griffey, 1975	.423
Tom Paciorek, 1976	.419
Mike Easler, 1984	.416
Scot Thompson, 1979	.413
Cecil Cooper, 1982	.412
Lloyd Moseby, 1983	.410
Luis Salazar, 1981	.408
Bill Buckner, 1984	.403
Chris Chambliss, 1981	.403
Alan Trammell, 1988	.403
Rick Manning, 1983	.402
Ken Griffey, 1986	.402
Cal Ripken, 1984	.398
Bill Buckner, 1978	.397
Will Clark, 1986	.397
Wade Boggs, 1985	.395
Tim Raines, 1987	.394
Rickey Henderson, 1983	.391

CAREER HOME RUN PCT. IN LATE-INNING PRESSURE SITUATIONS

Min. 10 Home Runs

Mark McGwire	8.24
Ken Phelps	8.09
Gary Alexander	7.80
Cory Snyder	7.56
Steve Balboni	7.14
Dave Kingman	6.90
Craig Kusick	6.78
Eddie Murray	6.07
Andre Thornton	6.01
Tony Armas	6.01
Dan Pasqua	5.68
Mike Schmidt	5.62
Eric Davis	5.60
Oscar Gamble	5.57
Reggie Smith	5.56
Darryl Strawberry	5.54
Graig Nettles	5.51
Bernie Carbo	5.41
Howard Johnson	5.38
Pedro Guerrero	5.36
Richie Zisk	5.32
Kirk Gibson	5.31
Willie Stargell	5.25
Cliff Johnson	5.24
Reggie Jackson	5.19

CAREER BATTING AVG. IN LATE-INNING PRESSURE SITUATIONS WITH RUNNERS IN SCORING POSITION

Min. 25 Hits

Eric Soderholm	.429
Jose Canseco	.418
Eddie Murray	.373
Wade Boggs	.358
Tim Raines	.356
Willie Montanez	.355
Lee May	.352
Pete Rose	.346
Oscar Gamble	.343
Dickie Thon	.342
Tony Gwynn	.342
Rickey Henderson	.342
Thurman Munson	.341
Bruce Bochte	.337
Mookie Wilson	.333
Mike Ivie	.333
Luis Salazar	.333
Reggie Smith	.333
Dave Chalk	.333
Gerald Perry	.333
Garth Iorg	.333
Cal Ripken	.331
Don Mattingly	.330
Cesar Geronimo	.330
Rod Carew	.328

CAREER BATTING AVERAGE IN LATE-INNING PRESSURE SITUATIONS WITH RUNNERS ON BASE

Min. 25 Hits

Mike Ivie	.370
Tim Raines	.357
Eddie Murray	.354
Tony Gwynn	.352
Kevin Seitzer	.352
Wade Boggs	.350
Dale Sveum	.348
Eric Soderholm	.348
Kurt Stillwell	.347
Thad Bosley	.347
Garth Iorg	.342
John Kruk	.342
Manny Mota	.342
Bill Buckner	.341
Ed Romero	.341
Cory Snyder	.337
Milt Thompson	.337
Jose Cardenal	.335
Alan Trammell	.335
Reggie Smith	.333
Dickie Thon	.333
Jose Canseco	.333
Dave Rader	.333
Pete Rose	.332
Gerald Perry	.331

SINGLE-SEASON BATTING AVERAGE IN LATE-INNING PRESSURE SITUATIONS WITH RUNNERS ON BASE

Min. 10 Hits

Rance Mulliniks, 1984	.684
Eddie Murray, 1985	.567
Bill Buckner, 1984	.563
Rey Quinones, 1987	.538
Rowland Office, 1975	.536
Rusty Staub, 1981	.536
Jack Clark, 1984	.526
Ron Oester, 1981	.524
Pedro Guerrero, 1980	.520
Manny Trillo, 1981	.520
Carl Yastrzemski, 1975	.500
Ken Griffey, 1975	.500
Bernie Carbo, 1976	.500
Mickey Rivers, 1977	.500
Ken Singleton, 1977	.500
Pete Rose, 1977	.500
Barry Foote, 1979	.500
Glenn Adams, 1979	.500
Dan Ford, 1983	.500
Rob Deer, 1987	.500
Paul Molitor, 1987	.500
Milt Thompson, 1988	.500
Rick Manning, 1983	.486
Cesar Geronimo, 1976	.485
Tim Raines, 1988	.484

CAREER BATTING AVERAGE IN LATE-INNING PRESSURE SITUATIONS WITH 2 OUTS AND RUNNERS ON BASE

Min. 15 Hits

Garth Iorg	.446
Eric Soderholm	.429
Marty Perez	.405
Tim Raines	.397
Mike Ivie	.387
Milt Thompson	.385
Dave Rader	.383
Wade Boggs	.367
Thurman Munson	.365
Vance Law	.365
Alan Trammell	.357
Oscar Gamble	.355
Eddie Murray	.353
Steve Henderson	.352
Jose Canseco	.351
Glenn Adams	.345
H. Pat Kelly	.344
Ed Ott	.343
Manny Sanguillen	.341
U.L. Washington	.338
Dave Revering	.333
Rico Carty	.333
Thad Bosley	.333
Donnie Hill	.333
Pete Rose	.332

CAREER BATTING AVG. IN LATE-INNING PRESSURE SITUATIONS WITH 2 OUTS AND RUNNERS IN SCORING POSITION

Min. 10 Hits

Eric Soderholm	.444
Garth Iorg	.441
Marty Perez	.435
Vance Law	.419
Jim Norris	.417
Rusty Staub	.405
Cesar Geronimo	.391
Thurman Munson	.387
Oscar Gamble	.381
Andres Thomas	.379
Jose Canseco	.378
Eddie Murray	.378
Willie Horton	.373
Pete Rose	.372
Gary Pettis	.367
Mike A. Marshall	.357
Bobby Bonilla	.357
Tim Raines	.356
Jose Cruz	.355
Lee May	.352
Wade Boggs	.352
Mike Ivie	.349
Don Mattingly	.345
Dave Chalk	.344
Dickie Thon	.343

HIGHEST CAREER RATIO OF GROUND OUTS TO AIR OUTS

Min. 1,000 PA

Milt Thompson	2.87
Wally Backman	2.53
Steve Jeltz	2.23
Willie McGee	2.22
Juan Bonilla	2.10
Gary Pettis	2.10
Steve Henderson	2.04
Duane Kuiper	2.02
Billy North	2.02
Steve Carlton	1.99
Steve Sax	1.92
Gene Richards	1.91
Rod Carew	1.89
Tony Gwynn	1.86
Alan Wiggins	1.84
Ron LeFlore	1.82
Miguel Dilone	1.82
Jackie Gutierrez	1.79
Pete Rose	1.79
Phil Bradley	1.76
Jerry Mumphrey	1.76
Lyman Bostock	1.73
Kevin Seitzer	1.72
Garry Templeton	1.72
Wayne Tolleson	1.71

LOWEST CAREER RATIO OF GROUND OUTS TO AIR OUTS

Min. 1,000 PA

Mark McGwire	0.59
Rob Deer	0.61
Gene Tenace	0.63
Jim Dwyer	0.63
Franklin Stubbs	0.65
Howard Johnson	0.65
Joe Morgan	0.65
Andre Thornton	0.65
Ken Phelps	0.66
Gary Redus	0.66
Darrell Evans	0.67
Don Baylor	0.67
Steve Balboni	0.69
Mark Salas	0.69
Joe Carter	0.69
Ron Kittle	0.70
Richie Hebner	0.70
Tom Brunansky	0.70
Mike Schmidt	0.71
Buck Martinez	0.71
Dave Revering	0.72
Tim Hulett	0.72
Bobby Murcer	0.73
Jerry White	0.74
Mike Greenwell	0.75

CAREER BATTING AVERAGE IN DAY GAMES

Min. 100 Hits

Rod Carew	.347
Wade Boggs	.345
Kevin Seitzer	.335
Don Mattingly	.330
Randy Ready	.327
Mike Greenwell	.326
George Brett	.323
Tony Gwynn	.322
Willie McGee	.320
Bake McBride	.316
Tim Raines	.315
Al Oliver	.315
Paul Molitor	.314
Lyman Bostock	.313
Ken Griffey	.312
Jerry Grote	.312
Wayne Krenchicki	.312
Kal Daniels	.312
Will Clark	.312
Thurman Munson	.311
Jose Morales	.311
Reggie Smith	.310
Gene Richards	.309
Andres Galarraga	.309
Carney Lansford	.308

CAREER BATTING AVERAGE IN NIGHT GAMES

Min. 100 Hits

Wade Boggs	.361
Tony Gwynn	.335
Kirby Puckett	.326
Mike Greenwell	.326
Don Mattingly	.326
Rod Carew	.324
Pedro Guerrero	.315
George Brett	.312
Kal Daniels	.311
Lyman Bostock	.310
Mickey Rivers	.309
Kevin Seitzer	.308
Al Oliver	.306
Tracy Jones	.306
Cecil Cooper	.304
Jim Rice	.303
Manny Sanguillen	.303
Tony Fernandez	.303
Rafael Palmeiro	.302
Bill Madlock	.302
Mike Easler	.301
Rick Peters	.301
Dion James	.300
Thurman Munson	.300
Luis Polonia	.299

CAREER BATTING AVERAGE ON GRASS SURFACES

Min. 150 Hits

Wade Boggs	.358
Tony Gwynn	.333
Rod Carew	.331
Don Mattingly	.324
Mike Greenwell	.320
Al Oliver	.318
Lyman Bostock	.313
Bobby Bonilla	.312
Keith Hernandez	.309
Pedro Guerrero	.309
Thurman Munson	.306
Bob Watson	.305
Jim Rice	.305
Kirby Puckett	.303
Bill Madlock	.303
Pat Tabler	.302
Tim Raines	.302
Julio Franco	.301
Steve Garvey	.301
Paul Molitor	.301
Will Clark	.301
Cecil Cooper	.301
Jose Cardenal	.300
Reggie Smith	.300
Andre Dawson	.299

CAREER BATTING AVERAGE ON ARTIFICIAL TURF

Min. 150 Hits

Wade Boggs	.346
Don Mattingly	.342
George Brett	.334
Rod Carew	.333
Kirby Puckett	.331
Kevin Seitzer	.330
Tony Gwynn	.326
Tracy Jones	.321
Kal Daniels	.320
Alan Trammell	.315
Al Bumbry	.314
Cal Ripken	.314
Mickey Rivers	.312
Von Joshua	.311
Lee Lacy	.308
Mickey Hatcher	.307
Mike Easler	.306
Ken Griffey	.306
Tim Raines	.306
Jim Gantner	.305
Pedro Guerrero	.304
Bill Madlock	.304
Chris Chambliss	.303
Dave Parker	.303
Tony Fernandez	.302

SINGLE-SEASON BATTING AVERAGE ON GRASS SURFACES

Min. 60 Hits

George Brett, 1980	.396
Rod Carew, 1977	.393
Paul Molitor, 1987	.376
Tony Gwynn, 1987	.374
Pete Rose, 1979	.373
Ray Knight, 1983	.370
Wade Boggs, 1987	.369
Ken Griffey, 1976	.368
Rod Carew, 1975	.367
Keith Hernandez, 1979	.366
Gary Gaetti, 1986	.364
Wade Boggs, 1983	.364
Wade Boggs, 1985	.363
Wade Boggs, 1988	.363
Cecil Cooper, 1980	.363
Oscar Gamble, 1979	.362
Pat Sheridan, 1984	.358
Dan Gladden, 1984	.357
Wade Boggs, 1982	.354
Wade Boggs, 1986	.352
Juan Beniquez, 1984	.352
Alan Trammell, 1987	.352
Bill Buckner, 1978	.351
Fred Lynn, 1979	.350
Tony Gwynn, 1984	.349

SINGLE-SEASON BATTING AVERAGE ON ARTIFICIAL TURF

Min. 60 Hits

Bill Madlock, 1975	.398
Steve Sax, 1986	.387
George Brett, 1980	.386
Hal McRae, 1976	.382
Kirby Puckett, 1988	.370
George Brett, 1979	.369
George Brett, 1976	.367
Keith Hernandez, 1985	.364
George Brett, 1978	.357
Lee Lacy, 1980	.356
Willie McGee, 1985	.356
George Brett, 1981	.356
Greg Gross, 1983	.356
Pete Rose, 1976	.354
Bake McBride, 1976	.354
George Brett, 1975	.352
Bill Madlock, 1981	.352
Kirby Puckett, 1986	.352
George Brett, 1985	.352
Mike Easler, 1980	.349
Kent Hrbek, 1984	.349
Willie Wilson, 1982	.349
Pete Rose, 1981	.348
Joe Morgan, 1975	.347
Pete LaCock, 1978	.347

CAREER ON-BASE AVERAGE LEADING OFF INNINGS

Min. 200 PA

Wade Boggs	.449
Mike Greenwell	.437
Fred McGriff	.422
Kal Daniels	.409
Tony Gwynn	.398
Rickey Henderson	.395
Rod Carew	.392
Willie Randolph	.385
Pepe Mangual	.384
Mike Hargrove	.382
Tony Solaita	.382
Greg Gross	.380
Mike Schmidt	.380
Tim Raines	.379
Bob Stinson	.377
Bobby Grich	.377
Jack Clark	.375
Gene Tenace	.375
Otto Velez	.375
Bernie Carbo	.374
Bobby Bonds	.374
Joe Morgan	.372
Pedro Guerrero	.372
Johnny Grubb	.372
Phil Bradley	.372

SINGLE-SEASON ON-BASE AVERAGE LEADING OFF INNINGS

Min. 100 PA

Rod Carew, 1982	.523
Andre Thornton, 1975	.519
Carlton Fisk, 1977	.504
Wade Boggs, 1983	.494
Toby Harrah, 1981	.491
Wade Boggs, 1988	.476
Joe Morgan, 1975	.470
Ozzie Smith, 1987	.469
Wade Boggs, 1985	.468
Ken Griffey, 1977	.466
Phil Bradley, 1987	.463
Kirby Puckett, 1987	.462
Fred McGriff, 1988	.460
Willie Randolph, 1980	.457
Wade Boggs, 1987	.457
Hal McRae, 1977	.456
Kirby Puckett, 1988	.453
Mike Hargrove, 1977	.453
Mitchell Page, 1977	.452
Cal Ripken, 1984	.452
Kal Daniels, 1987	.450
Willie Randolph, 1985	.448
Jose Cruz, 1979	.448
Richie Zisk, 1981	.447
Von Hayes, 1986	.444

CAREER WALK PCT. LEADING OFF INNINGS

Min. 25 Walks

Jim Wynn	19.71
Gene Tenace	15.78
Joe Morgan	15.34
Bernie Carbo	15.05
Fred McGriff	14.80
Pepe Mangual	14.76
Otto Velez	14.55
Glenn Borgmann	14.35
Ken Phelps	14.32
Jerry Hairston	14.18
Rickey Henderson	14.07
Dwayne Murphy	14.07
Tommy Hutton	14.00
Willie Randolph	13.95
Joe Ferguson	13.84
Mike Hargrove	13.67
Billy North	13.62
Bud Harrelson	13.56
Steve Jeltz	13.42
Lee Mazzilli	13.38
Merv Rettenmund	13.27
Toby Harrah	13.17
Tony Solaita	13.16
Rick Peters	13.13
John Cangelosi	13.02

SINGLE-SEASON WALK PCT. LEADING OFF INNINGS

Min. 15 Walks

John Cangelosi, 1987	24.77
Jim Wynn, 1975	23.85
Jack Clark, 1987	23.39
Dwayne Murphy, 1987	23.08
Lee Mazzilli, 1982	22.97
Lee Mazzilli, 1983	22.50
Joe Morgan, 1975	22.00
Gene Tenace, 1977	21.43
Dwayne Murphy, 1981	21.43
Andre Thornton, 1975	21.30
Carlton Fisk, 1977	21.17
Bernie Carbo, 1975	21.05
Jerry Hairston, 1984	20.55
Mike Scioscia, 1985	20.54
Gary Matthews, 1984	19.82
Toby Harrah, 1981	19.81
Steve Kemp, 1981	19.74
Toby Harrah, 1985	19.71
Johnny Briggs, 1975	19.15
Gene Tenace, 1979	19.05
Mike Hargrove, 1977	18.95
Willie Randolph, 1980	18.78
Darrell Porter, 1975	18.75
Willie Randolph, 1981	18.75
Jose Oquendo, 1987	18.75

CAREER BATTING AVERAGE WITH BASES LOADED

Min. 15 Hits

Pat Tabler	.578
Rudy Law	.469
Miguel Dilone	.436
Biff Pocoroba	.435
Rick Bosetti	.429
Lou Brock	.423
Ken Singleton	.417
Ellis Valentine	.417
Tony Gwynn	.417
Eric Davis	.413
Bill Madlock	.411
Eddie Murray	.409
Alan Trammell	.407
Rico Carty	.404
Lee May	.402
Jay Johnstone	.400
Denny Walling	.400
Larry Sheets	.395
Oscar Gamble	.392
Larry Hisle	.389
Rod Carew	.388
Candy Maldonado	.386
Dale Berra	.383
Richie Zisk	.382
Wade Boggs	.380

CAREER RRF RATIO (PER PA) WITH BASES LOADED

Min. 30 RBI

Wally Joyner	1.21
Pat Tabler	1.17
Darryl Motley	1.13
Devon White	1.11
John Milner	1.10
Cory Snyder	1.09
Eddie Murray	1.08
Biff Pocoroba	1.06
Ellis Burks	1.06
Terry Crowley	1.05
Mike Cubbage	1.04
Rick Leach	1.03
Dane Iorg	1.03
Greg Walker	1.02
Rico Carty	1.00
Lee Stanton	1.00
Roy Howell	0.99
Oscar Gamble	0.99
Jose Cruz	0.98
H. Pat Kelly	0.98
Dale Berra	0.98
Steve Garvey	0.98
Larry Sheets	0.98
Joe Rudi	0.98
Rob Deer	0.97

CAREER WALK PCT. WITH BASES LOADED

Min. 10 Walks

Oscar Gamble	17.65
Mike Hargrove	17.48
Sixto Lezcano	17.12
Gene Tenace	16.09
Gary Roenicke	15.91
Leon Durham	15.71
Pete Rose	15.57
Darrell Porter	15.32
Joe Morgan	14.55
Alvin Davis	14.49
Ken Oberkfell	13.33
Terry Puhl	13.16
Jeff Burroughs	12.90
Dave Winfield	12.77
Dan Driessen	12.40
Dwight Evans	12.37
Carl Yastrzemski	12.15
Jack Clark	11.97
Bobby Murcer	11.58
Rickey Henderson	11.54
Ken Singleton	11.48
Jim Gantner	11.24
Darrell Evans	11.11
Butch Wynegar	10.94
Dave Lopes	10.91

CAREER STRIKEOUT PCT. WITH BASES LOADED

Min. 50 PA

Rico Carty	1.43
Jim Spencer	1.89
Biff Pocoroba	1.92
Jerry Morales	2.02
Craig Reynolds	2.06
Ozzie Smith	2.24
Dave Cash	3.03
Bruce Benedict	3.66
Bill Buckner	3.66
Brett Butler	3.85
Dan Gladden	3.92
Lyman Bostock	3.92
Jose Cardenal	4.00
Ellis Valentine	4.00
Doug Flynn	4.08
Rich Dauer	4.35
Ken Oberkfell	4.44
Bill Madlock	4.46
Mike Scioscia	4.48
Lenny Randle	4.62
Frank Taveras	4.62
Jose Cruz	4.72
Larry Bowa	4.81
Pete O'Brien	5.17
Toby Harrah	5.19

CAREER PCT. OF RUNNERS DRIVEN IN FROM SCORING POSITION

Min. 100 RBI

Don Mattingly	.365
Wally Joyner	.355
Thurman Munson	.352
Dane Iorg	.352
Wade Boggs	.352
Broderick Perkins	.349
Al Oliver	.349
George Brett	.349
Rusty Staub	.349
Cecil Cooper	.347
Rod Carew	.346
Pat Tabler	.341
Lou Piniella	.341
Ted Simmons	.340
Keith Hernandez	.340
Rico Carty	.340
Dave Winfield	.340
Mike Hargrove	.340
Larry Hisle	.338
Kent Hrbek	.336
Mike Aldrete	.336
Bill Madlock	.335
Hal McRae	.335
Bill Buckner	.335
Lyman Bostock	.334

SINGLE-SEASON PCT. OF RUNNERS DRIVEN IN FROM SCORING POSITION

Min. 50 RBI

George Brett, 1980	.507
Bill Buckner, 1981	.476
Cecil Cooper, 1980	.470
Bill Madlock, 1976	.448
Dave Parker, 1976	.430
Eddie Murray, 1985	.428
Bill Buckner, 1978	.427
Richie Hebner, 1980	.422
Cecil Cooper, 1976	.420
Bake McBride, 1980	.419
Buddy Bell, 1984	.418
Larry Parrish, 1986	.415
John Milner, 1976	.412
Harold Baines, 1987	.412
Rod Carew, 1977	.411
Tony Gwynn, 1988	.410
Ted Simmons, 1983	.410
Tom Herr, 1985	.409
Rod Carew, 1975	.408
Joe Morgan, 1978	.408
Joe Morgan, 1976	.408
Pat Tabler, 1985	.407
Kent Hrbek, 1984	.405
Ray Knight, 1986	.403
Hal McRae, 1982	.402

CAREER PCT. OF RUNS BATTED IN FROM SCORING POSITION IN LATE-INNING PRESSURE SITUATIONS

Min. 20 RBI

Eric Soderholm	.427
Eddie Murray	.409
Jose Canseco	.406
Jim Essian	.403
Kevin Seitzer	.397
Jim Norris	.392
Pedro Guerrero	.380
Pete LaCock	.379
Lenn Sakata	.377
Ernest Riles	.370
Mike Hargrove	.369
Wade Boggs	.368
Eddie Milner	.367
Rico Carty	.364
Vance Law	.363
Don Mattingly	.361
Bill Melton	.361
Carmelo Martinez	.359
Rusty Staub	.357
Wally Joyner	.354
Reggie Smith	.354
Ellis Valentine	.352
Tony Gwynn	.350
Larry Sheets	.349
Oscar Gamble	.349

SINGLE-SEASON RBI OPPORTUNITIES FROM SCORING POSITION

Tony Perez, 1975	268
Willie McGee, 1987	260
Don Baylor, 1979	257
Jim Rice, 1986	250
Tim Wallach, 1987	247
Johnny Bench, 1975	246
George Foster, 1976	245
Julio Franco, 1985	244
George Foster, 1977	243
Bill Buckner, 1986	242
Keith Moreland, 1985	238
Jerry Morales, 1975	236
Bob Watson, 1976	236
Lance Parrish, 1983	235
Ruben Sierra, 1987	233
Tom Herr, 1985	232
Joe Carter, 1987	232
Greg Luzinski, 1975	230
Thurman Munson, 1976	229
Cecil Cooper, 1983	229
Mike Greenwell, 1988	229
Jim Rice, 1975	228
Jim Rice, 1984	228
Willie Montanez, 1975	227
Steve Garvey, 1978	227

CAREER PCT. OF RUNS BATTED IN FROM 3D BASE WITH LESS THAN 2 OUTS

Min. 40 RBI

Broderick Perkins	.753
Don Mattingly	.723
Rico Carty	.722
Wally Joyner	.720
Ed Kranepool	.720
Tony Solaita	.719
Rod Carew	.719
Wade Boggs	.708
Tony Gwynn	.708
Cal Ripken	.702
Jerry Hairston	.699
Manny Sanguillen	.695
Al Oliver	.692
Pat Tabler	.692
Mike Hargrove	.689
Rusty Staub	.686
George Brett	.686
R.J. Reynolds	.683
Wayne Krenchicki	.682
Mel Hall	.681
Steve Buechele	.681
Bill Madlock	.680
Pete Rose	.677
Dave Winfield	.677
Hal McRae	.675

SINGLE-SEASON PCT. OF RUNS BATTED IN FROM 3D BASE WITH LESS THAN 2 OUTS

Min. 15 RBI

Ben Oglivie, 1986	.913
Rod Carew, 1983	.900
Toby Harrah, 1981	.889
Bill Madlock, 1986	.880
Elliott Maddox, 1978	.875
Rickey Henderson, 1988	.870
Bill Madlock, 1976	.868
Dave Revering, 1979	.857
Kevin McReynolds, 1984	.852
Al Oliver, 1983	.846
Jerry Mumphrey, 1985	.846
Sid Bream, 1986	.846
Paul Molitor, 1978	.842
Dave Bergman, 1984	.842
Tom Foley, 1988	.842
Pat Tabler, 1985	.840
George Brett, 1980	.838
Richie Hebner, 1976	.833
Rich Dauer, 1978	.833
Denny Walling, 1978	.833
Brian Downing, 1982	.833
Alan Wiggins, 1984	.833
Juan Beniquez, 1987	.833
Jose Oquendo, 1987	.833
Herm Winningham, 1987	.833

CAREER PCT. OF RUNS BATTED IN FROM 1ST BASE

Min. 30 RBI

Willie Stargell	.110
Mark McGwire	.107
Darryl Strawberry	.102
Eric Davis	.102
Jose Canseco	.101
Glenn Davis	.099
Mike Schmidt	.097
Ken Phelps	.096
Danny Tartabull	.093
Alvin Davis	.092
Greg Luzinski	.092
Larry Hisle	.091
Dave Kingman	.091
Hal McRae	.089
Dave Parker	.088
Mike Greenwell	.088
Reggie Jackson	.087
Lance Parrish	.086
Oscar Gamble	.086
Bill Robinson	.086
Dale Murphy	.086
George Brett	.085
Steve Balboni	.085
Fred Lynn	.085
Cliff Johnson	.083

SINGLE-SEASON RUNS BATTED IN FROM 1ST BASE

Hal McRae, 1982	36
George Foster, 1977	31
Jim Rice, 1978	29
Don Mattingly, 1985	29
Greg Luzinski, 1977	28
Alvin Davis, 1984	28
Keith Hernandez, 1979	27
Joe Carter, 1986	26
Jim Rice, 1983	25
Fred Lynn, 1979	24
Steve Garvey, 1979	24
Dave Kingman, 1984	24
Jose Canseco, 1986	24
Mike Greenwell, 1988	24
Jeff Burroughs, 1977	23
Ron Cey, 1977	23
Jim Rice, 1979	23
Tony Armas, 1980	23
Tony Perez, 1980	23
Mike Schmidt, 1983	23
Eddie Murray, 1985	23
Darryl Strawberry, 1987	23
Fred Lynn, 1975	22
Johnny Bench, 1975	22
Bob Watson, 1977	22

CAREER OPP. BATTING AVERAGE VS. LEFT-HANDED BATTERS

Min. 400 PA

Player	AVG
Jesse Orosco	.191
Mark Langston	.196
Atlee Hammaker	.197
Pat Underwood	.201
Mark Davis	.201
Bob Lacey	.201
Juan Agosto	.202
Dave Dravecky	.203
Rod Scurry	.206
Nolan Ryan	.208
John Candelaria	.209
Sid Fernandez	.209
Willie Hernandez	.210
Bill Scherrer	.210
Jeff M. Robinson	.211
Frank DiPino	.213
Al Holland	.215
Mike Norris	.216
John Fulgham	.216
Joe Sambito	.218
Larry Gura	.218
Bob McClure	.218
Bob Shirley	.219
Craig Lefferts	.219
Bruce Sutter	.220

CAREER OPP. HOME RUN PCT. VS. LEFT-HANDED BATTERS

Min. 400 PA

Player	PCT
Mickey Lolich	0.46
Doug Sisk	0.47
Zane Smith	0.50
Bert Roberge	0.51
Dave Smith	0.55
Paul Mirabella	0.56
Jim Crawford	0.64
Bruce Berenyi	0.69
Joe Sambito	0.69
Doug Jones	0.75
Jeff Lahti	0.80
Gary Lavelle	0.82
Greg Minton	0.87
Ken Howell	0.89
Danny Jackson	0.91
Juan Agosto	0.92
Ricky Horton	0.92
Pedro Borbon	0.94
Andy Hassler	0.95
Frank Williams	0.96
Dwight Gooden	0.97
Jesse Orosco	0.98
Steve Trout	0.99
Bob Shirley	0.99
John Fulgham	1.03

CAREER OPP. WALK PCT. VS. LEFT-HANDED BATTERS

Min. 400 PA

Player	PCT
Steve Howe	3.06
Gary Nolan	3.23
Scott McGregor	4.16
Curt Young	4.47
Dick Bosman	4.75
Tom Burgmeier	4.80
Jim Kaat	5.13
Jon Matlack	5.14
Dan Quisenberry	5.24
John Tudor	5.31
Ted Higuera	5.32
Dave Tomlin	5.37
Oil Can Boyd	5.38
Will McEnaney	5.42
Frank Tanana	5.50
Bob Knepper	5.51
Bob Tewksbury	5.57
John Candelaria	5.59
Randy Jones	5.63
Atlee Hammaker	5.67
Bob Ojeda	5.68
Pedro Borbon	5.69
Rick Honeycutt	5.70
Ron Guidry	5.72
Frank Viola	5.78

CAREER OPP. STRIKEOUT PCT. VS. LEFT-HANDED BATTERS

Min. 100 Strikeouts

Player	PCT
Tom Henke	28.57
Sid Fernandez	27.67
Mark Davis	25.83
Nolan Ryan	24.70
Mark Langston	24.20
John Candelaria	23.95
Jesse Orosco	23.80
Dave Righetti	23.42
Al Holland	23.35
John Tudor	23.31
Joe Sambito	23.22
Ted Higuera	22.85
Frank DiPino	22.37
Rod Scurry	22.12
Matt Young	21.94
Tippy Martinez	21.48
Todd Worrell	21.48
Steve Carlton	21.31
Gary Lavelle	21.08
Dave Dravecky	21.03
Bob Ojeda	20.89
Bill Caudill	20.84
Roger Clemens	20.74
Atlee Hammaker	20.50
John Hiller	20.42

CAREER OPP. BATTING AVERAGE VS. RIGHT-HANDED BATTERS

Min. 600 PA

Player	AVG
J.R. Richard	.190
David Cone	.191
Jose DeLeon	.192
Floyd Youmans	.193
Tim Burke	.197
Mitch Williams	.199
Bobby Witt	.202
Luis DeLeon	.202
Mark Littell	.202
Rich Gossage	.202
Tom Henke	.203
Pat Perry	.206
Victor Cruz	.206
Sid Fernandez	.206
Mario Soto	.207
Eric Show	.208
Frank Williams	.209
Andy Messersmith	.209
Orel Hershiser	.209
Jeff Reardon	.209
Mark Eichhorn	.210
Roger Clemens	.211
Nolan Ryan	.212
Skip Lockwood	.213
Dan Warthen	.213

CAREER OPP. HOME RUN PCT. VS. RIGHT-HANDED BATTERS

Min. 600 PA

Player	PCT
Mark Fidrych	0.63
Rick Lysander	0.70
Steve Howe	0.80
Randy Niemann	0.93
Doug Sisk	0.95
J.R. Richard	0.98
Dave Heaverlo	1.00
Kent Tekulve	1.02
Dave Frost	1.09
Greg Minton	1.10
Mike Barlow	1.14
Pat Clements	1.14
Joe Magrane	1.15
Bill Swift	1.18
Pablo Torrealba	1.24
Ed Farmer	1.24
Mark Littell	1.26
Terry Forster	1.27
Jim Kern	1.28
Dale Murray	1.31
Dave Smith	1.31
Dave Tomlin	1.34
Steve Hargan	1.34
Carl Morton	1.35
John Urrea	1.36

CAREER OPP. WALK PCT. VS. RIGHT-HANDED BATTERS

Min. 600 PA

Player	PCT
Dan Quisenberry	2.24
LaMarr Hoyt	3.49
Gary Nolan	3.51
Bret Saberhagen	3.74
Bob Stanley	4.19
Bill Long	4.23
Lary Sorensen	4.43
Ferguson Jenkins	4.52
Tim Leary	4.52
Dick Bosman	4.65
Larry Andersen	4.72
Jim Barr	4.73
Luis DeLeon	4.83
Fernando Arroyo	4.84
Bill Wegman	4.85
Tim Burke	4.91
Dennis Leonard	4.95
Tom Hausman	4.96
Bill Gullickson	5.03
Rick Reuschel	5.04
Roger Erickson	5.08
Moose Haas	5.10
Rick Wise	5.12
Scott Sanderson	5.18
Ed Lynch	5.19

CAREER OPP. STRIKEOUT PCT. VS. RIGHT-HANDED BATTERS

Min. 150 Strikeouts

Player	PCT
Ken Howell	28.97
Tom Henke	27.50
Calvin Schiraldi	27.22
Roger Clemens	26.83
Jose DeLeon	26.77
Bobby Witt	26.38
Lee Smith	26.33
David Cone	26.19
J.R. Richard	26.06
Dwight Gooden	25.79
Jeff Reardon	25.00
Skip Lockwood	24.68
Nolan Ryan	24.60
Victor Cruz	24.38
Mark Clear	24.14
Cecilio Guante	24.12
Dan Plesac	23.64
Rich Gossage	23.44
Scott Garrelts	23.38
Luis DeLeon	23.00
Mark Littell	22.95
Mario Soto	22.80
Lance McCullers	22.70
Ron Robinson	22.67
Bill Caudill	22.56

SINGLE-SEASON OPP. BATTING AVERAGE VS. LEFT-HANDED BATTERS

Min. 125 PA

Bill Dawley, 1983	.142
Bob Lacey, 1977	.146
Mitch Williams, 1987	.146
Bryan Harvey, 1988	.147
Mark Clear, 1984	.147
Dave Smith, 1984	.152
Nolan Ryan, 1981	.153
Lance McCullers, 1988	.153
Ron Guidry, 1978	.156
Bob Shirley, 1978	.156
Larry McWilliams, 1983	.156
Matt Young, 1983	.158
Gary Lavelle, 1984	.158
Bill Scherrer, 1983	.158
Rich Wortham, 1979	.159
Larry Gura, 1983	.159
John Smiley, 1988	.159
Tom Burgmeier, 1980	.159
Mike Caldwell, 1978	.160
Sid Monge, 1979	.161
Andy Hassler, 1980	.162
Larry Gura, 1978	.164
Bob Knepper, 1981	.164
Gene Garber, 1978	.165
Jeff Musselman, 1987	.165

SINGLE-SEASON OPP. BATTING AVERAGE VS. RIGHT-HANDED BATTERS

Min. 175 PA

J.R. Richard, 1980	.124
Mark Eichhorn, 1986	.135
Dave LaRoche, 1976	.139
Rich Gossage, 1977	.140
Mario Soto, 1980	.147
Lance McCullers, 1986	.154
Hank Webb, 1975	.156
Mike Scott, 1986	.156
Mark Clear, 1979	.157
Don Carman, 1985	.161
Jim Kern, 1979	.161
Jeff Reardon, 1984	.161
Aurelio Lopez, 1983	.162
Tom Niedenfuer, 1983	.162
Luis DeLeon, 1982	.163
Sid Monge, 1978	.164
Frank Williams, 1985	.164
David Cone, 1988	.165
Frank Williams, 1984	.166
Tim Burke, 1985	.166
Cecilio Guante, 1985	.166
Jose DeLeon, 1984	.168
Mike Jackson, 1988	.169
Dwight Gooden, 1984	.170
Jose DeLeon, 1986	.171

CAREER OPP. BATTING AVERAGE IN HOME GAMES

Min. 500 PA

Sid Fernandez	.182
Jeff M. Robinson	.190
Nolan Ryan	.197
J.R. Richard	.197
Lance McCullers	.203
Mitch Williams	.206
John Smiley	.206
Dwight Gooden	.208
Tom Henke	.208
Scott Garrelts	.208
Bobby Witt	.211
Bert Roberge	.212
Floyd Youmans	.212
Steve Ontiveros	.213
David Cone	.214
Mike Armstrong	.215
Joe Cowley	.215
Mario Soto	.216
Todd Worrell	.216
Jose DeLeon	.217
Skip Lockwood	.217
Eric King	.218
Al Holland	.218
Rich Gossage	.219
Dave Righetti	.219

CAREER OPP. BATTING AVERAGE IN ROAD GAMES

Min. 500 PA

Mitch Williams	.177
Mark Littell	.203
John Fulgham	.208
Floyd Youmans	.209
Jesse Orosco	.212
Bruce Sutter	.219
Rich Gossage	.219
John Martin	.222
J.R. Richard	.223
Steve Bedrosian	.223
Lee Smith	.223
Dan Warthen	.224
Mario Soto	.224
Mark Eichhorn	.225
Nolan Ryan	.225
Roger Clemens	.226
Andy Messersmith	.226
Don Gullett	.227
Luis DeLeon	.227
Rod Scurry	.227
Tom Henke	.228
Bobby Witt	.228
Tim Burke	.228
Craig McMurtry	.228
Jose DeLeon	.228

CAREER OPP. BATTING AVERAGE ON GRASS SURFACES

Min. 500 PA

J.R. Richard	.195
Mitch Williams	.196
Sid Fernandez	.196
Danny Frisella	.199
Mark Littell	.211
Nolan Ryan	.212
Dan Warthen	.213
David Cone	.218
Dwight Gooden	.219
Jeff M. Robinson	.219
Frank Williams	.220
Rod Scurry	.221
DeWayne Buice	.221
Andy Messersmith	.221
Orel Hershiser	.221
Rich Gossage	.222
Bobby Witt	.222
Scott Garrelts	.222
Bill Laxton	.222
Cecilio Guante	.223
Joe Cowley	.223
Lance McCullers	.223
Brent Strom	.223
Gene Walter	.224
Mario Soto	.224

CAREER OPP. BATTING AVERAGE ON ARTIFICIAL TURF

Min. 500 PA

Jesse Orosco	.187
Mike Norris	.194
Mike Jackson	.197
Craig McMurtry	.199
Jeff Parrett	.205
Floyd Youmans	.205
Roger Clemens	.207
Nolan Ryan	.207
Rich Gossage	.211
Tom Henke	.211
Mark Littell	.212
Rob Murphy	.213
Jose DeLeon	.214
J.R. Richard	.215
Jim Kern	.216
Todd Worrell	.217
Mark Clear	.218
Mario Soto	.219
Pat Perry	.219
Al Holland	.220
Frank LaCorte	.222
Scott Garrelts	.223
Joe Sambito	.224
Len Barker	.226
Jeff Reardon	.226

CAREER OPP. BATTING AVERAGE IN DAY GAMES

Min. 250 PA

Eric Plunk	.199
Sid Fernandez	.202
Nolan Ryan	.204
Scott Garrelts	.206
Roger Clemens	.212
Mark Littell	.214
Joe Cowley	.214
Craig Lefferts	.215
Mario Soto	.216
Al Hrabosky	.216
Floyd Youmans	.216
Bob James	.218
Dave Smith	.218
Andy Messersmith	.221
Rich Gossage	.221
Rollie Fingers	.222
Steve Busby	.222
Frank Williams	.223
Steve Bedrosian	.223
Ted Higuera	.223
Bruce Berenyi	.223
Rod Scurry	.224
Tim Lollar	.225
Dave Righetti	.225
J.R. Richard	.226

CAREER OPP. BATTING AVERAGE IN NIGHT GAMES

Min. 250 PA

Mitch Williams	.189
J.R. Richard	.205
Floyd Youmans	.208
Dwight Gooden	.208
Sid Fernandez	.208
Mark Littell	.210
Jesse Orosco	.210
Nolan Ryan	.212
Jeff Lahti	.215
Rob Murphy	.216
Tom Henke	.216
Bobby Witt	.216
Jeff Parrett	.216
Jeff M. Robinson	.216
Lance McCullers	.217
Jose DeLeon	.218
Mike Norris	.218
Rich Gossage	.218
Mike Henneman	.218
Mike Jackson	.219
John Smiley	.219
Luis DeLeon	.220
Mark Eichhorn	.220
Tim Belcher	.221
Eric King	.221

CAREER OPP. BATTING AVERAGE IN LATE-INNING PRESSURE SITUATIONS

Min. 400 PA

Tom Henke	.196
Nolan Ryan	.198
Mark Davis	.201
Cecilio Guante	.205
Mitch Williams	.208
J.R. Richard	.209
Mark Littell	.214
Mario Soto	.218
Rob Murphy	.219
John Candelaria	.220
Rich Gossage	.220
Sid Monge	.221
Don Stanhouse	.222
Scott Garrelts	.222
Alejandro Pena	.223
John Franco	.223
Mike Boddicker	.223
Steve Bedrosian	.223
Jesse Orosco	.224
Skip Lockwood	.224
Frank LaCorte	.224
Aurelio Lopez	.225
Mark Eichhorn	.226
Gene Nelson	.226
Ron Darling	.226

SINGLE-SEASON OPP. BATTING AVERAGE IN LATE-INNING PRESSURE SITUATIONS

Min. 150 PA

Dave LaRoche, 1976	.142
Tom Niedenfuer, 1983	.146
Don Carman, 1985	.157
Tom Seaver, 1976	.163
Ron Davis, 1981	.166
Fernando Valenzuela, 1985	.167
Dennis Eckersley, 1977	.168
Bill Dawley, 1983	.169
Rich Gossage, 1977	.169
Tom Henke, 1986	.171
Randy Myers, 1988	.171
Aurelio Lopez, 1979	.173
Tom Henke, 1987	.174
Nolan Ryan, 1976	.174
Bill Caudill, 1982	.175
Manny Sarmiento, 1978	.176
Willie Hernandez, 1984	.176
Ed Farmer, 1979	.177
Jay Howell, 1988	.177
Skip Lockwood, 1976	.179
Roger Clemens, 1988	.179
J.R. Richard, 1976	.179
Cecilio Guante, 1986	.180
Steve Bedrosian, 1982	.181
Frank Tanana, 1976	.181

CAREER OPP. HOME RUN PCT. IN LATE-INNING PRESSURE SITUATIONS

Min. 400 PA

Doug Jones	0.24
Pat Clements	0.30
Steve Comer	0.61
Jim Todd	0.71
Jeff Lahti	0.73
Dave A. Roberts	0.75
Fernando Valenzuela	0.82
Doug Sisk	0.84
Don Stanhouse	0.84
Bill Gullickson	0.87
Frank Williams	0.88
Alejandro Pena	0.88
Ken Dayley	0.93
Dale Murray	0.96
Randy Jones	0.98
Clay Carroll	1.00
Steve Howe	1.00
Tommy John	1.01
Dave Giusti	1.04
Jay Howell	1.06
Don Carman	1.08
Darold Knowles	1.09
Rob Murphy	1.10
Juan Agosto	1.10
Pete Vuckovich	1.12

CAREER OPP. STRIKEOUT PCT. IN LATE-INNING PRESSURE SITUATIONS

Min. 100 Strikeouts

Tom Henke	30.08
Ken Howell	24.76
Mark Davis	24.59
Nolan Ryan	24.51
Scott Garrelts	24.10
Roger Clemens	23.86
Dwight Gooden	23.70
Mark Eichhorn	23.49
Lee Smith	23.22
Bill Caudill	22.94
Mitch Williams	22.82
Mark Clear	22.77
Skip Lockwood	22.56
Mark Littell	22.26
Rich Gossage	22.15
Dan Plesac	22.04
Ken Dayley	21.83
Rod Scurry	21.56
Paul Assenmacher	21.47
John Hiller	21.46
Steve Bedrosian	21.16
Victor Cruz	21.13
Todd Worrell	20.85
Jeff D. Robinson	20.84
Don Carman	20.64

CAREER OPP. BATTING AVERAGE IN LATE-INNING PRESSURE SITUATIONS WITH RUNNERS ON BASE

Min. 150 PA

Randy Myers	.144
Kevin Saucier	.160
Dave Tobik	.177
Cecilio Guante	.180
Steve McCatty	.197
Ron Darling	.197
Andy Hawkins	.198
Dave Dravecky	.203
Todd Worrell	.206
Steve Bedrosian	.206
Roger Clemens	.207
Rob Murphy	.207
Don Carman	.207
Nolan Ryan	.208
Sid Monge	.209
Jack Morris	.209
Alejandro Pena	.209
Danny Frisella	.210
Dock Ellis	.211
Jesse Orosco	.211
Randy Lerch	.211
Mark Eichhorn	.212
Bill Greif	.213
Bill Caudill	.213
Aurelio Lopez	.213

SINGLE-SEASON OPP. BATTING AVERAGE IN LATE-INNING PRESSURE SITUATIONS WITH RUNNERS ON BASE

Min. 60 PA

Frank Tanana, 1976	.116
Joe Sambito, 1981	.121
Randy Myers, 1988	.126
Dave LaRoche, 1976	.128
Jim Kern, 1976	.128
Bill Greif, 1976	.130
Dave Tobik, 1979	.130
Bud Black, 1986	.132
Joaquin Andujar, 1978	.133
Nolan Ryan, 1978	.134
Steve Bedrosian, 1982	.136
Kevin Saucier, 1981	.140
Tim Burke, 1987	.141
Mike Torrez, 1975	.143
George Frazier, 1982	.143
Tug McGraw, 1980	.146
Andy Hassler, 1980	.148
Dave Dravecky, 1984	.148
George Frazier, 1983	.149
Tom Niedenfuer, 1983	.150
Jeff Reardon, 1981	.151
Jesse Orosco, 1983	.152
Jose Rijo, 1988	.152
Richard Dotson, 1984	.153
Cecilio Guante, 1986	.153

CAREER OPP. HOME RUN PCT. IN LATE-INNING PRESSURE SITUATIONS WITH RUNNERS ON BASE

Min. 150 PA

Bill Lee	0.00
Steve Comer	0.00
Bob Ojeda	0.00
Charlie Williams	0.00
Ken Kravec	0.00
Mark L. Lee	0.00
Kevin Saucier	0.00
Dave Tomlin	0.41
Alejandro Pena	0.43
Steve Howe	0.43
Frank Williams	0.43
Andy McGaffigan	0.44
Doug Jones	0.44
Dave A. Roberts	0.45
Greg Minton	0.45
Vern Ruhle	0.47
Mark Eichhorn	0.47
Dwight Gooden	0.48
Bill Gullickson	0.53
Dave J. Schmidt	0.54
Pat Clements	0.60
Pete Vuckovich	0.62
Ron Darling	0.64
Ken Dayley	0.64
Fernando Valenzuela	0.64

CAREER OPP. STRIKEOUT PCT. IN LATE-INNING PRESSURE SITUATIONS WITH RUNNERS ON BASE

Min. 40 Strikeouts

Randy Myers	28.39
Calvin Schiraldi	27.63
Tom Henke	27.29
Mark Clear	24.06
Dwight Gooden	24.05
Roger Clemens	24.02
Bill Caudill	23.28
Mitch Williams	23.05
Scott Garrelts	22.83
Nolan Ryan	22.76
Ken Howell	22.11
Lee Smith	21.98
Skip Lockwood	21.50
Cecilio Guante	21.36
Mark Littell	21.19
Alejandro Pena	21.15
Jeff D. Robinson	20.80
Paul Assenmacher	20.42
Todd Worrell	20.27
Lance McCullers	20.13
Rod Scurry	20.09
John Hiller	20.00
Dave LaRoche	19.85
Victor Cruz	19.80
Mark Eichhorn	19.78

CAREER
OPP. BATTING AVERAGE WITH RUNNERS ON BASE

Min. 500 PA

Todd Worrell	.205
Mitch Williams	.205
Jesse Orosco	.205
Sid Fernandez	.211
Lance McCullers	.213
Jim Deshaies	.219
Jeff Reardon	.220
Rod Scurry	.222
Dwight Gooden	.222
Cecilio Guante	.222
Bill Caudill	.223
Mark Clear	.223
Nolan Ryan	.224
J.R. Richard	.224
Ron Darling	.225
Mark Littell	.225
Floyd Youmans	.225
Orel Hershiser	.226
Lee Smith	.227
Mario Soto	.228
Jose DeLeon	.228
Victor Cruz	.228
Craig Lefferts	.228
Roger Clemens	.228
Bruce Sutter	.228

SINGLE-SEASON
OPP. BATTING AVERAGE WITH RUNNERS ON BASE

Min. 175 PA

John D'Acquisto, 1978	.155
Gene Garber, 1978	.160
Jesse Orosco, 1984	.167
Bill Caudill, 1980	.173
Jesse Orosco, 1983	.175
Jeff M. Robinson, 1988	.175
Jose DeLeon, 1986	.175
Rich Gossage, 1977	.175
Willie Hernandez, 1984	.176
Al Holland, 1983	.177
Charlie Hough, 1976	.177
Lee Smith, 1983	.178
Mike Jackson, 1988	.179
Jim Deshaies, 1986	.180
Dwight Gooden, 1985	.180
Mitch Williams, 1987	.180
Doug Bair, 1978	.181
Mike Scott, 1986	.181
Tippy Martinez, 1983	.181
Sid Monge, 1979	.182
Bruce Sutter, 1977	.182
Jesse Orosco, 1986	.183
Mark Eichhorn, 1986	.183
Jose DeLeon, 1983	.185
Hal Dues, 1978	.185

CAREER
OPP. BATTING AVERAGE WITH RUNNERS IN SCORING POSITION

Min. 300 PA

Mitch Williams	.187
Jesse Orosco	.193
Sid Fernandez	.195
Steve Bedrosian	.196
Todd Worrell	.198
Cecilio Guante	.199
Floyd Youmans	.199
Bob Apodaca	.199
David Cone	.199
Jim Deshaies	.200
Tim Burke	.200
Lance McCullers	.200
Steve Busby	.206
Lee Smith	.208
Dwight Gooden	.209
Eric King	.211
Rich Gossage	.212
Jeff Lahti	.212
Craig Lefferts	.213
Stan Thomas	.213
Mark Eichhorn	.213
Joe Cowley	.214
Nolan Ryan	.215
Roger Clemens	.216
Orel Hershiser	.217

SINGLE-SEASON
OPP. BATTING AVERAGE WITH RUNNERS IN SCORING POSITION

Min. 125 PA

Jim Deshaies, 1986	.140
Rich Gossage, 1978	.143
Dwight Gooden, 1985	.144
Eric Show, 1986	.145
Tim Burke, 1985	.147
Joe Cowley, 1985	.148
Tom Hilgendorf, 1975	.149
John Candelaria, 1977	.149
Cecilio Guante, 1983	.151
Lance McCullers, 1988	.153
Don Sutton, 1980	.153
Gene Garber, 1982	.156
Bob Lacey, 1977	.157
Sid Fernandez, 1988	.157
Tom Hausman, 1975	.159
Rich Gossage, 1977	.159
Mike Scott, 1986	.159
Steve McCatty, 1981	.161
Joe Magrane, 1988	.161
Jeff D. Robinson, 1987	.161
Mitch Williams, 1987	.162
Tom Seaver, 1981	.163
Steve Bedrosian, 1986	.163
Bill Campbell, 1977	.165
Joaquin Andujar, 1978	.167

CAREER
OPP. BATTING AVERAGE WITH 2 OUTS AND RUNNERS ON BASE

Min. 250 PA

Eric King	.176
Bill Caudill	.186
Victor Cruz	.190
Pete Ladd	.190
Todd Worrell	.193
Floyd Youmans	.193
Dave Smith	.195
Mitch Williams	.195
Dwight Gooden	.195
Lance McCullers	.195
Jesse Orosco	.196
Cecilio Guante	.196
Pat Dobson	.196
Tim Burke	.196
Sid Fernandez	.197
Bobby Witt	.198
Ron Darling	.199
Terry Leach	.200
Bruce Sutter	.202
Dave Stewart	.202
J.R. Richard	.202
Rollie Fingers	.204
Jim Deshaies	.205
Craig Lefferts	.205
Jose DeLeon	.205

SINGLE-SEASON
OPP. BATTING AVERAGE WITH 2 OUTS AND RUNNERS ON BASE

Min. 100 PA

Bill Caudill, 1980	.103
Mike Scott, 1986	.109
Pat Dobson, 1976	.115
Jerry Ujdur, 1982	.122
Joe Magrane, 1988	.133
Jeff M. Robinson, 1988	.133
Eric Show, 1986	.138
Jose Rijo, 1988	.141
John Tudor, 1984	.143
Ed Whitson, 1984	.143
Ron Darling, 1986	.143
Jose DeLeon, 1985	.144
Bob Forsch, 1978	.147
Lance McCullers, 1986	.148
Eduardo Rodriguez, 1976	.149
Sparky Lyle, 1978	.149
Dan Warthen, 1975	.149
Bill Campbell, 1977	.149
Ron Darling, 1988	.150
Frank Tanana, 1977	.150
Fred Norman, 1978	.152
Scott Garrelts, 1985	.152
Tom Seaver, 1981	.153
Scott Sanderson, 1980	.154
Luis Tiant, 1978	.155

CAREER
OPP. BATTING AVERAGE WITH 2 OUTS AND RUNNERS IN SCORING POSITION

Min. 150 PA

Eric King	.161
Terry Leach	.162
Bob Apodaca	.165
Cecilio Guante	.172
Floyd Youmans	.175
Victor Cruz	.175
Todd Worrell	.175
Mitch Williams	.176
Tim Burke	.180
Dave Stewart	.181
Pete Ladd	.181
Lee Smith	.182
Craig Lefferts	.185
J.R. Richard	.185
Steve Busby	.186
Jesse Orosco	.186
Mark Eichhorn	.187
Bobby Witt	.188
Dave Smith	.188
Greg A. Harris	.188
Brian Fisher	.188
Sid Fernandez	.189
Tippy Martinez	.189
Dwight Gooden	.190
Joe Magrane	.190

SINGLE-SEASON
OPP. BATTING AVERAGE WITH 2 OUTS AND RUNNERS IN SCORING POSITION

Min. 75 PA

Jack Morris, 1987	.082
Joe Magrane, 1988	.097
Dan Warthen, 1975	.100
John Tudor, 1984	.110
Bobby Witt, 1987	.111
Luis Tiant, 1978	.113
Bill Gullickson, 1982	.118
Mike Scott, 1986	.119
Rich Gossage, 1978	.119
Ed Whitson, 1984	.119
Mike Krukow, 1986	.123
Brian Fisher, 1987	.125
Doug Corbett, 1980	.127
Ron Darling, 1986	.129
Mark Langston, 1988	.129
Frank Tanana, 1977	.130
Fred Norman, 1978	.130
Dwight Gooden, 1985	.133
Pat Dobson, 1976	.133
Tim Burke, 1985	.134
Frank Tanana, 1976	.135
Bill Campbell, 1977	.136
Tom Seaver, 1981	.138
Dave Freisleben, 1976	.143
Doug Rau, 1977	.143

SINGLE-SEASON DOUBLES ALLOWED

Dennis Leonard, 1978	62
Bruce Hurst, 1984	60
Rick Sutcliffe, 1983	58
Dennis Eckersley, 1986	58
Jim Barr, 1977	57
Jim Clancy, 1983	57
Bill Gullickson, 1983	56
Shane Rawley, 1987	56
Scott McGregor, 1983	55
John Montefusco, 1975	54
Dennis Leonard, 1980	54
Steve Rogers, 1983	54
Doyle Alexander, 1986	54
Mike Moore, 1987	54
Wilbur Wood, 1975	53
Mike Torrez, 1983	53
Ron Guidry, 1983	53
Doyle Alexander, 1984	53
Bob Knepper, 1985	53
Charlie Leibrandt, 1986	53
Ron Reed, 1975	52
Larry Christenson, 1977	52
Steve Carlton, 1977	52
Mike Flanagan, 1978	52
Jerry Koosman, 1980	52

SINGLE-SEASON TRIPLES ALLOWED

Larry Christenson, 1976	17
Paul Thormodsgard, 1977	16
Bret Saberhagen, 1988	16
Jim Barr, 1975	14
Jim Kaat, 1977	14
Jim Barr, 1977	14
Dave Goltz, 1977	14
Craig Swan, 1979	14
Randy Jones, 1979	14
Rick Sutcliffe, 1984	14
Ray Burris, 1976	13
Rick Reuschel, 1976	13
Luis Tiant, 1979	13
Dick Ruthven, 1980	13
Steve Carlton, 1980	13
Rich Gale, 1982	13
Tommy John, 1982	13
Mike Smithson, 1983	13
John Montefusco, 1975	12
Jim Kaat, 1976	12
Ken Holtzman, 1976	12
Ray Burris, 1978	12
Roger Erickson, 1979	12
Bob Forsch, 1979	12
Doc Medich, 1980	12

SINGLE-SEASON EXTRA-BASE HITS ALLOWED

Bert Blyleven, 1986	100
Phil Niekro, 1979	97
Dennis Leonard, 1978	94
Dennis Leonard, 1980	92
Rick Sutcliffe, 1983	92
Bert Blyleven, 1987	92
LaMarr Hoyt, 1984	91
Mike Witt, 1987	91
Doyle Alexander, 1988	91
Jerry Garvin, 1977	90
Mike Moore, 1987	90
Wilbur Wood, 1975	89
Jim Barr, 1977	89
Dan Petry, 1983	89
Mark Langston, 1986	89
Jim Clancy, 1983	88
Bill Gullickson, 1987	88
Ferguson Jenkins, 1979	87
Frank Viola, 1986	87
Willie Fraser, 1988	87
Luis Tiant, 1975	86
Ferguson Jenkins, 1975	86
Scott McGregor, 1983	86
Bruce Hurst, 1984	86
Charlie Hough, 1984	86

CAREER OPP. EXTRA-BASE HIT PCT. (PER 100 AB)

Min. 1,000 PA

Steve Howe	4.04
John Franco	4.67
Roger McDowell	4.69
Doug Sisk	4.84
Greg Minton	5.01
Scott Garrelts	5.08
Mark Fidrych	5.13
Alejandro Pena	5.20
Gary Lavelle	5.24
J.R. Richard	5.28
Dwight Gooden	5.29
Jesse Orosco	5.29
Jim Kern	5.35
Mark Littell	5.40
Orel Hershiser	5.40
Nolan Ryan	5.47
Dave Smith	5.51
Dave Righetti	5.52
Clay Carroll	5.56
Ernie Camacho	5.57
Rich Gossage	5.58
Kent Tekulve	5.59
Jaime Cocanower	5.64
Frank Williams	5.64
Lee Smith	5.75

HIGHEST CAREER RATIO OF GROUND OUTS TO AIR OUTS

Min. 1,000 PA

Roger McDowell	3.08
Doug Corbett	2.96
Doug Sisk	2.81
Juan Agosto	2.72
Ray Fontenot	2.53
Tommy John	2.52
Bill Swift	2.46
Bruce Ruffin	2.45
Jeff Dedmon	2.42
Greg Minton	2.41
Jim Todd	2.39
Jaime Cocanower	2.34
Dan Quisenberry	2.33
Dennis Lamp	2.32
Kent Tekulve	2.23
John Denny	2.21
Bob Stanley	2.18
Bill Castro	2.17
Gene Garber	2.17
Joe Magrane	2.16
Orel Hershiser	2.15
Randy Jones	2.13
Jim Winn	2.11
Steve Trout	2.08
Terry Forster	2.06

LOWEST CAREER RATIO OF GROUND OUTS TO AIR OUTS

Min. 1,000 PA

Sid Fernandez	0.49
Tom Niedenfuer	0.53
Jeff Reardon	0.55
Mike Armstrong	0.55
Keith Atherton	0.56
Don Carman	0.57
Victor Cruz	0.59
Jim Deshaies	0.59
Pete Ladd	0.60
Bill Caudill	0.60
Juan Berenguer	0.61
Dave LaRoche	0.61
Chris Knapp	0.62
Al Hrabosky	0.63
Cecilio Guante	0.65
Al Holland	0.65
Tom Browning	0.66
Skip Lockwood	0.66
Aurelio Lopez	0.67
Tim Conroy	0.67
Joe Price	0.67
Luis Tiant	0.67
John Henry Johnson	0.68
Tom Henke	0.69
Catfish Hunter	0.69

CAREER GROUND OUT PCT. (PER 100 PA)

Min. 1,000 PA

Roger McDowell	43.4
Dan Quisenberry	42.7
Randy Jones	41.3
Tommy John	41.2
Doug Sisk	40.4
Bill Castro	40.0
Doug Corbett	39.9
Juan Agosto	39.6
Greg Minton	39.3
Ray Fontenot	39.2
Jim Todd	38.6
Dennis Lamp	38.6
Bob Stanley	38.5
Kent Tekulve	38.5
Paul Hartzell	38.2
Fernando Arroyo	38.0
Bill Swift	37.9
Rob Dressler	37.8
Joe Magrane	37.7
Bruce Ruffin	37.6
Clay Carroll	37.5
Jaime Cocanower	37.4
Rick Matula	37.3
Jeff Dedmon	37.2
Dave Rozema	37.2

CAREER AIR OUT PCT. (PER 100 PA)

Min. 1,000 PA

Gary Nolan	36.0
Catfish Hunter	35.8
John Martin	35.2
Keith Atherton	35.1
Tom Browning	34.8
Mike Armstrong	34.8
Don Carman	34.5
Luis Tiant	34.3
Manny Sarmiento	34.2
Tom Niedenfuer	34.2
Scott McGregor	34.1
Larry Gura	33.6
Jeff Reardon	33.5
Jim Deshaies	33.5
Chris Knapp	33.3
Bill Wegman	33.3
Pete Ladd	33.3
Grant Jackson	33.2
Steve McCatty	33.1
Sid Fernandez	32.9
Brian Kingman	32.9
Craig Swan	32.9
Al Hrabosky	32.8
Ken Schrom	32.8
Pete Filson	32.8

CAREER OPP. ON-BASE AVERAGE LEADING OFF INNINGS

Min. 250 PA

Mike Armstrong	.252
Jeff M. Robinson	.253
Dan Quisenberry	.255
Tom Henke	.258
Brad Havens	.260
John Martin	.261
Dave Tobik	.262
Rich Gossage	.264
Dave J. Schmidt	.265
Steve Howe	.266
Tug McGraw	.269
Gary Nolan	.272
Jerry Reed	.272
Tom Niedenfuer	.272
Darold Knowles	.273
Jimmy Key	.278
Frank Tanana	.278
Gene Garber	.279
Pete Filson	.279
Marty Pattin	.279
Ron Reed	.279
Rawly Eastwick	.280
Doug Corbett	.281
Greg Swindell	.281
Rollie Fingers	.281

SINGLE-SEASON OPP. ON-BASE AVERAGE LEADING OFF INNINGS

Min. 100 PA

Greg A. Harris, 1985	.175
Dan Quisenberry, 1984	.188
Vern Ruhle, 1983	.191
Randy Martz, 1981	.202
Jeff D. Robinson, 1988	.211
Jeff D. Robinson, 1986	.212
Joe Price, 1983	.212
Dan Quisenberry, 1983	.215
Dave J. Schmidt, 1982	.217
John Tudor, 1985	.217
Rich Gossage, 1978	.219
Mike Armstrong, 1982	.220
Dan Schatzeder, 1984	.221
Don Sutton, 1975	.221
Dennis Eckersley, 1977	.223
Pat Underwood, 1982	.223
Ken Forsch, 1979	.223
Bob Forsch, 1977	.224
Marty Pattin, 1976	.224
Ron Guidry, 1981	.224
Vern Ruhle, 1981	.224
Rick Honeycutt, 1986	.225
Francisco Barrios, 1979	.225
Bryn Smith, 1987	.226
Jeff M. Robinson, 1987	.226

CAREER OPP. WALK PCT. LEADING OFF INNINGS

Min. 250 PA

Dan Quisenberry	2.38
Gene Garber	2.48
Gary Nolan	2.49
Dave J. Schmidt	2.96
Kevin Kobel	3.02
Atlee Hammaker	3.51
Ron Reed	3.54
Mark Fidrych	3.55
Steve Howe	3.58
Gary Lucas	3.78
Gary Ross	3.88
Pedro Borbon	3.95
Tommy John	4.01
Dave Rozema	4.04
Jim Barr	4.05
Bill Long	4.12
Kent Tekulve	4.12
Roger Erickson	4.16
Rick Reuschel	4.16
Dennis Eckersley	4.22
LaMarr Hoyt	4.25
Ferguson Jenkins	4.27
Bret Saberhagen	4.30
Ron Robinson	4.39
Scott Sanderson	4.41

SINGLE-SEASON OPP. WALK PCT. LEADING OFF INNINGS

Min. 100 PA

Gene Garber, 1982	0.00
Dan Quisenberry, 1983	0.00
Dan Quisenberry, 1985	0.00
Rick Langford, 1982	0.41
John Candelaria, 1988	0.62
Jim Barr, 1982	0.78
Tom Hausman, 1980	0.82
Bob Forsch, 1980	0.89
Dave J. Schmidt, 1982	0.94
Dennis Eckersley, 1987	0.94
Dennis Martinez, 1986	0.95
Jeff D. Robinson, 1986	0.96
Ron Reed, 1978	1.00
Mike Smithson, 1983	1.29
Gaylord Perry, 1981	1.29
Bryn Smith, 1987	1.29
Ferguson Jenkins, 1976	1.38
Glenn Abbott, 1983	1.45
Roger Clemens, 1984	1.45
Neal Heaton, 1987	1.48
Ron Guidry, 1981	1.49
Bob Shirley, 1980	1.50
Rick Rhoden, 1983	1.60
Atlee Hammaker, 1982	1.62
Gary Nolan, 1976	1.64

CAREER OPP. BATTING AVERAGE WITH BASES LOADED

Min. 50 PA

Eric Show	.143
Ed Figueroa	.147
Jesse Orosco	.147
Doug Rau	.152
Andy McGaffigan	.158
Dave LaRoche	.159
Charlie Lea	.159
Dave Lemanczyk	.167
Dave J. Schmidt	.169
Don Carman	.170
Cecilio Guante	.173
Mitch Williams	.173
Mike Smithson	.174
Ken Schrom	.175
Orel Hershiser	.176
Mark Thurmond	.178
Tom House	.179
Keith Atherton	.181
Jeff Dedmon	.182
Tippy Martinez	.183
Mark Gubicza	.185
Bruce Berenyi	.185
Ed Halicki	.185
Butch Metzger	.188
Tom Griffin	.188

CAREER MOST BATTERS FACED WITH BASES LOADED WITHOUT ALLOWING A GRAND-SLAM HOME RUN

Joaquin Andujar	158
Jim Kern	148
Mike Krukow	146
Bob Welch	130
Pat Zachry	128
Mike Moore	109
Jim Palmer	105
Greg A. Harris	97
Al Hrabosky	96
Andy Hassler	93
Jesse Jefferson	91
Joe Price	90
Juan Berenguer	89
Frank DiPino	88
Eric Show	88
Gene Nelson	86
Bruce Berenyi	84
Ed Figueroa	82
Doug Corbett	80
Mike Smithson	78
Dwight Gooden	76
Roy Thomas	75
Mike Boddicker	74
Don Hood	74
Rawly Eastwick	73

CAREER OPP. WALK PCT. WITH BASES LOADED

Min. 50 PA

Steve Crawford	0.00
Dave Heaverlo	0.81
Vern Ruhle	1.01
Steve McCatty	1.10
Matt Young	1.10
Ed Vande Berg	1.20
Craig Lefferts	1.30
Ed Lynch	1.39
Dave Tobik	1.43
Jim Gott	1.52
Dennis Eckersley	1.60
Mike G. Marshall	1.64
Fred Breining	1.72
John Butcher	1.75
Dave Dravecky	1.79
Larry Christenson	1.79
Ferguson Jenkins	1.82
Odell Jones	1.82
Mike Garman	1.82
Jay Tibbs	1.82
Jim Umbarger	1.82
Butch Metzger	1.82
Mike Parrott	1.89
Will McEnaney	1.89
Paul Reuschel	1.92

CAREER OPP. STRIKEOUT PCT. WITH BASES LOADED

Min. 15 Strikeouts

Bobby Witt	30.91
John Hiller	28.13
Nolan Ryan	27.78
Bruce Berenyi	27.38
Lance McCullers	26.98
Andy McGaffigan	26.56
Mark Littell	26.51
Tom Henke	25.86
Dave Smith	25.33
Dave LaRoche	25.20
Bill Caudill	25.00
Al Holland	24.14
Steve Carlton	24.11
Jeff Reardon	23.97
Ron Guidry	23.76
Sammy Stewart	23.61
Mario Soto	23.53
Orel Hershiser	23.47
Mitch Williams	23.29
Tippy Martinez	22.64
Rich Gossage	22.61
Dwight Gooden	22.37
Tom Seaver	22.29
Joe Sambito	22.12
Kevin Gross	21.74

VIII

Batter-Pitcher
Matchups

Batter-Pitcher Matchups

The Batter-Pitcher Matchup section lists, for the selected players, their performances against every pitcher or batter they have faced for at least five at bats in their careers. These statistics include all regular season appearances since the beginning of their careers.

Earl Weaver used to keep them on index cards. Dave Johnson maintains his on a PC. But until the past few years the public was largely unaware of the importance many managers place on specific matchup statistics in setting a lineup. The figures do not even out over the long run, and the differences can be massive. In this section, we expand the "Loves to Face" and "Hates to Face" matchups listed in the Batter and Pitcher Sections to take a look at the career performances of some of the most extraordinary players in the game.

Now you can see in detail just how few pitchers really give Kirby Puckett trouble. Or if anyone really has a book on Jose Canseco yet. Here, at last, are the answers.

Jose Canseco

Pitcher	AB	H	2B	3B	HR	BB	SO	BA	SA	OBA	Pitcher	AB	H	2B	3B	HR	BB	SO	BA	SA	OBA
Doyle Alexander	6	3	0	0	1	1	1	.500	1.000	.571	Eric King	16	3	1	0	0	1	5	.188	.250	.278
Neil Allen	15	3	0	0	0	0	3	.200	.200	.200	Mark Knudson	6	2	0	0	0	0	0	.333	.333	.333
Allan Anderson	8	3	1	0	1	2	1	.375	.875	.500	Pete Ladd	5	1	1	0	0	0	2	.200	.400	.200
Keith Atherton	9	2	2	0	0	0	3	.222	.444	.300	Mark Langston	22	5	0	0	2	3	8	.227	.500	.296
Don August	7	2	0	0	0	3	0	.286	.286	.500	Dave LaPoint	12	2	0	0	0	1	6	.167	.167	.231
Scott Bailes	10	2	0	0	1	1	1	.200	.500	.273	Tim Leary	6	3	0	0	1	1	0	.500	1.000	.625
Jeff Ballard	7	1	0	0	1	2	2	.143	.571	.333	Charlie Leibrandt	24	4	1	0	0	2	7	.167	.208	.231
Scott Bankhead	19	4	1	0	3	1	5	.211	.737	.286	Bill Long	10	2	0	0	0	0	5	.200	.200	.200
Floyd Bannister	16	5	3	0	2	0	5	.313	.875	.313	Gary Lucas	5	0	0	0	0	0	1	.000	.000	.000
Eric Bell	7	1	1	0	0	2	0	.143	.286	.333	Kirk McCaskill	22	4	2	0	0	4	8	.182	.273	.308
Juan Berenguer	6	1	1	0	0	1	2	.167	.333	.286	Jack McDowell	10	2	0	0	0	4	2	.200	.200	.429
Bud Black	7	0	0	0	0	0	0	.000	.000	.000	Scott McGregor	13	7	1	0	0	2	3	.538	.615	.600
Bert Blyleven	19	3	0	0	1	3	10	.158	.316	.273	Paul Mirabella	5	1	0	0	0	0	2	.200	.200	.200
Mike Boddicker	23	5	0	0	0	0	6	.217	.217	.208	Dale Mohorcic	13	3	0	0	2	0	1	.231	.692	.231
Rich Bordi	6	0	0	0	0	0	3	.000	.000	.000	Donnie Moore	6	1	0	0	0	0	3	.167	.167	.167
Chris Bosio	17	5	1	0	1	0	6	.294	.529	.294	Mike Moore	28	6	2	0	1	3	7	.214	.393	.290
Oil Can Boyd	19	8	1	0	4	2	2	.421	1.105	.476	Mike Morgan	12	3	1	0	0	4	3	.250	.333	.438
DeWayne Buice	5	1	0	0	0	2	3	.200	.200	.429	Jack Morris	15	2	0	0	2	5	5	.133	.533	.350
John Butcher	9	1	0	0	1	1	2	.111	.444	.200	Tom Niedenfuer	5	1	0	0	0	0	2	.200	.200	.200
John Candelaria	12	4	1	0	1	0	6	.333	.667	.333	Joe Niekro	10	2	0	0	1	2	2	.200	.500	.333
Tom Candiotti	21	4	0	0	1	7	4	.190	.333	.379	Phil Niekro	7	3	0	0	1	2	0	.429	.857	.556
Steve Carlton	13	4	0	1	1	1	1	.308	.692	.357	Scott Nielsen	9	3	0	0	1	0	0	.333	.667	.333
John Cerutti	16	7	0	0	3	2	4	.438	1.000	.500	Juan Nieves	11	6	2	0	0	0	3	.545	.727	.545
Jim Clancy	20	7	2	0	0	2	4	.350	.450	.391	Al Nipper	10	4	1	0	2	1	2	.400	1.100	.455
Terry Clark	5	0	0	0	0	1	4	.000	.000	.167	Melido Perez	9	5	1	0	2	1	0	.556	1.333	.600
Mark Clear	7	0	0	0	0	0	3	.000	.000	.000	Dan Plesac	6	2	0	0	0	0	3	.333	.333	.333
Roger Clemens	21	6	0	0	2	0	6	.286	.571	.286	Mark Portugal	6	4	1	0	0	0	1	.667	.833	.714
Stu Cliburn	7	3	0	0	0	0	1	.429	.429	.429	Dan Quisenberry	6	0	0	0	0	0	0	.000	.000	.000
Ed Correa	16	4	0	0	2	3	4	.250	.625	.368	Dennis Rasmussen	10	4	0	0	3	0	0	.400	1.300	.400
Joe Cowley	13	1	1	0	0	1	8	.077	.154	.143	Jeff Reardon	6	1	0	0	0	0	0	.167	.167	.167
Chuck Crim	8	1	0	0	1	0	1	.125	.500	.125	Jerry Reed	5	2	0	0	1	1	0	.400	1.000	.500
Danny Darwin	8	1	0	0	0	4	4	.125	.125	.125	Dave Righetti	8	4	1	0	0	0	2	.500	.625	.500
Joel Davis	8	2	0	0	1	1	2	.250	.625	.333	Jeff M. Robinson	18	4	0	0	1	1	3	.222	.389	.263
John Davis	5	1	1	0	0	1	0	.200	.400	.333	Ron Romanick	5	2	0	0	2	1	1	.400	1.600	.500
Storm Davis	9	1	0	0	0	0	2	.111	.111	.111	Jeff Russell	13	4	0	0	2	3	3	.308	.769	.438
Jose DeLeon	11	2	1	0	1	2	6	.182	.545	.308	Bret Saberhagen	37	9	0	0	1	2	8	.243	.324	.282
Ken Dixon	9	3	2	0	1	0	5	.333	.889	.333	Dave J. Schmidt	8	2	0	0	2	0	2	.250	1.000	.250
Richard Dotson	19	7	2	0	1	1	4	.368	.632	.429	Ken Schrom	13	3	2	0	1	0	0	.231	.385	.267
Mark Eichhorn	12	3	0	0	4	4	4	.250	.250	.438	Don Schulze	10	6	2	0	0	0	1	.600	.800	.600
Steve Farr	11	3	2	0	0	2	4	.273	.455	.385	Tom Seaver	6	1	0	0	0	0	1	.167	.167	.167
John Farrell	11	3	1	0	0	0	1	.273	.364	.273	Jeff Sellers	18	6	1	0	0	1	7	.333	.389	.400
Chuck Finley	9	5	3	0	1	1	1	.556	.889	.600	Steve Shields	8	0	0	0	0	0	2	.000	.000	.000
Mike Flanagan	14	2	0	0	0	2	1	.143	.143	.294	Bob Shirley	12	3	1	0	2	0	0	.250	.833	.231
Willie Fraser	8	3	1	0	2	0	3	.375	1.250	.375	Doug Sisk	7	2	1	0	0	0	1	.286	.429	.286
Wes Gardner	6	2	0	0	0	0	0	.333	.333	.333	Mike Smithson	18	2	0	0	1	2	4	.111	.278	.200
Mark Gubicza	24	4	2	0	0	4	10	.167	.250	.286	Nate Snell	8	0	0	0	0	0	2	.000	.000	.000
Lee Guetterman	6	4	0	0	1	0	0	.667	1.167	.667	Bob Stanley	17	8	2	0	1	3	3	.471	.588	.526
Ron Guidry	29	5	1	1	0	0	14	.172	.276	.172	Dave Stieb	21	9	6	0	2	1	6	.429	1.000	.458
Jose Guzman	23	9	0	0	3	3	7	.391	.783	.462	Tim Stoddard	8	0	0	0	0	1	3	.000	.000	.111
John Habyan	6	0	0	0	0	0	2	.000	.000	.000	Todd Stottlemyre	7	2	0	0	2	1	2	.286	1.143	.375
Greg A. Harris	10	0	0	0	0	0	7	.000	.000	.000	Don Sutton	8	0	0	0	0	0	4	.000	.000	.000
Brad Havens	8	2	1	0	1	0	2	.250	.750	.250	Bill Swift	9	1	0	0	0	1	2	.111	.111	.200
Tom Henke	9	3	1	0	1	1	4	.333	.778	.400	Greg Swindell	15	7	0	0	2	2	3	.467	.867	.529
Willie Hernandez	5	2	0	0	0	1	0	.400	.400	.571	Frank Tanana	22	7	2	0	0	1	6	.318	.409	.333
Ted Higuera	23	4	0	0	0	4	6	.174	.174	.323	Walt Terrell	24	9	1	1	1	4	6	.375	.625	.464
Ricky Horton	7	1	0	0	1	0	0	.143	.571	.143	Bobby Thigpen	9	1	0	0	0	0	5	.111	.111	.111
Charlie Hough	30	6	0	0	1	6	9	.200	.300	.333	Mark Thurmond	9	4	0	0	1	1	0	.444	.778	.444
Charles Hudson	9	2	0	0	1	0	1	.222	.556	.222	Jay Tibbs	13	6	2	0	1	0	4	.462	.846	.462
Mark Huismann	7	1	0	0	1	0	4	.143	.571	.143	Fred Toliver	5	2	0	0	0	0	0	.400	.400	.400
Bruce Hurst	23	4	1	0	3	0	9	.174	.609	.174	Steve Trout	8	3	0	1	0	1	0	.375	.625	.444
Danny Jackson	17	5	2	0	0	2	1	.294	.412	.368	Mike Trujillo	10	6	1	0	0	0	0	.600	.700	.600
Bob James	8	3	1	0	0	1	0	.375	.500	.364	Frank Viola	24	9	2	0	1	5	5	.375	.583	.483
Tommy John	22	6	3	0	0	0	4	.273	.409	.273	Bill Wegman	17	5	1	0	2	3	1	.294	.706	.400
Joe Johnson	10	4	1	0	1	0	0	.400	.800	.400	Mitch Williams	7	2	1	0	0	0	0	.286	.857	.286
Doug Jones	6	3	0	0	1	1	1	.500	1.000	.571	Mark Williamson	8	2	0	0	0	0	2	.250	.250	.333
Jimmy Key	16	7	0	0	0	2	3	.438	.438	.500	Bobby Witt	17	4	1	0	0	4	10	.235	.294	.381
Paul Kilgus	10	2	1	0	0	1	0	.200	.300	.273	Mike Witt	28	3	0	0	1	4	11	.107	.214	.235

Will Clark

Pitcher	AB	H	2B	3B	HR	BB	SO	BA	SA	OBA
Jim Acker	9	5	1	0	0	2	0	.556	.667	.636
Juan Agosto	10	1	0	0	0	1	2	.100	.100	.182
Rick Aguilera	13	4	1	0	2	2	1	.308	.846	.400
Doyle Alexander	12	2	0	0	1	0	2	.167	.417	.154
Jose Alvarez	6	0	0	0	0	3	3	.000	.000	.333
Larry Andersen	9	2	0	0	0	0	0	.222	.222	.222
Jack Armstrong	5	1	0	0	1	1	0	.200	.800	.333
Paul Assenmacher	8	6	2	0	0	1	0	.750	1.000	.778
Steve Bedrosian	7	2	0	0	1	0	1	.286	.714	.286
Tim Belcher	13	2	0	0	1	1	4	.154	.385	.214
Tom Browning	33	7	1	0	1	4	8	.212	.333	.293
Tim Burke	11	3	0	0	0	1	2	.273	.273	.333
Steve Carlton	6	1	0	0	0	0	2	.167	.167	.167
Don Carman	17	8	3	0	0	1	1	.471	.647	.500
Kevin Coffman	6	2	1	0	0	1	1	.333	.500	.429
David Cone	8	1	0	0	0	3	3	.125	.125	.364
Danny Cox	16	2	0	0	0	0	3	.125	.125	.125
Ron Darling	15	2	0	0	0	1	2	.133	.133	.188
Danny Darwin	18	6	1	0	1	2	4	.333	.556	.381
Mark Davis	9	5	2	0	0	0	1	.556	.778	.556
Storm Davis	6	1	0	0	0	0	1	.167	.167	.167
Ken Dayley	5	2	0	0	0	0	2	.400	.400	.400
Jose DeLeon	5	2	0	0	1	1	2	.400	1.000	.500
John Denny	6	1	0	0	0	0	0	.167	.167	.167
Jim Deshaies	19	6	2	0	1	3	3	.316	.579	.409
Doug Drabek	7	0	0	0	0	2	2	.000	.000	.200
Dave Dravecky	11	3	0	0	0	1	4	.273	.273	.308
Mike Dunne	13	4	2	0	0	1	0	.308	.462	.400
Sid Fernandez	9	2	2	0	0	0	3	.222	.444	.222
Bob Forsch	19	4	0	0	1	3	5	.211	.368	.304
John Franco	10	3	1	0	0	0	3	.300	.400	.300
Gene Garber	5	1	0	0	0	1	0	.200	.200	.333
Tom Glavine	7	1	0	0	0	1	1	.143	.143	.333
Dwight Gooden	22	4	1	0	0	2	9	.182	.227	.250
Mark Grant	7	2	0	0	1	1	0	.286	.714	.375
Kevin Gross	19	4	1	1	0	1	6	.211	.368	.250
Bill Gullickson	16	8	2	0	3	2	1	.500	1.188	.556
Andy Hawkins	23	9	3	0	2	3	3	.391	.783	.462
Jeff Heathcock	6	1	0	0	1	1	0	.167	.667	.286
Neal Heaton	10	2	1	0	1	0	1	.200	.600	.200
Orel Hershiser	28	5	0	0	0	3	12	.179	.179	.281
Joe Hesketh	7	2	0	0	0	0	3	.286	.286	.286
Guy Hoffman	8	4	1	0	0	0	1	.500	.625	.500
Rick Honeycutt	7	0	0	0	0	0	2	.000	.000	.000
Ricky Horton	6	1	0	0	0	1	2	.167	.167	.286
Danny Jackson	14	5	0	0	1	1	5	.357	.571	.400
Mike Jackson	5	2	0	0	0	0	0	.400	.400	.400
German Jimenez	5	1	1	0	0	1	0	.200	.400	.333
Barry Jones	5	0	0	0	0	2	0	.000	.000	.286
Jimmy Jones	9	4	2	0	0	0	1	.444	.667	.444
Bob Knepper	23	12	2	0	1	0	2	.522	.739	.522
Les Lancaster	9	2	0	0	0	1	1	.222	.222	.300
Bill Landrum	6	2	0	0	1	0	2	.333	.833	.333
Terry Leach	7	3	0	1	0	0	0	.429	.714	.429
Tim Leary	18	4	1	1	0	1	6	.222	.389	.263
Craig Lefferts	9	4	1	1	0	0	3	.444	.778	.444
Greg Maddux	11	5	1	0	1	3	1	.455	.818	.600
Joe Magrane	10	1	0	0	0	1	4	.100	.100	.167
Rick Mahler	36	12	4	0	0	3	7	.333	.444	.375
Dennis Martinez	16	3	2	0	0	4	5	.188	.313	.350
Lance McCullers	8	2	0	0	0	2	1	.250	.250	.364
Roger McDowell	9	2	1	0	0	0	1	.222	.333	.300
Andy McGaffigan	11	2	1	0	0	1	6	.182	.273	.250
Larry McWilliams	10	3	2	0	0	0	0	.300	.500	.300
Dave Meads	5	3	0	0	2	1	0	.600	1.800	.667
John Mitchell	5	2	0	0	0	0	0	.400	.400	.400
Jamie Moyer	15	2	0	0	0	1	3	.133	.133	.188
Rob Murphy	14	5	3	0	0	0	2	.357	.571	.357
Randy Myers	7	0	0	0	0	0	3	.000	.000	.000
Al Nipper	5	0	0	0	0	2	1	.000	.000	.286
Bob Ojeda	17	4	0	1	1	1	2	.235	.529	.278
Randy O'Neal	5	3	0	0	2	1	0	.600	1.800	.667
Jesse Orosco	8	2	0	0	0	1	2	.250	.250	.333
David Palmer	13	2	0	0	0	1	2	.154	.154	.214
Alejandro Pena	5	2	0	0	1	1	2	.400	1.000	.500
Pascual Perez	11	2	0	0	1	2	3	.182	.455	.308
Pat Perry	8	4	1	0	2	0	1	.500	1.375	.500
Dennis Powell	6	2	0	0	1	0	2	.333	.833	.333
Ted Power	6	3	0	0	2	2	0	.500	1.500	.625
Charlie Puleo	5	4	1	0	1	4	0	.800	1.600	.889
Dennis Rasmussen	12	3	0	1	0	0	0	.250	.417	.250
Shane Rawley	11	2	1	0	0	0	2	.182	.273	.182
Rick Reuschel	15	5	0	0	1	1	1	.333	.533	.375
Ron Robinson	13	8	1	1	1	3	0	.615	1.077	.688
Bruce Ruffin	9	3	1	0	0	2	2	.333	.444	.455
Nolan Ryan	36	12	2	0	6	3	12	.333	.889	.385
Scott Sanderson	8	2	0	1	0	1	0	.250	.500	.333
Mike Scott	28	8	2	0	3	6	4	.286	.679	.412
Eric Show	26	8	0	1	2	2	7	.308	.615	.357
John Smiley	13	0	0	0	0	0	5	.000	.000	.000
Bryn Smith	19	4	1	0	1	0	3	.211	.421	.211
Dave Smith	5	1	0	0	0	2	2	.200	.200	.375
Pete Smith	12	5	0	0	3	2	2	.417	1.167	.500
Zane Smith	13	4	0	0	0	0	1	.308	.308	.357
Mario Soto	10	7	0	1	2	2	0	.700	1.500	.750
Rick Sutcliffe	17	3	0	0	0	5	8	.176	.176	.364
Kent Tekulve	7	3	0	0	0	3	0	.429	.429	.600
Jay Tibbs	6	4	1	0	0	0	2	.667	.833	.667
Fred Toliver	5	1	0	0	0	0	2	.200	.200	.200
John Tudor	8	4	2	1	1	0	2	.500	1.375	.500
Fernando Valenzuela	35	11	4	0	0	3	8	.314	.429	.368
Ed Vande Berg	5	0	0	0	0	0	0	.000	.000	.000
Bob Walk	12	5	0	0	0	0	2	.417	.417	.462
Gene Walter	6	1	0	0	0	0	5	.167	.167	.167
Bob Welch	25	7	1	0	0	1	3	.280	.320	.308
Ed Whitson	20	9	2	0	2	1	3	.450	.850	.455
Ed Wojna	5	1	1	0	0	0	0	.200	.400	.333
Todd Worrell	8	4	1	0	1	2	2	.500	1.000	.600
Floyd Youmans	16	4	0	0	3	2	4	.250	.813	.333

Kirk Gibson

Pitcher	AB	H	2B	3B	HR	BB	SO	BA	SA	OBA
Don Aase	8	1	0	0	0	2	4	.125	.125	.300
Glenn Abbott	5	2	0	0	1	0	0	.400	1.000	.400
Jim Acker	11	3	0	0	1	2	2	.273	.545	.385
Juan Agosto	11	6	0	0	0	0	1	.545	.545	.545
Doyle Alexander	18	6	0	0	2	4	5	.333	.667	.455
Allan Anderson	9	3	0	0	0	1	1	.333	.333	.400
Bud Anderson	5	0	0	0	0	0	2	.000	.000	.000
Joaquin Andujar	15	5	0	0	3	1	0	.333	.933	.375
Mike Armstrong	7	1	0	0	0	1	4	.143	.143	.250
Paul Assenmacher	5	2	0	0	0	0	2	.400	.400	.500
Keith Atherton	9	1	1	0	0	0	6	.111	.222	.200
Scott Bailes	10	3	0	0	0	1	2	.300	.300	.364
Scott Bankhead	11	4	0	0	2	1	2	.364	.909	.417
Floyd Bannister	21	5	1	0	0	3	5	.238	.286	.360
Len Barker	17	6	2	1	0	1	3	.353	.588	.389
Salome Barojas	8	2	0	0	0	1	1	.250	.250	.300
Jim Beattie	18	4	0	0	1	0	3	.222	.389	.222
Joe Beckwith	7	2	0	1	0	0	0	.286	.571	.286
Rick Behenna	5	2	1	0	0	2	1	.400	.600	.571
Eric Bell	6	3	1	0	2	3	1	.500	1.667	.667
Tim Birtsas	12	2	1	1	0	2	4	.167	.417	.333
Bud Black	21	5	1	0	1	3	7	.238	.429	.360
Bert Blyleven	44	11	2	0	4	3	9	.250	.568	.306
Mike Boddicker	25	10	2	0	3	2	5	.400	.840	.444
Mark Bomback	6	1	0	0	0	1	1	.167	.167	.286
Rich Bordi	6	2	1	0	0	0	0	.333	.500	.333
Chris Bosio	9	3	2	0	1	3	1	.333	.889	.500
Oil Can Boyd	39	10	3	1	2	4	11	.256	.538	.318

Kirk Gibson continued

Pitcher	AB	H	2B	3B	HR	BB	SO	BA	SA	OBA
Tom Brennan	9	6	2	0	1	2	0	.667	1.222	.727
Mike G. Brown	8	6	1	0	2	1	1	.750	1.625	.778
Tom Browning	14	7	1	0	3	1	5	.500	1.214	.533
Tom Burgmeier	11	2	1	0	0	0	4	.182	.273	.182
Britt Burns	11	1	0	0	0	3	3	.091	.091	.267
Ray Burris	12	3	0	1	0	0	3	.250	.417	.357
John Butcher	24	8	1	0	3	1	5	.333	.750	.393
Mike Caldwell	20	3	0	0	0	0	2	.150	.150	.150
Ernie Camacho	7	1	1	0	0	2	1	.143	.286	.300
John Candelaria	6	0	0	0	0	2	5	.000	.000	.250
Tom Candiotti	10	5	0	1	1	2	1	.500	1.000	.583
Steve Carlton	5	2	1	0	0	0	1	.400	.600	.500
Don Carman	6	2	0	0	1	0	1	.333	.833	.286
Bill Caudill	9	0	0	0	0	2	5	.000	.000	.182
John Cerutti	9	2	0	0	1	2	1	.222	.556	.364
Jim Clancy	55	16	4	0	0	3	4	.291	.364	.322
Bryan Clark	11	3	1	0	1	0	2	.273	.636	.273
Mark Clear	14	9	1	0	1	1	0	.643	.929	.667
Roger Clemens	18	1	0	0	0	5	7	.056	.056	.250
Jaime Cocanower	11	1	0	0	0	1	2	.091	.091	.167
Chris Codiroli	26	4	1	0	0	0	6	.154	.192	.185
Steve Comer	8	3	0	0	0	0	1	.375	.375	.375
David Cone	7	1	0	0	0	0	5	.143	.143	.143
Tim Conroy	5	0	0	0	0	2	4	.000	.000	.286
Glen Cook	5	2	1	0	1	0	1	.400	1.200	.333
Doug Corbett	10	4	1	0	2	2	0	.400	1.100	.500
Ed Correa	8	2	1	0	0	2	3	.250	.375	.400
Joe Cowley	6	2	0	0	1	1	2	.333	.833	.429
Steve Crawford	7	2	1	0	1	2	2	.286	.857	.444
Ron Darling	6	1	1	0	0	1	4	.167	.333	.286
Danny Darwin	40	9	2	1	1	1	6	.225	.400	.244
Mark Davis	9	1	0	0	0	2	2	.111	.111	.111
Ron Davis	20	7	0	1	2	2	6	.350	.750	.409
Storm Davis	18	3	0	0	1	2	3	.167	.333	.250
Jose DeLeon	14	5	0	0	1	1	3	.357	.571	.400
Jim Deshaies	5	1	0	0	1	1	0	.200	.800	.333
Frank DiPino	6	1	0	0	0	0	1	.167	.167	.167
Ken Dixon	10	2	0	0	1	6	5	.200	.500	.500
John Dopson	9	3	1	0	1	2	0	.333	.778	.455
Richard Dotson	25	8	0	2	1	8	6	.320	.600	.500
Kelly Downs	6	0	0	0	0	2	2	.000	.000	.250
Doug Drabek	12	3	0	0	1	1	1	.250	.357	.357
Mike Dunne	7	3	0	0	0	2	0	.429	.429	.556
Jamie Easterly	13	4	2	0	0	0	4	.308	.462	.308
Dennis Eckersley	30	7	1	2	1	6	1	.233	.500	.378
Steve Farr	8	1	0	0	0	2	2	.125	.125	.300
Sid Fernandez	6	2	0	0	0	3	3	.333	.333	.333
Pete Filson	7	1	0	0	1	1	3	.143	.571	.250
Rollie Fingers	7	1	0	0	0	0	1	.143	.143	.143
Chuck Finley	10	3	1	0	0	0	1	.300	.400	.300
Brian Fisher	7	1	0	0	0	1	3	.143	.143	.250
Mike Flanagan	36	9	1	0	1	3	12	.250	.361	.325
Ray Fontenot	7	1	0	0	0	1	3	.143	.143	.333
Ken Forsch	13	2	0	0	0	2	1	.154	.154	.267
John Franco	5	2	1	0	0	1	2	.400	.600	.500
George Frazier	8	1	0	0	1	1	1	.125	.500	.222
Bob L. Gibson	10	2	0	0	0	1	2	.200	.200	.273
Tom Glavine	12	6	0	0	1	2	4	.500	.750	.533
Jerry Don Gleaton	5	1	0	0	0	0	1	.200	.200	.200
Dwight Gooden	12	3	0	0	1	0	5	.250	.500	.250
Rich Gossage	9	1	0	0	0	1	7	.111	.111	.200
Jim Gott	10	1	0	0	1	1	2	.100	.400	.182
Mike Griffin	5	0	0	0	0	1	2	.000	.000	.167
Kevin Gross	8	3	2	0	0	2	1	.375	.625	.500
Mark Gubicza	14	4	0	1	0	3	3	.286	.429	.389
Lee Guetterman	5	0	0	0	0	1	1	.000	.000	.167
Ron Guidry	26	6	1	0	2	3	9	.231	.500	.310
Larry Gura	13	2	0	0	1	1	4	.154	.385	.214
Jose Guzman	11	2	0	0	0	1	3	.182	.182	.250
Moose Haas	22	4	0	1	0	4	5	.182	.273	.296
John Habyan	11	3	0	0	0	0	0	.273	.273	.273
Greg A. Harris	9	4	0	0	1	5	1	.444	.778	.643
Brad Havens	12	2	1	0	0	1	5	.167	.250	.231
Andy Hawkins	10	3	1	0	0	0	1	.300	.400	.300
Neal Heaton	27	9	2	1	1	4	1	.333	.593	.419
Ted Higuera	17	6	2	0	1	2	5	.353	.647	.429
Rick Honeycutt	14	4	0	0	1	0	3	.286	.500	.286
Burt Hooton	10	4	1	0	1	0	2	.400	.800	.400
Charlie Hough	33	8	2	1	1	8	11	.242	.455	.405
Jay Howell	8	2	0	0	1	1	3	.250	.625	.400
LaMarr Hoyt	21	7	0	2	2	0	5	.333	.810	.333
Mark Huismann	5	1	0	0	0	0	2	.200	.200	.200
Bruce Hurst	26	9	0	0	1	2	6	.346	.462	.393
Danny Jackson	29	5	1	0	0	3	10	.172	.207	.242
Roy Lee Jackson	5	0	0	0	0	1	2	.000	.000	.167
Mike Jeffcoat	5	0	0	0	0	0	1	.000	.000	.000
Ferguson Jenkins	6	3	1	0	1	1	0	.500	1.167	.571
Tommy John	23	8	0	0	0	3	3	.348	.348	.423
John Henry Johnson	14	4	1	0	1	0	4	.286	.571	.286
Jeff A. Jones	5	0	0	0	0	0	1	.000	.000	.000
Mike Jones	10	6	1	0	2	3	0	.600	1.300	.643
Odell Jones	5	3	1	0	1	1	1	.600	1.400	.667
Curt Kaufman	7	3	0	0	2	0	2	.429	1.286	.429
Matt Keough	17	4	0	0	3	0	4	.235	.765	.235
Jimmy Key	24	2	0	0	0	4	9	.083	.083	.214
Bruce Kison	19	8	0	0	0	3	1	.421	.421	.500
Bob Knepper	9	1	1	0	0	1	4	.111	.222	.182
Jerry Koosman	11	5	0	1	0	0	3	.455	.636	.455
Bill Krueger	6	3	0	0	0	1	1	.500	.500	.571
Mike Krukow	5	1	0	0	0	1	1	.200	.200	.333
Pete Ladd	9	1	0	0	0	0	1	.111	.111	.111
Dennis Lamp	16	3	0	1	0	4	2	.188	.313	.333
Les Lancaster	6	3	0	0	2	0	1	.500	1.500	.500
Rick Langford	19	6	0	0	1	1	4	.316	.474	.350
Mark Langston	16	2	1	0	0	2	7	.125	.188	.222
Gary Lavelle	6	1	0	0	0	1	2	.167	.167	.286
Luis Leal	26	6	1	0	3	4	6	.231	.615	.313
Tim Leary	8	1	0	0	0	0	1	.125	.125	.125
Craig Lefferts	5	1	1	0	0	0	1	.200	.400	.200
Charlie Leibrandt	12	6	2	0	1	0	1	.500	.917	.500
Dave Leiper	5	1	0	0	1	0	1	.200	.200	.200
Dennis Leonard	21	9	1	1	2	1	4	.429	.857	.435
Randy Lerch	16	5	1	0	0	1	4	.313	.375	.353
Tim Lollar	6	1	0	0	0	0	5	.167	.167	.286
Gary Lucas	5	1	1	0	0	2	3	.200	.400	.429
Rick Lysander	10	2	0	0	1	0	1	.200	.500	.200
Greg Maddux	7	2	1	0	0	1	2	.286	.429	.375
Rick Mahler	17	5	0	0	0	2	4	.294	.294	.400
Dennis Martinez	43	14	2	1	0	5	7	.326	.419	.396
Tippy Martinez	18	5	0	0	1	0	4	.278	.444	.278
Mike Mason	7	2	0	0	0	3	1	.286	.286	.500
Jon Matlack	11	3	0	0	2	0	4	.273	.818	.273
Rudy May	8	2	0	0	1	0	1	.250	.625	.250
Kirk McCaskill	16	9	1	0	4	6	4	.563	1.375	.682
Steve McCatty	19	8	2	0	1	3	1	.421	.684	.500
Bob McClure	6	1	0	0	0	0	3	.167	.167	.375
Scott McGregor	36	14	3	0	4	0	7	.389	.806	.421
Joey McLaughlin	8	1	0	0	0	2	2	.125	.125	.300
Dale Mohorcic	5	2	1	0	0	0	0	.400	.600	.400
Sid Monge	6	3	1	0	0	0	2	.500	.667	.500
Donnie Moore	5	1	0	0	0	0	2	.200	.200	.200
Mike Moore	36	8	1	0	3	3	6	.222	.500	.300
Mike Morgan	6	2	0	0	0	1	1	.333	.333	.429
Jamie Moyer	10	4	1	0	0	0	1	.400	.500	.400
Rob Murphy	7	2	0	0	0	0	2	.286	.286	.286
Dale Murray	5	2	1	0	0	0	0	.400	.600	.500
Gene Nelson	14	4	1	0	0	0	4	.286	.357	.267
Joe Niekro	11	2	1	0	0	3	2	.182	.273	.357
Phil Niekro	26	12	3	0	4	2	1	.462	1.038	.483
Scott Nielsen	5	2	0	0	0	1	0	.400	.400	.500
Juan Nieves	16	5	0	0	0	0	4	.313	.313	.313
Al Nipper	27	7	1	0	1	1	4	.259	.407	.286
Dickie Noles	6	1	0	0	0	5	0	.167	.167	.545
Mike Norris	17	3	0	0	0	2	5	.176	.176	.300
Edwin Nunez	5	0	0	0	0	1	1	.000	.000	.167
Bob Ojeda	22	4	1	0	0	0	10	.182	.227	.217
Randy O'Neal	7	3	1	0	0	0	1	.429	.571	.429
Steve Ontiveros	8	6	0	0	2	0	1	.750	1.500	.750
Bob Owchinko	5	0	0	0	0	2	2	.000	.000	.000
Jim Palmer	17	4	0	0	0	1	7	.235	.235	.263

Kirk Gibson continued

Pitcher	AB	H	2B	3B	HR	BB	SO	BA	SA	OBA
Gaylord Perry	8	2	0	0	0	0	0	.250	.250	.250
Eric Plunk	5	2	0	0	1	1	1	.400	1.000	.500
Chuck Porter	10	4	0	0	2	3	0	.400	1.000	.538
Dan Quisenberry	24	6	0	0	2	3	3	.250	.500	.321
Chuck Rainey	5	2	0	0	0	2	0	.400	.400	.571
Dennis Rasmussen	27	7	0	0	1	2	5	.259	.370	.333
Shane Rawley	9	2	0	0	0	2	4	.222	.222	.333
Pete Redfern	17	6	1	0	1	1	5	.353	.588	.389
Steve Renko	10	3	1	0	0	1	1	.300	.400	.364
Rick Rhoden	7	3	1	0	1	0	0	.429	1.000	.429
Dave Righetti	15	4	0	0	1	1	5	.267	.467	.353
Jose Rijo	20	3	1	0	0	4	8	.150	.280	.280
Don Robinson	5	3	0	0	0	1	2	.600	.600	.667
Ron Robinson	5	1	0	0	0	1	2	.200	.200	.429
Ron Romanick	8	4	1	1	1	0	0	.500	1.250	.500
Bruce Ruffin	7	2	0	0	0	1	2	.286	.286	.375
Jeff Russell	6	3	0	0	0	0	1	.500	.500	.500
Nolan Ryan	12	3	1	0	1	3	4	.250	.583	.400
Bret Saberhagen	32	4	0	0	0	2	16	.125	.125	.176
Joe Sambito	7	2	1	0	0	1	0	.286	.429	.375
Luis Sanchez	9	2	1	0	0	1	1	.222	.333	.300
Calvin Schiraldi	12	3	0	0	1	0	3	.250	.500	.250
Dave J. Schmidt	10	2	0	0	0	1	5	.200	.200	.273
Ken Schrom	29	5	2	0	1	5	4	.172	.345	.294
Don Schulze	9	4	0	0	2	0	1	.444	1.111	.444
Mike Scott	13	3	0	0	1	2	3	.231	.462	.333
Ray Searage	5	1	0	0	0	4	1	.200	.200	.556
Tom Seaver	21	7	0	0	2	4	3	.333	.619	.440
Bob Shirley	16	3	0	0	1	0	5	.188	.375	.188
Eric Show	7	1	0	0	0	2	3	.143	.143	.364
Jim Slaton	15	4	1	0	1	2	2	.267	.533	.333
John Smiley	5	0	0	0	0	3	0	.000	.000	.375
Roy Smith	11	5	1	0	0	4	2	.455	.545	.600
Zane Smith	6	1	0	0	0	0	2	.167	.167	.167
Mike Smithson	18	7	2	0	1	1	5	.389	.667	.450
Nate Snell	7	2	0	0	0	0	0	.286	.286	.286
Lary Sorensen	20	6	0	1	0	0	2	.300	.400	.300
Dan Spillner	13	5	2	0	0	3	2	.385	.538	.500
Paul Splittorff	6	1	0	1	0	1	2	.167	.500	.286
Bob Stanley	16	6	2	2	0	0	0	.375	.750	.375
Dave Stewart	7	3	1	0	0	3	1	.429	.571	.600
Sammy Stewart	21	6	1	0	1	4	4	.286	.476	.400
Dave Stieb	46	11	1	0	2	6	13	.239	.391	.327
Bob Stoddard	6	2	1	0	0	2	2	.333	.500	.500
Tim Stoddard	6	0	0	0	0	0	1	.000	.000	.000
Steve Stone	6	1	0	0	1	2	1	.167	.667	.375
Les Straker	5	2	0	1	0	0	1	.400	.800	.400
Rick Sutcliffe	25	7	1	1	1	4	4	.280	.520	.379
Don Sutton	30	7	0	1	1	1	7	.233	.400	.281
Bill Swaggerty	7	4	2	0	0	0	0	.571	.857	.571
Frank Tanana	14	3	0	0	0	0	7	.214	.214	.267
Roy Thomas	8	1	0	0	0	2	1	.125	.125	.231
Mike Torrez	20	7	4	0	0	0	1	.350	.550	.350
Mike Trujillo	5	1	0	0	0	0	1	.200	.200	.200
John Tudor	18	7	2	0	2	0	4	.389	.833	.389
Tom Underwood	16	4	0	0	1	1	7	.250	.438	.294
Ed Vande Berg	15	2	0	0	0	3	1	.133	.133	.278
Frank Viola	18	3	1	0	1	1	5	.167	.389	.250
Pete Vuckovich	17	6	2	0	0	3	2	.353	.471	.450
Tom Waddell	9	1	0	0	0	2	1	.111	.111	.273
Rick Waits	11	3	0	1	0	1	2	.273	.455	.333
Bob Walk	7	0	0	0	0	1	0	.000	.000	.125
Curt Wardle	6	0	0	0	0	0	4	.000	.000	.000
Bill Wegman	20	7	0	0	3	1	1	.350	.800	.409
Ed Whitson	5	0	0	0	0	1	0	.000	.000	.167
Al Williams	16	1	0	0	0	0	3	.063	.063	.063
Mitch Williams	6	1	0	0	0	2	5	.167	.167	.375
Frank Wills	7	3	1	0	0	1	0	.429	.571	.500
Bobby Witt	6	1	0	0	0	1	3	.167	.167	.286
Mike Witt	38	12	1	0	0	4	8	.316	.342	.395
Rob Woodward	7	3	1	1	0	0	1	.429	.857	.429
Rich Yett	9	4	1	0	2	1	3	.444	1.222	.500
Curt Young	14	3	2	0	0	2	4	.214	.357	.353
Matt Young	8	1	1	0	0	0	4	.125	.250	.125
Geoff Zahn	9	3	0	0	0	0	1	.333	.333	.333

Mike Greenwell

Pitcher	AB	H	2B	3B	HR	BB	SO	BA	SA	OBA
Doyle Alexander	19	5	1	1	1	0	2	.263	.579	.263
Neil Allen	12	4	2	0	1	1	2	.333	.750	.385
Allan Anderson	5	1	0	0	0	0	0	.200	.200	.200
Joaquin Andujar	6	2	0	0	1	1	0	.333	.833	.429
Keith Atherton	6	3	1	1	1	3	0	.500	1.500	.667
Don August	6	1	0	0	0	1	0	.167	.167	.286
Scott Bailes	6	3	1	0	0	1	0	.500	.667	.571
Jeff Ballard	7	5	3	0	0	0	0	.714	1.143	.714
Scott Bankhead	18	7	4	0	1	0	3	.389	.778	.421
Floyd Bannister	8	1	0	0	0	0	1	.125	.125	.125
Jose Bautista	9	6	1	1	2	1	0	.667	1.667	.700
Juan Berenguer	8	1	1	0	0	6	0	.125	.250	.467
Bud Black	5	2	0	0	1	0	1	.400	1.000	.400
Bert Blyleven	12	5	1	0	0	2	2	.417	.500	.500
Chris Bosio	8	4	2	1	0	1	0	.500	1.000	.600
Mike Campbell	5	4	0	0	2	0	0	.800	2.000	.800
Tom Candiotti	15	4	1	0	1	1	0	.267	.533	.313
Jim Clancy	12	5	0	0	1	1	1	.417	.667	.462
Terry Clark	7	3	0	1	0	0	0	.429	.714	.429
John Davis	5	1	0	0	0	1	0	.200	.200	.333
Storm Davis	6	1	0	0	0	3	0	.167	.167	.444
Jose DeLeon	11	2	0	0	0	1	1	.182	.182	.250
Richard Dotson	11	2	0	0	0	1	1	.182	.182	.250
Dennis Eckersley	8	2	0	0	0	0	0	.250	.250	.333
Mark Eichhorn	8	2	1	0	0	0	1	.250	.375	.250
John Farrell	12	4	0	2	0	0	1	.333	.667	.333
Chuck Finley	12	6	0	0	0	0	0	.500	.500	.500
Mike Flanagan	7	2	0	0	0	2	0	.286	.286	.444
Paul Gibson	6	3	1	0	0	0	0	.500	.667	.500
Don Gordon	5	1	0	0	0	0	0	.200	.200	.200
Mark Gubicza	19	7	1	2	0	0	1	.368	.632	.368
Jose Guzman	10	2	0	0	1	1	1	.200	.500	.273
John Habyan	6	3	0	0	0	1	1	.500	.500	.571
Greg A. Harris	6	2	1	0	1	1	1	.333	1.000	.429
Mike Henneman	5	0	0	0	0	0	0	.000	.000	.000
Willie Hernandez	7	3	1	0	1	1	1	.429	1.000	.500
Ted Higuera	15	3	1	0	0	0	1	.200	.267	.235
Ricky Horton	6	3	0	0	0	0	0	.500	.500	.500
Charlie Hough	11	1	0	0	0	7	0	.091	.091	.444
Charles Hudson	15	3	1	0	1	1	1	.200	.267	.294
Mark Huismann	5	1	0	0	1	0	0	.200	.800	.200
Paul Kilgus	6	2	0	0	0	0	0	.333	.333	.429
Eric King	5	1	0	0	0	2	0	.200	.200	.429
Mark Langston	10	4	1	0	0	1	1	.400	.500	.455
Dave LaPoint	12	4	2	0	0	1	1	.333	.500	.385
Charlie Lea	7	3	1	0	1	0	0	.429	1.000	.429
Charlie Leibrandt	7	3	1	0	0	0	0	.429	.571	.429
Bill Long	10	5	1	2	0	0	0	.500	1.000	.500
Jack McDowell	6	2	0	0	1	1	0	.333	.833	.429
Jose Mesa	7	1	0	0	0	0	1	.143	.143	.143
Paul Mirabella	6	2	0	0	0	0	0	.333	.333	.333
Mike Moore	6	4	3	0	0	0	0	.667	1.167	.667
Jack Morris	14	4	0	0	1	4	2	.286	.500	.444
Jeff Musselman	8	2	1	0	0	0	0	.250	.375	.250
Juan Nieves	12	0	0	0	0	0	2	.000	.000	.000
Steve Ontiveros	9	2	0	0	1	1	1	.222	.556	.300
Dan Petry	11	1	0	0	0	0	3	.091	.091	.083
Mark Portugal	6	2	0	0	0	2	0	.333	.333	.500
Jerry Reed	7	1	0	0	0	0	0	.143	.143	.143
Rick Rhoden	8	3	0	1	0	1	0	.375	.750	.444
Dave Righetti	7	3	1	0	1	0	1	.429	1.000	.429
Jose Rijo	8	3	1	0	0	0	1	.375	.500	.444

Mike Greenwell continued

Pitcher	AB	H	2B	3B	HR	BB	SO	BA	SA	OBA
Jeff M. Robinson	12	4	3	0	0	1	1	.333	.583	.385
Jeff Russell	6	4	0	0	2	2	0	.667	1.667	.750
Bret Saberhagen	13	3	0	0	1	2	2	.231	.462	.313
Dan Schatzeder	5	2	0	0	0	0	1	.400	.400	.400
Dave J. Schmidt	10	5	0	0	2	1	0	.500	1.100	.545
Doug Sisk	7	2	0	0	0	1	0	.286	.286	.375
Dave Stewart	19	6	3	0	0	4	1	.316	.474	.435
Dave Stieb	7	4	2	0	0	3	1	.571	.857	.700
Les Straker	10	4	0	1	2	0	1	.400	1.200	.400
Bill Swift	6	2	0	0	0	1	0	.333	.333	.429
Walt Terrell	12	3	1	0	0	2	2	.250	.333	.357
Bobby Thigpen	5	2	0	0	0	0	1	.400	.400	.400
Jay Tibbs	7	3	0	0	1	0	1	.429	.857	.429
Frank Viola	13	3	0	0	0	1	0	.231	.231	.286
Bill Wegman	12	6	2	0	1	4	0	.500	.917	.625
Bill Wilkinson	5	0	0	0	0	0	0	.000	.000	.000
Mark Williamson	13	6	1	0	0	0	0	.462	.538	.462
Bobby Witt	8	2	0	0	0	5	1	.250	.250	.538
Mike Witt	18	4	1	0	0	1	2	.222	.278	.263
Rich Yett	12	4	0	1	0	0	0	.333	.500	.385

Kirby Puckett

Pitcher	AB	H	2B	3B	HR	BB	SO	BA	SA	OBA
Don Aase	9	3	0	0	0	1	1	.333	.333	.400
Jim Acker	5	2	0	0	0	0	0	.400	.400	.400
Darrel Akerfelds	8	5	1	0	2	1	0	.625	1.500	.667
Doyle Alexander	43	14	1	1	3	3	4	.326	.605	.383
Joaquin Andujar	5	2	1	1	0	3	0	.400	1.000	.625
Luis Aquino	6	1	1	0	0	1	0	.167	.333	.286
Mike Armstrong	7	3	0	0	1	0	3	.429	.857	.429
Keith Atherton	8	2	0	0	0	0	2	.250	.250	.250
Don August	5	0	0	0	0	0	3	.000	.000	.000
Scott Bailes	6	5	3	0	0	1	0	.833	1.333	.857
Doug Bair	15	4	1	0	0	0	3	.267	.333	.267
Jeff Ballard	6	4	0	0	0	0	0	.667	.667	.667
Scott Bankhead	9	4	0	0	0	0	2	.444	.444	.444
Floyd Bannister	36	11	0	0	2	0	4	.306	.472	.306
Len Barker	6	4	0	0	2	0	0	.667	1.667	.667
Salome Barojas	11	1	0	0	0	1	2	.091	.091	.167
Jim Beattie	12	7	1	1	0	1	1	.583	.833	.615
Joe Beckwith	7	4	0	1	0	0	0	.571	.857	.571
Eric Bell	10	3	0	0	0	1	1	.300	.300	.364
Mike Birkbeck	9	7	2	1	0	0	0	.778	1.222	.778
Bud Black	21	6	0	0	1	2	2	.286	.429	.348
Bert Blyleven	12	4	0	1	0	0	1	.333	.500	.333
Mike Boddicker	43	11	2	0	0	1	14	.256	.302	.273
Rich Bordi	6	1	0	0	0	0	0	.167	.167	.167
Chris Bosio	15	4	1	0	0	0	0	.267	.333	.250
Oil Can Boyd	24	9	2	1	1	2	1	.375	.667	.423
Mike G. Brown	6	1	0	0	0	0	2	.167	.333	.167
Britt Burns	18	8	2	0	0	0	4	.444	.556	.444
Ray Burris	14	4	0	0	1	0	3	.286	.500	.286
Marty Bystrom	6	2	0	0	0	1	1	.333	.333	.429
Mike Caldwell	11	5	2	1	0	0	0	.455	.818	.455
Ernie Camacho	6	3	0	0	0	0	1	.500	.500	.500
John Candelaria	22	2	1	0	0	4	6	.091	.136	.222
Tom Candiotti	29	8	3	0	0	0	2	.276	.379	.267
John Cerutti	12	3	0	0	1	0	1	.250	.500	.250
Jim Clancy	45	9	1	0	1	1	5	.200	.289	.217
Mark Clear	7	1	0	0	0	0	2	.143	.143	.125
Roger Clemens	43	11	2	1	0	1	12	.256	.349	.273
Stu Cliburn	6	1	0	0	0	0	2	.167	.167	.143
Jaime Cocanower	11	7	0	0	0	2	1	.636	.636	.692
Chris Codiroli	20	3	1	0	0	1	3	.150	.200	.190
Steve Comer	7	3	1	0	0	0	0	.429	.571	.429
Doug Corbett	8	3	0	0	0	0	1	.375	.375	.375
Ed Correa	8	5	1	0	1	0	2	.625	1.125	.625
Joe Cowley	20	2	0	0	0	1	9	.100	.100	.143
Steve Crawford	12	6	0	0	0	1	2	.500	.500	.538
Chuck Crim	12	6	3	0	0	0	2	.500	.750	.500
Danny Darwin	24	3	0	0	0	0	4	.125	.125	.120
Joel Davis	16	5	3	0	1	1	2	.313	.688	.353
Storm Davis	22	9	0	0	0	2	3	.409	.409	.458
Jose DeLeon	13	7	1	0	2	0	2	.538	1.077	.538
Ken Dixon	19	7	1	0	2	1	2	.368	.737	.400
Richard Dotson	28	10	1	2	0	3	6	.357	.536	.419
Doug Drabek	5	1	1	0	0	0	1	.200	.400	.200
Jamie Easterly	10	3	1	0	0	0	1	.300	.400	.300
Dennis Eckersley	5	0	0	0	0	0	1	.000	.000	.000
Mark Eichhorn	17	3	0	0	0	0	2	.176	.176	.176
Steve Farr	16	3	1	0	0	0	4	.188	.250	.176
John Farrell	14	5	1	0	0	0	2	.357	.429	.357
Chuck Finley	7	4	2	0	0	2	1	.571	.857	.667
Brian Fisher	11	3	0	0	0	1	3	.273	.273	.333
Mike Flanagan	27	8	0	0	2	2	4	.296	.519	.345
Ray Fontenot	5	0	0	0	0	0	0	.000	.000	.000
Willie Fraser	9	1	0	0	0	0	6	.111	.111	.100
Wes Gardner	11	4	2	0	1	1	1	.364	.818	.417
Bob L. Gibson	6	0	0	0	0	1	3	.000	.000	.143
Mark Gubicza	52	14	0	1	1	3	6	.269	.365	.321
Lee Guetterman	8	5	2	0	0	0	0	.625	.875	.667
Ron Guidry	23	4	0	1	0	1	2	.174	.261	.240
Jose Guzman	25	9	3	0	0	1	2	.360	.480	.385
Moose Haas	19	4	1	0	0	0	4	.211	.263	.211
Greg A. Harris	10	3	1	0	1	1	1	.300	.700	.364
Neal Heaton	26	8	2	0	0	0	1	.308	.385	.308
Tom Henke	11	3	2	0	0	2	1	.273	.455	.385
Willie Hernandez	8	4	0	0	1	1	0	.500	.875	.556
Ted Higuera	26	9	0	1	2	1	3	.346	.654	.370
Shawn Hillegas	7	1	1	0	0	0	1	.143	.286	.143
Charlie Hough	52	16	2	0	0	3	5	.308	.346	.357
Jay Howell	5	1	0	0	0	0	1	.200	.200	.200
LaMarr Hoyt	8	2	0	1	0	0	1	.250	.500	.250
Charles Hudson	6	1	0	0	0	0	1	.167	.167	.167
Mark Huismann	7	2	0	0	0	1	2	.286	.286	.375
Bruce Hurst	26	15	1	0	1	3	4	.577	.731	.621
Danny Jackson	32	12	4	1	0	1	3	.375	.563	.382
Roy Lee Jackson	5	0	0	0	0	0	0	.000	.000	.000
Bob James	8	0	0	0	0	0	2	.000	.000	.000
Tommy John	30	6	0	0	0	0	0	.200	.200	.200
Joe Johnson	6	2	0	0	0	0	0	.333	.333	.333
John Henry Johnson	9	3	0	0	0	0	4	.333	.333	.333
Odell Jones	6	2	1	0	1	0	0	.333	1.000	.333
Jimmy Key	14	4	0	0	1	0	2	.286	.500	.333
Paul Kilgus	11	2	0	0	0	1	0	.182	.182	.250
Eric King	9	3	1	0	0	0	2	.333	.444	.333
Bruce Kison	7	2	0	0	0	0	0	.286	.286	.375
Bill Krueger	12	3	1	0	0	0	1	.250	.333	.250
Pete Ladd	6	1	0	0	0	0	1	.167	.167	.167
Dennis Lamp	25	8	1	1	0	1	0	.320	.440	.346
Mark Langston	28	10	0	1	1	1	4	.357	.536	.379
Dave LaPoint	15	2	0	0	1	0	0	.133	.333	.133
Jack Lazorko	8	1	0	0	0	0	0	.125	.125	.125
Luis Leal	9	2	0	0	0	0	2	.222	.222	.300
Tim Leary	9	4	1	0	0	0	1	.444	.556	.444
Charlie Leibrandt	48	14	1	1	2	2	5	.292	.479	.320
Tim Lollar	7	2	0	1	0	0	2	.286	.571	.286
Bill Long	8	3	1	0	0	1	1	.375	.500	.444
Aurelio Lopez	6	1	0	0	0	0	1	.167	.167	.167
Dennis Martinez	10	4	0	0	0	0	0	.400	.400	.400
Mike Mason	23	3	0	0	0	0	5	.130	.130	.130
Kirk McCaskill	25	6	1	0	1	0	3	.240	.400	.240
Steve McCatty	10	1	1	0	0	0	0	.100	.200	.100
Bob McClure	7	2	1	0	0	1	0	.286	.429	.375
Jack McDowell	5	2	0	0	0	0	0	.400	.400	.500
Scott McGregor	26	11	4	1	1	1	1	.423	.769	.444
Dale Mohorcic	11	1	0	0	0	1	0	.091	.091	.167
Donnie Moore	11	4	0	0	1	2	4	.364	.636	.462
Mike Moore	43	17	3	0	2	1	7	.395	.605	.409

Kirby Puckett continued

Pitcher	AB	H	2B	3B	HR	BB	SO	BA	SA	OBA	Pitcher	AB	H	2B	3B	HR	BB	SO	BA	SA	OBA
Mike Morgan	27	11	0	0	3	3	2	.407	.741	.484	Steve Shields	6	5	0	0	2	0	0	.833	1.833	.833
Jack Morris	38	11	1	0	1	2	6	.289	.395	.317	Bob Shirley	7	4	1	0	0	1	0	.571	.714	.625
Gene Nelson	22	4	0	0	0	2	7	.182	.182	.250	Jim Slaton	22	7	2	0	0	0	1	.318	.409	.348
Phil Niekro	18	3	0	0	0	0	3	.167	.167	.167	Roy Smith	5	3	0	0	0	0	0	.600	.600	.600
Scott Nielsen	7	3	1	0	1	1	0	.429	1.000	.500	Nate Snell	8	2	0	0	0	1	1	.250	.250	.333
Juan Nieves	21	13	2	1	1	1	2	.619	.952	.636	Dan Spillner	8	3	0	0	0	0	0	.375	.375	.375
Al Nipper	12	5	0	0	1	2	3	.417	.667	.500	Bob Stanley	18	7	1	1	0	0	0	.389	.556	.421
Edwin Nunez	11	2	1	0	0	0	2	.182	.273	.182	Dave Stewart	38	12	2	0	0	0	4	.316	.368	.325
Bryan Oelkers	5	0	0	0	0	0	1	.000	.000	.000	Sammy Stewart	6	5	1	0	0	2	0	.833	1.000	.875
Bob Ojeda	12	6	0	1	0	0	1	.500	.667	.500	Dave Stieb	46	10	1	0	0	1	12	.217	.239	.250
Randy O'Neal	13	4	1	1	0	0	1	.308	.538	.286	Tim Stoddard	10	3	0	0	1	0	2	.300	.600	.364
Steve Ontiveros	8	3	0	0	0	0	0	.375	.375	.375	Don Sutton	33	11	0	0	2	1	3	.333	.515	.371
Oswaldo Peraza	6	3	0	0	1	0	1	.500	1.000	.500	Bill Swift	18	5	0	0	0	1	2	.278	.278	.316
Melido Perez	14	7	0	0	0	0	0	.500	.500	.500	Greg Swindell	25	10	3	1	0	0	6	.400	.600	.400
Dan Petry	25	6	1	0	2	1	6	.240	.520	.296	Frank Tanana	33	13	3	0	2	1	0	.394	.667	.400
Dan Plesac	6	1	0	0	1	0	2	.167	.667	.167	Tom Tellmann	7	4	0	0	0	0	0	.571	.571	.571
Eric Plunk	7	4	1	0	1	1	1	.571	1.143	.600	Walt Terrell	40	11	3	1	2	2	4	.275	.550	.310
Dan Quisenberry	13	2	0	0	0	0	0	.154	.154	.154	Bobby Thigpen	5	1	0	0	0	0	1	.200	.200	.200
Dennis Rasmussen	27	9	1	0	1	2	7	.333	.481	.379	Mike Trujillo	11	3	1	0	1	1	0	.273	.636	.333
Rick Rhoden	17	6	1	0	2	1	2	.353	.765	.389	Ed Vande Berg	10	2	0	0	0	0	2	.200	.200	.200
Dave Righetti	9	5	2	0	0	1	1	.556	.778	.600	Tom Waddell	5	0	0	0	0	0	0	.000	.000	.000
Jose Rijo	11	3	0	0	1	1	3	.273	.545	.333	Duane Ward	5	3	1	1	0	0	1	.600	1.200	.600
Jeff M. Robinson	11	2	0	0	0	0	2	.182	.182	.182	Bill Wegman	25	6	1	0	1	1	5	.240	.400	.269
Ron Romanick	7	6	1	0	1	0	0	.857	1.429	.857	Bob Welch	13	8	2	0	1	0	1	.615	.769	.643
Dave Rozema	5	1	0	0	0	0	0	.200	.200	.200	Ed Whitson	11	8	1	0	0	0	0	.727	.818	.727
Vern Ruhle	10	5	1	0	1	0	0	.500	.900	.500	Milt Wilcox	14	7	1	0	0	0	0	.500	.571	.500
Jeff Russell	16	4	0	0	0	3	3	.250	.250	.368	Mitch Williams	6	0	0	0	0	0	0	.000	.000	.000
Bret Saberhagen	38	16	2	1	1	0	3	.421	.605	.436	Frank Wills	8	4	1	0	1	0	1	.500	1.000	.500
Luis Sanchez	9	3	0	0	0	0	1	.333	.333	.333	Bobby Witt	24	5	1	0	0	1	9	.208	.250	.240
Calvin Schiraldi	7	1	0	0	0	0	4	.143	.143	.143	Mike Witt	38	13	1	0	0	0	3	.342	.368	.342
Dave J. Schmidt	24	8	0	0	3	0	1	.333	.708	.333	Rich Yett	7	3	1	0	1	0	2	.429	1.000	.429
Don Schulze	16	8	1	0	0	1	0	.500	.563	.556	Curt Young	31	13	4	1	2	0	2	.419	.806	.419
Tom Seaver	26	11	0	0	0	2	1	.423	.423	.483	Matt Young	13	6	0	1	2	0	2	.462	1.077	.462
Jeff Sellers	17	5	1	0	1	0	4	.294	.529	.294	Geoff Zahn	19	5	0	0	0	1	1	.263	.263	.300

John Franco

Batter	AB	H	2B	3B	HR	BB	SO	BA	SA	OBA	Batter	AB	H	2B	3B	HR	BB	SO	BA	SA	OBA
Luis Aguayo	7	2	1	0	0	2	3	.286	.429	.444	Len Dykstra	9	0	0	0	0	0	2	.000	.000	.000
Mike Aldrete	5	1	0	0	0	0	1	.200	.200	.200	Mike R. Fitzgerald	6	1	1	0	0	0	2	.167	.333	.167
Bill Almon	6	1	0	0	0	2	1	.167	.167	.375	Tim Flannery	7	0	0	0	0	0	0	.000	.000	.000
Dave Anderson	9	2	1	0	0	2	2	.222	.333	.364	George Foster	7	1	0	0	0	1	3	.143	.143	.250
Alan Ashby	9	0	0	0	0	1	1	.000	.000	.100	Phil Garner	13	1	0	0	0	3	2	.077	.077	.250
Kevin Bass	16	6	2	0	0	0	1	.375	.500	.375	Steve Garvey	14	4	1	0	0	4	1	.286	.357	.444
Bruce Benedict	7	2	0	0	0	0	0	.286	.286	.286	Kirk Gibson	5	2	1	0	0	1	2	.400	.600	.500
Kurt Bevacqua	8	4	0	0	0	1	2	.500	.500	.556	Ken Griffey	5	3	0	0	0	0	0	.600	.600	.600
Bruce Bochy	8	2	0	0	0	1	3	.250	.250	.333	Pedro Guerrero	15	4	1	0	0	1	2	.267	.333	.294
Barry Bonds	10	1	0	0	0	0	2	.100	.100	.100	Tony Gwynn	30	7	1	0	0	0	1	.233	.267	.226
Bobby Bonilla	9	1	0	0	0	0	1	.111	.111	.111	Albert Hall	6	1	0	0	0	0	0	.167	.167	.167
Sid Bream	5	1	1	0	0	0	2	.200	.400	.200	Jeff Hamilton	7	2	0	0	1	1	1	.286	.714	.375
Bob Brenly	8	1	1	0	0	2	3	.125	.250	.300	Terry Harper	6	1	0	0	0	1	0	.167	.167	.286
Greg Brock	6	1	0	0	0	0	2	.167	.167	.167	Billy Hatcher	6	1	0	0	0	0	0	.167	.167	.167
Hubie Brooks	9	3	0	0	0	0	1	.333	.333	.333	Mickey Hatcher	8	2	0	0	0	1	2	.250	.250	.333
Chris Brown	6	0	0	0	0	2	2	.000	.000	.250	Von Hayes	16	2	0	0	0	1	4	.125	.125	.176
Enos Cabell	10	2	0	0	1	3	0	.200	.500	.385	Keith Hernandez	9	0	0	0	0	2	1	.000	.000	.182
Casey Candaele	6	0	0	0	0	0	0	.000	.000	.000	Tom Herr	14	5	3	0	0	0	3	.357	.571	.357
Gary Carter	8	0	0	0	0	1	1	.000	.000	.111	Bob Horner	6	3	0	0	0	0	1	.500	.500	.500
Jack Clark	8	1	0	0	0	2	1	.125	.125	.300	Glenn Hubbard	9	3	0	0	0	3	2	.333	.333	.538
Will Clark	10	3	1	0	0	0	3	.300	.400	.300	Chris James	6	2	0	0	0	0	1	.333	.333	.333
Vince Coleman	14	4	0	0	0	0	2	.286	.286	.286	Stan Jefferson	5	0	0	0	0	1	1	.000	.000	.167
Jose Cruz	17	3	0	0	0	1	2	.176	.176	.222	Steve Jeltz	5	1	0	0	0	2	2	.200	.200	.429
Chili Davis	6	0	0	0	0	1	3	.000	.000	.143	Howard Johnson	15	3	1	0	0	1	5	.200	.267	.250
Glenn Davis	14	2	0	0	1	2	5	.143	.357	.250	Terry Kennedy	12	2	0	0	0	1	4	.167	.167	.231
Jody Davis	9	0	0	0	0	2	3	.000	.000	.182	Ray Knight	6	2	0	0	0	1	0	.333	.333	.429
Andre Dawson	8	6	0	0	0	0	0	.750	.750	.750	John Kruk	10	2	0	0	0	0	5	.200	.200	.200
Brian Dayett	6	3	1	0	0	0	0	.500	.667	.500	Ken Landreaux	8	3	0	0	1	0	0	.375	.750	.444
Ivan DeJesus	5	0	0	0	0	1	0	.000	.000	.167	Tito Landrum	11	3	0	0	0	1	3	.273	.273	.333
Bob Dernier	11	6	0	0	1	2	0	.545	.818	.615	Vance Law	7	1	1	0	0	2	3	.143	.286	.333
Bill Doran	16	6	0	1	0	4	2	.375	.500	.476	Jeffrey Leonard	5	2	1	0	0	0	1	.400	.600	.333
Mariano Duncan	9	4	0	0	0	2	2	.444	.444	.545	Garry Maddox	7	2	0	0	0	0	1	.286	.286	.286
Shawon Dunston	10	3	1	0	0	3	3	.300	.400	.300	Bill Madlock	8	3	0	1	0	2	0	.375	.750	.333
Leon Durham	7	1	1	0	0	0	2	.143	.286	.143	Candy Maldonado	15	4	0	0	1	2	2	.267	.467	.353

John Franco continued

Batter	AB	H	2B	3B	HR	BB	SO	BA	SA	OBA	Batter	AB	H	2B	3B	HR	BB	SO	BA	SA	OBA
Mike A. Marshall	14	2	0	0	0	3	5	.143	.143	.294	Ryne Sandberg	10	4	1	0	0	3	1	.400	.500	.538
Carmelo Martinez	16	2	1	0	0	2	6	.125	.188	.222	Rafael Santana	6	1	1	0	0	1	2	.167	.333	.286
Gary Matthews	6	4	0	0	1	0	1	.667	1.167	.667	Benito Santiago	9	2	0	0	1	1	1	.222	.556	.300
Lee Mazzilli	7	1	0	0	0	2	0	.143	.143	.333	Steve Sax	24	7	1	1	1	4	0	.292	.542	.393
Willie McGee	17	4	0	1	0	0	5	.235	.353	.235	Mike Schmidt	11	1	0	0	1	3	2	.091	.364	.286
Kevin McReynolds	11	3	1	0	1	2	1	.273	.636	.385	Rick Schu	5	1	0	0	0	1	0	.200	.200	.429
Bob Melvin	5	0	0	0	0	2	1	.000	.000	.286	Mike Scioscia	10	0	0	0	0	1	1	.000	.000	.091
Kevin Mitchell	8	2	0	0	1	0	2	.250	.250	.333	John Shelby	11	3	0	0	0	1	2	.273	.273	.333
Keith Moreland	7	1	0	0	0	1	0	.143	.143	.250	Ted Simmons	9	0	0	0	0	1	1	.000	.000	.100
Jim Morrison	13	2	1	0	0	1	4	.154	.231	.214	Ozzie Smith	12	4	0	0	0	1	3	.333	.333	.385
Jerry Mumphrey	9	4	1	0	0	0	1	.444	.556	.400	Chris Speier	11	2	0	0	1	0	4	.182	.455	.182
Dale Murphy	16	5	0	0	0	3	3	.313	.313	.421	Darryl Strawberry	10	2	0	0	2	4	4	.200	.800	.467
Graig Nettles	6	1	0	0	0	2	0	.167	.167	.333	Franklin Stubbs	6	2	0	0	0	1	0	.333	.333	.429
Tom Nieto	5	0	0	0	0	0	1	.000	.000	.000	Garry Templeton	21	7	1	0	0	2	5	.333	.381	.391
Ken Oberkfell	16	2	0	0	0	0	1	.125	.125	.125	Tim Teufel	5	0	0	0	0	0	1	.000	.000	.000
Jose Oquendo	8	1	0	0	0	1	0	.125	.125	.222	Andres Thomas	11	5	0	0	1	0	1	.455	.727	.455
Junior Ortiz	5	0	0	0	0	0	1	.000	.000	.000	Rob Thompson	7	1	0	0	0	0	1	.143	.143	.143
Jim Pankovits	8	1	0	0	1	1	1	.125	.500	.222	Dickie Thon	6	3	1	0	0	0	1	.500	.667	.500
Lance Parrish	6	0	0	0	0	0	2	.000	.000	.000	Alex Trevino	10	2	0	0	0	3	0	.200	.200	.385
Tony Pena	11	3	0	0	0	4	2	.273	.273	.467	Manny Trillo	5	1	0	0	0	1	3	.200	.200	.429
Terry Pendleton	8	4	1	0	0	1	0	.500	.625	.556	Jose Uribe	6	1	0	0	0	0	0	.167	.167	.167
Gerald Perry	6	0	0	0	0	1	2	.000	.000	.143	Andy Van Slyke	10	4	0	0	0	1	0	.400	.400	.417
Tim Raines	12	3	0	0	0	0	2	.250	.250	.250	Ozzie Virgil	10	6	0	1	0	6	1	.600	.800	.750
Rafael Ramirez	18	4	0	0	0	2	2	.222	.222	.300	Tony Walker	5	1	0	0	0	1	0	.200	.200	.333
Johnny Ray	15	6	1	0	0	1	2	.400	.467	.438	Tim Wallach	9	0	0	0	0	2	2	.000	.000	.182
Randy Ready	9	2	1	0	0	0	1	.222	.333	.222	Denny Walling	5	1	0	0	0	0	0	.200	.200	.200
Craig Reynolds	6	2	0	0	0	0	1	.333	.333	.333	Claudell Washington	11	3	0	0	0	0	2	.273	.273	.273
R.J. Reynolds	13	1	0	0	0	0	4	.077	.077	.077	Mitch Webster	9	1	0	0	0	1	2	.111	.111	.200
Jerry Royster	11	2	0	0	0	1	2	.182	.182	.250	Reggie Williams	5	0	0	0	0	0	0	.000	.000	.000
Bill Russell	12	3	1	0	0	0	3	.250	.333	.250	Glenn Wilson	8	2	0	0	0	1	1	.250	.250	.333
John Russell	7	3	0	0	0	1	1	.429	.429	.500	Mookie Wilson	8	2	0	0	0	1	0	.250	.250	.333
Luis Salazar	8	2	0	0	0	1	3	.250	.250	.333	Marvell Wynne	10	2	1	0	0	0	3	.200	.300	.200
Juan Samuel	14	4	0	0	0	2	3	.286	.286	.375	Joel Youngblood	9	3	0	0	1	0	2	.333	.667	.333

Orel Hershiser

Batter	AB	H	2B	3B	HR	BB	SO	BA	SA	OBA	Batter	AB	H	2B	3B	HR	BB	SO	BA	SA	OBA
Luis Aguayo	12	4	2	0	1	1	2	.333	.750	.385	Vince Coleman	21	6	2	1	0	2	5	.286	.476	.348
Mike Aldrete	31	9	1	0	0	5	3	.290	.323	.389	Dave Collins	9	3	1	0	0	0	1	.333	.444	.333
Bill Almon	9	3	0	0	0	0	4	.333	.333	.333	Dave Concepcion	21	1	0	0	0	2	5	.048	.048	.167
Roberto Alomar	7	2	0	0	0	0	0	.286	.286	.286	Joey Cora	9	4	0	0	0	1	2	.444	.444	.545
Alan Ashby	24	6	0	0	1	3	5	.250	.375	.333	Tim Corcoran	5	3	0	0	0	0	1	.600	.600	.600
Wally Backman	33	8	3	0	0	2	10	.242	.333	.286	Danny Cox	7	0	0	0	0	0	6	.000	.000	.000
Mark Bailey	14	2	0	0	0	0	2	.143	.143	.143	Jose Cruz	32	8	0	0	3	5	3	.250	.531	.351
Kevin Bass	50	12	4	0	3	10	0	.240	.320	.283	Kal Daniels	24	12	1	0	4	5	5	.500	1.042	.586
Buddy Bell	39	13	2	1	2	5	4	.333	.590	.409	Darren Daulton	15	4	0	0	1	1	3	.267	.467	.313
Rafael Belliard	22	8	0	0	0	3	4	.364	.364	.440	Chili Davis	32	8	1	0	0	0	6	.250	.281	.250
Bruce Benedict	14	0	0	0	0	1	3	.000	.000	.067	Eric Davis	34	9	1	0	0	6	8	.265	.294	.381
Dann Bilardello	12	2	0	0	0	0	2	.167	.167	.167	Glenn Davis	38	8	1	0	0	3	7	.211	.237	.279
Jeff Blauser	13	2	0	0	0	0	3	.154	.154	.214	Jody Davis	16	3	0	0	0	2	6	.188	.188	.278
Terry Blocker	9	2	0	0	0	1	1	.222	.222	.300	Andre Dawson	21	5	1	0	0	1	7	.238	.286	.304
Barry Bonds	31	9	0	0	3	1	9	.290	.581	.313	Rob Deer	6	0	0	0	0	3	5	.000	.000	.333
Bobby Bonilla	17	6	1	0	2	3	2	.353	.765	.450	Ivan DeJesus	5	2	0	0	0	0	0	.400	.400	.400
Thad Bosley	6	1	1	0	0	0	1	.167	.333	.167	Bob Dernier	16	6	0	0	0	2	4	.375	.375	.444
Larry Bowa	11	2	0	0	0	0	1	.182	.182	.182	Jim Deshaies	9	0	0	0	0	0	4	.000	.000	.000
Steve Braun	5	0	0	0	0	0	3	.000	.000	.000	Bo Diaz	24	2	0	0	1	0	4	.083	.208	.120
Sid Bream	34	6	1	0	0	4	4	.176	.206	.263	Bill Doran	55	13	0	0	1	5	7	.236	.291	.311
Bob Brenly	32	8	1	0	2	3	10	.250	.469	.306	Dave Dravecky	12	1	0	0	0	0	9	.083	.083	.083
Hubie Brooks	36	7	1	0	1	0	5	.194	.306	.189	Dan Driessen	14	3	1	0	0	0	3	.214	.286	.214
Chris Brown	20	4	0	1	0	1	1	.200	.300	.238	Shawon Dunston	10	4	0	0	0	2	3	.400	.400	.500
Tom Browning	7	2	0	0	0	1	2	.286	.286	.375	Leon Durham	26	9	2	0	0	2	6	.346	.423	.393
Tom Brunansky	6	3	0	0	1	1	1	.500	1.000	.571	Len Dykstra	14	5	2	1	0	1	0	.357	.643	.375
Sal Butera	8	2	0	0	0	0	0	.250	.250	.250	Nick Esasky	23	5	0	0	0	2	6	.217	.217	.280
Brett Butler	16	4	1	0	0	2	0	.250	.313	.333	Mike R. Fitzgerald	7	0	0	0	0	0	1	.000	.000	.000
Ken Caminiti	6	1	0	0	0	0	1	.167	.167	.167	Tim Flannery	31	8	0	0	1	0	0	.258	.355	.258
Casey Candaele	6	1	1	0	0	0	1	.167	.333	.286	Doug Flynn	6	0	0	0	0	0	1	.000	.000	.000
Gary Carter	25	8	0	1	1	1	3	.320	.520	.370	Tom Foley	36	7	3	1	0	4	4	.194	.333	.275
Cesar Cedeno	13	0	0	0	0	2	0	.000	.000	.133	Curt Ford	9	4	1	0	0	0	0	.444	.556	.444
Ron Cey	13	2	1	0	1	0	3	.154	.462	.214	George Foster	14	0	0	0	0	0	5	.000	.000	.000
Chris Chambliss	15	6	2	0	1	1	2	.400	.733	.438	Terry Francona	15	3	0	0	0	0	1	.200	.200	.200
Jack Clark	19	4	1	0	0	3	1	.211	.263	.318	Doug Frobel	12	0	0	0	0	0	4	.000	.000	.000
Will Clark	28	5	0	0	0	3	12	.179	.179	.281	Andres Galarraga	24	7	3	0	1	1	8	.292	.542	.320

Orel Hershiser continued

Batter	AB	H	2B	3B	HR	BB	SO	BA	SA	OBA
Ron Gant	11	3	1	0	0	1	4	.273	.364	.333
Damaso Garcia	8	0	0	0	0	0	3	.000	.000	.000
Phil Garner	15	4	0	0	0	2	2	.267	.267	.353
Steve Garvey	23	2	1	0	0	1	7	.087	.130	.125
Dan Gladden	24	7	1	0	0	0	3	.292	.333	.320
Tom Glavine	5	1	0	0	0	0	1	.200	.200	.200
David Green	9	1	0	0	0	0	5	.111	.111	.111
Ken Griffey	26	9	1	0	1	1	2	.346	.500	.370
Greg Gross	9	3	0	0	0	2	0	.333	.333	.455
Kevin Gross	9	2	0	0	0	0	2	.222	.222	.222
Brad Gulden	7	1	0	0	0	0	0	.143	.143	.143
Bill Gullickson	8	1	0	0	0	0	2	.125	.125	.125
Tony Gwynn	49	14	5	0	0	1	0	.286	.388	.300
Albert Hall	21	2	1	0	0	1	1	.095	.143	.136
Terry Harper	7	3	0	0	0	1	2	.429	.429	.500
Billy Hatcher	30	6	0	0	0	0	6	.200	.200	.200
Andy Hawkins	5	0	0	0	0	0	2	.000	.000	.000
Von Hayes	35	10	3	1	0	4	9	.286	.429	.359
Danny Heep	16	4	0	0	0	1	3	.250	.250	.294
Keith Hernandez	32	14	3	0	1	5	0	.438	.625	.514
Tom Herr	21	5	0	0	0	3	2	.238	.238	.333
Ron Hodges	5	1	0	0	0	1	0	.200	.200	.333
Bob Horner	22	8	1	0	2	3	3	.364	.682	.407
Glenn Hubbard	36	7	1	0	0	2	5	.194	.222	.237
Rex Hudler	7	1	0	0	0	0	3	.143	.143	.143
Chuck Jackson	5	1	0	0	0	0	3	.200	.200	.200
Chris James	8	1	0	0	0	0	0	.125	.125	.125
Dion James	32	6	0	0	0	2	5	.188	.188	.235
Stan Jefferson	7	2	0	0	1	0	2	.286	.714	.286
Steve Jeltz	19	4	0	0	0	0	5	.211	.211	.211
Howard Johnson	27	3	0	0	0	1	10	.111	.111	.143
Randy G. Johnson	6	0	0	0	0	1	1	.000	.000	.143
Wallace Johnson	7	2	0	0	0	0	0	.286	.286	.286
Jay Johnstone	8	2	1	0	0	0	1	.250	.375	.250
Tracy Jones	6	2	0	0	0	1	2	.333	.333	.429
Steve Kemp	7	2	1	0	0	0	2	.286	.429	.286
Terry Kennedy	25	5	0	0	0	0	3	.200	.200	.200
Alan Knicely	8	1	0	0	0	1	2	.125	.125	.182
Ray Knight	6	1	0	0	0	2	4	.167	.167	.375
Brad Komminsk	8	1	0	0	0	0	0	.125	.125	.125
Wayne Krenchicki	22	5	1	0	0	1	1	.227	.273	.250
John Kruk	17	3	0	0	0	5	1	.176	.176	.364
Mike Krukow	9	3	1	0	0	0	0	.333	.444	.400
Barry Larkin	29	8	1	0	0	3	2	.276	.310	.344
Mike LaValliere	17	4	0	0	0	3	1	.235	.235	.350
Vance Law	18	4	1	0	0	0	3	.222	.278	.222
Jeffrey Leonard	25	5	2	0	1	2	3	.200	.400	.259
Jose Lind	11	7	0	0	0	0	2	.636	.636	.636
Bill Madlock	9	2	0	0	0	1	1	.222	.222	.364
Dave Magadan	8	0	0	0	0	0	1	.000	.000	.000
Rick Mahler	8	1	0	0	0	1	2	.125	.125	.222
Candy Maldonado	27	9	1	0	1	1	7	.333	.481	.357
Carmelo Martinez	41	12	1	0	1	5	6	.293	.390	.370
Dave Martinez	12	4	0	0	0	1	1	.333	.333	.385
Gary Matthews	11	2	0	0	1	1	0	.182	.455	.250
Lee Mazzilli	7	0	0	0	0	3	4	.000	.000	.300
Willie McGee	30	9	0	2	0	2	3	.300	.433	.344
Terry McGriff	6	0	0	0	0	0	2	.000	.000	.000
Kevin McReynolds	35	7	1	1	0	2	2	.200	.286	.237
Bob Melvin	14	1	0	0	1	0	4	.071	.286	.067
Eddie Milner	41	6	1	0	0	4	0	.146	.171	.222
Kevin Mitchell	28	7	0	0	0	0	9	.250	.250	.250
Keith Moreland	25	4	2	0	0	1	3	.160	.240	.185
Omar Moreno	8	1	0	0	0	0	1	.125	.125	.125
Jim Morrison	16	1	0	0	0	2	4	.063	.063	.167
Jerry Mumphrey	20	7	1	1	1	1	4	.350	.650	.364
Dale Murphy	68	19	2	0	4	5	15	.279	.485	.338
Graig Nettles	29	4	1	0	1	6	0	.138	.276	.286
Al Newman	6	1	0	0	0	1	0	.167	.167	.286
Ken Oberkfell	41	5	1	0	0	5	4	.122	.146	.217
Ron Oester	46	13	1	0	1	4	9	.283	.370	.340
Al Oliver	9	0	0	0	0	1	1	.000	.000	.100
Paul O'Neill	25	6	2	0	1	1	3	.240	.440	.269
Jose Oquendo	8	1	0	0	0	0	1	.125	.125	.125
Joe Orsulak	11	3	1	2	0	0	1	.273	.727	.273

Batter	AB	H	2B	3B	HR	BB	SO	BA	SA	OBA
Junior Ortiz	5	0	0	0	0	0	0	.000	.000	.000
Rafael Palmeiro	7	4	1	0	0	1	0	.571	.714	.625
Dave Parker	41	7	1	0	0	6	6	.171	.195	.265
Lance Parrish	8	3	1	0	0	0	1	.375	.500	.375
Tony Pena	27	6	2	0	0	4	8	.222	.296	.323
Terry Pendleton	27	7	1	0	2	1	2	.259	.519	.286
Pascual Perez	6	0	0	0	0	1	5	.000	.000	.143
Gerald Perry	44	13	4	0	1	2	7	.295	.455	.326
Darrell Porter	8	2	1	0	0	1	3	.250	.375	.333
Terry Puhl	27	10	0	0	1	4	3	.370	.481	.452
John Rabb	5	2	0	0	1	0	0	.400	1.000	.400
Tim Raines	46	17	4	1	0	5	5	.370	.500	.431
Rafael Ramirez	46	11	1	0	1	1	7	.239	.326	.271
Johnny Ray	31	5	0	0	0	2	1	.161	.161	.212
Randy Ready	11	0	0	0	0	1	1	.000	.000	.083
Gary Redus	17	4	0	0	0	1	6	.235	.235	.278
Jeff Reed	14	5	1	0	0	1	2	.357	.429	.400
Rick Reuschel	7	0	0	0	0	0	6	.000	.000	.000
Craig Reynolds	34	10	4	1	0	0	2	.294	.471	.294
R.J. Reynolds	30	13	3	2	0	6	4	.433	.667	.528
Ronn Reynolds	6	0	0	0	0	0	4	.000	.000	.000
Ron Robinson	7	0	0	0	0	0	3	.000	.000	.000
Ron Roenicke	9	1	0	0	0	1	3	.111	.444	.200
Pete Rose	21	5	0	0	0	4	1	.238	.238	.385
Nolan Ryan	5	0	0	0	0	0	2	.000	.000	.000
Chris Sabo	14	7	2	0	0	3	0	.500	.643	.588
Juan Samuel	34	5	3	0	0	2	9	.147	.235	.237
Ryne Sandberg	26	9	2	1	0	2	4	.346	.500	.393
Scott Sanderson	5	1	0	0	0	0	3	.200	.200	.200
Rafael Santana	15	2	1	0	0	1	1	.133	.200	.188
Benito Santiago	18	4	0	0	0	0	3	.222	.222	.222
Nelson Santovenia	5	1	0	0	0	1	3	.200	.200	.333
Mike Schmidt	27	4	0	0	0	5	4	.148	.148	.303
Rick Schu	8	0	0	0	0	0	4	.000	.000	.111
Ted Simmons	5	1	0	0	0	3	0	.200	.200	.500
Lonnie Smith	9	4	0	0	0	1	1	.444	.444	.545
Ozzie Smith	25	8	0	0	0	4	0	.320	.320	.400
Zane Smith	5	0	0	0	0	0	1	.000	.000	.000
Chris Speier	11	5	0	0	1	0	0	.455	.727	.455
Harry Spilman	20	4	0	0	0	0	2	.200	.200	.200
Kurt Stillwell	13	5	2	1	0	2	1	.385	.692	.467
Jeff Stone	18	0	0	0	0	1	5	.000	.000	.053
Darryl Strawberry	25	7	2	0	1	5	6	.280	.480	.400
Garry Templeton	45	7	1	0	0	4	10	.156	.178	.224
Andres Thomas	24	7	3	0	0	2	3	.292	.417	.346
Derrel Thomas	6	1	0	0	0	1	1	.167	.167	.286
Jason Thompson	11	2	0	0	1	4	4	.182	.455	.400
Milt Thompson	25	3	0	0	0	3	9	.120	.120	.241
Rob Thompson	25	7	0	2	0	1	6	.280	.440	.308
Dickie Thon	15	3	0	0	0	0	4	.200	.200	.200
Jeff Treadway	12	5	2	0	1	3	0	.417	.833	.533
Alex Trevino	15	2	1	0	0	1	3	.133	.200	.188
John Tudor	5	1	0	0	0	0	3	.200	.200	.200
Jose Uribe	29	3	0	0	0	4	6	.103	.103	.212
Dave Van Gorder	6	0	0	0	0	0	2	.000	.000	.000
Andy Van Slyke	35	10	3	0	2	3	5	.286	.543	.333
Max Venable	12	5	2	0	0	0	2	.417	.583	.385
Ozzie Virgil	40	10	0	0	2	5	7	.250	.400	.348
Bob Walk	5	1	0	0	0	0	2	.200	.200	.200
Duane Walker	6	0	0	0	0	0	1	.000	.000	.000
Tim Wallach	38	11	2	0	2	2	5	.289	.500	.341
Denny Walling	28	5	2	0	0	4	2	.179	.250	.281
Claudell Washington	28	9	4	0	0	3	5	.321	.464	.387
Mitch Webster	23	10	1	0	0	5	1	.435	.478	.536
Brad Wellman	13	2	1	0	0	0	0	.154	.231	.154
Alan Wiggins	8	0	0	0	0	1	1	.000	.000	.111
Matt Williams	6	1	0	0	0	1	1	.167	.167	.250
Glenn Wilson	28	7	1	1	0	1	7	.250	.357	.276
Mookie Wilson	28	10	2	1	0	1	8	.357	.500	.379
Herm Winningham	27	4	1	0	0	1	6	.148	.185	.179
Mike Woodard	10	2	0	0	0	2	0	.200	.200	.333
Marvell Wynne	29	10	0	0	0	0	4	.345	.345	.345
Gerald Young	12	3	0	0	1	4	0	.250	.417	.438
Joel Youngblood	14	4	0	0	0	0	1	.286	.286	.286

Frank Viola

Batter	AB	H	2B	3B	HR	BB	SO	BA	SA	OBA
Willie Aikens	9	1	0	0	0	0	2	.111	.111	.111
Andy Allanson	9	1	1	0	0	0	3	.111	.222	.111
Rod Allen	6	2	0	0	0	0	1	.333	.333	.333
Gary Allenson	6	1	0	0	1	1	1	.167	.667	.286
Bill Almon	20	7	2	0	0	2	1	.350	.450	.391
Brady Anderson	6	2	0	0	0	0	1	.333	.333	.333
Tony Armas	45	16	3	1	3	0	4	.356	.667	.348
Benny Ayala	17	3	0	0	1	2	2	.176	.353	.263
Harold Baines	49	17	3	1	0	2	7	.347	.449	.373
Dusty Baker	18	5	0	0	0	1	2	.278	.278	.286
Steve Balboni	35	4	0	0	2	1	12	.114	.286	.139
Chris Bando	19	6	0	0	1	2	2	.316	.474	.381
Alan Bannister	10	3	1	1	0	3	1	.300	.600	.500
Jesse Barfield	50	13	4	0	2	8	13	.260	.460	.362
Marty Barrett	53	14	6	0	0	5	2	.264	.377	.328
Don Baylor	52	14	5	0	0	3	8	.269	.365	.356
Buddy Bell	21	5	1	0	0	3	0	.238	.286	.333
George Bell	41	8	1	0	4	6	6	.195	.512	.298
Juan Beniquez	39	11	0	1	1	2	3	.282	.410	.317
Todd Benzinger	10	0	0	0	0	0	2	.000	.000	.000
Tony Bernazard	42	13	4	0	1	4	7	.310	.476	.370
Dale Berra	7	1	0	0	0	0	1	.143	.143	.143
Buddy Biancalana	6	1	0	0	0	0	0	.167	.167	.167
Dante Bichette	5	2	2	0	0	0	0	.400	.800	.333
Wade Boggs	53	16	0	0	0	5	3	.302	.302	.362
Juan Bonilla	12	3	0	0	1	1	1	.250	.500	.308
Barry Bonnell	24	6	0	0	0	2	4	.250	.250	.308
Bob Boone	32	5	0	0	0	2	3	.156	.156	.206
Pat Borders	6	1	0	0	0	0	1	.167	.167	.167
Phil Bradley	31	7	0	1	0	0	5	.226	.290	.226
Glenn Braggs	13	4	0	0	1	0	4	.308	.538	.308
Mickey Brantley	13	1	0	0	0	0	1	.077	.077	.077
George Brett	34	8	0	0	2	1	3	.235	.412	.257
Greg Brock	7	4	1	0	0	3	0	.571	.714	.700
Tom Brookens	44	6	1	0	1	3	12	.136	.227	.191
Mark Brouhard	10	5	2	0	2	0	1	.500	1.300	.455
Bob Brower	16	3	0	0	0	3	3	.188	.188	.316
Mike C. Brown	10	1	0	0	0	1	4	.100	.100	.182
Jerry Browne	14	2	0	0	0	0	2	.143	.143	.143
Bill Buckner	37	11	1	0	0	1	3	.297	.324	.333
Steve Buechele	35	8	0	0	1	1	10	.229	.314	.250
Al Bumbry	5	1	0	0	0	1	0	.200	.200	.333
Ellis Burks	12	2	1	0	0	0	4	.167	.250	.154
Rick Burleson	13	1	0	0	0	2	3	.077	.077	.200
Jeff Burroughs	26	10	2	0	0	1	3	.385	.462	.407
Sal Butera	6	3	1	0	0	0	0	.500	.667	.500
Brett Butler	34	12	3	0	0	5	3	.353	.441	.436
Enos Cabell	11	4	0	0	1	1	1	.364	.636	.417
Ivan Calderon	28	8	4	0	1	1	7	.286	.536	.310
Bert Campaneris	5	1	0	0	0	2	0	.200	.200	.429
Sil Campusano	8	3	0	0	1	0	3	.375	.750	.375
John Cangelosi	5	1	0	0	0	2	1	.200	.200	.429
Jose Canseco	24	9	2	0	1	5	5	.375	.583	.483
Rod Carew	21	8	0	0	0	3	2	.381	.381	.458
Joe Carter	34	10	0	0	2	0	6	.294	.471	.294
Carmen Castillo	25	7	2	0	2	6	5	.280	.600	.419
Marty Castillo	13	2	1	0	0	2	0	.154	.231	.267
Rick Cerone	30	4	4	0	0	3	5	.133	.267	.212
Ron Cey	5	1	0	0	0	2	3	.200	.200	.429
Bobby Clark	11	4	0	0	0	1	2	.364	.364	.417
Jack Clark	6	1	0	0	0	1	4	.167	.167	.286
Darnell Coles	12	3	2	0	0	1	1	.250	.417	.308
Dave Collins	10	1	0	0	0	0	1	.100	.100	.100
Onix Concepcion	13	0	0	0	0	0	1	.000	.000	.000
Cecil Cooper	20	7	0	0	0	1	6	.350	.350	.381
Henry Cotto	12	1	1	0	0	0	4	.083	.167	.083
Al Cowens	27	9	2	0	0	0	4	.333	.407	.333
Julio Cruz	33	10	3	0	1	2	5	.303	.485	.343
Todd Cruz	12	3	2	0	0	1	3	.250	.417	.308
Rich Dauer	18	1	1	0	0	2	1	.056	.111	.150
Alvin Davis	33	6	4	0	0	1	6	.182	.303	.250
Chili Davis	8	2	0	0	0	0	2	.250	.250	.250
Mike Davis	26	5	1	0	0	2	7	.192	.231	.250
Brian Dayett	7	1	0	0	0	1	0	.143	.143	.250
Doug DeCinces	48	11	1	0	0	2	7	.229	.375	.245
Rob Deer	22	5	1	1	1	1	8	.227	.500	.261
Rick Dempsey	33	10	2	0	0	4	3	.303	.364	.378
Bucky Dent	5	2	0	0	0	2	0	.400	.400	.571
Mike Diaz	6	1	0	0	1	0	1	.167	.667	.167
Brian Downing	57	12	3	0	2	7	12	.211	.368	.292
Mike Easler	19	7	2	0	1	1	3	.368	.632	.429
Dave Edler	5	1	0	0	1	1	0	.200	.800	.333
Jim Essian	5	1	0	0	0	1	0	.200	.200	.333
Darrell Evans	14	2	0	0	1	0	3	.143	.357	.143
Dwight Evans	50	15	1	1	4	9	10	.300	.600	.407
Tony Fernandez	40	11	4	0	0	3	4	.275	.375	.333
Cecil Fielder	20	5	1	0	1	1	6	.250	.450	.286
Mike Fischlin	5	0	0	0	0	0	0	.000	.000	.000
Carlton Fisk	47	14	3	0	1	1	6	.298	.426	.313
Scott Fletcher	56	18	3	0	2	8	4	.321	.482	.406
Tim Foli	22	12	2	0	1	0	0	.545	.773	.545
Dan Ford	16	3	1	0	0	4	6	.188	.250	.350
Julio Franco	36	15	2	1	1	1	4	.417	.611	.432
Dave Gallagher	10	4	0	1	0	1	0	.400	.600	.455
Mike Gallego	8	3	1	0	1	0	1	.375	.875	.333
Jim Gantner	30	12	3	1	1	0	0	.400	.667	.400
Barbaro Garbey	25	8	2	0	2	0	0	.320	.640	.320
Damaso Garcia	44	9	2	0	0	0	7	.205	.250	.205
Rich Gedman	17	3	0	0	1	0	3	.176	.353	.176
Ken Gerhart	17	1	1	0	0	0	4	.059	.118	.059
Kirk Gibson	18	3	1	0	1	1	5	.167	.389	.250
Mike Greenwell	13	3	0	0	0	1	0	.231	.231	.286
Bobby Grich	32	9	1	0	3	5	3	.281	.594	.378
Ken Griffey	28	9	3	0	0	0	4	.321	.429	.321
Alfredo Griffin	49	13	2	0	0	0	4	.265	.306	.265
Kelly Gruber	20	6	2	1	0	1	6	.300	.500	.333
Ozzie Guillen	17	6	0	0	0	0	1	.353	.353	.353
Jackie Gutierrez	16	1	0	0	0	0	3	.063	.063	.063
Jerry Hairston	8	2	1	0	0	3	1	.250	.375	.455
Mel Hall	8	1	0	0	0	1	1	.125	.125	.222
Toby Harrah	16	4	1	0	0	2	4	.250	.313	.316
Ron Hassey	5	0	0	0	0	1	1	.000	.000	.167
Mike Heath	42	10	0	1	1	0	7	.238	.357	.238
Dave Henderson	40	12	1	0	2	3	8	.300	.475	.349
Rickey Henderson	46	14	1	1	2	8	9	.304	.500	.407
Steve Henderson	26	7	1	0	1	2	4	.269	.423	.321
George Hendrick	27	8	1	0	2	3	1	.296	.556	.367
Larry Herndon	52	15	4	0	1	3	8	.288	.423	.327
Donnie Hill	26	7	1	0	0	2	1	.269	.308	.310
Marc Hill	14	3	0	0	0	1	1	.214	.214	.267
Glenn Hoffman	13	3	0	0	0	1	3	.231	.231	.286
Dave Hostetler	12	3	0	0	0	2	4	.250	.250	.357
Jack Howell	8	2	2	0	0	0	2	.250	.500	.250
Tim Hulett	18	5	2	0	0	1	2	.278	.389	.316
Pete Incaviglia	35	6	1	0	1	1	18	.171	.286	.194
Garth Iorg	49	17	3	1	2	1	7	.347	.571	.360
Bo Jackson	12	2	1	0	1	0	6	.167	.500	.167
Reggie Jackson	14	1	0	0	1	0	5	.071	.286	.071
Ron Jackson	6	1	1	0	0	0	1	.167	.333	.167
Brook Jacoby	31	10	2	0	1	4	7	.323	.484	.400
Stan Javier	12	3	0	0	0	1	5	.250	.250	.308
Cliff Johnson	20	7	2	0	2	3	5	.350	.750	.440
Howard Johnson	7	1	1	0	0	0	3	.143	.286	.143
Lynn Jones	16	4	0	1	0	0	2	.250	.375	.250
Wally Joyner	30	9	0	0	1	1	3	.300	.400	.323
Ron Karkovice	6	0	0	0	0	0	3	.000	.000	.143
Bob Kearney	20	8	1	0	1	2	3	.400	.600	.478
Roberto Kelly	6	4	1	0	0	0	0	.667	.833	.667
Steve Kemp	14	3	0	0	0	1	4	.214	.214	.267
Terry Kennedy	5	1	0	0	0	0	3	.200	.200	.333
Dave Kingman	28	6	2	0	1	2	6	.214	.393	.267
Ron Kittle	37	8	1	0	3	3	14	.216	.486	.275
Ray Knight	17	2	0	0	1	0	3	.118	.294	.118
Jeff Kunkel	10	3	0	0	0	0	3	.300	.300	.300
Rusty Kuntz	10	2	1	0	0	0	1	.200	.300	.200
Lee Lacy	27	9	1	0	2	1	4	.333	.593	.357
Carney Lansford	50	10	0	0	1	2	7	.200	.260	.245
Vance Law	22	5	1	0	0	2	1	.227	.273	.292
Manny Lee	11	5	2	1	0	0	2	.455	.818	.455
Ron LeFlore	5	2	0	0	0	0	2	.400	.400	.400

Frank Viola continued

Batter	AB	H	2B	3B	HR	BB	SO	BA	SA	OBA
Chet Lemon	49	19	8	0	1	6	10	.388	.612	.455
Dave Lopes	21	8	1	0	2	2	4	.381	.714	.417
Greg Luzinski	19	8	4	0	1	1	1	.421	.789	.455
Fred Lynn	37	9	0	1	5	3	11	.243	.703	.300
Steve Lyons	12	1	1	0	0	0	5	.083	.167	.083
Scotti Madison	5	3	3	0	0	0	1	.600	1.200	.600
Rick Manning	10	1	0	0	0	0	2	.100	.100	.100
Fred Manrique	16	4	0	0	1	1	3	.250	.438	.294
Jerry Martin	7	2	0	0	0	0	4	.286	.286	.286
Buck Martinez	33	13	4	0	1	2	2	.394	.606	.429
Carlos Martinez	6	2	0	0	0	0	1	.333	.333	.333
John Marzano	5	1	0	0	0	0	1	.200	.200	.200
Gary Matthews	7	3	0	0	0	0	0	.429	.429	.429
Don Mattingly	38	8	5	0	0	1	1	.211	.342	.225
Lee Mazzilli	5	0	0	0	0	1	3	.000	.000	.167
Oddibe McDowell	17	4	0	1	1	0	4	.235	.529	.235
Fred McGriff	9	2	0	0	1	0	3	.222	.556	.222
Mark McGwire	12	2	0	0	0	4	7	.167	.167	.375
Mark McLemore	8	2	0	0	0	1	2	.250	.250	.333
Hal McRae	29	10	1	0	3	1	3	.345	.690	.367
Bobby Meacham	18	6	1	1	0	3	4	.333	.500	.455
Darrell Miller	19	5	0	1	0	1	6	.263	.368	.300
Paul Molitor	33	10	1	1	2	3	4	.303	.576	.361
Don Money	7	2	0	0	1	2	0	.286	.714	.444
Charlie Moore	20	4	1	0	0	1	2	.200	.250	.273
Russ Morman	9	3	0	0	0	0	2	.333	.333	.333
Jim Morrison	6	2	0	1	0	1	0	.333	.833	.333
Lloyd Moseby	47	18	2	1	4	2	5	.383	.723	.412
John Moses	11	2	0	0	0	0	2	.182	.182	.182
Darryl Motley	19	8	3	0	3	0	3	.421	1.053	.421
Jerry Mumphrey	7	1	0	0	0	1	2	.143	.143	.250
Dwayne Murphy	43	7	0	0	1	4	11	.163	.233	.234
Eddie Murray	59	13	1	0	1	4	12	.220	.288	.281
Graig Nettles	9	3	0	0	0	1	3	.333	.333	.400
Jeff Newman	11	2	0	0	0	1	2	.182	.182	.250
Reid Nichols	23	6	1	0	1	0	0	.261	.435	.261
Wayne Nordhagen	6	1	0	0	0	0	0	.167	.167	.167
Pete O'Brien	36	6	1	0	1	3	6	.167	.278	.231
Ben Oglivie	9	3	1	0	0	0	4	.333	.444	.333
Amos Otis	10	3	0	0	0	2	0	.300	.300	.417
Larry Owen	5	1	0	0	0	1	2	.200	.200	.333
Spike Owen	38	11	2	0	0	3	6	.289	.342	.341
Jim Paciorek	9	3	1	0	0	0	2	.333	.444	.333
Tom Paciorek	44	15	2	0	1	2	9	.341	.455	.370
Mike Pagliarulo	11	2	0	0	1	0	5	.182	.455	.182
Lance Parrish	29	6	1	0	2	3	4	.207	.448	.281
Larry Parrish	43	7	2	0	1	6	21	.163	.279	.265
Jack Perconte	13	5	0	0	0	1	1	.385	.385	.429
Gary Pettis	40	10	1	0	0	2	12	.250	.275	.286
Tony Phillips	28	9	2	0	0	7	2	.321	.393	.457
Lou Piniella	20	8	2	0	0	1	2	.400	.500	.429
Jim Presley	36	8	0	0	1	2	9	.222	.306	.263
Greg Pryor	7	2	0	0	0	0	1	.286	.286	.286
Pat Putnam	11	2	0	0	1	0	2	.182	.455	.182
Rey Quinones	16	3	0	0	1	1	6	.188	.375	.235
Domingo Ramos	10	2	1	0	0	2	0	.200	.300	.333
Willie Randolph	39	16	1	0	2	10	2	.410	.590	.531
Johnny Ray	11	3	1	0	0	1	0	.273	.364	.333
Floyd Rayford	18	4	0	0	1	3	4	.222	.389	.333
Randy Ready	6	2	0	0	1	2	1	.333	.833	.500
Gary Redus	16	4	0	0	2	0	1	.250	.625	.250
Jerry Remy	6	0	0	0	0	1	0	.000	.000	.143
Harold Reynolds	23	6	0	0	1	3	1	.261	.391	.346
Jim Rice	56	16	1	0	2	6	10	.286	.411	.355
Ernest Riles	9	2	0	0	1	0	1	.222	.556	.222
Billy Ripken	11	1	0	0	0	2	0	.091	.091	.231
Cal Ripken	61	20	6	0	3	7	5	.328	.574	.391
Leon Roberts	10	3	0	0	0	1	1	.300	.300	.364

Batter	AB	H	2B	3B	HR	BB	SO	BA	SA	OBA
Andre Robertson	16	7	4	0	0	0	3	.438	.688	.412
Gary Roenicke	30	9	0	0	2	4	4	.300	.500	.382
Ron Roenicke	6	3	0	0	1	0	0	.500	1.000	.500
Ed Romero	28	3	0	0	0	0	3	.107	.107	.107
Joe Rudi	5	1	0	0	1	0	1	.200	.800	.200
Lenn Sakata	16	5	1	0	0	2	2	.313	.375	.389
Luis Salazar	15	3	0	0	0	0	3	.200	.200	.200
Billy Sample	19	4	1	0	0	1	1	.211	.263	.250
Alejandro Sanchez	6	1	1	0	0	0	4	.167	.333	.167
Rafael Santana	6	1	0	0	0	2	1	.167	.167	.375
Dick Schofield	37	6	1	0	1	2	9	.162	.270	.200
Bill Schroeder	27	4	0	0	3	3	8	.148	.481	.233
Kevin Seitzer	12	3	0	0	0	2	2	.250	.250	.357
Larry Sheets	9	3	0	0	0	1	0	.333	.333	.455
John Shelby	27	5	1	0	1	0	6	.185	.333	.185
Ruben Sierra	41	10	3	0	0	0	4	.244	.317	.244
Nelson Simmons	5	2	0	0	0	0	0	.400	.400	.400
Ted Simmons	15	4	0	0	0	1	0	.267	.267	.313
Ken Singleton	7	5	0	0	1	2	1	.714	1.143	.778
Joel Skinner	8	1	1	0	0	0	2	.125	.250	.125
Don Slaught	22	2	0	0	0	1	7	.091	.091	.125
Roy Smalley	10	1	0	0	1	3	1	.100	.400	.308
Lonnie Smith	15	2	1	0	0	0	2	.133	.200	.133
Cory Snyder	16	3	1	0	1	0	6	.188	.438	.188
Pete Stanicek	5	0	0	0	0	2	2	.000	.000	.286
Mike Stanley	21	6	2	0	1	4	6	.286	.524	.400
Dave Stapleton	14	2	1	0	0	1	0	.143	.214	.200
Dave Stegman	7	2	0	1	0	1	2	.286	.571	.375
Bill Stein	6	4	1	0	0	1	1	.667	.833	.714
Terry Steinbach	15	4	0	0	0	1	0	.267	.267	.333
Marc Sullivan	11	2	0	0	0	1	4	.182	.182	.250
Jim Sundberg	23	7	0	0	1	0	2	.304	.435	.304
Dale Sveum	17	3	2	0	0	1	6	.176	.294	.211
Pat Tabler	31	9	1	1	0	1	3	.290	.387	.313
Danny Tartabull	17	7	1	0	2	4	5	.412	.824	.524
Mickey Tettleton	14	0	0	0	0	2	5	.000	.000	.125
Gorman Thomas	26	5	0	0	4	4	3	.192	.654	.300
Andre Thornton	26	5	1	0	2	2	3	.192	.462	.250
Wayne Tolleson	13	1	0	0	0	1	4	.077	.077	.143
Alan Trammell	52	15	3	1	5	5	4	.288	.673	.351
Willie Upshaw	39	11	2	0	3	2	7	.282	.564	.333
Ellis Valentine	8	0	0	0	0	0	1	.000	.000	.000
Dave Valle	17	6	0	0	1	1	3	.353	.529	.389
Greg Walker	32	7	4	0	2	4	8	.219	.531	.306
Gary Ward	40	6	2	2	0	3	10	.150	.300	.209
Claudell Washington	8	3	1	0	1	0	3	.375	.875	.375
U.L. Washington	6	1	1	0	0	1	2	.167	.333	.286
John Wathan	13	2	0	0	0	3	3	.154	.154	.313
Walt Weiss	5	3	0	0	0	0	0	.600	.600	.600
Lou Whitaker	37	13	2	1	1	5	9	.351	.541	.429
Devon White	13	2	0	0	1	0	4	.154	.385	.154
Frank White	38	11	2	0	2	2	6	.289	.500	.325
Alan Wiggins	20	9	2	0	0	0	1	.450	.550	.450
Curtis Wilkerson	15	3	1	0	0	1	2	.200	.267	.294
Jerry Willard	7	1	0	0	0	1	3	.143	.143	.250
Ken Williams	19	4	0	0	0	0	6	.211	.211	.250
Glenn Wilson	12	0	0	0	0	0	0	.000	.000	.000
Willie Wilson	46	16	2	1	1	1	11	.348	.500	.362
Dave Winfield	63	15	1	1	7	3	9	.238	.619	.273
John Wockenfuss	10	2	0	0	2	2	2	.200	.400	.333
George Wright	19	5	1	0	1	1	5	.263	.474	.333
Butch Wynegar	20	5	1	0	1	3	2	.250	.450	.348
Steve Yeager	6	1	0	0	0	0	0	.167	.167	.167
Ned Yost	9	3	1	0	0	0	2	.333	.444	.333
Mike Young	19	3	0	0	1	3	7	.158	.316	.261
Robin Yount	35	10	2	0	1	6	2	.286	.429	.390
Richie Zisk	14	5	1	0	2	1	4	.357	.857	.400

IX
Ballparks

Ballparks

The Ballparks section lists, for all 26 ballparks in use in the major leagues, a variety of statistics about the games played there over the past several years.

A ballpark's effect on performance has been a popular topic in recent years. Analysis that used to be limited to, "Gee, Fenway's a tough place for a lefty to pitch," has gotten increasingly sophisticated. Even the simplest conversation about an off-season trade now gets into such factors as the dimensions of a park, whether it has natural or artificial turf, the size of its foul territory, and how far it is above sea level. Our own analysis has led us to note in past editions those ballparks that promote doubles (like Fenway) or double plays (like Anaheim Stadium). This section takes a systematic look at the general effects of a given park.

A half page is devoted to each park. That half page is composed of two segments. The first is a box containing basic statistics for the games played there, as contrasted with that home team's games on the road. The totals listed are the complete statistics *for both teams* in those games. Totals and percentage differences are listed for the 1988 season, and for the five-year period from 1984 through 1988. (The differences, in many cases, don't reflect the change between the actual raw totals printed, but rather between related averages. For instance, we print the number of runs scored in home and road games, but compute the difference between the average number of runs *per game*. Since the statistics represent performance by the same set of players, the differences can be attributed to the peculiarities of the park. The significance or causes of these differences are "why" questions and are open to debate; the questions we're answering here are "what" and "how many."

The second set of tables highlights the performance of visiting players during the 1988 season. Listed are the top and bottom 10 in batting average, and the leaders in home runs and runs batted in. Qualifying for the batting average lists is based on a minimum of 3.1 plate appearances per game played by each player's team in that park.

Following the 13 pages of ballpark data are tables that rank the stadiums according to their effects on various elements of play. To illustrate, let's say that you find that the Oakland Coliseum reduced scoring by 17.5 percent over the past five seasons. You won't have to flip through the pages to check the corresponding figures for the 25 other stadiums to see where the Coliseum ranks. Just check the table at the end of the Ballparks section that ranks the 26 stadiums by their effect on scoring.

In addition to scoring, we've also included tables that rank the 26 parks by seven other categories. The fields with synthetic playing surfaces are indicated, giving you a quick read on what kind of impact plastic grass has on the category in question. For instance, if you check the table ranking the stadiums by their effect on stolen-base percentage, you'll see that the carpet has a nearly universal impact on base stealing.

Baltimore
Memorial Stadium

1988 Visiting Leaders

	1988 SEASON			1984 – 1988		
	Home Games	Road Games	Pct. Diff.	Home Games	Road Games	Pct. Diff.
G	80	81	− 1.2	403	405	− 0.5
AB	5451	5398	1.0	27458	27529	− 0.3
1B	966	997	− 4.1	4921	5020	− 1.7
2B	231	244	− 6.2	1147	1240	− 7.3
3B	18	35	− 49.1	82	193	− 57.4
HR	147	143	1.8	902	842	7.4
R	640	699	− 7.3	3570	3776	− 5.0
BA	.250	.263	− 5.0	.257	.265	− 3.1
SLG	.380	.401	− 5.2	.403	.416	− 3.1
XB%	.205	.219	− 6.3	.200	.222	− 10.0
E	107	107	1.2	593	595	0.2
SHO	11	10	11.4	45	41	10.3

BATTING AVG. (Top 10)

Baines, CHI	.500
White, KC	.500
Gagne, MIN	.417
Tartabull, KC	.417
Greenwell, BOS	.414
McGwire, OAK	.400
Walker, CHI	.381
Gladden, MIN	.375
Gruber, TOR	.375
2 players tied.	.364

HOME RUNS

McGwire, OAK	4
Baines, CHI	3
Evans, DET	3
Jackson, KC	3
Mattingly, NY	3
13 players tied.	2

BATTING AVG. (Bottom 10)

Snyder, CLE	.100
Reynolds, SEA	.105
Gantner, MIL	.111
Randolph, NY	.125
Hrbek, MIN	.136
Presley, SEA	.150
Wilson, KC	.174
Calderon, CHI	.176
Williams, CHI	.176
Franco, CLE	.182

RUNS BATTED IN

Evans, BOS	9
Greenwell, BOS	9
McGwire, OAK	9
Tartabull, KC	9
Jackson, KC	7
White, KC	7
Deer, MIL	6
Sheridan, DET	6
Sierra, TEX	6
Washington, NY	6

Boston
Fenway Park

1988 Visiting Leaders

	1988 SEASON			1984 – 1988		
	Home Games	Road Games	Pct. Diff.	Home Games	Road Games	Pct. Diff.
G	81	81	0.0	404	406	− 0.5
AB	5577	5441	2.5	28030	27829	0.7
1B	1064	1021	1.7	5422	5162	4.3
2B	335	233	40.3	1607	1242	28.5
3B	31	33	− 8.4	165	149	9.9
HR	141	126	9.2	755	801	− 6.4
R	816	686	19.0	4015	3738	7.9
BA	.282	.260	8.5	.284	.264	7.3
SLG	.429	.384	11.6	.433	.406	6.8
XB%	.256	.207	23.8	.246	.212	16.0
E	117	102	14.7	617	608	2.0
SHO	11	16	− 31.2	46	50	− 7.5

BATTING AVG. (Top 10)

Lansford, OAK	.600
Murray, BAL	.579
Washington, NY	.522
Brookens, DET	.471
Hrbek, MIN	.440
Brett, KC	.429
Liriano, TOR	.429
Seitzer, KC	.412
Weiss, OAK	.412
2 players tied.	.409

HOME RUNS

Gaetti, MIN	4
Buechele, TEX	3
Nokes, DET	3
8 players tied.	2

BATTING AVG. (Bottom 10)

Fletcher, TEX	.087
Franco, CLE	.100
B. Ripken, BAL	.111
Yount, MIL	.115
Gagne, MIN	.118
Sierra, TEX	.118
Clark, NY	.130
Jackson, KC	.136
Brock, MIL	.143
Deer, MIL	.148

RUNS BATTED IN

Whitt, TOR	11
Gruber, TOR	10
Gaetti, MIN	8
Nokes, DET	8
Trammell, DET	8
Bell, TOR	7
6 players tied.	6

California
Anaheim Stadium

1988 Visiting Leaders

BATTING AVG. (Top 10)　　　　HOME RUNS

Bush, MIN	.474	McGriff, TOR	3
Boggs, BOS	.458	McGwire, OAK	3
Snyder, CLE	.458	Parrish, BOS	3
Santana, NY	.450	10 players tied.	2
Puckett, MIN	.448		
Fernandez, TOR	.417		
Phelps, NY	.389		
Franco, CLE	.385		
Mattingly, NY	.385		
Brett, KC	.360		

BATTING AVG. (Bottom 10)　　　　RUNS BATTED IN

Hassey, OAK	.125	Puckett, MIN	10
Evans, DET	.136	Tabler, KC	10
Pettis, DET	.148	McGwire, OAK	7
Gedman, BOS	.150	Gruber, TOR	6
B. Ripken, BAL	.158	Lansford, OAK	6
Washington, NY	.174	McGriff, TOR	6
Sheridan, DET	.176	O'Brien, TEX	6
Javier, OAK	.182	Parrish, BOS	6
C. Ripken, BAL	.182	Sheffield, MIL	6
Tartabull, KC	.182	6 players tied.	5

	1988 SEASON			1984 – 1988		
	Home Games	Road Games	Pct. Diff.	Home Games	Road Games	Pct. Diff.
G	81	81	0.0	404	406	− 0.5
AB	5546	5604	− 1.0	27337	27966	− 2.2
1B	1051	1072	− 0.9	4909	5085	− 1.2
2B	228	283	− 18.6	1073	1336	− 17.8
3B	24	44	− 44.9	113	201	− 42.5
HR	129	130	0.3	835	745	14.7
R	701	784	− 10.6	3595	3761	− 3.9
BA	.258	.273	− 5.4	.254	.263	− 3.8
SLG	.378	.409	− 7.6	.393	.405	− 3.2
XB%	.193	.234	− 17.3	.195	.232	− 16.2
E	131	122	7.4	650	629	3.9
SHO	9	7	28.6	45	53	− 14.7

Chicago
Comiskey Park

1988 Visiting Leaders

BATTING AVG. (Top 10)　　　　HOME RUNS

Yount, MIL	.565	Burks, BOS	3
C. Ripken, BAL	.526	Canseco, OAK	3
Joyner, CAL	.500	Clark, NY	3
Knight, DET	.462	Laudner, MIN	3
Randolph, NY	.450	9 players tied.	2
Greenwell, BOS	.423		
Gagne, MIN	.421		
Davis, SEA	.409		
Winfield, NY	.409		
Brett, KC	.400		

BATTING AVG. (Bottom 10)　　　　RUNS BATTED IN

Wilson, KC	.095	Canseco, OAK	9
McDowell, TEX	.111	Burks, BOS	7
Presley, SEA	.115	C. Davis, CAL	7
Pagliarulo, NY	.125	Puckett, MIN	7
Sheets, BAL	.136	Sierra, TEX	7
Brantley, SEA	.167	Deer, MIL	6
Lansford, OAK	.167	Henderson, OAK	6
Leonard, MIL	.167	White, KC	6
Pettis, DET	.174	Yount, MIL	6
2 players tied.	.182	11 players tied.	5

	1988 SEASON			1984 – 1988		
	Home Games	Road Games	Pct. Diff.	Home Games	Road Games	Pct. Diff.
G	81	80	1.2	405	405	0.0
AB	5549	5420	2.4	27473	27417	0.2
1B	985	991	− 2.9	4820	4784	0.5
2B	253	226	9.3	1226	1178	3.9
3B	39	30	27.0	236	152	54.9
HR	119	151	− 23.0	732	798	− 8.5
R	684	704	− 4.0	3671	3425	7.2
BA	.252	.258	− 2.5	.255	.252	1.3
SLG	.376	.394	− 4.7	.397	.393	0.9
XB%	.229	.205	11.4	.233	.218	7.0
E	133	160	− 17.9	628	643	− 2.3
SHO	8	8	− 1.2	38	50	− 24.0

Cleveland
Cleveland Stadium

1988 Visiting Leaders

BATTING AVG. (Top 10)		HOME RUNS	
McDowell, TEX	.500	Greenwell, BOS	3
Javier, OAK	.480	Aguayo, NY	2
Greenwell, BOS	.458	Armas, CAL	2
C. Davis, CAL	.450	Burks, BOS	2
Orsulak, BAL	.440	Clark, NY	2
Cotto, SEA	.435	Gagne, MIN	2
Reynolds, SEA	.435	Rice, BOS	2
Lansford, OAK	.433	White, CAL	2
Sheets, BAL	.400	Williams, CHI	2
Rice, BOS	.385	Winfield, NY	2

BATTING AVG. (Bottom 10)		RUNS BATTED IN	
Brock, MIL	.077	Greenwell, BOS	9
C. Ripken, BAL	.080	Rice, BOS	9
Weiss, OAK	.091	Armas, CAL	8
Bell, TOR	.100	Burks, BOS	8
Lombardozzi, MIN	.111	Joyner, CAL	7
Stillwell, KC	.118	Canseco, OAK	6
Baines, CHI	.120	Clark, NY	6
Espy, TEX	.143	Diaz, SEA	6
Evans, DET	.158	Evans, BOS	6
Lynn, DET	.167	Sierra, TEX	6

	1988 SEASON			1984 – 1988		
	Home Games	Road Games	Pct. Diff.	Home Games	Road Games	Pct. Diff.
G	81	81	0.0	405	407	– 0.5
AB	5524	5536	– 0.2	28084	27938	0.5
1B	1089	1042	4.7	5589	5174	7.5
2B	227	254	– 10.4	1234	1310	– 6.3
3B	33	37	– 10.6	161	186	– 13.9
HR	114	140	– 18.4	752	782	– 4.3
R	712	685	3.9	3991	3894	3.0
BA	.265	.266	– 0.5	.275	.267	3.3
SLG	.380	.401	– 5.3	.411	.411	0.1
XB%	.193	.218	– 11.7	.200	.224	– 10.9
E	120	119	0.8	705	709	– 0.1
SHO	12	8	50.0	43	38	13.7

Detroit
Tiger Stadium

1988 Visiting Leaders

BATTING AVG. (Top 10)		HOME RUNS	
Allanson, CLE	.421	Benzinger, BOS	3
Cotto, SEA	.400	Brett, KC	3
Lee, TOR	.391	Hrbek, MIN	3
Anderson, BAL	.389	Phelps, NY	3
Brett, KC	.381	10 players tied.	2
Puckett, MIN	.375		
Ray, CAL	.375		
Sveum, MIL	.364		
3 players tied.	.348		

BATTING AVG. (Bottom 10)		RUNS BATTED IN	
Gagne, MIN	.045	Hrbek, MIN	8
Jackson, KC	.045	Benzinger, BOS	7
Tartabull, KC	.050	Barfield, TOR	6
Buckner, KC	.056	12 players tied.	5
Gladden, MIN	.080		
McDowell, TEX	.100		
Moseby, TOR	.100		
Brock, MIL	.125		
White, KC	.130		
C. Ripken, BAL	.136		

	1988 SEASON			1984 – 1988		
	Home Games	Road Games	Pct. Diff.	Home Games	Road Games	Pct. Diff.
G	81	81	0.0	406	403	0.7
AB	5384	5538	– 2.8	27484	27866	– 1.4
1B	912	1005	– 6.7	4671	4962	– 4.6
2B	196	253	– 20.3	1068	1336	– 18.9
3B	26	34	– 21.3	149	193	– 21.7
HR	159	134	22.1	919	820	13.6
R	631	730	– 13.6	3579	3814	– 6.9
BA	.240	.257	– 6.7	.248	.262	– 5.6
SLG	.375	.388	– 3.4	.398	.412	– 3.6
XB%	.196	.222	– 11.9	.207	.236	– 12.3
E	118	107	10.3	618	606	1.2
SHO	11	7	57.1	52	29	78.0

Kansas City
Royals Stadium

1988 Visiting Leaders

	1988 SEASON			1984 – 1988		
	Home Games	Road Games	Pct. Diff.	Home Games	Road Games	Pct. Diff.
G	80	81	− 1.2	405	404	0.2
AB	5490	5453	0.7	27730	27348	1.4
1B	1040	952	8.5	5010	4939	0.0
2B	302	233	28.7	1412	1147	21.4
3B	54	30	78.8	284	168	66.7
HR	92	131	− 30.2	545	742	− 27.6
R	689	663	5.2	3416	3354	1.6
BA	.271	.247	9.8	.261	.256	2.2
SLG	.396	.373	6.3	.392	.391	0.1
XB%	.255	.216	17.8	.253	.210	20.3
E	124	120	4.6	611	610	− 0.1
SHO	12	12	1.2	59	55	7.0

BATTING AVG. (Top 10)

		HOME RUNS	
Henderson, NY	.520	Bell, TOR	3
Reynolds, SEA	.500	Pasqua, CHI	3
Bell, TOR	.435	Franco, CLE	2
Barfield, TOR	.429	C. Ripken, BAL	2
Mattingly, NY	.423	Snyder, CLE	2
McGriff, TOR	.421	Winfield, NY	2
Trammell, DET	.412	23 players tied.	1
Downing, CAL	.400		
Evans, BOS	.391		
Fletcher, TEX	.391		

BATTING AVG. (Bottom 10)

		RUNS BATTED IN	
Incaviglia, TEX	.059	Winfield, NY	7
Orsulak, BAL	.105	Clark, NY	6
Phelps, NY	.133	Evans, BOS	6
Sveum, MIL	.136	Fletcher, TEX	6
Anderson, BAL	.143	10 players tied.	5
B. Ripken, BAL	.143		
Randolph, NY	.150		
Sheets, BAL	.150		
Surhoff, MIL	.158		
Lansford, OAK	.160		

Milwaukee
County Stadium

1988 Visiting Leaders

	1988 SEASON			1984 – 1988		
	Home Games	Road Games	Pct. Diff.	Home Games	Road Games	Pct. Diff.
G	81	81	0.0	403	404	− 0.2
AB	5514	5442	1.3	27744	27778	− 0.1
1B	995	996	− 1.4	5279	5213	1.4
2B	243	246	− 2.5	1257	1240	1.5
3B	24	22	7.7	180	157	14.8
HR	125	113	9.2	664	700	− 5.0
R	664	634	4.7	3651	3594	1.8
BA	.252	.253	− 0.6	.266	.263	1.1
SLG	.372	.369	1.0	.396	.395	0.4
XB%	.212	.212	− 0.2	.214	.211	1.2
E	126	112	12.5	679	645	5.5
SHO	8	14	− 42.9	44	39	13.1

BATTING AVG. (Top 10)

		HOME RUNS	
McGwire, OAK	.474	Hrbek, MIN	4
Hrbek, MIN	.435	Carter, CLE	3
Wilkerson, TEX	.421	McGwire, OAK	3
Allanson, CLE	.407	9 players tied.	2
Carter, CLE	.393		
O'Brien, TEX	.364		
Slaught, NY	.350		
Weiss, OAK	.350		
3 players tied.	.348		

BATTING AVG. (Bottom 10)

		RUNS BATTED IN	
Evans, BOS	.000	Carter, CLE	9
Reynolds, SEA	.042	McGwire, OAK	8
Winfield, NY	.059	Murray, BAL	7
Fletcher, TEX	.125	Ray, CAL	7
Puckett, MIN	.136	Bell, TOR	6
Brookens, DET	.143	Brett, KC	6
Whitaker, DET	.143	Hrbek, MIN	6
Buechele, TEX	.158	Hall, CLE	5
Lynn, DET	.158	13 players tied.	4
2 players tied.	.167		

Minnesota
Metrodome

1988 Visiting Leaders

1988 SEASON			1984 – 1988		
Home Games	Road Games	Pct. Diff.	Home Games	Road Games	Pct. Diff.
G	81	81	0.0	408	402	1.5
AB	5530	5457	1.3	28149	26991	4.3
1B	1031	1028	– 1.0	5024	4936	– 2.4
2B	301	253	17.4	1511	1215	19.2
3B	31	24	27.5	205	132	48.9
HR	155	142	7.7	870	807	3.4
R	756	675	12.0	3889	3549	8.0
BA	.275	.265	3.5	.270	.263	2.9
SLG	.424	.398	6.5	.431	.407	5.9
XB%	.244	.212	14.8	.255	.214	18.8
E	103	107	– 3.7	578	582	– 2.1
SHO	6	12	– 50.0	31	55	– 44.5

BATTING AVG. (Top 10)

Whitaker, DET	.444
Clark, NY	.438
Santana, NY	.409
Carter, CLE	.407
Brett, KC	.400
Gallagher, CHI	.400
C. Ripken, BAL	.400
Surhoff, MIL	.400
Wilson, KC	.393
Howell, CAL	.391

HOME RUNS

Carter, CLE	3
Moseby, TOR	3
Stillwell, KC	3
14 players tied.	2

BATTING AVG. (Bottom 10)

Quinones, SEA	.059
Greenwell, BOS	.100
Rice, BOS	.105
Downing, CAL	.111
Gerhart, BAL	.111
Jackson, KC	.120
Balboni, SEA	.143
Schofield, CAL	.143
Benzinger, BOS	.158
Tabler, KC	.158

RUNS BATTED IN

Carter, CLE	10
Stillwell, KC	9
Moseby, TOR	8
Murray, BAL	7
Winfield, NY	7
Brett, KC	6
Clark, NY	6
Henderson, NY	6
10 players tied.	5

New York
Yankee Stadium

1988 Visiting Leaders

1988 SEASON			1984 – 1988		
Home Games	Road Games	Pct. Diff.	Home Games	Road Games	Pct. Diff.
G	80	81	– 1.2	402	406	– 1.0
AB	5517	5730	– 3.7	27429	28215	– 2.8
1B	1002	1061	– 1.9	5089	5175	1.2
2B	257	314	– 15.0	1175	1385	– 12.7
3B	16	26	– 36.1	140	160	– 10.0
HR	152	153	3.2	797	829	– 1.1
R	723	797	– 8.2	3613	3924	– 7.0
BA	.259	.271	– 4.6	.263	.268	– 1.9
SLG	.394	.415	– 5.2	.403	.416	– 3.2
XB%	.214	.243	– 11.8	.205	.230	– 10.7
E	129	121	7.9	626	628	0.7
SHO	6	5	21.5	47	42	13.0

BATTING AVG. (Top 10)

Boggs, BOS	.478
Hubbard, OAK	.478
Hrbek, MIN	.444
Buechele, TEX	.429
McGriff, TOR	.421
Reynolds, SEA	.393
Downing, CAL	.385
Fernandez, TOR	.385
Schofield, CAL	.381
Wilson, KC	.381

HOME RUNS

Downing, CAL	5
Murray, BAL	3
14 players tied.	2

BATTING AVG. (Bottom 10)

McGwire, OAK	.000
Sveum, MIL	.069
Lemon, DET	.100
Trammell, DET	.120
Gaetti, MIN	.130
Calderon, CHI	.136
Canseco, OAK	.143
Carter, CLE	.143
Jacoby, CLE	.167
2 players tied.	.174

RUNS BATTED IN

Downing, CAL	9
Evans, BOS	8
Greenwell, BOS	7
Joyner, CAL	7
Kittle, CLE	6
Murray, BAL	6
Steinbach, OAK	6
Yount, MIL	6
4 players tied.	5

Oakland
Oakland-Alameda County Coliseum

	1988 SEASON			1984 – 1988		
	Home Games	Road Games	Pct. Diff.	Home Games	Road Games	Pct. Diff.
G	81	81	0.0	405	405	0.0
AB	5481	5689	– 3.7	27366	27975	– 2.2
1B	1027	1028	3.7	4897	5047	– 0.8
2B	211	261	– 16.1	1088	1358	– 18.1
3B	23	28	– 14.7	123	194	– 35.2
HR	114	158	– 25.1	719	897	– 18.1
R	656	764	– 14.1	3477	4107	– 15.3
BA	.251	.259	– 3.2	.249	.268	– 6.9
SLG	.360	.398	– 9.6	.377	.427	– 11.6
XB%	.186	.219	– 15.4	.198	.235	– 15.7
E	114	116	– 1.7	656	679	– 3.4
SHO	13	7	85.7	46	23	100.0

1988 Visiting Leaders

BATTING AVG. (Top 10)

		HOME RUNS	
Puckett, MIN	.516	Gaetti, MIN	3
Moses, MIN	.435	McGriff, TOR	3
McGriff, TOR	.429	Armas, CAL	2
Trammell, DET	.389	Clark, NY	2
Franco, CLE	.375	Gagne, MIN	2
Schofield, CAL	.368	Petralli, TEX	2
Snyder, CLE	.368	C. Ripken, BAL	2
Ray, CAL	.360	31 players tied.	1
Quinones, SEA	.346		
4 players tied.	.333		

BATTING AVG. (Bottom 10)

		RUNS BATTED IN	
Fisk, CHI	.059	Gaetti, MIN	8
Larkin, MIN	.087	McGriff, TOR	8
Espy, TEX	.095	Puckett, MIN	8
Santana, NY	.111	Winfield, NY	7
B. Ripken, BAL	.118	Hall, CLE	6
Parrish, BOS	.125	Ray, CAL	6
Lemon, DET	.130	Walker, CHI	6
Pagliarulo, NY	.136	7 players tied.	5
Henderson, NY	.143		
Howell, CAL	.143		

Seattle
Kingdome

	1988 SEASON			1984 – 1988		
	Home Games	Road Games	Pct. Diff.	Home Games	Road Games	Pct. Diff.
G	81	80	1.2	408	401	1.7
AB	5485	5359	2.4	27948	27166	2.9
1B	915	965	– 7.4	4925	5025	– 4.7
2B	295	266	8.4	1373	1299	2.7
3B	30	19	54.3	186	177	2.1
HR	178	114	52.6	912	661	34.1
R	767	641	18.2	3907	3608	6.4
BA	.259	.255	1.6	.265	.264	0.4
SLG	.421	.375	12.1	.425	.397	6.9
XB%	.262	.228	15.0	.240	.227	5.9
E	122	109	10.5	624	642	– 4.5
SHO	13	12	7.0	42	49	– 15.8

1988 Visiting Leaders

BATTING AVG. (Top 10)

		HOME RUNS	
Orsulak, BAL	.526	Canseco, OAK	6
Boggs, BOS	.500	Bell, TOR	3
Howell, CAL	.476	Fisk, CHI	3
Whitaker, DET	.458	Jackson, KC	3
McGriff, TOR	.429	McGriff, TOR	3
Fernandez, TOR	.400	10 players tied.	2
Winfield, NY	.391		
Salazar, DET	.375		
3 players tied.	.368		

BATTING AVG. (Bottom 10)

		RUNS BATTED IN	
Barfield, TOR	.059	Canseco, OAK	11
Pasqua, CHI	.087	Howell, CAL	9
White, KC	.105	Espy, TEX	8
Tettleton, BAL	.111	Baines, CHI	7
Wilson, KC	.111	C. Davis, CAL	7
Anderson, BAL	.118	McGriff, TOR	7
Henderson, NY	.120	Whitaker, DET	7
Buechele, TEX	.148	Winfield, NY	7
Brett, KC	.150	Yount, MIL	7
2 players tied.	.158	7 players tied.	6

Texas
Arlington Stadium

	1988 SEASON			1984 – 1988		
	Home Games	Road Games	Pct. Diff.	Home Games	Road Games	Pct. Diff.
G	81	80	1.2	403	404	– 0.2
AB	5431	5423	0.1	27536	27334	0.7
1B	1005	934	7.4	5098	4751	6.5
2B	224	226	– 1.0	1197	1217	– 2.4
3B	29	29	– 0.1	151	175	– 14.3
HR	125	116	7.6	780	753	2.8
R	704	668	4.1	3740	3590	4.4
BA	.255	.241	5.8	.262	.252	4.0
SLG	.376	.357	5.2	.402	.392	2.4
XB%	.201	.214	– 6.2	.209	.227	– 7.7
E	117	129	– 10.4	631	622	1.7
SHO	9	11	– 19.2	32	39	– 17.7

1988 Visiting Leaders

BATTING AVG. (Top 10)		HOME RUNS	
Henderson, OAK	.550	Canseco, OAK	4
Gallagher, CHI	.533	Gallagher, CHI	3
Canseco, OAK	.467	Henderson, OAK	3
Fernandez, TOR	.462	Jackson, KC	3
Snyder, CLE	.455	Snyder, CLE	3
Mattingly, NY	.407	Baines, CHI	2
Puckett, MIN	.391	Brett, KC	2
Brett, KC	.385	Jacoby, CLE	2
Lyons, CHI	.381	McGwire, OAK	2
Murray, BAL	.375	Puckett, MIN	2

BATTING AVG. (Bottom 10)		RUNS BATTED IN	
Gladden, MIN	.000	Tartabull, KC	11
White, KC	.080	Canseco, OAK	8
Howell, CAL	.091	Snyder, CLE	8
Parker, OAK	.091	Gruber, TOR	7
Surhoff, MIL	.091	Puckett, MIN	7
Hall, CLE	.105	7 players tied.	6
Valle, SEA	.111		
Javier, OAK	.118		
Schu, BAL	.130		
Balboni, SEA	.138		

Toronto
Exhibition Stadium

	1988 SEASON			1984 – 1988		
	Home Games	Road Games	Pct. Diff.	Home Games	Road Games	Pct. Diff.
G	81	81	0.0	404	407	– 0.7
AB	5526	5515	0.2	27599	28015	– 1.5
1B	1001	991	0.8	4742	5123	– 6.0
2B	255	266	– 4.3	1382	1247	12.5
3B	47	34	38.0	241	179	36.7
HR	151	150	0.5	801	806	0.9
R	715	728	– 1.8	3649	3629	1.3
BA	.263	.261	0.7	.260	.263	– 1.1
SLG	.408	.403	1.2	.414	.406	2.0
XB%	.232	.232	– 0.3	.255	.218	17.1
E	104	134	– 22.4	617	635	– 2.1
SHO	10	10	0.0	38	45	– 14.9

1988 Visiting Leaders

BATTING AVG. (Top 10)		HOME RUNS	
Howell, CAL	.545	Canseco, OAK	3
Salazar, DET	.500	Kittle, CLE	3
Winfield, NY	.483	Lynn, DET	3
C. Davis, CAL	.480	McGwire, OAK	3
Boggs, BOS	.474	10 players tied.	2
Guillen, CHI	.435		
Henderson, NY	.433		
Petralli, TEX	.412		
McGwire, OAK	.381		
Ray, CAL	.370		

BATTING AVG. (Bottom 10)		RUNS BATTED IN	
O'Brien, TEX	.043	Winfield, NY	11
Cotto, SEA	.053	McGwire, OAK	9
Jackson, KC	.053	Ray, CAL	8
Pettis, DET	.100	Canseco, OAK	7
Gladden, MIN	.111	C. Davis, CAL	7
Murray, BAL	.120	Greenwell, BOS	7
Sveum, MIL	.136	Brett, KC	6
Larkin, MIN	.158	Fletcher, TEX	6
McDowell, TEX	.158	Mattingly, NY	6
Gallagher, CHI	.160	Meyer, MIL	6

Atlanta
Atlanta-Fulton County Stadium

1988 Visiting Leaders

BATTING AVG. (Top 10)		HOME RUNS	
Dernier, PHI	.571	Esasky, CIN	4
Elster, NY	.524	Santiago, SD	4
Mitchell, SF	.448	Hernandez, NY	3
Oquendo, STL	.444	Strawberry, NY	3
Hatcher, HOU	.441	9 players tied.	2
Aldrete, SF	.417		
Marshall, LA	.400		
Clark, SF	.394		
Hayes, PHI	.391		
2 players tied.	.387		

	1988 SEASON			1984 – 1988		
	Home Games	Road Games	Pct. Diff.	Home Games	Road Games	Pct. Diff.
G	79	81	– 2.5	403	403	0.0
AB	5528	5440	1.6	27788	26927	3.2
1B	1056	1009	3.0	5288	4875	5.1
2B	250	221	11.3	1275	1133	9.0
3B	32	28	12.5	141	152	– 10.1
HR	112	92	19.8	700	567	19.6
R	686	610	15.3	3719	3187	16.7
BA	.262	.248	5.7	.266	.250	6.7
SLG	.380	.350	8.6	.398	.366	8.6
XB%	.211	.198	6.5	.211	.209	1.3
E	133	133	2.5	731	669	9.3
SHO	7	14	– 48.7	34	60	– 43.3

BATTING AVG. (Bottom 10)		RUNS BATTED IN	
Teufel, NY	.125	Aldrete, SF	10
Pena, STL	.130	Mitchell, SF	10
Kruk, SD	.154	Brooks, MTL	9
Lind, PIT	.167	Guerrero, STL	9
Pedrique, PIT	.167	Hernandez, NY	9
Thompson, SF	.167	Brenly, SF	8
Martinez, SD	.192	Butler, SF	8
Scioscia, LA	.192	Doran, HOU	8
O'Neill, CIN	.200	Marshall, LA	8
Raines, MTL	.217	Santiago, SD	8

Chicago
Wrigley Field

1988 Visiting Leaders

BATTING AVG. (Top 10)		HOME RUNS	
Thompson, PHI	.500	Bonilla, PIT	4
Perry, ATL	.478	Johnson, NY	4
Young, HOU	.458	Brunansky, STL	3
Bonilla, PIT	.432	Dykstra, NY	3
Van Slyke, PIT	.432	Gibson, LA	3
Galarraga, MTL	.429	Van Slyke, PIT	3
Jordan, PHI	.393	7 players tied.	2
Ramirez, HOU	.391		
Johnson, NY	.371		
2 players tied.	.357		

	1988 SEASON			1984 – 1988		
	Home Games	Road Games	Pct. Diff.	Home Games	Road Games	Pct. Diff.
G	82	81	1.2	403	404	– 0.2
AB	5748	5567	3.3	28041	27355	2.5
1B	1160	993	13.1	5341	4964	5.0
2B	226	286	– 23.5	1239	1317	– 8.2
3B	46	36	23.8	212	183	13.0
HR	129	99	26.2	859	576	45.5
R	719	635	11.8	3878	3293	18.1
BA	.272	.254	6.9	.273	.257	6.0
SLG	.394	.372	6.1	.424	.382	11.0
XB%	.190	.245	– 22.4	.214	.232	– 7.9
E	168	119	39.5	688	619	11.4
SHO	13	10	28.4	42	49	– 14.1

BATTING AVG. (Bottom 10)		RUNS BATTED IN	
Murphy, ATL	.045	Bonilla, PIT	12
Davis, HOU	.080	Van Slyke, PIT	10
Thomas, ATL	.130	Dykstra, NY	8
Shelby, LA	.136	Johnson, NY	8
Hatcher, HOU	.150	Ramirez, HOU	8
Magadan, NY	.154	McReynolds, NY	7
Sabo, CIN	.154	Reynolds, PIT	7
James, PHI	.172	8 players tied.	6
McGee, STL	.185		
Strawberry, NY	.188		

Cincinnati
Riverfront Stadium

1988 Visiting Leaders

BATTING AVG. (Top 10)		HOME RUNS	
Oberkfell, PIT	.476	Davis, HOU	5
'Grace, CHI	.450	R. Alomar, SD	3
Bonds, PIT	.400	Grace, CHI	3
Perry, ATL	.400	10 players tied.	2
Strawberry, NY	.400		
Brooks, MTL	.391		
Guerrero, STL	.370		
Bonilla, PIT	.368		
Clark, SF	.364		
R. Alomar, SD	.357		

	1988 SEASON			1984 – 1988		
	Home Games	Road Games	Pct. Diff.	Home Games	Road Games	Pct. Diff.
G	80	81	− 1.2	404	405	− 0.2
AB	5414	5377	0.7	27676	27253	1.6
1B	910	920	− 1.8	4920	4831	0.3
2B	250	228	8.9	1357	1155	15.7
3B	27	27	− 0.7	169	161	3.4
HR	146	97	49.5	739	625	16.4
R	645	592	10.3	3638	3300	10.5
BA	.246	.237	4.1	.260	.248	4.5
SLG	.383	.343	11.7	.401	.371	7.9
XB%	.233	.217	7.5	.237	.214	10.6
E	112	138	− 17.8	608	714	− 14.6
SHO	11	16	− 30.4	38	62	− 38.6

BATTING AVG. (Bottom 10)		RUNS BATTED IN	
McReynolds, NY	.059	Davis, HOU	13
Pendleton, STL	.083	Grace, CHI	10
Santiago, SD	.120	Hatcher, HOU	8
Brunansky, STL	.125	Ramirez, HOU	8
Maldonado, SF	.125	Marshall, LA	7
Young, PHI	.125	Bass, HOU	6
Galarraga, MTL	.136	Gwynn, SD	6
Sax, LA	.138	Moreland, SD	6
Uribe, SF	.152	Shelby, LA	6
Dawson, CHI	.174	Van Slyke, PIT	6

Houston
Astrodome

1988 Visiting Leaders

BATTING AVG. (Top 10)		HOME RUNS	
Oquendo, STL	.467	Clark, SF	3
Larkin, CIN	.448	Gant, ATL	3
Marshall, LA	.441	Bonds, PIT	2
Foley, MTL	.438	Daniels, CIN	2
Gwynn, SD	.393	Dawson, CHI	2
Dawson, CHI	.389	Larkin, CIN	2
Galarraga, MTL	.360	Marshall, LA	2
Clark, SF	.344	Parent, SD	2
Sabo, CIN	.343	Schmidt, PHI	2
4 players tied.	.333	30 players tied.	1

	1988 SEASON			1984 – 1988		
	Home Games	Road Games	Pct. Diff.	Home Games	Road Games	Pct. Diff.
G	81	81	0.0	405	405	0.0
AB	5418	5597	− 3.2	27342	27443	− 0.4
1B	937	978	− 1.0	4982	4851	3.1
2B	232	237	1.1	1134	1192	− 4.5
3B	37	37	3.3	197	193	2.4
HR	83	136	− 37.0	426	707	− 39.5
R	575	673	− 14.6	3065	3452	− 11.2
BA	.238	.248	− 4.1	.246	.253	− 2.6
SLG	.340	.376	− 9.6	.349	.388	− 10.0
XB%	.223	.219	1.9	.211	.222	− 5.1
E	115	142	− 19.0	624	699	− 10.7
SHO	19	10	90.0	72	44	63.6

BATTING AVG. (Bottom 10)		RUNS BATTED IN	
Coleman, STL	.050	Clark, SF	7
Samuel, PHI	.074	Dawson, CHI	6
Dunston, CHI	.080	Maldonado, SF	6
Guerrero, STL	.083	McReynolds, NY	6
Strawberry, NY	.087	Riles, SF	6
Carter, NY	.091	Schmidt, PHI	6
Murphy, ATL	.094	Uribe, SF	6
Lind, PIT	.105	6 players tied.	5
James, PHI	.125		
Van Slyke, PIT	.130		

Los Angeles
Dodger Stadium

1988 Visiting Leaders

1988 SEASON			1984 – 1988		
Home Games	Road Games	Pct. Diff.	Home Games	Road Games	Pct. Diff.

	Home Games	Road Games	Pct. Diff.	Home Games	Road Games	Pct. Diff.
G	81	81	0.0	405	405	0.0
AB	5403	5468	– 1.2	27458	27409	0.2
1B	1067	938	15.1	5260	4802	9.3
2B	185	211	– 11.3	968	1276	– 24.3
3B	26	27	– 2.5	89	166	– 46.5
HR	87	96	– 8.3	488	604	– 19.3
R	613	559	9.7	2991	3249	– 7.9
BA	.253	.233	8.6	.248	.250	– 0.8
SLG	.345	.334	3.3	.343	.375	– 8.5
XB%	.165	.202	– 18.4	.167	.231	– 27.5
E	153	134	14.2	754	746	1.1
SHO	16	18	– 11.1	79	65	21.5

BATTING AVG. (Top 10)

McGee, STL	.481
Bonilla, PIT	.458
Gwynn, SD	.455
Brunansky, STL	.450
Johnson, NY	.429
Hernandez, NY	.417
Bradley, PHI	.409
Doran, HOU	.406
Backman, NY	.400
Van Slyke, PIT	.393

HOME RUNS

Van Slyke, PIT	3
Brunansky, STL	2
Martinez, SD	2
Trevino, HOU	2
29 players tied.	1

BATTING AVG. (Bottom 10)

McReynolds, NY	.130
Pendleton, STL	.130
Dunston, CHI	.150
Thompson, PHI	.150
Coleman, STL	.154
Ramirez, HOU	.167
Murphy, ATL	.171
Hatcher, HOU	.172
Dawson, CHI	.174
Winningham, CIN	.179

RUNS BATTED IN

Hernandez, NY	8
Van Slyke, PIT	8
Bonilla, PIT	7
O'Neill, CIN	7
Pendleton, STL	7
Grace, CHI	6
Gwynn, SD	6
Santiago, SD	6
Davis, CIN	5
LaValliere, PIT	5

Montreal
Olympic Stadium

1988 Visiting Leaders

	Home Games	Road Games	Pct. Diff.	Home Games	Road Games	Pct. Diff.
G	81	82	– 1.2	404	404	0.0
AB	5581	5497	1.5	27328	27520	– 0.7
1B	947	961	– 2.9	4707	4967	– 4.6
2B	275	202	34.1	1294	1223	6.5
3B	55	41	32.1	222	181	23.5
HR	109	120	– 10.5	536	614	– 12.1
R	637	583	10.6	3174	3279	– 3.2
BA	.248	.241	3.1	.247	.254	– 2.6
SLG	.376	.358	5.0	.370	.378	– 2.3
XB%	.258	.202	28.0	.244	.220	10.5
E	140	127	11.6	645	652	– 1.1
SHO	10	14	– 27.7	55	52	5.8

BATTING AVG. (Top 10)

Dawson, CHI	.567
Bonilla, PIT	.455
Strawberry, NY	.419
Bream, PIT	.382
Bonds, PIT	.368
Davis, HOU	.360
Webster, CHI	.346
Gant, ATL	.333
Shelby, LA	.333
Pena, STL	.321

HOME RUNS

Bass, HOU	3
James, PHI	3
McReynolds, NY	3
Strawberry, NY	3
7 players tied.	2

BATTING AVG. (Bottom 10)

Mitchell, SF	.053
Esasky, CIN	.059
Parrish, PHI	.111
Murphy, ATL	.125
Sabo, CIN	.130
Santiago, SD	.143
Scioscia, LA	.150
Coleman, STL	.156
Brunansky, STL	.161
3 players tied.	.167

RUNS BATTED IN

Bream, PIT	13
Bonilla, PIT	9
McReynolds, NY	9
Davis, HOU	8
Strawberry, NY	7
Bass, HOU	6
Davis, ATL	6
Dawson, CHI	6
Samuel, PHI	6
Schmidt, PHI	6

New York
Shea Stadium

1988 Visiting Leaders

BATTING AVG. (Top 10)

		HOME RUNS	
Law, CHI	.424	Brooks, MTL	2
McGee, STL	.378	Da. Martinez, MTL	2
Hatcher, HOU	.360	Schmidt, PHI	2
Dunston, CHI	.343	28 players tied.	1
Santiago, SD	.333		
Van Slyke, PIT	.333		
Sabo, CIN	.320		
Thomas, ATL	.320		
Thompson, SF	.318		
Ramirez, HOU	.308		

BATTING AVG. (Bottom 10)

		RUNS BATTED IN	
Doran, HOU	.111	Hayes, PHI	6
Samuel, PHI	.132	James, PHI	6
Galarraga, MTL	.133	Sandberg, CHI	5
Kruk, SD	.133	Schmidt, PHI	5
Dawson, CHI	.143	Wallach, MTL	5
LaValliere, PIT	.143	8 players tied.	4
Esasky, CIN	.167		
Palmeiro, CHI	.172		
Sandberg, CHI	.179		
Sax, LA	.182		

	1988 SEASON			1984 – 1988		
	Home Games	Road Games	Pct. Diff.	Home Games	Road Games	Pct. Diff.
G	80	80	0.0	404	404	0.0
AB	5308	5437	− 2.4	27032	27867	− 3.0
1B	906	989	− 6.2	4824	5025	− 1.0
2B	199	261	− 21.9	1140	1256	− 6.4
3B	25	30	− 14.6	132	173	− 21.3
HR	101	129	− 19.8	600	664	− 6.8
R	531	704	− 24.6	3164	3544	− 10.7
BA	.232	.259	− 10.5	.248	.255	− 3.0
SLG	.336	.389	− 13.7	.366	.384	− 4.7
XB%	.198	.227	− 12.8	.209	.221	− 5.8
E	112	134	− 16.4	677	669	1.2
SHO	19	9	111.1	62	46	34.8

Philadelphia
Veterans Stadium

1988 Visiting Leaders

BATTING AVG. (Top 10)

		HOME RUNS	
R. Alomar, SD	.500	Bonilla, PIT	4
Dawson, CHI	.412	Bonds, PIT	3
Larkin, CIN	.389	McReynolds, NY	3
Coleman, STL	.387	Murphy, ATL	3
Moreland, SD	.381	9 players tied.	2
Bonds, PIT	.375		
Doran, HOU	.375		
Pena, STL	.370		
Raines, MTL	.370		
Diaz, CIN	.368		

BATTING AVG. (Bottom 10)

		RUNS BATTED IN	
Clark, SF	.056	Bonilla, PIT	14
Johnson, NY	.100	McReynolds, NY	9
Uribe, SF	.105	Bonds, PIT	8
Dunston, CHI	.108	Bream, PIT	8
Davis, LA	.118	Strawberry, NY	8
McGee, STL	.156	Daniels, CIN	7
Gwynn, SD	.158	Davis, HOU	7
Lind, PIT	.167	Moreland, SD	7
Oquendo, STL	.171	Sax, LA	7
Bass, HOU	.174	5 players tied.	6

	1988 SEASON			1984 – 1988		
	Home Games	Road Games	Pct. Diff.	Home Games	Road Games	Pct. Diff.
G	81	81	0.0	404	405	− 0.2
AB	5459	5414	0.8	27581	27530	0.2
1B	923	1022	− 10.4	4828	5002	− 3.7
2B	284	226	24.6	1369	1153	18.5
3B	30	32	− 7.0	241	179	34.4
HR	126	98	27.5	672	676	− 0.8
R	688	643	7.0	3613	3371	7.4
BA	.250	.255	− 1.9	.258	.255	1.2
SLG	.382	.362	5.4	.398	.383	3.9
XB%	.254	.202	25.9	.250	.210	18.9
E	114	148	− 23.0	668	679	− 1.4
SHO	12	10	20.0	49	41	19.8

Pittsburgh
Three Rivers Stadium

1988 Visiting Leaders

BATTING AVG. (Top 10)		HOME RUNS	
Thompson, SF	.520	Galarraga, MTL	4
Davis, HOU	.500	Johnson, NY	3
Pena, STL	.441	Mitchell, SF	3
Davis, LA	.409	8 players tied.	2
McGee, STL	.385		
Dunston, CHI	.382		
Thompson, PHI	.379		
Gwynn, SD	.375		
Foley, MTL	.370		
Thomas, ATL	.360		

	1988 SEASON			1984 – 1988		
	Home Games	Road Games	Pct. Diff.	Home Games	Road Games	Pct. Diff.
G	81	79	2.5	404	403	0.2
AB	5398	5371	0.5	27324	27300	0.1
1B	897	993	– 10.1	4771	4919	– 3.1
2B	268	220	21.2	1330	1237	7.4
3B	40	40	– 0.5	193	183	5.4
HR	106	112	– 5.8	569	580	– 2.0
R	624	643	– 5.4	3285	3270	0.2
BA	.243	.254	– 4.4	.251	.253	– 0.9
SLG	.366	.373	– 1.7	.376	.376	0.1
XB%	.256	.208	23.2	.242	.224	8.0
E	130	115	10.3	642	623	2.8
SHO	6	15	– 61.0	49	62	– 21.2

BATTING AVG. (Bottom 10)		RUNS BATTED IN	
Parrish, PHI	.040	Galarraga, MTL	11
Moreland, SD	.100	McGee, STL	8
O'Neill, CIN	.105	Pena, STL	8
Sandberg, CHI	.143	Davis, CIN	7
Johnson, NY	.154	Mitchell, SF	7
Maldonado, SF	.158	Dunston, CHI	6
Carter, NY	.172	Elster, NY	6
Sabo, CIN	.182	Gwynn, SD	6
Strawberry, NY	.182	Samuel, PHI	6
Brown, SD	.190	8 players tied.	5

St. Louis
Busch Stadium

1988 Visiting Leaders

BATTING AVG. (Top 10)		HOME RUNS	
Hatcher, HOU	.478	Clark, SF	3
Marshall, LA	.458	Marshall, LA	3
Gant, ATL	.444	Bream, PIT	2
Strawberry, NY	.444	Durham, CIN	2
Sax, LA	.435	Gibson, LA	2
Palmeiro, CHI	.424	Johnson, NY	2
Trevino, HOU	.412	McReynolds, NY	2
Dykstra, NY	.400	Wallach, MTL	2
Gibson, LA	.375	21 players tied.	1
Law, CHI	.375		

	1988 SEASON			1984 – 1988		
	Home Games	Road Games	Pct. Diff.	Home Games	Road Games	Pct. Diff.
G	81	81	0.0	405	404	0.2
AB	5573	5458	2.1	27310	27447	– 0.5
1B	1039	982	3.6	5000	5075	– 1.0
2B	257	246	2.3	1303	1177	11.3
3B	44	30	43.6	235	190	24.3
HR	68	94	– 29.2	406	526	– 22.4
R	632	579	9.2	3232	3298	– 2.2
BA	.253	.248	2.0	.254	.254	0.2
SLG	.351	.355	– 1.2	.364	.368	– 1.2
XB%	.225	.219	2.4	.235	.212	10.9
E	131	134	– 2.2	661	664	– 0.7
SHO	15	15	0.0	53	58	– 8.8

BATTING AVG. (Bottom 10)		RUNS BATTED IN	
Bass, HOU	.043	Clark, SF	9
Oberkfell, PIT	.125	Johnson, NY	9
Van Slyke, PIT	.139	Marshall, LA	8
Butler, SF	.148	Thomas, ATL	7
R. Alomar, SD	.150	Wilson, NY	7
James, ATL	.158	Gibson, LA	6
Murphy, ATL	.158	McReynolds, NY	6
Brooks, MTL	.161	Palmeiro, CHI	6
Thomas, ATL	.161	Perry, ATL	6
Samuel, PHI	.171	6 players tied.	5

San Diego
San Diego/Jack Murphy Stadium

1988 Visiting Leaders

				1988 SEASON				1984 – 1988		
		Home Games	Road Games	Pct. Diff.		Home Games	Road Games	Pct. Diff.		
G		81	80	1.2		405	404	0.2		
AB		5333	5428	– 1.8		27093	27477	– 1.4		
1B		950	999	– 3.2		4862	5198	– 5.1		
2B		191	247	– 21.3		1028	1216	– 14.3		
3B		27	37	– 25.7		167	164	3.3		
HR		112	94	21.3		689	558	25.2		
R		570	607	– 7.3		3211	3368	– 4.9		
BA		.240	.254	– 5.4		.249	.260	– 4.1		
SLG		.349	.365	– 4.3		.376	.377	– 0.3		
XB%		.187	.221	– 15.7		.197	.210	– 6.0		
E		131	116	11.5		682	647	5.1		
SHO		11	9	20.7		52	59	– 12.1		

BATTING AVG. (Top 10)

		HOME RUNS	
Palmeiro, CHI	.458	Brunansky, STL	5
Oberkfell, PIT	.435	Dawson, CHI	4
Grace, CHI	.409	Maldonado, SF	4
Strawberry, NY	.391	Bass, HOU	3
Dawson, CHI	.381	Clark, SF	3
O'Neill, CIN	.379	Davis, CIN	3
Clark, SF	.375	Galarraga, MTL	3
Coleman, STL	.360	Hayes, PHI	2
Thompson, PHI	.348	Murphy, ATL	2
Van Slyke, PIT	.348	27 players tied.	1

BATTING AVG. (Bottom 10)

		RUNS BATTED IN	
Young, HOU	.071	Maldonado, SF	11
Sax, LA	.091	Brunansky, STL	9
Law, CHI	.111	Dawson, CHI	9
Thompson, SF	.111	Clark, SF	8
Raines, MTL	.118	Murphy, ATL	7
Bonilla, PIT	.130	O'Neill, CIN	7
Bradley, PHI	.148	Thomas, ATL	6
Elster, NY	.158	6 players tied.	5
Perry, ATL	.161		
Hatcher, HOU	.179		

San Francisco
Candlestick Park

1988 Visiting Leaders

				1988 SEASON				1984 – 1988		
		Home Games	Road Games	Pct. Diff.		Home Games	Road Games	Pct. Diff.		
G		81	81	0.0		405	405	0.0		
AB		5400	5509	– 2.0		27333	27778	– 1.6		
1B		963	971	1.2		4821	5095	– 3.8		
2B		211	243	– 11.4		1139	1241	– 6.7		
3B		26	50	– 47.0		127	200	– 35.5		
HR		100	112	– 8.9		644	631	3.7		
R		602	694	– 13.3		3212	3571	– 10.1		
BA		.241	.250	– 3.6		.246	.258	– 4.6		
SLG		.345	.373	– 7.5		.368	.385	– 4.5		
XB%		.198	.232	– 14.8		.208	.220	– 5.7		
E		139	138	0.7		729	728	0.1		
SHO		14	13	7.7		58	45	28.9		

BATTING AVG. (Top 10)

		HOME RUNS	
Pendleton, STL	.389	Bell, HOU	2
Raines, MTL	.381	Dawson, CHI	2
Young, HOU	.364	Gant, ATL	2
Gant, ATL	.355	Parrish, PHI	2
Coles, PIT	.353	34 players tied.	1
Sandberg, CHI	.346		
Moreland, SD	.343		
Ramirez, HOU	.333		
Trillo, CHI	.318		
Larkin, CIN	.317		

BATTING AVG. (Bottom 10)

		RUNS BATTED IN	
Samuel, PHI	.091	Larkin, CIN	7
Thompson, PHI	.105	Sax, LA	7
Dunston, CHI	.120	Bell, HOU	6
Palmeiro, CHI	.120	Marshall, LA	6
Gwynn, SD	.128	8 players tied.	5
Strawberry, NY	.130		
Parrish, PHI	.136		
Shelby, LA	.138		
Dykstra, NY	.150		
Davis, HOU	.154		

Ranked by Effect on Runs

	1988 SEASON			1984 – 1988		
	Home Games	Road Games	Pct. Diff.	Home Games	Road Games	Pct. Diff.
Wrigley Field	719	635	11.8	3878	3293	18.1
Atlanta Stadium	686	610	15.3	3719	3187	16.7
*Riverfront Stadium	645	592	10.3	3638	3300	10.5
*Metrodome	756	675	12.0	3889	3549	8.0
Fenway Park	816	686	19.0	4015	3738	7.9
*Veterans Stadium	688	643	7.0	3613	3371	7.4
Comiskey Park	684	704	− 4.0	3671	3425	7.2
*Kingdome	767	641	18.2	3907	3608	6.4
Arlington Stadium	704	668	4.1	3740	3590	4.4
Cleveland Stadium	712	685	3.9	3991	3894	3.0
County Stadium	664	634	4.7	3651	3594	1.8
*Royals Stadium	689	663	5.2	3416	3354	1.6
*Exhibition Stadium	715	728	− 1.8	3649	3629	1.3
*Three Rivers Stadium	624	643	− 5.4	3285	3270	0.2
*Busch Stadium	632	579	9.2	3232	3298	− 2.2
*Olympic Stadium	637	583	10.6	3174	3279	− 3.2
Anaheim Stadium	701	784	− 10.6	3595	3761	− 3.9
San Diego Stadium	570	607	− 7.3	3211	3368	− 4.9
Memorial Stadium	640	699	− 7.3	3570	3776	− 5.0
Tiger Stadium	631	730	− 13.6	3579	3814	− 6.9
Yankee Stadium	723	797	− 8.2	3613	3924	− 7.0
Dodger Stadium	613	559	9.7	2991	3249	− 7.9
Candlestick Park	602	694	− 13.3	3212	3571	− 10.1
Shea Stadium	531	704	− 24.6	3164	3544	− 10.7
*Astrodome	575	673	− 14.6	3065	3452	− 11.2
Oakland Coliseum	656	764	− 14.1	3477	4107	− 15.3

Ranked by Effect on Home Runs

	1988 SEASON			1984 – 1988		
	Home Games	Road Games	Pct. Diff.	Home Games	Road Games	Pct. Diff.
Wrigley Field	129	99	26.2	859	576	45.5
*Kingdome	178	114	52.6	912	661	34.1
San Diego Stadium	112	94	21.3	689	558	25.2
Atlanta Stadium	112	92	19.8	700	567	19.6
*Riverfront Stadium	146	97	49.5	739	625	16.4
Anaheim Stadium	129	130	0.3	835	745	14.7
Tiger Stadium	159	134	22.1	919	820	13.6
Memorial Stadium	147	143	1.8	902	842	7.4
Candlestick Park	100	112	− 8.9	644	631	3.7
*Metrodome	155	142	7.7	870	807	3.4
Arlington Stadium	125	116	7.6	780	753	2.8
*Exhibition Stadium	151	150	0.5	801	806	0.9
*Veterans Stadium	126	98	27.5	672	676	− 0.8
Yankee Stadium	152	153	3.2	797	829	− 1.1
*Three Rivers Stadium	106	112	− 5.8	569	580	− 2.0
Cleveland Stadium	114	140	− 18.4	752	782	− 4.3
County Stadium	125	113	9.2	664	700	− 5.0
Fenway Park	141	126	9.2	755	801	− 6.4
Shea Stadium	101	129	− 19.8	600	664	− 6.8
Comiskey Park	119	151	− 23.0	732	798	− 8.5
*Olympic Stadium	109	120	− 10.5	536	614	− 12.1
Oakland Coliseum	114	158	− 25.1	719	897	− 18.1
Dodger Stadium	87	96	− 8.3	488	604	− 19.3
*Busch Stadium	68	94	− 29.2	406	526	− 22.4
*Royals Stadium	92	131	− 30.2	545	742	− 27.6
*Astrodome	83	136	− 37.0	426	707	− 39.5

*Playing surface is artificial turf.

Ranked by Effect on Batting Average

	1988 SEASON			1984 – 1988		
	Home Games	Road Games	Pct. Diff.	Home Games	Road Games	Pct. Diff.
Fenway Park	.282	.260	8.5	.284	.264	7.3
Atlanta Stadium	.262	.248	5.7	.266	.250	6.7
Wrigley Field	.272	.254	6.9	.273	.257	6.0
*Riverfront Stadium	.246	.237	4.1	.260	.248	4.5
Arlington Stadium	.255	.241	5.8	.262	.252	4.0
Cleveland Stadium	.265	.266	− 0.5	.275	.267	3.3
*Metrodome	.275	.265	3.5	.270	.263	2.9
*Royals Stadium	.271	.247	9.8	.261	.256	2.2
Comiskey Park	.252	.258	− 2.5	.255	.252	1.3
*Veterans Stadium	.250	.255	− 1.9	.258	.255	1.2
County Stadium	.252	.253	− 0.6	.266	.263	1.1
*Kingdome	.259	.255	1.6	.265	.264	0.4
*Busch Stadium	.253	.248	2.0	.254	.254	0.2
Dodger Stadium	.253	.233	8.6	.248	.250	− 0.8
*Three Rivers Stadium	.243	.254	− 4.4	.251	.253	− 0.9
*Exhibition Stadium	.263	.261	0.7	.260	.263	− 1.1
Yankee Stadium	.259	.271	− 4.6	.263	.268	− 1.9
*Olympic Stadium	.248	.241	3.1	.247	.254	− 2.6
*Astrodome	.238	.248	− 4.1	.246	.253	− 2.6
Shea Stadium	.232	.259	− 10.5	.248	.255	− 3.0
Memorial Stadium	.250	.263	− 5.0	.257	.265	− 3.1
Anaheim Stadium	.258	.273	− 5.4	.254	.263	− 3.8
San Diego Stadium	.240	.254	− 5.4	.249	.260	− 4.1
Candlestick Park	.241	.250	− 3.6	.246	.258	− 4.6
Tiger Stadium	.240	.257	− 6.7	.248	.262	− 5.6
Oakland Coliseum	.251	.259	− 3.2	.249	.268	− 6.9

Ranked by Effect on Slugging Percentage

	1988 SEASON			1984 – 1988		
	Home Games	Road Games	Pct. Diff.	Home Games	Road Games	Pct. Diff.
Wrigley Field	.394	.372	6.1	.424	.382	11.0
Atlanta Stadium	.380	.350	8.6	.398	.366	8.6
*Riverfront Stadium	.383	.343	11.7	.401	.371	7.9
*Kingdome	.421	.375	12.1	.425	.397	6.9
Fenway Park	.429	.384	11.6	.433	.406	6.8
*Metrodome	.424	.398	6.5	.431	.407	5.9
*Veterans Stadium	.382	.362	5.4	.398	.383	3.9
Arlington Stadium	.376	.357	5.2	.402	.392	2.4
*Exhibition Stadium	.408	.403	1.2	.414	.406	2.0
Comiskey Park	.376	.394	− 4.7	.397	.393	0.9
County Stadium	.372	.369	1.0	.396	.395	0.4
*Three Rivers Stadium	.366	.373	− 1.7	.376	.376	0.1
*Royals Stadium	.396	.373	6.3	.392	.391	0.1
Cleveland Stadium	.380	.401	− 5.3	.411	.411	0.1
San Diego Stadium	.349	.365	− 4.3	.376	.377	− 0.3
*Busch Stadium	.351	.355	− 1.2	.364	.368	− 1.2
*Olympic Stadium	.376	.358	5.0	.370	.378	− 2.3
Memorial Stadium	.380	.401	− 5.2	.403	.416	− 3.1
Anaheim Stadium	.378	.409	− 7.6	.393	.405	− 3.2
Yankee Stadium	.394	.415	− 5.2	.403	.416	− 3.2
Tiger Stadium	.375	.388	− 3.4	.398	.412	− 3.6
Candlestick Park	.345	.373	− 7.5	.368	.385	− 4.5
Shea Stadium	.336	.389	− 13.7	.366	.384	− 4.7
Dodger Stadium	.345	.334	3.3	.343	.375	− 8.5
*Astrodome	.340	.376	− 9.6	.349	.388	− 10.0
Oakland Coliseum	.360	.398	− 9.6	.377	.427	− 11.6

*Playing surface is artificial turf.

Ranked by Effect on Extra-Base Hit Percentage

	1988 SEASON			1984 – 1988		
	Home Games	Road Games	Pct. Diff.	Home Games	Road Games	Pct. Diff.
*Royals Stadium	.255	.216	17.8	.253	.210	20.3
*Veterans Stadium	.254	.202	25.9	.250	.210	18.9
*Metrodome	.244	.212	14.8	.255	.214	18.8
*Exhibition Stadium	.232	.232	– 0.3	.255	.218	17.1
Fenway Park	.256	.207	23.8	.246	.212	16.0
*Busch Stadium	.225	.219	2.4	.235	.212	10.9
*Riverfront Stadium	.233	.217	7.5	.237	.214	10.6
*Olympic Stadium	.258	.202	28.0	.244	.220	10.5
*Three Rivers Stadium	.256	.208	23.2	.242	.224	8.0
Comiskey Park	.229	.205	11.4	.233	.218	7.0
*Kingdome	.262	.228	15.0	.240	.227	5.9
Atlanta Stadium	.211	.198	6.5	.211	.209	1.3
County Stadium	.212	.212	– 0.2	.214	.211	1.2
*Astrodome	.223	.219	1.9	.211	.222	– 5.1
Candlestick Park	.198	.232	– 14.8	.208	.220	– 5.7
Shea Stadium	.198	.227	– 12.8	.209	.221	– 5.8
San Diego Stadium	.187	.221	– 15.7	.197	.210	– 6.0
Arlington Stadium	.201	.214	– 6.2	.209	.227	– 7.7
Wrigley Field	.190	.245	– 22.4	.214	.232	– 7.9
Memorial Stadium	.205	.219	– 6.3	.200	.222	– 10.0
Yankee Stadium	.214	.243	– 11.8	.205	.230	– 10.7
Cleveland Stadium	.193	.218	– 11.7	.200	.224	– 10.9
Tiger Stadium	.196	.222	– 11.9	.207	.236	– 12.3
Oakland Coliseum	.186	.219	– 15.4	.198	.235	– 15.7
Anaheim Stadium	.193	.234	– 17.3	.195	.232	– 16.2
Dodger Stadium	.165	.202	– 18.4	.167	.231	– 27.5

Ranked by Effect on Strikeout Percentage

	1988 SEASON			1984 – 1988		
	Home Games	Road Games	Pct. Diff.	Home Games	Road Games	Pct. Diff.
San Diego Stadium	.153	.143	6.7	.150	.134	12.0
*Metrodome	.146	.136	7.5	.143	.135	6.5
Shea Stadium	.169	.155	9.0	.166	.158	5.1
Memorial Stadium	.137	.123	11.0	.141	.135	4.5
*Exhibition Stadium	.149	.148	0.4	.148	.144	3.1
Tiger Stadium	.150	.133	13.1	.149	.144	3.1
Oakland Coliseum	.157	.146	8.2	.148	.144	2.7
Candlestick Park	.161	.150	7.6	.161	.158	2.1
*Astrodome	.156	.151	2.9	.158	.155	2.1
Anaheim Stadium	.141	.121	17.1	.141	.138	1.7
Wrigley Field	.147	.142	3.3	.153	.151	1.5
Fenway Park	.146	.146	0.4	.143	.142	1.0
*Olympic Stadium	.159	.163	– 2.2	.154	.153	0.9
*Veterans Stadium	.145	.153	– 5.3	.159	.158	0.8
*Kingdome	.142	.150	– 5.2	.151	.150	0.7
Yankee Stadium	.143	.143	0.2	.141	.140	0.6
County Stadium	.139	.149	– 6.7	.142	.141	0.3
Arlington Stadium	.149	.165	– 9.7	.156	.156	– 0.0
Comiskey Park	.137	.134	2.3	.144	.145	– 0.7
*Three Rivers Stadium	.141	.146	– 3.6	.147	.148	– 0.9
Dodger Stadium	.158	.169	– 6.7	.156	.161	– 3.1
*Riverfront Stadium	.156	.152	2.6	.147	.153	– 4.2
*Busch Stadium	.137	.140	– 1.8	.136	.143	– 5.3
Cleveland Stadium	.134	.141	– 4.6	.128	.138	– 7.0
Atlanta Stadium	.128	.143	– 10.7	.131	.145	– 9.6
*Royals Stadium	.131	.170	– 22.8	.133	.157	– 15.0

*Playing surface is artificial turf.

Ranked by Effect on Stolen Base Percentage

	1988 SEASON			1984 – 1988		
	Home Games	Road Games	Pct. Diff.	Home Games	Road Games	Pct. Diff.
*Metrodome	.720	.628	14.6	.698	.621	12.6
*Royals Stadium	.722	.725	− 0.5	.702	.647	8.5
*Astrodome	.781	.771	1.2	.760	.705	7.7
*Exhibition Stadium	.719	.709	1.4	.713	.664	7.4
*Kingdome	.663	.640	3.6	.667	.637	4.6
*Veterans Stadium	.707	.732	− 3.5	.744	.723	2.8
Comiskey Park	.712	.638	11.6	.691	.673	2.6
*Busch Stadium	.762	.704	8.2	.744	.727	2.3
*Riverfront Stadium	.738	.710	3.9	.720	.704	2.3
*Olympic Stadium	.718	.730	− 1.6	.739	.728	1.5
Tiger Stadium	.605	.710	− 14.8	.662	.657	0.9
Oakland Coliseum	.692	.644	7.5	.677	.674	0.5
San Diego Stadium	.665	.638	4.1	.677	.676	0.1
Memorial Stadium	.715	.621	15.1	.675	.679	− 0.5
Dodger Stadium	.686	.676	1.5	.657	.662	− 0.7
Candlestick Park	.667	.660	1.0	.638	.647	− 1.3
Wrigley Field	.647	.714	− 9.5	.672	.684	− 1.7
Arlington Stadium	.681	.749	− 9.0	.688	.706	− 2.6
Anaheim Stadium	.623	.603	3.4	.618	.640	− 3.3
County Stadium	.734	.700	4.8	.646	.668	− 3.3
Atlanta Stadium	.652	.635	2.7	.653	.677	− 3.5
*Three Rivers Stadium	.665	.716	− 7.1	.633	.660	− 4.2
Cleveland Stadium	.628	.686	− 8.6	.665	.701	− 5.2
Shea Stadium	.762	.773	− 1.4	.694	.759	− 8.6
Fenway Park	.616	.715	− 13.9	.589	.660	− 10.8
Yankee Stadium	.732	.807	− 9.4	.661	.743	− 11.0

Ranked by Effect on Errors

	1988 SEASON			1984 – 1988		
	Home Games	Road Games	Pct. Diff.	Home Games	Road Games	Pct. Diff.
Wrigley Field	168	119	39.5	688	619	11.4
Atlanta Stadium	133	133	2.5	731	669	9.3
County Stadium	126	112	12.5	679	645	5.5
San Diego Stadium	131	116	11.5	682	647	5.1
Anaheim Stadium	131	122	7.4	650	629	3.9
*Three Rivers Stadium	130	115	10.3	642	623	2.8
Fenway Park	117	102	14.7	617	608	2.0
Arlington Stadium	117	129	− 10.4	631	622	1.7
Tiger Stadium	118	107	10.3	618	606	1.2
Shea Stadium	112	134	− 16.4	677	669	1.2
Dodger Stadium	153	134	14.2	754	746	1.1
Yankee Stadium	129	121	7.9	626	628	0.7
Memorial Stadium	107	107	1.2	593	595	0.2
Candlestick Park	139	138	0.7	729	728	0.1
Cleveland Stadium	120	119	0.8	705	709	− 0.1
*Royals Stadium	124	120	4.6	611	610	− 0.1
*Busch Stadium	131	134	− 2.2	661	664	− 0.7
*Olympic Stadium	140	127	11.6	645	652	− 1.1
*Veterans Stadium	114	148	− 23.0	668	679	− 1.4
*Exhibition Stadium	104	134	− 22.4	617	635	− 2.1
*Metrodome	103	107	− 3.7	578	582	− 2.1
Comiskey Park	133	160	− 17.9	628	643	− 2.3
Oakland Coliseum	114	116	− 1.7	656	679	− 3.4
*Kingdome	122	109	10.5	624	642	− 4.5
*Astrodome	115	142	− 19.0	624	699	− 10.7
*Riverfront Stadium	112	138	− 17.8	608	714	− 14.6

*Playing surface is artificial turf.

X

1969 New York Mets: Looking Back 20 Years Later

1969 New York Mets:
Looking Back 20 Years Later

As we mentioned in the introduction to this year's *Analyst*, the most frustrating element of producing this book on an annual basis has been that it has made us aware of the limitations of baseball statistics in the pre computer era. Knowing how Don Mattingly performs against left-handed pitchers has only made us all the more eager to learn how Lou Gehrig did against them. We know what Jim Rice hits in Late-Inning Pressure situations, but what about Hall-of-Famer Sam Rice? Did Bob Feller or Ewell Blackwell enjoy the success against right-handed batters that J. R. Richard did throughout his career or David Cone did last season?

In this section, we take our first tentative steps toward reconstructing and applying to players of the past the type of information that we have compiled for contemporary players over the past 14 years. The guinea pigs are none other than the 1969 Mets, on the occasion of the 20th anniversary of their rags-to-riches championship, which captured the hearts of sports fans and non-fans alike.

We have assembled and processed play-by-play information for the 1969 Mets in a manner identical to the way that we now examine similar current data each season. The results are contained in this section, which is sort of a mini-*Analyst* dealing only with the '69 Mets.

First is a capsulized version of the Team Section. We have an essay on Gil Hodges's team, featuring a lot of new information developed by looking back at that team through the prism of statistics and techniques not previously available. The essay is followed by the Won-Lost Record by Starting Position chart, which lists, for each player on the team, the Mets' won-lost record in games started by that player at each position, in the leadoff spot in the lineup, and in games in which each pitcher appeared in relief.

The next charts that appear correspond to those that appear for contemporary players in the Batter and Pitcher sections. We have included the 15 Mets batters who had the most plate appearances in 1969, and the 10 Mets pitchers who faced the most opposing batters. In each case, the players are listed alphabetically, and following the last batter and the last pitcher are team totals for the Mets.

The "Loves to Face" and "Hates to Face" information listed for each player are based on statistics for the 1969 season only. And for pitchers, all earned-run averages are calculated using actual innings-pitched totals, rather than using rounded-off innings totals, as was done in 1969. (Actual innings totals didn't become the basis for ERA calculations until 1982, the year after the Steve McCatty-Sammy Stewart disputed ERA title controversy.)

Finally, we've concluded the section with a Time Line, something with which to put the events of the summer of '69 into further perspective. It was a remarkable year not only for the Mets, but also historically, politically, and socially. Sometimes, the melody of a song or the sound of a forgotten voice can act like a time machine, transporting us back instantly to some simple pleasure that otherwise would have been lost. We hope our day-by-day listings of what the Mets did each day that year, along with what else happened in baseball and in the world will serve that same purpose for those of us old enough to remember the Seattle Pilots, Babe Ruth's "715th home run", Jack Kemp as a quarterback, and cigarette ads on TV.

1969 New York Mets:
Looking Back 20 Years Later

Before the puddles of champagne dried on the locker-room floor, the 1969 New York Mets had become the embodiment of that overused cliche, a legend in their own time. Their World Series victory was a national event to rival that summer's triumphant return of the *Apollo 11* astronauts. At a time when sports events hit the front page about as often as Dear Abby, the Mets made headlines from coast to coast. And why not? The ultimate symbol of futility had become a celebrated source of national pride.

Twenty years later, the legend lives on. Our vision is no longer clouded by the glory of the moment or the social backdrop of assassination, war, and domestic unrest that made the Mets a welcome diversion. But enough time has passed to dull our memories of many of the events that made the Mets' season seem so magical. So a reexamination of those events was an enticing prospect.

Our analysis was designed to evaluate the common perceptions that still contribute to the aura of magic that surrounds the 1969 Mets. For instance: How abrupt was the team's turnaround from chumps to champs? Were there any precedents for such a talented, young pitching staff? Was the team's offense as anemic as it seemed, or were they terrors in the clutch? How did the team's second-half comeback compare with other great rebounds in major league history?

If all this sounds too clinical—well, frankly, we don't disagree. The romance that characterized the Mets' 1969 season was perhaps its most endearing quality, made all the more attractive by the changes that were soon to occur. Think of the championship teams that followed the '69 Mets—the powerful Weaver-led Orioles, the brash A's, the Big Red Machine. Consider the trends toward plastic grass, courtroom baseball, escalating salaries and ticket prices, and increasingly boorish behavior by management, players, and fans, and it's easy to support the theory that the 1969 season was actually the end of baseball's romantic era. It just might be that the wanton destruction of the Shea Stadium turf by celebrating fans in October 1969 was the symbolic welcoming party for the contemporary era.

But enough philosophizing. The simple fact is that over the past 20 years, baseball fans, like every other subset of society, have grown more sophisticated. If our analytical retrospective betrays the romance of the era, so be it. Now let's play ball.

Had the "Miracle of 1969" occured 20 years later, not only

would we have had to change its name, but we all would have been a lot less shocked by what transpired.

By one of the simplest but most discerning leading indicators that the past 10 years of statistical analysis has produced, we now see the 1969 Mets as a team poised for a dramatic turnaround. Had there been a *1969 Elias Baseball Analyst*, the Mets' poor record in one-run games a year earlier would have alerted us and our readers to the fact that almost anything was possible for a team that nevertheless was discounted from contention before the 1969 season even began. (The 1968 Mets posted a 26–37 record in games decided by one run.)

History has proven that you ignore teams with poor records in one-run contests at your own risk. In fact, had you bet ten bucks to win a division or league title on every team of the expansion era that had finished at least 10 games below the .500 mark in one-run games the previous season, you'd have shown a profit that any handicapper, card counter, or Wall Street trader would be proud of. You'd have collected at long odds not only on the 1969 Mets, but on the 1965 Minnesota Twins, and the 1967 Boston Red Sox as well. Take a look at the records of those teams in the seasons prior to their unexpected league championships:

Year	Team	W–L	Pos.	1-Run Games	Next Season
1964	Twins	79–83	6	28–38	102–60
1966	Red Sox	72–90	9	21–32	92–70
1968	Mets	73–89	9	26–37	100–62

All three finished at least 10 games below .500 in one-run games, and they all improved their overall marks by at least 20 wins the following season. Of course, they represent the three most outstanding recent examples of one-run games as a leading indicator, but they are also typical of the general trend.

Let's take a closer look. The table below classifies all teams of the modern era into two groups: those that lost at least 10 more one-run games than they won (column A), and all other teams (column B). The table profiles those groups according to (1) the likelihood that the teams would improve a year later, and (2) what degree they would improve. A "substantial improvement" indicates an increase in winning percentage corresponding to at least 10 wins over the course of a

435

162–game season; "dramatic improvement" means an increase in winning percentage corresponding to at least 20 wins:

	A	B
Included in group	175	1363
Improved the next season	134	623
Substantial improvement	86	247
Dramatic improvement	32	46

Now pay close attention—we're about to throw an awful lot of numbers at you, but they are all vital to an understanding of this important issue.

Only 11 percent of all teams played at least 10 games below .500 in one-run games, but that group accounted for 26 percent of the substantial improvements, and 41 percent of the dramatic increases. In fact, among the teams that played poorly in one-run games, nearly one in five moved up by the equivalent of 20 games the following season, compared to one in 30 among teams that didn't fare as badly in one-run games.

In retrospect, the 1968 Mets sent a signal that was as unintelligible to us 20 years ago as data on predicting tornadoes and earthquakes remain today. It's only over the last few years that we've all learned to interpret signals such as the one-run-game indicator, alerting us to the possibility of turnarounds like those of the Pittsburgh Pirates in 1987 and the Los Angeles Dodgers last season.

The 1969 Mets compounded the situation with a deceptively slow start. Right from the opening bell and for two months thereafter, the Mets gave no indication of what was to come. Their opening-day loss was, in fact, more characteristic of the team's bungling infancy. The Mets lost an 11–10 contest to the Montreal Expos, who were playing the first regular-season game in the franchise's history. It represented the fourth game in five years in which the Mets lost despite scoring in double figures. It's noteworthy that in 20 years since then, that's happened to them only once.

Things got only a little better over the next two months. The team straddled the .500 fence, never falling more than five games below or advancing more than one above the break-even point. They didn't even raise their record above the .500 mark for good until June 3. Those are unusual characteristics for a team about to make a major breakthrough. Of the 17 teams in modern major league history that played .600 or better following a losing season, 10 were at or above the .600 mark at the end of May. Only one team other than the 1969 Mets had a losing record at that point—the 1914 "Miracle" Braves.

After treading water for the first two weeks of June, the Mets made their only player trade of the entire season, and

it was a dandy. New York exchanged four minor leaguers—third baseman Kevin Collins and pitchers Steve Renko, Bill Carden, and Dave Colon for Montreal first baseman Donn Clendenon. Manager Gil Hodges immediately announced that his newest addition would platoon with Ed Kranepool. But, of course, Clendenon eventually won an everyday starting position during the Mets' September pennant drive and won the World Series MVP award as well.

What's truly noteworthy about the trade, in retrospect, is the timing with which the Mets front office abandoned its protectionist philosophy toward its pitchers in a bid to win a title that nearly everyone—fans, writers, and broadcasters—still considered a longshot.

For the first seven years of the team's existence, the Mets hoarded pitchers who showed even the slightest glimmer of major league potential, a strategy that helped give the 1969 Mets one of the finest young starting rotations in major league history. But until they dealt Renko (who eventually won 134 games during a 15–year major league career), only one of the 22 pitchers whom New York traded subsequently won even 25 games. And the exception, journeyman reliever Bob Miller, compiled a losing record after leaving the Mets. The list of those pitchers, and their major-league records after being traded:

Bob Miller	57–58	Jerry Arrigo	22–26
Larry Foss	—	Dennis Ribant	11–12
Ken MacKenzie	0–3	Jack Hamilton	12–12
Roger Craig	10–14	Rob Gardner	10–8
Jay Hook	—	Jack Lamabe	6–6
Frank Lary	2–0	Bob Shaw	0–2
Tracy Stallard	12–13	Bill Denehy	0–3
Tom Parsons	—	Joe Grzenda	13–9
Al Jackson	23–19	Jack Fisher	12–17
Gary Kroll	0–0	Billy Wynne	8–11

Lest you conclude that anyone who could spell *M-E-T-S* would have known that the motley crew listed above had little potential, consider some of the players the New York front office obtained for them: Jerry Grote (for Parsons), Don Cardwell (in a two-for-two deal for Ribant), and Tommie Agee and Al Weis (for Fisher and Wynne). They also acquired Hodges himself, surrendering Denehy as part of the settlement.

It's obvious that the Mets were able to seperate the potential *haves* (like Seaver, Koosman, Gentry, McGraw, McAndrew, and Ryan, to name half-a-dozen) from the *have-nots* with unerring accuracy. And to their additional credit, when the opportunity arose to acquire a player whom the front office believed could put the Mets over the top, they finally went for broke, trading the promising Renko for a set of World Series rings.

Did the Mets' 1969 staff include the best young starting

rotation in major league history? Consider the following: Jerry Koosman, at 26 years, four months, was the oldest of the Mets' young starters. We checked every team since 1901 and added up the number of wins by pitchers who were no older than the Kooz was in 1969. Only one team, the 1919 Boston Red Sox, accumulated more wins among its young pitchers than the 1969 Mets.

But such a method was obviously stacked in the Mets' favor. A question as general as which was the best young staff in major league history isn't easy to answer, so we constructed a rather simple statistical architecture to point us in the right direction. For every team in modern major-league history, we accumulated the number of games won by each of its pitchers *after that season*. Teams with poor staffs and those with old pitchers with most of their wins behind them fell by the wayside as we identified a handful of teams loaded with young pitchers on the brink of long, successful careers.

But as we studied those results, we noticed a flaw in that method as well. Consider the example of the 1964 Cleveland Indians, whose pitchers won more than 1000 games thereafter. More than one quarter of that total was drawn from a 21–year-old pitcher, Tommy John, who was only a minor contributor to that team, making just 14 starts. In fact, had John started only one game, he still would have contributed his nearly 300 subsequent wins to the team total.

So we altered our original method to weigh the contribution of each pitcher according to the number of games he started in the season in question. When that adjustment was made to the '64 Indians, Sam McDowell (24 starts at age 21), Luis Tiant (16 at 23), and John still contributed to an impressive figure. But the weighted team average of 84.8 "future wins" per starter was dwarfed by the top figures of the century. The following table shows the teams with the highest averages in modern history; "FW" indicates future wins, with each pitcher contributing a slice of the pie proportionate to the number of games he started:

Year	Team	FW
1903	Philadelphia Athletics	163.8
1903	New York Giants	148.9
1968	Chicago Cubs	139.1
1968	New York Mets	138.8
1970	St. Louis Cardinals	131.0
1912	Philadelphia Phillies	127.5
1919	Boston Red Sox	123.1
1909	Washington Senators	119.4
1967	Los Angeles Dodgers	119.0
1954	Milwaukee Braves	114.9

Well, it looks like we might have started a few more arguments than we settled. Not only wasn't the 1969 Mets staff the most promising in major league history by our measure, *it wasn't even the best of its year*. (Notice that the Mets actually compiled their highest average a year earlier, when

their young pitchers had an additional year ahead of them, and when Ryan started nearly twice as many games.)

We're not about to call our figures the final word. In fact, we'd like you to consider them simply as a launching pad, having defined the terms of the discussion. But you should know what the competition looks like, so we'll list the major contributors to the teams above along with their ages on July 1. And may the best team win:

1903	Phil. Athletics	Bender (20), Plank (27), Waddell (26)
1903	N.Y. Giants	Mathewson (22), Taylor (28)
1968	Chicago Cubs	Holtzman (22), Jenkins (24), J. Niekro (23)
1968	New York Mets	Koosman (25), Ryan (21), Seaver (23)
1970	St. L. Cardinals	Carlton (25), Reuss (21), Torrez (23)
1912	Phil. Phillies	Alexander (25), Rixey (21), Seaton (24)
1919	Boston Red Sox	Jones (26), Pennock (25), Russell (25)
1909	Wash. Senators	Johnson (21), Groom (24)
1967	L.A. Dodgers	Singer (23), Sutton (22)
1954	Milw. Braves	Buhl (25), Burdette (27)

The third Friday in August. The Mississippi Gulf Coast braced for the onslaught of Hurricane Camille. Hundreds of thousands of rock music fans headed for a three-day festival in a small town in upstate New York called Woodstock. Jerry Grote's wife Sharon gave birth to their third child, Jennifer. And the Mets returned home from a deflating 4–7 road trip only to be rained out at Shea, setting up consecutive double-headers with the Padres for Saturday and Sunday. That's how the Mets began their drive to the world championship.

From August 16 until they clinched the N.L. East title on September 24, the Mets won 34 of 44 games, and they did it with pitching. The staff ERA during that stretch was 2.03. Meanwhile, the offense was underwhelming. In fact, when the Mets defeated Montreal, 7–1, to move into first place on September 10, it marked the last time during the 1969 season that New York would score more than five runs in a game. Ironically, that streak of 29 consecutive games without scoring at least six runs (which extended slightly into the 1970 season) remains the longest in the franchise's history.

The following table compares the runs per game scored by the Mets and their opponents through mid-August with the averages of the 44–game run to the title. Notice that the team actually scored fewer runs per game during the 34–10 stretch than it had earlier in the season, while the pitching staff allowed 36 percent fewer runs:

	Games	Scored	Allowed	W–L
Through Aug. 13	113	3.94	3.76	62–51
Aug. 13–Sept. 24	44	3.86	2.41	34–10

For those who were looking for clues that something extraordinary was about to take place, they needed to look no further than the scores of those weekend doubleheaders with the Padres and that of the opening game of the series with the Giants that followed. The Mets won all five games, by scores of 2–0, 2–1, 3–2, 3–2, and 1–0. *Five consecutive wins without scoring more than three runs,* something that's happened only three other times in modern National League history. (The other teams were the 1902 Boston Braves, the 1910 Pittsburgh Pirates [who won six in a row], and the 1963 San Francisco Giants.)

During the six-week sprint to the N.L. East title, several of the Mets' pitchers were nearly unhittable. Don Cardwell, Tug McGraw, and Tom Seaver combined for 17 wins in 18 decisions and a 0.99 ERA, allowing 96 hits in 163.1 innings. But the improvement was staff-wide. The Mets allowed only 10 home runs in 44 games, and only two regular pitchers had higher ERAs during the stretch run than prior to it. One of those two, Jerry Koosman, went 7–1 during those six weeks anyway. The staff breakdown:

| | Through August 13 | | | | Aug. 16–Sept. 24 | | | |
Player	W	L	SV	ERA	W	L	SV	ERA
Cardwell	4	9	0	3.67	4	0	0	0.80
DiLauro	1	3	1	2.63	0	1	0	1.74
Gentry	9	10	0	3.81	3	2	0	2.73
Koonce	5	3	7	5.12	1	0	0	4.26
Koosman	9	8	0	2.24	7	1	0	2.43
McAndrew	3	5	0	4.82	3	2	0	1.98
McGraw	5	2	7	2.92	4	1	5	0.60
Ryan	4	1	1	3.41	2	2	0	3.74
Seaver	16	7	0	2.66	8	0	0	1.26
Taylor	6	3	10	3.03	2	1	2	1.88
Others	0	0	0	9.77	0	0	0	13.50
Totals	62	51	26	3.40	34	10	7	2.03

Another factor that hastened the Mets' climb to first place was the collapse of the Cubs. While the Mets were losing seven of 11 games on their early-August road trip, Chicago stretched its division lead to nine games with an 8–4 road trip of its own. But when both teams returned home, the Cubs started to fade. They split their last 18 games in August, then collapsed in September.

As the month began, the Cubs still led the division by four-and-a-half games. But it took the Mets less than two weeks to erase that lead. The Mets played so well during September and the Cubs so poorly that New York's gain of 12½ games during the month was the largest in modern major league history by a substantial margin. The largest September gains in games behind/ahead:

Year	Team	W–L	Gain
1969	New York Mets	23–7	12.5
1914	Boston Braves	26–5	10.5
1980	Minnesota Twins	17–7	10
1916	New York Giants	29–5	10
1983	Chicago White Sox	22–6	9

As a postscript to Chicago's collapse it should be noted that the 1969 Cubs were the only team in modern history to lead its league or division from opening day into September without winning a title.

Now that we've deified the pitchers, can we say anything good about the team's hitting? For years, the general perception has been that, if nothing else, the offense was especially potent in the clutch. But that notion, given popular credence by the team's great record in one-run games (41–23), has never been tested. Until now, that is.

The Mets scored an average of 3.90 runs per game. That beat only three teams in the league, including the expansion teams, Montreal and San Diego, which ranked next-to-last and last, respectively. Among the established teams, only St. Louis scored fewer runs than New York.

And while Shea Stadium subsequently became one of the National League's most biased pitchers' parks (see the table on page 423), that wasn't true in the 1960s. From 1965 through 1969, Shea reduced scoring by only 1.3 percent, an insignificant margin that fails to vindicate the Mets' weak attack.

But the clutch-hitting theory lives! The Mets batted .268 with runners in scoring position, 35 points higher than the team's average in other at-bats. Over the first 13 years that we computed those statistics on a league-wide basis (1975–1987), only three National League teams compiled wider gaps: the Cardinals in 1977 and 1978, and the 1982 Cubs. And while the 1969 Mets hit better in Late-Inning Pressure Situations than they did overall by a nine-point margin, the team's LIP Situations breakdown was even more impressive:

Bases Empty	.239
Runners on Base	.266
Runners in Scoring Position	.285
2 Outs/Runners on Base	.320
2 Outs/Runners in Scoring Pos.	.360

That last category—two outs and runners in scoring position in Late-Inning Pressure Situations—is the most focused and situation-specific yardstick of clutch hitting that we compile. And the Mets' mark of .360 is higher than the corresponding figure of any team during the 13 years from 1975 through 1987 with at least as many at-bats in those situations as the 1969 Mets (84). Of course, it's obvious that any ol' 84 at-bats during the course of a season probably won't substantially affect a team's overall performance. But it's equally true that by definition these particular 84 at-bats—with two outs and runners in scoring position in Late-Inning Pressure Situations—were among the Mets' most important swings of the season. There's little question that New York's success in those at bats greatly benefitted its overall record.

In retrospect, the phenomenon of the 1969 Mets was one of those once-in-a-lifetime events that seem to occur every few years or so in sports. Two factors combined to make the team's performance special: first, its rags-to-riches turnaround, bypassing the traditional period of mediocrity and boredom; and second, its remarkable second-half comeback.

If this look back has sharpened our vision of the past in any way, it may be this: In many ways, the team's performance was almost without precedent. The young pitching staff, the clutch hitting, the spectacular comeback were all the stuff of legends.

But maybe there's a more subtle lesson to be learned as well. Had the events of 1969 occurred 20 years later, we'd undoubtedly have been more prepared for the Mets' form reversal, and less shocked by what happened. The question is, are we really better off knowing what we know now?

WON-LOST RECORD BY STARTING POSITION

NEW YORK 100-62	C	1B	2B	3B	SS	LF	CF	RF	P	Leadoff	Relief	Starts
Tommie Agee	-	-	-	-	-	-	85-52	2-2	-	56-37	-	87-54
Ken Boswell	-	-	53-38	-	-	-	-	-	-	0-2	-	53-38
Don Cardwell	-	-	-	-	-	-	-	-	12-9	-	3-6	12-9
Ed Charles	-	-	-	24-21	-	-	-	-	-	-	-	24-21
Donn Clendenon	-	32-14	-	-	-	-	-	-	-	-	-	32-14
Kevin Collins	-	-	-	6-5	-	-	-	-	-	-	-	6-5
Jack DiLauro	-	-	-	-	-	-	-	-	1-3	-	6-13	1-3
Duffy Dyer	12-6	-	-	-	-	-	-	-	-	-	-	12-6
Danny Frisella	-	-	-	-	-	-	-	-	-	-	1-2	-
Wayne Garrett	-	-	20-14	42-21	0-1	-	-	-	-	2-0	-	62-36
Rod Gaspar	-	-	-	-	-	4-1	7-5	14-13	-	7-6	-	25-19
Gary Gentry	-	-	-	-	-	-	-	-	18-17	-	-	18-17
Jim Gosger	-	-	-	-	-	2-0	1-0	-	-	1-0	-	3-0
Jerry Grote	61-39	-	-	-	-	-	-	-	-	-	-	61-39
Bud Harrelson	-	-	-	-	72-43	-	-	-	-	31-14	-	72-43
Bob Heise	-	-	-	-	3-0	-	-	-	-	-	-	3-0
Jesse Hudson	-	-	-	-	-	-	-	-	-	-	0-1	-
Al Jackson	-	-	-	-	-	-	-	-	-	-	1-8	-
Bob Johnson	-	-	-	-	-	-	-	-	-	-	1-1	-
Cleon Jones	-	7-5	-	-	-	70-49	-	-	-	3-1	-	77-54
Cal Koonce	-	-	-	-	-	-	-	-	-	-	15-25	-
Jerry Koosman	-	-	-	-	-	-	-	-	22-10	-	-	22-10
Ed Kranepool	-	55-42	-	-	-	-	-	-	-	-	-	55-42
J.C. Martin	27-17	-	-	-	-	-	-	-	-	-	-	27-17
Jim McAndrew	-	-	-	-	-	-	-	-	13-8	-	1-5	13-8
Tug McGraw	-	-	-	-	-	-	-	-	3-1	-	24-14	3-1
Amos Otis	-	-	1-2	-	-	3-2	7-5	-	-	0-2	-	11-9
Bobby Pfeil	-	-	6-4	27-13	-	-	-	-	-	-	-	33-17
Les Rohr	-	-	-	-	-	-	-	-	-	-	0-1	-
Nolan Ryan	-	-	-	-	-	-	-	-	5-5	-	8-7	5-5
Tom Seaver	-	-	-	-	-	-	-	-	26-9	-	0-1	26-9
Art Shamsky	-	6-1	-	-	-	11-4	-	36-25	-	-	-	53-30
Ron Swoboda	-	-	-	-	-	10-6	-	48-22	-	-	-	58-28
Ron Taylor	-	-	-	-	-	-	-	-	-	-	27-32	-
Al Weis	-	-	21-6	-	25-18	-	-	-	-	-	-	46-24

Mets Batters

Tommie Agee

Bats Right

New York Mets	AB	H	2B	3B	HR	RBI	BB	SO	BA	SA	OBA
Season	565	153	23	4	26	76	59	137	.271	.464	.342
vs. Left-Handers	132	36	3	1	9	18	24	38	.273	.515	.385
vs. Right-Handers	433	117	20	3	17	58	35	99	.270	.448	.328
Home	282	71	9	1	14	40	37	67	.252	.440	.344
Road	283	82	14	3	12	36	22	70	.290	.488	.340
Day	265	75	10	1	16	45	27	59	.283	.509	.354
Night	300	78	13	3	10	31	32	78	.260	.423	.331
April	42	8	2	0	2	7	3	15	.190	.381	.244
May	74	23	4	1	5	14	8	17	.311	.595	.373
June	111	31	5	1	3	10	9	25	.279	.423	.331
July	105	29	4	2	6	17	9	21	.276	.524	.339
August	127	35	6	0	6	16	13	32	.276	.465	.343
Sept./Oct.	106	27	2	0	4	12	17	27	.255	.387	.368
Leading Off Inn.	201	64	9	2	11	11	24	41	.318	.547	.394
Runners On	179	49	8	2	6	56	17	43	.274	.437	.337
Runners/Scor. Pos.	98	29	8	2	1	46	10	21	.296	.449	.360
Runners On/2 Out	76	18	4	1	2	26	8	21	.237	.395	.310
Scor. Pos./2 Out	51	14	4	1	0	22	7	13	.275	.392	.362
Late Inning Pressure	76	20	4	0	2	12	7	19	.263	.395	.325
Leading Off	24	7	0	0	1	1	4	3	.292	.417	.393
Runners On	29	9	4	0	0	10	3	7	.310	.448	.375
Runners/Scor. Pos.	19	6	4	0	0	10	1	3	.316	.526	.350

RUNS BATTED IN	From 1B	From 2B	From 3B	Scoring Position
Totals	9/128	20/83	21/43	41/126
Percentage	7%	24%	49%	33%
Driving In Runners from 3B with Less than Two Out:		12/23		52%

Loves to face: Bill Hands (.333, 4-for-12, 2 HR)
Hates to face: Grant Jackson (0-for-10, 7 SO)
Fewest RBI to lead a division winner (excluding 1981): Norm Cash (61, Detroit, 1972), Agee (76, Mets, 1969), Rusty Staub (76, Mets, 1973).... Led team in RBI despite a streak of 34 consecutive plate appearances from June 10 through June 19 with nobody in scoring position.... Played 1,073 games in the outfield during his career, none at any other position. Other N.Y. outfielders in that club include Furillo, Maris, Mueller, Rivers, Snider, and Reggie.... Played at least 100 games in eight seasons. Of those, he batted .271 or better four times, .234 or lower four times, but never in between.

Ken Boswell

Bats Left

New York Mets	AB	H	2B	3B	HR	RBI	BB	SO	BA	SA	OBA
Season	362	101	14	7	3	32	36	47	.279	.381	.347
vs. Left-Handers	62	14	1	1	0	5	3	10	.226	.274	.273
vs. Right-Handers	300	87	13	6	3	27	33	37	.290	.403	.361
Home	181	51	7	5	2	15	18	26	.282	.409	.351
Road	181	50	7	2	1	17	18	21	.276	.354	.342
Day	167	53	9	2	2	15	19	19	.317	.431	.388
Night	195	48	5	5	1	17	17	28	.246	.338	.310
April	66	18	1	1	1	4	7	7	.273	.364	.351
May	86	20	2	1	7	5	10		.233	.337	.283
June	46	12	2	1	0	4	5	6	.261	.348	.333
July	63	14	2	0	1	5	2	12	.222	.302	.242
August	27	9	1	0	0	1	6	3	.333	.370	.455
Sept./Oct.	74	28	6	3	0	11	11	9	.378	.541	.459
Leading Off Inn.	71	23	3	2	1	1	4	8	.324	.465	.360
Runners On	154	50	6	3	0	29	15	19	.325	.403	.390
Runners/Scor. Pos.	79	22	4	0	0	24	11	12	.278	.329	.370
Runners On/2 Out	52	15	1	2	0	13	9	4	.288	.385	.393
Scor. Pos./2 Out	35	8	1	0	0	11	8	2	.229	.257	.372
Late Inning Pressure	60	14	1	1	0	7	5	4	.233	.283	.303
Leading Off	15	7	1	1	0	0	1	1	.467	.667	.500
Runners On	29	6	0	0	0	7	3	1	.207	.207	.303
Runners/Scor. Pos.	18	6	0	0	0	7	3	1	.333	.333	.455

RUNS BATTED IN	From 1B	From 2B	From 3B	Scoring Position
Totals	5/114	15/59	9/35	24/94
Percentage	4%	25%	26%	26%
Driving In Runners from 3B with Less than Two Out:		6/17		35%

Loves to face: Dick Selma (.625, 5-for-8, 1 HR)
Hates to face: Larry Dierker (0-for-13, 4 SO)
Career batting average of .266 through 1971, .225 in six seasons after that.... Established a career high with nine home runs in 1972, hit only four in 733 at bats thereafter.... Stranded seven consecutive runners at third base with less than two outs (May 15–July 18).... Grounded into 14 double plays, highest total on team, in 92 opportunities.... Mets allowed an average of 3.86 runs per nine innings with Boswell at second base, 2.67 with other second basemen.... Tied a record with three pinch hits in 1973 World Series. Co-holders: Dr. Bobby Brown, Dusty Rhodes, Carl Warwick, and Gonzalo Marquez.

Ed Charles

Bats Right

New York Mets	AB	H	2B	3B	HR	RBI	BB	SO	BA	SA	OBA
Season	169	35	8	1	3	18	18	31	.207	.320	.286
vs. Left-Handers	102	19	5	0	2	10	12	21	.186	.294	.276
vs. Right-Handers	67	16	3	1	1	8	6	10	.239	.358	.301
Home	96	21	5	1	2	12	11	16	.219	.354	.299
Road	73	14	3	0	1	6	7	15	.192	.274	.268
Day	97	22	4	1	2	13	10	20	.227	.361	.306
Night	72	13	4	0	1	5	6	9	.181	.278	.259
April	34	5	0	1	0	1	5	10	.147	.206	.256
May	30	4	2	0	1	5	4	4	.133	.300	.235
June	44	13	3	0	0	5	4	7	.295	.364	.360
July	17	3	1	0	1	3	2	6	.176	.412	.263
August	16	3	1	0	0	1	0	1	.188	.250	.188
Sept./Oct.	28	7	1	0	1	3	3	3	.250	.393	.323
Leading Off Inn.	35	5	0	1	0	0	4	6	.143	.200	.250
Runners On	70	20	3	0	2	17	9	9	.286	.414	.363
Runners/Scor. Pos.	40	11	2	0	1	15	7	6	.275	.400	.375
Runners On/2 Out	31	10	1	0	1	10	3	3	.323	.452	.382
Scor. Pos./2 Out	24	9	1	0	1	10	1	2	.375	.542	.400
Late Inning Pressure	29	3	0	0	0	0	3	10	.103	.103	.188
Leading Off	7	1	0	0	0	0	0	3	.143	.143	.143
Runners On	13	2	0	0	0	0	2	4	.154	.154	.267
Runners/Scor. Pos.	5	0	0	0	0	0	2	3	.000	.000	.286

RUNS BATTED IN	From 1B	From 2B	From 3B	Scoring Position
Totals	2/57	4/28	9/17	13/45
Percentage	4%	14%	53%	29%
Driving In Runners from 3B with Less than Two Out:		4/6		67%

Loves to face: Luke Walker (.429, 3-for-7, 1 HR)
Hates to face: Bob Gibson (0-for-4, 3 SO)
Played 386.2 innings at third base, just 26 percent of the team total, and only five-and-two-thirds more than Bobby Pfeil.... Hitless in seven at-bats with runners on base in postseason (all in World Series).... Batted .288 with 17 home runs and 20 stolen bases as a rookie with Kansas City Athletics in 1962, but never equalled any of those figures in seven seasons thereafter. He equalled or established career *lows* in each of those categories in 1969 (.207, 3 HR, 4 SB).... Spent four seasons at AAA level as second-best third baseman in organization whose best was Eddie Mathews.

Donn Clendenon

Bats Right

New York Mets	AB	H	2B	3B	HR	RBI	BB	SO	BA	SA	OBA
Season	202	51	5	0	12	37	19	62	.252	.455	.321
vs. Left-Handers	88	28	3	0	6	20	9	26	.318	.557	.384
vs. Right-Handers	114	23	2	0	6	17	10	36	.202	.377	.272
Home	90	19	2	0	4	12	7	36	.211	.367	.273
Road	112	32	3	0	8	25	12	26	.286	.527	.360
Day	99	25	5	0	2	15	10	30	.253	.364	.318
Night	103	26	0	0	10	22	9	32	.252	.544	.325
April	0	0	0	0	0	0	0	0	—	—	—
May	0	0	0	0	0	0	0	0	—	—	—
June	22	4	1	0	4	4	2	11	.182	.227	.250
July	56	16	3	0	2	13	3	13	.286	.446	.317
August	45	14	1	0	3	7	3	10	.311	.533	.367
Sept./Oct.	79	17	0	0	3	13	11	28	.215	.481	.319
Leading Off Inn.	34	9	0	0	0	2	4	.265	.324
Runners On	107	26	4	0	7	32	11	37	.243	.477	.317
Runners/Scor. Pos.	55	16	4	0	4	26	7	20	.291	.582	.365
Runners On/2 Out	49	12	1	0	5	16	6	19	.245	.571	.339
Scor. Pos./2 Out	28	7	1	0	2	10	2	11	.250	.500	.300
Late Inning Pressure	33	8	1	0	2	3	3	6	.242	.455	.306
Leading Off	5	1	0	0	0	0	0	1	.200	.200	.200
Runners On	17	3	1	0	1	2	2	3	.176	.412	.263
Runners/Scor. Pos.	8	1	1	0	0	2	2	1	.125	.250	.300

RUNS BATTED IN	From 1B	From 2B	From 3B	Scoring Position
Totals	6/82	9/40	10/27	19/67
Percentage	7%	23%	37%	28%
Driving In Runners from 3B with Less than Two Out:		6/11		55%

Loves to face: Gerry Arrigo (.800, 4-for-5, 1 HR)
Hates to face: Rick Wise (0-for-4, 4 SO)
Won the *Sport Magazine* World Series Most Valuable Player Award after not appearing in the League Championship Series.... Didn't start against Braves, who threw three right-handed starters in the L.C.S., although he started 14 of Mets last 22 games against right-handers prior to clinching the division title.... Struck out in 14 consecutive games (Sept. 3–17).... An early-day Kevin McReynolds: drove in more than 95 runs three times (1965, 1966, 1970), but never reached the 100-mark.... Stole 50 bases from 1962 through 1964—five more than Willie Mays—to rank ninth in N.L. during that time.

Wayne Garrett

Bats Left

New York Mets	AB	H	2B	3B	HR	RBI	BB	SO	BA	SA	OBA
Season	400	87	11	3	1	40	40	75	.218	.268	.290
vs. Left-Handers	29	6	0	1	0	3	4	5	.207	.276	.303
vs. Right-Handers	371	81	11	2	1	37	36	70	.218	.267	.289
Home	209	36	4	1	1	15	23	39	.172	.215	.256
Road	191	51	7	2	0	25	17	36	.267	.325	.329
Day	191	42	6	2	0	14	21	31	.220	.272	.296
Night	209	45	5	1	1	26	19	44	.215	.263	.284
April	15	4	2	0	0	0	3	7	.267	.400	.389
May	67	22	2	2	1	6	8	9	.328	.463	.400
June	72	13	0	0	0	7	7	11	.181	.181	.256
July	88	22	2	0	0	13	9	14	.250	.273	.316
August	75	12	3	0	0	6	4	19	.160	.200	.213
Sept./Oct.	83	14	2	1	0	8	9	15	.169	.217	.253
Leading Off Inn.	85	17	4	0	1	1	5	12	.200	.282	.253
Runners On	175	42	1	1	0	39	21	31	.240	.257	.320
Runners/Scor. Pos.	90	27	1	1	0	38	16	9	.300	.333	.393
Runners On/2 Out	62	13	0	0	0	12	10	10	.210	.210	.319
Scor. Pos./2 Out	36	10	0	0	0	12	7	4	.278	.278	.395
Late Inning Pressure	63	9	1	0	0	4	5	15	.143	.159	.214
Leading Off	18	3	0	0	0	0	2	4	.167	.167	.250
Runners On	28	4	0	0	0	4	2	4	.143	.143	.219
Runners/Scor. Pos.	13	1	0	0	0	3	1	1	.077	.077	.188

RUNS BATTED IN	From 1B	From 2B	From 3B	Scoring Position
Totals	1/122	14/66	24/47	38/113
Percentage	1%	21%	51%	34%
Driving In Runners from 3B with Less than Two Out:			18/28	64%

Loves to face: Pat Jarvis (.500, 5-for-10)
Hates to face: Ron Reed (0-for-9, 3 SO)

Started 98 games during regular season and four during post-season, but none against a left-handed starter.... Kept his batting average above .300 through June 13, batted .186 from that point on.... Had 90 at-bats without an extra-base hit from May 25 through July 2. ... Advanced 41 base runners on outs, highest total on team.... Drove in 12 consecutive runners from third base with less than two outs (June 6–July 25).... Mets' all-time leader in games at third base (709).... And incidentally, the Mets have now used 84 third basemen. Closest to the Mets' total since 1962: the Yankees, who have used 79.

Rod Gaspar

Bats Left and Right

New York Mets	AB	H	2B	3B	HR	RBI	BB	SO	BA	SA	OBA
Season	215	49	6	1	1	14	25	19	.228	.279	.313
vs. Left-Handers	76	20	1	0	1	3	10	6	.263	.316	.349
vs. Right-Handers	139	29	5	1	0	11	15	13	.209	.259	.293
Home	102	25	4	0	1	7	16	9	.245	.314	.353
Road	113	24	2	1	0	7	9	10	.212	.248	.274
Day	113	31	4	1	0	7	15	9	.274	.327	.362
Night	102	18	2	0	1	7	10	10	.176	.225	.257
April	56	12	2	0	0	1	7	4	.214	.250	.313
May	45	10	2	0	1	5	3	4	.222	.333	.280
June	31	9	1	1	0	3	5	1	.290	.387	.389
July	38	8	0	0	0	3	4	3	.211	.211	.286
August	28	5	0	0	0	2	1	5	.179	.179	.207
Sept./Oct.	17	5	1	0	0	3	5	2	.294	.353	.455
Leading Off Inn.	58	15	2	0	0	0	6	5	.259	.293	.328
Runners On	70	14	1	1	0	13	9	9	.200	.243	.296
Runners/Scor. Pos.	43	9	0	1	0	13	8	6	.209	.256	.327
Runners On/2 Out	35	8	1	1	0	7	5	5	.229	.314	.325
Scor. Pos./2 Out	24	5	0	1	0	7	4	4	.208	.292	.321
Late Inning Pressure	48	10	2	0	1	4	4	5	.208	.313	.264
Leading Off	14	3	0	0	0	0	0	1	.214	.214	.214
Runners On	16	3	1	0	0	3	2	2	.188	.250	.263
Runners/Scor. Pos.	8	1	0	0	0	3	1	2	.125	.125	.200

RUNS BATTED IN	From 1B	From 2B	From 3B	Scoring Position
Totals	0/51	8/37	5/14	13/51
Percentage	0%	22%	36%	25%
Driving In Runners from 3B with Less than Two Out:			3/5	60%

Loves to face: Steve Carlton (.571, 4-for-7)
Hates to face: Ferguson Jenkins (0-for-5)

Made his major league debut in 1969, appearing in 118 games, but played only 60 games in 1970s.... Didn't bat in 29 of those 118 games.... Only two N.L. players appeared in 100 games and had fewer at-bats: Ty Cline and Willie Smith.... One of three Mets to start each of first 10 games of season. Others: Agee and Jones.... Games started by month, April through September : 14, 9, 7, 6, 5, 3.... Four hits in 25 at-bats as a pinch hitter.... Hit the only HR of career off Mike McCormick on May 30.... Poured champagne on New York Mayor Lindsay, then running for reelection, during locker room celebration. Lindsay loved it.

Jerry Grote

Bats Right

New York Mets	AB	H	2B	3B	HR	RBI	BB	SO	BA	SA	OBA
Season	365	92	12	3	6	40	32	59	.252	.351	.313
vs. Left-Handers	119	28	4	0	1	16	9	15	.235	.294	.287
vs. Right-Handers	246	64	8	3	5	24	23	44	.260	.378	.325
Home	196	52	7	2	4	18	17	34	.265	.383	.326
Road	169	40	5	1	2	22	15	25	.237	.314	.297
Day	180	47	6	1	2	27	21	28	.261	.339	.338
Night	185	45	6	2	4	13	11	31	.243	.362	.286
April	51	12	4	0	0	8	3	6	.235	.314	.273
May	50	10	2	1	0	2	4	6	.200	.280	.273
June	65	16	2	1	1	9	6	13	.246	.354	.306
July	59	11	0	0	1	5	5	12	.186	.237	.250
August	58	21	1	1	2	11	8	7	.362	.517	.439
Sept./Oct.	82	22	3	0	2	5	6	15	.268	.378	.318
Leading Off Inn.	86	24	4	0	3	3	9	10	.279	.430	.347
Runners On	162	40	5	1	3	37	16	26	.247	.346	.315
Runners/Scor. Pos.	96	23	4	1	1	32	11	16	.240	.333	.312
Runners On/2 Out	80	21	3	0	2	16	6	10	.263	.375	.314
Scor. Pos./2 Out	51	13	2	0	1	11	5	7	.255	.294	.321
Late Inning Pressure	60	11	3	0	1	4	4	7	.183	.283	.242
Leading Off	13	3	1	0	1	0	0	0	.231	.538	.231
Runners On	24	5	1	0	0	3	3	3	.208	.250	.310
Runners/Scor. Pos.	14	2	0	0	0	2	1	1	.143	.143	.188

RUNS BATTED IN	From 1B	From 2B	From 3B	Scoring Position
Totals	5/120	14/70	15/49	29/119
Percentage	4%	20%	31%	24%
Driving In Runners from 3B with Less than Two Out:			13/24	54%

Loves to face: Larry Dierker (.429, 6-for-14)
Hates to face: Jim Merritt (0-for-12)

Opposing runners stole 31 bases, while 39 were caught stealing. Runners were combined 20-for-28 against Dyer and Martin.... Mets allowed an average of 3.15 runs per nine innings with Grote behind the plate, 3.59 with other catchers.... Set a career high with six home runs in 1969. Hit all six in the span of 128 at-bats from June 30 to Sept. 6.... Never played more than 126 games or drove in more than 40 runs in a season in his 16-year career.... Played on four division champions (Mets in 1969 and 1973, Dodgers in 1977 and 1978), and reached the World Series each time.

Bud Harrelson

Bats Left and Right

New York Mets	AB	H	2B	3B	HR	RBI	BB	SO	BA	SA	OBA
Season	395	98	11	6	0	24	54	54	.248	.306	.341
vs. Left-Handers	97	18	2	2	0	8	10	15	.186	.247	.259
vs. Right-Handers	298	80	9	4	0	16	44	39	.268	.326	.366
Home	217	62	8	4	0	12	30	30	.286	.359	.371
Road	178	36	3	2	0	12	24	24	.202	.242	.304
Day	177	50	7	3	0	10	21	26	.282	.356	.360
Night	218	48	4	3	0	14	33	28	.220	.266	.325
April	55	13	4	0	0	4	7	11	.236	.309	.323
May	68	22	1	1	0	6	12	15	.324	.368	.425
June	75	14	1	2	0	2	11	8	.187	.253	.299
July	22	6	1	0	0	0	6	1	.273	.318	.429
August	93	18	0	3	0	7	5	11	.194	.258	.232
Sept./Oct.	82	25	4	0	0	5	13	8	.305	.354	.406
Leading Off Inn.	140	27	2	1	0	12	16	19	.193	.221	.261
Runners On	128	39	2	4	0	24	27	20	.305	.383	.427
Runners/Scor. Pos.	69	23	1	4	0	24	21	10	.333	.464	.489
Runners On/2 Out	57	11	1	2	0	10	20	7	.193	.281	.403
Scor. Pos./2 Out	35	8	0	2	0	10	17	6	.229	.343	.481
Late Inning Pressure	54	19	2	3	0	5	12	8	.352	.500	.470
Leading Off	14	5	1	1	0	0	3	1	.357	.571	.471
Runners On	20	8	1	1	0	5	6	1	.400	.550	.538
Runners/Scor. Pos.	11	5	0	1	0	5	6	2	.455	.636	.647

RUNS BATTED IN	From 1B	From 2B	From 3B	Scoring Position
Totals	2/101	12/57	10/27	22/84
Percentage	2%	21%	37%	26%
Driving In Runners from 3B with Less than Two Out:			7/11	64%

Loves to face: Wayne Granger (.750, 3-for-4)
Hates to face: Ron Reed (0-for-10)

Mets allowed an average of 3.09 runs per nine innings with Harrelson at shortstop, 4.01 with Weis there.... Had one hit in 30 at-bats during a mid-June slump.... Stole only one base in 1969, compared to 51 over next two seasons.... At the end of 1969 season had one HR in 1473 career AB, an inside-the-parker misplayed by Al Luplow in 1967.... Career total of seven home runs in 4744 at-bats (one every 761 AB). Of all the players in major league history with as many at-bats, only three had lower home run rates: Jimmy Slagle (2 HR in 4996 AB), Eddie Foster (6 HR in 5652 AB), and Donie Bush (9 HR in 7206 AB).

Cleon Jones

New York Mets — Bats Right

New York Mets	AB	H	2B	3B	HR	RBI	BB	SO	BA	SA	OBA
Season	483	164	25	4	12	75	64	60	.340	.482	.422
vs. Left-Handers	130	44	5	2	7	24	21	11	.338	.569	.442
vs. Right-Handers	353	120	20	2	5	51	43	49	.340	.450	.414
Home	235	89	12	3	9	44	33	35	.379	.570	.458
Road	248	75	13	1	3	31	31	25	.302	.399	.387
Day	233	91	14	3	5	35	38	21	.391	.541	.476
Night	250	73	11	1	7	40	26	39	.292	.428	.369
April	78	32	5	1	2	14	6	10	.410	.577	.453
May	85	27	3	1	5	18	14	13	.318	.553	.406
June	88	30	4	2	2	16	15	16	.341	.500	.442
July	90	29	5	0	2	10	11	12	.322	.444	.413
August	98	36	8	0	1	14	11	4	.367	.480	.436
Sept./Oct.	44	10	0	0	0	3	7	5	.227	.227	.346
Leading Off Inn.	110	34	3	2	4	4	14	20	.309	.482	.397
Runners On	215	72	10	2	5	68	32	21	.335	.470	.427
Runners/Scor. Pos.	105	41	6	1	4	64	23	12	.390	.581	.496
Runners On/2 Out	87	27	3	2	1	19	19	11	.310	.425	.450
Scor. Pos./2 Out	44	17	2	1	0	16	13	5	.386	.477	.542
Late Inning Pressure	74	27	1	0	3	12	13	9	.365	.500	.466
Leading Off	18	7	0	0	1	1	1	1	.389	.556	.450
Runners On	34	11	1	0	2	11	7	3	.324	.529	.439
Runners/Scor. Pos.	15	5	1	0	1	9	7	1	.333	.600	.545

RUNS BATTED IN	From 1B	From 2B	From 3B	Scoring Position
Totals	11/164	24/74	28/50	52/124
Percentage	7%	32%	56%	42%
Driving In Runners from 3B with Less than Two Out:			22/29	76%

Loves to face: Denny Lemaster (.833, 5-for-6, 1 HR)
Hates to face: Claude Osteen (0-for-7)
Finished 3d in N.L. in batting average, highest rank in Mets history. Second highest: Keith Hernandez, 5th in 1986. ... Average never dropped below .332. ... Had six consecutive hits (April 11–12), and eight in a row vs. left-handers (May 10–25). ... Drove in 17 runs that gave Mets a lead, including 10 game-winners, highest totals on club. ... Last home run came on August 16. ... Hitless in 10 World Series at-bats with runners on base. ... Career batting average of .267 entering '69 season. ... Only 27 years old when he caught Davey Johnson's fly to end World Series, but he was oldest regular starter on team.

Ed Kranepool

New York Mets — Bats Left

New York Mets	AB	H	2B	3B	HR	RBI	BB	SO	BA	SA	OBA
Season	353	84	9	2	11	49	37	32	.238	.368	.307
vs. Left-Handers	35	3	0	0	0	1	5	5	.086	.086	.200
vs. Right-Handers	318	81	9	2	11	48	32	27	.255	.399	.319
Home	182	42	3	0	5	25	21	17	.231	.330	.306
Road	171	42	6	2	6	24	16	15	.246	.409	.309
Day	172	41	5	0	8	29	23	14	.238	.407	.327
Night	181	43	4	2	3	20	14	18	.238	.331	.288
April	58	18	3	1	2	15	5	3	.310	.500	.359
May	74	17	3	0	1	4	8	8	.230	.311	.305
June	70	12	1	0	4	11	5	5	.171	.357	.224
July	57	15	2	0	2	14	9	5	.263	.404	.353
August	58	14	0	1	1	3	6	9	.241	.328	.313
Sept./Oct.	36	8	0	0	1	2	4	2	.222	.306	.300
Leading Off Inn.	77	20	3	0	2	2	7	3	.260	.377	.321
Runners On	166	43	5	1	4	42	22	19	.259	.373	.339
Runners/Scor. Pos.	89	22	1	1	3	38	15	12	.247	.393	.343
Runners On/2 Out	61	19	4	0	1	18	15	6	.311	.426	.447
Scor. Pos./2 Out	38	13	2	0	1	17	10	4	.342	.474	.479
Late Inning Pressure	59	12	1	0	0	4	9	2	.203	.220	.309
Leading Off	17	3	0	0	0	0	2	0	.176	.176	.263
Runners On	28	7	1	0	0	4	5	1	.250	.286	.364
Runners/Scor. Pos.	14	3	0	0	0	3	3	0	.214	.214	.353

RUNS BATTED IN	From 1B	From 2B	From 3B	Scoring Position
Totals	6/133	10/63	22/45	32/108
Percentage	5%	16%	49%	30%
Driving In Runners from 3B with Less than Two Out:			13/25	52%

Loves to face: Bill Stoneman (.600, 6-for-10)
Hates to face: Nelson Briles (0-for-8)
Mets' all-time leader in extra-base hits, but not for much longer. Kranepool had 368, Strawberry has 357 entering the 1989 season. ... Led N.L. with 75 pinch hits during the 1970s. ... Set an all-time single-season record for pinch-hit batting average in 1974 (minimum: 15 hits): .485 (17-for-35). ... Made first major-league start the same day Maury Wills broke Ty Cobb's single-season record for steals. ... One of three players from 1969 team who wore a Mets uniform at the Polo Grounds. The others: Cleon Jones and Al Jackson. ... One day younger than Joe Niekro, three months younger than Graig Nettles.

J.C. Martin

New York Mets — Bats Left

New York Mets	AB	H	2B	3B	HR	RBI	BB	SO	BA	SA	OBA
Season	177	37	5	1	4	21	12	32	.209	.316	.257
vs. Left-Handers	17	4	1	1	1	2	0	3	.235	.588	.222
vs. Right-Handers	160	33	4	0	3	19	12	29	.206	.288	.260
Home	71	12	1	1	1	7	3	16	.169	.254	.197
Road	106	25	4	0	3	14	9	16	.236	.358	.296
Day	82	18	4	0	2	9	6	16	.220	.341	.267
Night	95	19	1	1	2	12	6	16	.200	.295	.248
April	20	2	1	0	0	1	2	3	.100	.150	.182
May	43	11	2	1	2	6	2	5	.256	.488	.283
June	35	8	0	0	0	3	3	7	.229	.229	.289
July	45	11	2	0	2	8	3	12	.244	.422	.292
August	20	4	0	0	0	3	1	2	.200	.200	.227
Sept./Oct.	14	1	0	0	0	0	1	3	.071	.071	.133
Leading Off Inn.	26	2	0	0	1	1	2	4	.077	.192	.143
Runners On	96	21	2	0	2	19	4	18	.219	.302	.245
Runners/Scor. Pos.	51	13	0	0	1	16	4	10	.255	.314	.298
Runners On/2 Out	42	12	1	0	2	11	3	7	.286	.452	.333
Scor. Pos./2 Out	24	7	0	0	1	8	3	3	.292	.417	.370
Late Inning Pressure	37	10	1	0	1	6	1	6	.270	.378	.289
Leading Off	6	1	0	0	0	1	1	1	.167	.167	.286
Runners On	22	6	0	0	1	6	0	3	.273	.409	.273
Runners/Scor. Pos.	12	4	0	0	1	6	0	2	.333	.583	.333

RUNS BATTED IN	From 1B	From 2B	From 3B	Scoring Position
Totals	2/71	5/36	10/26	15/62
Percentage	3%	14%	38%	24%
Driving In Runners from 3B with Less than Two Out:			6/14	43%

Loves to face: Mike Torrez (.500, 3-for-6)
Hates to face: Pat Jarvis (0-for-6)
Spent all or part of 14 seasons in majors, never had more than 294 at-bats. ... Had only one sacrifice bunt during season, and just 22 in his career, but had one memorable one in '69 World Series. ... Year by year batting averages, 1965 through 1970: .261, .255, .234, .225, .209, .156. ... Ever wonder who were the worst pinch-hitters ever? The lowest pinch-BAs (minimum: 100 AB): Ivan Murrell (.117), Charlie Gilbert (.122), Ted Kubiak (.122), Al Zarilla (.125), Woodie Held (.129), Lou Klimchock (.130), Roger Repoz (.145), J.C. Martin (.147), Dick Nen (.147), Hector Cruz (.148).

Bobby Pfeil

New York Mets — Bats Right

New York Mets	AB	H	2B	3B	HR	RBI	BB	SO	BA	SA	OBA
Season	211	49	9	0	0	10	7	27	.232	.275	.260
vs. Left-Handers	71	19	4	0	0	5	4	6	.268	.324	.316
vs. Right-Handers	140	30	5	0	0	5	3	21	.214	.250	.231
Home	100	21	6	0	0	3	3	13	.210	.270	.233
Road	111	28	3	0	0	7	4	14	.252	.279	.284
Day	104	22	4	0	0	5	4	9	.212	.250	.241
Night	107	27	5	0	0	5	3	18	.252	.299	.279
April	0	0	0	0	0	0	0	0	—	—	—
May	0	0	0	0	0	0	0	0	—	—	—
June	14	4	1	0	0	0	0	1	.286	.357	.286
July	55	12	3	0	0	3	4	5	.218	.273	.271
August	114	26	5	0	0	5	2	16	.228	.272	.241
Sept./Oct.	28	7	0	0	0	2	1	5	.250	.250	.300
Leading Off Inn.	43	7	2	0	0	0	1	3	.163	.209	.182
Runners On	82	15	3	0	0	10	0	14	.183	.220	.183
Runners/Scor. Pos.	38	9	3	0	0	10	0	5	.237	.316	.237
Runners On/2 Out	43	10	2	0	0	8	0	7	.233	.279	.233
Scor. Pos./2 Out	23	8	2	0	0	8	0	3	.348	.435	.348
Late Inning Pressure	24	6	2	0	0	3	0	2	.250	.333	.250
Leading Off	6	0	0	0	0	0	0	0	.000	.000	.000
Runners On	8	3	1	0	0	3	0	0	.375	.500	.375
Runners/Scor. Pos.	7	3	0	0	0	3	0	0	.429	.571	.429

RUNS BATTED IN	From 1B	From 2B	From 3B	Scoring Position
Totals	0/66	5/28	5/14	10/42
Percentage	0%	18%	36%	24%
Driving In Runners from 3B with Less than Two Out:			2/5	40%

Loves to pface: Tommie Sisk (.800, 4-for-5)
Hates to pface: Tom Griffin (0-for-8, 5 SO)
We're pretty sure he'd have loved to pface *Doug* Sisk too. ... Batted second in 46 of his 50 starts. ... Pfive hits in nine at-bats as a pinch-hitter. ... Didn't drive in a runner from pfirst base in 66 opportunities. ... Mets allowed an average of 2.55 runs per nine innings with Pfeil at third base, 3.58 with other third basemen. ... Played every position except pitcher and center pfield pfor Pfiladelphia in 1971, his only other season in the majors. ... Hit the only two home runs of his major league career in same game, off Larry Dierker on July 27, 1971.

Art Shamsky

New York Mets — Bats Left

New York Mets	AB	H	2B	3B	HR	RBI	BB	SO	BA	SA	OBA
Season	303	91	9	3	14	47	36	32	.300	.488	.375
vs. Left-Handers	22	9	0	0	1	3	0	3	.409	.545	.417
vs. Right-Handers	281	82	9	3	13	44	36	29	.292	.484	.372
Home	138	42	4	1	7	27	13	15	.304	.500	.363
Road	165	49	5	2	7	20	23	17	.297	.479	.384
Day	141	36	4	1	5	19	14	11	.255	.404	.329
Night	162	55	5	2	9	28	22	21	.340	.562	.414
April	0	0	0	0	0	0	0	0	—	—	—
May	30	7	1	0	0	4	2	7	.233	.267	.281
June	55	20	2	0	5	9	9	7	.364	.673	.446
July	68	24	3	1	3	12	12	5	.353	.559	.451
August	80	20	3	0	3	10	5	8	.250	.400	.294
Sept./Oct.	70	20	0	2	3	12	8	5	.286	.471	.361
Leading Off Inn.	71	17	2	0	3	3	9	10	.239	.394	.325
Runners On	152	50	5	1	4	37	18	16	.329	.454	.392
Runners/Scor. Pos.	83	25	1	0	2	29	10	14	.301	.386	.357
Runners On/2 Out	63	14	1	1	1	13	8	7	.222	.317	.310
Scor. Pos./2 Out	37	9	1	0	0	9	5	7	.243	.270	.333
Late Inning Pressure	40	15	1	0	2	9	9	0	.375	.550	.490
Leading Off	5	1	0	0	0	0	4	0	.200	.200	.556
Runners On	21	9	1	0	0	7	2	0	.429	.476	.480
Runners/Scor. Pos.	12	6	0	0	0	7	2	0	.500	.500	.533

RUNS BATTED IN	From 1B	From 2B	From 3B	Scoring Position
Totals	7/104	13/71	13/27	26/98
Percentage	7%	18%	48%	27%
Driving In Runners from 3B with Less than Two Out:	11/19			58%

Loves to face: Gary Nolan (3-for-3, 1 HR, 1 BB)
Hates to face: Juan Marichal (0-for-7)
Batted .296 during 1969–1970, .221 for the rest of his career. . . . Didn't start against a left-hander in 1969. . . . Drove in seven runners from scoring position in 13 opportunities in LIP Situations. . . . One of 13 players in major league history to hit home runs on four consecutive at bats. Of them, only Johnny Blanchard (67) hit fewer career HR than Shamsky (68). . . . Only player in major league history to hit 20+ home runs in a season in which he had only five other extra-base hits; he did that for 1966 Reds (same year he had four consecutive homers), when he hit career-high 21 homers in only 234 at-bats.

Ron Swoboda

New York Mets — Bats Right

New York Mets	AB	H	2B	3B	HR	RBI	BB	SO	BA	SA	OBA
Season	327	77	10	2	9	52	43	90	.235	.361	.326
vs. Left-Handers	120	29	5	1	4	24	17	28	.242	.400	.333
vs. Right-Handers	207	48	5	1	5	28	26	62	.232	.338	.322
Home	171	37	2	1	3	21	19	45	.216	.292	.297
Road	156	40	8	1	6	31	24	45	.256	.436	.357
Day	162	41	7	1	3	34	27	44	.253	.364	.359
Night	165	36	3	1	6	18	16	46	.218	.358	.291
April	50	16	2	0	1	9	3	11	.320	.420	.352
May	45	7	1	1	2	5	5	12	.156	.356	.235
June	47	8	0	1	0	3	5	19	.170	.213	.250
July	34	11	1	0	0	5	5	6	.324	.353	.410
August	62	16	5	0	3	17	8	15	.258	.484	.343
Sept./Oct.	89	19	1	0	3	13	17	27	.213	.326	.352
Leading Off Inn.	76	19	1	0	2	2	9	21	.250	.342	.329
Runners On	161	38	8	1	5	48	24	40	.236	.391	.332
Runners/Scor. Pos.	82	23	6	0	1	38	16	23	.280	.390	.390
Runners On/2 Out	71	14	1	1	0	17	11	20	.197	.239	.305
Scor. Pos./2 Out	45	11	1	0	0	16	6	11	.244	.267	.333
Late Inning Pressure	52	20	3	1	4	18	12	9	.385	.712	.500
Leading Off	17	5	1	0	1	1	5	3	.294	.529	.455
Runners On	25	12	1	0	3	17	4	4	.480	.880	.552
Runners/Scor. Pos.	12	7	1	0	1	13	2	3	.583	.917	.643

RUNS BATTED IN	From 1B	From 2B	From 3B	Scoring Position
Totals	8/138	20/69	15/33	35/102
Percentage	6%	29%	45%	34%
Driving In Runners from 3B with Less than Two Out:	9/18			50%

Loves to face: Ferguson Jenkins (.500, 3-for-6, 2 HR)
Hates to face: Bill Hands (0-for-9, 5 SO)
Had nine game-winning RBI, one fewer than team leader Cleon Jones, including seven from August 16 until pennant clinching (9-for-18 in LIP Situations during that span). . . . Batted .500 with bases loaded: 6-for-12, with four doubles, a home run, and four walks. . . . Yearly home runs for last seven seasons of career (1967–1973): 13, 11, 9, 9, 2, 1, 1. . . . One of four players on '69 Mets to bat as a designated hitter later in his career. The other three: Cleon Jones, Duffy Dyer, and Amos Otis. . . . One of 11 players to hit home runs for both the Mets and Yankees. Among the others: Gene Woodling and Marv Throneberry.

Al Weis

New York Mets — Bats Right

New York Mets	AB	H	2B	3B	HR	RBI	BB	SO	BA	SA	OBA
Season	247	53	9	2	2	23	15	51	.215	.291	.259
vs. Left-Handers	100	22	5	0	1	6	12	17	.220	.300	.301
vs. Right-Handers	147	31	4	2	1	17	3	34	.211	.286	.227
Home	94	20	4	1	0	7	6	21	.213	.277	.257
Road	153	33	5	1	2	16	9	30	.216	.301	.259
Day	126	31	5	2	2	16	7	24	.246	.365	.284
Night	121	22	4	0	0	7	8	27	.182	.215	.233
April	9	0	0	0	0	0	1	2	.000	.000	.100
May	17	3	0	0	0	1	1	4	.176	.176	.211
June	58	12	3	0	0	5	4	12	.207	.259	.258
July	78	20	4	1	2	11	6	13	.256	.410	.310
August	33	8	1	0	0	3	1	5	.242	.273	.265
Sept./Oct.	52	10	1	1	0	3	2	15	.192	.250	.222
Leading Off Inn.	67	14	1	1	1	3	3	12	.209	.299	.243
Runners On	106	27	5	1	1	22	6	22	.255	.349	.292
Runners/Scor. Pos.	55	17	4	1	1	22	6	8	.309	.473	.371
Runners On/2 Out	45	14	2	1	1	14	3	8	.311	.467	.354
Scor. Pos./2 Out	25	10	2	1	1	14	3	3	.400	.680	.464
Late Inning Pressure	30	7	1	0	0	1	1	6	.233	.267	.258
Leading Off	8	3	1	0	0	0	0	2	.375	.500	.375
Runners On	10	1	0	0	0	0	0	2	.100	.100	.100
Runners/Scor. Pos.	4	0	0	0	0	1	0	0	.000	.000	.000

RUNS BATTED IN	From 1B	From 2B	From 3B	Scoring Position
Totals	4/86	6/43	11/22	17/65
Percentage	5%	14%	50%	26%
Driving In Runners from 3B with Less than Two Out:	5/9			56%

Loves to face: Dick Selma (.600, 3-for-5, 1 HR)
Hates to face: Ferguson Jenkins (0-for-7)
His two home runs were hit in consecutive games at Chicago (July 15–16). . . . Grounded into only three DP in 55 opportunities. . . . Batted .191 in four years with Mets. Only two other Mets players with 500+ at-bats hit below .200: Koosman (.121) and Seaver (.150). . . . Ranked second in A.L. with 22 stolen bases in 1964, stole only 17 in seven seasons after that. . . . Hit his first major league home run off Tommy John in June 1964. . . . Early use of Batter-Pitcher Matchups? Weis's World Series HR was hit off Dave McNally, who had surrendered one of Weis's seven career regular-season homers back in '64.

New York Mets

New York Mets	AB	H	2B	3B	HR	RBI	BB	SO	BA	SA	OBA
Season	5427	1311	184	41	109	600	527	1089	.242	.351	.311
vs. Left-Handers	1382	329	45	11	34	157	150	278	.238	.360	.315
vs. Right-Handers	4045	982	139	30	75	443	377	811	.243	.348	.309
Home	2673	640	87	21	56	288	268	555	.239	.351	.311
Road	2754	671	97	20	53	312	259	534	.244	.351	.311
Day	2612	663	102	20	53	314	280	483	.254	.369	.328
Night	2815	648	82	21	56	286	247	606	.230	.334	.295
April	658	156	32	4	10	70	57	137	.237	.343	.299
May	802	198	27	10	20	90	84	146	.247	.380	.320
June	912	215	28	9	15	97	94	187	.236	.336	.307
July	946	236	34	4	22	121	94	178	.249	.364	.319
August	1049	257	36	5	20	111	77	199	.245	.346	.299
Sept./Oct.	1060	249	27	9	22	111	121	242	.235	.340	.318
Leading Off Inn.	1333	317	41	9	29	29	117	232	.238	.347	.303
Runners On	2300	587	73	18	44	535	248	472	.255	.360	.327
Runners/Scor. Pos.	1253	336	49	12	22	473	178	267	.268	.379	.354
Runners On/2 Out	994	236	30	11	19	229	136	215	.237	.347	.332
Scor. Pos./2 Out	615	161	21	6	8	198	100	130	.262	.354	.367
Late Inning Pressure	801	201	24	5	17	98	94	133	.251	.357	.333
Leading Off	203	53	5	2	4	4	24	26	.261	.365	.342
Runners On	349	93	13	1	8	89	44	54	.266	.378	.352
Runners/Scor. Pos.	186	53	8	1	4	78	33	27	.285	.403	.391

RUNS BATTED IN	From 1B	From 2B	From 3B	Scoring Position
Totals	73/1742	193/970	225/549	418/1519
Percentage	4%	20%	41%	28%
Driving In Runners from 3B with Less than Two Out:	151/281			54%

Love to face: Niekros (3–0 vs. Joe, 3–0 vs. Phil, 0–0 vs. Mom)
Hate to face: Larry Dierker (0–4 against him)
Batted .149 with runners on base in the World Series, .152 (5-for-33) with runners in scoring position, .217 with the bases empty. . . . Didn't make any double plays in Series—the only team that didn't turn a DP in a Series of any length. . . . Struck out 114 times fewer than in 1968 (when they set a major league record that still stands), but 1969 total is still No. 16 on the all-time un-hit list. . . . Stole more bases against Tim McCarver than against any other catcher (10 in 12 attempts). . . . Swept a doubleheader from Pirates on Sept. 12 by identical 1–0 scores with both runs driven in by pitchers.

Mets Pitchers

Don Cardwell — Throws Right

New York Mets	W-L	ERA	AB	H	HR	BB	SO	BA	SA	OBA
Season	8-10	3.01	576	145	15	47	60	.252	.392	.313
vs. Left-Handers			227	57	4	24	16	.251	.392	.328
vs. Right-Handers			349	88	11	23	44	.252	.393	.302
Home	4-6	2.50	311	78	6	23	37	.251	.370	.306
Road	4-4	3.62	265	67	9	24	23	.253	.419	.321
Day	5-8	2.89	412	107	9	35	38	.260	.396	.321
Night	3-2	3.32	164	38	6	12	22	.232	.384	.292
April	0-3	2.79	70	17	0	6	5	.243	.343	.312
May	1-3	2.90	119	28	6	6	14	.235	.437	.270
June	1-2	3.96	99	25	5	7	8	.253	.455	.302
July	1-1	5.16	93	31	2	6	11	.333	.527	.380
August	2-0	1.84	109	24	0	14	11	.220	.266	.317
Sept./Oct.	3-1	1.80	86	20	2	8	11	.233	.314	.305
Leading Off Inn.			146	38	3	8	19	.260	.363	.303
Runners On			228	54	5	24	15	.237	.377	.313
Runners/Scor. Pos.			109	29	1	20	11	.266	.376	.379
Runners On/2 Out			105	30	1	17	6	.286	.371	.390
Scor. Pos./2 Out			65	17	0	14	5	.262	.277	.400
Late Inning Pressure			81	20	0	3	11	.247	.370	.279
Leading Off			24	7	0	1	2	.292	.375	.320
Runners On			28	5	0	1	4	.179	.357	.200
Runners/Scor. Pos.			14	1	0	1	3	.071	.143	.125
First 9 Batters			231	61	6	20	30	.264	.407	.327
Second 9 Batters			170	45	7	16	13	.265	.441	.328
All Batters Thereafter			175	39	2	11	17	.223	.326	.279

Loves to face: Don Mason (0-for-10)
Hates to face: Vada Pinson (3-for-3, 2 BB)
Ground outs-to-air outs ratio: 1.59. . . . Additional statistics: 19 double-play ground outs in 105 opportunities, 26 doubles, 5 triples in 152.1 innings. . . . Mets' opening day starter in 1967. The next 10 openers belonged to Seaver. . . . Went 4–0 with a 0.80 ERA in his last six starts, before losing final game of season in relief. . . . One hit in 34 at-bats in day games, 7-for-13 in night games. . . . Had only two winning records in 14 seasons in majors (15–14 for Cubs in 1961, 13–10 for Pirates in 1965). . . . Compiled 4.38 ERA over first six seasons, 3.47 over last eight. . . . Only pitcher in major league history to pitch a no-hitter in his first start after a trade.

Jack DiLauro — Throws Left

New York Mets	W-L	ERA	AB	H	HR	BB	SO	BA	SA	OBA
Season	1-4	2.40	232	50	4	18	27	.216	.336	.269
vs. Left-Handers			77	14	0	4	10	.182	.247	.222
vs. Right-Handers			155	36	4	14	17	.232	.381	.291
Home	0-1	1.42	109	18	2	8	16	.165	.266	.220
Road	1-3	3.38	123	32	2	10	11	.260	.398	.311
Day	1-2	1.78	112	28	2	9	12	.250	.366	.303
Night	0-2	2.97	120	22	2	9	15	.183	.308	.237
April			0	0	0	0	0	—	—	—
May	0-0	0.00	26	5	0	3	3	.192	.269	.267
June	0-2	2.14	78	17	2	5	7	.218	.372	.262
July	1-1	4.30	56	14	1	2	6	.250	.375	.271
August	0-0	2.19	44	8	1	4	4	.182	.295	.250
Sept./Oct.	0-1	2.25	28	6	0	4	7	.214	.286	.313
Leading Off Inn.			60	16	1	1	3	.267	.383	.279
Runners On			92	17	2	11	13	.185	.293	.264
Runners/Scor. Pos.			57	10	1	9	9	.175	.281	.275
Runners On/2 Out			43	7	1	9	6	.163	.279	.308
Scor. Pos./2 Out			28	5	0	8	3	.179	.214	.361
Late Inning Pressure			31	3	1	0	6	.097	.129	.176
Leading Off			10	1	0	0	1	.100	.100	.100
Runners On			6	1	0	1	1	.167	.333	.286
Runners/Scor. Pos.			2	1	0	1	0	.500	1.000	.667
First 9 Batters			146	33	3	10	20	.226	.356	.272
Second 9 Batters			53	9	1	6	5	.170	.264	.250
All Batters Thereafter			33	8	0	2	2	.242	.364	.286

Loves to face: Bill Sudakis (0-for-5, 3 SO)
Hates to face: Curt Flood (.667, 4-for-6)
Ground outs-to-air outs ratio: 1.13. . . . Additional statistics: 5 double-play ground outs in 36 opportunities, 12 doubles, 2 triples in 63.2 innings. . . . Made four consecutive starts from June 4 through July 1, the only four of his 65-game major-league career. . . . ERA of 3.16 in four starts, 1.89 in 19 relief appearances. . . . Faced only five batters in the seventh inning or later while protecting a lead of no more than three runs. . . . Pitched in consecutive games only once (last two games of season). . . . Did not appear during postseason, although he was eligible. . . . Assigned to Tidewater after the Series, and drafted by Houston in December.

Gary Gentry — Throws Right

New York Mets	W-L	ERA	AB	H	HR	BB	SO	BA	SA	OBA
Season	13-12	3.43	863	192	24	81	154	.222	.342	.292
vs. Left-Handers			349	75	7	34	58	.215	.292	.289
vs. Right-Handers			514	117	17	47	96	.228	.375	.294
Home	5-6	3.31	466	102	12	49	81	.219	.333	.295
Road	8-6	3.57	397	90	12	32	73	.227	.353	.288
Day	7-6	4.22	414	100	13	37	72	.242	.386	.306
Night	6-6	2.74	449	92	11	44	82	.205	.301	.278
April	2-0	2.64	115	28	3	16	20	.243	.374	.336
May	2-4	4.70	144	35	7	15	28	.243	.424	.319
June	3-2	2.25	128	22	1	15	28	.172	.250	.262
July	2-3	4.87	154	37	8	13	26	.240	.429	.294
August	0-2	4.15	126	28	4	11	14	.222	.333	.295
Sept./Oct.	4-1	2.19	196	42	1	11	38	.214	.260	.260
Leading Off Inn.			221	55	5	18	30	.249	.339	.308
Runners On			329	73	7	35	64	.222	.313	.299
Runners/Scor. Pos.			161	42	4	22	34	.261	.385	.353
Runners On/2 Out			153	40	3	19	32	.261	.359	.343
Scor. Pos./2 Out			92	26	2	12	19	.283	.413	.365
Late Inning Pressure			94	16	2	14	11	.170	.266	.275
Leading Off			24	6	0	4	4	.250	.250	.400
Runners On			36	3	0	6	3	.083	.111	.209
Runners/Scor. Pos.			16	1	0	4	2	.063	.063	.238
First 9 Batters			281	50	5	24	63	.178	.260	.247
Second 9 Batters			265	66	13	26	47	.249	.445	.322
All Batters Thereafter			317	76	6	31	44	.240	.328	.306

Loves to face: Tim McCarver (.071, 1-for-14)
Hates to face: Ron Santo (.500, 7-for-14, 4 HR)
Ground outs-to-air outs ratio: 0.93. . . . Additional statistics: 16 double-play ground outs in 161 opportunities, 23 doubles, 4 triples in 223.2 innings. . . . Never again pitched more than 203 innings in a season. . . . Made five starts on three days' rest: 5–0, 2.38 ERA. . . . Faced 148 consecutive batters without allowing an extra-base hit, a streak that ended September 28 on a double by Phillies pitcher Jerry Johnson. . . . Walked at least one batter in each of his first 33 starts, none in either of his last two. . . . Hitless in 28 consecutive at-bats since Aug. 3 when he doubled in two runs off Jim Palmer in 2d inning of World Series Game 3.

Cal Koonce — Throws Right

New York Mets	W-L	ERA	AB	H	HR	BB	SO	BA	SA	OBA
Season	6-3	4.99	316	85	8	42	48	.269	.446	.358
vs. Left-Handers			129	35	1	20	18	.271	.434	.371
vs. Right-Handers			187	50	7	22	30	.267	.455	.349
Home	4-2	4.31	153	38	4	23	25	.248	.405	.358
Road	2-1	5.61	163	47	4	19	23	.288	.485	.359
Day	4-3	4.66	192	55	4	21	25	.286	.453	.361
Night	2-0	5.45	124	30	4	21	23	.242	.435	.354
April	0-2	6.10	39	9	2	13	5	.231	.462	.434
May	2-1	7.50	72	24	4	9	10	.333	.583	.410
June	0-0	1.93	36	8	1	3	7	.222	.389	.282
July	2-0	3.92	74	17	1	6	15	.230	.378	.284
August	2-0	3.94	59	15	0	8	9	.254	.339	.343
Sept./Oct.	0-0	6.23	36	12	0	3	2	.333	.528	.400
Leading Off Inn.			74	14	1	6	16	.189	.338	.250
Runners On			145	38	3	22	20	.262	.428	.363
Runners/Scor. Pos.			89	24	2	17	10	.270	.427	.391
Runners On/2 Out			61	11	1	10	9	.180	.295	.296
Scor. Pos./2 Out			39	8	0	8	5	.205	.282	.340
Late Inning Pressure			107	30	6	17	22	.280	.523	.384
Leading Off			25	3	0	2	9	.120	.160	.185
Runners On			47	12	3	10	6	.255	.532	.386
Runners/Scor. Pos.			26	8	2	8	1	.308	.577	.471
First 9 Batters			235	63	6	36	38	.268	.455	.370
Second 9 Batters			65	17	2	5	10	.262	.400	.314
All Batters Thereafter			16	5	0	1	0	.313	.500	.353

Loves to face: Fred Patek (0-for-3, 3 SO)
Hates to face: Jim Wynn (2-for-2, 1 HR, 3 BB)
Ground outs-to-air outs ratio: 2.75, highest on team. . . . Additional statistics: 10 double-play ground outs in 68 opportunities, 24 doubles, 4 triples in 83.0 innings. . . . Only pitcher on team to allow more hits than innings pitched (minimum: 10 games). . . . Only season of major league career in which he did not make a start. . . . Walked eight batters between strikeouts (April 17–27). . . . ERA of 6.99 through the end of May, 3.95 after that. . . . Didn't pitch during postseason. . . . Won 10 games as a rookie, never won more than seven in any season thereafter. . . . The "other rookie" on the 1962 Cubs, when Ken Hubbs was named Rookie of the Year.

Jerry Koosman — Throws Left

New York Mets	W–L	ERA	AB	H	HR	BB	SO	BA	SA	OBA
Season	17-9	2.28	864	187	14	68	180	.216	.309	.275
vs. Left-Handers			155	32	1	5	32	.206	.277	.230
vs. Right-Handers			709	155	13	63	148	.219	.316	.285
Home	9-3	2.25	419	91	8	35	99	.217	.310	.279
Road	8-6	2.30	445	96	6	33	81	.216	.308	.272
Day	5-3	3.28	311	71	6	32	55	.228	.341	.299
Night	12-6	1.88	553	116	8	36	125	.210	.291	.261
April	1-2	3.57	92	24	1	6	13	.261	.359	.303
May	0-1	1.06	57	7	1	3	21	.123	.228	.167
June	4-2	0.72	178	34	2	10	47	.191	.270	.234
July	3-1	3.14	173	41	5	19	31	.237	.353	.316
August	4-2	2.72	165	37	3	12	28	.224	.321	.283
Sept./Oct.	5-1	2.40	199	44	2	18	40	.221	.296	.285
Leading Off Inn.			228	53	3	14	61	.232	.307	.286
Runners On			330	69	2	32	61	.209	.279	.275
Runners/Scor. Pos.			171	32	1	23	38	.187	.263	.276
Runners On/2 Out			135	24	0	14	35	.178	.222	.255
Scor. Pos./2 Out			78	12	0	12	24	.154	.192	.267
Late Inning Pressure			151	30	4	9	31	.199	.325	.244
Leading Off			43	12	1	1	9	.279	.395	.295
Runners On			53	5	0	5	10	.094	.132	.172
Runners/Scor. Pos.			21	2	0	4	4	.095	.095	.240
First 9 Batters			251	62	1	25	70	.247	.311	.317
Second 9 Batters			245	47	5	19	48	.192	.306	.254
All Batters Thereafter			368	78	8	24	62	.212	.310	.261

Loves to face: Lou Brock (.083, 1-for-12, 5 SO)
Hates to face: Tim McCarver (.571, 4-for-7)
Ground outs-to-air outs ratio: 1.08. ... Additional statistics: 28 double-play ground outs in 178 opportunities, 30 doubles, 4 triples in 241.0 innings. ... Faced 36 consecutive batters with runners in scoring position without allowing a hit (April 16–June 13). ... Allowed more than one HR only once: July 8, vs. Cubs (Banks and Hickman). ... Ended a streak of 48 at-bats without a hit on August 22 against Clay Kirby. ... Pitched 13 shutouts in his first two full seasons with Mets, and another 13 during his other nine seasons with them. ... Posted a 48–30 (.615) record through 1970, but was sub-.500 during the remaining 15 years of his major league career (174–179).

Jim McAndrew — Throws Right

New York Mets	W–L	ERA	AB	H	HR	BB	SO	BA	SA	OBA
Season	6-7	3.47	497	112	12	44	90	.225	.374	.288
vs. Left-Handers			182	44	2	18	20	.242	.396	.315
vs. Right-Handers			315	68	10	26	70	.216	.362	.272
Home	4-4	3.06	288	65	4	28	51	.226	.351	.295
Road	2-3	4.04	209	47	8	16	39	.225	.407	.279
Day	1-0	5.45	129	35	4	19	19	.271	.450	.362
Night	5-7	2.82	368	77	8	25	71	.209	.348	.261
April	0-1	7.63	60	17	3	12	7	.283	.517	.403
May	0-1	4.50	23	7	1	2	7	.304	.522	.360
June	2-0	2.45	75	11	4	9	10	.147	.333	.235
July	0-1	13.50	33	14	1	3	4	.424	.545	.474
August	4-2	1.47	194	33	2	12	43	.170	.284	.217
Sept./Oct.	0-2	3.30	112	30	1	6	19	.268	.402	.306
Leading Off Inn.			132	33	6	7	20	.250	.462	.288
Runners On			166	40	5	27	37	.241	.392	.345
Runners/Scor. Pos.			95	25	3	19	20	.263	.421	.375
Runners On/2 Out			75	16	5	13	17	.213	.480	.337
Scor. Pos./2 Out			47	11	3	11	10	.234	.511	.390
Late Inning Pressure			60	13	2	12	8	.217	.367	.356
Leading Off			17	4	1	2	1	.235	.412	.316
Runners On			20	4	1	5	4	.200	.400	.385
Runners/Scor. Pos.			9	3	0	4	4	.333	.444	.538
First 9 Batters			201	59	8	18	37	.294	.517	.350
Second 9 Batters			148	26	2	11	30	.176	.277	.230
All Batters Thereafter			148	27	2	15	23	.182	.277	.262

Loves to face: Gary Sutherland (0-for-8)
Hates to face: Joe Torre (.500, 4-for-8, 2 HR, 2 BB)
Ground outs-to-air outs ratio: 0.92. ... Additional statistics: 6 double-play ground outs in 85 opportunities, 22 doubles, 8 triples (most on the team, and all after the All-Star break), in 135.0 innings. ... ERA breakdown in 21 starts: 5.05 in first 3 innings, 2.40 in middle three innings, 0.36 thereafter (one ER in 25 IP). ... Completed six innings in two of his first 10 starts, but 10 of his last 11. ... Compiled a 7.88 ERA in 8 innings of relief work. ... Walked 7.86 batters per nine innings in first 10 games, 1.74 in last 17 appearances. ... Started against Robin Roberts in RR's last pro start (June 17, 1967 in Eastern League).

Tug McGraw — Throws Left

New York Mets	W–L	ERA	AB	H	HR	BB	SO	BA	SA	OBA
Season	9-3	2.24	367	89	6	47	92	.243	.349	.328
vs. Left-Handers			103	31	1	11	17	.301	.427	.368
vs. Right-Handers			264	58	5	36	75	.220	.318	.312
Home	5-1	1.89	199	41	4	25	55	.206	.317	.295
Road	4-2	2.70	168	48	2	22	37	.286	.387	.366
Day	4-1	2.41	189	45	2	23	54	.238	.344	.321
Night	5-2	2.06	178	44	4	24	38	.247	.354	.335
April	2-0	1.46	42	9	0	5	15	.214	.286	.298
May	2-1	4.38	96	28	4	11	24	.292	.500	.361
June	0-0	4.26	50	14	1	6	11	.280	.400	.357
July	1-1	1.84	51	14	1	12	16	.275	.412	.413
August	2-1	0.48	63	11	0	8	11	.175	.190	.268
Sept./Oct.	2-0	0.52	65	13	0	5	15	.200	.231	.257
Leading Off Inn.			87	28	3	12	23	.322	.506	.404
Runners On			177	36	2	24	47	.203	.282	.297
Runners/Scor. Pos.			96	16	0	19	29	.167	.219	.302
Runners On/2 Out			67	12	1	13	22	.179	.254	.313
Scor. Pos./2 Out			41	4	0	10	17	.098	.122	.275
Late Inning Pressure			213	47	2	28	55	.221	.291	.311
Leading Off			52	15	1	6	15	.288	.404	.362
Runners On			98	17	0	16	26	.173	.204	.289
Runners/Scor. Pos.			56	5	0	12	16	.089	.107	.250
First 9 Batters			240	55	2	32	63	.229	.313	.320
Second 9 Batters			84	19	3	10	19	.226	.393	.309
All Batters Thereafter			43	15	1	5	10	.349	.465	.408

Loves to face: Ron Santo (0-for-6, 4 SO)
Hates to face: Randy Hundley (.571, 4-for-7)
Ground outs-to-air outs ratio: 1.06. ... Additional statistics: 12 double-play ground outs in 95 opportunities, 17 doubles, 2 triples in 100.1 innings. ... Won only four of 23 career decisions prior to 1969. ... 1–1, 5.23 ERA in four starts; 8–2, 1.47 ERA as a reliever. ... Allowed the leadoff batter to reach base safely in seven consecutive innings that he started (May 16-28). ... Faced 110 batters in the seventh inning or later protecting leads of three runs or less, twice as many as Ron Taylor. ... Allowed only two earned runs in his last 38 innings. ... One of three N.L. pitchers not to hit a batter in 100 or more innings. The others: Gary Nolan and Joe Niekro. ... Didn't pitch in the 1969 World Series.

Nolan Ryan — Throws Right

New York Mets	W–L	ERA	AB	H	HR	BB	SO	BA	SA	OBA
Season	6-3	3.53	317	60	3	53	92	.189	.265	.306
vs. Left-Handers			123	25	2	31	42	.203	.309	.359
vs. Right-Handers			194	35	1	22	50	.180	.237	.267
Home	3-1	4.23	138	29	3	19	45	.210	.319	.306
Road	3-2	3.00	179	31	0	34	47	.173	.223	.305
Day	3-1	3.74	162	31	3	27	46	.191	.284	.305
Night	3-2	3.30	155	29	0	26	46	.187	.245	.306
April	2-0	3.21	51	11	1	10	16	.216	.314	.344
May	0-0	0.00	24	4	0	2	4	.167	.208	.231
June	1-0	2.45	52	9	0	5	18	.173	.231	.254
July	0-1	7.56	60	13	2	15	18	.217	.400	.368
August	1-0	0.79	40	7	0	3	7	.175	.225	.233
Sept./Oct.	2-2	3.81	90	16	0	18	29	.178	.200	.315
Leading Off Inn.			73	11	0	18	25	.151	.192	.319
Runners On			141	33	2	24	36	.234	.355	.341
Runners/Scor. Pos.			79	17	2	13	24	.215	.316	.319
Runners On/2 Out			52	12	1	9	13	.231	.385	.344
Scor. Pos./2 Out			32	5	1	8	10	.156	.250	.325
Late Inning Pressure			39	9	0	8	9	.231	.231	.362
Leading Off			11	3	0	1	2	.273	.273	.333
Runners On			17	4	0	4	5	.235	.235	.381
Runners/Scor. Pos.			10	3	0	2	3	.300	.300	.417
First 9 Batters			158	22	3	33	54	.139	.228	.288
Second 9 Batters			92	17	0	12	23	.185	.250	.283
All Batters Thereafter			67	21	0	8	15	.313	.373	.382

Loves to face: John Bateman (0-for-7, 3 SO)
Hates to face: Larry Dierker (2-for-2, 1 2B, 1 HR)
Ground outs-to-air outs ratio: 0.82. ... Additional statistics: 6 double-play ground outs in 83 opportunities, 9 doubles, 3 triples in 89.1 innings. ... ERA breakdown in 10 starts: 2.89 in first 3 innings, 4.40 thereafter. ... Faced 34 consecutive left-handed batters without allowing a hit (Aug. 5–Sept. 10). ... Two of the three home runs he allowed were hit by Rusty Staub, the other by Larry Dierker. ... Saved Mets' first win of '69 season (April 9), his only save of season; also saved Game 3 of World Series. ... Only player on 1969 Mets still active in 1988. ... Made major league debut on Sept. 11, 1966; first strikeout victim: Braves pitcher Pat Jarvis.

Tom Seaver

New York Mets — Throws Right

	W–L	ERA	AB	H	HR	BB	SO	BA	SA	OBA
Season	25-7	2.21	975	202	24	82	208	.207	.331	.272
vs. Left-Handers			396	84	6	39	69	.212	.326	.280
vs. Right-Handers			579	118	18	43	139	.204	.335	.267
Home	12-3	2.02	481	89	12	38	112	.185	.312	.246
Road	13-4	2.40	494	113	12	44	96	.229	.350	.297
Day	10-5	2.48	487	108	9	51	113	.222	.339	.302
Night	15-2	1.97	488	94	15	31	95	.193	.324	.241
April	2-2	2.35	144	31	5	13	28	.215	.375	.278
May	5-1	2.68	168	38	2	13	25	.226	.321	.285
June	5-0	2.63	174	40	6	15	53	.230	.402	.298
July	3-3	2.32	153	33	3	9	39	.216	.314	.258
August	4-1	2.70	153	32	8	20	30	.209	.405	.309
Sept./Oct.	6-0	0.83	183	28	0	12	33	.153	.191	.209
Leading Off Inn.			260	57	8	14	55	.219	.369	.264
Runners On			343	70	5	38	67	.204	.303	.287
Runners/Scor. Pos.			185	34	1	23	42	.184	.222	.274
Runners On/2 Out			166	37	2	23	31	.223	.331	.321
Scor. Pos./2 Out			101	19	1	15	21	.188	.248	.293
Late Inning Pressure			170	33	3	10	28	.194	.294	.239
Leading Off			48	9	0	1	12	.188	.208	.204
Runners On			49	7	1	6	6	.143	.204	.236
Runners/Scor. Pos.			24	5	1	5	4	.208	.333	.345
First 9 Batters			274	57	6	30	79	.208	.339	.297
Second 9 Batters			277	60	10	20	54	.217	.354	.271
All Batters Thereafter			424	85	8	32	75	.200	.311	.257

Loves to face: Billy Williams (.118, 2-for-17, 5 SO)
Hates to face: Carl Taylor (.750, 3-for-4, 1 HR)
Ground outs-to-air outs ratio: 1.07. . . . Additional statistics: 20 double-play ground outs in 161 opportunities, 35 doubles, 7 triples in 273.1 innings. . . . Didn't allow a home run in his last seven starts, all complete-game wins. . . . Faced 35 consecutive batters with runners on base without allowing a hit (Aug. 5–Aug. 21). . . . Faced 13 batters with bases loaded. Struck out six, allowed no hits and only one run (on a sac fly by Jerry May). . . . Became winningest pitcher in Mets history with his 44th career win on June 29. . . . Jimmy Qualls's ninth-inning single to break up Seaver's perfect game (July 9) was his only career hit in six AB vs. Seaver.

Ron Taylor

New York Mets — Throws Right

	W–L	ERA	AB	H	HR	BB	SO	BA	SA	OBA
Season	9-4	2.72	268	61	7	24	42	.228	.351	.292
vs. Left-Handers			107	29	3	12	12	.271	.411	.350
vs. Right-Handers			161	32	4	12	30	.199	.311	.251
Home	6-3	2.28	152	33	2	10	26	.217	.322	.264
Road	3-1	3.31	116	28	5	14	16	.241	.388	.326
Day	5-1	2.06	132	20	3	13	22	.152	.258	.228
Night	4-3	3.44	136	41	4	11	20	.301	.441	.353
April	0-1	3.48	36	8	1	4	10	.222	.361	.300
May	0-0	4.50	38	11	3	2	7	.289	.526	.325
June	3-1	0.55	55	10	0	5	6	.182	.291	.246
July	2-0	5.02	51	10	3	5	9	.196	.392	.268
August	2-2	1.65	56	12	0	6	7	.214	.268	.297
Sept./Oct.	2-0	2.08	32	10	0	2	3	.313	.313	.353
Leading Off Inn.			61	15	1	3	10	.246	.328	.281
Runners On			116	27	5	15	12	.233	.397	.316
Runners/Scor. Pos.			68	19	5	14	7	.279	.515	.393
Runners On/2 Out			54	13	2	6	8	.241	.389	.317
Scor. Pos./2 Out			34	11	2	6	4	.324	.500	.425
Late Inning Pressure			162	34	3	16	26	.210	.327	.279
Leading Off			40	7	1	2	3	.175	.300	.214
Runners On			64	12	2	9	8	.188	.313	.284
Runners/Scor. Pos.			37	8	2	8	4	.216	.378	.348
First 9 Batters			266	61	7	24	41	.229	.353	.294
Second 9 Batters			2	0	0	0	1	.000	.000	.000
All Batters Thereafter			0	0	0	0	0	—	—	—

Loves to face: Randy Hundley (0-for-4, 3 SO)
Hates to face: Coco Laboy (.500, 2-for-4, 2 HR)
Ground outs-to-air outs ratio: 1.27. . . . Additional statistics: 7 double-play ground outs in 58 opportunities, 6 doubles, 3 triples in 76.0 innings. . . . Equalled his career highs in wins and saves (13). . . . Made his 12th save on August 12, then went six weeks before his last one. . . . Allowed two of the three grand slams hit against the Mets. The other: Cal Koonce. . . . Made 269 relief appearances with the Mets, the most among pitchers who never started for them. . . . Career ERA of 3.04 with the Mets, 4.65 with other teams. . . . Made major league debut with the 1962 Indians. Among his teammates: Tommie Agee and Ty Cobb's buddy, Barry Latman.

New York Mets

	W–L	ERA	AB	H	HR	BB	SO	BA	SA	OBA
Season	100-62	2.99	5369	1217	119	517	1012	.227	.349	.296
vs. Left-Handers			1873	437	29	204	299	.233	.351	.310
vs. Right-Handers			3496	780	90	313	713	.223	.348	.289
Home	52-30	2.77	2773	605	59	266	559	.218	.336	.288
Road	48-32	3.22	2596	612	60	251	453	.236	.363	.305
Day	45-30	3.30	2591	617	56	272	468	.238	.366	.313
Night	55-32	2.72	2778	600	63	245	544	.216	.333	.281
April	9-11	3.57	673	161	17	87	125	.239	.377	.328
May	12-12	3.74	794	198	28	68	147	.249	.414	.309
June	19-9	2.19	925	190	22	80	195	.205	.336	.270
July	15-12	4.30	919	232	28	93	180	.252	.402	.321
August	21-10	2.32	1009	207	18	98	164	.205	.307	.280
Sept./Oct.	24-8	2.31	1049	229	6	91	201	.218	.287	.283
Leading Off Inn.			1361	325	32	102	264	.239	.359	.295
Runners On			2119	478	38	260	385	.226	.337	.310
Runners/Scor. Pos.			1150	264	20	184	235	.230	.337	.333
Runners On/2 Out			937	214	17	139	184	.228	.344	.330
Scor. Pos./2 Out			580	128	9	108	122	.221	.317	.345
Late Inning Pressure			1122	240	23	121	211	.214	.329	.291
Leading Off			297	68	5	22	58	.229	.316	.282
Runners On			425	72	7	64	76	.169	.264	.278
Runners/Scor. Pos.			219	37	5	50	44	.169	.260	.320
First 9 Batters			2367	552	49	262	510	.233	.360	.312
Second 9 Batters			1411	311	43	126	254	.220	.361	.286
All Batters Thereafter			1591	354	27	129	248	.223	.322	.282

Starting pitchers: 72-51, 2.82 ERA
Relief pitchers: 28-11, 3.49 ERA
Ground outs-to-air outs ratio: 1.13./ . . . Didn't allow a home run in 23 consecutive games (Aug. 30–Sept. 19), longest streak in majors over past 30 years. The streak encompassed 220.1 innings, sandwiched between home runs by Bobby Bonds and Willie Stargell. . . . Pitched 28 shutouts, highest total of past 20 years. . . . Allowed only 91 fewer runs than they scored, smallest difference ever among 100-game winners. . . . Opposing batters hit .191 in LIP Situations from August 16 until they clinched the division title. . . . Only one of the 22 original "expansion Mets" appeared with team during 1969 season: Al Jackson pitched in nine early games before finishing his career with Reds.

1969 Time Line

DAY	NEW YORK METS	BASEBALL	OTHER NEWS
April 7		The Dodgers and Reds commemorated the 100th anniversary of organized baseball in the city where the Cincinnati Red Stockings were founded in 1869.	The Milwaukee Bucks formally made Lew Alcindor the first selection in the NBA's college draft.
April 8	The Mets lost their eighth consecutive opening-day game, 11–10 to Montreal, in a game that remains the highest-scoring one-run loss in team history.	Four expansion teams—Montreal Expos, San Diego Padres, Kansas City Royals, and Seattle Pilots—all won their opening-day games. . . . Billy Martin made his major league managerial debut for Minnesota, losing to Kansas City. Royals were paced by rookie Lou Piniella, who had four hits.	Comedian Dick Gregory entered Cook County jail in Chicago, vowing to fast until President Nixon released the Blakey report on organized crime in the U.S.
April 9	Tug McGraw earned his first victory since August 21, 1966 with 6.1 innings one one-run relief, beating the Expos, 9–5.	Royals became the second team in major league history to open a season with consecutive wins in games of 12 or more innings. . . . Tommy John of White Sox tossed a four-hit shutout vs. Oakland. John suffered torn ligaments in a fight with Dick McAuliffe in 1968, and had threatened a lawsuit if the injury hampered his career.	Three hundred students, led by Students for a Democratic Society, seized University Hall at Harvard University.
April 10	Gary Gentry won his major league debut, 4–2, supported by Tommie Agee's two home runs. Agee became the first player ever to hit a home run into the upper deck in left field at Shea Stadium.	Padres completed a three-game sweep of Astros behind combined two-hitter by Dick Kelley, Frank Reberger, and Billy McCool. San Diego wouldn't again stand three games over .500 until 1975.	Dr. Denton Cooley defended his implantation of a mechanical heart into Haskell Kemp, who died on April 7 after receiving a human heart to replace the artificial one.
April 11	Steve Carlton defeated Jerry Koosman, 6–5, giving the Cardinals their first victory of the season after three losses.	Pilots won their home opener at Sicks Stadium in Seattle behind Gary Bell's complete-game shutout and Don Mincher's 325–foot home run to right-center field.	The Defense Department recommended to President Nixon a lottery system for drafting Americans into military service.
April 12	Dave Giusti defeated Don Cardwell in a duel of six-hitters, scoring the game's only run in the third inning.	Hank Aaron tied Mel Ott for seventh place in major league history with his 511th home run. . . . Bill Mazeroski broke Frankie Frisch's N.L. mark for career assists by a second baseman, a record that would later be surpassed by Joe Morgan. . . . Dennis McLain suffered his first loss of the season, following 31 wins a year earlier.	Dallas Cowboys receiver Lance Rentzel married actress Joey Heatherton at St. Patrick's Cathedral in New York City.
April 13	Bob Gibson defeated Tom Seaver, 3–1, for his second win in two career matchups against him. Gibson would win just one of nine subsequent starts vs. Seaver.		George Archer won the Masters by one stroke over Billy Casper, George Knudson, and Tom Weiskopf.
April 14	The Mets dropped into a tie for last place with Philadelphia, losing to the Phillies, 5–1. Richie Allen had a single, a home run and two walks in his first appearance vs. New York since hitting home runs in last three at bats of 1968 season against them.	Montreal defeated St. Louis, 8–7, in the first major league game ever played outside the United States. . . . Tony Conigliaro drove in the game-winning run in his first appearance at Fenway Park following the beaning he suffered there in 1967.	Katherine Hepburn (*The Lion In Winter*) and Barbra Streisand (*Funny Girl*) shared the Academy Award for best actress.
April 15	Bud Harrelson had three hits and drove in three runs in the Mets' 6–3 win over Philadelphia.	Dodgers defeated Padres, 14–0, one run short of the largest shutout victory in the franchise's history to that point, a 15–0 win over Philadelphia in 1952.	A jury began deliberation in the trial of Sirhan Sirhan, accused assassin of Robert F. Kennedy.
April 16	Jerry Koosman was knocked out in the third inning of an 11–3 loss to Pittsburgh, his second loss in two starts.	Sal Bando hit the first grand-slam home run by an Oakland player in the team's 172d game since moving from Kansas City. . . . Billy Conigliaro hit a pair of home runs in his first major league start following strikeouts in his first two at bats.	U.S. Surgeon General William Stewart recommended that Congress require cigarette manufacturers to disclose the tar and nicotine content on their packaging.
April 17	Jim Bunning and Ron Kline combined to three-hit the Mets, 4–0. It was Don Cardwell's second start of the season, and the Mets failed to score in either game.	Bill Stoneman of the Expos pitched a no-hitter against Philadelphia.	Sirhan Sirhan was convicted of first-degree murder for the assassination of Robert Kennedy.
April 18	Off day.	Willie Mays became the all-time N.L. leader in games in the outfield, surpassing Max Carey's career total.	Bob Dylan released a new album, *Nashville Skyline*.

DAY	NEW YORK METS	BASEBALL	OTHER NEWS
April 19	Mets defeated St. Louis and Bob Gibson, 2–1, snapping a seven-game losing streak against Gibson, who entered the game with a career record of 22–3 against the Mets. Manager Gil Hodges shook up the Mets lineup, benching Tommie Agee and Rod Gaspar for Ron Swoboda and Kevin Collins.	Phil Niekro extended his scoreless streak to 24 consecutive innings, tossing his second straight shutout, 4–0, over the Reds. . . . Cubs ran their record to 10–1 with a 6–5 win over Expos in 30–degree weather in Montreal. . . . Boston traded Hawk Harrelson, Dick Ellsworth, and Juan Pizarro to Cleveland for Sonny Siebert, Joe Azcue, and Vicente Romo. Harrelson announced he wouldn't report to the Indians, and would retire instead.	About 40 black students seized the Cornell University Student Union to protest what they termed racist attitudes at Ivy League schools.
April 20	Kevin Collins hit his first home run of the season in an 11–3 rout of St. Louis. Cleon Jones had three hits, raising his batting average to .426, 12 points below the league leader, Coco Laboy of Montreal.	Donn Clendenon hit a three-run home run, leading Montreal to a 4–2 victory over Chicago, snapping the Cubs' winning streak at seven. . . . Les Rohr pitched a no-hitter for Memphis, the Mets' Texas League affiliate.	James Earl Jones and Jane Alexander (*The Great White Hope*), Jerry Ohrbach (*Promises, Promises*), and Angela Lansbury (*Mame*) won Tony Awards.
April 21	Gary Gentry tied a team record by walking seven batters, but reliever Ron Taylor allowed the winning run in the 11th inning of a 2–1 loss to Philadelphia.	After an 11–game game experiment as the Giants' leadoff hitter, Willie Mays returned to the number 3 spot in San Francisco's batting order.	The jury deciding the sentence for Sirhan Sirhan was sequestered at the end of its first day of deliberations.
April 22	The Mets and Phillies were postponed by rain at Shea.	Billy Martin was ejected for the first time as manager, by rookie umpire Larry Barnett for "excessive railing from the bench.". . .Oakland snapped Minnesota's seven-game winning streak, 7–0, behind the five-hit pitching of Rollie Fingers, making the first start of his major league career. . . .Following a closed-door meeting with Bowie Kuhn, Gabe Paul, and Dick O'Connell, Hawk Harrelson received a new two-year contract and agreed to report to Cleveland.	A team of surgeons at Houston's Methodist Hospital performed the world's first eye transplant.
April 23	Jerry Koosman pitched a five-hit shutout to defeat the Pirates, 2–0. Cleon Jones went 3–for–3 to take the N.L. lead with a .444 batting average.	Ted Williams returned to Fenway Park for the first time as manager of the Washington Senators, who defeated the Red Sox, 9–3.	Sirhan Sirhan was sentenced to death.
April 24	Rained out vs. Pittsburgh.	Reggie Jackson hit a pair of home runs, then was ejected from the game for fighting with Minnesota pitcher Dick Woodson after two knockdown pitches that failed to draw a warning from umpire Cal Drummond.	President Nixon asked Congress to increase the rate of first-class postage from six cents to seven cents.
April 25	The Cubs faced the Mets for the first time, defeating Tom Seaver, 3–1, on solo home runs by Ron Santo, Don Kessinger, and Ferguson Jenkins.	Reggie hit two home runs for the second game in a row. . . . Mel Stottlemyre became the major league's first five-game winner, cutting Baltimore's lead over the Yankees to two games with a 7–2 victory.	Group W Westinghouse announced it would accept no more ads for cigarettes on any of its five TV stations or seven radio stations, the first such ban in the U.S.
April 26	Bill Hands won his fifth career decision against the Mets without a loss, coasting to a 9–3 complete-game victory after the Cubs had built an 8–0 sixth-inning lead.	Rod Carew went 4–for–5, raising his average to .424, within seven points of A.L. leader Rico Petrocelli. . . . Carl Yastrzemski hit two home runs, giving the Red Sox an A.L. record with 26 over their past 10 games.	Groucho Marx faced Minnesota Fats on "Celebrity Billiards." . . . Sammy Davis, Jr., was the guest host on "Hollywood Palace." Other guests included Jo Anne Worley and Lola Falana.
April 27	The Mets lost their third straight to Chicago, blowing a two-run ninth inning lead when errors by Ken Boswell and Kevin Collins led to four unearned runs in the opening game of a doubleheader. In the nightcap, Cleon Jones broke a scoreless tie in the ninth inning with a three-run, game-winning homer.	Willie McCovey raised his league-leading totals to eight home runs and 21 RBI with three-run home runs in both ends of a doubleheader sweep over Houston, moving the Giants into a first-place tie with the Dodgers. . . . Frank Robinson drove in four runs in both games of Baltimore's sweep of the Yankees with a pair of homers, raising his totals to nine HR and 22 RBI, highest in the majors. . . . . Harmon Killebrew hit career home run number 400.	The research director for the National Audubon Society warned that unless a ban were imposed on the pesticide DDT, the American eagle would become extinct.
April 28	Off day.	Hank Aaron moved past former teammate Eddie Mathews into sixth place in major league history with the 513th home run of his career. . . . Don Drysdale was placed on the disabled list with a shoulder injury.	French President Charles de Gaulle resigned.
April 29	Ed Kranepool, rumored to be headed to Montreal in a deal for Donn Clendenon, beat the Expos, 2–0, with a pair of solo home runs. Jerry Koosman left the game in the fifth when his left arm "snapped like elastic." . . . Art Shamsky was reinstated from the disabled list and sent to Tidewater to play himself into shape; Kevin Collins was sent down.	Seattle's Marty Pattin lost his no-hit bid on a clean single to center by California catcher Tom Satriano with two out in the eighth.	Pete Rozelle announced that even under a proposed merger plan in which three NFL teams would join the AFL, the New York Giants would never switch leagues.

DAY	NEW YORK METS	BASEBALL	OTHER NEWS
April 30	Ken Boswell drove home Rod Gaspar with the game-winning run in the ninth inning, as Tom Seaver evened his record at 2–2 in a 2–1 victory over the Expos.	Jim Maloney pitched the second no-hitter of his career with a 13–strikeout win over Houston. . . . Juan Marichal's two-hit shutout over the Dodgers gave San Francisco sole possession of first place, a game over Los Angeles and Atlanta.	More than 100 members of Students for a Democratic Society seized two classrooms at Columbia University. . . . Willie Shoemaker suffered a fractured pelvis in a paddock accident at Hollywood Park.
May 1	Coco Laboy's ninth-inning sacrifice fly gave Montreal a 3–2 win. Elroy Face, signed by the Expos two days earlier after failing a tryout with the Mets, pitched 2.1 scoreless innings for the victory.	Don Wilson tossed the third no-hitter of the season, and the second in as many nights at Crosley Field, ending Houston's season-long streak of 13 consecutive road losses. . . . Don Sutton's no-hit bid was ended by Jim Davenport's double with one out in the eighth. . . . Stan Bahnsen of the Yankees held the Indians hitless until Max Alvis's leadoff double in the seventh.	It was reported that Goldie Hawn told the producers of "Rowan and Martin's Laugh-In" that she would leave the show at the end of the current season for a starring role in the movie *There's A Girl In My Soup*).
May 2	Chicago defeated the Mets, 6–4, despite Tommie Agee's 4-for-4 performance. Agee had been benched for two weeks on account of his sub-.200 batting average.	Rico Carty's pinch-hit sacrifice fly helped Atlanta defeat Los Angeles, 7–4, creating a three-way tie for first place. It was Carty's first plate appearance since 1967; he missed the 1968 season with tuberculosis, and the start of the 1969 season with a shoulder injury. . . . Al Lopez resigned as manager of the White Sox on account of illness.	Police were called to the campus of Queens College in New York City to quiet a disturbance among approximately 100 students. . . . Guests on "This Is Tom Jones" included Sonny and Cher, Herman's Hermits, and Henry Gibson.
May 3	Nolan Ryan, starting in place of the injured Jerry Koosman, left Chicago's 3–2 victory in the seventh inning with a strained groin muscle, leaving the Mets three starting pitchers short. (Jim McAndrew was forced out of a game on April 27 with a painful finger blister.) Phil Regan, who relieved Ferguson Jenkins in the eighth, became the N.L.'s first five-game winner.	San Diego set a team record that still stands today with nine runs in one inning—the first inning—including a grand slam by Ollie Brown off the Reds' Tony Cloninger, who failed to retire any of the five batters he faced.	*The Fantasticks* entered its tenth year at the Sullivan Street Playhouse. . . . Majestic Prince won the Kentucky Derby by a neck over Arts And Letters.
May 4	Tom Seaver and Tug McGraw, making his first start of the season, pitched complete-game victories for the Mets' first-ever doubleheader sweep at Wrigley Field. A beanball war broke out in the first game when Seaver decked Ron Santo. Bill Hands then hit Seaver with a pitch, and Seaver retaliated by hitting Hands.	Tony Cloninger made his second start in as many days against San Diego, and hit a home run in a 12–0 rout. . . . Oakland pitcher Blue Moon Odom hit a home run and drove in six runs in an 11–7 victory over Seattle. . . . Kansas City's Bob Oliver went 6-for-6. Official scorer Dave Distel, after consulting with umpire Larry Napp, changed a 7th-inning Aurelio Rodriguez error to a single. . . . Richie Scheinblum got his first hit of season, snapping an 0-for-34 streak.	Notre Dame announced plans to go co-ed in the fall.
May 5	Off day.	The Special Baseball Records Committee voted to reverse its prior ruling that credited Babe Ruth with an additional home run.	The Boston Celtics defeated the Los Angeles Lakers 108–106, in the deciding game of the NBA finals. Wilt Chamberlain left the game with five minutes to go with an injured ankle. . . . The New York Jets rewarded coach and general manager Weeb Ewbank for his victory in Super Bowl III with a new three-year contact.
May 6	Don Cardwell drove in more runs in one swing of the bat (a three-run home run) than the Mets had scored for him in his four previous starts (two) as the Mets defeated Cincinnati, 8–1. Wayne Garrett hit the first home run of his career.	The Cubs defeated Los Angeles, 7–1, for their 11th consecutive victory over Don Sutton. . . . Jim Hunter's eight-hitter and Reggie Jackson's two-run home run helped Oakland snap Washington's five-game winning streak. . . . Sam McDowell pitched his second consecutive three-hit shutout.	The Secretary of the Navy set aside the recommendation of a court of inquiry that called for a general court-martial for Lloyd Bucher, commander of the *USS Pueblo*.
May 7	Jim Merritt and Clay Carroll tossed a three-hit shutout. Merritt walked Cleon Jones on three pitches when John Kibler invoked the new 20–second rule that charged a ball when a pitcher failed to deliver in that time.	With Willie Mays, Willie McCovey, and Bobby Bonds on the bench, San Francisco snapped a five-game losing streak with a 5–3 victory over St. Louis.	The Treasury Department announced that it would evaluate a plan to reduce tax rates by eliminating the standard deduction and limiting all other deductions.
May 8	Off day.		Arsonists set a fire that nearly destroyed the Student Union at City College of New York.
May 9	Rained out vs. Houston.	Yankees committed five errors in fifth inning of 3–2 loss to Oakland, their 11th defeat in 13 games.	Pope Paul removed the feast days of 30 saints from the Roman Catholic calendar, including that of St. Christopher. . . . Bob Cousy signed a three-year contract to coach the Cincinnati Royals.
May 10	Tom Seaver pitched a four-hitter against Houston for his third consecutive win.	Reliever Jim Hardin kept Baltimore in first place with a game-winning ninth-inning home run off Kansas City's Moe Drabowsky.	The Baltimore Colts, the Cleveland Browns, and the Pittsburgh Steelers agreed to join 10 teams from American Football League in the 13–team American Football Conference of the new NFL, effective 1970.

DAY	NEW YORK METS	BASEBALL	OTHER NEWS
May 11	The Mets split a doubleheader with the Astros. Tommie Agee hit three home runs, and Cleon Jones raised his batting average to .411 with a 3–for–5 day.		The heaviest Saigon bombings of the year resulted in the deaths of six Vietnamese civilians.
May 12	Off day.	The Cubs got a scare when Glenn Beckert was hit on the jaw by a pitch from San Diego's Gary Ross. Beckert suffered a cut that required 15 stitches but no fracture. . . . Bob Gibson struck out the side (Len Gabrielson, Paul Popovich, and John Miller) on nine pitches in the seventh inning of his victory over the Dodgers.	White House counsel John Ehrlichman announced President Nixon's net worth as $596,000, and said that the Nixons had sold their Fifth Avenue apartment for $326,000.
May 13	Hank Aaron, Orlando Cepeda, and Bob Tillman drove in all of Atlanta's runs with home runs in a 4–3 win over Gary Gentry. Art Shamsky made his 1969 debut following rehab for a back injury. Nolan Ryan was placed on the disabled list.	The Cubs tied a National League for runs in a shutout victory in a 19–0 rout of San Diego. Ernie Banks had seven RBI, and Dick Selma pitched a three-hitter.	President Nixon called on Congress to adopt a plan to draft Americans into military service by lottery, starting with 19–year-olds.
May 14	The Mets scored eight runs in the eighth inning to defeat Atlanta, 9–3. . . . Jack DiLauro was recalled from Tidewater. Steve Chilcott, the first choice in the 1966 free agent draft, was placed on the voluntarily retired list. The Mets selected Chilcott over Reggie Jackson.	The Yankees snapped a six-game losing streak with a 5–4 victory over Seattle. Bobby Murcer drove in two runs to increase his major league leading total to 36. . . . St. Louis posted its 19th consecutive victory on a payday, defeating the Dodgers, 2–1.	President Nixon proposed a peace plan that included a provision calling for the withdrawal of U.S., allied, and North Vietnamese troops from South Vietnam. . . . The Dow Jones industrial average peaked at 952, which is now viewed as the end of the 1960s bull market.
May 15	Hank Aaron hit two home runs as Atlanta beat the Mets, 6–5. Felix Millan saved the game with two outs in the ninth with a leaping backhand catch of Cleon Jones's line drive with the bases loaded. After the game, Gil Hodges locked the clubhouse door and ripped his players for complancency and mental mistakes.	Another near no-hitter: Dave McNally lost his bid with one out in the ninth on a single to left-center by Cesar Tovar. . . . Luis Aparicio collected his 2000th career hit. . . . Willie Horton went AWOL, leaving the Tigers bench in the seventh inning of the game vs. Chicago.	Associate Justice Abe Fortas resigned from the U.S. Supreme Court following criticism of his financial ties to a convicted stock manipulator. He was the first justice ever to resign from the nation's highest court.
May 16	The Mets scored six runs during a seventh-inning downpour, and held on to defeat Cincinnati, 10–9. Wayne Garrett, Ed Kranepool, and Bud Harrelson each had three hits. Kranepool became involved in a wrestling match with Reds first-base coach Jimmy Bragan in the second inning.	The Cubs scored 10 runs in the seventh inning of an 11–0 rout of Houston at the Astrodome, with Ken Holtzman stretching his scoreless streak to 24 consecutive innings. . . . Mike Epstein hit three home runs in a losing effort for Washington.	The British bookmaking firm of William Hall closed the books on bets that man would land on the Moon. (In 1964, you could get odds of one thousand-to-one against a landing by Jan. 1, 1971.)
May 17	The Mets built a 10–0 lead after five innings and cruised to an 11–3 win over Cincinnati. Cleon Jones drove in four runs and Wayne Garrett raised his batting average to .358 with his second consecutive three-hit game.	Johnny Ellis made his major league debut memorable with an inside-the-park home run before the hometown fans at Yankee Stadium. . . . Rookie Jerry Nyman pitched a one-hit shutout for the White Sox in his first start of the season.	A South Vietnamese official said the U.S. would withdraw up to 50,000 troops by the end of the year if the Communist forces didn't escalate the war before then.
May 18	Rain washed out a 3–0 Cincinnati lead and Duffy Dyer's first start of the season when the game was called in the middle of the fourth. Jim Merritt had a perfect game through four innings when it was postponed.	Joe Pepitone hit late-inning, game-winning home runs in both games of a doubleheader sweep of California by the Yankees. . . . Cesar Tovar and Rod Carew stole home in the same inning against Mickey Lolich.	*Apollo 10* blasted off for the Moon in a test of procedures for the *Apollo 11* mission, set for July.
May 19	Off day.	The only game scheduled, Atlanta at Montreal, was postponed by rain.	The U.S. Supreme Court reversed the conviction of Dr. Timothy Leary on two narcotics violations.
May 20	Off day.	Ken Holtzman pitched his third consecutive shutout, a five-hitter, as the Cubs defeated the Dodgers, 7–0.	Dr. Timothy Leary announced he would run for governor of California as the "psychedelic" candidate against incumbent Ronald Reagan and Democratic challenger Jess Unruh.
May 21	The Mets reached .500 when Tom Seaver three-hit the Braves, 5–0. The latest any previous Mets team had reached the .500 mark was after eight games of the 1967 season. . . . Gil Hodges announced that Jerry Koosman would return to the starting rotation following an impressive outing at Memphis.	Reggie Jackson hit two home runs, including an inside-the-park blast to the 457–foot sign in Yankee Stadium's left-center field, but the Yankees won their seventh in a row, defeating the first-place A's, 6–5.	President Nixon nominated Warren Burger to succeed Earl Warren as chief justice of the United States.
May 22	The Braves increased their lead over Los Angeles to three-and-a-half games with a 15–3 win over the Mets. Mike Lum batted for Hank Aaron with the Braves leading 10–0 in the seventh, the only time Aaron was ever removed for a pinch hitter.		President Nixon revealed that four contenders voluntarily removed themselves from consideration as nominees for chief justice, among them John Mitchell.

DAY	NEW YORK METS	BASEBALL	OTHER NEWS
May 23	Tom Griffin pitched a five-hit shutout, struck out 13, and drove in three runs as Houston beat the Mets, 7–0, for their 15th victory in the last 19 games.	Mickey Lolich struck out 16 batters in a complete-game victory over California. . . . Rookie Al Oliver tied an N.L. record with three errors in one inning at first base.	Six hundred National Guardsmen swept the campus of North Carolina A&T, combatting rioting students with rifle fire, tear gas, and smoke bombs.
May 24	Jerry Koosman made his first start since April 29, allowing two runs in seven innings, but lost to Houston, 5–1. The Astros hit three home runs—two by Jim Wynn, the other by Curt Blefary.	Minnesota snapped the Yankees' seven-game winning streak, and tied Oakland for first place in the A.L. West. . . . Pete Rose began two weeks of summer training with the Army Reserve.	Eldridge Cleaver, who disappeared late in 1968 when faced with revocation of his parole, was found in Havana, Cuba.
May 25	Tom Seaver made his third start in eight days (including the washout on May 18) and lost to Houston, 6–3. Cleon Jones went 3-for-3 to regain the N.L. batting average lead from Hank Aaron.	Pittsburgh's Jim Bunning got his 200th career win with a five-hitter against San Francisco. . . . Johnny Podres pitched his first complete game in nearly four years, defeating the Cubs in the first game of a doubleheader split with San Diego.	Mexico eliminated Australia from the Davis Cup, the first time the Aussies had failed to reach the finals since 1937.
May 26	On an off day, Gil Hodges complained about the 31 Mets who struck out in the three-game sweep by Houston. "They all looked like wooden soldiers. They're just taking too many strikes."	Chief Noc-A-Homa's tepee caught fire after Clete Boyer hit a home run.	*Midnight Cowboy* made its world premiere with an X rating.
May 27	The Mets wasted a 12-hit attack by stranding 11 runners and lost their first-ever meeting with San Diego, 3–2. Jim McAndrew made his first start since April 27, allowing three runs in 5.2 innings, and lost.	Lefty Phillips replaced Bill Rigney as Angels manager, and broke his team's 10-game losing streak after restoring Alex Johnson to the starting lineup. . . . Billy Martin, following a loss to Ted Williams's Washington Senators, said that Williams wore the same uniform for 15 years "because he never bothered to slide to break up a double play."	Sam Yorty was elected to a third term as mayor of Los Angeles, defeating City Councilman Thomas Bradley in a runoff.
May 28	The Mets snapped a five-game losing streak with a 1–0 11-inning win over San Diego. Jerry Koosman pitched 10 scoreless innings and struck out 15 batters.	Rod Carew went 2-for-3, raising his average to .400. . . . Lee May took the major league lead in home runs with his third consecutive two-HR game.	Dave Stallworth was pronounced fit and signed with the Knicks after missing two seasons with heart problems.
May 29	Off day.	Denny McLain earned a complete-game win over Oakland, but committed a balk when the A's organist, Lloyd Fox, started playing as McLain took his stretch during a ninth-inning Oakland rally. McLain called the move "bush," but added, "The guy in Boston, now he's a real artist."	Senator Strom Thurmond of South Carolina denounced Supreme Court Justice William O. Douglass for "political activity" with liberal friends and called for his resignation.
May 30	Mike McCormick held the Mets hitless until Ron Swoboda's home run in the seventh. But Duffy Dyer, in only his third at bat since hitting a three-run home run on opening day, beat the Giants, 4–3, with a pinch-hit game-winning single in the eighth inning. Ron Taylor saved the win by striking out Willie Mays and Willie McCovey in the ninth.	Clay Carroll won the Reds' pool on the Indy 500, then hit a 10th-inning, game-winning home run off Bob Gibson.	Mario Andretti won the Indianapolis 500.
May 31	Ed Charles, playing against a right-handed pitcher only because Ken Boswell was fulfilling his military commitment, hit his first home run of the season and drove in all the Mets runs as they beat San Francisco, 4–2. Gil Hodges complained to umpire Frank Secory about a jelly-like substance that Gaylord Perry was using to doctor the baseballs.	Don Mincher's double with one out in the ninth was the only hit Detroit's Joe Sparma allowed in a 3–2 victory over Seattle. Sparma walked seven batters.	Physicist Edward Teller advocated a nuclear explosion on the Moon as the best source of seismographic data from which to learn about its interior.
June 1	The Mets completed a three-game sweep of the Giants with a 5–4 win when Joe Gibbon walked Ron Swoboda with the bases loaded in the bottom of the ninth.	The Cubs reduced Atlanta's lead in the N.L. West to a half-game over the Dodgers by beating the Braves, 13–4. Ernie Banks drove in two runs to tie the injured Bobby Murcer for the major league lead with 43.	National traffic deaths reached 550 for the Memorial Day weekend, an all-time high.
June 2	The Mets beat the Dodgers, 2–1, scoring both their runs in the fourth inning when third baseman Bill Sudakis misplayed Jerry Grote's two-out, wind-blown single in short left field and Al Weis followed with a double. Jerry Koosman pitched a five-hitter.	Hank Aaron moved past Ted Williams into fifth place in major league history with his 522d home run. . . . Orlando Cepeda hit a triple and a home run on his first two at bats at Busch Stadium following the off-season deal that sent him from St. Louis to Atlanta.	ABC Sports acquired the televison rights to a package of NFL regular-season games on Monday nights for 1970 through 1972.

DAY	NEW YORK METS	BASEBALL	OTHER NEWS
June 3	Ed Kranepool hit two home runs, leading the Mets to a 5–2 victory over Los Angeles. The win elevated the Mets above the .500 mark and past Pittsburgh into second place, eight-and-a-half games behind the division-leading Cubs.	Maury Wills announced his retirement, suddenly and without explanation. He returned, amid trade rumors, less than 48 hours later. . . . Roberto Clemente, on the occasion of his 2417th hit, moving him into third place in Pirates history: "I don't see how I can make it [to 3000 hits]. I don't expect to play four more years. I'd like to be home to see my kids grow up."	The Senate Judiciary Committee approved President Nixon's nomination of Warren Burger as U.S. chief justice.
June 4	Tommie Agee scored from first base with the game's only run in the 15th inning when Dodgers center fielder Willie Davis let Wayne Garrett's single roll under his glove all the way to the fence. Al Weis had preserved the scoreless tie in the top of the inning when he backhanded a ball that was deflected by Ron Taylor and threw Billy Grabarkewitz out at home on a play Gil Hodges called one of the greatest he'd ever seen. Jack DiLauro allowed two hits in nine innings in his first major league start.	Rookie Richie Hebner went 3-for-3 and took the N.L. batting lead from Cleon Jones, who went hitless in five at bats. . . . San Diego beat the Phillies for its sixth straight win, a streak that remained the Padres' longest until 1977.	Anthropologist Margaret Mead suggested that we had entered a "new phase in human history," in which girls were rebelling against being sex objects and boys were rebelling against having to support a wife.
June 5	Off day.	First two selections in free agent draft: Jeff Burroughs by Washington, J. R. Richard by Houston. Richard was considered a risk on account of the grant-in-aid he'd signed to play basketball at Southern University.	The NBA voted to add two new teams for the 1970–71 season. (Eventually, three franchises were awarded, to Buffalo, Cleveland, and Portland.)
June 6	The Mets set a team record with their eighth consecutive win, a 5–3 victory at San Diego. Pinch-hitter Art Shamsky broke a 3–3 tie with an eighth-inning single.	The Cubs maintained their lead with a 14–8 victory over Cincinnati, their seventh consecutive win, but second baseman Glenn Beckert fractured his right thumb and was placed on the disabled list. . . . Willie McCovey hit two home runs to take the major-league lead with 19, including 10 in his last 12 games.	Joe Namath announced that he would not sell his New York bar and restaurant, Bachelors III, as ordered by NFL Commissioner Pete Rozelle, and that he would retire from football.
June 7	Jerry Koosman struck out 11 batters in a 4–1 victory over the Padres.	The Dodgers beat the Expos, 9–5, cutting Atlanta's lead to a half-game. It was Montreal's 20th consecutive defeat, three short of the modern major league record set by Philadelphia in 1961.	Leonid Brezhnev warned a world Communist summit that China was planning a nuclear war against the Soviet Union.
June 8	Tom Seaver struck out 14 in seven innings and tied Ken Holtzman for the N.L. lead with his ninth victory, a 3–2 win over San Diego. Wayne Garrett drove in the winning run in the eighth inning, marking the sixth time during their 10-game winning streak that the Mets scored the game-winner in the eighth inning or later.	Mickey Mantle's number 7 is retired before more than 61,000 fans at Yankee Stadium. . . . Montreal snapped its losing streak at 20.	President Nixon announced that 25,000 U.S. troops would be withdrawn from South Vietnam by the end of August. . . . The U.S. government licensed the manufacture of a German measles vaccine.
June 9	Off day.	Rico Petrocelli became the first player to reach the 20 home-run mark.	The Senate confirmed the nomination of Warren Burger as chief justice of the United States.
June 10	The Mets won their 11th in a row, a streak they equalled in 1972 and 1986 but have never surpassed. Don Cardwell pitched a two-hitter for eight innings, and went 3-for-3 with a sacrifice fly at the plate.	Ken Holtzman became the major leagues' first 10-game winner. . . . Houston's Jesus Alou and Hector Torres were both carried from the field on stretchers after a collision. Both suffered concussions; Alou's was labeled "severe" and he fractured his jaw as well. . . . Maury Wills returned to Los Angeles when the Expos traded him to the Dodgers for Ron Fairly.	The House of Representatives voted to require U.S. astronauts to plant the American flag and no other on visits to the Moon or other planets.
June 11	Gaylord Perry stopped the Mets' winning streak with a four-hit victory, 7–2.	Joe Lahoud, who had four singles in his first 48 at-bats, hit three home runs as Boston defeated Minnesota, 13–5.	John L. Lewis, founder of the CIO, died at age 89. . . . California governor Ronald Reagan broke down as he eulogized actor Robert Taylor.
June 12	Off day.		A launch date of July 16 was confirmed for *Apollo 11*. . . . Connie Stevens was granted an uncontested divorce from Eddie Fisher.
June 13	Alan Foster of the Dodgers pitched the first complete game of his career, a seven-hitter, as Los Angeles beat the Mets, 1–0. The Dodgers scored the game's only run in the second after Manny Mota reached second when Art Shamsky misplayed his single. . . . Al Jackson, the last of the original Mets, was sold to Cincinnati.	Willie McCovey lost a 16–game hitting streak when he left the game after his first at-bat with pain in his arthritic knee.	California Governor Ronald Reagan defended the use of tear gas and weapons by the police and National Guard in coping with demonstrators at Berkeley.

DAY	NEW YORK METS	BASEBALL	OTHER NEWS
June 14	Tom Seaver won his 10th game of the season, defeating the Dodgers, 3–1. Cleon Jones was removed from the game with a bruised jaw and dizziness after he crashed into the left-field wall. Art Shamsky hit his first home run of the season.	Reggie Jackson drove in 10 runs, one short of the A.L. record, with five hits including a pair of home runs that gave him the major league lead with 22. Oakland defeated Boston, 21–7, and took over first place in the A.L. West.	Steffi Graf was born in Bruhl, West Germany.
June 15	Don Drysdale beat the Mets, 3–2, in his first appearance since being disabled April 28. "The shoulder felt fine and my arm didn't bother me at any time aside from getting tired." . . . The Mets acquired Donn Clendenon from the Expos for four players, including Kevin Collins and Steve Renko.	Don Kessinger set a major league record with his 54th consecutive errorless game at shortstop, but made an error in the second game of a doubleheader. . . . Reggie Jackson continued his hot hitting with a double, triple, home run, and four more RBI.	Georges Pompidou was elected President of France. . . . Orville Moody won the U.S. Open in Houston with a one-over-par 281.
June 16	Off day.	Denny McLain became the youngest active pitcher with 100 wins when he hit the century mark with a 3–2 victory over the Yankees. . . . Rod Carew tied an A.L. record with his sixth steal of home this season.	The Supreme Court ruled that the House of Representatives had illegally barred Adam Clayton Powell from taking his seat in 1967. The opinion, written by Chief Justice Warren, reversed the opinion of the Court of Appeals, written by Judge Warren Burger.
June 17	The Mets split a doubleheader with the Phillies, winning 1–0 on a two-hitter by Gary Gentry, and losing the nightcap, 7–3. They employed a four-man outfield against Richie Allen in the ninth inning of the opener, as Gentry fanned Allen.		Mayor John Lindsay of New York lost the Republican mayoral primary to John Marchi. Mario Procaccino won the Democratic primary. . . . Boris Spassky won the world chess championship from fellow Soviet player Tigran Petrosian.
June 18	Jerry Koosman pitched a four-hit shutout as the Mets beat the Phillies, 2–0. Since returning from the disabled list, Koosman has allowed only five runs in 51 innings.	Two more home runs—this time with President Nixon in attendance—prompted this Reggie Jackson classic: "Everyone knows who the president is. I wanted the president to know who Reggie Jackson is." Dick noticed and wrote Reggie, thanking him for his "generous comments with regard to hitting a homer in the presence of the president of the United States."	Lou Carnesecca was named coach of the New York Nets, effective with the 1970–71 season.
June 19	Art Shamsky hit a pair of home runs to compensate for an uncharacteristically poor performance by Tom Seaver. Ken Boswell drove in two runs with a ninth-inning single to beat the Phillies, 6–5.	Dave McNally pitched a two-hit shutout for his 10th victory without a defeat.	About 240 air traffic controllers "took ill" and refused to work, tying up air traffic throughout the nation.
June 20	The Mets beat the Cardinals, 4–3, before a crowd of 54,083 upon their return home from a successful road trip (8–4). Nolan Ryan, in his first start since May 3, defeated Bob Gibson, and Tug McGraw saved the victory by striking out Mike Shannon, Bob Johnson and Gibson—who'd homered in the seventh—to end the game. In attendance: concert pianist and Cardinals fan Vladimir Horowitz.	Don Drysdale pitched six scoreless innings to pick up his second straight win since coming off the disabled list June 13. But the Braves maintained their one-game lead over the Dodgers with a 12-inning win over the Giants on Bob Tillman's game-winning home run.	San Jose State's John Carlos ran the 100-yard dash in 9.1 seconds to win the national collegiate championship. The time equalled the world record, but wasn't recognized due to a six-MPH tailwind.
June 21	Tommie Agee made two base-running blunders in a 5–3 loss to St. Louis. He was picked off base following a double in the third, and was called out in the sixth when he advanced to third on a foul fly ball but failed to tag up after the catch.	Minnesota scored 11 runs in the 10th inning to defeat Oakland and move within one percentage point of the first-place A's. . . . Seattle's Gene Brabender lost his perfect game on a single by Kansas City's Pat Kelly with two out in the seventh.	Maureen Connolly Brinker, who won the Women's National tennis championships as a 16-year-old in 1951, died at age 34.
June 22	The Mets swept a doubleheader from the Cardinals, moving to within four-and-a-half games of the Cubs, their closest approach since April 23. Cleon Jones raised his batting average to .342 with a 3-for-3 performance and Ron Swoboda struck out five times in the first game. Jerry Koosman pitched another shutout in the nightcap, a 1–0 victory in which Rod Gaspar nailed Lou Brock at home in the eighth inning.	The Dodgers took sole possession of first place for the first time since April 25, as Bill Singer shut out the Reds on five hits while the Braves split a doubleheader with the Giants.	Judy Garland died at age 47 in London. . . . A man identified only as "Perez" hijacked an Eastern Airlines flight to Cuba. It was the 30th hijacking of the year, Eastern's eighth, and it was reported by *The New York Times* on page 78.
June 23	Off day.		Joe Frazier TKO'd Jerry Quarry in the eighth round of their heavyweight title fight at Madison Square Garden. On the same card, George Foreman made his pro debut with a three-round KO of Don Waldhelm.

DAY	NEW YORK METS	BASEBALL	OTHER NEWS
June 24	Richie Allen failed to show up for a doubleheader that the Mets swept from the Phillies by scores of 2–1 and 5–0. Phillies manager Bob Skinner announced that Allen would be suspended indefinitely. Jim McAndrew retired the first 16 batters in the second game and gained his first win of the season.	Bill Melton hit three home runs in the nightcap of Chicago's doubleheader sweep of the Pilots.	New York Consumer Affairs Commissioner Bess Myerson said that her department would enforce honesty and fairness in dealings between merchants and customers in the South Bronx.
June 25	Nolan Ryan retired the first 16 batters, including eight strikeouts. But the Phillies rallied from a 5–0 deficit to defeat the Mets, 6–5, on a 10th-inning home run by Dave Watkins.	Bill Lee, only a year removed from USC and the College World Series, made his debut for the Boston Red Sox. . . . Catfish Hunter of Oakland and George Culver of Cincinnati both lost no-hitters in the seventh inning.	In the longest match in Wimbledon history, both in time (5:12) and in games (112), 41–year-old Pancho Gonzalez defeated 25–year-old Charles Pasarell, 22–24, 1–6, 16–14, 6–3, 11–9.
June 26	Grant Jackson pitched a four-hit shutout and struck out 10 batters (including Ron Swoboda four times) as Philadelphia defeated the Mets, 2–0.	The Yankees lost their leading hitter when Roy White, batting .295, left the team for two weeks of Army summer training at Camp Drum in Watertown, N.Y.	Rep. Benjamin Rosenthal charged that the U.S. Army had subsidized John Wayne and his production company in the filming of *The Green Berets*. Wayne denied the charge.
June 27	The Mets trailed Pittsburgh, 3–1, with two on in the bottom the ninth when Gil Hodges elected to use Ron Swoboda (10 strikeouts in his last 12 plate appearances) as a pinch-*runner*. The manager sent Rod Gaspar and Ed Charles to the plate as pinch-hitters, and Joe Gibbon ended the rally and the game by retiring both.	Cleveland Indians announcer Herb Score presented Sam McDowell with a plaque on the occasion of his 1500th strikeout.	Salvador and Honduras completed a break in diplomatic relations in a dispute brought to a head by rioting following World Cup soccer games between the two nations.
June 28	The Pirates broke a 2–2 tie with five runs in the eighth and defeated the Mets, 7–4. It was New York's fourth straight defeat following 20 wins in 25 games.	The Dodgers, who defeated San Diego 15–0 in April, tied a six-week-old N.L. record for runs in a shutout by routing the Padres, 19–0. Don Drysdale pitched a five-hitter for his third consecutive win.	In the first football game of the season, the Coaches' All-America Game at Atlanta, the West beat the East, 14–10. Marty Domres of Columbia and Bobby Douglass of Kansas were the starting quarterbacks.
June 29	Tom Seaver became the winningest pitcher in Mets history at age 24 when he defeated the Pirates, 7–3, for the 44th victory of his career, one more than Al Jackson.	Billy Williams broke Stan Musial's N.L. record for consecutive games played. The Cubs swept a doubleheader from St. Louis, and stretched their lead over the second-place Mets to eight games.	For the first time in U.S. history, a rabbi, Louis Finkelstein, led a White House worship service. . . . Arthur Ashe disclosed that he had been denied a visa by South Africa when he sought to play in that country's tennis championships.
June 30	The Mets scored six times in the first inning of a 10–2 victory over St. Louis. Jim McAndrew pitched a complete-game three-hitter. Cleon Jones was benched after complaining of blurred vision.	Phil Niekro became the major leagues' first 13-game winner. . . . Bob Miller, an original Mets player who migrated to Minnesota, earned his first win in 84 appearances since 1967. (He won his next outing, four days later, as well.)	Miler Jim Ryun cancelled his European tour and all other competitions for the rest of the year, citing an emotional letdown.
July 1	Steve Carlton defeated Nolan Ryan in the first game of the Cardinals' sweep of the Mets by the scores of 4–1 and 8–5. It was the first-ever matchup between the major leagues' all-time strikeout kings.	Bowie Kuhn, addressing media representatives in Atlanta, said he foresaw no more expansion over the next 10 years, but conceded the likelihood of global baseball "in my lifetime."	Prince Charles, son of Queen Elizabeth II, was formally installed as prince of Wales.
July 2	Tug McGraw pitched six scoreless innings of relief in a 14-inning, 6–4 victory over St. Louis. Vic Davalillo had tied the game at 4–4 with a pinch-hit grand slam in the bottom of the eighth.	Reggie Jackson hit three home runs, giving him 33 in Oakland's first 72 games. . . . Five Atlanta batters were hit with pitches, including three in the same inning by Cincinnati pitcher Gerry Arrigo.	Senator George McGovern called for the withdrawal of all U.S. troops from Vietnam within 12 months.
July 3	The Mets defeated the Cardinals, 8–1, behind Gary Gentry's five-hitter. Tommie Agee hit a home run off Mudcat Grant's first pitch of the game.	Don Drysdale aggravated the injury to his right shoulder that had sidelined him earlier in the season. "I could feel something pop in the shoulder while I was warming up between the fifth and sixth innings."	Brian Jones, guitarist for the Rolling Stones, drowned in his swimming pool.
July 4	The Mets swept a doubleheader from Pittsburgh, 11–6 and 9–2. Cleon Jones went 4-for-10 to reclaim the N.L. batting lead with a .356 average. . . . Tug McGraw left for two weeks of duty with the Marine Corps reserve.	Baseball fans were treated to seven holiday doubleheaders. (An eighth was washed out by rain.) Baltimore (by 10 games), Oakland (four percentage points), Chicago (seven games), and Atlanta (one game) held the division leads at day's end.	The Federal Trade Commission gave the J. B. Williams Co. until July 25 to remove the word *power* from its TV ads ("Geritol adds iron power"), and to delete the references to "prevention of tiredness" from Geritol labels.
July 5	The Mets and Pirates were rained out in Pittsburgh.	Harmon Killebrew hit two home runs and drove in six runs as Minnesota defeated Oakland, 13–1, to take over first place, a position the Twins would hold for the remainder of the season.	Don Meredith announced his retirement from the Dallas Cowboys at age 31.
July 6	The Mets defeated Pittsburgh, 8–7, for their fifth consecutive win. It was the fourth straight game in which they scored at least eight runs. . . . Donn Clendenon hit his first home run since joining the team.	Montreal's Gary Waslewski pitched a one-hitter against Philadelphia. The only hit was a fifth-inning single by Rick Joseph. . . . St. Louis swept the Cubs to cut Chicago's lead over the Mets to five games.	A rock-throwing battle disrupted the performance of Sly and the Family Stone at the Newport Jazz Fesitval, prompting the producer to cancel the next evening's show by Led Zeppelin, the only rock band remaining on the festival schedule.

DAY	NEW YORK METS	BASEBALL	OTHER NEWS
July 7	The annual Mayor's Trophy Game between the Mets and Yankees was rained out and rescheduled for September 29.	Kansas City pitcher Jim Rooker hit two home runs in a 6–5 loss to Minnesota. . . . Washington's Frank Howard hit two home runs, raising his season total to 32, two fewer than major-league leader Reggie Jackson.	The Los Angeles Rams traded wide receiver Harold Jackson and defensive end John Zook to the Philadelphia Eagles for running back Israel Lang.
July 8	More than 55,000 fans filled Shea Stadium for the opener of a three-game series with the division-leading Cubs. The Mets—with only one hit off Ferguson Jenkins over the first eight innings—scored three runs in the bottom of the ninth to defeat Chicago, 4–3.		The National Association of Broadcasters recommended the elimination of cigarette ads on the three networks and their affiliate stations.
July 9	Tom Seaver defeated the Cubs, 4–0, allowing only one base runner—Jimmy Qualls, who singled to left-center with one out in the ninth—before the biggest baseball crowd ever at Shea (59,083).	Jim Bunning struck out three batters to move past Warren Spahn into third place in major league history with a career total of 2586.	The Department of Agriculture suspended the use of the pesticide DDT for 30 days, pending review of its side effects.
July 10	The Cubs defeated the Mets, 6–2, with a five-run fifth inning, and left town with a four-game lead.	Cincinnati moved into third place, two games behind the Dodgers, with a 10-inning win over Houston.	The U.S. command in Saigon announced that 153 Americans were killed in combat over the previous week, the *lowest* weekly total of the past six months.
July 11	Jim McAndrew suffered his second consecutive early knockout, as Montreal beat the Mets, 11–4.	San Francisco reclaimed third place and knocked the Dodgers out of first (if only for a day) with a 10-inning victory over Los Angeles. Two-and-a-half games separated the first four teams in the division.	The draft conspiracy conviction of Dr. Benjamin Spock was overturned in the U.S. Court of Appeals.
July 12	The Mets and Expos were postponed by rain.	The Cardinals won for the eighth time in their last nine games to reach the .500 mark for the first time since April, 10 games behind the Cubs.	Blind Faith, featuring Eric Clapton, Ginger Baker, and Steve Winwood, made its U.S. debut at Madison Square Garden.
July 13	Ed Kranepool and Ron Swoboda drove in the winning runs in the eighth and seventh innings, respectively, in a doubleheader sweep of the Expos. Swoboda had replaced Cleon Jones, to the boos of the Shea crowd, after Jones was ejected by umpire Frank Dezelan.	The Cubs kept pace with the Mets, sweeping the Phillies to take a four-and-a-half game lead into their series vs. New York at Wrigley Field. . . . Pittsburgh manager Larry Shepard was hospitalized complaining of chest pains after pitching batting practice in 95-degree heat. . . . Bob Gibson fanned Roberto Clemente for career strikeout number 2000.	The Soviet Union launched an unmanned spacecraft, *Luna 15*, toward the Moon in an apparent attempt to upstage the flight of *Apollo 11*.
July 14	Bill Hands outpitched Tom Seaver, and the Cubs defeated the Mets, 1–0. Don Kessinger scored the game's only run in the sixth inning, after reaching on a bunt single.		George Mikan resigned as commissioner of the American Basketball Association.
July 15	Al Weis hit the fifth home run of his eight-year major league career, and the Mets beat the Cubs, 5–4. Billy Williams and Ron Santo closed the gap with back-to-back solo home runs in the eighth before Ron Taylor preserved the win.	Lee May hit four home runs and drove in 10 runs as the Reds split a doubleheader with the Braves. . . . Ed Brinkman grounded into an around-the-horn triple play started by Detroit's Don Wert.	The House Ways and Means Committee approved the first increase in the tax rate for capital gains income in nearly 30 years.
July 16	The Mets scored six times in the first two innings, and Cal Koonce then pitched five innings of scoreless relief to defeat the Cubs, 9–5. Al Weis, Tommie Agee, and Art Shamsky homered. . . . J. C. Martin collapsed after the game, played in intense heat, and was treated at a local hospital.	Rod Carew stole home for the seventh time this season, tying Pete Reiser's major league record.	*Apollo 11* blasted off from Cape Kennedy, headed for the Moon.
July 17	Off day.	The Giants defeated the Dodgers, 14–13, to draw within one game of Los Angeles. The lead changed hands five times, and the Dodgers used a six-man infield against career .028-hitter Ron Herbel.	Promoters of a planned three-day music festival in Woodstock, N.Y., continued their preparations despite being denied permission to set up 100 temporary structures—a stage, dressing rooms, and toilet facilities.
July 18	The Mets beat Montreal, 5–2. Cleon Jones was ejected for the second time in a week, this time for fighting with Expos catcher Ron Brand following a home-plate collision.		Joe Namath agreed to sell his share of Bachelors III and return to the New York Jets. . . . Washington secretary Mary Jo Kopechne, a passenger in a car driven by Senator Edward Kennedy, was killed when the car plunged off a narrow bridge on Chappaquiddick Island into a pond.
July 19	Montreal knocked out Tom Seaver in the third inning of a 6–4 victory. Bill Stoneman pitched a complete game, striking out 10 for the Expos.		*Apollo 11* went into orbit around the Moon in preparation for landing.

DAY	NEW YORK METS	BASEBALL	OTHER NEWS
July 20	The Mets split a doubleheader with the Expos, losing 3–2, and winning 4–3. Tommie Agee was injured in the second game when he crashed into the center field wall.	The Cubs swept the Phillies to take a four-and-one-half-game lead at the All-Star break. . . . Atlanta routed San Diego, 10–0, to take a one-game lead over the Dodgers and Giants.	Neil Armstrong became the first man to walk on the Moon.
July 21	All-Star break.		The Soviet spacecraft *Luna 15* crashed onto the Moon's Sea of Crises, 500 miles from where the *Apollo 11* team had landed.
July 22	All-Star break.	The All-Star Game was rained out for the first time since its inception in 1933. President Nixon forfeited his spot in the rotation when he left Washington to attend the next day's splashdown of Apollo 11, so Vice President Agnew was scheduled to throw out the first pitch.	President Nixon predicted that by the year 2000 man will have found life on other planets.
July 23	All-Star break.	Denny McLain missed his scheduled All-Star Game start when he was late arriving in Washington from a dental appointment in Detroit. The N.L. beat the A.L., 9–3, with Willie McCovey hitting a pair of home runs.	Senator Edward Kennedy's driver's license was temporarily revoked after a preliminary report found him at fault in the accident in which Mary Jo Kopechne was killed.
July 24	The Mets matched single runs by Cincinnati in the sixth, eighth, and ninth innings, but lost 4–3 to the Reds in 12 innings. The victory went to Pedro Ramos and was the last of his major league career.	Richie Allen was reinstated by the Phillies one month after he was suspended for failing to show up for two games. . . . Manager Larry Shepard rejoined the Pirates. . . . Hank Aaron hit his 535th career home run to move past Jimmie Foxx into fourth place in major league history.	The *Apollo 11* astronauts splashed down. . . . Cassius Clay was sentenced to five years in prison and fined $1,000 for refusing induction into the armed forces in 1967. Clay was released on bail, and his attorney announced he would appeal the decision.
July 25	Tony Perez broke a 1–1 tie with a seventh-inning home run, but J. C. Martin hit a game-winning homer in the eighth to give the Mets a 4–3 victory over the Reds.	Bob Gibson pitched a 13–inning complete-game victory for St. Louis. . . . Ferguson Jenkins was removed for X-rays (which were negative) after Willie Crawford's line drive hit his right thumb.	In a nationally televised address, Edward Kennedy offered to resign from the U.S. Senate if his "irrational" and "indefensible" behavior impaired his standing in Massachusetts.
July 26	Tom Seaver pitched a complete-game victory over Cincinnati, 3–2. It was his first win in three starts since he experienced soreness in his right shoulder during his near-perfect game. He had taken anti-inflammation medication since then.	California reliever Hoyt Wilhelm turned 46.	"Honky Tonk Women" by the Rolling Stones reached the top of the U.S. singles chart.
July 27	Al Weis made a pair of fourth-inning errors that contributed to two runs, and Cincinnati defeated the Mets, 6–3.	The Dodgers defeated Ferguson Jenkins for the second time in three days. Don Drysdale struggled through five innings for the last victory of his career in his first appearance since July 3rd.	The federal government reported new evidence linking cigarette smoking with chronic bronchitis, coronary disorders, pulmonary emphysema, throat and respiratory cancer, and—in a new discovery—non cancerous mouth diseases.
July 28	Off day.	Roy Campanella, Stan Coveleski, Waite Hoyt, and Stan Musial were inducted into the Hall of Fame. . . . Plans were announced for the inclusion of stars from the Negro leagues into the Hall.	The U.S. government announced a surplus of more than three billion dollars for fiscal 1969.
July 29	Rain postponed a scheduled twi-night doubleheader between the Mets and Astros at Shea.	Reggie Jackson hit his 40th home run of the season in Oakland's 97th game, one game behind Roger Maris's pace in 1961, 23 ahead of Babe Ruth's in 1927.	*Mariner 6* transmitted to Earth the first-ever close-up look at Mars.
July 30	The Mets were routed by Houston in both ends of a doubleheader, 16–3 and 11–5 In an 11–run ninth inning of the first game, Denis Menke and Jim Wynn became the first teammates in N.L. history to hit grand slams in the same inning. Houston had another big inning in the nightcap, scoring 10 times in the third. During that inning, Gil Hodges walked to left field to remove Cleon Jones from the game for a lackadaisical play.	Dave McNally ran his record to 15–0, equalling the longest winning streak to start a season in A.L. history. . . . Hank Aaron hit his 537th career home run, to move past Mickey Mantle into third place in major league history. . . . Bob Tillman hit home runs in three consecutive at-bats.	Edward Kennedy announced he would retain his Senate seat and run for reelection in 1970. He ruled out a bid for the presidency in 1972.
July 31	Rookie Tom Griffin defeated Tom Seaver, 2–0. Houston scored both runs in the sixth, the first on a Jim Wynn home run.	Bo Belinsky was recalled by the Pirates. He had earned his return by winning nine consecutive decisions for Hawaii of the Pacific Coast League.	Boston Celtics player-coach Bill Russell revealed in an article in *Sports Illustrated* that he was retiring from the NBA as an active player.

DAY	NEW YORK METS	BASEBALL	OTHER NEWS
August 1	The Mets answered Atlanta's three first-inning runs with four of their own, and held on for a 5–4 victory. Cal Koonce pitched six-and-a-third innings in relief for the victory.	National Association President Phil Piton rejected the contract of Bernice Gera on the eve of her debut as the first female umpire in organized baseball. . . . Red Sox manager Dick Williams removed Carl Yastrzemski from a game and fined him five hundred dollars for loafing to first base. . . . Don Drysdale suffered a dislocated left thumb when struck by a line drive hit by his future ABC broadcast partner Tim McCarver.	Gregg Jefferies celebrated his second birthday.
August 2	Cleon Jones drove in the game's only run with a pinch single in the seventh as the Mets defeated Atlanta. Tug McGraw, in relief of Jim McAndrew, allowed five base runners but no runs over the final two innings.	Reggie Jackson moved five games ahead of Roger Maris's pace with his 41st home run, into the second tier at Oakland Coliseum.	Vince Lombardi made his debut as coach of the Washington Redskins, leading them to a 13–7 preseason win over Chicago.
August 3	Jerry Grote hit a game-winning home run in the 11th inning, after the Mets had tied the Braves with five runs in the sixth inning of a 6–5 victory.	Cincinnati scored 10 runs in the fifth inning and held on for a 19–17 victory over Philadelphia that gave the Reds a narrow lead in the N.L. West. The top five teams were separated by two games. . . . Minnesota's Rich Reese hit a pinch-hit grand slam to hand Dave McNally his first loss of the season after 15 wins. Earl Weaver was ejected in the first inning for the second straight game.	A group of 23 scientists recommended an ambitious program of unmanned space exploration, including missions beyond the planet Pluto.
August 4	The Reds defeated the Mets, 1–0, as Jim Maloney pitched a two-hitter with final-out help from Wayne Granger. Pete Rose saved the win with a wall-climbing catch of Art Shamsky's would-be home run in the eighth inning.	Tim McCarver and Julian Javier hit solo home runs in the seventh and ninth innings, respectively, to give the Cardinals their 21st win in 27 games, and move St. Louis to within two-and-a-half games of the Mets.	CBS extended its contract with the National Hockey League, announcing plans to televise a game of the week each Sunday afternoon starting in January 1970.
August 5	The Mets split a doubleheader with the Reds, losing 8–5 and winning 10–1. Tom Seaver left the first game after three innings with pain in his right shoulder. Nolan Ryan pitched his first complete game of the season in the nightcap. Plate umpire called Ryan's stuff "the best I've seen any pitcher have for nine innings this year."	Willie Stargell became the first player ever to hit a home run out of Dodger Stadium.	The debut edition of *Penthouse* magazine hit newsstands across the country.
August 6	The Mets squandered a 2–0 first-inning lead in a 3–2 loss to Cincinnati. Johnny Bench hit a game-winning home run off loser Jim McAndrew in the seventh.	Billy Martin knocked out Twins pitcher Dave Boswell following an altercation between Boswell and Bob Allison. Boswell was hospitalized for treatment of facial cuts that required 20 stitches.	A NASA official said that a manned space flight to Mars was likely during the 1980s.
August 7	Off day.	Bob Skinner resigned as manager of the Phillies, citing "a lack of support from the front office" in his dealings with Richie Allen.	The Justice Department announced it would not seek a reversal of the Supreme Court decision to acquit Dr. Benjamin Spock of conspiring to council draft evasion.
August 8	The Mets split with Atlanta. Jerry Koosman pitched a seven-hitter to win the first game, 4–1. Bob Tillman spoiled his shutout with a home run in the ninth. Atlanta won the nightcap, 1–0 in 10 innings. Gary Gentry and Ron Reed dueled through nine scoreless innings before Felipe Alou singled home the game-winner off loser Ron Taylor.	Thurman Munson made his major league debut and drove in two runs to help the Yankees to a 5–0 victory over Oakland. . . . Bill Singer pitched a two-hitter to halt the Cubs' seven-game winning streak.	The cover photo for the Beatles' album *Abbey Road* was shot.
August 9	Tom Seaver struggled into the eighth inning, but the Mets defeated Atlanta, 5–3, for his 16th victory.	Kansas City's Bill Butler shut out the Indians on one hit, a third-inning single by Eddie Leon. . . . Jim Palmer returned from six weeks on the disabled list and defeated Minnesota for his 10th win against two defeats.	O. J. Simpson ended his holdout and signed his first NFL contract, a four-year, no-cut agreement for an undisclosed sum. . . . Sharon Tate and four guests were brutally murdered at the actress's Hollywood home by four disciples of Charles Manson.
August 10	Three pitchers—Nolan Ryan, Don Cardwell and Tug McGraw—shut out the Braves, 3–0 on five hits. Ryan left the game in the third inning after straining a muscle in his thigh.	Mike Cuellar lost his no-hit bid when Cesar Tovar opened the ninth inning with Minnesota's only hit of the game. . . . Johnny Sain was fired as pitching coach of the Tigers. Denny McLain: "The club made a mistake." Mickey Lolich: "If I voiced my feeling, I'd get in trouble."	Manson followers murdered Mr. and Mrs. Leno LaBianca in Los Angeles.

DAY	NEW YORK METS	BASEBALL	OTHER NEWS
August 11	Tom Griffin shut the Mets out for eight innings, running his total to 25 consecutive scoreless innings against New York. Houston defeated the Mets, 3–0.	Don Drysdale announced his retirement from baseball. Doctors had told him that he had permanently lost the elasticity in his right shoulder. . . . White Sox outfielder Carlos May lost the top joint of his right thumb during firing exercises with his Marine Corps reserve unit.	New York Stock Exchange volume hit its lowest total in more than two years—6.68 million shares.
August 12	The Mets wasted Ed Kranepool's three-run home run during a five-run fourth inning, losing to Houston, 8–7.	Reggie Jackson hit his 42d home run—his first in 12 games. . . . The Yankees rose above the .500 mark for the first time since April 30 with a 10–3 victory over Minnesota.	Bill Shoemaker returned to racing following a three-month absence due to injury. He was shut out in three races at Arlington Park.
August 13	Houston completed a three-game sweep with an 8–2 victory. It was the Astros' ninth consecutive win over the Mets, and dropped New York into third place for the first time since early June, with its largest deficit of the season (nine-and-a-half games behind the Cubs). Curt Blefary drove in three runs, for a total of nine during the series.	By a unanimous vote of major league team owners, commissioner pro tem Bowie Kuhn was awarded a seven-year contract. . . . Roberto Clemente overtook Cleon Jones as the N.L. batting leader with a 4–for–5 performance that included three home runs. . . . Jim Palmer pitched a no-hitter against Oakland.	A national day of celebration for the *Apollo 11* astronauts included parades in New York and Chicago and a state dinner with President Nixon in Los Angeles.
August 14	Off day.	Joe Pepitone returned to the Yankees after missing two games with what manager Ralph Houk termed "personal problems. Pepi said his problem made it impossible to be at the Stadium."	Presidential press secretary Ron Zieglar said the increase in fighting might affect a decision on a second troop withdrawal from Vietnam, due later in the month.
August 15	The Mets at Padres were postponed by rain. Jennifer Michelle Grote was born to Jerry's wife, Sharon.	Grant Jackson five-hit the Astros for Philadelphia's third consecutive shutout victory, its longest streak in 15 years. . . . The Pirates traded Jim Bunning to the Dodgers.	The Woodstock Music and Arts Fair opened, drawing more than a half-million rock fans.
August 16	The Mets swept the Padres, 2–0 and 2–1. Tom Seaver pitched eight scoreless innings in the first game for his 17th win. Jerry Grote broke a 1–1 tie with a pinch single in the seventh inning of the nightcap. Tug McGraw saved the win for Jim McAndrew.	The Phillies tied a team record (one that still stands) when Rick Wise pitched their fourth consecutive shutout. . . . Bob Gibson became the first pitcher in N.L. history to strike out 200 or more batters in seven consecutive seasons.	Despite two years of remaining collegiate eligibility, 20-year-old Spencer Haywood signed a contract with the Denver Rockets of the ABA. The All-American from the University of Detroit had led the U.S. team to an Olympic title in 1968.
August 17	The Mets swept the Padres for the second day in a row, winning both games by 3–2 scores on Banner Day at Shea. Duffy Dyer hit a three-run home run in the first game. Bud Harrelson had the game-winner in the nightcap. a two-run triple to right- center over an outfield shifted around to left. . . . One banner read: "Cranberry, strawberry, we want Throneberry." We know the other guys, but who's this Cranberry character?		Hurricane Camille struck the coast of Mississippi, killing 400 persons and causing an estimated one billion dollars of damage over the next four days. . . . The Jets defeated the Giants, 37–14, in a pre-season game, the first ever meeting of New York's two pro football teams.
August 18	Off day.	Richie Allen, on a television program entitled "Rich Allen Tells All," announced, "I have no intention of returning [to the Phillies next season]. I have taken about as much as I can stand."	President Nixon nominated Clement Haynsworth, Jr., a conservative from South Carolina, to replace Abe Fortas on the Supreme Court.
August 19	Tommie Agee hit a game-winning home run in the 14th inning off starter Juan Marichal for a 1–0 Mets win. Cleon Jones saved the game with a leaping catch of Willie McCovey's blast to the wall in left-center in the 13th inning. Gary Gentry and Tug McGraw combined for a five-hitter.	Ken Holtzman pitched the fifth no-hitter of the season, and Ron Santo drove in the game's only runs with a three-run home run in the first as Chicago defeated Atlanta to maintain its lead over the Mets.	Lew Alcindor faced Wilt Chamberlain in the annual Maurice Stokes benefit game at Kutcher's Country Club. Alcindor outscored Wilt, 14 to 12. Chamberlain, who grabbed 16 rebounds to Alcindor's 10, said, "He's good. That's all that counts."
August 20	Jim McAndrew two-hit the Giants in a 6–0 Mets victory. Art Shamsky drove in four runs with a home run and double.	Los Angeles defeated Philadelphia, giving the Dodgers temporary custody of first place over the Reds, who lost to St. Louis.	The Beatles decided the running order of the songs on *Abbey Road*. It was the last time all four were together in a studio.
August 21	The Giants snapped New York's six-game winning streak with a 7–6 win in 11 innings. The Mets had tied the game with a two-out rally in the ninth. But Tommie Agee misplayed Ken Henderson's fly ball into a triple for the game-winner. Donn Clendenon took over as the Mets' everyday starting first baseman.	California's Steve Kealey pitched a seven-hit shutout over Baltimore in his first major league start.	The Al Aksa Mosque, a Moslem shrine in Jerusalem, was severely damaged in a fire set by a religious fanatic.
August 22	Making a rare start against a right-handed pitcher, Ron Swoboda hit his first home run since May 30, pacing the Mets to a 5–3 victory over Los Angeles.	Denny McLain became the majors' first 20-game winner. . . . Pittsburgh swept the Reds, reducing Cincinnati's lead in the N.L. West to one percentage point over the second-place Dodgers and only two games over fifth-place Houston.	National Hockey League owners agreed to fully fund the players' pension fund.

DAY	NEW YORK METS	BASEBALL	OTHER NEWS
August 23	The Mets defeated the Dodgers, 3–2. The winning run scored in the bottom of the ninth when, with Donn Clendenon running from first on a two-out, 3–2 pitch, Jerry Grote hit a pop-up behind second base. Willie Davis, Ted Sizemore, or Maury Wills could have caught the ball, but it fell as they all watched.	Jim Hickman drove in five runs and Ron Santo drove in three in Chicago's 11–5 win over Houston. Santo became the first N.L. player to reach the 100–RBI mark, and the Cubs maintained a five-and-a-half-game lead over the Mets.	A team from Taipeh was the surprise winner in the Little League World Series. It was the first time a team from Taiwan had won the event.
August 24	The Mets concluded a 9–1 home stand with a 7–4 victory over the Dodgers. Ron Swoboda's three-run double in the seventh was the game-winner.	Reggie Jackson hit two home runs in a doubleheader, raising his total for the season to 45 with 39 games to play.	The movie version of Arlo Guthrie's "Alice's Restaurant" opened in New York.
August 25	Off day.	The Cubs scored four times in the bottom of the ninth, but fell one run short when Paul Popovich lined out against Pedro Ramos, giving the Reds a 9–8 victory. Chicago's lead over the Mets was cut to four-and-a-half games. ... Billy Martin barred an NBC news crew from filming Vice President Humphrey in the Twins locker room following a loss. Martin said, "I don't care if it's President Nixon or the King of Italy."	The NBA broke off merger talks with the ABA, which announced that Billy Cunningham would jump to the ABA at the end of his current contract with the NBA's Philadelphia 76ers.
August 26	Tom Seaver and Jim McAndrew pitched complete games in the Mets' third doubleheader sweep of the Padres in 11 days, 8–4 and 3–0, cutting Chicago's lead to three games. Of McAndrew's performance, Gil Hodges said simply, "It's about time he delivered."	Cubs manager Leo Durocher was ejected from a loss to Cincinnati for kicking dirt on umpire Shag Crawford. ... Willie McCovey hit his 40th homer run of the season.	Promoters of the Woodstock Festival announced losses of up to two million dollars.
August 27	The Mets sliced another game off Chicago's lead with a 4–1 win over San Diego, their sixth in a row. Jerry Koosman allowed only two hits. ... Bowie Kuhn authorized the Mets to print tickets for the N.L.C.S.	All five contenders in the N.L. West won, leaving the Giants in first by a half-game over Cincinnati and Atlanta. The Dodgers remained a game behind, two games in front of Houston.	Bobby Seale was indicted on a charge of first-degree murder in the death of a former member of the Black Panther party.
August 28	Off day.	Jim Northrup went 6-for-6, including a game-winning home run in the 13th inning. ... Ferguson Jenkins snapped the Cubs' losing streak at four with a five-hit victory over Cincinnati.	A press conference was held to unveil *The Baseball Encyclopedia*, the first book ever to contain complete batting and pitching records of all major leaguers.
August 29	Juan Marichal pitched a four-hitter as the Giants beat the Mets, 5–0. It marked the first time in more than two weeks that the Mets lost ground to the Cubs. Willie Mays was sidelined with strained knee ligaments.	Jim Hickman's seventh-inning home run gave Chicago a 2–1 victory over Atlanta. ... Jim Bouton lost his first N.L. start, going all the way in Houston's 4–2, 10–inning loss to Pittsburgh. ... The Yankees announced that Joe Pepitone had been fined five hundred dollars for leaving the bench during a game. Upon learning of the fine, Pepitone left Yankee Stadium and was suspended.	A TWA flight from Rome, bound for Tel Aviv, was hijacked and diverted to Damascus. The flight, which originated in Los Angeles and made a stopover in New York, was the first U.S. plane ever hijacked outside the Western hemisphere.
August 30	Donn Clendenon hit a 10th-inning home run to defeat the Giants, 3–2. Rod Gaspar threw Bob Burda out at the plate in the ninth. Burda tried to score from first base on Willie McCovey's double down the left-field line against an outfield shifted to right. Ron Swoboda was made an everyday starter.	Ken Johnson, a knuckleballer acquired from the Yankees three weeks earlier, relieved Cubs starter Dick Selma in the first inning and pitched his team to a 5–4 win over Atlanta.	The National Academy of Sciences warned the federal government to counter the dangers of uncontrolled technology, such as nuclear war, pollution, and congested cities.
August 31	The Mets split two games with the Giants, winning 8–0 and losing 3–2, and fell four games behind the Cubs. Tom Seaver pitched a seven-hit shutout for his 19th victory in the opener. But Ron Taylor walked Jim Davenport with the bases loaded in the 11th inning of the nightcap. After a leadoff triple in the top of the inning, Bud Harrelson was thrown out trying to score on Tommie Agee's short fly to Bobby Bonds.	Ken Holtzman hit the first home run of his career as the Cubs defeated Atlanta, 8–4. ... Frank Howard pulled to within three home runs of major league leader Reggie Jackson with his 42nd of the season.	Rocky Marciano was killed in a plane crash near Des Moines, Iowa. ... Bob Dylan appeared at the Isle of Wight Festival, his first live performance since a 1966 motorcycle accident.
September 1	The Dodgers scored five times in the first inning, and defeated the Mets, 10–6. ... Steve Garvey made his major-league debut, striking out vs. Jack DiLauro.	San Francisco regained first place with a 12–2 win over Montreal. ... The Cubs were rained out in Cincinnati.	The International Federation of Airline Pilots Association called for a worldwide 24–hour air travel shutdown unless Syria released two Israeli hostages held since the hijacking of a TWA flight three days earlier.

DAY	NEW YORK METS	BASEBALL	OTHER NEWS
September 2	Tug McGraw struck out Willie Davis with two out in the ninth and the winning run on base in a 5–4 victory over the Dodgers. Gary Gentry gained his first victory since July 15. Earlier in the game, Davis had set a Dodgers record by hitting in his 30th consecutive game.	The Yankees announced the signing of manager Ralph Houk to a new three-year contract, the same day that Joe Pepitone was reinstated following a suspension. . . . The Cubs swept the Reds; the first game was the completion of a game suspended on June 15.	Hanoi officials reported that North Vietnamese President Ho Chi Minh was receiving around-the-clock medical care for an undisclosed illness.
September 3	Willie Davis hit a tie-breaking, ninth-inning double to extend his hitting streak to 31 games and defeat the Mets, 5–4. Tommie Agee and Donn Clendednon hit two-run home runs to tie the game in the eighth inning.	Jim Maloney shut the Cubs out on two hits.	North Vietnamese President Ho Chi Minh died.
September 4	Off day.	Willie Davis's hitting streak was snapped at 31 games, as the Dodgers lost to San Diego, 3–0.	First-term New York Rep. Edward Koch, an outspoken opponent of the Vietnam war, touched off an uproar in the House, saying "Ho Chi Minh is George Washington, Abraham Lincoln, and John Kennedy [to his people]. We must recognize that he was . . . a patriot in his own country."
September 5	Tom Seaver became the first 20–game winner in Mets history in a 5–1 win over Philadelphia. The Phillies won the second game, 4–2, scoring the winning run after a bad throw by Duffy Dyer allowed Johnny Callison to advance from first to third on a delayed steal.	Atlanta gained a game on the top three teams in the N.L. West with an 11–2 win over Cincinnati as the Dodgers and Giants were losing. . . . Mike Cuellar won his 20th game.	Dweezil Zappa was born.
September 6	Don Cardwell pitched six innings and Tug McGraw completed a 3–0 shutout of the Phillies, cutting Chicago's lead to three-and-a-half games.	The Pirates routed Ferguson Jenkins in the third inning of a 13–4 victory over the Cubs. . . . Minnesota stretched its lead over Oakland to seven-and-a-half games with an 18–inning victory over the A's.	The United States, France, and Great Britian announced recognition of the Revolutionary Command Council that overthrew Libyan King Idris. The Council leader: Col. Muhammad al-Khadafy.
September 7	The Mets broke a 3–3 tie with two runs in the seventh and four in the eighth to beat Philadelphia, 9–3, cutting the Cubs' lead to two-and-a-half games prior to a two-game series between the teams at Shea.	The Pirates beat the Cubs, scoring the winning run on Don Kessinger's error in the 11th inning. . . . Harmon Killebrew drove in seven runs with two home runs before leaving a 16–4 win over Oakland with a bruised knee.	Illinois Senator Everett Dirksen died.
September 8	The Mets cut Chicago's lead to a game-and-a-half with a 3–2 victory over the Cubs. Tommie Agee drove in the first two runs of the game with a third-inning home run, and scored the tie-breaker on Wayne Garrett's single in the sixth.	Cincinnati took over first place with a sweep of the Giants. . . . Cleon Jones regained the N.L. batting lead when Roberto Clemente went 0–for–5. . . . The Braves purchased Hoyt Wilhelm from the Angels.	Rod Laver completed a Grand Slam with his 7–9, 6–1, 6–2, 6–2 victory over Tony Roche in the men's singles final of the U.S. Open at Forest Hills.
September 9	Mets fans sang "Good-bye Leo" to the Cubs manager Durocher as New York beat Chicago, 7–1, for Tom Seaver's 21st victory. It was the Cubs' sixth straight loss, and reduced their lead to a half-game. Early in the game, a black cat ran onto the field and came to a halt in front of the Cubs' dugout.	Phil Niekro won his 20th game of the season, defeating the Dodgers as the Braves moved past Los Angeles into third place. The Giants beat the Reds to move back into first place.	A Swedish-American study on pairs of twins reported that twins who smoked had no higher mortality rates than those who didn't.
September 10	The Mets swept two games from the Expos to move into first place. They won the first game, 3–2, on Ken Boswell's two-out single in the 12th inning. Ron Taylor threw out Angel Hermoso at the plate in the top of the inning. Nolan Ryan pitched a three-hitter in the nightcap. The Mets scored six runs in the third inning.	At 10:13 p.m., Eastern Daylight Time, Philadelphia completed its 6–2 victory over Chicago, lifting the Mets into first place. Leo Durocher held a 10–minute closed door meeting after the game. Before the game, Ken Holtzman, responding to Jerry Koosman's admission that he purposely hit Ron Santo two nights earlier, threatened to retaliate when the teams met again.	Tom Landry announced that rookie running back Calvin Hill from Yale University had beaten out Craig Baynham for a starting spot.
September 11	Gary Gentry pitched a six-hitter as the Mets beat Montreal, 4–0. Cleon Jones had to leave the game with a torn rib muscle.	The Phillies scored three runs in the bottom of the eighth to hand Chicago its eighth straight defeat, 4–3. . . . The Reds took first place in the N.L. West by beating the Padres as Atlanta defeated San Francisco.	Lee Iacocca was named president of North American automobile operations for the Ford Motor Co.
September 12	The Mets won a pair of 1–0 games from Pittsburgh, and in both games the runs were driven in by pitchers—Jerry Koosman and Don Cardwell, respectively.	The Cubs snapped their losing streak, 5–1, over St. Louis. . . . Atlanta became the third different leader in three days in the N.L. West.	O. J. Simpson signed a long-term contract with ABC Sports to make appearances on "Wide World of Sports."

DAY	NEW YORK METS	BASEBALL	OTHER NEWS
September 13	Ron Swoboda broke an eight-inning tie with a grand-slam home run to give the Mets their 10th consecutive victory, a 5–2 win over Pittsburgh. Tom Seaver won his 22d game of the season.	Joe Torre and Tim McCarver had key hits to cap an eighth-inning rally that gave the Cardinals a 7–4 win over the Cubs, who fell three-and-a-half games behind the Mets. ... Felix Millan broke up Larry Dierker's no-hit bid with two out in the ninth inning of a scoreless tie. The Braves won the game with three runs in the top of the 13th, including the game-winner on a bases loaded walk to Bob Aspromonte. ... The Orioles clinched the A.L. East title.	Israeli Defense Minister Moshe Dayan said that a counterattack in response to an Egyptian air strike was designed to make Cairo "think twice" about attacks against Israeli positions along the Suez Canal.
September 14	After the Mets intentionally walked Fred Patek, Steve Blass hit a game-winning single in the bottom of the seventh to give Pittsburgh a 5–3 victory.	Rico Carty drove in all three runs with a pair of home runs in Atlanta's 3–2 win over Houston, its sixth straight, stretching its lead in the N.L. West to a game-and-a-half. ... Lou Brock's 10th inning home run gave St. Louis a 2–1 win over Ken Holtzman and the Cubs.	O. J. Simpson gained 35 yards rushing in his pro debut. The Buffalo Bills lost, 33–19 to the world champion Jets. Jack Kemp, in relief of James Harris and Tom Flores, was intercepted on each of Buffalo's last three drives.
September 15	Steve Carlton set a major-league record by striking out 19 batters, but the Mets defeated the Cardinals, 4–3, on a pair of two-run home runs by Ron Swoboda.	The Cubs lost to Montreal, 8–2, and fell four-and-a-half games behind. ... San Francisco beat Atlanta and Cincinnati beat the Dodgers, leaving the four teams separated by a game and a half.	Tom Heinsohn was named coach of the Boston Celtics, replacing Bill Russell.
September 16	The Mets and Cardinals were rained out in St. Louis. The game was rescheduled for September 22 in New York. ... New York lost ground to the Cubs for the first time since September 1.	Juan Marichal pitched a four-hit shutout against the Braves, lifting the Giants into first place. ... The Cubs beat Montreal for their second win in 13 games.	President Nixon announced that 35,000 more U.S. troops would be withdrawn from South Vietnam.
September 17	Jerry Koosman pitched his second consecutive shutout, a five-hitter, as New York beat Montreal, 5–0.	Ferguson Jenkins won his 20th game of the season as the Cubs defeated Philadelphia, 9–7.	Vice President Spiro Agnew announced a program to land a man on Mars in 1986 at a cost of 24 billion dollars.
September 18	Tom Seaver outdueled Bill Stoneman in a 2–0 victory over Montreal, his 23d. Ed Kranepool drove in both runs, the second with a home run.	Mike Ryan's single off Phil Regan was the game-winner in a three-run eighth-inning rally, as Philadelphia beat Chicago, 5–3. ... Carlton Fisk made his major league debut.	The House of Representatives approved a measure to determine the result of Presidential elections by popular vote.
September 19	Starters Nolan Ryan and Jim McAndrew were hit hard in Pittsburgh's sweep of the Mets, 8–2 and 8–0.	Ken Holtzman defeated Bob Gibson in the first game of a doubleheader, when Jim Hickman drove in the winning run with a disputed ground-rule double in the 10th inning; but Chicago lost the nightcap to St. Louis.	Alitalia announced a plan for a $299 round-trip tourist fare between New York and Rome.
September 20	Bob Moose pitched the sixth no-hitter of the 1969 season, as Pittsburgh defeated the Mets, 4–0. A large portion of the crowd of 38,874 stayed after the game until the Cubs' final was posted on the Shea scoreboard: St. Louis scored four times in the eighth to beat Chicago, 4–1.	The Braves and Giants (behind Juan Marichal's 20th) won, leaving San Francisco on top by a half-game, and putting some daylight between themselves and the Dodgers and Reds.	Assistant Attorney General William Rehnquist announced that Supreme Court nominee Clement Haynsworth had bought 1,000 shares of Brunswick stock between the time he issued a vote favorable to the company and the announcement of that decision.
September 21	The Mets swept the Pirates, 5–3 and 6–1, reducing their magic number to four. Jerry Koosman and Don Cardwell pitched complete games, the latter for his 100th career victory. Cleon Jones, still leading the league at .346, pinch-hit, his first appearance since September 11, and received a standing ovation.	Harmon Killebrew hit two home runs to tie Reggie Jackson and Frank Howard for the A.L. lead at 46. ... Los Angeles dropped three-and-a-half games behind San Francisco when Maury Wills let a grounder go through his legs with the bases loaded in the 10th inning against the Giants.	Wayne Maki of the St. Louis Blues fractured the skull of Boston Bruins defenseman Ted Green during a stick fight in a preseason game.
September 22	The Mets increased their lead to five games and reduced the magic number to three with a 3–1 victory over St. Louis. Tom Seaver went all the way for his 24th victory. During batting practice, Cleon Jones was injured when hit with a pitch.	Willie Mays became the second player in major league history to hit 600 home runs. He hit number 600 off Mike Corkins, pinch-hitting for rookie George Foster. ... Harmon Killebrew took the major league lead with his 47th home run as the Twins clinched the N.L. West.	The Army and Air Force announced that they would no longer offer beef stew on their chow lines.
September 23	The Mets clinched a tie in the N.L. East, beating St. Louis, 3–2, in 11 innings. They tied the game in the eighth, and won it on Bud Harrelson's single to left off Bob Gibson. Ron Swoboda, in a preview of his World Series catch, made a diving catch to save the game in the top of the eighth.	The Braves beat Jim Bouton and the Astros to regain the N.L. West lead, which they would not surrender again. ... Pete Rose went 6-for-10 in a doubleheader sweep of the Dodgers to draw within two points of Cleon Jones for the N.L. batting lead. ... Reggie Jackson hit his first home run in 18 games. ... Dick Williams was fired as manager of the Boston Red Sox.	A three-round exhibition between Cassius Clay and Joe Frazier—resulting from Clay's public challenge—was halted at the last minute by Frazier's manager, Yank Durham.

DAY	NEW YORK METS	BASEBALL	OTHER NEWS
September 24	The Mets scored five runs off Steve Carlton in the bottom of the first, and Gary Gentry pitched a four-hitter as the Mets defeated the Cardinals, 6–0, to clinch the N.L. East title. At 9:07 p.m., Joe Torre grounded into a game-ending double play—Harrelson to Weis to Clendenon—and thousands of spectators ran onto the field chanting, "We're number one!" All the runs scored on home runs—two by Donn Clendenon and one by Ed Charles.	Tony Gonzalez hit a home run—his eighth in 15 at-bats in the eighth inning to give Atlanta a 2–1 win over Houston. The Giants lost, 3–2, to San Diego, falling a game and a half behind the Braves.	*Butch Cassidy and the Sundance Kid* opened. . . . Jury selection began in the "Chicago 8" trial of Bobby Seale, Jerry Rubin, Abbie Hoffman, and five others.
September 25	Off day. The Mets signed Gil Hodges to a new three-year contract for $70,000 a season. . . . The Mets recorded an album of 10 songs at a Manhattan studio.	Pete Rose went 4-for-5 to take the N.L. batting lead from Cleon Jones, .347 to .343. . . . Dave McNally won his 20th game of the season. . . . Pilots chairman of the board William R. Daley announced the team would remain in Seattle in 1970.	Israeli Premier Golda Meir asked President Nixon and other U.S. officials for a long-term military and economic commitment to Israel.
September 26	Jerry Koosman shut out the Phillies on four hits. Donn Clendenon drove in two of New York's five runs with a first-inning home run. The Mets' lineup included Duffy Dyer, Bob Heise, Bobby Pfeil, and Amos Otis.	The Braves maintained a game-and-a-half lead over San Francisco with a 10–4 win over San Diego. Hoyt Wilhelm saved Phil Niekro's 22d victory.	"The Brady Bunch" made its debut on network television.
September 27	Tom Seaver pitched a three-hit shutout against the Phillies for his 25th win of the season. Bobby Pfeil drove in the game's only run with an eighth-inning single.	The Reds were eliminated from the pennant race when they lost to Houston.	It was reported that President Nixon privately called on Texas Representative George Bush to challenge that state's incumbent, Ralph Yarborough, for his seat in the Senate in 1970. Bush eventually ran, and lost—not to Yarborough, but to the man who defeated him in the Democratic primary, Lloyd Bentsen.
September 28	Gary Gentry, Nolan Ryan, and Ron Taylor combined to shut out the Phillies, 2–0. It was the Mets' fourth consecutive shutout.	Atlanta clinched a tie in the N.L. West by defeating San Diego. Clay Kirby became the majors' first 20-game loser. . . . Reds pitcher Wayne Granger tied a major league record by making his 89th appearance of the season.	Joe Kapp threw seven touchdown passes, tying an NFL record, leading the Minnesota Vikings to a 52–14 victory over the defending NFL champion Baltimore Colts.
September 29	The Mets defeated the Yankees, 7–6, in the annual Mayor's Trophy Game. For the first five innings, an experimental lively ball was used; 12 of the 13 runs were scored during the experiment.	Rico Petrocelli became the first shortstop in A.L. history to hit 40 home runs in a season.	A Harris poll reported that only 35 percent of Americans approved of President Nixon's handling of the Vietnam war.
September 30	Off day.	Atlanta clinched the N.L. West with a 3–2 win over Cincinnati. Rico Carty drove in the winning run in the bottom of the seventh, and Hoyt Wilhelm pitched two innings of perfect relief for the save.	Carl Stokes of Cleveland, the first black mayor of a major American city, won renomination in the city's Democratic primary.
October 1	The Mets won their 100th game of the season and ninth in a row, 6–5 in 12 innings over the Cubs at Wrigley Field. Only 10,136 fans attended the game.	Frank Howard batted leadoff, but it was Harmon Killebrew who broke the tie for the A.L. home run lead with his 49th of the season.	Testimony began in the "Chicago 8" trial. . . . The Concorde, an experimental jet, became the first commercial aircraft ever to break the sound barrier.
October 2	Chicago beat the Mets, 5–3. Gary Gentry left the game after being hit on the right wrist by a line drive hit by Paul Popovich. . . . Bobby Pfeil was cut from the Mets' postseason roster.	The Cardinals announced the retirement of Bill White. . . . Eddie Kasko was named manager of the Red Sox for 1970.	President Nixon reaffirmed his support of Supreme Court nominee Clement Haynsworth, despite growing opposition in the Senate.
October 3			The Beatles released *Abbey Road* in the U.S.
October 4	The Mets scored five runs in the eighth inning to defeat Atlanta, 9–5, in the first game of the first N.L.C.S. Cleon Jones scored the winning run on a throwing error by Orlando Cepeda.	Baltimore defeated Minnesota, 4–3, on Paul Blair's 12th-inning squeeze bunt. Boog Powell tied the game with a ninth-inning home run.	Joe Theismann threw three TD passes and scored another, leading Notre Dame to a 42–28 victory over previously undefeated Michigan State.
October 5	Tommie Agee, Ken Boswell, and Cleon Jones hit home runs in an 11–6 win over Atlanta, as the Mets took a 2–0 lead in the series.	Dave McNally pitched an 11-inning three-hitter, as Baltimore beat Minnesota, 1–0. Curt Motton drove in Boog Powell with the game's only run.	"The Forsyte Saga" made its American television debut.
October 6	Nolan Ryan pitched seven innings in relief of Gary Gentry as the Mets defeated Atlanta, 7–4, to sweep the Braves and win the N.L. title. Tommie Agee, Ken Boswell, and Wayne Garrett hit home runs.	The Orioles scored 11 runs on 18 hits to defeat the Twins for a three-game sweep of the A.L.C.S. Jim Palmer pitched a complete game for the win.	Nine members of Congress, including California Senator Alan Cranston and New York Rep. Allard Lowenstein, voiced their support of the upcoming student moritorium against the Vietnam war.
October 7		The Cardinals traded Curt Flood to the Phillies, starting the chain of events that led to Flood's challenge of the reserve clause.	Zelmo Beaty of the Atlanta Hawks jumped to the Utah Stars of the ABA.

DAY	NEW YORK METS	BASEBALL	OTHER NEWS
October 8			Congressional sources reported that Hubert Humphrey indicated to President Nixon his support for a systematic withdrawal of all U.S. combat troops from Vietnam.
October 9		The Reds fired manager Dave Bristol, and replaced him with Sparky Anderson.	The Senate Judiciary Committee upheld the nomination of Clement Haynsworth to the Supreme Court by a 10–7 vote.
October 10	Orioles manager Earl Weaver described the Mets as "two pitchers, some slap hitters, and a little speed."		The U.S. eased Operation Intercept, a campaign against the smuggling of marijuana into the country across the Mexican border.
October 11	Don Buford hit a leadoff home run in the first inning, pacing Baltimore to a 4–1 victory over Tom Seaver in the first game of the World Series.		The presidents of 79 colleges and universities called on President Nixon to accelerate his timetable for the withdrawal of U.S. troops from Vietnam.
October 12	Al Weis singled in the tie-breaking run in the top of the ninth, giving the Mets a 2–1 victory to even the Series at one game apiece. Jerry Koosman didn't allow a hit until Paul Blair singled leading off the seventh.		Sonia Henie died at age 57.
October 13		Billy Martin was fired as manager of the Minnesota Twins.	The Soviet Union launched its third manned Soyuz spacecraft into orbit in as many days with no comment on the purpose of the missions.
October 14	Gary Gentry and Nolan Ryan combined to four-hit Baltimore, and the Mets won, 5–0. Tommie Agee led off the bottom of the first with a home run, and made a pair of spectacular catches to save five runs.		Defendents in the "Chicago 8" trial were denied their request of a day off in observance of the war moratorium.
October 15	The Mets took a three-games-to-one lead in the Series with a 10-inning, 2–1 victory over Baltimore. The Orioles tied the game with a run in the ninth, and would have won it except for a game-saving catch by Ron Swoboda. The winning run scored on J. C. Martin's controversial bunt. Earl Weaver was ejected for arguing a strike call in the third inning.		A moratorium was observed nationwide in protest of the Vietnam war. . . . Rev. Fulton J. Sheen resigned as bishop of Rochester, New York.
October 16	The Mets won the World Series with a 5–3 victory. Ron Swoboda broke an eighth-inning tie with a double. The Mets had drawn to within one run in the sixth on a two-run homer by Donn Clendenon, driving in Cleon Jones. Jones reached base when umpire Lou DiMuro detected shoe polish on a ball and ruled Jones had been hit in the foot by a pitch.		The House Armed Services Committee unanimously approved the administration proposal for drafting Americans into military service by lottery.